A COMPENDIUM OF THE WAR OF THE REBELLION

COMPILED AND ARRANGED
FROM OFFICIAL RECORDS OF THE
FEDERAL AND CONFEDERATE ARMIES
REPORTS OF THE ADJUTANT GENERALS OF
THE SEVERAL STATES, THE ARMY REGISTERS
AND OTHER RELIABLE DOCUMENTS AND SOURCES

BY FREDERICK H. DYER
Late 7th Connecticut Volunteers

INCLUDING
IN THREE DEPARTMENTS
THE MATTER AS HERE OUTLINED

Organization of the several Military Divisions, Departments, Armies, Army Corps,
Divisions, Brigades and other important commands of the United States
Army formed during the War of the Rebellion, 1861–1865,
showing the Troops assigned to each and the
various Commanders of each Com-
mand from its formation
to its discon-
tinuance

A complete Record of the Battles, Engagements, Combats, Actions,
Skirmishes and Important Operations, tabulated by States and showing
the Union Troops engaged in each event

A
concise
History of each and
every Regiment, Battery,
Battalion and other Organizations
mustered by the several States for service
in the Union Army during the period referred to.

BROADFOOT PUBLISHING COMPANY
MORNINGSIDE PRESS
1994

Facsimile
46

☆

Copyright, 1908
By F. H. Dyer
Des Moines, Ia.

☆

ISBN-0-89029-046-X

New Materials Copyright 1978 by
Morningside Bookshop
P.O. Box 336, Forest Park Station
Dayton, Ohio 45405

PART III

Regimental Histories

Arrangement of Regimental and Other Histories

By States and Territories, alphabetically. Each state first presenting its Cavalry organizations, then Heavy Artillery, Light Artillery, Engineers, Sharpshooters and Infantry, in consecutive order of Regiments, Battalions, Companies, etc., for each branch of the service.

Regimental Histories

ALABAMA VOLUNTEERS.

1st REGIMENT CAVALRY.

Organized at Huntsville, Ala., and Memphis, Tenn., October, 1862. Attached to Cavalry Brigade, District of Corinth, 16th Army Corps, Dept. of Tennessee, January to March, 1863. Cavalry Brigade, District of Corinth, 2nd Division, 16th Army Corps, to June, 1863. 3rd Brigade, 1st Cavalry Division, 16th Army Corps, to August, 1863. 1st Brigade, 1st Division, 16th Army Corps, to April, 1864. Cavalry 4th Division, 16th Army Corps, to May, 1864. Headquarters 16th Army Corps to September, 1864. Unattached 15th Army Corps to November, 1864. Unattached 3rd Division, Cavalry Corps, Military Division Mississippi, to January, 1865. 3rd Brigade, Kilpatrick's 3rd Cavalry Division, Cavalry Corps, Military Division Mississippi, to June, 1865. District Northern Alabama, Dept. of the Cumberland, to October, 1865.

SERVICE.—Duty in District of Corinth, Miss., till June, 1863. Action at Cherokee Station, Ala., December 12, 1862. Chewalla, Tenn., January 20, 1863. Tuscumbia, Ala., February 22. Bear Creek March 3. Carroll County (Cos. "H" and "L") April 4. Glendale April 14. Dodge's Expedition to North Alabama April 15-May 8. Barton's Station April 16-17. Dickson, Great Bear Creek, Cherokee Station and Lundy's Lane April 17. Rock Cut, near Tuscumbia, April 22. Tuscumbia April 23. Town Creek April 28. Expedition to Tupelo, Miss., May 2-8. King's Creek, near Tupelo, May 5. Burnsville, Miss., June 11. Ripley Aug. 3. Vincent's Cross Roads and Bay Springs, Ala., October 26. Operations on Memphis & Charleston R. R. November 3-5. Colliersville, Tenn., November 3. Moscow, Miss., November 4. Camp Davies, Miss., November 22 (Detachment). Operations on Memphis & Charleston R. R. against Lee's attack November 28-December 10. Molino November 28. Wolf River Bridge December 4. Expedition toward Tuscumbia, Ala., December 9-24. Jack's Creek December 24. Expedition from Memphis to Wyatt's, Miss., February 6-18, 1864 (Detachment). Coldwater Ferry February 8. Near Senatobia February 8-9. Wyatt's February 13. Operations against Forrest, in West Tennessee and Kentucky, February 16-April 14. Reconnoissance down Tennessee River to Triana April 12-16 (Detachment). Decatur, Ala., April 17. Atlanta Campaign May to September. Movements on Dalton May 5-9. Snake Creek Gap May 10-12. Battle of Resaca May 13-15. Rome Cross Roads May 16. Battles about Dallas May 25-June 5. Operations about Marietta and against Kenesaw Mountain June 10-July 2. Nickajack Creek July 2-5. Chattahoochee River July 6-17. Cove Springs July 8. Expedition to Centre, Ala., July 11-13. Decatur July 19-22. Battle of Atlanta July 22. Siege of Atlanta July 22-August 25. Scout to Cedar Bluff, Ala., July 28-29. Expedition from Rome to Jacksonville, Ala., August 11-15. Buchanan August 15. Coreysville August 20. Flank movement on Jonesboro August 25-30. Battle of Jonesboro August 31-September 1. Bolensville September 3. Rome September 6. Reconnoissance from Rome on Cave Springs Road October 12-13. March to the sea November 15-December 10. Ball's Ferry, Oconee River, November 24-25. Waynesboro November 27-29. Briar Creek December 4. Little Ogeechee River December 4. Siege of Savannah December 10-21. Campaign of the Carolinas January to April, 1865. River's Bridge, S. C., February 7. Williston February 8. Near White Post February 8. Aiken February 11. Gunther's Bridge February 14. Rockingham, N. C., March 7. Monroe's Cross Roads March 10. Averysboro, Taylor's Hole Creek, March 16. Battle of Bentonville March 19-21. Faisson's Depot March 30-31. Roachland April 1. Mt. Pleasant April 11. Occupation of Raleigh April 13. Bennett's House April 26. Surrender of Johnston and his Army. Ordered to Dept. of the Cumberland May. Duty in

District of Northern Alabama and at Huntsville, Ala., till October. Mustered out October 20, 1865.

1st REGIMENT SIEGE ARTILLERY (AFRICAN DESCENT).

Organized at LaGrange, LaFayette and Memphis, Tenn., and Corinth, Miss., June 20, 1863. Attached to District of Corinth, 16th Army Corps, Dept. Tennessee, to November, 1863. Post of Corinth, 16th Army Corps, to January, 1864. Fort Pickering, District of Memphis, Tenn., 5th Division, 16th Army Corps, to April, 1864.

Served as Garrison at Corinth, Miss., till January, 1864, and at Fort Pickering, Memphis, Tenn., till March, 1864. 4 Cos. "A," "B," "C" and "D," Garrison at Fort Pillow, Tenn., and participated in the Massacre at that Post April 12, 1864.

Designation changed to 6th U. S. Colored Heavy Arty. March 11, 1864, and to 7th U. S. Colored Heavy Arty. April 26, 1864, which see.

1st REGIMENT INFANTRY (AFRICAN DESCENT).

Organized at Corinth, Miss., May 21, 1863. Attached to 2nd Division, 16th Army Corps, Dept. Tennessee, to November, 1863. Post of Corinth, Miss., 16th Army Corps, to January, 1864. 1st Colored Brigade, District of Memphis, 5th Division, 16th Army Corps, to March, 1864.

Served as Garrison at Corinth, Miss., till January, 1864, then on duty at Memphis, Tenn., till March, 1864.

Designation changed to 55th U. S. Colored Troops March 11, 1864, which see.

2nd REGIMENT INFANTRY (AFRICAN DESCENT).

Organized at Pulaski, Tenn., November 20, 1863. Attached to 2nd Division, 16th Army Corps, Dept. Tennessee, to January, 1864. Garrison at Pulaski, Tenn., Dept. of the Tennessee, to June, 1864.

Designation changed to 110th U. S. Colored Troops June 25, 1864, which see.

3rd REGIMENT INFANTRY (AFRICAN DESCENT).

Organized at Pulaski, Tenn., January 3, 1864. Attached to Garrison of Pulaski, Tenn., Dept. Tennessee, to June, 1864.

Garrison duty at Pulaski and Athens and as guard to Railroads in Northern Alabama till June, 1864.

Designation changed to 111th U. S. Colored Troops June 25, 1864, which see.

4th REGIMENT INFANTRY (AFRICAN DESCENT).

Organized at Decatur, Ala., March 31, 1864. Attached to Garrison at Pulaski, Tenn., to May, 1864. Designation changed to 106th U. S. Colored Troops May 16, 1864, which see.

ARKANSAS VOLUNTEERS.

1st REGIMENT CAVALRY.

Organized at Cassville and Springfield, Mo., June to August, 1862. Mustered in at Springfield, Mo., August 7, 1862. Attached to District of Southwest Missouri June to October, 1862. 1st Brigade, 3rd Division, Army of the Frontier, Dept. of Missouri, to December, 1862. Unattached Army of the Frontier, Dept. Missouri, to June, 1863. District Southwest Missouri, Dept. Missouri, to June, 1864. 3rd Brigade, Frontier Division, 7th Army Corps, Dept. of Arkansas, to February, 1865. 2nd Brigade, 3rd Division, 7th Army Corps, Dept. Arkansas, February, 1865. 1st Brigade, 3rd Division, 7th Army Corps, Dept. Arkansas, to August, 1865.

SERVICE.—Regiment organizing at Cassville, Mo., till July 1, 1862. Moved to Springfield, Mo., July 1. Schofield's Campaign in Missouri and Arkansas August to December. 1st Battalion with Gen. Blunt and engaged near Newtonia September 15. Skirmish at Cassville September 21. Near Newtonia October 13 (1st Battalion). 2nd Battalion joins Army of the Frontier

October 3. 1st and 2nd Battalions lead advance of Army during October. Stationed at Elkhorn Tavern and Cassville October 20 as outpost for 2nd and 3rd Divisions, Army Frontier. Huntsville November 5. Yocum Creek, Mo., November 15 (3 Cos.). 3rd Battalion join November 11 to December 3. Moved to join Gen. Blunt December 3-5. Illinois Creek December 7. Battle of Prairie Grove December 7. Middletown December 9. Expedition from Fayetteville to Huntsville, Ark., December 21-23. Duty at Fayetteville, Ark., to April 25, 1863. Defence of Springfield, Mo., January 8, 1863 (Detachment). Carrollton January 10. Expedition from Fayetteville to Van Buren January 23-27. Pope County January 25. Skirmishes at Vine Prairie, on White Oak River, and near mouth of Mulberry River, February 2-3. Skirmish, Pope County, February 5 (Detachment). Scout from Fayetteville to Arkansas River February 5-12. Threlkeld's Ferry February 6. Near Van Buren February 10. Arkadelphia February 15 (Detachment). White River March 6. Frog Bayou March 19. Washington and near White River March 22. Scouts from Fayetteville March 29-April 5. Cross Hollows March 30. Skirmishes in Carroll County, Mo., April 4 (Cos. "H" and "L"). White River April 9. Cabell's attack on Fayetteville April 18. Moved to Springfield, Mo., April 25-May 4. Elm Springs April 26. Duty at Springfield and Cassville till September, 1863. Skirmishes at Fayetteville June 4 and 15. Madison June 25. Near Cross Hollows July —. Cassville July 4. Near Elm Springs July 30. Pineville August 13. Washington August 30. Near Maysville September 5. Expedition from Springfield, Mo., into Arkansas and Indian Territory September 7-19. Near Enterprise September 15. Operations against Shelby's Raid into Arkansas and Missouri September 22-October 21. Reoccupation of Fayetteville September 22, and stationed there till February, 1865. Cassville, Mo., September 26, 1863. Demonstration on Fayetteville October 11-14. Cross Timbers October 15. Deer Creek October 16 (Detachment). Buffalo Mountain and Harrisonville October 24. Johnson County, Ark., October 26. Expedition to Frog Bayou, Ark., November 7-13. Near Huntsville November 9. Near Kingston November 10. Mt. Ida November 12. Scout from Fayetteville Dec. 16-31. Stroud's Store December 23. Buffalo River December 25. Searcy County December 31. Operations in Northwest Arkansas, Newton, Searcy, Izzard and Carroll Counties, against guerrillas January 16-February 15, 1864. Clear Creek and Tomahawk January 22. Bailey's Crooked Creek January 23. Rolling Prairie and near Burrowsville January 23. Crooked Creek February 5. White River February 7. Expedition against Freeman's Forces February 12-20. Black's Mills February 17. Carrollton March 13. Ben Brook's Mills March 27. Charlestown April 4. Skirmishes on Arkansas River and near Prairie Grove April 6-7. Rhea's Mills April 7. Washington May 28. Van Buren July 7. Operations in Central Arkansas August 9-15. Fayetteville August 14. Operations in Southwest Missouri and Northwest Arkansas August 15-24. Carrollton August 15. Richland Creek August 16. Expedition in Washington and Benton Counties August 21-27. Mud Town August 24. Fayetteville August 27. Richland September 6. Scout from Fayetteville to Huntsville September 12-15. Rodger's Crossing of White River and Huntsville September 14. Huntsville September 18 (Detachment). Skirmishes, Barry County, October 8 and 18. Fayetteville October 14. Crawford County October 19. Benton County October 20. Fayetteville and Van Buren October 20. Operations about Fayetteville October 25-November 4. Skirmishes at Bentonville and Newbeon Bridge October 25. Van Buren October 26. Fayetteville October 27-28. Duty about Fayetteville and at Fort Smith till August, 1865. Skirmish near Van Buren April 2, 1865. Mustered out August 20, 1865.

2d REGIMENT CAVALRY.

Organized at Helena, Ark., and Pilot Knob, Mo., July, 1862. Attached to Helena, Ark., District Southwest Missouri, Dept. Missouri, to December, 1862. 2nd Brigade, 3rd Cavalry Division, District Eastern Arkansas, to January, 1863. 2nd Brigade, 2nd Cavalry Division, 13th Army Corps, Dept. Tennessee, to April, 1863. 2nd Brigade, Cavalry Division, District of Eastern Arkansas, Dept. Tennessee, to May, 1863. District of Southwest Missouri, Dept. Missouri, to October, 1864. 3rd Brigade, Cavalry Division, Dept. Missouri, to January, 1865. Unattached Cavalry, District West Tennessee, to February, 1865. 1st Brigade, Cavalry Division, District West Tennessee, to August, 1865.

SERVICE.—Duty at Helena, Ark., till April, 1863. At Fayetteville, Ark., till July, 1863, and at Cassville, Mo., till September, 1864. (Co. "B" at Benton Barracks, Mo., June, 1863. At Cape Girardeau, Mo., July, 1863. Scout from Cape Girardeau to the Ash Hills and Poplar Bluff, Mo., August 9-18. Skirmish, Ash Hills, August 13. Expedition from Cape Girardeau to Pocahontas, Ark., August 18-26. Skirmishes, Pocahontas, August 22-23.) Elm Springs July 30. Near Fayette August 23 (Detachment). Jenny Lind September 1. Crawford County November 25. Barronsville, Searcy County, December 26. Waldron December 29. King's River January 10, 1864. Operations against Guerrillas in Northwest Arkansas, in Newton, Searcy, Izzard and Carroll Counties, January 16-February 15. Lewisburg January 17. Clear Creek and Tomahawk January 22. Bailey's or Crooked Creek January 23 (Co. "C"). Crooked Creek February 5. Tomahaw Gap February 9. Expedition from Rolling Prairie to Batesville February 19-April 4. Scouts from Yellville to Buffalo River March 13-26. Oil Trough Bottom March 24 (Detachment). Near White River March 25. Constant scouting and skirmishing with Guerrillas. Scouts from Bellefonte March 29-April 1. Whiteley's Mills April 5. Piney Mountain April 6. Osage Branch King's River April 16 (Co. "A"). Limestone Valley April 17. King's River April 19. Near mouth of Richland Creek May 3 and 5. Scout in Northern Arkansas May 17-22 (Co. "M"). Scout from Cassville to Cross Hollows June 9-14 and June 20-24. Near Maysville July 20. Operations in Southwest Missouri and Northwest Arkansas August 15-24. Scout from Ozark, Mo., to Dubuque Crossing and Sugar Loaf Prairie August 23-26 (Detachment). Expedition from Cassville, Mo., to Fayetteville, Ark., August 23-28 (Detachment). Gerald Mountain and Mud Town August 24. Operations against Price August 29-December 2. Moreau Creek, Jefferson City, October 7. Russellville October 9. California October 9. Near Booneville October 11-12. Fort Smith, Ark., October 14 (Detachment). Dover October 20. Little Blue October 21. Independence, Big Blue and State Line October 22. Big Blue and Westport October 23. Little Osage, Mine Creek, Marias des Cygnes, October 25. Engagement on the Marmiton, or Battle of Charlot, October 25. Newtonia October 28. Upshaw's Farm October 29. Expedition from Springfield, Mo., to Fort Smith, Ark., November 5-16. Near Cincinnati, Ark., November 6. Scout from Springfield to Huntsville and Yellville November 11-21. Ordered to Memphis, Tenn., January, 1865. Duty there and in District of West Tennessee till August. Mustered out August 20, 1865.

3rd REGIMENT CAVALRY.

Organized at Little Rock, Ark., February, 1864. Attached to Post of Little Rock, Ark., 7th Army Corps, Dept. Arkansas, to May, 1864. 3rd Brigade, 2nd Division, 7th Army Corps, to September, 1864. 4th Brigade, Cavalry Division, 7th Army Corps, to February, 1865. Post of Lewisburg, Ark., 7th Army Corps, to August, 1865.

SERVICE.—Operations in Northwest Arkansas January 16-February 15, 1864. Expedition from Batesville to near Searcy Landing January 30-February 3 (Detachment). Dardanelle March 15-17. Steele's Camden Expedition March 23-May 3. Skirmishes on Benton Road March 23-24. Rockport and Dover March 25. Quitman March 26. Arkadelphia March 29. Near Camden March 30. Spoonville and Terre Noir Creek April 2. Okolona

April 2-3. Elkin's Ferry, Little Missouri River, April 3-4. Prairie D'Ann April 9-12. Camden April 15-18. Mark's Mills April 25. Jenkins' Ferry, Saline River, April 30. Operations against Shelby North of Arkansas River May 13-31. Cypress Creek May 13. Princeton May 27. At Lewisburg till September. Lewisburg June 10. Scout from Lewisburg June 20-23. Operations against Guerrillas in Arkansas July 1-31. Searcy County July 4. Petit Jean, Arkansas River, July 10. Near Pine Bluff July 22 (Detachment). Scout in Yell County July 25-August 11 (Detachment). Operations in Central Arkansas and Skirmishes August 9-15. Near Dardanelle August 30. Near Beattie's Mill September 1. Near Quitman September 2. Operations about Lewisburg September 6-8. Norristown September 6. Point Remove September 7-8. Glass Village September 8. Scout to Norristown and Russellville September 9-12 (Co. "D"). Ordered to Little Rock September 10, and duty there till February, 1865. Expedition from Little Rock to Fort Smith September 25-October 13 (Detachment). Skirmishes at Clarksville September 28. White Oak Creek September 29. Clarksville October 9. Reconnoissance from Little Rock toward Monticello and Mt. Elba October 4-11. Expedition to Fort Smith November 5-23. Near Cypress Creek, Perry County, December 1 (Co. "C"). Perry County December 3. Operations in Arkansas January 1-27, 1865. Dardanelle January 14. Ivey's Ford January 17. Boggs' Mills January 24. Duty at Lewisburg and operations against Guerrillas in that vicinity till August. Near Lewisburg February 12. Scout from Lewisburg into Yell and Searcy Counties March 12-23. Mustered out August 20, 1865.

4th REGIMENT CAVALRY.

Organized at Little Rock December, 1863. Attached to Post of Little Rock, Ark., 7th Army Corps, Dept. of Arkansas, to May, 1864. 3rd Brigade, 1st Division, 7th Army Corps, Dept. of Ark., to September, 1864. 2nd Brigade, Cavalry Division, 7th Army Corps, to February, 1865. Unassigned, 7th Army Corps, to March, 1865. Cavalry Brigade, Little Rock, Ark., 7th Corps, to June, 1865.

SERVICE.—Duty at Little Rock, Ark., till June, 1865. Skirmish at Saline River, Ark., February 15, 1864. Cedar Glade March 1. Scout to Benton March 27-31. Mt. Elba March 30. Jenkins' Ferry, Camden, April 15. Dardanelle May 15-17. Operations in Arkansas against Guerrillas July 1-31. Near Benton July 6. Montgomery County July 11. Caddo Gap July 12. Fair's Mills and Bayou des Arc July 14. Saline River July 16. Scout to Benton September 6-7. Reconnoissance toward Monticello and Mt. Elba October 4-11. Reconnoissance to Princeton October 19-23. Skirmish, Hurricane Creek, October 23. Scout from Devall's Bluff to Searcy and Clinton November 9-15. Expedition from Little Rock to Fort Smith September 25-October 13. Skirmishes at Clarksville September 28 and October 9. White Oak Creek September 29. Scout from Little Rock to the Saline River April 26-29, 1865. Scout from Little Rock to Bayou Metoe and Little Bayou May 6-11. Mustered out June 30, 1865.

1st BATTERY LIGHT ARTILLERY.

Organized at Fayetteville, Ark., and Springfield, Mo., January to August, 1863. At Fayetteville, Ark., January to April, 1863. Moved to Springfield, Mo., April 25-May 4, and duty there till September 21. Expedition from Springfield into Arkansas and Indian Territory September 7-19. Near Enterprise, Mo., September 15. Moved to Fayetteville, Ark., September 21, and duty there till March, 1864. Attached to District of Southwest Missouri, Dept. Missouri, to March, 1864. 2nd Brigade, District of the Frontier, 7th Army Corps, Dept. of Arkansas, to January, 1865. Artillery, 3rd Division, 7th Army Corps, to February, 1865. 1st Brigade, 3rd Division, 7th Army Corps, to August, 1865.

SERVICE.—Actions at Cross Timbers, Mo., October 15 and 20, 1863. Moved to Fort Smith, Ark., March 19, 1864. Steele's Expedition to Camden March 23-May 3. Prairie D'Ann April 9-13. Van Buren April 12. Camden April 15. Poison Springs April 18. Jenkins' Ferry, Saline River, April 30. March to Fort Smith May 3-16. Garrison duty there and at Fort Gibson till August, 1865. Action at Prior Creek September 18, 1864. Mustered out August 10, 1864.

1st BATTERY LIGHT ARTILLERY (AFRICAN DESCENT).

Organized at Pine Bluff, Ark., June 4, 1864. Garrison duty at Pine Bluff, Ark. 7th Army Corps, Dept. of Arkansas, till December, 1864. Designation changed to Battery "H," 2nd U. S. Colored Light Artillery, December 13, 1864, which see.

1st REGIMENT INFANTRY.

Organized at Fayetteville, Ark., and mustered in March 25, 1863. Attached to District Southwest Missouri, Dept. Missouri, to December, 1863. 2nd Brigade, District of the Frontier, Dept. Missouri, to January, 1864. 2nd Brigade, District of the Frontier, 7th Army Corps, Dept. of Arkansas, to March, 1864. 1st Brigade, District of the Frontier, 7th Army Corps, to February, 1865. 1st Brigade, 3rd Division, 7th Army Corps, to August, 1865.

SERVICE.—Duty at Fayetteville, Ark., till April, 1863. Cabell's attack on Fayetteville April 18. March to Springfield, Mo., April 25-May 4, and duty there till July. Newton County June 14. Moved to Cassville July 6. Joined Army of the Frontier at Fort Gibson, C. N., August 17. Pursuit of Cabell to Perryville August 22-26. Perryville August 26. Devil's Back Bone, Back Bone Mountain, Fort Smith, September 1. Capture of Fort Smith September 1, and duty there till March, 1864. Moffatt's Station, Franklin County, September 27, 1863. Mt. Ida November 13. Scout from Waldron to Mt. Ida, Caddo Gap and Dallas December 2-7. Steele's Expedition to Camden March 23-May 3. Prairie D'Ann April 9-13. Moscow April 13. Camden April 15-18. Jenkins' Ferry, Saline River, April 30. March to Fort Smith May 1-16. Garrison duty at Fort Smith and escort and duty on the Frontier till August, 1865. Skirmish, Bates Township, November 2, and Newton County, November 15, 1864. Mustered out August 10, 1865.

1st BATTALION INFANTRY.

Organized at Helena, Ark., July 20, 1862. Attached to District of Eastern Arkansas and duty at Helena, Ark., till October. Moved to St. Louis, Mo., and duty at Benton Barracks, Mo., till December. Mustered out December 31, 1862.

1st REGIMENT INFANTRY (AFRICAN DESCENT).

Organized in Arkansas at large May 1, 1863. Attached to Post of Goodrich Landing, District of Northeast Louisiana, Dept. Tennessee, to January, 1864. 1st Colored Brigade, District of Vicksburg, Miss., to May, 1864.

SERVICE.—Moved to Lake Providence, La., May 8-10, 1863, thence to Goodrich Landing and Post duty there till January, 1864. Skirmish at Mound Plantation June 24, 1863. Lake Providence and Mound Plantation June 28. Action at Goodrich Landing June 29. Duty at Haines Bluff, District of Vicksburg, till May, 1864.

Designation of Regiment changed to 46th U. S. Colored Troops May 11, 1864, which see.

2nd REGIMENT INFANTRY.

Organized at Springfield, Mo., and Fort Smith, Ark., October, 1863, to March, 1864. Organization completed at Fort Smith March 13, 1864. Attached to District of the Frontier, Dept. of Missouri, to January, 1864. District of the Frontier, 7th Army Corps, Dept. of Arkansas, January, 1864. 2nd Brigade, District of the Frontier, 7th Army Corps, to March, 1864. 1st Brigade, District of the Frontier, 7th Corps, to May, 1864. 2nd Brigade, 2nd Division, 7th Corps, to December, 1864. 1st Brigade, District of the Frontier, 7th Corps, to February, 1865. 1st Brigade, 3rd Division, 7th Corps, to August, 1865.

SERVICE.—Skirmish at Clarksville December 15, 1863. Affair at Jacksonport, Ark., November 21, 1863.

At Fort Smith till March, 1864. Steele's Expedition to Camden March 23-May 3. Prairie D'Ann April 9-12. Moscow April 13. Limestone Valley April 17 (Detachment). Jenkins' Ferry, Saline River, April 30. Duty at Little Rock till July and at Lewisburg till September. Ordered to Little Rock September 10, and duty there till October 18. Escort train to Fort Smith October-November. Moved to Clarksville December 31, and duty there and at Fort Smith till August. Mustered out August 8, 1865.

2nd REGIMENT INFANTRY (AFRICAN DESCENT).

Organized in Arkansas at large September 4, 1863. Attached to District Eastern Arkansas, Dept. Arkansas, to January, 1864. District Eastern Arkansas, 7th Army Corps, Dept. Arkansas, January, 1864. Post of Little Rock, Ark., 7th Corps, to March, 1864.

SERVICE.—Post and Garrison duty at Helena, Ark., till January, 1864. Repulse of Holmes' attack on Helena July 4, 1863 (before muster in). Ordered to Little Rock, Ark., January, 1864, and Post duty there till March.

Designation of Regiment changed to 54th U. S. Colored Troops March 11, 1864, which see.

3rd REGIMENT INFANTRY.

Organization not completed.

3rd REGIMENT INFANTRY (AFRICAN DESCENT).

Organized at St. Louis, Mo., August 12, 1863. Attached to District of Eastern Arkansas, Dept. Arkansas, to January, 1864. Little Rock, Ark., 7th Army Corps, Dept. Ark., to March, 1864.

SERVICE.—Ordered to Helena, Ark., and Post duty there and at Little Rock till March, 1864. Expedition from Helena up White River February 4-8, 1864, and up St. Francis River February 13-14.

Designation of Regiment changed to 56th U. S. Colored Troops March 11, 1864, which see.

4th REGIMENT INFANTRY.

Organized at Batesville and Fort Smith, Ark., January to May, 1864. Attached to District of Northeast Arkansas, Dept. of Arkansas, to June, 1864. District of the Frontier, 7th Army Corps, to October, 1864.

SERVICE.—Operations in Northeast Arkansas January 1-30, 1864. Lunenburg January 19 (Detachment). Morgan's Mills, Spring River, White County, February 9. Waugh's Farm, near Batesville, February 19. Scout from Batesville February 25. At Clarksville till May 18. Moved to Fort Smith May 18, and duty there till July 21. Moved to Little Rock July 21, and duty there till October. Organization not completed and Regiment transferred to 2nd Arkansas Infantry October 28, 1864.

4th REGIMENT INFANTRY (AFRICAN DESCENT).

Organized at Devall's Bluff, Little Rock and Helena, Ark., December 2, 1863. Attached to District of Eastern Arkansas, 7th Corps, Dept. of Arkansas, to March, 1864, and on duty at Helena.

Designation of Regiment changed to 57th U. S. Colored Troops March 11, 1864, which see.

5th REGIMENT INFANTRY (AFRICAN DESCENT).

(See 112th U. S. C. T.)

6th REGIMENT INFANTRY (AFRICAN DESCENT).

(See 113th U. S. C. T.)

CALIFORNIA VOLUNTEERS.

1st REGIMENT CAVALRY.

Organized as a Battalion of 5 Companies at Camp Merchant, near Oakland, Cali., and mustered in as follows: Co. "A," August 16; Co. "B," October 31; Co. "C," October 31; Co. "D," September 9, and Co. "E," August 15, 1861. 7 new Companies organized and mustered in as follows: Co. "F," December 15; Co. "G," June 13; Co. "H," December 31; Co. "I," November 12; Co. "K," May 16; Co. "L," August 15, and Co. "M," May 16, 1863.

SERVICE.—Companies "A," "B," "C," "D," "E" moved to Southern California and duty at Los Angeles (3

Cos.) and at San Bernardino (2 Cos.) till March, 1862. Pursuit and capture of Showalter's party at Warner's Ranch, near San Jose Valley, November 20-29, 1861 (Detachment). Attached to Carlton's California Column, organized for an Expedition to recapture the Forts and Posts in Arizona and New Mexico, March, 1862. March to Stanwix Rancho, Arizona, March 1-16. Carlton's Expedition through Arizona to Northwest Texas and Indian Territory April 8-September 20. Led advance guard of the Column on its march across the Yuma and Colorado Deserts to the Rio Grande River. March to Picacho Pass April 8-15. Action at Picacho Pass April 15. March to Pimos Villages April 16-24. Expedition to Kenyon Station April 26-29. Duty at Pimos Villages till May 15. March to Tucson May 15-20. Occupation of Tucson May 20. Reoccupation of Fort Breckenridge, afterwards Fort Stanford, at Junction of the Gila and San Pedro Rivers, May 24, and duty there till June 17. Moved to Tucson, thence to Fort Thorne, Arizona, on the Rio Grande River, June 21-July 6. Reoccupation of Fort Thorne July 6. Expedition for the reoccupation of Mesilla, Fort Fillmore and Fort Bliss July 15-19. At Las Cruces till August 16. Expedition to Fort Bliss and Fort Quitman August 16-22. At Camp Johnson, Texas, till October. Affair at San Pedro Crossing, Arizona, September 21 (Detachment). At Mesilla, Arizona, till January, 1863. Expedition against Apache Indians November 15-December 31, 1862. White Mountains November 15. At Fort West, Dept. of New Mexico, till September, 1863. Skirmish at Bonito Rio, N. Mex., March 27 (Cos. "A," "B" and "L"). Skirmish near Fort Bowie, Arizona, April 25 (Detachment). Operations against Navajo Indians in New Mexico August 20-December 16, 1863. Skirmish at San Pedro Crossing, Arizona, August 22. Fort Bowie, Arizona, August 27 (Co. "E"). Duty at Las Cruces, N. Mex., till December, 1863. Companies scattered at various points and Posts in Districts of Arizona and California and Depts. of New Mexico and the Pacific till September, 1866. Skirmish at Oregon Mountains, Ore., January 28, 1864 (Co. "D"). Skirmish at Foot of Sierra Bonito, N. Mex. (Co. "C"). Doubtful Canon, N. Mex., May 4 (Co. "I"). Spencer's Ranch, near Presidio del Norte, N. Mex., May 15 (Co. "A"). Expedition from Fort Craig, N. Mex., to Fort Goodwin, Arizona, May 16-August 2. Expedition to Gila River May 25-July 13 (Cos. "C," "F" and "L"). Scout in Southeast Arizona July 6-24 (Co. "C"). Croton Springs, Arizona, July 14 (Co. "L"). Expedition to Pinal Mountains, Arizona, July 18-August 17 (Co. "E"). Company "I" at Fort Goodwin, Arizona, July, 1864, to November, 1865, and at Fort McDowell till April, 1866. Expedition to Southwest New Mexico July 23-October 10, 1864 (Co. "C"). Expedition from Fort Craig to Fort Goodwin, Arizona, October 1-November 27, 1864. St. Vrain's Old Fort, Canadian River, November 25, 1864 (Cos. "B," "K" and "M"). Fort Buchanan, Arizona, February 17, 1865. Scout from Fort Sumner May 10-19, 1865. Scout from Camp Nichols June 13-17, 1865 (Co. "F"). Skirmish, Santa Fe Road, N. Mex., June 14 (Co. "F"). Scout from Fort Sumner to Oscura Mountains June 15-22 (Detachment). Scout from Fort Bowie to Gila River, Arizona, June 26-July 6 (Cos. "F," "L" and "M"). Sacramento Mountains, N. Mex., July 1 (Cos. "G" and "H"). Cottonwood Creek July 3 (Cos. "F," "L" and "M"). Cavalry Canon July 4 (Cos. "F," "L" and "M"). Expedition from Fort Bowie to Maricopa Wells July 10-21 (Detachment). La Monica Springs, N. Mex., September 4, 1865 (Cos. "G" and "H"). Company "L" stationed at Camp Union, Cali., October, 1863, to January, 1864; Drum Barracks, Cali., February and March, 1864; Riventon, Arizona, April and May, 1864; Tubac, Arizona, to June, 1865; Fort Bowie, Arizona, to February, 1866; Fort McDowell, February, 1866. Regiment mustered out March 6 to October 19, 1866.

1st BATTALION CAVALRY.

Organized at large in California March, 1863, to July, 1864. Attached to Dept. of the Pacific. Company "A" at Presidio, San Francisco, to December, 1863. Ordered to District of Humboldt December 26. Arrive there January 12, 1864. Duty at Fort Gaston till March 6. Ordered to Camp Curtis March 6, and duty escorting trains to Arcate and Fort Humboldt to September 1, 1864. Ordered to Fort Humboldt September 1 and duty there till November 12, 1864. Ordered to Camp Wright and duty there till February, 1865. Ordered to Drum Barracks, District of Southern California, February 25, 1865, and duty there till May, 1865.

Company "B" on duty at the Presidio, San Francisco, till January, 1865. Ordered to San Juan, Monterey County, January 3, 1865, thence to Drum Barracks, District of Southern California, and duty there till May. Company "C" organized at Santa Barbara and ordered to Drum Barracks, District of Southern California, August 10, 1864, and duty there till May, 1865. Company "D" at Drum Barracks, District of Southern California, till May, 1865. Battalion assigned to duty in District of Arizona May, 1865, and operating against Indians in that District till April, 1866. Mustered out April 2, 1866.

2nd REGIMENT CAVALRY.

Organized at San Francisco September 5 to October 18, 1861. Company "A"—Ordered to Fort Churchill October 22, 1861, and duty there till July, 1862. March via Ruby Valley to Utah to protect Overland mail routes July to November, 1862. Duty in District of Utah at Camp Douglass and other points till November, 1864. Expedition from Camp Douglass to Cache Valley November 20-27, 1862. Skirmish at Cache Valley November 23, 1862. Engagement on Bear River, Utah, January 29, 1863. Expedition from Camp Douglass to Cedar Mountains, Utah, March 20-April 3. Skirmish, Cedar Fort, April 1. Expedition from Camp Douglass to Spanish Forks, Utah, April 11-20, 1863. Skirmish at Spanish Fork Canon April 15. Ordered to Camp Union, Sacramento, November, 1864. Duty there and in Districts of California and Nevada till muster out.

Company "B"—Moved to Southern California December, 1861. Duty at Los Angeles till March, 1862. Attached to Carlton's California Column on Expedition from Southern California through Arizona to Southwest Texas and New Mexico April 9-September 20, 1862. Occupation of Fort Quitman August 22. Duty at various points in Dept. of New Mexico till July, 1864. Operations against Navajo Indians in New Mexico August 20-December 16, 1863. Action at Pecos River, near Fort Sumner, January 5, 1864. Patrol Mojave Road between Camp Cady and Rock Springs, Southern California, July to September, 1864. Ordered to San Francisco September 26, thence to Camp Union, Sacramento, Cali., November 12. Duty in District of California and Nevada till mustered out. Expedition from Dun Glen to Fairbanks Station, Nev., June 13-26, 1865.

Company "C"—Ordered to Fort Creek October 22, 1861, and duty there till muster out. Expedition to Honey Lake Valley November 3-29, 1862.

Company "D"—Ordered to Los Angeles, Cali., December 28, 1861, and duty there till March, 1862. Ordered to Camp Latham March 10, 1862. Expedition to Owens River, Cali., March 19-April 28. Skirmish near Bishop's Creek, Owens River Valley, April 9. Expedition from Camp Latham to Owens River June 11-October 8, 1862. Skirmish, Owens Lake, June 24. Moved to Visalia September 29-October 7. At Camp Babbett, near Visalia, and Camp Independence, Cali., to July, 1863. Expedition to Keyesville April 12-24, 1863. Operations in Owens River Valley April 24-May 26. Moved to Fort Tejon, Cali., July 6-August 17. Ordered to Camp Union, Sacramento, Cali., January 6, 1864. At Drum Barracks June to December, 1864. At Camp Union, Sacramento, December, 1864, to June, 1865. Ordered to Calusa, Cali. Duty there and in District of California and Arizona till muster out.

Company "E"—Ordered to Fort Humboldt December, 1861. Operations in Humboldt District March 22-August 31, 1862. Skirmishes at Daley's Ferry and on Mad River June 6-7. Cutterback's House, on Van Dusen Creek, July 2. Ordered to San Francisco September, 1862, thence to Visalia December 29, 1862, and to Camp Independence, Owens River, March 11, 1863. Operations in Owens River Valley April 24-May 26. Moved to Fort Tejon, Cali., July 6-August 17, 1863, thence to Camp Babbitt, near Visalia, August 18-September 12. Expedition from Camp Babbitt to Keyesville April 23-24, 1864. Duty in District of California till muster out.

Company "F"—Ordered from San Francisco to Camp Union, Sacramento, December 6, 1862. Duty there and at Camp Bidwell till June, 1865. Skirmish on Eel River, near Fort Baker, April 26, 1862, and at Arcata, near Light Prairie, May 21, 1862. Ordered to Fort Crook June, 1865, and duty there and in the District of California and Nevada till muster out.

Company "G"—Ordered to Los Angeles December 28, 1861. Expedition from Camp Latham to Owens River, Cali., March 19-April 28, 1862. Skirmish at Bishop's Creek, Owens River Valley, April 9. Expedition from Camp Latham to Owens River June 11-October 8, 1862. Skirmish at Owens Lake June 24. At Camp Independence till July, 1863. Moved to Fort Tejon, Cali., July 6-August 17, and to Camp Babbitt December, 1863. Duty there till August, 1864. Ordered to Camp Union, Sacramento, August 18, 1864. Duty there and in the District of California till muster out.

Company "H"—Ordered to Fort Churchill October 22, 1861. Duty there till July, 1862. March via Ruby Valley to Utah to protect Overland mail route July to November, 1862. Expedition from Fort Ruby, Nev., to Camp Douglass, Utah, September 30-October 29. Affairs on Humboldt River October 11 and 15, 1862. Expedition from Camp Douglass to Cache Valley November 20-27, 1862. Skirmish at Cache Valley November 23. Engagement on Bear River, Utah, January 29, 1863. Expedition from Camp Douglass to Spanish Fork April 11-20. Spanish Fork Canon April 15. Duty in District of Utah till December, 1864. Expedition from Camp Douglass to Soda Springs, on Bear River, Idaho, May 5-30, 1863. At Camp Union, Sacramento, and in District of California from December, 1864, to muster out.

Company "I"—Ordered to Los Angeles, Cali., December 28, 1861. Expedition from Camp Latham to Antelope Creek April 5-18, 1862 (Detachment). Expedition from Camp Latham to Owens River, Cali., March 19-April 28, 1862. Skirmish, Bishop's Creek, Owens River Valley, April 9. Expedition from Camp Latham to Owens River June 11-October 8. Owens Lake June 24. Moved to Visalia September 29-October 9. At Camp Babbitt, near Visalia, till January, 1864. Ordered to Benicia Barracks January 6, 1864, thence to Camp Union, Sacramento, May 9. Moved to Chico, Cali., June 28-July 18. Duty there and at Camp Bidwell and in District of California till muster out.

Company "K"—Ordered to Utah July 5, 1862. March via Fort Churchill and Ruby Valley to Utah to protect Overland mail route July to November, 1862. Expedition from Fort Ruby, Nev., to Camp Douglass, Utah, September 30-October 29. Affairs on Humboldt River October 11 and 15. Expedition from Camp Douglass to Cache Valley November 20-27, 1862. Cache Valley November 23. Engagement on Bear River, Utah, January 29, 1863. At Fort Ruby and in District of Utah till December, 1864. At Camp Union, Sacramento, till May, 1865. Ordered to Fort Creek May 26, and duty there and in District of California till muster out.

Company "L"—At Fort Churchill December, 1862, to May, 1863. Ordered to Camp Independence May 21, 1863. At Fort Churchill and Fort Bridger till May, 1865. Moved to Fort Laramie, Dakota. Skirmish at Dead Man's Fork June 17. Powder River Expedition July to September, 1865. Garrison duty in District of Utah till muster out.

Company "M"—Ordered to Carson City, Nev., May, 1862. March via Fort Churchill and Ruby Valley to Utah to protect Overland mail route July to September, 1862. Expedition from Fort Ruby to Camp Douglass, Utah, September 30-October 29. Expedition from Camp

Douglass to Cache Valley November 20-27, 1862. Cache Valley November 23. Engagement on Bear River January 29, 1863. Expedition from Camp Douglass to Spanish Fork April 2-6. Action at Spanish Fork Canon April 4. Duty at Camp Douglass, Fort Bridger and Camp Connor till May, 1865. Moved to Fort Laramie, Dakota, May, 1865. Dead Man's Fork, Dakota, June 17. On Powder River Expedition July to September and garrison duty in Utah till muster out.

Mustered out July 12, 1866.

1st REGIMENT INFANTRY.

Organized at large August to October, 1861. Company "K" organized February 12, 1862. Attached to Depts. of the Pacific and New Mexico.

SERVICE.—In camp at Oakland till October, 1861, and near Los Angeles, Cali., till December, 1861. Pursuit and capture of Showalter's party at Warner's Ranch, San Jose Valley, November 20-29, 1861 (Cos. "F" and "G"). Moved to Fort Yuma December, 1861, and duty there till April, 1862 (Cos. "B," "D," "F," "H" and "I"). Company "D" at San Diego. Companies "A' and "C" at Camp Latham. Carleton's Expedition from Southern California through Arizona to Northwest Texas and New Mexico April 10-September 20, 1862. March from Fort Yuma to Pinos Villages, thence to Tucson, April 10-May 20. Expedition up the Gila River and engagement at Pechecho Pass April 15 (Co. "I"). March from Tucson, Ariz., across Desert to the Rio Grande River July 20-August 15. At La Mesilla till December 25. Moved to Fort Craig December 25-30. Duty by detachments at posts in New Mexico and Arizona, Las Cruces, Los Pinos, Franklin, Texas; Forts West, Craig, Selden, Union, Cummings, McRae, Whipple and Sumner, and operating against Indians in the Districts of New Mexico, Arizona and Utah, till October, 1866. Skirmish at Pinos Altas Mines January 29, 1863 (1 Co.). Company "G" at Camp Wright, Cali., January 1 to March 9, 1862. Moved to Fort Yuma and duty there till July 19. Moved to Tucson, Ariz., and duty there till December 2. At Messilla till April 20, 1863. At Franklin, Texas, till June 26. March to Fort McRae June 26-July 3. Rio de los Animos July 19. Expedition to Alamcito Mountains against Indians August 9-20, 1863. Expedition to Jornado del Muerta August 9-20, 1863. Expedition to Jornado del Muerta August 26-29. Operations against Navajo Indians August 20-December 16, 1863. Scout from Fort Wingate to Ojo Redendo September 15-October 5 (2 Cos.). Expedition against Indians in New Mexico November 5-15 and December 5-7, 1863. Scout in Southeastern Arizona July 6-24, 1864 (Co. "D"). Expedition from Fort Union August 4-September 15 (Detachment). Affair, San Andreas Mountains, August 12 (Detachment). Scout in Cimarron River, Northeast N. Mex., September 18-October 5. Engagement with Indians at Adobe Fort, on Canadian River, N. Mex., November 25 (Cos. "A" and "K"). Scout from Fort Cummings April 28-May 13, 1865 (Co. "G"). Duty in Districts of New Mexico, Arizona and Utah till October, 1866. Mustered out October 21, 1866.

1st BATTALION MOUNTAINEERS.

Organized at large May 30, 1863, to March 16, 1864, for special service in Humboldt County. Attached to Humboldt District, Dept. of the Pacific.

SERVICE.—Company "A"—Ordered to Fort Humboldt June, 1863. Stationed at Fort Humboldt, Fort Bager and Camps Curtis and Iaquia. Skirmish, Redwood Creek, February 29, 1864. Redwood Mountains March 1. Kneeland's Prairie May 1. Operations in Humboldt District till June, 1865.

Company "B"—Ordered to Fort Gaston. Duty there and at Camps Anderson and Curtis till June, 1865. Skirmish at Oak Camp June 6, 1863. Thomas' Ranch November 12. Trinity River November 13. Willow Creek November 17. Near Fort Gaston December 25-26. Skirmish near Boynton's Prairie May 6, 1864.

Scout from Camp Anderson to Bald Mountain August 8-12.

Company "C"—Ordered to Fort Gaston June, 1863. Duty there operating against Indians in Humboldt District till June, 1865. Redwood Creek July 9 and 11, 1863. Thomas' Ranch November 11. Trinity River November 13. Near Fort Gaston December 25-26. Thomas House, on Trinity River, May 27, 1864. Operations in Trinity Valley September 1-December 3, 1864.

Company "D"—Duty at Fort Gaston till June, 1865.

Company "E"—Duty at Camp Grant till June, 1865. Skirmish at Grouse Creek May 23, 1864. Matole May 26. Big Flat May 28. Expedition to North Fork Eel River September 1-29.

Battalion mustered out June 14, 1865.

2nd REGIMENT INFANTRY.

Organized at San Francisco and Carson City September 2, 1861, to December 30, 1862. Attached to Dept. of the Pacific.

SERVICE.—Companies "A," "B," "C," "D" and "E" ordered to District of Oregon October 17, 1861. Company "A"—At Fort Dalles, Ore., till March, 1862. At Fork Vancouver till May, 1862. At Fort Humboldt, Camp Lyon and Camp Wright till June, 1863. Skirmishes at Eel River March 21 and 24. Ordered to Benicia Barracks June 27, thence to Old Fort Miller August 11, and duty there till December, 1864. At Presidio till muster out.

Company "B"—At Fort Hoskins till March, 1862. At Fort Dalles till June, 1862. Ordered to Fort Vancouver June 27, thence to Fort Humboldt July, and duty there till June, 1863. Ordered to Benicia Barracks June 11, 1863, and duty there till December. Moved to Fort Tejon, Cali., and duty there till September, 1864. Ordered to San Francisco and duty at the Presidio till muster out.

Company "C"—At Fort Colville, Washington Territory, till June, 1862. Ordered to Humboldt District, Cali., and duty there till September, 1864. Ordered to San Francisco and duty at the Presidio till muster out.

Company "D"—At Fort Colville, Washington Territory, till June, 1862. Ordered to Humboldt District, Cali., and duty at Fort Bragg till December, 1863. Expedition to Keytesville April 12-24, 1863. Ordered to Camp Babbitt December, 1863. Operations in Humboldt District February 1 to June 30, 1864. Skirmish, Red Mountain, near Blue Rock Station, March 17. Eel River March 19. Bald Spring Canon March 22. On Eel River March 27. Big Bend, Eel River, April 28. Shelter Cove May 9. Ordered to San Francisco December, 1864, and duty at the Presidio till muster out.

Company "E"—At Fort Vancouver till May, 1862. At Fort Humboldt till December, 1862. Skirmish at Mad River May 14, 1862. Daly's Farm, Mad River, near Arcate, June 6-7, 1862. Mattole Valley June 7, 1862. Fawn Prairie, near Liscombe Hill, June 8, 1862. At Camp Curtis December, 1862, to June, 1863. Ordered to Benicia Barracks and duty there till December. Ordered to Humboldt District December, 1863, and duty there till December, 1864. Ordered to San Francisco and duty at the Presidio till muster out.

Company "F"—At San Francisco till December, 1861. Ordered to Fort Humboldt. Duty there and at Camps Anderson and Wright till June, 1865. Attack on Whitney's Ranch July 28, 1862. Alber's Ranch January 29. Crogan's Ranch May 7, 1862. Skirmish at Redwood September 8, 1862. Operations in Humboldt District March 10-July 10, 1863, and February 1-June 30, 1864. Expedition from Camp Wright to Williams Valley April 7-11, 1863. Skirmish, Williams Valley, April 9. Ordered to San Francisco June, 1865, and duty at the Presidio till muster out.

Company "G"—At Camp Lincoln, Humboldt District, till May, 1863. Ordered to Benicia Barracks May 30, 1863. Duty there and in San Francisco till muster out.

Company "H"—At Santa Barbara till April, 1862. Moved to San Francisco, thence to Forts Humboldt and

Gaston April 20. To Fort Humboldt July, 1862, and duty there till June, 1863. Ordered to Benicia Barracks June 11, and duty there till December. Duty in Humboldt District till December, 1864, and at Presidio, San Francisco, till muster out.

Company "I"—At Santa Barbara till April, 1862. Moved to San Francisco, thence to Fort Humboldt and to Fort Gaston April 20, 1862. Duty there till June, 1863. Skirmish at Fort Gaston August 6. Affair at Little River August 23, 1862. At Fort Humboldt and in Humboldt District till December, 1864. At Presidio, San Francisco, till muster out.

Company "K"—Ordered to Fort Humboldt December, 1861, thence to Fort Lyon and Fort Gaston, and duty there till June, 1863. Action, Weaversville Crossing, Mad River, July 2, 1862. Near Oak Camp April 30, 1863. Moved to Benicia Barracks June, 1863, thence to Chico, Cali., August 11. At Fort Miller till December, 1864. At Benicia Barracks, San Francisco, till muster out. Skirmishes at Yreka Road, near Fort Crook, September 21, 1862 (Detachment). Simmons' Ranch, near Hydesville, October 21, 1862 (Detachment). Scout from Fort Crook to Honey Lake Valley November 3-29, 1862 (Detachment).

Regiment mustered out July 2, 1866.

3rd REGIMENT INFANTRY.

Organized at Stockton and Benicia Barracks September 15 to December 3, 1861. Attached to Districts of California and Utah, Dept. of the Pacific. Duty at Benicia Barracks till July, 1862. Company "A"—At Fort Terwah and Fort Baker, Humboldt District, operating against Indians, October, 1861, to August, 1862. Ordered to San Francisco August 23, thence to Stockton and to Camp Union, Sacramento, November 17. To Fort Churchill and duty there till October, 1863. Ordered to Camp Douglass, Utah, and rejoin Regiment.

Company "B"—at Fort Bragg, Humboldt District, operating against Indians, October, 1861, to August, 1862. Ordered to San Francisco August 23, thence to Stockton, and to Camp Union, Sacramento, November 17, and duty there till June, 1863. Ordered to Camp Douglass, Utah, and rejoin Regiment.

Company "D"—At Fort Gaston, Humboldt District, operating against Indians, October, 1861, to August, 1862. Skirmish, Light Prairie, near Arcata, August 21, 1862. Ordered to San Francisco August 23, thence to Stockton and to Camp Union, Sacramento, November 17, and duty there till June, 1863. Ordered to Camp Douglass, Utah, and join Regiment.

Regiment at Benicia Barracks till July, 1862. March via Fort Churchill and Ruby Valley to Utah to protect Overland mail route July to November. Scouts from Fort Churchill, Nev., to Honey Lake Valley, Cali., November 3-29, 1862. Expedition from Fort Ruby, Nev., to Sierra Nevada Mountains November 22-27, 1862 (Co. "F"). Skirmish on Bear River, Utah, January 26, 1863 (Co. "K"). Engagement on Bear River January 29 (Co. "K"). Expedition from Camp Douglass to Soda Springs, on Bear River, Idaho, May 5-30, 1863 (Co. "H"). Duty at Camp Douglass, Camp Connor and in the District of Utah till July, 1866. Mustered out July 27, 1866.

4th REGIMENT INFANTRY.

Organized at Sacramento, Placerville and Auburn September to October, 1861. Attached to Dept. of the Pacific. Companies "A," "B," "C," "D" and "E" moved from San Francisco to Fort Vancouver, Washington Territory, October 29-November 4, 1861. Company "A"—At Fort Walla Walla till August, 1862. Ordered to San Francisco August 15 and duty at Benicia Barracks till March, 1863. Ordered to Camp Drum March 1, and duty there till June, 1864. At Santa Barbara till December, 1864. New Company "A"—Ordered to Fort Humboldt May 1, 1865. At Camp Iaqua till muster out.

Company "B"—At Fort Vancouver till March, 1862. At Fort Dalles to October, 1862. Ordered to San Francisco October 3, and duty at Benicia Barracks till March, 1863. Ordered to Camp Drum March 1, 1863,

thence to Fort Mojave April 29, and duty there till June, 1864. Ordered to Drum Barracks, and duty there till muster out. New Company "B"—Ordered to Fort Humboldt April 5, 1865, thence to Fort Gaston, and duty there till muster out.

Company "C"—At Fort Walla Walla, Washington Territory, till August, 1862. Ordered to San Francisco August 14, and duty at Benicia Barracks till March, 1863. At San Francisco till May. Ordered to Camp Drum May 28, 1863, and duty there till January, 1864. Occupation of Santa Catalina Island January 2, and duty there till December, 1864. At Drum Barracks till March, 1865, and at Fort Mojave till muster out.

Company "D"—At Fort Yamhill, Ore., till March, 1863. Ordered to Fort Hoskins March 25, and duty there till December, 1864. Expedition from Siletz Block House to Coos Bay April 21-May 12, 1864. At Fort Yamhill till muster out.

Company "E"—At Fort Steilacoom till October 3, 1862. Ordered to San Francisco, and duty at Benicia Barracks till May, 1863. Ordered to Drum Barracks May 28, and duty there till January, 1864. At Fort Yuma till June, 1865. At Drum Barracks till muster out.

Company "F"—At Camp Sigel, near Auburn, till January, 1862. Moved to Camp Union, Sacramento, thence to San Francisco April 28, and to Camp Latham, Southern California. At Camp Drum till March, 1863. Moved to Fort Yuma March 1, 1863; to LaPaz, Ariz., April 28, 1863; to Fort Yuma August 15, and to Drum Barracks November 7, 1864. New Company "F"—To Fort Humboldt May 1, 1865. Duty in Humboldt District till muster out.

Company "G"—At Camp Sigel, near Auburn, till January, 1862. Moved to Camp Union, Sacramento, thence to San Francisco April 28, 1862, and to Camp Latham, Southern California. Ordered to San Diego, Cali., and duty there till muster out.

Company "H"—At Camp Sigel, near Auburn, till January, 1862. Moved to Camp Union, Sacramento, thence to San Francisco April 28, and to Camp Latham, Southern California. Duty at Camp Latham and Camp Drum till March, 1863. Ordered to Fort Yuma March 1, and duty there till January, 1864. Moved to Drum Barracks January, 1864, thence to San Luis Obispo July 27, 1864. Return to Drum Barracks and duty there till muster out.

Company "I"—At Camp Sigel, near Auburn, till January, 1862. Moved to Camp Union, Sacramento, thence to San Francisco April 28, and duty at Benicia Barracks till November, 1862. To Fort Umpqua November 12. Duty there and at Benicia Barracks till March, 1863. Moved to Camp Drum March 6 and to Fort Mojave April 29, and duty there till muster out.

Company "K"—Moved to San Francisco April 28, 1862, and duty at Benicia Barracks till March, 1863. Moved to Camp Drum March 6, thence to Fort Yuma, and duty there till January, 1864. Moved to Drum Barracks, and duty there till muster out.

Regiment mustered out April 18, 1866.

5th REGIMENT INFANTRY.

Organized in California at large September to November, 1861. Attached to Depts. of the Pacific and New Mexico.

SERVICE.—Ordered to Camp Latham, Southern California, February 1, 1862. Carlton's Expedition from Southern California through Arizona to Northwest Texas and New Mexico April 13-September 20 (Cos. "D" and "G"). Regiment garrison posts in Southern California and Arizona. Company "D" at San Diego. Companies "C," "F," "H," "I" and "K" at Camp Wright and Fort Bowie. Companies "A" and "E" at Fort Barrett. Companies "B" and "G" at Tucson till December, 1862. Company — march to Tucson July 6, 1862. March from Tucson to the Rio Grande July 25-August 15, 1862 (Cos. "A," "B" and "G"). December, 1862, stationed at Tucson, Company "F"; at Fort Bowie, Companies "E" and "G"; at Fort Yuma, Companies "C" and "H"; at Camp Drum, Companies "D," "I" and "K." Engagement at Pinos

Altos Mines January 29, 1863 (Co. "A"). To Tucson and Messilla February, 1863 (Cos. "C" and "H"). Engagement at Cajou de Arivaypo, Apache Pass, April 25, 1863 (Co. "K"). Stationed May, 1863, at Fort Stanton (Co. "A"), Fort Bowie (Co. "E"), Tucson (Cos. "C," "F" and "H"), Fort Craig (Cos. "B," "D," "G," "I" and "K"). Skirmish, Cajou de Arivaypa, May 7, 1863. At Fort Stanton June, 1863. Crook's Canon, N. Mex., July 24, 1863 (Co. "E"). Skirmishes, Chiricahua Mountains, September 8-9, 1863. Skirmish, Gila River, November 5, 1863. Skirmish, San Andreas Mountains, January 26, 1864 (Detachment). Operations in New Mexico and Arizona February 1-March 7, 1864. Expedition from Camp Mimbres February 24-29, 1864 (Detachment). Pinos Altos, Ariz., February 27, 1864. Skirmish at foot of Sierra Bonita April 7, 1864 (Companies "F" and "I"). Doubtful Canon, N. Mex., May 4, 1864 (Company "I"). Gila River Expedition, Arizona, May 25-July 13, 1864 (Companies "E," "I" and "K"). Expedition from Fort Craig, N. Mex., to Fort Goodwin, Ariz., May 16-August 2, 1864 (Companies "A," "C" and "E"). At Fort Goodwin till October (Cos. "A," "C" and "E"). June, 1864, stationed at Camp Mimbres, Ariz. (Cos. "A" and "F"), at Fort Bowie (Co. "K"), at Franklin, Texas (Cos. "G" and "H"), at Tucson (Co. "D"), at Fort Cummings (Co. "I"). Scout in Southeastern Arizona July 16-24, 1864 (Co. "A"). Expedition to Pinal Mountains July 18-August 7, 1864 (Co. "E"). Expedition to Southwest New Mexico July 23-October 10, 1864 (Cos. "B" and "F"). Ordered to Las Cruces October 8, 1864 (Cos. "A," "C," "D," "E," "I" and "K"). Company "F" to Fort Cummings October, 1864. Mustered out November 27 to December 14, 1864.

6th REGIMENT INFANTRY.

Organized at San Francisco October 21, 1862. Attached to Dept. of the Pacific. Duty at Benicia Barracks, San Francisco. Company "A"—Ordered to Chico, Cali., August 20, 1863, and duty there till May, 1864. Ordered to Alcatraz Island May 30, and duty there till muster out.

Companies "C," "E" and "G"—Ordered to Fort Humboldt February 15, 1864. Companies "E" and "G" return to Benicia Barracks October 11, 1864. Company "C" returns May, 1865. Operations in Humboldt District February 1-June 30, 1864 (Cos. "C," "E" and "G"). Skirmish at Booth's Run May 1 (Co. "E"). Kneeland's Prairie May 2 (Co. "E"). Near Boynton's May 6 (Co. "C"). Grouse Creek May 23 (Cos. "E" and "G"). Regiment at Benicia Barracks till muster out.

Company "D"—at San Francisco till July, 1863. At Benicia Barracks till August 24. Moved to Butler County and at Camp Bidwell, near Chico, till October 24. At Benicia Barracks till June 1, 1864, and at Alcatraz Island till June, 1865. Companies "D" and "I" moved to Fort Churchill June 4, 1865. Regiment mustered out October 25 to December 20, 1865.

7th REGIMENT INFANTRY.

Organized at large October to December, 1864. Attached to Dept. of the Pacific. Companies "A," "C" and "K" ordered from San Francisco to Camp Drum, Southern California, March, 1865. Companies "A" and "K" to Fort Yuma. Company "C" to Fort Mojave. Regiment moved to District of Arizona June, 1865, and duty there, stationed at various posts, till June, 1866. Mustered out June 28, 1866.

8th REGIMENT INFANTRY.

Organized by Companies as follows: Company "A"—At Watsonville and mustered in November 17, 1864. Stationed at Fort Point, Cali., till February, 1865. At Cape Disappointment, mouth of the Columbia River, Washington Territory, till August 17, 1865, and at Fort Dalles, Ore., till October, 1865. Ordered to Fort Point, Cali., October, 1865. Company "B"—At Sacramento and mustered in December 5, 1864. Stationed at Fort Point, Cali., till April 17, 1865. Moved to Fort Stevens, Ore., April 17-26, and duty there till October 11. Ordered to

Fort Point, Cali. Company "C"—Organized at San Jose and mustered in January 28, 1865. At Fort Point, Cali., till October, 1865. Company "D"—Organized at San Francisco and mustered in February 14, 1865. Stationed at Fort Point, Cali., till October, 1865. Company "E"—Organized at San Francisco January 25, 1865. Stationed at Alcatraz Island till October, 1865. Company "F"—Organized at San Francisco February 14, 1865. Stationed at Point Blunt, Angel Island, till October, 1865. Company "G"—Organized at Marysville and mustered in January 5, 1865. Stationed at Alcatraz Island till October, 1865. Company "H"—Organized in Calaveras County and mustered in February 27, 1865, at San Francisco. Stationed at Alcatraz Island and Fort Point till October, 1865. Company "I"—Organized in Yuba and Sierra Counties and mustered in at San Francisco February 6, 1865. Stationed at Fort Point till October, 1865. Company "K"—Organized at Placerville and Sacramento and mustered in at San Francisco February 25, 1865. Stationed at Fort Point till October, 1865.

Regiment mustered out October 24, 1865.

COLORADO VOLUNTEERS.

1st REGIMENT CAVALRY.

Regiment organized from 1st Colorado Infantry November 1, 1862. Attached to District of Colorado, District of the Upper Arkansas and District of the Plains till November, 1865, operating against Indians and protecting stage routes. Stationed by detachments at Denver, Camps Collins, Curtis, Fillmore, Robbins, Weld and Canon City and at Forts Lyon and Garland.

SERVICE.—Skirmish at Grand Pass, Fort Halleck, Idaho, July 7, 1863 (Detachment). Expedition from Denver to Republican River, Kansas, April 8-23, 1864 (Co. "D"). Skirmish near Fremont Orchard, Colo., April 12 (Cos. "C" and "H"). Expedition from Camp Sanborn to Beaver Creek, Kansas, April 14-18 (Cos. "C" and "H"). Skirmish at Big Bushes, Smoky Hills, April 16 (Cos. "C" and "H"). Skirmish at Cedar Bluff, Colo., May 3 (Co. "C"). Scout from American Ranch to Cedar Bluff May 9-10. Scout from Fort Sumner August 3-November 4 (Cos. "A," "B" and "G"). Scout from Fort Union, N. Mex., August 4-September 5. Affair near Fort Lyon, Colo., August 7. Skirmish near Sand Creek August 11 (Cos. "D," "G," "K" and "L"). Scout on Fort Union Road, near Fort Garland, August 12-16 (Detachment). Skirmish, Atkins' Ranch, August 22. Skirmish, Walnut Creek, Kansas, September 25 (Cos. "L" and "M"). Skirmish, Fort Lyon, October 9. Affairs near Fort Lyon November 6-16. Pawnee Forks November 25 (1 Co.). Engagement with Indians at Sand Creek, Colo., November 29 (Cos. "C," "D," "E," "G," "H" and "K"). Company "B" at Fort Zarah, Kansas, August to October, 1864, then at Fort Garland. Skirmishes at Valley Station and Julesburg, Colo., January 7, 1865. Operations on Overland Stage Route between Denver and Julesburg January 14-25, 1865 (Co. "C"). Skirmish, Valley Station, Colo., January 14 (Co. "C"). Skirmish, Godfrey's Ranch, January 14 (Detachment). Skirmishes at Morrison's or American Ranch and Wisconsin Ranch January 15. Point of Rocks or Nine-Mile Ridge, near Fort Larned, January 20. Gittrell's Ranch January 25. Moore's Ranch January 26. Lillian Springs Ranch January 27. Near Valley Station January 28 (Co. "C"). Operations against Indians near Fort Collins, Colo., June 4-10 (Co. "D"). Expedition from Denver to Fort Halleck, Dakota, June 17-19 (Co. "D"). Operations about Rock Creek Station, Seven-Mile Creek, Dakota, June 24-30 (Cos. "A" and "D"). Mustered out at Leavenworth, Kansas, November 18, 1865.

2nd REGIMENT CAVALRY.

Organized at St. Louis, Mo., by consolidation of the 2nd and 3rd Regiments Infantry to date from October, 1863. Attached to District of Southeast Missouri, Dept. of Missouri, to December, 1863. District of St. Louis, Mo., Dept. Missouri, to January, 1864. District Central

Missouri, Dept. of the Missouri, to December, 1864. District of the Upper Arkansas to September, 1865.

SERVICE.—Organizing Regiment at Benton Barracks, Mo., till January, 1864. Companies "F," "G," "H" and "K" on duty in Colorado at Fort Lyon and other points till November 26, 1863. March to Fort Riley, Kansas, November 26-December 25, thence to Kansas City, Mo., January 6, 1864. Regiment moved from St. Louis, Mo., to Dresden January 16, 1864, thence to Kansas City February 15-20. Assigned to duty in 4th Sub-District of Central Missouri, consisting of Cass, Johnston, Bates and Vernon Counties, Mo., and engaged in protecting borders of Kansas and operations against guerrillas, with almost constant fighting by detachments, till October, 1864. Operating from Kansas City, Independence, Westport, Hickman's Mills, Pleasant Hill and Harrisonville. Skirmish at Dayton, Mo., April 27. Skirmishes in Johnson County April 28-30. Skirmish at Sni Hills April 29 and May 21. Affair at Blue River May 21 (Detachment). Pleasant Hill May 28. Scout on the Osage June 8-19 (Cos. "I" and "L"). Scout from Pleasant Hill June 14-16 (Cos. "D," "I," "K" and "M"). Expedition from Kansas City into Missouri June 18-20 (Cos. "I," "K" and "M"). Operations in Western Missouri July 6-30. Near the Little Blue, Jackson County, July 6 (Co. "C"). Camden Point July 13. Near Fredericksburg July 14. Fayette Road, near Helmsville, July 16. Fredericksburg July 17. Scout on South Platte River, Colo., July 17-28 (Detachment). Ragtown July 20. Camden Point July 22. Union Mills July 22. Pleasant Hill July 25. Near Independence August 1 (Detachment). Scout on Independence Road to Gunter's Mills August 1-3 (Cos. "F," "G," "I," "K" and "L"). Scout from Independence to Lafayette County August 2-8 (Detachment). Scout from Independence to Lafayette and Jackson Counties August 13-18 (Cos. "C," "D," "F," "I," "K" and "M"). Operations in Lafayette, Howard and Saline Counties Aug. 13-22. Engagement, Canadian River, I. T., August 21 (Detachment). Scouts in Jackson and Cass Counties August 25-29 (Co. "D"). Skirmish near Pleasant Hill August 26 (Co. "D"). Operations against Price's Invasion August 29-December 2. Scouts on Little Blue, Jackson County, September 2-10 (Co. "A"). Walnut Creek September 25. Skirmish near Pleasant Hill September 26. Regiment concentrated at Pleasant Hill October 1, and cover Independence and front of the Army of the Border. Near Lexington October 17 (Cos. "C," "E," "G," "K" and "L"). Lexington October 19. Battle of Little Blue October 21. Pursuit of Price October 21-28. Independence and State Line October 22. Big Blue and Westport October 23. Marias des Cygnes, Mine Creek, Little Osage River, October 25. Newtonia October 28. Moved to District of the Upper Arkansas December 22, and engaged in operations against Indians about Fort Riley, Fort Zarah, Fort Ellsworth and Fort Larned till September, 1865. Skirmish at Godfrey's Ranch, Colo., January 14, 1865 (Detachment). Operations on Overland Stage Route from Denver to Julesburg, Colo., January 14-25 (Detachment). Skirmish at Fort Zarah February 1 (Co. "C"). Scout from Fort Larned to Crooked Creek March 9 (Detachment). Near Fort Zarah April 23 (Detachment). Pawnee Rock May 20 (Detachment). Cow Creek Station, Plum Butte and Pawnee Rock June 12 (Detachments). Mustered out at Leavenworth, Kansas, September 23, 1865.

3rd REGIMENT CAVALRY.

Regiment organized at Denver, Colo., for 100 days' service August 20 to September 21, 1864. Duty at Denver till September 27. Operations against Arapahoe and Cheyenne Indians in the District of Colorado October to December. Company "G" at Camp Baxter, Company "A" at Camp Cass, Companies "E," "B," "I," "K," "L" and "M" at Camp Elbert, Company "F" at Junction Station, Company "C" at Latham Station, Company "B" at Old Fort Lupton and Company "D" at Valley Station. Skirmish near Valley Station October 10. Engagement with Indians at Sand Creek, Colo.,

November 29. Mustered out at Denver December 31, 1864.

M'LANE'S INDEPENDENT BATTERY LIGHT ARTILLERY.

Organized at Denver, Colo., December 15, 1862. Attached to District of Colorado to July, 1864. District of Upper Arkansas to December, 1864. District of South Kansas to April, 1865. District of North Kansas to August, 1865.

SERVICE.—Duty at Fort Lyon, Colo., operating against Indians, December, 1862, to July, 1863. At Camp Weld till December, 1863. Scout from Port Garland, Colo., October 12-16, 1863. At Denver December, 1863, to June, 1864. Expedition from Denver to Republican River, Kansas, April 8-23, 1864. Action at Big Bushes, Smoky Hill, Kansas, April 16. Ordered to District of Kansas June, 1864. At Fort Larned, District of South Kansas, till August, 1864. (A Detachment at Lawrence, Kansas.) Ordered to Lawrence August 9, and duty in District of Upper Arkansas. Stationed at Paola till October. Operations against Price's Invasion October-November. Actions at Little Blue October 21. Big Blue October 22. Westport October 23. Pursuit of Price October 24-December 2. Mine Creek, Marias des Cygnes, Charlot, October 25. Newtonia October 28. Cane Hill, November 6. At Paola, Kansas, till May, 1865. Ordered to Fort Scott and Fort Gibson, and duty in District of North Kansas till August. Mustered out August 31, 1865.

1st REGIMENT INFANTRY.

Organized at Camp Weld, near Denver, August 26 to December 14, 1861. 3 Companies sent to Fort Wise, afterwards Fort Lyon, and duty there till March, 1862, when marched from Fort Lyon to Fort Union, N. Mex., March 3-10, and rejoin Regiment. Regiment left Camp Weld February 22 and march to Fort Union, N. Mex. At Fort Union March 10-22. March toward Santa Fe, N. Mex. Actions at Apache Canon March 26. La Glorietta Pass, or Pigeon Ranch, March 28. Peralta April 15. At Fort Craig till July. Garrison at Fort Garland, Fort Union, Fort Craig, Fort Larned and Fort Lyon, Colo., till November. Designation changed to 1st Colorado Cavalry November 1, 1862, which see.

2nd REGIMENT INFANTRY.

Organized at Fort Garland, Canon City, Fort Lyon and Denver, Colo., December, 1861. Ford's Independent Company, organized at Canon City, Colo., August to December, 1861, assigned as Company "A." Company left Canon City December 12 and arrived at Fort Garland December 21, and mustered in December 24, 1861. Todd's Independent Company organized at Canon City August to December, 1861. Assigned as Company "B." Left Canon City December 7 and marched to Fort Garland. Mustered in December 14, 1861. Ford's Company at Fort Garland till February 4, 1862, then marched to Santa Fe, N. Mex., February 4-March 4, 1862, thence to Fort Union, N. Mex., March 5-11. Dodd's Company marched to Santa Fe, N. Mex., thence to Fort Craig and joined Canby. Skirmish at Fort Craig February 20 (Co. "B"). Engagement at Valverde February 21 (Co. "B"). Evacuation of Albuquerque and Santa Fe March 3-4. Skirmish at Albuquerque April 8. Action at Apache Canon March 26. La Glorietta Pass, or Pigeon Ranch, March 28. Peralta April 15. Apache Canon July 15. Duty at Fort Craig, Santa Fe and Fort Union till February, 1863. Expedition from Fort Union to Canadian River and Utah Creek October 29-November 23 (Co "C"). March to Fort Lyon, Colo. Duty there, at Denver and Fort Garland till March. Ordered to Camp Scott, Kansas. At Camp Leroy, Kansas, June. Fort Gibson, I. T., May 28. (Co. "C" at Council Grove, Kansas District of the Border, July, 1863.) Escort train from Fort Scott to Fort Smith, Ark., June-July (Cos. "A," "B.") Engagement at Cabin Creek, I. T., July 1-2, and at Elk Creek near Honey Springs, I. T., July 17. Duty in Cherokee Nation at Fort Blunt July, and at

Fort Smith, Ark., operating on line of the Arkansas River till November. Action at Perryville, I. T., August 26. Texas Prairie August 29 (Co. "F"). Skirmish at Webber Falls September 9. Ordered to Springfield, Mo., October, 1863, for consolidation with 3rd Colorado Infantry to form 2nd Colorado Cavalry, which see.

3RD REGIMENT INFANTRY.

Organized at Denver and Camp Weld, Colorado, September, 1862, to January, 1863. Attached to District of Colorado to March, 1863. District of Southeast Missouri, Department of Missouri, to October, 1863.

SERVICE.—March from Camp Weld, Denver, Colo., to Fort Leavenworth, Kansas, March 5-April 24, thence moved to St. Louis, Mo., via St. Jo and Hannibal, Mo., April 28-30. Ordered to Sulphur Springs, Mo., thence to Pilot Knob, Mo. Duty at Pilot Knob, Potosi and Ironton till October, 1863. Moved to St. Louis October, 1863, for consolidation with 2nd Colorado Infantry to form 2nd Colorado Cavalry, which see.

DENVER CITY HOME GUARD.

Organized at Denver August to October, 1861. Attached to District of Colorado. March from Denver to New Mexico January, 1862. Engagement at Valverde, N. Mex., February 21, 1862. Mustered out April 1, 1862.

CONNECTICUT VOLUNTEERS.

1st REGIMENT CAVALRY.

Organized at West Meriden as a battalion November 2, 1861. Moved to Wheeling, W. Va., February 20-24, 1862, and duty there till March 27. Attached to R. R. District, Mountain Department, to April, 1862. Schenck's Brigade, Mountain Department, to June, 1862. Cavalry Brigade, 1st Army Corps, Army of Va., to September, 1862. Cavalry Brigade, 11th Army Corps, Army Potomac, to January, 1863. Defences of Baltimore, Md. 8th Army Corps, Middle Dept., to July, 1863. Maryland Heights Division, Dept. of West Va., to October, 1863. Cavalry Brigade, 1st Division, Dept. West. Va. to January, 1864. Cavalry Reserve, 8th Army Corps, defences of Baltimore to March, 1864. 1st Brigade, 3rd Division, Cavalry Corps, Army of the Potomac and Army of the Shenandoah, Middle Military Division, to June, 1865. Cavalry Division, Dept. of Washington to August, 1865.

SERVICE.—Operations against guerrillas in Hardy County, W. Va., till May, 1862. Action at Moorefield, W. Va., April 3. March to relief of Milroy May 2-7. McDowell May 8. Franklin May 10-12. Strasburg May 24. Wosdensville May 28. Raid to Shaver River May 30. Strasburg June 1. New Market June 5. Harrisonburg June 7. Cross Keys June 8. Port Republic June 9. Movement down the valley to Madison C. H. June 10-July 28. Scout from Strasburg June 22-30 (Co. "B"). Scouting in vicinity of Madison C. H. till August. Pope's campaign in Northern Va. Aug. 16-Sept. 2. Provost duty during the Bull Run battles Aug. 27-30. Duty at Tennallytown, Fairfax C. H., Kalorama Heights and Hall's Farm till December. March to Fredericksburg, Va., and duty at Stafford C. H. till January, 1863. Kelly's Ford December 20-22, 1862. Moved to Baltimore, Md., and duty there, organizing as a regiment till March, 1864 (Cos. "A," "B," "C," "D" and "E"). Moved to Harper's Ferry, W. Va., July 5, 1863, and duty in that vicinity till January, 1864. Skirmish at Waterford Aug. 8, 1863 (Detachment). Berryville October 18. Expedition from Charlestown to New Market November 15-18. Operations in Hampshire and Hardy Counties, W. Va., January 27-February 7, 1864. Moorefield, February 4, 1864 (Detachment). Regimental organization completed at Baltimore January, 1864, and duty there till March. Moved to Annapolis Junction March 8, thence to Brandy Station, Va., March 15. Joined brigade March 15. Rappahannock April 1. Rapidan Campaign May-June. Craig's Meeting House May 5. Todd's Tavern May 5-6. Alsop's farm, Spottsylvania, May 8. Sheridan's raid to James River May 9-24. North Anna River May 9-10. Ground Squirrel Bridge and Yellow Tavern May 11.

Brook Church or fortifications of Richmond May 12. Strawberry Hill May 12. Demonstration on Little River May 26. Line of the Totopotomoy May 28-31. Mechump's Creek and Hanover C. H. May 31. Ashland June 1. Totopotomoy and Gaines' Mills June 2. Haw's Shop June 3. Cold Harbor June 3-12. Bethesda Church June 11. Long Bridge June 12. St. Mary's Church June 15. Cold Harbor June 18. Wilson's raid on south side and Danville R. R. June 20-30. Black and White Station and Nottaway C. H. June 23. Staunton Bridge or Roanoke Station June 25. Sappony Church or Stony Creek June 28-29. Ream's Station June 29. Siege of Petersburg till August. Sheridan's Shenandoah Valley Campaign August to December. Winchester August 17. Abraham's Creek September 13. Battle of Opequan, Winchester, September 19. Near Cedarville September 20. Front Royal Pike September 21. Milford September 22. Tom's Brook, "Woodstock Races," October 8-9. Battle of Cedar Creek October 10. Cedar Creek October 13. Cedar Run Church October 17. Newtown, Cedar Creek, November 12. Rude's Hill, near Mt. Jackson, November 22. Raid to Lacy Springs December 19-22. Lacy Springs December 21. Expedition from Winchester to Moorefield, W. Va., February 4-6, 1865. Sheridan's Raid February 27-March 25. Occupation of Staunton March 2. Waynesboro March 2. Charlottesville March 3. Ashland March 15. Appomattox Campaign March 28-April 9. Dinwiddie C. H. March 30-31. Five Forks April 1. Fall of Petersburg April 2. Namozine Church April 3. Sailor's Creek April 6. Appomattox Station April 8. Appomattox C. H., April 9. Surrender of Lee and his army. Expedition to Danville April 23-29. Moved to Washington, D. C., May. Grand review May 23. Provost duty at Washington till August. Mustered out August 2, 1865.

Regiment lost during service 4 Officers and 36 Enlisted men killed and mortally wounded, and 4 Officers and 149 Enlisted men by disease. Total 193.

1st REGIMENT HEAVY ARTILLERY.

Organized at Washington, D. C., from 4th Conn. Infantry, January 2, 1862. Attached to Military District of Washington to April, 1862. Siege artillery, Army Potomac, to May, 1862. 3rd Brigade, 2nd Division, 5th Army Corps, Army Potomac, to July, 1862. Siege artillery, Army Potomac, to August, 1862. Artillery defences Alexandria Military District of Washington, to February, 1863. Artillery defences of Alexandria, 22nd Army Corps, to April, 1863. 2nd Brigade, DeRussy's Division, defences south of the Potomac, 22nd Army Corps, to May, 1863. 3rd Brigade, DeRussy's Division, 22nd Corps, to December, 1863. 2nd Brigade, DeRussy's Division, 22nd Army Corps, to March, 1864. 4th Brigade, DeRussy's Division, 22nd Army Corps, to May, 1864. (Cos. "B" and "M" attached to Artillery Reserve, Army Potomac, October, 1862, to January, 1864.) Point of Rocks, Va., Dept., of Virginia and North Carolina to June, 1864. Seige artillery, Dept. of Virginia and North Carolina in the field, and siege artillery, Army Potomac, to May, 1865. Siege artillery, Dept. of Virginia, to July, 1865. 4th Brigade, DeRussy's Division, 22nd Army Corps, Dept. of Washington, to August, 1865. 3rd Brigade, Dept. of Washington, to September, 1865.

SERVICE.—Duty at Fort Richardson, defences of Washington, D. C., till April, 1862. Ordered to the Peninsula, Va., in charge of siege train Army Potomac, April 2. Siege of Yorktown April 12-May 4. Battle of Hanover C. H. May 27. Operations about Hanover C. H. May 27-29. Seven days before Richmond June 25-July 1. Gaines' Mill June 27. Malvern Hill July 1. At Harrison's Landing till August 15. Moved to Alexandria, Va., August 16-27. Duty in the defences of Washington, D. C., till May, 1864, as garrison at Fort Richardson. Cos. "B" and "M" detached with Army Potomac, participating in battle of Fredericksburg, Va., Dec. 12-15. Chancellorsville Campaign April 27-May 6. Battle of Chancellorsville May 1-5. Stafford Heights June 12. Battle of Gettysburg, Pa., July 1-3. Bristoe Campaign October 9-22. Advance to line of the Rappahannock November 7-8. Brandy Station November 8. Mine Run Campaign November 26-December 2. Rejoined regiment in defences of Washington January, 1864. Regiment ordered to Bermuda Hundred, Va., May 13, 1864. Engaged in fatigue duty and as garrison for batteries and forts on the Bermuda front and lines before Petersburg during siege operations against Petersburg and Richmond, May, 1864, to April, 1865. Occupy Fort Converse, Redoubt Dutton, Batteries Spofford, Anderson, Pruyn and Perry on the Bermuda front, and Forts Rice, Morton, Sedgwick and McGilvrey, and Batteries 1, 2, 3, 4, 5, 9, 10, 11, 12, 14, 15, 17, 18, 20, Burpee, Drake and Sawyer, on the Petersburg front, and at Dutch Gap, north of the James River. Assaults on Fort Dutton June 2 and 21, 1864 (Co. "L"). Attacks on the lines May 18, 19, 20, 21, 25, 27, 30, 31, June 1, 2, 5, 9, 18, 20 and 23. Mine explosion July 30, August 25, November 17, 18 and 28, 1864. Repulse of rebel fleet at Fort Brady on James River January 23-24, 1865. Expedition to Fort Fisher, N. C., January 3-15, 1865 (Cos. "B," "G," "L"). Capture of Fort Fisher January 15 (Cos. "B," "G," "L"). Assaults on and fall of Petersburg, Va., April 2, 1865. Duty in the Dept. of Va. till July 11. Moved to Washington, D. C., and duty in the defences of that city till September. Mustered out September 25, 1865.

Regiment lost during service 2 Officers and 49 Enlisted men killed and mortally wounded and 4 Officers and 172 Enlisted men by disease. Total 227.

2nd REGIMENT HEAVY ARTILLERY.

Organized at Washington, D. C., from 19th Conn. Infantry, November 23, 1863. Attached to 2nd Brigade, DeRussy's Division, 22nd Army Corps, Dept. of Washington, to February, 1864. 4th Brigade, DeRussy's Division, 22nd Army Corps, to May, 1864. 2nd Brigade, 1st Division, 6th Army Corps, Army Potomac, and Army Shenandoah, Middle Military Division, to June, 1865. 2nd Brigade, DeRussy's Division, 22nd Army Corps, Dept. of Washington, to August, 1865.

SERVICE.—Garrison duty at Forts Worth, Williams and Ellsworth, defences of Washington, D. C. South of the Potomac till May, 1864. Ordered to join Army of the Potomac in the field May 17. Moved to Spottsylvania C. H. May 17-19. Spottsylvania C. H. May 19-21. North Anna River May 23-26. On line of the Pamunkey May 26-28. Totopotomoy May 28-31. Hanover C. H. May 29. Cold Harbor May 31-June 12. Before Petersburg June 18-July 10. Jerusalem Plank Road June 22-23. Moved to Washington, D. C., July 10-12. Repulse of Early's attack on Washington July 12. Sheridan's Shenandoah Valley Campaign August to December. Battle of Opequan, Winchester, September 19. Fisher's Hill September 22. New Market September 23-24. Woodstock September 25. Battle of Cedar Creek October 19. Duty at Winchester and in the valley till December. Moved to Petersburg, Va., December 1-5. Siege of Petersburg December 5, 1864, to April 2, 1865. Dabney's Mills, Hatcher's Run Feb. 5-7, 1865. Appomattox Campaign March 28-April 9. Assault on and fall of Petersburg April 2. Pursuit of Lee April 3-9. Sailor's Creek April 6. Appomattox C. H. April 9. Surrender of Lee and his army. At Farmville and Burkesville till April 23. March to Danville April 23-27 and duty there till May 24. March to Richmond, thence to Washington, D. C., May 24-June 3. Corps review June 8. Duty at Washington till August. Mustered out August 18, 1865.

Regiment lost during service 12 Officers and 242 Enlisted men killed and mortally wounded and 2 Officers and 171 Enlisted men by disease. Total 427.

1st BATTERY LIGHT ARTILLERY.

Organized at West Meriden and mustered in October 26, 1861. Left State for Hilton Head, S. C., January 13, 1862. Attached to Sherman's expeditionary corps to April, 1862. 3rd Brigade, 2nd Division, Dept. of the South, to July, 1862. District of Beaufort, S. C., Dept.

of the South, to September, 1862. District of Beaufort, S. C., 10th Army Corps, Dept. of the South to June, 1863. United States forces Folly Island, S. C., 10th Corps, Dept. of the South, to April, 1864. Artillery, 1st Division, 10th Army Corps, Dept. of Virginia and North Carolina to August, 1864. Artillery Brigade, 10th Army Corps to December, 1864. Artillery Brigade, 25th Army Corps, Dept. of Virginia to June, 1865.

SERVICE.—Duty at Hilton Head, S. C., till May, 1862. Expedition to James Island and operations against Charleston, S. C., May 31-June 28. Battle of Secessionville June 16. Evacuation of James Island and movement to Hilton Head, S. C., May 28-July 7. Expedition to St. John's Bluff, Fla., September 30-October 13. Expedition to Pocotaligo October 21-23. Frampton's Plantation, Pocotaligo, October 22. Duty at Hilton Head and at Beaufort, S. C., till June, 1863. Moved to Folly Island, S. C. Expedition to James Island July 9-16. Williston Bluff, Pon Pon River July 10. Action on James Island July 16. Siege operations against Forts Wagner and Gregg, Morris Island and against Fort Sumter and Charleston, S. C., from Folly Island till April, 1864. Moved from Folly Island, S. C., to Gloucester Point, Va., April 18-23. Butler's operations on south side of the James and against Petersburg and Richmond May 4-June 21. Chester Station May 10. Operations against Fort Darling May 12-16. Battle of Drewry's Bluff May 14-16. Proctor's Creek May 14. On the Bermuda front May 17-June 21. Port Walthal June 16-17. Siege operations against Petersburg and Richmond June 16, 1864, to April 2, 1865. Moved to Deep Bottom, Va., June 21, 1864, and duty there till August 25. Actions at Deep Bottom July 21 and 27-28. Strawberry Plains, Deep Bottom, August 14-18. Moved to Petersburg front August 25 and duty in trenches before that city till September 28. Moved to Deep Bottom September 28. Battle of Chaffin's Farm, New Market Heights, September 29-30. Duty in trenches before Richmond till April, 1865. Occupation of Richmond April 3. Duty at Richmond and Manchester till June. Mustered out June 11, 1865.

Battery lost during service 1 Officer and 3 Enlisted men killed and mortally wounded and 21 Enlisted men by disease. Total 25.

2nd BATTERY LIGHT ARTILLERY.

Organized at Bridgeport September 10, 1862. Left State for Washington, D. C., October 15. Attached to 2nd Brigade, Casey's Division, Military District of Washington, to February, 1863. 2nd Brigade, Casey's Division, 22nd Army Corps, Dept. of Washington, to April, 1863. Artillery Abercrombie's Division, 22nd Corps, to June, 1863. 2nd Volunteer Brigade, Artillery Reserve Army Potomac to August, 1863. Artillery Dept. of the East to October, 1863. Camp Barry, Washington, D. C., 22nd Corps, to February, 1864. Defences of New Orleans, La., Dept. of the Gulf, to June, 1864. Artillery 4th Division, 13th Army Corps, Dept. of the Gulf, June, 1864. Defences of New Orleans, Dept. Gulf, to August, 1864. Unattached artillery 19th Army Corps, Dept. Gulf, to December, 1864. Artillery Reserve Corps Military Division West Mississippi to February, 1865. Artillery 2nd Division, Reserve Corps, February, 1865. Artillery 2nd Division, 13th Army Corps, Military Division West Mississippi, to August, 1865.

SERVICE.—Duty at Camp Barry, Defences of Washington, D. C., till January, 1863, and near Wolf Run Shoals, Va., to June, 1863. Battle of Gettysburg, Pa., July 1-4. Moved to Washington, D. C., and duty there till August 15. Moved to New York City August 15 and duty there and at various points in New York State till October 12. Moved to Washington October 12 and duty there till January, 1864. Moved to New Orleans, La., thence to Brashear City and duty there till June 17. At Algiers till July 31. Expedition to Mobile Bay July 31-September 8. Operations against Fort Gaines August 2-8 and against Fort Morgan August 9-23. Duty at Fort Gaines till September 8. Moved to Algiers September 8, thence to New Orleans September 19, and duty there till November 13. Moved to mouth of White River, Ark., November 13 and duty there till February, 1865. Moved to Kennerville, La., thence to Barrancas, Fla. Expedition to Fort Blakely, Mobile Bay, March 11-April 1. Occupation of Canoe Station March 27. Siege of Fort Blakely April 1-9. Assault on and capture of Fort Blakely April 9. Occupation of Mobile April 12. Duty at Mobile and Selma, Ala., till July. Moved to New Orleans, thence to New Haven, Conn., arriving there July 31. Mustered out August 9, 1865.

Battery lost during service 2 Enlisted men killed and 19 Enlisted men by disease. Total 21.

3rd BATTERY LIGHT ARTILLERY.

Organized at New Haven August to October, 1864. Moved to City Point, Va., November 16-19, 1864. Attached to defences of City Point, Va., Dept. of Virginia and North Carolina, to December, 1864. Siege artillery Army of the James and Army of the Potomac to June, 1865.

SERVICE.—Duty in the defences of City Point, Va. Occupying redoubts 2, 5, 7 and 8 till June, 1865. Repulse of attack on City Point by rebel ironclads January 24-25. Mustered out June 23, 1865.

Battery lost during service 4 Enlisted men killed and 1 Enlisted man by disease. Total 5.

1st REGIMENT INFANTRY.

Organized at Hartford April 22, 1861. Left State for Washington, D. C., May 18. Attached to Mansfield's command, Dept. of Washington, to June, 1861. Key's 1st Brigade, Tyler's Division, McDowell's Army of Northwestern Virginia, to August, 1861.

SERVICE.—Duty at Camp Corcoran. Defences of Washington, D. C., till June 1, 1861. Advance on Vienna and Falls Church, Va., June 1-8, and picket duty there till July 16. Advance on Manassas, Va., July 16-21. Occupation of Fairfax C. H. July 17. Battle of Bull Run July 21. Mustered out July 31, 1861.

2nd REGIMENT INFANTRY.

Organized at New Haven May 7, 1861. Left State for Washington, D. C., May 19. Attached to Mansfield's command, Dept. of Washington, to June, 1861. Key's 1st Brigade, Tyler's Division, McDowell's Army of Northeastern Virginia to August, 1861.

SERVICE.—At Camp Corcoran, defences of Washington, D. C., till June 1. Advance to Vienna and Falls Church, Va., June 1-3, and picket duty there till July 16. Advance on Manassas, Va., July 16-21. Occupation of Fairfax C. H. July 17. Battle of Bull Run July 21. Mustered out August 7, 1861.

3rd REGIMENT INFANTRY.

Organized at New Haven and mustered in May 14, 1861. Left State for Washington, D. C., May 19. Attached to Mansfield's command, Dept. of Washington, to June, 1861. Key's 1st Brigade, Tyler's 1st Division, McDowell's Army of Northeastern Virginia to August, 1861.

SERVICE.—Duty at Camp Corcoran, defences of Washington, D. C., till June 1, 1861. Advance to Vienna and Falls Church, Va., June 1-3, and picket duty there till July 16. Advance to Manassas, Va., July 16-21. Occupation of Fairfax C. H. July 17. Battle of Bull Run, Va., July 21. Mustered out August 12, 1861.

4th REGIMENT INFANTRY.

Organized at Hartford May 21, 1861. Left State for Washington, D. C., June 10. Attached to Abercrombie's 6th Brigade, 2nd Division, Dept. of Pennsylvania, to August, 1861. 2nd Brigade, Banks' Division, Army Potomac, to December, 1861. Defences of Washington to January, 1862.

SERVICE.—Duty at Chambersburg, Pa., and at Hagerstown, Md., till July 4, 1861, and at Williamsport till August 16. At Frederick, Md., till September 5. Moved to Darnestown September 5, thence to Fort Richardson. Defences of Washington, D. C., and duty there

till January, 1862. Designation of regiment changed to 1st Conn. Heavy Artillery January 2, 1862. (See 1st Heavy Artillery.)

5th REGIMENT INFANTRY.

Organized at Hartford July 26, 1861. Left State for Baltimore, Md., July 29, thence moved to Harper's Ferry, W. Va., July 30, and duty there till August 16. Attached to George H. Thomas' Brigade, Banks' Division, to October, 1861. Gordon's Brigade, Banks' Division, Army of the Potomac, to March, 1862. 1st Brigade, 1st Division, Banks' 5th Army Corps, and Dept. of the Shenandoah to June, 1862. 1st Brigade, 1st Division, 2nd Army Corps, Army of Virginia, to September, 1862. 1st Brigade, 1st Division, 12th Army Corps, Army of the Potomac and Army of the Cumberland to April, 1864. 2nd Brigade, 3rd Division, 20th Army Corps, Army of the Cumberland, April, 1864. 1st Brigade, 1st Division, 20th Army Corps to June, 1865. 2nd Brigade, Bartlett's Division, 22nd Army Corps, Dept. of Washington to July, 1865.

SERVICE.—Guard and outpost duty on the Upper Potomac till February, 1862. Operations near Edward's Ferry October 20-24, 1861. Operations about Dams Nos. 4 and 5 December 17-20. Advance on Winchester March 1-12, 1862. Near Winchester March 5. Occupation of Winchester March 12. Ordered to Manassas, Va., March 18, returning to Winchester March 19. Pursuit of Jackson March 24-April 27. Columbia Furnace April 17. At Strasburg till May 20. Retreat to Winchester May 20-25. Action at Front Royal May 23. Middletown May 24. Battle of Winchester May 24-25. Retreat to Martinsburg and Williamsport May 25-June 6. At Williamsport till June 10. Moved to Front Royal June 10-18. Reconnoissance to Luray June 29-30. Moved to Warrenton, Gordonsville and Culpeper, July, Reconnoissance to Raccoon Ford July 28 (Co. "I"). Pope's Campaign in Northern Virginia August 6-September 2. Battle of Cedar Mountain August 9. Battle of Bull Run August 29-30. Moved to Washington, D. C., thence to Frederick, Md., September 2-12. Duty at Frederick till December 10. March to Fairfax Station December 10-14, and duty there till January 19, 1863. Moved to Stafford C. H. January 19-23, and duty there till April 27. Chancellorsville Campaign April 27-May 6. Battle of Chancellorsville May 1-5. Gettysburg (Pa.) Campaign June 11-July 24. Battle of Gettysburg July 1-3. Funkstown, Md., July 12. Snicker's Gap, Va., July 21. Near Raccoon Ford, Va., till September 24. March to Brandy Station, thence to Bealeton and movement to Stevenson, Ala., September 24-October 3. Guard duty along Nashville and Chattanooga R. R. at Cowan and Cumberland Tunnel till April, 1864. Atlanta Campaign May to September. Demonstration on Rocky Faced Ridge May 8-11. Battle of Resaca May 14-15. Cassville May 19. New Hope Church May 25. Operations on line of Pumpkin Vine Creek and battles about Dallas, New Hope Church and Allatoona Hills May 26-June 5. Operations about Marietta and against Kenesaw Mountain June 10-July 2. Pine Mountain June 11-14. Lost Mountain June 15-17. Gilgal or Golgotha Church June 15. Muddy Creek June 17. Noyes Creek June 19. Kolb's Farm June 22. Assault on Kenesaw June 27. Ruff's Station, Smyrna Camp Ground July 4. Chattahoochee River July 5-17. Peach Tree Creek July 19-20. Siege of Atlanta July 22-August 25. Allatoona August 16. Operations at Chattahoochee River Bridge August 26-September 2. Occupation of Atlanta September 2-November 15. March to the sea November 15-December 10. Montieth Swamp December 9. Siege of Savannah December 10-21. Campaign of the Carolinas January to April, 1865. Thompson's Creek, near Chesterfield, S. C., March 2. Near Cheraw March 3. Averysboro, N. C., March 16. Battle of Bentonville March 19-21. Occupation of Goldsboro March 24. Advance on Raleigh April 9-13. Occupation of Raleigh April 14. Bennett's House April 26. Surrender of Johnston and his army. March to Washington, D. C., via Richmond, Va., April 29-May 20. Grand review

May 24. Mustered out (old members July 22, 1864) July 19, 1865.

Regiment lost during service 6 Officers and 104 Enlisted men killed and mortally wounded and 1 Officer and 82 Enlisted men by disease. Total 193.

6th REGIMENT INFANTRY.

Organized at New Haven September 12, 1861. Left State for Washington, D. C., September 17, thence moved to Annapolis, Md., October 5. Attached to Wright's 3rd Brigade, Sherman's Expeditionary Corps, to April, 1862. 1st Brigade, 1st Division, Dept. of the South, to July, 1862. District of Beaufort, S. C., Dept. of the South to September, 1862. District of Beaufort, S. C., 10th Army Corps, Dept. of the South, to March, 1863. Jacksonville, Fla., to April, 1863. District Hilton Head, S. C., 10th Corps, April, 1863. Folly Island, S. C., 10th Army Corps to June 1863. 2nd Brigade, United States forces, Folly Island, S. C., 10th Army Corps to July, 1863. 2nd Brigade, 2nd Division, Morris Island, S. C., 10th Army Corps, July, 1863. 1st Brigade, Morris Island, S. C., 10th Army Corps, July, 1863. District of Hilton Head, S. C., 10th Corps to April, 1864. 3rd Brigade, 1st Division, 10th Army Corps, Dept. of Va. and N. C. to May, 1864. 2nd Brigade, 1st Division, 10th Army Corps, Dept. Virginia and North Carolina, to December, 1864. 2nd Brigade, 1st Division, 24th Army Corps, to January, 1865. 2nd Brigade, 1st Division, Terry's Provisional Corps, Dept. of North Carolina, to March, 1865. 2nd Brigade, 1st Division, 10th Army Corps, Dept. North Carolina, to April, 1865. Abbott's Detached Brigade, Dept. North Carolina, to July, 1865.

SERVICE.—Sherman's Expedition to Port Royal, S. C., October 21-November 7, 1861. Capture of Forts Walker and Beauregard, Port Royal Harbor, November 7. Reconnoissance on Hilton Head Island November 8. Expedition to Braddock's Point November 10-11. Duty at Hilton Head, S. C., till January 20. Expedition to Warsaw Sound January 20-February 27. Duty at Hilton Head till March 20. Moved to Dafuskie Island and siege operations against Fort Pulaski, Ga., March 20-April 11. Bombardment and capture of Fort Pulaski April 10-11. Operations on James Island June 1-28. Grimball's Plantation June 10. Battle of Secessionville June 16. Evacuation of James Island and movement to Hilton Head June 28-July 7. Duty there till October. Expedition to Pocotaligo, S. C., October 21-23. Action at Frampton's Plantation, Pocotaligo, October 22. Duty at Beaufort, S. C., till March, 1863, and at Jacksonville, Fla., till April. Moved to Hilton Head, S. C., and duty there till June. Occupation of Folly Island, S. C., June 3-July 10. Attack on Morris Island, S. C., July 10. Assault on Fort Wagner, Morris Island, July 18. Moved to Hilton Head, S. C., July 25, and duty there till April, 1864. Moved to Gloucester Point April 27-May 1. Butler's operations on south side of James River and against Petersburg and Richmond May 4-28. Swift Creek or Arrowfield Church May 9-10. Chester Station May 10. Operations against Fort Darling May 12-16. Proctor's Creek May 13. Battle of Drewry's Bluff May 14-16. At Bermuda Hundred till August 13. Ware Bottom Church May 20. Petersburg June 9. Port Walthal June 16-17. Siege operations against Petersburg and Richmond June 16, 1864, to January 3, 1865. Ware Bottom Church June 20, 1864. Demonstration on north side of the James August 13-20. Battle of Strawberry Plains, Deep Bottom, August 14-18. Deep Run August 16. In trenches before Petersburg August 25-September 27. Moved to north side of the James September 27-28. Battle of Chaffin's Farm, New Market Heights, September 28-30. Darbytown and New Market Roads October 7. Darbytown Road October 13. Battle of Fair Oaks October 27-28. In front of Richmond October 31-November 2. Detached for duty at New York City during Presidential election of 1864, November 2-17. Duty in trenches before Richmond till January 3, 1865. Second expedition to Fort Fisher, N. C., January 3-15. Assault and capture of Fort Fisher January 15. Half Moon Battery January 19. Sugar Loaf Battery Feb-

ruary 11. Fort Anderson February 18. Capture of Wilmington February 22. North East Ferry February 22. Duty at Wilmington, N. C., till June and at Goldsboro till July. Mustered out August 21, 1865.

Regiment lost during service 8 Officers and 99 Enlisted men killed and mortally wounded and 4 Officers and 124 Enlisted men by disease. Total 235.

7th REGIMENT INFANTRY.

Organized at New Haven September 13, 1861. Left State for Washington, D. C., September 18, thence moved to Annapolis, Md., October 5. Attached to Wright's 3rd Brigade, Sherman's Expeditionary Corps, to April, 1862. 1st Brigade, 2nd Division, Dept. of the South to July, 1862. District of Hilton Head, S. C., Dept. of the South to September, 1862. District of Beaufort, S. C., 10th Army Corps, Dept. of the South, to January, 1863. Fernandina, Fla., to April, 1863. District of Hilton Head, S. C., 10th Corps to June, 1863 (Cos. "A," "B," "I," "K"). St. Helena Island, S. C., 10th Army Corps, June, 1863 (Cos. "A," "B," "I," "K"). 2nd Brigade, Folly Island, S. C., 10th Corps (Cos. "A," "B," "I," "K") to July, 1863. 2nd Brigade, 2nd Division, Morris Island, S. C., 10th Corps (Cos. "A," "B," "I," "K"), July, 1863. 1st Brigade, Morris Island, S. C., 10th Corps (Cos. "A," "B," "I," "K") to August, 1863. Regiment at St. Augustine, Fla., till August. 3rd Brigade, Morris Island, S. C., 10th Corps to October, 1863. St. Helena Island, S. C., 10th Corps to November, 1863. 1st Brigade, Morris Island, S. C., 10th Corps to December, 1863. St. Helena Island, S. C., 10th Corps to February, 1864. Hawley's Brigade, District of Florida, February, 1864. 2nd Brigade, Ames' Division, District of Florida, to April, 1864. 3rd Brigade, 1st Division, 10th Army Corps, Dept. of Virginia and North Carolina, to May, 1864. 2nd Brigade, 1st Division, 10th Army Corps to December, 1864. 2nd Brigade, 1st Division, 24th Army Corps to January, 1865. 2nd Brigade, 1st Division, Terry's Provisional Corps, Dept. of North Carolina to March, 1865. 2nd Brigade, 1st Division, 10th Army Corps, Dept. of North Carolina, to April, 1865. Abbott's Detached Brigade, Dept. of North Carolina, to July, 1865.

SERVICE.—Sherman's expedition to Port Royal, S. C., October 21-November 7, 1861. Capture of Forts Beauregard and Walker, Port Royal Harbor, November 7. Duty at Hilton Head, S. C., till December 18. Reconnoissance on Hilton Head Island November 8. Expedition to Braddock's Point November 10-11. Moved to Tybee Island, S. C., December 18 and engaged in fatigue duty building batteries for the reduction of Fort Pulaski till April 10, 1862 (Cos. "B," "G" and "I" on Dafuskie Island March 20 to April 11). Manned Batteries Totten, Halleck, Sherman, Lincoln and Stanton. Bombardment and capture of Fort Pulaski April 10-11. Garrison duty at Fort Pulaski till May 27. Operations on James Island, S. C., June 1-28. Battle of Secessionville June 16. Evacuation of James Island and movement to Hilton Head, S. C., June 28-July 7. Duty at Hilton Head till September 30. Expedition to St. John's Bluff, Fla., September 30-October 13. Expedition to Pocotaligo, S. C., October 21-23. Action at Frampton's Plantation, Pocotaligo, October 22. Duty at Hilton Head and Beaufort, S. C., till January 8, 1863. Moved to Fernandina, Fla., January 13, and duty there till April 12, and at St. Augustine, Fla., till August 2, then moved to Morris Island, S. C. Cos. "A," "B," "I" and "K" detached April, 1863, and moved to Hilton Head, S. C. Expedition against Charleston, S. C., April. Occupation of Folly Island, S. C., June 3. Attack on water batteries, Morris Island, S. C., July 10. Assault on Fort Wagner July 11. Siege of Fort Wagner July 11-September 7. Regiment joins from St. Augustine, Fla., August 5. Capture of Forts Wagner and Gregg, Morris Island, S. C., September 7. Operations against Fort Sumter and against Charleston till October 16. Man Batteries Stevens, Strong, Weed and Kearney. Moved to St. Helena Island, S. C., October 16. Boat duty at Folly Island October 29-November 17. At

1010 COMPENDIUM OF THE WAR OF THE REBELLION

St. Helena Island, S. C., till February, 1864. Veterans on furlough January 15 to February 27. Moved to Jacksonville, Fla., February 5-7. Expedition into Central Florida February 8-28. Battle of Olustee February 20. Duty at Jacksonville, Fla., till April 13. Moved to Gloucester Point, Va., April 13-20. Butler's operations on south side of the James and against Petersburg and Richmond, May 4-28. Swift Creek or Arrowfield Church May 9-10. Chester Station May 10. Operations against Fort Darling May 12-16. Proctor's Creek May 13. Battle of Drewery's Bluff May 14-16. On the Bermuda Hundred lines May 16-August 13. Attack on picket line June 2. Petersburg June 9. Bermuda Hundred June 14. Port Walthal June 16-17. Siege operations against Petersburg and Richmond June 16, 1864, to January 3, 1865. Demonstration on north side of the James August 13-20. Battle of Strawberry Plains Deep Bottom August 14-18. In trenches before Petersburg August 25 to September 28. Moved to north side of the James September 28. Battle of Chaffin's Farm, New Market Heights, September 28-30. Darbytown and New Market Roads October 7. Darbytown Road October 13. Battle of Fair Oaks October 27-28. Detached for duty at New York City during Presidential election of 1864, November 2-17. Duty in trenches before Richmond till January 3, 1865. Second expedition to Fort Fisher, N. C., January 3-15. Assault and capture of Fort Fisher January 15. Half Moon Battery January 19. Sugar Loaf Battery February 11. Fort Anderson February 18. Capture of Wilmington February 22. North East Ferry February 22. Duty at Wilmington, N. C., till June, and at Goldsboro till July. Mustered out July 20, 1865, and discharged at New Haven August 11, 1865.

Regiment lost during service 11 Officers and 157 Enlisted men killed and mortally wounded and 4 Officers and 192 Enlisted men by disease. Total 364.

8th REGIMENT INFANTRY.

Organized at Hartford September 21, 1861. Left State for Annapolis, Md., October 17. Attached to Parke's Third Brigade, Burnside's Expeditionary Corps, to April, 1862. 1st Brigade, 3rd Division, Dept. of North Carolina, to July, 1862. 2nd Brigade, 3rd Division, 9th Army Corps, Army of the Potomac, to April, 1863. 2nd Brigade, 2nd Division, 7th Army Corps, Department of Virginia, to July, 1863. 2nd Brigade, Getty's Division, United States forces, Portsmouth, Va., Dept. Virginia and North Carolina to January, 1864. Sub-District Albemarle, N. C., Dept. of Virginia and North Carolina, to April, 1864. 2nd Brigade, 1st Division, 18th Army Corps, Dept. of Virginia and North Carolina, to August, 1864. Provost Guard, 18th Army Corps to December, 1864. Provost Guard, 24th Army Corps, Dept. of Virginia to February, 1865. 2nd Brigade, 3rd Division, 24th Army Corps, to July, 1865. 2nd Provisional Brigade, 24th Army Corps, to August, 1865. Dept. of Virginia to December, 1865.

SERVICE.—Duty at Annapolis, Md., till January 6, 1862. Burnside's expedition to Hatteras Inlet and Roanoke Island, N. C., January 7-February 8, 1862. Battle of Roanoke Island February 8. At Roanoke Island till March 11. Moved to New Berne, N. C., March 11-13. Battle of Newberne March 14. Operations against Fort Macon March 23-April 26. Skirmish Fort Macon April 12. Capture of Fort Macon April 26. Duty at New Berne till July. Moved to Morehead City July 2, thence to Newport News, Va., July 3-5 and duty there till August 1. Moved to Fredericksburg, Va., August 1-5 and duty there till August 31. Moved to Brooks' Station, thence to Washington, D. C., August 31-September 3. Maryland Campaign September-October Frederick, Md., September 12. Turner's Gap, South Mountain, September 14. Battle of Antietam September 16-17. Duty in Pleasant Valley till October 27. Movement to Falmouth, Va., October 27-November 19. Battle of Fredericksburg, Va., December 12-15. Burnside's 2nd Campaign, "Mud March," January 20-24, 1863. Moved to Newport News February 6-9, thence to

Suffolk March 13. Siege of Suffolk April 12-May 4. Fort Huger, April 19. Edenton Road April 24. Nansemond River May 3. Siege of Suffolk raised May 4. Dix's Peninsula Campaign June 24-July 7. Expedition from White House to South Anna River July 1-7. Moved to Portsmouth, Va., and duty there till March, 1864. Expedition to South Mills October 12-14, 1863. Outpost duty at Deep Creek March 13 to April 18, 1864. Moved to Yorktown April 18-21. Butler's operations on south side of the James and against Petersburg and Richmond May 4-28. Occupation of City Point and Bermuda Hundred May 5. Port Walthal Junction, Chester Station, May 7. Swift Creek, or Arrowfield Church, May 9-10. Operations against Fort Darling May 12-16. Battle of Drewry's Bluff May 14-16. On Bermuda Hundred front May 17-27. Moved to White House Landing, thence to Cold Harbor, May 27-June 1. Battles about Cold Harbor June 1-12. Assaults on Petersburg June 15-18. Siege operations against Petersburg and Richmond June 16, 1864, to April 2, 1865. Mine explosion Petersburg, July 30, 1864 (Reserve). On Bermuda Hundred front August 25-September 27. Fort Harrison, New Market Heights, September 28-29. Chaffin's Farm, September 29-30. Duty in trenches before Richmond till April, 1865. Battle of Fair Oaks October 27-28, 1864. Occupation of Richmond April 3 and duty there and at Lynchburg, Va., till December. Mustered out December, 1865.

Regiment lost during service 8 Officers and 112 Enlisted men killed and mortally wounded and 3 Officers and 141 Enlisted men by disease. Total 264.

9th REGIMENT INFANTRY.

Organized at New Haven September 26, 1861. Moved to Lowell, Mass., November 4, thence to Boston and embarked on steamer "Constitution" for Ship Island, Miss., November 25, arriving there December 3. Duty at Ship Island till April 15, 1862. Attached to Butler's New Orleans Expeditionary Corps to April, 1862. Phelps' 1st Brigade, Dept. of the Gulf, to October, 1862. Defences of New Orleans, La., Dept. of the Gulf, to February, 1863. 1st Brigade, 3rd Division, 19th Army Corps, Dept. of the Gulf to March, 1863. 2nd Brigade, 2nd Division, 19th Corps, to August, 1863. 2nd Brigade, 4th Division, 19th Corps to February, 1864. 1st Brigade, 2nd Division, 19th Corps, to April, 1864. Dept. of the East to July, 1864. Bermuda Hundred, Va., 10th Corps, Dept. Virginia and North Carolina, July, 1864. 1st Brigade, 2nd Division, 19th Army Corps, Army of the Shenandoah, Middle Military Division, to January, 1865. 1st Brigade, Grover's Division, District of Savannah, Ga., Dept. of the South to March, 1865. 1st Brigade, 1st Division, 10th Army Corps, Dept. of North Carolina, to May, 1865. District of Port Royal, S. C., Dept. of the South, to August, 1865.

SERVICE.—Expedition to Biloxi and Pass Christian April 2-5, 1862. Biloxi April 3. Pass Christian April 4. Operations against Forts St. Phillip and Jackson, Miss. River April 15-28. Moved to New Orleans April 29-May 1. Occupation of New Orleans May 1. Expedition to New Orleans and Jackson R. R. May 9-10. Moved to Baton Rouge May 13. Reconnoissance to Warrenton May 14-29. Williams' expedition to Vicksburg, Miss., and operations against that city June 20-July 23. Ellis Cliff June 22. Hamilton Plantation, near Grand Gulf, June 24. Arrived at Vicksburg June 25. Fatigue duty on Vicksburg Canal till July 23. Moved to Baton Rouge July 23-26, and duty there till August 21. Battle of Baton Rouge August 5. Moved to Carrollton August 21-22. Expedition to St. Charles September 7-8. Near St. Charles Court House September 8. Duty in the defences of New Orleans till April, 1864, at New Orleans, Algiers, Mexican Gulf R. R. and mouth of the Mississippi and at Pass Manchac, Bonnet Carre, St. John Baptist District, October 19, 1862. Expedition to Ponchatoula March 21-30, 1863 (Detachment). Capture of Ponchatoula March 24 (Detachment). Action at Chackahoola Station, La., June 24 (Cos. "C," "E," "G," "I" and "K"). Expedition to Madisonville January 3,

1864. On veteran furlough in Connecticut April 15-July 16, 1864. Moved to Bermuda Hundred, Va., July 16-20. On Bermuda Hundred front July 20-28. Deep Bottom July 28-29. Moved to Washington, D. C., July 30-August 1, thence to Tenallytown August 1. Sheridan's Shenandoah Valley Campaign August to December. Battle of Opequan, Winchester, September 19. Fisher's Hill September 22. Battle of Cedar Creek October 19. Duty in the Shenandoah Valley till January, 1865. Moved to Savannah, Ga., January 6-20 and duty there till May 24. Moved to Hilton, S. C., May 24. Mustered out at Savannah, Ga., August 3, 1865.

Regiment lost during service 10 Enlisted men killed and mortally wounded and 3 Officers and 240 Enlisted men by disease. Total 253.

10th REGIMENT INFANTRY.

Organized at Hartford October 22, 1861. Left State for Annapolis, Md., October 31 and duty there till January 6, 1862. Attached to Foster's 1st Brigade, Burnside's Expeditionary Corps, to April, 1862. 2nd Brigade, 1st Division, Dept. of North Carolina to January, 1863. 2nd Brigade, 4th Division, 18th Army Corps, Dept. of N. C., to February, 1863. 2nd Brigade, 1st Division, 18th Corps, Dept. of the South to April, 1863. Stevenson's Brigade, Seabrook Island, S. C., 10th Army Corps, Dept. South to July, 1863. 1st Brigade, 1st Division, Morris Island, S. C., 10th Army Corps, Dept. South, July, 1863. 3rd Brigade, Morris Island, S. C., 10th Corps, to October, 1863. St. Augustine, Fla., Dept. South, to April, 1864. 2nd Brigade, 1st Division, 10th Army Corps, Dept. of Virginia and North Carolina, to May, 1864. 3rd Brigade, 1st Division, 10th Army Corps, to December, 1864. 3rd Brigade, 1st Division, 24th Army Corps, Dept. of Virginia, to July, 1865. 2nd Brigade, 1st Division, 24th Army Corps, to August, 1865.

SERVICE.—Burnside's expedition to Hatteras Inlet and Roanoke Island, N. C., January 7-February 8, 1862. Battle of Roanoke Island February 8. At Roanoke Island till March 11. Moved to Newberne March 11-13. Battle of New Berne March 14. Duty at New Berne till October. Expedition from Newberne October 30-November 12. Action at Rawle's Mills November 2. Foster's expedition to Goldsboro December 11-20. Kinston December 14. Whitehall December 16. Goldsboro December 17. Moved from Newberne to Hilton Head, S. C., January 26-29, 1863. Camp at St. Helena Island, S. C., till March 27 and at Seabrook Island, S. C., to July 6. Skirmish Edisto Island June 18. Expedition to James Island July 9-16. Battle of Secessionville July 16. Assault on Fort Wagner, Morris Island, S. C., July 18. Siege operations against Forts Wagner and Gregg, Morris Island, and against Fort Sumter and Charlestown, S. C., July 18-September 7. Capture of Forts Wagner and Gregg September 7. Operations against Forts Sumter and Charlestown till October 25. Moved to St. Augustine, Fla., October 26, and duty there till April, 1864. Ordered to Gloucester Point, Va., April 20. Butler's operations on south side of the James and against Petersburg and Richmond, Va., May 5-28. Occupation of Bermuda Hundred, Va., May 5. Port Walthal Junction, Chester Station, May 7. Operations against Fort Darling May 12-16. Battle of Drewry's Bluff May 14-16. On Bermuda Hundred front May 17-July 21. Action Bermuda Hundred June 2. Petersburg June 9. Walthal Junction June 16-17. Siege operations against Petersburg and Richmond June 16, 1864, to April 2, 1865. Demonstration on north side of the James July 27-29. Deep Bottom July 27-28 and August 1. Strawberry Plains August 14-18. Duty in trenches before Petersburg August 25-September 27. Movement to north of James September 27-28. Chaffin's Farm, New Market Heights, September 28-30. Darbytown and New Market Roads October 7. Reconnoissance on Darbytown Road October 13. Battle of Fair Oaks October 27-28. Johnston's Plantation October 29. Detached for duty at New York City during Presidential election of 1864, November 2-17. Duty in trenches before Rich-

mond November 17, 1864, to March 27, 1865. Movement to Hatcher's Run March 27-28. Appomattox Campaign March 28-April 9. Assault on and fall of Petersburg April 2. Pursuit of Lee April 3-9. Rice's Station April 6. Appomattox C. H. April 9. Surrender of Lee and his army. Duty at Richmond, Va., and in the Dept. of Va. till August. Mustered out August 15, 1865.

Regiment lost during service 13 Officers and 109 Enlisted men killed and mortally wounded and 5 Officers and 155 Enlisted men by disease. Total 282.

11th REGIMENT INFANTRY.

Organized at Hartford October 24 to November 14, 1861. Left State for Annapolis, Md., December 16, and duty there till January 6, 1862. Attached to Williams' Brigade, Burnside's Expeditionary Corps, to April, 1862. 2nd Brigade, 2nd Division, Dept. of North Carolina, to July, 1862. 2nd Brigade, 3rd Division, 9th Army Corps, Army of the Potomac, to April, 1863. 2nd Brigade, 2nd Division, 7th Army Corps, Dept. of Va., to July, 1863. 2nd Brigade, Getty's Division, Portsmouth, Va., Dept. of Va. and N. C., to October, 1863. United States forces, Yorktown, Va., Dept. Va. and N. C., to April, 1864. 2nd Brigade, 2nd Division, 18th Army Corps, Dept. Va. and N. C., to October, 1864. Provisional Division, Army of the James, to December, 1864. 1st Brigade, 3rd Division, 24th Army Corps, Dept. of Va., to July, 1865. 1st Independent Brigade, 24th Army Corps to August, 1865. Dept. of Virginia to December, 1865.

SERVICE.—Burnside's expedition to Hatteras Inlet and Roanoke Island, N. C., January 7-February 8, 1862. Battle of Roanoke Island February 8. At Roanoke Island till March 11. Moved to Newberne March 11-13. Battle of Newberne March 14. Duty at Newberne till July. Moved to Morehead City July 2, thence to Newport News, Va., July 3-5. Duty there till August 1. Moved to Fredericksburg August 1-6, and duty there till August 31. Moved to Brooks' Station, thence to Washington, D. C., August 31-September 3. Maryland Campaign September-October. Battle of South Mountain September 14. Battle of Antietam September 16-17. Duty at Pleasant Valley, Md., till October 27. Movement to Falmouth, Va., October 27-November 19. Battle of Fredericksburg, Va., December 12-15. Burnside's 2nd Campaign, "Mud March," January 20-24, 1863. Moved to Newport News, Va., February 6-9, thence to Suffolk March 13. Siege of Suffolk April 12-May 4. Edenton Road April 24. Providence Church Road and Nansemond River May 3. Siege of Suffolk raised May 4. Reconnoissance to the Chickahominy June 9-16. Dix's Peninsula Campaign June 24-July 7. Expedition from White House to South Anna River July 1-7. Moved to Portsmouth, Va., and duty there till October. Moved to Gloucester Point October 1 and duty there till April, 1864. Butler's operations on south side of the James River and against Petersburg and Richmond May 4-28. Occupation of Bermuda Hundred, Va., May 5. Port Walthal Junction, Chester Station, May 7. Swift Creek or Arrowfield Church May 9-10. Operations against Fort Darling May 12-16. Battle of Drewry's Bluff May 12-16. On Bermuda Hundred front May 17-27. Moved to White House, thence to Cold Harbor May 27-31. Battles about Cold Harbor June 1-12. Before Petersburg June 15-18. Siege operations against Petersburg and Richmond June 16, 1864, to April 2, 1865. Mine explosion Petersburg July 30, 1864 (Reserve). On Bermuda Hundred front August 25 to December, and on north side of the James before Richmond till April, 1865. Occupation of Richmond April 3. Duty at Richmond and Lynchburg, Va., till December. Mustered out December 21, 1865.

Regiment lost during service 8 Officers and 140 Enlisted men killed and mortally wounded and 1 Officer and 176 Enlisted men by disease. Total 325.

12th REGIMENT INFANTRY.

Organized at Hartford November 19 to December 3, 1861. Left State for Ship Island, Miss., February 24, 1862, arriving there March 9. Attached to 1st Brigade,

Dept. of the Gulf, to October, 1862. Weitzel's Reserve Brigade, Dept. of the Gulf, to January, 1863. 2nd Brigade, 1st Division, 19th Army Corps, Dept. of the Gulf, to August, 1863. 3rd Brigade, 1st Division, 19th Army Corps, to February, 1864. 2nd Brigade, 1st Division, 19th Army Corps, Dept. Gulf, to July, 1864, and Army of the Shenandoah, Middle Military Division, to April, 1865. 2nd Brigade, 1st Provisional Division, Army Shenandoah, April 1865. 2nd Brigade, Dwight's Division, Dept. of Washington, to June, 1865. District of Savannah, Dept. of the South, to August, 1865.

SERVICE.—Duty at Ship Island, Miss., till April 15, 1862. Operations against Fort St. Phillip and Jackson, Mississippi River, April 15-28. Occupation of New Orleans, La., May 1, the first regiment to land. Duty at Camp Parapet and Carrollton till October. Expedition to Lake Pontchartrain, Pass Manchac and up Tchefuncta and Pearl rivers July 25-August 2. Skirmishes at Madisonville and near Covington July 27. Operations in District of La Fourche October 24-November 6. Occupation of Donaldsonville October 25. Action at Georgia Landing, near Labadieville, October 27. Duty in District of La Fourche till February, 1863. Expedition to Bayou Teche January 13-15. Action with steamer "Cotton" January 14. Moved to Brashear City February and duty there till March. Operations against Port Hudson March 7-27. Pattersonville March 28 (Detachment). Operations in Western Louisiana April 9-May 14. Teche Campaign April 11-20. Port Bisland, near Centreville, April 12-13. Irish Bend April 14. Opelousas April 20. Expedition to Alexandria and Simsport May 5-18. Near Cheyneyville May 18. Movement to Bayou Sara, thence to Port Hudson May 22-25. Siege of Port Hudson May 25-July 9. Assaults on Port Hudson May 27 and June 14. Surrender of Port Hudson July 9. Operations in Western Louisiana July to September, 1863. Sabine Pass (Texas) Expedition September 4-11. Teche Campaign October 3-November 30. Duty at New Iberia till January, 1864. Move to New Orleans and on veteran furlough till May. Duty at Carrollton till July. Moved to Fortress Monroe, Va., thence to Washington, D. C., July 5-13. Snicker's Gap expedition July 14-23. Sheridan's Shenandoah Valley Campaign, August to December. Battle of Opequan, Winchester, September 19. Fisher's Hill September 22. Battle of Cedar Creek October 19. Duty at Winchester, Newtown and Summit Point till April, 1865. Moved to Washington, D. C., April 21, and duty there till June. Grand Review May 23-24. Moved to Savannah, Ga., June 1-5 and duty there till August. Mustered out August 12, 1865.

Regiment lost during service 6 Officers and 65 Enlisted men killed and mortally wounded and 8 Officers and 196 Enlisted men by disease. Total 273.

13th REGIMENT INFANTRY.

Organized at New Haven November 25, 1861, to January 7, 1862. Left State for Ship Island, Miss., March 17, 1862, arriving there April 13. Attached to 1st Brigade, Department of the Gulf, to September, 1862. Weitzel's Reserve Brigade, Dept. Gulf, to December, 1862. Grover's Division, Dept. of the Gulf, to January, 1863. 3rd Brigade, 3rd Division, 19th Army Corps, Dept. of the Gulf, January, 1863. 2nd Brigade, 4th Division, 19th Corps, to March, 1863. 3rd Brigade, 4th Division, 19th Corps, to August, 1863. 1st Brigade, 4th Division, 19th Corps, to February, 1864. 2nd Brigade, 2nd Division, 19th Corps, Dept. Gulf, to July, 1864, and Army of the Shenandoah, Middle Military Division, to January, 1865. District of Savannah, Ga., Dept. of the South, to March, 1865. 1st Brigade, 1st Division, 10th Army Corps, Dept. of North Carolina, to April, 1865. District of Georgia, Dept. of the South, to April, 1866.

SERVICE.—Operations against Forts St. Phillip and Jackson, Mississippi River, April 15-28, 1862. Occupation of New Orleans, La., May 1. Duty at Camp Parapet and Carrollton till October. Expedition to Pass Manchac and Ponchatoula September 13-15 (Detachment). Ponchatoula September 14-15. Operations in

District of La Fourche October 24-November 6. Occupation of Donaldsonville October 25. Action at Georgia Landing, near Labadieville, October 27. Thibodeauxville October 28. Duty at Thibodeauxville till December 27. Moved to Baton Rouge December 27, and duty there till March, 1863. Operations against Port Hudson March 7-27. Moved to Donaldsonville March 28. Operations in Western Louisiana April 9-May 14. Teche Campaign April 11-20. Porter's and McWilliams' Plantations at Indian Bend, April 13. Irish Bend April 14. Bayou Vermillion April 17. Expedition to Alexandria and Simsport May 5-18. Expedition from Barre's Landing toward Brashear City May 21-26. Siege of Port Hudson May 26-July 9. Assaults on Port Hudson May 27 and June 14. Brashear City June 21 (Detachment). Surrender of Port Hudson July 9. Moved to Donaldsonville July 11, thence to Thibodeauxville and duty there till March, 1864. Red River Campaign March 25-May 22. Monett's Bluff, Cane River Crossing April 28. Construction of dam at Alexandria April 30-May 10. Retreat to Morganza May 13-20. Mansura May 16. Duty at Morganza till July 3. Veterans on furlough July and August. Sheridan's Shenandoah Valley Campaign August to December. Battle of Opequan, Winchester, September 19. Fisher's Hill September 22. Battle of Cedar Creek October 19. Duty at Kernstown and Winchester till January, 1865. Moved to Savannah, Ga., January 5-22, and duty there till March 8. At Morehead City and New Berne, N. C., till May. Duty at Savannah, Augusta, Athens, Gainesville and District of Allatoona, Ga., till April, 1866. Mustered out at Fort Pulaski, Ga., April 25, 1866.

Regiment lost during service 2 Officers and 42 Enlisted men killed and mortally wounded and 3 Officers and 157 Enlisted men by disease. Total 204.

14th REGIMENT INFANTRY.

Organized at Hartford August 23, 1862. Left State for Washington, D. C., August 25. Attached to 2nd Brigade, 3rd Division, 2nd Army Corps, Army of the Potomac, to March, 1864. 3rd Brigade, 2nd Division, 2nd Army Corps, to May, 1865.

SERVICE.—Camp at Arlington, Va., till September 7, 1862. Moved to Rockville, Md., September 7-8. Battle of Antietam, Md., September 16-17. Moved to Harper's Ferry, W. Va., September 22 and duty there till October 30. Reconnoissance to Charlestown October 16-17. Advance up Loudon Valley and movement to Falmouth, Va., October 30-November 17. Battle of Fredericksburg December 12-15. Duty at Falmouth till April 27. Chancellorsville Campaign April 27-May 6. Battle of Chancellorsville May 1-5. Gettysburg (Pa.) Campaign June 11-July 24. Battle of Gettysburg July 1-4. Advance from the Rappahannock to the Rapidan September 13-17. Bristoe campaign October 9-22. Action at Bristoe Station October 14. Advance to line of the Rappahannock November 7-8. Mine Run Campaign November 26-December 2. At Stevensburg, Va., till April, 1864. Demonstration on the Rapidan February 6-7. Campaign from the Rapidan to the James May-June. Battles of the Wilderness May 5-7. Spottsylvania May 8-12. Laurel Hill May 8. Spottsylvania C. H. May 12-21. Assault on the Salient, Spottsylvania C. H., May 12. North Anna River May 23-26. Line of the Pamunkey May 26-28. Totopotomoy May 28-31. Cold Harbor June 1-12. Before Petersburg June 16-18. Siege of Petersburg June 16, 1864, to April 2, 1865. Jerusalem Plank Road June 22-23, 1864. Demonstration on north side of the James River July 27-29. Deep Bottom July 27-28. Strawberry Plains, Deep Bottom, August 14-18. Ream's Station August 25. Boydton Plank Road, Hatcher's Run October 27-28. Dabney's Mills February 5-7, 1865. Watkins' House March 25. Appomattox Campaign March 28-April 9. Crow's House March 31. Assault on and fall of Petersburg April 2. Sailor's Creek April 6. High Bridge and Farmville April 7. Appomattox C. H. April 9. Surrender of Lee and his army. At Burkesville till May 2. Moved to Washington, D. C., May 2-15. Grand review May 23. Old members mustered out

May 21, 1865. Veterans and recruits transferred to 2nd Conn. Heavy Artillery May 30, 1865.

Regiment lost during service 17 Officers and 188 Enlisted men killed and mortally wounded and 1 Officer and 191 Enlisted men by disease. Total 397.

15th REGIMENT INFANTRY.

Organized at New Haven August 25, 1862. Left State for Washington, D. C., August 28. Attached to Casey's Provisional Brigade, Military District of Washington, to October, 1862. 1st Brigade, Casey's Division, Military District Washington to December, 1862. 2nd Brigade, 3rd Division, 9th Army Corps, Army of the Potomac, to April, 1863. 2nd Brigade, 2nd Division, 7th Army Corps, Department of Virginia, to July, 1863. 2nd Brigade, Getty's Division, Portsmouth, Va., Dept. of Virginia and North Carolina, to January, 1864. District of the Albemarle, N. C., Dept. Virginia and North Carolina, to February, 1864. Defences of Newberne, N. C., Dept. Virginia and North Carolina, to January, 1865. Sub-district of Newberne, Dept. of North Carolina, to March, 1865. 2nd Brigade, 2nd Division, District of Beaufort, N. C., Dept. North Carolina, March, 1865. 1st Brigade, 1st Division, District of Beaufort and District of Newberne, to June, 1865.

SERVICE.—Duty in the Defences of Washington, D. C., till September 17, 1862. At Arlington Heights, Va., till November 3. At Fairfax Seminary, Va., till December 1. March to Fredericksburg, Va., December 1-6. Battle of Fredericksburg December 12-15. Burnside's 2nd Campaign, "Mud March," January 20-24, 1865. Moved to Newport News, Va., February 6-9, thence to Suffolk March 13. Siege of Suffolk April 12-May 4. Edenton Road April 24. Providence Church Road, Nansemond River, May 3. Siege of Suffolk raised May 4. Reconnoissance to the Chickahominy June 9-17. Dix's Peninsula Campaign June 24-July 7. Expedition from White House to South Anna River July 1-7. Moved to Portsmouth, Va., and duty there till January, 1864. (Five companies moved to South Mills September 20, 1863.) Skirmish Harrellsville January 20, 1864 (Detachment). Moved to New Berne, N. C., January 21, 1864, thence to Plymouth, N. C., January 24. Expedition up Roanoke River January 29 (Detachment). Windsor January 30 (Detachment). Moved to New Berne February 3 and duty there till March, 1865. Expedition to near Kinston June 20-23, 1864. Southwest Creek June 22. Battle of Wise's Forks March 8-10, 1865. Occupation of Kinston March 14. Provost duty at Kinston and at New Berne till June. Mustered out June 27, 1865. Dicharged at New Haven July 12, 1865.

Regiment lost during service 4 Officers and 34 Enlisted men killed and mortally wounded and 5 Officers and 142 Enlisted men by disease. Total 185.

16th REGIMENT INFANTRY.

Organized at Hartford August 24, 1862. Moved to Washington, D. C., August 29-31. Attached to 2nd Brigade, 3rd Division, 9th Army Corps, Army of the Potomac, to April, 1863. 2nd Brigade, 2nd Division, 7th Army Corps, Dept. of Virginia, to July, 1863. 2nd Brigade, Getty's Division, Portsmouth, Va., Dept. of Virginia and North Carolina, to January, 1864. District of Albemarle, N. C., Dept. Virginia and North Carolina, to April, 1864. Defences of Newberne, N. C., Dept. Virginia and North Carolina, to January, 1865. Roanoke Island, N. C., Dept. North Carolina, to June, 1865.

SERVICE.—Maryland Campaign September-October, 1862. Battle of Antietam, Md., September 16-17. Duty in Pleasant Valley, Md., till October 27. Movement to Falmouth, Va., October 27-November 17. Battle of Fredericksburg December 12-15. Burnside's 2nd Campaign, "Mud March," January 20-24, 1863. Moved to Newport News February 6-9, thence to Suffolk March 13. Siege of Suffolk April 12-May 4. Edenton Road April 24. Providence Church Road and Nansemond River May 3. Siege of Suffolk raised May 4. Reconnoissance to the Chickahominy June 9-17. Dix's Peninsula Campaign June 24-July 7. Expedition from White House

to South Anna River July 1-7. Moved to Portsmouth, Va. Duty there and at Norfolk till January, 1864. Skirmish at Harrellsville January 20 (Detachment). Moved to Morehead City, thence to Newberne and Plymouth January 24-28. Skirmish at Windsor January 30. Duty at Newberne February 2 to March 20, and at Plymouth, N. C., till April. Siege of Plymouth April 17-20. Captured April 20, and prisoners of war till March, 1865. Those not captured on duty at Newberne and Roanoke Island, N. C., till June, 1865. Mustered out June 24, 1865.

Regiment lost during service 6 Officers and 76 Enlisted men killed and mortally wounded and 3 Officers and 240 Enlisted men by disease. Total 325.

17th REGIMENT INFANTRY.

Organized at Bridgeport August 28, 1862. Left State for Baltimore, Md., September 3. Attached to Defences of Baltimore, Md., 8th Corps, Middle Dept., to October, 1862. 2nd Brigade, 1st Division, 11th Army Corps, Army of the Potomac, to August, 1863. 2nd Brigade, Gordon's Division, South End Folly Island, S. C., 10th Corps, Dept. South, to February, 1864. 1st Brigade, Ames' Division, District of Florida, Dept. South, to April, 1864. District of Florida, Dept. South, to October, 1864. 4th Separate Brigade, District Florida, Dept. South, to July, 1865.

SERVICE.—Duty at Fort Marshall, Defences of Baltimore, till October, 1862. At Tennallytown, building Fort Kearney, October 15-November 3. March to Thoroughfare Gap and Chantilly November 3-12. Duty at Brook's Station. Va., December, 1862, to April, 1863. "Mud March" January 20-24, 1863. Chancellorsville Campaign April 27-May 6. Battle of Chancellorsville May 1-5. Gettysburg (Pa.) Campaign June 11-July 24. Battle of Gettysburg July 1-3. Hagerstown, Md., July 11-13. Moved to Folly Island, S. C., August 1-12. Siege operations on Morris Island, S. C., against Forts Wagner and Gregg, and against Fort Sumter and Charleston August 15-September 7. Capture of Forts Wagner and Gregg September 7. Moved to Folly Island, S. C., and duty there, operating against Charleston, S. C., till February, 1864. Expedition to John's and James Islands February 6-14. Ordered to Jacksonville, Fla., February 22, and duty there till April 15. Moved to St. Augustine, Fla., April 15-17, and duty there till June, 1865. Action at Welaka May 19, 1864 (Detachment). Expedition to Camp Milton May 31-June 3. Action at Milton June 2. Whitesville July 24. Companies "A," "C," "I" and "K" at Picolata, St. Johns River, July 18, 1864, to February, 1865. Companies "A," "E," "F" and "H" moved to Jacksonville July 22, 1864, and participated in Expedition to Baldwin July 23-28. Expedition to Enterprise September 28, 1864. Companies "C," "F" and "H" at Lake City, Fla., and "G" and "I" at Tallahatchie May and June, 1865. Regiment moved from St. Augustine to Jacksonville June 9, and duty there till July 7. Mustered out July 19, 1865.

Regiment lost during service 5 Officers and 48 Enlisted men killed and mortally wounded and 1 Officer and 74 Enlisted men by disease. Total 128.

18th REGIMENT INFANTRY.

Organized at Norwich August 22, 1862. Left State for Baltimore, Md., August 22. Attached to Defences of Baltimore, Md., 8th Corps, Middle Dept., to January, 1863. 2nd Separate Brigade, 8th Corps, to February, 1863. 2nd Brigade, 2nd Division, 8th Army Corps, to June, 1863. Unattached, Scammon's Division, Dept. West Virginia, to December, 1863. 3rd Division, 1st Division, West Virginia, to April, 1864. 1st Brigade, 1st Division, West Virginia, to July, 1864. 2nd Brigade, 1st Division, West Virginia, to October, 1864. New Haven, Conn., to November, 1864. 1st Brigade, 3rd Division, West Virginia, to April, 1865. 1st Brigade, 2nd Division, West Virginia, to June, 1865.

SERVICE.—Duty at Forts McHenry and Marshall, Defences of Baltimore, till May, 1863. Moved to Winchester, Va., and joined Milroy's Command May 22.

Battle of Winchester June 13-15. Mostly captured June 15. Paroled July 2 and exchanged October 1, 1863. Moved to Martinsburg, Va., to join those not captured. Provost duty at Hagerstown, Md., till September 30, and at Martinsburg till March, 1864. At Bolivar Heights March 7-28. Reconnoissance toward Snicker's Gap March 16-18. On furlough March 28-April 9. Sigel's Expedition from Martinsburg to New Market April 29-May 17. Battle of New Market May 15. Hunter's Expedition to Lynchburg May 26-July 1. Advance on Staunton May 26-June 5. Action at Piedmont, Mount Crawford, June 5. Occupation of Staunton June 6. Lynchburg June 17-18. Moved to Camp Piatt, thence to Parkersburg, Cumberland, Md., Martinsburg, Harper's Ferry and Snicker's Ford July 1-18. Snicker's Ferry July 18. Battle of Kernstown, Winchester, July 24. Martinsburg July 25. At Charlestown, W. Va., till October, and at Martinsburg October 1-29. Moved to New Haven, Conn., and duty at Conscript Camp till November 11. Moved to Martinsburg, W. Va., November 11-13, thence to Halltown November 23, and duty there till March, 1865, and at Martinsburg till June. Mustered out at Harper's Ferry, W. Va., June 27, 1865.

Regiment lost during service 4 Officers and 67 Enlisted men killed and mortally wounded and 1 Officer and 80 Enlisted men by disease. Total 152.

19th REGIMENT INFANTRY.

Organized at Litchfield July 25 to September 9, 1862. Left State for Washington, D. C., September 15. Attached to Slough's Brigade, District of Alexandria, Defences of Washington, to January, 1863. Tyler's Command, Artillery, District of Alexandria, Military District of Washington, and 22nd Army Corps, Dept. of Washington, to April, 1863. 2nd Brigade, DeRussy's Division, 22nd Army Corps, to November, 1863.

SERVICE.—Guard and patrol duty at Alexandria, Va., till January 12, 1863. Garrison duty at Fort Worth till May, and at redoubts near Fort Lyon till November. (Cos. "B," "F" and "G" at Fort Ellsworth.) Designation of Regiment changed to 2nd Connecticut Heavy Artillery November 23, 1863. (See 2nd Heavy Artillery.)

20th REGIMENT INFANTRY.

Organized at New Haven September 8, 1862. Left State for Washington, D. C., September 11. Attached to 2nd Brigade, 1st Division, 12th Army Corps, Army of the Potomac, to May, 1863. 1st Brigade, 1st Division, 12th Army Corps, Army of the Potomac, to October, 1863, and Army of the Cumberland to April, 1864. 1st Brigade, 1st Division, 20th Army Corps, Army of the Cumberland, April, 1864. 2nd Brigade, 3rd Division, 20th Army Corps, to May, 1864. 3rd Brigade, 3rd Division, 20th Army Corps, to June, 1865.

SERVICE.—Duty in the Defences of Washington till September 29, 1862. Moved to Frederick, Md., September 29, thence to Sandy Hook October 2. March to Fredericksburg, Va., December 10. Duty at Fairfax Station, Va., December 14, 1862, to January 19, 1863. Moved to Stafford C. H. January 19-23, and duty there till April 27. Chancellorsville Campaign April 27-May 6. Battle of Chancellorsville May 1-5. Gettysburg (Pa.) Campaign June 11-July 24. Battle of Gettysburg July 1-3. Near Raccoon Ford till September 24. Moved to Brandy Station, thence to Bealeton and to Stevenson, Ala., September 24-October 3. Guard duty along Nashville & Chattanooga R. R. till April, 1864. Action at Tracy City, Tenn., January 20, 1864 (Co. "B"). Atlanta, Ga. Campaign May to September. Demonstration on Rocky Faced Ridge May 8-11. Buzzard's Roost Gap May 8-9. Boyd's Trail May 10. Battle of Resaca May 14-15. Cassville May 19. Guard Ordnance Trains May 24-June 13, and provost duty at Ackworth, Ga., till July 8. At Marietta till July 16. Peach Tree Creek July 19-20. Siege of Atlanta July 22-August 25. Operations at Chattahoochee River Bridge August 26-September 2. Occupation of Atlanta September 2-November 15. March to the sea November 15-December 10. Siege of Savannah December 10-21. At Hardee's Plantation January 4-16,

1865. Campaign of the Carolinas January to April. Lawtonville, S. C., February 2. Reconnoissance to Silver Run Creek, N. C., March 14. Averysboro or Taylor's Hole Creek March 16. Battle of Bentonville March 19-21. Occupation of Goldsboro March 24, and of Raleigh April 14. Bennett's House April 26. Surrender of Johnston and his army. March to Washington, D. C., via Richmond, Va., April 29-May 20. Grand Review May 24. Camp near Fort Lincoln till June 13. Mustered out June 13, 1865.

Regiment lost during service 4 Officers and 76 Enlisted men killed and mortally wounded and 3 Officers and 85 Enlisted men by disease. Total 168.

21st REGIMENT INFANTRY.

Organized at Norwich September 5, 1862. Left State for Washington, D. C., September 11. Attached to 2nd Brigade, 3rd Division, 9th Army Corps, Army of the Potomac, to January, 1863. 3rd Brigade, 3rd Division, 9th Army Corps, to April, 1863. 3rd Brigade, 2nd Division, 7th Army Corps, Dept. of Virginia, to July, 1863. 3rd Brigade, Getty's Division, Portsmouth, Va., Dept. of Virginia and North Carolina, to October, 1863. Heckman's Command, Newport News, Va., Dept. Virginia and North Carolina, to February, 1864. Defences of Newberne, N. C., Dept. Virginia and North Carolina, to March, 1864. Sub-District of the Pamlico, N. C., Dept. Virginia and North Carolina, to May, 1864. 3rd Brigade, 1st Division, 18th Army Corps, Dept. of Virginia and North Carolina, to December, 1864. 3rd Brigade, 3rd Division, 24th Army Corps, Dept. of Virginia, to June, 1865.

SERVICE.—Duty at Arlington Heights, Va., Defences of Washington, D. C., till November, 1862. March to Falmouth, Va., November 7-19. Battle of Fredericksburg, Va., December 12-15. Burnside's 2nd Campaign, "Mud March," January 20-24, 1863. Moved to Newport News, Va., February 6-9, thence to Suffolk, Va., March 13. Siege of Suffolk April 12-May 4. Chuckatuck and Reed's Ferry, Nansemond River, May 3. Siege of Suffolk raised May 4. Reconnoissance to Chickahominy June 9-16. Moved to Portsmouth, Va., June 16. Provost and guard duty at Portsmouth and Norfolk till November 10. Moved to Newport News November 10, and duty there till February, 1864. Expedition up James River to Fort Powhatan January 24-25. Smithfield February 1. Moved to Morehead City, N. C., February 3, thence to Newberne February 12, and duty there, at Plymouth and at Washington, N. C., till April. Near Blount's Creek April 5. Moved to Portsmouth, Va., April 28. Butler's operations on South Side of the James River and against Petersburg and Richmond May 10-28. Swift Creek, or Arrowfield Church, May 10. Operations against Fort Darling May 12-16. Battle of Drewry's Bluff May 14-16. At Bermuda Hundred May 17-27. Moved to White House, thence to Cold Harbor May 27-31. Battles about Cold Harbor June 1-12. Before Petersburg June 15-18. Siege operations against Petersburg and Richmond June 16, 1864, to April 2, 1865. Hare's Hill June 24-28, 1864. In trenches at Bermuda Hundred August 25-September 27, 1864. Chaffin's Farm, New Market Heights, September 28-30. Fair Oaks October 27-28. Duty in trenches before Richmond till March, 1865. Expedition to Fredericksburg March 5-8, and up the Potomac River March 11-13. Moved to White House March 13-18, thence to Signal Hill, before Richmond, March 24-26. Occupation of Richmond April 3. Moved to Columbia April 28, and duty there till June. Mustered out June 16, 1865.

Regiment lost during service 5 Officers and 55 Enlisted men killed and mortally wounded and 1 Officer and 114 Enlisted men by disease. Total 175.

22nd REGIMENT INFANTRY.

Organized at Hartford and mustered in September 20, 1862. Left State for Washington, D. C., October 2. Attached to 2nd Brigade, Abercrombie's Division, Military District of Washington, and 22nd Army Corps, Dept. of Washington, to April, 1863. 1st Brigade, 3rd

Division, 7th Army Corps, Dept. of Virginia, to May, 1863. 2nd Brigade, 2nd Division, 4th Army Corps, Dept. of Virginia, to July, 1863.

SERVICE.—Picket duty at Langley's, Va., on Washington and Leesburg Turnpike, Defences of Washington, D. C., till October 22, 1862. At Miner's Hill till February 12, 1863. Expedition to intercept Stuart's Cavalry December 29-30, 1862. Fatigue duty, building Forts Craig, McDowell and McClellan, Defences of Washington, till April 14, 1863. Moved to Suffolk, Va., April 14-16. Siege of Suffolk April 16-May 4. Siege of Suffolk raised May 4. Moved to West Point, York River, Va., May 5, and duty there till June 9. Reconnoissance to the Chickahominy June 9-10. Left Yorktown for home June 26. Mustered out July 7, 1863.

Regiment lost during service 20 Enlisted men by disease.

23rd REGIMENT INFANTRY.

Organized at New Haven November 14, 1862. Left State for East New York November 17, thence sailed for Ship Island, Miss., and New Orleans, La., November 29, arriving there December 17. (Part of Regiment did not reach New Orleans until January 16, 1863, having been stranded on Bahama Islands.) Attached to Defences of New Orleans and District of La Fourche, Dept. of the Gulf.

SERVICE.—Duty at Camp Parapet, Defences of New Orleans, till January 11, 1863. Moved to Algiers January 11, thence to Berwick Bay. Provost duty at Brashear City till February 9. Duty along Opelousas R. R. from Berwick Bay to Jefferson, Headquarters at La Fourche, till June, at following points: Company "D" at Jefferson, Company "G" at St. Charles, Company "I" at Boutte Station, Company "C" at Bayou des Allemands, Company "H" at Raceland, Company "B" at La Fourche till April 1, then at Napoleonville, Terre Bonne; Company "K" at Tigersville, Company "A" at Bayou Boeuf till March 1, thence moved to Bayou des Allemands and to Labadieville April 1; Company "E" at Bayou Romans till March 1, Companies "E" and "I" at La Fourche March 1. Duty at these points till June. Company "A" moved to Bayou Boeuf June 16, and Companies "B" and "E" to La Fourche. Other Companies to Brashear City. Action at Berwick June 1 (Cos. "C," "I," "G" and "K"). Regiment moved to La Fourche Crossing June 16. Action at La Fourche Crossing June 20-21. Bayou Boeuf June 22-23. Brashear City June 23. Companies "A," "C" and "H" captured June 23; paroled June 26. Regiment on guard duty in lowlands of Louisiana till August. Mustered out August 31, 1863.

Regiment lost during service 1 Officer and 10 Enlisted men killed and mortally wounded and 2 Officers and 46 Enlisted men by disease. Total 59.

24th REGIMENT INFANTRY.

Organized at Middletown and mustered in November 18, 1862. Left State for East New York November 18, thence sailed for New Orleans and Baton Rouge, La., November 29, arriving there December 17. Attached to Grover's Division, Dept. of the Gulf, to January, 1863. 2nd Brigade, 4th Division, 19th Army Corps, Dept. of the Gulf, to July, 1863. Defences of New Orleans to August, 1863.

SERVICE.—Duty at Baton Rouge till March, 1863. Operations against Port Hudson March 7-27. Moved to Donaldsonville March 28. Operations in Western Louisiana April 9-May 14. Teche Campaign April 11-20. Irish Bend April 14. Bayou Vermillion April 17. Expedition to Alexandria and Simsport May 5-18. Destruction of Salt Works, near New Iberia, May 18. Moved to Bayou Sara, thence to Port Hudson, May 22-25. Siege of Port Hudson May 25-July 9. Assaults on Port Hudson May 27 and June 14. Surrender of Port Hudson July 9. Ordered to Plaquemine District July 11, and duty there till September. Mustered out September 30, 1863.

Regiment lost during service 16 Enlisted men killed and mortally wounded and 2 Officers and 57 Enlisted men by disease. Total, 75.

25th REGIMENT INFANTRY.

Organized at Hartford and mustered in November 11, 1862. Left State for East New York November 14, thence sailed for New Orleans and Baton Rouge, La., November 29, arriving there December 17. Attached to Grover's Division, Dept. of the Gulf, to January, 1863. 3rd Brigade, 4th Division, 19th Army Corps, Dept. Gulf, to August, 1863.

SERVICE.—Duty at Baton Rouge till March, 1863. Operations against Port Hudson March 7-27. Moved to Donaldsonville March 28. Operations in Western Louisiana April 9-May 14. Teche Campaign April 11-20. Porter's and McWilliams' Plantation at Indian Bend April 13. Irish Bend April 14. Bayou Vermillion April 17. Expedition to Alexandria and Simsport May 5-18. Moved to Bayou Sara, thence to Port Hudson May 22-25. Siege of Port Hudson May 25-July 9. Assaults on Port Hudson May 27 and June 14. Surrender of Port Hudson July 9. Moved to Donaldsonville July 11. Duty in Plaquemine District till August. Mustered out August 26, 1863.

Regiment lost during service 3 Officers and 26 Enlisted men killed and mortally wounded and 4 Officers and 61 Enlisted men by disease. Total 94.

26th REGIMENT INFANTRY.

Organized at Norwich November 10, 1862. Left State for East New York November 12, thence sailed for Ship Island and New Orleans, La., November 29, arriving December 16. Attached to Sherman's Division, Dept. of the Gulf, to January, 1863. 1st Brigade, 2nd Division, 19th Army Corps, Dept. of the Gulf, to August, 1863.

SERVICE.—Duty at Camp Parapet till May, 1863. Moved to Springfield Landing May 20. Siege of Port Hudson May 24-July 9. Assaults on Port Hudson May 27 and June 14. Surrender of Port Hudson July 9. Mustered out August 17, 1863.

Regiment lost during service 4 Officers and 51 Enlisted men killed and mortally wounded and 1 Officer and 89 Enlisted men by disease. Total 145.

27th REGIMENT INFANTRY.

Organized at New Haven October, 1862. Left State for Washington, D. C., October 22. Attached to Military District of Washington to November, 1862. 3rd Brigade, 1st Division, 2nd Army Corps, Army of the Potomac, to April, 1863. 4th Brigade, 1st Division, 2nd Army Corps, to July, 1863.

SERVICE.—Duty in the Defences of Washington, D. C., till November 7, 1862. Advance to Falmouth, Va., November 7-19. Battle of Fredericksburg, Va., December 12-15. "Mud March" January 20-24, 1863. At Falmouth till April 27. Chancellorsville Campaign April 27-May 6. Battle of Chancellorsville May 1-5. Gettysburg (Pa.) Campaign June 11-July 24. Battle of Gettysburg July 1-3. Mustered out July 27, 1863.

Regiment lost during service 4 Officers and 42 Enlisted men killed and mortally wounded and 22 Enlisted men by disease. Total 68.

28th REGIMENT INFANTRY.

Organized at New Haven November 15, 1862. Left State for East New York November 17. Sailed for Ship Island, Miss., and New Orleans, La., December 3, arriving December 17. Duty at Camp Parapet, Carrollton, La., till February, and at Fort Barrancas, Fla., till May. Moved to Brashear City, La., May 10-12, thence to Port Hudson, La., May 23-26. Attached to 1st Brigade, 3rd Division, 19th Army Corps, Dept. of the Gulf, to July, 1863. 2nd Brigade, 3rd Division, 19th Corps, to August, 1863.

SERVICE.—Siege of Port Hudson, La., May 26-July 9, 1863. Assaults on Port Hudson May 27 and June 14. Surrender of Port Hudson July 9. Duty at Port Hudson till August 7. Mustered out August 28, 1863.

Regiment lost during service 2 Officers and 14 Enlisted men killed and mortally wounded and 3 Officers and 94 Enlisted men by disease. Total 113.

29th REGIMENT INFANTRY (COLORED).

Organized at Fair Haven and mustered in March 8, 1864. Left State for Annapolis, Md., March 19. Moved to Beaufort, S. C., April 8-13, and duty there till August 8. Attached to District of Beaufort, Dept. of the South, April to August, 1864. 1st Brigade, 3rd Division, 10th Army Corps, Army of the James, Dept. Virginia and North Carolina, to December, 1864. 2nd Brigade, 3rd Division, 25th Army Corps, to January, 1865. 2nd Brigade, 1st Division, 25th Army Corps, to April, 1865. District of St. Marys, 22nd Army Corps, Dept. of Washington, to May, 1865. 2nd Brigade, 1st Division, 25th Army Corps, Dept. of Texas, to October, 1865.

SERVICE.—Moved from Beaufort, S. C., to Bermuda Hundred, Va., August 8-13, 1864. Siege operations against Petersburg and Richmond August 13, 1864, to April 2, 1865. Demonstration on North Side of the James August 13-20, 1864. Deep Bottom, Strawberry Plains, August 14-18. Duty in the trenches before Petersburg August 25-September 24. New Market Heights and Fort Harrison September 28-29. Chaffin's Farm September 29-30. Darbytown Road October 13. Battle of Fair Oaks October 27-28. Duty in trenches before Richmond till April, 1865. Occupation of Richmond April 3. (First Infantry Regiment to enter city.) Moved to City Point April 18, thence to Point Lookout, Md., and duty there guarding prisoners till May 28. Moved to City Point May 28-30, thence sailed for Texas June 10, arriving at Brazos, Santiago, July 3. March to Brownsville and duty there till October. Mustered out October 24, 1865. At New Orleans October 27-November 11. Honorably discharged at New Haven, Conn., November 25, 1865.

Regiment lost during service 1 Officer and 44 Enlisted men killed and mortally wounded and 1 Officer and 152 Enlisted men by disease. Total 198.

30th REGIMENT INFANTRY (COLORED).

Organized at Fair Haven (4 Cos.) March, 1864. Moved to Annapolis, Md. Consolidated with 31st U. S. C. T. May 18, 1864. (See that Regiment.)

DAKOTA VOLUNTEERS.

1st BATTALION CAVALRY.

Organized, Company "A" at Yankton, D. T., April, 1862. Company "B" at Sioux City, Iowa, March 31, 1863.

Assigned to duty in the District of Iowa and Dakota Department of the Northwest, defending frontiers and operating against Indians. Participated in Sully's Expedition against hostile Sioux Indians in Dakota July 25 to Oct. 8, 1864, with engagements at Tah-kah-a-kuty July 28, and at Two Hills, Bad Lands, Little Missouri River August 8-9. Mustered out Co. A May 9, 1865, Co. B Nov. 15, 1865.

DELAWARE VOLUNTEERS.

1st REGIMENT CAVALRY.

Organized at Wilmington, Del., January 20, 1863. Attached to 1st Separate Brigade, 8th Army Corps, Middle Dept., to June, 1863. Cavalry Reserve, Defences of Baltimore, 8th Army Corps, to October, 1863. 3rd Separate Brigade, 8th Army Corps, to December, 1863. Cavalry Reserve, Defences of Baltimore, 8th Army Corps, to March, 1864. 3rd Separate Brigade, 8th Army Corps, to May, 1864. 1st Brigade, 1st Division, 6th Army Corps, Army of the Potomac, to July, 1864. 1st Separate Brigade, 8th Army Corps, to June, 1865.

SERVICE.—Duty at Wilmington, Del., till June, 1863, and in the Defences of Baltimore, Md. Engaged in provost duty at Baltimore City and in the surrounding country till June, 1864. Action at Westminster June 29, 1863. (Cos. "A" and "D" in District of Delaware to December, 1863. Cos. "D" and "E" in Delaware till March, 1864. Co. "E" at Havre de Grace April, 1864.) Regiment ordered to join Army of the Potomac in the field May 15, 1864. Reported and assigned to 6th Army Corps June 5. Operations about Cold Harbor June 5-12.

Before Petersburg June 17-July 10. Jerusalem Plank Road June 22-23. Ream's Station June 29. Assigned as guard to Artillery Brigade, 6th Army Corps, in movement to Baltimore and Washington, D. C., July 10-12. Ordered to Baltimore July 14. (Co. "A" remained with Army of the Potomac as guard to Reserve Artillery, 6th Army Corps, till September, 1864, when relieved and ordered to rejoin Regiment in Middle Department.) Duty on line of the Baltimore & Ohio R. R. Picket and outpost duty and guarding fords of the Potomac from Georgetown to Point of Rocks till November, 1864. (In Delaware during election of 1864.) Duty on Upper Potomac and on line of the Baltimore & Ohio R. R. till June, 1865. Operations in Montgomery County October 7-11, 1864. Mustered out June 30, 1865.

Regiment lost during service 2 Enlisted men killed and 2 Officers and 47 Enlisted men by disease. Total 51.

MILLIGAN'S INDEPENDENT CAVALRY COMPANY.

Organized at Wilmington, Del., for 30 days' service July 15, 1864. Assigned to 3rd Separate Brigade, 8th Army Corps, Middle Dept. Patrol duty from Middleburg to Hanover July 14-18. In Defences of Baltimore till July 30. Moved to Middleburg, and patrol duty about Middleburg, Liberty, Hanover and Westminster till August 10. Ordered to Wilmington, Del., August 10, and mustered out August 15, 1864.

AHL'S HEAVY ARTILLERY COMPANY.

Organized at Fort Delaware July 27, 1863, and garrison duty at Fort Delaware during entire service. Mustered out July 25, 1865.

NIELDS' INDEPENDENT BATTERY LIGHT ARTILLERY.

Organized at Wilmington, Del., August 30, 1862. Ordered to Washington, D. C., September, 1862. Attached to Camp Barry, Defences of Washington, D. C., to February, 1863. Camp Barry, Defences of Washington, 22nd Army Corps, to April, 1863. Unattached Artillery, 7th Army Corps, Dept. of Virginia, to June, 1863. Artillery, 1st Division, 7th Army Corps, to July, 1863. Camp Barry, 22nd Army Corps, to August, 1863. Dept. of the East to October, 1863. Camp Barry, 22nd Army Corps, to February, 1864. Defences of New Orleans, La., Dept. of the Gulf, to July, 1864. Artillery, 1st Division, 19th Army Corps, Dept. of the Gulf, to August, 1864. Artillery, 3rd Division, 19th Army Corps, Dept. of the Gulf, to November, 1864. Unassigned Artillery, Reserve Corps, Military Division West Mississippi, to December, 1864. Artillery, 2nd Division, 7th Army Corps, Dept. of Arkansas, to June, 1865.

SERVICE.—Duty in the Defences of Washington, D. C., till April, 1863. Ordered to Norfolk, Va., April 18. Siege of Norfolk April 21-May 4. Dix's Peninsula Campaign June 23-July 8. Ordered to Washington, D. C., July 8, and duty in the defences of that city till August. At New York City, Dept. of the East, till September 12, and at Light Artillery Camp of Instruction, Defences of Washington, till February, 1864. Ordered to Dept. of the Gulf, and at New Orleans, La., till March 2. Ordered to Franklin March 2. Red River Campaign March 10-May 22. Advance from Franklin to Alexandria, La., March 15-26. Battles of Sabine Cross Roads April 8 and Pleasant Hill April 9 (Reserve). At Grand Ecore April 10-22. Cane River Crossing April 23. At Alexandria April 26-May 13. Retreat to Morganza May 13-20. At Morganza till October 16. Ordered to mouth of White River and duty there and at Morganza till December. Ordered to Arkansas December 11. Duty at mouth of White River and at Little Rock, Ark., till June, 1865. Mustered out June 23, and discharged from service July 5, 1865.

Battery lost 6 by disease during service.

1st REGIMENT INFANTRY (3 MONTHS).

Organized at Wilmington, Del., May 22, 1861. Attached to Dix's Command and assigned to duty on line of the Philadelphia, Wilmington & Baltimore R. R. at

Havre de Grace, Elkton, Perryville, Bush River, Gunpowder, Northeast and Charlestown, guarding road and protecting bridges till August. Mustered out August 30, 1861.

1st REGIMENT INFANTRY (3 YEARS).

Organized at Wilmington, Del., September 10 to October 19, 1861. Moved to Fortress Monroe, Va., October 20-21, 1861. Attached to Fortress Monroe, Va., Dept. of Virginia, to May, 1862. . 2nd Brigade, 1st Division, Dept. of Virginia, to July, 1862. Weber's Brigade, Division at Suffolk, Va., 7th Army Corps, Dept. of Virginia, to September, 1862. 3rd Brigade, 3rd Division, 2nd Army Corps, Army of the Potomac, to May, 1863. 2nd Brigade, 3rd Division, 2nd Army Corps, to March, 1864. 3rd Brigade, 2nd Division, 2nd Army Corps, to July, 1865.

SERVICE.—Duty at Camp Hamilton, Va., till May, 1862. Engagement between "Monitor" and "Merrimac" in Hampton Roads, Va., March 8-9, 1862. Expedition to Norfolk May 9-10. Occupation of Norfolk May 10, and duty at Norfolk, Portsmouth and Suffolk till September 8. Moved to Washington, D. C., thence to Antietam, Md., September 8-16. Battle of Antietam, Md., September 16-17. Moved to Harper's Ferry, W. Va., September 22, and duty there till October 30. Reconnoissance to Charlestown October 16-17. Advance up Loudon Valley and movement to Falmouth, Va., October 30-November 17. Battle of Fredericksburg, Va., December 12-15. At Falmouth till April 27, 1863. "Mud March" January 20-24. Chancellorsville Campaign April 27-May 6. Battle of Chancellorsville May 1-6. Gettysburg (Pa.) Campaign June 11-July 24. Battle of Gettysburg July 1-3. Pursuit of Lee to Manassas Gap, Va., July 5-24. Williamsport, Md., July 13-14. Duty on line of the Rappahannock and Rapidan till October. Advance from the Rappahannock to the Rapidan September 13-17. Bristoe Campaign October 9-22. Auburn and Bristoe October 14. Blackburn's Ford October 15. Advance to line of the Rappahannock November 7-8. Mine Run Campaign November 26-December 2. At and near Stevensburg, Va., till May, 1864. Demonstration on the Rapidan February 6-7. Campaign from the Rapidan to the James May 3-June 15. Battles of the Wilderness May 5-7. Laurel Hill May 8. Spottsylvania May 8-12. Po River May 10. Spottsylvania Court House May 12-21. Assault on the Salient "Bloody Angle" May 12. North Anna River May 23-26. On line of the Pamunkey May 26-28. Totopotomoy May 28-31. Cold Harbor June 1-12. Before Petersburg June 16-18. Siege of Petersburg June 16, 1864, to April 2, 1865. Jerusalem Plank Road, Weldon R. R., June 22-23, 1864. Demonstration North of the James July 27-29. Deep Bottom July 27-28. Mine Explosion, Petersburg, July 30 (Reserve). Demonstration North of the James August 13-20. Strawberry Plains, Deep Bottom, August 14-18. Ream's Station August 25. Yellow House October 1-5. Boydton Plank Road, Hatcher's Run, October 27-28. Dabney's Mills, Hatcher's Run, February 5-7, 1865. Watkins' House March 25. Appomattox Campaign March 28-April 9. Boydton Road and White Oak Ridge March 29-31. Crow's House March 31. Fall of Petersburg April 2. Pursuit of Lee April 3-9. Sailor's Creek April 6. High Bridge, Farmville, April 7. Appomattox Court House April 9. Surrender of Lee and his army. At Burkesville till May 2. March to Washington, D. C., May 2-12. Grand review May 23. At Washington, D. C., till July. Mustered out July 12, 1865.

Regiment lost during service 12 Officers and 146 Enlisted men killed and mortally wounded and 3 Officers and 118 Enlisted men by disease. Total 279.

2nd REGIMENT INFANTRY.

Organized at Wilmington, Del., June 12 to October 7, 1861. Moved to Baltimore, Md., October, 1861. Attached to Dix's Command till June, 1862. 3rd Brigade, 1st Division, 2nd Army Corps, Army of the Potomac, to April, 1863. 4th Brigade, 1st Division, 2nd Army Corps, to June, 1864. 3rd Brigade, 2nd Division, 2nd Army Corps, to July, 1864.

SERVICE.—Duty at Baltimore, Md., till June, 1862. Expedition through Accomac County November 14-22, 1861. Ordered to join Army of the Potomac, on the Peninsula, Va., June, 1862. Seven days before Richmond June 25-July 1. Savage Station June 27. Battle of Gaines Mill June 27. Peach Orchard and Savage Station June 29. White Oak Swamp and Glendale June 30. Malvern Hill July 1. At Harrison's Landing to August 16. Movement to Fortress Monroe, thence to Centreville, August 16-30. Cover Pope's retreat from Bull Run August 31-September 2. Maryland Campaign September 6-22. Sharpsburg September 15. Battle of Antietam September 16-17. Moved to Harper's Ferry September 22, and duty there till October 30. Reconnoissance to Charlestown October 16-17. Advance up Loudon Valley and movement to Falmouth Va., October 30-November 17. Battle of Fredericksburg, Va., December 12-15. At Falmouth, Va., till April 27, 1863. "Mud March" January 20-24. Chancellorsville Campaign April 27-May 6. Battle of Chancellorsville May 1-5. Gettysburg (Pa.) Campaign June 11-July 24. Battle of Gettysburg July 1-3. Pursuit of Lee to Manassas Gap, Va., July 5-24. Duty on line of the Rappahannock and Rapidan till October. Advance from line of the Rappahannock to the Rapidan September 13-17. Bristoe Campaign October 9-22. Auburn and Bristoe October 14. Advance to line of the Rappahannock November 7-8. Mine Run Campaign November 26-December 2. New Hope Church November 29. Mine Run November 28-30. At and near Stevensburg till May, 1864. Demonstration on the Rapidan February 6-7. Campaign from the Rapidan to the James May 3-June 15. Battles of the Wilderness May 5-7. Spottsylvania May 8-12. Po River May 10. Spottsylvania Court House May 12-21. Assault on the Salient "Bloody Angle" May 12. North Anna River May 23-26. On line of the Pamunkey May 26-28. Totopotomoy May 28-31. Cold Harbor June 1-12. Before Petersburg June 16-July 1. Jerusalem Plank Road, Weldon R. R., June 22-23. Mustered out July 1, 1864, expiration of term. Veterans and Recruits transferred to 1st Delaware Infantry.

Regiment lost during service 6 Officers and 93 Enlisted men killed and mortally wounded and 1 Officer and 101 Enlisted men by disease. Total 201.

3rd REGIMENT INFANTRY.

Organized at Camden December 30, 1861, to May 15, 1862. Ordered to Washington, D. C., May, 1862. Attached to Slough's Brigade, Defences of Washington, D. C., May, 1862. Slough's 2nd Brigade, Sigel's Division, Dept. of the Shenandoah, to June, 1862. 2nd Brigade, 2nd Division, 2nd Army Corps, Army of Virginia, to August, 1862. 3rd Brigade, 2nd Division, 2nd Army Corps, Army of Virginia, to September, 1862. 3rd Brigade, 2nd Division, 12th Army Corps, Army of the Potomac, to October, 1862. Defences of Baltimore, Md., 8th Army Corps, Middle Dept., to January, 1863. 3rd Separate Brigade, 8th Army Corps, to October, 1864. 1st Separate Brigade, 8th Army Corps, to May, 1864. 2nd Brigade, 4th Division, 5th Army Corps, Army of the Potomac, to August, 1864. 3rd Brigade, 2nd Division, 5th Army Corps, to June, 1865.

SERVICE.—Defence of Harper's Ferry, W. Va., May 28-30, 1862. Operations in the Shenandoah Valley till August. Battle of Cedar Mountain August 9. Pope's Campaign in Northern Virginia August 16-September 2. Sulphur Springs August 23-24. Groveton August 29. Bull Run August 30. Sulphur Springs August 30. Chantilly September 1. Maryland Campaign September 6-22. Battles of South Mountain September 14. Antietam, Md., September 16-17. Duty at Frederick, Md.; Relay House, Md., and Elysville, Md., guarding R. R., and garrison duty in Middle Dept. till May, 1864. Ordered to join Army of the Potomac in the field May, 1864. Rapidan Campaign May 29-June 15. Totopotomoy May 29-31. Cold Harbor June 1-3. Before Petersburg June 16-18. Siege of Petersburg June 16, 1864, to April 2, 1865. Mine Explosion, Petersburg, July 30, 1864 (Reserve). Weldon R. R. August 18-21. Poplar Springs Church September 29-October 2. Boydton Plank Road, Hatcher's Run, October 27-28. Warren's Raid on Weldon R. R. December 7-12. Dabney's Mills, Hatcher's Run, February 5-7, 1865. Appomattox Campaign March 28-April 9. Lewis Farm, near Gravelly Run, March 29. Boydton and White Oak Roads March 30-31. Five Forks April 1. Fall of Petersburg April 2. Pursuit of Lee April 3-9. Appomattox Court House April 9. Surrender of Lee and his army. March to Washington, D. C., May 1-12. Grand review May 23. Mustered out June 3, 1865.

Regiment lost during service 7 Officers and 46 Enlisted men killed and mortally wounded and 2 Officers and 80 Enlisted men by disease. Total 135.

4th REGIMENT INFANTRY.

Organized at Wilmington, Del., June to November, 1862. Ordered to Baltimore, Md., September, 1862. Attached to Defences of Baltimore, 8th Army Corps, Middle Dept., to December, 1862. Busteed's Independent Brigade, 4th Army Corps, Dept. of Virginia, to May, 1863. King's Independent Brigade, 4th Army Corps, to June, 1863. Unattached, 4th Army Corps, to July. Unassigned, King's Division, 22nd Army Corps, Dept. of Washington, to January, 1864. Tyler's Division, 22nd Army Corps, to May, 1864. 2nd Brigade, 4th Division, 5th Army Corps, Army of the Potomac, to August, 1864. 3rd Brigade, 2nd Division, 5th Army Corps, to June, 1865.

SERVICE.—Duty in the Defences of Baltimore, Md., till December, 1862. Ordered to Yorktown, Va., arriving there December 28, and duty there till July, 1863. Expedition from Gloucester Point to Gloucester Court House April 7, 1863. Reconnoissance from Gloucester Point to Hickory Fork April 12. Expedition from Gloucester Point into Matthews County May 19-22. Expedition from Yorktown to Walkerton and Aylett's June 4-5. Dix's Peninsula Campaign June 24-July 7. Expedition from White House to South Anna River July 1-7. Baltimore Store July 2. Moved to Washington, D. C., July 8-14, and duty in the defences of that city and at Centreville and Fairfax Station till October, 1863. Guard Orange & Alexandria R. R. till November 16. Ordered to Delaware November 16. Duty in the District of Alexandria, Va., till May, 1864. Ordered to join Army of the Potomac in the field May, 1864. Rapidan Campaign May 29-June 15. Totopotomoy May 29-31. Cold Harbor June 1-12. Before Petersburg June 16-18. Siege of Petersburg June 16, 1864, to April 2, 1865. Mine Explosion, Petersburg, July 30, 1864. Reserve, Weldon R. R., August 18-21. Poplar Springs Church September 29-October 1. Yellow House October 1-3. Boydton Plank Road, Hatcher's Run, October 27-28. Warren's Raid on Weldon R. R. December 7-12. Dabney's Mills, Hatcher's Run, February 5-7, 1865. Appomattox Campaign March 28-April 9. Lewis Farm, near Gravelly Run, March 29. White Oak Road March 30. Gravelly Run March 31. Five Forks April 1. Fall of Petersburg April 2. Pursuit of Lee April 3-9. Appomattox Court House April 9. Surrender of Lee and his army. Moved to Washington, D. C., May 1-12. Grand review May 23. Mustered out June 3, 1865.

Regiment lost during service 4 Officers and 80 Enlisted men killed and mortally wounded and 1 Officer and 79 Enlisted men by disease. Total 164.

5th REGIMENT INFANTRY.

Organized in Delaware at large October 25 to November 26, 1862. Duty in Delaware and as garrison at Fort Delaware, and guard duty on line of the Philadelphia, Wilmington & Baltimore R. R. from Perryville to Baltimore, till August, 1863. Attached to District of Delaware, 8th Army Corps, Middle Dept., to July, 1863. 2nd Separate Brigade, 8th Army Corps, Middle Dept., to August. Mustered out August 12, 1863.

Regiment lost 3 by disease during service.

6th REGIMENT INFANTRY.

Organized in Delaware at large October 25 to December 18, 1862. Duty in District of Delaware, 8th Army Corps, Middle Dept., as R. R. guard on Philadelphia, Wilmington & Baltimore R. R. at Havre de Grace, Bush River, Gunpowder, Back River and Perrymansville till September, 1863. Mustered out September 5, 1863.

Regiment lost 10 by disease during service.

7th REGIMENT INFANTRY.

Organized at Wilmington, Del., for 30 days July 12, 1864. Guard duty on Philadelphia, Wilmington & Baltimore R. R. at Havre de Grace, Oconowingo Bridge, till July. Moved to Baltimore, Md., July 16, and duty in the defences of that city till August 12. Attached to 3rd Separate Brigade, 8th Army Corps, Middle Dept. Mustered out August 12, 1864.

Regiment lost 3 by disease during service.

8th REGIMENT INFANTRY.

Organized at Wilmington, Del., October, 1864. Ordered to City Point, Va., reporting there October 13, 1864. Attached to Engineer Brigade, Army of the Potomac, to January 12, 1865. Provost Guard, Army of the Potomac, to March, 1865. 3rd Brigade, 2nd Division, 5th Army Corps, Army of the Potomac, to June, 1865.

SERVICE.—Duty in the Defences of City Point, Va., and provost duty at General Army Headquarters till March 16, 1865. Joined 5th Army Corps March 18. Appomattox Campaign March 28-April 9. Lewis Farm, near Gravelly Run, March 29. White Oak Ridge March 31. Five Forks April 1. Fall of Petersburg April 2. Pursuit of Lee April 3-9. Appomattox Court House April 9. Surrender of Lee and his army. Moved to Washington, D. C., May 2-12. Grand review May 23. Mustered out June 5, 1865.

Regiment lost during service 3 Enlisted men killed and mortally wounded and 10 Enlisted men by disease. Total 13.

9th REGIMENT INFANTRY.

Organized at Wilmington, Del., for 100 days August 30, 1864. Assigned to duty guarding prisoners at Fort Delaware till January, 1865. Mustered out January 23, 1865.

Lost 11 by disease during service.

STERLING'S COMPANY INFANTRY.

Organized at Wilmington, Del., August 30, 1864. Guard Philadelphia, Wilmington & Baltimore R. R., and duty in District of Delaware till July, 1865. Mustered out July 17, 1865.

DISTRICT OF COLUMBIA VOLUNTEERS.

1st REGIMENT CAVALRY.

Organized (4 Cos. "A," "B," "C" and "E") at Washington, D. C., June to December, 1863, for special service in District of Columbia and to be subject only to orders of War Department. Attached to Defences of Washington, D. C., 22nd Army Corps, to January, 1864. Cavalry Brigade, U. S. Forces, Yorktown, Va., Dept. of Virginia and North Carolina, to April, 1864. (8 Cos. organized at Augusta, Me., January to March, 1864, and ordered to report at Norfolk, Va.) 1st Brigade, Kautz's Cavalry Division, Dept. of Virginia and North Carolina, to June, 1864. 2nd Brigade, Kautz's Cavalry Division, Dept. of Virginia and North Carolina, to January, 1865. 2nd Brigade, Cavalry Division, Dept. of Virginia, to August, 1865. Cavalry, Dept. of Virginia, to October, 1865.

SERVICE.—Duty in the Defences of Washington, D. C., till January, 1864. Skirmish near Annandale, Va., October 22, 1863 (Detachment). Bealeton, Va., October 24. Ordered to Dept. of Virginia and North Carolina, and on duty at Yorktown, and a portion of the Regiment at Portsmouth, till May, 1864, dismounted, till May, 1864. Kautz's Raid on Petersburg & Weldon R. R. May 5-11, 1864. Double Bridges May 5. Stony Creek Station May 7. White's Bridge, Nottaway Creek and Nottaway R. R. Bridge May 8. White's Bridge May 9.

Kautz's Raid on Richmond & Danville R. R. May 12-17. Belcher's Mills May 16. Petersburg June 9. Assaults on Petersburg June 15-19. Siege operations against Petersburg and Richmond June 16, 1864, to April 2, 1865. Wilson's Raid on Southside & Danville R. R. June 22-30, 1864. Staunton River Bridge, or Roanoke Station, June 25. Sappony Church, or Stony Creek, June 28-29. Ream's Station June 29-July 3. Demonstration on North Side of James River, with engagements at Deep Bottom, Darbytown and New Market Roads July 27-28. Sycamore Church August 9. Ream's Station August 21-23. Dinwiddie Road, near Ream's Station, August 23. Ream's Station August 24-25. (Cos. "D," "F," "G," "H," "I," "K" and "L" transferred to 1st Maine Cavalry August 27, 1864. Other Cos. consolidated to a Battalion of 2 Cos.) Prince George Court House September 1. Sycamore Church and Blackwater River September 3. Sycamore Church September 15. Cox's Mill September 15. Coggin's Point September 16. Darbytown Road October 7 and 13. Fair Oaks October 27-28. Russell's Mills November 23. Bellefield Raid December 7-12. Expedition to Fernsville and Smithfield February 11-15, 1865. Appomattox Campaign March 28-April 9, 1865. Dinwiddie Court House March 30-31. Five Forks April 1. Gravelly Ford on Hatcher's Run April 2. Near Amelia Court House April 4-5. Dinwiddie Road and Sailor's Creek April 6. Farmville and Prince Edward Court House April 7. Appomattox Station April 8. Appomattox Court House April 9. Surrender of Lee and his army. Expedition to Danville April 23-27. Duty in the Dept. of Virginia till October. Mustered out October 26, 1865.

OWENS' MILITIA CAVALRY COMPANY.

Organized at Washington, D. C., April 26, 1861, for the defence of the Capital. Mustered out July 19, 1861.

1st REGIMENT INFANTRY.

Organized at Washington, D. C., July 23 to October 25, 1861. Attached to Provisional Brigade, Casey's Division, Army of the Potomac, to November, 1861. Robinson's Brigade, Army of the Potomac, to December, 1861. Railroad guard, Bladensburg, Md., to May, 1862. Miles' Command, Harper's Ferry, W. Va., to June, 1862. 2nd Brigade, Sigel's Division, Dept. of the Shenandoah, to July, 1862. 2nd Brigade, 2nd Division, 2nd Army Corps, Army of Virginia, to August, 1862. 3rd Brigade, 2nd Division, 2nd Army Corps, Army of Virginia, to September, 1862. 3rd Brigade, 2nd Division, 12th Army Corps, Army of the Potomac, to October, 1862. District of Alexandria, Defences of Washington, D. C., to February, 1863. Slough's Command, Defences of Alexandria, 22nd Army Corps, Dept. of Washington, to February, 1865.

SERVICE.—Duty in the Defences of Washington, D. C., till December, 1861. Guard R. R. near Bladensburg, Md., till May, 1862. Ordered to Harper's Ferry, W. Va. Defence of Harper's Ferry, W. Va., May 24-30. Operations in the Shenandoah Valley, Va., till August. Battle of Cedar Mountain August 9. Pope's Campaign in Northern Virginia August 16-September 2. Fords of the Rappahannock August 28-26. Plains of Manassas August 27-29. Battle of Bull Run August 29-30 (Reserve). Moved to Washington, D. C., and duty in the defences of that city and Alexandria, Va., till February, 1865. Repulse of Early's attack on Washington July 11-13, 1864. Consolidated with 2nd Regiment District of Columbia Infantry February 28, 1865.

2nd REGIMENT INFANTRY.

Organized at Washington, D. C., February 26, 1862. Attached to Sturgis' Brigade, Military District of Washington, D. C., to February, 1863, and 22nd Army Corps, Dept. of Washington, to March, 1864. 1st Brigade, Tyler's Division, 22nd Army Corps, to May, 1864. District of Alexandria, 22nd Army Corps, to September, 1865.

SERVICE.—Duty in the Defences of Washington and Alexandria entire term except participated in the Maryland Campaign September 6-22, 1862. Attached temporarily to 2nd Brigade, 1st Division, 5th Army Corps, Army of the Potomac. Battle of Antietam September 16-17. Sharpsburg, Shepherdstown Ford and near Williamsport September 19. Near Shepherdstown September 20. Mustered out September 12, 1865.

2nd BATTALION INFANTRY.

Organized at Washington, D. C., for the defence of that city April, 1861. Attached to Mansfield's Command, Dept. of Washington, to June, 1861. Stone's Expedition to July, 1861.

SERVICE.—Duty in the Defences of Washington, D. C., till June, 1861. Expedition to Rockville, Md., June 10-July 7. Seneca Mills June 14. Great Falls July 7, 1861. Mustered out July, 1861.

3rd BATTALION INFANTRY.

Organized at Washington, D. C., for the defence of that city April, 1861. Attached to Mansfield's Command, Dept. of Washington, to June, 1861. Stone's Expedition to July, 1861.

SERVICE.—Duty in the Defences of Washington, D. C., till June, 1861. Expedition to Rockville, Md., June 10-July 7. Great Falls July 7. Mustered out July, 1861.

5th BATTALION INFANTRY.

Organized at Washington, D. C., for the defence of that city April, 1861. Attached to Mansfield's Command, Dept. of Washington, to June, 1861. Stone's Expedition to July, 1861.

SERVICE.—Duty in the Defences of Washington, D. C., till June, 1861. Expedition to Rockville, Md., June 10-July 7. Great Falls July 7. Mustered out July, 1861.

8th BATTALION INFANTRY.

Organized at Washington, D. C., for the defence of that city April, 1861. Attached to Mansfield's Command, Dept. of Washington, D. C., to June, 1861. Rockville Expedition to July, 1861.

SERVICE.—Duty in the Defences of Washington, D. C., till June, 1861. Expedition to Rockville, Md., June 10-July 7. Action at Seneca Mills June 17. Great Falls July 7. Mustered out July, 1861.

BOYD'S COMPANY MILITIA INFANTRY.

Organized at Washington, D. C., for defence of that city April 18, 1861. Mustered out July 16, 1861.

CALLAN'S COMPANY MILITIA INFANTRY.

Organized at Washington, D. C., for defence of that city April 22, 1861 Mustered out July 22, 1861.

CARRINGTON'S COMPANY MILITIA INFANTRY.

Organized at Washington, D. C., for the defence of that city April 13, 1861. Mustered out July 10, 1861.

CLARKE'S COMPANY MILITIA INFANTRY.

Organized at Washington, D. C., for defence of that city April 24, 1861. Mustered out July 24, 1861.

CROSS' COMPANY MILITIA INFANTRY.

Organized at Washington, D. C., for defence of that city April 22, 1861. Mustered out July 15, 1861.

DEGGE'S COMPANY MILITIA INFANTRY.

Organized at Washington, D. C., for defence of that city April 17, 1861. Mustered out July 17, 1861.

ELDER'S COMPANY MILITIA INFANTRY.

Organized at Washington, D. C., for defence of that city April 20, 1861. Mustered out July 20, 1861.

FERGUSON'S COMPANY MILITIA INFANTRY.

Organized at Washington, D. C., for defence of that city April 22, 1861. Mustered out July 22, 1861.

FLETCHER'S COMPANY MILITIA INFANTRY.

Organized at Washington, D. C., for defence of that city April 24, 1861. Mustered out July 24, 1861.

FOXWELL'S COMPANY MILITIA INFANTRY.

Organized at Washington, D. C., for defence of that city April 15, 1861. Mustered out July 15, 1861.

GERHARDT'S COMPANY MILITIA INFANTRY.

Organized at Washington, D. C., for defence of that city April 11, 1861. Mustered out July 11, 1861.

GODDARD'S COMPANY MILITIA INFANTRY.

Organized at Washington, D. C., for defence of that city April 17. 1861. Mustered out July 17, 1861.

GRINNELL'S COMPANY MILITIA INFANTRY.

Organized at Washington, D. C., for defence of that city April 22, 1861. Mustered out June 11, 1861.

KELLY'S COMPANY MILITIA INFANTRY.

Organized at Washington, D. C., for defence of that city April 11, 1861. Mustered out July 11, 1861.

KING'S COMPANY MILITIA INFANTRY.

Organized at Washington, D. C., for defence of that city April 15, 1861. Mustered out July 15, 1861.

KNIGHT'S COMPANY MILITIA INFANTRY.

Organized at Washington, D. C., for defence of that city April 18, 1861. Mustered out July 18, 1861.

KYRZANOWSKI'S COMPANY MILITIA INFANTRY.

Organized at Washington, D. C., for defence of that city April 22, 1861. Mustered out July 22, 1861.

LOEFFLER'S COMPANY MILITIA INFANTRY.

Organized at Washington, D. C., for defence of that city April 11, 1861. Mustered out July 11, 1861.

MARK'S COMPANY MILITIA INFANTRY.

Organized at Washington, D. C., for defence of that city April 17, 1861. Mustered out July 17, 1861.

MILLER'S COMPANY MILITIA INFANTRY.

Organized at Washington, D. C., for defence of that city April 17, 1861. Mustered out July 17, 1861.

MORGAN'S COMPANY MILITIA INFANTRY.

Organized at Washington, D. C., for the defence of that city April 17, 1861. Mustered out July 17, 1861.

MORRISON'S COMPANY MILITIA INFANTRY.

Organized at Washington, D. C., for defence of that city April 23, 1861. Mustered out July 16, 1861.

M'BLAIR'S COMPANY MILITIA INFANTRY.

Organized at Washington, D. C., for the defence of that city April 23, 1861. Mustered out July 23, 1861.

M'CLELLAND'S COMPANY MILITIA INFANTRY.

Organized at Washington, D. C., for defence of that city April 20, 1861. Mustered out July 20, 1861.

M'DERMOTT'S COMPANY MILITIA INFANTRY.

Organized at Washington, D. C., for defence of that city April 18, 1861. Mustered out July 18, 1861.

M'KIM'S COMPANY MILITIA INFANTRY.

Organized at Washington, D. C., for defence of that city April 11, 1861. Mustered out July 11, 1861.

NALLY'S COMPANY MILITIA INFANTRY.

Organized at Washington, D. C., for defence of that city April 11, 1861. Mustered out July 11, 1861.

POWELL'S COMPANY MILITIA INFANTRY.

Organized at Washington, D. C., for defence of that city April 20, 1861. Mustered out July 17, 1861.

RODIER'S COMPANY MILITIA INFANTRY.

Organized at Washington, D. C., for defence of that city April 13, 1861. Mustered out July 13, 1861.

RUTHERFORD'S COMPANY MILITIA INFANTRY.

Organized at Washington, D. C., for defence of that city pril 11, 1861. Mustered out July 11, 1861.

SMEAD'S COMPANY MILITIA INFANTRY.

Organized at Washington, D. C., for defence of that city April 15, 1861. Mustered out July 15, 1861.

THISTLETON'S COMPANY MILITIA INFANTRY.

Organized at Washington, D. C., for defence of that city April 11, 1861. Mustered out July 11, 1861.

WILLIAMS' COMPANY MILITIA INFANTRY.

Organized at Washington, D. C., for the defence of that city April 10, 1861. Mustered out July 10, 1861.

FLORIDA VOLUNTEERS.

1st REGIMENT CAVALRY.

Authorized by Gen. Banks October 29, 1863, and organized at Barrancas, Fla., December, 1863, to August, 1864. Attached to Pensacola, Fla., District West Florida, Dept. Gulf, to October, 1864. 2nd Brigade, District West Florida, to January, 1865. 3rd Brigade, District West Florida, to March, 1865. 2nd Brigade, Lucas' Cavalry Division, Steele's Command, to May, 1865. District of West Florida to November, 1865.

SERVICE.—Duty at Barrancas, Fla., till March, 1865. Expedition from Barrancas toward Pollard, Ala., July 21-25, 1864. Actions at Camp Gonzales July 22, and near Pollard July 23. Expedition from Barrancas August 13-14. Expedition from Barrancas to Mariana September 18-October 4. Euche Anna C. H. September 23. Mariana September 27. Vernon September 28. Expedition up Blackwater Bay October 25-28. Milton October 26. Expedition from Barrancas to Pine Barren Creek November 16-17. Pine Barren Creek and Bridge November 17. Expedition to Pollard, Ala., December 13-19. Bluff Springs and Pollard December 15. Escanabia Bridge December 15-16. Pine Barren Ford December 17-18. Expedition from Barrancas to Milton February 22-25, 1865. Milton February 23. Campaign against Mobile and its defences March 18-April 9. March to Blakely, Ala., March 18-31. (Dismounted men remain at Barrancas.) Expedition to Alabama & Florida R. R. March 18-25. Near Evergreen March 24. Muddy Creek, Ala., March 26. Siege of Fort Blakely March 31-April 9. Near Blakely April 1. Occupation of Mobile April 12. March to Montgomery April 13-25. Duty there and in Alabama till May. Ordered to Barrancas, Fla., and duty in Western and Middle Florida till November. Mustered out November 17, 1865.

2nd REGIMENT CAVALRY.

Organized at Cedar Keys and Key West, Fla., December, 1863, to June, 1864. Attached to District of Key West and Tortugas, Dept. of the Gulf, and Dept. of Florida, to November, 1865.

SERVICE.—Duty at Fort Myers, Cedar Keys and in District of Key West till June, 1865. Skirmishes at Pease Creek, Fla., February 13-14 and February 20, 1864. Attack on Fort Myers February 20. Affair at Tampa May 6. Operations on West Coast of Florida July 1-31. Expedition to Bayport July 1-4. Skirmish at Station Four, near Cedar Keys, July 6. Expedition to St. Andrews Bay July 20-29. Fort Myers August 26. Expedition to Bayport October 1, and to St. Andrews Bay October 20-29. Near Magnolia October 24. Expedition to Otter Creek, on Florida R. R., October 30-31. Braddock's Farm, near Welaka, February 5, 1865. Station Four, near Cedar Keys, February 13. Attack on Fort Myers February 20. Operations near St. Marks February 21-March 7. East River Bridge March 4-5. Newport Bridge March 5-6. Natural Bridge March 6. Occupation of Tampa May 27. Duty in District of Florida till November. Mustered out November 29, 1865.

GEORGIA VOLUNTEERS.

1st BATTALION INFANTRY.

Organized at Marietta, Ga., October 31, 1864. Served unattached, Dept. of the Cumberland, to March, 1865. 1st Brigade, 2nd Separate Division, District of the Etowah, Dept. of the Cumberland, to July.

SERVICE.—Railroad guard duty at Dalton, Ga., and in the District of the Etowah till July, 1865. Mustered out July 19, 1865.

ILLINOIS VOLUNTEERS.

1st REGIMENT CAVALRY.

Seven Companies, "A" to "G," organized at Alton, Ill., and mustered in July 3, 1861. (Cos. "I," "H" and "K" were not mustered with Regiment and never served with it.) Attached to Dept. of Missouri. Moved to St. Charles, Mo., thence to Jefferson City, Mexico, Hannibal and Lexington, Mo. Skirmish at Georgetown, Mo., August — (Co. "C"). Siege of Lexington, Mo., September 11-20. Surrendered September 20. Reorganizing at Benton Barracks, Mo., till June, 1862. Guard supply trains and depots at Rolla, Houston, West Plains, etc. Mustered out July 14, 1862.

Company "H" organized at Alton, Ill., June 12, 1861. Company "I" organized at Alton, Ill., July 9, 1861. Company "K" organized at Alton, Ill., December 9, 1861. Companies "H" and "I" attached to Military District of Cairo to February, 1862. 4th Brigade, 1st Division, Military District of Cairo, to March, 1862. Unattached, Army of Mississippi, to April, 1862. Cavalry Division, Army Mississippi, to June, 1862. District of Memphis, Tenn., to July, 1862.

SERVICE.—Skirmishes at Charleston, near Bird's Point, August 19-20, 1861. Fish Lake August 20. Underwood's Farm, near Bird's Point, October 14. Action at Belmont, Mo., November 7. At Cairo, Ill., and Bird's Point, Mo., till March, 1862. Operations against New Market, Mo., March 1-14, and against Island No. 10, Mississippi River, March 15-April 8. Duty at New Madrid till June, and at Memphis, Tenn., till July. Mustered out July 15, 1862.

Company "K" attached to Army of Southwest Missouri January to July, 1862. District of Eastern Arkansas, Dept. of Missouri, to October, 1862. Army of Southeast Missouri to December, 1862. Action at Warrensburg, Mo., March 28. Mustered out December 27, 1862.

Regiment lost during service 17 Enlisted men killed and mortally wounded and 26 Enlisted men by disease. Total 43.

2nd REGIMENT CAVALRY.

Organized at Camp Butler, Ill., and mustered in August 12, 1861. (Co. "M" mustered in December 30, 1861.) Moved to Fort Massac August 29, 1861; to Cairo, Ill., October 3, 1861 (6 Cos.), and to Paducah, Ky., November 1, 1861 (5 Cos.). Attached to Military District of Cairo, Dept. of Missouri, to February, 1862. Unattached, Army of Mississippi, to April, 1862 (Cos. "G," "H," "I" and "K"). District of Columbus, Ky., to November, 1862 (Cos. "E," "F," "G," "H," "I," "K" and "M"). (Cos. "A" and "B," 1st Brigade, 1st Division, Army Tennessee, to March, 1862. 2nd Division, Army Tennessee, to July, 1862.) Cavalry, District of Jackson, Tenn., to November, 1862 (Cos. "A," "B," "C" and "D"). Cavalry, 4th Division, Right Wing 13th Army Corps (Old), Dept. of the Tennessee, to December, 1862. 2nd Brigade, Cavalry Division, 16th Army Corps, to March, 1863. Unattached, 13th Army Corps, Army Tennessee, to August, 1863 (Detachment). District of Columbus, Ky., 6th Division, 16th Corps, to May, 1863 (Detachment). 4th Brigade, District of Memphis, Tenn., 5th Division, 16th Army Corps, to August, 1863 (Detachment). Cavalry Brigade, 13th Army Corps, Dept. of the Gulf, to September, 1863 (7 Cos.). 2nd Brigade, Cavalry Division, Dept. Gulf, to December, 1863 (7 Cos.). District of Columbus, Ky., 6th Division, 16th Army Corps, to December, 1863 (Detachment). Waring's Cavalry Brigade, Cavalry Division, 16th Army Corps, to January, 1864 (Detachment). 1st Brigade, 1st Cavalry Division, 16th Army Corps, to June, 1864 (Detachment). 3rd Brigade, Cavalry Division, Dept. of the Gulf, December, 1863, to January, 1864 (7 Cos.). 4th Brigade, Cavalry Division, Dept. of the Gulf, to June, 1864 (7 Cos.). Unattached, Defences of New Orleans, La., to August, 1864. 2nd Brigade, Cavalry Division, Dept. of the Gulf, to September, 1864. 3rd Brigade, Cavalry Division, Dept. of the Gulf, to February, 1865. Separate Cavalry Brigade, District of West Florida, to March, 1865. 2nd Brigade, Cavalry Division, District of West Florida, to April, 1865. 3rd Brigade, 1st Division, Cavalry Corps, Military Division West Mississippi, to June, 1865. Dept. of Mississippi to November, 1865.

SERVICE.—Duty in Military District of Cairo till February, 1862. Expedition to Belmont, Mo., November 6-7, 1861. Battle of Belmont November 7. Bertram, Mo., December 11. Charleston, Mo., December 13. Expedition to Camp Beauregard and Viola, Ky., December 28-31. Moved to Paducah, Ky., January 1, 1862. Expedition toward Fort Henry January 15-26. Operations against Fort Henry February 2-6 (Cos. "A" and "B"). Springfield February 12. Fort Donelson, Tenn., February 12-16 (Cos. "A" and "B"). Advance on Columbus, Ky., March 2 (6 Cos.). Operations against New Madrid and Island No. 10, Mo., February 28-April 8 (Cos. "G," "H," "I" and "K"). New Madrid March 2-3. Action, and capture of Columbus, Ky., March 3 (6 Cos.). Union City, Tenn., March 31 (Cos. "H" and "I"). Battle of Shiloh, Tenn., April 6-7 (Cos. "A" and "B"). Monterey April 28-29. Purdy April 29. Advance on and siege of Corinth April 29-May 30 (Cos. "A," "B," "C" and "D"). Expedition down Mississippi River to Fort Pillow, Tenn., May 19-23 (Cos. "G," "H," "I" and "K"). Expedition from Clifton in pursuit of Biffle's, Forest's and Newsome's Cavalry July 22-23. Gayoso, Tenn., August 4. Trenton, Tenn., August 7. Merriweather Ferry, Obeon River, August 16 (Co. "C"). White Oak Ridge August 19. Bolivar August 30 (4 Cos.). Somerville September 14. Battle of Iuka, Miss., September 19 (Detachment). Expedition from Bolivar to Grand Junction and LaGrange, and Skirmishes, September 20-22 (Cos. "C," "H," "K" and "M"). Expedition from Columbus, Ky., to Covington, Durhamsville and Fort Randolph, Ky., September 28-October 5 (Cos. "D" and "L"). Battle of Metamora, or Hatchie River, October 5 (Co. "A"). Island No. 10 October 17 (Co. "L"). Woodville October 21 (Detachment). Clarkson October 28 (Co. "D"). Grant's Central Mississippi Campaign October 31, 1862, to January 10, 1863. Reconnoissance from LaGrange to Colliersville, Tenn., November 5 (5 Cos.). Reconnoissance from LaGrange to Lamar, Miss., November 5 (2 Cos.). LaGrange November 6. Worsham's Creek, Miss., November 6 (2 Cos.). Carthage Road, near Hartsville, November 28 (Co. "H"). Holly Springs, Miss., December 20 (Cos. "C," "F," "G," "H," "I" and "K"). Ripley December 23 (Cos. "H" and "M"). Knob Creek, near Ripley January 8, 1863. Horn Lake Creek, February 8, 1863. Moscow Station, Tenn., February 14. Expedition from Young's Point, La., to Greenville, and Cypress Bend, Ark., February 14-29 (Detachment). Fish Lake, near Greenville, February 23 (Detachment). Expedition from Helena, Ark., to Yazoo Pass by Moon Lake, and Coldwater and Tallahatchie Rivers, February 24-April 8 (Co. "E"). Near Bloomington, on Hatchie River, February 27. Operations against Fort Pemberton and Greenwood March 13-April 5 (Co. "E"). Fort Pemberton March 24 (Co. "E"). Operations from Milliken's Bend, La., to New Carthage March 31-April 17 (Detachment). Roundaway Bayou, Richmond, March 31 (Detachment). Richmond April 4 (Detachment). Scout from LaGrange, Tenn., into Mississippi April 10-11 (Detachment). James' Plantation, near New Carthage, April 8 (Detachment). Dunbar's Plantation, Bayou Boeuf, April 15 (Detachment). Expedition from Perkins' Plantation to Hard Times Landing April 25-29. Fort Pillow April 26. Phelps' and Clark's Bayous April 26. Choctaw Bayou, on Lake Bruin, April 28. Turning Grand Gulf April 25-30 (4 Cos.). Battle of Port Gibson May 1. Willow Springs May 3 (Co. "C"). Near Black River May 5 (Detachment). Sandy Creek May 5 and 9 (Detachment). Utica May 9 and 10 (Cos. "A" and "E"). Coldwater May 11. Raymond May 12 (Cos. "A" and "E"). Hill's Ferry May 13 (Detachment). Jackson May 14 (Cos. "A" and "E"). Walnut Hill May 15. Champion's Hill May 16. Siege of Vicksburg May 18-July 4. Assaults on Vicksburg May 19 and 22. Haines Bluff May 23 (Detachment). Mechanicsburg May 29 (Detachment). Expedition to Satartia June 2-8. Satartia June 4. Coldwater, near Hernando, Miss., June 19. Hernando June 20. Moscow Station, Tenn., June 29. Advance on Jackson, Miss., July 5-10 (4 Cos.). Ripley July 7. Near Baker's Creek July 7. Bolton's Depot and near Clinton July 8. Near Jackson July 9. Brookhaven July 18. Scout from Fort Pillow, Tenn., August 3 (Detachment). Denmark August 3 (Detachment). Expedition from Fort Pillow to Jackson, Tenn., September 19-25 (5 Cos.). Moved to Dept. of the Gulf August, 1863 (7 Cos.). Sterling's Plantation on Bayou Fordoche, near Morganza, La., September 29. Western Louisiana Campaign October 3-November 30. Carrion Crow Bayou October 18. Opelousas and Barre's Landing October 21. Washington October 24. Carrion Crow Bayou November 3. Rogersville, Tenn., November 6 (Co. "M"). Carrion Crow Bayou and Vermillionville November 11. Obion River, near Union City, Tenn., November 19 (Detachment). Merriweather Ferry, near Union City, November 19 (Detachment). Camp Platt, La., November 20. Bayou Portage, La., November 23 (Detachment). Vermillionville, La., November 25. Camp Pratt November 25. St. Martinsville December 3 (Detachment). Okolona, Miss., December 9 (Detachment). Madrid Bend, La., December 9 (Detachment). Expedition from Union City to Trenton, Tenn., January 22-27, 1864 (1st Battalion). Smith's Expedition from Colliersville, Tenn., to Okolona, Miss., February 11-26 (5 Cos.). Prairie Station, Miss., and Okolona, Miss., February 21. Ivy's Hill, near Okolona, February 22. Hopefield, Ark., March 14. Red River Campaign March 14-May 22. Advance from Franklin to Alexandria, La., March 14-26. Bayou Rapides March 20. Monett's Ferry and Cloutiersville March 29-30. Natchitoches March 31. Crump's Hill, Piney Woods, April 2. Natchitoches April 5. Bayou de Paul April 8. Sabine Cross Roads April 8. About Cloutiersville April 22-24. Monett's Ferry, Cane River Crossing, April 23. Alexandria April 28 and May 2-9. Retreat to Morganza May 13-20. Near Alexandria May 14. Mansura May 16. Near Moreauville May 17. Yellow Bayou May 18. Steamer "City Belle" May 30. Regiment united at Baton Rouge, La., July, 1864. Operations near Baton Rouge July 3-25. Near Barton's Ferry, Amite River, July 25 (Detachment). Bayou Letsworth August 11. Expedition to Clinton August 23-29. Olive Branch, Comite River and Clinton August 25. Expedition from Baton Rouge to Clinton, Greensburg, Osyka and Camp Moore October 5-9. Clinton October 6. Lee's Expedition from Baton Rouge to Brookhaven, Miss., and Skirmishes, November 14-21. Davidson's Expedition from Baton Rouge against Mobile & Ohio R. R. November 27-December 13. Campaign against Mobile and its defences March 17-April 12, 1865. Steele's march from Barrancas, Fla., to Fort Blakely March 18-31. Near Evergreen March 24. Muddy Creek March 26. Near Blakely April 1. Operations against Fort Blakely April 1-9. Expedition from Blakely to Claiborne April 9-17. Expedition from Blakely to Georgetown, Ga., April 17-30. Moved to Mississippi May, thence to Shreveport, La., June 14-21; thence to San Antonia, Texas, July 9-August 2. Mustered out November 22, 1865. Discharged at Springfield, Ill., January 3, 1866.

Regiment lost during service 8 Officers and 50 Enlisted men killed and mortally wounded and 3 Officers and 173 Enlisted men by disease. Total 234.

3rd REGIMENT CAVALRY.

Organized at Camp Butler, Ill., and mustered in August 27, 1861. Moved to St. Louis, Mo., September 25, thence to Jefferson City, Mo., and to Warsaw, Mo., October 1-11. Attached to Dept. of the Missouri to January, 1862. 3rd Brigade, Army of Southwest Missouri, to February, 1862. 2nd Brigade, 4th Division, Army of Southwest Missouri, to May, 1862. 2nd Division, Army of Southwest Missouri, to July, 1862. District of Eastern Arkansas, Dept. of Missouri, to December, 1862. 3rd Brigade, Cavalry Division, District of Eastern Arkansas, December, 1862. Unattached, Sherman's Yazoo Expedition, to January, 1863 (Cos. "A," "E," "G," "K," "L" and "M"). Unattached, 13th Army Corps, Army of the Tennessee, Headquarters of Gen. McClernand and Gen. Osterhaus, to August, 1863. (5 Cos., "B," "C," "F," "H" and "I," 2nd Brigade, 1st Cavalry Division, 16th Army Corps, March to June, 1863. 1st Brigade, 1st Division Cavalry, 16th Army Corps, to August, 1863. 2nd Brigade, 1st Cavalry Division, 16th Army Corps, to January, 1864.) (Co. "D" at Headquarters 15th Army Corps to July, 1863, then with Arkansas Expedition to December, 1863.) Other Companies attached to Cavalry Brigade, 13th Army Corps, Dept. of the Gulf, to September, 1863. 2nd Brigade, Cavalry Division, Dept. of the Gulf, to December, 1863, when rejoined Regiment in 1st Brigade, 1st Cavalry Division, 16th Army Corps, to April, 1864. 3rd Brigade, 1st Cavalry Division, 16th Army Corps, to June, 1864. 1st Brigade, Cavalry Division, District of West Tennessee, to July, 1864. 1st Brigade, 1st Cavalry Division, District of West Tennessee, to November, 1864. 1st Brigade, 5th Division, Cavalry Corps, Military Division Mississippi, to May, 1865. Dept. of the Northwest to October, 1865.

SERVICE.—Fremont's Campaign against Springfield, Mo., October 23-November 2, 1861. Moved to Rolla November 13-19, and duty there till January, 1862. Curtis' advance on Springfield February 2-13. Marshfield, Mo., February 9. Pursuit of Price into Arkansas February 14-29. Pott's Hill, Sugar Creek, February 16. Sugar Creek February 17. Bentonville February 17. Battles of Pea Ridge March 6-8. Expedition to Fayetteville March 15. March to Batesville, Ark., April 5-May 3. Talbot's Ferry, White River, April 19. Fairview, Little Red River, June 7 (Co. "L"). Scouts from Batesville June 16-17. March to Helena, Ark., June 26-July 14. Helena July 14. Duty near Helena, Ark., till December. Expedition from Helena to Arkansas Post November 16-21. Expedition to Grenada, Miss., November 27-December 5. Oakland December 3. Sherman's Yazoo Expedition December 22, 1862, to January 3, 1863. Chickasaw Bayou December 26-28. Chickasaw Bluff December 29. Expedition to Arkansas Post, Ark., January 3-11, 1863. Capture of Fort Hindman, Arkansas Post, January 10-11. Milliken's Bend January 21. Richmond January 29. 5 Companies, "B," "C," "F," "H" and "I," ordered to Memphis, Tenn., February, 1863. Other Companies remained on duty with 13th Army Corps to August, 1863. Company "D" with 1st Division, 15th Army Corps, to July, then with Arkansas Expedition till December, 1863.

Companies "A," "E," "G," "K," "L" and "M"—Operations from Milliken's Bend to New Carthage March 31-April 17, 1863 (Cos. "A" and "K"). Near New Carthage April 5 (Cos. "A" and "K"). Movement on Bruinsburg and turning Grand Gulf April 25-30. Battle of Port Gibson May 1. Near Black River May 5 (Detachment). Battle of Champion's Hill May 16. Big Black Fiver Bridge May 17. Siege of Vicksburg May 18-July 4. Assaults on Vicksburg May 19 and 22. Edwards' Station June 10. Advance on Jackson, Miss., July 4-10. Edwards' Station July 6. Near Baker's Creek July 7. Bolton's Depot July 8. Near Clinton July 8. Near Jackson July 9. Siege of Jackson July 10-17. Brookhaven July 18. Moved to New Orleans, La., August. Campaign in Western Louisiana, operations in Teche Country October 3-November 30. Vermillion Bayou October 9-10. Opelousas and Barre Landing October 21. Washington October 24. Vermillionville November 5. Carrion Crow Bayou November 11. Vermillionville November 11. Camp Pratt November 20 and 25. Vermillionville November 25. Near Baton Rouge March 3, 1864 (Detachment). Jackson March 3, 1864 (Detachment). Livonia March 30. Near Port Hudson April 7 (Detachment). Companies rejoined Regiment at Memphis, Tenn., December, 1863.

Companies "B," "C," "F," "H" and "I"—Coldwater and Cochran's Cross Roads May 15, 1863. Expedition from LaGrange, Tenn., to Senatobia, Miss., May 21-26. Senatobia May 23. Operations in Northwest Mississippi June 15-25. Scout to Germantown July 8. Mt. Pleasant August 5. Expedition from Memphis to Grenada, Miss., August 12-23. Grenada August 17. Mt. Pleasant August 25. Expedition from LaGrange to Toon's Station September 11-16. Montezuma September 16. Operations against Chalmers' in North Mississippi and West Tennessee October 4-17. Lockhart's Mills October 6. Salem October 8. Ingraham's Mills, near Byhalia, October 12. Wyatts', Tallahatchie River, October 13. Operations on Memphis and Charleston R. R. November 3-5. Operations on Memphis and Charleston R. R. against Lee's attack November 28-December 10. Ripley December 1. Near Moscow December 3-4. Near Corinth Dec. 23 (Detachment).

Company "D."—Expedition to Greenville, Black Bayou and Deer Creek April 2-14, 1863. Jackson, Miss., May 14. Siege of Vicksburg May 18-July 4. Assaults on Vicksburg May 19 and 22. Advance on Jackson, Miss., July 4-10. Siege of Jackson July 10-17. Moved to Helena, Ark., July. Steele's Expedition to Little Rock, Ark., August 1-September 10. Bayou Fourche and capture of Little Rock September 10.

Regiment on Smith's Expedition from Colliersville, Tenn., to Okolona, Miss., February 11-26, 1864. Holly Springs, Miss., February 12. Near Pontotoc February 17. Houlka Swamp, near Houston, February 17. Near Okolona February 18. Ivey's Hill, near Okolona, February 22. New Albany February 23. Pontotoc February 24. Germantown May 9. Sturgis' Expedition from Memphis into Mississippi June 1-13. Brice's or Tishaming Creek, near Guntown, June 10. Ripley June 11. Near Holly Springs July 1. Smith's Expedition to Tupelo, Miss., July 5-21. Camargo's Cross Roads, near Harrisburg, July 13. Near Tupelo July 14-15. Old Town Creek July 15. Smith's Expedition to Oxford, Miss., August 1-30. Tallahatchie River August 7-9. Hurricane Creek and Oxford August 9. Hurricane Creek August 13-14 and 19. Forest's attack on Memphis, Tenn., August 21 (Detachment). Scout to Mayfield, Ky., and skirmish August 14-15 (Detachment). Moved to Clifton, Tenn., September 27. Operations in Tennessee and Alabama against Hood November-December. Expedition from Memphis to Moscow November 9-13. Shoal Creek, Ala., November 11. On line of Shoal Creek November 16-20. Duck River November 28. Franklin November 30. Battle of Nashville December 15-16. Pursuit of Hood December 17-28. West Harpeth River December 17. Richland Creek December 24. King's or Anthony's Gap, near Pulaski, December 25. At Gravelly Springs, Ala., till February, 1865. At Eastport, Miss., till May. Moved to St. Louis, Mo., thence to St. Paul, Minn. Operating against Indians in Minnesota and Dakota July 4 to October 1. Mustered out October 18, 1865.

Regiment lost during service 8 Officers and 50 Enlisted men killed and mortally wounded and 3 Officers and 173 Enlisted men by disease. Total 234.

4th REGIMENT CAVALRY.

Organized at Ottawa, Ills., and mustered in September 26, 1861. Moved to Cairo, Ills., October, 1861, and duty in that district till February, 1862. (Co. "A" detached as escort to General Grant, November, 1861, to August, 1863.) Attached to District of Cairo to February, 1862. 2nd Brigade, 1st Division, District of West Tennessee, to March, 1862. 2nd Division, Army of the Tennessee (Cos. "E," "F," "G," "H"). 4th Division, Army Tennessee (Cos. "I," "K," "L" and "M"). 1st Division, Army Tennessee (Cos. 'A," "B," "C," "D"), to April, 1862. 5th Division, Army Tennessee, to July, 1862 (Cos. "E," "F," "G," "H," "I," "K," "L," "M"). 1st Division, Army Tennessee, to July, 1862 (Cos. "A," "B," "C," "D"). 1st Division, District of Jackson, Tenn., to November, 1862 (Cos. "A," "B," "C," "D"). 5th Division, District of Memphis, Tenn., to November, 1862 (Cos. "E," "F," "G," "H," "I," "K," "L," "M"). Lee's

2nd Brigade, Cavalry Division, 13th Army Corps, (Old) Department of the Tennessee, to December, 1862, and 16th Army Corps to March, 1863. 2nd Brigade, 1st Cavalry Division, 16th Army Corps, to May, 1863. 1st Brigade, 1st Cavalry Division, 16th Army Corps, to August, 1863. Winslow's Cavalry Brigade, 15th Army Corps, December, 1863. Winslow's Cavalry Brigade, 17th Army Corps, and District of Vicksburg, Miss., to April, 1864. Post of Natchez, District of Vicksburg, Miss., to December, 1864. 3rd Brigade, Cavalry Division, District of West Tennessee, to June, 1865. 1st Brigade, Cavalry Division, District West Tennessee June 1865.

SERVICE.—Reconnoissance of Columbus Ky. December 1861. Reconnoissance from Paducah Ky. to Fort Henry Tenn. January 15-25 1862 (Detachment). Expedition from Cairo into Kentucky January 16-21. Operations against Fort Henry Tenn. February 2-6. Fort Donelson Tenn. February 12-16 (Co. "I"). Expedition from Paducah Ky. to Tennessee River and operations about Crump's Landing Tenn. March 8-14. Expedition from Savannah to Yellow Creek Miss. and occupation of Pittsburg Landing March 14-17. Black Jack Forest March 16 (Detachment). Battle of Shiloh Tenn. April 6-7. Corinth Road April 8. Expedition to Bear Creek, Ala., April 12-13 (Cos. "E," "G," "H," "L," "M"). Pea Ridge April 15. Corinth Road April 24-25. Pea Ridge April 27. Advance on and siege of Corinth, Miss., April 29-May 30. Raid on Mobile and Ohio R. R. April 29-May 14. March to Memphis, Tenn., June 1-July 21 (8 companies). Four companies operating in district of Jackson, Tenn., till November, and (eight companies) in District of Memphis, Tenn., till November. Tallahatchie Bridge, Miss., June 18. Near Holly Springs, Miss., July 1. Hatchie Bottom July 29. Grant's Central Mississippi Campaign October 31, 1862, to January 10, 1863. Double Bridges November 18. About Oxford December 1-3. Water Valley Station December 4. Coffeeville December 5. Expedition against Mobile and Ohio R. R. December 14-19. Ripley December 23. Bolivar and Middletown December 24. Scout duty in West Tennessee and North Mississippi, headquarters at Colliersville, Tenn., January to August, 1863. Centre Hill, near Germantown, January 27 (Detachment). Expedition from Colliersville March 8-12 (Detachment). Shelby County March 9. Expedition from Lagrange into Northern Mississippi April 29-May 5. Expedition from Lagrange to Senatobia May 21-26. Senatobia May 23. Operations in Northwest Mississippi June 15-25. Quinn's Mills and Coldwater June 16. Near Holly Springs June 16-17. Near Clinton July 8. Scout from Germantown July 16-20. Expedition from Memphis to Grenada, Miss., August 12-23. Craven's Plantation August 14 (Co. "M"). Grenada August 17. Moved to Vicksburg, Miss., August. Expedition from Vicksburg, Miss., to Monroe, La., August 20-September 2 (Battalion). Bayou Macon and Bayou Floyd August 24 (Battalion). Expedition from Big Black River to Yazoo City September 27-October 1 (Detachment). Morris Ford, near Benton, September 29 (Detachment). Ingraham's Plantation, near Port Gibson, October 10 (1st Battalion). Expedition toward Canton October 14-20. Canton Road, near Brownsville, October 15-16. Near Clinton and Vernon Cross Roads October 16. Bogue Chitto Creek October 17. Sartatia October 17. Robinson's Mill, near Livingston, October 17. Livingston Road, near Clinton, October 18. Expedition to Tallulah Court House November 10-13 (Detachment). Independence December 7 (Cos. "A," "B," "C," "D"). Moved to Natchez, Miss., December, 1863. Merriweather Ferry, Bayou Boeuf, December 13. Duty there and scouting in Southern Mississippi and Eastern Louisiana till December, 1864. Meridian Campaign February 3-March 2 1884. (Cos. "A," "B," "C," "D"). Chunky Station February 14. Washington March 29 (Detachment). Concordia July 25. Expedition from Natchez to Gillespie's Plantation August 4-6. Gillespie's Plantation August 5 (Detachment). Cross Bayou August 6. Bullitt's Bayou August 26. Consolidated to a Battalion of 5 companies October 14, 1864. Eight Mile Post, Natchez and Liberty Road

September 6 (Co. "L"). Expedition from Natchez to Buck's Ferry and skirmishes September 21-26. Expedition from Natchez to Woodville October 4-11 (Detachment). Woodville October 5-6. Ordered to Memphis, Tenn., December. Grierson's Raid on Mobile and Ohio R. R. December 21, 1864, to January 15, 1865. Franklin Creek December 21-22. Verona December 25, 1864. Egypt Station December 28. Franklin January 2, 1865. Duty at Memphis till June. Expedition from Memphis to Marion, Ark., January 19-22. Expedition from Memphis into Northern Mississippi February 3-11. Expedition from Memphis to Brownsville, Miss., April 23-26. Consolidated with 14th Illinois Cavalry June 14, 1865.

Regiment lost during service 1 Officer and 31 Enlisted men killed and mortally wounded and 1 Officer and 166 Enlisted men by disease. Total 199.

5th REGIMENT CAVALRY.

Organized at Camp Butler, Ills., August 31 to December 30, 1861. Moved to Benton Barracks, Mo., February 20, 1862. Thence to Pilot Knob, Mo., March 3. Moved to Doniphan March 27-April 1 and to Pocahontas April 17. Attached to Steele's Division, Army of Southeast Missouri, to May, 1862. Army of Southwest Missouri to July, 1862. District of Eastern Arkansas, Department of Missouri, to December, 1862. 1st Brigade 3rd (Cavalry) Division, District of Eastern Arkansas, to January, 1863. 1st Brigade, 2nd Cavalry Division, 13th Army Corps, Department of the Tennessee, to April, 1863. 1st Brigade, Cavalry Division, District of Eastern Arkansas, to June, 1863. Cavalry Herron's Division, 13th Army Corps to August, 1863. Winslow's Cavalry Brigade, 15th Army Corps to December, 1863. Winslow's Cavalry Brigade, 17th Army Corps, and District of Vicksburg, Miss., to January, 1865. 1st Brigade, Cavalry Division, District of West Tennessee to June, 1865. Departments of the Gulf and Texas to October, 1865.

SERVICE.—Action at Putnam's Ferry, Mo., April 1, 1862. Doniphan April 4. Pocahontas April 21. Scouting and skirmishing in Arkansas and Missouri till June. Smithville June 17 (Cos. "D," "F" and "L").. March to Helena, Ark., June 26-July 14. Hill's Plantation, Cache River, July 7. At Helena, Ark., till May, 1863. Expedition from Helena to Clarendon August 4-17, 1862. Clarendon August 15. Expedition from Helena to Jeffersonville and Mariana September 2-6. Expedition from Clarendon to Lawrenceville and St. Charles September 11-13. Near Helena October 22. Expedition from Helena to Arkansas Post November 16-21. Expedition from Helena to Grenada, Miss., November 27-December 5. Moved to Snyder's Bluff, Miss., May 31-June 1, 1863. Expedition to Satartia June 2-8 (Detachment). Satartia June 4 (Detachment). Raid to Brookhaven June 23-26 (Detachment). Expedition from Snyder's Bluff to Greenville June 25-July 1 (three companies). Rocky Creek, near Ellisville, June 26 (three Companies). Gaines' Landing, Ark., June 28. Advance on Jackson, Miss., July 5-10. Near Clinton July 8. Siege of Jackson July 10-17. Near Canton July 12. Holton's Depot July 16. Grant's Ferry, Pearl River, July 16. Briar Creek, near Canton, July 17. Canton July 18. Bolton's Depot July 24. Raid from Big Black River, on Mississippi Central R. R., and to Memphis, Tenn., August 10-22. Payne's Plantation, near Grenada, August 18. Panola August 20. Coldwater August 21. Moved from Memphis to Vicksburg, Miss., August 23-27, and duty in that District till January, 1865. Expedition from Big Black River to Yazoo City September 27-October 1, 1863 (Detachment). Brownsville September 28 (Detachment). Morris Ford, near Benton, September 29 (Detachment). Expedition to Canton October 14-20. Brownsville October 15. Canton Road, near Brownsville, October 15-16. Near Clinton and Vernon Cross Roads October 16. Bogue Chitto Creek October 17. Robinson's Mills, near Livingston, October 17. Livingston Road, near Clinton, October 18. Oak Ridge January 16, 1864. Meridian Campaign February 3-March 2. Champion's Hill February 4. Jackson February 5. Brandon February 7.

Morton February 8. About Meridian February 9 to 13. Hillsboro February 10. Meridian February 13-14. Marion Station February 16. Clinton April 3. Expedition from Vicksburg to Yazoo City May 4-21 (Detachment). Benton May 7-9. Yazoo River May 29. Expedition from Vicksburg to Pearl River July 2-10. Jackson July 7. Expedition from Vicksburg to Deer Creek September 21-26. Expedition to Rodney and Fayette September 29-October 3 (Detachment). Port Gibson September 30. Expedition from Natchez to Woodville October 4-11 (Detachment). Woodville October 5-6 (Detachment). Operations in Issaqueena and Washington Counties October 24-31. Expedition from Vicksburg to Gaines' Landing, Ark., and Bayou Macon, La., November 6-8. Expedition from Vicksburg to Yazoo City November 23-December 4. Franklin Creek, Miss., December 21-22. Moved to Memphis, Tenn., January 24, 1865. Expedition through Southern Arkansas and Northern Louisiana January 26-February 13. At Memphis, Tenn., till June. Expedition into Northern Mississippi March 3-11. Moved to Alexandria, La., via Red River, July 1, thence march to Hempstead, Texas, August 12, arriving August 26, and duty there till October. Moved to Springfield, Ills., October 6-17. Mustered out October 27, 1865.

Regiment lost during service 28 Enlisted men killed and mortally wounded and 5 Officers and 414 Enlisted men by disease. Total 447.

6th REGIMENT CAVALRY.

Organized at Camp Butler, Ills., November 19, 1861. Moved to Shawneetown, Ills., November 25, and duty there till February, 1862. Moved to Paducah, Ky., thence to Columbus, Ky. Regiment divided, five Companies, "A," "C," "D," "E" and "F," moved to Trenton, Tenn., March, 1862, and duty there operating against guerrillas till September, 1862. Action at Wood Springs, near Dyersburg, Tenn., August 7. Near Dyersburg August 18 (Co. "E"). Rejoined Regiment at Memphis, Tenn. 5 Companies, "G," "H," "I," "K" and "L," at Columbus, Ky., till June; then moved to Memphis, Tenn. 2 Companies, "B" and "M," at Paducah, Ky., and Bird's Point, Mo., till September, 1862. Rejoined Regiment at Memphis, Tenn. Attached to District of Columbus, Ky., and Memphis, Tenn., Department of the Tennessee to November, 1862. District of Memphis, Tenn., 13th Army Corps, (Old) Department of the Tennessee, to December, 1862. Grierson's First Brigade, Cavalry Division, Department of the Tennessee, to January, 1863. 1st Brigade, Cavalry Division, 16th Army Corps to March, 1863. 1st Brigade 1st Cavalry Division, 16th Army Corps to May, 1863. Cavalry Division 19th Army Corps, Department of the Gulf to August, 1863. 3rd Brigade, 1st Cavalry Division, 16th Army Corps, Department of the Tennessee to December, 1863. 2nd Brigade, 1st Cavalry Division, 16th Army Corps to April, 1864. 3rd Brigade, 1st Cavalry Division, 16th Army Corps to July, 1864. 2nd Brigade, 1st Cavalry Division, District of West Tennessee to November, 1864. 2nd Brigade, 5th Division Cavalry Corps, Military Division Mississippe to July, 1865. Department of Alabama to November, 1865.

SERVICE.—Action at Coldwater Station, Miss., June 21, 1862 (Cos. "G," "H," "I," "K," "L"). White Oak Bayou June 23. Expedition from Memphis to Cuba August 10-11 (2d Battalion). Scout toward Holly Springs September 5-6. Olive Branch September 6. Expedition from Memphis to Coldwater and Hernando, Miss., September 8-13. Coldwater Creek September 8. Cockrum's Cross Roads September 9. Coldwater Bridge September 10. Coldwater R. R. Bridge September 12. Scout to Colliersville, Tenn., October 21-24. Shelby Depot October 23. Grant's Central Mississippi Campaign November, 1862, to January, 1863. Tallahatchie march November 26-December 12, 1862. About Oxford December 1-3. Water Valley Station December 4. Coffeeville December 5. Ripley December 23. Middleburg, Tenn., and near Bolivar December 24. At Lagrange, Tenn., till April, 1863. Expedition to Covington,

Tenn., March 8-12. Covington March 9-10. Scout from Lagrange to Saulsbury March 21-23. Davis Mills Road, near Lagrange, March 24. Expedition from Lagrange to Macon March 28-April 3. Summerville and near Belmont March 29. Gierson's Raid from LaGrange to Baton Rouge, La., April 17-May 2. Garlandsville, Miss., April 24. Union Church April 28. Brookhaven April 29. Wall's Post Office May —. Robert's Ford, Comite River, May 2. Coldwater May 11 (Detachment). Salem May 14 (Detachment). Reconnoissance from Baton Rouge, La., May 13. Scouts on Clinton Road May 14. Expedition from Lagrange, Tenn., to Senatobia, Miss., May 21-26 (Detachment). Senatobia May 23 (Detachment). Action at Plains Store, La., May 21. Siege of Port Hudson, La., May 24-July 9. Clinton June 3-4. Near Holly Springs, Miss., June 16-17 (Detachment). Jackson Cross Roads, La., June 20. Moved from Port Hudson to Memphis, Tenn., July 19-28. Duty at Germantown, Tenn., till November 28. Expedition to Hernando, Miss., August 16-20 (2 Companies). Near Panola August 17. Operations against Chalmers, in North Mississippi and West Tennessee October 4-17. Germantown and Mt. Pleasant October 11. Ingraham's Mills, near Byhalia, Miss., October 12. Quinn and Jackson's Mill October 13. Wyatt's October 13. Germantown, Tenn., October 16. Expedition from Germantown to Chulahuma October 22-24. Operations on Memphis and Charleston R. R. November 3-5. Colliersville, Tenn., November 3. Moscow November 5. Operations against Lee's attack on Memphis and Charleston R. R. November 28-December 10. Louisville, Tenn., November 28. Saulsbury December 3. Wolf Bridge, near Moscow, December 3-4. Lafayette December 4. Scout from Memphis, Tenn., December 10 (Co. "M"). Operations against Forest and Chalmers till February, 1864. Colliersville, Tenn., December 27-28, 1863. Coldwater, Miss., December 29. Scout toward Hernando, Miss., January 3, 1864 (Cos. "I," "K"). Smith's Expedition from Colliersville, Tenn., to Okolona, Miss., February 11-26. West Point February 20. Okolona February 21. West Point February 21. Ivey's Hill, near Okolona, February 22. At Germantown till March 30. Regiment veteranized and Veterans on furlough March 30 to May 11. Moved to Memphis, Tenn., and duty there till July. Guard R. R. at Colliersville to July 10. Coldwater River July 22. Smith's Expedition to Oxford, Miss., August 1-30. Tallahatchie River August 7-9. Hurricane Creek and Oxford August 9. Hurricane Creek August 13-14 and 19. Repulse of Forest's attack on Memphis August 21 (Detachment). At White's Station, Tenn., till October 1. March through West Tennessee to Clifton October, thence to Pulaski, Tenn. Expedition from Memphis to Moscow November 9-13. Nashville Campaign November-December. Shoal Creek, Ala., November 11. On line of Shoal Creek November 16-20. Lawrenceburg, Tenn., November 22. Campbellsville November 24. Columbia, Duck River, November 24-27. Shelbyville November 28. Columbia Ford November 28-29. Mt. Carmel November 29. Franklin November 30. Expedition to Glasgow, Ky., December 5-13. Battle of Nashville December 15-16. Pursuit of Hood to the Tennessee River December 17-28. West Harpeth River December 17. Spring Hill December 18. Rutherford Creek December 19. Columbia December 20. Linnville, Buford's Station and Richland Creek, December 24. Anthony's Gap, near Pulaski, December 25. March to Gravelly Springs, Ala., and duty there till February, 1865, and at Eastport, Miss., till July. Moved to Nashville, Tenn., thence to Decatur and Montgomery, Ala., July 3-25. Duty at Demopolis, Montgomery, Opelika and Tuskegee, Ala., till November. Mustered out at Selma, Ala., November 5, and discharged at Springfield, Ills., November 20, 1865.

Regiment lost during service 5 Officers and 60 Enlisted men killed and mortally wounded and 8 Officers and 328 Enlisted men by disease. Total 401.

7th REGIMENT CAVALRY.

Organized at Camp Butler, Ills., and mustered in October 13, 1861. Companies "A," "C," "G" and "I" ordered to Bird's Point, Mo., October 30, 1861. Rest of regiment moved to Bird's Point December 24, thence to Cape Girardeau, Mo., and duty there till February, 1862. Attached to District of Cairo, Ills., to February, 1862. 4th Brigade, 1st Division, District Cairo, to March, 1862. Cavalry Division, Army of Mississippi, to April, 1862. 1st Brigade, Cavalry Division, Army Mississippi, November, 1862. Cavalry Right Wing 13th Army Corps (Old), Department of the Tennessee, to December, 1862. Grierson's First Brigade, Cavalry Division, Department of the Tennessee, to January, 1863. 1st Brigade, Cavalry Division, 16th Army Corps, to March, 1863. 1st Brigade, 1st Cavalry Division, 16th Army Corps to May, 1863. 4th Brigade, 1st Cavalry Division, 16th Corps (Detachment), June, 1863. Cavalry Brigade, 19th Army Corps, Department of the Gulf, to August, 1863. 3rd Brigade, 1st Cavalry Division, 16th Army Corps, to December, 1863. 2nd Brigade, 1st Cavalry Division, 16th Army Corps, to April, 1864. 3rd Brigade, 1st Cavalry Division, 16th Army Corps, to July, 1864. 1st Brigade, 1st Cavalry Division, District of West Tennessee, to November, 1864. 1st Brigade, 5th Division Cavalry Corps, Military Division Mississippi, to November, 1864. 2nd Brigade, 5th Division, Cavalry Corps Military Division Mississippi, to July, 1865. District of Alabama to October, 1865.

SERVICE.—Bird's Point, Mo., January 10, 1862. Expedition to Benton January 15-17. Expeditions to Bloomfield and Dallas January 15-17 (Detachments). Bloomfield February 6. Operations against New Madrid and Island No. 10 February 28-April 8. Four Companies join from Bird's Point, Mo., March. Actions at New Madrid, Mo., March 2-3-4. Expedition to Little River and action at Point Pleasant March 23. Capture of New Madrid March 14 and of Island No. 10 April 8. Expedition to Fort Pillow, Tenn., April 13-17. Moved to Hamburg Landing, Tenn., April 18-22. Advance on and siege of Corinth, Miss., April 29-May 30. Reconnoissance toward Corinth May 8. Reconnoissance on Alabama Road to Sharp's Mills May 10. Reconnoissances to Burnsville and Iuka May 22-23. Tuscumbia Creek May 30. Pursuit to Booneville May 30-June 12. Reconnoissance toward Baldwyn June 3. Blackland June 28 (Co. "K"). Guard Duty on Memphis and Charleston R. R. from Tuscumbia to Decatur, Ala., till December 1. Hatchie River July 5. Trinity, Ala., August 22 (Detachment). Reconnoissance toward Iuka September 16. Burnsville September 17. Battle of Corinth, Miss., October 3-4. Pursuit to Ripley October 5-12. Grant's Central Mississippi Campaign November, 1862, to January, 1863. Reconnoissance toward Colliersville November 5, 1862. Reconnoissance toward Lamar, Miss., November 5 (2 Cos.). Warsham's Creek November 6. Reconnoissance from Lagrange November 8-9. Lamar and Coldwater November 8. Holly Springs November 13. Near Summerville November 26. Waterword, or Lumpkin's Mills, November 29-30. About Oxford December 1-3. Prophet's and Springdale Bridges December 3. Water Valley Station December 4. Coffeeville December 5. Expedition against Mobile and Ohio R. R. December 14-19. Pontotoc December 18. Ripley December 23. Duty at Lagrange, Tenn., January to April, 1863. Scout toward Rocky Ford January 7 (3 Cos.). Scout toward Ripley, Miss., January 28-30. Reconnoissance near Saulsbury February 2-5. Expedition from Lagrange to Mt. Pleasant and Lamar, Miss., February 13-14. Expedition to Covington March 8-12. Scout to Saulsbury April 5-6 (Cos. "F," "H" and "M"). Scout from Lagrange into Mississippi April 10-11. Grierson's Raid from Lagrange to Baton Rouge, La., April 16-May 2. New Albany, Miss., April 18-19. Garlandsville April 24. Newton Station April 24. Brookhaven April 29. Tickfaw River and Walls' Post Office May 1. Robert's Ford, Comite River, May 2. Expedition from Lagrange to Panola, Miss., May 11-15 (Detachment). Reconnoissance from Baton Rouge, La., May 13. Scouts on Clinton Road, La., May 14. Advance on Port Hudson, La., May 18-24. Plain's Store May 21. Expedition from Lagrange, Tenn., to Senatobia, Miss., May 23 (Detachment). Siege of Port Hudson, La., May 24-July 9. Thompson's Creek, La., May 25. Clinton, La., June 3-4. Operations in Northwest Mississippi June 13-22. (Detachment). Near Holly Springs, Miss., June 16-17 (Detachment). Jackson's Cross Roads, La., June 20. Manchester, Tenn., June 24 (Detachment). Near Bradysville, Tenn., June 24 (Co. "C"). Regiment moved from Port Hudson, La., to Memphis, Tenn., July 19-28. Duty along Memphis and Charleston R. R. and at Germantown, Tenn., till September 30, 1864. Operations in North Mississippi and West Tennessee against Chalmers October 4-17. Salem October 8. Ingraham's Mills, near Byhalia, October 12. Wyatt's, Tallahatchie River, October 13. Scout to Chulahoma October 22-24. Quinn and Jackson's Mill, Coldwater River, November 1 and 3. Operations on Memphis and Charleston R. R. November 3-5. Colliersville, Tenn., November 3. Moscow November 5. Operations against Lee's attack on Memphis and Charleston R. R. November 28-December 10. Saulsbury December 3. Wolf Bridge, near Moscow, December 3-4. Lagrange December 13. Operating against Forest and Chalmers till February, 1864. Lamar December 19, 1863. Estenaula December 24. New Castle December 26. Somerville December 26. Lagrange, Tenn., January 2, 1864. Scout from Lagrange to Ripley, Miss., January 23. Smith's Expedition from Colliersville, Tenn., to West Point and Okolona, Miss., February 11-26. West Point February 20. Okolona February 21. Ivey's Hill, near Okolona, February 22. Tippah River February 24. Regiment veteranize at Germantown, Tenn., and Veterans on furlough April to June. Return to Memphis, Tenn. Non-Veterans on Sturgis' Expedition from Memphis, Tenn., into Mississippi June 1-14. Brice's or Tisamingo Creek, near Gintown, June 10. Ripley June 11. Cross Roads June 18. Okolona June 23. Smith's Expedition to Tupelo, Miss., July 5-21 (Detachment). Harrisonburg, near Tupelo, July 14-15. Smith's Expedition to Oxford, Miss., August 1-30 (Detachment). Tallahatchie River August 7-9. Hurricane Creek and Oxford August 9. Hurricane Creek August 13-14 and 19. Forest's attack on Memphis August 21 (Veterans). March to Clifton, Tenn., thence to Pulaski October 26, and to Shoal Creek, Ala., November 8. Expedition from Memphis to Moscow November 9-13. Nashville Campaign November-December. Shoal Creek, Ala., November 11. On line of Shoal Creek November 16-20. Lawrenceburg November 22. Campbellsville and Lynnville November 24. Columbia Duck River November 24-27. Mt. Carmel November 29. West Harpeth River, Franklin, November 30. Battle of Nashville December 15-16. Pursuit of Hood to the Tennessee River December 17-28. West Harpeth River, Franklin, December 17. Spring Hill December 18. Rutherford Creek December 19. Columbia December 20. Richland Creek and Lynnville December 24. Anthony's Gap, near Pulaski, December 25. March to Gravelly Springs, Ala., and duty there till February, 1865. At Eastport, Miss., till May. At Okolona, Miss., till July 1, and at Decatur, Ala., till October. Mustered out October 20, 1865, and discharged at Camp Butler, Ills., November 17, 1865.

Regiment lost during service 5 Officers and 59 Enlisted men killed and mortally wounded and 3 Officers and 267 Enlisted men by disease. Total 334.

8th REGIMENT CAVALRY.

Organized at St. Charles, Ills., and mustered in September 18, 1861. Moved to Washington, D. C., October 13-17. At Meridian Hill till December 17 and at Alexandria, Va., till March, 1862. Attached to Sumner's Division, Army of the Potomac, December, 1861, to March, 1862. Cavalry 2nd Army Corps, Army of the Potomac, to May, 1862. Stoneman's Light Brigade to June, 1862. Averill's Cavalry Brigade, 5th Army Corps, to July, 1862. 2nd Brigade, Stoneman's Cavalry Division, Army of the Potomac, to September, 1862. 1st Brigade, Pleasonton's Cavalry Division, Army of the Potomac, till February, 1863. 1st Brigade, 1st Division Cavalry Corps, Army of the Potomac, to April, 1864. 2nd Brigade, 3rd Division Cavalry Corps, Army Potomac, to June, 1864 (Detachment). Regiment Unattached Defences of Washington, D. C., 22nd Army Corps, to November, 1864. 1st Separate Brigade, 22nd Army Corps, Department of Washington, to July, 1865.

SERVICE.—Advance on Manassas, Va., March 10-19, 1862. Reconnoissance to Gainesville Madch 20. Operations on the Orange and Alexandria R. R. March 28-29. Warrenton Junction March 28. Bealeton Station March 28. Rappahannock Station March 29. Reconnoissance to the Rappahannock April 2. Moved to the Peninsula, Virginia, April 23-May 1. Near Williamsburg May 4. Battle of Williamsburg May 5. Mechanicsville May 23-24. Battle of Fair Oaks, Seven Pines, May 31-June 1. Seven days before Richmond June 25-July 1. Ashland June 25 (Detachment). Mechanicsville, Atlee's Station and near Hanover Court House, June 26. Hundley's Corners June 26-27. Garnett's Farm and Gaines' Mill June 27. Despatch Station June 28 (Cos. "E," "K"). Savage Station June 29. White Oak Swamp and Glendale June 30. Malvern Hill July 1. Reconnoissance from Harrison's Landing July 4. At Harrison's Landing till August 16. Malvern Hill July 5. Expedition to Malvern Hill July 20-22. Malvern Hill August 5. Movement to Fortress Monroe, thence to Alexandria August 16-23. Falls Church September 3-4. Poolesville, Md., September 7-8. Barnesville September 9. Monocacy Church and Nolansville September 9. Middletown September 10. Sugar Loaf Mountain September 11-12. Frederick September 12. Middletown September 13. Catoctin Mountain September 13. South Mountain September 14. Boonesborough September 15. Antietam September 16-17. Shephardstown Ford September 19. Reconnoissance from Sharpsburg to Shepardstown, W. Va., October 1. Martinsburg October 1. Pursuit of Stuart into Pennsylvania October 9-12. Mouth of Monocacy October 12. Sharpsburg and Hagerstown Pike October 16-17. Purcellsville and near Upperville October 29 (Detachment). Snickersville October 31. Philomont November 1-2. Upperville November 2-3. Union November 3. Barber's Cross Roads, Chester Gap and Markham November 5-6. Sperryville November 7. Little Washington November 8. Markham Station and Barber's Cross Roads November 10. Battle of Fredericksburg, Va., December 12-15. Turner's Mills January 30, 1863. Operations in Westmoreland and Richmond Counties February 10-16. Near Dumfries March 15 and 29. Zoar Church March 30. Chancellorsville Campaign April 27-May 8. Stoneman's Raid April 29-May 8. Rapidan Station May 1. Warrenton May 6. Lancaster May 20-21. Clendennin's Raid below Fredericksburg May 20-28. Brandy Station and Beverly Ford June 9. Aldie June 11. Goose Creek June 18. Upperville June 21. Battle of Gettysburg, Pa., July 1-3. Williamsport July 6-7. Funkstown, Md., July 8. Boonesborough July 8. Chester Gap and Benevola or Beaver Creek, July 9. At and near Funkstown, Md., July 10-13. Falling Waters July 15. Chester Gap July 21-22. Lovettsville July 22. Kelly's Ford July 31-August 1. Near Culpeper August 1-3. Brandy Station August 4. Weaversville August 2/. Brandy Station September 8. Raccoon Ford and Stevensburg September 10-11. Culpeper and Pony Mountain September 13. Reconnoissance across the Rapidan September 21-23. Liberty Mills September 21. Jack's Shop, Madison Court House, September 22. Mitchell's Ford October 7. Bristoe Campaign October 9-22. Culpeper October 9. Raccoon Ford October 10. Morton's Ford October 10. Stevensburg, near Kelly's Ford and Brandy Station, October 11. Fleetwood or Brandy Station October 12. Oak Hill October 15. Madison Court House October 16. Hazel River October 17. Bealeton October 27. Near Catlett's Station October 30. Advance to line of the Rappahannock November 7-8. Warrenton or Sulphur Springs, Jeffersonton and Hazel River November 8. Mine Run Campaign November 26-December 2. Parker's Store November 29. Jennings' Farm, near Ely's Ford, December 1. Reconnoissance to Madison Court House

January 31, 1864 (Detachment). Veterans on furlough January to March, 1864. Camp at Giesboro Point till May. Patrol duty at Washington, D. C., and scout duty at Fairfax, Va., till April, 1865, having numerous engagements with Mosby's guerrillas and the Black Horse Cavalry. A detachment with Army of the Potomac and participated in the Rapidan Campaign May-June, 1864. Craig's Meeting House, Va., May 5. Todd's Tavern May 5-6. Alsop's Farm May 8. Guinea Station May 18. Salem Church and Pole Cat Creek May 27. Cold Harbor June 1-12. Point of Rocks, Md., July 5. Noland's Ferry July 5. Middletown and Solomon's Gap July 7. Frederick July 7. Frederick July 8 (Detachment). Battle of Monocacy July 9. Rockville and Urbana July 9. Near Fort Stevens, D. C., July 11. Along northern defences of Washington, D. C., July 11-12. Rockville July 13. Cockeyville July 18. Philomont July 20. Snickersville July 21. Monocacy Junction July 30. Near Piedmont October 9. Near Rectortown October 10. White Plains October 11. Upperville October 28 (Detachment). Operations at Snicker's Gap October 28-29 (Detachment). Manassas Junction November 11. Fairfax Station November 26. Scout from Fairfax Court House to Hopewell Gap December 26-27. Scout from Fairfax Court House to Brentsville February 6-7, 1865, and to Aldie and Middleburg February 15-16 (Co. "B"). Operations about Warrenton, Bealeton Station, Sulphur Springs and Centreville March 3-8. Duty about Washington, D. C., till July. Ordered to St. Louis, Mo., thence to Chicago, Ill., and mustered out July 17, 1865.

Regiment lost during service 7 Officers and 68 Enlisted men killed and mortally wounded and 1 Officer and 174 Enlisted men by disease. Total 250.

9th REGIMENT CAVALRY.

Organized at Camp Douglas, Chicago, Ills., and mustered in November 30, 1861. Moved from Chicago to Benton Barracks, Mo., thence to Pilot Knob and to Reeve's Station on Big Black, February 16-27, 1862. Attached to Steele's Division, District of Southeast Missouri, to May, 1862. Unattached Cavalry Curtis' Army of Southwest Missouri, to July, 1862. District of Eastern Arkansas, Department of Missouri, to December, 1862. 2nd Brigade, 3rd (Cavalry) Division, District Eastern Arkansas, Department of the Tennessee to January, 1863. 2nd Brigade, 2nd Cavalry Division, 13th Army Corps, Dept. of the Tennessee, to April, 1863. 2nd Brigade, 1st Cavalry Division, 16th Army Corps, Department Tennessee to June, 1863. 1st Brigade, 1st Cavalry Division, 16th Army Corps to August, 1863. 2nd Brigade, 1st Cavalry Division, 16th Army Corps to April, 1864. 3rd Brigade, 1st Cavalry Division, 16th Army Corps to June, 1864. 1st Brigade, Cavalry Division, District West Tennessee, July, 1864. 2nd Brigade, 1st Cavalry Division, District of West Tennessee to November, 1864. 2nd Brigade, 5th Division Cavalry Corps, Military Division Mississippi to July, 1865. District of Alabama to October, 1865.

SERVICE.—Moved to Jacksonport, Ark., March, 1862, and duty there till June. Action at Cotton Plant May 14. Village Creek May 21. Reconnoissance from Jacksonport toward Augusta and Des Arc May 26-29. Cache River Bridge May 28. Galloway Farm, near Jacksonport, June 2. Waddell's Farm, Village Creek, June 2 (Cos. "A," "C," "K," "M"). Near Jacksonport June 12 (Detachment). Reconnoissance toward Augusta June 23 (Co. "F"). March to Helena, Ark., June 26-July 14. Stewart's Plantation, Village Creek, June 27. Duty at Helena till April, 1863. Expedition from Helena to Moro November 5-8, 1862 (Detachment). Clarendon August 13. Marianna November 7. Lagrange November 8. Expedition from Helena to Grenada, Miss., November 27-December 5. Yocknapatalfa, near Mitchell's Cross Roads, Miss., December 1. Oakland December 3. Expedition to Duvall's Bluff January 9-16, 1863. Moved to Memphis, thence to Germantown, Tenn., April 4-11. Expedition from Lagrange to Senatobia, Miss., May 21-26. Senatobia May 23 and 25. Operations in Northwest Mississippi June 15-25. Near Holly Springs, Miss., June

16-17. Jackson, Tenn., July 13. Scout from Germantown July 16-20. Coldwater July 28. Expedition from Memphis to Grenada, Miss., August 12-23. Grenada August 17. Expedition from LaGrange to Toon's Station September 11-16. Montezuma September 16. Operations in North Mississippi and West Tennessee against Chalmers October 4-17. Lockhart's Mills October 6. Salem October 8. Ingraham's Mills, near Byhalia, October 12. Wyatt's, Tallahatchie River, October 13. Operations on Memphis and Charleston R. R. November 3-5. Colliersville November 3. Moscow November 5. Operations on Memphis and Charleston R. R. against Lee's attack November 28-December 10. Saulsbury December 3. Wolf Bridge, near Moscow, December 3-4. Scout from Colliersville December 4. Near Colliersville December 13 (Detachment). Near Moscow December 27. Colliersville December 27-28. Oak Ridge January 16, 1864. Smith's Expedition from Colliersville to Okolona, Miss., February 11-26. Near Okolona February 18. Aberdeen February 18. New Albany February 18. West Point and New Albany February 20. Okolona February 21. Ivey's Hill, near Okolona, February 22. Regiment veteranized March 16, 1864, and Veterans on furlough till April 27. Sturgis' Expedition into Mississippi June 1-13 (Detachment). Brice's, or Tishamingo Creek, near Guntown, June 10. Ripley June 11. Smith's Expedition to Tupelo July 5-21. About Pontotoc July 11. Camargo's Cross Roads, Harrisburg, July 13. Tupelo July 14-15. Old Town Creek July 15. Smith's Expedition to Oxford, Miss., August 1-30. Tallahatchie River August 7-9. Hurricane Creek and Oxford August 9. Hurricane Creek August 13-14 and 19. Operations in West Tennessee and Alabama against Hood, and Nashville (Tenn.) Campaign November December. Expedition from Memphis to Moscow November 9-13. Shoal Creek November 11. On line of Shoal Creek November 16-20. Lawrenceburg November 22. Campbellsville November 24. Columbia, Duck River, November 24-27. Mt. Carmel November 28. Franklin November 30. Battle of Nashville December 15-16. Pursuit of Hood to the Tennessee River December 17-28. Brentwood and West Harpeth River December 17. Spring Hill December 18. Franklin Pike, Curtis Creek and Rutherford Creek December 19. Columbia December 20. Lynnville and Richland Creek December 24. Anthony's Gap, near Pulaski, December 25. Expedition from Eastport to Russellsville, Ala., February 19-23, 1865. Tuscumbia February 20. Duty at Huntsville and Florence, Ala., Eastport, Miss., and Gravelly Springs, Ala., till June. Moved to Iuka, Miss., June 23, thence to Decatur, Ala., July 4. To Montgomery and Selma, Ala., thence to Gainesville August 20. Duty in District of Montgomery, Ala., till October. Mustered out at Selma, Ala., October 31, 1865.

Regiment lost during service 1 Officer and 45 Enlisted men killed and mortally wounded and 6 Officers and 241 Enlisted men by disease. Total 293.

10th REGIMENT CAVALRY.

Organized at Camp Butler, Ill., and mustered in November 25, 1861. Moved to Quincy, Ill., December 20, thence to Benton Barracks, Mo., March 13, 1862. Moved to Springfield, Mo., April 4. Attached to District of Southwest Missouri, Dept. of Missouri, to October, 1862. 1st Brigade, 3rd Division, Army of the Frontier, Dept. of Missouri, to December, 1862. Unattached, Army of the Frontier, to February, 1863. 1st Brigade, 2nd Division, Army of the Frontier, to May, 1863. 2nd Brigade, 1st Cavalry Division, District of Southeast Missouri, to August, 1863. 2nd Brigade, 1st Cavalry Division, Arkansas Expedition, to December, 1863. 3rd Brigade, 1st Cavalry Division, Army of Arkansas, to January, 1864. 3rd Brigade, 1st Cavalry Division, 7th Army Corps, Dept. of Arkansas, to May, 1864. 3rd Brigade, 2nd Division, 7th Army Corps, to September, 1864. 3rd Brigade, Cavalry Division, 7th Army Corps, to February, 1865. 1st Brigade, Cavalry Division, 7th Army Corps, to April, 1865. 1st Brigade, 1st Cavalry Division, Military Division West Mississippi, to May, 1865. 2nd Brigade, 2nd

Cavalry Division, Military Division West Mississippi, to July, 1865. Dept. of Texas to November, 1865.

SERVICE.—Near Waynesville, Mo., May 31, 1862 (Co. "K"). Neosho May 31. Expedition to Keittsville, Mo., July 8-20. Near Fayetteville, Ark., July 15. Moved to Vera Cruz August 10, to Marshfield August 16, and duty there, operating from Springfield to Cane Hill, Ark., till November 13. Marshfield, Mo., October 20 (Detachment). Clark's Mills, Douglass County, November 7 (Co. "C"). Battle of Prairie Grove, Ark., December 7. 3rd Battalion (Cos. "C," "F," "I" and "M") moved to Fayetteville, Ark., December 8, and duty there till March, 1863, rejoining Regiment in Missouri. Expedition over Boston Mountains to Van Buren December 27-29, 1862 (Cos. "B," "E," "H" and "L"). 2nd Battalion (Cos. "B," "E," "H" and "L") moved to Huntsville January, 1863, and joined Totten. Moved to Flat Creek February, 1863, thence to Rolla, Mo. Scout from Fayetteville to Van Buren January 23-27, 1863 (3rd Battalion). Mulberry Springs January 27. Scout from Fayetteville to Arkansas River February 5-12 (3rd Battalion). Thelkelds' Ferry February 6. Near Van Buren February 10. Operations against Marmaduke April 17-May 2. Jackson April 26. At Pilot Knob till July. Steele's Campaign against Little Rock July 1-September 10. Bayou Metoe, or Reed's Bridge, August 27. Bayou LaFourche and capture of Little Rock September 10. Pursuit of Price September 11-13. Near Little Rock September 11. Duty at Little Rock till March, 1864. Steele's Expedition to Camden March 23-May 3. Elkins' Ferry April 3-4. Prairie D'Ann April 9-13. Jenkins' Ferry, Camden, April 15. Near Camden April 20. Jenkins' Ferry, Saline River, April 30. Operations against Shelby north of the Arkansas River May 13-31. Scouts from Huntersville and Clinton June 4-17. Operations in Arkansas July 1-31. Near Huntersville July 8 (Detachment). Near Little Rock July 10 (Detachment). Bayou des Arc July 14. Duty at Little Rock, Pine Bluff and Brownsville and in the Dept. of Arkansas to November, 1865. Expedition from Little Rock to Little Red River August 6-16, 1864. Expedition from Little Rock to Searcy, Fairview and Augusta in pursuit of Shelby August 27-September 6, 1864. Expedition from Pine Bluff September 9-12. Near Monticello September 10 (Detachment). Brewer's House September 11 (Detachment). Expedition from Brownsville to Cotton Plant October 26-November 2 (Detachment). Expedition from Brownsville to Fairview November 28-December 8. Duty in Arkansas till June 6, 1865. Moved to Shreveport, La., June 6-17, thence marched to San Antonio, Texas, July 8-August 1; duty there till November, 1865.

1st Battalion (Cos. "A," "D," "G" and "K") detached and ordered to join Gen. Curtis June 15, 1862. Reported at Jacksonport, Ark., July 4, 1862. Attached to Army of Southwest Missouri and District of Eastern Arkansas to December, 1862. 1st Brigade, 2nd Cavalry Division, 13th Army Corps, Dept. of the Tennessee, to May, 1863. Detached Brigade, District of Northeast Louisiana to June, 1863. Unattached, 13th Army Corps, to July, 1863.

SERVICE.—March to Helena, Ark., July 4-12, 1862. Action at Cotton Plant, Ark., July 7. Moved to Oldtown Landing August 6, and duty there till October. Moved to Helena October 6. Expedition to mouth of White River November 16-20. Washburn's Expedition to Oakland, Miss., November 27-December 7. Oakland December 3. Arkansas Post, Ark., January 11, 1863. Yazoo Pass Expedition February 24-April 8, 1863. Siege operations against Vicksburg, Miss., April to July. Near Richmond, La., June 6. Milliken's Bend and Young's Point, La., June 6-7. Expedition from Young's Point to Richmond June 14-16. Richmond June 16. Moved to Helena, Ark., July, and rejoined Regiment near Wittsburg, Ark., August 1, 1863. Regiment mustered out November 22, 1865.

Regiment lost during service 1 Officer and 24 Enlisted men killed and mortally wounded and 3 Officers and 262 Enlisted men by disease. Total 290.

11th REGIMENT CAVALRY.

Organized at Peoria, Ill., and mustered in December 20, 1861. Duty at Peoria till February, 1862. Moved to Benton Barracks, Mo., February 22-March 3, and duty there till March 28. Moved to Pittsburg Landing, Tenn., March 25-April 1. (1st Battalion to Crump's Landing and joined Lew Wallace's 3rd Division, Army Tennessee.) Attached to 3rd Division, Army Tennessee, to July, 1862. 6th Division, Army Tennessee, to July, 1862 (2nd and 3rd Battalions). District of Memphis, Tenn., to September, 1862, and District of Jackson, Tenn., to November, 1862 (1st Battalion). District of Corinth, Miss., to September, 1862, and District of Jackson, Tenn., to November, 1862 (2nd and 3rd Battalions). Cavalry Brigade, District of Jackson, Left Wing 13th Army Corps (Old), Dept. of the Tennessee, to December, 1862. Cavalry Brigade, District of Jackson, 16th Army Corps, to March, 1863. Mizner's Cavalry Brigade, 3rd Division, 16th Army Corps, to June, 1863. 4th Brigade, 1st Cavalry Division, 16th Army Corps, to August, 1863. Winslow's Cavalry Brigade, 15th Army Corps, to December, 1863. Winslow's Cavalry Brigade, 17th Army Corps, and District of Vicksburg, Miss., to December, 1864. 3rd Brigade, Cavalry Division, District of West Tennessee, to June, 1865. 1st Brigade, Cavalry Division, District of West Tennessee, to September, 1865.

SERVICE.—Battle of Shiloh, Tenn., April 6-7, 1862. Advance on and siege of Corinth, Miss., April 29-May 30. Purdy April 29. Pursuit to Booneville May 30-June 12. Coldwater Station, Miss., June 21 (3rd Battalion). Salisbury, Tenn., August 11. Bolivar, Tenn., August 30. Davis Bridge, Hatchie River, Tenn., September 25. Battle of Corinth, Miss., October 3-4. Pursuit to Hatchie River October 5-12. Grant's Central Mississippi Campaign November, 1862, to January, 1863. Lexington, Tenn., December 18, 1862. Salem Cemetery, near Jackson, Tenn., December 19. Huntington, Tenn., December 29-30. Parker's Cross Roads, Red Mound, December 30-31. Near Yorkville, Tenn., January 28, 1863. Dyersburg January 30. Operations in Northwest Mississippi June 15-25. Near Holly Springs, Miss., June 16-17. Hudsonville and on Helena Road, Miss., June 21. Bolivar, Tenn., July 10. Expedition from Memphis, Tenn., to Grenada, Miss., August 12-23. Grenada August 17. Expedition from LaGrange to Toone Station September 11-16. Ordered to Vicksburg, Miss., and duty in that District till December, 1864. Expedition from Big Black River to Yazoo City, Miss., September 27-October 1, 1863. Brownsville September 28. Morris Ford, near Benton, September 29. Expedition to Canton October 14-20. Canton Road near Brownsville October 15-16. Near Clinton and Vernon Roads October 16. Bogue, Chitto Creek, October 17. Robinson's Mills, near Livingston, October 17. Livingston Road, near Clinton, October 18. Near Natchez, Miss., December 7. Meridian Campaign February 3-March 2, 1864. Champion's Hill February 4. Jackson February 5. Hillsborough February 6. Brandon February 7. Morton February 8. Meridian February 9-13. Hillsborough February 10. Meridian February 13-14. Canton February 29 (Detachment). Brownsville March 3. Expedition from Vicksburg to Yazoo City May 4-21. (Detachment). Benton May 7 and 9. Expedition from Vicksburg to Pearl River July 2-10. Clinton July 5. Clinton and Jackson July 7. Expedition from Vicksburg to Rodney and Fayette September 29-October 3 (Detachment). Expedition from Natchez to Woodville October 4-11 (Detachment). Woodville October 5-6. Operations in Issaqueena and Washington Counties October 24-31. Expedition from Vicksburg to Gaines Landing, Ark., and Bayou Macon, La., November 6-8. Expedition from Vicksburg to Yazoo City November 23-December 4. Moved to Memphis, Tenn., December. Grierson's Raid on Mobile & Ohio R. R. December 21, 1864, to January 15, 1865. Franklin Creek December 21-22. Egypt Station December 28, 1864. Franklin January 2, 1865. Expedition from Memphis to Marion, Ark., January 19-22. Marion, Ark., January 20-21, 1865.

Duty on Memphis & Charleston R. R. between Memphis and Grand Junction, Headquarters at LaGrange, Tenn., January to September, 1865. Expedition from Memphis to Brownsville, Miss., April 23-26. Mustered out September 30, 1865.

Company "G" served detached as Headquarters Guard, 17th Army Corps, and participated in following: Movements on Bruinsburg and turning Grand Gulf April 25-30, 1863. Siege of Vicksburg, Miss., May 18-July 4. Messenger's Ferry, Big Black River, May 29-30 and July 4. Advance on Jackson, Miss., July 5-10. Siege of Jackson July 10-17. In Atlanta (Ga.) Campaign June 8 to September 8, 1864. About Marietta and against Kenesaw Mountain June 10-July 2. Assault on Kenesaw June 27. Chattahoochie River July 3-17. Battle of Atlanta July 22. Siege of Atlanta July 22-August 25. Flank movement on Jonesboro August 25-30. Battle of Jonesboro August 31-September 1. March to the sea November 15-December 10. Little Ogeechee River December 4. Station No. 5, Georgia Central R. R., December 4. Siege of Savannah December 10-21.

Regiment lost during service 2 Officers and 32 Enlisted men killed and mortally wounded and 8 Officers and 237 Enlisted men by disease. Total 279.

12th REGIMENT CAVALRY.

Companies "A," "B," "C," "D," "E" and "G" organized at Springfield, Ill., and mustered in February 24, 1862. Captain Gilmore's Company of Cavalry, Company "A," 32nd Illinois, organized at Camp Butler December 31, 1861; assigned as Company "F." Captain Sheerer's and Captain Barker's Companies, McClellan Dragoons, organized at Chicago, Ill., October, 1861; assigned as Company "H." Captain Brown's Company, McClellan Dragoons, organized at Chicago, Ill., October, 1861; assigned as Company "I." Companies "K," "L" and "M" organized at Springfield, Ill., December 30, 1863, to January 12, 1864. Duty at Camp Butler, Ill., guarding prisoners, till June, 1862. Ordered to Martinsburg, W. Va., June 25. Attached to District of Martinsburg, W. Va., to September, 1862. 1st Brigade, 2nd Division, 12th Army Corps, Army Potomac, to October, 1862. Defences Upper Potomac, 8th Army Corps, Middle Dept. to February, 1863. 2nd Brigade, 3rd Division, Cavalry Corps, Army of the Potomac, to June, 1863. 1st Brigade, 1st Division, Cavalry Corps, Army Potomac, to November, 1863. Chicago, Ill., to February, 1864. District of St. Louis, Mo., Dept. of Missouri, to March, 1864. 1st Brigade, Cavalry Division, 19th Army Corps, Dept. of the Gulf, to June, 1864. District of LaFourche, Dept. of the Gulf, to August, 1864. 4th Brigade, Cavalry Division, Dept. of the Gulf, August, 1864. 3rd Brigade, Cavalry Division, Dept. of the Gulf, to February, 1865. 2nd Brigade, Cavalry Division, District of West Tennessee, to July, 1865. Dept. of Texas to May, 1866.

SERVICE.—Duty at Martinsburg, W. Va., and on the Upper Potomac to September, 1862. Near Martinsburg September 3. Bunker Hill September 3-4. Martinsburg September 6. Darkesville September 7. Williamsport, Md., September 11. Martinsburg September 11-12. Defence of Harper's Ferry, W. Va., September 13-14. Regiment cut way through enemy's lines on night of September 14. Antietam, Md., September 16-18. Hagerstown, Md., September 20. Duty on Upper Potomac September 20 to December 8. Williamsport September 21. McCoy's or Russell's Ferry and near Green Springs Furnace October 10. Reconnoissance from Bolivar Heights to Rippon, W. Va., November 9. Dumfries, Va., December 26-27. At Falmouth, Va., till April 1863. Chancellorsville Campaign April 27-May 8. Stoneman's Raid April 29-May 8. Tunstall Station May 4. Aylett's May 5. Raid from Yorktown into Matthews County May 19-23. March to Falmouth, Va., Brandy Station and Beverly Ford June 9. Upperville June 21. Expedition from Yorktown to South Anna Bridge June 23-28 (Detachment). South Anna Bridge June 26 (Detachment). Battle of Gettysburg, Pa., July 1-3. Williamsport, Md., July 6. Bronsboro July 8. Benevola or Beaver Creek July 9. At and near Funkstown July 10-13. Falling

Waters July 14. Chester Gap July 26. Kelly's Ford July 31-August 1. Brandy Station August 1-4. Near Fairfax Court House August 6 (Detachment). Brandy Station and Culpeper Court House September 7-8. Near Bristoe Station September 12. Advance from the Rappahannock to the Rapidan September 13-17. Culpeper Court House September 13. Raccoon Ford September 14-16. Stevensburg September 17. Reconnoissance across the Rappahannock September 21-23. Jack's Shop, Madison Court House, September 22. Bristoe Campaign October 9-22. Raccoon and Morton's Fords October 10. Brandy Station October 11-12. Oak Hill October 15. Rappahannock Station October 27. Moved to Chicago, Ill., November 20-28, and duty there till February, 1864. Moved to St. Louis, Mo., February 9, thence moved to New Orleans, La., March 15-April 1. Moved to Red River April 20, arriving at Alexandria April 23. Actions at Alexandria April 28-May 5-8. Bayou Teche, La., May 5-8. Wilson's Landing May 14. Avoyelle's or Marksville Prairie May 15. Mansura May 16. Yellow Bayou May 17. Morganza May 20. Arrived at New Orleans, La., June 1. Moved to Napoleonville June 11, and duty there till October, engaged in picketing and scouting. Near Napoleonville July 29 (Co. "L"). Expedition from Paincoursville to Natchez, Miss., with skirmish August 15-21 (Cos. "I," "L"). Expedition to Grand Lake, Grand River and Lake Natchez September 7-11. Expedition from Napoleonville to Grand River and Bayou Pigeon September 26-30. Moved to Baton Rouge, La., and duty there till November 14. Liberty November 18. Davidson's Expedition against Mobile and Ohio R. R. November 27-December 13. Expedition from Baton Rouge to Clinton December 23-24. Moved to Vicksburg, Miss., thence to Memphis, Tenn., and to Gaines' Landing, Ark., January 7-26, 1865. Osban's Expedition through Southern Arkansas and Northern Louisiana January 27-February 14. Duty near Memphis, Tenn., till June. Expedition from Memphis, Tenn., into Northern Mississippi March 3-11. Moved to Alexandria, La., June 15-22, thence marched to Hempstead, Texas, August 8-26. Duty in Eastern Texas till May, 1866. Mustered out May 29, 1866.

Regiment lost during service 38 Enlisted men killed and mortally wounded and 4 Officers and 192 Enlisted men by disease. Total 234.

13th REGIMENT CAVALRY.

Eight Companies organized at Camp Douglass, Ill., October 30, 1861, to February 20, 1862. Consolidated to a Battalion of 3 Companies May 20, 1863. Seven new Companies assigned February, 1864. Regiment moved to Benton Barracks, Mo., December, 1861, and duty there till February, 1862. Attached to District of Southeast Missouri, Steele's Command, February to May, 1862. District of Southwest Missouri to October, 1862. Cavalry Brigade, District of Southeast Missouri, to February, 1863. 1st Brigade, 2nd Division, Army of Southeast Missouri, to March, 1863. District of Southeast Missouri to July, 1863. Reserve Brigade, 1st Cavalry Division, Army of Southeast Missouri, to August, 1863. Reserve Brigade, 1st Cavalry Division, Arkansas Expedition, to December, 1863. Unattached 2nd Division, Army of Arkansas, to January, 1864. 1st Brigade, 1st Cavalry Division, 7th Army Corps, Dept. of Arkansas, to May, 1864. Clayton's Cavalry Brigade, 7th Army Corps, to September, 1864. 1st Brigade, Cavalry Division, 7th Army Corps, to January, 1865. Post Pine Bluff, Ark., 7th Army Corps, to August, 1865.

SERVICE.—Duty in District of Southeast Missouri February to June, 1862. Joined Gen. Curtis at Jacksonport, Ark., June 1. March to Helena, Ark., June 1-July 14. Grand Haze, White River, July 4. Hill's Plantation, Cache River, Round Hill, Bayou De View July 7. Gaines' Landing, Pittman's Ferry July 20. Cotton Plant July 25. Scout in Wayne, Stoddard and Dunklin Counties, Mo., August 20-27 (Detachment). Union Mills August 22. Four Miles August 23. Bloomfield August 24. Camp Pillow August 29. Little River Bridge August 31 (Detachment). Bloomfield September

11. Davidson's Campaign in Southwest Missouri and Northwest Arkansas October, 1862, to May, 1863. Van Buren December 21, 1862. Operations against Marmaduke April 17-May 2. Jackson April 22. White River April 22. Bloomfield April 24. Union City and Chalk Bulffs April 25. Bushy Creek May 28. Near Doniphan June 1 (Detachment). Campaign against Little Rock, Ark., July 1-September 10. Harrison's Landing August 6. Near Helena August 8. Grand Prairie and White River August 17. Brownsville August 24-25. Reed's Bridge, Bayou Metoe August 27. Bayou Metoe August 30 and September 4. Austin August 31. Bayou Fourche and capture of Little Rock September 10. Pursuit of Price September 11-13. Near Little Rock September 11. Duty at Little Rock till July, 1864. Batesville October 22, 1863. Pine Bluff November 28. Steele's Expedition from Little Rock to Camden March 23-May 3, 1864. Little Missouri River April 4. Prairie d'Ann April 9-12. Jenkins' Ferry, Camden, April 15. Jenkins' Ferry, Saline River, April 30. Duty at Pine Bluff till August, 1865. Little Rock Road July 30, 1864. Near Pine Bluff July 30 (Detachment.) Pine Bluff September 11. Reconnoissance from Pine Bluff toward Monticello and Mt. Elba October 4-11. Scout from Pine Bluff toward Mt. Elba October 24-27 (Detachment). Near Half Way House October 25 (Detachment). Expedition from Helena to Friar's Point, Miss., December 1-5 (Detachment). Scout to Richland December 24-25 (Detachment). Scout from Pine Bluff to Simpson's Plantation December 27-28. Expedition from Pine Bluff January 7-9, 1865, and January 15-19. Expedition from Little Rock to Mt. Elba January 22-February 4. Expedition from Pine Bluff to Duvall's Bluff and skirmish February 9-19. Expedition to Arkansas River February 17-18 (Detachment). Near Bayou Metoe February 17. Scout to Douglass' Plantation February 21-22. Douglass' Plantation February 22. Near Voches February 23. Bayou Metoe February 24. Expedition to McMilley's Farm February 26-28 (Detachment). Skirmish McMilley's Farm February 27 (Detachment). Near Pine Bluff March 4 (Detachment). Expedition to Bass Plantation March 17-20 (Detachment). Expedition to Monticello March 21-23 (Detachment). Expedition to Bayou Bartholomew April 1-4 (Detachment). Scout from Pine Bluff to Rodgers' Plantation April 25 (Detachment). Scout from Pine Bluff to Noble's Plantation May 4-6 (Detachment). Scout from Pine Bluff to Johnson's Farm May 15-17. Skirmish on Monticello Road May 16 (Detachment). Scout to Monticello May 23-27. Monticello May 24. Mustered out August 31, 1865.

Regiment lost during service 21 Enlisted men killed and mortally wounded and 4 Officers and 360 Enlisted men by disease. Total 385.

14th REGIMENT CAVALRY.

Organized at Peoria, Ills., and mustered in 1st and 2nd Battalions, January 7, 1863. 3rd Battalion February 6, 1863. Moved to Louisville, Ky., March 28-30, 1863, thence to Glasgow, Ky., April 12-17. Attached to 1st Brigade, 3rd Division, 23rd Army Corps, Dept. of the Ohio, to August, 1863. 2nd Brigade, 4th Division, 23rd Army Corps, to October, 1863. 4th Brigade, 4th Division, 23rd Army Corps, to November, 1863. 2nd Brigade, 2nd Division Cavalry Corps, Dept. Ohio, to May, 1864. 3rd Brigade, Cavalry Division, District of Kentucky, Dept. Ohio, to June, 1864. 3rd Brigade, Cavalry Division, 23rd Army Corps, to August, 1864. Dismounted Cavalry Brigade, 23rd Army Corps, to September, 1864. 1st Brigade, Cavalry Division, 23rd Army Corps, to November, 1864. 2nd Brigade, 6th Division Cavalry Corps, Military Division Mississippi, to December, 1864. 1st Brigade, 6th Division Cavalry Corps, Military Division Mississippi, December, 1864. 2nd Brigade, 6th Division Cavalry Corps, Military Division Mississippi, to July, 1865.

SERVICE.—Scouting in the vicinity of Glasgow, Ky., till June 22, 1863. Action at Celina, Ky., April 19. Lafayette, Tenn., May 11. Kettle Creek May 25. Expedition from Glasgow to Burkesville and Tennessee State line June 8-10. Kettle Creek June 9. Moved to Tompkinsville, Ky., June 22. Pursuit of Morgan July 4-26. Buffington Island, Ohio, July 19. March from Louisville to Glasgow July 27-August 6. Burnside's Campaign in East Tennessee August 16-October 17. Occupation of Knoxville, Tenn., September 1. Expedition to Cumberland Gap September 4-9. Rheatown September 12. Kingsport September 18. Bristol September 19. Zollicoffer September 20-21. Jonesborough September 21. Hall's Ford, Watauga River, September 22. Carter's Depot and Blountsville September 22. Blue Springs October 10. Henderson's Mill and Rheatown October 11. Blountsville October 14. Bristol October 15. Warm Springs October 20 and 22. Knoxville Campaign November 4-December 23. Siege of Knoxville November 17-December 5. Near Maynardsville December 1. Walker's Ford, Clinch River, December 2. Reconnoissance to Powder Springs Gap December 2-3. Bean's Station December 14-15. Blain's Cross Roads December 16-19. Clinch River December 21. Dandridge December 24. Talbot's Station December 29. Operations about Dandridge January 16-17, 1864. Kimbrough's Cross Roads January 16. Dandridge January 17. Operations about Dandridge January 26-28. Fair Garden January 27. Fain's Island January 28. Expedition against Thompson's Legion of Whites and Cherokee Indians in North Carolina and action at Deep Creek, N. C., February 2. Flat Creek February 20. Duty in District of Kentucky till June. Action at Cittico May 27. Moved to join Stoneman June 13-19. Atlanta (Ga.) Campaign June 28-September 8. Sweetwater Bridge July 3. Raid to Macon July 27-August 6. Macon and Clinton July 30. Hillsboro, Sunshine, Church, July 30-31. Sunshine Church and Jug Tavern and Mulberry Creek August 3. Mostly captured. Duty at Marietta, Ga., August. Occupation of Atlanta September 2. Moved to Louisville, Ky., September 15, and duty there refitting till November. Actions at Hardison's Mills October 24. Henryville November 23. Mt. Pleasant November 23. Columbia, Duck River, November 24-27. Crossing of Duck River November 28. Franklin November 30. Battle of Nashville December 15-16. Pursuit of Hood to the Tennessee River December 17-28. Duty at Pulaski till July, 1865. Mustered out at Nashville, Tenn., July 31, 1865.

Regiment lost during service 2 Officers and 23 Enlisted men killed and mortally wounded and 190 Enlisted men by disease. Total 215.

15th REGIMENT CAVALRY.

Organized December 25, 1862, in the field and at Camp Butler, Ill., by assignment of Stewart's Independent Cavalry Battalion, organized at Jackson, Tenn., July, 1862, as Companies "A," "B," "C," "D," "E" and "F." Gilbert's Independent Cavalry Company, 52nd Illinois, organized at Geneva October 25, 1861, as Company "G." Kane County Independent Cavalry Company, organized September 1, 1861, as Company "H." Jenks' Company Dragoons, 36th Illinois, organized at Camp Hammond, Ill., September 23, 1861, as Company "I." Sherer's Company Dragoons, 36th Illinois, organized at Camp Hamilton, Ills., September 23, 1861, as Company "K." Ford's Cavalry Company, 53rd Illinois, organized at Ottawa, Ills., January 1, 1862, as Company "L." Company "K," 1st Illinois Cavalry, assigned as Company "M," but mustered out December 27, 1862.

Regiment attached to District of Columbus, 16th Army Corps, Dept. of the Tennessee, to March, 1863. Cavalry Brigade, District of Corinth, 16th Army Corps, to June, 1863. 3rd Brigade, 1st Cavalry Division, 16th Army Corps, to August, 1863. Detached Brigade, 1st Cavalry Division, 16th Army Corps, to December, 1863. Waring's Brigade, 1st Cavalry Division, 16th Army Corps, to January, 1864. District of Eastern Arkansas, 7th Army Corps, Dept. of Arkansas, to January, 1865.

SERVICE.—Bath Springs, Miss., January 1, 1863. Monterey, Tenn., January 4. Clifton January 10. Chambers' Creek, near Hamburg, January 13. Near Obion River April 9 (Co. "E"). Expedition from Corinth to Courtland, Ala., and North Alabama April 15-May 8.

Burnsville, Ala., April 14. Dickson's Station April 17. Great Bear Creek and Cherokee Station April 17. Dickson's Station April 19. Rock Cut, near Tuscumbia, April 22. Tuscumbia and Florence April 23. Town Creek April 28. Expedition from Burnsville to Tupelo, Miss., May 2-8. King's Creek, near Tupelo, May 5. Obion Plank Road Crossing May — (Co. "E"). Greenville, Miss., May 18 (Detachment). Expedition from Corinth to Florence, Ala., May 26-31. Florence May 28. Hamburg Landing May 30. Smith's Bridge, near Corinth, June 11 (Detachment). Iuka July 7. Duty about Memphis, Tenn., and Columbus, Ky., till January, 1864. Ordered to Helena, Ark. Post and garrison duty at Helena till January, 1865. Expedition from Helena up White River February 4-8, 1864. (Detachment.) Expedition up St. Francis River February 13-14 (Co. "G"). Expedition up White River February 20-26. Wallace's Ferry, Big Creek, July 26. Lamb's Plantation, near Helena, August 12 (Detachment). Operations in Eastern Arkansas August 1-5 (Co. "E"). Scout to Mt. Vernon August 22-25. Expedition up White River August 29-September 3 (Detachment). Kendall's Grist Mill September 3 (Detachment). Non-Veterans mustered out August 25, 1864. Veterans and Recruits consolidated to a Battalion, and consolidated with 10th Illinois Cavalry January 26, 1865.

Regiment lost during service 2 Officers and 12 Enlisted men killed and mortally wounded and 1 Officer and 122 Enlisted men by disease. Total 137.

Companies "F" and "I" detached and moved to Memphis, thence to Vicksburg, Miss., May 13-20, 1863. Attached to Herron's Division, 13th Army Corps, to July, 1863. Cavalry, 2nd Division, 13th Army Corps, to August, 1863. Cavalry Brigade, 13th Army Corps, Dept. of the Gulf, to September, 1863. 2nd Brigade, Cavalry Division, Gulf, to November, 1863. 3rd Brigade, Cavalry Division, Gulf, to December, 1863. Unattached Cavalry, Dept. Gulf, to January, 1864. Participated in Siege of Vicksburg, Miss., May 20-July 4, 1863. Engaged in outpost duty on Big Black River. Advance on Jackson, Miss., July 5-10. Siege of Jackson July 10-17. Assault on Jackson July 12. Ordered to Dept. of the Gulf with 13th Corps August 17. Western Louisiana Campaign and operations in the Teche Country October 3-November 30. Reconnoissance toward Opelousas October 20. Opelousas and Barre Landing October 21 (Co. "F"). Company "I" at New Iberia till January 5, 1864, then reported to Gen. Lee as escort. Companies ordered to Illinois on Veteran furlough February 11, and rejoined Regiment at Helena, Ark.

Company "H"—formerly Kane County Cavalry Company (which see)—served detached. Attached to 1st Brigade, 3rd (Cavalry) Division, District Eastern Arkansas, Dept. Tennessee, December, 1862. Sherman's Yazoo Expedition to January, 1863. Headquarters Gen. Blair, 15th Army Corps, to August, 1863. Headquarters Arkansas Expedition to January, 1864. Participated in Sherman's Yazoo Expedition December 22, 1862-January 3, 1863. Chickasaw Bayou December 26-28. Chickasaw Bluff December 29. Expedition to Arkansas Post, Ark., January 3-10, 1863. Fort Hindman January 10-11. Reconnoissance toward White River and St. Charles January 13. Moved to Young's Point, La. Duty there and at Milliken's Bend, operating against Vicksburg, Miss., till April. Expedition from Milliken's Bend to Greenville, Black Bayou and Deer Creek April 2-14. Deer Creek April 10. Battle of Jackson, Miss., May 14. Champion's Hill May 16. Siege of Vicksburg May 18-July 4. Advance on Jackson, Miss., July 4-10. Siege of Jackson July 10-17. Ordered to Helena, Ark., July 24. Steele's Expedition against Little Rock, Ark., August 1-September 10. Capture of Little Rock September 10, and duty there till January, 1864. Rejoined Regiment.

Company "K"—formerly Sherer's Independent Company (which see)—served detached at Headquarters, Right Wing 14th Army Corps, Dept. of the Cumberland, to January, 1863. Headquarters 20th Army Corps, Army Cumberland, to October, 1863. Headquarters 11th and 12th Army Corps to April, 1864. Headquarters 20th Army Corps, Army Cumberland, to June, 1865.

SERVICE.—At Murfreesboro, Tenn., till June, 1863. Actions at Rover, Tenn., March 15. Salem March 21. Near Murfreesboro March 22. Middle Tennessee or Tullahoma Campaign June 22-July 7. Occupation of Middle Tennessee till August 16. Passage of Cumberland Mountains and Tennessee River and Chickamauga (Ga.) Campaign August 16-September 22. Battle of Chickamauga, Ga., September 19-20. Chattanooga-Ringgold Campaign November 23-27. Battles of Lookout Mountain November 23-24. Mission Ridge November 25. Ringgold Gap, Taylor's Ridge, November 27. Atlanta (Ga.) Campaign May to September, 1864. Battle of Resaca May 13-14. Operations on line of Pumpkin Vine Creek and battles about Dallas, New Hope Church and Allatoona Hills May 25-June 5. Operations about Marietta and against Kenesaw Mountain June 10-July 2. Assault on Kenesaw June 27. Chattahoochie River July 3-17. Siege of Atlanta July 22-August 25. Operations at Chattahoochie River Bridge August 26-September 2. Occupation of Atlanta September 2-November 15. March to the sea November 15-December 10. Siege of Savannah December 10-21. Campaign of the Carolinas January to April, 1865. Mount Elon, S. C., February 27. Battle of Bentonville, N. C., March 19-21. Occupation of Goldsboro and Raleigh. Bennett's House April 26. Surrender of Johnston and his army. March to Washington, D. C., via Richmond, Va., April 29-May 19. Grand Review May 24.

16th REGIMENT CAVALRY.

Organized at Camp Butler, near Springfield, Ills., January to April, 1863, by assignment of Thielman's Independent Cavalry Battalion as Companies "A" and "B." Schambeck's Independent Cavalry Company as Company "C." Company "D" organized March 27, 1863. Company "E," originally organized for 17th Illinois Cavalry, assigned as Company "E." Company "F," organized January 2, 1863. Company "G," organized May 21, 1863. Company "H" organized February 17, 1863. McClellan's Body Guard, organized January 21 to April 16, 1863, assigned as Companies "I," "K" and "L." Company "M" organized May 19, 1863. Duty at Camp Butler, near Springfield, Ills., till October, 1863. (Cos. "A" and "B," Thielman's Battalion, and Co. "C," Schambeck's Company, served detached. For history, see these organizations.) Ordered to Covington, Ky., October 16, 1863, thence to Knoxville, Tenn. Attached to Cumberland Gap, Tenn., Left Wing forces, Dept. of Ohio, to January, 1864. District of the Clinch, Dept. Ohio, to February, 1864. Camp Nelson, Ky., 23rd Army Corps, Dept. of Ohio, to April, 1864. 3rd Brigade, 1st Division Cavalry Corps, Dept. Ohio, to May, 1864. 1st Brigade, Stoneman's Cavalry Division, 23rd Army Corps, Army Ohio, to June, 1864. Detached Cavalry Brigade, 3rd Division, 23rd Army Corps, to August, 1864. Dismounted Cavalry Brigade, Cavalry Division, 23rd Army Corps, to September, 1864. 1st Brigade, Cavalry Division, 23rd Army Corps, to November, 1864. 1st Brigade, 6th Division Cavalry Corps, Military Division Mississippi, to August, 1865.

SERVICE.—Moved to Cumberland Gap, Tenn., and garrison duty there till February, 1864. Actions at Jonesville, Va., December 13, 1863, and January 3, 1864. Near Stickleyville, Powell Run, December 13, 1863 (Co. "E"). At Camp Nelson, Ky., February to April, 1864. Moved to Red Clay, Ga., April 28-May 10. Atlanta (Ga.) Campaign, May to September. Action at Varnell Station May 12. Battle of Resaca May 13-15. Advance on Dallas May 18-25. Operations on line of Pumpkin Vine Creek and battles about Dallas, New Hope Church and Allatoona Hills, May 25-June 5. Operations about Marietta and against Kenesaw Mountain June 10-July 2. Lost Mountain June 15-17. Muddy Creek June 17. Noyes Creek June 19. Cheyney's Farm June 27. Olley's Creek June 26. Assault on Kenesaw June 27. (Assigned to 3rd Division, 23rd Army Corps, June 21.) Nickajack Creek July 2-5. Chattahoochie River July 6-17. Siege of Atlanta July 22-August 25. Detached as Provost Guard 23rd Army Corps, August 16. At Decatur till September 14. Ordered to Nicholasville, Ky., September 14, to refit. Moved to Nashville, Tenn., October 22, thence moved to Pulaski, Fayetteville and Waynesboro. Nashville Campaign November-December. Henrysville and Mt. Pleasant November 23. Columbia, Duck River, November 24-27. Maury's Mills and crossing of Duck River November 28. Battle of Franklin November 30. Battle of Nashville December 15-16. Pursuit of Hood to the Tennessee River December 17-28. Franklin and West Harpeth River December 17. Spring Hill December 18. Rutherford Creek December 19. Anthony's Gap, near Pulaski, December 25-26. At Pulaski till March, 1865, and at Springfield till May. Duty at Pulaski, Holton, Courtland and Decatur, Ala., till August. Mustered out August 19, 1865.

Regiment lost during service 3 Officers and 30 Enlisted men killed and mortally wounded and 1 Officer and 228 Enlisted men by disease. Total 262.

17th REGIMENT CAVALRY.

Organized at St. Charles, Ills., and 8 Companies mustered in January 28, 1864. Four Companies mustered in February 12, 1864. Moved to St. Louis, Mo., May 3, 1864. Equipped at Jefferson Barracks and moved to Alton, Ill. Guard prisoners there till August. 1st Battalion, Cos. "A," "B," "C," "D," ordered to St. Louis June, 1864, thence to District of North Missouri. Engaged in Escort and Provost duty at St. Joseph and Weston, Mo., till June, 1865. Cos. "C" and "D" moved to Jefferson City September, 1864. Defence of Jefferson City October 6-7. Joined Regiment. 2nd Battalion—"E," "F," "G" and "H"—ordered from Alton, Ills., to Glasgow, Mo., June, 1864, and duty there operating against Thornton's Command till September. Skirmish at Allen July 23 (Co. "G"). Huntsville July 24 (Co. "F"). Dripping Springs August 15-16 (Co. "F"). Columbia August 16 (Co. "F"). Rocheport August 20 (Co. "F"). Battalion moved to Rolla, Mo., arriving September 23, 1864. 3rd Battalion at Alton, Ills., till August, 1864. Moved to Benton Barracks, thence to Rolla, Mo., arriving there September 19. Operations against Price's invasion of Missouri September to November. Cover Ewing's retreat from Pilot Knob to Rolla, September 27-30. Moved to Jefferson City, Mo. Defence of Jefferson City October 6-7. Moreau Bottom October 7. Booneville October 9-12. Glasgow October 15. Little Blue October 21. Independence October 22. Hickman's Mill October 23. Mine Creek, Little Osage, Marias des Cygnes, Kansas, October 25. Returned to Springfield, Mo., thence moved to Cassville and Rolla, arriving November 15. Duty there till January, 1865. At Pilot Knob, Mo., till April, and at Cape Girardeau till June. Moved to Kansas and duty on the Plains till November. Mustered out Companies "C," "E," "I" and "M," November 23, and rest of Regiment December 15 to 22, 1865.

Regiment lost during service 7 Enlisted men killed and mortally wounded and 1 Officer and 86 Enlisted men by disease. Total 94.

STEWARTS INDEPENDENT CAVALRY BATTALION.

Organized at Jackson, Tenn., by consolidation of Stewart's Independent Company Cavalry, organized at Cape Girardeau, Mo., August 10, 1861, as Company "A;" Carmichael's Independent Cavalry Company, organized at Cairo, Ill., August 19, 1861, as Company "B;" Dollins' Independent Cavalry Company, organized at Cairo, Ill., August 27, 1861, as Company "C;" O'Harnett's Independent Cavalry Company, organized at Springfield, Ill., September 16, 1861, as Company "D"; Hutchins' Independent Cavalry Company, organized June 26, 1861, as Company "E." Attached to Districts of Jackson, Tenn., and Corinth, Miss., to November, 1862. District of Corinth, 13th Army Corps (Old), Department of the Tennessee, to December, 1862.

SERVICE.—Duty in the Districts of Jackson, Tenn., and Corinth, Miss., Dept. of the Tennessee, to December, 1862. Action at Toone's Station, on Lower Post

Ferry, Tenn., July 27, 1862. Near Humboldt, Tenn., July 28. Hatchie Bottom, near Denmark, July 29. Grant's Central Mississippi Campaign, November-December. Operations against Forrest in West Tennessee December 18, 1862, to January 3, 1863. Transferred to 15th Illinois Cavalry December 25, 1862, as Companies "A," "B," "C," "D," "E" and "F," which see.

THIELMAN'S INDEPENDENT CAVALRY BATTALION.

Organized at Smithland, Ky., December 9, 1861, by consolidation of Thielman's and Marx's Independent Cavalry Companies. Attached to District of Paducah, Ky., to March, 1862. 5th Division, Army of the Tennessee, to July, 1862. 5th Division, District of Memphis, Tenn., to November, 1862. 3rd Brigade, Cavalry, Right Wing 13th Army Corps (Old), Dept. of the Tennessee, to December, 1862. Cavalry, 2nd Division Sherman's Yazoo Expedition, to January, 1863. 2nd Division, 15th Army Corps, Army of the Tennessee, to May, 1863. Headquarters 15th Army Corps to December, 1863. Cumberland Gap, Dept. of the Ohio, to January, 1864.

SERVICE.—Duty at Paducah and Smithland, Ky., till March, 1862. Demonstration from Paducah to Columbus, Ky., November 7-9, 1861. Expedition to Camp Beauregard and Viola, Ky., December 28-31. Moved to Savannah, Tenn., March 6-10, 1862. Expedition to Yellow Creek and Occupation of Pittsburg Landing March 14-17. Battle of Shiloh, Tenn., April 6-7. Reconnoissance on Corinth and Purdy Roads April 13. Advance on and Siege of Corinth, Miss., April 29-May 30. March to Memphis, Tenn., June 3-July 21. Duty at Memphis till November. Grant's Central Mississippi Campaign, "Tallahatchie March," November 26-December 12. Sherman's expedition and operations against Vicksburg, Miss., December 20, 1862, to January 3, 1863. Chickasaw Bayou December 26-28. Chickasaw Bluff December 29. Expedition to Arkansas Post, Ark., January 3-10, 1863. Assault and capture of Fort Hindman, Arkansas Post, January 10-11. Moved to Young's Point, La., January 17, and duty there till April. Demonstrations on Haines' and Drumgould's Bluffs April 29-May 2. Movement to join army in rear of Vicksburg, Miss., May 2-14. Jackson May 14. Champion's Hill May 16. Siege of Vicksburg, Miss., May 18-July 4. Advance on Jackson, Miss., July 4-10. Siege of Jackson July 10-17. At Big Black River till September 26. Moved to Memphis, Tenn., thence to Chattanooga, Tenn., September 26-November 23. Operations on Memphis and Charleston R. R. in Alabama October 20-29. Chattanooga-Ringgold Campaign November 23-27. Battles of Chattanooga November 23-25. March to relief of Knoxville, Tenn., November 28-December 8. Joined Regiment at Cumberland Gap January, 1864. Battalion assigned to 16th Illinois Cavalry as Companies "A" and "B," January, 1863, but served detached till January, 1864. Ordered to Mt. Sterling, Ky., February, 1864. Duty at Lexington, Paris and Cynthiana, Ky.

BARKER'S DRAGOONS.

Organized at Chicago, Ills., April 19, 1861. Moved to Camp Defiance, Cairo, Ills., and duty there till June. Ordered to Clarksburg, W. Va., to join McClellan as escort, and arrived there June 23. Skirmish at Buckhannon June 30. West Virginia Campaign July 6-17. Battle of Rich Mountain July 10. Duty in West Virginia till September. Mustered out September, 1861.

CARMICHAEL'S INDEPENDENT CAVALRY COMP'Y.

Organized at Camp Butler, Ills., as Cavalry Company "B," 29th Illinois Infantry, and mustered in August 19, 1861. Attached to District of Cairo to February, 1862. 1st Brigade, 1st Division, Army Tennessee, to July, 1862.

SERVICE.—Duty in Military District of Cairo, Ills., till February, 1862. Expedition from Cairo into Kentucky January 16-21, 1862. Operations against Fort Henry, Tenn., February 2-6. Investment and capture of Fort Donelson, Tenn., February 12-16. Moved to Pittsburg Landing, Tenn., March 6-13. Battle of Shiloh, Tenn., April 6-7. Advance on and siege of Corinth, Miss., April 29-May 30. Raid on Mobile and Ohio R. R. and skirmish at Purdy May 4. March to Bethel and Jackson, Tenn., June 4-7, and duty there till July. Assigned to Stewart's Independent Cavalry Battalion as Company "B," July, 1862, which see.

DOLLINS' INDEPENDENT CAVALRY COMPANY.

Organized at Cairo, Ills., with 31st Illinois Infantry, and mustered in September 18, 1861. Attached to 1st Brigade, Military District of Cairo, to February, 1862. 1st Brigade, 1st Division, Army Tennessee, to July, 1862.

SERVICE.—Duty in District of Cairo, Ills., till February, 1862. Expedition from Bird's Point, Mo., to Belmont, Mo., November 6-7, 1861. Battle of Belmont, Mo., November 7. Expedition from Cairo into Kentucky January 16-21, 1862. Operations against Fort Henry, Tenn., February 2-6. Investment and capture of Fort Donelson, Tenn., February 12-16. Moved to Pittsburg Landing, Tenn., March 6-13. Battle of Shiloh, Tenn., April 6-7. Advance on and siege of Corinth, Miss., April 29-May 30. Raid on Mobile and Ohio R. R. April 29-May 14, and skirmish at Purdy, Tenn., May 4. March to Purdy and Jackson, Tenn., June 4-7, and duty there till July. Assigned to Stewart's Battalion, Illinois Cavalry, as Company "C," July, 1862, which see.

FORD'S INDEPENDENT CAVALRY COMPANY.

Organized at Ottawa, Ills., with 53rd Illinois Infantry, January 1, 1862. Attached to District of Columbus, Ky., to November, 1862. District of Corinth, Miss., 13th Army Corps (Old), Department of the Tennessee, to December, 1862.

SERVICE.—Duty in District of Columbus, Ky., till September, 1862, and in District of Corinth, Miss., till December. Action at Davis' Bridge, Hatchie River, September 25, 1862. Battle of Corinth October 3-4. Pursuit to Hatchie River October 5-12. At Corinth till December. Raid from Corinth to Tupelo, on Mobile and Ohio R. R., December 13-19. Assigned to 15th Illinois Cavalry as Company "L." December 25, 1862, which see.

GILBERT'S INDEPENDENT CAVALRY COMPANY.

Organized at Geneva, Ills., with 52nd Illinois Infantry, October 25, 1861. Attached to Dept. of Missouri to March, 1862. 2nd Division, Army of the Tennessee, to July, 1862. District of Corinth, Miss., to December, 1862.

SERVICE.—Moved to St. Louis, Mo., December 8, 1861; thence to Cairo, Ills., January 16, 1862, and to Smithland, Ky., January 24. Moved to Fort Donelson, Tenn., February 10-17. Guard prisoners from Fort Donelson to Chicago, Ills., February 18-March 6. Moved to St. Louis, Mo., March 6-7, thence to Pittsburg Landing, Tenn., March 20-30. Battle of Shiloh, Tenn., April 6-7. Advance on and siege of Corinth, Miss., April 29-May 30. Pursuit to Booneville May 30-June 12. Duty in District of Corinth till December. Battle of Corinth October 3-4. Pursuit to Ripley October 5-12. Assigned to 12th Illinois Cavalry as Company "H" August, 1862, but changed to 15th Illinois Cavalry as Company "G" December 25, 1862, which see.

HUTCHINS' INDEPENDENT CAVALRY COMPANY.

Organized with 27th Illinois Infantry August 10, 1861. Moved to Cairo, Ills., July 1. Duty in Military District of Cairo till March, 1862. Duty at Fort Holt, Ky. Expedition into Kentucky January 16-21, 1862. Occupation of Columbus March 3. Operations against New Madrid and Island No. 10 March and April. Expedition to Union City, Tenn., March 30-April 2. Moved to Humboldt, Tenn., thence to Corinth, Miss. Assigned to Stewart's Independent Battalion Illinois Cavalry as Company "E," July, 1862, which see.

JENKS' INDEPENDENT CAVALRY COMPANY.

Organized at Aurora, Ills., as Cavalry Company "A," 36th Illinois, and mustered in September 23, 1861. Moved to St. Louis, Mo., thence to Rolla, Mo., Septem-

ber 24-29, and duty there till January, 1862. Attached to 2nd Brigade, Army of Southwest Missouri, to June, 1862. Cavalry Army of Mississippi to October, 1862. 1st Brigade, 2nd Division, Army Mississippi, to November, 1862. District of Corinth, Miss., 13th Army Corps (Old), Dept. of the Tennessee, to December, 1862.

SERVICE.—Expedition against Freeman's Forces November 1-9, 1861. Curtis' Campaign in Missouri and Arkansas against Price, February and March, 1862. Advance on Springfield, Mo., February 2-13. Pursuit of Price into Arkansas February 14-29. Battles of Pea Ridge, Ark., March 6-8. At Keytesville till April 5. March to Batesville April 5-May 3. Moved to Cape Girardeau, Mo., May 11-22, thence to Hamburg Landing, Tenn., May 23-29. Occupation of Corinth, Miss., May 30, and pursuit to Booneville May 30-June 6. Duty at Rienzi till September. Battle of Iuka, Miss., September 19. Battle of Corinth, Miss., October 3-4. Pursuit to Hatchie River October 5-12. Grant's Mississippi Central Campaign November-December. Assigned to 15th Illinois Cavalry as Company "I," December 25, 1862. See 15th Cavalry.

DODSON'S KANE COUNTY INDEPENDENT COMPANY CAVALRY.

Organized September 1, 1861. Attached to Dept. of Missouri to April, 1862. Steele's Command, District of Southeast Missouri, to May, 1862. 1st Division, Army of Southwest Missouri, to July, 1862. District of Eastern Arkansas, Dept. of Missouri, to December, 1862. 1st Brigade, 3rd (Cavalry) Division, District of Eastern Arkansas, Dept. Tennessee, December, 1862.

SERVICE.—Duty in Missouri and guarding Iron Mountain R. R. till March, 1862. Ordered to Pilot Knob, Mo. Moved to Reeve's Station, Black River, March 23-27, thence to White River, Ark., April 19. March to Batesville, thence to Helena, Ark., May 25-July 15. Hill's Plantation, Cache River and Cotton Plant, July 7. Duty at Helena till December. Assigned to 15th Illinois Cavalry as Company "H," December 25, 1862, which see.

MARX'S INDEPENDENT CAVALRY COMPANY.

Organized December 9, 1861, and assigned to Thielman's Independent Cavalry Battalion as Company "B," which see.

McCLELLAN DRAGOONS.

Organized at Chicago, Ills., October, 1861. Assigned to 12th Illinois Cavalry as Companies "H" and "I," February, 1862, but served detached till February, 1863. Attached to Stoneman's Cavalry Command, Army of the Potomac, to March, 1862. Blake's Brigade, Cavalry Reserve, Army of the Potomac, to April, 1862. Headquarters Army Potomac to November, 1862. Provost Guard Army of the Potomac to February, 1863, and at Headquarters 3rd and 2nd Divisions Cavalry Corps, Army Potomac, to November, 1863, participating in the following service: Duty in the Defences of Washington, D. C., till March, 1862. Moved to the Peninsula, Virginia. Peninsula Campaign, April to August. Siege of Yorktown, Va., April 5-May 4. Near Williamsburg May 4. Battle of Williamsburg May 5. Reconnoissance to Hanover Court House May 26. Seven days before Richmond June 25-July 1. Battles of Mechanicsville June 26. Gaines' Mill June 27. Peach Orchard and Savage Station June 29. White Oak Swamp and Glendale June 30. Malvern Hill July 1. Campaign in Northern Virginia August 27-September 2. Maryland Campaign September-October. Battle of Antietam September 16-17. Movement to Falmouth, Va., October 29-November 17. Battle of Fredericksburg, Va., December 12-15. "Mud March," January 20-24, 1863. Chancellorsville Campaign April 27-May 6. Stoneman's Raid April 29-May 8. Brandy Station and Beverly Ford June 9. Upperville June 21. Battle of Gettysburg, Pa., July 1-3. Williamsport, Md., July 6. Boonsboro July 8. Benevola or Beaver Creek July 9. At and near Funkstown July 10-13. Falling Waters July 14. Chester Gap July 26. Kelly's Ford July 3-August 1. Brandy Station August 1-4 and

September 7-8. Bristoe Station September 12. Culpeper Court House September 13. Raccoon Ford September 14-16. Stevensburg September 17. Jack's Shop, Madison Court House, September 22. Bristoe Campaign October 9-22. Raccoon and Morton's Fords, October 10. Brandy Station October 11-12. Oak Hill October 15. Rejoined regiment and moved to Chicago, Ills., November 20-28, 1863. See 12th Illinois Cavalry.

McCLERNAND'S BODY GUARD.

Organized January 21 to April 16, 1863. Assigned to 16th Illinois Cavalry as Companies "I," "K" and "L," April, 1863.

NAUGHTON'S IRISH DRAGOONS.

Organized September 1, 1861, by authority of Gen. Fremont, to be attached to 23rd Illinois Infantry as a Cavalry Company. Expedition to Lexington, Mo., October 5-16. Lexington October 16. Johnstown October 24. Transferred to 3rd Missouri Cavalry as Company "L" and again to 5th Iowa Cavalry, "Curtis Horse," as Company "L," November, 1861.

O'HARNETT'S INDEPENDENT CAVALRY COMP'Y.

Organized at Camp Butler, Ills., with 30th Illinois Infantry, and mustered in August 28, 1861. Moved to Cairo, Ills., September 1, 1861. Attached to Military District of Cairo to February, 1862. 1st Brigade, 1st Division, Army of the Tennessee, to July, 1862.

SERVICE.—Duty in the Military District of Cairo, September, 1861, to February, 1862. Expedition from Cairo into Kentucky January 16-21, 1862. Operations against Fort Henry, Tenn., February 2-6. Investment and capture of Fort Donelson, Tenn., February 12-16. Moved to Pittsburg Landing March 6-13. Battle of Shiloh, Tenn., April 6-7. Advance on and Siege of Corinth, Miss., April 29-May 30. Raid on Mobile and Ohio R. R. and skirmish at Purdy, Tenn., May 7. Moved to Bethel and Jackson, Tenn., June 4-7 and duty there till July. Assigned to Stewart's Illinois Cavalry Battalion July, 1862, which see.

SCHAMBECK'S INDEPENDENT CAVALRY COMP'Y.

Organized at Chicago, Ills., July 8, 1861. Ordered to West Virginia and attached to 2nd Brigade, Army of Occupation, West Virginia, July to September, 1861. McCook's Brigade, District of the Kanawha, West Virginia, to October, 1861. 2nd Brigade, District of the Kanawha, to March, 1862. (Company assigned to Thielman's Cavalry Battalion as Company "C," December 9, 1861, and to 16th Illinois Cavalry as Company "C" December 25, 1862, but served detached from both these organizations during entire term.) 4th Brigade, Kanawha District, West Virginia, to August, 1862. 2nd Brigade, Kanawha Division, 9th Army Corps, Army Potomac, to October, 1862. Kanawha Division, District of West Virginia, Dept. Ohio, to March, 1863. Averill's 4th Separate Brigade, 8th Army Corps, Middle Department, to June, 1863. Averill's 4th Separate Brigade, West Virginia, to December, 1863. 2nd Brigade, 4th Division, West Virginia, to April, 1864. Reserve Division West Virginia to July, 1864.

SERVICE.—At New Creek, W. Va., till August, 1861. Battle of Carnifex Ferry, W. Va., September 10. Moved to Camp Lookout and Big Sewell Mountain September 15-23, thence to Camp Anderson October 6-9. Operations in Kanawha Valley and New River Region October 19-November 16. New River October 19-21. Moved to Gauley and duty there till May, 1862. Advance on Virginia and Tennessee R. R. May 10. Princeton May 11, 16, 17. Wolf Creek May 15. At Flat Top Mountain till August. Flat Top Mountain July 15. Blue Stone August 13-14. Movement to Washington, D. C., August 15-24. Maryland Campaign September 6-22. Frederick City, Md., September 12. South Mountain September 14. Battle of Antietam September 16-17. March to Clear Springs October 8, thence to Hancock October 9. March to the Kanawha Valley October 14-November 17. Duty in the Kanawha Valley till April, 1863. Scouting in Boone, Wyoming and Logan Counties December 1-10,

1862. At Buckhannon April, 1863. Operations against Imboden's Raid in West Virginia April 20-May 14. At Buckhannon, Bulltown, Clarksburg, Parkersburg and Weston May to July. Moved to Beverly July 2-7 and duty there till November. Beverly July 14. Shanghai July 16. Martinsburg July 18-19. Averill's Raid through Hardy, Pendleton, Highland, Bath, Greenbrier and Pocahontas Counties August 5-31. Rocky Gap, near White Sulphur Springs, August 25-26. Salt Lick Bridge October 14. Averill's Raid from Beverly to Lewisburg and Virginia and Tennessee R. R., November 1-17. Mill Point November 5. Droop Mountain November 6. Elk Mountain, near Hillsborough, November 10. Averill's Raid on Virginia and Tennessee R. R. December 8-25. March through Elk Mountain Pass to Beverly, December 13-17, and duty at Beverly till April, 1864, and at Harper's Ferry and on Baltimore R. R. till July. Baltimore and Ohio R. R., between Bloomfield and Piedmont, May 5, 1864. Mustered out July 16, 1864.

SHERER'S INDEPENDENT CAVALRY COMPANY.

Organized at Aurora, Ill., as Company "B" Cavalry, 36th Illinois Infantry, and mustered in September 23, 1861. Moved to St. Louis, Mo., thence to Rolla, Mo., September 24-29 and duty there till January, 1862. Attached to Army of the West to January, 1862. 2nd Brigade, Army of Southwest Missouri, to February, 1862. 2nd Brigade, 1st Division, Army of Southwest Missouri, to June, 1862. Cavalry, Army of Mississippi, to September, 1862. 9th Division, Army Ohio, to October, 1862. 9th Division, 3rd Army Corps, Army Ohio, to November, 1862. Headquarters Right Wing 14th Army Corps to December, 1862.

SERVICE.—Expedition against Freeman's forces November 1-9, 1861. Curtis' Campaign against Price in Missouri and Arkansas February and March, 1862. Advance to Springfield, Mo., February 2-13. Pursuit of Price into Arkansas February 14-29. Battles of Pea Ridge, Ark., May 6-8. At Keytesville till April 5. March to Batesville April 5-May 3. Moved to Cape Girardeau, Mo., May 11-22, thence to Hamburg Landing, Tenn., May 23-29. Occupation of Corinth, Miss., May 30. Pursuit to Booneville May 30-June 6. Duty at Rienzi till September 6. Moved to Covington, Ky., thence to Louisville, Ky., September 6-19. Pursuit of Bragg into Kentucky October 1-16. Battle of Perryville, Ky., October 8. Lancaster, Ky., October 16. March to Nashville, Tenn., October 16-November 7. Expedition from Edgefield to Harpeth Shoals and Clarksville November 25-December 1. Clarksville November 25. Advance on Murfreesboro, Tenn., December 26-30. Nolinsville, Knob Gap, November 26. Battle of Stone River, Tenn., December 30-31, 1862, and January 1-3, 1863. Company assigned to 15th Illinois Cavalry as Company K, December 25, 1862, which see.

SMITH'S INDEPENDENT CAVALRY COMPANY.

(See Sherer's Independent Cavalry Company.)

STEWART'S INDEPENDENT CAVALRY COMPANY.

Organized at Cape Girardeau, Mo., August 10, 1861, under authority of Gen. Fremont. Attached to District of Cairo to February, 1862. 1st Brigade, 1st Division, Army of the Tennessee, to July, 1862.

SERVICE.—Duty at Cape Girardeau, Bird's Point and Cairo till February, 1862. Skirmish at Huntley's Farm, near Belmont, Mo., September 26, 1861. Lucas Bend September 26. Operations about Ironton and Fredericktown October 12-25. Engagement at Fredericktown October 21. Expedition from Cairo into Kentucky January 10-21, 1862. Operations against Fort Henry, Tenn., February 2-6. Investment and capture of Fort Donelson, Tenn., February 12-16. Moved to Pittsburg Landing, Tenn., March 6-13. Battle of Shiloh, Tenn., April 6-7. Advance on and siege of Corinth, Miss., April 29-May 30. Raid on Mobile and Ohio R. R. and skirmish at Purdy, Tenn., May 4. Moved to Bethel and Jackson, Tenn., June 4-7 and duty there till July.

Assigned to Stewart's Independent Cavalry Battalion July, 1862, which see.

THIELMAN'S INDEPENDENT CAVALRY COMPANY.

Organized at Chicago, Ills., July 2, 1861. Duty in District of Paducah, Ky., Dept. of Missouri, to December, 1861. Demonstration from Paducah to Columbus, Ky., November 7-9. Assigned to Thielman's Independent Battalion Cavalry December 9, 1861, as Company "A," which see.

BATTERY "A," 1st REGIMENT LIGHT ARTILLERY.

First known as Smith's Chicago Light Artillery. Entered State service for three months, April 17, 1861, and moved to Cairo, Ills., with Swift's Cairo Expedition. Capture of steamers C. E. Hillman and J. D. Perry, and seizure of arms and munitions of war bound south, April 25. Duty at Cairo. Ills., till July. Reorganized at Cairo, Ill., for three years, July 16, 1861, as Battery "A," 1st Illinois Light Artillery. Attached to District of Cairo to February, 1862. 1st Brigade, 1st Division, District of Cairo, February, 1862. 3rd Brigade, 3rd Division, District of Cairo, March, 1862. 2nd Brigade, 2nd Division, Army of the Tennessee, to April, 1862. Artillery, 3rd Division, Army of the Tennessee, to July, 1862. Artillery, 5th Division, District of Memphis, Tenn., to November, 1862. Artillery, 5th Division, Right Wing 15th Army Corps (Old), Dept. of the Tennessee. November, 1862. Artillery, 2nd Division, District of Memphis, Tenn., 13th Army Corps, to December, 1862. Artillery, 2nd Division, Sherman's Yazoo Expedition, to January, 1863. Artillery, 2nd Division, 15th Army Corps, Army of the Tennessee, to November, 1864. Garrison Artillery Nashville, Tenn., to December, 1864. Artillery Reserve, Chattanooga, Tenn., Dept. of the Cumberland, to July, 1865.

SERVICE.—Duty in Military District of Cairo till February, 1862. Operations at Ironton-Fredericktown, Mo., October 12-25, 1861. Engagement at Fredericktown October 21. Expedition from Paducah, Ky., to Fort Henry, Tenn., January 15-25, 1862. Operations against Forts Henry and Heiman, Tenn., February 2-6. Investment and capture of Fort Donelson, Tenn., February 12-16. Expedition to Clarksville and Nashville, Tenn., February 22-March 1. Moved to Pittsburg Landing, Tenn., March 1-10. Battle of Shiloh, Tenn., April 6-7. Advance on and siege of Corinth, Miss., April 29-May 30. March to Memphis, Tenn., June 3-July 21. Duty at Memphis till November. Expedition from Memphis to Coldwater and Hernando, Miss., September 8-13. Grant's Central Mississippi Campaign November-December. "Tallahatchie March," November 26-December 12. Sherman's Yazoo Expedition December 20, 1862, to January 3, 1863. Chickasaw Bayou December 26-28. Chickasaw Bluff December 29. Expedition to Arkansas Post, Ark., January 3-10, 1863. Assault and capture of Fort Hindman, Arkansas Post, January 10-11. Moved to Young's Point, La., January 17, and duty there till March. Expedition to Rolling Fork, via Muddy, Steele's and Black Bayous and Deer Creek, March 14-27. Demonstration on Haines' and Drumgould's Bluffs, April 29-May 2. Movement to join army in rear of Vicksburg, Miss., via Richmond and Grand Gulf, May 2-14. Battle of Jackson, Miss., May 14. Champion's Hill May 16. Siege of Vicksburg, Miss., May 18-July 4. Assaults on Vicksburg May 19 and 22. Surrender of Vicksburg July 4. Advance on Jackson, Miss., July 5-10. Siege of Jackson, Miss., July 10-17. At Big Black till September 26. Movement to Memphis, thence march to Chattanooga, Tenn., September 26-November 20. Operations on Memphis and Charleston R. R. in Alabama October 20-29. Bear Creek, Tuscumbia, October 27. Chattanooga-Ringgold Campaign November 23-27. Tunnel Hill November 23-24. Mission Ridge November 25. March to relief of Knoxville, Tenn., November 28-December 17. At Scottsboro, Ala.. till May, 1864. Expedition from Scottsboro toward Rome, Ga., January 25-February 5, 1864. Atlanta (Ga.) Campaign May to September. Demonstration on Resaca May 8-13. Battle of Resaca

May 13-15. Advance on Dallas May 18-25. Operations on Pumpkin Vine Creek and battles about Dallas, New Hope Church and Allatoona Hills, May 25-June 5. Operations about Marietta and against Kenesaw Mountain June 10-July 2. Assault on Kenesaw June 27. Nickajack Creek July 2-5. Chattahoochie River July 6-17. Battle of Atlanta July 22. Siege of Atlanta July 22-August 25. Ezra Chapel, Hood's second sortie, July 28. Flank movement on Jonesboro August 25-30. Battle of Jonesboro August 31-September 1. Lovejoy Station September 2-6. Operations in North Georgia and North Alabama against Hood, September 29-October 28. Ordered to Nashville, Tenn., October 28, and garrison duty there and at Chattanooga. Tenn., till June, 1865. Mustered out at Chicago, Ills., July 3, 1865.

Battery lost during service 15 Enlisted men killed and mortally wounded and 22 Enlisted men by disease. Total 37.

BATTERY "B," 1st REGIMENT LIGHT ARTILLERY.

Organized at Chicago, Ills., for three months' service and mustered into United States service May 2, 1861. Moved to Cairo, Ills., June 1. Duty at Cairo and Bird's Point, Mo., till July. Reorganized for three years' service at Cairo, Ills., July 16, 1861. Attached to Military District of Cairo, Ills., to October, 1861. 3rd Brigade, Military District of Cairo, to February, 1862. 2nd Brigade, 1st Division, District of Cairo, February, 1862. Artillery, 1st Division, District of West Tennessee and Army of the Tennessee, to April, 1862. Artillery, 5th Division, Army Tennessee, to July, 1862. Artillery, 5th Division, District of Memphis, Tenn., to November, 1862. Artillery, 5th Division, District of Memphis, Right Wing 13th Army Corps (Old), Dept. of the Tennessee, to December, 1862. Artillery, District of Memphis, 2nd Division, 13th Army Corps, December, 1862. Artillery, 2nd Division Sherman's Yazoo Expedition, to January, 1863. Artillery, 2nd Division, 15th Army Corps, Army of the Tennessee, to July, 1864.

SERVICE.—Duty at Cairo, Ills., and Bird's Point, Mo., till February, 1862. Operations about Ironton and Fredericktown, Mo., October 12-25, 1861. Engagement at Fredericktown October 21. Expedition to Belmont November 6-7. Battle of Belmont, Mo., November 7. Reconnoissance of Columbus, Ky., January 10-22, 1862. Operations against Fort Henry, Tenn., February 2-6. Capture of Fort Henry February 6. Investment and capture of Fort Donelson, Tenn., February 12-16. Moved to Savannah, Tenn. Expedition to Yellow Creek and occupation of Pittsburg Landing, Tenn., March 14-17. Battle of Shiloh, Tenn., April 6-7. Corinth Road April 8. Advance on and siege of Corinth, Miss., April 26-May 30. Action at Russell House May 17. March to Memphis, Tenn., June 1-July 21. Duty at Memphis till November. Grant's Central Mississippi Campaign, "Tallahatchie March," November 25-December 14. Sherman's Yazoo Expedition December 20, 1862, to January 3, 1863. Chickasaw Bayou December 26-28. Chickasaw Bluff December 29. Expedition to Arkansas Post, Ark., January 3-10, 1863. Assault and capture of Fort Hindman, Arkansas Post, January 10-11. Moved to Young's Point, La., January 17, and duty there till March. Expedition to Rolling Fork, via Muddy, Steele's and Black Bayous and Deer Creek, March 14-27. Demonstrations on Haines' and Drumgould's Bluffs April 29-May 2. Movement to join army in rear of Vicksburg, Miss., via Richmond and Grand Gulf, May 2-14. Battle of Jackson, May 14. Battle of Champion's Hill May 16. Siege of Vicksburg, Miss., May 18-July 4. Assaults on Vicksburg May 19 and 22. Richmond, La., June 15. Surrender of Vicksburg July 4. At Big Black River till September 26. Movement to Memphis, Tenn., thence to Chattanooga, Tenn., September 26-November 21. Operations on Memphis & Charleston R. R. in Alabama October 20-29. Bear Creek, Tuscumbia, October 27. Chattanooga-Ringgold Campaign November 23-27. Tunnel Hill November 23-24. Mission Ridge November 25. March to relief of Knoxville, Tenn., November 28-December 17. Duty at Larkinsville, Ala., till May, 1864.

Atlanta (Ga.). Campaign May 1 to July 12. Demonstrations on Resaca May 8-13. Battle of Resaca May 14-15. Advance on Dallas May 18-25. Battles about Dallas May 25-June 5. Operations about Marietta and against Kenesaw Mountain June 10-July 2. Assault on Kenesaw June 27. Nickajack Creek July 2-5. Chattahoochie River July 6-12. Ordered to the rear for muster out July 12. Mustered out July 23, 1864, expiration of term. Veterans and Recruits transferred to Battery "A," 1st Light Artillery.

Battery lost during service 9 Enlisted men killed and mortally wounded and 1 Officer and 17 Enlisted men by disease. Total 27.

Battery reorganized March, 1865, by assignment of Bridges' Independent Battery Light Artillery. Attached to garrison artillery at Nashville, Tenn., Dept. of the Cumberland, to July, 1865. Mustered out July 6, 1865.

BATTERY "C," 1st REGIMENT LIGHT ARTILLERY ("HOUGHTAILING'S").

Organized at Ottawa, Ill., and mustered in October 31, 1861. Ordered to Cairo, Ill. Attached to Military District of Cairo to October, 1861. 3rd Brigade, District of Cairo, to February, 1862. 4th Brigade, 1st Division, District of Cairo, February, 1862. Artillery Division, Army of Mississippi, to April, 1862. Artillery 1st Division, Army Mississippi, to September, 1862. Artillery, 13th Division, Army Ohio, to November, 1862. 3rd Brigade, 3rd Division, Right Wing 14th Army Corps, Army of the Cumberland, to January, 1863. Artillery, 3rd Division, 20th Army Corps, Army of the Cumberland, to October, 1863. Artillery, 1st Division, 14th Army Corps, to July, 1864. Artillery Brigade, 14th Army Corps, to June, 1865.

SERVICE.—Duty in the Military District of Cairo, Ill., till February, 1862. Operations against New Madrid, Mo., and Island No. 10, Mississippi River, February 28-April 8. Action and capture at Tiptonville April 8. Expedition to Fort Pillow, Tenn., April 13-17. Moved to Pittsburg Landing, Tenn., April 17-23. Advance on and siege of Corinth, Miss., April 29-May 30. Action at Farmington May 3. Reconnoissance toward Corinth May 8. Engagement at Farmington May 9. Occupation of Corinth May 30, and pursuit to Booneville May 31-June 12. Reconnoissance toward Baldwyn June 3. At Corinth till July 21. Moved to Iuka, Miss., July 21, thence to Courtland, Ala., and duty along Memphis and Charleston R. R. till September 3. March to Nashville, Tenn., September 3-12. Action at Columbia September 9. Siege of Nashville September 12-November 7. Repulse of Forrest's attack on Edgefield November 5. Lavergne November 7. Advance on Murfreesboro December 26-30. Battle of Stone's River December 30-31, 1862, and January 1-3, 1863. Duty at Murfreesboro till June. Middle Tennessee or Tullahoma Campaign, June 23-July 7. Occupation of Middle Tennessee till August 16. Passage of Cumberland Mountains and Tennessee River and Chickamauga, Ga. Campaign August 16-September 22. Battle of Chickamauga, Ga., September 19-20. Siege of Chattanooga, Tenn., September 24-November 23. Chattanooga-Ringgold Campaign November 23-27. Mission Ridge November 24-25. At Rossville, Ga., till May, 1864. Atlanta (Ga.) Campaign May 1 to September 8. Rocky Faced Ridge May 8-11. Buzzard's Roost Gap May 8-9. Advance on Dallas May 18-25. Operations on line of Pumpkin Vine Creek and battles about Dallas, New Hope Church and Allatoona Hills May 25-June 5. Operations about Marietta and against Kenesaw Mountain June 10-July 2. Pine Hill June 11-14. Lost Mountain June 15-17. Assault on Kenesaw June 27. Ruff's Station and Vining Station July 4. Chattahoochie River July 6-17. Peach Tree Creek July 19-20. Siege of Atlanta July 22-August 25. Utoy Creek August 5-7. Flank movement on Jonesboro August 25-30. Battle of Jonesboro August 31-September 1. Lovejoy Station September 2-6. Pursuit of Hood into Alabama October 1-26. March to the sea November 15-December 10. Siege of Savannah December 10-21. Campaign of the Carolinas January to April, 1865. Bat-

tle of Bentonville, N. C., March 19-21. Occupation of Goldsboro March 24. Advance on Raleigh April 10-14. Occupation of Raleigh April 14. Bennett's House April 26. Surrender of Johnston and his army. March to Washington, D. C., via Richmond, Va., April 29-May 20. Grand Review May 24. Moved to Louisville, Ky., June. Mustered out June 14, 1865.

Battery lost during service 15 Enlisted men killed and mortally wounded and 19 Enlisted men by disease. Total 34.

BATTERY "D," 1st REGIMENT LIGHT ARTILLERY.

Organized at Cairo, Ill., and mustered in July 30, 1861. Ordered to Fort Holt, Ky., September 18, and duty there till February, 1862. Attached to 2nd Brigade, 1st Division, District of Cairo, February, 1862. 3rd Brigade, 1st Division, District of West Tennessee, and 1st Division, Army Tennessee, to July, 1862. 1st Division, District of Jackson, Tenn., to November, 1862. District of Jackson, 13th Army Corps (Old), Dept. of the Tennessee, November, 1862. Artillery, 3rd Division, Right Wing 13th Army Corps, to December, 1862. Artillery, 3rd Division, 17th Army Corps, Army of the Tennessee, to November, 1864. Artillery Reserve, Nashville, Tenn., to December, 1864. Garrison Artillery, Clarksville, Tenn. 5th Sub-District, District Middle Tennessee, to July, 1865.

SERVICE.—Operations against Fort Henry, Tenn., February 2-6, 1862. At Fort Henry February 6-12. Investment and capture of Fort Donelson, Tenn., February 12-16. Moved to Savannah, Tenn., March 5-13, thence to Pittsburg Landing, Tenn., March 23-25. Battle at Shiloh, Tenn., April 6-7. Advance on and siege of Corinth, Miss., April 29-May 30. March to Purdy and Jackson, Tenn., June 5-8, and duty in District of Jackson till November. Grant's Central Mississippi Campaign November 2, 1862, to January 10, 1863. At Memphis, Tenn., till February 20. Moved to Lake Providence, La., February 20-24, thence to Berry's Landing March 16, and to Milliken's Bend April 19. Advance on Bruinsburg and turning Grand Gulf April 25-30. Battle of Port Gibson May 1. Reserve, Raymond May 12. Jackson May 14. Battle of Champion's Hill May 16. Siege of Vicksburg, Miss., May 18-July 4. Assaults on Vicksburg May 19 and 22. Occupation of Vicksburg July 4 to November 6. Stevenson's Expedition to Monroe, La., August 20-September 2. Expedition to Canton October 14-20. Bogue Chitto Creek October 17. Duty at Big Black till February, 1864. Meridian Campaign February 3-March 3. Moved to Cairo, Ill., April 28, thence to Clifton, Tenn., April 30-May 5, March to Huntsville, Ala., May 5-23, thence to Ackworth, Ga., via Decatur and Warrenton, Ala., and Rome and Kingston, Ga., May 28-June 8. Atlanta (Ga.) Campaign June 8-September 8. Operations about Marietta and against Kenesaw Mountain June 10-July 2. Assault on Kenesaw June 27. Nickajack Creek July 2-5. Chattahoochie River July 6-17. Leggett's or Bald Hill July 20-21. Battle of Atlanta July 22. Siege of Atlanta July 22-August 25. Flank movement on Jonesboro August 25-30. Battle of Jonesboro August 31-September 1. Lovejoy Station September 2-6. Operations against Hood in North Georgia and North Alabama September 29-November 3. Ordered to Nashville, Tenn., and duty there till December. Battles of Nashville December 15-16. Ordered to Clarksville, Tenn., and duty there till July, 1865. Mustered out July 28, 1865.

Battery lost during service 1 Officer and 7 Enlisted men killed and mortally wounded and 28 Enlisted men by disease. Total 36.

BATTERY "E," 1st REGIMENT LIGHT ARTILLERY ("WATERHOUSE'S").

Organized at Chicago, Ill., and mustered in December 19, 1861. Moved to Cairo, Ill., February 13, 1862. Attached to District of Cairo, Ill., to March, 1862. Artillery, 5th Division, Army of the Tennessee, to July, 1862. Artillery, 5th Division, District of Memphis, Tenn., to November, 1862. Artillery, 5th Division, District of Memphis, Tenn., Right Wing 13th Army Corps (Old), Dept. of the Tennessee, November, 1862. Artillery, 1st Division, District of Memphis, Tenn., 13th Army Corps, to December, 1862. Artillery, 8th Division, 16th Army Corps, to March, 1863. Artillery, 3rd Division, 15th Army Corps, to December, 1863. Artillery, 1st Division, 16th Army Corps, to June, 1864. Artillery, 1st Division, Sturgis' Expedition, June, 1864. 1st Brigade, 1st Division, 16th Army Corps, to December, 1864. Artillery, 1st Division, Detachment Army of the Tennessee, Dept. of the Cumberland, to February, 1865. Artillery Reserve, Dept. of the Cumberland, Chattanooga, Tenn., to July, 1865.

SERVICE.—Duty at Paducah, Ky., till March, 1862. Expedition from Paducah to Tennessee River and operations about Crump's Landing, Tenn., March 8-14. Expedition to Yellow Creek, Miss., and occupation of Pittsburg Landing, Tenn., March 14-17. Battle of Shiloh, Tenn., April 6-7. Advance on and siege of Corinth, Miss., April 29-May 30. March to Memphis, Tenn., via Lagrange, Grand Junction and Holly Springs, June 1-July 21. Duty at Memphis, Tenn., till November. Grant's Central Mississippi Campaign, November 2, 1862, to January 10, 1863. Guard R. R. till March, 1863. Moved to Memphis, thence to Duckport, La., March 12-April 1. Demonstrations on Haines' and Snyder's Bluffs April 25-May 2. Movement to join army in rear of Vicksburg, via Richmond and Grand Gulf, May 2-14. Jackson, Miss., May 14. Siege of Vicksburg May 18-July 4. Assaults on Vicksburg May 19 and 22. Expedition to Mechanicsburg May 26-June 4. Advance on Jackson, Miss., July 4-10. Siege of Jackson July 10-17. Brandon Station July 19. Camp at Big Black till November. Expedition to Canton October 14-20. Bogue Chitto Creek October 17. Ordered to Memphis, Tenn., November 12, and duty guarding Railroad till January, 1864. Expedition to Tallahatchie River February 5-19. Coldwater Ferry February 8. Near Senatobia February 8-9. Wyatt's February 14. At Memphis till April. Sturgis' Expedition from Memphis to Ripley, Miss., April 30-May 9. Sturgis' Expedition from Memphis into Mississippi June 1-13. Brice's, or Tishamingo Creek, near Guntown, June 10. Smith's Expedition to Tupelo July 5-21. Camargo's Cross Roads, Harrisburg, July 13. Tupelo July 14-15. Old Town, or Tishamingo Creek, July 15. Smith's Expedition to Oxford, Miss., August 1-30. Tallahatchie River August 7-9. Oxford August 9. Abbeville August 23. Moved to Duvall's Bluff, Ark., September 1; thence march through Arkansas and Missouri. Light Artillery Reserve, Dept. of the Cumberland, to July, 1865. Mustered out July 15, 1865.

Battery lost during service 5 Enlisted men killed and mortally wounded and 25 Enlisted men by disease. Total 30.

BATTERY "F," 1st REGIMENT LIGHT ARTILLERY.

Organized at Camp Butler, Ill., and mustered in February 25, 1862. Ordered to Benton Barracks, Mo., March 15, thence moved to Pittsburg Landing, Tenn., April 1-9. Attached to 3rd Division, Army of the Tennessee, to July, 1862. Artillery, 5th Division. District of Memphis, Tenn., to November, 1862. Artillery, 5th Division, District of Memphis, Right Wing 13th Army Corps (Old), Dept. of the Tennessee, November, 1862. Artillery, 1st Division, 13th Army Corps, to December, 1862. Artillery, 1st Division, 17th Army Corps, to January, 1863. Artillery, 1st Division, 16th Army Corps, to July, 1863. Artillery, 4th Division, 15th Army Corps, to November, 1864. Artillery Reserve, District of Nashville, Tenn., to February, 1865.

SERVICE.—Advance on and Siege of Corinth, Miss., April 29-May 30, 1862. March to Memphis, Tenn., June 1-17, and duty there till November. Grant's Central Mississippi Campaign November, 1862, to January, 1863. Duty at Memphis and along Memphis and Charleston R. R. till June, 1863. Ordered to Vicksburg, Miss., June 9. Siege of Vicksburg, Miss., June 16-July 4. Advance on Jackson, Miss., July 4-10. Siege of Jackson July 10-17. Camp at Big Black till September

26. Moved to Memphis, Tenn., thence to Chattanooga, Tenn., September 28-November 21. Operations on Memphis & Charleston R. R. in Alabama October 20-29. Skirmish at Trenton, Ga., November 18. Chattanooga-Ringgold Campaign November 23-27. Tunnel Hill November 23-24. Mission Ridge November 25. March to relief of Knoxville, Tenn., November 28-December 17. At Scottsboro, Ala., till May, 1864. Atlanta (Ga.) Campaign May to September. Demonstrations on Resaca May 9-13. Snake Creek Gap May 10-12. Battle of Resaca May 13-15. Kingston May 19-22. Advance on Dallas May 23-25. Battles about Dallas, New Hope Church and Allatoona Hills May 25-June 5. Operations about Marietta and against Kenesaw Mountain June 10-July 2. Assault on Kenesaw June 27. Nickajack Creek July 2-5. Chattahoochie River July 6-17. Battle of Atlanta July 22. Siege of Atlanta July 22-August 25. Ezra Chapel, Hood's second sortie, July 28. Flank movement on Jonesboro August 25-30. Battle of Jonesboro August 31-September 1. Lovejoy Station September 2-6. Operations in North Georgia and North Alabama against Hood, September 29-November 3. Ordered to Nashville, Tenn., and garrison duty there till February, 1865. Battery discontinued February 22, 1865, and men transferred to other Batteries.

Battery lost during service 1 Officer and 7 Enlisted men killed and mortally wounded and 24 Enlisted men by disease. Total 32.

BATTERY "G," 1st REGIMENT LIGHT ARTILLERY.

Organized at Cairo, Ill., and mustered in February 28, 1862. Moved to Columbus, Ky., March 18, thence to Island No. 10, Mississippi River. Attached to Flotilla Brigade, Army of Mississippi, to April, 1862. Artillery Division, Army of Mississippi, to July, 1862. Artillery, District of Corinth, Miss., to November, 1862. Artillery, District of Corinth, 13th Army Corps (Old), Dept. of the Tennessee, to December, 1862. Artillery, District of Corinth, 17th Army Corps, to January, 1863. Artillery, District of Corinth, 16th Army Corps, to March, 1863. Artillery, 2nd Division, 16th Army Corps, to November, 1863. Post of Corinth, Miss., 16th Army Corps, to January, 1864. Fort Pickering, District of Memphis, 16th Army Corps, to June, 1864. 1st Brigade, Post and Defences of Memphis, District of West Tennessee, to December, 1864. Artillery Reserve, District of West Tennessee, to July, 1865.

SERVICE.—Operations against Island No. 10, Mississippi River, and garrison at New Madrid, Mo., March 20-April 11, 1862. Union City, Tenn., March 31. Action and capture at Tipton April 8. Moved to Columbus, Ky., April 11. Expedition to Fort Pillow, Tenn., April 13-17. Moved to Hamburg Landing, Tenn., April 17-22. Advance on and siege of Corinth, Miss., April 29-May 30. Occupation of Corinth and pursuit to Booneville May 30-June 12. Duty at Corinth, Miss., till January, 1864. Battle of Corinth October 3-4, 1862. Moved to Memphis, Tenn., January, 1864, and duty in the defences of that city and in the District of West Tennessee till July, 1865. Mustered out July 24, 1865.

Battery lost during service 1 Enlisted man killed and 11 Enlisted men by disease. Total 12.

BATTERY "H," 1st REGIMENT LIGHT ARTILLERY.

Organized at Chicago, Ill., and mustered in February 20, 1862. Moved to St. Louis, Mo., thence moved to Pittsburg Landing, Tenn., April 1-4. Served, unassigned, Army of the Tennessee, April, 1862. Artillery, 5th Division, Army Tennessee, to July, 1862. Artillery, 5th Division, District of Memphis, Tenn., to November, 1862. Artillery, 5th Division, Right Wing 13th Army Corps, Dept. of the Tennessee, November, 1862. Artillery, 1st Division, District of Memphis, 13th Army Corps, to January, 1863. Artillery, 2nd Division, 15th Army Corps, Army of the Tennessee, to September, 1864. Artillery Brigade, 15th Army Corps, to June, 1865.

SERVICE.—Battle of Shiloh, Tenn., April 6-7, 1862. Advance on and siege of Corinth, Miss., April 29-May

30. Russell's House May 17. Occupation of Corinth May 30. March to Memphis June 3 to July 21, and duty there till November. Grant's Central Mississippi Campaign November, 1862, to January, 1863. "Tallahatchie March" November 26-December 13. Moved to Young's Point, La., January, 1863, and duty there till March. Expedition to Rolling Fork, via Muddy, Steele's and Black Bayous and Deer Creek, March 14-27. Demonstration on Haines' and Drumgould's Bluffs April 29-May 2. Movement to join army in rear of Vicksburg, Miss., via Richmond and Grand Gulf, May 2-14. Battle of Champion's Hill May 16. Siege of Vicksburg May 18-July 4. Assaults on Vicksburg May 19 and 22. Advance on Jackson, Miss., July 4-10. Siege of Jackson July 10-17. At Big Black till September 25. Moved to Memphis, Tenn., thence to Chattanooga, Tenn., September 25-November 21. Operations on Memphis & Charleston R. R. in Alabama, October 20-29. Bear Creek, Tuscumbia, October 27. Chattanooga-Ringgold Campaign November 23-27. Tunnel Hill November 24-25. Mission Ridge November 25. Pursuit November 26-27. March to relief of Knoxville, Tenn., November 28-December 13. March to Chattanooga December 13-17, thence to Bridgeport, Ala. Duty at Bridgeport, Bellefonte and Larkinsville, Ala., to May, 1864. Atlanta (Ga.) Campaign May to September. Demonstrations on Resaca May 8-13. Battle of Resaca May 13-15. Advance on Dallas May 18-25. Battles about Dallas, New Hope Church and Allatoona Hills May 25-June 5. Operations about Marietta and against Kenesaw Mountain June 10-July 2. Assault on Kenesaw June 27. Nickajack Creek July 2-5. Chattahoochie River July 6-17. Battle of Atlanta July 22. Siege of Atlanta July 22-August 25. Ezra Chapel July 28. Flank movement on Jonesboro August 25-30. Battle of Jonesboro August 31-September 1. Lovejoly Station September 2-6. Operations against Hood in North Georgia and North Alabama September 29-November 3. March to the sea November 15-December 10. Siege of Savannah December 10-21. Campaign of the Carolinas January to April, 1865. Duck Branch, near Loper's Crossing, S. C., February 2. Salkehatchie Swamp February 3-6. Dillingham's Cross Roads, or Duck Branch, February 3. South Edisto River February 9. North Edisto River February 12-13. Congaree Creek February 15. Columbia February 16-17. Wateree Creek February 22. Battle of Bentonville, N. C., March 20-21. Occupation of Goldsboro March 24. Advance on Raleigh April 10-14. Occupation of Raleigh April 14. Bennett's House April 26. Surrender of Johnston and his army. March to Washington, D. C., via Richmond, Va., April 29-May 20. Grand review May 24. Moved to Louisville, Ky., June. Mustered out June 14, 1865.

Battery lost during service 1 Officer and 6 Enlisted men killed and mortally wounded and 27 Enlisted men by disease. Total 34.

BATTERY "I," 1st REGIMENT LIGHT ARTILLERY.

Organized at Camp Douglas, Chicago, Ill., and mustered in February 10, 1862. Moved to Benton Barracks, Mo., March 1. Thence to Pittsburg Landing, Tenn., April 1-4. Served unattached Army Tennessee, to May, 1862. Artillery, 5th Division, Army of the Tennessee, to July, 1862. Artillery, 5th Division, District of Memphis, Tenn., to November, 1862. Artillery, 5th Division, Right Wing 13th Army Corps (Old), Dept. of the Tennessee, November, 1862. 1st Division, Right Wing, 13th Army Corps, to December, 1862. 1st Division, 17th Army Corps, to January, 1863. 1st Division, 16th Army Corps, to July, 1863. 4th Division, 15th Army Corps, to April, 1864. Artillery Reserve, Nashville, Tenn., to November, 1864. Artillery, 5th Division, Cavalry Corps, Military Division Mississippi, to July, 1865.

SERVICE.—Battle of Shiloh, Tenn., April 6-7, 1862. Advance on and siege of Corinth, Miss., April 29-May 30. Russell House May 17. March to Memphis, Tenn., June 1-July 21, and duty there till November. Central Mississippi Campaign November, 1862, to January, 1863. "Tallahatchie March" November 26-December 12. At Mem-

phis and guarding Railroad till June, 1863. Action at Wall Hill May 11. Moved to Vicksburg, Miss., June 6-11. Siege of Vicksburg June 12-July 4. Advance on Jackson, Miss., July 4-10. Siege of Jackson July 10-17. At Big Black River till September 25. Moved to Memphis, Tenn., thence to Chattanooga, Tenn., September 25-November 23. Operations on Memphis and Charleston R. R. in Alabama October 20-29. Chattanooga-Ringgold Campaign November 23-27. Tunnel Hill November 24-25. Mission Ridge November 25. Pursuit to Graysville November 26-27. March to relief of Knoxville, Tenn., November 28-December 9. At Scottsboro, Ala., till April, 1864. Garrison duty at Nashville, Tenn., till November. Operations in Tennessee and Alabama and Nashville Campaign against Hood November-December. Columbia, Duck River, November 24-28. Franklin November 30. Battle of Nashville, Tenn., December 15-16. Pursuit of Hood to the Tennessee River December 17-19. West Harpeth River December 17. Rutherford Creek December 19. Lynnville and Rockland Creek December 24. Anthony's Gap, near Pulaski, December 25. At Huntsville, Ala.; Florence, Ala.; Eastport, Miss.; Iuka, Miss., and Gravelly Springs, Ala., till July, 1865. Moved to Chicago, Ill., and mustered out July 26, 1865.

Battery lost during service 1 Enlisted man killed and 13 Enlisted men by disease. Total 14.

BATTERY "K," 1st REGIMENT LIGHT ARTILLERY.

Organized at Shawneetown, Ill., and mustered in January 9, 1862. Ordered to Cairo, Ill., March, 1862. Attached to District of Columbus, Ky., to November, 1862. District of Columbus, Ky., 13th Army Corps (Old), Dept. of the Tennessee, to December, 1862. District of Columbus, Ky., 16th Army Corps, to March, 1863. District of Columbus, Ky., 6th Division, 16th Army Corps, to October, 1863. 3rd Brigade, 1st Cavalry Division, 16th Army Corps, to November, 1863. (A section of Battery detached with Grierson's Cavalry Brigade, 13th Army Corps (Old), Dept. of the Tennessee, November, 1862, to March, 1863. 1st Brigade, 1st Cavalry Division, 16th Army Corps, to May, 1863. Cavalry Brigade, 19th Army Corps, Dept. of the Gulf, to July, 1863. 3rd Brigade, 1st Cavalry Division, 16th Army Corps, to November, 1863.) 2nd Brigade, 1st Cavalry Division, 16th Army Corps, to June, 1864. 2nd Brigade, 1st Cavalry Division, District of West Tennessee, to November, 1864. 2nd Brigade, 5th Division Cavalry Corps, Military Division Mississippi, to December, 1864.

SERVICE.—Duty at Cairo, Ill.; Paducah, Ky., and in District of Columbus, Ky., till October, 1863. Grant's Central Mississippi Campaign November, 1862, to January, 1863 (Section). Reconnoissance from Lagrange toward Colliersville, Tenn., November 5, 1862 (Section). Action at Ripley, Miss., December 23 (Section). Middleburg and near Bolivar, Tenn., December 24 (Section). At Lagrange and Memphis, Tenn., till April, 1863 (Section). Expedition from Lagrange March 8-13, 1863. Skirmishes at Covington March 9-10 (Section). Grierson's Expedition from Lagrange to Baton Rouge, La., April 17-May 2 (Section). Palo Alto and Okolona, Miss., April 21-22 (Section). Garlandsville, Miss., April 24 (Section). Union Church April 28 (Section). Brookhaven April 29 (Section). Wall's Post Office, La., May 1 (Section). Robert's Ford, Comite River, La., May 2 (Section). Plain's Store, La., May 21 (Section). Siege of Port Hudson, La., May 24-July 9 (Section). Clinton June 3-4 (Section). Jackson Cross Roads June 20 (Section). Moved from Port Hudson, La., to Memphis, Tenn., July 18-28 (Section). Duty at Germantown, Tenn., till November. Operations in North Mississippi and West Tennessee against Chalmers October 4-17. Scout from Germantown to Tullahoma October 22-24. Operations on Memphis & Charleston R. R. November 3-5. Quinn and Jackson's Mills and Collersville November 3. Moscow and Lafayette November 5. Operations on Memphis & Charleston R. R. against Lee's attack November 28-December 10. Saulsbury December 3. Wolf Bridge, near Moscow, December 3-4. Lafayette December 4. Operations against Chalmers and

Forest till February, 1864. Colliersville December 27-28, 1863. Smith's Expedition from Colliersville to Okolona and West Point, Miss., February 11-26, 1864. West Point February 20-21. Okolona February 21. Ivey's Hill, near Okolona, February 22. At Germantown and Memphis till July. Smith's Expedition to Tupelo July 5-21. Near Tupelo July 14-15. Smith's Expedition to Oxford, Miss., August 1-30. Tallahatchie River August 7-9. Hurricane Creek and Oxford August 9. Hurricane Creek August 13, 14 and 19. Expedition into Middle Tennessee and North Alabama September 30-November 1. Campaign against Hood in North Alabama and Middle Tennessee November 1-December 10. Shoal Creek, Ala., November 11. On line of Shoal Creek November 16-20. Lawrenceburg November 22. Campbellsville November 24. Columbia, Duck River, November 24-27. Franklin November 30. Mustered out December 10, 1864. Veterans and Recruits transferred to Battery "E," 1st Illinois Light Artillery.

Battery lost while in service 11 Enlisted men by disease.

BATTERY "K," 1st REGIMENT LIGHT ARTILLERY, REORGANIZED.

Reorganized March, 1865, by assignment of Colvin's Independent Battery Light Artillery. Attached to 2nd Brigade, 4th Division, District of East Tennessee, and duty at Cumberland Gap and in District of East Tennessee till July. Mustered out July 15, 1865.

BATTERY "L," 1st REGIMENT LIGHT ARTILLERY.

Organized at Chicago, Ill., and mustered in February 22, 1862. Duty at Camp Douglas, Chicago, Ill., guarding prisoners till June, 1862. Ordered to Harper's Ferry, W. Va., June 14, thence to New Creek June 24. Attached to Railroad District, Mountain Dept., West Virginia, to July, 1862. Railroad District, 8th Army Corps, Middle Dept., to September, 1862. Railroad District, West Virginia, to January, 1863. Defences Upper Potomac to March, 1863. 5th Brigade, 1st Division, 8th Army Corps, to June, 1863. Mulligan's Brigade, Scammon's Division, West Virginia, to December, 1863. 2nd Brigade, 2nd Division, West Virginia, to April, 1864. Reserve Division, Harper's Ferry, W. Va., to January, 1865. Unattached, 3rd Division, West Virginia, to April, 1865. Unattached, 2nd Division, West Virginia, to July, 1865.

SERVICE.—Duty at New Creek, Petersburg, Romney, Cumberland, Md., Harper's Ferry and other points in West Virginia guarding line of the Baltimore & Ohio Railroad, June, 1862, to July, 1865. Action at Ridgville Road, near Petersburg, October 29, 1862. South Fork of the Potomac River November 9, 1862. Expedition to relief of Phillippi and Grafton April 25-27, 1863. Petersburg Gap September 4, 1863. Operations in Hampshire and Hardy Counties, W. Va., December 31, 1863, to January 5, 1864. Folck's Mills August 1, 1864. Attack on Cumberland, Md., August 1. New Creek August 4. Expedition from New Creek to Moorefield November 6-8. Moorefield, near New Creek, November 27-28. (1 Section at Grafton September 27 to November 15, 1864.) Mustered out July 10, 1865.

Battery lost during service 1 Officer and 10 Enlisted men by disease. Total 11.

BATTERY "M," 1st REGIMENT LIGHT ARTILLERY.

Organized at Camp Douglass, Chicago, Ill., and mustered in August 12, 1862. Moved to Louisville, Ky., September 27, 1862. Attached to District of Louisville, Ky., Dept. of Ohio, to October, 1862. 34th Brigade, 10th Division, Army Ohio, to November, 1862. 34th Brigade, 10th Division, District of West Kentucky, Dept. Ohio, to February, 1863. Reed's Brigade, Baird's Division, Army of Kentucky, Dept. of the Cumberland, to June, 1863. 1st Division, Reserve Corps, Army of the Cumberland, to October, 1863. Artillery, 2nd Division, 4th Army Corps, Army of the Cumberland, to July, 1864. Artillery Brigade, 4th Army Corps, to October, 1864. Unattached Artillery, Dept. of the Cumberland, to November, 1864. Garrison Artillery, Chattanooga,

Tenn., to April, 1865. Garrison Artillery, Cleveland, Tenn., Dept. of the Cumberland, to July, 1865.

SERVICE.—At Louisville, Ky., till October 11, 1862. Moved to Lebanon, Ky., October 11, thence to Columbia November 26, and to Lebanon, Ky., December 29. Operations against Morgan in Kentucky December 29, 1862-January 2, 1863. Moved to New Haven January 6, 1863, thence to Louisville, Ky., January 22, and to Nashville, Tenn., January 29-February 7. Moved to Franklin February 12, and duty there till June. Tullahoma Campaign June 23-July 7. At Shelbyville June 29-September 6. Chickamauga (Ga.) Campaign September 6-22. Battle of Chickamauga September 19-21. Rossville Gap September 21. Siege of Chattanooga, Tenn., September 24-November 23. Battles of Chattanooga November 23-25. Orchard Knob, Indian Hill, November 23-24. Mission Ridge November 25. March to relief of Knoxville November 28-December 17. Operations in East Tennessee December, 1863, to April, 1864. Moved to Cleveland, Tenn., April 18, 1864. Atlanta (Ga.) Campaign May to September. Demonstration on Rocky Faced Ridge May 8-11. Buzzard's Roost Gap, or Mill Creek, May 8-9. Battle of Resaca May 14-15. Adairsville May 17. Near Kingston May 18-19. Near Cassville May 19. Advance on Dallas May 22-25. Operations on line of Pumpkin Vine Creek and Battles about Dallas, New Hope Church and Allatoona Hills May 25-June 5. Operations about Marietta and against Kenesaw Mountain June 10-July 2. Pine Hill June 11-14. Lost Mountain June 15-17. Assault on Kenesaw June 27. Ruff's Station July 4. Chattahoochie River July 6-17. Buckhead, Nancy's Creek, July 18. Peach Tree Creek July 19-20. Siege of Atlanta July 22-August 25. Flank movement on Jonesboro August 25-30. Battle of Jonesboro August 31-September 1. Lovejoy Station September 2-6. Duty at Atlanta till November 1. Ordered to Chattanooga November 1. Garrison duty at Chattanooga, Cleveland and Charleston, Tenn., till July, 1865. Moved to Chicago, Ill., July 14 and mustered out July 24, 1865.

Battery lost 4 Enlisted men killed and mortally wounded and 1 Officer and 10 Enlisted men by disease. Total 15.

BATTERY "A," 2nd REGIMENT LIGHT ARTILLERY.

Organized at Peoria, Ill., and mustered into State service May 23, 1861. Moved to Alton, Ill., July 6, thence to St. Charles and Mexico, Mo., and duty in Northern Missouri till August. Ordered to Jefferson Barracks, Mo., and mustered in August 17, 1861. Moved to Jefferson City, Mo., thence to Booneville, Mo., October 1. Attached to Fremont's Army of the West and to Dept. of Missouri to February, 1862. 2nd Brigade, 3rd Division, Army of Southwest Missouri, to May, 1862. Artillery, 3rd Division, Army of Southwest Missouri, to July, 1862. District of Eastern Arkansas, Dept. of Missouri, to December, 1862, and Dept. of the Tennessee to January, 1863. Artillery, 12th Division, 13th Army Corps, Army of the Tennessee, to May, 1863. Artillery, 14th Division, 13th Army Corps, Army Tennessee, to July, 1863. 3rd Brigade, 1st Division, 13th Army Corps, Dept. of the Tennessee, to August, 1863, and Dept. of the Gulf to September, 1863. Artillery, 1st Division, 13th Army Corps, Dept. of the Gulf, to June, 1864. Defences of New Orleans, La., Dept. of the Gulf, to April, 1865. District of LaFourche, Dept. of the Gulf, to July, 1865.

SERVICE.—Fremont's Campaign against Springfield, Mo., October 21-November 8, 1861. At Ottersville, Mo., till January, 1862. Moved to Lebanon, Mo., January 25. Curtis' advance on Springfield, Mo., January 25-February 11. Pursuit of Price into Arkansas February 14-29. Battle of Pea Ridge, Ark., March 6-8. March to Sugar Creek March 10, thence to Cross Timbers March 15, and over Ozark Mountains to Batesville April 5-May 3. March to Helena, Ark., May 25-July 13. Duty at Helena till March, 1863. Ordered to Milliken's Bend, La., March 20, and duty there till April. Movement on Bruinsburg and turning Grand Gulf April 25-30. Battle of Thompson's Hill, Port Gibson, Miss., May 1. Battle of Champion's Hill May 16. Big Black River May 17. Siege of Vicksburg, Miss., May 18-July 4. Assaults on Vicksburg May 19 and 22. Advance on Jackson, Miss., July 5-10. Siege of Jackson July 10-17. At Big Black till August. Ordered to New Orleans, La., August 20. At Carrollton, Brashear City and Berwick till October. Western Louisiana Campaign October 3-November 30. Duty in District of LaFourche and Defences of New Orleans, La., till August, 1864. Operations in Mobile Bay against Forts Gaines and Morgan August 2-23. Siege and capture of Fort Gaines August 3-8. Siege and capture of Fort Morgan August 8-23. Duty in the Defences of New Orleans and District of LaFourche till July, 1865. (1st Section detached in District of Southwest Missouri to October, 1862. Attached to 1st Brigade, 2nd Division, Army of the Frontier, to June, 1863. District of Southeast Missouri. Advance on Fayetteville, Ark., October 11-December 3, 1862. March to relief of Gen. Blount December 3-6. Battle of Prairie Grove, Ark., December 7. At Fayetteville till December 27. Expedition over Boston Mountains to Van Buren, Ark., December 27-29. Duty at various points in Missouri till April, 1863. Operations against Marmaduke April 20-May 2. Moved to Pilot Knob, Mo. Duty in District of Southeast Missouri till July, 1863.) Battery mustered out July 28, 1865.

Battery lost during service 5 Enlisted men killed and mortally wounded and 1 Officer and 16 Enlisted men by disease. Total 22.

BATTERY "B," 2nd REGIMENT LIGHT ARTILLERY.

Organized at Springfield, Ill., June 20, 1861. Attached to Dept. of Missouri to April, 1862. Unattached Artillery, Army of the Tennessee, to May, 1862. Artillery, 4th Division, Army of the Tennessee, to July, 1862. 1st Division, District of Jackson, Tenn., to November, 1862. District of Jackson, 13th Army Corps (Old), Dept. of the Tennessee, to December, 1862. District of Corinth, 17th Army Corps, to January, 1863. District of Corinth, 16th Army Corps, to March, 1863. Artillery, 2nd Division, 16th Army Corps, to November, 1863. Post of Corinth, 16th Army Corps, to January, 1864. Fort Pickering, Post of Memphis, Tenn., to April, 1864. Artillery, 1st Division, 16th Corps, to June, 1864. 2nd Brigade, Sturgis' Expedition, June, 1864. Post of Memphis, Tenn., District of West Tennessee, to July, 1865.

SERVICE.—Duty in Dept. of Missouri till April, 1862. Moved to Pittsburg Landing, Tenn., April 1-4, 1862. Battle of Shiloh, Tenn., April 6-7. Advance on and siege of Corinth, Miss., April 29-May 30. Duty in Districts of Jackson and Corinth till October, 1862. Battle of Corinth October 3-4. Garrison duty at Corinth till January, 1864. Ordered to Memphis, Tenn., January 25, and duty at Fort Pickering, Defences of Memphis, till June, 1864. Expedition from Memphis to Wyatt's, Miss., February 6-18, 1864. Sturgis' Expedition to Guntown, Miss., June 1-13. Battle of Brice's or Tishamingo Creek, near Guntown, June 10. Duty at Memphis, Tenn., and in District of West Tennessee till July, 1865. Mustered out July 15, 1865.

Battery lost during service 3 Enlisted men killed and mortally wounded and 27 Enlisted men by disease. Total 30.

BATTERY "C," 2nd REGIMENT LIGHT ARTILLERY.

Organized at Cairo, Ill., August 5, 1861. Attached to District of Cairo, Ill., to March, 1862. District of Columbus, Ky., to November, 1862. District of Columbus, Ky., 13th Army Corps (Old), Dept. of the Tennessee, to December, 1862. District of Columbus, Ky., 6th Division, 16th Army Corps, to June, 1863. 3rd Division, Reserve Corps, Dept. of the Cumberland, to October, 1863. District of Clarksville and Fort Donelson, Tenn., Dept. of the Cumberland, to March, 1865. 5th Sub-District, District of Middle Tennessee, Dept. of the Cumberland, to August, 1865.

SERVICE.—Duty in District of Cairo till March, 1862. Ordered to Fort Donelson, Tenn., and garrison duty there and at Calrksville, Tenn., till August, 1865. Also engaged in mounted scout duty between the Cumber-

land and Tennessee Rivers. Expedition from Fort Donelson to Clarksville September 5-10, 1862. Action at New Providence September 6. Rickett's Hill, Clarksville, September 7. Near Waverly and Richland Creek October 23. Cumberland Iron Works, Fort Donelson, February 3, 1863. Mustered out August 3, 1865.

Battery lost during service 1 Officer and 3 Enlisted men killed and mortally wounded and 18 Enlisted men by disease. Total 22.

BATTERY "D," 2nd REGIMENT LIGHT ARTILLERY.

Organized at Cairo, Ill., and mustered in December 17, 1861. Attached to District of Cairo to February, 1862. 1st Division, District of Cairo, February, 1862. 3rd Brigade, 1st Division, District of West Tennessee, to April, 1862. Artillery, 1st Division, Army of the Tennessee, to July, 1862. Artillery, 1st Division, District of Jackson, Tenn., to November, 1862. District of Jackson, Tenn., 13th Army Corps (Old), Dept. of the Tennessee, to December, 1862. Artillery, 1st Division, 16th Army Corps, to May, 1863. 2nd Brigade, District of Memphis, Tenn., 5th Division, 16th Army Corps, to December, 1863. 3rd Brigade, 1st Cavalry Division, 16th Army Corps, to January, 1864. District of Memphis, Tenn., 16th Army Corps, January, 1864. Artillery, 4th Division, 16th Army Corps, to March, 1864. Decatur, Ala., District of Northern Alabama, Dept. of the Cumberland, to November, 1864.

SERVICE.—Duty at Cairo, Ill., till February, 1862. Expedition from Cairo into Kentucky January 16-21, 1862. Operations against Fort Henry, Tenn., February 2-6. Investment and capture of Fort Donelson, Tenn., February 12-16. Moved to Savannah, thence to Pittsburg Landing, Tenn., March 5-25. Battle of Shiloh, Tenn., April 6-7. Advance on and siege of Corinth, Miss., April 29-May 30. March to Jackson, Tenn., June 5-8, and duty there till November. Grant's Central Mississippi Campaign November and December. Action at Davis Mills, Wolf River, Miss., December 21. Post duty at Grand Junction till January, 1864. Expedition to Senatobia, Miss., May 21-26, 1863. Senatobia May 23. Moved to Memphis, Tenn., thence to Vicksburg, Miss., January, 1864. Meridian Campaign February 3-March 2. Ordered to Decatur, Ala., March, 1864, and duty there till November, 1864. Action at Pond Springs, near Courtland, May 27, and at Decatur June 1. Siege of Decatur October 26-29. Ordered to Louisville, Ky., November 1. Mustered out November 21, 1864. Veterans and Recruits transferred to Battery "K," 2nd Light Artillery.

Battery lost during service 6 Enlisted men killed and mortally wounded and 13 Enlisted men by disease. Total 19.

BATTERY "E," 2nd REGIMENT LIGHT ARTILLERY.

Organized at St. Louis, Mo., as Schwartz's Missouri Battery and mustered in August 20, 1861. Duty in North Missouri (1 Section) September 6 to December 29, 1861. Battery ordered to Cairo, Ill., September 14. Attached to District of Cairo and 1st Brigade, 1st Division, District of Cairo, to February, 1862. 3rd Brigade, 1st Division, District of West Tennessee, to April, 1862. Artillery, 1st Division, Army of the Tennessee, to July, 1862. 1st Division, District of Jackson, Tenn., to November, 1862. 3rd Division, 13th Army Corps (Old), Dept. of the Tennessee, to December, 1863. Artillery, 4th Division, 17th Army Corps, to January, 1863. Artillery, 4th Division, 16th Army Corps, to July, 1863. Artillery, 3rd Division, 13th Army Corps, Dept. of the Tennessee, to August, 1863, and Dept. of the Gulf to November, 1863. Plaquemine, District of Baton Rouge, La., Dept. of the Gulf, to June, 1864. Defences of New Orleans, La., to September, 1864.

SERVICE.—Duty at Cairo, Ill., Fort Holt and Jefferson, Ky., till February, 1862. Expedition to Bloomfield, Mo., November 1, 1861. Expedition into Kentucky January 10-21, 1862. Operations against Fort Henry, Tenn., February 2-6. Investment and capture of Fort Donelson, Tenn., February 12-16. Moved to Savannah, thence to Pittsburg Landing, Tenn., March. Battle of Shiloh,

Tenn., April 6-7. Advance on and siege of Corinth, Miss., April 29-May 30. March to Purdy, Bethel and Jackson June 5-8. Duty at Jackson till November. Action at Britton's Lane September 1. Grant's Central Mississippi Campaign November, 1862, to January, 1863. Reconnoissance from Lagrange November 8-9, 1862. March to Moscow, Tenn., December 24, 1862, to January 12, 1863, and duty there guarding Memphis & Charleston R. R. till March, 1863. Moved to Memphis, Tenn., and duty there till May. Moved to Vicksburg, Miss., May 12-22. Siege of Vicksburg May 22-July 4. Advance on Jackson, Miss., July 5-10. Siege of Jackson July 10-17. Assault on Jackson July 12. Ordered to New Orleans, La., August 13. Duty at Carrollton, Brashear and Berwick City till October. Western Louisiana Campaign October 3-November 30. Duty at Plaquemine, La., District of Baton Rouge, La., till June, 1864, and at New Orleans, La., till September. Mustered out September 29, 1864, expiration of term.

Battery lost during service 1 Officer and 6 Enlisted men killed and mortally wounded and 10 Enlisted men by disease. Total 17.

BATTERY "F," 2nd REGIMENT LIGHT ARTILLERY.

Organized at Cape Girardeau, Mo., and mustered in December 11, 1861. Attached to District of Cairo, Ill., Dept. of Missouri, to April, 1862. Unattached, Army Tennessee, April, 1862. Artillery, 6th Division, Army Tennessee, to July, 1862. Artillery, 6th Division, District of Corinth, Miss., to November, 1862. Artillery, 3rd Division, Right Wing 13 Army Corps (Old), Dept. of the Tennessee, to December, 1862. Artillery, 6th Division, 16th Army Corps, to January, 1863. Artillery, 6th Division, 17th Army Corps, to August, 1863. Artillery, 4th Division, 17th Army Corps, to November, 1864. Artillery Reserve, Nashville, Tenn., to March, 1865. 5th Sub-District, District of Middle Tennessee, to July, 1865.

SERVICE.—Duty at Cape Girardeau, Mo., as garrison of Forts "A" and "B" till March 14, 1862. Ordered to Pittsburg Landing, Tenn., March 14. Battle of Shiloh, Tenn., April 6-7. Advance on and siege of Corinth, Miss., April 29-May 30. Duty at Corinth till October. (1 Section at Bolivar, Tenn., and present at Battle of Hatchie River October 5, 1862.) Battle of Corinth, Miss., October 3-4. Pursuit to Ripley October 5-12. Grant's Central Mississippi Campaign November, 1862, to January, 1863. Reconnoissance from Lagrange November 8-9, 1862. At Moscow and Memphis, Tenn., January 12 to February 6, 1863. Moved to Lake Providence, La., February 6-10. Duty there till April 22. Moved to Milliken's Bend, La., April 22. Movement on Bruinsburg and turning Grand Gulf April 25-30. Siege of Vicksburg May 18-July 4. Assaults on Vicksburg May 19 and 22. Advance on Jackson, Miss., July 5-10. Siege of Jackson July 10-17. Moved to Natchez, Miss., August 15. Expedition from Natchez to Harrisonburg, La., September 1-7. Near Harrisonburg and capture of Fort Beauregard September 4. Duty at Natchez and Vicksburg till February, 1864. Meridian Campaign February 2-March 3. At Vicksburg till April. Moved from Vicksburg to Cairo, Ill., thence to Clifton, Tenn., and march to Ackworth, Ga., via Huntsville and Decatur, Ala., and Rome, Ga., April 28-June 8. Atlanta (Ga.) Campaign June 8 to September 8. Operations about Marietta and against Kenesaw Mountain June 10-July 2. Assault on Kenesaw June 27. Nickajack Creek July 2-5. Chattahoochie River July 6-17. Leggett's or Bald Hill July 20-21. Battle of Atlanta July 22. Siege of Atlanta July 22-August 25. Flank movement on Jonesboro August 25-30. Battle of Jonesboro August 31-September 1. Lovejoy Station September 2-6. Operations against Hood in North Georgia and North Alabama September 29-November 3. Shadow Church and Westbrook's, near Fairburn, October 2. Ordered to Nashville, Tenn., November, 1864, and duty there and in 5th Sub-District, Middle Tennessee, till July, 1865. Battle of Nashville, Tenn., December 15-16, 1864 (Reserve). Mustered out July 27, 1865.

Battery lost during service 5 Enlisted men killed and mortally wounded and 24 Enlisted men by disease. Total 29.

BATTERY "G," 2nd REGIMENT LIGHT ARTILLERY.

Organized at Camp Butler, Ill., and mustered in December 31, 1861. Attached to Fort Holt, Ky., Dept. of Missouri, to March, 1862. District of Columbus, Ky., to November, 1862. District of Jackson, 13th Army Corps (Old), Dept. of the Tennessee, to December, 1862. Artillery, 3rd Division, 17th Army Corps, Army of the Tennessee, to December, 1863. District of Columbus, Ky., 6th Division, 16th Army Corps, to June, 1864. Artillery, 3rd Division, 16th Army Corps, to December, 1864. 3rd Brigade, 2nd Division, Detachment Army of the Tennessee, Dept. of the Cumberland, to February, 1865. Artillery, 2nd Division, 16th Army Corps (New), Military Division of West Mississippi, to March, 1865. Artillery Brigade, 16th Army Corps, and Dept. of Alabama, to September, 1865.

SERVICE.—Duty at Fort Holt, Ky., till March, 1862, and in the District of Columbus, Ky., and in District of Jackson, Tenn., till November, 1862. Grant's Central Mississippi Campaign October 31, 1862, to January 10, 1863. About Oxford, Miss., December 1-3, 1862. Water Valley Station December 4. Coffeeville December 5. Moved to Memphis, Tenn., January, 1863, thence to Lake Providence, La., February 22, and to Milliken's Bend April 17. Movement on Bruinsburg and turning Grand Gulf April 25-30. While crossing river to Bruinsburg May 1 on Transport "Horizon" the boat was sunk in collision with Transport "Moderator" and guns and equipment lost. Battery sent to Memphis, Tenn., for re-equipment and rejoined for duty June 30, 1863. Siege of Vicksburg June 30-July 4. Surrender of Vicksburg July 4. Duty at Vicksburg till November. At Grand Junction, Tenn., till January, 1864, and in District of Columbus, Ky., till June, 1864. Operations in West Tennessee and Kentucky against Forest March 16-April 14. Smith's Expedition to Tupelo, Miss., July 5-21. Harrisburg, near Tupelo, July 14-15. Old Town, or Tishamingo Creek, July 15. Ellistown July 16. Smith's Expedition to Oxford, Miss., August 1-30. Moved to St. Louis, Mo., September. March through Missouri in pursuit of Price September to November. Moved to Nashville, Tenn., November 25-December 1. Battle of Nashville, Tenn., December 15-16. Pursuit of Hood December 17-28. Moved to Eastport, Miss., and duty there till February 6. Moved to New Orleans, La., February 6-22. Campaign against Mobile and its defences March 17-April 12. Siege of Spanish Fort and Fort Blakely March 26-April 8. Assault and capture of Fort Blakely April 9. Occupation of Mobile April 12. March to Montgomery April 13-25. Duty there and at various other points in District of Alabama till September. Mustered out September 4, 1865.

Battery lost during service 2 Enlisted men killed and mortally wounded and 25 Enlisted men by disease. Total 27.

BATTERY "H," 2nd REGIMENT LIGHT ARTILLERY.

Organized at Camp Butler, Ill., and mustered in December 31, 1861. Moved to Cairo, Ill., February 6, 1862. Attached to District of Cairo to March, 1862. District of Columbus, Ky., to November, 1862. District of Columbus, Ky., 13th Army Corps (Old), Dept. of the Tennessee, to January, 1863. District of Columbus, Ky., 16th Army Corps, to June, 1863. 3rd Division, Reserve Corps, Army of the Cumberland, to October, 1863. Posts of Fort Donelson and Clarksville, Tenn., Dept. of the Cumberland, to March, 1865. 5th Sub-District, District of Middle Tennessee., Dept. of the Cumberland, to July, 1865.

SERVICE.—Duty at Cairo, Ill., till March, 1862, and at Columbus, Ky., till August. Expedition to Fort Pillow, Tenn., April 13-17 (1 Section). Expedition to Henderson, Ky., in pursuit of Morgan August 18. (1 Section moved to Smithland, Ky., August 18, and 1 Section to Fort Heiman September 4, 1862.) Expedition from Fort Donelson, Tenn., to Clarksville, Tenn.,

September 5-20. Riggins' Hill, Clarksville, September 7. At Clarksville, Tenn., till March, 1863. Moved to Fort Donelson, Tenn., March 8. Action at Parker's Cross Road March 8. Duty at Fort Donelson, Tenn., till August. Moved to Clarksville, Tenn., August 26, and duty there as garrison and on mounted scouting between Cumberland and Tennessee Rivers and on Edgefield & Kentucky R. R. till July, 1865. Re-enlisted January 1, 1864, and Veterans on furlough March 5 to April 9, 1864. Action at Canton and Rockcastle Fords August 8, 1864. Mustered out July 29, 1865.

Battery lost during service 2 Enlisted men killed and 23 Enlisted men by disease. Total 25.

BATTERY "I," 2nd REGIMENT LIGHT ARTILLERY.

Organized at Camp Butler, Ill., and mustered in December 31, 1861. Moved to Cairo, Ill. Attached to District of Cairo to February, 1862. Flotilla Brigade, Army of Mississippi, to April, 1862. Artillery Division, Army Mississippi, to September, 1862. Artillery, 11th Division, Army of the Ohio, to October, 1862. Artillery, 11th Division, 3rd Corps, Army Ohio, to November, 1862. Artillery, 4th Division, Centre 14th Army Corps, Army of the Cumberland, to January, 1863. Artillery, 4th Division, 14th Army Corps, to June, 1863. Artillery, 2nd Division, Reserve Corps, Dept. of the Cumberland, to October, 1863. Artillery, 2nd Division, 14th Army Corps, to January, 1864. Artillery, 1st Division, 11th Army Corps, Army of the Cumberland, to April, 1864. Artillery, 2nd Division, 14th Army Corps, to July, 1864. Artillery Brigade, 14th Army Corps, to June, 1865.

SERVICE.—Duty at Cairo, Ill., till February, 1862. Operations against New Madrid February 28-March 14 and against Island No. 10 March 15-April 8. Action at Island No. 10 March 15-16. Action and capture at Tiptonville April 8. Expedition to Fort Pillow, Tenn., April 13-17. Moved to Hamburg Landing, Tenn., April 18-22. Advance on and siege of Corinth, Miss., April 29-May 30. Pursuit to Booneville May 31-June 12. Booneville June 3-4. At Big Springs June 14 to July 22. Moved to Iuka, Miss., thence to Courtland, Ala., and duty along Memphis & Charleston R. R. till September. March to Nashville, Tenn., September 3-12. Siege of Nashville September 12-November 7. Repulse of Forest's attack November 5. Duty at Nashville and Brentwood till June, 1863. Reconnoissance to Mill Creek November 27, 1862. Escort trains to Stone's River January 2-3, 1863. Stone's River January 3-5. Middle Tennessee or Tullahoma Campaign June 23-July 7. Occupation of Middle Tennessee till August 16. Passage of Cumberland Mountains and Tennessee River, and Chickamauga (Ga.) Campaign August 16-September 22. Battle of Chickamauga September 19-20. Rossville Gap September 21. Siege of Chattanooga, Tenn., September 24-November 23. Battles of Chattanooga November 23-25. Mission Ridge November 24-25. March to relief of Knoxville November 27-December 8. At Nashville and in Wauhatchie Valley, Tenn., till April, 1864. Atlanta (Ga.) Campaign May 1-September 8, 1864. Tunnel Hill May 6-7. Rocky Faced Ridge May 8-11. Buzzard's Roost Gap, or Mill Creek, May 8-9. Battle of Resaca May 14-15. Rome May 17-18. Operations on Pumpkin Vine Creek and battles about Dallas, New Hope Church and Allatoona Hills May 25-June 5. Operations about Marietta and against Kenesaw Mountain June 10-July 2. Pine Hill June 11-14. Lost Mountain June 15-17. Assault on Kenesaw June 27. Ruff's Station July 4. Chattahoochie River July 5-17. Peach Tree Creek July 19-20. Siege of Atlanta July 22-August 25. Utoy Creek August 5-7. Flank movement on Jonesboro August 25-30. Battle of Jonesboro August 31-September 1. Operations against Hood in North Georgia and North Alabama September 29-November 3. March to the sea November 15-December 10. Siege of Savannah December 10-21. Campaign of the Carolinas January to April, 1865. Averysboro, N. C., March 16. Battle of Bentonville March 19-21. Occupation of Goldsboro March 24. Advance on

Raleigh April 10-14. Occupation of Raleigh April 14. Bennett's House April 26. Surrender of Johnston and his army. March to Washington, D. C., via Richmond, Va., April 29-May 20. Grand Review May 24. Mustered out June 14, 1865.

Battery lost during service 1 Officer and 4 Enlisted men killed and mortally wounded and 10 Enlisted men by disease. Total 15.

BATTERY "K," 2nd REGIMENT LIGHT ARTILLERY.

Organized at Camp Butler, Ill., and mustered in December 31, 1861. Moved to Cairo, Ill., February 7, 1862, thence to Columbus, Ky., March, 1862. Attached to District of Columbus, Ky., to November, 1862. District of Columbus, Ky., 13th Army Corps (Old), Dept. of the Tennessee, November, 1862. Artillery, 4th Division, Right Wing 13th Army Corps, to December, 1862. Artillery, 4th Division, 17th Army Corps, to January, 1863. Artillery, 4th Division, 16th Army Corps, to July, 1863. Artillery, 4th Division, 13th Army Corps, to August, 1863. Artillery, 4th Division, 17th Army Corps, August, 1863. Post of Natchez, Miss., to October, 1864. Artillery, Cavalry Division, District of West Tennessee, to February, 1865. Unattached Artillery, District of West Tennessee, to July, 1865.

SERVICE.—Duty at Columbus, Ky., till June, 1862, and at Memphis, Tenn., till August. (1 Section to Fort Pillow, Tenn., June, 1862.) Return to Columbus, Ky., August. Duty there and at New Madrid, Mo., till November. Expedition from New Madrid to Clarkston, Mo., October. Actions at Clarkston, Mo., October 23 and 28. Moved to Memphis, Tenn., November, 1862. Grant's Central Mississippi Campaign November, 1862, to January, 1863. Duty on Memphis & Charleston R. R. till February, 1863, and at Memphis, Tenn., till May, 1863. Ordered to Vicksburg, Miss., May 13. Siege of Vicksburg May 22-July 4. Advance on Jackson, Miss., July 5-10. Siege of Jackson July 10-17. Assault on Jackson July 12. Moved to Natchez, Miss., August 20, and garrison duty there till October, 1864. Expedition from Natchez to Gillespie's Plantation, La., August 4-6, 1864. Expedition from Natchez to Woodville October 4-11 (Section). Action at Woodville October 5-6 (Section). Ordered to Vicksburg, Miss., October, 1864, and mounted. Expedition to Yazoo City November 26-December 4. Ordered to Memphis, Tenn., arriving December 11. Grierson's raid on Mobile & Ohio R. R. December 21, 1864-January 15, 1865. Egypt Station December 28. Duty at Memphis till July, 1865. Moved to Chicago, Ill., July 6-11. Mustered out July 14, 1865.

Battery lost during service 1 Officer and 10 Enlisted men by disease. Total 11.

BATTERY "L," 2nd REGIMENT LIGHT ARTILLERY.

Organized at Chicago, Ill., and mustered in February 28, 1862. Moved to Benton Barracks, Mo., March 11, thence to Pittsburg Landing, Tenn., April 8, 1862. Attached to 4th Division, Army of the Tennessee, to July, 1862. 4th Division, District of Jackson, Tenn., to November, 1862. 4th Division, 13th Army Corps (Old), Dept. of the Tennessee, to December, 1862. Artillery, 3rd Division, 17th Army Corps, to April, 1864. Artillery, 1st Division, 17th Army Corps, to September, 1864. Post and District of Vicksburg, Miss., to November, 1864. Artillery Reserve, District of Vicksburg, Dept. of Mississippi, to August, 1865.

SERVICE.—Battle of Shiloh, Tenn., April 6-7, 1862. Advance on and siege of Corinth, Miss., April 29-May 30. March to Memphis, Tenn., via Grand Junction, Lagrange, Holly Springs, Moscow and Germantown, June 1-July 21, and duty there till September. Moved to Bolivar September 6-14, and duty there till October 4. Battle of the Hatchie or Metamora October 5. Grant's Central Mississippi Campaign November, 1862, to January, 1863. Moved to Memphis, Tenn., January, 1863, thence to Lake Providence, La., February 22. Duty there and at Milliken's Bend, La., till April. Movements on Bruinsburg and turning Grand Gulf April 25-30. Battle of Port Gibson, Miss., May 1. Battles of Raymond May 12, Jackson May 14, Champion's Hill May 16.

Siege of Vicksburg, Miss., May 18-July 4. Assaults on Vicksburg May 19 and 22. Surrender of Vicksburg July 4, and garrison duty there till August, 1865. Expedition to Monroe, La., August 20-September 2, 1863. Expedition to Canton October 14-20. Action at Bogue Chitto Creek October 17. Expedition to Yazoo City May 4-21, 1864. Benton May 7 and 9. Vaughan May 12. Yazoo City May 13. Expedition from Vicksburg to Pearl River July 2-10. Near Jackson July 5. Jackson and Clinton July 7. At Vicksburg till August, 1865. Mustered out August 9, 1865.

Battery lost during service 4 Enlisted men killed and mortally wounded and 2 Officers and 32 Enlisted men by disease. Total 38.

BATTERY "M," 2nd REGIMENT LIGHT ARTILLERY.

Organized at Chicago, Ill., and mustered in June 6, 1862. Left State for Martinsburg, W. Va., June 16, 1862, arriving there June 24. Attached to R. R. Brigade, 8th Army Corps, Middle Dept., to September, 1862. Duty at Martinsburg, W. Va., June to September. Expedition to Darkesville August 24. Moved to Harper's Ferry, W. Va., September 12. Siege of Harper's Ferry September 12-15. Surrendered September 15. Paroled September 16 and moved to Annapolis, Md., thence to Camp Douglass, Chicago, Ill., and duty there till May, 1863. Ordered to Cincinnati, Ohio, May 12, thence to Covington, Ky. To Catlettsburg, Ky., May 24. To Louisa, Ky., June 2, and duty there till August. Expedition up Big Sandy Valley to Beaver Creek June 14-July 22. Expedition to Gladesville, Va., July (Section). Moved to Covington, Ky., thence to Camp Nelson, Ky., August 4-8. Attached to 1st Brigade, 4th Division, 23rd Army Corps, Army Ohio, to August, 1863. 2nd Brigade, 3rd Division, 23rd Army Corps, to December, 1863. District of North Central Kentucky, 1st Division, 23rd Army Corps, to January, 1864. District of Southwest Kentucky, 1st Division, 23rd Army Corps, to April, 1864.

SERVICE.—Burnside's Expedition over Cumberland Mountains into East Tennessee August 17-October 17, 1863. Occupation of Knoxville, Tenn., September 2. Action at Kingsport September 18. Bristol September 19. Zollicoffer September 20-21. Hall's Ford, Watauga River, September 22. Carter's Depot and Bluntsville September 22. Blue Springs October 10. Henderson's Mills and Rheatown October 11. Blountsville October 14. Bristol October 15. At Rodgersville October 19 to November 6. Rodgersville November 6. Guns captured. Siege of Knoxville November 17-December 5. Ordered to Camp Nelson, Ky., and duty there till April, 1864. Mustered out April 11, 1864. Men transferred to Batteries "C" and "H."

Battery lost during service 5 Enlisted men killed and mortally wounded and 16 Enlisted men by disease. Total 21.

BRIDGES' INDEPENDENT BATTERY LIGHT ARTILLERY.

Authorized January 1, 1863, and organized at Nashville, Tenn., January 14, 1863, from Company "G," 19th Illinois Infantry. Company "G," 19th Illinois Infantry, organized at Chicago, Ill., and mustered in June 17, 1861. Moved to Quincy, Ill., July 12-13, thence to Palmyra, Mo., July 14, and guard Hannibal & St. Joseph R. R. from Quincy to Palmyra and between Palmyra and Hannibal till July 27. Moved to Hannibal, thence to St. Louis, Mo., and to Bird's Point and Norfolk. Duty at Norfolk till August 14. Moved to Ironton August 14. Prentiss' Expedition toward Dallas and Jackson August 29-September 8. Moved to Cape Girardeau, Fort Holt, Ky., and Elliott's Mills, thence moved to Cairo, Ill., September 16, under orders for Washington, D. C. While en route east September 17, via Ohio & Mississippi R. R., Bridge No. 48, over Beaver Creek, 30 miles west of Cincinnati, Ohio, broke through, precipitating six passenger coaches a distance of 60 feet, killing and wounding 129 of the Regiment. At Camp Dennison, Ohio, till September 24. Moved to Louisville, Ky., September 24-25, thence to Lebanon, Ky.,

September 25, and duty there till October 22. Moved to Elizabethtown, Ky., and duty there and at Bacon Creek, Ky., till February 10, 1862. Attached to 8th Brigade, 3rd Division, Army of Ohio, to August. Advance on Bowling Green, Ky., February 10-15. Occupation of Bowling Green till February 22. Advance on Nashville, Tenn., February 22-25. Occupation of Nashville till March 18. Advance to Murfreesboro March 18, thence to Shelbyville, Tullahoma and McMinnville March 25-28. Advance on Huntsville, Ala., via Fayetteville, April 4-11. Occupation of Huntsville April 11. Advance on and capture of Decatur and Tuscumbia April 11-14. Action at Tuscumbia April 24. At Huntsville till May 26. Athens May 13. Moved to Fayetteville May 26-June 2. Negley's Expedition to Chattanooga, Tenn., June 2-10. Chattanooga June 7-8. Expedition to Larkinsville and Stevenson June 14-20. Winchester June 16. Guard Railroad bridges from Huntsville to Decatur till August. Richland Creek, near Pulaski, August 27. Retreat to Nashville August 27-29. Fitted out as a Battery at Nashville September. Siege of Nashville September 12 to November 7. At Gallatin, Tenn., till November 20, when turned in guns and moved to Nashville. March to Murfreesboro, Tenn., and rejoin Regiment January 2, 1863. Permanently detached as a Battery January 14, 1863. Fitted at Nashville. Ordered to Murfreesboro, Tenn., February 20, 1863. Attached to Pioneer Brigade, Army of the Cumberland, to June, 1863. 1st Brigade, 2nd Division, 14th Army Corps, Army of the Cumberland, to October, 1863. Artillery, 3rd Division, 4th Army Corps, to July, 1864. Artillery Brigade, 4th Army Corps, to November, 1864. Reserve Artillery, Nashville, Tenn., to December, 1864.

SERVICE.—Duty at Murfreesboro, Tenn., till June, 1863. Middle Tennessee or Tullahoma Campaign June 23-July 7. Occupation of Middle Tennessee till August 16. Passage of the Cumberland Mountains and Tennessee River, and Chickamauga (Ga.) Campaign, August 16-September 22. Davis' Cross Roads, near Dug Gap, September 11. Battle of Chickamauga, Ga., September 19-21. Siege of Chattanooga, Tenn., September 24-November 23. Chattanooga Ringgold Campaign November 23-27. Orchard Knob November 23-24. Mission Ridge November 25. Pursuit to Graysville November 26-27. March to relief of Knoxville November 28-December 8. Operations in East Tennessee December, 1863, to April, 1864. Reconnoissance from Marysville toward Seviersville February 1-2, 1864. Atlanta (Ga.) Campaign May 1 to September 8. Demonstrations on Rocky Faced Ridge and Dalton May 8-13. Buzzard's Roost Gap May 8-9. Battle of Resaca May 14-15. Adairsville May 17. Near Kingston May 18-19. Near Cassville May 19. Advance on Dallas May 22-25. Operations on Pumpkin Vine Creek and battles about Dallas, New Hope Church and Allatoona Hills May 25-June 5. Pickett's Mills May 27. Operations about Marietta and against Kenesaw Mountain June 10-July 2. Pine Hill June 11-14. Lost Mountain June 15-17. Assault on Kenesaw June 27. Ruff's Station, Smyrna Camp Ground, July 4. Chattahoochie River July 5-17. Peach Tree Creek July 19-20. Siege of Atlanta July 22-August 25. Flank movement on Jonesboro August 25-30. Battle of Jonesboro August 31-September 1. Lovejoy Station September 2-6. Operations against Hood in North Georgia and North Alabama September 29-November 3. Nashville Campaign November and December. Columbia, Duck River, November 24-27. Battle of Franklin November 30. Battle of Nashville December 15-16. Transferred to 1st Regiment Illinois Light Artillery as Battery "B," December 21, 1864, which date.

Battery lost during service 2 Officers and 7 Enlisted men killed and mortally wounded and 20 Enlisted men by disease. Total 29.

BUSTEED'S INDEPENDENT BATTERY LIGHT ARTILLERY.

"Chicago Light Artillery." Organized at Chicago, Ill., October 1, 1861. Moved to Washington, D. C., October

1-4. Disbanded and transferred to 1st New York Light Artillery November 9, 1861.

CHICAGO BOARD OF TRADE INDEPENDENT BATTERY LIGHT ARTILLERY.

Organized at Chicago, Ill., and mustered in August 1, 1862. Moved to Louisville, Ky., September 9-11. Attached to Dumont's 12th Division, Army Ohio, to November, 1862. Pioneer Brigade, Army of the Cumberland, to March, 1863. 2nd Brigade, 2nd Cavalry Division, Army of the Cumberland, to October, 1864. 2nd Division, Cavalry Corps, Military Division Mississippi, to June, 1865.

SERVICE.—Pursuit of Bragg into Kentucky October 1-16, 1862. Lawrenceburg October 11. Moved to Bowling Green, Ky., and duty there till December 4. March to Nashville, Tenn., December 4-7. Expedition on Franklin Pike and skirmish December 14. Advance on Murfreesboro, Tenn., December 26-30. Battle of Stone's River December 30-31, 1862, and January 1-3, 1863. Duty at Murfreesboro till June. Scouts on Manchester Pike June 13 (Section). Battery changed from Mounted Field to Flying Horse Artillery and assigned to 2nd Cavalry Division March, 1863. The only Battery of Flying Artillery in Western Armies. Middle Tennessee or Tullahoma Campaign June 23-July 7. Morris Ford, Elk River, July 2. Occupation of Middle Tennessee till August 16. Expedition to Huntsville July 13-22. Passage of Cumberland Mountains and Tennessee River, and Chickamauga (Ga.) Campaign, August 16-September 22. Alpine, Ga., September 3 and 8. Ringgold September 11. Reconnoissance from Lee and Gordon's Mills toward Lafayette and skirmish September 13. Pea Vine Ridge September 18. Reed's Bridge September 18. Battle of Chickamauga, Ga., September 19-21. Guarding fords above Chattanooga till October 1. Operations against Wheeler and Roddy October 1-17. Thompson's Cove October 3. McMinnville October 4. Murfreesboro October 5. Near Shelbyville and Farmington October 7. Sugar Creek October 9. March to Dechard, Tenn., October 10-15, thence to Maysville. At Maysville, Huntsville, Ala., and Pulaski, Tenn., till March, 1864. Refitted with 3-inch Parrotts February 24, 1864. Moved to Huntsville, Ala., March 10, thence to Columbia, Tenn., April 4-8. Atlanta (Ga.) Campaign May 1 to September 8. Movements on right flank of army May 11-17. Battle of Resaca May 14-15. Tanner's Bridge, Oostenaula River, May 15. Kingston May 19. Near Dallas May 24. Operations about Dallas May 25-June 5. Ackworth June 8. Near Big Shanty June 9. Operations about Marietta and against Kenesaw Mountain June 10-July 2. McAffee's Cross Roads June 11. Noonday Creek June 15 and 19. Powder Springs June 20. Noonday Creek June 27. Nickajack Creek July 2-5. Marietta and Rosswell July 3. Rottenwood Creek July 4. Chattahoochie River July 6-10. Raid to Atlanta & Augusta R. R. July 13-20. Raid to Covington July 22-24 (Centre Section). Decatur July 22. Garrard's Raid to South River July 27-31. Flat Rock Bridge July 28. Siege of Atlanta August 1-17. Kilpatrick's Raid around Atlanta August 18-22. Red Oak August 19. Flint River August 19. Jonesboro August 19. Lovejoy Station August 20. Operations at Chattahoochie River Bridge and Turner's Ferry August 26-September 2. At Cross Keys till September 21. Operations in North Georgia and North Alabama against Hood and Forest September 29-November 3. Near Lost Mountain October 4-7. New Hope Church October 5. Dallas October 7. Rome October 10-11. Narrows October 11. Coosaville Road, near Rome, October 13. Near Summerville October 17. Little River, Ala., October 20. Leesburg October 20-21. Ladiga, Terrapin Creek, October 28. Moved to Chattanooga, Tenn., November 3-5, thence to Nashville, Tenn., November 13. Line of Shoal Creek, Ala., November 16-20. Nashville Campaign November-December. Fouche Springs November 23. Columbia, Duck River, November 24-27. Occupation of Nashville during Hood's investment December 1-15. Battle of Nashville December 15-16. Pursuit of Hood to the Tennessee River December 17-28. Richland Creek December 24. Lynnville December 24. Pulaski December 25. At Gravelly Springs, Ala., till March, 1865. Wilson's Raid to Macon, Ga., March 22-April 24. Ebenezer Church, Ala., April 1. Selma April 2. Montgomery April 12. Capture of Columbus, Ga., April 16. Macon, Ga., April 20. Duty at Macon till May 23. Moved to Nashville, Tenn., thence to Chicago, Ill., June 23-27. Mustered out June 30, 1865.

Battery lost during service 10 Enlisted men killed and mortally wounded and 9 Enlisted men by disease. Total 19.

CHAPMAN'S PEORIA INDEPENDENT BATTERY LIGHT ARTILLERY.

Organized from 14th Illinois Infantry and attached to that Regiment till February, 1862, when designated Battery "B," 2nd Light Artillery, which see.

CHICAGO MERCANTILE INDEPENDENT BATTERY LIGHT ARTILLERY.

Organized at Chicago, Ill., and mustered in August 29, 1862. Duty at Camp Douglass, near Chicago, Ill., till November 8. Moved to Memphis, Tenn., November 8-11, 1862. Attached to 5th Division, District of Memphis, Tenn., 13th Army Corps (Old), Dept. of the Tennessee, and to 2nd Division, District of Memphis, Tenn., 13th Army Corps, to December, 1862. Artillery, 10th Division, Right Wing 13 Army Corps, December, 1862. Artillery, 1st Division, Sherman's Yazoo Expedition, to January, 1863. Artillery, 10th Division, 13th Army Corps, Army of the Tennessee, to August, 1863. Artillery, 4th Division, 13th Army Corps, Dept. of the Gulf, to March, 1864. Artillery, 1st Division, 13th Army Corps, to June, 1864. Defences of New Orleans, La., to July, 1864. Artillery Reserve, Dept. of the Gulf, to November, 1864. Artillery, Cavalry Division, Dept. of the Gulf, to May, 1865. Defences of New Orleans, La., to July, 1865.

SERVICE.—Grant's Central Mississippi Campaign November and December, 1862. "Tallahatchie March" November 24-December 12. Sherman's Yazoo Expedition December 20, 1862, to January 2, 1863. Chickasaw Bayou December 26-28. Chickasaw Bluff December 29. Expedition to Arkansas Post, Ark., January 3-10, 1863. Assault and capture of Fort Hindman. Arkansas Post, January 10-11. Moved to Young's Point, La., January 17, and duty there till March, and at Milliken's Bend, La., till April 25. Movement on Bruinsburg and turning Grand Gulf April 25-30. Battle of Magnolia Hills, or Port Gibson, May 1. Battle of Champion's Hill May 16. Big Black River Bridge May 17. Siege of Vicksburg, Miss., May 18-July 4. Assaults on Vicksburg May 19 and 22. Advance on Jackson, Miss., July 5-10. Siege of Jackson July 10-17. Ordered to New Orleans, La., August 6, thence to Brashear City. Western Louisiana Campaign October 3-November 30. Camp at Franklin till December 19. Moved to Algiers, La. Expedition to the Rio Grande, Texas, December 26, 1863-January 1, 1864. At Pass Cavallo, Texas, till March. Ordered to Berwick City, La. Red River Campaign March-April. Battle of Sabine Cross Roads April 8. Battery cut to pieces and guns captured. Retreat to Alexandria, thence to New Orleans, La., April 9-30. Duty at Camp Parapet, Defences of New Orleans, till November. Moved to Baton Rouge November 1. Davidson's Expedition against Mobile & Ohio R. R. November 27-December 13. Moved to New Orleans December 31, thence to Baton Rouge, and duty there till May, 1865. At New Orleans, La., till June, then ordered home for muster out. Mustered out at Chicago, Ill., July 10, 1865.

Battery lost during service 2 Officers and 5 Enlisted men killed and mortally wounded and 11 Enlisted men by disease. Total 18.

COGSWELL'S INDEPENDENT BATTERY LIGHT ARTILLERY.

Organized at Ottawa, Ill., and mustered in November 12, 1861, as Company "A" Artillery, 53rd Illinois Infantry. Moved to Chicago, Ill., February 28, 1862, and guard prisoners there till March 17. Detached as a Battery March 17, 1862, and ordered to St. Louis, Mo., March 23, thence embarked for Pittsburg Landing, Tenn., April 8. Attached to 3rd Division, Army of the Tennessee, to July, 1862. Artillery, 5th Division, District of Memphis, Tenn., to November, 1862. Artillery, 5th Division, District of Memphis, Tenn., Right Wing 13th Army Corps (Old), Dept. of the Tennessee, November, 1862. Artillery, 1st Division, District of Memphis, 13th Army Corps, to December, 1862. Artillery, 1st Division, 17th Army Corps, to January, 1863. Artillery, 1st Division, 16th Army Corps, to July, 1863. Artillery, 4th Division, 15th Army Corps, July, 1863. Artillery, 7th Division, 17th Army Corps, to September, 1863. Artillery, 2nd Division, 17th Army Corps, to December, 1863. Artillery, 3rd Division, 15th Army Corps, to April, 1864. Artillery Reserve, Nashville, Tenn., Dept. of the Cumberland, to December, 1864. 1st Brigade, 1st Division, Detachment Army of the Tennessee, Dept. of the Cumberland, to February, 1865. Artillery Brigade, 16th Army Corps (New), Military Division West Mississippi, to August, 1865.

SERVICE.—Advance on and siege of Corinth, Miss., April 29-May 30, 1862. March to Memphis, Tenn., June 1-14, and duty there till November. Grant's Central Mississippi Campaign November-December. "Tallahatchie March" November 24-December 12. At Grand Junction January 9 to March 8, 1863. At Lagrange till June 4. Moved to Memphis, Tenn., June 4, thence to Vicksburg, Miss., June 6-11. Siege of Vicksburg, Miss., June 11-July 4. Advance on Jackson, Miss., July 5-10. Siege of Jackson July 10-17. At Big Black till September 28. Moved to Memphis, Tenn., thence to Chattanooga, Tenn., September 28-November 23. Operations on Memphis & Charleston R. R. in Alabama October 20-29. Chattanooga-Ringgold Campaign November 23-27. Mission Ridge November 24-25. March to relief of Knoxville November 28-December 8. Garrison duty in Alabama till April, 1864. Moved to Nashville, Tenn., April 29, and garrison duty there till December. Battle of Nashville December 15-16. Pursuit of Hood to the Tennessee River December 17-28. Moved to Clifton, Tenn., and to Eastport, Miss. Duty at Eastport till February 5, 1865. Moved to New Orleans, La., February 5-22. Campaign against Mobile and its defences March 17-April 12. Siege of Spanish Fort and Fort Blakely March 26-April 8. Assault and capture of Fort Blakely April 9. Occupation of Mobile April 12. March to Montgomery April 13-25, and duty there till July. Mustered out August 14, 1865.

Battery lost during service 26 Enlisted men by disease.

COLVIN'S INDEPENDENT BATTERY LIGHT ARTILLERY.

Organized October 6, 1863, from men detached from 107th Illinois Infantry, 33rd Kentucky Infantry and 22nd Indiana Battery. Attached to 4th Brigade, 4th Division, 23rd Army Corps, Dept. of Ohio, to November, 1863. 2nd Division, Cavalry Corps, Dept. of Ohio, to April, 1864. 2nd Brigade, 4th Division, 23rd Army Corps, to February, 1865. 2nd Brigade, 4th Division, District of East Tennessee, Dept. of the Cumberland, to March, 1865.

SERVICE.—Knoxville Campaign November 4-December 23, 1863. Near Maynardsville December 1. Walker's Ford December 2. Mossy Creek, Talbot Station, December 29. Operations about Dandridge January 16-17, 1864. Kimbrough's Cross Roads January 16. Dandridge January 17. Operations about Dandridge January 26-28. Near Fair Garden January 27. Garrison duty at Knoxville, Tenn., till March, 1865. Operations against Wheeler's Raid in East Tennessee August 15-25, 1864. Strawberry Plains August 24. Battery transferred to 1st Illinois Light Artillery as Battery "K" March 23, 1865, which see.

Battery lost during service 14 by disease.

COOLEY'S INDEPENDENT BATTERY LIGHT ARTILLERY.

See Chicago Mercantile Battery.

RENWICK'S ELGIN INDEPENDENT BATTERY LIGHT ARTILLERY.

Organized at Elgin, Ill., and mustered in November 15, 1862. Ordered to Kentucky and attached to District of Western Kentucky, Dept. of the Ohio, to April, 1863. 1st Brigade, 3rd Division, 23rd Army Corps, Dept. Ohio, to August, 1863. 1st Brigade, 2nd Division, 23rd Army Corps, to April, 1864. 2nd Brigade, 4th Division, 23rd Army Corps, to February, 1865. 2nd Brigade, 4th Division, District of East Tennessee, Dept. of the Cumberland, February, 1865. Artillery, 1st Division, 23rd Army Corps, Dept. of North Carolina, to July, 1865.

SERVICE.—Duty at Bowling Green, Ky., till May, 1863, and at Glasgow and Tompkinsville till July. At Munfordsville July. Operations against Morgan in Kentucky July 2-26. Burnside's Campaign in East Tennessee August 16-October 17. At Loudon till November 9. Knoxville Campaign November 4-December 23. Moved to Kingston and duty there till December 4. Repulse of Wheeler's attack on Kingston November 24. Near Kingston December 4. March to Mossy Creek December 4-27. Action at Mossy Creek, Talbot's Station, December 29. At Mossy Creek till January, 1864. Post and garrison duty at Knoxville and other points in East Tennessee till February, 1865. Ordered to North Carolina. Campaign of the Carolinas March 1-April 26. Advance on Kinston and Goldsboro March 1-21. Battle of Wise's Forks, N. C., March 8-10. Occupation of Goldsboro March 21. Advance on Raleigh April 10-14. Occupation of Raleigh April 14. Bennett's House April 26. Surrender of Johnston and his army. Duty in Dept. of North Carolina till July. Mustered out July 18, 1865.

Battery lost during service 13 by disease.

HENSHAW'S INDEPENDENT BATTERY LIGHT ARTILLERY.

Organized at Ottawa, Ill., and mustered in December 3, 1862. Ordered to Kentucky and attached to District of Western Kentucky, Dept. of the Ohio, to June, 1863. 1st Brigade, 3rd Division, 23rd Army Corps, Dept. Ohio, to August, 1863. 2nd Brigade, 2nd Division, 23rd Army Corps, to April, 1864. 3rd Brigade, 4th Division, 23rd Army Corps, to October, 1864. 2nd Brigade, 4th Division, 23rd Army Corps, to February, 1865. 2nd Brigade, 4th Division, District of East Tennessee, Dept. of the Cumberland, to July, 1865.

SERVICE.—Duty at Louisville and other points in District of Western Kentucky till August, 1863. Operations against and pursuit of Morgan July 2-26. Action at Buffington Island, Ohio, July 19. Paris, Ky., July 29 and August 1. Burnside's Campaign in East Tennessee August 16-October 17. Duty at Loudon till November. Knoxville Campaign November 4-December 23. Actions at Huff's Ferry November 14. Lenoir Station November 14-15. Loudon November 15. Campbell's Station November 17. Siege of Knoxville November 17-December 5. Pursuit of Longstreet December 7-13. At Strawberry Plains till January, 1864, and at Mossy Creek till April. Garrison duty at Loudon, Tenn., and other points in District of East Tennessee till July, 1865. Mustered out July 18, 1865.

Battery lost during service 4 Enlisted men killed and 15 Enlisted men by disease. Total 19.

RENWICK'S INDEPENDENT BATTERY LIGHT ARTILLERY.

See Elgin Battery Light Artillery.

SMITH'S BATTERY CHICAGO LIGHT ARTILLERY.

Entered State service for three months April 17, 1861. Duty in District of Cairo, Ill., till July. Mustered out July 16, 1861. Became Battery "A," 1st Regiment Illinois Light Artillery.

SPRINGFIELD INDEPENDENT BATTERY LIGHT ARTILLERY ("VAUGHAN'S").

Organized at Springfield, Ill., and mustered in August 21, 1862. Duty at Camp Butler, near Springfield, till November 1, 1862. Moved to Bolivar, Tenn., November 1-8, 1862. Attached to District of Jackson, Tenn., 13th Army Corps (Old), Dept. of the Tennessee, to December, 1862. Post of Bolivar, Tenn., District of Jackson, 16th Army Corps, to March, 1863. 1st Brigade, 3rd Division, 16th Army Corps, to May, 1863. 3rd Brigade, 3rd Division, 16th Army Corps, to August, 1863. True's Brigade, Arkansas Expedition, to September, 1863. Artillery, 2nd Division, Army of Arkansas, to January, 1864. Artillery, 2nd Division, 7th Army Corps, Dept. of Arkansas, to March, 1864. 2nd Brigade, 1st Division, 7th Army Corps, to April, 1864. Artillery, 3rd Division, 7th Army Corps, to May, 1864. Artillery, 1st Division, 7th Army Corps, to June, 1865.

SERVICE.—Garrison duty at Bolivar, Tenn., till June 18, 1863. Guard Memphis & Charleston R. R. 1 Section at Moscow, 1 Section at Colliersville and 1 Section at Germantown, Tenn., till August 23. Moved to Helena, Ark., August 24-September 2. Steele's Expedition to Little Rock September 2-10. Bayou Fourche and capture of Little Rock September 10. Duty at Little Rock till March, 1864. (1 Section at Lewisburg October 19, 1863, to March 15, 1864.) Steele's Camden Expedition March 23-May 3. Okolona April 2-3. Prairie D'Ann April 9-12. Near Princeton April 28. Jenkins' Ferry, Saline River, April 30. Duty at Little Rock till June, 1865. Ordered to Springfield, Ill., June 25, and mustered out June 30, 1865.

Battery lost during service 1 Enlisted man killed and 22 Enlisted men by disease. Total 23.

STOKES' INDEPENDENT BATTERY LIGHT ARTILLERY.

See Chicago Board of Trade Battery Light Artillery.

VAUGHAN'S INDEPENDENT BATTERY LIGHT ARTILLERY.

See Springfield Independent Battery Light Artillery.

7th REGIMENT INFANTRY (3 MONTHS).

Organized at Camp Yates, Ill., and mustered in by Capt. John Pope, U. S. A., April 25, 1861. Duty at Alton, Cairo, Mound City, Ill., and St. Louis, Mo., till July. Expedition from Cairo to Little River June 22-23 (Cos. "E" and "G"). Mustered out July 25, 1861, expiration of term.

Regiment lost 5 by disease during service.

7th REGIMENT INFANTRY (3 YEARS).

Regiment organized at Cairo, Ill., July 25, 1861. Attached to District of Cairo to October, 1861. Cook's 4th Brigade, District of Cairo, to February, 1862. 3rd Brigade, 2nd Division, District of West Tennessee, and Army of the Tennessee, to July, 1862. 3rd Brigade, 2nd Division, District of Corinth, Dept. of the Tennessee, to November, 1862. 3rd Brigade, District of Corinth, Left Wing 13th Army Corps (Old), Dept. of the Tennessee, to December, 1862. 3rd Brigade, District of Corinth, 17th Army Corps, Army of the Tennessee, to January, 1863. 3rd Brigade, District of Corinth, 16th Army Corps, to March, 1863. 3rd Brigade, 2nd Division, 16th Army Corps, to September, 1864. 3rd Brigade, 4th Division, 15th Army Corps, to July, 1865.

SERVICE.—Moved to Ironton, Mo., thence to Cape Girardeau, Mo., August 23, 1861. Duty there and at Fort Holt, Ky., till February, 1862. Expedition toward Columbus, Ky., September 21-22, 1861. Skirmish at Mansfield's Creek September 22. Expedition to Elliott's Mills during Belmont November 6-7. Reconnoissance of Columbus, Ky., January 13-20, 1862. Movements against Fort Henry, Tenn., February 2-6. Investment and capture of Fort Donelson, Tenn., February 12-16. Expedition to Clarksville and Nashville, Tenn., February 19-21. Moved to Pittsburg Landing, Tenn., arriving there March 22. Battle of Shiloh, Tenn., April 6-7. Advance on and siege of Corinth, Miss., April 29-May 30.

Pursuit to Booneville May 31-June 11. Duty at Corinth, Miss., till October. Battle of Corinth October 3-4. Pursuit to Hatchie River October 5-12. Duty at Corinth till April, 1863. Dodge's Expedition to intercept Forest, and operations in West Tennessee, December 18, 1862, to January 3, 1863. Dodge's Expedition to Northern Alabama April 15-May 8. Iuka, Miss., April 16. Great Bear Creek, Cherokee Station and Lundy's Lane April 17. Rock Cut, near Tuscumbia, April 22. Tuscumbia April 23. Town Creek April 28. Guard Railroad from Bethel to Jackson, Tenn., May 12 to June 8. Regiment mounted June 18 and engaged in scout and patrol duty through West Tennessee till October, participating in numerous expeditions and skirmishes. Expedition from Corinth to Henderson, Tenn., September 11-16. Skirmish at Clark's Creek Church September 13. Henderson's Station September 14. Expedition into West Tennessee September 27-October 1. Swallow's Bluff September 30. At Chewalla October 4-26. Moved to Iuka October 26, thence marched to Pulaski, Tenn., November 1-12. Scout to Lawrenceburg November 17-19. Scout duty around Pulaski till December 22. Skirmishes near Florence December 1. Near Eastport December 2. Scout to Florence December 11-17. Shoal Creek, near Wayland Springs, December 12. Regiment Veteranize December 22 and mustered in as Veterans January 5, 1864. Veterans on furlough January and February, 1864. Return to Pulaski February 23-27. Duty at Florence, Ala., patrolling Tennessee River till June. At Florence, Sweetwater and Centre Store till June 14. Repulse of Roddy's attack on Florence May 7. Decatur May 8. Pulaski May 13. Regiment dismounted and moved to Chattanooga, Tenn., June 14-17, thence to Tilton, Ga., and patrol Railroad from Dalton to Resaca, Ga., till July 7. Moved to Rome, Ga., July 7, and duty there till October. (Non-Veterans mustered out July 29, 1864.) Action at Etowah River September 15. Operations against Hood September 29-November 3. Defence of Allatoona Pass October 4-5. Reconnoissance from Rome on Cave Springs Road and skirmishes October 12-13. March to the sea November 15-December 10. Regiment remounted November 21. Ogeechee Canal December 9. Siege of Savannah December 10-21. Hinesville December 16. Campaign of the Carolinas January to April, 1865. Hickory Hill, S. C., February 1. Salkehatchie Swamps February 2-5. Fishburn's Plantation, near Lane's Bridge, Salkehatchie, February 6. South Edisto River February 9. North Edisto River February 11-12. Columbia February 15-17. Lynch's Creek February 26. Cheraw March 2-3. Expedition from Cheraw to Florence and skirmishes March 4-6. Battle of Bentonville, N. C., March 19-21. Occupation of Goldsboro March 24, and of Raleigh April 14. Bennett's House April 26. Surrender of Johnston and his army. March to Washington, D. C., via Richmond, Va., April 29-May 19. Grand Review May 24. Moved to Louisville, Ky., June, and duty there till July. Mustered out July 9, 1865.

Regiment lost during service 8 Officers and 81 Enlisted men killed and mortally wounded and 3 Officers and 174 Enlisted men by disease. Total 266.

8th REGIMENT INFANTRY (3 MONTHS).

Organized at Springfield, Ill., and mustered in for three months' service April 25, 1861. Moved to Cairo, Ill., and duty there till July, 1861. Expedition from Cairo to Little River June 22-23 (Cos. "B" and "C"). Mustered out July 25, 1861.

Regiment lost 3 by disease during service.

8th REGIMENT INFANTRY (3 YEARS).

Organized at Cairo, Ill., for three years' service July 25, 1861. Attached to District of Cairo to October, 1861. 2nd Brigade, District of Cairo, to February, 1862. 1st Brigade, 1st Division, District of Cairo, February, 1862. 1st Brigade, 1st Division, District of West Tennessee, and Army of the Tennessee, to July, 1862. 1st Brigade, 1st Division, District of Jackson, Dept. of the Tennessee, to September, 1862. 4th Brigade, 1st Division, District of Jackson, to November, 1862. 4th Brigade, 3rd Division, Right Wing 13th Army Corps (Old), Dept. of the Tennessee, to December, 1862. 3rd Brigade, 3rd Division, 17th Army Corps, Army of the Tennessee, to April, 1864. Maltby's Brigade, District of Vicksburg, Miss., to August, 1864. 1st Brigade, 2nd Division, 19th Army Corps, Dept. of the Gulf, to December, 1864. 2nd Brigade, Reserve Division, Military Division West Mississippi, to February, 1865. 2nd Brigade, 1st Division, Reserve Corps, M. D. W. M., February, 1865. 2nd Brigade, 1st Division, 13th Army Corps (New), M. D. W. M., to June, 1865. Dept. of Louisiana to May, 1866.

SERVICE.—Duty at Cairo, Ill., till October, 1861. Moved to Bird's Point, Mo., and duty there till February, 1862. Expedition against Thompson's forces November 2-12, 1861. Expeditions toward Columbus, Ky., January 13-20, 1862. Advance on Fort Henry, Tenn., February 2-6. Investment and capture of Fort Donelson, Tenn., February 12-16. Moved to Pittsburg Landing, Tenn., March 6-13. Battle of Shiloh April 6-7. Advance on and siege of Corinth, Miss., April 29-May 30. Moved to Bethel June 4-6, thence to Jackson June 15. Duty there and guard duty at Toone's and Medon Stations till October. Grant's Central Mississippi Campaign October 31, 1862, to January 10, 1863. Ordered to Lagrange November, 1862. Reconnoissance from Lagrange November 8-9. March to Grand Junction January 4-9, 1863, and to Memphis, Tenn., January 12-19. Moved to Lake Providence, La., February 22, and duty there till April. Moved to Milliken's Bend, La., April 12. Movement on Bruinsburg and turning Grand Gulf April 25-30. Battles of Thompson's Hill, Port Gibson, May 1. South Fork Bayou Pierrie May 2. Raymond May 12. Jackson, Miss., May 14. Champion's Hill May 16. Siege of Vicksburg, Miss., May 18-July 4. Assaults on Vicksburg May 19 and 22. Surrender of Vicksburg July 4. Garrison duty at Vicksburg till July, 1864. Stevenson's Expedition from Vicksburg to Monroe, La., August 20-September 2, 1863. Expedition to Canton October 14-20. Bogue Chitto Creek October 17. Meridian Campaign February 3-March 5, 1864. Regiment Veteranize March 24, 1864. Expedition to Pearl River, Miss., July 2-10. Jackson July 7. Expedition to Morganza, La., July 29-September 3. Moved to mouth of White River September 3-8, and duty there till October 18. Movement to Memphis, Tenn., and return October 18-30. Moved to Duvall's Bluff November 9, thence to Memphis, Tenn., November 28. March to Moscow and return December 29-31. Moved to New Orleans, La., January 1-4, 1865. Campaign against Mobile and its defences February to April. Siege of Spanish Fort and Fort Blakely March 26-April 8. Assault and capture of Fort Blakely April 9. Occupation of Mobile April 12. Duty at Mobile till May 27. Moved to New Orleans, La., thence to Shreveport May 27-June 9. Moved to Marshall, Texas, and duty there till September. At Alexandria, La., till April, 1866. Mustered out at Baton Rouge May 4 and discharged at Springfield, Ill., May 13, 1866.

Regiment lost during service 6 Officers and 160 Enlisted men killed and mortally wounded and 155 Enlisted men by disease. Total 321.

9th REGIMENT INFANTRY (3 MONTHS).

Organized at Springfield, Ill., and mustered in for three months' service by Capt. John Pope, U. S. A., April 26, 1861. Moved to Cairo, Ill., and garrison duty there till July. Attached to Prentiss' Brigade. Expedition from Cairo to Little River June 22-23 (Cos. "C" and "H"). Mustered out July 26, 1861.

Regiment lost 9 by disease during service.

9th REGIMENT INFANTRY (3 YEARS).

Organized at Cairo, Ill., July 26 to August 31, 1861. Attached to District of Cairo to September, 1861. District of Paducah, Ky., to February, 1862. 1st Brigade, 2nd Division, District of Cairo, February, 1862. 1st Brigade, 2nd Division, District of West Tennessee, and Army of the Tennessee to March, 1862. 2nd Brigade, 2nd Division, Army Tennessee, to July, 1862. 2nd Brigade, 2nd Division, District of Corinth, to September, 1862. 3rd Brigade, 2nd Division, District of Corinth, to

October, 1862. 2nd Brigade, 2nd Division, District of Corinth, to November, 1862. 2nd Brigade, District of Corinth, 13th Army Corps (Old), Dept. of the Tennessee, to December, 1862. 2nd Brigade, District of Corinth, 17th Army Corps, to January, 1863. 2nd Brigade, District of Corinth, 16th Army Corps, to March, 1863. 2nd Brigade, 2nd Division, 16th Army Corps, to September, 1864. Unattached, 3rd Cavalry Division, Cavalry Corps, Army of the Cumberland, to November, 1864. Unattached, 3rd Division, Cavalry Corps, Military Division of the Mississippi, to July, 1865.

SERVICE.—Duty at Cairo, Ill., till September, 1861. Expedition to Paducah, Ky., September 5-6. Occupation of Paducah September 6, and duty there till February, 1862. Skirmish at Saratoga and Eddyville, Ky., October 26, 1861 (Cos. "B," "H" and "I"). Demonstration on Columbus, Ky., November 7-9. Reconnoissance to Fort Henry, Tenn., January 15-25, 1862. Operations against Forts Henry and Heiman February 5-6. Investment and capture of Fort Donelson, Tenn., February 12-16. Expedition to Clarksville and Nashville, Tenn., February 22-March 1. Moved to Pittsburg Landing, Tenn., March 1-10. Battle of Shiloh, Tenn., April 6-7. Advance on and siege of Corinth, Miss., April 29-May 30. Duty at Corinth till March, 1863. Battle of Corinth October 3-4, 1862. Pursuit to Ripley October 5-12. Grant's Central Mississippi Campaign November and December. Reconnoissance to Tupelo, Miss., December 13-19. Expedition to intercept Forest January 2-3, 1863. Regiment mounted March 15, 1863. Dodge's Expedition to Northern Alabama April 14-May 8. Burnsville April 14. Dickson and Lundy's Lane April 17. Dickson Station April 19. Rock Cut, near Tuscumbia, April 22. Florence April 23. Tuscumbia April 23. Town Creek April 28. Expedition from Burnsville to Tupelo, Miss., May 2-8. Tupelo May 4. King's Creek, near Tupelo, May 5. Expedition from Corinth, Miss., to Florence, Ala., May 26-31. Florence May 27-28. Hamburg Landing, Tenn., May 30. Moved to Pocahontas, Tenn., June 3. Expedition to Ripley, Miss., June 8-9. Raid to Ripley and New Albany, Miss., June 13-14. Forked Deer Creek and Orizaba June 13. Operations in Northwestern Mississippi June 15-25. New Albany June 19. Mud Creek Bottom June 20. Rocky Crossing, Tallahatchie River, June 20. Scout in West Tennessee July 8-15. Jackson, Tenn., July 13. Forked Deer Creek July 15. Scout through West Tennessee July 20-August 3. Expedition from Memphis, Tenn., to Grenada, Miss., August 12-23. Grenada August 17. Scouting in West Tennessee and North Mississippi September. Montezuma, Tenn., September 16. Bear Creek October 3. Operations in North Mississippi and West Tennessee against Chalmers October 4-17. Lockhart's Mills and Salem October 8. Ingraham's Mills, near Byhalia, October 12. Quinn and Jackson's Mill, Wyatt's, Tallahatchie River, October 13. Scouting in North Mississippi, North Alabama and Central Tennessee November. At Athens till February, 1864. Near Florence December 1, 1863. Athens, Ala., January 26, 1864. Near Tennessee River January 29. Near Moulton March 21. Near Decatur April 13. Flint River, Decatur, April 17. Atlanta (Ga.) Campaign May 1 to September 8, 1864. Conduct trains of 15th and 16th Army Corps from Huntsville, Ala., to Chattanooga, Tenn., May 1-5. Led advance of the Army of the Tennessee on Dalton, Ga., and scouting on flanks of army through the Atlanta Campaign, march to the sea and through the Carolinas. Demonstration on Dalton May 5-9. Snake Creek Gap May 9. Near Resaca May 10. Resaca May 13. Ley's Ferry, Oostenaula River, May 14-15. Rome Cross Roads May 16. Advance on Dallas May 19-25. Operations on line of Pumpkin Vine Creek and battles about Dallas, New Hope Church and Allatoona Hills May 25-June 5. Operations about Marietta and against Kenesaw Mountain June 10-July 2. Assault on Kenesaw June 27. Operations on line of Nickajack Creek July 2-5. Operations on line of the Chattahoochie River July 5-12. Peach Tree Creek July 19-20. Decatur and Battle of Atlanta July 22. Siege of Atlanta July 22-August 25. Flank movement on Jonesboro August 25-30,

Battle of Jonesboro August 31-September 1. Lovejoy Station September 2-6. Operations against Hood in North Georgia and Northern Alabama September 29-November 3. Skirmish on Cave Springs Road, near Rome, Ga., October 12-13. March to the sea November 15-December 10. Near Milledgeville November 23. Sandersville November 26. Siege of Savannah December 10-21. Campaign of the Carolinas January to April, 1865. Whippy Swamp Creek, S. C., February 1. Rivers' and Broxton's Bridges February 2. Salkehatchie Swamp February 2-5. Edisto R. R. Bridge February 7. Walker's or Valley Bridge, Edisto River, February 8. Binnaker's Bridge, South Edisto River, February 9. About Orangeburg, North Edisto River, February 11-12. Columbia February 15-17. Phillips' Cross Roads March 4. Expedition to Florence, S. C., and skirmishes March 4-6. Fayetteville, N. C., March 11. South River March 15. Averysboro March 16. Near Benton's Cross Roads March 18. Battle of Bentonville March 19-21. Occupation of Goldsboro March 24. Advance on Raleigh April 9-13. Near Raleigh April 12. Morrisville April 13. Near Chapel Hill April 15. Bennett's House April 26. Surrender of Johnston and his army. March to Washington, D. C., via Richmond, Va., April 29-May 19. Grand Review May 24. Mustered out July 9, 1865.

Regiment lost during service 5 Officers and 211 Enlisted men killed and mortally wounded and 1 Officer and 200 Enlisted men by disease. Total 417.

10th REGIMENT INFANTRY (3 MONTHS).

Regiment formed from first four Companies reporting at Springfield, Ill., April 20, 1861, which were ordered to Cairo, Ill., April 22. Regiment fully organized by the addition of three other Infantry Companies and three Artillery Companies and mustered in for three months' service by Capt. John Pope, U. S. A., April 29, 1861. Attached to Prentiss' Brigade and on garrison duty at Cairo, Ill., till July. Mustered out July 29, 1861.

Lost by disease 4 during service.

10th REGIMENT INFANTRY (3 YEARS).

Organized at Cairo, Ill., July 29, 1861. Attached to District of Cairo, Ill., to October, 1861. 1st Brigade, District of Cairo, to February, 1862. 4th Brigade, 1st Division, District of Cairo, February, 1862. 1st Brigade, 4th Division, Army of Mississippi, to April, 1862. 2nd Brigade, 1st Division, Army Mississippi, to September, 1862. 2nd Brigade, 13th Division, Army of the Ohio, to November, 1862. 1st Brigade, 4th Division, Centre 14th Army Corps, Army of the Cumberland, to January, 1863. 1st Brigade, 4th Division, 14th Army Corps, to June, 1863. 1st Brigade, 2nd Division, Reserve Corps, Army of the Cumberland, to October, 1863. 1st Brigade, 2nd Division, 14th Army Corps, to August, 1864. 3rd Brigade, 4th Division, 16th Army Corps, Army of the Tennessee, to September, 1864. 3rd Brigade, 1st Division, 17th Army Corps, to July, 1865.

SERVICE.—Moved to Mound City, Ill., and duty there till January, 1862. Expedition into Kentucky January 16-21. At Bird's Point, Mo., till March. Skirmish at Sykestown, Mo., March 1 (Detachment). Operations against New Madrid and Island No. 10 March 3-April 8. Actions at New Madrid March 12-14. Capture of New Madrid March 14. Island No. 10 April 6. Action and capture at Tiptonville April 8. Expedition to Fort Pillow, Tenn., April 13-17. Moved to Hamburg Landing, Tenn., April 17-24. Advance on and siege of Corinth, Miss., April 29-May 30. Engagement at Farmington May 3. Pursuit to Booneville May 30-June 12. Tuscumbia Creek May 31-June 1. Reconnoissance toward Baldwin June 3. At Clear Creek till July 21. Ordered to Tuscumbia, Ala., July 21, thence march to Nashville, Tenn., via Florence, Athens and Columbia August 28-September 15. Siege of Nashville September 15-November 6. Repulse of Morgan's attack on Edgefield November 5. Duty at Nashville and Edgefield till July, 1863. Moved to Murfreesboro July 20, 1863, thence to Bridgeport, Ala., August 24-September 12, and duty there till October. Pursuit of Wheeler up the Sequatchie Valley Oc-

tober 1-17. Action at Anderson's Cross Roads October 2. At Anderson's Cross Roads till October 24. Moved to Igo's Ferry October 24. Chattanooga-Ringgold Campaign November 23-27. Tunnel Hill November 24-25. Mission Ridge November 25. Chickamauga Station November 26. March to relief of Knoxville November 28-December 8. March to Columbus, thence to Chattanooga and to Rossville, Ga. Regiment Veteranize December 27, 1863. Veterans on furlough January 11 to February 22, 1864. At Rossville till May 2. Atlanta (Ga.) Campaign May 2-September 8. Demonstrations on Dalton May 5-13. Tunnel Hill May 6-7. Rocky Faced Ridge May 8-11. Buzzard's Roost Gap May 8-9. Battle of Resaca May 14-15. Rome, Ga., May 17-18. Operations on line of Pumpkin Vine Creek and battles about Dallas, New Hope Church and Allatoona Hills May 25-June 5. Operations about Marietta and against Kenesaw Mountain June 10-July 2. Pine Hill June 11-14. Lost Mountain June 15-17. Assault on Kenesaw June 27. Ruff's Station, Smyrna Camp Ground, July 4. Chattahoochie River July 5-17. Peach Tree Creek July 19-20. Siege of Atlanta July 22-August 25. Utoy Creek August 5-7. Flank movement on Jonesboro August 25-30. Battle of Jonesboro August 31-September 1. Lovejoy Station September 2-6. Pursuit of Hood into Alabama October 1-26. Action at Resaca, Ga., October 12-13. March to the sea November 15-December 10. Monteith Swamp December 9. Siege of Savannah December 10-21. Campaign of the Carolinas January to April, 1865. Moved to Beaufort, S. C., January 3, thence to Pocotaligo. Reconnoissance to Salkehatchie River January 20. Salkehatchie Swamp February 2-5. Rivers' and Broxton's Bridges February 2. Rivers' Bridge February 3. Binnaker's Bridge, South Edisto River, February 9. Orangeburg, North Edisto River, February 11-12. Columbia February 15-17. Fayetteville, N. C., March 11. Cape Fear March 18. Cox's Bridge, Neuse River, March 19-20. Battle of Bentonville March 20-21. Occupation of Goldsboro March 24. Advance on Raleigh April 10-14. Occupation of Raleigh April 14. Bennett's House April 26. Surrender of Johnston and his army. March to Washington, D. C., via Richmond, Va., April 29-May 19. Grand Review May 24. Moved to Louisville, Ky., June 4. Mustered out July 4, 1865, and discharged at Chicago, Ill., July 11, 1865.

Regiment lost during service 2 Officers and 48 Enlisted men killed and mortally wounded and 136 Enlisted men by disease. Total 186.

11th REGIMENT INFANTRY (3 MONTHS).

Organized at Springfield, Ill., and mustered in April 30, 1861, for three months' service by Capt. John Pope, U. S. A. Ordered to Villa Ridge, Ill., May 5, and duty there till June 20, and at Bird's Point, Mo., till July 30. Expedition from Cairo to Little River June 22-23 (Cos. "A" and "B"). Mustered out July 30, 1861.

Lost 10 by disease during service.

11th REGIMENT INFANTRY (3 YEARS).

Organized at Cairo, Ill., July 30, 1861. Attached to W. H. L. Wallace's 3rd Brigade, District of Cairo, to February, 1862. 2nd Brigade, 1st Division, District of Cairo, February, 1862. 2nd Brigade, 1st Division, District of West Tennessee, and Army of the Tennessee, to July, 1862. 2nd Brigade, 1st Division, District of Jackson, Tenn., to August, 1862. District of Cairo, Ill., to November, 1862. 2nd Brigade, 6th Division, Left Wing 13th Army Corps (Old), Dept. of the Tennessee, to December, 1862. 2nd Brigade, 6th Division, 16th Army Corps, to January, 1863. 2nd Brigade, 6th Division, 17th Army Corps, to September, 1863. 2nd Brigade, 1st Division, 17th Army Corps, to August, 1864. 1st Brigade, 2nd Division, 19th Army Corps, Dept. of the Gulf, to December, 1864. 2nd Brigade, Reserve Division, Military Division West Mississippi, to February, 1865. 2nd Brigade, 1st Division, Reserve Corps, M. D. W. M., February, 1865. 2nd Brigade, 1st Division, 13th Army Corps (New), M. D. W. M., to July, 1865.

SERVICE.—Expedition to Charleston, Mo., October 2, 1861. Expedition against Thompson's forces November 2-12. Skirmish at Charleston January 8, 1862. Reconnoissance of Columbus, Ky., under Gen. Grant January 25-28. Operations against Fort Henry February 2-6. Capture of Fort Henry February 6. Investment and capture of Fort Donelson, Tenn., February 12-16. Assault on Fort Donelson February 15. Moved to Fort Henry March 4-5, thence to Savannah, Tenn., March 5-13, and to Pittsburg Landing March 23-25. Battle of Shiloh, Tenn., April 6-7. Advance on and siege of Corinth, Miss., April 29-May 30. Moved to Jackson, Tenn., and duty there till August 2. Ordered to Cairo, Ill., August 2, and to Paducah, Ky., August 23. Expedition from Fort Donelson to Clarksville September 5-10. Riggin's Hill, Clarksville, September 7. Duty at Paducah, Ky., till November 20. Expeditions to Hopkinsville, Ky., October 31 to November 13. Moved to Lagrange, Tenn., November 20-24. Grant's Central Mississippi Campaign. Operations on Mississippi Central R. R. November 24, 1862, to January 10, 1863. Moved to Memphis, Tenn., January 12, 1863, thence to Young's Point, La., January 17-24, and to Lake Providence, La., February 11. Expedition to American Bend March 17-28. Passage of Vicksburg and Warrenton Batteries April 22 (Detachment). Movement on Bruinsburg and turning Grand Gulf April 25-30. Battle of Port Gibson May 1. Battles of Raymond May 12; Jackson, Miss., May 14; Champion's Hill May 16. Siege of Vicksburg, Miss., May 18-July 4. Assaults on Vicksburg May 19 and 22. Expedition from Haines' Bluff to Mechanicsburg May 26-June 4. Action at Mechanicsburg May 29. Surrender of Vicksburg July 4. Expedition to Natchez July 12-13. Occupation of Natchez July 13-October 12. Moved to Vicksburg, Miss., October 12, and duty there till July 29, 1864. Yazoo Expedition February 1-March 8. Liverpool Heights February 4. Capture of Yazoo City February 4. Satartia February 7. Occupation of Yazoo City till March 6. Action at Yazoo City March 5. At Black River Bridge till April 28. Expedition to Yazoo City May 4-21. Benton May 7-9. Vaughan May 12. Vaughan Station May 14. Expedition to Pearl River July 2-10. Jackson July 7. Clinton July 7. Moved to Morganza, La., July 29, and duty there till September 3. Expedition to Clinton, La., August 23-29. Moved to mouth of White River September 3, thence to Memphis, Tenn., October 8. Return to White River October 27. Expedition to Gaines' Landing November 6-7. Moved to Duvall's Bluff, Ark., November 8, thence to Memphis, Tenn., November 30-December 4. Expedition to Moscow, Tenn., December 20-31. Moved to Kenner, La., January 1-5, 1865. To Dauphin Island, Ala., February 4-7. Operations against Mobile, Ala., and its defences February 17-April 12. Siege of Spanish Fort and Fort Blakely March 26-April 8. Assault and capture of Fort Blakely April 9. Occupation of Mobile April 12. Duty there till May 27. Moved to New Orleans, thence to Alexandria. Moved to Baton Rouge, La., June 22. Mustered out July 14, 1865.

Regiment lost during service 7 Officers and 179 Enlisted men killed and mortally wounded and 1 Officer and 284 Enlisted men by disease. Total 471.

12th REGIMENT INFANTRY (3 MONTHS).

Organized at Springfield, Ill., and mustered in for three months' service May 2, 1861. Moved to Cairo, Ill., and garrison duty there till August. Mustered out August 1, 1861.

Lost 4 by disease during service.

12th REGIMENT INFANTRY (3 YEARS).

Organized at Cairo, Ill., August 1, 1861. Attached to District of Cairo, Ill., to October, 1861. 3rd Brigade, District of Cairo, to February, 1862. 1st Brigade, 2nd Division, District of Cairo, February, 1862. 2nd Brigade, 2nd Division, District of West Tennessee, and Army of the Tennessee, to July, 1862. 2nd Brigade,

2nd Division, District of Corinth, to September, 1862. 1st Brigade, 2nd Division, District of Corinth, to November, 1862. 2nd Brigade, District of Corinth, 13th Army Corps (Old), Dept. of the Tennessee, to December, 1862. 2nd Brigade, District of Corinth, 17th Army Corps, to January, 1863. 2nd Brigade, District of Corinth, 16th Army Corps, to March, 1863. 2nd Brigade, 2nd Division, 16th Army Corps, Army of the Tennessee, to September, 1864. 2nd Brigade, 4th Division, 15th Army Corps, to April, 1865. 1st Brigade, 1st Division, 15th Army Corps, to July, 1865.

SERVICE.—At Cairo, Ill., till September, 1861. Expedition to Belmont and Charleston September 2. Expedition to Paducah, Ky., September 5-6. Occupation of Paducah September 6, and duty there till February, 1862. (4 Cos. at Smithland, Ky., till January 25, 1862.) Demonstration on Columbus, Ky., November 8-9, 1861. Reconnoissance from Paducah to Fort Henry, Tenn., January 15-25, 1862. Demonstration on Columbus, Ky., January 25-28. Operations against Fort Henry, Tenn., February 5-6. Capture of Fort Henry February 6. Investment and capture of Fort Donelson, Tenn., February 12-16. Expedition to Clarksville and Nashville, Tenn., February 19-21. Moved to Pittsburg Landing, Tenn., March 1. Battle of Shiloh, Tenn., April 6-7. Advance on and siege of Corinth, Miss., April 29-May 30. Pursuit to Booneville May 31-June 6. Duty at Corinth, Miss., till September. March to Iuka September 16-18, thence to Burnsville September 19, and to Corinth October 2. Battle of Corinth October 3-4. Pursuit to Ripley October 5-12. Duty at Corinth till June, 1863. Grant's Central Mississippi Campaign November and December, 1862. Dodge's Expedition to Northern Alabama April 15-May 8, 1863. Rock Cut, near Tuscumbia, April 22. Tuscumbia April 23. Town Creek April 28. Moved to Pocahontas June 6, and duty there till October 29. March to Pulaski, Tenn., October 29-November 12. Moved to Richland Station November 25, and duty guarding Nashville & Decatur R. R. till January, 1864. Regiment Veteranize January 16, 1864. Veterans on furlough till March. Moved to Pulaski, Tenn. Atlanta (Ga.) Campaign May 1 to September 8. Demonstration on Resaca May 5-13. Near Resaca, Sugar Valley, May 9. Near Resaca May 13. Battle of Resaca May 14. Ley's Ferry, Oostenaula River, May 14-15. Rome Cross Roads May 16. (4 Cos. detached at Rome till June 24.) Operations on line of Pumpkin Vine Creek and battles about Dallas, New Hope Church and Allatoona Hills May 25-June 5. Operations about Marietta and against Kenesaw Mountain June 10-July 2. Assault on Kenesaw Mountain June 27. Nickajack Creek July 2-5. Ruff's Mills July 3-4. Chattahoochie River July 6-17. Decatur July 18-19. Battle of Atlanta July 22. Siege of Atlanta July 22-August 25. Utoy Creek August 5-7. Flank movement on Jonesboro August 25-30. Battle of Jonesboro August 31-September 1. Lovejoy Station September 2-6. Moved to Rome September 26, and duty there till November 11. Moved to Allatoona October 4. Battle of Allatoona October 5. Reconnoissance on Cave Springs Road and skirmishes October 12-13. March to the sea November 15-December 10. Ogeechee Canal December 9. Siege of Savannah December 10-21. Campaign of the Carolinas January to April, 1865. Salkehatchie Swamp, S. C., February 2-5. South Edisto River February 9. North Edisto River February 11-12. Columbia February 15-17. Camden February 24. Little Cohora Creek, N. C., March 16. Battle of Bentonville March 20-21. Occupation of Goldsboro March 24. Advance on Raleigh, N. C., April 9-14. Occupation of Raleigh April 14. Bennett's House April 26. Surrender of Johnston and his army. March to Washington, D. C., via Richmond, Va., April 29-May 19. Grand Review May 24. Moved to Louisville, Ky., June 3-6. Mustered out July 10, 1865, and discharged at Camp Butler, Ill., July 18, 1865.

Regiment lost during service 5 Officers and 143 Enlisted men killed and mortally wounded and 3 Officers and 109 Enlisted men by disease. Total 260.

13th REGIMENT INFANTRY.

Organized at Dixon, Ill., and mustered into State service April 21, 1861. Mustered into U. S. service by Capt. John Pope May 24, 1861, being the first three years Regiment from Illinois mustered into U. S. service. Moved to Caseyville, Ill., June 16, thence to Rolla, Mo., July 5-6, being first Regiment to cross Mississippi River into hostile Missouri. Attached to Fremont's Army of the West July to October, 1861. District of Rolla, Dept. of Missouri, to January, 1862. Unattached, Army of Southwest Missouri, to March, 1862. 1st Brigade, 2nd Division, Army of Southwest Missouri, to July, 1862. Helena, Ark., District of Eastern Arkansas, Dept. of Missouri, to November, 1862. 2nd Brigade, 2nd Division, District of Eastern Arkansas, Dept. of the Tennessee, to December, 1862. 2nd Brigade, 11th Division, 13th Army Corps (Old), Dept. of the Tennessee, December, 1862. 1st Brigade, 4th Division, Sherman's Yazoo Expedition, to January, 1863. 1st Brigade, 1st Division, 15th Army Corps, Army of the Tennessee, to April, 1864. Unassigned, 3rd Division, 15th Army Corps, to June, 1864.

SERVICE.—Duty at Rolla, Mo., till October 10, 1861. Fremont's advance on Springfield, Mo., October 10-November 7. Action at Wet Glaize October 13. Linn Creek October 15. Return to Rolla November 10, and duty there till March, 1862. Action at Salem, Mo., December 3, 1861. Ordered to join Curtis at Pea Ridge, Ark., March 6, 1862. March to Helena, Ark., April 8-July 14. Duty at Helena, Ark., till December. Sherman's Yazoo Expedition December 22, 1862-January 3, 1863. Chickasaw Bayou December 26-28. Chickasaw Bluffs December 29. Expedition to Arkansas Post, Ark., January 3-10, 1863. Assault and capture of Fort Hindman, Arkansas Post, January 10-11. Moved to Young's Point January 17, and duty there till March. Expedition to Greenville, Miss., February 14-26. Expedition from Milliken's Bend to Greenville, Black Bayou and Deer Creek, Miss., April 2-14. Demonstration against Haines' and Drumgould's Bluffs April 29-May 1. Moved to join army in rear of Jackson, Miss., via Richmond and Grand Gulf, May 2-14. Jackson May 14. Siege of Vicksburg, Miss., May 18-July 4. Assaults on Vicksburg May 19 and 22. Surrender of Vicksburg July 4. Advance on Jackson, Miss., July 5-10. Siege of Jackson July 10-17. Brandon July 19. Camp at Big Black till September 27. Movement to Memphis, thence to Chattanooga, Tenn., September 27-November 21. Operations on Memphis & Charleston R. R. in Alabama October 20-29. Cherokee Station October 21. Tuscumbia and Barton Station October 24-25. Bear Creek, Tuscumbia, October 27. Chattanooga-Ringgold Campaign November 23-27. Battles of Lookout Mountain November 23-24. Mission Ridge November 25. Captured flag of the 18th Alabama Infantry. Ringgold Gap, Taylor's Ridge, November 27. Stationed at Madison Station, Ala., till May, 1864. Action at Madison Station April 17. Resaca, Ga., May 13-15 (Detachment). Mustered out June 18, 1864.

Regiment lost during service 6 Officers and 61 Enlisted men killed and mortally wounded and 2 Officers and 123 Enlisted men by disease. Total 192.

14th REGIMENT INFANTRY.

Organized at Jacksonville, Ill., and mustered in May 25, 1861. Moved to Quincy, Ill., June 28, 1861. Attached to Dept. of Missouri to February, 1862. 2nd Brigade, 4th Division, District of West Tennessee, and Army of the Tennessee, to July, 1862. 2nd Brigade, 4th Division, District of Memphis, Tenn., to September, 1862. 2nd Brigade, 4th Division, District of Jackson, Tenn., to November, 1862. 2nd Brigade, 4th Division, Right Wing 13th Army Corps (Old), Dept. of the Tennessee, to December, 1862. 2nd Brigade, 4th Division, 17th Army Corps, Army of the Tennessee, to January, 1863. 2nd Brigade, 4th Division, 16th Army Corps, to July, 1863. 2nd Brigade, 4th Division, 13th Army Corps, to August, 1863. 2nd Brigade, 4th Division, 17th Army Corps, to November, 1864. 1st Brigade, 4th Division,

17th Army Corps, to April, 1865. 2nd Brigade, 4th Division, 17th Army Corps, to June, 1865. Dept. of Missouri to September, 1865.

SERVICE.—Moved to St. Charles, Mo., thence to Hannibal, Jefferson Barracks and Rolla, Mo., July-August, 1861. Advance toward Columbus August 29-September 8. Join Fremont's Army at Tipton, Mo., October 1. Fremont's advance on Springfield, Mo., October 13-November 3. Moved to Sedalia, thence to Otterville, and duty there till February, 1862. Moved to St. Louis, thence to Fort Donelson, Tenn., February 1-16. Capture of Fort Donelson February 16. Expedition to Crump's Landing and occupation of Pittsburg Landing, Tenn., March 14-17. Battle of Shiloh, Tenn., April 6-7. Advance on and siege of Corinth, Miss., April 29-May 30. March to Memphis, Tenn., via Grand Junction, Holly Springs and Lagrange, June 1-July 21. Duty at Memphis till September 6. March to Bolivar and forced march to Hatchie River September 6-October 4. Near Middletown October 4. Battle of the Hatchie, Metamora, October 5. Grant's Central Mississippi Campaign. Operations on the Mississippi Central R. R. from Bolivar to Coffeeville October 31, 1862, to January 10, 1863. Duty at Memphis, Tenn., till May, 1863. Ordered to Vicksburg, Miss., May 13. Siege of Vicksburg, Miss., May 22-July 4. Advance on Jackson, Miss., July 5-10. Siege of Jackson July 10-17. Assault on Jackson July 12. Moved to Natchez, Miss., August 15, and duty there till November 10. Expedition to Harrisonburg September 1-7. Near Harrisonburg and capture of Fort Beauregard September 4. Moved to Vicksburg November 10, and duty there till February 1, 1864. Meridian Campaign February 3-March 5. Champion's Hill, Baker's Creek, February 4. Movement to Cairo, Ill., thence to Clifton, Tenn., and march to Ackworth, Ga., via Huntsville and Decatur, Ala., and Rome, Ga., April 28-June 8. Atlanta (Ga.) Campaign June 8 to September 8. Assigned to garrison duty at Allatoona Pass, Ackworth, Big Shanty and Marietta, Ga., till November, 1864. Regiment consolidated with 15th Illinois Infantry July 1, 1864, as 14th and 15th Battalion Illinois Infantry. Action at Big Shanty October 3 (2 Cos.). Ackworth, Ga., October 4 (3 Cos.). Morris Station October 4 (Detachment). Allatoona Pass October 5 (Detachment). March to the sea November 15-December 10. Siege of Savannah December 10-21. Campaign of the Carolinas January to April, 1865. Pocotaligo, S. C., January 14-16. Salkehatchie Swamps February 2-5. Rivers' Bridge, Salkehatchie River, February 3. Binnaker's Bridge, South Edisto River, February 9. Orangeburg, North Edisto River, February 11-12. Columbia February 15-17. Cheraw March 3. Battle of Bentonville, N. C., March 19-21. Occupation of Goldsboro March 24, and of Raleigh April 14. Bennett's House April 26. Surrender of Johnston and his army. Regiment reorganized from 14th and 15th Battalion at Raleigh, N. C., April 28, 1865. March to Washington, D. C., via Richmond, Va., April 29-May 19. Grand Review May 24. Moved to Louisville, Ky., June 7-10, thence to St. Louis, Mo., and Fort Leavenworth, Kansas. March to Fort Kearney July 1-14, and duty on the plains till September 1. Ordered to Fort Leavenworth, Kansas, September 1. Mustered out at Fort Leavenworth, Kansas, September 18, 1865.

Regiment lost during service 62 Enlisted men killed and mortally wounded and 1 Officer and 160 Enlisted men by disease. Total 223.

15th REGIMENT INFANTRY.

Organized at Freeport, Ill., and mustered in May 24, 1861. Ordered to Alton, Ill., June 1, 1861, and duty there till July 15, 1861. Moved to St. Charles, Mo., thence to Hannibal, Jefferson Barracks and Rolla, Mo., July 15-August 7. Advance toward Columbus August 29-September 8. Join Fremont's Army at Tipton, Mo., October 1. Attached to Dept. of Missouri to February, 1862. 1st Brigade, 4th Division, District West Tennessee, to March, 1862. 2nd Brigade, 4th Division, District of West Tennessee, and Army of the Tennessee, to July, 1862. 2nd Brigade, 4th Division, District of Memphis, Tenn., to September, 1862. 2nd Brigade, 4th Division, District of Jackson, Tenn., to November, 1862. 2nd Brigade, 4th Division, Right Wing 13th Army Corps (Old), Dept. of the Tennessee, to December, 1862. 2nd Brigade, 4th Division, 17th Army Corps, Army of the Tennessee, to January, 1863. 2nd Brigade, 4th Division, 16th Army Corps, to July, 1863. 2nd Brigade, 4th Division, 13th Army Corps, to August, 1863. 2nd Brigade, 4th Division, 17th Army Corps, to November, 1864. 1st Brigade, 4th Division, 17th Army Corps, to April, 1865. 2nd Brigade, 4th Division, 17th Army Corps, to June, 1865. Dept. of Missouri to September, 1865.

SERVICE.—Fremont's advance on Springfield, Mo., October 13-November 3, 1861. Moved to Sedalia, thence to Otterville, and duty there till February, 1862. Moved to St. Louis, Mo.; thence to Fort Donelson, Tenn., February 1-16. Capture of Fort Donelson February 16. Expedition to Crump's Landing and occupation of Pittsburg Landing, Tenn., March 14-17. Battle of Shiloh, Tenn., April 6-7. Advance on and siege of Corinth, Miss., April 29-May 30. March to Memphis, Tenn., via Grand Junction, Holly Springs and Lagrange, June 1-July 21. Duty at Memphis till September 6. March to Bolivar and forced march to Hatchie River September 6-October 4. Battle of Hatchie River, or Metamora, October 5. Grant's Central Mississippi Campaign. Operations on the Mississippi Central R. R. from Bolivar to Coffeeville October 31, 1862, to January 10, 1863. Duty at Memphis, Tenn., till May, 1863. Ordered to Vicksburg, Miss., May 13. Siege of Vicksburg, Miss., May 22-July 4. Advance on Jackson, Miss., July 4-10. Siege of Jackson July 10-17. Assault on Jackson July 12. Reconnoissance to Pearl River July 15. Moved to Natchez, Miss., August 15, and duty there till November 10. Expedition to Harrisonburg September 1-7. Near Harrisonburg and capture of Fort Beauregard September 4. Moved to Vicksburg, Miss., November 10, and duty there till February, 1864. Meridian Campaign February 3-March 5. Champion's Hill, Baker's Creek, February 4. Movement to Cairo, Ill., thence to Clifton, Tenn., and march to Ackworth, Ga., via Huntsville and Decatur, Ala., and Rome, Ga., April 28-June 8. Atlanta Campaign June 8 to September 8. Assigned to garrison duty at Allatoona Pass, Ackworth, Big Shanty and Marietta till November. Regiment consolidated with 14th Illinois Infantry July 1, 1864, as 14th and 15th Illinois Battalion Infantry. Action at Big Shanty October 3 (2 Cos.). Ackworth October 4 (3 Cos.). Morris Station October 4 (Detachment). Allatoona Pass October 5 (Detachment). March to the sea November 15-December 10. Siege of Savannah December 10-21. Campaign of the Carolinas January to April, 1865. Pocotaliga, S. C., January 14-16. Combahee River January 25. Salkehatchie Swamps February 2-5. Rivers' Bridge, Salkehatchie River, February 3. South Edisto River, Binnaker's Bridge, February 9. Orangeburg, North Edisto River, February 11-12. Columbia February 15-17. Cheraw March 3. Battle of Bentonville March 19-21. Occupation of Goldsboro March 24, and of Raleigh April 14. Bennett's House April 26. Surrender of Johnston and his army. Regiment reorganized at Raleigh, N. C., April 28, 1865, from 14th and 15th Battalion Infantry. March to Washington, D. C., via Richmond, Va., April 29-May 19. Grand Review May 24. Moved to Louisville, Ky., June 7-10, thence to St. Louis, Mo., and Fort Leavenworth, Kansas. March to Fort Kearney July 1-14, and duty on the plains till September 1. Ordered to Fort Leavenworth, Kansas. Mustered out at Fort Leavenworth, Kansas, September 16, 1865.

Regiment lost during service 6 Officers and 81 Enlisted men killed and mortally wounded and 5 Officers and 135 Enlisted men by disease. Total 227.

16th REGIMENT INFANTRY.

Organized at Quincy, Ill., and mustered in May 24, 1861. Moved to Grand River, Mo., June 12, 1861, and duty as Railroad guard on Hannibal & St. Joseph R. R.

till September 10. Action at Monroe Station July 9 (Cos. "F" and "H"). Caldwell Station July 16. Operations about Kirksville August 16-21. Affairs at Hunnewell and Palmyra August 17. Operations in Northeast Missouri August 30-September 7. Expedition against Green's Guerrillas September 8-9. Moved to St. Joseph, Mo., September 10, and duty there till January 27, 1862. Skirmish at Platte City September 14, 1861. Attached to Dept. of Missouri to February, 1862. 4th Brigade, 1st Division, District of Cairo, February, 1862. 1st Brigade, 4th Division, Army of Mississippi, to April, 1862. 2nd Brigade, 1st Division, Army of Mississippi, to September, 1862. 2nd Brigade, 13th Division, Army of the Ohio, to November, 1862. 1st Brigade, 4th Division, Centre 14th Army Corps, Dept. of the Cumberland, to January, 1863. 1st Brigade, 4th Division, 14th Army Corps, Army of the Cumberland, to June, 1863. 1st Brigade, 2nd Division, Reserve Corps, Army of the Cumberland, to October, 1863. 1st Brigade, 2nd Division, 14th Army Corps, to July, 1865.

SERVICE.—Moved from St. Joseph, Mo., to Bird's Point, Mo., January 27, 1862, thence to New Madrid, Mo., March 3. Operations against New Madrid and Island No. 10 March 3-April 8. Actions at New Madrid March 12-14. Capture of New Madrid March 14. Island No. 10 April 6. Action and capture at Tiptonville April 8. Expedition to Fort Pillow, Tenn., April 13-17. Moved to Hamburg Landing, Tenn., April 17-24. Advance on and siege of Corinth, Miss., April 29-May 30. Action at Farmington May 3. Reconnoissance toward Corinth May 8. Pursuit to Booneville May 30-June 12. Tuscumbia Creek May 31-June 1. Reconnoissance toward Baldwyn June 3. At Clear Creek till July. March to Tuscumbia, Ala., July 20-25, thence to Nashville, Tenn., August 28-September 15. Action at Columbia September 10. Siege of Nashville September 15-November 6. Repulse of Forest's attack on Edgefield November 5. Duty at Nashville till July 20, 1863. Moved to Murfreesboro, Tenn., July 20, thence march to Columbia, Athens, Huntsville and Stevenson, Ala., August 24-September 7, and to Bridgeport, Ala., September 12. Duty there till October 1. Operations up the Sequatchie Valley against Wheeler October 1-17. Anderson's Cross Roads October 2. Moved to Waldron's Ridge, thence to Kelly's Ferry, and guard lines of transportation till January, 1864. Chattanooga-Ringgold Campaign November 23-27. Chickamauga Station November 26. Veterans on furlough January and February, 1864. Rejoined at Rossville, Ga. Demonstration on Dalton February 22-27. Tunnel Hill, Buzzard's Roost and Rocky Faced Ridge February 23-25. Atlanta Campaign May 1 to September 8. Demonstration on Rocky Faced Ridge May 5-11. Tunnel Hill May 6-7. Buzzard's Roost Gap May 8-9. Battle of Resaca May 14-15. Rome May 17-18. Operations on line of Pumpkin Vine Creek and battles about Dallas, New Hope Church and Allatoona Hills May 25-June 5. Operations about Marietta and against Kenesaw Mountain June 10-July 2. Pine Hill June 11-14. Lost Mountain June 15-17. Assault on Kenesaw June 27. Ruff's Station July 4. Chattahoochie River July 5-17. Vining Station July 17. Peach Tree Creek July 19-20. Siege of Atlanta July 22-August 25. Utoy Creek August 5-7. Flank movement on Jonesboro August 25-30. Battle of Jonesboro August 31-September 1. Operations in North Georgia and North Alabama against Forest and Hood September 29-November 3. Florence, Ala., October 6-7. March to the sea November 15-December 10. Sandersville November 26. Siege of Savannah December 10-21. Campaign of the Carolinas January to April, 1865. Fayetteville, N. C., March 11. Near Fayetteville March 13. Averysboro March 16. Battle of Bentonville March 19-21. Occupation of Goldsboro March 24. Advance on Raleigh April 10-14. Occupation of Raleigh April 14. Bennett's House April 26. Surrender of Johnston and his army. March to Washington, D. C., via Richmond, Va., April 29-May 19. Grand Review May 24. Moved to Louisville, Ky., June 12. Mustered out July 8, 1865.

Regiment lost during service 3 Officers and 54 Enlisted men killed and mortally wounded and 3 Officers and 110 Enlisted men by disease. Total 170.

17th REGIMENT INFANTRY.

Organized at Peoria, Ill., and mustered in May 24, 1861. Moved to Alton, Ill., June 17, 1861, thence to St. Charles and Warrenton, Mo., July 27. Moved to Bird's Point, Mo., August. Duty there, at Fort Holt, Ky., and Cape Girardeau, Mo., till February, 1862. Attached to District of Cairo to October, 1861. 5th Brigade, District of Cairo, to February, 1862. 3rd Brigade, 1st Division, District of Cairo, February, 1862. 3rd Brigade, 1st Division, District of West Tennessee, and Army of the Tennessee, to July, 1862. 3rd Brigade, 1st Division, District of Jackson, Tenn., to September, 1862. Unattached, District of Jackson, Tenn., to November, 1862. 4th Brigade, 3rd Division, Right Wing 13th Army Corps, Dept. of the Tennessee, November, 1862. 1st Brigade, 6th Division, 16th Army Corps, Army of the Tennessee, to January, 1863. 1st Brigade, 6th Division, 17th Army Corps, to July, 1863. 3rd Brigade, 3rd Division, 17th Army Corps, to April, 1864. Maltby's Brigade, District of Vicksburg, Miss., to June, 1864.

SERVICE.—Operations about Ironton and Fredericktown, Mo., against Thompson's forces October 12-25, 1861. Action at Fredericktown October 21. Expedition to Benton, Bloomfield and Dallas January 15-17, 1862. Operations against Fort Henry, Tenn., February 2-6. Investment and capture of Fort Donelson, Tenn., February 12-16. Moved to Savannah, thence to Pittsburg Landing, Tenn., March 5-25. Battle of Shiloh, Tenn., April 6-7. Advance on and siege of Corinth, Miss., April 29-May 30. March to Jackson June 5-8, and duty there till July 17. At Bolivar, Tenn., till November. Expedition to Iuka September 15-22. Grant's Central Mississippi Campaign November, 1862, to January, 1863. Reconnoissance from Lagrange November 8-9, 1862. Moved to Memphis, Tenn., January 12, 1863, thence to Lake Providence, La., January 17-24. Action at Richmond, La., January 29-30. Old River, Lake Providence, February 10. Moved to Milliken's Bend April 12. Movement on Bruinsburg and turning Grand Gulf April 25-30. Battles of Thompson's Hill, Port Gibson, May 1. Bayou Pierrie May 2. Raymond May 12. Jackson, Miss., May 14. Champion's Hill May 16. Big Black River May 17. Siege of Vicksburg, Miss., May 18-July 4. Assaults on Vicksburg May 19 and 22. Surrender of Vicksburg July 4. Garrison duty at Vicksburg till May, 1864. Expedition to Monroe, La., August 20-September 2, 1863. Expedition to Canton October 14-20. Bogue Chitto Creek October 17. Expedition from Vicksburg to Sunnyside Landing, Ark., January 10-16, 1864. Meridian Campaign February 3-March 2, 1864. Clinton February 5. Mustered out June 4, 1864, expiration of term. Veterans and Recruits transferred to 8th Illinois Infantry.

Regiment lost during service 3 Officers and 71 Enlisted men killed and mortally wounded and 1 Officer and 71 Enlisted men by disease. Total 146.

18th REGIMENT INFANTRY.

Organized at Aurora, Ill., and mustered into State service May 19, and into U. S. service May 28, 1861. Moved to Bird's Point, Mo., June 24, and duty there till August 26. Moved to Mound City August 26, and duty there till October 5. Moved to Cairo, Ill., October 5, and duty there till February, 1862. Attached to District of Cairo, to October, 1861. 1st Brigade, District of Cairo, to February, 1862. 1st Brigade, 1st Division, District of Cairo, February, 1862. 2nd Brigade, 1st Division, District of West Tenn., March, 1862. 1st Brigade, 1st Division, 1st District, West Tenn., and Army of the Tennessee, to July, 1862. 1st Brigade, 1st Division, District of Jackson, Tenn., to September, 1862. 2nd Brigade, 1st Division, District of Jackson, to November, 1862. District of Jackson, 13th Army Corps (Old), Dept. of the Tennessee, to December, 1862. 1st Brigade, District of Jackson, 16th Army Corps, to

March, 1863. 2nd Brigade, 3rd Division, 16th Army Corps, to May, 1863. 2nd Brigade, Kimball's Provisional Division, 16th Army Corps, to July, 1863. 2nd Brigade, Kimball's Provisional Division, District of Eastern Ark., to August, 1863. 1st Brigade, 2nd Division, Arkansas Expedition, to November, 1863. 3rd Brigade, 2nd Division, Arkansas Expedition, to January, 1864. 3rd Brigade, 2nd Division, 7th Army Corps, Dept. of Arkansas, to April, 1864. Post Pine Bluff, Ark., 7th Army Corps, to May, 1864. 1st Brigade, 2nd Division, 7th Army Corps, to January, 1865. Pontoneers, 7th Army Corps, to May, 1865. 1st Brigade, 1st Division, 7th Army Corps, to August, 1865. Dept. of Arkansas, to December, 1865.

SERVICE.—Expedition against Thompson's forces at Bloomfield, Mo., November 2-12, 1861. Expedition toward Columbus January 16-21, 1862. Operations against Fort Henry, Tenn., February 2-8. Capture of Fort Henry February 6. Investment and capture of Fort Donelson February 12-16. Moved to Pittsburg Landing, Tenn., March 11-23. Battle of Shiloh, Tenn., April 6-7. Advance on and siege of Corinth, Miss., April 29-May 30. Moved to Bethel June 4-6, thence to Jackson June 15, and duty there till May 30, 1863. Expedition to Bolivar and Brownville July 27-August 13, 1862. Grant's Central Mississippi Campaign October 31, 1862, to January 10, 1863. (Co. "K" left Regiment, December 11, 1862, to join Miss. Marine Brigade.) Operations against Forest, in West Tennessee December 18, 1862, to January 3, 1863. Clarksburg, Tenn., December 30, 1862 (Cos. "A" and "E"). Engagement at Red Mound, Parker's Cross Roads, December 30-31 (Detachment). Near Clifton January 3, 1863. Expedition to Huntington March 4-10. Scout to Trenton March 16-18. Expedition to Covington, Tenn., April 1-10, and to Summerville April 11-16. Moved to Vicksburg, Miss., May 30-June 2. Siege of Vicksburg, Miss., June 4-July 4. Occupation of Hickman, Ky., July 15-16 (Co. "K"). Moved to Helena, Ark., July 24-27. Steele's Expedition against Little Rock, Ark., August 1-September 10. Bayou Fourche and capture of Little Rock September 10. Duty at Little Rock, Pine Bluff and Duvall's Bluff, Ark., till December, 1865. Expedition from Pine Bluff to Mt. Elba and Longview March 27-31, 1864. Actions at Mt. Elba March 28 and 30. Non-Veterans mustered out May 28, 1864. Regiment mustered out at Little Rock, Ark., December 16, and discharged at Camp Butler, Ill., December 31, 1865.

Regiment lost during service 6 Officers and 99 Enlisted Men killed and mortally wounded and 7 Officers and 282 Enlisted men by disease. Total 394.

19th REGIMENT INFANTRY.

Four Chicago Companies mustered into State service at Camp Yates May 4, 1861. Regiment organized at Chicago, Ill., and mustered in June 17, 1861. Moved to Quincy, Ill., July 12-13, 1861. Thence to Palmyra, Mo., July 14, and guard Hannibal and St. Jo. R. R. from Quincy to Palmyra and between Palmyra and Hannibal till July 27. Moved to Hannibal, thence to St. Louis, Mo., and to Bird's Point and Norfolk, Mo., and duty at Norfolk till August 14. Moved to Ironton, Mo., August 14. Attached to Department of Missouri to September, 1861. Dept. of Kentucky to October, 1861. Elizabethtown, Ky., Dept. of the Cumberland, to November, 1861. 8th Brigade, Army of the Ohio, to December, 1861. 8th Brigade, 3rd Division, Army of the Ohio, to July, 1862. Unattached R. R. Guard, Army of the Ohio, to September, 1862. 29th Brigade, 8th Division, Army of the Ohio, to November, 1862. 2nd Brigade, 2nd Division, Centre 14th Army Corps, Army of the Cumberland, to January, 1863. 2nd Brigade, 2nd Division, 14th Army Corps, to October, 1863. 2nd Brigade, 1st Division, 14th Army Corps, October, 1863. 1st Brigade, 3rd Division, 14th Army Corps, to July, 1864.

SERVICE.—Prentiss' Expedition toward Dallas and Jackson, Mo., August 29-September 8, 1861. Moved to Cape Girardeau, Fort Holt, Ky., and Elliott's Mills, thence moved to Cairo, Ill., September 16, under orders for Washington, D. C. While en route East, September 17, via Ohio & Mississippi R. R., bridge No. 48, over Beaver Creek, 30 miles west of Cincinnati, Ohio, broke through, precipitating six passenger coaches a distance of 60 feet, killing and wounding 129 of the Regiment. At Camp Dennison, Ohio, till September 24. Moved to Louisville, Ky., September 24-25, thence to Lebanon, Ky., September 25, and duty there till October 22. Moved to Elizabethtown, Ky., October 22, and duty there and at Bacon Creek till February 10, 1862. Advance on Bowling Green, Ky., February 10-15. Occupation of Bowling Green February 15, thence advance to Nashville, Tenn., February 22-25. Occupation of Nashville February 25 to March 18. Advance to Murfreesboro, Tenn., March 18, thence to Shelbyville, Tullahoma and McMinnville March 25-28. Advance on Huntsville, Ala., via Fayetteville April 4-11. Occupation of Huntsville April 11. Advance on and capture of Decatur and Tuscumbia, Ala., April 11-14. Action at Tuscumbia April 24. Athens May 13. At Huntsville till May 26. Moved to Fayetteville May 26-June 2. Negley's Expedition to Chattanooga, Tenn., June 2-10. Chattanooga June 7-8. Expedition to Larkinsville and Stevenson, Ala., June 14-20. Winchester June 16. Guard R. R. and bridges from Huntsville to Decatur till August. Richland Creek, near Pulaski, August 27. Retreat to Nashville, Tenn., August 27-29. Siege of Nashville September 5-November 6. Repulse of Forest's attack on Edgefield November 5. At Nashville till December 26. Advance on Murfreesboro, Tenn., December 26-30. Battle of Stone River December 30-31, 1862, and January 1-3, 1863. At Murfreesboro till June. Middle Tennessee (or Tullahoma Campaign) June 24-July 7. Occupation of Middle Tennessee till August 16. Passage of Cumberland Mountains and Tennessee River and Chickamauga, Ga., Campaign August 16-September 22. Davis' Cross Roads, Ga., September 11. Battle of Chickamauga, Ga., September 18-21. Rossville Gap September 21. Siege of Chattanooga September 24-November 23. Chattanooga-Ringgold Campaign November 23-27. Orchard Knob November 23-24. Mission Ridge November 25. Pursuit to Ringgold, Ga., November 26-27. Pea Vine Valley and Graysville November 26. At Chattanooga till February 22, 1864. Demonstration on Dalton, Ga., February 22-27. Tunnel Hill, Buzzard's Roost Gap and Rocky Faced Ridge February 23-25. At Graysville till May 3. Atlanta (Ga.) Campaign May 3-June 8. Demonstration on Rocky Faced Ridge May 8-11. Battle of Resaca May 14-15. Kingston May 18-19. Advance on Dallas May 22-25. Operations on line of Pumpkin Vine Creek and battles about Dallas, New Hope Church and Allatoona Hills May 25-June 5. At Ackworth, Ga., till June 8. Moved to Chicago June 8-17. Mustered out July 9, 1864; expiration of term.

Regiment lost during service 4 Officers and 60 Enlisted men killed and mortally wounded and 4 Officers and 101 Enlisted men by disease. Total 169.

20th REGIMENT INFANTRY.

Organized at Joliet, Ill., and mustered in June 13, 1861. Moved to Alton, Ill., June 18, thence to St. Louis, Mo., July 6, and to Cape Girardeau, Mo., July 10, 1861. Attached to District of Cairo to October, 1861. Bird's Point, Mo., unattached to February, 1862. 2nd Brigade, 1st Division, District of Cairo, February, 1862. 2nd Brigade, 1st Division, District of West Tennessee, and Army of the Tennessee to July, 1862. 2nd Brigade, 1st Division, District of Jackson, Tenn., to September, 1862. 3rd Brigade, 1st Division, District of Jackson, to November, 1862. 1st Brigade, 3rd Division, Right Wing 13th Army Corps, Dept. of the Tennessee, to December, 1862. 1st Brigade, 3rd Division, 17th Army Corps, Army of the Tennessee, to July, 1864. Provost Guard, 3rd Division, 17th Army Corps, to April, 1865. 1st Brigade, 3rd Division, 17th Army Corps, to July, 1865.

SERVICE.—Duty at Cape Girardeau, Mo., till September 12, 1861. Expedition to Price's Landing, Commerce, Benton and Hamburg August 7-10 (Co. "F").

Expedition to Jackson August 28-September 5. Moved to Bird's Point, Mo., September 12, and duty there till February, 1862. Operations about Ironton and Fredericktown October 12-25, 1861. Action at Fredericktown October 21. Charleston January 8, 1862. Expedition toward Columbus, Ky., January 15-21. Operations against Fort Henry, Tenn., February 2-6, 1862. Occupation of Fort Henry February 6-12. Investment and capture of Fort Donelson, Tenn., February 12-16. Moved to Savannah March 5-13, thence to Pittsburg Landing March 23-25. Battle of Shiloh, Tenn., April 6-7. Advance on and siege of Corinth, Miss., April 29-May 30. March to Purdy, thence to Jackson, Tenn., June 5-8, and duty there till August 15. At Oustenaula, Tenn., till August 31. Medon Station, Mississippi Central R. R., August 31 (4 Companies). Toon's Station, Mississippi Central R. R., August 31 (Detachment). Britton's Lane September 1. At Jackson till October 22. Guard bridges along Mobile & Ohio R. R. till November 8. Grant's Central Mississippi Campaign November 8, 1862, to January 10, 1863. Reconnoissance from LaGrange November 8-9, 1862. Holly Springs, Miss., December 20 (Detachment). Moved to Memphis, Tenn., January 12, 1863, and duty there till February 20. Moved to Lake Providence, La., February 20-24, thence to Berry's Landing March 16. Moved to Milliken's Bend April 19. Passage of Vicksburg and Warrenton batteries April 22 (Detachment). Movement on Bruinsburg and turning Grand Gulf April 25-30. Battles of Thompson's Plantation, or Port Gibson, May 1. Raymond May 12. Jackson May 14. Champion's Hill May 16. Big Black River May 17. Siege of Vicksburg, Miss., May 18-July 4. Assaults on Vicksburg May 19-22 and June 25. Surrender of Vicksburg July 4. Occupation of Vicksburg July 4 to November 6. Stephenson's Expedition to Monroe, La., August 20-September 2. Expedition to Canton October 14-20. Bogue Chitto Creek October 17. At Big Black November 6 to February 4, 1864. Meridian Campaign February 4-March 1. Meridian February 13-14. Chunky Station February 14. Canton February 29. Veterans absent on furlough March 2 to April 22. Moved to Cairo, Ill., April 28, thence to Clifton, Tenn., April 30-May 5. March to Huntsville, Ala., May 5-23, thence to Ackworth, Ga., via Decatur and Warrenton, Ala., and Rome and Kingston, Ga., May 28-June 8. Atlanta (Ga.) Campaign June 8-September 8. Operations about Marietta and against Kenesaw Mountain June 10-July 2. Assault on Kenesaw June 27. Nickajack Creek July 2-5. Howell's Ferry July 5. Chattahoochie River July 6-17. Leggett's Bald Hill July 20-21. Battle of Atlanta July 22. Siege of Atlanta July 22-August 25. Flank movement on Jonesboro August 25-30. Battle of Jonesboro August 31-September 1. Lovejoy Station September 2-6. Operations in North Georgia and North Alabama against Hood September 28-November 3. March to the sea November 15-December 10. Siege of Savannah December 10-21. Campaign of the Carolinas January to April, 1865. Salkehatchie Swamp, S. C., February 1-5. Barker's Mills, Whippy Swamp, February 2. South Edisto River February 9. North Edisto River February 11-12. Columbia February 15-17. Fayetteville, N. C., March 13. Battle of Bentonville March 20-21. Occupation of Goldsboro March 24. Advance on Raleigh April 10-14. Occupation of Raleigh April 14. Bennett's House April 26. Surrender of Johnston and his army. March to Washington, D. C., via Richmond, Va., April 29-May 19. Grand Review May 24. Moved to Louisville, Ky., June 7-12. Mustered out July 16 and discharged at Chicago, Ill., July 24, 1865.

Regiment lost during service 7 Officers and 132 Enlisted men killed and mortally wounded and 1 Officer and 191 Enlisted men by disease. Total 331.

21st REGIMENT INFANTRY.

Organized at Mattoon, Ill., and mustered in June 28, 1861. Ordered to Ironton, Mo., July 3, 1861. Operations on line of Hannibal & St. Jo. R. R. at Mexico, Mo., till August. Reached Ironton, Mo., August 9.

Attached to Department of Missouri to March, 1862. Steele's Command, Army of Southeast Missouri, to May, 1862. 2nd Brigade, 4th Division, Army of Mississippi, to September, 1862. 31st Brigade, 9th Division, Army of the Ohio, to October, 1862. 31st Brigade, 9th Division, 3rd Army Corps, Army of the Ohio, to November, 1862. 2nd Brigade, 1st Division, Right Wing 14th Army Corps, Army of the Cumberland, to January, 1863. 2nd Brigade, 1st Division, 20th Army Corps, Army of the Cumberland, to October, 1863. 1st Brigade, 1st Division, 4th Army Corps, Army of the Cumberland, to June, 1865. 2nd Brigade, 1st Division, 4th Army Corps, to August, 1865. Department of Texas to December, 1865.

SERVICE.—Duty at Ironton, Mo., till January, 1862. Operations about Ironton, Mo., October 17-25, 1861. Action at Fredericktown October 21. March from Ironton to Greenville January 29, 1862, and duty there till March. Moved to Reeve's Station, on Black River, March 3-10, thence to Doniphan and Pocohontas, Ark., March 31-April 21. Action at Putnam Ferry April 1. March to Jacksonport, Ark., April 30-May 4, thence to Cape Girardeau, Mo., May 10-21, and to Hamburg Landing May 21-24. Siege of Corinth, Miss., May 26-30. Pursuit to Booneville May 31-June 12. March to Jacinto and Ripley June 29-July 4. At Corinth, till August 14. March through Alabama to Nashville, Tenn., and to Louisville, Ky., in pursuit of Bragg, August 14-September 26. Pursuit of Bragg into Kentucky October 1-16. Battle of Perryville October 8. Stanford October 14. March to Nashville, Tenn., October 16-November 9, and duty there till December 26. Advance on Murfreesboro December 26-30. Nolensville, Knob Gap, December 26. Battle of Stone River December 30-31, 1862, and January 1-3, 1863. At Murfreesboro till June. Reconnoissance from Murfreesboro March 6-7. Methodist Church, Shelbyville Pike, March 6. Reconnoissance to Versailles March 9-14. Middle Tennessee (or Tullahoma) Campaign June 24-July 7. Liberty Gap June 24-27. Occupation of Middle Tennessee till August 16. Passage of Cumberland Mountains and Tennessee River and Chickamauga (Ga.) Campaign August 16-September 22. Battle of Chickamauga, Ga., September 19-20. Siege of Chattanooga September 24-October 27. Reopening Tennessee River October 26-29. Duty at Bridgeport, Ala., till January 26, 1864. Moved to Ooltewah January 26. Veterans absent on furlough till June. Non-Veterans attached to 101st Ohio Infantry till June 4, when Veterans returned. Atlanta Campaign May to September, 1864. Tunnel Hill May 6-7. Demonstration on Rocky Faced Ridge May 8-11. Buzzard's Roost Gap May 8-9. Demonstrations on Dalton May 9-13. Battle of Resaca May 14-15. Near Kingston May 18-19. Near Cassville May 19. Advance on Dallas May 23-25. Operations on line of Pumpkin Vine Creek and battle about Dallas, New Hope Church and Allatoona Hills May 25-June 5. Operations about Marietta and against Kenesaw Mountain June 10-July 2. Pine Mount June 10. Pine Hill June 11-14. Lost Mountain June 15-17. Assault on Kenesaw June 27. Ruff's Station July 4. Chattahoochie River July 5-17. Peach Tree Creek July 19-20. Siege of Atlanta July 22-August 25. Flank movement on Jonesboro August 25-30. Battle of Jonesboro August 31-September 1. Lovejoy Station September 2-6. Pursuit of Hood into Alabama October 3-30. Nashville Campaign November-December. Columbia, Duck River, November 24-27. Spring Hill November 29. Battle of Franklin November 30. Battle of Nashville December 15-16. Pursuit of Hood to the Tennessee River December 17-28. March to Huntsville, Ala., and duty there till March 13, 1865. Operations in East Tennessee till April 11. At Nashville, Tenn., till June. Moved to New Orleans, La., June 17-25, thence to Indianola, Texas, July 12-15. Duty at San Antonio, Texas, till December. Mustered out at San Antonio, Texas, December 16, and discharged at Camp Butler, Ill., January 18, 1866.

Regiment lost during service 6 Officers and 124 Enlisted men killed and mortally wounded and 2 Officers and 140 Enlisted men by disease. Total 272.

22nd REGIMENT INFANTRY.

Organized at Belleville, Ill., and mustered in June 25, 1861. Moved to Bird's Point, Mo., July 11, 1861. Attached to District of Cairo to October, 1861. 2nd Brigade, District of Cairo, to February, 1862. 4th Brigade, 1st Division, District of Cairo, February, 1862. 2nd Brigade, 4th Division, Army of the Mississippi, to April, 1862. 1st Brigade, 1st Division, Army of the Mississippi, to September, 1862. 1st Brigade, 13th Division, Army of the Ohio, to November, 1862. 3rd Brigade, 3rd Division, Right Wing 14th Army Corps, Army of the Cumberland, to January, 1863. 3rd Brigade, 3rd Division, 20th Army Corps, Army of the Cumberland, to October, 1863. 3rd Brigade, 2nd Division, 4th Army Corps, to July, 1864.

SERVICE.—Duty at Bird's Point, Mo., till February, 1862. Charlestown-Bird's Point August 19-20, 1861 (Cos. "A," "B," "C," "D," "E"). Hunter's Farm, near Belmont and near Norfolk, September 26. Expedition to Belmont November 6-7. Battle of Belmont November 7. Expedition to Milford December 15-19. Milford December 18. Charlestown January 8, 1862. Operations against New Madrid and Island No. 10 February 28-April 8. Sykestown March 1. Actions at New Madrid March 13-14. Action and capture at Tiptonville April 8. Expedition to Fort Pillow, Tenn., April 13-17. Moved to Hamburg Landing, Tenn., April 17-23. Advance on and siege of Corinth, Miss., April 29-May 30. Action at Farmington May 3. Reconnoissance toward Corinth May 8. Action at Farmington May 9. Pursuit to Booneville May 31-June 12. At Corinth till July 20. March to Tuscumbia, Ala., July 20. Guard Memphis & Charleston R. R. in Alabama till August 26. March to Nashville, Tenn., August 26-September 12. Siege of Nashville, Tenn., September 12-November 6. Repulse of Forest's attack on Edgefield November 5. Duty at Nashville till December 26. Advance on Murfreesboro, Tenn., December 26-30. Battle of Stone's River, December 30-31, 1862, and January 1-3, 1863. Duty at Murfreesboro till June. Expedition to Columbia March 4-14. Middle Tennessee (or Tullahoma) Campaign June 24-July 7. Occupation of Middle Tennessee till August 16. Passage of Cumberland Mountains and Tennessee River and Chickamauga Campaign August 16-September 22. Battle of Chickamauga September 19-20. Siege of Chattanooga September 24-November 23. Battles of Chattanooga November 23-25. Orchard Knob November 23-24. Mission Ridge November 25. March to relief of Knoxville November 28-December 8. Operations in East Tennessee till February, 1864. Operations about Dandridge January 16-17, 1864. Veterans on furlough February 10 to March 30. At Cleveland, Tenn., till May. Atlanta (Ga.) Campaign May to July. Demonstrations on Rocky Faced Ridge May 8-11. Buzzard's Roost Gap May 8-9. Battle of Resaca May 14-15. Adairsville May 17. Near Kingston May 18-19. Near Cassville May 19. Advance on Dallas May 22-25. Operations on line of Pumpkin Vine Creek and battles about Dallas, New Hope Church and Allatoona Hills May 25-June 5. Operations about Marietta and against Kenesaw Mountain June 10-July 2. Pine Hill June 11-14. Lost Mountain June 15-17. Assault on Kenesaw June 27. Mustered out July 7, 1864, expiration of term. Veterans and Recruits transferred to 42nd Illinois Infantry.

Regiment lost during service 2 Officers and 145 Enlisted men killed and mortally wounded, and 2 Officers and 101 Enlisted men by disease. Total 250.

23rd REGIMENT INFANTRY ("IRISH BRIGADE").

Organized at Chicago, Ill., and mustered in June 15, 1861. Moved to Quincy, Ill., July 14, thence to St. Louis, Mo., and to Jefferson City July 21, and duty there till September 8. March to Lexington September 8-11. Siege of Lexington September 12-20. Captured by Price September 20 and paroled. Regiment mustered out by order of General Fremont October 8, 1861, but restored by order of General McClellan, December 10, 1861. Reassembled at Chicago and guard prisoners at Camp Douglas till June 14, 1862. Moved to Harper's Ferry, West Va., June 14. Attached to R. R. District, Mountain Department, Harper's Ferry and New Creek to July, 1862. R. R. District, 8th Army Corps, Middle Department, to September, 1862. R. R. District West Va. to January, 1863. New Creek, Va., Defences Upper Potomac, 8th Army Corps, Middle Department, to March, 1863. 5th Brigade, 1st Division, 8th Army Corps, to June, 1863. Mulligan's Brigade, Scammon's Division Dept. of West Virginia to December, 1863. 2nd Brigade, 2nd Division, West Virginia, to April, 1864. Kelly's Command, Reserve Division, West Virginia, to July, 1864. 1st Brigade, 3rd Infantry, Division West Virginia, to July, 1864. 3rd Brigade, 1st Infantry Division, West Virginia, to December, 1864. 2nd Brigade, Independent Division, 24th Army Corps, Army of the James, to June, 1865. 1st Brigade, Independent Division, 24th Army Corps, to July, 1865.

SERVICE.—Duty at New Creek, West Va., till April, 1863. Relief of Clarksburg, W. Va., September 1, 1862. Relief of Parkersburg September 3. Action at Moorefield, South Fork of the Potomac, November 9 (Cos. "B," "D," "K"). Relief of Colonel Washburn at Moorefield January 3-4, 1863. Moved to Grafton April 25, 1863. Skirmish at Greenland Gap April 25 (Co. "G"). Phillippi April 26. Altamont April 26 (Detachment). Rowlesburg April 28 (Cos. "B," "F," "I"). Fairmont April 29 (Co. "K"). Pursuit of Lee July, 1863. Hedgesville and Back Creek July 6. At Petersburg, W. Va., August 16. Petersburg Gap September 4. South Fork September 11 (Co. "I"). Moorefield November 8-9. Demonstration from Kanawha Valley, W. Va., December 8-25. Operations in Hampshire and Hardy Counties December 31, 1863, to January 5, 1864, and January 27 to February 7. Medley January 29-30. Regiment veteranize at New Creek April, 1864, and on furlough till June. Scout to Moorefield February 21-22 (Detachment). Raid on Baltimore & Ohio Railroad between Bloomfield and Piedmont May 5 (Non-Veterans). Leetown July 3. Operations about Harper's Ferry July 4-7. Bolivar Heights July 4-6. Maryland Heights July 6-7. Snicker's Ferry July 17-18 and July 20. Kernstown (or Winchester) July 24. Medley July 30. Sheridan's Shenandoah Valley Campaign August 7 to November 28. Cedar Creek August 12. Winchester August 17. Halltown August 22-23. Berryville September 3. Battle of Winchester September 19. Fisher's Hill September 22. Duty in the Shenandoah Valley till December. Moved to Petersburg front December 30. Siege operations against Petersburg and Richmond January to April, 1865. Duty in trenches before Richmond and on the Bermuda Hundred front till March 27. Moved to Hatcher's Run March 27-28. Appomattox Campaign March 28-April 9. Hatcher's Run March 30-31 and April 1. Assault on Fort Gregg and fall of Petersburg April 2. Pursuit of Lee April 3-9. Appomattox Court House April 9. Surrender of Lee and his army. Duty in the Department of Virginia till July. Mustered out at Richmond, Va., July 24, and discharged at Chicago, Ill., July 30, 1865.

Regiment lost during service 4 Officers and 50 Enlisted men killed and mortally wounded and 2 Officers and 93 Enlisted men by disease. Total 149.

24th REGIMENT INFANTRY ("1st HECKER REGT.")

Organized at Chicago, Ill., and mustered in July 8, 1861. Moved to Alton, Ill., July 10, 1861, thence to St. Charles and Mexico, Mo. Moved to Ironton, Mo., July 28. Reconnoissance from Ironton to Centreville August 2. Moved to Pilot Knob, Mo., August 8. Moved to Cape Girardeau, Mo., thence to Cairo, Ill., and ordered to Washington, D. C., September 15. Moved to Cincinnati, Ohio; thence ordered to Louisville, Ky., September 28. Attached to Thomas Command, Department of the Ohio, to November, 1861. 8th Brigade, Army of the Ohio, to December, 1861. 8th Brigade, 3rd Division, Army of the Ohio, to July, 1862. Unat-

tached R. R. Guard to September, 1862. 28th Brigade, 3rd Division, Army of the Ohio, to October, 1862. 28th Brigade, 3rd Division, 1st Army Corps, Army of the Ohio, to November, 1862. 3rd Brigade, 1st Division, Centre, 14th Army Corps, Army of the Cumberland, to January, 1863. 3rd Brigade, 1st Division, 14th Army Corps, Army of the Cumberland, to April, 1863. 2nd Brigade, 1st Division, 14th Army Corps, to October, 1863. 3rd Brigade, 1st Division, 14th Army Corps, to May, 1864. 1st Brigade, 3rd Division, 14th Army Corps, to August, 1864.

SERVICE.—Duty at Muldraugh's Hill, Ky., till November 30, 1861. At Elizabethtown, Ky., till December 22, and at Beacon Creek, Ky., till February 10, 1862. Advance on Bowling Green, Ky., February 10-15. Occupation of Bowling Green February 15-23. Advance on Nashville, Tenn., February 23-25. Occupation of Nashville February 25-March 18. Advance on Murfreesboro March 18-19. Reconnoissance to Shelbyville, Tullahoma and McMinnville March 25-28. Advance on Huntsville, Ala., April 4-11. Capture of Huntsville April 11. Advance on and capture of Decatur and Tuscumbia April 11-14. Occupation of Decatur April 13. Occupation of Tuscumbia till April 22. Moved to Jonesboro April 22-24, and to Decatur and Huntsville April 25-30. Moved to Athens May 1, and duty there till May 26. Negley's Expedition to Chattanooga, Tenn., May 26-June 11. Chattanooga June 7-8. March to Jasper June 11-16. Rankin's Ferry, near Jasper and Battle Creek, June 21. At Battle Creek till July 11, thence moved to Tullahoma and duty on Nashville & Chattanooga R. R. till September. March to Nashville, thence to Louisville, Ky., September 7-28. Pursuit of Bragg into Kentucky October 1-16. Battle of Perryville, Ky., October 8. Duty at Mitchellsville till December. March to Nashville December 7-9. Advance on Murfreesboro December 26-30. Action at Jefferson December 30. Battle of Stone's River December 31, 1862, and January 1-3, 1863. Duty at Murfreesboro till June. Expedition to McMinnville April 20-30. Middle Tennessee (or Tullahoma) Campaign June 24-July 7. Hoover's Gap June 24-26. Occupation of Middle Tennessee till August 16. Passage of Cumberland Mountains and Tennessee River and Chickamauga (Ga.) Campaign August 16-September 22. Dug Gap, Ga., September 11. Battle of Chickamauga September 19-21. Rossville Gap September 21. Siege of Chattanooga September 24-November 23. Chattanooga-Ringgold Campaign November 23-27. Orchard Knob November 23-24. Mission Ridge November 25. Pursuit to Stevens' Gap November 26-27. At Chattanooga till February, 1864. Scout from Chattanooga to Harrison and Ooltewah January 21, 1864. Demonstration on Dalton, Ga., February 22-27. Tunnel Hill, Buzzard's Roost Gap and Rocky Faced Ridge February 23-25. At Tyner's Station and Graysville, Ga., till May, 1864. Atlanta (Ga.) Campaign May 1-June 28. Demonstration against Rocky Faced Ridge May 8-11. Battle of Resaca May 14-15. Advance on Dallas May 22-25. Operations on line of Pumpkin Vine Creek and battles about Dallas, New Hope Church and Allatoona Hills May 25-June 5. Operations about Marietta and against Kenesaw Mountain June 10-28. Pine Hill June 11-14. Lost Mountain June 15-17. Assault on Kenesaw Mountain June 27. Sent to rear June 28 for muster out. Mustered out August 6, 1864. Expiration of term.

Regiment lost during service 3 Officers and 86 Enlisted men killed and mortally wounded and 2 Officers and 82 Enlisted men by disease. Total 173.

25th REGIMENT INFANTRY.

Organized at St. Louis, Mo., and mustered in August 4, 1861. Attached to Department of Missouri to January, 1862. 4th Brigade, Army of Southwest Missouri, to March, 1862. 1st Brigade, 1st Division, Army of Southwest Missouri, to June, 1862. 1st Brigade, 4th Division, Army of the Mississippi, to September, 1862. 32nd Brigade, 9th Division, Army of the Ohio, to October, 1862. 32nd Brigade, 9th Division, 3rd Army

Corps, Army of the Ohio, to November, 1862. 3rd Brigade, 1st Division, Right Wing, 14th Army Corps, Army of the Cumberland, to January, 1863. 3rd Brigade, 1st Division, 20th Army Corps, Army of the Cumberland, to October, 1863. 1st Brigade, 3rd Division, 4th Army Corps, to August, 1864.

SERVICE.—At St. Louis, Mo., till August 23, 1861. Moved to Jefferson City, Mo. Fremont's Campaign against Springfield, Mo., September 25-November 8. March to Rolla, Mo., November 13-19, and duty there till February, 1862. Advance on Springfield, Mo., February 2-13. Skirmish at Crane Creek February 14. Pursuit of Price, to Benton County, Arkansas. Battles of Pea Ridge, Ark., March 6-8. March to Batesville April 5-May 3. Moved to Cape Girardeau, Mo., May 11-20, thence to Pittsburg Landing, Tenn., May 22-26. Advance on and siege of Corinth, Miss., April 29-May 30. Pursuit to Boonesville May 31-June 6. Duty at Jacinto, Miss., till August 4. Reconnoissance to Bay Springs August 4-7. Skirmish at Bay Springs August 4. March to Nashville, Tenn., August 21-September 1, thence to Louisville, Ky., in pursuit of Bragg, September 2-26. Pursuit of Bragg into Kentucky October 1-15. Near Perryville October 6-7. Chaplin Hills, Perryville, October 8. Stanford October 14. March to Nashville, Tenn., October 17-November 7. Skirmish at White Range, Tenn., November 7. Expedition to Harpeth Shoals and Clarksville November 26-December 1. Reconnoissance toward Franklin December 9. Near Brentwood December 9. Advance on Murfreesboro December 26-30. Nolensville Knob Gap December 26. Battle of Stone's River December 30-31, 1862, and January 1-3, 1863. Duty at Murfreesboro till June. Reconnoissance to Salem and Versailles March 9-14. Operations on Edgeville Pike June 4. Middle Tennessee (or Tullahoma) Campaign June 24-July 7. Liberty Gap June 24-27. Occupation of Middle Tennessee till August 16. Passage of Cumberland Mountains and Tennessee River and Chickamauga (Ga.) Campaign August 16-September 22. Caperton's Ferry, near Bridgeport, August 29. Battle of Chickamauga September 19-20. Siege of Chattanooga September 24-October 26. Chattanooga-Ringgold Campaign November 23-26. Orchard Knob November 23-24. Mission Ridge November 25. March to relief of Knoxville November 28-December 8. Operations in East Tennessee till February, 1864. At Cleveland, Tenn., till June. Guard train to front June 4-7. Atlanta Campaign June 7-August 1. Operations about Marietta and against Kenesaw Mountain June 10-July 2. Pine Hill June 11-14. Lost Mountain June 15-17. Assault on Kenesaw June 27. Ruff's Station July 4. Chattahoochie River July 6-17. Peach Tree Creek July 19-20. Siege of Atlanta July 22-August 1. Sent to rear for muster out August 1, and mustered out at Camp Butler, Ill., September 5, 1864.

Regiment lost during service 3 Officers and 80 Enlisted men killed and mortally wounded and 1 Officer and 148 Enlisted men by disease. Total 232.

26th REGIMENT INFANTRY.

Organized at Camp Butler, Ill., and mustered in August 31, 1861. Moved September 1, 1861, to Quincy, Ill., without clothing, equipments, arms or subsistence. Detachments moved to Canton, LaGrange, Palmyra and Hannibal, Mo., and engaged in protecting line of the Hannibal & St. Jo. R. R. till February 19, 1862. Ordered to Commerce, Mo., February 19, 1862. Attached to 2nd Brigade, 5th Division, Army of the Mississippi, to April, 1862. 1st Brigade, 3rd Division, Army of the Mississippi, April, 1862. 2nd Brigade, 2nd Division, Army of the Mississippi, to November, 1862. 2nd Brigade, Left Wing, 13th Army Corps (Old), Dept. of the Tennessee, to December, 1862. 2nd Brigade, 8th Division, 16th Army Corps, Army of the Tennessee, December, 1862. 2nd Brigade, 1st Division, 17th Army Corps, to January, 1863. 2nd Brigade, 1st Division, 16th Army Corps, to March, 1863. 1st Brigade, 1st Division, 16th Army Corps, to July, 1863. 1st Brigade, 4th Division, 15th Army Corps, to August, 1864. 2nd Brigade,

4th Division, 15th Army Corps, to September, 1864. 2nd Brigade, 1st Division, 15th Army Corps, to July, 1865.

SERVICE.—Operations against New Madrid and Island No. 10, February 28-April 8, 1862. Actions at New Madrid March 3, 4 and 6. Union City March 31. Action and capture at Tiptonville April 8. Expedition to Fort Pillow, Tenn., April 13-17. Moved to Hamburg Landing, Tenn., April 17-23. Advance on and siege of Corinth, Miss., April 29-May 30. Reconnoissance toward Corinth May 8. Action at Farmington May 9. Occupation of Corinth May 30, and pursuit to Booneville May 31-June 12. At Clear Creek till June 23, and at Danville till August 18. March to Tuscumbia August 18-21, thence to Clear Creek September 8. Reconnoissance to Iuka and skirmish September 16. Battle of Iuka September 19. Battle of Corinth October 3-4. Pursuit to Ripley October 5-12. Grant's Central Mississippi Campaign. Operations on the Mississippi Central R. R. November, 1862, to January, 1863. Near Oxford December 4, 1862. Moved to LaGrange, Tenn., January 15 and duty there till March 8, 1863. At Colliersville, Tenn., till June 7. Moved to Memphis, Tenn., thence to Vicksburg, Miss., June 7-17. Siege of Vicksburg June 17-July 4. Surrender of Vicksburg July 4. Advance on Jackson, Miss., July 5-10. Siege of Jackson July 10-17. Camp at Big Black till September 28. Movement to Memphis, thence march to Chattanooga, Tenn., September 28-November 23. Operations on Memphis & Charleston R. R. in Alabama October 20-29. Chattanooga-Ringgold Campaign November 23-27. Tunnel Hill November 23-24. Mission Ridge November 25. March to the relief of Knoxville, Tenn., November 28-December 8. Regiment veteranize January 1, 1864, and Veterans on furlough January and February. At Scottsboro, Ala., till May. Atlanta (Ga.) Campaign May to September. Demonstrations on Resaca May 8-13. Battle of Resaca May 14-15. Near Kingston May 19-22. Advance on Dallas May 23-25. Operations on line of Pumpkin Vine Creek and battles about Dallas, New Hope Church and Allatoona Hills, May 25-June 5. Operations about Marietta and against Kenesaw Mountain June 10-July 2. Brush Mountain June 15. Assault on Kenesaw June 27. Nickajack Creek July 2-5. Chattahoochie River July 5-17. Battle of Atlanta July 22-August 25. Siege of Atlanta July 22-August 25. Ezra Chapel, Hood's second sortie, July 28. Flank movement on Jonesboro August 25-30. Battle of Jonesboro August 31-September 1. Lovejoy Station September 2-6. Pursuit of Hood into Alabama October 1-26. Reconnoissance from Gaylesville, Ala., to Turkeytown October 25. March to the sea November 15-December 10. Griswoldsville December 22. Siege of Savannah December 10-21. Campaign of the Carolinas January to April, 1865. Reconnoissance to Salkehatchie River, S. C., January 25. Salkehatchie Swamp February 2-5. South Edisto River February 9. North Edisto River February 11-12. Congaree Creek February 15. Columbia February 16-17. Battle of Bentonville, N. C., March 20-21. Neil Creek and Hannah's Creek March 22. Occupation of Goldsboro March 24. Advance on Raleigh April 10-14. Occupation of Raleigh April 14. Bennett's House April 26. Surrender of Johnston and his army. March to Washington, D. C., via Richmond, Va., April 29-May 19. Grand Review May 24. Moved to Louisville, Ky., June, and duty there till July. Mustered out July 20, and discharged at Springfield, Ill., July 28, 1865.

Regiment lost during service 2 Officers and 88 Enlisted men killed and mortally wounded and 2 Officers and 194 Enlisted men by disease. Total 286.

27th REGIMENT INFANTRY.

Organized at Camp Butler, Ill., August 10, 1861. At Jacksonville, Ill., till September 1. Moved to Cairo, Ill., September 1, and duty there till March, 1862. Attached to District of Cairo to February, 1862. 1st Brigade, 1st Division, District of Cairo, February, 1862. Flotilla Brigade, Army of the Mississippi, to April, 1862. 1st Brigade, 1st Division, Army of the Mississippi, to September, 1862. 1st Brigade, 13th Division,

Army of the Ohio, to November, 1862. 3rd Brigade, 3rd Division, Right Wing 14th Army Corps, Army of the Cumberland, to January, 1863. 3rd Brigade, 3rd Division, 20th Army Corps, Army of the Cumberland, to October, 1863. 3rd Brigade, 2nd Division, 4th Army Corps, to August, 1864.

SERVICE.—Expedition to Belmont, Mo., November 6-7, 1861. Battle of Belmont November 7. Expedition into Kentucky January 16-21, 1862. Occupation of Columbus, Ky., March 3. Skirmish at Columbus March 4. Operations against New Madrid and Island No. 10 March 14-April 8. Actions at Island No. 10 March 15-16 and 25. Expedition to Union City, Tenn., March 30-April 2. Union City March 30-31. Action and capture at Tiptonville April 8. Expedition to Fort Pillow, Tenn., April 13-17. Moved to Pittsburg Landing, Tenn., April 17-23. Advance on and siege of Corinth, Miss., April 29-May 30. Action at Farmington May 3. Reconnoissance toward Corinth May 8. Action at Farmington May 9. Pursuit to Booneville May 30-June 12. Tuscumbia Creek May 31-June 1. Reconnoissance toward Baldwyn June 3. Camp at Corinth till July 21. Moved to Iuka, Miss., thence to Courtland, Ala., and duty along Memphis & Charleston R. R. till September 3. March to Nashville, Tenn., September 3-12. Siege of Nashville September 12-November 6. Near La Vergne October 7. Repulse of Forest's attack on Edgefield November 5. Duty at Nashville till December 26. Advance on Murfreesboro December 26-30. Action at Nolensville, Knob Gap, December 26. Triune December 27-28. Battle of Stone's River December 30-31, 1862, and January 1-3, 1863. Duty at Murfreesboro till June. Expedition toward Columbia March 4-14. Middle Tennessee (or Tullahoma) Campaign June 24-July 7. Christiana June 24. Occupation of Middle Tennessee till August 16. Passage of Cumberland Mountains and Tennessee River and Chickamauga (Ga.) Campaign August 16-September 22. Battle of Chickamauga, (Ga.) September 19-20. Siege of Chattanooga, Tenn., September 24-November 23. Chattanooga-Ringgold Campaign November 23-27. Orchard Knob November 23-24. Mission Ridge November 25. March to relief of Knoxville and Campaign in East Tennessee November 28, 1863, to January 25, 1864. Operations about Dandridge January 16-17, 1864. At London, Tenn., till April 18. Atlanta (Ga.) Campaign May to August, 1864. Demonstration on Rocky Faced Ridge May 8-11. Buzzard's Roost Gap May 8-9. Demonstration on Dalton May 9-13. Battle of Resaca May 14-15. Near Calhoun May 16. Adairsville May 17. Near Kingston May 18-19. Near Cassville May 19. Advance on Dallas May 23-25. Operations on line of Pumpkin Vine Creek and battles about Dallas, New Hope Church and Allatoona Hills May 25-June 5. Operations about Marietta and against Kenesaw Mountain June 10-July 2. Pine Hill June 11-14. Lost Mountain June 15-17. Assault on Kenesaw June 27. Ruff's (or Neal Dow's) Station, Smyrna Camp Ground July 4. Chattahoochie River July 5-17. Buckhead Nancy's Creek July 18. Peach Tree Creek July 19-20. Siege of Atlanta July 22-August 25. Ordered to Springfield, Ill., August 25. Mustered out September 20, 1864, expiration of term. Veterans and Recruits transferred to 9th Illinois Infantry.

Regiment lost during service 7 Officers and 96 Enlisted men killed and mortally wounded and 2 Officers and 83 Enlisted men by disease. Total 188.

28th REGIMENT INFANTRY.

Organized at Camp Butler, Ill., and mustered in August 15, 1861. Moved to St. Louis, Mo., August 28, thence to Thebes and to Bird's Point, Mo., September 9. Attached to District of Cairo to October, 1861. 4th Brigade, District of Cairo, to February, 1862. 1st Brigade, 4th Division, District of Cairo, February, 1862. 1st Brigade, 4th Division, District of West Tennessee, and Army of the Tennessee to July, 1862. 1st Brigade, 4th Division, District of Memphis, Tenn., to September, 1862. 1st Brigade, 4th Division, District of Jackson, Tenn., to November, 1862. 3rd Brigade, 4th

Division, Right Wing 13th Army Corps (Old), Department of the Tennessee, to December, 1862. 3rd Brigade, 4th Division, 17th Army Corps, to January, 1863. 3rd Brigade, 4th Division, 16th Army Corps, to July, 1863. 3rd Brigade, 4th Division, 13th Army Corps, to August, 1863. 3rd Brigade, 4th Division, 17th Army Corps, August, 1863. Post of Natchez, Miss., to October, 1864. 3rd Brigade, 2nd Division, 19th Army Corps, Department of the Gulf, to December, 1864. 1st Brigade, Reserve Corps, Military Division West Mississippi, to February, 1865. 1st Brigade, 3rd Division, Reserve Corps, Military Division West Mississippi, February, 1865. 1st Brigade, 3rd Division, 13th Army Corps (New), Military Division West Mississippi, to July, 1865. Department of Texas to March, 1866.

SERVICE.—At Bird's Point, Mo., till October 2, 1861. Moved to Fort Holt, Ky., October 2, and duty there till January 31, 1862. Moved to Paducah, Ky., January 31. Operations against Forts Henry and Heiman February 2-6. Occupation of Fort Heiman February 6 to March 6. Moved to Pittsburg Landing, Tenn., March 6-22. Battle of Shiloh, Tenn., April 6-7. Advance on and siege of Corinth, Miss., April 29-May 30. March to Memphis, Tenn., via Grand Junction, LaGrange, Holly Springs, Moscow and Germantown, June 1-July 21, and duty there till September 6. Moved to Bolivar September 6-14. Duty there till October 4. Battle of the Hatchie, Metamora, October 5. Grant's Central Mississippi Campaign November 2, 1862, to January 10, 1863. Guard R. R. at Colliersville, Tenn., till May, 1863. Moved to Vicksburg, Miss., May 11-14. Duty at Grand Gulf till June 11. Siege of Vicksburg, Miss., June 11-July 4. Advance on Jackson, Miss., July 5-10. Siege of Jackson July 10-17. Assault on Jackson July 12. Duty at Vicksburg till August 15. Moved to Natchez, Miss., August 15, and duty there till October, 1864. Expedition to Harrisonburg, La., September 1-7, 1863. Near Harrisonburg and capture of Fort Beauregard September 4. Operations about Natchez December 1-10. Regiment veteranize January 4, 1864. Veterans absent on furlough May 18-July 8. Expedition to Gillespie's Plantation, Black Bayou, August 4-6. Expedition to Buck's Ferry and skirmishes September 9-22. Expedition to Sicily Island September 26-30. Expedition to Homachita River October 4-8. Moved to Morganza, La., October 10-12, thence to the mouth of White River November 3-7. Moved to Memphis, Tenn., November 20-22. Duty there till January, 1865. Expedition to Moscow December 21-31, 1864. Moved to Kennersville, La., January 3-6, 1865; thence to New Orleans February 12-15. Campaign against Mobile, Ala., and its defences February 17-April 12. Siege of Spanish Fort and Fort Blakely March 26-April 8. Assault and capture of Fort Blakely April 9. Occupation of Mobile, April 12. Whistler's Station April 13. Duty at Mobile till July. Moved to Brazos Santiago, Texas, July 2-3. To Clarksville July 7, to Brownsville August 2-3, and duty there till March, 1866. Mustered out March 15 and discharged at Camp Butler, Ill., May 13, 1866.

Regiment lost during service 9 Officers and 97 Enlisted men killed and mortally wounded and 2 Officers and 182 Enlisted men by disease. Total 290.

29th REGIMENT INFANTRY.

Organized at Camp Butler, Ill., and mustered in August 19, 1861. Ordered to Cairo, Ill., September 4, 1861. Attached to District of Cairo to October, 1861. 1st Brigade, District of Cairo, to February, 1862. 1st Brigade, 1st Division, District of Cairo, February, 1862. 1st Brigade, 1st Division, District of West Tennessee, to March, 1862. 3rd Brigade, 1st Division, Army of the Tennessee, to July, 1862. 3rd Brigade, 1st Division, District of Jackson, Tenn., to September, 1862. 2nd Brigade, 1st Division, District of Jackson, to November, 1862. District of Jackson, 13th Army Corps (Old), Department of the Tennessee, to December, 1862. 1st Brigade, District of Jackson, 16th Army Corps, December, 1862. 1st Brigade, 3rd Division, 17th Army Corps, Army of the Tennessee, July to December, 1863.

35

Post of Natchez, Miss., District of Vicksburg, Miss., to October, 1864. Paducah, Ky., to November, 1864. Memphis, Tenn., District of West Tennessee, to January, 1865. 1st Brigade, Reserve Corps, Military Division West Mississippi, to February, 1865. 3rd Brigade, 1st Division, Reserve Corps, Military Division West Mississippi, February, 1865. 3rd Brigade, 1st Division, 13th Army Corps (New), Military Division West Mississippi, to July, 1865. Department of Texas to November, 1865.

SERVICE.—Duty at Cairo, Ill., September, 1861, to February, 1862. Expedition to Bloomfield, Mo., October 22-24, 1861. Expedition against Thompson's Forces, November 2-12. Reconnoissance of Columbus, Ky., January 16-22, 1862. Operations against Fort Henry, Tenn., February 2-6. Capture of Fort Henry February 6. Investment and capture of Fort Donelson, Tenn., February 12-16. Moved to Savannah, thence to Pittsburg Landing, Tenn., March 5-25. Battle of Shiloh, Tenn., April 6-7. Advance on and siege of Corinth, Miss., April 29-May 30. March to Jackson, Tenn., June 5-8, and duty there till November. Expedition to Bolivar and Brownsville July 27-August 13. March to relief of Corinth and pursuit to Ripley, Miss., October 3-12. Actions at Chewalla and Big Hill October 5. Grant's Central Mississippi Campaign November 2 to December 20. Surrendered at Holly Springs, Miss., December 20, 1862. Paroled and sent to Benton Barracks, Mo. Duty there till July, 1863 (Cos. "D" and "K" escaped capture, having been sent to Jackson December 18, 1862. Attached to gunboats Tuscumbia, Tyler and Petrel, Mississippi Squadron, February, 1863. Passage of Grand Gulf batteries April 29, 1863. Regiment moved to Vicksburg, Miss., July, 1863, and duty there till December. Moved to Natchez, Miss., December 1, and duty there till October, 1864. Operations about Natchez December 2-10, 1863. Expedition to Gillespie's Plantation, Black Bayou, August 4-6, 1864. Expedition to Buck's Ferry and skirmishes September 19-22. Expedition to Fort Adams October 5-8. Moved to Memphis, Tenn., thence to Paducah, Ky., October 10-12, and duty there till November 26. Moved to Memphis, Tenn., November 26-29. Expedition from Memphis to Moscow December 21-31. Moved to Kennersville, La., January 1-5, 1865; thence to New Orleans, La., February 12-15. Campaign against Mobile, Ala., and its defences February 17-April 12. Siege of Spanish Fort and Fort Blakely March 26-April 8. Assault and capture of Fort Blakely April 9. Occupation of Mobile April 12, and duty there till June. Moved to Galveston, Texas, June 26-July 1. Duty at Millican, Hempstead, Brenham and Beaumont, on Texas Central R. R. till November. Mustered out November 6 and discharged from service November 28, 1865.

Regiment lost during service 5 Officers and 70 Enlisted men killed and mortally wounded and 3 Officers and 222 Enlisted men by disease. Total 300.

30th REGIMENT INFANTRY.

Organized at Camp Butler, Ill., and mustered in August 28, 1861. Moved to Cairo, Ill., September 1, 1861. Attached to District of Cairo to October, 1861. 1st Brigade, District of Cairo, to February, 1862. 1st Brigade, 1st Division, District of Cairo, February, 1862. 1st Brigade, 1st Division, District of West Tennessee and Army of the Tennessee, to July, 1862. 1st Brigade, 1st Division, District of Jackson, Tenn., to September, 1862. 3rd Brigade, 1st Division, District of Jackson, Tenn., to November, 1862. 1st Brigade, 3rd Division, Right Wing, 13th Army Corps (Old), Department of the Tennessee, to December, 1862. 2nd Brigade, 3rd Division, Right Wing, 13th Army Corps, December, 1862. 2nd Brigade, 3rd Division, 17th Army Corps, Army of the Tennessee, to December, 1863. 3rd Brigade, 3rd Division, 17th Army Corps, to April, 1864. 1st Brigade, 3rd Division, 17th Army Corps, to April, 1865. 1st Brigade, 4th Division, 17th Army Corps, to July, 1865.

SERVICE.—Duty at Cairo, Ill., till February, 1862.

Scout into Kentucky October 22-24, 1861. Expedition to Belmont November 6-7. Battle of Belmont November 7. Expedition toward Columbus, Ky., January 16-22, 1862. Operations against Forts Henry and Heiman February 2-6. Capture of Forts Henry and Heiman February 6. Investment and capture of Fort Donelson, Tenn., February 12-16. Garrison at Fort Donelson till April 22. Moved to Pittsburg Landing, Tenn., April 22-25. Advance on and siege of Corinth, Miss., April 29-May 30. Moved to Bethel, thence to Jackson, Tenn., June 4-7. Capture of Jackson June 7. Duty there till August 13. March to Estenaula August 13-14, and to Denmark August 31. Medon's Station, Britton's Lane, September 1. March to Jackson September 2-4, and duty there till November 2. Grant's Central Mississippi Campaign November 2, 1862, to January 10, 1863. Reconnoissance from LaGrange November 8-9, 1862. Moved to Memphis, Tenn., January 10, 1863. Moved to Lake Providence, La., February 22-24. Duty there till April 17, thence moved to Milliken's Bend, La. Flank movement on Bruinsburg and turning Grand Gulf April 25-30. Battle of Thompson's Plantation, Port Gibson, May 1. North Fork Bayou Pierre May 3. Hankinson's Ferry, near Black River, May 3-4. Battles of Raymond May 12, Jackson May 14, Champion's Hill May 16, Big Black River May 17. Siege of Vicksburg, Miss., May 18-July 4. Assaults on Vicksburg May 19-22 and June 25. Surrender of Vicksburg July 4. Duty at Vicksburg till February, 1864. Stephenson's Expedition to Monroe, La., August 20-September 2, 1863. Expedition toward Canton October 14-20. Bogue Chitto Creek October 17. Meridian Campaign February 3 to March 2. Veterans on furlough March 5-April 18. Moved to Cairo, Ill.; thence to Clifton, Tenn., April 18-30. March to Huntsville, Ala., thence to Decatur, Ala., Rome and Kingston, Ga., to Ackworth, Ga., May 5-June 8. Atlanta (Ga.) Campaign June 8 to September 8. Operations about Marietta and against Kenesaw Mountain June 10-July 2. Assault on Brushy Mountain June 15. Assault on Kenesaw Mountain June 27. Nickajack Creek July 2-5. Howell's Ferry July 5. Chattahoochie River July 5-17. Battle of Leggett's Bald Hill July 20-21. Battle of Atlanta July 22. Siege of Atlanta July 22-August 25. Ezra Chapel, Hood's Second Sortie, July 28. Flank Movement on Jonesboro August 25-30. Battle of Jonesboro August 31-September 1. Lovejoy Station September 2-6. Pursuit of Hood into Alabama October 1-26. March to the sea November 15-December 10. Siege of Savannah December 10-21. Campaign of the Carolinas January to April, 1865. Pocotaligo, S. C., January 14. Salkehatchie Swamps February 1-5. Barker's Mills, Whippy Swamp, February 3. Binnaker's Bridge, South Edisto River, February 9. Orangeburg, North Edisto River, February 11-12. Columbia February 15-17. Battle of Bentonville, N. C., March 20-21. Occupation of Goldsboro March 24. Advance on Raleigh April 10-14. Occupation of Raleigh April 14. Bennett's House April 26. Surrender of Johnston and his army. March to Washington, D. C., via Richmond, Va., April 29-May 19. Grand Review May 24. Moved to Louisville, Ky., June 9-12, and Provost duty there till July 16. Mustered out July 16 and discharged at Chicago, Ill., July 24, 1865.

Regiment lost during service 10 Officers and 115 Enlisted men killed and mortally wounded and 2 Officers and 218 Enlisted men by disease. Total 345.

31st REGIMENT INFANTRY.

Organized at Jacksonville, Ill., and mustered in at Cairo, Ill., September 18, 1861. Attached to District of Cairo to October, 1861. 1st Brigade, District of Cairo to February, 1862. 1st Brigade, 1st Division, District of Cairo, February, 1862. 1st Brigade, 1st Division, District of West Tennessee, and Army of the Tennessee, to July, 1862. 1st Brigade, 1st Division, District of Jackson, to September, 1862. 2nd Brigade, 1st Division, District of Jackson, to November, 1862. 1st Brigade, 3rd Division, Right Wing 13th Army Corps (Old), Department of the Tennessee, to December,

1862. 1st Brigade, 3rd Division, 17th Army Corps, to April, 1865. 2nd Brigade, 4th Division, 17th Army Corps, to July, 1865.

SERVICE.—Duty at Cairo, Ill., till February, 1862. Expedition to Belmont, Mo., November 6-7, 1861. Battle of Belmont November 7. Reconnoissance of Columbus, Ky., January 16-22, 1862. Operations against Forts Henry and Heiman February 2-6. Capture of Forts Henry and Heiman February 6. Investment and capture of Fort Donelson, Tenn., February 12-16. Garrison at Fort Donelson till April 22. Moved to Pittsburg Landing, Tenn., April 22-25. Advance on and siege of Corinth, Miss., April 29-May 30. Moved to Jackson, Tenn., June 4-7, and duty there till November. Action at Burnt Bridge, near Humboldt, Tenn., September 5. March to relief of Corinth and pursuit to Ripley October 3-12. Actions at Chewalla and Big Hill October 5. Grant's Central Mississippi Campaign November 2, 1862, to January 10, 1863. Reconnoissance from LaGrange November 8-9, 1862. Moved to La Grange, thence to Memphis, Tenn., January 10-19, 1863, and to Lake Providence, La., March 10. Moved to Milliken's Bend, La., April 17. Passage of Vicksburg and Warrenton batteries April 22 (Detachment). Movement on Bruinsburg and turning Grand Gulf April 25-30. Battle of Thompson's Plantation, or Port Gibson, May 1. North Fork Bayou Pierre and Ingraham's Heights May 3. Battles of Raymond, Miss., May 12. Jackson May 14. Champion's Hill May 16. Big Black River Bridge May 17. Siege of Vicksburg, Miss., May 18-July 4. Assaults on Vicksburg May 19-22 and June 25. Surrender of Vicksburg July 4. Duty there and at Big Black till February, 1864. Stephenson's Expedition to Monroe, La., August 20-September 2. Expedition toward Canton October 14-20. Bogue Chitto Creek October 17. Meridian Campaign February 3-March 2, 1864. Meridian February 13-14. Chunkey Station February 14. Meridian February 14-15. Brandon February 16. Canton February 29. Veterans on furlough March and April, 1864. Rendezvous at Carbondale, Ill., and moved to Cairo, Ill., thence to Clifton, Tenn., and march to Ackworth, Ga., via Huntsville and Decatur, Ala., and Rome, Ga., April 28-June 8. Atlanta (Ga.) Campaign June 8-September 8. Operations about Marietta and against Kenesaw Mountain June 10-July 2. Assault on Brushy Mountain June 15. Assault on Kenesaw June 27. Nickajack Creek July 2-5. Chattahoochie River July 5-17. Howell's Ferry July 5. Battle of Leggett's Bald Hill July 20-21. Battle of Atlanta July 22. Siege of Atlanta July 22-August 25. Ezra's Chapel, Hood's second sortie, July 28. Flank movement on Jonesboro August 25-30. Battle of Jonesboro August 31-September 1. Lovejoy Station September 2-6. Pursuit of Hood into Alabama October 1-26. March to the sea November 15-December 10. Siege of Savannah December 10-21. Campaign of the Carolinas January to April, 1865. Pocotaligo, S. C., January 14. Salkehatchie Swamps February 1-5. Barker's Mills, Whippy Swamp, February 3. Binnaker's Bridge, South Edisto River, February 9. Orangeburg, North Edisto River, February 11-12. Columbia February 15-17. Battle of Bentonville, N. C., March 20-21. Occupation of Goldsboro March 24. Advance on Raleigh April 10-14. Occupation of Raleigh April 14. Bennett's House April 26. Surrender of Johnston and his army. March to Washington, D. C., via Richmond, Va., April 29-May 19. Grand Review May 24. Moved to Louisville, Ky., June 8-11, and Provost duty there till July 19. Mustered out July 19 and discharged at Springfield, Ill., July 31, 1865.

Regiment lost during service 9 Officers and 166 Enlisted men killed and mortally wounded and 3 Officers and 293 Enlisted men by disease. Total 471.

32nd REGIMENT INFANTRY.

Organized at Camp Butler, Ill., and mustered in December 31, 1861. Moved to Cairo, Ill., January 28, 1862. Attached to District of Cairo, Ill., January to February, 1862. 4th Brigade, 1st Division, District of Cairo, February, 1862. 1st Brigade, 4th Division, District of West Tennessee, and Army of the Tennessee, to July, 1862. 1st Brigade, 4th Division, District of Memphis, Tenn., to September, 1862. 1st Brigade, 4th Division, District of Jackson, Tenn., to November 1862. 3rd Brigade, 4th Division, Right Wing 13th Army Corps (Old), Department of the Tennessee, to December, 1862. 3rd Brigade, 4th Division, 17th Army Corps, Army of the Tennessee, to January, 1863. 3rd Brigade, 4th Division, 16th Army Corps, to July, 1863. 3rd Brigade, 4th Division, 13th Army Corps, to August, 1863. 3rd Brigade, 4th Division, 17th Army Corps, to April, 1864. 1st Brigade, 4th Division, 17th Army Corps, to November, 1864. 3rd Brigade, 4th Division, 17th Army Corps, to April, 1865. 2nd Brigade, 4th Division, 17th Army Corps, to July, 1865. Department of the Missouri to September, 1865.

SERVICE.—Moved from Cairo, Ill., to Bird's Point, Mo., February 2, 1862; thence to Fort Henry, Tenn., February 8-9, and duty there till March 5 (Co. "A" at Fort Donelson, Tenn., February 13-15, and on Expedition to Eastport, Miss. Cos. "C" and "K" on gunboats "Tyler" and "Lexington," February, 1862. Action at Pittsburg Landing March 1.) Regiment moved from Fort Henry to Pittsburg Landing, Tenn., March 5-15. Battle of Shiloh, Tenn., April 6-7. Advance on and siege of Corinth, Miss., April 29-May 30. March to Memphis, Tenn., via Grand Junction, LaGrange, Holly Springs, Moscow and Germantown June 1-July 21, and duty there till September 6. Moved to Bolivar September 6-14, and duty there till October 3. March to relief of Corinth October 3. Battle of Metamora, or Hatchie River, October 5. Grant's Central Mississippi Campaign November 3, 1862, to January 10, 1863. Guard line of Memphis & Charleston R. R. till March 11, 1863. At Memphis, Tenn., till May. Moved to Young's Point, La., thence to Grand Gulf May 11-16, and duty there till June 8. Ordered to Vicksburg, Miss. Siege of Vicksburg, Miss., June 12-July 4. Advance on Jackson, Miss., July 4-10. Siege of Jackson July 10-17. Assault on Jackson July 12. Reconnoissance to Pearl River July 15. At Vicksburg till August 15. Moved to Natchez, Miss., August 15, and duty there till November 24. Expedition to Harrisonburg September 1-7. Near Harrisonburg and capture of Fort Beauregard September 4. Moved to Vicksburg November 24, and returned to Natchez December 1. Operations about Natchez December 2-10. Near Fayette December 21-22. Moved to Hebron's Plantation, near Vicksburg, January 23, 1864. Meridian Campaign February 3-March 2. Clinton February 5. Near Canton February 27-28. Canton February 28-29. Veterans on furlough March and April. Moved to Bird's Point, thence to Clifton, Tenn., and march to Ackworth, Ga., via Huntsville and Decatur, Ala., and Rome, Ga., April 28-June 8. Atlanta (Ga.) Campaign June 8 to September 8. Operations about Marietta and against Kenesaw Mountain June 10-July 2. Assault on Kenesaw Mountain June 27. Nickajack Creek July 2-5. Chattahoochie River July 5-17. Turner's Ferry July 5. Duty at Marietta July 18 to November 3. Action at Kenesaw Water Tank October 3. March to the sea November 15-December 10. Oconee River November 26. Siege of Savannah December 10-21. Campaign of the Carolinas January to April, 1865. Pocotaligo, S. C., January 14. Salkehatchie Swamps February 1-5. River's Bridge, Salkehatchie River, February 3. Binnaker's Bridge, South Edisto River, February 9. Orangeburg, North Edisto River, February 11-12. Columbia February 15-17. Cheraw March 3. Fayetteville, N. C., March 11. Battle of Bentonville March 20-21. Occupation of Goldsboro March 24. Advance on Raleigh April 10-14. Occupation of Raleigh April 14. Bennett's House April 26. Surrender of Johnston and his army. March to Washington, D. C., via Richmond, Va., April 29-May 19. Grand Review May 24. Moved to Louisville, Ky., June 6. Thence to St. Louis, Mo., and Fort Leavenworth, Kansas. March to Fort Kearney July 1-14, and duty on the Plains till September 1. Ordered to Fort Leavenworth, Kansas, and there mustered out September 16, 1865.

Regiment lost during service 8 Officers and 90 Enlisted men killed and mortally wounded and 2 Officers and 168 Enlisted men by disease. Total 268.

33rd REGIMENT INFANTRY.

Organized at Camp Butler, Ill., and mustered in September 3, 1861. Moved to Ironton, Mo., September 20, 1861. Attached to Department of Missouri to March, 1862. 2nd Brigade, Steele's Army of Southeast Missouri, to May, 1862. 1st Division, Army of Southwest Missouri, to July, 1862. 1st Division, District of Eastern Arkansas, Dept. of Missouri, to November, 1862. 1st Brigade, 1st Division, Army of Southeast Missouri, to March, 1863. 1st Brigade, 14th Division, 13th Army Corps, Dept. of the Tennessee, to July, 1863. 1st Brigade, 1st Division, 13th Army Corps, Dept. of the Tennesee, to August, 1863, and Dept. of the Gulf, to June, 1864. District of LaFourche, Dept. of the Gulf, to February, 1865. 1st Brigade, 1st Division, 16th Army Corps, Military Division West Mississippi, to June, 1865. Dept. of Mississippi, to November, 1865.

SERVICE.—Duty at Ironton, Mo., till March, 1862. Expedition to Fredericktown, Mo., October 12-25, 1861. Skirmish at Big River Bridge, near Potosi, October 15. Action at Fredericktown October 21. Moved to Reeve's Station March 3, 1862. Steele's Expedition to White River, Ark., March 23-May 10. March to Batesville, Ark., April 5-May 3, thence to Helena, Ark., May 25-July 14. Action at Hill's Plantation, Cache River, July 7. Duty at and near Helena, Ark., till September 1, participating in numerous expeditions. Action at Totten's Plantation August 2. Prentiss and Bolivar September 24. Friar's Point September 28. Moved to Pilot Knob, Mo., thence to Van Buren, Ark. November 15. Campaign in Southeast Missouri December, 1862, to March, 1863. Ordered to St. Genevieve March 5, and thence to Milliken's Bend, La. Duty there till April 25. Movement on Bruinsburg and turning Grand Gulf April 25-30. Battle of Port Gibson May 1. Battle of Champion's Hill, Miss., May 16. Big Black River Bridge May 17. Siege of Vicksburg, Miss., May 18-July 4. Assaults on Vicksburg May 19 and 22. Surrender of Vicksburg July 4. Advance on Jackson, Miss., July 5-10. Siege of Jackson July 10-17. Duty at Vicksburg till August 20. Ordered to New Orleans, La., August 20. Duty at Carrollton, Brashear City and Berwick till October. Western Louisiana Campaign October 3-November 10. Ordered to New Orleans, La., November 10, thence to Texas November 12. Capture of Mustang Island, Matagorda Bay, November 17. Fort Esperanza November 27-30. Duty at Indianola and Lavacca, Texas, till March, 1864. Veterans on furlough March and April. Moved to New Orleans, La., April 18-29, thence to Brashear City May 17, and duty there and in the District of LaFourche, till February, 1865. Companies "F," "C" and "K," at Bayou Boeuf; Company "I" at Bayou L'Ours; Companies "A" and "D" at Tigerville; Company "G" at Chacahoula; Company "E" at Terre Bonne; Company "B" at Bayou LaFourche, and Bayou des Allemands; Company "H" at Boutte, till March, 1865. Non-Veterans moved north in charge of prisoners via New York September 17, 1864. Mustered out October 11, 1864. Campaign against Mobile and its defences March 18-April 12, 1865. Siege of Spanish Fort and Fort Blakely March 26-April 8. Assault and capture of Fort Blakely April 9. Occupation of Mobile April 12. March to Montgomery April 13-25. Moved to Selma May 10, thence to Meridian, Miss., May 17. Duty at Meridian and Vicksburg till November. Mustered out November 24 and discharged at Chicago, Ill., December 6, 1865.

Regiment lost during service 2 Officers and 56 Enlisted men killed and mortally wounded and 1 Officer and 250 Enlisted men by disease. Total 309.

34th REGIMENT INFANTRY.

Organized at Camp Butler, Ill., and mustered in September 7, 1861. Moved to Lexington, Ky., October 2, 1861, thence to Louisville and Camp Nevin, Ky., and duty there till February, 1862. Attached to Johnson's 3rd Brigade, McCook's Command, at Nolin, Ky., to November, 1861. 5th Brigade, Army of the Ohio, to December, 1861. 5th Brigade. 2nd Division, Army Ohio, to September, 1862. 5th Brigade, 2nd Division, 1st Corps, Army Ohio, to November, 1862. 2nd Brigade, 2nd Division, Right Wing 14th Army Corps, Army of the Cumberland, to January, 1863. 2nd Brigade, 2nd Division, 20th Army Corps, Army of the Cumberland, to October, 1863. Unattached, Dept. of the Cumberland, to November, 1863. 2nd Brigade, 2nd Division, 14th Army Corps, Army of the Cumberland, to July, 1865.

SERVICE.—Advance on Bowling Green, Ky., and Nashville, Tenn., February 14-March 2, 1862. March to Savannah, Tenn., thence moved to Pittsburg Landing, Tenn., March 16-April 6. Battle of Shiloh, Tenn., April 6-7. Advance on and siege of Corinth, Miss., April 29-May 30. Pursuit to Booneville May 31-June 6. Buell's operations on line of Memphis and Tennessee R. R. in Northern Alabama and Middle Tennessee June to August. March to Nashville, Tenn., thence in pursuit of Bragg, to Louisville, Ky., August 21-September 26. Pursuit of Bragg into Kentucky October 1-16. Action at Floyd's Fork October 1, near Clay Village October 4. Battle of Perryville October 8 (Reserve). March to Nashville, Tenn., October 16-November 7, and duty there till December 26. Reconnoissance toward Lavergne November 19. Reconnoissance to Lavergne November 26-27. Lavergne, Scrougesville November 27. Advance on Murfreesborough December 26-30. Triune December 27-28. Battle of Stone's River December 30-31, 1862, and January 1-3, 1863. Duty at Murfreesboro till June. Middle Tennessee or Tullahoma Campaign June 24-July 7. Liberty Gap June 24-27. Occupation of Middle Tennessee till August 16. Moved to Bellefonte, Ala., August 16, and detailed as Provost Guard. Moved to Caperton's Ferry, Tennessee River, August 30, and guard pontoon bridge there till September 18. Moved boats to Battle Creek September 18. Moved to Anderson's Cross Roads October 20, thence to Harrison's Landing, Tennessee River, November 8. Joined Brigade at Chattanooga November 15. Battles of Chattanooga November 23-25; Tunnel Hill November 24-25; Missionary Ridge November 25; Chickamauga Station November 26. March to relief of Knoxville, Tenn., November 28-December 17. At Rissville, Ga., till May, 1864. Veterans on furlough January 8 to March 7, 1864. Atlanta (Ga.) Campaign May to September, 1864. Tunnel Hill May 6-7. Demonstration on Rocky Faced Ridge May 8-11. Buzzard's Roost Gap May 8-9. Demonstration on Dalton May 9-13. Battle of Resaca May 14-15. Rome May 17-18. Operations on line of Pumpkin Vine Creek and battles about Dallas, New Hope Church and Allatoona Hills May 25-June 5. Operations about Marietta and against Kenesaw Mountain June 10-July 2; Pine Hill June 11-14; Lost Mountain June 15-17. Assault on Kenesaw June 27. Ruff's Station, Smyrna Camp Ground, July 4. Chattahoochie River July 5-17. Peach Tree Creek July 19-20. Siege of Atlanta July 22-August 25. Flank movement on Jonesboro August 25-30. Battle of Jonesboro August 31-September 1. Lovejoy Station September 2-6. Pursuit of Forest and operations against Hood in North Georgia and North Alabama September 29-November 3. March to the sea November 15-December 10. Siege of Savannah December 10-21. Campaign of the Carolinas January to April, 1865. Averysboro, Taylor's Hole Creek March 16. Bushy Swamp March 18. Battle of Bentonville March 19-21. Occupation of Goldsboro March 24. Advance on Raleigh April 10-14. Occupation of Raleigh April 14. Bennett's House April 26. Surrender of Johnston and his army. March to Washington, D. C., via Richmond, Va., April 29-May 19. Grand Review May 24. Moved to Louisville, Ky., June 12. Mustered out July 12 and discharged at Chicago, Ill., July 17, 1865.

Regiment lost during service 11 Officers and 129 Enlisted men killed and mortally wounded and 2 Officers and 119 Enlisted men by disease. Total 261.

35th REGIMENT INFANTRY.

Organized at Decatur, Ill., July 3, 1861, and accepted by the Secretary of War as G. A. Smith's Independent Regiment July 23, 1861. Moved to Jefferson Barracks, Mo., August 4-5. Mustered in at St. Louis, Mo., August 28, 1861. Moved to Jefferson City, Mo., September 15, thence to Otterville September 25, and to Sedalia October 15. Fremont's Campaign against Springfield, Mo., October 15-November 8. Attached to Dept. of Missouri to January, 1862. 1st Brigade, Army of Southwest Missouri, to March, 1862. 1st Brigade, 4th Division, Army of the Southwest Missouri, to June, 1862. 1st Brigade, 4th Division, Army of Mississippi, to September, 1862. 32nd Brigade, 9th Division, Army of the Ohio, to October, 1862. 32nd Brigade, 9th Division, 3rd Army Corps, Army Ohio, to November, 1862. 3rd Brigade, 1st Division, Right Wing 14th Army Corps, Army of the Cumberland, to January, 1863. 3rd Brigade, 1st Division, 20th Army Corps, Army of the Cumberland, to October, 1863. 1st Brigade, 3rd Division, 4th Army Corps, to September, 1864.

SERVICE.—Moved from Springfield to Rolla, Mo., November 13-19, 1861, and duty there till January, 1862. Curtis' Campaign in Missouri and Arkansas. Advance on Springfield, Mo. and pursuit of Price to Cross Hollows, Ark., January 23-February 21. Battles of Pea Ridge March 6-8. March to Batesville, Ark., April 5-May 8. March to Cape Girardeau, Mo., May 10-21, thence moved to Hamburg Landing, Tenn., May 22-25. Advance on and siege of Corinth, Miss., May 27-30. Pursuit to Booneville May 31-June 12. March to Jacinto June 21-22, thence to Holly Springs June 27-29. At Jacinto till August 8. Guard Bear Creek Bridge till August 21. March to Nashville, Tenn., August 21-September 1, thence to Louisville, Ky., in pursuit of Bragg, September 2-26. Pursuit of Bragg into Kentucky October 1-15. Near Perryville October 6-7. Chaplin Hills, Perryville October 8. March to Nashville, Tenn., October 17-November 7 and duty there till December 26. Expedition from Edgefield to Harpeth Shoals and Clarksville November 26-December 1. Advance on Murfreesboro December 26-30. Nolensville Knob Gap December 26. Battle of Stone River December 30-31, 1862, and January 1-3, 1863. Duty at Murfreesboro till June. Scout to Franklin January 31-February 12. Reconnoissance to Salem and Versailles March 9-14. Operations on Edgeville Pike June 4; Middle Tennessee or Tullahoma Campaign June 24-July 7; Liberty Gap June 24-27. Occupation of Middle Tennessee till August 16. Passage of Cumberland Mountains and Tennessee River and Chickamauga (Ga.) Campaign August 16-September 22. Battle of Chickamauga, Ga., September 19-20. Siege of Chattanooga, Tenn., September 24-November 23. Chattanooga-Ringgold Campaign November 23-27. Orchard Knob November 23-24. Mission Ridge November 25. March to relief of Knoxville, Tenn., November 28-December 8. Operations in East Tennessee till January, 1864. At Loudon, Tenn., January 22-April 13. Atlanta (Ga.) Campaign May 1-August 26. Demonstration on Rocky Faced Ridge May 8-11. Buzzard's Roost Gap May 8-9. Demonstrations on Dalton May 9-13. Battle of Resaca May 14-15. Adairsville May 17. Near Kingston May 18-19. Near Cassville May 19. Advance on Dallas May 23-25. Operations on line of Pumpkin Vine Creek and battles about Dallas, New Hope Church and Allatoona Hills May 25-June 5. Pickett's Mills May 27. Operations about Marietta and against Kenesaw Mountain June 10-July 2; Pine Hill June 11-14; Lost Mountain June 15-17. Assault on Kenesaw June 27. Ruff's Station, Smyrna Camp Ground, July 4. Chattahoochie River July 5-17. Peach Tree Creek July 19-20. Siege of Atlanta July 22-August 25. Moved to Chattanooga, Tenn., August 26-27, thence to Springfield, Ill., August 31. Mustered out September 27, 1864, expiration of term.

Regiment lost during service 7 Officers and 91 Enlisted men killed and mortally wounded and 5 Officers and 164 Enlisted men by disease. Total 267.

36th REGIMENT INFANTRY.

Organized at Aurora, Ill., and mustered in September 23, 1861. Moved to St. Louis, Mo., thence to Rolla, Mo., September 24-29, 1861. Attached to Dept. of Missouri to January, 1862. 2nd Brigade, Army of Southwest Missouri, to March, 1862. 2nd Brigade, 1st Division, Army of Southwest Missouri, to June, 1862. 1st Brigade, 5th Division, Army Mississippi, to September, 1862. 37th Brigade, 11th Division, Army of the Ohio, to October, 1862. 37th Brigade, 11th Division, 3rd Corps, Army Ohio, to November, 1862. 1st Brigade, 3rd Division, Right Wing, 14th Army Corps, Army of the Cumberland, to January, 1863. 1st Brigade, 3rd Division, 20th Army Corps, Army of the Cumberland, to October, 1863. 1st Brigade, 2nd Division, 4th Army Corps, to August, 1865. Dept. of Texas, to September, 1865.

SERVICE.—Duty at Rolla, Mo., till January 14, 1862. Expedition against Freeman's forces November 1-9, 1861. Curtis' Campaign against Price in Missouri and Arkansas January to March, 1862. Advance on Springfield February 2-13. Pursuit of Price into Arkansas February 14-29. Battles of Pea Ridge, Ark., March 6-8. At Keitsville, Mo., till April 5. March to Batesville, Ark., April 5-May 3. Moved to Cape Girardeau, Mo., May 11-22, thence to Hamburg Landing, Tenn., May 23-29. Occupation of Corinth, Miss., May 30. Pursuit to Booneville May 31-June 6. Duty at Rienzi till September 6. Moved to Covington, Ky., thence to Louisville, Ky., September 6-19. Pursuit of Bragg into Kentucky October 1-16. Battle of Perryville, October 8. March to Nashville, Tenn., October 16-November 7. Duty there till December 26. Reconnoissance toward Clarksville November 15-20. Reconnoissance to Mill Creek November 27. Advance on Murfreesboro, Tenn., December 26-30. Battle of Stone's River December 30-31, 1862, and January 1-3, 1863. At and near Murfreesboro till June. Expedition toward Columbia March 4-14. Middle Tennessee or Tullahoma Campaign June 24-July 7. Occupation of Middle Tennessee till August 15. Passage of Cumberland Mountains and Tennessee River and Chickamauga (Ga.) Campaign August 16-September 22. Battle of Chickamauga, Ga., September 19-20. Siege of Chattanooga September 24-November 23. Chattanooga-Ringgold Campaign November 23-27. Orchard Knob November 23-24. Mission Ridge November 25. Pursuit to Graysville November 26-27. March to relief of Knoxville November 28-December 8. Operations in East Tennessee till January, 1864. Regiment Veteranize January 1, 1864, and Veterans on furlough till March. Atlanta (Ga.) Campaign May 1 to September 8. Demonstration on Rocky Faced Ridge May 8-11. Buzzard's Roost Gap May 8-9. Demonstration on Dalton May 9-13. Battle of Resaca May 14-15. Adairsville May 17. Near Kingston May 18-19. Cassville May 19. Advance on Dallas May 22-25. Operations on line of Pumpkin Vine Creek and battles about Dallas, New Hope Church and Allatoona Hills May 25-June 5. Operations about Marietta and against Kenesaw Mountain June 10-July 2. Pine Hill June 11-14. Lost Mountain June 15-17. Assault on Kenesaw June 27. Ruff's Station, Smyrna Camp Ground, July 4. Chattahoochie River July 5-17. Buckhead, Nancy's Creek, July 18. Peach Tree Creek July 19-20. Siege of Atlanta July 22-August 25. Flank movement on Jonesboro August 25-30. Battle of Jonesboro August 31-September 1. Lovejoy Station September 2-6. Pursuit of Hood, into Alabama October 1-26. Nashville Campaign November-December. Columbia, Duck River, November 24-27. Spring Hill November 29. Battle of Franklin November 30. Battle of Nashville December 15-16. Pursuit of Hood to the Tennessee River December 17-28. At Huntsville, Ala., till March, 1865. Operations in East Tennessee March 15-April 22. Moved to Nashville and duty there till June. Moved to New Orleans, La., June 15-23. Duty at Headquarters of General P. H. Sheridan, Commanding Dept. of the Gulf, to October. Mustered out October 8 and discharged at Springfield, Ill., October 27, 1865.

Regiment lost during service 11 Officers and 193 Enlisted men killed and mortally wounded and 1 Officer and 127 Enlisted men by disease. Total 332.

37th REGIMENT INFANTRY ("FREMONT RIFLES").

Organized at Chicago, Ill., and mustered in September 18, 1861. Moved to St. Louis, Mo., September 19, thence to Booneville, Mo., October 2, 1861. Attached to Dept. of Missouri to February, 1862. 2nd Brigade, 3rd Division, Army of Southwest Missouri, to May, 1862. Cassville, Mo., District of Southwest Missouri, to September, 1862. 2nd Brigade, 2nd Division, Army of the Frontier, Dept. of Missouri, to June, 1863. 1st Brigade, Herron's Division, 13th Army Corps, Army of the Tennessee, to July, 1863. 1st Brigade, 2nd Division, 13th Army Corps, Dept. of the Tennessee, to August, 1863, and Dept. of the Gulf to June, 1864. 1st Brigade, 3rd Division, 19th Army Corps, Dept. of the Gulf, to December, 1864. 4th Brigade, Reserve Corps, Military Division West Mississippi, to February, 1865. 3rd Brigade, 2nd Division, Reserve Corps, M. D. W. M., February, 1865. 3rd Brigade, 2nd Division, 13th Army Corps, M. D. W. M., to July, 1865. Dept. of Texas to May, 1866.

SERVICE.—Expedition to Arrow Rock, Mo., October 10-14, 1861 (Cos. "C" and "K"). Fremont's Campaign against Springfield, Mo., October 13-November 3 (Cos. "C" and "H," at Rolla, Mo., till February, 1862). At Lamine River till February, 1862. Curtis' Campaign against Price in Missouri and Arkansas February and March. Springfield February 12. Sugar Creek and Bentonville February 17. Battles of Pea Ridge, Ark., March 6-8. At Cassville, Mo., guarding frontier in Southwest Missouri, and operating against guerrillas till September 29, 1862. Cassville June 11 (Detachment). Expedition from Ozark to Forsyth August 14-17 (Cos. "A" and "K"). March to Osage Springs September 29-October 24. Occupation of Newtonia October 4. Expedition from Osage Springs to Fayetteville, Ark., October 27-30. March to relief of Blunt, December 3-7. Battle of Prairie Grove, Ark., December 7. Expedition over Boston Mountains to Van Buren, Ark., December 27-29. Operations against Marmaduke in Missouri April 17-May 2, 1863. Action at Cape Girardeau, April 26. Chalk Bluffs May 2. Moved to St. Louis, Mo., thence to Vicksburg, Miss., June 3-14. Siege of Vicksburg June 14-July 4. Surrender of Vicksburg July 4. Expedition to Yazoo City, Miss., July 12-21. Capture of Yazoo City July 13. Moved to Port Hudson, La., July 24, thence to New Orleans, La., August 13. Expedition after Taylor's and Green's forces, west of the Atchafalaya River September 8-October 11. Action at Sterling's Farm on Bayou Fordoche September 29. Moved to the Rio Grande, Texas, October 24-November 4. At Brownsville and guarding Rio Grande to Ringgold Barracks till February, 1864. Expedition to Rio Grande City November 23-December 2, 1863. Regiment veteranize February 28, 1864. Veterans on furlough till April. Moved to Memphis, Tenn. Expedition from Memphis, Tenn., to Ripley, Miss., April 30-May 9. Moved to Atchafalaya Bayou, La. Construct Steamboat Bridge across Bayou for Banks' forces. At Morganza, La., till July 12. Moved to St. Charles on White River, Ark., July 12 and duty there till October. Non-Veterans mustered out September 20. Duty at Duvall's Bluff, Ark., October 7, 1864, to January 4, 1865. Moved to New Orleans, La., thence to Barrancas, Fla. March to Pensacola, Fla., March 11. March to Fort Blakely, Ala., March 20-April 1. Occupation of Canoe Station March 27. Siege of Spanish Fort April 2-8. Assault and capture of Fort Blakely April 9. Occupation of Mobile April 12. Moved to Montgomery April 20-29, thence to Selma May 1. Moved to Mobile and duty there May 15 to June 28. Moved to Galveston, Texas, June 28-July 1, and to Sabine Pass July 1-5. To Houston July 17. Railroad guard duty in that vicinity till May, 1866. Mustered out May 15, 1866.

Regiment lost during service 4 Officers and 60 Enlisted men killed and mortally wounded and 1 Officer and 168 Enlisted men by disease. Total 233.

38th REGIMENT INFANTRY.

Organized at Camp Butler, Ill., and mustered in August 15, 1861. Ordered to Pilot Knob, Mo., September 20, 1861. Attached to Dept. of Missouri to March, 1862. 1st Brigade, Steele's Army of Southeast Missouri, to June, 1862. 2nd Brigade, 4th Division, Army of Mississippi, to September, 1862. 31st Brigade, 9th Division, Army of the Ohio, to October, 1862. 31st Brigade, 9th Division, 3rd Corps, Army Ohio, to November, 1862. 2nd Brigade, 1st Division, Right Wing 14th Army Corps, Army of the Cumberland, to January, 1863. 2nd Brigade, 1st Division, 20th Army Corps, Army of the Cumberland, to October, 1863. 1st Brigade, 1st Division, 4th Army Corps, to June, 1865. 2nd Brigade, 1st Division, 4th Army Corps, to August, 1865. Dept. of Texas to December, 1865.

SERVICE.—Duty at Pilot Knob till March, 1862. Operations about Fredericktown, Mo., October 12-25, 1861. Action at Fredericktown October 21. Expedition against Thompson's forces November 2-12. Moved to Reeve's Station on Black River March 3-10, 1862, thence to Doniphan and Pocahontas March 31-April 21. Action at Putnam's Ferry, Mo., April 1. March to Jacksonport, Ark., April 30-May 4, thence to Cape Girardeau, Mo., May 10-21, and to Hamburg Landing, Tenn., May 21-24. Siege of Corinth, Miss., May 26-30. Pursuit to Booneville May 31-June 12. March to Jacinto and Ripley June 29-July 4. At Corinth, Miss., till August 14. March through Alabama to Nashville, Tenn., thence to Louisville, Ky., in pursuit of Bragg, August 14-September 26. Pursuit of Bragg into Kentucky October 1-16. Battle of Perryville October 8. Manchester, Ky., October 14. Stanford, Ky., October 14. March to Nashville, Tenn., October 16-November 9, and duty there till December 26. Reconnoissance toward Clarksville November 15-30. Advance on Murfreesboro, Tenn., December 26-30. Nolensville, Knob Gap, December 26. Battle of Stone's River December 30-31, 1862, and January 1-3, 1863. At Murfreesboro till June. Reconnoissance from Murfreesboro March 6-7. Methodist Church on Shelbyville Pike March 6. Reconnoissance to Versailles March 9-14. Operations on Edgeville Pike June 4. Middle Tennessee or Tullahoma Campaign June 24-July 7. Liberty Gap June 24-27. Occupation of Middle Tennessee till August 16. Passage of Cumberland Mountains and Tennessee River and Chickamauga (Ga.) Campaign August 16-September 22. Battle of Chickamauga, Ga., September 19-20. Siege of Chattanooga September 24-October 27. Reopening Tennessee River October 26-29. Duty at Bridgeport, Ala., till January 26, 1864. Moved to Ooltewah January 26. Re-enlisted February 29, 1864. Veterans on furlough March 28 to June 9, rejoining at Ackworth, Ga. Non-Veterans attached to 101st Ohio Infantry during this time. Atlanta (Ga.) Campaign May to September, 1864. Tunnel Hill May 6-7. Demonstration on Rocky Faced Ridge May 8-11. Buzzard's Roost Gap May 8-9. Demonstration on Dalton May 9-13. Battle of Resaca May 14-15. Near Kingston May 18-19. Near Cassville May 19. Advance on Dallas May 22-25. Operations on line of Pumpkin Vine Creek and battles about Dallas, New Hope Church and Allatoona Hills May 25-June 5. Operations about Marietta and against Kenesaw Mountain June 10-July 2. Pine Hill June 11-14. Lost Mountain June 15-17. Assault on Kenesaw June 27. Ruff's Station July 4. Chattahoochie River July 5-17. Peach Tree Creek July 19-20. Siege of Atlanta July 22-August 25. Flank movement on Jonesboro August 25-30. Battle of Jonesboro August 31-September 1. Lovejoy Station September 2-6. Pursuit of Hood into Alabama October 3-30. Nashville Campaign November-December. Columbia, Duck River, November 24-27. Spring Hill November 29. Battle of Franklin November 30. Battle of Nashville December 15-16. Pursuit of Hood, to the Tennessee River, December 17-28. March to Huntsville, Ala., and duty there till March 13, 1865. Operations in East Tennessee till April 11. Moved to Nashville, Tenn., and duty there till June. Moved to New Orleans, La., June

17-25, thence to Indianola, Texas, July 12-15, and to Victoria, Texas. Duty there till December, 1865. Mustered out December 31, 1865.

Regiment lost during service 7 Officers and 107 Enlisted men killed and mortally wounded and 3 Officers and 177 Enlisted men by disease. Total 294.

39th REGIMENT INFANTRY ("YATES PHALANX").

Organized at Chicago, Ill., and mustered in October 11, 1861. Left state for St. Louis, Mo., October 13, thence ordered to Williamsport, Md., October 29, 1861. Attached to R. R. Guard, Dept. of West Virginia, to January, 1862. 1st Brigade, Lander's Division, Army of the Potomac, to March, 1862. 2nd Brigade, Shields' 2nd Division, Banks' 5th Army Corps, to April, 1862, and Department of the Shenandoah to May, 1862. 2nd Brigade, Shields' Division, Dept. of the Rappahannock, to July, 1862. 3rd Brigade, 2nd Division, 4th Army Corps, Army of the Potomac, to September, 1862. Ferry's Brigade, Division at Suffolk, Va., 7th Army Corps, Dept. of Virginia, to December, 1862. 1st Brigade, 3rd Division, 18th Army Corps, Dept. of North Carolina, to February, 1863. 3rd Brigade, 2nd Division, 18th Army Corps, Dept. of the South, to April, 1863. U. S. Forces, Folly Island, S. C., 10th Army Corps, Dept. of the South, to June, 1863. 2nd Brigade, Folly Island, S. C., 10th Army Corps, June, 1863. 1st Brigade, Folly Island, S. C., 10th Army Corps, to July, 1863. 1st Brigade, 2nd Division, Morris Island, S. C. 10th Army Corps, July, 1863. 1st Brigade, Morris Island, S. C., 10th Army Corps, to October, 1863. Howell's Brigade, Gordon's Division, Folly Island, S. C., to December, 1863. District of Hilton Head, S. C., 10th Army Corps, to April, 1864. 1st Brigade, 1st Division, 10th Army Corps, Army of the James, Dept. of Virginia and North Carolina, to December, 1864. 1st Brigade, 1st Division, 24th Army Corps, to August, 1865. District of Eastern Virginia, Dept. of Virginia, to December, 1865.

SERVICE.—Moved from Williamsport, Md., to Hancock, Md., December 11, 1861, and guard duty on Baltimore and Ohio R. R. till January, 1862. Action near Bath January 3, 1862 (Cos. "D," "I," and "K"). Great Cacapon Bridge January 3 (Co. "G"). Alpine Station January 3 Companies "A," "B," "C," "E," "F" and "H." Retreat to Cumberland, Md., January 5. Moved to New Creek, Va., thence to Patterson's Creek and duty there till March. Advance on Winchester, Va., March 7-15. Reconnoissance to Strasburg March 18. Action at Kernstowy March 22. Battle of Winchester March 23. Pursuit to New Market. Mt. Jackson March 25. Strasburg March 27. Woodstock April 1. Edenburg April 2. Occupation of Mt. Jackson, April 17. In Luray Valley till May, guarding bridges over South branch Shenandoah River. March to Fredericksburg, Va., May 12-21, thence to Front Royal March 25-30. Moved to Alexandria, thence to Harrison's Landing, Va., June 29-July 2. Chickahominy Swamps July 3-4. At Harrison's Landing till August 16. Moved to Fortress Monroe, Va., August 16-22, and duty there till September 1. Moved to Suffolk, Va., and duty there till January, 1863. Skirmishes on the Blackwater October 9-25-29-30. Expedition from Suffolk December 1-3, 1862. Action near Franklin on the Blackwater December 2. Zuni October 20 and 25 and December 12, 1862. Moved to New Berne, N. C., January 23, thence to Port Royal, S. C., January 28-February 1. Camp at St. Helena Island, S. C., till April. Expedition against Charleston April 7-13. Occupation of Folly Island, S. C., April 13 to July 10. Attack on Morris Island, S. C., July 10. Assaults on Fort Wagner, Morris Island, S. C., July 11 and 18. Siege of Forts Wagner and Gregg, Morris Island, S. C., and operations against Fort Sumpter and Charleston July 18-September 7. Capture of Forts Wagner and Gregg, September 7. Siege operations against Charleston, S. C., till October. Duty at Folly Island, S. C., till December and at Hilton Head, S. C., till April, 1864. Veterans on furlough January 1 to February 3, 1864, then moved from Chicago to Washington, D. C., thence to Yorktown, Va. Butler's operations on south side of the James River and against

Petersburg and Richmond May 5-June 15. Occupation of Bermuda Hundred and City Point May 5. Chester Station June 6-7. Weir Bottom Church May 9. Swift Creek or Arrowfield Church May 9-10. Proctor's and Palmer's Creeks and Drury's Bluff May 12-16. Defences of Bermuda Hundred, May 16-June 15. Weir Bottom Church, May 20. Bermuda Hundred June 2 and 14. Bermuda Front June 16-17. Siege operations against Petersburg and Richmond June 16, 1864, to April 2, 1865. On the Bermuda Hundred front till August 14, 1864. Demonstration north of the James August 14-18. Strawberry Plains, Deep Bottom, August 14-18. Deep Run August 16. In trenches before Petersburg August 25-September 27. Chaffin's Farm, New Market Heights, September 28-30. Darbytown Road October 13. Battle of Fair Oaks October 27-28. In trenches before Richmond till March 27, 1865. Moved to Hatcher's Run March 27-28. Appomattox Campaign March 28-April 9. Hatcher's Run March 29-31. Assaults on Petersburg April 1-2. Assault on Fort Gregg and fall of Petersburg, April 2. Pursuit of Lee April 3-9. Appomattox Court House April 9. Surrender of Lee and his army. Duty at Richmond till August, and at Norfolk, Va., till December. Mustered out December 6 and Discharged at Chicago, Ill., December 16, 1865.

Regiment lost during service 12 Officers and 129 Enlisted men killed and mortally wounded and 2 Officers and 130 Enlisted men by disease. Total 273.

40th REGIMENT INFANTRY.

Organized at Springfield, Ill., and mustered in August 10, 1861. Moved to Jefferson Barracks, Mo., August 13, 1861, thence to Bird's Point, Mo., August 30, and to Paducah, Ky., September 8. Attached to District of Paducah, Ky., to March, 1862. 1st Brigade, 5th Division, Army of the Tennessee, to May, 1862. 2nd Brigade, 5th Division, Army Tennessee, to July, 1862. 2nd Brigade, 5th Division, District of Memphis, Tenn., to November, 1862. 2nd Brigade, District of Memphis, Right Wing 13th Army Corps (Old), Dept. of the Tennessee, November, 1862. 1st Brigade, 1st Division, 13th Army Corps, to December, 1862. 1st Brigade, 1st Division, 17th Army Corps, Army of the Tennessee, to January, 1863. 2nd Brigade, 1st Division, 16th Army Corps, to July, 1863. 2nd Brigade, 4th Division, 15th Army Corps, to September, 1864. 2nd Brigade, 1st Division, 15th Army Corps, to July, 1865.

SERVICE.—Duty at Paducah, Ky., till March, 1862. Demonstrations on Columbus, Ky., November 7-9, 1861. Moved to Savannah, Tenn., March 10-14, 1862. Expedition to Yellow Creek, Miss., and occupation of Pittsburg Landing, Tenn., March 14-17. Battle of Shiloh, Tenn., April 6-7. Corinth Road April 8. Advance on and siege of Corinth, Miss., April 29-May 30. March to Memphis, Tenn., via LaGrange Grand Junction and Holly Springs, June 1 to July 21. Duty at Memphis till November 21. Sherman's Tallahatchie March November 26-December 12. At Davis' Mills and scouting in Northern Mississippi till April, 1863. Expedition through Northern Mississippi, April 17-26. Guarding Memphis and Charleston R. R. till June. Moved to Vicksburg, Miss., June 8-14. Siege of Vicksburg June 14-July 4. Advance on Jackson, Miss., July 4-10. Birdsong Ferry, Black River, July 4-6. Siege of Jackson, Miss., July 10-17. At Big Black River till September 25. Moved to Memphis, thence march to Chattanooga, Tenn., September 25-November 22. Operations on Memphis and Charleston R. R. in Alabama October 20-29. Battles of Chattanooga November 23-25. Tunnel Hill November 23-24. Mission Ridge November 25. Pursuit to Graysville November 26-27. March to relief of Knoxville, Tenn. November 28-December 9. At Scottsboro till May, 1864. Regiment veteranize January 1, 1864. Veterans on furlough March to May. Atlanta (Ga.) Campaign, May to September. Joined army June 3. Operations about Marietta and against Kenesaw Mountain June 10-July 2. Brush Mountain June 15. Assault on Kenesaw June 27. Nickajack Creek July 2-5. Chattahoochie River July 5-17. Battle of Atlanta July 22. Siege of Atlanta July 22-August 25.

Ezra Chapel, Hood's 2nd sortie, July 28. Flank movement on Jonesboro August 25-30. Battle of Jonesboro August 31-September 1. Lovejoy Station September 2-6. Pursuit of Hood into Alabama October 3-26. March to the sea November 15-December 10. Griswoldsville November 22. Ogeechee River December 7-9. Siege of Savannah December 10-21. Campaign of the Carolinas January to April, 1865. Reconnaissance to Salkehatchie River January 25. Combahee River, S. C., January 28. Salkehatchie Swamps February 2-5. South Edisto River February 9. North Edisto River February 11-12. Savannah Creek and Congaree Creek February 15. Columbia February 15-17. Battle of Bentonville, N. C., March 20-21. Mill Creek March 22. Occupation of Goldsboro March 24. Advance on Raleigh April 10-14. Occupation of Raleigh April 14. Bennett's House April 26. Surrender of Johnston, and his army. March to Washington, D. C. via Richmond April 29-May 19. Grand Review May 24. Moved to Louisville, Ky., June 6. Mustered out July 24, 1865.

Regiment lost during service 6 Officers and 119 Enlisted men killed and mortally wounded and 4 Officers and 117 Enlisted men by disease. Total 246.

41st REGIMENT INFANTRY.

Organized at Decatur, Ill., and mustered in August 5, 1861. Moved to St. Louis, Mo., August 8, 1861, thence to Bird's Point, Mo., August 29, and to Paducah, Ky., September 8. Attached to District of Cairo to December, 1861. 1st Brigade, 2nd Division, District of Cairo, to February, 1862. 1st Brigade, 4th Division, District of West Tennessee and Army of the Tennessee, to July, 1862. 1st Brigade, 4th Division, District of Memphis, to September, 1862. 1st Brigade, 4th Division, District of Jackson, to November, 1862. 1st Brigade, 4th Division, Right Wing 13th Army Corps (Old), Dept. of the Tennessee to December, 1862. 1st Brigade, 4th Division, 17th Army Corps, Army of the Tennessee to January, 1863. 1st Brigade, 4th Division, 16th Army Corps, to July, 1863. 1st Brigade, 4th Division, 13th Army Corps to August, 1863. 1st Brigade, 4th Division, 17th Army Corps, to March, 1864. 1st Brigade, Provisional Division, 17th Army Corps, Dept. of the Gulf, to June, 1864 (Non-Veterans). 4th Brigade, 1st Division, 16th Army Corps, to August, 1864 (Non-Veterans). 2nd Brigade, 4th Division, 17th Army Corps, to November, 1864. 1st Brigade, 4th Division, 17th Army Corps, to December, 1864.

SERVICE.—Duty at Paducah, Ky. (Cos. "B" and "I," at Smithland, Ky.), till February, 1862. Demonstration on Columbus, Ky., November 7-9, 1861. Operations against Forts Henry and Heiman, Tenn., February 3-6. Fort Heiman February 7. Investment and capture of Fort Donelson, Tenn., February 12-16. Expedition to Clarksville, Tenn., February 19-21. Moved to Pittsburg Landing, Tenn., March 10-16. Battle of Shiloh, Tenn., April 6-7. Advance on and siege of Corinth, Miss., April 29-May 30. March to Memphis, Tenn., via LaGrange, Grand Junction, Holly Springs and Germantown, June 1-July 21. Duty there till September 6. Moved to Bolivar, Tenn. March to relief of Corinth October 4. Battle of Hatchie River or Metamora, October 5. Pursuit to Ripley October 5-12. Grant's Central Mississippi Campaign, November 2, 1862, to January 10, 1863. Reconnoissance from LaGrange to Lamar, Miss., November 5, 1862. Worsham Creek November 16. Guard R. R. at Moscow, Tenn., January to March, 1863. Skirmish at Moscow February 18 (Detachment). Moved to Memphis, Tenn., March, and duty there till May. Expedition to the Coldwater, Miss., April 18-24. Hernando April 18. Coldwater April 19. Moved to Vicksburg, Miss., June 12-22. Siege of Vicksburg June 22-July 4. Surrender of Vicksburg July 4. Advance on Jackson, Miss., July 5-10. Siege of Jackson, July 10-17. Assault on Jackson July 12. At Vicksburg till November. Moved to Natchez, Miss., November 18 and return to Vicksburg, December 16. Duty there till February, 1864. Meridian Campaign February 3-March 2. Pearl River February 27. Veterans on furlough March to May, 1864. Non-Veterans on Red River Campaign March 10-May 22.

Fort DeRussy March 14. Battle of Pleasant Hill, La., April 9. Pleasant Hill Landing April 12-13. About Cloutiersville April 22-24. At Alexandria April 30-May 13. Boyce's Plantation May 6. Well's Plantation May 6. Bayou Boeuf May 7. Retreat to Morganza May 13-22. Mansura May 16. Yellow Bayou May 18. Moved to Vicksburg, thence to Memphis, Tenn., May 22-June 10. Action at Lake Chicot, Ark., June 6-7. Smith's Expedition to Tupelo, Miss., July 5-21. Harrisburg near Tupelo July 14-15. Smith's Expedition to Oxford, Miss., August 1-30. Veterans moved to Cairo, Ill., thence to Nashville, Tenn., and to Tunnel Hill May, 1864. Assigned to duty guarding R. R. at Tunnel Hill, Moon Station, Big Shanty, Marietta and Kenesaw Mountain till November. March to the sea November 15-December 10. Siege of Savannah December 10-21. Consolidated with 53d Illinois Infantry December 23, 1864.

Regiment lost during service 8 Officers and 107 Enlisted men killed and mortally wounded and 3 Officers and 107 Enlisted men by disease. Total 225.

42nd REGIMENT INFANTRY.

Organized at Chicago, Ill., July 22, 1861. Left state for St. Louis, Mo., September 20, 1861. Attached to Dept. of Missouri, to February, 1862. Flotilla Brigade, Army of Mississippi, to April, 1862. 1st Brigade, 1st Division, Army Miss., to September, 1862. 1st Brigade, 13th Division, Army of the Ohio, to November, 1862. 3rd Brigade, 3rd Division, Right Wing 14th Army Corps, Army of the Cumberland to January, 1863. 3rd Brigade, 3rd Division, 20th Army Corps, Army of the Cumberland, to October, 1863. 3rd Brigade, 2nd Division, 4th Army Corps to June, 1865. 2nd Brigade, 2nd Division, 4th Army Corps, to August, 1865. Dept. of Texas, to December, 1865.

SERVICE.—Joined Fremont at Tipton, Mo., October 18, 1861. Fremont's Campaign against Springfield, Mo., October 18-November 9. Duty at Smithton, Mo., December 13, 1861, to February 3, 1862. March to St. Charles, Mo., thence moved to Fort Holt, Ky., February 3-20, 1862. Operations against New Madrid, Mo., and Island Number 10, Mississippi River, February 28-April 8. Engagement at New Madrid, March 3-4. Actions at Island Number 10, March 15-16 and 25. Action and capture at Tiptonville April 8. Expedition to Fort Pillow, Tenn., April 13-17. Moved to Hamburg Landing, Tenn., April 17-22. Advance on and siege of Corinth, Miss., April 29-May 30. Action at Farmington May 3. Reconnoissance toward Corinth May 8. Action at Farmington May 9. Pursuit to Booneville May 31-June 12. Skirmish at Rienzi June 3 (Detachment). Reconnoissance toward Baldwyn June 3. Camp at Big Springs June 14 to July 22. Moved to Iuka, Miss., July 22, thence to Courtland, Ala. Skirmish at Courtland August 22. Duty along line of Memphis and Charleston R. R. till September 2. March to Nashville, Tenn., September 3-12. Action at Columbia, Tenn., September 9. Siege of Nashville September 12-November 6. Repulse of Forest's attack on Edgefield November 5. Duty at Nashville till December 26. Hardin Pike near Nashville December 3. Advance on Murfreesboro December 26-30. Battle of Stone's River December 30-31, 1862, and January 1-3, 1863. Expedition to Columbia March 5-14. Middle Tennessee or Tullahoma Campaign June 24-July 7. Occupation of Middle Tennessee till August 16. Passage of Cumberland Mountains and Tennessee River and Chickamauga, Ga. Campaign August 16-September 22. Battle of Chickamauga September 19-20. Siege of Chattanooga, Tenn., September 24-November 23. Chattanooga-Ringgold Campaign November 23-27. Orchard Knob November 23-24. Mission Ridge November 25. March to relief of Knoxville, Tenn., and Campaign in East Tennessee November 28, 1863, to January 15, 1864. Camp at Stone's Mill, Tenn., December 27, 1862, to January 15, 1864. Regiment veteranize January 1, 1864. Moved to Dandridge, Tenn., January 15, 1864. Operations about Dandridge January 16-17. Moved to Chattanooga January 21. Veterans on furlough February 21 to April 27. Atlanta, (Ga.) Campaign May 1 to

September 8. Demonstration against Rocky Faced Ridge May 8-11. Buzzard's Roost Gap May 8-9. Battle of Resaca May 14-15. Calhoun May 16. Adairsville May 17. Kingston May 18-19. Near Cassville May 19. Advance on Dallas May 22-25. Operations on line of Pumpkin Vine Creek and battles about Dallas, New Hope Church and Allatoona Hills May 25-June 5. Operations about Marietta and against Kenesaw Mountain June 10-July 2. Pine Hill June 11-14. Lost Mountain June 15-17. Assault on Kenesaw June 27. Ruff's Station Smyrna, Camp Ground, July 4. Chattahoochie River July 5-17. Peach Tree Creek July 19-20. Siege of Atlanta July 22-August 25. Flank movement on Jonesboro August 25-30. Battle of Jonesboro August 31-September 1. Lovejoy's Station September 2-6. Moved to Bridgeport, Ala., September 28. March to Chattanooga, thence to Alpine, Ga., and return October 19-30. Nashville Campaign November-December. Columbia, Duck River, November 24-27. Spring Hill November 29. Battle of Franklin November 30. Battle of Nashville December 15-16. Pursuit of Hood, to the Tennessee River, December 17-28. Duty at Huntsville and Decatur, Ala., till April 1, 1865. Expedition to Bull's Gap April 1-22. Moved to Nashville, Tenn., and duty there till June 15. Moved to New Orleans, La., June 15-18, thence to Fort Lavacca, Texas, July 18-23, thence to Camp Irwin and duty there till August 17. Post duty at Port Lavacca till December. Mustered out at Camp Irwin December 16 and discharged at Springfield, Ill., January 10, 1866.

Regiment lost during service 13 Officers and 168 Enlisted men killed and mortally wounded and 5 Officers and 201 Enlisted men by disease. Total 387.

43rd REGIMENT INFANTRY.

Organized at Camp Butler, Ill., and mustered in October 12, 1861. Moved to Benton Barracks, Mo., October 13, thence to Tipton and Otterville, November 3-4. Attached to Dept. of Missouri to February, 1862. 3rd Brigade, 1st Division, District of Cairo, February, 1862. 3rd Brigade, 1st Division, District of West Tennessee and Army of the Tennessee, to July, 1862. 3rd Brigade, 1st Division, District of Jackson to September, 1862. Unattached District of Jackson to November, 1862. Post of Bolivar, District of Jackson, 13th Army Corps (Old), Dept. of the Tennessee, to December, 1862. Post of Bolivar, District of Jackson, 16th Army Corps, to March, 1863. 1st Brigade, 3rd Division, 16th Army Corps, to May, 1863. 1st Brigade, Kimball's Provisional Division, 16th Army Corps, to July, 1863. 1st Brigade, Kimball's Provisional Division, District of Eastern Arkansas, to August, 1863. 1st Brigade, 2nd Division, Arkansas Expedition to November, 1863. 2nd Brigade, 2nd Division, Arkansas Expedition, to January, 1864. 2nd Brigade, 2nd Division, 7th Army Corps, Dept. of Arkansas, to March, 1864. 3rd Brigade, 3rd Division, 7th Army Corps, to May, 1864. 2nd Brigade, 1st Division, 7th Army Corps. garrison at Little Rock, Ark., to January, 1865. 1st Brigade, 1st Division, 7th Army Corps, to August, 1865. Dept. of Arkansas, to November, 1865.

SERVICE.—Duty at Otterville, Mo., till December 30, 1861. March to Tipton December 30-31, thence to Benton Barracks January 20-21, 1862. Moved to Fort Henry, Tenn., February 6-8, and to Fort Donelson February 25-26, thence to Savannah, Tenn., March 4-12. Expedition to Pinhook March 18-19. Moved to Pittsburg Landing, Tenn., March 22. Battle of Shiloh, Tenn., April 6-7. Advance on and siege of Corinth, Miss., April 29-May 30. March to Bethel, thence to Jackson, Tenn., June 4-16, and to Bolivar July 17-19, and duty there till May, 1863. March to support of Rosecrans at Iuka, Miss., September 15-23, 1862. March to LaGrange and return October 9-10. Grant's Central Mississippi Campaign October 31, 1862, to January 10, 1863. Operations against Forest in West Tennessee December 18, 1862, to January 3, 1863. Salem Cemetery, near Jackson, December 19, 1862. Scouting in West Tennessee and post duty at Bolivar till May, 1863. Expedition to Wesley Camp, Somerville, May 26-29. Movement to Memphis, Tenn., thence to Vicksburg, Miss., May 31-June 3. Expedition up the Yazoo to Satartia June 2-8. Action at Mechanicsburg, Satartia, June 4. Moved to Haines' Bluff June 6. Siege of Vicksburg June 9-July 4. Moved to Big Black July 12, thence to Snyder's Bluff July 22, and to Helena, Ark., July 29-August 1. Steele's Expedition to Little Rock, Ark., August 1-September 10. Engagement at Bayou Fourche and capture of Little Rock September 10. Duty at Little Rock till March, 1864. Steele's Expedition to Camden March 23-May 3. Okolona April 2-3. Prairie D'Ann April 9-13. Camden April 15. Princeton April 28. Saline Bottom April 29. Jenkin's Ferry April 30. Garrison duty at Little Rock till November, 1865. Princeton May 27, 1864. Scouts from Pine Bluff toward Camden and Monticello January 26-31, 1865. Mustered out November 30 and discharged at Camp Butler, Ill., December 14, 1865.

Regiment lost during service 8 Officers and 75 Enlisted men killed and mortally wounded and 2 Officers and 161 Enlisted men by disease. Total 246.

44th REGIMENT INFANTRY.

Organized at Chicago, Ill., and mustered in September 13, 1861. Moved to St. Louis, Mo., September 14-15, thence to Jefferson City, Mo., September 22-25. Attached to Sigel's Division, Dept. of Missouri, and Dept. of Missouri, to January, 1862. 4th Brigade, Army of Southwest Missouri, to February, 1862. 1st Brigade, 1st Division, Army of Southwest Missouri, to June, 1862. 1st Brigade, 5th Division, Army of Mississippi, to September, 1862. 35th Brigade, 11th Division, Army of the Ohio, to October, 1862. 35th Brigade, 11th Division, 3rd Army Corps, Army of the Ohio, to November, Division, 3rd Army Corps, Army of the Ohio, to November, 1862. 2nd Brigade, 3rd Division, Right Wing 14th Army Corps, Army of the Cumberland, to January, 1863. 2nd Brigade, 3rd Division, 20th Army Corps, Army of the Cumberland, to October, 1863. 1st Brigade, 2nd Division, 4th Army Corps, to August, 1865. Department of Texas to September, 1865.

SERVICE.—Fremont's advance on Springfield, Mo., October 13-November 8, 1861. March to Rolla November 8-19, and duty there till February, 1862. Curtis' advance on Springfield, Mo., February 2-13. Pursuit of Price into Arkansas February 13-29. Battles of Pea Ridge, Bentonville, Leetown and Elkhorn Tavern March 6-8. March to Batesville, Ark., April 5-May 3. Moved to Cape Girardeau, Mo., thence to Pittsburg Landing May 11-26. Siege of Corinth, Miss., May 29-30. Pursuit to Booneville May 31-June 12. At Rienzi, Miss., till August 26. Moved to Cincinnati, Ohio, August 26-September 1, thence to Louisville, Ky., September 17-19. Pursuit of Bragg into Kentucky October 1-16. Battle of Perryville, Ky., October 8. March to Nashville, Tenn., October 16-November 7, and duty there till December 26. Reconnoissance to Milk Creek November 27. Advance on Murfreesboro December 26-30. Battle of Stone's River December 30-31, 1862, and January 1-3, 1863. At Murfreesboro till June. Expedition toward Columbia March 4-14. Middle Tennessee (or Tullahoma) Campaign June 24-July 7. Fairfield June 27. Occupation of Middle Tennessee till August 16. Passage of the Cumberland Mountains and Tennessee River and Chickamauga (Ga.) Campaign August 16-September 22. Battle of Chickamauga September 19-20. Siege of Chattanooga, Tenn., September 24-November 23. Chattanooga-Ringgold Campaign November 23-27. Orchard Knob November 23-24. Mission Ridge November 25. Pursuit to Graysville November 26-27. March to relief of Knoxville, Tenn., November 28-December 8. Campaign in East Tennessee December, 1863, to February, 1864. March to Chattanooga, thence to Cleveland, Tenn., and duty there till May. Veterans on furlough February 18 to April 14. Atlanta (Ga.) Campaign May 1 to September 8. Demonstrations against Rocky Faced Ridge May 8-11. Buzzard's Roost Gap May 8-9. Demonstration on Dalton May 9-13. Battle of Resaca May 14-15. Adairsville May 17. Near Kingston May 18-19. Near

Cassville May 19. Advance on Dallas May 22-25. Operations on line of Pumpkin Vine Creek and battles about Dallas, New Hope Church and Allatoona Hills May 25-June 5. Operations about Marietta and against Kenesaw Mountain June 10-July 2. Pine Hill June 11-14. Lost Mountain June 15-17. Assault on Kenesaw June 27. Ruff's Station, Smyrna Camp Ground, July 4. Chattahoochie River July 5-17. Buckhead, Nancy's Creek, July 18. Peach Tree Creek, July 19-20. Siege of Atlanta July 22-August 25. Flank movement on Jonesboro August 25-30. Battle of Jonesboro August 31-September 1. Lovejoy Station September 2-6. Operations against Hood and Forrest in North Georgia and North Alabama September 29-November 3. Nashville (Tenn.) Campaign November-December. Columbia, Duck River, November 24-27. Spring Hill November 29. Battle of Franklin November 30. Battle of Nashville December 15-16. Pursuit of Hood to the Tennessee River December 17-28. March to Huntsville, Ala., and duty there till March, 1865. Operations in East Tennessee March 28-April 19. Moved to Nashville, Tenn., and duty there till June. Moved to New Orleans, La., June 15-22, thence to Port Lavaca, Texas, July 16-23. Camp on La Placido River till September 25. Mustered out September 25, 1865.

Regiment lost during service 6 Officers and 129 Enlisted men killed and mortally wounded and 1 Officer and 156 Enlisted men by disease. Total 292.

45th REGIMENT INFANTRY ("WASHBURN LEAD MINE REGIMENT").

Organized at Galena, Ill., and mustered in at Camp Douglas, Ill., December 25, 1861. Moved to Cairo, Ill., January 12, 1862, and duty there till February 2. Attached to District of Cairo to February, 1862. 2nd Brigade, 1st Division, District of West Tennessee, and Army of the Tennessee, to March, 1862. 2nd Brigade, 1st Division, Army of the Tennessee, to July, 1862. 2nd Brigade, District of Jackson, to September, 1862. 3rd Brigade, District of Jackson, to November, 1862. 1st Brigade, 3rd Division, Right Wing 13th Army Corps (Old), Department of the Tennessee, to December, 1862. 1st Brigade, 3rd Division, 17th Army Corps, Army of the Tennessee, to July, 1865.

Operations against Fort Henry, Tenn., February 2-6, 1862. Capture of Fort Henry February 6. Investment and capture of Fort Donelson, Tenn., February 12-16. Duty at Fort Donelson till March 4. Moved to Savannah, Tenn., March 4-11. Expedition to Pin Hook March 18-19. Moved to Pittsburg Landing, Tenn., March 25. Battle of Shiloh, Tenn., April 6-7. Advance on and siege of Corinth, Miss., April 29-May 30. Moved to Bethel, thence to Jackson, Tenn., June 4-8. Guard R. R. there till August 11. Action at Medon August 3. Guard Mississippi Central R. R. August 11 to September 17 (4 companies at Medon, 5 companies at Toon's, Co. "G" at Treager's). Actions with Armstrong at Meadon, Toon's and Treager's August 31 (Co. "G" captured at Treager's). Duty at Jackson, Tenn., till November 2. Grant's Central Mississippi Campaign. Operations on the Mississippi Central R. R. to the Yockna River, Miss., November 2, 1862, to January 10, 1863. Capture of Henderson Station November 25, 1862 (Co. "B"). At Memphis, Tenn., till February, 1863. Moved to Lake Providence, La., February 22-24. Moved to Barry's Landing March 16 and to Milliken's Bend April 19 (a detachment ran batteries on transports April 22, the whole Regiment volunteering). Movement on Bruinsburg and turning Grand Gulf April 25-30. Battle of Thompson's Plantation (or Port Gibson) May 1. North Fork Bayou Pierre May 3. Ingraham's Heights May 3. Battles of Raymond May 12, Jackson May 14, Champion's Hill May 16, Big Black River May 17. Siege of Vicksburg, Miss., May 18-July 4. Assaults on Vicksburg May 19-22 and June 25. Surrender of Vicksburg July 4. Provost duty at Vicksburg till October. Expedition toward Canton October 14-20. Bogue Chitto Creek and Robinson's Mill October 17. At Big Black till February, 1864. Meridian Campaign February 3-

March 2. Meridian February 13-14. Chunky Station February 14. Chunkyville Station February 29. Moved to Memphis, Tenn., March 17. Veterans on furlough till May. Moved to Cairo, Ill., thence to Clifton, Tenn., April 28-May 5. March to Huntsville, Ala., May 5-23, thence to Ackworth, Ga., via Decatur and Warrenton, Ala., and Rome and Kingston, Ga., May 28-June 8. Atlanta (Ga.) Campaign June 8-September 8. Operations about Marietta and against Kenesaw Mountain June 10-July 2. Assault on Kenesaw June 27. Nickajack Creek July 2-5. Chattahoochie River July 5-17. Howell's Ferry July 5. Leggett's, Bald Hill, July 20-21. Battle of Atlanta July 22. Siege of Atlanta July 22-August 25. Flank movement on Jonesboro August 25-30. Battle of Jonesboro August 31-September 1. Lovejoy Station September 2-6. Operations against Hood in North Georgia and North Alabama September 28-November 3. March to the sea November 15-December 10. Siege of Savannah December 10-21. Campaign of the Carolinas January to April, 1865. Salkehatchie Swamp, S. C., February 1-5. Barker's Mills, Whippy Swamp, February 2. South Edisto River February 9. North Edisto River February 11-12. Columbia February 15-17. Fayetteville, N. C., March 13. Battle of Bentonville March 20-21. Occupation of Goldsboro March 24. Advance on Raleigh April 10-14. Occupation of Raleigh April 14. Bennett's House April 26. Surrender of Johnston and his army. March to Washington, D. C., via Richmond, Va., April 29-May 19. Grand Review May 24. Moved to Louisville, Ky., June 6-8. Mustered out July 12, 1865.

Regiment lost during service 9 Officers and 76 Enlisted men killed and mortally wounded and 2 Officers and 136 Enlisted men by disease. Total 223.

46th REGIMENT INFANTRY.

Organized at Camp Butler, Ill., December 28, 1861, and duty there till February 11, 1862. Moved to Cairo, Ill., thence to Fort Donelson, Tenn., February 11-14. Attached to 2nd Brigade, 3rd Division, District of Cairo, February, 1862. 2nd Brigade, 4th Division, District of West Tennessee, and Army of the Tennessee to July, 1862. 2nd Brigade, 4th Division, District of Memphis, Tenn., to September, 1862. 2nd Brigade, 4th Division, District of Jackson, Tenn., to November, 1862. 2nd Brigade, 4th Division, Right Wing 13th Army Corps (Old), Department of the Tennessee, to December, 1862. 2nd Brigade, 4th Division, 17th Army Corps, to January, 1863. 2nd Brigade, 4th Division, 16th Army Corps, to July, 1863. 2nd Brigade, 4th Division, 13th Army Corps, to August, 1863. 2nd Brigade, 4th Division, 17th Army Corps, to April, 1864. 2nd Brigade, 1st Division, 17th Army Corps, to August, 1864. 1st Brigade, 2nd Division, 19th Army Corps, Department of the Gulf, to December, 1864. 2nd Brigade, Reserve Division, Military Division West Mississippi, to February, 1865. 2nd Brigade, 1st Division, Reserve Corps, Military Division West Mississippi, February, 1865. 2nd Brigade, 1st Division, 13th Army Corps, Military Division West Mississippi, to June, 1865. Department of Louisiana to January, 1866.

SERVICE.—Investment and capture of Fort Donelson, Tenn., February 14-16, 1862. Occupation of Fort Henry, Tenn., February 19 to March 6. Moved to Pittsburg Landing, Tenn., March 6-18. Battle of Shiloh, Tenn., April 6-7. Advance on and siege of Corinth, Miss., April 29-May 30. March to Memphis, Tenn., via LaGrange, Grand Junction, Holly Springs, etc., June 10-July 21. Duty at Memphis, Tenn., till September 6. March to Bolivar and Hatchie River September 6-14. March to relief of Corinth, Miss., October 3. Battle of the Hatchie or Metamora October 5. Grant's Central Mississippi Campaign. Operations on the Mississippi Central R. R. November 2, 1862, to January 10, 1863. Garrison duty at Moscow, Tenn., January 13-February 5. Moved to LaFayette, thence to Memphis, Tenn., March 9. Expedition to Hernando, Miss., April 2-24. Moved to Young's Point, La., May 13-15. Siege of Vicksburg, Miss., May 18-July 4. Assaults on Vicksburg May 19 and 22. Advance on Jackson, Miss., July 5-10. Siege of Jackson, Miss., July 10-17. Assault on Jackson July 12. Reconnoissance to Pearl River July 15. Duty at Vicksburg till August 12. Moved to Natchez, Miss., August 12. Expedition to Harrisonburg, La., September 1-7. Action near Harrisonburg and capture of Fort Beauregard September 4. Moved to Vicksburg, Miss., September 16, and duty there till January 12, 1864. Red River October 14. Expedition from Natchez to Red River October 20. Regiment veteranize January 4, 1864. Veterans on furlough January 27 to March 2. Return to Vicksburg March 2. Duty there and at Big Black till July. Expedition to Benton and Yazoo City May 4-22. Actions at Benton May 7 and 9. Luce's Plantation May 13. Yazoo City May 13. Expedition to Pearl River, Miss., July 2-10. Near Jackson July 5. Jackson July 7. Ordered to Morganza, La., July 29, and duty there till August 23. Expedition to Port Hudson and Clinton, La., August 23-29. Moved to mouth of White River, Ark., September 3-8. Non-Veterans mustered out September 13. Moved to Duvall's Bluff, Ark., October 7-9. Thence to Memphis, Tenn., November 28-December 1, and duty there till December 21. Expedition to Germantown, Moscow and Wolf River, Tenn., December 21-31. Moved to Kennersville, La., January 2, thence to Fort Gaines, Dauphin Island, Ala., February 8-10, 1865. Campaign against Mobile and its defences March 18-April 12. Siege of Spanish Fort and Fort Blakely March 26-April 8. Assault and capture of Fort Blakely April 9. Capture of Mobile April 12. Expedition to Meridian, Miss., May 12-21. Moved to New Orleans, La., May 27-28, thence to Alexandria, Natchitoches and Shreveport, La., on Red River. Moved to Grand Ecore, La., June 19, and duty there till November 20. Moved to Shreveport November 20, thence to Baton Rouge, La., December 27. Mustered out at Baton Rouge, La., January 20, 1866, and discharged at Springfield, Ill., February 1, 1866.

Regiment lost during service 7 Officers and 74 Enlisted men killed and mortally wounded and 1 Officer and 253 Enlisted men by disease. Total 335.

47th REGIMENT INFANTRY.

Organized at Peoria, Ill., and mustered in August 16, 1861. Moved to St. Louis, Mo., September 23; thence to Jefferson City, Mo., October 9, and duty there till December 22, 1861. Attached to Dept. of the Missouri to February, 1862. 2nd Brigade, 2nd Division, Army of the Mississippi, to March, 1862. 1st Brigade, 5th Division, Army of the Mississippi, to April, 1862. 1st Brigade, 3rd Division, Army of the Mississippi, April, 1862. 2nd Brigade, 2nd Division, Army of the Mississippi, to November, 1862. 2nd Brigade, 8th Division, Left Wing 13th Army Corps (Old), Dept. of the Tennessee, to December, 1862. 2nd Brigade, 8th Division, 16th Army Corps, to April, 1863. 2nd Brigade, 3rd Division, 15th Army Corps, to December, 1863. 2nd Brigade, 1st Division, 16th Army Corps, to March, 1864. 2nd Brigade, 1st Division, 16th Army Corps, Detachment Army of the Tennessee, Department of the Gulf, to June, 1864. 2nd Brigade, 1st Division, 16th Army Corps, Dept. of the Tennessee, to November, 1864. Chicago, Ill., to December, 1864. 2nd Brigade, 2nd Division, District of Kentucky, to January, 1865. 2nd Brigade, 1st Division, Detachment Army of the Tennessee, Dept. of the Cumberland, to February, 1865. 2nd Brigade, 1st Division, 16th Army Corps (New), Military Division West Mississippi, to August, 1865. District of Alabama, Dept. of the Gulf, to January, 1866.

SERVICE.—Moved from Jefferson City, Mo., to Otterville, Mo., December 22, 1861, and duty there till February, 1862. Moved to Commerce, Mo., February 2. Operations against New Madrid, Mo., and Island No. 10, Mississippi River, February 28-April 8. New Madrid March 5. Point Pleasant March 7. Action and capture of Tiptonville April 8. Expedition to Fort Pillow, Tenn., April 13-17. Moved to Hamburg Landing, Tenn., April 17-22. Advance on and siege of Corinth, Miss., April

29-May 30. Reconnoissance toward Corinth May 8. Action at Farmington, Miss., May 9. Near Corinth May 28. Pursuit to Booneville May 31-June 12. Moved to Rienzi July 3, and duty there till August 18. March to Tuscumbia, Ala., August 18-22. March to Clear Creek September 8-14. Reconnoissance to Iuka, Miss., and skirmish September 16. Battle of Iuka September 19. Battle of Corinth October 3-4. Pursuit to Ripley October 5-14. Grant's Central Mississippi Campaign. Operations on the Mississippi Central R. R. November 2, 1862-January 10, 1863. March from Grand Junction to Corinth, Miss., January 8-14, 1863, thence to Ridgway Station January 26 and duty there guarding R. R. till March 12. Moved to Memphis, Tenn., thence to Duckport, La., March 12-April 1. Demonstration on Haines' and Snyder's Bluffs April 25-May 2. Movement to Jackson, Miss., via Grand Gulf May 2-14. Mississippi Springs May 13. Jackson May 14 and May 16. Siege of Vicksburg, Miss., May 18-July 4. Assaults on Vicksburg May 19 and 22. Expedition to Satartia and Mechanicsburg June 2-8. Satartia June 4. Expedition from Young's Point to Richmond, La., June 14-16. Richmond, La., June 15. Advance toward Jackson, Miss., July 5. Guard duty at Black River Bridge till July 22. At Bear Creek till October. Expedition to Canton October 14-20. Bogue Chitto Creek October 17. Moved to Memphis, Tenn., November 14-20; thence to LaGrange, Tenn., and guard Memphis & Charleston R. R., and scouting after Forrest till January 26, 1864. Skirmish at Saulsbury December 3, 1863. Moved to Vicksburg, Miss., January 26-February 3. Meridian Campaign February 3-March 2. At Black River Bridge till February 23. March to Canton and return to Vicksburg February 23-March 7. Red River Campaign March 10-May 22. Fort DeRussy March 14. Occupation of Alexandria March 16. Henderson's Hill March 21. Grand Ecore April 2. Campti April 3. Battle of Pleasant Hill April 9. About Cloutiersville, Cane River, April 22-24. At Alexandria April 26-May 13. Muddy Bayou May 2-6. Well's Plantation, near Alexandria, May 2-13. Retreat to Morganza May 13-20. Mansura May 16. Moved to Vicksburg, Miss., May 22-24, thence to Memphis, Tenn., June 4-10. Action at Lake Chicot, Ark., June 6. Defeat of Marmaduke. Veterans on furlough till August. Smith's Expedition to Tupelo, Miss., July 5-21. Near Camargo's Cross Roads July 13. Harrisburg, near Tupelo, July 14-15. Tishamingo (or Old Town) Creek July 15. Expedition to Oxford, Miss., August 1-30. Abbeville August 23. Non-Veterans muster out October 11, 1864. Mower's Expedition to Brownsville, Ark., September 2-10. March through Arkansas and Missouri in pursuit of Price September 17-November 4. Ordered to Chicago November 9, thence moved to Springfield, Ill., and to Louisville, Ky., December 3. Duty at Louisville and Bowling Green, Ky., till January 27, 1865. Moved to Eastport, Miss., via Nashville, Tenn., January 27-February 1, thence to New Orleans, La., February 6-22. Campaign against Mobile and its defences March 7-April 12. Siege of Spanish Fort and Fort Blakely March 26-April 8. Assault and capture of Fort Blakely April 9. Occupation of Mobile April 12. March to Montgomery April 13-25. Duty there and at Selma till January, 1866. Mustered out January 21, 1866.

Regiment lost during service 5 Officers and 58 Enlisted men killed and mortally wounded and 3 Officers and 184 Enlisted men by disease. Total 250.

48th REGIMENT INFANTRY.

Organized at Camp Butler, Ill., September, 1861. Moved to Cairo, Ill., November 11, 1861, and duty there till February, 1862. Attached to District of Cairo to February, 1862. 2nd Brigade, 1st Division, District of Cairo, to March, 1862. 2nd Brigade, 1st Division, District of West Tennessee, and Army of the Tennessee to July, 1862. 2nd Brigade, 1st Division, District of Jackson, Tenn., to September, 1862. Post of Bethel, District of Jackson, Tenn., to November, 1862. Post of Bethel, District of Jackson, 13th Army Corps (Old), Department of the Tennessee, to December, 1862. Post of Bethel, District of Jackson, 16th Army Corps, to March, 1863. 4th Brigade, 1st Division, 16th Army Corps, to July, 1863. 4th Brigade, 4th Division, 15th Army Corps, to September, 1863. 3rd Brigade, 4th Division, 15th Army Corps, to August, 1864. 1st Brigade, 4th Division, 15th Army Corps, to September, 1864. 3rd Brigade, 2nd Division, 15th Army Corps, to August, 1865.

SERVICE.—Grant's Expedition into Kentucky January 16-21, 1862. Operations against Fort Henry, Tenn., February 2-6. Capture of Fort Henry February 6. Investment and capture of Fort Donelson, Tenn., February 12-16. Duty at Fort Donelson till March 4. Moved to Savannah, Tenn., March 4-11, thence to Pittsburg Landing, Tenn., March 25. Battle of Shiloh, Tenn., April 6-7. Advance on and siege of Corinth, Miss., April 29-May 30. Moved to Bethel, Tenn., June 4, and garrison duty at that post till May, 1863. Operations against Forest in West Tennessee December 18, 1862-January 3, 1863. Germantown May 22. Moved from Germantown to Memphis, Tenn., thence to Vicksburg, Miss., June 9-17. Siege of Vicksburg June 17-July 4. Advance on Jackson, Miss., July 4-10. Birdsong Ferry, Big Black River, July 4-6. Jones' Ford, Messenger's Ferry, Big Black River, July 6. Quinn's Hill July 7. Siege of Jackson July 10-17. Camp at Big Black till September 28. Movement to Memphis, Tenn.; thence march to Chattanooga, Tenn., September 28-November 23. Operations on Memphis & Charleston R. R. in Alabama October 20-29. Chattanooga-Ringgold Campaign November 23-27. Tunnel Hill November 23-24. Mission Ridge November 25. March to relief of Knoxville November 28-December 8. At Scottsboro, Ala., till May, 1864. Atlanta (Ga.) Campaign May 1-September 8. Demonstrations on Resaca May 8-13. Near Resaca May 13. Battle of Resaca May 14-15. Near Kingston May 19-22. Advance on Dallas May 22-25. Operations on line of Pumpkin Vine Creek and battles about Dallas, New Hope Church and Allatoona Hills May 25-June 5. Operations about Marietta and against Kenesaw Mountain June 10-July 2. Brush Mountain June 15. Assault on Kenesaw Mountain June 27. Nickajack Creek July 2-5. Chattahoochie River July 5-17. Battle of Atlanta July 22. Siege of Atlanta July 22-August 25. Ezra Chapel, Hood's second sortie, July 28. Flank movement on Jonesboro August 25-30. Battle of Jonesboro August 31-September 1. Lovejoy Station September 2-6. Pursuit of Hood into Alabama October 1-26. Reconnoissance from Rome on Cave Springs Road October 12-13. March to the sea November 15-December 10. Griswoldsville November 22. Near Bryan's Court House December 8. Siege of Savannah December 10-21. Assault on and capture of Fort McAllister December 13. Campaign of the Carolinas January to April, 1865. Salkehatchie Swamp, S. C., February 2-5. Dillingham's Cross Roads, or Duck Branch, February 3. South Edisto River February 9. North Edisto River February 11-12. Columbia February 15-17. Battle of Bentonville, N. C., March 20-21. Occupation of Goldsboro March 24. Advance on Raleigh April 10-14. Occupation of Raleigh April 14. Bennett's House April 26. Surrender of Johnston and his army. March to Washington, D. C., via Richmond, Va., April 29-May 19. Grand Review May 24. Moved to Louisville, Ky., June 2, thence to Little Rock, Ark., June 25. Mustered out August 15, 1865.

Regiment lost during service 10 Officers and 113 Enlisted men killed and mortally wounded and 6 Officers and 251 Enlisted men by disease. Total 380.

49th REGIMENT INFANTRY.

Organized at Camp Butler, Ill., and mustered in December 31, 1861. Moved to Cairo, Ill., thence to Fort Henry, Tenn., February 8-10, 1862. Attached to 3rd Brigade, 1st Division, District of Cairo, February, 1862. 3rd Brigade, 1st Division, District of West Tennessee, and Army of the Tennessee, to July, 1862. 3rd Brigade, District of Jackson, Tenn., to November, 1862. Post of Bethel, District of Jackson, 13th

Army Corps (Old), Department of the Tennessee, to December, 1862. Post of Bethel, District of Jackson, 16th Army Corps, to March, 1863. 4th Brigade, 1st Division, 16th Army Corps, to May, 1863. 4th Brigade, District of Memphis, Tenn., 5th Division, 16th Army Corps, to July, 1863. 3rd Brigade, 3rd Division, 16th Army Corps, to August, 1863. True's Brigade, Arkansas Expedition, to November, 1863. Gilbert's Brigade, District of Memphis, Tenn., 5th Division, 16th Army Corps, to January, 1864. 3rd Brigade, 3rd Division, 16th Army Corps, to March, 1864. 3rd Brigade, 3rd Division, 16th Army Corps, Dept. of the Gulf, to June, 1864, and Dept. of the Tennessee to November, 1864. 3rd Brigade, 2nd Division, Smith's Detachment, Army of the Tennessee, Dept. of the Cumberland, to December, 1864. Garrison, Paducah, Ky., Dept. of Kentucky, to September, 1865.

SERVICE.—Investment and capture of Fort Donelson, Tenn., February 12-16, 1862. Moved to Savannah, thence to Pittsburg Landing, Tenn., March 5-25. Battle of Shiloh, Tenn., April 6-7. Advance on and siege of Corinth, Miss., April 29-May 30. March to Bethel, Tenn., June 4, and Post duty there till March, 1863. Moved to Germantown and White's Station, Tenn., March 10-12, and guard R. R. till August 10. Moved to Memphis, Tenn., thence to Helena and Brownsville, Ark., August 21-September 2. Steele's Expedition against Little Rock September 2-10. Bayou Fourche and capture of Little Rock September 10. Moved to Duvall's Bluff, thence to Memphis, Tenn., November 15-21, and duty there till January, 1864. Regiment veteranize January 15, 1864. Moved to Vicksburg, Miss., January 27-February 2. Meridian Campaign February 3-March 2. Red River Campaign March 10-May 22. Fort DeRussy March 14. Occupation of Alexandria March 16. Battle of Pleasant Hill April 9. About Cloutiersville, Cane River, April 22-24. Occupation of Alexandria April 26-May 13. Governor Moore's Plantation and Bayou Roberts May 3-7 and 11. Retreat to Morganza May 13-20. Mansura May 16. Yellow Bayou May 18. Moved to Vicksburg, Miss., thence to Memphis, Tenn., May 22-June 10. Old River Lake (or Lake Chicot), Ark., June 6. Skirmish near Lafayette June 29. Smith's Expedition to Tupelo, Miss., July 5-21. Near Camargo's Cross Roads, Harrisburg, July 13. Harrisburg, near Tupelo, July 14-15. Tishamingo Creek (or Old Town), July 15. Expedition to Oxford, Miss., August 1-30. Hurricane Creek August 13-14. Abbeville August 23. Moved to Jefferson Barracks, Mo., and in pursuit of Price through Missouri September to November. Franklin, Mo., October 1 and October 30. Moved from St. Louis, Mo., to Nashville, Tenn., November 21-December 1. Battle of Nashville, Tenn., December 15-16. Pursuit to Tennessee River December 17-28. Ordered to Paducah, Ky., December 29, and garrison duty there till September, 1865. Mustered out September 9, 1865.

Regiment lost during service 7 Officers and 72 Enlisted men killed and mortally wounded and 5 Officers and 170 Enlisted men by disease. Total 254.

50th REGIMENT INFANTRY.

Organized at Quincy, Ill., and mustered in September 12, 1861. Moved to Hannibal, Mo., October 9, thence to Chillicothe October 19. To St. Joseph, Mo., November 27; to Palmyra, Mo., December 19, and to St. Joseph, December 24. Attached to Department of Missouri October, 1861, to February, 1862. 3rd Brigade, 2nd Division, District of Cairo, February, 1862. 3rd Brigade, 2nd Division, District of West Tennessee, and Army of the Tennessee to July, 1862. 3rd Brigade, 2nd Division, District of Corinth, Miss., to November, 1862. 3rd Brigade, 2nd Division, District of Corinth, Miss., 13th Army Corps (Old), Department of the Tennessee, to December, 1862. 3rd Brigade, District of Corinth, 17th Army Corps, to January, 1863. 3rd Brigade, District of Corinth, 16th Army Corps, to March, 1863. 3rd Brigade, 2nd Division, 16th Army Corps, to September, 1864. 3rd Brigade, 4th Division, 15th Army Corps, to July, 1865.

SERVICE.—Moved from St. Joseph, Mo., to Cairo, Ill., and Smithland, Ky., January 21-28, 1862. Operations against Fort Henry, Tenn., February 2-6. Capture of Fort Henry February 6. Investment and capture of Fort Donelson, Tenn., February 12-16. Expedition to Clarksville and Nashville, Tenn., February 19-March 1. Moved to Pittsburg Landing, Tenn., March 25-31. Battle of Shiloh, Tenn., April 6-7. Advance on and siege of Corinth, Miss., April 29-May 30. Duty at Corinth till November, 1863. Reconnoissance to Bay Springs August 4-7, 1862 (two Companies). Battle of Corinth October 3-4, 1862. Pursuit to Hatchie River October 5-12. Grant's Central Mississippi Campaign November, 1862, to January, 1863. Expedition against Forest in West Tennessee December 18, 1862-January 3, 1863. Dodge's Expedition to Northern Alabama April 15-May 3, 1863. Great Bear Creek and Cherokee Station April 17. Rock Cut, near Tuscumbia, April 22. Tuscumbia April 23. Town Creek April 28. Moved to LaGrange, Tenn., and return to Corinth October 11-17. Moved to Eastport, Pulaski and Lynnville November 6-12, and duty there till March, 1864. Regiment mounted November 17, and Veteranize January 1, 1864. Veterans on furlough till March 5. Atlanta (Ga.) Campaign May 1-September 8. Demonstration on Resaca May 8-13. Sugar Valley, near Resaca, May 9. Near Resaca May 13. Battle of Resaca May 14-15. Lay's Ferry, Oostenaula River, May 14-15. Rome Cross Roads May 16. Assigned to garrison duty at Rome, Ga., till November. Battle of Allatoona October 5. Cave Springs Road October 12-13. March to the sea November 15-December 10. Ogeechee Canal December 9. Siege of Savannah December 10-21. Campaign of the Carolinas January to April, 1865. Salkehatchie Swamps, S. C., February 2-5. South Edisto River February 9. North Edisto River February 11-12. Columbia February 15-17. Battle of Bentonville, N. C., March 20-21. Occupation of Goldsboro March 24. Advance on Raleigh April 10-14. Occupation of Raleigh April 14. Bennett's House April 26. Surrender of Johnston and his Army. March to Washington, D. C., via Richmond, Va., April 29-May 19. Grand Review May 24. Moved to Louisville, Ky., June 3-8. Mustered out July 13, 1865.

Regiment lost during service 2 Officers and 60 Enlisted men killed and mortally wounded and 129 Enlisted men by disease. Total 191.

51st REGIMENT INFANTRY.

Organized at Camp Douglas, Chicago, Ill., and mustered in December 24, 1861. Moved to Cairo, Ill., February 14, 1862. Duty there and at Camp Cullum, Ky., till March 4, 1862. Attached to 2nd Brigade, 4th Division, Army of Mississippi, to April, 1862. 1st Brigade, 1st Division, Army of the Mississippi, to September, 1862. 1st Brigade, 13th Division, Army of the Ohio, to November, 1862. 3rd Brigade, 3rd Division, Right Wing 14th Army Corps, Army of the Cumberland, to January, 1863. 3rd Brigade, 3rd Division, 20th Army Corps, Army of the Cumberland, to October, 1863. 3rd Brigade, 2nd Division, 4th Army Corps, to August, 1865. Department of Texas to September, 1865.

SERVICE.—Operations against New Madrid, Mo., and Island No. 10, Mississippi River, March 7-April 8, 1862. Actions at New Madrid March 13-14. Action and capture at Tiptonville April 8. Expedition to Fort Pillow, Tenn., April 13-17. Moved to Hamburg Landing, Tenn., April 17-23. Advance on and siege of Corinth, Miss., April 29-May 30. Action at Farmington May 3. Reconnoissance toward Corinth May 8. Action at Farmington May 9. Pursuit to Booneville May 31-June 12. Reconnoissance toward Baldwyn June 3. At Corinth till July 20. Moved to Tuscumbia, Ala., July 20. Guard R. R. from Hillsboro to Decatur, Ala. Stationed at Decatur till September 4. March to Nashville, Tenn., September 4-12. Siege of Nashville, Tenn., September 12-November 6. Repulse of Forest's attack on Edgefield November 5. Duty at Nashville till December 26. Advance on Murfreesboro December 26-30. Battle of Stone's River December 30-31, 1862, and January 1-3,

1863. Duty at Murfreesboro till June. Expedition to Columbia March 4-14. Middle Tennessee (or Tullahoma) Campaign June 24-July 7. Occupation of Middle Tennessee till August 16. Passage of the Cumberland Mountains and Tennessee River and Chickamauga (Ga.) Campaign August 16-September 22. Battle of Chickamauga, Ga., September 19-20. Siege of Chattanooga, Tenn., September 24-November 23. Chattanooga-Ringgold Campaign November 23-27. Orchard Knob November 23-24. Mission Ridge November 25. March to relief of Knoxville and operations in East Tennessee November 28-January 15, 1864. Moved to Chattanooga, thence to Cleveland, Tenn., and duty there till May, 1864. Veterans on furlough February 10-March 30. Atlanta (Ga.) Campaign May 1 to September 8. Demonstrations on Rocky Faced Ridge May 8-11. Buzzard's Roost Gap May 8-9. Battle of Resaca May 14-15. Adairsville May 17. Near Kingston May 18-19. Near Cassville May 19. Advance on Dallas May 22-25. Operations on line of Pumpkin Vine Creek and battles about Dallas, New Hope Church and Allatoona Hills May 25-June 5. Operations about Marietta and against Kenesaw Mountains June 10-July 2. Pine Hill June 11-14. Lost Mountain June 15-17. Assault on Kenesaw June 27. Ruff's Station, Smyrna Camp Ground, July 4. Chattahoochie River July 5-17. Buckhead, Nancy's Creek, July 18. Peach Tree Creek July 19-20. Siege of Atlanta July 22-August 25. Flank movement on Jonesboro August 25-30. Battle of Jonesboro August 31-September 1. Moved to Chattanooga, Tenn., September 28, thence to Bridgeport, Ala., and duty there till October 18. Moved to Chattanooga October 18. Nashville Campaign November-December. Columbia, Duck River, November 24-27. Spring Hill November 29. Battle of Franklin November 30. Battle of Nashville December 15-16. Pursuit of Hood to the Tennessee River December 17-28. Moved to Huntsville, Ala., and duty there till March, 1865. Operations in East Tennessee March and April. Moved to Nashville, Tenn., and duty there till June. Moved to New Orleans, La., June 16-22, thence to Texas July 28-31. At Camp Placider, Texas, till September. Mustered out at Camp Irwin September 25 and discharged at Chicago, Ill., October 15, 1865.

Regiment lost during service 9 Officers and 106 Enlisted men killed and mortally wounded and 1 Officer and 134 Enlisted men by disease. Total 250.

52nd REGIMENT INFANTRY.

Organized at Geneva, Ill., and mustered in November 19, 1861. Moved to Benton Barracks, Mo., November 28, thence to St. Joseph, Mo., December 8, 1861. Attached to Department of the Missouri to February, 1862. 3rd Brigade, 2nd Division, District of Cairo, February, 1862. 3rd Brigade, 1st Division, District of West Tennessee, to March, 1862. 2nd Brigade, 4th Division, District of West Tennessee, March, 1862. 3rd Brigade, 2nd Division, Army of the Tennessee, to July, 1862. 3rd Brigade, 2nd Division, District of Corinth, Miss., to September, 1862. 1st Brigade, 2nd Division, District of Corinth, to November, 1862. 3rd Brigade, District of Corinth, 13th Army Corps (Old), Department of the Tennessee, to December, 1862. 1st Brigade, District of Corinth, 17th Army Corps, to January, 1863. 1st Brigade, District of Corinth, 16th Army Corps, to March, 1863. 1st Brigade, 2nd Division, 16th Army Corps, to September, 1864. 1st Brigade, 4th Division, 15th Army Corps, to July, 1865.

SERVICE.—Moved from St. Joseph, Mo., to Cairo, Ill., and Smithland, Ky., January 16-24, 1862. Duty there till February 10. Moved to Fort Donelson, Tenn., February 10-17. Duty escorting prisoners from Fort Donelson, Tenn., to Chicago, Ill., February 18-March 5. Moved to St. Louis March 6-7, thence to Pittsburg Landing, Tenn., March 13-20. Battle of Shiloh, Tenn., April 6-7. Advance on and siege of Corinth, Miss., April 29-May 30. Pursuit to Booneville May 31-June 6. At Corinth, Miss., till August, 1863. Battle of Corinth October 3-4, 1862. Pursuit to Ripley October 5-12. Action at Little Bear Creek November 28. Dodge's Expedition into Alabama December 9-14. Dodge's Expedition to intercept Forest, and operations in West Tennessee December 18, 1862-January 3, 1863. Expedition to Hamburg, Tenn., January 26-28, 1863. Expedition to Jacinto, Miss., February 25-March 6. Dodge's Expedition to Northern Alabama April 15-May 8. Rock Cut, near Tuscumbia, April 22. Tuscumbia April 23. Town Creek April 27-28. At Corinth till August 18. Moved to Germantown, Tenn., August 18, and duty there guarding R. R. till October 29. March to Pulaski, Tenn., October 29-November 11. Duty at Pulaski till April 30, 1864. Regiment veteranize January 9, 1864. Veterans on furlough January 9 to February 24, returning to Pulaski from Chicago February 24-29. Moved to Chattanooga April 30-May 2. Atlanta (Ga.) Campaign May 2 to September 8. Demonstrations on Resaca May 8-13. Snake Creek Gap May 9-12. Near Resaca May 13. Battle of Resaca May 14-15. Ley's Ferry, Oostenaula River, May 15. Rome Cross Roads May 16. Rome May 17-18. Advance on Dallas May 20-25. Operations on line of Pumpkin Vine Creek and battles about Dallas, New Hope Church and Allatoona Hills May 25-June 5. Operations about Marietta and against Kenesaw Mountain June 10-July 2. Assault on Kenesaw June 27. Ruff's Mills July 3-4. Chattahoochie River July 5-17. Decatur and Battle of Atlanta July 22. Siege of Atlanta July 22-August 25. Flank movement on Jonesboro August 25-30. Battle of Jonesboro August 31-September 1. Moved to Rome, Ga., September 26, and duty there till November. Reconnoissance on Cave Springs Road and skirmishes October 12-13. March to the sea November 15-December 10. Little Ogeechee River December 4. Jenks' Bridge December 7. Eden Cross Roads December 7-9. Siege of Savannah December 10-21. Campaign of the Carolinas January to April, 1865. Salkehatchie Swamps, S. C., February 2-5. South Edisto River February 9. North Edisto River February 11-12. Columbia February 15-17. Lynch's Creek February 25-26. Cheraw March 2-3. Reconnoissance from Fayetteville, N. C., and skirmish on Raleigh Road to Silver Run Creek March 14. Averysboro, Taylor's Hole Creek, March 16. Battle of Bentonville March 20-21. Occupation of Goldsboro March 24. Advance on Raleigh April 10-14. Occupation of Raleigh April 14. Bennett's House April 26. Surrender of Johnston and his army. March to Washington, D. C., via Richmond, Va., April 29-May 19. Grand Review May 24. Moved to Louisville, Ky., June 2. Mustered out July 5 and discharged at Chicago, Ill., July 12, 1865.

Regiment lost during service 2 Officers and 59 Enlisted men killed and mortally wounded and 119 Enlisted men by disease. Total 180.

53rd REGIMENT INFANTRY.

Organized at Ottawa, Ill., January, 1862. Moved to Chicago, Ill., February 27, 1862, and duty there till March 23, guarding prisoners. Moved to St. Louis, Mo., thence to Pittsburg Landing, Tenn., March 23-April 7. Attached to 1st Brigade, 4th Division, Army of the Tennessee, to July, 1862. 1st Brigade, 4th Division, District of Memphis, Tenn., to September, 1862. 1st Brigade, 4th Division, District of Jackson, Tenn., to November, 1862. 1st Brigade, 4th Division, Right Wing 13th Army Corps (Old), Department of the Tennessee, to December, 1862. 1st Brigade, 4th Division, 17th Army Corps, to January, 1863. 1st Brigade, 4th Division, 16th Army Corps, to July, 1863. 1st Brigade, 4th Division, 13th Army Corps, to August, 1863. 1st Brigade, 4th Division, 17th Army Corps, to April, 1864. 2nd Brigade, 4th Division, 17th Army Corps, to July, 1864. 1st Brigade, 4th Division, 17th Army Corps, to July, 1865.

SERVICE.—Battle of Shiloh, Tenn., April 7, 1862. Advance on and siege of Corinth, Miss., April 29-May 30. March to Memphis, Tenn., via Grand Junction, La Grange, Holly Springs, etc., June 1-July 21, and duty at Memphis till September 6. Moved to Bolivar, Tenn., September 6-13. March to relief of Corinth, Miss.,

October 4. Battle of Hatchie River (or Metamora) October 5. Grant's Central Mississippi Campaign. Operations on the Mississippi Central R. R. November 2, 1862, to January 10, 1863. Reconnoissance from La Grange to Lamar, Miss., November 5. Worsham Creek November 6. At Moscow, Tenn., and guarding Memphis & Charleston R. R. January to March, 1863. Skirmishes near Moscow February 9 and 18. Moved to Memphis, Tenn., March 11, and duty there till May 17. Moved to Young's Point, La., May 17-20. Siege of Vicksburg May 20-July 4. Advance on Jackson, Miss., July 4-10. Siege of Jackson July 10-17. Assault on Jackson July 12. Duty at Vicksburg till August 15. Moved to Natchez, Miss., August 15, and duty there till November 30. Moved to Vicksburg November 30. At Milldale till February 1, 1864. Meridian Campaign February 3-March 2. Pearl River February 27. Regiment veteranize January 1, 1864. Veterans on furlough March and April. Moved to Bird's Point, thence to Clifton, Tenn., and march to Ackworth, Ga., via Huntsville and Decatur, Ala., and Rome, Ga., April 28-June 8. Ordered to Allatoona Pass June 8, and duty there building fortifications till July 13. Rejoined army at Marietta and duty there till November. Skirmish at Decatur July 20-21. Shadna Church and Westbrook's October 2. March to the sea November 15-December 10. Oconee River November 26. Siege of Savannah December 10-21. Campaign of the Carolinas January to April, 1865. Salkehatchie Swamps, S. C., February 2-5. River's Bridge, Salkehatchie River, February 3. Binnaker's Bridge, South Edisto River, February 9. Orangeburg, North Edisto River, February 11-12. Columbia February 15-17. Cheraw March 3. Fayetteville, N. C., March 11. Battle of Bentonville March 20-21. Occupation of Goldsboro March 24. Advance on Raleigh April 10-14. Bennett's House April 26. Surrender of Johnston and his army. March to Washington, D. C., via Richmond, Va., April 29-May 19. Grand Review May 24. Moved to Louisville, Ky., June 6. Mustered out July 22, 1865.

Regiment lost during service 8 Officers and 80 Enlisted men killed and mortally wounded and 2 Officers and 137 Enlisted men by disease. Total 227.

54th REGIMENT INFANTRY.

Organized at Camp Dubois, Anna, Ill., as a part of the Kentucky Brigade, and mustered in February, 1862. Moved to Cairo, Ill., February 24, 1862. Attached to District of Cairo to March, 1862. District of Columbus, Ky., to September, 1862. District of Jackson, Tenn., to November, 1862. Unattached, District of Jackson, Tenn., 13th Army Corps (Old), to December, 1862. Unattached, District of Jackson, Tenn., 16th Army Corps, to January, 1863. 1st Brigade, District of Jackson, 16th Army Corps, to March, 1863. 2nd Brigade, 3rd Division, 16th Army Corps, to May, 1863. 2nd Brigade, Kimball's Provisional Division, 16th Army Corps, to July, 1863. 2nd Brigade, Kimball's Division, District of Eastern Arkansas, to August, 1863. 1st Brigade, 2nd Division, Arkansas Expedition, to November, 1863. 3rd Brigade, 2nd Division, Arkansas Expedition, to January, 1864. 3rd Brigade, 2nd Division, 7th Army Corps, Department of Arkansas, to May, 1864. 1st Brigade, 2nd Division, 7th Army Corps, to August, 1865. Dept. of Arkansas to October, 1865.

SERVICE.—Moved from Cairo to Columbus, Ky., March 4, 1862, and duty there till December 18, 1862. Three Companies at Humboldt, Tenn. Expedition down Mississippi River to Fort Pillow, Tenn., May 19-23 (2 Cos). Merriwether Ferry, Obion River, Tenn., August 16. Moved to Jackson, Tenn., December 18, and duty there till May, 1863. (2 Cos. at Mendon Station and 2 Cos. at Toone's Station January to April, 1863.) Operations against Forest in West Tennessee December 20-28, 1862. Union City, Tenn., December 21, 1862 (Detachment). Captured by Forest. Moved to Vicksburg, Miss., May 30-June 2, 1863. Siege of Vicksburg, Miss., June 2-July 4. Moved to Helena, Ark., July 24. Steele's Expedition to Little Rock, Ark., August 1-September 10. Bayou Fourche and capture of Little Rock September 10. Duty at Little Rock till March, 1864. Veterans on furlough March and April. Riot at Charleston, Ill., March 28. Veterans. Moved to Little Rock April 12-30, thence to Brownsville May 18. Pursuit of Shelby May 19-31. Moved to Duvall's Bluff and Clarendon June 25-29. Action at Clarendon June 25-26. Guard Memphis and Little Rock R. R. till August 24. Actions with Shelby, at Jones' Hay Station, Long Prairie and Ashley's Station August 24. Regiment mostly captured, except Companies "F" and "H." Paroled at Jacksonport, Ark., and reached Benton Barracks, Mo., September 9. Exchanged December 5, 1864. Arrived at Hickory Station, on Memphis & Little Rock R. R., January 18, 1865. On railroad guard duty till June 6. Moved to Pine Bluff June 6-9, and duty there till August 18. March to Fort Smith, Ark., August 18-30. Moved to Little Rock, Ark., October 4-6. Mustered out October 15, 1865, and discharged at Camp Butler, Ill.

Regiment lost during service 1 Officer and 11 Enlisted men killed and mortally wounded and 2 Officers and 171 Enlisted men by disease. Total 185.

55th REGIMENT INFANTRY.

Organized at Camp Douglas, Chicago, Ill., and mustered in October 31, 1861. Moved to Benton Barracks, Mo., November 9-11, 1861, and duty there till January 12, 1862. Moved to Paducah, Ky., January 12-22. Attached to District of Paducah, Ky., to March, 1862. 2nd Brigade, 5th Division, Army of the Tennessee, to May, 1862. 1st Brigade, 5th Division, Army of the Tennessee, to July, 1862. 1st Brigade, 5th Division, District of Memphis, Tenn., to November, 1862. 4th Brigade, 5th Division, District of Memphis, Right Wing 13th Army Corps (Old), Department of the Tennessee, November, 1862. 2nd Brigade, 2nd Division, District of Memphis, 13th Army Corps, to December, 1862. 2nd Brigade, 2nd Division, Sherman's Yazoo Expedition, to January, 1863. 2nd Brigade, 2nd Division, 15th Army Corps, Army of the Tennessee, to September, 1863. 1st Brigade, 2nd Division, 15th Army Corps, to August, 1865.

SERVICE.—Action at and occupation of Columbus, Ky., March 3, 1862. Moved from Paducah, Ky., to Savannah, Tenn., March 6-10. Expedition to Yellow Creek, Miss., and occupation of Pittsburg Landing, Tenn., March 14-17. Battle of Shiloh, Tenn., April 6-7. Corinth Road April 8. Advance on and siege of Corinth, Miss., April 29-May 30. Russell's House May 17. Occupation of Corinth May 30. March to Memphis, Tenn., June 3-July 21, and duty there till November 26. Expedition from Memphis to Coldwater and Hernando, Miss., September 8-13. Sherman's Tallahatchie March November 26-December 13. Sherman's Yazoo Expedition December 20, 1862, to January 2, 1863. Chickasaw Bayou December 26-28. Chickasaw Bluff December 29. Expedition to Arkansas Post, Ark., January 3-10, 1863. Assault and capture of Fort Hindman, Arkansas Post, January 10-11. Moved to Young's Point, La., January 17, and duty there till March. Expedition to Rolling Fork, via Muddy, Steele's and Black Bayous and Deer Creek March 14-27. Demonstration on Haines' and Drumgould's Bluffs April 29-May 2. Haines' Bluff May 1. At Milliken's Bend till May 5. Moved to join Army in rear of Vicksburg, Miss., May 7-16. Battle of Champion's Hill May 16. Siege of Vicksburg, Miss., May 18-July 4. Assaults on Vicksburg May 19 and 22. Advance on Jackson, Miss., July 5-10. Siege of Jackson July 10-17. Brandon Station July 19. At Big Black till September 25. Moved to Memphis, Tenn., thence march to Chattanooga, Tenn., September 25-November 21. Operations on Memphis & Charleston R. R. in Alabama October 20-29. Bear Creek, Tuscumbia, October 27. Chattanooga-Ringgold Campaign November 23-27. Brown's Ferry November 23. Foot of Missionary Ridge November 24. Tunnel Hill November 24-25. Mission Ridge November 25. Pursuit to Graysville November 26-27. March to relief of Knoxville November 28-December 5. Expedition to Tellico Plains

December 6-13. March to Chattanooga December 13-17, thence to Bridgeport, Ala., December 19, and to Bellefonte, Ala., December 26. To Larkinsville, Ala., January 6, 1864, and duty there till April. Expedition toward Rome, Ga., January 25-February 5. Veterans on furlough April 16-June 10. Rejoined Army at Big Shanty June 19. Non-Veterans attached to 116th Illinois Infantry. Atlanta (Ga.) Campaign May 1-September 8. Demonstration on Resaca May 8-13. Near Resaca May 13. Battle of Resaca May 14-15. Movements on Dallas May 18-25. Operations on line of Pumpkin Vine Creek and battles about Dallas, New Hope Church and Allatoona Hills May 25-June 5. Operations about Marietta and against Kenesaw Mountain June 10-July 2. Assault on Kenesaw Mountain June 27. Nickajack Creek July 2-5. Chattahoochie River July 5-17. Battle of Atlanta July 22. Siege of Atlanta July 22-August 25. Ezra Chapel, Hood's second sortie, July 28. Flank movement on Jonesboro August 25-30. Battle of Jonesboro August 31-September 1. Lovejoy Station September 2-6. Pursuit of Hood into Alabama October 3-26. Non-Veterans mustered out October 30, 1864. March to the sea November 15-December 10. Near Clinton November 21-23. Oconee River November 25. Statesborough December 3. Siege of Savannah December 10-21. Assault and capture of Fort McAllister December 13. Campaign of the Carolinas January to April, 1865. Duck Creek February 2. Salkehatchie Swamps, S. C., February 3-5. Holmes' Bridge, South Edisto River, February 9. North Edisto River February 11-12. Congaree Creek February 15. Columbia February 16-17. Fayetteville, N. C., March 11. Battle of Bentonville, N. C., March 20-21. Occupation of Goldsboro March 24. Advance on Raleigh April 10-14. Occupation of Raleigh April 14. Bennett's House April 26. Surrender of Johnston and his army. March to Washington, D. C., via Richmond, Va., April 29-May 19. Grand Review May 24. Moved to Louisville, Ky., June 2, thence to Memphis, Tenn., and Duvall's Bluff and Little Rock, Ark., June 30-July 6. Mustered out August 14, 1865.

Regiment lost during service 9 Officers and 149 Enlisted men killed and mortally wounded and 2 Officers and 127 Enlisted men by disease. Total 286.

56th REGIMENT INFANTRY.

Organized at Shawneetown, Ill., and mustered in February 27, 1862. Left State for Paducah, Ky., February 27, and duty there till April 20. Attached to District of Paducah, Ky., to April, 1862. 2nd Brigade, 3rd Division, Army of Mississippi, to November, 1862. 2nd Brigade, 7th Division, Left Wing 13th Army Corps (Old), Department of the Tennessee, to December, 1862. 2nd Brigade, 7th Division, 16th Army Corps, to January, 1863. 2nd Brigade, 7th Division, 17th Army Corps, to September, 1863. 2nd Brigade, 2nd Division, 17th Army Corps, to December, 1863. 2nd Brigade, 3rd Division, 15th Army Corps, to April, 1865. 2nd Brigade, 1st Division, 15th Army Corps, to August, 1865.

SERVICE.—Moved from Paducah, Ky., to Hamburg Landing, Tenn., April 20-25, 1862. Advance on and siege of Corinth, Miss., April 29-May 30. Pursuit to Booneville May 31-June 12. Expedition to Ripley June 22-23. At Camp Clear Creek till October, 1862. Battle of Corinth October 3-4. Pursuit to Ripley October 5-12. Grant's Central Mississippi Campaign November 4 to December 30. Reconnoissance from LaGrange November 8-9. Guard Memphis & Charleston R. R. till March 1, 1863. Yazoo Pass Expedition March 1-April 5. Fort Pemberton March 22. Moved to Milliken's Bend, La., April 13. Movement on Bruinsburg and turning Grand Gulf April 25-30. At Grand Gulf guarding transportation lines and base of supplies May 1-13. Battle of Champion's Hill May 16. Big Black River May 17. Siege of Vicksburg, Miss., May 18-July 4. Assaults on Vicksburg May 19 and 22 and June 25. Surrender of Vicksburg July 4. Moved to Helena, Ark., August 20; thence to Memphis, Tenn., and march to Chattanooga, Tenn., September 20-November 23. Operations on Memphis & Charleston R. R. in Alabama October 20-29.

Chattanooga-Ringgold Campaign November 23-27. Tunnel Hill November 24-25. Mission Ridge November 25. Pursuit to Graysville November 26-27. Guard railroad and duty at Whitesburg, on Tennessee River, till May, 1864. Atlanta (Ga.) Campaign May to September. Guard Memphis & Charleston R. R. and Chattanooga & Atlanta R. R. and fords of the Etowah; stationed at Mud Creek, Calhoun and Adairsville, Ga., till October. Defence of Resaca October 12-13. Company "F" at surrender of Dalton, Ga., October 13. Adairsville October 22. March to the sea November 15-December 10. Siege of Savannah December 10-21. Campaign of the Carolinas January to April, 1865. Salkehatchie Swamp, S. C., February 2-5. Fishburn's Plantation, near Lane's Bridge, Salkehatchie River, February 6. South Edisto River February 9. North Edisto River February 11-12. Columbia February 15-17. Cox's Bridge, Neuse River, February 19-20. Battle of Bentonville, N. C., March 20-21. Occupation of Goldsboro March 24. Advance on Raleigh, N. C., April 10-14. Occupation of Raleigh April 14. Bennett's House April 26. Surrender of Johnston and his army. March to Washington, D. C., via Richmond, Va., April 29-May 19. Grand Review May 24. Moved to Louisville, Ky., June; thence to Little Rock, Ark., and duty there till August. Mustered out August 12, 1865.

Regiment lost during service 2 Officers and 25 Enlisted men killed and mortally wounded and 14 Officers and 348 Enlisted men by disease. Total 389.

57th REGIMENT INFANTRY.

Organized at Camp Douglas, Chicago, Ill., and mustered in December 26, 1861. Moved to Cairo, Ill.; thence to Fort Donelson, Tenn., February 8-14, 1862. Attached to 2nd Brigade, 3rd Division, District of Cairo, February, 1862. 3rd Brigade, 2nd Division, District of West Tennessee and Army of the Tennessee, to July, 1862. 3rd Brigade, 2nd Division, District of Corinth, to November, 1862. 3rd Brigade, District of Corinth, 13th Army Corps (Old), Department of the Tennessee, to December, 1862. 3rd Brigade, District of Corinth, 17th Army Corps, to January, 1863. 3rd Brigade, District of Corinth, 16th Army Corps, to March, 1863. 3rd Brigade, 2nd Division, 16th Army Corps, to September, 1864. 3rd Brigade, 4th Division, 15th Army Corps, to July, 1865.

SERVICE.—Investment and capture of Fort Donelson, Tenn., February 14-16, 1862. Moved to Fort Henry, Tenn., February 17; thence to Crump's Landing, Tenn., March 8-13, and to Pittsburg Landing March 28. Battle of Shiloh, Tenn., April 6-7. Advance on and siege of Corinth, Miss., April 29-May 30. Pursuit to Booneville May 31-June 6. Duty at Corinth, Miss., till November, 1863. Battle of Corinth October 3-4, 1862. Pursuit of enemy to Hatchie River October 5-12. At Corinth till April, 1863. Grant's Central Mississippi Campaign November, 1862, to January, 1863. Operations against Forest in West Tennessee December 18, 1862, to January 3, 1863. Dodge's Expedition to Northern Alabama April 15-May 2, 1863. Great Bear Creek, Cherokee Station and Lundy's Lane April 17. Rock Cut, near Tuscumbia, April 22. Tuscumbia April 23. Town Creek April 28. At Corinth till November. Grand Junction, Tenn., July 30; 1863. Moved to Eastport, Pulaski and Lynnville November 6-12, and duty there till March, 1864. Atlanta (Ga.) Campaign May to September, 1864. Demonstrations on Resaca May 8-13. Sugar Valley, near Resaca, May 9. Near Resaca May 13. Battle of Resaca May 14-15. Ley's Ferry, Oostenaula River, May 14-15. Rome Cross Roads May 16. Operations on line of Pumpkin Vine Creek and battles about Dallas, New Hope Church and Allatoona Hills May 25-June 5. Operations about Marietta and against Kenesaw Mountain June 10-July 2. Assault on Kenesaw June 27. Ruff's Mills July 3-4. Chattahoochie River July 5-17. Decatur and battle of Atlanta July 22. Siege of Atlanta July 22-August 25. Scout from Rome to Cedar Bluffs, Ala., July 28-29 (Detachment). Flank movement on Jonesboro August 25-30. Battle of Jonesboro August 31-September 1. Lovejoy Station September 2-6. Moved to Rome September 26, and duty there till November 11. Battle of Allatoona October 5 (Cos. "A," "B"). Reconnoissance on Cave Springs Road and skirmishes October 12-13. March to the sea November 15-December 10. Ogeechee River and Canal December 9. Siege of Savannah December 10-21. Campaign of the Carolinas January to April, 1865. Salkehatchie Swamp, S. C., February 2-5. South Edisto River February 9. North Edisto River February 11-12. Congaree Creek February 15. Columbia February 16-17. Battle of Bentonville, N. C., March 20-21. Occupation of Goldsboro March 24. Advance on Raleigh April 10-14. Occupation of Raleigh April 14. Bennett's House April 26. Surrender of Johnston and his army. March to Washington, D. C., via Richmond, Va., April 29-May 19. Grand Review May 24. Moved to Louisville, Ky., June 3. Mustered out July 7, 1865.

Regiment lost during service 3 Officers and 65 Enlisted men killed and mortally wounded and 4 Officers and 108 Enlisted men by disease. Total 180.

58th REGIMENT INFANTRY.

Organized at Camp Douglas, Chicago, Ill., February 11, 1862. Moved to Cairo, Ill., thence to Fort Donelson, Tenn., February 11-13. Attached to 2nd Brigade, 3rd Division, District of Cairo, February, 1862. 3rd Brigade, 2nd Division, District of West Tennessee, and Army of the Tennessee, to May, 1862. 1st Brigade, 2nd Division, Army of the Tennessee, to July, 1862 (Detachment). 1st Brigade, 2nd Division, District of Corinth, Miss., to November, 1862. 1st Brigade, 2nd Division, District of Corinth, 13th Army Corps (Old), Department of the Tennessee, to December, 1862. Springfield, Ill., to June, 1863. District of Columbus, Ky., 6th Division, 16th Army Corps, Dept. of the Tennessee, to January, 1864. 1st Brigade, 3rd Division, 16th Army Corps, Army of the Tennessee, to March, 1864, and Dept. of the Gulf to June, 1864. 1st Brigade, 3rd Division, 16th Army Corps, Dept. of the Tennessee, to November, 1864. 2nd Brigade, 2nd Division, 16th Army Corps, to December, 1864. 2nd Brigade, 2nd Division (Detachment), Army of the Tennessee, Department of the Cumberland, to February, 1865. 2nd Brigade, 2nd Division, 16th Army Corps (New), Military Division of West Mississippi, to March, 1865. 3rd Brigade, 2nd Division, 16th Army Corps, to August, 1865. District of Alabama to April, 1866.

SERVICE.—Investment and capture of Fort Donelson, Tenn., February 14-16. Occupation of Fort Henry February 18-March 6. Moved to Savannah, thence to Pittsburg Landing, Tenn., March 6-25. Battle of Shiloh, Tenn., April 6-7. Mostly captured. Regiment consolidated into four Companies and organized with remnants of the 2nd, 7th, 12th and 14th Iowa Infantry into a body known as the Union Brigade, Army of the Tennessee. Advance on and siege of Corinth, Miss., April 29-May 30. Pursuit to Booneville May 31-June 6. Duty at Corinth till October. March to Iuka September 18-20. Battle of Corinth, Miss., October 3-4. Pursuit to Ruckersville October 5-12. The several detachments of Regiment concentrated at Camp Butler, Ill., in December, 1862, and on duty guarding prisoners till June, 1863. Ordered to Cairo, Ill. Garrison duty at Cairo and Mound City, Ill., Paducah and Mayfield, Ky., till January, 1864. Action at Mayfield November 2, 1863. Skirmish Obion River, near Union City, Tenn., November 19, 1863 (Cos. "G," "H," "I," "K"). Ordered to Vicksburg, Miss., January 21. Meridian Campaign February 3-March 2. Red River Campaign March 10-May 22. Fort DeRussy March 14. Occupation of Alexandria March 16. Battle of Pleasant Hill April 9. Natchitoches April 20-21. About Cloutiersville April 22-24. At Alexandria April 26-May 13. Retreat to Morganza May 13-20. Mansura May 16. Yellow Bayou May 18. Moved to Vicksburg, Miss.; thence to Memphis, Tenn., May 22-June 10. Lake Chicot, Ark., June 6. Defeat of Marmaduke. Smith's Expedition to Tupelo, Miss., July 5-21. Near Camargo's Cross Roads July 13. Harrisburg, near Tupelo, July 14-15. Old Town (or Tishamingo Creek), July 15. Smith's Expedition to Oxford, Miss., August 1-31. Tallahatchie River August 7-9. Abbeville August 23. Mower's Expedition to Brownsville, Ark., September 2-10. March through Arkansas and Missouri in pursuit of Price September 17-November 19. Moved to Nashville, Tenn., November 21-December 1. Battle of Nashville December 15-16. Pursuit of Hood to the Tennessee River December 17-28. Moved to Eastport, Miss., and duty there till February, 1865. Expedition from Eastport to Iuka January 9, 1865. Movement to New Orleans, La., February 8-26; thence to Dauphin Island, Ala., March 6. Campaign against Mobile and its defences March 17-April 12. Siege of Spanish Fort and Fort Blakely March 26-April 8. Assault and capture of Fort Blakely April 9. Occupation of Mobile April 12. March to Montgomery April 13-25. Duty at Montgomery and in the District of Alabama till April, 1866. Mustered out April 15, 1866.

Regiment lost during service 8 Officers and 75 Enlisted men killed and mortally wounded and 4 Officers and 211 Enlisted men by disease. Total 298.

59th REGIMENT INFANTRY.

Organized at St. Louis, Mo., as 9th Missouri Infantry, September 18, 1861 (Cos. "A," "B," "C" at Cape Girardeau from August 6, 1861). Regiment moved to Jefferson Barracks, Mo., September 21, 1861; thence to Booneville, Mo., September 30. Attached to Kelton's Brigade, Pope's Division, Fremont's Army of the West, to November, 1861. Department of Missouri to February, 1862. (Designation of Regiment changed to 59th Illinois Infantry February 12, 1862.) 2nd Brigade, 3rd Division, Army of Southwest Missouri, to June, 1862. 1st Brigade, 4th Division, Army of Mississippi, to September, 1862. 30th Brigade, 9th Division, Army of the Ohio, to October, 1862. 30th Brigade, 9th Division, 3rd Corps, Army of the Ohio, to November, 1862. 1st Brigade, 1st Division, Right Wing 14th Army Corps, Army of the Cumberland, to January, 1863. 1st Brigade, 1st Division, 20th Army Corps, Army of the Cumberland, to October, 1863. 2d Brigade, 1st Division, 4th Corps, October, 1863. 3rd Brigade, 1st Division, 4th Army Corps, to May 1864. 2nd Brigade, 1st Division, 4th Army Corps, to August, 1864. 3rd Brigade, 1st Division, 4th Army Corps, August, 1864. 2nd Brigade, 3rd Division, 4th Army Corps, to August, 1865. Department of Texas to December, 1865.

SERVICE.—Fremont's advance on Springfield, Mo., October 13-November 3, 1861. March to Syracuse November 9-17, thence to LaMine River December 7 and to Georgetown, Mo., December 15. To LaMine Bridge December 23 and duty there till January 25, 1862. Curtis' advance on Springfield, Mo., January 25-February 11. Campaign against Price February and March. Battles of Pea Ridge, Ark., March 6-8. March to Sugar Creek March 10, thence to Cross Timbers. March to Batesville April 5-May 3. Moved to Cape Girardeau, Mo., thence to Pittsburg Landing, Tenn., May 11-24. Advance on and siege of Corinth, Miss., May 26-30. Pursuit to Booneville June 1-16. Duty at Jacinto, Miss., till August 4. Reconnoissance to Bay Springs, Miss., August 4-7. Bay Springs August 5. March to Murfreesboro, Tenn., August 8-September 1, thence to Louisville, Ky., in pursuit of Bragg, September 3-26. Pursuit of Bragg into Kentucky October 1-15. Battle of Perryville, Ky., October 8. Lancaster October 15. March to Nashville, Tenn., October 17-November 7 and duty there till December 26. Wilson's Creek Pike December 25. Advance on Murfreesboro, Tenn., December 26-30. Nolensville, Knob Gap, November 26. Triune December 27. Battle of Stone's River December 30-31, 1862, and January 1-3, 1863. At Murfreesboro till June. Reconnoissance to Versailles March 9-14. Operations on Edgeville Pike June 4. Middle Tennessee or Tullahoma Campaign June 24-July 7. Liberty Gap June 24-27. Occupation of Middle Tennessee till August 16. Passage of the Cumberland

Mountains and Tennessee River and Chickamauga (Ga.) Campaign August 16-September 22. Guard supply trains over Mountain in rear of Bragg's army during battle of Chickamauga. Siege of Chattanooga, Tenn., September 24-October 27. Reopening Tennessee River October 26-29. Chattanooga-Ringgold Campaign November 23-27. Battles of Lookout Mountain November 23-24. Mission Ridge November 25. Taylor's Ridge, Ringgold Gap, November 27. At Whiteside, Ala., till January 27, 1864. Regiment veteranize January 12, 1864. Veterans on furlough January 27-March 19. Moved to Cleveland, Tenn., and duty there till May. Atlanta (Ga.) Campaign May 1 to September 8, 1864. Tunnel Hill May 6-7. Demonstration on Rocky Faced Ridge May 8-11. Buzzard's Roost Gap May 8-9. Demonstration against Dalton May 9-13. Battle of Resaca May 14-15. Near Kingston May 18-19. Near Cassville May 19. Advance on Dallas May 22-25. Operations on line of Pumpkin Vine Creek and battles about Dallas, New Hope Church and Allatoona Hills May 25-June 5. Operations about Marietta and against Kenesaw Mountain June 10-July 2. Pine Hill June 11-14. Lost Mountain June 15-17. Assault on Kenesaw June 27. Ruff's Station, Smyrna Camp Ground, July 4. Chattahoochie River July 5-17. Peach Tree Creek July 19-20. Siege of Atlanta July 22-August 25. Flank movement on Jonesboro August 25-30. Red Oak August 28-29. Rough and Ready August 31. Battle of Jonesboro August 31-September 1. Lovejoy Station September 2-6. Pursuit of Hood, into Alabama, October 3-26. Nashville Campaign November-December. Columbia, Duck River, November 24-27. Battle of Franklin November 30. Battle of Nashville December 15-16. Pursuit of Hood, to the Tennessee River, December 17-28. Moved to Huntsville, Ala., and duty there till March, 1865. Expedition to Bull's Gap and operations in East Tennessee March 15-April 22. At Nashville, Tenn., till June. Moved to New Orleans, La., June 16, thence to Indianola, Texas, July 7. Duty at San Antonio and at New Braunfels, Texas, till December. Mustered out December 8, 1865.

Regiment lost during service 4 Officers and 105 Enlisted men killed and mortally wounded and 4 Officers and 117 Enlisted men by disease. Total 230.

60th REGIMENT INFANTRY.

Organized at Camp Dubois, Anna, Ill., and mustered in February 17, 1862. Moved to Cairo, Ill., February 22, 1862, thence to Island No. 10, Mississippi River, March 14. Attached to District of Cairo to March, 1862. 2nd Brigade, 1st Division, Army of Mississippi, to September, 1862. 2nd Brigade, 13th Division, Army of the Ohio, to November, 1862. 1st Brigade, 4th Division, Centre 14th Army Corps, Army of the Cumberland, to January, 1863. 1st Brigade, 4th Division, 14th Army Corps, to June, 1863. 1st Brigade, 2nd Division, Reserve Corps, Army of the Cumberland, to October, 1863. 1st Brigade, 2nd Division, 14th Army Corps, to July, 1865.

SERVICE.—Operations against Island Number 10, Mississippi River, March 14-April 8. Return to Columbus, Ky., and Cairo, Ill., thence moved to Hamburg Landing, Tenn., May 7-12. Advance on and siege of Corinth, Miss., May 12-30. Pursuit to Booneville May 31-June 12. At Clear Creek till July. March to Tuscumbia, Ala., July 20-25, thence to Nashville, Tenn., August 28-September 15. Action at Columbia September 10. Siege of Nashville September 15-November 6. Repulse of Forest's attack on Edgefield November 5. Duty at Nashville, Tenn., till July 20, 1863. Skirmish at Edgefield November 7, 1862. Skirmish near Nashville January 3, 1863. Moved to Murfreesboro, Tenn., July 20, thence march to Columbia, Athens, Huntsville and Stevenson, Ala., August 24-September 7, and to Bridgeport, Ala., September 12. Duty there till October 1. Operations up the Sequatchie Valley against Wheeler October 1-17. Anderson's Cross Roads October 2 (Detachment). Moved to Waldron's Ridge, thence to Kelly's Ferry and guard lines of transportation till

January, 1864. Chattanooga-Ringgold Campaign November 23-27, 1863. Chickamauga Station November 26. March to relief of Knoxville, Tenn., November 28-December 24. At Rossville, Ga., till May, 1864. Demonstration on Dalton, Ga., February 22-27, 1864. Tunnel Hill, Buzzard's Roost and Rocky Faced Ridge February 23-25. Atlanta (Ga.) Campaign May 1-September 8. Near Tunnel Hill May 5. Tunnel Hill May 6-7. Demonstration on Rocky Faced Ridge May 8-11. Buzzard's Roost Gap May 8-9. Battle of Resaca May 14-15. Rome May 17-18. Operations on line of Pumpkin Vine Creek and battles about Dallas, New Hope Church and Allatoona Hills May 25-June 5. Operations about Marietta and against Kenesaw Mountain June 10-July 2. Pine Hill June 11-14. Lost Mountain June 15-17. Assault on Kenesaw June 27. Ruff's or Vining Station July 4. Chattahoochie River May 5-17. Peach Tree Creek July 19-20. Siege of Atlanta July 22-August 25. Utoy Creek August 5-7. Flank movement on Jonesboro August 25-30. Battle of Jonesboro August 31-September 1. Lovejoy Station September 2-6. Operations in North Georgia and North Alabama against Forest and Hood September 29-November 3. Florence, Ala., October 6-7. March to the sea November 15-December 10. Siege of Savannah December 10-21. Campaign of the Carolinas January to April, 1865. Fayetteville, N. C., March 13. Averysboro, Taylor's Hole Creek, March 16. Battle of Bentonville March 19-21. Occupation of Goldsboro March 24. Advance on Raleigh April 10-14. Occupation of Raleigh April 14. Bennett's House April 26. Surrender of Johnston and his army. March to Washington, D. C., via Richmond, Va., April 29-May 19. Grand Review May 24. Moved to Louisville, Ky., June 12. Provost guard at headquarters 14th Army Corps till July 31. Mustered out July 31, 1865.

Regiment lost during service 2 Officers and 44 Enlisted men killed and mortally wounded and 4 Officers and 225 Enlisted men by disease. Total 275.

61st REGIMENT INFANTRY.

Organized at Carrollton, Ill., and mustered in February 5, 1862. Moved to Benton Barracks, Mo., February 21, and duty there till March 26. Moved to Pittsburg Landing, Tenn., March 26-30. Attached to 2nd Brigade, 6th Division, Army of the Tennessee, to April, 1862. 1st Brigade, 3rd Division, Army Tennessee, to July, 1862. 3rd Brigade, 1st Division, District of Jackson, Tenn., to September, 1862. Unattached, District of Jackson, Tenn., to November, 1862. Post of Bolivar, District of Jackson, Tenn., 13th Army Corps (Old), Dept. of the Tennessee, to December, 1862. Post of Bolivar, District of Jackson, 16th Army Corps, to March, 1863. 1st Brigade, 3rd Division, 16th Army Corps, to May, 1863. 1st Brigade, Kimball's Provisional Division, 16th Army Corps, to July, 1863. 1st Brigade, Kimball's Division, District of Eastern Arkansas, to August, 1863. 1st Brigade, 2nd Division, Arkansas Expedition, to November, 1863. 3rd Brigade, 2nd Division, Arkansas Expedition, to January, 1864. 3rd Brigade, 2nd Division, 7th Army Corps, Dept. of Arkansas, to May, 1864. 1st Brigade, 2nd Division, 7th Army Corps, August, 1864. Veteran furlough, Dept. of Missouri, October-November, 1864. Veterans. 1st Brigade, Nashville and Chattanooga R. R., Dept. of the Cumberland, to February, 1865. Veterans, Unattached, 4th Division, 20th Army Corps, Dept. of the Cumberland, to March, 1865. 2nd Sub-District, Middle Tennessee, Dept. of the Cumberland, to September, 1865.

SERVICE.—Battle of Shiloh, Tenn., April 6-7, 1862. Advance on and siege of Corinth, Miss., April 29-May 30. Moved to Bethel, thence to Jackson and Bolivar, Tenn., June 6-17. Duty at Bolivar till May, 1863. March to support of Rosecrans, at Iuka, Miss., September 16-22, 1862. Grant's Central Mississippi Campaign. Operations against Forest, in West Tennessee, December 18, 1862-January 3, 1863. Action at Salem Cemetery, near Jackson, December 19, 1862. Moved to Memphis, Tenn., thence to Vicksburg, Miss., May 31-June 3, 1863. Expedition up the Yazoo to Satartia

June 2-8. Action at Satartia, Mechanicsburg, June 4. Moved to Haines' Bluff June 6. Siege of Vicksburg, Miss., June 9-July 4. Moved to Black River Bridge July 17, thence to Helena, Ark., July 27-31. Steele's Expedition against Little Rock, Ark., August 1-September 10. Bayou Fourche and capture of Little Rock September 19. Duty at Little Rock and Duvall's Bluff, Ark., till August, 1864. Expedition to Clarendon, Ark., June 25-29, 1864. Action at Clarendon June 25-26. Veterans on furlough August 14 to September. Company "K" joined Regiment from Camp Butler, Ill., March 20, 1864, and remained with Recruits at Duvall's Bluff, Ark., till February, 1865. Joined Regiment at Murfreesboro, Tenn., February 4, 1865. Veterans halted at St. Louis while returning to Arkansas. Companies "B," "D" and "G" guard river at Chester, Ill., till October 14, then joined Regiment at St. Louis. March through Missouri in pursuit of Price October 16-November 6. Moved to Paducah, Ky., November 6-11, thence to Nashville and Murfreesboro, Tenn., November 24-28. Action at Overall's Creek December 4. Hood's attack on Murfreesboro December 5-12. Wilkinson's Pike, near Murfreesboro, "The Cedars," December 7. Action with Forest near Murfreesboro December 15. Duty at Murfreesboro till March 21, 1865. Moved to Franklin, Tenn., and duty there till September. Mustered out at Nashville, Tenn., September 8 and discharged at Camp Butler, Ill., September 27, 1865.

Regiment lost during service 3 Officers and 34 Enlisted men killed and mortally wounded and 4 Officers and 183 Enlisted men by disease. Total 224.

62nd REGIMENT INFANTRY.

Organized at Camp Dubois, Anna, Ill., April 10, 1862. Moved to Cairo, Ill., April 22, thence to Paducah, Ky., May 7 and to Columbus, Ky., June 7, 1862. Attached to District of Columbus, Ky., District of West Tennessee, to September, 1862. District of Jackson, Tenn., to November, 1862. District of Jackson, Tenn., 13th Army Corps (Old), Dept. of the Tennessee, to December, 1862. 1st Brigade, District of Jackson, Tenn., 16th Army Corps, to March, 1863. 3rd Brigade, 3rd Division, 16th Army Corps, to August, 1863. True's Brigade, Arkansas Expedition, to January, 1864. Unattached, 2nd Division, 7th Army Corps, Dept. of Arkansas, to May, 1864. 2nd Brigade, 2nd Division, 7th Army Corps, to July, 1865. Fort Gibson, Cherokee Nation, Dept. of Arkansas, to March, 1866.

SERVICE.—Assigned to duty in Tennessee as railroad guard on Mobile and Ohio R. R., near Crockett's Station, headquarters at Kenton, till December, 1862. Moved to Jackson, Tenn., thence to Grand Junction and Holly Springs and return to Jackson, Tenn., December 7-16. Operations against Forest in West Tennessee December 18, 1862-January 3, 1863. Action at Salem Cemetery, near Jackson, December 19, 1862. Holly Springs, Miss., December 20 (Detachment). Detachment captured. Duty at Jackson, Tenn., till April 18, 1863. Moved to LaGrange, Tenn., April 18, and duty there till August. Moved to Memphis, Tenn., thence to Helena, Ark., August 19-28. Steele's Campaign against Little Rock, Ark., August 28-September 10. Bayou Fourche and capture of Little Rock September 10. Duty at Little Rock till April 25, 1864, and at Pine Bluff till July 28, 1865. Veterans on furlough August 12 to November 25, 1864. Moved to Fort Gibson, Cherokee Nation, July 28, 1865, and duty there till March, 1866. Mustered out March 6, 1866.

Regiment lost during service 3 Enlisted men killed and mortally wounded and 9 Officers and 251 Enlisted men by disease. Total 263.

63rd REGIMENT INFANTRY.

Organized at Camp Dubois, Anna, Ill., and mustered in April 10, 1862. Moved to Cairo, Ill., April 27, 1862. Attached to District of Cairo, Ill., till September, 1862. 4th Brigade, 1st Division, District of Jackson, Tenn., to November, 1862. 4th Brigade, 3rd Division, Right

Wing 13th Army Corps (Old), Dept. of the Tennessee, to December, 1862. 3rd Brigade, 3rd Division, 17th Army Corps, to January, 1863. District of Memphis, Tenn., 16th Army Corps, to March, 1863. 4th Brigade, District of Memphis, 5th Division, 16th Army Corps, to May, 1863. Detached Brigade, District of Northeast Louisiana, to June, 1863. 2nd Brigade, 6th Division, 17th Army Corps, to July, 1863. 1st Brigade, 7th Division, 17th Army Corps, to September, 1863. 1st Brigade, 2nd Division, 17th Army Corps, to December, 1863. 1st Brigade, 3rd Division, 15th Army Corps, to April, 1865. 2nd Brigade, 4th Division, 15th Army Corps, to July, 1865.

SERVICE.—Duty at Cairo, Ill., till July 12, 1862. Moved to Columbus, Ky., thence to Jackson, Tenn., August 4, and duty there till November 10. Grant's Central Mississippi Campaign November 10, 1862, to January 10, 1863. Reconnoissance from LaGrange November 8-9, 1862. Duty at LaGrange, Tenn., till May 10, 1863. Burning of Hopewell February 19, 1863 (Cos. "C," "D," "E," "F"). Moved to Vicksburg, Miss., May 10-17. Siege of Vicksburg May 21-July 4. Expedition from Young's Point, La., to Richmond, La., June 14-16. Action at Richmond June 15. Post duty at Vicksburg, Miss., July 5 to September 12. Moved to Helena, Ark., September 12, thence to Memphis, and march to Chattanooga, Tenn., September 28-November 20. Operations on Memphis and Charleston R. R. in Alabama October 20-29. Chattanooga-Ringgold Campaign November 23-27. Tunnel Hill November 24-25. Mission Ridge November 25. Pursuit to Ringgold, Ga., November 26-27. Moved to Bridgeport, Ala., December 3, thence to Huntsville, Ala., December 21-26, and duty there till May, 1864. Regiment veteranize January 1, 1864. Veterans on furlough April 3-May 21. Moved to Triune, Tennessee River, May 23, thence to Huntsville June 15, and to Kingston June 23. Railroad guard duty between Chattanooga and Atlanta till November 11. March to the sea November 15-December 10. Siege of Savannah December 10-21. Campaign of the Carolinas January to April, 1865. Salkehatchie Swamp, S. C., February 2-5. South Edisto River February 9. North Edisto River February 11-12. Columbia February 15-17. West's Cross Roads, S. C., February 25. Lynch's Creek February 25-26. Battle of Bentonville, N. C., March 20-21. Occupation of Goldsboro March 24. Advance on Raleigh April 10-14. Occupation of Raleigh April 14. Bennett's House April 26. Surrender of Johnston and his army. March to Washington, D. C., via Richmond, Va., April 29-May 19. Grand Review May 24. Moved to Louisville, Ky., June 3-6. Mustered out July 13, 1865.

Regiment lost during service 5 Enlisted men killed and mortally wounded and 4 Officers and 135 Enlisted men by disease. Total 144.

64th REGIMENT INFANTRY ("YATES' SHARP-SHOOTERS").

Organized at Camp Butler, Ill., as a Battalion of 4 Companies, December, 1861. Two more Companies mustered in December 31, 1861. Moved to Quincy, Ill., January 10, 1862, thence to Cairo, Ill., February 15, and to New Madrid, Mo., March 4, 1862. Attached to Army of Mississippi, unassigned, to April, 1862. 2nd Brigade, 1st Division, Army Mississippi, to May, 1862. Unattached, Army Mississippi, to November, 1862. Unattached, District of Corinth, 13th Army Corps (Old), Dept. of the Tennessee, to December, 1862. Unattached, District of Corinth, 17th Army Corps, to January, 1863. Unattached, District of Corinth, 16th Army Corps, to March, 1863. Unattached, 2nd Division, 16th Army Corps, to November, 1863. Fuller's Brigade, 2nd Division, 16th Army Corps, to March, 1864. 1st Brigade, 4th Division, 16th Army Corps, to September, 1864. 1st Brigade, 1st Division, 17th Army Corps, to July, 1865.

SERVICE.—Operations against New Madrid, Mo., and Island No. 10, Mississippi River, March 4-April 8, 1862. Action at New Madrid March 12. Capture of New

Madrid March 14. Capture of Island No. 10 April 8. Expedition to Fort Pillow, Tenn., April 13-17. Moved to Hamburg Landing, Tenn., April 17-22. Advance on and siege of Corinth, Miss., April 29-May 30. Action at Farmington, Miss., May 3. Reconnoissance toward Corinth May 8. Action at Farmington May 9. Pursuit to Booneville May 31-June 12. Tuscumbia Creek May 31-June 1. Reconnoissance toward Baldwyn June 3. At Big Springs and on guard duty at Headquarters of General Rosecrans, Commanding Army Mississippi, till November 27. Reconnoissance to Iuka and skirmish September 16. Battle of Iuka September 19. Battle of Corinth, Miss., October 3-4. Pursuit to the Hatchie River October 5-12. On Outpost duty at Glendale, Miss., November 27, 1862, to November 4, 1863. Moved to Iuka, thence to Pulaski, Tenn., November 4-11, and duty there till January, 1864, and at Decatur, Ala., till May. Veterans on furlough January 15 to March 17, 1864. Four new Companies, "G," "H," "I" and "K," organized February and March, 1864. Moved to Decatur, Ala., March 17-23. Atlanta (Ga.) Campaign May 1-September 8. Demonstrations on Resaca May 8-13. Near Resaca May 13. Battle of Resaca May 14-15. Advance on Dallas May 18-25. Operations on line of Pumpkin Vine Creek and battles about Dallas, New Hope Church and Allatoona Hills May 25-June 5. Near New Hope Church June 5. Operations about Marietta and against Kenesaw Mountain June 10-July 2. Assault on Kenesaw June 27. Nickajack Creek July 2-5. Ruff's Mills July 3-4. Chattahoochie River July 6-17. Nance's Creek July 17. Decatur July 19-22. Battle of Atlanta July 22. Siege of Atlanta July 22-August 25. Flank movement on Jonesboro August 25-30. Battle of Jonesboro August 31-September 1. Lovejoy Station September 2-6. Reconnoissance to Fairburn October 1-3. Pursuit of Hood into Alabama October 4-29. Snake Creek Gap October 15-16. March to the sea November 15-December 10. Montieth Swamp December 9. Siege of Savannah December 10-21. Campaign of the Carolinas January to April, 1865. Reconnoissance to Salkehatchie River, S. C., January 20. Salkehatchie Swamps February 1-5. Rivers' and Broxton's Bridges, Salkehatchie River, February 2. Rivers' Bridge February 3. South Edisto River February 9. North Edisto River February 11-12. Columbia February 15-17. Juniper Creek near Cheraw, March 2. Cheraw March 3-4. Battle of Bentonville, N. C., March 20-21. Occupation of Goldsboro March 24. Advance on Raleigh April 10-14. Occupation of Raleigh April 14. Bennett's House April 26. Surrender of Johnston and his army. March to Washington, D. C., via Richmond, Va., April 29-May 19. Grand Review May 24. Moved to Louisville, Ky., June 6. Mustered out July 11 and discharged at Chicago, Ill., July 18, 1865.

Regiment lost during service 6 Officers and 106 Enlisted men killed and mortally wounded and 2 Officers and 131 Enlisted men by disease. Total 242.

65th REGIMENT INFANTRY ("SCOTCH REGIMENT").

Organized at Camp Douglas, Chicago, Ill., and mustered in May 1, 1862. Ordered to Martinsburg, W. Va. Attached to Railroad District, Mountain Department, to July, 1862. Railroad District, 8th Army Corps, Middle Department, to September, 1862.

SERVICE.—Duty at Martinsburg, W. Va., till September, 1862. Action at Darkesville September 7. Moved to Harper's Ferry September 11-12. Siege of Harper's Ferry September 12-15. Surrender September 15. Paroled September 16 and sent to Annapolis, Md., thence to Chicago, Ill. Duty there till April, 1863. Declared exchanged and ordered to Kentucky. Attached to District of Central and Eastern Kentucky, Dept. of Ohio, to June, 1863. 1st Brigade, 4th Division, 23rd Army Corps, Dept. Ohio, to August, 1863. 2nd Brigade, 3rd Division, 23rd Army Corps, to February, 1865. 2nd Brigade, 3rd Division, 23rd Army Corps, Dept. of North Carolina, to July, 1865.

SERVICE.—Duty in Eastern and Central Kentucky till August, 1863. Expedition from Beaver Creek, Ky., to Southwest Virginia, Pound Gap Expedition, July 3-11. Action at Pond Creek July 5. Burnside's Campaign in East Tennessee August 16-October 17. Siege of Knoxville November 17-December 5. Operations about Dandridge January 16-17, 1864. At Knoxville and operations in East Tennessee till May, 1864. Atlanta (Ga.) Campaign June 4-September 8. Operations about Marietta and against Kenesaw Mountain June 10-July 2. Lost Mountain June 15-17. Muddy Creek June 17. Noyes Creek June 19. Cheyney's Farm June 22. Olley's Farm June 26-27. Assault on Kenesaw June 27. On line of Nickajack Creek June 2-5. On line of the Chattahoochie July 5-17. Isham's Ford July 8. Siege of Atlanta July 22-August 25. Utoy Creek August 5-7. Flank movement on Jonesboro August 25-30. Rough and Ready August 31. Battle of Jonesboro August 31-September 1. Lovejoy Station September 2-6. Operations against Hood in North Georgia and North Alabama September 29-November 3. Nashville Campaign November and December. Columbia, Duck River, November 24-28. Franklin November 30. Battle of Nashville December 15-16. Pursuit of Hood to the Tennessee River December 17-28. At Clifton, Tenn., till January 15, 1865. Movement to Washington, thence to Fort Fisher, N. C., January 15-February 7. Cape Fear Intrenchments February 10-13. Sugar Loaf Battery February 11. Fort Anderson February 18. Capture of Fort Anderson February 19. Town Creek February 19-20. Capture of Wilmington February 22. Advance on Goldsboro March 6-21. Occupation of Goldsboro March 21. Advance on Raleigh April 10-14. Occupation of Raleigh April 14. Bennett's House April 26. Surrender of Johnston and his army. At Greensboro, N. C., till July. Mustered out July 13 and discharged at Chicago, Ill., July 26, 1865.

Regiment lost during service 1 Officer and 30 Enlisted men killed and mortally wounded and 1 Officer and 97 Enlisted men by disease. Total 129.

66th REGIMENT INFANTRY.

Organized at Benton Barracks, Mo., as Birge's Western Sharpshooters under authority of General Fremont, September and October, 1861. Mustered in as 14th Missouri Infantry November 23, 1861. Attached to Dept. of Missouri to February, 1862. 1st Brigade, 2nd Division, District of West Tennessee, February, 1862. 4th Brigade, 2nd Division, District West Tennessee, to March, 1862. 2nd Brigade, 2nd Division, Army of the Tennessee to July, 1862. 2nd Brigade, 2nd Division, District of Corinth, Miss., to November, 1862. Unattached, District of Corinth, Miss., 13th Army Corps (Old), Dept. of the Tennessee, to December, 1862. Unattached, District of Corinth, 17th Army Corps, to January, 1863. Unattached, District of Corinth, 16th Army Corps, to March, 1863. Unattached, 2nd Division, 16th Army Corps, to November, 1863. 2nd Brigade, 2nd Division, 16th Army Corps, to September, 1864. 2nd Brigade, 4th Division, 15th Army Corps, to April, 1865. 3rd Brigade, 1st Division, 15th Army Corps, to July, 1865.

SERVICE.—Moved to Centralia, Mo., December 12-14, 1861. Operating against Bushwhackers of Price's Army, December 14-28. Silver Creek December 25. Capture of Columbia December 26. Mt. Zion Church December 28. Moved to Sturgeon, Mo., December 29. Duty there and scouting about Renick, Macon and Centralia till February, 1862. Moved to St. Louis, Mo., thence to Cairo, Ill., Paducah, Ky., and Fort Henry, Tenn., February 4-9. Investment and capture of Fort Donelson, Tenn., February 12-16. Moved to Savannah, thence to Pittsburg Landing, Tenn., March 5-17. Battle of Shiloh, Tenn., April 6-7. Advance on and siege of Corinth, Miss., April 29-May 30. Phillips' Creek May 21. Occupation of Corinth May 30. Pursuit to Booneville June 1-8. Duty at headquarters General Grant, Corinth, Miss., till August 25. Expedition to Bethel, Tenn., August 28-30. Burnsville September 17. March

to Glendale and Iuka September 18-21. Battle of Iuka September 19. Battle of Corinth, Miss., October 3-4. Pursuit to Hatchie River October 5-12. Skirmish at Hatchie River October 9. Scout to Hatchie River November 2-5. At Rienzi till November 26. Moved to the Tuscumbia Hills and established Camp Davies, and duty there till November, 1863. Designation of Regiment changed to 66th Illinois Infantry November 20, 1862. Skirmishes at Tuscumbia Bridge December 19, 1862. Danville December 20. Hatchie River December 30. Rienzi January 7, 1863. Danville, Tuscumbia Bridge and Rienzi January 24-25. Danville February 8. Ripley Cross Roads March 25. Booneville April 1. Glendale April 14. Jumpertown May 12. Kossuth May 24. Cartersville June 6. Yellow Creek June 8. Seward House and Jumpertown July 11. Jacinto August 9. Rienzi August 11. Seward House August 19. Whitesides Farm September 9. Relieved at Camp Davies November 1, and march to Pulaski, Tenn., November 1-12. Duty there till April 29, 1864. Veterans on furlough January 16-March 8. Atlanta Campaign May 1 to September 8. Demonstrations on Resaca May 8-13. Snake Creek Gap and Sugar Valley, near Resaca, May 9. Near Resaca May 13. Battle of Resaca May 14-15. Ley's Ferry, Ooostenaula River, May 14-15. Rome Cross Roads May 16. Advance on Dallas May 18-25. Operations on line of Pumpkin Vine Creek and battles about Dallas, New Hope Church and Allatoona Hills May 25-June 5. Operations about Marietta and against Kenesaw Mountain June 10-July 2. Assault on Kenesaw June 27. Nickajack Creek July 2-5. Ruff's Mills July 3-4. Chattahoochie River July 6-17. Decatur July 20-21. Battle of Atlanta July 22. Siege of Atlanta July 22-August 25. Non-Veterans mustered out August 26, 1864. Flank movement on Jonesboro August 25-30. Battle of Jonesboro August 31-September 1. Lovejoy Station September 2-6. Moved to Rome, Ga., September 26, and duty there till November 10. Reconnoissance from Rome on Cave Springs Road and skirmishes October 12-13. March to the sea November 15-December 10. Waynesboro November 27-28. Wrightstown November 29. Ogeechee Canal and Wilmington Cross Roads December 9. Siege of Savannah December 10-21. Campaign of the Carolinas January to April, 1865. Salkehatchie Swamp, S. C., February 2-5. South Edisto River February 9. North Edisto River February 11-12. Columbia February 15-17. Camden February 24. Battle of Bentonville, N. C., March 20-21. Occupation of Goldsboro March 24. Advance on Raleigh April 10-14. Occupation of Raleigh April 14. Bennett's House April 26. Surrender of Johnston and his army. March to Washington, D. C., via Richmond, Va., April 29-May 19. Grand Review May 24. Moved to Louisville, Ky., June 3-8. Mustered out July 7, 1865.

Regiment lost during service 6 Officers and 73 Enlisted men killed and mortally wounded and 2 Officers and 146 Enlisted men by disease. Total 227.

67th REGIMENT INFANTRY.

Organized at Camp Douglass, Chicago, Ill., June 13, 1862, for three months. Assigned to guard duty at Camp Douglass till October. Mustered out October 6, 1862.

Regiment lost 12 by disease during service.

68th REGIMENT INFANTRY.

Organized at Camp Butler, June 16, 1862, for three months. Moved to Wheeling, W. Va., July 5-7, thence to Washington, D. C., July 9-10. Camp at Soldiers' Retreat and near Alexandria, Va., till August 24. Provost duty at Alexandria, Va., till September 17. Moved to Camp Butler, Ill., September 17-21. Mustered out September 27, 1862.

Regiment lost 25 by disease during service.

69th REGIMENT INFANTRY.

Organized at Camp Douglass, Chicago, Ill., and mustered in June 14, 1862, for three months. Assigned to guard duty at Camp Douglass till September. Mustered out September 27, 1862.

Regiment lost 13 by disease during service.

70th REGIMENT INFANTRY.

Organized at Camp Butler and mustered in July 4, 1862, for three months. Assigned to guard duty at Camp Butler, Ill., till October. Mustered out October 23, 1862.

Regiment lost 19 by disease during service.

71st REGIMENT INFANTRY.

Organized at Camp Douglass, Chicago, Ill., July 26, 1862, for three months. Moved to Cairo, Ill., July 27, thence to Columbus, Ky., August 6. Guard railroad and bridges by detachments, at Big Muddy Bridge, Illinois Central R. R. (2 Cos.); at Mound City, Ill., (2 Cos.); at Moscow, Ky. (3 Cos.), and at Little Obion bridge (3 Cos.), till October. Mustered out October 29, 1862.

Regiment lost 23 by disease during service.

72nd REGIMENT INFANTRY ("CHICAGO BOARD OF TRADE REGIMENT").

Organized at Chicago, Ill., and mustered in August 23, 1862. Moved to Cairo, Ill., August 23-24, 1862. Attached to District of Cairo to September, 1862. District of Columbus, Ky., to November, 1862. 1st Brigade, 7th Division, Left Wing 13th Army Corps (Old), Dept. of the Tennessee, to December, 1862. 1st Brigade, 7th Division, 16th Army Corps, to January, 1863. 1st Brigade, 7th Division, 17th Army Corps, to May, 1863. 2nd Brigade, 6th Division, 17th Army Corps, to September, 1863. 1st Brigade, 1st Division, 17th Army Corps, to November, 1864. Unassigned, 23rd Army Corps, Army of the Ohio, to December, 1864. 1st Brigade, 3rd Division, Detachment Army Tennessee, Dept. of the Cumberland, to February, 1865. 1st Brigade, 3rd Division, 16th Army Corps (New), Military Division West Mississippi, to August, 1865.

SERVICE.—Duty at Cairo, Ill., till September 6, 1862. Moved to Paducah, Ky., September 6, thence to Columbus, Ky., September 17, and duty there till November 21. Expedition from Columbus to Covington, Durhamsville and Fort Randolph September 28-October 5. Expedition to Clarkson, Mo., October 6. Expedition to New Madrid, Mo., October 21. Skirmishes at Clarkson, Mo., October 23 and 28. Moved to Moscow, Miss., November 21, and join Quinby's Command. Grant's Central Mississippi Campaign. Operations on the Mississippi Central R. R. November 21-December 30. Duty on line of the Memphis and Charleston R. R. till January 10, 1863. At Memphis, Tenn., till February 24. Yazoo Pass Expedition, by Moon Lake, Yazoo Pass and the Coldwater and Tallahatchie Rivers February 24-April 8. Operations against Fort Pemberton and Greenwood March 13-April 5. Fort Pemberton near Greenwood March 11-16-25-April 2 and 4. Moved to Milliken's Bend, La., and guard duty from Milliken's Bend to New Carthage till April 25. Duty at Richmond, La., April 25-May 10. Battle of Champion's Hill May 16. Siege of Vicksburg, Miss., May 18-July 4. Assaults on Vicksburg May 19 and 22. Expedition to Mechanicsburg May 26-June 4. Surrender of Vicksburg July 4. Moved to Natchez, Miss., July 12-13, and duty there till October 17. Action at St. Catherine's Creek July 28 and September 1. Moved to Vicksburg, Miss., October 17, and Provost duty there till October 30, 1864. Expedition to Waterproof, La., January 29-February 23, 1864. Waterproof February 14-15. Yazoo City Expedition May 4-21. Actions at Benton May 7 and 9. Vaughan May 12. Luce's Plantation May 13. Vaughan Station May 14. Expedition to Grand Gulf July 10-17. Port Gibson July 13. Grand Gulf July 16. Moved to Nashville, Tenn., October 30-November 13, thence to Columbia, Tenn., November 13-21. Nashville Campaign November-December. Columbia, Duck River, November 24-27. Spring Hill November 29. Battle of Franklin November 30. Skirmish near Nashville December 7. Battle of Nashville December 15-16. Pursuit of Hood to the Tennes-

see River December 17-28. Moved to Clifton, Tenn., thence to Eastport, Miss., and duty there till February 9, 1865. Moved to New Orleans, La., February 9-21, and duty there till March 12. Campaign against Mobile, Ala., and its defences March 17-April 12. Expedition from Dauphin Island to Fowl River Narrows March 18-22. Siege of Spanish Fort and Fort Blakely March 26-April 8. Assault and capture of Fort Blakely April 9. Capture of Mobile April 12. March to Montgomery April 14-25, and duty there till May 23. Moved to Union Springs, Ala., May 23, and duty there till July 19. Moved to Vicksburg, Miss., July 19. Mustered out August 7, 1865.

Regiment lost during service 7 Officers and 79 Enlisted men killed and mortally wounded and 3 Officers and 145 Enlisted men by disease. Total 234.

73rd REGIMENT INFANTRY.

Organized at Camp Butler, Ill., and mustered in August 21, 1862. Moved to Louisville, Ky., August 23-25, thence moved to Covington, Ky., and duty there during Kirby Smith's threatened attack on Cincinnati, Ohio, September 1-17. Attached to 35th Brigade, 11th Division, Army of the Ohio, to October, 1862. 35th Brigade, 11th Division, 3rd Corps, Army Ohio, to November, 1862. 2nd Brigade, 3rd Division, Right Wing 14th Army Corps, Army of the Cumberland, to January 1863. 2nd Brigade, 3rd Division, 20th Army Corps, Army of the Cumberland, to October, 1863. 1st Brigade, 2nd Division, 4th Army Corps, to June, 1865.

SERVICE.—Pursuit of Bragg into Kentucky October 1-16, 1862. Battle of Perryville, Ky., October 8. March to Nashville, Tenn., October 16-November 7. Duty at Nashville till December 26. Reconnoissance to Mill Creek November 27. Advance on Murfreesboro, Tenn., December 26-30. Battle of Stone's River December 30-31, 1862, and January 1-3, 1863. At Murfreesboro till June. Expedition toward Columbia March 4-14. Middle Tennessee or Tullahoma Campaign June 24-July 7. Fairfield June 27. Occupation of Middle Tennessee till August 16. Passage of Cumberland Mountains and Tennessee River and Chickamauga (Ga.) Campaign August 16-September 22. Battle of Chickamauga, Ga., September 19-20. Siege of Chattanooga September 24-November 23. Chattanooga-Ringgold Campaign November 23-27. Orchard Knob November 23-24. Missionary Ridge November 25. Pursuit to Graysville November 26-27. March to relief of Knoxville, Tenn., November 28-December 8. Operations in East Tennessee till February, 1864. Moved to Chattanooga, thence to Cleveland, Tenn., and duty there till May. Atlanta (Ga.) Campaign May 1-September 8. Demonstration on Rocky Faced Ridge May 8-11. Buzzard's Roost Gap May 8-9. Demonstrations against Dalton May 9-13. Battle of Resaca May 14-15. Adairsville May 17. Near Kingston May 18-19. Near Cassville May 19. Advance on Dallas May 22-25. Operations on line of Pumpkin Vine Creek and battle about Dallas, New Hope Church and Allatoona Hills May 25-June 5. Operations about Marietta and against Kenesaw Mountain June 10-July 2. Pine Hill June 11-14. Lost Mountain June 15-17. Assault on Kenesaw June 27. Ruff's Station July 4. Chattahoochie River July 5-17. Buckhead, Nancy's Creek, July 18. Peach Tree Creek July 19-20. Siege of Atlanta July 22-August 25. Flank movement on Jonesboro August 25-30. Battle of Jonesboro August 31-September 1. Lovejoy Station September 2-6. Operations in North Georgia and North Alabama against Hood and Forest September 29-November 3. Nashville Campaign November-December. Columbia, Duck River, November 24-27. Spring Hill November 29. Battle of Franklin November 30. Battle of Nashville December 15-16. Pursuit of Hood to the Tennessee River December 17-28. Moved to Huntsville, Ala., and duty there till March, 1865. Operations in East Tennessee March 28-April 19. Moved to Nashville, Tenn., and duty there till June. Mustered out June 12, 1865.

Regiment lost during service 5 Officers and 109 Enlisted men killed and mortally wounded and 167 Enlisted men by disease. Total 281.

74th REGIMENT INFANTRY.

Organized at Rockford, Ill., and mustered in September 4, 1862. Moved to Louisville, Ky., September 28-30. Attached to 30th Brigade, 9th Division, Army of the Ohio, to October, 1862. 30th Brigade, 9th Division, 3rd Corps, Army Ohio, to November, 1862. 1st Brigade, 1st Division, Right Wing 14th Army Corps, Army of the Cumberland, to January, 1863. 1st Brigade, 1st Division, 20th Army Corps, Army of the Cumberland, to October, 1863. 1st Brigade, 2nd Division, 4th Army Corps, to June, 1865.

SERVICE.—Pursuit of Bragg into Kentucky October 1-16, 1862. Chaplin Hills near Perryville October 6-7. Battle of Perryville October 8. Lancaster October 15. March to Nashville, Tenn., October 16-November 7, and duty there till December 26. Wilson's Creek Pike December 25. Advance on Murfreesboro, Tenn., December 26-30. Nolensville, Knob Gap, December 26. Battle of Stone's River December 30-31, 1862, and January 1-3, 1863. At Murfreesboro till June. Reconnoissance from Salem to Versailles March 9-14. Operations on Edgeville Pike June 4. Middle Tennessee or Tullahoma Campaign June 22-July 7. Liberty Gap June 22-24, and June 24-27. Occupation of Middle Tennessee till August 16. Passage of Cumberland Mountains and Tennessee River and Chickamauga (Ga.) Campaign August 16-September 22. Guard supply trains over mountains in rear of Bragg's army during battle of Chickamauga. Near Chattanooga September 22-24. Siege of Chattanooga September 24-November 23. Chattanooga-Ringgold Campaign November 23-27. Orchard Knob November 23-24. Mission Ridge November 25. Pursuit to Graysville November 26-27. March to relief of Knoxville, Tenn., November 28-December 8. Operations in East Tennessee till February, 1864. Moved to Chattanooga and thence to Cleveland, Tenn. Duty there till May. Atlanta (Ga.) Campaign May 1-September 8. Tunnel Hill May 6-7. Demonstration on Rocky Faced Ridge May 8-11. Buzzard's Roost Gap May 8-9. Demonstration on Dalton May 9-13. Battle of Resaca May 14-15. Adairsville May 17. Near Kingston May 18-19. Near Cassville May 19. Advance on Dallas May 22-25. Operations on Line of Pumpkin Vine Creek and battle about Dallas, New Hope Church and Allatoona Hills May 25-June 5. Operations about Marietta and against Kenesaw Mountain June 10-July 2. Pine Hill June 11-14. Lost Mountain June 15-17. Assault on Kenesaw June 27. Ruff's Station July 4. Chattahoochie River June 5-17. Buckhead, Nancy's Creek, July 18. Peach Tree Creek July 19-20. Siege of Atlanta July 22-August 25. Flank movement on Jonesboro August 25-30. Battle of Jonesboro August 31-September 1. Lovejoy Station September 2-6. Operations against Hood and Forest in North Georgia and North Alabama September 29-November 3. Nashville Campaign November-December. Columbia, Duck River, November 24-27. Spring Hill November 29. Battle of Franklin November 30. Battle of Nashville December 15-16. Pursuit of Hood to the Tennessee River December 17-28. Moved to Huntsville, Ala., and duty there till March, 1865. Operations in East Tennessee March 28-April 19. Moved to Nashville, Tenn., and duty there till June. Mustered out June 10, 1865.

Regiment lost during service 5 Officers and 78 Enlisted men killed and mortally wounded and 3 Officers and 116 Enlisted men by disease. Total 202.

75th REGIMENT INFANTRY.

Organized at Dixon, Ill., and mustered in September 2, 1862. Left state for Jeffersonville, Ind., September 27, 1862. Attached to 30th Brigade, 9th Division Army of the Ohio, to October, 1862. 30th Brigade, 9th Division, 3rd Corps, Army Ohio, to November, 1862. 1st Brigade, 1st Division, Right Wing 14th Army Corps, Army of the Cumberland, to January, 1863. 1st Bri-

gade, 1st Division, 20th Army Corps, Army of the Cumberland, to October, 1863. 3rd Brigade, 1st Division, 4th Army Corps, to June, 1865.

SERVICE.—Pursuit of Bragg, into Kentucky October 1-16, 1862. Battle of Perryville, Ky., October 8. Action at Stanford, Ky., October 14. March to Nashville, Tenn., October 16-November 7, and duty there till December 26. Wilson's Creek Pike December 25. Advance on Murfreesboro December 26-30. Nolensville, Knob Gap, November 26. Battle of Stone's River December 30-31, 1862, and January 1-3, 1863. At Murfreesboro till June. Shelbyville Pike January 21. Reconnoissance from Salem to Versailles March 9-14. Operations on Edgeville Pike June 4. Middle Tennessee or Tullahoma Campaign June 24-July 7. Liberty Gap June 24-27. Occupation of Middle Tennessee till August 16. Passage of Cumberland Mountains and Tennessee River and Chickamauga (Ga.) campaign August 16-September 22. Guard supply trains over mountains in rear of Bragg's army during battle of Chickamauga. Siege of Chattanooga September 24-November 23. Reopening Tennessee River October 26-29. Chattanooga-Ringgold Campaign November 23-27. Lookout Mountain November 23-24. Mission Ridge November 25. Taylor's Ridge, Ringgold Gap, November 27. March to relief of Knoxville November 27-December 8. At Whitesides, Tyner's Station and Blue Springs till May, 1864. Demonstration on Dalton, Ga., February 22-27. Near Dalton, Ga., February 23. Tunnel Hill, Rocky Faced Ridge and Buzzard's Roost Gap February 23-25. Atlanta (Ga.) Campaign May 1-September 8. Tunnel Hill May 6-7. Demonstration on Rocky Faced Ridge May 8-11. Buzzard's Roost Gap May 8-9. Demonstration on Dalton May 11-13. Near Dalton May 13. Battle of Resaca May 14-15. Adairsville May 17. Near Kingston May 18-19. Near Cassville May 19. Advance on Dallas May 22-25. Operations on line of Pumpkin Vine Creek and battles about Dallas, New Hope Church and Allatoona Hills May 25-June 5. Operations about Marietta and against Kenesaw Mountain June 10-July 2. Pine Hill June 11-14. Lost Mountain June 15-17. Assault on Kenesaw June 27. Ruff's Station, Smyrna Camp Ground, July 4. Chattahoochie River July 5-17. Peach Tree Creek July 19-20. Siege of Atlanta July 22-August 25. Flank movement on Jonesboro August 25-30. Battle of Jonesboro August 31-September 1. Lovejoy Station September 2-6. Operations against Hood and Forest in North Georgia and North Alabama September 29-November 3. Nashville Campaign November-December. Columbia, Duck River, November 24-27. Spring Hill November 29. Battle of Franklin November 30. Battle of Nashville December 15-16. Pursuit of Hood to the Tennessee River December 17-28. Moved to Huntsville, Ala., and duty there till March, 1865. Expedition to Bull's Gap and operations in East Tennessee March 15-April 22. Moved to Nashville, Tenn., and duty there till June. Mustered out at Nashville, Tenn., June 12, and discharged at Chicago, Ill., July 1, 1865.

Regiment lost during service 3 Officers and 94 Enlisted men killed and mortally wounded and 5 Officers and 103 Enlisted men by disease. Total 205.

76th REGIMENT INFANTRY.

Organized at Kankakee, Ill., and mustered in August 22, 1862. Moved to Columbus, Ky., August 22-29, 1862, and duty there till October 4. Attached to District of Columbus, Ky., to October, 1862. 2nd Brigade, 4th Division, District of Jackson, to November, 1862. 2nd Brigade, 4th Division, Right Wing 13th Army Corps, Department of the Tennessee, to December, 1862. 2nd Brigade, 4th Division, 17th Army Corps, to January, 1863. 2nd Brigade, 4th Division, 16th Army Corps, to July, 1863. 2nd Brigade, 4th Division, 13th Army Corps, to August, 1863. 2nd Brigade, 4th Division, 17th Army Corps, to April, 1864. 2nd Brigade, 1st Division, 17th Army Corps, to August, 1864. 1st Brigade, 2nd Division, 19th Army

Corps, Dept. of the Gulf, to December, 1854. 2nd Brigade, Reserve Division, Military Division West Mississippi, to February, 1865. 2nd Brigade, 2nd Division, Reserve Corps, Military Division West Mississippi, February, 1865. 2nd Brigade, 2nd Division, 13th Army Corps (New), Military Division West Mississippi, to July, 1865.

SERVICE.—Moved from Columbus, Ky., to Bolivar, Tenn., October 4-5, 1862, and duty there till November 3. Moved to LaGrange November 3 and duty there till November 28. Grant's Central Mississippi Campaign. Operations on the Mississippi Central R. R. November 28, 1862, to January 5, 1863. Moved to Moscow, Tenn., January 10, 1863, thence to La Fayette February 5, and to Memphis, Tenn., March 10. Duty there till May 13. Moved to Vicksburg, Miss., May 13-17. Siege of Vicksburg, Miss., May 18-July 4. Assaults on Vicksburg May 19-22. Surrender of Vicksburg July 4. Advance on Jackson, Miss., July 4-10. Big Black River July 4-5. Siege of Jackson, Miss., July 10-17. Assault on Jackson July 12. Reconnoissance to Pearl River July 15. Duty at Vicksburg till August 11. Moved to Natchez, Miss., August 11-12, and duty there till November 28. Expedition to Harrisonburg, La., September 1-7. Near Harrisonburg and capture of Fort Beauregard September 4. Moved to Vicksburg, Miss., November 28, and duty there till February, 1864. Meridian Campaign February 3-March 5. Champion's Hill February 5. Meridian February 14-15. Duty at Big Black till April 27. Yazoo City Expedition May 4-21. Actions at Benton May 7 and 9. Vaughan, Big Black River Bridge, May 12. Yazoo City May 13. At Vicksburg till July. Expedition to Pearl River July 2-10. Action at Jackson, Miss., July 7. Ordered to Morganza, La., July 29, and duty there till September 3. Expedition to Clinton, La., August 23-29. Moved to mouth of White River, Ark., September 3 and duty there till October 18. Moved to Memphis, Tenn., thence to Duvall's Bluff, Ark. Camp at Memphis, Tenn., November 28-December 31. Moved to New Orleans, La., December 31, 1864-January 4, 1865; thence to Mobile Point, Ala., February 12, and to Barrancas, Fla., and duty there till March 11. Steele's Expedition from Pensacola, Fla., to Blakely, Ala., March 20-31. Occupation of Pollard March 26. Siege of Spanish Fort and Fort Blakely April 1-8. Assault and capture of Fort Blakely April 9. Occupation of Mobile April 12. Expedition to Selma, Ala., April 22-28. Duty at Selma till May 11. Moved to Mobile, thence to Galveston, Texas, and duty there till July. Mustered out July 22 and discharged at Chicago, Ill., August 4, 1865.

Regiment lost during service 1 Officer and 51 Enlisted men killed and mortally wounded and 2 Officers and 205 Enlisted men by disease. Total 259.

77th REGIMENT INFANTRY.

Organized at Peoria, Ill., and mustered in September 3, 1862. Moved to Covington, Ky., October 4, 1862. Attached to 3rd Division, Army of Kentucky, Dept. of the Ohio, October, 1862. 2nd Brigade, 1st Division, Army of Kentucky, to November, 1862. 2nd Brigade, 10th Division, 13th Army Corps (Old), Department of the Tennessee, to December, 1862. 2nd Brigade, 1st Division, Sherman's Yazoo Expedition, to January, 1863. 2nd Brigade, 10th Division, 13th Army Corps, Army of the Tennessee, to August, 1863. 2nd Brigade, 4th Division, 13th Army Corps, Dept. of the Tennessee and Army of the Gulf, to January, 1864. 1st Division, 4th Division, 13th Army Corps, Dept. of the Gulf, to June, 1864. Defences of New Orleans, La., Dept. of the Gulf, June, 1864. 3rd Brigade, 3rd Division, 19th Army Corps, Dept. of the Gulf, to October, 1864. Defences of New Orleans, La., to February, 1865. 1st Brigade, 3rd Division, Reserve Corps, Military Division West Mississippi, February, 1865. 1st Brigade, 3rd Division, 13th Army Corps (New), Military Division West Mississippi, to July, 1865.

SERVICE.—March to Lexington, Ky., thence to Richmond, Ky., October 17-November 2, 1862. March to Louisville, Ky., November 11-17, thence to Memphis, Tenn., November 20-27, and duty there till December 20. Sherman's Yazoo Expedition December 20, 1862, to January 2, 1863. Chickasaw Bayou December 26-28. Chickasaw Bluff December 29, 1862. Expedition to Arkansas Post, Ark., January 3-10, 1863. Assault and capture of Fort Hindman, Arkansas Post, January 10-11. Moved to Young's Point, La., January 14-22, thence to Milliken's Bend March 9. Movement on Bruinsburg and turning Grand Gulf April 25-30. Battle of Port Gibson May 1. Battle of Champion's Hill May 16. Big Black River May 17. Siege of Vicksburg, Miss., May 18-July 4. Assaults on Vicksburg May 19 and 22. Surrender of Vicksburg July 4. Advance on Jackson, Miss., July 4-10. Siege of Jackson July 10-17. Duty at Vicksburg till August 25. Ordered to New Orleans August 25, and duty there till October 3. Western Louisiana Campaign October 3-November 30. At New Iberia till December 6. Moved to New Orleans December 6, thence to Pass Cavallo, Texas, December 8-20, and duty there till February, 1864. Reconnoissance on Matagorda January 21, 1864. Moved to New Orleans February, 1864. Red River Campaign March 10-May 22. Advance from Franklin to Alexandria March 14-26. Battle of Sabin Cross Roads April 8. Pleasant Hill April 9. Cane River Crossing April 23. At Alexandria and constructing dam across Red River April 26-May 13. Retreat to Morganza May 13-20. Mansura May 16. Moved to Baton Rouge, La., and duty there till August 1. Operations in Mobile Bay against Forts Gaines and Morgan August 2-23. Siege and capture of Fort Gaines August 3-8. Siege and capture of Fort Morgan August 8-23. At Morganza Bend, Mississippi River, till October, and Provost duty at New Orleans, La., till March, 1865. Campaign against Mobile, Ala., and its defences March 17-April 12. Siege of Spanish Fort and Fort Blakely March 26-April 8. Assault and capture of Fort Blakely April 9. Occupation of Mobile April 12. Expedition to Tombigbee River and McIntosh Bluffs April 13-May 9. At Mobile till July. Mustered out July 10, 1865.

Regiment lost during service 2 Officers and 66 Enlisted men killed and mortally wounded and 1 Officer and 137 Enlisted men by disease. Total 206.

78th REGIMENT INFANTRY.

Organized at Quincy, Ill., and mustered in September 1, 1862. Left State for Louisville, Ky., September 19, 1862. Attached to 39th Brigade, 12th Division, Army of the Ohio, to November, 1862. Gilbert's Command, District of Western Kentucky, Department of the Ohio, to February, 1863. Franklin, Tenn., Army of Kentucky, Dept. of the Cumberland, to June, 1863. 2nd Brigade, 1st Division Reserve Corps, Army of the Cumberland, to October, 1863. 2nd Brigade, 2nd Division, 14th Army Corps, to June, 1865.

SERVICE.—Moved to Shephardstown, Ky., October 5, 1862, and guard Louisville & Nashville R. R. from Elizabethtown to New Haven, with Headquarters at New Haven, till January 30, 1863. Action at Muldraugh's Hill December 28, 1862 (Cos. "B" and "C," captured by Morgan). New Haven December 30 (Co. "H"). Moved to Nashville, Tenn., January 30-February 7, 1863. Repulse of Forest's attack on Fort Donelson, Tenn., February 3. Moved to Franklin, Tenn., February 12, and duty there till June 23. Actions at Franklin March 4, April 10 and June 4-5. March to Triune, Murfreesboro and thence to Army near Shelbyville, June 24-28. Middle Tennessee (or Tullahoma) Campaign June 28-July 7. Occupation of Shelbyville July 1. Occupation of Middle Tennessee till August 16. Passage of Cumberland Mountains and Tennessee River and Chickamauga (Ga.) Campaign August 16-September 22. Battle of Chickamauga September 19-20. Siege of Chattanooga, Tenn., September 24-November 23. Chattanooga-Ringgold Campaign November 23-27. Tunnel Hill November 23-24. Mission Ridge November 24-25. Chickamauga Station November 26 (Regiment temporarily attached to 15th Army Corps, November 24). March to relief of Knoxville November 29-December 17. Duty at Rossville, Ga., till May, 1864. Demonstration on Dalton, Ga., February 22-27. Tunnel Hill, Buzzard's Roost Gap and Rocky Faced Ridge February 23-25. Reconnoissance from Rossville to La Fayette April 11-13. Atlanta (Ga.) Campaign May 1-September 8. Tunnel Hill May 6-7. Demonstration on Rocky Faced Ridge May 8-11. Buzzard's Roost Gap May 8-9. Demonstration on Dalton May 9-13. Battle of Resaca May 14-15. Rome May 17-18. Advance on Dallas May 19-25. Operations on line of Pumpkin Vine Creek and battles about Dallas, New Hope Church and Allatoona Hills May 25-June 5. Operations about Marietta and against Kenesaw Mountain June 9-July 2. Pine Mountain June 11-14. Lost Mountain June 15-17. Assault on Kenesaw June 27. Ruff's Station, Smyrna Camp Ground, July 4. Chattahoochie River July 5-17. Battle of Peach Tree Creek July 19-20. Siege of Atlanta July 22-August 25. Utoy Creek August 5-7. Flank movement on Jonesboro August 25-30. Battle of Jonesboro August 31-September 1. Lovejoy Station September 2-6. Operations in North Georgia and North Alabama against Forest and Hood September 29-November 3. Florence October 6-8. March to the sea November 15-December 10. Siege of Savannah December 10-21. Campaign of the Carolinas January to April, 1865. Averysboro, Taylor's Hole Creek, N. C., March 16. Battle of Bentonville March 19-21. Occupation of Goldsboro March 24. Advance on Raleigh April 10-14. Occupation of Raleigh April 14. Bennett's House April 26. Surrender of Johnston and his army. March to Washington, D. C., via Richmond, Va., April 29-May 19. Grand Review May 24. Mustered out June 7, 1865.

Regiment lost during service 9 Officers and 95 Enlisted men killed and mortally wounded and 117 Enlisted men by disease. Total 221.

79th REGIMENT INFANTRY.

Organized at Mattoon, Ill., and mustered in August 28, 1862. Ordered to Louisville, Ky. Attached to 3rd Brigade, Cruft's Division, Army of Kentucky, to September 13, 1862. 4th Brigade, 2nd Division, Army of the Ohio, to October 1, 1862. 5th Brigade, 2nd Division, 1st Corps, Army of Ohio, to November, 1862. 2nd Brigade, 2nd Division, Right Wing 14th Army Corps, Army of the Cumberland, to January, 1863. 2nd Brigade, 2nd Division, 20th Army Corps, Army of the Cumberland, to October, 1863. 3rd Brigade, 2nd Division, 4th Army Corps, to June, 1865.

SERVICE.—Pursuit of Bragg into Kentucky October 1-16, 1862. Near Clay Village October 4. Battle of Perryville October 8. March to Nashville, Tenn., October 16-November 7, and duty there till December 26. Reconnoissances toward Lavergne November 19, and November 26-27. Lavergne, Scrougesville, November 27. Advance on Murfreesboro December 26-30. Battle of Stone's River December 30-31, 1862, and January 1-3, 1863. At Murfreesboro till June. Middle Tennessee (or Tullahoma) Campaign June 24-July 7. Liberty Gap June 24-27. Occupation of Middle Tennessee till August 16. Passage of Cumberland Mountains and Tennessee River and Chickamauga (Ga.) Campaign August 16-September 22. Battle of Chickamauga, Ga., September 19-20. Siege of Chattanooga, Tenn., September 24-November 23. Chattanooga-Ringgold Campaign November 23-27. Orchard Knob November 23-24. Mission Ridge November 25. Pursuit to Graysville November 26-27. March to relief of Knoxville November 28-December 7. Operations in East Tennessee till April, 1864. Atlanta (Ga.) Campaign May 1-September 8. Demonstrations on Rocky Faced Ridge May 8-11. Buzzard's Roost Gap May 8-9. Battle of Resaca May 14-15. Adairsville May 17. Near Kingston May 18-19. Near Cassville May 19. Advance on Dallas May 22-25. Operations on Pumpkin Vine Creek and battles about Dallas, New Hope Church and Allatoona Hills May 25-June 5. Operations about Marietta and against Ken-

esaw Mountain June 10-July 2. Pine Hill June 11-14. Lost Mountain June 15-17. Assault on Kenesaw June 27. Ruff's Station July 4. Chattahoochie River July 5-17. Peach Tree Creek July 19-20. Siege of Atlanta July 22-August 25. Flank movement on Jonesboro August 25-30. Battle of Jonesboro August 31-September 1. Lovejoy Station September 2-6. Moved to Chattanooga, Tenn., September 25, thence to Bridgeport, Ala., and duty there till October 19. Moved to Chattanooga, Tenn., October 19, to Alpine, Ga., October 22, and to Pulaski, Tenn., October 30-November 2. Nashville Campaign November-December. Columbia, Duck River, November 24-27. Spring Hill November 29. Battle of Franklin November 30. Battle of Nashville December 15-16. Pursuit of Hood to the Tennessee River December 17-28. At Decatur, Ala., January 6 to March 30, 1865. Moved to Bull's Gap March 30, thence to Nashville April 22, and duty there till June. Mustered out June 12 and discharged at Camp Butler, Ill., June 23, 1865.

Regiment lost during service 4 Officers and 81 Enlisted men killed and mortally wounded and 1 Officer and 211 Enlisted men by disease. Total 297.

80th REGIMENT INFANTRY.

Organized at Centralia, Ill., and mustered in August 25, 1862. Moved to Louisville, Ky., September 4, 1862. Attached to 33rd Brigade, 10th Division, Army of the Ohio, to October, 1862. 33rd Brigade, 10th Division, 1st Army Corps, Army of the Ohio, to November, 1862. 1st Brigade, 5th Division, Centre, 14th Army Corps, Army of the Cumberland, to January, 1863. 1st Brigade, 5th Division, 14th Army Corps, to April, 1863. Streight's Independent Brigade, Dept. of the Cumberland to May, 1863. 2nd Brigade, 4th Division, 14th Army Corps, Army of the Cumberland, June to October, 1863. 3rd Brigade, 3rd Division, 11th Army Corps, Army of the Cumberland, to December, 1863. 3rd Brigade, 1st Division, 4th Army Corps, Army of the Cumberland, to June, 1864.

SERVICE.—Pursuit of Bragg into Kentucky October 1-16, 1862. Battle of Perryville, Ky., October 8. March to Munfordsville, Ky., October 12-18, and duty there till November 30. Expedition to Cave City October 31-November 26. Moved to Bledsoe Creek November 30. Pursuit of Morgan to Bear Wallow December 26, 1862-January 2, 1863. Moved to Nashville, thence to Murfreesboro, Tenn., January 3-10, and duty at Murfreesboro till April. Expedition to Auburn, Liberty and Alexandria February 3-5. Expedition to Woodbury March 3-8. Vaught's Hill, Milton, March 20. Moved to Nashville, Tenn., April 7, and attached to Streight's Provisional Brigade. Moved to Eastport, Miss., April 12-19, thence march to Tuscumbia, Ala., and Regiment mounted. Streight's Raid from Tuscumbia toward Rome, Ga., April 26-May 3. Day's Gap April 28. Sand Mountain April 30. Crooked Creek, Hog Mountain, April 30. East Branch Black Warrior Creek May 1. Blount's Farm May 2. Near Centre May 2. Cedar Bluffs May 3. Surrendered to vastly superior forces under Forest. Paroled. Moved to Atlanta, Ga., thence to Richmond, Va., and Annapolis, Md., May 4-17. Moved to Camp Chase, Ohio, May 19. Declared exchanged June 23, and moved to St. Louis, Mo., thence to Nashville, Tenn., and Stevenson, Ala., June 29-September 8. Moved to Battle Creek, Tenn., October 16, and to Bridgeport, Ala., October 23. Reopening Tennessee River October 26-29. Battle of Wauhatchie, Tenn., October 28-29. Duty in Lookout Valley till November 23. Chattanooga-Ringgold Campaign November 23-27. Orchard Knob November 23. Tunnel Hill November 24-25. Mission Ridge November 25. Pursuit to Graysville November 26-27. March to relief of Knoxville November 28-December 17. Duty at Whitesides, Tyner's Station and Blue Springs till May, 1864. Demonstration on Dalton, Ga., February 22-27, 1864. Tunnel Hill, Buzzard's Roost Gap and Rocky Faced Ridge February 23-25. Near Dalton February 23. Atlanta (Ga.) Campaign May 1-September 8. Tunnel Hill

May 6-7. Demonstration on Rocky Faced Ridge May 8-11. Buzzard's Roost Gap May 8-9. Demonstration on Dalton May 9-13. Near Dalton May 13. Battle of Resaca May 14-15. Near Kingston May 18-19. Near Cassville May 19. Advance on Dallas May 22-25. Operations on line of Pumpkin Vine Creek and battles about Dallas, New Hope Church and Allatoona Hills May 25-June 5. Operations about Marietta and against Kenesaw Mountain June 10-July 2. Pine Hill June 11-14. Lost Mountain June 15-17. Assault on Kenesaw June 27. Ruff's Station, Smyrna Camp Ground, July 4. Chattahoochie River July 5-17. Peach Tree Creek July 19-20. Siege of Atlanta July 22-August 25. Flank movement on Jonesboro August 25-30. Battle of Jonesboro August 31-September 1. Lovejoy Station September 2-6. Pursuit of Hood into Alabama October 3-26. Nashville Campaign November-December. Columbia, Duck River, November 24-27. Spring Hill November 29. Battle of Franklin November 30. Battle of Nashville December 15-16. Pursuit of Hood to the Tennessee River December 17-28. Moved to Huntsville, Ala., and duty there till March, 1865. Expedition to Bull's Gap and operations in East Tennessee March 15 to April 22. Moved to Nashville, Tenn., and duty there till June. Mustered out June 10, 1865.

Regiment lost during service 6 Officers and 52 Enlisted men killed and mortally wounded and 160 Enlisted men by disease. Total 218.

81st REGIMENT INFANTRY.

Organized at Anna, Ill., and mustered in August 26, 1862. Ordered to Cairo, Ill., and thence to Humboldt, Tenn., October 8, 1862. Attached to District of Columbus, Ky., Department of the Tennessee, to November, 1862. 1st Brigade, 3rd Division, Right Wing 13th Army Corps (Old), Department of the Tennessee to December, 1862. 4th Brigade, 3rd Division, 13th Corps, to December, 1862. 3rd Brigade, 3rd Division, 17th Army Corps, Army of the Tennessee, to March, 1864. 2nd Brigade, Provisional Detachment 17th Army Corps, Department of the Gulf, to June, 1864 (Non-Veterans). 2nd Brigade, Sturgis' Expedition, June, 1864. Detached Brigade, 17th Army Corps, June, 1864 (Non-Veterans). 4th Brigade, 1st Division, 16th Army Corps, to December, 1864 (Non-Veterans). 3rd Brigade, 3rd Division, 17th Army Corps, to December, 1864 (Veterans). 2nd Brigade, 3rd Division, Detachment Army of the Tennessee, Department of the Cumberland, to February, 1865. 3rd Brigade, 3rd Division, 16th Army Corps, Military Division West Mississippi, to July, 1865.

SERVICE.—Grant's Central Mississippi Campaign November 2, 1862, to January 10, 1863. Reconnoissance from LaGrange November 8-9, 1862. Moved to Memphis, Tenn., January 12-19, thence to Lake Providence, La., February 20-23, and duty there till April 17. Moved to Milliken's Bend, La., April 17. Movement on Bruinsburg and turning Grand Gulf April 25-30. Battles of Port Gibson, Miss., May 1. Raymond May 12. Jackson May 14. Champion's Hill May 16. Big Black River May 17. Siege of Vicksburg, Miss., May 18-July 4. Assaults on Vicksburg May 19 and 22 and June 25. Surrender of Vicksburg July 4, and duty there till March, 1864. Stephenson's Expedition to Monroe, La., August 20-September 2, 1863. Expedition toward Canton October 14-20. Bogue Chitto Creek October 17. Expedition to Sunnyside Landing, Ark., January 10-16, 1864. Non-Veterans on Red River Campaign March 10-May 22. Fort DeRussy March 14. Battle of Pleasant Hill April 9. Pleasant Hill Landing April 12-13. About Cloutiersville April 22-24. At Alexandria April 26-May 13. Bryce's Plantation May 6. Wells' Plantation May 6. Bayou Boeuf May 7. Retreat to Morganza May 13-20. Mansura May 16. Yellow Bayou May 18. Moved to Vicksburg, Miss., May 21-24, thence to Memphis, Tenn., May 28-30. Sturgis' Expedition to Guntown June 1-13. Brice's (or Tishamingo) Creek, near Guntown, June 10. Ripley June 11. Moved to St. Charles, Ark., August 3-6, thence to Duvall's Bluff

September 1 and to Brownsville September 8. March through Arkansas and Missouri in pursuit of Price September 17-November 21. Moved to Nashville, Tenn., November 23-30. Battle of Nashville December 15-16. Pursuit of Hood to the Tennessee River December 17-28. Moved to Eastport, Miss., and duty there till February 6, 1865.

Veterans joined 3rd Brigade, 3rd Division, 17th Army Corps, at Cairo, Ill., thence moved to Clifton, Tenn., and march to Ackworth, Ga., via Huntsville and Decatur, Ala., and Rome, Ga., May 4-June 8, 1864. Atlanta (Ga.) Campaign June 8 to September 8. Operations about Marietta, Ga., and against Kenesaw Mountain June 10-July 2. Assault on Kenesaw June 27. Nickajack Creek July 2-5. Howell's Ferry July 5. On line of the Chattahoochie River July 6-17. Leggett's Bald Hill July 20-21. Battle of Atlanta July 22. Siege of Atlanta July 22-August 25. Flank movement on Jonesboro August 25-30. Battle of Jonesboro August 31-September 1. Battle of Lovejoy Station September 2-6. Operations against Hood in North Georgia and North Alabama September 29-November 3. Rejoined Regiment at Nashville, Tenn.

Moved to New Orleans, La., February 6-21, 1865, and duty there till March 12. Campaign against Mobile and its defences March 21-April 12. Siege of Spanish Fort and Fort Blakely March 26-April 8. Assault and capture of Fort Blakely April 9. Occupation of Mobile April 12. March to Montgomery April 14-25. Duty there till July. Moved to Chicago, Ill., via Meridian and Vicksburg, Miss., July 19-August 5. Mustered out August 5, 1865.

Regiment lost during service 8 Officers and 66 Enlisted men killed and mortally wounded and 3 Officers and 292 Enlisted men by disease. Total 369.

82nd REGIMENT INFANTRY ("2nd HECKER REGT.).

Organized at Springfield, Ill., and mustered in October 23, 1862. Moved to Washington, D. C., November 3-9. Attached to 1st Brigade, 3rd Division, 11th Army Corps, Army of the Potomac, to October, 1863. 3rd Brigade, 3rd Division, 11th Army Corps, Army of the Cumberland, to April, 1864. 3rd Brigade, 1st Division, 20th Army Corps, Army of the Cumberland and Army of Georgia, to June, 1865.

SERVICE.—Moved to Fairfax Court House, Va., November 19, 1862, thence to Stafford Court House December 11. Near Aquia Creek, Va., December 19 to January 20, 1863. "Mud March," January 20-24, 1863. At Stafford Court House, Va., till April 27. Chancellorsville Campaign April 27-May 6. Battle of Chancellorsville May 1-5. Gettysburg (Pa.) Campaign June 12-July 24. Battle of Gettysburg, Pa., July 1-3. Pursuit to Manassas Gap July 5-24. Hagerstown July 12. Duty along Orange & Alexandria R. R. till September. Movement to Bridgeport, Ala., September 25-October 4. Operations in Lookout Valley October 19-26. Reconnoissance to Trenton October 20. Reopening Tennessee River October 26-29. Battle of Wauhatchie, Tenn., October 28-29. Duty in Lookout Valley, Tenn., till November 23. Chattanooga-Ringgold Campaign November 23-27. Orchard Knob November 23. Tunnel Hill November 24-25. Mission Ridge November 25. Pursuit to relief of Knoxville November 26-27. March to relief of Knoxville November 29-December 17. At Whitesides, Tenn., till May 3, 1864. Atlanta (Ga.) Campaign May 3-September 8. Demonstration on Rocky Faced Ridge May 8-11. Battle of Resaca May 14-15. Near Cassville May 19. New Hope Church May 25. Battles about Dallas, New Hope Church and Allatoona Hills May 26-June 5. Operations about Marietta and against Kenesaw Mountain June 10-July 2. Pine Hill June 11-14. Lost Mountain June 15-17. Gilgal (or Golgotha) Church June 15. Muddy Creek June 17. Noyes' Creek June 19. Kolb's Farm June 22. Assault on Kenesaw June 27. Smyrna Camp Ground July 4. Chattahoochie River July 5-17. Peach Tree Creek July 19-20. Siege of Atlanta July 22-August 25. Operations at Chattahoochie River Bridge August 26-September 2. Occupation of

Atlanta September 2-November 15. Expedition to Tuckum's Cross Roads October 26-29. March to the sea November 15-December 10. Milledgeville November 22. Montieth Swamp December 9. Siege of Savannah December 10-21. Campaign of the Carolinas January to April, 1865. Averysboro, Taylor's Hole Creek, N. C., March 16. Battle of Bentonville March 19-21. Occupation of Goldsboro March 24. Advance on Raleigh April 10-14. Occupation of Raleigh April 14. Bennett's House April 26. Surrender of Lee and his Army. March to Washington, D. C., via Richmond, Va., April 29-May 19. Grand Review May 24. Mustered out June 16, 1865.

Regiment lost during service 4 Officers and 98 Enlisted men killed and mortally wounded and 60 Enlisted men by disease. Total 162.

83rd REGIMENT INFANTRY.

Organized at Monmouth, Ill., and mustered in August 21, 1862. Moved to Cairo, Ill., August 25-29, thence to Fort Henry September 3, and to Fort Donelson, Tenn., September 5. Attached to garrison of Forts Henry, Donelson and Heiman, District of Columbus, Dept. of the Tennessee, to November, 1862. District of Columbus, 13th Army Corps (Old), Dept. of the Tennessee, to January, 1863. District of Columbus, 16th Army Corps, to June, 1863. 1st Brigade, 3rd Division, Reserve Corps, Dept. of the Cumberland, to October, 1863. Garrison of Clarksville, Tenn., Dept. of the Cumberland, to April, 1864. Unassigned, 4th Division, 20th Army Corps, Dept. of the Cumberland, to March, 1865. 5th Sub-District, Middle Tennessee, Dept. of the Cumberland, to June, 1865.

SERVICE.—Garrison duty at Forts Heiman (2 Companies), Henry (3 Companies) and Donelson, Tenn., till September 20, 1863. Expedition from Fort Donelson to Waverly, Tenn., October 22-25, 1862. Near Waverly and Richland Creek October 23. Cooley's Mill October 23. Near Garrettsburg, Ky., November 6. Fort Donelson Road January 2, 1863. Cumberland Iron Works, repulse of Forest's attack on Fort Donelson, February 3. Right wing moved to Clarksville, Tenn., September 20, 1863. Garrison duty at Clarksville and Fort Donelson and operating against guerrillas in Northwest Tennessee and Southwest Kentucky till December, 1864. Action at Budd's Creek, Clarksville, October 28, 1863. Pine Bluff, Tennessee River, August 19-20, 1864. Garrison duty at Nashville till June, 1865. Mustered out at Nashville, Tenn., June 26, and discharged at Chicago, Ill., July 5, 1865.

Regiment lost during service 4 Officers and 34 Enlisted men killed and mortally wounded and 1 Officer and 82 Enlisted men by disease. Total 121.

84th REGIMENT INFANTRY.

Organized at Quincy, Ill., and mustered in September 1, 1862. Left State for Louisville, Ky., September 23. Attached to 10th Brigade, 4th Division, 2nd Army Corps, Army of the Ohio, to November, 1862. 3rd Brigade, 2nd Division, Left Wing 14th Army Corps, Army of the Cumberland, to January, 1863. 3rd Brigade, 2nd Division, 21st Army Corps, Army of the Cumberland, to October, 1863. 3rd Brigade, 1st Division, 4th Army Corps, to May, 1865. 2nd Brigade, 1st Division, 4th Army Corps, to June, 1865.

SERVICE.—Pursuit of Bragg into Kentucky October 1-16, 1862. Battle of Perryville, Ky., October 8. Pursuit to Loudon October 10-22. March to Nashville, Tenn., October 22-November 7. Duty at Nashville till December 26. Advance on Murfreesboro, Tenn., December 26-30. Battle of Stone's River December 30-31, 1862, and January 1-3, 1863. At Murfreesboro till June. Woodbury January 24. Middle Tennessee (or Tullahoma) Campaign June 24-July 7. Occupation of Middle Tennessee till August 16. Passage of Cumberland Mountains and Tennessee River and Chickamauga (Ga.) Campaign August 16-September 22. Reconnoissance from Rossville September 17. Ringgold, Ga., September 17. Battle of Chickamauga, Ga., Septem-

ber 19-20. Siege of Chattanooga, Tenn., September 24-November 23. Chattanooga-Ringgold Campaign November 23-27. Lookout Mountain November 23-24. Mission Ridge November 25. Pursuit to Ringgold, Ga., November 26-27. Ringgold Gap, Taylor's Ridge, November 27. March to relief of Knoxville November 28-December 17. At Whiteside, Tyner's Station and Blue Springs till May, 1864. Demonstration on Dalton, Ga., February 22-27, 1864. Near Dalton February 23. Tunnel Hill, Buzzard's Roost Gap, and Rocky Faced Ridge February 23-25. Atlanta (Ga.) Campaign May to September. Tunnel Hill May 6-7. Demonstration on Rocky Faced Ridge May 8-11. Buzzard's Roost Gap May 8-9. Demonstration on Dalton May 9-13. Battle of Resaca May 14-15. Kingston May 18-19. Near Cassville May 19. Advance on Dallas May 22-25. Operations on line of Pumpkin Vine Creek and battles about Dallas, New Hope Church and Allatoona Mills May 25-June 5. Operations about Marietta and against Kenesaw Mountain June 10-July 2. Pine Hill June 11-14. Lost Mountain June 15-17. Assault on Kenesaw June 27. Ruff's Station, Smyrna Camp Ground, July 4. Chattahoochie River July 5-17. Peach Tree Creek July 19-20. Siege of Atlanta July 22-August 25. Flank movement on Jonesboro August 25-30. Battle of Jonesboro August 31-September 1. Lovejoy Station September 2-6. Operations against Hood in North Georgia and North Alabama September 29-November 3. Nashville Campaign November-December. Columbia, Duck River, November 24-27. Battle of Franklin November 30. Battle of Nashville December 15-16. Pursuit of Hood to the Tennessee River December 17-28. Moved to Huntsville, Ala., and duty there till March, 1865. Expedition to Bull's Gap and operations in East Tennessee March 15-April 22. Moved to Nashville, Tenn., and duty there till June. Mustered out at Nashville, Tenn., June 8, and discharged June 16, 1865.

Regiment lost during service 4 Officers and 120 Enlisted men killed and mortally wounded and 1 Officer and 144 Enlisted men by disease. Total 269.

85th REGIMENT INFANTRY.

Organized at Peoria, Ill., and mustered in August 27, 1862. Moved to Louisville, Ky., September 6, 1862. Attached to 36th Brigade, 11th Division, Army of the Ohio, to October, 1862. 36th Brigade, 11th Division, 3rd Army Corps, Army of the Ohio, to November, 1862. 2nd Brigade, 4th Division, Centre 14th Army Corps, Army of the Cumberland, to January, 1863. 2nd Brigade, 4th Division, 14th Army Corps, Army of the Cumberland, to June, 1863. 2nd Brigade, 2nd Division, Reserve Corps, Army of the Cumberland, to October, 1863. 3rd Brigade, 2nd Division, 14th Army Corps, Army of the Cumberland and Army of Georgia, to June, 1865.

SERVICE.—Pursuit of Bragg into Kentucky October 1-16, 1862. Battle of Perryville, Ky., October 8. March to Nashville, Tenn., October 16-November 7. Post duty at Nashville till March, 1863. Conduct ammunition trains to Army of the Cumberland at Stone's River December 28, 1862-January 2, 1863. Battle of Stone's River January 3, 1863. Expedition to Franklin March 9. At Brentwood till June 5, and at Murfreesboro till July 15. At Nashville, Tenn., till August 20. March to Bridgeport, Ala., via Franklin, Columbia, Athens and Huntsville August 20-September 14. Battle of Chickamauga, Ga., September 19-21. Siege of Chattanooga September 24-November 23. Chattanooga-Ringgold Campaign November 23-27. Orchard Knob November 23. Tunnel Hill November 24-25. Mission Ridge November 25. Pursuit to Graysville November 26-27. March to relief of Knoxville, Tenn., November 28-December 18. At North Chickamauga and McAffee's Church, Ga., till May, 1864. Demonstration on Dalton, Ga., February 22-27, 1864. Tunnel Hill, Buzzard's Roost Gap and Rocky Faced Ridge February 23-25. Atlanta (Ga.) Campaign May to September. Tunnel Hill May 6-7. Demonstration on Rocky Faced Ridge May 8-11. Buzzard's Roost Gap May 8-9. Battle of Resaca

May 14-15. Rome May 17-18. Operations on line of Pumpkin Vine Creek and battles about Dallas, New Hope Church and Allatoona Hills May 25-June 5. Operations about Marietta and against Kenesaw Mountain June 10-July 2. Pine Hill June 11-14. Lost Mountain June 15-17. Assault on Kenesaw June 27. Ruff's Station, Smyrna Camp Ground, July 4. Chattahoochie River July 5-17. Peach Tree Creek July 19-20. Siege of Atlanta July 22-August 25. Utoy Creek August 5-7. Flank movement on Jonesboro August 25-30. Battle of Jonesboro August 31-September 1. Lovejoy Station September 2-6. Operations in North Georgia and North Alabama against Hood and Forest September 29-November 3. March to the sea November 15-December 10. Siege of Savannah December 10-21. Campaign of the Carolinas January to April, 1865. Averysboro, Taylor's Hole Creek, N. C., March 16. Battle of Bentonville March 19-21. Occupation of Goldsboro March 24. Advance on Raleigh April 10-14. Occupation of Raleigh April 14. Bennett's House April 26. Surrender of Johnston and his army. March to Washington, D. C., via Richmond, Va., April 29-May 19. Grand Review May 24. Mustered out June 5, 1865.

Regiment lost during service 4 Officers and 86 Enlisted men killed and mortally wounded and 1 Officer and 131 Enlisted men by disease. Total 222.

86th REGIMENT INFANTRY.

Organized at Peoria, Ill., and mustered in August 27, 1862. Moved to Louisville, Ky., September 7, 1862, and duty there till October 1. Attached to 36th Brigade, 11th Division, Army of the Ohio, to October, 1862. 36th Brigade, 11th Division, 3rd Army Corps, Army of the Ohio, to November, 1862. 2nd Brigade, 4th Division, Centre 14th Army Corps, Army of the Cumberland, to January, 1863. 2nd Brigade, 4th Division, 14th Army Corps, Army of the Cumberland, to June, 1863. 2nd Brigade, 2nd Division, Reserve Corps, Army of the Cumberland, to October, 1863. 3rd Brigade, 2nd Division, 14th Army Corps, Army of the Cumberland, and Army of Georgia to June, 1865.

SERVICE.—Pursuit of Bragg into Kentucky October 1-16. Battle of Perryville, Ky., October 8. March to Nashville, Tenn., October 16-November 7. Post duty at Nashville till June 30, 1863. Moved to Murfreesboro, Tenn., June 30. Return to Nashville July 18, and duty there till August 20. March to Chattanooga, Tenn., via Brentwood, Columbia, Tenn., Huntsville and Bridgeport, Ala., August 20-September 16. Battle of Chickamauga, Ga., September 19-21. Siege of Chattanooga, Tenn., September 24-November 23. Chattanooga-Ringgold Campaign November 23-27. Orchard Knob November 23. Tunnel Hill November 24-25. Mission Ridge November 25. Pursuit to Graysville November 26-27. March to relief of Knoxville, Tenn., November 28-December 17. At Lee and Gordon's Mills, Ga., till May, 1864. Demonstration on Dalton, Ga., February 22-27, 1864. Tunnel Hill, Buzzard's Roost Gap and Rocky Faced Ridge February 23-25. Atlanta (Ga.) Campaign May to September. Tunnel Hill May 6-7. Demonstration against Rocky Faced Ridge May 8-11. Buzzard's Roost Gap May 8-9. Battle of Resaca May 14-15. Rome May 17-18. Operations on line of Pumpkin Vine Creek and battles about Dallas, New Hope Church and Allatoona Hills May 25-June 5. Operations about Marietta and against Kenesaw Mountain June 10-July 2. Pine Hill June 11-14. Lost Mountain June 15-17. Assault on Kenesaw June 27. Ruff's Station, Smyrna Camp Ground, July 4. Chattahoochie River July 5-17. Peach Tree Creek July 19-20. Siege of Atlanta July 22-August 25. Utoy Creek August 5-7. Flank movement on Jonesboro August 25-30. Battle of Jonesboro August 31-September 1. Lovejoy Station September 2-6. Operations in North Georgia and North Alabama against Hood and Forest September 29-November 3. March to the sea November 15-December 10. Louisville November 30. Cuyler's Plantation December 9. Siege of Savannah December 10-21. Campaign of the Carolinas January to April, 1865. Averysboro, Taylor's Hole Creek, N. C., March 16. Battle of Bentonville March 19-21. Occupation of Goldsboro March 24. Advance on Raleigh April 10-14. Occupation of Raleigh April 14. Bennett's House April 26. Surrender of Johnston and his army. March to Washington, D. C., via Richmond, Va., April 29-May 19. Grand Review May 24. Mustered out June 6 and discharged at Chicago, Ill., June 21, 1865.

Regiment lost during service 3 Officers and 73 Enlisted men killed and mortally wounded and 1 Officer and 93 Enlisted men by disease. Total 175.

87th REGIMENT INFANTRY.

Organized at Shawneetown, Ill., and mustered in October 3, 1862. Moved to Memphis, Tenn., January 31-February 4, 1863. Attached to District of Memphis, Tenn., 16th Army Corps, Department of the Tennessee, to March, 1863. 3rd Brigade, District of Memphis, Tenn., 5th Division, 16th Army Corps, to June, 1863. 2nd Brigade, 12th Division, 13th Army Corps, Army of the Tennessee, to July, 1863. 2nd Brigade, 3rd Division, 13th Army Corps, Dept. of the Tennessee, to August, 1863, and Department of the Gulf to September, 1863. Unattached Cavalry, Dept. of the Gulf, to November, 1863. 1st Brigade, Cavalry Division, Dept. of the Gulf, to January, 1864. 3rd Brigade, Cavalry Division, Dept. of the Gulf, to July, 1864. Cavalry Brigade, 19th Army Corps, Dept. of the Gulf, to December, 1864. Cavalry Brigade, Reserve Division, Military Division West Mississippi, to February, 1865. Cavalry District of Eastern Arkansas, 7th Army Corps, Dept. of Arkansas, to June, 1865.

SERVICE.—Duty at Memphis, Tenn., till May, 1863. Moved to Vicksburg, Miss., May 9-11. Siege of Vicksburg, Miss., May 18-July 4. Assault on Vicksburg May 22. Surrender of Vicksburg July 4. Advance on Jackson, Miss., July 4-10. Siege of Jackson July 10-17. Moved to Natchez, Miss., July 25; thence to New Orleans, La., August 10. Western Louisiana Campaign October 3-November 30. Regiment mounted in November. Washington, La., October 31. Grand Coteau November 3. Vermillionville November 11. Camp Pratt November 20. Grosse Tete Bayou February 19, 1864. Banks' Red River Campaign March 10-May 22, 1864. Advance from Franklin to Alexandria March 14-26. Monett's Ferry and Cloutiersville March 29-30. Natchitoches March 31. Wilson's Farm April 7. Sabine Cross Roads April 8. Pleasant Hill April 9. Retreat to Alexandria April 10-26. About Cloutiersville April 22-24. Monett's Ferry, Cane River Crossing, April 23. Occupation of Alexandria April 26-May 13. Wilson's Landing May 2. Retreat to Morganza May 13-20. Avoyelle, or Marksville Prairie, May 15. Mansura May 16. Yellow Bayou May 18. At Morganza, and on steamer Baltic, Marine Brigade, May to September. Scouting in Bayous between Mississippi, Atchafalaya and Red Rivers and Bayou Plaquemine. Expedition from Morganza to the Atchafalaya May 30-June 5. Livonia May 30. Near Morganza June 4. Bayou Grosse Tete June 19. Atchafalaya July 21. Scout from Morganza August 10-12. Bayou Letsworth August 11. Operations near Morganza September 16-25. Williamsport September 16. Moved to mouth of White River, Ark., September 4, and duty there till January, 1865. 3 Companies at St. Charles. Moved to Helena, Ark., and duty there till June. Scout from Helena to Madison, Ark., February 8-13. Friar's Point February 10. Skirmish near Madison February 12. Scout from Helena to Clark's Store February 24 (Detachment). Mustered out June 16, 1865.

Regiment lost during service 1 Officer and 15 Enlisted men killed and mortally wounded and 3 Officers and 219 Enlisted men by disease. Total 238.

88th REGIMENT INFANTRY ("2nd BOARD OF TRADE REGIMENT").

Organized at Camp Douglas, Chicago, Ill., and mustered in September 4, 1862. Ordered to Louisville, Ky., September 4, 1862. Attached to 37th Brigade,

11th Division, Army of the Ohio, to October, 1862. 37th Brigade, 11th Division, 3rd Corps, Army of the Ohio, to November, 1862. 1st Brigade, 3rd Division, Right Wing 14th Army Corps, Army of the Cumberland, to January, 1863. 1st Brigade, 3rd Division, 20th Army Corps, Army of the Cumberland, to October, 1863. 1st Brigade, 2nd Division, 4th Army Corps, Army of the Cumberland, to June, 1865.

SERVICE.—Pursuit of Bragg into Kentucky October 1-16, 1862. Battle of Perryville, Ky., October 8. March to Nashville, Tenn., October 17-November 7, and duty there till December 26. Reconnoissance to Mill Creek November 27. Advance on Murfreesboro December 26-30. Lavergne December 30. Battle of Stone River December 30-31, 1862, and January 1-3, 1863. Duty at and near Murfreesboro till June. Expedition toward Columbia March 4-14. Middle Tennessee (or Tullahoma) Campaign June 24-July 7. Occupation of Middle Tennessee till August. Passage of the Cumberland Mountains and Tennessee River and Chickamauga (Ga.) Campaign August 16-September 22. Battle of Chickamauga, Ga., September 19-20. Siege of Chattanooga September 24-November 23. Chattanooga-Ringgold Campaign November 23-27. Orchard Knob November 23-24. Mission Ridge November 25. March to relief of Knoxville, Tenn., November 28-December 8. Campaign in East Tennessee December, 1863, to February, 1864. At Loudon, Tenn., till April and at Cleveland till May. Atlanta (Ga.) Campaign May to September. Movements on Dalton May 5-9. Demonstration on Rocky Faced Ridge May 8-11. Buzzard's Roost Gap May 8-9. Demonstration on Dalton May 9-13. Battle of Resaca May 14-15. Adairsville May 17. Near Kingston May 18-19. Near Cassville May 19. Advance on Dallas May 22-25. Operations on line of Pumpkin Vine Creek and battles about Dallas, New Hope Church and Allatoona Hills May 25-June 5. Operations about Marietta and against Kenesaw Mountain June 10-July 2. Pine Mountain June 11-14. Lost Mountain June 15-17. Assault on Kenesaw June 27. Ruff's Station, Smyrna Camp Ground, July 4. Chattahoochie River July 5-17. Buckhead, Nancy's Creek, July 18. Peach Tree Creek July 19-20. Siege of Atlanta July 22-August 25. Flank movement on Jonesboro August 25-30. Battle of Jonesboro August 31-September 1. Lovejoy Station September 2-6. Operations against Hood in North Georgia and North Alabama September 29-November 3. Nashville Campaign November-December. Columbia, Duck River, November 24-27. Spring Hill November 29. Battle of Franklin November 30. Battle of Nashville December 15-16. Pursuit of Hood to the Tennessee River December 17-28. Moved to Huntsville, Ala., and duty there till March, 1865. Expedition to Bull's Gap and operations in East Tennessee March 15-April 22. Moved to Nashville, Tenn., and duty there till June. Mustered out at Nashville, Tenn., June 9, and discharged at Chicago, Ill., June 22, 1865.

Regiment lost during service 5 Officers and 98 Enlisted men killed and mortally wounded and 4 Officers and 84 Enlisted men by disease. Total 191.

89th REGIMENT INFANTRY ("RAILROAD REGT.").

Organized at Chicago, Ill., and mustered in August 27, 1862. Moved to Louisville, Ky., September 4, 1862. Attached to Army of Kentucky September, 1862. 6th Brigade, 2nd Division, 1st Army Corps, Army of the Ohio, to November, 1862. 1st Brigade, 2nd Division, Right Wing, 14th Army Corps, Army of the Cumberland, to January, 1863. 1st Brigade, 2nd Division, 20th Army Corps, Army of the Cumberland, to October, 1863. 1st Brigade, 3rd Division, 4th Army Corps, to June, 1865.

SERVICE.—Pursuit of Bragg into Kentucky October 1-15, 1862. Skirmish at Lawrenceburg, Ky., October 7. Battle of Perryville, Ky., October 8. March to Bowling Green, Ky., and Nashville, Tenn., October 16-November 7. Duty at Nashville, Tenn., till December 26. Advance on Murfreesboro December 26-30. Nolensville, Knob Gap December 26. Battle of Stone's River Decem-

ber 30-31, 1862, and January 1-3, 1863. Duty at Murfreesboro till June. Reconnoissance from Murfreesboro March 6-7. Middle Tennessee (or Tullahoma) Campaign June 22-July 7. Liberty Gap June 22-27. Occupation of Middle Tennessee till August 16. Passage of the Cumberland Mountains and Tennessee River and Chickamauga (Ga.) Campaign August 16-September 22. Battle of Chickamauga, Ga., September 19-20. Siege of Chattanooga September 24-November 23. Chattanooga-Ringgold Campaign November 23-27. Orchard Knob November 23-24. Mission Ridge November 25. Pursuit to Graysville November 26-27. March to relief of Knoxville November 28-December 8. Operations in East Tennessee December, 1863, to April, 1864. Atlanta (Ga.) Campaign May to September. Demonstration on Rocky Faced Ridge May 8-11. Buzzard's Roost Gap May 8-9. Demonstration on Dalton May 9-13. Battle of Resaca May 14-15. Adairsville May 17. Near Kingston May 18-19. Near Cassville May 19. Advance on Dallas May 22-25. Operations on line of Pumpkin Vine Creek and battles about Dallas, New Hope Church and Allatoona Hills May 25-June 5. Pickett's Mills May 27. Operations about Marietta and against Kenesaw Mountain June 10-July 2. Pine Hill June 11-14. Lost Mountain June 15-17. Assault on Kenesaw June 27. Ruff's Station, Smyrna Camp Ground, July 4. Chattahoochie River July 5-17. Peach Tree Creek July 19-20. Siege of Atlanta July 22-August 25. Flank movement on Jonesboro August 25-30. Battle of Jonesboro August 31-September 1. Lovejoy Station September 2-6. Operations against Hood in North Alabama and North Georgia September 29-November 3. Nashville (Tenn.) Campaign November-December. Columbia, Duck River, November 24-27. Battle of Franklin November 30. Battle of Nashville December 15-16. Pursuit of Hood to the Tennessee River December 17-28. Moved to Huntsville, Ala., and duty there till March, 1865. Operations in East Tennessee March 15-April 22. Moved to Nashville and duty there till June. Mustered out June 10 and discharged at Camp Douglas, Chicago, Ill., June 24, 1865.

Regiment lost during service 12 Officers and 121 Enlisted men killed and mortally wounded and 1 Officer and 172 Enlisted men by disease. Total 306.

90th REGIMENT INFANTRY.

Organized at Chicago, Ill., and mustered in September 7, 1862. Engaged in guard duty at Camp Douglass, Chicago, Ill., till November 27, 1862. Moved to Cairo, Ill., thence to Columbus, Ky., and LaGrange, Tenn., November 27-December 2. Attached to R. R. Guard, 13th Army Corps (Old), Dept. of the Tennessee, to January, 1863. 3rd Brigade, 1st Division, 16th Army Corps. Dept. of the Tennessee, to March, 1863. 1st Brigade, 1st Division, 16th Army Corps, to July, 1863. 1st Brigade, 4th Division, 15th Army Corps, to September, 1864. 3rd Brigade, 2nd Division, 15th Army Corps, to June, 1865.

SERVICE.—Grant's Central Mississippi Campaign December 5, 1862, to January 10, 1863. Guard bridges at Coldwater. Action at Holly Springs and Coldwater December 20, 1862. Duty at LaGrange and LaFayette, on Memphis & Charleston R. R., till June, 1863. Moved to Memphis, Tenn., thence to Vicksburg, Miss., June 7-17. Siege of Vicksburg June 17-July 4. Advance on Jackson July 4-10. Siege of Jackson, Miss., July 10-17. At Big Black till September 27. Movement to Memphis, Tenn., thence march to Chattanooga, Tenn., September 27-November 23. Operations on Memphis & Charleston R. R. in Alabama October 20-29. Chattanooga-Ringgold Campaign November 23-27. Tunnel Hill November 23-24. Mission Ridge November 25. Pursuit to Graysville November 26-27. March to relief of Knoxville, Tenn., November 28-December 17. At Scottsboro, Ala., till May, 1864. Atlanta (Ga.) Campaign May to September. Demonstrations on Resaca May 8-13. Battle of Resaca May 14-15. Near Kingston May 19-22. Advance on Dallas May 22-25. Operations on line of Pumpkin Vine Creek and battles about Dallas,

New Hope Church and Allatoona Hills May 25-June 5. Operations about Marietta and against Kenesaw Mountain June 10-July 2. Brush Mountain June 15. Assault on Kenesaw June 27. Nickajack Creek July 2-5. Chattahoochee River July 5-17. Battle of Atlanta July 22. Siege of Atlanta July 22-August 25. Ezra Chapel, Hood's second sortie, July 28. Flank movement on Jonesboro August 25-30. Battle of Jonesboro August 31-September 1. Lovejoy Station September 2-6. Operations against Hood in North Georgia and North Alabama September 29-November 3. Rome and Gadsden October 4. Reconnoissance on Cave Springs Road and skirmishes October 12-13. Reconnoissance from Gaylesville, Ala., to Turkeytown October 25. March to the sea November 15-December 10. Jenks' Bridge, Ogeechee River, December 7. Near Bryant's Court House December 8. Siege of Savannah December 10-21. Assault and capture of Fort McAllister December 13. Campaign of the Carolinas January to April, 1865. Salkehatchie Swamps, S. C., February 2-5. South Edisto River February 9. North Edisto River February 12-13. Columbia February 15-17. Battle of Bentonville, N. C., March 20-21. Occupation of Goldsboro March 24. Advance on Raleigh April 10-14. Occupation of Raleigh April 14. Bennett's House April 26. Surrender of Johnston and his army. March to Washington, D. C., via Richmond, Va., April 29-May 19. Mustered out June 10, 1865.

Regiment lost during service 2 Officers and 58 Enlisted men killed and mortally wounded and 1 Officer and 87 Enlisted men by disease. Total 148.

91st REGIMENT INFANTRY.

Organized at Camp Butler, Ill., and mustered in September 8, 1862. Moved to Shephardsville, Ky., October 1-7, 1862. Attached to Railroad Guard, Department of the Ohio, to December, 1862. District of St. Louis, Mo., February to July, 1863. 2nd Brigade, Herron's Division, 13th Army Corps, Department of the Tennessee, July, 1863. 2nd Brigade, 2nd Division, 13th Army Corps, Dept. of the Tennessee, to August, and Dept. of the Gulf to October, 1863. 1st Brigade, 2nd Division, 13th Army Corps, to June, 1864. U. S. forces Texas, Dept. of the Gulf, to August, 1864. Garrison Brazos Santiago, Texas, to December, 1864. Defences of New Orleans, La., Dept. of the Gulf, to February, 1865. 2nd Brigade, 3rd Division, 13th Army Corps, Military Division West Mississippi, to July, 1865.
SERVICE.—Guarding Louisville & Nashville R. R. and scouting through Kentucky after Morgan October 7 to December 27, 1862. Actions with Morgan at Nolin Station and Bacon Creek December 26, and at Elizabethtown, Ky., December 27. Regiment captured and paroled December 28. On duty as paroled prisoners of war at Benton Barracks, Mo., February 28 to June 5, 1863. Exchanged June 5, 1863. Moved to Vicksburg, Miss., July 8-15, thence to Port Hudson, La., July 24-25 and to New Orleans, La., August 13. At New Orleans till September 5. Moved to Morganza Bend September 5-6. Action at Morgan's Ferry, Atchafalaya River, September 7. Morganza September 8. Duty at Morganza till October 10. Moved to New Orleans, La., October 10-11; thence to Point Isabel, Texas, October 23-November 3. March to Brownsville November 6-9, and frontier duty there till July 28, 1864. Raid to Salt Lake December 31, 1862-January 9, 1864. Moved to Brazos Santiago July 28-30, and garrison duty there till December 24, 1864. Operations near Brazos Santiago August 4-15. Palmetto Ranch September 6. Action Bagdad September 11. Bocca Chica Pass October 14. Moved to New Orleans December 24-29 and duty there till February 21, 1865. Campaign against Mobile, Ala., and its defences February 21-April 12. Siege of Spanish Fort and Fort Blakely March 26-April 8. Assault on and capture of Fort Blakely April 9. Occupation of Mobile April 12. Whistler's Station April 13. March to Nanahubba Bluffs, Tombigbee River, and duty there till May 9. Moved to Mobile and duty there till July. Mustered

out July 12 and discharged at Chicago, Ill., July 28, 1865.
Regiment lost during service 12 Enlisted men killed and mortally wounded and 1 Officer and 131 Enlisted men by disease. Total 144.

92nd REGIMENT INFANTRY.

Organized at Rockford, Ill., and mustered in September 4, 1862. Moved to Cincinnati, Ohio, and Covington, Ky., October 10, 1862. Moved to Mt. Sterling, Ky., October 19, thence to Nicholasville, Ky., November 16-18 and to Danville, Ky., November 26. Attached to 2nd Brigade, 3rd Division, Army of Kentucky, Dept. of the Ohio, to February, 1863. 2nd Brigade, Baird's 3rd Division, Army of Kentucky, Dept. of the Cumberland, to June, 1863. 1st Brigade, 1st Division, Reserve Corps, Dept. of the Cumberland, to July, 1863. 1st Brigade, 4th Division, 14th Army Corps, Dept. of the Cumberland, to October, 1863. Wilder's Mounted Brigade, Army of the Cumberland, to December, 1863. 3rd Brigade, 2nd Division, Cavalry Corps, Army of the Cumberland, to April, 1864. 3rd Brigade, Kilpatrick's 3rd Division, Cavalry Corps, Army of the Cumberland, to October, 1864. 3rd Brigade, 3rd Division, Cavalry Corps, Military Division Mississippi, to November, 1864. 2nd Brigade, 3rd Division Cavalry Corps, Military Division Mississippi, to June, 1865.
SERVICE.—Duty at Danville, Ky., till December 26, 1862. Expedition to intercept Morgan on Louisville & Nashville R. R. December 26, 1862-January 2, 1863. Moved to Louisville, Ky., thence to Nashville, Tenn., January 26-February 6, 1863. Repulse of Forest's attack on Fort Donelson, Tenn., February 4, 1863. Duty at Nashville, Tenn., till March 5, 1863. Moved to Franklin, Tenn., March 5, and pursuit of Van Dorn March 5-12. Operations about Columbia March 9-10. At Brentwood till April 8. Repulse of Van Dorn's attack on Franklin April 10. At Franklin till June 2. Moved to Triune June 2. Action with Wheeler at Triune June 11. Middle Tennessee (or Tullahoma) Campaign June 24-July 7. Occupation of Shelbyville July 1. March to Wartrace July 3. Detached from Brigade July 6 and attached to Wilder's Mounted Infantry Brigade July 10. Mounted July 22. Occupation of Middle Tennessee till August 16. Passage of Cumberland Mountains and Tennessee River and Chickamauga (Ga.) Campaign August 16-September 22. Rossville and Ringgold, Ga., September 11. Lee and Gordon's Mills September 11-13. Leet's Tan Yard, or Rock Springs, September 12-13. Alexander's Bridge and Dyer's Ford September 18. Battle of Chickamauga, Ga., September 19-21. Operations against Wheeler and Roddy September 30-October 17. Hill's Gap, Thompson's Cove, near Beersheba, October 3. Murfreesboro Road October 4. Near McMinnville October 4-5. Farmington October 7. Sim's Farm, near Shelbyville, October 7. Guard Tennessee River north of Chattanooga till October 27. Moved to Bridgeport, Ala., and duty there till January 15, 1864. Ringgold Gap, Ga., November 27, 1863 (Co. "E"). Operations in North Alabama January 23-29. Bainbridge Ferry January 25 (Co. "I"). Sweetwater and Florence January 25. At Huntsville, Ala., till April 6. Moved to Ringgold, Ga., April 6. Nickajack Trace (or Gap) April 23. Reconnoissance from Ringgold toward Tunnel Hill April 29. Skirmish at Tunnel Hill April 29. Stone Church May 1. Leet's Cross Roads May 2. Atlanta (Ga.) Campaign May to September. Near Ringgold Gap May 2. Near Nickajack Gap May 7. Demonstrations on Resaca May 8-13. Near Resaca May 13. Battle of Resaca May 14-15. Calhoun May 15. Operations on line of Pumpkin Vine Creek and battles about Dallas, New Hope Church and Allatoona Hills May 25-June 5. Operations about Marietta and against Kenesaw Mountain June 10-July 2. Assault on Kenesaw June 27. Operations on line of Chattahoochie River July 3-17. Siege of Atlanta July 22-August 25. Fairburn August 15. Sandtown August 15. Kilpatrick's Raid around Atlanta August 18-22. Jonesboro August 19. Lovejoy Station

August 20. Flank movement on Jonesboro August 25-30. Fairburn August 27-28. Jonesboro August 30. Flint River Station August 30. Battle of Jonesboro August 31-September 1. Lovejoy Station September 2-6. Glass Bridge September 2. Operations against Hood and Forest in North Georgia and North Alabama September 29-November 3. Camp Creek September 30. Sweetwater and Noyes Creek, near Powder Springs, October 1-3. Van Wert October 9-10. March to the sea November 15-December 10. Bear Creek Station November 16. Near Clinton and Walnut Creek November 20. East Macon November 20. Near Macon November 21. Near Waynesboro November 27-28. Thomas' Station December 3. Waynesboro December 4. Ebenezer Creek December 8. Siege of Savannah December 10-21. Campaign of the Carolinas January to April, 1865. Near Barnwell, S. C., February 6. Aiken and Johnson's Station February 11. Phillips' Cross Roads March 4. Averysboro, Taylor's Hole Creek, N. C., March 16. Bentonville March 19-21. Occupation of Goldsboro March 26, and of Raleigh April 14. Bennett's House April 26. Surrender of Johnston and his army. Duty in Department of North Carolina till June. Mustered out at Concord, N. C., June 21, and discharged at Chicago, Ill., July 10, 1865. Recruits transferred to 65th Illinois Infantry, June 21, 1865.

Regiment lost during service 1 Officer and 51 Enlisted men killed and mortally wounded and 2 Officers and 127 Enlisted men by disease. Total 181.

93rd REGIMENT INFANTRY.

Organized at Chicago, Ill., and mustered in October 13, 1862. Moved to Memphis, Tenn., November 9-14, 1862. Attached to 5th Brigade, 5th Division, District of Memphis, Tenn., 13th Army Corps (Old), Dept. of the Tennessee, November, 1862. 3rd Brigade, 1st Division, District of Memphis, 13th Army Corps, to December, 1862. 3rd Brigade, 7th Division, 16th Army Corps, to January, 1863. 3rd Brigade, 7th Division, 17th Army Corps, to September, 1863. 3rd Brigade, 2nd Division, 17th Army Corps, to December, 1863. 3rd Brigade, 3rd Division, 15th Army Corps, to August, 1864. 1st Brigade, 3rd Division, 15th Army Corps, to April, 1865. 1st Brigade, 1st Division, 15th Army Corps, to June, 1865.

SERVICE.—Grant's Central Mississippi Campaign November, 1862, to January, 1863. Tallahatchie March November 26-December 12, 1862. At Ridgway, Tenn., January to March, 1863. Moved to Lake Providence, La., March 3, thence to Helena, Ark., March 10. Expedition to Yazoo Pass by Moon Lake, Yazoo Pass and Coldwater and Tallahatchie Rivers March 13-April 5. Operations against Fort Pemberton and Greenwood March 13-April 5. Moved to Milliken's Bend, La., April 13. Movement on Bruinsburg and turning Grand Gulf April 25-30. Battle of Port Gibson, Miss., May 1 (Reserve). Battles of Raymond May 12; near Raymond May 13; Jackson May 14; Champion's Hill May 16; Big Black River May 17. Siege of Vicksburg May 18-July 4. Assaults on Vicksburg May 19 and 22. Surrender of Vicksburg July 4. Moved to Jackson, Miss., July 13-15. Siege of Jackson July 15-17. At Vicksburg till September 12. Moved to Helena, Ark., September 12, thence to Memphis, Tenn., September 30. March to Chattanooga, Tenn., October 3-November 19. Operations on the Memphis and Charleston R. R. in Alabama October 20-29. Chattanooga-Ringgold Campaign November 23-27. Tunnel Hill November 23-24. Mission Ridge November 25. Pursuit to Graysville November 26-27. Moved to Bridgeport, Ala., December 3. To Larkinsville, Ala., December 22, and to Huntsville, Ala., January 17, 1864. Duty there till June. Demonstration on Dalton, Ga., February 22-27. Tunnel Hill, Buzzard's Roost Gap and Rocky Faced Ridge February 23-25. Moved to Decatur, Ala., June 12, thence march to Stevenson, Ala., June 14-25. To Kingston, Ga., June 27-28, thence to Etowah and guard bridge and crossing till July 11. At Kingston till August 2. March to Allatoona August 2-3. Pursuit of

Wheeler to Spring Place August 15-18. At Resaca and Allatoona till November. Battle of Allatoona October 5. March to the sea November 15-December 10. Siege of Savannah December 10-21. Campaign of the Carolinas January to April, 1865. Salkehatchie Swamps, S. C., February 2-5. South Edisto River February 9. North Edisto River February 12-13. Columbia February 15-17. West's Cross Roads February 25 (Detachment). Battle of Bentonville, N. C., March 20-21. Occupation of Goldsboro March 24. Advance on Raleigh April 10-14. Occupation of Raleigh April 14. Bennett's House April 26. Surrender of Johnston and his army. March to Washington, D. C., via Richmond, Va., April 29-May 19. Grand Review May 24. Mustered out June 23 and discharged at Chicago, Ill., July 7, 1865.

Regiment lost during service 4 Officers and 147 Enlisted men killed and mortally wounded and 1 Officer and 142 Enlisted men by disease. Total 294.

94th REGIMENT INFANTRY ("THE McLEAN REGIMENT").

Organized in McLean County and mustered in August 20, 1862. Moved to Benton Barracks, Mo., August 25, 1862, thence to Rolla, Mo., September 10, and march to Springfield, Mo., September 16-24. Duty there till October 11. Attached to 2nd Brigade, 3rd Division, Army of the Frontier, Dept. of Missouri, to June, 1863. 2nd Brigade, Herron's Division, 13th Army Corps, Dept. of the Tennessee, to July, 1863. 2nd Brigade, 2nd Division, 13th Army Corps, Dept. of the Tennessee, to August, 1863, and Dept. of the Gulf, to June, 1864. U. S. Forces Brownsville, Texas, to August, 1864. U. S. Forces Mobile Bay, Dept. of the Gulf, to December, 1864. District of Southern Alabama, Dept. of the Gulf, to February, 1865. 1st Brigade, 2nd Division, Reserve Corps, Military Division West Mississippi, February, 1865. 1st Brigade, 2nd Division, 13th Army Corps (New), Military Division West Mississippi, to July, 1865.

SERVICE.—March from Springfield to Cassville, Mo., October 11-14, 1862. Expedition to Cross Hollows, Ark., over Boston Mountains, October 17-24. March to Wilson's Creek November 4-22. Forced march to relief of General Blunt, December 3-6. Battle of Prairie Grove, Ark., December 7. At Prairie Grove till December 27. Expedition over Boston Mountains to Van Buren, White River, December 27-31. March through Missouri to near Rolla and duty there till June, 1863. Moved to St. Louis, Mo., thence to Vicksburg, Miss., June 3-10. Siege of Vicksburg, Miss., June 10-July 4. Surrender of Vicksburg July 4. Expedition to Yazoo City, Miss., July 12-21. Moved to Port Hudson, La., July 24, thence to Carrollton, La., August 28, and duty there till September 5. Expedition to Morganza September 5-October 11. Action at Morgan's Ferry, Atchafalaya River, September 7. Moved to the Rio Grande, Texas, October 23-November 4. Moved to Brownsville November 5-9, and duty at Fort Brown till July 28, 1864. Moved to Carrollton, La., August 1-5, thence to Mobile Bay, Ala. Operations against Fort Morgan, Mobile Bay, August 9-23. Capture of Fort Morgan August 23. At Navy Cove near Fort Morgan till December 14. Expedition to Pascagoula December 14-31. Franklin, Miss., December 22. Duty at Navy Cove till March, 1865. Campaign against Mobile and its defences March 17-April 12. Siege of Spanish Fort and Fort Blakely March 26-April 8. Assault and capture of Fort Blakely April 9. Conducted prisoners to Ship Island, then on duty at Mobile till June 22. Moved to Galveston, Texas, and duty there till July 17. Mustered out July 17, 1865.

Regiment lost during service 9 Enlisted men killed and mortally wounded and 4 Officers and 162 Enlisted men by disease. Total 175.

95th REGIMENT INFANTRY.

Organized at Rockford, Ill., and mustered in September 4, 1862. Moved to Jackson, Tenn., November 4-12, 1862. Attached to 1st Brigade, 6th Division, Left Wing 13th Army Corps (Old), Dept. of the Tennessee, to December, 1862. 1st Brigade, 6th Division, 16th Army Corps, to January, 1863. 1st Brigade, 6th Division, 17th Army Corps, to May, 1863. 2nd Brigade, 6th Division, 17th Army Corps, to September, 1863. 2nd Brigade, 1st Division, 17th Army Corps, to March, 1864. 2nd Brigade, Provisional Division, 17th Army Corps, Dept. of the Gulf, to June, 1864 (Non-Veterans). 2nd Brigade, Sturgis' Expedition, June, 1864 (Non-Veterans). Detached Brigade, 17th Army Corps, June, 1864 (Non-Veterans). 4th Brigade, 1st Division, 16th Army Corps, to December, 1864 (Non-Veterans). 3rd Brigade, 3rd Division, 17th Army Corps, April to December, 1864 (Veterans). 2nd Brigade, 3rd Division, Detachment, Army of the Tennessee, Dept. of the Cumberland, to February, 1865. 3rd Brigade, 3rd Division, 16th Army Corps (New), Military Division West Mississippi, to August, 1865.

SERVICE.—Grant's Central Mississippi Campaign November, 1862, to January, 1863. At Memphis January 13-20, 1863. Moved to Lake Providence, La., January 20-26, and duty there till April. Skirmish at Old River, Lake Providence, February 10. Moved to Milliken's Bend, La., April 12. Movement on Bruinsburg and turning Grand Gulf April 25-30. Battles of Fort Gibson, Miss., May 1; Raymond May 12; Jackson May 14; Champion's Hill May 16; Big Black River May 17. Siege of Vicksburg May 18-July 4. Assaults on Vicksburg May 19-22 and June 25. Expedition to Mechanicsburg May 26-June 4. Surrender of Vicksburg July 4. Moved to Natchez, Miss., July 12-13, and duty there till October 17. Moved to Vicksburg October 17 and duty there till February, 1864. Meridian Campaign February 3-25. Veterans on furlough March-April. Red River Campaign March 10-May 22. Fort DeRussy March 14. Battle of Pleasant Hill, Pleasant Hill Landing, April 12-13. About Cloutiersville April 22-24. Natchitoches April 22. At Alexandria April 26-May 13. Boyce's Plantation and Wells' Plantation May 6. Twelve Mile Bayou and Bayou Boeuf May 7. Retreat to Morganza May 13-20. Mansura May 16. Yellow Bayou May 18. Moved to Vicksburg, Miss., May 21-24, thence to Memphis, Tenn., May 28-30. Sturgis' Expedition to Guntown June 1-13. Brice's or Tishamingo Creek near Guntown June 10. Ripley June 11. Moved to St. Charles, Ark., August 3-6, thence to Duvall's Bluff September 1, and to Brownsville September 8. March through Arkansas and Missouri in pursuit of Price September 17-November 21. Moved to Nashville, Tenn., November 23-30. Battle of Nashville December 15-16. Pursuit of Hood to the Tennessee River December 17-28. Moved to Eastport, Miss., and duty there till February 6, 1865. (Veterans joined 3rd Brigade, 3rd Division, 17th Army Corps, at Cairo, Ill., thence moved to Clifton, Tenn., and march to Ackworth, Ga., via Huntsville and Decatur, Ala., and Rome, Ga., April 28-June 8, 1864. Atlanta (Ga.) Campaign June 8 to September 8. Operations about Marietta and against Kenesaw Mountain June 10-July 2. Assault on Kenesaw Mountain June 27. Nickajack Creek July 2-5. Howell's Ferry July 5. On line of the Chattahoochie River July 6-17. Leggett's Bald Hill July 20-21. Battle of Atlanta July 22. Siege of Atlanta July 22-August 25. Flank movement on Jonesboro August 25-30. Battle of Jonesboro August 31-September 1. Lovejoy Station September 2-6. Operations against Hood in North Georgia and North Alabama September 29-November 3. Rejoined Regiment at Nashville, Tenn.)

Moved to New Orleans, La., February 6-21, 1865, and duty there till March 12. Campaign against Mobile and its defences March 21-April 12. Siege of Spanish Fort and Fort Blakely March 26-April 8. Assault and capture of Fort Blakely April 9. Occupation of Mobile April 12. March to Montgomery, Ala., April 13-25, and duty there till July. Moved to Meridian and Vicksburg, Miss. Mustered out August 17, 1865. Recruits transferred to 47th Illinois Infantry.

Regiment lost during service 7 Officers and 77 Enlisted men killed and mortally wounded and 1 Officer and 204 Enlisted men by disease. Total 289.

96th REGIMENT INFANTRY.

Organized at Rockford, Ill., and mustered in September 6, 1862. Moved to Cincinnati, Ohio, October 8-10, 1862. Attached to 2nd Brigade, 3rd Division, Army of Kentucky, Dept. of the Ohio, to February, 1863. 2nd Brigade, Baird's 3rd Division, Army of Kentucky, Dept. of the Cumberland, to June, 1863. 1st Brigade, 1st Division, Reserve Corps, Army of the Cumberland, to October, 1863. 3rd Brigade, 1st Division, 4th Army Corps, October, 1863. 2nd Brigade, 1st Division, 4th Army Corps, to June, 1865.

SERVICE.—Moved to Covington, Ky., October 10, 1862, and duty there till October 29. Operating against Kirby Smith's threatened attack on Cincinnati, Ohio (Cos. "A," "E," "F," "G" and "H" escort train to Lexington, Ky., October 19-25). Moved to Lexington, Ky., October 29-November 6. Duty at Lexington till November 14 and at Harrodsburg, Ky., till November 28. (Cos. "A" and "E" at Lexington till January, 1863.) Moved to Danville November 28 and duty there till January 26, 1863. Pursuit of Morgan to Lebanon Junction December 26-31, 1862. Moved to Louisville, Ky., January 26-31, thence to Nashville, Tenn., January 31-February 8. Repulse of Wheeler's attack on Fort Donelson, Tenn., February 4. At Nashville till March 5. Moved to Franklin, Tenn., and pursuit of Van Dorn March 5-12. Spring Hill March 10. At Brentwood March 27-April 8. Return to Franklin April 8, and repulse of Van Dorn's attack April 10. At Franklin till June 2. Moved to Triune June 2. Action at Triune with Wheeler June 11. Middle Tennessee or Tullahoma Campaign June 24-July 7. At Wartrace July 3 to August 12, and at Elk River near Estill Springs till September 7. Chickamauga (Ga.) Campaign September 7-22. Ringgold September 17. Spring Creek September 18. Battle of Chickamauga September 19-20. Moved to Moccasin Point September 23 and duty there till November 1, and at Shellmound till November 20. Chattanooga-Ringgold Campaign November 23-27. Lookout Mountain November 23-24. Mission Ridge November 25. Taylor's Ridge, Ringgold Gap, November 27. At Lookout Mountain till December 1. At Nickajack Cove till January 26, 1864. Duty on East Tennessee R. R. till February 22. Demonstration on Dalton, Ga., February 22-27. Tunnel Hill, Buzzard's Roost Gap and Rocky Faced Ridge February 23-25. At Cleveland, Tenn., March 1-April 22. Atlanta (Ga.) Campaign May 1-September 8. Tunnel Hill May 6 7. Demonstration on Rocky Faced Ridge May 8-11. Buzzard's Roost Gap May 8-9. Demonstration on Dalton May 11-13. Battle of Resaca May 14-15. Near Kingston May 18-19. Near Cassville May 19. Advance on Dallas May 22-25. Operations on line of Pumpkin Vine Creek and battles about Dallas, New Hope Church and Allatoona Hills May 25-June 5. Operations about Marietta and against Kenesaw Mountain June 10-July 2. Pine Hill June 11-14. Lost Mountain June 15-17. Assault on Kenesaw June 27. Ruff's Station, Smyrna Camp Ground, July 4. Chattahoochie River July 5-17. Peach Tree Creek July 19-20. Siege of Atlanta July 22-August 25. Flank movement on Jonesboro August 25-30. Battle of Jonesboro August 31-September 1. Lovejoy Station September 2-6. Operations against Hood in North Georgia and North Alabama September 28-November 3. Nashville Campaign November-December. Columbia, Duck River, November 24-27. Battle of Franklin November 30. Battle of Nashville December 15-16. Pursuit of Hood to the Tennessee River December 17-28. Moved to Huntsville, Ala., and duty there till March, 1865. Expedition to Bull's Gap and operations in East Tennessee March 20-April 22. Moved to Nashville, Tenn., and duty there till June. Mustered out June 10, 1865.

Regiment lost during service 5 Officers and 111 Enlisted men killed and mortally wounded and 1 Officer and 124 Enlisted men by disease. Total 241.

97th REGIMENT INFANTRY.

Organized at Camp Butler, Ill., and mustered in September 16, 1862. Moved to Covington, Ky., October 1, 1862. Attached to 2nd Brigade, 1st Division, Army of Kentucky, Dept. of the Ohio, to November, 1862. 2nd Brigade, 10th Division, 13th Army Corps (Old), Dept. of the Tennessee, to December, 1862. 2nd Brigade, Sherman's Yazoo Expedition, to January, 1863. 2nd Brigade, 10th Division, 13th Army Corps, Army of the Tennessee, to August, 1863. 2nd Brigade, 4th Division, 13th Army Corps, Dept. of the Gulf, to December, 1863. 2nd Brigade, 4th Division, 19th Army Corps, Dept. of the Gulf, to February, 1864. 2nd Brigade, 4th Division, 13th Army Corps, to June, 1864. 2nd Brigade, 3rd Division, 19th Army Corps, Dept. of the Gulf, to December, 1864. District of Southern Alabama and 3rd Brigade, Reserve Corps, Military Division West Mississippi, to February, 1865. 2nd Brigade, 2nd Division, Reserve Corps, Military Division West Mississippi, February, 1865. 2nd Brigade, 2nd Division, 13th Army Corps (New), Military Division West Mississippi, to July, 1865.

SERVICE.—March to Lexington, thence to Nicholsville, Ky., October 17-November 2, and Louisville, Ky., November 11-17. Moved to Memphis, Tenn., November 20-27, and duty there till December 20. Sherman's Yazoo Expedition December 20, 1862-January 2, 1863. Chickasaw Bayou December 26-28, 1862. Chickasaw Bluff December 29. Expedition to Arkansas Post, Ark., January 3-10, 1863. Assault and capture of Fort Hindman, Arkansas Post, January 10-11. Moved to Young's Point, La., January 14-22, thence to Milliken's Bend, La., March 9. Movement on Bruinsburg and turning Grand Gulf April 25-30. Battles of Port Gibson may 1; Champion's Hill May 16; Big Black River May 17. Siege of Vicksburg, Miss., May 18-July 4. Assaults on Vicksburg May 19 and 22. Surrender of Vicksburg July 4. Advance on Jackson, Miss., July 5-10. Siege of Jackson July 10-17. Reconnoissance to Pearl River July 11. At Vicksburg till August 25. Moved to New Orleans, La., August 25 and duty there till October. Western Louisiana Campaign October 3-November 1. Ordered to New Orleans, La., and provost duty there till May, 1864. Moved to Morganza, La., and duty there till September. Atchafalaya Bayou September 16-17 and 19, and October 5. Moved to Pascagoula and duty there till February 1, 1865. Moved to Barrancas, Fla., February 1, and duty there till March 20. Steele's Expedition to Mobile, Ala., March 20-31. Occupation of Pollard March 26 and Canoe Station March 27. Siege of Fort Blakely April 1-8. Assault and capture of Fort Blakely April 9. Occupation of Mobile April 12. Expedition to Selma April 22-28, and to Cahawba May 1-2. Moved to Mobile May 11, thence to Galveston, Texas, and duty there till July. Mustered out July 29, 1865.

Regiment lost during service 2 Officers and 28 Enlisted men killed and mortally wounded and 3 Officers and 200 Enlisted men by disease. Total 233.

98th REGIMENT INFANTRY.

Organized at Centralia, Ill., and mustered in September 3, 1862. Moved to Louisville, Ky., September 8, 1862, thence to Jeffersonville September 9, and to Shepherdsville September 19. Attached to 40th Brigade, 12th Division, Army of the Ohio, to November, 1862. 2nd Brigade, 5th Division, Centre 14th Army Corps, Army of the Cumberland, to January, 1863. 2nd Brigade, 5th Division, 14th Army Corps, Army of the Cumberland, to June, 1863. 1st Brigade, 4th Division, 14th Army Corps, to October, 1863. Wilder's Mounted Infantry Brigade, Army of the Cumberland, to November, 1863. 3rd Brigade, 2nd Division, Cavalry Corps, Army of the Cumberland, November, 1863. 2nd Brigade, 2nd Division, Cavalry Corps, Army of the Cumberland, to December, 1863. 3rd Brigade, 2nd Division, Cavalry Corps, Army of the Cumberland, to November, 1864. 1st Brigade, 2nd Division, Cavalry Corps, Military Division Mississippi, to June, 1865.

SERVICE.—Moved to Elizabethtown, Ky., thence to Frankfort and Versailles September 30-October 13, 1862. March to Bowling Green, Ky., October 26-November 3, thence to Scottsboro November 10. To Gallatin November 26, and to Castillian Springs November 28. To Bledsoe Creek December 14. Operations against Morgan in Kentucky December 22-January 2, 1863. Moved to Cave City, thence to Murfreesboro, Tenn., January 2-8, and duty there till June. Expedition to Auburn, Liberty and Alexandria February 3-5. Regiment mounted March 8. Expedition to Woodbury March 3-8. Expedition to Lebanon, Carthage and Liberty April 1-8. Expedition to McMinnville April 20-30. Reconnoissance to the front May 23. Armed with Spencer Carbines May 31. Liberty Road June 4. Liberty June 10. Middle Tennessee or Tullahoma Campaign June 24-July 7. Hoover's Gap June 24-26. Occupation of Manchester June 27. Dechard June 29. Pelham and Elk River Bridge July 2. Occupation of Middle Tennessee till August 16. Passage of the Cumberland Mountains and Tennessee River and Chickamauga (Ga.) Campaign August 16-September 22. Friar's Island September 9. Lee and Gordon's Mills September 11-13. Ringgold September 11. Leet's Tan Yard September 12-13. Pea Vine Ridge September 18. Alexander's Bridge September 18. Battle of Chickamauga September 19-21. Operations against Wheeler and Roddy September 30-October 17. Hill's Gap, Thompson's Cove, near Beersheba October 3. Murfreesboro Road near McMinnville and McMinnville October 4. Farmington October 7. Sims' Farm near Shelbyville October 7. Chattanooga-Ringgold Campaign November 23-27. Raid on East Tennessee and Georgia R. R. November 24-27. Charleston November 26. Cleveland November 27. March to relief of Knoxville and operations in East Tennessee November 28, 1863, to January 6, 1864. Near Loudon December 2, 1863. Expedition to Murphey, N. C., December 6-11. Operations in North Alabama January 23-29, 1864. Florence January 25. Demonstration on Dalton, Ga., February 22-27. Tunnel Hill, Buzzard's Roost Gap and Rocky Faced Ridge February 23-25. Near Dalton February 23. Atlanta (Ga.) Campaign May 1-September 8. Battle of Resaca May 13-15. Rome May 17-18. Near Dallas May 24. Operations on line of Pumpkin Vine Creek and battles about Dallas, New Hope Church and Allatoona Hills May 25-June 5. Near Big Shanty June 9. Operations about Marietta and against Kenesaw Mountain June 10-July 2. Noonday Creek June 19-20. Powder Springs, Lattimer's Mills, June 20. Noonday Creek and assault on Kenesaw June 27. Nickajack Creek July 2-5. Rottenwood Creek July 4. Chattahoochie River July 5-17. Garrard's Raid to Covington July 22-24. Siege of Atlanta July 22-August 25. Garrard's Raid to South River July 27-31. Flat Rock Bridge July 28. Kilpatrick's Raid around Atlanta August 20-22. Operations at Chattahoochie River Bridge August 26-September 2. Operations against Hood in North Georgia and North Alabama September 29-November 3. Near Lost Mountain October 4-7. New Hope Church October 5. Dallas October 7. Rome October 10-11. Narrows October 11. Near Rome October 13. Near Summerville October 18. Little River, Ala., October 20. Leesburg October 21. Ladiga, Terrapin Creek, October 28. Moved to Nashville, Tenn., thence to Louisville, Ky., November 2-15, and duty there refitting till December 26. March to Nashville, Tenn., December 26, 1864, to January 12, 1865, thence to Gravelly Springs, Ala., and duty there till March 13. Wilson's Raid to Macon, Ga., March 22-April 24. Summerville April 2. Selma April 2. Montgomery April 12. Columbus, Ga., April 16. Macon April 20. Provost duty at Macon till May 23. Moved to Edgefield and duty there till June, 1865. Mustered out June 27 and discharged at Springfield, Ill., July 7, 1865.

Regiment lost during service 30 Enlisted men killed and mortally wounded and 5 Officers and 136 Enlisted men by disease. Total 171.

99th REGIMENT INFANTRY.

Organized at Florence, Ill., and mustered in August 23, 1862. Moved to St. Louis, Mo., August 23-24, 1862. At Benton Barracks, Mo., till September 8. Moved to Rolla September 8. Attached to District of Rolla, Dept. of the Missouri, to November, 1862. 1st Brigade, 1st Division, District of Southeast Missouri, Dept. of Missouri, to February, 1863. 1st Brigade, 14th Division, 13th Army Corps, Dept. of the Tennessee, to August, 1863. 1st Brigade, 1st Division, 13th Army Corps, Dept. of the Gulf, to June, 1864. District of LaFourche, Dept. Gulf, to August, 1864. 2nd Brigade, 2nd Division, 19th Army Corps, Dept. Gulf, to December, 1864. 1st Brigade, Reserve Corps, Military Division West Mississippi, to February, 1865. 1st Brigade, 1st Division, Reserve Corps, Military Division West Mississippi, February, 1865. 1st Brigade, 1st Division, 13th Army Corps (New), Military Division West Mississippi, to July, 1865.

SERVICE.—Moved from Rolla to Salem, Mo., September 17, 1862, and duty there till November 20. Moved to Houston, Mo., November 20, and duty there till January 27, 1863. Action at Beaver Creek, Texas County, November 24, 1862. Hartsville, Wood's Forks, January 11, 1863. Moved to West Plains, Mo., January 27, and duty there till March 3. Moved to Milliken's Bend, La., March 3-15, and duty there till April 11. To New Carthage April 11-12 and duty there till April 25. Movement on Bruinsburg and turning Grand Gulf April 25-30. Battles of Port Gibson, Miss., May 1; Champion's Hill May 16; Big Black River Bridge May 17. Siege of Vicksburg May 18-July 4. Assaults on Vicksburg May 19 and 22. Surrender of Vicksburg July 4. Advance on Jackson, Miss., July 5-10. Siege of Jackson July 10-17. Duty at Vicksburg till August 20. Ordered to New Orleans, La., August 20. Duty at Carrollton, Brashear City and Berwick till October. Western Louisiana Campaign October 3-November 9. Moved to New Orleans November 9-12, thence to Mustang Island, Texas, November 16-25. Duty at Indianola till June, 1864. Moved to Algiers, La., June 16. Duty at Kennersville, Algiers, and Morganza till September. Moved to St. Charles, Ark., September 3-11, and duty there till October 23. Expedition to Duvall's Bluff October 23-November 12. Moved to Litle Rock, thence to Memphis, Tenn., November 12-25. At Germantown, Tenn., guarding railroad till December 28. Moved to Memphis, Tenn., December 28, thence to New Orleans, La., January 1-9, 1865. Campaign against Mobile, Ala., and its defences February 1-April 12. Siege of Spanish Fort and Fort Blakely March 26-April 8. Assault and capture of Fort Blakely April 9. Occupation of Mobile April 12. Moved to New Orleans, thence to Shreveport, La., May 28-June 6. To Baton Rouge July 19. Mustered out July 31 and discharged at Springfield, Ill., August 9, 1865.

Regiment lost during service 4 Officers and 47 Enlisted men killed and mortally wounded and 1 Officer and 120 Enlisted men by disease. Total 172.

100th REGIMENT INFANTRY.

Organized at Joliet, Ill., and mustered in August 30, 1862. Left state for Louisville, Ky., September 2, 1862. Attached to 1st Brigade, 2nd Division, Army of Kentucky, Dept. of the Ohio, to October, 1862. 15th Brigade, 6th Division, 2nd Army Corps, Army of the Ohio, to November, 1862. 1st Brigade, 1st Division, Left Wing 14th Army Corps, Army of the Cumberland, to January, 1863. 1st Brigade, 1st Division, 21st Army Corps, Army of the Cumberland, to October, 1863. 2nd Brigade, 2nd Division, 4th Army Corps, to June, 1865.

SERVICE.—Pursuit of Bragg into Kentucky October 1-18. Battle of Perryville, Ky., October 8 (Reserve). Nelson's Cross Roads October 18. March to Nashville, Tenn., October 18-November 26, and duty there till December 26. Advance on Murfreesboro December 26-30. Lavergne December 26-27. Battle of Stone's River December 30-31, 1862, and January 1-3, 1863. At Murfreesboro till June. Middle Tennessee or Tulla-

homa Campaign June 24-July 7. Occupation of Middle Tennessee till August 16. Passage of Cumberland Mountains and Tennessee River and Chickamauga (Ga.) Campaign August 16-September 22. Expedition from Tracy City to Tennessee River August 22-24. Near Lee and Gordon's Mills September 17-18. Battle of Chickamauga, Ga., September 19-20. Siege of Chattanooga, Tenn., September 24-November 23. Chattanooga-Ringgold Campaign November 23-27. Battles of Orchard Knob November 23-24; Mission Ridge November 25. March to relief of Knoxville and operations in East Tennessee December 28-February 1, 1864. At Athens, Tenn., February to April. Atlanta (Ga.) Campaign May 1-September 8. Demonstration on Rocky Faced Ridge May 8-11. Buzzard's Roost Gap May 8-9. Demonstrations on Dalton May 9-13. Battle of Resaca May 14-15. Adairsville May 17. Near Kingston May 18-19. Near Cassville May 19. Advance on Dallas May 22-25. Operations on line of Pumpkin Vine Creek and battles about Dallas, New Hope Church and Allatoona Hills May 25-June 5. Operations about Marietta and against Kenesaw Mountain June 10-July 2. Pine Mountain June 11-14. Lost Mountain June 15-17. Assault on Kenesaw June 27. Ruff's Station, Smyrna Camp Ground, July 4. Chattahoochie River July 5-17. Buckhead, Nancy's Creek, July 18. Peach Tree Creek July 19-20. Siege of Atlanta July 22-August 25. Flank movement on Jonesboro August 25-30. Battle of Jonesboro August 31-September 1. Lovejoy Station September 2-6. Operations against Hood in North Georgia and North Alabama September 28-November 3. Nashville (Tenn.) Campaign November-December. Columbia, Duck River, November 24-27. Spring Hill November 29. Battle of Franklin November 30. Battle of Nashville December 15-16. Pursuit of Hood to the Tennessee River December 17-28. Moved to Huntsville, Ala., and duty there till March, 1865. Expedition to Bull's Gap and operations in East Tennessee March 20-April 22. Moved to Nashville, Tenn., and duty there till June. Mustered out at Nashville, Tenn., June 12, and discharged at Chicago, Ill., June 15, 1865.

Regiment lost during service 7 Officers and 73 Enlisted men killed and mortally wounded and 134 Enlisted men by disease. Total 214.

101st REGIMENT INFANTRY.

Organized at Jacksonville, Ill., and mustered in September 2, 1862. Moved to Cairo, Ill., October 6-7, 1862. Attached to District of Cairo, Dept. of the Tennessee, to November, 1862. 2nd Brigade, 4th Division, Right Wing 13th Army Corps (Old), Dept. of the Tennessee, to December, 1862. 2nd Brigade, 4th Division, 17th Army Corps, to January, 1863. 2nd Brigade, 4th Division, 16th Army Corps, January, 1863. District of Memphis, Tenn., 16th Army Corps, to March, 1863. Ram Fleet, Mississippi Squadron, to June, 1863. District of Columbus, Ky., 6th Division, 16th Army Corps, to July, 1863. 1st Brigade, 6th Division, 16th Army Corps, to October, 1863. 1st Brigade, 3rd Division, 11th Army Corps, Army of the Cumberland, to April, 1864. 3rd Brigade, 1st Division, 20th Army Corps, Army of the Cumberland and Army of Georgia, to June, 1865.

SERVICE.—Duty at Cairo, Ill., October 7, to November 26, 1862. Moved to Columbus, Ky., thence to Davis Mills, Miss., November 26-27. Grant's Central Mississippi Campaign. March to Lumpkin's Mills, thence to Holly Springs, Miss., November 28-December 3. Provost and garrison duty there till December 20. (Co. "A" guard prisoners to Cairo, Ill., Vicksburg, Miss., and Alton, Ill., December 13, 1862, to February 1, 1863. Returned to Memphis, Tenn.) Action and capture at Holly Springs, Miss., December 20, 1862. Companies "B," "C," "E," "F" and "I" captured, paroled and sent to Memphis, Tenn., thence to Benton Barracks, Mo., and duty there as paroled prisoners of war till June, 1863. Companies "D," "G," "H," "I" and "K" on duty guarding railroad, fell back to Coldwater, December 20, 1862, and assisted in repulse of Van Dorn's attack December 20. Companies "D," "G," "H" and "K" formed temporarily into a Battalion and attached to 14th Illinois Infantry till March, 1863. Operations on Mississippi Central Railroad and scouting till February, 1863. At Memphis till March. Company "A" rejoined at Memphis February, 1863. Ordered to Vicksburg, Miss., March, 1863. Battalion broken up. Company "K" assigned as provost guard at General Grant's headquarters; Company "G" to ram "Switzerland;" Company "D" to "Rattler" and "Cricket;" Company "A" to "General Bragg;" Company "H" to "Lafayette," so serving till September, 1863. Rejoined Regiment at Union City, Tenn. Regiment exchanged June 7, 1863. Moved to New Madrid, Mo., and duty there till July 11. Moved to Columbus, Ky., and duty there scouting till August. At Union City, Tenn., August 25 to September 24. Moved to Louisville, Ky., September 24-27, thence to Bridgeport, Ala., September 30-October 2, and duty there till October 27. Reopening Tennessee River October 27-29. Battle of Wauhatchie, Tenn., October 28-29. Duty in Lookout Valley till November 23. Chattanooga-Ringgold Campaign November 23-27. Orchard Knob November 23. Tunnel Hill November 24-25. Mission Ridge November 25. Pursuit to Cleveland November 26-27. March to relief of Knoxville, Tenn., November 28-December 17. At Whiteside till May, 1864. Atlanta (Ga.) Campaign May 3-September 8. Demonstration on Rocky Faced Ridge May 8-11. Battle of Resaca May 14-15. Near Cassville May 19. New Hope Church May 25. Operations on line of Pumpkin Vine Creek and battles about Dallas, New Hope Church and Allatoona Hills May 25-June 5. Operations about Marietta and against Kenesaw Mountain June 10-July 2. Pine Hill June 11-14. Lost Mountain June 15-17. Gilgal or Gulgotha Church June 15. Muddy Creek June 17. Noyes Creek June 19. Kolb's Farm June 22. Assault on Kenesaw June 27. Ruff's Station, Smyrna Camp Ground, July 4. Chattahoochie River July 6-17. Peach Tree Creek July 19-20. Siege of Atlanta July 22-August 25. Operations at Chattahoochie River Bridge August 26-September 2. Occupation of Atlanta September 2-November 15. Expedition from Atlanta to Tuckum's Cross Roads October 26-29. March to the sea November 15-December 10. Near Sandersville November 26. Montieth Swamp December 9. Siege of Savannah December 10-21. Campaign of the Carolinas January to April, 1865. Averysboro, Taylor's Hole Creek, N. C., March 16. Battle of Bentonville March 19-21. Occupation of Goldsboro March 24. Advance on Raleigh April 10-14. Occupation of Raleigh April 14. Bennett's House April 26. Surrender of Johnston and his army. March to Washington, D. C., via Richmond, Va., April 29-May 19. Grand Review May 24. Mustered out June 7 and discharged at Springfield, Ill., June 21, 1865.

Regiment lost during service 3 Officers and 47 Enlisted men killed and mortally wounded and 1 Officer and 118 Enlisted men by disease. Total 169.

102nd REGIMENT INFANTRY.

Organized at Knoxville, Ill., and mustered in September 1, 1862. Moved to Peoria, Ill., September 22, thence to Louisville, Ky., October 1. Attached to Ward's Brigade, Dumont's 12th Division, Army of the Ohio, to November, 1862. Ward's Brigade, Post of Gallatin, Tenn., Dept. of the Cumberland, to June, 1863. 2nd Brigade, 3rd Division, Reserve Corps, Army of the Cumberland, to August, 1863. Ward's Brigade, Post of Nashville, Tenn., Dept. of the Cumberland, to January, 1864. 1st Brigade, 1st Division, 11th Army Corps, Army of the Cumberland, to April, 1864. 1st Brigade, 3rd Division, 20th Army Corps, Army of the Cumberland, and Army of Georgia, to June, 1865.

SERVICE.—March in pursuit of Bragg through Kentucky October 1-16, 1862. March to Gallatin, Tenn., via Frankfort, Bowling Green and Scottsville October 16-November 26. Duty at Gallatin till June 6, 1863. Action at Woodbury April 27, 1863. Moved to Lavergne, Tenn., and on railroad guard duty at Lavergne and Stewart's Creek till February, 1864. (5 Companies

mounted August, 1863.) Moved to Wauhatchie Valley, Tenn., February 25, 1864. Scout from Lookout Valley to Deer Head Cove, Ga., March 29-31. Atlanta (Ga.) Campaign May 1-September 8. Movement on Dalton May 5-8. Demonstration on Rocky Faced Ridge May 8-11. Battle of Resaca May 14-15. Near Cassville May 19. Advance on Dallas May 22-25. New Hope Church May 25. Operations on line of Pumpkin Vine Creek and battles about Dallas, New Hope Church and Allatoona Hills May 26-June 5. Big Shanty June 1. Operations about Marietta and against Kenesaw Mountain June 10-July 2. Pine Hill June 11-14. Lost Mountain June 15-17. Gilgal or Golgotha Church June 15. Muddy Creek June 17. Noyes Creek June 19. Kolb's Farm June 22. Assault on Kenesaw June 27. Ruff's Station, Smyrna Camp Ground, July 4. Chattahoochie River July 5-17. Peach Tree Creek July 19-20. Siege of Atlanta July 22-August 25. Operations at Chattahoochie River Bridge August 26-September 2. Occupation of Atlanta September 2-November 15. March to the sea November 15-December 10. Occupation of Milledgeville November 22. Ogeechee River November 29. Siege of Savannah December 10-21. Campaign of the Carolinas January to April, 1865. Occupation of Hardeeville January 3, 1865. Occupation of Lawtonville, S. C., February 2. Rockingham, N. C., March 7. Fayetteville, N. C., March 11. Averysboro, Taylor's Hole Creek, March 16. Battle of Bentonville March 19-21. Moccasin Creek March 24. Occupation of Goldsboro March 24. Advance on Raleigh April 10-14. Occupation of Raleigh April 14. Bennett's House April 26. Surrender of Johnston and his army. March to Washington, D. C., via Richmond, Va., April 30-May 19. Grand Review May 24. Mustered out June 6 and discharged at Chicago, Ill., June 14, 1865.

Regiment lost during service 51 Enlisted men killed and mortally wounded and 68 Enlisted men by disease. Total 119.

103rd REGIMENT INFANTRY.

Organized at Peoria, Ill., and mustered in October 2, 1862. Moved to Cairo, Ill., thence to Bolivar, Tenn., October 30-November 2, 1862. Attached to 1st Brigade, 4th Division, Right Wing 13th Army Corps (Old), Department of the Tennessee, to December, 1862. 2nd Brigade, District of Jackson, 16th Army Corps, to March, 1863. 2nd Brigade, 1st Division, 16th Army Corps, to July, 1863. 2nd Brigade, 4th Division, 15th Army Corps, to September, 1864. 2nd Brigade, 1st Division, 15th Army Corps, to June, 1865.

SERVICE.—Grant's Central Mississippi Campaign November 2-December 31, 1862. Moved to LaGrange, Tenn., November 3, and duty there till November 28. Reconnoissance from LaGrange to Lamar, Miss., November 5. Wirsham Creek November 6. Garrison at Waterford, Miss., December 1-31. Moved to Jackson, Tenn., December 31, and duty there till March 10, 1863. Moved to LaGrange, Tenn., March 10, 1863, and duty there till June 5. Expedition to Holly Springs and Waterford, Miss., and Colliersville, Tenn., April 17-26. Moved to Memphis, Tenn., June 5-6; thence to Vicksburg, Miss., June 8-13. Siege of Vicksburg, Miss., June 14-July 4. Advance on Jackson, Miss., July 4-10. Birdsong Ferry, Big Black River, July 4-6. Siege of Jackson July 10-17. At Big Black River till September 28. Moved to Memphis, Tenn.; thence march to Chattanooga, Tenn., September 28-November 23. Operations on Memphis & Charleston R. R. in Alabama October 20-29. Chattanooga-Ringgold Campaign November 23-27. Tunnel Hill November 24-25. Mission Ridge November 25. Pursuit to Graysville November 26-27. March to relief of Knoxville and return to Bridgeport, Ala., November 28-December 19. Moved to Stevenson, Ala., December 24, thence to Scottsboro, Ala., December 26-28, and duty there till February 8, 1864. Moved to Cleveland, Tenn., February 8-14. Demonstration on Dalton, Ga., February 22-27. Tunnel Hill, Buzzard's Roost Gap and Rocky Faced

Ridge February 23-25. At Cleveland till May. Atlanta (Ga.) Campaign May to September. Demonstrations on Resaca May 8-13. Near Resaca May 13. Battle of Resaca May 14-15. Advance on Dallas May 18-25. Operations on line of Pumpkin Vine Creek and battles about Dallas, New Hope Church and Allatoona Hills May 25-June 5. Operations about Marietta and against Kenesaw Mountain June 10-July 2. Brush Mountain June 15. Assault on Kenesaw June 27. Nickajack Creek July 2-5. Ruff's Mills July 4. Chattahoochie River July 6-17. Battle of Atlanta July 22. Siege of Atlanta July 22-August 25. Ezra Chapel, Hood's second sortie, July 28. Flank movement on Jonesboro August 25-30. Battle of Jonesboro August 31-September 1. Lovejoy Station September 2-6. Operations against Hood in North Georgia and North Alabama September 29-November 3. March to the sea November 15-December 10. Griswoldsville November 22. Ogeechee River December 7-9. Siege of Savannah December 10-21. Campaign of the Carolinas January to April, 1865. Reconnoissance to Salkehatchie River, S. C., January 25. Combahee River January 28. Salkehatchie Swamps February 2-5. South Edisto River February 9. North Edisto River February 12-13. Congaree Creek February 15. Columbia February 16-17. Battle of Bentonville, N. C., March 20-21. Mill Creek March 22. Occupation of Goldsboro March 24. Advance on Raleigh April 9-13. Occupation of Raleigh April 14. Bennett's House April 26. Surrender of Johnston and his army. March to Washington, D. C., via Richmond, Va., April 29-May 19. Grand Review May 24. Moved to Louisville, Ky., June 2-4. Mustered out June 14 and discharged at Chicago, Ill., July 9, 1865.

Regiment lost during service 8 Officers and 87 Enlisted men killed and mortally wounded and 1 Officer and 153 Enlisted men by disease. Total 249.

104th REGIMENT INFANTRY.

Organized at Ottawa, Ill., and mustered in August 27, 1862, and ordered to Louisville, Ky. Attached to 39th Brigade, 12th Division, Army of the Ohio, to November, 1862. District of Western Kentucky, Dept. of the Ohio, to December, 1862. Prisoners of war to April, 1863. 1st Brigade, 2nd Division, 14th Army Corps, Army of the Cumberland, to October, 1863. 1st Brigade, 1st Division, 14th Army Corps, to June, 1865.

SERVICE.—Moved from Louisville to Frankfort, Ky., September, 1862, and duty there till October 25. Moved to Hartsville, Tenn., October 26-December 1. Action at Hartsville December 7. Regiment captured and paroled. Sent to Camp Douglas, Chicago, Ill., and duty there as paroled prisoners of war till April, 1863, when declared exchanged. Ordered to Brentwood, Tenn.; thence to Murfreesboro, Tenn., and duty there till June. Middle Tennessee (or Tullahoma) Campaign June 24-July 7. Elk River July 3. Occupation of Middle Tennessee till August 16. Passage of the Cumberland Mountains and Tennessee River and Chickamauga (Ga.) Campaign August 16-September 22. Davis Cross Roads, near Dug Gap, September 11. Battle of Chickamauga September 19-21. Rossville Gap September 21. Siege of Chattanooga, Tenn., September 24-November 23. Chattanooga-Ringgold Campaign November 23-27. Lookout Mountain November 24. Mission Ridge November 25. Pea Vine Valley and Graysville November 26. Taylor's Ridge, Ringgold Gap, November 27. At Chattanooga till February, 1864. Moved to Nashville, Tenn., February 10, and duty there till March 15. Moved to Chattanooga March 15-19. Atlanta (Ga.) Campaign May 1-September 8. Demonstration of Rocky Faced Ridge May 8-11. Buzzard's Roost Gap May 8-9. Near Resaca May 13. Battle of Resaca May 14-15. Advance on Dallas May 18-25. Operations on line of Pumpkin Vine Creek and battles about Dallas, New Hope Church and Allatoona Hills May 25-June 5. Pickett's Mills May 27. Operations about Marietta and against Kenesaw Mountain June 10-July 2. Pine Mountain June 11-14. Lost Mountain

June 15-17. Assault on Kenesaw June 27. Ruff's Station, Smyrna Camp Ground, July 4. Chattahoochie River July 5-18. Peach Tree Creek June 19-20. Siege of Atlanta July 22-August 25. Utoy Creek August 5-7. Flank movement on Jonesboro August 25-30. Near Red Oak August 29. Battle of Jonesboro August 31-September 1. Operations against Hood in North Georgia and North Alabama September 29-November 3. March to the sea November 15-December 10. Siege of Savannah December 10-21. Campaign of the Carolinas January to April, 1865. Near Stroud's Mills, S. C., February 26. Cloud's House February 26. Near Rocky Mount February 28. Averysboro, Taylor's Hole Creek, N. C., March 16. Battle of Bentonville March 19-21. Occupation of Goldsboro March 24. Advance on Raleigh April 10-14. Occupation of Raleigh April 14. Bennett's House April 26. Surrender of Johnston and his army. March to Washington, D. C., via Richmond, Va., April 29-May 19. Grand Review May 24. Mustered out June 6 and discharged at Chicago, Ill., July 11, 1865.

Regiment lost during service 6 Officers and 110 Enlisted men killed and mortally wounded and 2 Officers and 76 Enlisted men by disease. Total 194.

105th REGIMENT INFANTRY.

Organized at Dixon, Ill., and mustered in September 2, 1862. Moved from Dixon to Camp Douglas, Ill., September 8, 1862; thence to Louisville, Ky., September 30-October 2. Attached to Ward's Brigade, Dumont's 12th Division, Army of the Ohio, to November, 1862. Ward's Brigade, Post of Gallatin, Tenn., Dept. of the Cumberland, to June, 1863. 2nd Brigade, 3rd Division, Reserve Corps, Dept. of the Cumberland, to August, 1863. Ward's Brigade, Post of Nashville, Tenn., Dept. of the Cumberland, to January, 1864. 1st Brigade, 1st Division, 11th Army Corps, Army of the Cumberland, to April, 1864. 1st Brigade, 3rd Division, 20th Army Corps, Army of the Cumberland, and Army of Georgia to June, 1865.

SERVICE.—March to Frankfort, Ky., October 3-9, 1862; thence to Lawrenceburg in pursuit of Morgan, October 10-13. Moved to Bowling Green, Ky., October 26-November 4. To Scottsville November 11, to Gallatin, Tenn., November 25; to South Tunnel December 11 and duty there till February 1, 1863. At Gallatin till June 1. Moved to Lavergne, thence to Murfreesboro July 2. Return to Lavergne July 29; thence moved to Nashville, Tenn., August 19, and duty there till February 24, 1864. March to Wauhatchie Valley, Tenn., February 24-March 10, and duty there till May 2. Atlanta (Ga.) Campaign May 2-September 8. Demonstrations on Resaca May 8-13. Battle of Resaca May 14-15. Cassville May 19. Advance on Dallas May 23-25. Burnt Hickory May 25. Operations on line of Pumpkin Vine Creek and battles about Dallas, New Hope Church and Allatoona Hills May 26-June 5. Operations about Marietta and against Kenesaw Mountain June 10-July 2. Pine Hill June 11-14. Lost Mountain June 15-17. Gilgal (or Golgotha Church) June 15. Muddy Creek June 17. Noyes Creek June 19. Kolb's Farm June 22. Assault on Kenesaw June 27. Ruff's Station, Smyrna Camp Ground, July 4. Chattahoochie River July 5-17. Peach Tree Creek July 19-20. Siege of Atlanta July 22-August 25. Operations at Chattahoochie River Bridge August 26-September 2, Occupation of Atlanta September 2-November 15. March to the sea November 15-December 10. Siege of Savannah December 10-21. Campaign of the Carolinas January to April, 1865. Near Hardeesville, S. C., January 3. Lawtonville, S. C., February 2. Salkehatchie February 3-5. Averysboro, Taylor's Hole Creek, N. C., March 16. Battle of Bentonville March 19-21. Occupation of Goldsboro March 24. Advance on Raleigh April 10-14. Bennett's House April 26. Surrender of Johnston and his army. March to Washington, D. C., via Richmond, Va., April 29-May 19. Grand Review May 24. Mustered out June 7 and discharged at Chicago, Ill., July 17, 1865.

Regiment lost during service 2 Officers and 49 Enlisted men killed and mortally wounded and 137 Enlisted men by disease. Total 188.

106th REGIMENT INFANTRY.

Organized at Lincoln, Ill., and mustered in September 18, 1862. Moved to Columbus, Ky., November 7-10; thence to Jackson, Tenn. Attached to District of Jackson, Tenn., Left Wing 13th Army Corps (Old), Department of the Tennessee, to December, 1862. 4th Brigade, District of Jackson, 16th Army Corps, to March, 1863. 1st Brigade, 3rd Division, 16th Army Corps, to May, 1863. 1st Brigade, Kimball's Provisional Division, 16th Army Corps, to July, 1863. 1st Brigade, Kimball's Division, District of Eastern Arkansas, to August, 1863. 1st Brigade, 2nd Division, Arkansas Expedition, to November, 1863. 3rd Brigade, 2nd Division, Army of Arkansas, to January, 1864. 3rd Brigade, 2nd Division, 7th Army Corps, Dept. of Arkansas, to May, 1864. 2nd Brigade, 2nd Division, 7th Army Corps, to July, 1865.

SERVICE.—Assigned to Provost duty at Jackson, Tenn., and as railroad guard along Mobile & Ohio R. R. till March, 1863. Repulse of Forest's attack on Jackson December 20, 1862. Railroad crossing Forked Deer River December 20 (Cos. "H," "I" and "K"). Moved to Bolivar, Tenn., March, 1863; thence to Vicksburg, Miss., May 31. Siege of Vicksburg, Miss., June 9-July 4. Surrender of Vicksburg July 4. Ordered to Helena, Ark., July 29; thence moved to Clarendon, Ark., August 13, and to Duvall's Bluff August 22. Steele's Expedition against Little Rock, Ark., September 1-10. Bayou Fourche and capture of Little Rock September 10. Duty there till October 26. Pursuit of Marmaduke's Forces October 26-November 1. Duty at Little Rock, Duvall's Bluff, Hot Springs, Lewisburg, St. Charles, Dardanelles and Brownsville, Ark., till July, 1865. Operations against Shelby north of the Arkansas River May 13-31, 1864. Action at Clarendon June 25-26. Scouts from Pine Bluff toward Camden and Monticello January 26-31, 1865. Expedition from Little Rock to Mt. Elba January 22-February 4, 1865. Mustered out July 12 and discharged at Springfield, Ill., July 24, 1865.

Regiment lost during service 3 Enlisted men killed and mortally wounded and 7 **Officers and** 188 **En**listed men by disease. Total 198.

107th REGIMENT INFANTRY.

Organized at Camp Butler, Ill., and mustered in September 4, 1862. Moved to Jeffersonville, Ind., September 30-October 1, 1862, and to Louisville, Ky., October 12. Attached to railroad guard Louisville & Nashville R. R., Dept. of the Ohio, to November, 1862. District of West Kentucky, Dept. of the Ohio, to June, 1863. 1st Brigade, 3rd Division, 23rd Army Corps, Army of the Ohio, to August, 1863. 2nd Brigade, 2nd Division, 23rd Army Corps, Army of the Ohio, to February, 1865; and Dept. of North Carolina to June, 1865.

SERVICE.—Moved to Elizabethtown, Ky., October 18, 1862, and duty there till December, 1862. Moved to Mumfordsville, Ky., December 3, and duty there till March, 1863. Moved to Glasgow, Ky., and duty there till June 18. Pursuit of Morgan June 18-July 26. Return to Lebanon, Ky. Burnside's Campaign in East Tennessee August 16-October 17. Knoxville Campaign November 4-December 23. Huff's Ferry November 14. Near Loudon November 15. Campbell's Station November 16. Siege of Knoxville November 17-December 5. Pursuit of Longstreet December 5-22. At Knoxville till April, 1864. Expedition to Flat Creek February 1. March to Calhoun, Tenn., April 27-30. Atlanta (Ga.) Campaign May 1-September 8. Demonstration on Dalton May 8-13. Rocky Faced Ridge May 8-11. Battle of Resaca May 14-15. Operations on line of Pumpkin Vine Creek and battles about Dallas, New Hope Church and Allatoona Hills May 25-June 5. Operations about Marietta and against Kenesaw Mountain June 10-July 5. Lost Mountain June 15-17.

Muddy Creek June 17. Noyes' Creek June 19. Kolb's Farm June 22. Assault on Kenesaw June 27. On line of the Nickajack Creek July 2-5. On line of the Chattahoochie July 5-17. Siege of Atlanta July 22-August 25. Utoy Creek August 5-7. Flank movement on Jonesboro August 25-30. Lovejoy Station September 2-6. Operations in North Georgia and North Alabama against Hood September 29-November 3. Nashville, Tenn., Campaign November-December. Columbia, Duck River, November 24-27. Battle of Franklin November 30. Battle of Nashville December 15-16. Pursuit of Hood to the Tennessee River December 17-20. At Clifton, Tenn., till January 26, 1865. Moved to Washington, D. C., January 26-February 2, thence to Fort Fisher, N. C., February 11-15. Occupation of Wilmington, N. C., February 22. Campaign of the Carolinas March 1-April 26. Advance on Goldsboro, N. C., March 6-21. Occupation of Goldsboro March 21. Advance on Raleigh April 10-14. Occupation of Raleigh April 14. Bennett's House April 26. Surrender of Johnson and his army. Duty at Saulsbury, N. C., till June 21. Mustered out June 21, 1865.

Regiment lost during service 3 Officers and 27 Enlisted men killed and mortally wounded and 122 Enlisted men by disease. Total 152.

108th REGIMENT INFANTRY.

Organized at Peoria, Ill., and mustered in August 28, 1862. Moved to Nicholasville, Ky., October 17-November 1, 1862. Attached to 2nd Brigade, 1st Division, Army of Kentucky, Dept. of the Ohio, to November, 1862. 2nd Brigade, 10th Division, 13th Army Corps (Old), Department of the Tennessee, to December, 1862. 2nd Brigade, 1st Division, Sherman's Yazoo Expedition, to January, 1863. 2nd Brigade, 10th Division, 13th Army Corps, Army of the Tennessee, to May, 1863. Detached Brigade, District of Northeast Louisiana, to August, 1863. 1st Brigade, 2nd Division, 16th Army Corps, to November, 1863. Post of Corinth, Miss., 2nd Division, 16th Army Corps, to January, 1864. 2nd Brigade, District of Memphis, Tenn., to June, 1864. 2nd Brigade, Sturgis' Expedition, June, 1864. 1st Brigade, Memphis, Tenn., District of West Tennessee, to February, 1865. 3rd Brigade, 3rd Division, 16th Army Corps (New), Military Division of West Mississippi, to August, 1865.

SERVICE.—March to Louisville, Ky., November 14-19, 1862; thence moved to Memphis, Tenn., November 21-26, and duty there till December 20. Sherman's Yazoo Expedition December 20, 1862, to January 2, 1863. Chickasaw Bayou December 26-28, 1862. Chickasaw Bluff December 29. Expedition to Arkansas Post, Ark., January 3-10, 1863. Assault and capture of Fort Hindman, Arkansas Post, January 10-11. Moved to Young's Point, La., January 17-24, and duty there till March 10. At Milliken's Bend, La., till April 25. Movement on Bruinsburg and turning Grand Gulf April 25-30. Battles of Port Gibson, Miss., May 1. Champion's Hill May 16. Detached to guard prisoners from Big Black River to Memphis, Tenn., May 16-30. At Young's Point, La., during siege of Vicksburg and until July 18. Moved to Vicksburg July 18, thence to Memphis, Tenn., July 26-29, and to LaGrange, Tenn., August 5. Duty there till October 28, and at Pocahontas till November 9. At Corinth, Miss., till January 25, 1864. Moved to Memphis, Tenn., and duty there till February, 1865. Sturgis' Expedition to Guntown, Miss., June 1-13, 1864. Brice's (or Tishamingo) Creek, near Guntown, June 10. Ripley June 11. Repulse of Forest's attack on Memphis August 21, 1864. Moved to New Orleans, La.; thence to Dauphin Island, Ala., February 28-March 16. Operations against Mobile and its defences March 16-April 12. Siege of Spanish Fort and Fort Blakely March 26-April 8. Assault and capture of Fort Blakely April 9. Occupation of Mobile April 12. March to Montgomery April 13-25. Duty there till July 18. Moved to Vicksburg, Miss., July 18-August 5. Mustered out August 5, 1865.

Regiment lost during service 1 Officer and 8 Enlisted men killed and mortally wounded and 3 Officers and 202 Enlisted men by disease. Total 214.

109th REGIMENT INFANTRY.

Organized at Camp Anna, Ill., and mustered in September 11, 1862. Moved to Columbus, Ky., October 20-25, 1862; thence to Bolivar, Tenn. Attached to District of Jackson, Tenn., 13th Army Corps (Old), Department of the Tennessee, to December, 1862. District of Jackson, 16th Army Corps, to January, 1863. District of Memphis, Tenn., 16th Army Corps, to April, 1863.

SERVICE.—Grant's Central Mississippi Campaign November, 1862, to January, 1863. At Memphis till March, 1863. Moved to Lake Providence, La. Regiment disbanded April 10, 1863, having lost 237 by desertion and officers (excepting those of Company "K") having proved themselves utterly incompetent. Company "K" transferred to 11th Illinois Infantry.

Regiment lost by disease 2 Officers and 92 Enlisted men during its service.

110th REGIMENT INFANTRY.

Organized at Anna, Ill., and mustered in September 11, 1862. Moved to Louisville, Ky., September 23-25, 1862. Attached to 19th Brigade, 4th Division, 2nd Army Corps, Army of the Ohio, to November, 1862. 2nd Brigade, 2nd Division, Left Wing 14th Army Corps, Army of the Cumberland, to January, 1863. 2nd Brigade, 2nd Division, 21st Army Corps, Army of the Cumberland, to May, 1863. Unattached, 21st Army Corps to October, 1863. 3rd Brigade, 2nd Division, 14th Army Corps, to June, 1865.

SERVICE.—Pursuit of Bragg into Kentucky October 1-22, 1862. Battle of Perryville, Ky., October 8. Danville October 11. Pursuit to Loudon October 11-22. Wild Cat Mountain, near Crab Orchard and Big Rockcastle River October 15-16. Mt. Vernon October 16. Wild Cat Mountain October 17. March to Nashville, Tenn., October 22-November 7. Duty there till December 26. Advance on Murfreesboro December 26-30. Stewart's Creek December 27. Battle of Stone's River December 30-31, 1862, and January 1-3, 1863. At Murfreesboro and Readyville till Junc. Woodbury January 24. Expedition to Woodbury April 2-6. Regiment consolidated May, 1863. Middle Tennessee (or Tullahoma) Campaign June 24-July 7. Near Bradysville June 24. Occupation of Middle Tennessee till August 16. Passage of the Cumberland Mountains and Tennessee River and Chickamauga (Ga.) Campaign August 16-September 22. Lee and Gordon's Mills September 11-13. Battle of Chickamauga, Ga., September 19-20. Skirmishes before Chattanooga September 22-26. Siege of Chattanooga September 24-November 23. Chattanooga-Ringgold Campaign November 23-27. Orchard Knob November 23. Tunnel Hill November 24-25. Mission Ridge November 25. Pursuit to Graysville November 26-27. March to relief of Knoxville November 28-December 18. At North Chickamauga and McAfee's Church till May, 1864. Demonstration on Dalton, Ga., February 22-27. Tunnel Hill, Buzzard's Roost Gap and Rocky Faced Ridge February 23-25. Atlanta (Ga.) Campaign May 1 to September 8. Tunnel Hill May 6-7. Demonstrations on Rocky Faced Ridge May 8-11. Battle of Resaca May 14-15. Guard trains of the Army till July 20. Siege of Atlanta July 22-August 25. Utoy Creek August 5-7. Flank movement on Jonesboro August 25-30. Battle of Jonesboro August 31-September 1. Lovejoy Station September 2-6. Operations in North Georgia and North Alabama against Hood September 29-November 3. March to the sea November 15-December 10. Siege of Savannah December 10-21. Campaign of the Carolinas January to April, 1865. Averysboro, Taylor's Hole Creek, N. C., March 16. Battle of Bentonville March 19-21. Occupation of Goldsboro March 24. Advance on Raleigh April 10-14. Occupation of Raleigh April 14. Bennett's House April 26. Surrender of Johnston and his army. March to Wash-

ington, D. C., via Richmond, Va., April 29-May 19. Grand Review May 24. Mustered out June 5 and discharged at Chicago, Ill., June 15, 1865.

Regiment lost during service 1 Officer and 13 Enlisted men killed and mortally wounded and 2 Officers and 212 Enlisted men by disease. Total 228.

111th REGIMENT INFANTRY.

Organized at Salem, Ill., and mustered in September 18, 1862. At Camp Marshall, Salem, till October 31, 1862. Moved to Cairo, Ill., October 31; thence to Columbus, Ky., November 1, and Post and garrison duty there till March, 1863. Attached to District of Columbus,, 13th Army Corps (Old), Department of the Tennessee, November to December, 1862. District of Columbus, Ky., 16th Army Corps, to November, 1863. 2nd Brigade, 2nd Division, 16th Army Corps, to March, 1864. 1st Brigade, 2nd Division, 15th Army Corps, to August, 1864. 2nd Brigade, 2nd Division, 15th Army Corps, to June, 1865.

SERVICE.—Moved from Columbus, Ky., to Fort Heiman, Ky., March 12-13, 1863, and garrison duty there till May 28. Moved to Paducah, Ky., May 28 and duty there till October. Expedition to Conyersville, Tenn., September 1-10, and to McLemoresville, Tenn., September 20-30. Moved to Eastport, Miss.; thence to Gravelly Springs, Ala., and Pulaski, Tenn., October 31-November 12. Duty at Pulaski and Decatur, Ala., till February 25, 1864. Moved to Decatur Junction February 25-27. Capture of Decatur March 7. Moved to Huntsville, Ala., March 16-18. At Larkinsville till May 1. Atlanta Campaign May 1-September 8. Demonstrations on Resaca, Ga., May 8-13. Near Resaca May 13. Battle of Resaca May 14-15. Advance on Dallas May 17-25. Operations on line of Pumpkin Vine Creek and battles about Dallas, New Hope Church and Allatoona Hills May 25-June 5. Operations about Marietta and against Kenesaw Mountain June 10-July 2. Assault on Kenesaw June 27. Nickajack Creek July 2-5. Chattahoochie River July 6-17. Battle of Atlanta July 22. Siege of Atlanta July 22-August 25. Ezra Chapel, Hood's second sortie, July 28. Flank movement on Jonesboro August 25-30. Battle of Jonesboro August 31-September 1. Lovejoy Station September 2-6. Operations against Hood in North Georgia and North Alabama September 29-November 3. Bull's Gap, Ala., October 23. Turkeytown and Gadsden Road October 25. March to the sea November 15-December 10. Siege of Savannah December 10-21. Assault on and capture of Fort McAllister December 13. Campaign of the Carolinas January to April, 1865. Salkehatchie Swamps February 2-5. Cannon's Bridge, South Edisto River, February 8. North Edisto River February 12-13. Congaree Creek February 15. Columbia February 16-17. Fayetteville, N. C., March 11. Battle of Bentonville March 20-21. Occupation of Goldsboro March 24. Advance on Raleigh April 10-14. Occupation of Raleigh April 14. Bennett's House April 26. Surrender of Johnston and his army. March to Washington, D. C., via Richmond, Va., April 29-May 19. Grand Review May 24. Mustered out June 7 and discharged at Springfield, Ill., June 27, 1865.

Regiment lost during service 7 Officers and 75 Enlisted men killed and mortally wounded and 2 Officers and 166 Enlisted men by disease. Total 250.

112th REGIMENT INFANTRY.

Organized at Peoria, Ill., and mustered in September 20, 1862. Moved to Covington, Ky., October 8, 1862. Attached to 1st Brigade, 2nd Division, Army of Kentucky, Dept. of the Ohio, to January, 1863. 3rd Brigade, District of Central Kentucky, Dept. of the Ohio, to April, 1862. 2nd Brigade, District of Central Kentucky, Dept. of the Ohio, to June, 1863. 1st Brigade, 1st Division, 23rd Army Corps, Army of the Ohio, to August, 1863. 1st Brigade, 4th Division, 23rd Army Corps, to October, 1863. 2nd Brigade, 4th Division, 23rd Army Corps, to November, 1863. 2nd Brigade,

1st Cavalry Division, 23rd Army Corps, to May, 1864. 1st Brigade, 3rd Division, 23rd Army Corps, to August, 1865. 3rd Brigade, 3rd Division, 23rd Army Corps, Army of the Ohio, to February, 1865; and Dept. of North Carolina to June, 1865.

SERVICE.—Moved to Falmouth, Ky., October 18, 1862. Escort supply train to Big Eagle, Ky., October 19-21, thence moved to Georgetown and Lexington, Ky. October 23-24. Duty at Lexington till March, 1863. Moved to Danville, Ky., March 21; thence to Nicholasville, Camp Dick Robinson, Lancaster and Crab Orchard, Stanford and Milledgeville, Ky. Duty at Milledgeville till April 26. Regiment mounted at Milledgeville. Moved to Somerset April 26. Operations against Pegram's forces in Southeast Kentucky April 26-May 12. Action at Monticello May 1. Duty at Somerset, Ky., till July. Saunders' Raid in East Tennessee June 14-24 (Detachment). Knoxville June 19-20. Strawberry Plains June 20. Rogers' Gap June 20. Powder Springs Gap June 21. Pursuit of Scott's forces July 9-13. Operations in Eastern Kentucky against Scott July 26-August 6. Battle of Richmond July 28. Burnside's Campaign in East Tennessee August 16-October 16. Winker's Gap August 31. Action at Cleveland September 18. Athens, Calhoun and Charleston September 25. Calhoun September 26. Athens September 27. About Kingston October 16-24. Philadelphia October 25-26. Lieper's Ferry, Holston River, October 28. Knoxville Campaign November 4-December 23. Holston River November 15. Campbell's Station November 16. Near Knoxville November 16. Siege of Knoxville November 17-December 5. Skirmishes about Bean's Station December 9-13. Bean's Station December 10 and 14. Blain's Cross Roads December 16-19. Bend of Chucky Road, near Dandridge, January 16, 1864. Operations about Dandridge January 16-17. Dandridge January 17. Operations about Dandridge January 26-28. Flat and Muddy Creek January 26. Near Fair Garden January 27. Kelly's Ford January 27-28. Moved to Marysville, thence to Knoxville and dismounted, thence moved to Mount Sterling, Ky., February, 1864. Duty at Mt. Sterling February 22-April 6. Moved to Camp Nelson, Ky., April 6, thence to Knoxville, Tenn., arriving May 3. Movement to Tunnel Hill, Ga., May 3-5. Atlanta (Ga.) Campaign May 5-September 8. Demonstrations on Dalton May 9-13. Battle of Resaca May 14-15. Cartersville May 18. Advance on Dallas May 18-25. Operations on line of Pumpkin Vine Creek and battles about Dallas, New Hope Church and Allatoona Hills May 25-June 5. Operations about Marietta and against Kenesaw Mountain June 10-July 2. Lost Mountain June 15-17. Muddy Creek June 17. Noyes' Creek June 19. Cheyney's Farm June 22. Olley's Creek June 26-27. Assault on Kenesaw June 27. Line of Nickajack Creek July 2-5. Chattahoochie River July 5-17. Siege of Atlanta July 22-August 25. Utoy Creek August 5-7. Flank movement on Jonesboro August 25-30. Battle of Jonesboro August 31-September 1. Lovejoy Station September 2-6. Operations against Hood and Forest in North Georgia and North Alabama September 29-November 3. Nashville Campaign November-December. Columbia, Duck River, November 24-27. Battle of Franklin November 30. Battle of Nashville December 15-16. Pursuit of Hood to the Tennessee River December 17-29. At Clifton, Tenn., till January 15, 1865. Movement to Washington, D. C., thence to Fort Fisher, N. C., January 18-February 9. Operations against Hoke February 11-14. Fort Anderson February 18. Capture of Fort Anderson February 19. Town Creek February 19-20. Capture of Wilmington February 22. Campaign of the Carolinas March 1-April 26. Advance on Goldsboro March 6-21. Occupation of Goldsboro March 21. Gurley's March 31. Advance on Raleigh April 10-14. Occupation of Raleigh April 14. Bennett's House April 26. Surrender of Johnston and his army. Duty at Greensboro, N. C., till June 20. Mustered out at Greensboro, N. C., June 20 and discharged at Chicago, Ill., July 7, 1865.

Regiment lost during service 4 Officers and 76 Enlisted men killed and mortally wounded and 1 Officer and 153 Enlisted men by disease. Total 234.

113th REGIMENT INFANTRY.

Organized at Camp Hancock, near Chicago, Ill., and mustered in October 1, 1862. Ordered to Memphis, Tenn., November 6, 1862. Attached to 1st Brigade, District of Memphis, Tenn., Right Wing 13th Army Corps (Old), Department of the Tennessee, November, 1862. 1st Brigade, 2nd Division, District of Memphis, 13th Army Corps, to December, 1862. 1st Brigade, 2nd Division, Sherman's Yazoo Expedition to January, 1863. 1st Brigade, 2nd Division, 15th Army Corps, Army of the Tennessee, to August, 1863. 3rd Brigade, 2nd Division, 16th Army Corps, to November, 1863. Post of Corinth, Miss., 2nd Division, 16th Army Corps, to January, 1864. 2nd Brigade, District of Memphis, Tenn., 16th Army Corps, to June, 1864. 2nd Brigade, Sturgis' Expedition, June, 1864. 1st Brigade, Post of Memphis, District of West Tennessee, to February, 1865. Unattached, Post of Memphis, District of West Tennessee, to June, 1865.

SERVICE.—Grant's Central Mississippi Campaign. "Tallahatchie March," November 26-December 12, 1862. Sherman's Yazoo Expedition December 20, 1862-January 2, 1863. Chickasaw Bayou December 26-28. Chickasaw Bluff December 29. Expedition to Arkansas Post, Ark., January 3-10. Assault and capture of Fort Hindman, Arkansas Post, January 10-11. (Cos. "C," "D," "F," "I" and "K" guard prisoners North after Arkansas Post, and retained in Illinois on guard duty till October, 1864, when rejoined Regiment at Memphis, Tenn.) Moved to Young's Point, La., January 17-22, and duty there till March. Expedition to Rolling Fork, Miss., via Muddy, Steele's and Black Bayous and Deer Creek March 14-27. Near Deer Creek March 22. Demonstration on Haines' and Drumgould's Bluffs April 29-May 2. Movement to Jackson, Miss., via Grand Gulf, May 2-14. Jackson May 14. Champion's Hill May 16. Siege of Vicksburg, Miss., May 18-July 4. Assaults on Vicksburg May 19 and 22. Surrender of Vicksburg July 4. Advance on Jackson, Miss., July 4-10. Siege of Jackson July 10-17. Ordered to Memphis, Tenn.; thence to Corinth, Miss., and Post duty there till January, 1864. At Memphis, Tenn., till June, 1865. Sturgis' Expedition into Mississippi June 1-13, 1864. Near Colliersville, Tenn., June 10. Brice's (or Tishamingo) Creek, near Guntown, Miss., June 10. Ripley June 11. Repulse of Forrest's attack on Memphis August 21, 1864. Eastport, Miss., October 10, 1864. Mustered out June 20, 1865.

Regiment lost during service 1 Officer and 25 Enlisted men killed and mortally wounded and 4 Officers and 273 Enlisted men by disease. Total 303.

114th REGIMENT INFANTRY.

Organized at Camp Butler, Ill., and mustered in September 18, 1862. Moved to Memphis, Tenn., November 8-16, 1862. Attached to the 5th Brigade, 5th Division, District of Memphis, Right Wing 13th Army Corps (Old), Dept. of the Tennessee, November, 1862. 3rd Brigade, 1st Division, District of Memphis, 13th Army Corps, to December, 1862. 3rd Brigade, 8th Division, 16th Army Corps, to April, 1863. 1st Brigade, 3rd Division, 15th Army Corps, to December, 1863. 1st Brigade, 1st Division, 16th Army Corps, to June, 1864. 1st Brigade, Sturgis' Expedition, June, 1864. 1st Brigade, 1st Division, 16th Army Corps, to December, 1864. 1st Brigade, 1st Division, Detachment Army of the Tennessee, Dept. of the Cumberland, to February, 1865. Pontoneers 16th Army Corps (New), Military Division West Mississippi, to August, 1865.

SERVICE.—Grant's Central Mississippi Campaign. "Tallahatchie March" November 26-December 12, 1862. Moved to Jackson, Tenn., December 23, and duty there till February 9, 1863. Expedition to Wyatt's, Miss., February 9-18. Guard duty on Memphis & Charleston R. R. till March 17. Moved to Young's

Point, La., March 17-April 2. Operations against Vicksburg April 2-July 4. At Ducksport, La., till May 2. Movement to Jackson, Miss., via Grand Gulf, May 2-14. Mississippi Springs May 13. Jackson May 14. Siege of Vicksburg, Miss., May 18-July 4. Assault on Vicksburg May 19 and 22. Expedition to Mechanicsburg May 26-June 4. Surrender of Vicksburg July 4. Advance on Jackson, Miss., July 4-10. Birdsong Ferry, Big Black River, July 4-6. Siege of Jackson July 10-17. Brandon Station July 19. At Vicksburg till September 3, and at Oak Ridge till October 14. Expedition toward Canton October 14-20. Bogue Chitto Creek October 17. Moved to Memphis, Tenn., November 20-26. Expedition to Tallahatchie River February 5-19, 1864. Coldwater Ferry February 8. Near Senatobia February 8-9. Wyatt's, Tallahatchie River, February 13. Provost duty at Memphis, Tenn., till June. Sturgis' Expedition from Memphis to Ripley, Miss., April 30-May 9. Sturgis' Expedition to Guntown, Miss., June 1-13. Battle of Brice's Cross Roads (or Tishamingo Creek), near Guntown, June 10. Ripley June 11. Davis' Mills June 12. Smith's Expedition to Tupelo, Miss., July 5-21. Camargo's Cross Roads, near Harrisburg, July 13. Harrisburg, near Tupelo, July 14-15. Old Town (or Tishamingo Creek) July 15. Smith's Expedition to Oxford, Miss., August 1-30. Tallahatchie River August 7-9. Abbeville August 23. Moved to Duvall's Bluff, Ark., September 2. March through Arkansas and Missouri in pursuit of Price September 24-November 16. Moved to Nashville, Tenn., November 24-30. Battle of Nashville December 15-16. Pursuit of Hood to the Tennessee River December 17-28. Moved to Eastport, Miss., and duty there till February, 1865. Moved to New Orleans, La.; thence to Dauphin Island, Ala., February 9-March 3. Campaign against Mobile and its defences March 3-April 12. Siege of Spanish Fort and Fort Blakely March 26-April 9. Fort Blakely April 9. Occupation of Mobile April 12. March to Montgomery, Ala., April 13-24, and duty there till July. Moved to Vicksburg, Miss., July 17. Mustered out August 3 and discharged August 15, 1865.

Regiment lost during service 2 Officers and 45 Enlisted men killed and mortally wounded and 4 Officers and 159 Enlisted men by disease. Total 210.

115th REGIMENT INFANTRY.

Organized at Camp Butler, Ill., and mustered in September 13, 1862. Moved to Cincinnati, Ohio, and Covington, Ky., October 4-6, 1862. Attached to 2nd Brigade, 3rd Division, Army of Kentucky, Dept. of the Ohio, to February, 1862. 2nd Brigade, Baird's 3rd Division, Army of the Kentucky, Dept. of the Cumberland, to June, 1863. 1st Brigade, 1st Division, Reserve Corps, Army of the Cumberland, to October, 1863. 1st Brigade, 2nd Division, 4th Army Corps, October, 1863. 2nd Brigade, 1st Division, 4th Army Corps, to June, 1865.

SERVICE.—Duty at Covington, Ky., till October 20, 1862, operating against Kirby Smith's threatened attack on Cincinnati. March to Richmond, Ky., October 20-25, thence to Danville December 21, and duty there till January 26, 1863. Pursuit of Morgan to Lebanon Junction December 26-31, 1862. Moved to Louisville, Ky., January 26-31, 1863; thence to Nashville, Tenn., January 31-February 8. Repulse of Wheeler's attack on Fort Donelson, Tenn., February 4. At Nashville till March 5. Moved to Franklin, Tenn., and pursuit of Van Dorn March 5-12. Spring Hill March 10. At Brentwood March 27-April 8. Return to Franklin April 8, and repulse of Van Dorn's attack April 10. At Franklin till June 2. Moved to Triune June 2. Action at Triune with Wheeler June 11. Middle Tennessee (or Tullahoma) Campaign June 24-July 7. At Wartrace July 3-August 12, and at Elk River till September 7. Chickamauga (Ga.) Campaign September 7-22. Ringgold, Ga., September 17. Battle of Chickamauga, Ga., September 19-20. Siege of Chattanooga September 24-October 26. Reopening Tennessee River October 26-29. Battle of Wauhatchie, Tenn.,

October 28-29. Duty in Lookout Valley till December 1. At Nickajack Cove, Ga., till February, 1864. Demonstration on Dalton, Ga., February 22-27. Tunnel Hill, Buzzard's Roost Gap and Rocky Faced Ridge February 23-25. At Cleveland, Tenn., March and April. Atlanta (Ga.) Campaign May 1-September 8. Tunnel Hill May 6-7. Demonstration on Rocky Faced Ridge May 8-11. Buzzard's Roost Gap May 8-9. Demonstrations on Dalton May 9-13. Battle of Resaca May 14-15. Near Kingston May 18-19. Near Cassville May 19. Advance on Dallas May 22-25. Operations on line of Pumpkin Vine Creek and battles about Dallas, New Hope Church and Allatoona Hills May 25-June 5. Operations about Marietta and against Kenesaw Mountain June 10-July 2. Pine Hill June 11-14. Lost Mountain June 15-17. Assault on Kenesaw June 27. Ruff's Station, Smyrna Camp Ground, July 4. Chattahoochie River July 5-17. Peach Tree Creek July 19-20. Siege of Atlanta July 22-August 25. Flank movement on Jonesboro August 25-30. Battle of Jonesboro August 31-September 1. Lovejoy Station September 2-6. Operations against Hood in North Georgia and North Alabama September 29-November 3. Buzzard's Roost Block House October 13 (1 Company). Nashville Campaign November-December. Columbia, Tenn., December 23. Columbia, Duck River, November 24-27. Battle of Franklin November 30. Battle of Nashville December 15-16. Pursuit of Hood to the Tennessee River December 17-28. Moved to Huntsville, Ala., and duty there till March, 1865. Expedition to Bull's Gap and operations in East Tennessee March 20-April 22. Moved to Nashville, Tenn., and duty there till June. Mustered out at Nashville June 11 and discharged at Camp Butler, Ill., June 23, 1865.

Regiment lost during service 6 Officers and 58 Enlisted men killed and mortally wounded and 2 Officers and 147 Enlisted men by disease. Total 213.

116th REGIMENT INFANTRY.

Organized at Decatur, Ill., and mustered in September 30, 1862. Left State for Memphis, Tenn., November 8, 1862. Attached to 4th Brigade, 5th Division, District of Memphis, 13th Army Corps (Old), Department of the Tennessee, November, 1862. 2nd Brigade, 2nd Division, District of Memphis, 13th Army Corps, to December, 1862. 1st Brigade, 2nd Division, Sherman's Yazoo Expedition, to January, 1863. 1st Brigade, 2nd Division, 15th Army Corps, Army of the Tennessee, to June, 1865.

SERVICE.—At Memphis, Tenn., till November 26, 1862. Grant's Central Mississippi Campaign. "Tallahatchie March" November 26-December 12. Sherman's Yazoo Expedition December 20, 1862, to January 2, 1863. Chickasaw Bayou December 26-28, 1862. Chickasaw Bluff December 29. Expedition to Arkansas Post, Ark., January 3-10, 1863. Assault on and capture of Fort Hindman, Arkansas Post, January 10-11. Moved to Young's Point, La., January 17-22, and duty there till March. Expedition to Rolling Fork, Miss., via Muddy, Steele's and Black Bayous, and Deer Creek, March 14-27. Demonstrations against Haines' and Drumgould's Bluffs April 29-May 2. Movement to Jackson, Miss., via Grand Gulf, May 2-14. Jackson May 14. Champion's Hill May 16. Siege of Vicksburg May 18-July 4. Assaults on Vicksburg May 19 and 22. Surrender of Vicksburg July 4. Advance on Jackson, Miss., July 4-10. Siege of Jackson July 10-17. At Big Black till September 22. Moved to Memphis, Tenn.; thence march to Chattanooga September 26-November 20. Operations on Memphis & Charleston R. R. in Alabama October 20-29. Bear Creek, Tuscumbia, October 27. Chattanooga-Ringgold Campaign November 23-27. Foot of Missionary Ridge November 24. Tunnel Hill November 24-25. Mission Ridge November 25. Pursuit to Graysville November 26-27. March to relief of Knoxville November 28-December 8. Moved to Larkinsville, Ala., and duty there till May, 1864. Expedition toward Rome, Ga., January 25-February 5. Atlanta (Ga.) Campaign May 1-September 8. Demonstrations on Resaca May 8-13. Near Resaca May 13. Battle of Resaca May 14-15. Advance on Dallas May 18-25. Operations on line of Pumpkin Vine Creek and battles about Dallas, New Hope Church and Allatoona Hills May 25-June 5. Operations about Marietta and against Kenesaw Mountain June 10-July 2. Assault on Kenesaw June 27. Nickajack Creek July 2-5. Chattahoochie River July 5-17. Battle of Atlanta July 22. Siege of Atlanta July 22-August 25. Ezra Chapel, Hood's second sortie, July 28. Flank movement on Jonesboro August 25-30. Battle of Jonesboro August 31-September 1. Lovejoy Station September 2-6. Operations against Hood in North Georgia and North Alabama September 29-November 3. March to the sea November 15-December 10. Clinton November 21-23. Ball's Ferry and Georgia Central R. R. Bridge, Oconee River, November 23-25. Statesboro December 4. Siege of Savannah December 10-21. Fort McAllister December 13. Campaign of the Carolinas January to April, 1865. Salkehatchie Swamps, S. C., February 2-5. South Edisto River February 9. North Edisto River February 12-13. Columbia February 16-17. Battle of Bentonville, N. C., March 20-21. Occupation of Goldsboro March 24. Advance on Raleigh April 10-14. Occupation of Raleigh April 14. Bennett's House April 26. Surrender of Johnston and his army. March to Washington, D. C., via Richmond, Va., April 29-May 19. Grand Review May 24. Mustered out June 7, 1865.

Regiment lost during service 7 Officers and 49 Enlisted men killed and mortally wounded and 7 Officers and 232 Enlisted men by disease. Total 295.

117th REGIMENT INFANTRY.

Organized at Camp Butler, Ill., and mustered in September 19, 1862. Moved to Memphis, Tenn., November 11-17, 1862. Attached to Reserve Brigade, District of Memphis, Tenn., 13th Army Corps (Old), Department of the Tennessee, to January, 1863. District of Memphis, 16th Army Corps, to March, 1863. 1st Brigade, 5th Division, District of Memphis, 16th Army Corps, to January, 1864. 3rd Brigade, 3rd Division, 16th Army Corps, to December, 1864. 3rd Brigade, 2nd Division, Detachment Army of the Tennessee, Dept. of the Cumberland, to February, 1865. 2nd Brigade, 2nd Division, 16th Army Corps (New), Military Division West Mississippi, to August, 1865.
SERVICE.—Duty at Memphis, Tenn., till July 5, 1863. Affairs near Memphis June 17-18, 1863 (Detachment). Moved to Helena, Ark., July 5, and return to Memphis. Duty there till December 29, 1863. Expedition after Forest December 24-31, 1863 (Detachment). Grierson's Bridge and near Moscow and LaFayette December 27. Ordered to Vicksburg, Miss. Meridian Campaign February 3-March 2, 1864. Clinton February 5. Meridian February 9-13. Red River Campaign March 10-May 22. Fort DeRussy March 14. Occupation of Alexandria March 16. Battle of Pleasant Hill April 9. About Cloutiersville April 22-24. At Alexandria April 26-May 13. Governor Moore's Plantation and Bayou Roberts May 3-7 and 11. Retreat to Morganza May 13-20. Mensura May 16. Yellow Bayou May 18. Moved to Vicksburg, Miss.; thence to Memphis, Tenn., May 21-June 10. Action at Lake Chicot, Ark., June 6. March to relief of Gen. Sturgis June 14-16. Near LaFayette June 23. Smith's Expedition to Tupelo, Miss., July 5-21. Camargo's Cross Roads, near Harrisburg, July 13. Harrisburg, near Tupelo, July 14-15. Old Town (or Tishamingo) Creek July 15. Smith's Expedition to Oxford, Miss., August 1-30. Hurricane Creek August 13-14. Abbeville August 23. Moved to Jefferson Barracks, Mo., and in pursuit of Price through Missouri September to November. Action at Franklin, Mo., October 1. Moved from St. Louis to Nashville, Tenn., November 21-December 1. Battle of Nashville December 15-16. Pursuit of Hood to the Tennessee River December 17-28. Moved to Clifton, Tenn., and Eastport, Miss., and duty there till February, 1865. Moved to New Orleans, La., February 6-17. Campaign against Mobile and its defences March 17-April 12. Siege of Spanish Fort

and Fort Blakely March 26-April 8. Assault and capture of Fort Blakely April 9. Occupation of Mobile April 12. March to Montgomery April 13-25, and duty there till August. Mustered out August 5, 1865.

Regiment lost during service 11 Enlisted men killed and mortally wounded and 4 Officers and 115 Enlisted men by disease. Total 130.

118th REGIMENT INFANTRY.

Organized at Camp Butler, Ill., August to October, 1862. Mustered in November 7, 1862. Duty at Camp Butler and guarding prisoners till December. Left State for Memphis, Tenn., December 1, 1862. Attached to 1st Brigade, 9th Division, Right Wing 13th Army Corps (Old), Department of the Tennessee, December, 1862. 1st Brigade, 3rd Division, Sherman's Yazoo Expedition, to January, 1863. 1st Brigade, 9th Division, 13th Army Corps, Army of the Tennessee, to July, 1863. 3rd Brigade, 1st Division, 13th Army Corps, Army of the Tennessee, to August, 1863, and Dept. of the Gulf to September, 1863. 1st Brigade, Cavalry Division, Dept. of the Gulf, to November, 1863. 2nd Brigade, Cavalry Division, Dept. of the Gulf, to July, 1864. 1st Brigade, Cavalry Division, Dept. of the Gulf, to September, 1864. 2nd Brigade, Cavalry Division, Dept. of the Gulf, to February, 1865. Cavalry Brigade, District of Baton Rouge, Dept. of the Gulf, to July, 1865. Dept. of Texas to October, 1865.
SERVICE.—Sherman's Yazoo Expedition December 20, 1862, to January 2, 1863. Chickasaw Bayou December 26-28, 1862. Chickasaw Bluffs December 29. Yazoo River January 2, 1863. Expedition to Arkansas Post, Ark., January 3-10. Assault and capture of Fort Hindman January 10-11. Moved to Young's Point, La., January 17-23, and duty there till March 9. Moved to Milliken's Bend, La., March 9. Operations from Milliken's Bend to New Carthage March 31-April 17. Movement on Bruinsburg and turning Grand Gulf April 25-30. Thompson's Hill, Port Gibson, May 1. Champion's Hill May 16. Big Black River May 17. Siege of Vicksburg, Miss., May 18-July 4. Assaults on Vicksburg May 19 and 22. At Black River Bridge May 24-July 6. Regiment mounted June 10. Edwards' Ferry July 1 (Detachment). Advance on Jackson, Miss., July 6-10. Near Clinton July 8 (Detachment). Near Jackson July 9. Siege of Jackson July 10-17. Raid to Brookhaven July 17-20. Brookhaven July 18. At Vicksburg July 25-August 8. Moved to Port Hudson August 8-9, thence to Carrollton, La., August 15-16, and to Bayou Boeuf September 5-7. To Brashear City September 16. Western Louisiana Campaign October 3-November 30. Regiment mounted October 11, 1863. Vermillionville October 15. Carrion Crow Bayou October 16-20. Grand Coteau October 19. Reconnoissance toward Opelousas October 20. Barrie's Landing, Opelousas, October 21. Scouting and skirmishing about Opelousas October 22-30. Washington October 24. Bayou Bourbeaux November 2. Carrion Crow Bayou November 3. Bayou Sara November 9. Near Vermillionville November 11. At New Iberia November 15-December 18. Camp Pratt November 20. Scout to Vermillion Bayou November 22-23. Scout to St. Martinsville December 2-3. Moved to Donaldsonville December 18-23, thence to Port Hudson January 3-7, and duty there till July 3, 1864. On scout January 12. Capture of Jackson, Miss., February 10. Skirmish February 16. Raid to Bayou Sara and skirmish February 22. Raid to Jackson March 3. Skirmishes March 26-28, April 1 and 5, May 15, June 13 and 17. Bayou Grosse Tete March 30 and April 2. Plains Store April 7. Redwood Bayou May 3. Moved to Baton Rouge July 3. Operations about Baton Rouge July 3-25. Expedition to Davidson's Ford, near Clinton, July 17-18. Olive Branch August 5. Lee's Expedition to Clinton August 23-29. Comite River and Clinton August 25. Hodge's Plantation September 11. Expedition to Amite River, New River and Bayou Manchac October 2-8. Expedition to Clinton, Greensburg, etc., October 5-9. Lee's Expedition to Brookhaven, Miss., November 14-

21. Liberty November 18. Davidson's Expedition to West Pascagoula against Mobile & Ohio R. R. November 27-December 13. Outpost duty at Baton Rouge till May 22, 1865. Expedition west of Mississippi River February 2-3. Expedition to Olive Branch, La., March 1-10. Provost duty at Baton Rouge till October. Expedition to Clinton and Comite River March 30-April 2. Mustered out October 1. Moved to Camp Butler, Ill., October 2-10. Discharged October 13, 1865.

Regiment lost during service 3 Officers and 21 Enlisted men killed and mortally wounded and 1 Officer and 182 Enlisted men by disease. Total 207.

119th REGIMENT INFANTRY.

Organized at Quincy, Ill., and mustered in October 7, 1862. Ordered to Columbus, Ky., thence to Jackson, Tenn., and duty along Mobile & Ohio R. R. till December, 1862. Attached to District of Jackson, Tenn., 13th Army Corps (Old), Department of the Tennessee, to December, 1862. District of Columbus, Ky., 16th Army Corps, to January, 1863. 3rd Brigade, District of Jackson, 16th Army Corps, to March, 1863. 4th Brigade, 1st Division, 16th Army Corps, to May, 1863. 4th Brigade, District of Memphis, Tenn., 5th Division, 15th Army Corps, to January, 1864. 1st Brigade, 3rd Division, 16th Army Corps, to December, 1864. 1st Brigade, 2nd Division, Detachment Army of the Tennessee, Dept. of the Cumberland, to February, 1865. 1st Brigade, 2nd Division, 16th Army Corps (New), Military Division West Mississippi, to August, 1865.

SERVICE.—Company "G" captured at Rutherford Station and Company "K" at Dyer's Station December 21, 1862. Duty at Columbus, Ky., and at Union City, Tenn., till February, 1863. Moved to Humboldt, Huntington and Memphis, Tenn., and guard railroad near Memphis till May 30. Moved to Memphis and Post duty there till January, 1864. Ordered to Vicksburg, Miss., January 21, 1864. Meridian Campaign February 3-March 2. Queen Hill February 4. Meridian February 14-15. Red River Campaign March 10-May 22. Fort DeRussy March 14. Occupation of Alexandria, La., March 16. Battle of Pleasant Hill April 9. Natchitoches April 20-21. About Cloutiersville April 22-24. At Alexandria April 26-May 13. Bayou La Mourie May 7. Retreat to Morganza May 13-20. Mansura May 16. Yellow Bayou May 18. Moved to Vicksburg, Miss., thence to Memphis, Tenn., May 21-June 10. Lake Chicot, Ark., June 6. Defeat of Marmaduke. Smith's Expedition to Tupelo, Miss., July 5-21. Camargo's Cross Roads, near Harrisburg, July 13. Harrisburg, near Tupelo, July 14-15. Old Town (or Tishamingo) Creek July 15. Smith's Expedition to Oxford, Miss., August 1-30. Tallahatchie River August 7-9. Abbeville August 23. Mower's Expedition to Brownsville, Ark., September 2-10. March through Arkansas and Missouri in pursuit of Price September 17-November 19. Moved to Nashville, Tenn., November 21-December 1. Battle of Nashville December 15-16. Pursuit of Hood to the Tennessee River December 17-28. Moved to Eastport, Miss., and duty there till February, 1865. Movement to New Orleans, La., February 8-26. To Dauphin Island March 6. Campaign against Mobile and its defences March 17-April 12. Siege of Spanish Fort and Fort Blakely March 26-April 8. Assault and capture of Fort Blakely April 9. Occupation of Mobile April 12. March to Montgomery April 13-25. Return to Mobile and duty there till August. Mustered out August 26, 1865.

Regiment lost during service 2 Officers and 22 Enlisted men killed and mortally wounded and 3 Officers and 130 Enlisted men by disease. Total 157.

120th REGIMENT INFANTRY.

Organized at Camp Butler, Ill., by consolidation of 7 Companies recruited for 120th Infantry at Vienna, Ill., and 3 Companies recruited for the 132nd Infantry at Shawneetown, Ill. Mustered in October 28, 1862. Guard railroad bridge at Jimtown till November 9, 1862. Moved to Alton, Ill., November 9; thence to Memphis, Tenn. Attached to 1st Brigade, District of Memphis, Tenn., 13th Army Corps (Old), Dept. of the Tennessee, November, 1862. 1st Brigade, 2nd Division, District of Memphis, 13th Army Corps, to December. District of Memphis, Tenn., 16th Army Corps, to March, 1863. 2nd Brigade, District of Memphis, 5th Division, 16th Army Corps, to May, 1863. Detached Brigade, District of Northeast Louisiana, to August, 1863. 3rd Brigade, 2nd Division, 16th Army Corps, to December, 1863. Post of Corinth, Miss., 2nd Division, 16th Army Corps, to January, 1864. 2nd Brigade, District of Memphis, Tenn., 16th Army Corps, to June, 1864. 2nd Brigade, Sturgis' Expedition, June, 1864. 1st Brigade, Post of Memphis, District of West Tennessee, to February, 1865. Unassigned Post of Memphis, Tenn., to June, 1865. 1st Infantry Brigade, District of West Tennessee, to September, 1865.

SERVICE.—Garrison and Provost duty at Memphis, Tenn., November 14, 1862, till May, 1863. Expedition to Marion, Ark., January 13-15, 1863. Moved to Vicksburg, Miss., May. Siege operations against Vicksburg May to July. Greenville, Miss., May 12. Moved to La Grange, Tenn., July 28-August 2; thence to Memphis, Tenn., and duty there till November. Expedition into Mississippi October 10-21. Guard train to Corinth, Miss., October 30-November 5. Moved to Corinth November 7, and Post duty there till January 25, 1864. Moved to Memphis, Tenn., January 25, and Provost duty there till June. Sturgis' Expedition to Guntown June 1-13. Brice's (or Tishamingo) Creek, near Guntown, June 10. Ripley June 11. At Memphis, Tenn., till September 30. Repulse of Forrest's attack on Memphis August 21. Moved to Cairo, Ill., September 30-October 1; thence to Paducah, Ky., October 2-3. Moved to Clifton, Tenn., October 3-6; to Florence October 8. Moved to Pittsburg Landing, thence to Johnsonville October 8-11. Moved to Memphis October 21-23, and Provost duty there till September, 1865. Mustered out September 7, 1865.

Regiment lost during service 20 Enlisted men killed and mortally wounded and 4 Officers and 261 Enlisted men by disease. Total 285.

121st REGIMENT INFANTRY.

Failed to complete organization.

122nd REGIMENT INFANTRY.

Organized at Carlinville, Ill., and mustered in September 4, 1862. Moved to Columbus, Ky., thence to Trenton, Tenn., October 8-12, 1862, and duty there till December 18. Attached to District of Jackson, Tenn., 13th Army Corps (Old), Dept. of the Tennessee, to December, 1862. 4th Brigade, District of Jackson, 16th Army Corps, to February, 1863. 2nd Brigade, District of Corinth, 16th Army Corps, to March, 1863. 2nd Brigade, 2nd Division, 16th Army Corps, to December, 1863. District of Columbus, Ky., 6th Division, 16th Army Corps, to June, 1864. 2nd Brigade, 3rd Division, 16th Army Corps, to November, 1864. 1st Brigade, 3rd Division, 16th Army Corps, to December, 1864. 1st Brigade, 2nd Division, Detachment Army of the Tennessee, Dept. of the Cumberland, to February, 1865. 1st Brigade, 2nd Division, 16th Army Corps (New), Military Division West Mississippi, to July, 1865.

SERVICE.—Right Wing of Regiment moved from Trenton, Tenn., to Humboldt, Tenn., November 12, 1862, to hold Mobile & Ohio R. R. from Trenton to Jackson. Regiment moved to Jackson, Tenn., December 18, 1862. Operations against Forest in West Tennessee December 18, 1862, to January 3, 1863. Action at Salem Cemetery, near Jackson, December 19, 1862. Parker's Cross Roads December 30. Battle of Red Mound (or Parker's Cross Roads) December 31. At Trenton, Tenn., till February 17. Moved to Corinth, Miss., February 17, and duty there till June 25. Dodge's Expedition to Northern Alabama April 15-May 8. Rock Creek, near Tuscumbia, April 22. Tuscumbia April 23. Town Creek April 28. Guard Memphis & Charleston R. R. from Middletown to Grand Junction, with Headquarters at Salisbury, Tenn., June 25 to October 31, 1863. Moved to Iuka, Miss., October 31-November 1; thence to Eastport, Miss., November 5, and duty there till December 8. Moved to Paducah, Ky., December 8, and duty there till January 18, 1864. Moved to Cairo, Ill., January 18, and duty there till June. Operations against Forest in West Tennessee and Kentucky March 16-April 14. Repulse of Forest's attack on Paducah, Ky., March 25 (Cos. "C," "H," "K"). Moved to LaGrange, Tenn., June 26-July 3. Smith's Expedition to Tupelo, Miss., and return to Memphis, Tenn., July 5-21. Battle of Harrisburg, near Tupelo, July 14-15. Old Town Creek July 15. Smith's Expedition to Oxford, Miss., August 1-30. Moved to St. Louis, Mo., September 8. Pursuit of Price through Missouri September to November. Moved to Nashville, Tenn., November 25-December 1. Battles of Nashville December 15-16. Pursuit of Hood to the Tennessee River December 17-28. Moved to Eastport, Miss., and duty there till February, 1865. Movement to New Orleans. La., February 9-21; thence to Dauphin Island, Ala., March 6. Campaign against Mobile and its defences March 22-April 12. Siege of Spanish Fort and Fort Blakely March 26-April 8. Assault and capture of Fort Blakely April 9. March to Montgomery April 13-26, and duty there till June 5. Moved to Mobile June 5, and duty there till July 15. Mustered out at Mobile July 15 and discharged at Springfield, Ill., August 4, 1865.

Regiment lost during service 2 Officers and 38 Enlisted men killed and mortally wounded and 121 Enlisted men by disease. Total 161.

123rd REGIMENT INFANTRY.

Organized at Mattoon, Ill., and mustered in September 6, 1862. Left State for Louisville, Ky., September 19, 1862. Attached to 33rd Brigade, 10th Division, Army of the Ohio, to October, 1862. 33rd Brigade, 10th Division, 1st Corps, Army of the Ohio, to November, 1862. 1st Brigade, 5th Division, Centre 14th Army Corps, Army of the Cumberland, to January, 1863. 1st Brigade, 5th Division, 14th Army Corps, to June, 1863. 1st Brigade, 4th Division, 14th Army Corps, to October, 1863. 3rd Brigade, 2nd Division, Cavalry Corps, Army of the Cumberland, to November, 1864, and Military Division Mississippi, to June, 1865.

SERVICE.—Duty at Louisville, Ky., till October 1, 1862. Pursuit of Bragg into Kentucky October 1-12. Battle of Perryville, Ky., October 8. March to Munfordsville October 12-18, and duty there till November 30. Expedition to Cave City October 31-November 26. Moved to Bledsoe Creek November 30. Pursuit of Morgan to Bear Wallow December 26, 1862, to January 2, 1863. March to Nashville, thence to Murfreesboro, Tenn., January 3-10, 1863. Duty at Murfreesboro till June. Action at Woodbury January 24. Expedition to Auburn, Liberty and Alexandria February 3-5. Cainsville February 15. Expedition to Woodbury March 3-8. Breed's Hill March 4. Vaught's Hill, near Milton, March 20. Expedition to Lebanon, Carthage and Liberty April 1-8. Expedition to McMinnville April 20-30. Regiment mounted and armed with Spencer carbines May 6. Attached to Wilder's Mounted Brigade, Smithville, June 5. Middle Tennessee (or Tullahoma) Campaign June 24-July 7. Big Spring Branch June 24. Hoover's Gap June 24-26. Occupation of Manchester June 27. Estill Springs July 2. Occupation of Middle Tennessee till August 16. Expedition to Columbia and Centreville July. Expedition from Decherd, Tenn., August 5-9. Passage of the Cumberland Mountains and Tennessee River and Chickamauga (Ga.) Campaign August 16-September 22. Ringgold, Ga., September 11. Lee and Gordon's Mills September 11-13. Leet's Tan Yard (or Rock Springs) September 12-13. Alexander and Reed's Bridges September 18. Pea Vine Creek September 18. Crawfish Springs and Dyer's Ford September 18. Battle of Chickamauga September 19-21. Operations against Wheeler and Roddy September 30-October 17. Hill's Gap, Thompson's Cove, near Beersheeba, October 3. Murfreesboro Road October 4. Near McMinnville October 4-5. Farmington October 7. Sim's Farm, near Shelbyville. October 7. Camp at Maysville, Ala., October 19-December 21. Moved to Pulaski December 21, thence to Mooresville, Ala., January 12, 1864, and guard Tennessee River till April. Moved to Columbia, Tenn., thence to join army near Dalton, Ga., reporting May 11. Atlanta (Ga.) Campaign May 11-September 8. Battle of Resaca May 13-15. Near Dallas May 24. Operations on Pumpkin Vine Creek and battles about Dallas, New Hope Church and Allatoona Hills May 25-June 5. Near Big Shanty June 9. Operations about Marietta and against Kenesaw Mountain June 10-July 2. Noonday Creek June 19. Powder Springs, Lattimer's Mills, Noonday Creek, June 20. Noonday Creek and assault on Kenesaw June 27. Nickajack Creek July 2-5. Rottenwood Creek July 4. Chattahoochie River June 5-17. Stone Mountain Station July 19. Garrard's Raid to Oxford and Covington July 22-24. Garrard's Raid to South River July 27-31. Snapfinger Creek July 27. Flat Rock Bridge July 28. Siege of Atlanta August 1-13. Operations about Chattahoochie River Bridge, Pace's and Turner's Ferries August 26-September 2. Occupation of Atlanta September 2. Operations against Hood in North Georgia and North Alabama September 29-November 3. Near Lost Mountain October 4-7. New Hope Church October 7. Dallas October 7. Rome October 10-11. Narrows October 11. Coosaville Road, near Rome, October 13. Near Summerville October 18. Little River October 20. Leesburg, Blue Pond, October 21. Ladiga, Terrapin Creek, October 28. Dismounted November 1, and ordered to Louisville, Ky. Refitting at Louisville till December 28. Moved to Gravelly Springs, Ala., December 28, 1864-January 20, 1865. Wilson's Raid on Selma, Ala., and Macon, Ga., March 22-April 24. Selma April 2. Montgomery April 12. Columbus, Ga., April 16. Macon, Ga., April 20. Moved to Chattanooga, Tenn., May 23; thence to Nashville and duty there till June 27. Mustered out June 27 and discharged at Springfield, Ill., July 11, 1865

Regiment lost during service 3 Officers and 82 Enlisted men killed and mortally wounded and 1 Officer and 133 Enlisted men by disease. Total 219.

124th REGIMENT INFANTRY.

Organized at Camp Butler, Ill., and mustered in September 10, 1862. Moved to Jackson, Tenn., October 6-9, 1862, and duty there till November 2. Attached to 1st Brigade, 3rd Division, Right Wing 13th Army Corps (Old), Dept. of the Tennessee, to December, 1862. 1st Brigade, 3rd Division, 17th Army Corps, Army of the Tennessee to April, 1864. Maltby's Brigade, District of Vicksburg, Miss., to October, 1864. 1st Brigade, 2nd Division, 19th Army Corps, Dept. of the Gulf, October, 1864. Maltby's Brigade, District of Vicksburg, Miss., to February, 1865. 3rd Brigade, 3rd Division, 16th Army Corps (New), Military Division West Mississippi, to August, 1865.

SERVICE.—Grant's Central Mississippi Campaign. Operations on the Mississippi Central R. R. to the Tallahatchie and Yocknapatafa Rivers November, 1862, to January, 1863. Reconnoissance from LaGrange November 8-9, 1862. Moved to Memphis, Tenn., January 12-21, 1863; thence to Lake Providence, La., February 21, and to Milliken's Bend, La., April 17. Movement on Bruinsburg and turning Grand Gulf April 25-30. Battle of Thompson's Hill, Port Gibson, May 1. North Fork Bayou Pierre May 3. Battles of Raymond, Miss., May 12. Jackson May 14. Champion's Hill May 16. Siege of Vicksburg May 18-July 4. Assaults on Vicksburg May 19 and 22 and June 25. Surrender of Vicksburg July 4. Occupation of Vicksburg till November, 1863. Stephenson's Expedition to Monroe, La., August 20-September 2, 1863. Expedition toward Canton October 14-20. Bogue Chitto Creek October 17. At Big

Black November 7, 1863, to February, 1864. (Regiment won the "Excelsior Prize Banner," tendered by Gen. M. D. Leggett, Commanding the Division, to the best drilled and finest Regiment in the Division. Awarded by the unanimous vote of the committee, and presented to the Regiment by Gen. J. B. McPherson January 23, 1864, and carried by the Regiment till April 5, 1864, when, through reassignment outside the Division, it was turned over to the Division-Commander,) Expedition to Sunnyside Landing, Ark., January 10-16, 1864. Meridian Campaign February 3-March 2. Clinton February 5. Meridian February 13-14. Chunky Creek February 14. Canton February 29. Duty at Vicksburg, Miss., till February 25, 1865. Expedition to Benton and Yazoo City, Miss., May 4-21, 1864. Benton May 7 and 9. Big Black River Bridge May 12. Vaughan Station May 14. Expedition to Pearl River, Miss., July 2-10. Clinton July 4. Clinton and Jackson July 7. Movement to Memphis and return October 13-26. Moved to New Orleans, La., February 25-27, 1865; thence to Dauphin Island, Ala., March 11-16. Canby's Campaign against Mobile, Ala., and its defences March 17-April 12. Siege of Spanish Fort and Fort Blakely March 26-April 9. Capture of Mobile April 12. March to Montgomery April 13-25. and Provost duty there till July 16. Moved to Vicksburg, Miss.; thence to Chicago, Ill., July 16-August 3. Mustered out at Vicksburg, Miss., July 28, and discharged at Chicago, Ill., August 16, 1865.

Regiment lost during service 1 Officer and 40 Enlisted men killed and mortally wounded and 2 Officers and 147 Enlisted men by disease. Total 190.

125th REGIMENT INFANTRY.

Organized at Danville, Ill., and mustered in September 3, 1862. Moved to Covington, Ky., September 25, 1862. Attached to 36th Brigade, 11th Division, Army of the Ohio, to October, 1862. 36th Brigade, 11th Division, 3rd Army Corps, Army of the Ohio, to November, 1862. 2nd Brigade, 4th Division, Centre 14th Army Corps, Army of the Cumberland, to January, 1863. 2nd Brigade, 4th Division, 14th Army Corps, to June, 1863. 2nd Brigade, 2nd Division, Reserve Corps, Army of the Cumberland, to October, 1863. 3rd Brigade. 2nd Division, 14th Army Corps, Army of the Cumberland, and Army of Georgia, to June, 1865.

SERVICE.—Pursuit of Bragg into Kentucky October 1-16, 1862. Battle of Perryville, Ky., October 8. March to Nashville, Tenn., October 16-November 7, and duty at Nashville till June 30, 1863. Moved to Murfreesboro, Tenn., June 30. Return to Nashville July 18 and duty there till August 20. Moved to Chattanooga, Tenn., via Brentwood, Columbia, Huntsville, Ala., and Bridgeport, Ala., August 20-September 16. Battle of Chickamauga, Ga., September 19-21. Siege of Chattanooga, Tenn., September 24-November 23. Ringgold September 26. Chattanooga-Ringgold Campaign November 23-27. Orchard Knob November 23. Tunnel Hill November 24-25. Mission Ridge November 25. Pursuit to Graysville November 26-27. March to relief of Knoxville, Tenn., November 28-December 17. At Lee and Gordon's Mills till May, 1864. Demonstration on Dalton, Ga., February 22-27, 1864. Tunnel Hill, Buzzard's Roost Gap and Rocky Faced Ridge February 23-25. Atlanta (Ga.) Campaign May 1-September 8. Tunnel Hill May 6-7. Demonstration on Rocky Faced Ridge May 8-11. Buzzard's Roost Gap May 8-9. Battle of Resaca May 14-15. Rome May 17-18. Operations on line of Pumpkin Vine Creek and battles about Dallas, New Hope Church and Allatoona Hills May 25-June 5. Operations about Marietta and against Kenesaw Mountain June 10-July 2. Pine Hill June 11-14. Lost Mountain June 15-17. Assault on Kenesaw June 27. Ruff's Station, Smyrna Camp Ground, July 4. Chattahoochie River July 5-17. Peach Tree Creek July 19-20. Siege of Atlanta July 22-August 25. Utoy Creek August 5-7. Flank movement on Jonesboro August 25-30. Battle of Jonesboro August 31-September 1. Lovejoy Station September 2-6. Operations against Hood and Forest in North Georgia and North Alabama Sep-

tember 29-November 3. March to the sea November 15-December 10. Louisville November 30. Cuyler's Plantation December 9. Siege of Savannah December 10-21. Campaign of the Carolinas January to April, 1865. Averysboro, Taylor's Hole Creek, N. C., March 16. Battle of Bentonville March 19-21. Occupation of Goldsboro March 24. Advance on Raleigh April 10-14. Occupation of Raleigh April 14. Bennett's House April 26. Surrender of Johnston and his army. March to Washington, D. C., via Richmond, Va., April 29-May 19. Grand Review May 24. Mustered out June 9, 1865, and discharged from service.

Regiment lost during service 9 Officers and 88 Enlisted men killed and mortally wounded and 3 Officers and 104 Enlisted men by disease. Total 204.

126th REGIMENT INFANTRY.

Organized at Alton, Ill., and mustered in September 4. 1862. Moved to Columbus. Ky., thence to Bolivar and LaGrange, Tenn., November 20-28, 1862. Attached to District of Jackson, 13th Army Corps (Old), Department of the Tennessee, to December, 1862. 3rd Brigade, District of Jackson, 16th Army Corps, to March, 1863. 2nd Brigade, 3rd Division, 16th Army Corps, to May, 1863. 2nd Brigade, Kimball's Provisional Division, 16th Army Corps, to July, 1863. 2nd Brigade, Kimball's Division, District of Eastern Arkansas, to August, 1863. 2nd Brigade, 2nd Division, Arkansas Expedition, to January, 1864. 2nd Brigade, 2nd Division, 7th Army Corps, Dept. of the Arkansas. to March, 1864. 3rd Brigade, 3rd Division, 7th Army Corps, to February, 1865. Unattached, 7th Army Corps, mouth of White River, Ark., to July, 1865.

SERVICE.—Duty at LaGrange, Tenn., till January, 1863. (6 Companies moved to Jackson, Tenn., December 19, 1862; thence moved to Humboldt, Tenn. R. R. crossing at Fork Deer River December 20. Action at Humboldt December 21.) 4 Companies on duty at Jackson, Tenn., and 6 Companies at Humboldt, Tenn., January to March 25; then at Jackson till May 25, 1863. Moved to Vicksburg, Miss., May 25-28. Siege of Vicksburg May 28-July 4. Moved to Helena. Ark., July 24. Expedition against Little Rock, Ark., August 1-September 10. Bayou Fourche and capture of Little Rock September 10. Moved to Duvall's Bluff October 24, and duty there till August 19, 1864. Action at Clinton June 25-26. Moved to Pine Bluff, Ark., August 19, and duty there till February 12, 1865. Scouts from Pine Bluff toward Camden and Monticello January 26-31. At mouth of White River, Ark., till June 12, and at Pine Bluff till July 12. Mustered out July 12, 1865.

Regiment lost during service 6 Enlisted men killed and mortally wounded and 4 Officers and 192 Enlisted men by disease. Total 202.

127th REGIMENT INFANTRY.

Organized at Camp Douglas, Ill., and mustered in September 6, 1862. Moved to Memphis, Tenn., November 9-13, 1862. Attached to 4th Brigade, 5th Division, District of Memphis, 13th Army Corps (Old), Dept. of the Tennessee, November, 1862. 2nd Brigade, 2nd Division, 13th Army Corps, to December, 1862. 2nd Brigade, 2nd Division, Sherman's Yazoo Expedition, to January, 1863. 2nd Brigade, 2nd Division, 15th Army Corps, Army of the Tennessee, to September, 1863. 1st Brigade, 2nd Division, 15th Army Corps, to June, 1865.

SERVICE.—Duty at Camp Douglas, Ill., guarding prisoners, September 6 to November 9, 1862. Grant's Mississippi Central Campaign. "Tallahatchie March" November 26-December 13. Sherman's Yazoo Expedition December 20, 1862, to January 3 1863. Chickasaw Bayou December 26-28, 1862. Chickasaw Bluff December 29. McClernand's Expedition to Arkansas Post, Ark., January 3-10, 1863. Assault and capture of Fort Hindman, Arkansas Post, January 10-11. Moved to Young's Point, La., January 22, and duty there till March. Expedition to Rolling Fork, via Muddy, Steele's and Black Bayous and Deer Creek March 14-27. Deer Creek March 22. Demonstrations on Haines' and

Drumgould's Bluffs April 29-May 2. Movement to Jackson, Miss., via Grand Gulf, May 2-14. Jackson May 14. Champion's Hill May 16. Siege of Vicksburg, Miss., May 18-July 4. Assaults on Vicksburg May 19 and 22. Surrender of Vicksburg July 4. Advance on Jackson, Miss., July 4-10. Siege of Jackson July 10-17. At Big Black till September 22. Moved to Memphis, Tenn.; thence march to Chattanooga, Tenn., September 22-November 20. Operations on Memphis & Charleston R. R. in Alabama October 20-29. Bear Creek, Tuscumbia, Ala., October 27. Chattanooga-Ringgold Campaign November 23-27. Foot of Missionary Ridge November 24. Tunnel Hill November 24-25. Mission Ridge November 25. Pursuit to Graysville November 26-27. March to relief of Knoxville November 28-December 8. At Larkinsville, Ala., till May, 1864. Atlanta (Ga.) Campaign May to September. Demonstration on Resaca May 8-13. Battle of Resaca May 14-15. Movement on Dallas May 18-25. Operations on line of Pumpkin Vine Creek and battles about Dallas, New Hope Church and Allatoona Hills May 25-June 5. Operations about Marietta and against Kenesaw Mountain June 10-July 2. Assault on Kenesaw June 27. Nickajack Creek July 2-5. Chattahoochie River July 6-17. Battle of Atlanta July 22. Siege of Atlanta July 22-August 25. Ezra Chapel, Hood's second sortie, July 28. Flank movement on Jonesboro August 25-30. Battle of Jonesboro August 31-September 1. Lovejoy Station September 2-6. Operations against Hood in North Georgia and North Alabama September 29-November 3. March to the sea November 15-December 10. Clinton November 23. Siege of Savannah December 10-21. Assault and capture of Fort McAllister December 13. Campaign of the Carolinas January to April, 1865. Salkehatchie Swamps, S. C., February 2-5. South Edisto River February 9. North Edisto River February 12-13. Columbia February 16-17. Battle of Bentonville, N. C., March 20-21. Occupation of Goldsboro March 24. Advance on Raleigh April 10-14. Occupation of Raleigh April 14. Bennett's House April 26. Surrender of Johnston and his army. March to Washington, D. C., via Richmond, Va., April 29-May 19. Grand Review May 24. Mustered out June 4 and discharged at Chicago, Ill., June 17, 1865

Regiment lost during service 2 Officers and 47 Enlisted men killed and mortally wounded and 1 Officer and 168 Enlisted men by disease. Total 218.

128th REGIMENT INFANTRY.

Organized at Camp Butler, Ill., and mustered in November 4, 1862. Attached to District of Columbus, Ky., 16th Army Corps, Dept. of the Tennessee. Disbanded April 1, 1863, by order of Gen. Grant, having lost in 5 months over 700 men, principally by desertion, and the Officers having proved themselves utterly incompetent, were mustered out of service. The few remaining men were consolidated into a Detachment and consolidated with 9th Illinois Infantry April 1, 1863.

Regiment lost during service by disease 1 Officer and 34 men. Total 35:

129th REGIMENT INFANTRY.

Organized at Pontiac and mustered in September 8, 1862. Moved to Louisville, Ky., September 22. Attached to 38th Brigade, 12th Division, Army of the Ohio, to November, 1862. Bowling Green, Ky., District of West Kentucky, Dept. of the Ohio, to June, 1863. 2nd Brigade, 3rd Division, Reserve Corps, Army of the Cumberland, June, 1863. Garrison Gallatin, Tenn., to August, 1863. Ward's Brigade, District of Nashville, Tenn., Dept. of the Cumberland, to January, 1864. 1st Brigade, 1st Division, 11th Army Corps, Dept. of the Cumberland, to April, 1864. 1st Brigade, 3rd Division, 20th Army Corps, Army of the Cumberland, and Army of Georgia to June, 1865.

SERVICE.—Pursuit of Bragg into Kentucky October 1-16, 1862. March to Bowling Green, Ky., October 20-25; thence moved to Mitchellsville, Ky., November 21,

and Garrison duty there till December. Guard R. R. from Bowling Green, Ky., to Gallatin, Tenn., till June 1, 1863. Skirmish at Richland Station March 19. Garrison Fort Thomas at Gallatin June 1 to August 22. March to Nashville, Tenn., August 22, and duty there till February 24, 1864. Expedition from Nashville to Creelsboro December 28, 1863, to January 4, 1864. March to Wauhatchie Valley, Tenn., February 24-March 12, and duty there till May 2. Atlanta (Ga.) Campaign May 2-September 8. Demonstration on Resaca May 8-13. Battle of Resaca May 14-15. Cassville May 19. Advance on Dallas May 22-25. Burnt Hickory and New Hope Church May 25. Operations on line of Pumpkin Vine Creek and battles about Dallas, New Hope Church and Allatoona Hills May 26-June 5. Operations about Marietta and against Kenesaw Mountain June 10-July 2. Pine Hill June 11-14. Lost Mountain June 15-17. Gilgal (or Golgotha Church) June 15. Muddy Creek June 17. Noyes Creek June 19. Kolb's Farm June 22. Assault on Kenesaw June 27. Ruff's Station, Smyrna Camp Ground, July 4. Chattahoochie River July 5-17. Peach Tree Creek July 19-20. Siege of Atlanta July 22-August 25. Operations at Chattahoochie River Bridge August 26-September 2. Occupation of Atlanta September 2-November 15. March to the sea November 15-December 10. Siege of Savannah December 10-21. Near Hardeesville, S. C., January 3, 1865. Campaign of the Carolinas January to April, 1865. Averysboro, Taylor's Hole Creek, N. C., March 16. Battle of Bentonville March 19-21. Occupation of Goldsboro March 24. Advance on Raleigh April 10-14. Occupation of Raleigh April 14. Bennett's House April 26. Surrender of Johnston and his army. Moved to Washington, D. C., via Richmond, Va., April 29-May 19. Grand Review May 24. Mustered out June 8, 1865.

Regiment lost during service 50 Enlisted men killed and mortally wounded and 2 Officers and 128 Enlisted men by disease. Total 180.

130th REGIMENT INFANTRY.

Organized at Camp Butler, Springfield, Ill., and mustered in October 25, 1862. Moved to Memphis, Tenn., November 11-17, 1862. Attached to Reserve Brigade, District of Memphis, 13th Army Corps (Old), Dept. of the Tennessee, to December, 1862. District of Memphis, 16th Army Corps, to March, 1863. 2nd Brigade, 10th Division, 13th Army Corps, Army of the Tennessee, to July, 1863. 2nd Brigade, 4th Division, 13th Army Corps, Dept. of the Tennessee, to August, 1863, and Dept. of the Gulf to June, 1864. 3rd Brigade, 3rd Division, 19th Army Corps, Dept. of the Gulf, to October, 1864. Defences of New Orleans, La., to January, 1865. Consolidated with 77th Illinois Infantry January 25, 1865. Regiment revived June 23, 1865. 1st Brigade, 3rd Division, 13th Army Corps (New), Military Division West Mississippi, to August, 1865.

SERVICE.—Duty at Fort Pickering, Memphis, Tenn., till March 27, 1863. Moved to Milliken's Bend, La., March 27-31, and duty there till April 25. Movement on Bruinsburg and turning Grand Gulf April 25-30. Battle of Magnolia Hills, Port Gibson, May 1. Champion's Hill May 16. Big Black River Bridge May 17. Siege of Vicksburg, Miss., May 18-July 4. Assaults on Vicksburg May 19 and 22. Advance on Jackson, Miss., July 5-10. Siege of Jackson July 10-17. Reconnoissance to Pearl River July 11. Camp at Big Black till August 13. Ordered to New Orleans, La., August 13, and duty there till October. Western Louisiana Campaign October 3-November 30. At New Iberia till December 6. Moved to New Orleans, thence to Pass Cavallo, Texas, December 6-20, and duty there till February, 1864. Reconnoissance on Matagorda Peninsula January 21. Moved to Algiers, thence to Franklin, La. Red River Campaign March 10-May 22. Advance from Franklin to Alexandria, La., March 14-26. Bayou De Paul, Carroll's Mills, April 8. Battle of Sabine Cross Roads April 8. Regiment mostly captured at Sabine Cross Roads and confined at Tyler, Texas, 13 months. Retreat to Morganza May 13-20.

Garrison duty at New Orleans, La., June, 1864, to January, 1865. With 77th Illinois Infantry in Campaign against Mobile and its defences February to April. Siege of Spanish Fort and Fort Blakely March 26-April 9. Assault and capture of Fort Blakely April 9. Occupation of Mobile April 12. Expedition to Tombigbee River and McIntosh Bluffs April 13-May 9. At Mobile till July. Regiment reorganized at Mobile July 11, 1865. Ordered to New Orleans and mustered out August 15, 1865.

Regiment lost during service 2 Officers and 18 Enlisted men killed and mortally wounded and 4 Officers and 153 Enlisted men by disease. Total 177.

131st REGIMENT INFANTRY.

Organized at Old Fort Massac and mustered in November 13, 1862. Moved to Cairo, Ill.; thence to Memphis, Tenn., December 2-7, 1862. Attached to 2nd Brigade, 10th Division, 13th Army Corps (Old), Dept. of the Tennessee, December, 1862. 2nd Brigade, 1st Division, Sherman's Yazoo Expedition, to January, 1863. 2nd Brigade, 10th Division, 13th Army Corps, Army of the Tennessee, to March, 1863. District of Memphis, Tenn., 5th Division, 16th Army Corps, to May, 1863. Detached Brigade, District of Northeast Louisiana, to July, 1863. Paducah, Ky., District of Columbus, Ky., 6th Division, 16th Army Corps, to October, 1863. 1st Brigade, 3rd Division, 17th Army Corps, to November, 1863.

SERVICE.—At Memphis, Tenn., till December 20, 1862. Sherman's Yazoo Expedition December 20, 1862, to January 3, 1863. Chickasaw Bayou December 26-28. Chickasaw Bluffs December 29. Expedition to Arkansas Post, Ark., January 3-10, 1863. Assault and capture of Fort Hindman, Arkansas Post, January 10-11. Moved to Young's Point, La., January 15-22, and duty there till March 2. Moved to Memphis, Tenn., March 2-6, and duty there till May 9. Moved to Vicksburg, Miss., May 10-12. Near Island No. 82. Mississippi River, May 11. At Milliken's Bend, La., guarding supplies till May 24. At Sherman's Landing till July 4. Moved to Paducah, Ky., July 20-27, and duty there till October 15. Consolidated to a Battalion of 4 Companies September 16. Expedition to Mayfield and Murray, Ky., October 15-20. Moved to Vicksburg, Miss., October 20-29. Regiment consolidated with 29th Illinois Infantry November 15, 1863.

Regiment lost during service 1 Enlisted man killed and 11 Officers and 282 Enlisted men by disease. Total 294.

132nd REGIMENT INFANTRY.

Organized at Camp Fry, Chicago, Ill., and mustered in for 100 days June 1, 1864. Moved to Columbus, Ky., June 3. Attached to District of Columbus, Ky., 6th Division, 16th Army Corps, Dept. of the Tennessee, to August, 1864. District of Columbus, Ky., Dept. of the Ohio, to October, 1864.

SERVICE.—Garrison duty at Paducah, Ky., till October. Expedition from Paducah to Hadix Ferry July 25-27. Action near Haddix Ferry July 27. Mustered out October 17, 1864.

Regiment lost during service 12 by disease. Total 12.

133rd REGIMENT INFANTRY.

Organized at Camp Butler, Ill., and mustered in for 100 days May 31, 1864. Moved to Rock Island Barracks, Ill., June 3, and duty there guarding prisoners of war till September, 1864. Mustered out September 24, 1864.

Regiment lost during service 16 by disease.

134th REGIMENT INFANTRY.

Organized at Camp Fry, Chicago, Ill., and mustered in for 100 days May 31, 1864. Moved to Columbus, Ky., June 6-8. Attached to District of Columbus, Ky. and Garrison duty at Columbus till October. Mustered out October 5, 1864.

Regiment lost during service 1 Officer and 20 Enlisted men by disease. Total 21.

135th REGIMENT INFANTRY.

Organized at Mattoon, Ill., and mustered in for 100 days June 6, 1864. Moved to Benton Barracks, Mo., June 10. Assigned to guard duty on Iron Mountain R. R. at the Gasconade and Osage crossings of the Missouri Pacific R. R., and at Jefferson City, Mo. Mustered out September 28, 1864.

Regiment lost 2 Enlisted men killed and 17 Enlisted men by disease during service. Total 19.

136th REGIMENT INFANTRY.

Organized at Centralia, Ill., and mustered in for 100 days June 1, 1864. Moved to Cairo, Ill.; thence to Columbus, Ky. Attached to District of Columbus, Ky., Dept. of the Tennessee, to August, 1864, and Department of the Ohio to September, 1864. Assigned to Garrison duty at Columbus, Ky., till September 26. Expedition to Mayfield, Ky., August 12-16. Re-enlisted for 15 days' service against Price's Invasion of Missouri, and on duty at various points about St. Louis, Mo., till October 15. Mustered out at Camp Butler, Ill., October 22, 1864.

Regiment lost during service 2 Enlisted men killed and 2 Officers and 40 Enlisted men by disease. Total 44.

137th REGIMENT INFANTRY.

Organized at Camp Wood, Quincy, Ill., and mustered in for 100 days June 5, 1864. Ordered to Memphis, Tenn., June 9. Attached to 4th Brigade, District of Memphis, Tenn., District of West Tennessee. Transferred to 3rd Brigade, District of Memphis, July 9. Assigned to guard and picket duty at and about Memphis till September. Repulse of Forrest's attack on Memphis August 21. Mustered out September 4, 1864.

Regiment lost during service 1 Officer and 17 Enlisted men killed and mortally wounded and 1 Officer and 31 Enlisted men by disease. Total 50.

138th REGIMENT INFANTRY.

Organized at Camp Wood, Quincy, Ill., and mustered in for 100 days June 21, 1864. Moved to Fort Leavenworth, Kansas, June 26, and duty there till October. (Cos. "C" and "F" at Weston, Mo., July 7 to August 3.) Mustered out October 14, 1864.

Lost 13 by disease during service.

139th REGIMENT INFANTRY.

Organized at Peoria, Ill., and mustered in for 100 days June 1, 1864. Moved to St. Louis, Mo., June 8-10; thence to Columbus, Ky. Moved to Cairo, Ill., June 20, and on Garrison duty there till September. Attached to District of Columbus, Ky., Dept. of the Tennessee, to August, and Dept. of the Ohio to September. Moved to Peoria September 25-28. Volunteered for service during Price's Invasion of Missouri and moved to St. Louis. March into Missouri toward Franklin in pursuit of Price, October. Mustered out October 25, 1864.

Lost by disease during service 16.

140th REGIMENT INFANTRY.

Organized at Camp Butler, Ill., and mustered in for 100 days June 18, 1864. Moved to Cairo, Ill., thence to Memphis, Tenn., June 18-22. Attached to 3rd Brigade, Memphis, Tenn., District of West Tennessee. March from Memphis to Wolf River and guard R. R. by detachments between Wolf River and Holly Springs, Miss., till August. Action at LaFayette June 26 and August 8. Moved to Memphis, Tenn., and Post duty there till October. Repulse of Forrest's attack on Memphis August 21. Near Memphis August 25. Ordered to Camp Fry, Chicago, Ill. Mustered out October 29, 1864. (Volunteered for the defence of Missouri during Price's Invasion.)

Regiment lost during service 5 Enlisted men killed and mortally wounded and 24 Enlisted men by disease. Total 29.

141st REGIMENT INFANTRY.

Organized at Elgin, Ill., and mustered in for 100 days June 16, 1864. Moved to Columbus, Ky., and Garrison duty in that District till October. Mustered out October 10, 1864.

Regiment lost by disease during service 21.

142nd REGIMENT INFANTRY.

Organized at Freeport, Ill., and mustered in for 100 days June 18, 1864. Moved to Memphis, Tenn., June 21-24. Attached to R. R. District, Memphis, Tenn., District of West Tennessee, and assigned to duty on Memphis & Charleston R. R. at White's Station till October. Mustered out October 27, 1864.

Regiment lost by disease during service 30.

143rd REGIMENT INFANTRY.

Organized at Mattoon, Ill., and mustered in for 100 days June 11, 1864. Moved to Memphis, Tenn., June 16-19. Attached to 3rd Brigade, Memphis, Tenn., District of West Tennessee. Transferred to 3rd Brigade July 12. Duty at Memphis, Tenn., till July 27. Moved to Helena, Ark., District of Eastern Arkansas, July 27-28, and duty there till September 10. Mustered out September 26, 1864.

Regiment lost by disease during service 55.

144th REGIMENT INFANTRY.

Organized at Alton, Ill., and mustered in for 1 year October 21, 1864. Ordered to St. Louis, Mo., and duty in that District till July, 1865. Mustered out July 14, 1865.

Regiment lost during service by disease 69.

145th REGIMENT INFANTRY.

Organized at Camp Butler and mustered in for 100 days June 9, 1864. Ordered to St. Louis, Mo., June 12, and duty in that District till September. Mustered out at Camp Butler September 23, 1864.

Regiment lost during service by disease 40.

146th REGIMENT INFANTRY.

Organized at Camp Butler, Ill., and mustered in for 1 year September 18, 1864. Assigned to duty in Illinois. Guarding drafted men at Camp Butler. Cos. "B" and "C" at Brighton, Cos. "D" and "E" at Quincy, and Co. "F" at Jacksonville. Mustered out July 5, 1865.

Regiment lost during service by disease 38.

147th REGIMENT INFANTRY.

Organized at Camp Fry, Chicago, Ill., for 1 year February 18, 1865. Moved to Louisville, Ky., thence to Nashville, Tenn., February 21-25, and to Chattanooga, Tenn., and Dalton, Ga., February 27-28. Attached to 1st Brigade, 2nd Separate Division, District of the Etowah, Dept. of the Cumberland, to July, 1865. Dept. of Georgia to January, 1866.

SERVICE.—Duty at Dalton, Ga., and operating against guerrillas till May 1, 1865. Expedition to Mill Creek March 14-16. Action near Dalton March 14. Expedition to Spring Place March 20-22, and to Ringgold March 28-29. Moved to Resaca May 1-2, thence to Calhoun June 26, to Dalton July 2-3. To Marietta, Macon and Albany July 27-31. Duty there and at Americus and Smithville till November. Moved to Macon and Hawkinsville November 4-6, thence to Savannah November 25-December 3. (Cos. "F" and "I" at Hawkinsville till November 28. Joined Regiment at Savannah December 5.) Duty at Savannah till January 23, 1866. Mustered out January 20, 1866. Moved to Springfield, Ill., January 23-31. Discharged February 8, 1866.

Regiment lost during service 3 Enlisted men killed and 31 Enlisted men by disease. Total 34.

149th REGIMENT INFANTRY.

Organized at Camp Butler, Ill., and mustered in February 21, 1865. Moved to Nashville, Tenn., February 22-25, thence to Tullahoma, Tenn., March 1. Attached

to 1st Brigade, Defences Nashville & Chattanooga R. R. to April, 1865. 2nd Brigade, 1st Sub-District, District of Middle Tennessee, Dept. of the Cumberland, to June, 1865. 3rd Brigade, 1st Sub-District, District of Middle Tennessee, to September, 1865.

SERVICE.—Duty at Tullahoma, Tenn., till June 18, 1865; then distributed 5 Companies at Decherd, 1 Company at McMinnville and 4 Companies guarding Nashville & Chattanooga R. R. from Lombardy to Anderson's Station till September. Mustered out at Nashville, Tenn., September 5, 1865.

Regiment lost during service 2 Enlisted men killed and 1 Officer and 70 Enlisted men by disease. Total 73.

149th REGIMENT INFANTRY.

Organized at Camp Butler, Ill., and mustered in for 1 year February 11, 1865. Moved to Nashville, Tenn., February 14-17, 1865; thence to Chattanooga, Tenn. Attached to 2nd Brigade, 2nd Separate Division, District of the Etowah, Dept. of the Cumberland, to July, 1865. Dept. of Georgia to January, 1866.

SERVICE.—Provost Guard duty at Chattanooga, Tenn., and guarding R. R. till May 2. Moved to Dalton, Ga., May 2; thence to Atlanta, Ga., July 6. Guard duty in 4th Sub-District, District of Allatoona, till January, 1866. Mustered out January 27, 1866.

Regiment lost during service by disease 31.

150th REGIMENT INFANTRY.

Organized at Camp Butler, Ill., and mustered in for 1 year's service February 14, 1865. Moved to Bridgeport, Ala., February 18-27, 1865. Attached to 2nd Brigade, 2nd Separate Division, District of the Etowah, Dept. of the Cumberland, to July, 1865. Dept. of Georgia to January, 1866.

SERVICE.—Garrison duty at Bridgeport, Ala., at Forts 3 and 4 and Block Houses on Nashville & Chattanooga R. R. from Bridgeport, Ala., to Chattanooga, Tenn., till March 24. Moved to Cleveland, Tenn., March 24-25. To Dalton, Ga., May 2-3, and duty there till July 7. (Left Wing at Spring Place till July 1.) Moved to Atlanta July 7-8, thence to Griffin, Ga., August 14. Duty in 2nd Sub-District, District of Allatoona, till December, 1865. Cos. "A" and "E" at Griffin. Co. "D" at LaGrange, Co. "C" at West Point, Co. "F" at Newnan, Cos. "B" and "G" at Atlanta, "Co. "K" at Greenville, Co. "H" at Franklin, and Co. "I" at Atlanta. Assigned to District of Atlanta December 31. Mustered out January 16, 1866.

Regiment lost during service by disease 58.

151st REGIMENT INFANTRY.

Organized at Quincy, Ill., and mustered in for 1 year's service February 23, 1865. Moved to Springfield, Ill.; thence to Nashville, Murfreesboro and Chattanooga, Tenn., and Dalton, Ga., February 23-March 13, 1865. Attached to 1st Brigade, 2nd Separate Division, District of the Etowah, Dept. of the Cumberland, to July, 1865. Dept. of Georgia to January, 1866.

SERVICE.—Duty at Dalton, Ga., till May 2, 1865. Moved to Resaca, Calhoun and Kingston, Ga., May 2-12. Surrender of Warford May 13-14-15. At Kingston, Ga., till July 28. Detachments at Adairsville, Rome and Cartersville. Moved to Columbus, Ga., July 28-31, and duty there till January, 1866. Mustered out January 24, 1866. Discharged February 8, 1866. Regiment lost during service by disease 51.

152nd REGIMENT INFANTRY.

Organized at Camp Butler, Ill., and mustered in for 1 year February 18, 1865. Moved to Nashville, Tenn.; thence to Tullahoma, Tenn., February 20-28, 1865. Attached to 2nd Brigade, Defences Nashville & Chattanooga R. R., Dept. of the Cumberland, to April, 1865. 2nd Brigade, 1st Sub-District, District of Middle Tennessee, to July, 1865. 1st Infantry Brigade, District of West Tennessee, to September, 1865.

SERVICE.—Assigned to duty as railroad guard on the Nashville & Chattanooga R. R. till July, 1865. Moved to Memphis, Tenn., and duty there till September. Mustered out September 9, 1865.

Regiment lost during service by disease 76.

153rd REGIMENT INFANTRY.

Organized at Camp Fry, Chicago, Ill., and mustered in for 1 year February 27, 1865. Moved to Nashville, Tenn.; thence to Tullahoma, Tenn., March 4-10. Attached to 2nd Brigade, Defences of Nashville & Chattanooga R. R., Dept. of the Cumberland, to April, 1865. 2nd Brigade, 1st Sub-District, District of Middle Tennessee, to July, 1865. 1st Infantry Brigade, District of West Tennessee, to September, 1865.

SERVICE.—Assigned to guard duty on Nashville & Chattanooga R. R. till July, 1865. Moved to Memphis, Tenn., July 1, and duty there till September. Mustered out September 15, 1865, and discharged September 24, 1865.

Regiment lost during service by disease 37.

154th REGIMENT INFANTRY.

Organized at Camp Butler and mustered in February 21, 1865. Moved to Louisville, Ky.; thence to Nashville and Murfreesboro, Tenn., February 24-March 3, 1865. Attached to 1st Brigade, Defences Nashville & Chattanooga R. R., Dept. of the Cumberland, to April, 1865. 1st Brigade, 1st Sub-District, District of Middle Tennessee, to September, 1865.

SERVICE.—Duty at Murfreesboro, Tenn., till May 13, 1865. Moved to Tullahoma, Tenn., May 13-15; thence to Nashville June 11 and Garrison duty there till September. Mustered out September 18, 1865.

Regiment lost during service by disease 76.

155th REGIMENT INFANTRY.

Organized at Camp Butler and mustered in February 28, 1865. Moved to Louisville, Ky.; thence to Nashville and Tullahoma, Tenn., March 2-10, 1865. Attached to 2nd Brigade, Defences Nashville & Chattanooga R. R., Dept. of the Cumberland, to April, 1865. 2nd Brigade, 1st Sub-District, District of Middle Tennessee, to September, 1865.

SERVICE.—Guard Block Houses on Nashville & Chattanooga R. R. by Detachments from Nashville to Duck River till September. Mustered out September 4, 1865.

Regiment lost during service by disease 71.

156th REGIMENT INFANTRY.

Organized February 16, 1865. Moved to Nashville, Tenn., and attached to 3rd Brigade, 2nd Separate Division, District of the Etowah, Department of the Cumberland.

SERVICE.—Engaged in guarding R. R. and Post duty in Department of the Cumberland till September. Mustered out September 20, 1865. Regiment lost during service 2 Enlisted men killed and 24 Enlisted men by disease. Total 26.

FIRST TROOPS IN SERVICE—ON EXPEDITION TO CAIRO.

CHICAGO LIGHT ARTILLERY COMPANY.—Organized April 21. Discharged May 2, 1861.

LOCKPORT ARTILLERY COMPANY.—Organized April 22. Discharged July 31, 1861.

CHICAGO ZOUAVES, COMPANY "A."—Organized April 19. Discharged May 3, 1861.

CHICAGO ZOUAVES, COMPANY "B."—Organized April 15. Discharged April 29, 1861.

CHICAGO LIGHT INFANTRY COMPANY.—Organized April 19. Discharged May 3, 1861.

TURNER UNION CADETS.—Organized April 15. Discharged April 29, 1861.

LINCOLN RIFLES.—Organized April 15. Discharged April 29, 1861.

LIGHT ARTILLERY COMPANY.—Organized April 21. Discharged April 29, 1861.

HOUGHTAILING'S OTTAWA COMPANY.—Organized April 18. (Co. "F," 110th Illinois Infantry. 3 Mos.)

CAIRO SANDWICH COMPANY.—Organized April 19. (Co. "C," 10th Illinois Infantry. 3 Mos.)

Participating in Swift's Cairo Expedition, April 21-29, 1861.

STURGIS' RIFLES.

Organized at Chicago, Ill., April —, and mustered in May 6, 1861. Ordered to West Virginia June 15 and reported at Parkersburg, W. Va. Assigned to duty as Body Guard to Gen. George B. McClellan, Commanding Army of West Virginia. West Virginia Campaign July 6-17. Battle of Rich Mountain July 10-11. Moved with Gen. McClellan to Washington, D. C., July 25 and guard duty at Headquarters Army of the Potomac till November, 1862. Participating in the Virginia Peninsula Campaign March to August, 1862. Siege of Yorktown. Battles of the seven days before Richmond. Maryland Campaign, Battle of Antietam, Md., and movement to Falmouth, Va. Mustered out November 25, 1862.

INDIANA VOLUNTEERS.

1st REGIMENT CAVALRY.

(28th Regiment Volunteers.)

Organized at Evansville, Ind., and mustered in August 20, 1861. Left State for St. Louis, Mo., August 21; thence moved to Ironton, Mo. Duty at and near Ironton till February, 1862. Skirmish at Black River, Ironton, September 12, 1861. Operations about Ironton and Fredericktown October 12-21. Skirmish at Fredericktown October 18. Action at Fredericktown October 21. Attached to Dept. of Missouri to February, 1862. District of Southeast Missouri to May, 1862. 1st Division, Army of Southwest Missouri, to July, 1862. District of Eastern Arkansas, Dept. of Missouri, to December, 1862. 1st Brigade, 3rd (Cavalry) Division, District of Eastern Arkansas, Dept. of the Tennessee, to April, 1863. 1st Brigade, 2nd Cavalry Division, 13th Army Corps, Dept. of the Tennessee, to April, 1863. 1st Brigade, Cavalry Division, District of Eastern Arkansas, to June, 1863. Clayton's Independent Cavalry Brigade, District of Eastern Arkansas, to July, 1863. Clayton's Cavalry Brigade, 13th Division, 16th Army Corps, to August, 1863. Clayton's Cavalry Brigade, Arkansas Expedition, to January, 1864. Clayton's Cavalry Brigade, 7th Army Corps, Dept. of Arkansas, to September, 1864. 1st Brigade, Cavalry Division, 7th Army Corps, to February, 1865. Mouth of White River, Ark., and St. Charles, Ark. 7th Army Corps to June, 1865. Company "C" detached and with 12th Division, 13th Army Corps, Army of the Tennessee, to August, 1863. Cavalry Brigade, 13th Army Corps, Dept. of the Gulf, to September, 1863. 2nd Brigade, Cavalry Division, Dept. of the Gulf, to November, 1863. 3rd Brigade, Cavalry Division, Dept. of the Gulf, to December, 1863. Defences of New Orleans, La., Dept. of the Gulf, to July, 1864. Rejoined Regiment at Pine Bluff, Ark.

(For Companies "I" and "K" see Stewart's and Bracken's Cavalry Companies.)

SERVICE.—Scouting and skirmishing in Missouri and Arkansas February to June, 1862. Reconnoissance from Greenville to St. Francisville February 23-25 (Detachment). Mingo Creek, near St. Francisville, February 24 (Detachment). Moved to Doniphan March 27-April 1, and to Pocahontas April 17. Litchfield, Ark., May 2. Eleven Points June 1. Operations in Fulton County, Mo., June 1-5. March to Helena, Ark., June 26-July 14. Hill's Plantation, Cache River, July 7. Duty at Helena till July, 1863. Expedition from Helena to Clarendon August 4-17, 1862. Expedition from Clarendon to Lawrenceville and St. Charles September 11-13. Expedition from Helena to Moro November 5-8 (Detachment). Expedition from Helena to Arkansas Post November 16-21. Expedition from Helena to Grenada, Miss., November 27-December 5. Junction Coldwater and Tallahatchie Rivers November 29. Tallahatchie River November 30 (Detachment). Near Mitchell's Cross Roads December 1. Oakland December 3. Near Coldwater River February 19, 1863. Near Yazoo Pass February 19 (Detachment). Coldwater March 14. Languelle Creek May 11. Taylor's Creek and Crowley's Ridge May 11. Expedition from Helena to Napoleonville May 23-26 (Detachment). Near Island No. 65, Mississippi River, May 25 (Detachment). Repulse of Holmes' Attack on Helena July 4. Steele's Expedition to Little Rock August 1-September 14. Action at Bayou Fourche and capture of Little Rock September 10. Pursuit of Price September 11-14. Near Little Rock September 11. Moved to Pine Bluff September 14, and duty there till March, 1864. Tulip October 12, 1863. Pine Bluff October 25. Branchville, Ivey's Ford, Pine Bluff, January 19, 1864. Steele's Expedition to Camden February 23-May 3. Branchville March 27. Expedition from Pine Bluff to Mt. Elba and Longview March 27-31. Longview March 29. Mt. Elba and pursuit to Big Creek March 30. Marks' Mills April 25 (Detachment). At Pine Bluff and Little Rock till October, 1864. Walter's Plantation June 7. Expedition from Pine Bluff September 9-11 (Detachment). Near Monticello September 10. Brewer's Lane September 11. Near Pine Bluff September 13 (2 Companies). Reconnoissance from Little Rock to Monticello and Mt. Elba October 4-11. Veterans and Recruits consolidated to a Battalion of 2 Companies, and duty at Pine Bluff till January, 1865. Moved to mouth of White River and duty there till March 20, 1865. At St. Charles till June, 1865. Mustered out May 31 and discharged June 22, 1865.

Company "C" detached as escort to Gen. Hovey, February to July, 1863. Expedition to Yazoo Pass February 24-April 8, 1863. Moved to Milliken's Bend, La., April 12. Advance on Bruinsburg and turning Grand Gulf April 25-30. Battle of Port Gibson May 1. Fourteen-Mile Creek May 12-13. Battle of Champion's Hill May 16. Siege of Vicksburg May 18-July 4. Advance on Jackson, Miss., July 4-10. Siege of Jackson July 10-17. Ordered to New Orleans, La., August, thence to Brashear City and Berwick; Western Louisiana "Teche" Campaign October 3-November 30. Reconnoissance toward Opelousas October 20. Opelousas and Barre Landing October 21. Bayou Portage October 23. Moved to New Orleans, La., and duty there till July 7, 1864. Cypress Creek March 8, 1864. Rejoined Regiment at Pine Bluff, Ark.

Regiment lost during service 4 Officers and 32 Enlisted men killed and mortally wounded and 3 Officers and 148 Enlisted men by disease. Total 187.

2nd REGIMENT CAVALRY.
(41st Regiment Volunteers.)

Organized at Indianapolis, Ind., September 20, 1861. Left State for Louisville, Ky., December 15, 1861; thence moved to Camp Wickliffe, Ky. Attached to Cavalry 4th Division, Army of the Ohio, to June, 1862. Cavalry Brigade, Army of the Ohio, to September, 1862. 1st Brigade, Cavalry Division, Army of the Ohio, to November, 1862. 1st Brigade, Cavalry Division, Army of the Cumberland, to January, 1863. 2nd Brigade, 1st. Cavalry Division, Army of the Cumberland, to October, 1864. 2nd Brigade, 1st Division, Wilson's Cavalry Corps, Military Division of the Mississippi, to July, 1865.

SERVICE.—Action at Bowling Green, Ky., February 1, 1862 (Co. "H"). Movement to Nashville, Tenn., February 14-25. Occupation of Nashville February 25. March to Pittsburg Landing, Tenn., March 10-April 8. Reconnoissance in force April 22. Advance on and siege of Corinth, Miss., April 29-May 30. Tuscumbia Creek May 31-June 1. Pursuit to Booneville June 1-3. Osborn and Wolf's Creeks June 4. Buell's Campaign in North Alabama and Middle Tennessee June to August. Raid on Louisville & Nashville R. R. August 19-21 (Detachment). Humboldt Road, near Gallatin, August 21. Murfreesboro, Tenn., August 20-25-27 and September 7. Crab Orchard, Ky., September 10. Vinegar Hill September 22. Near Nashville October 1. Near Perryville, Ky., October 6-7. Chaplin Hills,

Perryville, October 8. Near Mountain Gap, Ky., October 14-16. Big Rockcastle River, near Mt. Vernon, October 16. New Haven October 29. Capture of 3rd Georgia Cavalry. Hartsville, Tenn., November 28 and December 7. Regiment complimented in special field orders for recapture of Government train and 200 prisoners. Advance on Murfreesboro December 26-30 (Co. "M"). Lavergne December 26-27 (Co. "M"). Operations near Lavergne December 29-31 (Co. "M"). Battle of Stone's River December 30-31, 1862, and January 1-3, 1863 (Co. "M"). Duty near Nashville, Tenn., till June, 1863. Murfreesboro March 10. Shelbyville Pike, near Murfreesboro, June 6. Triune June 9 and 11. Middle Tennessee (or Tullahoma) Campaign June 23-July 7. Middleton June 24. Guy's Gap, Fosterville and Shelbyville June 27. Bethpage Bridge, Elk River, July 1. Occupation of Middle Tennessee till August 16. Expedition to Huntsville July 13-22. Passage of Cumberland Mountains and Tennessee River and Chickamauga (Ga.) Campaign August 16-September 22. Reconnoissance toward Rome September 11. Alpine September 12. Dirt Town, LaFayette Road, near Chattooga River, September 12. Reconnoissance from Lee and Gordon's Mills toward LaFayette and skirmish September 13. Near Stevens' Gap September 18. Battle of Chickamauga, Ga., September 19-21. Missionary Ridge and Shallow Ford Gap September 22. Operations against Wheeler and Roddy September 30-October 17. Fayetteville October 13-14. Duty along Nashville & Chattanooga R. R. till December. Operations about Dandridge and Mossy Creek December 24-28. Peck's House, near New Market, December 24. Mossy Creek December 26. Talbot Station December 28. Mossy Creek, Talbot Station, December 29. Regiment re-enlisted January 10, 1864. Near Mossy Creek January 11-12. Operations about Dandridge January 16-17. Bend of Chucky Road, near Dandridge, January 16. Dandridge January 17. Operations about Dandridge January 26-28. Fair Garden January 27. Swann's Island January 28. Near Marysville February 8. Atlanta (Ga.) Campaign May 1 to September 8. Varnell's Station May 7 and 9. Demonstrations on Dalton May 9-13. Tilton May 13. Battle of Resaca May 14-15. Cassville May 19. Stilesborough May 23. Burnt Hickory May 24. Battles about Dallas May 25-June 5. Ackworth June 3-4. Big Shanty June 6. Operations about Marietta and against Kenesaw Mountain June 10-July 2. Lost Mountain June 15-17. Assault on Kenesaw June 27. Nickajack Creek July 2-5. Chattahoochie River July 5-17. Siege of Atlanta July 22-August 25. McCook's Raid on Atlanta & West Point R. R. July 27-31. Lovejoy Station July 29-30. Clear Creek July 30. Newnan July 30. Expedition to Jasper August 11-15. Flank movement on Jonesboro August 25-30. Rousseau's pursuit of Wheeler September 1-8. Consolidated to a Battalion of 4 Companies September 14. Cartersville September 20. Camp Creek September 30. Operations against Hood in North Georgia and North Alabama October. Moved to Louisville, Ky., to refit. Pursuit of Lyon from Paris, Ky., to Hopkinsville, Ky., December 6, 1864, to January 15, 1865. Hopkinsville, Ky., December 16, 1864. Moved to Nashville, Tenn., duty there till February, 1865, and at Waterloo, Ala., till March. Wilson's Raid from Chickasaw, Ala., to Macon, Ga., March 22-April 24. Near Scottsville and Selma April 2. Near Hinton April 10. Montgomery April 12. Columbus Road, near Tuskegee, April 14. West Point and near Opelika April 16. Capture of Macon April 20. Duty at Macon and in the Dept. of Georgia till June. Moved to Nashville, Tenn., and there mustered out July 12, 1865.

Regiment lost during service 4 Officers and 38 Enlisted men killed and mortally wounded and 3 Officers and 211 Enlisted men by disease. Total 256.

3rd REGIMENT CAVALRY (45th REGIMENT VOLUNTEERS).

Right Wing (Cos. "A," "B," "C," "D," "E" and "F") organized at Madison, Ind., August 22, 1861, for 1st

Cavalry. Moved to Washington, D. C., September, 1861. Designated 3rd Cavalry October 22, 1861. Attached to Hooker's Division, Army of the Potomac, to March, 1862. Lower Maryland, Middle Department, to May, 1862. Geary's Independent Brigade, Dept. of the Rappahannock, to June, 1862. Shields' Division, Dept. of the Rappahannock, to July, 1862. Farnsworth's 2nd Brigade, Pleasanton's Cavalry Division, Army of the Potomac, to November, 1862. 2nd Brigade, Cavalry Division, Army of the Potomac, to February, 1863. 1st Brigade, 1st Division, Cavalry Corps, Army of the Potomac, to April, 1864. 2nd Brigade, 3rd Division, Cavalry Corps, Army of the Potomac, and Army of the Shenandoah, Middle Military Division, to June, 1865. Louisville, Ky., to August, 1865.

SERVICE.—Duty at Budd's Ferry, Md., till December, 1861. Assigned to duty in Lower Maryland by Detachments till May, 1862. Capture of Sloop "Victory," December 15, 1861. Companies "A," "B" and "F" in St. Mary's County December, 1861, to April, 1862. Company "E" at Maryland Point and Port Tobacco December, 1861, to April, 1862. Regiment moved to Washington, D. C., May 3; thence to Thoroughfare Gap, Va., May 25. Action at Wardensville May 28. Joined Shield's Command at Luray June 16, and movement to Front Royal. At Bristoe Station till July 7 and at Falmouth, Va., till August 25. Action at Mt. Carmel Church July 23. Reconnoissance to Orange Court House July 24-26. Expedition to Frederick's Hall Station and Spottsylvania Court House August 5-8. Thornburg's Mills and Massaponax Church August 5-6. Pope's Campaign in Northern Virginia. Centreville August 26. Battle of Bull Run August 29-30. Centreville and Chantilly August 31. Maryland Campaign September-October. Poolesville, Md., September 7-8. Nolansville September 9. Barnesville and Monocacy Church September 9. Sugar Loaf Mountain September 10-11. Catoctin Mountain and Middletown September 13. South Mountain September 14. Battle of Antietam September 16-17. Shepherdstown Ford September 19. Reconnoissance to Martinsburg and Shephardstown, W. Va., October 1. Pursuit of Stuart into Pennsylvania October 9-12. Mouth of Monocacy October 12. Philomont November 1-2. Union November 2-3. Upperville and Bloomfield November 2-3. Barber's Cross Roads November 5-6. Waterloo Bridge November 7. Little Washington November 8. Battle of Fredericksburg, Va., December 12-15. "Mud March" January 20-24, 1863. Chancellorsville Campaign April 27-May 6. Stoneman's Raid April 29-May 8. Rapidan Station May 1. Brandy Station and Beverly Ford June 9. Upperville and Middleburg June 21. Battle of Gettysburg, Pa., July 1-3. Williamsport, Md., July 6. Boonsboro July 8. Benevola (or Beaver Creek) July 9. Funkstown July 10-13. Falling Waters July 14. Chester Gap, July 21-22. Kelly's Ford July 31-August 1. Brandy Station August 1-3 and August 4. Advance from the Rappahannock to the Rapidan September 13-17. Culpeper Court House September 13. Raccoon Ford September 14-16. Reconnoissance across the Rapidan September 21-23. Jack's Shop, Madison Court House, September 22. Raccoon Ford September 22. Rapidan Campaign October 9-22. Raccoon and Morton's Fords October 10. Stevensburg, near Kelly's Ford, and Brandy Station October 11. Brandy Station, or Fleetwood, October 12. Oak Hill October 15. Near Bealeton October 25-26. Catlett's Station November 1. Advance to line of the Rappahannock November 7-8. Muddy Run, Culpeper, November 8. Mine Run Campaign November 26-December 2. Parker's Store November 29. Scout from Culpeper to Madison Court House January 20, 1864. Demonstration on the Rapidan February 6-7. Barnett's Ford February 6-7. Kilpatrick's Raid to Richmond February 28-March 4. Fortifications of Richmond, Hanover Junction and Ashland March 1. Rapidan Campaign May-June. Near Chancellorsville May 4. Craig's Meeting House May 5. Wilderness May 5-7. Alsop's Farm, Spottsylvania, May 8. Sheridan's Raid to the James River May 9-24.

North Anna River May 9-10. Ground Squirrel Church and Yellow Tavern May 11. Brook Church (or Richmond Fortifications) May 12. Demonstration on Little Run May 26. On line of the Pamunkey May 26-28. Salem Church May 27. Totopotomoy May 28-31. Mechump's Creek May 31. Cold Harbor June 1-12. Totopotomoy, Gaines' Mill, Salem Church and Haw's Shop June 2. Haw's Shop and near Via's House June 3. Long Bridge June 12. Riddell's Shop June 13. White Oak Swamp June 13. Siege of Petersburg till August. Ream's Station June 22. Wilson's Raid to Southside & Danville R. R. June 22-30. Nottaway Court House and Black and White Station June 23. Staunton River Bridge (or Roanoke Station) June 25. Sappony Church (or Stony Creek) June 28-29. Ream's Station June 29. Jarrett's Station June 30. Ream's Station June 30-July 3. Ream's Station July 7 and 22. Sheridan's Shenandoah Valley Campaign August 7-November 28. Winchester August 17. Near Kearneysville August 25. Near Brucetown and Winchester September 7. Battle of Opequan, Winchester, September 19. Near Cedarville September 20. Front Royal September 21. Milford September 22. Waynesboro September 29 and October 2. Back Road, near Strasburg, October 7. Near Kernstown November 10. Newtown November 12. Cedar Creek and Rude's Hill, near New Market, November 22. Expedition from Kernstown to Lacey Springs December 19-22. Lacey Springs December 21. Sheridan's Raid from Winchester February 27-March 25, 1865. Waynesboro March 2. Ashland March 15. Appomattox Campaign March 28-April 9. Dinwiddie Court House March 30-31. Five Forks April 1. Deep Creek April 3. Sailor's Creek April 5. Appomattox Station April 8. Appomattox Court House April 9. Surrender of Lee and his army. Grand Review at Washington, D. C., May 23. Moved to Louisville, Ky. Mustered out August 7, 1865.

3rd REGIMENT CAVALRY, LEFT WING.

Companies "G," "H," "I" and "K," Left Wing, organized at Madison, Ind., October 1, 1861. Never joined Regiment. Company "L" organized October, 1862. Joined Left Wing in East Tennessee. Company "M" organized December 11, 1862. Joined Left Wing in East Tennessee. Left Wing moved to Kentucky October, 1861. Company "G" attached to 1st Division, Army of the Ohio, to June, 1862. Company "H" to 2nd Division, Army of the Ohio, to June, 1862. Company "I" to 4th Division, Army of the Ohio, to June, 1862, and Company "K" to Dumont's Independent Brigade, Army of the Ohio, to June, 1862. Cavalry Brigade, Army of the Ohio, to September, 1862. Cavalry, 1st Corps, Army of the Ohio, to November, 1862. Cavalry, Right Wing, 14th Army Corps, Army of the Cumberland, to January, 1863. 1st Brigade, 2nd Cavalry Division, Army of the Cumberland, to April, 1864. 1st Brigade, Kilpatrick's 3rd Cavalry Division, Army of the Cumberland, to November, 1864, and 2nd Brigade, Kilpatrick's 3rd Division, Cavalry Corps, Military Division Mississippi, to December, 1864.

SERVICE.—Duty at Camp Wickliffe, Ky., till February, 1862. Advance on Nashville, Tenn., February 10-March 2. March to Savannah, Tenn., March 16-April 6. Battle of Shiloh, Tenn., April 7. Advance on and siege of Corinth, Miss., April 29-May 30. Pursuit to Booneville May 30-June 12. Shelbyville June 21. Sparta, Tenn., June 28. Buell's Campaign in North Alabama and Middle Tennessee June to August. (Co. "K" Garrison at Nashville and scout duty till August. Dumont's Expedition over Cumberland Mountains, June.) March to Louisville, Ky., in pursuit of Bragg August 21-September 26. Pursuit of Bragg into Kentucky October 1-22. March to Nashville, Tenn., and duty there till December 26. (Cos. "L" and "M" on duty at Indianapolis, Ind., till December, 1863; then joined in East Tennessee.) Reconnoissance to Lavergne November 26-27. Lavergne, Scrougesville November 27. Kimbrough's Mills, Mill Creek, December 6. Near Nashville December 23. Advance on Murfreesboro December 26-30. Triune and Nolensville December 27. Battle of Stone's River December 30-31, 1862, and January 1-3, 1863. Lytle's Creek and Manchester Pike January 5. Expedition to Auburn, Liberty and Alexandria February 3-5. Christiana and Middleton March 6. Methodist Church, Shelbyville Pike, March 6. Middleton March 7. Franklin April 10. Shelbyville Pike April 23. Expedition to Middleton May 21-22. Middleton May 21-22. Near Murfreesboro June 3. Scout on Middleton and Eaglesville Pike June 10. Scout on Manchester Pike June 13. Expedition to Lebanon June 15-17. Lebanon June 16. Middle Tennessee (or Tullahoma) Campaign June 23-July 7. Guy's Gap, Fosterville and Shelbyville June 27. University Depot July 4. Expedition to Huntsville July 13-22. Reconnoissance to Rock Island Ferry August 4-5. Sparta August 9. Calf Killer River August 17. March over Cumberland Mountains, passage of Tennessee River and Chickamauga (Ga.) Campaign August 17-September 22. Reed's Bridge September 18. Battle of Chickamauga September 19-21. Rossville Gap September 21. Operations against Wheeler and Roddy September 30-October 17. Cottonport September 30. McMinnville October 4. Chattanooga-Ringgold Campaign November 23-27. March to Relief of Knoxville, Tenn., November 28-December 8. Kingston December 4. Campaign in East Tennessee December, 1863, to April, 1864. Expedition from Marysville up Little Tennessee River January 11-12, 1864. Somerville Road, near Knoxville, February 20. Chucky Bend March 12. Bent Creek and Spring Hill March 13. Bull's Gap March 15. Near Greenville April 15. Rheatown April 16. Expedition from Bull's Gap to Watauga River April 25-27. Watauga Bridge April 25-26. Atlanta (Ga.) Campaign May to September. Lee's Cross Roads and near Ringgold Gap May 2. Demonstrations on Resaca May 8-13. Near Resaca May 13. Battle of Resaca May 14-15. Advance on Dallas May 18-25. Operations on line of Pumpkin Vine Creek and battles about Dallas, New Hope Church and Allatoona Hills May 25-June 5. Operations about Marietta and against Kenesaw Mountain June 10-July 2. Calhoun June 10. Lost Mountain June 15-17. Assault on Kenesaw June 27. On line of the Chattahoochie River July 5-18. Siege of Atlanta July 22-August 25. Sandtown and Fairburn August 15. Flank movement on Jonesboro August 25-30. Fairburn August 27-28. Flint River Station August 30. Battle of Jonesboro August 31-September 1. Lovejoy Station September 2-6. Operations against Hood in North Georgia and North Alabama September 29-November 3. Camp Creek September 30. Van Wert October 9-10 and 14. March to the sea November 15-December 10. Siege of Savannah December 10-21. Transferred to 8th Indiana Cavalry December, 1864.

Regiment lost during service 1 Officer and 62 Enlisted men killed and mortally wounded and 1 Officer and 130 Enlisted men by disease. Total 194.

4th REGIMENT INFANTRY (77th REGIMENT VOLUNTEERS).

Organized at Indianapolis, Ind., and mustered in August 22, 1862. 4 Companies ordered to Henderson, Ky. Regiment to Louisville, Ky. Served Unattached Army of Kentucky, Dept. of the Ohio, to November, 1862. District of Western Kentucky, Dept. of the Ohio, to March, 1863. 2nd Brigade, 1st Cavalry Division, Army of the Cumberland, to October, 1864. 2nd Brigade, 1st Division Cavalry Corps, Military Division Mississippi, to June, 1865. (Co. "C" served detached at Headquarters of Gen. A. J. Smith, October, 1862, to August, 1863.) Cavalry Brigade, 13th Army Corps, Dept. of the Gulf, to September, 1863. 2nd Brigade, Cavalry Division, Dept. of the Gulf, to November, 1863. 3rd Brigade, Cavalry Division, Dept. of the Gulf, to January, 1864. 1st Brigade, Cavalry Division, Dept. of the Gulf, to June, 1864. Unattached Dept. of the Gulf to September, 1864.

SERVICE.—Actions at Madisonville, Ky., August 25 and September 5, 1862 (4 Companies). Lebanon Junction, Ky., September 21. Floyd's Forks October 1. Bardstown Pike, near Mt. Washington, Ky., October 1. Madisonville October 5. Duty in Western Kentucky till January, 1863. Operations against Morgan December 22, 1862, to January 2, 1863. Bear Wallow December 23. Munfordsville December 25. Burksville Road, near Green's Chapel, December 25. Ordered to Murfreesboro, Tenn., January, 1863. Near Murfreesboro January 21. Expedition to Auburn, Liberty and Alexandria February 3-5. Franklin April 10. Triune June 9 and 11. Middle Tennessee (or Tullahoma) Campaign June 23-July 7. Eaglesville and Rover June 23. Middleton June 24. Guy's Gap, Fosterville and Shelbyville June 27. Bethpage Bridge, Elk River, July 1. Expedition to Huntsville July 13-22. Chickamauga (Ga.) Campaign August 16-September 22. Reconnoissance toward Rome, Ga., September 11. Alpine September 12. Dirt Town, Lafayette road, near Chattooga River September 13. Reconnoissance from Lee and Gordon's Mills toward Lafayette, and Skirmish, September 13. Near Summerville September 13. Near Stevens' Gap September 18. Battle of Chickamauga September 19-21. Operations against Wheeler and Roddy September 29-October 17. Valley Road, near Jasper, October 2. Scout to Fayetteville October 29-November 2. Fayetteville November 1. Chattanooga-Ringgold Campaign November 23-27. March to relief of Knoxville November 28-December 8. Mossy Creek Station December 24. Peck's House, near New Market, December 24. Operations about Dandridge and Mossy Creek December 24-28. Mossy Creek December 26. Talbot's Station December 28. Mossy Creek, Talbot's Station, December 29. Near Mossy Creek January 11-12, 1864 (Detachment). Operations about Dandridge January 16-17, 1864. Bend of Chucky Road, near Dandridge, January 16. Dandridge January 17. Operations about Dandridge January 26-28. Fair Garden January 27. Swann's Island January 28. Reconnoissance toward Seviersville February 1-2. Dandridge February 17. Atlanta (Ga.) Campaign May to September. Demonstrations on Dalton May 9-13. Tilton May 13. Battle of Resaca May 14-15. Advance on Dallas May 18-25. Stilesboro May 23. Burnt Hickory May 24. Operations on line of Pumpkin Vine Creek and battles about Dallas, New Hope Church and Allatoona Hills May 25-June 5. Near Burned Church May 26 and May 30-June 1. Ackworth June 3-4. Big Shanty June 6. Ackworth June 10. Operations about Marietta and against Kenesaw Mountain June 10-July 2. Allatoona June 15. Lost Mountain June 15-17. Assault on Kenesaw June 27. On line of Nickajack Creek July 2-5. Chattahoochie River July 5-17. Siege of Atlanta July 22-August 25. McCook's Raid on Atlanta and West Point R. R. July 27-31. Campbellton July 28. Lovejoy Station July 29. Clear Creek and Newnan's July 30. Expedition to Jasper August 11-15. Flank movement on Jonesboro August 25-30. Rousseau's pursuit of Wheeler September 24-October 1. Pulaski September 26-27. Operations against Hood till November. Ordered to Louisville, Ky., and duty there refitting till December. Pursuit of Lyons from Paris to Hopkinsville, Ky., December 6, 1864, to January 15, 1865. Action at Hopkinsville December 16, 1864. At Nashville, Tenn., till February, 1865, and at Waterloo, Ala., till March. Wilson's Raid to Macon, Ga., March 22-April 24. Centreville April 2. Selma April 2. Montgomery April 12. Columbus Road, near Tuskegee, April 14. Fort Tyler, West Point, April 16. Near Opelika April 16. Near Barnesville April 19. Capture of Macon April 20. Duty at Macon till May and at Nashville and Edgefield, Tenn., till June. Mustered out June 29, 1865.

Company "C" served detached from Regiment at Headquarters of Gen. A. J. Smith, Commanding 10th Division, 13th Army Corps, Army of the Tennessee, December, 1862, to August, 1863, participating in the following service: Movement to Memphis, Tenn., November, 1862. Sherman's Yazoo Expedition December

20, 1862, to January 3, 1863. Chickasaw Bayou and Bluff December 26-29. Expedition to Arkansas Post, Ark., January 3-10, 1863. Capture of Fort Hindman, Arkansas Post, January 10-11. Reconnoissance to White River and St. Charles January 13, 1863. Moved to Young's Point, La., January 17. Duty there and at Milliken's Bend till April. Movement on Bruinsburg and turning Grand Gulf April 25-30. Battle of Port Gibson May 1. Battle of Champion's Hill May 16. Siege of Vicksburg, Miss., May 18-July 4. Advance on Jackson, Miss., July 4-10. Near Baker's Creek July 7. Bolton's Depot and near Clinton July 8. Jackson July 9. Siege of Jackson July 10-17. Brookhaven July 18. Moved to New Orleans, La., August. Western Louisiana Campaign October 3-November 30. Reconnoissance toward Opelousas October 20. Opelousas and Barre Landing October 21. Grand Coteau November 3. Duty in defences of New Orleans till September 1, 1864.

Regiment lost during service 3 Officers and 25 Enlisted men killed and mortally wounded and 5 Officers and 193 Enlisted men by disease. Total 226.

5th REGIMENT CAVALRY (90th REGIMENT VOLUNTEERS).

Organized at Indianapolis, Ind., August 22 to October 30, 1862. Companies "C" and "F" at Carrollton, Ky. Company "I" at Rising Sun, Ind. Companies "A" and "G" at Newburg, Ind. Company "B" at Rockport, Ind. Companies "D" and "L" at Manckport, Ind. Companies "E" and "H" at Cannelton, Ind. Company "K" at Mt. Vernon, Ind., and Company "M" at Evansville, Ind., December, 1862, to February, 1863. Regiment moved to Louisville, Ky., February 28, 1863; thence to Glasgow, Ky., March 4-11. (Cos. "C," "F" and "I" moved to Louisville, Ky., December, 1862; thence to Munfordsville, Ky., and joined Regiment at Glasgow, Ky., March, 1863.) Attached to District of Western Kentucky, Dept. of the Ohio, to June, 1863. 1st Brigade, 3rd Division, 23rd Army Corps, Dept. of the Ohio, to August, 1863. 2nd Brigade, 4th Division, 23rd Army Corps, to October, 1863. 4th Brigade, 4th Division, 23rd Army Corps, to November, 1863. 2nd Brigade, 2nd Division, Cavalry Corps, Dept. of the Ohio, to May, 1864. 1st Brigade, Cavalry Division, 23rd Army Corps, to July, 1864. 2nd Brigade, Cavalry Division, 23rd Army Corps, to August, 1864. Dismounted Cavalry Brigade, Cavalry Division 23rd Army Corps, to September, 1864. 1st Brigade, Cavalry Division, 23rd Army Corps, to September, 1864. Louisville, Ky., to November, 1864. 1st Brigade, 6th Division, Wilson's Cavalry Corps, Military Division Mississippi, to December, 1864. 2nd Brigade, 6th Division, Cavalry Corps, Military Division Mississippi, to June, 1865.

SERVICE.—Operations against Morgan in Kentucky December 22, 1862, to January 2, 1863 (Cos. "C," "F," "I"). Action Burkesville Road, near Green's Chapel, December 25, 1862 (Cos. "C," "F," "I"). Scout duty from Glasgow, Ky., toward the Cumberland River till April 17, 1863. Expedition to the Cumberland River April 18-22. Skirmish at Cumberland River April 18. Celina April 19. Scouting in the vicinity of Glasgow till June 22. Marrow Bone Creek, Tenn., May 18. Near Edmonton, Ky., June 7. Expedition from Glasgow to Burkesville and Tennessee State line June 8-10. Kettle Creek June 9. Moved to Tompkinsville June 22. Pursuit of Morgan July 4-26. Buffington Island, Ohio, July 19. March from Louisville to Glasgow July 27-August 8. Burnside's Campaign in East Tennessee August 16-October 17. Occupation of Knoxville, Tenn., September 2. Rheatown September 12. Kingsport September 18. Bristol, Va., September 19. Zollicoffer September 20-21. Jonesborough September 21. Hall's Ford, Watauga River, September 22. Carter's Depot and Blountsville September 22. Blue Springs October 10. Henderson's Mill October 11. Rheatown October 11. Blountsville October 14. Bristol October 15. Warm Springs October 20 and 26. Knoxville Campaign November 4-December 23. Siege of Knoxville November

17-December 5. Log Mountain December 3. Walker's Ford, Clinch River, December 5. Bean's Station December 14. Blain's Cross Roads December 16-19. Clinch River December 21. Morristown Road January 16, 1864. Kimbrough's Mills January 16. Operations about Dandridge January 16-17 and January 26-28. Near Fair Garden January 27. March to Knoxville, thence to Cumberland Gap January 29-February 10. March to Mt. Sterling, Ky., February 17-26. Duty at Mt. Sterling, Paris and Nicholasville, Ky., till May 1. March to Tunnel Hill, Ga., May 1-12. Atlanta (Ga.) Campaign May to September. Varnell's Station May 7 and 9. Demonstration on Dalton May 9-13. Battle of Resaca May 14-15. Cassville May 19. Operations on line of Pumpkin Vine Creek and battles about Dallas, New Hope Church and Allatoona Hills May 25-June 5. Mt. Zion Church May 27-28. Stoneman's Hill May 29. Operations about Marietta and against Kenesaw Mountain June 10-July 2. Lost Mountain June 15-17. Allatoona June 23-25 and 30. Nickajack Creek July 2-5. Mitchell's Cross Roads July 4. Chattahoochie River July 5-17. Campbellton July 10. Marietta July 19. Stoneman's Raid to Macon July 27-August 6. Clinton and Macon July 30. Sunshine Church, Hillsboro, July 30-31 (most of Regiment captured). Dismounted men on guard duty at Decatur and Atlanta till September 13. Ordered to Louisville, Ky., and guard duty there till January, 1865. March to Pulaski, Tenn., January 17-February 12. Post duty at Pulaski and operations against guerrillas in that vicinity till June. Expedition from Pulaski to New Market, Ala., May 5-13. Mustered out June 16, 1865.

Regiment lost during service 1 Officer and 40 Enlisted men killed and mortally wounded and 1 Officer and 188 Enlisted men by disease. Total 230.

6th REGIMENT CAVALRY (71st REGIMENT VOLUNTEERS).

Organized at Indianapolis, Ind., February 23, 1863, from the 71st Indiana Infantry. Company "L" organized September 1, 1863. Company "M" organized October 12, 1863. Regiment left State for Kentucky August 26, 1863. Attached to 1st Division, 23rd Army Corps, Lexington, Ky. Dept. of the Ohio to September, 1863. Wilcox's Command, Left Wing forces 23rd Army Corps, Dept. of the Ohio, to January, 1864. District of the Clinch, Dept. of the Ohio, to April, 1864. 2nd Brigade, 1st Division Cavalry Corps, Dept. of the Ohio, to May, 1864. 1st Brigade, Cavalry Division, 23rd Army Corps, to July, 1864. 2nd Brigade, Cavalry Division, 23rd Army Corps, to August, 1864. Dismounted Brigade, Cavalry Division, 23rd Army Corps, to September, 1864. 1st Brigade, Cavalry Division, 23rd Army Corps, to November, 1864. 2nd Brigade, 6th Division, Wilson's Cavalry Corps, Military Division Mississippi, to June, 1865. District of Middle Tennessee, Dept. of the Cumberland, to September, 1865.

SERVICE.—Reconnoissance to Olympian Springs, Ky., October 8-11, 1863. Moved to Cumberland Gap, Tenn. Knoxville Campaign November 4-December 23. Action at Lenoir Station November 14-15. Campbell's Station November 16. Siege of Knoxville November 17-December 5. Been's Station December 14. Lee County, Va., December 24. Big Springs January 19, 1864 (Detachment). Tazewell January 24. Duty at Mt. Sterling and Nicholasville, Ky., till April. March from Nicholasville to Dalton, Ga., April 29-May 11. Atlanta (Ga.) Campaign May to August. Demonstrations on Dalton May 9-13. Varnell's Station May 12. Battle of Resaca May 14-15. Pine Log Creek May 18. Etowah River, near Cartersville, May 20. Operations on line of Pumpkin Vine Creek and battles about Dallas, New Hope Church and Allatoona Hills May 25-June 5. Allatoona Pass June 1-2. Lost Mountain June 9. Pine Mountain June 10. Operations about Marietta and against Kenesaw Mountain June 10-July 2. Lost Mountain June 11-17. Cheyney's Farm June 27. Assault on Kenesaw June 27. Nickajack Creek July 2-5. Chattahoochie River July 5-17. Sandtown July 6-7,

Campbellton July 12-14. Turner's Ferry July 16 and 22. Siege of Atlanta July 22-August 25. Sweetwater July 23. Stoneman's Raid to Macon July 27-August 6. Macon and Clinton July 30. Hillsborough Sunshine Church July 30-31. Jug Tavern, Mulberry Creek, August 3. Moved to Nashville, Tenn., August 28. Pursuit of Wheeler September 24-October 18. Pulaski, Tenn., September 26-27. Waterloo, Ala., October 3. Moved to Dalton, Ga., November 1, and return to Nashville, Tenn., November 26. Battle of Nashville December 15-16. Duty at Nashville till April 1, 1865. At Pulaski, Tenn., and in Middle Tennessee till September. Non-Veterans mustered out June 17, 1865. Regiment mustered out September 15, 1865.

Regiment lost during service 4 Officers and 66 Enlisted men killed and mortally wounded and 2 Officers and 201 Enlisted men by disease. Total 273.

7th REGIMENT CAVALRY (119th REGIMENT VOLUNTEERS).

Organized at Indianapolis, Ind., and mustered in October 1, 1863. Left State for Union City, Tenn., December 6, 1863. Attached to District of Columbus, Ky. 6th Division, 16th Army Corps, Army of the Tennessee, December, 1863. Waring's Cavalry Brigade, 16th Army Corps, to January, 1864. 1st Brigade, 1st Cavalry Division, 16th Army Corps, to June, 1864. 1st Brigade, 2nd Cavalry Division, District of West Tennessee, to November, 1864. 2nd Brigade, Wilson's Cavalry Corps, Military Division Mississippi, to December, 1864. 1st Brigade, Cavalry Division, District of West Tennessee, to June, 1865. Dept. of Texas to February, 1866.

SERVICE.—Expedition to Paris, Tenn., December 14-23, 1863. Action at Huntington, Tenn., December 27. Expedition from Union City to Trenton January 22-24, 1864. Bolivar February 6 (Detachment). Smith's Expedition to Okolona, Miss., February 11-26. West Point February 20-21. Okolona February 21-22. Ivey's Hill February 22. Hudsonville February 25. Regiment complimented by Generals Smith and Grierson for soldierly bearing and conduct during the Expedition. Near Raleigh, Tenn., April 3. Wolf River April 8. Near Raleigh April 9 (Detachment). Cypress Swamp April 10. Sturgis' Expedition to Ripley, Miss., April 30-May 9. Sturgis' Expedition to Guntown, Miss., June 1-13. Ripley June 7. Brice's Cross Roads (or Tishamingo Creek), near Guntown, June 10. Ripley June 11. White's Station June 20 and 26. Byhalia Road, near Colliersville, July 2. Action at Port Gibson, Miss., July 17. Grand Gulf July 19. Expedition to Oxford, Miss., August 1-30. Tallahatchie River August 7-9. Hurricane Creek August 9-13-14 and 19. Oxford August 9 and 11. Lamar August 14. Colliersville August 28. White Station October 4. Near Memphis October 4 (1 Company). Memphis, Tenn., October 20 and 24. Nonconah Creek October 29 (Co. "F"). March through Arkansas and Missouri in pursuit of Price September-November. Action at Little Blue, Mo., October 21. Independence October 22. Big Blue and State Line October 22. Westport October 23. Mine Creek, Marias des Cygnes, October 25. At the Marmiton, or Battle of Charlot, October 25. Grierson's Expedition from Memphis to destroy Mobile & Ohio R. R. December 21, 1864, to January 15, 1865. Capture of Verona December 25, 1864. Egypt Station December 28. Lexington January 2, 1865. Duty at Memphis and along Memphis & Charleston R. R. till June, 1865. Expedition from Memphis to Marion, Ark., January 19-22 (Detachment). Expedition from Memphis into Northern Mississippi March 3-11, 1865. Moved to Alexandria, La., June 6-16. Consolidated to 6 Companies July 21. March to Hempstead, Texas, August 5-26. Duty there and at Austin, Texas, till February, 1866. Mustered out at Austin, Texas, February 18, 1866.

Regiment lost during service 1 Officer and 47 Enlisted men killed and mortally wounded and 3 Officers and 243 Enlisted men by disease. Total 294.

8th REGIMENT CAVALRY.

Organized at Indianapolis, Ind., as 39th Regiment Infantry, August 29, 1861. Ordered to Kentucky and duty at Muldraugh's Hill, Camp Nevin, Nolin Creek and Green River till February, 1862. Attached to Wood's Brigade, McCook's Command, at Nolin, Army of the Ohio, October-November, 1861. 6th Brigade, Army of the Ohio, to December, 1861. 6th Brigade, 2nd Division, Army of the Ohio, to September, 1862. 6th Brigade, 2nd Division, 1st Army Corps, Army of the Ohio, to November, 1862. 1st Brigade, 2nd Division, Right Wing 14th Army Corps, Army of the Cumberland, to January, 1863. 1st Brigade, 2nd Division, 20th Army Corps, Army of the Cumberland, to April, 1863. Unassigned Cavalry Corps, Army of the Cumberland, to October, 1863. Designation changed to 8th Cavalry October 15, 1863. 1st Brigade, 2nd Division, Cavalry Corps, Army of the Cumberland, to April, 1864. 2nd Brigade, Kilpatrick's 3rd Division, Cavalry Corps, Army of the Cumberland, to October, 1864. 2nd Brigade, 3rd Division, Wilson's Cavalry Corps, Military Division Mississippi, to November, 1864. 1st Brigade, 3rd Division, Cavalry Corps, Military Division Mississippi, to July, 1865.

SERVICE.—Action at Upton's Hill, Ky., October 12, 1861. March to Bowling Green, Ky.; thence to Nashville, Tenn., February 14-March 2, 1862. March to Savannah, Tenn., March 16-April 6. Battle of Shiloh, Tenn., April 6-7. Advance on and siege of Corinth, Miss., April 29-May 30. Pursuit to Booneville May 31-June 6. Buell's Campaign in Northern Alabama and Middle Tennessee June to August. March to Nashville, Tenn.; thence to Louisville, Ky., in pursuit of Bragg August 20-September 26. Pursuit of Bragg into Kentucky October 1-15. Dog Walk October 8-9. March to Bowling Green, Ky.; thence to Nashville, Tenn., October 16-November 7, and duty there till December 26. Advance on Murfreesboro December 26-30. Battle of Stone's River December 30-31, 1862, and January 1-3, 1863. Duty at Murfreesboro till April. Reconnoissance to Middleton March 6-7. Christiana and Middleton March 6. Regiment mounted and changed to mounted infantry April, 1863. Expedition to Middleton May 21-22. Middleton May 22. Shelbyville Pike June 4. Operations on Eaglesville Pike June 4. Near Murfreesboro June 6. Middle Tennessee (or Tullahoma) Campaign June 22-July 7. Christiana June 24. Liberty Gap June 24-27. Tullahoma June 29-30. Occupation of Middle Tennessee till August 16. Passage of Cumberland Mountains and Tennessee River and Chickamauga (Ga.) Campaign August 16-September 22. Davis Ford, Chickamauga Creek, September 17. Battle of Chickamauga September 19-20. Mission Ridge September 22. Shallow Ford Road September 22. Companies "L" and "M" join September, 1863. Expedition to East Tennessee after Champ Ferguson September-October. Designation changed from 39th Infantry to 8th Cavalry October 15, 1863. Courier duty between Chattanooga, Tenn., and Ringgold, Ga., November-December. Operations about Sparta January 4-14, 1864. Mill Creek Gap February 25. Leet's Tan Yard March 5. Near Nickajack Gap March 9. Regiment Veteranize February 22, and Veterans on furlough April-May. Atlanta Campaign July to September. Rousseau's Raid July 10-22, 1864. Ten Island Ford, Coosa River, Ala., July 14. Near Greenpoint July 14. Chehaw Station and Notasulga July 18. Siege of Atlanta July 22-August 25. McCook's Raid to Atlanta & West Point R. R. July 27-31. Lovejoy Station July 29. Clear Creek and near Newnan July 30. Dalton August 14-15. Sandtown August 15. Fairburn August 15. Kilpatrick's Raid around Atlanta August 18-22. Camp Creek August 18. Jonesboro August 19-20. Lovejoy Station August 20. Flank movement on Jonesboro August 25-30. Camp Creek and Flint River Station August 30. Jonesboro August 31-September 1. Lovejoy Station September 2-6. Campbellton September 10. Operations against Hood in North Georgia and North Alabama September 29-November 3. Van Wert October 9-10. March to the sea November 15-December 10. Jonesboro November 15. Lovejoy Station November 16. Griswoldsville November 22. Milledgeville November 23. Sylvan Grove November 27. Waynesborough November 27-28. Near Waynesborough November 28. Buckhead Creek November 28 (Cos. "E," "G"). Buckhead Creek (or Reynolds' Plantation) November 28. Near Louisville November 29. Millen Grove December 1. Waynesboro December 4. Near Springfield December 10. Siege of Savannah December 10-21. Campaign of the Carolinas January to April, 1865. Blackville, S. C., February 7. Williston February 8. Johnson's Station February 10-11. Aiken February 11. Phillip's Cross Roads, N. C., March 4. Taylor's Hole Creek, Averysboro, March 16. Battle of Bentonville March 19-21. Occupation of Goldsboro March 24. Advance on Raleigh April 9-13. Raleigh April 13. Morristown April 13. Bennett's House April 26. Surrender of Johnston and his army. Duty in the Dept. of North Carolina till July. Mustered out July 20, 1865. Dismounted detachment left in Tennessee. Action at Pulaski September 26-27, 1864. Sparta November 29. Franklin November 30. Nashville December 15-16. Pulaski December 25-26.

Regiment lost during service 9 Officers and 138 Enlisted men killed and mortally wounded and 1 Officer and 250 Enlisted men by disease. Total 398.

9th REGIMENT CAVALRY (121st REGIMENT VOLUNTEERS).

Organized at Indianapolis, Ind., December 7, 1863, to March 29, 1864. Left State for Pulaski, Tenn., May 3, 1864. Attached to District of North Alabama, Dept. of the Cumberland, to November, 1864. 1st Brigade, 7th Division, Wilson's Cavalry Corps, Military Division Mississippi, to March, 1865. Dept. of Mississippi to August, 1865.

SERVICE.—Post duty at Pulaski, Tenn., till November 23, 1864. Actions at Florence, Ala., September 1 and 12. Elk River September 2. Lynnville September 4. Sulphur Branch Trestle September 25. Richland Creek, near Pulaski, September 26. Pulaski September 26-27. Nashville Campaign November-December. Owen's Cross Roads December 1. Franklin December 10. Battle of Nashville December 15-16. Pursuit of Hood to the Tennessee River December 17-28. West Harpeth River and Hollow Tree Gap December 17. Franklin December 17. Lynnville December 23. Anthony's Hill, Pulaski, December 25. Sugar Creek December 25-26. At Gravelly Springs January 16 to February 6, 1865. Moved to Vicksburg, Miss.; thence to New Orleans, La., February 6-March 10. Return to Vicksburg, Miss., and duty there March 25 to May 3. Expedition from Rodney to Port Gibson May 3-6. Garrison duty at various points in Mississippi May 3 to August 22. Mustered out August 28, 1865.

Regiment lost during service 4 Officers and 28 Enlisted men killed and mortally wounded and 204 Enlisted men by disease. Total 236.

10th REGIMENT CAVALRY (125th REGIMENT VOLUNTEERS).

Organized at Columbus, Vincennes, Terre Haute, New Albany and Indianapolis, Ind., December 30, 1863, to April 30, 1864. Left State for Nashville, Tenn., May 3, 1864; thence moved to Pulaski, Tenn., June 1. Attached to District of Northern Alabama, Dept. of the Cumberland, to November, 1864. 1st Brigade, 7th Division, Wilson's Cavalry Corps, Military Division Mississippi, to March, 1865. 2nd Brigade, Grierson's 1st Cavalry Division, Military Division West Mississippi, to May, 1865. 3rd Brigade, 1st Cavalry Division, Military Division West Mississippi, to June, 1865. District of Vicksburg, Miss., Dept. of Mississippi, to August, 1865.

SERVICE.—Duty at Pulaski, Tenn., and Decatur, Ala., guarding Northern Alabama R. R. by detachments till November 26, 1864. Action at Elk River

September 2. Sulphur Branch Trestle September 25. Richland Creek, near Pulaski, September 26. Repulse of Forest's attack on Pulaski September 26-27. Athens October 1-2. A Detachment at Decatur, Ala. Siege of Decatur October 26-29. A Detachment moved to Murfreesboro, Tenn., and participated in the Siege of Murfreesboro December 5-17. "The Cedars" December 5-8. Murfreesboro December 13-14. Moved to Nashville, Tenn., November 26. Owen's Cross Roads December 1. Battle of Nashville, Tenn., December 15-16. Pursuit of Hood to the Tennessee River December 17-28. Franklin and Hollow Tree Gap December 17. Sugar Creek, Pulaski, December 25-26. Decatur, Ala., December 27-28 (Detachment). Pond Springs, Ala., December 29 (Detachment). Russellville December 31 (Detachment). Detachments brought together February, 1865. Moved to Vicksburg, Miss.; thence to New Orleans, La., and to Mobile Bay, Ala., February 12-March 22. Campaign against Mobile and its defences March 22-April 12. Siege of Spanish Fort and Fort Blakely March 26-April 9. Capture of Mobile April 12. March to Montgomery April 13-20. March to Columbus and Vicksburg, Miss., and Provost duty in Holmes and Attalla Counties till August. Mustered out at Vicksburg, Miss., August 31, 1865. 3 Paroled Officers and 35 men lost on Steamer "Sultana" April 28, 1865.

Regiment lost during service 1 Officer and 20 Enlisted men killed and mortally wounded and 4 Officers and 157 Enlisted men by disease. Total 182.

11th REGIMENT CAVALRY (126th REGIMENT VOLUNTEERS).

Organized at Lafayette, Kokomo and Indianapolis, Ind., November 10, 1863, to April 2, 1864. Left State for Nashville, Tenn., May 1, 1864. Attached to District of Northern Alabama, Dept. of the Cumberland, to November, 1864. 1st Brigade, 5th Division, Cavalry Corps, Military Division Mississippi, to May, 1865. District of Kansas, Dept. of Missouri, to September, 1865.

SERVICE.—Duty at Nashville, Tenn., May 7 to June 1, 1864. Guard duty along line of Memphis & Charleston R. R. in Alabama. Headquarters at Larkinsville, Ala., till October 16. Defence of Huntsville, Ala., against Buford's attack September 30-October 1. Moved to Nashville, Tenn., October 16. Siege of Decatur, Ala., October 26-29 (Detachment). Nashville Campaign November-December. On line of Shoal Creek November 16-20. Near Maysville and near New Market November 17 (Detachment). In front of Columbia November 24-27. Crossing of Duck River November 28. Battle of Franklin November 30. Near Paint Rock Bridge, Ala., December 7 (Detachment). Battle of Nashville December 15-16. Pursuit of Hood to the Tennessee River December 17-28. West Harpeth River December 17. Richland Creek December 24. Pulaski December 25-26. Hillsboro, Ala., December 29 (Detachment). Near Leighton, Ala., December 30 (Detachment). Duty at Gravelly Springs, Ala., January 7 to February 7, 1865, and at Eastport, Miss., till May 12. Moved to St. Louis, Mo., May 12-17; to Rolla, Mo., June 20-26, and to Fort Riley, Kansas, June 29-July 8. Moved to Council Grove and assigned to duty along Santa Fe route across the plains, Headquarters at Cottonwood Crossing till September 1. March to Fort Leavenworth, Kansas, September 1-11, and there mustered out September 19, 1865.

Regiment lost during service 2 Officers and 11 Enlisted men killed and mortally wounded and 1 Officer and 160 Enlisted men by disease. Total 174.

12th REGIMENT CAVALRY (126th REGIMENT VOLUNTEERS).

Organized at Kendallville, Ind., and Michigan City, Ind., December 10, 1863, to April 28, 1864. Left State for Nashville, Tenn., May 6, 1864. Attached to District of Northern Alabama, Dept. of the Cumberland, to September, 1864. Tullahoma, Tenn.; defences of

Nashville & Chattanooga R. R., Dept. of the Cumberland, to November, 1864. 2nd Brigade, 7th Division, Cavalry Corps, Military Division Mississippi, to February, 1865. 1st Brigade, 1st Cavalry Division, Military Division West Mississippi, to April, 1865. 2nd Brigade, Cavalry Division, Dept. of the Gulf, to May, 1865. Dept. of Mississippi to November, 1865.

SERVICE.—Duty at Nashville, Tenn., till May 29, 1864. Moved to Huntsville, Ala., May 29, and duty there and guarding Railroad from Decatur to Paint Rock, Ala. Headquarters at Huntsville and Brownsborough till September 15. Action at Big Cove Valley June 27. Near Vienna July 8. Scout in Clear Springs and Sink Springs Valleys July 18-21 (Detachment). Flint River, Ala., July 25. Paint Rock Station July 30. Moore's Hill August 11. Operations in Madison County August 12-14. Near Lynchburg September 29 (Detachment). Repulse of Buford's attack on Huntsville September 30-October 1 and October 18 (Cos. "C," "D" and "H"). Regiment moved to Tullahoma, Tenn., September 15, and duty there till November 26. Siege of Decatur, Ala., October 26-29 (Detachment). Near Maysville, Ala., and near New Market, Ala., November 17 (Detachment). Moved to Murfreesboro, Tenn., November 26. Overall's Creek December 4. Siege of Murfreesboro December 5-12. Wilkinson's Pike December 7. Paint Rock Bridge, Ala., December 7 (Detachment). Murfreesboro December 13-14. Near Murfreesboro December 15 (Detachment). Moved to Nashville, Tenn., and duty there till February, 1865. Action at Hillsboro, Ala., December 29, 1864 (Detachment). Near Leighton, Ala., December 30 (Detachment). Moved to Vicksburg, Miss.; thence to New Orleans, La., and to Mobile Bay, Ala., February 11-March 22. Campaign against Mobile and its defences March 22-April 12. Siege of Spanish Fort and Fort Blakely March 26-April 9. Grierson's Raid through Alabama, Georgia and Mississippi April 17-May 20. Duty at Columbus, Miss., till July. At Grenada and Austin, Miss., till November. Mustered out at Vicksburg, Miss., November 10, 1865.

Regiment lost during service 16 Enlisted men killed and mortally wounded and 1 Officer and 154 Enlisted men by disease. **Total 171.**

13th REGIMENT CAVALRY (131st REGIMENT VOLUNTEERS).

Organized at Indianapolis, Kokomo and New Albany, Ind., December 23, 1863, to April 29, 1864. Left State for Nashville, Tenn., April 30, 1864. Attached to District of Northern Alabama, Dept. of the Cumberland, to November, 1864. 2nd Brigade, 7th Division, Wilson's Cavalry Corps, Military Division Mississippi, to February, 1865. 2nd Brigade, 1st Cavalry Division, Military Division West Mississippi, to May, 1865. Dept. of Mississippi to November, 1865.

SERVICE.—Duty at Nashville, Tenn., till May 31, 1864. Moved to Huntsville, Ala., May 31, and Garrison duty there till November. Repulse of Buford's attack on Huntsville September 30-October 1. Companies "A," "C," "D," "F," "H" and "I" moved to Louisville, Ky., October 16, to draw horses and equipment; thence moved to defence of Paducah, Ky. Duty at Paducah till November 1. Moved to Louisville, Ky.; thence to Nashville, Tenn., and to Lavergne November 30. To Murfreesboro December 1. Owens' Cross Roads December 1. Siege of Murfreesboro December 5-12. Murfreesboro December 8-9 and 13-14. Near Paint Rock Bridge, Ala., December 7 (Detachment). Moved to Nashville December 19. Companies "B," "E," "G," "K" and "L" participated in the Siege of Decatur, Ala., October 26-29. Battles of Nashville, Tenn., December 15-16, Hillsboro December 29 and Leighton December 30. Regiment moved to Vicksburg, Miss.; thence to New Orleans, La., and to Mobile Bay February 11-March 23, 1865. Campaign against Mobile and its defences March 23-April 12. Siege of Spanish Fort and Fort Blakely March 26-April 9. Capture of Mobile **April 12.** Grierson's Raid through Alabama, Georgia

and Mississippi April 17-May 22. Garrison duty in Dept. of Mississippi till November. Mustered out at Vicksburg, Miss., November 18, 1865.

Regiment lost during service 1 Officer and 14 Enlisted men killed and mortally wounded and 2 Officers and 125 Enlisted men by disease. Total 142.

STEWART'S INDEPENDENT COMPANY CAVALRY.

Organized at Terre Haute, Ind., for one year's State service April 25, 1861. Mustered in for three years' service July 4, 1861. Assigned to 1st Indiana Cavalry as Company "L," August 20, 1861, but served detached from Regiment entire term. Served in Dept. of West Virginia as Escort to Gen. Rosecrans July to November, 1861. At Headquarters Dept. of Western Virginia to March, 1862; and Dept. of the Mountains to June, 1862. At Headquarters 1st Corps, Army of Virginia, to September, 1862. At Headquarters 11th Army Corps, Army of the Potomac, to September, 1863, and at Headquarters Army of the Potomac to May, 1865. Participated in all the services of these headquarters. Old members mustered out July 3, 1864. Veterans and Recruits mustered out May 31, 1865.

BRACKEN'S INDEPENDENT COMPANY CAVALRY.

Organized at Indianapolis, Ind., June 20, 1861, and mustered in July 9, 1861. Assigned to 1st Indiana Cavalry as Company "K," August 20, 1861, but served detached from Regiment entire time. Served in the Dept. of West Virginia as Escort to Gen. Rosecrans July to November, 1861. At Headquarters Dept. of Western Virginia and Dept. of the Mountains to June, 1862. At Headquarters 1st Army Corps, Army of Virginia, to September, 1862. At Headquarters 11th Army Corps, Army of the Potomac, to September, 1863, and at Headquarters Army of the Potomac to May, 1865, participating in all the services of these headquarters. Old members mustered out June 23, 1864. Veterans and Recruits mustered out May 31, 1865.

Camp Allegheny, Greenbrier, W. Va., December 13, 1861. Expedition to Huntersville December 31, 1861-January 6, 1862. Huntersville January 3, 1862. Charge into Fredericksburg, Va., November 9, 1862. Duty at Glymont, Md., on lower Potomac, January to May, 1864. Joined Army of the Potomac at White House, and duty at Headquarters of Gen. Meade till mustered out.

INDEPENDENT COMPANY MOUNTED SCOUTS.

Organized at Leavenworth, Kansas, August 13, 1863. Mustered out April 23, 1864.

1st REGIMENT HEAVY ARTILLERY.

Organized at Indianapolis, Ind., July 24, 1861, as 21st Indiana Infantry. Left State for Baltimore, Md., July 31, and duty in the Defences of that city till February 19, 1862. Attached to Dix's Division, Baltimore, Md., to February, 1862. Butler's New Orleans Expedition to March, 1862. 2nd Brigade, Dept. of the Gulf, to October, 1862. Independent Command, Dept. of the Gulf, to January, 1863. Unattached, 1st Division, 19th Army Corps, Dept. of the Gulf, to February, 1863. Designation changed to 1st Heavy Artillery February, 1863. Artillery, 1st Division, 19th Army Corps, to August, 1863. District of Baton Rouge, La., Dept. of the Gulf, to June, 1864. Unattached, 19th Army Corps, and Unattached, Dept. of the Gulf, to January, 1866.

SERVICE.—Expedition to Eastern Shore of Maryland November 14-22, 1861. Moved to Newport News, Va., February 19, 1862; thence sailed on Steamer "Constitution" for Ship Island, Miss., March 4-13. Duty at Ship Island till April 14. Operations against Forts St. Phillip and Jackson April 14-28. Occupation of New Orleans May 1 (first Regiment to land). Camp at Algiers till May 30. Expedition to New Orleans and Jackson R. R. May 9-10. Moved to Baton Rouge May 30, and duty there till August 20. Battle of Baton Rouge, La., August 5. Evacuation of Baton Rouge

August 20. Camp at Carrollton till October. Action at Bayou des Allemands September 4-5. Expedition from Carrollton to St. Charles Court House September 7-8. Skirmish near St. Charles Court House September 8. Expedition from Carrollton to Donaldsonville and skirmish October 21-25. Duty at Berwick Bay till February, 1863. Bayou Teche November 3, 1862. Action with Steamer "Cotton" Bayou Teche January 14, 1863. Operations in Western Louisiana April 9-May 19. Teche Campaign April 11-20. Fort Bisland April 12-14. Advance on Port Hudson May 20-24. Siege of Port Hudson May 24-July 9. Assaults on Port Hudson May 27 and June 14. Lafourche Crossing June 20-21 (Co. "F"). Brashear City June 23 (Co. "F"). Expedition to Sabine Pass, Texas, September 4-11 (Detachment). Garrison duty at New Orleans, Baton Rouge and at various points in the Dept. of the Gulf till February, 1865. Companies "L" and "M" organized August 12 to November 2, 1863. Red River Campaign March to May, 1864 (Cos. "G" and "H"). Blair's Landing April 12-13 (Detachment). Monett's Ferry, Cane River Crossing, April 23 (Detachment). Retreat to Morganza May 13-20. Operations in Mobile Bay, Ala., against Forts Gaines and Morgan August 2-23 (Cos. "B," "F," "H" and "K"). Siege and capture of Fort Gaines August 3-8. Siege and capture of Fort Morgan August 8-23. At New Orleans, La., till March, 1865. Campaign against Mobile, Ala., and its defences March 17-April 12, 1865. Siege of Spanish Fort and Fort Blakely March 26-April 8. Fort Blakely April 9. Occupation of Mobile April 12, and duty there till June 24. Garrison duty till January, 1866. Companies "B" and "C" at Fort Morgan, "H" and "K" at Fort Gaines, "F" and "L" at Barrancas, Fla.; "I" and "M" at Fort Pickens, Fla.; "A," "E" and "G" at Baton Rouge, La., and "D" at Port Hudson, La. Mustered out at Baton Rouge, La., January 10, 1866.

Regiment lost during service 7 Officers and 60 Enlisted men killed and mortally wounded and 3 Officers and 320 Enlisted men by disease. Total 390.

1st INDEPENDENT BATTERY LIGHT ARTILLERY.

Organized at Evansville, Ind., August 5, 1861. Mustered in at Indianapolis, Ind., August 16, 1861. Moved to St. Louis, Mo. Attached to Fremont's Army of the West and Dept. of Missouri to January, 1862. Artillery, 1st Brigade, 3rd Division, Army of Southwest Missouri, Dept. of Missouri, to May, 1862. Artillery, 1st Division, Army of Southwest Missouri, to July, 1862. District of Eastern Arkansas, Dept. of Missouri, to October, 1862. Artillery, 1st Division, District of Southeast Missouri, Dept. of Missouri, to March, 1863. Artillery, 14th Division, 13th Army Corps, Army of the Tennessee, to July, 1863. Artillery, 1st Division, 13th Army Corps, Dept. of the Tennessee, to August, 1863, and Dept. of the Gulf to September, 1863. District of Lafourche, Dept. of the Gulf, to February, 1864. Artillery, 1st Division, 13th Army Corps, Dept. of the Gulf, to March, 1864. Artillery, 4th Division, 13th Army Corps, to July, 1864. Artillery, Reserve Dept. of the Gulf, to February, 1865. Artillery Brigade, 16th Army Corps, Military Division West Mississippi, to August, 1865.

SERVICE.—Fremont's Advance on Springfield, Mo., September 27-October 3, 1861. Camp at LaMine till January, 1862. Advance on Springfield, Mo., in pursuit of Price January 25-February 14. Pursuit of Price into Arkansas February 15-29. Battles of Pea Ridge, Ark., March 6-8. March to Sugar Creek March 10, thence to Cross Timbers March 15. March to Batesville April 5-May 3. March to Helena, Ark., May 25-July 14, and duty there till October. Moved to Ironton, Pilot Knob, Mo., and operations in Southeast Missouri till March, 1863. Ordered to St. Genevieve, Mo., March 5; thence to Milliken's Bend, La., March 14-25, and duty there till April 25. Movement on Bruinsburg and turning Grand Gulf April 25-30. Battle of Thompson's Hill, Port Gibson, May 1. Battle of Champion's

Hill May 16. Big Black River May 17. Siege of Vicksburg, Miss., May 18-July 4. Assaults on Vicksburg May 19 and 22. Advance on Jackson, Miss., May 4-10. Siege of Jackson July 10-17. Duty at Vicksburg till August 20. Ordered to New Orleans, La. Duty there and at Brashear City till October. Western Louisiana Campaign October 3-November 30. Duty in the District of LaFourche, La., till March, 1864. Red River Campaign March 10-May 22. Battle of Sabine Cross Roads April 8. Cane River Crossing April 23. At Alexandria April 27-May 13. Retreat to Morganza May 13-20. Moved to New Orleans and duty there till March, 1865. Campaign against Mobile, Ala., and its defences March 17-April 12. Siege of Spanish Fort and Fort Blakely March 26-April 8. Fort Blakely April 9. Capture of Mobile April 12. March to Montgomery April 13-25, and duty there till August. Mustered out August 22, 1865.

Battery lost during service 3 Enlisted men killed and mortally wounded and 1 Officer and 31 Enlisted men by disease. Total 35.

2nd INDEPENDENT BATTERY LIGHT ARTILLERY.

Organized at Indianapolis, Ind., and mustered in August 9, 1861. Left State for St. Louis, Mo., September 5, 1861. Attached to Fremont's Army of the West to November, 1861. District of Fort Scott, Kansas, Dept. of Kansas, to June, 1862. Solomon's 3rd Brigade, Dept. of Kansas, to October, 1862. 3rd Brigade, 1st Division, Army of the Frontier, to January, 1863. Springfield, Mo., Dept. of Missouri, to July, 1863. District of the Frontier, Dept. of Missouri, to December, 1863. 2nd Brigade, District of the Frontier, to January, 1864. 2nd Brigade, District of the Frontier, 7th Army Corps, Dept. of Arkansas, to September, 1864. Indianapolis, Ind., to October, 1864. Post and District of Nashville, Tenn., Dept. of the Cumberland, to February, 1865. Garrison Artillery, Murfreesboro, Tenn., Dept. of the Cumberland, to July, 1865.

SERVICE.—Camp at St. Louis, Mo., September 6-25, 1861. Fremont's advance on Springfield, Mo., October 4-November 2. Moved to Fort Leavenworth, Kansas; thence to Fort Scott, Kansas, and duty there till May, 1862. Moved to Iola, Kansas, May 23. Expedition into Indian Territory May 25-July 8. Action at Round Grove, I. T., June 5. Capture of Fort Gibson July 18. Blount's Campaign in Missouri and Arkansas September to December. Old Fort Wayne, or Beattie's Prairie, near Maysville, October 22. Between Fayetteville and Cane Hill November 9. Cane Hill, Boston Mountains, November 28. Capture of Fort Davis Dec. Battle of Prairie Grove December 7. Moved to Springfield, Mo., January, 1863, and duty there till June, 1863. Operations in Indian Territory and Arkansas July to September. Action at Perryville, C. N., August 26. Cotton Gap, Devil's Backbone, Fort Smith September 1. Dardanelle September 9. Creek Agency, I. T., October 15 and 25. Duty at Waldron and Fort Smith and operations in Western Arkansas till March, 1864. Scout from Waldron to Mt. Ida, Caddo Gap and Dallas December 2-7, 1863. Niobrara December 4, 1863. Steele's Expedition to Camden March 23-May 3, 1864. Prairie D'Ann April 9-12. Moscow April 13. Camden April 16-18. Poison Springs April 18. Jenkins' Ferry, Saline River, April 30. Duty at Fort Smith till September. Mazzard's Prairie, near Fort Smith, July 27. Defence of Fort Smith July 29-31. Ordered to Indiana September, and Non-Veterans mustered out September 14, 1864. Battery reorganized at Indianapolis, Ind., October 14, 1864. Moved to Nashville, Tenn., and assigned to duty there as Garrison Artillery November, 1864, to June, 1865. Battle of Nashville December 15-16, 1864. Ordered to Indiana June, 1865, and mustered out at Indianapolis, Ind., July 3, 1865.

Battery lost during service 1 Officer and 13 Enlisted men killed and mortally wounded and 14 Enlisted men by disease. Total 28.

3rd INDEPENDENT BATTERY LIGHT ARTILLERY.

Organized at Connersville, Ind., and mustered in at Indianapolis, Ind., August 24, 1861. Moved to St. Louis, Mo., September. Attached to Fremont's Army of the West and Dept. of the Missouri to February, 1862. Jefferson City, Mo., Dept. of Missouri, to March, 1862. Central District of Missouri, Dept. of Missouri, to February, 1863. District of Southwest Missouri, Dept. of Missouri, to June, 1863. District of Rolla, Mo.; Department of Missouri, to July, 1863. District of St. Louis, Mo., Department of Missouri, to January, 1864. Artillery, 3rd Division, 16th Army Corps, Army of the Tennessee, to December, 1864. 2nd Brigade, 2nd Division, Detachment Army of the Tennessee, Dept. of the Cumberland, to February, 1865. Artillery, 1st Division, 16th Army Corps (New), Military Division West Mississippi, to August, 1865.

SERVICE.—Fremont's advance on Springfield, Mo., September 23-November 2, 1861. Duty at Tipton and LaMine, Mo., till February, 1862. Duty at Jefferson City, Mo., till November, 1862. Expedition in Moniteau County and Skirmish March 25-28. Campaign against Porter's and Poindexter's guerrillas July 20-September 10. Actions at Moore's Mills July 28; Kirkesville August 6; near Stockton August 9; Lone Jack August 16. Duty at Springfield, Rolla and St. Louis, Mo., November, 1862, to December, 1863. Re-enlisted November 30, 1863. Moved to Columbus, Ky. Smith's Campaign in Western Tennessee against Forest December 20-26. Moved to Vicksburg, Miss., January 23, 1864. Meridian Campaign February 3-March 2. Red River Campaign March 10-May 22. Fort DeRussy March 14. Occupation of Alexandria April 16. Battle of Pleasant Hill April 9. About Cloutiersville April 22-24. Cotile Landing April 25. Red River May 3-7. Retreat to Morganza May 13-20. Mansura May 16. Yellow Bayou May 18. Moved to Vicksburg May 19-24, thence to Memphis, Tenn., May 25-June 10. Old River Lake or Lake Chicot June 6. Smith's Expedition to Tupelo, Miss., July 5-21. Harrisburg, near Tupelo, July 14-15. Old Town (or Tishamingo Creek) July 15. Smith's Expedition to Oxford, Miss., August 1-30. Moved to Jefferson Barracks, Mo., September 8-19. Expedition to De Soto September 20-October 1. March through Missouri in pursuit of Price October 2-November 19. Moved to Nashville, Tenn., November 25-December 1. Battle of Nashville December 15-16. Pursuit of Hood to the Tennessee River December 17-28. Moved to Eastport, Miss., and duty there till February, 1865. Expedition from Eastport to Iuka January 9, 1865. Moved to New Orleans, La., February 7-22. Campaign against Mobile and its defences March 17-April 12. Siege of Spanish Fort and Fort Blakely March 26-April 8. Fort Blakely April 9. Capture of Mobile April 12. March to Montgomery April 13-25. Duty at Montgomery and Selma till July 30. Ordered home July 30, and mustered out at Indianapolis, Ind., August 21, 1865.

Battery lost during service 1 Officer and 10 Enlisted men killed and mortally wounded and 18 Enlisted men by disease. Total 29.

4th INDEPENDENT BATTERY LIGHT ARTILLERY.

Organized at Indianapolis, Ind., and mustered in September 30, 1861. Ordered to Louisville, Ky., October 4. Duty at New Haven and Munfordsville, Ky., till February, 1862. Served unattached, Army of the Ohio, to June, 1862. Artillery Reserve, Army of the Ohio, to July, 1862. 7th Independent Brigade, Army of the Ohio, to August, 1862. 28th Brigade, 3rd Division, Army of the Ohio, to September, 1862. 28th Brigade, 3rd Division, 1st Corps, Army of the Ohio, to November, 1862. 1st Brigade, 3rd Division, Right Wing 14th Army Corps, Army of the Cumberland, to January, 1863. Artillery, 3rd Division, 20th Army Corps, Army of the Cumberland, to October, 1863. Artillery, 1st Division, 14th Army Corps, October, 1863. 2nd Division, Artillery Reserve, Dept. of the Cumberland, to November, 1863. Garrison Artillery, Chattanooga, Tenn., Dept. of the Cumberland, to October, 1864. Garrison Artillery, Nashville, Tenn., Dept. of the Cumberland, to December, 1864, and at Murfreesboro, Tenn., till July, 1865.

SERVICE.—Advance on Nashville, Tenn., February 10-March 3, 1862. March to Savannah, Tenn., March 17-April 7. Advance on and siege of Corinth, Miss., April 29-May 30. Pursuit to Booneville May 31-June 6. Buell's Campaign in Northern Alabama and Middle Tennessee June to August. March to Louisville, Ky., in pursuit of Bragg August 21-September 26. Pursuit of Bragg into Kentucky October 1-15. Battle of Perryville, Ky., October 8. March to Nashville, Tenn., October 20-November 9, and duty there till December 26. Advance on Murfreesboro December 26-30. Battle of Stone's River December 30-31, 1862, and January 1-3, 1863. Duty at Murfreesboro till June. Expedition toward Columbia March 4-14. Middle Tennessee (or Tullahoma) Campaign June 23-July 7. Hoover's Gap June 24-26. Occupation of Middle Tennessee till August 16. Passage of Cumberland Mountains and the Tennessee River and Chickamauga (Ga.) Campaign August 16-September 22. Davis Cross Rroads or Dug Gap September 21. Battle of Chickamauga September 19-20. Rossville Gap September 21. Siege of Chattanooga, Tenn., September 24-November 23. Chattanooga-Ringgold Campaign November 23-27. Garrison duty at Chattanooga till September, 1864. Veterans and Recruits transferred to 7th Indiana Battery September 21, 1864. Old members mustered out October 6, 1864. Battery reorganized October 14, 1864. Moved to Nashville, Tenn., October 28 and duty there till December. Battle of Nashville December 15-16. Moved to Murfreesboro, Tenn., and garrison duty at Fortress Rosecrans till July, 1865. Moved to Nashville, Tenn.; thence to Indianapolis, Ind., July 19. Mustered out August 1, 1865.

Battery lost during service 12 Enlisted men killed and mortally wounded and 1 Officer and 15 Enlisted men by disease. Total 28.

5th INDEPENDENT BATTERY LIGHT ARTILLERY (SIMONSON'S).

Organized at Indianapolis, Ind., and mustered in November 22, 1861. Left state for Louisville, Ky., November 27. Attached to 3rd Division, Army of the Ohio, to September, 1862. 9th Brigade, 3rd Division, 1st Corps, Army of the Ohio, to November, 1862. 3rd Brigade, 2nd Division, Right Wing 14th Army Corps, Army of the Cumberland, to January, 1863. Artillery, 2nd Division, 20th Army Corps, Army of the Cumberland, to October, 1863. Artillery, 1st Division, 4th Army Corps, Army of the Cumberland, to July, 1864. Artillery Brigade, 4th Army Corps, to September, 1864. Garrison Artillery, Chattanooga, Tenn., Dept. of the Cumberland, to November, 1864.

SERVICE.—Duty at Camp Gilbert, Louisville, Ky., till December 20, 1861, and at Bacon Creek, Ky., till February, 1862. Advance on Bowling Green, Ky., and Nashville, Tenn., February 10-25. Occupation of Bowling Green, Ky., February 15, and of Nashville February 25. Moved to Murfreesboro, Tenn., March 18. Reconnoissance to Shelbyville, Tullahoma and McMinnville March 25-28. Advance on Fayetteville and Huntsville, Ala., April 7-11. Capture of Huntsville April 11. Advance on and capture of Decatur April 11-14. Duty at Bridgeport, Ala. (Detachment), and along Nashville & Chattanooga R. R. till August. Moved to Stevenson, Ala., August 24. Moved to Nashville, Tenn.; thence to Louisville, Ky., in pursuit of Bragg, August 31-September 26. Pursuit of Bragg into Kentucky October 1-15. Battle of Perryville, Ky., October 8. March to Nashville, Tenn., October 20-November 9, and duty there till December 26. Advance on Murfreesboro, Tenn., December 26-30. Battle of Stone's River December 30-31, 1862, and January 1-3, 1863. Duty at Murfreesboro till June. Middle Tennessee (or Tullahoma) Campaign June 22-July 7. Liberty Gap June 22-24. Occupation of Middle Tennessee till August 16. Passage of the Cumberland Mountains and Tennessee River and Chickamauga (Ga.) Campaign

August 16-September 22. Battle of Chickamauga September 19-20. Siege of Chattanooga, Tenn., September 24-October 26. Reopening Tennessee River October 26-29. Outpost duty at Shellmound till February, 1864. Demonstrations on Dalton February 22-27. Tunnel Hill, Buzzard's Roost Gap and Rocky Faced Ridge February 23-25. Stone Church, near Catoosa Platform, February 27. Atlanta (Ga.) Campaign May 1 to September 8. Tunnel Hill May 6-7. Demonstration on Rocky Faced Ridge and Dalton May 8-13. Buzzard's Roost Gap May 8-9. Near ·Dalton May 13. Battle of Resaca May 14-15. Near Kingston May 18-19. Near Cassville May 19. Advance on Dallas May 22-25. Operations on line of Pumpkin Vine Creek and battles about Dallas, New Hope Church and Allatoona Hills May 25-June 5. Operations about Marietta and against Kenesaw Mountain June 10-July 2. Pine Hill June 11-14. Lost Mountain June 15-17. Assault on Kenesaw June 27. Ruff's Station July 4. Chattahoochie River July 5-17. Peach Tree Creek July 19-20. Siege of Atlanta July 22-August 25. Flank movement on Jonesboro August 25-30. Battle of Jonesboro August 31-September 1. Lovejoy Station September 2-6. Ordered to Chattanooga, Tenn., September 20. Veterans and Recruits transferred to 7th Indiana Battery. Mustered out November 26, 1864.

Battery lost during service 1 Officer and 11 Enlisted men killed and mortally wounded and 24 Enlisted men by disease. Total 36.

6th INDEPENDENT BATTERY LIGHT ARTILLERY.

Organized at Evansville, Ind., and mustered in at Indianapolis, Ind., September 7, 1861. Left State for Henderson, Ky., October 2. Attached to District of Paducah, Ky., to March, 1862. Artillery, 5th Division, Army of the Tennessee, to July, 1862. Artillery, 5th Division, District of Memphis, Tenn., to November, 1862. Artillery, 1st Division, Right Wing 13th Army Corps (Old), Dept. of the Tennessee, to December, 1862. Artillery, 1st Division, 17th Army Corps, to January, 1863. Artillery, 1st Division, 16th Army Corps, to July, 1863. Artillery, 3rd Division, 15th Army Corps, to December, 1863. Artillery, 1st Division, 16th Army Corps, to June, 1864. 1st Brigade, Sturgis' Expedition, June, 1864. Artillery, 1st Division, 16th Army Corps, to November, 1864. 1st Brigade, Post and Defences of Memphis, Tenn., District of West Tennessee, to December, 1864. Artillery Reserve, District of West Tennessee, to July, 1865.

SERVICE.—Duty at Henderson, Calhoun, South Carrollton, Owensburg and Paducah, Ky., till March, 1862. Moved from Paducah to Savannah, Tenn., March 6-10. Expedition to Yellow Creek, Miss., and occupation of Pittsburg Landing, Tenn., March 14-17. Battle of Shiloh, Tenn., April 6-7. Advance on and siege of Corinth, Miss., April 29-May 30. March to Memphis, Tenn., June 1-July 21, via Lagrange, Grand Junction and Holly Springs. Action near Holly Springs July 1. Duty at Memphis, Tenn., till November 26. Grant's Central Mississippi Campaign November 26, 1862, to January 10, 1863. Duty at Lagrange, Lafayette and Colliersville, Tenn., till June, 1863. Moved to Memphis, Tenn., June 9; thence to Vicksburg, Miss. Siege of Vicksburg, Miss. Siege of Vicksburg June 12-July 4. Advance on Jackson, Miss., July 4-10. Siege of Jackson July 10-17. Camp at Oak Ridge and Bear Creek till October 14. Expedition to Canton October 14-20. Bogue Chitto Creek October 17. Moved to Memphis, Tenn., November; thence to Lagrange and Pocahontas, and duty there till January, 1864. Veteranize January 1, 1864. Moved to Vicksburg, Miss., January 31-February 3. Meridian Campaign February 3-March 2. Return to Memphis and duty there till June. Sturgis' Expedition to Guntown, Miss., June 1-13. Brice's (or Tishamingo) Creek, near Guntown, June 10. Smith's Expedition to Tupelo, Miss., July 5-21. Camargo's Cross Roads, near Harrisburg, July 13. Harrisburg, near Tupelo, July 14-15. Smith's Expedition to Oxford, Miss., August 1-30. Tallahatchie River August 7-9. Assigned to duty

at Memphis, Tenn., as garrison September, 1864, to July, 1865. Mustered out July 22, 1865.

Battery lost during service 1 Officer and 1 Enlisted man killed and 15 Enlisted men by disease. Total 17.

7th INDEPENDENT BATTERY LIGHT ARTILLERY.

Organized at Indianapolis, Ind., and mustered in December 2, 1861. Left State for ·Louisville, Ky., December 6. Attached to Artillery, 4th Division, Army of the Ohio, to June, 1862. Artillery, 1st Division, Army of the Ohio, to September, 1862. Artillery, 5th Division, 2nd Corps, Army of the Ohio, to November, 1862. Artillery, 3rd Division, Left Wing 14th Army Corps, Army of the Cumberland, to January, 1863. Artillery, 3rd Division, 21st Army Corps, Army of the Cumberland, to October, 1863. Artillery, 3rd Division, 14th Armp Corps, to July, 1864. Artillery Brigade, 14th Army Corps, to October, 1864. Garrison Artillery, Chattanooga, Tenn., Dept. of the Cumberland, to April, 1865. 2nd Brigade, 4th Division, District of East Tennessee, Dept. of the Cumberland, to July, 1865.

SERVICE.—Duty at Camp Wickliffe, Ky., till February, 1862. Advance on Nashville, Tenn., February 14-25. Occupation of Nashville, February 25 to March 17. March to Savannah, Tenn., March 17-April 6. Battle of Shiloh, Tenn., April 6-7. Advance on and siege of Corinth, Miss., April 29-May 30. Pursuit to Booneville May 31-June 12. Buell's Campaign in North Alabama and Middle Tennessee June to August. March to Louisville, Ky., in pursuit of Bragg August 21-September 26. Pursuit of Bragg to Loudon, Ky., October 1-20. Battle of Perryville, Ky., October 8. Reserve. Nelson's Cross Roads October 18. March to Nashville, Tenn., October 20-November 7 and duty there till December 26. Dobbin's Ferry, near Lavergne, December 9. Advance on Murfreesboro December 26-30. Battle of Stone's River December 30-31, 1862, and January 1-3, 1863. Duty at Murfreesboro till June. Middle Tennessee (or Tullahoma) Campaign June 23-July 7. Occupation of Middle Tennessee till August 16. Passage of the Cumberland Mountains and Tennessee River and Chickamauga (Ga.) Campaign August 16-September 22. Battle of Chickamauga September 19-20. Siege of Chattanooga, Tenn., September 24-November 23. Lookout Mountain November 23-24. Mission Ridge November 25. Duty at Chattanooga and Ringgold, Ga., till May, 1864. Reconnoissance from Ringgold toward Tunnel Hill April 29. Atlanta (Ga.) Campaign May to September. Demonstrations on Rocky Faced Ridge May 8-11. Battle of Resaca May 14-15. Advance on Dallas May 18-25. Operations on line of Pumpkin Vine Creek and battles about Dallas, New Hope Church and Allatoona Hills May 25-June 5. Operations about Marietta and against Kenesaw Mountain June 10-July 2. Pine Hill June 11-14. ⸱ Lost Mountain June 15-17. Assault in Kenesaw June 27. Ruff's Station July 4. Chattahoochie River July 5-17. Peach Tree Creek July 19-20. Siege of Atlanta July 22-August 25. Utoy Creek August 5-7. Flank movement on Jonesboro August 25-30. Battle of Jonesboro August 31-September 1. Ordered to Chattanooga, Tenn., September 20, and post duty there till December. Old members mustered out December 7, 1864. Veterans and Recruits on duty at Chattanooga, Tenn., till July, 1865. Mustered out July 20, 1865.

Battery lost during service 1 Officer and 6 Enlisted men killed and mortally wounded and 22 Enlisted men by disease. Total 29.

8th INDEPENDENT BATTERY LIGHT ARTILLERY.

Organized at Indianapolis, Ind., and mustered in December 13, 1861. Left State for Louisville, Ky., January 24, 1862. Attached to Artillery, 4th Division, Army of the Ohio, to March, 1862. Artillery, 6th Division, Army of the Ohio, to September, 1862. 15th Brigade, 6th Division, 2nd Corps, Army of the Ohio, to November, 1862. 1st Brigade, 1st Division, Left Wing 14th Army Corps, Army of the Cumberland, to January, 1863. Artillery, 1st Division, 21st Army Corps, Army of the

Cumberland, to October, 1863. 2nd Division, Artillery Reserve, Dept. of the Cumberland, to November, 1863. Garrison Artillery, Chattanooga, Tenn., to January, 1865.

SERVICE.—Movement to Nashville, Tenn., February 10-25, 1862. Occupation of Nashville February 25 to March 17. March to Savannah, Tenn., March 17-April 6. Battle of Shiloh, Tenn., April 7 (Reserve). Advance on and siege of Corinth, Miss., April 29-May 30. Pursuit to Booneville May 31-June 12. Buell's Campaign in Northern Alabama and Middle Tennessee June to August. Action at Little Pond, near McMinnville, August 30. March to Louisville, Ky., in pursuit of Bragg August 30-September 26. Pursuit of Bragg to Loudon, Ky., October 1-22. Battle of Perryville, Ky., October 8 (Reserve). Nelson's Cross Roads October 18. March to Nashville, Tenn., October 22-November 7, and duty there till December 26. Murfreesboro Pike November 9. Advance on Murfreesboro December 26-30. Lavergne December 26-27. Battle of Stone's River December 30-31, 1862, and January 1-3, 1863. Duty at Murfreesboro till June. Middle Tennessee (or Tullahoma) Campaign June 23-July 7. Occupation of Middle Tennessee till August 16. Passage of the Cumberland Mountains and Tennessee River and Chickamauga, (Ga.) Campaign August 16-September 22. Lee and Gordon's Mills September 11-13 and September 17-18. Battle of Chickamauga September 19-20. Siege of Chattanooga, Tenn., September 24-November 23. Chattanooga-Ringgold Campaign November 23-27. Duty at Chattanooga till March, 1865. (A detachment at Resaca, Ga., till November, 1864, participating in the repulse of Hood's attack on Resaca October 12. Rejoined Battery at Chattanooga November, 1864.) Non-Veterans mustered out January 25, 1865. Veterans and Recruits consolidated with 7th Indiana Battery March 13, 1865.

Battery lost during service 5 Enlisted men killed and mortally wounded and 10 Enlisted men by disease. Total 15.

9th INDEPENDENT BATTERY LIGHT ARTILLERY.

Organized at Indianapolis, Ind., and mustered in December 20, 1861. Duty at Indianapolis, Ind., till January 27, 1862. Moved to Cairo, Ill., January 27, and duty there till March 27. Remustered February 25, 1862. Attached to Military District of Cairo to April, 1862. Artillery, 3rd Division, Army of the Tennessee, to July, 1862. Artillery, 1st Division, District of Jackson, Tenn., to September, 1862. Artillery, 4th Division, District of Jackson to November, 1862. Artillery, 4th Division, District of Jackson, Right Wing 13th Army Corps (Old), Dept. of the Tennessee, to December, 1862. Artillery, 4th Division, 17th Army Corps, to January, 1863. Artillery, 4th Division, 16th Army Corps, to March, 1863. Artillery, District of Columbus, Ky., 6th Division, 16th Army Corps, to July, 1863. 1st Brigade, District of Columbus, 6th Division, 16th Army Corps, to January, 1864. Artillery, 3rd Division, 16th Army Corps, to December, 1864. 1st Brigade, 2nd Division (Detachment), Army of the Tennessee, Dept. of the Cumberland, to January, 1865. Indiana to March, 1865. Camp Butler, Ill., to June, 1865.

SERVICE.—Moved to Pittsburg Landing, Tenn., March 27, 1862. Battle of Shiloh, Tenn., April 6-7. Advance on and siege of Corinth, Miss., April 29-May 30. Moved to Bolivar, Tenn., and duty there till November, 1862. Action at Bolivar August 30. Grant's Central Mississippi Campaign November, 1862, to January, 1863. Duty at Tallahatchie River December 24, 1862, to January 20, 1863. Moved to Colliersville, Tenn., thence to Memphis, Tenn., and to Columbus, Ky., March, 1863. Duty there till July 10. Expedition to Cape Girardeau April 29-May 4. Moved to Clinton, Ky., July 10. Campaign against Roddy's forces July 15-August 4. Duty at Union City, Tenn., August 4, 1863, to January 23, 1864. Pursuit of Forest December 20-26, 1863. Ordered to Vicksburg, Miss., January 23. Meridian Campaign February 3-March 2. Red River

Campaign March 10-May 22. Fort DeRussy March 14. Occupation of Alexandria March 16. Henderson's Hill March 21. Battle of Pleasant Hill April 9. About Cloutiersville April 22-24. Alexandria April 30-May 13. Bayou LaMourie May 6-7. Retreat to Morganza May 13-20. Avoyelle's Prairie, Marksville, May 16. Yellow Bayou May 18. Moved to Vicksburg, Miss., May 19-24; thence to Memphis, Tenn., May 25-June 10. Lake Chicot, Ark., June 6-7. Smith's Expedition to Tupelo, Miss., July 5-21 (Non-Veterans). Harrisburg, near Tupelo, July 14-15. Old Town (or Tishamingo Creek) July 15. Smith's Expedition to Oxford, Miss., October 1-30. Moved to Jefferson Barracks, Mo., September 8-19. Expedition to DeSoto September 20-October 1. March through Missouri in pursuit of Price October 2-November 19. Moved to Nashville, Tenn., November 25-December 1. Battles of Nashville December 15-16. Pursuit of Hood to the Tennessee River December 17-28. Ordered to Indiana January 25, 1865; blown up on Steamer "Eclipse" at Johnsonville January 27, 1865, and out of 70 Officers and men but 10 escaped unhurt. Non-Veterans mustered out March 6, 1865. Veterans and Recruits on duty at Camp Butler, Springfield, Ill., till June. Mustered out June 25, 1865.

Battery loss during service 6 Enlisted men killed and mortally wounded and 55 Enlisted men by disease. Total 61.

10th INDEPENDENT BATTERY LIGHT ARTILLERY.

Organized at Indianapolis, Ind., January 25, 1862, and ordered to Louisville, Ky. Attached to Artillery, 4th Division, Army of the Ohio, to June, 1862. Reserve Artillery Army of the Ohio to July 1862. Artillery, 6th Division, Army of the Ohio, to September, 1862. 21st Brigade, 6th Division, 2nd Corps, Army of the Ohio, to November, 1862. 2nd Brigade, 1st Division, Left Wing 14th Army Corps, Army of the Cumberland, to January, 1863. Artillery, 1st Division, 21st Army Corps, Army of the Cumberland, to October, 1863. Artillery, 2nd Division, 4th Army Corps, Army of the Cumberland, to March, 1864. Garrison Artillery, Chattanooga, Tenn., Dept. of the Cumberland, to April, 1864. Unattached Artillery, Dept. of the Cumberland, to August, 1864. District of North Alabama, Dept. of the Cumberland, to July, 1865.

SERVICE.—Advance on Nashville, Tenn., February 10-25, 1862. Occupation of Nashville February 25-March 17. March to Savannah, Tenn., March 17-April 6. Battle of Shiloh April 6-7 (Reserve). Advance on and siege of Corinth, Miss., April 29-May 30. Occupation of Corinth May 30. Pursuit to Booneville May 31-June 12. Buell's Campaign in Northern Alabama and Middle Tennessee June to August. March to Louisville, Ky., in pursuit of Bragg August 21-September 26. Pursuit of Bragg to Loudon, Ky., October 1-22. Battle of Perryville, Ky., October 8 (Reserve). March to Nashville, Tenn., October 22-November 7, and duty there till December 26. Advance on Murfreesboro December 26-30. Battle of Stone's River December 30-31, 1862, and January 1-3, 1863. Duty at Murfreesboro till June. Reconnoissance to Nolensville and Versailles January 13-15. Expedition to McMinnville April 20-30. Middle Tennessee (or Tullahoma) Campaign June 23-July 7. Occupation of Middle Tennessee till August 16. Chickamauga (Ga.) Campaign August 16-September 22. Occupation of Chattanooga, Tenn., September 9. Assigned to duty as garrison. Siege of Chattanooga September 24-November 24. Chattanooga-Ringgold Campaign November 23-27. Lookout Mountain November 24. Mission Ridge November 25. Garrison duty at Chattanooga till March, 1864. 88 men transferred to 5th and 18th Indiana Batteries March 1864. Balance assigned to duty on Gunboat "Stone River" and at Decatur, Ala., till June 19, 1865. Fletcher's Ferry May 18, 1864. Battery brought together June, 1865, and duty at Huntsville, Ala., till July 2. Moved to Indianapolis, Ind., July 2-6 and mustered out July 10, 1865.

Battery lost during service 5 Enlisted men killed and mortally wounded and 22 Enlisted men by disease. Total 27.

11th INDEPENDENT BATTERY LIGHT ARTILLERY.

Organized at Indianapolis, Ind., and mustered in December 17, 1861. Ordered to Louisville, Ky., December 20, 1861. Served unattached, Army of Ohio, to June, 1862. Reserve Artillery Army of the Ohio to September, 1862. Post and Defences of Nashville, Tenn., Army of the Ohio, to November, 1862. Reserve Artillery (Center), 14th Army Corps, Army of the Cumberland, to January, 1863. Garrison Artillery, District of Nashville, Tenn., Dept. of the Cumberland, to June, 1863. Artillery, 3rd Division, 20th Army Corps, Army of the Cumberland, to October, 1863. 2nd Division, Artillery Reserve, Dept. of the Cumberland, to November, 1863. Garrison Artillery, Chattanooga, Tenn., Dept. of the Cumberland. Siege Artillery, Army of the Cumberland, to October, 1864. Garrison Artillery, Chattanooga, Tenn., to November, 1864.

SERVICE.—Buell's advance on Nashville, Tenn., February 10-25, 1862. March to Savannah, Tenn., to reinforce Army of the Tennessee March 16-April 7. Advance on and siege of Corinth, Miss., April 29-May 30. Pursuit to Booneville May 31-June 6. Buell's Campaign in Northern Alabama and Middle Tennessee June to August. Assigned to Post and Garrison duty at Nashville, Tenn., September, 1862, to January, 1863. Siege of Nashville, Tenn., September 12-November 7, 1862. Ordered to Murfreesboro, Tenn., January, 1863, and duty there till June. Middle Tennessee (or Tullahoma) Campaign June 23-July 7. Occupation of Tullahoma July 1. Guard Railroad from Dechard, Tenn., to Stevenson, Ala., July-August. Crossing Cumberland Mountains and Tennessee River and Chickamauga (Ga.) Campaign August 16-September 22. Battle of Chickamauga September 19-20. Siege of Chattanooga, Tenn., September 24-November 23. Battles of Chattanooga November 23-25. Orchard Knob November 23-24. Mission Ridge November 25. Duty at Chattanooga till April, 1864. Atlanta (Ga.) Campaign May to September. Operations about Tunnel Hill, Buzzard's Roost Gap and Rocky Faced Ridge May 5-11. Battle of Resaca May 14-15. Operations on line of Pumpkin Vine Creek and battles about Dallas, New Hope Church and Allatoona Hills May 25-June 5. Operations about Marietta and against Kenesaw Mountain June 10-July 2. Pine Hill June 11-14. Lost Mountain June 15-17. Assault on Kenesaw June 27. Ruff's Station July 4. Chattahoochie River July 5-17. Peach Tree Creek July 19-20. Siege of Atlanta July 22-August 25. Utoy Creek August 5-7. Flank movement on Jonesboro August 25-30. Battle of Jonesboro August 31-September 1. Ordered to Chattanooga, Tenn., and garrison duty there till November. Battery Consolidated with 18th Indiana Battery November 21, 1864.

Battery lost during service 6 Enlisted men killed and mortally wounded and 1 Officer and 18 Enlisted men by disease. Total 25.

12th INDEPENDENT BATTERY LIGHT ARTILLERY.

Organized at Jeffersonville and Indianapolis and mustered in January 25, 1862. Left State for Louisville, Ky., January 25, 1862. Served unattached, Army of the Ohio, to June, 1862. Reserve Artillery, Army of the Ohio, to September, 1862. Post and Defences of Nashville, Tenn., Dept. of the Ohio, to November, 1862, and Dept. of the Cumberland to July, 1865.

SERVICE.—Movement to Nashville, Tenn., February 14-March 6, 1862, thence march to Savannah, Tenn., March 20-April 7. Advance on and siege of Corinth, Miss., April 29-May 30. Buell's Campaign in Northern Alabama and Middle Tennessee June to August. Assigned to duty as garrison at Fort Negley, Defences of Nashville, Tenn., August 18, 1862, to July, 1865. Siege of Nashville, Tenn., September 12-November 6, 1862. Repulse of attack on Nashville by Breckenridge, Forest and Morgan November 5, 1862. One half of Battery ordered to Chattanooga November, 1863, and participated in the battles of Chattanooga November 23-25, 1863. Battle of Nashville December 15-16, 1864. Non-

Veterans mustered out December 23, 1864. Battery mustered out July 7, 1865.

Battery lost during service 2 Officers and 22 Enlisted men by disease. Total 24.

13th INDEPENDENT BATTERY LIGHT ARTILLERY.

Organized at Indianapolis, Ind., and mustered in February 22, 1862. Left State for Louisville, Ky., February 23. Served unassigned in Kentucky, Army of the Ohio, to September, 1862. Artillery, 12th Division, Army of the Ohio, to November, 1862. Ward's Brigade, Post of Gallatin, Tenn., Dept. of the Cumberland, to June, 1863. Garrison Artillery, Gallatin, Tenn., Dept. of the Cumberland, to January, 1865. Garrison Artillery, Chattanooga, Tenn., Dept. of the Cumberland, to July, 1865.

SERVICE.—Served as Cavalry in Kentucky from February, 1862, to January, 1863. Skirmish at Monterey, Owen County, Ky., June 11. Operations against Morgan July 4-28. Paris, Ky., July 19. Siege of Munfordsville September 14-17. Frankfort October 9. Hartsville, Tenn., December 7. Garrison Fort Thomas, Gallatin, Tenn., January, 1863, to January, 1865, and garrison duty at Chattanooga, Tenn., till July, 1865. Mustered out July 10 1865.

Battery lost during service 7 Enlisted men killed and mortally wounded and 19 Enlisted men by disease. Total 26.

14th INDEPENDENT BATTERY LIGHT ARTILLERY.

Organized at Indianapolis, Ind., and mustered in March 24, 1862. Moved to Pittsburg Landing, Tenn., April 11-21, 1862. Attached to 1st Division, Army of the Tennessee, to July, 1862. Artillery, 1st Division, District of Jackson, Tenn., to November, 1862. Artillery, District of Jackson, Tenn., 13th Army Corps (Old), Dept. of the Tennessee, to December, 1862. Artillery, District of Jackson, 16th Army Corps, to March, 1863. Artillery, 3rd Division. 16th Army Corps, to June, 1863. District of Corinth, Miss., 2nd Division, 16th Army Corps, to November, 1863. Post of Corinth, 2nd Division, 16th Army Corps, to January, 1864. Artillery, 3rd Division, 16th Army Corps, to June, 1864. Unattached Artillery, District of West Tennessee, to December, 1864. Artillery, 3rd Division Detachment, Army of the Tennessee, Dept. of the Cumberland, to February, 1865. Artillery, 3rd Division, 16th Army Corps (New), Military Division West Mississippi, to March, 1865. Artillery Brigade, 16th Army Corps, Military Division West Mississippi, to August, 1865.

SERVICE.—Advance on and siege of Corinth, Miss., April 29-May 30, 1862. Moved to Jackson, Tenn., and duty there till June, 1863. Action at Lexington, Tenn., December 18, 1862. (Detachment captured.) Parker's Cross Roads, near Jackson, December 30. Red Mound (or Parker's) Cross Roads December 31, 1862. Duty at LaGrange, Tenn., June to October, 1863. Moved to Pocahontas October 11, and duty there till November 23. Moved to Corinth, Miss., November 23, and duty there till January 25, 1864. Ordered to Memphis, Tenn., thence to Vicksburg, Miss. Meridian Campaign February 3-March 2, 1864. Queen Hill February 4. Return to Memphis, Tenn., March, and duty there till November 16. Veterans on furlough May and June. Sturgis' Expedition from Memphis to Guntown, Miss., June 1-13 (Non-Veterans). Battle of Brice's Cross Roads, near Guntown, June 10. (Guns captured.) Smith's Expedition to Tupelo, Miss., July 5-21. Harrisburg, near Tupelo, July 14-15. Smith's Expedition to Oxford, Miss., August 1-30. Duty at Memphis, Tenn., till November 16. Moved to Nashville, Tenn., November 16-December 1. Battle of Nashville December 15-16. Pursuit of Hood to the Tennessee River December 17-28. At Eastport, Miss., till February 7, 1865. Moved to New Orleans, La., February 7-22. Campaign against Mobile, Ala., and its Defences March 17-April 12. Siege of Spanish Fort and Fort Blakely March 26-April 8. Fort Blakely April 9. Occupation of Mobile April 12. March to Montgomery April 13-25. Duty there till

August. Ordered to Indianapolis, Ind., August 15, and mustered out September 1, 1865.

Battery lost during service 4 Enlisted men killed and mortally wounded and 1 Officer and 23 Enlisted men by disease. Total 28.

15th INDEPENDENT BATTERY LIGHT ARTILLERY.

Organized at Indianapolis, Ind., March 11, 1862, and mustered in July 5, 1862. Left State for Harper's Ferry, W. Va., July 5. Attached to D'Utassy's Brigade, White's Division, Army of Virginia, to September, 1862. Miles' Command, Harper's Ferry, September, 1862. Camp Douglas, Ill., and Indianapolis, Ind., to April, 1863. District of Central Kentucky, Dept. of the Ohio, to June, 1863. 2nd Brigade, 4th Division, 23rd Army Corps, Army of Ohio, to July, 1863. 2nd Brigade, 1st Division, 23rd Army Corps, to August 1863. 1st Brigade, 4th Division, 23rd Army Corps, to October, 1863. 2nd Brigade, 4th Division, 23rd Army Corps, to November, 1863. 2nd Brigade, 1st Cavalry Division, Dept. of Ohio, to December, 1863. Artillery, 2nd Division, 9th Army Corps, Dept. of Ohio, to April 1864. Artillery, 3rd Division, 23rd Army Corps, to December, 1864. Artillery, 2nd Division, 23rd Army Corps, Army of Ohio, to February, 1865, and Dept. of North Carolina to June, 1865.

SERVICE.—Duty at Martinsburg and Harper's Ferry, W. Va., till September, 1862. Defence of Harper's Ferry September 13-15. Bolivar Heights September 14. Surrendered September 15. Paroled September 16 and sent to Annapolis, Md., thence to Camp Douglas, Chicago, Ill. Duty at Camp Douglas and Indianapolis, Ind., till March, 1863. Ordered to Louisville, Ky. Pursuit of Morgan in Kentucky April, 1863. Action at Paris, Ky., April 16. Pursuit of Morgan through Indiana and Ohio July 1-26. New Lisbon, Ohio, July 26. Paris, Ky., July 29. Burnside's Campaign in East Tennessee August 16-October 17. Winter's Gap August 31. Actions at Athens, Calhoun and Charleston September 25. Philadelphia September 27 and October 24. Knoxville Campaign November 4-December 23. Loudon November 14. Lenoir November 14-15. Campbell's Station November 16. Siege of Knoxville November 17-December 5. Kingston November 24. Bean's Station December 10. Blain's Cross Roads December 16-19. Duty at Knoxville till January 19, 1864. March to Red Clay, Ga. Atlanta Campaign May 1-September 8. Demonstration on Rocky Faced Ridge May 8-11. Battle of Resaca May 14-15. Cartersville May 20. Operations on line of Pumpkin Vine Creek and battles about Dallas, New Hope Church and Allatoona Hills May 25-June 5. Operations about Marietta and against Kenesaw Mountain June 10-July 2. Lost Mountain June 15-17. Muddy Creek June 17. Noyes Creek June 19. Cheyney's Farm June 22. Olley's Farm June 26-27. Assault on Kenesaw June 27. Nickajack Creek July 2-5. Chattahoochie River July 5-17. Siege of Atlanta July 22-August 25. Utoy Creek August 5-7. Flank movement on Jonesboro August 25-30. Battle of Jonesboro August 31-September 1. Lovejoy Station September 2-6. Pursuit of Hood into Alabama October 1-26. Nashville Campaign November-December. Columbia, Duck River, November 24-27. Columbia Ford November 28-29. Battle of Franklin November 30. Battle of Nashville December 15-16. Pursuit of Hood, to the Tennessee River, December 17-28. At Clifton, Tenn., till January 16, 1865. Movement to Washington, D. C., thence to Fort Fisher, N. C., January 16-February 9. Operations against Hoke February 11-14. Fort Anderson February 18-19. Town Creek February 19-20. Capture of Wilmington February 22. Campaign of the Carolinas March 1-April 26. Advance on Goldsboro March 6-21. Occupation of Goldsboro March 21. Advance on Raleigh April 10-14. Occupation of Raleigh April 14. Bennett's House April 26. Surrender of Johnston and his army. Duty at Greensboro, N. C., till June. Ordered to Indianapolis, Ind., and there mustered out June 30, 1865.

Battery lost during service 1 Enlisted man killed and 1 Officer and 12 Enlisted men by disease. Total 14.

16th INDEPENDENT BATTERY LIGHT ARTILLERY.

Organized at Lafayette, Ind., and mustered in at Indianapolis, Ind., March 24, 1862. Left State for Washington, D. C., June 1. Duty at Capital Hill till June 26. Attached to Military District of Washington, D. C., June, 1862. Artillery, 2nd Army Corps, Army of Virginia, to September, 1862. Artillery, 2nd Division, 12th Army Corps, Army of the Potomac, to October, 1862. Artillery, 2nd Brigade, Defences North of the Potomac, Defences of Washington, D. C., to February, 1863. Fort Washington, Defences of Washington, North of the Potomac, 22nd Army Corps, to May, 1864. 2nd Brigade, DeRussy's Division, 22nd Army Corps, to July, 1864. 3rd Brigade, DeRussy's Division, 22nd Army Corps, to December, 1864. 1st Brigade, DeRussy's Division, 22nd Army Corps, to July, 1865.

SERVICE.—Ordered to join Banks in the Shenandoah Valley June 26, 1862. Pope's Campaign in Northern Virginia July to September. Battle of Cedar Mountain August 9. Fords of the Rappahannock August 21-23. Battles of Groveton August 29 and Bull Run August 30. Maryland Campaign September 6-22. Battle of Antietam, Md., September 16-17 (Reserve). Ordered to Washington, D. C., and duty in the Defences of that city North and South of the Potomac till June, 1865. Repulse of Early's attack on Washington July 11-12, 1864. Ordered to Indianapolis, Ind., June, 1865, and there mustered out July 5, 1865.

Battery lost during service 11 Enlisted men by disease.

17th INDEPENDENT BATTERY LIGHT ARTILLERY.

Organized at Indianapolis, Ind., and mustered in May 20, 1862. Left State for Baltimore, Md., July 5, 1862. Attached to Defences of Baltimore, Md., 8th Army Corps, Middle Department, to January, 1863. Defences, Upper Potomac, 8th Army Corps, to March, 1863. 1st Brigade, 1st Division, 8th Army Corps, to June, 1863. Maryland Brigade, French's Command, 8th Army Corps, to July. 2nd Brigade, Maryland Heights Division, Dept. of West Virginia, July, 1863. 1st Brigade, Maryland Heights Division, West Virginia, to December, 1863. 1st Brigade, 1st Division, West Virginia, to January, 1864. Wheaton's Brigade, 1st Division, West Virginia, to April, 1864. Reserve Division, Harper's Ferry, W. Va., to August, 1864. Reserve Artillery, 19th Army Corps, Army of the Shenandoah, Middle Military Division, to October, 1864. Garrison Artillery, Frederick City, Md., and Winchester, Va., to December, 1864. Artillery Brigade, 19th Army Corps, Army of the Shenandoah, to March 1865. Artillery Reserve, Army of the Shenandoah, to July, 1865.

SERVICE.—Garrison duty at Baltimore, Md., July 7 to December 27, 1862. Moved to Harper's Ferry, W. Va., December 27, and garrison duty there till July, 1863. Evacuation of Harper's Ferry July 1, 1863. Reoccupation of Harper's Ferry and Maryland Heights July 7, 1863, and garrison duty there till July, 1864. Action at Berryville, Va., October 18, 1863. Well's Demonstration from Harper's Ferry December 10-24, 1863. Sheridan's Shenandoah Valley Campaign August 7-November 28, 1864. Battle of Opequan, Winchester, September 19. Strasburg September 21. Fisher's Hill September 22. Battle of Cedar Creek October 19. Garrison duty at Frederick City, Md., and at Winchester, Va., till June 19, 1865. Ordered to Indianapolis, Ind., June 19, and there mustered out July 8, 1865.

Battery lost during service 4 Enlisted men killed and mortally wounded and 2 Officers and 10 Enlisted men by disease. Total 16.

18th INDEPENDENT BATTERY LIGHT ARTILLERY.

Organized at Indianapolis, Ind., and mustered in August 20, 1862. Ordered to Louisville, Ky., September. Attached to Artillery, 12th Division, Army of the Ohio, to November, 1862. Artillery, 5th Division (Center), 14th Army Corps, Army of the Cumberland, to January, 1863. Artillery, 5th Division, 14th Army Corps, Army of the Cumberland, to June, 1863. Artillery, 4th Division, 14th Army Corps, June, 1863. Artillery, Wilder's Mounted Brigade, Army of the Cumberland, to November, 1863. 3rd Brigade, 2nd Cavalry Division, Army of the Cumberland, to January, 1864. Artillery, 1st Cavalry Division, Army of the Cumberland, to October, 1864. Artillery, 1st Division, Wilson's Cavalry Corps, Military Division, Mississippi, to June, 1865.

SERVICE.—Campaign against Bragg in Kentucky October 3-26, 1862. March to Bowling Green, Ky., October 26-November 3, thence to Scottsboro, Ky., and Gallatin, Tenn., November 11-26. Pursuit of Morgan December 22, 1862-January 2, 1863. Moved to Murfreesboro, Tenn., January 2-8, 1863, and duty there till June. Expedition to Auburn, Liberty and Alexandria February 3-5. Expedition to Woodbury March 3-8. Expedition to Lebanon, Carthage and Liberty April 1-8. Expedition to McMinnville April 20-30. Middle Tennessee (or Tullahoma) Campaign June 23-July 7. Hoover's Gap June 24-26. Occupation of Middle Tennessee till August 16. Passage of the Cumberland Mountains and Tennessee River and Chickamauga (Ga.) Campaign August 16-September 22. Bombardment of Chattanooga August 21. Ringgold, Ga., September 11. Lee and Gordon's Mills September 11. Leet's Tan Yard or Rock Springs September 12-13. Alexander's and Reed's Bridges September 17. Battle of Chickamauga September 19-21. Operations against Wheeler and Roddy September 30-October 17. Hill's Gap, Thompson's Cove, near Beersheba, October 3. Murfreesboro Road October 4. McMinnville October 4-5. Farmington October 7. Moved to Huntsville, Ala., and duty there till November. Moved to relief of Knoxville, Tenn., November 28-December 8. Dandridge December 24. Operations about Dandridge and Mossy Creek December 24-28. Mossy Creek Station December 26. Talbot's Station December 28. Mossy Creek, Talbot's Station, December 29. Operations about Dandridge January 16-17, 1864. Bend of Chucky River, near Dandridge, January 16. Dandridge January 17. Operations about Dandridge January 26-28. Near Fair Garden January 27. Atlanta (Ga.) Campaign May 1-September 8. Demonstrations on Dalton, Ga., May 9-13. Tilton May 13. Battle of Resaca May 14-15. Cassville May 19. Statesborough May 23. Burnt Hickory May 24. Battles about Dallas, New Hope Church and Allatoona Hills May 25-June 5. Ackworth June 8. Operations about Marietta and against Kenesaw Mountain June 10-July 2. Lost Mountain June 15-17. Assault on Kenesaw June 27. Chattahoochie River July 5-17. Siege of Atlanta July 22-August 25. McCook's Raid on Atlanta & West Point R. R. July 27-31. Lovejoy Station July 29. Newnan's July 30-31. Flank movement on Jonesboro August 25-30. Pursuit of Wheeler September 24-October 18. Ordered to Louisville, Ky., and duty there refitting till December. Pursuit of Lyons from Paris, Ky., to Hopkinsville, Ky., December 8-January 15, 1865. Hopkinsville, Ky., December 16, 1864. Moved to Nashville, Tenn. Duty there till February 1865, and at Waterloo, Ala., till March. Wilson's Raid to Macon, Ga., March 22-April 24. Selma, Ala., April 2. Montgomery April 12. Fort Tyler, West Point, April 16. Capture of Macon April 20. Duty at Macon, Chattanooga and Nashville till June. Mustered out June 23, 1865.

Battery lost during service 1 Officer and 11 Enlisted men killed and mortally wounded and 31 Enlisted men by disease. Total 43.

19th INDEPENDENT BATTERY LIGHT ARTILLERY.

Organized at Indianapolis, Ind., and mustered in August 5, 1862. Ordered to Louisville, Ky., and attached to 34th Brigade, 10th Division, Army of the Ohio, September, 1862. 34th Brigade, 10th Division, 1st Army Corps, Army of Ohio, to November, 1862. Artillery, 5th Division (Center), 14th Army Corps, Army of the Cumberland, to January, 1863. Artillery, 5th Division, 14th Army Corps, Army of the Cumberland,

to June, 1863. Artillery, 4th Division, 14th Army Corps, to October, 1863. Artillery, 3rd Division, 14th Army Corps, to July, 1864. Artillery Brigade, 14th Army Corps, to June, 1865.

SERVICE.—Pursuit of Bragg into Kentucky October 1-15, 1862. Battle of Perryville, Ky., October 8. March to Lebanon and Woodsonville October 16-28, and duty there till December. Operations against Morgan, in Kentucky, December 22, 1862-January 2, 1863. March to Nashville, Tenn., thence to Murfreesboro, Tenn., January, 1863, and duty there till June. Expedition to Auburn, Liberty and Alexandria February 3-5. Expedition to Woodbury March 3-8. Action at Vaught's Hill, near Woodbury, March 20. Expedition to Lebanon, Carthage and Liberty April 1-8. Expedition to McMinnville April 20-30. Middle Tennessee (or Tullahoma) Campaign June 23-July 7. Hoover's Gap June 24-26. Occupation of Middle Tennessee till August 16. Passage of the Cumberland Mountains and Tennessee River and Chickamauga (Ga.) Campaign August 16-September 22. Shellmound August 21. Narrows, near Shellmound, August 28. Reconnoissance toward Chattanooga August 30-31. Battle of Chickamauga, Ga., September 19-21. Siege of Chattanooga September 24-November 23. Chattanooga-Ringgold Campaign November 23-27. Battles of Orchard Knob November 23-24. Mission Ridge November 25. Demonstrations on Dalton, Ga., February 22-27, 1864. Tunnel Hill, Buzzard's Roost Gap and Rocky Faced Ridge February 23-25. Atlanta (Ga.) Campaign May 1 to September 8. Demonstrations on Rocky Faced Ridge May 8-11. Battle of Resaca May 14-15. Advance on Dallas May 18-25. Operations on Pumpkin Vine Creek and battles about Dallas, New Hope Church and Allatoona Hills May 25-June 5. Ackworth June 2. Operations about Marietta and against Kenesaw Mountain June 10-July 2. Pine Hill June 11-14. Lost Mountain June 15-17. Assault on Kenesaw June 27. Ruff's Station July 4. Chattahoochie River July 5-17. Peach Tree Creek July 19-20. Siege of Atlanta July 22-August 25. Utoy Creek August 5-7. Flank movement on Jonesboro August 25-30. Battle of Jonesboro August 31-September 1. Operations against Hood in North Georgia and North Alabama September 29-November 3. March to the sea November 15-December 10. Siege of Savannah December 10-21. Campaign of the Carolinas January to April, 1885. Fayetteville, N. C., March 11. Taylor's Hole Creek, Averysboro, March 16. Battle of Bentonville March 19-21. Occupation of Goldsboro March 24. Advance on Raleigh April 10-14. Occupation of Raleigh April 14. Bennett's House April 26. Surrender of Johnston and his army. March to Washington, D. C., via Richmond, Va., April 29-May 19. Grand Review May 24. Mustered out June 10, 1865.

Battery lost during service 1 Officer and 10 Enlisted men killed and mortally wounded and 21 Enlisted men by disease. Total 32.

20th INDEPENDENT BATTERY LIGHT ARTILLERY.

Organized at Indianapolis, Ind., and mustered in September 19, 1862. Left State for Henderson, Ky., December 17, 1862. Attached to District of Western Kentucky, Dept. of the Ohio, to May, 1863. Post and District of Nashville, Tenn., Dept. of the Cumberland, to January, 1864. Artillery, 1st Division, 11th Army Corps, Army of the Cumberland, to April, 1864. Unattached, 4th Division, 20th Army Corps, Dept. of the Cumberland, to July, 1864. Artillery Brigade, 14th Army Corps, Army of the Cumberland, to November, 1864. Artillery, Provisional Division, District of the Etowah, Dept. of the Cumberland, to January, 1865. Garrison Artillery, Chattanooga, Tenn., Dept. of the Cumberland, to June, 1865.

SERVICE.—Duty at Henderson Ky., and in the District of Western Kentucky till May, 1863. Ordered to Nashville, Tenn., and duty there till October 5, 1863. Refitted and assigned to guard duty along Nashville & Chattanooga R. R. till March 5, 1864. Moved to Bridgeport, Ala., March 5, and garrison duty there till

July. Ordered to the field and joined 14th Army Corps, Army of the Cumberland, south of the Chattahoochie River, Georgia. Siege of Atlanta July 22-August 25. Flank movement on Jonesboro August 25-30. Battle of Jonesboro August 31-September 1. Pursuit of Hood into Alabama October 1-26. Action near Atlanta October 30. Moved to Chattanooga, Tenn., November 5, thence to Nashville, Tenn. Battles of Nashville December 15-16. Duty at Courtland, Ala., and Chattanooga, Tenn., till June, 1865. Mustered out June 28, 1865.

Battery lost during service 7 Enlisted men killed and mortally wounded and 24 Enlisted men by disease. Total 25.

21st INDEPENDENT BATTERY LIGHT ARTILLERY.

Organized at Indianapolis, Ind., and mustered in September 9, 1862. Left State for Covington, Ky., September 9. Attached to 2nd Division, Army of Kentucky, Dept. of the Ohio, October 1862. Unassigned, Army of Kentucky, Dept. of the Ohio, to December, 1862. Artillery, 3rd Division, Army of Kentucky, Dept. of the Ohio, to February, 1863. Crook's Brigade, Baird's Division, Army of Kentucky, Dept. of the Cumberland, to June, 1863. Artillery, 4th Division, 14th Army Corps, Army of the Cumberland, to October, 1863. 2nd Division, Artillery Reserve, Dept. of the Cumberland, to March, 1864. Garrison Artillery, Columbia, Tenn., Dept. of the Cumberland, to November, 1864. Garrison Artillery, Nashville, Tenn., Dept. of the Cumberland, to March, 1865. 2nd Sub-District, District of Middle Tennessee, Dept. of the Cumberland, to June, 1865.

SERVICE.—Duty at Lexington, Richmond, Danville and Louisville, Ky., till February 2, 1863. Ordered to Nashville, Tenn., February 2; thence moved to Cathage, Tenn., and duty there till June. Moved to Murfreesboro June 3. Middle Tennessee (or Tullahoma) Campaign June 23-July 7. Hoover's Gap June 24-26. Occupation of Middle Tennessee till August 16. Passage of the Cumberland Mountains and Tennessee River and Chickamauga (Ga.) Campaign August 16-September 22. Catlett's Gap, Pigeon Mountain, September 15-18. Battle of Chickamauga September 19-21. Siege of Chattanooga, Tenn., September 24-November 23. Battles of Chattanooga November 23-25. Duty at Chattanooga till March 26, 1864, and at Columbia, Tenn., till November 24. Moved to Nashville, Tenn., November 24. Battle of Nashville December 15-16. Garrison duty at Nashville till June, 1865. Mustered out June 26, 1865.

Battery lost during service 4 Enlisted men killed and mortally wounded and 24 Enlisted men by disease. Total 28.

22nd INDEPENDENT BATTERY LIGHT ARTILLERY.

Organized at Indianapolis, Ind., and mustered in December 15, 1862. Left State for Louisville, Ky., March, 1863. Served unassigned, Army of Kentucky, Dept. of the Ohio, to June, 1863. 1st Brigade, 2nd Division, 23rd Army Corps, Army of Ohio, to August, 1863. Russellsville, Ky., 1st Division, 23rd Army Corps, to December, 1863. District of Southwest Kentucky, 1st Division, 23rd Army Corps, to April, 1864. Camp Burnside, Ky., District of Kentucky, Dept. of the Ohio, to June, 1864. Artillery, 2nd Division, 23rd Army Corps, to November, 1864. Garrison Artillery, Nashville, Tenn., Dept. of the Cumberland, to December, 1864. Artillery, 1st Division, 23rd Army Corps, Army of Ohio, to February, 1865, and Dept. of North Carolina to April, 1865. Artillery, 1st Division, 10th Army Corps, Dept. of North Carolina, to June, 1865.

SERVICE.—Duty at Louisville, Bowling Green and Russellville, Ky., till December, 1863. Pursuit of Morgan July 2-26, 1863. Moved to Point Burnside, Ky., December, 1863, and duty there till May, 1864. Ordered to join Army of the Ohio in the field. Atlanta (Ga.) Campaign June 29-September 8. Nickajack Creek July 2-5. Chattahoochie River July 5-17. Decatur July 19. Howard House July 20. Siege of Atlanta July 22-

August 25. Utoy Creek August 5-7. Flank movement on Jonesboro August 25-30. Lovejoy Station September 2-6. Pursuit of Hood into Alabama October 1-26. Nashville Campaign November-December. Battle of Franklin November 30. Battle of Nashville December 15-16. Pursuit of Hood to the Tennessee River December 17-28. At Clifton, Tenn., till January 16, 1865. Movement to Washington, D. C., thence to Morehead City, N. C., January 16-February 20. Campaign of the Carolinas March 1-April 26. Advance on Kinston and Goldsboro March 6-21. Battle of Wise's Forks March 8-10. Occupation of Kinston March 14. Occupation of Goldsboro March 21. Advance on Raleigh April 10-14. Occupation of Raleigh April 14. Bennett's House April 26. Surrender of Johnston and his army. Duty in North Carolina till June. Ordered to Indianapolis, Ind., and there mustered out July 7, 1865.

Battery lost during service 1 Officer and 1 Enlisted man killed and 11 Enlisted men by disease. Total 13.

23rd INDEPENDENT BATTERY LIGHT ARTILLERY.

Organized at Indianapolis, Ind., and mustered in November 8, 1862. On duty at Indianapolis, Ind., guarding Confederate prisoners till July, 1863. Ordered to Louisville, Ky., July 4. Attached to District of Louisville, Ky., Dept. of the Ohio, to September, 1863. Artillery, Willcox's Left Wing forces, 23rd Army Corps, Dept. of the Ohio, to January, 1864. District of the Clinch, Dept. of the Ohio, to April, 1864. Artillery, 1st Division, 23rd Army Corps, Dept. of the Ohio, to August, 1864. Artillery, 3rd Division, 23rd Army Corps, Army of the Ohio, to February, 1865, and Dept. of North Carolina to June, 1865.

SERVICE.—Operations against Morgan in Kentucky July, 1863. Duty at Indianapolis, Ind., till September. Left State for Camp Nelson, Ky., September 16. March to Cumberland Gap September 24-October 3, thence to Morristown October 6-8. March to Greenville and duty there till November 6. Moved to Bull's Gap and duty there till December. March across Clinch Mountain to Clinch River December. Duty in District of the Clinch till April, 1864. Atlanta (Ga.) Campaign May 1-September 8. Demonstrations on Rocky Faced Ridge and Dalton, Ga., May 8-13. Battle of Resaca May 14-15. Operations on line of Pumpkin Vine Creek and battles about Dallas, New Hope Church and Allatoona Hills May 25-June 5. Operations about Marietta and against Kenesaw Mountain June 10-July 2. Lost Mountain June 15-17. Muddy Creek June 17. Assault on Kenesaw June 27. Nickajack Creek July 2-5. Chattahoochie River July 5-17. Siege of Atlanta July 22-August 25. Utoy Creek August 5-7. Flank movement on Jonesboro August 25-30. Lovejoy Station September 2-6. Pursuit of Hood into Alabama October 1-26. Nashville Campaign November-December. Columbia, Duck River, November 24-27. Columbia Ford November 28-29. Battle of Franklin November 30. Battle of Nashville December 15-16. Pursuit of Hood to the Tennessee River December 17-28. At Clifton, Tenn., till January 16, 1865. Movement to Washington, D. C., thence to Fort Fisher, N. C., January 16-February 9. Operations against Hoke February 11-14. Fort Anderson February 18-19. Capture of Wilmington February 22. Campaign of the Carolinas March 1-April 26. Advance on Goldsboro March 6-21. Occupation of Goldsboro March 21. Advance on Raleigh April 10-14. Occupation of Raleigh April 14. Bennett's House April 26. Surrender of Johnston and his army. Duty at Greensboro till June. Mustered out July 2, 1865.

Battery lost during service 2 Enlisted men killed and mortally wounded and 17 Enlisted men by disease. Total 19.

24th INDEPENDENT BATTERY LIGHT ARTILLERY.

Organized at Indianapolis, Ind., and mustered in November 29, 1862. Left State for Louisville, Ky., March 13, 1863. Attached to District of Western Kentucky, Dept. of the Ohio, to June, 1863. 2nd Brigade, 3rd Division, 23rd Army Corps, Dept. of the Ohio, to August, 1863. 2nd Brigade, 4th Division, 23rd Army Corps, to

October, 1863. Artillery Reserve, 23rd Army Corps, to April, 1864. Artillery, 1st Division, 23rd Army Corps, to July, 1864. Artillery, Cavalry Division, 23rd Army Corps, to August, 1864. Artillery, 2nd Division, 23rd Army Corps, to October, 1864. Garrison Artillery, Nashville, Tenn., Dept. of the Cumberland, to January, 1865. Garrison Artillery, Louisville, Ky., to July, 1865.

SERVICE.—Expedition to Monticello and operations in Southeast Kentucky April 25-May 12, 1863. Horse Shoe Bend May 11. Duty at Columbia June 5-22, and at Glasgow till August. Pursuit of Morgan July 1-26. Marrow Bone, Burkesville, July 2. Burnside's Campaign in East Tennessee August 16-October 17. Philadelphia October 20. Knoxville Campaign November 4-December 23. Huff's Ferry November 14. Campbell's Station November 16. Siege of Knoxville November 17-December 5. Duty at Knoxville till April, 1864. March to Charleston April 5-24. Atlanta (Ga.) Campaign May 1 to September 8, 1864. Demonstrations on Rocky Faced Ridge and Dalton May 8-13. Battle of Resaca May 14-15. Operations on line of Pumpkin Vine Creek and battles about Dallas, New Hope Church and Allatoona Hills May 25-June 5. Operations about Marietta and against Kenesaw Mountain June 10-July 2. Lost Mountain June 15-17. Muddy Creek June 17. Assault on Kenesaw June 27. Transferred to Stoneman's Cavalry Division July 1. Nickajack Creek July 2-5. Chattahoochie River July 5-17. Stoneman's Raid to Macon July 27-August 6. Clinton and Macon July 30. Hillsboro, Sunshine Church, July 30-31. Mostly captured. Siege of Atlanta August 6-25. Flank movement on Jonesboro August 25-30. Lovejoy Station September 2-6. Pursuit of Hood into Alabama October 1-26. Garrison duty at Nashville, Tenn., till January, 1865. Battle of Nashville December 15-16. Ordered to Louisville, Ky., January 18, and Post duty there till July 28. Mustered out August 3, 1865.

Battery lost during service 31 Enlisted men by disease.

25th INDEPENDENT BATTERY LIGHT ARTILLERY.

Organized at Indianapolis, Ind., September 4 to November 28, 1864. Left State for Nashville, Tenn., November 28. Attached to Artillery Brigade, 4th Army Corps, Army of the Cumberland, to February, 1865. Unattached Artillery, Dept. of the Cumberland, to March, 1865. Garrison Artillery, Decatur, Ala., to July, 1865.

SERVICE.—Battle of Nashville, Tenn., December 15-16, 1864. Pursuit of Hood to the Tennessee River December 17-28. Duty at Huntsville, Ala., January 4 to February 3, 1865. Moved to Decatur, Ala., February 3, and garrison duty there till July 11. Ordered to Indiana July 11. Mustered out at Indianapolis, Ind., July 20, 1865.

Battery lost during service 1 Enlisted man killed and 6 Enlisted men by disease. Total 7.

WILDER'S OR RIGBY'S INDEPENDENT BATTERY LIGHT ARTILLERY.

(26th INDEPENDENT BATTERY.)

Organized May, 1861, but not accepted. Mustered in as Company "A," 17th Indiana Infantry, June 12, 1861. Left State for Parkersburg, W. Va., July 2. Attached to Reynolds' Cheat Mountain District, West Virginia, to November, 1861. Milroy's Command, Cheat Mountain, W. Va., to March, 1862. Milroy's Cheat Mountain Brigade, Dept. of the Mountains, to June, 1862. Milroy's Independent Brigade, 1st Army Corps, Army of Virginia, to July, 1862. Piatt's Brigade, Winchester, Va., to August, 1862. Trimble's Brigade, White's Division, Winchester, Va., to September, 1862. Miles' Command, Harper's Ferry, W. Va., September, 1862. Camp Douglas, Ill., and Indianapolis, Ind., to March, 1863. Central District of Kentucky, Dept. of the Ohio, to June, 1863. 2nd Brigade, 1st Division, 23rd Army Corps, Army of the Ohio, to July, 1863. 2nd Brigade, 4th Division, 23rd Army Corps, to August, 1863. Reserve Artillery, 23rd Army Corps, to October, 1863.

2nd Brigade, 3rd Division, 23rd Army Corps, to April, 1864. 2nd Brigade, 4th Division, 23rd Army Corps, to February, 1865. 2nd Brigade, 4th Division, District of East Tennessee, Dept. of the Cumberland, to March, 1865. 1st Brigade, 4th Division, District of East Tennessee, to July, 1865.

SERVICE.—Moved from Parkersburg, W. Va., to Oakland July 23, 1861; thence to Camp Pendleton and duty there till August 7. Moved to Cheat Mountain Pass and Elkwater August 7-13. Operations on Cheat Mountain September 11-17. Petersburg September 11-13. Cheat Mountain Pass September 12. Elkwater September 13. Greenbrier River October 3-4. Expedition to Camp Baldwin December 11-14. Allegheny Mountain December 13. Duty at Beverly till April, 1862. Expedition on the Seneca April 1-12. Monterey April 12. Battle of McDowell May 8. Franklin May 10-12. Strasburg and Staunton Road June 1-2. Battle of Cross Keys June 8. Duty at Winchester till September 1. Defence of Harper's Ferry September 12-15. Bolivar Heights September 14. Surrendered September 15. Paroled and sent to Annapolis, Md., thence to Camp Douglas, Ill.; duty there. At Camp Butler, Springfield, Ill., and at Indianapolis, Ind., till March, 1863. Left State for Lexington, Ky., March 18. Duty in Central District of Kentucky till August. Operations against Pegram March 22-April 1. Action at Danville, Ky., March 24. Hickman's Heights March 28. Dutton's Hill, Monticello, May 1. Burnside's Campaign in East Tennessee August 16-September 17. Carter's Depot September 20-21. Jonesboro September 21. Knoxville Campaign November 4-December 23. Siege of Knoxville November 17-December 5. Garrison duty at Knoxville till March, 1865. Stoneman's Raid through East Tennessee into North Carolina March and April, 1865. Duty at Greenville, East Tennessee, till July. Mustered out July 19, 1865.

Battery lost during service 1 Officer and 12 Enlisted men by disease. Total 13.

6th REGIMENT INFANTRY.—(3 MONTHS.)

Organized at Indianapolis, Ind., April 22-27, 1861. Left State for Grafton, W. Va., May 30. Attached to Kelly's Command. Action at Philippi June 3. Morris' Indiana Brigade, Army of West Virginia, July. West Virginia Campaign July 6-16. Carrick's Ford July 12-14. Pursuit of Garnett's forces July 15-16. Mustered out August 2, 1861. Lost 3 by disease.

6th REGIMENT INFANTRY.—(3 YEARS.)

Regiment organized at Madison, Ind., and mustered in September 20, 1861. Ordered to Louisville, Ky., September 20. Duty at Muldraugh's Hill till October 14. Moved to Nolin River, Ky. Duty at Bacon Creek and Green River till February, 1862. Attached to 1st Brigade, McCook's Command, at Nolin, Ky., October-November, 1861. 4th Brigade, Army of the Ohio, to December, 1861. 4th Brigade, 2nd Division, Army of the Ohio, to September, 1862. 4th Brigade, 2nd Division, 1st Corps, Army of the Ohio, to November, 1862. 3rd Brigade, 2nd Division, Right Wing 14th Army Corps, Army of the Cumberland, to January, 1863. 3rd Brigade, 2nd Division, 20th Army Corps, Army of the Cumberland, to October, 1863. 2nd Brigade, 3rd Division, 4th Army Corps, Army of the Cumberland, to September, 1864.

SERVICE.—March to Nashville, Tenn., February 14-March 3, 1862. March to Duck River, thence to Savannah, Tenn., March 16-April 6. Battle of Shiloh, Tenn., April 6-7. Advance on and siege of Corinth, Miss., April 29-May 30. Duty at Corinth till June 10. March to Iuka, Miss., thence to Tuscumbia, Florence, Huntsville and Stevenson, Ala., June 10-July 5. Expedition to Tullahoma July 14-18. March to Pelham July 24, thence to Altamont August 28. Reconnoissance toward Sequatchie Valley August 29-30. March to Louisville, Ky., in pursuit of Bragg, August 30-September 26. Pursuit of Bragg into Kentucky October 1-15. March to Nashville, Tenn., October 16-November 7, and duty there till December 26. Advance on Murfreesboro December 26-30. Battle of Stone's River December 30-31, 1862, and January 1-3, 1863. Duty at Murfreesboro till June. Middle Tennessee (or Tullahoma) Campaign June 23-July 7. Liberty Gap June 24-27. (Guard Ammunition Trains through Liberty Gap.) Occupation of Middle Tennessee till August 16. Passage of the Cumberland Mountains and Tennessee River and Chickamauga (Ga.) Campaign August 16-September 22. Battle of Chickamauga September 19-20. Siege of Chattanooga, Tenn., September 24-November 23. Reopening Tennessee River October 26-29. Brown's Ferry October 27. Chattanooga-Ringgold Campaign November 23-27. Orchard Knob November 23-24. Mission Ridge November 25. March to relief of Knoxville, Tenn., November 28-December 8. Operations in East Tennessee December, 1863, to April, 1864. Atlanta (Ga.) Campaign May 1 to August 22. Demonstrations on Rocky Faced Ridge and Dalton May 8-13. Battle of Resaca May 14-15. Adairsville May 17. Near Kingston May 18-19. Near Cassville May 19. Advance on Dallas May 22-25. Operations on line of Pumpkin Vine Creek and battles about Dallas, New Hope Church and Allatoona Hills May 25-June 5. Pickett's Mills May 27. Operations about Marietta and against Kenesaw Mountain June 10-July 2. Pine Hill June 11-14. Lost Mountain June 15-17. Assault on Kenesaw June 27. Ruff's Station, Smyrna Camp Ground, July 4. Chattahoochie River July 5-17. Pace's Ferry July 5. Peach Tree Creek July 19-20. Siege of Atlanta July 22-August 22. Ordered to Chattanooga, Tenn., August 22. Mustered out September 22, 1864. Expiration of term. Veterans and Recruits transferred to 68th Indiana Infantry.

Regiment lost during service 9 Officers and 116 Enlisted men killed and mortally wounded and 2 Officers and 140 Enlisted men by disease. Total 267.

7th REGIMENT INFANTRY.—(3 MONTHS.)

Organized at Indianapolis, Ind., April 21-27, 1861. Left State for West Virginia May 29. At Grafton, W. Va., June 1. Attached to Kelly's Command. Action at Philippi June 3. Attached to Morris' Indiana Brigade Army of West Virginia, July. West Virginia Campaign July 6-17. Laurel Hill July 7. Bealington July 8. Carrick's Ford July 12-14. Pursuit of Garnett's forces July 15-17. Mustered out August 2, 1863.

Regiment lost during service 1 Enlisted man killed and 2 Enlisted men by disease.

7th REGIMENT INFANTRY.—(3 YEARS.)

Organized at Indianapolis, Ind., and mustered in September 13, 1861. Ordered to Cheat Mountain, W. Va., September, 1861. Attached to Cheat Mountain District, West Virginia, to January, 1862. 3rd Brigade, Landers' Division, Army of the Potomac, to March, 1862. 3rd Brigade, Shields' 2nd Division, Banks' 5th Army Corps, and Dept. of the Shenandoah, to May, 1862. 4th Brigade, Shields' Division, Dept. of the Rappahannock, to June, 1862. 4th Brigade, 2nd Division, 3rd Army Corps, Army of Virginia, to September, 1862. 2nd Brigade, 1st Division, 3rd Corps, Army of Virginia, September, 1862. 2nd Brigade, 1st Division, 1st Army Corps, Army of the Potomac, to March, 1864. 2nd Brigade, 4th Division, 5th Army Corps, Army of the Potomac, to April, 1864. 1st Brigade, 4th Division, 5th Army Corps, to August, 1864. 3rd Brigade, 3rd Division, 5th Army Corps, to September, 1864.

SERVICE.—Duty in Cheat Mountain District, West Virginia, to December, 1861. Action at Greenbrier October 3-4. Scouting Expedition through the Kanawha District October 27-November 7. Expedition to Camp Baldwin December 11-14. Moved to Green Springs Run December 18, and duty there till March, 1862. Advance on Winchester March 5-13. Middletown March 18. Battle of Winchester March 22-23. Mt. Jackson March 25. Occupation of Mt. Jackson April 17. March to Fredericksburg, Va., May 12-21, and return to Front Royal May 25-30. Burner's Springs, near Front Royal, May 31. Battle of Port Republic June 9. March to Cloud's Mills, near Alexandria, June 10-26, and duty there till

July 24. Pope's Campaign in Northern Virginia August 6-September 2. Fords of the Rappahannock August 21-23. Thoroughfare Gap August 28. Battles of Groveton August 29; Bull Run August 30. Maryland Campaign September 6-22. Battles of South Mountain, Md., September 14; Antietam September 16-17. Movement to Falmouth, Va., October 29-November 17. Battle of Fredericksburg, Va., December 12-15. "Mud March" January 20-24, 1863. At Falmouth till April 27. Expedition to Mattox Creek February 12-14. Chancellorsville Campaign April 27-May 6. Operations at Pollock's Mill Creek April 29-May 2. Fitzhugh's Crossing April 29-30. Battle of Chancellorsville May 2-5. Gettysburg (Pa.) Campaign June 11-July 24. Battle of Gettysburg July 1-3. Duty on line of the Rappahannock and Rapidan to October, 1863. Bristoe Campaign October 9-22. Advance to line of the Rappahannock November 7-8. Mine Run Campaign November 26-December 2. Demonstration on the Rapidan February 6-7, 1864. Campaign from the Rapidan to the James River May 4-June 15. Battles of the Wilderness May 5-7; Laurel Hill May 8; Spottsylvania May 8-12; Spottsylvania Court House May 12-21. Assault on the Salient May 12. North Anna River May 23-26. Jericho Ford May 23. On line of the Pamunkey May 26-28. Totopotomoy May 28-31. Cold Harbor June 1-12. Bethesda Church June 1-3. Before Petersburg June 16-18. Siege of Petersburg June 16-September 20. Weldon R. R. August 18-21. Non-Veterans mustered out September 20, 1864. Veterans and Recruits transferred to 19th Indiana Infantry September 23, 1864.

Regiment lost during service 8 Officers and 108 Enlisted men killed and mortally wounded and 2 Officers and 111 Enlisted men by disease. Total 229.

8th REGIMENT INFANTRY.—(3 MONTHS.)

Organized at Indianapolis, Ind., April 21-27, 1861. Ordered to West Virginia June 19. Attached to Rosecrans' Brigade, McClellan's Provisional Army of West Virginia. Moved to Clarksburg, W. Va., June 19; thence march to Buckhannon June 29. Occupation of Buchannon June 30. West Virginia Campaign July 6-17. Battle of Rich Mountain July 11. Mustered out August 6, 1861.

Regiment lost during service 4 Enlisted men killed and mortally wounded and 3 Enlisted men by disease. Total 7.

8th REGIMENT INFANTRY.—(3 YEARS.)

Organized at Indianapolis, Ind., August 20-September 5, 1861. Ordered to St. Louis, Mo., September 10. Attached to Fremont's Army of the West and Dept. of Missouri to January, 1862. 1st Brigade, 3rd Division, Army of Southwest Missouri, Dept. of Missouri, to May, 1862. 1st Division, Army of Southwest Missouri, to July, 1862. District of Eastern Arkansas, Dept. of Missouri, to October, 1862. 2nd Brigade, 1st Division, District of Southeast Missouri, Dept. of Missouri, to March, 1863. 1st Brigade, 14th Division, 13th Army Corps, Army of the Tennessee, to July, 1863. 1st Brigade, 1st Division, 13th Army Corps, Dept. of the Tennessee, to August, 1863, and Dept. of the Gulf to June, 1864. District of LaFourche, Dept. of the Gulf, to August, 1864. 3rd Brigade, 2nd Division, 19th Army Corps, Army of the Shenandoah, Middle Military Division, to August, 1864. 4th Brigade, 2nd Division, 19th Army Corps, to December, 1864. 1st Brigade, 2nd Division, 19th Army Corps, to January, 1865. 1st Brigade, Grover's Division, District of Savannah, Ga., Dept. of the South, to August, 1865.

SERVICE.—Fremont's advance on Springfield, Mo., September 22-October 15. Camp at Otterville till January 25, 1862. Expedition to Milford December 15-19, 1861. Action at Milford, Blackwater or Shawnee Mound December 18. Curtis' advance on Springfield January 25-February 14, 1862. Pursuit of Price to Cassville, Ark. Battle of Pea Ridge March 6-8. At Sulphur Rock till May. March to Batesville, Ark.; thence to Helena, Ark., May 25-July 14. Action at Hill's Plantation, Cache River, July 7. Expedition to Coldwater,

Miss., July 22-25 (Cos. "B," "E"). White Oak Bayou July 24 (Cos. "B," "E"). Austin, Tunica County, August 2. At Helena till October. Ordered to Pilot Knob, Mo., and operations in Southeast Missouri till March 5, 1863. Moved to Helena, Ark., thence to Milliken's Bend, La. Movement on Bruinsburg and turning Grand Gulf April 25-30. Battle of Port Gibson May 1. Battle of Champion's Hill May 16. Big Black River May 17. Siege of Vicksburg, Miss., May 18-July 4. Assaults on Vicksburg May 19 and 22. Advance on Jackson, Miss., July 4-10. Siege of Jackson, Miss., July 10-17. Duty at Vicksburg till August 20. Ordered to New Orleans, La. Duty at Carrollton, Brashear City and Berwick till October. Western Louisiana "Teche" Campaign October 3-November 8. Moved to New Orleans, La., November 8, thence to Texas November 12. Capture of Mustang Island November 17. Fort Esperanza November 27-30. Duty at Matagorda Bay till February, 1864. Duty at Indianola and Lavacca, Tex., till April. Veterans on furlough April and May. Duty in District of LaFourche, La., till July. Ordered to Washington, D. C. Sheridan's Shenandoah Valley Campaign August 7 to November 28. Berryville, Va., September 3. Battle of Opequan, Winchester, September 19. Fisher's Hill September 22. Battle of Cedar Creek October 19. Duty in the Shenandoah Valley, Virginia, till January, 1865. Moved to Baltimore, Md., January 6-7, 1865; thence to Savannah, Ga., January 14-20. Duty there and at various points in Georgia and South Carolina till August. Mustered out August 28, 1865.

Regiment lost during service 7 Officers and 84 Enlisted men killed and mortally wounded and 5 Officers and 166 Enlisted men by disease. Total 258.

9th REGIMENT INFANTRY.—(3 MONTHS.)

Organized at Indianapolis, Ind., April 22-27, 1861. Ordered to Grafton, W. Va., May 29. Attached to Kelly's Command, West Virginia, to July. Action at Philippi June 3. Attached to Morris' Indiana Brigade, West Virginia, July. West Virginia Campaign July 6-17. Laurel Hill July 7-8. Bealington July 10. Carrick's Ford July 12-14. Pursuit of Garnett's forces July 14-17. Mustered out August 2, 1861.

Regiment lost 3 Enlisted men killed and mortally wounded and 2 Enlisted men by disease. Total 5.

9th REGIMENT INFANTRY.—(3 YEARS.)

Organized at Laporte September 5, 1861. Ordered to Cheat Mountain, West Virginia, September 10. Attached to Cheat Mountain District, West Virginia, to March, 1862. 19th Brigade, 4th Division, Army of the Ohio, to September, 1862. 19th Brigade, 4th Division, 2nd Corps, Army of the Ohio, to November, 1862. 2nd Brigade, 2nd Division, Left Wing 14th Army Corps, Army of the Cumberland, to January, 1863. 2nd Brigade, 2nd Division, 21st Army Corps, Army of the Cumberland, to October, 1863. 3rd Brigade, 1st Division, 4th Army Corps, Army of the Cumberland, to June, 1865. 2nd Brigade, 1st Division, 4th Army Corps, to August, 1865. Dept. of Texas to September, 1865.

SERVICE.—Duty at Cheat Mountain, West Virginia, till January 9, 1862. Action at Greenbrier River October 3-4, 1861. Expedition to Camp Baldwin December 11-13. Greenbrier River December 12. Camp Allegheny December 13. Moved to Fetterman, W. Va., January 9, 1862, and duty there till February 19. Ordered to Louisville, Ky., February 19; thence march to Nashville, Tenn. March to Savannah, Tenn. March 18-April 6. Battle of Shiloh, Tenn., April 6-7. Advance on and siege of Corinth, Miss., April 29-May 30. Occupation of Corinth May 30, and pursuit to Booneville May 31-June 12. March to Iuka, Miss., thence to Tuscumbia, Florence and Athens, Ala., June 12-July 8. Duty at Athens till July 17, and at Murfreesboro, Tenn., till August 17. March to Louisville, Ky., in pursuit of Bragg August 17-September 26. Pursuit of Bragg, to Loudon, Ky., October 1-22. Battle of Perryville, Ky., October 8. Danville October 11. Wild Cat Mountain, near Crab Orchard, Big Rockcastle River and near Mt. Vernon October 16. Wild Cat October 17. Rockcastle

River and Nelson's Cross Roads October 18. Pittman's Forks October 20. March to Nashville, Tenn., October 22-November 5, and duty there till December 26. Advance on Murfreesboro December 26-30. Lavergne December 26-27. Stewart's Creek December 27. Battle of Stone's River December 30-31, 1862, and January 1-3, 1863. Duty at Murfreesboro and Readyville till June. Woodbury January 24. Expedition from Readyville to Woodbury April 2. Middle Tennessee (or Tullahoma) Campaign June 23-July 7. At Manchester till August 16. Passage of the Cumberland Mountains and Tennessee River and Chickamauga (Ga.) Campaign August 16-September 22. Lee and Gordon's Mills, Ga., September 11-13. Battle of Chickamauga September 19-20. Siege of Chattanooga September 22-November 23. Before Chattanooga September 22-27. Reopening Tennessee River October 26-29. Chattanooga-Ringgold Campaign November 23-27. Lookout Mountain November 23-24. Mission Ridge November 25. Ringgold Gap, Taylor's Ridge, November 27. At Whitesides, Ala., till March, 1864, and at Cleveland, Tenn., till May. Atlanta (Ga.) Campaign May 1-September 8. Tunnell Hill May 6-7. Demonstration on Rocky Faced Ridge and Dalton May 8-13. Buzzard's Roost Gap May 8-9. Near Dalton May 13. Battle of Resaca May 14-15. Near Kingston May 18-19. Cassville May 19 and May 24. Operations on line of Pumpkin Vine Creek and battles about Dallas, New Hope Church and Allatoona Hills May 25-June 5. Operations about Marietta and against Kenesaw Mountain June 10-July 2. Pine Hill June 11-14. Lost Mountain June 15-17. Assault on Kenesaw June 27. Ruff's Station Smyrna Camp Ground July 4. Chattahoochie River July 5-17. Peach Tree Creek July 19-20. Siege of Atlanta July 22-August 25. Flank movement on Jonesboro August 25-30. Battle of Jonesboro August 31-September 1. Lovejoy Station September 2-6. Operations against Hood in North Georgia and North Alabama, September 29-November 3. Nashville Campaign November-December. Columbia Duck River November 24-27. Battle of Franklin November 30. Battle of Nashville December 15-16. Pursuit of Hood to the Tennessee River December 17-28. Moved to Huntsville, Ala., and duty there till March, 1865. Operations in East Tennessee March 15-April 22. Duty at Nashville till June. Ordered to New Orleans, La., June 16; thence to Indianola, Tex., July 7. Duty at San Antonio and at New Braunfels till September. Mustered out September 28, 1865.

Regiment lost during service 11 Officers and 120 Enlisted men killed and mortally wounded and 2 Officers and 220 Enlisted men by disease. Total 353.

10th REGIMENT INFANTRY.—(3 MONTHS.)

Organized at Indianapolis, Ind., April 22-25, 1861. Duty near Evansville, Ind., till June 7. Ordered to West Virginia June 7. Attached to Rosecrans' Brigade, McClellan's Army of West Virginia. Occupation of Buckhannon June 30. West Virginia Campaign July 6-17. Battle of Rich Mountain July 11. Duty at Beverly till July 24. Mustered out August 2, 1861.

Regiment lost during service 4 Enlisted men killed and mortally wounded and 2 Enlisted men by disease. Total 6.

10th REGIMENT INFANTRY.—(3 YEARS.)

Organized at Indianapolis, Ind., September 18, 1861. Ordered to Louisville, Ky., September 22. Attached to Thomas' Command, Army of the Ohio, October-November, 1861. 2nd Brigade, Army of the Ohio, to December, 1861. 2nd Brigade, 1st Division, Army of the Ohio, to September, 1862. 2nd Brigade, 1st Division, 3rd Corps, Army of the Ohio, to November, 1862. 2nd Brigade, 3rd Division (Center), 14th Army Corps, Army of the Cumberland, to January, 1863. 2nd Brigade, 3rd Division, 14th Army Corps, Army of the Cumberland, to October, 1863. 3rd Brigade, 3rd Division, 14th Army Corps, to December, 1863. Garrison, Chattanooga, Tenn., Dept. of the Cumberland, to April, 1864. 3rd Brigade, 3rd Division, 14th Army Corps, to September, 1864.

SERVICE.—At Bardstown, Ky., October and November, 1861. Advance on Camp Hamilton, Ky., January 1-15, 1862. Action at Logan's Cross Roads January 19. Mill Springs January 19-20. Moved to Louisville, Ky., thence to Nashville, Tenn., February 11-March 2. March to Savannah, Tenn., March 20-April 7. Expedition to Bear Creek, Ala., April 12-13. Advance on and siege of Corinth, Miss., April 29-May 30. Pursuit to Booneville May 30-June 12. March to Iuka, Miss., thence to Tuscombia, Ala., and duty there till August. March to Louisville, Ky., in pursuit of Bragg August 20-September 26. Pursuit of Bragg into Kentucky October 1-15. Battle of Perryville, Ky., October 8 (Reserve). March to Gallatin, Tenn., and duty there till January 13, 1863. Operations against Morgan December 22, 1862, to January 2, 1863. Boston December 29, 1862. Action at Rolling Fork December 30. Moved to Nashville, Tenn., January 13, 1863; thence to Murfreesboro, Tenn., and duty there till June. Expedition toward Columbia March 4-14. Middle Tennessee (or Tullahoma) Campaign June 23-July 7. Hoover's Gap June 24-26. Tullahoma June 29-30. Occupation of Middle Tennessee till August 16. Passage of the Cumberland Mountains and Tennessee River and Chickamauga (Ga.) Campaign August 16-September 22. Battle of Chickamauga September 19-21. Siege of Chattanooga, Tenn., September 24-November 23. Chattanooga-Ringgold Campaign November 23-27. Orchard Knob November 23-24. Mission Ridge November 25. Demonstration on Dalton, Ga., February 22-27, 1864. Tunnel Hill, Buzzard's Roost Gap and Rocky Faced Ridge February 23-25. Atlanta (Ga.) Campaign May 1 to September 8. Demonstrations on Rocky Faced Ridge May 8-11. Battle of Resaca May 14-15. Advance on Dallas May 18-25. Operations on line of Pumpkin Vine Creek and battles about Dallas, New Hope Church and Allatoona Hills May 25-June 5. Operations about Marietta and against Kenesaw Mountain June 10-July 2. Pine Hill June 11-14. Lost Mountain June 15-17. Assault on Kenesaw June 27. Ruff's Station July 4. Vining Station July 4-5. Chattahoochie River July 5-17. Peach Tree Creek July 19-20. Siege of Atlanta July 22-August 25. Utoy Creek August 5-7. Flank movement on Jonesboro August 25-30. Battle of Jonesboro August 31-September 1. Veterans and Recruits transferred to 58th Indiana Infantry September 8, 1864. Old members mustered out September 19, 1864.

Regiment lost during service 3 Officers and 64 Enlisted men killed and mortally wounded and 5 Officers and 114 Enlisted men by disease. Total 186.

11th REGIMENT INFANTRY.—(3 MONTHS.)

Organized at Indianapolis, Ind., April 21-25, 1861. Duty picketing the Ohio River, near Evansville, Ind., till June 7. Moved to Cumberland, Md., June 7-9. Action at Romney June 13. Seneca Mills June 14. Frankfort and Patterson Creek June 27. March to Bunker Hill July 8 and joined Patterson's command. Expedition to Romney July 11-13. Moved to Indianapolis, Ind., July 29. Mustered out August 2, 1861. Regiment lost 1 Enlisted man by disease during service.

11th REGIMENT INFANTRY.—(3 YEARS.)

Organized at Indianapolis, Ind., August 31, 1861. Moved to Paducah, Ky., September 6, and duty there till February 5, 1862. Attached to 5th Brigade, 2nd Division, Army of the Tennessee, February, 1862. 1st Brigade, 3rd Division, Army of the Tennessee, to July, 1862. Helena, Ark., District of East Arkansas, Dept. of Missouri, to December, 1862. 2nd Brigade, 2nd Division, District of Eastern Arkansas, Dept. of the Tennessee, to January, 1863. 3rd Brigade, 12th Division, 13th Army Corps, Army of the Tennessee, to February, 1863. 1st Brigade, 12th Division, 13th Army Corps, to July, 1863. 1st Brigade, 3rd Division, 13th Army Corps, Army of the Tennessee, to August, 1863, and Dept. of the Gulf to June, 1864. 2nd Brigade, 2nd Division, 19th Army Corps, to August, 1864. 2nd Brigade, 2nd Division, 19th Army Corps, Army of the Shenandoah, Middle Military Division, to January, 1865. 2nd Separate Brigade, 8th Army Corps, Middle Department, to July, 1865.

SERVICE.—Operations against Forts Henry and Heiman, Tenn., February 2-6, 1862. Investment and capture of Fort Donelson, Tenn., February 12-16. Expedition to Clarksville, Tenn., February 19-21. Expedition toward Purdy and operations about Crump's Landing, Tenn., March 9-14. Battle of Shiloh, Tenn., April 6-7. Advance on and siege of Corinth, Miss., April 29-May 30. Occupation of Corinth and pursuit to Booneville May 30-June 3. March to Memphis, Tenn., June 3-20, and duty there till July 24. Ordered to Helena, Ark., July 24, and duty there till April, 1863. Expedition from Helena to Arkansas Post, Ark., November 16-21, 1862. Expedition from Helena to Grenada, Miss., November 27-December 5. Tallahatchie November 30. Mitchell's Cross Roads December 1. Moved to Milliken's Bend, La., April 14. Movement on Bruinsburg and turning Grand Gulf April 25-30. Battle of Port Gibson May 1. 14-Mile Creek May 12-13. Battle of Champion's Hill May 16. Siege of Vicksburg, Miss., May 18-July 4. Assaults on Vicksburg May 19 and 22. Advance on Jackson, Miss., July 4-10. Siege of Jackson July 10-17. Duty at Vicksburg till August 6. Ordered to New Orleans, La., August 6; thence to Brasher City, and duty there till October. Western Louisiana Campaign October 3-November 30. Bayou Cortableau October 21. Carrion Crow Bayou November 3. Regiment Veteranize January 1, 1864. Veterans on furlough March 4 to May 8. Duty in District of LaFourche and Defences of New Orleans, La., till May. At New Orleans, La., till July 19. Ordered to Washington, D. C., July 19. Sheridan's Shenandoah Valley Campaign August 7-November 28. Battle of Opequan, Winchester, September 19. Fisher's Hill September 22. Woodstock September 23. Mt. Jackson September 23-24. Battle of Cedar Creek October 19. Duty in the Shenandoah Valley till January, 1865. Duty at Fort Marshall, Baltimore, Md., January 7 to July 26, 1865. Mustered out July 26, 1865.

Regiment lost during service 1 Officer and 114 Enlisted men killed and mortally wounded and 3 Officers and 170 Enlisted men by disease. Total 288.

12th REGIMENT INFANTRY.—(1 YEAR.)

Organized at Indianapolis, Ind., for one year's State service May 11, 1861. Moved to Evansville, Ind., June 11. Transferred to U. S. service July 18, 1861. Left State for Baltimore, Md., July 23; thence moved to Sandy Hook, Md., July 28. Attached to Abercrombie's Brigade, Banks' Dept. of the Shenandoah, to October, 1861. Abercrombie's Brigade, Bank's Division, Army of the Potomac, to March, 1862. 2nd Brigade, Williams' 1st Division, Banks' 5th Army Corps, to April, 1862, and Dept. of the Shenandoah to May, 1862.

SERVICE.—Duty at Harper's Ferry, W. Va., Williamsport and Sharpsburg, Md., till March, 1862. Advance on Winchester, Va., March 1-12. Skirmish at Stephenson's Station, near Winchester, March 11. Operations in the Shenandoah Valley till April. Duty at Warrenton Junction, Va., April 3-May 5. Reconnoissance to Rappahannock River and skirmish at Rappahannock Crossing April 18. March to Washington, D. C., May 5, and mustered out May 14, 1862. Expiration of term. Regiment lost during service 24 Enlisted men by disease.

12th REGIMENT INFANTRY.—(3 YEARS.)

Organized at Indianapolis, Ind., May 27 to August 27, 1862, and mustered in August 17, 1862. Left State for Kentucky August 21. Attached to Cruft's Brigade, Army of Kentucky, and moved to Richmond, Ky. Battle of Richmond, Ky., August 30. Regiment mostly captured. Paroled and sent to Indianapolis, Ind., for reorganization. Action at Lexington, Ky., September 2 (Detachment). Regiment left Indianapolis, Ind., for Memphis, Tenn., November 23, 1862. Attached to 2nd Brigade, District of Memphis, Tenn., 13th Army Corps (Old), to December, 1862. 1st Brigade, 1st Division, District of Memphis, 13th Army Corps, December, 1862.

1st Brigade, 1st Division, 17th Army Corps, Army of the Tennessee, to January, 1863. 1st Brigade, 1st Division, 16th Army Corps, to July, 1863. 1st Brigade, 4th Division, 15th Army Corps, to September, 1864. 1st Brigade, 1st Division, 15th Army Corps, to June, 1865.

SERVICE.—Grant's Central Mississippi Campaign November-December, 1862. Action at Holly Springs, Miss., December 20, 1862. Duty at Grand Junction and Colliersville, Tenn., guarding Memphis & Charleston R. R. till June, 1863. Ordered to Vicksburg, Miss., June 9. Siege of Vicksburg June 12-July 4. Advance on Jackson, Miss., July 4-10. Siege of Jackson July 10-17. Duty at Big Black till September 28. Moved to Memphis, Tenn., thence march to Chattanooga, Tenn., September 28-November 20. Operations on the Memphis & Charleston R. R. in Alabama October 20-29. Chattanooga-Ringgold Campaign November 23-27. Tunnel Hill November 23-25. Missionary Ridge November 25. March to relief of Knoxville, Tenn., November 28-December 8. Duty at Scottsboro, Ala., till May, 1864. Atlanta Campaign May 1-September 8. Demonstrations on Resaca May 8-13. Near Resaca May 13. Battle of Resaca May 14-15. Movements on Dallas May 18-25. Battles about Dallas, New Hope Church and Allatoona Hills May 25-June 5. Operations about Marietta and against Kenesaw Mountain June 10-July 2. Brush Mountain June 15. Assault on Kenesaw June 27. Nickajack Creek July 2-5. Chattahoochie River July 5-17. Battle of Atlanta July 22. Siege of Atlanta July 22-August 25. Ezra Chapel, Hood's 2nd sortie, July 28. Flank movement on Jonesboro August 25-30. Battle of Jonesboro August 31-September 1. Lovejoy Station September 2-6. Operations against Hood in North Georgia and North Alabama September 29-November 3. March to the sea November 15-December 10. Siege of Savannah December 10-21. Campaign of the Carolinas January to April, 1865. Reconnoissance to Salkehatchie River, South Carolina, January 25. Salkehatchie Swamp February 2-5. South Edisto River February 9. North Edisto River February 12-13. Congaree Creek February 15. Columbia February 16-17. Battle of Bentonville, N. C., March 20-21. Occupation of Goldsboro March 24. Advance on Raleigh April 10-14. Occupation of Raleigh April 14. Bennett's House April 26. Surrender of Johnston and his army. March to Washington, D. C., via Richmond, Va., April 29-May 20. March and review June 24, 1865. Veterans and Recruits transferred to the 48th and 59th Indiana Infantry.

Regiment lost during service 8 Officers and 92 Enlisted men killed and mortally wounded and 2 Officers and 193 Enlisted men by disease. Total 295.

13th REGIMENT INFANTRY.

Organized at Indianapolis, Ind., for one year's service May, 1861, but reorganized for three years and mustered in June 19, 1861. Left State for West Virginia July 4. Attached to Rosecrans' Brigade, McClellan's Army of West Virginia, July 1861. 1st Brigade, Army of Occupation, West Virginia, to September, 1861. Reynolds' Cheat Mountain Brigade, West Virginia, to November, 1861. Milroy's Command, Cheat Mountain District, W. Va., to January, 1862. 2nd Brigade, Landers' Division, to March, 1862. 2nd Brigade, Shields' 2nd Division, Banks' 5th Army Corps and Dept. of the Shenandoah to May, 1862. 2nd Brigade, Shields' Division, Dept. of the Rappahannock, to July, 1862. Ferry's 2nd Brigade, 2nd Division, 4th Army Corps, Army of the Potomac. to September, 1862. Ferry's Brigade, Division at Suffolk, Va., 7th Army Corps, Dept. of Virginia, September, 1862. Foster's Provisional Brigade, Division at Suffolk, 7th Army Corps, to April, 1863. 2nd Brigade, 1st Division, 7th Army Corps, to July, 1863. 1st Brigade, Vogdes' Division, Folly Island, S. C., 10th Army Corps, Dept. of the South, to January, 1864. 1st Brigade, Vogdes Division, Folly Island, S. C., Northern District, Dept. of the South, to February, 1864. 1st Brigade, Vogdes' Division, District of

Florida, to April, 1864. 2nd Brigade, 3rd Division, 10th Army Corps, Army of the James, Dept. of Virginia and North Carolina, to May, 1864. 2nd Brigade, 3rd Division, 18th Army Corps, to June, 1864. 3rd Brigade, 2nd Division, 18th Army Corps, to December, 1864. 3rd Brigade, 2nd Division, 24th Army Corps, to January, 1865. 3rd Brigade, 2nd Division, Terry's Provisional Corps, Dept. of North Carolina, to March, 1865. 3rd Brigade, 2nd Division, 10th Army Corps, Dept. of North Carolina, to September, 1865.

SERVICE.—Campaign in West Virginia July 7-17, 1861. Battle of Rich Mountain July 11. Moved to Beverly July 13, thence to Cheat Mountain Pass. Operations on Cheat Mountain September 11-17. Cheat Mountain Pass September 12. Greenbrier River October 3-4. Scouting Expedition through the Kanawha District October 29-November 7. Expedition to Camp Baldwin December 11-14. Action at Camp Allegheny December 13. Moved to Green Springs Run December 18, and duty there till March, 1862. Skirmishes at Bath, Hancock, Great Cacapon Bridge, Alpine Station and Sir John's Run January 1-4. Advance on Winchester, Va., March 5-15. Kernstown March 22. Battle of Winchester March 23. Occupation of Mt. Jackson April 17. Summerville Heights May 7. March to Fredericksburg May 12-21, and return to Front Royal May 25-30. Battle of Port Republic June 9. Moved to the Peninsula, Va., June 29-July 2. At Harrison's Landing till August 16. Moved to Fortress Monroe August 16-23, thence to Suffolk, Va., August 30, and duty there till June 27, 1863. Reconnoissance to Franklin on the Blackwater October 3, 1862. Franklin October 3. Zuni Minor's Ford December 12. Expedition toward Blackwater January 8-10, 1863. Action at Deserted House January 30. Leesville April 4. Siege of Suffolk April 12-May 4. Edenton, Providence Church and Somerton Roads April 13. Suffolk April 17. Edenton Road April 24. Siege of Suffolk raised May 4. Foster's Plantation May 20. Dix's Peninsula Campaign June 24-July 7. Expedition from White House to South Anna Bridge July 1-7. South Anna Bridge July 4. Moved to Folly Island, S. C., July 28-August 3. Siege operations against Fort Wagner, Morris Island and against Fort Sumpter and Charleston, S. C., till February, 1864. Capture of Forts Wagner and Gregg September 7, 1863. Stationed at Folly Island October, 1863, to February, 1864. Re-enlisted December, 1863. Moved to Jacksonville, Fla., February 23, 1864, and duty there till April 17. Ordered to Hilton Head, S. C.; thence to Gloucester Point, Va. Butler's operations on Southside of the James River and against Petersburg and Richmond, Va., May 4-28. Occupation of Bermuda Hundred May 5. Port Walthal Junction May 6-7. Swift Creek May 9-10. Operations against Fort Darling May 12-16. Battle of Drury's Bluff May 14-16. Bermuda Hundred May 16-28. Moved to White House, thence to Cold Harbor May 28-June 1. Battles about Cold Harbor June 1-12; before Petersburg June 15-18. Siege operations against Petersburg and Richmond June 16, 1864, to December 6, 1864. Mine Explosion, Petersburg, July 30, 1864. Non-Veterans left front June 19. Mustered out June 24, 1864. Demonstration north of the James at Deep Bottom August 13-20. Battle of Strawberry Plains August 14-18. Chaffin's Farm, New Market Heights, September 28-30. Battle of Fair Oaks October 27-28. Detached duty at New York City during Election of 1864 November 4-17. Expedition to Fort Fisher, N. C., December 7-27. 2nd Expedition to Fort Fisher, N. C., January 3-15, 1865. Assault and capture of Fort Fisher January 15. Town Creek February 19-20. Capture of Wilmington February 22. Campaign of the Carolinas March 1-April 26. Advance on Goldsboro March 6-21. Occupation of Goldsboro March 21. Advance on Raleigh April 10-14. Occupation of Raleigh April 14. Bennett's House April 26. Surrender of Johnston and his army. Duty at various points in North Carolina till September. Mustered out September 5, 1865.

Regiment lost during service 3 Officers and 104 Enlisted men killed and mortally wounded and 2 Officers and 146 Enlisted men by disease. Total 255.

14th REGIMENT INFANTRY.

Organized at Terre Haute, Ind., for one year's service May, 1861. Reorganized for three years' service and mustered in June 7, 1861. (1st three years Regiment organized in Indiana.) Moved to Indianapolis, Ind., June 24, thence to Clarksburg, W. Va., July 5. Attached to 1st Brigade, Army of Occupation, West Virginia, to September, 1861. Reynolds' Cheat Mountain District, W. Va., to December, 1861. 1st Brigade, Lander's Division, Army of the Potomac, to March, 1862. 1st Brigade, Shields' 2nd Division, Banks' 5th Army Corps, to April, 1862, and Dept. of the Shenandoah to May 1862. 1st Brigade, Shields' Division, Dept. of the Rappahannock, to June, 1862. Kimball's Independent Brigade, 2nd Army Corps, Army of the Potomac, to September, 1862. 1st Brigade, 3rd Division, 2nd Army Corps, to March, 1864. 3rd Brigade, 2nd Division, 2nd Army Corps, to June, 1864.

SERVICE.—Campaign in West Virginia July 7-17, 1861. Battle of Rich Mountain July 11 (Reserve). Moved to Cheat Mountain July 13, and duty there till October. Operations on Cheat Mountain September 11-17. Cheat Mountain Summit September 12. Action at Greenbrier River October 3-4. Duty at Huttonsville, Philippi and Romney till January 10, 1862. Expedition to Blue's Gap January 6-7. Hanging Rock, Blue's Gap, January 7. Moved to Paw Paw Tunnel January 10, and duty there till March 5. Advance on Winchester, Va., March 5-15. Battle of Winchester March 23. Columbia Furnace April 16. Occupation of Mt. Jackson April 17. March to Fredericksburg May 12-21, and return to Front Royal May 25-30. Front Royal May 30. Expedition to Luray June 3-7. Forced march to Port Republic June 8-9. Battle of Port Republic June 9 (Reserve). Moved to Alexandria June 29, thence to Harrison's Landing June 30-July 2. Chickahominy Swamps July 3-5. Saxall's, Herring Creek, Harrison's Landing July 4. At Harrison's Landing till August 15. Moved to Alexandria, thence to Centreville August 16-29. In works at Centreville and cover Pope's retreat to Washington August 29-September 2. Maryland Campaign September 6-22. Battles of South Mountain September 14; Antietam September 16-17. Moved to Harper's Ferry, W. Va., September 22, and duty there till October 30. Reconnoissance to Leesburg October 1-2. Berry's Ford Gap November 1. March to Falmouth, Va., October 30-November 19. Battle of Fredericksburg, Va., December 12-15. "Mud March" January 20-24, 1863. At Falmouth till April. Chancellorsville Campaign April 27-May 6. Battle of Chancellorsville May 1-5. Gettysburg (Pa.) Campaign June 11-July 24. Battle of Gettysburg July 2-4. Pursuit of Lee to Manassas Gap, Va., July 5-24. Detached on duty at New York City during draft disturbances August 16 to September 6. Bristoe Campaign October 9-22. Auburn and Bristoe October 14. Blackburn's Ford October 15. Advance to line of the Rappahannock November 7-8. Mine Run Campaign November 26-December 2. Robertson's Tavern or Locust Grove November 27. Demonstration on the Rapidan February 6-7, 1864. Morton's Ford February 6-7. Campaign from the Rapidan to the James River May 4-June 15. Battle of the Wilderness May 5-7. Laurel Hill May 8. Spottsylvania May 8-12. Po River May 10. Spottsylvania Court House May 12-21. Assault on the Salient "Bloody Angle" May 12. North Anna River May 23-26. On line of the Pamunkey May 26-28. Totopotomoy May 28-31. Cold Harbor June 1-6. Left front June 6. Mustered out June 16, 1864, expiration of term. Veterans and Recruits transferred to 20th Indiana Infantry.

Regiment lost during service 11 Officers and 139 Enlisted men killed and mortally wounded and 72 Enlisted men by disease. Total 222.

15th REGIMENT INFANTRY.

Organized at Lafayette, Ind., for one year's service

May, 1861. Reorganized for three years' service and mustered in June 14, 1861. Moved to Indianapolis, Ind., thence to Clarksburg, W. Va., July 1-6. West Virginia Campaign July 6-17. Attached to 1st Brigade, Army of Occupation, West Virginia, July to September, 1861. Reynolds' Cheat Mountain District, W. Va., to November, 1861. 15th Brigade, Army of the Ohio, to December, 1861. 15th Brigade, 4th Division, Army of the Ohio, to March, 1862. 15th Brigade, 6th Division, Army of the Ohio, March, 1862. 21st Brigade, 6th Division, Army of the Ohio, to September, 1862. 21st Brigade, 6th Division, 2nd Corps, Army of the Ohio, to November, 1862. 2nd Brigade, 1st Division, Left Wing 14th Army Corps, Army of the Cumberland, to January, 1863. 2nd Brigade, 1st Division, 21st Army Corps, Army of the Cumberland, to October, 1863. 2nd Brigade, 2nd Division, 4th Army Corps, Army of the Cumberland, to February, 1864. Garrison, Chattanooga, Tenn., Dept. of the Cumberland, to June, 1864.

SERVICE.—Duty in Elkwater Valley, W. Va., July to November, 1861. Operations on Cheat Mountain September 11-17. Elkwater September 11. Cheat Mountain Pass September 12. Greenbrier River October 3-4. Ordered to Louisville November 19. Duty at Bardstown and Lebanon, Ky., till February, 1862. March to Nashville, Tenn., February 17-March 13, and to Savannah, Tenn., March 21-April 6. Battle of Shiloh April 6-7. Advance on and siege of Corinth, Miss., April 29-May 30. Pursuit to Booneville May 30-June 12. Buell's Campaign in Northern Alabama and Middle Tennessee June to August. March to Louisville, Ky., in pursuit of Bragg August 21-September 26. Pursuit of Bragg into Kentucky October 1-22. Battle of Perryville, Ky., October 8 (Reserve). March to Nashville, Tenn., October 22-November 7, and duty there till December 26. Lavergne December 11. Advance on Murfreesboro December 26-30. Battle of Stone's River December 30-31, 1862, and January 1-3, 1863. Duty at Murfreesboro till June. Reconnoissance to Nolensville and Versailles January 13-15. Middle Tennessee or Tullahoma Campaign June 23-July 7. Camp at Pelham till August 17. Passage of the Cumberland Mountains and Tennessee River and Chickamauga (Ga.) Campaign August 17-September 22. Occupation of Chattanooga September 9, and assigned to duty there as garrison. Siege of Chattanooga, Tenn., September 24-November 23. Chattanooga-Ringgold Campaign November 23-27. Orchard Knob November 23-24. Mission Ridge November 25. Pursuit to Graysville November 26-27. March to relief of Knoxville, Tenn., November 28-December 8. Duty at Knoxville and vicinity till February, 1864. Ordered to Chattanooga, Tenn., and garrison duty there till June. Mustered out June 16, 1864 (expiration of term). Veterans and Recruits transferred to 17th Indiana Infantry.

Regiment lost during service 4 Officers and 103 Enlisted men killed and mortally wounded and 76 Enlisted men by disease. Total 183.

16th REGIMENT INFANTRY.—(1 YEAR.)

Organized at Richmond, Ind., for one year's service May, 1861. Transferred to United States service July 23, 1861, and left State for Baltimore, Md.; thence moved to Sandy Hook, Md., July 28. Attached to Abercrombie's Brigade, Dept. of the Shenandoah, to October, 1861. Abercrombie's Brigade, Banks' Division, Army of the Potomac, to March, 1862. 2nd Brigade, 1st Division, Banks' 5th Army Corps, to April, 1862. 2nd Brigade, 1st Division, Dept. of the Shenandoah, to May, 1862.

SERVICE.—Duty at Pleasant Valley, Md., till August 17, 1861, and at Darnestown till October 21. Operations about Ball's Bluff October 21-24. Action at Goose Creek and near Edward's Ferry October 22. Camp at Seneca Creek till December 2, and at Frederick City till February, 1862. Moved to Harper's Ferry, W. Va., February 27, and to Charleston March 1. March to Winchester March 10-12. Strasburg March 27. Operations in the Shenandoah Valley till April. Duty at

Warrenton, Va., April 2 to May 22. Reconnoissance to the Rappahannock River April 7. Ordered to Washington, D. C., May 12, and mustered out May 14, 1862.

Regiment lost during service 1 Enlisted man killed and 15 Enlisted men by disease. Total 16.

16th REGIMENT INFANTRY.—(3 YEARS.)

Organized at Indianapolis, Ind., May 27 to August 19, 1862. Mustered in August 19, 1862. Moved to Louisville, Ky., August 19, and to Richmond, Ky. Attached to Manson's Brigade, Army of Kentucky. Battle of Richmond, Ky., August 30. Regiment captured. Paroled and sent to Indianapolis, Ind. Exchanged November 1, 1862. Ordered to Memphis, Tenn., November 20. Attached to 1st Brigade, 10th Division, Right Wing 13th Army Corps (Old), Dept. of the Tennessee, to December, 1862. 1st Brigade, 1st Division, Sherman's Yazoo Expedition to January, 1863. 1st Brigade, 10th Division, 13th Army Corps, Army of the Tennessee, to July, 1863. 1st Brigade, 4th Division, 13th Army Corps, Dept. of the Tennessee, to August, 1863, and Dept. of the Gulf to September, 1863. Unattached Cavalry Division, Dept. of the Gulf, to November, 1863. 1st Brigade, Cavalry Division, Dept. of the Gulf, to June, 1864. 4th Brigade, Cavalry Division, Dept. of the Gulf, to August, 1864. District of LaFourche, Dept. of the Gulf, to June, 1865.

SERVICE.—Sherman's Yazoo Expedition December 20, 1862, to January 3, 1863. Expedition to Texas and Shreveport R. R. December 25-26. Chickasaw Bayou December 26-28. Chickasaw Bluff December 29. Expedition to Arkansas Post, Ark., January 3-10, 1863. Assault and capture of Fort Hindman, Arkansas Post, January 10-11. Moved to Young's Point, La., January 17-21. Duty there and at Milliken's Bend till April. Expedition to Greenville, Miss., and Cypress Bend, Ark., February 14-29. Action at Cypress Bend, Ark., February 19. Fish Lake, near Greenville, February 23. Movement on Bruinsburg and turning Grand Gulf April 25-30. Battle of Port Gibson, Miss., May 1. Battle of Champion's Hill May 16. Big Black River May 17. Siege of Vicksburg May 18-July 4. Assaults on Vicksburg May 19 and 22. Advance on Jackson, Miss., July 4-10. Siege of Jackson July 10-17. Duty at Vicksburg till August 24. Ordered to New Orleans, La., August 24. Regiment mounted and assigned to duty along Eastern shore of the Mississippi, protecting transportation to New Orleans and points along the coast till October. Expedition to New and Amite Rivers September 24-29. Western Louisiana "Teche" Campaign October 3-November 30. Action at Grand Coteau November 3. Vermillionville November 8. Camp Piatt November 20. Ordered to New Orleans to refit. Action at Franklin February 22, 1864. Red River Campaign March 10-May 22. Advance from Franklin to Alexandria March 14-26. Bayou Rapides March 20. Henderson's Hill March 21. Monett's Ferry and Cloutiersville March 29-30. Crump's Hill April 2. Wilson's Plantation, near Pleasant Hill, April 7. Bayou de Paul Carroll's Mills April 8. Battle of Sabine Cross Roads April 8. Pleasant Hill April 9. Grand Ecore April 16. Natchitoches April 22. About Cloutiersville April 22-24. Cane River Crossing April 23. Alexandria April 28. Hudnot's Plantation May 1. Alexandria May 1-8. Retreat to Morganza May 13-20. Wilson's Landing May 14. Avoyelle's Prairie May 15. Mansure May 16. Morganza May 28. Ordered to report to General Cameron, and assigned to frontier and patrol duty in District of Lafourche, Dept. of the Gulf, till June, 1865. Action at Berwick August 27, 1864. Expedition to Natchez Bayou August 30-September 2. Near Gentilly's Plantation September 1. Expedition to Grand Lake, Grand River, Lake Fosse Point, Bayou Pigeon and Lake Natchez September 7-11. Labadieville September 8. Bayou Corn September 9. Expedition from Terre Bonne to Bayou Grand Caillou November 19-27. Bayou Grand Caillou November 23. Expedition from Morganza to Morgan's Ferry, Archafalaya River, December 13-14. Expedition from Brashear City to Amite River Febru-

ary 10-13, 1865. Expedition to Grand Glaze and Bayou Goula February 14-18 (Cos. "B," "F," "K"). Scout to Bayou Goula March 23-24 (Co. "K"). Skirmish Grand Bayou April 4. Expedition to Bayou Goula April 19-25 (Cos. "B," "K"). Operations about Brashear City April 21-22. Skirmish Brown's Plantation May 11. Mustered out June 30, 1865. Veterans and Recruits transferred to 13th Indiana Cavalry.

Regiment lost during service 3 Officers and 82 Enlisted men killed and mortally wounded and 212 Enlisted men by disease. Total 297.

17th REGIMENT INFANTRY.

Organized at Indianapolis, Ind., and mustered in June 12, 1861. Left State for Parkersburg, W. Va., July 1. Attached to District of the Kanawha, West Virginia, to September, 1861. Cheat Mountain District, W. Va., to November, 1861. 15th Brigade, Army of the Ohio, to January, 1862. 15th Brigade, 4th Division, Army of the Ohio, January, 1862. 15th Brigade, 6th Division, Army of the Ohio, to September, 1862. 15th Brigade, 6th Division, 2nd Corps, Army of the Ohio, to November, 1862. 1st Brigade, 1st Division, Left Wing 14th Army Corps, Army of the Cumberland, to December, 1862. 2nd Brigade, 5th Division (Center), 14th Army Corps, to January, 1863. 2nd Brigade, 5th Division, 14th Army Corps, to June, 1863. 1st Brigade, 4th Division, 14th Army Corps, to October, 1863. Wilder's Mounted Brigade, Army of the Cumberland, to November, 1863. 2nd Brigade, 2nd Cavalry Division, Army of the Cumberland, November, 1863. 3rd Brigade, 2nd Cavalry Division, Army of the Cumberland, to October, 1864. 1st Brigade, 2nd Division, Wilson's Cavalry Corps, Military Division Mississippi, to August, 1865.

SERVICE.—Moved to Oakland, W. Va., July 23, 1861; thence to Camp Pendleton and duty there till August 7. Moved to Cheat Mountain Pass and Elkwater August 7-13. Operations on Cheat Mountain September 11-17. Elkwater September 11. Point Mountain Turnpike September 11-12. Cheat Mountain Pass September 12. Elkwater September 14. Action at Greenbrier River October 3-4. Moved to Louisville, Ky., November 19 and duty there till December 10. At Camp Wickliffe, Ky., till February 10, 1862. Advance on Bowling Green, Ky., and Nashville, Tenn., February 10-March 12. March to Savannah, Tenn., March 29-April 7. Lawrenceburg April 4. Arrive at Pittsburg Landing April 7. Advance on and siege of Corinth, Miss., April 29-May 30. Pursuit to Booneville May 31-June 6. Buell's Campaign in Northern Alabama and Middle Tennessee June to August. Little Pond, near McMinnville, Tenn., August 30. March to Louisville, Ky., in pursuit of Bragg September 3-26. (Siege of Munfordsville, Ky., September 16-21. A detachment of recruits en route to join Regiment captured September 21.) Moved to Bardstown, Ky., October 1 and duty there till October 18. March to Nashville, Tenn., via Lebanon, Columbia, Glasgow, Ky., and Gallatin, Tenn., October 18-November 26. Duty at Nashville till February 1, 1863. Moved to Murfreesboro, Tenn., February 1 and duty there till June. Expedition to Auburn, Liberty and Alexandria February 3-8. Regiment mounted February 12, and assigned to duty as Mounted Infantry. Expedition to Woodbury March 3-8. Action at Woodbury March 6. Expedition to Liberty, Carthage and Lebanon April 1-8. Expedition to McMinnville April 20-30. Armed with Spencer Carbines May 18. Middle Tennessee (or Tullahoma) Campaign June 23-July 7. Big Spring Gap June 24. Hoover's Gap June 24-26. Occupation of Manchester June 27. Raid on Bragg's communications July 1-August 16. Captured depot of supplies at Dechard. Passage on the Cumberland Mountains and Tennessee River and Chickamauga (Ga.) Campaign August 16-September 22. Capture of Chattanooga September 9. Ringgold, Ga., September 11. Lee and Gordon's Mills September 12. Leet's Tan Yard September 12-13. Alexander's Bridge and Hall's House September 18. Vinyard's House September 19. Battle of

Chickamauga September 19-21. Widow Glen's House September 20. Operations against Wheeler and Roddy September 29-October 17. Thompson's Cove, near Beersheba October 3. Glass Cocks October 4. Murfreesboro Road, near McMinnville, October 4. Farmington October 7. Sim's Farm, near Shelbyville, October 7. Shelbyville October 10. Expedition from Maysville to Whitesburg and Decatur November 14-17. Chattanooga-Ringgold Campaign November 23-27. Raid on East Tennessee & Georgia R. R. November 24-27. Charleston and Cleveland November 26. March to relief of Knoxville, Tenn., November 28-December 8. Duty at Pulaski, Charleston and Nashville, Tenn., till May, 1864. Regiment re-enlisted January 4, 1864. Veterans on furlough January 22 to April 2. Atlanta (Ga.) Campaign May 1 to September 8. Joined Sherman May 10. Battle of Resaca May 14-15. Movements on Dallas May 18-25. Near Dallas May 24. Operations on line of Pumpkin Vine Creek and battles about Dallas, New Hope Church and Allatoona Hills May 25-June 5. Big Shanty June 9. Operations about Marietta and against Kenesaw Mountain June 10-July 2. Noonday Creek June 19. Powder Springs June 20-27. Rottenwood Creek July 4. Chattahoochie River July 5-17. Covington July 22. Siege of Atlanta July 22-August 25. Garrard's Raid to South River July 27-31. Flat Rock Bridge July 28. Lovejoy Station July 29-30. Newnan's July 30. Operations at Chattahoochie River Bridge August 26-September 2. Operations against Hood in North Georgia and North Alabama September 29-November 1. Near Lost Mountain October 4-7. New Hope Church October 5. Dallas October 7. Rome October 10-11. Narrows October 11. Coosaville Road, near Rome, October 13. Near Summerville October 18. Little River October 20. Leesburg and Grove Road Crossing, Ala., October 21. Goshen October 28. Dismounted November 1 and ordered to Louisville, Ky. Duty there till December 28. Moved to Nashville, Tenn., thence to Gravelly Springs, Ala., and duty there till March, 1865. Wilson's Raid to Macon, Ga., March 22-April 24. Plantersville, Ala., April 1. Selma April 2. Montgomery April 12. Columbia April 16. Spring Hill, Mimm's Mills, Tobasofkee Creek, Montpelier Springs and Rocky Creek Bridge, near Macon, April 20. Capture of Macon April 20. Post duty at Macon till August. Mustered out August 8, 1865.

Regiment lost during service 3 Officers and 90 Enlisted men killed and mortally wounded and 1 Officer and 143 Enlisted men by disease. Total 237.

18th REGIMENT INFANTRY.

Organized at Indianapolis, Ind., and mustered in August 16, 1861. Left State for St. Louis, Mo., August 17. March to relief of Colonel Mulligan at Lexington, Mo., September. Action at Glasgow Mountain September 19. Attached to Fremont's Army of the West and Dept. of Missouri to January, 1862. 1st Brigade, 3rd Division, Army of Southwest Missouri, to May, 1862. 1st Division, Army of Southwest Missouri, to July, 1862. District of Eastern Arkansas, Dept. of Missouri, to October, 1862. 2nd Brigade, 1st Division, District of Southeast Missouri, Dept. of Missouri, to March, 1863. 1st Brigade, 14th Division, 13th Army Corps, Army of the Tennessee, to July, 1863. 1st Brigade, 1st Division, 13th Army Corps, Army of the Tennessee, to August, 1863, and Dept. of the Gulf to June, 1864. 3rd Brigade, 2nd Division, 19th Army Corps, to August, 1864. 4th Brigade, 2nd Division, 19th Army Corps, Army of the Shenandoah Middle Military Division, to December, 1864. 1st Brigade, 2nd Division, 19th Army Corps, to January, 1865. 1st Brigade, Grover's Division, District of Savannah, Ga., Dept. of the South, to August, 1865.

SERVICE.—Fremont's advance on Springfield, Mo., September 22-October 15, 1861. March to Otterville, Mo., November, and duty there till January, 1862. Expedition to Milford December 15-19, 1862. Action at Shawnee Mound or Milford on the Blackwater, and capture of 1,300 prisoners December 18. Advance on Springfield, Mo., January 25-February 14. Pursuit of

Price to Cassville, Ark. Battles of Pea Ridge, Ark., March 6-8. At Sulphur Rock till May. March to Batesville, thence to Helena, Ark., May 25-July 14. Duty at Helena till October. Ordered to Pilot Knob, Mo., and operations in Southeast Missouri till March 5, 1863. Moved to Helena, Ark., March 5, thence to Milliken's Bend, La., and duty there till April. Movement on Bruinsburg and turning Grand Gulf April 25-30. Battle of Port Gibson May 1. Battle of Champion's Hill May 16. Big Black River Bridge May 17. Siege of Vicksburg, Miss., May 18-July 4. Assaults on Vicksburg May 19 and 22. Advance on Jackson, Miss., July 4-10. Siege of Jackson July 10-17. Duty at Vicksburg till August 20. Ordered to New Orleans, La., August 20. Duty at Carrollton, Brashear City and Berwick till October. Western Louisiana Campaign October 3-November 8. Moved to New Orleans November 8, thence to Texas November 12. Capture of Mustang Island November 17. Fort Esperanza November 27-30. Duty at Mustang Island and Indianola till March, 1864. Regiment re-enlisted January 1, 1864. Near Baton Rouge, La., March 8-May 3. Veteran furlough and duty in Indiana June 4 to July 16. Moved to Bermuda Hundred, Va., July 16; thence to Washington, D. C., August 5. March to Shenandoah Valley August 10-19. Sheridan's Shenandoah Valley Campaign August to November. Battle of Opequan, Winchester, September 19. Fisher's Hill September 22. Battle of Cedar Creek October 19. Duty in the Shenandoah Valley till January, 1865. Moved to Baltimore, Md., thence to Savannah, Ga., January 6-20. Duty there till May 3. At Augusta, Ga., till June 7. Provost duty in Southern Georgia till August. Mustered out August 28, 1865.

Regiment lost during service 5 Officers and 68 Enlisted men killed and mortally wounded and 1 Officer and 130 Enlisted men by disease. Total 204.

19th REGIMENT INFANTRY.

Organized at Indianapolis, Ind., and mustered in July 29, 1861. Left State for Washington, D. C., August 5. Attached to 3rd Brigade, McDowell's Division, Army of the Potomac, to March, 1862. 1st Brigade, King's 3rd Division, 1st Army Corps, Army of the Potomac, to April, 1862. 3rd Brigade, King's Division, Dept. of the Rappahannock, to June, 1862. 4th Brigade, 1st Division, 3rd Army Corps, Army of Virginia, to September, 1862. 4th Brigade, Iron Brigade, 1st Division, 1st Army Corps, Army of the Potomac, to June, 1863. 1st Brigade, 1st Division, 1st Army Corps, to March, 1864. 1st Brigade, 4th Division, 5th Army Corps, to August, 1864. 3rd Brigade, 3rd Division, 5th Army Corps, to September, 1864. 1st Brigade, 3rd Division, 5th Army Corps to October.

SERVICE.—Affair at Lewinsville, Va., September 11, 1861. Reconnoissance to Lewinsville September 25. Occupation of Falls Church September 28. Duty at Fort Craig, Va., till March, 1862. Advance on Manassas, Va., March 10-16. Camp at Upton's Hill till April 9. Advance on Falmouth, Va., April 9-19. Duty at Falmouth and Fredericksburg till May 25. McDowell's advance on Richmond May 25-29. Operations against Jackson June 1-21. At Warrenton till August 5. Reconnoissance to Orange Court House July 24-27. Reconnoissance to Frederick's Hall Station and Spottsylvania Court House August 5-8. Thornburg's Mills August 5-6. Pope's Campaign in Northern Virginia August 16-September 2. Fords of the Rappahannock August 21-23. Sulphur Springs August 26. Gainesville August 28. Groveton August 29. Bull Run August 30. Maryland Campaign September 6-22. Battle of South Mountain September 14. Battle of Antietam September 16-17. At Sharpsburg till October 30. Movement to Warrenton, thence to the Rappahannock October 30-November 19. Battle of Fredericksburg, Va., December 12-15. Burnside's 2nd Campaign ("Mud March,") January 20-24, 1863. Duty at Falmouth till April. Chancellorsville Campaign April 27-May 6. Operations at Pollock's Mill Creek April 29-May 2. Fitzhugh's Crossing April 29-30. Battle of Chancellorsville May 2-5.

Expedition to Westmoreland County and operations on Northern Neck May 20-26. Gettysburg (Pa.) Campaign June 11-July 24. Battle of Gettysburg July 1-3. Pursuit of Lee to Manassas Gap July 5-24. At Rappahannock Station and Culpeper August 1 to October. Bristoe Campaign October 9-22. Advance to line of the Rappahannock November 7-8. Mine Run Campaign November 26-December 2. Demonstration on the Rapidan February 6-7. 1864. Campaign from the Rapidan to the James River May 4-June 15. Battles of the Wilderness May 5-7; Laurel Hill May 8. Spottsylvania May 8-12. Spottsylvania Court House May 12-21. Assault on the Salient May 12. North Anna River May 23-26. Jericho Ford May 23. On line of the Pamunkey May 26-29. Totopotomoy May 28-31. Cold Harbor June 1-12. Bethesda Church June 1-3. Bottom's Bridge June 12. Before Petersburg June 16-18. Siege of Petersburg June 16 to October 18. Non-Veterans mustered out July 28, 1864. Weldon R. R. August 18-21. Consolidated with 20th Indiana Infantry October 18, 1864.

Regiment lost during service 5 Officers and 194 Enlisted men killed and mortally wounded and 1 Officer and 116 Enlisted men by disease. Total 316.

20th REGIMENT INFANTRY.

Organized at Lafayette, Ind., and mustered in July 22, 1861. Left State for Baltimore, Md., August 2. Stationed at Cockeysville, Md., guarding Northern Central R. R. to Pennsylvania line till September. Expedition to Hatteras Inlet, N. C., September 24-27. At fortifications North end of Hatteras bank till November. Action at Chickamacomico October 4. Ordered to Fortress Monroe, Va., November 9, and duty there till March, 1862. Attached to Fortress Monroe, Va., Dept. of Virginia, to May, 1862. Robinson's Brigade, Dept. of Virginia, to June, 1862. 1st Brigade, 3rd Division, 3rd Army Corps, Army of the Potomac, to August, 1862. 1st Brigade, 1st Division, 3rd Army Corps, to March, 1864. 1st Brigade, 3rd Division, 2nd Army Corps, to July, 1865.

SERVICE.—Engagement at Newport News, Va., between Ram "Merrimac" and United States Ships "Cumberland" and "Congress" and the "Monitor" March 8-9, 1862. Occupation of Norfolk and Portsmouth May 10. Joined Army of the Potomac on the Peninsula June 8. Charles City Cross Roads June 19. Seven days before Richmond June 25-July 1. Battles of Oak Grove ("The Orchards") June 25; White Oak Swamp and Glendale June 30; Jordan's Ford June 30; Malvern Hill July 1 and July 5. At Harrison's Landing till August 16. Movement to Fortress Monroe, thence to Centreville August 16-28. Pope's Campaign in Virginia August 28-September 2. Battles of Groveton August 29; Bull Run August 30; Chantilly September 1. Duty at Arlington Heights till October. At Poolesville till October 29. Movement to Falmouth, Va., October 29-November 19. Battle of Fredericksburg, Va., December 12-15. Burnside's 2nd Campaign ("Mud March") January 20-24, 1863. At Falmouth till April. Chancellorsville Campaign April 27-May 6. Battle of Chancellorsville May 1-5. (Captured 23rd Georgia.) Gettysburg (Pa.) Campaign June 11-July 24. Battle of Gettysburg July 1-3. Pursuit of Lee to Manassas Gap, Va., July 5-24. Wapping Heights, Va., July 23. Detached at New York City during draft disturbances August-September. Advance to line of the Rappahannock November 7-8. Kelly's Ford November 7. Mine Run Campaign November 26-December 2. Payne's Farm November 27. Regiment veteranize January 1, 1864. Demonstration on the Rapidan February 6-7. Campaign from the Rapidan to the James River May 4-June 15. Battles of the Wilderness May 5-7; Laurel Hill May 8; Spottsylvania May 8-12; Po River May 10; Spottsylvania Court House May 12-21. Assault on the Salient ("Bloody Angle") May 12. Harris Farm (or Fredericksburg) Road May 19. North Anna River May 23-26. On line of the Pamunken May 26-28. Totopotomoy May 28-31. Cold Harbor June 1-12. Before Petersburg June 16-18. Siege of Petersburg June 16, 1864 to April 2, 1865.

Jerusalem Plank Road, Weldon R. R., June 22-23, 1864. Demonstration on North side of the James July 27-29. Deep Bottom July 28-29. Demonstration on North side of the James at Deep Bottom August 13-20. Strawberry Plains August 14-18. Ream's Station August 25. The Chimneys September 10. Poplar Springs Church September 29-October 2. Yellow House October 2-5. Boydton Plank Road, Hatcher's Run, October 27-28. Raid on Weldon Railroad December 7-12. Dabney's Mills, Hatcher's Run, February 5-7, 1865. Watkins' House March 25. Appomattox Campaign March 28-April 9. Vaughan Road, near Hatcher's Run, March 29. Crow's House March 31. Fall of Petersburg April 2. Sailor's Creek April 6. Farmville April 7. Appomattox Court House April 9. Surrender of Lee and his army. March to Washington, D. C., May 2-12. Grand Review May 23. Moved to Louisville, Ky., June 14-21 and duty there till July 12. Mustered out July 12, and discharged at Indianapolis, Ind.

Regiment lost during service 15 Officers and 186 Enlisted men killed and mortally wounded and 113 Enlisted men by disease. Total 314.

21st REGIMENT INFANTRY.

See 1st Regiment Heavy Artillery.

22nd REGIMENT INFANTRY.

Organized at Madison, Ind., and mustered in at Indianapolis, Ind., August 15, 1861. Moved to St. Louis, Mo., August 17. March to relief of Colonel Mulligan at Lexington, Mo., September. Action at Glasgow, Mo., September 19. Fremont's advance on Springfield, Mo., September 22-October 15. Duty at Otterville, Mo., till January, 1862. Attached to Army of the West and Dept. of Missouri September, 1861, to January, 1862. 1st Brigade, 3rd Division, Army of Southwest Missouri, to May, 1862. 1st Brigade, 4th Division, Army of Mississippi, to September, 1862. 30th Brigade, 9th Division, Army of the Ohio, September, 1862. 30th Brigade, 9th Division, 3rd Corps, Army of the Ohio, to November, 1862. 1st Brigade, 1st Division, Right Wing 14th Army Corps, Army of the Cumberland, to January, 1863. 1st Brigade, 1st Division, 20th Army Corps, Army of the Cumberland, to October, 1863. 2nd Brigade, 1st Division, 4th Army Corps, Army of the Cumberland, October, 1863. 1st Brigade, 2nd Division, 4th Army Corps, to April, 1864. 3rd Brigade, 2nd Division, 14th Army Corps, to July, 1865.

SERVICE.—Pope's Expedition to Milford, Mo., December 15-19, 1861. Action at Milford (or Shawnee) Mound on Blackwater Creek and capture of 1,300 prisoners December 18. Advance on Springfield, Mo., January 24-February 14. Pursuit of Price to Cassville, Ark. Battles of Pea Ridge, Ark., March 6-8. March to Batesville, Ark., April 5-May 3. Moved to Cape Girardeau, Mo., thence to Corinth, Miss., May 20-28. Siege of Corinth, Miss., May 28-30. Pursuit to Booneville May 31-June 6. Duty at Jacinto and other points in Northern Mississippi till August 17. To Louisville, Ky., August 17-September 26. Pursuit of Bragg into Kentucky October 1-15. Battle of Perryville, Ky., October 8. Lancaster October 14. March to Nashville, Tenn., October 16-November 28. Scout to Harpeth Shoals November 26-30. At Nashville till December 26. Wilson's Creek Pike December 25. Advance on Murfreesboro December 26-30. Nolensville December 26-27. Battle of Stone's River December 30-31, 1862, and January 1-3, 1863. Duty at Murfreesboro till June. Operations on Edgeville Pike, near Murfreesboro, June 4. Middle Tennessee (or Tullahoma) Campaign June 23-July 7. Liberty Gap June 24-27. Occupation of Middle Tennessee till August 16. Passage of the Cumberland Mountains and Tennessee River and Chickamauga (Ga.) Campaign August 16-September 22. Guard supply trains over Mountains in rear of Bragg's army during battle of Chickamauga. Siege of Chattanooga, Tenn., September 22-November 23. Before Chattanooga September 22-26. Chattanooga-Ringgold Campaign November 23-27. Orchard Knob November 23-24. Mission Ridge November 25. Pursuit to Graysville

November 26-27. March to relief of Knoxville, Tenn., November 28-December 8. Re-enlisted at Blain's Cross Roads December 23, 1863. Operations in East Tennessee till February, 1864. Veterans on furlough February and March. Atlanta (Ga.) Campaign May 1-September 8. Tunnel Hill May 6-7. Demonstration on Rocky Faced Ridge May 8-11. Buzzard's Roost Gap May 8-9. Battle of Resaca May 14-15. Rome May 17-18. Advance on Dallas May 18-25. Operations on line of Pumpkin Vine Creek and battles about Dallas, New Hope Church and Allatoona Hills May 25-June 5. Operations about Marietta and against Kenesaw Mountain June 10-July 2. Pine Hill June 11-14. Lost Mountain June 15-17. Assault on Kenesaw June 27. Ruff's Station July 4. Chattahoochie River July 5-17. Peach Tree Creek July 19-20. Siege of Atlanta July 22-August 25. Utoy Creek August 5-7. Flank movement on Jonesboro August 25-30. Battle of Jonesboro August 31-September 1. Operations against Hood in North Georgia and North Alabama September 29-November 3. March to the sea November 15-December 10. Louisville November 30. Siege of Savannah December 10-21. Campaign of the Carolinas January to April, 1865. Taylor's Hole Creek, Averysboro, N. C., March 16. Battle of Bentonville March 19-21. Occupation of Goldsboro March 24. Advance on Raleigh April 10-14. Occupation of Raleigh April 14. Bennett's House April 26. Surrender of Johnston and his army. March to Washington, D. C., via Richmond, Va., April 29-May 19. Grand Review May 24. Moved to Louisville, Ky., June and duty there till July. Mustered out July 24, 1865.

Regiment lost during service 14 Officers and 139 Enlisted men killed and mortally wounded and 190 Enlisted men by disease. Total 343.

23rd REGIMENT INFANTRY.

Organized at New Albany, Ind., and mustered in July 29, 1861. Left State for Paducah, Ky., August 15. Attached to District of Paducah, Ky., to February, 1862. 3rd Brigade, 3rd Division, Army of the Tennessee, to March, 1862. 2nd Brigade, 3rd Division, Army of the Tennessee, to July, 1862. Unattached, District of Jackson, Tenn., to November, 1862. 2nd Brigade, 3rd Division, Left Wing 13th Army Corps (Old), Dept. of the Tennessee, to December, 1862. 1st Brigade, 3rd Division, 13th Army Corps, December, 1862. 1st Brigade, 3rd Division, 17th Army Corps, Army of the Tennessee, to January, 1864. 3rd Brigade, 4th Division, 17th Army Corps, to April, 1864. 1st Brigade, 4th Division, 17th Army Corps, to July, 1865.

SERVICE.—Duty at Paducah, Ky., till February, 1862. Demonstration from Paducah on Columbus, Ky., November 7-9, 1861. Moved to Fort Donelson, Tenn., February 12-15, 1862. Expedition toward Purdy and operations about Crump's Landing, Tenn., March 9-14. Battle of Shiloh, Tenn., April 6-7. Advance on and siege of Corinth, Miss., April 29-May 30. March to Purdy, thence to Bolivar, Tenn., and duty there till September. March to Iuka, Miss., September 1-20. Duty in District of Jackson till November. Grant's Central Mississippi Campaign November 2, 1862, to January 10, 1863. Reconnoissance from LaGrange November 8-9, 1862. Moved to Memphis, Tenn., January 20, 1863; thence to Lake Providence, La., February 21, and to Milliken's Bend, La., April 17. Passage of Vicksburg and Warrenton Batteries April 22 (Detachment). Movement on Bruinsburg and turning Grand Gulf April 25-30. Battle of Port Gibson, Miss., May 1. Bayou Pierrie, May 3. Ingraham's Heights May 3. Bruinsburg May 6. Battle of Raymond May 12. Jackson May 14. Battle of Champion's Hill May 16. Siege of Vicksburg May 18-July 4. Assaults on Vicksburg May 19 and 22. Surrender of Vicksburg July 4, and duty there till February, 1864. Expedition to Monroe, La., August 20-September 2, 1863. Operations about Natchez, Miss., December 1-10. Meridian Campaign February 3-March 2, 1864. Veterans on furlough March and April. Moved to Bird's Point, Mo.; thence to Clifton, Tenn.; thence march to Ackworth, Ga., May 5-June 8. Atlanta (Ga.)

Campaign June 9 to September 8. Operations about Marietta and against Kenesaw Mountain June 10-July 2. Assault on Kenesaw June 27. Nickajack Creek July 2-5. Chattahoochie River July 5-17. Nickajack Creek July 6-8. Leggett's (or Bald) Hill July 20-21. Battle of Atlanta July 22. Siege of Atlanta July 22-August 25. Flank movement on Jonesboro August 25-30. Battle of Jonesboro August 31-September 1. Lovejoy Station September 2-6. Operations against Hood in North Georgia and North Alabama September 29-November 3. Shadow Church and Westbrook, near Fairburn, October 1-3. March to the sea November 15-December 10. Ball's Ferry and Georgia Central Railroad Bridge, Oconee River, November 23-25. Siege of Savannah December 10-21. Campaign of the Carolinas January to April, 1865. Pocotaligo, S. C., January 14. Salkehatchie Swamp February 2-5. Rivers Bridge February 3. South Edisto River February 9. Orangeburg February 12-13. Columbia February 16-17. Fayetteville, N. C., March 11. Battle of Bentonville March 19-21. Occupation of Goldsboro March 24. Advance on Raleigh April 10-14. Occupation of Raleigh April 14. Bennett's House April 26. Surrender of Johnston and his army. March to Washington, D. C., via Richmond, Va., April 29-May 19. Grand Review May 24. Moved to Louisville June, and duty there till July 23. Mustered out July 23, 1865.

Regiment lost during service 4 Officers and 68 Enlisted men killed and mortally wounded and 2 Officers and 143 Enlisted men by disease. Total 217.

24th REGIMENT INFANTRY.

Organized at Vincennes, Ind., and mustered in July 31, 1861. Left State for St. Louis, Mo., August 19. Moved to Jefferson City, Mo., September 14; thence to Syracuse and to Georgetown. Attached to Army of the West and Dept. of Missouri to February, 1862. 1st Brigade, 3rd Division, Army of the Tennessee, to July, 1862. Helena, Ark., District of Eastern Arkansas, Dept. of the Missouri, to November, 1862. 3rd Brigade, 2nd Division, District of Eastern Arkansas, Dept. of the Tennessee, to January, 1863. 3rd Brigade, 12th Division, 13th Army Corps, Army of the Tennessee, to February, 1863. 1st Brigade, 12th Division, 13th Army Corps, to July, 1863. 1st Brigade, 3rd Division, 13th Army Corps, Dept. of the Tennessee, to August, 1863, and Dept. of the Gulf to June, 1864. 2nd Brigade, 3rd Division, 19th Army Corps, Dept. of the Gulf, to December, 1864. 3rd Brigade, Reserve Corps, Military Division, West Mississippi, to February, 1865. 2nd Brigade, 2nd Division, Reserve Corps, Military Division West Mississippi, February, 1865. 2nd Brigade, 2nd Division, 13th Army Corps (New), Military Division West Mississippi, to July, 1865. Dept. of Texas to November, 1865.

SERVICE.—Expedition to Big Springs, Mo., September 7, 1861. Fremont's advance on Springfield, Mo., September 27-November 2. Duty at Tipton till December. Expedition to Milford, Mo., December 15-19. Shawnee Mound (or Milford) December 18. Camp near Otterville till February 7, 1862. Moved to Jefferson City February 7-10, thence to St. Louis, Mo., Paducah, Ky., and Fort Henry, Tenn., February 15-17. Duty at Fort Henry till March. Moved to Pittsburg Landing, Tenn. Expedition toward Purdy and operations about Crump's Landing March 9-14. Battle of Shiloh, Tenn., April 6-7. Advance on and siege of Corinth, Miss., April 29-May 30. March to Memphis, Tenn., June 3-20. Expedition up White River, Ark., June 26-July 14. Grand Prairie July 6-7. Near Duvall's Bluff July 7. Aberdeen July 9. Moved to Helena, Ark., July 14, and duty there till April, 1863. Expedition to Clarendon August 4-17, 1862. Expedition to Arkansas Post November 16-21, 1862. Expedition to Grenada, Miss., November 27-December 5. Mitchell's Cross Roads December 1. Expedition to White River and Duvall's Bluff January 13-19, 1863. Duvall's Bluff, Des Arc, January 16. Occupation of Des Arc January 18. Expedition to St. Francis and Little Rivers March 5-12. Madison March 9.

Moved to Milliken's Bend, La., April 14. Movement on Bruinsburg and turning Grand Gulf April 25-30. Battle of Port Gibson May 1. Fourteen-Mile Creek May 12-13. Battle of Champion's Hill May 16. Siege of Vicksburg, Miss., May 18-July 4. Assaults on Vicksburg May 19 and 24. Advance on Jackson July 4-10. Siege of Jackson July 10-17. Ordered to New Orleans, La., August 5. Duty at Carrollton, Brashear City and Berwick till October. Western Louisiana Campaign October 3-November 30. Opelousas and Berre Landing October 21. Grand Coteau November 3. Moved to New Orleans December 17, and duty at Algiers till January, 1864. Re-enlisted January 1, 1864. Duty at various points in Louisiana till January, 1865. Moved to Pensacola, Fla., January 31, and duty there till March 14. Moved to Barrancas, Fla., thence march through Florida and Southern Alabama to Blakely, Ala., March 20-April 1. Occupation of Pollard March 26. Siege of Spanish Fort and Fort Blakely April 1-9. Assault and capture of Fort Blakely April 9. March to Selma April 13-22, and duty there till June. Ordered to Galveston, Tex., and duty there till November. Old members mustered out July 19, 1865. Regiment mustered out November 15, 1865.

Regiment lost during service 8 Officers and 80 Enlisted men killed and mortally wounded and 3 Officers and 204 Enlisted men by disease. Total 295.

25th REGIMENT INFANTRY.

Organized at Evansville, Ind., and mustered in August 19, 1861. Moved to St. Louis, Mo., August 26; thence to Jefferson City, Mo., September 14; thence to Georgetown, Mo. Attached to Army of the West and Dept. of Missouri to December, 1861. St. Louis, Mo., to February, 1862. 4th Brigade, 2nd Division, Military District of Cairo, February, 1862. 2nd Brigade, 4th Division, Army of the Tennessee, to July, 1862. 2nd Brigade, 4th Division, District of Memphis, Tenn., to September, 1862. 2nd Brigade, 4th Division, District of Jackson, Tenn., to November, 1862. 3rd Brigade, 4th Division, Right Wing 13th Army Corps (Old), Dept. of the Tennessee, to December, 1862. 3rd Brigade, 4th Division, 17th Army Corps, Army of the Tennessee, to January, 1863. District of Memphis, Tenn., 16th Army Corps, to March, 1863. 2nd Brigade, District of Memphis, 5th Division, 16th Army Corps, to December, 1863. 3rd Brigade, Cavalry Division, 16th Army Corps, to January, 1864. 2nd Brigade, 4th Division, 16th Army Corps, to March, 1864. 3rd Brigade, 4th Division, 16th Army Corps, to September, 1864. 3rd Brigade, 1st Division, 17th Army Corps, to July, 1865.

SERVICE.—Fremont's Campaign against Springfield, Mo., September 22-November 3, 1861. Duty at Otterville and at LaMine Bridge till December. Pope's Expedition to Warrensburg December 16-20. Action on the Blackwater, Milford, December 18. Conduct prisoners to St. Louis, and duty at Benton Barracks till February 2, 1862. Expedition up the Tennessee against Fort Donelson, Tenn., February 2-11. Investment and capture of Fort Donelson February 12-16. Expedition to Clarksville, Tenn., March 19-21. Moved to Pittsburg Landing, Tenn., March 5-18. Battle of Shiloh, Tenn., April 6-7. Advance on and siege of Corinth, Miss., April 29-May 30. March to Memphis, Tenn., via Grand Junction June 1-July 21. Duty at Memphis till September 6. Action at Nonconah Creek August 3. Forced march to Bolivar, Tenn., September 6-9, and duty there till October 4. Battle of Hatchie River, Metamora, October 5. Grant's Central Mississippi Campaign November, 1862, to January, 1863. Action with Van Dorn at Davis Mills December 21 (Cos. "A," "C," "D," "F," "H" and "I"). Moved from Davis Mills to Memphis, Tenn., January 14, 1863. Provost duty there till November, 1863. Railroad guard duty from Grand Junction to Moscow November, 1863, to January, 1864. Moved to Memphis January 28; thence moved to Vicksburg, Miss. Meridian Campaign February 3-March 2. Marion Station February 15-17. Re-enlisted at Canton February 29. Veterans on furlough March and April.

Moved to Decatur, Ala., April 24, and duty there till August. Action at Fletcher's Ferry, Flint River, May 18. Pond Springs near Courtland, Ala., May 27. Pond Springs June 29. Expedition to Moulton July 25-28. Decatur July 27. Moved to Atlanta, Ga., August 4-8. Atlanta campaign August 8-September 8. Siege of Atlanta August 8-25. Flank movement on Jonesboro August 25-30. Battle of Jonesboro August 31-September 1. Lovejoy Station September 2-6. Operations against Hood in North Georgia and North Alabama September 29-November 3. March to the sea November 15-December 10. Montieth Swamp December 9. Siege of Savannah December 10-21. Campaign of the Carolinas January to April, 1865. Reconnoissance to Salkehatchie River January 20. Salkehatchie Swamp, S. C., February 2-3. River's and Broxton's Bridges, Salkehatchie River, February 2. Binnaker's Bridge February 9. Orangeburg February 11-12. Columbia February 16-17. Battle of Bentonville, N. C., March 19-21. Occupation of Goldsboro March 24. Advance on Raleigh April 10-14. Occupation of Raleigh April 14. Bennett's House April 26. Surrender of Johnston and his army. March to Washington, D. C., via Richmond, Va., April 29-May 19. Grand Review May 24. Moved to Louisville, Ky., June 5, and duty there till July 17. Mustered out July 17, 1865.

Regiment lost during service 7 Officers and 81 Enlisted men killed and mortally wounded and 3 Officers and 270 Enlisted men by disease. Total 361.

26th REGIMENT INFANTRY.

Regiment organized at Indianapolis, Ind., August 31, 1861. Left State for St. Louis, Mo., September 7. Attached to Army of the West and Dept. of Missouri, to January, 1862. Sedalia, Mo., Dept. of Missouri, to June, 1862. District of Southwest Missouri, Dept. Missouri, to October, 1862. 1st Brigade, 2nd Division, Army of the Frontier, Dept. of Missouri, to June, 1863. 1st Brigade, Herron's Division, 13th Army Corps, Army of the Tennessee, to July, 1863. 1st Brigade, 2nd Division, 13th Army Corps, Dept. of the Tennessee, to August, and Dept. of the Gulf, to June, 1864. District of LaFourche, Dept. of the Gulf, to February, 1865. 1st Brigade, 1st Division, 16th Army Corps (New), Military Division West Mississippi, to August, 1865. Dept. of Mississippi to January, 1866.

SERVICE.—Fremont's advance on Springfield, Mo., September 22-November 3, 1861. Duty at Sedalia, Mo., guarding Pacific Railroad till July, 1862. Near Shiloh, Mo., April 11 (Detachment). Moved to Springfield, Mo. Schofield's campaign and operations in Southwest Missouri till December. Occupation of Newtonia October 4. Advance on Fayetteville October 11-December 3. March to relief of Gen. Blount December 3-6. Battle of Prairie Grove, Ark., December 7. At Fayetteville till December 27. Expedition over Boston Mountains to Van Buren, Ark., December 27-29. Capture of Van Buren December 29. Duty at various points in Southwest Missouri till June. Ordered to Vicksburg, Miss., June 3. Siege of Vicksburg June 11-July 4. Expedition to Yazoo City, Miss., July 12-21. Capture of Yazoo City July 14. Moved to Port Hudson July 23, thence to Carrollton, La., August 28. Expedition to Morganza September 5-12. Atchafalaya River September 9-10. Sterling's Farm September 12. Battle of Sterling's Farm on Bayou Fordoche, near Morganza, September 29. Mostly captured. Moved to Carrollton October 10. Expedition to the Rio Grande, Texas, October 27-December 2. Duty at Mustang Island, Brazos Santiago and Brownsville, Texas, till March, 1864. Regiment veteranize February 1, 1864. Furlough April and May. Garrison duty at Fort Butler, Donaldsville, La., June, 1864, to March, 1865. Campaign against Mobile and its defences March 17-April 12. Siege of Spanish Fort and Fort Blakely March 26-April 9. Occupation of Mobile April 12. Duty at Mobile, Ala., Meridian and Macon, Miss., till January, 1866. Mustered out January 15, 1866.

Regiment lost during service 96 Enlisted men killed and mortally wounded and 3 Officers and 265 Enlisted men by disease. Total 364.

27th REGIMENT INFANTRY.

Organized at Indianapolis, Ind., and mustered in September 12, 1861. Left State for Washington, D. C., September 15. Attached to Stile's Brigade, Banks' Division, Army of the Potomac, to March, 1862. 3rd Brigade, 1st Division, Banks' 5th Army Corps, to April, 1862, and Dept. of the Shenandoah to June, 1862. 3rd Brigade, 1st Division, 2nd Corps, Army of Virginia, to September, 1862. 3rd Brigade, 1st Division, 12th Army Corps, Army of the Potomac, to October, 1863, and Army of the Cumberland to April, 1864. 2nd Brigade, 1st Division, 20th Army Corps, Army of the Cumberland, to November, 1864.

SERVICE.—Operations in District of the Upper Potomac and camp at Frederick City, Md., till March, 1862. Movement into the Shenandoah Valley, Va., and occupation of Winchester, Va., March 3-9. Smithfield March 13. Advance toward Manassas March 23-25. Pursuit of Jackson up the Shenandoah Valley. Operations in the Shenandoah Valley May 15-June 17. Buckton Station, Middletown and Front Royal May 23. Newtown May 24. Battle of Winchester May 25. Retreat to Williamsport, Md., May 25-26. Duty at Front Royal till July 6, and at Little Washington till August 6. Battle of Cedar Mountain August 9. Pope's Campaign in Northern Virginia August 16-September 2. Guard trains of the army during battles of Bull Run August 28-30. Maryland Campaign September 6-22. Battle of Antietam September 16-17. Moved to Harper's Ferry, W. Va. Picket duty from Harper's Ferry to Opequan Creek and duty at Fairfax Station and Stafford Court House till December. March to Fredericksburg, Va., December 12-16. Burnside's 2nd Campaign, "Mud March," January 20-24, 1863. At Stafford Court House till April 27. Chancellorsville Campaign April 27-May 6. Germania Ford April 29. Battle of Chancellorsville May 2-5. Gettysburg, Pa., Campaign, June 11-July 24. Battle of Gettysburg July 1-3. Pursuit of Lee, to Manassas Gap, Va., July 5-24. On detached duty in New York during draft disturbances August 15-September 5. Movement to Bridgeport, Ala., September 24-October 3. Guarding Nashville and Chattanooga Railroad at Elkwater Bridge and Tullahoma, Tenn., till April, 1864. Regiment Veteranize at Tullahoma, Tenn., January 24, 1864. Atlanta (Ga.) Campaign May 1 to September 8. Demonstration on Rocky Faced Ridge May 8-11. Battle of Resaca May 14-15. Near Cassville May 19. New Hope Church May 25. Operations on line of Pumpkin Vine Creek and battles about Dallas, New Hope Church and Allatoona Hills, May 25-June 5. Operations about Marietta and against Kenesaw Mountain June 10-July 2. Pine Hill June 11-14. Lost Mountain June 15-17. Gilgal or Golgotha Church June 15. Muddy Creek June 17. Noyes Creek June 19. Kolb's Farm June 22. Assault on Kenesaw June 27. Ruff's Station, Smyrna Camp Ground, July 4. Chattahoochie River July 5-17. Peach Tree Creek July 19-20. Siege of Atlanta July 25-August 25. Operations at Chattahoochie River Bridge August 26-September 2. Occupation of Atlanta September 2-November 4. Mustered out November 4, 1864. Veterans and Recruits transferred to 70th Indiana Infantry.

Regiment lost during service 10 Officers and 159 Enlisted men killed and mortally wounded and 2 Officers and 131 Enlisted men by disease. Total 302.

28th REGIMENT VOLUNTEERS.

See 1st Regiment Cavalry.

28th REGIMENT INFANTRY (COLORED).

Organized at Indianapolis, Ind., December 24, 1863. (See 29th U. S. Colored Troops.)

29th REGIMENT INFANTRY.

Organized at Laporte, Ind., and mustered in August 27, 1861. Ordered to Kentucky and joined General Rousseau at Camp Nevin October 9, 1861. Attached to Wood's Brigade, McCook's Command at Nolin, Ky., to November, 1861. 5th Brigade, Army of the Ohio, to December, 1861. 5th Brigade, 2nd Division, Army of the Ohio, to September, 1862. 5th Brigade, 2nd Division, 1st Corps, Army of the Ohio, to November, 1862. 2nd Brigade, 2nd Division, Right Wing 14th Army Corps, Army of the Cumberland, to January, 1863. 2nd Brigade, 2nd Division, 20th Army Corps, Army of the Cumberland, to October, 1863. 1st Brigade, 1st Division, 4th Army Corps, Army of the Cumberland, to April, 1864. 1st Separate Brigade, Garrison at Chattanooga, Tenn., Dept. of the Cumberland, to January, 1865. 2nd Brigade, 1st Separate Division, District of the Etowah, Dept. of the Cumberland, to May, 1865. 2nd Brigade, 2nd Separate Division, District of the Etowah, Dept. of the Cumberland, and Dept. of Georgia, to December, 1865.

SERVICE.—Camp at Nolin River, Ky., till December, 1861, and at Munfordsville, Ky., till February, 1862. March to Bowling Green, Ky., thence to Nashville, Tenn., February 14-March 3, and to Savannah, Tenn., March 16-April 6. Battle of Shiloh, Tenn., April 6-7. Advance on and siege of Corinth, Miss., April 29-May 30. Near Corinth May 9. Pursuit to Booneville May 31-June 6. Buell's Campaign in Northern Alabama and Middle Tennessee June to August. Gallatin August 13. March to Louisville, Ky., in pursuit of Bragg, August 21-September 26. Pursuit of Bragg into Kentucky October 1-15. Near Clay Village October 4. Dog Walk October 9. March to Nashville, Tenn., October 16-November 7. Reconnoissance to Lavergne November 26-27. Lavergne, Scrougesville November 27. Duty at Nashville till December 26. Advance on Murfreesboro December 26-30. Battle of Stone's River December 30-31, 1862, and January 1-3, 1863. Duty at Murfreesboro till June. Action at Triune June 11. Middle Tennessee or Tullahoma Campaign June 23-July 7. Liberty Gap June 24-27. Occupation of Middle Tennessee till August 16. Passage of the Cumberland Mountains and Tennessee River and Chickamauga (Ga.) Campaign August 16-September 22. Battle of Chickamauga September 19-20. Reopening Tennessee River October 26-29. Duty at Bridgeport, Ala., till January, 1864. Garrison duty at Chattanooga till May, 1865. Action at Dalton, Ga., August 14-15, 1864. Garrison duty at Marietta and Dalton, Ga., till December. Mustered out December 2, 1865.

Regiment lost during service 4 Officers and 56 Enlisted men killed and mortally wounded and 4 Officers and 240 Enlisted men by disease. Total 304.

30th REGIMENT INFANTRY.

Organized at Fort Wayne, Ind., and mustered in September 24, 1861. Ordered to Camp Nevin, Ky., and reported to General Rousseau October 9. Attached to Wood's 2nd Brigade, McCook's Command, at Nolin, Ky., to November, 1861. 5th Brigade, Army of the Ohio, to December, 1861. 5th Brigade, 2nd Division, Army of the Ohio, to September, 1862. 5th Brigade, 2nd Division, 1st Corps, Army of the Ohio, to November, 1862. 2nd Brigade, 2nd Division, Right Wing 14th Army Corps, Army of the Cumberland, to January, 1863. 2nd Brigade, 2nd Division, 20th Army Corps, Army of the Cumberland, to October, 1863. 3rd Brigade, 1st Division, 4th Army Corps, Army of the Cumberland, to June, 1865. 2nd Brigade, 1st Division, 4th Army Corps, to August, 1865. Dept. of Texas to November, 1865.

SERVICE.—Camp at Nolin River, Ky., till February, 1862. March to Bowling Green, Ky., thence to Nashville, Tenn., February 14-March 3. March to Savannah, Tenn., March 16-April 6. Battle of Shiloh, Tenn., April 6-7. Advance on and siege of Corinth, Miss., April 29-May 30. Pursuit to Booneville May 31-June 6. Buell's Campaign in Northern Alabama and Middle Tennessee June to August. March to Louisville, Ky., in pursuit of Bragg, August 21-September 26. Pursuit of Bragg into Kentucky October 1-22. Near Clay Village October 4. Battle of Perryville, Ky., October 8 (Reserve). March to Nashville, Tenn., October 22-November 7, and duty there till December 26. Reconnoissance toward

Lavergne November 19. Reconnoissance to Lavergne November 26-27. Lavergne, Scrougesville November 27. Advance on Murfreesboro December 26-30. Battle of Stone's River December 30-31, 1862, and January 1-3, 1863. Duty at Murfreesboro till June. Middle Tennessee or Tullahoma Campaign June 23-July 7. Liberty Gap June 24-27. Occupation of Middle Tennessee till August 16. Passage of the Cumberland Mountains and Tennessee River and Chickamauga (Ga.) Campaign August 16-September 22. Battle of Chickamauga September 19-20. Duty at Whiteside, Tyner's Station and Blue Springs, Tenn., till April, 1864. Demonstration on Dalton, Ga., February 22-27, 1864. Near Dalton February 23. Tunnel Hill, Buzzard's Roost Gap and Rocky Faced Ridge February 23-25. Atlanta (Ga.) Campaign May 1-September 3. Tunnel Hill May 6-7. Demonstrations on Rocky Faced Ridge and Dalton May 8-13. Buzzard's Roost Gap May 8-9. Battle of Resaca May 14-15. Near Kingston May 18-19. Near Cassville May 19. Advance on Dallas May 22-25. Operations on line of Pumpkin Vine Creek and battles about Dallas, New Hope Church and Allatoona Hills May 25-June 5. Operations about Marietta and against Kenesaw Mountain June 10-July 2. Pine Hill June 11-14. Lost Mountain June 15-17. Assault on Kenesaw June 27. Ruff's Station, Smyrna Camp Ground, July 4. Chattahoochie River July 5-17. Peach Tree Creek July 19-20. Siege of Atlanta July 22-August 25. Flank movement on Jonesboro August 25-30. Battle of Jonesboro August 31-September 1. Lovejoy Station September 2-6. Operations against Hood in North Georgia and North Alabama September 20-November 3. Consolidated to a battalion of 7 companies October 3. Nashville Campaign November-December. Columbia, Duck River, November 24-27. Battle of Franklin November 30. Battle of Nashville December 15-16. Pursuit of Hood to the Tennessee River December 17-28. Moved to Huntsville, Ala., and duty there till March, 1865. Operations in East Tennessee March 15-April 22. Duty at Nashville till June. Moved to New Orleans, La., June 16, thence to Texas July, and duty at various points till November. Mustered out November 25, 1865.

Regiment lost during service 4 Officers and 133 Enlisted men killed and mortally wounded and 1 Officer and 274 Enlisted men by disease. Total 412.

31st REGIMENT INFANTRY.

Organized at Terre Haute, Ind., and mustered in September 15, 1861. Ordered to Kentucky and camp at Green River till February, 1862. Attached to 13th Brigade, Army of the Ohio, to December, 1861. 13th Brigade, 5th Division, Army Ohio, to February, 1862. 1st Brigade, 3rd Division, Army of the Tennessee, to March, 1862. 3rd Brigade, 4th Division, Army of the Tennessee, to April, 1862. 22nd Brigade, 4th Division, Army of the Ohio, to September, 1862. 22nd Brigade, 4th Division, 2nd Army Corps, Army of the Ohio, to November, 1862. 1st Brigade, 2nd Division, Left Wing 14th Army Corps, Army of the Cumberland, to January, 1863. 1st Brigade, 2nd Division, 21st Army Corps, Army of the Cumberland, to October, 1863. 1st Brigade, 1st Division, 4th Army Corps, Army of the Cumberland, to August, 1865. Dept. of Texas to December, 1865.

SERVICE.—Moved to Fort Donelson, Tenn., February 11-13, 1862. Investment and capture of Fort Donelson February 14-16. Expedition to Crump's Landing, Tenn., March 9-14. Battle of Shiloh, Tenn., April 6-7. Advance on and siege of Corinth, Miss., April 29-May 30. Phillips' Creek, Widow Serratt's, May 21. Bridge Creek before Corinth May 28. Occupation of Corinth May 30. Pursuit to Booneville May 31-June 12. Buell's Campaign in Northern Alabama and Middle Tennessee June to August. March to Louisville, Ky., in pursuit of Bragg, August 21-September 26. Pursuit of Bragg to Loudon, Ky., October 1-22. Battle of Perryville, October 8. Wild Cat October 17. March to Nashville, Tenn., October 22-November 8. Destruction of Goose Creek Salt Works October 23-24. Duty at Nashville till De-

cember 26. Advance on Murfreesboro December 26-30. Lavergne December 26-27. Battle of Stone's River December 30-31, 1862, and January 1-3, 1863. Duty at Murfreesboro and Cripple Creek till June. Action at Spring Hill, Woodbury, April 2. Middle Tennessee or Tullahoma Campaign June 23-July 7. Occupation of Middle Tennessee to August 16. Passage of the Cumberland Mountains and Tennessee River and Chickamauga (Ga.) Campaign August 16-September 22. Lee and Gordon's Mills September 11-13. Battle of Chickamauga September 19-20. Siege of Chattanooga, Tenn., September 24-October 26. Reopening Tennessee River October 26-29. At Bridgeport, Ala., October 28, 1863, to January, 1864. Regiment Veteranize January 1, 1864, and on furlough February and March. At Ooltewah till May. Atlanta (Ga.) Campaign May 1-September 8. Tunnel Hill May 6-7. Demonstrations on Rocky Faced Ridge and Dalton, Ga., May 8-13. Buzzard's Roost Gap May 8-9. Battle of Resaca May 14-15. Near Kingston May 18-19. Near Cassville May 19. Advance on Dallas May 22-25. Operations on line of Pumpkin Vine Creek and battles about Dallas, New Hope Church and Allatoona Hills May 25-June 5. Operations about Marietta and against Kenesaw Mountain June 10-July 2. Pine Hill June 11-14. Lost Mountain June 15-17. Assault on Kenesaw June 27. Ruff's Station, Smyrna Camp Ground, July 4. Chattahoochie River July 5-17. Vining Station July 7. Peach Tree Creek July 19-20. Siege of Atlanta July 22-August 25. Flank movement on Jonesboro August 25-30. Battle of Jonesboro August 31-September 1. Lovejoy Station September 2-6. Operations against Hood in North Georgia and North Alabama September 29-November 3. Nashville Campaign November-December. Columbia, Duck River, November 24-27. Battle of Franklin November 30. Battle of Nashville December 15-16. Pursuit of Hood to the Tennessee River December 17-28. Moved to Huntsville, Ala., and duty there till March, 1865. Operations in East Tennessee March 15-April 22. Duty at Nashville till June. Moved to New Orleans, La., June 16, thence to Texas, July. Duty at Green Lake and San Antonio till December. Mustered out December 8, 1865.

Regiment lost during service 5 Officers and 115 Enlisted men killed and mortally wounded and 5 Officers and 253 Enlisted men by disease. Total 378.

32nd REGIMENT INFANTRY ("1st GERMAN REGIMENT").

Organized at Indianapolis, Ind., and mustered in August 24, 1861. Left State for Louisville, Ky., September 28, thence moved to New Haven, Ky., and to Camp Nevin, Ky., and duty there till December 9. Picketing south side of Green River and protecting working parties. Action at Rowlett's Station, Woodsonville, December 17. Regiment specially complimented by General Buell for its gallantry. At Munfordsville, Ky., till February, 1862. Attached to Johnson's Brigade, McCook's Command at Nolin, Ky., October-November, 1861. 6th Brigade, Army of the Ohio, to December, 1861. 6th Brigade, 2nd Division, Army of the Ohio, to September, 1862. 6th Brigade, 2nd Division, 1st Corps, Army of the Ohio, to November, 1862. 1st Brigade, 2nd Division, Right Wing 14th Army Corps, Army of the Cumberland, to January, 1863. 1st Brigade, 2nd Division, 20th Army Corps, Army of the Cumberland, to October, 1863. 1st Brigade, 3rd Division, 4th Army Corps, to October, 1864. Post of Chattanooga, Tenn., Dept. of the Cumberland, to November, 1864. 2nd Brigade, 1st Separate Division, District of the Etowah, Dept. of the Cumberland, to June, 1865. 1st Brigade, 3rd Division, 4th Army Corps, to August, 1865. Dept. of Texas to December, 1865.

SERVICE.—March to Bowling Green, Ky., thence to Nashville, Tenn., February 10-March 3, 1862. March to Savannah, Tenn., March 16-April 6. Battle of Shiloh, Tenn., April 6-7. Advance on and siege of Corinth, Miss., April 29-May 30. Pursuit to Booneville May 31-June 12. Buell's Campaign in Northern Alabama and Middle Tennessee June to August. March to Louisville, Ky., in pursuit of Bragg August 21-September 26. Pursuit of Bragg into Kentucky October 1-15. Chesser's Store October 9. March to Nashville, Tenn., October 16-November 7, and duty there till December 26. Advance on Murfreesboro December 26-30. Battle of Stone's River December 30-31, 1862, and January 1-3, 1863. Duty at Murfreesboro till June. Reconnoissance from Murfreesboro March 6-7. Christiana and Middleton March 6. Middle Tennessee or Tullahoma Campaign June 22-July 7. Liberty Gap June 22-24, and June 24-27. Occupation of Middle Tennessee till August 16. Passage of the Cumberland Mountains and Tennessee River and Chickamauga (Ga.) Campaign August 16-September 22. Battle of Chickamauga September 19-20. Siege of Chattanooga, Tenn., September 24-November 23. Reopening Tennessee River October 26-29. Chattanooga-Ringgold Campaign November 23-27. Orchard Knob November 23-24. Mission Ridge November 25. Pursuit to Graysville November 26-27. March to relief of Knoxville, Tenn., November 28-December 8. Operations in East Tennessee till April, 1864. Atlanta (Ga.) Campaign May 1-September 8. Demonstrations on Rocky Faced Ridge and Dalton May 8-13. Buzzard's Roost Gap May 8-9. Battle of Resaca May 14-15. Adairsville May 17. Near Cassville May 19. Advance on Dallas May 22-25. Operations on line of Pumpkin Vine Creek, and battles about Dallas, New Hope Church and Allatoona Hills, May 25-June 5. Pickett's Mills May 27. Operations about Marietta and against Kenesaw Mountain June 10-July 2. Pine Hill June 11-14. Lost Mountain June 15-17. Assault on Kenesaw June 27. Ruff's Station, Smyrna Camp Ground, July 4. Chattahoochie River July 5-17. Peach Tree Creek July 19-20. (Non-Veterans ordered home July, participated in expedition from Mt. Vernon, Ind., into Kentucky, August 16-22. Skirmishes at White Oak Springs August 17. Gouger's Lake August 18. Smith's Mills August 19. Mustered out September 7, 1864.) Siege of Atlanta July 22-August 25. Flank movement on Jonesboro August 25-30. Battle of Jonesboro August 31-September 1. Lovejoy Station September 2-6. Veterans and Recruits consolidated to a Battalion of four Companies, and ordered to Chattanooga, Tenn., September 6. Duty there till June, 1865. Ordered to New Orleans, La., June 16, thence to Texas, July. Duty at Green Lake and San Antonio till December. Mustered out December 4, 1865.

Regiment lost during service 7 Officers and 174 Enlisted men killed and mortally wounded and 1 Officer and 96 Enlisted men by disease. Total 268.

33rd REGIMENT INFANTRY.

Organized at Indianapolis and mustered in September 16, 1861. Moved to Louisville, Ky., September 28, thence to Camp Dick Robinson, Ky., and duty there till October 13. Attached to Thomas' Command, Army of the Ohio, to November, 1861. 1st Brigade, Army of the Ohio, to December, 1861. 1st Brigade, 1st Division, Army of Ohio, to February, 1862. 27th Brigade, 7th Division, Army of the Ohio, to October, 1862. 1st Brigade, 3rd Division, Army of Kentucky, Dept. of Ohio, to February, 1863. Coburn's Brigade, Baird's Division, Army of Kentucky, Dept. of the Cumberland, to June, 1863. 3rd Brigade, 1st Division, Reserve Corps, Army of the Cumberland, to October, 1863. Coburn's Brigade, Post of Murfreesboro, Tenn., Dept. of the Cumberland, to January, 1864. 2nd Brigade, 1st Division, 11th Army Corps, Army of the Cumberland, to April, 1864. 2nd Brigade, 3rd Division, 20th Army Corps, Army of the Cumberland, to July, 1865.

SERVICE.—Moved to Camp Wild Cat, Ky., October 13, 1861. Action at Camp Wild Cat, Rockcastle Hills, October 21. At Crab Orchard, Ky., November 15, 1861, to January 3, 1862. Operations about Mill Springs, Somerset, Ky., December 1-13, 1861. At Lexington, Ky., January 3 to April 11, 1862. Cumberland Gap Campaign March 28-June 18. Occupation of Cumberland Gap June 18 to September 17. Retreat to the Ohio River September 17-October 3. Duty at Covington, Lexington, Nicholasville and Danville, Ky., till January 26, 1863.

Moved to Louisville, Ky., thence to Nashville, Tenn., January 26-February 7. Moved to Franklin February 21. Action at Franklin March 4. Battle of Thompson's Station March 4-5. Most of Regiment captured by Van Dorn's forces nearly 18,000 strong. Exchanged May 5, 1863. Brentwood March 25 (Detachment). Middle Tennessee or Tullahoma Campaign June 23-July 7. Duty at Guy's Gap and Murfreesboro till September 5. At Manchester, Estill Springs, Cowan, Dechard, Tracy City, Christiana City and along Nashville & Chattanooga R. R. till April, 1864. Regiment re-enlisted at Christiana City, January, 1864. On Veteran furlough February and March. Atlanta Campaign May 1-September 8. Demonstrations on Rocky Faced Ridge May 8-11. Battle of Resaca May 14-15. Cassville May 19. Advance on Dallas May 22-25. New Hope Church May 25. Operations on line of Pumpkin Vine Creek and battles about Dallas, New Hope Church and Allatoona Hills May 25-June 5. Operations about Marietta and against Kenesaw Mountain June 10-July 2. Pine Hill June 11-14. Lost Mountain June 15-17. Gilgal or Golgotha Church June 15. Muddy Creek June 17. Noyes Creek June 19. Kolb's Farm June 22. Assault on Kenesaw June 27. Ruff's Station, Smyrna Camp Ground, July 4. Chattahoochie River July 5-17. Peach Tree Creek July 19-20. Siege of Atlanta July 22-August 25. Operations at Chattahoochie River Bridge August 26-September 2. Occupation of Atlanta September 2-November 15. McDonough Road near Atlanta November 6. March to the sea November 15-December 10. Siege of Savannah December 10-21. Campaign of the Carolinas January to April, 1865. Lawtonville, S. C., February 2. Fayetteville, N. C., March 11. Averysboro March 16. Battle of Bentonville March 19-21. Occupation of Goldsboro March 24. Advance on Raleigh April 10-14. Occupation of Raleigh April 14. Bennett's House April 26. Surrender of Johnston and his army. March to Washington, D. C., via Richmond, Va., April 29-May 20. Grand Review May 24. Ordered to Louisville, Ky., June, and duty there till July 21. Mustered out July 21, 1865.

Regiment lost during service 4 Officers and 112 Enlisted men killed and mortally wounded and 2 Officers and 180 Enlisted men by disease. Total 298.

34th REGIMENT INFANTRY.

Organized at Anderson, Ind., and mustered in September 16, 1861. Moved to Jeffersonville, Ind., October 10, thence to New Haven, Ky., November 15, and duty there till December 14. Moved to Camp Wickliffe, Ky., December 14, and duty there till February 7, 1862. Attached to 10th Brigade, Army of the Ohio, November-December, 1861. 10th Brigade, 4th Division, Army of the Ohio, to February, 1862. 1st Brigade, 2nd Division, Army of Mississippi, to April, 1862. 1st Brigade, 3d Division, Army Mississippi. Garrison at New Madrid, Mo., to July, 1862. Helena, Ark., District of Eastern Arkansas, Dept. of Missouri, to November, 1862. 3rd Brigade, 2nd Division, District of Eastern Arkansas, Dept. of the Tennessee, to January, 1863. 3rd Brigade, 12th Division, 13th Army Corps, Army of the Tennessee, to February, 1863. 1st Brigade, 12th Division, 13th Army Corps, to July, 1863. 1st Brigade, 3rd Division, 13th Army Corps, Army of the Tennessee, to August, 1863, and Dept. of the Gulf to March, 1864. Defences of New Orleans, La., to December, 1864. Brazos, Santiago, Texas, U. S. Forces, Texas, to June, 1865. Dept. of Texas to February, 1866.

SERVICE.—Moved to Green River, Ky., February 7, 1862, thence to the Ohio River February 14, and to Cairo, Ill., with Nelson's Division, Army of the Ohio, February 17-20. Detached from Division and moved to Commerce, Mo., February 27-March 3. Siege of New Madrid, Mo., March 5-14. Siege and capture of Island No. 10, Mississippi River, March 15-April 8. Riddell's Point March 17. Garrison duty at New Madrid, Mo., April 7 to June 14. Expedition down Mississippi River to Fort Pillow, Tenn., May 19-23 (Detachment). Capture of Fort Pillow June 5 (Detachment). Moved to Memphis, Tenn., June 14-15. Expedition up White

River, Ark., June 26-July 14. Action at Grand Prairie July 6-7. Near Duvall's Bluff July 7. Aberdeen July 9. Arrived at Helena July 14, and duty there till April, 1863. Expedition to Arkansas Post November 16-22, 1862. Ordered to Milliken's Bend, La., April 14. Movement on Bruinsburg and turning Grand Gulf April 25-30. Battle of Port Gibson May 1. Fourteen-Mile Creek May 12-13. Battle of Champion's Hill May 16. Siege of Vicksburg, Miss., May 18-July 4. Assaults on Vicksburg May 19 and 22. Advance on Jackson, Miss., July 4-10. Siege of Jackson July 10-17. Ordered to New Orleans, La., August 4, thence to Brashear City September 12. Western Louisiana Campaign October 3-November 30. Grand Coteau October 19. Carrion Crow Bayou November 3. At New Iberia till December 19. Regiment re-enlisted at New Iberia December 15. Moved to Pass Cavallo, Texas, December 23, 1863-January 8, 1864, and duty there till February 21. Moved to New Orleans, La., February 21, and duty there till March 20. Veterans on furlough till May. Garrison duty at New Orleans till December 18. Ordered to Brazos, Santiago, Texas, December 18, and duty there till June 16, 1865. Expedition from Brazos, Santiago, May 11-14, 1865. Action at Palmetto Ranch May 12-13, 1865 (last action of the war). White's Ranch May 13. March to Ringgold Barracks, 260 miles up the Rio Grande June 16-28. Duty at Ringgold Barracks till July 24, and at Brownsville till February, 1866. Mustered out February 3, 1866.

Regiment lost during service 2 Officers and 32 Enlisted men killed and mortally wounded and 5 Officers and 204 Enlisted men by disease. Total, 243.

35th REGIMENT INFANTRY.

Organized at Indianapolis, Ind., and mustered in December 11, 1861. Ordered to Kentucky December 13, and duty at Bardstown till February, 1862. Attached to Negley's 7th Independent Brigade, Army of the Ohio, to July, 1862. 23rd Independent Brigade, Army of the Ohio, to September, 1862. 23rd Brigade, 5th Division, 2nd Corps, Army of the Ohio, to November, 1862. 3rd Brigade, 3rd Division, Left Wing 14th Army Corps, Army of the Cumberland, to January, 1863. 3rd Brigade, 3rd Division, 21st Army Corps, Army of the Cumberland, to October, 1863. 2nd Brigade, 1st Division, 4th Army Corps, to August, 1865. Dept. of Texas to September, 1865.

SERVICE.—Movement to Nashville, Tenn., February 10-March 12, 1862. Duty there till April 5. At Shelbyville till May 10. Negley's Expedition to Chattanooga, Tenn., May 28-June 15. Chattanooga June 7. Guard duty along Memphis and Charleston Railroad till August. March to Louisville, Ky., in pursuit of Bragg, August 21-September 26. Pursuit of Bragg to Loudon, Ky., October 1-22. Battle of Perryville, Ky., October 8. March to Nashville, Tenn., October 22-November 12, and duty there till December 26. Murfreesboro Pike November 9. Dobbin's Ferry, near Lavergne, December 9. Advance on Murfreesboro December 26-30. Battle of Stone's River December 30-31, 1862, and January 1-3, 1863. Duty at Murfreesboro till June. Middle Tennessee or Tullahoma Campaign June 23-July 7. Occupation of Middle Tennessee till August 16. Passage of the Cumberland Mountains and Tennessee River and Chickamauga (Ga.) Campaign August 16-September 22. Battle of Chickamauga September 19-20. Siege of Chattanooga September 24-November 23. Reopening Tennessee River October 26-29. Chattanooga-Ringgold Campaign November 23-27. Lookout Mountain November 23-24. Mission Ridge November 25. Ringgold Gap, Taylor's Ridge, November 27. Regiment re-enlisted at Shellmound, Tenn., December 16, 1863. Veterans on furlough January and February, 1864. At Blue Springs, Tenn., till May. Atlanta (Ga.) Campaign May 1-September 8. Tunnel Hill June 6-7. Demonstrations on Rocky Faced Ridge and Dalton, Ga., May 8-13. Buzzard's Roost Gap May 8-9. Battle of Resaca May 14-15. Near Kingston May 18-19. Near Cassville May 19. Advance on Dallas May 22-25. Operations on line

of Pumpkin Vine Creek and battles about Dallas, New Hope Church and Allatoona Hills May 25-June 5. Operations about Marietta and against Kenesaw Mountain June 10-July 2. Pine Hill June 11-14. Lost Mountain June 15-17. Assault on Kenesaw June 27. Ruff's Station, Smyrna Camp Ground, July 4. Chattahoochie River July 5-17. Peach Tree Creek July 19-20. Siege of Atlanta July 22-August 25. Flank movement on Jonesboro August 25-30. Battle of Jonesboro August 31-September 1. Lovejoy Station September 2-6. Operations against Hood in North Georgia and North Alabama September 29-November 3. Nashville Campaign November-December. Columbia, Duck River, November 24-27. Battle of Franklin November 30. Battle of Nashville December 15-16. Pursuit of Hood to the Tennessee River December 17-28. Moved to Huntsville, Ala., and duty there till March, 1865. Operations in East Tennessee March 15-April 22. At Nashville, Tenn., till June. Ordered to New Orleans June 16, thence to Texas, July, and duty there till September. Mustered out September 30, 1865 Discharged at Indianapolis, Ind., October 23, 1865.

Regiment lost during service 5 Officers and 82 Enlisted men killed and mortally wounded and 164 Enlisted men by disease. Total 251.

36th REGIMENT INFANTRY.

Organized at Richmond, Ind., and mustered in September 16, 1861. Ordered to Kentucky and duty at Camp Wickliffe, Ky., till February, 1862. Attached to 10th Brigade, Army of the Ohio, October-November, 1861. 10th Brigade, 4th Division, Army of the Ohio, to September, 1862. 10th Brigade, 4th Division, 2nd Corps, Army of the Ohio, to November, 1862. 3rd Brigade, 2nd Division, Left Wing 14th Army Corps, Army of the Cumberland, to January, 1863. 3rd Brigade, 2nd Division, 21st Army Corps, Army of the Cumberland, to October, 1863. 3rd Brigade, 1st Division, 4th Army Corps, Army of the Cumberland, to June, 1865. 2nd Brigade, 1st Division, 4th Army Corps, to July, 1865.

SERVICE.—Expedition down Ohio River to reinforce General Grant at Fort Donelson, Tenn., thence to Nashville, Tenn., February 14-25, 1862. Occupation of Nashville February 25. March to Savannah, Tenn., March 17-April 6. Battle of Shiloh, Tenn., April 6-7. Advance on and siege of Corinth, Miss., April 29-May 30. Occupation of Corinth May 30. Pursuit to Booneville May 31-June 12. Buell's Campaign in Northern Alabama and Middle Tennessee June to August. Round Mountain, near Woodbury, August 28. March to Nashville, Tenn., thence to Louisville, Ky., in pursuit of Bragg, August 21-September 26. Pursuit of Bragg to Wild Cat, Ky., October 1-20. Wild Cat, Ky., October 17. March to Nashville, Tenn., October 20-November 9, and duty there till December 26. Advance on Murfreesboro December 26-30. Battle of Stone's River December 30-31, 1862, and January 1-3, 1863. Duty at Murfreesboro till June. Action at Woodbury January 24. Middle Tennessee or Tullahoma Campaign June 23-July 7. At Manchester till August 16. Passage of the Cumberland Mountains and Tennessee River and Chickamauga (Ga.) Campaign August 16-September 22. Battle of Chickamauga September 19-20. Siege of Chattanooga, Tenn., September 24-November 23. Reopening Tennessee River October 26-29. Chattanooga-Ringgold Campaign November 23-27. Lookout Mountain November 23-24. Mission Ridge November 25. Pigeon Hill November 26. Ringgold Gap, Taylor's Ridge, November 27. Duty at Whiteside, Tyner's Station and Blue Springs till May, 1864. Demonstration on Dalton, Ga., February 22-27. Near Dalton February 23. Tunnel Hill, Buzzard's Roost Gap and Rocky Faced Ridge February 23-25. Atlanta (Ga.) Campaign May 1 to September 8. Tunnel Hill May 6-7. Demonstrations on Rocky Faced Ridge and Dalton May 8-13. Buzzard's Roost Gap May 8-9. Battle of Resaca May 14-15. Near Kingston May 18-19. Near Cassville May 19. Advance on Dallas May 22-25. Operations on line of Pumpkin Vine Creek and battles about Dallas, New Hope Church and Allatoona Hills May 25-

June 5. Operations about Marietta and against Kenesaw Mountain June 10-July 2. Pine Hill June 11-14. Lost Mountain June 15-17. Assault on Kenesaw June 27. Ruff's Station, Smyrna Camp Ground, July 4. Chattahoochie River July 5-17. Peach Tree Creek July 19-20. Siege of Atlanta July 22-August 25. Non-Veterans mustered out August 13, 1864. Veterans and Recruits consolidated to a Battalion. Flank movement on Jonesboro August 25-30. Battle of Jonesboro August 31-September 1. Lovejoy Station September 2-6. Pursuit of Hood into Alabama October 3-26. Nashville Campaign November-December. Columbia, Duck River, November 24-27. Battle of Franklin November 30. Battle of Nashville December 15-16. Pursuit of Hood to the Tennessee River December 17-28. Moved to Huntsville, Ala., and duty there till March, 1865. Operations in East Tennessee March 15-April 22. At Nashville, Tenn., till June. Ordered to New Orleans, La., June 16. Transferred to 30th Indiana Battalion Infantry July 12, 1865.

Regiment lost during service 11 Officers and 102 Enlisted men killed and mortally wounded and 2 Officers and 130 Enlisted men by disease. Total 245.

37th REGIMENT INFANTRY.

Organized at Lawrenceburg, Ind., and mustered in September 18, 1861. Ordered to Kentucky October, and duty at mouth of Salt River and at Bacon Creek till February, 1862. Attached to 8th Brigade, Army of the Ohio, October to December, 1861. 8th Brigade, 3rd Division, Army of the Ohio, to July, 1862. Unattached, Army of the Ohio, Railroad Guard to September, 1862. 7th Brigade, 8th Division, Army of the Ohio, to November, 1862. 3rd Brigade, 2nd Division, Center 14th Army Corps, Army of the Cumberland, to January, 1863. 3rd Brigade, 2nd Division, 14th Army Corps, to October, 1863. 3rd Brigade, 1st Division, 14th Army Corps, to October, 1864. 3rd Brigade, 2nd Division, 14th Army Corps, to July, 1865.

SERVICE.—Advance on Bowling Green, Ky., and Nashville, Tenn., February 10-25, 1862. Moved to Murfreesboro March 18. Reconnoissance to Shelbyville, Tullahoma and McMinnville March 25-28. Moved to Fayetteville April 7. Expedition to Huntsville, Ala., April 10-11. Capture of Huntsville April 11. Advance on and capture of Decatur April 11-14. Guard duty on Nashville & Chattanooga Railroad till August. Elkins' Station, near Athens, May 9 (Co. "E"). Moved to Nashville August 29-September 2, and duty there till December 26. Siege of Nashville September 12-November 7. Advance on Murfreesboro, Tenn., December 26-30. Battle of Stone's River December 30-31, 1862, and January 1-3, 1863. Duty at Murfreesboro till June. Middle Tennessee or Tullahoma Campaign June 23-July 7. Occupation of Middle Tennessee till August 16. Passage of the Cumberland Mountains and Tennessee River and Chickamauga (Ga.) Campaign August 16-September 22. Davis Cross Roads or Dug Gap September 11. Battle of Chickamauga September 19-21. Rossville Gap September 21. Siege of Chattanooga, Tenn., September 24-November 23. Chattanooga-Ringgold Campaign November 23-27. Lookout Mountain November 23-24. Mission Ridge November 25. Duty at Rossville, Ga., and Chattanooga, Tenn., till May, 1864. Mulberry Village December 23, 1863 (Detachment). Scout from Chattanooga to Harrison and Ooltewah January 21, 1864 (Detachment). Demonstration on Dalton, Ga., February 22-27, 1864. Tunnel Hill, Buzzard's Roost Gap and Rocky Faced Ridge February 23-25, 1864. Atlanta (Ga.) Campaign May 1-September 8. Demonstrations on Rocky Faced Ridge May 8-11. Buzzard's Roost Gap May 8-9. Battle of Resaca May 14-15. Advance on Dallas May 18-25. Operations on line of Pumpkin Vine Creek and battles about Dallas, New Hope Church and Allatoona Hills May 25-June 5. Pickett's Mill May 27. Operations about Marietta and against Kenesaw Mountain June 10-July 2. Pine Hill June 11-14. Lost Mountain June 15-17. Assault on Kenesaw June 27. Ruff's Station, Smyrna Camp Ground, July 4.

Chattahoochie River July 5-17. Peach Tree Creek July 19-20. Siege of Atlanta July 22-August 25. Utoy Creek August 5-7. Flank movement on Jonesboro August 25-30. Battle of Jonesboro August 31-September 1. Pursuit of Hood into Alabama October 1-26. March to the sea November 15-December 10. Non-Veterans mustered out October 27, 1864. Veterans and Recruits consolidated to a Battalion of two Companies. Near Sandersville November 26. Siege of Savannah December 10-21. Campaign of the Carolinas January to April, 1865. Averysboro, N. C., March 16. Battle of Bentonville March 19-21. Occupation of Goldsboro March 24. Advance on Raleigh April 10-14. Occupation of Raleigh April 14. Bennett's House April 26. Surrender of Johnston and his army. March to Washington, D. C., via Richmond, Va., April 29-May 20. Grand Review May 24. Moved to Louisville, Ky., June, and there mustered out July 25, 1865.

Regiment lost during service 5 Officers and 80 Enlisted men killed and mortally wounded and 1 Officer and 140 Enlisted men by disease. Total 226.

38th REGIMENT INFANTRY.

Organized at New Albany, Ind., and mustered in September 18, 1861. Ordered to Elizabethtown, Ky., September 21, and duty at Camp Nevin on Green River till February, 1862. Attached to Wood's Brigade, McCook's Command, at Nolin, Ky., October-November, 1861. 7th Brigade, Army of the Ohio, to December, 1861. 7th Brigade, 2nd Division, Army of the Ohio, to March, 1862. 7th Independent Brigade, Army of the Ohio, to July, 1862. 9th Brigade, 3rd Division, Army of the Ohio, to September, 1862. 9th Brigade, 3rd Division, 1st Corps, Army of the Ohio, to November, 1862. 1st Brigade, 1st Division, Center 14th Army Corps, Army of the Cumberland, to January, 1863. 1st Brigade, 1st Division, 14th Army Corps, to April, 1864. 3rd Brigade, 1st Division, 14th Army Corps, to June, 1865. 1st Brigade, 1st Division, 14th Army Corps, to July, 1865.

SERVICE.—Advance on Bowling Green, Ky., and Nashville, Tenn., February 10-March 6, 1862. Moved to Franklin March 25, thence to Columbia and Shelbyville. Duty at Shelbyville till May 11. Action at Rogersville May 13. Expedition to Chattanooga May 28-June 16. Chattanooga June 7. Guard duty at Shelbyville and Stevenson till August. Moved to Dechard August 17, thence march to Louisville, Ky., in pursuit of Bragg, August 21-September 26. Pursuit of Bragg into Kentucky October 1-15. Battle of Perryville October 8. March to Nashville, Tenn., October 16-November 7, and duty there till December 26. Advance on Murfreesboro December 26-30. Battle of Stone's River December 30-31, 1862, and January 1-3, 1863. Duty at Murfreesboro till June. Middle Tennessee or Tullahoma Campaign June 24-July 7. Hoover's Gap June 24-26. Occupation of Middle Tennessee till August 16. Passage of the Cumberland Mountains and Tennessee River and Chickamauga (Ga.) Campaign August 16-September 22. Davis Cross Roads, Dug Gap, September 11. Battle of Chickamauga September 19-21. Rossville Gap September 21. Siege of Chattanooga, Tenn., September 24-November 23. Chattanooga-Ringgold Campaign November 23-27. Lookout Mountain November 23-24. Mission Ridge November 25. Pea Vine Creek and Graysville November 26. Ringgold Gap, Taylor's Ridge, November 27. Duty at Rossville, Ga., and Chattanooga, Tenn., till February, 1864, and at Tyner's Station and Graysville till May. Atlanta (Ga.) Campaign May 1 to September 8. Demonstration on Rocky Faced Ridge May 8-11. Buzzard's Roost Gap May 8-9. Battle of Resaca May 14-15. Advance on Dallas May 18-25. Operations on Pumpkin Vine Creek and battles about Dallas, New Hope Church and Allatoona Hills May 25-June 5. Pickett's Mills May 27. Operations about Marietta and against Kenesaw Mountain June 10-July 2. Pine Hill June 11-14. Lost Mountain June 15-17. Assault on Kenesaw June 27. Ruff's Station, Smyrna Camp Ground, July 4. Chattahoochie River July 5-17. Peach Tree Creek July 19-20. Siege of Atlanta July 22-August 25. Utoy Creek August 5-7. Flank movement on Jonesboro August 25-30. Battle of Jonesboro August 31-September 1. Pursuit of Hood into Alabama October 3-26. March to the sea November 15-December 10. Siege of Savannah December 10-21. Campaign of the Carolinas January to April, 1865. Averysboro, N. C., March 16. Battle of Bentonville March 19-21. Occupation of Goldsboro March 24. Advance on Raleigh April 10-14. Occupation of Raleigh April 14. Bennett's House April 26. Surrender of Johnston and his army. March to Washington, D. C., via Richmond, Va., April 29-May 20. Grand Review May 24. Moved to Louisville, Ky., June, and there mustered out July 15, 1865.

Regiment lost during service 9 Officers and 147 Enlisted men killed and mortally wounded and 1 Officer and 254 Enlisted men by disease. Total 411.

39th REGIMENT INFANTRY.

See 8th Regiment Cavalry for service.

40th REGIMENT INFANTRY.

Organized at Lafayette and Indianapolis, Ind., and mustered in December 30, 1861. Ordered to Kentucky and duty at Bardstown, Ky., till February, 1862. Attached to 21st Brigade, Army of the Ohio, January, 1862. 21st Brigade, 6th Division, Army of the Ohio, to September, 1862. 21st Brigade, 6th Division, 2nd Army Corps, Army of the Ohio, to November, 1862. 2nd Brigade, 1st Division, Left Wing 14th Army Corps, Army of the Cumberland, to January, 1863. 2nd Brigade, 1st Division, 21st Army Corps, Army of the Cumberland, to October, 1863. 2nd Brigade, 2nd Division, 4th Army Corps, Army of the Cumberland, to June, 1865. 1st Brigade, 2nd Division, 4th Army Corps, to August, 1865. Dept. of Texas, to December, 1865.

SERVICE.—March to Bowling Green, Ky., and Nashville, Tenn., February 10-March 13, 1862, and to Savannah, Tenn., March 29-April 6. Battle of Shiloh, Tenn., April 6-7. Advance on and siege of Corinth, Miss., April 29-May 30. Pursuit to Booneville May 31-June 12. Buell's Campaign in Northern Alabama and Middle Tennessee June to August. March to Louisville, Ky., in pursuit of Bragg August 21-September 26. Pursuit of Bragg to Loudon, Ky., October 1-22. Battle of Perryville, Ky., October 8. March to Nashville, Tenn., October 22-November 7, and duty there till December 26. Advance on Murfreesboro December 26-30. Lavergne December 26-27. Battles of Stone's River December 30-31, 1862, and January 1-3, 1863. Duty at Murfreesboro till June. Reconnoissance to Nolensville and Versailles January 13-15. Middle Tennessee or Tullahoma Campaign June 23-July 7. Occupation of Middle Tennessee till August 16. March over Cumberland Mountains to Chattanooga, Tenn., August 16-September 9. Occupation of Chattanooga September 9 and garrison duty there during Chickamauga (Ga.) Campaign. Siege of Chattanooga September 24-November 23. Chattanooga-Ringgold Campaign November 23-27. Orchard Knob November 23-24. Mission Ridge November 25. Pursuit to Graysville November 26-27. March to relief of Knoxville November 28-December 8. Operations in East Tennessee December, 1863, to April, 1864. Operations about Dandridge January 16-17. Atlanta Campaign May 1 to September 8. Demonstrations on Rocky Faced Ridge and Dalton May 8-13. Buzzard's Roost Gap May 8-9. Battle of Resaca May 14-15. Adairsville May 17. Near Kingston May 18-19. Near Cassville May 19. Advance on Dallas May 22-25. Operations on line of Pumpkin Vine Creek and battles about Dallas, New Hope Church and Allatoona Hills May 25-June 5. Operations about Marietta and against Kenesaw Mountain June 10-July 2. Pine Hill June 11-14. Lost Mountain June 15-17. Assault on Kenesaw June 27. Ruff's Station, Smyrna Camp Ground, July 4. Chattahoochie River July 5-17. Buckhead, Nancy's Creek, July 18. Peach Tree Creek July 19-20. Siege of Atlanta July 22-August 25. Flank movement on Jonesboro August 25-30. Battle of Jonesboro August 31-September 1. Operations

against Hood in North Georgia and North Alabama September 29-November 3. Nashville Campaign November-December. Columbia, Duck River, November 24-27. Spring Hill November 29. Battle of Franklin November 30. Battle of Nashville December 15-16. Pursuit of Hood to the Tennessee River December 17-28. Moved to Huntsville, Ala., and duty there till March, 1865. Operations in East Tennessee March 15-April 22. At Nashville till June. Ordered to New Orleans, La., June 16, thence to Texas, July. Duty at Green Lake and San Antonio and at Port Lavacca till December. Mustered out December 21, 1865.

Regiment lost during service 5 Officers and 143 Enlisted men killed and mortally wounded and 5 Officers and 206 Enlisted men by disease. Total 359.

41st REGIMENT VOLUNTEERS.

See 2nd Regiment Cavalry.

42nd REGIMENT INFANTRY.

Organized at Evansville, Ind., and mustered in October 9, 1861. Ordered to Kentucky, and duty at Henderson, Calhoun and Owensboro, Ky., till February, 1862. Attached to 14th Brigade, Army of the Ohio, October to December, 1861. 14th Brigade, 5th Division, Army of the Ohio, to April, 1862. 17th Brigade, 3rd Division, Army of the Ohio, to September, 1862. 17th Brigade, 3rd Division, 1st Corps, Army of the Ohio, to November, 1862. 2nd Brigade, 1st Division, Center 14th Army Corps, Army of the Cumberland, to January, 1863. 2nd Brigade, 1st Division, 14th Army Corps, Army of the Cumberland, to April, 1863. 1st Brigade, 2nd Division, 14th Army Corps to October, 1863. 1st Brigade, 1st Division, 14th Army Corps, to July, 1865.

SERVICE.—Advance on Nashville, Tenn., February 10-25, 1862. Occupation of Shelbyville and Fayetteville and advance on Huntsville, Ala., March 28-April 11. Action at Wartrace April 11. Advance on and capture of Decatur, Ala., April 11-14. Action at West Bridge near Bridgeport, Ala., April 29. Duty at Huntsville, Ala., till August. March to Nashville, Tenn., thence to Louisville, Ky., in pursuit of Bragg, August 27-September 26. Pursuit of Bragg into Kentucky October 1-15. Battle of Perryville, Ky., October 8. March to Nashville, Tenn., October 16-November 7, and duty there till December 26. Advance on Murfreesboro December 26-30. Battle of Stone's River December 30-31, 1862, and January 1-3, 1863. Duty at Murfreesboro till June. Reconnoissance to Versailles March 9-14. Middle Tennessee or Tullahoma Campaign June 23-July 7. Elm River June 29. Occupation of Middle Tennessee till August 16. Passage of the Cumberland Mountains and Tennessee River and Chickamauga (Ga.) Campaign August 16-September 22. Davis Cross Roads or Dug Gap September 11. Battle of Chickamauga September 19-21. Rossville Gap September 21. Siege of Chattanooga, Tenn., September 24-November 23. Chattanooga-Ringgold Campaign November 23-27. Lookout Mountain November 23-24. Mission Ridge November 25. Pea Vine Creek and Graysville November 26. Ringgold Gap, Taylor's Ridge November 27. Regiment re-enlisted January 1, 1864. Atlanta (Ga.) Campaign May 1-September 8, 1864. Demonstrations on Rocky Faced Ridge May 8-11. Buzzard's Roost Gap May 8-9. Battle of Resaca May 14-15. Advance on Dallas May 18-25. Operations on Pumpkin Vine Creek and battles about Dallas, New Hope Church and Allatoona Hills May 25-June 5. Pickett's Mill May 27. Operations about Marietta and against Kenesaw Mountain June 10-July 2. Pine Hill June 11-14. Lost Mountain June 15-17. Assault on Kenesaw June 27. Ruff's Station, Smyrna Camp Ground, July 4. Chattahoochie River July 5-17. Buckhead, Nancy's Creek, July 18. Peach Tree Creek July 19-20. Siege of Atlanta July 22-August 25. Utoy Creek August 5-7. Flank movement on Jonesboro August 25-30. Near Red Oak August 29. Battle of Jonesboro August 31-September 1. Operations against Hood in North Georgia and North Alabama September 29-November 3. March to the sea November 15-December 10. Siege of

Savannah December 10-21. Campaign of the Carolinas January to April, 1865. Averysboro, N. C., March 16. Battle of Bentonville March 19-21. Occupation of Goldsboro March 24. Advance on Raleigh April 10-14. Occupation of Raleigh April 14. Bennett's House April 26. Surrender of Johnston and his army. March to Washington, D. C., via Richmond, Va., April 29-May 19. Grand Review May 24. Moved to Louisville, Ky., June and there mustered out July 21, 1865.

Regiment lost during service 5 Officers and 108 Enlisted men killed and mortally wounded and 1 Officer and 196 Enlisted men by disease. Total 310.

43rd REGIMENT INFANTRY.

Organized at Terre Haute, Ind., and mustered in September 27, 1861. Left State for Calhoun, Ky., October 1, and duty there till February, 1862. Attached to 14th Brigade, Army of the Ohio, to December, 1861. 14th Brigade, 5th Division, Army of the Ohio, to February, 1862. 1st Brigade, 2nd Division, Army of Mississippi, to April, 1862. 1st Brigade, 3rd Division, Army of Mississippi, to July, 1862. Helena, Ark., District of Eastern Arkansas, Dept. of Missouri, to December, 1862. 1st Brigade, 2nd Division, District of Eastern Arkansas, Dept. of the Tennessee, to January, 1863. 1st Brigade, 12th Division, 13th Army Corps, Army of the Tennessee, to February, 1863. 1st Brigade, 13th Division, 13th Army Corps, to July, 1863. 1st Brigade, 13th Division, 16th Army Corps, July, 1863. 1st Brigade, 13th Division, 16th Army Corps, Arkansas Expedition, to August, 1863. 1st Brigade, 3rd Division, Arkansas Expedition, to January, 1864. 1st Brigade, 3rd Division, 7th Army Corps, Dept. of Arkansas, to April, 1864. 2nd Brigade, 3rd Division, 7th Army Corps, to May, 1864. 2nd Brigade, 1st Division, 7th Army Corps, to July, 1864. Camp Morton, Ind., to June, 1865.

SERVICE.—Ordered to Commerce, Mo., February 19, 1862. Siege of New Madrid, Mo., March 5-14. Siege and capture of Island No. 10 March 15-April 8. Riddell's Point March 17. Expedition to Fort Pillow, Tenn., April 13-17. Operations against Fort Pillow April 15-June 5. Capture of Fort Pillow June 5. Occupation of Memphis, Tenn., June 6. Expedition up White River, Ark., June 10-July 14. Adam's Bluff June 30. Grand Prairie July 6-7. Near Duvall's Bluff July 7. Aberdeen July 9. Duty at Helena, Ark., till August, 1863. Near Helena October 18 and 20, 1862. Expedition to Arkansas Post, Ark., November 16-21. Expedition to Yazoo Pass, by Moon Lake, Yazoo Pass and Coldwater and Tallahatchie Rivers February 24-April 8, 1863. Operations against Fort Pemberton and Greenwood March 13-April 5. Battle of Helena July 4. Repulse of Holmes' attack. Steele's Expedition to Little Rock August 11-September 10. Bayou Fourche and capture of Little Rock September 10. Pursuit of Marmaduke's forces October 26-November 1. Duty at Little Rock till March, 1864. Regiment re-enlisted January 1, 1864. Steele's Expedition to Camden March 23-May 3. Elkins' Ford Crossing, Little Missouri River, April 3-4. Prairie D'Ann April 9-12. Camden April 16-18. Marks' Mills April 25. Jenkin's Ferry, Saline River, April 30. Duty at Pine Bluff and Little Rock till June. Veterans on furlough June-July. Volunteered for duty at Frankford, Ky., during Morgan's operations, and invasion of Central Kentucky. Assigned to guard duty at Camp Morton guarding Confederate prisoners till June, 1865. Mustered out June 14, 1865.

Regiment lost during service 2 Officers and 41 Enlisted men killed and mortally wounded and 5 Officers and 200 Enlisted men by disease. Total 248.

44th REGIMENT INFANTRY.

Organized at Fort Wayne, Ind., and mustered in November 22, 1861. Moved to Henderson, Ky., December. Attached to 13th Brigade, Army of the Ohio, December, 1861. 13th Brigade, 5th Division, Army of the Ohio, to February, 1862. 1st Brigade, 3rd Division, Army of the Tennessee, to March, 1862. 3rd Brigade, 4th Division, Army of the Tennessee, to April, 1862.

14th Brigade, 5th Division, Army of the Ohio, to September, 1862. 14th Brigade, 5th Division, 2nd Corps, Army of the Ohio, to November, 1862. 2nd Brigade, 3rd Division, Left Wing 14th Army Corps, Army of the Cumberland, to January, 1863. 2nd Brigade, 3rd Division, 21st Army Corps, Army of the Cumberland, to October, 1863. 3rd Brigade, 3rd Division, 4th Army Corps, to November, 1863. Post of Chattanooga, Tenn., Dept. of the Cumberland, to April, 1864. 1st Separate Brigade, Post of Chattanooga, Tenn., to January, 1865. 2nd Brigade, 1st Separate Division, District of the Etowah, Dept. of the Cumberland, to May, 1865. 2nd Brigade, 4th Division, District of East Tennessee, Dept. of the Cumberland, to September, 1865.

SERVICE.—Duty at Calhoun, Green River, Ky., January-February, 1862. Moved to Fort Donelson, Tenn., February 11-12. Investment and capture of Fort Donelson February 14-16. Expedition to Crump's Landing, Tenn., March 9-14. Battle of Shiloh, Tenn., April 6-7. Advance on siege of Corinth, Miss., April 29-May 30. Pursuit to Booneville May 31-June 12. Buell's Campaign in Northern Alabama and Middle Tennessee June to August. March to Louisville, Ky., in pursuit of Bragg August 21-September 26. Pursuit of Bragg to Loudon, Ky., October 1-22. March to Nashville, Tenn., October 22-November 7, and duty there till December 26. Lavergne November 23. Advance on Murfreesboro, Tenn., December 26-30. Battle of Stone's River December 30-31, 1862, and January 1-3, 1863. Duty at Murfreesboro till June. Middle Tennessee (or Tullahoma) Campaign June 23-July 7. Occupation of Middle Tennessee till August 16. Passage of the Cumberland Mountains and Tennessee River and Chickamauga (Ga.) Campaign August 16-September 22. Battle of Chickamauga September 19-20. Mission Ridge September 22. Before Chattanooga September 22-26. Siege of Chattanooga September 26-November 23. Assigned to Provost duty at Chattanooga November 8. Chattanooga-Ringgold Campaign November 23-27. Mission Ridge November 25. On Provost duty at Chattanooga, Tenn., till September, 1864. At Tullahoma September 28 to October 2. Return to Chattanooga, Tenn., October 15, and Provost duty there till September, 1865. Mustered out September 14, 1865.

Regiment lost during service 4 Officers and 76 Enlisted men killed and mortally wounded and 9 Officers and 220 Enlisted men by disease. Total 309.

45th REGIMENT VOLUNTEERS.

See 3rd Regiment Cavalry.

46th REGIMENT INFANTRY.

Organized at Logansport, Ind., and mustered in December 11, 1861. Ordered to Kentucky and duty at Camp Wickliffe till February, 1862. Attached to 19th Brigade, Army of the Ohio, January, 1862. 19th Brigade, 4th Division, Army of Ohio, to February, 1862. 1st Brigade, 2nd Division, Army of Mississippi, to April, 1862. 2nd Brigade, 3rd Division, Army of Mississippi, to July, 1862. Helena, Ark., District of Eastern Arkansas, Dept. of the Missouri, to December, 1862. 1st Brigade, 2nd Division, District of Eastern Arkansas, Dept. of the Tennessee, to January, 1863. 1st Brigade, 12th Division, 13th Army Corps, Army of the Tennessee, to February, 1863. 1st Brigade, 13th Division, 13th Army Corps, to March, 1863. 1st Brigade, 12th Division, 13th Army Corps, to July, 1863. 1st Brigade, 3rd Division, 13th Army Corps, Army of Tennessee, to August, 1863, and Dept. of the Gulf to July, 1864. 4th Brigade, 1st Division, District of Kentucky, Dept. of the Ohio, to December, 1864. Garrison, Lexington, Ky., District of Kentucky, Dept. of the Ohio, to February, 1865, and District of Kentucky to September, 1865.

SERVICE.—Ordered to Commerce, Mo., February 16, 1862. Siege of New Madrid, Mo., March 5-14. Siege and capture of Island No. 10, Mississippi River, March 15-April 8. Expedition to Fort Pillow, Tenn., April 13-17. Operations against Fort Pillow April 17-June 5. Capture of Fort Pillow June 5. Occupation of Memphis, Tenn., June 6. Expedition up White River, Ark., June 10-July 14. St. Charles June 17. Grand Prairie July 6-7. Duvall's Bluff July 7. Duty at Helena, Ark., till April, 1863. Expedition to Arkansas Post November 16-22, 1862. Expedition to Yazoo Pass by Moon Lake, Yazoo Pass and Coldwater and Tallahatchie Rivers February 24-April 5. Operations against Fort Pemberton and Greenwood March 11-April 5. Fort Pemberton March 11. Moved to Milliken's Bend, La., April 12. Movement on Bruinsburg and turning Grand Gulf April 25-30. Battle of Port Gibson, Miss., May 1-14. Mile Creek April 12-13. Battle of Champion's Hill May 16. Siege of Vicksburg May 18-July 4. Assaults on Vicksburg May 19 and 22. Advance on Jackson July 4-10. Near Jackson July 9. Siege of Jackson July 10-17. Ordered to New Orleans, La., August 10. Duty at Carrollton, Brashear City and Berwick till October. Western Louisiana "Teche" Campaign October 3-November 30. Grand Coteau November 3. Moved to New Orleans, La., December 17. Regiment re-enlisted January 2, 1864. Red River Campaign March 10-May 22. Advance from Franklin to Alexandria March 14-26. Battle of Sabine Cross Roads April 8. Monett's Ferry, Cane River Crossing, April 23. Alexandria April 30-May 10. Graham's Plantation May 6. Retreat to Morganza May 13-20. Mansura May 16. Expedition to the Atchafalaya May 30-June 5. Moved to New Orleans, La., thence home on Veteran furlough June 12. Expedition down the Ohio River toward Shawneetown, Ill., to suppress insurrection, and from Mt. Vernon, Ind., into Kentucky against Confederate Recruiting parties August 16-22. White Oak Springs August 17. Gouger's Lake August 18. Smith's Mills August 19. Moved to Lexington, Ky., to resist Buckner's invasion of Kentucky. Burbridge's Expedition to Saltsville, Va., September 17-October 19. Garrison, Prestonburg and Catlettsburg, Ky., during the Expedition. Return to Lexington and garrison duty there till September, 1865. Moved to Louisville, Ky., and there mustered out September 4, 1865.

Regiment lost during service 4 Officers and 66 Enlisted men killed and mortally wounded and 3 Officers and 191 Enlisted men by disease. Total 264.

47th REGIMENT INFANTRY.

Organized at Anderson and Indianapolis, Ind., November 2 to December 13, 1861. Left State for Bardstown, Ky., December 13, 1861; thence moved to Camp Wickliffe, Ky., and duty there till February, 1862. Attached to 19th Brigade, Army of the Ohio, to January, 1862. 19th Brigade, 4th Division, Army of the Ohio, to February, 1862. 1st Brigade, 2nd Division, Army of Mississippi, to April, 1862. 2nd Brigade, 3rd Division, Army of Mississippi, to July, 1863. Helena, Ark., District of Eastern Arkansas, Dept. of the Missouri, to December, 1862. 1st Brigade, 2nd Division, District of Eastern Arkansas, Dept. of the Tennessee, to January, 1863. 1st Brigade, 12th Division, 13th Army Corps, Army of the Tennessee, to February, 1863. 1st Brigade, 13th Division, 13th Army Corps, to March, 1863. 2nd Brigade, 12th Division, 13th Army Corps, to July, 1863. 2nd Brigade, 3rd Division, 13th Army Corps, Dept. of the Tennessee, to August, 1863, and Dept. of the Gulf to June, 1864. District of LaFourche, Dept. of the Gulf, to July, 1864. 2nd Brigade, 2nd Division, 19th Army Corps, Dept. of the Gulf, to December, 1864. 1st Brigade, Reserve Division, Military Division, West Mississippi, to February, 1865. 1st Brigade, 1st Division, Reserve Corps, Military Division, West Mississippi, February, 1865. 1st Brigade, 1st Division, 13th Army Corps (New), Military Division, West Mississippi, to May, 1865. Dept. of Louisiana to October, 1865.

SERVICE.—Ordered to Commerce, Mo., February 14, 1862. New Madrid, Mo., February 24. Siege of New Madrid, Mo., March 5-14. Siege and capture of Island No. 10, Mississippi River, March 15-April 8. Expedition to Fort Pillow, Tenn., April 13-17. Duty at Tiptonville till May 19. Expedition down Mississippi River

to Fort Pillow May 19-23. Moved to Memphis, Tenn., June, and duty there till July 24. Moved to Helena, Ark., July 24 and duty there till February, 1863. Brown's Plantation, Miss., August 11, 1862. Expedition to Arkansas Post November 16-21. Expedition to Yazoo Pass by Moon Lake, Yazoo Pass and Coldwater and Tallahatchie Rivers February 24-April 8. Fort Pemberton March 11. Operations against Fort Pemberton and Greenwood March 13-April 5. Moved to Milliken's Bend, La., April 12. Movement on Bruinsburg and turning Grand Gulf April 25-30. Battle of Port Gibson, Miss., May 1. 14-Mile Creek May 12-13. Battle of Champion's Hill May 16. Siege of Vicksburg, Miss., May 18-July 4. Assault on Vicksburg May 19 and 22. Advance on Jackson, Miss., July 4-10. Siege of Jackson July 10-17. Ordered to New Orleans, La., August 10. At Carrollton, Brashear City and Berwick till October. Western Louisiana "Teche" Campaign October 3-November 30. Duty at New Iberia till December 17. Moved to New Orleans, La., December 17, thence to Madisonville January 7, 1864, and duty there till March. Red River Campaign March 10-May 22. Advance from Franklin to Alexandria March 14-26. Battle of Sabine Cross Roads April 8. Monett's Ferry, Cane River Crossings, April 23. Alexandria April 30-May 10. Muddy Bayou May 2-6. Graham's Plantation May 5. Retreat to Morganza May 13-20. Mansura May 16. Expedition to the Atchafalaya May 30-June 6. Duty at Morganza till September. Expedition to Clinton August 23-29. At St. Charles, Ark., September 3-October 23. Expedition to Duvall's Bluff October 23-November 12. Moved to Little Rock, Ark.; thence to Memphis, Tenn., November 25, and duty there till January, 1865. Expedition to Moscow December 21-31, 1864. Ordered to New Orleans, La., January 1, 1865. Campaign against Mobile and its Defences March 17-April 12. Near Spanish Fort March 26. Siege of Spanish Fort and Fort Blakely March 26-April 8. Assault on and capture of Fort Blakely April 9. Occupation of Mobile April 12 to May 26. Moved to New Orleans, La., May 26; thence to Shreveport, La., and duty there till October. Mustered out October 23, 1865, and discharged at Indianapolis, Ind., November 2, 1865.

Regiment lost during service 2 Officers and 80 Enlisted men killed and mortally wounded and 4 Officers and 250 Enlisted men by disease. Total 336.

48th REGIMENT INFANTRY.

Organized at Goshen, Ind., December 5, 1861, to January 28, 1862. Left State for Paducah, Ky., February 1, 1862. Attached to District of Paducah, Ky., to May, 1862. 2nd Brigade, 3rd Division, Army of Mississippi, May, 1862. 1st Brigade, 3rd Division, Army of Mississippi, to November, 1862. 1st Brigade, 7th Division, Left Wing 13th Army Corps (Old), Dept. of the Tennessee, to December, 1862. 1st Brigade, 7th Division, 16th Army Corps, to January, 1863. 1st Brigade, 7th Division, 17th Army Corps, to September, 1863. 1st Brigade, 2nd Division, 17th Army Corps, to December, 1863. 1st Brigade, 3rd Division, 15th Army Corps, to April, 1865. 2nd Brigade, 4th Division, 15th Army Corps, to July, 1865.

SERVICE.—Duty at Paducah, Ky., till May, 1862. Moved to Pittsburg Landing, Tenn. Siege of Corinth, Miss., May 13-30. Pursuit to Booneville May 30-June 12. Duty at Clear Creek till August 6, and at Jacinto till September 7. Battle of Iuka, Miss., September 19. Battle of Corinth October 3-4. Pursuit to Ripley October 5-12. Grant's Central Mississippi Campaign. Operations on the Mississippi Central Railroad November, 1862, to January, 1863. Reconnoissance from Lagrange November 8-9, 1862. Moved to Memphis, Tenn., January 10, 1863, and duty there till February. Expedition to Yazoo Pass by Moon Lake, Yazoo Pass and Coldwater and Tallahatchie Rivers February 24-April 8. Operations against Fort Pemberton and Greenwood March 13-April 5. Moved to Milliken's Bend, La., April 13. Movement on Bruinsburg and turning Grand Gulf April 25-30. Battle of Port Gibson May 1 (Reserve). Jones'

Cross Roads and Willow Springs May 3. Forty Hills and Hankinson's Ferry May 3-4. Battle of Raymond May 12. Jackson May 14. Battle of Champion's Hill May 16. Siege of Vicksburg, Miss., May 18-July 4. Assaults on Vicksburg May 19 and 22. Surrender of Vicksburg July 4. Duty at Vicksburg till September 13. Moved to Helena, Ark., thence to Memphis, Tenn., and march to Chattanooga, Tenn., September 13-November 20. Operations on Memphis & Charleston Railroad in Alabama October 20-29. Chattanooga-Ringgold Campaign November 23-27. Tunnel Hill November 23-24. Mission Ridge November 25. Pursuit to Graysville November 26-27. Duty at Huntsville, Ala., till June, 1864. Re-enlisted at Huntsville January, 1864, and Veterans on furlough February and March. Duty at Cartersville, Ga., protecting Railroad till October. March to the sea November 15-December 10. Siege of Savannah December 10-21. Campaign of the Carolinas January to April, 1865. Salkehatchie Swamps, S. C., February 2-5, 1865. North Edisto River February 12-13. Columbia February 16-17. West's Cross Roads February 25. Battle of Bentonville, N. C., March 19-21. Occupation of Goldsboro March 24. Advance on Raleigh April 10-14. Occupation of Raleigh April 14. Bennett's House April 26. Surrender of Johnston and his army. March to Washington, D. C., via Richmond, Va., April 29-May 19. Grand Review May 24. Moved to Louisville, Ky., June, and there mustered out July 15, 1865.

Regiment lost during service 88 Enlisted men killed and mortally wounded and 4 Officers and 175 Enlisted men by disease. Total 267.

49th REGIMENT INFANTRY.

Organized at Jeffersonville, Ind., and mustered in November 21, 1861. Moved to Bardstown, Ky., December 11-13, and duty there till January 12, 1862. Attached to 12th Brigade, Army of the Ohio, December, 1861. 12th Brigade, 1st Division, Army of the Ohio, to March, 1862. 24th Brigade, 7th Division, Army of the Ohio, to October, 1862. 3rd Brigade, Cumberland Division, District of West Virginia, Dept. of the Ohio, to November, 1862. 2nd Brigade, 9th Division, Right Wing 13th Army Corps (Old), Dept. of the Tennessee, to December, 1862. 2nd Brigade, Sherman's Yazoo Expedition, to January, 1863. 2nd Brigade, 9th Division, 13th Army Corps, Army of the Tennessee, to February, 1863. 1st Brigade, 9th Division, 13th Army Corps, to July, 1863. 3rd Brigade, 1st Division, 13th Army Corps, Dept. of the Tennessee, to August, 1863, and Dept. of the Gulf to March, 1864. 2nd Brigade, 1st Division, 13th Army Corps, to July, 1864. 4th Brigade, 1st Division, District of Kentucky, to February, 1865. Dept. of Kentucky to September, 1865.

SERVICE.—March to Cumberland Ford January 12-February 15, 1862. Flat Lick Ford, Cumberland River, February 14. Skirmishes at Big Creek Gap and Jacksborough March 14 (Detachment). Reconnoissance toward Cumberland Gap and skirmishes March 21-23. Duty at Cumberland Ford till June. Cumberland Gap Campaign March 28 to June 18. Occupation of Cumberland Gap June 18 to September 16. Tazewell July 22 (Detachment). Evacuation of Cumberland Gap and retreat to the Ohio River September 17-October 3. Expedition to Charleston, W. Va., October 21-November 10. Moved to Memphis, Tenn., November 10, and duty there till December 20. Sherman's Yazoo Expedition December 20, 1862, to January 3, 1863. Chickasaw Bayou December 26-28. Chickasaw Bluff December 29. Expedition to Arkansas Post, Ark., January 3-10, 1863. Assault and capture of Fort Hindman, Arkansas Post, January 10-11. Moved to Young's Point, La., January 15; thence to Milliken's Bend March 8. Operations from Milliken's Bend to New Carthage March 31-April 17. James' Plantation, near New Carthage, April 6 and 8. Dunbar's Plantation, Bayou Vidal, April 15. Expedition from Perkins' Plantation to Hard Times Landing April 25-29. Phelps' and Clark's Bayous April 26. Choctaw Bayou on Lake Bruin April 28. Battle of Thompson's Hill, Port Gibson, May 1. Battle of Champion's

Hill May 16. Big Black River Bridge May 17. Siege of Vicksburg, Miss., May 18-July 4. Assaults on Vicksburg May 19 and 22. Advance on Jackson, Miss., July 4-10. Near Clinton July 8. Siege of Jackson July 10-17. Ordered to New Orleans, La., August 13. Duty at Carrollton, Brashear City and Berwick till October. Western Louisiana "Teche" Campaign October 3-November 30. Moved to New Orleans, thence to DeCrow's Point, Tex., December 10-14. Duty at Matagorda Island and Indianola till April, 1864. Ordered to New Orleans April 19, thence to Alexandria April 23. Red River Campaign April 26-May 22. Action at Graham's Plantation May 5. Retreat to Morganza May 13-20. Expedition to the Atchafalaya May 30-June 6. Duty at Morganza till July. Moved to New Orleans, thence home on Veteran furlough July and August. Ordered to Lexington, Ky., and garrison duty there till September 7, 1865. Moved to Louisville, Ky., September 7, and there mustered out September 13, 1865.

Regiment lost during service 1 Officer and 40 Enlisted men killed and mortally wounded and 3 Officers and 192 Enlisted men by disease. Total 236.

50th REGIMENT INFANTRY.

Organized at Seymour, Ind., and mustered in September 12, 1861. Moved to New Albany, Ind., October 25; thence to Bardstown, Ky., December 25. Attached to 15th Brigade, 4th Division, Army of the Ohio, to June, 1862. Unassigned Railroad Guard, Army of the Ohio, to September, 1862. District of Louisville, Ky., Dept. of the Ohio, to November, 1862. District of Jackson, Tenn., 13th Army Corps (Old), Dept. of the Tennessee, to December, 1862. 2nd Brigade, District of Jackson, Tenn., 16th Army Corps, to March, 1863. 2nd Brigade, 3rd Division, 16th Army Corps, to August, 1863. True's Brigade, Arkansas Expedition, to January, 1864. Unassigned, 2nd Division, 7th Army Corps, Dept. of Arkansas, to April, 1864. 1st Brigade, 3rd Division, 7th Army Corps, to May, 1864. 1st Brigade, 1st Division, 7th Army Corps, to February, 1865. 2nd Brigade, 3rd Division, 13th Army Corps (New), Military Division West Mississippi, to April, 1865. 2nd Brigade, 2nd Division, 16th Army Corps, Military Division West Mississippi, to May, 1865.

SERVICE.—Duty at Bardstown, Ky., till February, 1862. Advance on Bowling Green, Ky., and Nashville, Tenn., February 10-March 3. Guard duty along Nashville & Chattanooga Railroad till September, 1862. Operations against Morgan July 4-28. Near Edgefield Junction August 20 (Detachment). Pilot Knob August 20. Siege of Munfordsville, Ky., September 14-17 (Cos. "A," "B," "D," "F" and "H"). Captured September 17. Paroled and sent to Indianapolis, Ind., and duty there till November. Moved to Jackson, Tenn., November 1-10. Operations against Forest in West Tennessee December 18, 1862, to January 3, 1863. Huntington December 29-30. Parker's Cross Roads, near Jackson, December 30. Clarksburg December 30 (Detachment). Red Mound (or Parker's) Cross Roads December 31. Duty at Jackson, Colliersville and Memphis, Tenn., till August, 1863. Moved to Helena, Ark., August 28. Steele's Expedition to Little Rock September 1-10. Bayou Fourche and capture of Little Rock September 10. Garrison duty at Lewisburg, Ark., till March, 1864. Re-enlisted March 2, 1864. Steele's Expedition to Camden March 23-May 3. Antoine and Terre Noir Creek April 2. Prairie D'Ann April 9-12. Camden April 15. Liberty Postoffice April 15-16. Camden April 16-18. Red Mound April 17. Jenkins' Ferry, Saline River, April 30. Duty at Little Rock till July. Non-Veterans till December. Veterans absent on furlough July-August. Duty at Little Rock till January, 1865. Carr's Expedition to Saline River January 22-February 4. Moved to Mobile Point, Ala., February, 1865. Campaign against Mobile and its defences March 17-April 12. Siege of Spanish Fort and Fort Blakely March 26-April 8. Assault and capture of Fort Blakely April 9. Capture of Mobile April 12. Whistler's Station April 13. March to Montgomery April 13-22. Consolidated with 52nd Indiana Infantry May 25, 1865.

Regiment lost during service 3 Officers and 54 Enlisted men killed and mortally wounded and 3 Officers and 158 Enlisted men by disease. Total 218.

51st REGIMENT INFANTRY.

Organized at Indianapolis, Ind., and mustered in December 14, 1861. Moved to Louisville, Ky., December 14; thence to Bardstown, Ky., and duty there till February, 1862. Attached to 20th Brigade, Army of the Ohio, to January, 1862. 20th Brigade, 6th Division, Army of the Ohio, to September, 1862. 20th Brigade, 6th Division, 2nd Army Corps, Army of the Ohio, to November, 1862. 3rd Brigade, 1st Division, Left Wing 14th Army Corps, Army of the Cumberland, to January, 1863. 3rd Brigade, 1st Division, 21st Army Corps, Army of the Cumberland, to April, 1863. Streight's Provisional Brigade, Army of the Cumberland, to May, 1863. Prisoners of war till December, 1863. Post of Chattanooga, Tenn., Dept. of the Cumberland, to April, 1864. 1st Separate Brigade, Chattanooga, Tenn., Dept. of the Cumberland, to September, 1864. 2nd Brigade, 2nd Division, 4th Army Corps, Army of the Cumberland, to November, 1864. 1st Brigade, 3rd Division, 4th Army Corps, to August, 1865. Dept. of Texas to December, 1865.

SERVICE.—March to Nashville, Tenn., February 7-March 13, 1862, and to Savannah, Tenn., March 29-April 6. Battle of Shiloh, Tenn., April 6-7. Advance on and siege of Corinth, Miss., April 29-May 30. Pursuit to Booneville May 31-June 12. Buell's Campaign in Northern Alabama and Middle Tennessee June to August. Guarding Memphis & Charleston Railroad. March to Louisville, Ky., in pursuit of Bragg August 21-September 26. Pursuit of Bragg to Loudon, Ky., October 1-22. Battle of Perryville October 8 (Reserve). March to Nashville, Tenn., October 22-November 7, and duty there till December 26. Prim's Blacksmith Shop, Edmonson Pike, December 25. Advance on Murfreesboro December 26-30. Battle of Stone's River December 30-31, 1862, and January 1-3, 1863. Duty at Murfreesboro till April. Reconnoissance to Nolensville and Versailles January 13-15. Streight's Raid to Rome, Ga., April 26-May 3. Dug Gap, Sand Mountain, Crooked Creek and Hog Mountain April 30. East Branch Black Warrior Creek May 1. Blount's Farm and near Centre May 2. Galesville (Cedar Bluff) May 3. Regiment captured. Exchanged November, 1863. Reorganized at Indianapolis, Ind., and rejoined army at Nashville, Tenn., December, 1863. (A detachment on Tullahoma Campaign June 23-July 7.) Assigned to duty as guard on Railroad, between Nashville and Chattanooga, till April, 1864. Duty at Chattanooga, Tenn., till September, 1864, and at Atlanta, Ga., till October. Action at Dalton, Ga., August 14-15. Pursuit of Hood into Alabama October 3-26. Nashville Campaign November-December. Columbia, Duck River, November 24-27. Battle of Franklin November 30. Battle of Nashville December 15-16. Pursuit of Hood to the Tennessee River December 17-28. Columbia December 21. Duck River December 22. Non-Veterans mustered out December 14, 1864. Moved to Huntsville, Ala., and duty there till March, 1865. Operations in East Tennessee March 15-April 22. At Nashville till June. Ordered to New Orleans, La., June 16; thence to Texas, July. Duty at Green Lake and San Antonio till December. Mustered out at San Antonio December 13, 1865.

Regiment lost during service 1 Officer and 55 Enlisted men killed and mortally wounded and 6 Officers and •202 Enlisted men by disease. Total 264.

52nd REGIMENT INFANTRY.

Organized at Rushville and Indianapolis, Ind., February 1, 1862. Left State for Fort Donelson, Tenn., February 7. Attached to 1st Brigade, 3rd Division, Army of the Tennessee, to March, 1862. Garrison Forts Henry and Donelson, Tenn., to April, 1862. 1st Brigade, 4th Division, Army of the Tennessee, to May, 1862. 2nd Brigade, 4th Division, Army of the Tennes-

see, to July, 1862. 2nd Brigade, 4th Division, District of Memphis, Tenn., to September, 1862. Garrison Fort Pillow, Tenn., to November, 1862. District of Columbus, Ky., 13th Army Corps (Old), Dept. of the Tennessee, to January, 1863. District of Columbus, Ky., 6th Division, 16th Army Corps, to January, 1864. 3rd Brigade, 3rd Division, 16th Army Corps, to December, 1864. 3rd Brigade, 2nd Division (Detachment), Army of the Tennessee, Dept. of the Cumberland, to February, 1865. 3rd Brigade, 2nd Division,. 16th Army Corps (New), Military Division West Mississippi, to August, 1865.

SERVICE.—Investment and capture of Fort Donelson, Tenn., February 12-16, 1862. Garrison at Forts Henry and Heiman till April 18. Action at Paris March 11 (Detachment). Moved to Pittsburg Landing, Tenn., April 18. Advance on and siege of Corinth, Miss., April 29-May 30. March to Memphis, Tenn., via Grand Junction, LaGrange and Holly Springs, June 1-July 21. Duty at Memphis till September. Action near Memphis September 2. Durhamsville September 17. Garrison duty at Fort Pillow, Tenn., and operations against guerillas in Tennessee and Arkansas September 30, 1862, to·January 18, 1864. Expedition to Jackson September 19-25, 1863 (Detachment). Expedition to Covington, Durhamsville and Fort Randolph September 28-October 5, 1863. Scout from Fort Pillow November 21-22. Ordered to Vicksburg, Miss., January 18, 1864. Meridian Campaign February 3-March 2. Clinton February 5. Meridian February 14-15. Veterans absent on furlough March and April. Left Vicksburg March 4, arriving home March 17. Left for field April 23. Reached Columbus, Ky., April 26. Moved to Morganza, La., thence to Vicksburg, Miss. Non-Veterans temporarily attached to 89th Indiana Infantry. Red River Campaign March 10-May 22. Fort DeRussy March 14. Bayou Rapides March 21. Battle of Pleasant Hill April 9. Cane River Crossing April 23. At Alexandria April·26-May 13. Moore's Plantation May 3. Bayou LeMourie May 6. Retreat to Morganza May 13-20. Mansura May 16. Yellow Bayou May 18. Moved to Vicksburg, Miss., thence to Memphis, Tenn., May 20-June 10. Lake Chicot, Ark., June 6-7. Colliersville, Tenn., June 23. Near Lafayetteville June 23. Smith's Expedition to Tupelo July 5-21. About Pontotoc July 11-12. Harrisburg, near Tupelo, July 14-15. Old Town (or Tishamingo) Creek July 15. Smith's Expedition to Oxford, Miss., August 1-30. March through Missouri in pursuit of Price·September 26-November 19. Moved to Nashville, Tenn., November 26-December 1. Battle of Nashville December 15-16. Pursuit of Hood to the Tennessee River December 17-23. Duty at Clifton, Tenn., and Eastport, Miss., till February, 1865. Moved to New Orleans February 6-17. Campaign against Mobile and its defences March 17-April 12. Siege of Spanish Fort and Fort Blakely March 26-April 8. Assault and capture of Fort Blakely April 9. Occupation of Mobile April 12. March to Montgomery April 13-25, and duty there till July 14. At Tuskeegee till August 28. Mustered out September 10, 1865.

Regiment lost during service 2 Officers and 26 Enlisted men killed and mortally wounded and 2 Officers and 175 Enlisted men by disease. Total 205.

53rd REGIMENT INFANTRY.

Organized at New Albany and Indianapolis, Ind., February 19 to March 6, 1862. Guard prisoners at Indianapolis till March 15. Ordered to Savannah, Tenn., March 15. Attached to 2nd Brigade, 4th Division, Army of the Tennessee, to July, 1862. 2nd Brigade, 4th Division, District of Memphis, Tenn., to September, 1862. 2nd Brigade, 4th Division, District of Jackson, Tenn., to November, 1862. 3rd Brigade, 4th Division, District of Jackson, Tenn., 13th Army Corps (Old), Dept. of the Tennessee, to December, 1862. 3rd Brigade, 4th Division, 17th Army Corps, to January, 1863. 3rd Brigade, 4th Division, 16th Army Corps, to July, 1863. 3rd Brigade, 4th Division, 13th Army Corps, to August, 1863. 3rd Brigade, 4th Division, 17th Army

Corps, to May, 1864. 1st Brigade, 4th Division, 17th Army Corps, to July, 1865.

SERVICE.—Advance on and siege of Corinth, Miss., April 29-May 30, 1862. March to Memphis, Tenn., via Grand Junction, LaGrange and Holly Springs, June 1-July 21, and duty there till September 6. March to Jackson and Bolivar, Tenn., September 6-14. Battle of Metamora, Hatchie River, October 5. Grant's Central Mississippi Campaign. Operations on the Mississippi Central Railroad November, 1862, to January, 1863. Duty at Colliersville and Memphis till April. Ordered to Young's Point, La., thence to Grand Gulf, Miss., and duty there till June 12. Siege of Vicksburg, Miss., June 15-July 4. Advance on Jackson, Miss., July 4-10. Siege of Jackson July 10-17. Reconnoissance to Pearl River July 15. Duty at Vicksburg till August 15. Ordered to Natchez, Miss., August 15, and duty there till November 24. Expedition to Harrisonburg September 1-8. Near Harrisonburg and capture of Fort Beauregard September 4. Ordered to Vicksburg, Miss., November 24, and duty there till February, 1864. Meridian Campaign February 3-March 2. Veterans on furlough March and April. Moved to Bird's Point, Mo., April 28; thence to Clifton, Tenn., and march to Ackworth, Ga., via Huntsville and Decatur, Ala., and Rome, Ga., May 5-June 9. Atlanta (Ga.) Campaign June 9-September 8. Operations about Marietta and against Kenesaw Mountain June 10-July 2. Assault on Kenesaw June 27. Nickajack Creek July 2-5. Turner's Ferry July 5. Chattahoochie River July 5-17. Leggett's or Bald Hill July 20-21. Battle of Atlanta July 22. Siege of Atlanta July 22-August 25. Flank movement on Jonesboro August 25-31. Battle of Jonesboro August 31-September 1. Lovejoy Station September 2-6. Operations against Hood in North Georgia and North Alabama September 29-November 3. Shadow Church and Westbrook's, near Fairburn, October 1-3. March to the sea November 15-December 10. Ball's Ferry and Georgia Central Railroad Bridge, Oconee River, November 23-25. Siege of Savannah December 10-21. Campaign of the Carolinas January to April, 1865. Salkehatchie Swamps, S. C., February 2-5. Rivers Bridge, Salkehatchie River, February 3. South Edisto River February 9. North Edisto River February 12-13. Columbia February 16-17. Fayetteville, N. C., March 11. Averysboro March 16. Battle of Bentonville March 19-21. Occupation of Goldsboro March 24. Advance on Raleigh April 10-14. Occupation of Raleigh April 14. Bennett's House April 26. Surrender of Johnston and his army. March to Washington, D. C., via Richmond, Va., April 29-May 20. Grand Review May 24. Moved to Louisville, Ky., June, and there mustered out July 21, 1865.

Regiment lost during service 9 Officers and 98 Enlisted men killed and mortally wounded and 4 Officers and 248 Enlisted men by disease. Total 359.

54th REGIMENT INFANTRY.—(3 MONTHS.)

Organized at Indianapolis, Ind., May 30 to June 10, 1862. Duty at Camp Morton, Ind., guarding prisoners till August 17. Ordered to Kentucky August 17 to repel threatened invasion by Kirby Smith, and duty in Central Kentucky till September. Skirmish at Shepherdsville, Ky., September 7 (Co. "C"). Mustered out October 4, 1862.

Regiment lost 2 by disease during service.

54th REGIMENT INFANTRY.—(1 YEAR.)

Regiment organized at Indianapolis, Ind., and mustered in November 16, 1862. Left State for Memphis, Tenn., December 9, 1862. Attached to 3rd Brigade, 9th Division, Right Wing 13th Army Corps (Old), Dept. of the Tennessee, to December, 1862. 3rd Brigade, 3rd Division, Sherman's Yazoo Expedition, to January, 1863. 3rd Brigade, 9th Division, 13th Army Corps, Army of the Tennessee, to February, 1863. 2nd Brigade, 9th Division, 13th Army Corps, to July, 1863. 4th Brigade, 1st Division, 13th Army Corps, Dept. of the Tennessee, to August, 1863, and Dept. of the Gulf to September,

1863. 3rd Brigade, 1st Division, 13th Army Corps, Dept. of the Gulf, to December, 1863.

SERVICE.—Sherman's Yazoo Expedition December 20, 1862, to January 3, 1863. Chickasaw Bayou December 26-28, 1862. Chickasaw Bluff December 29. Expedition to Arkansas Post, Ark., January 3-10, 1863. Assault and capture of Fort Hindman, Arkansas Post, January 10-11. Moved to Young's Point, La., January 15. Moved to Milliken's Bend, La., March 8. Operations from Milliken's Bend to New Carthage March 31-April 17. Movement on Bruinsburg and turning Grand Gulf April 25-30. Battle of Port Gibson May 1. Garrison at Raymond and escorting prisoners to Yazoo River May 12 to June 3. Siege of Vicksburg, Miss., June 3-July 4. Advance on Jackson, Miss., July 4-10. Near Clinton July 8. Siege of Jackson July 10-17. Ordered to New Orleans August 13. Duty at Carrollton, Brashear City and Berwick till October. Western Louisiana, "Teche" Campaign, October 3-November 30. Moved to New Orleans December 1. Mustered out December 8, 1863.

Regiment lost during service 2 Officers and 44 Enlisted men killed and mortally wounded and 2 Officers and 222 Enlisted men by disease. Total 270.

55th REGIMENT INFANTRY.

Organized at Indianapolis, Ind., for three months June 16, 1862. Duty at Camp Morton, Ind., guarding prisoners till August. Operations against Morgan July 4-28. Ordered to Kentucky, August, and attached to Manson's Brigade, Army of Kentucky, District of Central Kentucky. Battle of Richmond, Ky., August 30. Mostly captured. Paroled and sent to Indianapolis, Ind. Mustered out September 6 to October 23, 1862.

Regiment lost while in service 1 Officer and 9 Enlisted men killed and mortally wounded and 3 Enlisted men by disease. Total 13.

56th REGIMENT INFANTRY.

Failed to complete organization and Regiment merged into 52nd Indiana Infantry January 20, 1862.

57th REGIMENT INFANTRY.

Organized at Richmond, Ind., and mustered in November 18, 1861. At Indianapolis, Ind., till December 23. Left State for Kentucky December 23, and duty at Bardstown and Lebanon, Ky., till February, 1862. Attached to 21st Brigade, Army of the Ohio, January, 1862. 21st Brigade, 6th Division, Army of the Ohio, to September, 1862. 21st Brigade, 6th Division, 2nd Army Corps, Army of the Ohio, to November, 1862. 2nd Brigade, 1st Division, Left Wing 14th Army Corps, Army of the Cumberland, to January, 1863. 2nd Brigade, 1st Division, 21st Army Corps, Army of the Cumberland, to October, 1863. 2nd Brigade, 2nd Division, 4th Army Corps, Army of the Cumberland, to June, 1865. 1st Brigade, 2nd Division, 4th Army Corps, to August, 1865. Dept. of Texas to December, 1865.

SERVICE.—March through Central Kentucky to Nashville, Tenn., February 10-March 13, 1862. March to Savannah, Tenn., March 21-April 6. Battle of Shiloh, Tenn., April 6-7. Advance on and siege of Corinth, Miss., April 29-May 30. Pursuit to Booneville May 31-June 6. Buell's Campaign in Northern Alabama and Middle Tennessee, along Memphis & Charleston Railroad June to August. March to Louisville, Ky., in pursuit of Bragg August 21-September 26. Pursuit of Bragg to Loudon, Ky., October 1-22. Battle of Perryville, Ky., October 8. March to Nashville, Tenn., October 22-November 7, and duty there till December 26. Near Nashville December 11. Advance on Murfreesboro December 26-30. Battle of Stone's River December 30-31, 1862, and January 1-3, 1863. Duty at Murfreesboro till June. Reconnoissance to Nolensville and Versailles January 13-15. Middle Tennessee (or Tullahoma) Campaign June 23-July 7. Camp near Pelham till August 17. Passage of the Cumberland Mountains and Tennessee River and Chickamauga (Ga.) Campaign August 17-September 22. Occupation of Chattanooga, Tenn., September 9, and garrison duty there during Chickamauga (Ga.) Campaign. Siege of Chattanooga, Tenn., September 22-November 23. Chattanooga-Ringgold Campaign November 23-27. Orchard Knob November 23-24. Mission Ridge November 25. Pursuit to Graysville November 26-27. March to relief of Knoxville November 28-December 8. Operations in East Tennessee till April, 1864. Operations about Dandridge January 16-17. Atlanta (Ga.) Campaign May 1 to September 8. Demonstrations on Rocky Faced Ridge and Dalton May 8-13. Buzzard's Roost Gap May 8-9. Battle of Resaca May 14-15. Adairsville May 17. Near Kingston May 18-19. Near Cassville May 19. Advance on Dallas May 22-25. Operations on line of Pumpkin Vine Creek and battles about Dallas, New Hope Church and Allatoona Hills May 25-June 5. Operations about Marietta and against Kenesaw Mountain June 10-July 2. Pine Hill June 10-14. Lost Mountain June 15-17. Assault on Kenesaw June 27. Ruff's Station, Smyrna Camp Ground, July 4. Chattahoochie River July 5-17. Buckhead, Nancy's Creek, July 18. Peach Tree Creek July 19-20. Siege of Atlanta July 22-August 25. Flank movement on Jonesboro August 25-30. Battle of Jonesboro August 31-September 1. Lovejoy Station September 2-6. Operations against Hood in North Georgia and North Alabama September 29-November 3. Nashville Campaign November-December. Columbia, Duck River, November 24-27. Spring Hill November 29. Battle of Franklin November 30. Battle of Nashville December 15-16. Pursuit of Hood to the Tennessee River December 17-28. Moved to Huntsville, Ala., and duty there till March, 1865. Operations in East Tennessee March 15-April 22. At Nashville till June. Ordered to New Orleans, La., June 16; thence to Texas July. Duty at Green Lake and San Antonio till December. Mustered out December 14, 1865.

Regiment lost during service 6 Officers and 97 Enlisted men killed and mortally wounded and 2 Officers and 170 Enlisted men by disease. Total 275.

58th REGIMENT INFANTRY.

Organized at Princeton and Indianapolis, Ind., November 12 to December 22, 1861. Ordered to Kentucky December 29, and duty at Bardstown and Lebanon, Ky., till February, 1862. Attached to 21st Brigade, Army of the Ohio, January, 1862. 21st Brigade, 6th Division, Army of the Ohio, to September, 1862. 15th Brigade, 6th Division, 2nd Corps, Army of the Ohio, to November, 1862. 1st Brigade, 1st Division, Left Wing 14th Army Corps, Army of the Cumberland, to January, 1863. 1st Brigade, 21st Division, 21st Army Corps, Army of the Cumberland, to October, 1863. 2nd Brigade, 2nd Division, 4th Army Corps, Army of the Cumberland, to April, 1864. Unattached Pontooneers, Army of the Cumberland and Army of Georgia, till July, 1865.

SERVICE.—March through Central Kentucky to Nashville, Tenn., February 10-March 1, 1862. March to Savannah, Tenn., March 18-April 6. Battle of Shiloh, Tenn., April 6-7. Advance on and siege of Corinth, Miss., April 29-May 30. Pursuit to Booneville May 31-June 12. Buell's Campaign in Northern Alabama and Middle Tennessee along line of the Memphis & Charleston Railroad June to August. Little Pond, near McMinnville, August 30. March to Louisville, Ky., in pursuit of Bragg August 30-September 26. Pursuit of Bragg to Loudon, Ky., October 1-22. March to Nashville, Tenn., October 22-November 7, and duty there till December 26. Advance on Murfreesboro December 26-30. Lavergne December 26-27. Battle of Stone's River December 30-31, 1862, and January 1-3, 1863. Duty at Murfreesboro till June. Middle Tennessee (or Tullahoma) Campaign June 23-July 7. Occupation of Middle Tennessee till August 16. Passage of the Cumberland Mountains and Tennessee River and Chickamauga (Ga.) Campaign August 16-September 22. Expedition from Tracy City to the Tennessee River August 22-24 (Detachment). Occupation of Chattanooga, Tenn., September 9. Near Lee and Gordon's Mills September 17-18. Battle of Chickamauga September 19-20. Siege of

Chattanooga September 24-November 23. Chattanooga-Ringgold Campaign November 23-27. Orchard Knob November 23-24. Mission Ridge November 25. Pursuit to Graysville November 26-27. March to relief of Knoxville, Tenn., November 28-December 8. Operations in East Tennessee till April, 1864. Re-enlisted January 24, 1864. Assigned to duty in charge of the Pontoon Trains of General Sherman's Army April, 1864, and performed all the bridging from Chattanooga to Atlanta, from Atlanta to the sea, and in the Campaign through the Carolinas. Atlanta Campaign May 1 to September 8, 1864. Demonstrations on Rocky Faced Ridge May 8-11. Battle of Resaca May 14-15. About Dallas May 25-June 5. About Marietta and Kenesaw Mountain June 10-July 2. Nickajack Creek July 2-5. Chattahoochie River July 5-17. Peach Tree Creek July 19-20. Siege of Atlanta July 22-August 25. Flank movement on Jonesboro August 25-30. Battle of Jonesboro August 31-September 1. Pursuit of Hood into Alabama October. March to the sea November 15-December 10. Siege of Savannah December 10-21. Campaign of the Carolinas January to April, 1865. Non-Veterans mustered out December 31, 1864. March to Washington, D. C., via Richmond, Va., April 29-May 20. Grand Review May 24. Moved to Louisville, Ky., June, and there mustered out July 25, 1865.

Regiment lost during service 4 Officers and 60 Enlisted men killed and mortally wounded and 2 Officers and 192 Enlisted men by disease. Total 258.

59th REGIMENT INFANTRY.

Organized at Gosport and Indianapolis, Ind., February 11, 1862. Moved to Commerce, Mo., February 18-22, the first Regiment to report to General Pope for duty with the Army of Mississippi. Attached to 1st Brigade, 2nd Division, Army of Mississippi, to April, 1862. 2nd Brigade, 3rd Division, Army of Mississippi, April, 1862. 1st Brigade, 3rd Division, Army of Mississippi, to November, 1862. 1st Brigade, 7th Division, Left Wing 13th Army Corps, Dept. of the Tennessee, to December, 1862. 1st Brigade, 7th Division, 16th Army Corps, to January, 1863. 1st Brigade, 7th Division, 17th Army Corps, to September, 1863. 1st Brigade, 2nd Division, 17th Army Corps, to December, 1863. 1st Brigade, 3rd Division, 15th Army Corps, to April, 1865. 2nd Brigade, 4th Division, 15th Army Corps, to July, 1865.

SERVICE.—Siege operations against New Madrid, Mo., March 3-14, 1862. Siege and capture of Island No. 10, Mississippi River, March 15-April 8. Expedition to Fort Pillow, Tenn., April 13-17. Moved to Hamburg Landing, Tenn., April 18-22. Advance on and siege of Corinth, Miss., April 29-May 30. Pursuit to Booneville May 30-June 12. Duty at Clear Creek till August 6, and at Jacinto till September 18. March to Iuka, Miss., September 18-20. Battle of Corinth October 3-4. Pursuit to Ripley October 5-12. Grant's Central Mississippi Campaign. Operations on Mississippi Central Railroad November 2, 1862, to January 10, 1863. Reconnoissance from LaGrange November 8-9, 1862. Duty at Memphis January 12 to February 24, 1863. Yazoo Pass Expedition by Moon Lake, Yazoo Pass and Coldwater and Tallahatchie Rivers February 24-April 8. Operations against Fort Pemberton and Greenwood March 13-April 5. Moved to Milliken's Bend, La., April 13. Movement on Bruinsburg and turning Grand Gulf April 25-30. Battle of Port Gibson May 1 (Reserve). Jones' Cross Roads and Willow Springs May 3. Battles of Raymond May 12; Jackson May 14; Champion's Hill May 16. Siege of Vicksburg May 18-July 4. Assaults on Vicksburg May 19 and 22. Surrender of Vicksburg July 4. Duty there till September 13. Movement to Memphis, Tenn., thence march to Chattanooga, Tenn., September 13-November 20. Operations on Memphis & Charleston Railroad in Alabama October 20-29. Chattanooga-Ringgold Campaign November 23-27. Tunnel Hill November 23-25. Mission Ridge November 25. Pursuit to Graysville November 26-27. Duty at Bridgeport and Huntsville, Ala., December 18, 1863, to June

22, 1864. Re-enlisted January 1, 1864. Guard Bridge at Etowah River July 13-August 26. Ordered to Chattanooga, Tenn., August 26. Pursuit of Wheeler August 27-31. Duty at Chattanooga till September 21, and at Etowah River till November 12. March to the sea November 15-December 10. Siege of Savannah December 10-21. Campaign of the Carolinas January to April, 1865. Salkehatchie Swamp, S. C., February 2-5. South Edisto River February 9. North Edisto River February 12-13. Columbia February 16-17. Battle of Bentonville, N. C., March 19-21. Occupation of Goldsboro March 24. Advance on Raleigh April 10-14. Occupation of Raleigh April 14. Bennett's House April 26. Surrender of Johnston and his army. March to Washington, D. C., via Richmond, Va., April 29-May 19. Grand Review May 24. Moved to Louisville, Ky., June, and there mustered out July 17, 1865.

Regiment lost during service 1 Officer and 36 Enlisted men killed and mortally wounded and 229 Enlisted men by disease. Total 266.

60th REGIMENT INFANTRY.

Organized at Evansville and Indianapolis, Ind., February 19 to March 21, 1862. Duty at Camp Morton, Indianapolis, Ind., guarding prisoners February 22 to June 20, 1862. Left State for Louisville, Ky., June 20; thence moved to Munfordsville, Ky., and duty there till September. Attached to Garrison of Munfordsville, Ky., Dept. of the Ohio, to September, 1862. Reorganizing Indianapolis, Ind., to November, 1862. 1st Brigade, 10th Division, Right Wing 13th Army Corps (Old), Dept. of the Tennessee, to December, 1862. 1st Brigade, 1st Division, Sherman's Yazoo Expedition, to January, 1863. 1st Brigade, 10th Division, 13th Army Corps, Army of the Tennessee, to August, 1863. 1st Brigade, 4th Division, 13th Army Corps, Dept. of the Gulf, to June, 1864. District of LaFourche, Dept. of the Gulf, to December, 1864. District of Southern Alabama, Dept. of the Gulf, to February, 1865. 1st Brigade, 2nd Division, Reserve Corps, Military Division West Mississippi, February, 1865. 1st Brigade, 2nd Division, 13th Army Corps (New), Military Division West Mississippi, February, 1865.

SERVICE.—Siege of Munfordsville, Ky., September 14-17, 1862. Seven Companies captured September 17, paroled and ordered to Indianapolis, Ind. Three Companies which escaped capture being detached guarding Railroad Bridge over Rolling Fork, near Lebanon; also ordered to Indianapolis. Regiment reorganizing at Indianapolis to November. Ordered to Memphis, Tenn., and duty there till December 20. Sherman's Yazoo Expedition December 20, 1862, to January 3, 1863. Expedition from Milliken's Bend, La., to Dallas Station and Delhi December 25-26. Chickasaw Bayou December 26-28. Chickasaw Bluff December 29. Expedition to Arkansas Post, Ark., January 3-10, 1863. Assault and capture of Fort Hindman, Arkansas Post, January 10-11. Moved to Young's Point, La., January 17. Expedition to Greenville, Miss., and Cypress Bend, Ark., February 14-29. Duty at Young's Point and Milliken's Bend till April. Movement on Bruinsburg and turning Grand Gulf April 25-30. Battle of Port Gibson May 1. Battle of Champion's Hill May 16. Siege of Vicksburg, Miss., May 18-July 4. Assaults on Vicksburg May 19 and 22. Advance on Jackson, Miss., July 4-10. Siege of Jackson July 10-17. Moved to New Orleans, La., August 24. Expedition to New and Amite Rivers September 24-29. Western Louisiana "Teche" Campaign October 3-November 30. Action at Grand Coteau November 3. Moved to Algiers December 13, thence to Texas December 18. Duty at Du Crow's Point and Pass Cavallo till March, 1864. Moved to Algiers, La., thence to Alexandria, La. Red River Campaign April 26-May 20. Retreat to Morganza May 13-20. Duty at Thibodeaux till November, and at Algiers till February 24, 1865. Veterans and Recruits transferred to 26th Indiana Infantry February 24. Regiment mustered out March 11, 1865.

Regiment lost during service 2 Officers and 43 Enlisted men killed and mortally wounded and 3 Officers and 165 Enlisted men by disease. Total 213.

61st REGIMENT INFANTRY.

Failed to complete organization and enlisted men transferred to 35th Indiana Infantry May 22, 1862.

62nd REGIMENT INFANTRY.

Failed to complete organization and enlisted men transferred to 53rd Indiana Infantry February 26, 1862.

63rd REGIMENT INFANTRY.

Organized at Lafayette, Ind., as a Battalion of 4 Companies, "A," "B," "C," "D," February 21, 1862. Duty as prison guard at Lafayette and at Camp Morton, Indianapolis, Ind., till May. Left State for Washington, D. C., May 27. Attached to Piatt's Brigade, Sturgis' Command, Defences of Washington, to August, 1862. Piatt's Brigade, Army of the Potomac, to October, 1862.

SERVICE.—Duty in the defences of Washington, D. C., till August, 1862. Pope's Campaign in Northern Virginia August 16-September 2. Ordered to Indianapolis, Ind., October 3. Completing organization of Regiment and prison guard at Camp Morton and Indianapolis till December 25, 1862. Ordered to Shepherdsville, Ky., December 25, and guard duty along Louisville & Nashville Railroad till January 16, 1864. Operations against Morgan July 2, 1863. Cummings Ferry July 8. Attached to Railroad Guard, District of Western Kentucky, Dept. of Ohio, to June, 1863. Unattached, 2nd Division, 23rd Army Corps, Dept. of the Ohio, to August, 1863. New Haven, Ky., 1st Division, 23rd Army Corps, to October, 1863. District South Central Kentucky, 1st Division, 23rd Army Corps, to January, 1864. District Southwest Kentucky, 1st Division, 23rd Army Corps, to April, 1864. 2nd Brigade, 3rd Division, 23rd Army Corps, to August, 1864. 3rd Brigade, 3rd Division, 23rd Army Corps, Army of the Ohio, to February, 1865, and Dept. of North Carolina to June, 1865.

SERVICE.—At Camp Nelson, Ky., January 16 to February 25, 1864. March over mountains to Knoxville, Tenn., February 25-March 15; thence moved to Mossy Creek and to Bull's Gap April 1. Expedition toward Jonesboro and destruction of Tennessee & Virginia Railroad April 23-28. Atlanta (Ga.) Campaign May 1 to September 8. Demonstrations on Rocky Faced Ridge and Dalton May 8-13. Battle of Resaca May 14-15. Cartersville May 20. Operations on line of Pumpkin Vine Creek and battles about Dallas, New Hope Church and Allatoona Hills May 25-June 5. Operations about Marietta and against Kenesaw Mountain June 10-July 2. Lost Mountain June 15-17. Muddy Creek June 17. Noyes Creek June 19. Cheyney's Farm June 22. Olley's Farm June 26-27. Assault on Kenesaw June 27. Nickajack Creek July 2-5. Ruff's Mills July 3-4. Chattahoochie River July 5-17. Isham's Ford July 8. Siege of Atlanta July 22-August 25. Utoy Creek August 5-7. Flank movement on Jonesboro August 25-30. Battle of Jonesboro August 31-September 1. Lovejoy Station September 2-6. Pursuit of Hood into Alabama October 3-26. Nashville Campaign November-December. Columbia, Duck River, November 24-27. Columbia Ford November 29. Battle of Franklin November 30. Battle of Nashville December 15-16. Pursuit of Hood to the Tennessee River December 17-28. At Clifton, Tenn., till January 16, 1865. Movement to Washington, D. C., thence to Fort Fisher, N. C., January 16-February 9. Operations against Hoke February 12-14. Fort Anderson February 18-19. Town Creek February 19-20. Capture of Wilmington February 22. Campaign of the Carolinas March 1-April 26. Advance on Goldsboro March 6-21. Occupation of Goldsboro March 24. Gulley's March 31. Advance on Raleigh April 10-14. Occupation of Raleigh April 14. Bennett's House April 26. Surrender of Johnston and his army. At Raleigh till May 5. At Greensboro till June 21. Companies "A," "B," "C" and "D" mustered out May 3, 1865. Regiment mustered out June 21, 1865.

Regiment lost during service 3 Officers and 53 Enlisted men killed and mortally wounded and 2 Officers and 130 Enlisted men by disease. Total 188.

64th REGIMENT VOLUNTEERS.

Intended for 1st Regiment Light Artillery, but organization not completed.

65th REGIMENT INFANTRY.

Organized at Princeton, Ind., and mustered in August 18, 1862. Company "K" mustered in September 10, 1862, and joined Regiment at Madisonville, Ky. Left State for Henderson, Ky., August 20, 1862. Served unassigned, District of Western Kentucky, Dept. of Ohio, to June, 1863. 1st Brigade, 2nd Division, 23rd Army Corps, Army of Ohio, to August, 1863. 2nd Brigade, 4th Division, 23rd Army Corps, to October, 1863. 4th Brigade, 4th Division, 23rd Army Corps, to November, 1863. 2nd Brigade, 2nd Cavalry Division, Dept. of the Ohio, to April, 1864. 2nd Brigade, 3rd Division, 23rd Army Corps, Army of the Ohio, to February, 1865, and Dept. of North Carolina to June, 1865.

SERVICE.—Action at Madisonville, Ky., August 25, 1862. Guard duty along line of Louisville & Nashville Railroad till August, 1863. Skirmish at Bradenburg, Ky., September 12, 1862, and at Henderson, Ky., September 14, 1862 (Co. "D"). Regiment mounted April, 1863. Action at Cheshire, Ohio, July 21, 1863. Dixon July 29 (Co. "E"). Burnside's Campaign in East Tennessee August 16-October 17. Occupation of Knoxville September 2. Action at Greenville September 11. Kingsport September 18. Bristol September 19. Zollicoffer September 20-21. Carter's Depot September 20-21. Jonesborough September 21. Hall's Ford, Watauga River, September 22. Carter's Depot September 22. Blue Springs October 10. Henderson's Mill and Rheatown October 11. Blountsville October 14. Bristol October 15. Knoxville Campaign November 4-December 23. Mulberry Gap November 19. Walker's Ford, Clinch River, December 2. Near Maynardsville December 12. Bean's Station December 14. Blain's Cross Roads December 16-19. Kimbrough's Cross Roads January 16, 1864. Operations about Dandridge January 16-17 and January 26-28. Dandridge January 17. Scout to Chucky Bend March 12. Regiment dismounted April 21, 1864. Atlanta (Ga.) Campaign May 1-September 8. Demonstrations on Rocky Faced Ridge and Dalton May 8-13. Battle of Resaca May 14-15. Cartersville May 20. Operations on line of Pumpkin Vine Creek and battles about Dallas, New Hope Church and Allatoona Hills May 25-June 5. Operations about Marietta and against Kenesaw Mountain June 10-July 2. Lost Mountain June 15-17. Muddy Creek June 17. Cheyney's Farm June 22. Olley's Farm June 26-27. Assault on Kenesaw June 27. Nickajack Creek July 2-5. Chattahoochie River July 5-17. Isham's Ford July 8. Siege of Atlanta July 22-August 25. Utoy Creek August 5-7. Flank movement on Jonesboro August 25-30. Near Rough and Ready August 31. Lovejoy's Station September 2-6. Decatur September 28. Pursuit of Hood into Alabama October 3-26. Nashville Campaign November-December. Columbia, Duck River, November 24-27. Battle of Franklin November 30. Battle of Nashville December 15-16. Pursuit of Hood to the Tennessee River December 17-28. At Clifton, Tenn., till January 16, 1865. Movement to Washington, D. C., thence to Fort Fisher, N. C., January 16-February 9. Operations against Hoke February 11-14. Sugar Loaf Battery February 11. Fort Anderson February 18-19. Town Creek February 19-20. Capture of Wilmington February 22. Campaign of the Carolinas March 1-April 26. Advance on Goldsboro March 6-21. Advance on Raleigh April 10-14. Occupation of Raleigh April 14. Bennett's House April 26. Surrender of Johnston and his army. Duty at Raleigh and Greensboro till June. Mustered out June 22, 1865.

Regiment lost during service 34 Enlisted men killed and mortally wounded and 4 Officers and 216 Enlisted men by disease. Total 254.

66th REGIMENT INFANTRY.

Organized at New Albany and mustered in August 19, 1862. Left State for Lexington, Ky., August 19; thence moved to Richmond, Ky. Attached to Cruft's Brigade, Army of Kentucky. Battle of Richmond August 30. Regiment mostly captured, paroled and sent to New Albany, Ind.; those not captured marched to New Albany; arrived September 10. Regiment moved to Indianapolis, Ind., November 18; thence to Corinth, Miss., December 10, 1862. Attached to 1st Brigade, District of Corinth, Miss., 13th Army Corps (Old), Dept. of the Tennessee, December, 1862. 1st Brigade, District of Corinth, 17th Army Corps, to January, 1863. 1st Brigade, District of Corinth, 16th Army Corps, to March, 1863. 1st Brigade, 2nd Division, 16th Army Corps, to September, 1864. 1st Brigade, 4th Division, 15th Army Corps, to June, 1865.

SERVICE.—Garrison duty at Corinth, Miss., December, 1862, to August, 1863. Dodge's Expedition into Northern Alabama April 15-May 2, 1863. Rock Cut, near Tuscumbia, April 22. Tuscumbia April 23. Town Creek April 28. Moved to Colliersville, Tenn., August 18, and duty there till October 29. Action at Colliersville October 11 (Cos. "B," "C," "D," "E," "G," "I"). March to Pulaski October 29-November 11 and duty there till April 29, 1864. Atlanta (Ga.) Campaign May 1-September 8. Demonstrations on Resaca May 8-13. Sugar Valley, near Resaca, May 9. Battle of Resaca May 14-15. Ley's Ferry, Oostenaula River, May 15. Rome Cross Roads May 16. Advance on Dallas May 18-25. Operations on line of Pumpkin Vine Creek and battles about Dallas, New Hope Church and Allatoona Hills May 25-June 5. Operations about Marietta and against Kenesaw Mountain June 10-July 2. Assault on Kenesaw June 27. Nickajack Creek July 2-5. Ruff's Mills July 3-4. Chattahoochie River July 5-17. Battle of Atlanta July 22. Siege of Atlanta July 22-August 25. Flank movement on Jonesboro August 25-30. Battle of Jonesboro August 31-September 1. Lovejoy Station September 2-6. Operations against Hood in North Georgia and North Alabama September 29-November 3. Reconnoissance from Rome on Cave Springs Road and skirmishes October 12-13. March to the sea November 15-December 10. Little Ogeechee River December 4. Jenk's Bridge and Eden Station December 7. Siege of Savannah December 10-21. Campaign of the Carolinas January to April, 1865. Salkehatchie Swamps, S. C., February 2-5. South Edisto River February 9. North Edisto River February 12-13. South River February 15. Columbia February 16-17. Little Congaree Creek February 16. Battle of Bentonville, N. C., March 19-21. Occupation of Goldsboro March 14. Advance on Raleigh April 10-14. Occupation of Raleigh April 14. Bennett's House April 26. Surrender of Johnston and his army. March to Washington, D. C., via Richmond, Va., April 29-May 19. Grand Review May 24. Mustered out at Washington, D. C., June 3, 1865.

Regiment lost during service 3 Officers and 62 Enlisted men killed and mortally wounded and 1 Officer and 184 Enlisted men by disease. Total 250.

67th REGIMENT INFANTRY.

Organized at Madison, Ind., and mustered in August 20, 1862. Ordered to Louisville, Ky., and attached to 1st Brigade, 2nd Division, Army of Kentucky, Dept. of the Ohio. Siege of Munfordsville, Ky., September 14-17. Captured September 17, paroled and sent to Indianapolis, Ind. Reorganizing at Indianapolis till December. Ordered to Memphis, Tenn., December 10. Attached to 1st Brigade, 10th Division, Right Wing 13th Army Corps (Old), Dept. of the Tennessee, December, 1862. 1st Brigade, 1st Division, Sherman's Yazoo Expedition, to January, 1863. 1st Brigade, 10th Division, 13th Army Corps, Army of the Tennessee, to August, 1863. 1st Brigade, 4th Division, 13th Army Corps, Dept. of the Gulf, to June, 1864. 3rd Brigade, 3rd Division, 19th Army Corps, Dept. of the Gulf, to December, 1864. 2nd Brigade, Reserve Division, Military Division West Mississippi, December, 1864.

SERVICE.—Sherman's Yazoo Expedition December 20, 1862, to January 3, 1863. Expedition from Milliken's Bend to Dallas Station and Delhi December 25-26. Chickasaw Bayou December 26-28. Chickasaw Bluff December 29. Expedition to Arkansas Post, Ark., January 3-10, 1863. Assault and capture of Fort Hindman, Arkansas Post, January 10-11. Moved to Young's Point, La., January 17, and duty there till March 8. Expedition to Greenville, Miss., and Cypress Bend, Ark., February 14-29. Moved to Milliken's Bend, La., March 8, and duty there till April 25. Movement on Bruinsburg and turning Grand Gulf April 25-30. Battle of Port Gibson May 1. Battle of Champion's Hill May 16. Big Black River Bridge May 17. Siege of Vicksburg, Miss., May 18-July 4. Assaults on Vicksburg May 19 and 22. Advance on Jackson, Miss., July 4-10. Siege of Jackson July 10-17. Ordered to New Orleans, La., August 24. Duty at Carrollton, Brashear City and Berwick till October. Expedition to New and Amite Rivers September 24-29. Western Louisiana "Teche" Campaign October 3-November 30. Action at Grand Coteau November 3. Moved to Algiers December 13, thence to Texas December 18. Duty at Du Crow's Point, Matagorda Bay, till March, 1864. Reconnoissance on Matagorda Peninsula January 21, 1864. Moved to Algiers, La., March 1. Red River Campaign March 10-May 22. Advance from Franklin to Alexandria March 14-26. Battle of Sabine Cross Roads April 8. Monett's Ferry, Cane River Crossing, April 23. Constructing dam at Alexandria April 30-May 10. Retreat to Morganza May 13-20. At Morganza and Baton Rouge till August. Operations in Mobile Bay against Forts Gaines and Morgan August 2-23. Siege and surrender of Fort Gaines August 3-8. Capture of Fort Morgan August 23. Duty at Morganza till December. Expedition to mouth of White River November 12-20. Consolidated with 24th Indiana Infantry December 21, 1864.

Regiment lost during service 1 Officer and 52 Enlisted men killed and mortally wounded and 2 Officers and 194 Enlisted men by disease. Total 249.

68th REGIMENT INFANTRY.

Organized at Indianapolis, Ind., and mustered in August 19, 1862. Left State for Louisville, Ky., August 20. Attached to 1st Brigade, 2nd Division, Army of Kentucky, Dept. of the Ohio. Moved to Lebanon, Ky., August 25; thence to Munfordsville, Ky. Siege of Munfordsville, Ky., September 14-17. Regiment captured September 17. Paroled and sent to Indianapolis, Ind. Reorganized at Indianapolis till December 25. Moved to Louisville, Ky., December 26; thence to Murfreesboro, Tenn., January 1, 1863. Attached to 2nd Brigade, 4th Division, 14th Army Corps, Army of the Cumberland, to October, 1863. 2nd Brigade, 3rd Division, 14th Army Corps, October, 1863. 1st Brigade, 3rd Division, 4th Army Corps, Army of the Cumberland, to April, 1864. Garrison at Chattanooga, Tenn., Dept. of the Cumberland, to November, 1864. 2nd Brigade, 1st Separate Division, District of the Etowah, Dept. of the Cumberland, to June, 1865.

SERVICE.—Duty at Murfreesboro, Tenn., January to June, 1863. Expedition to McMinnville April 20-30. Middle Tennessee (or Tullahoma) Campaign June 23-July 7. Hoover's Gap June 24-26. Tullahoma June 29-30. Occupation of Middle Tennessee till August 16. Passage of the Cumberland Mountains and Tennessee River and Chickamauga (Ga.) Campaign August 16-September 22. Shellmound August 21. Reconnoissance from Shellmound toward Chattanooga August 30-31. Battle of Chickamauga, Ga., September 19-21. Before Chattanooga September 22-26. Siege of Chattanooga September 22-November 23. Chattanooga-Ringgold Campaign November 23-27. Orchard Knob November 23-24. Mission Ridge November 25. March to relief of Knoxville November 28-December 8. Operations in East Tennessee till April, 1864. Operations

about Dandridge January 16-17. Garrison duty at Chattanooga April to September, 1864. Relief of Dalton, Ga., August 14-15. March to Cleveland, Charleston, Athens and Madisonville August 18-20. Moved to Tullahoma September 1, thence to Chattanooga and Decatur, Ala., October 27. Defence of Decatur, Ala., October 29-31. Duty at Resaca, Ga., November 13-29; thence moved to Nashville, Tenn. Battle of Nashville, Tenn., December 15-16. Pursuit of Hood to the Tennessee River December 17-28. Moved to Chattanooga, Tenn., and garrison duty there till June, 1865. Moved to Nashville, Tenn., June 16, and there mustered out June 20, 1865.

Regiment lost during service 4 Officers and 35 Enlisted men killed and mortally wounded and 111 Enlisted men by disease. Total 150.

69th REGIMENT INFANTRY.

Organized at Richmond, Ind., and mustered in August 19, 1862. Left State for Lexington, Ky., August 20. Attached to Manson's Brigade, Army of Kentucky, Dept. of the Ohio. Battle of Richmond, Ky., August 30. Regiment captured August 30; paroled and sent to Indianapolis, Ind. Reorganizing at Indianapolis till November 27, 1862. Left State for Memphis, Tenn., November 27, 1862. Attached to 1st Brigade, 9th Division, Right Wing 13th Army Corps (Old), Dept. of the Tennessee, to December, 1862. 1st Brigade, 3rd Division, Sherman's Yazoo Expedition, to January, 1863. 1st Brigade, 9th Division, 13th Army Corps, Army of the Tennessee, to July, 1863. 3rd Brigade, 1st Division, 13th Army Corps, Army of the Tennessee, to August, 1863, and Dept. of the Gulf to March, 1864. 2nd Brigade, 1st Division, 13th Army Corps, to June, 1864. 2nd Brigade, 3rd Division, 19th Army Corps, Dept. of the Gulf, to December, 1864. District of Southern Alabama, Dept. of the Gulf, December, 1864. 3rd Brigade, Reserve Corps, Military Division West Mississippi, to February, 1865. 2nd Brigade, 2nd Division, Reserve Corps, Military Division West Mississippi, February, 1865. 2nd Brigade, 2nd Division, 13th Army Corps (New), Military Division West Mississippi, to July, 1865.

SERVICE.—Sherman's Yazoo Expedition December 20, 1862, to January 3, 1863. Chickasaw Bayou December 26-28. Chickasaw Bluff December 29. Expedition to Arkansas Post, Ark., January 3-10, 1863. Assault and capture of Fort Hindman, Arkansas Post, January 10-11. Moved to Young's Point, La., January 17, and duty there till March 8. Moved to Milliken's Bend, La., March 8, and duty there till April 25. Roundaway Bayou, Richmond, March 31. Operations from Milliken's Bend to New Carthage March 31-April 17. James' Plantation, near New Carthage, April 6. Movement on Bruinsburg and turning Grand Gulf April 25-30. Battle of Port Gibson May 1. Battle of Champion's Hill May 16. Big Black Bridge May 17. Siege of Vicksburg May 18-July 4. Assaults on Vicksburg May 19 and 22. Advance on Jackson, Miss., July 4-10. Near Clinton July 8. Near Jackson July 9. Siege of Jackson July 10-17. Moved to New Orleans, La., August 13. Duty at Carrollton, Brashear City and Berwick till October. Western Louisiana "Teche" Campaign October 3-November 30. Ordered to Algiers December 13, thence moved to Texas December 18. Duty at Matagorda Bay and Indianola till February, 1864, and at Matagorda Island till April 19. Moved to New Orleans, thence to Alexandria, La., April 19-27. Red River Campaign April 27-May 22. Actions at Alexandria April 29 and May 2 to 9. Graham's Plantation May 5. Retreat to Morganza May 13-20. Duty at Morganza till December. Expedition to the Atchafalaya May 30-June 6. Expedition to mouth of White River and St. Charles, Ark., September 13-20. Moved to Dauphin Island, Mobile Bay, December 7. Granger's Pascagoula Expedition December 14, 1864, to January 1, 1865. Duty at Pascagoula till January 31. Consolidated to a Battalion of 4 Companies January 22. Moved to Barrancas, Fla., January 31; thence to Pensacola, Fla., March 14. Steele's march through Florida to Mobile March 20-

April 1. Occupation of Pollard March 26. Siege of Spanish Fort and Fort Blakely April 1-9. Assault and capture of Fort Blakely April 9. March to Montgomery and Selma April 13-22. Return to Mobile May 3 and duty there till July. Mustered out July 5, 1865.

Regiment lost during service 3 Officers and 77 Enlisted men killed and mortally wounded and 3 Officers and 248 Enlisted men by disease. Total 331.

70th REGIMENT INFANTRY.

Organized at Indianapolis, Ind., July 22 to August 8, 1862. Left State for Louisville, Ky., August 13. Attached to District of Louisville, Ky., Dept. of the Ohio, to November, 1862. Ward's Brigade, Dumont's 12th Division, Army of the Cumberland, to December, 1862. Ward's Brigade, Post of Gallatin, Tenn., Dept. of the Cumberland, to June, 1863. 2nd Brigade, 3rd Division Reserve Corps, Dept. of the Cumberland, to October, 1863. Ward's Brigade, Post and District of Nashville, Tenn., Dept. of the Cumberland, to January, 1864. 1st Brigade, 1st Division, 11th Army Corps, Army of the Cumberland, to April, 1864. 1st Brigade, 3rd Division, 20th Army Corps, Army of the Cumberland, to June, 1865.

SERVICE.—Moved from Louisville, Ky., to Bowling Green, Ky., August, 1862. Duty there and along line of the Louisville & Nashville Railroad till November. Skirmishes at Russellville and Glasgow September 30. Moved to Scottsville November 10, thence to Gallatin, Tenn., November 24, and duty along Louisville & Nashville Railroad from Gallatin to Nashville, Tenn., till February 9, 1863. Garrison duty at Gallatin till June 1. Moved to Lavergne June 1, thence to Murfreesboro, Tenn., June 30. Duty at Fortress Rosecrans, Murfreesboro, till August 19. Moved to Nashville, Tenn., August 19, and picket and fatigue duty at that point till February 24, 1864. Skirmish at Tullahoma, Tenn., October 23, 1863. March to Wauhatchie, Tenn., February 24-March 10. Atlanta (Ga.) Campaign May 1-September 8. Demonstrations on Rocky Faced Ridge May 8-11. Battle of Resaca May 14-15. Near Cassville May 19-24. Combat at New Hope Church May 25. Operations on line of Pumpkin Vine Creek and battles about Dallas, New Hope Church and Allatoona Hills May 25-June 5. Operations about Marietta and against Kenesaw Mountain June 10-July 2. Pine Mountain June 11-14. Lost Mountain June 15-17. Gilgal or Golgotha Church June 15. Muddy Creek June 17. Noyes Creek June 19. Kolb's Farm June 22. Assault on Kenesaw June 27. Ruff's or Neal Dow Station, Smyrna Camp Ground, July 4. Chattahoochie River July 5-17. Peach Tree Creek July 19-20. Siege of Atlanta July 22-August 25. Operations at Chattahoochie River Bridge August 26-September 2. Occupation of Atlanta September 2-November 15. Near Turner's and Howell's Ferries, Chattahoochie River, October 19 (Detachment). March to the sea November 15-December 10. Siege of Savannah December 10-21. Campaign of the Carolinas January to April, 1865. Lawtonville, S. C., February 2. Taylor's Hole Creek, Averysboro, N. C., March 16. Battle of Bentonville March 19-21. Occupation of Goldsboro March 24. Advance on Raleigh April 10-14. Occupation of Raleigh April 14. Bennett's House April 26. Surrender of Johnston and his army. March to Washington, D. C., via Richmond, Va., April 29-May 19. Grand Review May 24. Mustered out June 8, 1865. Recruits transferred to 33rd Indiana Infantry.

Regiment lost during service 2 Officers and 96 Enlisted men killed and mortally wounded and 2 Officers and 103 Enlisted men by disease. Total 203.

71st REGIMENT INFANTRY.

Organized at Terre Haute, Ind., July 21 to August 18, 1862. Mustered in at Indianapolis August 18, 1862, and left State for Lexington, Ky., August 18. Battle of Richmond, Ky., August 30. Regiment mostly captured, paroled and sent to Indianapolis, Ind. Reorganizing at Indianapolis till December, 1862. Ordered to Kentucky. Action at Muldraugh's Hill, Ky., December 27, 1862. Regiment again captured. Paroled and sent to Indianapolis, and on duty there till August 26, 1863. Designation of Regiment changed to 6th Indiana Cavalry February 22, 1863. (See 6th Indiana Cavalry.)

72nd REGIMENT INFANTRY.

Organized at Lafayette, Ind. Moved to Indianapolis, Ind., August 11, and there mustered in August 16, 1862. Left State for Lebanon, Ky., August 17. Attached to 40th Brigade, 12th Division, Army of the Ohio, to November, 1862. 2nd Brigade, 5th Division, Center 14th Army Corps, Army of the Cumberland, to January, 1863. 2nd Brigade, 5th Division, 14th Army Corps, to June, 1863. 1st Brigade, 4th Division, 14th Army Corps, to October, 1863. Wilder's Mounted Infantry Brigade, Cavalry Corps, Army of the Cumberland, to December, 1862. 3rd Brigade, 2nd Cavalry Division, Army of the Cumberland, to January, 1864. 3rd Brigade, Grierson's Cavalry Division, 16th Army Corps, Army of the Tennessee, to March, 1864. 3rd Brigade, 2nd Cavalry Division, Army of the Cumberland, to October, 1864. 1st Brigade, 2nd Division, Wilson's Cavalry Corps, Military Division Mississippi, to June, 1865.

SERVICE.—Duty at Lebanon Junction, Ky., September 6-22, 1862. Moved to Louisville September 22, and to Elizabethtown, West Point, September 30-October 5. Pursuit of Bragg and operations against Morgan October 6-20. March to Bowling Green, Ky., October 26-November 3, thence to Scottsboro November 10. To Gallatin November 26 and to Castillian Springs November 28. To Bledsoe Creek December 14. Operations against Morgan December 22, 1862-January 2, 1863. Moved to Cave City, thence to Murfreesboro, Tenn., January 2-8, 1863, and duty there till June. Scout to Woodbury March 3-8. Regiment mounted March 17. Expedition to Carthage, Lebanon and Liberty April 1-8. Expedition to McMinnville April 20-30. Occupation of McMinnville April 22. Woodbury May 24. Liberty June 4. Middle Tennessee or Tullahoma Campaign June 23-July 7. Bay Spring Branch June 24. Hoover's Gap June 24-26. Occupation of Manchester June 27. Raid on Bragg's communications June 28-30. Dechard June 29. Raid to Lynchburg July 16-17. At Dechard July 27-August 16. Passage of the Cumberland Mountains and Tennessee River and Chickamauga (Ga.) Campaign August 16-September 22. Sequatchie River August 19. Wild Cat Trace August 20. Friar's Island August 25 and September 9. Capture of Chattanooga September 9. Lee and Gordon's Mills September 11. Ringgold September 11. Leet's Tan Yard September 12-13. Pea Vine Bridge and Alexander's Bridge September 17. Reed's Bridge and Dyer's Bridge September 18. Battle of Chickamauga September 19-21. Operations against Wheeler and Roddy September 29-October 17. Thompson's Cove, Cumberland Mountains, October 3. Murfreesboro Road, near McMinnville, and McMinnville October 4. Sims' Farm, near Shelbyville, and Farmington October 7. Shelbyville Pike October 7. Expedition from Maysville to Whitesburg and Decatur November 14-17. Moved from Pulaski to Colliersville, Tenn., December 31, 1862-January 14, 1864. Shoal Creek, Ala., January 24 (Detachment). Florence January 24. Athens January 25 (Detachment). Smith's Expedition from Colliersville to Okolona, Miss., February 10-26. Raiford's Plantation near Byhalia February 10. Ivey's Hill near Okolona February 22. Moved to Mooresville March 5-26, thence to Columbia April 3-8. March to Lafayette, Ga., April 30-May 9. Atlanta Campaign May to September, 1864. Battle of Resaca May 14-15. Near Dallas May 24. About Dallas May 25-June 5. Big Shanty June 9. Operations about Marietta and against Kenesaw Mountain June 10-July 2. Noonday Creek and Powder Springs June 19-20. Assault on Kenesaw June 27. On line of Nickajack Creek July 2-5. Rottenwood Creek June 4. Chattahoochie River July 5-17. Garrard's Raid to Covington July 22-24. Garrard's Raid to South River July 27-31. Flat Rock July 28. Siege of Atlanta August 1-25. Operations at Chattahoochie River Bridge August 26-September 2. Operations in Northern Georgia and North Alabama against Hood September

29-November 3. Skirmishes near Lost Mountain October 4-7. New Hope Church October 5. Dallas October 7. Near Rome October 10-11. Narrows October 11. Coosaville Road near Rome October 12-13. Near Summerville October 18. Blue Pond and Little River, Ala., October 21. King's Hill October 23. Ladiga, Terrapin Creek, October 28. Dismounted November 1, and ordered to Nashville, thence to Louisville, Ky., and duty there till December 28. March to Nashville, Tenn., December 28, 1864, to January 8, 1865, thence to Gravelly Springs, Ala., and duty there till March, 1865. Wilson's Raid from Chickasaw. Ala., to Macon, Ga., March 22-April 24. Plantersville and near Randolph April 1. Selma April 2. Montgomery April 12. Columbia April 16. Capture of Macon April 20. Pursuit of Jeff Davis May 6-10. Moved to Nashville, Tenn., May 23-June 15. Mustered out June 26, 1865.

Regiment lost during service 2 Officers and 26 Enlisted men killed and mortally wounded and 2 Officers and 130 Enlisted men by disease. Total 160.

73rd REGIMENT INFANTRY.

Organized at South Bend, Ind., and mustered in August 16, 1862. Ordered to Lexington, Ky. Evacuation of Lexington August 31. Attached to 20th Brigade, 6th Division, Army of the Ohio, September, 1862. 20th Brigade, 6th Division, 2nd Corps, Army of the Ohio, to November, 1862. 3rd Brigade, 1st Division, Left Wing 14th Army Corps, Army of the Cumberland, to January, 1863. 3rd Brigade, 1st Division, 21st Army Corps, Army of the Cumberland, to April, 1863. Streight's Provisional Brigade, Dept. of the Cumberland, to May, 1863. Prisoners of war to December, 1863. Post and District of Nashville, Tenn., Dept. of the Cumberland, to January, 1864. 1st Brigade, District of Nashville, Tenn., Dept. of the Cumberland, January, 1864. 1st Brigade, Rousseau's 3rd Division, 12th Army Corps, Army of the Cumberland, to April, 1864. 1st Brigade, 4th Division, 20th Army Corps, Dept. of the Cumberland, to March, 1865. District of Northern Alabama, Dept. of the Cumberland, to June, 1865.

SERVICE.—Pursuit of Bragg to Loudon, Ky., October 1-22, 1862. Battle of Perryville, Ky., October 8. March to Nashville, Tenn., October 22-November 9, and duty there till December 26. Advance on Murfreesboro, Tenn., December 26-30. Battle of Stone's River December 30-31, 1862, and January 1-3, 1863. Duty at Murfreesboro till April. Reconnoissance to Nolensville and Versailles January 13-15. Streight's Raid to Rome, Ga., April 26-May 3. Day's Gap, Sand Mountain, Crooked Creek and Hog Mountain April 30. East Branch, Black Warrior Creek, May 1. Blount's Farm and Center May 2. Cedar Bluff May 3. Regiment captured. Re-organized and rejoined army at Nashville, Tenn., December, 1863. Guard duty along Nashville & Chattanooga Railroad, and picketing Tennessee River from Draper's Ferry to Limestone Point. Headquarters at Triana till September, 1864. Paint Rock Bridge April 8, 1864. Scout from Triana to Somerville July 29 (Detachment). Action at Athens, Ala., October 1-2. Defence of Decatur October 26-29. Duty at Stevenson, Ala., till January, 1865. At Huntsville, Ala., and along Mobile & Charleston Railroad till July. Gurley's Tank February 16, 1865 (Detachment). Mustered out July 1, 1865.

Regiment lost during service 3 Officers and 41 Enlisted men killed and mortally wounded and 191 Enlisted men by disease. Total 241.

74th REGIMENT INFANTRY.

Organized at Fort Wayne, Ind., and mustered in August 21, 1862. Moved to Louisville, Ky., August 22, thence to Bowling Green, Ky., and duty there till September 5. Attached to 2nd Brigade, 1st Division, Army of the Ohio, September, 1862. 2nd Brigade, 1st Division, 3rd Corps, Army of the Ohio, to November, 1862. 2nd Brigade, 3rd Division, Center 14th Army Corps, Army of the Cumberland, to January, 1863. 2nd Brigade, 3rd Division, 14th Army Corps, to October, 1863.

3rd Brigade, 3rd Division, 14th Army Corps, to June, 1865.

SERVICE.—Moved to Louisville, Ky., September 5, 1862. (Companies "C" and "K" at siege of Munfordsville, Ky., September 14-17. Captured September 17. Exchanged November 17, and rejoined Regiment at Castillian, Tenn., December 4, 1862.) Pursuit of Bragg into Kentucky October 1-15. Battle of Perryville, Ky., October 8. March to Gallatin, Tenn., and duty there and at Castillian till January, 1863. Operations against Morgan December 22, 1862, to January 2, 1863. Boston December 29, 1862. Moved to Nashville, Tenn., January 13, 1863, thence to Murfreesboro, and duty there till June. Expedition toward Columbia March 4-14. Middle Tennessee or Tullahoma Campaign June 23-July 7. Hoover's Gap June 24-26. Tullahoma June 29-30. Occupation of Middle Tennessee till August 16. Passage of the Cumberland Mountains and Tennessee River and Chickamauga (Ga.) Campaign August 16-September 22. Battle of Chickamauga September 19-21. Siege of Chattanooga, Tenn., September 24-November 23. Before Chattanooga September 22-26. Chattanooga-Ringgold Campaign November 23-27. Orchard Knob November 23-24. Mission Ridge November 25. Pursuit to Ringgold November 26-27. Demonstration on Dalton, Ga., February 22-27, 1864. Tunnel Hill, Buzzard's Roost Gap, and Rocky Raced Ridge, February 23-25. Atlanta (Ga.) Campaign May 1-September 8. Demonstrations on Rocky Faced Ridge May 8-11. Battle of Resaca May 14-15. Advance on Dallas May 18-25. Operations on Pumpkin Vine Creek and battles about Dallas, New Hope Church and Allatoona Hills May 25-June 5. Operations about Marietta and against Kenesaw Mountain June 10-July 2. Pine Hill June 11-14. Lost Mountain June 15-17. Assault on Kenesaw June 27. Ruff's Station July 4. Chattahoochie River July 5-17. Peach Tree Creek July 19-20. Siege of Atlanta July 22-August 25. Utoy Creek August 5-7. Flank movement on Jonesboro August 25-30. Battle of Jonesboro August 31-September 1. Lovejoy Station September 2-6. Operations against Hood in North Georgia and North Alabama September 29-November 3. Kingston, Ga., November 8 and 10. March to the sea November 15-December 10. Siege of Savannah December 10-21. Campaign of the Carolinas January to April, 1865. Fayetteville, N. C., March 11. Averysboro March 16. Battle of Bentonville March 19-21. Occupation of Goldsboro March 24. Advance on Raleigh April 10-14. Occupation of Raleigh April 14. Bennett's House April 26. Surrender of Johnston and his army. March to Washington, D. C., via Richmond, Va., April 29-May 19. Grand Review May 24. Mustered out at Washington, D. C., June 9, 1865.

Regiment lost during service 5 Officers and 86 Enlisted men killed and mortally wounded and 2 Officers and 181 Enlisted men by disease. Total 274.

75th REGIMENT INFANTRY.

Organized at Wabash, Ind., and mustered in August 19, 1862. Left State for Louisville, Ky., August 21, thence moved to Lebanon, Ky. Attached to 40th Brigade, 12th Division, Army of the Ohio, to November, 1862. 2nd Brigade, 5th Division, Center 14th Army Corps, Army of the Cumberland, to January, 1863. 2nd Brigade, 5th Division, 14th Army Corps, to June, 1863. 2nd Brigade, 4th Division, 14th Army Corps, to October, 1863. 2nd Brigade, 3rd Division, 14th Army Corps, to June, 1865.

SERVICE.—Pursuit of Bragg into Kentucky October 1-20, 1862. Battle of Perryville, Ky., October 8. March to Bowling Green, Ky., October 26-November 3, thence to Scottsville November 10, and to Gallatin, Tenn., November 25. Pursuit of Morgan to Glasgow, Ky., December 22, 1862, to January 2, 1863. Moved to Cave City January 2, thence to Nashville and Murfreesboro, Tenn. Duty at Murfreesboro till June. Expedition to Auburn, Liberty and Alexandria February 3-5. Expedition to Woodbury March 3-8. Expedition to Lebanon, Carthage and Liberty April 1-8. Expedition to McMinnville April 20-30. Middle Tennessee or Tullahoma Campaign June 23-July 7. Hoover's Gap June 24-26. Tullahoma June 29-30. Occupation of Middle Tennessee till August 16. Passage of the Cumberland Mountains and Tennessee River and Chickamauga (Ga.) Campaign August 16-September 22. Shellmound August 21. Narrows near Shellmound August 28. Reconnoissance from Shellmound toward Chattanooga August 30-31. Battle of Chickamauga September 19-21. Siege of Chattanooga September 22-November 23. Chattanooga-Ringgold Campaign November 23-27. Mission Ridge November 23-24. Mission Ridge November 25. Pursuit to Graysville November 26-27. Duty at Chattanooga and Ringgold, Ga., till May, 1864. Reconnoissance from Ringgold toward Tunnel Hill April 29. Atlanta (Ga.) Campaign May 1 to September 8. Demonstrations on Rocky Faced Ridge May 8-11. Battle of Resaca May 14-15. Advance on Dallas May 18-25. Operations on line of Pumpkin Vine Creek and battles about Dallas, New Hope Church and Allatoona Hills May 25-June 5. Operations about Marietta and against Kenesaw Mountain June 10-July 2. Pine Hill June 11-14. Lost Mountain June 15-17. Assault on Kenesaw June 27. Ruff's Station, Smyrna Camp Ground, July 4. Chattahoochie River July 5-17. Peach Tree Creek July 19-20. Siege of Atlanta July 22-August 25. Utoy Creek August 5-7. Flank movement on Jonesboro August 25-30. Battle of Jonesboro August 31-September 1. Operations against Hood in North Georgia and North Alabama September 29-November 3. March to the sea November 15-December 10. Siege of Savannah December 10-21. Campaign of the Carolinas January to April, 1865. Fayetteville, N. C., March 11. Averysboro March 16. Battle of Bentonville March 19-21. Occupation of Goldsboro March 24. Advance on Raleigh April 10-14. Occupation of Raleigh April 14. Bennett's House April 26. Surrender of Johnston and his army. March to Washington, D. C., via Richmond, Va., April 29-May 19. Grand Review May 24. Mustered out at Washington, D. C., June 8, 1865.

Regiment lost during service 1 Officer and 43 Enlisted men killed and mortally wounded and 2 Officers and 186 Enlisted men by disease. Total 232.

76th REGIMENT INFANTRY.

Organized at Indianapolis, Ind., for 30 days State service July 20, 1862. Duty at Evansville, Ind., and at Henderson, Ky., operating against guerrillas and protecting steamboats on the Ohio River till August 20. Mustered out August 20, 1862.

77th REGIMENT VOLUNTEERS.

See 4th Regiment Cavalry.

78th REGIMENT INFANTRY.

Organized at Indianapolis, Ind., for 60 days State service and mustered in August 5, 1862. Guard duty at Evansville, Ind., and operations against guerrillas in Kentucky till October 3. Part of Regiment engaged at Uniontown September 1, and Company "K" at siege of Munfordsville, Ky., September 14-17. Mustered out October 3, 1862.

Regiment lost 1 Officer and 1 Enlisted man killed and 3 Enlisted men by disease. Total 5.

79th REGIMENT INFANTRY.

Organized at Indianapolis, Ind., August 20 to September 2, 1862. Mustered in September 2, 1862, and moved to Louisville, Ky. Attached to 11th Brigade, 5th Division, Army of the Ohio, September, 1862. 11th Brigade, 5th Division, 2nd Corps, Army of the Ohio, to November, 1862. 1st Brigade, 3rd Division, Left Wing 14th Army Corps, Army of the Cumberland, to January, 1863. 1st Brigade, 3rd Division, 21st Army Corps, Army of the Cumberland, to October, 1863. 3rd Brigade, 3rd Division, 4th Army Corps, Army of the Cumberland, to June, 1865.

SERVICE.—Pursuit of Hood to Loudon, Ky., October 1-22, 1862. Battle of Perryville, Ky., October 8 (Reserve). March to Nashville, Tenn., October 22-Novem-

ber 7, and duty there till December 26. Advance on Murfreesboro, Tenn., December 26-30. Battle of Stone's River December 30-31, 1862, and January 1-3, 1863. Duty at Murfreesboro till June. Middle Tennessee or Tullahoma Campaign June 23-July 7. Occupation of Middle Tennessee till August 16. Passage of the Cumberland Mountains and Tennessee River and Chickamauga (Ga.) Campaign August 16-September 22. Battle of Chickamauga September 19-20. Siege of Chattanooga, Tenn., September 24-November 23. Chattanooga-Ringgold Campaign November 23-27. Orchard Knob November 23-24. Mission Ridge November 25. Pursuit to Graysville November 26-27. March to relief of Knoxville, Tenn., November 28-December 8. Operations in East Tennessee December, 1863, to April, 1864. Atlanta (Ga.) Campaign May 1 to September 8. Demonstrations on Rocky Faced Ridge and Dalton, Ga., May 8-13. Battle of Resaca May 14-15. Adairsville May 17. Near Kingston May 18-19. Near Cassville May 19. Advance on Dallas May 22-25. Operations on line of Pumpkin Vine Creek and battles about Dallas, New Hope Church and Allatoona Hills May 25-June 5. Pickett's Mills May 27. Operations about Marietta and against Kenesaw Mountain June 10-July 2. Pine Hill June 11-14. Lost Mountain June 15-17. Assault on Kenesaw June 27. Ruff's Station, Smyrna Camp Ground, July 4. Chattahoochie River July 5-17. Peach Tree Creek July 19-20. Siege of Atlanta July 22-August 25. Flank movement on Jonesboro August 25-30. Battle of Jonesboro August 31-September 1. Lovejoy Station September 2-6. Operations against Hood in North Georgia and North Alabama September 29-November 3. Nashville Campaign November-December. Columbia, Duck River, November 24-27. Battle of Franklin November 30. Battle of Nashville December 15-16. Pursuit of Hood to the Tennessee River December 17-28. Moved to Huntsville, Ala., and duty there till March, 1865. Expedition from Whitesburg February 17, 1865. Operations in East Tennessee March 15-April 22. At Nashville till June. Mustered out June 7, 1865.

Regiment lost during service 3 Officers and 50 Enlisted men killed and mortally wounded and 2 Officers and 147 Enlisted men by disease. Total 202.

80th REGIMENT INFANTRY.

Organized at Princeton and Indianapolis, Ind., and mustered in September 8, 1862. Left State for Covington, Ky., September 9, thence moved to Louisville, Ky. Attached to 34th Brigade, 10th Division, Army of the Ohio, September, 1862. 34th Brigade, 10th Division, 1st Corps, Army of the Ohio, to November, 1862. District of Western Kentucky, Dept. of the Ohio, to June, 1863. 2nd Brigade, 3rd Division, 23rd Army Corps, Dept. Ohio, to August, 1863. 1st Brigade, 2nd Division, 23rd Army Corps, Army Ohio, to June, 1864. 2nd Brigade, 2nd Division, 23rd Army Corps, Army Ohio, to February, 1865, and Dept. of North Carolina to June, 1865.

SERVICE.—Pursuit of Bragg into Kentucky October 1-15, 1862. Battle of Perryville, Ky., October 8. Moved to Lebanon, Ky., and duty there till December. Pursuit of Morgan to the Cumberland River December 22, 1862, to January 2, 1863. Duty at Elizabethtown, Ky., till March, and at Woodsonville till August. Pursuit of Morgan June 20-July 5. Burnside's Campaign in East Tennessee August 16-October 17. March over Cumberland Mountains to Knoxville August 16-September 3. Duty at Kingston till December 5. Action at Kingston November 24. Moved to Nashville, Tenn., December 6, thence march to Blain's Cross Roads and Mossy Creek. Mossy Creek, Talbot Station, December 29. Operations in East Tennessee till April, 1864. Atlanta (Ga.) Campaign May 1 to September 8. Demonstrations on Rocky Faced Ridge and Dalton, Ga., May 9-13. Battle of Resaca May 14-15. Advance on Dallas May 18-25. Operations on line of Pumpkin Vine Creek and battles about Dallas, New Hope Church and Allatoona Hills May 25-June 5. Operations about Marietta and against Kenesaw Mountain June 10-July 2. Pine Hill June 11-14. Lost Mountain June 15-17. Muddy

Creek June 17. Noyes Creek June 19. Kolb's Farm June 22. Assault on Kenesaw June 27. Chattahoochie River July 3-17. Decatur July 19. Howard House July 20. Siege of Atlanta July 22-August 25. Flank movement on Jonesboro August 25-30. Battle of Jonesboro August 31-September 1. Lovejoy Station September 2-6. Pursuit of Hood into Alabama October 3-26. Nashville Campaign November-December. Columbia, Duck River, November 24-27. Battle of Franklin November 30. Battle of Nashville December 15-16. Pursuit of Hood to the Tennessee River December 17-28. At Clifton, Tenn., till January 16, 1865. Movement to Washington, D. C., thence to Fort Fisher, N. C., January 16-February 9. Operations against Hoke February 11-14. Fort Anderson February 18-19. Town Creek February 19-20. Capture of Wilmington February 22. Campaign of the Carolinas March 1-April 26. Advance on Goldsboro March 6-21. Occupation of Goldsboro March 21. Advance on Raleigh April 10-14. Occupation of Raleigh April 14. Bennett's House April 26. Surrender of Johnston and his army. Duty at Salisbury till June. Mustered out June 22, 1865. Recruits transferred to 129th Indiana Infantry.

Regiment lost during service 6 Officers and 64 Enlisted men killed and mortally wounded and 1 Officer and 171 Enlisted men by disease. Total 242.

81st REGIMENT INFANTRY.

Organized at New Albany, Ind., and mustered in August 29, 1862. Ordered to Louisville, Ky., August 29. Attached to 32nd Brigade, 9th Division, Army of the Ohio, September, 1862. 32nd Brigade, 9th Division, 3rd Corps, Army Ohio, to November, 1862. 3rd Brigade, 1st Division, Right Wing 14th Army Corps, Army of the Cumberland, to January, 1863. 3rd Brigade, 1st Division, 20th Army Corps, Army of the Cumberland, to March, 1863. 2nd Brigade, 1st Division, 20th Army Corps, to October, 1863. 1st Brigade, 1st Division, 4th Army Corps, Army of the Cumberland, to June, 1865.

SERVICE.—Pursuit of Bragg into Kentucky October 1-15, 1862. Battle of Perryville, Ky., October 8. March to Nashville, Tenn., October 16-November 7, and duty there till December 26. Reconnoissance toward Franklin December 9. Near Brentwood December 9. Advance on Murfreesboro December 26-30. Nolensville December 26-27. Battle of Stone's River December 30-31, 1862, and January 1-3, 1863. Duty at Murfreesboro till June. Reconnoissance from Salem to Versailles March 9-14. Operations on Eaglesville Pike near Murfreesboro June 4. Middle Tennessee or Tullahoma Campaign June 23-July 7. Liberty Gap June 22-27. Duty at Winchester till August. Passage of the Cumberland Mountains and Tennessee River and Chickamauga (Ga.) Campaign August 16-September 22. Battle of Chickamauga September 19-20. Siege of Chattanooga, Tenn., September 24-October 25. Reopened Tennessee River October 26-29. Duty at Bridgeport, Ala., till January 26, 1864, and at Ooltewah till May, 1864. Atlanta (Ga.) Campaign May 3 to September 8, 1864. Tunnel Hill May 6-7. Demonstrations on Rocky Faced Ridge and Dalton May 8-13. Buzzard's Roost Gap May 8-9. Battle of Resaca May 14-15. Near Kingston May 18-19. Near Cassville May 19. Advance on Dallas May 22-25. Operations on line of Pumpkin Vine Creek and battles about Dallas, New Hope Church and Allatoona Hills May 25-June 5. Operations about Marietta and against Kenesaw Mountain June 10-July 2. Pine Hill June 11-14. Lost Mountain June 15-17. Assault on Kenesaw June 27. Ruff's Station, Smyrna Camp Ground, July 4. Chattahoochie River July 5-17. Peach Tree Creek July 19-20. Siege of Atlanta July 22-August 25. Flank movement on Jonesboro August 25-30. Battle of Jonesboro August 31-September 1. Lovejoy Station September 2-6. Operations against Hood in North Georgia and North Alabama September 29-November 3. Nashville Campaign November-December. Columbia, Duck River, November 24-27. Battle of Franklin November 30. Battle of Nashville December 15-16. Pursuit of Hood to the Tennessee River December 17-28. Moved to

Huntsville, Ala., and duty there till March, 1865. Operations in East Tennessee March 15-April 22. At Nashville till June. Mustered out June 13, 1865.

Regiment lost during service 4 Officers and 52 Enlisted men killed and mortally wounded and 1 Officer and 188 Enlisted men by disease. Total 245.

82nd REGIMENT INFANTRY.

Organized at Indianapolis and Camp Emerson and mustered in August 30, 1862. Ordered to Louisville, Ky., September 1. Attached to 1st Brigade, 1st Division, Army of the Ohio, September, 1862. 1st Brigade, 1st Division, 3rd Corps, Army of the Ohio, to November, 1862. 1st Brigade, 3rd Division, Center 14th Army Corps, Army of the Cumberland, to January, 1863. 1st Brigade, 3rd Division, 14th Army Corps, to June, 1865.

SERVICE.—Pursuit of Bragg into Kentucky October 1-15, 1862. Battle of Perryville, Ky., October 8. March to Nashville, Tenn., October 16-November 7, and duty there till December 26. Advance on Murfreesboro December 26-30. Battle of Stone's River December 30-31, 1862, and January 1-3, 1863. Duty at Murfreesboro till June. Expedition toward Columbia March 4-14. Middle Tennessee or Tullahoma Campaign June 23-July 7. Hoover's Gap June 24-26. Occupation of Middle Tennessee till August 16. Passage of the Cumberland Mountains and Tennessee River and Chickamauga (Ga.) Campaign August 16-September 22. Battle of Chickamauga September 19-21. Siege of Chattanooga, Tenn., September 24-November 23. Reopening Tennessee River November 26-29. Brown's Ferry October 27. Chattanooga-Ringgold Campaign November 23-27. Orchard Knob November 23-24. Mission Ridge November 25. Pursuit to Graysville November 26-27. Demonstrations on Dalton, Ga., February 22-27, 1864. Tunnel Hill, Buzzard's Roost Gap and Rocky Faced Ridge February 23-25. Atlanta (Ga.) Campaign May 1-September 8. Demonstrations on Rocky Faced Ridge May 8-11. Battle of Resaca May 14-15. Advance on Dallas May 18-25. Operations on line of Pumpkin Vine Creek and battles about Dallas, New Hope Church and Allatoona Hills May 25-June 5. Operations about Marietta and against Kenesaw Mountain June 10-July 2. Pine Hill June 10-14. Lost Mountain June 15-17. Assault on Kenesaw June 27. Ruff's Station, Smyrna Camp Ground, July 4. Chattahoochie River July 5-17. Peach Tree Creek July 19-20. Siege of Atlanta July 22-August 25. Utoy Creek August 5-7. Flank movement on Jonesboro August 25-30. Battle of Jonesboro August 31-September 1. Lovejoy Station September 2-6. Operations in North Georgia and North Alabama against Hood September 29-November 3. March to the sea November 15-December 10. Siege of Savannah December 10-21. Campaign of the Carolinas January to April, 1865. Fayetteville, N. C., March 11. Averysboro March 16. Battle of Bentonville March 19-21. Occupation of Goldsboro March 24. Advance on Raleigh April 10-14. Occupation of Raleigh April 14. Bennett's House April 26. Surrender of Johnston and his army. March to Washington, D. C., via Richmond, Va., April 29-May 19. Grand Review May 24. Mustered out June 9, 1865.

Regiment lost during service 3 Officers and 65 Enlisted men killed and mortally wounded and 6 Officers and 170 Enlisted men by disease. Total 244.

83rd REGIMENT INFANTRY.

Organized at Lawrenceburg, Ind., September 4 to November 5, 1862. Ordered to Memphis, Tenn., and attached to 4th Brigade, 5th Division, District of Memphis, Tenn., 13th Army Corps (Old), Dept. of the Tennessee, November, 1862. 2nd Brigade, 2nd Division, District of Memphis, 13th Army Corps, to December, 1862. 2nd Brigade, 2nd Division, Sherman's Yazoo Expedition, to January, 1863. 2nd Brigade, 2nd Division, 15th Army Corps, Army of the Tennessee, to June, 1865.

SERVICE.—Duty at Memphis, Tenn., to November 26, 1862. "Tallahatchie March" November 26-December 13, 1862. Sherman's Yazoo Expedition December 20, 1862, to January 3, 1863. Chickasaw Bayou December 26-28. Chickasaw Bluff December 29. Expedition to Arkansas Post, Ark., January 3-10, 1863. Assault and capture of Fort Hindman, Arkansas Post, January 10-11. Moved to Young's Point, La., January 17, and duty there till April. Black Bayou March 24-25. Demonstration on Haines' and Drumgould's Bluffs April 29-May 2. Movement to join army in rear of Vicksburg, Miss., May 2-14. Battle of Champion's Hill May 16. Siege of Vicksburg May 18-July 4. Assaults on Vicksburg May 19 and 22. Advance on Jackson, Miss., July 4-10. Siege of Jackson July 10-17. Camp at Big Black to Chattanooga, Tenn., September 26-November 20. Operations on the Memphis & Charleston Railroad in Alabama October 20-29. Cherokee Station, Ala., October 21. Bear Creek, Tuscumbia, October 27. Chattanooga-Ringgold Campaign November 23-27. Tunnel Hill November 23-25. Mission Ridge November 25. Pursuit to Graysville November 26-27. March to relief of Knoxville, Tenn., November 28-December 8. Garrison duty in Alabama till May, 1864. Atlanta Campaign May 1 to September 8. Demonstrations on Resaca May 8-13. Near Resaca May 13. Battle of Resaca May 14-15. Advance on Dallas May 18-25. Operations on line of Pumpkin Vine Creek and battles about Dallas, New Hope Church and Allatoona Hills May 25-June 5. Operations about Marietta and against Kenesaw Mountain June 10-July 2. Assault on Kenesaw June 27. Ruff's Mills July 3-4. Chattahoochie River July 6-17. Battle of Atlanta July 22. Siege of Atlanta July 22-August 25. Ezra Chapel, Hood's second sortie, July 28. Flank movement on Jonesboro August 25-30. Battle of Jonesboro August 31-September 1. Lovejoy Station September 2-6. Operations in North Georgia and North Alabama against Hood September 29-November 3. Turkeytown and Gadsden Road, Ala., October 25. March to the sea November 15-December 10. Siege of Savannah, Ga., December 10-21. Fort McAllister December 13. Campaign of the Carolinas January to April, 1865. Cannon's Bridge, South Edisto River, S. C., February 8. Orangeburg February 11-12. North Edisto River February 12-13. Columbia February 16-17. Battle of Bentonville, N. C., March 19-21. Occupation of Goldsboro March 24. Advance on Raleigh April 10-14. Occupation of Raleigh April 14. Bennett's House April 26. Surrender of Johnston and his army. March to Washington, D. C., via Richmond, Va., April 29-May 20. Grand Review May 24. Mustered out June 3, 1865.

Regiment lost during service 5 Officers and 56 Enlisted men killed and mortally wounded and 3 Officers and 220 Enlisted men by disease. Total 284.

84th REGIMENT INFANTRY.

Organized at Richmond and Indianapolis, Ind., and mustered in September 3, 1862. Ordered to Covington, Ky., September 8, and duty in the defences of Covington and Cincinnati, Ohio, during Kirby Smith's threatened attack on Cincinnati. Moved to Point Pleasant, W. Va., October 1. Attached to 3rd Brigade, Kanawha Division, District of West Virginia, Dept. of Ohio, to November, 1862. District of Eastern Kentucky, Dept. of Ohio, to February 18, 1863. 2nd Brigade, Baird's 3rd Division, Army of Kentucky, Dept. Ohio, February, 1863. Baird's Division, Franklin, Tenn., Dept. of the Cumberland, to June, 1863. 1st Brigade, 1st Division, Reserve Corps, Dept. of the Cumberland, to October, 1863. 2nd Brigade, 1st Division, 4th Army Corps, Army of the Cumberland, to August, 1864. 3rd Brigade, 1st Division, 4th Army Corps, to June, 1865.

SERVICE.—Moved from Point Pleasant, W. Va., to Guyandotte October 13, 1862, and duty there till November 14. Ordered to Kentucky November 14. Duty at Catlettsburg and Cassville, Ky., till February 7, 1863. Moved to Nashville, Tenn., February 7-20, thence to Franklin, Tenn., March 5, and duty there till June 3. Pursuit of Van Dorn March 9-12. Repulse of Van Dorn's attack on Franklin April 10. Moved to Triune June 3. Repulse of Forest's attack on Triune June 11. Middle Tennessee or Tullahoma Campaign June 23-July 7.

Occupation of Shelbyville July 1. At Wartrace till August 12. Chickamauga (Ga.) Campaign August-September. Battle of Chickamauga September 19-21. Siege of Chattanooga, Tenn., September 24-October 26. Near Chattanooga October 2. Reopening Tennessee River October 26-29. At Whiteside till February, 1864. Near Kingston December 4, 1863. Demonstration on Dalton, Ga., February 22-27, 1864. Tunnel Hill, Buzzard's Roost Gap and Rocky Faced Ridge February 23-25. Atlanta (Ga.) Campaign May 1 to September 8. Tunnel Hill May 6-7. Demonstrations on Rocky Faced Ridge and Dalton May 8-13. Buzzard's Roost Gap May 8-9. Battle of Resaca May 14-15. Near Kingston May 18-19. Near Cassville May 19. Advance on Dallas May 22-25. Operations on line of Pumpkin Vine Creek and battles about Dallas, New Hope Church and Allatoona Hills May 25-June 5. Operations about Marietta and against Kenesaw Mountain June 10-July 2. Pine Hill June 11-14. Lost Mountain June 15-17. Assault on till September 26. Moved to Memphis, thence march Chattahoochie River July 5-17. Peach Tree Creek July 19-20. Siege of Atlanta July 22-August 25. Flank movement on Jonesboro August 25-30. Battle of Jonesboro August 31-September 1. Lovejoy Station September 2-6. Operations against Hood in North Georgia and North Alabama September 29-November 3. Nashville Campaign November-December. Columbia, Duck River, November 24-27. Battle of Franklin November 30. Battle of Nashville December 15-16. Pursuit of Hood to the Tennessee River December 17-28. Moved to Huntsville, Ala., and duty there till March, 1865. Operations in East Tennessee March 15-April 22. At Nashville, Tenn., till June. Mustered out June 14, 1865. Recruits transferred to 57th Indiana Infantry.

Regiment lost during service 5 Officers and 82 Enlisted men killed and mortally wounded and 2 Officers and 145 Enlisted men by disease. Total 234.

85th REGIMENT INFANTRY.

Organized at Terre Haute, Ind., September 2, 1862. Ordered to Kentucky and duty at Covington, Lexington, Nicholasville and Danville, Ky., till January 26, 1863. Attached to 1st Brigade, 2nd Division, Army of Kentucky, Dept. of Ohio, September-October, 1862. 1st Brigade, 3rd Division, Army of Kentucky, Dept. of Ohio, to February, 1863. Coburn's Brigade, Baird's Division, Army of Kentucky, Dept. of the Cumberland, to June, 1863. 3rd Brigade, 1st Division, Reserve Corps, Army of the Cumberland, to October, 1863. Coburn's unattached Brigade, Post Murfreesboro, Tenn., Dept. of the Cumberland, to January, 1864. 2nd Brigade, 1st Division, 11th Army Corps, Army of the Cumberland, to April, 1864. 2nd Brigade, 3rd Division, 20th Army Corps, Army of the Cumberland, to June, 1865.

SERVICE.—Moved to Louisville, Ky., thence to Nashville, Tenn., January 26-February 1. Moved to Brentwood Station, Tenn., February 21, thence to Franklin. Action at Franklin March 4, and at Thompson's Station, Spring Hill, March 4-5. Regiment captured by Van Dorn, comanding Bragg's Cavalry forces, nearly 18,-000 strong. Exchanged May 5, 1863. Regiment reorganizing at Indianapolis, Ind., till June 12. Ordered to Nashville, Tenn., June 12, and guard duty along Nashville & Chattanooga Railroad at Franklin and Murfreesboro till April, 1864. Garrison's Creek near Fosterville and Christiana October 6, 1863 (Detachment). March to Lookout Valley, Tenn., April 20-28. Atlanta (Ga.) Campaign. Demonstration on Rocky Faced Ridge May 8-11. Battle of Resaca May 14-15. Cassville May 19. Advance on Dallas May 22-25. New Hope Church May 25. Operations on line of Pumpkin Vine Creek and battles about Dallas, New Hope Church and Allatoona Hills May 25-June 5. Pine Mount June 5. Operations about Marietta and against Kenesaw Mountain June 10-July 2. Pine Hill June 11-14. Lost Mountain June 15-17. Gilgal or Golgotha Church June 15. Muddy Creek June 17. Noyes Creek June 19. Kolb's Farm June 22. Assault on Kenesaw June 27. Ruff's Station, Smyrna Camp Ground, July 4. Chattahoochie River

July 5-17. Peach Tree Creek July 19-20. Siege of Atlanta July 22-August 25. Operations at Chattahoochie River Bridge August 26-September 2. Occupation of Atlanta September 2-November 15. March to the sea November 15-December 10. Siege of Savannah December 10-21. Campaign of the Carolinas January to April, 1865. Lawtonville, S. C., February 2. Battle of Bentonville, N. C., March 19-21. Occupation of Goldsboro March 24. Advance on Raleigh April 10-14. Occupation of Raleigh April 14. Bennett's House April 26. Surrender of Johnston and his army. March to Washington, D. C., via Richmond, Va., April 29-May 19. Grand Review May 24. Mustered out June 12, 1865.

Regiment lost during service 2 Officers and 40 Enlisted men killed and mortally wounded and 3 Officers and 190 Enlisted men by disease. Total 235.

86th REGIMENT INFANTRY.

Organized at Lafayette, Ind., and mustered in September 4, 1862. Ordered to Cincinnati, Ohio, September 5, thence to Covington, Ky., and to Louisville, Ky., September 30. Duty there till October 1. Attached to 14th Brigade, 5th Division, Army of the Ohio, September, 1862. 14th Brigade, 5th Division, 2nd Corps, Army of the Ohio, to November, 1862. 2nd Brigade, 3rd Division, Left Wing 14th Army Corps, Army of the Cumberland, to January, 1863. 2nd Brigade, 3rd Division, 21st Army Corps, Army of the Cumberland, to October, 1863. 3rd Brigade, 3rd Division, 4th Army Corps, Army of the Cumberland, to June, 1865.

SERVICE.—Pursuit of Bragg to Loudon, Ky., October 1-22, 1862. Battle of Perryville, Ky., October 8 (Reserve). March to Nashville, Tenn., October 22-November 7, and duty there till December 26. Advance on Murfreesboro December 26-30. Battle of Stone's River December 30-31, 1862, and January 1-3, 1863. Duty at Murfreesboro till June. Middle Tennessee or Tullahoma Campaign June 23-July 7. Occupation of Middle Tennessee till August 16. Passage of the Cumberland Mountains and Tennessee River and Chickamauga (Ga.) Campaign August 16-September 22. Battle of Chickamauga September 19-20. Siege of Chattanooga September 24-November 23. Chattanooga-Ringgold Campaign November 23-27. Orchard Knob November 23-24. Mission Ridge November 25. Pursuit to Graysville November 26-27. March to relief of Knoxville November 28-December 8. Operations in East Tennessee December, 1863, to April, 1864. Atlanta (Ga.) Campaign May 1 to September 8. Demonstrations on Rocky Faced Ridge and Dalton May 8-13. Battle of Resaca May 14-15. Adairsville May 17. Near Kingston May 18-19. Near Cassville May 19. Cassville May 24. Operations on line of Pumpkin Vine Creek and battles about Dallas, New Hope Church and Allatoona Hills May 25-June 5. Pickett's Mills May 27. Operations about Marietta and against Kenesaw Mountain June 10-July 2. Pine Hill June 11-14. Lost Mountain June 15-17. Assault on Kenesaw June 27. Ruff's or Neal Dow Station, Smyrna Camp Ground, July 4. Chattahoochie River July 5-17. Peach Tree Creek July 19-20. Siege of Atlanta July 22-August 25. Flank movement on Jonesboro August 25-30. Battle of Jonesboro August 31-September 1. Lovejoy Station September 2-6. Operations against Hood in North Georgia and North Alabama September 29-November 3. Nashville Campaign November-December. Columbia, Duck River, November 24-27. Columbia Ford November 29. Battle of Franklin November 30. Battle of Nashville December 15-16. Pursuit of Hood to the Tennessee River December 17-28. Moved to Huntsville, Ala., and duty there till March, 1865. Expedition from Whitesburg February 17, 1865. Operations in East Tennessee March 15-April 22. At Nashville till June. Mustered out June 6, 1865.

Regiment lost during service 2 Officers and 70 Enlisted men killed and mortally wounded and 1 Officer and 176 Enlisted men by disease. Total 249.

87th REGIMENT INFANTRY.

Organized at South Bend, Ind., and mustered in August 31, 1862. Ordered to Louisville, Ky., August 31. At-

tached to 3rd Brigade, 1st Division, Army of the Ohio, September, 1862. 3rd Brigade, 1st Division, 3rd Army Corps, Army of the Ohio, to November, 1862. 3rd Brigade, 3rd Division, Center 14th Army Corps, Army of the Cumberland, to January, 1863. 3rd Brigade, 3rd Division, 14th Army Corps, Army of the Cumberland, to October, 1863. 2nd Brigade, 3rd Division, 14th Army Corps, to June, 1865.

SERVICE.—Pursuit of Bragg to Crab Orchard, Ky., October 1-15, 1862. Battle of Perryville, Ky., October 8. March to Nashville, Tenn., October 16-November 7. Duty South Tunnel, Pilot Knob and Gallatin, Tenn., November 8-26, and guarding fords of the Cumberland till January 29, 1863. Duty at Nashville, Tenn., till March 6. Duty at Triune till June. Expedition toward Columbia, Tenn., March 4-14. Franklin June 4-5. Middle Tennessee or Tullahoma Campaign June 23-July 7. Hoover's Gap June 24-26. Occupation of Middle Tennessee till August 16. Passage of the Cumberland Mountains and Tennessee River and Chickamauga (Ga.) Campaign August 16-September 22. Battle of Chickamauga September 19-21. Siege of Chattanooga, Tenn., September 24-November 23. Chattanooga-Ringgold Campaign November 23-27. Orchard Knob November 23-24. Mission Ridge November 25. Demonstration on Dalton, Ga., February 22-27, 1864. Tunnel Hill, Buzzard's Roost Gap and Rocky Faced Ridge February 23-25. Reconnoissance from Ringgold toward Tunnel Hill April 29. Atlanta (Ga.) Campaign May 1 to September 8. Demonstration on Rocky Faced Ridge May 8-11. Battle of Resaca May 14-15. Advance on Dallas May 18-25. Operations on line of Pumpkin Vine Creek and battles about Dallas, New Hope Church and Allatoona Hills May 25-June 5. Operations about Marietta and against Kenesaw Mountain June 10-July 2. Pine Hill June 11-14. Lost Mountain June 15-17. Assault on Kenesaw June 27. Ruff's or Neal Dow Station July 4. Chattahoochie River July 5-17. Peach Tree Creek July 19-20. Siege of Atlanta July 22-August 25. Utoy Creek August 7. Flank movement on Jonesboro August 25-30. Battle of Jonesboro August 31-September 1. Operations against Hood in North Georgia and North Alabama September 29-November 3. March to the sea November 15-December 10. Siege of Savannah December 10-21. Campaign of the Carolinas January to April, 1865. Fayetteville, N. C., March 11. Averysboro March 16. Battle at Bentonville March 19-21. Occupation of Goldsboro March 24. Advance on Raleigh April 10-14. Occupation of Raleigh April 14. Bennett's House April 26. Surrender of Johnston and his army. March to Washington, D. C., via Richmond, Va., April 29-May 19. Grand Review May 24. Mustered out June 10, 1865.

Regiment lost during service 10 Officers and 81 Enlisted men killed and mortally wounded and 2 Officers and 190 Enlisted men by disease. Total 283.

88th REGIMENT INFANTRY.

Organized at Fort Wayne, Ind., and mustered in August 29, 1862. Ordered to Louisville, Ky., August 29, and duty there till October 1. Attached to 17th Brigade, 3rd Division, Army of the Ohio, September, 1862. 17th Brigade, 3rd Division, 1st Corps, Army Ohio, to November, 1862. 2nd Brigade, 1st Division, Center 14th Army Corps, Army of the Cumberland, to January, 1863. 2nd Brigade, 1st Division, 14th Army Corps, Army of the Cumberland, to April, 1863. 1st Brigade, 2nd Division, 14th Army Corps, to October, 1863. 1st Brigade, 1st Division, 14th Army Corps, to June, 1865.

SERVICE.—Pursuit of Bragg into Kentucky October 1-15, 1862. Battle of Perryville, Ky., October 8. March to Nashville, Tenn., October 16-November 7, and duty there till December 26. Advance on Murfreesboro December 26-30. Battle of Stone's River December 30-31, 1862, and January 1-3, 1863. Duty at Murfreesboro till June. Middle Tennessee or Tullahoma Campaign June 23-July 7. Occupation of Middle Tennessee till August 16. Passage of the Cumberland Mountains and Tennessee River and Chickamauga (Ga.) Campaign August 16-September 22. Davis Cross Roads or Dug

Gap September 11. Battle of Chickamauga September 19-21. Rossville Gap September 21. Siege of Chattanooga, Tenn., September 24-November 23. Chattanooga-Ringgold Campaign November 23-27. Lookout Mountain November 23-24. Mission Ridge November 25. Pea Vine Creek and Graysville November 26. Ringgold Gap, Taylor's Ridge, November 27. March to Charleston December 30, 1863, to January 10, 1864. Demonstration on Dalton, Ga., February 22-27, 1864. Tunnel Hill, Buzzard's Roost Gap and Rocky Faced Ridge February 23-25. Atlanta (Ga.) Campaign May 1-September 8. Demonstration on Rocky Faced Ridge May 8-11. Buzzard's Roost Gap, May 8-9. Battle of Resaca May 14-15. Advance on Dallas May 18-25. Operations on line of Pumpkin Vine Creek and battles about Dallas, New Hope Church and Allatoona Hills May 25-June 5. Operations about Marietta and against Kenesaw Mountain June 10-July 2. Pine Hill June 11-14. Lost Mountain June 15-17. Assault on Kenesaw June 27. Ruff's Station July 4. Chattahoochie River July 5-17. Buckhead, Nancy's Creek, July 18. Peach Tree Creek July 19-20. Siege of Atlanta July 22-August 25. Utoy Creek August 5-7. Flank movement on Jonesboro August 25-30. Near Red Oak August 30. Battle of Jonesboro August 31-September 1. Operations aginst Hood in North Georgia and North Alabama September 29-November 3. March to the sea November 15-December 10. Siege of Savannah December 10-21. Campaign of the Carolinas January to April, 1865. Averysboro, N. C., March 16. Battle of Bentonville March 19-21. Occupation of Goldsboro March 24. Advance on Raleigh April 10-14. Occupation of Raleigh April 14. Bennett's House April 26. Surrender of Johnston and his army. March to Washington, D. C., via Richmond, Va., April 29-May 19. Grand Review May 24. Mustered out June 7, 1865.

Regiment lost during service 9 Officers and 55 Enlisted men killed and mortally wounded and 3 Officers and 147 Enlisted men by disease. Total 214.

89th REGIMENT INFANTRY.

Organized at Indianapolis, Ind., and mustered in August 28, 1862. Left State for Louisville, Ky., thence moved to Munfordsville, Ky., September 2. Siege of Munfordsville September 14-17. Regiment captured September 17 and paroled. March to Brandenburg, thence to Jeffersonville, Ind. Duty at Indianapolis, Ind., saw June 27. Ruff's Station July 4. Chattahoochie December 5-8. Attached to District of Memphis, Tenn., 16th Army Corps, Dept. of the Tennessee, to March, 1863. 1st Brigade, District of Memphis, Tenn., 5th Division, 16th Army Corps, to January, 1864. 1st Brigade, 3rd Division, 16th Army Corps, to December, 1864. 1st Brigade, 2nd Division (Detachment), Army of the Tennessee, Dept. of the Cumberland, to February, 1865. 1st Brigade, 2nd Division, 16th Army Corps (New), Military Division West Mississippi, to July, 1865.

SERVICE.—Guard and fatigue duty at Fort Pickering, Memphis, Tenn., December 21, 1862, to October 18, 1863. Expedition to Hernando, Miss., August 16-20, 1863. Garrison and picket duty at Memphis, Tenn., till January 26, 1864. Expedition after Forest December 24-31, 1863. Lafayette and Grierson's Bridge December 27 (Detachment). Moscow December 27 (Detachment). Moved to Vicksburg, Miss., January 26-31, 1864. Big Black River February 2. Meridian Campaign February 3-March 2. Queen Hill February 4. Meridian February 14-15. Decatur February 22. Red River Campaign March 10-May 22. Fort DeRussy March 14. Occupation of Alexandria March 16. Henderson's Hill March 21. Battle of Pleasant Hill April 9. Fort Bisland April 12. Natchitoches April 20-21. At Alexandria April 26-May 13. Bayou LaMouri May 7. Retreat to Morganza May 13-20. Mansura May 16. Yellow Bayou May 18. Moved to Vicksburg May 20-24, and to Memphis, Tenn., June 4-9. Old River Lake or Lake Chicot, Ark., June 6. Smith's Expedition to Tupelo, Miss., July 5-21. Harrisburg, near Tupelo, July 14-15. Smith's Expedition to Oxford, Miss., August 1-30. Moved to Jefferson Barracks, Mo., September 8-19. Expedition to DeSoto September 20-October 1. March through Missouri in pursuit of Price October 2-November 19. Greenton November 1. Moved to Nashville, Tenn., November 25-December 1. Battle of Nashville December 15-16. Pursuit of Hood to the Tennessee River December 17-28. Moved to Eastport, Miss., January 1, 1865, and duty there till February 9. Moved to Vicksburg, Miss., thence to New Orleans, La., February 9-21. Campaign against Mobile and its defences March 17-April 12. Siege of Spanish Fort and Fort Blakely March 26-April 9. Assault and capture of Fort Blakely April 9. Occupation of Mobile April 12. March to Montgomery April 13-27, and duty there till June 1. Moved to Mobile June 1 and duty there till July 19. Mustered out July 19, 1865.

Regiment lost during service 6 Officers and 55 Enlisted men killed and mortally wounded and 3 Officers and 188 Enlisted men by disease. Total 252.

90th REGIMENT VOLUNTEERS.

See 5th Regiment Cavalry.

91st REGIMENT INFANTRY.

Organized as a Battalion of seven Companies at Evansville, Ind., and mustered in October 1, 1862. Left State for Henderson, Ky., October 10. Attached to District of Western Kentucky, Dept. of the Ohio, to June, 1863. 1st Brigade, 2nd Division, 23rd Army Corps, Army Ohio, to August, 1863. Russellville, Ky., 1st Division, 23rd Army Corps, to October, 1863. District of Southwest Kentucky, Dept. of the Ohio, October, 1863. District of Somerset, Ky., 1st Division, 23rd Army Corps, to January, 1864. District of the Clinch, Dept. of the Ohio, to April, 1864. 1st Brigade, 4th Division, 23rd Army Corps, to June, 1864. 1st Brigade, 2nd Division, 23rd Army Corps, to August, 1864. 3rd Brigade, 2nd Division, 23rd Army Corps, Army Ohio, to February, 1865, and Dept. of North Carolina, to June, 1865.

SERVICE.—Duty at Henderson, Madisonville and Smithlands, Ky., till June, 1863. Pursuit of Morgan to Burkesville June 15-23. (Cos. "H," "G" and "K" organized September, 1863.) Duty at Russellville till September 25. (Cos. "G," "H" and "K" joined at Russellville.) Ordered to Nashville, Tenn., September 25. Duty at Nashville, Tenn., Camp Nelson, Ky., and Camp Burnside, Ky., till January, 1864. At Cumberland Gap January to May, 1864. Wyerman's Mills February 22, 1864 (Co. "A"). Cumberland Gap February 22 (Detachment). March to Kingston, Ga., May 17-June 3, thence to Ackworth, Ga. Atlanta (Ga.) Campaign June 8-September 8. Operations about Marietta and against Kenesaw Mountain June 10-July 2. Lost Mountain June 15-17. Muddy Creek June 17. Noyes Creek June 19. Kolb's Farm June 22. Assault on Kenesaw June 27. Chattahoochie River July 3-17. Decatur July 19. Howard House July 20. Siege of Atlanta July 22-August 25. October 27 to December 5. Moved to Memphis, Tenn., Flank movement on Jonesboro August 25-30. Battle of Jonesboro August 31-September 1. Lovejoy Station September 2-6. Operations against Hood in North Georgia and North Alabama September 29-November 3. Nashville Campaign November-December. Columbia, Duck River, November 24-27. Spring Hill November 29. Battle of Franklin November 30. Battle of Nashville December 15-16. Pursuit of Hood to the Tennessee River December 17-23. Duty at Clifton, Tenn., till January 16, 1865. Movement to Washington, D. C., thence to Fort Fisher, N. C., January 16-February 9. Operations against Hoke February 11-14. Fort Anderson February 18-19. Town Creek February 19-20. Capture of Wilmington February 22. Campaign of the Carolinas March 1-April 26. Advance on Goldsboro March 6-21. Capture of Goldsboro March 21. Advance on Raleigh April 10-14. Occupation of Raleigh April 14. Bennett's House April 26. Surrender of Johnston and his army. Duty at Raleigh till May 3 and at Salisbury till June 26. Mustered out June 26, 1865. Recruits transferred to 120th, 124th and 128th Regiments, Indiana Infantry.

Regiment lost during service 2 Officers and 18 Enlisted men killed and mortally wounded and 2 Officers and 114 Enlisted men by disease. Total 136.

92nd REGIMENT INFANTRY.

Failed to complete organization. Enlisted men merged into 93rd Indiana Infantry.

93rd REGIMENT INFANTRY.

Organized at Madison, Indianapolis and New Albany, Ind., August 16 to October 31, 1862. Left State for Memphis, Tenn., November 9, 1862. Attached to 5th Brigade, District of Memphis, Tenn., 13th Army Corps (Old). Dept of the Tennessee, November, 1862. 3rd Brigade, 1st Division, District of Memphis, 13th Army Corps, to December, 1862. 3rd Brigade, 8th Division, 16th Army Corps, to April, 1863. 1st Brigade, 3rd Division, 15th Army Corps, to December, 1863. 1st Brigade, 1st Division, 16th Army Corps, to December, 1864. 1st Brigade, 1st Division (Detachment), Army of the Tennessee, Dept. of the Cumberland, to February, 1865. 1st Brigade, 1st Division, 16th Army Corps (New), Military Division West Mississippi, to August, 1865.

SERVICE.—"Tallahatchie March" November 26-December 20, 1862. Duty at Lagrange, Tenn., Corinth, Miss., and at Memphis, Tenn., till March, 1863. Moved to Helena, Ark., March 13, thence to Young's Point, La. At Ducksport, La., till May 3. Movement to join army in rear of Vicksburg, Miss., via Richmond and Grand Gulf, May 3-14. Mississippi Springs May 13. Jackson May 14. Siege of Vicksburg May 18-July 4. Expedition to Mechanicsburg May 26-June 4. Advance on Jackson, Miss., July 4-10. Siege of Jackson July 10-17. Camp at Big Black River till September 5 and at Oak Ridge till October 14. Expedition to Canton October 14-20. Bogue, Chitto Creek, October 17. Moved to Memphis, Tenn., November 7, and provost duty there till May 10, 1864. Expedition from Memphis to Wyatt's, Miss., February 6-18, 1864. Coldwater Ferry February 8. Near Senatobia February 8-9. Wyatt's February 13. Sturgis' Expedition to Ripley, Miss., April 30-May 9. Sturgis' Expedition to Guntown, Miss., June 1-13. Battle of Brice's Cross Roads or Tishamingo Creek near Guntown June 10. Ripley June 11. Smith's Expedition to Tupelo, Miss., July 5-21. Camargo's Cross Roads, Harrisburg, July 13. Harrisburg near Tupelo July 14-15. Old Town or Tishamingo Creek July 15. Smith's Expedition to Oxford, Miss., August 1-30. Tallahatchie River August 7-9. Abbeville August 23. Moved to Duvall's Bluff, Ark., September 2. March through Arkansas and Missouri in pursuit of Brice September 24-November 18. Moved to Nashville, Tenn., November 25-December 1. Battle of Nashville December 15-16. Pursuit of Hood to the Tennessee River December 17-28. Moved to Eastport, Miss., and duty there till February 9, 1865. Moved to Vicksburg, Miss., thence to New Orleans, La., and to Dauphin Island, Ala., February 9-March 3. Campaign against Mobile and its defences March 17-April 12. Siege of Spanish Fort and Fort Blakely March 26-April 8. Assault and capture of Fort Blakely April 9. Capture of Mobile April 12. March to Montgomery April 13-25, and duty there till May 10. At Selma and Gainesville till August. Mustered out at Gainesville, Ala., August 10, 1865.

Regiment lost during service 1 Officer and 37 Enlisted men killed and mortally wounded and 3 Officers and 250 Enlisted men by disease. Total 291.

94th REGIMENT INFANTRY.

Failed to complete organization.

95th REGIMENT INFANTRY.

Failed to complete organization.

96th REGIMENT INFANTRY.

Failed to complete organization. Three Companies raised and merged into 99th Regiment Indiana Infantry.

97th REGIMENT INFANTRY.

Organized at Terre Haute, Ind., and mustered in September 20, 1862. Ordered to Louisville, Ky., thence to Memphis, Tenn., and duty there till December, 1862. Attached to District of Louisville, Ky., Dept. of Ohio, to November, 1862. 3rd Brigade, District of Memphis, Tenn., 13th Army Corps (Old), Dept. of the Tennessee, November, 1862. 2nd Brigade, 1st Division, District of Memphis, 13th Army Corps, to December, 1862. 2d Brigade, 1st Division, 17th Army Corps, to January, 1863. 2nd Brigade, 1st Division 16th Army Corps, to March, 1863. 3rd Brigade, 1st Division, 16th Army Corps, to July, 1863. 3rd Brigade, 4th Division, 15th Army Corps, to April, 1864. 2nd Brigade, 4th Division, 15th Army Corps, to August, 1864. 2nd Brigade, 1st Division, 15th Army Corps, to June, 1865.

SERVICE.—Grant's Central Mississippi Campaign. Operations on the Mississippi Central Railroad November, 1862, to January, 1863. Guard duty along Memphis & Charleston Railroad at LaGrange and Moscow, Tenn., till June, 1863. Ordered to Young's Point, La., June 9. Siege of Vicksburg, Miss., June 14-July 4. Advance on Jackson, Miss., July 4-10. Siege of Jackson July 10-17. Camp at Big Black till September 26. Moved to Memphis, Tenn., thence march to Chattanooga, Tenn., September 26-November 20. Operations on Memphis & Charleston Railroad in Alabama October 20-29. Chattanooga-Ringgold Campaign November 23-27. Tunnel Hill November 23-24. Mission Ridge November 25. March to relief of Knoxville, Tenn., November 27-December 8. Moved to Scottsboro, Ala., and duty there till May, 1864. Demonstration on Dalton, Ga., February 22-27, 1864. Tunnel Till, Buzzard's Roost Gap and Rocky Faced Ridge February 23-25. Atlanta (Ga.) Campaign May 1, to September 8. Demonstrations on Resaca May 8-12. Near Resaca May 13. Battle of Resaca May 14-15. Movements on Dallas May 18-25. Operations on line of Pumpkin Vine Creek and battles about Dallas, New Hope Church and Allatoona Hills May 25-June 5. Operations about Marietta and against Kenesaw Mountain June 10-July 2. Brushy Mountain June 15. Assault on Kenesaw June 27. Nickajack Creek July 2-5. Ruff's Mills July 3-4. Chattahoochie River July 5-17. Battle of Atlanta July 22. Siege of Atlanta July 22-August 25. Ezra Chapel, Hood's second sortie, July 28. Flank movement on Jonesboro August 25-30. Battle of Jonesboro August 31-September 1. Lovejoy Station September 2-6. Operations against Hood in North Georgia and North Alabama September 29-November 3. March to the sea November 15-December 10. Griswaldsville November 22. Siege of Savannah December 10-21. Campaign of the Carolinas January to April, 1865. Reconnoissance to Salkehatchie River January 25, 1865. Congaree Creek, S. C., February 15. Columbia February 16-17. Battle of Bentonville, N. C., March 19-21. Mill Creek March 22. Occupation of Goldsboro March 24. Advance on Raleigh April 10-14. Occupation of Raleigh April 14. Bennett's House April 26. Surrender of Johnston and his army. March to Washington, D. C., via Richmond, Va., April 29-May 20. Grand Review May 24. Mustered out June 9, 1865.

Regiment lost during service 3 Officers and 51 Enlisted men killed and mortally wounded and 6 Officers and 172 Enlisted men by disease. Total 232.

98th REGIMENT INFANTRY.

Failed to complete organization. Two Companies organized, transferred to 100th Regiment Indiana Infantry.

99th REGIMENT INFANTRY.

Organized at South Bend, Ind., and mustered in October 21, 1862. Ordered to Louisville, Ky., thence to Memphis, Tenn. Attached to District of Louisville, Ky., Dept. Ohio, to November, 1862. 3rd Brigade, District of Memphis, Tenn., 13th Army Corps (Old), Dept. of the Tennessee, November, 1862. 2nd Brigade, 1st Division, District of Memphis, Tenn., 13th Army Corps, to December, 1862. 2nd Brigade, 1st Division, 17th Army Corps, to January, 1863. 2nd Brigade, 1st Division, 16th Army Corps, to March, 1863. 3rd Brigade, 1st Division, 16th Army Corps, to July, 1863. 3rd Brigade, 4th Division, 15th Army Corps, to August, 1864. 1st Brigade 4th Division 15th Army Corps, to September, 1864. 3rd Brigade, 2nd Division, 15th Army Corps, to June, 1865.

SERVICE.—Grant's Central Mississippi Campaign November 26, 1862, to January 10, 1863. Duty along Memphis & Charleston Railroad till June, 1863. Ordered to Vicksburg, Miss., June 9. Siege of Vicksburg June 14-July 4. Advance on Jackson, Miss., July 4-10. Bolton's Ferry, Big Black River, July 4-6. Siege of Jackson July 10-17. Camp at Big Black till September 26. Moved to Memphis, Tenn., thence march to Chattanooga, Tenn., September 26-November 20. Operations on Memphis & Charleston Railroad in Alabama October 20-29. Chattanooga-Ringgold Campaign November 23-27. Tunnel Hill November 23-25. Mission Ridge November 25. March to relief of Knoxville November 27-December 8. At Scottsboro, Ala., December 17, 1863, to May, 1864. Demonstration on Dalton, Ga., February 22-27, 1864. Tunnel Hill, Buzzard's Roost Gap and Rocky Faced Ridge, February 23-25. Atlanta (Ga.) Campaign May 1 to September 8. Demonstrations on Resaca May 8-13. Near Resaca May 13. Battle of Resaca May 14-15. Movements on Dallas May 18-25. Operations on line of Pumpkin Vine Creek and battles about Dallas, New Hope Church and Allatoona Hills May 25-June 5. Operations about Marietta and against Kenesaw Mountain June 10-July 2. Brushy Mountain June 15. Assault on Kenesaw Mountain June 27. Nickajack Creek July 2-5. Ruff's Mills July 3-4. Chattahoochie River July 5-17. Nickajack Creek July 6-8, and July 9-10. Battle of Atlanta July 22. Siege of Atlanta July 22-August 25. Ezra Chapel, Hood's second sortie, July 28. Flank movement on Jonesboro August 25-30. Battle of Jonesboro August 31-September 1. Lovejoy Station September 2-6. Operations against Hood in North Georgia and North Alabama September 29-November 3. Reconnoissance from Rome, Ga., on Cave Springs Road and skirmishes October 12-13. March to the sea November 15-December 10. Near Statesboro December 4. Siege of Savannah December 10-21. Fort McAllister December 13. Campaign of the Carolinas January to April, 1865. Columbia, S. C., February 15-17. Battle of Bentonville, N. C., March 19-21. Occupation of Goldsboro March 24. Advance on Raleigh April 10-14. Occupation of Raleigh April 14. Bennett's House April 26. Surrender of Johnston and his army. March to Washington, D. C., via Richmond, Va., April 29-May 20. Grand Review May 24. Mustered out June 6, 1865.

Regiment lost during service 45 Enlisted men killed and mortally wounded and 5 Officers and 147 Enlisted men by disease. Total 197.

100th REGIMENT INFANTRY.

Organized at Fort Wayne, Ind., and mustered in September 10, 1862. Left State for Memphis, Tenn., November 11. Attached to 2nd Brigade, District of Memphis, Tenn., 13th Army Corps (Old), Dept. of the Tennessee, November, 1862. 1st Brigade, 1st Division, District of Memphis, 13th Army Corps, to December, 1862. 1st Brigade, 1st Division, 17th Army Corps, to January, 1863. 1st Brigade, 1st Division, 16th Army Corps, to July, 1863. 1st Brigade, 4th Division, 15th Army Corps, to August, 1864. 2nd Brigade, 4th Division, 15th Army Corps, to September, 1864. 2nd Brigade, 1st Division, 15th Army Corps, to June, 1865.

SERVICE.—Grant's Central Mississippi Campaign. Operations on the Mississippi Central Railroad November 26, 1862, to January 10, 1863. Duty at Colliersville, Tenn., and along the Memphis & Charleston Railroad till June 7. Ordered to Vicksburg, Miss., June 7. Siege of Vicksburg June 14-July 4. Advance on Jackson, Miss., July 4-10. Siege of Jackson July 10-17. Camp at Big Black till September 28. Moved to Memphis, Tenn., thence march to Chattanooga, Tenn., September 28-November 20. Operations on the Memphis & Charleston Railroad in Alabama October 20-29. Chattanooga-Ringgold Campaign November 23-27. Tunnel Hill November 23-24. Mission Ridge November 25. March to relief of Knoxville, Tenn., November 28-December 8.

Moved to Scottsboro, Ala., and duty there December 17, 1863, to May, 1864. Atlanta (Ga.) Campaign May 1 to September 8. Demonstration on Resaca May 8-13. Near Resaca May 13. Battle of Resaca May 14-15. Movement on Dallas May 18-25. Operations on line of Pumpkin Vine Creek and battles about Dallas, New Hope Church and Allatoona Hills May 25-June 5. Operations about Marietta and against Kenesaw Mountain June 10-July 2. Brushy Mountain June 15. Assault on Kenesaw June 27. Nickajack Creek July 2-5. Chattahoochie River July 5-17. Battle of Atlanta July 22. Siege of Atlanta July 22-August 25. Ezra Chapel, Hood's second sortie, July 28. Flank movement on Jonesboro August 25-30. Battle of Jonesboro August 31-September 1. Lovejoy Station September 2-6. Operations against Hood in North Georgia and North Alabama September 29-November 3. March to the sea November 15-December 10. Griswoldsville November 22. Siege of Savannah December 10-21. Campaign of the Carolinas January to April, 1865. Reconnoissance to Salkehatchie River, S. C., January 25, 1865. Congaree Creek, S. C., February 15. Columbia February 16-17. Battle of Bentonville, N. C., March 19-21. Mill Creek March 22. Occupation of Goldsboro March 24. Advance on Raleigh April 10-14. Occupation of Raleigh April 14. Bennett's House April 26. Surrender of Johnston and his army. March to Washington, D. C., via Richmond, Va., April 29-May 20. Grand Review May 24. Mustered out July 8, 1865. Recruits transferred to 48th Indiana Infantry.

Regiment lost during service 2 Officers and 56 Enlisted men killed and mortally wounded and 3 Officers and 173 Enlisted men by disease. Total 234.

101st REGIMENT INFANTRY.

Organized at Wabash, Ind., and mustered in September 7, 1862. Left State for Covington, Ky., September 7, and duty there till September 23. Moved to Louisville, Ky., September 23. Attached to 33rd Brigade, 10th Division, Army of the Ohio, September, 1862. 33rd Brigade, 10th Division, 1st Corps, Army of the Ohio, to November, 1862. 2nd Brigade, 5th Division (Centre), 14th Army Corps, Army of the Cumberland, to January, 1863. 2nd Brigade, 5th Division, 14th Army Corps, Army of the Cumberland, to June, 1863. 2nd Brigade, 4th Division, 14th Army Corps, to October, 1863. 2nd Brigade, 3rd Division, 14th Army Corps, to June, 1865. 1st Brigade, 3rd Division, 14th Army Corps, to June, 1865.

SERVICE.—Pursuit of Bragg into Kentucky October 1-15, 1862. Escort Division trains to Springfield, Ky. March to Munfordsville, Ky., October 12, and duty there till November 30. Expedition to Cave City October 31-November 26. Moved to Bledsoe Creek November 30. Pursuit of Morgan December 22, 1862, to January 2, 1863. March to Nashville, Tenn., thence to Murfreesboro, Tenn., January 3-11, and duty there till June. Expedition to Auburn, Liberty and Alexandria February 3-5. Reconnoissance to Woodbury March 3-8. Action at Vaught's Hill, near Milton, March 20. Expedition to Lebanon, Carthage and Liberty April 1-8. Expedition to McMinnville April 20-30. Middle Tennessee (or Tullahoma) Campaign June 23-July 7. Hoover's Gap June 24-26. Camp at Dechard till August 17. Passage of the Cumberland Mountains and Tennessee River and Chickamauga (Ga.) Campaign August 17-September 22. Shellmound August 21. Narrows, near Shellmound, August 28 (Detachment). Reconnoissance from Shellmound toward Chattanooga August 29-30. Battle of Chickamauga September 19-21. Siege of Chattanooga, Tenn., September 22-November 23. Before Chattanooga September 22-26. Chattanooga-Ringgold Campaign November 23-27. Orchard Knob November 23-24. Mission Ridge November 25. Duty at Chattanooga and Ringgold, Ga., till May, 1864. Reconnoissance from Ringgold, Ga., toward Tunnel Hill April 29. Atlanta (Ga.) Campaign May 1 to September 8. Demonstrations on Rocky Faced Ridge May 8-11. Battle of Resaca May 14-15. Advance on Dallas May 18-25. Operations on line of Pumpkin Vine Creek and battles about Dallas, New Hope Church and Allatoona Hills May 25-June 5. Allatoona Pass June 1-2. Operations about Marietta and against Kenesaw Mountain June 10-July 2. Pine Hill June 10-14. Lost Mountain June 15-17. Assault on Kenesaw June 27. Ruff's Station July 4. Chattahoochie River July 5-17. Peach Tree Creek July 19-20. Siege of Atlanta July 22-August 25. Utoy Creek August 5-7. Flank movement on Jonesboro August 25-30. Battle of Jonesboro August 31-September 1. Lovejoy Station September 2-6. Operations against Hood in North Georgia and North Alabama September 29-November 3. March to the sea November 15-December 10. Cypress Swamp, near Sister's Ferry, December 7. Siege of Savannah December 10-21. Campaign of the Carolinas January to April, 1865. Fayetteville, N. C., March 11. Taylor's Hole Creek, Averysboro, March 16. Battle of Bentonville March 19-21. Occupation of Goldsboro March 24. Advance on Raleigh April 10-14. Bennett's House April 26. Surrender of Johnston and his army. March to Washington, D. C., via Richmond, Va., April 29-May 19. Grand Review May 24. Moved to Louisville, Ky., and there mustered out June 24, 1865.

Regiment lost during service 3 Officers and 47 Enlisted men killed and mortally wounded and 1 Officer and 169 Enlisted men by disease. Total 220.

102nd REGIMENT INFANTRY.

Organized to repel Morgan's Raid July 10, 1863. Left Indianapolis, Ind., for Vernon July 11. Duty at Vernon, Dupont, Osgood and Sauman's Station till July 17. Mustered out July 17, 1863.

103rd REGIMENT INFANTRY.

Organized at Indianapolis, Ind., July 10, 1863, to repel the Morgan Raid. Left Indianapolis for Vernon, Ind., July 11. Pursuit of Morgan from Vernon to Harrison and Batavia, Ohio, July 12-15. March to Sauman's Station July 15, thence to Indianapolis, Ind. Mustered out July 16, 1863.

104th REGIMENT INFANTRY.

Organized July 10, 1863, to repel the Morgan Raid. Pursuit of Morgan July 11-18. Mustered out July 18, 1863.

105th REGIMENT INFANTRY.

Organized July 12, 1863, to repel the Morgan Raid. Mustered out July 18, 1863.

106th REGIMENT INFANTRY.

Organized July 10, 1863, to repel the Morgan Raid. Mustered out July 18, 1863.

107th REGIMENT INFANTRY.

Organized July 10, 1863, to repel the Morgan Raid. Mustered out July 18, 1863.

108th REGIMENT INFANTRY.

Organized July 12, 1863, to repel the Morgan Raid. Mustered out July 18, 1863.

109th REGIMENT INFANTRY.

Organized July 10, 1863, to repel the Morgan Raid. Mustered out July 17, 1863.

110th REGIMENT INFANTRY.

Organized July 12, 1863, to repel the Morgan Raid. Mustered out July 15, 1863.

111th REGIMENT INFANTRY.

Organized July 13, 1863, to repel the Morgan Raid. Mustered out July 15, 1863.

112th REGIMENT INFANTRY.

Organized July 10, 1863, to repel the Morgan Raid. Mustered out July 17, 1863.

113th REGIMENT INFANTRY.

Organized July 10, 1863, to repel the Morgan Raid. Mustered out July 16, 1863.

114th REGIMENT INFANTRY.

Organized July 9, 1863, to repel the Morgan Raid. Engaged in the pursuit of Morgan July 11-21. Mustered out July 21, 1863.

115th REGIMENT INFANTRY.

Organized at Indianapolis, Ind., and mustered in for 6 months' service August 13, 1863. Moved to Nicholasville, Ky., September 16. Attached to Mahan's 1st Brigade, Willcox's Left Wing Forces, Dept. of the Ohio, to February, 1864.

SERVICE.—March from Nicholasville, Ky., to Cumberland Gap September 24-October 3, 1863, and to Morristown October 6-8. Action at Blue Springs October 10. Duty at Greenville till November 6. Moved to Bull's Gap November 6, and duty there till December. March across Clinch Mountain to Clinch River. Action at Walker's Ford December 2. Guard and patrol duty in East Tennessee till February. 1864. Mustered out February 25, 1864.

Regiment lost during service 1 Enlisted man killed and 69 Enlisted men by disease. Total 70.

116th REGIMENT INFANTRY.

Organized at Lafayette, Ind., and mustered in for 6 months' service August 17, 1863. Moved to Dearborn, Mich., August 31, and guard arsenal till September 16. Moved to Nicholasville, Ky., September 16. Attached to Mahan's 1st Brigade, Willcox's Left Wing Forces, Dept. of the Ohio, to October, 1863. 2nd Brigade, Willcox's Division, Left Wing Forces, Dept. of the Ohio, to January, 1864. District of the Clinch, Dept. of the Ohio, to February, 1864.

SERVICE.—March from Nicholasville, Ky., to Cumberland Gap September 24-October 3, 1863, and to Morristown October 6-8. Action at Blue Springs October 10. March to Greenville and duty there till November 6; thence march to Bull's Gap and across Clinch Mountain to Clinch River November-December. Action at Walker's Ford, Clinch River, December 2. Duty at Tazewell, Maynardsville and in East Tennessee till February, 1864. Action at Tazewell January 24. Mustered out February 29 to March 2, 1864.

Regiment lost during service 1 Enlisted man killed and 64 Enlisted men by disease. Total 65.

117th REGIMENT INFANTRY.

Organized at Indianapolis, Ind., and mustered in for 6 months' service September 17, 1863. Left State for Nicholasville, Ky., September 17. Attached to Mahan's 1st Brigade, Willcox's Left Wing Forces, Dept. of the Ohio, to December, 1863. 1st Brigade, 3rd Division, 23rd Army Corps, to January, 1864. District of the Clinch, Dept. of the Ohio, to February, 1864.

SERVICE.—March from Nicholasville, Ky., to Cumberland Gap September 24-October 3, 1863; thence to Morristown October 6-8. Action at Blue Springs October 10. March to Greenville and duty there till November 6. Moved to Bean's Station November 6. Action at Clinch Mountain Gap November 14. Duty at Tazewell, Maynardsville and Cumberland Gap till February, 1864. Action at Tazewell January 24, 1864. Mustered out February 23-27, 1864.

Regiment lost during service 95 Enlisted men by disease. Total 95.

118th REGIMENT INFANTRY.

Organized at Wabash, Ind., July and August, 1863, for 6 months' service. Left State for Nicholasville, Ky., September 16. Attached to Mahan's 1st Brigade, Willcox's Left Wing Forces, Dept. of the Ohio, to October, 1863. 2nd Brigade, Willcox's Left Wing Forces, Dept. of the Ohio, to January, 1864. District of the Clinch, Dept. of the Ohio, to March, 1864.

SERVICE.—March from Nicholasville, Ky., to Cumberland Gap September 24-October 3, and to Morristown October 6-8. Action at Blue Springs October 10. March to Greenville and duty there till November 6. March across Clinch Mountain to Clinch River. Action at Walker's Ford, Clinch River, December 2. Duty at Tazewell, Maynardsville and Cumberland Gap till February, 1864. Action at Tazewell January 24. Mustered out March 1-4, 1864.

Regiment lost during service 3 Enlisted men killed and mortally wounded and 1 Officer and 86 Enlisted men by disease. Total 90.

119th REGIMENT VOLUNTEERS.
See 7th REGIMENT CAVALRY.

120th REGIMENT INFANTRY.
Organized at Columbus, Ind., December, 1863, to March, 1864. Left State for Louisville, Ky., March 20, 1864; thence moved to Nashville, Tenn. Attached to 1st Brigade, 1st Division, 23rd Army Corps, Army of the Ohio, to June, 1864. 4th Brigade, 3rd Division, 23rd Army Corps, to August, 1864. 3rd Brigade, 3rd Division, 23rd Army Corps, to December, 1864. 1st Brigade, 1st Division, 23rd Army Corps, Army of the Ohio, to February, 1865, and Dept. of North Carolina to August, 1865. Dept. of North Carolina to February, 1866.

SERVICE.—March to Charleston, Tenn., April 7-24, 1864. Atlanta (Ga.) Campaign May 1 to September 8, 1864. Demonstrations on Dalton May 8-13. Rocky Faced Ridge May 8-11. Battle of Resaca May 14-15. Movements on Dallas May 18-25. Operations on line of Pumpkin Vine Creek and battles about Dallas, New Hope Church and Allatoona Hills May 25-June 5. Cassville May 27. Operations about Marietta and against Kenesaw Mountain June 10-July 2. Lost Mountain June 15-17. Muddy Creek June 17. Noyes Creek June 19. Assault on Kenesaw June 27. Nickajack Creek July 2-5. Chattahoochie River July 5-17. Siege of Atlanta July 22-August 25. Utoy Creek August 5-7. Flank movement on Jonesboro August 25-30. Lovejoy Station September 2-6. Operations in North Georgia and North Alabama against Hood September 29-November 3. Nashville Campaign November-December. In front of Columbia November 24-27. Battle of Franklin November 30. Battle of Nashville December 15-16. Pursuit of Hood to the Tennessee River December 17-28. At Clifton, Tenn., till January 15, 1865. Movement to Washington, D. C., thence to Morehead City, N. C., January 15-February 24. Campaign of the Carolinas March 1-April 26. Advance on Kinston and Goldsboro March 1-21. Battle of Wise's Forks March 8-10. Kinston March 11. Occupation of Goldsboro March 21. Advance on Raleigh April 10-14. Occupation of Raleigh April 14. Bennett's House April 26. Surrender of Johnston and his army. Duty at Raleigh till May 10. At Charlotte and Greensboro, N. C., till August 21, and at Raleigh till January, 1866. Mustered out January 8, 1866.

Regiment lost during service 1 Officer and 26 Enlisted men killed and mortally wounded and 1 Officer and 140 Enlisted men by disease. Total 168.

121st REGIMENT VOLUNTEERS.
See 9th REGIMENT CAVALRY.

122nd REGIMENT INFANTRY.
Failed to complete organization. Enlisted men merged into 120th Regiment Indiana Infantry.

123rd REGIMENT INFANTRY.
Organized at Greensburg, Terre Haute and Indianapolis, Ind., December 25, 1863, to March 7, 1864. Left State for Nashville, Tenn., March 18, 1864. Attached to 2nd Brigade, 1st Division, 23rd Army Corps, Army of the Ohio, to June, 1864. 4th Brigade, 3rd Division, 23rd Army Corps, to August, 1864. 3rd Brigade, 2nd Division, 23rd Army Corps, to December, 1864. 2nd Brigade, 1st Division, 23rd Army Corps, Army of the Ohio, to February, 1865, and Dept. of North Carolina to August, 1865.

SERVICE.—March to Charleston, Tenn., April 7-24, 1864. Atlanta (Ga.) Campaign May 1 to September 8. Demonstrations on Dalton, Ga., May 8-13. Rocky Faced Ridge May 8-11. Battle of Resaca May 14-15. Movements on Dallas May 18-25. Operations on Pumpkin Vine Creek and battles about Dallas, New Hope Church

and Allatoona Hills May 25-June 5. Operations about Marietta and against Kenesaw Mountain June 10-July 2. Lost Mountain June 15-17. Muddy Creek June 17. Noyes Creek June 19. Assault on Kenesaw June 27. Nickajack Creek July 2-5. Ruff's Mills July 3-4. Chattahoochie River July 5-17. Siege of Atlanta July 22-August 25. Utoy Creek August 5-7. Flank movement on Jonesboro August 25-30. Lovejoy Station September 2-6. Operations against Hood in North Georgia and North Alabama September 29-November 3. Nashville Campaign November-December. In front of Columbia November 24-27. Battle of Franklin November 30. Battle of Nashville December 15-16. Pursuit of Hood to the Tennessee River December 17-28. At Clifton, Tenn., till January 15, 1865. Movement to Washington, D. C.; thence to Morehead City, N. C., January 15-February 24. Campaign of the Carolinas March 1-April 26. Advance on Kinston and Goldsboro March 1-21. Battle of Wise's Forks March 6-8. Kinston March 14. Occupation of Goldsboro March 21. Advance on Raleigh April 10-14. Occupation of Raleigh April 14. Bennett's House April 26. Surrender of Johnston and his army. Duty at Charlotte and Raleigh, N. C., till August. Mustered out August 25, 1865.

Regiment lost during service 4 Officers and 47 Enlisted men killed and mortally wounded and 1 Officer and 131 Enlisted men by disease. Total 183.

124th REGIMENT INFANTRY.
Organized at Richmond, Terre Haute and Indianapolis, Ind., November, 1863, to March, 1864. Mustered in March 10, 1864. Left State for Louisville, Ky., March 19; thence moved to Nashville, Tenn. Attached to 1st Brigade, 1st Division, 23rd Army Corps, Army of the Ohio, to June, 1864. 4th Brigade, 3rd Division, 23rd Army Corps, to August, 1864. 2nd Brigade, 3rd Division, 23rd Army Corps, to December, 1864. 1st Brigade, 1st Division, 23rd Army Corps, Army of the Ohio, to February, 1865, and Dept. of North Carolina to August, 1865.

SERVICE.—March to Charleston, Tenn., April 5-24. Atlanta (Ga.) Campaign May 1 to September 8. Demonstrations on Dalton, Ga., May 8-13. Rocky Faced Ridge May 8-11. Battle of Resaca May 14-15. Movements on Dallas May 18-25. Operations on line of Pumpkin Vine Creek and battles about Dallas, New Hope Church and Allatoona Hills May 25-June 5. Operations about Marietta and against Kenesaw Mountain June 10-July 2. Lost Mountain June 15-17. Muddy Creek June 17. Noyes Creek June 19. Assault on Kenesaw June 27. Nickajack Creek July 2-5. Chattahoochie River July 5-17. Siege of Atlanta July 22-August 25. Utoy Creek August 5-7. Flank movement on Jonesboro August 25-30. Near Rough and Ready August 31. Lovejoy Station September 2-6. Operations against Hood in North Georgia and North Alabama September 29-November 3. Nashville Campaign November-December. In front of Columbia November 24-27. Columbia Ford November 29. Battle of Franklin November 30. Battle of Nashville December 15-16. Pursuit of Hood to the Tennessee River December 17-28. At Clifton, Tenn., till January 15, 1865. Movement to Washington, D. C.; thence to Morehead City, N. C., January 15-February 24. Campaign of the Carolinas March 1-April 26. Advance on Kinston and Goldsboro March 1-21. Battle of Wise's Forks March 8-10. Kinston March 14. Occupation of Goldsboro March 21. Advance on Raleigh April 10-14. Occupation of Raleigh April 14. Bennett's House April 26. Surrender of Johnston and his army. Duty at Raleigh, Greensboro and Charlotte, N. C., till August. Mustered out August 31, 1865.

Regiment lost during service 2 Officers and 24 Enlisted men killed and mortally wounded and 1 Officer and 128 Enlisted men by disease. Total 155.

125th REGIMENT VOLUNTEERS.
See 10th REGIMENT CAVALRY.

126th REGIMENT VOLUNTEERS.
See 11th REGIMENT CAVALRY.

127th REGIMENT VOLUNTEERS.
See 12th REGIMENT CAVALRY.

128th REGIMENT INFANTRY.

Organized at Michigan City, Ind., December 15, 1863, to March 7, 1864. Mustered in March 18, 1864. Left State for Nashville, Tenn., March 23. Attached to 1st Brigade, 1st Division, 23rd Army Corps, Army of the Ohio, to June, 1864. 4th Brigade, 3rd Division, 23rd Army Corps, to August, 1864. 3rd Brigade, 3rd Division, 23rd Army Corps, to December, 1864. 1st Brigade, 1st Division, 23rd Army Corps, Army of the Ohio, to February, 1865, and Dept. of North Carolina to August, 1865. Dept. of North Carolina to April, 1866.

SERVICE.—March to Charleston, Tenn., April 5-24, 1864. Atlanta (Ga.) Campaign May 1 to September 8. Demonstrations on Dalton, Ga., May 8-13. Rocky Faced Ridge May 8-11. Battle of Resaca May 14-15. Movements on Dallas May 18-25. Operations on line of Pumpkin Vine Creek and battles about Dallas, New Hope Church and Allatoona Hills May 25-June 5. Allatoona Pass June 1-2. Operations about Marietta and against Kenesaw Mountain June 10-July 2. Lost Mountain June 15-17. Muddy Creek June 17. Noyes Creek June 19. Assault on Kenesaw June 27. Nickajack Creek July 2-5. Chattahoochie River July 5-17. Siege of Atlanta July 22-August 25. Utoy Creek August 5-7. Flank movement on Jonesboro August 25-30. Lovejoy Station September 2-6. Operations against Hood in North Georgia and North Alabama September 29-November 3. Nashville Campaign November-December. In front of Columbia November 24-27. Battle of Franklin November 30. Battle of Nashville December 15-16. Pursuit of Hood to the Tennessee River December 17-28. At Clifton, Tenn., till January 15, 1865. Movement to Washington, D. C.; thence to Morehead City, N. C., January 15-February 24. Campaign of the Carolinas March 1 to April 26. Advance on Kinston and Goldsboro March 1-21. Battle of Wise's Forks March 8-10. Kinston March 14. Occupation of Goldsboro March 21. Advance on Raleigh April 10-14. Occupation of Raleigh April 14. Bennett's House April 26. Surrender of Johnston and his army. Duty at Goldsboro and Raleigh till April, 1866. Mustered out April 10, 1866.

Regiment lost during service 4 Officers and 27 Enlisted men killed and mortally wounded and 1 Officer and 112 Enlisted men by disease. Total 144.

129th REGIMENT INFANTRY.

Organized at Kendallsville and Michigan City, Ind., December 16, 1863, to March 1, 1864. Mustered in March 1, 1864. Duty at Michigan City till March 30. Moved to Nashville, Tenn., March 30-April 7. Attached to 2nd Brigade, 1st Division, 23rd Army Corps, Army of the Ohio, to June, 1864. 4th Brigade, 2nd Division, 23rd Army Corps, to August, 1864. 2nd Brigade, 2nd Division, 23rd Army Corps, to December, 1864. 2nd Brigade, 1st Division, 23rd Army Corps, Army of the Ohio, to February, 1865, and Dept. of North Carolina to August, 1865.

SERVICE.—March to Charleston, Tenn., April 7-24, 1864. Atlanta (Ga.) Campaign May 1 to September 8. Demonstrations on Dalton, Ga., May 8-13. Rocky Faced Ridge May 8-11. Battle of Resaca May 14-15. Movements on Dallas May 18-25. Cartersville May 24. Operations on line of Pumpkin Vine Creek and battles about Dallas, New Hope Church and Allatoona Hills May 25-June 5. Operations about Marietta and against Kenesaw Mountain June 10-July 2. Lost Mountain June 15-17. Muddy Creek June 17. Noyes Creek June 19. Assault on Kenesaw June 27. Nickajack Creek July 2-5. Ruff's Mills July 3-4. Chattahoochie River July 5-17. Siege of Atlanta July 22-August 25. Utoy Creek August 5-7. Flank movement on Jonesboro August 25-30. Lovejoy Station September 2-6. Operations against Hood in North Georgia and North Alabama

September 29-November 3. Nashville Campaign November-December. In front of Columbia November 24-27. Columbia Ford November 29. Battle of Franklin November 30. Battle of Nashville December 15-16. Pursuit of Hood to the Tennessee River December 17-28. At Clifton, Tenn., till January 15, 1865. Movement to Washington, D. C.; thence to Morehead City, N. C., January 15-February 24. Campaign of the Carolinas March 1-April 26. Advance on Kinston and Goldsboro March 1-21. Battle of Wise's Forks March 8-10. Kinston March 14. Occupation of Goldsboro March 21. Advance on Raleigh April 10-14. Occupation of Raleigh April 14. Bennett's House April 26. Surrender of Johnston and his army. Provost duty at Charlotte, N. C., May 9 to August 29. Mustered out at Charlotte, N. C., August 29, 1865.

Regiment lost during service 2 Officers and 19 Enlisted men killed and mortally wounded and 2 Officers and 166 Enlisted men by disease. Total 189.

130th REGIMENT INFANTRY.

Organized at Kokomo, Ind., December, 1863, to March, 1864. Mustered in March 12, 1864. Left State for Nashville, Tenn., March 16. Attached to 2nd Brigade, 1st Division, 23rd Army Corps, Army of the Ohio, to June, 1864. 4th Brigade, 2nd Division, 23rd Army Corps, to August, 1864. 1st Brigade, 2nd Division, 23rd Army Corps, to December, 1864. 2nd Brigade, 1st Division, 23rd Army Corps, Army of the Ohio, to February, 1865, and Dept. of North Carolina to August, 1865. Dept. of North Carolina to December, 1865.

SERVICE.—March to Charleston, Tenn., April 5-24, 1864. Atlanta (Ga.) Campaign May 1 to September 8. Demonstrations on Dalton, Ga., May 8-13. Rocky Faced Ridge May 8-11. Battle of Resaca May 14-15. Movement on Dallas May 18-25. Operations on Pumpkin Vine Creek and battles about Dallas, New Hope Church and Allatoona Hills May 25-June 5. Operations about Marietta and against Kenesaw Mountain June 10-July 2. Lost Mountain June 15-17. Muddy Creek June 17. Noyes Creek June 19. Assault on Kenesaw June 27. Nickajack Creek July 2-5. Ruff's Mills July 3-4. Chattahoochie River July 5-17. Siege of Atlanta July 22-August 25. Utoy Creek August 5-7. Flank movement on Jonesboro August 25-30. Lovejoy Station September 2-6. Operations against Hood in North Georgia and North Alabama September 29-November 3. Nashville Campaign November-December. In front of Columbia November 24-27. Centreville November 27. Battle of Franklin November 30. Battle of Nashville December 15-16. Pursuit of Hood to the Tennessee River December 17-28. At Clifton, Tenn., till January 15, 1865. Movement to Washington, D. C.; thence to Morehead City, N. C., January 15-February 24. Campaign of the Carolinas March 1-April 26. Advance on Kinston and Goldsboro March 1-21. Battle of Wise's Forks March 6-8. Kinston March 14. Occupation of Goldsboro March 21. Advance on Raleigh April 10-14. Occupation of Raleigh April 14. Bennett's House April 26. Surrender of Johnston and his army. Duty at Charlotte, N. C., May 8 to December 2. Mustered out December 2, 1865.

Regiment lost during service 2 Officers and 36 Enlisted men killed and mortally wounded and 1 Officer and 146 Enlisted men by disease. Total 185.

131st REGIMENT VOLUNTEERS.
See 13th Regiment Cavalry.

132nd REGIMENT INFANTRY.

Organized at Indianapolis, Ind., and mustered in May 18, 1864. Ordered to Tennessee May 18, and assigned to duty as Railroad Guard in Tennessee and Alabama, Dept. of the Cumberland, till September. Duty at Stevenson, Ala., till July, and at Nashville, Tenn., till September. Mustered out September 7, 1864. Lost during service 12 by disease.

133rd REGIMENT INFANTRY.

Organized at Indianapolis, Ind., and mustered in May 17, 1864. Ordered to Tennessee and assigned to duty at Bridgeport, Ala., and as Railroad Guard, Dept. of the Cumberland, till September. Mustered out September 5, 1864. Lost during service 17 by disease.

134th REGIMENT INFANTRY.

Organized at Indianapolis, Ind., and mustered in May 25, 1864. Ordered to Tennessee and assigned to Railroad Guard duty in Tennessee and Alabama, Dept. of the Cumberland, till September, 1864. Mustered out September 2, 1864. Lost during service 32 by disease.

135th REGIMENT INFANTRY.

Organized at Indianapolis, Ind., and mustered in May 23, 1864. Ordered to Tennessee and assigned to duty as Railroad Guard in Tennessee and Alabama, Dept. of the Cumberland, till September. Mustered out September 29, 1864. Lost during service 28 by disease.

136th REGIMENT INFANTRY.

Organized at Indianapolis, Ind., and mustered in May 21, 1864. Ordered to Tennessee and assigned to duty as Railroad Guard in Tennessee and Alabama, Dept. of the Cumberland, till September. Mustered out September 2, 1864. Lost during service 8 by disease.

137th REGIMENT INFANTRY.

Organized at Indianapolis, Ind., and mustered in May 26, 1864. Ordered to Tennessee and assigned to duty as Railroad Guard in Tennessee and Alabama, Dept. of the Cumberland, till September, 1864. Mustered out September 21, 1864. Lost during service 17 by disease.

138th REGIMENT INFANTRY.

Organized at Indianapolis, Ind., and mustered in May 27, 1864. Ordered to Tennessee and assigned to Railroad Guard duty in Tennessee and Alabama, Dept. of the Cumberland, to September. Mustered out September 22, 1864. Lost during service 8 by disease.

139th REGIMENT INFANTRY.

Organized at Indianapolis, Ind., and mustered in June 5, 1864. Ordered to Tennessee and assigned to Railroad Guard duty in Tennessee and Alabama, Dept. of the Cumberland, till September. Mustered out September 29, 1865. Lost during service 11 by disease.

140th REGIMENT INFANTRY.

Organized at Indianapolis, Ind., and mustered in October 24, 1864. Left State for Nashville, Tenn., November 15; thence moved to Murfreesboro, Tenn. Attached to 1st Brigade, Defences Nashville & Chattanooga Railroad, Dept. of the Cumberland, to January, 1865. 3rd Brigade, 3rd Division, 23rd Army Corps, Army of the Ohio, to February, 1865, and Dept. of North Carolina to July, 1865.

SERVICE.—Siege of Murfreesboro, Tenn., December 5-12, 1864. Near Murfreesboro December 13-14. March to Columbia December 24-28, thence to Clifton, Tenn., January 2-6, 1865. Movement to Washington, D. C.; thence to Fort Fisher, N. C., January 16-February 7. Arrive at Fort Fisher, N. C., February 7. Operations against Hoke February 11-14. Fort Anderson February 18-19. Town Creek February 19-20. Capture of Wilmington February 22. Campaign of the Carolinas March 1-April 26. Advance on Goldsboro March 6-21. Occupation of Goldsboro March 21. Gulley's March 31. Advance on Raleigh April 10-14. Occupation of Raleigh April 14. Bennett's House April 26. Surrender of Johnston and his army. Duty at Raleigh till May 6, and at Greensboro till July. Mustered out July 11, 1865.

Regiment lost during service 2 Enlisted men killed and 1 Officer and 111 Enlisted men by disease. Total 114.

141st REGIMENT INFANTRY.

Failed to complete organization. Enlisted men transferred to 140th Indiana Infantry.

142nd REGIMENT INFANTRY.

Organized at Indianapolis, Ind., and mustered in November 3, 1864. Left State for Nashville, Tenn., November 18. Attached to 2nd Brigade, 4th Division, 20th Army Corps, Dept. of the Cumberland, to March, 1865. Garrison, Nashville, Tenn., Dept. of the Cumberland, to July, 1865.

SERVICE.—Assigned to post duty at Nashville, Tenn., November, 1864, to July, 1865. Battle of Nashville December 15-16, 1864. Mustered out July 14, 1865.

Regiment lost during service 1 Officer and 1 Enlisted man killed and 70 Enlisted men by disease. Total 72.

143rd REGIMENT INFANTRY.

Organized at Indianapolis, Ind., and mustered in February 21, 1865. Left State for Nashville, Tenn., February 24; thence moved to Murfreesboro, Tenn., and duty there till May 13. Attached to 1st Brigade, 1st Sub-District, District of Middle Tennessee, Dept. of the Cumberland. Moved to Tullahoma, Tenn., May 13, and duty there till June 26. Garrison duty at Nashville, Clarksville and Fort Donelson, Tenn., till October. Mustered out at Nashville, Tenn., October 17, 1865.

Regiment lost 1 Enlisted man killed and 92 Enlisted men by disease. Total 93.

144th REGIMENT INFANTRY.

Organized at Indianapolis, Ind., and mustered in March 6, 1865. Left State for Harper's Ferry, W. Va., March 9. Attached to 1st Brigade, 2nd Provisional Division, Army of the Shenandoah. Duty at Halltown, Charleston, Winchester, Stevenson's Depot and Opequan Creek till August. Mustered out August 5, 1865. Lost by disease 47 during service.

145th REGIMENT INFANTRY.

Organized at Indianapolis, Ind., and mustered in February 16, 1865. Moved to Nashville, Tenn., February 18-21; thence to Chattanooga, Tenn., February 22-23, and to Dalton, Ga., February 23. Skirmish Spring Place February 27 and April 20. On Railroad Guard duty at Dalton, Marietta and Cuthbert, Ga., till January, 1866. Skirmish near Tunnel Hill March 3, 1865 (Detachment). Mustered out January 21, 1866. Lost during service 70 Enlisted men by disease.

146th REGIMENT INFANTRY.

Organized at Indianapolis, Ind., and mustered in March 9, 1865. Left State for Harper's Ferry, W. Va., March 11. Attached to 1st Brigade, 2nd Provisional Division, Army of the Shenandoah. Duty at Charleston, Winchester, Stevenson's Depot, Jordan's Springs and Summit Point till July 27. Ordered to Baltimore, Md., July 27, and assigned to duty in the Military District of Delaware by detachments. Mustered out at Baltimore, Md., August 31, 1865. Lost during service 31 by disease.

147th REGIMENT INFANTRY.

Organized at Indianapolis, Ind., and mustered in March 13, 1865. Left State for Harper's Ferry, W. Va., March 16. Attached to 1st Brigade, 3rd Provisional Division, Army of the Shenandoah, and guard duty at Charleston, Stevenson's Station and Summit Point, Berryville, Harper's Ferry and Maryland Heights till August. Mustered out August 4, 1865. Lost during service 44 Enlisted men by disease.

148th REGIMENT INFANTRY.

Organized at Indianapolis, Ind., and mustered in February 25, 1865. Left State for Nashville, Tenn., February 28. Duty there and as guard and garrison in District of Middle Tennessee, Dept. of the Cumberland, to September. Mustered out September 5, 1865. Lost during service 2 Enlisted men killed and 34 Enlisted men by disease. Total 36.

149th REGIMENT INFANTRY.

Organized at Indianapolis, Ind., and mustered in March 1, 1865. Left State for Nashville, Tenn., March

3; thence moved to Decatur, Ala., and garrison and guard duty there till September. Regiment received the surrender of Generals Roddy and Warren. Mustered out September 27, 1865. Lost during service 43 by disease.

150th REGIMENT INFANTRY.

Organized at Indianapolis, Ind., and mustered in March 9, 1865. Left State for Harper's Ferry, W. Va., March 13. Duty at Charleston, Winchester, Stevenson's Station and Jordan's Springs, Va., till August. Mustered out August 5, 1865. Lost during service 35 by disease.

151st REGIMENT INFANTRY.

Organized at Indianapolis, Ind., and mustered in March 3, 1865. Left State for Nashville, Tenn., March 6; thence moved to Tullahoma, Tenn., March 14, and duty there till June 14. Moved to Nashville, Tenn., June 14, and garrison duty there till September. Mustered out September 19, 1865. Lost during service 66 by disease.

152nd REGIMENT INFANTRY.

Organized at Indianapolis, Ind., and mustered in March 16, 1865. Left State for Harper's Ferry, W. Va., March 18. Duty at Charleston, Stevenson's Station, Summit Point and Clarksburg, W. Va., till August. Mustered out August 30, 1865. Lost during service 49 by disease.

153rd REGIMENT INFANTRY.

Organized at Indianapolis, Ind., March 1, 1865. Left State for Nashville, Tenn., March 5. Stopped at Louisville, Ky., while en route and sent to Russellsville, Ky. Operating against guerillas in vicinity of Russellsville till June. Lyons County April 29 (Detachment). Moved to Louisville, Ky., June 16, and duty at Taylor's Barracks till September. Mustered out September 4, 1865. Lost during service 3 Enlisted men killed and 46 Enlisted men by disease. Total 49.

154th REGIMENT INFANTRY.

Organized at Indianapolis, Ind., April 20, 1865. Left State for Parkersburg, W. Va., April 30; thence moved to Stevenson's Station, Shenandoah Valley, Va., May 2-4. Duty at Stevenson's Station till June 27, and at Opequan Creek till August 4. Mustered out August 4, 1865. Lost during service 1 Enlisted man killed and 40 Enlisted men by disease. Total 41.

155th REGIMENT INFANTRY.

Organized at Indianapolis April 18, 1865. Left State for Washington, D. C., April 26. Assigned to Provisional Brigade, 3rd Division, 9th Army Corps. Moved to Dover, Del., May 3. Duty in Delaware and Maryland by Detachments till August. Mustered out August 4, 1865. Lost during service 19 by disease.

156th REGIMENT INFANTRY.

Organized at Indianapolis, Ind., April 12, 1865. Left State for Harper's Ferry, W. Va., April 27. Guard and patrol duty at various points in the Shenandoah Valley till August. Mustered out August 4, 1865. Lost during service 17 by disease.

157th REGIMENT INFANTRY.

Failed to complete organization.

158th REGIMENT INFANTRY.

Failed to complete organization.

IOWA VOLUNTEERS.

1st REGIMENT CAVALRY.

Organized at Davenport August and September, 1861. Accepted by the United States Government June 13, 1861. Owned its own horses and equipment, and was first Regiment of three years' Cavalry accepted into United States Volunteers. Ordered to St. Louis, Mo., September 26, 1861; thence moved to Benton Barracks and to Otterville, Mo., October. Attached to Fremont's Army of the West and Dept. of Missouri to March, 1862. District of Central Missouri, Dept. of Missouri, to October, 1862. 2nd Brigade, 3rd Division, Army of the Frontier, Dept. of Missouri, to November, 1862. 1st Brigade, 3rd Division, Army of the Frontier, to June, 1863. 2nd Brigade, 1st Cavalry Division, Army of Southeast Missouri, to August, 1863. 2nd Brigade, Davidson's 1st Cavalry Division, Arkansas Expedition, to January, 1864. 3rd Brigade, 1st Cavalry Division, 7th Army Corps, Dept. of Arkansas, to September, 1864. 2nd Brigade, Cavalry Division, 7th Corps, to February, 1865. (Veterans in Dept. of Missouri June to December, 1864.) 1st Brigade, Cavalry Division, 7th Corps, February, 1865. 2nd Brigade, Cavalry Division, District of West Tennessee, Dept. of Tennessee, to June, 1865. Dept. of the Gulf to August, 1865. Dept. of Texas to February, 1866.

SERVICE.—Fremont's Campaign against Springfield, Mo., October 21-November 2, 1861. Moved to Sedalia and Georgetown November 9-16. (3rd Battalion, Cos. "I," "K," "L" and "M," at Benton Barracks, Mo., till March 6, 1862; then moved to Sedalia, Mo.) Pope's Expedition to Warrensburg and Milford, Mo., December 5-27, 1861. Action at Shawnee Mound, Milford, on the Blackwater December 18. Expedition against Poindexter January 6-10, 1862. Action at Silver Creek January 8 (Cos. 'A," "F," "G" and "I"). Raid on Warsaw January 15 (Cos. "A," "F," "G" and "I"). Patrol and scout duty in Central District of Missouri till October. Action at Lexington, Lafayette County, March 10 (Cos. "B" and "D"). Expedition toward Osage and operations in Johnson, St. Clair and Henry Counties, March 18-30. Action at Louisville March 19. Monaghan Springs March 25. Musgrove Ferry March 28. On Blackwater, near Warrensburg, March 29 (Cos. "A," "F," "G"). Near Clinton March 30 (Detachment). Scouts on Marias des Cygnes and Elk Fork Rivers April 4-14. Near Shiloh April 11 (Cos. "D" and "K"). Scout to Montevallo April 13-14 (Cos. "D" and "K"). On Osage, near Montevallo, April 14 (Cos. "D" and "K"). Near Blackwater April 16 (Cos. "D" and "K"). Butler, Bates County, May 15 (Co. "D"). Butler, Bates County, May 26. Monaghan Springs May 27. Deep Water June 11. Guerilla Campaign against Quantrell's, Porter's and Poindexter's forces July to September. Pleasant Hill July 8 (Co. "K"). Expeditions in Cass County July 9 (Detachment). Lotspeach Farm July 9 (Cos. "E," "G," "H" and "L"). Clinton July 9. Sears House and Big Creek Bluff, near Pleasant Hill, July 11 (Cos. "H" and "L"). Clear Creek, near Tabersville, August 2 (Cos. "A," "G," "H" and "L"). Kirksville August 6 (Cos. "A," "G," "H" and "L"). Near Stockton August 9 (Detachment). Regiment reunites at Clinton, Mo., August 8. Big Creek September 9. Newtonia October 4 and 7. Oxford Bend, near Fayetteville, October 27-28. Expedition to Yellville November 25-30. March to join General Blunt December 3-6. Battle of Prairie Grove, Ark., December 7. Expedition over Boston Mountains to Van Buren, Ark., December 27-30. Dripping Springs December 28. Expedition from Huntsville to Buffalo River January 9-12, 1863. At Lake Springs till April, 1863. Operations against Marmaduke in Southeastern Missouri April 17-May 3. Jackson, Mo., April 27. Castor River, near Bloomfield, April 29. Bloomfield April 30. Chalk Bluffs, St. Francis River, April 30-May 1. At Lake Springs till July. Expedition against Little Rock, Ark., July 1-September 10. Expedition from Greensborough to Helena, Ark., July (Detachment). Brownsville, Ark., August 25. Near Bayou Metoe August 26. Reed's Bridge or Bayou Metoe August 27. Austin August 31. Ashley's Mills September 7. Bayou Fourche and capture of Little Rock September 10. Elizabethtown October 1. Vance's Store October 2. Expedition to Arkadelphia November 26-December 1. Reconnoissance from Little Rock December 5-13. Princeton December 6. Expedition to Camden December 15. Steele's Expedition to Shreveport, La., March 23-May 3, 1864. Antoine and Wolf Creeks April 2. Elkins' Ferry, Little Missouri River,

April 3-4. Prairie D'Anna April 9-12. White Oak Creek April 14. Camden Cross Roads April 15. Occupation of Camden April 16-18. Camden April 20. Marks Mills April 25. Moro Bottom April 25-26. Jenkins' Ferry, Saline River, April 30. Veterans on furlough May and June. Non-Veterans on duty at Little Rock till February, 1865. Expedition to Fort Smith, Ark., September 25-October 13, 1864 (Detachment). Reconnoissance to Princeton October 19-23. Hurricane Creek October 23. Expedition to Saline River November 17-18 (Detachment). Veterans moved from Iowa to Missouri June 20, 1864. Operating against guerrillas, headquarters at Macon, Mo., till October. Scout in Boone and Howard Counties September 6-12. Skirmishes in Boone County September 7-8. Scout in Randolph, Boone and Howard Counties September 15-19 (Detachment). Skirmishes at Columbia September 16. Massacre at Centralia, North Missouri Railroad, September 27. Moved to Jefferson City, Mo., October. Skirmish at California October 9. Booneville October 9-12. Campaign against Price October-November. (Served as body guard to General Rosecrans.) Marias des Cygnes, Osage River, October 25. Moved to Warrensburg, thence to St. Louis, Mo., and to Helena, Ark., November-December. Operations in Arkansas January 1-27, 1865. Action at Dardanelle January 14. Expedition from Little Rock to Mt. Elba January 22-February 4. Ordered to Memphis, Tenn., February 17, and duty there till June. Expedition into Northern Mississippi March 3-11. Moved to Alexandria, La., June 15-22; thence to Hemstead, Tex., August 8-26. Moved to Austin, Tex., October 20-November 4, and duty there till February, 1866. Mustered out February 15, 1866. Moved to Iowa February 19-March 12, and discharged March 16, 1866.

Regiment lost during service 2 Officers and 56 Enlisted men killed and mortally wounded and 2 Officers and 233 Enlisted men by disease. Total 293.

2nd REGIMENT CAVALRY.

Organized at Davenport August and September, 1861. Left State for Benton Barracks, Mo., December 7, 1861, and duty there till February, 1862. Attached to Dept. of Missouri December, 1861, to March, 1862. Unassigned, Army of the Mississippi, to April, 1862. 2nd Brigade, Cavalry Division, Army of Mississippi, to June, 1862. Cavalry, 5th Division, Army of Mississippi, to September, 1862. 2nd Brigade, Cavalry Division, Army of Mississippi, to November, 1862. Grierson's Cavalry Brigade, Left Wing 13th Army Corps (Old), Dept. of the Tennessee, to December, 1862. 1st Brigade, Cavalry Division, 16th Army Corps, Dept. of Tennessee, to March, 1863. (District of Memphis, Tenn., 16th Corps, January to March, 1863—6 Companies.) 1st Brigade, 1st Cavalry Division, 16th Corps, to May, 1863. 2nd Brigade, 1st Cavalry Division, 16th Corps, to August, 1863. 3rd Brigade, 1st Cavalry Division, 16th Corps, to December, 1863. 2nd Brigade, 1st Cavalry Division, 16th Corps, to July, 1864. 2nd Brigade, 1st Cavalry Division, District of West Tennessee, to November, 1864. 2nd Brigade, 5th Division, Wilson's Cavalry Corps, Military Division Mississippi, to June, 1865. Dept. of Mississippi to September, 1865.

SERVICE.—Moved to Bird's Point, Mo., February 17, 1862. Expedition against Thompson's forces February 25-29. Moved to New Madrid, Mo., March 4. Actions at New Madrid March 13-14. Operations against Island No. 10 March 16-April 8. Expedition to Fort Pillow, Tenn., April 12-17. Moved to Hamburg Landing, Tenn., April 22. Action at Birmingham April 24. Monterey April 28-29. Advance on and siege of Corinth, Miss., April 29-May 30. Reconnoissance to Memphis & Charleston Railroad April 30. Glendale May 8. Farmington May 9. Near Farmington May 12. Reconnoissance to Memphis & Charleston Railroad May 13-15. Expedition to Booneville May 28-30. Booneville May 29. Occupation of Corinth and pursuit to Booneville May 30-June 12. Tuscumbia Creek May 31-June 1. Blackland June 4. Reconnoissance toward Baldwyn June 6. Reconnoissance to Guntown, Baldwyn, etc., June 9-10. Booneville July 1. Brown Springs July 21. At Rienzi till September. Rienzi August 26. Payton's Mills September 19. Iuka September 19-20. Battle of Corinth, Miss., October 3-4. Pursuit to Ripley October 5-12. Capture of Ripley and Orizaba November 2. Grant's Central Mississippi Campaign November, 1862, to January, 1863. Warsham's Creek November 6, 1862. LaGrange November 8-9. Coldwater November 8. Hudsonville November 9. Reconnoissance to Holly Springs November 12-14. Holly Springs November 13-14. Expedition to Ripley November 19-20. Ripley November 20. Waterford or Lumpkin's Mill November 29-30. Tallahatchie River November 30. About Oxford December 1-3. Yocana River and Spring Dale Bridge December 3. Water Valley December 4. Coffeeville December 5. Expedition against Mobile & Ohio Railroad December 14-19. Ripley December 23-25. Prairie Station February 21, 1863. Davis Mills March 14 (Detachment). Expedition to Mt. Pleasant, Miss., April 5-7. Grierson's Raid from LaGrange to Baton Rouge, La., April 17-May 2 (Detachment). Pontototoc, Miss., April 19. Palo Alto and Okolona April 21-22. Birmingham, Miss., April 24 (Detachment). Scout from LaGrange into Northern Mississippi April 29-May 5. Expedition from LaGrange to Panola, Miss., May 11-15. Walnut Hill and Pigeon Roost May 15. Tuskahoma May 15. Expedition from LaGrange to Senatobia, Miss., May 21-26. Senatobia May 23. Hernando May 28. Operations in West Mississippi June 15-22. Near Holly Springs June 16-17. Coldwater Bridge June 18 (Detachment). Matthews Ferry, Coldwater River, June 20 (Detachment). Jackson July 13. LaGrange July 16. Expedition from Memphis to Grenada, Miss., August 14-23. Grenada August 14. Expedition from Memphis to Hernando, Miss., October 10-11 (4 Cos.). Operations on Memphis & Charleston Railroad November 3-5. Colliersville, Tenn., and Coldwater, Miss., November 3. Moscow November 5. Operations on Memphis & Charleston Railroad against Lee's attack November 28-December 10. Salisbury December 3. Wolf Bridge, near Moscow, December 3-4. Pursuit of Forrest December 22-30. Colliersville, Tenn., December 27-28. At Memphis till February 5, 1864. Smith's Raid from Colliersville to Okolona, Miss., February 11-26. Wall Hill February 12. West Point, Miss., February 20-21. Okolona February 21. Ellis Bridge February 21. Ivy's Hill, near Okolona, February 22. Veterans on furlough April-May. Smith's Expedition to Tupelo, Miss., July 5-21. Near Ripley July 7. Camargo's Cross Roads, near Harrisburg, July 13. Tupelo July 14-15. Old Town Creek July 15. Smith's Expedition to Oxford, Miss., August 1-30. Tallahatchie River August 7-9. Hurricane Creek and Oxford August 9. Hurricane Creek August 13-14 and 19. Oxford August 19. Operations in Tennessee and Alabama against Hood, and Nashville Campaign October to January, 1865. Eastport, Miss., October 10, 1864 (Detachment). Near Hernando October 11 (Detachment). Expedition from Memphis to Moscow November 9-13. Shoal Creek November 11. On line of Shoal Creek November 16-20. Butler Creek November 22. Campbellsville and Lynnville November 24. In front of Columbia November 24-27. Lawrenceburg November 27. Mt. Carmel November 29. Battles of Franklin November 30; Nashville December 15-16. Pursuit of Hood December 17-29. West Harpeth River December 17. Spring Hill December 18. Rutherford Creek and Curtis Creek December 19. Lawrenceburg December 22. Lynnville and Richland Creek December 24. Richland Creek December 25. King's Gap, near Pulaski, December 25. Egypt Station, Miss., December 28 (Co. "E"). Tuscumbia February 20, 1865. Duty at Huntsville and Florence, Ala., Eastport, Miss., and Gravelly Springs, Ala., till June, 1865. Expedition to Russellville, Ala., February 19-23, 1865, and in the Dept. of Mississippi till September. Mustered out September 19, 1865.

Regiment lost during service 1 Officer and 59 Enlisted men killed and mortally wounded and 2 Officers and 207 Enlisted men by disease. Total 269.

3rd REGIMENT CAVALRY.

Organized at Keokuk August 30 to September 14, 1861. Moved to Benton Barracks, Mo., November 4-6, and duty there till February 4, 1862. (Cos. "E," "F" "G" and "H" detached to Jefferson City, Mo., December 12, 1861, and duty in Northern and Southern Missouri till July, 1863. See service following that of Regiment.) Cos. "A," "B," "C," "D," "I," "K," "L" and "M" moved to Rolla, Mo., February 4-6, 1862. (Cos. "I" and "K" detached to garrison, Salem, Mo., February 11, 1862. Scout to Mawameck February 12. Expedition to Mt. Vernon February 18-19. Action at West Plains February 20. Scouting after Coleman's guerillas till April. Actions near Salem February 28 and March 18. Rejoin Regiment near Forsythe April, 1862.) Regiment march to join General Curtis February 14-18. (Co. "L" detached at Springfield, Mo.) Attached to Curtis' Army of Southwest Missouri, Dept. of Missouri, February to May, 1862. 3rd Brigade, 1st Division, Army of Southwest Missouri, to July, 1862. District of Eastern Arkansas, Dept. of Missouri, to October, 1862. 3rd Brigade, 4th Division, District of Eastern Arkansas, to December, 1862. 2nd Brigade, Cavalry Division, District of Eastern Arkansas, Dept. of Tennessee, to January, 1863. 2nd Brigade, 2nd Cavalry Division, 13th Corps, Dept. of Tennessee, to April, 1863. 2nd Brigade, Cavalry Division, District of Eastern Arkansas, Dept. of Tennessee, to June, 1863. Bussy's Cavalry Brigade, Herron's Division, Dept. of Tennessee, to August, 1863. Reserve Cavalry Brigade, Army of Arkansas, to January, 1864. 1st Brigade, 1st Division, 7th Army Corps, Dept. of Arkansas, to May, 1864. 2nd Brigade, Cavalry Division, 16th Corps, Dept. of Tennessee, to June, 1864. 2nd Brigade, 2nd Cavalry Division, District of West Tennessee, to December, 1864. 2nd Brigade, Cavalry Division, District of West Tennessee, to February, 1865. 1st Brigade, 4th Division, Wilson's Cavalry Corps, Military Division Mississippi, to June, 1865. District of Georgia to August, 1865.

SERVICE.—Expedition to Fayetteville, Ark., February 22, 1862. Battles of Pea Ridge March 6-8. (Cos. "D" and "M" escort prisoners to Rolla, Mo., March 12-31.) March to Batesville via Cassville, Forsythe, Osage and West Plains April 6-May 1. (Cos. "L" and "M" detached at Lebanon, Mo., operating against guerillas till November, 1862; then join Cos. "E," "F," "G" and "H".) (Co. "D" guard train to Rolla, Mo., May 25 to June 20.) Action at Kickapoo Bottom, near Sylamore, May 29. Sylamore May 30. Foraging and scouting at Sulphur Rock June 1-22. Waddell's Farm, Village Creek, June 12. March from Batesville to Clarendon on White River June 25-July 9. Waddell's Farm June 27 (Co. "K"). Stewart's Plantation, Village Creek, June 27. Bayou Cache July 6 (Co. "I"). Hill's Plantation, Cache River, July 7. March to Helena July 11-14. Duty there and scouting from White River to the St. Francis till June, 1863.. Expedition from Clarendon to Lawrenceville and St. Charles September 11-13, 1862. LaGrange September 11. Marianna and LaGrange November 8. Expedition to Arkansas Post November 16-21. Expedition to Grenada, Miss., November 27-December 5. Oakland, Miss., December 3. Expedition up St. Francis and Little Rivers March 5-12, 1863 (Detachment). Expedition to Big and Little Creeks and skirmishes March 6-10. Madison, Ark., March 9 (Detachment). Madison, Ark., April 14 (Detachment). LaGrange May 1. Polk's Plantation, Helena, May 25. Moved to Vicksburg, Miss., June 4-8. Siege of Vicksburg June 8-July 4. Advance on Jackson, Miss., July 5-10. Near Clinton July 8. Siege of Jackson July 10-17. Near Canton July 12. Canton, Bolton's Depot and Grant's Ferry, Pearl River, July 16. Bear Creek, near Canton, July 17. Canton July 18. At Flowers' Plantation till August 10. Raid from Big Black on Mississippi Central Railroad and to Memphis, Tenn., August 10-22.

Payne's Plantation, near Grenada, August 18. Panola August 20. Coldwater August 21. Moved to Helena, Ark., August 26; thence moved to Little Rock, arriving October 1. Duty at Berton, Ark., October 1 to December 20. Expedition to Mt. Ida November 10-18. Near Benton December 1. Expedition to Princeton December 8-10. Ordered to Little Rock December 20. Regiment Veteranize January 5, 1864. Veterans on furlough January 6 to February 5. At St. Louis, Mo., February 6 to April 26. Ordered to Memphis, Tenn., April 26. Operations against Forest May to August. Sturgis' Expedition to Guntown, Miss., June 1-13. Near Guntown June 10. Ripley June 11. Smith's Expedition to Tupelo, Miss., July 5-21. Saulsbury July 2. Near Kelly's Mills July 8. Cherry Creek July 10. Huston Road July 12. Okolona July 12-13. Harrisburg, near Tupelo, July 14-15. Old Town or Tishamingo Creek July 15. Ellistown July 16 and 21. Smith's Expedition to Oxford, Miss., August 1-30. Tallahatchie River August 7-9. Holly Springs August 8. Hurricane Creek and Oxford August 9. Hurricane Creek August 13, 14 and 19. College Hill August 21. Hurricane Creek August 22. Repulse of Forrest's attack on Memphis August 21 (Detachment). Moved to Brownsville, Ark., September 2. Campaign against Price in Arkansas and Missouri September-November. Independence, Big Blue and State Line October 22. Westport October 23. Battles of Charlot, Marias des Cygnes, Mine Creek, Little Osage River October 25. White's Station, Tenn., December 4 (Detachment). Grierson's Raid from Memphis on Mobile & Ohio Railroad December 27, 1864, to January 6, 1865 (Detachment). Near White's Station December 25. Okolona December 27. Egypt Station, Miss., December 28. Mechanicsburg January 3, 1865. At the Pond January 4. Moved from Vicksburg, Miss., to Memphis, Tenn.; thence to Louisville, Ky., January 6-15, 1865, and rejoin Regiment. Regiment at St. Louis, Mo., and Louisville, Ky., till February, 1865. Moved to Chickasaw, Ala.; Wilson's Raid to Macon, Ga., March 22-April 24. Montevallo March 31. Six-Mile Creek March 31. Maplesville April 1 (Co. "L"). Ebeneezer Church, near Maplesville, April 1. Selma April 2. Fike's Ferry, Cahawba River, April 7 (Co. "B"). Montgomery April 12. Columbus, Ga., April 16. Capture of Macon April 20. Duty at Macon and at Atlanta, Ga., till August. Mustered out August 9, 1865.

Regiment lost during service 5 Officers and 79 Enlisted men killed and mortally wounded and 4 Officers and 230 Enlisted men by disease. Total 318.

Companies "E," "F," "G" and "H" ordered to Jefferson City, Mo., December 12, 1861. Attached to Army of Southwest Missouri to February, 1862. District of North Missouri to August, 1862. District of Southwest Missouri to November, 1862. Cavalry Brigade, District of Southeast Missouri, to June, 1863. Reserve Cavalry Brigade, Army of Southeast Missouri, to August, 1863. Reserve Brigade, 1st Cavalry Division, Arkansas Expedition, to October, 1863.

SERVICE.—Engaged in operations against guerillas about Booneville, Glasgow, Fulton and in North Missouri at Lebanon, and in Southwest Missouri covering frontier from Iron Mountain to Boston Mountains till June, 1863. Companies "L" and "M" joined November, 1862. Actions at Florida, Mo., May 22, 1862. Salt River, near Florida, May 31. Boles' Farm, Florida, July 22 and 24. Santa Fe July 24-25. Brown Springs July 27. Moore's Mills, near Fulton, July 28. Kirksville August 26. Occupation of Newtonia December 4. Hartsville, Wood's Fork, January 11, 1863. Operations against Marmaduke April 17-May 2. Cape Girardeau April 26. Near Whitewater Bridge April 27. Castor River, near Bloomfield, April 29. Bloomfield April 30. Chalk Bluffs, St. Francis River, April 30-May 1. Davidson's march to Clarendon, Ark., August 1-8. Steele's Expedition to Little Rock August 8-September 10. Reed's Bridge or Bayou Metoe August 27. Shallow Ford, Bayou Metoe, August 30. Bayou Fourche and capture of Little Rock September 10. Rejoined Regiment at Little Rock October 1, 1863.

4th REGIMENT CAVALRY.

Organized at Camp Harlan, Mount Pleasant, September to November, 1861. Companies muster in "A," "E" and "F" November 23, "B," "C," "D," "I," "K" and "M" November 25, "G" November 27, "L" December 24, and "H" January 1, 1862. Duty at Camp Harlan till February, 1862. 1st Battalion moved to St. Louis, Mo., February 26, 2nd Battalion February 28 and 3rd Battalion March 3, 1862. At Benton Barracks, Mo., till March 10. Ordered to Rolla, Mo., March 10; thence to Springfield, Mo., and duty there till April 14. Attached to 2nd Division, Army of Southwest Missouri, Dept. of Missouri, to July, 1862. District of Eastern Arkansas, Dept. of Missouri, to December, 1862. 2nd Brigade, 1st Cavalry Division, District of Eastern Arkansas, Dept. of Tennessee, to January, 1863. 2nd Brigade, 2nd Cavalry Division, 13th Corps, Dept. of Tennessee, to May, 1863. Unattached, 15th Army Corps, Army of Tennessee, to August, 1863. Winslow's Cavalry Brigade, 17th Corps, to May, 1864. 2nd Brigade, 1st Cavalry Division, 16th Corps, to July, 1864. 2nd Brigade, 2nd Cavalry Division, District of West Tennessee, to November, 1864. 1st Brigade, 4th Division, Wilson's Cavalry Corps, Military Division Mississippi, to December, 1864. 2nd Brigade, Cavalry Division, District of West Tennessee, to February, 1865. 1st Brigade, 4th Division, Cavalry Corps, Military Division Mississippi, to June, 1865. Dept. of Georgia to August, 1865.

SERVICE.—Expedition to Salem, Mo., March 12-19, 1862 (Cos. "F" and "L"). Ordered to join Curtis at Batesville, Ark., April 14. Skirmish at Nitre Cave, White River, April 18 (Detachment Cos. "G" and "K"). Talbot's Farm, White River, April 19 (Detachment Cos. "E," "F," "G" and "K"). Skirmish, White River, May 6. Little Red River June 5. (Co. "F" detached for duty with Chief Commissary and as provost guard at Helena, Ark., May, 1862, to April, 1863.) Mt. Olive June 7, 1862 (Co. "F"). Gist's Plantation July 14, 1862 (Co. "F"). March to Helena, Ark., June 11-July 14. Duty at Helena till April, 1863. Polk's Plantation September 20, 1862 (Detachment Co. "D"). Expedition from Helena to LaGrange September 26 (2 Cos.). Jones' Lane or Lick Creek October 11 (Detachment Cos. "A," "G" and "H"). Marianna and LaGrange November 8. Expedition from Helena to Arkansas Post November 16-21, and to Grenada, Miss., November 27-December 5. Oakland, Miss., December 3. Expedition to Big and Little Creeks March 6-12, 1863. Big Creek March 8. St. Charles and St. Francis Counties April 8. Moved to Milliken's Bend, La., April 28-30. Reconnoissance to Bayou Macon May 1-4. March to New Carthage May 5-8. (Co. "G" detached on courier duty at Young's Point, La., during May.) Fourteen-Mile Creek May 12-13. Mississippi Springs May 13. Hall's Ferry May 13 (Detachment). Baldwyn's Ferry May 13 (Detachment). Jackson May 14. Haines Bluff May 18 (Co. "B"). Siege of Vicksburg, Miss., May 18-July 4. Engaged in outpost duty against Johnston between Big Black and Yazoo Rivers. Mechanicsburg May 24 and 29. Expedition from Haines Bluff to Satartia and Mechanicsville June 2-8 (Detachment). Barronsville June 18. Bear Creek or Jones' Plantation June 22 (Cos. "A," "F," "I" and "K"). Big Black River, near Birdsong Ferry, June 22 (Detachment). Hill's Plantation, near Bear Creek, June 22. Messenger's Ferry, Big Black River, June 26. Advance on Jackson July 5-10. Siege of Jackson July 10-17. Near Canton July 12. Bolton's Depot July 16. Bear Creek, Canton, July 17. Canton July 18. Raid from Big Black on Mississippi Central Railroad and to Memphis, Tenn., August 10-22. Payne's Plantation, near Grenada, August 18. Panola August 20. Coldwater August 21. Expedition to Yazoo City September 21-October 1 (Detachment). Brownsville September 28. Morris Ford, near Burton, September 29. Expedition toward Canton October 14-20. Brownsville October 15. Canton Road, near Brownsville, October 15-16. Near Clinton and Vernon Cross

Roads October 16. Bogue Chitto Creek October 17. Robinson's Mills, near Livingston, October 17. Louisville Road, near Clinton and Brownsville, October 18. Expedition to Natchez December 4-17 (Detachment Cos. "C," "H," "I," "K," "L" and "M"). Near Natchez December 7. Meridian Campaign February 3-28, 1864. Big Black River Bridge February 3. Raymond Road, Edwards Ferry, Champion's Hill, Baker's Creek and near Bolton's Depot February 4. Jackson and Clinton February 5. Brandon February 7. Morton February 8. Meridian February 9-13. Hillsborough February 10. Tallahatta February 13. Meridian February 14. Near Meridian February 19. Veterans on furlough March 4 to April 24. Reported at Memphis, Tenn., April 24. Non-Veterans at Vicksburg, Miss., till April 29; then moved to Memphis. Sturgis' Campaign against Forrest April 30-May 12. Sturgis' Expedition to Guntown, Miss., June 1-13. Ripley June 7. Brice's Cross Roads, near Guntown, June 10. Ripley June 11. Smith's Expedition to Tupelo, Miss., July 5-21. Near Ripley July 7. Cherry Creek July 10. Plentitude July 10. Harrisburg Road July 13. Tupelo July 14-15. Old Town or Tishamingo Creek July 15. Smith's Expedition to Oxford, Miss., August 1-30. Tallahatchie River August 7-9. Hurricane Creek and Oxford August 9. Hurricane Creek August 13, 14 and 19. College Hill August 21. Oxford August 22. (Forrest's attack on Memphis August 21—Co. "G.") Moved to Little Rock, Ark., September 2-9. Campaign against Price in Arkansas and Missouri September 17-November 30. Moved to Batesville and Pocahontas, Ark.; thence to Cape Girardeau, St. Louis, Jefferson City and Independence, Mo., Trading Post and Fort Scott, Kansas, Pea Ridge and Fayetteville, Ark., Tahlequah and Webber's Falls, Ind. Ter., returning via Pea Ridge, Springfield and Rolla to St. Louis. Engaged at Brownsville September 28. Morris Bluff September 29 (Co. "D"). Little Blue October 21. Independence October 22. Westport, Big Blue and State Line October 23. Trading Post October 25. Marias des Cygnes, Osage, Mine Creek October 25. Charlot Prairie October 25. At St. Louis till December 9; then at Louisville, Ky., till February, 1865. (A detachment at Memphis, Tenn., September 1 to December 20, 1864. Scout near Memphis November 10. Skirmish on Germantown Pike, near Memphis, December 14, Detachments of Cos. "A" and "B." Grierson's Raid on Mobile & Ohio Railroad December 21, 1864, to January 5, 1865. Okolona, Miss., December 27, 1864. Egypt Station December 28. Franklin January 2, 1865. Rejoined Regiment at Louisville, Ky., January 15, 1865.) Dismounted men of Regiment moved from Memphis, Tenn., to Louisville, Ky., January 2, 1865. Moved to Gravelly Springs, Ala., February, 1865, and duty there till March 20. Expedition to Florence March 1-6. Wilson's Raid to Macon, Ga., March 20 to May 10. (Co. "G" escort to General Upton, Commanding Division.) Montevallo March 30. Near Montevallo March 31. Six-Mile Creek March 31. Ebenezer Church April 1. Selma April 2. Fike's Ferry, Cahawba River, April 7. Wetumpka April 13. Columbus, Ga., April 16. Capture of Macon April 20. Duty at Macon and Atlanta, Ga., till August. Mustered out at Atlanta August 10, 1865, and discharged at Davenport, Ia., August 24, 1865.

Regiment lost during service 4 Officers and 51 Enlisted men killed and mortally wounded and 5 Officers and 194 Enlisted men by disease. Total 254.

5th REGIMENT CAVALRY.

Organized as Curtis Horse by order of General Fremont. Cos. "A," "B," "C" and "D" organized at Omaha, Neb., September 14 to November 13, 1861; "E" at Dubuque, Ia.; "F" in Missouri, as Fremont Hussars, October 25, 1861; "H" at Benton Barracks, Mo., December 28, 1861; "G," "I" and "K" as 1st, 2nd and 3rd Independent Companies, Minnesota Cavalry, at Fort Snelling, Minn., October 29 to December 20, 1861; "L" as Naughton's Irish Dragoons at Jefferson City, Mo., and "M" as Osage Rifles at St. Louis, Mo., November 1, 1861. Duty at Benton Barracks, Mo., till February,

1862. Moved to Fort Henry, Tenn., February 8-11. Patrol duty during battle of Fort Donelson. Expedition to destroy railroad bridge over Tennessee River February 14-16. Attached to Dept. of the Tennessee, Unassigned, to November, 1862. District of Columbus, Ky., 13th Corps, Dept. of Tennessee, to December, 1862. District of Columbus, 16th Corps, to June, 1863. 1st Brigade, 2nd Division, Cavalry Corps, Army of the Cumberland, to August, 1863. 3rd Brigade, 2nd Division, Cavalry Corps, Cumberland, to November, 1863. 1st Brigade, 2nd Division, Cavalry Corps, Cumberland, to April, 1864. 1st Brigade, 3rd Division Cavalry Corps, Cumberland, to November, 1864. 2nd Brigade, 6th Division, Wilson's Cavalry Corps, Military Division Mississippi, to December, 1864. 1st Brigade, 6th Division, Cavalry Corps, Military Division Mississippi, December, 1864. 2nd Brigade, 6th Division, Cavalry Corps, Military Division Mississippi, to February, 1865. 2nd Brigade, 4th Division, Wilson's Cavalry Corps, to June, 1865. Dept. of Georgia to August, 1865.

SERVICE.—Garrison duty at Forts Henry and Heiman till February 5, 1863. Skirmish, Agnew's Ferry, March 25, 1862 (Detachment of Co. "K"). Moved to Savannah, Tenn., March 28-April 1 (Cos. "G," "I" and "K"). Moved toward Nashville, Tenn., repairing roads and erecting telegraph lines April 3-6. Advance on and siege of Corinth, Miss., April 29-May 30. Acting as escort to Telegraph Corps. Expedition from Trenton to Paris and Dresden May 2-9. Dresden May 5. Lockridge's Mills May 5. Occupation of Corinth May 30. Pursuit to Booneville May 31-June 12. Designated 5th Iowa Cavalry June, 1862. Duty at Humboldt, Tenn., till August. Companies "G," "I" and "K" rejoin Regiment. Paris, Tenn., March 11, 1862 (1st Battalion). Expedition to Paris March 31-April 2 (Co. "F"). Near Fort Donelson August 23 (Detachment). Fort Donelson August 23. Cumberland Iron Works August 26. Expedition to Clarksville September 5-10. New Providence September 6 (Cos. "G," "I" and "K"). Clarksville September 7. Operations about Forts Donelson and Henry September 18-23. Near Lexington Landing October 1 (Detachment). Scout toward Eddyville October 29-November 10 (Cos. "G," "I" and "K"). Garrettsburg, Ky., November 6. Expedition from Fort Heiman December 18-28 (Cos. "G," "I" and "K"). Waverly January 16, 1863. Cumberland Iron Works, Fort Donelson, February 3, 1863. Moved to Fort Donelson February 5, and duty there till June 5. Destruction of Bridge, Mobile & Ohio Railroad, February 15. Paris, Tenn., March 14. Waverly April 10 (Detachment). Stewartsborough April 12 (1 Co.). Moved to Murfreesboro and Nashville, Tenn., June 5-11. Scout on Middletown and Eaglesville Pike June 10. Expedition to Lebanon June 15-17. Lebanon June 16. Middle Tennessee (or Tullahoma) Campaign June 23-July 7. Guy's Gap, Fosterville, June 25. Fosterville June 27. Expedition to Huntsville July 13-22. Moved to McMinnville September 6-8, and operating against Guerillas till October. Wartrace September 6. Operations against Wheeler and Roddy September 30-October 17. Garrison Creek near Fosterville October 6. Wartrace October 6. Sugar Creek October 9. Tennessee River October 10. At Maysville till January, 1864. Expedition from Maysville to Whitesburg and Decatur November 14-17, 1863, to destroy boats on the Tennessee River. Outpost duty on line of the Tennessee River, from south of Huntsville to Bellefonte November and December. Veteranize January, 1864. On Veteran furlough January 7 to April 24. Non-Veterans at Nashville, Tenn., till May. Companies "G," "I" and "K" detached February 25, 1864, and designated Brackett's Battalion, Minnesota Cavalry. Moved from Nashville to Pulaski and guard Nashville & Decatur Railroad till July. Moved to Decatur July 5. Rousseau's Raid from Decatur on West Point & Montgomery Railroad July 10-22. Near Coosa River July 13. Ten Island Ford, Coosa River, July 14. Chehaw Station, West Point & Montgomery Railroad July 18. Siege of Atlanta July 22-August 25. McCook's Raid on Atlanta & West Point

Railroad July 27-31. Lovejoy Station July 29. Clear Creek July 30. Near Newnan August 15. Flank movement on Jonesboro August 25-30. Flint River Station August 30. Jonesboro Aug. 31-September 1. (5th Iowa Infantry consolidated with Regiment as Companies "G" and "I" September 1, 1864.) Lovejoy Station September 2-6. Operations against Hood in North Georgia and North Alabama September 29-November 3. Camp Creek September 30. Sweetwater and Noyes Creek, near Powder Springs October 1-3. Van Wert October 9. Nashville Campaign November-December. Columbia, Duck River, November 24-27. Crossing of Duck River November 28. Columbia Ford November 28-29. Battle of Nashville December 15-16. Pursuit of Hood December 17-28. Franklin and West Harpeth River December 17. Spring Hill December 18. Richland Creek December 24. King's Gap near Pulaski December 25. At Gravelly Springs, Ala., till March, 1865. Wilson's Raid on Macon, Ga., March 22-April 24. Near Elyton March 28. Near Montevallo March 31. Ebenezer Church, near Maysville April 1. Selma April 2. Montgomery April 12. Columbus, Ga., April 16. Capture of Macon April 20. Duty in North Georgia and at Nashville, Tenn., till August. Mustered out August 11, 1865.

Regiment lost during service 7 Officers 58 Enlisted men killed and mortally wounded and 2 Officers and 179 Enlisted men by disease. Total 246.

6th REGIMENT CAVALRY.

Organized at Davenport January 31 to March 5, 1863. Moved to Sioux City, Dakota, March 16-April 26, 1863. Operations against hostile Indians about Fort Randall May and June. Moved to Fort Pierre, and duty there till July. Sully's Expedition against hostile Sioux Indians August 13-September 11. Actions at White Stone Hill September 3 and 5. Duty at Fort Sully, Fort Randall and Sioux City till June, 1864. Sully's Expedition against hostile Sioux Indians June 26-October 8. Engagement at Tah kah a kuty July 28. Two Hills, Bad Lands, Little Missouri River, August 8. Expedition from Fort Rice to relief of Fisk's Emigrant train September 11-30. Fort Rice September 27. Duty by Detachments at Fort Randall, Sioux City, Fort Berthold, Yankton and the Sioux and Winnebago Indian Agencies till October, 1865. Mustered out October 17, 1865.

Regiment lost during service 1 Officer and 21 Enlisted men killed and mortally wounded and 1 Officer and 74 Enlisted men by disease. Total 97.

7th REGIMENT CAVALRY.

Organized at Davenport April 27 to July 13, 1863, Companies "A" to "H." Company "I" organized as Sioux City Cavalry November 14, 1861, and three Companies organized for 41st Iowa Battalion assigned as Companies "K," "L" and "M." Regiment moved to Omaha, Neb., June, 1863, and assigned to duty at various points in Nebraska and Dakota, as garrison, guarding lines of telegraph and travel, escorting trains and protecting Emigrants, having frequent combats with Indians in the Departments of Missouri, Kansas and the Northwest. Sully's Expedition against hostile Sioux Indians August 13-September 11, 1863. Actions at Whitestone Hill September 3 and 5. Niobrara December 4, 1863 (1 Co.). Sully's Expedition against hostile Sioux Indians July 25-October 8, 1864. Actions at Tah kah a kuty July 25. (Cos. "K" and "M"). Two Hills, Bad Lands, Little Missouri River, August 8 (Cos. "K" and "M"). Scout on Smoky Hill Fork, Kansas, August 1-5 (Co. "H"). Smoky Hill Crossing August 16 (Co. "H"). Operations against Indians in Nebraska August 11-November 24, 1864. Fort Cottonwood August 28 and September 18 (Co. "B"). Near Fort Cottonwood September 20. Detachment of Company "C." Operations against Indians in Nebraska and Colorado Territories September 29-November 30 (1st Battalion). Cow Creek near Fort Zarah December 4 (Detachment). Julesburg, Indian Territory, January 7, 1865 (Co. "F"). Rush Creek

February 8 (Co. "D"). Mud Springs February 8-9. Rush Creek February 9. Boyd's Station June 3 (Co. "E"). Cow Creek Station, Kansas, June 12 (Co. "G"). Horse Creek, Dakota Ter., June 14 (Cos. "B" and "D"). Tongue River August 29 (Co. "F"). Duty on the plains till June, 1866. Mustered out June 22, 1866.

Killed and mortally wounded 1 Officer 29 Enlisted men; by disease 1 Officer 93 Enlisted men. Total 124.

8th REGIMENT CAVALRY.

Organized at Davenport September 30, 1863. Moved to Chattanooga, Tenn., October 17-22, thence to Nashville, Tenn., November 14-16. Attached to Defences of Nashville & Northwestern Railroad, Dept. of the Cumberland, to March, 1864. 1st Brigade, 1st Division, Cavalry Corps, Army Cumberland, and to November, 1864. 1st Brigade, 1st Division, Cavalry Corps, Military Division Mississippi, to June, 1865. Dept. of Georgia to August, 1865.

SERVICE.—Guard and garrison duty and operating against guerrillas at Waverly and points west of Nashville till March, 1864. Moved to Nashville, Tenn., March 13-17, thence to Chattanooga and Cleveland, Tenn., April 1-15. Atlanta (Ga.) Campaign May to September. Varnell's Station May 7. Demonstration on Rocky Faced Ridge and Dalton May 8-13. Battle of Resaca May 14-15. Near Cassville May 19. Stilesborough May 23. Burnt Hickory May 24. Operations on line of Pumpkin Vine Creek and battles about Dallas, New Hope Church and Allatoona Hills May 25-June 5. Near Burned Church May 26. Ackworth June 3-4. Operations about Marietta and against Kenesaw Mountain June 9-July 2. Lost Mountain June 15-17. Assault on Kenesaw June 27. Nickajack Creek July 2-5. Chattahoochie River July 6-17. McCook's Raid on Atlanta & West Point Railroad July 27-31. Lovejoy Station July 29. Clear Creek and near Newnan July 30. At Kingston, Ga., till Sept. 17. Pursuit of Wheeler Sept. 1-8. Moved to Nashville, Tenn., Sept. 17, thence to Franklin, Tenn. Pursuit of Forest September 25-October 10. Pulaski September 27. Florence, Ala., October 6-7. Muscle Shoals near Florence October 30. Near Shoal Creek October 31. Nashville Campaign November-December. Shoal Creek near Florence November 5-6 and 9. On line of Shoal Creek November 16-20. Fouche Springs November 23. Campbellsville November 24. Front of Columbia November 24-27. Franklin November 30. Battle of Nashville December 15-16. Lynnville December 24-25. Pulaski December 25-26. Expedition into Mississippi January 5-21, 1865. Wilson's Raid to Macon, Ga., March 22-May 1. Northport near Tuscaloosa April 3. Occupation of Tuscaloosa April 4. Occupation of Talladega April 22. Munford's Station April 23. Rejoined Wilson at Macon May 1. Duty at Macon and in Georgia till August. Mustered out August 13, 1865.

Regiment lost during service 15 Enlisted men killed and mortally wounded and 3 Officers and 176 Enlisted men by disease. Total 194.

9th REGIMENT CAVALRY.

Organized at Davenport and mustered in November 30, 1863. Moved to St. Louis, Mo., December 8-11, thence to Benton Barracks, Mo., December 16, and duty there till April, 1864. Attached to District of St. Louis, Mo., Dept. Missouri, to May, 1864. 3rd (Cavalry) Brigade, 2nd Division, 7th Army Corps, Dept. of Arkansas, to September, 1864. 3rd Brigade, Cavalry Division, 7th Corps, to February, 1865. Cavalry Brigade, Little Rock, 1st Division, 7th Corps, to August, 1865. Dept. of Arkansas to March, 1866.

SERVICE.—Moved to Rolla, Mo., and return to Jefferson Barracks April 14-19, 1864. Duty there till May 15. Moved to Duvall's Bluff, Ark., May 15-23, and duty there till September. West Point June 16. Clarendon June 25-26. Expedition from Little Rock to Little Red River August 6-16. Jones' Hay Station August 24. Long Prairie August 24. Brownsville August 25. Bull Bayou August 26. Expedition in pursuit of Shelby August 27-September 6. Searcy September 6. At Austin and

Brownsville till November 4. Brownsville October 30. Pursuit of Price November 4-18. Expedition from Brownsville to Des Arc, and skirmish December 6 (Detachment). Expedition to Fort Smith November 2-24 (Detachment). At Brownsville till June, 1865. Expedition from Brownsville to Augusta January 4-27. Moved to Lewisburg June 11. Duty there and at various points in Arkansas till March, 1866. Mustered out March 23, 1866.

1st BATTERY LIGHT ARTILLERY.

Organized at Burlington August 17, 1861, and duty there till December. Ordered to Benton Barracks, Mo.; thence to Rolla, Mo., and joined General Curtis. Attached to 1st Brigade, Army of Southwest Missouri, to February, 1862. 1st Brigade, 4th Division, Army of Southwest Missouri, to May, 1862. Artillery, 2nd Division, Army of Southwest Missouri, to July, 1862. District of Eastern Arkansas, Dept. of Missouri, to December, 1862. 3rd Brigade, 11th Division, Right Wing 13th Army Corps (Old), Dept. of the Tennessee, December, 1862. 3rd Brigade, 4th Division, Sherman's Yazoo Expedition, to January, 1863. Artillery, 1st Division, 15th Army Corps, Army of the Tennessee, to April, 1864. Artillery, 4th Division, 15th Corps, to September, 1864. Artillery, 1st Division, 15th Corps, to November, 1864. Artillery Reserve, Nashville, Tenn., to July, 1865.

SERVICE.—Curtis' advance on Springfield, Mo., January 22-February 12, 1862. Pursuit of Price in Arkansas February 14-29. Battle of Pea Ridge, Ark., March 6-8. March to Batesville, Ark., April 5-May 3; thence to Helena, Ark., May 25-July 14. Expedition from Helena to mouth of White River, August 6-8. Expedition from Helena to Eunice August 28-September 3. Expedition from Helena to Arkansas Post November 16-21, and to Grenada, Miss., November 27-December 7. Mitchell's Cross Roads December 1. Sherman's Yazoo Expedition December 22, 1862, to January 2, 1863. Chickasaw Bayou December 26-28, 1862. Chickasaw Bluffs December 29. Expedition to Arkansas Post, Ark., January 3-10, 1863. Assault on and capture of Fort Hindman, Arkansas Post, January 10-11. Moved to Young's Point, La., January 17-23, and duty there till April. Expedition to Greenville, Black Bayou and Deer Creek April 5-14. Demonstration on Haines and Drumgould's Bluffs April 29-May 2. Moved to join army in rear of Vicksburg, via Richmond and Grand Gulf, May 2-14. Jackson, Miss., May 14. Siege of Vicksburg May 18-July 4. Assaults on Vicksburg May 19 and 22. Advance on Jackson, Miss., July 5-10. Siege of Jackson July 10-17. At Big Black till September 22. Moved to Memphis, Tenn.; thence to Chattanooga September 22-November 21. Operations on Memphis & Charleston Railroad in Alabama October 20-29. Cherokee Station October 21 and 29. Cane Creek October 26. Tuscumbia October 26-27. Battles of Chattanooga November 23-27. Lookout Mountain November 23-24. Mission Ridge November 25. Ringgold Gap, Taylor's Ridge, November 27. Garrison duty in Alabama till April, 1864. Atlanta (Ga.) Campaign May 1 to August 8. Demonstration on Resaca May 8-13. Battle of Resaca May 14-15. Advance on Dallas May 18-25. Battles about Dallas, New Hope Church and Allatoona Hills May 25-June 5. Operations about Marietta and Kenesaw Mountain June 10-July 2. Assault on Kenesaw June 27. Nickajack Creek July 2-5. Chattahoochie River July 6-17. Battle of Atlanta July 22. Siege of Atlanta July 22-August 25. Ezra Chapel, Hood's second sortie, July 28. Flank movement on Jonesboro August 25-30. Battle of Jonesboro August 31-September 1. Lovejoy Station September 2-6. Operations against Hood in North Georgia and North Alabama October 1-26. Turkeytown, Ala., October 25. Ordered to Nashville, Tenn., and garrison duty there till July, 1865. Battle of Nashville, Tenn., December 15-16, 1864 (Reserve). Mustered out July 5, 1865.

Battery lost during service 10 Enlisted men killed and mortally wounded and 1 Officer and 50 Enlisted men by disease. Total 61.

2nd BATTERY LIGHT ARTILLERY.

Organized in Iowa at large and mustered in at Council Bluffs, Ia., August 18, 1861. Ordered to St. Louis, Mo., October, 1861, and duty at Benton Barracks till February, 1862. Attached to Dept. of Missouri to March, 1862. Artillery Division, Army of Mississippi, to April, 1862. 3rd Division, Army of Mississippi, to April, 1862. Artillery, 2nd Division, Army of Mississippi, to October, 1862. Artillery, District of Corinth, to November, 1862. Artillery, 2nd Brigade, 8th Division, 13th Corps (Old), Dept. of the Tennessee, to December, 1862. Artillery, 2nd Brigade, 8th Division, 16th Corps, to April, 1863. Artillery, 3rd Division, 15th Corps, to December, 1863. Artillery, 1st Division, 16th Corps, to December, 1864. Artillery, 2nd Brigade, 1st Division (Detachment), Army of Tennessee, Dept. of the Cumberland, to February, 1865. Artillery, 1st Division, 16th Corps, Military Division West Mississippi, to March, 1865. Artillery Brigade, 16th Corps, to August, 1865.

SERVICE.—Moved to Commerce, Mo., February 26, 1862. Operations against New Madrid, Mo., March 6-15. Actions at New Madrid March 3-4 and 13. Operations against Island No. 10 and pursuit to Tiptonville March 15-April 8. Riddell's Point March 18. Tiptonville April 8. Expedition to Fort Pillow, Tenn., April 13-17. Moved to Hamburg Landing, Tenn., April 18-22. Advance on and siege of Corinth, Miss., April 29-May 30. Action at Farmington May 9. Occupation of Corinth and pursuit to Booneville May 30-June 12. Expedition to Rienzi June 30-July 1. Duty there till August 18. March to Tuscumbia August 18-22. Moved to Iuka September 8-12. Battle of Iuka September 19. Battle of Corinth October 3-4. Pursuit to Ripley October 5-12. At Corinth till November 2. Moved to Grand Junction November 2. Grant's Central Mississippi Campaign November, 1862, to January, 1863. At LaGrange and Germantown, Tenn., till March 14. Moved to Memphis, thence to Young's Point, La., March 14-29. At Duckport till May. Moved to join army in rear of Vicksburg, Miss., May 2-14. Mississippi Springs May 13. Jackson May 14. Siege of Vicksburg May 18-July 4. Assaults on Vicksburg May 19 and 22. Expedition to Mechanicsburg May 26-June 4. Satartia June 4. Advance on Jackson July 5-10. Siege of Jackson July 10-17. At Big Black till November. Expedition to Canton October 14-20. Bogue Chitto Creek October 17. Ordered to Memphis, Tenn., November 7, and guard Memphis & Charleston Railroad at LaGrange till February, 1864. Ordered to Vicksburg, Miss. Meridian Campaign February 6-March 2. Return to Memphis and duty there till September. Sturgis' Expedition to Ripley April 30-May 9. Smith's Expedition to Tupelo, Miss., July 5-21. Camargo's Cross Roads, near Harrisburg, July 13. Harrisburg, near Tupelo, July 14-15. Old Town Creek July 15. Smith's Expedition to Oxford, Miss., August 1-30. Tallahatchie River August 7-9. Hurricane Creek August 13-14. Mower's Expedition up White River to Duvall's Bluff, Ark., September 1-7. March through Arkansas and Missouri in pursuit of Price September 17-November 16. Moved to Nashville, Tenn., November 24-December 1. Battle of Nashville December 15-16. Pursuit of Hood December 17-28. At Eastport, Miss., till February, 1865. Moved to New Orleans, La., February 9-22. Campaign against Mobile and its defences March 17-April 12. Siege of Spanish Fort and Fort Blakely March 26-April 8. Fort Blakely April 9. Occupation of Mobile April 12. March to Montgomery April 13-25. Duty there and at Meridian, Miss., till August. Mustered out August 7, 1865.

Battery lost during service 3 Enlisted men killed and mortally wounded and 29 Enlisted men by disease. Total 32.

3rd BATTERY LIGHT ARTILLERY ("DUBUQUE BATTERY").

Organized at Dubuque and mustered in September 24, 1861. Moved to St. Louis, Mo., September 26-30. Attached to Dept. of Missouri to January, 1862. Un-

attached, Army of Southwest Missouri, to February, 1862. 2nd Brigade, 4th Division, Army of Southwest Missouri, to May, 1862. Artillery, 2nd Division, Army of Southwest Missouri, to July, 1862. Artillery, District of Eastern Arkansas, Dept. of Missouri and Dept. of the Tennessee, to January, 1863. Artillery, 13th Division, 13th Army Corps, Dept. of the Tennessee, to July, 1863. Artillery, 13th Division, 16th Corps, to August, 1863. Artillery, 3rd Division, Arkansas Expedition, to January, 1864. Artillery, 3rd Division, 7th Army Corps, Dept. of Arkansas, to May, 1864. Artillery, 1st Division, 7th Corps, to August, 1865. Dept. of Arkansas to October, 1865.

SERVICE.—Moved to Pacific City, Mo., November 13, 1861, and duty there guarding Railroad till January 25, 1862. Moved to Rolla, Mo.; thence to Lebanon January 28-February 4. Curtis' advance on Springfield February 9-13. Pursuit of Price to Cassville February 13-16. Action at Sugar Creek February 17. Expedition toward Huntsville March 4. Battles of Pea Ridge March 6-8. March to Batesville April 5-May 10, thence to Helena May 25-July 14. Duty at Helena till August, 1863. Expedition from Helena to Grenada, Miss., November 27-December 5, 1862. Expedition up White River January 13-19, 1863. Expedition from Helena to Yazoo Pass by Moon Lake, Yazoo Pass, Coldwater and Tallahatchie Rivers and operations against Fort Pemberton and Greenwood February 24-April 8. Repulse of Holmes' attack on Helena July 4. Steele's Expedition to Little Rock August 11-September 10. Near Bayou Metoe August 26. Bayou Fourche and capture of Little Rock September 10. Rice's Expedition to Arkadelphia November 10-18. Duty at Little Rock till August, 1865. Expedition to Fort Smith September 25-October 13, 1864 (Detachment). Moved to Fort Smith August, 1865, thence to Davenport, Iowa, October. Mustered out Oct. 23, 1865.

Battery lost during service 3 Enlisted men killed and mortally wounded and 34 Enlisted men by disease. Total 37.

4th BATTERY LIGHT ARTILLERY.

Organized at Davenport November 23, 1863. Attached to the Dept. of the Northwest, to February, 1864. Defences of New Orleans, Dept. Gulf, to June, 1864. District of LaFourche, Dept. of the Gulf, to July, 1865.

SERVICE.—Garrison duty in the Dept. of the Northwest till February, 1864. Ordered to New Orleans, La., and duty in the Defences of that city and at Thibodeaux, La., District of LaFourche till July, 1865. Mustered out July 14, 1865.

Battery lost during service 5 Enlisted men by disease.

1st REGIMENT INFANTRY.

Organized at Keokuk for three months and mustered in May 14, 1861. Left State for Missouri June 13. Moved from Macon City to Renick and Booneville June 15-21. Lyons' advance on Springfield, Mo., June-July. Expedition to Forsyth July 20-25. Action at Forsyth July 22. Dug Springs August 2. Battle of Wilson's Creek August 10. Retreat to Springfield, thence to Rolla. Mustered out August 20, 1861.

Regiment lost during service 1 Officer and 19 Enlisted men killed and mortally wounded, and 8 Enlisted men by disease. Total 28.

1st REGIMENT INFANTRY COLORED.

Organized at Keokuk and mustered in Companies "A," "B," "C," "D," "E" and "F," October 11, 1863. Company "G" organized at St. Louis and mustered in October 15, 1863. Company "H" organized at St. Louis and mustered in November 21, 1863. Company "I" mustered in November 27, 1863, and Company "K" December 4, 1863. Moved to Helena, Ark., December 19-22, 1863. Attached to District of Eastern Arkansas, 7th Corps, Dept. of Arkansas. On post and garrison duty at Helena till March, 1864. Designation changed to 60th U. S. Colored Troops March 11, 1864, which see.

2nd REGIMENT INFANTRY.

Organized at Keokuk and mustered in May 27, 1861. Left State for Northern Missouri June 13. Attached to Dept. of Missouri, to October, 1861. 3rd Brigade, District of Cairo, October, 1861. District of St. Louis, Mo., Dept. Missouri, to February, 1862. 4th Brigade, 2nd Division, District of Cairo, February, 1862. 1st Brigade, 2nd Division, Army of the Tennessee, to July, 1862. 1st Brigade, 2nd Division, District of Corinth, to September, 1862. 3rd Brigade, 2nd Division, District Corinth, to October, 1862. 2nd Brigade, 2nd Division, District Corinth, to November, 1862. 1st Brigade, 2nd Division, District of Corinth, 13th Army Corps (Old), Dept. Tennessee, to December, 1862. 1st Brigade, District of Corinth, 17th Army Corps, to January, 1863. 1st Brigade, District of Corinth, 16th Army Corps, to March, 1863. 1st Brigade, 2nd Division, 16th Army Corps, to September, 1862. 1st Brigade, 4th Division, 15th Army Corps, to July, 1865.

SERVICE.—Guarding railroad with headquarters at St. Joseph, Mo., till July 26, 1861. At Bird Point, Mo., till August 14. At Ironton, Pilot Knob, till August 27. At Jackson, Mo., till September 8. At Fort Jefferson, Ky., till September 23, and at Bird's Point till October 2. Expedition to Charleston October 2-12. At St. Louis, Mo., till February 10, 1862. Moved to Fort Donelson, Tenn., February 10-14. Investment and capture of Fort Donelson February 14-16. Duty at Fort Donelson till March 5. Moved to Pittsburg Landing, Tenn., March 5-17. Battle of Shiloh, Tenn., April 6-7. Advance on and siege of Corinth, Miss., April 29-May 30. Duty at Corinth till September. March to Iuka September 18-22. Battle of Corinth October 3-4. Pursuit to Ruckerville October 5-12. Duty at Corinth till April, 1863. Skirmish at Little Brier Creek November 28, 1862. Expedition to intercept Forest December 9-14. Little Briar Creek December 12. Dodge's Expedition to intercept Forest December 18, 1862, to January 3, 1863. Expedition to Hamburg January 26, 1863, and to Jacinto February 25-27. Dodge's Expedition into Northern Alabama April 15-May 2. Bear Creek April 16-17. Tuscumbia April 23-24. Town Creek April 27-28. Duty at Corinth till August, and at LaGrange till November 1. March to Pulaski, Tenn., November 1-11. Duty there and along Nashville & Decatur Railroad, and at Decatur till May, 1864. Atlanta (Ga.) Campaign May 1-September 8. Movements on Resaca May 5-13. Snake Creek Gap May 10-12. Battle Resaca May 14-15. Ley's Ferry, Oostenaula River, May 15. Rome Cross Roads May 16. Operations on line of Pumpkin Vine Creek and battles about Dallas, New Hope Church and Allatoona Hills May 25-June 5. Operations about Marietta and against Kenesaw Mountain June 10-July 2. Nickajack Creek July 4. Chattahoochie River July 6-17. Decatur July 19. Battle of Atlanta July 22. Siege of Atlanta July 22-August 25. Skirmish on picket line Auguse 4. Flank movement on Jonesboro August 25-30. Action Flint River Station August 30. Battle of Jonesboro August 31-September 1. Lovejoy Station September 2-6. Moved to Rome September 26, and duty there till November 10. Reconnoissance and skirmishes on Cave Springs Road October 12-13. March to the sea November 15-December 10. Little Ogeechee River December 4. Jenks' Station December 7. Siege of Savannah December 10-21. Campaign of the Carolinas January to April, 1865. Sister's Ferry, Savannah River, January 31-February 5. South Edisto River February 9. North Edisto River February 12-13. Congaree Creek February 15. Columbia February 16-17. Lynch's Creek February 26. Battle of Bentonville, N. C., March 20-21. Occupation of Goldsboro March 24. Advance on Raleigh April 10-13. Occupation of Raleigh April 14. Bennett's House April 26. Surrender of Johnston and his army. March to Washington, D. C., via Richmond, Va., April 29-May 20. Grand Review May 24. Moved to Louisville, Ky., June. Mustered out July 12 and discharged at Davenport, Iowa, July 20, 1865.

Regiment lost during service 12 Officers and 108 Enlisted men killed and mortally wounded and 4 Officers and 159 Enlisted men by disease. Total 283.

3rd REGIMENT INFANTRY.

Organized at Keokuk and mustered in June 8, 1861. Left State for Hannibal, Mo., June 29. Attached to Dept. of Missouri, to March, 1862. 1st Brigade, 4th Division, Army of the Tennessee, to July, 1862. 1st Brigade, 4th Division, District of Memphis, Tenn., Dept. of Tennessee, to September, 1862. 1st Brigade, 4th Division, District of Jackson, Dept. Tennessee, to November, 1862. 1st Brigade, 4th Division, Right Wing 13th Army Corps, Dept. Tennessee, to December, 1862. 1st Brigade, 4th Division, 17th Army Corps, Army Tennessee, to January, 1863. 1st Brigade, 4th Division, 16th Corps, to July, 1863. 1st Brigade, 4th Division, 13th Corps, to August, 1863. 1st Brigade, 4th Division, 17th Corps, to March, 1864. (1st Brigade, Provisional Division, 17th Corps, Dept. of the Gulf, to June, 1864. Non-Veterans.) 1st Brigade, 4th Division, 17th Corps, Army Tennesee, to November, 1864.

SERVICE.—March into Missouri July 1-12, 1861. Skirmish at Utica July 3. Hagar's Woods July 8 (3 Cos.). Monroe Station July 9 and 11 (Cos. "A," "F," "H" and "K"). At Chillicothe, Mo., and guarding Hannibal & St. Joseph R. R. till August 7. Moved to Brookfield August 7 (7 Cos.), and against Green's forces at Kirksville August 15-21. (3 Cos. on Expedition to Paris, August.) Operations against guerrillas in North Central Missouri August 30-September 7. Action at Shelbina September 4. Expedition to Fonda against Green's forces September 8-9. Moved to Liberty September 12. Action at Blue Mills September 17. Operations in North Missouri till October 18. At Quincy, Ill., November. Regiment reunite. Moved to Benton Barracks and duty there till December 26. Guard duty at Mexico and on Northern Missouri R. R. till march, 1862. Ordered to Pittsburg Landing, Tenn. Battle of Shiloh April 6-7. Advance on and siege of Corinth, Miss., April 29-May 30. March to Memphis, Tenn., June 2-July 21, and duty there till September 6. Moved to Bolivar September 6. Skirmishes at Bolivar and Middleburg September 21. Duty at Bolivar till October 4. Battle of the Hatchie, Metamora, October 5. Grant's Central Mississippi Campaign November, 1862, to January, 1863. Worsham's Creek November 6. Guard Memphis & Charleston Railroad till March, 1863. Duty at Memphis till May. Expedition to the Coldwater April 18-24. Moved to Vicksburg, Miss., May 17-20. Attack on Steamer Crescent City, near Island 82, Mississippi River, May 18. Siege of Vicksburg, Miss., May 22-July 4. Advance on Jackson, Miss., July 5-10. Siege of Jackson July 10-17. Assault on Jackson July 12. Duty at Vicksburg till November. Moved to Natchez, Miss., November 18. Return to Vicksburg December 16, and duty there till February, 1864. Meridian Campaign February 3-March 2. Veterans on furlough March to May. Non-Veterans on Red River Campaign March 10-May 22. Fort DeRussy March 14. Pleasant Hill April 9. Pleasant Hill Landing April 12-13. About Cloutiersville April 22-24. At Alexandria April 30-May 13. Boyce's and Wells' Plantation May 6. Bayou Boeuf May 7. Retreat to Morganza May 13-20. Mansura May 16. Yellow Bayou May 18-19. Non-Veterans mustered out June, 1864. Veterans moved to Cairo, Ill., thence to Clifton, Tenn. March to Ackworth, Ga., via Huntsville and Decatur, Ala., and Rome, Ga., May 5-June 10. Atlanta (Ga.) Campaign June 10-September 8. Operations about Marietta and against Kenesaw Mountain June 10-July 2. Assault on Kenesaw June 27. Nickajack Creek July 2-5. Chattahoochie River July 6-12. Leggett's, Bald Hill, July 20-21. Battle of Atlanta July 22. Siege of Atlanta July 22-August 25. Flank movement on Jonesboro August 25-30. Battle of Jonesboro August 31-September 1. Lovejoy Station September 2-6. Pursuit of Hood into Alabama October 1-26. Shadow Church and Westbrooks, near Fairburn, October 1-3. Veterans consolidated to a Battalion of three Companies

July, 1864. Transferred to 2nd Iowa Infantry as Companies "A," "F" and "I," November 4, 1864.

Regiment lost during service 8 Officers and 119 Enlisted men killed and mortally wounded and 122 Enlisted men by disease. Total 249.

4th REGIMENT INFANTRY.

Organized at Council Bluffs and mustered in August 8, 1861. Moved to St. Louis, thence to Rolla, thence August 9-24. Attached to Dept. of Missouri, to December, 1861. 1st Brigade, Army of Southwest Missouri, to February, 1862. 1st Brigade, 4th Division, Army Southwest Missouri, to May, 1862. 2nd Division, Army Southwest Missouri, to July, 1862. District of Eastern Arkansas, Dept. Missouri, to November, 1862. 2nd Brigade, 2nd Division, District Eastern Arakansas, to December, 1862. 3rd Brigade, 11th Division, Right Wing 13th Army Corps (Old), Dept. Tennessee, to December, 1862. 3rd Brigade, 4th Division, Sherman's Yazoo Expedition, to Janauary, 1863. 3rd Brigade, 1st Division, 15th Army Corps, Army Tennessee, to September, 1863. 2nd Brigade, 1st Division, 15th Corps, to September, 1864. 3rd Brigade, 1st Division, 15th Corps, to July, 1865.

SERVICE.—Duty at Rolla, Mo., August 24, 1861, to January 22, 1862. Expedition to Houston and Salem against Freeman's forces November 1-9, 1861. March from Rolla to Lebanon January 22-31, 1862. Advance on Springfield, Mo., February 10-13. Near Springfield February 12. Pursuit of Price to Cassville February 13-17. Cane Creek February 14. Sugar Creek February 17. Blackburn's Mills February 27. Battles of Pea Ridge March 6-8. March to Batesville April 5-May 3, thence to Helena, Ark., May 25-July 14. Expedition from Helena to Arkansas Post November 16-21. Duty at Helena till December 22. Sherman's Yazoo Expedition December 22, 1862, to January 2, 1863. Chickasaw Bayou December 26-28. Chickasaw Bluffs December 29. (By command of Gen. Grant, Regiment authorized to inscribe upon its banners "1st at Chickasaw Bayou.") Expedition to Arkansas Post, Ark., January 3-10, 1863. Assault on and capture of Fort Hindman, Arkansas Post, January 10-11. Moved to Young's Point, La., January 17-23, and duty there till April. Expedition to Greenville, Black Bayou and Deer Creek April 5-14. Black Bayou April 10. Demonstration on Haines and Droumgould's Bluffs April 25-May 2. Snyder's Bluff April 30. March to join army in rear of Vicksburg, Miss., via Richmond and Grand Gulf, May 2-14. Jackson May 14. Siege of Vicksburg May 18-July 4. Assaults on Vicksburg May 19 and 22. Advance on Jackson July 5-10. Siege of Jackson July 10-17. At Big Black till September 22. Moved to Memphis, thence march to Chattanooga, Tenn., September 22-November 22. Operations on Memphis & Charleston Railroad in Alabama October 20-29. Cherokee Station October 21 and 29. Cane Creek October 26. Tuscumbia October 26-27. Battles of Chattanooga November 23-27. Lookout Mountain November 23-24. Mission Ridge November 25. Ringgold Gap, Taylor's Ridge, November 27. March to relief of Knoxville November 28-December 8. Duty at Woodville and other points in Alabama till May, 1864. Claysville, Ala., March 14 (Non-Veterans). Atlanta (Ga.) Campaign May 1-September 8. Demonstration on Resaca May 8-13. Battle of Resaca May 14-15. Operations on line of Pumpkin Vine Creek and battles about Dallas, New Hope Church and Allatoona Hills May 25-June 5. Operations about Marietta and against Kenesaw Mountain June 10-July 2. Assault on Kenesaw June 27. Nickajack Creek July 2-5. Chattahoochie River July 6-17. Battle of Atlanta July 22. Siege of Atlanta July 22-August 25. Ezra Chapel, Hood's second sortie, July 28. Flank movement on Jonesboro August 25-30. Battle of Jonesboro August 31-September 1. Lovejoy Station September 2-6. Pursuit of Hood into Alabama October 1-26. Snake Creek Gap October 15. Ships Gap October 16. March to the sea November 15-December 10. Griswoldsville November 22. Ogeechee River December 7-9. Siege of Savannah December 10-21. Campaign of the Carolinas January to April, 1865. Reconnoissance to Salkehatchie River, S. C., January 25. Salkehatchie Swamps, S. C., February 3-5. South Edisto River February 9. North Edisto River February 12-13. Congaree Creek February 15. Columbia February 16-17. Lynch's Creek February 25-26. Battle of Bentonville, N. C., March 20-21. Occupation of Goldsboro March 24. Advance on Raleigh April 10-13. Occupation of Raleigh April 14. Bennett's House April 26. Surrender of Johnston and his army. March to Washington, D. C., via Richmond, Va., April 29-May 19. Grand Review May 24. Moved to Louisville, Ky., June, and duty there till July. Mustered out July 24, 1865.

Regiment lost during service 6 Officers and 109 Enlisted men killed and mortally wounded and 2 Officers and 285 Enlisted men by disease. Total 402.

5th REGIMENT INFANTRY.

Organized at Burlington July 15, 1861. Moved to Keokuk, Iowa, August 2, thence to St. Louis, Mo., August 11. Attached to Fremont's Army of the West and Dept. of Missouri, to March, 1862. 1st Brigade, 2nd Division, Army Mississippi, to April, 1862. 2nd Brigade, 3rd Division, Army Mississippi, April, 1862. 1st Brigade, 3rd Division, Army Mississippi, to November, 1862. 3rd Brigade, 7th Division, Left Wing 13th Army Corps (Old), Dept. Tennessee, to December, 1862. 3rd Brigade, 7th Division, 16th Army Corps, to January, 1863. 3rd Brigade, 7th Division, 17th Army Corps, to September, 1863. 3rd Brigade, 2nd Division, 17th Army Corps, to December, 1863. 3rd Brigade, 3rd Division, 15th Army Corps, to August, 1864.

SERVICE.—Expedition to Northeastern Missouri August, 1861. Detachment moved to St. Louis, Mo., August 11, thence to Jefferson City, Mo., August 14. Expedition toward Columbia September 2. Moved to Booneville September 14, thence to Glasgow September 25. Return to Booneville October 2. Fremont's Campaign against Springfield, Mo., October 4-November 8. Guard railroad and duty at Booneville and Syracuse till February, 1862. Moved to Cairo, Ill., February 6, thence to Benton, Mo. Operations against New Madrid, Mo., February 28-March 15, and against Island No. 10. March 15-April 8. Expedition to Fort Pillow March 13-17. Moved to Hamburg Landing, Tenn., April 18-22. Advance on and siege of Corinth, Miss., April 29-May 30. Pursuit to Booneville May 31-June 6. At Clear Creek till August 5. Expedition to Holly Springs June 27-July 10. Moved to Jacinto August 5. March to Iuka September 18-19. Battle of Iuka September 19. Moved to Corinth October 1. Battle of Corinth October 3-4. Pursuit to Ripley October 5-12. Grant's Central Mississippi Campaign November, 1862, to January, 1863. Reconnoissance from LaGrange November 8-9, 1862. Duty at Memphis, Tenn., January to March, 1863. Expedition up Yazoo and operations about Fort Pemberton and Greenwood March 13-April 5. Fort Pemberton March 25. Moved to Milliken's Bend, La., April 13. Movement on Bruinsburg and turning Grand Gulf April 25-30. Battle of Port Gibson May 1. South Fork Bayou Pierrie May 2. Battles of Raymond May 12. Near Raymond May 13. Jackson May 14. Champion's Hill May 16. Siege of Vicksburg May 18-July 4. Assaults on Vicksburg May 19 and 22. Surrender of Vicksburg July 4. Duty at Vicksburg till September 13. Moved to Memphis, thence march to Chattanooga, Tenn., September 13-November 20. Operations on Memphis & Charleston railroad in Alabama October 20-29. Battles of Chattanooga November 23-25. Tunnel Hill November 24-25. Mission Ridge, November 25. Pursuit to Graysville November 26-27. March to relief of Knoxville November 28-December 17. Duty at Bridgeport and Huntsville, Ala., till April, 1864. Veterans on furlough April-May. Non-Veterans guard railroad till June 15. Mustered out July 30. Moved to Huntsville, thence to Kingston, Ga., June 23. Guard duty there and at Etowah River till July 30. Consolidated with 5th Iowa Cavalry August 8, 1864.

Regiment lost during service 9 Officers and 108 Enlisted men killed and mortally wounded and 2 Officers and 131 Enlisted men by disease. Total 250.

6th REGIMENT INFANTRY.

Organized at Burlington and mustered in July 17, 1861. Moved to Keokuk August 3, thence to St. Louis, Mo., August 9, and duty there till September 19. Attached to Dept. of Missouri, to March, 1862. 1st Brigade, 5th Division, Army Tennessee, to May, 1862. 2nd Brigade, 5th Division, Army Tennessee, to July, 1862, and District of Memphis, to November, 1862. 2nd Brigade, 5th Division, District of Memphis, 13th Army Corps (Old), Dept. of Tennessee, November, 1862. 1st Brigade, 1st Division, District of Memphis, 13th Corps, to December, 1862. 1st Brigade, 1st Division, 17th Army Corps, to January, 1863. 1st Brigade, 1st Division, 16th Army Corps, to March, 1863. 2nd Brigade, 1st Division, 16th Corps, to May, 1863. 4th Brigade, 1st Division, 16th Corps, to July, 1863. 4th Brigade, 4th Division, 15th Corps, to September, 1863. 2nd Brigade, 4th Division, 15th Corps, to September, 1864. 2nd Brigade, 1st Division, 15th Corps, to July, 1865.

SERVICE.—Moved to Jefferson City, Mo., September 19, 1861. Fremont's Campaign against Springfield, Mo., October 7-November 9. At Sedalia till December 9. Moved to Lamine Bridge November 9, thence to Tipton January 22, 1862, and duty there till March 7. Expedition to Crump's Landing, Tennessee River, and operations there March 7-14. Expedition from Savannah to Yellow Creek, Miss., and occupation of Pittsburg Landing, Tenn., March 14-17. Battle of Shiloh April 6-7. Advance on and siege of Corinth, Miss., April 29-May 30. March to Memphis, Tenn., via LaGrange, Grand Junction and Holly Springs June 2-July 21. Skirmish with Forest July 2. Provost duty at Memphis till November. Grant's Central Mississippi Campaign November, 1862, to January, 1863. Tallahatchie march November 2-December 12. At Grand Junction and duty along Memphis & Charleston railroad till June, 1863. Regiment mounted. Expedition to Hernando, Miss., April 17-26, 1863. Holly Springs April 17. Scout from LaGrange into Northern Mississippi April 29-May 5. Salem May 20. Expedition to Senatobia, Miss., May 21-26. Moved to Vicksburg, Miss., June 9-14. Siege of Vicksburg June 14-July 4. Advance on Jackson, Miss., July 4-10. Birdsong Ferry, Big Black River, July 4-6. Jones' Ford and Messenger's Ferry July 6. Queen Hill July 7. Siege of Jackson July 10-17. At Big Black till September 25. Moved to Memphis, thence march to Chattanooga, Tenn., September 25-November 20. Operations on Memphis & Charleston railroad in Alabama October 20-29. Battles of Chattanooga November 23-25. Tunnel Hill November 23-24. Mission Ridge November 25. Pursuit to Graysville November 26-27. March to relief of Knoxville November 28-December 17. At Scottsboro, Ala., till April, 1864. Atlanta (Ga.) Campaign May 1-September 8. Demonstration on Resaca May 8-13. Near Resaca May 14. Battle of Resaca May 14-15. Operations on line of Pumpkin Vine Creek and battles about Dallas, New Hope Church and Allatoona Hills May 25-June 5. Operations about Marietta and against Kenesaw Mountain June 10-July 2. Assault on Kenesaw June 27. Nickajack Creek July 2-5. Chattahoochie River July 6-17. Battle of Atlanta July 22. Siege of Atlanta July 22-August 25. Ezra Chapel, Hood's second sortie, July 28. Flank movement on Jonesboro August 25-30. Battle of Jonesboro August 31-September 1. Lovejoy Station September 2-6. Pursuit of Hood into Alabama October 1-26. Snake Creek Gap October 15. Ships Gap October 16. March to the sea November 15-December 10. Griswoldsville November 22. Ogeechee River December 7-9. Siege of Savannah December 10-21. Campaign of the Carolinas January to April, 1865. Salkehatchie Swamps, S. C., February 3-5. South Edisto River February 9. North Edisto River February 12-13. Congaree Creek February 15. Columbia February 16-17. Lynch's Creek February 25-26. Battle of Bentonville, N. C., March 20-21.

Occupation of Goldsboro March 24. Advance on Raleigh April 9-13. Occupation of Raleigh April 14. Bennett's House April 26. Surrender of Johnston and his army. March to Washington, D. C., via Richmond, Va., April 29-May 20. Grand Review May 24. Moved to Louisville, Ky., June. Mustered out July 21, 1865.

Regiment lost during service 8 Officers and 144 Enlisted men killed and mortally wounded and 2 Officers and 126 Enlisted men by disease. Total 280.

7th REGIMENT INFANTRY.

Organized at Burlington July 24 to August 4, 1861. Moved to St. Louis, Mo., August 6; thence to Pilot Knob, Mo. Attached to District of Cairo to February, 1862. 4th Brigade, 2nd Division, District of Cairo, February, 1862. 1st Brigade, 2nd Division, District of West Tennessee and Army of Tennessee, to July, 1862. 1st Brigade, 2nd Division, District of Corinth, Dept. of the Tennessee to September, 1862. 3rd Brigade, 2nd Division, District of Corinth, to October, 1862. 2nd Brigade, 2nd Division, District of Corinth, to November, 1862. 1st Brigade, District of Corinth, 13th Army Corps (Old), Dept. of the Tennessee, to December, 1862. 1st Brigade, District of Corinth, 17th Army Corps, Dept. of the Tennessee, to January, 1863. 1st Brigade, District of Corinth, 16th Army Corps, to March, 1863. 1st Brigade, 2nd Division, 16th Army Corps, to September, 1864. 1st Brigade, 4th Division, 15th Army Corps, to July, 1865.

SERVICE.—Duty at Pilot Knob, Jackson, Cape Girardeau County, Norfolk, Fort Jefferson, Bird's Point, Mo., Fort Holt, Ky., and Cairo, Ill., till November, 1861. Affair at Elliott's Mills, Camp Crittenden, September 22. Expedition to Belmont November 6-7. Battle of Belmont November 7. Moved from Bird's Point to St. Louis, Mo., November 10, and duty there till January, 1862. Expedition to Fort Henry, Tenn., January 15-25. Operations against Fort Henry February 2-6. Investment of Fort Donelson February 12-16. Capture of Fort Donelson February 16. Expedition to Clarksburg, Tenn., February 19-21. Moved to Pittsburg Landing March 5-18. Battle of Shiloh April 6-7. Advance on and siege of Corinth, Miss., April 29-May 30. Pursuit May 31-June 6. Duty at Corinth till October. Expedition to Iuka, Miss., September 18-22. Battle of Iuka September 19. Battle of Corinth October 3-4. Pursuit October 5-7. Moved to Rienzi October 7; thence to Boneyard and duty there till November. Little Bear Creek November 28 and December 12. Duty at Corinth till March, 1863. Expedition against Forest December 18, 1862, to January 3, 1863. Moved to Bethel, Tenn., March 1863, and duty there till June 1. Moved to Corinth June 1; thence to Moscow and duty there till August. At LaGrange till October. March to Pulaski October 30-November 11 and duty there till March, 1864. Veterans on furlough January and February. At Prospect, Tenn., till April. Atlanta (Ga.) Campaign May 1 to September 8. Demonstration on Resaca May 8-13. Sugar Valley May 9. Battle of Resaca May 13-14. Ley's Ferry, Oostenaula River, May 15. Rome Cross Roads May 16. Operations on line of Pumpkin Vine Creek and battles about Dallas, New Hope Church and Allatoona Hills May 25-June 5. Operations about Marietta and against Kenesaw Mountain June 10-July 2. Assault on Kenesaw June 27. Ruff's Mill July 3-4. Chattahoochie River July 5-17. Battle of Atlanta July 22. Siege of Atlanta July 22-August 25. Flank movement on Jonesboro August 25-30. Flint River Station August 30. Battle of Jonesboro August 31-September 1. Lovejoy Station September 2-6. Pursuit of Hood into Alabama October 1-26. Reconnoissance and skirmishes on Cave Springs Road, near Rome, October 12-13. March to the sea November 15-December 10. Little Ogeechee River December 4. Eden Station and Jenks Bridge December 7. Siege of Savannah December 10-21. Campaign of the Carolinas January to April, 1865. Salkehatchie Swamps, S. C., February 3-5. South Edisto River February 9. North Edisto River February 12-13. Congaree Creek February 15. Columbia

February 16-17. Lynch's Creek February 25-26. Expedition to Florence, S. C., March 4-6. Battle of Bentonville March 20-21. Occupation of Goldsboro March 24. Advance on Raleigh April 9-13. Occupation of Raleigh April 14. Bennett's House April 26. Surrender of Johnston and his army. March to Washington, D. C., via Richmond, Va., April 29-May 20. Grand Review May 24. Moved to Louisville, Ky., June. Mustered out July 12, 1865.

Regiment lost during service 7 Officers and 134 Enlisted men killed and mortally wounded and 4 Officers and 160 Enlisted men by disease. Total 305.

8th REGIMENT INFANTRY.

Organized at Davenport August and September, 1861. Left State for St. Louis, Mo., September 25. Attached to Dept. of Missouri to March, 1862. 3rd Brigade, 2nd Division, Army of Tennessee, to April, 1862. 1st Brigade, 2nd Division, Army of Tennessee, to July, 1862, and District of Corinth, Dept. of the Tennessee, to November, 1862. 1st Brigade, District of Corinth, 13th Army Corps (Old), Dept. of the Tennessee, to December, 1862. Davenport, Ia., to January, 1863. District of St. Louis, Mo., Dept. of the Missouri, to April, 1863. 3rd Brigade, 3rd Division, 15th Army Corps, Army of Tennessee, to December, 1863. 3rd Brigade, 1st Division, 16th Army Corps, to June, 1864. Unassigned, District of Memphis, Tenn., District of West Tennessee, to February, 1865. 3rd Brigade, 3rd Division, 16th Army Corps, Military Division West Mississippi, to August, 1865. Dept. of Alabama to April, 1866.

SERVICE.—Moved to Syracuse, Mo., October 15, 1861. Fremont's Campaign against Springfield, Mo., October 21-November 8. Duty at Sedalia, Mo., till March, 1862. Expedition to Milford, Mo., December 15-19, 1861. Action at Shawnee Mound, Milford on the Blackwater, December 18. (Cos. "E" and "K" detached to guard train to Fort Leavenworth, Kansas, November 21, 1861, and duty on Border till March, 1862. Rejoin Regiment at Sedalia.) Moved from Sedalia to St. Louis; thence to Pittsburg Landing, Tenn., March 11-21. Battle of Shiloh, Tenn., April 6-7. Most of Regiment captured. Men confined at Macon, Ga.; Officers at Selma, Ala., and Madison, Ga. Paroled October 18, 1862. Exchanged November 10, 1862. Those not captured attached to Union Brigade and participated in advance on and siege of Corinth, Miss., April 29-May 30. Duty at Corinth till August. Moved to Danville, Miss., August 15, and duty there till October. Battle of Corinth October 3-4. Pursuit to Ripley October 5-12. Duty at Corinth till December 18. Ordered to rejoin Regiment at Davenport, Iowa, December 18. While en route participated in the defence of Jackson, Tenn., December 20, 1862, to January 4, 1863. Arrived at Davenport January 7, 1863. Regiment reorganizing at Davenport, Iowa, and St. Louis, Mo., and duty at Rolla, Mo., till April, 1863. Ordered to Young's Point, La., April 9. Duty there and at Duckport till May 2. Moved to join army in rear of Vicksburg, Miss., May 2-14. Mississippi Springs May 13. Jackson, Miss., May 14. Siege of Vicksburg May 18-July 4. Assaults on Vicksburg May 19 and 22. Expedition to Mechanicsburg May 26-June 4. Advance on Jackson, Miss., July 5-10. Siege of Jackson July 10-17. At Bear Creek till October. Expedition toward Canton, Miss., October 14-20. Bogue Chitto Creek October 17. Moved to Memphis, thence to Pocohontas, Tenn. Duty there and guarding Memphis & Charleston railroad till January 31, 1864. Moved to Vicksburg, Miss., February 1-6. Expedition to Canton February 25-March 4. Red River Campaign March 10-May 22. Fort DeRussy March 14. Henderson's Hill March 21. Campti March 26 and April 4. Grand Ecore April 5. Battle of Pleasant Hill April 9. Retreat to Natchitoches April 22-23. Cane River Crossing April 23. Cloutiersville April 23-24. At Alexandria, La., April 27-May 13. Bayou La Mourie May 6-7. Retreat to Morganza May 13-20. Mansura May 16. Yellow Bayou May 18-19. Moved to Vicksburg, Miss.; thence to Memphis, Tenn., May 20-June 10. Lake

Chicot, Ark., June 5-6. Provost duty at Memphis till February, 1865. Repulse of Forest's attack on Memphis August 21. Moved to New Orleans, La., February, 1865. Campaign against Mobile and its Defences March 7-April 13. Siege of Spanish Fort and Fort Blakely March 26-April 8. Fort Blakely April 9. Capture of Mobile April 12. March to Montgomery, Ala., April 13-22. Provost duty there till August and at Tuscaloosa and Selma till April, 1866. Mustered out April 20, 1866.

Regiment lost during service 4 Officers and 98 Enlisted men killed and mortally wounded and 4 Officers and 170 Enlisted men by disease. Total 276.

9th REGIMENT INFANTRY.

Organized at Dubuque and mustered in September 24, 1861. Ordered to St. Louis, Mo. Attached to Dept. of Missouri October, 1861, to January, 1862. Unattached, Army of Southwest Missouri, to February, 1862. 2nd Brigade, 4th Division, Army of Southwest Missouri, to May, 1862. 2nd Division, Army of Southwest Missouri, to July, 1862. District of Eastern Arkansas, Dept. of Missouri, to November, 1862. 3rd Brigade, 1st Division, District of Eastern Arkansas, Dept. of Tennessee, to December, 1862. 3rd Brigade, 11th Division, Right Wing 13th Army Corps (Old), Dept. of Tennessee, to December, 1862. 3rd Brigade, 4th Division, Sherman's Yazoo Expedition, to January, 1863. 3rd Brigade, 1st Division, 15th Army Corps, Army of Tennessee, to September, 1863. 2nd Brigade, 1st Division, 15th Army Corps, to September, 1864. 3rd Brigade, 1st Division, 15th Army Corps, to July, 1865.

SERVICE.—Moved to Franklin, Mo., October 11, 1861, and duty there guarding railroad till January, 1862. Curtis' advance on Springfield, Mo., January 23-February 12, 1862. Pursuit of Price to Cassville, Ark., February 13-16. Sugar Creek February 17. Battles of Pea Ridge, Ark., March 6, 7 and 8. March to Batesville April 5-May 3, and to Helena, Ark., May 25-July 14. Duty at Helena till December. Expedition from Helena to Arkansas Post November 16-21. Sherman's Yazoo Expedition December 22, 1862, to January 2, 1863. Chickasaw Bayou December 26-28, 1862. Chickasaw Bluffs December 29. Expedition to Arkansas Post, Ark., January 3-10, 1863. Assault on and capture of Fort Hindman, Arkansas Post, January 10-11. Moved to Young's Point, La., January 17-23, and duty there till April. Expedition to Greenville, Black Bayou and Deer Creek April 5-14. Black Bayou April 10. Demonstration on Haines and Drumgould's Bluffs April 25-May 2. Snider's Bluff April 30. Moved to join army in rear of Vicksburg, Miss., May 2-14. Battle of Jackson May 14. Siege of Vicksburg, Miss., May 18-July 4. Assaults on Vicksburg May 19 and 22. Advance on Jackson, Miss., July 5-10. Siege of Jackson July 10-17. Brandon Station July 19. At Big Black till September 22. Moved to Memphis, thence march to Chattanooga, Tenn., September 22-November 20. Operation on the Memphis & Charleston Railroad in Alabama October 20-29. Cherokee Station October 21 and 29. Cane Creek October 26. Tuscumbia October 26-27. Battles of Chattanooga November 23-27; Lookout Mountain November 23-24; Mission Ridge November 25; Taylor's Ridge, Ringgold Gap, November 27. March to relief of Knoxville November 28-December 17. At Woodville, Ala., till April, 1864. Atlanta (Ga.) Campaign May 1-September 8. Demonstration on Resaca May 8-13. Battle of Resaca May 14-15. Operations on line of Pumpkin Vine Creek and battles about Dallas, New Hope Church and Allatoona Hills May 25-June 5. Operations about Marietta and against Kenesaw Mountain June 10-July 2. Assault on Kenesaw June 27. Nickajack Creek July 2-5. Chattahoochie River July 6-17. Battle of Atlanta July 22. Siege of Atlanta July 22-August 25. Ezra Chapel, Hood's second sortie, July 28. Flank movement on Jonesboro August 25-30. Battle of Jonesboro August 31-September 1. Lovejoy Station September 2-6. Pursuit of Hood into Alabama October 1-26. Snake Creek Gap October 15. Ship Gap October 16. March to the sea November 15-December 10. Griswoldsville November 22. Ogeechee River December 7-9. Siege of Savannah December 10-21. Campaign of the Carolinas January to April, 1865. Reconnoissance to Salkehatchie River January 25, 1865. Salkehatchie Swamps, S. C., February 3-5. South Edisto River February 9. North Edisto River February 12-13. Congaree Creek February 15. Columbia February 16-17. Battle of Bentonville, N. C., March 20-21. Occupation of Goldsboro March 24. Advance on Raleigh April 10-13. Occupation of Raleigh April 14. Bennett's House April 26. Surrender of Johnston and his army. March to Washington, D. C., via Richmond, Va., April 29-May 20. Grand Review May 24. Moved to Louisville, Ky., June. Mustered out July 18, 1865.

Regiment lost during service 12 Officers and 142 Enlisted men killed and mortally wounded and 2 Officers and 230 Enlisted men by disease. Total 386.

10th REGIMENT INFANTRY.

Organized at Iowa City and Montezuma August and September, 1861. Ordered to St. Louis, Mo., September 6; thence to Cape Girardeau, Mo., October 1. Attached to District of Cairo October, 1861. 5th Brigade, Military District of Cairo, to February, 1862. 4th Brigade, 1st Division, District of Cairo, February, 1862. 2nd Brigade, 2nd Division, Army of Mississippi, to April, 1863. 2nd Brigade, 3rd Division, Army of Mississippi, to April, 1862. 1st Brigade, 3rd Division, Army of Mississippi, to May, 1862. 2nd Brigade, 3rd Division, Army of Mississippi, to November, 1862. 3rd Brigade, 7th Division, Left Wing 13th Army Corps (Old), Dept. of Tennessee, to December, 1862. 3rd Brigade, 7th Division, 16th Army Corps, to January, 1863. 3rd Brigade, 7th Division, 17th Army Corps, to September, 1863. 3rd Brigade, 2nd Division, 17th Army Corps, to December, 1863. 3rd Brigade, 3rd Division, 15th Army Corps, to August, 1864. 2nd Brigade, 3rd Division, 15th Corps, to April, 1865. 1st Brigade, 2nd Division, 15th Corps, to August, 1865.

SERVICE.—At Cape Girardeau, Mo., till November, 1861. Expedition against Thompson's forces November 2-12. Action at Bloomfield November 10. Moved to Bird's Point, Mo., November 12. Action at Charleston January 8, 1862. Moved to New Madrid, Mo., March 4. Operations against New Madrid, Mo., March 6-15, and against Island No. 10 March 15-April 8. Pursuit and capture at Tiptonville April 8. Expedition to Fort Pillow, Tenn., April 13-17. Moved to Hamburg Landing, Tenn., April 18-22. Advance on and siege of Corinth, Miss., April 29-May 30. Actions at Farmington May 9 and 26. Occupation of Corinth and pursuit to Booneville May 30-June 12. At Clear Creek till July 29. Moved to Jacinto July 29. Expedition to Iuka September 18-19. Battle of Iuka September 19. Moved to Corinth October 1. Battle of Corinth October 3-4. Pursuit to Ripley October 5-12. Grant's Central Mississippi Campaign November, 1862, to January, 1863. Reconnoissance to Holly Springs November 8-9, 1862. Duty near Memphis guarding Memphis & Charleston Railroad January to March, 1863. Yazoo Pass Expedition and operations against Fort Pemberton and Greenwood March 13-April 5. Moved to Milliken's Bend, La., April 13. Movement on Bruinsburg and turning Grand Gulf April 25-30. Battle of Port Gibson May 1. South Fork of Bayou Pierrie May 2. Battles of Raymond May 12. Near Raymond May 13. Jackson May 14. Champion's Hill May 16. Big Black River May 17. Siege of Vicksburg May 18-July 4. Assaults on Vicksburg May 19 and 22. Surrender of Vicksburg July 4 and duty there till September 13. Moved to Memphis, thence march to Chattanooga, Tenn., September 13-November 20. Operations on Memphis & Charleston Railroad in Alabama October 20-29. Battles of Chattanooga November 23-25; Tunnel Hill November 23-24; Mission Ridge November 25. Pursuit to Graysville November 26-27. March to relief of Knoxville November 28-December 8. Duty at Bridgeport and Huntsville, Ala., till April 30, 1864. Moved to Decatur, Ala., April 30. Veterans on furlough June 15-

August 1. Duty at Kingston, Ga., till November. Non-Veterans mustered out September 28, 1864. Operations against Wheeler October. March to the sea November 15-December 10. Siege of Savannah December 10-21. Campaign of the Carolinas January to April, 1865. Salkehatchie Swamps, S. C., February 3-5. Fishburn's Plantation, near Lane's Bridge, Salkehatchie, February 6. South Edisto River February 9. North Edisto River February 12-13. Congaree Creek February 15. Columbia February 16-17. Lynch's Creek February 25-26. Cox's Bridge, N. C., March 19-20. Battle of Bentonville March 20-21. Occupation of Goldsboro March 24. Advance on Raleigh April 9-13. Occupation of Raleigh April 14. Bennett's House April 26. Surrender of Johnston and his army. March to Washington, D. C., via Richmond, Va., April 29-May 30. Grand Review May 24. Moved to Louisville, Ky., June. Duty there and at Little Rock, Ark., till August. Mustered out August 15, 1865.

Regiment lost during service 6 Officers and 95 Enlisted men killed and mortally wounded and 134 Enlisted men by disease. Total 235.

11th REGIMENT INFANTRY.

Organized at Davenport September 28 to October 18, 1861. Ordered to St. Louis, Mo., November 1. Attached to Dept. of Missouri to March, 1862. 1st Brigade, 1st Division, Army of Tennessee, to April, 1862. 3rd Brigade, 6th Division, Army of Tennessee, to July, 1862, and District of Corinth to November, 1862. 3rd Brigade, 6th Division, Left Wing 13th Army Corps (Old), Dept. of Tennessee, to December, 1862. 3rd Brigade, 6th Division, 16th Army Corps, Army of the Tennessee, to January, 1863. 3rd Brigade, 6th Division, 17th Army Corps, to September, 1863. 3rd Brigade, 1st Division, 17th Corps, to April, 1864. 3rd Brigade, 4th Division, 17th Corps, to July, 1865.

SERVICE.—Moved to Jefferson City, Mo., November, 1861, and duty there till March, 1862. Expedition to Booneville December 8, 1861, and to Providence and Booneboro December 14. Moved to Pittsburg Landing, Tenn., March 10, 1862. Battle of Shiloh, Tenn., April 6-7. Advance on and siege of Corinth, Miss., April 29-May 30. Duty at Corinth and Bolivar till November. Battle of Corinth October 3-4. Pursuit to Ripley October 5-12. Grant's Central Mississippi Campaign November, 1862, to January, 1863. Moved to Memphis, Tenn., January 12, 1863; thence to Lake Providence, La., January 18. Expedition to Richmond, La., January 29-31. Richmond January 30. Duty at Lake Providence till April. Movement on Bruinsburg and turning Grand Gulf April 25-30. Battle of Port Gibson May 1 (Reserve). Battles of Raymond May 12. Jackson May 14. Champion's Hill May 16. Big Black River Crossing May 17. Siege of Vicksburg May 18-July 4. Assaults on Vicksburg May 19 and 22. Expedition to Mechanicsburg May 26-June 4. Surrender of Vicksburg July 4. Advance on Jackson July 5-10. Guard ammunition and subsistance trains at Vicksburg till February, 1864. Expedition to Monroe, La., August 20-September 2, 1863. Expedition to Canton October 14-20. Meridian Campaign February 3-March 6. Veterans on furlough March and April. Non-Veterans garrison duty at Mound City, Ill. Moved to Clifton, Tenn.; thence march to Ackworth, Ga., via Huntsville and Decatur, Ala., and Rome, Ga., April 21-June 8. Atlanta (Ga.) Campaign June 8-September 8. Operations about Marietta and against Kenesaw Mountain June 10-July 2. Bushy Mountain June 15-17. Assault on Kenesaw June 27. Nickajack Creek July 2-5. Chattahoochie River July 6-17. Leggett's or Bald Hill July 20-21. Battle of Atlanta July 22. Siege of Atlanta July 22-August 25. Flank movement on Jonesboro August 25-30. Battle of Jonesboro August 31-September 1. Lovejoy Station September 2-6. Pursuit of Hood into Alabama October 1-26. Snake Creek Gap October 15-16. March to the sea November 15-December 10. Siege of Savannah December 10-21. Campaign of the Carolinas January to April, 1865. Pocotaligo, S.

C., January 14-16. Salkehatchie Swamps February 3-5. River's Bridge February 3. Edisto Railroad Bridge February 7. South Edisto River February 9. Orangeburg February 11-12. Columbia February 15-17. Cheraw March 3. Fayetteville, N. C., March 11. Battle of Bentonville March 20-21. Occupation of Goldsboro March 24. Advance on Raleigh April 9-13. Occupation of Raleigh April 14. Bennett's House April 26. Surrender of Johnston and his army. March to Washington, D. C., via Richmond, April 29-May 20. Grand Review May 24. Moved to Louisville, Ky., June. Mustered out July 15, 1865.

Regiment lost during service 5 Officers and 86 Enlisted men killed and mortally wounded and 2 Officers and 166 Enlisted men by disease. Total 259.

12th REGIMENT INFANTRY.

Organized at Dubuque and mustered in November 25, 1861. Moved to St. Louis, Mo., November 28-30. Attached to Dept. of Missouri till February, 1862. 3rd Brigade, 2nd Division, District of Cairo, February, 1862. 1st Brigade, 2nd Division, Army of Tennessee, to April, 1862. (1st Union Brigade, 2nd Division, Army of Tennessee and District of Corinth, to December, 1862, Detachment.) Davenport, Iowa, to January, 1863. District of St. Louis, Mo., Dept. of Missouri, to April, 1863. 3rd Brigade, 3rd Division, 15th Army Corps, Army of Tennessee, to December, 1863. 3rd Brigade, 1st Division, 16th Army Corps, to December, 1864. 3rd Brigade, 1st Division (Detachment), Army of Tennessee, Dept. of the Cumberland, to February, 1865. 3rd Brigade, 1st Division, 16th Corps, Military Division West Mississippi, to August, 1865. District of Alabama, Dept. of the Gulf, to January, 1866.

SERVICE.—Duty at Benton Barracks, Mo., till January 27, 1862. Moved to Cairo, Ill.; thence to Smithland, Ky., January 27-31. Reconnoissance to Fort Henry, Tenn., January 15-25. Expedition up the Tennessee River February 5-6. Capture of Fort Henry February 6. Investment of Fort Donelson February 12-16. Capture of Fort Donelson February 16. Moved to Pittsburg Landing, Tenn., March 14-17. Battle of Shiloh, Tenn., April 6-7. Most of Regiment captured. Paroled October 26. Exchanged November 10. Those not captured attached to Union Brigade and participated in the advance on and siege of Corinth, Miss., April 29-May 30. Pursuit to Booneville May 30-June 12. Duty at Corinth till August. At Danville, Miss., till October 1. Battle of Corinth October 3-4. Pursuit to Ripley October 5-12. Duty at Corinth till December 12. Ordered to Davenport, Iowa, December 12 to rejoin Regiment. While en route participated in the Defence of Jackson, Tenn., December 20, 1862, to January 4, 1863. Arrived at Davenport January 7. Reorganizing at Davenport and St. Louis, Mo., till April, 1863. Moved to Duckport, La., April 9-14. Duty there till May 2. Moved to join army in rear of Vicksburg, Miss., May 2-14. Mississippi Springs May 13. Jackson May 14. Siege of Vicksburg May 18-July 4. Assaults on Vicksburg May 19 and 22. Expedition to Mechanicsburg May 26-June 4. Advance on Jackson, Miss., July 4-10. Siege of Jackson July 10-17. Assault on Jackson July 12. Duty at Big Black till November. Expedition toward Canton October 14-20. Bogue Chitto Creek October 17. Moved to Memphis, Tenn., November 7-12, and guard duty at Chewalla and along Memphis & Charleston Railroad till February, 1864. Moved to Vicksburg, Miss., February 1-6. Expedition to Canton February 25-March 4. Return to Memphis, Tenn.; duty there and at mouth of White River, Ark., till June. Skirmish at White River Station June 23 (Detachment). Smith's Expedition to Tupelo, Miss., July 5-21. Pontotoc July 11. Camargo's Cross Roads, near Harrisburg, July 13. Tupelo July 14-15. Old Town Creek July 15. Smith's Expedition to Oxford, Miss., August 1-30. Tallahatchie River August 7-9. Abbeville and Oxford August 12. Abbeville August 23. Mower's Expedition up White River to Duvall's Bluff September 1-7. March in pursuit of Price through Arkansas and Missouri Sep-

tember 17-November 15. Moved to Nashville, Tenn., November 23-December 1. Battle of Nashville, Tenn., December 15-16. Pursuit of Hood to the Tennessee River December 17-28. At Clifton and Eastport, Miss., till February, 1865. Moved to Vicksburg, Miss.; thence to New Orleans, La., February 6-25, and to Dauphin Island, Ala., March 7-8. Campaign against Mobile and its defences March 8-April 12. Siege of Spanish Fort and Fort Blakely March 26-April 8. Fort Blakely April 9. Capture of Mobile April 12. March to Montgomery, Ala., April 13-22, and duty there till May 11. At Selma till September 23, and in the District of Talladega till December 26. Moved to Memphis, Tenn., December 26. Mustered out January 20, 1866.

Regiment lost during service 4 Officers and 76 Enlisted men killed and mortally wounded and 8 Officers and 260 Enlisted men by disease. Total 348.

13th REGIMENT INFANTRY.

Organized at Davenport October 18 to November 2, 1861. Ordered to St. Louis, Mo., November 20, 1861. Attached to Dept. of Missouri to February, 1862. 1st Brigade, 1st Division, Army of Tennessee, to April, 1862. 3rd Brigade, 6th Division, Army of Tennessee, to July, 1862, and District of Corinth, Dept. of Tennessee, to November, 1862. 3rd Brigade, 6th Division, Left Wing 13th Army Corps (Old), Dept. of Tennessee, to December, 1862. 3rd Brigade, 6th Division, 16th Army Corps, Army of Tennessee, to January, 1863. 3rd Brigade, 6th Division, 17th Army Corps, to September, 1863. 3rd Brigade, 1st Division, 17th Army Corps, to April, 1864. 3rd Brigade, 4th Division, 17th Army Corps, to July, 1865.

SERVICE.—Moved to Jefferson City, Mo., December 13, 1861, and duty there till March, 1862. Moved to St. Louis, Mo.; thence to Pittsburg Landing, Tenn., March 8-23. Battle of Shiloh, Tenn., April 6-7. Advance on and siege of Corinth, Miss., April 29-May 30. Duty at Corinth and Bolivar till November. Battle of Corinth October 3-4. Pursuit to Ripley October 5-12. Grant's Central Mississippi Campaign November, 1862, to January, 1863. Moved to Memphis, Tenn., January 12; thence to Lake Providence, La., January 18, and duty there till April. Expedition to Richmond, La., January 29-31. Richmond January 30. Movement on Bruinsburg and turning Grand Gulf April 25-30. Battle of Port Gibson May 1 (Reserve). Battles of Raymond May 12. Jackson May 14. Champion's Hill May 16. Big Black River May 17. Siege of Vicksburg May 18-July 4. Assaults on Vicksburg May 19 and 22. Expedition to Mechanicsburg May 26-June 4. Messenger's Ferry June 29-30 (Cos. "A," "D," "F" and "H"). Surrender of Vicksburg July 4. Advance on Jackson, Miss., July 5-10. Guard Ammunition and Subsistance trains. Duty at Vicksburg till February, 1864. Stevenson's Expedition to Monroe, La., August 20-September 12, 1863. Expedition to Canton October 14-20. Meridian Campaign February 3-March 6, 1864. Veterans on furlough March and April. Non-Veterans' garrison at Mound City, Ill. Moved to Clifton, Tenn.; thence to Ackworth, Ga., via Huntsville and Decatur, Ala., and Rome, Ga., April 21-June 8. Atlanta Campaign June 8 to September 8. Operations about Marietta and against Kenesaw Mountain June 10-July 2. Bushy Mountain June 15-17. Assault on Kenesaw June 27. Nickajack Creek July 2-5. Chattahoochie River July 6-17. Leggett's or Bald Hill July 20-21. Battle of Atlanta July 22. Siege of Atlanta July 22-August 25. Flank movement on Jonesboro August 25-30. Battle of Jonesboro August 31-September 1. Lovejoy Station September 2-6. Pursuit of Hood into Alabama October 1-21. Snake Creek Gap October 15-16. March to the sea November 15-December 10. Siege of Savannah December 10-21. Campaign of the Carolinas January to April, 1865. Pocotaligo, S. C., January 14-16. Salkehatchie Swamps February 3-5. River's Bridge February 3. South Edisto River February 9. Orangeburg February 11-12. Columbia February 15-17. Cheraw March 3. Fayetteville, N. C., March 11. Battle of Bentonville March 20-21. Occupation of Goldsboro March 24. Advance on Raleigh April 9-13. Occupation of Raleigh April 14. Bennett's House April 26. Surrender of Johnston and his army. March to Washington, D. C., via Richmond, Va., April 29-May 20. Grand Review May 24. Moved to Louisville, Ky., June. Mustered out July 21, 1865.

Regiment lost during service 5 Officers and 114 Enlisted men killed and mortally wounded and 4 Officers and 205 Enlisted men by disease. Total 328.

14th REGIMENT INFANTRY.

Organized at Davenport November and mustered in November 6, 1861. Ordered to St. Louis, Mo., December, 1861. Attached to Dept. of Missouri to February, 1862. 4th Brigade, 2nd Division, District of Cairo, February, 1862. 1st Brigade, 2nd Division, Army of Tennessee, to April, 1862. Union Brigade, 2nd Division, Army of Tennessee, to July, and District of Corinth, Dept. of Tennessee, to December, 1862. Davenport, Iowa, and St. Louis, Mo., to April, 1863. Cairo, Ill., District of Columbus, 6th Division, 16th Army Corps, Dept. of Tennessee, to January, 1864. 2nd Brigade, 3rd Division, 16th Army Corps, to December, 1864. Springfield, Ill., to August, 1865.

SERVICE.—Cos. "A," "B" and "C" detached October, 1861, by order of General Fremont and sent to Fort Randall, Dakota Territory. Permanently detached September 18, 1862. (See 41th Iowa.) Reconnoissance to Fort Henry, Tenn., January 15-25. Operations against Fort Henry February 2-6. Investment of Fort Donelson February 12-16. Capture of Fort Donelson February 16. Expedition to Clarksville, Tenn., February 19-21. Moved to Pittsburg Landing, Tenn., March 2-14. Battle of Shiloh, Tenn., April 6-7. Held center at "Hornet's Nest" and Regiment mostly captured. Paroled October 12, 1862. Exchanged November 19, 1862. Those not captured assigned to Union Brigade and participated in the advance on and sieze of Corinth, Miss., April 29-May 30. Pursuit to Booneville May 31-June 12. Duty at Corinth till August, and at Danville, Miss., till October. Battle of Corinth October 3-4. Pursuit to Ripley October 5-12. At Corinth till December 18. Ordered to rejoin Regiment at Davenport, Iowa, December 18. While en route participated in the defence of Jackson, Tenn., December 20, 1862, to January 4, 1863. Arrived at Davenport January 7. Reorganizing Regiment at Davenport, Iowa, and at St. Louis, Mo., till April. Moved to Cairo, Ill., April 10, and duty there till January, 1864. Moved to Vicksburg, Miss. Meridian Campaign February 3 to March 5. Meridian February 14-15. Marion February 15-17. Canton February 28. Red River Campaign March 10-May 22. Fort DeRussy March 14. Occupation of Alexandria March 16. Henderson's Hill March 21. Battle of Pleasant Hill April 9. Cloutiersville and Cane River Crossing April 22-24. At Alexandria April 27-May 13. Moore's Plantation May 5-7. Bayou Boeuf May 7. Bayou La Mourie May 12. Retreat to Morganza May 13-20. Mansura May 16. Yellow Bayou May 18-19. Moved to Vicksburg, Miss., thence to Memphis, Tenn., May 20-June 10. Lake Chicot, Ark., June 6-7. Smith's Expedition to Tupelo July 5-21. Pontotoc July 11. Camargo's Cross Roads, near Harrisburg, July 13. Tupelo July 14-15. Old Town Creek July 15. Smith's Expedition to Oxford, Miss., August 1-30. Tallahatchie River August 7-9. Abbeville and Oxford August 12. Abbeville August 23. Mower's Expedition up White River to Duvall's Bluff September 1-7. March through Arkansas and Missouri in pursuit of Price September 17-October 25. (4 Cos. sent to Pilot Knob, Mo., and participated in actions at Ironton, Shut in Gap and Arcadia September 26. Fort Davidson, Pilot Knob, September 26-27. Leesburg or Harrison September 28-29.) Regiment assembled at St. Louis, Mo., November 2 and mustered out November 16, 1864. Veterans and recruits consolidated to two Companies and assigned to duty at Springfield, Ill., till August, 1865. Mustered out August 8, 1865.

Regiment lost during service 5 Officers and 59 Enlisted men killed and mortally wounded and 1 Officer and 138 Enlisted men by disease. Total 203.

15th REGIMENT INFANTRY.

Organized at Keokuk February 22, 1862. Moved to St. Louis, Mo., March 19; thence to Pittsburg Landing, Tenn. Attached to 3rd Brigade, 6th Division, Army of Tennessee, to July, 1862. 3rd Brigade, 6th Division, District of Corinth, Dept. of Tennessee, to November, 1862. 3rd Brigade. 6th Division, Left Wing 13th Army Corps (Old), Dept. of Tennessee, to December, 1862. 3rd Brigade, 6th Division, 16th Army Corps, to January, 1863. 3rd Brigade, 6th Division, 17th Corps, to September, 1863. 3rd Brigade, 1st Division, 17th Corps, to April, 1864. 3rd Brigade, 4th Division, 17th Corps, to July, 1865.

SERVICE.—Battle of Shiloh, Tenn., April 6-7, 1862. Advance on and siege of Corinth, Miss., April 29-May 30. Duty at Corinth and Bolivar till November. Battle of Corinth October 3-4. Pursuit to Ripley October 5-12. Grant's Central Mississippi Campaign November 2, 1862, to January 12, 1863. Moved to Memphis, Tenn., thence to Lake Providence, La., January 18, and duty there till April. Movement on Bruinsburg and turning Grand Gulf April 25-30. Battle of Port Gibson May 1 (Reserve). Battles of Raymond May 12; Jackson May 14; Champion's Hill May 16; Big Black River Crossing May 17. Siege of Vicksburg May 18-July 4. Assaults on Vicksburg May 19 and 22. Expedition to Mechanicsburg May 26-June 4. Messenger's Ferry, Big Black, July 3 (Co. "G"). Advance on Jackson, Miss., July 5-10. Guarding Ammunition and Subsistance trains. Duty at Vicksburg till February, 1864. Expedition to Monroe, La., August 20-September 2, 1863. Expedition to Canton October 14-20. Meridian Campaign February 3-March 6, 1864. Veterans on furlough March and April. Moved to Clifton, Tenn., thence march to Ackworth, Ga., via Huntsville and Decatur, Ala., and Rome, Ga., April 21-June 8. Atlanta (Ga.) Campaign June 8 to September 8. Operations about Marietta and against Kenesaw Mountain June 10-July 2. Bushy Mountain June 15-17. Assault on Kenesaw June 27. Nickajack Creek July 2-5. Chattahoochie River July 6-17. Leggett's, Bald Hill, July 20-21. Battle of Atlanta July 22. Siege of Atlanta July 22-August 25. Flank movement on Jonesboro August 25-30. Battle of Jonesboro August 31-September 1. Lovejoy Station September 2-6. Pursuit of Hood into Alabama October 1-26. Snake Creek Gap October 15-16. March to the sea November 15-December 10. Siege of Savannah December 10-21. Campaign of the Carolinas January to April, 1865. Pocotaligo, S. C., January 14-16. Salkehatchie Swamps February 3-5. River's Bridge February 3. South Edisto River February 9. Orangeburg February 11-12. Columbia February 15-17. Cheraw March 3. Fayetteville, N. C., March 11. Battle of Bentonville March 20-21. Occupation of Goldsboro March 24. Advance on Raleigh April 9-13. Occupation of Raleigh April 14. Bennett's House April 26. Surrender of Johnston and his army. March to Washington, D. C., via Richmond, Va., April 29-May 20. Grand Review May 24. Moved to Louisville, Ky., June. Mustered out July 24, 1865.

Regiment lost during service 8 Officers and 118 Enlisted men killed and mortally wounded and 1 Officer and 260 Enlisted men by disease. Total 387.

16th REGIMENT INFANTRY.

Organized at Davenport December 10, 1861, to March, 1862. Left State for St. Louis, Mo., March 20, 1862; thence moved to Pittsburg Landing, Tenn. Attached to 2nd Brigade, 6th Division, Army of Tennessee, to April, 1862. 2nd Brigade, 6th Division, Army of Tennessee and District of Corinth, Dept. of the Tennessee, to November, 1862. 3rd Brigade, 6th Division, Left Wing 13th Army Corps (Old), Dept. of Tennessee, to December, 1862. 3rd Brigade, 6th Division, 16th Army Corps, to January, 1863. 3rd Brigade, 6th Division, 17th

Corps, to September, 1863. 3rd Brigade, 1st Division, 17th Corps, to April, 1864. 3rd Brigade, 4th Division, 17th Corps, Army of Tennessee, to July, 1865.

SERVICE.—Battle of Shiloh, Tenn., April 6-7, 1862. Advance on and siege of Corinth, Miss., April 29-May 30. Duty at Corinth and Bolivar till November. Battle of Corinth October 3-4. Pursuit to Ripley October 5-12. Grant's Central Mississippi Campaign November 2, 1862, to January 12, 1863. Moved to Memphis, Tenn., thence to Lake Providence, La., January 18, and duty there till April, 1863. Movement on Bruinsburg and turning Grand Gulf April 25-30. Battle of Port Gibson May 1 (Reserve). Battles of Raymond May 12; Jackson May 14; Champion's Hill May 16; Big Black River Crossing May 17. Siege of Vicksburg, Miss., May 18-July 4. Expedition to Mechanicsburg May 26-June 4. Jones' Ferry, Big Black, June 28. Surrender of Vicksburg July 4. Advance on Jackson, Miss., July 5-10. Guarding Ammunition and Subsistance trains. Duty at Vicksburg till February, 1864. Expedition to Monroe, La., August 20-September 2, 1863. Expedition to Canton October 14-20. Meridian Campaign February 3-March 5, 1864. Veterans on furlough March and April. Moved to Clifton, Tenn., thence march to Ackworth, Ga., via Huntsville and Decatur, Ala., and Rome, Ga., April 21-June 8. Atlanta (Ga.) Campaign June 8 to September 8. Operations about Marietta and against Kenesaw Mountain June 10-July 2. Bushy Mountain June 15-17. Assault on Kenesaw June 27. Nickajack Creek July 2-5. Chattahoochie River July 6-17. Leggett's Bald Hill July 20-21. Battle of Atlanta July 22. Siege of Atlanta July 22-August 25. Flank movement on Jonesboro August 25-30. Lovejoy Station September 2-6. Pursuit of Hood into Alabama October 1-26. March to the sea November 15-December 10. Siege of Savannah December 10-21. Campaign of the Carolinas January to April, 1865. Pocotaligo, S. C., January 14-16. Salkehatchie Swamps February 3-5. River's Bridge February 3. South Edisto River February 9. Orangeburg February 11-12. Columbia February 15-17. Cheraw March 3. Fayetteville, N. C., March 11. Battle of Bentonville March 20-21. Occupation of Goldsboro March 24. Advance on Raleigh April 9-13. Occupation of Raleigh April 14. Bennett's House April 26. Surrender of Johnston and his army. March to Washington, D. C., via Richmond, Va., April 29-May 20. Grand Review May 24. Moved to Louisville, Ky., June. Mustered out July 19, 1865.

Regiment lost during service 7 Officers and 94 Enlisted men killed and mortally wounded and 3 Officers and 219 Enlisted men by disease. Total 323.

17th REGIMENT INFANTRY.

Organized at Keokuk March 21 to April 16, 1862, and mustered in April 16, 1862. Left State for St. Louis, Mo., April 19. Attached to 2nd Brigade, 3rd Division, Army of Mississippi, to November, 1862. 2nd Brigade, 7th Division, Left Wing 13th Army Corps (Old), Dept. of Tennessee, to December, 1862. 2nd Brigade, 7th Division, 16th Army Corps, to January, 1863. 2nd Brigade, 7th Division, 17th Army Corps, to September, 1863. 2nd Brigade, 2nd Division, 17th Army Corps, to December, 1863. 2nd Brigade, 3rd Division, 15th Army Corps, to April, 1865. 3rd Brigade, 2nd Division, 15th Army Corps, to July, 1865.

SERVICE.—Duty at Benton Barracks, Mo., till May 5, 1862. Moved to Hamburg Landing, Tenn., May 5-7. Advance on and siege of Corinth, Miss., May 8-30. Action on Corinth Road May 29. Pursuit to Booneville May 31-June 12. Camp at Clear Creek, near Corinth, till August 15. Expedition to Ripley, Miss., June 27-July 1. Moved to Jacinto August 15, and duty there till October 2. Expedition to Iuka, Miss., September 18-20. Battle of Iuka September 19. Moved to Corinth October 2. Battle of Corinth October 3-4. Pursuit to Ripley October 5-13. Grant's Central Mississippi Campaign November 2, 1862, to January 10, 1863. Duty at Bray's Station guarding Memphis & Charleston Railroad till February 8. March to Memphis, thence moved

to Helena, Ark., March 2-3. Yazoo Pass Expedition and operations against Fort Pemberton and Greenwood March 13-April 5. Moved to Richmond, La., April 17-20. Movement on Bruinsburg and turning Grand Gulf April 25-30. Battles of Port Gibson May 1; Raymond May 12; Jackson May 14; Champion's Hill May 16; Big Black River Crossing May 17. Siege of Vicksburg, Miss., May 18-July 4. Assaults on Vicksburg May 19 and 22. Fort Hill Bastion June 25. Surrender of Vicksburg July 4, and occupation of that city till September 9. Moved to Helena, Ark., September 9; thence to Memphis, Tenn., September 29, and march to Chattanooga, Tenn., October 10-November 19. Battles of Chattanooga November 23-25; Tunnel Hill November 23-24; Mission Ridge November 25. Pursuit to Graysville November 26-27. Provost and guard duty at Huntsville, Ala., December 22, 1863, to June, 1864. (Veterans on furlough April and May.) At Tilton, Ga., July 2 to October 13. Attack on Tilton October 13. Regiment captured. Remnant joined Sherman at Savannah, Ga., January, 1865. Campaign of the Carolinas January to April, 1865. Salkehatchie Swamps, S. C., February 3-5. South Edisto River February 9. North Edisto River February 12-13. Columbia February 15-17. Lynch's Creek February 25-26. Cox's Bridge, N. C., March 19-20. Battle of Bentonville March 20-21. Occupation of Goldsboro March 24. Advance on Raleigh April 9-13. Occupation of Raleigh April 14. Bennett's House April 26. Surrender of Johnston and his army. March to Washington, D. C., via Richmond, Va., April 29-May 20. Grand Review May 24. Moved to Louisville, Ky., June. Mustered out July 25, 1865.

Regiment lost during service 5 Officers and 66 Enlisted men killed and mortally wounded and 2 Officers and 121 Enlisted men by disease. Total 194.

18th REGIMENT INFANTRY.

Organized at Clinton and mustered in August 6, 1862. Moved to Sedalia, Mo., August 11. Attached to District of Southwest Missouri, Dept. of Missouri, to October, 1862. 1st Brigade, 2nd Division, Army of the Frontier, Dept. of Missouri, to June, 1863. District of Southwest Missouri, Dept. of Missouri, to October, 1863. District of the Frontier, Dept. of Missouri, to December, 1863. 2nd Brigade, District of the Frontier, Dept. of Missouri, to January, 1864. 2nd Brigade, District of the Frontier, 7th Army Corps, Dept. of Arkansas, to March, 1864. 1st Brigade, District of the Frontier, 7th Corps, to January, 1865. 1st Brigade, 3rd Division, 7th Corps, to July, 1865.

SERVICE.—Moved to Springfield, Mo., arriving September 13, 1862. Operations in Southwest Missouri September to November, 1862. Duty at Springfield, Mo., November 14, 1862, to September 22, 1863. Defence of Springfield January 7-8, 1863. Affair at Quincy September 4, 1863 (Detachment). Expedition from Springfield into Arkansas and Indian Territory September 7-19. Near Enterprise September 15. Operations against Shelby September 22-October 31. Arriving at Fort Smith October 31. Action at Cross Timbers October 15-16 (Cos. "D" and "F"). Garrison duty at Fort Smith, Ark., till March, 1864. Steele's Campaign against Camden March 22-May 15. Prairie D'Ann April 9-12. Moscow April 13. Poison Springs April 18. Jenkins Ferry, Saline River, April 30. Garrison duty at Fort Smith till July, 1865. (4 Cos. at Van Buren February 26 to July 6, 1865.) Ordered to Little Rock and mustered out July 20, 1865.

Regiment lost during service 2 Officers and 33 Enlisted men killed and mortally wounded and 1 Officer and 131 Enlisted men by disease. Total 167.

19th REGIMENT INFANTRY.

Organized at Keokuk and mustered in August 25, 1862. Ordered to St. Louis, Mo. Attached to District of Southwest Missouri, Dept. of Missouri, to October, 1862. 2nd Brigade, 3rd Division, Army of the Frontier, Dept. of Missouri, to June, 1863. 2nd Brigade, Herron's Division, 13th Army Corps, Army of Tennessee, to

July, 1863. 2nd Brigade, 2nd Division, 13th Army Corps, Dept. of the Tennessee, to August, 1863, and Dept. of the Gulf to June, 1864. 2nd Brigade, United States Forces, Texas, Dept. of the Gulf, to August, 1864. District of West Florida, Dept. of the Gulf, to December, 1864. District of Southern Alabama, Dept. of the Gulf, to February, 1865. 1st Brigade, 2nd Division, Reserve Corps, Military Division West Mississippi, February, 1865. 1st Brigade, 2nd Division, 13th Army Corps, Military Division West Mississippi, to July, 1865.

SERVICE.—Moved to Rolla, Mo., September 11, 1862; thence to Springfield, Mo., September 16, and to Cassville October 11. Blunt's Campaign October 17-December 27. Battle of Prairie Grove, Ark., December 7. Expedition over Boston Mountains to Van Buren December 27-28. Capture of Van Buren December 28. Duty at Forsythe February 15 to April 22, 1863. March to Hartsville and Salem April 22-May 2, and to Rolla June 2. Moved to Vicksburg, Miss., June 6-14. Siege of Vicksburg June 14-July 4. Expedition from Vicksburg to Yazoo City July 12-21. Capture of Yazoo City July 14. Moved to Port Hudson July 23 and to Carrollton, La., August 12-13. Expedition to Morganza September 5-12. Atchafalaya River September 9-10. Battle of Sterling's Plantation September 29. At Morganza till October 10, then moved to Carrollton. Expedition to Brazos, Santiago, Texas, October 27-December 2. Advance to Brownsville November 2-6 and duty there till July 24, 1864. Moved to New Orleans, La., July 24-August 7. Ordered to Pensacola, Fla., August 14, and duty at Barrancas, Fla., till December. Action at Milton, Fla., October 18. Expedition to Blackwater Bay October 25-28. Milton October 26. Moved to Fort Gaines, Dauphin Island, Ala., December 6, and duty there till March 17, 1865. Campaign against Mobile and its Defences March 17-April 12. Siege of Spanish Fort and Fort Blakely March 26-April 9. Fatigue duty dismantling Rebel Defences till May 4. Duty at Mobile till July 10. Mustered out July 10, 1865.

Regiment lost during service 6 Officers and 86 Enlisted men killed and mortally wounded and 2 Officers and 98 Enlisted men by disease. Total 192.

20th REGIMENT INFANTRY.

Organized at Clinton and mustered in August 25, 1862. Moved to St. Louis, Mo., September 5; thence to Springfield, Mo., arriving September 24. Attached to 2nd Brigade, 2nd Division, Army of the Frontier, Dept. of Missouri, to June, 1863. 1st Brigade, Herron's Division, 13th Army Corps, Dept. of Tennessee, to July, 1863. 1st Brigade, 2nd Division, 13th Army Corps, Dept. of Tennessee, to August, 1863, and Dept. of the Gulf to October, 1863. 2nd Brigade, 2nd Division, 13th Corps, Dept. of the Gulf, to January, 1864. 2nd Brigade, 4th Division, 13th Corps, to February, 1864. 2nd Brigade, 2nd Division, 13th Corps, to June, 1864. 1st Brigade, United States Forces, Texas, Dept. of the Gulf, to August, 1864. United States Forces, Mobile Bay, Dept. of the Gulf, to September, 1864. 1st Brigade, 3rd Division, 19th Corps, Dept. of the Gulf, to December, 1864. 4th Brigade, Reserve Corps, Military Division West Mississippi, to February, 1865. 3rd Brigade, 2nd Division, Reserve Corps, February, 1865. 3rd Brigade, 2nd Division, 13th Army Corps, Military Division West Mississippi, to July, 1865.

SERVICE.—Schofield's Campaign in Southwest Missouri October, 1862, to January, 1863. Occupation of Newtonia October 4. Battle of Prairie Grove, Ark., December 7. March over Boston Mountains to Van Buren, Ark., December 27-31. March to Huntsville, Ark., January 2-18, 1863, to Elk Creek January 22-February 15, and to St. Louis, arriving April 24. Guard Arsenal till May 15. (Cos. "A" and "F" at Defence of Cape Girardeau.) At Pilot Knob till June 3. Moved to St. Genevieve June 3, and to Vicksburg, Miss., June 6-14. Siege of Vicksburg June 14-July 4. Expedition to Yazoo City July 12-22. Capture of Yazoo City July 14. Moved to Port Hudson July 24 and to Carrollton,

La., August 16. Expedition to Morganza September 5-12. Atchafalaya River September 9-10. Sterling's Plantation September 29. At Morganza October 10, then moved to Carrollton. Expedition to Rio Grande, Texas, October 27-December 2. Brazos, Santiago, November 4. Point Isabel November 6. Duty at Brownsville, Point Isabel and Mustang Island till June 24, 1864. Moved to Brazos Santiago, thence to Brownsville, and duty there till August 2. Moved to New Orleans, thence to Mobile May August 2-7. Siege of Fort Morgan August 9-23. Capture of Fort Morgan September 23. Moved to Morganza September 7-12, thence to Duvall's Bluff, Ark., October 12, and duty there and at Brownsville till January, 1865. Moved to New Orleans January 28, thence to Barrancas, Fla., February 17. Campaign against Mobile and its Defences March and April. Steele's march from Pensacola, Fla., to Blakely, Ala., March 20-April 2. Occupation of Canoe Station March 27. Siege of Fort Blakely April 2-9. Assault and capture of Fort Blakely April 9. Moved to Mobile April 14, and duty there till July. Mustered out July 8, 1865.

Regiment lost during service 1 Officer and 13 Enlisted men killed and mortally wounded and 2 Officers and 157 Enlisted men by disease. Total 173.

21st REGIMENT INFANTRY.

Organized at Dubuque August, 1862. Moved to St. Louis, Mo., September 16. Attached to District of Rolla, Dept. of Missouri, to October, 1862. Warren's Brigade, District of Southeast Missouri, Dept. of Missouri, to January, 1863. 2nd Brigade, 2nd Division, Army of Southeast Missouri, Dept. of Missouri, to March, 1863. 2nd Brigade, 14th Division, 13th Army Corps, Dept. of Tennessee, to July, 1863. 2nd Brigade, 1st Division, 13th Army Corps, Dept. of Tennessee, to August, 1863, and Dept. of the Gulf to March, 1864. 1st Brigade, 1st Division, 13th Army Corps, Dept. of the Gulf, to June, 1864. District of LaFourche, Dept. of the Gulf, to August, 1864. 2nd Brigade, 2nd Division, 19th Army Corps, Dept. of the Gulf, to December, 1864. 1st Brigade, Reserve Corps, Military Division West Mississippi, to February, 1865. 1st Brigade, 1st Division, Reserve Corps, Military Division West Mississippi, February, 1865. 1st Brigade, 1st Division, 13th Army Corps, Military Division West Mississippi, to July, 1865.

SERVICE.—Moved from St. Louis to Rolla, Mo., September 22, 1862, and duty there till October 18. Moved to Salem October 18-20, and duty there till November. Moved to Houston and Hartsville. Action at Beaver Creek, Texas County, Mo., November 24 (Detachment). Moved to Houston December, and duty there till January 27, 1863. March to relief of Springfield, Mo., January 9-17. Action at Hartsville, Wood's Fork, January 11. Moved to West Plains January 27-February 2, thence to Iron Mountain February 9-25, and to St. Genevieve March 9-11. Moved to Milliken's Bend, La., March 15-22, and duty there till April 25. Movement on Bruinsburg and turning Grand Gulf April 25-30. Battle of Port Gibson May 1. Bayou Pierrie May 2-3. Battle of Champion's Hill May 16. Big Black River May 17. Siege of Vicksburg, Miss., May 18-July 4. Assaults on Vicksburg May 19 and 22. Advance on Jackson, Miss., July 5-10. Siege of Jackson July 10-17. Ordered to Dept. of the Gulf August 13. Duty at Carrollton, Brashear City and Berwick till October 3. Western Louisiana Campaign October 3-November 17. Expedition to New Iberia October 3-6 and to Vermillion Bayou October 8-30. Moved to Brazos, Santiago, Texas, November 22-26. At Matagorda Island and Indianola till March, 1864, and at Matagorda Island till June. Moved to New Orleans, La., and provost duty at Algiers, Carrollton and Thibodeaux till July 26. Moved to Morganza July 26, and duty there till September 3. Moved to mouth of White River, Ark., September 3. Duty there and at St. Charles and Duvall's Bluff till December. At Memphis, Tenn., till January, 1865. Ordered to New Orleans, La., January 1, thence to Kennersville Station, and duty there till February 5. Moved to Dauphin Island. Ala.,

February 5. Campaign against Mobile and its defences March 17 to April 12. Siege of Spanish Fort and Fort Blakely March 26-April 8. Assault on and capture of Fort Blakely April 9. Occupation of Mobile April 12 to May 26. Moved to Shreveport, La., May 26-June 8, and duty there and in District of LaFourche till July. Mustered out July 25, 1865.

Regiment lost during service 4 Officers and 77 Enlisted men killed and mortally wounded and 1 Officer and 168 Enlisted men by disease. Total 250.

22nd REGIMENT INFANTRY.

Organized at Iowa City and mustered in September 9, 1862. Moved to St. Louis, Mo., September 14-18, thence to Rolla, Mo., September 22-23. Attached to District of Rolla, Dept. of Missouri, to February, 1863. 2nd Brigade, 2nd Division, Army of Southeast Missouri, to March, 1863. 2nd Brigade, 14th Division, 13th Army Corps, Dept. Tennessee, to July, 1863. 2nd Brigade, 1st Division, 13th Army Corps, Dept. Tennessee, to August, 1863, and Dept. of the Gulf to March, 1864. 1st Brigade, 1st Division, 13th Corps, Dept. Gulf, to June, 1864. Defences of New Orleans, La., to August, 1864. 2nd Brigade, 2nd Division, 19th Army Corps, Dept. Gulf and Army of the Shenandoah, Middle Military Division, to January, 1865. 2nd Brigade, Grover's Division, District of Savannah, Ga., Dept. South, to March, 1865. 1st Brigade, 1st Division, 10th Army Corps, Army Ohio, to April, 1865. District of Savannah, Ga., Dept. South, to July, 1865.

SERVICE.—Garrison duty at Rolla, Mo., till January 27, 1863. Moved to West Plains January 27-February 2, 1863. March to Eminence, thence to Iron Mountain, Mo., February 9-26. Moved to St. Genevieve March 9-12, thence to Milliken's Bend, La., March 22-27, and duty there till April 25. Movement on Bruinsburg and turning Grand Gulf April 25-30. Anderson's Hill April 30. Battle of Port Gibson May 1. Bayou Pierrie May 2-3. Battle of Champion's Hill May 16. Big Black River May 17. Siege of Vicksburg, Miss., May 18-July 4. Assaults on Vicksburg May 19 and 22. Advance on Jackson, Miss., July 5-10. Siege of Jackson July 10-17. Ordered to Dept. of the Gulf August 13. Duty at Carrollton, Brashear City and Berwick till October 3. Western Louisiana Campaign October 3-November 17. Expedition to New Iberia October 3-7 and to Vermillion Bayou October 8-30. Moved to Brazos Santiago, Texas, November 17-23. Fort Esperanza November 27-30. Duty at DeCrow's Point till January 3, 1864, and at Indianola till March 13. Affair at Lamar February 11 (Detachment). At Matagorda Island till April. Affair Corpus Christi March 24 (Detachment). Moved to Baton Rouge, La., and duty there till July. Moved to Fort Monroe, thence to City Point, Va., July 6-17. Duty at Bermuda Hundred and on north side of the James at Deep Bottom till July 30. Moved to Washington, D. C., July 30-August 1. Sheridan's Shenandoah Valley Campaign August 7-November 28. Berryville September 3-4. Battle of Opequan, Winchester, September 19. Fisher's Hill September 22. Woodstock September 23. Battle of Cedar Creek October 19. Duty at Kernstown, Winchester and in the Shenandoah Valley till January, 1865. Moved to Savannah, Ga., January 5-22, 1865, and duty there till March. Moved to Newberne and Morehead City, N. C., thence to Augusta, Ga., April 11. Duty there and at Savannah, Ga., till July. Mustered out July 25, 1865.

Regiment lost during service 6 Officers and 108 Enlisted men killed and mortally wounded and 1 Officer and 135 Enlisted men by disease. Total 250.

23rd REGIMENT INFANTRY.

Organized at Des Moines and mustered in September 19, 1862. Ordered to St. Louis, Mo. Attached to Dept. Missouri to February, 1863. 2nd Brigade, 2nd Division, Army of Southeast Missouri, Dept. Missouri, to March, 1863. 2nd Brigade, 14th Division, 13th Army Corps, Dept. Tennessee, to July, 1863. 2nd Brigade, 1st Division, 13th Army Corps, Dept. Tennessee, to August, 1863, and Dept. of the Gulf to March, 1864. 1st

Brigade, 1st Division, 13th Army Corps, Dept. Gulf, to June, 1864. 1st Brigade, 3rd Division, 19th Army Corps, Dept. Gulf, to August, 1864. 4th Brigade, 2nd Division, 19th Corps, Dept. Gulf, to December, 1864. 4th Brigade, Reserve Corps, Military Division West Mississippi, to February, 1865. 1st Brigade, 2nd Division, Reserve Corps, Middle Division West Mississippi, February, 1865. 1st Brigade, 2nd Division, 13th Army Corps, Military Division West Mississippi, to July, 1865.

SERVICE.—Duty at St. Louis, Camp Patterson and West Plains, Mo., till February, 1863. March via Thomasville and Eminence to Iron Mountain, Mo., February 9-26, and duty there till March 9. Moved to St. Genevieve March 9-12, thence to Milliken's Bend, La., March 22-27, and duty there till April 25. Movement on Bruinsburg and turning Grand Gulf April 25-30. Anderson's Hill April 30. Battle of Port Gibson May 1. Bayou Pierrie May 2-3. Battle of Champion's Hill May 16. Big Black River May 17. (A detachment of Regiment guard prisoners to Memphis, Tenn., May 18-June 10, and while en route to rejoin Brigade at Vicksburg, reinforced garrison at Milliken's Bend, La., June 5, and participated in repulse of McCullough's attack on Milliken's Bend June 6-7.) Siege of Vicksburg May 18-July 4. Advance on Jackson July 5-10. Siege of Jackson July 10-17. Ordered to the Dept. of the Gulf August 13. Duty at Carrollton, Brashear City and Berwick till October 3. Western Louisiana Campaign October 3-November 17. Expedition to New Iberia October 3-7, and to Vermillion Bayou October 8-30. Moved to Brazos Santiago, Texas, November 17-23. Fort Esperanza November 27-30. Duty at Indianola till March, and at Matagorda Island till May 4. Moved to New Orleans, La., thence to join Banks on Red River, May 4-15. Joined at Simsport and retreat to Morganza May 16-22. Duty at Morganza till October. Simsport October 6. Moved to Duvall's Bluff October 12, and duty there and in Arkansas till January, 1865. Ordered to New Orleans, La., thence to Barrancas, Fla., February 17. Campaign against Mobile and its defences March and April. Steele's march from Pensacola, Fla., to Blakely, Ala., March 21-April 2. Occupation of Canoe Station March 27. Siege of Fort Blakely April 2-9. Assault and capture of Fort Blakely April 9. Occupation of Mobile April 12, and duty there till June. At Columbus till July. Mustered out July 26, 1865.

Regiment lost during service 6 Officers and 69 Enlisted men killed and mortally wounded and 1 Officer and 208 Enlisted men by disease. Total 284.

24th REGIMENT INFANTRY.

Organized at Muscatine and mustered in September 18, 1862. Moved to Helena, Ark., October 20-28. Attached to District of Eastern Arkansas, Dept, Missouri, to December, 1862. 3rd Brigade, 1st Division, District of Eastern Arkansas, December, 1862. 2nd Brigade, 2nd Division, District of Eastern Arkansas, Dept. Tennessee, to February, 1863. 2nd Brigade, 12th Division, 13th Army Corps, Dept. Tennessee, to July, 1863. 2nd Brigade, 3rd Division, 13th Army Corps, Dept. Tennessee, to August, 1863, and Dept. of the Gulf to June, 1864. District of LaFourche, Dept. Gulf, to July, 1864. 3rd Brigade, 2nd Division, 19th Army Corps, Dept. of the Gulf and Army of the Shenandoah, Middle Military Division, to August, 1864. 4th Brigade, 2nd Division, 19th Army Corps, Army Shenandoah, to December, 1864. 3rd Brigade, 2nd Division, 19th Army Corps, Army Shenandoah, to January, 1865. 3rd Brigade, Grover's Division, District of Savannah, Dept. South, to March, 1865. 1st Brigade, 1st Division, 10th Army Corps, Army Ohio, to April, 1865. District of Savannah, Ga., Dept. South, to July, 1865.

SERVICE.—Expedition from Helena, Ark., to Arkansas Post, November 16-21, 1862. Expedition to Grenada, Miss., November 27-December 5. Gorman's Expedition up White River January 13-19, 1863. Expedition up St. Francis and Little Rivers March 5-12. Skirmish at Madison March 9. Yazoo Pass Expedition and operations against Fort Pemberton and Greenwood March

13-April 5. Moved to Milliken's Bend April 13. Movement on Bruinsburg and turning Grand Gulf April 25-30. Battle of Port Gibson May 1. Bayou Pierrie May 2-3. Fourteen Mile Creek May 12-13. Battle of Champion's Hill May 16. Big Black River Bridge May 17. Siege of Vicksburg, Miss., May 18-July 4. Assaults on Vicksburg May 19 and 22. Advance on Jackson, Miss., July 5-10. Siege of Jackson July 10-17. Ordered to New Orleans, La., August 2. Duty at Carrollton and Brashear City till October. Western Louisiana Campaign October 3-November 20. Vermillionville, Carrion Crow Bayou, November 3. At New Iberia till January 17, 1864. Moved to New Orleans January 17, thence to Madisonville and duty there till March. Red River Campaign March 14-May 22. Advance from Franklin to Alexandria March 14-26. Battle of Sabine Cross Roads April 8. Pleasant Hill April 9. Cane River Crossing April 22-23. At Alexandria April 26-May 13. Construction of dam at Alexandria April 30-May 10. Graham's Plantation May 5. Retreat to Morganza May 13-22. Mansura May 16. Expedition from Morganza to the Atchafalaya River May 30-June 6. Moved to Fort Monroe, Va., thence to Washington, D. C., July 2-13. Sheridan's Shenandoah Valley Campaign August 7-November 28. Battle of Opequan, Winchester, September 19. Fisher's Hill September 22. Battle of Cedar Creek October 19. Duty in the Shenandoah Valley till January, 1865. Moved to Baltimore, Md., January 6-7, thence to Savannah, Ga., January 14-20. To Hilton Head, S. C., March 4. To Wilmington, N. C., March 6. To Morehead City and Newberne March 8-10. To Morehead City March 12. To Goldsboro April 9 and to Savannah May 1-6. Moved to Hamburg, S. C., May 11, to Augusta May 31 and to Savannah June 20. Moved to Davenport, Iowa, July 20-August 2. Mustered out at Savannah, Ga., July 17, 1865.

Regiment lost during service 9 Officers and 119 Enlisted men killed and mortally wounded and 3 Officers and 212 Enlisted men by disease. Total 343.

25th REGIMENT INFANTRY.

Organized at Mount Pleasant and mustered in September 27, 1862. Ordered to Helena, Ark., November. Attached to District of Eastern Arkansas, Dept. Missouri, to December, 1862. 3rd Brigade, 1st Division, District of Eastern Arkansas, Dept. Tennessee, December, 1862. 2nd Brigade, 11th Division, Right Wing 13th Army Corps, Dept. Tennessee, December, 1862. 2nd Brigade, 4th Division, Sherman's Yazoo Expedition, to January, 1863. 2nd Brigade, 1st Division, 15th Army Corps, Army Tennessee, to December, 1863. 3rd Brigade, 1st Division, 15th Corps, to April, 1864. 2nd Brigade, 1st Division, 15th Corps, to September, 1864. 3rd Brigade, 1st Division, 15th Corps, to June, 1865.

SERVICE.—Expedition from Helena to mouth of White River, November 17-24, 1862. Sherman's Yazoo Expedition December 22, 1862, to January 2, 1863. Chickasaw Bayou December 26-28, 1862. Chickasaw Bluff December 29. Expedition to Arkansas Post, Ark., January 3-10, 1863. Assault on and capture of Fort Hindman, Arkansas Post, January 10-11. Moved to Young's Point, La., January 17-23, and duty there till April. Expedition to Greenville, Black Bayou and Deer Creek April 2-14. Demonstration against Haines and Snyder's Bluffs April 28-May 2. Moved to join army in rear of Vicksburg, Miss., via Richmond and Grand Gulf May 2-14. Fourteen-Mile Creek May 12-13. Jackson May 14. Siege of Vicksburg May 18-July 4. Assaults on Vicksburg May 19 and 22. Advance on Jackson, Miss., July 5-10. Siege of Jackson July 10-17. Briar Creek near Canton July 17. Canton July 18. Duty at Big Black till September 22. Moved to Memphis, thence march to Chattanooga, Tenn., September 22-November 21. Operations on Memphis & Charleston Railroad in Alabama October 10-29. Cherokee Station October 21 and 29. Cane Creek October 26. Tuscumbia October 26-27. Battles of Chattanooga November 23-27; Lookout Mountain November 23-24; Mission Ridge November 25; Ringgold Gap, Taylor's Ridge,

November 27. March to relief of Knoxville November 28-December 8. Garrison duty in Alabama till May, 1864. Atlanta (Ga.) Campaign May 1 to September 8. Demonstration on Resaca May 8-13. Snake Creek Gap May 10-12. Battle of Resaca May 14-15. Operations on Pumpkin Vine Creek and battles about Dallas, New Hope Church and Allatoona Hills May 25-June 5. Operations about Marietta and against Kenesaw Mountain June 10-July 2. Bushy Mountain June 15-17. Assault on Kenesaw June 27. Nickajack Creek July 2-5. Chattahoochie River July 6-17. Battle of Atlanta July 22. Siege of Atlanta July 22-August 25. Ezra Chapel, Hood's second sortie, July 28. Flank movement on Jonesboro August 25-30. Battle of Jonesboro August 31-September 1. Lovejoy Station September 2-6. Pursuit of Hood into Alabama October 1-26. March to the sea November 15-December 10. Clinton November 22. Griswoldsville November 23. Statesboro December 4. Siege of Savannah December December 10-21. Campaign of the Carolinas January to April, 1865. Reconnoissance to Salkehatchie River, S. C., January 25. Salkehatchie Swamps, S. C., February 3-5. South Edisto River February 9. North Edisto River February 12-13. Columbia February 15-17. Lynch's Creek February 25-26. Battle of Bentonville, N. C., March 20-21. Occupation of Goldsboro March 24. Advance on Raleigh April 9-13. Occupation of Raleigh April 14. Bennett's House April 26. Surrender of Johnston and his army. March to Washington, D. C., via Richmond, Va., April 29-May 20. Grand Review May 24. Mustered out June 6, 1865.

Regiment lost during service 2 officers and 63 Enlisted men killed and mortally wounded and 2 Officers and 207 Enlisted men by disease. Total 274.

26th REGIMENT INFANTRY.

Organized at Clinton and mustered in September 30, 1862. Moved to St. Louis, Mo., thence to Helena, Ark., October, 1862. Attached to District of Eastern Arkansas, Dept. Missouri, to November, 1862. 2nd Brigade, 1st Division, District of Eastern Arkansas, Dept. Tennessee, to December, 1862. 3rd Brigade, 11th Division, Right Wing, 13th Army Corps (Old), Dept. Tennessee, December, 1862. 3rd Brigade, 4th Division, Sherman's Yazoo Expedition to January, 1863. 3rd Brigade, 1st Division, 15th Army Corps, Army Tennessee, to September, 1863. 2nd Brigade, 1st Division, 15th Army Corps, to December, 1863. 1st Brigade, 1st Division, 15th Army Corps, to April, 1865. 3rd Brigade, 1st Division, 15th Army Corps, to June, 1865.

SERVICE.—Expedition from Helena, Ark., to mouth of White River November 16-21, 1862. Sherman's Yazoo Expedition December 22, 1862, to January 2, 1863. Chickasaw Bayou December 26-28, 1862. Chickasaw Bluffs December 29. Expedition to Arkansas Post, Ark., January 3-10, 1863. Assault on and capture of Fort Hindman, Arkansas Post, January 10-11. Moved to Young's Point, La., January 17-23, and duty there till April. Expedition to Greenville, Black Bayou and Deer Creek April 2-14. Demonstration on Haines and Snyder's Bluffs April 28-May 2. Moved to join army in rear of Vicksburg, Miss., May 2-14. Jackson, Miss., May 14. Siege of Vicksburg May 18-July 4. Assaults on Vicksburg May 19 and 22. Advance on Jackson, Miss., July 5-10. Siege of Jackson July 10-17. Brandon Station May 19. At Big Black till September 22. Moved to Memphis; thence march to Chattanooga, Tenn., September 22-November 21. Operations on Memphis & Charleston Railroad in Alabama October 20-29. Cherokee Station October 21 and 29. Cane Creek October 26. Tuscumbia October 26-27. Battles of Chattanooga November 23-27. Lookout Mountain November 23-24. Mission Ridge November 25. Ringgold Gap, Taylor's Ridge, November 27. March to relief of Knoxville November 28-December 8. Garrison duty in Alabama till April, 1864. Harrison's Gap April 21 (Detachment). Atlanta (Ga.) Campaign May 1 to September 8. Demonstration on Resaca May 8-13. Snake Creek Gap May 10-12. Battle of Resaca May 14-15. Operations on line of

Pumpkin Vine Creek and battles about Dallas, New Hope Church and Allatoona Hills May 25-June 5. Operations about Marietta and against Kenesaw Mountain June 10-July 2. Bushy Mountain June 15-17. Assault on Kenesaw June 27. Nickajack Creek July 2-5. Chattahoochie River July 6-17. Battle of Atlanta July 22. Siege of Atlanta July 22-August 25. Ezra Chapel, Hood's second sortie, July 28. Flank movement on Jonesboro August 25-30. Lovejoy Station September 2-6. Pursuit of Hood into Alabama October 1-26. Kingston October 12. Ship's Gap, Taylor's Ridge, October 16. March to the sea November 15-December 10. Griswoldsville October 23. Siege of Savannah December 10-21. Campaign of the Carolinas January to April, 1865. Reconnoissance to Salkehatchie River, S. C., January 25, 1865. Hickory Hill February 1. Salkehatchie Swamps, S. C., February 3-5. South Edisto River February 9. North Edisto River, Columbia, February 15-17. Lynch's Creek February 25-26. Battle of Bentonville, N. C., March 20-21. Occupation of Goldsboro March 24. Advance on Raleigh April 9-13. Occupation of Raleigh April 14. Bennett's House April 26. Surrender of Johnston and his army. March to Washington, D. C., via Richmond, Va., April 29-May 20. Grand Review May 24. Mustered out June 6, 1865.

Regiment lost during service 6 Officers and 70 Enlisted men killed and mortally wounded and 4 Officers and 213 Enlisted men by disease. Total 293.

27th REGIMENT INFANTRY.

Organized at Dubuque and mustered in October 3, 1862. Moved to St. Paul, Minn., October 11, 1862, Companies "A," "B," "C," "E," "F" and "G." Moved to Mille Lac's, Minn., October 17, thence moved to Cairo, Ill., November 4. Companies "D," "I," "H" and "K" at Fort Snelling, Minn., till November 1. Moved to Cairo, Ill., November 1. Regiment moved to Memphis, Tenn., November 20. Attached to District of Memphis, Dept. Tennessee, to December, 1862, District of Jackson, Tenn., 16th Army Corps, Army Tennessee, to March, 1863. 3rd Brigade, 3rd Division, 16th Army Corps, to August, 1863. True's Brigade, Arkansas Expedition to November, 1863. Gilbert's Brigade, District of Memphis, 5th Division, 16th Corps, to January, 1864. 2nd Brigade, 3rd Division, 16th Army Corps, to December, 1864. 2nd Brigade, 2nd Division (Detachment), Army Tennessee, Dept. of the Cumberland, to February, 1865. 2nd Brigade, 2nd Division, 16th Army Corps, Military Division West Mississippi, to August, 1865.

SERVICE.—Duty at Jackson, Tenn., and guard railroad from Corinth, Miss., to Memphis, Tenn., till June 2, 1863. Guard Memphis & Charleston Railroad at Moscow till August 20. Moved to Memphis, thence to Helena and Brownsville, Ark., August 20-24. Steele's Arkansas Expedition August 24-September 10. Bayou LaFourche and capture of Little Rock September 10. At Little Rock till November 15. Moved to Memphis, Tenn., November 15, and duty there till January 28, 1864. Moved to Vicksburg, Miss., January 28. Meridian Campaign February 3-March 5. Meridian February 14-15. Marion February 15-17. Union February 21-22. Canton February 28. Red River Campaign March 10-May 22. Fort DeRussy March 14. Occupation of Alexandria March 16. Henderson's Hill March 21. Battle of Pleasant Hill April 9. Cloutiersville and Cane River Crossing April 22-24. At Alexandria April 27-May 13. Moore's Plantation May 5-7. Bayou Boeuf May 7. Bayou LaMourie April 12. Retreat to Morganza May 13-20. Mansura May 16. Yellow Bayou May 18-19. Moved to Vicksburg, Miss.; thence to Memphis, Tenn., May 20-June 10. Action at Lake Chicot, Ark., June 6-7. Smith's Expedition to Tupelo July 5-21. Poctotoc July 11. Camargo's Cross Roads, near Harrisburg, July 13. Tupelo July 14-15. Old Town Creek July 15. Smith's Expedition to Oxford, Miss., August 1-30. Tallahatchie River August 7-9. Abbeville and Oxford August 12. Abbeville August 13. Mower's Expedition up White River to Duvall's Bluff, Ark., September 1-6. March through Arkansas and Missouri in pursuit of Price September

17-November 18. Moved to Nashville, Tenn., November 25-December 1. Battle of Nashville, Tenn., December 15-16. Pursuit of Hood to the Tennessee River December 17-28. At Eastport, Miss., till February 9, 1865. Expedition from Eastport to Iuka January 9. Moved to New Orleans, La., February 9-22. Campaign against Mobile and its Defences March 8-April 12. Siege of Fort Blakely and Spanish Fort March 26-April 8. Assault and capture of Fort Blakely April 9. Occupation of Mobile April 12. March to Montgomery April 13-25, and duty there till July. Moved to Vicksburg, Miss., July 14; thence to Clinton, Iowa, July 15-August 3. Mustered out August 8, 1865.

Regiment lost during service 1 Officer and 23 Enlisted men killed and mortally wounded and 2 Officers and 167 Enlisted men by disease. Total 193.

28th REGIMENT INFANTRY.

Organized at Iowa City and mustered in October 10, 1862. Ordered to Helena, Ark., arriving there November 20, 1862. Attached to 2nd Brigade, 1st Division, District of Eastern Arkansas, Dept. of Missouri, to December, 1862. 2nd Brigade, 2nd Division, District of Eastern Arkansas, Dept. of the Tennessee, to January, 1863. 2nd Brigade, 12th Division, 13th Army Corps, Dept. of the Tennessee, to July, 1863. 2nd Brigade, 3rd Division, 13th Corps, Dept. of the Tennessee, to August, 1863, and Dept. of the Gulf to June, 1864. District of LaFourche, Dept. of the Gulf, to July, 1863. 3rd Brigade, 2nd Division, 19th Army Corps, Dept. of the Gulf, to August, 1864. 4th Brigade, 2nd Division, 19th Corps, Army of the Shenandoah, Middle Military Division, to December, 1864. 2nd Brigade, 2nd Division, 19th Corps, to January, 1865. 2nd Brigade, Grover's Division, District of Savannah, Ga., Dept. of the South, to March, 1865. 1st Brigade, 1st Division, 10th Army Corps, Army of Ohio, to April, 1865. District of Savannah, Dept. of the South, to July, 1865.

SERVICE.—Hovey's Expedition from Helena, Ark., to Grenada, Miss., November 27-December 5, 1862. Gorman's Expedition up White River January 13-19, 1863. Expedition from Helena to Yazoo Pass by Moon Lake, Yazoo Pass and Coldwater and Tallahatchie Rivers February 14-April 5. Operations against Fort Pemberton and Greenwood March 13-April 5. Expedition to St. Francis River April 5-11. Moved to Milliken's Bend, La., April 11-13. Movement on Bruinsburg and turning Grand Gulf April 25-30. Battle of Port Gibson May 1. Bayou Pierrie May 2-3. Fourteen-Mile Creek May 12-13. Battle of Champion's Hill May 16. Big Black River May 17. Siege of Vicksburg, Miss., May 18-July 4. Assaults on Vicksburg May 19 and 22. Advance on Jackson, Miss., July 5-10. Siege of Jackson July 10-17. Ordered to New Orleans, La., August 2. At Carrollton and Brashear City till October. Western Louisiana Campaign October 3-November 30. Vermillionville, Carrion Crow Bayou, November 3. At New Iberia till December 17. Moved to New Orleans December 17, thence to Madisonville January 7, 1864, and duty there till March. Red River Campaign March 14-May 22. Advance from Franklin to Alexandria March 14-26. Battle of Sabine Cross Roads April 8. Pleasant Hill April 9. Cane River Crossing April 23-24. At Alexandria April 26-May 13. Graham's Plantation May 5. Retreat to Morganaza May 13-20. Mansura May 16. Expedition from Morganza to the Atchafalaya May 30-June 6. Moved to Fortress Monroe, thence to Washington, D. C., July. Sheridan's Shenandoah Valley Campaign August 7-November 28. Battle of Opequan, Winchester, September 19. Fisher's Hill September 22. Battle of Cedar Creek October 19. Duty in the Shenandoah Valley till January, 1865. Moved to Baltimore, Md.; thence to Savannah, Ga., January 6-20. Moved to Hilton Head, S. C., March 4; to Wilmington, N. C., March 6; to Morehead City and New Berne March 8-10; to Morehead City March 12; to Goldsboro April 9, and to Savannah, Ga., May 14. Duty in Georgia and South Carolina till July. Mustered out July 31, 1865.

Regiment lost while in service 6 Officers and 76 Enlisted men killed and mortally wounded and 3 Officers and 186 Enlisted men by disease. Total 271.

29th REGIMENT INFANTRY.

Organized at Camp Dodge, Council Bluffs, and mustered in December 1, 1862. March to St. Joseph, Mo., December 5-9; thence to Benton Barracks, Mo., December 19-20. Attached to District of St. Louis, Mo., Dept. of Missouri, to January, 1862. 2nd Brigade, 13th Division, 13th Army Corps, Dept. of Tennessee, to July, 1863. 2nd Brigade, 13th Division, 16th Army Corps, to August, 1863. 2nd Brigade, 3rd Division, Arkansas Expedition, to January, 1864. 2nd Brigade, 3rd Division, 7th Army Corps, Dept. of Arkansas, to March, 1864. 1st Brigade, 3rd Division, 7th Corps, to May, 1864. 1st Brigade, 1st Division, 7th Army Corps, to November, 1864. 2nd Brigade, 2nd Division, 7th Corps, to February, 1865. 2nd Brigade, 3rd Division, Reserve Corps, Military Division West Mississippi, to February, 1865. 2nd Brigade, 3rd Division, 13th Army Corps, Military Division West Mississippi, to July, 1865. Dept. of Texas to August, 1865.

SERVICE.—Guard Prison at Benton Barracks, Mo., till December 25, 1862. Moved to Columbus, Ky., en route to Helena, Ark., December 25-29. Duty there till January 8, 1863. Moved to Helena, Ark., January 8, and duty there till March. Gorman's Expedition up White River January 11-26. Yazoo Pass Expedition and operations against Fort Pemberton and Greenwood March 13-April 5. Duty at Helena till August. Repulse of Holmes' attack on Helena July 4. Steele's Expedition to Little Rock August 1-September 10. Bayou LaFourche and capture of Little Rock September 10. Duty at Little Rock till March, 1864. Steele's Expedition to Camden March 23 to May 3. Antoine or Terre Noir Creek April 2. Elkin's Ferry, Little Missouri River, April 3-4 Prairie D'Ann April 9-12. Liberty Postoffice April 15-16. Jenkins Ferry, Saline River, April 30. Duty at Little Rock till July, and at Lewisburg till September. At Little Rock till February, 1865. Moved to New Orleans, La., February 9-16. Campaign against Mobile and its Defences March 17-April 12. Siege of Spanish Fort and Fort Blakely March 26-April 9. Occupation of Mobile April 12. Whistler's or Eight-Mile Bridge April 13. March to Mt. Vernon and duty at Mt. Vernon Arsenal till June. Moved to Brazos Santiago, Texas, and duty there till July. Moved to New Orleans, La.; thence home and mustered out August 10, 1865.

Regiment lost during service 1 Officer and 42 Enlisted men killed and mortally wounded and 1 Officer and 266 Enlisted men by disease. Total 310.

30th REGIMENT INFANTRY.

Organized at Keokuk and mustered in September 20, 1862. Moved to St. Louis, Mo., October 25, 1862; thence to Helena, Ark. Attached to District of Eastern Arkansas, Dept. of Missouri, to December, 1862. 2nd Brigade, 1st Division, District of Eastern Arkansas, Dept. of Tennessee, December, 1862. 3rd Brigade, 11th Division, Right Wing 13th Army Corps (Old), Dept. of Tennessee, to December, 1862. 3rd Brigade, 4th Division, Sherman's Yazoo Expedition, to January, 1863. 3rd Brigade, 1st Division, 15th Army Corps, Dept. of Tennessee, to September, 1863. 2nd Brigade, 1st Division, 15th Corps, to December, 1863. 1st Brigade, 1st Division, 15th Corps, to September, 1864. 3rd Brigade, 1st Division, 15th Corps, to July, 1865.

SERVICE.—Expedition from Helena, Ark., to Arkansas Post November 16-21, 1862. Hovey's Expedition to Grenada, Miss., November 27-December 5. Mitchell's Cross Roads December 1. Sherman's Yazoo Expedition December 22, 1862, to January 2, 1863. Chickasaw Bayou December 26-28, 1862. Chickasaw Bluffs December 29. Expedition to Arkansas Post, Ark., January 3-10, 1863. Assault on and capture of Fort Hindman, Arkansas Post, January 10-11. Moved to Young's Point, La., January 17-23, and duty there till April. Expedition to Greenville, Black Bayou and Deer Creek April 2-14. Demonstration on Haines and Snyder's Bluffs April 28-May

2. Moved to join army in rear of Vicksburg, Miss., via Richmond and Grand Gulf May 2-14. Jackson, Miss., May 14. Siege of Vicksburg May 18-July 4. Assaults on Vicksburg May 19 and 22. Advance on Jackson July 5-10. Siege of Jackson July 10-17. Brandon Station July 17-19. Duty at Big Black till September 22. Moved to Memphis, thence march to Chattanooga, Tenn., September 22-November 21. Operations on Memphis & Charleston Railroad in Alabama October 20-29. Cherokee Station October 21 and 29. Cane Creek October 26. Tuscumbia October 26-27. Battles of Chattanooga November 23-27; Lookout Mountain November 23-24; Mission Ridge November 25; Ringgold Gap, Taylor's Ridge, November 27. March to relief of Knoxville November 28-December 8. Garrison duty in Alabama till April, 1864. Atlanta Campaign May 1 to September 8. Demonstration on Resaca May 8-13. Snake Creek Gap May 10-12. Battle of Resaca May 14-15. Operations on line of Pumpkin Vine Creek and battles about Dallas, New Hope Church and Allatoona Hills May 25-June 5. Operations about Marietta and against Kenesaw Mountain June 10-July 2. Bushy Mountain June 15-17. Assault on Kenesaw June 27. Nickajack Creek July 2-5. Chattahoochie River July 6-17. Battle of Atlanta July 22. Siege of Atlanta July 22-August 25. Ezra Chapel, Hood's second sortie, July 28. Flank movement on Jonesboro August 25-30. Battle of Jonesboro August 31-September 1. Lovejoy Station September 2-6. Pursuit of Hood into Alabama October 1-26. March to the sea November 15-December 10. Griswoldsville November 23. Siege of Savannah December 10-21. Campaign of the Carolinas January to April, 1865. Reconnoissance to Salkehatchie River, S. C., January 25. Salkehatchie Swamps, S. C., February 3-5. South Edisto River February 9. North Edisto River February 12-13. Columbia February 15-17. Lynch's Creek February 25-26. Battle of Bentonville, N. C., March 20-21. Occupation of Goldsboro March 24. Advance on Raleigh April 9-13. Occupation of Raleigh April 14. Bennett's House April 26. Surrender of Johnston and his army. March to Washington, D. C., via Richmond April 29-May 20. Grand Review May 24. Mustered out June 5, 1865.

Regiment lost during service 8 Officers and 65 Enlisted men killed and mortally wounded and 3 Officers and 241 Enlisted men by disease. Total 317.

31st REGIMENT INFANTRY.

Organized at Davenport and mustered in October 13, 1862. Moved to Helena, Ark., November 1-20, 1862. Attached to 3rd Brigade, 1st Division, District of Eastern Arkansas, Dept. of Tennessee, to December, 1862. 2nd Brigade, 11th Division, Right Wing 13th Army Corps (Old), Dept. of Tennessee, to December, 1862. 2nd Brigade, 4th Division, Sherman's Yazoo Expedition, to January, 1863. 2nd Brigade, 1st Division, 15th Army Corps, Dept. of Tennessee, to September, 1864. 3rd Brigade, 1st Division, 15th Army Corps, to June, 1865.

SERVICE.—Hovey's Expedition from Helena, Ark., to Coldwater, Miss., November 27-December 5, 1862. Sherman's Yazoo Expedition December 22, 1862, to January 2, 1863. Chickasaw Bayou December 26-28, 1862. Chickasaw Bluffs December 29. Expedition to Arkansas Post January 3-10, 1863. Assault on and capture of Fort Hindman, Arkansas Post, January 10-11. Moved to Young's Point, La., January 17-23, and duty there till April. Expedition to Greenville, Black Bayou and Deer Creek April 2-14. Deer Creek April 7. Black Bayou April 10. Demonstration on Haines and Snyder's Bluffs April 28-May 2. Moved to join army in rear of Vicksburg, Miss., via Richmond and Grand Gulf May 2-14. Fourteen-Mile Creek May 12-13. Jackson, Miss., May 14. Siege of Vicksburg May 18-July 4. Assaults on Vicksburg May 19 and 22. Advance on Jackson, Miss., July 5-10. Siege of Jackson July 10-17. Briar Creek, near Canton, July 17. At Big Black till September 22. Moved to Memphis, thence march to Chattanooga, Tenn., September 23-November 21. Operations on the Memphis & Charleston Railroad in Alabama October 20-29. Cherokee Station October 21 and 29. Cane Creek October

26. Tuscumbia October 26-27. Battles of Chattanooga November 23-27; Lookout Mountain November 23-24; Mission Ridge November 25; Ringgold Gap, Taylor's Ridge, November 27. March to relief of Knoxville November 28-December 8. Garrison duty in Alabama till April, 1864. Atlanta Campaign May 1 to September 8. Demonstration on Resaca May 8-13. Snake Creek Gap May 10-12. Battle of Resaca May 14-15. Operations on the line of Pumpkin Vine Creek and battles about Dallas, New Hope Church and Allatoona Hills May 25-June 5. Operations about Marietta and against Kenesaw Mountain June 10-July 2. Bushy Mountain June 15-17. Assault on Kenesaw June 27. Nickajack Creek July 2-5. Chattahoochie River July 6-17. Battle of Atlanta July 22. Siege of Atlanta July 22-August 25. Ezra Chapel, Hood's second sortie, July 28. Flank movement on Jonesboro August 25-30. Battle of Jonesboro August 31-September 1. Lovejoy Station September 2-6. Pursuit of Hood into Alabama October 1-26. Ships Gap October 16. March to the sea November 15-December 10. Griswoldsville November 23. Siege of Savannah December 10-21. Campaign of the Carolinas January to April, 1865. Reconnoissance to Salkehatchie River January 25. Salkehatchie Swamps, S. C., February 3-5. South Edisto River February 9. North Edisto River February 12-13. Columbia February 15-17. Lynch's Creek February 25-26. Battle of Bentonville, N. C., March 20-21. Occupation of Goldsboro March 24. Advance on Raleigh April 9-13. Occupation of Raleigh April 14. Bennett's House April 26. Surrender of Johnston and his army. March to Washington, D. C., via Richmond, Va., April 29-May 20. Grand Review May 24. Mustered out June 27, 1865.

Regiment lost during service 1 Officer and 27 Enlisted men killed and mortally wounded and 3 Officers and 272 Enlisted men by disease. Total 303.

32nd REGIMENT INFANTRY.

Organized at Dubuque and mustered in October 6, 1862. Moved to Davenport, Iowa, October 15-16; thence to St. Louis, Mo., November 21-23. Attached to District of Columbus, 13th Army Corps (Old), Dept. of Tennessee, to January, 1863. District of Columbus, 6th Division, 16th Army Corps, Dept. of Tennessee, to January, 1864. 2nd Brigade, 3rd Division, 16th Corps, to March, 1864. 2nd Brigade, 3rd Division, 16th Corps, Dept. of the Gulf, to June, 1864. 2nd Brigade, 3rd Division, 16th Corps, Dept. of Tennessee, to December, 1864. 2nd Brigade, 2nd Division (Detachment), Army of Tennessee, Dept. of the Cumberland, to February, 1865. 2nd Brigade, 2nd Division, 16th Corps, Military Division West Mississippi, to August, 1865.

SERVICE.—Companies "B," "C," "E," "H", "I" and "K" moved from St. Louis, Mo., to New Madrid, Mo., November 25-28, 1862, and duty there till December 28. Expedition to Clarkston, Mo., December 17-21 (Cos. "C" and "I"). Evacuation of New Madrid December 28, and moved to Fort Pillow, Tenn., December 28-29. Duty there till June 20, 1863. (Co. "F" at Fulton April 1 to June.) Ordered to Columbus, Ky., June 20, and duty there till January 20, 1864. Expedition to Rickman, Ky., August 1, 1863 (Cos. "B" and "I"). (Co. "C" mounted July 1, 1863, and attached to 4th Missouri Cavalry till January 15, 1864, when rejoined Regiment.) Companies "H" and "I" ordered to Island No. 10 September 1, 1863. Action at Island No. 10 October 16 (Cos. "H" and "I"). Expedition to Tiptonville November 21 (Co. "H"). All Companies moved to Vicksburg, Miss., January 20-26, 1864. Meridian Campaign February 3-March 2. Meridian February 16. Near Canton February 27-28. Canton February 28. (Cos. "A," "D," "F" and "G" detached from Regiment and moved to Cape Girardeau, Mo., November 25-28, 1862. Attached to District of Southeast Missouri to July, 1863. Reserve Brigade, 1st Cavalry Division, Army of Southeast Missouri, to August, 1863. Reserve Brigade, 1st Cavalry Division, Arkansas Expedition, to December, 1863. 1st Brigade, 1st Cavalry Division, Dept. of Arkansas, to January, 1864.

SERVICE.—Garrison duty at Cape Girardeau, Mo.,

till March 14, 1863. Moved to Bloomfield March 14 and return to Cape Girardeau April 21. Action at Cape Girardeau April 28. Pursuit of Marmaduke to Castor April 28-May 5. At Cape Girardeau till July. Moved to Bloomington July 10, thence march to Clarendon, Ark., July 19-August 8. Steele's Expedition to Little Rock August 8-September 10. Expedition up White and Little Red Rivers August 13-16. West Point, White River, August 14. Harrison's Landing August 16. Reed's Bridge, Bayou Metoe, August 27. Shallow Ford, Bayou Metoe, August 30. Bayou LaFourche and capture of Little Rock September 10. Duty at Little Rock till January, 1864. Expedition to Mt. Ida November 10-18, 1863. Moved to Memphis, Tenn., January 31-February 5, 1864; thence to Vicksburg, Miss., February 7-9, and duty there till March, when rejoined Regiment. (Red River Campaign March 10-May 22, 1864. Fort DeRussy March 14. Battle of Pleasant Hill April 9. Cane River Crossing April 22-24. At Alexandria April 26-May 13. Alexandria May 2-9. Retreat to Morganza April 13-20. Mansura May 15-16. Mellow Bayou May 18. Moved to Vicksburg, Miss., thence to Memphis, Tenn., May 20-June 10. Lake Chicot, Ark., June 6-7. Smith's Expedition to Tupelo, Miss., July 5-21. Harrisburg July 13. Tupelo July 14-15. Old Town Creek July 15. Smith's Expedition to Oxford, Miss., August 1-30. Tallahatchie River August 7-9. Abbeville August 23. Moved to St. Louis, Mo., September 16; thence to Desota, Mo., September 25. March through Missouri in pursuit of Price September 25-November 19. Moved to Nashville, Tenn., November 21-December 1. Battles of Nashville, Tenn., December 15-16. Pursuit of Hood December 17-28. At Eastport, Miss., till February, 1865. Expedition from Eastport to Iuka January 9, 1865. Moved to New Orleans, La., February 9-22; thence to Dauphin Island, Ala. Campaign against Mobile and its Defences March 8-April 12. Siege of Spanish Fort and Fort Blakely March 26-April 18. Assault and capture of Fort Blakely April 9. Occupation of Mobile April 12. March to Montgomery April 13-25, and duty there and in District of Alabama till August. Mustered out August 24, 1865.

Regiment lost during service 6 Officers and 101 Enlisted men killed and mortally wounded and 2 Officers and 213 Enlisted men by disease. Total 322.

33rd REGIMENT INFANTRY.

Organized at Oskaloosa and mustered in October 4, 1862. Left State for St. Louis, Mo., November 20. Attached to Dept. of Missouri to January, 1862. 1st Brigade, 13th Division, 13th Army Corps, Dept. of Tennessee, to February, 1863. 2nd Brigade, 13th Division, 13th Corps, to July, 1863. 2nd Brigade, 13th Division, 16th Corps, to August, 1863. 2nd Brigade, 3rd Division, Army of Arkansas, to January, 1864. 2nd Brigade, 3rd Division, 7th Corps, Dept. of Arkansas, to March, 1864. 1st Brigade, 3rd Division, 7th Corps, to May, 1864. 1st Brigade, 1st Division, 7th Corps, to February, 1865. 3rd Brigade, 3rd Division, Reserve Corps, Military Division West Mississippi, to February, 1865. 3rd Brigade, 3rd Division, 13th Corps, to July, 1865.

SERVICE.—Duty at St. Louis, Mo., till December 21, 1862. Moved to Columbus, Ky., December 21-24; thence to Union City, Tenn., January 1-3, 1863, and to Helena, Ark., January 8. Duty there till August. Yazoo Pass Expedition by Moon Lake, Yazoo Pass and Tallahatchie and Coldwater Rivers and operations against Ft. Pemberton and Greenwood February 14-April 8. Yazoo Pass April 16. Expedition from Helena May 6-13. Repulse of Holmes' attack on Helena July 4. Steele's Expedition to Little Rock August 11-September 10. Bayou Fourche and capture of Little Rock September 10. Duty at Little Rock till March, 1864. Expedition to Benton October 25-26, 1863. Steele's Expedition to Camden March 23-May 3, 1864. Antoine or Terre Noir Creek April 2. Elkins' Ferry, Little Missouri River, April 3-4. Prairie D'Ann April 9-12. Jenkins Ferry and Camden April 15. Occupation of Camden April 15-23. Moro Bottom April 25-26. Jenkins Ferry, Saline River, April 30. At Little Rock till February, 1865. Expedition to

Fort Smith October 30-December 8, 1864. Expedition to Mt. Elba January 22-February 4, 1865. Moved to New Orleans, La., February 14-18. Campaign against Mobile and its Defences March 17-April 12. Siege of Spanish Fort and Fort Blakely March 26-April 8. Assault on and capture of Fort Blakely April 9. Occupation of Mobile April 12. Whistler's Station April 13. At McIntosh's Bluff April 19 to June 1. Moved to Mobile, thence to Brazos Santiago, Texas, June 1-7, and duty there till July 4. Ordered to New Orleans July 4. Mustered out July 17, 1865, and discharged at Rock Island, Ill., August 7, 1865.

Regiment lost during service 3 Officers and 65 Enlisted men killed and mortally wounded and 1 Officer and 215 Enlisted men by disease. Total 284.

34th REGIMENT INFANTRY.

Organized at Burlington and mustered in October 15, 1862. Moved to Helena, Ark., November 22-December 5, 1862. Attached to 2nd Brigade, 1st Division, District of Eastern Arkansas, Dept. of Tennessee, to December, 1862. 3rd Brigade, 11th Division, Right Wing 13th Army Corps (Old), Dept. of Tennessee, to December, 1862. 3rd Brigade, 4th Division, Sherman's Yazoo Expedition, to January, 1863. 3rd Brigade, 1st Division, 15th Army Corps, Army of Tennessee, to April, 1863. District of St. Louis, Mo., Dept. of Missouri, to June, 1863. 1st Brigade, Herron's Division, 13th Army Corps, to July, 1863. 1st Brigade, 2nd Division, 13th Army Corps, Army of Tennessee, to August, 1863, and Dept. of the Gulf to December, 1863. 3rd Brigade, 2nd Division, 13th Army Corps, to January, 1864. 2nd Brigade, 4th Division, 13th Army Corps, to March, 1864. 2nd Brigade, 1st Division, 13th Army Corps, to April, 1864. 2nd Brigade, 4th Division, 13th Army Corps, to June, 1864. Defences of New Orleans, Dept. of the Gulf, to August, 1864. 3rd Brigade, 3rd Division, 19th Army Corps, Dept. of the Gulf, to December, 1864. 3rd Brigade, Reserve Corps, Military Division West Mississippi, to February, 1865. 3rd Brigade, 2nd Division, Reserve Corps, Military Division West Mississippi, February, 1865. 3rd Brigade, 2nd Division, 13th Army Corps, Military Division West Mississippi, to July, 1865. Dept. of Texas to August, 1865.

SERVICE.—Sherman's Yazoo Expedition December 22, 1862, to January 2, 1863. Chickasaw Bayou December 26-28, 1862. Chickasaw Bluffs December 29. Expedition to Arkansas Post, Ark., January 3-10, 1863. Assault on and capture of Fort Hindman, Arkansas Post, January 10-11. Moved to Chicago, Ill., with prisoners January 17-February 5. At St. Louis, Mo., till April 1. Guard prisoners to City Point, Va., April 1-20. Moved to Pilot Knob, Mo., and duty there till June 3. Moved to Vicksburg, Miss., June 3-10. Siege of Vicksburg June 10-July 4. Expedition to Yazoo City July 12-21. Occupation of Yazoo City July 14. Moved to Port Hudson, thence to Carrollton, La., August 20-24. Expedition to Morganza through swamps of the Atchafalaya September 9-10. Sterling's Plantation September 29. Moved to Carrollton October 10. Expedition to the Rio Grande, Texas, October 24-November 8. Brazos Santiago, November 2-3. Advance on Brownsville November 3-6. Expedition to Arkansas November 14-21. Mustang Island November 17. Fort Esperanza November 27-30. Duty on Matagorda Island till April. Moved to Alexandria, La., April 20-27. Red River Campaign April 27-May 22. Construction of dam at Alexandria April 30-May 10. Graham's Plantation May 5. Retreat to Morganza May 13-20. Mansure May 15-16. Expedition from Morganza to the Atchafalaya May 30-June 6. Moved to Baton Rouge and duty there till July. Operations against Fort Gaines, Mobile Bay, August 2-8, and against Fort Morgan August 9-23. Capture of Fort Morgan August 23. Moved to Morganza August 7-11. Duty there and at mouth of White River, Ark., till January 25, 1865. Expedition to Morgan's Ferry December 13-14, 1864. Moved to New Orleans, La., January 25, 1865; thence to Barrancas, Fla., January 26-28, and to Pensacola, Fla., March 11. March to Fort Blakely, Ala.,

March 20-April 2. Occupation of Canoe Station March 27. Siege of Fort Blakely April 2-9. Capture of Fort Blakely April 9. Duty at Mobile and Selma, Ala., till May. Ordered to Texas May 12. Duty at Galveston and Houston, Texas, till August. Mustered out August 15, 1865.

Regiment lost during service 1 Officer and 11 Enlisted men killed and mortally wounded and 2 Officers and 244 Enlisted men by disease. Total 258.

35th REGIMENT INFANTRY.

Organized at Muscatine and mustered in September 18, 1862. Duty at Camp Strong till November 22. Moved to Cairo, Ill., November 22. Attached to District of Columbus, 13th Army Corps (Old), Dept. of Tennessee, to January, 1863. District of Columbus, 6th Division, 16th Army Corps, Dept. of Tennessee, to April, 1863. 3rd Brigade, 3rd Division, 15th Army Corps, to December, 1863. 3rd Brigade, 1st Division, 16th Army Corps, to December, 1864. 3rd Brigade, 1st Division (Detachment), Army of Tennessee, Dept. of the Cumberland, to February, 1865. 3rd Brigade, 1st Division, 16th Army Corps, Military Division West Mississippi, to August, 1865.

SERVICE.—Duty at Cairo and Mound City, Ill., till December 19, 1862. Moved to Columbus, Ky., and duty there till January 3, 1863. Moved to Cairo, Ill., February 3-5, and provost duty there till March 14. Ordered to Young's Point, La., March 14; thence to Duckport and duty there till May 2. Moved to join army in rear of Vicksburg, via Richmond and Grand Gulf, May 2-14. Jackson, Miss., May 14. Siege of Vicksburg May 18-July 4. Assaults on Vicksburg May 19 and 22. Expedition to Mechanicsburg May 26-June 4. Advance on Jackson July 5-10. Siege of Jackson July 10-17. Camp at Bear Creek till October 14. Expedition to Canton October 14-20. Bogue Chitto Creek October 17. Camp near Vicksburg till November 7. Moved to Memphis, Tenn., November 7-12; thence to LaGrange November 19, and duty there and along Memphis & Charleston Railroad till January, 1864. Middletown January 14. Moved to Vicksburg, Miss., February 1-6. Expedition to Canton February 25-March 4. Red River Campaign March 10-May 22. Fort DeRussy March 14. Henderson's Hill March 21. Campti March 26 and April 4. Grand Ecore April 5. Battle of Pleasant Hill April 9. About Cloutiersville and Cane River Crossing April 22-23. At Alexandria April 27-May 13. Bayou LaMourie May 6-7. Retreat to Morganza May 13-20. Mansure May 16. Yellow Bayou May 18. Moved to Vicksburg, Miss., thence to Memphis, Tenn., May 20-June 10. Action at Lake Chicot, Ark., June 5-6. Smith's Expedition to Tupelo July 5-21. Camargo's Cross Roads, near Harrisburg, July 13. Tupelo July 14-15. Old Town Creek July 15. Smith's Expedition to Oxford, Miss., August 1-30. Tallahatchie River August 7-9. Mower's Expedition up White River to Duvall's Bluff, Ark., September 1-6. March through Arkansas and Missouri in pursuit of Price September 7-November 15. Moved to Nashville, Tenn., November 23-December 1. Battle of Nashville December 15-16. Pursuit of Hood December 17-28. At Clifton, Tenn., and Eastport, Miss., till February, 1865. Moved to New Orleans, La., February 6-21. Campaign against Mobile and its Defences March 17-April 12. Siege of Spanish Fort and Fort Blakely March 26-April 8. Assault and capture of Fort Blakely April 9. Occupation of Mobile April 12. March to Montgomery April 13-22. Duty there and at Selma till August. Mustered out August 10, 1865.

Regiment lost during service 5 Officers and 44 Enlisted men killed and mortally wounded and 3 Officers and 185 Enlisted men by disease. Total 237.

36th REGIMENT INFANTRY.

Organized at Keokuk and mustered in October 4, 1862. Ordered to Memphis, Tenn., December, 1862; thence to Helena, Ark. Attached to 1st Brigade, 13th Division, 13th Army Corps, Dept. of Tennessee, to February, 1863. 2nd Brigade, 13th Division, 13th Army Corps, to July, 1863. 2nd Brigade, 13th Division, 16th Army Corps, to

August, 1863. 1st Brigade, 13th Division, 16th Army Corps, to August, 1863. 1st Brigade, 3rd Division, Arkansas Expedition, to December, 1863. 1st Brigade, 3rd Division, 7th Army Corps, Dept. of Arkansas, to March, 1864. 2nd Brigade, 3rd Division, 7th Army Corps, to May, 1864. 2nd Brigade, 1st Division, 7th Army Corps, to February, 1865. 1st Brigade, 1st Division, 7th Army Corps, to March, 1865. 1st Brigade, 2nd Division, 7th Army Corps, to August, 1865.

SERVICE.—Duty at Helena, Ark., till February 24, 1863. Yazoo Pass Expedition by Moon Lake, Yazoo Pass and Coldwater and Tallahatchie Rivers, and operations against Fort Pemberton and Greenwood February 24-April 5. Fort Pemberton April 4. Post duty at Helena till August 10. Repulse of Holmes' attack on Helena July 4. (A detachment on expedition to Napoleonville May 23-26, and engaged near Island No. 65 May 25.) Steele's Expedition to Little Rock August 10-September 10. Bayou Fourche and capture of Little Rock September 10. Duty at Little Rock till October 26. Pursuit of Marmaduke's forces October 26-November 1. Duty at Pine Bluff and Little Rock till March 23, 1864. Steele's Expedition to Camden March 23-May 3. Elkin's Ford, Little Missouri River, April 4-6. Prairie D'Ann April 10-13. Jenkins Ferry and Camden April 15. Occupation of Camden April 15-23. Battle of Marks Mill April 25; most of Regiment captured. Confined at Camp Tyler, Texas, till March, 1865. Rejoined Regiment at St. Charles on White River, Ark., April, 1865. Action at Jenkins Ferry, Saline River, April 30, 1864. Duty at Little Rock till March, 1865; at St. Charles till May, and at Duvall's Bluff till August, 1865. Mustered out August 24, 1865.

Regiment lost during service 1 Officer and 64 Enlisted men killed and mortally wounded and 6 Officers and 232 Enlisted men by disease. Total 303.

37th REGIMENT INFANTRY.—("GREYBEARD REGIMENT").

Organized at Muscatine and mustered in December 15, 1862. Moved to St. Louis, Mo., January 1, 1863. Attached to District of St. Louis, Mo., Dept. of Missouri, to May, 1863. Alton, Ill., to January, 1864. Rock Island, Ill., to June, 1864. Memphis, Tenn., District of West Tennessee, to August, 1864. Indianapolis, Ind., Cincinnati, Columbus and Gallipolis, Ohio, to May, 1865. Provost guard duty at St. Louis, Mo., and guarding Military Prisons till May 1, 1863. Guard Pacific Railroad from St. Louis to Jefferson City, Mo. Headquarters at Franklin till July 29. Moved to Alton, Ill., and guard Military Prison till January 16, 1864, and at Rock Island, Ill., till June 5. Ordered to Memphis, Tenn., June 6, and duty there till August 27. Moved to Indianapolis, Ind., August 27-31. Guard prisoners at Camp Morton (5 Cos.) and Military Prisons at Cincinnati, Ohio (5 Cos.), till May, 1865. Detachments also at Columbus, Ohio, and at Gallipolis, Ohio. Mustered out May 24, 1865.

38th REGIMENT INFANTRY.

Organized at Dubuque and mustered in December 4, 1862. Moved to St. Louis, Mo., December 15; thence to Columbus, Ky., December 28-30. Attached to District of Columbus, Ky., 16th Army Corps, Dept. of Tennessee, to June, 1863. 1st Brigade, Herron's Division, 13th Army Corps, Army of Tennessee, to July, 1863. 1st Brigade, 2nd Division, 13th Army Corps, Army of Tennessee, to August, 1863, and Dept. of the Gulf to June, 1864. United States Forces, Texas, to August, 1864. United States Forces, Mobile Bay, to October, 1864. District of LaFourche, Dept. of the Gulf to December, 1864. 3rd Brigade, Reserve Corps, Military Division West Mississippi, to December, 1864.

SERVICE.—Expedition to Union City, Tenn., December 31, 1862-January 1, 1863. Moved to New Madrid, Mo., January 1, 1863, and duty there till June. Moved to Vicksburg, Miss., June 6-15. Siege of Vicksburg June 15-July 4. Expedition to Yazoo City July 12-21. Occupation of Yazoo City July 14. Moved to Port Hud-

son, La., July 24-27; thence to Carrollton, La., August 15. Expedition to the Rio Grande, Texas, October 23-November 4. Advance on Brownsville November 6. Duty at Brownsville till July 31, 1864. Moved to New Orleans, La., July 31-August 5; thence to Mobile Bay August 7-9. Siege of Fort Morgan August 9-23. Capture of Fort Morgan August 23. Moved to New Orleans, La., September 8-11. Duty at Donaldsonville till December. Consolidated with 34th Iowa Infantry December 12, 1864.

Regiment lost during service 2 Enlisted men killed and mortally wounded and 4 Officers and 311 Enlisted men by disease. Total 317.

39th REGIMENT INFANTRY.

Organized at Des Moines and Davenport and mustered in November 24, 1862. Moved to Cairo, Ill., December 12-14; thence to Columbus, Ky., December 16. Attached to 3rd Brigade, District of Corinth, 17th Army Corps, Dept. of Tennessee, to January, 1863. 3rd Brigade, District of Corinth, 16th Army Corps, to March, 1863. 3rd Brigade, 2nd Division, 16th Army Corps, to September, 1864. 3rd Brigade, 4th Division, 15th Army Corps, to August, 1865.

SERVICE.—Defence of Jackson, Tenn., and pursuit of Forest December 18, 1862, to January 3, 1863. Parker's Cross Roads December 30-31, 1862. Moved to Corinth, Miss., January 6, 1863, and duty there till November, 1863. Dodge's Expedition into Northern Alabama April 15-May 8. Great Bear Creek and Cherokee Station April 17. Tuscumbia April 22-23. Town Creek April 28. March to Pulaski, Tenn., November 2-12. Guard duty at Reynolds Station and along railroad till January 21, 1864, and at Pulaski till March 12. Moved to Athens, Ala., March 12, and to Chattanooga, Tenn., April 30. Atlanta (Ga.) Campaign May 1 to September 8. Demonstration on Resaca May 8-13. Snake Creek Gap and Sugar Valley May 9-10. Battle of Resaca May 13-14. Ley's Ferry, Oostenaula River, May 14-15. Rome Cross Roads May 16. Kingston May 19. Moved to Rome May 22 and duty there till August 15. Expedition after Wheeler August 15-September 16. Moved to Allatoona October 4. Battle of Allatoona October 5. Moved to Rome October 9. Reconnoissance and skirmishes on Cave Springs Road October 12-13. Etowah River October 13. March to the sea November 15-December 10. Ogeechee Canal December 9. Siege of Savannah December 10-21. Campaign of the Carolinas January to April, 1865. Salkehatchie Swamps, S. C., February 3-5. South Edisto River February 9. North Edisto River February 12-13. Columbia February 15-17. Lynch's Creek February 25-26. Battle of Bentonville, N. C., March 20-21. Occupation of Goldsboro March 24. Advance on Raleigh April 9-13. Occupation of Raleigh April 14. Bennett's House April 26. Surrender of Johnston and his army. March to Washington, D. C., via Richmond, Va., April 29-May 30. Grand Review May 24. Moved to Louisville, Ky., June. Mustered out August 2, 1865.

Regiment lost during service 6 Officers and 58 Enlisted men killed and mortally wounded and 2 Officers and 134 Enlisted men by disease. Total 200.

40th REGIMENT INFANTRY.

Organized at Iowa City and mustered in November 15, 1862. Moved to Columbus, Ky., December 17. Attached to District of Columbus, Ky., 16th Army Corps, Dept. of Tennessee, to June, 1863. Kimball's Provisional Division, 16th Army Corps, to July, 1863. Kimball's Provisional Division, District of Eastern Arkansas, to August, 1863. 2nd Brigade, 2nd Division, Arkansas Expedition, to January, 1864. 2nd Brigade, 2nd Division, 7th Army Corps, Dept. of Arkansas, to March, 1864. 3rd Brigade, 3rd Division, 7th Army Corps, to May, 1864. 2nd Brigade, 1st Division, 7th Army Corps, to February, 1865. 1st Brigade, 1st Division, 7th Army Corps, February, 1865. 1st Brigade, 3rd Division, 7th Army Corps, to June, 1865.

SERVICE.—Duty at Columbus, Ky., till March 3, 1863. Moved to Paducah, Ky., and duty there till May 31.

Moved to Vicksburg, Miss., May 31-June 3. Siege of Vicksburg June 3-July 4. Moved to Helena, Ark., July 23. Steele's Expedition to Little Rock August 1-September 10. Bayou Fourche and capture of Little Rock September 10. Duty at Little Rock till March, 1864. Steele's Expedition to Camden March 23-May 3. Okalona April 2-3. Prairie D'Ann April 9-12. Camden April 16-18. Moro Bottom April 25. Near Princeton April 28. Jenkins Ferry, Saline River, April 30. Duty at Little Rock till August 24. At Brownsville Station August 24-September 4. At Little Rock till February, 1865. Expedition to Mt. Elba January 22-February 4. At Fort Smith and Fort Gibson, Cherokee Nation, till June. Mustered out June 5, 1865.

Regiment lost during service 19 Enlisted men killed and mortally wounded and 2 Officers and 184 Enlisted men by disease. Total 205.

41st REGIMENT INFANTRY.

Originally organized at Companies "A," "B," "C," 14th Iowa Infantry, October, 1861. Detached by order of General Fremont, and march from Davenport, via Des Moines, Council Bluffs and Sioux City, to Fort Randall, Dakota Territory, arriving December 5, 1861, and on special duty at that point till April, 1863. Permanently detached from 14th Iowa Infantry September 18, 1862, and designated 41st Iowa Battalion Infantry. Transferred to 7th Iowa Cavalry as Companies "K," "L" and "M."

42nd REGIMENT INFANTRY.

Failed to complete organization.

43rd REGIMENT INFANTRY.

Failed to complete organization.

44th REGIMENT INFANTRY.

Organized at Davenport June 1, 1864. Ordered to Memphis, Tenn., and assigned to guard duty in that district till September, 1864. Mustered out September 15, 1864.

45th REGIMENT INFANTRY.

Organized at Keokuk May 25, 1864. Moved to St. Louis, Mo., thence to Memphis and Moscow, Tenn., and assigned to duty guarding Memphis & Charleston Railroad till September, 1864. Mustered out September 16, 1864.

Lost 21 Enlisted men by disease.

46th REGIMENT INFANTRY.

Organized at Davenport June 10, 1864. Ordered to Memphis, Tenn., June 20, and to Colliersville, Tenn., June 27. Assigned to guard duty on Memphis & Charleston Railroad till September, 1864. Action near Colliersville, Tenn., July 24 (Detachment of Company "I"). Repulse of Forest's attack on Memphis August 21 (Detachment). Mustered out September 23, 1864.

Regiment lost during service 1 Enlisted man killed and 27 Enlisted men by disease. Total 28.

47th REGIMENT INFANTRY.

Organized at Davenport July 13, 1864. Ordered to Helena, Ark., and duty there and in District of Eastern Arkansas, 7th Army Corps, Dept. of Arkansas, to September. Ordered to Davenport, Iowa, September 1. Mustered out September 28, 1864.

Regiment lost during service 57 Enlisted men by disease.

KANSAS VOLUNTEERS.

2nd REGIMENT CAVALRY.

Organized at Kansas City as 12th Kansas Infantry. At Fort Leavenworth, Kansas, designation changed to 9th Kansas Infantry February 4, 1862, and to 2nd Cavalry March 5, 1862. Attached to Dept. of Kansas November, 1861, to August, 1862. 2nd Brigade, Dept. of Kansas, to October, 1862. 2nd Brigade, 1st Division, Army of the Frontier, Dept. of Missouri, to February, 1863. District of Southwest Missouri, Dept. of Missouri, to December, 1863. 2nd Brigade, District of the Frontier, to January, 1864. 2nd Brigade, District of the Frontier, 7th Corps, Dept. of Arkansas, to March, 1864. 1st Brigade, District of the Frontier, 7th Corps, to April, 1864. 3rd Brigade, District of the Frontier, 7th Corps, to January, 1865. 2nd Brigade, 3rd Division, 7th Corps, to February, 1865. Unattached, 7th Corps, to August, 1865.

SERVICE.—Moved to Quindaro, Wyandotte County, January 20, 1862; thence to Shawneetown March 12. Expedition to Little Santa Fe, Mo., against guerrillas March 22-25 (Cos. "D" and "E"). Independence, Little Santa Fe, March 22. Moved to Lawrence, thence to Topeka, Kansas, April 20-26, and to Fort Riley May 1-4 to join New Mexico Expedition. Companies "A" and "D" detached as escort to Paymaster Fisk to Fort Lyon, Colo., and return to Fort Larned May 20-June 22. Companies "B" and "C" detached as garrison at Fort Riley June 11-22. March to relief of Fort Larned June 22-28. Regiment moved from Fort Riley to Emporia June 11-14; thence to Iola June 23-26. Duty there till July 14. Moved to Fort Scott July 14-15; thence to Baxter Springs July 18-20. Expedition to Park Hill August 1-3. March to Fort Scott August 13. Expedition against Coffey August 13-25. Coon Creek, near Lamar, August 24 (Cos. "A," "B," "C" and "D"). Rejoin September 20. Scout from Fort Scott September 27-30. March to Sarcoxie and Newtonia October 1-4. Occupation of Newtonia October 4. Near Newtonia October 5. Hazel Bottom October 14 (Cos. "B" and "M"). Expedition to Sugar Creek, Cross Hollows and Mud Town October 16-20. Elkhorn Tavern October 16. Shell's Mill October 16 (Co. "B"). Sugar Creek October 17. Cross Hollows October 18. Boonsboro November 7. Cove Creek November 8. Between Fayetteville and Cane Hill November 9. (Guard supply train from Fort Scott November 17-26 Detachment). Pineville November 19. Beattie's Prairie, near Maysville, November 19 (Cos. "C" and "M"). Carthage November 27. Cane Hill, Boston Mountains, November 28. Scouting and skirmishing in Boston Mountains December 4-6. Reed Mountains December 6. Battle of Prairie Grove December 7. Picket duty at Cane Hill till December 26. Expedition over Boston Mountains to Van Buren December 27-29. Dripping Springs December 29. Moved to Springfield, Mo., January 11-16, 1863, and duty there till July. Scout to Stanwood May 5-9 (Detachment). Expedition through Northwest Arkansas to Newton and Jasper Counties May 21-30. Bentonville May 22 (Cos. "H" and "M"). Carthage, Mo., May 26. Bentonville June 22. Cabin Creek, Cherokee Nation, July 2-3. Elk Creek, near Honey Springs, July 12. Moved to Cassville July 23, thence march to Fort Gibson, Cherokee Nation, August 11-21. Bentonville August 15. Fayetteville August 23. Operations against Cabbel, Jenny Lind and Devil's Backbone September 1. Duty at Fort Smith September 2 to November 30. Operations in Cherokee Nation September 9-25. Dardanelle September 9 and 12. Newtonia September 27 (Cos. "E" and "M"). (A detachment at Dardanelle November 6 to December 23.) Choctaw Nation November 9. Fouche le Aix Mountains November 11. Roseville November 12 (Cos. "D" and "M"). Clarksville November 24. Moved to Waldron November 30-December 1 and duty there till March 22, 1864. Scout from Waldron to Mount Ida, Caddo Gap and Dallas December 2-7, 1863 (Cos. "B" and "M"). Caddo Gap December 4 (Cos. "B" and "M"). Caddo Mill December 14 (Cos. "G" and "K"). Waldron December 29 (Detachment). Scout from Waldron to Baker Springs and Caddo Gap January 21-25, 1864. Baker's Springs January 24-25. Sulphur Springs January 25 (Cos. "G" and "M"). Little Missouri River January 25 (Cos. "A," "D" and "M"). Caddo Gap January 26. Dallas January 28. Waldron February 1. Mountain Fork February 4. Scott's Farm, Caddo Gap, February 12-14. Caddo Gap February 16. Steele's Expedition to Camden March 22-May 3. Danville March 28. Roseville March 29 (Cos. "B," "E" and "M"). Prairie D'Ann April 9-13. Roseville April 15 (Cos. "A" and

"M"). Camden April 16-18. Poison Springs April 18. Jenkins Ferry, Saline River, April 30. Moved to Fort Smith May 5-14, thence to Clarksville June 1 (Cos. "E" and "D" garrison at Roseville April 1-May 5; Roseville April 4-5, Cos. "E" and "D.") Duty at Clarksville till July 28. Moved to Fort Smith and duty there till December 27. Fort Smith July 29. Crawford County August 11. Van Buren August 12. Fort Smith September 1. Fort Gibson September 16 and 18. Cabin Creek September 19 (Cos. "C," "D," "E," "F," "G" and "I"). Moved to Fort Leavenworth, Kansas, December 25. Balance of Regiment moved to Clarksville December 27, and duty there till March 3, 1865. Dardanelle January 14-15 (Cos. "A," "B" and "M"). Moved to Lewisburg March 3-7 and duty there till May 13. Moved to Fort Gibson, Cherokee Nation, May 13-20 and duty there till July 2. Moved to Lawrence, Kansas, July 2-14. Mustered out August 17, 1865.

Regiment lost during service 2 Officers and 62 Enlisted men killed and mortally wounded and 1 Officer and 116 Enlisted men by disease. Total 181.

5th REGIMENT CAVALRY.

Organized at Leavenworth City July 12, 1861, to January 22, 1862. (Cos. "L" and "M" organized April to July, 1862.) Attached to Dept. of Kansas to June, 1862. Unattached, Army of Southwest Missouri, Dept. of Missouri, to July, 1862. District of Eastern Arkansas, Dept. of Missouri, to December, 1862. 2nd Brigade, 3rd Cavalry Division, District of Eastern Arkansas, Dept. of Missouri, to January, 1863. 2nd Brigade, 2nd Cavalry Division, 13th Army Corps, Army of Tennessee, to April, 1863. 2nd Brigade, District of Eastern Arkansas, Dept. of Tennessee, to June, 1863. Clayton's Independent Brigade, District of Eastern Arkansas, Dept. of Tennessee, to August, 1863. Clayton's Cavalry Brigade, Arkansas Expedition, to January, 1864. Pine Bluff, Ark., 7th Corps, Dept. of Arkansas, to September, 1864. 1st Brigade, Cavalry Division, 7th Corps, to February, 1865. Post St. Charles, 7th Corps, to August, 1865.

SERVICE.—Companies "A" and "F" moved to Kansas City, Mo., July 17, 1861. Expedition to Harrisonville July 20-25. Skirmish at Harrisonville July 25 (Cos. "A" and "F"). Regiment moved to Fort Scott, Kansas, as escort to a supply train and duty there till September 17, 1861. (Cos. "B," "C" and "E" joined at Fort Scott.) Ball's and Morse's Mills August 28-29. Fort Scott September 1. Drywood Creek, Fort Scott, September 2. Fort Scott September 3. Papinsville September 5. Morristown September 17. Moved to West Point, Mo., September 17; thence with 3rd and 4th Kansas to Osceola. Actions with Price at Osceola September 20, 21 and 22. Butler October 1. West Point October 5. Moved to Kansas City, Mo., thence to Springfield, Mo., and join Fremont. Little Santa Fe November 6. Moved to Fort Scott, Ossawatomee, and Fort Lincoln, Kansas, and duty at Camp Denver, near Barnesville, till February, 1862. Camp near Fort Scott till March 17. March to Carthage, Mo., March 17-19. Duty there till April 10. Moved to Springfield, Mo., April 10-12. Turnback Creek April 26. Moved to Houston May 25-27, thence to Rolla, Mo. March to join Curtis June 17. Eminence June 17. March to Helena, Ark., June 17-July 12. (Cos. "A," "D" and "K" escort train June 25-July 14.) Salem July 6. Jacksonport, Black River, July 8. Duty at Helena, Ark., till August, 1863. Operations against Quantrell in Kansas August 20-28, 1862 (Detachment). Washburne's Expedition from Helena against Mobile & Ohio Railroad July 24-26, 1862 (Co. "C"). Expedition to Oldtown and Trenton July 28-31 (Co. "C"). Clayton's Expedition toward Clarendon August 4-17. Expedition to Johnsonville and Marianna September 26 (Detachment). Action at Trenton October 14. Expedition to Moro November 5-8 (Detachment). Expedition against Arkansas Post November 16-26. Expedition to Grenada, Miss., November 27-December 5. Oakland, Miss., December 3. Expedition to Big and Little Creeks and skirmishes March 6-10, 1863 (Detachment). Little Rock Road April 2 (Co.

"G"). Mount Vernon May 11. Polk's Plantation, near Helena, May 25. Repulse of Holmes' attack on Helena July 4. Steele's Expedition to Little Rock August 1-September 10. Bayou Metoe August 27. Bayou Fourche and capture of Little Rock September 10. Near Brownsville September 12. Moved to Pine Bluff September 14 and duty there till March 27, 1864. Tulip October 10, 1863. Pine Bluff October 25. Scout to Monticello January 13-14, 1864. Monticello January 16. Branchville, Ivy's Ford, January 19. Expedition to Mount Elba and Longview March 27-31. Branchville March 27 (Detachment). Longview March 29-30. Action at Mount Elba and pursuit to Big Creek March 30. Swan Lake April 23. Mark's Mills April 25 (Detachment). Duty at Pine Bluff and Little Rock till October, 1864. Monticello Road, near Pine Bluff, June 17. Reconnoissance from Pine Bluff July 13. Scout on Arkansas River, near Pine Bluff, and skirmishes August 27-28. Expedition from Pine Bluff September 9-11 (Detachment). Near Monticello September 10. Brewer's Lane September 11. Reconnoissance from Little Rock toward Monticello and Mount Elba October 4-11. Expedition from Kansas into Missouri June 16-20, 1864 (Co. "L"). Pursuit of Price through Arkansas and Missouri September-October. Lexington, Mo., October 19. Little Blue October 21. Independence October 22. Big Blue and State Line October 22. Westport October 23. Mine Creek, Little Osage River and Marias des Cygnes October 25. Battle of Charlot October 25. Mound City and Fort Lincoln October 25. Newtonia October 28. Scout to Richland December 24 (Detachment). Near Oxford January 13, 1865. Non-Veterans mustered out (Cos. "A" to "H") August 11 to December 8, 1864. Companies "I" and "K" mustered out June 22, 1865. Companies "L" and "M" consolidated with 15th Kansas Cavalry August 22, 1865.

Regiment lost during service 2 Officers and 45 Enlisted men killed and mortally wounded and 2 Officers and 219 Enlisted men by disease. Total 268.

6th REGIMENT CAVALRY.

Organized at Fort Scott July, 1861. Attached to Dept. of Kansas to August, 1862. 2nd Brigade, Dept. of Kansas, to October, 1862. 2nd Brigade, 1st Division, Army of the Frontier, Dept. of Missouri, to February, 1863. 1st Brigade, 1st Division, Army of the Frontier, to June, 1863. District of the Frontier, Dept. of Missouri, to January, 1864. District of the Frontier, 7th Corps, Dept. of Arkansas, to March, 1864. 3rd Brigade, District of the Frontier, 7th Corps, to January, 1865. 2nd Brigade, 3rd Division, 7th Corps, to February, 1865. 1st Brigade, 2nd Division, 7th Corps, to August, 1865.

SERVICE.—Duty at Fort Scott till March, 1862. Drywood Creek, Fort Scott, September 1, 1861. Morristown September 17. Osceola September 20, 21 and 22. (The 3 original Cos. march to Fort Lincoln September 1, 1861; thence return to Fort Scott.) Little Santa Fe, Mo., November 6. Regiment reorganized March 27, 1862, and "A," "B" and "C," original Companies, mustered out. Duty at Fort Scott till May. Carthage, Mo., March 23. Diamond Grove April 14. Lost Creek April 15. Companies "C," "H" and "K" moved to Carthage, Mo., with 15th Kansas, rejoining May. Regiment stationed at various points on southern line of Kansas; Headquarters at Paoli till June. Concentrated at Fort Scott. Expedition into Indian Territory May 25-July 8 (Cos. "C," "H" and "K"). Reconnoissance from Grand River to Fort Gibson, Tahliquah and Park Hill, and skirmishes June 14-17. Regiment joined June 20. Expedition into Cherokee Country July 2-August 1. Stan Wattie's Mill July 4 (2 Cos.). Expedition from Fort Leavenworth to Independence August 12-14 (1 Co.). Clear Creek August 19. Taboursville August 20. Osage River August 21. Coon Creek and Lamar, and Lamar, August 24. Operations in Southwest Missouri September to December. Expedition through Jackson, Cass, Johnson and Lafayette Counties, Mo., September 8-23 (1 Co.). Hickory Grove September 19. Granby September 24. Newtonia September 30. Occupation of Newtonia October 4. Old Fort Wayne or Beattie's Prairie, near Maysville, October 22. Operations in Jackson County against Quantrell November 1-5. Drywood, Boston Mountains, November 9. Reconnoissance toward Van Buren and Fort Smith November 20. Near Cane Hill November 25. Cane Hill November 28. Battle of Prairie Grove, Ark., December 7. Expedition over Boston Mountains to Van Buren December 27-29. Dripping Springs December 29. (1st Battalion, Cos. "A," "C," "F" and "H" camp on Crane Creek, near Springfield, Mo., till March, 1863.) Operations in Newton and Jasper Counties March 5-13 (Cos. "A" and "C"). Near Sherwood March 9 (Cos. "A" and "C"). Companies "F" and "H" march from Westbrook to Salem, thence to Rolla May 7; thence to Fort Scott June 21-July 4. Webber Falls, Cherokee Nation, April 21-23 (3rd Battalion). Big Creek, near Pleasant Hill, May 15 (Co. "E"). Fort Gibson May 22 and 25. Greenleaf Prairie June 16. Cabin Creek July 1-2. Elk Creek, near Honey Springs, July 17. Perryville August 26. Operations in Cherokee Nation September 11-25. Webber Falls October 12. Moved to Fort Smith November 13-18 and duty there till March, 1864. Scout to Baker's Springs January 21-25. Baker's Springs, Caddo Gap, January 24. Steele's Expedition to Camden March 31-May 3 (Cos. "A," "C,"' "G," "K" and "M"). Roseville April 4-5 (Detachment). Stone's Ferry April 5 (Detachment). Prairie D'Ann April 9-12. Moscow April 13. Dutch Mills April 14. Camden April 16-18. Poison Springs April 18 (Detachment). Saline Bottom April 29. Jenkins Ferry, Saline River, April 30. Moved to Dardanelle, thence to Fort Smith May 6-16. Dardanelle May 10. Clarksville May 18. Fayetteville May 19. Roseville June 4-5 (Detachment). Hahn's Farm, near Waldron, and Iron Bridge June 19. Balance of Regiment near Fort Smith and duty there till September. Mazzard's Prairie July 27 (Cos. "B," "D," "E" and "H"). Near Fort Smith July 31. Lee's Creek August 1 (Detachment). Van Buren August 12. Fort Smith August 27. March to Cabin Creek, Cherokee Nation, September 14-19. Fort Scott October 22. Cow Creek October 23 (Detachment. Non-Veterans') Training Post October 24. Moved from Fort Smith to Clarksville December 29 and duty there till February 16, 1865. Moved to Little Rock and duty there till June. Consolidated to a Battalion April 18, 1865. Moved to Duvall's Bluffs June 5, thence to Fort Leavenworth, Kansas, July 27-August 11. Mustered out August 27, 1865.

Regiment lost during service 4 Officers and 81 Enlisted men killed and mortally wounded and 3 Officers and 140 Enlisted men by disease. Total 228.

7th REGIMENT CAVALRY.

Organized at Fort Leavenworth October 28, 1861. Attached to Dept. of Kansas to June, 1862. 5th Division, Army of Mississippi, to September, 1862. 2nd Brigade, Cavalry Division, Army of Mississippi, to November, 1862. 1st Brigade, Cavalry Division, 13th Corps, Dept. of the Tennessee, to December, 1862. 2nd Brigade, Cavalry Division, 16th Army Corps, Army of Tennessee, to March, 1863. Cavalry Brigade, District of Corinth, 2nd Division, 16th Army Corps, to June, 1863. 3rd Brigade, 1st Cavalry Division, 16th Army Corps, to August, 1863. 1st Brigade, 1st Cavalry Division, 16th Corps, to February, 1864. Unattached, 1st Cavalry Division, 16th Corps, to June, 1864. 1st Brigade, 1st Cavalry Division, District of West Tennessee, to September, 1864. District of St. Louis, Mo., Dept. of Missouri, to July, 1865. Dept. of Kansas to September, 1865.

SERVICE.—Duty in Western Missouri till January 31, 1862. Spring Hill, Mo., October 21, 1861 (1 Co.). Little Blue November 11, 1861 (Cos. "A," "B" and "H"). Little Santa Fe November 20. Independence, Little Blue, November 20 (Detachment). Columbus, Mo., January 9, 1862. Moved to Humboldt, Kansas, January 31, and duty there till March 25. Moved to Fort Leavenworth, Kansas, March 25; thence to Columbus, Ky., May 18-June 2, and to Corinth, Miss., June 7, escorting working parties on Mobile & Ohio Railroad and arriv-

ing at Corinth July 10; thence moved to Jacinto and Rienzi, Miss., July 18-23. Expedition from Rienzi to Ripley, Miss., July 27-29. Reconnoissance to Jacinto and Bay Springs and skirmish August 4-7. Reconnoissance from Rienzi to Hay Springs August 18-21. Marietta and Bay Springs August 20. Kossuth August 27. Rienzi September 9 and 18. Battle of Iuka, Miss., September 19 (Cos. "B" and "E"). Ruckersville October 1 (Detachment). Baldwin October 2. Battle of Corinth October 3-4. Pursuit to Ripley October 5-12. Ruckersville October 6. Grant's Central Mississippi Campaign October 31, 1862, to January 10, 1863. Capture of Ripley November 2, 1862. Orizaba November 2. Jumpertown November 5. Reconnoissance from LaGrange November 8-9. Lamar and Coldwater November 8. Holly Springs November 13, 28 and 29. Waterford or Lumpkin's Mill November 26-30. About Oxford December 1-3. Tallahatchie December 2. Water Valley December 4. Coffeeville December 5. Moved to Moscow, Tenn., December 31, and duty on line of Memphis & Charleston Railroad at Germantown, Tenn., till April 14, 1863. Joinerville January 3, 1863. Near Germantown January 27. Near Yorkville January 28 (1 Co.). Tuscumbia, Ala., February 22. Expedition to Colliersville and to LaFayette and Moscow March 8-16. Lafayette Depot March 15. Moscow March 16. Germantown April 1. Scout in Beaver Creek Swamp April 2-6. Moved to Corinth April 14-17. Dodge's Expedition into Northern Alabama April 15-May 8. Rock Cut, near Tuscumbia, April 22. Tuscumbia, Dickson Station and Leighton April 23. Town Creek April 27. Expedition from Burnsville to Tupelo, Miss., May 2-8. Tupelo May 5. At Corinth, Miss., May 8, 1863, to January 8, 1864. Expedition to Florence May 26-31, 1863. Florence May 28. Hamburg Landing May 30. Iuka, Miss., July 9 and 14. Near Corinth August 16. Expedition into West Tennessee August 27-October 1. Swallow Bluff September 30 (Cos. "A" and "C"). Operations in North Mississippi and West Tennessee against Chalmers October 4-17. Ingraham's Mills, near Byhalia, October 12. Wyatts, Tallahatchie River, October 13. Operations on Memphis & Charleston Railroad November 3-5. Operations on Memphis & Charleston Railroad against Lee's attack November 28-December 10. Molino November 28. Ripley December 1 and 4. Jack's Creek December 24. Moved to Memphis, Tenn., January 18, 1864. Veterans on furlough February 4-March 4; then moved to St. Louis, Mo., March 12. Moved to Memphis June 6. Near Memphis May 2 (Detachment). LaFayette June 9. Smith's Expedition to Tupelo, Miss., July 5-18. King's Creek July 9. Pontotoc July 11-12. Tupelo July 13-14. Oldtown Creek July 15. Ellistown July 16. Tupelo July 25. Smith's Expedition to Oxford, Miss., August 1-30. Tallahatchie River August 7-9. Hurricane Creek, Oxford, August 9. Hurricane Creek August 13, 14, 16 and 19. Moved to St. Louis, Mo., arriving September 17. Pursuit of Price through Missouri September 20-November 26. Little Blue October 21. Independence October 22. Big Blue and State Line, Westport, October 23. Mine Creek, Little Osage River, October 25. Duty by Detachments in St. Louis District till July 18, 1865. Moselle Bridge, near Franklin, December 7, 1864 (Co. "E"). Expedition from Bloomfield into Dunklin County March 3-7, 1865. Skirmishes near Bloomfield March 3 and 7. Dunklin County March 4. Skirmish, McKinzie's Creek, near Patterson, April 15. Ordered to Omaha, Neb., July 18; thence to Fort Kearney and duty there till September. Moved to Fort Leavenworth, Kansas, arriving September 14. Mustered out September 29, 1865.

Regiment lost during service 3 Officers and 55 Enlisted men killed and mortally wounded and 1 Officer and 164 Enlisted men by disease. Total 223.

9th REGIMENT CAVALRY.

Organized at Fort Leavenworth by consolidation of Independent Battalions, Squadrons and Detachments originally formed for other Regiments March 27, 1862. Company "A" organized as Company "D," 8th Kansas,

September 13 to October 14, 1861; Company "B" as Company "H," 8th Kansas, September 21 to November 20, 1861; Company "C" as Company "C," 3rd Kansas, July 24, 1861; Company "D" as Company "D," 1st Battalion Cavalry, October 19, 1861, to January 16, 1862; Company "E" as Company "E," 1st Battalion Cavalry, October 19, 1861, to January 16, 1862. Company "F" organized as Home Guard October 19, 1861, to January 16, 1862, and on scout and patrol duty at Paola. Company "G" for 1st Battalion Cavalry September 9, 1861, to January 16, 1862. Company "H" for 1st Battalion Cavalry October 22, 1861. Company "I" mustered in March 6, 1862. Company "K" mustered in July 11, 1862. Company "L" mustered in May 2, 1863, and Company "M" mustered in June 11 to August 2, 1863.

SERVICE.—Company "C" had participated in skirmish at Medoc, Mo., August 23, 1861; Ball's and Morse's Mills August 28-29; Drywood Creek, Fort Scott, September 2; Morristown, Mo., September 17, and Osceola, Mo., September 22. Companies "G" and "H" on Expedition from Morristown to Dayton and Rose Hill, Mo., January 1-3, 1862. Operations in Johnson and LaFayette Counties, Mo., January 5-12. Columbus, Mo., January 9. Regiment attached to Dept. of Kansas to August, 1862. 1st Brigade, Dept. of Kansas, to October, 1862. 1st Brigade, 1st Division, Army of the Frontier, Dept. of Missouri, to June, 1863. District of the Frontier, Dept. of Missouri, to July, 1864. District of the Border, Dept. of Missouri, to January, 1864. Dept. of Kansas to May, 1864. 3rd Brigade, District of the Frontier, 7th Corps, Dept. of Arkansas, to September, 1864. 4th Brigade, Cavalry Division, 7th Corps, to January, 1865. Unattached, 7th Corps, Little Rock, Ark., to July, 1865. Companies "A," "B," "C," "G" and "I" detached June 10, 1862. Company "A" on escort duty to Fort Union, New Mexico. Company "B" in Mountains near Denver and built Fort Halleck. Company "C" to Fort Riley, Kansas; Company "G" to Fort Lyon, Colorado, and Company "I" to Fort Laramie. Locust Grove, Cherokee Nation, July 3, 1862 (Cos. "D," "E," "F" and "H"). Operations against Coffey August. March to Sarcoxie. Blunt's Campaign in Missouri and Arkansas August to December. Reconnoissance to Newtonia September 28-29. Newtonia September 30. Occupation of Newtonia October 4. Cane Hill, Boston Mountains, November 28. Battle of Prairie Grove, Ark., December 7. Expedition over Boston Mountains to Van Buren December 27-31. Cane Hill January 2, 1863 (Co. "H"). Spring River, Mo., February 19 (Co. "D"). Fort Halleck, Dakota Territory, February 20 (Co. "B"). Regiment moved to Fort Scott escorting trains February, 1863. Stationed along borders of Kansas operating against guerrillas March, 1863, to March, 1864 (Cos. "A," "D," "E," "F" and "K"). Expedition from Humboldt to Cottonwood April 10, 1863 (Co. "G"). Scout in Bates and Cass Counties May 3-11. Hog Island May 18 (Cos. "C," "E" and "K"). Westport June 17 (Cos. "E" and "K"). Blue River June 18 (Co. "K"). Cabin Creek July 1-2. Grand Pass, Indian Territory, July 7 (Co. "B"). Honey Springs, Kansas, July 17 (Co. "C"). Taylor's Farm, Little Blue, August 1. Brooklyn, Kansas, August 21 (Co. "K"). At Trading Post (Cos. "E" and "G"), Harrisonville, Aubrey County (Co. "K"), Pleasant Hill (Co. "D") and Westport (Co. "H") operating against guerillas. Company "C" rejoin from Fort Riley August, 1863. Pursuit of Quantrell August 20-28. Brooklyn August 28. Scout from Coldwater Grove to Pleasant Hill and Big Creek and skirmishes September 4-7 (Cos. "D," "E" and "G"). Jackson County September 15. Baxter Springs October 10. Pursuit of Shelby toward Warrensburg. Harrisonville October 24 (Co. "G"). Carthage October 18. Regiment assembled and ordered to Fort Smith via Springfield, Mo., April 3, 1864. Duty at Fort Smith till July. (Co. "F" stationed at Van Buren May 23.) Hahn's Farm, near Waldron, June 19. Near Fayetteville June 24 (Co. "C"). Operations in Arkansas July 1-31. Frog Bayou July 1. Moved to Little Rock July 2-14. Duty there and at Duvall's Bluff till July, 1865. Bull's Bayou August 26, 1864. Bull Creek August 27 (Co. "I").

Expedition in pursuit of Shelby August 27-September 6. Whittier's Mills October 8. Reconnoissance from Little Rock to Princeton October 19-23. Hurricane Creek October 23. Expedition from Brownsville to Cotton Plant October 26-November 3. Scout from Duvall's Bluff to West Point November 16-18. Expedition from Duvall's Bluff up White River December 13-15. Duty in Arkansas till July, 1865. Mustered out July 17, 1865.

Regiment lost during service 1 Officer and 52 Enlisted men killed and mortally wounded and 2 Officers and 140 Enlisted men by disease. Total 195.

11th REGIMENT CAVALRY.

Organized at Kansas City April 1863, from 11th Kansas Infantry. Attached to District of the Border and District of Kansas, Dept. of Missouri, till February, 1865. District of Upper Arkansas to March, 1865. 2nd Brigade, 2nd Division, 7th Corps, Dept. of Arkansas, to April, 1865. District of the Plains, Dept. of Missouri, to September, 1865.

SERVICE.—Assigned to duty on eastern border of Kansas till October, 1864. Expedition from Salem to Mulberry Creek, Kansas, August 8-11, 1863 (Detachment). Scout on Republican River, Kansas, August 19-24, 1863 (Detachment). Operations against Quantrell on his raid into Kansas August 20-28. Independence, Mo., August 25. (Cos. "C" and "F" duty on Southern border of Kansas December, 1863, to August, 1864.) Company "L" stationed at Fort Riley; Company "G" at Fort Leavenworth as body guard to General Curtis. Action at Scott's Ford, Mo., October 14, 1863. Deep Water Creek, Mo., October 15. Expedition into Missouri June 16-20, 1864. Scout from Salem to Mulberry Creek August 8-11 (Detachment). Operations against Indians in Nebraska August 11-November 28 (1 Co.). Operations against Price in Missouri and Kansas. Lexington October 19. Little Blue October 21. Independence, Big Blue and State Line October 22. Westport October 23. Cold Water Grove October 24. Mine Creek, Little Osage River, October 25. Regiment ordered to Fort Riley December, 1864. Companies "C" and "E" to Fort Larned February, 1865. Regiment moved to Fort Kearney, Neb., February 20-March 4, thence moved to Fort Laramie March 6-April 9, and to Platte Bridge. Duty guarding telegraph lines and operating against Indians till June. Sage Creek, Dakota Ter., April 21. Deer Creek May 21. Platte Bridge, Dakota Ter., June 3. Companies "A," "B," "E," "F," "L" and "M" moved to Fort Halleck June 11-24. Protect stage route from Camp Collins, Colorado, to Green River till August 13. White River, Dakota Ter., June 17. Rock Creek July 1. Fort Halleck July 4 and 26. Moved to Kansas and mustered out September 26, 1865.

Regiment lost during service 61 Enlisted men killed and mortally wounded and 2 Officers and 110 Enlisted men by disease. Total 173.

14th REGIMENT CAVALRY.

Organized at Fort Scott and Leavenworth April, 1863, as a Battalion of 4 Companies for escort to General Blunt. Regiment organized at Fort Scott, December, 1863. Attached to District of the Frontier, Dept. of Missouri, April, 1863, to January, 1864. Unattached, District Frontier, 7th Corps, Dept. Arkansas, to March, 1864. 3rd Brigade, Frontier Division, 7th Corps, to January, 1865. 2nd Brigade, 3rd Division, 7th Corps, to February, 1865. Unattached, 7th Corps, Pine Bluff, Ark., to June, 1863.

SERVICE.—Cabin Creek, C. N., July 1-2, 1863 (Co. "B"). Operations against Quantrell in Kansas August 20-28. Massacre at Lawrence August 21 (Detachment). Operations in Cherokee Nation September 11-25. Waldron September 11. Baxter Springs October 6 (Co. "B"). Regiment moved to Fort Smith, Ark., November 20-December 3. Duty there scouting and foraging till February 23, 1864. Expedition into Choctaw County February 1-21. Moved to Ozark February 26-28, and duty there till April 6. Flint Creek March 6. Steele's Expedition against Camden April 6-May 3. Prairie D'Ann

April 9-12. Poison Springs April 18 (Detachment). Jenkins' Ferry, Saline River, April 30 (Cos. 'F" and "G"). Return to Fort Smith May and duty there till January, 1865. Hahn's Farm near Waldron June 19, 1864. Ozark July 14-15. Scout on Republican River August 19-24. Camp Verdegris September 2. Cabin Creek September 19. Vache Grass September 26. (Co. "E" with Blunt's headquarters during Brice's Raid in Missouri and Kansas October-November. Big Blue and State Line October 22. Westport October 23. Mine Creek, Little Osage River, and Battle of Charlot October 25. Newtonia October 28.) Moved to Clarksville January 1, 1865, thence to Pine Bluff February 25-27, and duty there till May. Moved to Fort Gibson and duty there till June. Mustered out June 25, 1865.

Regiment lost during service 2 Officers and 51 Enlisted men killed and mortally wounded and 2 Officers and 114 Enlisted men by disease. Total 169.

15th REGIMENT CAVALRY.

Organized at Leavenworth September and October, 1863. Attached to District of the Border, Dept. of Missouri, to January, 1864. Dept. of Kansas to June, 1864. Districts of North and South Kansas, Dept. Missouri, to October, 1865.

SERVICE.—Assigned to duty at Leavenworth and at various points in Southern Kansas, at Olathe, Paola, Coldwater Grove, Trading Post, Fort Scott, Osage Mission and Humboldt by detachments (Co. "H" at Fort Riley) till October, 1864. Skirmish at Clear Creek, Mo., May 16, 1864 (Detachments of Companies "D" and "L"). Scout from Fort Leavenworth to Weston, Mo., June 13-16, 1864. Expedition into Missouri June 16-20 (Cos. "B," "C" and "G"). Price's Raid in Missouri and Kansas September to November. Lexington October 19. Little Blue October 21. Independence, Big Blue and State Line October 22. Westport October 23. Coldwater Grove, Osage, October 24. Mine Creek, Little Osage River, and battle of Charlot October 25. Newtonia October 28. Duty in Dept. of Kansas and Dept. of the Missouri till October, 1865. Mustered out October 19, 1865. Company "H" mustered out December 7, 1865.

Regiment lost during service 2 Officers and 19 Enlisted men killed and mortally wounded and 2 Officers and 77 Enlisted men by disease. Total 100.

16th REGIMENT CAVALRY.

Organized at Leavenworth City November, 1863, to May, 1864. Attached to District of Kansas, Dept. Missouri, to April, 1865. District of the Plains, Dept. Missouri, to December, 1865.

SERVICE.—Duty in the District of North Kansas at Fort Leavenworth till September, 1864. Company "D" at Fort Scott, 1st Brigade, District South Kansas. Companies "A" and "L" at Paola, 2nd Brigade, District South Kansas. Company "B" at Shawnee Mission and Company "C" at Olathe, 2nd Brigade, District of South Kansas. Companies "F" and "G" at Lawrence August, 1864. Action at Ridgley, Mo., June 11, 1864 (Co. "E"). Scout from Leavenworth to Weston, Mo., June 13-16, and from Kansas into Missouri June 16-29. Camden Point July 13 (Co. "F"). Near Lexington October 17 (Co. "H"). Lexington October 19. Operations against Price October. Battle of Little Blue October 21. Pursuit of Price October 21-28. Independence and State Line October 22. Big Blue and Westport October 23. Mine Creek, Little Osage River and Marias des Cygnes October 25. Battle of Charlot October 25. Mound City and Fort Lincoln October 25 (Cos. "A," "D"). Newtonia October 28. Operations on Upper Arkansas January 28-February 9, 1865. Protecting country against Indians till June. Powder River Expedition, march to Powder River and Fort Connor, July 11-September 20. Actions with Indians September 2-5. Powder River, Mouth of Dry Ford, September 8. Mustered out December 6, 1865.

Regiment lost during service 1 Officer and 10 Enlisted men killed and mortally wounded and 1 Officer and 98 Enlisted men by disease. Total 110.

39

1st BATTERY LIGHT ARTILLERY.

Organized at Mound City July 24, 1861. Attached to Dept. of Kansas to August, 1862. 2nd Brigade, Dept. of Kansas, to October, 1862. 1st Brigade, 1st Division, Army of the Frontier, Dept. Missouri, to February, 1863. District of Rolla, Dept. of Missouri, to June, 1863. District of Columbus, Ky., 6th Division, 16th Army Corps, Dept. Tennessee, to November, 1863. Defences of the Nashville & Northwestern Railroad, District of Nashville, Dept. of the Cumberland, and 2nd Brigade, 4th Division, 20th Army Corps, Dept. of the Cumberland, to November, 1864. 2nd Colored Brigade, District of the Etowah, Dept. Cumberland, to January, 1865. Reserve Artillery, District of Nashville, Dept. Cumberland, to July, 1865.

SERVICE.—Attached to Lane's Kansas Brigade and operations about Fort Scott, and on line of the Marmiton August and September, 1861. Actions at Ball's Mills August 28. Morse's Mill August 29. Dogwood Creek near Fort Scott September 2. Morristown September 17. Osceola September 21-22. Duty at Fort Scott till May, 1862. Expedition into Indian Country May 25-August 15. Action at Grand River June 6. Locust Grove July 3. Bayou Bernard July 27. Blunt's Campaign in Missouri and Arkansas September 17-December 3. Expedition to Sarcoxie September 28-30. Action at Newtonia September 29-30. Occupation of Newtonia October 4. Old Fort Wayne or Beattie's Prairie near Maysville October 22. Cane Hill November 28. Battle of Prairie Grove, Ark., December 7. Expedition over Boston Mountains to Van Buren December 27-31. Moved to Springfield, Mo., January, 1863, and duty there till February 17. Moved to Forsyth, Mo., thence to Fort Scott, Kansas. Duty in Missouri and Kansas, District of Rolla, till July, 1863. Ordered to St. Louis, Mo., July 5, thence to Cairo, Ill., July 18. Duty in District of Columbus, Ky., till November. Ordered to Nashville, Tenn., and assigned to duty on line of the Nashville & Northwestern Railroad till November, 1864. Moved to Nashville, Tenn. Battles of Nashville December 15-16. Post duty at Nashville till January, 1865, and at Chattanooga, Tenn., till July. Mustered out July 17, 1865.

Regiment lost during service 2 Enlisted men killed and 1 Officer and 23 Enlisted men by disease. Total 26.

2nd BATTERY LIGHT ARTILLERY.

Organized at Fort Scott and mustered in September 10, 1862. Attached to Dept. of Kansas to September, 1862. 1st Brigade, Dept. of Kansas, to October, 1862. 2nd Brigade, 1st Division, Army of the Frontier, Dept. of Missouri (1 Section), to February, 1863. District of Southwest Missouri, Dept. Missouri, to June, 1863. District of the Frontier, Dept. Missouri, to January, 1864. Unattached, District of the Frontier, 7th Corps, Dept. Arkansas, to May, 1864. 1st Brigade, District of the Frontier, 7th Corps, to February, 1865. 1st Brigade, 3rd Division, 7th Corps, to July, 1865.

SERVICE.—Duty at Fort Scott, Kansas, till June, 1863. (1st Section moved to Greenfield, Mo., September 1-3, 1862. Action at Newtonia September 30. Occupation of Newtonia October 4. Cane Hill November 28. 2nd Section moved from Fort Scott to Pea Ridge, Ark., October 12-19, 1862, returning to Fort Scott December 3-10, 1862.) Scout from Creek Agency to Jasper County, Mo., May 16-19, 1863 (1 Section). Sherwood May 19. (1 Section moved to Baxter Springs May 6, returning to Fort Scott June 24.) Fort Gibson May 22. Near Fort Gibson May 28. Operations about Fort Gibson June 6-20. Greenleaf Prairie June 16. 1 Section moved to Fort Gibson with supply train June 19-July 4. Action at Cabin Creek July 1-2 and 5. Battery moved to Fort Gibson July 5-12. Elk Creek near Honey Springs July 17. Duty at Fort Gibson till August 22. Near Sherwood August 14. Campaign to Perryville, C. N., August 22-31. At Fort Gibson till November. Ordered to Fort Smith, Ark., arriving November 15, and duty there till July, 1865. Near Fort Smith July 31, 1864. (1 Section at Clarksville June and July, 1864. 1 Section remained at Fort Scott and participated in the pursuit of Price.) Battle of Westport October 23, and pursuit beyond Fort Scott. Joined Battery at Fort Smith June, 1865. Action at Dardanelle, Ark., January 14, 1865. Battery mustered out August 11, 1865.

Battery lost during service 3 Enlisted men killed and 18 Enlisted men by disease. Total 21.

3rd BATTERY LIGHT ARTILLERY.

Organized as Company "B," 2nd Kansas Cavalry, December 9, 1861. Organized as a Battery October 27, 1862, with guns captured at Old Fort Wayne, and designated as Hopkins' Kansas Battery. Designated 3rd Battery October 1, 1863. Attached to 3rd Brigade, 1st Division, Army of the Frontier, Dept. Missouri, October, 1862, to February, 1863. District of Northwest Arkansas, Dept. Missouri, to June, 1863. District of the Frontier, Dept. Missouri, to December, 1863. 3rd Brigade, District Frontier, Dept. Missouri, to January, 1864. 3rd Brigade, District of the Frontier, 7th Corps, Dept. Arkansas, to January, 1865.

SERVICE.—Occupation of Newtonia October 4, 1862. Hazel Bottom October 14. Shell's Mill October 16. Cane Hill November 28. Battle of Prairie Grove, Ark., December 7. Expedition over Boston Mountains to Van Buren December 27-31. At Rhea's Mills January 1, 1863. Ordered to Fort Gibson February, arriving March 1, and duty there till July 17, 1863. Action at Webber's Falls April 28. Honey Springs July 1. At Webber's Falls and Scullyville till September. March to Van Buren September 2, and duty there till January 1865. (A detachment of 60 men sent to Little Rock to receive new Battery and duty there till January, 1865. Attached to Battery "G," 1st Missouri Light Artillery. September 13, 1864, to January 1, 1865.) Mustered out January 19, 1865. Veterans and Recruits transferred to 2nd Kansas Battery.

Battery lost during service 2 Enlisted men killed and 18 by disease. Total 20.

ARMSTRONG'S BATTERY LIGHT ARTILLERY.
Attached to 1st Kansas Colored Infantry.

HOPKINS' BATTERY LIGHT ARTILLERY.
Attached to 2nd Kansas Cavalry. See 3rd Battery.

OPDYKE'S BATTERY LIGHT ARTILLERY.
Attached to 9th Kansas Cavalry.

STOVER'S BATTERY LIGHT ARTILLERY.
Attached to 2nd Kansas Cavalry.

ZISCH'S MILITIA BATTERY LIGHT ARTILLERY.
Duty at Fort Leavenworth, Kansas, October, 1864.

1st REGIMENT INFANTRY.

Organized at Camp Lincoln, Fort Leavenworth, May 20 to June 3, 1861. Moved to Wyandotte, thence to Kansas City and Clinton, Mo., to join General Lyon, June 7-July 13, 1861. Attached to Dietzler's Brigade, Lyon's Army of the West. Advance on Springfield July. Action at Dug Springs August 2. At Springfield, Mo., till August 7. Battle of Wilson's Creek August 10. March to Rolla, Mo., August 11-22, thence to St. Louis, Mo., and duty on the Hannibal & St. Joseph Railroad till October. Attached to Dept. of Missouri to February, 1862. Dept. of Kansas to June, 1862. District of Columbus, Ky., Dept. Tennessee, to September, 1862. 1st Brigade, 6th Division, District of Corinth, Dept. Tennessee, to November, 1862. 1st Brigade, 6th Division, Left Wing 13th Army Corps, Dept. of the Tennessee, to December, 1862. 1st Brigade, 6th Division, 16th Army Corps, Army Tennessee, to January, 1863. 1st Brigade, 6th Division, 17th Army Corps, to July, 1863. District of Vicksburg, Miss., to September, 1863. 1st Brigade, 1st Division, 17th Army Corps, to August, 1864. Unattached, 2nd Division, 19th Army Corps, Dept. of the Gulf, to December, 1864. District of Eastern Arkansas, 7th Army Corps, Dept. of Arkansas, to January, 1865. Dept. Headquarters, Dept. of Arkansas, to August, 1865.

SERVICE.—Duty at Tipton, Mo., October, 1861, to January, 1862. Expedition to Milford, Mo., December 15-19, 1861. Shawnee Mound, Milford, December 18. At Lexington till February, 1862. Moved to Fort Leavenworth, Kansas. New Mexico Expedition April and May. Ordered to Columbus, Ky., and duty guarding Mobile & Ohio Railroad. Headquarters at Trenton, Tenn., till September. Moved to Jackson, Tenn., and duty there till November. Brownsburg September 4. Trenton September 17. March to relief of Corinth, Miss., October 3-5. Pursuit to Ripley October 5-12. Actions at Chewalla and Big Hill October 5. Moved to Grand Junction November 2. Grant's Central Mississippi Campaign. Operations on the Mississippi Central Railroad to the Yocknapatalfa River November, 1862, to January, 1863. Moved to Moscow, thence to Memphis, Tenn., and to Young's Point, La., January 17, 1863. Regiment mounted February 1, 1863. Moved to Lake Providence February 8, and provost duty there till July. Actions at Old River, Hood's Lane, Black Bayou and near Lake Providence February 10. Pin Hook and Caledonia, Bayou Macon, May 10. Expedition to Mechanicsburg May 26-June 4. Repulse of attack on Providence June 9. Baxter's Bayou and Lake Providence June 10. Bayou Macon June 10. Richmond June 16. Lake Providence June 29. Moved to Natchez July 12-13, and duty there till October. Expedition to Harrisonburg, La., September 1-8. Cross Bayou September 14. Moved to Vicksburg, Miss., October, and duty at Big Black and near Haynes' Bluff till June, 1864. Big Black River October 8, 1863. Scout from Bovina Station to Baldwyn's Ferry November 1. Scout to Baldwyn's Ferry January 14, 1864. Expedition up Yazoo River April 19-23. McArthur's Expedition to Yazoo City May 4-21. Benton May 7-9. Luce's Plantation May 13. Non-Veterans ordered to Fort Leavenworth, Kans., June 1, 1864. Attacked near Columbus, Ky., June 2. Mustered out June 19, 1864. Veterans on duty in District of Vicksburg, Miss., till August, 1864. Ordered to Morganza, La., July 29. Operations in vicinity of Morganza September 16-25. Near Alexandria September 20. Atchafalaya October 5. Ordered to White River, Ark., October 7, thence to Little Rock, Ark., December 7. Duty there as Headquarters Guard and escort, Dept. of Arkansas, till August, 1865. Mustered out August 30, 1865.

Regiment lost during service 7 Officers and 120 Enlisted men killed and mortally wounded and 3 Officers and 122 Enlisted men by disease. Total 252.

1st REGIMENT COLORED INFANTRY.

Organized at Fort Scott and mustered in as a Battalion January 13, 1863. Attached to Dept. of Kansas to June, 1863. District of the Frontier, Dept. Missouri, to January, 1864. Unattached, District of the Frontier, 7th Corps, Dept. of Arkansas, to March, 1864. 2nd Brigade, District of the Frontier, 7th Corps, to December, 1864.

SERVICE.—Duty in the Dept. of Kansas October, 1862, to June, 1863. Action at Island Mound, Mo., October 27, 1862. Island Mound, Kansas, October 29. Butler, Mo., November 28. Ordered to Baxter Springs May, 1863. Scout from Creek Agency to Jasper County, Mo., May 16-19 (Detachment). Sherwood, Mo., May 18. Bush Creek May 24. Near Fort Gibson May 28. Shawneetown, Kan., June 6 (Detachment). March to Fort Gibson, C. N., June 27-July 5, with train. Action at Cabin Creek July 1-2. Elk Creek near Honey Springs July 17. At Fort Gibson till September. Lawrence, Kan., July 27 (Detachment). Near Sherwood August 14. Moved to Fort Smith, Ark., October, thence to Roseville December, and duty there till March, 1864. Horse Head Creek February 12, 1864. Roseville Creek March 20. Steele's Camden Expedition March 23-May 3. Prairie D'Ann April 9-12. Poison Springs April 18. Jenkins' Ferry April 30. March to Fort Smith, Ark., May 3-16, and duty there till December. Fort Gibson, C. N., September 16. Cabin Creek September 19. Timber Hill November 19. Designation of Regiment changed to 79th U. S. Colored Troops December 13, 1864, which see.

1st REGIMENT MILITIA INFANTRY.

Called into service October 9, 1864, to repel Price's Invasion. Disbanded October 29, 1864.

2nd REGIMENT INFANTRY.

Organized at Lawrence for three months May, 1861. Mustered in at Kansas City June 20, 1861. Moved to Clinton, Mo., to join Lyon. Attached to Deitzler's Brigade, Lyon's Army of the West. Advance on Springfield, Mo., June 29-July 5. Expedition from Springfield to Forsyth July 20-25. Action at Forsyth July 22. Dug Springs August 2. Battle of Wilson's Creek August 10. March to Rolla, thence to St. Louis August 11-22. Operations in Northeast Missouri August 30-September 7. Paris September 2. Shelbina September 4. Iatan September 4. Capture of St. Jo September 13. Moved to Wyandotte, Kan., to resist Price's invasion. Mustered out October 31, 1861.

Regiment lost during service 1 Officer and 12 Enlisted men killed and mortally wounded and 1 Officer and 3 Enlisted men by disease. Total 17.

2nd REGIMENT COLORED INFANTRY.

Organized at Fort Scott and Fort Leavenworth August 11 to October 17, 1863. Attached to District of the Frontier, Dept. Missouri, to January, 1864. Unattached, District of the Frontier, 7th Corps, Dept. of Arkansas, to March, 1864. 2nd Brigade, District of the Frontier, 7th Corps, to December, 1864.

SERVICE.—Action at Baxter Springs, Ark., October 6, 1863 (Co. "B"). Moved from Fort Scott, Kan., to Fort Smith, Ark., October 19, 1863, as escort to train. Duty at Fort Smith till March, 1864. Steele's Expedition to Camden March 23-April 30. Prairie D'Ann April 9-13. Jenkins' Ferry April 30, and May 4 and 8. Return to Fort Smith and duty there till December. Designation of Regiment changed to 83rd U. S. Colored Troops (New), December 13, 1864, which see.

2nd REGIMENT MILITIA INFANTRY.

Called into service October 9, 1864, to resist Price's invasion. Disbanded October 29, 1864.

3rd REGIMENT INFANTRY.

Organization not completed. Consolidated with 4th Kansas Infantry to form 10th Kansas Infantry April 3, 1862.

3rd REGIMENT MILITIA INFANTRY.

Called into service October 9, 1864, to repel Price's invasion. Disbanded October 29, 1864.

4th REGIMENT INFANTRY.

Organization not completed. Consolidated with 3rd Kansas Infantry to form 10th Kansas Infantry April 3, 1862.

4th REGIMENT MILITIA INFANTRY.

Called into service October 9, 1864, to repel Price's invasion. Action at Byram's Ford, Big Blue, October 22. Westport October 23. Mine Creek, Little Osage River, Marias des Cygnes, October 25. Disbanded October 29, 1864.

5th REGMENT INFANTRY.

Two Companies organized at Fort Scott. Attached to Lane's Kansas Brigade. Operations about Fort Scott September and October, 1861. Action at Morristown September 17. Osceola September 21-22. Discontinued and merged into other organizations.

5th REGIMENT MILITIA INFANTRY.

Called into service October 9, 1864, to repel Price's invasion. Action at Byram's Ford, Big Blue, October 22. Westport October 23. Mine Creek, Little Osage River, Marias des Cygnes, October 25. Newtonia October 28. Disbanded October 29, 1864.

6th REGIMENT MILITIA INFANTRY.

Called into service October 9, 1864, to repel Price's invasion. Action at Byram's Ford, Big Blue, October 22. Westport October 23. Mine Creek, Little Osage River, Marias des Cygnes, October 25. Disbanded October 29, 1864.

7th REGIMENT MILITIA INFANTRY.

Called into service to repel Price's invasion. Duty at Fort Leavenworth and Kansas City. Disbanded October 29, 1864.

8th REGIMENT INFANTRY.

Regiment organized for service in the State and along border August, 1861. Companies "A," "D," "G" and "H" at Lawrence, Kan., October, 1861. Companies "A" and "G" march to West Point, Mo., December 16-19, and Companies "D" and "H," to same place November 23-25, 1861. Companies "A," "F" and "G" moved to Fort Kearney, Neb., February 16, 1862. Companies "D," "H" and "K" to Osawatomie, Kan., February 22, thence to Fort Leavenworth March 12. Companies "A," "D" and "G" at Fort Kearney, Neb. Companies "B" and "F" at Fort Leavenworth, Kan. Company "C" at Fort Riley till April, then at Fort Leavenworth, Kan. Companies "E" and "K" at Aubrey, Kan. Company "H" at Fort Leavenworth, Kan., till April, then at Fort Riley, and Company "I" at Leavenworth City. All till May, 1862. Companies "B," "E," "H," "I" and "K" moved from Leavenworth to Columbus, Ky., May 28-June 2, and to Union City, Tenn., June 8-11. To Trenton, Tenn., June 16-17. To Humboldt, Tenn., June 26, and to Corinth, Miss., July 2-3. Attached to 2nd Brigade, 4th Division, Army Mississippi, to September, 1862. 32nd Brigade, 9th Division, Army Ohio, to October, 1862. 32nd Brigade, 9th Division, 3rd Corps, Army Ohio, to November, 1862. 3rd Brigade, 1st Division, Right Wing 14th Army Corps, Dept. of the Cumberland, to January, 1863. Post of Nashville, Dept. of the Cumberland, to June, 1863. 3rd Brigade, 1st Division, 20th Army Corps, Army Cumberland, to October, 1863. 1st Brigade, 3rd Division, 4th Army Corps, Army Cumberland, to August, 1865. Dept. of Texas to November, 1865.

SERVICE.—Companies "B," "E," "H," "I" and "K" moved from Corinth, Miss., to Jacinto July 22, 1862, and to Eastport, Miss., August 3-5. March to Nashville, Tenn., August 18-September 4, thence to Louisville, Ky., in pursuit of Bragg September 11-26. Pursuit of Bragg into Kentucky October 1-16. Near Perryville October 6-7. Battle of Perryville October 8. Lancaster October 14. March to Nashville, Tenn., October 16-November 7. Reconnoissance toward Franklin December 9. Near Brentwood December 9. Assigned to provost duty at Nashville December 18, 1862, to June 9, 1863. Company "G" stationed at Leavenworth till February, 1863. Joined Regiment at Nashville, Tenn., March 29, 1863. Companies "A," "D" and "F" at Fort Kearney till June, 1862, then at Leavenworth, Kan., till February, 1863. Company "C" at Leavenworth, Kan., till February, 1863. Skirmish with Gordon's guerrillas at Hickory Grove, Mo., August 7, 1862 (Cos. "A," "D" and "F"). Scout from Fort Leavenworth to Independence, Mo., August 12-14, 1862 (Cos. "A" and "F"). Hickory Grove August 23 (Cos. "A," "C" and "F"). Expedition through Jasper, Cass, Johnson and LaFayette Counties, Mo., September 8-23 (Cos. "C" and "F"). Companies "A," "C," "D" and "F" joined Regiment at Nashville, Tenn., February 22, 1863. Regiment moved from Nashville to Murfreesboro, Tenn., June 9, 1863. Middle Tennessee or Tullahoma Campaign June 23-July 7. Liberty Gap June 24-27. Passage of Cumberland Mountains and Tennessee River, and Chickamauga (Ga.) Campaign August 16-September 22. Caperton's Ferry, Bridgeport, August 29. Battle of Chickamauga, Ga., September 19-20. Siege of Chattanooga September 24-October 27. Battles of Chattanooga November 23-25; Orchard Knob November 23-24; Missionary Ridge November 25. Pursuit to Graysville November 26-27. March to relief of Knoxville, Tenn., November 28-December 8. Campaign in East Tennessee till February, 1864. Veterans on furlough February 17-April 5. Moved to Nashville, Tenn., April 20-28. Escort train from Nashville to Sherman's army May 1 to June 17. Rejoined Brigade before Kenesaw Mountain June 28. Operations against Kenesaw Mountain June 28-July 2. Ruff's Station, Smyrna Camp Ground, July 4. Chattahoochie River July 5-17. Battle of Peach Tree Creek July 19-20. Siege of Atlanta July 22-August 25. Flank movement on Jonesboro August 25-30. Battle of Jonesboro August 31-September 1. Lovejoy's Station September 2-6. Operations against Hood in North Georgia and North Alabama October 1-26. Moved to Nashville, thence to Pulaski, Tenn. Nashville Campaign November-December. Columbia, Duck River, November 24-27. Spring Hill November 29. Battle of Franklin November 30. Battles of Nashville December 15-16. Pursuit of Hood to the Tennessee River December 17-28. March to Huntsville, Ala., December 1, 1864, to January 5, 1865, duty there till February 1. Moved to Nashville and back to Huntsville February 1-6, and duty there till March 15. Bull's Gap Expedition and operations in East Tennessee March 15-April 22. Moved to Nashville April 22 and duty there till June 15. Moved to New Orleans, La., June 15-29, thence to Indianola, Texas, July 6-9. March to Green Lake July 9, and duty there till August 10. Moved to San Antonio August 10-23, and duty there till November 29. Mustered out November 29, 1865. Moved to Fort Leavenworth, Kan., November 30, 1865-January 6, 1866, and honorably discharged January 9, 1866.

Regiment lost during service 3 Officers and 94 Enlisted men killed and mortally wounded and 3 Officers and 144 Enlisted men by disease. Total 244.

8th REGIMENT MILITIA INFANTRY.

Called into service October 9, 1864, to repel Price's invasion. Disbanded October 29, 1864.

9th REGIMENT MILITIA INFANTRY.

Called into service to repel Price's invasion. Duty at Fort Leavenworth and Kansas City. Disbanded October 29, 1864.

10th REGIMENT INFANTRY.

Organized at Paola by consolidation of 3rd and 4th Kansas Infantry April 3, 1862. Attached to Dept. of Kansas to August, 1862. 2nd Brigade, Dept. of Kansas, to October, 1862. 2nd Brigade, 1st Division, Army of the Frontier, Dept. Missouri, to February, 1863. District of Rolla, Dept. Missouri, to June, 1863. District of St. Louis, Mo., Dept. Missouri, to August, 1863. District of Kansas, Dept. of Missouri, to January, 1864. Alton, Ill., to August, 1864. District of St. Louis, Mo., Dept. Missouri, to November, 1864. Nashville, Tenn., Dept. of the Cumberland, to December, 1864. 2nd Brigade, 2nd Division (Detachment), Army Tennessee, to February, 1865. 2nd Brigade, 2nd Division, 16th Army Corps, Military Division West Mississippi, to August, 1865.

SERVICE.—Moved to Fort Scott, Kan., April, 1862, and duty there till June 4. Companies on Expedition into Indian Territory with 2nd Ohio Cavalry June 13-August 15. Locust Grove, C. N., July 3. Reconnoissance from Grand River to Fort Gibson, Tahlequah and Park Hill, and skirmishes July 14-17. Campaign against Coffey and Cockrell in Missouri August. Jackson County, Mo., September 15. Newtonia September 30. Occupation of Newtonia October 4. Old Fort Wayne or Beattie's Prairie near Maysville October 22. Cane Hill October 28. Battle of Prairie Grove, Ark., December 7. Expedition over Boston Mountains to Van Buren December 27-31. Moved to Springfield, Mo., January, 1863, and duty there till February 27. Near Mount Vernon till March 15. Operations against Shelby till April. Moved to Rolla, Mo., April 27, thence to St. Louis, Mo., June 4-8. Moved to Indianapolis, Ind., and return to St. Louis July 18. Moved to Kansas City, Mo., August,

and duty there till January, 1864. Skirmish with Quantrell at Paola August 21, 1863 (Detachment). Company "I" detached at St. Louis, Mo., as provost guard July and August, 1863, rejoining at Kansas City. Company "K" at Topeka, Kan., September to November, 1863. Regiment moved to St. Louis, Mo., January, 1864, thence to Alton, Ill., and guard Military Prison there till August, 1864. Non-Veterans moved to St. Louis, Mo., and mustered out August 19-20, 1864. Veterans and Recruits consolidated to a Battalion of four Companies August 15, 1864. On duty at St. Louis, Mo., till October 20. Moved to Pilot Knob October 20-24, thence to Paducah, Ky., November 2-12, and to Nashville, Tenn., November 28-29. Temporarily attached to 4th Army Corps, Army of the Cumberland. Battle of Franklin November 30. Battle of Nashville December 15-16. Pursuit of Hood to the Tennessee River December 17-28. Moved to Eastport, Miss., January 4-7, 1865. Reconnoissance to Iuka, Miss., January 9. Moved to New Orleans, La., February 8-21. Campaign against Mobile, Ala., and its defences March 17-April 12. Siege of Spanish Fort and Fort Blakely March 26-April 8. Assault and capture of Fort Blakely April 9. Occupation of Mobile April 12. March to Montgomery April 13-25. Duty there and in the District of Alabama till August. Mustered out August 30, 1865, and discharged at Fort Leavenworth, Kan., September 20, 1865.

Regiment lost during service 2 Officers and 26 Enlisted men killed and mortally wounded and 4 Officers and 114 Enlisted men by disease. Total 146.

10th REGIMENT MILITIA INFANTRY.

Called into service October 9, 1864, to repel Price's invasion. Action at Byram's Ford, Big Blue, October 22. Westport October 23. Mine Creek, Little Osage River, Marias des Cygnes, October 25. Newtonia October 28. Disbanded October 29, 1864.

11th REGIMENT INFANTRY.

Organized at Camp Lyon near Fort Leavenworth August 29 to September 14, 1862. Moved to Fort Scott, Kan., October 4-9, 1862, thence to Pea Ridge, Ark., October 15-19. Attached to 1st Brigade, 1st Division, Army of the Frontier, Dept. Missouri, to February, 1863. District of Rolla, Dept. Missouri and District of Kansas, Dept. Missouri, to April, 1863.

SERVICE.—Action at Old Fort Wayne or Beattie's Prairie, near Maysville, October 22, 1862. Cane Hill, Boston Mountains, November 28. Boston Mountains December 4-6. Reed's Mountain December 6. Battle of Prairie Grove December 7. Expedition over Boston Mountains to Van Buren December 27-31. Moved to Springfield, Mo., January, 1863, and duty there till February 17. Moved to Forsyth, Mo., thence to Fort Scott, Kan. On furlough March. Moved from Fort Scott to Salem, Mo., thence to Kansas City, Mo., April 6-20. Regiment mounted and designation changed to 11th Kansas Cavalry April, 1863, which see.

11th REGIMENT MILITIA INFANTRY.

Called into service October 9, 1864, to repel Price's invasion. Protect border from Coldwater Grove to Fort Scott. Disbanded October 29, 1864.

12th REGIMENT INFANTRY.

Organized at Paola September, 1862. Attached to Dept. of Kansas to June, 1863. Unattached, District of the Border, Dept. Missouri, to January, 1864. Unattached, District of the Border, 7th Corps, Dept. of Arkansas, to March, 1864. 2nd Brigade, Frontier Division, 7th Corps, to May, 1864. 1st Brigade, District of the Frontier, 7th Corps, to February, 1865. 1st Brigade, 3rd Division, 7th Corps, February, 1865. 1st Brigade, 1st Division, 7th Corps, to June, 1865.

SERVICE—Regiment assigned to duty by detachments on line between Kansas and Missouri till November, 1863. At Olathe, Paola, Wyandotte, Mound City, Shawnee Trading Post, Fort Scott, Leavenworth and Fort Riley, Kan. Company "H" at Fort Larned till January, 1864, then rejoined regiment at Fort Smith,

Ark., also occupy Kansas City, Westport and Hickman's Mills, Mo., guarding trains and operating against guerillas. Operations in Jackson County against Quantrell November 2-5, 1862 (Co. "A"). Baxter Springs October 6, 1863 (Detachment). Companies "B," "E" and "F" escort train to Fort Smith, Ark., October 28-November 17, 1863. Companies "A," "C," "D," "G," "I" and "K" concentrated at Fort Scott November, 1863, and march to Fort Smith, Ark., December 13-28, 1863. Duty there till March, 1864. Steele's Expedition to Camden March 23-May 3, 1864. Prairie D'Ann April 9-13. Jenkins' Ferry, Saline River, April 29-30. Return to Fort Smith May 3-16, and duty there till February, 1865. Fort Smith September 11, 1864. Moved to Little Rock February 24, 1865, and duty there till June. Mustered out June 3, 1865.

Regiment lost during service 2 Officers and 10 Enlisted men killed and mortally wounded and 2 Officers and 121 Enlisted men by disease. Total 135.

12th REGIMENT MILITIA INFANTRY.

Called into service October 9, 1864, to repel Price's invasion. Action at Big Blue October 22. Westport October 23. Disbanded October 29, 1864.

13th REGIMENT INFANTRY.

Organized at Atchison and mustered in September 20, 1862. Attached to 2nd Brigade, 1st Division, Army of the Frontier, Dept. Missouri, to February, 1863. District of Southwest Missouri, Dept. Missouri, to June, 1863. District of the Frontier, Dept. Missouri, to December, 1863. 3rd Brigade, District of the Frontier, Dept. Missouri, to January, 1864. 3rd Brigade, District of the Frontier, 7th Corps, Dept. of Arkansas, to February, 1865. 1st Brigade, 3rd Division, 7th Corps, February, 1865. 1st Brigade, 2nd Division, 7th Corps, February, 1865. 1st Brigade, 1st Division, 7th Corps, to June, 1865.

SERVICE—Action at Newtonia, Mo., September 29, 1862. Occupation of Newtonia October 4. March to Old Fort Wayne, arriving October 29. Cane Hill November 28. Battle of Prairie Grove, Ark., December 7. Expedition over Boston Mountains to Van Buren, Ark., Dec. 27-31. Capture of Van Buren December 29. March to Springfield, Mo., January 7, 1863, and duty there till May. March to Fort Scott, Kan., May 19-29, thence to Drywood, and duty there till August. Blunt's Campaign August 3-31. Capture of Fort Smith. To Webber Falls, C. N., arriving August 31, and duty there till September 15. March to Scullyville, C. N., and outpost and scout duty there till October 1. March to Van Buren, Ark., and duty there till February, 1865. (Cos. "B," "E" and "F," garrison at Fort Smith March, 1864, to February, 1865.) Companies "A," "C," "D," "G," "H" and "I" ordered to Little Rock February 3, 1865, and provost and garrison duty there till June, 1865. Mustered out June 26, 1865, and discharged at Fort Leavenworth, Kan., July 13, 1865.

Regiment lost during service 3 Officers and 19 Enlisted men killed and mortally wounded and 1 Officer and 106 Enlisted men by disease. Total 129.

13th REGIMENT MILITIA INFANTRY.

Called into service October 9, 1864, to repel Price's invasion. Action at Byram's Ford, Big Blue, October 22. Westport October 23. Disbanded October 29, 1864.

14th REGIMENT MILITIA INFANTRY.

Called into service October 9, 1864, to repel Price's invasion. Disbanded October 29, 1864.

15th REGIMENT MILITIA INFANTRY.

Called into service to resist Price's invasion. Action at Big Blue October 22. Westport October 23. Disbanded October 29, 1864.

16th REGIMENT MILITIA INFANTRY.

Called into service to repel Price's invasion. Action at Big Blue October 22. Westport October 23. Disbanded October 29, 1864.

17th REGIMENT INFANTRY.

Organized at Fort Leavenworth July 28, 1864, for 100 days. Attached to District of North Kansas. Company "A" ordered to Fort Riley, Company "C" to Cottonwood Falls and Company "D" at Lawrence. Operations against Price October-November. March to relief of Mound City. Mustered out November 16, 1864.

Regiment lost 4 by disease.

17th REGIMENT MILITIA INFANTRY.

Called into service October 9, 1864, to repel Price's invasion. Disbanded October 29, 1864.

18th REGIMENT MILITIA INFANTRY.

Called into service October 9, 1864, to repel Price's invasion. Action at Little Blue October 21. Disbanded October 29, 1864.

19th REGIMENT MILITIA INFANTRY.

Called into service to repel Price's invasion October 9, 1864. Action at Byram's Ford, Big Blue, October 22. Westport October 23. Disbanded October 29, 1864.

20th REGIMENT MILITIA INFANTRY.

Called into service October 9, 1864, to repel Price's invasion. Action at Byram's Ford, Big Blue, October 22. Westport October 23. Disbanded October 29, 1864.

21st REGIMENT MILITIA INFANTRY.

Called into service October 9, 1864, to resist Price's invasion. Action at Big Blue October 22. Westport October 23. Disbanded October 29, 1864.

22nd REGIMENT MILITIA INFANTRY.

Called into service October 9, 1864, to repel Price's invasion. Disbanded October 29, 1864.

LEAVENWORTH COLORED MILITIA INFANTRY.

Called into service October 9, 1864, to repel Price's invasion. Duty at Fort Leavenworth. Disbanded October 29, 1864.

LEAVENWORTH STATE GUARD.

Called into service October 9, 1864, to repel Price's invasion. Duty at Fort Leavenworth. Disbanded October 29, 1864.

KENTUCKY VOLUNTEERS.

1st REGIMENT CAVALRY.

Organized at Liberty, Burkeville and Monticello, Ky., October, 1861, and mustered in October 28, 1861. Attached to Thomas' Command, Camp Dick Robinson, Ky., to December, 1861. 1st Division, Army of the Ohio, to March, 1862. (5 Cos. attached to Garfield's 18th Brigade, Army Ohio, December, 1861, to March, 1862.) Unattached, Army Ohio, to September, 1862. 1st Brigade, Cavalry Division, Army Ohio, to November, 1862. Post Gallatin, Tenn., Dept. of the Cumberland, to April, 1863. District of Central Kentucky, Dept. Ohio, to June, 1863. 1st Brigade, 1st Division, 23rd Army Corps, Army Ohio, to August, 1863. Independent Cavalry Brigade, 23rd Army Corps, to November, 1863. 1st Brigade, 1st Division, Cavalry Corps, Army Ohio, to May, 1864. Independent Brigade, Cavalry Division, 23rd Army Corps, to August, 1864. 4th Brigade, 1st Division, District of Kentucky, Dept. of Ohio, to December, 1864. Camp Nelson, Military District of Kentucky, to September, 1865.

SERVICE—Near Rockcastle Hills October 18, 1861. Camp Wild Cat October 21. Fishing Creek December 8. (5 Cos. sent to Prestonburg, Ky., December 10 and join Garfield. Garfield's operations against Humphrey Marshall December 23, 1861, to January 20, 1862. Middle Creek, near Prestonburg, January 10, 1862.) Near Logan's Cross Roads, Mill Springs, on Fishing Creek, January 19-20, 1862. Near Cumberland Gap February 14 (Detachment). Big Creek Gap and Jacksboro March 14 (Detachment). Reconnoissance to Cumberland Gap March 21-23 (1st Battalion). Moved to Nashville, Tenn., April. Purdy and Lebanon May 5. Duty at Shelbyville, Columbia, Mt. Pleasant, Lawrenceburg, Pulaski and Murfreesboro, Tenn., till August. March to Louisville, Ky., in pursuit of Bragg August 21-September 26. Capture of 3rd Georgia Cavalry at New Haven September 29. Pursuit of Bragg into Kentucky October 1-22. Near Perryville October 6-7. Battle of Perryville October 8. Danville October 11. Near Mountain Gap October 14 and 16. March to Nashville, Tenn., October 22-November 7. Ordered to Kentucky November. Operations against Morgan December, 1862, to January, 1863. Operations against Pegram March 22-April 1. Danville March 24. Dutton's Hill, near Somerset, March 30. Expedition to Monticello and operations in Southeast Kentucky April 25-May 12. Howe's Ford, Weaver's Store, April 28. Monticello May 1. Neal Springs May. Near Mill Springs May 29. Monticello and Rocky Gap June 9. Saunders' raid in East Tennessee June 14-24. Lenoir June 19. Knoxville June 19-20. Strawberry Plains and Rogers' Gap June 20. Powder Springs Gap June 21. Columbia and Creelsborough June 29. Pursuit of Morgan July 2-26. Marrowbone, Burkesville, July 2. Columbia July 3. Martin's Creek July 10. Buffington's Island, Ohio, July 19. Near Lisbon July 26. Operation against Scott in Eastern Kentucky. Lancaster and Paint Lick Bridge July 31. Lancaster August 1. Smith's Shoals, Cumberland River, August 1. Burnside's campaign in East Tennessee August 16-October 17. Calhoun and Charleston September 25. Near Philadelphia September 27 and October 15. Philadelphia October 20. Motley's Ford, Little Tennessee River, November 4. Knoxville Campaign November 4-December 23. Marysville November 14. Little River November 14-15. Stock Creek November 15. Near Knoxville November 16. Siege of Knoxville November 17-December 5. Pursuit of Longstreet December 5-23. About Bean Station December 9-13. Operations about Dandridge January 16-17, 1864. Bend of Chucky River, near Dandridge, January 16. Dandridge January 17. Flat and Muddy Creek January 26. Seviersville January 26. Near Fair Garden January 27. Moved to Mt. Sterling, Ky., February 17-26, and duty there reorganizing till April. March to Tunnel Hill, Ga., May 1-12. Atlanta Campaign May to September. Demonstrations on Dalton May 9-13. Operations on line of Pumpkin Vine Creek and battles about Dallas, New Hope Church and Allatoona Hills May 25-June 5. Operations about Marietta and against Kenesaw Mountain June 10-July 2. Lost Mountain June 10 and 15-17. Assault on Kenesaw June 27. Operations on line of Nickajack Creek July 2-5. Campbellton July 4. On line of the Chattahoochie River July 5-17. About Atlanta July 22-27. Stoneman's raid to Macon July 27-August 6. Macon and Clinton July 30. Sunshine Church July 30-31. Ordered to Mt. Sterling, Ky., September. Duty at Camp Nelson, Ky., and at other points in Kentucky till December. Mustered out December 31, 1864. Veterans and recruits consolidated to a Battalion of 3 Companies and on duty at various points in Kentucky, operating against guerrillas and quieting country, till September, 1865. Mustered out September 20, 1865.

Regiment lost during service 5 Officers and 56 Enlisted men killed and mortally wounded and 1 Officer and 282 Enlisted men by disease. Total 344.

2nd REGIMENT CAVALRY.

Organized at Camp Joe Holt and Muldraugh's Hill, Ky., September 9, 1861, to February 13, 1862. Attached to Rousseau's Brigade, McCook's Command, Army of the Ohio, October, 1861, to December, 1861. 2nd Division, Army of the Ohio, to September, 1862. Unattached Cavalry, 1st Corps, Army Ohio, to November, 1862. Cavalry, 1st Division, Centre 14th Army Corps, Army of the Cumberland, to January, 1863. 2nd Brigade, 2nd Cavalry Division, Army of the Cumberland, to April, 1864. 2nd Brigade, 3rd Division, Cavalry Corps, Army of the Cumberland, to October, 1864. 2nd Brigade, 3rd Division, Cavalry Corps, Military Division Mississippi, to November, 1864. 1st Brigade, 3rd Division, Cavalry Corps, M. D. M., to July, 1865.

SERVICE—At Bacon Creek and Green River, Ky., till February, 1862. March to Nashville, Tenn., February 10-25, thence to Savannah, Tenn., March 31-April 7. Battle of Shiloh, Tenn., April 7-8. Advance on and siege of Corinth, Miss., April 29-May 30. Duty at Corinth till June 10. Buell's Campaign in Northern Alabama and Middle Tennessee June to August. March to Louisville, Ky., in pursuit of Bragg August 21-September 26. Woodburn, Ky., September 10. Pursuit of Bragg into Kentucky October 1-22. Near Bardstown October 4. Battle of Perryville October 8. Pursuit to Loudon October 10-22. Bloomfield October 18. March to Nashville, Tenn., October 22-November 7. Duty there till December 26. Nolensville December 26. Advance on Murfreesboro December 26-30. Battle of Stone's River December 30-31, 1862, and January 1-3, 1863. At Murfreesboro till June. Expedition to McMinnville April 20-30. Wartrace Road June 13. Middle Tennessee or Tullahoma Campaign June 24-July 7. Near Hillsborough June 29. Tullahoma July 1. Bob's Cross Roads July 1. Moore's Ford and Rock Creek Ford, Elk River, July 2. Boiling Fork, near Winchester, July 3. Expedition to Huntsville July 13-22. Passage of Cumberland Mountains and Tennessee River, and Chickamauga (Ga.) Campaign August 16-September 22. Alpine, Ga., September 3 and 8. Reconnoissance toward LaFayette September 10. Neal's Gap September 17. Battle of Chickamauga September 19-21. Near Philadelphia September 27. Operations against Wheeler and Roddy September 30-October 17. Pitt's Cross Roads, Sequatchie Valley, October 2. Hill's Gap, Thompson's Cove, October 3. Murfreesboro Road, near McMinnville, October 4. McMinnville October 4. Farmington October 7. Sim's Farm, near Shelbyville, October 7. Lookout Mountain November 24 (Detachment). Mission Ridge November 25 (Detachment). March to relief of Knoxville November 28-December 8. At Bridgeport, Ala., till May, 1864. Scouts to Caperton's Ferry March 28 (Detachment). Atlanta Campaign May to September. Near Resaca May 13. Battle of Resaca May 14-15. Kingston May 24. Dalton May 27. Rousseau's Raid from Decatur on West Point & Montgomery Railroad July 10-22. Ten Island Ford, Coosa River, July 14. Siege of Atlanta July 22-August 25. McCook's Raid on Atlanta and West Point and Macon & Western Railroad July 27-31. Lovejoy Station and Smith's Cross Roads July 29. Clear Creek and near Newman's July 30. Kilpatrick's Raid around Atlanta August 18-22. Camp Creek August 18. Jonesboro August 19. Lovejoy Station August 20. Flank movement on Jonesboro August 25-30. Flint River Station August 30. Battle of Jonesboro August 31-September 1. Lovejoy's Station September 2-6. Operations against Hood in North Carolina and North Alabama September 29-November 3. Camp Creek September 30. Sweetwater and Noyes Creek, near Powder Springs, October 1-3. Van Wert October 9-10. Marietta November 6. March to the sea November 15-December 10. Lovejoy Station November 16. Griswoldsville November 22. Sylvan Grove and near Waynesboro November 27. Waynesboro November 27-28. Near Waynesboro November 28. Near Louisville November 30. Millen or Shady Grove December 1. Waynesboro December 4. Siege of Savannah December 10-21. Campaign of the Carolinas January to April, 1865. Blackville, S. C., February 7. Williston February 8. Johnson's Station February 10. Phillips Cross Roads, N. C., March 4. Monroe's Cross Roads March 8. Averysboro, Taylor's Hole Creek, N. C., March 16. Battle of Bentonville March 19-21. Occupation of Raleigh and Moresville April 13. Chapel Hill April 15. Bennett's House April 26. Surrender of Johnston and his army. Duty at Mt. Olive, Lexington and Durham, N. C., till July. Mustered out at Camp Joe Holt, Ky., July 9-27, 1865.

Regiment lost during service 5 Officers and 51 Enlisted men killed and mortally wounded and 1 Officer and 122 Enlisted men by disease. Total 179.

3rd REGIMENT CAVALRY.

Organized in Calhoun and McLean Counties, Ky., December 13, 1861. Attached to 5th Division, Army of the Ohio, to June, 1862. Cavalry Brigade, Army of the Ohio, to September, 1862. 1st Brigade, Cavalry Division, Army Ohio, to November, 1862. 1st Brigade, Cavalry Division, Army of the Cumberland, to January, 1863. 1st Brigade, 1st Cavalry Division, Army Cumberland, to March, 1863. . District of Western Kentucky, Dept. Ohio, to June, 1863. 1st Brigade, 2nd Division, 23rd Army Corps, Dept. Ohio, to August, 1863. Unattached, Hopkinsville, Ky., 1st Division, 23rd Army Corps, to October, 1863. District of South Central Kentucky, 1st Division, 23rd Army Corps, to November, 1863. District of Nashville, Tenn., Dept. of the Cumberland, to April, 1864. 3rd Brigade, 3rd Division, Cavalry Corps, Army of the Cumberland, to October, 1864. 1st Brigade, 3rd Division, Cavalry Corps, Military Division Mississippi, to July, 1865.

SERVICE.—Action at Woodbury, Ky., October 29, 1861. Brownsville, Ky., November 21. Sacramento December 28. Moved to Nashville, Tenn., February 15-March 8, 1862, and to Savannah, Tenn., March 18-April 6. Battle of Shiloh April 6-7. Advance on and siege of Corinth, Miss., April 29-May 30. Pursuit to Booneville May 31-June 12. Buell's Campaign in Northern Alabama and Middle Tennessee June to August. Columbia and Kinderhook August 11 (Detachment). Mt. Pleasant August 14. March to Louisville, Ky., in pursuit of Bragg August 21-September 26. Mumfordsville, Ky., September 22. Ashbysburg September 25. New Haven September 29. Capture of 3rd Georgia Cavalry. Pursuit of Bragg into Kentucky October 1-22. Near Perryville October 6-7. Near Mountain Gap October 14 and 16. Expedition to Big Hill and Richmond October 21. March to Nashville, Tenn., October 25-November 7. Duty there till December 26. Reconnoissance to Franklin December 11-12. Wilson's Creek Pike December 11. Franklin December 12. Advance on Murfreesboro December 26-30. Lavergne December 26-27. Battle of Stone's River December 30-31, 1862, and January 1-3, 1863. Overall's Creek and Wilkinson's Cross Roads December 31. Lytle's Creek, Manchester Pike, January 5, 1863. Expedition to Franklin January 31-February 13. Unionville and Rover January 31. Rover February 13. Ordered to Kentucky February. Duty at Hopkinsville and Russellville and in District of West Kentucky till December, 1863. Action at Russellville June 28. Pursuit of Morgan July 2-26. Buffington Island, Ohio, July 19. Near Volney October 22. Lafayette November 27 (Detachment). Ordered to Nashville December 17. Smith's Expedition from Nashville, Tenn., to Corinth, Miss., December 28, 1863, to January 18, 1864. Ringgold, Ga., April 27. Reconnoissance from Ringgold, Ga., toward Tunnel Hill April 29. Atlanta (Ga.) Campaign May 1-September 8. Near Tunnel Hill and Ringgold Gap May 2. Near Nickajack Gap May 7. Near Resaca May 13. Battle of Resaca May 14-15. Calhoun May 15. Operations on line of Pumpkin Vine Creek and battles about Dallas, New Hope Church and Allatoona Hills May 25-June 5. Operations about Marietta and against Kenesaw Mountain June 10-July 2. Assault on Kenesaw June 27. On line of the Chattahoochie River July 2-12. Adairsville July 7. Siege of Atlanta July 22-August 25. Expedition to Pickens County July. Fairburn and Sandtown August 15. Kilpatrick's Raid around Atlanta August 18-22. Lovejoy Station August 20. Flank movement on Jonesboro August 25-30. Flint River Station August 30. Battle of Jonesboro August 31-September 1. Lovejoy Station September 2-6. Operations against Hood in North Georgia and North Alabama September 29-November 3. Camp Creek and near Atlanta September 30. Sweetwater and Noyes Creek near Powder Springs October 1-3. Van Wert October 9-10. March to the sea November 15-December 10. East Macon November 20. Griswoldsville November 22. Sylvan Grove November 27. Waynesboro November 27-28. Near Waynesboro No-

vember 28. Near Louisville November 30. Millen or Shady Grove December 1. Rocky Creek Church December 2. Waynesboro December 4. Siege of Savannah December 10-21. Campaign of the Carolinas January to April, 1865. Blacksville, S. C., February 7. Williston February 8. Johnston's Station February 10. About Columbia February 15-17. Lancaster February 27. Phillips' Cross Roads, N. C., March 4. Rockingham March 7. Monroe's Cross Roads March 10. Averysboro, Taylor's Hole Creek March 16. Battle of Bentonville March 19-21. Occupation of Goldsboro March 24. Morrisville and occupation of Raleigh April 13. Chapel Hill April 15. Bennett's House April 26. Surrender of Johnston and his army. Duty at Lexington, N. C., and in the Dept. of North Carolina till July. Mustered out July 15, 1865.

Regiment lost during service 3 Officers and 41 Enlisted men killed and mortally wounded and 3 Officers and 168 Enlisted men by disease. Total 215.

4th REGIMENT CAVALRY.

Organized at Louisville, Ky., December 24, 1861. Moved to Bardstown, Ky., January 6, 1862, and duty there till March. Unattached Cavalry, Army of the Ohio, to September, 1862. 1st Brigade, Cavalry Division, Army Ohio, to October, 1862. District of Louisville, Ky., Dept. Ohio, to November, 1862. District of Western Kentucky, Dept. of the Ohio, to January, 1863. 1st Brigade, 1st Cavalry Division, Army of the Cumberland, to July, 1863. 3rd Brigade, 1st Division, Cavalry Corps, Army of the Cumberland, to November, 1864. 3rd Brigade, 1st Division, Cavalry Corps, Military Division Mississippi, to January, 1865. 2nd Brigade, 1st Division, Cavalry Corps, Military Division Mississippi, to August, 1865.

SERVICE.—Moved from Bardstown, Ky., to Nashville, Tenn., March 26, 1862, thence to Wartrace, Tenn., April 8, and duty in that vicinity till July. Action at Lebanon May 5. Readyville June 7. Rankin's Ferry near Jasper June 18. Shell Mountain June 21. Battle Creek June 21 and July 5. Murfreesboro July 13 (4 Cos.). Moved to Tullahoma July 13, and duty there till August. Sparta August 4 (Detachment). Raid on Louisville & Nashville Railroad August 19-21 (Detachment). March to Louisville, Ky., in pursuit of Bragg August 22-September 26. Pursuit of Bragg into Kentucky October 1-22. Near Perryville October 6-7. Near Mountain Gap October 14 and 16. Duty on southern border of Kentucky till February, 1863. Ordered to Nashville, Tenn., February 9, thence to Murfreesboro and Franklin, Tenn. Expedition to Spring Hill March 4-5. Franklin March 4. Thompson's Station, Spring Hill, March 5. Expedition from Franklin to Columbia March 8-12. Thompson's Station March 9. Rutherford Creek March 10-11. Spring Hill March 19. Near Thompson's Station March 23. Little Harpeth March 25. Near Franklin March 31. Thompson's Station May 2. Franklin June 4. Triune June 9. Middle Tennessee or Tullahoma Campaign June 23-July 7. Uniontown and Rover June 23. Middleton June 24. Fosterville, Guy's Gap and Shelbyville June 27. Expedition to Huntsville July 13-22. Passage of Cumberland Mountains and Tennessee River and Chickamauga (Ga.) Campaign August 16-September 22. Maysville, Ala., August 21 and 28. Reconnoissance from Alpine, Ga., toward Summerville September 10. Skirmishes at Summerville September 10 and 15. Battle of Chickamauga September 19-21. Moved to Bellefonte, Ala., September 25-30. Operations against Wheeler and Roddy September 30-October 2. Moved to Caperton's Ferry October 2, and duty there till December 2. Moved to Rossville, Ga., December 2-5, and duty there till January 6, 1864. Scout toward Dalton December 12, 1863. Skirmish at Lafayette December 12. Scout to Lafayette December 21-23. Veterans on furlough January to March, 1864. **Near Chattanooga till May.** Atlanta (Ga.) Campaign May to September. Duty in rear of army covering and protecting railroad at Wauhatchie, Lafayette, Calhoun, Dalton and Resaca. At Wauhatchie May 5 to June 18.

(A detachment at Lexington, Ky., June 10, 1864.) At Lafayette till August 4. Actions at Lafayette June 24 and 30. At Calhoun August 4 to October 12. Pine Log Creek and near Fairmount August 14. Resaca October 12-13. Near Summerville October 18. Little River, Ala., October 20. Leesburg October 21. Ladiga, Terrapin Creek, October 28. Moved to Louisville, Ky., November 3-9. Operations against Lyon in Kentucky December 6-28. Hopkinsville, Ky., December 16. At Nashville, Tenn. ,till January 9, 1865. Moved to Gravelly Springs, Ala., and duty there till March. Wilson's Raid from Chickasaw, Ala., to Macon, Ga., March 22-May 1. Six-Mile Creek March 31. Selma April 2. Montgomery April 12. Wetumpka April 13. Fort Tyler, West Point, April 16. Capture of Macon April 20. Duty at Macon and in the Dept. of Georgia till August. Mustered out August 21, 1865.

Regiment lost during service 1 Officer and 30 Enlisted men killed and mortally wounded and 1 Officer and 148 Enlisted men by disease. Total 180.

5th REGIMENT CAVALRY.

Organized at Columbus, Ky., December, 1861, to February, 1862, and mustered in at Gallatin, Tenn., March 31, 1862. Served with Unattached Cavalry, Army Ohio, to September, 1862. 2nd Brigade, Cavalry Division, Army Ohio, to November, 1862. 4th Division, Center 14th Army Corps, Army of the Cumberland, to January, 1863. 2nd Brigade, 1st Division, Cavalry Corps, Army of the Cumberland, to July, 1863. (District Central Kentucky, Dept. of the Ohio, April to June, 1863; 2nd Brigade, 4th Division, 23rd Army Corps, to July, 1863; 4 Cos.) 3rd Brigade, 1st Division, Cavalry Corps, Army of the Cumberland, to January, 1864. 3rd Brigade, 1st Cavalry Division, 16th Army Corps, Army Tennessee, to April, 1864. 3rd Brigade, 3rd Division, Cavalry Corps, Army of the Cumberland, to October, 1864. 3rd Brigade, 3rd Division, Cavalry Corps, Military Division Mississippi, to November, 1864. 1st Brigade, 3rd Division, Cavalry Corps, Military Division Mississippi, to January, 1865. 3rd Brigade, 3rd Division, Cavalry Corps, Military Division Mississippi, to May, 1865.

SERVICE.—Duty at and near Columbia scouting and operating against guerrillas on border till February, 1862. Gradysville, Ky., December 12, 1861. Moved to Gallatin, Tenn., February, 1862, and duty there and in Tennessee till September. Lebanon, Tenn., May 5. Lamb's Ferry May 10. Expedition to Rodgersville, Ala., 13-14. Lamb's Ferry May 14. Sweeden's Cove June 4. Chattanooga June 7. Raid on Louisville & Nashville Railroad August 12-21 (Detachment). Hartsville Road near Gallatin August 21 (Detachment). March to Louisville, Ky., in pursuit of Bragg, August 22-September 26. Glasgow, Ky., September 18. Pursuit of Bragg into Kentucky October 1-22. Burksville November 8. Kimbrough's Mills, Mill Creek, December 6. Operations against Cluke's forces in Central Kentucky February 18-March 5, 1863. Duty at Franklin and in Middle Tennessee till June. Near Nashville May 4. University Depot and Cowan July 4. Expedition to Huntsville July 13-22. Expedition to Athens, Ala., August 2-8. Passage of Cumberland Mountains and Tennessee River and Chickamauga (Ga.) Campaign August 16-September 22. Reconnoissance from Alpine to Summerville and skirmish September 10. Battle of Chickamauga September 19-21. Operations against Wheeler and Roddy September 30-October 17. Smith's Expedition from Nashville to Corinth, Miss., December 28, 1863, to January 8, 1864. Smith's Expedition to Okolona, Miss., February 11-26. Okolona, Ivey's Hill, February 22. New Albany February 23. Atlanta (Ga.) Campaign May to September. Scout from Alpine to Summerville May, —. Near Nickajack Gap May 7. Near Resaca May 13. Battle of Resaca May 14-15. Adairsville May 17. Operations on line of Pumpkin Vine Creek and battles about Dallas, New Hope Church and Allatoona Hills May 25-June 4. Operations about Marietta and against Kenesaw Mountain June 10-July 2. On line of the Nickajack July 2-5. On line of the Chattahoochie

July 5-17. Summerville July 7. Sandtown and Fairburn August 15. Siege of Atlanta July 22-August 25. Kilpatrick's Raid around Atlanta July 18-22. Lovejoy Station August 20. Flank movement on Jonesboro August 25-30. Flint River Station August 30. Battle of Jonesboro August 31-September 1. Lovejoy Station September 2-6. Operations against Hood in North Georgia and North Alabama September 29-November 3. Camp Creek September 30. Sweetwater and Noyes Creek near Powder Springs October 1-3. Van Wert October 9-10. March to the sea November 15-December 10. Jonesboro November 15. Towallaga Bridge November 16. East Macon November 20. Griswoldsville November 22. Sylvan Grove and near Waynesboro November 27. Waynesboro November 27-28. Near Waynesboro November 28. Near Louisville November 30. Millen Grove and Louisville December 1. Rocky Creek Church December 2. Waynesboro December 4. Siege of Savannah December 10-21. Campaign of the Carolinas January to April, 1865. Blackville, S. C., February 7. Near White Post February 8. Williston February 8. Johnson's Station, February 11. About Columbia February 15-17. Lancaster February 27. Phillips' Cross Roads, N. C., March 4. Rockingham March 7. Monroe's Cross Roads March 10. Averysboro, Taylor's Hole Creek, March 16. Battle of Bentonville March 19-21. Occupation of Goldsboro March 24. Advance on Raleigh April 8-13. Morrisville and occupation of Raleigh April 13. Chapel Hill April 15. Bennett's House April 26. Surrender of Johnston and his army. Mustered out May 3, 1865.

Regiment lost during service 4 Officers and 32 Enlisted men killed and mortally wounded and 5 Officers and 172 Enlisted men by disease. Total 213.

6th REGIMENT CAVALRY.

Organized in Central Kentucky July to October, 1862. Munday's 1st Battalion Cavalry assigned as Companies "A," "B," "C," "D" and "E." Attached to District of Central Kentucky to October, 1862. District of Louisville, Ky., Dept. Ohio, to November, 1862. District Central Kentucky, Dept. Ohio, to January, 1863. 1st Brigade, 1st Division Cavalry, Army of the Cumberland, to July, 1863. 3rd Brigade, 1st Division, Cavalry Corps, Army of the Cumberland, to November, 1864. 3rd Brigade, 1st Division, Cavalry Corps, Military Division Mississippi, to January, 1865. 1st Brigade, 1st Division, Cavalry Corps, Middle Division Mississippi, and District of Middle Tennessee, Dept. of the Cumberland, to September, 1865.

SERVICE.—Skirmish Flat Lick August 17 (Detachment). Skirmish at Slaughterville, Ky., September 3, 1862 (Detachment). Mumfordsville September 20-21 (Detachment). Pursuit of Bragg through Kentucky October 1-22. 1st Battalion to Litchfield and skirmish with Bragg. 2nd Battalion to Bardstown and skirmish with Wheeler. 3rd Battalion to Stanford. 1st Battalion ordered to Louisa, Ky., November 14, thence to Mt. Sterling, Ky., December 9. Regiment concentrated at Lebanon, Ky., December, 1862. Operations against Morgan December 22, 1862, to January 2, 1863. Near Huntington December 27. Parker's Mills on Elk Fork December 28. Affair Springfield December 30 (Detachment). Muldraugh's Hill near New Market December 31. Ordered to Nashville, Tenn., January 30, thence to Franklin, Tenn., and duty there till June. Expedition from Franklin to Columbia March 8-12. Thompson's Station March 9. Rutherford Creek March 10-11. Near Thompson's Station March 23. Little Harpeth River March 25. Near Franklin March 31. Franklin April 27. Thompson's Station May 2. Moved to Triune June 2-4. Franklin June 4. Triune June 9. Middle Tennessee or Tullahoma Campaign June 23-July 7. University Depot July 4. Expedition to Huntsville July 13-22. Expedition to Athens, Ala., August 2-8. Passage of Cumberland Mountains and Tennessee River and Chickamauga (Ga.) Campaign August 16-September 22. Alpine, Ga., September 5. Summerville September 6-7 and 10. Battle of Chickamauga September 19-21.

Buell's Ford September 28. Operations against Wheeler and Roddy September 30-October 17. At Caperton's Ferry till January, 1864. Lafayette, Ga., December 12, 1863. Ringgold December 13. Scout to Lafayette December 21-23. Regiment veteranize January, 1864, and Veterans on furlough till March. Near Chattanooga, Tenn., till May. Atlanta (Ga.) Campaign May to September. Guarding railroad in rear of the army at Wauhatchie, Lafayette, Calhoun, Dalton and Resaca. At Wauhatchie, Tenn., May 5 to June 18. At Lafayette, Ga., June 18 to August 4. Summerville July 7. Actions at Lafayette June 24 and 30. Scouting about Calhoun, Adairsville and Resaca till October 12. Pine Log Creek near Fairmount August 14. Rousseau's pursuit of Wheeler September 1-8. Resaca October 12-13. Near Summerville October 18. Little River, Ala., October 20. Leesburg October 21. Ladiga, Terrapin Creek, October 28. Moved to Louisville, Ky., November 3-9. McCook's pursuit of Lyon December 6-28. Hopkinsville, Ky., December 16. At Nashville, Tenn., till January 9. Moved to Gravelly Springs, Ala., and duty there till March. Wilson's Raid from Chickasaw, Ala., to Macon, Ga., March 22-April 24. Centerville April 1. Trion April 1. Selma April 2. Northport near Tuscaloosa April 4. Lapier's Mills, Sipsey Creek, April 6. King's Store April 6 (Co. "D"). Occupation of Talladega April 22. Munford's Station April 23. At Macon till June. Moved to Nashville, Tenn., and duty in District of Middle Tennessee till September. Non-Veterans mustered out at Edgefield July 14, 1865. Regiment mustered out September 6, 1865.

Regiment lost during service 2 Officers and 31 Enlisted men killed and mortally wounded and 4 Officers and 251 Enlisted men by disease. Total 288.

7th REGIMENT CAVALRY.

Organized at large and mustered in at Paris, Ky., August 16, 1862. Attached to Army of Kentucky, unassigned, Dept. of Ohio, to November, 1862. District of Central Kentucky, Dept. Ohio, to March, 1863. 1st Brigade, 1st Division, Cavalry Corps, Army of the Cumberland, to July, 1863. 3rd Brigade, 1st Division, Cavalry Corps, Army of the Cumberland, to November, 1864. 3rd Brigade, 1st Division, Cavalry Corps, Military Division Mississippi, to January, 1865. 2nd Brigade, 1st Division, Cavalry Corps, M. D. M., to July, 1865.

SERVICE—Before muster participated in operations against Morgan July 4-28, 1862. Cynthiana, Ky., July 17 (Detachment). Paris July 19. Big Hill, Madison County, August 23. Richmond August 30. Moved to Tennessee December, 1862. Hartsville December 7. Scouting at Castillian Springs till March, 1863. Moved to Franklin, Tenn. Expedition from Franklin to Columbia March 8-12. Thompson's Station March 9. Rutherford Creek March 10-11. Spring Hill March 18-19. Columbia Pike April 1. Thompson's Station May 2. Moved to Triune June 2-4. Franklin June 4. Middle Tennessee or Tullahoma Campaign June 23-July 7. Expedition to Huntsville July 13-22. Detached at Bridgeport, Caperton's Ferry and Nashville till December. Operations about Mossy Creek and Dandridge, Tenn., December 24-28. Mossy Creek Station December 24. Peck's House, near New Market, December 24. Mossy Creek December 26. Talbot's Station December 26-28. Mossy Creek December 29. Moved to Morristown. Kimbrough' Cross Roads and bend of Chucky River January 16, 1864. Operations about Dandridge January 16-17. Dandridge January 17. Pigeon River, near Fair Garden, January 27. Swann's Bridge, Paris Ford, January 28. At Cleveland, Tenn., till May. Atlanta (Ga.) Campaign May to September. Guarding railroad in rear of army, at Wauhatchie, Tenn., May 5 to June 18. At Lee and Gordon's Mills and Lafayette till August 4. Action at Lafayette June 24. Actions at Lost Mountain July 1-2. At Calhoun and Dalton till October 12. Pine Log Creek and near Fairmount August 14. Dalton August 14-15 (Co. "B"). Rousseau's pursuit of Wheeler September 1-8. Resaca October

12-13. Surrender of Dalton October 13 (Co. "B"). Near Summerville October 18. Little River, Ala., October 20. Leesburg October 21. Ladiga, Terrapin Creek, October 28 (Detachment). Moved to Louisville, Ky., November 3-9. McCook's pursuit of Lyon December 6-28. Hopkinsville, Ky., December 16. At Nashville, Tenn., till January 9, 1865. Moved to Gravelly Springs, Ala., and duty there and at Waterloo till March. Wilson's Raid from Chickasaw, Ala., to Macon, Ga., March 22-April 24. Selma April 2. Montgomery April 12. Columbus Road, near Tuskegee, April 14. Fort Tyler, West Point, April 16. Capture of Macon April 20. Duty at Macon till June and at Nashville, Tenn., till July. Mustered out July 10, 1865.

Regiment lost during service 2 Officers and 22 Enlisted men killed and mortally wounded and 5 Officers and 118 Enlisted men by disease. Total 147.

8th REGIMENT CAVALRY.

Organized at Russellville, Ky., and mustered in August 13, 1862. Attached to District of Louisville, Ky., Dept. of the Ohio, to November, 1862. Unattached, Bowling Green, District of Western Kentucky, Dept. Ohio, to June, 1863. 1st Brigade, 2nd Division, 23rd Army Corps, Army of Ohio, to August, 1863. Unassigned, Bowling Green, Ky. 1st Division, 23rd Army Corps, to September, 1863.

SERVICE—Duty at Russellsville, Bowling Green and Hopkinsville, Ky., District of West Kentucky, and at Clarksville, Tenn., operating against guerrillas, till September, 1863. Actions at Morganfield, Ky., August 3, 1862. Madisonville August 25. Morganfield September 1. Geiger's Lake September 3. Near Madisonville September 4. Ashbysburg September 25. Henderson County November 1. Greenville Road November 5. Garrettsburg November 6. Rural Hill, Tenn., November 18. Near Nashville, Tenn., January 28, 1863. Expedition from Bowling Green, Ky., to Tennessee State Line May 2-6. Operations against Morgan July 2-26. Buffington's Island, Ohio, July 19. Mustered out September 23, 1863.

Regiment lost during service 1 Officer and 8 Enlisted men killed and mortally wounded and 4 Officers and 104 Enlisted men by disease. Total 117.

9th REGIMENT CAVALRY.

Organized at Emminence, Ky., August 22, 1862. Attached to 3rd Brigade, Cavalry Division, Army Ohio, to November, 1862. District of Western Kentucky, Dept. of the Ohio, to June, 1863. 2nd Brigade, 3rd Division, 23rd Army Corps, Army Ohio, to August, 1863. Emminence, Ky., 1st Division, 23rd Army Corps, to September, 1863.

SERVICE—Advance toward Richmond, Ky., August, 1862. Retreat to Shelbyville August 30-September 1. Pursuit of Bragg into Kentucky October 1-22. Near Clay Village October 4. Near Perryville October 6-7. Battle of Perryville October 8. Lawrenceburg October 8. Dog Walk, Chesser's Store, October 9. Capture of Harrodsburg October 11. Moved to Cumberland River and operating against Champ Ferguson till December. Operations against Morgan's Raid in Kentucky December 22, 1862, to January 2, 1863. Springfield, Ky., December 30 (Detachment). Operations against Pegram March 22-April 1. Danville March 22 and 28. Expedition to Monticello and operations in Southeastern Kentucky April 26-May 12. Cumberland River May 9. Pursuit of Morgan July 2-26. Marrowbone-Burkesville July 2. New Lisbon, Ohio, July 26. Duty at Emminence till September. Mustered out September 11, 1863.

Regiment lost during service 5 Enlisted men killed and mortally wounded and 1 Officer and 101 Enlisted men by disease. Total 107.

10th REGIMENT CAVALRY.

Organized at Covington, Lexington and Crab Orchard, Ky., for one year's service, September 8 to November 11, 1862. Attached to Cavalry, 1st Division, Army of Kentucky, Dept. of the Ohio, to November, 1862. Unattached, Army of Kentucky, November, 1862. **District** of Central Kentucky, Dept. Ohio, to April, 1863. 2nd Brigade, District Central Kentucky, Dept. Ohio, to June, 1863. 2nd Brigade, 4th Division, 23rd Army Corps, Dept. of Ohio, to July, 1863. 2nd Brigade, 1st Division, 23rd Army Corps, to August, 1863. Mt. Sterling, Ky., 1st Division, 23rd Army Corps, to September, 1863. (2nd Battalion attached to District of Eastern Kentucky to June, 1863. 1st Brigade, 4th Division, 23rd Army Corps, to August, 1863.)

SERVICE—Duty about Mt. Sterling, Ky., and in the District of Central Kentucky, scouting and operating against guerrillas and protecting that part of the State, till September, 1863. Skirmish near Florence, Ky., September 8, 1862. Expedition to East Tennessee December 24, 1862, to January 1, 1863. Parker's Mills, on Elk Fork, December 28, 1862. Operations against Cluke's forces February 18-March 5, 1863. Coomb's Ferry February 22. Slate Creek, near Mt. Sterling, and Stoner's Bridge, February 24. Slate Creek, near Mt. Sterling, March 2. Operations against Pegram March 22-April 1. Mt. Sterling March 22. Operations against Everett's Raid in Eastern Kentucky June 13-23. Triplett's Bridge, Flemming County, June 16. Operations against Scott's forces July 25-August 6. Richmond July 28. Lancaster and Paint Creek Bridge July 31-August 1. Smith's Shoals, Cumberland River, August 1. Duty at Mt. Sterling till September. (2nd Battalion served detached in District Eastern Kentucky. Expedition from Beaver Creek into Southwest Virginia July 3-11, 1863. Gladesville, Va., July 7.) Regiment mustered out September 17, 1863.

Regiment lost during service 13 Enlisted men killed and mortally wounded and 1 Officer and 61 Enlisted men by disease. Total 75.

11th REGIMENT CAVALRY.

Companies "A," "C," "D" and "F" organized at Harrodsburg, Ky., July, 1862. Balance at Louisville, Ky., September 26, 1862. Attached to District of Western Kentucky, Dept. Ohio, to June, 1863. 2nd Brigade, 3rd Division, 23rd Army Corps, Dept. Ohio, to August, 1863. Independent Cavalry Brigade, 23rd Army Corps, to November, 1863. 1st Brigade, 1st Division, Cavalry Corps, Army Ohio, to April, 1864. 3rd Brigade, Cavalry Division, District Kentucky, Dept. Ohio, to May, 1864. Independent Brigade, Cavalry Division, 23rd Army Corps, to September, 1864. Military District Kentucky, Dept. Ohio, to March, 1865. 2nd Brigade, Cavalry Division, District of East Tennessee, Dept. of the Cumberland, to July, 1865.

SERVICE.—Companies "A," "C," "D" and "F" moved to Frankfort, Ky., July 22, 1862, thence to Louisville, Ky., and join Regiment. Regiment moved to Frankfort, Ky., November, 1862. Duty there and at Bowling Green, Scottsville and Gallatin, Tenn., till December 25, 1862. Hartsville, Tenn., December 7 (Co. "E"). Moved to Glasgow, Ky., December 25, and duty there and at various points in Western Kentucky till August, 1863. Action at Creelsburg, Ky., April 19. Expedition to Monticello and operations in Southeast Kentucky April 26-May 12. Scottsville June 11. Pursuit of Morgan July 2-26. Buffington Island, Ohio, July 19. New Lisbon, Ohio, July 26. Burnside's Campaign in East Tennessee August 16-October 17. Calhoun and Charleston September 25. Philadelphia October 20. Knoxville Campaign November 4-December 23. Marysville November 14. Little River November 14-15. Stock Creek November 15. Near Loudon November 15. Near Knoxville November 16. Siege of Knoxville November 17-December 5. About Bean's Station December 9-13. Operations about Dandridge January 16-17, 1864. Bend of Chucky Road near Dandridge January 16. Dandridge January 17. Flat and Muddy Creeks January 26. Near Fair Garden January 27. French Broad January 28. Moved to Mt. Sterling, Ky., February 3-12, and duty there till April. March from Nicholasville, Ky., to Dalton, Ga., April 29-May 11. Atlanta (Ga.) Campaign May to August. Varnell Station May 11. Demonstration on Dalton May 11-13. Battle of Resaca May 14-15.

Operations on line Pumpkin Vine Creek and battles about Dallas, New Hope Church and Allatoona Hills May 25-June 5. Burnt Church May 26-27. Mt. Zion Church May 27-28. Allatoona May 30. Operations about Marietta and against Kenesaw Mountain June 10-July 2. Pine Hill June 11-14. Lost Mountain June 15-17. Muddy Creek June 17. Noyes Creek June 19. Cheyney's Farm June 22. Olley's Creek June 26-27. Assault on Kenesaw June 27. On line of Nickajack Creek July 2-5. On line of Chattahoochie River July 6-17. Siege of Atlanta July 22-August 25. Stoneman's Raid to Macon July 27-August 6. Macon and Clinton July 30. Sunshine Church July 30-31. Ordered to Kentucky August 31, and operating against guerrillas in Green River counties till September. Burbridge's Expedition into Southwest Virginia September 20-October 17. Saltsville, Va., October 2. Sandy Mountain October 3. Stoneman's Raid into Southwest Virginia December 10-29. Bristol December 14. Abington, Va., December 15. Marion, Va., December 16. Near Marion December 17-18. Capture of Saltsville, Va., December 20-21. Jonesboro December 23. Clinch River December 24. At Lexington, Ky., till February, 1865. Moved to Louisville, thence to Knoxville, Tenn., February 27-March 9, and to Strawberry Plains March 15. Stoneman's Raid into Southwest Virginia and Western North Carolina March 21-April 25, 1865. Statesville, N. C., April 10-11. Shallow Ford, N. C., April 11. Salisbury April 12. Catawba River near Morgantown April 17. Howard's Gap, Blue Ridge, April 22. Hendersonville April 23. Asheville April 25. Moved to Atlanta, Ga., thence to Louisa, Ky. Mustered out July 12 to 17, 1865.

Regiment lost during service 1 Officer and 23 Enlisted men killed and mortally wounded and 2 Officers and 236 Enlisted men by disease. Total 262.

12th REGIMENT CAVALRY.

Organized at Caseyville and Owensboro, Ky., November 17, 1862. Attached to District of West Kentucky, Dept. Ohio, to June, 1863. 2nd Brigade, 3rd Division, 23rd Army Corps, Army of the Ohio, to August, 1863. Independent Cavalry Brigade, 23rd Army Corps, to November, 1863. 1st Brigade, 1st Division, Cavalry Corps, Dept. Ohio, to April, 1864. 3rd Brigade, Cavalry Division, District Kentucky, Dept. Ohio, May, 1864. 1st Brigade, Cavalry Division, 23rd Army Corps, to June, 1864. Detached Cavalry Brigade, 3rd Division, 23rd Army Corps, to August, 1864. Dismounted Brigade, Cavalry Division, 23rd Army Corps, to September, 1864. 1st Brigade, Cavalry Division, 23rd Army Corps, September, 1864. District of Louisville, Ky., to November, 1864. 2nd Brigade, 4th Division, 23rd Army Corps, to March, 1865. 2nd Brigade, Cavalry Division, District East Tennessee, to July, 1865. Cavalry Brigade, District East Tennessee, to August, 1865.

SERVICE.—Action at Owensboro, Ky., September 18, 1862. Sutherland Farm September 19. Action at Calhoun, Ky., November 25, 1862. Operations against Morgan's Raid into Kentucky December 22, 1862, to January 2, 1863. Bear Wallow, Ky., December 23, 1862. Near Glasgow December 24. Bear Wallow and near Munfordsville December 25. Bacon Creek near Munfordsville December 26. Johnson's Ferry, Hamilton's Ford, Rolling Fork, December 29. Boston, Ky., December 29. Duty in District of Western Kentucky till April, 1863. Creelsborough April 19. Expedition to Monticello and operations in Southeastern Kentucky April 26-May 12. Narrows, Horse Shoe Bottom, April 28-29. Horse Shoe Bend, Greasy Creek, May 10. Pursuit of Morgan through Kentucky, Indiana and Ohio July 2-26. Marrowbone July 2. Buffington's Island, Ohio, July 19. Surrender of Morgan near Cheshire, Ohio, July 20. New Lisbon, Ohio, July 26. Ordered to Glasgow, Ky., August 4. Burnside's march into East Tennessee August 16-October 17. Operations about Cumberland Gap September 7-10. Carter's Station September 20-21. Jonesboro September 21. Watauga River Bridge September 21-22. Philadelphia October 20. Knoxville Campaign November 4-December 23. Little River November 14-

15. Stock Creek November 15. Near Knoxville November 16. Siege of Knoxville November 17-December 4. Clinch Mountain December 6. Rutledge December 7. Bean's Station December 9-17. Rutledge December 16. Blain's Cross Roads December 16-19. Bean's Station and Rutledge December 18. Bend of Chucky Road near Dandridge January 16-17. About Dandridge January 16-17. Dandridge January 17. About Dandridge January 26-28. Flat Creek and Muddy Creek January 26. Fair Garden January 27. Dandridge January 28. Moved to Lebanon, Ky., February 3-12. At Mt. Sterling till April. March from Nicholsville, Ky., to Dalton, Ga., April 29-May 11. Atlanta (Ga.) Campaign May 11-September 8. Vernell Station May 11. Battle of Resaca May 14-15. Pine Log Creek May 18. Cassville May 19-22. Eutaw River May 20. About Dallas May 25-June 5. Burned Church May 26-27. Mt. Zion Church May 27-28. Allatoona May 30. Pine Mountain June 10. Operations about Marietta and against Kenesaw Mountain June 10-July 2. Lost Mountain June 11-17. Muddy Creek June 17. Noyes Creek June 19. McAffee's Cross Roads June 20. Cheyney's Farm June 22. Olley's Cross Roads June 26-27. Assault on Kenesaw June 27. Lost Mountain July 1-2. Nickajack Creek July 2-5. Chattahoochie River July 6-17. Siege of Atlanta July 22-August 25. Flank movement on Jonesboro August 25-30. Battle of Jonesboro August 31-September 1. Ordered to Louisville, Ky., September 14. Duty there at Lexington and Camp Nelson, Ky., till November. Rally Hill November 29. Burbridge's Saltsville Expedition December 10-29. Kingsport December 13. Bristol December 14. Near Glade Springs December 15. Marion and capture of Wytheville, Va., December 16. Mt. Airey December 17. Near Marion December 17-18. Capture and destruction of Salt works at Saltsville, Va., December 20-21. Operations against Sue Monday's guerrillas near Elizabethtown, Ky., and in Green River Counties January and February, 1865. Moved to Knoxville, Tenn., March 20 and join General Stoneman. Stoneman's Raid in Southwest Virginia and Western North Carolina March 20-April 27. Boone, N. C., March 28. Statesville April 10-11. Shallow Ford and near Mocksville April 11. Grant's Creek and Salisbury April 12. Catawba River near Morgantown April 17. Howard's Gap, Blue Ridge Mountains, April 22. Near Hendersonville April 23. Asheville April 25. Return to East Tennessee and duty at Sweetwater till August. Mustered out August 23, 1865.

Regiment lost during service 3 Officers and 22 Enlisted men killed and mortally wounded and 4 Officers and 204 Enlisted men by disease. Total 233.

13th REGIMENT CAVALRY.

Organized at Columbia, Ky., December 22, 1863. Attached to District of South Central Kentucky, 1st Division, 23rd Army Corps, Dept. of the Ohio, to January, 1864. District of Southwest Kentucky, Dept. Ohio, to April, 1864. 2nd Brigade, 1st Division, District of Kentucky, Dept. Ohio, to July, 1864. 1st Brigade, 1st Division, District of Kentucky, to January, 1865.

SERVICE—Duty at Lebanon and protecting country south of Lebanon till June, 1864. Cumberland River, Ky., November 26, 1863. Creelsborough and Celina December 7. Cumberland River March 19, 1864. Obey's River March 28 (Detachment). Expedition to Obey's River April 18-20. Wolf River May 18. Operations against Morgan May 31-June 30. Cynthiana June 12. Liberty June 17. Canton and Roaring Springs August 22. At Camp Burnside August 26-September 16. Ordered to Mt. Sterling September 16. Burbridge's Expedition into Southwest Virginia September 20-October 17. Saltsville, Va., October 2. At Mt. Sterling, Lexington and Crab Orchard, Ky., till December 17. At Camp Nelson, Ky., till January 10, 1865. Mustered out January 10, 1865.

Regiment lost during service 1 Officer and 9 Enlisted men killed and mortally wounded and 1 Officer and 83 Enlisted men by disease. Total 94.

14th REGIMENT CAVALRY.

Companies "A," "B," "C" and "D" organized at Mt. Sterling, Ky., and mustered in November 6, 1862. Other Companies organized at Irvine, Ky., August 21, 1862, to February 13, 1863. Attached to District of Central Kentucky, Dept. Ohio, to June, 1863. 2nd Brigade, 4th Division, 23rd Army Corps, to July, 1863. 2nd Brigade, 1st Division, 23rd Army Corps, to August, 1863. District North Central Kentucky, 1st Division, 23rd Army Corps, to January, 1864. District Southwest Kentucky to March, 1864.

SERVICE—Assigned to duty scouting in mountains of Eastern Kentucky and operating against guerrillas till January, 1864. Owensburg September 19-20, 1862. Brookville September 28. Operations in Bath, Estill, Powell, Clark, Montgomery and Boonsborough Counties October 16-25. Perry County, Kentucky River, November 8. Johnson County December 1. Floyd County December 4. Powell County December 26, 1862, and January 26, 1863. Mt. Sterling March 22. Slate Creek, near Mt. Sterling, June 11. Mud Lick Springs, Bath County, June 13. Operations against Everett's Raid in East Kentucky June 13-23. Triplett's Bridge June 16. Operations against Scott in Eastern Kentucky July 25-August 6. Irvine, Estill County, July 30. Lancaster and Paint Lick Bridge July 31. Lancaster August 1. Mustered out September 16, 1863, to March 24, 1864.

Regiment lost during service 14 Enlisted men killed and mortally wounded and 2 Officers and 64 Enlisted men by disease. Total 80.

15th REGIMENT CAVALRY.

Organized at Owensborough, Ky., October, 1862. Ordered to Paducah, Ky., October, 1862. Attached to District of Columbus, Dept. of the Tennessee, to November, 1862. District of Columbus, Ky., 13th Army Corps, Dept. of the Tennessee, to January, 1863. District of Columbus, Ky., 16th Army Corps, to August, 1863. Detached Brigade, District of Columbus, Ky., 6th Division, 16th Army Corps, to October, 1863.

SERVICE—Garrison duty at Paducah, Ky., and at various points in District of Columbus till October, 1863. Scout from Fort Heiman into Tennessee May 26-June 2, 1863 (Cos. "A" and "D"). Spring Creek, Tenn., June 29. Lexington, Tenn., June 29. Expedition from Clifton in pursuit of Biffle's, Forest's and Newsome's Cavalry July 22-27. Expedition from Paducah, Ky., to McLemoresville, Tenn., September 20-30. Mustered out October 6 to 29, 1863.

Regiment lost during service 1 Officer and 2 Enlisted men killed and mortally wounded and 1 Officer and 54 Enlisted men by disease. Total 58.

16th REGIMENT CAVALRY.

Organized at Paducah, Ky., September, 1863. Attached to 2nd Brigade, 2nd Division, Cavalry Corps, Dept Ohio, to May, 1864. 1st Cavalry Brigade, District of Kentucky, 5th Division, 23rd Army Corps, Dept. Ohio, to October, 1864.

SERVICE—Duty at Paducah, Ky., till April, 1864. Fort Anderson, Paducah, March 25-26, 1864. Ordered to Louisville, Ky., April 12. Operations against Morgan May 31-June 30. Cynthiana June 12. At Nicholasville, Ky., June to August. Cleveland, Tenn., August 17. Gillem's Expedition from East Tennessee toward Southwest Virginia September 20-October 17. Leesburg September 28. Near Rheatown, Duvall's Ford, Watauga River, September 30. Consolidated with 12th Kentucky Cavalry October 15, 1864.

Regiment lost during service 3 Enlisted men killed and 1 Officer and 54 Enlisted men by disease. Total 58.

17th REGIMENT CAVALRY.

Organized at Russellsville, Ky., April 25, 1865. Attached to Military Dept. of Kentucky and assigned to duty at Hopkinsville, Ky., and in Southern Kentucky, along Louisville & Nashville Railroad. Mustered out September 20, 1865.

MUNDAY'S 1st BATTALION CAVALRY.

Organized at Lexington, Ky., December, 1861, to January, 1862. Attached to 12th Brigade, Army of the Ohio, to February, 1862. 7th Division, Army Ohio, to October, 1862.

SERVICE—Ordered to Lebanon, Ky., thence to Loudon January 8, 1862. Expedition from Central Kentucky to the Cumberland River January 31-February 12. Flat Lick Ford, Cumberland River, February 14. Cumberland Gap Campaign March 28-June 18. Occupation of Cumberland Gap June 18 to September 17. Tazewell July 26. Operations about Cumberland Gap August 2-17. Tazewell August 6. Rogers' Gap August 16. Pine Mountain August 17. Red Bird Creek August 25. Richmond, Ky., August 30. Retreat from Cumberland Gap to the Ohio River September 17-October 3. Assigned to 6th Kentucky Cavalry as Companies "A," "B," "C," "D" and "E" October, 1862. (See 6th Cavalry.)

BATTERY "A" LIGHT ARTILLERY (STONE'S).

Organized at Camp Joe Holt, Ky., from Louisville Legion July, 1861, as Stone's Battery, and mustered in at Camp Muldraugh's Hill, Ky., September 27, 1861. Attached to Rousseau's Brigade, McCook's Command, at Nolin, to December, 1861. Artillery, 2nd Division, Army Ohio, to August, 1862. 28th Brigade, 3rd Division, Army Ohio, to October, 1862. Artillery, 3rd Division, 3rd Corps, Army Ohio, to November, 1862. 3rd Brigade, 1st Division, Centre 14th Army Corps, Army of the Cumberland, to January, 1863. Artillery, 1st Division, 14th Army Corps, Army Cumberland, to October, 1863. Unassigned, Army of the Cumberland, to December, 1863. Post of Murfreesboro, Tenn., Dept. of the Cumberland, to March, 1864. 2nd Division, Artillery Reserve, Dept. of the Cumberland, to November, 1864. Artillery Brigade, 4th Army Corps, to August, 1865. Dept. of Texas to November, 1865.

SERVICE—Moved to Muldraugh's Hill, Ky., September 17, 1861. At Camp Muldraugh's Hill and Nolin till February, 1862. Advance on Bowling Green, Ky., and Nashville, Tenn., February 10-March 2. March to Savannah, Tenn., March 16-April 7. Advance on and siege of Corinth, Miss., April 29-May 30. Buell's Campaign in Northern Alabama and Middle Tennessee June to August. March to Louisville, Ky., in pursuit of Bragg August 20-September 26. Pursuit of Bragg into Kentucky October 1-16. Battle of Perryville, Ky., October 8. March to Nashville, Tenn., October 16-November 7, and duty there till December 26. Advance on Murfreesboro, Tenn., December 26-30. Jefferson December 30. Battle of Stone's River December 30-31, 1862, and January 1-3, 1863. At Murfreesboro till June. Expedition to McMinnville March 20-30. Middle Tennessee (or Tullahoma) Campaign June 23-July 7. Hoover's Gap June 24-26. Occupation of Tullahoma July 1. Occupation of Middle Tennessee till August 16. Passage of Cumberland Mountains and Tennessee River, and Chickamauga (Ga.) Campaign August 16-September 22. Davis Cross Roads, near Dug Gap, September 11. Battle of Chickamauga September 19-21. At Murfreesboro, Tenn., till March, 1864, and at Nashville, Tenn., as Garrison Artillery, till November, 1864. Nashville Campaign November-December. Columbia, Duck River, November 24-27. Battle of Franklin November 30. Battle of Nashville December 15-16. Warfield's, near Columbia, December 23. At Huntsville, Ala., till March, 1865. Expedition to Bull's Gap and operations in East Tennessee March 15-April 22. At Nashville till June. Moved to New Orleans, La., thence to Texas June-July. Duty at San Antonio, Texas, and at Victoria, Texas, till November. Mustered out November 17, 1865.

Battery lost during service 10 Enlisted men killed and mortally wounded and 1 Officer and 21 Enlisted men by disease. Total 32.

BATTERY "B" LIGHT ARTILLERY "HEWITT'S."

Organized at Camp Dick Robinson, Ky., as Company "D," 3rd Kentucky Infantry, but mustered in as a Battery October 8, 1861. Attached to Thomas' Command, Camp Dick Robinson, Ky., to December, 1861. Artillery, 1st Division, Army Ohio, to March, 1862. Unattached Artillery, Army Ohio, March, 1862. 23rd Independent Brigade, Army Ohio, to September, 1862. Artillery, 8th Division, Army Ohio, to November, 1862. Artillery, 2nd Division, Center 14th Army Corps, Army of the Cumberland, to January, 1863. Artillery, 2nd Division, 14th Army Corps, to October, 1863. Unattached Army of the Cumberland, to December, 1863. Artillery Brigade, 12th Army Corps, Army Cumberland, to April, 1864. Unattached Artillery, Dept. Cumberland, to August, 1864. Defences Nashville & Northwestern Railroad to October, 1864. Artillery Brigade, 4th Army Corps, to November, 1864.

SERVICE.—At Campbellsville, Ky., December, 1861. At Beech Grove, Ky., January, 1862. March to relief of Thomas at Mill Springs, Ky., January 19-21. Moved to Louisville, Ky., thence to Nashville, Tenn., February 10-March 2. Advance on Murfreesboro March 17-19. Duty at Murfreesboro, Columbia, Shelbyville and Elk River Bridge guarding line of Chattanooga Railroad till July. Negley's Expedition to Chattanooga June 1-15 (Section). Chattanooga June 7-8. Battle of Murfreesboro July 13. Hewett and 4 guns captured. At Manchester August (1 Section), and at Nashville till December. Siege of Nashville September 12-November 7. Franklin Pike, near Nashville, December 14. Advance on Murfreesboro December 26-30. Battle of Stone's River December 30-31, 1862, and January 1-3, 1863. At Murfreesboro till June. Middle Tennessee (or Tullahoma) Campaign June 23-July 7. Hoover's Gap June 24-26. Occupation of Tullahoma July 1. Elk River Bridge July 3 and 14. Stationed at Elk River Bridge guarding line of Nashville & Chattanooga Railroad till February, 1864. At Decherd Station till April and at Tullahoma, Tenn., till November. Ordered to Louisville, Ky., and mustered out November 16, 1864.

Battery lost during service 2 Enlisted men killed and 20 Enlisted men by disease. Total 22.

BATTERY "C" LIGHT ARTILLERY.

Commenced organizing at Lebanon, Ky., May, 1863. Morgan's attack on Lebanon, Ky., July 3, 1863. Battery captured. Reorganized at Louisville, Ky., September 10, 1863. Attached to District of Louisville, Ky., 1st Division, 23rd Army Corps, Dept. of Ohio, to October, 1863. District of South Central Kentucky, Dept. of Ohio, to January, 1864. District of Southwest Kentucky, Dept. of Ohio, to April, 1864. 3rd Brigade, 1st Division, District of Kentucky, 5th Division, 23rd Army Corps, Dept. of Ohio, to December, 1864. Mt. Sterling, District of Kentucky, to February, 1865. Little Rock, Ark., Dept. of Arkansas, to July, 1865.

SERVICE.—Duty in District of Louisville till October, 1863, and in South Central Kentucky till January, 1864. Ordered to Southwest Kentucky and duty there till March, 1864. Reported at Paris, Ky., March 1. At Mt. Sterling, Ky., till May. Ordered to mouth of Beaver on Big Sandy May 3. Operations against Morgan May 31-June 30. Action at Mt. Sterling June 9. Cynthiana June 12. Duty in Eastern Kentucky till December. Stoneman's Raid to Southwest Virginia December 10-29. Marion December 17-18. Saltsville December 20-21. Duty in Eastern Kentucky till February, 1865. Ordered to Little Rock, Ark., and post duty there till July. Mustered out July 26, 1865.

Battery lost during service 4 Enlisted men killed and mortally wounded and 16 Enlisted men by disease. Total 20.

BATTERY "D" LIGHT ARTILLERY.

Failed to complete organization.

BATTERY "E" LIGHT ARILLERY.

Organized at Camp Nelson, Ky., October to December, 1863. Attached to District of North Central Kentucky, 1st Division, 23rd Army Corps, Dept. of Ohio, to November, 1863. District of Somerset, Ky., 1st Division, 23rd Army Corps, to January, 1864. District of Southwest Kentucky, Dept. of Ohio, to April, 1864.

4th Brigade, 1st Division, District of Kentucky, 5th Division, 23rd Army Corps, to December, 1864. Garrison, Lexington, Ky., District of Kentucky, to August, 1865.

SERVICE.—Garrison duty at Camp Nelson and Camp Burnside, Ky., till June, 1864. Re-enlisted February, 1864. Duty at Lexington, Ky., till November, 1864. Stoneman's Raid to Southwest Virginia December 10-29. Kingsport December 13. Near Marion December 16-17. Saltsville, Va., December 20-21. Duty at Lexington and Camp Nelson, Ky., till August, 1865. Mustered out August 1, 1865.

Battery lost during service 10 by disease.

SIMMONDS' BATTERY LIGHT ARTILLERY.

Organized at Pendleton, Ohio, from Company "E," 1st Kentucky Infantry, June 3, 1861. Permanently detached January, 1862. Attached to District of the Kanawha, West Virginia, to March, 1862. 2nd Brigade, Kanawha Division West Virginia, to September, 1862. 2nd Brigade, Kanawha Division, 9th Army Corps, Army of the Potomac, to October, 1862. District of the Kanawha, West Virginia, Dept. of the Ohio, to March, 1863. 1st Brigade, 3rd Division, 8th Army Corps, Middle Department, to June, 1863. 1st Brigade, Scammon's Division, Dept. of West Virginia, to December, 1863. 3rd Brigade, 3rd Division West Virginia, to April, 1864. Artillery, 2nd Infantry Division West Virginia, to July, 1864. Reserve Division, Harper's Ferry, W. Va., to April, 1865. 2nd Brigade, 1st Infantry Division West Virginia, to July, 1865.

SERVICE.—Duty at Pendleton, Ohio, till July, 1861. Ordered to the Kanawha Valley, W. Va., July 10. March from Mt. Pleasant to Charleston, W. Va., July 11-25. Action at Scarry Creek July 17. Tyler Mountain July 24. Capture of Charleston July 25. Advance to Gauley July 26-August 1. Moved to Camp Piatt, arriving August 25. Gauley Bridge August 28. Boone Court House September 1. Peytonia September 12. Moved to Raleigh September 20-27. Chapmansville September 25. Return to Gauley, arriving there October 10. Cotton Hill October 13. Operations in Kanawha Valley October 19-November 16. Gauley Bridge October 23. Attack on Gauley by Floyd's Batteries November 1-9. Movement on Cotton Mountain and pursuit of Floyd November 1-18. Duty at Gauley Bridge till April, 1862. Advance on Princeton April 22-May 4. At Flat Top Mountain till August. Wolf Creek May 15. Moved to Washington, D. C., August 14-23. Maryland Campaign September 6-22. Frederick, Md., September 12. Battles of South Mountain September 14, and Antietam September 16-17. Moved to Clarksburg, Suttonville, Summerville, Gauley Bridge and Kanawha Falls, W. Va., October 8-November 14, and duty there till April, 1863, and at Camp White, Charleston, W. Va., till July. At Gauley Bridge till September. At Camp Toland, Charleston, W. V., till January, 1864. Scout to Boone Court House October 21-22, 1863. Expedition from Charleston to Lewisburg November 3-13. Capture of Lewisburg November 7. At Fayetteville till April, 1864. Crook's Expedition against Virginia & Tennessee Railroad May 2-19. Action at Cloyd's Mountain May 9. New River Bridge May 10. Hunter's Raid on Lynchburg May 26-July 1. Lexington June 11. Diamond Hill June 17. Lynchburg June 17-18. Buford's Gap June 20. Salem June 21. At Camp Piatt and Harper's Ferry till August, and at Camp Fuller, Va., till June, 1865. Mustered out July 20, 1865.

Battery lost during service 3 Enlisted men killed and mortally wounded and 10 Enlisted men by disease. Total 13.

PATTERSON'S INDEPENDENT COMPANY.

Organized at Camp Haskins, Ky., October, 1861. Served unattached, Army Ohio, to March, 1862. Engineers, 7th Division, Army Ohio, to October, 1862. Cumberland Division, District of West Virginia, Dept. Ohio, to November, 1862. 9th Division, Right Wing 13th Army Corps (Old), Dept. of the Tennessee, to December, 1862. Unattached, Sherman's Yazoo Expedition, to January, 1863. Unattached, 9th Division, 13th Army Corps, to July, 1863. Unattached, 13th Army Corps, Army Tennessee and Dept. of the Gulf, to October, 1863. Unattached, 13th Army Corps, Texas, to July, 1864. Engineer Brigade, Dept. of the Gulf, to January, 1865.

SERVICE.—Constructing defences for Camp Haskins and Somerset, Ky., till January, 1862. Action at Mill Springs, Ky., January 19. Repair roads from Somerset to Stanford, Ky., till April 12. Moved to Cumberland Ford April 2-20, repairing roads en route. Cumberland Gap Campaign May 1-June 18. Occupation of Cumberland Gap June 18-September 17. Retreat to Greenup on the Ohio River September 17-October 3. Expedition to Charleston, W. Va., October 21-November 10. Moved to Memphis, Tenn., November 10-15. At Memphis, Tenn., till December 20. Sherman's Yazoo Expedition December 20, 1862, to January 3, 1863. Chickasaw Bayou December 26-28. Chickasaw Bluff December 29. Expedition to Arkansas Post, Ark., January 3-10, 1863. Assault and capture Fort Hindman, Arkansas Post, January 10-11. Moved to Young's Point, La., January 14-22, and engineer duty there till March 30. Moved to Richmond, La., March 30. Built floating bridge across Bayou Roundaway April 1. Movement on Bruinsburg and turning Grand Gulf April 25-30. Battle of Port Gibson May 1. Took advance of Logan's 3rd Division, 17th Army Corps, and built bridge over Bayou Pierrie May 2-3. Battles of Raymond May 12; Champion's Hill May 16; Big Black River May 27. Siege of Vicksburg May 18-July 4. Assaults on Vicksburg May 19 and 22. Advance on Jackson, Miss., July 4-10. Siege of Jackson July 10-17. Moved to New Orleans August 5-27, and duty there till October 5. Western Louisiana Campaign October 5-November 1. Vermillion Bayou October 3 and 10. Moved to New Orleans November 1, thence to Brazos, Santiago, Texas, November 15-20, and to Aransas Pass November 21. Advance up coast to Pass Cavallo November 22-December 7. Constructed bridge 300 yards long across Cedar Bayou on November 25. At Pass Cavallo till April 19, 1864, building hospitals, signal stations, warehouses and wharves. Moved to Alexandria, La., April 19-29. Construction of dam at Alexandria April 29-May 10. Retreat to Morganza May 13-20. Mansura May 16. Yellow Bayou May 18-19. Moved to New Orleans, La., June 1, and reported to Engineer Department July 3. Engaged in working lumber in Cypress Swamp till November 7. Ordered to New Orleans, thence moved to Louisville, Ky., November 23-December 1. Mustered out January 22, 1865.

Company lost during service 8 by disease.

1st REGIMENT INFANTRY.

First organized at Pendleton, Ohio, for three months April and May, 1861, but not recognized by Kentucky till June, when reorganized for three years. Duty at Pendleton, Ohio, April to July, 1861. Ordered to the Kanawha Valley, W. Va., July 10, 1861. Attached to Kanawha Brigade, West Virginia, to October, 1861. District of the Kanawha, W. Va., to January, 1862. 22nd Brigade, Army of Ohio, to February, 1862. 22nd Brigade, 4th Division, Army of Ohio, to September, 1862. 22nd Brigade, 4th Division, 2nd Corps, Army of Ohio, to November, 1862. 1st Brigade, 2nd Division, Left Wing 14th Army Corps, Army of the Cumberland, to January, 1863. 1st Brigade, 2nd Division, 21st Army Corps, Army of the Cumberland, to October, 1863. 1st Brigade, 1st Division, 4th Army Corps, to June, 1864.

SERVICE.—Campaign in West Virginia July to October, 1861. March to Sissonville in rear of Wise, returning via Ravenswood and Charleston July 14-26. Moved to Gauley, arriving August 1. Moved to Camp Piatt, arriving August 25. Gauley Bridge August 28. Boone Court House September 1. Peytonia September 12. Moved to Raleigh September 20-27. Chapmansville September 25. Return to Gauley, arriving October

10. Operations in the Kanawha Valley October 19-November 16. Skirmish at Gauley Bridge October 23. Attack on Gauley by Floyd's Batteries November 1-9. Pursuit of Floyd November 10. Duty at Charleston December 4 to January 5, 1862. Ordered to Kentucky January 5, 1862. Camp near Bardstown January 24-February 13. March to Nashville, Tenn., February 14-March 12, and to Savannah, Tenn., March 13-April 5. Battle of Shiloh, Tenn., April 6-7. Advance on and siege of Corinth, Miss., April 29-May 30. Phillips Creek, Widow Serratt's, May 21. Bridge Creek, before Corinth, May 28. Occupation of Corinth May 30. Pursuit to Booneville May 31-June 6. Buell's Campaign in Northern Alabama and Middle Tennessee June to August. March to Louisville, Ky., in pursuit of Bragg, August 21-September 25. Pursuit of Bragg to Loudon, Ky., October 1-22. Battle of Perryville, Ky., October 8. Camp Wild Cat October 17. Nelson's Cross Roads October 18. Destruction of Salt Works at Goose Creek October 23-24. March to Nashville, Tenn., October 24-November 9, and duty there till December 26. Advance on Murfreesboro December 26-30. Lavergne December 26-27. Battle of Stone's River December 30-31, 1862, and January 1-3, 1863. Duty at Cripple Creek till June. Epedition to Woodbury April 2. Snow Hill, Woodbury,, April 3. Middle Tennessee (or Tullahoma) Campaign June 24-July 7. At Manchester July 9 to August 16. Passage of Cumberland Mountains and Tennessee River, and Chickamauga (Ga.) Campaign August 16-September 22. Pea Vine Creek September 10. Lee and Gordon's Mills September 11-13. Battle of Chickamauga September 19-20. Siege of Chattanooga September 24-October 27. Reopening Tennessee River October 26-29. Duty at Bridgeport, Ala., till January 26, 1864. At Ooltewah, Ga., till May 17, and at Resaca till May 29. Ordered to Kentucky May 29. Operations against Morgan's Invasion of Kentucky May 31-June 18. Mt. Sterling June 9. Mustered out June 18, 1864.

Regiment lost during service 60 Enlisted men killed and mortally wounded and 1 Officer and 82 Enlisted men by disease. Total 143.

2nd REGIMENT INFANTRY.

Organized at Pendleton, Ohio, May and June, 1861. Moved to the Kanawha Valley, West Va., July 10. Attached to Kanawha Brigade, West Va., to October, 1861. District of the Kanawha, West Va., to January, 1862. 22nd Brigade, Army of the Ohio, to February, 1862. 22nd Brigade, 4th Division, Army of the Ohio, to September, 1862. 22nd Brigade, 4th Division, 2nd Corps, Army of the Ohio, to November, 1862. 1st Brigade, 2nd Division, Left Wing 14th Army Corps, Army of the Cumberland, to January, 1863. 1st Brigade, 2nd Division, 21st Army Corps, Army of the Cumberland, to October, 1863. 1st Brigade, 1st Division, 4th Army Corps, to June, 1864.

SERVICE.—Campaign in West Virginia July to October, 1861. Red House July 13 (Cos. "A," "B," "D," "F" and "K"). Barboursville July 16. Scarrytown July 17. Gauley's Bridge September 1. Operations in Kanawha Valley October 19-November 16. Attack on Gauley by Floyd's Batteries November 1-9. Gauley Bridge November 10. At Charlestown, W. Va., December 4 to January 25, 1862. Moved to Louisville, Ky.; thence to Bardstown February 5. March to Nashville, Tenn., February 14-March 12. March to Savannah, Tenn., March 13-April 5. Battle of Shiloh April 6-7. Advance on and siege of Corinth, Miss., April 29-May 30. Phillips' Creek, Widow Serratt's, May 21. Bridge Creek, before Corinth, May 28. Occupation of Corinth May 30. Pursuit to Booneville May 31-June 6. Buell's Campaign in North Alabama and Middle Tennessee June to August. March to Louisville, Ky., in pursuit of Bragg August 21-September 25. Pursuit of Bragg to Loudon, Ky., October 1-22. Battle of Perryville October 8. Camp Wild Cat October 17. Destruction of Salt Works at Goose Creek October 23-24. March to Nashville, Tenn., October 24-November 9. Duty at Nashville till December 26. Advance on Murfreesboro December 26-30. Lavergne December 26-27. Battle of Stone's River December

30-31, 1862, and January 1-3, 1863. Duty at Murfreesboro and Cripple Creek till June. Expedition to Woodbury April 2. Action at Snow Hill, Woodbury, April 3. Middle Tennessee (or Tullahoma) Campaign June 24-July 7. At Manchester July 9 to August 16. Passage of Cumberland Mountains and Tennessee River and Chickamauga (Ga.) Campaign August 16-September 22. Pea Vine Creek, Ga., September 10. Lee and Gordon's Mills September 11-13. Battle of Chickamauga, Ga., September 19-20. Siege of Chattanooga September 24-October 27. Reopening of Tennessee River October 26-29. At Bridgeport, Ala., October 28, 1863, to January 26, 1864. (A Detachment at Ringgold Gap, Ga., November 27, 1863, and on Demonstration on Dalton February 22-27, 1864. Near Dalton February 23. Tunnel Hill, Buzzard's Roost Gap and RockyFaced Ridge February 23-25.) At Ooltewah, Ga., till May 17, and at Resaca till June 3. Ordered home June 3. Operations against Morgan in Kentucky till June 19. Mt. Sterling June 9. Mustered out June 19, 1864.

Regiment lost during service 3 Officers and 74 Enlisted men killed and mortally wounded and 1 Officer and 87 Enlisted men by disease. Total 165.

3rd REGIMENT INFANTRY.

Organized at Camp Dick Robinson, Ky., October 8, 1861. Attached to Thomas' Command to November, 1861. 11th Brigade, Army of the Ohio, to December, 1861. Unattached, Loudon, Ky., Army of the Ohio, to March, 1862. 15th Brigade, 4th Division, Army of the Ohio, March, 1862. 20th Brigade, 6th Division, Army of the Ohio, March, 1862. 15th Brigade, 6th Division, Army of the Ohio, to September, 1862. 15th Brigade, 6th Division, 2nd Army Corps, Army of the Ohio, to November, 1862. 1st Brigade, 1st Division, Left Wing 14th Army Corps, Army of the Cumberland, to January, 1863. 1st Brigade, 1st Division, 21st Army Corps, Army of the Cumberland, to April, 1863. 3rd Brigade, 1st Division, 21st Army Corps, to October, 1863. 3rd Brigade, 2nd Division, 4th Army Corps, to January, 1865.

SERVICE.—Moved to Lexington, Ky., September, 1861, and duty there till October 1. Moved to Camp Dick Robinson, Ky., October 1. Duty there, at Round Stone Creek, Crab Orchard, Somerset and Columbia till January, 1862. Moved to Renick's Creek, near Burkesville, January 7, and to mouth of Greasy Creek January 17. Moved to Nashville, Tenn., March 18-25; thence march to Savannah, Tenn., and to Shiloh March 29-April 7. Advance on and siege of Corinth, Miss., April 29-May 30. Pursuit to Booneville May 30-June 6. Buell's Campaign in North Alabama and Middle Tennessee June to August. March to Nashville, Tenn., and Louisville, Ky., in pursuit of Bragg, August 19-September 26. Pursuit of Bragg into Kentucky October 1-18. Batttle of Perryville October 8. Nelson's Cross Roads, Ky., October 18. March to Nashville, Tenn., October 18-November 7, and duty there till December 26. Advance on Murfreesboro December 26-30. Stewart's Creek December 29. Battle of Stone's River December 30-31, 1862, and January 1-3, 1863. Duty at Murfreesboro till June. Reconnoissance to Nolensville and Versailles January 13-15. Middle Tennessee (or Tullahoma) Campaign June 23-July 7. Occupation of Middle Tennessee till August 16. Passage of Cumberland Mountains and Tennessee River and Chickamauga (Ga.) Campaign August 16-September 22. Reconnoissance toward Chattanooga September 7. Lookout Valley September 7-8. Occupation of Chattanooga September 9. Lee and Gordon's Mills September 11-13. Near Lafayette September 14. Battle of Chickamauga September 19-20. Siege of Chattanooga September 24-October 26. Reopening Tennessee River October 26-29. Chattanooga-Ringgold Campaign November 23-27. Orchard Knob November 23-24. Mission Ridge November 25. Pursuit to Graysville November 26-27. March to relief of Knoxville November 28-December 8. Campaign in East Tennessee till April, 1864. March to Charleston April 18-26. Atlanta (Ga.) Campaign May to September. Demonstrations on Rocky Faced Ridge and Dalton May 5-13. Tunnel Hill May 6-7. Buzzard's Roost Gap May 8-9. Rocky Faced Ridge May 8-11. Battle of Resaca May 14-15. Near Calhoun May 16. Adairsville May 17. Near Kingston May 18-19. Near Cassville May 19. Advance on Dallas May 22-25. Operations on line of Pumpkin Vine Creek and battles about Dallas, New Hope Church and Allatoona Hills May 25-June 5. Operations about Marietta and against Kenesaw Mountain June 10-July 2. Pine Hill June 11-14. Lost Mountain June 15-17. Assault on Kenesaw June 27. Ruff's Station, Smyrna Camp Ground, July 4. Chattahoochie River July 5-17. Buckhead, Nancy's Creek, July 18. Peach Tree Creek July 19-20. Siege of Atlanta July 22-August 25. Flank movement on Jonesboro August 25-30. Battle of Jonesboro August 31-September 1. Lovejoy Station September 2-6. Moved to Nashville, Tenn., September 9-12; thence to Louisville, Ky., October 6. Mustered out by Companies October 13, 1864, to January 10, 1865.

Regiment lost during service 6 Officers and 103 Enlisted men killed and mortally wounded and 192 Enlisted men by disease. Total 301.

4th REGIMENT INFANTRY.

Organized at Camp Dick Robinson, Ky., October 9, 1861. Attached to Thomas' Command, Army of Ohio, to November, 1861. 2nd Brigade, Army of Ohio, to December, 1861. 2nd Brigade, 1st Division, Army of Ohio, to September, 1862. 2nd Brigade, 1st Division, 3rd Corps, Army of Ohio, to November, 1862. 2nd Brigade, 3rd Division (Centre), 14th Army Corps, Army of the Cumberland, to January, 1863. 2nd Brigade, 3rd Division, 14th Army Corps, to October, 1863. 3rd Brigade, 3rd Division, 14th Army Corps, to June, 1864. 1st Brigade, 1st Division, Cavalry Corps, Army of the Cumberland, to November, 1864. 1st Brigade, 1st Division, Cavalry Corps, Military Division Mississippi, to August, 1865.

SERVICE.—Moved to Crab Orchard, Ky., October 28, 1861; thence to Lebanon, Ky., and duty there till January, 1862. Advance on Camp Hamilton January 1-15. Action at Logan's Cross Roads on Fishing Creek January 19. Battle of Mill Springs January 19-20. Duty at Mill Springs till February 11. Moved to Louisville, Ky., thence to Nashville, Tenn., February 11-March 2. March to Savannah, Tenn., March 20-April 7. Expedition to Bear Creek, Ala., April 12-13. Advance on and siege of Corinth, Miss., April 29-May 30. Buell's Campaign in Northern Alabama and Middle Tennessee June to August. Action at Decatur August 7. March to Nashville, Tenn., thence to Louisville, Ky., in pursuit of Bragg August 20-September 26. Pursuit of Bragg into Kentucky October 1-16. Battle of Perryville October 8. March to Gallatin, Tenn., and duty there till January 13, 1863. Operations against Morgan December 22, 1862-January 2, 1863. Action at Boston December 29, 1862. Moved to Nashville, Tenn., January 13, 1863, and duty there till June. Expedition toward Columbia March 4-14. Middle Tennessee (or Tullahoma) Campaign June 24-July 7. Hoover's Gap June 24-26. Tullahoma June 29-30. Elk River July 3. Occupation of Middle Tennessee till August 16. Passage of Cumberland Mountains and Tennessee River and Chickamauga (Ga.) Campaign August 16-September 22. Battle of Chickamauga, Ga., September 19-21. Siege of Chattanooga, Tenn., September 24-November 23. Chattanooga-Ringgold Campaign November 23-27. Orchard Knob November 23-24. Mission Ridge November 25. Veterans on furlough January and February, 1864. Regiment changed to Mounted Infantry and reorganized at Lexington, Ky. Moved to Lafayette, Ga., May 16-June 11. At Villenow Valley and Snake Creek Gap, Ga., guarding railroad till July. Lafayette June 24. Near Atlanta June 26. Chattahoochie River July 6-17. McCook's Raid on Atlanta & West Point Railroad and Macon & Western Railroad July 27-31. Lovejoy Station July 29. Near Newnan July 30. At Kingston, Ga., till September 17. Moved to Nashville, Tenn., thence to Franklin and pursuit of Forest September 25-October 10. Pulaski,

Tenn., September 26, 27 and 29. Muscle Shoals, near Florence, Ala., October 30. Near Shoal Creek, Ala., October 31. Nashville Campaign November-December. Shoal Creek, near Florence, November 5-6. On line of Shoal Creek November 16-20. Fouche Springs November 23. Campbellsville November 24. In front of Columbia November 24-27. Battle of Franklin November 30. Battle of Nashville December 15-16. Lynnville and Richland Creek December 24-25. Pulaski December 25-26. Expedition into Mississippi January 15-21, 1865. Wilson's Raid to Macon, Ga., March 22-May 1. Trion, Ala., April 1. Northport, near Tuscaloosa, April 3. Occupation of Tuscaloosa April 4. Occupation of Talladega April 22. Munford's Station April 23. Rejoin Wilson at Macon May 1. Duty at Macon and in Georgia till August. Mustered out August 17, 1865.

Regiment lost during service 1 Officer and 118 Enlisted men killed and mortally wounded and 4 Officers and 326 Enlisted men by disease. Total 459.

5th REGIMENT INFANTRY.—("LOUISVILLE LEGION.")

Organized at Camp Joe, Holt, Ky., September 9, 1861. Attached to Rousseau's 1st Brigade, McCook's Command, at Nolin to November, 1861. 4th Brigade, Army of Ohio, to December, 1861. 4th Brigade, 2nd Division, Army of Ohio, to September, 1862. 4th Brigade, 2nd Division, 1st Army Corps, Army of Ohio, to November, 1862. 3rd Brigade, 2nd Division, Right Wing 14th Army Corps, Army of the Cumberland, to January, 1863. 3rd Brigade, 2nd Division, 20th Army Corps, Army of the Cumberland, to October, 1863. 2nd Brigade, 3rd Division, 4th Army Corps, to July, 1864. Unattached, 4th Division, 20th Army Corps, to September, 1864.

SERVICE.—Moved to Muldraugh's Hill, Ky., September 17, 1861, and duty there till October 14. Duty at Bacon Creek and Green River till February, 1862. March to Nashville, Tenn., February 17-March 3; thence march to Savannah, Tenn., March 16-April 6. Battle of Shiloh, Tenn., April 6-7. Advance on and siege of Corinth, Miss., April 29-May 30. Bridge Creek May 27. Duty at Corinth till June 10. Buell's Campaign in Northern Alabama and Middle Tennessee June to August. March to Louisville, Ky., in pursuit of Bragg August 21-September 26. Pursuit of Bragg into Kentucky October 1-15. Dog Walk, Ky., October 8-9. March to Nashville, Tenn., October 16-November 7, and duty there till December 26. Kimbrough's Mills December 6. Advance on Murfreesboro, Tenn., December 26-30. Nolensville December 26-27. Battle of Stone's River December 30-31, 1862, and January 1-3, 1863. At Murfreesboro till June. Middle Tennessee (or Tullahoma) Campaign June 22-July 7. Liberty Gap June 22-27. Occupation of Middle Tennessee till August 16. Passage of Cumberland Mountains and Tennessee River and Chickamauga (Ga.) Campaign August 16-September 22. Battle of Chickamauga, Ga., September 19-20. Siege of Chattanooga September 24-November 23. Reopening Tennessee River October 26-29. Brown's Ferry October 27. Battles of Chattanooga November 23-25. Orchard Knob November 23-24. Mission Ridge November 25. Pursuit to Graysville November 26-27. March to relief of Knoxville November 28-December 8. Campaign in East Tennessee December, 1863, to April, 1864. Atlanta (Ga.) Campaign May 1 to July 25. Demonstration on Rocky Faced Ridge and Dalton May 5-13. Battle of Resaca May 14-15. Adairsville May 17. Near Kingston May 18-19. Near Cassville May 19. Advance on Dallas May 22-25. Operations on line of Pumpkin Vine Creek and battles about Dallas, New Hope Church and Allatoona Hills May 25-June 5. Pickett's Mills May 27. Operations about Marietta and against Kenesaw Mountain June 10-July 2. Pine Hill June 11-14. Lost Mountain June 15-17. Assault on Kenesaw June 27. Ruff's Station, Smyrna Camp Ground, July 4. Pace's Ferry July 5. Chattahoochie River July 6-17. Peach Tree Creek July 19-20.

Siege of Atlanta July 22-25. Ordered to Nashville, Tenn., July 25; thence to Louisville, Ky. Mustered out September 14, 1864. (Veterans moved to Nashville July 25 and duty there till January, 1865. Battle of Nashville, Tenn., December 15-16. Pursuit of Hood December 17-28. Moved to Louisville, Pittsburg, Philadelphia, New York and Hilton Head, S. C., and rejoin Sherman at Raleigh, N. C., April, 1865. Bennett's House April 26. Surrender of Johnston and his army. March to Washington, D. C., via Richmond, Va., April 29-May 19. Grand Review May 24. Moved to Louisville, Ky., June. Mustered out July 25, 1865.)

Regiment lost during service 8 Officers and 149 Enlisted men killed and mortally wounded and 2 Officers and 143 Enlisted men by disease. Total 302.

6th REGIMENT INFANTRY.

Organized at Sigel, Muldraugh's Hill and Shepherdsville, Ky., September 9 to December 24, 1861. Attached to Rousseau's 1st Brigade, McCook's Command, at Nolin, Ky., to November, 1861. 12th Brigade, Army of Ohio, to December, 1861. 12th Brigade, 1st Division, Army of Ohio, to January, 1862. 19th Brigade, 4th Division, Army of Ohio, to September, 1862. 19th Brigade, 4th Division, 2nd Corps, Army of Ohio, to November, 1862. 2nd Brigade, 2nd Division, Left Wing 14th Army Corps, Army of the Cumberland, to January, 1863. 2nd Brigade, 2nd Division, 21st Army Corps, to October, 1863. 2nd Brigade, 3rd Division, 4th Army Corps, to August, 1864. 1st Brigade, Defences of Nashville & Chattanooga Railroad, to September, 1864. Unattached, 4th Division, 20th Army Corps, to November, 1864. District of Kentucky to January, 1865.

SERVICE.—Engaged in the Defence of Eastern Kentucky before muster. Moved to Lebanon, Ky., November 28, 1861. Skirmish at Bagdad, Selby County, Ky., December 12, 1861. At Camp Wyckliffe, Ky., till February, 1862. Advance on Nashville, Tenn., February 14-25. Occupation of Nashville February 25-March 18. March to Savannah, Tenn., March 18-April 6. Battle of Shiloh, Tenn., April 7. Advance on and siege of Corinth, Miss., April 29-May 30. Occupation of Corinth May 30, and pursuit to Booneville May 31-June 12. Buell's Campaign in Northern Alabama and Middle Tennessee June to August. Flat Lick, Tenn., August 17 (Detachment). March to Louisville, Ky., in pursuit of Bragg August 17-September 26. Pursuit of Bragg to Loudon, Ky., October 1-22. Battle of Perryville, Ky., October 8. Danville October 11. Near Crab Orchard October 15. Wild Cat Mountain, near Crab Orchard, and Big Rockcastle River, near Mt. Vernon, October 18. Pittman's Cross Roads October 19. March to Nashville, Tenn., October 23-November 6, and duty there till December 26. Advance on Murfreesboro, Tenn., December 26-30. Springfield, Ky., December 30 (Detachment). Battle of Stone's River December 30-31, 1862, and January 1-3, 1863. At Murfreesboro till June. Woodbury January 24. Expedition to Woodbury April 2. Snow Hill, Woodbury, April 3. Middle Tennessee (or Tullahoma) Campaign June 24-July 7. Liberty Gap June 24-27. Occupation of Middle Tennessee till August 16. Passage of Cumberland Mountains and Tennessee River and Chickamauga (Ga.) Campaign August 16-September 22. Lee and Gordon's Mills, Ga., September 11-13. Battle of Chickamauga, Ga., September 19-20. Siege of Chattanooga, Tenn., September 24-November 23. Reopening Tennessee River October 26-29. Brown's Ferry October 27. Chattanooga-Ringgold Campaign November 23-27. Orchard Knob November 23-24. Mission Ridge November 25. March to relief of Knoxville November 28-December 8. Operations in East Tennessee December, 1863, to April, 1864. Atlanta Campaign May 1 to August 19, 1864. Demonstrations on Rocky Faced Ridge and Dalton May 8-13. Battle of Resaca May 14-15. Adairsville May 17. Near Kingston May 18-19. Near Cassville May 19. Advance on Dallas May 22-25. Operations on line of Pumpkin Vine Creek and battles about Dallas, New Hope Church and Allatoona Hills May 25-June 5. Pickett's Mills May 27. Operations about Mari-

etta and against Kenesaw Mountain June 10-July 2. Pine Hill June 11-14. Lost Mountain June 15-17. Assault on Kenesaw June 27. Ruff's Station, Smyrna Camp Ground, July 4. Pace's Ferry July 5. Chattahoochie River July 6-17. Peach Tree Creek July 19-20. Siege of Atlanta July 22-August 19. Ordered to Chattanooga, Tenn., August 19. Garrison duty there and at Bridgeport, Ala., till November 2. Moved to Nashville, Tenn.; thence ordered to Louisville, Ky. Mustered out September 23, 1864, to January 2, 1865.

Regiment lost during service 10 Officers and 105 Enlisted men killed and mortally wounded and 5 Officers and 96 Enlisted men by disease. Total 216.

7th REGIMENT INFANTRY.

"One of the first Recruited in the State. Old 3rd." Organized at Camp Dick Robinson, Ky., September 22, 1861. Attached to Thomas' Command, Army of the Ohio, to January, 1862. 12th Brigade, 1st Division, Army of the Ohio, to March, 1862. 24th Brigade, 7th Division, Army of the Ohio, to October, 1862. 3rd Brigade, District of West Virginia, Dept. of the Ohio, to November, 1862. 2nd Brigade, 9th Division, Right Wing 13th Army Corps (Old), Dept. of the Tennessee, to December, 1862. 2nd Brigade, 3rd Division, Sherman's Yazoo Expediton, to January, 1863. 2nd Brigade, 9th Division, 13th Army Corps, Army of the Tennessee, to February, 1863. 1st Brigade, 9th Division, 13th Army Corps, to July, 1863. 3rd Brigade, 1st Division, 13th Army Corps, Dept. of the Tennessee, to August, 1863; and Dept. of the Gulf to November, 1863. Plaquemine, District of Baton Rouge, La., Dept. of the Gulf, to March, 1864. 2nd Brigade, 1st Division, 13th Army Corps, to June, 1864. 1st Brigade, 3rd Division, 19th Army Corps, to December, 1864. District of Baton Rouge, La., to April, 1865. Provisional Brigade, District of Baton Rouge, Dept. of the Gulf, to March, 1866.

SERVICE.—Moved to Mt. Vernon, Ky., October, 1861, and duty there till March, 1862. Action at Camp Wild Cat, or Rockcastle Hills, October 21, 1861. Reconnoissance toward Cumberland Gap and skirmishes March 21-23, 1862. Cumberland Gap Campaign March 28-June 18. Occupation of Cumberland Gap June 18 to September 16. Evacuation of Cumberland Gap and retreat to Greenupsburg, in the Ohio River, September 16-October 3. Expedition to Charleston, West Va., October 21-November 10. Ordered to Memphis, Tenn., November 10; duty there till December 20. Sherman's Yazoo Expedition December 20, 1862, to January 2, 1863. Chickasaw Bayou December 26-28. Chickasaw Bluff December 29. Expedition to Arkansas Post, Ark., January 3-10, 1862. Assault on and capture of Fort Hindman, Arkansas Post, January 10-11. Moved to Young's Point, La., January 15-23, and duty there till March. Moved to Milliken's Bend March 8. Operations from Milliken's Bend to New Carthage March 31-April 17. James Plantation, near New Carthage, April 6 and 8. Dunbar's Plantation, Bayou Vidal, April 15. Expedition from Perkins' Plantation to Hard Times Landing April 25-29. Phelps' and Clark's Bayous April 26. Choctaw Bayou and Lake Bruin April 28. Battle of Thompson's Hill, Port Gibson, May 1. Champion's Hill May 16. Big Black River Bridge May 17. Siege of Vicksburg May 18-July 4. Assaults on Vicksburg May 19 and 22. Advance on Jackson July 5-10. Near Clinton July 8. Near Jackson July 9. Siege of Jackson July 10-17. Ordered to New Orleans, La., August 13. Duty at Carrollton, Brashear City and Berwick till October. Western Louisiana Campaign October 3-November 20. Duty at Plaquemine till March, 1864. Moved to Baton Rouge, La., March 23, and duty there till October. At mouth of White River and Duvall's Bluff, Ark., October 6-November 10. At Baton Rouge till May 1, 1865; and at Clinton till March, 1866. Mustered out March 11, 1866.

Regiment lost during service 3 Officers and 40 Enlisted men killed and mortally wounded and 2 Officers and 274 Enlisted men by disease. Total 319.

8th REGIMENT INFANTRY.

Organized at Estill Springs and Lebanon, Ky., October, 1861. Attached to Thomas' Command to January, 1862. 16th Brigade, Army of the Ohio, to February, 1862. 23rd Independent Brigade, Army of the Ohio, to September, 1862. 23rd Brigade, 5th Division, Army of the Ohio, September, 1862. 23rd Brigade, 5th Division, 2nd Army Corps, Army of the Ohio, to November, 1862. 3rd Brigade, 3rd Division, Left Wing 14th Army Corps, Army of the Cumberland, to January, 1863. 3rd Brigade, 3rd Division, 21st Army Corps, Army of the Cumberland, to October, 1863. 2nd Brigade, 1st Division, 4th Army Corps, to April, 1864. 1st Separate Brigade, Post of Chattanooga, Tenn., Dept. of the Cumberland, to November, 1864. 2nd Brigade, District of the Etowah, Dept. of the Cumberland, to February, 1865.

SERVICE.—Duty at Estill Springs, Ky., till November 28, 1861. March to Lebanon, Ky., November 28-December 3, and duty there till March, 1862. Moved to Nashville, Tenn., March 10-23; thence to Murfreesboro, Tenn., April 3-4, and to Wartrace May 3. Duty there till June 11. Dumont's Expedition over Cumberland Mountains June 11-19. Moved to Elk River Bridge July 4; thence to Tullahoma July 9, and join Nelson. March to Louisville, Ky., in pursuit of Bragg August 21-September 26. Russellville and Glasgow September 30. Pursuit of Bragg into Kentucky October 1-22. Battle of Perryville October 8. Nelson's Cross Roads October 18. Reconnoissance on Madison Road October 19. March to Nashville, Tenn., October 22-November 12, and duty there till December 26. Murfreesboro Pike November 9. Dobbins' Ferry, near Lavergne, December 9. Advance on Murfreesboro December 26-30. Battle of Stone's River December 30-31, 1862, and January 1-3, 1863. At Murfreesboro till June. Middle Tennessee (or Tullahoma) Campaign June 23-July 7. Liberty Gap June 25-26. At McMinnville till August 16. Passage of Cumberland Mountains and Tennessee River and Chickamauga (Ga.) Campaign August 16-September 22. Ringgold, Ga., September 11. Battle of Chickamauga September 19-20. Siege of Chattanooga September 24-November 23. Reopening Tennessee River October 26-29. Chattanooga-Ringgold Campaign November 23-27. Lookout Mountain November 23-24. Mission Ridge November 25. Taylor's Ridge, Ringgold Gap, November 27. At Shellmound, Tenn., till March, 1864. Demonstration on Dalton, Ga., February 22-27. Buzzard's Roost Gap and Rocky Faced Ridge February 23-25. Moved to Chattanooga, Tenn., March 1, and garrison duty there till September 26, 1864. Moved to Elk River Bridge September 26 and duty there till October 20. At Chattanooga till November 28 and at Bridgeport, Ala., till January, 1865. Mustered out February, 1865. Veterans and Recruits transferred to 4th Kentucky Mounted Infantry.

Regiment lost during service 4 Officers and 56 Enlisted men killed and mortally wounded and 1 Officer and 144 Enlisted men by disease. Total 205.

9th REGIMENT INFANTRY.

Organized at Camp Boyle, Adair County, Ky., and mustered in November 20, 1861. Attached to Thomas' Command, Army of Ohio, November, 1861. 11th Brigade, Army of Ohio, to December, 1861. 11th Brigade, 1st Division, Army of Ohio, to March, 1862. 11th Brigade, 5th Division, Army of Ohio, to September, 1862. 11th Brigade, 5th Division, 2nd Army Corps, Army of Ohio, to November, 1862. 1st Brigade, 3rd Division, Left Wing 14th Army Corps, Army of the Cumberland, to January, 1863. 1st Brigade, 3rd Division, 21st Army Corps, Army of the Cumberland, to October, 1863. 3rd Brigade, 3rd Division, 4th Army Corps, to December, 1864.

SERVICE.—Duty at Columbia, Ky., till February, 1862. March to Bowling Green, Ky., thence to Nashville, Tenn., February 15-March 8. March to Savannah, Tenn., March 18-April 6. Battle of Shiloh, Tenn., April 7. Advance on and siege of Corinth, Miss., April 29-May 30. Engaged May 21, 28 and 29. Occupation of Corinth May 30, and pursuit to Booneville May 31-

June 1. March to Stevenson, Ala., via Iuka, Miss., Tuscumbia, Florence, Huntsville and Athens, Ala., June 12-July 24; thence to Battle Creek, Tenn., and duty there till August 20. March to Louisville, Ky., in pursuit of Bragg August 20-September 26. Pursuit of Bragg to Loudon, Ky., October 1-22. Battle of Perryville, Ky., October 8 (Reserve). Nelson's Cross Roads October 18. March to Nashville, Tenn., October 22-November 7 and duty there till December 26. Advance on Murfreesboro December 26-30. Battle of Stone's River December 30-31, 1862, and January 1-3, 1863. At Murfreesboro till June. Middle Tennessee (or Tullahoma) Campaign June 23-July 7. At McMinnville till August 16. Passage of Cumberland Mountains and Tennessee River and Chickamauga (Ga.) Campaign August 16-September 22. Battle of Chickamauga September 19-20. Siege of Chattanooga September 24-November 23. Chattanooga-Ringgold Campaign November 23-27. Orchard Knob November 23-24. Mission Ridge November 25. Pursuit to Graysville November 26-27. March to relief of Knoxville November 28-December 8. Operations in East Tennessee December, 1863, to April, 1864. Atlanta (Ga.) Campaign May 1 to September 8. Demonstrations on Rocky Faced Ridge and Dalton, Ga., May 8-13. Battle of Resaca May 14-15. Adairsville May 17. Near Kingston May 18-19. Near Cassville May 19. Advance on Dallas May 22-25. Operations on line of Pumpkin Vine Creek and battles about Dallas, New Hope Church and Allatoona Hills May 25-June 5. Pickett's Mills May 27. Operations about Marietta and against Kenesaw Mountain June 10-July 2. Pine Hill June 11-14. Lost Mountain June 15-17. Assault on Kenesaw June 27. Ruff's Station, Smyrna Camp Ground, July 4. Chattahoochie River July 6-17. Peach Tree Creek July 19-20. Siege of Atlanta July 22-August 25. Flank movement on Jonesboro August 25-30. Battle of Jonesboro August 31-September 1. Lovejoy Station September 2-6. Operations against Hood in North Georgia and North Alabama October 1-26. Moved to Nashville, thence to Pulaski, Tenn. Ordered to Kentucky November 22. Mustered out December 15, 1864.

Regiment lost during service 8 Officers and 96 Enlisted men killed and mortally wounded and 3 Officers and 250 Enlisted men by disease. Total 357.

10th REGIMENT INFANTRY.

Organized at Lebanon, Ky., November 21, 1861. Attached to 2nd Brigade, Army of Ohio, to December, 1861. 2nd Brigade, 1st Division, Army of Ohio, to September, 1862. 2nd Brigade, 1st Division, 3rd Corps, Army of Ohio, to November, 1862. 2nd Brigade, 3rd Division (Centre), 14th Army Corps, Army of the Cumberland, to January, 1863. 2nd Brigade, 3rd Division, 14th Army Corps, to October, 1863. 3rd Brigade, 3rd Division, 14th Army Corps, to December, 1864.

SERVICE.—Advance on Camp Hamilton, Ky., January 1-15, 1862. Action at Logan's Cross Roads on Fishing Creek January 19. Battle of Mill Springs January 19-20. Duty at Mill Springs till February 11. Moved to Louisville, thence to Nashville, Tenn., February 11-March 2. March to Savannah, Tenn., March 20-April 7. Expedition to Bear Creek, Ala., April 12-13. Advance on and siege of Corinth, Miss., April 29-May 30. Buell's Campaign in Northern Alabama and Middle Tennessee June to August. Courtland Bridge July 25 (Cos. "A" and "H"). Decatur August 7. March to Nashville, Tenn., thence to Louisville, Ky., in pursuit of Bragg August 20-September 26. Pursuit of Bragg into Kentucky October 1-16. Battle of Perryville, Ky., October 8. March to Gallatin, Tenn., and duty there till January 13, 1863. Operations against Morgan December 22, 1862, to January 2, 1863. Moved to Nashville, Tenn., January 13, 1863; thence to Murfreesboro and duty there till June. Expedition toward Columbia March 4-14. Middle Tennessee (or Tullahoma) Campaign June 23-July 7. Hoover's Gap June 24-26. Occupation of Middle Tennessee till August 16. Passage of Cumberland Mountains and Tennessee River and

Chickamauga (Ga.) Campaign August 16-September 22. Battle of Chickamauga September 19-21. Before Chattanooga September 22-26. Siege of Chattanooga September 26-November 23. Chattanooga-Ringgold Campaign November 23-27. Orchard Knob November 23-24. Mission Ridge November 25. Reconnoissance of Dalton, Ga., February 22-27, 1864. Tunnel Hill, Buzzard's Roost Gap and Rocky Faced Ridge February 23-25. Atlanta (Ga.) Campaign May 1-September 8. Demonstration on Rocky Faced Ridge and Dalton May 8-13. Buzzard's Roost Gap May 8-9. Battle of Resaca May 14-15. Advance on Dallas May 18-25. Operations on line of Pumpkin Vine Creek and battles about Dallas, New Hope Church and Allatoona Hills May 25-June 5. Operations about Marietta and against Kenesaw Mountain June 10-July 2. Pine Hill June 11-14. Lost Mountain June 15-17. Near Marietta June 19. Assault on Kenesaw June 27. Ruff's Station July 4. Chattahoochie River July 5-17. Vining Station July 9-11. Peach Tree Creek July 19-20. Siege of Atlanta July 22-August 25. Flank movement on Jonesboro August 25-30. Battle of Jonesboro August 31-September 1. Moved to Ringgold, Ga., thence to Chattanooga, Tenn., and duty there till November. Ordered to Kentucky November 14. Mustered out December 6, 1864.

Regiment lost during service 2 Officers and 70 Enlisted men killed and mortally wounded and 5 Officers and 144 Enlisted men by disease. Total 221.

11th REGIMENT INFANTRY.

Organized at Camp Calhoun, Ky., December 9, 1861. Attached to 14th Brigade, Army of Ohio, December, 1861. 14th Brigade, 5th Division, Army of Ohio, to September, 1862. 14th Brigade, 5th Division, 2nd Army Corps, Army of Ohio, to November, 1862. 1st Brigade, 3rd Division, Left Wing 14th Army Corps, Army of the Cumberland, to January, 1863. 1st Brigade, 3rd Division, 21st Army Corps, Army of the Cumberland, to April, 1863. District of Western Kentucky, Dept. of Ohio, to June, 1863. 3rd Brigade, 3rd Division, 23rd Army Corps, Army of Ohio, to August, 1863. Unattached, Bowling Green, Ky., 1st Division, 23rd Army Corps, to October, 1863. 1st Brigade, 4th Division, 23rd Army Corps, to November, 1863. 3rd Brigade, 1st Division, Cavalry Corps, Dept. of Ohio, to April, 1864. 3rd Brigade, 4th Division, 23rd Army Corps, to June, 1864. 3rd Brigade, 3rd Division, 23rd Army Corps, to August, 1864. 1st Brigade, 3rd Division, 23rd Army Corps, to December, 1864.

SERVICE.—Duty at Calhoun, Ky., till February, 1862. Advance on Bowling Green, Ky., and Nashville, Tenn., February 10-25. Occupation of Nashville February 25. March to Savannah, Tenn., March 17-April 6. Battle of Shiloh April 7. Advance on and siege of Corinth, Miss., April 29-May 30. Buell's Campaign in Northern Alabama and Middle Tennessee June to August. March to Louisville, Ky., in pursuit of Bragg August 21-September 26. Pursuit of Bragg into Kentucky October 1-20. Battle of Perryville, Ky., October 8 (Reserve). Nelson's Cross Roads and Rural Hill October 18. March to Nashville, Tenn., October 20-November 7, and duty there till December 26. Advance on Murfreesboro December 26-30. Nolensville December 26-27. Battle of Stone's River December 30-31, 1862, and January 1-3, 1863. Ordered to Kentucky January 8, 1863. Duty at Bowling Green, Ky., till July. Regiment mounted and operating against guerrillas. Expedition to Tennessee State Line May 2-6. Woodburn and South Union May 13. At Glasgow, Ky., July to September. March to Knoxville, Tenn., and Burnside's Campaign in East Tennessee September to November. Philadelphia October 24. Leiper's Ferry, Holston River, October 27. Knoxville Campaign November 4 to December 23. Rockford and near Loudon November 14. Lenoir Station, Stock Creek and Holston River November 15. Near Knoxville November 16. Siege of Knoxville November 17-December 5. About Bean's Station December 9-13. Russellville December 10. Bean's Station December 13, 14 and 15. Rutledge

December 16. Blain's Cross Roads December 16-19. Scout to Bean's Station December 29-30. About Dandridge January 26-28, 1864. Fair Garden January 27. Moved to Mt. Sterling, Ky., February, 1864. Dismounted and march to Knoxville, Tenn. Duty there and at Crossing of the Hiawassee operating against Wheeler and guarding Sherman's communications till June. Joined Sherman at Kingston, Ga. Operations about Marietta and against Kenesaw Mountain June 10-July 2. Lost Mountain June 15-17. Muddy Creek June 17. Noyes Creek June 19. Cheyney's Farm June 22. Olley's Creek June 26-27. Assault on Kenesaw June 27. Nickajack Creek July 2-5. Chattahoochie River July 6-17. Peach Tree Creek July 19-20. Siege of Atlanta July 22-August 25. Utoy Creek August 5-7. Flank movement on Jonesboro August 25-30. Battle of Jonesboro August 31-September 1. Lovejoy Station September 2-6. Operations against Hood in North Georgia and North Alabama October 1-26. Moved to Nashville, thence to Pulaski, Tenn. Ordered to Louisville, Ky., November 14; thence to Bowling Green, Ky., and duty there till December. Mustered out December 16, 1864.

Regiment lost during service 2 Officers and 45 Enlisted men killed and mortally wounded and 3 Officers and 214 Enlisted men by disease. Total 264.

12th REGIMENT INFANTRY.

Company "A" organized at Camp Dick Robinson, Ky., September 26, 1861, and other companies near Waitsboro, Pulaski County, Ky., October, 1861, to January, 1862. Attached to Thomas' Command, Camp Dick Robinson, Kentucky, to November, 1861. 1st Brigade, Army of the Ohio, to December, 1861. 1st Brigade, 1st Division, Army of the Ohio, to September, 1862. 1st Brigade, 1st Division, 3rd Corps, Army of the Ohio, to November, 1862. 1st Brigade, 3rd Division, Centre 14th Army Corps, Army of the Cumberland, to December, 1862. District of Western Kentucky, Dept. of the Ohio, to June, 1863. 1st Brigade, 2nd Division, 23rd Army Corus, Army of the Ohio, to August, 1863. 1st Brigade, 3rd Division, 23rd Army Corps, to June, 1864. 3rd Brigade, 3rd Division, 23rd Army Corps, to August, 1864. 1st Brigade, 3rd Division, 23rd Army Corps, Army of the Ohio, to February, 1865, and Dept. of North Carolina to July, 1865.

SERVICE.—Actions at Albany and Travisville, Ky., September 29, 1861 (Co. "A"). Operations in Wayne and Clinton Counties and at Mill Springs, Ky., November, 1861. At Camp Hoskins till December. Operations about Mill Springs December 1-13. Action with Zollicoffer December 2. Moved to Somerset and duty there till January, 1862. Battle of Mill Springs January 19-20. Regiment mustered in at Clio, Ky., January, 1862. Moved to Louisville, Ky.; thence to Nashville, Tenn., February 11-March 2. March to Savannah, Tenn., March 20-April 8. Advance on and Siege of Corinth, Miss., April 29-May 30. Pursuit to Booneville June 1-6. Buell's Campaign in North Alabama and Middle Tennessee June to August. March to Nashville, Tenn.; thence to Louisville, Ky., in pursuit of Bragg, August 20-September 25. Pursuit of Bragg into Kentucky October 1-15. Battle of Perryville, Ky., October 8 (Reserve). March to Lebanon, Ky., and duty there till April, 1863. Operations against Morgan December 22, 1862, to January 2, 1863. Moved to Bowling Green, Ky., April 10. Duty there and at Rusellville till August. Moved to Camp Nelson and Danville and join Gen. Burnside. Burnside's march over Cumberland Mountains and Campaign in East Tennessee August 16-October 17. Occupation of Knoxville September 3. Watauga River, Blue Springs, October 10. Knoxville Campaign November 4-December 23. Siege of Knoxville November 17-December 5. Blain's Cross Roads December 15-16. At Strawberry Plains till January, 1864. Regiment veteranize and moved to Louisville, Ky. Veterans on furlough till April 1. At Burnside's Point till May. March to Chattanooga, Tenn.; thence to Burnt Hickory, Ga., May 1-24. Burnt Hickory May 25. Battles about Dallas, New Hope Church and Allatoona Hills May 25-June 5. Raccoon Bottom June

2. Operations about Marietta and against Kenesaw Mountain June 10-July 2. Burnt Hickory June 13. Lost Mountain June 15-17. Muddy Creek June 17. Noyes Creek June 19. Cheyney's Farm June 22. Near Marietta June 23. Olley's Farm June 26-27. Assault on Kenesaw June 27. Nickajack Creek July 2-5. Chattahoochie River July 6-17. Peach Tree Creek July 19-20. Siege of Atlanta July 22-August 25. Utoy Creek August 5-7. Flank movement on Jonesboro August 25-30. Battle of Jonesboro August 31-September 1. Lovejoy Station September 2-6. Operations against Hood in North Georgia and North Alabama September 29-November 3. Cedar Bluff, Ala., October 27. Moved to Nashville, thence to Pulaski. Nashville Campaign November-December. Columbia, Duck River, November 24-27. Columbia Ford November 29. Battle of Franklin November 30. Battle of Nashville December 15-16. Pursuit of Hood to the Tennessee River December 17-28. At Clifton, Tenn., till January 16. Moved to Washington, D. C.; thence to Federal Point, N. C., January 16-February 9. Operations against Hoke February 12-14. Fort Anderson February 18-19. Town Creek February 19-20. Capture of Wilmington February 22. Campaign of the Carolinas March 1-April 26. Advance on Goldsboro March 6-21. Occupation of Goldsboro March 21. Advance on Raleigh April 10-13. Occupation of Raleigh April 14. Bennett's House April 26. Surrender of Johnston and his army. Duty at Greensboro, N. C., till July. Mustered out July 11, 1865.

Regiment lost during service 1 Officer and 40 Enlisted men killed and mortally wounded and 5 Officers and 193 Enlisted men by disease. Total 239.

13th REGIMENT INFANTRY.

Organized at Camp Hobson, near Greensburg, Ky., and mustered in at Green River December 10, 1861. Attached to 16th Brigade, Army of the Ohio, December, 1861. 11th Brigade, 1st Division, Army of the Ohio, to March, 1862. 11th Brigade, 5th Division, Army of the Ohio, to September, 1862. 11th Brigade, 5th Division, 2nd Army Corps, Army of the Ohio, to November, 1862. 1st Brigade, 3rd Division, Left Wing 14th Army Corps, Army of the Cumberland, to December, 1862. District of West Kentucky, Dept. of the Ohio, to June, 1863. 2nd Brigade, 3rd Division, 23rd Army Corps, Army of the Ohio, to August, 1863. 2nd Brigade, 2nd Division, 23rd Army Corps. to April, 1864. 1st Brigade, 2nd Division, 23rd Army Corps, to June, 1864. 2nd Brigade, 2nd Division, 23rd Army Corps, to January, 1865.

SERVICE.—Duty on Green River, Ky., till February, 1862. March to Bowling Green, Ky.; thence to Nashville, Tenn., February 15-March 8, and to Savannah, Tenn., March 18-April 6. Battle of Shiloh, Tenn., April 7. Advance on and siege of Corinth, Miss., April 29-May 30. Pursuit to Booneville May 30-June 12. Buell's Campaign in Northern Alabama and Middle Tennessee June to August. March to Nashville, Tenn.; thence to Louisville, Ky., in pursuit of Bragg, August 21-September 26. Pursuit of Bragg into Kentucky October 1-22. Nelson's Cross Roads October 18. Duty at Munfordsville and other points in Kentucky November, 1862, to August, 1863. Operations against Morgan December 22, 1862, to January 2, 1863. Boston December 29, 1862. Burnside's march over Cumberland Mountains and campaign in East Tennessee August 16-October 17. At Loudon, Tenn., September 4 to November 14. Ruff's Ferry November 14. Near Loudon and Holston River November 15. Siege of Knoxville November 17-December 5. Near Lexington December 15. Scott's Mill Road, near Knoxville, January 27, 1864. Duty in East Tennessee till April. March to Chattanooga, Tenn., April. Atlanta (Ga.) Campaign May 1-September 8. Demonstration on Rocky Faced Ridge and Dalton May 5-13. Buzzard's Roost Gap May 8-9. Dalton May 9. Battle of Resaca May 14-15. Cassville May 19. Battles about Dallas, New Hope Church and Allatoona Hills May 25-June 5. Ackworth June 2. Operations about Marietta and against Kenesaw Mountain June 10-July 2. Lost Mountain June 15-17. Muddy Creek June 17. Noyes' Creek June 19.

Kolb's Farm June 22. Assault on Kenesaw June 27. Nickajack Creek July 2-5. Chattahoochie River July 6-17. Decatur July 19. Howard House July 20. Battle of Atlanta July 22. Siege of Atlanta July 22-August 25. Utoy Creek August 5-7. Flank movement on Jonesboro August 25-30. Battle of Jonesboro August 31-September 1. Lovejoy Station September 2-6. Ordered to Kentucky September, and duty at Bowling Green till January, 1865. Ordered to Louisville, Ky., and mustered out January 12, 1865.

Regiment lost during service 8 Officers and 50 Enlisted men killed and mortally wounded and 6 Officers and 181 Enlisted men by disease. Total 245.

14th REGIMENT INFANTRY.

Organized at Camp Wallace, Lawrence County, Ky., December 10, 1861. Attached to 18th Brigade, Army of the Ohio, to March, 1862. 27th Brigade, 7th Division, Army of the Ohio, to October, 1862. 2nd Brigade, 3rd Division, Army of Kentucky, Dept. of the Ohio, to February, 1863. District of Eastern Kentucky, Dept. of the Ohio, to June, 1863. 1st Brigade, 4th Division, 23rd Army Corps, Dept. of the Ohio, to September, 1863. Louisa, Ky., District of Eastern Kentucky, 1st Division, 23rd Army Corps, to April, 1864. 1st Brigade, 1st Division, District of Kentucky, 5th Division, 23rd Army Corps, Dept. of the Ohio, to May, 1864. 3rd Brigade, 2nd Division, 23rd Army Corps, to August, 1864. 1st Brigade, 2nd Division, 23rd Army Corps, to December, 1864. Military District of Kentucky and Dept. of Kentucky to September, 1865.

SERVICE.—Engaged in operations on borders of Virginia and participated in action at Ivey's Mountain November 8, 1861, before muster. Garfield's Campaign against Humphrey Marshall December 23, 1861, to January 30, 1862. Advance on Paintsville, Ky., December 31, 1862, to January 7, 1862. Occupation of Paintsville January 8. Abbott's Hill January 9. Middle Creek, near Prestonburg, January 10. At Paintsville till February 1. Expedition to Little Sandy and Piketon January 24-30. Cumberland Gap Campaign March 28-June 18. Cumberland Mountain April 28. Occupation of Cumberland Gap June 18-September 16. Tazewell July 26. Operations about Cumberland Gap August 2-6. Big Springs August 3. Tazewell August 6 and 9. Big Hill, Henderson County, August 23. Richmond September 5. Evacuation of Cumberland Gap and retreat to Greenup, on the Ohio River, September 17-October 3. Expedition to Charleston, West Va., October 21-November 10. Duty in Eastern Kentucky till May, 1864. Johnson County December 1, 1862. Floyd County December 4-5. Louisa March 12, 1863. Near Louisa March 25-26. Operations in Eastern Kentucky March 28-April 16. Bushy Creek April 7. Expedition from Beaver Creek into Southwest Virginia July 3-11 (1 Co.). Actions at Saylersville Oct. 10, 30; November 30 and December 1. Rock House and Laurel Creek, Wayne County, February 12, 1864. Laurel Creek Gap February 15. Forks of Beaver March 31. Quicksand Creek April 5 (Co. "I"). Paintsville April 13. Half Mountain, Magoffin County, April 14. Louisa April 16. Pound Gap May 9. Ordered to join Sherman in the field and reported at Burnt Hickory, Ga., May 24. Atlanta (Ga.) Campaign May 24-September 8. Kingston May 24. Battles about Dallas, New Hope Church and Allatoona Hills May 25-June 5. Allatoona Pass June 1-2. Operations about Marietta and against Kenesaw Mountain June 10-July 2. Pine Mountain June 11-14. Lost Mountain June 15-17. Muddy Creek June 17. Noyes' Creek June 19. Kolb's Farm June 22. Assault on Kenesaw June 27. Nickajack Creek July 2-5. Chattahoochie River July 6-17. Decatur July 19. Howard House July 20. Battle of Atlanta July 22. Siege of Atlanta July 22-August 25. Utoy Creek August 5-7. Flank movement on Jonesboro August 25-30. Battle of Jonesboro August 31-September 1. Lovejoy Station September 2-6. At Decatur till October 4. Operations against Hood in North Alabama and Middle Tennessee October 4-26. Ordered to Kentucky November 15; at Bowling Green, Ky., till December 30, and at Louisa, Ky., protecting Virginia line till September, 1865. Mustered out September 15, 1865.

Regiment lost during service 5 Officers and 49 Enlisted men killed and mortally wounded and 5 Officers and 142 Enlisted men by disease. Total 201.

15th REGIMENT INFANTRY.

Organized at New Haven, Ky., December 14, 1861. Attached to 16th Brigade, Army of Ohio, to December, 1861. 17th Brigade, Army of Ohio, to January, 1862. 17th Brigade, 3rd Division, Army of Ohio, to September, 1862. 17th Brigade, 3rd Division, 1st Army Corps, Army of Ohio, to November, 1862. 2nd Brigade, 1st Division (Center), 14th Army Corps, Army of the Cumberland, to January, 1863. 2nd Brigade, 1st Division, 14th Army Corps, to April, 1863. 1st Brigade, 2nd Division, 14th Army Corps, to October, 1863. 1st Brigade, 1st Division, 14th Army Corps, to November, 1863. Post of Chattanooga to April, 1864. 1st Brigade, 1st Division, 14th Army Corps, to November, 1864.

SERVICE.—Duty at New Haven and Bacon Creek, Ky., till February, 1862. Advance on Bowling Green, Ky., February 10-15. Occupation of Bowling Green February 15-22. Advance on Nashville, Tenn., February 22-25. Advance on Murfreesboro, Tenn., March 17-19. Occupation of Shelbyville, Fayetteville and advance on Huntsville, Ala., March 18-April 11. Capture of Huntsville April 11. Advance on Decatur, Ala., April 11-14. Action at West Bridge, near Bridgeport, Ala., April 29. At Huntsville till August. Guntersville and Law's Landing July 28. Old Deposit Ferry July 29. March to Louisville, Ky., in pursuit of Bragg August 27-September 26. Pursuit of Bragg into Kentucky October 1-15. Battle of Perryville October 8. March to Nashville, Tenn., October 16-November 7, and duty there till December 26. Bacon Creek, near Munfordsville, Ky., December 26 (Detachment). Advance on Murfreesboro December 26-30. Battle of Stone's River December 30-31, 1862, and January 1-3, 1863. At Murfreesboro till June, 1863. Middle Tennessee (or Tullahoma) Campaign June 23-July 7. Hoover's Gap June 24-26. Occupation of Tullahoma July 1. Occupation of Middle Tennessee till August 16. Passage of Cumberland Mountains and Tennessee River and Chickamauga (Ga.) Campaign August 16-September 22. Steven's Gap September 6. Davis Cross Roads or Dug Gap September 11. Battle of Chickamauga, Ga., September 19-21. Rossville Gap September 21. Siege of Chattanooga September 24-November 23. Chattanooga-Ringgold Campaign November 23-27. Mission Ridge November 25. In reserve. Post duty at Chattanooga, Tenn., till April, 1864. Atlanta (Ga.) Campaign May 1-September 8. Demonstration on Rocky Faced Ridge May 8-11. Buzzard's Roost Gap May 8-9. Battle of Resaca May 14-15. Advance on Dallas May 18-25. Operations on line of Pumpkin Vine Creek and battles about Dallas, New Hope Church and Allatoona Hills May 25-June 5. Operations about Marietta and against Kenesaw Mountain June 10-July 2. Pine Hill June 11-14. Lost Mountain June 15-17. Assault on Kenesaw June 27. Ruff's Station July 4. Chattahoochie River July 6-17. Buckhead, Nancy's Creek, July 18. Battle of Peach Tree Creek July 19-20. Siege of Atlanta July 22-August 25. Flank movement on Jonesboro August 25-30. Red Oak August 29. Battle of Jonesboro August 31-September 1. Lovejoy Station September 2-6. Operations in North Georgia and North Alabama against Hood October 1-26. Duty at Chattanooga, Tenn., and Bridgeport, Ala., till December. Ordered to Louisville, Ky., and mustered out January 14, 1865.

Regiment lost during service 9 Officers and 128 Enlisted men killed and mortally wounded and 1 Officer and 113 Enlisted men by disease. Total 251.

16th REGIMENT INFANTRY.

Organized at Camp Kenton in fall of 1861 and mustered in January 27, 1862. Attached to 18th Brigade, Army of Ohio, to March, 1862. Unattached, Army of Ohio, to November, 1862. District of West Kentucky, Dept. of Ohio, to June, 1863. 2nd Brigade, 3rd Division,

23rd Army Corps, Army of Ohio, to August, 1863. 1st Brigade, 2nd Division, 23rd Army Corps, to April, 1864. 1st Brigade, 3rd Division, 23rd Army Corps, to March, 1865. 1st Brigade, 3rd Division, 23rd Army Corps, Dept. of North Carolina, to July, 1865.

SERVICE.—Nelson's Expedition into Eastern Kentucky November, 1861. Action at Ivy Mountain November 8. Piketon November 8-9. Returned to Camp Kenton and duty there and near Maysville, Ky., till March 2, 1862. Moved to Piketon March 2 and duty there till June 13. Moved to Prestonburg June 13, thence to Louisa July 15, and duty there till August. Moved to Covington, Louisville and Bowling Green, Ky., August. Duty there, at Shepherdsville, West Point and Munfordsville till December. Operations against Morgan December 22, 1862, to January 2, 1863. Duty at Lebanon, Munfordsville and Glasgow, Ky., till August, 1863. Operations against Morgan July 2-26. Burnside's march over Cumberland Mountains and Campaign in East Tennessee August 16-October 17. At Loudon September 4 to November 14. Knoxville Campaign November 4-December 23. Kingston November 7. Lenoir November 14-15. Campbell's Station November 16. Siege of Knoxville November 17-December 5. Near Kingston November 24-December 4. Mossy Creek, Talbot Station, December 29. (Regiment re-enlisted at Mossy Creek December 27, 1863.) Moved to Kentucky January, 1864, and Veterans on furlough February and March. Ordered to Camp Nelson, Ky., April 16; thence march to Knoxville, Tenn., and to Red Clay, Ga., and joined Sherman. Atlanta (Ga.) Campaign May to September. Demonstration on Rocky Faced Ridge and Dalton May 8-13. Battle of Resaca May 14-15. Cartersville May 20. Operations on line of Pumpkin Vine Creek and battles about Dallas, New Hope Church and Allatoona Hills May 25-June 5. Operations about Marietta and against Kenesaw Mountain June 10-July 2. Lost Mountain June 11-17. Muddy Creek June 17. Noyes Creek June 19. Cheyney's Farm June 22. Olley's Creek June 26-27. Assault on Kenesaw June 27. Nickajack Creek July 2-5. Chattahoochie River July 6-17. Peach Tree Creek July 19-20. Siege of Atlanta July 22-August 25. Utoy Creek August 5-7. Flank movement on Jonesboro August 25-30. Battle of Jonesboro August 31-September 1. Lovejoy Station September 2-6. Operations in North Georgia and North Alabama against Hood September 29-November 3. Moved to Nashville, thence to Pulaski, Tenn. Nashville Campaign November-December. Columbia, Duck River, November 24-27. Columbia Ford November 29. Battle of Franklin November 30. Battle of Nashville December 15-16. Pursuit of Hood to the Tennessee River December 17-28. At Clifton, Tenn., till January 15, 1865. Moved to Washington, D. C., thence to Smithville, N. C., January 15-February 9. Operations against Hoke February 12-14. Near Smithville February 16. Fort Anderson February 18-19. Town Creek February 19-20. Eagle Island February 21. Capture of Wilmington February 22. Campaign of the Carolinas March 1-April 26. Advance on Goldsboro, N. C., March 6-21. Occupation of Goldsboro March 21. Advance on Raleigh April 10-13. Occupation of Raleigh April 14. Bennett's House April 26. Surrender of Johnston and his army. Duty at Greensburg, N. C., till July. Mustered out July 15, 1865.

Regiment lost during service 2 Officers and 50 Enlisted men killed and mortally wounded and 5 Officers and 131 Enlisted men by disease. Total 188.

17th REGIMENT INFANTRY.

Organized at Hartford and Calhoun, Ky., September to December, 1861. Attached to 13th Brigade, Army of Ohio, to December, 1861. 13th Brigade, 5th Division, Army of Ohio, to February, 1862. 1st Brigade, 3rd Division, Army of the Tennessee, to March, 1862. 3rd Brigade, 4th Division, Army of the Tennessee, to April, 1862. 10th Brigade, 4th Division, Army of the Ohio, to July, 1862. 9th Brigade, 3rd Division, Army of Ohio, to September, 1862. District of Western Kentucky, Dept. of Ohio, to November, 1862. Post of Clarksville, Tenn., Dept. of the Cumberland, to March, 1863. 1st Brigade, 3rd Division, 21st Army Corps, Army of the Cumberland, to October, 1863. 3rd Brigade, 3rd Division, 4th Army Corps, to January, 1865.

SERVICE.—Duty at Calhoun, Ky., till February, 1862. Action at Woodbury, Ky., October 29, 1861. Morgantown October 31. Moved to Fort Donelson, Tenn., February 11-13. Investment and capture of Fort Donelson, Tenn., February 13-16. Expedition to Crump's Landing, Tenn., March 14-17. Battle of Shiloh, Tenn., April 6-7. Advance on and siege of Corinth, Miss., April 29-May 30. Bridge Creek before Corinth May 28. Pursuit to Booneville May 31-June 12. Buell's Campaign in Northern Alabama and Middle Tennessee June to August. March to Nashville, Tenn., thence to Louisville, Ky., in pursuit of Bragg August 21-September 26. Moved to Bowling Green, Ky., thence to Russellville, Ky., and duty there till December. Ordered to Clarksville, Tenn., and duty there till March, 1863. Moved to Nashville, Tenn., thence to Murfreesboro, Tenn., and duty there till June. Middle Tennessee (or Tullahoma) Campaign June 23-July 7. At McMinnville till August 16. Passage of Cumberland Mountains and Tennessee River and Chickamauga (Ga.) Campaign August 16-September 22. Battle of Chickamauga September 19-20. Siege of Chattanooga, Tenn., September 24-November 23. Chattanooga-Ringgold Campaign November 23-27. Orchard Knob November 23-24. Mission Ridge November 25. March to relief of Knoxville November 28-December 8. Operations in East Tennessee December, 1863, to April, 1864. Moved to Cleveland, Tenn. Atlanta (Ga.) Campaign May to September. Demonstration on Rocky Faced Ridge May 8-11. Battle of Resaca May 14-15. Adairsville May 17. Near Kingston May 18-19. Near Cassville May 19. Advance on Dallas May 22-25. Operations on Pumpkin Vine Creek and battles about Dallas, New Hope Church and Allatoona Hills May 25-June 5. Pickett's Mills May 27. Ackworth June 6. Operations about Marietta and against Kenesaw Mountain June 10-July 2. Pine Hill June 11-14. Lost Mountain June 15-17. Assault on Kenesaw June 26. Ruff's Station July 4. Chattahoochie River July 5-17. Peach Tree Creek July 19-20. Siege of Atlanta July 22-August 25. Flank movement on Jonesboro August 25-30. Battle of Jonesboro August 31-September 1. Lovejoy Station September 2-6. Operations against Hood in North Georgia and North Alabama September 29-November 3. Moved to Nashville and Pulaski, Tenn. Columbia, Duck River, November 24-27. Battle of Franklin November 30. Ordered to Louisville, Ky., December, and mustered out January 23, 1865.

Regiment lost during service 7 Officers and 128 Enlisted men killed and mortally wounded and 5 Officers and 158 Enlisted men by disease. Total 298.

18th REGIMENT INFANTRY.

Organized at large and mustered in February 8, 1862. Served unattached, Army of Ohio, to August, 1862. Cruft's Brigade, Nelson's Division, Richmond, Ky., Army of Kentucky, to September, 1862. 1st Brigade, 2nd Division, Army of Kentucky, Dept. of Ohio, to October, 1862. Unattached, Army of Kentucky, Dept. of Ohio, to December, 1862. 1st Brigade, 2nd Division, Army of Kentucky, to February, 1863. Crook's Brigade, Baird's Division, Army of Kentucky, Dept. of the Cumberland, to June, 1863. 3rd Brigade, 4th Division, 14th Army Corps, Army of the Cumberland, to October, 1863. 3rd Brigade, 3rd Division, 14th Army Corps, to June, 1865. 1st Brigade, 3rd Division, 14th Army Corps, to July, 1865.

SERVICE.—Duty guarding Covington & Lexington Railroad. Headquarters at Falmouth, Ky., till April 16, 1862, and at Lexington, Ky., till August 20, 1862. Affairs in Owen County June 20 and 23. Operations in Kentucky against Morgan July 4-28. Action at Cynthiana July 17. Paris July 19. Mt. Sterling, Ky., July 29. Moved to Richmond, Ky., August 20. Battle of

Richmond, Ky., August 30. Regiment mostly captured; those not captured retreat to Louisville, Ky.; thence moved to Covington, Ky., September 28; thence to Paris, Ky., and duty there till December 5. Moved to Lexington, Ky., December 5; thence to Louisville, Ky., January 27, 1863, and to Nashville, Tenn., February 2. Moved to Carthage and duty there till June 2. Moved to Murfreesboro, Tenn., June 2-7. Middle Tennessee (or Tullahoma) Campaign June 23-July 7. Hoover's Gap June 24-26. Occupation of Tullahoma July 1. Occupation of Middle Tennessee till August 16. Passage of Cumberland Mountains and Tennessee River and Chickamauga (Ga.) Campaign August 16-September 22. Catlett's Gap, Pigeon Mountain, September 15-18. Battle of Chickamauga September 19-21. Rossville Gap September 21. Siege of Chattanooga, Tenn., September 22-November 23. Reopening Tennessee River October 26-29. Brown's Ferry October 27. Chattanooga-Ringgold Campaign November 23-27. Orchard Knob November 23-24. Mission Ridge November 25. Duty at Chattanooga till January, 1864. Regiment Veteranize January 5, and Veterans on leave till March. Moved to Nashville, Tenn., March 12; thence march to Ringgold, Ga., March 22-May 7. Atlanta (Ga.) Campaign May to September. Assigned May 10 to post duty at Ringgold, Ga. Relieved September 25 and moved to Atlanta, Ga. Operations against Hood in North Georgia and North Alabama October 3-26. March to the sea November 10. Siege of Savannah December 10-21. Campaign of the Carolinas January to April, 1865. Fayetteville, N. C., March 11. Battle of Bentonville, N. C., March 19-21. Occupation of Goldsboro March 24. Non-Veterans mustered out April 4, 1865. Advance on Raleigh, N. C., April 10-14. Occupation of Raleigh April 14. Bennett's House April 26. Surrender of Johnston and his army. March to Washington, D. C., via Richmond, Va., April 29-May 30. Grand Review May 24. Moved to Louisville, Ky., June. Mustered out July 18, 1865.

Regiment lost during service 5 Officers and 85 Enlisted men killed and mortally wounded and 1 Officer and 152 Enlisted men by disease. Total 243.

19th REGIMENT INFANTRY.

Organized at Camp Harwood, Harrodsburg, Ky., and mustered in January 2, 1862. Attached to 20th Brigade, Army of Ohio, to February, 1862. 20th Brigade, 6th Division, Army of Ohio, to March, 1862. 27th Brigade, 7th Division, Army of Ohio, to October, 1862. 2nd Brigade, 1st Division, Army of Kentucky, Dept. of Ohio, to November, 1862. 2nd Brigade, 10th Division, Right Wing 13th Army Corps, Army of the Tennessee, to December, 1862. 2nd Brigade, 1st Division, Sherman's Yazoo Expedition, to January, 1863. 2nd Brigade, 10th Division, 13th Army Corps, Army of Tennessee, to August, 1863. 2nd Brigade, 4th Division, 13th Army Corps, Dept. of the Gulf, to March, 1864. 1st Brigade, 4th Division, 13th Army Corps, to June, 1864. Defences of New Orleans, La., June, 1864. District of Baton Rouge, La., to January, 1865.

SERVICE.—Moved to Somerset, Ky., January, 1862, and duty there till April. Cumberland Gap Campaign March 28-June 18. At Cumberland Ford till June. Occupation of Cumberland Gap June 18-September 16. Evacuation of Cumberland Gap and retreat to Greenup on the Ohio River September 16-October 3. Expedition to Charleston, W. Va., October 21-November 10. Moved to Memphis, Tenn., November 10-15, and duty there till December 20. Sherman's Yazoo Expedition December 20, 1862, to January 3, 1863. Chickasaw Bayou December 26-28. Chickasaw Bluff December 29. Expedition to Arkansas Post, Ark., January 3-10, 1863. Assault and capture of Fort Hindman, Arkansas Post, January 10-11. Moved to Young's Point, La., January 15-22, and duty there till March 10. Expedition to Fort Pemberton and Greenwood March 10-April 5. Moved to Milliken's Bend, La., April 5-8. Movement on Bruinsburg and turning Grand Gulf April 25-30. Battles of Port Gibson, Miss., May 1; Champion's Hill May 16; Big Black River Bridge May 17. Siege of Vicksburg May 18-July 4. Assaults on Vicksburg May 19 and 22. Surrender of Vicksburg July 4. Advance on Jackson, Miss., July 5-10. Siege of Jackson July 10-17. Camp at Big Black till August 13. Ordered to New Orleans, La., August 13. Duty at Carrollton, Brashear City and Berwick till October. Western Louisiana Campaign October 3-November 30. Grand Coteau November 3. At New Iberia till December 19. Moved to New Orleans December 19, thence to Madisonville January 19, and duty there till March. Red River Campaign March 10-May 22. Advance from Franklin to Alexandria March 14-26. Battle of Sabine Cross Roads April 8. Bayou de Paul April 8. Battle of Pleasant Hill April 9. Cane River Crossing April 22-23. At Alexandria April 27-May 13. Near Alexandria May 2-9. Retreat to Morganza April 13-20. Mansura May 16. Moved to Baton Rouge, La., May 29, and duty there till January, 1865. Ordered to Louisville, Ky., and there mustered out January 26, 1865.

Regiment lost during service 1 Officer and 42 Enlisted men killed and mortally wounded and 3 Officers and 152 Enlisted men by disease. Total 198.

20th REGIMENT INFANTRY.

Organized at Lexington, Camp Dick Robinson, and Smithland, Ky., and mustered in January 6, 1862. Attached to 22nd Brigade, Army of Ohio, to February, 1862. 22nd Brigade, 4th Division, Army of Ohio, to September, 1862. 22nd Brigade, 4th Division, 2nd Army Corps, Army of Ohio, to November, 1862. 1st Brigade, 2nd Division, Left Wing 14th Army Corps, Army of the Cumberland, to December, 1862. District of Western Kentucky, Dept. of Ohio, to June, 1863. Unassigned, 2nd Division, 23rd Army Corps, Dept. of Ohio, to August, 1863. District of Louisville, Ky., 1st Division, 23rd Army Corps, to April, 1864. 2nd Brigade, 2nd Division, District of Kentucky, 5th Division, 23rd Army Corps, to May, 1864. 3rd Brigade, 2nd Division, 23rd Army Corps, to December, 1864. Unattached, District of Kentucky, to January, 1865.

SERVICE.—Regiment united at Smithland and ordered to Louisville, Ky.; thence to Bardstown, Ky., January, 1862, and duty there till February. March to Nashville, Tenn., February 23-March 12; thence march to Savannah, Tenn., March 13-April 6. Battle of Shiloh, Tenn., April 6-7. Advance on and siege of Corinth, Miss., April 29-May 30. Phillips' Creek, Widow Serratt's, May 21. Bridge Creek, before Corinth, May 28. Occupation of Corinth May 30 and pursuit to Booneville May 31-June 6. Buell's Campaign in Northern Alabama and Middle Tennessee June to August. March to Nashville, Tenn.; thence to Louisville, Ky., in pursuit of Bragg, August 20-September 26. Pursuit of Bragg into Kentucky October 1-22. Glasgow, Ky., October 5. Battle of Perryville October 8. Camp Wild Cat October 17. March to Nashville, Tenn., October 22-November 9, and duty there till December 19. Ordered to Bowling Green, Ky., December 19, and duty there and guarding railroad at various points in Kentucky till July, 1863. Morgan's attack on Lebanon July 5. Regiment mostly captured. At Camp Nelson till July 28. Ordered to Louisville, Ky., and provost duty there till May 15, 1864. Ordered to join Sherman's army in the field May 15. Operations and battles about Dallas, New Hope Church and Allatoona Hills May 30-June 5. Ackworth June 3-4. Operations about Marietta and against Kenesaw Mountain June 10-July 2. Pine Hill June 11-14. Lost Mountain June 15-17. Muddy Creek June 17. Noyes' Creek June 19. Kolb's Farm June 22. Assault on Kenesaw June 27. Nickajack Creek July 2-5. Chattahoochie River July 6-17. Decatur July 19. Howard House July 20. Siege of Atlanta July 22-August 25. Utoy Creek August 5-7. Flank movement on Jonesboro August 25-30. Battle of Jonesboro August 31-September 1. Lovejoy Station September 2-6. Ordered to Louisville, Ky., September, and guard duty there till January, 1865. Mustered out January 17, 1865.

Regiment lost during service 36 Enlisted men killed and mortally wounded and 3 Officers and 194 Enlisted men by disease. Total 233.

21st REGIMENT INFANTRY.

Organized at Camps Hobson and Ward, Ky., and mustered in December 31, 1861, and January 2, 1862, at Green River Bridge, Ky. Attached to 11th Brigade, 1st Division, Army of the Ohio, to March, 1862. 11th Brigade, 5th Division, Army of the Ohio, to June, 1862. 7th Independent Brigade, Army of the Ohio, to July, 1862. 23rd Independent Brigade, Army of the Ohio, to August, 1862. 23rd Brigade, 5th Division, Army of the Ohio, to September, 1862. 23rd Brigade, 5th Division, 2nd Army Corps, Army of the Ohio, to November, 1862. 3rd Brigade, 3rd Division, Left Wing 14th Army Corps, Army of the Cumberland, to January, 1863. 3rd Brigade, 3rd Division, 21st Army Corps, Army of the Cumberland, to October, 1863. Unattached, Army of the Cumberland, to January, 1864. 2nd Brigade, 1st Division, 4th Army Corps, to June, 1865. 1st Brigade, 1st Division, 4th Army Corps, to August, 1865. Dept. of Texas to December, 1865.

SERVICE.—Duty at Green River Bridge, Ky., till March, 1862. Moved to Creelsboro; thence to Nashville, Tenn., and duty there till April 1. Moved to Columbia, Tenn., April 1-2; thence march to Shelbyville April 24, and duty there till June 11. Dumont's Expedition to Cumberland Mountain June 11-14. Expedition to Wartrace June 17-19. Moved to Tullahoma July 2, thence to Duck Bridge July 4. March to Louisville, Ky., in pursuit of Bragg August 20-September 19. Pursuit of Bragg into Kentucky October 1-22. Battle of Perryville October 8 (Reserve). Nelson's Cross Roads October 18. Pittman's Cross Roads October 19. Reconnoissance on Madison Road October 20. March to Nashville, Tenn., October 22-November 12, and duty there till December 26. Dobbins' Ferry, near Lavergne, December 9. Advance on Murfreesboro December 26-30. Battle of Stone River December 30-31, 1862, and January 1-3, 1863. At Murfreesboro till June. Middle Tennessee (or Tullahoma) Campaign June 23-July 7. Liberty Gap June 25-26. Occupation of Middle Tennessee till August 16. Passage of Cumberland Mountain and Tennessee River and Chickamauga (Ga.) Campaign August 16-September 22. Ringgold, Ga., September 11. Catlett's Gap September 15. At Whitesides during battle of Chickamauga September 19-20. At Chattanooga, Tenn., till October 1. Action at Anderson's (or Mountain Gap), near Smith's Cross Roads, October 1. Anderson's Cross Roads October 2. Duty in Sequatchie Valley till November 19. Chattanooga-Ringgold Campaign November 23-27. Tunnel Hill, Mission Ridge, November 24-25. Pursuit to Graysville November 26-27. Chickamauga Station November 26. March to relief of Knoxville November 28-December 18. At Chattanooga and Shellmound, Tenn., till January, 1864. Regiment veteranize January 11, 1864, and Veterans on furlough till March 30. Moved to Cleveland, thence to Blue Springs, Tenn., April 26. Atlanta (Ga.) Campaign May to September. Tunnel Hill May 6-7. Demonstrations on Rocky Faced Ridge and Dalton May 8-13. Buzzard's Roost Gap May 8-9. Battle of Resaca May 14-15. Near Kingston May 18-19. Near Cassville May 19. Advance on Dallas May 22-25. Operations on Pumpkin Vine Creek and battles about Dallas, New Hope Church and Allatoona Hills May 25-June 5. Burnt Hickory May 25. Operations about Marietta and against Kenesaw Mountain June 10-July 2. Pine Hill June 11-14. Lost Mountain June 15-17. Assault on Kenesaw June 27. Ruff's Station, Smyrna Camp Ground, July 4. Chattahoochie River July 5-17. Peach Tree Creek July 19-20. Siege of Atlanta July 22-August 25. Flank movement on Jonesboro August 25-30. Battle of Jonesboro August 31-September 1. Lovejoy Station September 2-6. Jonesboro September 5 and 12. Operations in North Georgia and North Alabama against Hood October 1-26. Moved to Nashville, Tenn.; thence to Pulaski, Tenn. Nashville Campaign November-December. Columbia, Duck River, November

24-27. Spring Hill November 29. Battle of Franklin November 30. Battle of Nashville December 15-16. Pursuit of Hood to the Tennessee River December 17-28. Moved to Huntsville, Ala., and duty there till March, 1865. Expedition to Bull's Gap and operations in East Tennessee March 15-April 22. At Nashville, Tenn., till June. Ordered to New Orleans, La., June 19; thence moved to Texas. Duty at Indianola and Victoria till December. Mustered out December 9, 1865.

Regiment lost during service 3 Officers and 57 Enlisted men killed and mortally wounded and 6 Officers and 152 Enlisted men by disease. Total 218.

22nd REGIMENT INFANTRY.

Organized at Louisa, Ky., January 20, 1862. Attached to 18th Brigade, Army of the Ohio, to March, 1862. 26th Brigade, 7th Division, Army of the Ohio, to October, 1862. 4th Brigade, District of West Virginia, Dept. of the Ohio, to November, 1862. 3rd Brigade, 9th Division, Right Wing 13th Army Corps (Old), Dept. of the Tennessee, to December, 1862. 3rd Brigade, 3rd Division, Sherman's Yazoo Expedition to January, 1863. 3rd Brigade, 9th Division, 13th Army Corps, to February, 1863. 2nd Brigade, 9th Division, 13th Army Corps, to July, 1863. 4th Brigade, 1st Division, 13th Army Corps, Army of the Tennessee, to August, 1863; and Dept. of the Gulf to September, 1863. 3rd Brigade, 1st Division, 13th Army Corps, to November, 1863. Plaquemine, District of Baton Rouge, La., Dept. of the Gulf, to March, 1864. 2nd Brigade, 1st Division, 13th Army Corps, to June, 1864. 2nd Brigade, 3rd Division, 19th Army Corps, Dept. of the Gulf, to December, 1864.
SERVICE.—Operations in Eastern Kentucky till March, 1862. Garfield's Campaign against Humphrey Marshall December 23, 1861, to January 30, 1862. Advance on Paintsville, Ky., December 30, 1861, to January 7, 1862. Jennie's Creek January 7. Occupation of Paintsville October 8. Abbott's Hill January 9. Middle Creek, near Prestonburg, January 10. Occupation of Prestonburg January 11. Expedition to Pound Gap, Cumberland Mountains, March 14-17. Pound Gap March 16. Cumberland Gap Campaign March 28-June 18. Cumberland Mountain April 28. Occupation of Cumberland Gap June 18-September 16. Operations about Cumberland Gap August 2-6. Tazewell August 6. Evacuation of Cumberland Gap and retreat to Greenup, on the Ohio River, September 16-October 3. West Liberty September 24. Expedition to Charleston, W. Va., October 21-November 10. Moved to Memphis, Tenn., November 10-15, and duty there till December 20. Sherman's Yazoo Expedition December 20, 1862, to January 3, 1863. Chickasaw Bayou December 26-28. Chickasaw Bluff December 29. Expedition to Arkansas Post, Ark., January 3-10, 1863. Assault and capture of Fort Hindman. Arkansas Post, January 10-11. Moved to Young's Point, La., January 17-22 and duty there till March. Operations from Milliken's Bend to New Carthage March 31-April 17. Movement on Bruinsburg and turning Grand Gulf April 25-30. Battle of Port Gibson May 1. Battle of Champion's Hill May 16. Big Black River Bridge May 17. Siege of Vicksburg May 18-July 4. Assaults on Vicksburg May 19 and 22. Advance on Jackson, Miss., July 5-10. Near Clinton July 8. Siege of Jackson July 10-17. At Big Black till August 13. Ordered to New Orleans, La., August 13. Duty at Carrollton, Brashear City and Berwick till October. Western Louisiana Campaign October 3-November 21. Duty at Plaquemine November 21, 1863, to March 24, 1864; and at Baton Rouge till April. Ordered to Alexandria, reporting there April 26. Red River Campaign April 26-May 22. Graham's Plantation May 5. Retreat to Morganza May 13-20. Mansura May 16. Expedition to the Atchafalaya May 31-June 6. Duty at Morganza, at mouth of the White River, Ark., and at Baton Rouge, La., till January, 1865. Mustered out January 20, 1865. Veterans and Recruits transferred to 7th Kentucky Infantry.

Regiment lost during service 3 Officers and 48 Enlisted men killed and mortally wounded and 3 Officers and 145 Enlisted men by disease. Total 199.

23rd REGIMENT INFANTRY.

Organized at Camp King, Lexington, Ky., and mustered in January 2, 1862. Attached to District of Kentucky, Dept. of the Ohio, to March, 1862. 23rd Independent Brigade, Army of the Ohio, to July, 1862. 10th Brigade, 4th Division, Army of the Ohio, to September, 1862. 10th Brigade, 4th Division, 2nd Corps, Army of the Ohio, to November, 1862. 3rd Brigade, 2nd Division, Left Wing 14th Army Corps, Army of the Cumberland, to January, 1863. 3rd Brigade, 2nd Division, 21st Army Corps, Army of the Cumberland, to October, 1863. 2nd Brigade, 3rd Division, 4th Army Corps, to August, 1864. 2nd Brigade, 1st Division, 4th Army Corps, to June, 1865. 1st Brigade, 1st Division, 4th Army Corps, to August, 1865. Dept. of Texas to December, 1865.
SERVICE.—Garrison and guard duty in Southern Kentucky and Middle Tennessee January to August, 1862. Round Mountain, near Woodbury, Tenn., August 27. March to Louisville, Ky., in pursuit of Bragg, September 1-26. Pursuit of Bragg into Kentucky October 1-16. Battle of Perryville October 8 (Reserve). March to Nashville, Tenn., October 17-November 7, and duty there till December 26. Advance on Murfreesboro December 26-30. Lavergne December 27. Battle of Stone's River December 30-31, 1862, and January 1-3, 1865. Woodbury January 24. At Murfreesboro till June. Scout from Clarksville May 20-22. Middle Tennessee (or Tullahoma) Campaign June 23-July 7. At Manchester till August 16. Passage of Cumberland Mountains and Tennessee River and Chickamauga (Ga.) Campaign August 16-September 22. Ringgold September 11. Lee and Gordon's Mills September 12-13. Battle of Chickamauga September 19-20. Siege of Chattanooga, Tenn., September 24-November 23. Reopening Tennessee River October 26-29. Brown's Ferry October 27. Chattanooga-Ringgold Campaign November 23-27. Orchard Knob November 23-24. Mission Ridge November 25. Pursuit to Graysville November 26-27. March to relief of Knoxville November 28-December 8. Charlestown December 28. Operations in East Tennessee December, 1863, to April, 1864. Regiment Veteranize at Blain's Cross Roads, Tenn., January 5, 1864. Atlanta (Ga.) Campaign May 1 to September 8, 1864. Demonstrations on Rocky Faced Ridge and Dalton, Ga., May 5-13. Battle of Resaca May 14-15. Adairsville May 17. Near Kingston May 18-19. Near Cassville May 19. Operations on line of Pumpkin Vine Creek and battles about Dallas, New Hope Church and Allatoona Hills May 25-June 5. Pickett's Mills May 27. Operations about Marietta and against Kenesaw Mountain June 10-July 2. Pine Hill June 11-14. Lost Mountain June 15-17. Assault on Kenesaw June 27. Ruff's Station, Smyrna Camp Ground, July 4. Pace's Ferry July 5. Chattahoochie River July 6-17. Peach Tree Creek July 19-20. Siege of Atlanta July 22-August 25. Utoy Creek August 5-7. Flank movement on Jonesboro August 25-30. Battle of Jonesboro August 31-September 1. Lovejoy Station September 2-6. Operations against Hood in North Georgia and North Alabama October 1-26. Nashville Campaign November-December. Columbia, Duck River, November 24-27. Battle of Franklin November 30. Battle of Nashville December 15-16. Pursuit of Hood to the Tennessee River December 17-29. Moved to Huntsville, Ala., and duty there till March, 1865. Expedition to Bull's Gap and operations in East Tennessee March 15-April 22. At Nashville, Tenn., till June. Ordered to New Orleans, La., June 6; thence moved to Texas July. Duty at Indianola, Green Lake and Victoria till December. Mustered out December 27, 1865.

Regiment lost during service 5 Officers and 84 Enlisted men killed and mortally wounded and 102 Enlisted men by disease. Total 191.

24th REGIMENT INFANTRY.

Organized at Lexington, Ky., December 31, 1861. Attached to 21st Brigade, Army of the Ohio, to January, 1862. 21st Brigade, 6th Division, Army of the Ohio, to September, 1862. 21st Brigade, 6th Division, 2nd Corps, Army of the Ohio, to November, 1862. 2nd Brigade, 1st

Division, Left Wing 14th Army Corps, Army of the Cumberland, to December, 1862. 2nd Brigade, 2nd Division, Army of Kentucky, Dept. of the Ohio, to January, 1863. 1st Brigade, District of Central Kentucky, Dept. of the Ohio, to June, 1863. 2nd Brigade, 1st Division, 23rd Army Corps, Army of the Ohio, to July, 1863. 2nd Brigade, 4th Division, 23rd Army Corps, to August, 1863. 2nd Brigade, 3rd Division, 23rd Army Corps, to December, 1864. Louisa, Ky., Military District of Kentucky, to January, 1865.

SERVICE.—Moved to Louisville, Ky., January 1, 1862; thence to Bardstown, Spring Garden (on Salt River), Lebanon and Munfordsville, Ky. March to Nashville, Tenn., February 17-25. March to Savannah, Tenn., March 21-April 6. Battle of Shiloh April 7. Advance on and siege of Corinth, Miss., April 29-May 30. Pursuit to Booneville May 31-June 12. Buell's Campaign in Northern Alabama and Middle Tennessee June to August. March to Nashville, Tenn.; thence to Louisville, Ky., in pursuit of Bragg, August 21-September 26. Pursuit of Bragg into Kentucky October 1-22. Battle of Perryville, Ky., October 8. March to Nashville, Tenn., October 22-November 7. Ordered to Frankfort, Ky., November 24 and duty there till January, 1863. Moved to Louisville, Ky.; thence to Nashville, Tenn. Owing to smallpox breaking out on boat Regiment quarantined above Nashville till February; then moved to Winchester, Ky., and duty there till March. At Mt. Vernon and Wild Cat engaged in outpost duty till June 1. Moved to Lancaster, thence to Camp Nelson, Ky. Burnside's March over Cumberland Mountains and campaign in East Tennessee August 16-October 17. Carter's Depot September 20-21. Jonesboro September 21. Watauga September 25. Knoxville Campaign November 4-December 23. Siege of Knoxville November 17-December 5. Armstrong's Hill November 25. Longstreet's assault on Fort Saunders November 29. Blain's Cross Roads December 17. Operations about Dandridge January 16-17, 1864. Strawberry Plains January 22. Operations in East Tennessee till April. Moved to Cleveland, Tenn., and Red Clay, Ga. Atlanta (Ga.) Campaign May to September. Demonstrations on Rocky Faced Ridge and Dalton May 8-13. Battle of Resaca May 14-15. Cartersville May 20. Battles about Dallas, New Hope Church and Allatoona Hills May 25-June 5. Near Marietta June 1-9. Operations about Marietta and against Kenesaw Mountain June 10-July 2. Lost Mountain June 15-17. Muddy Creek June 17. Noyes' Creek June 20. Cheyney's Farm June 22. Olley's Creek June 26-27. Assault on Kenesaw June 27. Nickajack Creek July 2-5. Chattahoochie River July 6-17. Isham's Ford, Chattahoochie River, July 8. Decatur July 19. Siege of Atlanta July 22-August 25. Utoy Creek August 5-7. Flank movement on Jonesboro August 25-30. Near Rough and Ready August 31. Battle of Jonesboro August 31-September 1. Lovejoy Station September 2-6. At Decatur till October. Ordered to Lexington, Ky., and duty there till January, 1865. Mustered out January 31, 1865.

Regiment lost during service 2 Officers and 28 Enlisted men killed and mortally wounded and 3 Officers and 174 Enlisted men by disease. Total 207.

25th REGIMENT INFANTRY.

Organized at Calhoun, Ky., January 1, 1862. Attached to 13th Brigade, Army of the Ohio, to December, 1861. 13th Brigade, 5th Division, Army of the Ohio, to February, 1862. 1st Brigade, 3rd Division, Army of the Tennessee, to March, 1862. 3rd Brigade, 4th Division, Army of the Tennessee, to April, 1862.

SERVICE.—Duty at Calhoun, Ky., till February, 1862. Moved to Fort Donelson, Tenn., February 11-13. Investment and capture of Fort Donelson, Tenn., February 13-16. Expedition to Crump's Landing, Tenn., March 14-17. Battle of Shiloh, Tenn., April 6-7. Consolidated with 17th Kentucky Infantry April 13, 1862.

26th REGIMENT INFANTRY.

Organized at Owensboro, Ky., July to November, 1861, and mustered in at Nashville, Tenn., March 5,

1862. Attached to 14th Brigade, Army of Ohio, November, 1861, to December, 1861. 14th Brigade, 5th Division, Army of Ohio, to September, 1862. 14th Brigade, 5th Division, 2nd Corps, Army of Ohio, to November, 1862. 2nd Brigade, 3rd Division, Left Wing 14th Army Corps, Army of the Cumberland, November, 1862. District of Western Kentucky, Dept. of Ohio, to June, 1863. Unattached, 2nd Division, 23rd Army Corps, Army of Ohio, to August, 1863. Unattached, Bowling Green, Ky., 1st Division, 23rd Army Corps, to October, 1863. District of Southwest Kentucky, 1st Division, 23rd Army Corps, to April, 1864. 2nd Brigade, 2nd Division, District of Kentucky, 5th Division, 23rd Army Corps, to December, 1864. 1st Brigade, 2nd Division, 23rd Army Corps, Army of Ohio, to February, 1865, and Dept. of North Carolina to July, 1865.

SERVICE.—Action at Woodbury, Ky., October 29, 1861. Morgantown, Ky., October 31, 1861. Moved from Owensboro to Calhoun, Ky., November, 1861, and duty there till February, 1862. Action at Whippoorwill Creek, Ky., December 1, 1861. Moved to South Carrollton, thence to Calhoun, Owensboro and Nashville, Tenn., February, 1862. March to Savannah, Tenn., March 17-April 6. Battle of Shiloh, Tenn., April 7. Advance on and siege of Corinth, Miss., April 29-May 30. Buell's Campaign in Northern Alabama and Middle Tennessee June to August. March to Nashville, Tenn., thence to Louisville, Ky., in pursuit of Bragg August 21-September 26. Pursuit of Bragg into Kentucky October 1-22. Battle of Perryville, Ky., October 8. Nelson's Cross Roads October 18. March to Nashville, Tenn., October 22-November 7. Ordered to Bowling Green, Ky., November 22, and duty there till January, 1864. Action at Woodbury, Ky., July 5, 1863. Regiment veteranize at Camp Nelson, Ky., January, 1861, and on furlough till March. Duty at Bowling Green, Ky. Mounted and engaged in post duty and scouting from Bowling Green to the Ohio River, and from western part of State to Lexington till December, 1864. Burbridge's Expedition into Southwest Virginia September 20-October 17. Saltsville, Va., October 2. At Bowling Green till December. Ordered to Nashville, Tenn., December 7. Battle of Nashville, Tenn., December 15-16. Pursuit of Hood to the Tennessee River December 17-28. At Clifton, Tenn., till January 15, 1865. Moved to Washington, D. C., thence to Fort Fisher, N. C., January 15-February 12. Fort Anderson February 18-19. Town Creek February 20. Capture of Wilmington February 22. Campaign of the Carolinas March 1-April 26. Advance on Goldsboro March 6-21. Occupation of Goldsboro March 21. Advance on Raleigh April 10-14. Occupation of Raleigh April 14. Bennett's House April 26. Surrender of Johnston and his army. Duty at Saulsbury, N. C., till July. Ordered to Louisville, Ky. Mustered out July 10, 1865.

Regiment lost during service 2 Officers and 27 Enlisted men killed and mortally wounded and 2 Officers and 142 Enlisted men by disease. Total 173.

27th REGIMENT INFANTRY.

Organized at Rochester, Ky., December 16, 1861, to March 21, 1862. Attached to 19th Brigade, 4th Division, Army of Ohio, to September, 1862. 19th Brigade, 4th Division, 2nd Army Corps, Army of Ohio, to November, 1862. 2nd Brigade, 2nd Division, Left Wing 14th Army Corps, Army of the Cumberland, November, 1862. District of Western Kentucky, Dept. of Ohio, to June, 1863. Unattached, 2nd Division, 23rd Army Corps, Army of Ohio, to August, 1863. Unattached, Munfordsville, Ky., 1st Division, 23rd Army Corps, to October, 1863. 1st Brigade, 4th Division, 23rd Army Corps, to November, 1863. 3rd Brigade, 1st Division, Cavalry Corps, Dept. of Ohio, to April, 1864. 3rd Brigade, 4th Division, 23rd Army Corps, to June, 1864. 3rd Brigade, 2nd Division, 23rd Army Corps, to December, 1864. 2nd Division, District of Kentucky and Dept. of Kentucky, to March, 1865.

SERVICE.—At Elizabethtown and Grayson Springs, Ky., till March, 1862. Ordered to Nashville, Tenn., thence march to Savannah, Tenn. Battle of Shiloh, Tenn., April 7. Advance on and siege of Corinth, Miss., April 29-May 30. Occupation of Corinth May 30 and pursuit to Booneville May 31-June 12. Buell's Campaign in Northern Alabama and Middle Tennessee June to August. At Athens, Ala., till July 17, and at Murfreesboro, Tenn., till August 17. March to Louisville, Ky., in pursuit of Bragg August 21-September 26. Pursuit of Bragg into Kentucky October 1-22. Battles of Perryville October 8; Danville October 11. Near Crab Orchard October 15. Big Rockcastle River October 16. March to Nashville, Tenn., October 22-November 7. Ordered to Munfordsville, Ky., November 24, and post duty there and guarding line of the Louisville & Nashville Railroad till September, 1863. Operations against Morgan December 22, 1862, to January 2, 1863. Joined Manson at Glasgow, Ky., and march to Knoxville, Tenn., September, 1863. Burnside's Campaign in East Tennessee October 4-17. Duty at Loudon, Tenn., till November 14. Knoxville Campaign November 4-December 23. Action at Philadelphia October 24. Leiper's Ferry, Holston River, October 26-28. Rockford November 14. Stock Creek and Holston River November 15. Kingston and near Knoxville November 16. Siege of Knoxville November 17-December 5. About Bean's Station December 9-13. Russellville December 10. Bean's Station December 13-15. Rutledge December 16. Blain's Cross Roads December 16-19. Scout to Bean Station December 29-30. Operations about Dandridge January 26-28, 1864. Fair Garden January 27. Ordered to Mt. Sterling, Ky., February, 1864. March to Kingston, Ga., and join Sherman's Army May 23. Atlanta (Ga.) Campaign May 23-September 8. Kingston May 24. Battles about Dallas, New Hope Church and Allatoona Hills May 25-June 5. Operations about Marietta and against Kenesaw Mountain June 10-July 2. Pine Mountain June 11-14. Lost Mountain June 15-17. Muddy Creek June 17. Noyes Creek June 19. Kolb's Farm June 22. Assault on Kenesaw June 27. Nickajack Creek July 2-5. Chattahoochie River July 6-17. Decatur July 19. Howard House July 20. Siege of Atlanta July 22-August 25. Utoy Creek August 5-7. Flank movement on Jonesboro August 25-30. Battle of Jonesboro August 31-September 1. Lovejoy Station September 2-6. Operations against Hood in North Georgia and North Alabama September 29-November 3. Ordered to Kentucky November 14. Duty at Louisville and at Owensboro, Ky., operating against guerrillas till March, 1865. Mustered out March 29, 1865.

Regiment lost during service 1 Officer and 34 Enlisted men killed and mortally wounded and 1 Officer and 181 Enlisted men by disease. Total 217.

28th REGIMENT INFANTRY.

Organized at Louisville and New Haven, Ky., October 10, 1861, to May 9, 1862. Attached to 16th Brigade, Army of Ohio, January-February, 1862. 23rd Independent Brigade, Army of Ohio, to August, 1862. Dumont's Independent Brigade, Army of Ohio, to October, 1862. District of Louisville, Ky., Dept. of Ohio, to November, 1862. Clarksville District, Western Kentucky, Dept. of Ohio, to June, 1863. 1st Brigade, 3rd Division, Reserve Corps, Army of the Cumberland, to October, 1863. Unattached, Dept. of the Cumberland, to April, 1864. 1st Brigade, 2nd Division, 4th Army Corps, Army of the Cumberland, to May, 1864. 2nd Brigade, 2nd Division, 4th Army Corps, to August, 1865. Dept. of Texas to December, 1865.

SERVICE.—Duty at Shepherdsville, Ky., October to December, 1861. Moved to New Haven, Ky., and guard Louisville & Nashville Railroad and Lebanon Branch and at Bowling Green, Ky., and Franklin, Ky., till July, 1862. (A Detachment at Gallatin.) Operations against Morgan July 4-28. Lebanon July 12. Attack on Gallatin August 12 (Cos. "A," "B," "D," "E" and "F"). Guarding railroad and operating against guer-

rillas between Green River and the Cumberland River and Louisville & Nashville Railroad till December, 1862. Munfordsville and Woodsonville, Ky., September 14-17 (Co. "I"). Garrison at Clarksville, Tenn., December, 1862, to August, 1863. Regiment mounted and engaged in scouting about Clarksville with many skirmishes. Ordered to Columbia August 25. Scouting and outpost duty on flanks of the army and about Chattanooga till January, 1864. Action at Railroad Tunnel, near Cowan, October 9, 1863 (Detachment). Reconnoissance toward Dalton, Ga., January 21-23, 1864. Near Dalton January 22. Picketing roads south of Chattanooga toward Lafayette, Resaca and Dalton, Ga., till March. Demonstration on Dalton, Ga., February 22-27. Rocky Faced Ridge and Buzzard's Roost Gap February 23-25. At Pulaski, Tenn., till April. At Lee and Gordon's Mills till April 20. Dismounted April 20 and joined 4th Army Corps. Atlanta (Ga.) Campaign May 1 to September 8. Demonstrations on Rocky Faced Ridge and Dalton May 8-13. Buzzard's Roost Gap May 8-9. Battle of Resaca May 14-15. Adairsville May 17. Near Kingston May 18-19. Near Cassville May 19. Advance on Dallas May 22-25. Operations on line of Pumpkin Vine Creek and battles about Dallas, New Hope Church and Allatoona Hills May 25-June 5. Operations about Marietta and against Kenesaw Mountain June 10-July 2. Pine Hill June 11-14. Lost Mountain June 15-17. Assault on Kenesaw June 27. Ruff's Station or Smyrna Camp Ground July 4. Chattahoochie River July 5-17. Buckhead or Nancy's Creek July 18. Peach Tree Creek July 19-20. Siege of Atlanta July 22-August 25. Flank movement on Jonesboro August 25-30. Battle of Jonesboro August 31-September 1. Lovejoy Station September 2-6. Operations against Hood in North Georgia and North Alabama September 29-November 3. Nashville Campaign November-December. In front of Columbia November 24-27. Spring Hill November 29. Battle of Franklin November 30. Battle of Nashville December 15-16. Pursuit of Hood to the Tennessee River December 17-28. Moved to Huntsville, Ala., and duty there till March, 1865. Expedition to Bull's Gap and operations in East Tennessee March 15-April 22. Moved to Nashville, Tenn., and duty there till June. Moved to New Orleans, La., thence to Texas June and July. Duty at San Antonio and Victoria till December. Mustered out December 14, 1865.

Regiment lost during service 1 Officer and 36 Enlisted men killed and mortally wounded and 1 Officer and 74 Enlisted men by disease. Total 112.

29th REGIMENT INFANTRY.

Regiment failed to complete organization.

30th REGIMENT MOUNTED INFANTRY.

Organized at Somerset and Frankfort, Ky. Companies "A," "B," "E" and "F" mustered in at Frankfort February 19, 1864; Company "G" March 29, 1864, and Companies "C," "D," "H," "I" and "K" at Camp Burnside, Ky., April 5, 1864. Attached to 4th Brigade, 1st Division, District of Kentucky, 5th Division, 23rd Army Corps, Dept. of the Ohio, to August, 1864. 2nd Brigade, 1st Division, District of Kentucky, Dept. of Ohio, to April, 1865.

SERVICE.—Operating against guerrillas in Kentucky till April, 1865. Action at Lexington, Ky., June 10, 1864. Cynthiana June 12. Sibley County, Ky., September 3. Burbridge's Expedition to Southwest Virginia September 20-October 17. Laurel Creek Gap and Clinch Mountain October 1. Saltsville, Va., October 2. Kingsport, Tenn., October 6. Ordered to Paris, Ky., October 25. Owen County, Ky., November 15. Stoneman's Expedition to Southwest Virginia December 10-29. Brush Creek, Tenn., December 12. Kingsport, Tenn., December 13. Marion, Va., December 17-18. New Market December 18. Saltsville December 20-21. At Louisa, Ky., December 31. At Camp Nelson, Ky., January 6, 1865. Duty in Green, Taylor and Barron Counties operating against guerrillas till April. Action at

Charleston January 30. Bradfordsville February 8. Mustered out April 18, 1865.

Regiment lost during service 2 Officers and 21 Enlisted men killed and mortally wounded and 71 Enlisted men by disease. Total 94.

31st REGIMENT INFANTRY.

Regiment failed to complete organization.

32nd REGIMENT INFANTRY.

Organized at Frankfort and Camp Burnside, Ky., August, 1862. Attached to District of Western Kentucky, Dept. of Ohio, to April, 1863. 2nd Brigade, District of Western Kentucky, Dept. of Ohio, to June, 1863. 1st Brigade, 1st Division, 23rd Army Corps, Army of Ohio, to August, 1863.

SERVICE.—Engaged in guard and scouting duty at various points in District of Western Kentucky, principally at Hopkinsville, Camp Burnside, Danville, Lexington, Somerset, Stanford and Lebanon. A part of the Regiment participated in the defence of Kentucky against Bragg's invasion and subsequent pursuit, being present at the battle of Perryville, Ky., October 8, 1862, with Garrard's Detachment. Mustered out May 28 to August 12, 1863.

Regiment lost during service 1 Officer and 42 Enlisted men by disease. Total 43.

33rd REGIMENT INFANTRY.

Organized at Munfordsville, Ky., September 13, 1862. Attached to District of Western Kentucky, Dept. of the Ohio, to April, 1863. 2nd Brigade, District of Central Kentucky, Dept. of Ohio, to June, 1863. Unattached, Munfordsville, Ky., 1st Division, 23rd Army Corps, Army of Ohio, to August, 1863. Unattached, 2nd Division, 23rd Army Corps, to October, 1863. District of South Central Kentucky, 1st Division, 23rd Army Corps, to January, 1864. District of Southwest Kentucky, Dept. of Ohio, to April, 1864.

SERVICE.—Companies "C" and "G" participated in the siege of Munfordsville, Ky., and Woodsonville, Ky., September 13-17, 1862, and captured. Regiment on duty at Munfordsville, Ky., and on line of the Louisville & Nashville Railroad and Lebanon Branch Railroad till April, 1864. Consolidated with 26th Kentucky Infantry April 1, 1864.

Regiment lost during service 22 by disease.

34th REGIMENT INFANTRY.

Organized at Louisville, Ky., October, 1862, from Louisville Provost Guard. Attached to District of Western Kentucky, Dept. of the Ohio, to June, 1863. Unattached, Bowling Green, Ky., 2nd Division, 23rd' Army Corps, Dept. of Ohio, to October, 1863. District of South Central Kentucky, 1st Division, 23rd Army Corps, to October, 1863. Left Wing Forces, Cumberland Gap, to January, 1864. District of the Clinch, Dept. of Ohio, to April, 1864. 1st Brigade, 4th Division, 23rd Army Corps, to December, 1864. 2nd Brigade, 4th Division, 23rd Army Corps, to January, 1865. 1st Brigade, 4th Division, 23rd Army Corps, to February, 1865. 1st Brigade, 4th Division, District of East Tennessee, Dept. of the Cumberland, to March, 1865. 2nd Brigade, 4th Division, District of East Tennessee, to June, 1865.

SERVICE.—Provost Guard duty at Louisville, Ky., till May 8, 1863. (Co. "K" at Munfordsville, Ky., September 14-17, 1862.) Ordered to Bowling Green, Ky., May 8, 1863, and duty there till July 1. Moved to Glasgow, Ky., July 1, and operations against Morgan July 1-26. Garrison duty at Glasgow, Ky., till September 28. March to Knoxville, Tenn., thence to Morristown September 28-October 6. Action at Blue Springs October 10. At Morristown till December 5. Moved to Tazewell, Tenn., December 5, and duty there till January 26, 1864. Attack on Tazewell January 24. Moved to Cumberland Gap and duty there till November 8. Powell River Bridge February 22, 1864 (Cos. "A" and "D"). Moved to Knoxville November 8-18, and provost duty there till February 2, 1865. At Cum-

berland Gap till April 24. Expedition to Gibson's Mills April 20-22. Received surrender of Colonels Pridemore, Slump, Richmond and Wicher and their commands (2,713 men). Ordered to Knoxville April 24, thence to Loudon, Tenn., and garrison duty there till June 20. Mustered out at Knoxville, Tenn., June 24, 1865.

Regiment lost during service 3 Enlisted men killed and 2 Officers and 64 Enlisted men by disease. Total 69.

35th REGIMENT INFANTRY.

Organized at Owensboro, Ky., September 26, 1863. Mustered in October 20, 1863. Attached to District of Southwest Kentucky, Dept. of the Ohio, to April, 1864. 2nd Brigade, 2nd Division, District of Kentucky, 5th Division, 23rd Army Corps, Dept. of Ohio, to July, 1864. 1st Brigade, 1st Division, District of Kentucky, 5th Division, 23rd Army Corps. to December, 1864.

SERVICE.—March to Henderson, Ky., October 10, 1863; thence to Hopkinsville, Ky., and duty guarding country between Green and Cumberland Rivers from guerrillas till August, 1864. Saylersville, Ky., November 30, 1863. Greenville, Ky., December 3, 1863. Scout in Meade and Breckenridge Counties May 5, 1864 (Co. "B"). Morganfield May 6 and June 25. Slaughtersville July. Scout to Big Springs July 13-15 (Detachment). Operations in Webster and Union Counties July 14-18. Pursuit of Adam Johnson's forces August, 1864 (Co. "A"). Canton and Roaring Springs August 22. Burbridge's Expedition into Southwest Virginia September 20-October 17. Action at Saltsville, Va., October 2. At Lexington, Ky., till November 5. Ordered to Louisville November 5, and mustered out December 29, 1864.

Regiment lost during service 8 Enlisted men killed and mortally wounded and 49 Enlisted men by disease. Total 57.

36th REGIMENT INFANTRY.

Regiment failed to complete organization.

37th REGIMENT MOUNTED INFANTRY.

Organized at Glasgow, Ky., September 17 to December 22, 1863. Attached to District of South Central Kentucky, 1st Division, 23rd Army Corps, Dept. of Ohio, to January, 1864. District of Southwest Kentucky, 1st Division, 23rd Army Corps, to April, 1864. 3rd Brigade, 1st Division, District of Kentucky, 5th Division, 23rd Army Corps, Dept. of Ohio, to December, 1864.

SERVICE.—Duty at Glasgow, Ky., and in District of South Central Kentucky, operating against guerrillas and protecting public property till March, 1864. Attack on Camp at Glasgow October 6, 1863. Moved to Columbia March, 1864. Operations against Morgan May 31-June 20. Mt. Sterling, Ky., June 9. Cynthiana June 12. Operations in Eastern Kentucky till September. Bettier's Gap August 23. Burbridge's Expedition into Southwest Virginia September 20-October 17. McCormick's Gap September 20. Saltsville, Va., October 2. Bloomfield November 5. Owen County November 15. Mustered out December 29, 1864.

Regiment lost during service 8 Enlisted men killed and mortally wounded and 98 Enlisted men by disease. Total 106.

38th REGIMENT INFANTRY.

Regiment failed to complete organization.

39th REGIMENT INFANTRY.

Organized at Peach Orchard, Ky., November 18, 1862, and mustered in February 16, 1863. Attached to District of Eastern Kentucky, Dept. of Ohio, to June, 1863. 1st Brigade, 4th Division, 23rd Army Corps, Dept. of Ohio, to August, 1863. District of Eastern Kentucky, 1st Division, 23rd Army Corps, to April, 1864. 1st Brigade, 1st Division, District of Kentucky, 5th Division, 23rd Army Corps, to July, 1864. 3rd Brigade, 1st Division, District of Kentucky, to December, 1864. Louisa (Ky.) District and Dept. of Kentucky, to September, 1865.

SERVICE.—Action near Piketon, Ky., November 5, 1862. Wireman's Shoals, Big Sandy River, December 4. Skirmishes in Floyd County December 4 and near Prestonburg December 4-5. Near Prestonburg December 31. Near Louisa, Ky., March 25-26, 1863. Piketon April 13 and 15. Beaver Creek, Floyd County, June 27. Mouth of Coal Run, Pike County, July 2. Expedition from Beaver Creek into Southwest Virginia July 3-11. Pond Creek July 6. Clark's Neck and Carter County August 27. Marrowbone Creek September 22. Terman's Ferry January 9, 1864. Laurel Creek, W. Va., February 12. Operations in Eastern Kentucky March 28-April 16. Forks of Beaver March 31. Brushy Creek April 7. Paintsville April 13. Half Mountain, Magoffin County, April 14. Saylersville April 16. Expedition from Louisa to Rockhouse Creek May 9-13 (Co. "B"). Pond Creek, Pike County, May 16. Pike County May 18. Operations against Morgan May 31-June 20. Mt. Sterling June 9. Cynthiana June 12. Burbridge's Expedition into Southwest Virginia September 20-October 17. Saltsville October 2. Stoneman's Expedition into Southwest Virginia December 10-29. Bristol, Tenn., December 13. Abington, Va., December 15. Near Marion, Va., December 17-18. Saltsville, Va., December 20-21. Capture and destruction of salt works. Duty in the Sandy Valley and in Eastern Kentucky guarding and protecting the country till September, 1865. Mustered out September 15, 1865.

Regiment lost during service 3 Officers and 24 Enlisted men killed and mortally wounded and 3 Officers and 194 Enlisted men by disease. Total 234.

40th REGIMENT INFANTRY.

Organized at Grayson and Falmouth, Ky., July 30, 1863. Attached to District of North Central Kentucky, 1st Division, 23rd Army Corps, Dept. of Ohio, to April, 1864. 1st Brigade, 2nd Division, District of Kentucky, 5th Division, 23rd Army Corps, Dept. of Ohio, to July, 1864. 1st Brigade, 1st Division, District of Kentucky, to December, 1864.

SERVICE.—Scout duty in North Central Kentucky till December, 1863. Actions at Mt. Sterling December 3 and 10, 1863. Scouting in Eastern Kentucky till May, 1864. Near Paintsville, Ky., April 14, 1864. Operations against Morgan May 31-June 20. Mt. Sterling June 9. Cynthiana June 12. Duty in Eastern Kentucky till September. Near New Haven August 2 (Co. "C"). Canton and Roaring Springs August 22. Burbridge's Expedition to Southwest Virginia September 10-October 17. Action at Saltsville, Va., October 2. Duty in Eastern Kentucky till December. Mustered out December 30, 1864.

Regiment lost during service 9 Enlisted men killed and mortally wounded and 2 Officers and 91 Enlisted men by disease. Total 102.

41st REGIMENT INFANTRY.

Regiment failed to complete organization.

42nd REGIMENT INFANTRY.

Regiment failed to complete organization.

43rd REGIMENT INFANTRY.

Regiment failed to complete organization.

44th REGIMENT INFANTRY.

Regiment failed to complete organization.

45th REGIMENT MOUNTED INFANTRY.

Organized at large October 10, 1863. Attached to District of North Central Kentucky, 1st Division, 23rd Army Corps, Dept. of Ohio, to January, 1864. District of Southwest Kentucky, 1st Division, 23rd Army Corps, to April, 1864. 4th Brigade, 1st Division, District of Kentucky, 5th Division, 23rd Army Corps, Dept. of Ohio, to July, 1864. 2nd Brigade, 1st Division, District of Kentucky, to January, 1865. Unattached, District of Kentucky, February, 1865.

SERVICE.—First organized as a Battalion for service in Eastern Counties of Kentucky and on the Virginia border, and so served till October, 1863. At Mt. Sterling, Ky., and cover front from Cumberland Gap to Louisa till March, 1864. Action at Saylersville, Ky., November 30, 1863. Moved to Flemmingsburg March, 1864; thence to Irvine, Ky., and operating south of that point till July. Pound Gap April 19 (Detachment). Troublesome Creek April 27. Morganfield May 5. Operations against Morgan May 31-June 20. Near Pound Gap June 1. Mt. Sterling June 9. Cynthiana June 12. Operations against guerrillas in Owens and Trimble Counties July and August. Burbridge's Expedition into Southwest Virginia September 20-October 17. Action at Saltsville October 2. Stoneman's Raid into Southwest Virginia December 10-29. Briston, Va., December 13. Abington, Va., December 15. Near Marion December 17-18. Saltsville December 20-21. Capture and destruction of salt works. Mustered out Companies "A," "B," "C," "D," "E" and "F" December 24, 1864, and Companies "G," "H," "I" and "K" February 14, 1865.

Regiment lost during service 10 Enlisted men killed and mortally wounded and 1 Officer and 102 Enlisted men by disease. Total 113.

46th REGIMENT INFANTRY.

Regiment failed to complete organization.

47th REGIMENT MOUNTED INFANTRY.

Organized at Irvine and Camp Nelson, Ky., October 5, 1863, to January, 1864. Attached to District of North Central Kentucky, 1st Division, 23rd Army Corps, Dept. of Ohio, to January, 1864. District of Southwest Kentucky, 1st Division, 23rd Army Corps, to April, 1864. 4th Brigade, 1st Division, District of Kentucky, 5th Division, 23rd Army Corps, to July, 1864. Camp Nelson (Ky.) District and Dept. of Kentucky to April, 1865.

SERVICE.—Scout and patrol duty in Eastern Kentucky till June, 1864. Operations against Morgan May 31-June 20. Mt. Sterling, Ky., June 9. Keller's Bridge, near Cynthiana, June 11. Cynthiana June 12. Duty at Camp Nelson, Ky., and on line of Kentucky Central Railroad till April, 1865. Mustered out Companies "A" to "H" at Lexington, Ky., December 26, 1864, and Companies "I" and "K" April 12, 1865.

Regiment lost while in service 1 Enlisted man killed and 4 Officers and 68 Enlisted men by disease. Total 73.

48th REGIMENT MOUNTED INFANTRY.

Organized at Princeton, Ky., October 26, 1863. Attached to District of Southwest Kentucky, 1st Division, 23rd Army Corps, Dept. of Ohio, to April, 1864. 1st Brigade, 2nd Division, District of Kentucky, 5th Division, 23rd Army Corps, Dept. of Ohio, to December, 1864.

SERVICE.—Duty at Princeton, Ky., till December 1, 1863. Moved to Russellsville December 1 and duty there (Cos. "B," "F," "G" and "H") and at Bowling Green, Ky. (Cos. "A," "D," "I" and "K"), till April 6, 1864. Guard duty on line of Louisville & Nashville Railroad from Cave City to Louisville, Ky. Company "A" at Elizabethtown; Companies "B," "F" and "H" and headquarters at Munfordsville; Companies "C" and "K" at Fort Boyle, Colesburg; Company "D" at Cave City; Company "E" at Shepherdsville; Company "I" at Louisville, and Company "G" at Smithland till July 8, 1864. Action at Salem August 8 (Detachments from Companies "B" and "C"). Regiment relieved and mounted. Moved to Calhoun August 13-19 and join Hobson's operations against Adam Johnson August 19-24. Canton, Ky., August 24. Moved to Cadiz, thence to Princeton, Ky., and operating against guerrillas in Counties bordering on the Cumberland River till December 1. Skirmish in Union County August 31 (Detachment). Weston September 14. Action with Lyon's forces November 6 (Detachment Cos. "F" and "K"). Eddyville October 17. Providence November 21. Mustered out December 19, 1864.

Regiment lost during service 7 Enlisted men killed and mortally wounded and 1 Officer and 96 Enlisted men by disease. Total 104.

49th REGIMENT MOUNTED INFANTRY.

Organized at Camp Nelson, Ky., September 19, 1863. Attached to District of Somerset, Ky., 1st Division, 23rd Army Corps, Dept. of Ohio, to January, 1864. District of Southwest Kentucky, 1st Division, 23rd Army Corps, to April, 1864. 4th Brigade, 1st Division, District of Kentucky, 5th Division, 23rd Army Corps, Dept. of Ohio, to July, 1864. Camp Nelson, District of Kentucky, to December, 1864.

SERVICE.—Moved to Somerset, Ky., October 28, 1863, and duty in that vicinity till January, 1864. Moved to Camp Burnside, Ky., January 3-4, and duty there till August, 1864. At Lexington August and at Camp Nelson till October. Ordered to Tennessee October 1 and railroad guard duty near Murfreesboro and between Wartrace and Mill Creek till November. At Lexington, Ky., till December. Mustered out December 26, 1864.

Regiment lost during service 1 Enlisted man killed and 1 Officer and 74 Enlisted men by disease. Total 76.

50th REGIMENT INFANTRY.

Regiment failed to complete organization.

51st REGIMENT INFANTRY.

Regiment failed to complete organization.

52nd REGIMENT MOUNTED INFANTRY.

Organized at Franklin and Scottsville, Ky. Companies "A," "B," "C" and "E" mustered in at Scottsville October 16, 1863; Company "D" October 17, 1863; Company "F" November 12, 1863, and Company "G" December 21, 1863. Companies "H," "I" and "K" mustered in at Franklin March 3, 1864. Attached to 3rd Brigade, 1st Division, District of Kentucky, Dept. Ohio, to July, 1864. 2nd Brigade, 2nd Division, District of Kentucky, Dept. Ohio, to October, 1864. 1st Brigade, 2nd Division, District of Kentucky, 5th Division, 23rd Army Corps, Dept. Ohio, to January, 1865.

SERVICE.—Operations against guerrillas in Southern and Central Kentucky, guarding and protecting public property, and protecting lines of communication with the army operating at the front till March, 1864. Operations against Forest's Raid into Kentucky March 23-April 19, and against Morgan in Eastern Kentucky May 31-June 20. Action at New Hope March 28. Mt. Sterling June 9. Cynthiana June 12. Operations in Western Kentucky July-August. Action at Bell Mines July 13. Operations in Webster and Union counties July 14-18. Morganfield July 14. Geiger's Lake July 15. Operations against Adam Johnson about Uniontown August. Grubb's Cross Roads August 21. Canton and Roaring Springs August 22. Moved to Lexington August 27, thence to Bowling Green August 30, and to Nashville, Tenn. Scottsville December 8 (1 Co.). Mustered out January 17, 1865.

Regiment lost during service 1 Officer and 10 Enlisted men killed and mortally wounded and 48 Enlisted men by disease. Total 59.

53rd REGIMENT MOUNTED INFANTRY.

Organized at Covington, Ky., September, 1864. Attached to Military District of Kentucky, Dept. Ohio, and Dept. of Kentucky, to September, 1865.

SERVICE.—Guard Kentucky Central Railroad between Lexington and Cincinnati. Scouting in Central Kentucky and operating against guerrillas till November, 1864. Moved to Crab Orchard, Ky., November 24, and joined General Stoneman. Stoneman's Raid into Southwest Virginia December 10-29. Near Marion, Va., December 17-18. Saltsville, Va., December 20-21. Capture and destruction of salt works. Operating against guerrillas at various points in Kentucky by detachments till September, 1865. Mustered out September 17, 1865.

Regiment lost during service 1 Officer and 8 Enlisted men killed and mortally wounded and 40 Enlisted men by disease. Total 49.

54th REGIMENT MOUNTED INFANTRY.

Organized at New Castle, Ky., September, 1864. Attached to Military District of Kentucky and Dept. of Kentucky, to September, 1865.

SERVICE.—Operating against guerrillas in Henry County, Ky., till December, 1864. Stoneman's Raid into Southwest Virginia December 10-29. Near Marion, Va., December 17-18. Saltsville, Va., December 20-21. Capture and destruction of salt works. Provost duty in country about Lexington, Ky., and operating against guerrillas till September, 1865. Mustered out September 1, 1865.

Regiment lost during service 1 Enlisted man killed and 29 Enlisted men by disease. Total 30.

55th REGIMENT MOUNTED INFANTRY.

Organized at Covington November, 1864. Attached to Military District of Kentucky, Dept. Ohio and Dept. of Kentucky, to September, 1865. Regiment mounted and assigned to duty in counties bordering on the Kentucky Central Railroad till December, 1864. Stoneman's Raid into Southwest Virginia December 10-29. Near Marion December 17-18. Saltsville December 20-21. Capture and destruction of salt works. Operating against guerrillas in counties west of the Kentucky Central Railroad and the Counties of Campbell, Bracken, Mason, Fleming, Nicholas, Harrison and Pendleton, east of the Kentucky Central Railroad till September, 1865. Mustered out September 19, 1865.

Regiment lost during service 7 Enlisted men killed and mortally wounded and 2 Officers and 29 Enlisted men by disease. Total 38.

LOUISIANA VOLUNTEERS.

1st REGIMENT CAVALRY.

Organized at New Orleans, La., August, 1862. Attached to Weitzel's Reserve Brigade, Dept. of the Gulf, to January, 1863. Unassigned, 1st Division, 19th Army Corps, Dept. Gulf, to May, 1863. Cavalry Command, 19th Army Corps, to August, 1863. Defences of New Orleans, La., to September, 1863. 1st Brigade, Cavalry Division, Dept. Gulf, to January, 1864. 3rd Brigade, Cavalry Division, Dept. Gulf, to July, 1864. Separate Cavalry Brigade, 19th Army Corps, Dept. Gulf, to August, 1864. Morganza, La., to December, 1864. Separate Cavalry Brigade, Reserve Corps, Military Division West Mississippi, to February, 1865. Separate Cavalry Brigade, District West Florida, to March, 1865. 1st Brigade, Lucas' Cavalry Division, Steele's Command, Military Division West Mississippi, to April, 1865. 3rd Brigade, Cavalry Division, Dept. Gulf, to July, 1865. Dept. of the Gulf to December, 1865.

SERVICE—Duty in the Defences of New Orleans, La., till October, 1862. Operations in District of La Fourche October 24-November 6. Capture of Donaldsonville October 25. Georgia Landing, near Labadieville, October 27. Engagement on Bayou Teche and capture of Gunboat "Cotton" January 14, 1863. Skirmish at Indian Village January 28. Operations on Bayou Plaquemine and the Atchafalaya River February 12-28. Operations against Port Hudson March 7-27. Skirmish, Brashear City, March 18. Operations in Western Louisiana April 9-May 4. Teche Campaign April 10-20. Pattersonville April 11. Fort Bisland, Bayou Teche, April 12-13. Porter's and McWilliams' Plantations, Indian Bend, April 13. Irish Bend April 14. Jeanerette April 14. Vermillion Bayou April 17. Expedition to Breaux Bridge and Opelousas April 17-21. Occupation of Opelousas and Washington April 20. Expedition from Opelousas to Barre Landing April 21-26 (Co. "F"). Skirmishes at Bayou Boeuf and near Washington April 22 (Co. "F"). Near Washington May 1. Reconnoissance from Baton Rouge May 2 (1 Co.). Scouts from Merritt's Plantation on Clinton Road May 14. Boyce's Bridge, Cotile Landing, May 14. Advance on Port Hudson May 16-24. Operations about Merritt's Plantation and on Bayou Sara Road May 18-19. Near Cheyneyville May 18 and 20. Plain's Store May 21. Siege of Port Hudson May

24-July 9. Assault on Port Hudson May 27. Expedition to Clinton June 3-8. Pretty Creek, near Clinton, June 3. La Fourche Crossing June 20-21. Surrender of Port Hudson July 9. Engagement, Bayou La Fourche, near Donaldsonville, July 12-13. Moved to Thibodeaux August 2. Affair at Thibodeaux August 29-30. Western Louisiana Campaign October 3-November 30. Bayou Vermillion October 9-10. Grand Coteau October 16 and 19. Washington October 24 and 31. Opelousas October 30. Bayou Bourbeaux, Buzzard's Prairie, near Grand Coteau, November 2. Carrion Crow Bayou November 3. Vermillion Bayou November 8. Camp Pratt November 20. At New Iberia till December and at New Orleans and Franklin till March, 1864. Red River Campaign March 10-May 22. Marksville Prairie March 15. Monett's Ferry, Cloutiersville, March 29-30. Natchitoches March 31. Crump's Plantation April 2. Wilson's Farm, near Pleasant Hill, April 7. Sabine Cross Roads April 8. Pleasant Hill April 9. Grand Ecore April 16. About Cloutiersville and Cane River Crossing April 22-24. At Alexandria April 27-May 13. Retreat to Morganza April 13-20. Avoyelle's Prairie May 15. Mansura May 16. Yellow Bayou May 18-19. Expedition from Morganza to the Atchafalaya May 30-June 5. Livonia May 30. Duty at Morganza till November. (A detachment there till January, 1865.) Expedition to Clinton August 23-29. Olive Branch and Comite River August 25. Operations about Morganza September 16-25. Williamsport September 16. Moved to Baton Rouge November 19 and duty there till January, 1865. (Co. "K" detached in District of La Fourche till May, 1865. Expedition from Thibodeaux to Lake Veret and Bayou Planton January 30-31, 1865 (Co. "K"). Lake Veret January 30 (Co. "K"). Expedition to Lake Veret February 10-13 (Co. "K"). Scout from Bayou Boeuf to Bayou Chemise March 24. Expedition from Bayou Boeuf and Thibodeaux to Lake Veret, Grand Bayou and the Park April 2-10 (Co. "K"). Grand Bayou May 4. Expedition from Bayou Boeuf to Bayou De Large May 25-27.) Regiment, Davidson's Expedition from Baton Rouge against Mobile & Ohio Railroad November 27-December 13. Expedition from Morganza to Morgan's Ferry December 13-14 (Detachment). Moved to Barrancas, Fla., February, 1865. Campaign against Mobile, Ala., and its defences March 18-April 9. March from Pensacola to Blakely, Ala., March 20-April 1. College Hill, Fla., March 21. Pine Barren Creek March 23. Canoe Creek March 25. Mitchell's Creek March 25. Pollard, Ala., March 26. Siege of Fort Blakely April 1-9. Expedition from Blakely to Claiborne April 9-17. Near Mt. Pleasant April 11. Duty in District of Alabama and in Dept. of the Gulf till December, 1865. Mustered out December 18, 1865.

2nd REGIMENT CAVALRY.

Organized at New Orleans, La., November 25, 1863, as 3rd Louisiana Infantry. Attached to Defences of New Orleans, Dept. of the Gulf.

SERVICE— Duty in the Defences of New Orleans, La., at Brashear City, Baton Rouge and Port Hudson, La., till September, 1864. Skirmish at Spanish Hill, La., April 2, 1864. Bayou Boeuf May 7. Wilson's Landing May 14. Expedition to Clinton August 23-29. Skirmishes at Olive Branch, Comite River and Clinton August 25. Consolidated with 1st Louisiana Cavalry September 7, 1864.

1st REGIMENT HEAVY ARTILLERY (AFRICAN DESCENT).

Organized at New Orleans, La., November 29, 1862. Attached to Defences of New Orleans and duty as Garrison Artillery till November, 1863. Designation of Regiment changed to 1st Corps de Afrique Heavy Artillery November 19, 1863, which see.

1st BATTERY LIGHT ARTILLERY (AFRICAN DESCENT).

Organized at Hebron's Plantation, Miss., November 6, 1863. Attached to 1st Brigade, U. S. Colored Troops, District of Vicksburg, to April, 1864. On duty at Good-

rich Landing and Vicksburg till April, 1864. Designation of Battery changed to Battery "C," 2nd U. S. Colored Light Artillery, April 26, 1864, which see.

2nd BATTERY LIGHT ARTILLERY (AFRICAN DESCENT).

Organized at Black River Bridge, Miss., December 21, 1863. Attached to Post of Vicksburg, Miss., District of Vicksburg, to March, 1864. Post Goodrich Landing, District of Vicksburg, to April, 1864. Designation of Battery changed to Battery "D," 2nd U. S. Colored Light Artillery, April 26, 1864, which see.

3rd BATTERY LIGHT ARTILLERY (AFRICAN DESCENT).

Organized at Helena, Ark., December 1, 1863. Attached to District of Eastern Arkansas, 7th Army Corps, Dept. of Arkansas, and duty at Helena, Ark., till April, 1864. Designation of Battery changed to Battery "E," 2nd U. S. Colored Light Artillery, April 26, 1864, which see.

1st REGIMENT INFANTRY.

Organized at New Orleans, La., July 30, 1862. Attached to Weitzel's Reserve Brigade, Dept. of the Gulf, to January, 1863. Grover's Division, 19th Army Corps, Dept. of the Gulf, January, 1863. 2nd Brigade, 1st Division, 19th Army Corps, to March, 1863. 1st Brigade, 4th Division, 19th Army Corps, to August, 1863. 2nd Brigade, 4th Division, 19th Army Corps, to October, 1863. District of La Fourche to February, 1864. 2nd Brigade, 2nd Division, 19th Army Corps, to June, 1864. District of La Fourche, Dept. Gulf, to August, 1864. 2nd Brigade, 2nd Division, 19th Army Corps, Dept. Gulf, to November, 1864. District of La Fourche to July, 1865.

SERVICE—Duty in the Defences of New Orleans and District of La Fourche till January, 1863, and at Baton Rouge till March. Operations against Port Hudson March 7-27. Moved to Donaldsonville March 26, thence to Brashear City. Operations in Western Louisiana April 9-May 14. Teche Campaign April 11-20. Porter's and McWilliams' Plantations, Indian Bend, April 13. Irish Bend April 14. Moved to Franklin April 15. Bayou Vermillion April 17. Expedition to Breux Bridge and Opelousas April 17-21. Moved to New Iberia April 25; to Washington May 6, thence to Brashear City May 11-27, and to Port Hudson May 28. Siege of Port Hudson May 30-July 9. Surrender of Port Hudson July 9. Cox's Plantation, near Donaldsonville, Bayou La Fourche, July 12-13. Duty at Donaldsonville and in District of La Fourche till March, 1864. Red River Campaign March 25-May 22. Monett's Bluff, Cane River Crossing, April 23. At Alexandria April 27-May 13. Construction of dam at Alexandria April 30-May 10. Retreat to Morganza April 13-20. Mansura May 16. At Morganza till June. Expedition to the Atchafalaya May 30-June 5. Livonia May 31. In District of La Fourche till September. Ordered to Morganza September 2, and duty there till February, 1865. At Donaldsonville and in the District of La Fourche till July. Mustered out July 12, 1865.

1st REGIMENT NEW ORLEANS INFANTRY.

Organized at New Orleans, La., March 6, 1864. Attached to Defences of New Orleans to April, 1865. District of La Fourche and Dept. of the Gulf to May, 1866.

SERVICE—Garrison and guard duty in the Defences of New Orleans and in District of La Fourche, Dept. of the Gulf, entire term. Mustered out May, 1866.

2nd REGIMENT INFANTRY.

Organized at New Orleans, La., September 29, 1862. Attached to Grover's Division, Dept. of the Gulf, to January, 1863. 3rd Brigade, 1st Division, 19th Army Corps, Dept. Gulf, to May, 1863. 1st Brigade, 1st Division, 19th Army Corps, to July, 1863. District of Baton Rouge, La., to September, 1863. Unattached, Cavalry Division, Dept. Gulf, to November, 1863. 3rd Brigade, Cavalry Division, Dept. of the Gulf, to January, 1864. 1st Brigade, Cavalry Division, Dept. Gulf, to August, 1864. District of Port Hudson, La., to September, 1864. District of Baton Rouge, La., to April, 1865. Provisional Brigade, District of Baton Rouge, La., Dept. Gulf, to September, 1865.

SERVICE.—Duty in the Defences of New Orleans, La., till January, 1863. Moved to Baton Rouge, La., January 13-14, and duty there till May. Reconnoissance to False River March 19. Reconnoissance from Baton Rouge May 13. Advance on Port Hudson May 14-24. Operations about Monett's Plantation and on Bayou Sara Road May 18-19. Action at Plain's Store May 21. Siege of Port Hudson May 24-July 9. Assaults on Port Hudson May 27 and June 14. Surrender of Port Hudson July 9. Cox's Plantation, Donaldsonville, July 12-13. Moved to Baton Rouge and duty there till September 2. Sabine Pass Expedition September 2-11. Regiment mounted September, 1863. Western Louisiana Campaign October 3-November 30. Washington October 24 and 31. Bayou Bourbeaux November 3. Grand Coteau, Carrion Crow Bayou, November 3. Vermillion Bayou November 12. Camp Pratt November 20. Bayou Portage November 23. At New Iberia till December and at New Orleans and Franklin till March, 1864. Expedition to Madisonville January 3 (Co. "D"). Red River Campaign March 14-May 20. Advance from Franklin to Alexandria March 14-26. Bayou Rapides March 20. Henderson's Hill March 21. Monett's Ferry and Cloutiersville March 29-30. Natchitoches March 31. Crump's Hill April 2. Wilson's Plantation near Pleasant Hill April 7. Sabine Cross Roads April 8. Pleasant Hill April 9. Grand Ecore April 16. Natchitoches April 22. About Cloutiersville and Cane River Crossing April 22-24. At Alexandria April 28-May 13. Retreat to Morganza April 13-20. Avoyelle's Prairie and Mansura May 15-16. Yellow Bayou May 18-19. At Morganza till June. At New Orleans till August. At Baton Rouge till July, 1865, and at New Orleans till September. Mustered out September 11, 1865.

2nd REGIMENT NEW ORLEANS INFANTRY.

Organization not completed. Duty in the Defences of New Orleans, La., till August, 1864. Operations in Calcasseu Pass May 6-10, 1864. Disbanded August 4, 1864, and transferred to 1st New Orleans Infantry.

1st REGIMENT NATIVE GUARD INFANTRY.

Organized at New Orleans, La., September 27, 1862. Attached to Defences of New Orleans, Dept. of the Gulf, to December, 1862. Independent Command, Dept. of the Gulf, to January, 1863. Unattached, 1st Division, 19th Army Corps, Dept. of the Gulf, to June, 1863.

SERVICE.—Operations in La Fourche District October 24-November 6, 1862. Capture of Donaldsonville October 25. Action at Georgia Landing near Labadieville October 27. Duty at Baton Rouge and in the District of La Fourche till May, 1863. Advance on Port Hudson May 20-24. Siege of Port Hudson May 24-July 9. Assaults on Port Hudson May 27 and June 14. Designation of Regiment changed to 1st Corps de Afrique June 6, 1863, which see.

2nd REGIMENT NATIVE GUARD INFANTRY.

Organized at New Orleans, La., October 19, 1862. Attached to Defences of New Orleans to December, 1862. Independent Command, Dept. Gulf, to January, 1863. Defences of New Orleans to June, 1863.

SERVICE.—Operations in La Fourche District October 24-November 6, 1862. Capture of Donaldsonville October 25. Georgia Landing near Labadieville October 27. Duty in La Fourche District and Defences of New Orleans till January, 1863. Garrison at Ship Island, Miss., January 9 to June, 1863. East Pascagouga, Miss., April 9, 1863. Designation of Regiment changed to 2nd Regiment, Corps de Afrique, June 6, 1863, which see.

3rd REGIMENT NATIVE GUARD INFANTRY.

Organized at New Orleans, La., November 24, 1862. Attached to Independent Command, Dept. of the Gulf,

to January, 1863. Unattached, 1st Division, 19th Army Corps, Dept. of the Gulf, to June, 1863.

SERVICE.—Duty in the Defences of New Orleans and District of La Fourche till May, 1863. Advance on Port Hudson May 20-24. Siege of Port Hudson May 24-July 9. Assaults on Port Hudson May 27 and June 14. Designation of Regiment changed to 3rd Regiment, Corps de Afrique, June 6, 1863, which see.

4th REGIMENT NATIVE GUARD INFANTRY.

Organized at New Orleans, La., February 10, 1863. Attached to 1st Division, 19th Army Corps, Dept. Gulf, to June, 1863.

SERVICE.—Duty in the Defences of New Orleans, La., till March, 1863, and at Baton Rouge, La., till May. Siege of Port Hudson May 24-July 9. Assaults on Port Hudson May 27, and June 14. Designation of Regiment changed to 4th Regiment, Corps de Afrique, June 6, 1863.

5th REGIMENT INFANTRY (AFRICAN DESCENT).

Failed to complete organization.

6th REGIMENT INFANTRY (AFRICAN DESCENT).

Organized at New Orleans, La., for 60 days, July 4, 1863. Duty at New Orleans. Mustered out August 13, 1863.

7th REGIMENT INFANTRY (AFRICAN DESCENT).

Organized at New Orleans, La., for 60 days, July 10, 1863. Duty at New Orleans. Mustered out August 6, 1863.

7th REGIMENT INFANTRY (AFRICAN DESCENT).

Organized at Memphis, Tenn., Holly Springs, Miss., and Island No. 10, Mo., December 1, 1863. Attached to District of Vicksburg, Miss., to March, 1864. Unattached, 1st Division, United States Colored Troops, District of Vicksburg, Miss., March, 1864.

SERVICE.—Post duty at Vicksburg, Miss., till March, 1864. (A Detachment near Memphis, Tenn.) Skirmish at Vidalia, La., February 7, 1864. Designation of Regiment changed to 64th U. S. Colored Troops March 11, 1864, which see.

8th REGIMENT INFANTRY (AFRICAN DESCENT).

Organized at Lake Providence, La., May 5, 1863. Attached to African Brigade, District of Northeast Louisiana, to July, 1863. Post of Vicksburg, District of Vicksburg, Miss., to March, 1864. 2nd Brigade, 1st Division, United States Colored Troops, District of Vicksburg, March, 1864.

SERVICE.—Duty at Lake Providence, La., till July, 1863. Post duty at Vicksburg, Miss., till March, 1864. Expedition up Yazoo River February 1-March 8, 1864. Liverpool Heights February 4. Capture of Yazoo City February 4. Satartia February 7. Occupation of Yazoo City February 9-March 6. Skirmish Yazoo City March 5. Designation of Regiment changed to 47th U. S. Colored Troops March 11, 1864, which see.

9th REGIMENT INFANTRY (AFRICAN DESCENT).

Organized at Vicksburg, Miss., May 1, 1863. Attached to African Brigade, District of Northeast Louisiana, May to July, 1863. Post of Vicksburg, Miss., to September, 1863.

SERVICE.—Duty at Milliken's Bend, La., till July, 1863. Action at Milliken's Bend and Young's Point, La., June 6-7. Battle at Milliken's Bend June 25. Duty at Vicksburg, Miss., till September. Designation of Regiment changed to 1st Mississippi Heavy Artillery, African Descent, September 26, 1863, which see.

Re-organized at Vicksburg, Miss., and Memphis, Tenn., August 7, 1863, to January 17, 1864. Attached to Post of Vicksburg, Miss., to January, 1864, and to Post of Natchez, Miss., to March, 1864. (A detachment at Memphis, Tenn., attached to 5th Division, 16th Army Corps.) Designation of Regiment changed to 63rd U. S. Colored Troops March 11, 1864, which see.

10th REGIMENT INFANTRY (AFRICAN DESCENT).

Organized at Lake Providence and Goodrich Landing, La., May 6 to August 8, 1863. Attached to Post of Goodrich Landing, La., District Northeast Louisiana, to January, 1864. 1st Brigade, U. S. Colored Troops, District of Vicksburg, Miss., to March, 1864.

SERVICE.—Duty at Lake Providence and Goodrich Landing, La., till January, 1864. Tensas Bayou May 9 and August 10, 1863. Duty at Vicksburg, Miss., till March, 1864. Designation of Regiment changed to 48th U. S. Colored Troops March 11, 1864, which see.

11th REGIMENT INFANTRY (AFRICAN DESCENT).

Organized at Milliken's Bend, La., May 23 to August 22, 1863. Attached to African Brigade, District of Northeast Louisiana, to July, 1863. Post Goodrich Landing, District of Vicksburg, Miss., to January, 1864. 1st Brigade, U. S. Colored Troops, District Vicksburg, to March, 1864.

SERVICE.—Duty at Milliken's Bend till January, 1864. Action at Milliken's Bend June 7. Post duty at Vicksburg, Miss., January to March, 1864. Expedition to Waterproof January 29-February 23. Waterproof February 14-15. Designation of Regiment changed to 49th U. S. Colored Troops March 11, 1864, which see.

12th REGIMENT INFANTRY (AFRICAN DESCENT).

Organized May to July, 1863. Attached to African Brigade, District Northeast Louisiana, to July, 1863. Post of Vicksburg, District of Vicksburg, Miss., to March, 1864.

Duty at Milliken's Bend and Vicksburg till March, 1864. Designation of Regiment changed to 50th U. S. Colored Troops March 11, 1864, which see.

MAINE VOLUNTEERS.

1st REGIMENT CAVALRY.

Organized at Augusta and mustered in November 5, 1861. Companies "A," "D," "E" and "F" moved to Washington, D. C., March 14-19, 1862; Companies "B," "I," "H" and "M" March 19-24, and Companies "C," "G," "K" and "L" to Washington March 19-28, 1862. Attached to Miles' Railroad Brigade, Army of Potomac, to May, 1862 (Cos. "A," "B," "E," "H" and "M"). Hatch's Cavalry Brigade, Banks' 5th Army Corps, and Dept. of the Shenandoah, to July, 1862 (Cos. "A," "B," "E," "H" and "M"). Abercrombie's Brigade, Williams' Division, Banks' 5th Army Corps, and Dept. of the Shenandoah, March to May, 1862 (Cos. "C," "D," "F," "G," "I," "K" and "L"). Bayard's Cavalry Brigade, Dept. of the Rappahannock, to July, 1862 (Cos. "C," "D," "F," "G," "I," "K" and "L"). Bayard's Cavalry Brigade, Army of Virginia, to September, 1862. Bayard's Cavalry Brigade, Cavalry Division, Army of the Potomac, to January, 1863. 1st Brigade, 3rd Division, Cavalry Corps, Army of the Potomac, to June, 1863. 2nd Brigade, 2nd Division, Cavalry Corps, June, 1863. 3rd Brigade, 2nd Division, Cavalry Corps, to October, 1863. 2nd Brigade, 2nd Division, Cavalry Corps, to October, 1864. 3rd Brigade, 2nd Division, Cavalry Corps, to August, 1865.

SERVICE.—Companies "A," "B," "E," "H" and "M" ordered to Harper's Ferry, W. Va., March, 1862, and guard duty along Baltimore & Ohio Railroad till May 19. Moved to Strasburg and operations in the Shenandoah Valley May 15-June 17. Action at Woodstock May 21, Strasburg May 22 (Cos. "H" and "M"), Middletown May 24, Winchester May 25. Retreat to Williamsport May 25-26. Winchester June 3. Milford June 24. Reconnoissance to Front Royal June 29-30. Luray June 30. Rejoin Regiment at Warrenton July 10. Companies "C," "D," "F," "G," "I," "K" and "L" moved to Warrenton March, 1862. Reconnoissance to the Rappahannock April 16 (Co. "C"). Reconnoissance to Liberty Church April 16 (Detachment). Reconnoissance to Culpeper Court House May 4-5. Brandy Station May 5. Join McDowell at Manassas Junction May 25. Milford July 2. Winchester July 3. Sperryville July

5. Regiment scouting on the Rappahannock during July. Reconnoissance to James City July 22-24. Slaughter House August 7. Robinson River August 8. Battle of Cedar Mountain August 9. Pope's Campaign in Northern Virginia August 16-September 2. Stevensburg, Raccoon Ford and Brandy Station August 20. Beverly Ford August 20. Fords of the Rappahannock August 21-23. Rappahannock Station August 24-25. Sulphur Springs August 27. Thoroughfare Gap August 28. Groveton August 29. Bull Run August 30. Mountsville, Centerville, Chantilly and Germantown August 31. Chantilly September 1. Frederick, Md., September 7 and 12. South Mountain September 14. Antietam September 16-17. At Frederick, Md., till November 2. Manassas Junction October 24. Middleburg October 30. Aldie October 31. Salem, New Baltimore and near Warrenton November 4. Rappahannock Station November 7-9. Battle of Fredericksburg December 12-15. Dumfries December 28. "Mud March" January 20-24, 1863. Rappahannock Bridge April 14. Stoneman's Raid April 29-May 8. Kelly's Ford April 29. Louisa Court House May 1-2. South Anna Bridge near Ashland May 3. Bealton May 10. Operations on Northern Neck May 20-26 (Detachment). Brandy Station and Beverly Ford June 9. Aldie June 17. Middleburg June 18-19. Upperville June 21. Hanover, Pa., June 30. Battle of Gettysburg, Pa., July 1-3. Steven's Furnace July 5. Hagerstown July 11. Funkstown, Md., July 12. Shephardstown and near Harper's Ferry July 14. Halltown and Charlestown July 15. Shephardstown July 16. Little Washington August 5. Beverly Ford August 15. Brandy Station September 6. Advance from the Rappahannock to the Rapidan September 13-17. Culpeper Court House September 13. Hazel River September 13. Raccoon Ford September 14. Culpeper September 20. White's Ford September 21-22. Bristoe Campaign October 9-22. Gaines' Cross Roads October 12. Warrenton or White Sulphur Springs October 12-13. Auburn and Bristoe October 14. St. Stephen's Church October 14. Blackburn's Ford October 15. Culpeper October 20. Near Bealton October 22. Rappahannock Crossing October 22. Rappahannock Station October 23. Advance to line of the Rappahannock November 7-8. Mine Run Campaign November 26-December 2. Morton's Ford November 26. New Hope Church November 27. Parker's Store November 29. Expedition to Luray December 21-23. Reconnoissance to Front Royal January 1-4, 1864. Near Salem January 3 (Detachment). Kilpatrick's Raid to Richmond February 28-March 4. Beaver Dam Station February 29. Fortifications of Richmond March 1. Brook's Turnpike March 1. Old Church March 2. Near Tunstall Station March 2. Rapidan Campaign May 3-June 15. Battles of Todd's Tavern May 5-6; Wilderness May 6-7; Todd's Tavern May 7-8. Sheridan's Raid May 9-24. North Anna River May 9-10. Ground Squirrel Church and Yellow Tavern May 11. Diamond Hill May 11. Brook Church or Fortifications of Richmond May 12. Meadow Bridge May 12. Jones' Bridge May 17. Haxall's Landing May 18. Milford May 20. Haw's Shop May 28. Old Church May 29-30. Cold Harbor May 31-June 1. About Cold Harbor June 1-7. Sumner's Upper Bridge and McGee's Mills June 2. Sheridan's Trevillian Raid June 7-24. Elliott's Mills June 8. Trevillian Station June 11-12. Black Creek, Tunstall Station, June 21. White House, St. Peter's Church, June 21. St. Mary's Church June 24. Second Swamp June 28. Siege operations against Petersburg and Richmond June, 1864, to April, 1865. Warwick Swamp and Lee's Mill July 12. Deep Bottom July 27-28. New Market July 28. Malvern Hill July 29. Lee's Mills July 30. Near Sycamore Church August 9. Gravel Hill August 14. Strawberry Plains August 14-18. Deep Run August 16. Nelson's Farm August 18. Ream's Station August 23-25. Dinwiddie Road near Ream's Station August 23. Yellow Tavern September 2. Stony Creek Station September 15. Belcher's Mills September 17. Lee's Mills September 18. Vaughan Road September 26. Wyatt's Farm September 29. Poplar Springs Church September 29-Oc-

tober 1. Vaughan and Duncan Road October 1. Boyd-ton Plank Road or Hatcher's Run October 27-28. Old members mustered out November 4, 1864. Stony Creek Station December 1. Bellefield Raid December 7-11. Bellefield December 9-10. Dabney's Mills, Hatcher's Run, February 5-7, 1865. Appomattox Campaign March 28-April 9. Dinwiddie Court House March 30-31. Five Forks April 1. Namozine Church and Jettersville April 3. Fame's Cross Roads and Amelia Springs April 5. Sailor's Creek and Deatonville Road April 6. Briery Creek and Farmville April 7. Appomattox Station April 8. Appomattox Court House April 9. Surrender of Lee and his army. Duty at Petersburg and in the Dept. of Virginia till August. Mustered out August 1, 1865.

This Regiment lost greatest number killed in action of any Cavalry Regiment in the entire army: 15 Officers and 159 Enlisted men killed and mortally wounded; 3 Officers and 341 Enlisted men died of disease, a total of 518.

2nd REGIMENT CAVALRY.

Organized at Augusta November 30, 1863, to January 2, 1864. Left State for Dept. of the Gulf April, 1864. Attached to District of La Fourche, Dept. of the Gulf, to July, 1864. Pensacola, Fla., District of West Florida, Dept. Gulf, to October, 1864. 2nd Brigade, District of West Florida, Dept. Gulf, to February, 1865. 2nd Brigade, Lucas' Cavalry Division, Steele's Command, Military Division of West Mississippi, to April, 1865. District of Florida to December, 1865.

SERVICE—Duty in the Defences of New Orleans, La., till May 26, 1864. Moved to Thibodeaux, La., May 26. Duty there and scout and picket duty in the District of La Fourche by detachments till July 27. (Cos. "A," "D" and "G" detached and moved to Alexandria, La., April 16-21. Red River Campaign April 21-May 22. Duty at Alexandria, La., till May 13. Retreat to Morganza May 13-22. Marksville or Avoyelle's Prairie May 15. Mansura May 16. Yellow Bayou May 18. Rejoined Regiment at Thibodeaux June 1.) Moved to Algiers, thence to Pensacola, Fla., July 27-August 11, and duty there till March, 1865. Milton, Fla., August 25, 1864. Expedition from Barrancas to Marianna September 18-October 4. Euche Anna C. H. September 23. Marianna September 27. Expedition up Blackwater Bay October 25-28. Milton October 26. Expedition from Barrancas to Pine Barren Creek November 16-17. Pine Barren Creek November 17. Expedition to Pollard, Ala., December 13-19. Bluff Springs and Pollard December 15. Escanabia Bridge December 15-16. Pine Barren Ford December 17-18. (A detachment at Pascagoula, Miss., December, 1864, to February 6, 1865.) Expedition from Barrancas to Milton February 22-25, 1865. Milton February 23. Steele's march to Mobile, Ala., March 18-31. (Dismounted men remain at Barrancas, Fla.) Near Evergreen March 24. Muddy Creek, Ala., March 26. Near Blakely April 1. Siege of Fort Blakely April 1-9. Assault and capture of Fort Blakely April 9. Occupation of Mobile April 12. March to Montgomery April 13-25. Duty in Alabama with 16th Corps till August, and in Western and Middle Florida by detachments to December. Mustered out December 6 and discharged at Augusta, Me., December 21, 1865.

Death losses during service: Two Officers and 8 Enlisted men killed and mortally wounded; 334 Enlisted men died of disease. Total 344.

1st REGIMENT HEAVY ARTILLERY.

Organized at Bangor as 18th Infantry and mustered in August 21, 1862. Left State for Washington, D. C., August 24. Designation changed to 1st Heavy Artillery January 6, 1863. Company "L" organized January, 1864, and Company "M" February, 1864. Attached to Defences of Washington August, 1862, to February, 1863. 2nd Brigade, Haskins' Division, 22nd Army Corps. Defences North of the Potomac to May, 1864. 2nd Brigade, 4th Division, 2nd Army Corps, Army of the Potomac, to May 24, 1864. 1st Brigade, 3rd Division, 2nd

Army Corps, to July, 1864. 2nd Brigade, 3rd Division, 2nd Army Corps, to June, 1865. 3rd Brigade, Hardin's Division, 22nd Corps, to September, 1865.

SERVICE—Duty in the Defences of Washington, building and garrisoning Batteries and Forts. Eight Companies at Fort Alexandria, Company "E" at Batteries Vermont and Mattox, Company "K" at Batteries Cameron and Parrott, August 26, 1862, to May 15, 1864. Moved to Belle Plains, Va., May 15, 1864, as a part of Tyler's Heavy Artillery Division. Rapidan Campaign May 18 to June 15. Harris' Farm, Fredericksburg Road, May 19. (82 killed, 394 wounded, 5 missing; total 481.) On line of North Anna May 20-23. North Anna May 23-26. On line of the Pamunkey River May 26-28. Totopotomoy May 28-31. Cold Harbor June 1-5. Barker's Mills June 5-12. Before Petersburg June 16-19. Hare's House, Assault on Petersburg, June 18. (Sustained greatest loss of any one Regiment in any one action of the war. 635 killed and wounded out of 900 engaged.) Siege of Petersburg June 16, 1864, to April 2, 1865. Weldon Railroad June 22-23, 1864. Picket duty at Deserted House till July 23. Demonstration on north side of James River July 27-29. Deep Bottom July 27-28. Duty at Hare's House till August 12. Demonstration on north side of James River August 13-20. Strawberry Plains August 14-18. Near Fort Sedgwick till September 30. Poplar Springs Church September 30-October 2. Yellow House October 1. Squirrel Level Road October 2. At Fort Sedgwick October 6-24. Boydton Plank Road, Hatcher's Run, October 27-28. Warren's Hicksford Raid December 7-12. Hatcher's Run February 5-7, 1865. Armstrong House March 25. Appomattox Campaign March 28-April 9. South Side Railroad March 29. Boydton Road and White Oak Ridge March 29-31. Fall of Petersburg April 2. Jettersville April 5. Amelia Springs and Sailor's Creek April 6. Farmville April 7. Appomattox C. H. April 9. Surrender of Lee and his army. Moved to Washington, D. C., May 9-16. Grand Review May 23. Garrison Forts in the Defences of Washington from Fort Washington to Fort Mahone June 27 to September 11. Mustered out September 11 and ordered to Bangor, Me. Discharged September 20, 1865.

Of all Regiments in army this Regiment sustained greatest loss in battle. 23 Officers and 400 Enlisted men killed and mortally wounded; 260 died of disease, etc. Total 683.

1st BATTERY LIGHT ARTILLERY ("A").

Organized at Portland and mustered in December 18, 1861. Moved to Lowell, Mass., December 19, and duty there till February, 1862. Moved to Boston February 2, and there embarked on Steamer "Idaho" for Ship Island, Miss., February 8, arriving there March 10. Duty at Ship Island till May 8. Attached to 3rd Brigade, Dept. of the Gulf, to September, 1862. Weitzel's Reserve Brigade, Dept. Gulf, to January, 1863. Artillery, 1st Division, 19th Army Corps, Dept. Gulf, to January, 1864. Artillery, 2nd Division, 19th Army Corps, to April, 1864. Camp Barry, Defences of Washington, 22nd Army Corps, to July, 1864. Artillery, 2nd Division, 19th Army Corps, Army of the Shenandoah, Middle Military Division, to February, 1865. 2nd Division, Army Shenandoah, to July.

SERVICE—Moved from Ship Island, Miss., to New Orleans, La., May 8-15, and provost duty there till September, 1862. Duty at Camp Parapet September 1-October 24. Operations in La Fourche District October 24-November 6. Action at Georgia Landing, Labadieville, October 27. At Thibodeauxville till January, 1863. Expedition up the Teche January 11-18. Action with Steamer "Cotton," Bayou Teche, January 14. At Camp Stevens, Brashear City and Bayou Boeuf till April. Operations in Western Louisiana April 9-May 14. Teche Campaign April 11-20. Fort Bisland, near Centreville, April 12-13. Jeanerette April 14. Expedition from Opelousas to Barre Landing April 21. Siege of Port Hudson May 23-July 8. Thompson's Creek May 25. Assaults on Port Hudson May 27 and June 14. Surrender of Port Hudson July 8. Koch's Plantation, Donaldsonville,

July 12-13. Moved to Baton Rouge August 3, and duty there till September 18. Western Louisiana Campaign October 3-November 18. At New Iberia till January 7, 1864. Moved to Franklin January 7, thence to Brashear City and New Orleans January 18-20. On Veteran furlough February and March. Moved to Annapolis, Md., April 15-19, thence to Camp Barry, Washington, D. C., April 20. Duty there and at Forts Smith and Strong, Defences of Washington, till July. Repulse of Early's attack on Washington July 11-12. At Camp Barry till July 30. Ordered to Tennallytown July 30, and join 19th Army Corps at Monocacy Junction August 1. Sheridan's Shenandoah Valley Campaign August 7-November 28. March to Middletown August 6-15; to Winchester, thence to Berryville August 15-17, and to Halltown August 21. At Berryville August 28-September 18. Battle of Opequan, Winchester, September 19. Fisher's Hill September 22. Battle of Cedar Creek October 19. Duty near Cedar Creek till November 9, and near Winchester till December 30. At Stevenson's Depot till January 14, 1865; at Manchester till April 14, and at Winchester till July 9. Moved to Portland, Me., July 9-13. Mustered out July 15, 1865.

Battery lost during service 2 Officers and 13 Enlisted men killed and mortally wounded, and 28 Enlisted men by disease. Total 43.

2nd BATTERY LIGHT ARTILLERY ("B").

Organized at Augusta and mustered in November 30, 1861. Duty at Augusta till March 10, 1862, and at Fort Preble, Portland, Me., till April 2. Ordered to Washington, D. C., April 2, and camp at Capital Hill till April 20. Attached to 2nd Brigade, 2nd Division (McDowell's), Dept. of the Rappahannock, to June, 1862. Artillery, 2nd Division, 3rd Army Corps, Army of Virginia, to September, 1862. Artillery, 2nd Division, 1st Army Corps, Army of the Potomac, to June, 1863. Artillery Brigade, 1st Army Corps, to November, 1863. Camp Barry, Defences of Washington, D. C., 22nd Army Corps, to April, 1864. Artillery, 1st Division, 9th Army Corps, Army Potomac, to July, 1864. Artillery Brigade, 9th Army Corps, to August, 1864. Artillery Reserve, Army Potomac, to May, 1865.

SERVICE—Moved to Potomac Creek, Va., thence to Belle Plains April 20-27, 1862. Moved to Falmouth May 9, thence to Manassas and Front Royal May 25-30. Moved to Manassas June 16, to Warrenton July 5, to Waterloo July 9, thence to Culpeper C. H. August 5. Battle of Cedar Mountain August 9. Pope's Campaign in Northern Virginia August 16-September 2. Fords of the Rappahannock August 21-23. Plains of Manassas August 25-27. Thoroughfare Gap August 28. Battle of Groveton August 29. Bull Run August 30. Centreville September 1. Duty in the Defences of Washington September 11-October 13. Operations in Maryland and Virginia October 13-November 23. Camp at Brooks Station November 23-December 9. Battle of Fredericksburg December 12-15. "Mud March" January 20-24, 1863. Camp near Fletcher's Chapel till April 28. Chancellorsville Campaign April 28-May 8. Operations at Fitzhugh's Crossing April 29-May 2. Battle of Chancellorsville May 2-5. Battle of Gettysburg, Pa., July 1-3. At Norman's Ford August 2-September 16. Moved to Culpeper, thence to the Rapidan River. Ordered to Camp Barry, Washington, D. C., November 5, and duty there till April 25, 1864. Joined 9th Army Corps April 25. Rapidan Campaign May 3-June 15. Battles of the Wilderness May 5-7. Spottsylvania May 8-12. Ny River May 10. Spottsylvania C. H. May 12-21. North Anna River May 23-26. On line of the Pamunkey River May 26-28. Totopotomoy May 28-31. Cold Harbor June 1-12. Bethesda Church June 1-3. Before Petersburg June 15-September 17, 1864. Mine Explosion, Petersburg, July 30. Moved to City Point September 17, and duty in the defences at that point till May 3, 1865. Defence of City Point September 18, 1864, and April 2, 1865. Moved to Alexandria, Va., May 3, thence to Augusta May 31. Mustered out June 16, 1865.

Battery lost during service 1 Officer and 4 Enlisted

40

men killed and mortally wounded, and 26 Enlisted men by disease. Total 31.

3rd BATTERY LIGHT ARTILLERY ("C").

Organized at Augusta and mustered in December 11, 1861. Duty at Augusta till March 19, 1862, and at Portland, Me., till April 1. Moved to Washington, D. C., April 1-8. Camp at Capital Hill till April 14. Assigned to duty as Pontooneers, McDowell's Dept. of the Rappahannock, April to June, 1862. Pontooneers, 3rd Army Corps, Army of Virginia, to September, 1862. 1st Brigade, Haskins' Division, Defences of Washington, to February, 1863. Battery assigned to 1st Maine Heavy Artillery as Company "M" March 28, 1863. Attached to Haskins' Division, 22nd Army Corps, to February, 1864. Detached from 1st Maine Heavy Artillery and reorganized as 3rd Battery February 23, 1864. Attached to Camp Barry, Defences of Washington, 22nd Corps, April to July, 1864. Artillery, 3rd Division, 9th Army Corps, Army Potomac, to August, 1864. Artillery Reserve, Army Potomac, to June, 1865.

SERVICE—Duty with Pontoon Train at Falmouth, Va., Washington, D. C., and at Alexandria, Va., April to November, 1862. Pope's Campaign in Northern Virginia August 16-September 2. Battle of Bull Run August 30. At Fort Lincoln, Defences of Washington, till March 28, 1863, and in the Defences with 1st Maine Heavy Artillery till January, 1864. On Veteran furlough January and February. Moved to Camp Barry March 25, and duty there till July 5. Moved to City Point, thence to Petersburg front July 5-9. Siege of Petersburg July 9-October 25. Moved to City Point, Va., October 25, and duty in the defences at that point till May 3, 1865. Moved to Washington, D. C., May 3-17. At Fairfax Seminary till June 2. Ordered to Augusta, Me., and mustered out June 17, 1865.

Battery lost during service 3 Enlisted men killed and mortally wounded and 14 Enlisted men by disease. Total 17.

4th BATTERY LIGHT ARTILLERY ("D").

Organized at Augusta and mustered in December 21, 1861. Duty at Augusta till March 14, 1862, and at Portland till April 1. Moved to Washington, D. C., April 1-3, and duty in the defences of that city till June 28. Ordered to Harper's Ferry, W. Va., June 28, and attached to 2nd Division, 2nd Army Corps, Army of Virginia, to September, 1862. Artillery, 3rd Division, 3rd Army Corps, Army Potomac, to May, 1863. Artillery Brigade, 3rd Army Corps, to September, 1863. Artillery, 2nd Division, 3rd Army Corps, to April, 1864. Artillery Brigade, 6th Army Corps, to August, 1864. Artillery Reserve, Army Potomac, to March, 1865. Artillery Reserve, Army Potomac, to June, 1865.

SERVICE—Battle of Cedar Mountain, Va., August 9. Pope's Campaign in Northern Virginia August 16-September 2. Fords of the Rappahannock August 20-23. Sulphur Springs August 24. Battles of Groveton August 29, and Bull Run August 30. Battle of Antietam, Md., September 16-17. Duty at Maryland Heights till October 13, and on the Upper Potomac till December 10. At Bolivar Heights till April 7, and at Maryland Heights till June 30. Moved to Monocacy Junction, thence to South Mountain, Md., June 30-July 6. Pursuit of Lee July 6-24. Wapping Heights, Va., July 23. Camp near Bealton August 1-September 15, and on Culpeper and Warrenton Pike till October 10. Bristoe Campaign October 10-22. Culpeper October 12-13. McLean's Ford October 15. Kelly's Ford November 7. Mine Run Campaign November 26-December 2. Payne's Farm November 27. At Brandy Station till March 31, 1864. Rapidan Campaign May 4-June 15. Battle of the Wilderness May 5-7. Spottsylvania May 8-12. Spottsylvania C. H. May 12-21. North Anna River May 23-27. Totopotomoy May 28-31. Cold Harbor June 1-12. Siege of Petersburg, Va., June 17, 1864, to April 2, 1865. Mine Explosion, Petersburg, July 30, 1864. Duty in the trenches before Petersburg at various points from the James River to the Weldon Railroad till April, 1865. Fall of

Petersburg April 2. Sailor's Creek April 6. Appomattox C. H. April 9. Surrender of Lee and his army. Mustered out June 17, 1865.

Battery lost during service 5 Enlisted men killed and mortally wounded and 1 Officer and 22 Enlisted men by disease. Total 28.

5th BATTERY LIGHT ARTILLERY ("E").

Organized at Augusta and mustered in December 4, 1861. Duty at Augusta till March 10, 1862, and at Fort Preble, Portland, Me., till April 1. Moved to Washington, D. C., April 1-3. Camp on Capital Hill till May 19. Moved to Aquia Creek, thence to Fredericksburg, Va., May 19-22. Attached to 2nd Division, Dept. of the Rappahannock, to June, 1862. 2nd Division, 3rd Army Corps, Army of Virginia, to September, 1862. 2nd Division, 1st Corps, Army Potomac, to May, 1863. Artillery Brigade, 1st Army Corps, to April, 1864. Artillery Brigade, 5th Army Corps, to June, 1864. Artillery Brigade, 6th Army Corps, to December, 1864. Artillery Brigade, Army of the Shenandoah, to July, 1865.

SERVICE—Moved to Front Royal, Va., May 25, 1862, and to Manassas June 17. At Warrenton July 4-22. March to Waterloo July 22, thence to Culpeper August 4. Battle of Cedar Mountain August 9. Pope's Campaign in Northern Virginia August 16-September 2. Fords of the Rappahannock August 20-23. Thoroughfare Gap August 28. Battle of Groveton August 29, and Bull Run August 30. Ordered to Washington September 7, to refit, and duty there till October 24. Moved to Berlin October 24, and thence to Lovettsville October 30. Reconnoissance from Bolivar Heights to Rippon, W. Va., November 9. Battle of Fredericksburg December 12-15. "Mud March" January 20-24, 1863. At Fletcher's Chapel till April 28. Chancellorsville Campaign April 28-May 6. Operations at Fitzhugh's Crossing April 29-May 2. Battle of Chancellorsville May 2-5. Battle of Gettysburg, Pa., July 1-3. Bristoe Campaign October 9-22. Advance to line of the Rappahannock November 7-8. Mine Run Campaign November 26-December 2. Rapidan Campaign May 4-June 15, 1864. Battles of the Wilderness May 5-7. Spottsylvania May 8-12. Ny River May 10. Spottsylvania C. H. May 12-21. North Anna River May 23-26. Line of the Pamunkey May 26-28. Totopotomoy May 28-31. Cold Harbor June 1-12. Before Petersburg June 17-19. Siege of Petersburg June 17-July 9, 1864. Ordered to Washington, D. C. Sheridan's Shenandoah Valley Campaign August 7-November 28. Battle of Opequan, Winchester, September 19. Fisher's Hill September 22. Battle of Cedar Creek October 19. Duty at Strasburg till November 10. Near Winchester till December 28, and at Stevenson's Depot till January 10, 1865. At Frederick, Md., till April 4. At Winchester till June 21. Ordered to Augusta, Me., June 21, and there mustered out July 6, 1865.

Battery lost during service 2 Officers and 16 Enlisted men killed and mortally wounded and 15 Enlisted men by disease. Total 33.

6th BATTERY LIGHT ARTILLERY ("F").

Organized at Augusta and mustered in January 1, 1862. Duty at Augusta till March and at Portland, Me., till April 1. Moved to Washington, D. C., April 1-3. Camp at East Capital Hill and at Forts Buffalo and Ramsey, and at Falls Church, Va., till June. Ordered to report to General Banks at Harper's Ferry, W. Va. Attached to 2nd Division, 2nd Army Corps, Army of Virginia, to August, 1862. 3rd Division, 3rd Army Corps, Army Potomac, August, 1862. Artillery, 1st Division, 3rd Army Corps, to September, 1862. Artillery, 2nd Division, 12th Corps, Army Potomac, to June, 1863. 4th Volunteer Brigade, Artillery Reserve, Army Potomac, to September, 1863. 1st Volunteer Brigade, Artillery Reserve, to April, 1864. Artillery Brigade, 2nd Army Corps, to November, 1864. Artillery Reserve, Army Potomac, to June, 1865.

SERVICE.—Duty at Harper's Ferry, Cedar Creek and Little Washington, Va., June to August, 1862. Battle of Cedar Creek August 9. Pope's Campaign in Northern Virginia August 16-September 2. Fords of the

Rappahannock August 20-26. Battles of Groveton August 29, and Bull Run August 30. Chantilly September 1. Maryland Campaign September-October. Crampton's Pass, South Mountain, Md., September 14. Battle of Antietam, Md., September 16-17. Duty at Sandy Hook, Md., and at Harper's Ferry, W. Va., till December. Reconnoissance to Winchester December 2-6. Action at Dumfries December 27. Duty at Dumfries till May 27, 1863, and at Falmouth till June 13. Gettysburg (Pa.) Campaign June-July. Battle of Gettysburg July 1-3. Pursuit to Williamsport, Md., July 7-14. Frederick, Md., July 13. March to Warrenton Junction, Va., July 18-August 2, and duty there till September 16. At Culpeper till October 12. Bristoe Campaign October 12-22. Culpeper October 12-13. Bristoe October 14. Advance to line of Rappahannock November 7-8. Mine Run Campaign November 26-December 2. Mine Run November 28-30. Campaign from the Rapidan to James River May 3-June 15, 1864. Battles of the Wilderness May 5-7; Spottsylvania May 8-12; Spottsylvania C. H. May 12-21; "Bloody Angle," Spottsylvania C. H., May 12. North Anna River May 23-26. On line of the Pamunkey May 26-28. Totopotomoy May 28-31. Cold Harbor June 1-12. Before Petersburg June 16-19. Siege of Petersburg June 16, 1864, to April 2, 1865. Jerusalem Plank Road June 22-23, 1864. Deep Bottom July 27-28. Mine Explosion July 30 (Reserve). Strawberry Plains, Deep Bottom, August 14-18. Garrison, Fort Davis, till October 20. At Fort McGilvrey and Battery 9 till March 15, 1865. At Fort Sampson till April 3. Assault on and capture of Petersburg April 2-3. Ordered to Reserve Artillery at City Point April 3. Duty there till May 3. Ordered to Alexandria and duty there to June 4. Ordered to Augusta, Me., and mustered out June 7, 1865.

Battery lost during service 13 Enlisted men killed and mortally wounded and 27 Enlisted men by disease. Total 40.

7th BATTERY LIGHT ARTILLERY ("G").

Organized at Augusta and mustered in December 30, 1863. Left State for Washington, D. C., February 1, 1864. Duty at Camp Barry till April 25. Attached to 3rd Division, 9th Army Corps, Army Potomac, to August, 1864. Artillery Brigade, 9th Army Corps, to June, 1865.

SERVICE.—Campaign from the Rapidan to the James River, Va., May 3-June 15, 1864. Battles of the Wilderness May 5-7; Spottsylvania May 8-12; Spottsylvania C. H. May 12-21; North Anna May 23-26. Ox Ford May 23-24. Line of the Pamunkey May 26-28. Totopotomoy May 28-31. Cold Harbor June 1-12. Bethesda Church June 1-3. Before Petersburg June 16-18. Siege of Petersburg June 16, 1864, to April 2, 1865. Mine Explosion, Petersburg, July 30, 1864. Ream's Station August 25. Poplar Springs Church September 29-October 2. Pegram's Farm October 2. Garrison, Fort Welsh, till November 30, and Fort Sedgwick (Fort Hell) and Battery 21 till April 3, 1865. Assault on and capture of Petersburg April 2-3. Pursuit of Lee April 4-9. At Farmville April 10-20. Moved to Washington, D. C., April 20-28, and camp near Fairfax Seminary to June 5. Grand Review May 24. Moved to Augusta, Me., June 5-8, and mustered out June 21, 1865.

Battery lost during service 13 Enlisted men killed and mortally wounded and 27 Enlisted men by disease. Total 40.

GARRISON ARTILLERY.

Companies "A," "B" and "C" organized November, 1861, for service as Garrison Artillery in State of Maine. Mustered out September, 1862, failing to complete organization.

MAINE COMPANY SHARPSHOOTERS.

Organized at Augusta and mustered in November 2, 1861. Left State for Washington, D. C., with 11th Infantry. Attached to 2nd Regiment, Berdan's U. S. Sharpshooters, as Company "D," which see.

1st BATTALION SHARPSHOOTERS.

Organized at Augusta from October 27 to December 29, 1864. Companies "A" and "B" left State for City Point, Va., November 12, 1864. Assigned to duty at that point till January, 1865. Company "C" organized November 29, 1864. Moved to Galloupe's Island, Boston Harbor, thence moved to City Point, Va., January 1-5, 1865. Company "D" organized December 2. Company "E" organized November 28, and Company "F" organized December 29, 1864, all moved to City Point, Va., and joined other Companies. Ordered to Petersburg front and attached to 3rd Brigade, 1st Division, 5th Army Corps, Army Potomac, January to June, 1865.

SERVICE.—Siege of Petersburg January 5 to April 2, 1865. Dabney's Mills, Hatcher's Run, February 5-7. Fort Fisher, Petersburg, March 25. Appomattox Campaign March 28-April 9. White Oak Road March 29. Quaker Road March 30. Boydton Road March 30-31. Five Forks April 1. Amelia C. H. April 5. High Bridge April 6. Appomattox C. H. April 9. Surrender of Lee and his army. Moved to Washington, D. C., May 2-12. Grand Review May 23 Transferred to 20th Maine Infantry June 21, 1865.

Regiment lost during service 7 Enlisted men killed and mortally wounded and 12 Enlisted men by disease. Total 19.

1st REGIMENT INFANTRY.

Organized at Portland and mustered in for three months April 28, 1861. Ordered to Washington, D. C., June 1. Duty in the Defences of that city till August 1. Mustered out at Portland, Me., August 5, 1861.

1st REGIMENT VETERAN INFANTRY.

Organized at Charleston, Va., by consolidation of the Veterans of the 5th, 6th and 7th Regiments of Maine Volunteer Infantry August 21, 1864. Attached to 3rd Brigade, 2nd Division, 6th Army Corps, Armies of the Shenandoah and Potomac, to June, 1865.

SERVICE.—Skirmishes near Charleston, Va., August 21-22, 1864. Demonstration on Gilbert's Ford, Opequan, September 13. Battle of Opequan, Winchester, September 19. Fisher's Hill September 22. Battle of Cedar Creek October 19. Duty at Kernstown and vicinity till December. March to Washington, D. C., December 9, thence moved to Petersburg, Va. Siege of Petersburg December 12, 1864, to April 2, 1865. Fort Fisher, Petersburg, March 25-27, 1865. Assault on and fall of Petersburg April 2. Sailor's Creek April 6. Appomattox C. H. April 9. Surrender of Lee and his army. March to Danville, Va., and provost duty there till June. Moved to Washington, D. C. Corps Review June 9. Mustered out June 28, 1865.

Regiment lost during service 6 Officers and 40 Enlisted men killed and mortally wounded and 40 Enlisted men by disease. Total 86.

1st BATTALION INFANTRY.

Organized at Augusta and Portland February and March, 1865, from 21st, 24th, 25th and 26th Unassigned Companies of Infantry. Ordered to Summit Point, Va. Attached to 2nd Brigade, Dwight's Division, Army of the Shenandoah to May, 1865. 2nd Brigade, Dwight's Division, Dept. of Washington, to June, 1865. Dwight's Division, Dept. of the South, to July, 1865. 4th Sub-District, District of South Carolina, Dept. of the South, to August, 1865. 3rd Sub-District, Dept. of the South, to April, 1866.

SERVICE.—Moved from the Shenandoah Valley to Washington, D. C., May 1, 1865, and duty there till June 1. Moved to Savannah, Ga., June 1, thence to Georgetown, S. C., June 15. To Florence, S. C., July 6-9. Duty in Eastern South Carolina till August 19. At Charleston till August 29, and in 3rd Sub-District, Western South Carolina, till April, 1866. Mustered out April 5, 1866.

Lost by disease during service 40.

2nd REGIMENT INFANTRY.

Organized at Bangor for three months' service. Left State for Willett's Point, N. Y., May 14, 1861. Mustered into U. S. service for two and three years May 28, 1861. Moved to Washington, D. C., May 30. Attached to Keyes' Brigade, Tyler's Division, McDowell's Army of Northeastern Virginia, June to August, 1861. Fort Corcoran, Division of the Potomac, to October, 1861. Martindale's Brigade, Fitz-John Porter's Division, Army Potomac, to March, 1862. 1st Brigade, 1st Division, 3rd Army Corps, Army Potomac, to May, 1862. 1st Brigade, 1st Division, 3rd Army Corps, to June, 1863.

SERVICE—Camp on Meridian Hill, Defences of Washington, D. C., till July 1, 1861. Moved to Falls Church, Va., July 1, and duty there till July 16. Advance on Manassas, Va., July 16-21. Occupation of Fairfax C. H. July 17. Battle of Bull Run July 21. Duty at Arlington Heights, Va., and at Fort Corcoran till October, and at Hall's Hill, Defences of Washington, till March, 1862. Moved to the Peninsula March. Warwick Road and near Lee's Mills April 5. Siege of Yorktown April 5-May 4. New Bridge May 24. Hanover C. H. May 27. Operations about Hanover C. H. May 27-29. Seven days before Richmond June 25-July 1. Battles of Mechanicsville June 26; Gaines' Mill June 27; Peach Orchard and Savage Station June 29; Turkey Bridge or Malvern Cliff June 30; Malvern Hill July 1. At Harrison's Landing till August 15. Retreat from the Peninsula and movement to Centreville August 16-27. Pope's Campaign in Northern Virginia August 27-September 2. Battle of Groveton August 29. Bull Run August 30. Battle of Antietam, Md., September 16-17. Shephardstown Ford September 19. Shephardstown September 20. Battle of Fredericksburg, Va., December 12-15. Expedition to Richards and Ellis Fords December 29-30. "Mud March" January 20-24, 1863. At Falmouth till April. Chancellorsville Campaign April 27-May 6. Battle of Chancellorsville May 1-5. Ordered home May 20. Three-year men transferred to 20th Maine Infantry. Mustered out June 9, 1863.

Regiment lost during service 4 Officers and 65 Enlisted men killed and mortally wounded and 70 Enlisted men by disease. Total 139.

3rd REGIMENT INFANTRY.

Organized at Augusta and mustered in June 4, 1861. Left State for Washington, D. C., June 5. Attached to Howard's Brigade, Heintzelman's Division, McDowell's Army of Northeastern Virginia, to August, 1861. Howard's Brigade, Division of the Potomac, to October, 1861. Sedgwick's Brigade, Heintzelman's Division, Army of the Potomac, to March, 1862. 2nd Brigade, 3rd Division, 3rd Army Corps, Army Potomac, to July, 1862. 2nd Brigade, 1st Division, 3rd Army Corps, to March, 1864. 1st Brigade, 3rd Division, 2nd Army Corps, to June, 1864.

SERVICE—Camp on Meridian Hill, Defences of Washington, D. C., till July 16, 1861. Advance on Manassas, Va., July 16-21. Battle of Bull Run July 21. Duty in the Defences of Washington till March, 1862. Advance on Manassas, Va., March 10-15. Virginia Peninsula Campaign April to August. Siege of Yorktown April 5-May 4. Battle of Williamsburg May 5. Battle of Seven Pines or Fair Oaks May 31-June 1. Near Richmond June 18. Seven days before Richmond June 25-July 1. Oak Grove June 25. Jordan's Ford June 27. Peach Orchard and Savage Station June 29. Charles City Cross Roads and Glendale June 30. Malvern Hill July 1. At Harrison's Landing till August 16. Retreat from the Peninsula and movement to Centreville August 16-27. Pope's Campaign in Northern Virginia August 27-September 2. Battles of Groveton August 29, and Bull Run August 30. Chantilly September 1. Guard fords from Monocacy River to Conrad's Ferry till October 11. March to Leesburg, thence to Falmouth, Va., October 11-November 23. Battle of Fredericksburg December 12-15. "Mud March" January 20-24, 1863. At Falmouth till April 27. Chancellorsville Campaign April

27-May 6. Battle of Chancellorsville May 1-5. Gettysburg (Pa.) Campaign June 13-July 24. Battle of Gettysburg July 1-3. Pursuit of Lee July 5-24. Wapping Heights, Va., July 23. Bristoe Campaign October 9-22. Advance to line of the Rappahannock November 7-8. Kelly's Ford November 7. Mine Run Campaign November 26-December 2. Payne's Farm November 27. Demonstration on the Rapidan February 5-7, 1864. Campaign from the Rapidan to the James River May 3-June 5. Battles of the Wilderness May 5-7. Laurel Hill May 8. Spottsylvania May 8-12. Po River May 10. Spottsylvania C. H. May 12-21. Bloody Angle, Assault on the Salient, May 12. Harris Farm, Fredericksburg Road, May 19. North Anna River May 23-26. On line of the Pamunkey May 26-28. Totopotomoy May 28-31. Cold Harbor June 1-5. Ordered to the rear June 5. Mustered out June 28, 1864. Veterans and recruits transferred to 17th Regiment Maine Infantry.

Regiment lost during service 10 Officers and 124 Enlisted men killed and mortally wounded and 1 Officer and 148 Enlisted men by disease. Total 283.

4th REGIMENT INFANTRY.

Organized at Rockland and mustered in June 15, 1861. Left State for Washington, D. C., June 20. Attached to Howard's Brigade, Heintzelman's Division, McDowell's Army of Northeastern Virginia, to August, 1861. Heintzelman's Brigade, Division of the Potomac, to October, 1861. Sedgwick's Brigade, Heintzelman's Division, Army of the Potomac, to March, 1862. 2nd Brigade, 3rd Division, 3rd Army Corps, Army Potomac, to July, 1862. 2nd Brigade, 1st Division, 3rd Army Corps, to March, 1864. 2nd Brigade, 3rd Division, 2nd Corps, to May, 1864. 1st Brigade, 3rd Division, 2nd Army Corps, to June, 1864.

SERVICE—Camp on Meridian Hill, Defences of Washington, till July 16, 1861. Advance on Manassas, Va., July 16-21. Battle of Bull Run July 21. Duty in the Defences of Washington, D. C., till March, 1862. Advance on Manassas, Va., March 10-15. Moved to the Peninsula March 17. Peninsula Campaign April to August. Siege of Yorktown April 5-May 4. Battle of Williamsburg May 5. Battle of Seven Pines or Fair Oaks May 31-June 1. Near Richmond June 18. Seven days before Richmond June 25-July 1. Oak Grove June 25. Charles City Cross Roads and Glendale June 30. Malvern Hill July 1. At Harrison's Landing till August 16. Retreat from the Peninsula and movement to Centreville August 16-27. Pope's Campaign in Northern Virginia August 27-September 2. Battles of Groveton August 29; Bull Run August 30; Chantilly September 1. Guard fords from Monocacy River to Conrad's Ferry till October 11. March to Leesburg, thence to Falmouth, Va., October 11-November 23. Mouth of Monocacy, White's Ford, October 12. Battle of Fredericksburg, Va., December 12-15. "Mud March" January 20-24, 1862. At Falmouth till April 27. Chancellorsville Campaign April 27-May 6. Battle of Chancellorsville May 1-5. Gettysburg (Pa.) Campaign June 13-July 24. Battle of Gettysburg July 1-3. Pursuit of Lee July 5-23. Wapping Heights, Va., July 23. Bristoe Campaign October 9-22. Advance to line of the Rappahannock November 7-8. Kelly's Ford November 7. Mine Run Campaign November 26-December 2. Payne's Farm November 27. Demonstration on the Rapidan February 6-7, 1864. Campaign from the Rapidan to the James River May 3-June 15. Battles of the Wilderness May 5-7. Laurel Hill May 8. Spottsylvania May 8-12. Po River May 10. Spottsylvania C. H. May 12-21. "Bloody Angle," Assault on the Salient, May 12. Harris Farm, Fredericksburg Road, May 19. North Anna River May 23-26. On line of the Pamunkey May 26-28. Totopotomoy May 28-31. Cold Harbor June 1-12. Before Petersburg June 15. Ordered to the rear June 15. Mustered out July 19, 1864, expiration of term. Veterans and recruits transferred to 19th Maine Infantry.

Regiment lost during service 14 Officers and 156 Enlisted men killed and mortally wounded and 2 Officers and 135 Enlisted men by disease. Total 307.

5th REGIMENT INFANTRY.

Organized at Portland and mustered in June 24, 1861. Left State for Washington, D. C., June 26. Attached to Howard's Brigade, Heintzelman's Division, McDowell's Army of Northeastern Virginia, to August, 1861. Heintzelman's Brigade, Division of the Potomac, to October, 1862. Slocum's Brigade, Franklin's Division, Army of the Potomac, to March, 1862. 2nd Brigade, 1st Division, 1st Army Corps, Army Potomac and Dept. of the Rappahannock, to May, 1862. 2nd Brigade, 1st Division, 6th Army Corps, Army Potomac, to June, 1864.

SERVICE.—Camp at Meridian Hill till July 16, 1861. Advance on Manassas, Va., July 16-21. Battle of Bull Run July 21. Duty in the Defences of Washington till March, 1862. Expedition to Pohick Church, Va., October 3, 1861. Advance on Manassas, Va., March 10-15, 1862. McDowell's advance on Fredericksburg, Va., April 4-12. Ordered to the Peninsula April 22. Siege of Yorktown (on Transports) April 24-May 4. West Point May 7-8. Seven days before Richmond June 25-July 1. Gaines' Mill June 27. Golding's Farm June 28. Savage Station June 29. Charles City Cross Roads and Glendale June 30. Malvern Hill July 1. At Harrison's Landing till August 15. Retreat from the Peninsula and movement to Centreville August 15-27. In works at Centreville August 27-31. Assist in checking Pope's rout at Bull Run and cover retreat to Fairfax C. H., September 1. Maryland Campaign September-October. Crampton's Pass, South Mountain, September 14. Battle of Antietam September 16-17. At Hagerstown, Md., September 26 to October 29. Movement to Falmouth, Va., October 29-November 19. Battle of Fredericksburg December 12-15. "Mud March" January 20-24, 1863. Chancellorsville Campaign April 27-May 6. Operations at Franklin's Crossing April 29-May 2. Maryes Heights, Fredericksburg, May 3. Salem Heights May 3-4. Banks' Ford May 4. Operations about Deep Run Ravine June 6-13. Battle of Gettysburg, Pa., July 2-4. Near Funkstown, Md., July 10-13. Hagerstown July 13. Bristoe Campaign October 9-22. Advance to line of the Rappahannock November 7-8. Rappahannock Station November 7. Mine Run Campaign November 26-December 2. Campaign from the Rapidan to the James River May 3 to June 15. Battles of the Wilderness May 5-7; Laurel Hill May 8; Spottsylvania May 8-12; Spottsylvania C. H. May 12-21. "Bloody Angle," assault on the Salient, May 12. North Anna River May 23-26. On line of the Pamunkey May 26-28. Totopotomoy May 28-31. Cold Harbor June 1-12. Before Petersburg June 19-22. Ordered to the rear for muster out. Mustered out July 27, 1864, expiration of term. Veterans and Recruits transferred to 6th Maine Infantry.

Regiment lost during service 8 Officers and 99 Enlisted men killed and mortally wounded and 1 Officer and 76 Enlisted men by disease. Total 184.

6th REGIMENT INFANTRY.

Organized at Portland and mustered in July 15, 1861. Left State for Washington, D. C., July 17. Attached to W. F. Smith's Brigade, Division of the Potomac, to October, 1861. 2nd Brigade, Smith's Division, Army of the Potomac, to March, 1862. 1st Brigade, 2nd Division, 4th Army Corps, Army Potomac, to May, 1862. 1st Brigade, 2nd Division, 6th Army Corps, to February, 1863. Light Division, 6th Army Corps, to May, 1863. 3rd Brigade, 1st Division, 6th Corps, to August, 1864.

SERVICE.—Duty in the defences of Washington, D. C., till March, 1862. Advance on Manassas, Va., March 10-15, 1862. Ordered to the Peninsula March 16. Advance toward Yorktown April 4-5. Siege of Yorktown April 5-May 4. Reconnoissance toward Yorktown April 6. Reconnoissance toward Lee's Mills April 28. Battle of Williamsburg May 5. Duty at White House till May 18. Duty near Richmond till June 6 and picket on the Chickahominy till June 25. Seven days before Richmond June 25-July 1. Gaines' Mill June 26. Golding's Farm June 27. Savage Station June 29. White Oak Swamp Bridge June 30. Malvern Hill July 1.

Duty at Harrison's Landing till August 15. Retreat from the Peninsula and movement to Centreville August 15-27. In works at Centreville August 27-31. Assist in checking Pope's rout at Bull Run August 30, and cover retreat to Fairfax C. H. September 1. Maryland Campaign September-October. Sugar Loaf Mountain, Md., September 11-12. Crampton's Pass, South Mountain, September 14. Battle of Antietam September 16-17. Duty in Maryland till October 29. Movement to Falmouth, Va., October 29-November 19. Battle of Fredericksburg December 12-15. "Mud March" January 20-24, 1863. At Falmouth till April. Chancellorsville Campaign April 27-May 6. Operations at Franklin's Crossing April 29-May 2. Maryes Heights, Fredericksburg, May 3. Salem Heights May 3-4. Banks' Ford May 4. Operations about Franklin's Crossing or Deep Run Ravine June 5-13. Brandy Station and Beverly Ford June 9. Battle of Gettysburg, Pa., July 2-4. Near Funkstown, Md., July 10-13. Bristoe Campaign October 9-22. Advance to line of the Rappahannock November 7-8. Rappahannock Station November 7. Mine Run Campaign November 26-December 2. Mine Run November 28-30. Campaign from the Rapidan to the James River May 3 to June 15, 1864. Battles of the Wilderness May 5-7; Spottsylvania May 8-12; Spottsylvania C. H. May 12-21. "Bloody Angle," assault on the Salient, May 12. North Anna May 23-26. On line of the Pamunkey May 26-28. Totopotomoy May 28-31. Cold Harbor June 1-12. Before Petersburg June 17-July 10. Jerusalem Plank Road June 22-23. Destruction of Weldon Railroad June 30. Ordered to rear for muster out July 10. Volunteered for 30 days' service in defence of Washington. Repulse of Early's attack on Washington July 12-13. Mustered out August 15, 1864, expiration of term. Veterans and Recruits transferred to 7th Maine.

Regiment lost during service 12 Officers and 141 Enlisted men killed and mortally wounded and 2 Officers and 100 Enlisted men by disease. Total 255.

7th REGIMENT INFANTRY.

Organized at Augusta and mustered in August 21, 1861. Left State for Baltimore, Md., August 23. Attached to Dix's Division, August to October, 1861. Davidson's Brigade, W. F. Smith's Division, Army of the Potomac, to March, 1862. 3rd Brigade, 2nd Division, 4th Army Corps, Army Potomac, to May, 1862. 3rd Brigade, 2nd Division, 6th Army Corps, to August, 1864.

SERVICE.—Duty at Baltimore, Md., till October 25, 1861. Moved to Washington, D. C. Duty at Georgetown Heights till November 7, and at Lewinsville, Va., till March, 1862. Advance on Manassas, Va., March 10-15. Return to Alexandria, thence moved to Fortress Monroe, Va., March 23-24. Reconnoissance to Watt's Creek March 27-31. Siege of Yorktown April 5-May 4. Battle of Williamsburg May 5. Advance up the Peninsula May 9-13. At White House till May 19. Mechanicsville May 23-24. Seven days before Richmond June 25-July 1. Garnett's and Golding's Farms June 27-28. Savage Station June 29. White Oak Swamp Bridge and Glendale June 30. Malvern Hill July 1. At Harrison's Landing till August 15. Movement to Fortress Monroe, thence to Centreville, August 15-27. In works at Centreville August 27-31. Assist in checking Pope's rout at Bull Run August 30, and cover retreat to Fairfax C. H. September 1. Maryland Campaign September-October. Crampton's Pass, South Mountain, September 14. Battle of Antietam September 16-17. Ordered home to recruit October, and at Portland, Me., till January 21, 1863. Joined Brigade and Division at White Oak Church, Va., January 25. Chancellorsville Campaign April 27-May 6. Operations at Franklin's Crossing April 29-May 2. Maryes Heights, Fredericksburg, May 3. Salem Heights May 3-4. Banks' Ford May 4. (Co. "F" joined May 23.) Operations at Franklin's Crossing June 5-13. Battle of Gettysburg, Pa., July 2-4. Fairfield July 5. Near Funkstown, Md., July 10-13. Bristoe Campaign October 9-22. Advance to line of the Rappahannock November 7-8. Rappahan-

nock Station November 7. Mine Run Campaign November 26-December 2. Campaign from the Rapidan to the James River May 3-June 15, 1864. Battles of the Wilderness May 5-7; Spottsylvania May 8-12; Spottsylvania C. H. May 12-21. "Bloody Angle," assault on the Salient, May 12. North Anna River May 23-26. On line of the Pamunkey May 26-28. Totopotomoy May 28-31. Cold Harbor June 1-12. Before Petersburg June 17-July 9. Jerusalem Plank Road June 22-23. Moved to Washington, D. C., July 9-11. Repulse of Early's attack on Washington, D. C., July 11-12. Sheridan's Shenandoah Valley Campaign August 7-21. Mustered out at Charlestown, Va., August 21, 1864. Veterans and Recruits transferred to 1st Maine Veteran Infantry.

Regiment lost during service 15 Officers and 113 Enlisted men killed and mortally wounded and 3 Officers and 209 Enlisted men by disease. Total 340.

8th REGIMENT INFANTRY.

Organized at Augusta and mustered in September 7, 1861. Left State for New York September 10, thence moved to Washington, D. C. Attached to Viele's 1st Brigade, Sherman's South Carolina Expeditionary Corps, October, 1861, to April, 1862. 1st Brigade, 1st Division, Dept. of the South, to November, 1862. District of Beaufort, S. C., 10th Corps, Dept. South, to April, 1863. District of Hilton Head, S. C., 10th Corps, Dept. South, to November, 1863. District of Beaufort, S. C., 10th Corps, to April, 1864. 2nd Brigade, 3rd Division, 10th Army Corps, Army of the James, Dept. of Virginia and North Carolina, to May, 1864. 1st Brigade, 3rd Division, 10th Army Corps, to June, 1864. 2nd Brigade, 2nd Division, 18th Army Corps, to December, 1864. 4th Brigade, 1st Division, 24th Army Corps, to May, 1865. 2nd Brigade, 1st Division, 24th Corps, May, 1865. 2nd Brigade, 1st Division, 24th Corps, to August, 1865. Dept. of Virginia to January, 1866.

SERVICE—Moved to Annapolis, Md., October 6, 1861. Expedition to Port Royal, S. C., October 21-November 7. Capture of Forts Walker and Beauregard, Port Royal Harbor, November 7. Hilton Head November 8-9. Duty at Hilton Head till February, 1862. Five Companies ordered to Dafuskie Island, S. C., February 14. Siege operations against Fort Pulaski till April 11. Bombardment and capture of Fort Pulaski April 10-11. Duty at Hilton Head and Beaufort, S. C., till March, 1863. Expedition to Jacksonville, Fla., March 18-23. Operations near Jacksonville March 23-31. Reconnoissance toward Baldwin March 25. Skirmish near Jacksonville March 25. Moved to Beaufort, S. C., March 31-April 1. Expedition against Charleston April 3-12. Moved to Hilton Head, S. C., April 16, and duty there till November 14. Moved to Beaufort, S. C., November 14, and duty there till April, 1864. Veterans on furlough March and April. Moved to Fortress Monroe, Va., April 14. Butler's operations on south side of James River and against Petersburg and Richmond May 4-28. Occupation of City Point and Bermuda Hundred May 5. Port Walthall May 6-7. Swift Creek May 9-10. Arrowfield Church, Chester Station, May 10. Operations against Fort Darling May 12-16. Drury's Bluff May 14-16. Bermuda Hundred front May 17-28. Moved to White House Landing May 28-June 1. Rapidan Campaign June 1-15. Cold Harbor June 1-12. Before Petersburg June 15-19. Siege of Petersburg and Richmond June 16, 1864, to April 2, 1865. Mine Explosion, Petersburg, July 30, 1864 (Reserve). Non-Veterans left front September 4, 1864, and mustered out September 15, 1864. Chaffin's Farm September 28-30. Battle of Fair Oaks October 27-28. Duty in trenches north of James River before Richmond till March 27, 1865. Moved to Hatcher's Run March 27-28. Appomattox Campaign March 28-April 9. White Oak Road March 30-31. Assault and capture of Forts Gregg and Baldwin April 2. Fall of Petersburg April 2. Pursuit of Lee April 3-9. Rice's Station April 6. Appomattox C. H. April 9. Surrender of Lee and his army. Duty at Richmond, Va., till August; at Manchester till November, and at Fortress Monroe till January, 1866. Mustered out January 18, 1866.

Regiment lost during service 6 Officers and 128 Enlisted men killed and mortally wounded and 4 Officers and 243 Enlisted men by disease. Total 381.

9th REGIMENT INFANTRY.

Organized at Augusta and mustered in September 22, 1861. Left State for Washington, D. C., September 24, and camp at Bladensburg, Defences of Washington, September 26-October 8. Moved to Annapolis, Md., October 8. Attached to Wright's 3rd Brigade, Sherman's South Carolina Expeditionary Corps, to February, 1862. Fernandina, Fla., Dept. of the South, to January, 1863. District of Hilton Head, S. C., 10th Corps, Dept. South, to June, 1863. St. Helena Island, S. C., to July, 1863. 2nd Brigade, Folly Island, S. C., 10th Corps, July, 1863. 2nd Brigade, Morris Island, S. C., 10th Corps, to August, 1863. 1st Brigade, Morris Island, S. C., 10th Corps, to April, 1864. 1st Brigade, 3rd Division, 10th Army Corps, Army of the James, Dept. of Virginia and North Carolina, to May, 1864. 2nd Brigade, 3rd Division, 18th Corps, to June, 1864. 3rd Brigade, 2nd Division, 10th Army Corps, to December, 1864. 3rd Brigade, 2nd Division, 24th Army Corps, to March, 1865. 3rd Brigade, 2nd Division, 10th Army Corps, Army Ohio, to July, 1865.

SERVICE.—Expedition to Port Royal, S. C., October 21-November 7, 1861. Capture of Forts Walker and Beauregard, Port Royal Harbor, November 7. Hilton Head November 8. Duty at Hilton Head till January 29, 1862. Expedition to Warsaw Sound January 29-March 1. Expedition to Florida February 25-March 5. Occupation of Fernandina, Fla., March 5, and duty there till January, 1863. Near Fernandina April 10, 1862 (Co. "I"). Moved to Hilton Head, S. C., January, 1863, and duty there till June, and at St. Helena Island till July. Moved to Folly Island, S. C., July 4. Attack on Morris Island July 10. Assaults on Fort Wagner, Morris Island, July 11 and 18. Siege operations against Forts Wagner and Gregg, Morris Island, and Fort Sumter and Charleston July 11-September 7. Capture of Forts Wagner and Gregg September 7. Occupation of Black Island till January, 1864. Veterans on furlough February and March. Non-Veterans duty on Morris Island till April, then moved to Gloucester Point, Va. Veterans rejoin April 28. Butler's operations on south side of James River and against Petersburg and Richmond May 4-27. Occupation of City Point and Bermuda Hundred, Va., May 5. Port Walthal Junction, Chester Station, May 6-7. Arrowfield Church May 9. Operations against Fort Darling May 12-16. Drury's Bluff May 14-16. Bermuda Hundred May 16-27. Moved to White House, thence to Cold Harbor May 27-June 1. Cold Harbor June 1-12. Before Petersburg June 15-19. Siege of Petersburg and Richmond June 16, 1864, to February, 1865. Mine Explosion, Petersburg, July 30, 1864. Demonstration north of James River August 13-20. Strawberry Plains, Deep Bottom, August 14-18. Bermuda Hundred August 24-25. In trenches before Petersburg till September 25. Non Veterans left front September 21 and mustered out September 27, 1864. New Market Heights September 28-29. Chaffin's Farm September 29-30. Charles City Cross Roads October 1. Fair Oaks October 27-28. Duty on north side of James till February, 1865. Rejoined Brigade at Fort Fisher, N. C. Cape Fear Intrenchments February 11-12. Fort Anderson February 18-20. Capture of Wilmington February 22. Advance on Goldsboro March 6-21. Occupation of Goldsboro March 21. Advance on Raleigh April 10-13. Occupation of Raleigh April 14. Bennett's House April 26. Surrender of Johnson and his army. Duty in North Carolina till July. Mustered out July 13, 1865.

Regiment lost during service 10 Officers and 172 Enlisted men killed and mortally wounded and 3 Officers and 236 Enlisted men by disease. Total 421.

10th REGIMENT INFANTRY.

Organized at Portland and mustered in October 4,

1861. Left State for Baltimore, Md., October 6. Attached to Dix's Division to November, 1861. Railroad Brigade, Army Potomac, to April, 1862. 1st Brigade, Williams' Division, Dept. of the Shenandoah, to June, 1862. 1st Brigade, 1st Division, 2nd Army Corps, Army of Virginia, to September, 1862. 1st Brigade, 1st Division, 12th Army Corps, Army of the Potomac, to April, 1863. Headquarters 12th Army Corps, Armies of the Potomac and Cumberland, to November, 1863.

SERVICE.—Duty at Baltimore, Md., till November 4, 1861. At Relay House till November 27, and at Baltimore till February 27, 1862. Guard duty by detachments along Baltimore & Ohio Railroad between Martinsburg and Charleston, W. Va., till May. Company "D" at Harper's Ferry till May 24, then moved to Winchester. Company "F" at Harper's Ferry till May 9, then moved to Winchester. Company "H" at Duffield's till May 24, then moved to Winchester. Company "K" at Kearneysville till May 24, then moved to Winchester. Company "C" at Van Obeiseville till May 9, then moved to Winchester. Company "A" at Opequan Bridge till May 24, then moved to Winchester. Company "B" at Martinsburg till May 24, then moved to Winchester. Company "E" at Halitown till May 9, then moved to Winchester. Companies "G" and "I" at Charleston till May 9, then moved to Winchester. All Companies at their stations from March 28. Operations in Shenandoah Valley May 15-June 17. Middletown May 24. Winchester May 25. Retreat to Williamsport May 25-27. Reconnoissance toward Martinsburg May 28. Reconnoissance to Luray C. H. June 29-30. Battle of Cedar Mountain August 9. Pope's Campaign in Northern Virginia August 16-September 2. Guarding trains during Bull Run Battles. Battle of Antietam, Md., September 16-17. Duty at Berlin, Md., October 3-December 10. March to Fairfax Station December 10-14, and duty there till January 19, 1863. March to Stafford C. H. January 19-23, and duty there till April 27. Ordered to rear for muster out April 27. Three-year men formed into a Battalion of three Companies and assigned to duty at Headquarters 12th Army Corps April 26. Old members mustered out May 8, 1863. Chancellorsville Campaign April 27-May 6. Battle of Chancellorsville May 1-5. Gettysburg (Pa.) Campaign June 13-July 24. Battle of Gettysburg July 1-3. Along the Rapidan August 1-September 24. Moved to Nashville, Tenn., September 24-October 2; to Murfreesboro, Tenn., October 5, thence to Shelbyville and Wartrace. Reopening Tennessee River October 26-29. Provost duty at Headquarters 12th Corps till November. Transferred to 29th Maine Infantry November 1, 1863.

Regiment lost during service 8 Officers and 74 Enlisted men killed and mortally wounded and 1 Officer and 53 Enlisted men by disease. Total 136.

11th REGIMENT INFANTRY.

Organized at Augusta and mustered in November 12, 1861. Left State for Washington, D. C., November 13. Attached to Davis' Provisional Brigade, Army Potomac, to January, 1862. 1st Brigade, Casey's Division, Army Potomac, to March, 1862. 1st Brigade, 3rd Division, 4th Army Corps, Army Potomac, to June, 1862. 1st Brigade, 2nd Division, 4th Corps, to December, 1862. Naglee's Brigade, Dept. North Carolina, to January, 1863. 2nd Brigade, 2nd Division, 18th Corps, to February, 1863. 1st Brigade, 2nd Division, 18th Corps, Port Royal, S. C., Dept. South, to April, 1863. District of Beaufort, S. C., 10th Corps, Dept. South, to June, 1863. Fernandina, Fla., Dept. of the South, to October, 1863. 1st Brigade, Morris Island, S. C., 10th Corps, Dept. South, to April, 1864. 2nd Brigade, 1st Division, 10th Army Corps, Army of the James, Dept. Virginia and North Carolina, to May, 1864. 3rd Brigade, 1st Division, 10th Corps, to December, 1864. 3rd Brigade, 1st Division, 24th Army Corps, to July, 1865. 2nd Brigade, 1st Division, 24th Corps, to August, 1865. Dept. of Virginia, to February, 1866.

SERVICE.—Duty in the defences of Washington, D. C., till March, 1862. Advance on Manassas, Va., March

10-15. Moved to Newport News March 28. Siege of Yorktown April 5-May 4. Battle of Williamsburg May 5. Operations about Bottom's Bridge May 20-23. Battle of Fair Oaks, Seven Pines, May 31-June 1. Guard Bottom's Bridge June 13-26. Seven days before Richmond June 25-July 1. Destruction of railroad bridge over Chickahominy June 27. Bottom's Bridge June 28-29. White Oak Swamp June 30. Malvern Hill July 1. At Harrison's Landing till August 15. Moved to Yorktown August 16-22, and duty there till December 26. Expedition to Matthews County December 11-15. Moved to Morehead City, N. C., December 26-January 1, 1863, thence to Port Royal, S. C., January 28-31. To St. Helena Island February 10, and duty there till April 4. Expedition against Charleston April 4-12. At Beaufort, S. C., till June. Moved to Fernandina, Fla., June 4-6, and duty there till October 6. (A detachment acting as Artillery on Morris Island, S. C., during siege of Fort Wagner, and operations against Charleston, July to October, 1863.) Regiment moved to Morris Island October 6 and siege operations against Charleston till April, 1864, then ordered to Gloucester Point, Va. Butler's operations on south side of James River and against Petersburg and Richmond May 4-June 15. Occupation of City Point and Bermuda Hundred May 5. Port Walthal May 6-7. Ware Bottom Church May 9. Swift Creek or Arrowfield Church May 9-10. Operations against Fort Darling May 12-16. Drury's Bluff May 14-16. Bermuda Hundred May 17-June 20. Action at Bermuda Hundred June 2 and 14. Port Walthal, Bermuda Front, June 16-17. Siege operations against Petersburg and Richmond June 16, 1864, to April 2, 1865. Deep Bottom June 20 and 25. Grover House, Deep Bottom, July 21. New Market Heights, Deep Bottom, July 27-28. Strawberry Plains August 14-18. In trenches before Petersburg August 27-September 26. New Market Heights September 28-29. Chaffin's Farm September 29-30. Darbytown and New Market Roads October 7. Darbytown Road October 13. Fair Oaks October 27-28. Chaffin's and Johnson's Farms October 29. Non-Veterans left front for muster out November 7. Duty on north side of James River before Richmond till March 27, 1865. (Detached for duty at New York City during election of 1864, November 5-17, 1864.) Moved to Hatcher's Run March 27-29. Appomattox Campaign March 28-April 9. Assault and capture of Forts Gregg and Baldwin and fall of Petersburg April 2. Pursuit of Lee to Appomattox April 3-9. Rice's Station April 6. High Bridge April 7. Clover Hill, Appomattox C. H., April 9. Surrender of Lee and his army. Duty at Richmond, Va., April 24 to November 24, and at Fredericksburg, Va., till January 19, 1866. Mustered out at City Point, Va., February 2, 1866.

Regiment lost during service 7 Officers and 115 Enlisted men killed and mortally wounded and 4 Officers and 233 Enlisted men by disease. Total 259.

12th REGIMENT INFANTRY.

Organized at Portland and mustered in November 16, 1861. Left State for Lowell, Mass., November 24, thence moved to Boston December 30 and embarked on Steamer "Constitution" for Ship Island, Miss., January 2, 1862, arriving there February 12. Attached to Butler's Expeditionary Corps January to March, 1862. 3rd Brigade, Dept. of the Gulf, to November, 1862. Grover's Division, Baton Rouge, La., Dept. Gulf, to January, 1863. 2nd Brigade, 4th Division, 19th Army Corps, Dept. Gulf, to February, 1864. 1st Brigade, 2nd Division, 19th Corps, Dept. Gulf, to July, 1864, and Army of the Shenandoah, Middle Military Division, to January, 1865. District of Savannah, Ga., Dept. of the South, to March, 1865. 1st Brigade, 1st Division, 10th Army Corps, Army Ohio, to April, 1865. District of Savannah, Dept. South, to April, 1866.

SERVICE.—Duty at Ship Island, Miss., to May 4, 1862. Moved to New Orleans, La., and duty at U. S. Mint till October, 1862. Expedition to Pass Manchac June 16-20. Pass Manchac June 17. Expedition to Ponchatoula (Cos. "C," "D," "F") September 13-18.

Ponchatoula September 15. Moved to Camp Parapet October 21, and duty there till November 19. Moved to Baton Rouge, La., and duty there till March, 1863. Operations against Port Hudson March 7-27. Moved to Donaldsville. Operations in Western Louisiana April 9-May 14. Teche Campaign April 11-20. Porter's and McWilliams' Plantation at Indian Head April 13. Irish Bend April 14. Destruction of salt works at New Iberia April 18. Advance to the Red River April 20-May 20. Advance on Port Hudson May 21-24. Siege of Port Hudson May 24-July 8. Assaults on Port Hudson May 27 and June 14. Thibodeaux June 20 (Detachment). Surrender of Port Hudson July 9. Donaldsville July 13. Moved to New Orleans August 12, thence to Ship Island, Miss., and duty there till October. At Camp Parapet till January 3, 1864. Expedition to Madisonville (Cos. "B," "F," "I," "K") January 3-7. Capture of Madisonville January 7, and duty there till March 11. Ordered to New Orleans March 11. Veterans on furlough April to June 16. Non-Veterans at Camp Parapet till June 16. Veterans moved from Portland to New Orleans May 27, thence Regiment moved to Morganza, La., and duty there till July 3. Moved to Algiers, thence to Fort Monroe, Va., July 13-20, thence to Bermuda Hundred, Va., July 21. Duty in trenches at Bermuda Hundred till July 25. Demonstration on north side of James River July 27-29. Deep Bottom July 27-28. Moved to Washington, D. C., July 31, hence to Tennallytown, Md., August 2. Sheridan's Shenandoah Valley Campaign August 7-November 28. Berryville September 3-4. Battle of Opequan, Winchester, September 19. Fisher's Hill September 22. Battle of Cedar Creek October 19. Duty at Cedar Creek till November 9 and at Opequan till November 19. Non-Veterans left front November 19, and mustered out December 7, 1864. Veterans consolidated to a Battalion of four Companies. Ordered to Savannah, Ga., January 3, 1865, and duty there till April, 1866. Six new Companies organized February and March, 1865, and assigned as "E," "F," "G," "H," "I," "K." Mustered out in February and March, 1866. Regiment mustered out April 18, 1866.

Regiment lost during service 3 Officers and 49 Enlisted men killed and mortally wounded and 2 Officers and 237 Enlisted men by disease. Total 291.

13th REGIMENT INFANTRY.

Organized at Augusta and mustered in December 13, 1861. Moved to Boston, Mass., February 8, 1862. Companies "A," "B," "E" and "I" embark on Steamer "Mississippi" for Ship Island, Miss., February 20, arriving March 20. Regiment moved to New York February 21, and there embark February 27 on Steamer "Fulton" for Ship Island, Miss., arriving there March 8. Attached to Butler's Expeditionary Corps January to March, 1862. 3rd Brigade, Dept. of the Gulf, to July, 1862. Independent Command, Dept. of the Gulf, to December, 1862. Defences of New Orleans, La., Dept. Gulf, to August, 1863. 2nd Brigade, 4th Division, 19th Army Corps, Dept. Gulf, to December, 1863. 3rd Brigade, 2nd Division, 13th Corps, Dept. Gulf, to January, 1864. 2nd Brigade, 4th Division, 13th Corps, Dept. Gulf, to February, 1864. 2nd Brigade, 1st Division, 19th Corps, Dept. Gulf, to July, 1864, and Army of the Shenandoah, Middle Military Division, to December, 1864.

SERVICE.—Duty at Ship Island, Miss., till July 5, 1862. Company "C" moved to Fort Pike July 5, thence to Fort Macomb, and duty there till August 30, 1863. Moved to New Orleans. Company "A" moved to quarantine station July 8, and duty there till August 7, then at Fort St. Phillip till August, 1863. Moved to New Orleans. Companies "G," "H" and "I" moved to Fort Jackson July 8, and to Fort St. Phillip August 24. Duty there till August, 1863. Expedition to Pass Manchac February 8-11, 1863 (Detachment). Moved to New Orleans. Companies "B" and "E" moved to New Orleans July 11, thence to Fort St. Phillip July 15, and duty there till August, 1863. Moved to New Orleans. Companies "D" and "F" at Ship Island till January 23, 1863, and at Forts Jackson and St. Phillip till August, 1863. Moved to New Orleans August 1. Company 'K" moved to Fort Macomb July 5, and duty there till August 30, 1863. Moved to New Orleans. Region on duty at New Orleans August to October, 1863. Expedition to the Rio Grande, Texas, October 27-December 2. Advance on Brownsville, Texas, November 3-6. Occupation of Fort Brown November 6. Expedition to Aransas Pass November 17. Capture of Mustang Island November 17. Fort Esperanza November 25-27. Matagorda Bay December 29-30. Companies "C," "H" and "K" duty at Pass Cavallo, Matagorda Island, till February, 1864. Moved to Franklin, La., February 12-16, and duty there till March 15. Red River Campaign March 15-May 22. Advance from Franklin to Alexandria March 15-26, thence to Natchitoches March 26-April 2. Battle of Sabine Cross Roads April 8. Pleasant Hill April 9. Cane River Crossing April 23. At Alexandria April 25-May 13. Retreat to Morganza May 13-22. Mansura May 16. Duty at Morganza till July 1. Moved to Fortress Monroe, Va., thence to Washington, D. C., July 1-13. Expedition to Snicker's Gap, Va., July 13-23. Veterans on furlough August-September, Non-Veterans duty at Harper's Ferry, W. Va., till October 5. Regiment ordered to Martinsburg, W. Va., and duty there till December 25. Non-Veterans left front for muster out December 25. Mustered out January 5, 1865. Veterans and Recruits consolidated to a Battalion and transferred to 30th Maine Infantry December 25, 1864.

Regiment lost during service 1 Officer and 13 Enlisted men killed and mortally wounded and 3 Officers and 178 Enlisted men by disease. Total 195.

14th REGIMENT INFANTRY.

Organized at Augusta and mustered in December 31, 1861. Left State for Boston, Mass., February 5, 1862, and there embarked February 6 on Steamer "North America" for Ship Island, Miss., arriving March 8. Attached to Butler's New Orleans Expeditionary Corps, January to March, 1862. 3rd Brigade, Dept. of the Gulf, to December, 1862. Sherman's Division, Dept. Gulf, to January, 1863. 3rd Brigade, 2nd Division, 19th Army Corps, Dept. Gulf, to July, 1863. 1st Brigade, 3rd Division, 19th Corps, July, 1863. 2nd Brigade, 3rd Division, 19th Corps, to February, 1864. 1st Brigade, 2nd Division, 19th Corps, Dept. Gulf, to July, 1864, and Army Shenandoah, Middle Military Division, to January, 1865. District of Savannah, Ga., Dept. South, to March, 1865. 1st Brigade, 1st Division, 10th Army Corps, Army Ohio, to April, 1865. District of Savannah, Dept. of the South, to August, 1865.

SERVICE.—Duty at Ship Island, Miss., till May 19, 1862. Moved to New Orleans, May 19-25, and duty there till July 7. Moved to Baton Rouge, La., July 7. Expedition to Amite River July 23-25 (Cos. "F" and "K"). Battle of Baton Rouge August 5. Moved to Carrollton August 20, and duty there till December 13. Bayou des Allemands September 4-5. Expedition to St. Charles C. H. September 7 8. St. Charles C. H. September 8. Moved to Bonnet Carre December 13, and duty there till May 7, 1863. Company "H" detached at Frenier December 14, 1862, to January 6, 1863. Company "B" detached at Frenier December 14, 1862, to February 20, 1863. Company "E" detached at Frenier January 6 to April 11. Scout to Pass Manchac February 8-11, 1863 (Detachment). Expedition to Ponchatoula March 21-24. Capture of Ponchatoula March 24 (Co. "E"). Expedition to Amite River March 24-30 (Cos. "A," "B," "C," "D," "G," "H" and "I"). Expedition to Amite River May 7-19. Civiques Ferry May 10. Moved to Baton Rouge, thence to Port Hudson May 20-22. Siege of Port Hudson May 24-July 8. Assaults on Port Hudson May 27 and June 14. Surrender of Port Hudson July 8. Moved to Baton Rouge July 22. Sabine Pass Expedition September 4-11. Western Louisiana ("Teche") Campaign October 3-November 30. Duty at New Iberia till January 7, 1864. Moved to Franklin January 7, thence to New Orleans Janu-

ary 16. Duty at Camp Parapet till May 5. Veterans on furlough February 10 to April 19. Moved to Baton Rouge May 5, and duty there till June 1. Moved to Morganza, La., and duty there till July 3. Moved to Algiers, thence to Fort Monroe and Bermuda Hundred, Va., July 3-22. In trenches at Bermuda Hundred till July 28. Demonstration north of James River July 28-29. Deep Bottom July 28-30. Moved to Washington, D. C., July 31, thence to Tennallytown, Md., August 2. Sheridan's Shenandoah Valley Campaign August 7-November 28. Berryville September 3-4. Battle of Opequan, Winchester, September 19. Fisher's Hill September 22. Battle of Cedar Creek October 19. At Cedar Creek till November 9. At Kernstown till November 24. Guard train to Martinsburg. Moved to Camp Russell December 1, and duty there till December 22. Non-Veterans left front for muster out December 22. Mustered out January 13, 1865. Veterans and Recruits consolidated to a Battalion of four Companies, and duty at Stevenson's Depot till January 6, 1865. Moved to Savannah, Ga., January 6-20, and provost duty there till May 6. (Two new unassigned Companies joined March 30, and four Companies joined April 10. Assigned as "E," "F," "G," "H," "I" and "K.") March to Augusta, Ga., May 6-14, and to Savannah May 31-June 7. Moved to Darien June 9-10, and duty there till August 28. (Co. "B" at Walthamville and Co. "H" at Brunswick.) Mustered out August 28, 1865.

Regiment lost during service 5 Officers and 81 Enlisted men killed and mortally wounded and 2 Officers and 330 Enlisted men by disease. Total 418.

15th REGIMENT INFANTRY.

Organized at Augusta December 6-31, 1861, and mustered in January 23, 1862. Moved to Portland February 25, and there embarked for Ship Island, Miss., March 6. Attached to Butler's New Orleans Expeditionary Corps January to March, 1862. 3rd Brigade, Dept. of the Gulf, to September, 1862. District of West Florida, Dept. Gulf, to June, 1863. 2nd Brigade, 4th Division, 19th Army Corps, Dept. Gulf, to December, 1863. 3rd Brigade, 2nd Division, 13th Corps, Dept. Gulf, to January, 1864. 2nd Brigade, 4th Division, 13th Corps, Dept. Gulf, to February, 1864. 2nd Brigade, 1st Division, 19th Corps, Dept. Gulf, to July, 1864, and Army Shenandoah, Middle Military Division, to April, 1865. 1st Brigade, 1st Division, Dept. of Washington, to June, 1865. 2nd Separate Brigade, District of South Carolina, Dept. of the South, to July, 1866.

SERVICE.—Duty at Ship Island, Miss., till May, 1862, and at Camp Parapet and Carrollton May 19-September 8. Moved to Pensacola, Fla., September 8, and duty there till June, 1863. Action at Fifteen Mile House, Fla., February 25, 1863, and at Arcadia March 6. Ordered to New Orleans June 21, thence to La Fourche Landing. Expedition to Thibodeaux June 23-25. At Camp Parapet till August, and provost duty in New Orleans till October. Expedition to the Rio Grande, Texas, October 27-December 2. Advance on Brownsville November 3-6. Occupation of Brownsville November 6. Expedition to Aransas November 14-21. Aransas Pass and capture of Mustang Island November 17. Fort Esperanza November 25-27. Cedar Bayou November 23 (Detachment). Duty at Pass Cavallo, Matagorda Island, till February 28, 1864. Moved to Franklin, La., March 1-5. Red River Campaign March 10-May 22. Advance from Franklin to Alexandria March 14-26, thence to Natchitoches March 26-April 2. Battle of Sabine Cross Roads April 8. Pleasant Hill April 9. Cane River Crossing April 23. At Alexandria April 26-May 13. Retreat to Morganza May 13-22. Mansura May 16. Duty at Morganza till July. Moved to Fort Monroe, thence to Bermuda Hundred, Va., July 1-17 (6 Cos.). Duty in trenches at Bermuda Hundred till July 28. Deep Bottom July 28-30. Moved to Washington, D. C., thence to Monocacy, Md. (4 Cos., under Murray and Drew, moved from Morganza to Washington, D. C., July 1-12. Pursuit of Early July 14-24. Rejoin Regiment at Monocacy, Md., August 4.) Veterans on furlough August 5-

October 1. Non-Veterans temporarily attached to 13th Maine Infantry, and duty at Harper's Ferry till October 5. Regiment moved to Martinsburg October 5, and duty there till January 7, 1865. Moved to Stevenson's Depot, and operations in the Shenandoah Valley till April. Moved to Washington, D. C., April 19-23, and duty there till May 31. On provost duty during Grand Review May 23-24. Moved to Savannah, Ga., May 31-June 4, thence to Georgetown, S. C., June 13-14. Duty at Georgetown, Darlington, Cheraw, Chesterfield C. H., Bennettsville, Columbia and in Districts of Chester, Lancaster, York, Spartanburg and Union till July, 1866. Mustered out July 5, 1866. Non-Veterans mustered out January 15, 1865.

Regiment lost during service 5 Enlisted men killed and mortally wounded and 3 Officers and 340 Enlisted men by disease. Total 348.

16th REGIMENT INFANTRY.

Organized at Augusta and mustered in August 14, 1862. Left State for Washington, D. C., August 19, and camp at Arlington Heights till September 6. Attached to 3rd Brigade, 2nd Division, 1st Army Corps, Army Potomac, to November, 1862. 1st Brigade, 2nd Division, 1st Corps, to March, 1864. 1st Brigade, 2nd Division, 5th Corps, to June, 1865. 1st Brigade, 3rd Division, 5th Corps, to September, 1864. 2nd Brigade, 3rd Division, 5th Corps, to June, 1865.

SERVICE.—March into Maryland September 6-16, 1862. Battle of Antietam September 16-17. Duty near Sharpsburg, Md., till October 28. Moved to Warrenton, Va., October 28-November 7. Forced march to Rappahannock Station November 11. Duty there till November 19, and at Brooks Station till December 11. Battle of Fredericksburg December 12-15. "Mud March" January 20-24, 1863. At Falmouth and Belle Plains till April 27. Chancellorsville Campaign April 27-May 6. Fitzhugh's Crossing April 29-30. Battle of Chancellorsville May 1-5. Gettysburg (Pa.) Campaign June 13-July 24. Battle of Gettysburg July 1-3. Pursuit of Lee July 5-24. Bristoe Campaign October 9-22. Advance to line of the Rappahannock November 7-8. Mine Run Campaign November 26-December 2. Demonstration on the Rapidan February 6-7, 1864. Campaign from the Rapidan to the James May 3-June 15. Battles of the Wilderness May 5-7. Laurel Hill May 8. Spottsylvania May 8-12. Spottsylvania C. H. May 12-21. North Anna River May 23-26. Jericho Ford May 23. Line of the Pamunkey May 26-28. Totopotomoy May 28-31. Cold Harbor June 1-12. Bethesda Church June 1-3. White Oak Swamp June 13. Before Petersburg June 16-19. Siege of Petersburg June 16, 1864, to April 2, 1865. Jerusalem Plank Road June 22-23, 1864. Mine Explosion, Petersburg, July 30 (Reserve). Weldon Railroad August 18-21. Reconnoissance toward Dinwiddie C. H. September 15. Garrison Fort Wadsworth till December 5. Warren's Hicksford Raid December 7-12. Dabney's Mills February 5-7, 1865. Appomattox Campaign March 28-April 9. White Oak Road March 29-30. Gravelly Run March 31. Five Forks April 1. Fall of Petersburg April 2. Sailor's Creek April 6. Appomattox C. H. April 9. Surrender of Lee and his army. At Black and White Station April 21-May 1. Moved to Manchester, thence marched to Washington, D. C., May 1-12. Grand Review May 23. Duty at Ball's Cross Roads till June 5. Mustered out June 5, 1865. Recruits transferred to 20th Maine Infantry.

Regiment lost during service 9 Officers and 172 Enlisted men killed and mortally wounded and 2 Officers and 257 Enlisted men by disease. Total 440.

17th REGIMENT INFANTRY.

Organized at Camp King, Cape Elizabeth, and mustered in August 18, 1862. Left State for Washington, D. C., August 21. Attached to Defences of Washington to October, 1862. 3rd Brigade, 1st Division, 3rd Army Corps, Army Potomac, to March, 1864. 2nd Brigade, 3rd Division, 2nd Army Corps, to June, 1864. 1st Brigade, 3rd Division, 2nd Corps, to March, 1865. 2nd Brigade, 3rd Division, 2nd Corps, to June, 1865.

SERVICE.—Garrison duty in the Defences of Washington August 23-October 7, 1862. At Upton's Hill, Va., till October 12. At Edwards Ferry October 12-28. Advance to Warrenton, thence to Falmouth, Va., October 28-November 22. Battle of Fredericksburg December 12-15. "Mud March" January 20-24, 1863. Chancellorsville Campaign April 27-May 6. Battle of Chancellorsville May 1-5. Gettysburg (Pa.) Campaign June 13-July 24. Battle of Gettysburg July 1-3. Pursuit of Lee July 5-24. Wapping Heights July 23. Bristoe Campaign October 9-22. Auburn and Bristoe October 14. Advance to line of the Rappahannock November 7-8. Kelly's Ford November 7. Mine Run Campaign November 26-December 2. Payne's Farm November 27. Mine Run November 28-30. Demonstration on the Rapidan February 6-7, 1864. Campaign from the Rapidan to the James May 3-June 15. Battles of the Wilderness May 5-7. Laurel Hill May 8. Spottsylvania May 8-12. Po River May 10. Spottsylvania C. H. May 12-21. "Bloody Angle," Assault on the Salient, May 12. Harris Farm, Fredericksburg Road, May 19. North Anna May 23-26. Line of the Pamunkey May 26-28. Totopotomoy May 28-31. Cold Harbor June 1-12. Before Petersburg June 16-19. Siege of Petersburg June 16, 1864, to April 2, 1865. Jerusalem Plank Road June 22-23, 1864. Deep Bottom, north of the James, July 27-28. Mine Explosion, Petersburg, July 30. Demonstration north of the James August 13-20. Strawberry Plains August 14-18. Ream's Station August 25. Poplar Springs Church September 29-October 2. Boydton Plank Road, Hatcher's Run, October 27-28. Raid on Weldon Railroad December 7-11. Dabney's Mills February 5-7, 1865. Appomattox Campaign March 28-April 9. South Side Railroad March 29. Boydton Road and White Oak Ridge March 30-31. Fall of Petersburg April 2. Jettersville April 5. Sailor's Creek April 6. High Bridge April 6-7. Farmville April 7. Appomattox C. H. April 9. Surrender of Lee and his army. At Burkesville April 11-May 1. March to Washington, D. C., May 1-15. Grand Review May 23. Mustered out at Bailey's Cross Roads June 4, 1865. Recruits transferred to 1st Maine Heavy Artillery. Discharged at Portland, Me., June 10, 1865.

Regiment lost during service 12 Officers and 195 Enlisted men killed and mortally wounded and 4 Officers and 159 Enlisted men by disease. Total 370.

18th REGIMENT INFANTRY.

Organized at Bangor and mustered in August 21, 1862. Left State for Washington, D. C., August 24, and duty in the defences of that city till January 6, 1863. Designation of Regiment changed to 1st Maine Heavy Artillery January 6, 1863, which see.

19th REGIMENT INFANTRY.

Organized at Bath and mustered in August 25, 1862. Left State for Washington, D. C., August 27. Attached to Defences of Washington to October, 1862. 1st Brigade, 2nd Division, 2nd Army Corps, Army of the Potomac, to June, 1865.

SERVICE.—Duty in the Defences of Washington, D. C., till September 30, 1862. Moved to Harper's Ferry, W. Va., September 30-October 4. Advance to Warrenton, Va., October 30-November 9. March to Falmouth November 15-17. Battle of Fredericksburg December 12-15. "Mud March" January 20-24, 1863. Duty at Falmouth till April, 1863. Chancellorsville Campaign April 27-May 6. Maryes Heights, Fredericksburg, May 3. Salem Heights May 3-4. Banks Ford May 4. Gettysburg (Pa.) Campaign June 13-July 24. Haymarket June 25. Battle of Gettysburg July 1-3. Pursuit of Lee July 5-24. Bristoe Campaign October 9-22. Bristoe Station October 14. Advance to line of the Rappahannock November 7-8. Mine Run Campaign November 26-December 2. Demonstration on the Rapidan February 6-7, 1864. Morton's Ford February 6-7. Campaign from the Rapidan to the James May 3-June 15. Battles of the Wilderness May 5-7. Laurel Hill May 8. Spottsylvania May 8-12. Po River May 9-10. Spottsylvania C. H. May 12-21. "Bloody Angle," Assault on the Salient, May 12.

North Anna River May 23-26. Line of the Pamunkey May 26-28. Totopotomoy May 28-31. Cold Harbor June 1-12. Before Petersburg June 16-19. Siege of Petersburg June 16, 1864, to April 2, 1865. Jerusalem Plank Road June 22-23, 1864. Deep Bottom, north of the James, July 27-28. Mine Explosion, Petersburg, July 30 (Reserve). Demonstration north of the James August 13-20. Strawberry Plains, Deep Bottom, August 14-18. Ream's Station August 25. Boydton Plank Road, Hatcher's Run, October 27-28. Dabney's Mills February 5-7, 1865. Appomattox Campaign March 28-April 9. Boydton Road March 30-31. Fall of Petersburg April 2. Sailor's Creek April 6. High Bridge April 6-7. Farmville April 7. Appomattox C. H. April 9. Surrender of Lee and his army. At Burkesville April 11-May 2. March to Washington, D. C., May 2-15. Grand Review May 23. Mustered out May 31 and discharged June 7, 1865. Recruits transferred to 1st Maine Heavy Artillery.

Regiment lost during service 3 Officers and 189 Enlisted men killed and mortally wounded and 2 Officers and 182 Enlisted men by disease. Total 376.

20th REGIMENT INFANTRY.

Organized at Portland and mustered in August 29, 1862. Left State for Alexandria, Va., September 3. Attached to 1st Brigade, 1st Division, 5th Army Corps, Army Potomac, to October, 1862. 3rd Brigade, 1st Division, 5th Army Corps, to July, 1865.

SERVICE.—Battle of Antietam, Md., September 16-17, 1862. Shephardstown September 19. Advance to Falmouth, Va., October-November. Battle of Fredericksburg, Va., December 12-15. Expedition to Richards and Ellis Fords December 20-30. "Mud March" January 20-24, 1863. Chancellorsville Campaign April 27-May 6. Battle of Chancellorsville May 1-5. Gettysburg (Pa.) Campaign June 12-July 24. Aldie June 17. Upperville and Upperville June 21. Middleburg June 24. Battle of Gettysburg July 1-3. Pursuit of Lee to Manassas Gap, Va., July 5-24. Bristoe Campaign October 9-22. Advance to line of the Rappahannock November 7-8. Rappahannock Station November 7. Mine Run Campaign November 26-December 2. Campaign from the Rapidan to the James May 3-June 15, 1864. Battles of the Wilderness May 5-7. Laurel Hill May 8. Spottsylvania May 8-12. Spottsylvania C. H. May 12-21. North Anna River May 23-26. Jericho Mills May 23. Line of the Pamunkey May 26-28. Totopotomoy May 28-31. Cold Harbor June 1-3. Bethesda Church June 1-3. Before Petersburg June 16-19. Siege of Petersburg June 16, 1864, to April 2, 1865. Weldon Railroad June 21-23, 1864. Mine Explosion, Petersburg, July 30 (Reserve). Six Mile House, Weldon Railroad, August 18-21. Poplar Springs Church, Peeble's Farm, September 29-October 2. Hatcher's Run October 27-28. Warren's Hicksford Raid December 7-11. Dabney's Mills, Hatcher's Run, February 5-7, 1865. Appomattox Campaign March 28-April 9. White Oak Road March 29. Quaker Road March 30. Boydton Road March 30-31. Five Forks April 1. Amelia C. H. April 5. High Bridge April 6. Appomattox C. H. April 9. Surrender of Lee and his army. March to Washington, D. C., May 2-12. Grand Review May 23. Mustered out—Old members, June 4; Regiment, July 16, 1865.

Regiment lost during service 9 Officers and 138 Enlisted men killed and mortally wounded and 1 Officer and 145 Enlisted men by disease. Total 293.

21st REGIMENT INFANTRY.

Organized at Augusta and mustered in for nine months' service October 14, 1862. Left State for Washington, D. C., October 21. Ordered on reaching Trenton, N. J., to return to New York, and duty at East New York till January, 1863. Embarked for New Orleans, La., January 9. Companies "A," "C," "E," "F," "H" and "K," on Steamer "Onward," reach New Orleans January 31, and moved to Baton Rouge, La., February 3. Balance of Regiment arrive at Baton Rouge February 11. Attached to 1st Brigade, 1st Division, 19th Army Corps, Dept. of the Gulf, to July, 1863.

SERVICE.—Operations against Port Hudson March 7-20, 1863. Duty at Baton Rouge till May. Advance on Port Hudson May 20-24. Action at Plains Store May 21. Siege of Port Hudson May 24-July 8. Assaults on Port Hudson May 27 and June 14. Surrender of Port Hudson July 8. Ordered home July 24. Mustered out August 25, 1863, expiration of term.

Regiment lost during service 1 Officer and 26 Enlisted men killed and mortally wounded and 1 Officer and 144 Enlisted men by disease. Total 172.

22nd REGIMENT INFANTRY.

Organized at Bangor and mustered in for nine months' service October 10, 1862. Left State for Washington, D. C., October 21. Duty at Arlington Heights, Va., till November 3. Moved to Fortress Monroe, Va., November 3, thence to Ship Island, Miss., and New Orleans, La., December 2-15. Attached to Grover's Division, Dept. of the Gulf, to January, 1863. 1st Brigade, 4th Division, 19th Army Corps, Army Gulf, to July, 1863.

SERVICE.—Moved to Baton Rouge, La., January 16, 1863. Duty there till March. Operations against Port Hudson, La., March 7-20. Moved to Donaldsonville March 26, thence to Brashear City. Operations in Western Louisiana April 9-May 14. Teche Campaign April 11-20. Porter's and McWilliams' Plantations at Indian Bend April 13. Irish Bend April 14. Moved to Franklin April 15. Bayou Vermillion April 17. Moved to New Iberia April 25; to Washington May 6, thence to Brashear City May 11-27. Moved to Port Hudson May 28. Siege of Port Hudson June 1-July 8. Assault at Port Hudson June 14. Surrender of Port Hudson July 8. Ordered home July 24. Mustered out August 14, 1863, expiration of term.

Regiment lost during service 1 Officer and 8 Enlisted men killed and mortally wounded and 2 Officers and 169 Enlisted men by disease. Total 180.

23rd REGIMENT INFANTRY.

Organized at Portland and mustered in for nine months' service September 29, 1862. Left State for Washington, D. C., October 18. Attached to Grover's Brigade, Defences of Washington, to February, 1863. Jewett's Brigade, 22nd Corps, to June, 1863. Slough's Brigade, Defences of Alexandria, 22nd Corps, to July, 1863.

SERVICE.—Camp at East Capital Hill till October 25, 1862. Moved to Seneca, Md., October 25, and guard duty along the Potomac River till April 19, 1863. Stationed at Edwards Ferry December, 1862, to April, 1863. Moved to Poolesville April 19, thence to Washington May 5, and to Alexandria May 24. Moved to Poolesville, Md., June 17, thence to Harper's Ferry, W. Va. Mustered out July 15, 1863, expiration of term.

Regiment lost during service 56 Enlisted men by disease.

24th REGIMENT INFANTRY.

Organized at Augusta and mustered in for nine months' service October 16, 1862. Left State for New York City October 29. Duty at East New York till January 12, 1863. Moved to Fortress Monroe, Va., thence to New Orleans, La., January 12-February 14. Attached to 3rd Brigade, 2nd Division, 19th Army Corps, Dept. of the Gulf, to July, 1863.

SERVICE.—Moved to Bonnet Carre, La., February 26, 1863, and duty there till May. Expedition to Ponchatoula and Amite River March 21-30. Capture of Ponchatoula March 24. Amite River March 28. Expedition to Amite River May 7-21. Civiques Ferry May 10. Advance on Port Hudson May 21-24. Siege of Port Hudson May 24-July 8. Assaults on Port Hudson, May 27 and June 14. Surrender of Port Hudson July 8. Ordered home July 24, and mustered out August 25, 1863, expiration of term.

Regiment lost during service 1 Enlisted man killed and 5 Officers and 185 Enlisted men by disease. Total 191.

25th REGIMENT INFANTRY.

Organized at Portland and mustered in for nine months' service September 29, 1862. Left State for Washington, D. C., October 16. Attached to Casey's Division, Defences of Washington, to February, 1863. 1st Brigade, Casey's Division, 22nd Corps, to April, 1863. 1st Brigade, Abercrombie's Division, 22nd Corps, to July, 1863.

SERVICE.—Garrison duty in the Defences of Washington, D. C., October 18, 1862, to March 24, 1863. Moved to Chantilly, Va., March 24, and picket duty there till June 26. (Temporarily attached to 12th Army Corps, Army Potomac.) Moved to Arlington Heights June 26, thence ordered home June 30. Mustered out July 10, 1863, expiration of term.

Regiment lost during service 20 Enlisted men by disease.

26th REGIMENT INFANTRY.

Organized at Bangor and mustered in for nine months' service October 11, 1862. Left State for Washington, D. C., October 26. Duty in the defences of that city till November 16. Moved to Fortress Monroe, Va., 16, thence sailed for New Orleans, La., December 2. Attached to Grover's Division, Dept. of the Gulf, to January, 1863. 3rd Brigade, 4th Division, 19th Army Corps, Dept. Gulf, to July, 1863.

SERVICE.—Duty at Camp Chalmette, La., till January 8, 1863. Occupation of Baton Rouge, La., December 17, 1862 (part of Regiment). Rest of Regiment moved to Baton Rouge January 8, 1863, and duty there till March 13. Operations against Port Hudson March 13-20. Moved to Donaldsonville March 28, thence to Thibodeauxville and Brashear City. Operations in Western Louisiana April 9-May 14. Bayou Teche Campaign April 11-20. Irish Bend April 14. Bayou Vermillion April 17. Conduct train from Alexandria to Brashear City, a march of 300 miles, May 21-26. Moved to Algiers May 27, thence to Port Hudson May 29. Siege of Port Hudson May 30-July 8. Assault on Port Hudson June 14. Surrender of Port Hudson July 8. Ordered home July 25 and mustered out August 17, 1863, expiration of term.

Regiment lost during service 34 Enlisted men killed and mortally wounded and 1 Officer and 130 Enlisted men by disease. Total 165.

27th REGIMENT INFANTRY.

Organized at Portland and mustered in for nine months' service September 30, 1862. Left State for Washington, D. C., October 20. Attached to Casey's Division, Defences of Washington, to February, 1863. 1st Brigade, Casey's Division, 22nd Corps, to April, 1863. 1st Brigade, Abercrombie's Division, 22nd Corps, to July, 1863.

SERVICE.—Duty at Arlington Heights, Va., October 23 to December 12, 1862, and at Hunting Creek till March, 1863. Moved to Chantilly, Va., March 24, and duty there till June 23. Ordered to rear for muster out June 26. Volunteered to remain beyond its time in the defences of Washington during the Gettysburg (Pa.) Campaign. Left Washington for home July 4. Mustered out July 17, 1863.

Regiment lost during service 1 Officer and 21 Enlisted men by disease. Total 22.

28th REGIMENT INFANTRY.

Organized at Augusta and mustered in for nine months' service October 18, 1862. Left State for Washington, D. C., October 26. Stopped at New York and duty at Fort Schuyler till November 26, and at East New York till January 17, 1863. Moved to Fortress Monroe, Va., January 17-22, thence to New Orleans, La., January 22-29. Attached to 2nd Brigade, 2nd Division, 19th Army Corps, Dept. of the Gulf, to May, 1863. 3rd Brigade, 2nd Division, 19th Corps, Dept. Gulf, to July, 1863 (6 Cos.).

SERVICE.—Duty at Chalmette, La., till February 15, 1863. Moved to Pensacola, Fla., February 15, returning to New Orleans March 22, thence moved to Don-

aldsonville and duty there and at Plaquemine till May 27. (Six Companies ordered to Port Hudson May 27. Siege of Port Hudson May 30-July 8. Assault on Port Hudson June 14. Ordered to Donaldsonville July 4, and duty there till July 12.) Four Companies remained on duty at Donaldsonville May 27 to July 12. Action at Donaldsonville June 28 (4 Cos.). Moved to Baton Rouge July 12, thence to Cairo, Ill., August 6, and home. Mustered out August 31, 1863.

Regiment lost during service 1 Officer and 10 Enlisted men killed and mortally wounded and 3 Officers and 140 Enlisted men by disease. Total 154.

29th REGIMENT INFANTRY.

Organized at Augusta and mustered in December 17, 1863. (Cos. "A" and "D" transferred from 10th Maine Battalion.) Left State for New Orleans, La., January 31, arriving February 16, 1864. Attached to 2nd Brigade, 1st Division, 19th Army Corps, Dept. of the Gulf, to July, 1864. 1st Brigade, 1st Division, 19th Corps, Dept. Gulf and Army Shenandoah, Middle Military Division, to March, 1865. 1st Brigade, 1st Division, Army Shenandoah, to April, 1865. 1st Brigade, 1st Division, Dept. of Washington, to June, 1865. District of South Carolina, Dept. South, to June, 1866.

SERVICE.—Moved to Brashear City, La., February 20, 1864; thence to Franklin February 21. Red River Campaign March 10-May 22. (10th Maine Battalion join May 30.) Advance from Franklin to Alexandria March 14-26. Battle of Sabine Cross Roads April 8. Pleasant Hill April 9. Monett's Bluff, Cane River Crossing, April 23. At Alexandria April 25-May 13. Construction of dam at Alexandria April 30-May 10. Retreat to Morganza May 13-22. Mansura May 16. Duty at Morganza till July 2. Moved to New Orleans, thence to Washington, D. C., July 2-13. Snicker's Gap Expedition July 14-23. Sheridan's Shenandoah Valley Campaign August 7-November 28. Berryville August 21 and September 3-4. Battle of Opequan, Winchester, September 19. Fisher's Hill September 22. Battle of Cedar Creek October 19. Duty near Middletown till November 9. At Newton till December 30, and at Stevenson's Depot till April, 1865. Moved to Washington, D. C., and duty there April 22 to June 1. Provost duty during Grand Review May 23-24. Moved to Savannah, Ga., June 1-5, thence to Georgetown, S. C., June 14-15. Duty at various points in South Carolina, with headquarters at Darlington till March, 1865. Moved to Hilton Head, S. C., March 27, and duty there till June 21. (A Detachment at Helena and Seabrook Islands.) Mustered out Company "A" October 18, 1864; Regiment June 21, 1866.

Regiment lost during service 2 Officers and 40 Enlisted men killed and mortally wounded, and 4 Officers and 191 Enlisted men by disease. Total 237.

30th REGIMENT INFANTRY.

Organized at Augusta and mustered in January 8, 1864. Left State for New Orleans, La., January 31, 1864, arriving February 16. Attached to 3rd Brigade, 1st Division, 19th Army Corps, Dept. of the Gulf, to July, 1864; and Army of the Shenandoah, Middle Military Division, to December, 1864. Garrison of Winchester, Va., Army of the Shenandoah, to April, 1865. Dept. of Washington to June, 1865. District of Savannah, Ga., Dept. of the South, to August, 1865.

SERVICE.—Duty at Algiers, La., February 16-18, 1864. Moved to Franklin February 18, and duty there till March 15. Red River Campaign March 15-May 22. Advance to Alexandria March 15-26, and to Natchitoches March 29-April 2. Battle of Sabine Cross Roads April 8. Pleasant Hill April 9. Cane River Crossing April 23. Construction of dam at Alexandria April 30-May 10. Retreat to Morganza May 13-20. Mansura May 16. At Morganza till July 2. Moved to New Orleans, thence to Fortress Monroe and Bermuda Hundred, Va., July 2-18. Duty at Deep Bottom till July 31. Moved to Washington, D. C., thence to Harper's Ferry, W. Va. Sheridan's Shenandoah Valley Campaign August 7-November 28. On detached duty, guarding trains, stores, etc., till October 26. Bunker Hill October 25. Duty near Middletown till November, and at Newtown till January, 1865. At Winchester and Stevenson's Depot till April, 1865. Moved to Washington, D. C., April 20, and duty there till June 30. Provost guard during Grand Review May 23-24. Moved to Savannah, Ga., June 30-July 7, and duty there till August. Mustered out August 20, 1865.

Regiment lost during service 3 Officers and 31 Enlisted men killed and mortally wounded and 2 Officers and 254 Enlisted men by disease. Total 290.

31st REGIMENT INFANTRY.

Organized at Augusta March and April, 1864. Left State for Washington, D. C., April 18, 1864. Attached to 2nd Brigade, 2nd Division, 9th Army Corps, Army of the Potomac, to July, 1865.

SERVICE—Campaign from the Rapidan to the James River, Va., May 3-June 15, 1864. Battles of the Wilderness May 5-7. Spottsylvania May 8-12. Spottsylvania C. H. May 12-21. North Anna River May 23-26. On line of the Pamunkey May 26-28. Totopotomoy May 28-31. Cold Harbor June 1-12. Bethesda Church June 1-3. Before Petersburg June 16-19. Siege of Petersburg June 16, 1864, to April 2, 1865. Mine Explosion, Petersburg, July 30, 1864. Weldon R. R. August 18-21. Poplar Springs Church September 29-October 2. Boydton Plank Road, Hatcher's Run, October 27-28. Fort Steadman March 25, 1865. Assault on Fort Davis April 1. Assault on Fort Mahone April 2. Fall of Petersburg April 2. Occupation of Petersburg April 3-20. Moved to Alexandria April 20-27. Grand Review May 23. Mustered out July 15, 1865.

Regiment lost during service 18 Officers and 161 Enlisted men killed and mortally wounded and 176 Enlisted men by disease. Total 359.

32nd REGIMENT INFANTRY.

Organized at Augusta March 3 to May 6, 1864. 6 Companies left State for Washington, D. C., April 20. 4 Companies left State for Washington May 11 and joined Regiment at North Anna River, Va., May 26. Attached to 2nd Brigade, 2nd Division, 9th Army Corps, Army of the Potomac, to December, 1864.

SERVICE—Campaign from the Rapidan to the James River, Va., May 3-June 15, 1864. Battles of the Wilderness May 5-7. Spottsylvania May 8-12. Spottsylvania C. H. May 12-21. North Anna River May 23-26. On line of the Pamunkey May 26-28. Totopotomoy May 28-31. Cold Harbor June 1-12. Bethesda Church June 1-3. Before Petersburg June 16-19. Siege of Petersburg June 16, 1864, to December 12, 1864. Mine Explosion, Petersburg, July 30. Weldon R. R. August 18-21. Poplar Springs Church September 29-October 2. Boydton Plank Road, Hatcher's Run, October 27-28. Consolidated with 31st Maine Infantry December 12, 1864.

Regiment lost during service 4 Officers and 81 Enlisted men killed and mortally wounded, and 3 Officers and 114 Enlisted men by disease. Total 202.

COAST GUARD INFANTRY.

Company "A" mustered in at Belfast March 18, 1864. Stationed at Fort Washington, Md. Mustered out May 25, 1865.

Company "B" mustered in at Augusta April 27, 1864. Stationed at Fort Foote, Md. Mustered out June 24, 1865.

Company "C" mustered in at Eastport May 16, 1864. Stationed at Fort Sullivan, Eastport, Me. Mustered out September 6, 1865.

Company "D" mustered in at Augusta January 6, 1865. Stationed at Machiasport, Me. Mustered out September 6, 1865.

Company "E" mustered in at Augusta January 7, 1865. Stationed at Rockland, Me. Mustered out July 7, 1865.

Company "F" mustered in at Augusta January 6, 1865. Stationed at Belfast, Me. Mustered out July 7, 1865.

Company "G" mustered in at .... March 1, 1865. Stationed at Calais, Me. Mustered out July 6, 1865.

MARYLAND VOLUNTEERS.

1st REGIMENT CAVALRY.

Organized at Baltimore and Williamsport, Md., Pittsburg, Pa., and Washington, D. C., August, 1861, to June, 1862. Companies "A," "B," "C," "D," "E" and "F" organized at Baltimore, Md. Company "G" organized at Pittsburg, Pa., as Patterson's Union Cavalry April 5, 1861. Companies "H" and "I" organized in Washington and Allegheny Counties, Pa. Company "K" organized at Allegheny City, Pa., as Morehead's Cavalry Company August 19, 1861. Companies "L" and "M" organized at Washington, D. C., May, 1862. Companies "G," "H," "I" and "K" were attached to 1st Virginia Union Cavalry August, 1861, to January, 1862, when assigned to 1st Maryland Cavalry. Regiment attached to Dix's Command, Baltimore, Md., to March, 1862 (Cos. "A," "B," "C," "D," "E" and "F"). Department of West Virginia to March, 1862 (Cos. "G," "H," "I," "K"). (Co. "K" ordered to Washington, D. C., August 19, 1861. Attached to Landers' Command, Army of the Potomac, to March, 1862. Duty at Williamsport, Hancock and Cumberland, Md.) Hatch's Cavalry Brigade, Dept. of the Shenandoah, to June, 1862. Cavalry Brigade, 2nd Corps, Pope's Army of Virginia, to September, 1862. Cavalry Brigade, 11th Army Corps, Army of the Potomac, to February, 1863. Defences Upper Potomac, 8th Army Corps, Middle Department, February, 1863. 2nd Brigade, 3rd Division, Cavalry Corps, Army of the Potomac, to June, 1863. 1st Brigade, 2nd Division, Cavalry Corps, to October, 1863. Provost Marshal General's Command, Army of the Potomac, to February, 1864. 3rd Separate Brigade, 8th Army Corps, Middle Dept., to June, 1864. 3rd Brigade, 1st Division, 10th Army Corps, Army of the James, Dept. of Virginia and North Carolina, to October, 1864. 3rd Brigade, Cavalry Division, Dept. of Virginia and North Carolina, to April, 1865. Cavalry, Dept. of Virginia, to August, 1865.

SERVICE—Skirmishes at Edward's Ferry September 3-4, 1861 (Co. "K"). Action at Greenbrier, W. Va., October 3, 1861 (Co. "G"). Ball's Bluff, Va., October 21, 1861 (Detachment). Stone's Cross Roads, Ball's Bluff, Bath and Alpine Station, January 4, 1862 (Cos. "G," "H" and "I"). Hancock January 5-6 (Co. "K"). Bloomery Gap January 7 and February 14 (Co. "I"). Regiment at Baltimore, Md., till March, 1862. Operations in Shenandoah Valley March to June. Advance on Winchester March 7-15. Pursuit of Jackson up the Valley. Retreat to Williamsport, Md., May 24-26. Middletown May 24 (Cos. "A," "B," "C," "G" and "I"). (Cos. "D," "F," "H," "K" and "L" arrive at Harper's Ferry, W. Va., May 25.' Winchester May 25 (Cos. "A," "B," "C," "G" and "I"). Charlestown May 28. Defence of Harper's Ferry May 28-30 (Cos. "D," "F," "H," "K" and "L"). Near Harper's Ferry June 9. Expedition to Madison Court House, Culpeper and Orange Court Houses July 12-17. Near Culpeper July 12. Rapidan Station July 13. Madison Court House August 8. Battle of Cedar Creek August 9. Pope's Campaign in Northern Virginia August 16-September 2. Fords of the Rappahannock August 21-23. Fauquier, White Sulphur Springs, August 23-24. Gainesville August 28. Groveton August 29. Bull Run August 30. Chantilly September 1. Evacuation of Winchester September 2 (Cos. "H," "I"). Frederick, Md., September 6. Boonsboro, Md., September 7. Near Boonsboro September 10. Maryland Heights and Harper's Ferry September 12-13 (Cos. "H," "I"). Cut way through enemy's lines September 14 (Cos. "H" and "I"). Culpeper September 14. Sharpsburg September 15. Capture of Longstreet's trains (Cos. "H," "I"). Rapidan Station September 16. Duty in the Defences of the Upper Potomac covering Washington, D. C., till December. Manassas, Va., October 23-24. Affair opposite Williamsport October 29 (Detachment). Reconnoissance from Bolivar Heights to Rippon, W. Va., November 9 (2 Cos.). Reconnoissance to Winchester December 2-6 (Detachment). Battle of Fredericksburg December 12-15. Dumfries December 27. Duty in the defences of the Upper Potomac till April, 1863; near

Cumberland, Md., Grove Church, near Morrisville, January 26. Chancellorsville Campaign April 27-May 6. Stoneman's Raid April 27-May 8. South Anna Bridge, near Ashland, May 3. Brandy Station, or Fleetwood, and Beverly Ford, June 9. Aldie June 17. Frederick, Md., June 21 (Detachment). Upperville June 23. Middleburg June 25. Westminster June 30. Battle of Gettysburg, Pa., July 1-3. Emmettsburg July 4-6. Middletown July 5. Leitersburg July 7. Cavetown July 8. Hagerstown and Old Antietam Forge, near Leitersburg, July 10. Shepherdstown July 14 and 16. Beverly Ford September 6. Advance from the Rappahannock to the Rapidan September 13-17. Culpeper Court House September 13. Rapidan Station September 13 and 15-16. Raccoon Ford September 15. White's Ford September 21. Bristoe Campaign October 9-22. Germania Ford and James City October 10. Near Warrenton October 11. White Sulphur Springs October 12-13. Bristoe Station October 14. Near Centreville and Brentsville October 14. Advance to line of the Rappahannock November 7-8. Mine Run Campaign November 26-December 2. Grove Church, near Morrisville, November 26. Parker's Store November 29. Duty in Middle Department till June, 1864. Princeton May 6. Jeffersonville May 8. Wier Bottom Church, on Bermuda Hundred Front, Va., June 16-17. Richmond and Petersburg R. R. June 19. Deep Bottom July 21. New Market Heights July 27-28. Strawberry Plains, north of the James, August 14-18. Flusser's Mills August 14. Deep Run August 16-18. Siege of Petersburg August 25-September 27. Battle of Chaffin's Farm September 28-30. New Market Heights October 7. Darbytown Road October 13. Fair Oaks October 27-28. Smithfield December 7. Duty before Richmond to March, 1865. Scout to Long and Bottom's Bridge January 30, 1865. Expedition to Fearnsville and Smithfield February 11-15. Appomattox Campaign March 28-April 9. Dinwiddie Court House March 30-31. Five Forks April 1. Sutherland Station April 2. Burgess Mills April 3. Deep Creek April 4. Amelia Court House April 5. Sailor's Creek and Harper's Farm April 6. Farmville April 6-7. Appomattox Court House April 9. Surrender of Lee and his army. March to Danville April 23-29. Duty in the Department of Virginia till August. Mustered out August 8, 1865.

Regiment lost during service 3 Officers and 65 Enlisted men killed and mortally wounded and 3 Officers and 130 Enlisted men by disease. Total 201.

1st REGIMENT POTOMAC HOME BRIGADE CAVALRY.—(COLE'S.)

Originally organized at Cole's (Co. "A"), Furey's (Co. "B"), Horner's (Co. "C") and Currie's (Co. "D"). Independent Cavalry Companies organized at Frederick, Md., August 10 to November 27, 1861. Served unattached, Dept. of West Virginia, to January, 1862. Lander's Division, Army of the Potomac, to March, 1862 (Cos. "A," "C" and "D"). Unattached, West Virginia, to August, 1862 (Co. "B"). Hatch's Cavalry Brigade, Banks' 5th Army Corps, and Dept. of the Shenandoah to June, 1862. Cavalry Brigade, 2nd Corps, Pope's Army of Virginia, to August, 1862, and participated in the following service: South Branch Bridge, W. Va., October 26, 1861 (Co. "B"); Hancock, Md., January 5-6, 1862 (Cos. "A," "C" and "D"); Bloomery Gap February 14. Advance on Winchester March 2-12. Martinsburg March 3. Bunker Hill March 5 (Co. "A"). Between Bunker Hill and Winchester March 7. Stephenson's Depot March 7-8. Winchester March 12. Kernstown March 22. Winchester March 23. Edenburg April 1. Grass Lick, W. Va., April 23 (Co. "B"). Wardensville, W. Va., May 7 (Co. "B"). Charlestown May 28. Companies consolidated to a Battalion August 1, 1862, and designated Cole's Battalion, Potomac Home Brigade Cavalry. Attached to Railroad Brigade, 8th Army Corps, Middle Department, to September, 1862. Cavalry, 12th Army Corps, Army of the Potomac, to November, 1862. Defences of Upper Potomac, 8th Army Corps, Middle Department, to March, 1863. 3rd Brigade, 1st Division, 8th Army Corps, to July, 1863. 2nd Brigade, Maryland Heights Division West

Virginia, to December, 1863. Cavalry Brigade, 1st Division West Virginia, to April, 1864. 1st Brigade, 1st Cavalry Division, West Virginia, to August, 1864. 3rd Brigade, 1st Division, Cavalry Corps, Army of the Shenandoah, to October, 1864. Reserve Division, Harper's Ferry, W. Va., to January, 1865. 3rd Brigade, 3rd Division West Virginia, to February, 1865. 1st Brigade, 2nd Division West Virginia, to June, 1865.

SERVICE.—Leesburg, Va., September 2, 1862. Edwards' Ferry, Md., September 4. Monocacy Creek September 4. Reconnoissance to Lovettsville September 4. Maryland Heights and siege of Harper's Ferry September 12-14. Cut through enemy's lines September 14. Capture of Longstreet's train at Sharpsburg September 15. Hyattstown, Md., October 12. Charleston November 14. Berryville December 1. Charlestown December 2. Winchester December 5. Halltown December 20. Near Charlestown May 16, 1863. Berryville June 13. Martinsburg June 14. Winchester June 15 (Co. "B"). Williamsport June 15. Catoctin Creek June 17. Frederick, Md., June 21. Sharpsburg July —. Fountain Dale, Pa., July 1. Gettysburg, Pa., July 1-3. Near Emmittsburg July 4. Falling Waters July 6. Harper's Ferry July 6. Smithfield August 23. Scouts into Loudoun County August 25 and September 12-16 and September 21-26. Catoctin Mountain September 14. Loudoun Valley, Va., September 25. Loudoun Valley and Summit Point October 7. Charleston October 7 (Co. "B"). Snickersville, Leesburg, Rector's Cross Roads and Bloomfield September 14. Upperville September 25. Berryville October 18. Near Annandale October 22. Expedition from Charleston to New Market November 15-18. Mt. Jackson November 16. Ashby's Gap November —. Upperville December 10. Edenburg December 17. New Market December 18. Harrisonburg and Staunton December 21. Five Points, Rectortown, January 1, 1864. Loudoun Heights January 10. Romney, Moorfield and Mechanicsville Gap February 4. Regiment re-enlisted February 13, 1864. Upperville February 20. Veterans on furlough till April. Authority given to increase Battalion to a Regiment, and Companies "E," "F," "G," "H," "I," "K," "L" and "M" organized at Baltimore and Frederick February 9 to April 23, 1864. Sigel's Expedition from Martinsburg, W. Va., to New Market April 30-May 16. New Market May 13-15. Hunter's Expedition to Lynchburg May 26-July 1. Harrisonburg June 3. Piedmont June 5. Occupation of Staunton June 6. Tye River June 12. Lexington June 13. Buckhannon June 14. Lynchburg June 17-18. Catawba Mountains and near Salem June 21. Leetown and Shepardstown July 3 (Detachment). Keedysville July 5. Frederick, Md., July 11-12. Maryland Heights, Brownsville, Crampton's Gap and Herndon July —. Purcellsville July 16. Snicker's Ferry July 17-18. Ashby's Gap and Winchester July 19. Kernstown July 23-24. Winchester, Bunker Hill and Martinsburg July 25. Snicker's Gap July 25. Falling Waters July 26. Hagerstown July 29-30. Keedysville August 5. Winchester August 17. Opequan Creek August 18, 19 and 20. Near Berryville August 21. Near Charlestown August 21-22. Antietam August 22. Williamsport August 26. Summit Point August 30. White Post September 3. Winchester September 19. Fisher's Hill September 22. Battle of Cedar Creek October 19. Duty in West Virginia operating against Moseby and guarding Baltimore & Ohio Railroad till June, 1865. Mustered out June 28, 1865.

Regiment lost during service 2 Officers and 45 Enlisted men killed and mortally wounded and 2 Officers and 120 Enlisted men by disease. Total 169.

2nd REGIMENT CAVALRY.

Organized at Baltimore and Annapolis, Md., July 1 to August 12, 1863, for 6 months. Assigned to provost duty in Anne Arundel and Calvert counties and at Annapolis, Md., during entire term. Mustered out Companies "A" and "B" January 26, 1864; Companies "C" and "D" February 6, 1864; Company "E" January 31, 1864.

Lost 13 by disease during service.

3rd REGIMENT CAVALRY.—("BRADFORD DRAGOONS.")

Organized at Baltimore, Md., August 8, 1863, to January 9, 1864. Attached to Cavalry Reserve, 8th Army Corps, Middle Department, to January, 1864. Unattached, Defences of New Orleans, La., Dept. of the Gulf, to March, 1864. District of LaFourche, Dept. of the Gulf, to June, 1864. District of Morganza, Dept. of the Gulf, to August, 1864. United States forces, Mobile Bay, Dept. of the Gulf, to December, 1865. District of Southern Alabama, Military Division of West Mississippi, to May, 1865. 1st Brigade, 2nd Division, Cavalry Corps, West Mississippi, to June, 1865. Dept. of Mississippi to September, 1865.

SERVICE.—Duty in the Defences of Baltimore, Md., till January, 1864. Ordered to New Orleans, La., thence to Madisonville, La., and duty there till March, 1864. Expedition to Franklinton February 1-3. Flemming's Ford, Madisonville, February 11. Ordered to Brashear City March 14 and duty there till June. At Morganza till July. Expedition to the Atchafalaya May 30-June 5. Morgan's Ferry Road June 9. Ordered to New Orleans, La., July 1. Dismounted July 7. Sailed from Algiers for Mobile Bay, Ala., August 5. Siege operations against Fort Morgan August 9-23. Capture of Fort Morgan August 23. Post duty at Dauphin's Island and in District of Southern Alabama till March, 1865. Campaign against Mobile March and April. Garrison duty at Fort Gaines till April 30. Ordered to New Orleans, La., April 30, and duty there till June. Ordered to Natchez, Miss., June 20. Duty there and in the Dept. of Mississippi till September. Mustered out at Vicksburg, Miss., September 7, 1865.

PURNELL LEGION CAVALRY.

Companies "A" and "B" organized at Pikesville September to November, 1861. Company "C" organized at Baltimore, Md., September, 1862. Company "A" attached to Dix's Command, Baltimore, Md., Middle Department, to July, 1862. Lockwood's Brigade, District of the Eastern Shore, 8th Army Corps, Middle Department, to January, 1863. 1st Separate Brigade, 8th Army Corps, to June, 1863. 3rd Separate Brigade, 8th Army Corps, to December, 1863. 1st Separate Brigade, 8th Army Corps, to July, 1865.

SERVICE.—Duty on the eastern shore of Maryland and in St. Mary's County, Md., till July, 1865. Near Harper's Ferry, W. Va., July 14, 1863. Mustered out July 28, 1865.

Company "B" attached to Dix's Command, Baltimore, Md., Middle Department, to July, 1862. Unattached, 8th Army Corps, Maryland and Delaware, to January, 1863. Annapolis, Md., to May, 1864. 2nd Brigade, 2nd Division, 5th Army Corps, Army of the Potomac, to October, 1864.

SERVICE.—On special service in Maryland and Delaware and at Annapolis, Md., till May, 1864. Dismounted May 28 and joined Purnell Legion Infantry in Army of the Potomac June 7, 1864. Battles about Cold Harbor June 7-12. Before Petersburg June 16-19. Siege of Petersburg June 16-October 26, 1864. Jerusalem Plank Road June 22-23. Mine Explosion, Petersburg, July 30 (Reserve). Weldon Railroad August 18-21. Poplar Springs Church September 29-October 2. Chapel House October 2-5. Peeble's Farm October 7-8. Mustered out October 26, 1864. Veterans and Recruits transferred to 8th Maryland Infantry November 17, 1864.

Company "C" attached to Defences of Baltimore, Md., 8th Corps, Middle Department, to January, 1863. 1st Separate Brigade, 8th Army Corps, to June, 1863. 3rd Separate Brigade, 8th Army Corps, to July, 1863. District of Delaware, Middle Department, to May, 1864. 2nd Brigade, 2nd Division, 5th Army Corps, Army of the Potomac, to October, 1864.

SERVICE.—At Camp Bradford till February 5, 1863. Moved to Harper's Ferry, W. Va.; thence to Drummondsville, Va., and to Wilmington, Del., and duty there till May, 1864. Dismounted May 28 and joined Purnell Legion Infantry in Army of the Potomac June 7, 1864. Battles about Cold Harbor June 7-12. Before Petersburg, Va., June 16-19. Siege of Petersburg June 16 to October 26, 1864. Jerusalem Plank Road June 22-23. Mine Explosion, Petersburg, July 30 (Reserve). Weldon Railroad August 18-21. Poplar Springs Church September 29-October 2. Chapel House October 2-5. Peeble's Farm October 7-8. Mustered out October 26, 1864. Veterans and Recruits transferred to 8th Maryland Infantry November 17, 1864.

Legion lost while in service 7 Enlisted men killed and mortally wounded and 24 Enlisted men by disease. Total 31.

SMITH'S INDEPENDENT COMPANY CAVALRY.

Organized at Snow Hill October 15, 1862. Attached to Lockwood's District of Eastern Shore, 8th Army Corps, Middle Department, to January, 1863. 1st Separate Brigade, 8th Army Corps, to June, 1863. Unattached, Eastern Shore, 8th Army Corps, to April, 1864. 3rd Separate Brigade, 8th Army Corps, to October, 1864. 1st Separate Brigade, 8th Army Corps, to June, 1865.

SERVICE.—On special duty on eastern shore of Maryland; stationed at Snow Hill, Newton, Point Lookout, Eastville, Drummondtown, Salisbury, Relay House and Barnesville till June, 1865. Mustered out June 30, 1865.

RIGBY'S BATTERY "A" LIGHT ARTILLERY.

Organized at Baltimore, Md., with Purnell Legion August and September, 1861. Attached to Dix's Command, Baltimore, Md., to May, 1862. 4th Brigade, Artillery Reserve, 5th Army Corps, Army of the Potomac, to September, 1862. Artillery, 1st Division, 6th Army Corps, to May, 1863. 4th Volunteer Brigade, Artillery Reserve, Army of the Potomac, to July, 1863. 3rd Volunteer Brigade, Artillery Reserve, Army of the Potomac, to October, 1863. Artillery Brigade, 1st Army Corps, Army of the Potomac, to March, 1864. Camp Barry, Defences of Washington, 22nd Army Corps, to May, 1864. 1st Brigade, DeRussy's Division, 22nd Army Corps, to July, 1864. Reserve Division, Harper's Ferry, W. Va., to January, 1865. 3rd Brigade, 3rd Division, West Virginia, to March, 1865.

SERVICE.—Duty at Baltimore, Md., and on eastern shore of Maryland till May, 1862. Joined Army of the Potomac on the Virginia Peninsula. Peninsula Campaign June to August. Seven days before Richmond June 25-July 1. Battles of Mechanicsville June 26. Savage Station June 29. White Oak Swamp June 30. Malvern Hill July 1. At Harrison's Landing till August 15. Movement to Fortress Monroe and Alexandria August 15-22. Maryland Campaign September 6-22. Battles of Crampton's Pass, South Mountain, Md., September 14. Antietam September 16-17. At Downsville, Md., till October 29. Movement to Falmouth, Va., October 29-November 19. Battle of Fredericksburg, Va., December 12-15. "Mud March" January 20-24, 1863. At White Oak Church till April 27. Chancellorsville Campaign April 27-May 6. Operations at Franklin's Crossing April 29-May 2. Battle of Maryes Heights, Fredericksburg, May 3. Salem Heights May 3-4. Banks' Ford May 4. Gettysburg (Pa.) Campaign June 11-July 24. Battle of Gettysburg July 1-3. Duty on line of the Rappahannock and Rapidan till October. Bristoe Campaign October 9-22. Advance to line of the Rappahannock November 7-8. Mine Run Campaign November 26-December 2. Demonstration on the Rapidan February 6-7, 1864. Morton's Ford February 6-7. At Camp Barry and in the Defences of Washington March to July, 1864. Dismounted and ordered to Harper's Ferry, W. Va., July 3 as Infantry. Duty in District of Harper's Ferry, W. Va., till March, 1865. Consolidated with Battery "B," Maryland Light Artillery, March 11, 1865.

Battery lost during service 6 Enlisted men killed and mortally wounded and 28 Enlisted men by disease. Total 34.

BATTERY "A" JUNIOR LIGHT ARTILLERY.

Organized at Baltimore, Md., for 6 months' service July 14, 1863. Duty in the Defences of Baltimore and attached to Artillery Reserve, 8th Army Corps, to January, 1864. Mustered out January 19, 1864.

SNOW'S BATTERY "B" LIGHT ARTILLERY.

Organized at Baltimore, Md., with the Purnell Legion September and October, 1861. Attached to Dix's Command, Baltimore, Md., Middle Department, to May, 1862. 4th Brigade, Artillery Reserve, 5th Army Corps, Army of the Potomac, to September, 1862. Artillery, 2nd Division, 6th Army Corps, Army of the Potomac, to May, 1863. Unattached, Artillery Reserve, Army of the Potomac, to June, 1863. Camp Barry, Washington, D. C., 22nd Army Corps, to August, 1863. 2nd Brigade, Maryland Heights Division, West Virginia, to December, 1863. 2nd Brigade, 1st Division West Virginia, to April, 1864. Artillery, 1st Division West Virginia, to May, 1864. Artillery Brigade, West Virginia, to July, 1864. Reserve Division, Harper's Ferry, W. Va., to April, 1865. 2nd Brigade, 1st Division, West Virginia, to July, 1865.

SERVICE.—Duty at Baltimore, Md., and in the eastern shore of Maryland till May, 1862. Joined Army of the Potomac on Virginia Peninsula. Peninsula Campaign May to August, 1862. New Bridge June 5. Seven days before Richmond June 25-July 1. Battles of Mechanicsville June 26; Savage Station June 29; White Oak Swamp June 30; Malvern Hill July 1. At Harrison's Landing till August 15. Movement to Fortress Monroe, thence to Alexandria August 15-22. Maryland Campaign September 6-22. Battles of Crampton's Pass, Md., September 14; Antietam September 16-17. At Hagerstown, Md., till October 29. Movement to Falmouth, Va., October 29-November 19. Battle of Fredericksburg, Va., December 12-15. "Mud March" January 20-24, 1863. Chancellorsville Campaign April 27-May 6. With Provost Guard, Army of the Potomac. Ordered to Washington, D. C., June 25, and duty at Camp Barry till July 5. Ordered to Frederick, Md., with Briggs' occupation of Harper's Ferry, W. Va., July 8. Duty in District of Harper's Ferry till April, 1864. Moved to Martinsburg April 17. Sigel's Expedition from Martinsburg to New Market April 30-May 16. Battle of New Market May 15. Hunter's Raid to Lynchburg May 24-July 1. Advance to Staunton May 24-June 6. Piedmont June 5. Occupation of Staunton June 6. Near Lynchburg June 14. Diamond Hill June 17. Lynchburg June 17-18. Liberty June 19. Buford's Gap June 20. Catawba Mountains and about Salem June 21. Duty in District of Harper's Ferry till July, 1865. One section in operations in the Shenandoah Valley July 27 to August 8, 1864. At Cumberland, Md., and in action at Falck's Mills, near Cumberland, August 1, 1864.

Battery lost during service 5 Enlisted men killed and mortally wounded and 27 Enlisted men by disease. Total 32.

BATTERY "B" JUNIOR LIGHT ARTILLERY.

Organized at Baltimore, Md., July 14, 1863, for 6 months' service. Duty in the Defences of Baltimore. Attached to Artillery Reserve, 8th Army Corps, to January, 1864. Mustered out January 16, 1864.

BATTERY "D" LIGHT ARTILLERY.

Organized at Baltimore, Md., February 29, 1864. Attached to 3rd Separate Brigade, 8th Army Corps, Middle Department, to June, 1864. 3rd Brigade, DeRussy's Division, 22nd Army Corps, Defences of Washington, D. C., 4th Brigade, DeRussy's Division, 22nd Army Corps, to October, 1864. 3rd Brigade, ReRussy's Division, 22nd Army Corps, to February, 1865. 1st Brigade, DeRussy's Division, 22nd Army Corps, to June, 1865.

SERVICE.—Duty in the Defences of Baltimore, Md., till June, 1864, and in the Defences of Washington south of the Potomac. Stationed at Forts Tillinghast, Lyon, Willard, Richardson, Ward, Barnard, C. F. Smith and Whipple till June, 1865. Mustered out June 24, 1865.

BALTIMORE INDEPENDENT BATTERY LIGHT ARTILLERY.

Organized at Baltimore, Md., and mustered in August 18, 1862. Ordered to Monocacy, Md., September 18, 1862. Attached to Kenly's Maryland Brigade, Defences Upper Potomac, Middle Department, to March, 1863. 3rd Brigade, 2nd Division, 8th Army Corps, Middle Department, to June, 1863. French's Division, 8th Army Corps, to July, 1863. Defences of Baltimore, 8th Army Corps, to October, 1863. 3rd Separate Brigade, 8th Army Corps, to December, 1863. Artillery Reserve, 8th Army Corps, to July, 1864. Reserve Division, District of Harper's Ferry, W. Va., to January, 1865. Camp Barry, Washington, D. C., 22nd Army Corps, to June, 1865.

SERVICE.—Defence of Williamsport, Md., September 20-21, 1862. Duty at Williamsport till December. Moved to Maryland Heights December 11-12, and duty there till March, 1863. Moved to Berryville, Va., March 28, 1863, and duty there till June. Action at Berryville June 13. Opequan Creek June 13. Retreat to Winchester June 13. Battle of Winchester June 14-15. Battery mostly captured. Reorganizing battery and duty in the Defences of Baltimore, Md., till June, 1864. Operations against Early's invasion June and July. Middletown, Solomon's Gap and Catoctin Mountains July 7. Frederick, Md., July 7-8. Battle of Monocacy July 9. Pursuit of Early till July 30. Duty in the Defences of Harper's Ferry, W. Va., till January, 1865, and at Camp Barry, Defences of Washington, D. C., till June. Mustered out June 17, 1865.

Battery lost during service 1 Enlisted man killed and 7 Enlisted men by disease. Total 8.

1st REGIMENT HEAVY ARTILLERY.

Organization not completed. Company "A" on duty in the Defences of Baltimore, Md.

1st REGIMENT INFANTRY.

Organized at Baltimore, Md., and mustered in: Company, "A" May 10; Companies "B," "C," May 11; Company "D," May 16, 1861. Moved to Relay House, Md., May 24, 1861. Company "E" mustered in May 25, and Companies "F," "G," "H," "I" and "K" mustered in at Relay House May 27, 1861. Camp at Relay House, on Baltimore & Ohio Railroad till June 6. Moved to Camp Carroll, near Baltimore, June 6; thence to Frederick City, Md., June 7. March to Middletown and Downsville July 7-10, and to Williamsport July 23. Duty guarding fords and ferries of Upper Potomac, from Williamsport to mouth of Antietam, till October 16. Attached to Defences Upper Potomac, Dept. of the Shenandoah, to October, 1861. Gordon's Brigade, Banks' Division, Army of the Potomac, to March, 1862. 1st Brigade, 1st Division, Banks' 5th Army Corps, to April, 1862. 1st Brigade, 1st Division, Dept. of the Shenandoah, to June, 1862. Baltimore, Md., Middle Dept., to September, 1862. Maryland Brigade, Defences Upper Potomac. Middle Dept., to March, 1863. 1st Brigade, 1st Division, 8th Army Corps, to June, 1863. Maryland Brigade, French's Division, 8th Army Corps, to July, 1863. 3rd Brigade, 3rd Division, 1st Army Corps, Army of the Potomac, to December, 1863. 2nd Brigade, 3rd Division, 1st Army Corps, to March, 1864. 3rd Brigade, 2nd Division, 5th Army Corps, to June, 1864. 2nd Brigade, 2nd Division, 5th Army Corps, to July, 1865.

SERVICE.—Action at Shepherdstown, Md., September 3, 1861 (Cos. "E," "G"). March to Darnestown October 16-19. Operations at Conrad's and Edwards' Ferries October 21-26. At Darnestown till December 2. March to Frederick City December 2, thence to Williamsport, Md., December 18, and guard crossing Upper Potomac till January 7, 1862. (Cos. "B," "C," "E" and "G" at Four

Locks. Co. "F" at Dam No. 5; then at Four Locks. Co. "A" at Cherry Run, Co. "H" at Old Fort Frederick Cos. "I" and "K" near Fogal's Ferry.) Operations about Dams Nos. 4 and 5 December 17-20, 1861. Skirmishes at Old Fort Frederick December 25 (Co. "H"). Cherry Run December 25 (Co. "A"). Dam No. 5 December 25 (Co. "F"). Forced march to relief of Hancock, Md., January 7. 1862. Duty on Upper Potomac till February 28, 1862 (Cos. "A," "B," "C" and "G" at Millstone Point, "D" at Old Fort Frederick, "F" at Four Locks, "H" at Cherry Run, "I" at Bevan's Hill, "K" at Licking Creek Bridge, and "C" at Baer's School House. March to Williamsport February 28-March 1. Advance on Winchester March 2-12. Skirmish at Bunker Hill March 5. Near Winchester March 8 and 11. Occupation of Winchester March 12. March to Castleman's Ferry and return March 22-23. (Co. "B" detached at Winchester and in battle of March 23.) Pursuit of Jackson to Strasburg March 23-25. Reconnoissance toward Columbia Furnace April 9. Pursuit of Jackson April 17-25. Harrisonburg April 22. March to Strasburg May 1-9. Moved to Front Royal May 16. Operations in the Shenandoah Valley May 16-June 17. Action at Front Royal May 23, mostly captured. Middletown May 24 (Detachment). Winchester May 25 (Detachment). Company "E" at Linden Station. Retreat to Manassas Junction May 23-28; thence moved to Baltimore, Md., and duty there till September. Prisoners exchanged August, 1862. Regiment reorganized at Baltimore and duty there till September 18. Moved to the Antietam September 18. Defence of Williamsport September 20-21. Duty between Williamsport and Hagerstown till December 11. Moved to Maryland Heights December 11-12, and duty there till April 9, 1863. At Bolivar Heights till April 30. Moved to Grafton and Clarksburg, W. Va., to repel Rebel invasion April 30-May 1. Operations against Jones and Imboden May 1-26. Return to Maryland Heights May 26, and duty there till June 30. Retreat to Frederick, Md., and guard bridges over the Monocacy July 6. Recapture of Maryland Heights July 7. Joined 1st Army Corps near Boonsboro July 10. Pursuit of Lee to Warrenton, Va., July 10-24. Funkstown, Md., July 12-13. At Warrenton Junction July 25-27. Duty near Rappahannock Station August 4 to September 16. Advance to the Rapidan September 16-18. Bristoe Campaign October 9-22. Bristoe Station October 14. Haymarket October 19. Guard Orange and Alexandria R. R. October 24-November 23. Mine Run Campaign November 26-December 2. Near Culpeper till May, 1864. Demonstration on the Rapidan February 6-7. Veterans on furlough April and May. Campaign from the Rapidan to the James May 4-June 15. Battles of the Wilderness May 5-7. Laurel Hill May 8. Spottsylvania May 8-12. Spottsylvania Court House May 12-21. "Bloody Angle" May 12. Non-Veterans left front for muster out May 19. 1864. Mustered out May 28, 1864. Harris Farm, Fredericksburg Road, May 19. North Anna River May 23-26. Jericho Ford May 23. On line of the Pamunkey May 26-28. Totopotomoy May 28-31. Cold Harbor June 1-12. Bethesda Church June 1-3. Before Petersburg June 16-18. Siege of Petersburg June 16, 1864, to April 2, 1865. Jerusalem Plank Road June 22-23, 1864. Mine Explosion, Petersburg, July 30 (Reserve). Weldon Railroad August 18-21, Poplar Springs Church September 29-October 2. Yellow House October 2-5. Peeble's Farm November 7-8. Hatcher's Run October 27-28. Warren's Raid on Weldon R. R. December 7-12. Dabney's Mills, Hatcher's Run, February 5-7, 1865. Appomattox Campaign March 28-April 9. Lewis Farm, near Gravelly Run, March 29. White Oak Road March 31. Five Forks April 1. Fall of Petersburg April 2. Pursuit of Lee, Appomattox Court House. April 9. Surrender of Lee and his army. March to Washington, D. C., May 1-12. Grand Review May 23. Camp at Arlington Heights, Va., till July. Mustered out July 2, 1865.

Regiment lost during service 8 Officers and 110 Enlisted men killed and mortally wounded and 1 Officer and 148 Enlisted men by disease. Total 267.

1st REGIMENT POTOMAC HOME BRIGADE INFANTRY.

Organized at Frederick City, Md., August 15 to December 13, 1861. Attached to Banks' Division, Army of the Potomac, to March, 1862. Unassigned, Banks' 5th Corps, and Dept. of the Shenandoah to May, 1862. Railroad District, Middle Department, to July, 1862. Railroad District, 8th Army Corps, Middle Dept., to September, 1862. Annapolis, Md., 8th Army Corps, to March, 1863. 1st Separate Brigade, 8th Army Corps, to June, 1863. Lockwood's Brigade, 8th Army Corps, to July, 1863. 2nd Brigade, 1st Division, 12th Army Corps, Army of the Potomac, July, 1863. 2nd Brigade, Maryland Heights, Division West Virginia, to December, 1863. 2nd Brigade, 1st Division, West Virginia, to April, 1864. Reserve Division, Harper's Ferry, W. Va., to January, 1865. 3rd Brigade, 3rd Division, West Virginia, to April, 1865.

SERVICE.—Railroad guard duty till March, 1862. Advance on Winchester, Va., March 7-12. Strasburg March 27. Guarding Baltimore & Ohio Railroad till May. Concentrated at Harper's Ferry May 24, and action at Loudon Heights May 27. Defence of Harper's Ferry May 28-30. Guard Baltimore & Ohio Railroad till September. Action at Monocacy Aqueduct September 4. Poolesville September 5. Concentrated at Sandy Hook and march to Harper's Ferry. Siege of Harper's Ferry September 12-15. Maryland Heights September 13. Harper's Ferry September 14-15. Surrendered September 15 and paroled September 16. Sent to Annapolis, Md., and when exchanged assigned to duty on the Potomac in Southern Maryland to June, 1863. Martinsburg June 14. At point Lookout June—Joined Lockwood's Brigade and march to Gettysburg, Pa., June 25-July 2. Battle of Gettysburg July 2-3. Pursuit of Lee July 5-24. Guard duty on Baltimore & Ohio Railroad in Maryland and Virginia till May, 1864. Operations against Early's invasion of Maryland June and July. Duffield Station June 29. Battle of Monocacy July 9. Moved from Monocacy to Harper's Ferry, W. Va., and duty in that district till April, 1865. Mustered out August to December, 1864. Recruited to a full Regiment and designation changed to 13th Maryland Infantry April 8, 1865, which see.

Regiment lost during service 3 Officers and 42 Enlisted men killed and mortally wounded and 1 Officer and 85 Enlisted men by disease. Total 131.

1st REGIMENT EASTERN SHORE INFANTRY.

Organized at Cambridge, Md., September, 1861. Attached to Dix's Division, Army of the Potomac, to November. 1861. Eastern Shore Maryland and Virginia, Middle Department, to July, 1862. District Eastern Shore, 8th Army Corps, Middle Dept., to January, 1863. 1st Separate Brigade, 8th Army Corps, to June, 1863. Lockwood's Brigade, 8th Army Corps, to July, 1863. 2nd Brigade, 1st Division, 12th Army Corps, Army of the Potomac, July, 1863. 2nd Brigade, Maryland Heights, Division West Virginia, to October, 1863. 3rd Separate Brigade, 8th Army Corps, to June, 1864. 1st Separate Brigade, 8th Army Corps, to September, 1864. Reserve Division, Harper's Ferry, W. Va., to February, 1865.

SERVICE.—Duty at Baltimore, Md., till November, 1861. Expedition to Accomac and Northampton counties November 14-23, 1861. Duty at Baltimore and on the Eastern Shore till June, 1863. Moved with Lockwood to Gettysburg, Pa., June 25-July 2. Battle of Gettysburg July 2-3. Pursuit of Lee July 5-24. Duty at Maryland Heights, W. Va., July 17 to October 5, 1863. Ordered to the Eastern Shore of Maryland and duty there till February, 1865. Company "A" mustered out by order of the War Department August 16, 1862. Regiment consolidated with 11th Maryland Infantry February 23, 1865.

Regiment lost during service 9 Enlisted men killed and mortally wounded and 52 Enlisted men by disease. Total 61.

2nd REGIMENT INFANTRY.

Organized at Baltimore, Md., June to September, 1861. Duty at Baltimore, Md., till March, 1862. Attached to Dix's Division, Army of the Potomac, to March, 1862. 1st Brigade, 2nd Division, Department of North Carolina, to July, 1862. 1st Brigade, 2nd Division, 9th Army Corps, Army of the Potomac, to April, 1863. 1st Brigade, 2nd Division, 9th Army Corps, Army of the Ohio, to June, 1863. Unassigned, 1st Division, 23rd Army Corps, Army of the Ohio, to October, 1863. 1st Brigade, 2nd Division, 9th Army Corps, Army of the Ohio, to January, 1864. 2nd Brigade, 2nd Division, 9th Army Corps, Army of the Ohio, to March, 1864. 1st Brigade, 2nd Division, 9th Army Corps, Army of the Potomac, to April, 1864. 2nd Brigade, 3rd Division, 9th Army Corps, to June 5, 1864. 2nd Brigade, 2nd Division, 9th Army Corps, to July, 1865.

SERVICE.—Duty at Baltimore, Md., till March, 1862. Ordered to North Carolina March. Duty at Roanoke Island, N. C., till June. Battle of Camden South Mills April 19. Expedition toward Trenton May 15-16. Skirmish at Young's Cross Roads May 15. Expedition to New Berne June 18-July 2. Moved to Newport News, Va., July 6-10; thence to Aquia Creek and Fredericksburg, Va., August 2-7. Pope's Campaign in Northern Virginia August 16-September 2. Battles of Groveton August 29. Bull Run August 30. Chantilly September 1. Maryland Campaign September 6-22. Battles of South Mountain, Md., September 14. Antietam September 16-17. Stone Bridge September 17. Duty in Pleasant Valley till October 27. Movement to Falmouth, Va., October 27-November 19. Battle of Fredericksburg, Va., December 12-15. Burnside's 2nd Campaign ("Mud March") January 20-24, 1863. Moved to Newport News February 11, thence to Lexington, Ky., March 26-April 1. Duty at Frankfort, Ky., till September. Rejoined Corps September 10. March to Knoxville, Tenn., September 12-20. Action at Blue Springs October 10. Operations in East Tennessee till November 14. Knoxville Campaign November 4-December 23. Loudon November 15. Campbell's Station November 16. Siege of Knoxville November 17-December 4. Repulse of Longstreet's assault on Fort Saunders November 29. Pursuit of Longstreet December 5-29. Duty in East Tennessee till March, 1864. Moved to Annapolis, Md., March 30-April 7. Campaign from the Rapidan to the James May 4-June 15. Battles of the Wilderness May 5-7. Spottsylvania May 8-12. Po River May 10. Spottsylvania Court House May 12-21. Assault on the Salient May 12. North Anna River May 23-26. On line of the Pamunkey May 26-28. Totopotomoy May 28-31. Cold Harbor June 1-12. Bethesda Church June 1-3. Before Petersburg June 16-18. Siege of Petersburg June 16, 1864, to April 2, 1865. Mine Explosion, Petersburg, July 30, 1864. Weldon Railroad August 18-21. Poplar Springs Church September 29-October 2. Boydton Plank Road, Hatcher's Run, October 27-28. Fort Steadman March 25, 1865. Appomattox Campaign March 28-April 9. Assault on and fall of Petersburg April 2. March to Farmville April 4-10. March to City Point April 20-24, thence moved to Alexandria April 24-28. Grand Review May 23. Duty in the Department of Washington till July. Mustered out July 7, 1865.

Regiment lost during service 5 Officers and 84 Enlisted men killed and mortally wounded and 3 Officers and 134 Enlisted men by disease. Total 226.

2nd REGIMENT POTOMAC HOME BRIGADE INFANTRY.

Organized at Cumberland, Md., August 27 to October 31, 1861. Attached to Railroad District West Virginia to February, 1862. District of Cumberland, Mountain Department, to April, 1862. Railroad District, Dept. of the Mountains, to July, 1862. Railroad District, 8th Army Corps, Middle Department, to September, 1862. Railroad Division, District of West Virginia, Dept. of the Ohio, to January, 1863. Cumberland, Md., Defences Upper Potomac, 8th Army Corps, Middle Dept., to March, 1863. 5th Brigade, 1st Division, 8th Army Corps, to June, 1863. Mulligan's Brigade, Scammon's Division, Army of West Virginia, to December, 1863. 2nd Brigade, 2nd Division West Virginia, to April, 1864. Reserve Division, Kelly's Command, West Virginia, to April, 1865. 2nd Brigade, 1st Division West Virginia, to May, 1865. (Co. "F," Cavalry, Martinsburg, W. Va.; 8th Army Corps, January to March, 1863. 3rd Brigade, 1st Division, 8th Army Corps, to June, 1863. 1st Brigade, Maryland Heights, Division West Virginia, to December, 1863. Cavalry, 1st Division West Virginia.)

SERVICE.—Duty on Baltimore & Ohio Railroad. At Patterson Creek and Romney, W. Va., till March, 1862. Skirmishes at Springfield, W. Va., August 23, 1861. Blue House August 26. South Branch Bridge, Mill Creek Mills, Romney and Springfield, October 26. Great Cacapon Bridge January 4, 1862. Duty at Charlestown, New Creek and Cumberland guarding Railroad between and to the Ohio River till March, 1863; and from Monocacy Bridge to the Ohio River till April, 1864. Action at Vance's Ford, near Romney, September 17, 1862. Charlestown. W. Va., May 15, 1863. Perryville June 14, 1863 (Co. "F"). Point of Rocks June 17 (Co. "F"). Summit Point October 7, 1863 (Co. "F"). Charlestown, W. Va., October 18, 1863. Burlington November 16. Salem December 16, 1863. Jackson River, near Covington, December 19, 1863. Ridgeville, Va., January 4, 1864. Moorefield Junction January 8, 1864. Medley January 30, 1864. Hunter's Raid on Lynchburg May 26-July 1, 1864. Lynchburg June 17-18. Salem June 21. Salem Branch Bridge July 4. Sir John's Run July 6. Snicker's Gap July 18. Kernstown, Winchester July 24. Martinsburg July 25. Back Creek Bridge July 27. Hancock, Md., July 31. Green Springs Run August 2. Guard duty in West Virginia till May, 1865. Mustered out May 29, 1865.

Regiment lost during service 1 Officer and 9 Enlisted men killed and mortally wounded and 84 Enlisted men by disease. Total 94.

2nd REGIMENT EASTERN SHORE INFANTRY.

Organized at Charlestown, Kent County, Md., October 2 to December 28, 1861. Attached to Dix's Division, Army of the Potomac, to March, 1862. Eastern Shore Maryland and Virginia Middle Department to July, 1862. District of Eastern Shore, 8th Army Corps, Middle Department, to March, 1863. 1st Separate Brigade, 8th Army Corps, to June, 1863. Lockwood's Brigade, 8th Army Corps, to July, 1863. 2nd Brigade, 1st Division, 12th Army Corps, Army of the Potomac, July, 1863. 2nd Brigade, Maryland Heights, Division West Virginia, to December, 1863. 2nd Brigade, 1st Division, West Virginia, to April, 1864. 1st Brigade, 1st Infantry, Division of West Virginia, to July, 1864. 2nd Brigade, 1st Infantry Division of West Virginia, to October, 1864. Reserve Division, District of Harper's Ferry, West Virginia, to February, 1865.

SERVICE.—Duty on eastern shore of Maryland till March, 1862, and at Baltimore till October, 1862. On eastern shore of Maryland till June, 1863. At Baltimore June, 1863. Joined Lockwood's Brigade at Frederick, Md., July 6, 1863. Pursuit of Lee July 6-14. Falling Waters July 14. Assigned to duty at Maryland Heights July 17. Duty there and guarding Baltimore & Ohio Railroad till April, 1864. Hunter's Expedition to Lynchburg, Va., May 26-July 1. Advance on Staunton May 26-June 6. Action at Piedmont and Mt. Crawford June 5. Occupation of Staunton June 6. Lexington June 12. Buchanan June 14. Liberty June 16. Lynchburg June 17-18. Retreat to the Ohio River June 19-July 1. Salem June 21. Moved to Shenandoah Valley July 1-17. Snicker's Gap July 18. Battle of Winchester July 24. Martinsburg July 25. Strasburg August 14-15. Bolivar Heights August 24. Berryville September 3. Guard duty in West Virginia till February, 1865. Consolidated with 1st Eastern Shore Infantry February 23, 1865.

Regiment lost during service 10 Enlisted men killed and mortally wounded and 1 Officer and 62 Enlisted men by disease. Total 73.

3rd REGIMENT INFANTRY.

Organized at Baltimore and Williamsport, Md., June 18, 1861, to February 17, 1862. Companies "A," "B," "C," "D" and "H" organized at Baltimore August, 1861, to February 16, 1862. 4 Companies organized at Williamsport in summer of 1861; assigned as Companies "A," "B," "C" and "I." Original Companies "A," "B," "C" and "D" designated Companies "D," "E," "F" and "G." Companies "E," "F," "H" and "I" broken up May 11, 1862, and distributed among Companies "A," "B," "C," "D" and "G." 2 Companies recruited for 4th Maryland Infantry and assigned as Companies "E" and "H." 2 Companies recruited for Dix's Light Infantry and assigned as Companies "I" and "K." Company "F" organized October 15, 1862, at Euston, Md., for 9 months; assigned February, 1863, and mustered out September 2, 1863.

Regiment attached to Dix's Division, Baltimore, Md., to May, 1862. 1st Brigade, Sigel's Division, Dept. of the Shenandoah, to June, 1862. 2nd Brigade, 2nd Division, 2nd Corps, Pope's Army of Virginia, to August, 1862. 1st Brigade, 2nd Division, 2nd Army Corps, Army of Virginia, to September, 1862. 2nd Brigade, 2nd Division, 12th Army Corps, Army of the Potomac, to October, 1862. 2nd Brigade, 1st Division, 12th Army Corps, to May, 1863. 1st Brigade, 1st Division, 12th Army Corps, Army of the Potomac, to September, 1863, and Army of the Cumberland to April, 1864. (1st Brigade, 1st Division, 20th Army Corps, Army of the Cumberland, April to October, 1864. Non-Veterans.) Regiment, 2nd Brigade, 1st Division, 9th Army Corps, Army of the Potomac, April to June 1, 1864. 1st Brigade, 1st Division, 9th Army Corps, to July, 1864. 2nd Brigade, 1st Division, 9th Army Corps, to September, 1864. 3rd Brigade, 1st Division, 9th Army Corps, to July, 1865.

SERVICE.—Duty at Baltimore, Md., till May 24, 1862. Moved to Harper's Ferry, W. Va., May 24. Defence of Harper's Ferry May 28-30. Operations in the Shenandoah Valley till August. Battle of Cedar Mountain August 9. Pope's Campaign in Northern Virginia August 16-September 2. Fords of the Rappahannock August 21-23. Sulphur Springs August 24. Plains of Manassas August 28-29 (Reserve). Battle of Bull Run August 30 (Reserve). Maryland Campaign September 6-22. Battle of Antietam, Md., September 16-17. Duty at Bolivar Heights September 22 to December 10. Reconnoissance to Rippon, W. Va., November 9. Expedition to Winchester December 2-6. Moved to Fredericksburg December 10-14. At Stafford's Court House December 14, 1862, to April 27, 1863. "Mud March" January 20-24, 1863. Chancellorsville Campaign April 27-May 6. Battle of Chancellorsville May 1-5. Gettysburg (Pa.) Campaign June 11-July 24. Battle of Gettysburg July 1-3. Pursuit of Lee July 5-24. At Raccoon Ford till September. Moved to Brandy Station, thence to Bealeton and to Stevenson, Ala., September 24-October 4. Guard duty on Nashville & Chattanooga Railroad till April, 1864. Veterans on furlough March and April. Old members participated in Atlanta (Ga.) Campaign May 1 to September 8, 1864. Demonstration on Rocky Faced Ridge May 8-11. Battle of Resaca May 14-15. Near Cassville May 19. Advance on Dallas May 22-25. New Hope Church May 25. Battles about Dallas, New Hope Church and Allatoona Hills May 26-June 5. Operations about Marietta and against Kenesaw Mountain June 10-July 2. Pine Mountain June 11-14. Lost Mountain June 15-17. Gilgal or Golgotha Church June 15. Muddy Creek June 17. Noyes Creek June 19. Kolb's Farm June 22. Assault on Kenesaw June 27. Ruff's Station, Smyrna Camp Ground, July 4. Chattahoochie River July 5-17. Peach Tree Creek July 19-20. Siege of Atlanta July 22-August 25. Operations at Chattahoochie River Bridge August 26-September 2. Occupation of Atlanta September 2. Regiment joined 9th Army Corps, Army of the Potomac, April, 1864. Campaign from the Rapidan to the James May 3-June 15. Battles of the Wilderness May 5-7; Spottsylvania May 8-12; Nye River May

10; Spottsylvania Court House May 12-21. Assault on Salient May 12. Ox Ford May 21. North Anna River May 23-26. On line of the Pamunkey May 26-28. Totopotomoy May 28-31. Cold Harbor June 1-12. Bethesda Church June 1-3. Before Petersburg June 16-18. Siege of Petersburg June 16, 1864, to April 2, 1865. Mine Explosion, Petersburg, July 30, 1864. Weldon Railroad August 18-21. Poplar Grove Church September 29-October 2. Boydton Plank Road, Hatcher's Run, October 27-28. Fort Steadman, Petersburg, March 25, 1865. Appomattox Campaign March 28-April 9. Assault on and fall of Petersburg April 2. Occupation of Petersburg April 3. March to Farmville April 3-9. Moved to Petersburg and City Point April 20-24, thence to Alexandria April 26-28. Grand Review May 23. Duty in the Dept. of Washington till July. Mustered out July 31, 1865.

Regiment lost during service 8 Officers and 83 Enlisted men killed and mortally wounded and 4 Officers and 130 Enlisted men by disease. Total 225.

3rd REGIMENT POTOMAC HOME BRIGADE INFANTRY.

Organized at Cumberland, Hagerstown and Baltimore, Md., October 31, 1861, to May 20, 1862. Companies "I" and "K" organized at Ellicott's Mills and Monrovia April and May, 1864. Regiment attached to Railroad District West Virginia to January, 1862. Lander's Division, Army of the Potomac, to March, 1862. Railroad District, Mountain Department, to July, 1862. Railroad Brigade, 8th Army Corps, Middle Department, to September, 1862. Harper's Ferry, W. Va., September, 1862. Annapolis (Md.) 8th Army Corps to July, 1863. 3rd Separate Brigade, 8th Army Corps, to October, 1863. 1st Separate Brigade, 8th Army Corps, to July, 1864. Kenly's Independent Brigade, 6th Army Corps, Army of the Shenandoah, to August, 1864. Kenly's Brigade, Reserve Division, West Virginia, to October, 1864. Reserve Division, West Virginia, to April, 1865. 1st Brigade, 1st Division, West Virginia, to May 29, 1865.

SERVICE.—Assigned to duty as railroad guard on Upper Potomac in Maryland and Virginia. Action at Grass Lick, W. Va., April 23, 1862. Wardensville May 7. Franklin May 10-12. Moorefield June 29. Siege of Harper's Ferry, W. Va., September 12-15. Surrendered September 15. Paroled September 16 and sent to Annapolis, Md. Duty at Annapolis and in the Defences of Baltimore till June, 1863. Guard Washington Branch, Baltimore & Ohio Railroad, June 28-July 10. At Annapolis, Relay Station, Annapolis Junction and Monocacy till July, 1864. Operations against Early's invasion of Maryland July, 1864. Frederick City July 7-8. Battle of Monocacy July 9. Pursuit of Early till July 30. Snicker's Gap July 18. Bolivar Heights August 6. Halltown August 8. Charlestown August 9. Berryville August 13. Duty in the District of Harper's Ferry, W. Va., till May, 1865. Ordered to Baltimore, Md., May 12, and mustered out May 29, 1865.

Regiment lost during service 1 Officer and 8 Enlisted men killed and mortally wounded and 1 Officer and 73 Enlisted men by disease. Total 83.

4th REGIMENT INFANTRY.

Organized at Baltimore, Md., July and August, 1862. Left Baltimore for the Antietam, Md., September 18, 1862. Attached to Kenly's Maryland Brigade, Defences of the Upper Potomac, 8th Army Corps, Middle Department, to March, 1863. 1st Brigade, 1st Division, 8th Army Corps, to June, 1863. Maryland Brigade, French's Division, 8th Army Corps, to July, 1863. 3rd Brigade, 3rd Division, 1st Army Corps, Army of the Potomac, to December, 1863. 2nd Brigade, 3rd Division, 1st Army Corps, to March, 1864. 3rd Brigade, 2nd Division, 5th Army Corps, to June, 1864. 2nd Brigade, 2nd Division, 5th Army Corps, to May, 1865.

SERVICE.—Defence of Williamsport, Md., September 20-21, 1862. Duty between Williamsport and Hagerstown till December 11. Moved to Maryland Heights

December 11-12 and duty there till April 9, 1863. At Bolivar Heights to April 30. Moved to Grafton and Clarksburg, W. Va., April 30-May 1 to repel invasion. Operations against Jones and Imboden May 1-26. Reported at Maryland Heights May 26 and duty there till June 30. Retreat to Frederick, Md., June 30, and guard bridges on the Monocacy till July 6. Reoccupation of Maryland Heights July 7. Joined 1st Army Corps near Boonsborough, Md., July 10. Pursuit of Lee to Warrenton, Va., July 12-24. At Warrenton Junction July 25-27, and near Rappahannock Station August 4 to September 16. Advance to the Rapidan September 16-18. Bristoe Campaign October 9-22. Bristoe Station October 14. Haymarket October 19. Guard Orange & Alexandria Railroad October 24-November 23. Mine Run Campaign November 26-December 2. Duty near Culpeper till May, 1864. Demonstration on the Rapidan February 6-7, 1864. Campaign from the Rapidan to the James May 3-June 15. Battles of the Wilderness May 5-7; Laurel Hill May 8; Spottsylvania May 8-12; Spottsylvania Court House May 12-21. Assault on the Salient May 12. Harris Farm or Fredericksburg Road May 19. North Anna River May 23-26. Jericho Ford May 23. On line of the Pamunkey May 26-28. Totopotomoy May 28-31. Cold Harbor June 1-12. Bethesda Church June 1-3. Before Petersburg June 16-18. Siege of Petersburg June 16, 1864, to April 2, 1865. Jerusalem Plank Road, Weldon Railroad, June 22-24, 1864. Mine Explosion, Petersburg, July 30 (Reserve). Weldon Railroad August 18-21. Poplar Grove Church September 29-October 2. Yellow House October 2-5. Peeble's Farm October 7-8. Davis House October 8. Boydton Plank Road, Hatcher's Run, October 27-28. Warren's Raid on Weldon Railroad December 7-12. Dabney's Mills, Hatcher's Run, February 5-7, 1865. Appomattox Campaign March 28-April 9. Boydton Plank Road and White Oak Road March 29-31. Five Forks April 1. Fall of Petersburg April 2. Pursuit of Lee April 3-9. Appomattox Court House April 9. Surrender of Lee and his army. March to Washington, D. C., May 1-12. Grand Review May 23. Mustered out May 31, 1865.

Regiment lost during service 3 Officers and 32 Enlisted men killed and mortally wounded and 1 Officer and 72 Enlisted men by disease. Total 108.

4th REGIMENT POTOMAC HOME BRIGADE INFANTRY.

Organization not completed. 3 Companies organized and on duty guarding Baltimore & Ohio Railroad between Martinsburg and Harper's Ferry, W. Va., till August, 1862. Consolidated with 3rd Regiment, Potomac Home Brigade Infantry, August 11, 1862.

5th REGIMENT INFANTRY.

Organized at Baltimore, Md., September, 1861. Attached to Dix's Division, Baltimore, Md., to March, 1862. Fort Monroe, Va., to July, 1862. Weber's Brigade, Division at Suffolk, Va., 7th Army Corps, Dept. of Virginia, to September, 1862. 3rd Brigade, 3rd Division, 2nd Army Corps, Army of the Potomac, to December, 1862. Point of Rocks Defences, Upper Potomac, 8th Army Corps, Middle Department, to March, 1863. 2nd Brigade, 1st Division, 8th Army Corps, to July, 1863. Defences of Baltimore, Md., 8th Army Corps, to January, 1864. District of Delaware, 8th Army Corps, to June, 1864. 3rd Brigade, 2nd Division, 18th Army Corps, Army of the James, to August, 1864. 2nd Brigade, 1st Division, 18th Army Corps, to December, 1864. 2nd Brigade, 3rd Division, 24th Army Corps, to July, 1865. 2nd Independent Brigade, 24th Army Corps, to September, 1865.

SERVICE.—Camp at LaFayette Square, Baltimore, Md., till March, 1862. Ordered to Fortress Monroe, Va., March 11, 1862. Duty there and at Suffolk, Va., to September, 1862. Moved to Washington, D. C., thence to Antietam, Md., September 8-16. Battle of Antietam, Md., September 16-17. Moved to Harper's Ferry September 22 and duty there till January, 1863.

Reconnoissance to Charleston October 16-17. At Point of Rocks and Maryland Heights protecting Baltimore & Ohio Railroad till June, 1863. Moved to Winchester, Va., June 2. Battle of Winchester June 13-15; mostly captured; those not captured at Bloody Run, Pa., and Loudon, Pa., till July. Duty in the Defences of Baltimore, Middle Department, till January, 1864, and in the District of Delaware, Middle Department, till June, 1864. Ordered to join Army of the Potomac in the field June 4, 1864. Siege operations against Petersburg and Richmond, Va., June 16, 1864, to April 2, 1865. Mine Explosion, Petersburg, July 30, 1864 (Reserve). Duty in trenches before Petersburg till September 27. Battle of Chaffin's Farm, New Market Heights, September 28-30. Battle of Fair Oaks October 27-28. Duty in trenches before Richmond till April, 1865. Occupation of Richmond April 3. Pursuit of Lee to Appomattox Court House April 3-9. Appomattox Court House April 9. Surrender of Lee and his army. Duty in the Dept. of Virginia till September. Mustered out September 1, 1865, at Fredericksburg, Va.

Regiment lost during service 1 Officer and 63 Enlisted men killed and mortally wounded and 6 Officers and 91 Enlisted men by disease. Total 161.

6th REGIMENT INFANTRY.

Organized at Baltimore, Md., August 12 to September 3, 1862. Moved to join Army of the Potomac in Western Maryland September 20, 1862. Attached to Kenly's Brigade, Defences Upper Potomac, 8th Army Corps, Middle Department, to March, 1863. 3rd Brigade, 2nd Division, 8th Army Corps, to June, 1863. Elliott's Command, 8th Army Corps, to July, 1863. 2nd Brigade, 3rd Division, 3rd Army Corps, Army of the Potomac, to March, 1864. 2nd Brigade, 3rd Division, 6th Army Corps, Army of the Potomac and Army of the Shenandoah, to June, 1865.

SERVICE.—Defence of Williamsport, Md., September 20-21, 1862. Duty between Williamsport and Hagerstown, Md., till December 11. Moved to Maryland Heights December 11-12 and duty there till March 28, 1863. Moved to Berryville March 28. Action at Kelly's Ford June 10. Berryville June 13. Opequan Creek June 13. Retreat to Winchester June 13. Battle of Winchester June 14-15. Retreat to Harper's Ferry, W. Va., June 15-16; thence to Washington, D. C., July 1-4. Join Army of the Potomac July 5. Pursuit of Lee to Manassas Gap, Va., July 5-24. Wapping Heights, Va., July 23. Duty on line of the Rappahannock till August 15. Detached for duty in New York during draft disturbances till September 5. Bristoe Campaign October 9-22. Culpeper Court House October 11. Bristoe Station October 14. Advance to line of the Rappahannock November 7-8. Kelly's Ford November 7. Brandy Station November 8. Mine Run Campaign November 26-December 2. Payne's Farm November 27. Demonstration on the Rapidan February 6-7, 1864. Campaign from the Rapidan to the James River May 3-June 15. Battles of the Wilderness May 5-7. Spottsylvania May 8-12. Spottsylvania Court House May 12-21. Assault on the Salient, "Bloody Angle," May 12. North Anna River May 23-26. On line of the Pamunkey May 26-28. Totopotomoy May 28-31. Cold Harbor June 1-12. Before Petersburg June 18-July 6. Jerusalem Plank Road June 22-23. Ream's Station June 29. Moved to Baltimore, Md., July 6-8. Battle of the Monocacy July 9. Pursuit of Early to Snicker's Gap July 14-24. Snicker's Ferry July 17-18. Sheridan's Shenandoah Valley Campaign August 6-November 28. Charleston August 29. Battle of Winchester September 19. Fisher's Hill September 22. Battle of Cedar Creek October 19. Duty at Kernstown till December. Moved to Washington, D. C., thence to Petersburg, Va., December 3-6. Siege of Petersburg December 6, 1864, to April 2, 1865. Fort Fisher, Petersburg, March 25, 1865. Appomattox Campaign March 28-April 9. Assault on and fall of Petersburg April 2. Pursuit of Lee April 3-9. Appomattox Court House April 9. Surrender of Lee and his army. March to Danville, Va., April 23-27, and duty there till May 18. March to Richmond, Va., thence to Washington, D. C., May 18-June 3. Corps Review June 8. Mustered out June 20, 1865.

Regiment lost during service 8 Officers and 120 Enlisted men killed and mortally wounded and 1 Officer and 107 Enlisted men by disease. Total 236.

7th REGIMENT INFANTRY.

Organized at Baltimore, Md., August and September, 1862. Moved to the Antietam September 18, 1862. Attached to Kenly's Maryland Brigade, Defences Upper Potomac, 8th Army Corps, Middle Department, to March, 1863. 1st Brigade, 1st Division, 8th Army Corps, to June, 1863. Maryland Brigade, French's Division, 8th Army Corps, to July, 1863. 3rd Brigade, 3rd Division, 1st Army Corps, Army of the Potomac, to December, 1863. 2nd Brigade, 3rd Division, 1st Army Corps, to March, 1864. 3rd Brigade, 2nd Division, 5th Army Corps, to June, 1864. 2nd Brigade, 2nd Division, 5th Army Corps, to May, 1865.

SERVICE.—Defence of Williamsport, Md., September 20-21, 1862. Duty between Williamsport and Hagerstown till December 11. Moved to Maryland Heights December 11-12, and duty there till April 9, 1863. At Bolivar Heights till April 30. Moved to Grafton and Clarksburg, W. Va., to repel invasion. Operations against Jones and Imboden May 1-26. Return to Maryland Heights May 26, and duty there till June 30. Retreat to Frederick, Md., June 30. Guard bridges over Monocacy till July 6. Reoccupation of Maryland Heights July 7. Joined 1st Army Corps, Army of the Potomac, near Boonsborough, Md., July 10. Pursuit of Lee to Warrenton, Va., July 12-24. Funkstown July 12-13. At Warrenton Junction July 25-27. Near Rappahannock Station August 4 to September 16. Advance to the Rapidan September 16-18. Bristoe Campaign October 9-22. Bristoe Station October 14. Haymarket October 19. Guard Orange and Alexandria Railroad October 24 to November 23. Mine Run Campaign November 26-December 2. Near Culpeper till May, 1864. Demonstration on the Rapidan February 6-7. Campaign from the Rapidan to the James May 3-June 15. Battles of the Wilderness May 5-7. Laurel Hill May 8. Spottsylvania May 8-12. Spottsylvania Court House May 12-21. Assault on the Salient May 12. Harris Farm, or Fredericksburg Road, May 19. North Anna River May 23-26. Jericho Ford May 23. On line of the Pamunkey May 26-28. Totopotomoy May 28-31. Cold Harbor June 1-12. Bethesda Church June 1-3. Before Petersburg June 16-18. Siege of Petersburg June 16, 1864, to April 2, 1865. Jerusalem Plank Road June 22-23, 1864. Mine Explosion, Petersburg, July 30. Reserve, Weldon Railroad August 18-21. Poplar Grove Church September 29-October 2. Yellow House October 2-5. Peeble's Farm October 7-8. Davis House October 8. Boydton Plank Road, Hatcher's Run, October 27-28. Warren's Raid on Weldon R. R. December 7-12. Dabney's Mills, Hatcher's Run, February 5-7, 1865. Appomattox Campaign March 28-April 9. Lewis Farm, near Gravelly Run, March 29. Boydton and White Oak Roads March 30-31. Five Forks April 1. Fall of Petersburg April 2. Pursuit of Lee April 3-9. Appomattox Court House April 9. Surrender of Lee and his army. March to Washington, D. C., May 1-12. Grand Review May 23. Mustered out May 31, 1865.

Regiment lost during service 1 Officer and 78 Enlisted men killed and mortally wounded and 1 Officer and 109 Enlisted men by disease. Total 189.

8th REGIMENT INFANTRY.

Organized at Baltimore, Md., August, 1862. Moved from Baltimore to the Antietam, Md., September 18, 1862. Attached to Kenly's Maryland Brigade, Defences Upper Potomac, 8th Army Corps, Middle Department, to March, 1863. 1st Brigade, 1st Division, 8th Army Corps, to June, 1863. Maryland Brigade, French's Command, 8th Army Corps, to July, 1863. 3rd Brigade, 3rd Division, 1st Army Corps, Army of the Potomac, to December,

1863. 2nd Brigade, 3rd Division, 1st Army Corps, to March, 1864. 3rd Brigade, 2nd Division, 5th Army Corps, to June, 1864. 2nd Brigade, 2nd Division, 5th Army Corps, to May, 1865.

SERVICE.—Defence of Williamsport, Md., September 20-21, 1862. Duty between Williamsport and Hagerstown, Md., till December 11. Moved to Maryland Heights December 11-12, and duty there till April 9, 1863. At Bolivar Heights till April 30. Moved to Grafton and Clarksburg, W. Va., to repel invasion. Operations against Jones and Imboden May 1-26. Return to Maryland Heights May 26, and duty there till June 30. Retreat to Frederick, Md., June 30, and guard bridges over the Monocacy till July 6. Reoccupation of Maryland Heights July 7. Joined 1st Army Corps, Army of the Potomac, near Boonsborough, Md., July 10. Pursuit of Lee to Warrenton, Va., July 12-24. At Warrenton Junction, Va., July 25-27. Near Rappahannock Station August 4-September 16. Advance to the Rapidan September 16-18. Bristoe Campaign October 9-22. Bristoe Station October 14. Haymarket October 19. Guard Orange & Alexandria Railroad October 24-November 23. Mine Run Campaign November 26-December 2. Near Culpeper till May, 1864. Demonstration on the Rapidan February 6-7. Campaign from the Rapidan to the James May 3-June 15. Battles of the Wilderness May 5-7. Laurel Hill May 8. Spottsylvania May 8-12. Spottsylvania Court House May 12-21. Assault on the Salient ("Bloody Angle") May 12. Harris Farm, or Fredericksburg Road, May 19. North Anna River May 23-26. Jericho Ford May 23. On line of the Pamunkey May 26-28. Totopotomoy May 28-31. Cold Harbor June 1-12. Bethesda Church June 1-3. Before Petersburg June 16-18. Siege of Petersburg June 16, 1864, to April 2, 1865. Jerusalem Plank Road June 22-23, 1864. Mine Explosion, Petersburg, July 30 (Reserve). Weldon Railroad August 18-21. Poplar Grove Church September 29-October 2. Yellow House October 2-5. Peeble's Farm October 7-8. Davis House October 8. Boydton Plank Road, Hatcher's Run, October 27-28. Warren's Raid on Weldon Railroad December 7-12. Dabney's Mills, Hatcher's Run, February 5-7, 1865. Appomattox Campaign March 28-April 9. Lewis Farm near Gravelly Run, March 29. White Oak Road March 31. Five Forks April 1. Fall of Petersburg April 2. Pursuit of Lee April 3-9. Appomattox Court House April 9. Surrender of Lee and his army. March to Washington, D. C., May 1-12. Grand Review May 23. Mustered out May 31, 1865.

Regiment lost during service 3 Officers and 54 Enlisted men killed and mortally wounded and 70 Enlisted men by disease. Total 127.

9th REGIMENT INFANTRY.

Organized at Baltimore, Md., June and July, 1863, for six months. Moved from Baltimore to Western Maryland July 6, 1863. Attached to 1st Brigade, Maryland Heights, Division of West Virginia, to December, 1863. 1st Brigade, 1st Division, West Virginia, to February, 1864.

SERVICE.—Occupation of Maryland Heights July 7, 1863. At Loudon Heights till August. Guard duty on Baltimore & Ohio Railroad. Company "B" at Duffield Station, Company "C" at Brown's Crossing, Companies "A" and "B" provost duty at Harper's Ferry, Companies "D," "E," "F," "G," "H" and "I" at Charleston, W. Va., till October 18. Attacked by Imboden and captured. Companies "A," "B" and "C" on duty in West Virginia till February, 1864. Moved to Baltimore, Md., and mustered out February 24, 1864.

Regiment lost during service 2 Enlisted men killed and mortally wounded and 124 Enlisted men by disease. Total 126.

10th REGIMENT INFANTRY.

Organized at Baltimore, Md., June and July, 1863, for six months. Ordered to Harper's Ferry, W. Va., July 16, and guard lines of the Upper Potomac till January, 1864. Attached to 2nd Brigade, Maryland Heights Division of West Virginia, July, 1863. 1st Brigade, Maryland Heights Division of West Virginia, to December, 1863. 1st Brigade, 1st Division, West Virginia, to January, 1864. Mustered out January 29, 1864.

Regiment lost 22 by disease during service.

11th REGIMENT INFANTRY.

Organized at Baltimore, Md., for 100 days, June 16, 1864. Moved to Monocacy Junction July 1, 1864. Attached to 3rd Separate Brigade, 8th Army Corps, Middle Department, to July, 1864. 1st Separate Brigade, 8th Army Corps, to October, 1864.

SERVICE.—Guard duty at Monocacy and Mt. Airy, Md., till October 1, 1864. Battle of Monocacy July 9. Mustered out October 1, 1864.

Regiment reorganized for 1 year December, 1864. 3 Companies ("A," "B" and "C") were consolidated with 1st Eastern Shore Regiment January, 1865. Company "C" on detached service at Relay House, Baltimore, & Ohio Railroad. Company "I" at Baltimore. Rest of Regiment at Fort Delaware. Mustered out June 15, 1865.

Regiment lost 29 by disease during service.

12th REGIMENT INFANTRY.

Organized at Baltimore, Md., for 100 days, July 30, 1864. Attached to 1st Separate Brigade, 8th Army Corps, to September, 1864. Reserve Division West Virginia to November, 1864.

On guard duty along Baltimore & Ohio Railroad between Baltimore, Md., and Kearneysville, Va., till November, 1864. Mustered out November 14, 1864.

Lost 2 by disease during service.

13th REGIMENT INFANTRY.

Organized from Veterans 1st Potomac Home Brigade Infantry March 1, 1865. Designated 13th Regiment Infantry April 8, 1865. Attached to 1st Brigade, 2nd Infantry Division, West Virginia. Assigned to duty at Martinsburg, W. Va., and on Baltimore & Ohio Railroad from Martinsburg to Harper's Ferry. Mustered out May 29, 1865.

PURNELL LEGION INFANTRY.

Organized at Pikesville, Md., near Baltimore, under special authority of the Secretary of War, October 31 to December 31, 1861. Attached to Dix's Division, Baltimore, Md., to March, 1862. Lockwood's Brigade, Middle Department, to May, 1862. 2nd Brigade, Sigel's Division, Department of the Shenandoah, to June, 1862. 2nd Brigade, 2nd Division, 2nd Army Corps, Pope's Army of Virginia, to August, 1862. 3rd Brigade, 2nd Division, 2nd Corps, Army of Virginia, to September, 1862. 3rd Brigade, 2nd Division, 12th Army Corps, Army of the Potomac, to October, 1862. 2nd Brigade, 2nd Division, 12th Army Corps, to December, 1862. Frederick, Md., 8th Army Corps, Middle Department, to February, 1863. 3rd Separate Brigade, 8th Army Corps, to June, 1863. 1st Separate Brigade, 8th Army Corps, to May, 1864. 3rd Brigade, 2nd Division, 5th Army Corps, Army of the Potomac, to June, 1865. 2nd Brigade, 2nd Division, 5th Army Corps, to October, 1864.

SERVICE.—Expedition through Accomac and Northampton Counties, Va., November 14-22, 1861. Duty at Baltimore and with Lockwood on Eastern Shore, Va., till May 25, 1862. Ordered to Harper's Ferry, W. Va., May 25. Defence of Harper's Ferry May 28-30. Operations in Shenandoah Valley, Va., till August. Battle of Cedar Mountain August 9. Pope's Campaign in Northern Virginia August 16-September 2. Fords of the Rappahannock August 21-23. Catlett's Station August 22. Plains of Manassas August 27-29 (Reserve). Battle of Bull Run August 30 (Reserve). Maryland Campaign September 6-22. Battles of South Mountain September 14 (Reserve). Antietam September 16-17. Moved to Bolivar Heights September 22, and duty there till December 10. Reconnoissance to Rippon, W. Va., November 9. Detached and assigned to duty at Frederick, Md., and in the Middle Department till May 26, 1864. Joined Army of the Potomac in the field May 26. Rap-

idan Campaign May 30-June 15. Shady Grove May 30. Cold Harbor June 1-12. Bethesda Church June 1-3. Before Petersburg June 16-18. Siege of Petersburg June 16 to October 24, 1864. Jerusalem Plank Road June 21-23. Mine Explosion, Petersburg, July 30. Weldon Railroad August 18-21. Poplar Springs Church September 29-October 2. Yellow House October 2-5. Peeble's Farm October 7-8. Mustered out October 24, 1864. Veterans and Recruits transferred to 1st Maryland Infantry.

Regiment lost during service 1 Officer and 42 Enlisted men killed and mortally wounded and 1 Officer and 73 Enlisted men by disease. Total 117.

BALTIMORE (OR DIX) LIGHT GUARD INFANTRY.

Organized at Baltimore November and December, 1861. Attached to Dix's Command and duty at Baltimore, Md., till May, 1862. Transferred to 3rd Maryland Infantry May 24, 1862.

PATAPSCO GUARD.

Organized at Ellicott's Mills, Md., September 25, 1861. Attached to Dix's Command, Baltimore, Md., to March, 1862. Railroad Brigade, Middle Department, to July, 1862. Railroad Bridge, 8th Army Corps, Middle Department, to September, 1862. Unassigned, 8th Army Corps, to January, 1863. 2nd Separate Brigade, 8th Army Corps, to June, 1863. York, Pa., Dept. of the Susquehanna, to December, 1863. Dept. of the Susquehanna to August, 1865.

SERVICE.—Guard duty on the Philadelphia, Wilmington & Baltimore Railroad till September, 1862. Duty at York, Pa., till June, 1863. Moved to Shippensburg, Pa., June 17; thence to Columbia. Defence of bridge at Wrightsville June 29. At Harrisburg, Pa., till August. At York, Pa., till December, 1863. At Harrisburg and Carlisle, Pa., till July, 1864. At Chambersburg, Pottsville and Phillipsburg, Pa., till March, 1865. Action at Chambersburg July 29-30, 1864. In Juniata District till August, 1865. Mustered out August 17, 1865.

MASSACHUSETTS VOLUNTEERS.

1st REGIMENT CAVALRY.

Organized at Camp Brigham, Reedville, and duty there till December 25, 1861. Companies "A," "B," "C" and "D" left State for Annapolis, Md., December 25, 1861; thence moved to Hilton Head, S. C., February, 1862, and join Regiment. Second Battalion left State for New York December 27, and Third Battalion December 29 for same point; thence sailed for Hilton Head, S. C., January 13, arriving January 20, 1862. Attached to Department of the South to April, 1862. 3rd Brigade, 1st Division, Dept. of the South, to August, 1862. Companies "A" to "H" moved to Fort Monroe August 19, 1862; thence to Washington, D. C., and join Pleasanton's Cavalry, Army of the Potomac, at Tenallytown, September 3. Attached to Pleasanton's Cavalry, Army of the Potomac, to October, 1862. Averill's Brigade, Cavalry Division, Army of the Potomac, to January, 1863. 1st Brigade, 2nd Division, Cavalry Corps, Army of the Potomac, to April, 1865. (4 new Companies, "I," "K," "L," "M," organized December 5, 1863, to January 14, 1864.) Provost Marshal's Command, Army of the Potomac, to May, 1865. Headquarters, Army of the Potomac, to June, 1865.

SERVICE.—Duty at Hilton Head, S. C., till May, 1862. Moved to Edisto Island, S. C., May (Cos. "E" to "M"). Operations on James Island, S. C., June 1-28. Action James Island June 8. Battle of Secessionville June 16 (Co. "H"). Evacuation of James Island and movement to Hilton Head June 28-July 7. Poolesville, Md., September 4-5. Sugar Loaf Mountain September 10-11. South Mountain September 14. Battle of Antietam September 16-17. Shepherdstown, W. Va., September 19. Kearneysville, Shephardstown and Smithfield October 16-17. 4 Companies with 5th Corps October 30-November 25. 4 Companies near Hagerstown, Md., till November 16, thence moved to Washington November 16-25, and duty there refitting till December 13. Bloomfield November 2-3. Snicker's Gap November 3-4.

Markham Station November 4. Manassas Gap November 5-6. Reconnoissance to Grove Church December 1. Battle of Fredericksburg, Va., December 12-15. Reconnoissance toward Warrenton December 21-22. Expedition to Richard's and Ellis' Fords December 29-30. Reconnissance to Catlett's and Rappahannock Station January 8-10, 1863. Elk Run, Catlett's Station, January 9. Near Grove Church January 9. Destruction of Rappahannock Bridge February 5. Hartwood Church February 25. Kelly's Ford March 17. Bealeton March 17. Chancellorsville Campaign, Stoneman's Raid, April 29-May 6. Rapidan Station May 1. Near Fayetteville June 3. Kelly's Ford, Brandy Station and Stevensburg June 9. Aldie June 17. Upperville June 21. Battle of Gettysburg, Pa., July 2-3. Emmettsburg July 4. Williamsport July 6-7. Near Harper's Ferry, W. Va., July 14. Old Antietam Forge, near Leitersburg, July 10. Jones' Cross Roads July 12. Shepherdstown July 16. Near Aldie July 31. Scout to Hazel River August 4. Rixeyville August 5. Welford's Ford August 9. Scout to Barbee's Cross Roads August 24. Scout to Middleburg September 10-11. Advance from the Rappahannock to the Rapidan September 13-17. Culpeper C. H. September 13. Rapidan Station September 13-14-15. Bristoe Campaign October 9-22. Warrenton (or White Sulphur Springs) October 12. Auburn and Bristoe October 14. Brentsville October 14. Picket near Warrenton till November 22. Mine Run Campaign November 26-December 2. New Hope Church November 27. Scout and picket duty at Warrenton till April 21, 1864. Kilpatrick's Raid on Richmond February 28-March 4. Fortifications of Richmond March 1. (Cos. "C," "D" at Headquarters Army of the Potomac, April, 1864, to muster out.) Rapidan Campaign May-June. Todd's Tavern May 5-6. Wilderness May 6-7. Todd's Tavern May 7-8. Corbin's Bridge, Spottsylvania, May 8. Davenport Ford May 9. Sheridan's Raid to James River May 9-24. North Anna River May 9-10. Ground Squirrel Church, Ashland and Yellow Tavern May 11. Brooks' Church, or Richmond Fortifications, May 12. Line of the Pamunkey May 26-28. Totopotomoy May 28-31. Cold Harbor May 31-June 1. About Cold Harbor June 1-7. Sumner's Upper Bridge June 2. Sheridan's Trevillian Raid June 7-24. Trevillian Station June 11-12. Newark, or Mallory's Cross Roads, June 12. Black Creek, or Tunstall Station, and White House, or St. Peter's Church, June 21. St. Mary's Church June 24. Camp at Prince George Court House June 27-July 13. Weldon Railroad and Warwick Swamp July 12. At Lee's Mills till July 26. Demonstration on north side of James River July 27-29. Deep Bottom July 27-28. Malvern Hill July 28. Lee's Mills July 30. Scouting duty till August 14. Demonstration north of James River August 14-18. Gravel Hill August 14. Strawberry Plains August 14-18. Charles City Cross Roads August 18. Weldon Railroad August 19-21. Dinwiddie Road, near Ream's Station, August 23. Ream's Station August 25. Hawkinsville September 14. Jerusalem Plank Road September 16. Belcher's Mills September 17. Poplar Grove Church September 29-October 2. Davis' Farm September 30. Arthur's Swamp September 30-October 1. Vaughan Road October 1. (Old members left front for Massachusetts October 25, 1864.) Boydton Plank Road, Hatcher's Run, October 27-28. At McCann's Station till November 18. Reconnoissance toward Stony Creek November 7. At Westbrook House till December 1. Stony Creek Station December 1. Bellefield Raid December 7-12. Bellefield December 9-10. At Westbrook House till March 17, 1865. Dabney's Mills, Hatcher's Run, February 5-7. Provost duty at City Point till April 2. Fall of Petersburg April 2. Provost duty till May 27. Duty in the Defences of Washington till June 26. Mustered out June 29, 1865, and discharged at Readville, Mass., July 24, 1865.

3rd Battalion.—(Cos. "I," "K," "L" and "M.") Duty in District of Beaufort, S. C., till August, 1862. Action at Pocotaligo, S. C., May 22, 1862 (Detachment). Patrol and guard duty and picketing Broad River. Expedition to St. John's Bluff, Fla., September 30-October

13, 1862. Expedition to Pocotaligo, S. C., October 21-23. Pocotaligo Bridge October 21. Caston and Frampton's Plantation October 22. Attached to 10th Army Corps, Dept. of the South. Company "M" at Hilton Head, S. C., and outpost duty at Lawton's Plantation till August, 1863. A Detachment of Company "I" at Folly Island, S. C., till July, 1863, and Morris Island, S. C., to August, 1863. Balance of Company "I" on outpost duty at Hilton Head, S. C., June to August, 1863. Permanently detached from 1st Cavalry by S. C. 346, War Department, August 4, 1863, and designated Independent Battalion, Massachusetts Cavalry (which see).

Regiment lost during service 6 Officers and 93 Enlisted men killed and mortally wounded and 140 Enlisted men by disease. Total 239.

2nd REGIMENT CAVALRY.

Company "A" organized at San Francisco, Cal., December 10, 1862. Arrived at Readville, Mass., January 4, 1863. Companies "B," "C," "D," "G," "H," "I" and "K" organized at Camp Meigs, Readville, Mass. Companies "E," "F," "L" and "M" organized at San Francisco, Cal., February and March, 1863. Left San Francisco for Readville, Mass., March 21 and joined Regiment at Readville, Mass., as California Battalion April 16, 1863.

Companies "A," "B," "C," "D" and "K" left Massachusetts for Baltimore, Md.; thence moved to Fortress Monroe, Va., February 12-18, 1863; thence moved to Gloucester Point, Va., February 19. Attached to Cavalry Command, 4th Army Corps, Dept. of Virginia. Engaged in picket and outpost duty and scouting till July, 1863. Reconnoissance from Gloucester March 30. Expedition to Gloucester Court House April 7. Companies "A" and "B" moved to Williamsburg, Va., and reconnoissance to White House April 27-May 14. Expedition to King and Queen County May 6. Companies "C," "D" and "K" moved to West Point May 15 and duty there till June 1. Dix's Peninsula Campaign June 24-July 7. Expedition to South Anna Bridge June 23-28. Action at Hanovertown and South Anna Bridge June 26. Expedition from White House to South Anna River July 1-7. Expedition to Gloucester Court House July 25. Moved to Washington, D. C., July 27-29, and joined Regiment at Centreville, Va., August 6.

Companies "E," "F," "G," "H," "I," "L" and "M" moved from Readville, Mass., to Washington, D. C., May 11-16, 1863. Attached to Casey's Provisional Troops, 22nd Corps, to August, 1863. King's Division, 22nd Corps, to September, 1863. Cavalry Brigade, 22nd Corps, to August, 1864. Reserve Cavalry Brigade, 1st Division, Cavalry Corps, Army of Shenandoah, Middle Military Division, to September, 1864. 3rd (Reserve) Brigade, 1st Division, Cavalry Corps, Army of Shenandoah and Army of the Potomac, to July, 1865.

SERVICE.—Duty at East Capital Hill, Defences of Washington, D. C., till May 30, 1863, and at Camp Brightwood June 1-11. Moved to Poolesville, Md., June 23, and patrol duty in rear of the Army of the Potomac June 23-July 3. Brockville July 1. Scout near Dawsonville July 3-9. Reconnoissance to Ashby's Gap July 11-14. Action at Ashby's Gap July 12. Rockville, Md., July 13. Reconnoissance to Warrenton July 20-21. Skirmishes at Warrenton July 21 and 31. Operations about Fairfax Court House July 28-August 3. Near Aldie July 30. Duty at Centreville, Va., operating against Moseby till October 6. Companies "C," "F," "G" and "I" detached at Muddy Branch September 15, 1863, to March 8, 1864. Warrenton Pike August 17. Coyle's Tavern, near Fairfax Court House, August 24. Expeditions from Centreville August 15-19, September 18-20 and October 2-5. Ordered to Fairfax Court House October 6, thence to Vienna October 9 and duty there till May 24, 1864. Scout to Gum Springs October 12-13, 1863. Near Annandale October 22. Tyson's Cross Roads November 14. Reconnoissance to Blue Ridge Mountains November 18-26. Picket attacks December 12-23. Affair at Germantown December 13 (Detachment). Scout from Vienna to Middleburg December 18-20. Skirmish with Moseby December 29. Near Ellis and Ely's Fords January 17, 1864. Ellis Ford January 26. Scout to Aldie February 4-6. Aldie February 5. Near Circlesville February 21. Dranesville February 22. Scout to Farmwell February 25-26. Companies "B," "D," "E" and "M" relieve Companies "C," "F," "G" and "I" at Muddy Branch March 8. Expedition to Faquier and Loudoun Counties April —. Affair Leesburg April 19 (Detachment). Action with Moseby near Leesburg April 28. Scout to Upperville April 28-May 1. Patrol duty on Orange & Alexandria Railroad May —. Moved to Fall's Church May 24. Escort wounded from the Wilderness June 8-14. Point of Rocks July 5. Action with Moseby at Mt. Zion Church, near Aldie, July 6. Frederick Pike July 7-8. Tennallytown July 10. Fort Reno and near Fort Stevens July 11. Fort Stevens and about Northern Defences of Washington July 11-12. Rockville, Md., July 13. Poolesville, Md., July 14. Pursuit of Early to Snicker's Gap July 14-23. Snicker's Gap July 17-18. At Rockville July 26-August 9. Sheridan's Shenandoah Valley Campaign August to November. Shepherdstown August 10. White Post August 12. Strasburg August 15. Winchester August 17 and 18. Opequan Creek August 18. Near Opequan Creek August 19. Berryville Pike August 20. Summit Point August 21. Charleston August 21-22. Halltown August 22-24. Summit Point August 25-27. Smithfield August 29. Berryville September 3-4. Berryville Pike September 4. Opequan Creek September 7. Locke's Ford, Opequan Creek, September 13. Sevier's Ford, Opequan Creek, September 15. Battle of Opequan, Winchester, September 19. Front Royal and Snake Mountain September 20. Fisher's Hill September 21. Milford September 22. Mill's Ford September 23. Toll Gate, near Front Royal, September 23. Luray Valley September 24. Port Republic September 26-27. Rockfish Gap September 28. Waynesboro September 28, 29 and 30 and October 2. Mt. Crawford October 2. Tom's Brook, "Woodstock Races," October 8-9. Battle of Cedar Creek October 19. Guarding Winchester & Potomac Railroad November 3-28. Near Kernstown November 11. Expedition to Loudoun and Faquier Counties November 28-December 3. Expedition to Gordonsville December 19-28. Madison Court House December 20. Gordonsville December 23. Charlottesville December 24. At Camp Russell, near Winchester, January 1 to February 27, 1865. Sheridan's Raid to White House Landing February 27-May 25. Occupation of Staunton March 2. Waynesborough March 2. Duguidsville March 8. South Anna Bridge March 14. Destruction of Virginia Central Railroad and James River Canal. Appomattox Campaign March 28-April 9. White Oak Road, near Five Forks, March 30. Dinwiddie Court House March 30-31. Five Forks April 1. Scott's Cross Roads April 2. Tabernacle Church or Beaver Pond Creek April 4. Sailor's Creek April 6. Appomattox Station April 8. Appomattox Court House April 9. Surrender of Lee and his army. At Nottaway Station till April 19. Expedition to Danville April 23-29. Near Petersburg to May 10. March to Washington, D. C., May 10-16. Grand Review May 23. Near Cloud's Mills May 29-June 26, and at Fairfax Court House till July 20. Mustered out July 20, 1865.

Regiment lost during service 8 Officers and 82 Enlisted men killed and mortally wounded and 3 Officers and 138 Enlisted men by disease. Total 231.

2nd BATTALION CAVALRY.

Organized at Camp Chase, Lowell, Mass. Company "A" November 15, Company "B" December 27 and Company "C" December 6, 1861. Moved to Boston January 2, 1862; thence sailed to Fortress Monroe, Va., and Ship Island, Miss., January 13, arriving at Ship Island February 12. Attached to Phelp's 1st Brigade (Co. "A"), Williams' 2nd Brigade (Co. "B") and Shipley's 3rd Brigade (Co. "C"), Dept. of the Gulf, to September, 1862. Sherman's 2nd Division, 19th Army Corps, Dept. of the Gulf (Co. "A"), to June, 1863. Weitzel's Reserve Brigade, Dept. of the Gulf, to January, 1863 (Co. "B"). 1st Division, 19th Army Corps, Dept. of the Gulf, to June, 1863 (Co. "B"). Defences New Orleans, Dept. of the Gulf, to May, 1863 (Co. "C"). Cavalry Brigade, 19th Army Corps, Dept. of the Gulf, to June, 1863 (Co. "C").

SERVICE.—At Ship Island, Miss., till April, 1862. Occupation of New Orleans, La., May. Battle of Baton Rouge, La., August 5 (Co. "B"). St. Charles Court House August 29 (Co. "B"). Operations in LaFourche District October 24-November 6 (Co. "B"). Affair at Plaquemine December 31 (Co. "C"). Operations on Bayou Plaquemine and the Black and Atchafalaya Rivers February 12-28, 1863 (Co. "B"). Operations against Port Hudson March 7-27. Expedition to Hermitage Landing March 24 (Co. "B"). Operations in Western Louisiana April 9-May 14. Teche Campaign April 11-20. Fort Bisland April 12-13. Jeanerette April 14. Near Washington May 1. Boyce's Bridge, Cotile Landing, May 14. Siege of Port Hudson May 24-June 17. Expedition to Clinton June 3-8 (Co. "C"). Assigned to 3rd Massachusetts Cavalry June 17, 1863. Companies "A" and "B" as Company "M," and Company "C" as Company "L." (See 3rd Massachusetts Cavalry.)

3rd REGIMENT CAVALRY.

Organized as 41st Massachusetts Infantry. Designation changed to 3rd Cavalry June 17, 1863. Company "A," 33rd Massachusetts Infantry, assigned as Company "I." 2nd Battalion, Massachusetts Cavalry, assigned as Companies "L" and "M." Attached to 2nd Brigade, 4th Division, 19th Army Corps, Army of the Gulf, to June, 1863. Cavalry Brigade, Dept. of the Gulf, to July, 1863. Defences of New Orleans to August, 1863. Cavalry Brigade, District of Port Hudson, La., Dept. of the Gulf, to October, 1863. Unattached, Cavalry Division, Dept. of the Gulf, to January, 1864. 4th Brigade, Cavalry Division, Dept. of the Gulf, to June, 1864. 2nd Brigade, 2nd Division, 19th Army Corps, Dept. of the Gulf and Army of Shenandoah, Middle Military Division, to February, 1865. Reserve Cavalry Brigade, Army of Shenandoah, to April, 1865. Defences of Washington, D. C., 22nd Army Corps, to June, 1865. Dept. of Missouri to September, 1865.

SERVICE.—Siege of Port Hudson, La., June 17-July 9, 1863. Duty at Port Hudson till January, 1864, scouting, outpost and patrol duty. Action at Jackson August 3, 1863. Plain's Store November 30. Ordered to New Orleans, La., January 2, 1864. Duty at Carrollton till February 29. March to Berwick and Brashear City February 29-March 10. Red River Campaign March 10-May 22. Advance from Franklin to Alexandria March 14-26. Monett's Ferry and Cloutiersville March 29-30. Natchitoches March 31. Crump's Hill, Piney Woods, April 2. Bayou de Paul, Carroll's Mills, April 8. Sabine Cross Roads April 8. Pleasant Hill April 9. Natchitoches April 19. Monett's Bluff, Cane River Crossing, April 23. Hudnot's Plantation and Alexandria May 1. Mansura May 4. Retreat to Morganza May 13-20. Mansura May 16. Moreauville May 17. Yellow Bayou May 18. Dismounted June 25 and equipped as Infantry. Moved from Morganza to New Orleans, La., July 3; thence to Fortress Monroe, Va., and Washington, D. C., July 15-28. Moved to Monocacy, Md., July 29; thence to Harper's Ferry, W. Va., August 4. Sheridan's Shenandoah Valley Campaign August 7-November 28. Battle of Opequan, Winchester, September 19. Fisher's Hill September 22. Battle of Cedar Creek October 19. At Cedar Creek till November 9. At Opequan Creek, near Winchester, till December 25. Moved to Stephenson's Landing, thence to Remount Camp, Pleasant Valley, Md., December 25-28, and duty there till February 24, 1865. Again mounted and equipped as Cavalry February 15. Moved to Opequan Creek March 8. Scout to Front Royal March 16. Scout to Woodstock April 1. Duty at Cedar Creek, Edinburg, Winchester and Berryville till April 20. Moved to Washington, D. C., April 20-22, and duty at

Fall's Church till May 22. Grand Review May 23-24. Old members mustered out May 20, 1865. Company "L" mustered out December 27, 1864, and Company "M" January 31, 1865. Duty at Bladensburg and Cloud's Mills till June 14. Moved to St. Louis, Mo., June 14-20; thence to Fort Leavenworth, Kansas, June 21-25. Regiment consolidated to 6 Companies July 21. March to Fort Kearney, Neb., July 27-August 16. March to Cottonwood Springs, Colo., August 23-28; thence to Fort Kearney August 29-September 1, and to Fort Leavenworth September 8-18. Mustered out September 28, 1865. Moved to Boston, Mass., September 29-October 5, and discharged October 8, 1865.

Regiment lost during service 5 Officers and 101 Enlisted men killed and mortally wounded and 2 Officers and 180 Enlisted men by disease. Total 288.

4th REGIMENT CAVALRY.

Organized at Readville December 26, 1863, to February 8, 1864. 1st Battalion formerly Independent Battalion, Massachusetts Cavalry, was assigned as Companies "I," "K," "L" and "M" February 12, 1864. Attached to Light Brigade, District of Florida, 10th Corps, Dept. of the South, to April, 1864. Unattached, Dept. of Virginia and North Carolina, 10th, 18th and 24th Army Corps, and 25th Army Corps, Dept. of Virginia and North Carolina, to August, 1865. Dept. of Virginia to November, 1865.

SERVICE.—Expedition from Jacksonville, Fla., to Lake City, Fla., February 7-22, 1864. Battle of Olustee, Fla., February 20. McGrath's Creek, Cedar Run, March 1. Cedar Run April 2. Ordered to Bermuda Hundred, Va., arriving there May 8. Operations against Fort Darling April 12-16. Bermuda Hundred May 20-30. Jordan's Crossing and Petersburg June 9. Siege operations against Petersburg and Richmond June 16, 1864, to April 2, 1865. At Headquarters, Dept. of Virginia and North Carolina, June 21 to August 15, 1864. At Headquarters, 10th Army Corps, till December, 1864. Demonstration on north side of the James August 13-20. Strawberry Plains August 14-18. Flusser's Mills August 18-19. (Co. "M" detached at Harrison's Landing on outpost duty August 23, 1864, to March, 1865.) Before Petersburg August 24 to September 28. Chaffin's Farm, New Market Heights, September 28-30. Harrison's Landing October 13 (Co. "M"). Fair Oaks October 27-28. Expedition into Charles City and Henrico Counties November 1-5. Duty before Richmond till March, 1865. At Headquarters, Dept. of Virginia and North Carolina, December, 1864, to April, 1865 (Cos. "I," "L" and "M"). At Headquarters, 24th Army Corps, December, 1864, to April, 1865 (Co. "K"). Appomattox Campaign March 28-April 9, 1865. Fall of Petersburg April 2. High Bridge, Farmville, April 6-7. Appomattox Court House April 9. Surrender of Lee and his army. Duty at Richmond till November —.

2nd Battalion.—(Cos. "A," "B," "C" and "D.") Sailed from Boston for Hilton Head, S. C., on Steamer "Western Metropolis" March 20, 1864, arriving April 1. Picket and outpost duty at Hilton Head till June. Expedition to Ashepoo River May 22-26 (2 Cos.). 2 Companies moved to Jacksonville, Fla., June 6-8, and duty there till January, 1865, participating in skirmish at Front Creek July 15, 1864. Raid from Jacksonville upon Baldwin July 23-28. Skirmish at South Fork, Black Creek, July 24. St. Mary's Trestle July 26. Raid on Florida Railroad August 15-19. Gainesville August 17. Magnolia October 24. Gum Swamp October 24. 2 Companies on duty at Hilton Head, S. C., June to November, 1864. Expedition to John's Island, S. C., July 2-10. Operations against Battery Pringle July 4-9. Expedition to Boyd's Neck November 29-30. Battle of Honey Hill November 30. Expedition to Deveaux's Neck December 1-6. March to Charleston January 15-February 23, 1865. Potter's Expedition to Camden, S. C., April 5-25. Statesburg April 15. Occupation of Camden April 17. Boykin's Mills April 18. Denkin's Mills April 19. Beech Creek, near Statesburg, April 19. Duty in the Dept. of the South till mustered out.

3rd Battalion.—(Cos. "E," "F," "G" and "H.") Sailed from Boston for Hilton Head, S. C., on Steamer "Western Metropolis" April 23, 1864, arriving April 27. Moved to Newport News, Va., May 1-3; thence to City Point May 23, and duty there scouting, picketing and on the fortifications till June 16. Duty at Bermuda Hundred till August 23. Companies "E" and "H" at Headquarters of 18th Army Corps June 16-December 4, and at Headquarters of 25th Army Corps December, 1864, to April, 1865. Company "F" at Headquarters of 24th Army Corps December, 1864, to April, 1865. Company "G" detached at Yorktown and Williamsburg, Va., August 23, 1864, to April, 1865. Occupation of Richmond April 3, 1865 (Cos. "E" and "H"). Company "F" on Appomattox Campaign March 28-April 9. High Bridge, Farmville, April 6-7. Appomattox Court House April 9. Surrender of Lee and his army. Regiment mustered out November 14, 1865. Discharged at Boston November 26, 1865.

Regiment lost during service 4 Officers and 28 Enlisted men killed and mortally wounded and 2 Officers and 128 Enlisted men by disease. Total 162.

5th REGIMENT CAVALRY.—(COLORED.)

Organized at Camp Meigs, Readville. 1st Battalion moved to Washington, D. C., May 5-8, 1864. At Camp Stoneman, Giesboro Point, Md., May 8-12. Dismounted and moved to Camp Casey, near Fort Albany, May 12. 2nd Battalion moved to Washington May 6-8, and to Camp Casey May 9. 3rd Battalion moved to Washington May 8-10, and to Camp Casey May 11. Regiment moved to Fortress Monroe, Va., thence to City Point, Va., May 13-16. Attached to Rand's Provisional Brigade, 18th Army Corps, Dept. of Virginia and North Carolina, May, 1864. Hinks' Colored Division, 18th Army Corps, to June, 1864. 1st Brigade, 3rd Division, 18th Army Corps, to July, 1864. Point Lookout, Md., District of St. Mary's, 22nd Army Corps, to March, 1865. Unattached, 25th Army Corps, Dept. of Virginia, to June, 1865. Dept. of Texas to October, 1865.

SERVICE.—Duty at City Point, Va., as Infantry till June 16, 1864. Before Petersburg June 16-19. Siege of Petersburg June 16-28. Moved to Point Lookout, Md., June 30, and duty there guarding prisoners till March, 1865. Ordered to the field and duty near Richmond, March; near Petersburg, April; near City Point, May, and at Camp Lincoln till June 16. Ordered to Texas and duty at Clarksville till October. Mustered out October 31, 1865.

Regiment lost during service 7 Enlisted men killed and 116 Enlisted men by disease. Total 123.

DEVINS' BATTALION MOUNTED RIFLES.

Organized at Worcester and at Baltimore, Md., April 19, 1861. Attached to the Defences of Baltimore, Md. Mustered out August 3, 1861.

INDEPENDENT BATTALION CAVALRY.

Organized by detachment of Companies "I," "K," "L" and "M," 1st Massachusetts Cavalry, August 4, 1863. Duty at Beaufort and Hilton Head, S. C., till February, 1864. Company "I" (a Detachment) at Morris Island, S. C., August to December, 1863. Siege operations against Sumpter and Charleston. Expedition from Hilton Head, S. C., to Jacksonville, Fla., February 5-7, 1864. Capture of Jacksonville February 7. Ten-Mile Run, near Camp Finnegan, February 8. Barber's Place February 10. Lake City February 11. Assigned to 4th Massachusetts Cavalry as Companies "I," "K," "L" and "M" February 12, 1864.

1st REGIMENT HEAVY ARTILLERY.

Organized as 14th Massachusetts Infantry July 5, 1861. Designation changed to 1st Heavy Artillery January 1, 1862. Attached to Wadsworth's Command, Military District of Washington, January to May, 1862. Whipple's Brigade, Military District of Washington, to December, 1862. Artillery, District of Alexandria, Defences of Washington, to February, 1863. Artillery, District of Alexandria, 22nd Army Corps, to April, 1863.

SEE CORRECTION SHEET, PG. 1750

1st Brigade, DeRussy's Division, 22nd Army Corps, to April, 1864. 2nd Brigade, DeRussy's Division, 22nd Army Corps, to May, 1864. 2nd Brigade, Tyler's Heavy Artillery Division, Army of the Potomac, to May, 1864. 2nd Brigade, 3rd Division, 2nd Army Corps, Army of the Potomac, to May, 1865. Defences of Washington, 22nd Army Corps, to August, 1865. (Cos. "B," "C," "H" and "I" attached to Defences of Upper Potomac, 8th Army Corps, Middle Department, October, 1862, to March, 1863. 2nd Brigade, 1st Division, 8th Army Corps, Middle Department, to June, 1863. Maryland Brigade, French's Command, 8th Army Corps, to July, 1863. Artillery Reserve, Army of the Potomac, to August, 1863. Unattached, Maryland Heights Division, Dept. of West Virginia, to December, 1863.)

SERVICE.—Garrison duty in the Defences of Washington at Forts Albany, Runyon, Scott, Richardson, Barnard, Craig and Tillinghast till August 23, 1862. Moved to Cloud's Mills August 23. March to Manassas. Va., August 26-30. Return to Washington and garrison Forts Albany, Craig, Tillinghast, Woodbury and DeKalb, Defences South of the Potomac till May, 1864. (Cos. "H" and "I" detached September 27, 1862, and moved to Harper's Ferry, W. Va. Co. "C" ordered to Harper's Ferry October 27, 1862. Co. "B" ordered to Harper's Ferry, W. Va., December 23, 1862; garrison duty there till July 1, 1863. Co. "I" moved to Winchester June 10, 1863, and participated in the Battle of Winchester June 13-15, and retreat to Harper's Ferry. Defence of Harper's Ferry June 16-July 1. Evacuation of Harper's Ferry and march to Frederick, Md., July 1-2. Duty with Artillery Reserve, Army of the Potomac, to July 11-22. Moved to Harper's Ferry July 22 and duty there till December 1, when ordered to Washington and rejoin Regiment.) Regiment moved to join Army of the Potomac at Belle Plain, Va., May 15-16, 1864. Harris Farm, Fredericksburg Road, May 19. Spottsylvania Court House May 19-21. North Anna River May 23-26. Line of the Pamunkey May 26-28. Totopotomoy May 28-31. Cold Harbor June 1-12. Before Petersburg June 16-19. Siege of Petersburg June 16, 1864, to April 2, 1865. Jerusalem Plank Road June 22-23, 1864. Deep Bottom July 27-28. Mine Explosion, Petersburg, July 30 (Reserve). Strawberry Plains August 14-18. Peeble's Farm September 29-October 2. Boydton Plank Road, Hatcher's Run, October 27-28. Expedition to Weldon Railroad December 7-12. Dabney's Mills, Hatcher's Run, February 5-7, 1865. Appomattox Campaign March 28-April 9. Crow's House March 31. Fall of Petersburg April 2. Sailor's Creek April 6. High Bridge, Farmville, April 7. Appomattox Court House April 9. Surrender of Lee and his army. March to Burkesville April 11-13 and duty there till May 2. March to Washington May 2-15. Camp at Bailey's Cross Roads till June 15. Grand Review May 23. Duty at Forts Ethan, Allen and Marcy till June 27. At Forts C. F. Smith and Strong till July 19, and at Fort Bunker Hill till August 17. Mustered out August 16, 1865, and discharged at Gallop's Island, Boston Harbor, August 25, 1865.

Regiment lost during service 9 Officers and 232 Enlisted men killed and mortally wounded and 2 Officers and 241 Enlisted men by disease. Total 484.

1st BATTALION HEAVY ARTILLERY.

Organized April, 1865, from 1st, 2nd and 4th Unattached Companies Heavy Artillery. 5th Unattached Company Heavy Artillery added June, 1863. Organized for Coast Defence. Company "A" on duty at Fort Warren, Boston Harbor, till December 24, 1864. At Champlain, N. Y., till May 13, 1865, and at Fort Warren till October, 1865. Mustered out October 20, 1865.

Company "B" at Fort Warren till August, 1864, and at New Bedford, Mass., till June, 1865. Mustered out June 29, 1865.

Company "C" on duty at Fort Warren till October, 1865. Mustered out October 20, 1865.

Company "D" at Fort Independence to September, 1865. Mustered out September 12, 1865.

Companies "E" and "F" organized August 15, 1864, for one year. On duty at Fort Warren. Mustered out June 28, 1865.

Companies "A," "C" and "D" also furnished detachments for duty at Plymouth, Provincetown, Gloucester, Marblehead, Newburyport, Fairhaven, etc.

2nd REGIMENT HEAVY ARTILLERY.

Organized at Readville and mustered in: Company "A" July 28, 1863; Company "B" July 29, 1863; Company "C" August 4, 1863; Company "D" August 22, 1863, and left State for New Berne, N. C., September 5, 1863. Company "E" October 5, 1863, and Company "F" October 8, 1863. Left State for New Berne, N. C., November 7, 1863. Company "G" December 7, 1863. Company "H" December 7, 1863. Company "I" December 11, 1863. Companies "K" and "L" December 22, 1863, and Company "M," December 24, 1863. Left State for Fortress Monroe, Va., January 8, 1864. Assigned to garrison duty in Department of Virginia and North Carolina. Company "A" at Fort Macon, N. C., to July, 1864; at New Berne to December, 1864; at Plymouth till March, 1865. Company "B" at Newport Barracks to December, 1864, and at New Berne till March, 1865. Company "C" at Morehead City till July, 1864, and at New Berne till March, 1865. Company "D" at Fort Macon till July, 1864; at New Berne till November, 1864, and at Plymouth till March, 1865. Company "E" at Fort Totten to July, 1864; at New Berne till November, 1864, and at Plymouth till March, 1865. Company "F" at Fort Totten till April, 1864; at Fort Levinson till July, 1864, and at New Berne till March, 1865. Company "G" at Plymouth till April, 1864. Siege of P-ymlouth April 17-20. Captured. At New Berne till April, 1865, and at Fort Macon till June, 1865. Company "H" at Plymouth till April, 1864. Siege of Plymouth April 17-20. Captured. At New Berne till November, 1864, and at Plymouth till March, 1865. Company "I" at Norfolk and Portsmouth, Va., till July, 1864, and at New Berne, N. C., till March, 1865. Companies "K" and "L" at Norfolk and Portsmouth, Va., and other points in Virginia till April, 1865; and at New Berne, N. C., till June, 1865. Company "M" at Norfolk and Portsmouth, Va., to May, 1864, and at New Berne, N. C., to March, 1865. Regimental Headquarters at Norfolk and Portsmouth, Va., to May, 1864, and at New Berne, N. C., to July, 1865. Expedition to Columbia, N. C., February 13-15, 1865 (Cos. "A," "D," "E" and "H" attached to 1st Brigade, 1st Division, District of Beaufort, N. C., Dept. of North Carolina, March, 1865, and ordered to the field March 3. Expedition to Kinston, N. C., March 3-14. Southwest Creek March 7. Battle of Wise's Forks March 8-10. Occupation of Kinston March 14. Provost duty at Kinston till June.) Regiment concentrated at New Berne June, 1865, and assigned to duty at Wilmington and in the Defences of Cape Fear River, including Forts Fisher and Caswell, and duty at Smithville till September. Moved to Boston September 2-16. Mustered out September 23, 1865.

Regiment lost during service 15 Enlisted men killed and mortally wounded and 4 Officers and 363 Enlisted men by disease. Total 382.

3rd REGIMENT HEAVY ARTILLERY.

Organized for one year August, 1864, by consolidation of 3rd, 6th, 7th, 8th, 9th, 10th, 11th, 12th, 13th, 14th, 15th and 16th Unattached Companies Heavy Artillery. Attached to 2nd Brigade, Hardin's Division, 22nd Army Corps, Dept. of Washington, and engaged in garrison duty in the Defences of Washington, north of the Potomac, to September, 1865. (For Co. "I," 13th Unattached Company, see 13th Unattached Company.) Mustered out September 18, 1865.

Regiment lost during service 2 Enlisted men killed and 1 Officer and 38 Enlisted men by disease. Total 41.

4th REGIMENT HEAVY ARTILLERY.

Organized November 12, 1864, by consolidation of the 17th, 18th, 19th, 20th, 21st, 22nd, 23rd, 24th, 25th, 26th, 27th and 28th Unattached Companies Heavy Artillery.

Organized August, 1864, for one year's service. Consolidated to a Regiment November 12, 1864. Attached to 3rd Brigade, DeRussy's Division, 22nd Army Corps, Dept. of Washington. . Garrison duty in the Defences of Washington, south of the Potomac, till June, 1865. Mustered out June 17, 1865.

Lost during service 2 Officers and 23 Enlisted men by disease. Total 25.

UNASSIGNED COMPANIES HEAVY ARTILLERY.

First—Organized February 26, 1862, for garrison duty in the forts of Boston Harbor, and on duty at Fort Warren till April, 1863, when assigned to 1st Battalion Heavy Artillery as Company "A."

Second—Organized November 3, 1862, for garrison duty in the forts of Boston Harbor, and on duty at Fort Warren till April, 1863, when assigned to 1st Battalion Heavy Artillery as Company "B."

Third—Organized January 10, 1863, for garrison duty in the forts of Boston Harbor. Ordered to Washington, D. C., March, 1864. Attached to 2nd Brigade, De Russy's Division, 22nd Corps, Dept. of Washington, to July, 1864. 3rd Brigade, DeRussy's Division, 22nd Corps, to August. Assigned to 3rd Heavy Artillery as Company "A" August, 1864.

Fourth—Organized April 22, 1863. Assigned to 1st Battalion Heavy Artillery April, 1863, as Company "C."

Fifth—Organized June 6, 1863. Assigned to 1st Battalion Heavy Artillery as Company "D" June, 1863.

Sixth—Organized May 9, 1863, for garrison of forts in Boston Harbor. Ordered to Washington, D. C., and garrison duty there till August, 1864. Attached to Third Brigade, Hardin's Division, 22nd Army Corps, May to August, 1864. Assigned to 3rd Heavy Artillery as Company "B" August, 1864.

Seventh—Organized August 14, 1863, for garrison of forts in Boston Harbor. Ordered to Washington, D. C., and garrison duty in the defences of that city till August, 1864. Attached to 3rd Brigade, Hardin's Division, 22nd Army Corps, Dept. of Washington, May to August, 1864. Assigned to 3rd Heavy Artillery as Company "C" August, 1864.

Eighth—Organized August 14, 1863, for garrison of forts in Boston Harbor. Ordered to Washington, D. C., and garrison duty there in the defences of that city till August, 1864. Attached to 3rd Brigade, Hardin's Division, 22nd Army Corps, Dept. of Washington, May to August, 1864. Assigned to 3rd Heavy Artillery as Company "D" August, 1864.

Ninth—Organized August 27, 1863, for garrison of forts in Boston Harbor. Ordered to Washington, D. C., and garrison duty in the Defences of that city till August, 1864. Attached to 3rd Brigade, Hardin's Division, 22nd Army Corps, Dept. of Washington, May to August, 1864. Asigned to 3rd Heavy Artillery August, 1864, as Company "E."

Tenth—Organized September 16, 1863, for garrison of forts in Boston Harbor. Ordered to Washington, D. C., and garrison duty in the Defences of that city till August, 1864. Attached to 3rd Brigade, Hardin's Division, 22nd Army Corps, Dept. of Washington, May to August, 1864. Assigned to 3rd Heavy Artillery as Company "F" August, 1864.

Eleventh—Organized October 20, 1863, for garrison of forts in Boston Harbor. Ordered to Washington, D. C., and garrison duty in the Defences of that city till August, 1864. Attached to 3rd Brigade, Hardin's Division, 22nd Army Corps, Dept. of Washington, May to August, 1864. Assigned to 3rd Heavy Artillery as Company "G" August, 1864.

Twelfth—Organized November 20, 1863, for garrison of forts in Boston Harbor. Ordered to Washington, D. C., and garison duty in the Defences of that city till August, 1864. Attached to 3rd Brigade, Hardin's Division, 22nd Army Corps, Dept. of Washington, May to August, 1864. Assigned to 3rd Heavy Artillery as Company "H" August, 1864.

Thirteenth—Organized February 10, 1864, for garrison of forts in Boston Harbor. Left Boston for Fortress Monroe, Va., March 7, 1864. Placed in charge of the pontoon train, Army of the James, and participated in the Campaign of Gen. Butler against Petersburg and Richmond, Va., May, 1864. Built and maintained bridges across the Appomattox, connecting Army of the Potomac and Army of the James, and the bridges across James River used in the frequent crossings of the Federal armies during the siege of Petersburg. In the Appomattox Campaign built the pontoon bridge at Farmville by which the 2nd and 6th Corps crossed in pursuit of Lee, and built the bridge at Richmond, Va., by which all the Union Armies crossed the James River on their way to Washington after close of the war. Assigned to 3rd Massachusetts Heavy Artillery as Company "I," but remained detached. Mustered out September 26, 1865.

Fourteenth—Organized May 12, 1864. Sailed from Gallop's Island for Washington, D. C., June 23, 1864, and garrison duty in the Defences of that city till August, 1864. Attached to 3rd Brigade, Hardin's Division, 22nd Army Corps, Dept. of Washington, June to August, 1864. Assigned to 3rd Heavy Artillery August, 1864, as Company "K."

Fifteenth—Organized May 20, 1864. Sailed from Gallop's Island for Washington, D. C., June 23, 1864, and garrison duty in the Defences of that city till August, 1864. Attached to 3rd Brigade, Hardin's Division, 22nd Army Corps, Dept. of Washington, June to August, 1864. Assigned to 3rd Heavy Artillery August, 1864, as Company "L."

Sixteenth—Organized August, 1864. Assigned to 3rd Heavy Artillery as Company "M" August, 1864. Sailed for Washington, D. C., September 22, 1864.

Seventeenth, Eighteenth, Nineteenth, Twentieth, Twenty-first, Twenty-second, Twenty-third, Twenty-fourth, Twenty-fifth, Twenty-sixth, Twenty-seventh and Twenty-eighth Companies organized August, 1864, and left State for Washington, D. C., September 11 to September 16, 1864. Assigned to 4th Heavy Artillery November 12, 1864.

Twenty-ninth—Organized September 20, 1864. Ordered to Washington October 29, 1864, and garrison duty in the Defences of Washington, D. C., till June, 1865. Attached to 1st Brigade, DeRussy's Division, 22nd Army Corps. Mustered out June 16, 1865.

Thirtieth—Organized September 1, 1864. Ordered to Washington, D. C., September 26, 1864, and garrison duty in the Defences of that city till June, 1865. Attached to 1st Brigade, DeRussy's Division, 22nd Army Corps. Mustered out June 16, 1865.

COOK'S BATTERY BOSTON LIGHT ARTILLERY.

Left State with 5th Massachusetts Volunteer Militia April 21, 1861, for Fortress Monroe, Va., arriving April 23; thence moved to Annapolis, Md., April 23-24. Quartered in Naval School Building till May 4. At Relay House May 6 to June 13. Mustered into United States service May 18, 1861, for three months. Duty at Camp Clare, near Baltimore, Md., and in Monument Square till August 2. Mustered out August 2, 1861.

1st BATTERY LIGHT ARTILLERY.

Organized at Camp Cameron August 27, 1861. Left State for Washington, D. C., October 3. Attached to Franklin's Division, Army of the Potomac, to March, 1862. Artillery, 1st Division, 1st Army Corps, Army of the Potomac, to April, 1862. Artillery, 1st Division, Dept. of the Rappahannock, to April, 1862. Artillery, 1st Division, 6th Army Corps, Army of the Potomac, to June, 1863. Artillery Brigade, 6th Army Corps, Army of the Potomac and Army of the Shenandoah, to October, 1864.

SERVICE.—Duty in the Defences of Washington, D. C., till March, 1862. Advance on Manassas, Va., March 10-15, 1862. McDowell's advance on Fredericksburg, Va., April 4-12. Ordered to the Peninsula, Va. Siege of Yorktown, Va., April 23-May 4 (on transports). West Point May 7-8. Mechanicsville June 12. Seven days before Richmond June 25-July 1. Mechanicsville June 26. Gaines Mill June 27. Golding's Farm and Fort

Davidson June 28. Charles City Cross Roads June 30. Malvern Hill July 1. At Harrison's Landing till August 16. Retreat from the Peninsula and movement to Centreville August 16-27. In works at Centreville August 27-31. Assist in checking Pope's rout at Bull Run August 30, and cover retreat to Fairfax Court House September 1. Maryland Campaign September-October. Crampton's Gap, Md., September 14. Battle of Antietam September 16-17. At Downsville, Md., till October 29. Movement to Falmouth, Va., October 29-November 19. Battle of Fredericksburg, Va., December 11-15. Burnside's Second Campaign, "Mud March," January 20-24, 1863. At White Oak Church till April. Chancellorsville Campaign April 27-May 6. Operations at Franklin's Crossing April 29-May 2. Maryes Heights, Fredericksburg, May 3. Salem Heights May 3-4. Franklin's Crossing, Deep Run, June 5-13. Battle of Gettysburg, Pa., July 2-4. Moved to Boonsboro, Williamsport, Berlin and Warrenton, Va., July 5-25. Camp at Warrenton till September 15, and at Stone House Mountain till October 5. Bristoe Campaign October 9-22. Advance to line of the Rappahannock November 7-8. Rappahannock Station November 7. Mine Run Campaign November 26-December 2. Camp at Brandy Station till May, 1864. Campaign from the Rapidan to the James May 3-June 15. Battles of the Wilderness May 5-7. Spottsylvania May 8-12. Spottsylvania C. H. May 12-21. "Bloody Angle" May 12. North Anna River May 23-26. Line of the Pamunkey May 26-28. Totopotomoy May 28-31. Cold Harbor June 1-12. Before Petersburg June 17-July 9. Jerusalem Plank Road June 22-23. Moved to Washington, D. C., July 9-12. Repulse of Early's attack on Washington July 12. Sheridan's Shenandoah Valley Campaign August-October. Battle of Opequan, Winchester, September 19. Fisher's Hill September 22. Moved to Boston October 2-12. Mustered out October 19, 1864, expiration of term.

Battery lost during service 6 Enlisted men killed and mortally wounded and 15 Enlisted men by disease. Total 21.

2nd BATTERY LIGHT ARTILLERY.

Organized at Quincy and mustered in July 31, 1861. Moved to Baltimore, Md., August 8-11. Attached to Dix's Command to February, 1862. New Orleans (La.) Expedition to March, 1862. 2nd Brigade, Dept. of the Gulf, to December, 1862. Artillery, Grover's Division, Dept. of the Gulf, to January, 1863. Artillery, 4th Division, 19th Army Corps, Dept. of the Gulf, to August, 1863. Artillery Reserve, Dept. of the Gulf, to September, 1863. Artillery, Cavalry Division, Dept. Gulf, to August, 1864. Unattached Artillery, Dept. Gulf, to October, 1864. Separate Cavalry Brigade, 19th Army Corps, to December, 1864. Artillery Brigade, Reserve Corps, Dept. Gulf, to February, 1865. Lucas' Cavalry Division, Steele's Command, District of West Florida, to April, 1865. 3rd Brigade, Cavalry Division, Dept. Gulf, to June, 1865. Dept. of Mississippi to August, 1865.

SERVICE.—Duty at Baltimore, Md., till February, 1862. Lockwood's Expedition to Eastern Shore of Maryland November 4-December 15, 1861. Moved to Fortress Monroe, Va., February 25-26, 1862, and camp at Old Point Comfort till April 19. Moved to New Orleans, La., April 19-May 11, thence to Baton Rouge, La., May 31-June 2. Expedition from Baton Rouge June 7-9. Williams' Expedition to Vicksburg, Miss., June 19, and operations against that place till July 24. Action at Ellis Cliff June 22. Hamilton's Plantation, Grand Gulf, June 24. Moved to Baton Rouge July 24-26, and duty there till August 21. Battle of Baton Rouge August 5. Moved to Carrollton August 21-22, thence to New Orleans Race Course August 24, and duty there till September 2. Bayou Des Allemands September 4-5. Duty at New Orleans till December 17. Moved to Baton Rouge December 17-18, and duty there till March, 1863. Operations against Port Hudson March 7-27. Moved to Donaldsonville March 28. Operations in Western Louisiana April 9-May 14. Teche Campaign April 9-20. Fort Bisland, near Centreville, April 12-13. Irish Bend April

14. Bayou Vermillion April 17. Moved to Barre Landing April 22-28. Expedition to Alexandria May 2-7. Boyce's Bridge, near Cotile Bayou, May 14. Movement from Alexandria to Port Hudson May 17-30. Near New Iberia May 18. Expedition toward Berwick City May 21-26. Franklin May 25. Siege of Port Hudson May 30-July 9. Clinton June 3-4. Assault on Port Hudson June 14. Surrender of Port Hudson July 9. Moved to Baton Rouge, thence to Donaldsonville and Carrollton July 11-August 1. Moved to Algiers September 17, thence to Brashear City and Berwick. Western Louisiana ("Teche") Campaign October 3-November 30. Reconnoissance toward Opelousas October 20. Opelousas and Barre Landing October 21. Washington October 24. Carrion Crow Bayou November 3. Bayou Sara November 9. Camp Pratt November 20. At New Iberia till January 8, 1864. Moved to Franklin January 8-11, and duty there till March 13. Red River Campaign March 10-May 22. Advance from Franklin to Alexandria March 14-26. Bayou Rapides March 20. Monett's Ferry and Cloutiersville March 29-30. Natchitoches March 31. Wilson's Farm April 7. Bayou de Paul, Carroll's Mill, April 8. Sabine Cross Roads April 8 (guns captured). Moved to New Orleans April 19-20, thence to Carrollton May 10 and to Apollo Stables, New Orleans, July '8. Moved to Morganza September 2, and duty there till March, 1865. Expedition to Simsport September 16-18, 1864. Expedition to the Atchafalaya September 21. Expedition to Bayou Sara October 3-6. Jackson October 5. Epedition to Morgan's Ferry December 13-14. Moved to Greenville, La., March 3-5, 1865; to New Orleans, thence to Barrancas, Fla., March 7-10. March to Mobile Bay March 18-April 1. Siege of Fort Blakely April 1-9. Storming of Fort Blakely April 9. Expedition to Claiborne, Ala., April 9-17. Daniel's Plantation, near Mt. Pleasant, April 11. Grierson's Raid through Alabama and Georgia April 17-30. Moved to Columbus, Miss., May 17-24, thence to Vicksburg, Miss., May 27-June 4, and duty there till July 22. Moved to Boston, Mass., July 22-August 4. Mustered out August 11, 1865.

Lost during service 4 Enlisted men killed and mortally wounded and 26 Enlisted men by disease. Total 30.

3rd BATTERY LIGHT ARTILLERY.

Organized at Boston September 5, 1861. Moved to Washington, D. C., September 5-11. Attached to Porter's Division, Army of the Potomac, to March, 1862. Artillery, 1st Division, 3rd Army Corps, Army Potomac, to May, 1862. Artillery, 1st Division, 5th Army Corps, Army Potomac, to June, 1863. Artillery Brigade, 5th Army Corps, to September, 1864.

SERVICE—At Hall's Hill, Va., Defences of Washington, till March, 1862. Advance on Manassas, Va., March 10-15. Moved to Fortress Monroe March 21-24. Reconnoissance to Big Bethel March 27. Warwick Road April 5. Siege of Yorktown April 5-May 4. Hanover C. H. May 27. Operations about Hanover C. H. May 27-29. Seven days before Richmond June 25-July 1. Battles of Mechanicsville June 26; Gaines' Mill June 27; White Oak Swamp and Turkey Bridge June 30; Malvern Hill July 1. At Harrison's Landing till August 15. Movement to Fortress Monroe, thence to Manassas, Va., August 15-28. Pope's Campaign in Northern Virginia August 28-September 2. Groveton August 29. Bull Run August 30. Maryland Campaign September-October. Battle of Antietam, Md., September 16-17 (Reserve). Shephardstown September 19. At Sharpsburg till October 30. Reconnoissance to Leetown October 16-17. Leetown October 17. Movement to White Plains and Falmouth, Va., October 30-November 19. Battle of Fredericksburg December 11-15. "Mud March" January 20-24, 1863. Duty at Falmouth till April. Chancellorsville Campaign April 27-May 6. Battle of Chancellorsville May 1-5. Gettysburg (Pa.) Campaign June 13-July 24. Battle of Gettysburg, Pa., July 1-3. Bristoe Campaign October 9-22. Rappahannock Station November 7. Mine Run Campaign November 26-December 2. Camp near Rappahannock Station December 4, 1863, to May 1, 1864. Campaign from the Rapidan to the James May-

June. Battles of the Wilderness May 5-7. Spottsylvania May 8-12. Spottsylvania C. H. May 12-21. Bloody Angle May 12. North Anna River May 23-26. Line of the Pamunkey May 26-28. Totopotomoy May 28-31. Cold Harbor June 1-12. Bethesda Church June 1-3. Before Petersburg June 16-19. Siege of Petersburg June 16-September 5. Six Mile House, Weldon Railroad, August 18-21. Left front September 4. Veterans and recruits transferred to 5th Massachusetts Battery August 30. Moved to Boston September 5-9. Mustered out September 16, 1864.

Battery lost during service 9 Enlisted men killed and mortally wounded and 10 Enlisted men by disease. Total 19.

4th BATTERY LIGHT ARTILLERY.

Organized at Lowell November 17, 1861. Moved to Boston November 20, thence sailed on Steamer "Constitution" for Ship Island, Miss., arriving December 3. Attached to Ship Island Expedition to March, 1862. 1st Brigade, Dept. of the Gulf, to October, 1862. Independent Command, Dept. of the Gulf, to January, 1863. Artillery, 3rd Division, 19th Army Corps, Dept. of the Gulf, to November, 1863. Artillery, 1st Division, 19th Army Corps, Dept. Gulf, to March, 1864. Defences of New Orleans, La., Dept. of the Gulf, to September, 1864. Unattached Artillery, Gulf, to December, 1864. Unattached Artillery, Reserve Corps, Dept. Gulf, to February, 1865. Artillery, 1st Division, Reserve Corps, Dept. Gulf, February, 1865. Artillery, 1st Division, 13th Army Corps, Dept. Gulf, to July, 1865. Dept. of Texas to November, 1865.

SERVICE.—Garrison duty at Fort Massachusetts, Ship Island, Miss., till April 15, 1862. Operations against Forts St. Phillip and Jackson April 15-28. Occupation of Forts St. Phillip and Jackson April 28. Moved to New Orleans, La., April 30-May 2. Duty at Carrollton till July 10. Expedition to Pass Manchac June 15-20. Manchac Pass June 17. Moved to Baton Rouge July 10-12. Duty there till August 21. Battle of Baton Rouge August 5. Moved to Carrollton August 21, and duty there till October 26. Two Sections moved to Fort Pike October 28, and garrison duty there till January 24, 1863, participating in numerous Expeditions along the coast and up the bayous leading into Lake Pontchartrain. Action at Bayou Bonfonca November 26, 1862. Expedition to Bay St. Louis and Pass Christian December 9-10. Moved to New Orleans January 24, 1863. (One Section remained at New Orleans, attached to Weitzel's Reserve Brigade, and participated in the Expedition to Bisland January 12-15, 1863, and action with Steamer "Cotton" January 14.) Battery at New Orleans January 24-March 1, 1863. Moved to Baton Rouge March 1. Operations against Port Hudson March 17-27. Advance on Port Hudson May 21-24. Siege of Port Hudson May 24-July 9. Assaults on Port Hudson May 27 and June 14. Surrender of Port Hudson July 9. Moved to Baton Rouge July 11-12, thence to Donaldsonville July 16. Moved to Port Hudson August 4-5, and duty there till August 22. Moved to Baton Rouge August 22-24. Moved to Brashear City, thence to Berwick September 19-23. Western Louisiana ("Teche") Campaign October 3-November 30. Vermillionville November 11. Bonfonca November 26. At New Iberia till January 7, 1864. Moved to Franklin January 7-9, thence to New Orleans January 26-28. Absent on Veteran furlough February 11-March 22. Moved from Boston to New York, thence to New Orleans March 25-April 6. Duty at New Orleans as Infantry till June 30. At Apollo Stables till September 5. Moved to Morganza September 5-6, and duty there till November 10. Atchafalaya River September 16-17. Expedition to Atchafalaya River September 20-23. Moved to Bayou Sara October 3, and Expedition to Clinton October 3-7. Jackson October 5. Moved to White River, Ark., November 10-15, thence to Duvall's Bluff November 16-17, and to Memphis, Tenn., November 23-28. Duty there till January 1, 1865. Expedition to Colliersville, Tenn., December 21-31, 1864. Moved to Kennersville, La., Jan-

uary 3-5, 1865; to Dauphin's Island, Ala., February 9-11. Campaign against Mobile and its defences March 17-April 12. Siege of Spanish Fort and Fort Blakely March 26-April 8. Storming of Fort Blakely April 9. Occupation of Mobile April 12, and duty there till July 1. Moved to Galveston, Tex., July 1-5, thence to Houston July 8-9, and duty there till October. Moved to Galveston, thence to New Orleans, Port Royal, S. C., and Boston, Mass., October 5-November 3. Mustered out November 10, 1865.

Battery lost during service 1 Enlisted man killed in action and 50 Enlisted men by disease. Total 51.

5th BATTERY LIGHT ARTILLERY.

Organized at Lynnfield and Reedville and mustered in December 10, 1861. Moved to Washington, D. C., December 25-27. Attached to Porter's Division, Army of the Potomac, to March, 1862. Artillery, 1st Division, 3rd Army Corps, Army Potomac, to May, 1862. Artillery, 1st Division, 5th Army Corps, Army Potomac, to June, 1863. 1st Volunteer Brigade, Artillery Reserve, Army Potomac, to July, 1863. Artillery Brigade, 5th Army Corps, to June, 1865.

SERVICE.—At Capital Hill, Defences of Washington, D. C., till February 15, 1862, and at Hall's Hill till March 18. Moved to Alexandria and Fortress Monroe, Va., March 18-24. Warwick Road April 5. Siege of Yorktown April 5-May 4. Hanover C. H. May 27. Operations about Hanover C. H. May 27-29. Seven days before Richmond June 25-July 1. Battles of Mechanicsville June 26; Gaines' Mill June 27; White Oak Swamp and Turkey Bridge June 30; Malvern Hill July 1. At Harrison's Landing till August 16. Movement to Fortress Monroe, thence to Manassas August 15-28. Battle of Bull Run August 30. Duty in the Defences of Washington till October 8, and at Sharpsburg, Md., till October 30. Reconnoissance to Smithfield October 16-17. Kearneysville and Shephardstown October 16-17. Movement to Warrenton and Falmouth, Va., October 30-November 19. Battle of Fredericksburg December 11-15. "Mud March" January 20-24, 1863. Chancellorsville Campaign April 27-May 6. Battle of Chancellorsville May 1-5. Battle of Gettysburg, Pa., July 2-4. Kelly's Ford July 31-August 1. Brandy Station August 1-3. At Beverly Ford and Culpeper C. H. till October. Bristoe Campaign October 9-22. Advance to the Rappahannock November 7-8. Rappahannock Station November 7. Mine Run Campaign November 26-December 2. At Rappahannock Station December 6, 1863, to May 1, 1864. Rapidan Campaign May 3-June 12, 1864. Battles of the Wilderness May 5-7. Laurel Hill May 8. Spottsylvania May 8-12. Spottsylvania C. H. May 12-21. Assault on the Salient May 12. North Anna River May 23-26. Jericho Mills May 23. Line of the Pamunkey May 26-28. Totopotomoy May 28-31. Cold Harbor June 1-12. Bethesda Church June 1-3. Before Petersburg June 16-19. Siege of Petersburg June 16, 1864, to April 2, 1865. Six Mile House, Weldon Railroad, August 18-21, 1864. Non-Veterans mustered out October 3, 1864. Boydton Plank Road, Hatcher's Run, October 27-28. Warren's Raid on Weldon Railroad December 7-12. Dabney's Mills February 5-7, 1865. Appomattox Campaign March 28-April 9. Assaults on and fall of Petersburg April 2. Moved to City Point April 4, and duty there till May 3. March to Washington, D. C., May 3-13. Grand Review May 23. Moved to Readville, Mass., June 4-6, and there mustered out June 12, 1865.

Battery lost during service 1 Officer and 18 Enlisted men killed and mortally wounded and 11 Enlisted men by disease. Total 30.

6th BATTERY LIGHT ARTILLERY.

Organized at Camp Chase, Lowell, and mustered in January 20, 1862. Sailed from Boston for Ship Island, Miss., on Steamer "Idaho" February 8, 1862, arriving there March 8. Attached to 2nd Brigade, Dept. of the Gulf, to October, 1862. Reserve Brigade, Dept. of the Gulf, to January, 1863. Artillery, 1st Division, 19th Army Corps, Dept. Gulf, to August, 1863. Reserve Artillery, Dept. of the Gulf, to October, 1863. Artillery, 1st Division, 19th Army Corps, to June, 1864. Reserve Artillery, Dept. of the Gulf, Defences of New Orleans, La., to July, 1865.

SERVICE.—Duty at Ship Island, Miss., till April 15, 1862. Expedition to Biloxi and Pass Christian April 2-5. Biloxi April 3. Pass Christian April 4. Operations against Forts St. Phillip and Jackson April 15-28. Occupation of New Orleans May 1. Epedition to New Orleans & Opelousas Railroad May 9-10. Moved to Baton Rouge May 12. (One Section on duty at Algiers till June.) Reconnoissance to Warrenton May 14-29. Williams' Expedition to Vicksburg, Miss., and operations against that place June 20-July 26. Ellis Cliff June 22. Hamilton Plantation, near Grand Gulf, June 24. Duty at Baton Rouge till August 21. Battle of Baton Rouge August 5. Evacuation of Baton Rouge and movement to Carrollton August 21-22. Duty there till October. Operations in La Fourche District October 24-November 10. Capture of Donaldsonville October 25. Georgia Landing, near Labadieville, October 27. Duty near Thibodeaux till February 22, 1863. Expedition to Bayou Teche January 11-15. Action with Steamer "Cotton" January 14. Moved to Brashear City February 22, thence to Bayou Boeuf and duty there till April 2. Operations in Western Louisiana April 9-May 14. Teche Campaign April 11-20. Fort Bisland, near Centreville, April 12-13. Jeanerette April 14. Pursuit to Opelousas April 14-20. Expedition to Alexandria May 4-17. Moved from Alexandria to Port Hudson May 17-25. Siege of Port Hudson May 25-July 9. Assaults on Port Hudson May 27-June 14. Surrender of Port Hudson July 9. Moved to Donaldsonville July 11 and duty there till July 30. Cox's Plantation July 12-13. Duty at Thibodeaux July 31-September 25. Moved to Algiers September 25, thence to Berwick October 6. Western Louisiana "Teche" Campaign October 11-November 7. Rejoined Division at Carrion Crow Bayou. Duty at New Iberia November 17, 1863, to January 7, 1864. Moved to Franklin January 7 and duty there till March 3. Moved to New Orleans March 3, thence to Boston, Mass., April 13-20. Moved from Boston to New Orleans May 23-June 8. Assigned to duty in the Defences of New Orleans till July, 1865. Moved to Readville, Mass., July 21-August 1, and there mustered out August 7, 1865.

Battery lost during service 6 Enlisted men killed and mortally wounded and 1 Officer and 50 Enlisted men by disease. Total 57.

7th BATTERY. LIGHT ARTILLERY.

Organized at Lowell as Richardson's Light Guard; an Independent Infantry Company and mustered in May 21, 1861. Left State for Fortress Monroe, Va., May 22, and garrison duty there as Infantry till December 25, 1861. Detached on Light Artillery duty December 25, 1861, and duty at Fort Monroe till May, 1862. Designated 7th Massachusetts Battery March 17, 1862. Attached to Dept. of Virginia to June, 1862. Newport News, Va., Dept. of Virginia, to July, 1862. Yorktown, Va., Dept. of Virginia, to September, 1862. Artillery Division at Suffolk, 7th Army Corps, Dept. of Virginia, to June, 1863. Artillery, 1st Division, 7th Army Corps, Dept. of Virginia, to July, 1863. Camp Barry, 22nd Army Corps, Dept. of Washington, to January, 1864. Artillery, 2nd Division, 19th Army Corps, Dept. of the Gulf, to November, 1864. Reserve Artillery, Reserve Corps, Military Division West Mississippi, to February, 1865. Artillery, 1st Division, 13th Army Corps, Military Division West Mississippi, to April, 1865. Artillery, 1st Division, U. S. C. T., Military Division West Mississippi, to July, 1865. Dept. of Texas to November, 1865.

SERVICE.—Occupation of Norfolk and Portsmouth, Va., May 10, 1862. Duty at Fort Monroe May 13 to June 19, and at Newport News, Va., till July 25. Moved to Yorktown, Va., and duty there till September 29. Moved to Suffolk September 29-October 2, and duty there till June, 1863. Expedition from Suffolk De-

cember 1-3, 1862. Action on the Blackwater, near Franklin, December 2. Action at Deserted House, Va., January 30, 1863, and at Franklin on the Blackwater March 17. Siege of Suffolk April 11-May 4. Actions at Blackwater April 12 and 14. Somerton Road April 15. Providence Church Road May 3. Siege of Suffolk raised May 4. Expedition to Carrsville May 13-17. Holland House May 15-16. At Portsmouth till June. Dix's Peninsula Campaign June 24-July 7. Expedition from White House to South Anna River July 1-7. South Anna Bridge July 4. March to Fort Monroe July 5-14, thence to Portsmouth July 15. Moved to Washington, D. C., July 20-22, and duty at Camp Marshall till August 18. Moved to Alexandria, thence to New York August 18-21. Duty in New York during draft troubles till September 11. Moved to Washington, D. C., September 11, and duty at Camp Barry till January 24, 1864. Moved to Baltimore, Md., thence sailed on Steamer "Arago" to New Orleans January 24-February 5. At Apollo Stables till March 18. Moved to Algiers, thence to Alexandria, La., March 19-31. Red River Campaign April 1-May 22. (1 Section stationed at Pineville April 29 to May 11.) Retreat to Morganza May 13-20. Mansura May 16. At Morganza till July 13. Expedition to Atchafalaya River May 30-June 6. Moved to White River, Ark.; thence to St. Charles July 13-23. Moved to Morganza August 6-13. Expedition to White River and St. Charles September 3-11. Duty there till October 23. Moved to Duvall's Bluff October 23-24 and duty there till January 10, 1865. Moved to Kennersville, La., January 10-15; thence to Dauphin Island, Ala., February 9-11. Campaign against Mobile and its Defences March 17-April 12. Siege of Spanish Fort and Fort Blakely March 26-April 9. Storming of Fort Blakely April 9. Moved from Mobile to Selma, Ala., April 20-27; thence to Montgomery April 27-30. Moved to Mobile May 9-16 and duty there till June 30. Moved to Galveston, Texas, June 30-July 3, thence to Houston July 9, and duty there till October. Moved to Boston, Mass., via Galveston, Texas, New Orleans, Port Royal, S. C., and New York, October 1-November 3. Mustered out November 10, 1865.

Battery lost during service 3 Enlisted men killed and mortally wounded and 1 Officer and 36 Enlisted men by disease. Total 40.

8th BATTERY LIGHT ARTILLERY.

Organized at North Cambridge for six months' service June 24, 1862. Left State for Washington, D. C., arriving June 27. Attached to Cook's Brigade, Sturgis' Reserve Corps, Military District of Washington, to August, 1862. Artillery, 1st Division, 9th Army Corps, Army of the Potomac, to November, 1862.

SERVICE.—Camp near Fairfax Seminary, Va., July 1 to August 8, 1862. Moved to Alexandria, thence to Aquia Creek and Falmouth August 8-11. Pope's Campaign in Northern Virginia August 16-September 2. Battles of Groveton August 29; Bull Run August 30; Chantilly September 1; South Mountain, Md., September 14. Battle of Antietam September 16-17. At Antietam Creek till October 6. Moved to Washington, D. C., to refit October 5-9; thence to Pleasant Valley, Md., October 21-26. Movement to Falmouth, Va., October 26-November 19. Mustered out November 29, 1862.

Lost 1 Enlisted man killed and 10 Enlisted men by disease. Total 11.

9th BATTERY LIGHT ARTILLERY.

Organized at Camp Meigs, Readville, and mustered in August 10, 1862. Left State for Washington, D. C., September 3. Attached to Abercrombie's Division, Military District of Washington, D. C., to February, 1863. 2nd Brigade, Abercrombie's Division, 22nd Army Corps, Dept. of Washington, to May, 1863. Barry's Command, 22nd Army Corps, to July, 1863. 1st Volunteer Brigade, Artillery Reserve, Army of the Potomac, to December, 1863. 2nd Volunteer Brigade, Artillery

Reserve, to April, 1864. 3rd Volunteer Brigade, Artillery Reserve, to May, 1864. Artillery Brigade, 5th Army Corps, Army of the Potomac, to June, 1865.

SERVICE.—Duty in the Defences of Washington, D. C., September, 1862, to June, 1863. At Camp Seymour, Capital Hill, September 7-22, 1862; at Camp Chase till October 27; at Camp Barry till November 19; at Forts Ramsey and Buffalo, Upton's Hill, Va., till April 17, 1863. Moved to Centreville, Va., April 17; thence to Fairfax C. H. and Edward's Ferry June 25. To Frederick City, Md., June 27; to Middleburg June 29; to Tanneytown June 30, and to Gettysburg, Pa., July 1. Battle of Gettysburg July 2-4. Supported 3rd Corps in battle of July 2, and was the last of five Batteries to withdraw, firing by prolonge when the Corps was obliged to fall back. After retiring 400 yards it was ordered to make a stand close to the Throstle house and hold that point at all hazards, until a line of Artillery could be formed. It was immediately charged by Col. Humphrey's 21st Mississippi Regiment, which entered the Battery and were fought hand to hand by the Cannoneers until they had suffered a loss of 28 men killed and wounded and 65 horses, when it was ordered to fall back, having sacrificed itself for the safety of the line. At Warrenton August 1-September 16, and at Culpeper C. H. till October 11. Bristoe Campaign October 11-22. Advance to line of the Rappahannock November 7-8. Mine Run Campaign November 26-December 2. At Brandy Station December 13, 1863, to May 4, 1864. Rapidan Campaign May-June. Battles of the Wilderness May 5-7. Laurel Hill May 8, Spottsylvania May 8-12. Spottsylvania C. H. May 12-21. North Anna River May 23-26. Line of the Pamunkey River May 26-28. Totopotomoy May 28-31. Cold Harbor June 1-12. Bethesda Church June 1-3. Before Petersburg June 16-18. Siege of Petersburg June 16, 1864, to April 2, 1865. Built and occupied Fort Davis June 24 to August 14, 1864. Weldon Railroad August 18-21. Garrison Fort Duschene and Fort Howard till October 27. Boydton Plank Road, Hatcher's Run, October 27-28. Warren's Raid on Weldon Railroad December 7-12. Garrison Fort Rice till February 5, 1865. Dabney's Mills, Hatcher's Run, February 5-7. Fort Stedman March 25. Appomattox Campaign March 28-April 9. Assault on and fall of Petersburg April 2. Duty at City Point till May 3. Moved to Washington, D. C., May 3-13. Grand Review May 23. Mustered out at Gallop's Island, Boston Harbor, June 6, 1865.

Battery lost during service 2 Officers and 13 Enlisted men killed and mortally wounded and 4 Enlisted men by disease. Total 19.

10th BATTERY LIGHT ARTILLERY.

Organized at Lynnfield and mustered in September 9, 1862. Left State for Washington, D. C., October 14. Attached to Grover's Brigade, Military District of Washington, to February, 1863. Jewett's Brigade, 22nd Army Corps, Dept. of Washington, to June, 1863. French's Command, 8th Army Corps, to July, 1863. Artillery Brigade, 3rd Army Corps, Army of the Potomac, to March, 1864. Artillery Brigade, 2nd Army Corps, Army of the Potomac, to June, 1865.

SERVICE.—Duty at Camp Barry, Defences of Washington, October 17 to December 26, 1862. Moved to Poolesville, Md., December 26-28, and duty there till June 24, 1863. Removed to Maryland Heights June 24, thence to Frederick City and Frederick Junction June 30-July 1. March to Williamsport July 8-11. Near Antietam Bridge July 12-14. Operations in Loudoun Valley July 17-31. Wapping Heights July 23. Near Warrenton July 26-31. At Sulphur Springs July 31-September 15. Near Culpeper September 17-October 10. Bristoe Campaign October 10-22. Auburn October 13. Near Fairfax Station October 15-19. At Catlett's Station October 21-30. At Warrenton Junction till November 6. Kelly's Ford November 7. At Brandy Station November 9-25. Mine Run Campaign November 26-December 2. Payne's Farm November 27. At Brandy Station December 3, 1863, to April 8, 1864, and at Stevensburg till May 3. Rapidan

Campaign May-June. Battles of the Wilderness May 5-7. Spottsylvania May 8-12. Spottsylvania C. H. May 12-21. Assault on the Salient, Spottsylvania C. H., May 12. Harris Farm, Fredericksburg Road, May 19. North Anna River May 23-26. Line of the Pamunkey May 26-28. Totopotomoy May 28-31. Cold Harbor June 1-12. Before Petersburg June 16-18. Siege of Petersburg June 16, 1864, to April 2, 1865. Jerusalem Plank Road June 22-23, 1864. Demonstration north of James River July 27-29. Deep Bottom July 27-28. Strawberry Plains, Deep Bottom, August 14-18. Ream's Station August 25. In trenches before Petersburg in Battery 14 September 24 to October 24. Boydton Plank Road, Hatcher's Run, October 27-28. In Forts Stevenson, Blaisdell and Welch till November 29. Movement to Hatcher's Run December 9-10. In Forts Emery and Siebert till February 5, 1865. Dabney's Mills, Hatcher's Run, February 5-7. Watkins' House March 25. Appomattox Campaign March 28-April 9. Moved to Dabney's Mills March 30. Fall of Petersburg April 2. Pursuit of Lee April 8-9. Sailor's Creek April 6. Cover crossing of 2nd Corps at High Bridge, Farmville, April 7. Appomattox C. H. April 9. Surrender of Lee and his army. March to Burkesville April 11-14. March to Washington, D. C., May 2-13. Grand Review May 23. Mustered out June 9 and discharged from service June 14, 1865.

Battery lost during service 2 Officers and 6 Enlisted men killed and mortally wounded and 16 Enlisted men by disease. Total 24.

11th BATTERY LIGHT ARTILLERY.

Organized at Boston and mustered in at Readville for nine months' service August 25, 1862. Left State for Washington, D. C., November 3. Attached to Casey's Provisional Division, Military District of Washington, to February, 1863. Casey's Division, 22nd Army Corps, Dept. of Washington, to April, 1863. Abercrombie's Division, 22nd Corps, to May, 1863.

SERVICE.—Duty at Camp Barry, Defences of Washington, D. C., till November 19, 1862. At Hall's Hill, Va., till November 27. Moved to Fairfax Station, Va., November 27-28; thence to Union Mill, and duty along Potomac from Wolf Run Shoals to Centreville till February, 1863. In forts on Centreville Heights till April. Ordered to Upton's Hill April 18. Duty at Forts Ramsey and Buffalo till May 23. Moved to Boston May 25-28, and there mustered out May 29, 1863.

11th BATTERY LIGHT ARTILLERY.

Organized at Readville and mustered in for three years January 2, 1864. Left State for Washington, D. C., February 5. Attached to Defences of Washington, 22nd Army Corps, to April, 1864. Artillery, 2nd Division, 9th Army Corps, Army of the Potomac, to July, 1864. Temporarily attached to Artillery Brigade, 2nd Army Corps, May, 1864. Artillery Brigade, 9th Army Corps, to June, 1865. Temporarily attached to Artillery Brigade, 5th Army Corps, August, 1864.

SERVICE.—Duty in the Defences of Washington, D. C., till April 9, 1864. Rapidan Campaign May-June, 1864. Battles of the Wilderness May 5-7. Spottsylvania May 8-12. Spottsylvania C. H. May 12-21. Assault on the Salient, Spottsylvania C. H., May 12. Stannard's Mills May 21. North Anna River May 23-26. Line of the Pamunkey May 26-28. Totopotomoy May 28-31. Cold Harbor June 1-12. Bethesda Church June 1-3. Before Petersburg June 16-18. Siege of Petersburg June 16, 1864, to April 2, 1865. Mine Explosion, Petersburg, July 30, 1864. Weldon Railroad August 18-21. Poplar Springs Church, Peeble's Farm, September 29-October 2. Dabney's Mills, Hatcher's Run, February 5-7, 1865. Fort Stedman March 25. Appomattox Campaign March 28-April 9. Assault on and fall of Petersburg April 2. Pursuit of Lee to Appomattox C. H. April 3-9. Moved to Washington, D. C., April 20-27. Grand Review May 23. Mustered out June 16, 1865.

Battery lost during service 3 Enlisted men killed and mortally wounded and 12 Enlisted men by disease. Total 15.

12th BATTERY LIGHT ARTILLERY.

Organized at Readville October 3 to December 29, 1862. Sailed from Boston for New Orleans, La., on ship "E. W. Farley," January 3, 1863, arriving February 3. Attached to 1st Division, 19th Army Corps, Dept. of the Gulf, to July, 1863. Artillery Reserve, 19th Army Corps, to October, 1863. Garrison Port Hudson, La., Dept. of the Gulf, to December, 1863. Artillery, 1st Division, Corps de Afrique, Dept. of the Gulf, to March, 1864. Garrison Artillery, Port Hudson, La., to July, 1865.

SERVICE.—Duty at Apollo Stables, New Orleans, La., till February 24, 1863. Moved to Baton Rouge, La., and duty there till March 28. Moved to New Orleans March 28, and duty at Metaire Race Course till April 17. Moved to Brashear City April 17, and engaged in the defence of transports moving up with troops and supplies, till May 23. Moved to New Orleans May 23, and duty in the defence of that city till October 15. Moved to Port Hudson, La., October 15, and garrison duty there till June, 1865. Action at Tunica November 11, 1863. Foraging Expedition up the river December 31, 1863-January 4, 1864. Action near Port Hudson May 6. Expedition to Clinton August 24-28. Action near Clinton August 24. Mustered out July 25, 1865.

Battery lost during service 25 Enlisted men by disease.

13th BATTERY LIGHT ARTILLERY.

Organized at Readville and mustered in December 13, 1862. Left State for Dept. of the Gulf January 20, 1863. Attached to Defences of New Orleans, La., to June, 1863. Artillery, 4th Division, 19th Army Corps, Dept. of the Gulf, to August, 1863. Defences of New Orleans to March, 1864. Artillery, 1st Division, 19th Army Corps, to June, 1864. Defences of New Orleans to July, 1865.

SERVICE.—Duty at Apollo Stables, New Orleans, till June 5, 1863. Moved to Port Hudson, La., June 5. Siege of Port Hudson June 6 to July 9. Assault on Port Hudson June 14. Surrender of Port Hudson July 9. Duty at Port Hudson till August 31. Ordered to New Orleans and duty there till September 17. Battery attached to 2nd Massachusetts Battery September 18, 1863, to February 17, 1864. To 6th Massachusetts Battery till March 6, 1864, and to Battery "L," 1st United States Artillery, to June 28, 1864. Duty in the Defences of New Orleans June 30, 1864, to July, 1865. Mustered out July 28, 1865.

Battery lost during service 26 Enlisted men by disease.

14th BATTERY LIGHT ARTILLERY.

Organized at Readville and mustered in February 27, 1864. Left State for Annapolis, Md., April 4, 1864; thence ordered to Camp Marshall, Washington, D. C. Ordered to join 9th Army Corps, Army of the Potomac, in the field, and moved to Rappahannock Station, Va., April 26-30. Attached to Artillery, 1st Division, 9th Army Corps, to July, 1864. Artillery Brigade, 9th Army Corps, to August, 1864. Artillery Reserve, Army of the Potomac, to June, 1865. Duty with 2nd Army Corps October, 1864; with Artillery Brigade, 6th Army Corps, January to March, 1865; with Artillery Brigade, 9th Army Corps, to June, 1865.

SERVICE.—Rapidan Campaign May-June, 1864. Battles of the Wilderness, Va., May 5-7. Spottsylvania May 8-12. Spottsylvania C. H. May 12-21. Assault on the Salient, Spottsylvania C. H., May 12. North Anna River May 23-26. Line of the Pamunkey May 26-28. Totopotomoy May 28-31. Cold Harbor June 1-12. Bethesda Church June 1-3. Before Petersburg June 16-18. Siege of Petersburg June 16, 1864, to April 2, 1865. Actions on the Petersburg line June 21, 22, 23, 24, July 10, 11, 12, 13, 14, 15, 16 and 17. Mine Explosion July 30. Weldon Railroad August 18-21. Action on Petersburg line October 11. Duty at Fort Merriam, Defences of City Point, Va., October 25, 1864, to January 15, 1865. Ordered to Petersburg front January 15. Assault on and capture of Petersburg April 2. At City Point April 4 to May 3. March to Fairfax C. H. May 3-13, and duty there till June 4. Moved to Readville, Mass., June 4-6. Mustered out June 16, 1865.

Battery lost during service 1 Officer and 9 Enlisted men killed and mortally wounded and 9 Enlisted men by disease. Total 19.

15th BATTERY LIGHT ARTILLERY.

Organized at Lowell and Fort Warren and mustered in February 17, 1863. Sailed from Boston on steamer "Zouave" for New Orleans, La., March 9, arriving there April 9. Attached to Defences of New Orleans, Dept. of the Gulf, to July, 1864. Reserve Artillery, Dept. of the Gulf, to February, 1865. Artillery, 2nd Division, 13th Army Corps, Military Division West Mississippi, to August, 1865.

SERVICE.—Duty at Apollo Stables, New Orleans, till May 20, 1863. Moved to Brashear City May 20, thence to New Orleans May 29. Assigned to duty as garrison at forts at Bayou St. John and at Gentilly June 3 to December 29. Moved to Lakeport December 29-31. Expedition to Madisonville on steamer "Kate Dale," serving as a gunboat January 3-15, 1864. Moved to New Orleans January 20, and duty there till October 17, 1864. At Wood's Yard till March 5, and at Terrell's Press till October 17. Moved to White River, Ark., October 17; thence to Devall's Bluff November 7, and to Memphis, Tenn., November 27-December 2. Duty there till January 1, 1865. Moved to Kennersville, La., January 1-5; thence to Greenville February 13, and to Pensacola, Fla. March to Fort Blakely, Ala., March 20-April 1. Occupation of Canoe Station March 27. Siege of Fort Blakely April 2-9. Storming of Fort Blakely April 9. Moved to Selma, Ala., April 20, and duty there till May 11. Moved to Mobile and duty there till June 30. At Fort Gaines till July 20. Moved to Readville, Mass., July 20-August 1. Mustered out August 4, 1865.

Battery lost during service 1 Enlisted man killed and 27 Enlisted men by disease. Total 28.

16th BATTERY LIGHT ARTILLERY.

Organized at Camp Meigs, Readville, and mustered in April 4, 1864. Left State for Washington, D. C., April 17. Attached to Camp Barry, 22nd Army Corps, Dept. of Washington, to June, 1864. 2nd Brigade, DeRussy's Division, 22nd Army Corps, to July, 1864. Camp Barry, 2nd Corps, to November, 1864. 1st Separate Brigade, 22nd Army Corps, to July, 1865.

SERVICE.—Duty at Camp Barry, Washington, D. C., till May 14, 1864. At Fort Thayer till May 22. At Fort Lyon till July 10. At Fort Kearney during Early's attack on Washington, July 11-12. At Camp Barry till September 5. Ordered to Albany, N. Y., September 5, and duty at Troy Road Barracks till November 16. Moved to Washington November 16, thence to Fairfax C. H., Va., December 6. Duty at Fairfax C. H., and Station, and at Vienna till June 17, 1865. Ordered to Massachusetts and mustered out July 13, 1865.

Lost by disease 6.

1st COMPANY SHARPSHOOTERS.

Organized at Lynnfield and mustered in September 2, 1861. Left State for Washington, D. C., September 2. Attached to 15th Massachusetts Infantry to July, 1864, and to 19th Massachusetts Infantry to September, 1864. (See these Regiments.) Mustered out September 6, 1864.

Company lost during service 3 Officers and 21 Enlisted men killed and mortally wounded and 15 Enlisted men by disease. Total 39.

2nd COMPANY SHARPSHOOTERS.

Organized at Lynnfield September 3, 1861. Left State for Washington, D. C. Attached to 22nd Massachusetts Infantry. (See this Regiment.) Mustered out October 17, 1864.

Company lost during service 11 Enlisted men killed and mortally wounded and 12 Enlisted men by disease. Total 23.

1st BATTALION INFANTRY.

Organized by consolidation of Clark's Company. Organized April 19, 1861, and mustered in for three years May 21, 1861. Moved to Fortress Monroe, Va., May

22-26, and attached to 4th Massachusetts Militia Infantry as Company "M." Tyler's Company organized April 17, 1861. Moved to Fortress Monroe, Va., May 10-13, and attached to 3rd Massachusetts Militia Infantry as Company "M." Mustered in for three years May 14, 1861. Leach's Company organized May 1, 1861. Moved to Boston May 17, thence to Fortress Monroe, Va., May 19-23. Mustered in for three years May 22, 1861, and attached to 4th Massachusetts Militia Infantry as Company "L." Chipman's Company organized May 6, 1861. Moved to Fortress Monroe, Va., May 19-21. Mustered in for three years May 22, 1861, and attached to 3rd Massachusetts Militia Infantry as Company "D." Doten's Company, Plymouth Rock Guards, organized May 6, 1861. Moved to Fortress Monroe, Va., May 19-21. Mustered in for three years May 22, 1861, and attached to 3rd Massachusetts Militia Infantry as Company "E." Chamberlin's Company, "Union Guards," organized April 18, 1861. Moved to Fortress Monroe, Va., May 19-23. Mustered in for three years May 14, 1861, and assigned to 3rd Massachusetts Militia Infantry as Company "I." Barnes' Company, "Greenough Guards," organized April 25, 1861. Moved to Fortress Monroe, Va., May 19-21. Mustered in for three years May 22 and attached to 4th Massachusetts Militia Infantry as Company "K." Battalion organized at Fort Monroe, Va., July, 1861. Company "M," 4th Militia, designated as Rifles; Company "M," 3rd Militia, designated as "M": Company "L," 4th Militia, designated as "L"; Company "D," 3rd Militia. designated as "D": Company "E." 4th Militia. designated as "E"; Company "I," 4th Militia, designated as "I"; Company "K," 4th Militia, designated as "K." Companies "L" and "M" detached for duty at Fort Wool, Rip Raps, July 16 and 26 to November 3. Rejoined Regiment at Newport News. Five Companies at Hampton till July 30, then garrison duty at Fortress Monroe till August 5. Moved to Camp Hamilton August 5, thence to Newport News August 18 and duty there till December. —. Action on Warwick Road October 21. Battalion transferred to 29th Massachusetts Infantry December 13, 1861. Rifles as Company "A," Company "M" as Company "B," Company "L" as Company "C," Company "D" as Company "D," Company "E" as Company "E," Company "I" as Company "I" and Company "K" as Company "K."

1st REGIMENT INFANTRY.

Organized at Boston and mustered in Companies "A," "B," "G" and "H" May 23; Companies "D," "F," "K" and "I" May 24; Company "E" May 25, and Company "C" May 27, 1861. Left State for Washington, D. C., June 15, arriving June 17. Attached to Richardson's Brigade, Tyler's Division, McDowell's Army of Northeast Virginia, to August, 1861. Hooker's Brigade, Division of the Potomac, to October, 1861. 1st Brigade, Hooker's Division, Army of the Potomac, to March, 1862. 1st Brigade, 2nd Division, 3rd Army Corps, Army of the Potomac, to March, 1864. 1st Brigade, 4th Division, 2nd Army Corps, to May, 1864.

SERVICE.—Duty at Camp Banks, Georgetown, D. C., till July 16, 1861. Advance on Manassas, Va., July 16-21. Occupation of Fairfax Court House July 17. Battle of Bull Run July 21. At Fort Albany till August 15. Moved to Bladensburg August 15 and duty there till September 7. Expedition to Lower Maryland September 7-October 7. Moved to Posey's Plantation October 25-27. Duty there and at Shipping Point till April 5, 1862. Affair at Mattawoman Creek November 14, 1861. Ordered to Fortress Monroe, Va., April 7, 1862; thence to Yorktown. Siege of Yorktown April 16-May 4. Affair at Yorktown April 26 (Cos. "A," "H" and "I"). Battle of Williamsburg May 5. Battle of Fair Oaks, Seven Pines, May 31-June 1. Seven days before Richmond June 25-July 1. Battles of Oak Grove June 25; Savage Station June 29; White Oak Swamp and Glendale June 30; Malvern Hill July 1. At Harrison's Landing till August 15. Movement to Fortress Monroe, thence to Centreville August 15-26.

Bristoe Station or Kettle Run August 27. Catlett's Station August 28. Battles of Groveton August 29, and Bull Run August 30. Duty in the Defences of Washington till December —. At Fort Lyon till September 13. Near Fairfax Seminary till October 20, and at Munson's Hill till November 1. Duty at Fairfax Station November 2-25. Operations on Orange & Alexandria Railroad November 10-12. Battle of Fredericksburg, Va., December 12-15. "Mud March" January 20-24, 1863. At Falmouth till April 27. Operations at Rappahannock Bridge and Grove Church February 5-7. Chancellorsville Campaign April 27-May 6. Battle of Chancellorsville May 1-5. Gettysburg (Pa.) Campaign June 11-July 24. Battle of Gettysburg July 1-3. Pursuit of Lee till July 24. Moved to New York July 30-August 1. Duty at Governor's Island, Ricker's Island and David's Island, New York Harbor, till October 15. Moved to Washington October 15, thence to Union Mills, Va., and rejoin Corps October 17. Advance to line of the Rappahannock November 7-8. Kelly's Ford November 7. Mine Run Campaign November 26-December 2. Payne's Farm November 27. Duty near Brandy Station till May, 1864. Demonstration on the Rapidan February 6-7. Rapidan Campaign May 3-20. Battles of the Wilderness May 5-7; Spottsylvania May 8-12; Spottsylvania Court House May 12-21. Assault on the Salient at Spottsylvania Court House May 12. Harris Farm or Fredericksburg Road May 19. Ordered home for muster out May 20. Veterans and Recruits transferred to 11th Massachusetts Infantry May 20. Mustered out May 25, 1864. Expiration of term.

Regiment lost during service 8 Officers and 134 Enlisted men killed and mortally wounded and 1 Officer and 78 Enlisted men by disease. Total 221.

2nd REGIMENT INFANTRY.

Organized at Camp Andrew, West Roxbury, and mustered in May 25, 1861. Left State for Hagerstown, Md., July 8; thence moved to Williamsport and Martinsburg, Va., July 11-12. Attached to Abercrombie's Brigade, Patterson's Army, July, 1861. Abercrombie's Brigade, Banks' Division, Dept. of the Shenandoah, to August, 1861. Gordon's Brigade, Banks' Division, Army of the Potomac, to March, 1862. Gordon's 3rd Brigade, Williams' 1st Division, Banks' 5th Army Corps, to April, 1862. 3rd Brigade, 1st Division, Dept. of the Shenandoah, to June, 1862. 3rd Brigade, 1st Division, 2nd Army Corps, Army of Virginia, to September, 1862. 3rd Brigade, 1st Division, 12th Army Corps, Army of the Potomac, to October, 1863. 3rd Brigade, 1st Division, 12th Army Corps, Army of the Cumberland, to April, 1864. 2nd Brigade, 1st Division, 20th Army Corps, Army of the Cumberland, to July, 1865.

SERVICE.—Duty at Harper's Ferry, W. Va., August to October, 1861. At Conrad's Ferry October 23-24, and picket duty at Seneca Mills till December 4. Duty at Frederick, Md., till February 27, 1862. Reconnoissance to Charleston February 27-28. Occupation of Winchester March 12. Pursuit of Jackson up the Shenandoah Valley March 24-April 27. Strasburg March 27. Woodstock April 1. Edenburg April 1-2. Operations in Shenandoah Valley May 15-June 17. Buckton Station May 23. Retreat to Martinsburg and Williamsport May 23-June 6. Middletown and Newtown May 24. Battle of Winchester May 25. (Rear guard May 24-25.) At Williamsport till June 10. Moved to Front Royal June 10-18, thence to Warrenton and Little Washington July 11-17. Pope's Campaign in Northern Virginia August 6-September 2. Battle of Cedar Mountain August 9. Fords of the Rappahannock August 19-23. Guarding trains during battles of Bull Run August 28-30. Battle of Antietam, Md., September 16-17. Duty at Maryland Heights September 19-October 29. Picket duty at Blackford's Ford and Sharpsburg, Md., till December. March to Fredericksburg December 12-16. "Mud March" January 20-24, 1863. At Stafford Court House till April 27. Chancellorsville Campaign April 27-May 6. Germania Ford April 29. Battle of

Chancellorsville May 1-5. Brandy Station and Beverly Ford June 9. Gettysburg (Pa.) Campaign June 11-July 24. Battle of Gettysburg, Pa., July 1-3. Pursuit to Warrenton Junction, Va., July 5-26. Detached duty in New York City August 16 to September 13. Movement to Stevenson, Ala., September 24-October 3. Guarding Nashville & Chattanooga Railroad at Elkwater Bridge and Tullahoma till April, 1864. Regiment veteranize December 31, 1863, and Veterans on furlough January 10 to March 1, 1864. Atlanta (Ga.) Campaign May 1 to September 9. Demonstration against Rocky Faced Ridge May 8-11. Battle of Resaca May 14-15. Cassville May 19. (Non-Veterans left front for muster out May 22, and mustered out at Chattanooga, Tenn., May 25, 1864.) New Hope Church May 25. Operations on line of Pumpkin Vine Creek, and battles about Dallas, New Hope Church and Allatoona Hills May 25-29. Guard trains to Kingston and back May 29-June 8. Raccoon Creek June 6. Operations about Marietta and against Kenesaw Mountain June 10-July 2. Pine Hill June 11-14. Gilgal or Golgotha Church June 15. Lost Mountain June 15-17. Muddy Creek June 17. Noyes Creek June 19. Kolb's Farm June 22. Assault on Kenesaw June 27. Ruff's Mills, Smyrna Camp Ground, July 4. Chattahoochie River July 5-17. Peach Tree Creek July 19-20. Siege of Atlanta July 22-August 25. Operations at Chattahoochie River Bridge August 26-September 2. Occupation of Atlanta September 2-November 15. March to the sea November 15-December 10. Monteith Swamp December 9. Siege of Savannah December 10-21. Campaign of the Carolinas January to April, 1865. Thompson's Creek, near Chesterfield, March 2. Thompson's Creek, near Cheraw, S. C., March 3. Averysboro, N. C., March 16. Battle of Bentonville March 19-21. Occupation of Goldsboro March 24. Advance on Raleigh April 9-13. Occupation of Raleigh April 14. Bennett's House April 26. Surrender of Johnston and his army. March to Washington, D. C., via Richmond, Va., April 29-May 19. Grand Review May 24. Provost duty at Washington till July. Mustered out July 11, and discharged at Boston, Mass., July 26, 1865.

Regiment lost during service 14 Officers and 176 Enlisted men killed and mortally wounded and 2 Officers and 96 Enlisted men by disease. Total 288.

3rd REGIMENT INFANTRY.—(MILITIA 3 MONTHS.)

Left Boston on Steamer "S. R. Spaulding" for Fortress Monroe, Va., April 17, 1861. Arrived April 20, and ordered on board United States Sloop of War "Pawnee" April 20. Moved to Norfolk April 20, and destruction of navy yard April 20. Expedition to Hampton May 13. Fatigue and garrison duty at Fortress Monroe till July 1, and at Hampton till July 16. Ordered home July 16, and mustered out July 22, 1861. Expiration of term.

3rd REGIMENT INFANTRY.—(MILITIA 9 MONTHS.)

Organized at Lakeville September, 1862. Moved to Boston October 22, thence embarked on Steamers "Merrimac" and "Mississippi" for New Berne, N. C., arriving there October 26. Attached to 3rd Brigade, 1st Division, Dept. of North Carolina, to December, 1862. Heckman's Brigade, Dept. of North Carolina, to January, 1863. 2nd Brigade, 5th Division, 18th Army Corps, Dept. of North Carolina, to April, 1863. Jourdan's Independent Brigade, Defences of Newberne, Dept. of North Carolina, to June, 1863.

SERVICE.—Duty at New Berne, N. C., till December, 1862. (Co. "I" detached at Plymouth and Elizabeth City November 30, 1862, to April, 1863.) Action at Plymouth December 10, 1862 (Co. "I"). Foster's Expedition to Goldsboro December 11-22. Action at Kinston December 14. Whitehall December 16. Goldsboro December 17. Duty at New Berne till June, 1863. Expedition to Trenton, Pollocksville, Young's Cross Roads and Swansborough March 6-10. Reconnoissance to Pollocksville March 15-16. Expedition to relief of Little Washington April 7-10. Expedition toward

Kinston April 16-21 and to Batchelor's Creek May 23-24. Moved to Boston June 11-16. Mustered out June 26, 1863.

Regiment lost 1 Enlisted man killed and 17 Enlisted men by disease. Total 18.

3rd BATTALION RIFLES.

Organized at Worcester. Moved to New York April 20, 1861; thence to Annapolis, Md., April 21-24, and duty there till May 2. Moved to Baltimore, Md., and garrison duty at Fort McHenry till August —. Company "D" organized at Boston. Ordered to Washington, D. C., via Fortress Monroe and the Potomac River May 2, 1861; thence moved to Baltimore and joined Battalion at Fort McHenry. Mustered out August 3, 1861.

4th REGIMENT INFANTRY.—(MILITIA 3 MONTHS.)

Left Boston for Fortress Monroe, Va., on Steamer "State of Maine" April 17, 1861, arriving there April 20. Fatigue and garrison duty at Fortress Monroe till May 27. At Newport News till July 11. Movement on Great Bethel June 9-10. Battle of Big Bethel June 10. Moved to Boston July 15-17, and mustered out July 22, 1861.

Lost 1 Enlisted man killed.

4th REGIMENT INFANTRY.—(MILITIA 9 MONTHS.)

Organized at Camp Joe Hooker, Lakeville, and mustered in September 23, 1862. Moved to New York December 27-28, thence to New Orleans and Carrollton, La., January 3-February 13, 1863. Attached to 1st Brigade, 3rd Division, 19th Army Corps, Dept. of the Gulf, to August, 1863.

SERVICE.—Moved to Baton Rouge, La., March 7, 1863. Expedition to Port Hudson March 13-20. Moved to Algiers April 3, thence to Brashear City April 8, and duty there till May 30. Skirmish at Barre Landing, Bayou Teche, May 22 (Co. "B"). Moved to Port Hudson May 30. Siege of Port Hudson June 3-July 9. Assault on Port Hudson June 14. Brashear City June 23 (Detachment). Surrender of Port Hudson July 9. Garrison duty at Port Hudson till August 4. Moved to Cairo, Ill., on Steamer "North America," thence by rail to Boston, Mass., August 4-17. Mustered out August 28, 1863.

Regiment lost during service 1 Officer and 19 Enlisted men killed and mortally wounded and 2 Officers and 129 Enlisted men by disease. Total 151.

4th BATTALION INFANTRY.—(MILITIA.)

Organized at Boston May 27, 1862. Mustered out May 31, 1862.

5th REGIMENT INFANTRY.—(MILITIA 3 MONTHS.)

Tendered services to the government April 15, 1861. Left State for Washington, D. C., April 21, and there mustered in for three months May 1. Moved to Alexandria, Va., May 25. Duty at Camp Andrew till July 16. Attached to Franklin's Brigade, Heintzelman's Division, McDowell's Army of Northeast Virginia. Advance on Manassas, Va., July 16-21. Battle of Bull Run July 21. Ordered to Boston July 29, and there mustered out August 1, 1861.

Lost during service 9 Enlisted men killed and mortally wounded and 2 Enlisted men by disease. Total 11.

5th REGIMENT INFANTRY.—(MILITIA 9 MONTHS.)

Tendered services to government for nine months August 14, 1862. Organized at Camp Lander, Wenham, and mustered in by Company. Company "A" October 8; Companies "B," "D" and "K" September 19; Companies "C," "E," "G," "H" and "I" September 16, and Company "F" September 23, 1862. Moved to Boston October 22, thence on Steamer "Mississippi" to New Berne, N. C., October 22-27, and to Washington, N. C., October 30-31. Attached to 3rd Brigade, 1st Division, Dept. of North Carolina, to December, 1862. Lee's Brigade, Dept. of North Carolina, to January,

1863. 2nd Brigade, 1st Division, 18th Army Corps, Dept. of North Carolina, to June, 1863.

SERVICE.—Foster's Expedition to Williamston November 2-12, 1862. Duty at New Berne till December 10. Foster's Expedition to Goldsboro December 11-20. Action at Kinston December 14. Whitehall December 16. Goldsboro December 17. Duty at New Berne till June, 1863. Deep Gully, New Berne, March 13-14. (Co. "G" detached at Forts Hatteras and Clark, Hatteras Inlet, February 21 to June 22, 1863.) (Co. "D" at Plymouth February 21 to May 4.) Operations on the Pamlico April 4-6. Expedition to the relief of Washington April 7-10. Expedition toward Kinston April 27-May 1. Wise's Cross Roads April 28. Demonstration on Kinston May 20-23. Gum Swamp May 22. Moved to Boston June 22-25, and there mustered out July 2, 1863.

Lost by disease 16 Enlisted men.

5th REGIMENT INFANTRY.—(MILITIA 100 DAYS.)

Tendered services to the government for 100 days July, 1864. Left State for Baltimore, Md., July 28, 1864. Camp at Mankin's Woods and garrison duty at Forts McHenry, Marshall, Carroll and other points in and about the Defences of Baltimore till November. Attached to 8th Army Corps, Middle Department. Ordered home November 6. Mustered out November 16, 1864.

Lost by disease 9 Enlisted men.

6th REGIMENT INFANTRY.—(MILITIA 3 MONTHS.)

Tendered services to government January 21, 1861. Moved from Lowell to Boston in response to call of the President April 15, 1861. Left Boston for Washington, D. C., April 17 via New York and Philadelphia and to Baltimore April 19. Attacked in streets of Baltimore April 19. Reached Washington April 19 and camp in Capitol Buildings. Moved to Relay House May 5 and to Baltimore May 13, returning to Relay House May 16. Guard railroad till June 13. Duty at Baltimore and Relay House till July 29. Relieved from duty July 29, and mustered out August 2, 1861.

Lost 4 Enlisted men killed and mortally wounded.

6th REGIMENT INFANTRY (MILITIA, 9 MONTHS).

Organized at Camp Wilson, Lowell, and mustered in August 31, 1862. Moved to Washington, D. C., September 9-12; thence moved to Suffolk, Va., September 14-15. Attached to Foster's Provisional Brigade, Division at Suffolk, 7th Army Corps, Dept. of Virginia, to April, 1863. 2nd Brigade, 1st Division, 7th Army Corps, Dept. of Virginia, to June, 1863.

SERVICE.—Duty at Suffolk till May, 1863. Expedition to Western Branch Church October 3-4, 1862. Expedition to Blackwater October 24-26 and November 17-19. Skirmish at Lawrence's Plantation November 17. Expedition to Beaver Dam Church December 1-3. Action on the Blackwater near Franklin December 2. Expedition to Zuni December 11-13. Action at Zuni December 11. Action at Deserted House January 30, 1863. Siege of Suffolk April 12-May 4. Siege of Suffolk raised May 4. Operations on Seaboard & Roanoke Railroad May 12-26. Holland House May 15-16. Moved to Boston May 26-29, and there mustered out June 3, 1863.

Regiment lost during service 2 Officers and 11 Enlisted men killed and mortally wounded and 18 Enlisted men by disease. Total 31.

6th REGIMENT INFANTRY (MILITIA, 100 DAYS).

Organized at Readville and mustered in July 14-19, 1864. Left State for Washington, D. C., July 20, arriving there July 22. Assigned to garrison duty at Fort C. F. Smith on Arlington Heights till August 21. Moved to Fort Delaware, on Pea Patch Island, relieving 157th Ohio Infantry from guard duty. Guarding Rebel prisoners there till October 19. Moved to Boston October 19-21. Mustered out October 27, 1864.

Lost 10 Enlisted men by disease.

7th REGIMENT INFANTRY.

Organized at Taunton and mustered in June 15, 1861. Ordered to Washington, D. C., July 14-15, and camp at Kalorama Heights till August 6. Attached to Couch's Brigade, Division of the Potomac, to October, 1861. Couch's Brigade, Buell's (Keyes') Division, Army of the Potomac, to March, 1862. 1st Brigade, 1st Division, 4th Army Corps, Army of the Potomac, to September, 1862. 1st Brigade, 3rd Division, 6th Army Corps, Army of the Potomac, to October, 1862. 2nd Brigade, 3rd Division, 6th Army Corps, to January, 1864. 4th Brigade, 2nd Division, 6th Army Corps, to July, 1864.

SERVICE.—At Camp Brightwood, Defences of Washington, D. C., till March 11, 1862. March to Prospect Hills, Va., March 11-15. Embarked at Alexandria for the Peninsula March 25. Siege of Yorktown April 5-May 4. Battle of Williamsburg May 5. Bottom's Bridge May 19-21. Reconnoissance toward Richmond May 23. Battle of Fair Oaks, Seven Pines, May 31-June 1. Seven days before Richmond June 25-July 1. Oak Grove, near Seven Pines, June 25. James River Road, near Fair Oaks, June 29. Malvern Hill July 1. At Harrison's Landing till August 16. Reconnoissance to Turkey Island August 5-6, and to Haxall's Station August 8-11. Movement to Alexandria August 16-September 1; thence march into Maryland September 3-18. Battle of Antietam September 18. At Downsville September 23-October 20. Movement to Stafford C. H. October 20-November 19, and to Belle Plains December 5. Battle of Fredericksburg December 12-15. "Mud March" January 20-24, 1863. Chancellorsville Campaign April 27-May 6. Operations at Franklin's Crossing April 29-May 2. Maryes Heights, Fredericksburg, May 3. Salem Heights May 3-4. Banks' Ford May 4. Deep Run Ravine June 5-13. Battle of Gettysburg, Pa., July 2-4. Pursuit of Lee July 5-23. At Warrenton, Va., till September 15. Bristoe Campaign October 9-22. Advance to the Rappahannock November 7-8. Rappahannock Station November 7. Mine Run Campaign November 26-December 2. Duty at Brandy Station till May, 1864. Rapidan Campaign May-June. Battles of the Wilderness May 5-7. Spottsylvania May 8-12. Spottsylvania C. H. May 12-21. "Bloody Angle" May 12. North Anna River May 23-26. Line of the Pamunkey May 26-28. Totopotomoy May 28-31. Cold Harbor June 1-12. March to James River June 12-14. Moved to Taunton, Mass., June 16-20, and there mustered out July, 1864, expiration of term.

Regiment lost during service 4 Officers and 76 Enlisted men killed and mortally wounded and 2 Officers and 72 Enlisted men by disease. Total 154.

8th REGIMENT INFANTRY (MILITIA, 3 MONTHS).

One of the first four Regiments to respond to the call after opening of hostilities. Gathered at Boston April 16, 1861. Left State for Washington April 18. Moved from Philadelphia to Annapolis, Md., via Perryville, April 20-21; thence march to Washington, D. C., April 24-26, and duty there till May 15. At Relay House till July 29. Moved to Boston July 29-30, and mustered out August 1, 1861.

8th REGIMENT INFANTRY (MILITIA, 9 MONTHS).

Organized at Camp Lander, Wenham. Moved to Boston November 25, 1862; thence on steamer "Mississippi" to Morehead City, N. C., November 25-30, and to New Berne November 30. Attached to 2nd Brigade, 1st Division, Dept. of North Carolina, to December, 1862. Heckman's Brigade, Dept. of North Carolina, to January, 1863. 2nd Brigade, 5th Division, 18th Army Corps, Dept. of North Carolina, to April, 1863. Jourdan's Independent Brigade, Defences of New Berne, N. C., to June, 1863. 8th Army Corps, Middle Department, to July, 1863.

SERVICE.—Garrison duty at New Berne till June, 1863. (Cos. "A" and "E" detached as garrison at Roanoke Island, N. C., December 4, 1862, to July 12, 1863.) Companies "G" and "K" garrison Fort Totten till June 24, 1863. Expedition up Currituck Sound against guerrillas and to destroy Salt Works February 1-6, 1863. Companies "B" and "F" detached February 7 for garrison duty at Roanoke Island. Company "B" ordered to Elizabeth City February 10, and duty there till April 16, when rejoined Regiment. Reconnoissance toward Trenton March 16-17. Expedition to relief of Washington April 7-10. Reconnoissance toward Kinston April 16-21. Duty in the Defences of New Berne, at Fort Totten, Camp Coffin, Fort Thompson and Camp Jourdan till June 24. Moved to Fortress Monroe June 24-27, thence to Baltimore, Md., June 30-July 1. At Camp Bradford till July 6. Moved to Monocacy Junction, thence to Sandy Hook and Maryland Heights July 6-8. Moved to reinforce Army of the Potomac at Funkstown, Md., July 12-13. Movements to Rappahannock July 16-22. Ordered home July 26 and mustered out August 7, 1863.

Lost 11 Enlisted men by disease.

8th REGIMENT INFANTRY (MILITIA, 100 DAYS).

Organized at Readville July 13 to 26, 1864. Left State for Baltimore, Md., July 26. Attached to 3rd Separate Brigade, 8th Army Corps, Middle Department.

SERVICE.—Camp at Mankin's Woods till August 15. Company "B" on duty at hospitals August 12 to October 28. Companies "A" to "K" on Provost duty in Baltimore August 12 to October 28. Companies "D," "E," "G" and "H" at Camp Bradford, near Baltimore. Draft Rendezvous for Maryland and Delaware August 12 to October 28. Companies "C," "F" and "I" guard Northern Central Railroad. Headquarters at Cockeyville, Md., August 15 to September 25, then at Camp Bradford. Moved to Massachusetts October 28, and mustered out November 10, 1864.

Lost by disease 4 Enlisted men.

9th REGIMENT INFANTRY.

Organized at Boston June 11, 1861. Left State for Washington, D. C., June 27. Attached to Sherman's Brigade, Division of the Potomac, to October, 1861. Morrell's Brigade, Porter's Division, Army of the Potomac, to March, 1862. 2nd Brigade, 1st Division, 3rd Army Corps, Army of the Potomac, to May, 1862. 2nd Brigade, 1st Division, 5th Army Corps, Army of the Potomac, to June, 1864.

SERVICE.—Duty at Arlington Heights and Munson's Hill, Defences of Washington, D. C., till March 10, 1862. Moved to the Peninsula, Virginia, March 16. Skirmish at Howard's Bridge April 4. Warwick Road April 5. Siege of Yorktown April 5-May 4. Battle of Hanover C. H. May 27. Operations about Hanover C. H. May 27-29. Seven days before Richmond June 25-July 1. Battle of Mechanicsville June 26. Gaines' Mill June 27. White Oak Swamp and Turkey Bridge June 30. Malvern Hill July 1. Duty at Harrison's Landing till August 16. Movement to Fortress Monroe, thence to Centreville August 16-28. Pope's Campaign August 28-September 2. Battles of Groveton August 29. Bull Run August 30. Battle of Antietam, Md., September 16-17. Blackford's Ford September 19. Shepherdstown, W. Va., September 20. Reconnoissance toward Smithville, W. Va., October 16-17. Battle of Fredericksburg, Va., December 12-15. Expedition to Richard's and Ellis' Fords December 29-30. "Mud March" January 20-24, 1863. Chancellorsville Campaign April 27-May 6. Battle of Chancellorsville May 1-5. Gettysburg (Pa.) Campaign June 11-July 24. Battle of Gettysburg July 1-3. Bristoe Campaign October 9-22. Rappahannock Station November 7. Mine Run, Campaign November 26-December 2. At Bealeton and guard Orange & Alexandria Railroad till April 30, 1864. Bealeton January 14, 1864 (1 Company). Rapidan Campaign May-June. Battles of the Wilderness May 5-7. Laurel Hill May 8. Spottsylvania May 8-12. Spottsylvania C. H. May 12-21. Assault on the Salient at Spottsylvania C. H. May 12. North Anna River May 23-26. Jericho Mills May 24. Line of the Pamunkey May 26-28. Totopotomoy May 28-31. Cold Harbor June 1-10. Left front June 10 and ordered home for muster out. Mustered out June 21, 1864.

Regiment lost during service 15 Officers and 194 Enlisted men killed and mortally wounded and 3 Officers and 66 Enlisted men by disease. Total 278.

10th REGIMENT INFANTRY.

Organized at Springfield June 21, 1861. Moved to Washington, D. C., July 25-28. Attached to Couch's Brigade, Division of the Potomac, to October, 1861. Couch's Brigade, Buell's (Keyes') Division, Army of the Potomac, to March, 1862. 1st Brigade, 1st Division, 4th Army Corps, Army of the Potomac, to September, 1862. 1st Brigade, 3rd Division, 6th Army Corps, to October, 1862. 2nd Brigade, 3rd Division, 6th Army Corps, to January, 1864. 4th Brigade, 2nd Division, 6th Army Corps, to July, 1864.

SERVICE.—Duty at Kalorama Heights and Camp Brightwood, Defences of Washington, D. C., till March, 1862. March to Prospect Hill, Va., March 11-15. Embarked at Alexandria for the Peninsula, Virginia, March 25. Siege of Yorktown April 5-May 4. Battle of Fair Oaks, Seven Pines, May 31-June 1. Seven days before Richmond June 25-July 1. Oak Grove, near Seven Pines, June 25. White Oak Swamp June 30. Malvern Hill July 1. At Harrison's Landing till August 16. Reconnoissance to Turkey Island August 5-6, and to Haxall's Landing August 8-11. Movement to Alexandria August 16-September 1, thence march into Maryland September 3-18. Battle of Antietam September 18. At Downsville September 18-October 20. Movement to Stafford C. H. October 20-November 18, and to Belle Plains December 5. Battle of Fredericksburg, Va., December 12-15. "Mud March" January 20-24, 1863. Chancellorsville Campaign April 27-May 6. Operations at Franklin's Crossing April 29-May 2. Maryes Heights, Fredericksburg, May 3. Salem Heights May 3-4. Banks' Ford May 4. Franklin's Crossing June 6-7. Battle of Gettysburg, Pa., July 2-4. Bristoe Campaign October 9-22. Rappahannock Station November 7. Mine Run Campaign November 26-December 2. At Brandy Station till May 1, 1864. Reconnoissance to Madison C. H. February 27-March 2. Rapidan Campaign May-June. Battles of the Wilderness May 5-7. Spottsylvania May 8-12. Spottsylvania C. H. May 12-21. Assault on the Salient at Spottsylvania C. H. May 12. North Anna River May 23-26. Line of the Pamunkey June 26-28. Totopotomoy May 28-31. Cold Harbor June 1-12. Before Petersburg June 17-19. Ordered home for muster out June 19. Mustered out July 6, 1864.

Regiment lost during service 10 Officers and 124 Enlisted men killed and mortally wounded and 1 Officer and 55 Enlisted men by disease. Total 190.

11th REGIMENT INFANTRY.

Organized at Readville and mustered in June 13, 1861. Left State for Washington, D. C., June 24. Attached to Franklin's Brigade, Heintzelman's Division, McDowell's Army of Northeast Virginia, to August, 1861. Hooker's Brigade, Division of the Potomac, to October, 1861. 1st Brigade, Hooker's Division, Army of the Potomac, to March, 1862. 1st Brigade, 2nd Division, 3rd Army Corps, Army of the Potomac, to March, 1864. 2nd Brigade, 4th Division, 2nd Army Corps, Army of the Potomac, to May, 1864. 4th Brigade, 3rd Division, 2nd Army Corps, to June, 1864. 3rd Brigade, 3rd Division, 2nd Army Corps, to June, 1865.

SERVICE.—Advance on Manassas, Va., July 16-21, 1861. Battle of Bull Run July 21. Moved to Bladensburg August 10, thence to Budd's Ferry October 27. Duty in that vicinity till April, 1862. Ordered to Fortress Monroe, Va., April 7. Siege of Yorktown, Va., April 16-May 4. Affair at Yorktown April 26 (Cos. "A" and "G"). Battle of Williamsburg May 5. Battle of Fair Oaks, Seven Pines, May 31-June 1. Seven days before Richmond June 25-July 1. Oak Grove, near Fair Oaks, June 25. Savage Station June 29. White Oak Swamp and Glendale June 30. Malvern Hill July 1 and August 5. At Harrison's Landing till August 15. Movement to Fortress Monroe, thence to Centreville August 15-26. Bristoe Station August 26-27. Kettle Run August 27. Catlett's Station August 28. Groveton August 29. Bull Run August 30. Chantilly September 1. Camp near Fort Lyon till September 13, and near Fairfax Seminary till October 20. At Munson's Hill till November. At Fairfax Station November 2-25. Operations on Orange & Alexandria R. R. November 10-12. Rappahannock Campaign December, 1862, to June, 1863. Battle of Fredericksburg, Va., December 12-15. "Mud March" January 20-24, 1863. Operations at Rappahannock Bridge and Grove Church February 5-7. At Falmouth till April 27. Chancellorsville Campaign April 27-May 6. Battle of Chancellorsville May 1-5. Gettysburg (Pa.) Campaign June 11-July 24. Battle of Gettysburg July 1-4. Wapping Heights July 23. Moved to New York July 30-August 1, and duty there till October. Rejoin Corps at Union Mills October 17. Advance to the Rappahannock November 7-8. Kelly's Ford November 7. Mine Run Campaign November 26-December 2. Payne's Farm November 27. Duty near Brandy Station till May, 1864. Demonstration on the Rapidan February 6-7. Rapidan Campaign May-June. Battles of the Wilderness May 5-7. Spottsylvania May 8-12. Spottsylvania C. H. May 12-21. Assault on the Salient at Spottsylvania C. H. May 12. Harris Farm, Fredericksburg Road, May 19. North Anna River May 23-26. Line of the Pamunkey May 26-28. Totopotomoy May 28-31. Cold Harbor June 1-12. (Old members left front June 12. Mustered out June 24, 1864.) Veterans and Recruits consolidated to a Battalion of 5 Companies June 12. Before Petersburg June 16-18. Siege of Petersburg June 16, 1864, to April 2, 1865. Jerusalem Plank Road June 22-23, 1864. Demonstration on north side of the James July 27-29. Deep Bottom July 27-28. Mine Explosion, Petersburg, July 30 (Reserve). Demonstration on north side of the James River August 13-20. Strawberry Plains August 14-18. Peeble's Farm, Poplar Grove Church, September 29-October 2. Boydton Plank Road, Hatcher's Run, October 27-28. In front of Fort Morton November 5. Expedition to Weldon Railroad December 7-11. Watkin's House March 25, 1865. Appomattox C. H. March 28-April 9. Crow's House March 31. Fall of Petersburg April 2. Sailor's Creek April 6. High Bridge and Farmville April 7. Appomattox C. H. April 9. Surrender of Lee and his army. March to Burkesville April 11-13, and duty there till May 2. March to Washington, D. C., May 2-15. Grand Review May 23. Mustered out June 14, 1865.

Regiment lost during service 11 Officers and 153 Enlisted men killed and mortally wounded and 2 Officers and 95 Enlisted men by disease. Total 261.

12th REGIMENT INFANTRY.

Organized at Fort Warren and mustered in June 26, 1861. Moved to Sandy Hook, Md., July 23-27. Attached to George H. Thomas' Brigade, Dept. of the Shenandoah, to October, 1861. Abercrombie's Brigade, Banks' Division, Army of the Potomac, to March, 1862. 2nd Brigade, Williams' 1st Division, Banks' 5th Army Corps and Dept. of the Shenandoah, to May, 1862. 3rd Brigade, 2nd Division, Dept. of the Rappahannock, to June, 1862. 3rd Brigade, 2nd Division, 3rd Army Corps, Army of Virginia, to September, 1862. 3rd Brigade, 2nd Division, 1st Army Corps, Army of the Potomac, to November, 1862. 2nd Brigade, 2nd Division, 1st Army Corps, to March, 1864. 2nd Brigade, 2nd Division, 5th Army Corps, to May, 1864. 2nd Brigade, 3rd Division, 5th Army Corps, to July, 1864.

SERVICE.—Operations on the Upper Potomac August, 1861, to February, 1862. Operations opposite Edward's Ferry October 21-24, 1861. Operations in the Shenandoah Valley March 24-April 27. Strasburg March 27. Edenburg April 1-2. Rappahannock Crossing April 18. Battle of Cedar Mountain August 9. Pope's Campaign in Northern Virginia August 16-September 2. Rappahannock Station August 20-23. Thoroughfare Gap August 28. Bull Run August 30. Chantilly September 1. Maryland Campaign September-October. Battles of South Mountain September 14, and Antietam September 16-17. Duty at Sharpsburg till October 30. Movement to Warrenton, thence to Falmouth, Va., October 30-November 19. Battle of Fredericksburg December 12-15. "Mud March" January 20-24, 1863. At Falmouth and Belle Plain, Va., till April 27.

Chancellorsville Campaign April 27-May 6. Operations at Pollock's Mill Creek April 29-May 2. Fitzhugh's Crossing April 29-30. Battle of Chancellorsville May 1-5. Gettysburg (Pa.) Campaign June 11-July 24. Battle of Gettysburg July 1-3. Picket duty on the Rapidan till October. Bristoe Campaign October 9-22. Advance to line of the Rappahannock November 7-8. Mine Run Campaign November 26-December 2. Demonstration on the Rapidan February 6-7, 1864. Campaign from the Rapidan to the James May-June, 1864. Battles of the Wilderness May 5-7; Laurel Hill May 8; Spottsylvania May 8-12; Spottsylvania Court House May 12-21. Assault on the Salient May 12. North Anna River May 23-26. Jericho Ford May 23. Line of the Pamunkey May 26-28. Totopotomoy May 28-31. Cold Harbor June 1-12. Bethesda Church June 1-3. White Oak Swamp June 13. Before Petersburg June 16-18. Ordered home for muster out June 25. Mustered out July 8, 1864.

Regiment lost during service 18 Officers and 175 Enlisted men killed and mortally wounded and 83 Enlisted men by disease. Total 276.

13th REGIMENT INFANTRY.

Organized at Fort Independence June 16, 1861. Left State for Washington, D. C., July 30. Attached to Stile's Brigade, Banks' Division, Army of the Potomac, to October, 1861. Abercrombie's Brigade, Banks' Division, to March, 1862. 2nd Brigade, 1st Division, Banks' 5th Army Corps and Dept. of the Shenandoah, to May, 1862. 3rd Brigade, 2nd Division, Dept. of the Rappahannock, to June, 1862. 3rd Brigade, 2nd Division, 3rd Army Corps, Army of Virginia, to September, 1862. 3rd Brigade, 2nd Division, 1st Army Corps, Army of the Potomac, to May, 1863. 1st Brigade, 2nd Division, 1st Army Corps, to March, 1864. 1st Brigade, 2nd Division, 5th Army Corps, to June, 1864. 1st Brigade, 3rd Division, 5th Army Corps, to July, 1864.

SERVICE.—Patrol and outpost duty on the Upper Potomac till March, 1862. Action at Beller's Mill, near Harper's Ferry, W. Va., September 2, 1861. Pritchard's Mills September 18 (2 Cos.). Bolivar Heights, near Harper's Ferry, October 16. (Cos. "C," "D," "I" and "K" detached at Hancock, Md., January 5-30, 1862.) Operations in the Shenandoah Valley March and April. Occupation of Winchester, Va., March 12. Pursuit of Jackson up the Valley March 24-April 27. Guard duty on the Orange & Alexandria Railroad May 3-18. Battle of Cedar Mountain August 9. Pope's Campaign in Northern Virginia August 16-September 2. Thoroughfare Gap August 28. Battle of Bull Run August 30. Chantilly September 1. Maryland Campaign September-October. Battles of South Mountain September 14, and Antietam September 16-17. At Sharpsburg till October 30. Movement to Warrenton, thence to Falmouth, Va., October 30-November 19. Battle of Fredericksburg December 12-15. "Mud March" January 20-24, 1863. At Falmouth and Belle Plain till April 27. Chancellorsville Campaign April 27-May 6. Operations at Pollock's Mill Creek April 29-May 2. Fitzhugh's Crossing April 29-30. Battle of Chancellorsville May 2-5. Gettysburg (Pa.) Campaign June 11-July 24. Battle of Gettysburg July 1-3. Picket duty along the Rapidan till October —. Bristoe Campaign October 9-22. Advance to line of the Rappahannock November 7-8. Mine Run Campaign November 26-December 2. Duty on the Orange & Alexandria Railroad till April, 1864. Demonstrations on the Rapidan February 6-7. Campaign from the Rapidan to the James May-June. Battles of the Wilderness May 5-7; Spottsylvania May 8-12; Spottsylvania Court House May 12-21. Assault on the Salient May 12. North Anna River May 23-26. Jericho Ford May 23. Line of the Pamunkey June 26-28. Totopotomoy May 28-31. Cold Harbor June 1-12. Bethesda Church June 1-3. White Oak Swamp June 13. Before Petersburg June 16-18. Siege of Petersburg June 16-July 14. Mustered out August 1, 1864.

Regiment lost during service 4 Officers and 117 Enlisted men killed and mortally wounded and 40 Enlisted men by disease. Total 161.

14th REGIMENT INFANTRY.—("ESSEX COUNTY REGIMENT.")

Organized at Fort Warren and mustered in July 5, 1861. Left State for Washington, D. C., August 7. At Camp Kalorama till August 18. Moved to Fort Albany. Garrison duty in the Defences of Washington till January, 1862. Designation of Regiment changed by order of the War Department to 1st Massachusetts Heavy Artillery January 1, 1862. (See 1st Heavy Artillery.)

15th REGIMENT INFANTRY.

Organized at Worcester and mustered in June 12, 1861. Moved to Washington, D. C., August 8-11. Attached to Gorman's Brigade, Stone's (Sedgwick's) Division, Army of the Potomac, to March, 1862. 1st Brigade, 2nd Division, 2nd Army Corps, Army of the Potomac, to July, 1864.

SERVICE.—At Camp Kalorama till August 25, 1861. March to Poolesville, Md., August 25-27. Picket and outpost duty on the Upper Potomac from Conrad's Ferry to Harrison's Island till October 20. Operations on the Potomac October 21-24. Battle of Ball's Bluff October 21. At Harper's Ferry and Bolivar Heights till March 7, 1862. At Charlestown till March 10. At Berryville till March 13. Movement toward Winchester and return to Bolivar Heights March 13-15. Moved to Fortress Monroe March 22-April 1. Siege of Yorktown April 5-May 4. Battle of Fair Oaks, Seven Pines, May 31-June 1. Seven days before Richmond June 25-July 1. Peach Orchard and Savage Station June 29. White Oak Swamp and Glendale June 30. Malvern Hill July 1. At Harrison's Landing till August 15. Movement to Alexandria August 15-28, and to Centreville August 29-30. Cover Pope's retreat August 31-September 1. Battle of Antietam, Md., September 16-17. Moved to Harper's Ferry September 22 and duty there till October 30. Movement to Falmouth, Va., October 30-November 20. Battle of Fredericksburg December 12-15. "Mud March" January 20-24, 1863. Chancellorsville Campaign April 27-May 6. Maryes Heights, Fredericksburg, May 3. Salem Heights May 3-4. Banks' Ford May 4. Battle of Gettysburg, Pa., July 2-4. Advance from the Rappahannock to the Rapidan September 13-17. Bristoe Campaign October 9-22. Bristoe Station October 14. Advance to line of the Rappahannock November 7-8. Mine Run Campaign November 26-December 2. Robertson's Tavern or Locust Grove November 27. Morton's Ford February 6-7, 1864. Picketing Rapidan till May, 1864. Campaign from the Rapidan to the James May-June. Battles of the Wilderness May 5-7; Laurel Hill May 8; Spottsylvania May 8-12; Po River May 10; Spottsylvania Court House May 12-21. Assault on the Salient at Spottsylvania Court House May 12. North Anna River May 23-26. Line of the Pamunkey May 26-28. Totopotomoy May 28-31. Cold Harbor June 1-12. Before Petersburg June 16-18. Siege of Petersburg June 16-July 12. Jerusalem Plank Road June 22-23. Left the front July 12. Mustered out July 28, 1864. Veterans and Recruits transferred to 20th Massachusetts.

Regiment lost during service 14 Officers and 227 Enlisted men killed and mortally wounded and 1 Officer and 121 Enlisted men by disease. Total 363.

16th REGIMENT INFANTRY.

Organized at Camp Cameron, Cambridge, June 29, 1861. Left State for Old Point Comfort, Va., August 17. Attached to Fortress Monroe, Dept. of Virginia, to May, 1862. 1st Brigade, 1st Division, Dept. of Virginia, to June, 1862. 1st Brigade, 2nd Division, 3rd Army Corps, Army of the Potomac, to March, 1864. 1st Brigade, 4th Division, 2nd Army Corps, to May, 1864. 3rd Brigade, 3rd Division, 2nd Army Corps, to July, 1864.

SERVICE.—Garrison duty at Fortress Monroe, Va., September 1, 1862, to May 8, 1862. Occupation of Norfolk May 10. Moved to Suffolk May 17, and joined Army of the Potomac at Fair Oaks June 13. Nine-Mile Road, near Richmond, June 18. Seven days before Richmond June 25-July 1. Oak Grove, near Fair Oaks, June 25. White Oak Swamp and Glendale June 30. Malvern Hill July 1 and August 5. Duty at Harrison's Landing till August 15. Movement to Fortress Monroe, thence to Centreville August 15-26. Bristoe Station, Kettle Run, August 27. Battles of Groveton August 29; Bull Run August 30; Chantilly September 1. Duty at Fort Lyon and at Fairfax Station, Defences of Washington, till October 30, and at Munson's Hill till November 2. At Fairfax Station till November 25. Operations on Orange & Alexandria Railroad November 10-12. Rappahannock Campaign December, 1862, to June, 1863. Battle of Fredericksburg, Va., December 12-15. "Mud March" January 20-24, 1863. At Falmouth till April 27. Chancellorsville Campaign April 27-May 6. Battle of Chancellorsville May 1-5. Gettysburg (Pa.) Campaign June 11-July 24. Battle of Gettysburg, Pa., July 1-3. Wapping Heights, Va., July 23. Bristoe Campaign October 9-22. Advance to the Rappahannock November 7-8. Kelly's Ford November 7. Mine Run Campaign November 26-December 2. Payne's Farm November 27. Demonstration on the Rapidan February 6-7, 1864. Duty near Brandy Station till May, 1864. Rapidan Campaign May-June. Battles of the Wilderness May 5-7; Spottsylvania May 8-12; Spottsylvania Court House May 12-21. Assault on the Salient, Spottsylvania Court House, May 12. Harris' Farm, Fredericksburg Road, May 19. North Anna River May 23-26. Ox Ford May 23-24. On line of the Pamunkey May 26-28. Totopotomoy May 28-31. Cold Harbor June 1-12. Before Petersburg June 16-18. Siege of Petersburg June 16-July 11. Jerusalem Plank Road June 22-23. Left front for muster out July 11. Veterans and Recruits transferred to the 11th Massachusetts Infantry. Mustered out July 27, 1864.

Regiment lost during service 16 Officers and 134 Enlisted men killed and mortally wounded and 2 Officers and 93 Enlisted men by disease. Total 245.

17th REGIMENT INFANTRY.

Organized at Lynnfield July 22, 1861. Left State for Baltimore, Md., August 23. Attached to Dix's Command, Baltimore, Md., to March, 1862. Foster's 1st Brigade, Burnside's Expeditionary Corps, to April, 1862. 1st Brigade, 1st Division, Dept. of North Carolina, to December, 1862. Amory's Brigade, Dept. of North Carolina, to January, 1863. 1st Brigade, 1st Division, 18th Army Corps, Dept. of North Carolina, to July, 1863. Defences of New Berne, N. C., Dept. of Virginia and North Carolina, to July, 1864. Sub-District of Beaufort, N. C., Dept. of Virginia and North Carolina, to January, 1865. Sub-District of Beaufort, N. C., Dept. of North Carolina, to March, 1865. 3rd Brigade, 2nd Division, District of Beaufort, N. C., Dept. of North Carolina, to March, 1865. 1st Brigade, Division District of Beaufort, to April, 1865. 3rd Brigade, 3rd Division, 23rd Army Corps, to July, 1865.

SERVICE.—Duty at Baltimore, Md., till March, 1862. Ordered to New Berne, N. C., March 12, and duty there till December. Reconnoissance toward Trenton May 15-16. Trenton Bridge May 15. Trenton and Pollocksville Road May 22 (Co. "I"). Expedition to Trenton and Pollocksville July 24-28. Demonstration on New Berne November 11. Foster's Expedition to Goldsboro December 11-20. Kinston December 14. Whitehall December 16. Goldsboro December 17. Provost duty at and near New Berne till April, 1863. March to relief of Washington, N. C., April 7-10. Blount's Creek April 9. Expedition to Washington April 17-19. Expedition toward Kinston April 27-May 1. Wise's Cross Roads and Dover Road April 28. Expedition to Thenton July 4-8. Quaker Bridge July 6. Raid on Weldon July 25-August 1. Duty at New Berne till February, 1864. Operations about New Berne against Whiting January 18-February 10, 1864. Skirmishes at Beech Creek and Batchelor's Creek February 1-3. Expedition to Washington April 18-22. Washington April 27-28. Duty at New Berne and vicinity till July 27, and at Newport Barracks till September 23. Veterans on furlough till November 10. Duty at Newport Barracks November 20, 1864, to March 4, 1865. Moved to Core Creek. Battle of Wise's Forks March 8-10, 1865. Occupation of Kinston March 15. Occupation of Goldsboro March 21. Advance on Raleigh April 9-14. Occupation of Raleigh April 14. Duty at Greensboro May 5-July 11. Mustered out at Greensboro, N. C., July 11, 1865.

Regiment lost during service 21 Enlisted men killed and mortally wounded and 4 Officers and 147 Enlisted men by disease. Total 172.

18th REGIMENT INFANTRY.

Organized at Readville and Boston and mustered in August 27, 1861. Left State for Washington, D. C., August 28. Attached to Fort Corcoran, Defences of Washington, to October, 1861. Martindale's Brigade, Porter's Division, Army of the Potomac, to March, 1862. 1st Brigade, 1st Division, 3rd Army Corps, Army of the Potomac, to May, 1862. 1st Brigade, 1st Division, 5th Army Corps, Army of the Potomac, to March, 1864. 3rd Brigade, 1st Division, 5th Army Corps, to October, 1864.

SERVICE.—Duty at Fort Corcoran, Defences of Washington, D. C., till September 26, 1861, and at Hall's Hill, Va., till March 10, 1862. Advance on Manassas, Va., March 10-16, 1862. Moved to Alexandria, thence to Fortress Monroe March 16-23. Reconnoissance to Great Bethel March 27. Warwick Road April 5. Siege of Yorktown April 5-May 4. Battle of Hanover Court House May 27. Operations about Hanover Court House May 27-29. Seven days before Richmond June 25-July 1. Operations about White House Landing June 26-July 2. At Harrison's Landing till August 15. Retreat from the Peninsula and movement to Centreville August 15-28. Battle of Bull Run August 30. Battle of Antietam, Md., September 16-17. Shepherdstown Ford September 19. Shepherdstown, W. Va., September 20. At Sharpsburg till October 30. Movement to Falmouth, Va., October 30-November 19. Battle of Fredericksburg December 12-15. Expedition to Richards and Ellis Fords December 29-30. "Mud March" January 20-24, 1863. Duty at Falmouth till April 27. Chancellorsville Campaign April 27-May 6. Battle of Chancellorsville May 1-5. Gettysburg (Pa.) Campaign June 11-July 24. Ashby's Gap June 21. Battle of Gettysburg July 1-3. Williamsport, Md., July 14. At Warrenton and Beverly Ford July 27 to September 17, and at Culpeper till October 11. Bristoe Campaign October 11-22. Advance to line of the Rappahannock November 7-8. Rappahannock Station November 7. Mine Run Campaign November 26-December 2. At and near Brandy Station and Stevensburg till May, 1864. Campaign from the Rapidan to the James May-June. Battles of the Wilderness May 5-7; Laurel Hill May 8; Spottsylvania May 8-12; Spottsylvania Court House May 12-21. Assault on the Salient May 12. North Anna River May 23-26. Jericho Ford May 23. On line of the Pamunkey May 26-28. Totopotomoy May 28-31. Cold Harbor June 1-12. Bethesda Church June 1-3. Before Petersburg June 16-18. Siege of Petersburg June 16 to October 21. Weldon Railroad June 21-23. Old members left front July 20 and mustered out September 2, 1864. Veterans and Recruits consolidated to a Battalion. Poplar Springs' Church, Peeble's Farm, September 30-October 2. Consolidated with 32nd Massachusetts Infantry October 21, 1864.

Regiment lost during service 9 Officers and 114 Enlisted men killed and mortally wounded and 2 Officers and 127 Enlisted men by disease. Total 252.

19th REGIMENT INFANTRY.

Organized at Lynnfield August 28, 1861. Left State for Washington, D. C., August 30. Attached to Lander's Brigade, Division of the Potomac, to October, 1861. Lander's Brigade, Stone's (Sedgwick's) Division, Army of the Potomac, to March, 1862. 3rd Brigade, 2nd Division, 2nd Army Corps, Army of the Potomac,

to March, 1864. 1st Brigade, 2nd Division, 2nd Army Corps, to June, 1865.

SERVICE.—Camp at Meridian Hill till September 12, 1861. Moved to Poolesville, Md., September 12-15. Guard duty on the Upper Potomac till December. Operations on the Potomac October 21-24. Action at Ball's Bluff October 21. Moved to Muddy Run December 4, and duty there till March 12, 1862. Moved to Harper's Ferry, thence to Charlestown and Berryville March 12-15. Ordered to Washington, D. C., March 24, and to the Peninsula March 27. Siege of Yorktown April 5-May 4. West Point May 7-8. Battle of Fair Oaks, Seven Pines, May 31-June 1. Seven days before Richmond June 25-July 1. Oak Grove, near Fair Oaks, June 25. Peach Orchard and Savage Station June 29. White Oak Swamp and Glendale June 30. Malvern Hill July 1. Harrison's Landing July 8. At Harrison's Landing till August 15. Movement to Alexandria August 15-28, thence to Fairfax C. H. August 28-31. Cover Pope's retreat from Bull Run August 31-September 1. Maryland Campaign September-October. Battle of South Mountain September 14 (Reserve). Battle of Antietam September 16-17. Moved to Harper's Ferry September 22, and duty there till October 30. Advance up Loudon Valley and movement to Falmouth, Va., October 30-November 17. Battle of Fredericksburg December 11-15. (Forlorn hope to cross Rappahannock at Fredericksburg December 11.) Duty at Falmouth, Va., till April, 1863. Chancellorsville Campaign April 27-May 6. Maryes' Heights, Fredericksburg, May 3. Salem Heights May 3-4. Gettysburg (Pa.) Campaign June 11-July 24. Battle of Gettysburg July 2-4. Advance from the Rappahannock to the Rapidan September 13-17. Bristoe Campaign October 9-22. Bristoe Station October 14. Advance to line of the Rappahannock November 7-8. Mine Run Campaign November 26-December 2. Robertson's Tavern, or Locust Grove, November 27. At Stevensburg till May, 1864. Demonstration on the Rapidan February 6-7. Campaign from the Rapidan to the James May-June. Battles of the Wilderness May 5-7. Laurel Hill May 8. Spottsylvania May 8-12. Po River May 10. Spottsylvania C. H. May 12-21. Assault on the Salient May 12. North Anna River May 23-26. On line of the Pamunkey May 26-28. Totopotomoy May 28-31. Cold Harbor June 1-12. Before Petersburg June 16-18. Siege of Petersburg June 16, 1864, to April 2, 1865. Jerusalem Plank Road June 22-23, 1864. Demonstration north of the James July 27-29. Deep Bottom July 27-28. Strawberry Plains, Deep Bottom, August 14-18. Ream's Station August 25. Boydton Plank Road, Hatcher's Run, October 27-28. Dabney's Mills, Hatcher's Run, February 5-7, 1865. Watkin's House March 25. Appomattox Campaign March 28-April 9. Crow's House March 31. Fall of Petersburg April 2. Sailor's Creek April 6. High Bridge and Farmville April 7. Appomattox C. H. April 9. Surrender of Lee and his army. At Burkesville till May 2. March to Washington May 2-13. Grand Review May 23. Duty at Washington till June 30. Mustered out June 30 and discharged July 22, 1865.

Regiment lost during service 14 Officers and 147 Enlisted men killed and mortally wounded and 133 Enlisted men by disease. Total 294.

20th REGIMENT INFANTRY.

Organized at Readville August 29 to September 4, 1861. Left State for Washington, D. C., September 4. Attached to Lander's Brigade, Division of the Potomac, to October, 1861. Lander's Brigade, Stone's (Sedgwick's) Division, Army of the Potomac, to March, 1862. 3rd Brigade, 2nd Division, 2nd Army Corps, Army of the Potomac, to March, 1864. 1st Brigade, 2nd Division, 2nd Army Corps, to July, 1865.

SERVICE.—Moved to Poolesville, Md., September 12-15, 1861. Guard duty along Upper Potomac till December. Operations on the Potomac October 21-24. Action at Ball's Bluff October 21. Near Edwards' Ferry October 22. Moved to Muddy Branch December 4, and duty there till March 12, 1862. Moved to Harper's Ferry, thence to Charlestown and Berryville, March 12-15.

Ordered to Washington, D. C., March 24, and to the Peninsula March 27. Siege of Yorktown April 5-May 4. West Point May 7-8. Battle of Fair Oaks, Seven Pines, May 31-June 1. Seven days before Richmond June 25-July 1. Oak Grove, near Fair Oaks, June 25. Peach Orchard and Savage Station July 29. White Oak Swamp and Glendale June 30. Malvern Hill July 1 and August 5. At Harrison's Landing till August 15. Movement to Alexandria August 15-28, thence march to Fairfax C. H. August 28-31. Cover retreat of Pope's army from Bull Run August 31-September 1. Maryland Campaign September-October. South Mountain, Md., September 14 (Reserve). Battle of Antietam September 16-17. Moved to Harper's Ferry September 22, and duty there till October 30. Reconnoissance to Charlestown October 16-17. Advance up Loudon Valley and movement to Falmouth, Va., October 30-November 17. Battles of Fredericksburg December 11-15. (Forlorn hope to cross Rappahannock December 11.) Duty at Falmouth till April. Chancellorsville Campaign April 27-May 6. Maryes Heights, Fredericksburg, May 3. Salem Heights May 3-4. Gettysburg (Pa.) Campaign June 11-July 24. Battle of Gettysburg July 2-4. Advance from the Rappahannock to the Rapidan September 13-17. Bristoe Campaign October 9-22. Bristoe Station October 14. Advance to line of the Rappahannock November 7-8. Mine Run Campaign November 26-December 2. Demonstration on the Rapidan February 6-7, 1864. At Stevensburg till May. Campaign from the Rapidan to the James May-June. Battles of the Wilderness May 5-7. Laurel Hill May 8. Spottsylvania May 8-12. Po River May 10. Spottsylvania C. H. May 12-21. Assault on the Salient May 12. North Anna River May 23-26. Line of the Pamunkey May 26-28. Totopotomoy May 28-31. Cold Harbor June 1-12. Before Petersburg June 16-18. Siege of Petersburg June 16, 1864, to April 2, 1865. Jerusalem Plank Road June 22-23, 1864. Demonstration north of the James July 27-29. Deep Bottom July 27-28. Strawberry Plains, Deep Bottom, August 14-18. Ream's Station August 25. Boydton Plank Road, Hatcher's Run, October 27-28. Dabney's Mills, Hatcher's Run, February 5-7, 1865. Watkins' House March 25. Appomattox Campaign March 28-April 9. Crow's House March 31. Fall of Petersburg April 2. Sailor's Creek April 6. High Bridge and Farmville April 7. Appomattox C. H. April 9. Surrender of Lee and his army. At Burkesville till May 2. March to Washington, D. C., May 2-15. Grand Review May 23. Duty at Washington till July 15. Mustered out July 16 and discharged July 28, 1865.

Regiment lost during service 17 Officers and 243 Enlisted men killed and mortally wounded and 1 Officer and 148 Enlisted men by disease. Total 409.

21st REGIMENT INFANTRY.

Organized at Worcester July 19 to August 19, 1861. Moved to Baltimore, Md., August 23-25; thence to Annapolis, Md., August 29; and duty there till January 6, 1862. Attached to Reno's 2nd Brigade, Burnside's Expeditionary Corps, to April, 1862. 2nd Brigade, 2nd Division, Dept. of North Carolina, to July, 1862. 2nd Brigade, 2nd Division, 9th Army Corps, Army of the Potomac, to April, 1863. 2nd Brigade, 2nd Division, 9th Army Corps, Dept. of the Ohio, to June, 1863. Unassigned, 1st Division, 23rd Army Corps, Dept. of the Ohio, to October, 1863. 1st Brigade, 2nd Division, 9th Army Corps, Dept. of the Ohio, to April, 1864. 2nd Brigade, 1st Division, 9th Army Corps, Army of the Potomac, to June, 1863. 1st Brigade, 1st Division, 9th Army Corps, to September, 1864. 2nd Brigade, 1st Division, 9th Army Corps, to October, 1864.

SERVICE.—Burnside's Expedition to Hatteras Inlet January 6-February 7, 1862. Battle of Roanoke Island February 8. At Roanoke Island till March 11. Moved to New Berne March 11-13. Battle of New Berne March 14. Expedition to Elizabeth City April 17-19. Battle of Camden, South Mills, April 19. Duty at New Berne till July 6. Expedition to Pollocksville to relief of 2nd Maryland, May 17. Moved to Newport News, Va., July 6-9; thence to Fredericksburg August 2-4. March to re-

lief of Gen. Pope August 12-15. Pope's Campaign in Northern Virginia August 16-September 2. Battles of Groveton August 29. Bull Run August 30, and Chantilly September 1. Maryland Campaign September-October. Battles of South Mountain September 14, and Antietam September 16-17. At Pleasant Valley, Md., till October 27. Movement to Falmouth, Va., October 27-November 17. Warrenton, Sulphur Springs, November 15. Battle of Fredericksburg December 12-15. "Mud March" January 20-24, 1863. At Falmouth till February 19. Moved to Newport News, Va., and duty there till March 26. Moved to Covington, Ky., March 26-April 1. At Paris, Ky., April 1-5. At Mt. Sterling till July 6, and at Camp Nelson till September 12. March to Knoxville September 12-20. Operations in East Tennessee October 22-November 4. Knoxville Campaign November 4-December 23. Campbell's Station December 16. Siege of Knoxville November 17-December 4. Pursuit of Longstreet December 5-29. Re-enlisted December 29. Veterans absent on furlough January to March, 1864. Moved to Annapolis, Md., and join 9th Army Corps. Campaign from the Rapidan to the James May-June. Battles of the Wilderness May 5-7. Spottsylvania May 8-12. Ny River May 10. Spottsylvania C. H. May 12-21. Assault on the Salient May 12. North Anna River May 23-26. Ox Ford May 24. Line of the Pamunkey May 26-28. Totopotomoy May 28-31. Cold Harbor June 1-12. Bethesda Church June 1-3. Before Petersburg June 16-18. Siege of Petersburg June 16-October 21. Mine Explosion, Petersburg, July 30. Non-Veterans left front August 18 and mustered out August 30, 1864. Weldon Railroad August 18-21. Poplar Springs Church, Peeble's Farm, September 29-October 2. Veterans and Recruits transferred to 36th Massachusetts Infantry October 21, 1864.

Regiment lost during service 11 Officers and 148 Enlisted men killed and mortally wounded and 2 Officers and 89 Enlisted men by disease. Total 250.

22nd REGIMENT INFANTRY.

Organized at Lynnfield September 4 to October 6, 1861. Moved to Washington, D. C., October 8-11. Attached to Martindale's Brigade, Porter's Division, Army of the Potomac, to March, 1862. 1st Brigade, 1st Division, 3rd Army Corps, Army of the Potomac, to May, 1862. 1st Brigade, 1st Division, 5th Army Corps, to March, 1864. 2nd Brigade, 1st Division, 5th Army Corps, to October, 1864.

SERVICE.—Duty at Hall's Hill, Va. Defences of Washington till March, 1862. Advance on Manassas, Va., March 10-16. Moved to Alexandria, thence to Fortress Monroe, Va., March 16-23. Warwick Road April 5. Siege of Yorktown April 5-May 4. Hanover C. H. May 27. Operations about Hanover C. H. May 27-29. Seven days before Richmond June 25-July 1. Mechanicsville June 26. Gaines' Mill June 27. White Oak Swamp and Turkey Bridge June 30. Malvern Hill July 1. At Harrison's Landing till August 15. Retreat from the Peninsula and movement to Centreville August 15-28. Battle of Bull Run August 30. Battle of Antietam, Md., September 16-17. Shepherdstown September 19. At Sharpsburg till October 30. Movement to Falmouth, Va., October 30-November 19. Battle of Fredericksburg, Va., December 12-15. Expedition to Richards' and Ellis' Fords December 29-30. "Mud March" January 20-24, 1863. At Falmouth till April 27. Chancellorsville Campaign April 27-May 6. Battle of Chancellorsville May 1-5. Gettysburg (Pa.) Campaign June 11-July 24. Battle of Gettysburg July 2-4. At Warrenton and Beverly Ford till September 17. At Culpeper till October 11. Bristoe Campaign October 11-22. Advance to line of the Rappahannock November 7-8. Rappahannock Station November 7. Mine Run Campaign November 26-December 2. At Beverly Ford till May, 1864. Campaign from the Rapidan to the James May-June. Battles of the Wilderness May 5-7. Laurel Hill May 8. Spottsylvania May 8-12. Spottsylvania C. H. May 12-21. Assault on the Salient May 12. North Anna River May 23-26. Line of the Pamunkey May 26-28. Totopotomoy May 28-31.

Cold Harbor June 1-12. Bethesda Church June 1-3. Before Petersburg June 16-18. Siege of Petersburg June 16 to August 8. Relieved August 8 and guard duty at City Point till October 5. Mustered out October 17, 1864.

Regiment lost during service 9 Officers and 207 Enlisted men killed and mortally wounded and 1 Officer and 102 Enlisted men by disease. Total 319.

23rd REGIMENT INFANTRY.

Organized September 28, 1861. Left State for Annapolis, Md., November 11, and duty there till January 6, 1862. Attached to Foster's 1st Brigade, Burnside's Expeditionary Corps, to April, 1862. 1st Brigade, 1st Division, Dept. of North Carolina, to December, 1862. Heckman's Brigade, Dept. of North Carolina, to January, 1863. 1st Brigade, 2nd Division, 18th Army Corps, Dept. of North Carolina, to February, 1863. 1st Brigade, 1st Division, 18th Army Corps, Dept. of the South, to April, 1863. District of Beaufort, N. C., Dept. of North Carolina, to July, 1863. Defences of New Berne, N. C., Dept. of Virginia and North Carolina, to October, 1863. Heckman's Command, Newport News, Va., Dept. of Virginia and North Carolina, to January, 1864. 3rd Brigade, United States Forces, Portsmouth, Va., Dept. of Virginia and North Carolina, to April, 1864. 1st Brigade, 2nd Division, 18th Army Corps, Dept. of Virginia and North Carolina, to September, 1864. Defences of New Berne, N. C., Dept. of Virginia and North Carolina, to February, 1865. 1st Brigade, 1st Division, District of Beaufort, N. C., Dept. of North Carolina, to March, 1865. District of Beaufort, Dept. of North Carolina, to June, 1865.

SERVICE.—Burnside's Expedition to Hatteras Inlet and Roanoke Island, N. C., January 6-February 7, 1862. Battle of Roanoke Island February 8. On transports off Roanoke Island till March 11. Moved to New Berne, N. C., March 11-13. Battle of New Berne March 14. Duty at New Berne till April 11, and at Batchelor's Creek till May 4. Batchelor's Creek April 29. Provost duty at New Berne, N. C., till November 22. Expedition from New Berne November 2-12. Action at Rawle's Mill November 2 (Cos. "B," "C," "D," "G" and "I"). Demonstration on New Berne November 11. Picket and outpost duty in vicinity of New Berne till December 10. Foster's Expedition to Goldsboro December 11-20. Southwest Creek December 13-14. Kinston December 14. Whitehall December 16. Goldsboro December 17. Moved to Carolina City January 13, 1863; thence to Morehead City and Hilton Head, S. C., January 19-February 2. Camp at St. Helena Island, S. C., February 11-April 3. Expedition against Charleston April 3-10. Moved to New Berne April 12-16. March to relief of Little Washington April 17-19. Moved to Carolina City, N. C., April 25, and duty there till July 2. (Co. "D" detached at Fort Spinola June 26). Reconnoissance toward Swansboro June 27 (Co. "H"). Expedition to Trenton and Pollocksville July 4-8 (Cos. "C," "G," "H" and "K"). Action at Quaker Bridge July 6 (Cos. "A," "B," "E," "F" and "I"). Ordered to New Berne July 2, and duty in the Defences of the city till October 16. Expedition from Newport Barracks to Cedar Point July 13-16. Moved to Newport News, Va., October 16-18, and duty there till January 22, 1864. Moved to Portsmouth, Va., January 22. Duty there and at Getty's Station, on Norfolk & Suffolk Railroad, till April 26. Demonstration on Portsmouth March 1-5. Expedition to Isle of Wight County April 13-15. Action at Smithfield, Cherry Grove, April 14. Moved to Yorktown April 26. Butler's operations on south side of James River and against Petersburg and Richmond May 4-28. Port Walthal Junction, Chester Station, May 6-7. Swift's Creek, Arrowfield Church, May 9-10. Operations against Fort Darling May 12-16. Drury's Bluff May 14-16. Bermuda Hundred May 16-28. Moved to White House, thence to Cold Harbor, May 28-June 1. Battles about Cold Harbor June 1-12. Before Petersburg June 15-18. Siege of Petersburg June 15-September 4. Mine Explosion July 30 (Reserve). Duty in the trenches at Bermuda Hun-

dred, Va., August 25-September 4. Moved to New Berne, N. C., September 4-10. Picket, guard and patrol duty there till March 3, 1865. Affair at Currituck Bridge September 9 (Detachment). Non-Veterans mustered out September 28, 1864. Movements on Goldsboro March 3-14. Southwest Creek March 7. Battle of Wise's Forks March 8-10. Occupation of Kinston March 14, and duty there till May 2. Moved to New Berne May 2, and duty there till June 25. Mustered out June 25, 1865.

Regiment lost during service 4 Officers and 80 Enlisted men killed and mortally wounded and 2 Officers and 132 Enlisted men by disease. Total 218.

24th REGIMENT INFANTRY.

Organized at Readville September to December, 1861. Left State for Annapolis, Md., December 9, 1861. Attached to Foster's 1st Brigade, Burnside's Expeditionary Corps, to April, 1862. 2nd Brigade, 1st Division, Dept. of North Carolina, to January, 1863. 2nd Brigade, 4th Division, 18th Army Corps, Dept. of North Carolina, to February, 1863. 2nd Brigade, 1st Division, 18th Army Corps, Dept. of the South, to April, 1863. Stevenson's Brigade, Seabrook Island, S. C., 10th Army Corps, Dept. of the South, to July, 1863. 1st Brigade, 1st Division, Morris Island, S. C., 10th Army Corps, Dept. of the South, July, 1863. 3rd Brigade, Morris Island, S. C., 10th Army Corps, to September, 1863. St. Augustine, Fla., Dept. of the South, to February, 1864. Jacksonville, Fla., Dept. of the South, February, 1864. 1st Brigade, Hodges' Division, District of Florida, Dept. of the South, to April, 1864. 2nd Brigade, 1st Division, 10th Army Corps, Dept. of Virginia and North Carolina, to May, 1864. 3rd Brigade, 1st Division, 10th Army Corps, to December, 1864. 3rd Brigade, 1st Division, 24th Army Corps, Dept. of Virginia, to July, 1865. 2nd Brigade, 1st Division, 24th Army Corps, to August, 1865. Dept. of Virginia to January, 1866.

SERVICE.—Burnside's Expedition to Hatteras Inlet and Roanoke Island, N. C., January 6-February 7, 1862. Battles of Roanoke Island February 8. Expedition to Columbia March 8-9, and to New Berne, N. C., March 11-13. Battle of New Berne March 14. Guard, picket and outpost duty at New Berne till January 22, 1863. Reconnoissance toward Beaufort and Expedition to Washington March 20-21, 1862. Company "A" ordered to Washington May 1, and Company "C" to same point May 12. Action at Tranter's Creek June 5. Action at Washington September 6. Expedition from New Berne November 2-12. Rawle's Mills November 2. Demonstration on New Berne November 11. Foster's Expedition to Goldsboro December 11-20. Kinston December 14. Whitehall December 16. Goldsboro December 17. Moved from New Berne to Hilton Head, S. C., January 22-31, 1863; thence to St. Helena Island, S. C., February 9, and duty there till March 27. Moved to Seabrook Island, S. C., March 27-28, and duty there till July 6. Expedition to and operations on James Island, S. C., July 9-16. Battle of Secessionville July 16. Assault on Fort Wagner, Morris Island, S. C., July 18. (Cos. "C," "E," "F" and "I" remained at Seabrook Island till July 16.) Siege of Fort Wagner and Battery Gregg, Morris Island, July 18-September 7. Assault on Rifle Pits August 26. Capture of Forts Wagner and Gregg September 7. Moved to St. Augustine, Fla., September 30-October 4, and duty there till February, 1864. Reconnoissance to St. Johns River November 7-9, 1863. Skirmish near St. Augustine December 30 (Detachment). Veterans on furlough February to April, 1864. Non-Veterans moved to Jacksonville, Fla., February 18, and Provost duty there till April 24. Moved to Gloucester Point, Va., April 24-May 1. Butler operations on south side of James River and against Petersburg and Richmond May 4-28. Port Walthal Junction, Chester Station, May 7. Swift Creek May 9-10. Operations against Fort Darling May 12-16. Drewry's Bluff May 15-16. Bermuda Hundred line May 16-June 20. Port Walthal June 16-17. Siege operations against Petersburg and Richmond June 16, 1864, to April 2, 1865. At Deep Bottom June to August, 1864.

Demonstration north of James July 27-28. Strawberry Plains, Deep Bottom, August 14-18. Before Petersburg August 28-September 26. Chaffin's Farm, New Market Heights, September 28-30. Darbytown and New Market Roads October 7. Reconnoissance on Darbytown Road October 13. Non-Veterans mustered out December 4, 1864. Duty at Four-Mile Church before Richmond till December 18, and at Bermuda Hundred till April 8, 1865. Guard duty at Richmond, Va., till January, 1866. Mustered out January 20, 1866.

Regiment lost during service 7 Officers and 90 Enlisted men killed and mortally wounded and 1 Officer and 122 Enlisted men by disease. Total 220.

25th REGIMENT INFANTRY.

Organized at Worcester September 1 to October 31, 1861. Moved to Annapolis, Md., October 31-November 1, and duty there till January 7, 1862. Attached to Foster's 1st Brigade, Burnside's Expeditionary Corps, to April, 1862. 1st Brigade, 1st Division, Dept. of North Carolina, to December, 1862. Lee's Brigade, Dept. of North Carolina, to January, 1863. 2nd Brigade, 1st Division, 18th Army Corps, Dept. of North Carolina, to June, 1863. 2nd Brigade, 1st Division, Defences of New Berne, N. C., Dept. of North Carolina, to August, 1863. District of the Pamlico, N. C., Dept. of Virginia and North Carolina, to September, 1863. Defences of New Berne, N. C., Dept. of Virginia and North Carolina, to October, 1863. Heckman's Brigade, Newport News, Va., Dept. of Virginia and North Carolina, to January, 1864. Unattached, United States Forces, Portsmouth, Va., Dept. of Virginia and North Carolina, to March, 1864. 2nd Brigade, United States Forces, Portsmouth, Va., to April, 1864. 1st Brigade, 2nd Division, 18th Army Corps, Dept. of Virginia and North Carolina, to September, 1864. Defences of New Berne, N. C., District of North Carolina, Dept. of Virginia and North Carolina, to March, 1865. 3rd Brigade, 2nd Division, District of Beaufort, N. C., Dept. of North Carolina, to March, 1865. 2nd Brigade Division, District of Beaufort, N. C., Dept. of North Carolina, to April, 1865. 3rd Brigade, 1st Division, 23rd Army Corps, Dept. of North Carolina, to July, 1865.

SERVICE.—Burnside's Expedition to Hatteras Inlet and Roanoke Island, N. C., January 7-February 7, 1862. Battle of Roanoke Island February 8. Expedition to New Berne March 11-13. Battle of New Berne March 14. Provost duty at New Berne till May 9. Reconnoissance toward Trenton May 15-16. Trenton Bridge May 15. Picket and outpost duty till July. Expedition to Trenton and Pollocksville July 24-28. Guard, picket and outpost duty at New Berne till December 10. Demonstration on New Berne November 11. Foster's Expedition to Goldsboro December 10-20. Kinston December 14. Whitehall December 16. Goldsboro December 17. Duty at New Berne till October, 1863. Demonstration on Kinston March 6-8. Core Creek March 7. Skirmishes at Deep Gully, New Berne, March 13-14. Demonstration on Kinston May 20-23. Gum Swamp May 22. Expedition to Swift Creek July 17-20, and to Winton July 25-31. Moved to Newport News October 16-18 and duty there till January 22, 1864. Moved to Portsmouth January 22, 1864, and duty in the Defences of that city till April 26. Moved to Yorktown April 26. Butler's operations on south side of the James and against Petersburg and Richmond May 4-28. Occupation of City Point and Bermuda Hundred May 5. Port Walthal, Chester Station, May 6-7. Swift Creek or Arrowfield Church May 9-10. Operations against Port Darling May 12-16. Drury's Bluff May 14-16. Bermuda Hundred front May 17-28. Moved to White House, thence to Cold Harbor May 28-June 1. Battles about Cold Harbor June 1-12; before Petersburg June 15-18. Siege of Petersburg and Richmond June 16 to September 4. In trenches at Bermuda Hundred August 25-September 4. Moved to New Berne, N. C., September 4-10, and duty there till March, 1865. Non-Veterans ordered home October 5, 1864, and mustered out October 20, 1864. Demonstration from New Berne on

Kinston December 9-13, 1864. Operations against Goldsboro, N. C., March 3-21. Battle of Wise's Forks March 8-10. Occupation of Kinston March 14. Moved to Goldsboro March 22-23, and duty there till April 3. Advance on Raleigh April 9-13. Occupation of Raleigh April 14. Moved to Greensboro May 3-7, thence to Charlotte May 12-13, and duty there till July 13. Moved to Readville, Mass., July 13-21. Mustered out July 28, 1865.

Regiment lost during service 7 Officers and 154 Enlisted men killed and mortally wounded and 169 Enlisted men by disease. Total 330.

26th REGIMENT INFANTRY.

Organized at Camp Cameron, Cambridge, August 28, 1861. Moved to Camp Chase, Lowell, September 23, and to Boston November 19. Sailed on Steamer "Constitution" to Ship Island, Miss., November 21, arriving there December 3. Duty at Ship Island till April 15, 1862. Attached to Ship Island Expedition to March, 1862. 2nd Brigade, Dept. of the Gulf, to October, 1862. Defences of New Orleans, Dept. of the Gulf, to January, 1863. 2nd Brigade, 2nd Division, 19th Army Corps, Dept. of the Gulf, to July, 1863. 2nd Brigade, 3rd Division, 19th Army Corps, Dept. of the Gulf, to February, 1864. 2nd Brigade, 2nd Division, 19th Army Corps, Dept. of the Gulf, to June, 1864. 1st Brigade, 2nd Division, 19th Army Corps, Dept. of the Gulf, to July, 1864, and Army of the Shenandoah, Middle Military Division, to January, 1865. 2nd Brigade, 1st Division, 19th Army Corps, Army of the Shenandoah, to April, 1865. 2nd Brigade, 1st Provisional Division, Army of the Shenandoah, to April, 1865. 2nd Brigade, 1st Division, Dept. of Washington, 22nd Army Corps, to June, 1865. Dept. of the South to August, 1865.

SERVICE.—Occupation of Ship Island, Miss., December 3, 1861, to April 15, 1862. Skirmish at Mississippi City March 8, 1862. Movement to the passes of the Mississippi River April 15-18. Operations against Forts St. Phillip and Jackson April 18-28. Occupation of Forts St. Phillip and Jackson April 28 to July —. Moved to New Orleans, La., and duty there till June 20, 1863. Expedition to Pass Manchac and Ponchatoula September 13-15, 1862 (1 Co.). Ponchatoula September 14-15 (1 Co.). Moved to LaFourche Crossing June 20, 1863. Action at LaFourche Crossing, Thibodeaux, June 20-21. Moved to Bontee Station June 26, and to Jefferson Station June 30. Moved to New Orleans July 15, and Provost duty there till August 28. Moved to Baton Rouge August 28-29. Sabine Pass Texas Expedition, September 4-11. At Algiers till September 16. Moved to Brashear City and Berwick City September 16, and to Camp Bisland September 23. Western Louisiana "Teche" Campaign October 3-November 30. At New Iberia till January 7, 1864. Moved to Franklin January 7-9 and duty there till February 24. Moved to New Orleans February 24-25 and duty there till March 22. (Veterans on leave March 22 to May 20.) Camp at Carrollton till June 8. Moved to Morganza June 8 and duty there till July 3. Moved to New Orleans July 3-4, thence to Fortress Monroe and Bermuda Hundred, Va., July 11-21. On the Bermuda Hundred front July 22-28. Demonstration on north side of the James July 28-30. Deep Bottom July 28-29. Moved to Washington, D. C., July 30-August 1; thence to Tennallytown August 1. Sheridan's Shenandoah Valley Campaign August to December. Battle of Opequan, Winchester, September 19. Fisher's Hill September 22. Battle of Cedar Creek October 19. Non-Veterans left front October 19 and mustered out November 7, 1864. Provost duty at Headquarters of Middle Military Division and Army of the Shenandoah at Winchester, till May 1, 1865. Moved to Washington, D. C., May 1-2, and camp there till June 3. Moved to Savannah, Ga., June 3-7, and Provost duty there till August 2. Mustered out August 26, 1865. Moved to Boston, Mass., September 12-18, and there discharged from service.

Regiment lost during service 3 Officers and 61 Enlisted men killed and mortally wounded and 3 Officers and 182 Enlisted men by disease. Total 249.

27th REGIMENT INFANTRY.

Organized at Springfield and mustered in September 20, 1861. Moved to Annapolis, Md., November 2-5, and duty there till January 6, 1862. Attached to Foster's 1st Brigade, Burnside's Expeditionary Corps, to April, 1862. 2nd Brigade, 1st Division, Dept. of North Carolina, to July, 1862. 2nd Brigade, 1st Division, 9th Army Corps, Army of the Potomac, to August, 1862. 1st Brigade, 1st Division, Dept. of North Carolina, to November, 1862. 3rd Brigade, 1st Division, Dept. of North Carolina, to December, 1862. Lee's Brigade, Dept. of North Carolina, to January, 1863. 2nd Brigade, 1st Division, 18th Army Corps, Dept. of North Carolina, to June, 1863. 2nd Brigade, 1st Division, Defences of New Berne, N. C., to October, 1863. Heckman's Brigade, Newport News, Va., Dept. of Virginia and North Carolina, to January, 1864. Unattached, United States Forces, Portsmouth, Va., Dept. of Virginia and North Carolina, to March, 1864. 2nd Brigade, United States Forces, Portsmouth, Va., to April, 1864. 1st Brigade, 2nd Division, 18th Army Corps, Dept. of Virginia and North Carolina, to September, 1864. District of Beaufort, N. C., Dept. of Virginia and North Carolina, to January, 1865. Sub-District, New Berne, N. C., Dept. of North Carolina, to March, 1865. 2nd Brigade, 2nd Division, District of Beaufort, Dept. of North Carolina, to March, 1865. District of New Berne, N. C., Dept. of North Carolina, to June, 1865.

SERVICE.—Burnside's Expedition to Hatteras Inlet and Roanoke Island, N. C., January 7-February 7, 1862. Battle of Roanoke Island February 8. Moved to New Berne March 11-13. Battle of New Berne March 14. Duty at New Berne till May; at Batchelor's Creek till June 1, and at New Berne till September 22. Expedition to Trenton and Pollocksville July 24-28. Expedition on Neuse River Road July 28 (Cos. "D," "G" and "H"). Companies "A," "C" and "I" at Washington, N. C., and five Companies at Newport Barracks September 9 to October 30. Expedition from New Berne November 2-12. Kinston Road November 11. Foster's Expedition to Goldsboro December 11-20. Kinston December 14. Whitehall December 16. Goldsboro December 17. Moved to Washington, N. C., January 4-5, 1863, and duty there till April 24. Near Washington February 13. (Cos. "G" and "H" detached for duty at Plymouth January 27 to May 8, then rejoined Regiment at New Berne.) Demonstration on Plymouth March 10-13. Siege of Little Washington March 30-April 20. Rodman's Point April 4-5 (2 Cos.). Moved to New Berne April 24. Expedition toward Kinston April 27-May 1. Dover Road and Wise's Cross Roads April 28. Demonstration on Kinston May 20-23. Gum Swamp May 22. Provost duty at New Berne June 5 to October 1. Expedition to Trenton July 4-8. Quaker Bridge July 6. Expedition to Swift Creek July 17-20, and to Winton July 25-30. Moved to Newport News, Va., October 16-18, thence to Norfolk November 18, and Provost duty there till March 22, 1864. Companies "A," "D" and "K" at Portsmouth, and "F" at Norfolk till April 15. Demonstration against Portsmouth March 4-5. Expedition to Isle of Wight County April 13-15. Smithfield, Cherry Grove, April 14. Camp near Julian Creek till April 26. Moved to Yorktown April 26. Butler's operations on south side of the James and against Petersburg and Richmond May 4-28. Port Walthal Junction, Chester Station, May 6-7. Swift Creek or Arrowfield Church May 9-10. Operations against Fort Darling May 12-16. Drewry's Bluff May 14-16. On Bermuda Hundred front May 17-28. Moved to White House, thence to Cold Harbor May 28-June 1. Battles about Cold Harbor June 1-12. Before Petersburg June 15-18. Siege of Petersburg June 15-August 24. On Bermuda front August 24 to September 17. Moved to Carolina City, N. C., September 17-21, and duty there till November 28. Moved to Beaufort,

N. C., November 28; thence to New Berne December 4, and to Plymouth December 7 and duty there till January, 1865. Moved to New Berne January 8-11 and duty there till March 3. Moved to Core Creek March 4. Movements on Kinston March 4-12. Southwest Creek March 7. Wise's Forks March 8-10. Ordered to New Berne March 12 and duty there till June —. Mustered out June 26, 1865. Old members mustered out September 27, 1864.

Regiment lost during service 9 Officers and 128 Enlisted men killed and mortally wounded and 3 Officers and 261 Enlisted men by disease. Total 401.

28th REGIMENT INFANTRY.

Organized at Cambridge and Boston December 12, 1861. Left State for New York January 11, 1862. Duty at Fort Columbus, New York Harbor, till February 14. Sailed on Steamer "Erickson" for Hilton Head, S. C., February 14, arriving there February 23. Attached to Dept. of the South to April, 1862. 1st Brigade, 2nd Division, Dept. of the South, to July, 1862. 1st Brigade, 1st Division, 9th Army Corps, Army of the Potomac, to December, 1862. 2nd Brigade, 1st Division, 2nd Army Corps, Army of the Potomac, to June, 1864. 1st Brigade, 1st Division, 2nd Army Corps, to November, 1864. 2nd Brigade, 1st Division, 2nd Army Corps, to June, 1865.

SERVICE.—Moved to Dafuskie Island, S. C., April 7, 1862, and duty there till May —. (Cos. "A" and "K" detached at Jones and Bird Islands April 18-May 6. Cos. "A," "C," "D," "F" and "K" moved to Tybee Island May 12 and duty there till May 28. Cos. "B," "E," "G," "H" and "I" moved to Dafuskie Island and to Hilton Head May 28.) Operations on James Island, S. C., June 1-28. Skirmishes on James Island June 3-4. Battle of Secessionville June 16. Evacuation of James Island June 28-July 7. Moved from Hilton Head to Newport News, Va., July 14-18; thence to Aquia Creek and Fredericksburg August 3-6. Operations in support of Pope August 6-16. Pope's Campaign in Northern Virginia August 16-September 2. Battles of Groveton August 29. Bull Run August 30. Chantilly September 1. Maryland Campaign September-October. Battles of South Mountain September 14. Antietam September 16-17. March to Pleasant Valley September 19-October 2 and duty there till October 25. Movement to Falmouth, Va., October 25-November 19. Battle of Fredericksburg December 12-15. "Mud March" January 20-24, 1863. At Falmouth till April 27. Chancellorsville Campaign April 27-May 6. Battle of Chancellorsville May 1-5. Gettysburg (Pa.) Campaign June 11-July 24. Battle of Gettysburg July 2-4. Advance from the Rappahannock to the Rapidan September 13-17. Bristoe Campaign October 9-22. Auburn and Bristoe October 14. Advance to line of the Rappahannock November 7-8. Mine Run Campaign November 26-December 2. At Stevensburg till May, 1864. Demonstration on the Rapidan February 6-7. Campaign from the Rapidan to the James May-June. Battles of the Wilderness May 5-7; Spottsylvania May 8-12; Po River May 10; Spottsylvania Court House May 12-21. Assault on the Salient May 12. North Anna River May 23-26. On line of the Pamunkey May 26-28. Totopotomoy May 28-31. Cold Harbor June 1-12. Before Petersburg June 16-19. Siege of Petersburg June 16, 1864, to April 2, 1865. Jerusalem Plank Road June 22-23, 1864. Demonstration on north side of the James July 27-29. Deep Bottom July 27-28. Strawberry Plains, Deep Bottom, August 14-18. Ream's Station August 25. Boydton Road, Hatcher's Run, October 27-28. Dabney's Mills, Hatcher's Run, February 5-7, 1865. Watkin's House March 25. Appomattox Campaign March 28-April 9. Hatcher's Run or Boydton Road March 31. White Oak Road March 31. Sutherland Station and fall of Petersburg April 2. Sailor's Creek April 6. High Bridge and Farmville April 7. Appomattox Court House April 9. Surrender of Lee and his army. At Burkesville till May 2. March to Washington, D. C., May 2-15. Grand Review May 23. Duty at Washington till June 25. Mustered out June 29, 1865.

Regiment lost during service 15 Officers and 235 Enlisted men killed and mortally wounded and 1 Officer and 136 Enlisted men by disease. Total 387.

29th REGIMENT INFANTRY.

Organized at Newport News, Va., December, 1861, from 1st Battalion Massachusetts Infantry (7 Cos.) and 3 new Companies ("F," "G" and "H") organized December 13-17, 1861, which joined Regiment at Newport News, Va., January 17, 1862. Attached to Newport News, Va., Dept. of Virginia, to May, 1862. 1st Brigade, 1st Division, Dept. of Virginia, to June, 1862. 2nd Brigade, 1st Division, 2nd Army Corps, Army of the Potomac, to December, 1862. 2nd Brigade, 1st Division, 9th Army Corps, Army of the Potomac, to April, 1863. 2nd Brigade, 1st Division, 9th Army Corps, Dept. of the Ohio, to June, 1863. 3rd Brigade, 2nd Division, 9th Army Corps, Army of the Tennessee, to August, 1863. 2nd Brigade, 1st Division, 9th Army Corps, Dept. of the Ohio, to March, 1863. 3rd Brigade, 1st Division, 5th Army Corps, Army of the Potomac, May to June, 1864. 2nd Brigade, 1st Division, 9th Army Corps, Army of the Potomac, to July, 1864. 1st Brigade, 1st Division, 9th Army Corps, to September, 1864. 3rd Brigade, 1st Division, 9th Army Corps, to July, 1865.

SERVICE.—Duty at Newport News, Va., till May, 1862. Sinking of the "Cumberland" and "Congress" by the Merrimac March 8, 1862. Battle between "Monitor" and "Merrimac" March 9. Occupation of Norfolk and Portsmouth May 10. Duty there till June 2. Moved to Suffolk, thence to Portsmouth and White House Landing June 6-7. March to Fair Oaks June 8. Near Seven Pines June 15. Fair Oaks June 24. Seven days before Richmond June 25-July 1. Gaines' Mill June 27. Peach Orchard and Savage Station June 29. White Oak Swamp and Glendale June 30. Malvern Hill July 1. At Harrison's Landing till August 16. Movement to Fortress Monroe, thence to Alexandria and Centreville August 16-30. Cover retreat of Pope's army from Bull Run August 31-September 1. Battle of Antietam, Md., September 16-17. At Harper's Ferry, W. Va., till October 29. Advance up Loudoun Valley and movement to Falmouth October 29-November 19. Battle of Fredericksburg December 12-15. "Mud March" January 20-24, 1863. Moved to Newport News February 12-14, thence moved to Kentucky March 21-26. Duty at Paris, Ky., till April 26. Moved to Nicholasville, Lancaster and Stanford April 27-29. March to Somerset May 6-8. Movement through Kentucky to Cairo, Ill., June 4-10; thence to Vicksburg, Miss., June 14-17. Siege of Vicksburg June 17-July 4. Advance on Jackson, Miss., July 4-10. Siege of Jackson July 10-17. At Milldale till August 12. Moved to Covington, Ky., August 12-23. Burnside's Campaign in East Tennessee August to October. Action at Blue Springs October 10. At Lenois till November 14. Knoxville Campaign November-December. Campbell's Station November 16. Siege of Knoxville November 17-December 4. Pursuit of Longstreet December 7-28. Operations in East Tennessee till March, 1864. Veterans march to Nicholasville, Ky., March 21-31; thence moved to Covington, Ky.; Cincinnati, Ohio, and to Boston, Mass., March 31-April 9. On furlough till May 16. Moved to Washington, D. C.; thence to Belle Plain, Va., March 16-20. Joined Army of the Potomac May 28. Non-Veterans attached to 36th Massachusetts Infantry February 1 to May 16. Rapidan Campaign May-June. Totopotomoy May 28-31. Cold Harbor June 1-12. Bethesda Church June 1-3. Before Petersburg June 15-19. Siege of Petersburg June 16, 1864, to April 2, 1865. Mine Explosion, Petersburg, July 30, 1864. Weldon Railroad August 18-21. Poplar Springs Church, Peeble's Farm, September 29-October 2. Reconnoissance on Vaughan and Squirrel Level Roads October 8. Boydton Plank Road, Hatcher's Run, October 27-28. Fort Stedman March 25, 1865. Assault on and fall of Petersburg April 2. Occupation of Petersburg April 3. Moved to Washington, D. C., April 21-28. Grand Review May 23. Provost duty at Washington and Alexandria till July. Mustered out July 29, 1865.

Regiment lost during service 4 Officers and 53 Enlisted men killed and mortally wounded and 4 Officers and 95 Enlisted men by disease. Total 156.

30th REGIMENT INFANTRY.

Organized as "Eastern Bay State Regiment" at Camp Chase, Lowell, by Gen. B. F. Butler, December 31, 1861. Moved to Boston January 2, 1862. Mustered into United States service as 30th Massachusetts Infantry January 4, 1862. Sailed from Boston on steamer "Constitution" for Fortress Monroe, Va., January 13, arriving January 16; thence sailed for Ship Island, Miss., February 6, arriving there February 12, and duty there till April 15. (Co. "K" joined March 9.) Attached to 3rd Brigade, Dept. of the Gulf, to October, 1862. Defences of New Orleans to January, 1863. 3rd Brigade, 1st Division, 19th Army Corps, Dept. of the Gulf, to August, 1863. 1st Brigade, 1st Division, 19th Army Corps, Dept. of the Gulf, to July, 1864, and Army of the Shenandoah, Middle Military Division, to March, 1865. 1st Brigade, 1st Provisional Division, Army of the Shenandoah, to April, 1865. Dept. of Washington to June, 1865. Dept. of the South to December, 1865.

SERVICE.—Operations against Forts St. Phillip and Jackson, Mississippi River, April 15-28, 1862. Occupation of Fort St. Phillip April 28. Moved to New Orleans April 29-30. Occupation of New Orleans May 1. Expedition to New Orleans & Jackson Railroad May 9-10. Moved to Baton Rouge May 30-31. Expedition from Baton Rouge June 7-9. Williams' Expedition to Vicksburg, Miss., and operations in that vicinity June 18-July 23. Ellis Cliff June 22. Hamilton Plantation, near Grand Gulf, June 24. Moved to Baton Rouge July 23-26, and duty there till August 21. Battle of Baton Rouge August 5. Moved to Carrollton August 21-22, and duty there till November 4. Garrison duty at New Orleans till January 13, 1863. Moved to Baton Rouge January 13-14. Expedition to Port Hudson March 7-27. Operations against Port Hudson May 12-24. Monett's Plantation and on Bayou Sara Road May 18-19. Plain's Store May 24. Siege of Port Hudson May 24-July 9. Assaults on Port Hudson May 27 and June 14. Surrender of Port Hudson July 9. Cox's Plantation, Donaldsonville, July 12-13. Camp at Baton Rouge August 1-September 2. Sabine Pass Expedition September 4-11. Moved from Algiers to Brashear City September 16, thence to Berwick and to Camp Bisland September 26. Western Louisiana ("Teche") Campaign October 3-November 30. At New Iberia till January 7, 1864, and at Franklin till February 18. Veterans on leave February 18-May 3. Moved to New Orleans May 3-16, and to Morganza June 13. Moved to New Orleans, thence to Fortress Monroe, Va., and Washington, D. C., July 2-13. Snicker's Gap Expedition July 14-23. Sheridan's Shenandoah Valley Campaign August to December. Battle of Opequan, Winchester, September 19. Fisher's Hill September 22. Mt. Jackson September 23-24. Battle of Cedar Creek October 19. Duty at Winchester, Kernstown and Stephenson's Depot till April 1, 1865. Moved to Washington, D. C., April 21-22, and duty there till June 1. Grand Review May 23-24. Moved to Savannah, Ga., June 2-6, thence to Georgetown, S. C., June 13, and to Florence June 27. To Sumpter July 9. Duty in 3rd Sub-District Eastern South Carolina till December. Mustered out December 1, 1865.

Regiment lost during service 4 Officers and 57 Enlisted men killed and mortally wounded and 2 Officers and 341 Enlisted men by disease. Total 404.

31st REGIMENT INFANTRY.

"Western Bay State Regiment," organized at Pittsfield, November 20, 1861, to February 20, 1862. Duty at Camp Chase, Lowell, till February, 1862. Moved to Boston February 19, thence sailed on steamer "Mississippi" for Ship Island, Miss. Detained at Hilton Head, S. C., repairing vessel, March 1-13. Arrived at Ship Island March 23, and duty there till April 18. Attached to 2nd Brigade, Dept. of the Gulf, to October, 1862. Sherman's Division, Dept. of the Gulf, to January, 1863. 3rd

Brigade, 3rd Division, 19th Army Corps, Dept. of the Gulf, to July, 1862. 2nd Brigade, 1st Division, 19th Army Corps, Dept. of the Gulf, to December, 1863. 4th Brigade, Cavalry Division, Dept. of the Gulf, to June, 1864. Defences of New Orleans to September, 1864. 1st Brigade, Cavalry Division, Dept. of the Gulf, to October, 1864. Defences of New Orleans to March, 1865. 1st Brigade, Lucas' Cavalry Division, Steele's Command, Military Division West Mississippi, to April, 1865. District of Mobile, Ala., to September, 1865.

SERVICE.—Operations against Forts St. Phillip and Jackson, Mississippi River, April 18-28, 1862. Moved to New Orleans April 29-30. Occupation of New Orleans May 1. (The first Union Regiment to enter city.) Provost duty at New Orleans till August. Garrison duty at Forts St. Phillip and Jackson till January, 1863. (3 Cos. at Fort Pike till September, 1863. Rejoined Regiment September 9.) Skirmish at Bayou Bontecou November 21, 1862, and Deserted Station December 10. Moved to Carrollton January, 1863, and duty there till March 6. Moved to Baton Rouge March 6-7. Expedition to Port Hudson March 7-27. Moved to Algiers April 1, thence to Berwick City April 9. Operations in Western Louisiana April 9-May 14. Teche Campaign April 11-20. Fort Bisland April 12-13. March from Opelousas to Alexandria and Simsport May 5-18. Moved to Bayou Sara, thence to Port Hudson May 22-25. Siege of Port Hudson May 25-July 9. Skirmish at Thompson's Creek May 25 (Detachment). Assaults on Port Hudson May 27 and June 14. Expedition to Clinton June 3-8. Surrender of Port Hudson July 9. Moved to Baton Rouge July 11, thence to Donaldsonville July 15-August 1. Moved to Baton Rouge September 1 and duty there till December 9. Moved to New Orleans December 9 and there converted into a Cavalry Regiment known as 6th Massachusetts Cavalry. Bonfonca November 26. Duty at Carrollton till February 29, 1864. March to Berwick Bay and Brashear City February 29-March 9. Red River Campaign March 10-May 22. Advance to Alexandria March 11-26. Bayou Rapides March 20. Monett's Ferry and Cloutiersville March 29-30. Natchitoches March 31. Crump's Hill, Piney Woods, April 2. Wilson's Farm April 7. Bayou de Paul, Carroll's Mill and Sabine Cross Roads April 8. Pleasant Hill April 9. Monett's Bluff, Cane River Crossing, April 23. Hudnot's Plantation May 1. Near Alexandria May 2-9. Retreat to Morganza May 13-20. Near Alexandria May 14. Mansura May 16. Near Moreauville May 17. Yellow Bayou May 18. At Morganza till July 3. Expedition to the Atchafalaya May 30-June 6. Expedition to Tunica Bend June 19-21. Moved to New Orleans July 3. Veterans absent on furlough July 21 to September 19. Non-Veterans guard prisoners at New Orleans till September —. Duty in Defences of New Orleans till March, 1865. Non-Veterans mustered out November 19, 1864. Ordered to Donaldsonville November 27, and operating against guerrillas till February, 1865. Operations near Hermitage Plantation December 14, 1864, to January 5, 1865. Expedition from Plaquemine to the Park January 26 to February 4 (Detachment). Skirmish at the Park February 4 (Detachment). Consolidated to a Battalion of five Companies. Ordered to Carrollton February 9, 1865; thence moved to Barrancas, Fla., March 6-9. March to Fort Blakely, Mobile Bay, March 20-April 1. Siege of Fort Blakely April 1-9. Occupation of Mobile April 12 and duty there till September. Mustered out September 9, 1865. Moved to Boston September 11-24, and discharged September 30, 1865.

Regiment lost during service 52 Enlisted men killed and mortally wounded and 3 Officers and 150 Enlisted men by disease. Total 205.

32nd REGIMENT INFANTRY.

Organized as a Battalion of 6 Companies for garrison duty at Fort Warren, Boston Harbor, November 25, 1861. Duty at Fort Warren till May, 1862. Moved to Washington, D. C., May 26-28. Attached to Military

district of Washington to July, 1862. 1st Brigade, 1st Division, 5th Army Corps, Army of the Potomac, to September, 1862. 2nd Brigade, 1st Division, 5th Army Corps, to October, 1864.

SERVICE.—At Capital Hill, Defences of Washington, till June 24, 1862. Moved to Harrison's Landing, Va., June 25-July 3. (1 Co. join at Harrison's Landing July 23, and 3 Cos. at Minor's Hill, Va., September 4, 1862.) At Harrison's Landing till August 15. Movement to Fortress Monroe, thence to Centreville August 15-28. Pope's Campaign in Northern Virginia August 28-September 2. Battle of Bull Run August 30. Battle of Antietam, Md., September 16-17. Blackford's Ford September 19. At Sharpsburg, Md., till October 30. Reconnoissance to Smithfield, W. Va., October 16-17. Movement to Falmouth October 30-November 19. Battle of Fredericksburg, Va., December 12-15. Expedition to Richards' and Ellis Fords December 29-30. "Mud March" January 20-24, 1863. At Falmouth till April 27. Chancellorsville Campaign April 27-May 6. Battle of Chancellorsville May 1-5. Gettysburg (Pa.) Campaign June 11-July 24. Battle of Gettysburg July 1-4. Pursuit of Lee July 5-24. At Warrenton and Beverly Ford till September 17. At Culpeper till October 11. Bristoe Campaign October 11-22. Advance to line of the Rappahannock November 7-8. Mine Run Campaign November 26-December 2. At Bealeton, Va., till May, 1864. Campaign from the Rapidan to the James May-June. Battles of the Wilderness May 5-7; Laurel Hill May 8; Spottsylvania May 8-12; Spottsylvania Court House May 12-21. Assault on the Salient May 12. North Anna River May 23-26. Jericho Mills May 23. On line of the Pamunkey May 26-28. Totopotomoy May 28-31. Cold Harbor June 1-12. Bethesda Church June 1-3. Before Petersburg June 16-18. Siege of Petersburg June 16, 1864, to April 2, 1865. Mine Explosion, Petersburg, July 30, 1864 (Reserve). Six-Mile House, Weldon Railroad, August 18-21. Poplar Springs Church September 29-October 2. Boydton Plank Road, Hatcher's Run, October 27-28. Expedition to Weldon Railroad December 7-12. Dabney's Mills, Hatcher's Run, February 5-7, 1865. Appomattox Campaign March 28-April 9. Lewis Farm, near Gravelly Run, March 29. White Oak Road March 31. Five Forks April 1. Appomattox Court House April 9. Surrender of Lee and his army. March to Washington, D. C., May 1-12. Grand Review May 23. Duty at Washington till June 29. Mustered out June 29, and discharged July 11, 1865.

Regiment lost during service 5 Officers and 139 Enlisted men killed and mortally wounded and 2 Officers and 143 Enlisted men by disease. Total 289.

33rd REGIMENT INFANTRY.

Organized at Springfield August 6, 1862. Moved to Washington, D. C., August 14-17. Attached to Military District of Washington to October, 1862. 2nd Brigade, 2nd Division, 11th Army Corps, Army of the Potomac, to October, 1863, and Army of the Cumberland to April, 1864. 3rd Brigade, 3rd Division, 20th Army Corps, Army of the Cumberland, to June, 1865.

SERVICE.—Duty in the Defences of Washington, D. C., and Provost at Alexandria, Va., till October 10, 1862. Moved to Fairfax Station October 10, thence to Fairfax Court House and duty there till November 1. Moved to Warrenton, thence to Germantown November 1-20. March to Fredericksburg December 10-15. Camp at Falmouth till January 20, 1863. "Mud March" January 20-24, 1863. At Falmouth till April 27. Chancellorsville Campaign April 27-May 6. Battle of Chancellorsville May 1-5. Brandy Station and Beverly Ford June 9. Gettysburg (Pa.) Campaign June 11-July 24. Battle of Gettysburg July 1-4. At Bristoe Station August 3-September 24. Movement to Bridgeport, Ala., September 24-October 3. March along line of Nashville & Chattanooga Railroad to Lookout Valley, Tenn., October 25-28. Battle of Wauhatchie, Tenn., October 28-29. Chattanooga-Ringgold Campaign November 23-27. Tunnel Hill November 24-25. Mission

Ridge November 25. March to relief of Knoxville November 28-December 17. Duty in Lookout Valley till May, 1864. Atlanta (Ga.) Campaign May to September. Demonstration on Rocky Faced Ridge May 5-11. Buzzard's Roost Gap May 8-9. Battle of Resaca May 14-15. Cassville May 19. Advance on Dallas May 22-25. Battle of New Hope Church May 25. Operations on line of Pumpkin Vine Creek and battles about Dallas, New Hope Church and Allatoona Hills May 25-June 5. Operations about Marietta and against Kenesaw Mountain June 10-July 2. Pine Hill June 11-14. Lost Mountain June 15-17. Gilgal or Golgotha Church June 15. Muddy Creek June 17. Noyes Creek June 19. Kolb's Farm June 22. Assault on Kenesaw June 27. Ruff's Station or Smyrna Camp Ground July 4. Chattahoochie River July 5-17. Duty as Division Train Guard July 17 to August 27. Battle of Peachtree Creek July 19-20. Siege of Atlanta July 22-August 25. Operations at Chattahoochie River Bridge August 26-September 2. Occupation of Atlanta September 2-November 15. March to the sea November 15-December 10. Siege of Savannah December 10-21. Campaign of the Carolinas January to April, 1865. Lawtonville, S. C., February 2. Skirmish, Raleigh Road, near Fayetteville, N. C., March 14. Averysboro March 16. Battle of Bentonville March 19-21. Occupation of Goldsboro March 24. Advance on Raleigh April 10-13. Occupation of Raleigh April 14. Bennett's House April 26. Surrender of Johnston and his army. March to Washington, D. C., via Richmond, Va., April 29-May 20. Grand Review May 24. Duty at Washington till June 11. Mustered out June 11 and discharged from service July 2, 1865.

Regiment lost during service 7 Officers and 104 Enlisted men killed and mortally wounded and 77 Enlisted men by disease. Total 188.

34th REGIMENT INFANTRY.

Organized at Worcester August 1, 1862. Moved to Washington, D. C., August 15-17. Attached to Military District of Washington and Alexandria to February; 1863. Tyler's Brigade, District of Alexandria, 22nd Army Corps, Dept. of Washington, to April, 1863. 2nd Brigade, DeRussy's Division, Defences South of the Potomac, 22nd Army Corps, to June, 1863. Martindale's Command, Garrison of Washington, 22nd Army Corps, to July, 1863. 1st Brigade, Maryland Heights Division, Dept. of West Virginia, to December, 1863. 1st Brigade, 1st Division, Dept. of West Virginia, to January, 1864. Unattached, 1st Division, West Virginia, to April, 1864. 2nd Brigade, 1st Infantry Division, West Virginia, to June, 1864. 1st Brigade, 1st Infantry Division, West Virginia, to December, 1864. 1st Brigade, Independent Division, 24th Army Corps, Army of the James, to June, 1865.

SERVICE.—At Arlington Heights, Va., till August 22, 1862. Moved to Alexandria, Va., August 22, and duty on line of Orange & Alexandria Railroad till September 10. At Fort Lyon, Defences of Washington, D. C., September 15, 1862, to June 2, 1863. Provost and guard duty in Washington till July 9. Moved to Maryland Heights July 9. Occupation of Harper's Ferry, W. Va., July 14. Duty at Harper's Ferry and Bolivar till December 10. Action at Berryville October 18. Raid to Harrisonburg December 10-24. At Harper's Ferry till February 1, 1864. Operations in Hampshire and Hardy Counties, W. Va., January 27-February 7. Moved to Cumberland, Md., February 15. Return to Harper's Ferry, thence moved to Monocacy, Md., March 5, to Martinsburg, W. Va., March 7 and to Harper's Ferry April 2. Moved to Martinsburg, W. Va., April 17. Sigel's Expedition from Martinsburg to New Market April 13-May 16. Rude's Hill May 14. New Market May 14-15. Advance to Staunton May 24-June 5. Piedmont, Mount Crawford, June 5. Occupation of Staunton June 6. Hunter's Raid on Lynchburg June —. Lynchburg June 17-18. Retreat to the Gaul June 18-29. Moved to the Shenandoah Valley July 5-17. Snicker's Ferry July 17-18. Kernstown or Winchester July 23-24. Martinsburg July 25. Sheridan's Shenandoah Valley Campaign August to December. Berryville September 3. Battle of Opequan, Winchester, September 19. Fisher's Hill September 22. Cedar Creek October 13. Battle of Cedar Creek October 19. Duty at Kernstown till December. Moved to Washington, D. C., thence to Bermuda Hundred, Va., December 19-23. Siege operations against Richmond and Petersburg December 25, 1864, to April 2, 1865. In trenches north of the James before Richmond till March, 1865. Appomattox Campaign March 28-April 9. Assault on and fall of Petersburg April 2. Pursuit of Lee April 3-9. Rice's Station April 6. Appomattox Court House April 9. Surrender of Lee and his army. March to Lynchburg April 12-15, thence to Farmville and Burkesville Junction April 15-19, and to Richmond April 22-25. Duty there till June. Mustered out June 16, 1865.

Regiment lost during service 7 Officers and 128 Enlisted men killed and mortally wounded and 2 Officers and 132 Enlisted men by disease. Total 269.

35th REGIMENT INFANTRY.

Organized at Worcester August 1, 1862. Left State for Washington, D. C., August 22. Attached to 2nd Brigade, 2nd Division, 9th Army Corps, Army of the Potomac, to April, 1863; Dept. of the Ohio to June, 1863; Army of the Tennessee to August, 1863, and Dept. of the Ohio to April, 1864. 1st Brigade, 1st Division, 9th Army Corps, Army of the Potomac, to May, 1864. Acting Engineers, 1st Division, 9th Army Corps, to July, 1864. 1st Brigade, 1st Division, 9th Army Corps, to September, 1864. 1st Brigade, 2nd Division, 9th Army Corps, to June, 1865.

SERVICE.—March into Maryland September 6-12, 1862. Battles of South Mountain, Md., September 14, and Antietam September 16-17. Duty at Pleasant Valley till October 27. Movement to Falmouth, Va., October 27-November 19. Warrenton, Sulphur Springs, November 15. Battle of Fredericksburg December 12-15. "Mud March" January 20-24, 1863. At Falmouth till February 19. Moved to Newport News, Va., February 19, thence to Covington, Ky., March 26-30. Moved to Paris April 1, and to Mt. Sterling April 3. To Lancaster May 6-7, thence to Crab Orchard May 23, and to Stanford May 25. Movement to Vicksburg, Miss., June 3-14. Siege of Vicksburg June 14-July 4. Advance on Jackson, Miss., July 5-10. Siege of Jackson July 10-17. At Milldale till August 6. Moved to Cincinnati, Ohio, August 6-14. At Covington, Ky., till August 18. March to Nicholasville August 18-25, and to Crab Orchard September 9-11. March over Cumberland Mountains to Knoxville, Tenn., thence to Lenoir Station October 2-29. Knoxville Campaign November 4-December 23. At Lenoir Station till November 14. Campbell's Station November 16. Siege of Knoxville November 17-December 4. Pursuit of Longstreet December 5-19. Operations in East Tennessee till March 20, 1864. Movement to Annapolis, Md., March 20-April 7. Rapidan Campaign May-June. Battles of the Wilderness May 5-7; Spottsylvania May 8-12; Ny River May 10; Spottsylvania C. H. May 12-21. Assault on the Salient May 12. North Anna River May 23-26. On line of the Pamunkey May 26-28. Totopotomoy May 28-31. Cold Harbor June 1-12. Bethesda Church June 1-3. Before Petersburg June 16-18. Siege of Petersburg June 16, 1864, to April 2, 1865. Mine Explosion, Petersburg, July 30, 1864. Weldon Railroad August 18-21. Poplar Springs Church September 29-October 2. Boydton Plank Road, Hatcher's Run, October 27-28. Fort Stedman March 25, 1865. Appomattox Campaign March 28-April 9. Assault on and fall of Petersburg April 2. Occupation of Petersburg April 3. March to Farmville April 4-10. Moved to City Point, thence to Alexandria April 20-28. Grand Review May 23. Mustered out June 9, and discharged from service June 27, 1865.

Regiment lost during service 10 Officers and 138 Enlisted men killed and mortally wounded and 1 Officer and 100 Enlisted men by disease. Total 249.

36th REGIMENT INFANTRY.

Organized at Worcester and mustered in August 30, 1862. Left State for Washington, D. C., September 2, thence moved to Leesburg, Md., September 9, and to Pleasant Valley. Attached to 3rd Brigade, 1st Division, 9th Army Corps, Army Potomac, to April, 1863, and Dept. Ohio, to June, 1863. 1st Brigade, 1st Division, 9th Army Corps, Dept. Ohio, and Army Tennessee, to August, 1863, and Dept. Ohio, to April, 1864. 1st Brigade, 2nd Division, 9th Army Corps, Army Potomac, to June, 1865.

SERVICE.—Duty at Pleasant Valley, Md., till October 26. March to Lovettsville, Va., October 26-29, and to Warrenton October 29-November 19. Battle of Fredericksburg, Va., December 12-15. "Mud March" January 20-24, 1863. Moved to Newport News, Va., February 10, thence to Lexington, Ky., March 19-23. Duty at Camp Dick Robinson, Ky., April 9-30, and at Middleburg till May 23. March to Columbia May 23-26. Expedition toward Cumberland River after Morgan May 27-30. Jamestown June 2. Moved to Vicksburg, Miss., June 7-14. Siege of Vicksburg, Miss., June 14-July 4. Advance on Jackson, Miss., July 5-10. Siege of Jackson July 10-17. At Milldale till August 5. Moved to Covington, Ky., August 5-12, and to Crab Orchard August 17-18. March across Cumberland Mountains to East Tennessee September 10-22. Near Knoxville September 27-October 3. Action at Blue Springs October 10. At Lenoir October 29-November 14. Knoxville Campaign November-December. Lenoir Station November 14-15. Campbell's Station November 17. Siege of Knoxville November 17-December 4. Pursuit of Longstreet December 5-19. Operations in East Tennessee till March 21, 1864. Strawberry Plains January 21-22. Moved from Knoxville, Tenn., to Covington, Ky., thence to Annapolis, Md., March 21-April 6. Rapidan Campaign May-June. Battles of the Wilderness May 5-7; Spottsylvania May 8-12; Spottsylvania C. H. May 12-21. Assault on the Salient May 12. Stannard's Mills May 21. North Anna River May 23-26. On line of the Pamunkey May 26-28. Totopotomoy May 28-31. Cold Harbor June 1-12. Bethesda Church June 1-3. Before Petersburg June 16-18. Siege of Petersburg June 16, 1864, to April 2, 1865. Mine Explosion, Petersburg, July 30, 1864. Weldon Railroad August 18-21. Poplar Springs Church September 29-October 2. Boydton Plank Road, Hatcher's Run, October 27-28. At Fort Rice till April, 1865. Appomattox Campaign March 28-April 9. Assault on and fall of Petersburg April 2. March to Farmville April 3-9. Moved to Petersburg and City Point, thence to Alexandria April 20-28. Grand Review May 23. Mustered out June 8, 1865, and discharged from service June 21, 1865.

Regiment lost during service 6 Officers and 105 Enlisted men killed and mortally wounded and 3 Officers and 160 Enlisted men by disease. Total 274.

37th REGIMENT INFANTRY.

Organized at Pittsfield August 30, 1862. Left State for Washington, D. C., September 7. Attached to 2nd Brigade, 3rd Division, 6th Army Corps, Army of the Potomac, to March, 1864. 4th Brigade, 2nd Division, 6th Army Corps, Army of the Potomac, to July, 1864. 3rd Brigade, 1st Division, 6th Army Corps, Army of the Shenandoah, and Army of the Potomac, to June, 1865.

SERVICE.—At Downsville, Md., till October 20. Movement to Stafford C. H., Va., October 20-November 19, and to Belle Plains December 5. Battle of Fredericksburg, Va., December 12-15. "Mud March" January 20-24, 1863. Chancellorsville Campaign April 27-May 6. Operations at Franklin's Crossing April 29-May 2. Maryes Heights, Fredericksburg, May 3. Salem Heights May 3-4. Banks' Ford May 4. Battle of Gettysburg, Pa., July 2-4. Detached for duty at New York and duty at Fort Hamilton, N. Y. Harbor, July 30 to October 17. Rejoined army at Chantilly, Va., October 17. Advance to line of the Rappahannock November 7-8. Rappahannock Station November 7. Mine Run Campaign November 26-December 2. At Brandy Station till April,

1864. Rapidan Campaign May-June. Battles of the Wilderness May 5-7; Spottsylvania May 8-12; Spottsylvania C. H. May 12-21. Assault on the Salient May 12. North Anna River May 23-26. Line of the Pamunkey May 26-28. Totopotomoy May 28-31. Cold Harbor June 1-12. Before Petersburg June 16-18. Siege of Petersburg to July 9. Jerusalem Plank Road June 22-23. Moved to Washington, D. C., July 9-11. Repulse of Early's attack on Fort Stevens and the Northern Defences of Washington July 11-12. Sheridan's Shenandoah Valley Campaign August to December. Near Charlestown August 21-22. Battle of Opequan, Winchester, September 19. Provost duty at Winchester till December 13. Moved to Petersburg, Va., December 13-16. Siege of Petersburg December 16, 1864, to April 2, 1865. Appomattox Campaign March 28-April 9. Assault on and fall of Petersburg April 2. Pursuit of Lee April 3-9. Appomattox C. H. April 9. Surrender of Lee and his army. Moved to Danville, Va., April 23-27. Moved to Wilson's Station May 3; thence march to Washington, D. C., May 18-June 2. Corps Review June 8. Moved to Readville, Mass., June 22-23. Mustered out June 30, 1865.

Regiment lost during service 4 Officers and 165 Enlisted men killed and mortally wounded and 92 Enlisted men by disease. Total 261.

38th REGIMENT INFANTRY.

Organized and mustered in August 24, 1862. Moved to Baltimore, Md., August 26-28, 1862. Attached to Defences of Baltimore, Md., 8th Army Corps, Middle Dept. to January, 1863. 3rd Brigade, 3rd Division, 19th Army Corps, Dept. of the Gulf, to August, 1863. 2nd Brigade, 1st Division, 19th Army Corps, to February, 1864. 3rd Brigade, 2nd Division, 19th Army Corps, Dept. of the Gulf, and Army of the Shenandoah, Middle Military Division, to January, 1865. 3rd Brigade, Grover's Division, District of Savannah, Dept. of the South, to March, 1865. 3rd Brigade, 1st Division, 10th Army Corps, Dept. of North Carolina, to April, 1865. District of Savannah, Ga., Dept. of the South, to June, 1865.

SERVICE.—Duty at Baltimore, Md., till September 8, 1862; at Powhattan Dam till October 12, and at Baltimore till November 10. Embarked on steamer "Baltic" for Ship Island, Miss., November 10, arriving there December 14. Moved to New Orleans, La., December 29-31, and camp at Carrollton till February 11, 1863. Expedition to Plaquemine February 11-19. At Carrollton till March 6. Moved to Baton Rouge March 6-7. Operations against Port Hudson March 7-27. Moved to Algiers April 1, thence to Berwick City April 9. Operations in Western Louisiana April 9-May 14. Teche Campaign April 11-20. Fort Bisland April 12-13. Expedition from Opelousas to Alexandria and Simsport May 5-14. Moved to Bayou Sara, thence to Port Hudson May 22-25. Siege of Port Hudson May 25-July 9. Assaults on Port Hudson May 27 and June 14. Expedition to Clinton June 3-8. Surrender of Port Hudson July 9. Moved to Baton Rouge July 11, with Artillery train; thence to Donaldsonville July 15, and duty there till August 1. At Baton Rouge till March 23, 1864. Red River Campaign March 23-May 22. At Alexandria till April 12. Monett's Bluff, Cane River Crossing, April 23. Construction of dam at Alexandria April 30-May 10. Retreat to Morganza May 11-20. At Morganza till July 3. Reconnoissance to Atchafalaya May 30-June 6. Moved to New Orleans, La., thence to Fortress Monroe, Va., and Washington, D. C., July 3-29. Sheridan's Shenandoah Valley Campaign August to December. Battle of Opequan, Winchester, September 19. Fisher's Hill September 22. Battle of Cedar Creek October 19. At Kernstown and Winchester till January 5, 1865. Moved to Savannah, Ga., January 5-22, and duty there till March 5. Moved to Wilmington, N. C., March 5; thence to Morehead City March 10, and duty there till April 8. Moved to Goldsboro April 8, and duty there till May 2. Moved to Savannah, Ga., May 2-7, and duty there till June 30. Mustered out June 30, 1865. Moved to Boston Mass., June 30-July 5. Discharged July 13, 1865.

Regiment lost during service 4 Officers and 73 Enlisted men killed and mortally wounded and 151 Enlisted men by disease. Total 228.

39th REGIMENT INFANTRY.

Organized at Lynnfield August 13 to Septembr 2, 1862. Left State for Washington, D. C., September 6. Attached to Grover's Brigade, Defences of Washington, to February, 1863. Jewett's Independent Brigade, 22nd Army Corps, Dept. of Washington, to May, 1863. District of Washington, 22nd Army Corps, to July, 1863. 1st Brigade, 2nd Division, 1st Army Corps, Army Potomac, to March, 1864. 1st Brigade, 2nd Division, 5th Army Corps, to June, 1864. 1st Brigade, 3rd Division, 5th Army Corps, to September, 1864. 2nd Brigade, 3rd Division, 5th Army Corps, to June, 1865.

SERVICE.—Duty in the Defences of Washington from Fort Tillinghast to Fort Craig, till September 14, 1862. Guard Potomac from Edward's Ferry to Conrad's Ferry and Seneca Creek till October 20. At Muddy Branch till November 10. At Offutt's Cross Roads, Md., till December 21, and at Poolesville, Md., till April 15, 1863. Moved to Washington, D. C., April 15-17 and guard and patrol duty there till July 9. Moved to Harper's Ferry and Maryland Heights July 9-10, thence to Funkstown, Md., July 12-13. Pursuit of Lee July 14-27. Duty along the Rapidan till October. Bristoe Campaign October 9-22. Advance to line of the Rappahannock November 7-8. Rappahannock Station November 7. Mine Run Campaign November 26-December 2. Duty on Orange & Alexandria Railroad till May, 1864. Demonstration on the Rapidan February 6-7. Rapidan Campaign May-June. Battles of the Wilderness May 5-7; Laurel Hill May 8; Spottsylvania May 8-12; Spottsylvania C. H. May 12-21. Assault on the Salient May 12. North Anna River May 23-26. Jericho Ford May 23. On line of the Pamunkey May 26-28. Totopotomoy May 28-31. Cold Harbor June 1-12. Bethesda Church June 1-3. White Oak Swamp June 13. Before Petersburg June 16-18. Siege of Petersburg June 16, 1864, to April 2, 1865. Mine Explosion, Petersburg, July 30, 1864 (Reserve). Weldon Railroad August 18-21. Reconnoissance toward Dinwiddie C. H. September 15. Warren's Raid on Weldon Railroad December 7-12. Dabney's Mills February 5-7, 1865. Appomattox Campaign March 28-April 9. Davis Farm near Gravelly Run March 29. White Oak Road March 31. Five Forks April 1. Fall of Petersburg April 2. Pursuit of Lee April 3-9. Appomattox C. H. April 9. Surrender of Lee and his army. At Black and White Station till May 1. Moved to Manchester, thence march to Washington, D. C., May 1-15. Grand Review May 23. Mustered out June 1, 1865.

Regiment lost during service 5 Officers and 91 Enlisted men killed and mortally wounded and 183 Enlisted men by disease. Total 279.

40th REGIMENT INFANTRY.

Organized at Lynnfield August, 1862. Moved to Washington, D. C., September 8-11. Attached 2nd Brigade, Abercrombie's Division, Military District of Washington, to February, 1863. 2nd Brigade, Abercrombie's Division, 22nd Army Corps, Dept. of Washington, to April, 1863. 1st Brigade, 3rd Division, 7th Army Corps, Dept. of Virginia, to May, 1863. 2nd Brigade, 2nd Division, 4th Army Corps, Dept. of Virginia, to July, 1863. 2nd Brigade, 1st Division, 11th Army Corps, Army of the Potomac, to August, 1863. 2nd Brigade, Gordon's Division, South End of Folly Island, S. C., 10th Army Corps, Dept. of the South, to January, 1864. 2nd Brigade, Gordon's Division, Folly Island, S. C., Northern District, 10th Army Corps, Dept. South, January, 1864. 1st Brigade, District of Hilton Head, S. C., 10th Army Corps, to February, 1864. Light Brigade, District of Florida, Dept. of the South, to April, 1864. 1st Brigade, 2nd Division, 10th Army Corps, Dept. of Virginia and North Carolina, to May, 1864. 3rd Brigade, 1st Division, 18th Army Corps, to December, 1864. 3rd Brigade, 3rd Division, 24th Army Corps, Dept. of Virginia, to June, 1865.

SERVICE.—Duty in the Defences of Washington, D. C., till April, 1863. Expedition to Mill's Cross Roads after Stuart's Cavalry December 28-29, 1862. Picket duty on the Columbia Pike February 12 to March 30, 1863, and at Vienna till April 11. Moved to Norfolk, thence to Suffolk April 15-17. Siege of Suffolk April 17-May 4. Siege of Suffolk raised May 4. Moved to West Point May 5, thence to Yorktown May 31. Raid to Jamestown Island June 10-13. Dix's Peninsula Campaign June 24-July 7. Expedition from White House to Bottom's Bridge July 1-7. Baltimore Cross Roads July 2. Moved to Washington, D. C., July 10-11. March in pursuit of Lee, to Berlin, Md., July 13-22. Moved to Alexandria August 6, thence sailed to Folly Island, S. C., August 7-13. Siege operations on Folly and Morris Islands against Forts Wagner and Gregg, and against Fort Sumpter and Charleston, August 15-November 13. Expedition to Seabrook Island November 13-15. Duty at Folly Island till January 16, 1864. Moved to Hilton Head, S. C., January 16. Expedition to Jacksonville, Fla., February 4-7, and to Lake City, Fla., February 7-22. Ten Mile Run near Camp Finnegan February 8. Barber's Place February 10. Lake City February 11. Gainesville February 14 (Cos. "C," "G," "H"). Battle of Olustee February 20. McGirt's Creek March 1. Cedar Creek March 1. Duty at Jacksonville till April 22. Moved to Gloucester Point April 22-28. Expedition to West Point April 30-May 5. Butler's operations on south side of James River and against Petersburg and Richmond May 5-28. Swift Creek or Arrowfield Church May 9-10. Operations against Fort Darling May 12-16. Battle of Drewry's Bluff May 14-16. On Bermuda Hundred Front May 17-28. Moved to White House, thence to Cold Harbor May 28-June 1. Cold Harbor June 1-12. Before Petersburg June 15-18. Siege operations against Petersburg and Richmond June 16, 1864, to April 2, 1865. Hares Hill June 24 and 28. Mine Explosion, Petersburg, July 30, 1864 (Reserve). In trenches before Petersburg till August 27. Moved to Bermuda Front August 27, thence to Bermuda Landing August 28, and provost duty there till September 29. On the Bermuda Front till October 24. Moved to Chaffin's Farm on north side of the James, and duty there till March, 1865. Expedition to Fredericksburg March 5-8, and up the Potomac River to the Yecomico, and to Kinsel's Landing March 11-13, thence to White House March 13-18. March to Signal Hill before Richmond March 24-26. Occupation of Richmond April 3. Moved to Manchester April 25 and provost duty there till June 16. Mustered out June 16, and discharged at Reedville, Mass., June 30, 1865.

Regiment lost during service 5 Officers and 67 Enlisted men killed and mortally wounded and 125 Enlisted men by disease. Total 197.

41st REGIMENT INFANTRY.

Organized at Lynnfield August 31 to November 1, 1862. Left State for New York November 5. Sailed for New Orleans, La., on Steamer "North Star" December 4, arriving December 15. Moved to Baton Rouge December 16-17. Attached to Grover's Division, Dept. of the Gulf, to January, 1863. 2nd Brigade, 4th Division, 19th Army Corps, Dept. of the Gulf, to June, 1863.

SERVICE.—Duty at Baton Rouge to March 28, 1863. Expedition to Comite River March 9-10. Moved to Donaldsville March 28. Operations in Western Louisiana April 9-May 14. Teche Campaign April 11-20. Irish Bend April 14. Destruction of salt works near Iberia April 18. Provost duty at Opelousas till May 11. Moved to Barre Landing May 11, thence with trains to Berwick May 21-26. Actions at Franklin and Centreville May 25. Moved to Algiers, thence to Port Hudson May 26-June 3. Designation of Regiment changed to 3rd Massachusetts Cavalry June 17, 1863. (See 3rd Massachusetts Cavalry.)

42nd REGIMENT INFANTRY.

Organized at Camp Meigs, Reedville, November 11, 1862. Left State for New York November 11, thence to

East New York November 22. Sailed December 2 for New Orleans, La. (Cos. "D," "G" and "I"), on Steamer "Saxon," arriving at Ship Island December 14, and at New Orleans December 16. Companies "A," "B" and "F" on Steamer "Quincy," arriving at Hilton Head, S. C., December 11, at Tortugas, Fla., December 20, at Ship Island, Miss., December 26, and at New Orleans, December 29. Companies "C" and "H" on Steamer "Shetucket," arriving at New Orleans January 1, 1863. Companies "E" and "K" on Steamer "Chas. Osgood," arriving at New Orleans January 1, 1863. Attached to Sherman's Division, Dept. of the Gulf, to January, 1863. 2nd Brigade, 2nd Division, 19th Army Corps, Dept. of the Gulf, to August, 1863.

SERVICE.—Companies "D," "G" and "I" moved on Steamer "Saxon" to Galveston, Texas, December 19-24, 1862. Occupation of Galveston December 24 (Cos. "D," "G," "I"). Action at Galveston January 1, 1863. Captured and paroled at Alexandria, La., February 18, 1863, and rejoined Regiment at New Orleans February 22. Assigned to duty at Paroled Camp Bayou, Gentilly, till July. Companies "A," "B," "E," "F" and "K" at Carrollton, La., till January 26, 1863. Moved to Bayou Gentilly on Ponchartrain Railroad, and duty there till July. Companies "C" and "H" detached from Regiment January 15, and assigned to duty with Engineer Corps, Dept. of the Gulf, at Camp Parapet, and erecting fortifications for the Defence of New Orleans till June. Rejoined Regiment at Camp Farr June 5. Company "K" detached February 16 for Engineer duty. Moved to New Orleans February 18, and placed in charge of a pontoon train. Moved to Bayou Montesino March 10 and laid bridge, returning to Baton Rouge March 15. Expedition up Mississippi River March 19-22. Moved to New Orleans March 23-24, thence to Brashear City April 6. Expedition to Bayou Teche with bridge 300 feet long, which was placed across Bayou Teche April 12. Removed torpedoes and obstructions to Indian Bend April 12-15. Removed obstructions to wreck of Steamer "Cotton" April 15-23. Moved to Brashear City April 23, thence to Washington on Courtableaux River. Expedition to Alexandria and Simsport April 27-May 21. Ordered to Port Hudson May 21. Siege of Port Hudson May 26-July 9. Laid bridge at Sandy Creek May 26. LaFourche June 21-22. Brashear June 23. Expedition to Donaldsville July 13-21 and laid bridge across Bayou LaFourche 280 feet long. Relieved from duty as Engineers and rejoined Regiment at New Orleans. Regiment engaged in outpost and picket duty from Bayou St. John to Point Aux Herbs. Company "A" at battery on Bayou St. John till July 28. Company "F" at Lakeport April 6 to July 28. Regiment concentrated and moved to Boston July 31-August 10. Mustered out August 20, 1863.

Regiment lost during service 4 Enlisted men killed and mortally wounded and 2 Officers and 44 Enlisted men by disease. Total 50.

42nd REGIMENT INFANTRY (MILITIA).

Organized at Reedville for 100 days July 22, 1864. Mustered out November 11, 1864.

43rd REGIMENT INFANTRY.

Organized at Camp Meigs, Readville, September 12 to October 23, 1862. Left State for Newberne, N. C., October 24. Attached to 1st Brigade, 1st Division, Dept. of North Carolina, to December, 1862. Amory's Brigade, Dept. North Carolina, to January, 1863. 1st Brigade, 1st Division, 18th Army Corps, Dept. North Carolina, to June, 1863. 1st Brigade, Maryland Heights, Division West Virginia, to July, 1863.

SERVICE.—Duty at Newberne, N. C., till December 10, 1862. (Co. "C" detached at Beaufort, N. C., November 30, 1862, to March 4, 1863.) Foster's Expedition to Goldsboro December 11-20, 1862. Kinston December 14. Whitehall December 16. Goldsboro December 17. At Newberne till January 17, 1863. Companies "A," "D" and "E" detached on outpost duty at Batchelor's Creek December 31, 1862, to January 11, 1863. Com-

pany "I" detached on picket duty at Evans' Mills January 11 to March 2. Expedition toward Trenton January 17-22. At Newberne till March 14. Expedition to Rocky Run March 14-16. At Newberne till April 7. March to relief of Little Washington April 7-10. Blount's Creek April 9. Moved to Little Washington April 17-18, and duty there till April 24. Moved to Newberne April 24-25. Expedition to Core Creek April 27-May 1. At Newberne till June 24. Moved to Fort Monroe, thence to White House, Pamunkey River, June 24-28. Moved to Baltimore, Md., June 29-July 3. Moved to Sandy Hook, Md., July 7-9, and duty there till July 18. Moved to Boston, Mass., July 18-21. Mustered out July 30, 1863.

Regiment lost during service 3 Enlisted men killed and mortally wounded and 12 Enlisted men by disease. Total 15.

44th REGIMENT INFANTRY.

Organized at Readville and mustered in September 12, 1862. Moved to Newberne, N. C., October 22-27. Attached to 2nd Brigade, 1st Division, Dept. of North Carolina, to January, 1863. 2nd Brigade, 4th Division, 18th Army Corps, Dept. North Carolina, to May, 1863. Lee's Brigade, Defences of Newberne, Dept. North Carolina, to June, 1863.

SERVICE.—Expedition from Newberne November 2-12, 1862. Action at Rawle's Mills November 2. Demonstration on Newberne November 11. Foster's Expedition to Goldsboro December 11-20. Kinston December 14. Whitehall December 16. Goldsboro December 17. At Newberne till February 10, 1863. Moved to Plymouth, N. C., February 10, and duty there till March 15. (Cos. "B" and "F" detached on outpost duty at Batchelor's Creek February 10 to May 1.) Skirmishes Deep Gully, Newberne, March 13-14 (2 Cos.). Regiment moved to Washington March 15. Siege of Washington March 30-April 20. Skirmish at Washington March 30 (Cos. "A" and "G"). Skirmishes at Washington April 3 and 15. Expedition from Newberne to relief of Little Washington April 7-10 (2 Cos.). Regiment moved to Newberne April 22-24, and duty there till June 6. Expedition toward Kinston April 27-May 1. Dover Road April 28. Moved to Boston, Mass., June 6-10. Mustered out June 18, 1863.

Regiment lost during service 11 Enlisted men killed and mortally wounded and 1 Officer and 29 Enlisted men by disease. Total 41.

45th REGIMENT INFANTRY ("CADET REGIMENT").

Organized at Camp Meigs, Readville, September 26-October 28, 1862. Moved to Morehead City, N. C., on Steamer "Mississippi" November 5-14. Attached to 3rd Brigade, 1st Division, Dept. of North Carolina, to January, 1863. 2nd Brigade, 4th Division, 18th Army Corps, Dept. of North Carolina, to May, 1863. Lee's Brigade, Defences of Newberne, N. C., to June, 1863.

SERVICE.—Camp on banks of the Trent near Newberne till December 12, 1862. Foster's Expedition to Goldsboro December 12-20. Kinston December 14. Whitehall December 16. Goldsboro December 17. Reconnoissance toward Trenton January 17-22, 1863. Duty as post guard at Newberne January 26 to April 25. Moved to mouth of the Trent, south side of the Neuse River, April 25. Expedition toward Kinston, up the Atlantic & N. C. Railroad, April 27-May 1. Dover Road and Wise's Cross Roads April 28. Camp near Fort Spinola, mouth of Trent, till June 24. Company "C" detached at Morehead City November 29, 1862, to January 3, 1863. Company "G" at Fort Macon till April 25. Company "I" at Morehead City January 3 to April 25, and at Fort Spinola till June 24. Regiment moved to Morehead City June 24 and embarked for Boston, Mass., arriving at Fortress Monroe June 26, and at Boston June 30. Mustered out July 8, 1863.

Regiment lost during service 19 Enlisted men killed and mortally wounded and 32 Enlisted men by disease. Total 51.

46th REGIMENT INFANTRY.

Organized at Springfield September 25-October 30, 1862. Moved to Boston November 5 and there embarked for Newberne, N. C., arriving November 15. Attached to 3rd Brigade, 1st Division, Dept. of North Carolina, to January, 1863. 2nd Brigade, 1st Division, 18th Army Corps, Dept. of North Carolina, to June, 1863. 8th Army Corps, Middle Dept., July, 1863. Temporarily to 1st Army Corps, Army Potomac.

SERVICE.—Duty at Newberne, N. C., till December 10, 1862. (Co. "A" detached at Newport Barracks November 18, 1862, to January 23, 1863.) Foster's Expedition to Goldsboro December 11-20. Kinston December 14. Whitehall December 16. Goldsboro December 17. Duty at Newberne till March 26, 1863. Skirmishes at Deep Gully, Newberne, March 13-14. Moved to Plymouth March 26, and duty there till May. (Cos. "A" and "I" remain at Newberne.) Expedition toward Kinston April 27-May 1. Dover Road April 28. Moved to Newberne May 7-8. Demonstration on Kinston May 20-23. Gum Swamp May 22. Batchelor's Creek May 23. Duty at Newberne till June 24. Moved to Fortress Monroe June 24-28, thence to Baltimore, Md., June 30-July 1. Moved to Monocacy Junction, thence to Frederick, Sandy Hook and Maryland Heights July 6-7. Occupation of Harper's Ferry July 8. March to Funkstown July 12-13, and join 1st Army Corps. Pursuit of Lee July 14-15. Moved to Boston July 15-17, thence to Springfield and there mustered out July 29, 1863.

Regiment lost during service 1 Enlisted man killed and 35 by disease. Total 36.

47th REGIMENT INFANTRY.

Organized at Boxford and Readville October 16, 1862. Moved to New York November 29, thence sailed on Steamer "Mississippi" for Ship Island, Miss., and New Orleans, La., December 21, arriving at New Orleans December 31. Moved to Carrollton January 1, 1863. Attached to 2nd Brigade, 2nd Division, 19th Army Corps, Dept of the Gulf, to July, 1863.

SERVICE.—Duty at Carrollton, U. S. Barracks, Lower Cotton Press, Metarre Race Course and at Camp Parapet, Defences of New Orleans, till August, 1863. Skirmishes at Amite River April 17, and at LaFourche Crossing June 20-21 (Detachments). Moved to Boston, Mass., August 3-18, and mustered out September 1, 1863.

Regiment lost during service 1 Enlisted man killed and 1 Officer and 36 Enlisted men by disease. Total 38.

48th REGIMENT INFANTRY.

Organized at Wenham and mustered in October 29, 1862. Moved to New York December 27. Embarked on Steamer "Constitution" and sailed for New Orleans, La., December 29, arriving February 1, 1863. Moved to Baton Rouge, La., February 3. Attached to 1st Brigade, 1st Division, 19th Army Corps, Dept. of the Gulf, to August, 1863.

SERVICE.—Reconnoissance toward Port Hudson March 13-20, 1863. Duty at Baton Rouge till May 18. Operations against Port Hudson May 18-24. Action at Plain's Store May 21. Siege of Port Hudson May 25-July 9. Assaults on Port Hudson May 27 and June 14. Surrender of Port Hudson July 9. Moved to Donaldsonville July 9-10, and duty there till August 1. Action at Cox's Plantation, Donaldsonville, July 12-13. Moved to Boston, Mass., via Cairo, Ill., August 9-23. Mustered out September 3, 1863.

Regiment lost during service 2 Officers and 17 Enlisted men killed and mortally wounded and 50 Enlisted men by disease. Total 59.

49th REGIMENT INFANTRY.

Organized at Pittsfield and mustered in October 28, 1862. Moved to New York November 21, and provost duty there till January 24, 1863. Embarked for New Orleans, La., on Steamer "Illinois" January 24, arriving there February 3, thence moved to Carrollton and Baton Rouge, La. Attached to 1st Brigade, 1st Division, 19th Army Corps, Dept. of the Gulf, to August, 1863.

SERVICE.—Reconnoissance toward Port Hudson March 13-20, 1863. At Baton Rouge till May 18. Operations against Port Hudson May 18-24. Action at Plain's Store May 21. Siege of Port Hudson May 24-July 9. Assaults on Port Hudson May 27 and June 14. Surrender of Port Hudson July 9. Moved to Donaldsonville July 9-10, and duty there till August 1. Action at Cox's Plantation, Donaldsonville, July 12-13. Moved to Baton Rouge August 1, thence to Pittsfield, Mass., August 8-21. Mustered out September 1, 1863.

Regiment lost during service 2 Officers and 28 Enlisted men killed and mortally wounded and 84 Enlisted men by disease. Total 114.

50th REGIMENT INFANTRY (7th MASSACHUSETTS VOLUNTEER MILITIA).

Organized at Boxford. Moved to New York November 19-20, 1862, thence sailed for New Orleans, La. (Cos. "A," "E" and "K"), on Steamer "Jersey Blue," December 11. Transferred to "Guerrilla" at Hilton Head, S. C., and arrived at New Orleans January 20, 1863. Company "I" sailed on Steamer "New Brunswick" December 1, arriving at Baton Rouge, La., December 16, and temporarily attached to 30th Massachusetts. Companies "B," "C," "D," "F," "G" and "H" sailed on Steamer "Niagara" December 13, but returned to Philadelphia, Pa., December 16. Again sailed from Philadelphia January 9, 1863, on Ship "Jenny Lind," arriving at Fortress Monroe, Va., January 13, where Companies "B," "D" and "H" were transferred to Ship "Monticello," and arrived at New Orleans January 27, but were detained at Quarantine till April, joining Regiment at Baton Rouge April 2. Companies "C," "F" and "G" arrived at New Orleans February 9 and at Baton Rouge February 14. Attached to 3rd Brigade, 1st Division, 19th Army Corps, Dept. of the Gulf, to July, 1863.

SERVICE.—Duty at Baton Rouge till March 14, 1863. Reconnoissance toward Port Hudson March 7-27. Expedition to Bayou Montecino April 19. At Baton Rouge till May 12. At White's Bayou May 12-26 (Cos. "A," "B," "C" and "I"). Siege of Port Hudson May 26-July 9. Assaults on Port Hudson May 27 and June 14. Surrender of Port Hudson July 9. Garrison duty at Port Hudson till July 29. Moved to Boston, Mass., via Cairo, Ill., July 29-August 11. Mustered out August 24, 1863.

Regiment lost during service 2 Enlisted men killed and 1 Officer and 100 Enlisted men by disease. Total 103.

51st REGIMENT INFANTRY.

Organized at Worcester September 25 to October 30, 1862. Moved to Boston, thence to Newberne, N. C., November 25-30. Attached to 1st Brigade, 1st Division, Dept. of North Carolina, to December, 1862. Amory's Brigade, Dept. North Carolina, to January, 1863. 1st Brigade, 1st Division, 18th Army Corps, Dept. of North Carolina, to June, 1863. 8th Army Corps, Middle Dept., July, 1863. Temporary to 1st Army Corps, Army Potomac, July, 1863.

SERVICE.—Foster's Expedition to Goldsboro December 11-20, 1862. Kinston December 14. Whitehall December 16. Goldsboro December 17. Duty at Newberne till March, 1863. Expedition to Trenton, Pollocksville, Young's Cross Roads and Onslow, January 17-21, 1863. Companies "A," "B," "C," "D," "H," "I," "K" guard and outpost duty by detachments on railroad between Newberne and Morehead City March 2 to May 4. Companies "A" and "C" at Morehead City. (Co. "C" at Fort Macon March 30 to May 5.) "B," "D," "H" and "I" at Newport. "K" at Evans' Mills. "E" and "F" at Beaufort and "G" at Brice's Ferry. Headquarters at Beaufort. Moved to Newberne May 4, and duty there till June 24. Moved to Fort Monroe, Va., thence to White House June 24-28. Moved to Baltimore, Md., June 29-July 1. To Monocacy Junction, Frederick and Sandy Hook July 6-7. Occupation of Harper's Ferry July 8. March to Funkstown, Md., July

12-13, and join 1st Army Corps. Pursuit of Lee. March to Berlin July 15-17, thence moved to Worcester, Mass., July 17-21. Mustered out July 27, 1863.

Regiment lost during service 44 Enlisted men by disease.

52nd REGIMENT INFANTRY.

Organized at Greenfield October, 1862. Ordered to New York November 19, thence moved to New Orleans and Baton Rouge, La., and duty there till March, 1863. Attached to 2nd Brigade, 4th Division, 19th Army Corps, Dept. of the Gulf, to July, 1863.

SERVICE.—Reconnoissance to Port Hudson, La., March 13-20. Moved to Donaldsonville March 27. Operations in Western Louisiana April 9-May 14. Teche Campaign April 11-20. Irish Bend April 14. Bayou Vermillion April 17. March to Opelousas April 19-20, thence to Barre Landing April 26, and duty there till May 21. Companies "A," "E," "F" and "G" on provost duty at New Iberia April 17-May 19. Expedition toward Berwick City May 21-26. Moved to Algiers, thence to Port Hudson May 26-30. Siege of Port Hudson May 30-July 9. Assault on Port Hudson June 14. Jackson Cross Roads June 20 (Detachment). Surrender of Port Hudson July 9, and duty there till July 23. Moved to Massachusetts July 23-August 3. Mustered out August 14, 1863.

Regiment lost during service 1 Officer and 10 Enlisted men killed and mortally wounded and 101 Enlisted men by disease. Total 112.

53rd REGIMENT INFANTRY.

Organized at Groton Junction October 17 to November 6, 1862. Moved to New York November 18, and duty there till January 17, 1863. Embarked on Steamer "Continental" for New Orleans, La., January 17, arriving there January 30. Attached to 3rd Brigade, 3rd Division, 19th Army Corps, Dept. of the Gulf, to August, 1863.

SERVICE.—Duty at Carrollton, La., January 30 to March 6, 1863. Moved to Baton Rouge March 6-7. Operations against Port Hudson March 7-27. Moved to Brashear and Berwick City April 1-9. Operations in Western Louisiana April 9-May 14. Teche Campaign April 11-20. Fort Bisland near Centreville April 12-13. Expedition from Opelousas to Alexandria and Simsport May 5-18. Moved to Bayou Sara May 22, thence to Port Hudson. Siege of Port Hudson May 24-July 9. Assaults on Port Hudson May 27 and June 14. Expedition to Clinton June 3-8. Surrender of Port Hudson July 9. Moved to Baton Rouge July 11-12, and to Donaldsonville July 15. Duty there and at Baton Rouge till August 12. Moved to Cairo, Ill., August 12-19, thence to Fitchburg, Mass., August 19-24. Mustered out September 2, 1863. Losses, 5 Officers and 28 Enlisted men killed and mortally wounded and 144 Enlisted men by disease. Total 177.

54th REGIMENT INFANTRY ("COLORED").

Organized at Readville and mustered in May 13, 1863. Left Boston on Steamer "De Molay" for Hilton Head, S. C., May 28, arriving there June 3. Attached to U. S. Forces, St. Helena Island, S. C., 10th Army Corps, Dept. of the South, to July, 1863. 3rd Brigade, 1st Division, Morris Island, S. C., 10th Army Corps, July, 1863. 3rd Brigade, Morris Island, S. C., to August, 1863. 4th Brigade, Morris Island, S. C., to November, 1863. 3rd Brigade, Morris Island, S. C., to January, 1864. Montgomery's Brigade, District of Hilton Head, S. C., to February, 1864. Montgomery's Brigade, District of Florida, February, 1864. 3rd Brigade, Ames' Division, District of Florida, to April, 1864. Folly and Morris Islands, S. C., Northern District, Dept. South, to October, 1864. 1st Separate Brigade, Dept. South, to November, 1864. 2nd Brigade, Coast Division, Dept. South, to February, 1865. 1st Separate Brigade, Northern District, Dept. South, to March, 1865. 1st Separate Brigade, District of Charleston, S. C., Dept. South, to June, 1865. 3rd Sub-District, District of Charleston, Dept. South Carolina, to August, 1865.

SERVICE.—At Thompson's Plantation near Beaufort, S. C., June 4-8, 1863. Moved to St. Simon's Island June 8-9. Expedition up Altamaha River June 10-11. At St. Simon's Island June 12-24. At St. Helena Island June 25-July 8. To Stono Inlet July 8. Expedition against James Island July 9-16. Affair Legaresville July 13. Secessionville July 16. Moved to Morris Island July 16-18. Assault on Fort Wagner July 18. Siege operations against Forts Wagner and Gregg, Morris Island, July 18-September 7, and against Fort Sumpter and Charleston September 7, 1863, to January 28, 1864. Capture of Forts Wagner and Gregg September 7, 1863. Moved to Hilton Head, S. C., January 28, 1864. Expedition to Jacksonville, Fla., February 5-7. Capture of Jacksonville February 6. Expedition to Lake City, Fla., February 7-22. Battle of Oolustee February 20. Duty at Jacksonville till April 17. Moved to Morris Island April 17-18. Duty on Morris and Folly Islands, S. C., till November, 1864. Expedition to James Island June 30-July 10. Actions on James Island July 2, 9 and 10. Six Companies in charge of rebel prisoners under fire of Charleston Batteries September 7 to October 20. Eight Companies moved to Hilton Head, November 27. (Cos. "B" and "F" at Morris Island till February, 1865.) Expedition to Boyd's Neck, S. C., November 29-30. Boyd's Landing November 29. Battle of Honey Hill November 30. Demonstration on Charleston & Savannah Railroad December 6-9. Moved to Graham's Neck December 20. Connect with Sherman's Army at Pocotaligo, S. C., January 15, 1865. March to Charleston January 15-February 23, skirmishing all the way. (Cos. "B" and "F" occupy Charleston February 18.) Regiment on duty at Charleston February 27 to March 12. At Savannah, Ga., March 13-27. At Georgetown, S. C., March 31-April 5. Potter's Expedition to Camden April 5-25. Seven Mile Bridge April 6. Destruction of Eppes' Bridge, Black River, April 7. Dingle's Mills April 9. Destruction of Rolling Stock at Wateree Junction April 11. Singleton's Plantation April 12. Statesburg April 15. Occupation of Camden April 17. Boykin's Mills April 18. At Georgetown April 25. Duty at Georgetown, Charleston, and various points in South Carolina April 25 to August 17. Mustered out at Mount Pleasant, S. C., August 20, 1865. Discharged at Boston, Mass., September 1, 1865.

Regiment lost during service 5 Officers and 104 Enlisted men killed and mortally wounded and 1 Officer and 160 Enlisted men by disease. Total 270.

55th REGIMENT INFANTRY (COLORED).

Organized at Readville and mustered in June 22, 1863. Left State for Newberne, N. C., July 21, 1863, arriving there July 25, thence moved to Folly Island, S. C., July 30-August 3. Attached to Wild's African Brigade, Vodge's Division, North End, Folly Island, S. C., 10th Army Corps, Dept. of the South, to October, 1863. 3rd Brigade, Vodge's Division, Folly Island, 10th Army Corps, to February, 1864. 3rd Brigade, Ames' Division, District of Florida, to April, 1864. Folly and Morris Islands, S. C., Northern District, Dept. of the South, to November, 1864. 2nd Brigade, Coast Division, Dept. South, to January, 1865. 1st Separate Brigade, Dept. of the South, to March, 1865. 1st Separate Brigade, District of Charleston, Dept. South, to June, 1865. District of Charleston, S. C., Dept. South Carolina, to August, 1865.

SERVICE.—Fatigue duty on north end of Folly Island, S. C., and in trenches on Morris Island August 9 to September 5, 1863. Fatigue duty on Forts Wagner and Gregg, Morris Island, S. C., and operations against Fort Sumpter and Charleston September 17-October 28. Camp on Folly Island till February, 1864. Expedition to John's Island February (Co. "F"). Moved to Jacksonville, Fla., February 13-16, and Provost duty there till March 11. Advance to Baldwin February 19-20. (Co. "F" detached as garrison at Fort Fribley, Jacksonville, February to April.) Companies "B" and "I" at Yellow Bluff February 28 to April 17. Regiment ordered to Palatka, Fla., March 11, and duty there till

April 17. Moved to Folly Island, S. C., April 17-18. Duty there till November 27. Demonstration on James Island May 21-22. Expedition to James Island June 30-July 10. Action on James Island July 2. Moved to Hilton Head, S. C., November 27-28. (Co. "G" detached at Battery on Long Island, and Co. "H" at Fort Delafield, Stono Inlet, till February 12, 1865.) Hatch's Expedition up Broad River to Boyd's Neck November 29-30. Battle of Honey Hill November 30. Demonstration on Charleston & Savannah Railroad December 6-9. Deveaux's Neck December 6. At Boyd's Landing till January 11, 1865. Moved to Hilton Head, thence to Fort Thunderbolt, near Savannah, Ga., January 11-13. Duty at Forts Jackson, Bartow and Battery Lee till February 1. Moved to Hilton Head, S. C., thence to Beaufort, S. C., February 1. Expedition up South Edisto River February 1-6. Moved to Stono Inlet February 6. Expedition to James Island February 9-10. Expedition to Bull's Bay February 11-15. Moved to Mount Pleasant February 19-20. Expedition to Santee River February 21-March 10. Duty at and near Charleston till May 7. Expedition to Eutaw Springs April 6-12. Moved to Sumpterville May 7-8, thence to Orangeburg May 19, and Provost duty there till August. Mustered out August 29, 1865. Discharged at Boston, Mass., September 23, 1865.

Regiment lost during service 3 Officers and 64 Enlisted men killed and mortally wounded and 2 Officers and 128 Enlisted men by disease. Total 197.

56th REGIMENT INFANTRY.

Organized at Readville December 26, 1863, to February 24, 1864. Left State for Annapolis, Md., March 21; thence moved to Washington and Alexandria April 23. Attached to 1st Brigade, 1st Division, 9th Army Corps, Army of the Potomac, to September, 1864. 2nd Brigade, 2nd Division, 9th Army Corps, to July, 1865.

SERVICE.—Campaign from the Rapidan to the James May 3-June 15, 1864. Battles of the Wilderness May 5-7; Spottsylvania May 8-12; Ny River May 10; Spottsylvania Court House May 12-21. Assault on the Salient May 12. North Anna River May 23-26. On line of the Pamunkey May 26-28. Totopotomoy May 28-31. Cold Harbor June 1-12. Bethesda Church June 1-3. Before Petersburg June 16-18. Siege of Petersburg June 16, 1864, to April 2, 1865. Mine Explosion, Petersburg, July 30, 1864. Weldon Railroad August 18-21. Poplar Springs Church or Peeble's Farm September 29-October 2. Boydton Plank Road, Hatcher's Run, October 27-28. At Fort Hays January 1 to April 1, 1865. Fort Stedman March 25. Appomattox Campaign March 28-April 9. Assault on and fall of Petersburg April 2. Occupation of Petersburg April 3. Pursuit of Lee April 3-9. March to Petersburg and City Point April 18-22, thence moved to Alexandria April 23-25. Grand Review May 23. Duty at Washington and Alexandria till July —. Mustered out July 12, 1865.

Regiment lost during service 6 Officers and 120 Enlisted men killed and mortally wounded and 100 Enlisted men by disease. Total 226.

57th REGIMENT INFANTRY.

Organized at Worcester and Readville and mustered in April 6, 1864. Moved to Annapolis, Md., thence to Washington and Alexandria April 18-20. Attached to 1st Brigade, 1st Division, 9th Army Corps, Army of the Potomac, to September, 1864. 3rd Brigade, 1st Division, 9th Army Corps, to July, 1865.

SERVICE.—Campaign from the Rapidan to the James May 3-June 15, 1864. Battles of the Wilderness May 5-7; Spottsylvania May 8-12; Ny River May 10; Spottsylvania Court House May 12-21. Assault on the Salient May 12. North Anna River May 23-26. On line of the Pamunkey May 26-28. Totopotomoy May 28-31. Cold Harbor June 1-12. Bethesda Church June 1-3. Before Petersburg June 16-18. Siege of Petersburg June 16, 1864, to April 2, 1865. Mine Explosion, Petersburg, July 30, 1864. Weldon Railroad August 18-21. Poplar Springs Church or Peeble's Farm September 29-October

2. Reconnoissance on Vaughan and Squirrel Level Roads October 8. Boydton Plank Road, Hatcher's Run, October 27-28. Fort Stedman March 25, 1865. Appomattox Campaign March 28-April 9. Assault on and fall of Petersburg April 2. Occupation of Petersburg April 3. Pursuit of Lee April 4-9. Moved to City Point, thence to Alexandria April 20-28, and duty there till July —. Grand Review May 23. Mustered out July 30, 1865.

Regiment lost during service 10 Officers and 191 Enlisted men killed and mortally wounded and 86 Enlisted men by disease. Total 287.

58th REGIMENT INFANTRY.

Organized at Readville April 25, 1864. Moved to Alexandria, Va., April 28-30. Attached to 1st Brigade, 2nd Division, 9th Army Corps, Army of the Potomac, to July, 1865.

SERVICE.—Moved to Bristoe Station, Va., and join 9th Army Corps May 1-2, 1864. Campaign from the Rapidan to the James May 3-July 15. Battles of the Wilderness May 5-7; Spottsylvania May 8-12; Ny River May 10; Spottsylvania Court House May 12-21. Assault on the Salient May 12. Stannard's Mills May 21. North Anna River May 23-26. On line of the Pamunkey May 26-28. Totopotomoy May 28-31. Cold Harbor June 1-12. Bethesda Church June 1-3. Before Petersburg June 16-18. Siege of Petersburg June 16, 1864, to April 2, 1865. Mine Explosion, Petersburg, July 30, 1864. Weldon Railroad August 18-21. Poplar Springs Church or Peeble's Farm September 29-October 2. Boydton Plank Road, Hatcher's Run, October 27-28. Fort Stedman March 25, 1865. Appomattox Campaign March 28-April 9. Assault on and fall of Petersburg April 2. Occupation of Petersburg April 3. Pursuit of Lee April 3-9. At Farmville till April 20. Moved to City Point, thence to Alexandria April 20-28. Duty there till July 15. Grand Review May 23. Mustered out July 14. Moved to Readville July 15-18, and discharged July 26, 1865.

Lost during service 10 Officers and 129 Enlisted men killed and mortally wounded and 156 Enlisted men by disease. Total 295.

59th REGIMENT INFANTRY.—(4th VETERAN.)

Organized at Readville December 3, 1863, to April 20, 1864. Moved to Washington, D. C., April 26-28, thence to Rappahannock Station, Va., April 29-May 2, and join Army of the Potomac. Attached to 1st Brigade, 1st Division, 9th Army Corps, Army of the Potomac, to September, 1864. 3rd Brigade, 1st Division, 9th Army Corps, to May, 1865.

SERVICE.—Campaign from the Rapidan to the James May 3-June 15, 1864. Battles of the Wilderness May 5-7; Spottsylvania May 8-12; Ny River May 10; Spottsylvania Court House May 12-21. Assault on the Salient May 12. North Anna River May 23-26. On line of the Pamunkey May 26-28. Totopotomoy May 28-31. Cold Harbor June 1-12. Bethesda Church June 1-3. Before Petersburg June 16-18. Siege of Petersburg June 16, 1864, to April 2, 1865. Mine Explosion, Petersburg, July 30, 1864. Weldon Railroad August 18-21. Poplar Springs Church or Peeble's Farm September 29-October 2. Reconnoissance on Vaughan and Squirrel Level Road October 8. Boydton Plank Road, Hatcher's Run, October 27-28. Fort Stedman March 25, 1865. Appomattox Campaign March 28-April 9. Assault on and fall of Petersburg April 2. Occupation of Petersburg April 3. Pursuit of Lee April 3-9. Moved to City Point, thence to Alexandria April 20-28. Grand Review May 23. Consolidated with 57th Massachusetts Infantry May 26, 1865.

Regiment lost during service 7 Officers and 83 Enlisted men killed and mortally wounded and 1 Officer and 93 Enlisted men by disease. Total 184.

60th REGIMENT INFANTRY.

Organized for 100 days August 1, 1864. Left State for Washington, D. C., August 1. Stopped at Baltimore, Md., and duty at Relay House till August 9, and at Carroll Hill till August 16. Ordered to Indianapolis, Ind., and duty guarding Confederate prisoners till November. Mustered out November 30, 1864. Lost 11 by disease.

61st REGIMENT INFANTRY.

Organized at Gallop's Island, Boston Harbor, August to October, 1864. A Battalion of 5 Companies, "A," "B," "C," "D" and "E." Moved to City Point, Va., October 7-12, 1864. Attached to Benham's Engineer Brigade, Dept. of Virginia and North Carolina, and Army of the Potomac to March, 1865. Independent Brigade, 9th Army Corps, Army of the Potomac, to April, 1865. 1st Brigade, 2nd Division, 5th Army Corps, Army of the Potomac, to July, 1865.

SERVICE.—Engaged in Engineer duty erecting fortifications at City Point, Va., and picket duty at that point till March, 1865. Company "F" reported to Regiment November 17, 1864; Company "G" January 5, 1865; Company "H" February 15, 1865; Companies "I" and "K" March 15, 1865. Ordered to Petersburg March 28, 1865. Appomattox Campaign March 28-April 9. Assault on and fall of Petersburg April 2. Occupation of Petersburg April 3. Pursuit of Lee April 3-9. Moved to City Point April 12, thence march to Burkerville April 16-20. March to Washington, D. C., May 1-12. Grand Review May 23. Companies "A" to "E" moved to Reedville, Mass, June 6-8, and discharged June 17, 1865. Companies "F" to "K" organized as a Battalion and attached to 3rd Brigade, 3rd Division, Provisional Corps. Duty at Washington, D. C., till July 20. Mustered out July 16. Moved to Reedville, Mass., July 20-22, and discharged August 1, 1865.

Regiment lost during service 1 Officer and 5 Enlisted men killed and mortally wounded and 20 Enlisted men by disease. Total 26.

62nd REGIMENT INFANTRY.

Organization commenced April, 1865, but not completed, and mustered out May 5, 1865.

1st Unattached Company Infantry—Mustered in for 90 days' service April 29, 1864. Duty at Fort Independence, Boston Harbor. Mustered out August 1, 1864.

2nd Unattached Company Infantry—Mustered in for 90 days' service May 3, 1864. Duty at Eastern Point, Gloucester, till August 6. Re-enlisted for 100 days and mustered in August 7, 1864. Stationed at Gallop's Island, Boston Harbor, till November. Again enlisted for one year and mustered in November 16, 1864. At Gallop's Island, Boston Harbor, till July, 1865. Mustered out July 7, 1865.

3rd Unattached Company Infantry—Mustered in for 90 days' service May 3, 1864, and on duty at Fort Pickering, Salem, Mass. Mustered out August 5, 1864.

4th Unattached Company Infantry—Organized at Readville, Mass., and mustered in for 90 days' service May 3, 1864. On duty at Fort Clark's Point, New Bedford. Mustered out August 6, 1864.

5th Unattached Company Infantry—Organized at Readville, Mass., and mustered in for 90 days' service May 4, 1864. Duty at Camp Meigs, Readville, and at Beach Street Barracks. Mustered out August 2, 1864.

6th Unattached Company Infantry.—Organized at Readville and mustered in for 90 days' service May 4, 1864. Duty at Readville. Mustered out August 2, 1864.

7th Unattached Company Infantry—Organized at Readville and mustered in for 90 days' service May 4, 1864. Duty at Gallop's Island, Boston Harbor. Mustered out August 5, 1864.

8th Unattached Company Infantry—Organized at Readville and mustered in for 90 days' service May 10, 1864. At Gallop's Island, Boston Harbor, till August. Mustered out August 11, 1864.

9th Unattached Company Infantry—Organized at Readville and mustered in for 90 days' service May 10, 1864. Stationed at Gallop's Island, Boston Harbor. Mustered out August 11, 1864.

10th Unattached Company Infantry—Organized at Readville and mustered in for 90 days' service May 10, 1864. Stationed at Fort Warren, Boston Harbor. Mustered out August 8, 1864.

11th Unattached Company Infantry—Organized at Readville and mustered in for 90 days' service May 16, 1864. Duty at Forts Sewell and Eastern Point, Gloucester, and at Marblehead, Mass. Mustered out August 15, 1864.

12th Unattached Company Infantry—Organized at Readville and mustered in for 90 days' service. Duty at Long's Point, Provincetown. Mustered out August 15, 1864.

13th Unattached Company Infantry—Organized at Readville and mustered in for 90 days' service May 16, 1864. Duty at Fort Clark's Point, New Bedford, Mass. Mustered out August 15, 1864.

15th Unattached Company Infantry—Organized at Readville and mustered in for 90 days' service July 29, 1864. Stationed at Fort Warren, Boston Harbor. Mustered out November 15, 1864.

16th Unattached Company Infantry—Organized at Readville and mustered in for 90 days' service August 6, 1864. Duty at Gallop's Island, Boston Harbor. Mustered out November 14, 1864.

17th Unattached Company Infantry—Organized at Readville and mustered in for 90 days' service August 5, 1864. Duty at Fort Pickering, Salem, Mass. Mustered out November 12, 1864. Again mustered in for one year at Salem. Mustered out June 30, 1865.

18th Unattached Company Infantry—Organized at Readville and mustered in for 100 days August 6, 1864. Duty at Camp Meigs, Readville. Mustered out November 14, 1864. Re-enlisted and mustered in for one year December 6, 1864. Duty at Camp Meigs, Readville. Mustered out May 12, 1865.

19th Unattached Company Infantry—Organized at Readville and mustered in for 100 days August 9, 1864. Stationed at Fort Warren, Boston Harbor. Mustered out November 16, 1864. Reorganized and mustered in for one year November 25, 1864. Stationed at Fort Winthrop. Mustered out June 27, 1865.

20th Unattached Company Infantry—Organized at Readville and mustered in for 100 days August 11, 1864. Stationed at Fort Sewell, Marblehead, Mass. Mustered out November 18, 1864. Again mustered in for one year November 17, 1864. Stationed at Salisbury Beach. Mustered out June 29, 1865.

21st Unattached Company Infantry—Organized at Readville and mustered in for 100 days August 11, 1864. Stationed at Long's Point, Provincetown. Mustered out November 18, 1864. Reorganized at Fall River, Mass., for one year, and mustered in November 23, 1864. Stationed at Provincetown. Mustered out June 28, 1865.

22nd Unattached Company Infantry—Organized at Readville and mustered in for 100 days' service August 18, 1864. Duty at Camp Meigs, Readville. Mustered out November 2, 1864.

23rd Unattached Company Infantry—Organized at Readville and mustered in for 100 days August 18, 1864. Duty at Camp Meigs, Readville. Mustered out November 26, 1864.

24th Unattached Company Infantry—Organized at Plymouth and mustered in for one year's service December 16-22, 1864. Duty at Camp Meigs, Readville. Mustered out May 12, 1865.

25th Unattached Company Infantry—Organized at Salem and mustered in for one year's service December 9, 1864. Stationed at Fort Miller, Marblehead. Mustered out June 29, 1865.

26th Unattached Company Infantry—Organized at New Bedford and mustered in for one year's service December 13, 1864. Duty at Camp Meigs, Readville. Mustered out May 12, 1865.

Boston Cadets—Mustered in May 26, 1862. Stationed at Fort Warren, Boston Harbor. Mustered out July 2, 1862.

Salem Cadets—Mustered in May 26, 1862. Stationed at Fort Warren, Boston Harbor. Mustered out October 11, 1862.

MICHIGAN VOLUNTEERS.

1st REGIMENT CAVALRY.

Organized at Detroit, Mich., August 21 to September 6, 1861. Mustered in September 13, and left State for Washington, D. C., September 29, 1861. Attached to Cavalry Brigade, Army of the Potomac, to December, 1861. Cavalry, Banks' Division, Army of the Potomac, to March, 1862. Cavalry, 1st Division, Banks' 5th Corps, to April, 1862. Hatch's Cavalry Brigade, Dept. of the Shenandoah, to June, 1862. Cavalry Brigade, 2nd Corps, Army of Virginia, to September, 1862. Unassigned, Alexandria, Va., September, 1862. Price's Cavalry Brigade, Military District of Washington, to February, 1863, and 22nd Army Corps, Dept. of Washington, to March, 1863. 1st Brigade, Stahel's Cavalry Division, 22nd Army Corps, to June, 1863. 2nd Brigade, 3rd Division, Cavalry Corps, Army of the Potomac, to March, 1864. 1st Brigade, 1st Division, Cavalry Corps, Army of the Potomac, to August, 1864. Army of the Shenandoah, Middle Military Division, to March, 1865, and Army of the Potomac to June, 1865. Dept. of Missouri to August, 1865. District of the Plains, Dept. of Missouri, to September, 1865. District of Dakota, Dept. of Missouri, to December, 1865. District of Utah, Dept. of Missouri, to March, 1866. SERVICE.—Operations in Loudoun County, Va., February 25-May 6, 1862. Occupation of Loudoun Heights February 27. Berryville March 6 (Detachment). Capture of Leesburg March 8. Reconnoissance to Snicker's Gap March 12. Battle of Winchester March 23. Strasburg March 27. Advance from Strasburg to Woodstock and Edenburg April 1-2. Salem and Woodstock April 1. Edenburg April 1-2. Thoroughfare Gap April 2. Greenwich April 3. Catlett's Station April 4. Warrenton April 5. Columbia Furnace April 7. White Plains April 11. Rectortown April 14. Piedmont, Mt. Jackson and New Market April 17. McGaheysville April 27. Linden May 15. Operations in the Shenandoah Valley May 15-June 17. Middletown May 24. Retreat to Williamsport May 24-26. Winchester May 25. Expedition from Gainesville June 7-8. Milford June 24. Strasburg Pike June 26. Reconnoissance to Front Royal June 29-30. Luray June 30. Culpeper Court House July 12. Orange Court House July 15. Reconnoissance to Madison Court House July 17. Reconnoissance to Orange Court House under Crawford August 2. Battle of Cedar Mountain August 9. Reconnoissance to Orange Court House August 13, and to Louisa Court House August 16. Pope's Campaign in Northern Virginia August 16-September 2. Fords of the Rappahannock August 21-23. Lewis Ford and Bull Run August 30. Duty in the Defences of Washington, D. C., till June, 1863. Mouth of Monocacy September 5. Reconnoissance to Berryville November 28-30, 1862. Snicker's Ferry, Berryville, November 30. Expedition to Catlett's and Rappahannock Station January 8-10, 1863. Brentsville January 9. Near Union Mills February 14 (Detachment). Hanover, Pa., June 30. Battle of Gettysburg July 1-3. Hunterstown July 2. Fairfield Gap July 4. Smithburg July 5. Hagerstown and Williamsport, Md., July 6. Boonsboro July 8. Hagerstown July 11-13. Falling Waters July 14. Ashby's Gap July 20. Battle Mountain, near Newby's Cross Roads, July 24. Barbee's Cross Roads July 25. King George Court House August 24. Expedition to Port Conway September 1-3. Lamb's Creek Church, near Port Conway, September 1. Advance from the Rappahannock to the Rapidan September 13-17. Stevensburg and Pony Mountain September 13. Culpeper Court House September 13. Somerville Ford September 14-16. Reconnoissance across the Rapidan September 21-23. White's Ford September 21-22. Robertson's Ford and near Liberty Mills September 23. Bristoe Campaign October 8-22. James City October 8-9-10. Bethesda Church October 10. Near Culpeper and Brandy Station October 11. Gainesville October 14. Groveton October 17-18. Gainesville, Catlett's Station and Buckland's Mills October 19. Advance to line of the Rappahannock November 7-8. Mine Run Campaign November 26-October 2. Morton's Ford November 26. Raccoon Ford November 26-27. (4 new Companies or-

ganized October 13 to December 29, 1863.) Demonstration on the Rapidan February 6-7, 1864. Regiment consolidated to 8 Companies February 15, 1864. Kilpatrick's Raid on Richmond February 28-March 4. Fortifications of Richmond March 1. Campaign from the Rapidan to the James River May 3-June 24. Todd's Tavern May 5-6. Wilderness May 5-7. The Furnaces and Brock Road May 6. Todd's Tavern May 7-8. Sheridan's Raid to James River May 9-24. Beaver Dam Station May 9. Ground Squirrel Church and Yellow Tavern May 11. Meadow Bridge May 12. Hanover Court House May 21. On line of the Pamunkey May 26-28. Dabney's Ferry, Hanovertown Ferry, Hanovertown and Crump's Creek May 27. Haw's Shop and Aenon Church May 28. Totopotomoy May 28-31. Old Church and Mattadequin Creek May 30. Bethesda Church, Cold Harbor, May 31-June 1. Sheridan's Trevillian Raid June 7-24. Trevillian Station June 11-12. Newark, or Mallory's Cross Roads, June 12. Black Creek, or Tunstall's Station, and White House, or St. Peter's Church, June 21. Jones' Bridge June 23. Demonstration north of the James River July 27-29. Deep Bottom July 27-28. Ordered to Washington, D. C., August. Sheridan's Shenandoah Valley Campaign August 7-November 28. Winchester and Toll Gate near White Post August 11. Cedarville, or Front Royal, August 16 and 18. Kearneysville August 23. Near Kearneysville August 25. Shephardstown August 25. Leetown and Smithfield August 28. Smithfield Crossing of the Opequan August 29. Berryville September 4. Locke's Ford, Opequan Creek, September 13. Sevier's Ford, Opequan Creek, September 15. Battle of Opequan, Winchester, September 19. Fisher's Hill September 21. Milford September 22. Luray September 24. Port Republic September 26-28. Mt. Crawford October 2. Luray Valley October 8. Tom's Brook October 8-9. Battle of Cedar Creek October 19. Near Kernstown November 11. Expedition into Loudoun and Faquier Counties November 28-December 3. Middleburg December 2. Raid to Gordonsville December 19-28. Madison Court House December 21. Liberty Mills December 22. Jack's Shop, near Gordonsville, December 23. Expedition from Edenburg to Little Fort Valley, February 13-17, 1865. Sheridan's Raid from Winchester February 27-March 25. Occupation of Staunton March 2. Waynesboro March 2. Duguidsville March 8. Hanover Court House March 15. Appomattox Court House March 28-April 9. Dinwiddie Court House March 30-31. Five Forks April 1. Scott's Cross Roads April 2. Tabernacle Church, or Beaver Creek Pond, April 4. Sailor's Creek April 6. Appomattox Station April 8. Appomattox Court House April 9. Surrender of Lee and his army. Expedition to Danville April 23-29. March to Washington May. Grand Review May 23. Moved to Fort Leavenworth, Kansas, June 1. Powder River Expedition and operations against Indians in District of the Plains and Dakota July to November, 1865. Duty in District of Utah till March, 1866. Mustered out March 10, 1866. (Company "D" served detached as Provost Guard at Alexandria November 25, 1862, till June, 1863.) (Regiment absent on furlough December 21, 1863, to March 1, 1864. Returned to Camp Stoneman, D. C., and duty there till April, 1864.)

Regiment lost during service 14 Officers and 150 Enlisted men killed and mortally wounded and 6 Officers and 244 Enlisted men by disease. Total 414.

2nd REGIMENT CAVALRY.

Organized at Detroit, Mich., and mustered in October 2, 1861. Left State for St. Louis, Mo., November 14. Duty at Benton Barracks, Mo., till February 21, 1862. Ordered to Commerce, Mo., February 21. Attached to Cavalry Division, Army of Mississippi, to April, 1862. 2nd Brigade, Cavalry Division, Army of Mississippi, to September, 1862. 2nd Brigade, Cavalry Division, Army of the Ohio, to November, 1862. Unattached, District of Central Kentucky, Dept. of the Ohio, to March, 1863. 1st Brigade, 1st Cavalry Division, Army of the Cumberland, to June, 1864. District of Nashville, Tenn., Dept. of the Cumberland, to October, 1864. 1st Brigade, 1st Division, Cavalry Corps, Army of the Cumberland, to November, 1864. 1st Brigade, 1st Division, Wilson's Cavalry Corps, Military Division Mississippi to August, 1865.

SERVICE.—Siege operations against New Madrid, Mo., March 3-14, 1862. New Mardrid March 4. Siege and capture of Island No. 10, Mississippi River, March 15-April 8. Moved to Hamburg Landing, Tenn., April 17-22. Atkins' Mills, Tenn., April 26. Monterey April 28-29. Siege of Corinth, Miss., April 29-May 30. Reconnoissance to Memphis & Charleston R. R. May 3. Farmington, Miss., May 3 and 9. Glendale May 8. Near Farmington May 12. Reconnoissance to Memphis & Charleston R. R. May 15. Expedition to Mobile & Ohio Railroad May 28-29. Booneville May 29. Osborn and Wolf's Creek, near Lackland, June 4. Reconnoissance toward Baldwyn June 6. Baldwyn June 6. Reconnoissance toward Guntown, Baldwyn, etc., June 9-10. Booneville July 1. Rienzi August 26. Ordered to Louisville, Ky., September. Near Louisville September 30. Pursuit of Bragg to Wild Cat, Ky., October 1-7. Near Perryville October 6-7. Battle of Perryville October 8. Lancaster October 14. Duty in Central Kentucky till December. Carter's Raid from Winchester and Nicholasville, Ky., into East Tennessee and Southwest Virginia December 20, 1862, to January 5, 1863. Bear Wallow December 23. Glasgow December 24 (Cos. "C," "H," "L," "M"). Near Munfordsville and Bacon Creek December 26 (Cos. "C," "H," "L," "M"). Passage of Moccasin Gap December 29. Watauga Bridge, Carter's Station, December 30. Holston River December 30. Dandridge, Tenn., January 6, 1863. Near Auburn February 15. Vaught's Hill, Milton, Tenn., February 18. Thompson's Station March 4-5 (Detachment). Expedition from Franklin to Columbia March 8-12. Thompson's Station March 9. Rutherford Creek March 10-11. Spring Hill March 19. Near Thompson's Station March 23. Little Harpeth March 25. Near Franklin March 31. Franklin June 4-5. Expedition to Thompson's Station May 2. Triune June 9. Middle Tennessee (or Tullahoma) Campaign June 23-July 7. Shelbyville, Eaglesville and Rover June 23. Middleton June 24. Fosterville, Guy's Gap and Shelbyville June 27. Bethpage Bridge, Elk River, July 1. Occupation of Middle Tennessee till August 16. Passage of the Cumberland Mountains and Tennessee River, and Chickamauga (Ga.) Campaign August 16-September 22. Rawlinsville, Ala., September 5. Destruction of Salt Works. Reconnoissance from Alpine toward Rome, Ga., September 10-11. Alpine September 12. Dirt Town, Lafayette Road, near Chattooga River, September 12. Reconnoissance from Lee and Gordon's Mills towards Lafayette September 13. Battle of Chickamauga September 19-21. Operations against Wheeler and Roddy September 29-October 17. Sparta November 26. Operations about Dandridge and Mossy Creek December 24-28. Dandridge, Tenn., December 24. Talbot's Station, Mossy Creek, December 29. Operations about Dandridge January 16-17, 1864. Bend of Chucky Road, near Dandridge, January 16. Dandridge January 17. Operations about Dandridge January 26-28. McNutt's Bridge January 27. Fair Garden January 27-28. Swann's Island January 28. Regiment re-enlisted March 28, 1864, and on Veteran furlough April to June. Atlanta Campaign May 1-June 29 (Non-Veterans). Varnell's Station May 7. Demonstrations on Dalton May 9-13. Tilton May 13. Battle of Resaca May 14-15. Near Cassville May 19. Stilesboro May 23. Burnt Hickory May 24. About Dallas May 25-June 5. Burned Church May 30-June 1. Operations about Marietta and against Kenesaw June 10-29. Lost Mountain June 15-17. Moved to Franklin, Tenn., June 29. Duty Railroad Defences of the District of Nashville till August 29. Rousseau's Pursuit of Wheeler September 1-3. Lavergne September 1. Pursuit of Forrest September 25-October 1. Pulaski September 26-27. Muscle Shoals October 30. Near Shoal Creek October 31. Shoal Creek, near Florence, November 5-6. On line of Shoal Creek November 16-20. Fouche Springs November 23. Battle of Franklin November 30. Nashville December 15-16. Lynnville and Richland Creek December 24. Pulaski December 25-26.

Raid through Mississippi January 17-21, 1865. At Waterloo, Ala., till March 11. Wilson's Raid to Macon, Ga., March 22-April 24. Trion April 1. Selma April 2. North Port, near Tuscaloosa, April 3. Occupation of Tuscaloosa April 4. Lanier's Mills, Sipsey Creek, April 6. Talladega April 22. Mumford's Station April 23. Camp at Macon May 1 to July 17. Mustered out August 17, 1865.

Regiment lost during service 4 Officers and 70 Enlisted men killed and mortally wounded and 2 Officers and 266 Enlisted men by disease. Total 342.

3rd REGIMENT CAVALRY.

Organized at Grand Rapids, Mich., August 24 to November 28, 1861. Left State for St. Louis, Mo., November 28, 1861. Duty at Benton Barracks, Mo., till February 21, 1862. Ordered to Commerce, Mo., February 21. Attached to Cavalry Division, Army of the Mississippi, to April, 1862. 1st Brigade, Cavalry Division, Army of the Mississippi, to June, 1862. 5th Division, Army of the Mississippi, to September, 1862. 2nd Brigade, Cavalry Division, Army of the Mississippi to November, 1862. 3rd Brigade, Cavalry Division, 13th Army Corps (Old), Dept. of the Tennessee, to December, 1862. Cavalry Brigade, District of Jackson, Tennessee, 16th Army Corps, to March, 1863. Mizner's Cavalry Brigade, 3rd Division, 16th Army Corps, to June, 1863. 2nd Brigade, 1st Cavalry Division, 16th Army Corps, to August, 1863. 1st Brigade, 1st Cavalry Division, 16th Army Corps, to January, 1864. District of St. Louis, Mo., Dept. of Missouri, March to May, 1864. 3rd Brigade, 2nd Division, 7th Army Corps, Dept. of Arkansas, to August, 1864. 4th Brigade, Cavalry Division, 7th Army Corps, Dept. of Arkansas, to February, 1865. 1st Brigade, Cavalry Division, 7th Army Corps, to April, 1865. 1st Brigade, 1st Cavalry Division, Military Division of West Mississippi, to May, 1865. 2nd Brigade, 2nd Cavalry Division, West Mississippi, to August, 1865. Dept. of Texas to February, 1866.

SERVICE.—Siege of New Madrid, Mo., March 3-14, 1862. Siege and capture of Island No. 10, Mississippi River, March 15-April 8. Moved to Hamburg Landing, Tenn., April 17-22. Advance on and siege of Corinth, Miss., April 29-May 30. Action at Farmington May 1. Farmington Heights May 4 (Cos. "A," "E," "I," "K"). Reconnoissance toward Corinth May 8. Reconnoissance on Alabama Road toward Sharp's Mills May 10. Reconnoissance to Memphis & Charleston Railroad May 13. Near Farmington May 19 (3rd Battalion). Near Farmington May 22 (Co. "G"). Reconnoissance to Burnsville and Iuka May 22-23. Tuscumbia Creek May 30. Pursuit to Booneville May 30-June 12. Reconnoissance toward Baldwyn June 3. Action at Booneville June 3-4. Clear Creek, near Baldwyn, June 14. Blackland June 28. Ripley June 29. Hatchie Bottom July 20 (Co. "H"). Booneville July 26. Spangler's Mills July 28 (Cos. "H," "L," "M"). Iuka September 19. Battle of Corinth October 3-4. Pursuit to the Hatchie River October 5-12. Grant's Central Mississippi Campaign November 2, 1862, to January 10, 1863. Capture of Ripley and Orizaba November 2, 1862. Reconnoissance from Lagrange November 8-9. Coldwater and Lamar November 8. Holly Springs November 13. Expedition from Grand Junction to Ripley, Miss., November 19-20 (Detachment). Holly Springs November 29 and December 20. Orizaba November 29. Waterford, Lumpkin's Mills, November 29-30. About Oxford December 1-3. Water Valley Station December 4. Coffeeville December 5. Water Valley Station December 18. Ripley December 23. Bolivar December 24. Expedition from Lexington to Clifton February 17-21, 1863 (Cos. "A," "B," "K," "L"). Clifton February 20. Scout from Lexington to mouth of Duck River March 31-April 1. Trenton April 19. Cotton Grove April 25. Forked Deer Creek June 13. Operations in Northwest Mississippi June 15-25. Near Holly Springs June 16-17. Lagrange June 17. Belmont and Coldwater Bridge June 18. Near Panola June 19-20. Senatobia June 20. Matthews' Ferry, on Coldwater River, June 20. Lamar July 5. Forked Deer Creek July

15. Jackson, Tenn., July 17. Expedition to Grenada, Miss., August 12-23. Grenada August 13. Operations in Northern Mississippi and Western Tennessee against Chalmers October 4-17. New Albany October 5. Salem October 8. Ingraham's Mills, near Byhalia, October 12. Wyatt's Ford, Tallahatchie River, October 13. Smith's Bridge October 19. Corinth, Miss., November 2. Operations on Memphis & Charleston Railroad November 3-5. Corinth, Miss., November 12. Operations on Memphis & Charleston Railroad against Lee's attack November 28-December 10. Danville November 14-15. Ripley November 27. Molino November 28. Ripley December 1 and 4. Regiment veteranize January 19, 1864. At Lagrange till January 29. Lagrange January 25. On Veteran furlough till March. Provost duty at St. Louis, Mo., March 22-May 18, and at Little Rock, Ark., May 24 to August 1. Clarendon, Ark., June 25-26. Remount Camp and Lake Bluff August 5. Bull Creek August 6. Expedition from Little Rock to Little Red River August 6-16. Hatch's Ferry August 9 (Detachment). Augusta August 10 (Detachment). Duvall's Bluff August 23. Searcy August 29. Brownsville September 4. Scout and patrol duty September-October. At Brownsville Station, Memphis & Little Rock Railroad, November, 1864, to February, 1865. Expedition from Brownsville to Arkansas Post December 7-13, 1864 (Cos. "A," "H," "K," "L," "M"). Near Dudley's Lake December 16 (Cos. "E," "F" and "G"). Moved to Carrollton, La., March 14-23, 1865; thence to Mobile, Ala. Siege operations against Forts Blakely and Spanish Fort March 26-April 9. Occupation of Mobile April 12. Citronelle, Ala., May 4. Surrender of Gen. Dick Taylor (Regiment acted as escort to Gen. Canby). Moved to Mobile, thence to Baton Rouge, La., May 8-22, and to Shreveport June 10. March from Shreveport to San Antonio, Texas, July 10-August 2. Garrison duty at San Antonio and scouting along frontier to Rio Grande till February 12, 1866. Mustered out February 12 and discharged at Jackson, Mich., March 15, 1866.

Regiment lost during service 3 Officers and 27 Enlisted men killed and mortally wounded and 4 Officers and 380 Enlisted men by disease. Total 414.

4th REGIMENT CAVALRY.

Organized at Detroit, Mich., and mustered in August 28, 1862. Left State for Louisville, Ky., September 26. Attached to 1st Brigade, Cavalry Division, Army of the Ohio, to November, 1862. 1st Brigade, Cavalry Division, Army of the Cumberland, to January, 1863. 1st Brigade, 2nd Cavalry Division, Army of the Cumberland, to October, 1863. 2nd Brigade, 2nd Cavalry Division, Army of the Cumberland, to November, 1863. 1st Brigade, 2nd Cavalry Division, Army of the Cumberland, to November, 1864. 1st Brigade, 2nd Division, Wilson's Cavalry Corps, Military Division Mississippi, to November, 1864. 2nd Brigade, 2nd Division, Cavalry Corps, Military Division Mississippi, to July, 1865.

SERVICE.—Advance on Stanford, Ky., October 10-14, 1862. Action at Stanford October 14. March to Gallatin, Tenn., November 1-8. Cumberland River, near Gallatin, November 8. Lebanon November 11. Franklin Pike, near Hollow Tree Gap, December 4. Reconnoissance from Nashville to Trenton December 11-12. Wilson's Creek Pike December 11. Franklin December 12. Near Murfreesboro December 15. Reconnoissance from Rural Hill December 20. Wilson's Creek Pike December 21 (Cos. "A" and "B"). Advance on Murfreesboro December 26-30. Lavergne December 26-27. Stewart's Creek Bridge, Jefferson Pike, December 27 (Cos. "B," "E," "H" and "L"). Battle of Stone River December 30-31, 1862, and January 1-3, 1863. Overall's Creek December 31. Lavergne and Stewart's Creek January 1 (Cos. "A," "D," "E" and "G"). Lytle's Creek January 5, 1863. Reconnoissance to Harpeth River and Cumberland Shoals January 13-19. Woodbury January 24. Unionville and Rover January 31. Expedition to Franklin January 31-February 13. Rover February 13. Manchester Pike February 22 (Detachment). Unionville and Rover March 4. Expedition to-

ward Columbia March 4-14. Thompson's Station March 9. Rutherford Creek March 10-11. Expedition from Murfreesboro to Auburn, Liberty, Snow Hill, etc., April 2-6. Snow Hill, Woodbury and Liberty April 3. Franklin April 10. Expedition to McMinnville April 20-30. Hickory Creek April 21. Expedition to Middleton May 21-22. Middleton May 22. Near Murfreesboro June 3. Scout on Middleton and Eaglesville Pike June 10. Scout on Salem Pike June 12. Expedition to Lebanon June 15-17. Lebanon June 16. Middle Tennessee (or Tullahoma) Campaign June 23-July 7. Fosterville and Guy's Gap June 27. Shelbyville June 27. Reconnoissance to Rock Island Ferry August 4-5. Sparta August 9. Passage of the Cumberland Mountains and Tennessee River and Chickamauga (Ga.) Campaign August 16-September 22. Calf Killer River August 17. Pea Vine Bridge and Reed's Bridge September 18. Battle of Chickamauga September 19-21. Rossville Gap September 21. Operations against Wheeler and Roddy September 30-October 17. McMinnville October 4. Chattanooga-Ringgold Campaign November 23-27. Raid on East Tennessee & Georgia Railroad November 24-27. Charleston and Cleveland November 26. March to relief of Knoxville November 28-December 8. On courier duty between Headquarters of General Grant and General Burnside during December. Cleveland December 22 (Detachment). Scout from Rossville toward Dalton, Ga., January 21-23, 1864. Near Dalton January 22. Ringgold, Ga., February 18. Demonstrations on Dalton, Ga., February 22-27. Tunnel Hill and near Dalton February 23. Buzzard's Roost Gap and Rocky Faced Ridge February 23-25. Stone Church, near Catoosa Platform, February 27. Atlanta (Ga.) Campaign May 1-September 8. Tanner's Bridge May 15. Near Rome May 15. Arundel Creek and Floyd's Springs May 16. Near Ringston May 18. Near Dallas May 24. Operations on line of Pumpkin Vine Creek and battles about Dallas, New Hope Church and Allatoona Hills May 25-June 5. Big Shanty June 9. Operations about Marietta and against Kenesaw Mountain June 10-July 2. McAffee's Cross Roads June 11. Noonday Creek June 20. Powder Springs or Lattimer's Mills June 20. Noonday Creek June 27. Assault on Kenesaw June 27. Tunnel Hill June 28. On line of Nickajack Creek July 2-5. Rottenwood Creek July 4. Chattahoochie River July 5-17. Flint Hill Church July 20. Garrard's Raid to Covington July 22-24. Garrard's Raid to South River July 27-31. Flat Rock Bridge July 28. Siege of Atlanta August 1-16. Kilpatrick's Raid around Atlanta August 18-22. Red Oak August 19. Flint River and Jonesboro August 19. Lovejoy Station August 20. Operations at Chattahoochie River Bridge August 26-September 2. Sandtown August 29. Roswell September 28. Operations against Hood in North Georgia and North Alabama September 29-November 3. Lost Mountain October 4-7. New Hope Church October 5. Dallas October 7. Near Rome October 10-11. Narrows October 11. Coosaville Road, near Rome, October 13. Little River October 20. Blue Pond and Leesburg October 21. Ordered to Nashville, Tenn., October 26; thence to Louisville, Ky., to refit. At Louisville till December 28. March from Louisville, Ky., to Gravelly Springs, Ala., December 28, 1864, to January 25, 1865, and duty there till March —. Wilson's Raid from Chickasaw, Ala., to Macon, Ga., March 22-April 24. Selma, Ala., April 2. Montgomery April 12. Pleasant Hill and Double Bridges April 18. Capture of Macon April 20. Pursuit and capture of Jeff Davis at Irwinsville, Ga., May 10 (Detachment). Duty at Macon and Nashville till July. Mustered out July 1, 1865.

Regiment lost during service 3 Officers and 48 Enlisted men killed and mortally wounded and 2 Officers and 341 Enlisted men by disease. Total 394.

5th REGIMENT CAVALRY.

Regiment organized at Detroit, Mich., and mustered in August 30, 1862. Left State for Washington, D. C., December 4, 1862. Attached to Provisional Cavalry

Brigade, Military District of Washington, to February, 1863. Provisional Cavalry Brigade, Casey's Division, 22nd Army Corps, Dept. of Washington, to March, 1863. 1st Brigade, Stahel's Cavalry Division, 22nd Army Corps, to June, 1863. 2nd Brigade, 3rd Division, Cavalry Corps, Army of the Potomac, to March, 1864. 1st Brigade, 1st Division, Cavalry Corps, Army of the Potomac and Middle Military Division, to June, 1865.

SERVICE.—Duty in the Defences of Washington, D. C., till June, 1863. Scout from Centreville to Falmouth, Va., February 27-28, 1863. Hauxhurst Mills April 13. On Lawyer's Road, near Fairfax Court House and Frying Pan, June 4. Ordered to join Army of the Potomac in the field June 25. Reconnoissance up the Catoctin Valley June 27-28. Occupation of Gettysburg, Pa., June 28. Action at Hanover, Pa., June 30. Battle of Gettysburg, Pa., July 1-3. Hunterstown July 2. Monterey July 4. Smithburg July 5. Williamsport and Hagerstown July 6. Boonsboro July 8. Hagerstown July 11-13. Falling Waters July 14. Williamsport July 14. Snicker's Gap July 17. Ashby's Gap July 17, 18 and 20. Battle Mountain, near Newby's Cross Roads, July 24. Expedition from Warrenton Junction between Bull Run and Blue Ridge Mountains August 1-8. King George Court House August 24. Hartwood Church August 25. Expedition to Port Conway September 1-3. Lamb's Creek Church, near Port Conway, September 1. Advance from the Rappahannock to the Rapidan September 13-17. Culpeper Court House September 13. Raccoon Ford September 14-16. Somerville Ford September 15. Reconnoissance across the Rapidan September 21-23. Madison Court House September 21. White's Ford September 21-22. Robertson's Ford September 23. Woodville September 30. Bristoe Campaign October 8-22. James City October 8-10. Bethesda Church October 11. Brandy Station October 11. Near Culpeper October 11. Hartwood Church October 12. Grove Church October 14. Gainesville October 14. Groveton October 17-18. Gainesville, Catlett's Station and Buckland's Mill October 19. Advance to line of the Rappahannock November 7-8. Stevensburg November 7. Mine Run Campaign November 26-December 2. Morton's Ford November 26. Raccoon Ford November 26-27. Demonstration on the Rapidan February 6-7, 1864. Kilpatrick's Raid on Richmond February 28-March 4. Fortification of Richmond March 1. Brooks' Turnpike March 1. Near Tunstall's Station March 3 (Detachment). Campaign from the Rapidan to the James River May 3-June 24. Todd's Tavern May 5-6. Brock Road and the Furnaces May 6. Wilderness May 6-7. Todd's Tavern May 7-8. Sheridan's Raid to James River May 9-24. Beaver Dam Station May 9. Ground Squirrel Church and Yellow Tavern May 11. Meadow Bridge and fortifications of Richmond May 12. Hanover Court House May 21. Haw's Shop May 24. On line of the Pamunkey May 26-28. Hanovertown Ferry, Hanovertown, and Crump's Creek May 27. On line of the Totopotomoy May 28-31. Haw's Shop and Aenon Church May 28. Old Church and Mattadequin Creek May 30. Bethesda Church, Cold Harbor, May 31-June 1. Sheridan's Trevillian Raid June 7-24. Trevillian Station June 11-12. Newark or Mallory's Cross Roads June 12. Black Creek or Tunstall's Station June 21. White House or St. Peter's Church June 21. Jones' Bridge June 23. Demonstration north of the James River July 27-29. Deep Bottom July 27-28. Ordered to Washington, D. C., August —. Sheridan's Shenandoah Valley Campaign August 7-November 28. Toll Gate, near White Post and Winchester, August 11. Cedarville or Front Royal August 16. Snicker's Gap Pike August 19. Near Berryville August 19-20. Kearneysville and Shepherdstown August 25. Leetown-Smithfield August 29. Smithfield Crossing, Opequan, August 29. Locke's Ford, Opequan Creek, September 13. Sevier's Ford, Opequan Creek, September 15. Battle of Opequan-Winchester September 19. Fisher's Hill September 21. Milford September 22. Luray September 24. Port Republic September 26-28. Mt. Crawford October 2. Luray Valley October 8. Tom's

Brook, "Woodstock Races," October 8-9. Battle of Cedar Creek October 19. Near Kernstown November 11. Loudon County November 18. Expedition into Loudoun and Faquier Counties November 28-December 3. Raid to Gordonsville December 19-28. Madison Court House December 21. Liberty Mills December 22. Near Gordonsville December 23. Expedition to Little Fort Valley February 13-17, 1865. Sheridan's Expedition from Winchester February 27-March 25. Occupation of Staunton and Waynesboro March 2. Duguidsville March 8. Appomattox Campaign March 28-April 9. Dinwiddie Court House March 30-31. Five Forks April 1. Scott's Cross Roads April 2. Tabernacle Church or Beaver Pond Creek April 4. Sailor's Creek April 6. Appomattox Station April 8. Appomattox Court House April 9. Surrender of Lee and his army. Expedition to Danville April 23-29. March to Washington, D. C., May —. Grand Review May 23. Moved to Fort Leavenworth, Kansas, June 1. Mustered out June 23, 1865. Veterans and Recruits transferred to 1st Michigan Cavalry.

Regiment lost during service 6 Officers and 135 Enlisted men killed and mortally wounded and 3 Officers and 322 Enlisted men by disease. Total 366.

6th REGIMENT CAVALRY.

Organized at Grand Rapids, Mich., May 28 to October 13, 1862. Mustered in October 13, 1862. Duty at Grand Rapids, Mich., till December 10. Left State for Washington, D. C., December 10, 1862. Attached to Provisional Cavalry Brigade, Casey's Division, Military District of Washington, to February, 1863. Provisional Cavalry Brigade, Casey's Division, 22nd Army Corps, Dept. of Washington, to March, 1863. 1st Brigade, Stahel's Cavalry Division, 22nd Army Corps, to June, 1863. 2nd Brigade, 3rd Division, Cavalry Corps, Army of the Potomac, to March, 1864. 1st Brigade, 1st Division, Cavalry Corps, Army of the Potomac and Middle Military Division, to June, 1865. District of the Plains, Dept. of Missouri, to September, 1865. tered out November 24, 1865.
District of Dakota, Dept. of Missouri, to November, 1865.

SERVICE.—Duty in the Defences of Washington, D. C., till June, 1863. Scout from Centreville, Va., to Falmouth, Va., February 27-28, 1863. Marstellar's Place, near Warrenton Junction, May 14. Reconnoissance up the Catoctin Valley June 27-28. Occupation of Gettysburg, Pa., June 28. Action at Hanover, Pa., June 30. Battle of Gettysburg, Pa., July 1-3. Hunterstown, Pa., July 2. Monterey July 4. Smithburg July 5. Williamsburg and Hagerstown July 6. Boonsboro July 8. Hagerstown July 11-13. Falling Waters July 14. Ashby's Gap July 17, 18 and 20. Berry's Ford July 20. Battle Mountain, near Newby's Cross Roads, July 24. King George Court House August 24. Expedition to Port Conway September 1-3. Advance from the Rappahannock to the Rapidan September 13-17. Culpeper Court House September 13. Somerville Ford September 14. Raccoon Ford September 14-16. Somerville Ford September 15. Reconnoissance across the Rapidan September 21-23. Madison Court House September 21. White's Ford September 21-22. Robertson's Ford September 23. Bristoe Campaign October 8-22. James City October 8-10. Bethesda Church October 10. Near Culpeper and Brandy Station October 11. Gainesville October 14. Manassas Junction October 15. Groveton October 17-18. Gainesville, Catlett's Station and Buckland's Mills October 19. Advance to line of the Rappahannock November 7-8. Stevensburg November 8. Mine Run Campaign November 26-December 2. Morton's Ford November 26. Raccoon Ford November 26-27. Demonstration on the Rapidan February 6-7, 1864. Kilpatrick's Raid on Richmond February 28-March 4. Fortifications of Richmond March 1. Campaign from the Rapidan to the James River May 3-June 24. Battles of the Wilderness May 5-7; Todd's Tavern May 5-6; Brock Road and the Furnaces May 6; Todd's Tavern May 7-8. Sheridan's Raid to James

River May 9-24. Beaver Dam Station May 9. Ground Squirrel Church and Yellow Tavern May 11. Meadow Bridge and fortifications of Richmond May 12. Hanover Court House May 21. On line of the Pamunkey May 26-28. Hanovertown Ferry, Hanovertown, and Crump's Creek May 27. Haw's Shop and Aenon Church May 28. Totopotomoy May 28-31. Old Church and Mattadequin Creek May 30. Bethesda Church, Cold Harbor, May 31-June 1. Bottom's Bridge June 1. Sheridan's Trevillian Raid June 7-24. Trevillian Station June 11-12. Newark or Mallory's Cross Roads June 12. Black Creek or Tunstall's Station and White House or St. Peter's Church June 21. Jones' Bridge June 23. Muddy Branch, Md., July 26 (Detachment). Demonstration north of the James River July 27-29. Deep Bottom July 27-28. Ordered to Washington, D. C. Sheridan's Shenandoah Valley Campaign August 7-November 28. Toll Gate, near White Post and Winchester, August 11. Cedarville or Front Royal August 16. Kearneysville and Shephardstown August 25. Leetown and Smithfield August 28. Smithfield Crossing, Opequan, August 29. Berryville September 4. Charlestown September 9. Locke's Ford, Opequan Creek, September 13. Sevier's Ford, Opequan Creek, September 15. Battle of Opequan, Winchester, September 19. Fisher's Hill September 21. Clifford September 22. Luray September 24. Port Republic September 26-28. Mt. Crawford October 2. Luray Valley October 8. Tom's Brook "Woodstock Races" October 8-9. Battle of Cedar Creek October 19. Edenburg November 7. Near Kernstown November 11. Expedition into Loudoun and Faquier Counties November 28-December 3. Raid to Gordonsville December 19-28. Madison Court House December 21. Liberty Mills December 22. Near Gordonsville December 23. Expedition to Little Fort Valley February 13-17, 1865. Sheridan's Raid from Winchester to James River February 27-March 25. Occupation of Staunton and action at Waynesboro March 2. Duguidsville March 8. Appomattox Campaign March 28-April 9. Dinwiddie Court House March 30-31. Five Forks April 1. Scott's Cross Roads April 2. Tabernacle Church or Beaver Pond Creek April 4. Sailor's Creek April 6. Appomattox Station April 8. Appomattox Court House April 9. Surrender of Lee and his army. Expedition to Danville April 23-29. March to Washington, D. C., May —. Grand Review May 23. Moved to Fort Leavenworth, Kansas, June 1. Powder River Expedition and operations against Indians on the plains till November. Consolidated with 1st Michigan Cavalry November 7, 1865. Old members mustered

Companies "I" and "M" served detached from Regiment February, 1863, to May, 1864. Attached to Jewett's Corps of Observation February to June, 1863. Guard and patrol duty along the Potomac to prevent blockade running across that river to Baltimore, Md. Stationed at and operating about Rockville, Great Falls, Edward's Ferry, Poolesville and White's Ford, Md., till June, 1863. Skirmish at Oakland, Md., April 26 (Co. "I"). Skirmish with Moseby at Seneca Mills, Md., June 10. Gettysburg (Pa.) Campaign June-July. Forced march during night of July 3 from Fredericksburg, Va., and action with Lee's Bridge Guard at Falling Waters July 4. Detachment of 140 men surprised and dispersed a much larger force guarding Lee's Pontoon Bridge swinging on the Virginia side of the Potomac, capturing men and ammunition and completely destroying the pontoons and trains which General Lee admitted delayed his army seven days. Occupation of Harper's Ferry July 7. Attached to Well's Brigade, Maryland Heights Division, Dept. of West Virginia. Operating from Harper's Ferry and having almost continuous Raids, Expeditions and skirmishes in the Shenandoah Valley, Mechanicsville Gap and Moorefield Valley till April, 1864. Skirmish near Harper's Ferry July 14, 1863. Halltown July 15. Waterford August 8. Skirmishes at Charleston and on the Berryville Pike October 18. Expedition from Charleston to near New Market November 13-18. Skirmishes at Woodstock, Edenburg and Mt. Jackson No-

vember 16. Operations in Hampshire and Hardy Counties, W. Va., January 27-February 7, 1864. Skirmishes near Romney February 2, Moorefield February 4 and Smithfield February 5. Ordered to rejoin Regiment in Army of the Potomac April 25, and joined May 3, 1864.

Regiment lost during service 7 Officers and 128 Enlisted men killed and mortally wounded and 251 Enlisted men by disease. Total 386.

7th REGIMENT CAVALRY.

Organized at Grand Rapids, Mich., October, 1862, to June, 1863. 1st Battalion left State for Washington, D. C., February 20, 1863. Balance of Regiment May, 1863. Attached to Provisional Cavalry Brigade, Casey's Division, Defences of Washington, 22nd Army Corps, to April, 1863. 1st Brigade, Stahel's Cavalry Division, 22nd Army Corps, Dept. of Washington, to June, 1863. 2nd Brigade, 3rd Division, Cavalry Corps, Army of the Potomac, to March, 1864. 1st Brigade, 1st Division, Cavalry Corps, Army of the Potomac and Middle Military Division, to June, 1865. District of the Plains, Dept. of Missouri, to September, 1865. District of Dakota to December, 1865.

SERVICE.—Duty in the Defences of Washington, D. C., till June, 1863. Action at Thoroughfare Gap, Va., May 21, 1863. Greenwich May 30. Expedition up the Catoctin Valley June 27-28. Occupation of Gettysburg, Pa., June 28. Hanover, Pa., June 30. Battle of Gettysburg, Pa., July 1-3. Huntersville July 2. Monterey July 4. Smithburg July 5. Williamsport and Hagerstown July 6. Boonsboro July 8. Hagerstown July 11-13. Falling Waters July 14. Snicker's Gap July 19. Expedition from Warrenton Junction, between Bull Run and Blue Ridge Mountains, August 1-8. Hartwood Church August 15. King George Court House August 24. Expedition to Port Conway September 1-3. Advance from the Rappahannock to the Rapidan September 13-17. Culpeper Court House September 13. Raccoon Ford September 14-16. Raccoon Ford September 17. Reconnoissance across the Rapidan September 21-23. White's Ford September 21-22. Orange Court House September 22. Bristoe Campaign October 8-22. Robertson's River October 8. Jams City October 8-10. Bethesda Church October 10. Near Culpeper and Brandy Station October 11. Gainesville October 14. Groveton October 17-18. Gainesville, Catlett's Station and Buckland's Mills October 19. Near Falmouth November 6. Advance to line of the Rappahannock November 7-8. Stevensburg November 8. Mine Run Campaign November 26-December 2. Morton's Ford November 26. Raccoon Ford November 26-27. Demonstration on the Rapidan February 6-7, 1864. Kilpatrick's Raid on Richmond February 28-March 4. Fortifications of Richmond and Atlee's March 1. Campaign from the Rapidan to the James River May 3-June 24. Battles of the Wilderness May 5-7. Todd's Tavern May 5-6. Brook Road and the Furnaces May 6. Todd's Tavern May 7-8. Sheridan's Raid to the James River May 9-24. Beaver Dam Station May 9. Ground Squirrel Church and Yellow Tavern May 11. Meadow Bridge and fortifications of Richmond May 12. Malvern Hill May 16. Hanover Court House May 21. On line of the Pamunkey May 26-28. Hanovertown Ferry, Hanovertown and Crump's Creek May 27. On line of the Totopotomoy May 28-31. Haw's Shop and Aenon Church May 28. Old Church and Mattadequin Creek May 30. Bethesda Church, Cold Harbor, May 21-June 1. Bottom's Bridge June 1. Sheridan's Trevillian Raid June 7-24. Trevillian Station June 11-12. Newark, or Mallory's Cross Roads, June 12. Black Creek, or Tunstall's Station, and White House, or St. Peter's Church, June 21. Jones' Bridge June 23. Fort Stevens and along Northern Defences of Washington July 11-12 (Detachment). Demonstration North of the James River July 27-29. Deep Bottom July 27-29. Ordered to Washington, D. C., August. Sheridan's Shenandoah Valley Campaign August 7-November 28. Toll Gate, near White Post, and near Winchester August 11. Cedarville, or Front Royal, August 16. Kearneysville August 23. Kearneysville and Shephardstown August 25. Leetown and Smithfield

August 28. Smithfield Crossing of the Opequan September 29. Locke's Ford, Opequan Creek, September 13. Sevier's Ford, Opequan, September 15. Battle of Opequan, Winchester, September 19. Fisher's Hill September 21. Milford September 22. Luray September 24. Port Republic September 26-28. Mt. Crawford October 2. Salem Church October 6. Luray Valley October 8. Tom's Brook ("Woodstock Races") October 8-9. Battle of Cedar Creek October 19. Edenburg November 7. Near Kernstown November 11. Expedition into Loudoun and Faquier Counties November 28-December 3. Raid to Gordonsville December 19-28. Madison Court House December 21. Liberty Mills December 22. Near Gordonsville December 23. Expedition to Little Fort Valley February 13-17, 1865. Sheridan's Raid from Winchester to James River February 28-March 25. Occupation of Staunton and action at Waynesboro March 2. Duguidsville March 8. Appomattox Campaign March 28-April 9. Dinwiddie Court House March 30-31. Five Forks April 1. Scott's Cross Roads April 2. Tabernacle Church, or Beaver Bend Creek, April 4. Sailor's Creek April 6. Appomattox Station April 8. Appomattox Court House April 9. Surrender of Lee and his army. Expedition to Danville April 23-27. March to Washington, D. C., May. Grand Review May 23. Moved to Leavenworth, Kansas, June 1. Powder River Expedition and operations against Indians in District of the Plains and Dakota till December. Regiment mustered out December 15, 1865. Veterans and Recruits transferred to 1st Michigan Cavalry.

Regiment lost during service 4 Officers and 81 Enlisted men killed and mortally wounded and 2 Officers and 256 Enlisted men by disease. Total 343.

8th REGIMENT CAVALRY.

Organized at Mt. Clemens, Mich., December 30, 1862, to May 2, 1863. Left State for Covington, Ky., May 12, 1863; thence moved to Hickman's Bridge, Ky., June 1-4, and to Mt. Sterling, Ky. Attached to 2nd Brigade, 4th Division, 23rd Army Corps, to July, 1863. 2nd Brigade, 1st Division, 23rd Army Corps, to August, 1863. 1st Brigade, 4th Division, 23rd Army Corps, to October, 1863. 2nd Brigade, 4th Division, 23rd Army Corps, to November, 1863. 2nd Brigade, 1st Cavalry Division, Dept. of the Ohio, to May, 1864. 3rd Brigade, Cavalry Division, District of Kentucky, Dept. of the Ohio, to June, 1864. 3rd Brigade, Cavalry Division, 23rd Army Corps, Army of the Ohio, to November, 1864. 1st Brigade, 6th Division, Wilson's Cavalry Corps, Military Division Mississippi, to June, 1865. Cavalry District West Tennessee to September, 1865.

SERVICE.—Operations against Everett in Eastern Kentucky June 13-23, 1863. Action at Triplett's Bridge, Ky., June 16. Pursuit of Morgan June 27-July 25. Buffington Island, Ohio, July 19. New Lisbon, Ohio, July 22. Operations against Scott in Eastern Kentucky July 25-August 6. Lancaster and Paint Lick Bridge July 31-August 1. Burnside's Campaign in East Tennessee August 16-October 17. March across Cumberland Mountains to Knoxville, Tenn., August 16-September 2. Winter's Gap August 31.. Cleveland September 18. Calhoun, Athens and Charleston September 25. Calhoun September 26. Sweetwater October 26-27. Knoxville Campaign November 4-December 23. Lenoir Station November 14-15. Campbell's Station November 16. Near Knoxville November 16. Siege of Knoxville November 17-December 5. Near Bean's Station December 9-13. Bean's Station December 14. Blain's Cross Roads December 16-19. Operations about Dandridge January 16-17, 1864. Bend of Chucky Road, near Dandridge, January 16. Dandridge January 17. Operations about Dandridge January 26-28. Seviersville and Flat and Muddy Creeks January 26. Near Fair Garden January 27. Moved to Knoxville February 3, thence march to Mt. Sterling, Ky., February 6-24, and duty there till June 3. March to Big Shanty June 3-28. Spring Place June 25. Atlanta Campaign June 28-September 8. Kenesaw Mountain July 1. Sweetwater July 3. Chattahoochie River July 6-17. Dark Corners July 7. Campbellton July 18. Stoneman's Raid

on Macon July 27-August 6. Clinton and Macon July 30. Hillsborough, Sunshine Church, July 30-31. Eatonton August 1. Regiment refused to surrender with Gen. Stoneman, and cut their way through the rebel lines, but were afterwards surprised at Mulberry Creek and Jug Tavern August 3, and mostly captured. Picket duty at Turner's Ferry and Marietta till September 14. Moved to Nicholasville, Ky., September 14-21, and duty there till October 19. March to Nashville, Tenn., October 19-26; thence moved to Pulaski, Tenn. Scout to Lawrenceburg November 6, and to Waynesboro November 12. Nashville Campaign November-December. Near Eastport November 15. Henrysville November 23. Mt. Pleasant November 23. Duck River November 24-27. Columbia Ford November 28-29. Franklin November 30. Battle of Nashville December 15-16. Moved to Pulaski January 18, 1865, and engaged in scout and patrol duty in that section till September 22. Scout from Pulaski to Rogersville, Ala., April 23-26 (Detachment). Mustered out at Nashville, Tenn., September 22, 1865.

Regiment lost during service 1 Officer and 41 Enlisted men killed and mortally wounded and 2 Officers and 290 Enlisted men by disease. Total 334.

9th REGIMENT CAVALRY.

Organized at Coldwater, Mich., January 8 to May 19, 1863. Left State for Covington, Ky., May 20, 1863; thence moved to Hickman's Bridge, Ky., June 1-4, and to Mt. Sterling, Ky. Attached to 3rd Brigade, 1st Division, 23rd Army Corps, Army of the Ohio, to August, 1863. 3rd Brigade, 4th Division, 23rd Army Corps, to November, 1863. 1st Brigade, 2nd Cavalry Division, Dept. of the Ohio, to May, 1864. 1st Brigade, Cavalry Division, District of Kentucky, Dept. of the Ohio, to July, 1864. 1st Brigade, Cavalry Division, 23rd Army Corps, to August, 1864. Mounted Brigade, Cavalry Division, 23rd Army Corps, to September, 1864. 2nd Brigade, Cavalry Division, 23rd Army Corps, to November, 1864. 2nd Brigade, Kilpatrick's 3rd Division, Cavalry Corps, Military Division Mississippi, to July, 1865.

SERVICE.—Operations against Everett in Eastern Kentucky June 13-23, 1863. Action at Triplett's Bridge, Ky., June 16. Pursuit of Morgan June 27-July 25. Action at Lebanon, Ky., July 5. Cumming's Ferry July 8 (Cos. "B," "D," "H"). Buffington Island, Ohio, July 19. Operations in Eastern Kentucky against Scott July 25-August 6. Salinesville July 26. Lancaster and Paint Lick Bridge, Ky., July 31. Lancaster August 1. Burnside's Campaign in East Tennessee August 16-October 17. March across Cumberland Mountains to Knoxville, Tenn., August 16-September 2. Winter's Gap August 31. Expedition to Cumberland Gap September 4-7. Operations about Cumberland Gap September 7-10. Capture of Cumberland Gap September 9. Carter's Station September 22. Zollicoffer September 24. Jonesborough September 28. Leesburg September 29. Blue Springs October 5 and 10. Sweetwater October 10-11. Rheatown October 11. Spurgeon's Mill October 19. Knoxville Campaign November 4-December 23. Stock Creek November 15. Siege of Knoxville November 17-December 5. Rutledge December 7. Morristown December 10. Cheek's Cross Roads December 12. Russellville December 12-13. Bean's Station December 14. Rutledge December 15-16. Blain's Cross Roads December 16-19. Stone's Mill December 19. Dandridge December 24. Mossy Creek December 26. Operations about Dandridge January 16-17, 1864. Kimbrough's Cross Roads January 16. Bull's Gap January 16-17. Dandridge January 17. Operations about Dandridge January 26-28. Near Fair Garden January 27. Island Ford January 28. Strawberry Plains February 20. Cheek's Cross Roads March 13. Moved to Nicholasville, Ky., and duty there till July. Operations against Morgan May 31-June 20, 1864 (Detachment). Mt. Sterling June 9. Cynthiana June 12. March to Marietta, Ga., July 4-27. Atlanta Campaign July 27-September 8. Siege of Atlanta August 1-September 2. Sandtown and Fairburn August 15. Stone Mountain October 2. Expedition from Atlanta to Tuckum's Cross Roads October 26-29. Tuckum's Ferry October 27. Near Lawrenceville, Stone Mountain, October 27. March to the sea November 15-December 10. Jonesborough November 15. Bear Creek Station November 16. East Macon and Walnut Creek November 20. Griswoldsville November 20 (Cos. "B," "C," "D"). Waynesboro November 27-28. Near Waynesboro November 28. Buckhead Creek, or Reynolds' Plantation, November 28. Waynesboro December 4. Cypress Swamp, near Sister's Ferry, December 7. Buck Creek December 7. Ebenezer Creek December 8. Seige of Savannah December 10-21. Campaign of the Carolinas January to April, 1865. Aiken and Blackville, S. C., February 11. Johnson's Station February 11. South Edisto River February 11-12. Gunter's Bridge, North Edisto, February 14. Phillips' Cross Roads and Wadesboro, N. C., March 4. Monroe's Cross Roads March 10. Near Smith's Mill, Black River, March 15. Taylor's Hole Creek, Averysboro, March 16. Battle of Bentonville March 19-21. Raleigh & Smithfield Railroad April 10-11. Raleigh April 12-13. Morrisville April 13. Bennett's House April 26. Surrender of Johnston and his army. Duty at Concord, N. C., May 14 to July 21. Mustered out July 21, 1865.

Regiment lost during service 2 Officers and 26 Enlisted men killed and mortally wounded and 2 Officers and 154 Enlisted men by disease. Total 184.

10th REGIMENT CAVALRY.

Organized at Grand Rapids, Mich., September 18 to November 23, 1863. Mustered in November 18, 1863. Left State for Lexington, Ky., December 1, 1863. Attached to District of North Central Kentucky, 1st Division, 23rd Army Corps, Dept. of the Ohio, to April, 1864. 2nd Brigade, 4th Division, 23rd Army Corps, to February, 1865. 2nd Brigade, 4th Division, District of East Tennessee, Dept. of the Cumberland, to July, 1865. Cavalry Brigade, District of East Tennessee, Dept. of the Cumberland, to November, 1865.

SERVICE.—Duty at Lexington, Ky., till January 25, 1864. Moved to Burnside's Point January 14, and duty there till February 25. March from Burnside's Point to Knoxville, Tenn., February 25-March 6. Action at Flat Creek Valley March 15. Moved to Morristown March 16. Expedition to Carter's Station April 24-28. Rheatown April 24. Jonesboro and Johnsonville April 25. Expedition from Bull's Gap to Watauga River April 25-27. Watauga Bridge April 25. Powder Springs Gap April 29. Newport May 2. Dandridge May 19. Reconnoissance from Strawberry Plains to Bull's Gap and Greenville May 28-31. Greenville May 30. Bean's Station June 14. Wilsonville June 16. Scout from Strawberry Plains to Greenville August 1-5. Morristown August 2. Gillem's Expedition into East Tennessee August 17-31 (Cos. "E," "F" and "I" remained at Knoxville.) Blue Springs August 23 (Co. "A"). Bull's Gap August 24. Strawberry Plains and Flat Creek Bridge August 24. Park's Gap, Greenville, September 4. (Morgan killed.) Expedition from East Tennessee toward Southwest Virginia September 20-October 17. Carter's Station September 30-October 1. Thorn Hill, near Bean Station, October 10. Mossy Creek October 15. Sweetwater October 23. Morristown November 13. Russellsville November 14. Strawberry Plains November 16-17. Flat Creek November 17. Stoneman's Raid into Southwest Virginia December 10-29. Bristol December 14. Near Marion and Wytheville December 17-18. Saltsville, Va., December 20-21. Expedition from Strawberry Plains to Clinch Mountain and skirmish January 28-31, 1865 (Co. "M"). Duty at Knoxville till March 21. Stoneman's Expedition from East Tennessee into Southwest Virginia and Western North Carolina March 21-April 25. Brabson's Mills March 25. Boonesville, N. C., March 27. Henry Court House, Va., April 8. Abbott's Creek April 10. High Point April 11. Salisbury April 12. Statesville April 14. Catawba River April 17. Howard's Gap, Blue Ridge Mountains, April 22. Asheville April 26. Duty at Lenoir Station and Sweetwater till August, and in West Tennessee till November. Mustered out November 11, 1865.

Regiment lost during service 2 Officers and 29 Enlisted

men killed and mortally wounded and 240 Enlisted men by disease. Total 271.

11th REGIMENT CAVALRY.

Organized at Kalamazoo and Detroit, Mich., October 7 to December 10, 1863. Moved to Lexington, Ky., December 10-22, 1863, and duty there till April 28, 1864. Attached to District of Lexington, Ky., 23rd Army Corps, Army of the Ohio, to April, 1864. 1st Brigade, 1st Division, District of Kentucky, 5th Division, 23rd Army Corps, Dept. of the Ohio, to August, 1864. 4th Brigade, District of Kentucky, Dept. of the Ohio, to February, 1865. 2nd Brigade, Cavalry Division, District of East Tennessee, Dept. of the Cumberland, to July, 1865.

SERVICE.—Moved from Lexington to Louisa, Ky., April 28-May 3, 1864, and duty scouting and patrolling in Eastern Kentucky till May 25. Expedition from Louisa to Rockhouse Creek May 9-13 (Cos. "A," "F"). Pound Gap May 9 (Cos. "A," "F"). Pursuit of Morgan May 25-June 20. Mt. Sterling June 9. Duty at Lexington, Ky., till August 23. Moved to Camp Burnside, on the Cumberland River, August 23, and duty protecting southern borders of Kentucky till September 16. Burbridge's Expedition to Saltsville, Va., September 17-October 20. McCormack's Farm September 23. Laurel Mountain, Va., September 29. Cedar Bluffs September 30. Bowen's Farm September 30-October 1. Saltsville October 2. Sandy Mountain October 3. Regiment complimented by Gen. Burbridge for gallant conduct in cutting its way through greatly superior numbers when completely surrounded by the forces of Gen. Cerro Gordo Williams. Operations against guerrillas near Mt. Sterling till November 17. Moved to Crab Orchard November 17-20, thence to Cumberland Gap, Tenn. Scout to Morristown December 1-4. Stoneman's Raid to Southwest Virginia December 10-29. Paperville and Kingsport December 13. Bristol December 14. Abington, Va., December 15. Wytheville December 16. Marion December 17-18. Saltsville December 20-21. Duty at Lexington, Ky., till February 23, 1865. Moved to Knoxville, Tenn., February 23-March 15. Stoneman's Expedition from East Tennessee in Southwet Virginia and Western North Carolina March 21-April 25. Boone N. C., March 28. Danbury, N. C., April 9. Shallow Ford and near Mocksville April 11. Salisbury April 12. Catawba River, near Morgantown, April 17. Blue Ridge Mountains, Howard's Gap, April 22. Hudsonville April 23. Asheville April 25. Moved to Pulaski, Tenn., June 24, and duty there till July. Consolidated with 8th Michigan Cavalry July 20, 1865.

Regiment lost during service 4 Officers and 24 Enlisted men killed and mortally wounded and 114 Enlisted men by disease. Total 142.

1st UNITED STATES LANCERS.

Organized at Detroit, Saginaw and St. John, Mich., November 30, 1861, to February 20, 1862. Mustered out March 20, 1862.

CHANDLER'S HORSE GUARD.

Organized at Coldwater, Mich., September 19, 1861. Mustered out November 22, 1861.

6th REGIMENT HEAVY ARTILLERY.

See 6th Regiment Infantry.

BATTERY "A" 1st REGIMENT LIGHT ARTILLERY. ("LOOMIS' BATTERY," "COLDWATER ARTILLERY.")

Attached to State Militia. Tendered its services to the government as an organization and accepted by the government April 23, 1861. On duty at Fort Wayne, Detroit, Mich. Battery reorganized for three years' service and mustered in May 28, 1861. Left State for Cincinnati, Ohio, May 31. Duty at Camp Dennison, Ohio, till June 12. Ordered to West Virginia June 12. Attached to McCook's Brigade, Army of Occupation, West Virginia, to August, 1861. Reynolds' Cheat Mountain District, West Virginia, to December, 1861. Artillery, 3rd Division, Army of the Ohio, to September, 1862. 17th Brigade, 3rd Division, 1st Corps, Army of the Ohio, to November, 1862. 2nd Brigade, 1st Division, Center 14th Army Corps, Army of the Cumberland, to January, 1863. Artillery, 1st Division, 14th Army Corps, Army of the Cumberland, to December, 1863. Garrison Artillery, Chattanooga, Tenn., Dept. of the Cumberland, to July, 1865.

SERVICE.—At Clarksburg, W. Va., June 28, 1861. March to Buckhannon June 28-July 1. Middle Fork Bridge July 6. Camp Garnett, Rich Mountain, July 10. Battle of Camp Garnett, Rich Mountain, July 10-11. Battery remounted with six 10-lb. Parrotts by order of the General commanding. At Beverly July 12. Moved to Cheat Mountain Pass July 13, thence to Elkwater August 14 and duty there till October 30. Operations on Cheat Mountain September 11-17. Point Mountain Turnpike and Cheat Mountain Pass September 13. Elkwater September 14. Greenbrier River October 3-4. Moved to Huttonsville October 30, thence to Phillippi December 6. Ordered to Louisville, Ky., December 16; thence to Bacon Creek December 31 and duty there till February, 1862. Advance on Bowling Green, Ky., February 14-15. Occupation of Bowling Green February 15. Advance on Nashville, Tenn., February 22-25. Occupation of Nashville February 25. Engaged in scout and patrol duty in Northern Alabama by detachments and at Edgefield, Tenn., till August. Action at Bridgeport, Ala., April 29. Gunter's Landing May 15 (Detachment). Athens May 29 (Detachment). Whitesboro June 13 (Detachment). Expedition from Woodville to Guntersville July 27-30 (Section). March to Nashville, Tenn., thence to Louisville, Ky., in pursuit of Bragg August 21-September 26. Pursuit of Bragg to Crab Orchard, Ky., October 1-15. Battle of Perryville, Ky., October 8. March to Nashville, Tenn., October 16-November 7, and duty there till December 26. Advance on Murfreesboro, Tenn., December 26-30. Battle of Stone River December 30-31, 1862, and January 1-3, 1863. Duty at Murfreesboro till June. Expedition to McMinnville April 20-30. Middle Tennessee (or Tullahoma) Campaign June 23-July 7. Hoover's Gap June 24-26. Occupation of Tullahoma July 1. Occupation of Middle Tennessee till August 16. Passage of the Cumberland Mountains and Tennessee River and Chickamauga (Ga.) Campaign August 16-September 22. Davis Cross Roads, near Dug Gap, September 11. Battle of Chickamauga September 19-21; 5 pieces captured after 27 Officers and men and 50 horses had been killed and disabled; one with 3 caissons was recaptured on September 19, and two more on the 20th, but all were unfit for duty and the Battery was ordered to Chattanooga; one gun was recaptured at Mission Ridge and the last at Atlanta. Siege of Chattanooga, Tenn., September 24-November 23. Battles of Chattanooga November 23-25. Battery stationed at Chattanooga as garrison till July, 1865. Demonstration on Dalton February 22-27, 1864 (Section). Tunnel Hill, Buzzard's Roost Gap and Rocky Faced Ridge February 23-25, 1864. Mustered out July 12, 1865, and discharged at Jackson, Mich., July 28, 1865.

Battery lost during service 1 Officer and 11 Enlisted men killed and mortally wounded and 28 Enlisted men by disease. Total 40.

BATTERY "B" 1st REGIMENT LIGHT ARTILLERY.

Organized at Grand Rapids and Detroit, Mich., September 10 to December 14, 1861. Left State for St. Louis, Mo., December 17, 1861. Duty in District of West Tennessee till March, 1862. Attached to Hurlburt's 4th Division, Army of the Tennessee, to April, 1862. Moved to Pittsburg Landing, Tenn., March —. Battle of Shiloh, Tenn., April 6-7. Battery overwhelmed and captured except Lang's Section, which was attached to Mann's Battery "C", 1st Missouri Artillery, April, 1862, to January, 1863. Battery reorganized at Detroit, Mich., December, 1862, and left State for Columbus, Ky., December 25, 1862. Attached to District of Corinth, Miss., 16th Army Corps, Dept. of the Tennessee, to

March, 1863. Artillery, 2nd Division, 16th Army Corps, to September, 1864. Artillery Brigade, 15th Army Corps, to July, 1865.

SERVICE.—Moved from Columbus, Ky., to Corinth, Miss., January 4-9, 1863, and duty there till March 9. (Lang's Section joined at Corinth January, 1863.) March to Bethel, Tenn., March 9, and duty there till June 7. Moved to Corinth, Miss., June 7, and duty there till October 29. March to Pulaski, Tenn., October 29-November 12, and duty there till April 21, 1864. Veterans on furlough January 7-February 26, 1864. Moved to Athens, Ala., April 21. Atlanta (Ga.) Campaign May 1 to September 8. Demonstrations on Resaca May 8-13. Sugar Valley, near Resaca, May 9. Near Resaca May 13. Battle of Resaca May 14-15. Lay's Ferry, Oostenaula River, May 14-15. Rome Cross Roads May 16. Duty at Rome, Ga., till October 14. Reconnoissance from Rome on Cave Springs Road and skirmishes October 12-13. Turkey Creek, Ala., October 25. March to the sea November 15-December 10. Griswoldsville November 22. Jones' Bridge, Ogeechee River, December 7. Siege of Savannah December 10-21. Campaign of the Carolinas January to April, 1865. Salkehatchie Swamps, S. C., February 2-5. South Edisto River February 9. North Edisto River February 11-12. Congaree Creek February 15. Bates' Ferry, Congaree Creek, February 15. Columbia February 16-17. Near Falling Creek, N. C., March 20. Battle of Bentonville March 20-21. Mill Creek March 22. Occupation of Goldsboro March 24. Advance on Raleigh April 10-14. Occupation of Raleigh April 14. Bennett's House April 26. Surrender of Johnston and his army. March to Washington, D. C., via Richmond, Va., April 29-May 19. Grand Review May 24. Moved to Detroit, Mich., June 1-6, and mustered out June 14, 1865.

Battery lost during service 1 Officer and 1 Enlisted man killed and 35 Enlisted men by disease. Total 37.

BATTERY "C" 1st REGIMENT LIGHT ARTILLERY.

Organized at Grand Rapids, Mich., November 23 to December 17, 1861. Mustered in November 28, 1861. Left State for St. Louis, Mo., December 17, 1861, and duty there till February, 1862. Ordered to Commerce, Mo. Attached to Artillery Division, Army of Mississippi, to April, 1862. Artillery, 2nd Division, Army of Mississippi, to November, 1862. 1st Brigade, 8th Division, 13th Army Corps (Old), Dept. of the Tennessee, to December, 1862. 1st Brigade, 8th Division, 16th Army Corps, to March, 1863. 4th Brigade, 2nd Division, 16th Army Corps, to May, 1863. 3rd Brigade, District of Memphis, Tenn., 5th Division, 16th Army Corps, to November, 1863. Fuller's Brigade, 2nd Division, 16th Army Corps, to March, 1864. Artillery, 4th Division, 16th Army Corps, to September, 1864. Artillery, 1st Division, 27th Army Corps, to November, 1864. Artillery Brigade, 17th Army Corps, to June, 1865.

SERVICE.—Siege of New Madrid, Mo., March 3-14, 1862. Siege and capture of Island No. 10, Mississippi River, March 15-April 8. Expedition to Fort Pillow, Tenn., April 13-17. Moved to Hamburg Landing, Tenn., April 17-22. Action at Monterey April 29. Advance on and siege of Corinth, Miss., April 29-May 30. Reconnoissance toward Corinth May 8. Action at Farmington May 9. Near Corinth May 24. Occupation of Corinth May 30. Pursuit to Booneville May 31-June 12. Duty at Corinth till November. Reconnoissance from Burnsville toward Iuka and action September 16. Battle of Iuka September 19. Battle of Corinth October 3-4. Pursuit to Ripley October 5-12. Grant's Central Mississippi Campaign November 2, 1862, to January 10, 1863. Duty at Corinth till April, 1863. Dodge's Expedition to Northern Alabama April 15-May 2. Rock Cut, near Tuscumbia, April 22. Tuscumbia April 23. Town Creek April 28. Moved to Memphis, Tenn., May 13, and duty there till October 18. At Iuka, Miss., till November. Moved to Prospect, Tenn., and duty there till March, 1864. At Decatur, Ala., till May. Atlanta (Ga.) Campaign May 1 to September 8. Demonstrations on Resaca May 8-13. Sugar Valley, near Resaca,

May 9. Near Resaca May 13. Battle of Resaca May 14-15. Advance on Dallas May 18-25. Operations on line of Pumpkin Vine Creek and battles about Dallas, New Hope Church and Allatoona Hills May 25-June 5. Operations about Marietta and against Kenesaw Mountain June 10-July 2. Assault on Kenesaw June 27. Nickajack Creek July 2-5. Ruff's Mills July 3-4. Chattahoochie River July 5-17. Sandtown July 6-7. Decatur and battle of Atlanta July 22. Siege of Atlanta July 22-August 25. Duty at Marietta till October. Pursuit of Hood into Alabama October 3-26. March to the sea November 15-December 10. Siege of Savannah December 10-21. Campaign of the Carolinas January to April, 1865. Fishburn's Plantation, near Lane's Bridge, Salkehatchie River, S. C., February 6. Binnaker's Bridge February 9. Orangeburg February 11-12. Columbia February 16-17. Cheraw February 28. Fayetteville, N. C., March 11. Battle of Bentonville March 19-21. Occupation of Goldsboro March 24. Advance on Raleigh April 10-14. Occupation of Raleigh April 14. Bennett's House April 26. Surrender of Johnston and his army. March to Washington, D. C., via Richmond, Va., April 29-May 19. Grand Review May 24. Mustered out at Detroit, Mich., June 22, 1865.

Battery lost during service 3 Enlisted men killed and mortally wounded and 34 Enlisted men by disease. Total 37.

BATTERY "D" 1st REGIMENT LIGHT ARTILLERY.

Organized at White Pigeon, Mich., September 17 to December 7, 1861. Left State for Kentucky December 9, 1861. Attached to 1st Division, Army of the Ohio, to September, 1862. Artillery, 1st Division, 3rd Corps, Army of the Ohio, to November, 1862. Artillery, 3rd Division, Center 14th Army Corps, Army of the Cumberland, to January, 1863. Artillery, 3rd Division, 14th Army Corps, Army of the Cumberland, to October, 1863. Artillery, 2nd Division, Artillery Reserve, Dept. of the Cumberland, to March, 1864. Garrison Artillery, Murfreesboro, Tenn., Dept. of the Cumberland, to July, 1864. 1st Brigade, Defences of Nashville & Chattanooga Railroad, Dept. of the Cumberland, to March, 1865. 1st Brigade, 1st Sub-District, District of Middle Tennessee, Dept. of the Cumberland, to August, 1865.

SERVICE.—Duty at Camp Dick Robinson and Somerset, Ky., till January, 1862. Advance on Camp Hamilton, Ky., January 1-17. Mill Springs, Fishing Creek, January 19. Moved to Nashville, Tenn., February 10-March 2. March to Savannah, Tenn., March 20-April 8. Advance on and siege of Corinth, Miss., April 29-May 30. Pursuit to Booneville May 31-June 12. Duty at Iuka, Miss., and Tuscumbia, Ala., till August. March to Louisville, Ky., in pursuit of Bragg August 21-September 26. Pursuit of Bragg to Crab Orchard, Ky., October 1-15. Battle of Perryville, Ky., October 8. March to Nashville, Tenn., October 16-November 7, and duty there till December 26. Advance on Murfreesboro December 26-30. Battle of Stone River December 30-31, 1862, and January 1-3, 1863. Duty at Murfreesboro till June. Middle Tennessee (or Tullahoma) Campaign June 23-July 7. Hoover's Gap June 24-26. Occupation of Middle Tennessee till August 16. Passage of the Cumberland Mountains and Tennessee River and Chickamauga (Ga.) Campaign August 16-September 22. Battle of Chickamauga September 19-21. Siege of Chattanooga, Tenn., September 24-November 23. Battles of Chattanooga November 23-25. Occupied Fort Negley and supported General Hooker's assault on Lookout Mountain November 24. Mission Ridge November 25. Ordered to Nashville, Tenn., December 5, and garrison duty there till March 30, 1864. Moved to Murfreesboro March 30, and garrison duty at Fort Rosecrans till July, 1865. Siege of Murfreesboro December 5-12, 1864. Moved from Murfreesboro to Jackson, Mich., July 15-22. Mustered out August 3, 1865.

Battery lost during service 2 Enlisted men killed and 39 Enlisted men by disease. Total 41.

BATTERY "E" 1st REGIMENT LIGHT ARTILLERY.

Organized at Grand Rapids, Albion and Marshall, Mich., and mustered in December 6, 1861. Left State for Louisville, Ky., thence moved to Bacon Creek, Ky., and duty there till February, 1862. Attached to Artillery, 5th Division, Army of the Ohio, to June, 1862. Artillery Reserve, Army of the Ohio, to August, 1862. Post of Nashville, Tenn., Dept. of the Ohio and Cumberland, to June, 1863. 2nd Brigade, 3rd Division, Reserve Corps, Army of the Cumberland, to October, 1863. Garrison Artillery, Nashville, Tenn., Dept. of the Cumberland, to December, 1864. Artillery Brigade, 4th Army Corps, to February, 1865. Unattached, District of North Alabama, Dept. of the Cumberland, to July, 1865.

SERVICE.—Advance on Nashville, Tenn., February 10-March 3, 1862. March to Savannah, Tenn., March 17-April 7. Advance on and siege of Corinth, Miss., April 29-May 30. Occupation of Corinth and pursuit to Booneville May 30-June 12. Buell's Campaign in Northern Alabama and Middle Tennessee June to August. Garrison duty at Nashville, Tenn., till June, 1863. Siege of Nashville, Tenn., September 12-November 7, 1862. Moved to Murfreesboro, Tenn., June 1, 1863, and duty there till October. Return to Nashville, Tenn., and garrison duty there till December, 1864. Rousseau's Raid into Alabama and Georgia July 10-22, 1864 (1 Section). Ten Islands, Coosa River, July 14. Stone's Ferry, Tallapoosa River, July 15. Nontasulga July 18. Chewa Station July 18. Opelika July 18. McCook's Raid on Atlanta & West Point Railroad and Macon & Western Railroad July 27-31 (1 Section). Lovejoy's Station July 29. Newnan's July 30. Battle of Nashville, Tenn., December 15-16, 1864. Pursuit of Hood to the Tennessee River December 17-28. Duty at Nashville till February, 1865. Ordered to Decatur, Ala., and garrison duty there till July. Mustered out July 30, 1865.

Battery lost during service 33 by disease.

BATTERY "F" 1st REGIMENT LIGHT ARTILLERY.

Organized at Detroit and Coldwater, Mich., and mustered in January 9, 1862. Left State for Kentucky March 3, 1862. Attached to garrison at West Point, Ky., Dept. of the Ohio, to June, 1862. Unattached, Dept. of the Ohio, to August, 1862. Cruft's Brigade, Richmond, Ky., Dept. of the Ohio, to September, 1862. 2nd Brigade, 2nd Division, Army of Kentucky, Dept. of the Ohio, to October, 1862. District of Louisville, Ky., Dept. of the Ohio, to December, 1862. Bowling Green, Ky., District of Western Kentucky, Dept. of the Ohio, to June, 1863. Unattached, 2nd Division, 23rd Army Corps, Dept. of the Ohio, to August, 1863. Munfordsville, Ky., 1st Division, 23rd Army Corps, Dept. of the Ohio, to August, 1863. District of South Central Kentucky, 1st Division, 23rd Army Corps, to January, 1864. Unattached, 2nd Division, 23rd Army Corps, to May, 1864. Artillery, 2nd Division, 23rd Army Corps, to November, 1864. District of Nashville, Tenn., Dept. of the Cumberland, to December, 1864. Artillery, 1st Division, 23rd Army Corps, Dept. of the Ohio, to February, 1865, and Dept. of North Carolina to April, 1865. Post of New Berne, N. C., Dept. of North Carolina, to July, 1865.

SERVICE.—Garrison at West Point, Ky., till June, 1862. Action at Henderson, Ky., June 30. At Richmond, Ky., till September 1. Battle of Richmond August 29-30. Guns captured. Duty at Louisville, Bowling Green and Munfordsville, Ky., till October, 1863. Action at Shepherdsville July 7, 1863. At Glasgow, Ky., October to December, 1863. March across Cumberland Mountains to Knoxville, Tenn., January 14-22, 1864, and garrison duty at Knoxville till April 24, 1864. March to Cleveland, Tenn., April 24-May 1. Atlanta (Ga.) Campaign May 1 to September 8. Demonstrations on Rocky Faced Ridge and Dalton, Ga., May 8-13. Battle of Resaca May 14-15. Cassville May 19-22. Operations on line of Pumpkin Vine Creek and battles about Dallas, New Hope Church and Allatoona

Hills May 25-June 5. Operations about Marietta and against Kenesaw Mountain June 10-July 2. Lost Mountain June 15-17. Muddy Creek June 17. Noyes Creek June 19. Kolb's Farm June 22. Assault on Kenesaw Mountain June 27. Nickajack Creek July 2-5. Chattahoochie River July 5-17. Decatur July 19. Howard House July 20. Battle of Atlanta July 22. Siege of Atlanta July 22-August 25. Utoy Creek August 5-7. Flank movement on Jonesboro August 25-30. Battle of Jonesboro August 31-September 1. Lovejoy Station September 2-6. At Decatur September 8 to October 4. At Chattanooga, Tenn., till November 2, and at Johnsonville till November 24. Nashville Campaign November-December. March to Nashville, Tenn., December 1-8. Battle of Nashville, Tenn., December 15-16. Movement to Washington, D. C., thence to Fort Fisher, N. C., January 19-February 24, 1865, and to Beaufort and New Berne, N. C., February 25-26. Carolina Campaign March 1-April 26. Advance on Kinston and Goldsboro March 3-21. Battle of Wise's Forks March 8-10. Kinston March 14. Occupation of Goldsboro March 21 and duty there till April 8. Ordered to New Berne, N. C., April 8, and duty there till June. Ordered to Jackson, Mich., arriving there June 24. Mustered out July 1, 1865.

Battery lost during service 1 Officer and 9 Enlisted men killed and mortally wounded and 23 Enlisted men by disease. Total 33.

BATTERY "G" 1st REGIMENT LIGHT ARTILLERY.

Organized at Kalamazoo, Mich., and mustered in January 17, 1862. Moved to Louisville, Ky., February 12-14; thence to West Point, Ky., March 3-5, and duty there till April 1. Attached to Artillery, 7th Division, Army of the Ohio, to October, 1862. Artillery, Cumberland Division, District of West Virginia, Dept. of the Ohio, to November, 1862. Artillery, 9th Division, Right Wing 13th Army Corps (Old), Dept. of the Tennessee, to December, 1862. Artillery, 3rd Division, Sherman's Yazoo Expedition, to January, 1863. Artillery, 9th Division, 13th Army Corps, Army of the Tennessee, to July, 1863. Artillery, 1st Division, 13th Army Corps, Army of the Tennessee, to August, 1863, and Dept. of the Gulf to June, 1864. Defences of New Orleans, La., Dept. of the Gulf, to August, 1864. Artillery Reserve, Dept. of the Gulf, to October, 1864. United States Forces, Mobile Bay, Dept. of the Gulf, to December, 1864. District of Southern Alabama, Dept. of the Gulf, to July, 1865.

SERVICE.—Cumberland Gap Campaign March 28-June 18, 1862. Occupation of Cumberland Gap June 18 to September 16. Evacuation of Cumberland Gap and retreat to the Ohio River June 17-October 3. Expedition to Charleston, Gauley River, W. Va., October 21-November 10. Moved to Memphis, Tenn., November 20, and duty there till December 20. Sherman's Yazoo Expedition December 20, 1862, to January 3, 1863. Chickasaw Bayou December 26-28, 1862. Chickasaw Bluff December 29. Expedition to Arkansas Post, Ark., January 3-10, 1863. Assault and capture of Fort Hindman, Arkansas Post, January 10-11. Moved to Young's Point, La., January 17, and duty there till March 8. Moved to Milliken's Bend, La., March 8. Operations from Milliken's Bend to New Carthage March 31-April 17. James' Plantation, near New Carthage, April 8. Expedition from Perkins' Plantation to Hard Times Landing April 25-29. February, 1863. Price's Cavalry Brigade, 22nd Army Phelps' and Clark's Bayous April 26. Choctaw Bayou, on Lake Bruin, April 28. Battle of Port Gibson May 1. Battle of Champion's Hill May 16. Big Black River May 17. Siege of Vicksburg, Miss., May 18-July 4. Assaults on Vicksburg May 19 and 22. Advance on Jackson, Miss., July 4-10. Near Clinton July 8. Near Jackson July 9. Siege of Jackson July 10-17. Moved to Carrollton, La., August 13, and duty there till November 13. Moved to Brazos Santiago and Aransas, Texas, November 13-20. Fort Esperanza November 27-30. Duty at Fort Esperanza till December 15. At DeCrow's Point till January 4, 1864. At Indianola till May 28, and at

Fort Esperanza till June 13. Moved to Carrolton, La., June 13-19, and duty there till October 9. Moved to Fort Morgan, Mobile Bay, October 9-11, and garrison and outpost duty there till April 10, 1865. Operations against Mobile April 10-12. Capture of Mobile April 12. Garrison bay batteries Defences of Mobile till July 19. Moved to Jackson, Mich., July 19-August 2. Mustered out August 6, 1865.

Battery lost during service 4 Enlisted men killed and mortally wounded and 1 Officer and 41 Enlisted men by disease. Total 46.

BATTERY "H," 1st REGIMENT LIGHT ARTILLERY ("DE GOLYER'S BATTERY").

Organized at Monroe, Mich., and mustered in March 6, 1862. Left State for St. Louis, Mo., March 13; thence moved to New Madrid, Mo. Attached to Artillery Division, Army of the Mississippi, to July, 1862. District of Columbus, Ky., Dept. of the Tennessee, to November, 1862. Artillery, 3rd Division, Right Wing 13th Army Corps (Old), Dept. of the Tennessee, to December, 1862. Artillery, 3rd Division, 17th Army Corps, Army of the Tennessee, to October, 1864. Post of Chattanooga, Tenn., Dept. of the Cumberland, October, 1864. Post of Nashville, Tenn., Dept. of the Cumberland, to February, 1865. Post of Chattanooga, Tenn., Dept. of the Cumberland, to July, 1865.

SERVICE.—Operations against Island No. 10, Mississippi River, March 15-April 8, 1862. Expedition down the Mississippi River to Fort Pillow, Tenn., May 19-23. Duty in District of Columbus, Ky., till November. Expedition from Columbus, Ky., to Covington, Durhamsville and Fort Randolph September 28-October 5. Grant's Central Mississippi Campaign November 2, 1862, to January 10, 1863. Reconnoissance from Lagrange November 8-9, 1862. Moved to Memphis, Tenn., January, 1863; thence to Lake Providence, La., February 22. Duty there and at Milliken's Bend, La., till April 25. Movement on Bruinsburg and turning Grand Gulf April 25-30. Battle of Thompson's Hill, Port Gibson, Miss., May 1. South Fork, Bayou Pierrie, May 2. Forty Hills and Hankinson's Ferry May 3-4. Battles of Raymond May 12, Jackson May 14, and Champion's Hill May 16. Siege of Vicksburg, Miss., May 18-July 4. Assaults on Vicksburg May 19 and 22. Surrender of Vicksburg July 4. Duty at Vicksburg till February, 1864. Expedition to Monroe, La., August 20-September 2, 1863. Expedition to Canton October 14-20. Bogue Chitto Creek October 17. Duty at Big Black November 8, 1863, to February, 1864. Meridian Campaign February 3-March 2. Clinton February 5. Meridian February 14-15. Moved to Clifton, Tenn., April; thence march to Ackworth, Ga., May 5-June 8. Atlanta (Ga.) Campaign June 8-September 8. Operations about Marietta and against Kenesaw Mountain June 10-July 2. Assault on Kenesaw June 27. Nickajack Creek July 2-5. Howell's Ferry July 5. Chattahoochie River July 5-17. Leggett's (or Bald Hill) July 20-21. Battle of Atlanta July 22. Siege of Atlanta July 22-August 25. Flank movement on Jonesboro August 25-30. Battle of Jonesboro August 31-September 1. Lovejoy Station September 2-6. Duty near Atlanta till October. Reconnoissance from Rome, on Cave Springs Road, and skirmishes October 12-13. Guard Railroad near Chattanooga, Tenn., till November. Moved to Nashville, Tenn., November 15-18, and duty there till February, 1865. Battle of Nashville December 15-16, 1864 (Reserve). Moved to Chattanooga February 16-19, 1865, and duty there till July. Ordered to Jackson, Mich.. and there mustered out July 22, 1865.

Battery lost during service 2 Officers and 3 Enlisted men killed and mortally wounded and 42 Enlisted men by disease. Total 47.

BATTERY "I," 1st REGIMENT LIGHT ARTILLERY.

Organized at Detroit, Mich., and mustered in August 29, 1862. Moved to Washington, D. C., December 4-11. Attached to Camp Berry, Defences of Washington, to to Triplett's Bridge June 16, 1863. Action at Triplett's Corps, Dept. of Washington, to March, 1863. Artillery,

Stahel's Cavalry Division, 22nd Army Corps, to June, 1863. 1st Brigade, Horse Artillery, Army of the Potomac, to August, 1863. 2nd Brigade, Horse Artillery, Army of the Potomac, to November, 1863. Artillery Brigade, 11th Army Corps, Army of the Cumberland, to March, 1864. Artillery, 3rd Division, 11th Army Corps, to April, 1864. Artillery, 3rd Division, 20th Army Corps, Army of the Cumberland, to July, 1864. Artillery Brigade, 20th Army Corps, to October, 1864. Unattached Artillery, Dept. of the Cumberland, to November, 1864. Reserve Artillery, Chattanooga, Tenn., Dept. of the Cumberland, to July, 1865.

SERVICE.—Duty in the Defences of Washington, D. C., till June, 1863. At Fairfax Court House, Va., till June 24. March to Gettysburg, Pa., June 24-July 2. Battle of Gettysburg July 2-3. March to Warrenton, Va., July 8-24; thence to Culpeper Court House. Moved to Nashville, Tenn., October 27-November 12, and duty there till March 7, 1864. March to Whiteside, Tenn., March 7-17, and duty there till April 28. Atlanta (Ga.) Campaign May 1 to September 8. Demonstrations on Rocky Faced Ridge May 8-11. Battle of Resaca May 14-15. Cassville May 19. New Hope Church May 25. Operations on line of Pumpkin Vine Creek and battles about Dallas, New Hope Church and Allatoona Hills May 25-June 5. Operations about Marietta and against Kenesaw Mountain June 10-July 2. Pine Hill June 11-14. Lost Mountain June 15-17. Gilgal (or Golgotha Church) June 15. Muddy Creek June 17. Noyes' Creek June 19. Assault on Kenesaw June 27. Ruff's Station July 4. Chattahoochie River July 5-17. Peach Tree Creek July 19-20. Siege of Atlanta July 22-August 25. Operations at Chattahoochie River Bridge August 26-September 2. Occupation of Atlanta September 2-November 1. Ordered to Chattanooga, Tenn., November 1, and garrison duty there as Reserve Artillery till July, 1865. Ordered to Jackson, Mich., and there mustered out July 14, 1865.

Battery lost during service 5 Enlisted men killed and mortally wounded and 27 Enlisted men by disease. Total 32.

BATTERY "K," 1st REGIMENT LIGHT ARTILLERY.

Organized at Grand Rapids, Mich., November 21, 1862, to February 20, 1863. Left State for Washington, D. C., February 28, arriving there March 1. Attached to Camp Barry, Defences of Washington, 22nd Army Corps, to April, 1863. 1st Brigade, DeRussy's Division, 22nd Army Corps, to June, 1863. Camp Barry, Defences of Washington, D. C., to November, 1863. Artillery Brigade, 11th Army Corps, Army of the Cumberland, to March, 1864. Garrison Artillery, Chattanooga, Tenn., Dept. of the Cumberland, to March, 1865. 2nd Brigade, 4th Division, District of East Tennessee, Dept. of the Cumberland, to July, 1865.

SERVICE.—Duty at Washington, D. C., till May 23, 1863. Garrison Forts Ramsey and Buffalo, Upton's Hill, Defences of Washington, to June. At Camp Barry till October. Moved to Nashville, Tenn., October 28-November 12, and Reserve Artillery duty there till March 6, 1864. March to Chattanooga, Tenn., March 6-19, and Reserve Artillery duty there till March 31, 1865. One detachment attached to 13th New York Battery and one detachment to Battery "I," 1st Michigan Artillery, serving in the 20th Army Corps during 1864. Battery moved to Riceville, Tenn., March 31, 1865, and duty there till July. Ordered to Detroit, Mich., and there mustered out July 22, 1865.

Battery lost during service 3 Officers and 1 Enlisted man killed and mortally wounded and 14 Enlisted men by disease. Total 18.

BATTERY "L" 1st REGIMENT LIGHT ARTILLERY.

Organized at Coldwater, Mich., and mustered in April 11, 1863. Left State for Covington, Ky., May 20, and duty there till June 4, 1863. Moved to Camp Nelson, Ky., June 4; thence to Mt. Sterling, Ky., June 12. Attached to Artillery, 3rd Division, 23rd Army Corps, Dept. of the Ohio, to September, 1863. Willcox's Division, Cumberland Gap, Left Wing Forces, Dept. of the Ohio, to January, 1864. District of the Clinch, Dept. of the Ohio, to April, 1864. 1st Brigade, 4th Division, 23rd Army Corps, Dept. of the Ohio, to August, 1864. 2nd Brigade, 4th Division, 23rd Army Corps, to February, 1865. 2nd Brigade, 4th Division, District of East Tennessee, Dept. of the Cumberland, to August, 1865.

SERVICE.—Reconnoissance from Mt. Sterling, Ky., Bridge June 16. Moved to Lebanon, Ky., July 4. Action with Morgan at Lebanon July 5. Pursuit of Morgan July 6-29. Buffington Island, Ohio, July 19 (Section). Steubenville, Ohio, July 26 (Section). Burnside's Campaign in East Tennessee August 16-October 17. March across Cumberland Mountains to Knoxville, Tenn., August 16-September 2. Winter's Gap August 31. Moved to Morristown September 4. Operations about Cumberland Gap September 7-10. Carter's Depot September 22. Zollicoffer September 24. Jonesboro September 28. Blue Springs October 5 and 10. Sweetwater October 10-11. Moved to Bean's Station November 9 and to Tazewell November 12. To Cumberland Gap November 18. Return to Tazewell December 25, thence to Evans' Ford, Clinch River, December 26. To Cumberland Gap January 12, 1864, and duty there till June 27. Moved to Knoxville June 27-July 1 and duty there till August, 1865. (One Section detached to guard railroad at Strawberry Plains December 6, 1864, to April 10, 1865.) Ordered to Jackson, Mich., August 15, and there mustered out August 22, 1865.

Battery lost during service 1 Enlisted man killed and 1 Officer and 27 Enlisted men by disease. Total 29.

BATTERY "M" 1st REGIMENT LIGHT ARTILLERY.

Organized at Detroit, Mt. Clemens and Dearborn, and organization completed May 30, 1863. Moved to Indianapolis, Ind., July 9-11; thence to Cincinnati, Ohio, July 13, and return to Indianapolis, Ind., July 17. Duty there till September 18. Moved to Camp Nelson, Ky., September 18-20. Attached to Willcox's Division, Left Wing Forces, 23rd Army Corps, Dept. of the Ohio, to January, 1864. District of the Clinch, Dept. of the Ohio, to April, 1864. 1st Brigade, 4th Division, 23rd Army Corps, Dept. of the Ohio, to February, 1865. 1st Brigade, 4th Division, District of East Tennessee, Dept. of the Cumberland, to March, 1865. 2nd Brigade, 4th Division, District of East Tennessee, to July, 1865.

SERVICE.—March from Camp Nelson, Ky., to Cumberland Gap, Tenn., September 24-October 3, 1863, and to Morristown, Tenn., October 6. Moved to Bull's Gap October 17, thence to Bean's Station October 19, and to Tazewell October 21, and to Cumberland Gap October 22. Garrison duty at Cumberland Gap till May 10, 1865. Action at Walker's Ford, Clinch River, December 2, 1863. Tazewell January 24, 1864. Moved to Knoxville, Tenn., May 10, 1865; thence to Strawberry Plains and duty there till July 7. Moved to Jackson, Mich., July 7-12, and there mustered out August 1, 1865.

Battery lost during service 3 Enlisted men killed and mortally wounded and 15 Enlisted men by disease. Total 18.

13th INDEPENDENT BATTERY LIGHT ARTILLERY.

Organized at Grand Rapids, Mich., and mustered in January 20, 1864. Left State for Washington, D. C., February 3. Attached to Camp Barry, Defences of Washington, D. C., 22nd Army Corps, to May, 1864. 1st Brigade, Hardin's Division, Defences North of the Potomac, 22nd Army Corps, to July, 1864. Fort Foote, Defences North of the Potomac, 22nd Army Corps, to October, 1864. 1st Brigade, Hardin's Division, 22nd Army Corps, to June, 1865.

SERVICE.—Duty at Camp Barry, Defences of Washington, D. C., till May 14, 1864. Garrison Fort Slemmer, Defences of Washington, till July, 1864, and Fort Stevens during July. Repulse of Early's attack on Fort Stevens and the Northern Defences of Washington July 11-12. Duty at Fort Foote till October, and at Fort Sumner till December. Garrison Fort Reno till February, 1865. Battery mounted February 27, 1865, and engaged in operations against guerrillas and patrol duty in Maryland till June, headquarters of the Battery remaining at Fort Reno. Dismounted June 15 and ordered to Jackson, Mich. Mustered out July 1, 1865.

Battery lost during service 1 Enlisted man killed and 13 Enlisted men by disease. Total 14.

14th INDEPENDENT BATTERY LIGHT ARTILLERY.

Organized at Kalamazoo, Mich., and mustered in January 5, 1864. Left State for Washington, D. C., February 1. Attached to Camp Barry, Defences of Washington, 22nd Army Corps, to May, 1864. 1st Brigade, Hardin's Division, Defences of Washington North of the Potomac, 22nd Army Corps, to August, 1864. 2nd Brigade, Hardin's Division, 22nd Army Corps, to December, 1864. 3rd Brigade, Hardin's Division, 22nd Army Corps, to June, 1865.

SERVICE.—Duty at Camp Barry, Defences of Washington, February 5 to April 20, 1864. Mounted and duty at Fort Bunker Hill May 15-22. Dismounted May 22 and ordered to Camp Barry, thence moved to Fort Slocum May 25. Duty as Heavy Artillery at Forts Bunker Hill, Totten, Slemmer, Snyder, Carroll and Greble, Defences of Washington North of the Potomac, till June 17, 1865. Repulse of Early's attack on the Northern Defences of Washington July 11-13, 1864. Moved to Jackson, Mich., June 17-21, 1865, and mustered out July 1, 1865.

Battery lost during service 9 by disease.

1st REGIMENTS ENGINEERS AND MECHANICS.

Organized at Marshall, Mich., September 12, 1861, and mustered in to date October 29, 1861. Left State for Louisville, Ky., December 17, 1861. Assigned to duty by Detachments as follows: Companies "D," "F" and "G" with Thomas' 1st Division, Army of the Ohio; Companies "B," "E" and "I" with McCook's 2nd Division, Army of the Ohio; Companies "C" and "H" with Mitchell's 3rd Division, Army of the Ohio, and Companies "A" and "K" with Nelson's 4th Division, Army of the Ohio, to June, 1862. Unattached, Army of the Ohio, to November, 1862. Unattached, Dept. of the Cumberland, to muster out.

SERVICE.—Companies "D," "F" and "G" with Thomas at Camp Dick Robinson and Somerset, Ky., constructing roads to Mill Springs. Action at Mill Springs January 19, 1862. Other Companies on Green River, Ky., building storehouses, fortifications, etc., till February, 1862. Advance on Bowling Green, Ky., February 14-15. Occupation of Bowling Green February 15 (Cos. "C" and "H"). Advance on Nashville, Tenn., February 14-28. Engaged in building railroad bridges at Franklin, Columbia, Murfreesboro, etc., till April. 8 Companies moved to Shiloh, Tenn., April 3-15, building bridges and repairing roads. 2 Companies remained with Mitchell and engaged in running trains, etc., on Memphis & Charleston Railroad and Nashville & Decatur Railroad during May. Regiment engaged in advance on and siege of Corinth, Miss., April 29-May 30. Skirmish near Corinth May 9. Buell's Campaign on line of the Memphis & Charleston Railroad in Northern Alabama and Middle Tennessee June to August, building bridges, repairing railroad, etc. At Huntsville, Ala., and building bridges, repairing track and running trains on the Tennessee & Alabama Railroad and the Memphis & Charleston Railroad till August. Companies "C," "F," "I" and "K" at Stevenson, Ala., till August; rejoining Regiment near Gallatin till September. Companies "A," "B," "D," "G" and "H" moved to Nashville, Tenn., August 20-22, and building bridges on the Louisville & Nashville Railroad till September 16. March in advance of the Army to Louisville, Ky., September 16-26. Pursuit of Bragg into Kentucky October 1-22. Battle of Perryville October 8 (Cos. "A," "C" and "H"). March to Nashville, Tenn., October 22-November 7, and to Mill Creek, near Nashville, November 22. Duty

there till December 31. Battle of Stone River December 31, 1862, and January 1-3, 1863. Lavergne January 1, 1863. Repulse of Forest's attack. Duty at Lavergne, Murfreesboro, etc., till June 29 building bridges, magazines, repairing railroad and other engineering work. Repairing line of the Nashville & Chattanooga Railroad from Murfreesboro to Bridgeport, Ala., till September. Engineering duty at Chattanooga, Bridgeport, Stevenson and on line of the Nashville & Chattanooga Railroad, Nashville & Northwestern Railroad, Tennessee & Alabama Railroad and Memphis & Charleston Railroad building block houses, etc., till May, 1864. Chattanooga October 6, 1863. Reopening Tennessee River October 26-29, 1863. Brown's Ferry October 27, 1863. 1 Battalion at Chattanooga May, 1864. 1 Battalion on Memphis & Charleston Railroad building block houses from Decatur to Stevenson, Ala., till June. Companies "L" and "M" at Stevenson, Ala., till November 28, 1864. Regiment on duty on the Atlantic & Western Railroad building block houses, etc., till September. Ordered to Atlanta, Ga., September 25. Old members mustered out October 31, 1864. Duty at Atlanta September 28 to November 15. March to the sea destroying railroad track, bridges and repairing and making roads November 15-December 10. Siege of Savannah December 10-21. Carolina Campaign January to April, 1865. South Edisto River, S. C., February 9. North Edisto River February 12-13. Columbia February 16-17. Fayetteville, N. C., March 11. Averysboro March 16. Battle of Bentonville March 19-21. Occupation of Goldsboro March 24. (Cos. "L" and "M" detached at Stevenson, Ala., working on fortifications there and on Nashville & Chattanooga Railroad building block houses, etc., till December, 1864; then at Nashville, Tenn., till March, 1865. Participated in siege of Murfreesboro, Tenn., December 5-12, 1864. Near Murfreesboro December 15. Co. "L" captured. Rejoined Regiment at Goldsboro, N. C., March 25, 1865.) Advance on Raleigh April 10-14. Occupation of Raleigh April 14. Bennett's House April 26. Surrender of Johnston and his army. March to Washington, D. C., via Richmond, Va., April 29-May 20. Grand Review May 24. Ordered to Louisville, Ky., June 6; thence to Nashville, Tenn. Duty at Nashville July 1 to September 22. Mustered out September 22, and discharged at Jackson, Mich., October 1, 1865.

Regiment lost during service 1 Officer and 12 Enlisted men killed and mortally wounded and 351 Enlisted men by disease. Total 364.

HOWLAND'S COMPANY ENGINEERS.

Organized at Battle Creek, Mich., September 16, 1861. Mustered out January 8, 1862.

1st REGIMENT SHARPSHOOTERS.

Organized at Kalamazoo and Dearborn, Mich., April 14 to October 7, 1863. 6 Companies mustered in July 7, 1863, and ordered to Indianapolis, Ind.; thence to Seymour, Ind., to repel the Morgan Raid. Action with Morgan at North Vernon, Ind., July 13, and at Pierceville July 14. Returned to Dearborn, Mich., and duty there till August 16. Moved to Chicago, Ill., August 16, and duty guarding prisoners at Camp Douglas till March 17, 1864. Ordered to Annapolis, Md., March 17. Attached to 2nd Brigade, 3rd Division, 9th Army Corps, Army of the Potomac, to September; 2nd Brigade, 1st Division, 9th Army Corps, to July, 1865.

SERVICE.—Duty at Annapolis, Md., till April 23, 1864. Campaign from the Rapidan to the James River, Va., May 4-June 15. Battles of the Wilderness May 5-7; Spottsylvania May 8-12; Ny River May 10; Spottsylvania Court House May 12-21. Assault on the Salient May 12. North Anna River May 23-26. Ox Ford May 23-24. On line of the Pamunkey May 26-28. Totopotomoy May 28-31. Cold Harbor June 1-12. Bethesda Church June 1-3. Before Petersburg June 16-18. Siege of Petersburg June 16, 1864, to April 2, 1865. Mine Explosion, Petersburg, July 30, 1864. Weldon Railroad August 18-21. Poplar Springs Church September 29-

October 2. Reconnoissance on Vaughan and Squirrel Level Roads October 8. Boydton Plank Road, Hatcher's Run October 27-28. Fort Stedman, Petersburg, March 25, 1865. Appomattox Campaign March 28-April 9. Assault on and fall of Petersburg April 2. Occupation of Petersburg April 3. Pursuit of Lee April 3-9. Moved to Washington, D. C., April 22-27. Grand Review May 23. Camp near Washington, D. C., till July 28. Mustered out July 28, 1865.

Regiment lost during service 6 Officers and 131 Enlisted men killed and mortally wounded and 165 Enlisted men by disease. Total 362.

HALL'S INDEPENDENT BATTALION SHARPSHOOT-
ERS.

Organized at Marshall, Mich., August 27 to November 2, 1864. Attached to 16th Michigan Infantry and consolidated with that Regiment April 10, 1865.

BRADY'S INDEPENDENT COMPANY SHARPSHOOT-
ERS.

Organized at Detroit, Mich., February 3, 1862. Attached to 16th Michigan Infantry (which see).

DYGERT'S INDEPENDENT COMPANY SHARP-
SHOOTERS.

Organized February, 1862. Attached to 16th Michigan Infantry (which see).

JARDINE'S INDEPENDENT COMPANY SHARP-
SHOOTERS.

Organized at Saginaw, Mich., May 3, 1864. Attached to 16th Michigan Infantry (which see).

COMPANY "C" 1st UNITED STATES SHARPSHOOT-
ERS.

Organized August 21, 1861. (See 1st United States Sharpshooters.)

COMPANY "I" 1st UNITED STATES SHARPSHOOT-
ERS.

Organized March 4, 1862. (See 1st United States Sharpshooters.)

COMPANY "K" 1st UNITED STATES SHARPSHOOT-
ERS.

Organized March 30, 1862. (See 1st United States Sharpshooters.)

COMPANY "B" 2nd UNITED STATES SHARPSHOOT-
ERS.

Organized October 4, 1861. (See 2nd United States Sharpshooters.)

1st REGIMENT INFANTRY.—(3 MONTHS.)

Organized at Fort Wayne, Detroit, Mich., and mustered into United States service May 1, 1861 (the only three-months Regiment from Michigan). Left State for Washington, D. C., May 13. Occupation of Arlington Heights, Va., May 24. Attached to Willcox's Brigade, Heintzelman's Division, McDowell's Army of Northeast Virginia. Duty in the Defences of Washington, D. C., till July 16. Action at Arlington Mills June 1 (Co. "E"). Advance on Manassas, Va., July 16-21. Battle of Bull Run July 21. Mustered out August, 7, 1861.

1st REGIMENT INFANTRY.—(3 YEARS.)

Organized at Detroit, Mich., and mustered in September 16, 1861. Left State for Washington, D. C., September 16. Attached to 1st Brigade, Hooker's Division, Army of the Potomac, to February, 1862. Railroad Brigade, Army of the Potomac, to March, 1862. 1st Brigade, 2nd Division, 3rd Army Corps, Army of the Potomac, to March, 1862. Camp Hamilton, Va., Dept. of Virginia, to May, 1862. Robinson's Brigade, Dept. of Virginia, to June, 1862. 1st Brigade, 1st Division, 5th Army Corps, Army of the Potomac, to March, 1864. 3rd Brigade, 1st Division, 5th Army Corps, to July, 1865.

SERVICE.—Duty at Bladensburg, Md., October, 1861, and at Annapolis Junction guarding Washington &

Baltimore Railroad till March, 1862. Duty at Camp Hamilton, Fortress Monroe, Va., to June. Ordered to join Army of the Potomac in the field. Seven days before Richmond, Va., June 25-July 1. Battles of Mechanicsville June 26; Gaines Mill June 27; Peach Orchard and Savage Station June 29; Glendale and Turkey Bridge June 30; Malvern Hill July 1. At Harrison's Landing till August 16. Movement to Fortress Monroe, thence to Centreville, Va., August 16-27. Gainesville August 28. Battle of Bull Run August 30. Maryland Campaign September 6-22. Battle of Antietam, Md., September 16-17. Shepherdstown Ford September 19. Shepherdstown September 20. Movement to Falmouth, Va., October 29-November 19. Battle of Fredericksburg, Va., December 12-15. Expedition from Potomac Creek to Richards and Ellis Fords, Rappahannock River, December 29-30. "Mud March" January 20-24, 1863. At Falmouth till April 27. Chancellorsville Campaign April 27-May 6. Battle of Chancellorsville May 1-5. Gettysburg (Pa.) Campaign June 11-July 24. Battle of Gettysburg July 1-3. Pursuit of Lee to Manassas Gap July 5-24. At Warrenton and Beverly Ford July 27 to September 17. Provost duty at Culpeper till October 11. Bristoe Campaign October 11-22. Advance to line of the Rappahannock November 7-8. Rappahannock Station November 7. Mine Run Campaign November 26-December 2. Duty near Culpeper till May, 1864. Campaign from the Rapidan to the James River May 4-June 15. Battles of the Wilderness May 5-7; Laurel Hill May 8; Spottsylvania May 8-12; Spottsylvania Court House May 12-21. Assault on the Salient May 12. North Anna River May 23-26. Jericho Mills May 23. Totopotomoy May 28-31. Cold Harbor June 1-12. Bethesda Church June 1-3. Before Petersburg June 16-18. Siege of Petersburg June 16, 1864, to April 2, 1865. Mine Explosion, Petersburg, July 30, 1864 (Reserve). Six-Mile House, Weldon Railroad, August 18-21. Poplar Springs Church September 29-October 2. Boydton Road, Hatcher's Run, October 27-28. Warren's Expedition to Weldon Railroad December 7-12. Dabney's Mills, Hatcher's Run, February 5-7, 1865. Appomattox Campaign March 28-April 9. Junction, Quaker and Boydton Roads March 29. Lewis' Farm, near Gravelly Run, March 29. White Oak Road March 30-31. Five Forks April 1. Fall of Petersburg April 2. Pursuit of Lee April 3-9. Appomattox Court House April 9. Surrender of Lee and his army. Duty at City Point, Va., till May 16. Moved to Alexandria May 16-18. Grand Review May 23. Ordered to Louisville, Ky., June 16, and mustered out July 9, 1865.

Regiment lost during service 15 Officers and 172 Enlisted men killed and mortally wounded and 1 Officer and 149 Enlisted men by disease. Total 337.

1st REGIMENT COLORED INFANTRY.

Organized at Detroit, Mich., August, 1863, to February, 1864. Mustered in February 17, 1864. Moved to Annapolis, Md., March 29, and joined 9th Army Corps. At Annapolis, Md., till April 15. Ordered to Hilton Head, S. C., April 15. Picket and outpost duty on Hilton Head and St. Helena Islands, S. C., and garrison at Port Royal till June 15. Designation of Regiment changed to 102nd United States Colored Troops May 23, 1864. (See 102nd U. S. C. T.)

2nd REGIMENT INFANTRY.

Organized at Detroit, Mich., May 25, 1861. ("The first three-years Regiment from Michigan.") Moved to Washington, D. C., June 6-10. Attached to Richardson's Brigade, Tyler's Division, McDowell's Army of Northeastern Virginia, to August, 1861. Richardson's Brigade, Division of the Potomac, to October, 1861. Richardson's Brigade, Heintzelman's Division, Army of the Potomac, to March, 1862. 3rd Brigade, 3rd Division, 3rd Army Corps, Army of the Potomac, to August, 1862. 3rd Brigade, 1st Division, 3rd Army Corps, to November, 1862. 1st Brigade, 1st Division, 9th Army Corps, Army of the Potomac, to April, 1863, and Army of the Ohio to June,

1863. 3rd Brigade, 1st Division, 9th Army Corps, Army of the Tennessee, to August, 1863, and Army of the Ohio to January, 1864. 2nd Brigade, 1st Division, 9th Army Corps, Army of the Ohio, to April, 1864. 1st Brigade, 3rd Division, 9th Army Corps, Army of the Potomac, to July, 1864. 2nd Brigade, 3rd Division, 9th Army Corps, to September, 1864. 2nd Brigade, 1st Division, 9th Army Corps, to July, 1865.

SERVICE.—Duty in the Defences of Washington, D. C., June 10 to July 16, 1861. Advance on Manassas, Va., July 16-21. Occupation of Fairfax Court House July 17. Action at Blackburn's Ford July 18. Battle of Bull Run July 21. Duty in the Defences of Washington, D. C., till March, 1862. Reconnoissance to Occoquan October 21-24, 1861. Reconnoissance to Pohick Church, Va., November 12-14. Moved to the Virginia Peninsula March 17, 1862. Siege of Yorktown, Va., April 5-May 4. Battle of Fair Oaks, or Seven Pines, May 31-June 1. Reconnoissance beyond Seven Pines June 1-2. Seven days before Richmond June 25-July 1. Oak Grove June 25. Savage Station June 29. Glendale and Charles City Cross Roads June 30. Malvern Hill July 1. Duty at Harrison's Landing till August 15. Movement to Fortress Monroe, thence to Centreville, Va., August 15-28. Battles of Groveton August 29. Bull Run August 30. Chantilly September 1. Duty in the Defences of Washington, D. C., September 3 to October 11. March up the Potomac to Leesburg, thence to Falmouth, Va., October 11-November 19. Battle of Fredericksburg, Va., December 12-15. "Mud March" January 20-24, 1863. Moved to Newport News, Va., February 10, and duty there till March 19. Movement to Kentucky March 19-23. Duty at Camp Dick Robinson, Ky., April 9-30, and at Columbia till June. Moved to Vicksburg, Miss., June 7-14. Siege of Vicksburg June 14-July 4. Advance on Jackson, Miss., July 4-10. Siege of Jackson July 10-17. Destruction of Mississippi Central Railroad at Madison Station July 18-22. Duty at Milldale till August 4. Moved to Covington, Ky., August 4-12, and to Crab Orchard, Ky., August 17-18. Burnside's Campaign in East Tennessee August 18-October 17. March to Knoxville, Tenn., over the Cumberland Mountains September 10-26. Duty near Knoxville September 27-October 3. Action at Blue Springs October 10. Knoxville Campaign November 4-December 23. Action at Campbell's Station November 16. Siege of Knoxville November 17-December 5. Assault on Confederate works November 23. Repulse of Longstreet's assault on Fort Saunders November 29. Granger's Mills December 14. Operation in East Tennessee till February, 1864. Veterans on furlough February 4 to April 4, when rejoined Corps at Annapolis, Md. Campaign from the Rapidan to the James River May 4-June 15. Battles of the Wilderness May 5-7. Spottsylvania May 8-12. Ny River May 10. Spottsylvania Court House May 12-21. Assault on the Salient May 12. North Anna River May 23-26. Ox Ford May 23-24. On line of the Pamunkey May 26-28. Totopotomoy May 28-31. Cold Harbor June 1-12. Bethesda Church June 1-3. Before Petersburg June 16-18. Siege of Petersburg June 16, 1864, to April 2, 1865. Mine Explosion, Petersburg, July 30, 1864. Weldon Railroad August 18-21. Ream's Station August 25. Poplar Springs Church, Pegram's Farm, September 29-October 2. Reconnoissance on Vaughan and Squirrel Level Roads October 8. Boydton Road, Hatcher's Run, October 27-28. Fort Stedman, Petersburg, March 25, 1865. Appomattox Campaign March 28-April 9. Assault on and fall of Petersburg April 2. Occupation of Petersburg April 3. Pursuit of Lee April 3-9. Moved to Washington, D. C., April 22-28, and duty there till July. Grand Review May 23. Mustered out July 29, and discharged at Detroit, Mich., August 1, 1865.

Regiment lost during service 11 Officers and 214 Enlisted men killed and mortally wounded and 4 Officers and 143 Enlisted men by disease. Total 372.

3rd REGIMENT INFANTRY.

Organized at Grand Rapids, Mich., and mustered into State service May 21, 1861. Mustered into United States

service June 10, 1861. Left State for Washington, D. C., June 13. Attached to Richardson's Brigade, Tyler's Division, McDowell's Army of Northeastern Virginia, to August, 1861. Richardson's Brigade, Division of the Potomac, to October, 1861, Richardson's Brigade, Heintzelman's Division, Army of the Potomac, to March, 1862. 3rd Brigade, 3rd Division, 3rd Army Corps, Army of the Potomac, to August, 1862. 3rd Brigade, 1st Division, 3rd Army Corps, to March, 1864. 2nd Brigade, 3rd Division, 2nd Army Corps, to June, 1864.

SERVICE.—Duty in the Defences of Washington, D. C., till July 16, 1861. Advance on Manassas, Va., July 16-21. Occupation of Fairfax Court House, Va., July 17. Action at Blackburn's Ford July 18. Battle of Bull Run July 21. Duty in the Defences of Washington, D. C., till March, 1862. Reconnoissance to Occoquan October 21-24, 1861. Reconnoissance to Occoquan Village February 3, 1862 (Cos. "H," "I"). Moved to the Virginia Peninsula March 17, 1862. Siege of Yorktown April 5-May 4. Battle of Fair Oaks or Seven Pines May 31-June 1. Reconnoissance beyond Seven Pines June 1-2. Seven days before Richmond June 25-July 1. Oak Grove June 25. Savage Station and Peach Orchard June 29. Charles City Cross Roads and Glendale June 30. Malvern Hill July 1. Duty at Harrison's Landing till August 15. Moved to Fortress Monroe, thence to Centreville August 16-27. Battles of Groveton August 29, Bull Run August 30, Chantilly September 1. Duty in the Defences of Washington, D. C., till October 11. March up the Potomac to Leesburg, thence to Falmouth, Va., October 11-November 23. Battle of Fredericksburg, Va., December 12-15. "Mud March" January 20-24, 1863. At Falmouth till April 27. Chancellorsville Campaign April 27-May 6. Battle of Chancellorsville May 1-5. Gettysburg (Pa.) Campaign June 11-July 24. Battle of Gettysburg, Pa., July 1-3. Pursuit of Lee to Manassas Gap July 5-24. Action at Wapping Heights July 23. Duty at New York and at Troy, N. Y., during the draft disturbances August 17-September 17. Bristoe Campaign October 9-22. Auburn October 3. Advance to line of the Rappahannock November 7-8. Kelly's Ford November 8. Mine Run Campaign November 26-December 2. Payne's Farm November 27. Demonstration on the Rapidan February 6-7, 1864. Campaign from the Rapidan to the James May 4-June 9. Battles of the Wilderness May 5-7. Laurel Hill May 6. Spottsylvania May 8-12. Po River May 10. Spottsylvania Court House May 12-21. Assault on the Salient ("Bloody Angle") May 12. Harris Farm, Fredericksburg Road, May 19. North Anna River May 21-23. On line of the Pamunkey May 26-28. Tototopotomoy May 28-31. Cold Harbor June 1-9. Left front June 9. Non-veterans mustered out June 10, 1864. Veterans and Recruits transferred to 5th Michigan Infantry June 13, 1864.

Regiment lost during service 4 Officers and 154 Enlisted men killed and mortally wounded and 2 Officers and 89 Enlisted men by disease. Total 249.

3rd REGIMENT INFANTRY (REORGANIZED).

Organized at Grand Rapids, Adrian and Pontiac, Mich., August 24 to October 12, 1864. Mustered in October 15, 1864. Left State for Decatur, Ala., October 20. Attached to District of Northern Alabama, Dept. of the Cumberland, to November, 1864. 1st Brigade, Defences of Nashville & Chattanooga Railroad, Dept. of the Cumberland, to January, 1865. 3rd Brigade, 3rd Division, 4th Army Corps, to June, 1865. 2nd Brigade, 3rd Division, 4th Army Corps, to August, 1865. Dept. of Texas to May, 1866.

SERVICE.—Defence of Decatur, Ala., against Hood's attack October 26-30, 1864. Duty at Decatur till November 25. Moved to Murfreesboro, Tenn., November 25-27, and duty there till January 16, 1865. Hood's attack on Murfreesboro December 5-12, 1864. Moved to Huntsville, Ala., January 16, 1865; thence to Nashville, Tenn., January 31, and to Huntsville, Ala., February 6. Expedition to Bull's Gap and operations in East Tennessee March 16-April 17. Moved to Nashville, Tenn., April 20-24, and duty there till June 15. Moved to New Orleans, La.,

June 15-July 5; thence to Indianola, Texas, July 6-10. March to Green Lake and duty there till September 12. March to San Antonio September 12-26. Guard and provost duty at San Antonio, Gonzales and Victoria till May, 1866. Mustered out at Victoria May 26 and discharged at Detroit, Mich., June 10, 1866.

Regiment lost during service 1 Enlisted man killed and 1 Officer and 163 Enlisted men by disease. Total 165.

4th REGIMENT INFANTRY.

Organized at Adrian, Mich., and mustered in June 20, 1861. Left State for Washington, D. C., June 26. Attached to Wilcox's Brigade, Heintzelman's Division, McDowell's Army of Northeastern Virginia, to August, 1861. Sherman's Brigade, Division of the Potomac, to October, 1861. Morell's Brigade, Porter's Division, Army of the Potomac, to March, 1862. 2nd Brigade, 1st Division, 3rd Army Corps, Army of the Potomac, to May, 1862. 2nd Brigade, 1st Division, 5th Army Corps, Army of the Potomac, to June, 1864.

SERVICE.—Advance on Manassas, Va., July 16-21, 1861. Battle of Bull Run, Va., July 21. Duty in the defences of Washington, D. C., till March, 1862. Moved to the Virginia Peninsula March 16. Action at Howard's Mills April 4. Warwick Road April 15. Siege of Yorktown April 5-May 4. Hogan's, near New Bridge, and Ellison's Mills, near Mechanicsville, May 23. New Bridge May 24. Battle of Hanover Court House May 27. Operations about Hanover Court House May 27-29. Seven days before Richmond June 25-July 1. Battle of Mechanicsville June 26. Gaines' Mill June 27. Malvern Hill July 1. Duty at Harrison's Landing till August 16. Movement to Fortress Monroe, thence to Centreville August 16-28. Battle of Bull Run August 30. Maryland Campaign September 6-22. Battle of Antietam, Md., September 16-17. Blackford's Ford September 19. Shephardstown September 20. Reconnoissance toward Smithfield, W. Va., October 16-17. Movement to Falmouth, Va., October 29-November 17. Battle of Fredericksburg, Va., December 12-15. Expedition from Potomac Creek to Richards' and Ellis Fords, Rappahannock River, December 29-30. At Falmouth, Va., till April 27. "Mud March" January 20-24, 1863. Chancellorsville Campaign April 27-May 6. Battle of Chancellorsville May 1-5. Gettysburg (Pa.) Campaign June 11-July 24. Battle of Gettysburg, Pa., July 1-3. Pursuit of Lee to Manassas Gap, Va., July 5-24. Duty on line of the Rappahannock and Rapidan till October. Bristoe Campaign October 9-22. Advance to line of Rappahannock November 7-8. Rappahannock Station November 7. Mine Run Campaign November 26-December 2. Duty at Bealeton, Va., till May, 1864. Campaign from the Rapidan to the James River May 4-June 15. Battle of the Wilderness May 5-7. Laurel Hill May 8. Spottsylvania May 8-12. Spottsylvania Court House May 12-21. Assault on the Salient May 12. North Anna River May 23-26. Jericho Mills May 23. On line of the Pamunkey May 26-28. Totopotomoy May 28-31. Cold Harbor June 1-12. Bethesda Church June 1-3. Before Petersburg June 16-19. Relieved from duty in the trenches June 19. Mustered out June 30, 1864. Veterans and Recruits transferred to 1st Michigan Infantry.

Regiment lost during service 12 Officers and 177 Enlisted men killed and mortally wounded and 1 Officer and 107 Enlisted men by disease. Total 297.

4th REGIMENT INFANTRY (REORGANIZED).

Organized at Adrian and Hudson, Mich., and mustered in October 14, 1864. Left State for Nashville, Tenn., October 22; thence moved to Decatur, Ala., October 26. Attached to District of Northern Alabama, Dept. of the Cumberland, to November, 1864. 1st Brigade, Defences of the Nashville & Chattanooga Railroad, Dept. of the Cumberland, to January, 1865. 3rd Brigade, 3rd Division, 4th Army Corps, Army of the Cumberland, to June, 1865. 2nd Brigade, 3rd Division, 4th Army Corps, to August, 1865. Dept. of Texas to May, 1866.

SERVICE.—Defence of Decatur against Hood's attack October 28-30, 1864. Duty at Decatur till November 25.

Actions near Maysville and near New Market, Ala., November 17. Duckett's Place, near Paint Rock River, November 19. Moved to Murfreesboro November 25-27. Hood's attack on Murfreesboro December 5-12. Picket duty and guarding supply trains till January 15, 1865. Moved to Huntsville, Ala., January 15, and duty there till March 23. Duty at Knoxville, Strawberry Plains, Bull's Gap, Jonesboro and Nashville, Tenn., till June 16. Moved to New Orleans, La., June 16-July 5; thence to Indianola, Texas, July 6-10. March to Green Lake and duty there till September 12. March to San Antonio September 12-24. Camp at Salada Creek till November. Provost duty at San Antonio and other points in Texas till May, 1866. Mustered out at Houston, Texas, May 26, and discharged at Detroit, Mich., June 10, 1866.

Regiment lost during service 7 Enlisted men killed and mortally wounded and 141 Enlisted men by disease. Total 148.

5th REGIMENT INFANTRY.

Organized at Detroit, Mich., and mustered in August 28, 1861. Left State for Washington, D. C., September 11. Attached to Richardson's Brigade, Heintzelman's Division, Army of the Potomac, to March, 1862. Berry's 3rd Brigade, Kearny's 3rd Division, 3rd Army Corps, Army of the Potomac, to August, 1862. 3rd Brigade, 1st Division, 3rd Army Corps, to March, 1864. 2nd Brigade, 3rd Division, 2nd Army Corps, to July, 1865.

SERVICE.—Duty in the Defences of Washington, D. C., September 13, 1861, to March 10, 1862. Reconnoissance to Occoquan October 21-24, 1861. Pohick Run, Va., January 9, 1862. Advance to Manassas, Va., March 10-15. Moved to the Virginia Peninsula March 17. Peninsula Campaign March to August. Siege of Yorktown, Va., April 5-May 4. Battle of Fair Oaks, or Seven Pines, May 31-June 1. Seven days before Richmond June 25-July 1. Oak Grove June 25. Savage Station and Peach Orchard June 29. Charles City Cross Roads and Glendale June 30. Malvern Hill July 1. Duty at Harrison's Landing till August 16. Movement to Fortress Monroe, thence to Centreville August 16-26. Battles of Groveton August 29, Bull Run August 30, Chantilly September 1. Duty in the Defences of Washington, D. C., till October 11. March up the Potomac to Leesburg, and thence to Falmouth October 11-November 23. Battle of Fredericksburg, Va., December 12-15. "Mud March" January 20-24, 1863. At Falmouth till April 27. Chancellorsville Campaign April 27-May 6. Battle of Chancellorsville May 1-5. Gettysburg (Pa.) Campaign June 11-July 24. Battle of Gettysburg July 1-3. Pursuit of Lee to Manassas Gap, Va., July 5-24. Action at Wapping Heights, Va., July 23. On detached duty at New York City and at Troy, N. Y., August 16-September 17. Bristoe Campaign October 9-22. Auburn October 13. Advance to line of the Rappahannock November 7-8. Kelly's Ford November 7. Mine Run Campaign November 26-December 2. Payne's Farm November 27. Veterans on furlough January 4 to February 14, 1864. Demonstration on the Rapidan February 6-7. Campaign from the Rapidan to the James River May 4-June 15, 1864. Battles of the Wilderness May 5-7, Laurel Hill May 8, Spottsylvania May 8-12, Po River May 10, Spottsylvania Court House May 12-21. Assault on the Salient ("Bloody Angle") May 12. Harris Farm, Fredericksburg Road, May 19. North Anna River May 23-26. On line of the Pamunkey May 26-28. Totopotomoy May 28-31. Cold Harbor June 1-12. Before Petersburg June 16-18. Siege of Petersburg June 16, 1864, to April 2, 1865. Jerusalem Plank Road, Weldon Railroad, June 22-23, 1864. Demonstration on north side of the James July 27-29. Deep Bottom July 27-28. Demonstration on north side of the James at Deep Bottom August 13-20. Strawberry Plains August 14-18. Poplar Springs Church September 29-October 2. Boydton Plank Road, Hatcher's Run, October 27-28. Warren's Raid on Weldon Railroad December 7-12. Dabney's Mills, Hatcher's Run, February 5-7, 1865. Watkins' House March 25. Appomattox Campaign March 28-April 9. White Oak Road March 30-31. Crow's House March 31. Fall of

Petersburg April 2. Pursuit of Lee April 3-9. Sailor's Creek April 6. High Bridge April 7. Appomattox Court House April 9. Surrender of Lee and his army. March to Washington, D. C., May 2-12. Grand Review May 23. Moved to Louisville, Ky., June 10-14. At Jeffersonville, Ind., till July 5. Mustered out July 5, 1865.

Regiment lost during service 16 Officers and 247 Enlisted men killed and mortally wounded and 3 Officers and 188 Enlisted men by disease. Total 454.

6th REGIMENT INFANTRY AND HEAVY ARTILLERY.

Organized at Kalamazoo, Mich., and mustered in August 20, 1861. Left State for Baltimore, Md., August 30, and duty there till February 22, 1862. Attached to Dix's Command, Baltimore, Md., to February, 1862. Butler's New Orleans Expedition to March, 1862. 2nd Brigade, Dept. of the Gulf, to November, 1862. Sherman's Division, Dept. of the Gulf, to January, 1863. 1st Brigade, 2nd Division, 19th Army Corps, Dept. of the Gulf, to August, 1863. Designation of Regiment changed to 6th Regiment Heavy Artillery July 28, 1863. District of Port Hudson, La., Dept. of the Gulf, to June, 1864. Bailey's Engineer Brigade, Dept. of the Gulf, to August, 1864. U. S. Forces, Mobile Bay, Dept. of the Gulf, to December, 1864. District Southern Alabama, Dept. of the Gulf, to August, 1865.

SERVICE.—Expedition to eastern shore of Maryland November 11-December 8, 1861. Ordered to Fortress Monroe, Va., February 22, 1862. Sailed with Gen. Butler's Expedition against New Orleans, La., on Transport "Constitution" March 4 and arrived at Ship Island, Miss., March 13. Duty there till April 14. Operations against Forts St. Phillip and Jackson April 25-28. Occupation of New Orleans May 2 (one of the first Regiments to occupy the city). Expedition to New Orleans & Jackson Railroad May 9-10. Moved to Baton Rouge, La., May 13. Reconnoissance to Warrenton May 14-29. Grand Gulf May 16. Vicksburg May 20. Grand Gulf May 27. Camp at Baton Rouge till August 20. Expedition to Camp Moore July 20-30. Battle of Baton Rouge August 5. Evacuation of Baton Rouge August 20. Guard duty at Metaria Ridge August 22-December 6. Expedition to Bayou Teche January 12-15, 1863. Action with Steamer "Cotton" January 14. Duty at Camp Parapet and Kenner till March. Expedition to Ponchatoula March 21-30 (1 Co.). Capture of Ponchatoula March 24. Skirmish at Ponchatoula March 26. Manchac Pass, Amite River, April 12. Raid on Amite River & Jackson Railroad May 9-18, destroying over $400,000 worth of property. Ponchatoula May 13. Camp Moore May 15. Moved to New Orleans, thence to Port Hudson May 21-23. Siege of Port Hudson May 24-July 9. Assaults on Port Hudson May 27 and June 14. Surrender of Port Hudson July 9. Regiment received thanks of Gen. Banks for gallant and efficient services during the siege and was by his orders, on July 10, 1863, converted into a Regiment of Heavy Artillery, to retain its Infantry number, and to have the organization pay and equipment prescribed by law for troops of the Artillery arms. Order approved by Secretary of War July 30, 1863. Regiment on garrison duty at Port Hudson, La., till June 6, 1864. Action at Tunica Bayou, La., November 8, 1863. Moved to Morganza, La., June 6, and duty there as Infantry till June 24. At Vicksburg, Miss., till July 23. Moved to mouth of White River, thence to St. Charles, Ark. Ashton, Ark., July 24. Ordered to Mobile Bay, Ala., August, and assigned to duty as follows: Companies "A," "B," "D," "G" and "K" garrison at Fort Morgan August 23, 1864, to July 9, 1865. (Co. "B" detached on Granger's Expedition to Mobile December 23, 1864, to January 31, 1865, then returned to Fort Morgan.) Companies "C," "E," "F," "H" and "I" garrison at Fort Gaines August 23, 1864, to July 9, 1865. (Cos. 'C," "E," "F" and "H" on Granger's Expedition to Mobile, December 23, 1864, to January 31, 1865.) Companies "A" and "K" detached from Fort Morgan March 31, 1865. Siege of Spanish Fort March 31-April 8, and of Forts Huger and Tracy April 8-9, then garrison Fort Blake-

ly till April 20, and return to Fort Morgan. Company "B" detached from Fort Morgan to Navy Cove April 10 to July 9. Company "E" detached from Fort Gaines at Fort Powell April 10 to July 9. Regiment ordered to New Orleans, La., July 9, and duty there till August 20. Mustered out August 20 and discharged at Jackson, Mich., September 5, 1865.

Regiment lost during service 2 Officers and 76 Enlisted men killed and mortally wounded and 6 Officers and 498 Enlisted men by disease. Total 582.

7th REGIMENT INFANTRY.

Organized at Monroe, Mich., and mustered in August 22, 1861. Left State for Washington, D. C., September 5. Attached to Lander's Brigade, Stone's Division, Army of the Potomac, to March, 1862. 3rd Brigade, 2nd Division, 2nd Army Corps, Army of the Potomac, to December, 1863. 1st Brigade, 2nd Division, 2nd Army Corps, to July, 1865.

SERVICE.—Guard duty along the upper Potomac till December, 1861. Near Edward's Ferry October 22. Moved to Muddy Branch December 4, and duty there till March, 1862. Moved to Harper's Ferry, thence to Charleston and Berryville March 12-15. To Harper's Ferry, thence to Washington, D. C., March 24, and to the Virginia Peninsula March 27. Peninsula Campaign April to August. Siege of Yorktown April 5-May 4. West Point May 7-8. Battle of Fair Oaks or Seven Pines May 31-June 1. Seven days before Richmond June 25-July 1. Peach Orchard and Savage Station June 29. White Oak Swamp and Glendale June 30. Malvern Hill July 1. Duty at Harrison's Landing till August 16. Action at Malvern Hill August 5. Movement from Harrison's Landing to Alexandria August 15-28, thence to Fairfax Court House August 28-31. Cover Pope's retreat from Bull Run to Washington. Maryland Campaign September 6-22. Battle of Antietam September 16-17. Moved to Harper's Ferry, W. Va., September 22, and duty there till October 30. Advance up the Loudon Valley and movement to Falmouth, Va., October 30-November 17. Battle of Fredericksburg, Va., December 11-15. Forlorn hope to cross the Rappahannock at Fredericksburg December 11. Duty at Falmouth, Va., till April, 1863. Chancellorsville Campaign April 27-May 6. Maryes Heights, Fredericksburg, May 3. Salem Heights May 3-4. Gettysburg (Pa.) Campaign June 11-July 24. Battle of Gettysburg July 1-3. Pursuit of Lee to Manassas Gap, Va., July 5-24. On detached duty at New York City during draft disturbances August 20-September 12. Rejoined army at Culpeper, Va. Bristoe Campaign October 9-22. Bristoe Station October 14. Advance to line of the Rappahannock November 7-8. Mine Run Campaign November 26-December 2. At Stevensburg till May,, 1864. Campaign from the Rapidan to the James River May 4-June 15. Battles of the Wilderness May 5-7; Laurel Hill May 8; Spottsylvania May 8-12; Po River May 10; Spottsylvania Court House May 12-21. Assault on the Salient, "Bloody Angle," May 12. North Anna River May 23-26. On line of the Pamunkey May 26-28. Totopotomoy May 28-31. Cold Harbor June 1-12. Before Petersburg June 16-18. Siege of Petersburg June 16, 1864, to April 2, 1865. Jerusalem Plank Road, Weldon Railroad, June 22-23, 1864. Demonstration on north side of the James River July 27-29. Deep Bottom July 27-28. Demonstration north of James at Deep Bottom August 13-20. Strawberry Plains August 14-18. Ream's Station August 25. Boydton Plank Road, Hatcher's Run, October 27-28. Dabney's Mills, Hatcher's Run, February 5-7, 1865. Watkins' House March 25. Appomattox Campaign March 28-April 9. Boydton Road March 30-31. Crow's House March 31. Fall of Petersburg April 2. Pursuit of Lee April 3-9. Sailor's Creek April 6. High Bridge and Farmville April 7. Appomattox Court House April 9. Surrender of Lee and his army. At Burkesville till May 2. Moved to Washington, D. C., May 2-12. Grand Review May 23. Moved to Louisville, Ky., June 16-22, thence to Jeffersonville, Ind. Mustered out July 5, 1865.

Regiment lost during service 11 Officers and 197 Enlisted men killed and mortally wounded and 3 Officers and 186 Enlisted men by disease. Total 397.

8th REGIMENT INFANTRY.

Regiment organized at Grand Rapids and at Fort Wayne, Detroit, Mich., and mustered in September 23, 1861. Left State for Washington, D. C., September 27. Camp at Meridian Hill till October 9. Moved to Annapolis, Md., October 9, and attached to Stevens' 2nd Brigade, Sherman's South Carolina Expeditionary Corps, to April, 1862. 1st Brigade, 2nd Division, Dept. of the South, to July, 1862. 1st Brigade, 1st Division, 9th Army Corps, Army of the Potomac, to September, 1862. 2nd Brigade, 1st Division, 9th Army Corps, to December, 1862. 1st Brigade, 1st Division, 9th Army Corps, Army of the Potomac, to March, 1863, and Army of the Ohio to June, 1863. 1st Brigade, 1st Division, 9th Army Corps, Army of the Tennessee, to August, 1863. 1st Brigade, 1st Division, 9th Army Corps, Army of the Ohio, to March, 1864. 1st Brigade, 3rd Division, 9th Army Corps, Army of the Potomac, to September, 1864. 1st Brigade, 1st Division, 9th Army Corps, to April, 1865. 2nd Brigade, 1st Division, 9th Army Corps, to July, 1865.

SERVICE.—Sherman's Expedition to Port Royal, S. C., October 19-November 7, 1861. Capture of Forts Walker and Beauregard, Port Royal Harbor, November 7. Hilton Head, S. C., November 8. Occupation of Beaufort, S. C., December 7. Chisholm Island December 17. Port Royal Ferry, Coosaw River, January 1, 1862. Guard and picket duty at Beaufort till April. Reconnoissance up Bull River February 23-26 (Detachment). Duty at Battery Halleck, Tybee Island, during siege of Fort Pulaski April 1-12. Bombardment and capture of Fort Pulaski April 10-11. Reconnoissance to Wilmington and Whitmarsh Islands and action April 16. Duty on Port Royal Island till June. Pocotaligo May 29 (1 Co.). Operations on James Island, S. C., June 1-28. Battle of Secessionville June 16. Evacuation of James Island June 28-July 7. Moved from Hilton Head, S. C., to Newport News, Va., July 12-17, thence to Fredericksburg, Va., August 4-6. Operations on the Rapidan and Rappahannock Rivers till August 27. Pope's Campaign in Northern Virginia August 27-September 2. Battles of Groveton August 29; Bull Run August 30; Chantilly September 1. Maryland Campaign September 6-22. Battles of South Mountain September 14; Antietam September 16-17. March up the Potomac to Leesburg, Va., thence to Falmouth, Va., October 11-November 18. Battle of Fredericksburg, Va., December 12-15. "Mud March" January 20-24, 1863. Moved to Newport News, Va., February 13, thence to Kentucky March 19-23, and duty at various points in that State till June. Moved to Vicksburg, Miss., June 7-14. Siege of Vicksburg June 14-July 4. Advance on Jackson, Miss., July 4-10. Siege of Jackson July 10-17. Destruction of Mississippi Central Railroad at Madison Station July 18-22. Camp at Milldale till August 4. Moved to Covington, Ky., thence to Crab Orchard, Ky., August 4-18. Burnside's Campaign in East Tennessee. March to Knoxville, Tenn., September 10-26, and duty there till October 3. Action at Blue Springs October 10. Knoxville Campaign November 4-December 24. Lenoir November 15. Campbell's Station November 16. Siege of Knoxville November 17-December 5. Camp at Blain's Cross Roads till January 8, 1864. Veterans marched over Cumberland Mountains to Nicholasville, Ky., over 200 miles, in midwinter, and reached Detroit January 25. Ordered to Annapolis, Md., March 9, and duty there till April 23. Campaign from the Rapidan to the James River May 4-June 15. Battles of the Wilderness May 5-7; Spottsylvania May 8-12; Ny River May 10; Spottsylvania Court House May 12-21. Assault on the Salient May 12. North Anna River May 23-26. Ox Ford May 23-24. On line of the Pamunkey May 26-28. Totopotomoy May 28-31. Cold Harbor June 1-12. Bethesda Church June 1-3. Before Petersburg June 16-19. Siege of Petersburg June 16, 1864, to April 2, 1865. Mine Explosion. Pe-

tersburg, July 30, 1864. Weldon Railroad August 18-21. Poplar Springs Church September 29-October 2. Reconnoissance on Vaughan and Squirrel Level Roads October 8. Boydton Plank Road, Hatcher's Run, October 27-28. Fort Stedman, Petersburg, March 25, 1865. Assault on and fall of Petersburg April 2. Fort Mahone April 2. Occupation of Petersburg April 3. Guard Southside Railroad till April 20. Moved to Alexandria April 20-23. Grand Review May 23. Guard and patrol duty at Washington, D. C., till July 30. Mustered out July 30, 1865.

Regiment lost during service 11 Officers and 212 Enlisted men killed and mortally wounded and 3 Officers and 223 Enlisted men by disease. Total 449.

9th REGIMENT INFANTRY.

Organized at Detroit, Mich., and mustered in October 15, 1861. Moved to Jeffersonville, Ind., October 25, thence to West Point and to Muldraugh's Hill, Ky., and duty there constructing bridges and earthworks till January 4, 1862. Attached to Thomas' Command, Dept. of the Ohio, November, 1861. 16th Brigade, Army of the Ohio, to March, 1862. 23rd Independent Brigade, Army of the Ohio, to November, 1862. Headquarters 14th Army Corps, Army of the Cumberland, to February, 1864. Headquarters Dept. of the Cumberland in the field to May, 1864. Reserve Brigade, Dept. of the Cumberland, to October, 1864. Headquarters Dept. of the Cumberland, Chattanooga, Tenn., to June, 1865. Nashville, Tenn., to September, 1865.

SERVICE.—March to Elizabethtown, Ky., January 4-6, 1862 (Cos. "A," "B," "C," "D," "F" and "K"), and duty there till March 11. (Cos. "E" and 'G' at West Point till January 15, 1862, then moved to Elizabethtown. Co. 'I' at West Point till March 9, then moved to Elizabethtown. Co. "F" at Nolin Bridge January 9 to March 9, 1862.) March to West Point March 11-12, thence to Nashville, Tenn., March 19-23, and duty there till May 28. Expedition to Middle Tennessee in pursuit of Morgan May 3-7. Negley's Expedition to Chattanooga, Tenn., May 28-June 17. Chattanooga June 7. Forest's attack on Murfreesboro July 13. (Six Companies, "A," "B," "C," "G," "H" and "K" captured.) Companies "E," "D," "F" and "I" at Tullahoma till August. Short Mountain Cross Roads near McMinnville August 29 (Co. "D"); Tyree Springs September 11. Companies "E," "D," "F" and "I" at Bowling Green, Ky., District of Louisville, Dept. Ohio, to October. March to Nashville, Tenn., October 16-November 7. Regiment detailed as special guard at Headquarters of General Thomas, and also as provost guard for 14th Army Corps, October. Advance on Murfreesboro December 26-30. Battle of Stone's River December 30-31, 1862, and January 1-3, 1863. Overall's Creek December 31, 1862. Duty at and near Murfreesboro till June. Middle Tennessee or Tullahoma Campaign June 23-July 7. Occupation of Middle Tennessee till August 16. Passage of the Cumberland Mountains and Tennessee River and Chickamauga (Ga.) Campaign August 16-September 22. Battle of Chickamauga September 19-21. Siege of Chattanooga, Tenn., September 24-November 23. Chattanooga-Ringgold Campaign November 23-27. Battles of Chattanooga November 23-25. Reconnoissance toward Dalton February 22-27, 1864. Atlanta (Ga.) Campaign May 1 to September 8. Demonstrations on Rocky Faced Ridge and Dalton May 8-13. Battle of Resaca May 14-15. Advance on Dallas May 18-25. Operations on line of Pumpkin Vine Creek and battles about Dallas, New Hope Church and Allatoona Hills May 25-June 5. Operations about Marietta and against Kenesaw Mountain June 10-July 2. Pine Hill June 11-14. Lost Mountain June 15-17. Assault on Kenesaw June 27. Ruff's Station July 4. Chattahoochie River July 5-17. Peach Tree Creek July 19-20. Siege of Atlanta July 22-August 25. Utoy Creek August 5-7. Flank movement on Jonesboro August 25-30. Battle of Jonesboro August 31-September 1. Provost duty at Atlanta, Ga., till October 30. Moved to Chattanooga October 30-November 6, and duty there at Headquarters Dept. of the Cumberland till March 27, 1865. Moved to Nashville, Tenn., March 27, and duty at Headquarters Dept. of the Cumberland; also guarding military prisons till September. Mustered out September 15 and discharged at Detroit, Mich., September 26, 1865.

Regiment lost during service 2 Officers and 22 Enlisted men killed and mortally wounded and 4 Officers and 281 Enlisted men by disease. Total 309.

10th REGIMENT INFANTRY.

Organized at Flint, Mich., and mustered in February 6, 1862. Left State for Pittsburg Landing, Tenn., April 22. Attached to 2nd Brigade, 1st Division, Army Mississippi, to September, 1862. 2nd Brigade, 13th Division, Army of the Ohio, to November, 1862. 1st Brigade, 4th Division, Center 14th Army Corps, Army of the Cumberland, to January, 1863. 1st Brigade, 4th Division, 14th Army Corps, Army of the Cumberland, to June, 1863. 1st Brigade, 2nd Division, Reserve Corps, Army of the Cumberland, to October, 1863. 2nd Brigade, 1st Division, 14th Army Corps, to July, 1865.

SERVICE.—Advance on and siege of Corinth, Miss., April 29-May 30, 1862. Actions at Farmington, Miss., May 3 and 9. Reconnoissance toward Corinth May 8. Occupation of Corinth May 30. Pursuit to Booneville May 31-June 12. Tuscumbia Creek May 31-June 1. Reconnoissance toward Baldwyn June 3. In camp near Corinth till July 20. Moved to Tuscumbia July 20-25, and duty there till September. March to Nashville, Tenn., September 3-15. Siege of Nashville, Tenn., September 15-November 7. Duty at Nashville, Tenn., till January, 1863. Guard trains to Murfreesboro, Tenn., January 2-3, 1863. Duty at Murfreesboro till August. Mill Creek near Murfreesboro January 25 (Co. "I"). Antioch Station April 10. March to Columbia, Tenn., thence via Athens and Huntsville to Stevenson, Ala., August 19-September 7. Moved to Bridgeport, Ala., September 20, thence to Anderson's Cross Roads October 1, and to Smith's Ferry, Tenn., October 18-26. Chattanooga-Ringgold Campaign November 23-27. Tunnel Hill November 24-25. Mission Ridge November 25. Chickamauga Station November 26. March to relief of Knoxville, Tenn., November 28-December 19. At Chattanooga December 19. Demonstration on Dalton February 22-27, 1864. Tunnel Hill, Buzzard's Roost Gap, and Rocky Faced Ridge, February 23-25. (Regiment participated in this demonstration and actions while awaiting Veteran furlough, suffering a loss of over 60 men killed, wounded and missing.) Veterans absent on furlough till May 11. Atlanta (Ga.) Campaign May 11-September 8. Rome May 17-18. Advance on Dallas May 18-25. Operations on line of Pumpkin Vine Creek and battles about Dallas, New Hope Church and Allatoona Hills May 25-June 5. Operations about Marietta and against Kenesaw Mountain June 10-July 2. Pine Hill June 11-14. Lost Mountain June 15-17. Assault on Kenesaw June 27. Ruff's Station July 4. Chattahoochie River July 5-17. Peach Tree Creek July 19-20. Siege of Atlanta July 22-August 25. Utoy Creek August 5-7. Flank movement on Jonesboro August 25-30. Battle of Jonesboro August 31-September 1. Pursuit of Hood October 2-10. Florence October 6-7. At Chattanooga, Tenn., October 13-18, and at Rome, Ga., till October 31. March to Atlanta via Kingston and Cartersville, destroying railroad and bridges the entire distance, November 1-15. March to the sea November 15-December 10. Louisville November 30. Siege of Savannah December 10-21. Campaign of the Carolinas January to April, 1865. Near Fayetteville, N. C., March 13. Averysboro March 16. Battle of Bentonville March 19-21. Occupation of Goldsboro March 24. Advance on Raleigh April 10-14. Occupation of Raleigh April 14. Bennett's House April 26. Surrender of Johnston and his army. March to Washington, D. C., via Richmond, Va., April 29-May 17. Grand Review May 24. Moved to Louisville, Ky., June 13, and duty there till July 19. Mustered out July 19, and discharged at Jackson, Mich., August 1, 1865.

Regiment lost during service 7 Officers and 95 Enlisted men killed and mortally wounded and 2 Officers and 223 Enlisted men by disease. Total 327.

11th REGIMENT INFANTRY.

Organized at White Pigeon, Mich., and mustered in September 24, 1861. Left State for Bardstown, Ky., December 9, and duty there till March, 1862. Attached to Railroad Guard, Unattached, Dept. of the Ohio, to September, 1862. 29th Brigade, 8th Division, Army of the Ohio, to November, 1862. 2nd Brigade, 2nd Division, Center 14th Army Corps, Army of the Cumberland, to January, 1863. 2nd Brigade, 2nd Division, 14th Army Corps, Army of the Cumberland, to October, 1863. 2nd Brigade, 1st Division, 14th Army Corps, to September, 1864.

SERVICE.—Guard duty along Louisville & Nashville Railroad March to July, 1862. Operations against Morgan July 4-28. Paris, Ky., July 19. Action with Morgan at Gallatin, Tenn., August 13. Ordered to Nashville, Tenn., August, and duty there till December 26. Siege of Nashville September 12-November 7. Neeley's Bend, Cumberland River, October 5. Advance on Murfreesboro December 26-30. Battle of Stone's River December 26-30, 1862, and January 1-3, 1863. Duty at Murfreesboro till June. Middle Tennessee or Tullahoma Campaign June 23-July 7. Occupation of Middle Tennessee, and at Dechard, Ala., till August 16. Passage of the Cumberland Mountains and Tennessee River and Chickamauga (Ga.) Campaign August 16-September 22. Davis Cross Roads near Dug Gap September 11. Battle of Chickamauga September 19-21. Rossville Gap September 21. Siege of Chattanooga, Tenn., September 24-November 23. Chattanooga-Ringgold Campaign November 23-27. Lookout Mountain November 24. Mission Ridge November 25. Pea Vine Valley and Graysville November 26. Outpost duty at Rossville till March 15, 1864. Atlanta (Ga.) Campaign May 1-August 27. Demonstrations on Rocky Faced Ridge May 8-11. Battle of Resaca May 14-15. Advance on Dallas May 18-25. Operations on line of Pumpkin Vine Creek and battles about Dallas, New Hope Church and Allatoona Hills May 25-June 5. Pickett's Mills May 27. Operations about Marietta and against Kenesaw Mountain June 10-July 2. Pine Hill June 11-14. Lost Mountain June 15-17. Assault on Kenesaw June 27. Ruff's Station July 4. Chattahoochie River July 5-17. Peach Tree Creek July 19-20. Siege of Atlanta July 22-August 25. Utoy Creek August 5-7. Ordered to Chattanooga August 27. Pursuit of Wheeler to Huntsville, Ala., August 30-September 13. Moved to Michigan September 18-25. Mustered out September 30, 1864. Recruits formed into a detachment and transferred to 11th Regiment reorganized.

Regiment lost during service 5 Officers and 107 Enlisted men killed and mortally wounded and 2 Officers and 194 Enlisted men by disease. Total 308.

11th REGIMENT INFANTRY (REORGANIZED).

Organized at Jackson, Mich., January 4 to February 26, 1865. Four Companies left State for Nashville, Tenn., March 4, 1865, and duty there till April 1, then ordered to Chattanooga, Tenn. Six Companies left State for Chattanooga, Tenn., April 1. Attached to 3rd Brigade, 2nd Separate Division, District of the Etowah, Dept. of the Cumberland, to July, 1865. 2nd Brigade, 4th Division, District of East Tennessee, Dept. of the Cumberland, to September, 1865. Regiment moved to East Tennessee April 23, 1865, and duty guarding Chattanooga & Knoxville Railroad with Headquarters at Cleveland, Tenn., till July. Moved to Knoxville and duty there till August 3. Moved to Nashville, Tenn., August 3 and mustered out September 16, 1865.

Regiment lost during service 96 Enlisted men by disease.

12th REGIMENT INFANTRY.

Organized at Niles, Dowagiac and Buchanan, Mich., December 9, 1861, to March 1, 1862. Mustered in March 5, 1862. Left State for St. Louis, Mo., March 5, thence moved to Pittsburg Landing, Tenn. Attached to 1st Brigade, 6th Division, Army of the Tennessee, April, 1862. 1st Brigade, 1st Division, Army Tennessee, to July, 1862. 1st Brigade, 1st Division, District of Jackson, Tenn., to November, 1862. Unattached, District of Jackson, 13th Army Corps (Old), Dept. of the Tennessee, to December, 1862. Post of Bolivar, District of Jackson, 16th Army Corps, to March, 1863. 1st Brigade, 3rd Division, 16th Army Corps, to May, 1863. 1st Brigade, Kimball's Provisional Division, 13th Army Corps, to July, 1863. 1st Brigade, Kimball's Provisional Division, District of Eastern Arkansas, to August, 1863. 1st Brigade, 2nd Division, Arkansas Expedition, to November, 1863. 3rd Brigade, 2nd Division, Army of Arkansas, to January, 1864. 3rd Brigade, 2nd Division, 7th Army Corps, Dept. of Arkansas, to May, 1864. 1st Brigade, 2nd Division, 7th Army Corps, to July, 1865. Dept. of Arkansas to February, 1866.

SERVICE.—Battle of Shiloh, Tenn., April 6-7, 1862. Advance on and siege of Corinth, Miss., April 29-May 30. Pursuit to Booneville June 1-6. Moved to Bethel June 5, thence to Jackson, Tenn., June 13, and duty there till August. At Bolivar till November. Guard duty along Mississippi Central Railroad from Hickory Valley to near Bolivar with Headquarters at Middleburg, Tenn., till May, 1863. Action at Middleburg December 24, 1862. Regiment complimented by General Grant in General Order No. 3 for gallant and efficient services on successfully defending their post against a force of 3,000 Confederates under Van Dorn. Moved to Memphis, Tenn., thence to Vicksburg, Miss., May 31-June 3, 1863. Siege of Vicksburg, Miss., June 4-July 4. Surrender of Vicksburg July 4. Moved to Helena, Ark., July 25-27, thence to Clarendon August 13, and to Duvall's Bluff August 22. Steele's Expedition to Little Rock September 1-10. Engagement at Bayou Fourche and capture of Little Rock September 10. Duty at Little Rock till January 14, 1864. Veterans on furlough till February 21. March to Pine Bluff April 26-28. Train guard to Steele's army till April 30. Duty at Little Rock till June 22. Operations against Shelby north of the Arkansas River May 13-31. Expedition to Clarendon June 25-29. Clarendon June 25-26. Duty at Duvall's Bluff till August 30. Expedition in pursuit of Shelby August 27-September 6. Gregory's Landing, White River, September 4. Duty at Duvall's Bluff, guarding railroad, provost and fatigue duty till June 6, 1865. Hazen's Farm near Duvall's Bluff November 2, 1864 (Detachment). Moved to Little Rock June 6, thence march to Washington June 13-22. Guard public property at several points by detachments, with Headquarters at Camden till January 28, 1866. Companies "A," "B," "C" and "F" march from Washington to Camden July 8-22, 1865. Company "E" to Arkadelphia July 19-22, 1865. Companies "H" and "K" to Camden September 26, 1865, and Companies "D," "G" and "I" to Camden November 1, 1865. Company "F" assigned to duty at Paraclifta September 30. Regiment assembled at Camden and mustered out February 15, 1866.

Regiment lost during service 1 Officer and 52 Enlisted men killed and mortally wounded and 3 Officers and 372 Enlisted men by disease. Total 428.

13th REGIMENT INFANTRY.

Organized at Kalamazoo, Mich., and mustered in January 17, 1862. Left State for Nashville, Tenn., February 12. Attached to 15th Brigade, 4th Division, Army of the Ohio, to March, 1862. 20th Brigade, 6th Division, Army of the Ohio, to September, 1862. 20th Brigade, 6th Division, 2nd Corps, Army of the Ohio, to November, 1862. 3rd Brigade, 1st Division, Left Wing 14th Army Corps, Army of the Cumberland, to January, 1863. 3rd Brigade, 1st Division, 21st Army Corps, to April, 1863. 1st Brigade, 1st Division, 21st Army Corps, to October, 1863. 2nd Brigade, 2nd Division, 4th Army Corps, Army of the Cumberland, to November, 1863. Engineer Brigade, Dept. of the Cumberland, to October, 1864. 2nd Brigade, 1st Division,

14th Army Corps, Army of the Cumberland, to July, 1865.

SERVICE.—March from Nashville, Tenn., to Savannah, Tenn., to reinforce Army of the Tennessee, March 29-April 7, 1862. Battle of Shiloh April 7. Advance on and siege of Corinth, Miss., April 29-May 30. Pursuit to Booneville June 1-12. Buell's operations in Northern Alabama and Middle Tennessee on line of the Memphis & Charleston Railroad June to August. Duty at Stevenson, Ala., July 18 to August 31, building forts and stockades and guarding the railroad. March to Louisville, Ky., in pursuit of Bragg August 31-September 26. Pursuit of Bragg to Wild Cat, Ky., October 1-16. Nelson's Cross Roads October 18. March to Nashville, Tenn., October 22-November 7. Duty at Nashville, Tenn., till December 26. Advance on Murfreesboro December 26-30. Battle of Stone's River December 30-31, 1862, and January 1-3, 1863. Duty at Murfreesboro till June. Middle Tennessee or Tullahoma Campaign June 23-July 7. At Hillsboro, Tenn., till August 16. Passage of the Cumberland Mountains and Tennessee River and Chickamauga (Ga.) Campaign August 16-September 22. Expedition from Tracy City to Tennessee River August 22-24 (Detachment). Occupation of Chattanooga September 9. Lee and Gordon's Mills September 17-18. Battle of Chickamauga, Ga., September 19-20. Siege of Chattanooga September 24-November 23. Chattanooga-Ringgold Campaign November 23-27. Battles of Chattanooga November 23-25. Stationed on the Chickamauga; engaged in picket duty and cutting timber for warehouses in Chattanooga till February 17, 1864. Engineer duty at Chattanooga and stationed at Lookout Mountain constructing military hospitals till September, 1864. Relieved from Engineer duty and pursuit of Forest into Northern Alabama September 25-October 17. Joined Sherman's army at Kingston, Ga., November 7. March to the sea November 15-December 10. Skirmishes at Dalton, Ga., November 30 and December 5 (Detachments). Siege of Savannah December 10-21. Campaign of the Carolinas January to April, 1865. Averysboro, N. C., March 16. Battle of Bentonville March 19-21. Occupation of Goldsboro March 24. Advance on Raleigh April 10-14. Occupation of Raleigh April 14. Bennett's House April 26. Surrender of Johnston and his army. March to Washington, D. C., via Richmond, Va., April 29-May 19. Grand Review May 24. Moved to Louisville, Ky., June 9-15. Mustered out July 25, 1865.

Regiment lost during services 4 Officers and 68 Enlisted men killed and mortally wounded and 2 Officers and 314 Enlisted men by disease. Total 388.

14th REGIMENT INFANTRY.

Organized at Ypsilanti and Detroit, Mich., January 7 to February 18, 1862. Mustered in February 13, 1862. Left State for St. Louis, Mo., April 17, thence moved to Pittsburg Landing, Tenn. Attached to 2nd Brigade, 1st Division, Army of Mississippi, to September, 1862. 2nd Brigade, 13th Division, Army of the Ohio, to November, 1862. 1st Brigade, 4th Division, Center 14th Army Corps, Army of the Cumberland, to January, 1863. 1st Brigade, 4th Division, 14th Army Corps, Army of the Cumberland, to June, 1863. 1st Brigade, 2nd Division, Reserve Corps, Army of the Cumberland, to October, 1863. 1st Brigade, 2nd Division, 14th Army Corps, Army of the Cumberland, to December, 1863. Columbia, Tenn., Dept. of the Cumberland, to May, 1864. 1st Brigade, 2nd Division, 14th Army Corps, Army of the Cumberland, to July, 1865.

SERVICE.—Advance on and siege of Corinth, Miss., April 29-May 30, 1862. Actions at Farmington, Miss., May 3 and 9. Reconnoissance toward Corinth May 8. Pursuit to Booneville May 31-June 12. Reconnoissance toward Baldwyn June 3. Buell's operations along Memphis & Charleston Railroad in Northern Alabama and Middle Tennessee June 13-July 18. At Tuscumbia, Ala., till September 1. March to Nashville, Tenn., September 1-6, and duty there till December 26. Siege of Nashville September 12-November 7. Near Nashville

November 5. Near Lavergne November 7. Advance on Murfreesboro December 26-30. Guard trains to Murfreesboro January 2-3, 1863. Duty at Murfreesboro till March 8. At Brentwood till July 3 guarding line between Nashville and Franklin. Duty at Nashville, Franklin and Columbia till May, 1864. Action at Weem's Springs August 19, 1863 (Co. "C"). Regiment mounted September 8, 1863, and armed with Spencer carbines. Engaged in scout and patrol duty through Lawrence, Giles and Maury Counties, operating against guerrillas of that section. Action at Lawrenceburg, Tenn., November 4, 1863. Specially complimented by General Gordon Granger in General Order No. 38, dated November 8, 1863, for efficient services. March to join Sherman at Dallas, Ga., May 21-June 4, 1864. Atlanta Campaign June 4 to September 8, 1864. Operations about Marietta and against Kenesaw Mountain June 10-July 2. Pine Hill June 11-14. Lost Mountain June 15-17. Assault on Kenesaw June 27. Ruff's Station July 4. Chattahoochie River July 5-17. Peach Tree Creek July 19-20. Siege of Atlanta July 22-August 25. Utoy Creek August 5-7. Flank movement on Jonesboro August 25-30. Battle of Jonesboro August 31-September 1. Operations against Hood in North Georgia and North Alabama September 29-November 3. March to the sea November 15-December 10. Siege of Savannah December 10-21. Campaign of the Carolinas January to April, 1865. Averysboro, N. C., March 16. Battle of Bentonville March 19-21. Occupation of Goldsboro March 24. Advance on Raleigh April 10-14. Occupation of Raleigh April 14. Bennett's House April 26. Surrender of Johnston and his army. March to Washington, D. C., via Richmond, Va., April 29-May 19. Grand Review May 24. Moved to Louisville, Ky., June 13. Mustered out July 18, 1865.

Regiment lost during service 1 Officer and 58 Enlisted men killed and mortally wounded and 3 Officers and 184 Enlisted men by disease. Total 246.

15th REGIMENT INFANTRY.

Organized at Detroit, Monroe and Grand Rapids, Mich., October 16, 1861, to March 13, 1862. Mustered in March 20, 1862. Moved to Benton Barracks, Mo., thence to Pittsburg Landing, Tenn., March 27-April 5. Attached to 2nd Brigade, 6th Division, Army of the Tennessee, to July, 1862. 2nd Brigade, 6th Division, District of Corinth, Miss., to November, 1862. 2nd Brigade, 6th Division, Left Wing 13th Army Corps (Old), Dept. of the Tennessee, to December, 1862. Unattached, 1st Division, 17th Army Corps, to January, 1863. Unattached, 1st Division, 16th Army Corps, to June, 1863. 2nd Brigade, 1st Division, 16th Army Corps, to July, 1863. 2nd Brigade, 4th Division, 15th Army Corps, to January, 1864. Unattached, 4th Division, 15th Army Corps, to April, 1864. 3rd Brigade, 4th Division, 15th Army Corps, to August, 1864. 1st Brigade, 1st Division, 15th Army Corps, to September, 1864. 3rd Brigade, 2nd Division, 15th Army Corps, to August, 1865.

SERVICE.—Battle of Shiloh, Tenn., April 6-7, 1862. Advance on and siege of Corinth, Miss., April 29-May 30. Duty at Corinth till July 18. Moved to Bolivar, Tenn., July 18, and duty there till August 16, then moved to Corinth, Miss. Battle of Corinth, Miss., October 3-4. Pursuit to Ripley October 5-12. Garrison and provost duty at Grand Junction and LaGrange November 19, 1862, to June 5, 1863. Ordered to Vicksburg, Miss., June 5. Siege of Vicksburg, Miss., June 11-July 4. Advance on Jackson, Miss., July 4-10. Siege of Jackson July 10-17. Camp at Big Black till September. Moved to Memphis, thence march to Chattanooga, Tenn., September 28-November 20. Operations on Memphis & Charleston Railroad in Alabama October 20-29. Chattanooga-Ringgold Campaign November 23-27. March to relief of Knoxville November 28-December 8. At Scottsboro, Ala., till February, 1864. Expedition toward Rome, Ga., January 25-February 5, 1864. Veterans on furlough till April. Action at Guntersville, Ala., March 2 (Non-Veterans). Atlanta (Ga.) Campaign May 1 to September 8. Demonstration on Resaca May

8-13. Near Resaca May 13. Battle of Resaca May 14-15. Advance on Dallas May 18-25. Operations on line of Pumpkin Vine Creek and battles about Dallas, New Hope Church and Allatoona Hills May 25-June 5. Operations about Marietta and against Kenesaw Mountain June 10-July 2. Brush Mountain June 15. Assault on Kenesaw June 27. Nickajack Creek July 2-5. Chattahoochie River July 5-17. Battle of Atlanta July 22. Siege of Atlanta July 22-August 25. Ezra Chapel, Hood's second sortie, July 28. Flank movement on Jonesboro August 25-30. Battle of Jonesboro August 31-September 1. Lovejoy Station September 2-6. Operations against Hood in North Georgia and North Alabama September 29-November 3. Reconnoissance from Rome on Cave Springs Road and skirmishes October 12-13. March to the sea November 15-December 10. Clinton November 21-23. Near Bryan's Court House December 8. Siege of Savannah December 10-21. Fort McAllister December 13. Campaign of the Carolinas January to April, 1865. Salkehatchie Swamps, S. C., February 2-5. North Edisto River February 12-13. Columbia February 16-17. Battle of Bentonville, N. C., March 19-21. Occupation of Goldsboro March 24. Advance on Raleigh April 10-14. Occupation of Raleigh April 14. Bennett's House April 26. Surrender of Johnston and his army. March to Washington, D. C., via Richmond, Va., April 29-May 20. Grand Review May 24. Moved to Louisville, Ky., June 1-6, thence moved to Little Rock, Ark., June 28, and duty there till August 13. Mustered out August 18, 1865.

Regiment lost during service 3 Officers and 60 Enlisted men killed and mortally wounded and 4 Officers and 268 Enlisted men by disease. Total 335.

16th REGIMENT INFANTRY ("STOCKTON'S INDEPENDENT REGIMENT").

Organized at Plymouth and Detroit, Mich., July to September, 1861. Left State for Washington, D. C., September 16, 1861. Attached to Butterfield's Brigade, Fitz John Porter's Division, Army of the Potomac, to March, 1862. 3rd Brigade, 1st Division, 3rd Army Corps, Army of the Potomac, to May, 1862. 3rd Brigade, 1st Division, 5th Army Corps, Army of the Potomac, to July, 1865.

SERVICE.—Camp at Hall's Hill, Defences of Washington, D. C., till March, 1862. Advance on Manassas, Va., March 10. Moved to the Virginia Peninsula March 22-24. Reconnoissance to Big Bethel March 30. Warwick Road April 5. Siege of Yorktown April 5-May 4. Reconnoissance up the Pamunkey May 10. Battle of Hanover Court House May 27. Operations about Hanover Court House May 27-29. Seven days before Richmond June 25-July 1. Battles of Mechanicsville June 26; Gaines' Mill June 27; Savage Station June 29; Turkey Bridge or Malvern Cliff June 30; Malvern Hill July 1. Duty at Harrison's Landing till August 16. Movement to Fortress Monroe, thence to Centreville August 16-28. Battle of Bull Run August 30. Maryland Campaign September 6-22. Battle of Antietam September 16-17. Shepherdstown Ford September 19. At Sharpsburg till October. Movement to Falmouth, Va., October 29-November 17. Battle of Fredericksburg, Va., December 12-15. Expedition from Potomac Creek to Richards and Ellis Fords, Rappahannock River, December 29-30. "Mud March" January 20-24, 1863. At Falmouth till April 27. Chancellorsville Campaign April 27-May 6. Battle of Chancellorsville May 1-5. Aldie June 17. Middleburg and Upperville June 21. Battle of Gettysburg, Pa., July 1-3. Pursuit of Lee to Manassas Gap, Va., July 5-24. Duty at Warrenton, Beverly Ford and Culpeper till October. Bristoe Campaign October 9-22. Advance to line of the Rappahannock November 7-8. Rappahannock Station November 7. Mine Run Campaign November 26-December 2. Veterans absent on furlough January 2 to February 17, 1864. At Bealeton Station till May. Campaign from the Rapidan to the James River May 4-June 15. Battles of the Wilderness May 5-7; Laurel Hill May 8; Spottsylvania May 8-12; Spottsylvania Court House May 12-

21. Assault on the Salient May 12. North Anna May 23-26. Jericho Mills May 23. On line of the Pamunkey May 26-28. Totopotomoy May 28-31. Cold Harbor June 1-12. Bethesda Church June 1-3. Before Petersburg June 16-18. Siege of Petersburg June 16, 1864, to April 2, 1865. Six Mile House, Weldon Railroad, August 18-21, 1864. Poplar Springs Church, Peeble's Farm, September 29-October 2. Boydton Plank Road, Hatcher's Run, October 27-28. Warren's Raid on Weldon Railroad December 7-12. Dabney's Mills, Hatcher's Run, February 5-7, 1865. Appomattox Campaign March 28-April 9. Junction of Quaker and Boydton Roads and Lewis Farm near Gravelly Run March 29. White Oak Road March 30-31. Five Forks April 1. Fall of Petersburg April 2. Pursuit of Lee April 3-9. Appomattox Court House April 9. Surrender of Lee and his army. March to Washington, D. C., May 3-12. Grand Review May 23. Moved to Louisville, Ky., June 16-22, thence to Jeffersonville, Ind. Mustered out July 8, 1865.

Regiment lost during service 12 Officers and 235 Enlisted men killed and mortally wounded and 143 Enlisted men by disease. Total 390.

17th REGIMENT INFANTRY ("STONEWALL REGIMENT").

Organized at Detroit, Mich., August 8 to 22, 1862. Left State for Washington, D. C., August 27. Attached to 1st Brigade, 1st Division, 9th Army Corps, Army of the Potomac, to April, 1863. Army of the Ohio to June, and Army of the Tennessee to August, 1863. 3rd Brigade, 1st Division, 9th Army Corps, Army of the Ohio, to January, 1864. 2nd Brigade, 1st Division, 9th Army Corps, Army Ohio, and Army Potomac, to April, 1864. 1st Brigade, 3rd Division, 9th Army Corps, Army Potomac, to May, 1864. Acting Engineers, 3rd Division, 9th Army Corps, to September, 1864. Acting Engineers, 1st Division, 9th Army Corps, to April, 1865. 1st Brigade, 1st Division, 9th Army Corps, to June, 1865.

SERVICE.—Maryland Campaign September 6-22, 1862. Battle of South Mountain September 14. (Regiment afterwards designated the "Stonewall Regiment" for its achievements in this battle.) Battle of Antietam September 16-17. Duty in Maryland till October 30. Movement to Falmouth, Va., October 30-November 18. Battle of Fredericksburg, Va., December 12-15. "Mud March" January 20-24, 1863. Moved to Newport News, Va., February 14, thence to Louisville, Ky., March 19. To Bardstown, Ky., March 29. To Lebanon April 3. To Columbia April 29, and thence to Jameston, Ky., and duty there till June 4. Moved to Vicksburg, Miss., June 4-12. Siege of Vicksburg June 14-July 4. Advance on Jackson, Miss., July 4-10. Siege of Jackson July 10-17. Destruction of Mississippi Central Railroad at Madison Station July 18-20. At Milldale till August 3. Moved to Covington and Crab Orchard, Ky., August 3-24. March to Knoxville, Tenn., September 10-26. Action at Blue Springs October 10. Duty at Lenoir October 20 to November 14. Knoxville Campaign November 4-December 24. Lenoir Station November 14. Action at Campbell's Station November 16. Siege of Knoxville November 17-December 5. Repulse of Longstreet's assault on Fort Saunders November 29. Operations in East Tennessee till March, 1864. Moved to Nicholasville, Ky., thence to Annapolis, Md., March 17-April 5. Campaign from the Rapidan to the James River May 4-June 15. Battles of the Wilderness May 5-7; Spottsylvania May 8-12; Ny River May 10; Spottsylvania Court House May 12-21. Assault on the Salient May 12. North Anna River May 23-26. Ox Ford May 23-24. On line of the Pamunkey May 26-28. Totopotomoy May 28-31. Cold Harbor June 1-12. Bethesda Church June 1-3. Before Petersburg June 16-18. Siege of Petersburg June 16, 1864, to April 2, 1865. Mine Explosion, Petersburg, July 30, 1864. Six Mile House, Weldon Railroad, August 18-21. Poplar Springs Church, September 29-October 2. Reconnoissance on Vaughan and Squirrel Level Roads October 8. Boydton Plank Road, Hatcher's Run, October 27-28. Fort Stedman, Petersburg, March 25, 1865.

Appomattox Campaign March 28-April 9. Assault on and fall of Petersburg April 2. Occupation of Petersburg April 3. Pursuit of Lee April 3-9. Moved to Alexandria, Va., April 24-27. Grand Review May 23. Mustered out June 3, 1865.

Regiment lost during service 7 Officers and 128 Enlisted men killed and mortally wounded and 154 Enlisted men by disease. Total 289.

18th REGIMENT INFANTRY.

Organized at Hillsdale, Mich., and mustered in August 26, 1862. Left State for Cincinnati, Ohio, September 4. Attached to 2nd Brigade, 1st Division, Army of Kentucky, Dept. of the Ohio, to November, 1862. 1st Brigade, 2nd Division, Army of Kentucky, Dept. Ohio, to January, 1863. 3rd Brigade, District of Central Kentucky, Dept. of Ohio, to April, 1863. Garrison at Nashville, Tenn., Dept. of the Cumberland, to June, 1863. 3rd Brigade, 2nd Division, Reserve Corps, Dept. of the Cumberland, to October, 1863. Unattached, Nashville, Tenn., Dept. of the Cumberland, to January, 1864. 1st Brigade, District of Nashville, Dept. of the Cumberland, January, 1864. 1st Brigade, Roussau's 3rd Division, 12th Army Corps, Army of the Cumberland, to April, 1864. 1st Brigade, 4th Division, 20th Army Corps, Dept. of the Cumberland, to March, 1865. District of North Alabama, Dept. of the Cumberland, to June, 1865.

SERVICE.—Duty at Lexington, Ky., October, 1862, to February, 1863. March to Danville, Ky., February 21-22. Retreat to the Kentucky River February 24-27. Duty at Lexington, Ky., till March 21. Operations against Pegram's forces March 22-April 1. Action at Danville, Ky., March 24. Heckman's Bridge March 24-27. Moved to Stanford, Ky., April 2, thence to Lebanon, Ky., and to Nashville, Tenn., April 7-14. Duty at Nashville, Tenn., till June 11, 1864. Moved to Decatur, Ala., June 11-12, and duty there till September 1. Operations in District of North Alabama June 24-August 30. Action at Curtiss Wells June 24. Pond Springs June 28. Expedition from Decatur to Moulton July 25. Courtland, Ala., July 25 and 27. Expedition to relief of Athens September 1-8. Athens September 2. Pursuit of Wheeler to Shoal Creek September 8-11. Action with Wheeler near Athens September 23-24 (Detachment captured). At Decatur till November 25. Defence of Decatur against Hood's attack October 26-29. March to Stevenson November 25-December 2, and duty there till December 19. Garrison duty at Decatur and along line of the Memphis & Charleston Railroad till January 11, 1865. Moved to Huntsville, Ala., January 11, and post duty there till June 20. Scout from Huntsville to New Market, etc., April 5-7. Moved to Nashville, Tenn., and there mustered out June 26, 1865.

Regiment lost during service 18 Enlisted men killed and mortally wounded and 293 Enlisted men by disease. Total 311.

19th REGIMENT INFANTRY.

Organized at Dowagiac and mustered in September 5, 1862. Left State for Cincinnati, Ohio, September 14, and duty at Covington, Ky., till October 7. Moved to Georgetown, Lexington, Sandersville and to Nicholasville, Ky., October 7-November 13. Attached to 1st Brigade, 3rd Division, Army of Kentucky, Dept. of Ohio, October, 1862, to February, 1863. Coburn's Brigade, Baird's Division, Army of Kentucky, Dept. of the Cumberland, to June, 1863. 3rd Brigade, 1st Division, Reserve Corps, Dept. of the Cumberland, to October, 1863. Coburn's unattached Brigade, Dept. of the Cumberland, to December, 1863. Post of Murfreesboro, Tenn., Dept. of the Cumberland, to January, 1864. 2nd Brigade, 1st Division, 11th Army Corps, Army of the Cumberland, to April, 1864. 2nd Brigade, 3rd Division, 20th Army Corps, Army of the Cumberland, to June, 1865.

SERVICE.—Moved to Danville, Ky., December 12, 1862, and duty there till January 26, 1863. Moved to Louisville, Ky., thence to Nashville, Tenn., January 26-

February 7, and to Brentwood Station February 21. To Franklin February 23. Reconnoissance toward Spring Hill March 3-5. Action at Spring Hill, Thompson's Station, March 4-5. Regiment mostly captured by Bragg's Cavalry forces, nearly 18,000 strong, under Van Dorn. Little Harpeth and Brentwood March 25 (Detachment). Exchanged May 25, 1863. Regiment reorganized at Camp Chase, Ohio, during June. Moved to Nashville, Tenn., June 8-11. Middle Tennessee or Tullahoma Campaign June 23-July 7. Moved to Murfreesboro, Tenn., July 23, and garrison duty there till October 25. Stockade near Murfreesboro Bridge, Stone's River, October 4 (Co. "D"). Moved to McMinnville October 25, and duty there till April 21, 1864. Ordered to join Corps in Lookout Valley. Atlanta (Ga.) Campaign May 1-September 8. Demonstrations on Rocky Faced Ridge May 8-11. Boyd's Trail May 9. Battle of Resaca May 14-15. Cassville May 19. New Hope Church May 25. Operations on line of Pumpkin Vine Creek and battles about Dallas, New Hope Church and Allatoona Hills May 25-June 5. Operations about Marietta and against Kenesaw Mountain June 10-July 2. Pine Hill June 11-14. Lost Mountain June 15-17. Gilgal or Golgotha Church June 15. Muddy Creek June 17. Noyes Creek June 19. Kolb's Farm June 22. Assault on Kenesaw June 27. Ruff's Station July 4. Chattahoochie River July 5-17. Peach Tree Creek July 19-20. Siege of Atlanta July 22-August 25. Operations at Chattahoochie River Bridge August 26-September 2. Occupation of Atlanta September 2-November 15. March to the sea November 15-December 10. Campaign of the Carolinas January to April, 1865. Lawtonville, S. C., February 2. Averysboro, N. C., March 16. Battle of Bentonville March 19-21. Occupation of Goldsboro March 24. Advance on Raleigh April 10-14. Occupation of Raleigh April 14. Bennett's House April 26. Surrender of Johnston and his army. March to Washington, D. C., via Richmond, Va., April 29-May 19. Grand Review May 24. Mustered out June 10, 1865.

Regiment lost during service 7 Officers and 88 Enlisted men killed and mortally wounded and 160 Enlisted men by disease. Total 255.

20th REGIMENT INFANTRY.

Organized at Jackson, Mich., August 15-19, 1862. Left State for Washington, D. C., September 1, thence march to Leesburg, Va., September 8, and to Sharpsburg, Md., September 18-22. Attached to 1st Brigade, 1st Division, 9th Army Corps, Army of the Potomac, to April, 1863, and Army of the Ohio, to June, 1863. 3rd Brigade, 1st Division, 9th Army Corps, Army of the Tennessee, to August, 1863, Army of the Ohio to January, 1864. 1st Brigade, 1st Division, 9th Army Corps, Army Ohio, to April, 1864. 2nd Brigade, 3rd Division, 9th Army Corps, Army of the Potomac, to September, 1864. 2nd Brigade, 1st Division, 9th Army Corps, to May, 1865.

SERVICE.—Duty at Sharpsburg, Md., September 22 to October 6, 1862, and at Pleasant Valley, Md., till October 14. At Nolen's Ford to October 30. Advance on Culpeper November 2-15, and to Falmouth, Va., November 16-19. Battle of Fredericksburg, Va., December 12-15. "Mud March" January 20-24, 1863. At Falmouth till February 19. Moved to Newport News, Va., February 19, thence to Kentucky March 19-23. Duty at various points in Kentucky till June. Expedition to Monticello and operations in Southeast Kentucky April 26-May 12. Skirmish Alcorn's Distillery near Monticello May 9 (Detachment). Horse Shoe Bend, Ky., May 10. Moved to Vicksburg, Miss., June 3-14. Siege of Vicksburg June 14-July 4. Advance on Jackson, Miss., July 4-10. Siege of Jackson July 10-17. Destruction of Mississippi Central Railroad at Madison Station July 18-22. Camp at Milldale till August 4. Moved to Covington, Ky., thence to Crab Orchard, Ky., August 4-30. March to Knoxville, Tenn., September 10-26. Action at Blue Springs October 10. Duty at Lenoir Station till November 14. Knoxville Campaign November 4-December 24. Campbell's Station

November 16. Siege of Knoxville November 17-December 5. Repulse of Longstreet's assault on Fort Saunders November 29. Pursuit of Longstreet to Bean's Station December 5-18. Strawberry Plains January 21-22, 1864. Advance to Morristown January 24-March 2. Reconnoissance to Chucky River March 14. Moved from Knoxville to Nicholasville, Ky., thence to Annapolis, Md., March 23-30. Campaign from the Rapidan to the James River May 4-June 15. Battles of the Wilderness May 5-7; Spottsylvania May 8-12; Ny River May 10; Spottsylvania Court House May 12-21. Assault on the Salient May 12. North Anna River May 23-26. Ox Ford May 23-24. On line of the Pamunkey May 26-28. Totopotomoy May 28-31. Cold Harbor June 1-12. Bethesda Church June 1-3. Before Petersburg June 16-18. Siege of Petersburg June 16, 1864, to April 2, 1865. Mine Explosion, Petersburg, July 30, 1864. Weldon Railroad August 18-21. Poplar Springs Church September 29-October 2. Reconnoissance on Vaughan and Squirrel Level Roads October 8. Boydton Plank Road, Hatcher's Run, October 27-28. Fort Stedman, Petersburg, March 25, 1865. Appomattox Campaign March 28-April 9. Assault on and capture of Petersburg April 2. Occupation of Petersburg April 3. Pursuit of Lee April 3-9. Moved to Alexandria April 20-24. Grand Review May 23. Mustered out May 30, 1865.

Regiment lost during service 13 Officers and 111 Enlisted men killed and mortally wounded and 3 Officers and 175 Enlisted men by disease. Total 302.

21st REGIMENT INFANTRY.

Organized at Ionia and Grand Rapids and mustered in September 9, 1862. Left State for Louisville, Ky., September 12, 1862. Attached to 37th Brigade, 11th Division, Army of the Ohio, September, 1862. 37th Brigade, 11th Division, 3rd Corps, Army of the Ohio, to November, 1862. 1st Brigade, 3rd Division, Right Wing 14th Army Corps, Army of the Cumberland, to January, 1863. 1st Brigade, 3rd Division, 20th Army Corps, Army of the Cumberland, to October, 1863. 1st Brigade, 2nd Division, 4th Army Corps, Army of the Cumberland, to November, 1863. Engineer Brigade, Army of the Cumberland, to November, 1864. 2nd Brigade, 1st Division, 14th Army Corps, to June, 1865.

SERVICE.—Pursuit of Bragg to Crab Orchard, Ky., October 1-16, 1862. Battle of Perryville October 8. March to Bowling Green, Ky., thence to Nashville, Tenn., October 17-November 12. Duty at Nashville till December 26. Advance on Murfreesboro, Tenn., December 26-30. Battle of Stone's River December 30-31, 1862, and January 1-3, 1863. Duty at Murfreesboro till June. Middle Tennessee or Tullahoma Campaign June 23-July 7. Occupation of Middle Tennessee till August 16. Passage of the Cumberland Mountains and Tennessee River and Chickamauga (Ga.) Campaign August 16-September 22. Battle of Chickamauga September 19-20. Siege of Chattanooga September 24-November 23. Battles of Chattanooga November 23-25. Stationed near Chattanooga, engaged in Engineer duty, building bridges, erecting storehouses, etc., till June 11, 1864, and at Lookout Mountain building hospitals, running mills, etc., till September 20. Relieved from duty with Engineer Brigade September 20. Pursuit of Forest to Florence, Ala., September 28-October 11. Garrison duty at Dalton, Ga., October 18-30. Ordered to join 14th Army Corps at Kingston, Ga. March to the sea November 15-December 10. Siege of Savannah December 10-21. Campaign of the Carolinas January to April, 1865. Averysboro, N. C., March 16. Battle of Bentonville March 19-21. Occupation of Goldsboro March 24. Advance on Raleigh April 10-14. Occupation of Raleigh April 14. Bennett's House April 26. Surrender of Johnston and his army. March to Washington, D. C., via Richmond, Va., April 29-May 17. Grand Review May 24. Mustered out June 8, 1865.

Regiment lost during service 3 Officers and 80 Enlisted men killed and mortally wounded and 3 Officers and 291 Enlisted men by disease. Total 377.

22nd REGIMENT INFANTRY.

Organized at Pontiac, Mich., and mustered in August 29, 1862. Left State for Kentucky September 4. Attached to 3rd Brigade, 1st Division, Army of Kentucky, Dept. of the Ohio, to November, 1862. 1st Brigade, 2nd Division, Army of Kentucky, Dept. Ohio, to January, 1863. 3rd Brigade, District of Central Kentucky, Dept. Ohio, to April, 1863. District of Nashville, Tenn., Dept. of the Cumberland, to June, 1863. 3rd Brigade, 2nd Division, Reserve Corps, Dept. of the Cumberland, to September, 1863. 1st Brigade, 1st Division, Reserve Corps, to October, 1863. 2nd Brigade, 2nd Division, 14th Army Corps, Army of the Cumberland, to November, 1863. Engineer Brigade, Dept. of the Cumberland, to May, 1864. Reserve Brigade, Dept. of the Cumberland, to April, 1865. 3rd Brigade, 2nd Separate Division, District of the Etowah, Dept. of the Cumberland, to June, 1865.

SERVICE.—Operations in Central Kentucky September to November, 1862. Duty at Lexington, Ky., till February 21, 1863. Moved to Danville, Ky., February 21-22, and return to Lexington February 23-24, and duty there till March 21. Operations against Pegram March 21-April 2. Action at Danville March 24. Hickman's Bridge March 24-27. At Stanford till April 8. March to Lebanon April 8-10, thence moved to Nashville, Tenn., April 12-14. Duty at Nashville and guarding railroad April 14 to September 5, 1863. Moved to Bridgeport, Ala., September 5-6; to Rossville, Ga., September 13-14. Reconnoissance to Ringgold, Ga., and skirmish September 17. Battle of Chickamauga September 19-21. Siege of Chattanooga, Tenn., September 24-November 23. Duty at Moccasin Point; engaged in Engineer duty till October 28. At Wauhatchie, Tenn., October 28-30. Regiment attached to Engineer Brigade November 2, and engaged in building road from Chattanooga to Brown's Ferry November 2-21. Laid pontoon bridge for crossing of Sherman's army November 22. Battles of Chattanooga November 23-25. Moved to Lookout Mountain December 1, and engaged in repairing railroad till December 16. Building storehouses in Chattanooga, cutting and rafting timber and similar Engineer duty till May 26, 1864. March to Brown's Mill Creek May 26-31 and joined Headquarters, Army of the Cumberland. Assigned to provost duty at Headquarters, Army of the Cumberland, participating in the following service: Atlanta (Ga.) Campaign June 1 to September 8. Operations about Marietta and against Kenesaw Mountain June 10-July 2. Pine Hill July 11-14. Lost Mountain June 15-17. Assault on Kenesaw June 27. Ruff's Station or Smyrna Camp Ground July 4. Chattoochie River July 5-17. Building bridges at Pace's Ferry July 18-21. Peach Tree Creek July 19-20. Siege of Atlanta July 22-August 25. Utoy Creek August 5-7. Flank movement on Jonesboro August 25-30. Battle of Jonesboro August 31-September 1. Provost duty at Atlanta September 9-October 31. Escort to Gen. Thomas' Headquarters from Marietta, Ga., to Chattanooga, Tenn., October 31-November 6. Provost duty at Chattanooga till April 1, 1865. Transferred to the District of the Etowah April 1. Duty at Chattanooga till June 20. Mustered out at Nashville, Tenn., June 26, 1865.

Regiment lost during service 3 Officers and 86 Enlisted men killed and mortally wounded and 4 Officers and 306 Enlisted men by disease. Total 399.

23rd REGIMENT INFANTRY.

Organized at East Saginaw, Mich., and mustered in September 13, 1862. Left State for Louisville, Ky., September 18. Attached to 38th Brigade, 12th Division, Army of the Ohio, to November, 1862. District of Western Kentucky, Dept. of the Ohio, to June, 1863. 1st Brigade, 3rd Division, 23rd Army Corps, Army Ohio, to August, 1863. 2nd Brigade, 2nd Division, 23rd Army Corps, Army Ohio, to February, 1865, and Dept. of North Carolina, to June, 1865.

SERVICE.—Pursuit of Bragg's forces from Louisville to Crab Orchard, Ky., October 1-16, 1862. Moved to

Bowling Green October 16-19, and duty there till May 29, 1863. Moved to Glasgow, Ky., May 29-31, thence to Tompkinsville, Ky., and duty there till July. Pursuit of Morgan July 4-26. Action at Paris, Ky., July 29. Burnside's Campaign in East Tennessee August 16-October 17. March into East Tennessee August 16-September 4. At Loudon till November. Knoxville Campaign November 4-December 23. Action at Ruff's Ferry November 14. Near Loudon November 15. Campbell's Station November 16. Siege of Knoxville November 17-December 5. Pursuit of Longstreet December 7-13. Duty at Strawberry Plains till January 14, 1864. Scott's Mill Road near Knoxville January 27. Expedition to Flat Creek February 1. Duty at Mossy Creek till April 26. March to Charleston April 26-30. Atlanta (Ga.) Campaign May 1-September 8. Demonstrations on Dalton, Ga., May 9-13. Battle of Resaca May 14-15. Advance on Dallas May 18-25. Operations on line of Pumpkin Vine Creek and battles about Dallas, New Hope Church and Allatoona Hills May 25-June 5. Operations about Marietta and against Kenesaw Mountain June 10-July 2. Lost Mountain June 15-17. Muddy Creek June 17. Noyes Creek June 19. Kolb's Farm June 22. Assault on Kenesaw June 27. Nickajack Creek July 2-5. Chattahoochie River July 5-17. Decatur July 19. Howard House July 20. Battle of Atlanta July 22. Siege of Atlanta July 22-August 25. Utoy Creek August 5-7. Flank movement on Jonesboro August 25-30. Battle of Jonesboro August 31-September 1. Lovejoy Station September 2-6. Pursuit of Hood into Alabama October 4-26. At Johnsonville till November 20. Nashville Campaign November-December. Battle of Franklin November 30. Battle of Nashville December 15-16. Pursuit of Hood to the Tennessee River December 17-28. At Clifton, Tenn., till January 16, 1865. Movement to Washington, D. C., thence to Fort Fisher, N. C., January 16-February 16. Capture of Wilmington February 22. Campaign of the Carolinas March 1-April 26. Advance on Goldsboro March 6-21. Occupation of Goldsboro March 21. Advance on Raleigh April 10-14. Occupation of Raleigh April 14. Bennett's House April 26. Surrender of Johnston and his army. Duty at Raleigh, Greensboro and Salisbury to June. Mustered out June 28, 1865.

Regiment lost during service 3 Officers and 70 Enlisted men killed and mortally wounded and 4 Officers and 257 Enlisted men by disease. Total 334.

24th REGIMENT INFANTRY.

Organized at Detroit, Mich., and mustered in August 15, 1862. Moved to Washington, D. C., August 29, 1862. Attached to Defences of Washington, D. C., to October, 1862. 1st Brigade, 1st Division, 1st Army Corps, Army of the Potomac, to November, 1862. 4th Brigade, 1st Division, 1st Army Corps, to June, 1863. 1st Brigade, 1st Division, 1st Army Corps, to March, 1864. 1st Brigade, 4th Division, 5th Army Corps, to August, 1864. 3rd Brigade, 3rd Division, 5th Army Corps, to September, 1864. 1st Brigade, 3rd Division, 5th Army Corps, to February, 1865. Springfield, Ill., Northern Department, to June, 1865.

SERVICE.—Duty in the Defences of Washington, D. C., till October 1, 1862. Moved to Frederick, Md., October 1, thence to Sharpsburg, Md., October 6, and to Warrenton, Va., October 20-November 6. Guard Richmond, Fredericksburg & Aquia Creek Railroad November 25-December 6. Advance to Falmouth December 6-11. Battle of Fredericksburg December 12-15. "Mud March" January 20-24, 1863. At Belle Plain till April. Expedition to Port Royal and Port Conway April 22-23. Chancellorsville Campaign April 27-May 6. Operations at Pollock's Mill Creek April 29-May 2. Fitzhugh's Crossing April 29-30. Battle of Chancellorsville May 2-5. Operations on Northern Neck May 20-26. Gettysburg (Pa.) Campaign June 11-July 24. Battle of Gettysburg, Pa., July 1-3. (Division was first Infantry force under fire, and Regiment lost in first day's fight 316 killed, wounded and missing, out of 496.) Pursuit of

Lee to Manassas Gap, Va., July 5-24. Duty on line of the Rappahannock and Rapidan till October. Bristoe Campaign October 9-22. Haymarket October 19. Advance to line of the Rappahannock November 7-8. Mine Run Campaign November 26-December 2. Demonstration on the Rapidan February 6-7, 1864. Campaign from the Rapidan to the James River May 4-June 15. Battles of the Wilderness May 5-7; Spottsylvania May 8-12; Laurel Hill May 8; Spottsylvania Court House May 12-21. Assault on the Salient May 12. North Anna River May 23-26. Jericho Mills May 23. On line of the Pamunkey May 26-28. Totopotomoy May 28-31. Cold Harbor June 1-12. Bethesda Church June 1-3. Before Petersburg June 16-18. Siege of Petersburg June 16, 1864, to February 11, 1865. Weldon Railroad August 18-21, 1864. Boydton Plank Road, Hatcher's Run, October 27-28. Warren's Raid on Weldon Railroad December 7-12. Dabney's Mills February 5-7, 1865. Ordered to Baltimore, Md., for special duty February 11, 1865. Moved to Springfield, Ill., February 15, and assigned to garrison and guard duty there at Draft Rendezvous till June 19. Regiment selected as escort at funeral of President Lincoln. Mustered out June 30, 1865.

Regiment lost during service 12 Officers and 177 Enlisted men killed and mortally wounded and 3 Officers and 136 Enlisted men by disease. Total 328.

25th REGIMENT INFANTRY.

Organized at Kalamazoo, Mich., and mustered in September 22, 1862. Left State for Louisville, Ky., September 29. Attached to District of Louisville, Dept. of the Ohio, to December, 1862. District of Western Kentucky, Dept. of the Ohio, to June, 1863. Unattached, 2nd Division, 23rd Army Corps, Army of the Ohio, to August, 1863. 1st Brigade, 2nd Division, 23rd Army Corps, Army of the Ohio, to February, 1865, and Dept. of North Carolina, to June, 1865.

SERVICE.—Duty at Louisville, Ky., till December 9, 1862. Moved to Munfordsville December 9, and duty there till January 8, 1863. Operations against Morgan December 22, 1862, to January 2, 1863. Action at Bacon Creek, near Munfordsville, December 26, 1862. Moved to Bowling Green, Ky., January 8, 1863, and duty there till March 26. Moved to Lebanon, Ky., March 26, and operations against Pegram's forces March 26-April 3. Provost and guard duty at Louisville till August. (Cos. "D," "E" "F.," "I" and "K" moved to Lebanon June 10, thence to Green River Bridge. Action at Green River Bridge, Tebb's Bend, July 4. Successfully repulse Gen. John Morgan and his command of 4,000 with a loss of 50 killed and 200 wounded.) Moved to Lebanon, Ky., August 17. Burnside's Campaign in East Tennessee August 17-October 17. March over Cumberland Mountains to Knoxville, Tenn., August 17-September 4. Duty at Loudon till November 9. Knoxville Campaign November 4-December 23. Moved to Kingston November 9, and duty there till December 4. Repulse of Wheeler's attack on Kingston November 24. Near Kingston December 4. March to Mossy Creek December 4-27. Action at Mossy Creek, Talbot Station, December 29. Duty at Mossy Creek till January 18, 1864. Moved to Knoxville January 18-21 and duty there till February 24. Advance to Morristown February 24-March 12. To Mossy Creek March 18 thence march to Red Clay, Ga., March 25-May 4. Atlanta (Ga.) Campaign May 4-September 8. Demonstrations on Dalton May 9-13. Battle of Resaca May 14-15. Advance on Dallas May 18-25. Operations on line of Pumpkin Vine Creek and battles about Dallas, New Hope Church and Allatoona Hills May 25-June 5. Pickett's Mills May 27. Operations about Marietta and against Kenesaw Mountain June 10-July 2. Lost Mountain June 15-17. Muddy Creek June 17. Noyes' Creek June 19. Kolb's Farm June 22. Assault on Kenesaw June 27. Nickajack Creek July 2-5. Chattahoochie River July 5-17. Decatur July 19. Howard House July 20. Battle of Atlanta July 22. Siege of Atlanta July 22-August 25. Utoy Creek August 5-7. Flank movement on Jonesboro August 25-30. Lovejoy Station September 2-6.

Pursuit of Hood into Alabama October 4-26. Moved to Johnsonville, Tenn., November 2-5, thence to Centreville and guard fords of Duck River till November 28. Battle of Franklin November 30. Battle of Nashville December 15-16. Pursuit of Hood to the Tennessee River December 17-28. At Clifton, Tenn., till January 16, 1865. Moved to Washington, D. C., thence to Fort Fisher, N. C., January 16-February 15. Fort Anderson February 18-19. Town Creek February 19-20. Capture of Wilmington February 22. Campaign of the Carolinas March 1-April 26. Advance on Goldsboro March 6-21. Occupation of Goldsboro March 21. Advance on Raleigh April 10-14. Occupation of Raleigh April 14. Bennett's House April 26. Surrender of Johnston and his army. Duty at Salisbury, N. C., till June. Mustered out June 24, 1865.

Regiment lost during service 1 Officer and 34 Enlisted men killed and mortally wounded and 2 Officers and 141 Enlisted men by disease. Total 178.

26th REGIMENT INFANTRY.

Organized at Jackson, Mich., September 10 to December 12, 1862. Mustered in December 12, 1862. Left State for Washington, D. C., December 13. Attached to District of Alexandria, Defences of Washington, D. C., to February, 1863. Slough's Brigade, Garrison of Alexandria, Va., 22nd Army Corps, to April, 1863. Ferry's 1st Brigade, Corcoran's 1st Division, 7th Army Corps, Dept. of Virginia, to July, 1863. New York, Dept. of the East, to October, 1863. 1st Brigade, 1st Division, 2nd Army Corps, Army of the Potomac, to June, 1865.

SERVICE.—Provost duty at Alexandria, Va., till April 20, 1863. Ordered to Suffolk, Va., April 20. Siege of Suffolk, Va., April 22-May 4. Siege of Suffolk raised May 4. Windsor May 23. Dix's Peninsula Campaign June 24-July 8. Expedition to Bottom's Bridge July 1-7. Ordered to New York City July 12. Duty there and at Fort Richmond, N. Y. Harbor, July 14 to October 13. Ordered to join Army of the Potomac in the field. Advance to line of the Rappahannock November 7-8. Mine Run Campaign November 26-December 2. Demonstration on the Rapidan February 6-7, 1864. Campaign from the Rapidan to the James River May 4-June 15. Battles of the Wilderness, Corbin's Bridge, May 8. Spottsylvania May 8-12. Po River May 10. Spottsylvania Court House May 12-21. Assault on the Salient ("Bloody Angle") May 12. North Anna River May 23-26. On line of the Pamunkey May 26-28. Totopotomoy May 28-31. Cold Harbor June 1-12. (Co. "F" detached in Slough's Brigade, Defences of Washington, D. C., 22nd Army Corps, June, 1864, to June, 1865.) Before Petersburg June 16-18. Siege of Petersburg June 16, 1864, to April 2, 1865. Jerusalem Plank Road, Weldon Railroad, June 22-23, 1864. Demonstration north of the James July 27-29. Deep Bottom July 27-28. Demonstration north of the James at Deep Bottom August 13-20. Strawberry Plains August 14-18. Ream's Station August 25. Reconnoissance to Hatcher's Run December 9-10. Dabney's Mills, Hatcher's Run, February 5-7, 1865. Watkin's House March 25. Appomattox Campaign March 28-April 9. On line of Hatcher's and Gravelly Runs March 29-30. Hatcher's Run (or Boydton Road) and White Oak Road March 31. Sutherland Station April 2. Fall of Petersburg April 2. Pursuit of Lee April 3-9. Sailor's Creek April 6. Flat Creek, near Amelia Springs, April 6. High Bridge April 7. Appomattox Court House April 9. Surrender of Lee and his army. Regiment specially detailed to remain at Appomattox Court House until the paroling of Lee's army was accomplished. Moved to Washington, D. C., May 2-13. Grand Review May 23. Mustered out June 4, 1865.

Regiment lost during service 3 Officers and 115 Enlisted men killed and mortally wounded and 3 Officers and 159 Enlisted men by disease. Total 280.

27th REGIMENT INFANTRY.

Organized at Port Huron, Ovid and Ypsilanti, Mich., and mustered in April 10, 1863. (Co. "I" December 13, 1863; Co. "K" January 4, 1864.) Left State for Kentucky April 12, 1863. Attached to 2nd Brigade, 1st Division, 9th Army Corps, Army of the Ohio, to June, 1863. 1st Brigade, 1st Division, 9th Army Corps, Army of the Tennessee, to August, 1863. 2nd Brigade, 1st Division, 9th Army Corps, Army of the Ohio, to April, 1864. 1st Brigade, 3rd Division, 9th Army Corps, Army of the Potomac, to September, 1864. 1st Brigade, 1st Division, 9th Army Corps, to July, 1865.

SERVICE.—Duty at various points in Kentucky April to June, 1863. Action at Jamestown, Ky., June 2. Moved to Vicksburg, Miss., June 4-12. Siege of Vicksburg, Miss., June 14-July 4. Advance on Jackson, Miss., July 4-10. Siege of Jackson July 10-17. Destruction of Mississippi Central Railroad at Madison Station July 18-22. At Milldale till August 4. Moved to Covington, thence to Crab Orchard, Ky., August 4-30. March to Knoxville, Tenn., September 10-26. Action at Blue Springs October 10. Duty at Lenoir till November 14. Knoxville Campaign November 4-December 23. Loudon Station November 14. Campbell's Station November 16. Siege of Knoxville November 17-December 5. Repulse of Longstreet's assault on Fort Saunders November 29. Pursuit of Longstreet December 6-18. Operations in East Tennessee till March, 1864. Armstrong's Ferry January 22. Advance on Morristown January 24-March 2. (Cos. "I" and "K" join Regiment at Mossy Creek, Tenn., March, 1864.) Moved from Knoxville, Tenn., to Nicholasville, Ky.; thence to Annapolis, Md., March 17-April 5. Campaign from the Rapidan to the James River May 4-June 15. Battles of the Wilderness May 5-7. Spottsylvania May 8-12. Ny River May 10. Spottsylvania May 12-21. Assault on the Salient May 12. North Anna River May 23-26. Ox Ford May 23-24. On line of the Pamunkey May 26-28. Totopotomoy May 28-31. Cold Harbor June 1-12. Bethesda Church June 1-3. Before Petersburg June 16, 1864, to April 2, 1865. Mine Explosion, Petersburg, July 30, 1864. Weldon Railroad August 18-21. Poplar Springs Church September 29-October 2. Reconnoissance on Vaughan and Squirrel Level Roads October 8. Boydton Plank Road, Hatcher's Run, October 27-28. Fort Stedman March 25, 1865. Appomattox Campaign March 28-April 9. Assault on Fort Mahone and fall of Petersburg April 2. Occupation of Petersburg April 3. Pursuit of Lee April 3-9. Moved to Washington, D. C., April 20-24. Grand Review May 23. Duty at Washington and Alexandria till July. Mustered out July 26, 1865.

Regiment lost during service 10 Officers and 215 Enlisted men killed and mortally wounded and 3 Officers and 204 Enlisted men by disease. Total 432.

28th REGIMENT INFANTRY.

Organized at Kalamazoo and Marshall, Mich., by consolidation of 28th and 29th Michigan Infantry on October 26, 1864. Moved to Louisville, Ky., October 26-29, and duty there till November 10. Moved to Camp Nelson, Ky.; thence guard trains to Nashville, Tenn., November 10-December 5. Attached to Post of Nashville, Tenn., Dept. of the Cumberland, to January, 1865. 2nd Brigade, 1st Division, 23rd Army Corps, Army of the Ohio to February, 1865, and Dept. of North Carolina to April, 1865. District of Raleigh, N. C., Dept. of North Carolina, to August, 1865. District of Wilmington, N. C., Dept. of North Carolina, to January, 1866. District of New Berne, N. C., to June, 1865.

SERVICE.—Occupation of Nashville, Tenn., during Hood's investment, December 5-14, 1864. Battle of Nashville December 15-16. Pursuit of Hood December 17-28. At Clifton, Tenn., till January 11, 1865. Moved to Louisville, Ky., January 11-18, thence to Alexandria, Va., January 18-25. Duty there till February 19. Moved to Morehead City, thence to Newberne, N. C., February 19-25. Campaign of the Carolinas March 1-April 26. Advance on Kinston and Goldsboro March 1-21. Battle of Wise's Forks March 8-10. Kinston March 14. Occupation of Goldsboro March 21. Advance on Raleigh April 10-14. Occupation of Raleigh April 14. Bennett's House April 26. Surrender of Johnston and his army. Duty in District of Raleigh, Hardin County, N. C., till August. In District of Wilmington, Crook County, N.

C., to October, and in District of Newberne, N. C., till June, 1866. Mustered out June 6, 1866.

Regiment lost during service 1 Officer and 5 Enlisted men killed and mortally wounded and 1 Officer and 126 Enlisted men by disease. Total 133.

29th REGIMENT INFANTRY.

Organized at East Saginaw, Mich., and mustered in October 3, 1864. Ordered to Nashville, Tenn., thence to Decatur, Ala., October, 1864. Attached to District of North Alabama, Dept. of the Cumberland, to November, 1864. 1st Brigade, Defences Nashville & Chattanooga Railroad, Dept. of the Cumberland, to December, 1864. 3rd Brigade, Defences Nashville & Chattanooga Railroad, to February, 1865. Unattached, 4th Division, 20th Army Corps, Dept. of the Cumberland, to March, 1865. 3rd Brigade, 1st Sub-district, Middle Tennessee, Dept. of the Cumberland, to September, 1865.

SERVICE.—Defence of Decatur against Hood's attack October 26-29, 1864. Garrison duty at Decatur, Ala., till November 24. Moved to Murfreesboro, Tenn., November 24-27. Siege of Murfreesboro December 5-12. Winchester Church December 12. Near Murfreesboro December 13. Murfreesboro December 13-14. Moved to Anderson December 27 and assigned to duty guarding Nashville & Chattanooga Railroad till July, 1865. Moved to Dechard, thence to Murfreesboro, Tenn., and garrison duty there till September 6. Mustered out September 6 and discharged at Detroit, Mich., September 12, 1865.

Regiment lost during service 1 Officer and 5 Enlisted men killed and mortally wounded and 1 Officer and 65 Enlisted men by disease. Total 72.

30th REGIMENT INFANTRY.

Organized at Detroit, Mich., for 12 months' service in the State and mustered in January 9, 1865. Engaged in frontier duty in Michigan along the Detroit and St. Clair Rivers till June, 1865. Mustered out June 30, 1865.

Regiment lost during service 18 by disease.

STANTON GUARD.

Organized at Detroit, Mich., May 10, 1862. Duty at Mackinac Island, Mich., till September. Mustered out September 25, 1862.

INDEPENDENT COMPANY (PROVOST GUARD).

Organized at Detroit, Mich., January 3, 1863. Duty at Detroit Barracks till May, 1865. Mustered out May 9, 1865.

MINNESOTA VOLUNTEERS.

1st REGIMENT CAVALRY ("MOUNTED RANGERS").

Organized at St. Cloud, St. Peters and Fort Snelling, Minn., October 9 to December 30, 1862. Organized for frontier duty against Indians. 1st Battalion engaged in frontier duty till June, 1863. Sibley's Expedition against Indians in Dakota Territory June 16-September 14.

Battle of Big Mound, D. T., July 24. Dead Buffalo Lake July 26. Stony Lake July 28. Missouri River July 28-30. 1st Battalion on duty at Fort Ripley, and rest of Regiment at Fort Snelling, Minn., till December. Mustered out October 20 to December 7, 1863.

Regiment lost during service 2 Officers and 4 Enlisted men killed and mortally wounded and 31 Enlisted men by disease. Total 37.

2nd REGIMENT CAVALRY.

Organized at Fort Snelling, Minn., December 5, 1863, to January 5, 1864. Duty there and garrison posts on Minnesota frontier till May, 1864. March to Fort Ridgley May 24-28, 1864. Sully's Expedition against hostile Indians west of the Missouri River June 5 to October 15, 1864. March to Fort Sully, Missouri River, June 5-July 1. Pursuit of Indians to the Bad Lands July 5-28. Battle of Tah kah a kuty or Killdeer Mountain July 28. Passage of the Bad Lands August 3-18. Action at Two Hills, Bad Lands, Little Missouri River, August 8-9. Rescue of Fiske's Emigrant train September 10-30. Engaged in frontier and patrol duty between Forts Wadsworth, Abercrombie, Ripley and Ridgley, Headquarters at Fort Snelling, till May, 1866. Mustered out Companies "B," "C," "D," "E," "F," "G," "I" and "M" November 17 to December 29. 1865, Company "A" April 2, 1866, Company "H" April 28, 1866, and Companies "K" and "L" May 4, 1866.

Regiment lost during service 4 Enlisted men killed and 3 Officers and 56 Enlisted men by disease. Total 63.

BRACKETT'S BATTALION CAVALRY.

Companies "A," "B" and "C" organized at Fort Snelling, Minn., as 1st, 2nd and 3rd Companies, Minnesota Light Cavalry, September to November, 1861. Ordered to Benton Barracks, Mo., November, 1861, and attached to Curtis Horse, an Independent Regiment of Cavalry, which was later designated 5th Iowa Cavalry. Assigned as Companies "G," "I" and "K." Duty at Benton Barracks, Mo., till February, 1862. Moved to Fort Henry, Tenn., February 8-11. Served unassigned, Dept. of the Tennessee, to November, 1862. District of Columbus, Ky., 13th Army Corps, Dept. of the Tennessee, to December, 1862. District of Columbus, Ky., 16th Army Corps, Dept. Tennessee, to June, 1863. 1st Brigade, Turchin's 2nd Cavalry Division, Army of the Cumberland, to October, 1863. 3rd Brigade, 2nd Division, Cavalry Corps, Army of the Cumberland, to December, 1863. 1st Brigade, 2nd Division, Cavalry Corps, Army Cumberland, to January, 1864.

SERVICE.—Engaged in patrol duty during battle of Fort Donelson, Tenn. Expedition to destroy railroad bridge over Tennessee River February 14-16, 1862. Duty at Forts Henry and Heiman, Tenn., till February 5, 1863, and at Fort Donelson, Tenn., till June 5, 1863. Moved from Fort Henry to Savannah, Tenn., March 25-April 1, 1862. Moved toward Nashville, Tenn., repairing roads and erecting telegraph lines April 3-6. Advance on and siege of Corinth, Miss., April 29-May 30. Acting as escorts to Telegraph Corps, Lockridge Mills, May 5. Occupation of Corinth May 30, and pursuit to Booneville May 31-June 12. Duty at Humboldt till August, 1862. Scouting and protecting railroad. Action at Fort Donelson, Tenn., August 25. Cumberland Iron Works August 26. Expedition to Clarksville September 5-9. New Providence September 6. Clarksville September 7. Scout toward Eddyville October 29-November 10. Expedition from Fort Heiman December 18-28. Fort Donelson February 3, 1863. Duty at Fort Donelson till June. Moved to Murfreesboro and Nashville, Tenn., June 5-11. Scout on Middleton and Eagleville Pike June 10. Expedition to Lebanon June 15-17. Lebanon June 16. Middle Tennessee or Tullahoma Campaign June 23-July 7. Guy's Gap, Fosterville, June 25. Guy's Gap. Fosterville and Shelbyville, June 27. Occupation of Middle Tennessee till September. Moved to McMinnville September 6-8, and operating against guerrillas till October. Operations against Wheeler and Roddy September 30-October 17. Garrison Creek near Fosterville and Wartrace October 6. Sugar Creek October 9. Tennessee River October 10. At Maysville till January, 1864. Expedition from Maysville to Whitesburg and Decatur November 14-17, 1863, to destroy boats on the Tennessee River. Outpost duty on line of Tennessee River from south of Huntsville to Bellefonte, Ala., November and December, 1863. Veteranized January 1, 1864. Battalion moved to Minnesota January 7. Detached from 5th Iowa Cavalry February 25, 1864, and designated Brackett's Battalion, Minnesota Cavalry. Duty at Fort Snelling, Minn., to May, 1864. March from Fort Snelling to Sioux City May 2-25. Sully's Expedition against hostile Indians west of the Missouri River June 4 to November 10, 1864. March to Fort Sully June 4-15. March to Fort Rice June 28-July 7. Pursuit of Indians to the Bad Lands July 19-28. Battle of Tah kah a kuty or Killdeer Mountain July 28. Passage of the Bad Lands of. Dakota Territory August 3-18. Action at Two Hills, Bad Lands, Little Missouri River, August 8-9. Relief

of Fiske's Emigrant train September 10-30. At Fort Ridgley, Minn., till spring of 1865. Sully's operations against Indians May to October, 1865. Patrol duty from Sioux City to Fort Randall. Headquarters at Sioux City, October, 1865, to May, 1866. Mustered out June 1, 1866.

Regiment lost during service 4 Enlisted men killed and 1 Officer and 6 Enlisted men by disease. Total 11.

HATCH'S INDEPENDENT BATTALION CAVALRY.

Organized at Fort Snelling and St. Paul, Minn. Companies "A," "B," "C," "D" July 25 to September, 1863. Company "E" mustered August 31, 1864, and Company "F" mustered September 1, 1864.

Companies "A," "B," "C," "D" march to Pembina October 5-November 13. 1863, and frontier duty there till May, 1864. Moved to Fort Abercrombie May 5-16, 1864. Assigned to duty Companies "A" and "B" as garrison at Fort Abercrombie, Company "C" at Alexandria and Pomme de Terre. Company "D" on patrol duty from Fort Abercrombie to Pembina. Companies "E" and "F" on frontier duty. Mustered out April 26 to June 22, 1866.

Battalion lost during service by disease 21.

1st REGIMENT HEAVY ARTILLERY.

Organized at St. Paul and Rochester, Minn., September, 1864, to February, 1865. Companies ordered to Chattanooga, Tenn., as fast as organized and garrison duty there till September, 1865. Mustered out September 27, 1865.

Regiment lost during service by disease 87.

1st INDEPENDENT BATTERY LIGHT ARTILLERY.

Organized at Fort Snelling, Minn., November 21, 1861. Ordered to St. Louis, Mo., and duty there till February, 1862. Moved to Cairo, Ill., thence to Pittsburg Landing, Tenn. Attached to Buckland's Brigade, Sherman's 5th Division, Army of the Tennessee, to April, 1862. 2nd Brigade, 6th Division, Army of the Tennessee, to July, 1862. Artillery, 6th Division, District of Corinth, Miss., to November, 1862. 6th Division, Left Wing 13th Army Corps (Old), Dept. of the Tennessee, to December, 1862. Artillery, 6th Division, 16th Army Corps, to January, 1863. Artillery, 6th Division, 17th Army Corps, to September, 1863. Artillery, 1st Division, 17th Army Corps, to April, 1864. Artillery, 4th Division, 17th Army Corps, to October, 1864. Artillery Brigade, 17th Army Corps, to July, 1865.

SERVICE.—Expedition to Eastport, Miss., and Chickasaw, Ala., April 1, 1862. Battle of Shiloh, Tenn., April 6-7. Advance on and siege of Corinth, Miss., April 29-May 30. Duty at Corinth till October. Battle of Corinth October 3-4. Pursuit to Ripley October 5-12. Grant's Central Mississippi Campaign November, 1862, to January, 1863. At Moscow and Memphis, Tenn., to February 6, 1863. Moved to Lake Providence, La., February 6-10, and duty there till April 22. Movement on Bruinsburg and turning Grand Gulf April 25-30. Siege of Vicksburg May 18-July 4. Assaults on Vicksburg May 19 and 22. Surrender of Vicksburg July 4. Duty at Vicksburg till April, 1864. Veterans on furlough February 20 to April 17, 1864. Moved to Cairo, Ill., April 4-17. Moved to Clifton, Tenn., to Big Shanty, Ga., via Huntsville and Decatur, Ala., and Kingston and Rome, Ga., April 28-June 9. Atlanta (Ga.) Campaign June 9-September 8. Operations about Marietta and against Kenesaw Mountain June 10-July 2. Assault on Kenesaw June 27. Nickajack Creek July 2-5. Howell's Ferry July 5. Chattahoochie River July 6-17. Leggett's or Bald Hill July 20-21. Battle of Atlanta July 22. Siege of Atlanta July 22-August 25. Ezra Chapel, Hood's second sortie, July 28. Flank movement on Jonesboro August 25-30. Battle of Jonesboro August 31-September 1. Lovejoy Station September 2-6. Operations in North Georgia and North Alabama against Hood September 29-November 3. March to the sea November 15-December 10. Ball's Ferry and Georgia Central Railroad Bridge, Oconee River, November 23-25. Siege of Savannah December 10-21. Campaign of the Carolinas January to April, 1865. Salkehatchie Swamps, S. C., February 2-5. South Edisto River February 9. Orangeburg February 11-12. About Columbia February 15-17. Cheraw March 3. Battle of Bentonville, N. C., March 20-21. Occupation of Goldsboro March 24. Advance on Raleigh April 10-14. Bennett's House April 26. Surrender of Johnston and his army. March to Washington, D. C., via Richmond, Va., April 29-May 30. Grand Review May 24. Moved to St. Paul, Minn., June 12. Mustered out July 1, 1865.

Battery lost during service 1 Officer and 7 Enlisted men killed and mortally wounded and 1 Officer and 29 Enlisted men by disease. Total 38.

2nd INDEPENDENT BATTERY LIGHT ARTILLERY.

Organized at Fort Snelling, Minn., March 21, 1862. Moved to St. Louis, Mo., April 21-25, 1862. Duty at Benton Barracks till May 18. Moved to Pittsburg Landing, Tenn., May 21-25. Attached to 2nd Brigade, 4th Division, Army of Mississippi, to September, 1862. 31st Brigade, 9th Division, Army Ohio, to October, 1862. 31st Brigade, 9th Division, 3rd Corps, Army Ohio, to November, 1862. 2nd Brigade, 1st Division, Right Wing 14th Army Corps, Army of the Cumberland, to January, 1863. Artillery, 1st Division, 20th Army Corps, Army of the Cumberland, to October, 1863. Artillery, 2nd Division, 14th Army Corps, to April, 1864. Unattached, Dept. of the Cumberland, to October, 1864. Garrison Artillery, Post of Chattanooga, Tenn., Dept. of the Cumberland, to April, 1865. 2nd Brigade, 4th Division, District of East Tennessee, to August, 1865.

SERVICE.—Siege of Corinth, Miss., May 27-30, 1862. Pursuit to Booneville May 30-June 3. March to Jacinto and Ripley June 29-July 4. March through Alabama to Nashville, Tenn., August 14-September 8, thence to Louisville, Ky., in pursuit of Bragg September 11-26. Pursuit of Bragg into Kentucky October 1-16. Battle of Perryville October 8. Perryville October 9. Stanford October 14. March to Nashville, Tenn., October 16-November 7. Duty at Nashville till December 26. Advance on Murfreesboro December 26-30. Nolensville, Knob Gap, December 26. Battle of Stone's River December 30-31, 1862, and January 1-3, 1863. At Murfreesboro till June. Reconnoissance from Murfreesboro March 6-7. Methodist Church, Shelbyville Pike, March 6. Reconnoissance from Salem to Versailles February 9-14. Operations on Edgeville Pike June 4. Middle Tennessee or Tullahoma Campaign June 23-July 7. Liberty Gap June 24-27. Occupation of Tullahoma July 1. Winchester July 3. Occupation of Middle Tennessee till August 16. Passage of the Cumberland Mountains and Tennessee River and Chickamauga (Ga.) Campaign August 16-September 22. Battle of Chickamauga September 19-20. Siege of Chattanooga, Tenn., September 24-November 23. Chattanooga-Ringgold Campaign November 23-27. Tunnel Hill November 23-24. Mission Ridge November 25. Pursuit to Ringgold November 26-27. Chickamauga Creek November 26. At Rossville, Ga., till March 21, 1864. Demonstration on Dalton, Ga., February 22-27, 1864. Tunnel Hill, Buzzard's Roost Gap and Rocky Faced Ridge February 23-25. Battery Veteranized March 21. Veterans on furlough April 11 to June 5. Non-Veterans attached to Battery "I," 2nd Illinois Light Artillery. Battery mounted at Nashville, Tenn., and escort cattle and horses to army in the field till July 14, 1864. Moved to Chattanooga, Tenn., July 14-18. Mounted and engaged in scouting till October. Duty as Infantry at Fort Irwin, Defences of Chattanooga, till March 30, 1865. Moved to Philadelphia, Tenn., and garrison duty there till July. Ordered to St. Paul, Minn., and mustered out August 16, 1865.

Battery lost during service 1 Officer and 5 Enlisted men killed and mortally wounded and 19 Enlisted men by disease. Total 25.

3rd INDEPENDENT BATTERY LIGHT ARTILLERY.

Organized at Fort Snelling, Minn., from the enlisted men of the 6th, 7th, 8th, 9th and 10th Regiments, Minnesota Infantry, February 2 to May 1, 1863. Sibley's Expedition against hostile Indians in Dakota June 16-September 12, 1863. Actions at Big Hills, D. T., July 24. Dead Buffalo Lake July 26. Stony Lake July 28. Missouri River July 29-30. 4th Section moved as escort to Gen. Ramsey, U. S. Commissioner, from Sauk Centre to Fort Abercrombie to treat with Chippewa Indians at Red Lake River Crossing, then stationed at Fort Ripley till May, 1864. 2nd Section at Pembina October, 1863, to May, 1864. 3rd Section at Fort Ridgly till May, 1864. 1st Section at Fort Snelling till May, 1864. Sully's Expedition against hostile Indians west of the Missouri River June 5 to October 15, 1864. Battle of Tah kah a kuty or Killdeer Mountain July 28. Two Hills, Bad Lands, Little Missouri River August 8. 1st Section stationed at Fort Ripley, 3rd Section at Fort Sisseton, 2nd and 4th Sections at Fort Ridgly till May, 1865. Expedition against hostile Indians in Dakota June to October, 1865 (1st, 2nd and 4th Sections). 1st Section at Fort Abercrombie, rest of Battery at Fort Wadsworth till February, 1866. Mustered out February 27, 1866.

Lost by disease during service 4.

1st COMPANY SHARPSHOOTERS.

Organized under authority of the Secretary of War at Fort Snelling, Minn., and mustered in October 5, 1861. Moved to Washington, D. C., October 6-10, 1861, and reported to Col. Berdan, at Camp of Instruction. Assigned as Company "A," 2nd United States Sharpshooters, February 10, 1862 (See 1st U. S. Sharpshooters).

2nd COMPANY SHARPSHOOTERS.

Organized at St. Paul, Minn., November 23, 1861, to March 17, 1862, and mustered in March 20, 1862. Moved to Washington, D. C., April 21-26, 1862, thence to Virginia Peninsula May 3-5. Attached to 1st U. S. Sharpshooters as Company "I" till May 30, 1862. Assigned to duty with 1st Minnesota Infantry, May 30 to November 23, 1863. Attached to 1st Brigade, 2nd Division, 2nd Army Corps, Army of the Potomac.

SERVICE.—New Bridge May 24, 1862. Operations about Hanover Court House May 27-29. Joined 1st Minnesota Infantry June 3. Seven days before Richmond June 25-July 1. Peach Orchard, Allen's Farm, and Savage Station June 29. White Oak Swamp and Glendale June 30. Malvern Hill July 1 and August 5. At Harrison's Landing till August 16. Moved to Alexandria August 16-28, thence march to Centreville August 30. Cover Pope's retreat to Washington, D. C., September 1-2. Near Chantilly and Flint Hill September 1. Vienna September 2. Maryland Campaign September 6-22. Battles of South Mountain September 14. Antietam September 16-17. Moved to Harper's Ferry September 22, and duty there till October 30. Reconnoissance to Charlestown October 16-17. March up Loudoun Valley and to Falmouth, Va., October 30-November 17. Battle of Fredericksburg, Va., December 12-15. At Falmouth till April, 1863. Chancellorsville Campaign April 27-May 6. Operations about Franklin's Crossing April 29-May 2. Battle of Maryes Heights, Fredericksburg May 3. Salem Heights May 3-4. Gettysburg (Pa.) Campaign June 11-July 24. Haymarket June 25. Battle of Gettysburg, Pa., July 1-3. Pursuit of Lee to Manassas Gap, Va., July 5-24. At Kelly's Ford, Va., July 31-August 15. Detached for duty in New York during draft disturbances August 15-September 16. Rejoined Brigade, near Culpeper, Va., September 16. Bristoe Campaign October 9-22. Bristoe Station October 14. Advance to line of the Rappahannock November 7-8. At Kelly's Ford till November 26. Detailed November 23, 1863, as provost guard at Headquarters of 2nd Division, 2nd Army Corps. Mine Run Campaign November 26-December 2. Camp at Stevensburg till May, 1864. Campaign from the Rapidan to the James River May 3-June 15. Battles of the Wilderness May 5-7; Spottsylvania May 8-12; Spottsylvania Court House May 12-21; North Anna River May 23-26. On line of the Pamunkey May 26-

28. Totopotomoy May 28-31. Cold Harbor June 1-12. Movement to Petersburg June 12-15. Assault on Petersburg June 16-18. Siege of Petersburg June 16, 1864, to March 19, 1865. Jerusalem Plank Road June 22-23, 1864. Demonstration north of the James July 27-29. Battle of Deep Bottom July 27-28. Demonstration north of the James August 13-20. Strawberry Plains August 14-18. Ream's Station August 25. Boydton Plank Road, Hatcher's Run, October 27-28. Raid on Weldon Railroad December 7-11. Dabney's Mills, Hatcher's Run, February 5-7, 1865. Mustered out March 19, 1865. Veterans transferred to 1st Minnesota Battalion Infantry.

1st REGIMENT INFANTRY.

The first Regiment tendered to the government, April 14, 1861. Organized under first call at Fort Snelling, Minn., and mustered in April 29, 1861, for three months. Reorganized for three years May 10, 1861, to date from April 29, 1861. Companies "B" and "G" moved to Fort Ridgly, Minn., May 28. Company "A" moved to Fort Ripley May 29. Company "E" moved to Fort Ripley June 6, and Companies "C" and "D" moved to Fort Abercrombie June 10. Rejoined Regiment at Fort Snelling under orders for Washington, D. C., June 21. Moved to Washington, D. C., June 22-26, and to Alexandria July 3. Attached to Franklin's Brigade, Heintzelman's Division, McDowell's Army of Northeast Virginia, to August, 1861. Stone's Brigade, Division of the Potomac, to October, 1861. Gorman's Brigade, Stone's (Sedgwick's) Division, Army of the Potomac, to March, 1862. 1st Brigade, 2nd Division, 2nd Army Corps, Army of the Potomac, to February, 1864, Dept. of the Northwest to May, 1864. 1st Brigade, 2nd Division, 2nd Army Corps, Army Potomac, to July, 1865.

SERVICE.—Advance on Manassas, Va., July 16-21, 1861. Battle of Bull Run July 21. Moved to Seneca Mills, Md., August 2-7, thence to near Edward's Ferry, August 16, and duty guarding Upper Potomac till February, 1862. Operations about Ball's Bluff October 11-23. Battle of Ball's Bluff October 21. Leesburg Road October 21 (2 Cos.). Goose Creek and near Edward's Ferry October 22. Advance toward Winchester, February 25-March 15. At Bolivar Heights till March 22. Moved to Washington and Alexandria, thence to Hampton, Va., March 22-April 1. Siege of Yorktown April 5-May 4. West Point May 7. Advance to the Chickahominy May 9-23. Built Grape Vine Bridge May 27-28. Battle of Fair Oaks May 31-June 1. Seven days before Richmond June 25-July 1. Peach Orchard, Allen's Farm and Savage Station June 29. White Oak Swamp and Glendale June 30. Malvern Hill July 1 and August 5. At Harrison's Landing till August 16. Moved to Alexandria August 16-28, thence march to Centreville August 30. Cover Pope's retreat to Washington September 1-2. Near Chantilly and Flint River September 1. Vienna September 2. Maryland Campaign September 6-22. Battles of South Mountain September 14 and Antietam September 16-17. March to Harper's Ferry, W. Va., September 22, and duty there till October 30. Reconnoissance to Charlestown October 16-17. March up Loudon Valley and to Falmouth, Va., October 30-November 17. Battle of Fredericksburg, Va., December 12-15. At Falmouth till April, 1863. Chancellorsville Campaign April 27-May 6. Operations about Franklin's Crossing April 29-May 2. Battle of Maryes Heights, Fredericksburg, May 3. Salem Heights May 3-4. Banks' Ford May 4. Gettysburg (Pa.) Campaign June 12-July 24. Haymarket June 25. Battle of Gettysburg July 1-3. Pursuit of Lee to Manassas Gap, Va., July 5-24. At Kelly's Ford, Va., July 31-August 15. Detached for duty in New York during draft disturbances August 15-September 16. Rejoined Brigade near Culpeper September 16. Bristoe Campaign October 9-22. Bristoe Station October 14. Advance to line of the Rappahannock November 7-8. At Kelly's Ford till November 26. Mine Run Campaign November 26-December 2. Robertson's Tavern November 27.

Mine Run November 28-30. Camp at Stevensburg, Va., till February 5, 1864. Ordered home for muster out February 5. Moved to Fort Snelling, Minn., and duty there till April 29. Mustered out April 29, 1864, expiration of term. Veterans and Recruits organized into two Companies as 1st Minnesota Battalion Infantry. At Fort Snelling, Minn., and duty there till May 16. Moved to Washington, D. C., May 16-22, thence to White House May 30-June 1. Assigned to 1st Brigade, 2nd Division, 2nd Army Corps, and joined Brigade at Cold Harbor, Va., June 12. Moved to Petersburg, Va., July 12-15. Assaults on Petersburg June 16-18. Siege of Petersburg June 16, 1864, to April 2, 1865. Jerusalem Plank Road June 22-23, 1864. Demonstration north of the James July 27-29. Deep Bottom July 27-28. Demonstration north of the James August 13-20. Strawberry Plains August 14-18. Weldon Railroad August 25. Boydton Plank Road, Hatcher's Run, October 27-29. Raid on Weldon Railroad December 7-11. Dabney's Mills, Hatcher's Run, February 5-7, 1865. Watkins' House March 25. Appomattox Campaign March 28-April 9. Hatcher's Run, Boydton Road, March 29-31. Crow's House March 31. Sutherland Station and fall of Petersburg April 2. Pursuit of Lee April 3-9. Sailor's Creek April 6. High Bridge and Farmville April 7. Appomattox Court House April 9. Surrender of Lee and his army. March to Washington, D. C., May 2-12. Grand Review May 23. Moved to Louisville June 6-9, and duty there till July 15. Mustered out July 15, 1865.

Regiment lost during service 10 Officers and 177 Enlisted men killed and mortally wounded and 2 Officers and 97 Enlisted men by disease. Total 286.

2nd REGIMENT INFANTRY.

Organized at Fort Snelling, Minn., and mustered in by Companies as follows: "A" and "B" June 26, "D" and "E" July 5, "F" and "G" July 8, "H" July 15, "I" July 20, and "K" August 23, 1861. Companies "A" and "F" sent to Fort Ripley on the Upper Mississippi, "B" and "C" to Fort Abercrombie on the Upper Red River, and "D" and "E" to Fort Ridgly on the Upper Minnesota River, and garrison duty at these points till September 20, 1861. Regiment concentrated at Fort Snelling and left State for Louisville, Ky., October 14, arriving there October 22. Moved to Lebanon Junction, Ky., October 22, and duty there till December 8. Attached to R. L. McCook's Brigade, Army of the Ohio, to December, 1861. 3rd Brigade, 1st Division, Army Ohio, to September, 1862. 3rd Brigade, 1st Division, 3rd Army Corps, Army Ohio, to November, 1862. 3rd Brigade, 3rd Division, Center 14th Army Corps, Army of the Cumberland, to January, 1863. 3rd Brigade, 3rd Division, 14th Army Corps, to October, 1863. 2nd Brigade, 3rd Division, 14th Army Corps, to June, 1865. 1st Brigade, 3rd Division, 14th Army Corps, to July, 1865.

SERVICE.—Moved to Lebanon, Ky., December 8, 1861, and duty there till January 1, 1862. Expedition to Somerset January 1-18. Battle of Mill Springs January 19-20. At Somerset till February 10. March to Louisville, Ky., February 10-25, thence moved to Nashville, Tenn., February 26-March 2. Moved to Savannah, Tenn., and Pittsburg Landing, Tenn., March 20-April 9. Advance on and siege of Corinth, Miss., April 29-May 30. Pursuit to Booneville May 31-June 12. At Corinth till June 22. March to Iuka, Miss., June 22-25, thence to Tuscumbia, Ala., June 27-29, and duty there till July 26. March to Athens, Ala., and Winchester, Tenn., July 26-August 7, thence to Dechard and Pelham Gap, Tenn., August 19-31, and to Manchester, Murfreesboro and Nashville, Tenn., September 1-7. March to Louisville, Ky., in pursuit of Bragg September 14-26. Pursuit of Bragg into Kentucky October 1-20. Battle of Perryville, Ky., October 8. March to Bowling Green, Ky., October 20-November 2, thence to Mitchellsville November 6-7. Guard Tunnel till November 23. Moved to Cunningham's Ford, Cumberland River, November 23-25, and guard duty there till December 22, and at Gallatin till January 29, 1863. Moved to Murfreesboro, Tenn., January 29, and duty there till March 2. Nolensville February 15. Moved to Triune March 2. Nolensville Ford, Harpeth River, March 4. Expedition toward Columbia March 4-14. Chapel Hill March 5. At Triune till June 23. Franklin June 4-5. Middle Tennessee or Tullahoma Campaign June 23-July 7. Hoover's Gap June 24-26. Occupation of Tullahoma July 1. At Winchester, Tenn., till August 16. Passage of Cumberland Mountains and Tennessee River and Chickamauga (Ga.) Campaign August 16-September 22. Battle of Chickamauga, Ga., September 19-20. Rossville Gap September 21. Siege of Chattanooga, Tenn., September 24-November 23. Chattanooga-Ringgold Campaign November 23-27. Mission Ridge November 24-25. Pursuit to Ringgold November 26-29. Regiment Veteranize December 29, 1863. Veterans on furlough January 8 to April 9, 1864. Non-Veterans on duty as provost guard at Division Headquarters till April, 1864. Reconnoissance from Ringgold, Ga., toward Tunnel Hill April 29. Atlanta (Ga.) Campaign May 1-September 8. Tunnel Hill May 6-7. Rocky Faced Ridge May 8-11. Battle of Resaca May 13-15. Guard trains May 21-June 2. About Dallas June 2-5. Operations about Marietta and against Kenesaw Mountain June 10-July 2. Pine Hill June 11-14. Lost Mountain June 15-17. Assault on Kenesaw June 27. Ruff's Station July 4. Garrison duty at Marietta till July 13. Assigned as provost and depot guard at Marietta July 15-August 19. March to Atlanta August 19-20. Siege of Atlanta August 20-25. Flank movement on Jonesboro August 25-30. Battle of Jonesboro August 31-September 1. Operations in North Georgia and North Alabama against Hood September 29-November 3. March to the sea November 15-December 10. Waynesboro December 4. Ebenezer Creek December 8. Siege of Savannah December 10-21. Campaign of the Carolinas January to April, 1865. Fayetteville, N. C., March 11. Battle of Bentonville March 19-21. Occupation of Goldsboro March 24. Advance on Raleigh April 10-14. Occupation of Raleigh April 14. Bennett's House April 26. Surrender of Johnston and his army. March to Washington, D. C., via Richmond, Va., April 30-May 19. Grand Review May 24. Moved to Louisville, Ky., June 14-20. Mustered out July 11, 1865.

Regiment lost during service 2 Officers and 91 Enlisted men killed and mortally wounded and 2 Officers and 186 Enlisted men by disease. Total 281.

3rd REGIMENT INFANTRY.

Organized at Fort Snelling, Minn., October 2 to November 14, 1861. Left State for Louisville, Ky., November 17-20, 1861. Attached to 16th Brigade, Army Ohio, to March, 1862. 23rd Independent Brigade, Army Ohio, to August, 1862, Dept. of the Northwest to February, 1863. District of Columbus, Ky., 6th Division, 16th Army Corps, Dept. of the Tennessee, to May, 1863. 3rd Brigade, Kimball's Provisional Division, 16th Army Corps, Army of the Tennessee, to July, 1863. 3rd Brigade, Kimball's Division, District of Eastern Arkansas, to August, 1863. 2nd Brigade, 2nd Division, Arkansas Expedition, to November, 1863. 3rd Brigade, 2nd Division, Army of Arkansas, to January, 1864. 3rd Brigade, 2nd Division, 7th Army Corps, Dept. of Arkansas, to May, 1864. 1st Brigade, 2nd Division, 7th Army Corps, to September, 1865.

SERVICE.—Moved to Louisville, Ky., November 17-20, 1861. At Camp Jenkins till December 6, and at Shepherdsville, Lebanon Junction and Belmont, Ky., guarding Louisville & Nashville Railroad till March, 1862. Moved to Nashville, Tenn., March 11-24, and duty there till April 27. Moved to Murfreesboro, Tenn., April 27, and garrison duty there till July. Dumont's Expedition to Pikesville June 11-18. Forest's attack on Murfreesboro July 13. Regiment surrendered, paroled and sent to Benton Barracks, Mo., Company "C" being on detached duty was not captured. Joined 2nd Minnesota at Nashville, Tenn., and with it till September 30, when left for Minnesota. March to Wartrace July 13, thence to Tullahoma July 15, and to Murfreesboro

July 22. To Nashville, Tenn., with prisoners August. Regiment declared exchanged August 27. Moved to Minnesota August 28-September 4. March to Fort Ridgly to join Sibley September 5-13. Sibley's Campaign against hostile Sioux Indians September 13-November 14. Battle of Wood Lake, Yellow Medicina, September 23. A detachment of Regiment march from Fort Snelling to relief of Fort Abercrombie on Red River September 11-October 5, then joined Regiment at Camp Release. Duty at Fort Snelling reorganizing till January 16, 1863. Moved to Cairo, Ill., January 16-26, 1863, thence to Columbus, Ky., February 3, and duty there till March 12. Expedition to Fort Heiman March 12-14. Duty at Fort Heiman and operations against guerrillas till June 2. Expedition into Tennessee May 26-June 2 (Cos. "B," "D," "G" and "H"). Moved to Columbus, Ky., thence to Vicksburg, Miss., June 2-9. Siege of Vicksburg, Miss., June 9-July 4. Moved to Oak Ridge July 5, and duty there till July 21. Moved to Helena, Ark., July 24-26. Steele's Expedition to Little Rock August 13-September 10. Bayou Fourche and capture of Little Rock September 10. Garrison duty at Little Rock till April 28, 1864. Regiment veteranize January, 1864. Expedition up White River to Augusta March 30-April 3. Battle of Fitzhugh's Woods April 1 (Cos. "B," "C," "E," "G," "H" and "I"). Moved to Pine Bluff April 28, and duty there till October 10. Veterans of Companies "B," "C," "E," "G," "H" and "I" on furlough August 14-October 17. Rejoined at Duvall's Bluff. Non-Veterans moved to Duvall's Bluff October 10, and duty there till May 13, 1865. Moved to Batesville May 13-20. Companies assigned to duty as follows: "D" and "G" at Batesville, "A" and "F" at Searcy, "E" and "H" at Augusta, "B," "C," "I" and "K" at Jacksonport, Companies "C" and "I" moved to Powhatan July 19. Regiment concentrated at Jacksonport and moved to Duvall's Bluff August 29. Mustered out September 2 and discharged at Fort Snelling, Minn., September 16, 1865.

Regiment lost during service 17 Enlisted men killed and mortally wounded and 4 Officers and 275 Enlisted men by disease. Total 296.

4th REGIMENT INFANTRY.

Organized by Companies at Fort Snelling, Minn., as follows: Company "A" mustered in October 4, 1861, and Company "B" October 2, 1861. Moved to Fort Ridgly, Minn., and garrison duty there till March, 1862. Company "C" mustered in October 7, 1861. Also moved to Fort Ridgly and garrison duty there till March, 1862. Company "D" mustered in October 10, 1861. Moved to Fort Abercrombie, D. T., and duty there till March, 1862. Company "E" mustered in November 27, 1861. Company "F" mustered in October 11, 1861. Company "G" mustered in November 22, 1861. Moved to Fort Abercrombie and duty there till March, 1862. Company "H" mustered in December 20, 1861. Company "I" mustered in December 23, 1861. Company "K" mustered in December 23, 1861. Regiment concentrated at Fort Snelling March, 1862, and moved to Benton Barracks, Mo., April 20-23, 1862. Moved to Hamburg Landing, Tenn., May 2-14. Attached to 1st Brigade, 3rd Division, Army of Mississippi, May to November, 1862. 1st Brigade, 7th Division, Left Wing 13th Army Corps (Old), Dept. of the Tennessee, to December, 1862. 1st Brigade, 7th Division, 16th Army Corps, to January, 1863. 1st Brigade, 7th Division, 17th Army Corps, to September, 1863. 1st Brigade, 2nd Division, 17th Army Corps, to December, 1863. 1st Brigade, 3rd Division, 15th Army Corps, to April, 1865. 1st Brigade, 1st Division, 15th Army Corps, to July, 1865.

SERVICE.—Advance on and siege of Corinth, Miss., May 18-30. Pursuit to Booneville May 31-June 12. Duty at Clear Creek till August. Expedition to Rienzi and Ripley June. Moved to Jacinto August 5, and duty there till September 18. March to Iuka, Miss., September 18-19. Battle of Iuka September 19. Moved to Corinth October 1. Battle of Corinth October 3-4. Pursuit to Ripley October 5-12. Grant's Central Mississippi Campaign November, 1862, to January, 1863. Reconnoissance from Lagrange November 8-9, 1862. Duty at White's Station and Memphis, Tenn., till February, 1863. Expedition to Yazoo Pass by Moon Lake, Yazoo Pass and Coldwater and Tallahatchie Rivers February 24-April 8. Operations against Fort Pemberton and Greenwood March 13-April 5. Moved to Milliken's Bend, La., April 13-15. Movement on Bruinsburg and turning Grand Gulf April 25-30. Battle of Port Gibson, Miss., May 1. Jones' Cross Roads and Willow Springs May 3. Battles of Raymond May 12; Jackson May 14; Champion's Hill May 16; Big Black River May 17. Siege of Vicksburg May 18-July 4. Assaults on Vicksburg May 19 and 22. Expedition to Mechanicsburg May 26-June 4. Surrender of Vicksburg July 4. Garrison duty at Vicksburg till September 12. Moved to Helena, Ark., September 12, thence to Memphis, Tenn., and Corinth, Miss., and march to Chattanooga, Tenn., October 6-November 20. Operations on Memphis & Charleston Railroad in Alabama October 20-29. Chattanooga-Ringgold Campaign November 23-27. Tunnel Hill November 24-25. Mission Ridge November 25. Pursuit to Graysville November 26-27. At Bridgeport and Huntsville, Ala., till June, 1864. Operations about Whitesburg, Ala., February 2, 1864. Veterans on furlough March 5 to May 4, 1864. Moved from Huntsville, Ala., to Stevenson, Ala., thence to Kingston, Ga., June 22-25, thence to Allatoona July 5-6, and garrison duty there till November. Battle of Allatoona October 5. March to the sea November 15-December 10. Siege of Savannah, Ga., December 10-21. Campaign of the Carolinas January to April, 1865. Salkehatchie Swamps, S. C., February 2-5. South Edisto River February 9. North Edisto River February 12-13. About Columbia February 15-17. Cheraw March 3. Battle of Bentonville, N. C., March 19-21. Occupation of Goldsboro March 24. Advance on Raleigh April 10-14. Occupation of Raleigh April 14. Bennett's House April 26. Surrender of Johnston and his army. March to Washington, D. C., via Richmond, Va., April 29-May 20. Grand Review May 24. Moved to Louisville, Ky., June 2-3. Duty there till July 19. Mustered out July 19 and discharged at St. Paul, Minn., August 7, 1865.

Regiment lost during service 3 Officers and 58 Enlisted men killed and mortally wounded and 3 Officers and 175 Enlisted men by disease. Total 239.

5th REGIMENT INFANTRY.

Organized at Fort Snelling, Minn., March 15 to April 30, 1862. Company "D" moved to Fort Abercrombie, D. T., March 15-29, and garrison duty there (with a detachment at Georgetown till August 20) till November, 1862. Action at Fort Abercrombie June 20. Defence of Fort Abercrombie September 3-26. Actions with Sioux Indians September 3-6. Company ordered to join Regiment and joined at Germantown, Tenn., February 14, 1863. Company "C" moved to Fort Ripley March, 1862, and garrison duty there till November, 1862. Rejoined Regiment near Oxford, Miss., December 12, 1862. (Part of Company under Lieut. T. J. Shehan, marched to Fort Ridgly June 19-28, 1862.) Company "B" moved to Fort Ridgly March 22-25, 1862, and garrison duty there till November, 1862. Companies "B" and "C" march to Sioux Agency on Yellow Medicine River June 30-July 2, to preserve order during annuity payment to Indians. Sioux outbreak August, 1862. Battle of Redwood August 18 (Co. "B"). Defence of Fort Ridgly August 20-22 (Cos. "B" and "C"). (A detachment of Co. "C" moved to Fort Ripley September 18.) Company "B" marched for Fort Snelling November 9 as escort to captured Indians. Rejoined Regiment near Oxford, Miss., December 12, 1862. Regiment moved to Mississippi May 10-24, 1862. Attached to 2nd Brigade, 2nd Division, Army of Mississippi, to November, 1862. 2nd Brigade, 8th Division, Left Wing 13th Army Corps (Old), Dept. of the Tennessee, to December, 1862. 2nd Brigade, 8th Division, 16th Army Corps, Army of the Tennessee, to April, 1863. 2nd Brigade, 3rd Division, 15th Army Corps, to December, 1863. 2nd Brigade, 1st Division, 16th Army Corps, to

November, 1864. 2nd Brigade, 1st Division (Detachment), Army of the Tennessee, Dept. of the Cumberland, to February, 1865. 2nd Brigade, 1st Division, 16th Army Corps, Military Division West Mississippi, to September, 1865.

SERVICE.—Siege of Corinth, Miss., May 26-30, 1862. Action near Corinth May 28. Occupation of Corinth May 30 and pursuit to Booneville May 31-June 12. At Camp Clear Creek till July 3. Moved to Rienzi July 3, thence to Tuscumbia, Ala., August 18-22, and duty there till September 13. Moved to Clear Creek September 13-14, thence to Iuka, Miss., September 16. Skirmish at Iuka September 16. Battle of Iuka September 19. Battle of Corinth October 3-4. Pursuit to Ripley October 5-12. Grant's Central Mississippi Campaign November, 1862, to January, 1863. At Jackson, Tenn., till March 12, 1863. Moved to Memphis, Tenn., thence to Duckport, La., March 12-April 1. Demonstration on Haines and Drumgould's Bluffs April 29-May 2. Movement to join army in rear of Vicksburg, Miss., via Richmond and Grand Gulf May 2-14. Mississippi Springs May 13. Jackson May 14. Siege of Vicksburg May 18-July 4. Expedition to Mechanicsburg and Satartia June 2-8. Satartia June 4. Expedition from Young's Point to Richmond, La., June 14-16. Richmond, La., June 15. Advance toward Jackson July 5. Guard duty at Black River Bridge till July 22. At Bear Creek till October. Expedition to Canton October 14-20. Bogue Chitto Creek October 17. Moved to Memphis, Tenn., November 14-20, thence to LaGrange, Tenn., and guard Memphis & Charleston Railroad and scouting after Forest till January 26, 1864. Moved to Vicksburg, Miss., January 26-February 3. Meridian Campaign February 3-March 2. At Black River Bridge till February 23. March to Canton and return to Vicksburg February 23-March 7. Regiment veteranize February 12, 1864. Red River Campaign March 10-May 22. Fort DeRussy March 14. Occupation of Alexandria March 16. Henderson's Hill March 21. Grand Ecore April 2. Campti April 3. Battle of Pleasant Hill April 9. About Cloutiersville, Cane River, April 22-24. At Alexandria April 26-May 13. Moore's Plantation May 3. Bayou LaMourie May 6-7. Bayou Roberts May 7. Retreat to Morganza May 13-20. Mansura May 16. Yellow Bayou May 18. Moved to Vicksburg, Miss., May 22-24, thence to Memphis, Tenn., June 4-10. Action at Lake Chicot June 6. Defeat of Marmaduke. Veterans on furlough June 17-August 17. Smith's Expedition to Tupelo July 5-21 (Non-Veterans). Camargo's Cross Roads July 13. Harrisburg, near Tupelo, July 14-15. Tishamingo or Old Town Creek July 15. Smith's Expedition to Oxford, Miss., August 1-30. Abbeville August 23. Mower's Expedition to Brownsville, Ark., September 2-10. March through Arkansas and Missouri in pursuit of Price September 17-November 15. Moved to Nashville, Tenn., November 24-30. Battle of Nashville December 15-16. Pursuit of Hood to the Tennessee River December 17-28. Moved to Eastport, Miss., and duty there till February, 1865. Moved to New Orleans, La., February 6-22. Campaign against Mobile, Ala., and its Defences March 7-April 12. Siege of Spanish Fort and Fort Blakely March 26-April 8. Assault and capture of Fort Blakely April 9. Occupation of Mobile April 12. March to Montgomery April 13-25. Duty at Montgomery, Selma and Demopolis, Ala., till August. Mustered out September 6, 1865.

Regiment lost during service 4 Officers and 86 Enlisted men killed and mortally wounded and 4 Officers and 175 Enlisted men by disease. Total 269.

6th REGIMENT INFANTRY.

Organized at Camp Release and Fort Snelling, Minn., September 29 to November 20, 1862. Campaign against the Sioux Indians in Minnesota August 20 to November 14, 1862. Sibley's march to relief of Fort Ridgly August 24-28. Engagement at Birch Coolie September 1, 2 and 3 (Co. "A"). Engagement at Wood Lake September 23. At Camp Release September 26. Regiment mustered in at Camp Release. Companies "A," "B,"

"F" and "G" October 1; Company "C" October 13; Company "D" September 29; Company "E" October 5; Company "I" October 4; Company "K" October 10, and Company "H" at Fort Snelling November 20, 1862. Garrison duty at Fort Snelling, Companies "A," "B," "G," "H" and "K"; at Glencoe, Companies "C," "F" and "I"; at Forest City, Company "D"; at Kingston, Company "E," till February, 1863. Companies "A," "G" and "K" at Glencoe; Company "B" at Forest City; Companies "C," "D," "F" and "I" at Fort Snelling; Company "E" at Clearwater, and Company "H" at Kingston, till April, 1863. At Camp Pope till June, 1863. Sibley's Expedition against hostile Indians in Dakota June 16 to September 12, 1863. Action at Big Hills, Dakota Territory, July 24. Dead Buffalo Lake July 26. Stony Lake July 28. Missouri River July 29-30. On frontier duty in Minnesota till June, 1864. Company "A" at Fort Ridgly September, 1863, to June, 1864. Company "B" at Fort Snelling September, 1863; Swan Lake and Fort Ridgly to January, 1864, and at Fort Snelling till June, 1864. Company "C" at Fairmont September, 1863, to June, 1864. Company "D" at Kingston September, 1863; at Fort Snelling to November, 1863. Escort trains to agencies on the Missouri River November 6 to December 29, 1863; at Kingston till June, 1864. Company "E" at Lake Hanska September to November, 1863; escort trains to agencies on the Missouri River November 6-December 29; at Fort Ridg-

Organized at Anoka, Forest City, Stillwater, Lake ly till June, 1864. Company "F" at Fort Ridgly September, 1863; at Lake Hanska till June, 1864. Company "G" at Wautowan River September, 1863, to January, 1864; at Madelia till June, 1864. Company "H" at Buffalo Creek September-October, 1863; at Fort Ridgly to November, 1863; escort supply trains to agencies on the Missouri River November 6-December 29, 1863; at Fort Ridgly till June, 1864. Company "I" at Forest City September, 1863, to June, 1864. Company "K" at Fort Snelling September, 1863, to June, 1864. Regiment concentrated at Fort Snelling June 9, 1864. Moved to Helena, Ark., June 14-23, and duty there till November 4. Attached to District of Eastern Arkansas, 7th Army Corps, Dept. of Arkansas, June to November, 1864. District of St. Louis, Mo., Dept. of Missouri, to February, 1865. 2nd Brigade, 2nd Division, 16th Army Corps (New), Military District of West Mississippi, to August, 1865.

SERVICE.—Expedition from Helena, Ark., to Buck Island July 13-16, 1864 (Cos. "E" and "F"). Moved to St. Louis, Mo., November 4-11, and Provost duty there till January 29, 1865. Moved to New Orleans January 29-February 7, and duty there till March 5. Moved to Dauphin Island, Mobile Bay, Ala., March 5-8. Campaign against Mobile, Ala., and its Defences March 8-April 12. Siege of Spanish Fort and Fort Blakely March 26-April 8. Assault and capture of Fort Blakely April 9. Occupation of Mobile April 12. March to Montgomery April 13-25. Duty there till July. Moved to St. Paul, Minn., and mustered out August 19, 1865.

Regiment lost during service 12 Enlisted men killed and mortally wounded and 4 Officers and 161 Enlisted men by disease. Total 177.

7th REGIMENT INFANTRY.

Organized at Camp Release, Fort Snelling and St. Peter, Minn., August 16 to October 30, 1862. (Co. "D" at Fort Abercrombie August, 1862, to July, 1863.) Sibley's Campaign against Sioux Indians in Minnesota August 20-November 14, 1862 (Cos. "A," "B," "F," "G" and "H"). March to relief of Fort Ridgly August 24-28. Action at Birch Cooley September 3. Engagement at Wood Lake September 23. At Camp Release September 26. Frontier duty in Minnesota at Mankato and other points till May, 1863. March to Camp Pope at mouth of Redwood River May 30. Sibley's Expedition against hostile Indians in Dakota June 16-September 12. Actions at Big Mound, Dakota Territory, July 24. Dead Buffalo Lake July 26. Stony Lake July 28. Moved to St. Louis, Mo., October 7-11, and duty there

till April 20, 1864. Attached to Dept. of Missouri, District of St. Louis, October, 1863, to April, 1864. Paducah, Ky., Dept. of the Tennessee, to June, 1864. 3rd Brigade, 1st Division, 16th Army Corps, to December, 1864. 3rd Brigade, 1st Division (Detachment), Army of the Tennessee, Dept. of the Cumberland, to February, 1865. 3rd Brigade, 1st Division, 16th Army Corps (New), Military Division West Mississippi, to August, 1865.

SERVICE.—Moved from St. Louis, Mo., to Paducah, Ky., April 20-22, 1864, and duty there till June 19. Moved to Memphis, Tenn., June 19-22. Moved to Moscow, thence to Lagrange June 23-27. Smith's Expedition to Tupelo, Miss., July 5-20. Near Camargo's Cross Roads July 13. Harrisburg, near Tupelo, July 14-15. Smith's Expedition to Oxford, Miss., August 1-30. Tallahatchie River August 7-9. Abbeville August 23. Mower's Expedition to Duvall's Bluff, Ark., September 3-10. March through Arkansas and Missouri in pursuit of Price September 17-November 15. Moved to Nashville, Tenn., November 24-30. Battle of Nashville December 15-16. Pursuit of Hood to the Tennessee River December 17-28. Moved to Clifton, Tenn., thence to Eastport, Miss., December 29-January 4, 1865. Duty at Eastport, Miss., till February 6. Moved to New Orleans, La., February 6-21. Campaign against Mobile, Ala., and its Defences March 17-April 12. Siege of Spanish Fort and Fort Blakely March 26-April 8. Assault and capture of Fort Blakely April 9. Occupation of Mobile April 12. March to Montgomery April 13-25 and duty there till May 10. Moved to Selma, Ala., and duty there till July 20. Moved to St. Paul, Minn., July 20-August 8. Mustered out August 16, 1865.

Regiment lost during service 2 Officers and 31 Enlisted men killed and mortally wounded and 138 Enlisted men by disease. Total 171.

8th REGIMENT INFANTRY.

3, then join Sibley and assist in guarding Indian pris-City, St. Paul and Fort Snelling June 2 to September 1, 1862. On frontier duty at various points in Minnesota August, 1862, to May, 1864. At Anoka, Princeton, Monticello, Kingston, Manannah, Paynesville, Fort Ripley, Sauk Centre, Pomme de Terre, Alexandria and Fort Abercrombie guarding Sioux frontier. Concentrated at Paynesville May 24, 1864. Mounted and march to Fort Ridgly May 24-28. Sibley's Expedition against hostile Indians west of the Missouri River June 5-October 15, 1864. Battle of Tah kah a kuty or Killdeer Mountain July 28. Two Hills, Bad Lands, Little Missouri River, August 8. Moved to Murfreesboro, Tenn., October 26-November 7, 1864. Attached to Defences of Nashville & Northwestern Railroad, Dept. of the Cumberland, to January, 1865. 3rd Brigade, 1st Division, 23rd Army Corps, Dept. of the Ohio, to February, 1865, and Dept. of North Carolina to July, 1865.

SERVICE.—Siege of Murfreesboro, Tenn., December 5-12. Wilkinson's Pike, near Murfreesboro, December 7. Moved to Clifton, Tenn., and join 23rd Army Corps. Moved from Clifton, Tenn., to Washington, D. C., January 17-29, 1865, and duty there till February 21. Moved to Fort Fisher, N. C., thence to Morehead City and New Berne, N. C., February 21-26. Advance on Kinston and Goldsboro March 1-21. Battle of Wise's Forks March 6-9. Kinston March 14. Occupation of Goldsboro March 21. Advance on Raleigh April 10-14. Occupation of Raleigh April 14. Bennett's House April 26. Surrender of Johnston and his army. Duty at Raleigh, Greensboro and Charlotte, N. C., till July. Mustered out July 11, 1865.

Regiment lost during service 1 Officer and 26 Enlisted men killed and mortally wounded and 56 Enlisted men by disease. Total 83.

9th REGIMENT INFANTRY.

Organized at Camp Release, Hutchinson, St. Peter, Fort Snelling, Glencoe and Fort Ridgly August 15 to October 31, 1862. Company "A" participated in Campaign against Sioux Indians in Minnesota August 20-November 14, 1862. Joined 6th Minnesota August 25, and march to relief of Fort Ridgly August 25-28. Action at Birch Coolie September 2-3. Wood Lake September 23. At Camp Release September 26. Mustered in at Camp Release October 2, 1862. At Fort Ridgly till April, 1863. Company "B" participated in Campaign against Sioux Indians in Minnesota August and September, 1862. March to Glencoe. Action at Glencoe September 3. Defence of Hutchinson September 3-4. Duty at Hutchinson till April, 1863. Moved to Hanska Lake and duty there till September, 1863. Company "C" participated in Sibley's Campaign against Sioux Indians in Minnesota August to November, 1862. March to New Ulm, then join Sibley and attached to 7th Minnesota Infantry. Battle of Wood Lake September 23. At Camp Release September 26. Mustered in October 5, 1862. At Fort Ridgly till April, 1863, then on garrison duty at frontier posts till September, 1863. Company "D" moved to St. Peter and duty there till April, 1863. Mustered in September 23, 1862. Present as guard at hanging of Indians at Mankato December 26, 1862. Frontier duty at Judson, Fairmount and Chanyaska Lake till September, 1863. Company "E" organized at Mankato and duty there; at Lake Crystal, Judson, till April, 1863. Present as guard at hanging of Indians at Mankato December 26, 1862. Mustered in November 14, 1862. Frontier post service at Hutchinson, Forest City, Long Lake and Pipe Lake till September, 1863. Company "F" organized at Fort Snelling. Moved to Glencoe and duty there till December, 1862. Mustered in September 24, 1862. At Fort Ridgly till September, 1863. Company "G" organized at St. Cloud. Moved to Fort Abercrombie September 3, 1862, and duty there till September, 1863. Action at Fort Abercrombie September 26, 1862. Mustered in October 30, 1862. Company "H" organized in Carver County. Moved to Glencoe, thence to relief of Hutchinson. Action at Hutchinson September 4. At Glencoe till April, 1863. Guard at hanging of Indians at Mankato December 26, 1862. At Fort Abercrombie till October, 1863. Company "I" participated in Indian Campaign of 1862. Moved to Glencoe, thence to St. Peter and to Fort Ridgly, and duty there till April, 1863. Mustered in October 12, 1862. At Camp Pope April to June, 1863; at Fort Ridgly till July, and at St. Paul till September, 1863. Company "K" organized at Fort Snelling August, 1862. Duty there till November oners at South Bend till February 27, 1863. Moved to New Ulm and Madelia and duty there till September, 1863. Sibley's Expedition against hostile Indians in Dakota June 16-September 12, 1863 (Cos. "A" and "H"). Actions at Big Mound July 24. Dead Buffalo Lake July 26. Stony Lake July 28. Missouri River July 29-30. Regiment concentrated September, 1863, and furloughed September 23 to October 3. Moved to St. Louis, Mo., October 8-12, 1863. Attached to Dept. of the Missouri to May, 1864. 2nd Brigade, 1st Division, 16th Army Corps, Dept. of the Tennessee, to December, 1864. 2nd Brigade, 1st Division (Detachment), Army of the Tennessee, Dept. of the Cumberland, to February, 1865. 2nd Brigade, 1st Division, 16th Army Corps (New), Military Division West Mississippi, to August, 1865.

SERVICE.—Moved from St. Louis, Mo., to Jefferson City, Mo., October 13, 1863. Assigned duty guarding railroad from Kansas Line to near St. Louis till May, 1864. Stationed at Rolla, Jefferson City, LaMine Bridge, Warrensburg, Independence, Knob Noster, Kansas City, Waynesville, Franklin, etc. Headquarters at Jefferson City till April 14, 1864, and at Rolla till May 18. Companies "G" and "H" reached St. Louis November, 1863, and duty there till May, 1864. Regiment concentrated at St. Louis, Mo., May 15 to 26, and moved to Memphis, Tenn., May 29-31. Sturgis' Expedition to Guntown, Miss., June 1-13. Ripley June 7. Brice's or Tishamingo Creek, near Guntown, June 10. Ripley June 11. Davis Mills June 12. Smith's Expedition to Tupelo, Miss., July 5-21. Near Camargo's Cross Roads July 13. Near Tupelo July 14-15. Smith's Raid to Oxford, Miss., August 1-30. Tallahatchie River August 7-9. Abbeville August 23. Mower's Expedition to Duvall's Bluff,

Ark., September 3-9. March through Arkansas and Missouri in pursuit of Price September 17-November 15. Moved to Nashville, Tenn., November 24-30. Battle of Nashville, Tenn., December 15-16. Pursuit of Hood to the Tennessee River December 17-28. Moved to Clifton, Tenn., thence to Eastport, Miss., December 29-January 4, 1865, and duty there till February 6, 1865. Moved to New Orleans, La., February 6-21. Campaign against Mobile, Ala., and its Defences March 17-April 12. Skirmish, Deer Park Road, March 25. Siege of Spanish Fort and Fort Blakely March 26-April 8. Assault and capture of Fort Blakely April 9. Occupation of Mobile April 12. March to Montgomery April 13-25. Duty at Montgomery and Selma till July. Moved to St. Paul July 26-August 11. Mustered out August 24, 1865.

Regiment lost during service 6 Officers and 41 Enlisted men killed and mortally wounded and 3 Officers and 224 Enlisted men by disease. Total 274.

10th REGIMENT INFANTRY.

Organized at Garden City, Winnebago Agency, Fort Snelling and St. Paul, Minn., August 12 to November 15, 1862. Sibley's Campaign against Sioux Indians in Minnesota August 20 to November 14, 1862. Defence of New Ulm August 24-25, 1862 (Detachment of Cos. "G" and "I"). Fort Ridgly August 20-22 (Detachment of Co. "I"). Birch Coolie September 2-3 (Detachment of Co. "I"). Wood Lake, Yellow Medicine, September 23 (Detachment of Co. "I"). Regiment after organization was stationed as follows: Company "A" at Garden City, Company "B" at Winnebago Agency, Company "C" at Fort Ridgly, Company "D" at Henderson, Company "E" at Henderson, Company "F" at Winnebago Agency, Company "G" at La Seur, Company "H" at Swan Lake and Vernon Centre, Company "I" at La Seur and Company "K" at Norwegian Lake till June, 1863. Companies "A," "B," "F," "G," "H" and "K" at Indian execution, Mankato, December 26, 1862. Sibley's Expedition against Sioux Indians in Dakota Territory June 16-September 12, 1863. (Co. "I" stationed at Manannah.) Big Mound, Dakota Territory, July 24. Dead Buffalo Lake July 26. Stony Lake July 28. Missouri River July 29-30. Regiment moved to St. Louis, Mo., October 7-12, 1863. Attached to District of St. Louis, Mo., Dept. of Missouri, to April, 1864. District of Columbus, Ky., Dept. of the Tennessee, to June, 1864. 1st Brigade, 1st Division, 16th Army Corps, Dept. of the Tennessee, to December, 1864. 1st Brigade, 1st Division (Detachment), Army of the Tennessee, Dept. of the Cumberland, to February, 1865. 1st Brigade, 1st Division, 16th Army Corps (New), Military Division West Mississippi, to July, 1865.

SERVICE.—Garrison and Provost duty at Benton Barracks, Mo., October, 1863, to April, 1864. Moved to Columbus, Ky., April 22, and duty there till June 19. (Cos. "E" and "D" detached at Island No. 10 April 27 to June 15.) Moved to Memphis, Tenn., June 19-20. Smith's Expedition to Tupelo, Miss., July 5-21. Pontotoc July 11. Near Camargo's Cross Roads July 13. Near Tupelo July 14-15. Old Town or Tishamingo Creek July 15. Smith's Expedition to Oxford, Miss., August 1-30. Tallahatchie River August 7-9. Abbeville August 23. Mower's Expedition to Duvall's Bluff, Ark., September 2-9. March through Arkansas and Missouri in pursuit of Price September 17-November 15. Moved to Nashville, Tenn., November 24-30. Battle of Nashville December 15-16. Pursuit of Hood to the Tennessee River December 17-28. Moved to Clifton, Tenn., thence to Eastport, Miss., December 29-January 4, 1865. Duty at Eastport, Miss., till February 6. Moved to New Orleans, La., February 6-21. Campaign against Mobile, Ala., and its Defences March 17-April 12. Siege of Spanish Fort and Fort Blakely March 26-April 8. Assault and capture of Fort Blakely April 9. Occupation of Mobile April 12. March to Montgomery April 13-25 and duty there till May. Moved to Meridian, Miss., and duty there till July. Moved to St. Paul, Minn., and mustered out August 18, 1865.

Regiment lost during service 2 Officers and 35 Enlisted men killed and mortally wounded and 4 Officers and 111 Enlisted men by disease. Total 152.

11th REGIMENT INFANTRY.

Organized at Fort Snelling, Minn., August and September, 1864. Moved to Chicago, St. Louis, Mo., and Nashville, Tenn., September 20-October 5, 1864. Attached to railroad guard Louisville & Nashville Railroad, Dept. of the Cumberland, to March, 1865. 4th Sub-District, District of Middle Tennessee, Dept. of the Cumberland, to June, 1865.

SERVICE.—Assigned to duty guarding line of the Louisville & Nashville Railroad from Nashville to the Kentucky line. Companies "E," "G" and "I" at Gallatin, Tenn.; Company "A" at Duck Lodge; Company "B" at Edgefield Junction; Company "C" at Richland; Company "D" at Sandersville; Companies "F" and "K" at ——————, and Company "H" at Mitchellsville October, 1864, to June, 1865. Moved to St. Paul June 26-July 5. Mustered out June 26, 1865, and discharged at St. Paul July 11, 1865.

Regiment lost during service 3 Enlisted men killed and 1 Officer and 21 Enlisted men by disease. Total 25.

MISSOURI VOLUNTEERS.

1st REGIMENT CAVALRY.

Organized at Jefferson Barracks, Mo., September 6, 1861. Moved to Benton Barracks September 12, thence to Jefferson City, Mo., September 21 (5 Cos.). Other Companies moved to Jefferson City October 4 and joined Regiment at Tipton, Mo., October 19. Expedition to Lexington October 5-16 (Cos. "C" and "L"). Capture of Lexington October 16 (Cos. "C" and "L"). Warrensburg October 18. Fremont's advance on Springfield, Mo., October 20-26. 1st Battalion (Cos. "A," "C," "D" and "E") moved to Sedalia, Mo., as escort to General Hunter, November; thence to Fort Leavenworth, Kansas, and duty there till May, 1862. Attached to Dept. of Kansas November, 1861, to May, 1862. District of Southwest Missouri, Dept. of Missouri, to October, 1862. 2nd Brigade, 2nd Division, Army of the Frontier, Dept. of Missouri, to February, 1863. 2nd Brigade, 3rd Division, Army of the Frontier, to June, 1863. 1st Brigade, 1st Cavalry Division, District of Southeast Missouri, Dept. of Missouri, to August, 1863. Reserve Brigade, 1st Cavalry Division, Arkansas Expedition, to December, 1863. 1st Brigade, 1st Division Cavalry, Army of Arkansas, to January, 1864. 1st Brigade, 1st Cavalry Division, 7th Army Corps, Dept. of Arkansas, to May, 1864. 3rd Brigade, 1st Division, 7th Army Corps, to September, 1864. (Regiment consolidated to 7 Cos. September 10, 1864.) 2nd Brigade, Cavalry Division, 7th Army Corps, to March, 1865. Separate Brigade, 7th Army Corps, to September, 1865.

SERVICE.—Operations about Atchison, Kansas, January 20-24, 1862 (Co. "E"). Pink Hill March 31 (Cos. "C" and "D"). Moved to Independence, Mo., May, 1862, and operating against guerrillas till September, 1862. Scout to Little Blue May 15-17 (Detachment). Independence May 16 (Detachment). Near Sedalia June 5 (Cos. "A," "C" and "E"). Operations in Johnson County June 28-29. Expedition toward Blackwater and Chapel Hill July 6-9. Expedition in Cass County July 9-11. Lotspeach Farm, near Wadesburg, July 9. Sear's House and Big Creek Bluffs, near Pleasant Hill, August 8 (Cos. "A," "C" and "D"). Joined Herron's Division September —. At Rolla, Mo., till June, 1863. Moved to Pilot Knob and join Davidson's Cavalry Division. Expedition against Little Rock, Ark., July 1-September 10. Pocohontas August 24. Shallow Ford, Bayou Metoe, August 30. Near Shallow Ford September 2. Bayou Fourche and capture of Little Rock September 10. Expedition from Benton to Mt. Ida November 10-18, Caddo Gap November 11. Near Benton December 1, Reconnoissance from Little Rock December 5-13. At Little Rock till March, 1864. Carter's Creek January 23, 1864. Steele's Expedition to Camden March 23-May

3. Rockport March 25. Arkadelphia March 29. Spoonville April 2. Little Missouri River April 6. Prairie D'Ann April 9-12. Camden April 15. Jenkins' Ferry, Saline River, April 30. Operations against Shelby north of Arkansas River May 18-31. Osceola August 2. Benton August 18. Near Pine Bluff August 18. Scout to Benton September 6-7. Reconnoissance to Princeton October 19-23. Expedition to Saline River November 17-18. Expedition to Mt. Elba January 22-February 4, 1865. At Little Rock till September. Mustered out September 1, 1865.

2nd Battalion—(Cos. "B," "H," "I" and "L.") Moved to Otterville, Mo., November, 1861, and duty there till February, 1862. Expedition to Milford December 15-19. Shawnee Mound, Milford, Blackwater River, December 19. Roan's Tan Yard, Silver Creek, January 8, 1862. Joined 3rd Battalion at Lebanon February 9. Attached to 3rd Brigade, Army of Southwest Missouri, Dept. of Missouri, to February, 1862. 2nd Brigade, 3rd Division, Army of Southwest Missouri, to April, 1862. Cassville, Mo., District of Southwest Missouri, to October, 1862. (Detached from 3rd Battalion at Cassville, Mo., April 7.) Unattached, 2nd Division, Army of the Frontier, to January, 1863; then same as 1st Battalion. Advance on Springfield, Mo., February 13-16. Pursuit of Price to Fayetteville, Ark., February 13-16. Skirmish with Price's Rear Guard February 14-15. Bentonville February 17. Sugar Creek February 18. Reconnoissance to Berryville March 3-7. Battles of Pea Ridge March 7-8. Leetown March 7. Elkhorn Tavern March 8. Operations against Stan Wattee March 19-23. At Cross Timbers till April 6. Moved to Cassville April 6-7. Santa Fe Road April 14. Neosho April 26. Near Newtonia August 8. Union Mills August 20. Occupation of Newtonia October 4. Battle of Prairie Grove, Ark., December 7. Expedition over Boston Mountains December 27-29. Dripping Springs and capture of Van Buren December 28. (See 1st Battalion.)

3rd Battalion—(Cos. "F," "G," "K" and "M.") Moved to Rolla, Mo., November, 1861. Expedition against Sam Freeman December —. Stein's Creek, LaClede County, January 1, 1862. Scouting on the Gasconade till January 15, 1862. Attached to 3rd Brigade, Army of Southwest Missouri, Dept. of Missouri, to April, 1862. 2nd Division, Army of Southwest Missouri, to July, 1862. District of Eastern Arkansas, Dept. of Missouri, to December, 1862. 1st Brigade, 3rd Cavalry Division, District of Eastern Arkansas, to January, 1863. Helena, Ark., District of Eastern Arkansas, 13th Army Corps, Dept. of Tennessee, to January, 1863. District of Memphis, Tenn., 16th Army Corps, to March, 1863. 4th Brigade, District of Memphis, 5th Division, 16th Army Corps, to June, 1863. Dept. of Missouri to December, 1863. New Madrid, Mo., to September, 1864.

SERVICE.—Curtis' Campaign in Southwest Missouri January 15-February 16, 1862. Occupation of Lebanon January 26, 1862. Reconnoissance beyond Bolivar February 6-9. Bolivar February 8. Advance on Springfield, Mo., February 10-13. Pursuit of Price to Fayetteville, Ark., February 13-16. Skirmish with Price's Rear Guard February 14-15. Bentonville February 17. Sugar Creek February 18. Reconnoissance to Berryville March 3-7. Battles of Pea Ridge March 6-9. Leetown March 7. Elkhorn Tavern March 8. Operations against Stan Wattee March 19-23. At Cross Timbers till April 6. Advance to Forsyth, thence to Batesville April 7-May 5. (Co. "F" detached as escort to General Jeff C. Davis May 10, 1862, and moved to Army of the Tennessee.) March to Helena, Ark., May 25-July 14. Big Indian Creek, White County, May 23. Searcy, White County, May 27. Taberville August 11. Lagrange September 6. Expedition to Lawrenceville and St. Charles September 11-13. Expedition from Helena to Lagrange September 26. Near Helena October 11. Expedition from Helena to Moro November 5-8. At Helena, Ark., till January 29, 1863. Moved to Memphis, Tenn., and duty there till June. Carter's Creek Pike April 27. Expedition to Hernando May 23-24 and May 26 (Detachments). Scouts toward Hernando May 27-28 (Detachment). Operations in Northwest Mississippi June 15-25. Coldwater, near Hernando, June 19 (Detachment). Hernando June 20. Moved to St. Louis, Mo., June 30-July 3; thence to Cape Girardeau escorting train July 20-27. March to Bloomfield and return to Cape Girardeau August 1-6. Expedition to Pocohontas August 17-27. Pocohontas August 24. At Cape Girardeau and Pilot Knob till October 23, and at Bloomfield till December 14. Moved to New Madrid, Mo., and duty there till September, 1864. In swamps of Little River April 6, 1864. Scout to Gainesville, Ark., May 10-25. Expedition to Carruthersville July 5-10. Operations in Southeast Missouri and Northeast Arkansas July 18-August 6.

Company "F" served detached as escort to General Jeff C. Davis, commanding 4th Division, Army of Mississippi, to September, 1862; then with Headquarters, 9th Division, 3rd Corps, Army of Ohio, to November, 1862. 1st Division, Right Wing 14th Army Corps, Army of the Cumberland, to January, 1863. 1st Division, 20th Army Corps, Army of the Cumberland, to October, 1863. At Headquarters, Dept. of Missouri, to August, 1864. Siege of Corinth, Miss., April 29-May 30, 1862. Campaign against Bragg in Kentucky October, 1862. Stone River Campaign December, 1862-January, 1863. Weem's Springs August 19, 1863.

Regiment lost during service 2 Officers and 51 Enlisted men killed and mortally wounded and 2 Officers and 179 Enlisted men by disease. Total 234.

1st REGIMENT STATE MILITIA CAVALRY.

Organized in Missouri at large February 3 to April 9, 1862. Companies "A" and "B" in Davies County, Company "C" in Sullivan County, "D" in Putnam County, "E" in Gentry County, "F" in Linn County, "H" in DeKalb County, "I" in Harrison County and "K" in Lundy County. Company "L" organized in Andrew and Buchanan Counties and attached May, 1863. Company "M" organized in Worth and Gentry Counties and attached July, 1863. Regiment attached to District of Central Missouri, Dept. of Missouri, to July, 1863. District of the Border, Dept. of Missouri, to January, 1864. District of Central Missouri, Dept. of Missouri, to July, 1865. Headquarters at Lexington till March, 1863. (4 Cos. at Sedalia, Mo., November, 1862, to April, 1863.) At Independence till April, 1863. At Harrisonville till May, 1863. At Warrensburg till June, 1863. At Lexington till October, 1863. At Warrensburg till July, 1865, operating against Cash's, Davis', Kirk's, Merrick's, Marchbank's, Ballou's, Porter's, Poindexter's, Quantrell's and Cockrell's guerrillas.

SERVICE.—Expedition to Spring Hill May 24, 1862 (Cos. "G" and "K"). Sear's House and Big Creek Bluffs, near Pleasant Hill, July 11 (Cos. "A," "C" and "D"). Clark's Mills July 30 (2 Cos.). Grand River August 1 (Battalion). Operations on Missouri River August — (Detachment). Near Cravensville August 5. Kirksville August 5-6. Panther Creek and Walnut Creek August 8. Near Stockton August 8 (Detachment). Sear's Ford, Chariton River, August 9 (Detachment). Expedition from Camp Gamble against guerrillas August 12-18. Putnam September 1. Strother's Fork of Black River September 13. Syracuse October 14. Expedition from Independence to Greenton, Chapel Hill and Hopewell October 24-26 (Cos. "E" and "H"). Operations in Jackson and Lafayette Counties October 26-29 (Detachment). Blue Springs, near Independence, March 22. Sedalia April 9, 1863. Hog Island May 18 (Detachment). Near Wellington June 17. Near Papinsville June 23 (Detachment). Saline County July 30. Near Lexington July 30 (Cos. "C," "I" and "K"). Stumptown August 2 (Cos. "F," "G" and "H"). Scout from Lexington to Hopewell August 6-9 (Detachment). Dayton August 10 (Detachment). Near Wellington August 14 (Detachment). Operations against Quantrell's Raid into Kansas August 20-28. Big Creek, near Pleasant Hill, August 22. Scouts in Lafayette County and skirmishes September 22-25 (Cos. "B," "H," "L" and "M"). Operations against Shelby September 22-October 26. Booneville October 11-12. Jones-

borough October 12. Merrill's Crossing and Dug Ford, near Jonesborough, October 12. Marshall, Arrow Rock, Blackwater, October 13. Syracuse October 14. Greenton Valley, near Hopewell, October 21 (Detachment of Co. "B"). Near Lexington November 4 (Detachment). Scouts in Jackson County January 15-17, 1864 (Detachment). Lexington February 22. Operations about Warrensburg February 22-24 (Detachment). Scout from Lexington March 19-22. Scouts in Jackson and Lafayette Counties and skirmishes March 20-30 (Detachments). Deep Water Township March 27. Near Greenton March 30 (Co. "F"). Offett's Knob April 28. Skirmishes in Johnson County April 28-30 (Cos. "D" and "M"). Scout from Warrensburg May 23-25. Near Shanghai May 27 (Detachment). Scout from Warrensburg to North Blackwater River June 5-9 (Co. "I"). Near Kingsville June 12 (Detachment). Lexington June 14 (Cos. "F" and "I"). Lafayette County June 14 (Detachment). Attack on Arrow Rock July 20. Operations in Lafayette and Johnson Counties and skirmishes July 20-31 (Co. "E"). Scout in Saline County August 6-9 (Detachment). Arrow Rock August 7 (Detachment). Saline County August 13 (Co. "H"). Operations in Lafayette, Saline and Howard Counties August 13-22. Near Lexington August 19 (Co. "A"). Dover August 20. Davis Creek August 22. The Tabo August 22. Operations on Texas Prairie, Jackson County, August 25-30. Near Warrensburg September 9 (Detachment). Near Lexington September 18 (Detachment). Near Longwood September 22 (Detachment). Blackwater September 23 (1st Battalion). Prince's Shoals, Osage River, Cole County, October 5-6. Moreau Bottom, Jefferson City, October 7. Near Jefferson City October 8. California October 9. Booneville October 9-12. Sedalia October 15. Little Blue October 21. Independence, Big Blue and State Line October 23. Westport October 23. Mine Creek, Little Osage River, Marias des Cygnes, October 25. Engagement at the Marmiton or Battle of Charlot October 25. Escort prisoners from Fort Scott to Warrensburg, Mo., October 26-November 1. Near Fort Scott October 28. At Warrensburg and Pleasant Hill, Cass County, operating against guerrillas in Central District of Missouri till July, 1865. Scout from Warrensburg to Greenton Valley November 29-December 3, 1864 (Detachment). Near Lexington January 11, 1865. Scout from Camp Grover to Texas Prairie January 12-15. Scout from Warrensburg to Snibar Hills January 18-22 (Detachment). Scout from Warrensburg to Wagon Knob, etc., February 1-5 (Detachment). Old members mustered out February and March, 1865. Recruits consolidated to a Battalion of 2 Companies. Near Lone Jack March 12 (Detachment). Scout from Lexington March 20-22 (Detachment). Near Pleasant Hill May 3 (Detachment). Mustered out July 12, 1865.

Regiment lost during service 2 Officers and 71 Enlisted men killed and mortally wounded and 2 Officers and 67 Enlisted men by disease. Total 142.

1st BATTALION STATE MILITIA CAVALRY. ("KREKEL'S.")

Organized at St. Charles, Mo., March 26, 1862. Attached to District of Central Missouri, Dept. of Missouri. Duty at St. Charles and in District of Central Missouri operating against guerrillas till November, 1862. Skirmish at Bob's Creek March 7. Big Creek March 9. Scouts in Calloway County September 4. Prairie Station September 4. Portland October 16. Broken up November 11, 1862.

Battalion lost during service 1 Enlisted man killed and 12 Enlisted men by disease. Total 13.

1st BATTALION MISSISSIPPI MARINE BRIGADE CAVALRY.

Organized at Jefferson Barracks, Mo., January and February, 1863, for duty in Western Waters. Attached to District of Northeast Louisiana, Dept. of the Tennessee, October, 1863, to April, 1864. District of Vicksburg, Miss., to August, 1864.

SERVICE.—Action at Little Rock Landing April 26, 1863. Beaver Dam Lake, near Austin, May 24 and 28. Expedition from Young's Point, La., to Richmond, La., June 14-16. Richmond June 15. Grand Luxe, Ark., June 16. Expedition from Snyder's Bluff to Greenville June 29-30. Bayou Tensas June 30. Expedition from Goodrich Landing to Griffin's Landing, Cat Fish Point, Miss., October 24-November 10. Operations about Natchez December 1-10. Rodney December 17. Fayette December 22. Rodney December 24. Port Gibson December 26. Grand Gulf January 16-18, 1864. Expedition to Grand Gulf February 15-March 6. Lima Landing, Ark., February 22. Red River Campaign March 10-May 22. Fort DeRussy March 14. Worthington's and Sunnyside Landings, Fish Bayou, June 5. Old River Lake or Lake Chicot June 6. Indian Bayou June 8. Coleman's Plantation, Port Gibson, July 4. Port Gibson July 7. Consolidated with 1st Infantry, Mississippi Marine Brigade, August, 1864.

Battalion lost during service 2 Officers and 15 Enlisted men killed and mortally wounded and 1 Officer and 38 Enlisted men by disease. Total 56.

1st BATTALION ENROLLED MILITIA COMPANY.

Called into service September 25, 1864, to resist Price's invasion of Missouri. Relieved from active service October 31, 1864.

2nd REGIMENT CAVALRY.—("MERRILL HORSE.")

Organized at Benton Barracks, Mo., by Captain Lewis Merrill, U. S. A., under authority of General Fremont, September 3 to December 11, 1861. (Co. "L" organized at St. Louis, Mo., January 1, 1863, and Co. "M" at Warrenton June 30, 1863.) Before organization of Regiment was completed ordered to march to Springfield, Mo., September, 1861. Fremont's Campaign against Springfield, Mo., September-October. At Sedalia, Mo., till January, 1862. Scout through Saline County December 3-12, 1861. Expedition to Milford December 15-19. Shawnee Mound or Milford, Blackwater River, December 18. Roan's Tan Yard, Silver Creek, January 8, 1862. Knobnoster January 22. Attached to Dept. of Missouri September, 1861, to January, 1862. District of Northeast Missouri, Dept. of Missouri, to June, 1863. District of Southeast Missouri, Dept. of Missouri, to August, 1863. 1st Brigade, 1st Cavalry Division, Arkansas Expedition, to December, 1863. 2nd Brigade, 1st Cavalry Division, Army of Arkansas, to January, 1864. 2nd Brigade, 1st Cavalry Division, 7th Army Corps, Dept. of Arkansas, to May, 1864. 3rd Brigade, 2nd Division, 7th Army Corps, to September, 1864. 2nd Brigade, Cavalry Division, 7th Army Corps, to February, 1865. 2nd Brigade, Cavalry Division, District of West Tennessee, to muster out. SERVICE.—Moved to Northern Missouri and duty at Columbia, Glasgow, Sturgeon, Paris, Huntsville, Palmyra and Warrenton, operating against guerrillas January, 1862, to June, 1863. Expedition into Schuyler and Scotland Counties, Porter's and Poindexter's guerrillas, July 12-August 8, 1862. Near Memphis, Mo., July 18. Brown Springs July 27. Moore's Mills, near Fulton, July 28. Kirksville August 6 (Detachment). Pursuit of Poindexter August 8-15, with skirmishes at Grand River, Lee's Ford, Chariton River and Walnut Creek, near Stockton, August 9. Switzler's Mill August 10. Little Compton Ferry, Yellow Creek, August 11. Roanoke September 6 (Detachment). Scotland and Boone Counties September 30 (Detachment). Joined Davidson's Cavalry Division at Pilot Knob June, 1863. Expedition to Little Rock, Ark., July 1-September 10. Grand Prairie August 17. Brownsville August 25. Bayou Metoe or Reed's Bridge August 27. Reconnoissance from Brownsville August 29. Bear Skin Lake, Ashby's Mills, September 7. Bayou Fourche and capture of Little Rock September 10. Pursuit of Price September 11-13. Near Little Rock September 11. Duty at Little Rock till March, 1864. Steele's Expedition to Camden March 23-May 3. Benton Road March 23-24. Okolona April 2-3. Prairie D'Ann April 9-12. Camden

April 15-18. Moro Bottom April 25-26. Jenkins' Ferry, Saline River, April 30. Scatterville July 28. Duty in Arkansas till September. Operating against Price September and October. Booneville, Mo., October 9-12. Little Blue October 21. Big Blue, State Line, October 22. Westport October 23. Battle of Charlot October 25. Mine Creek, Osage River, Marias des Cygnes, October 25. Grierson's Expedition from Memphis against Mobile & Ohio Railroad December 21, 1864, to January 15, 1865 (Co. "E"). Near Memphis February 9 (Detachment). Moved to Chattanooga, Tenn., and duty operating against guerrillas in Georgia and Alabama and escorting trains from Chattanooga to Atlanta January to September, 1865. Mustered out September 19, 1865.

Regiment lost during service 3 Officers and 53 Enlisted men killed and mortally wounded and 1 Officer and 205 Enlisted men by disease. Total 262.

2nd REGIMENT STATE MILITIA CAVALRY.

Organized in Missouri at large December, 1861, to April, 1862, and by consolidation of original 2nd and 11th Regiments, State Militia Cavalry. Attached to District of Northern Missouri, Dept. of Missouri, to March, 1863. District of St. Louis, Mo., Dept. of Missouri, to June, 1863. District of Southeast Missouri, Dept. of Missouri, to July, 1863. District of St. Louis, Mo., Dept. of Missouri, to April, 1865. SERVICE.—Walkerville, Mo., April 2 and 14, 1862. Cherry Grove June 26. Near Newark July 7. Whaley's Mills August 1. Kirksville August 6 (Detachment). Near Stockton August 8 (Detachment). Near Bragg's Farm September 13. Bloomfield March 1-2, 1863. Expedition from Bloomfield to Chalk Bluff, Ark., and to Gum Slough, etc., Mo., and skirmishes March 9-15. Chalk Bluff March 9 and 15. Gum Slough March 16. Scout to Doniphan March 19-23. Near Doniphan March 21. Scouts from Bloomfield to Scatterville, Ark., March 25-April 1. Chalk Bluff April 1. Operations against Marmaduke April 21-May 2. Cape Girardeau April 26. Castor River, near Bloomfield, April 29. Bloomfield April 29-30. Chalk Bluff, St. Francis River, April 30-May 1. Round Ponds August 1 (Detachment). Scout from Cape Girardeau to Poplar Bluff August 9-18 (1st Battalion). Ash Hill August 3 (Detachment). Expedition from Cape Girardeau to Pilot Knob and Pocohontas, Ark., August 17-26. Pocohontas, Ark., August 22-23. Expedition to Big Lake, Mississippi County, Ark., September 7-30. Expedition from Pilot Knob to Oregon County and to Pocohontas, Ark., September 29-October 6 (Detachment). Scout from Cape Girardeau to Doniphan and Pocohontas October 26-November 12. Expedition from Cape Girardeau to Clarkton October 26-November 15 (Detachment). Attack on Bloomfield and pursuit to Brown's Ferry, Ark., November 29-30. Halcom Island February 2, 1864 (Detachment). Cape Girardeau February 5. Near Charleston February 15 (Detachment). Near Bloomfield April 1. Scout from Bloomfield May 6. Sykestown June 7. Near St. James June 10. Expedition from New Madrid to Carruthersville July 5-10 (Detachment). Bloomfield July 14. Operations in Southeast Missouri and Northeast Arkansas July 18-August 6. Scatterville, Ark., July 28 (Detachment). Osceola, Ark., August 2. Elkchute August 4 (Detachment). Near Homersville and Gayoso September 8 (Detachment). Sykestown September 22. Ironton September 26. Shut in Gap and Arcadia Valley September 26. Fort Davidson, Pilot Knob, September 26-27 (Co. "K"). Leesburg or Harrison September 28-29 and October 1. Scout in Pemiscot County and skirmish October 10-12 (Detachment). Little Blue October 21. Independence, Big Blue and State Line October 22. Westport October 23. Engagement at the Marmiton or battle of Charlot October 25. Mine Creek, Little Osage River, Marias des Cygnes, October 25. West Point October 26. Operations in Mississippi County, Ark., November 5-6 (Detachment). Sikestown November 6 (Detachment). Scout in Pemiscot County and skirmish November 13-16 (Detachment). Near New Madrid December 3 (Detachment). Cypress Swamp, near Cape Girardeau, December 14 (Detachments). Expedition from Cape Girardeau and Dallas to Cherokee Bay and St. Francis River, Ark., with skirmish, December 20, 1864-January 4, 1865. Near Carruthersville December 30, 1864. Expedition from Bloomfield to Poplar Bluff January 4-16 (Detachment). Expedition from Cape Girardeau to Eleven Points River, Ark., January 24-February 22. Mississippi County February 13 (Co. "B"). Expedition from Bloomfield into Dunklin County March 3-7 (Detachment). Near Bloomfield March 3. Dunklin County March 4. Bloomfield March 7 (Detachment). Scout from Cape Girardeau to Bolinger, Stoddard and Wayne Counties March 9-15 (Co. "F"). Mustered out April 20, 1865.

Regiment lost during service 18 Enlisted men killed and mortally wounded and 1 Officer and 88 Enlisted men by disease. Total 107.

2nd BATTALION STATE MILITIA CAVALRY.

Organized at Harrisville and Kansas City, Mo., March 17 to May 5, 1862. Attached to District of Central Missouri, Dept. of Missouri.

Scout to Little Manqua, near Quincy, and skirmish April, 1862. Scout to Monticello, Vernon County, and to Shiloh Camp, on Boyle's Run, April 9-16. Pink Hill April 11. Montevallo April 14. Near Independence May 15-17. Surrender of Independence August 11 (Detachment). Action at Lone Jack August 16. At Lexington and in District of Central Missouri till March, 1863. Grand Prairie October 24. Expedition into Southeast Missouri and North Arkansas November 8-13. Affairs in Jackson and Lafayette Counties November 26-29. Mustered out March 31, 1863.

Battalion lost during service 3 Officers and 48 Enlisted men killed and mortally wounded and 1 Officer and 109 Enlisted men by disease. Total 161.

3rd REGIMENT CAVALRY.

Organized at Palmyra, Mo., and St. Louis, Mo., October 15, 1861, to March 6, 1862. Attached to District of Rolla, Dept. of Missouri, to December, 1862. Cavalry Brigade, Army of Southeast Missouri, Dept. of Missouri, to June, 1863. 2nd Brigade, 1st Cavalry Division, Army of Southeast Missouri, Dept. of Missouri, to August, 1863. 2nd Brigade, 1st Cavalry Division, Arkansas Expedition, to December, 1863. 3rd Brigade, 1st Cavalry Division, Army of Arkansas, to January, 1864. 3rd Brigade, 1st Cavalry Division, 7th Army Corps, Dept. of Arkansas, to March, 1865. Separate Cavalry Brigade, 7th Army Corps, to June, 1865.

SERVICE.—Duty in Southeast Missouri and District of Rolla, Mo., till December, 1862, under Prentiss and McNeil. Action near Hallsville, Mo., December 27, 1861. Mt. Zion Church December 28. Inman's Hollow July 7, 1862 (Cos. "B," "D," "G," "H"). Mountain Store, Big Piney, July 25-26 (Cos. "E," "F"). Scout in Sinking Creek and skirmish August 4-11 (Detachment). Salem August 9. Wayman's Mills and Spring Creek August 23. Scout from Salem to Current River August 24-28 (Co. "E"). Beaver Creek, Texas County, November 24. Expedition from Rolla to Ozark Mountains November 30-December 6 (Cos. "A," "B"). Ozark December 2 (Cos. "A," "B"). Wood's Creek January 11, 1863. Hartsville, Wood's Fork, January 11. Batesville, Ark., February 4. Operations against Marmaduke April 17-May 2. Castor River, near Bloomfield, April 29. Bloomfield April 30. Coal Bluff, St. Francis River, April 30-May 1. Expedition against Little Rock, Ark., July 1-September 10. Moved from Wittsburg to Clarendon August 1-8. Near Bayou Metoe August 26. Bayou Metoe (or Reed's Bridge) August 27. Advance on Little Rock September 1-10. Bayou Fourche and capture of Little Rock September 10. Brownsville September 16. At Jacksonport, Ark., November, 1863, to March, 1864. Affair at Jacksonport November 21, 1863 (Co. "E"). Reconnoissance from Little Rock December 5-13, 1863. Jacksonport December 23. Scouts from Brownsville January 17-19, 1864. Hot Springs February 4. Steele's Expedition to Camden March 23-May 3. Elkins' Ferry, Little Missouri River, April 3-4. Mark's

Mills April 5. Little Missouri River April 6. Prairie D'Ann April 9-12. Camden April 15, 16, 18 and 24. Mt. Elba Ferry April 26. Princeton April 29. Operations against Shelby, north of Arkansas River, May 18-31. At Little Rock till June, 1865. Benton Road, near Little Rock, July 19, 1864. Benton July 25 (Co. "C"). Scatterville July 28 (Detachment). Expedition from Little Rock to Little Red River August 6-16. At Tannery, near Little Rock, September 2 (Detachment). Expedition Little Rock to Fort Smith September 25-October 13 (Detachment). Reconnoissance from Little Rock toward Monticello and Mt. Elba October 4-11. Reconnoissance from Little Rock to Princeton October 19-23. Princeton October 23. Expedition from Little Rock to Saline River November 17-18 (Detachment). Expedition from Little Rock to Benton November 27-30 (Detachment). Mustered out June 14, 1865. (Co. "M" at Headquarters Dept. of Missouri, St. Louis, Mo., November, 1862, to June, 1863.)

Regiment lost during service 3 Officers and 37 Enlisted men killed and mortally wounded and 1 Officer and 172 Enlisted men by disease. Total 213.

3rd REGIMENT STATE MILITIA CAVALRY (OLD).

Organized at Louisiana, Pike County, Mo., May 5, 1862. Guard line of the North Missouri Railroad and operations in Northeast Missouri against Porter till February, 1863. Prairie Jackson, Mo., April 9, 1862 (Cos. "A," "B," "C"). Near Fayetteville, Ark., July 15. Moore's Mills, near Fulton, July 24. Greenville July 26. Dallas August 24. Newtonia September 13. Monroe County September 16 and October 4. Operations against Marmaduke in Missouri December 31, 1862, to January 25, 1863. Springfield January 8, 1863. Regiment disbanded February 4. 1863.

Regiment lost during service 7 Enlisted men killed and mortally wounded and 3 Officers and 62 Enlisted men by disease. Total 72.

3rd REGIMENT STATE MILITIA CAVALRY (NEW).

Reorganized from 10th Regiment State Militia Cavalry February 2, 1863. Attached to District of St. Louis, Mo., Dept. of Missouri, to June, 1863. District of Southeast Missouri, Dept. of Missouri, to July, 1863. District of St. Louis, Mo., Dept. of Missouri, to July, 1865.

SERVICE.—Moved from Pilot Knob to Patterson, Mo., March 16, 1863. Operations against Marmaduke April 20-May 1, 1863. Patterson April 20. Fredericktown April 22. Castor River, near Bloomfield, April 29. Bloomfield April 29-30. Chalk Bluff, St. Francis River, April 30-May 1. Near Doniphan June 1 (Detachment). Expedition from Cape Girardeau and Pilot Knob to Pocahontas, Ark., August 17-26. Oregon County October 23. Scout from Cape Girardeau to Doniphan and Pocahontas, Ark., October 26-November 12 (Detachment). Scout from Pilot Knob to Doniphan, Ark., October 29-November 5 (Detachment). Reeve's attack on Centreville December 23. Pursuit of Reeves December 23-25. Puliam's December 25. Bolinger County January 14, 1864. Scout from Patterson to Cherokee Bay, Ark., January 20-27 (Detachment). Poplar Bluff February 27. Scout from Pilot Knob to Arkansas line, and skirmishes March 16-25 (Detachment). Oregon County March 19. Wayne County April 26. Scout from Patterson May 6-11 (Co. "A"). Randolph County May 8. Cherokee Bay, Ark., May 8 (Co. "A"). Near St. James June 10. Scout from Patterson to Buffalo July 8-12 (Detachment). Operations in Southeast Missouri and Northeast Arkansas July 18-August 6. Scatterville, Ark., July 28 (Detachment). Osceola August 2. Elkchute August 4. Near Rocheport September 3 (Detachment). Caledonia September 12 (Detachment). Scout in Randolph, Howard and Boone Counties September 15-19 (Detachment). Columbia September 16 (Detachment). Doniphan September 19. Ponder's Mill, Little Black River, September 20. Near Rocheport September 23 (Detachment). Ironton September 26. Shut-in Gap and Arcadia Valley September 26. Fort Davidson, Pilot Knob, September 26-27. Arcadia Valley September 27 (Detachment). Caledonia September 28 (Co. "C"). Leesburg October 1. Ponder's Mills October 3. Moreau Bottom, Jefferson City, October 7. Independence October 22 and 26. Pilot Knob October 26. Leesburg October 28. Duty at Weston, St. Joe, Liberty, Parksville, Pleasant Hill and Lone Jack, operating against guerrillas January to July, 1865. Mustered out July 13, 1865.

Regiment lost during service 4 Officers and 57 Enlisted men killed and mortally wounded and 1 Officer and 102 Enlisted men by disease. Total 164.

4th REGIMENT CAVALRY.

Organized February, 1862, by consolidation of Fremont Hussars and three Companies Hollan Horse. Attached to 3rd Brigade, Army of Southwest Missouri, Dept. of Missouri, to March, 1862. Cavalry, 2nd Division, Army of Southwest Missouri, Dept. of Missouri, to May, 1862. Cavalry 3rd Division, Army of Southwest Missouri, to July, 1862. District of Eastern Arkansas, Dept. of Missouri, to October, 1862. Cavalry Brigade, Army of Southeast Missouri, Dept. of Missouri, till April, 1863. District of Columbus, Ky., 6th Division, 16th Army Corps, Dept. of Tennessee, to December, 1863. Waring's Detached Brigade, Dist. of Columbus, to January, 1864. 1st Brigade, 1st Cavalry Division, 16th Army Corps, to June, 1864. 1st Brigade, Cavalry Division, Sturgis' Expedition, June, 1864. 1st Brigade, 2nd Cavalry Division, Dist. of West Tennessee, to December, 1864. 1st Brigade, Cavalry Division, District of West Tennessee, to June, 1865. 2nd Brigade, 2nd Division Cavalry Corps, Military Division West Mississippi, and Dept. of Texas to November, 1865.

SERVICE.—Curtis' Campaign in Missouri and Arkansas January to April, 1862. Occupation of Springfield, Mo., February 14. Pierson's and Crane's Creeks February 14. Flat Creek February 15. Cross Timbers February 16. Sugar Creek, Ark., February 17. Bentonville February 19. Occupation of Fayetteville February 23. Scout through LaClede, Wright and Douglass Counties, Mo., March 1-11 (Co. "F"). Battles of Pea Ridge, Ark., March 6-8; Fox Creek March 7 (Cos. "E" and "F"); Mountain Grove March 9 (Cos. "E" and "F"). March to Keitsville, thence to Forsyth March 19-April 10. Forsyth April 11. March to White Plains and Batesville April 15-May 3. Batesville May 3. Little Red River May 17 (Detachment). Scout to Grand Glaze May 14. Searcy Landing, Little Red River, May 19. Expedition from Searcy Landing to West Point, Searcy and Des Arc May 27. Searcy May 27. Expedition to Grand Glaze May 31 (Detachment). Scouts from Batesville June 16-17. March to Helena July 5-14. Round Hill July 7. Occupation of Helena till October. Expedition from Clarendon to Lawrenceville and St. Charles September 11-13. Battle of Iuka, Miss., September 19 (Co. "C"). Expedition to LaGrange September 26 (Detachment). Moved with Davidson to Southeast Missouri and operations against Marmaduke October, 1862, to May, 1863. (Battle of Corinth, Miss., October 3-4, 1862 (Co. "C"). Grant's Central Mississippi Campaign October 31, 1862, to January 10, 1863 (Co. "C").) Batesville, Ark., February 4, 1863. Moved to Columbus, Ky., May, 1863, and duty there till January, 1864. (Raymond, Miss., May 12, 1863 (Co. "F"); Jackson, Miss., May 14 (Co. "F"); Champion's Hill, Miss., May 16 (Co. "F").) Siege of Vicksburg, Miss., May 18-July 4, 1863 (Co. "F"). Near Lexington, Tenn., June 29, 1863 (Detachment). Union City, Tenn., July 10 (Cos. "C" and "E"). Occupation of Hickman, Ky., July 15-16. Expedition from Clifton in pursuit of Biffle's, Forest's and Newsome's Cavalry July 22-27. Expedition from Columbus to Hickman, Ky., August 1 (1 Co.). Scout from Fort Pillow, Tenn., August 3 (Detachment). Expedition from Union City to Conyersville September 1-10. Conyersville September 5. Como September 19. Expedition from Paducah, Ky., to McLemoresville, Tenn., September 20-30. Pillowville November 5. Attack on Bloomfield, Mo., November 29-30. Expedition from Union City to Trenton January 22-24, 1864. Smith's Expedition from Colliersville, Tenn., to Okolona, Miss., February 11-26. Prairie Station Febru-

ary 20. Okolona February 21. Ivy's Hill, near Okolona, February 22. Operations against Forest in West Tennessee March 16-April 14. Sturgis' Expedition from Memphis, Tenn., to Ripley, Miss., April 30-May 9. Near Mt. Pleasant May 22 (Detachment). Holly Springs, Miss., May 24. Sturgis' Expedition to Guntown, Miss., June 1-13. Brice's or Tishamingo Creek, near Guntown, June 10. Ripley and Salem June 11. Expedition to Grand Gulf, Miss., July 4-24. Grand Gulf July 16. Smith's Expedition from Lagrange, Tenn., to Oxford, Miss., August 1-30. Operations against Price in Missouri September-October. Little Blue, Mo., October 21. Big Blue and State Line October 22. Westport October 23. Engagement at the Marmiton or battle of Charlot October 25. Mine Creek, Osage River, Marias des Cygnes, October 25. Grierson's Expedition to destroy Mobile & Ohio Railroad December 21, 1864, to January 15, 1865. Verona December 25. Egypt Station December 28. At Memphis and along Memphis & Charleston Railroad till June, 1865. Moved to Alexandria, thence to Shreveport, La. Moved to Texas July 10-August 2. Garrison duty at San Antonio and scouting along the Rio Grande, Texas, till November, 1865. Mustered out November 13, 1865.

Regiment lost during service 4 Officers and 56 Enlisted men killed and mortally wounded and 6 Officers and 177 Enlisted men by disease. Total 243.

4th REGIMENT STATE MILITIA CAVALRY.

Organized at St. Joseph, Mo., January 28 to May 14, 1862. Ordered to Kansas City, Mo., May, 1862, and duty there fitting out till August. Skirmish on Little Blue June 2. Ordered to Southwest Missouri August, 1862, and reported to General Egbert B. Brown. Attached to District of Southwest Missouri, Dept. of Missouri, to December, 1862. District of Central Missouri, Dept. of Missouri, to July, 1863. District of the Border, Dept. of Missouri, to January, 1864. District of Central Missouri, Dept. of Missouri, to July, 1865.

SERVICE.—Pursuit of Coffee August 8-September 1, 1862. Between Stockton and Humansville and near Stockton August 12. Duty at Mt. Vernon till September 30. Joined Totten's Division, Army of the Frontier. Oxford Bend, near Fayetteville, Ark., October 27-28. Expedition from Greenfield into Jasper and Barton Counties November 24-26. Operations against Marmaduke in Missouri December 31, 1862-January 25, 1863. Defence of Springfield, Mo., January 8, 1863. Duty in Central Missouri and guarding Missouri Pacific Railroad, with Headquarters at LaMine Bridge, Jefferson City, Tipton, Sedalia and Warrensburg, Mo., till October, 1864. Operations about Princeton May 4, 1863. Waverly June 1 (Cos. "B" and "C"). Sibley June 23 (4 Cos.). Marshall July 28. Saline County July 30. Operations against Quantrell August 20-28. Operations against Shelby September 22-October 26. Tipton and Syracuse October 10 (Cos. "A," "B," "E" and "F"). Booneville October 11-12. Merrill's Landing and Dug Ford, near Jonesborough, October 12. Marshall, Arrow Rock, Blackwater, October 13. Operations about Warrensburg February 22-24, 1864. Scout from Sedalia to Blackwater June 3-5 (Co. "M"). Near Sedalia and Marshall Road June 26 (Co. "E"). Huntsville July 16. Scout from Independence to Lafayette County August 7-8 (Detachment). Operations in Lafayette and Saline Counties August 13-22 (Detachment). Near Rocheport August 28 (Detachment). Howard County August 28 (Co. "E"). Moved to Defence of Jefferson City October 1. Campaign against Price October —. Moreau Bottoms October 7. California October 9. Booneville October 9-12. Little Blue October 21. Independence, Big Blue and State Line October 22. Westport October 23. Engagement at the Marmiton or battle of Charlot October 25. Mine Creek, Little Osage River, Marias des Cygnes, October 25. At Sedalia, Mo., November 1864, to April, 1865. Scout in Calloway County November 6-7, 1864 (Detachment). Moved to St. Louis April, 1865, and most of Regiment mustered out April 18, 1865. Balance mustered out July 8, 1865.

Regiment lost during service 2 Officers and 34 Enlisted men killed and mortally wounded and 2 Officers and 86 Enlisted men by disease. Total 124.

5th REGIMENT CAVALRY.

Organized by consolidation of Benton Hussars and 3 Companies of Hollan Horse February 14, 1862. Served unattached, 2nd Division, Army of Southwest Missouri, Dept. of Missouri, to October, 1862. Army of Southeast Missouri, Dept. of Missouri, to November, 1862.

SERVICE.—Curtis' Campaign in Missouri and Arkansas against Price February-March, 1862. Battles of Pea Ridge, Ark., March 6-8. Duty in District of Southwest Missouri till October. Expedition to Blue Mountains June 19. Near Knight's Cove June 19. Expedition from Clarendon to Lawrenceville and St. Charles September 11-13. Ordered to Pilot Knob October. Consolidated with 4th Missouri Cavalry November 15, 1862.

Regiment lost during service 1 Officer and 4 Enlisted men killed and mortally wounded and 1 Officer and 36 Enlisted men by disease. Total 42.

5th REGIMENT STATE MILITIA CAVALRY.—(OLD.)

Organized at St. Joseph, Mo., March and April, 1862. Attached to District of Central Missouri, Dept. of Missouri, to February, 1863.

SERVICE.—Duty in Central District of Missouri till February, 1863. Operations in Carroll, Ray and Livingston Counties July 27-August 4, 1862. Grand River August 1. Near Barry Section August 14. Iron County September 11. Liberty and Sibley's Landing October 6 (Cos. "A," "B," "D" and "K"). California House October 18. Independence February 3, 1863. (See 5th Regiment State Militia Cavalry (New) for further service.)

Lost 21 Enlisted men killed and mortally wounded and 1 Officer and 47 Enlisted men by disease. Total 69.

5th REGIMENT STATE MILITIA CAVALRY.—(NEW.)

Organized February 2, 1863, from 13th Regiment, State Militia Cavalry. Attached to District of Rolla, Dept. of Missouri, to June, 1863. District of the Border, Dept. of Missouri, to October, 1863. District of Rolla, Dept. of Missouri, to muster out.

SERVICE.—Independence, Mo., February 8, 1863 (Cos. "C," "D," "F"). Blue Springs March 22. Independence March 23. Headquarters at Waynesville. Scouts from Waynesville June 20-23 (Co. "H"). Scout from Salem and skirmish July 3 (Co. "D"). Scout from Houston to Spring River Mills and skirmish August 6-11 (Cos. "B," "C," "F" and "G"). Jack's Ford August 14 (Detachment). Warrensville August 25 (Detachment). Texas County September 11-12 (Detachment). Near Houston September 12 (Detachment). Near Salem September 13 (Cos. "C," "M"). Near Man's Creek October 14 (Detachment). King's House, near Waynesville, October 26 (Co. H). Scout from Houston to Jack's Fork November 4-6 (Cos. "B," "G," "I"). Scouts from Houston November 23-29 (Detachment), and December 9-19. Scouts from Salem December 26-29 (Cos. "C," "M"). Scout from Houston into Arkansas, with skirmishes February 5-17, 1864 (Detachment). Independence April 23. Scouts from Big Piney July 5-6. Scout in Shannon County July 18-21 (Detachment). Rolla August 1. Scouts in Moniteau and Morgan Counties September 11-18 (Detachment). Scout in Texas County September 14-21 (Detachment). Thomasville September 18. Waynesville September 30 (Co. "B"). Moreau Bottom, Jefferson City, October 7. Booneville October 9. Lexington October 19. Independence October 22. Big Blue and State Line October 22. Westport October 23. Engagement on the Marmiton, or battle of Charlot, October 25. Mine Creek, Little Osage River, Marias des Cygnes, October 25. Near Centreville November 2 (Co. "K"). Operations near Waynesville December 1-3 (Detachment). Big Piney December 2 (Detachment). Scouting and escort duty in District of Rolla till July, 1865. McCartney's Mills January, 1865 (Detachment). Scout in Shannon County January 2-7 (Cos. "C," "D," "M"). Operations about Waynesville January 16-22. Scouts from Salem and Licking to Spring River, Ark.,

and skirmishes February 23-March 2. Scouts from Waynesville to Hutton Valley, Rolla and Lebanon March 5-12. Near Rolla March 24 (Co. "E"). Mustered out July 8, 1865.

Regiment lost during service 19 Enlisted men killed and mortally wounded and 2 Officers and 93 Enlisted men by disease. Total 114.

6th REGIMENT CAVALRY.

Organized February 14, 1862, by consolidation of Wright's, Wood's and Hawkins' Battalions. Attached to District of Southwest Missouri, Dept. of Missouri, to July, 1862. District of Eastern Arkansas, Dept. of Missouri, to December, 1862. 1st Brigade, 3rd (Cavalry) Division, District of Eastern Arkansas, to January, 1863 (6 Companies). 1st Brigade, 2nd Cavalry Division, 13th Army Corps, Dept. of Tennessee, to April, 1863 (6 Companies). Headquarters 13th Army Corps, Army of the Tennessee, to August, 1863 (6 Cos.). Cavalry Brigade, 13th Army Corps, Dept. of the Gulf, to November, 1863 (6 Cos.). 3rd Brigade, Cavalry Division, Dept. of the Gulf, to January, 1864 (7 Cos.). 1st Brigade, Cavalry Division, Dept. of the Gulf, to December, 1864. District of Southern Alabama, Dept. of the Gulf, to February, 1865. Separate Brigade, District of Baton Rouge, La., Dept. of the Gulf, February, 1865 (7 Cos.). Cavalry Brigade, District of Baton Rouge, La., to July, 1865. Dept. of Texas to September, 1865. Cos. "A," "D," "E" and "L" attached to District of Southwest Missouri, Dept. of Missouri, to October, 1862. 2nd Brigade, 2nd Division, Army of the Frontier, Dept. of Missouri, to June, 1863. District of Southeast Missouri, Dept. of Missouri, to October, 1863. District of St. Louis, Mo., Dept. of Missouri, to muster out.

SERVICE.—Curtis' Campaign in Southwest Missouri and Arkansas February-March, 1862. Marshfield, Mo., February 9. Sugar Creek, Ark., February 17. Bentonville February 17. West Plains, Mo., February 17. Keytesville February 25. Battles of Pea Ridge, Ark., March 6-8. Spring River March 13. Salem Spring River March 18 (Detachment). Scout through Gadfly, Newtonia, Granby, Neosho and Valley of Indian Creek and skirmish April 8. Scout from Batesville, Ark., June 16-17 (4 Cos.). White Oak Bayou, Miss., June 23 (Battalion). Near Fayetteville, Ark., July 15. Expedition to Coldwater, Miss., July 22-25 (Battalion). White Oak Bayou, Miss., July 29 (Battalion). Chariton Bridge, Mo., August 3. Montevallo August 7. Between Stockton and Humansville August 12. Stockton August 12. Neosho August 21. Hickory Grove August 23 (Co. "B"). Expedition from Clarendon, Ark., to Lawrenceville and St. Charles September 11-13. Occupation of Newtonia, Mo., October 4 (2nd Battalion). Expedition from Helena, Ark., to Grenada, Miss., November 27-December 5. Oakland, Miss., December 3. Cane Hill, Boston Mountains, Ark. (2nd Battalion). Battle of Prairie Grove, Ark., December 7 (2nd Battalion). Near Helena, Ark., December 14 (Co. "E"). Sherman's Yazoo Expedition December 20, 1862-January 3, 1863. Expedition from Milliken's Bend to Dallas Station and Delhi December 25-26, 1862. Expedition over Boston Mountains to Van Buren, Ark., December 27-29 (2nd Battalion). Reconnoissance toward White River and St. Charles January 13, 1863 (Squadron). Carthage January 23, 1863. Expedition from Young's Point, La., to Greenville, Miss., and Cypress Bend, Ark., February 14-29. Cypress Bend, Ark., February 19 (Detachment). Fish Lake, near Greenville, Miss., and Deer Creek, near Greenville, February 23 (Detachment). Operations from Milliken's Bend, La., to New Carthage March 31-April 17 (1st Battalion). Near Dunbar's Plantation, Bayou Vidal, April 7 (Detachment). Movement on Bruinsburg and turning Grand Gulf April 25-30. Port Gibson May 1. Near Black River May 5. Raid on New Orleans & Jackson Railroad, near Crystal Springs, May 11. Jackson May 14. Champion's Hill May 16. Near Bridgeport May 17. Siege of Vicksburg May 18-July 4. Assaults on Vicksburg May 19 and 22. Mason's Ford, Big Black River, June 9. Advance on Jackson, Miss., July 4-10. Near Baker's Creek July 7. Bolton's Station July 8 (Detachment). Near Clinton July 8 (Detachment). Near Jackson and near Clinton July 9 (Detachment). Siege of Jackson July 10-17. Brookhaven July 18 (Detachment). Moved to the Dept. of the Gulf August. Near Morganza, La., September 8. Atchafalaya September 8-9. Hornersville, Mo., September 20 (2nd Battalion). Sterling's Farm, on Bayou Fordoche, near Morganza, September 27. Western Louisiana Campaign October 3-November 30. Reconnoissance toward Opelousas October 20. Opelousas, Barre Landing, October 21. Washington October 24. Bayou Bourbeaux November 2. Carrion Crow Bayou November 18. Bayou Portage, Grand Lake, November 23. Attack on Bloomfield, Mo., and pursuit to Brown's Ferry November 29-30 (2nd Battalion). Near Vermillionville, La., November 30. Branchville, Ark., January 17, 1864 (Detachment). Branchville, Ivey's Ford, Pine Bluff, January 19 (Detachment). Red River Campaign March 10-May 22. Advance from Franklin to Alexandria March 14-26. Bayou Rapides March 20. Henderson's Hill March 21. Monett's Ferry and Cloutiersville March 29-30. Natchitoches March 31. Crump's Hill, Piney Woods, April 2. Wilson's Farm April 7. Bayou de Paul, Carroll's Mill, April 8. Battle of Sabine Cross Roads April 8. Pleasant Hill April 9. About Cloutiersville April 22-24. Bayou Rapides Bridge and McNutt's Hill, Alexandria, April 27-28. Scout from Pilot Knob, Mo., to Gainesville, Ark., May 10-25 (2nd Battalion). Retreat to Morganza April 13-20. Wilson's Landing May 14. Avoyelle's (or Marksville Prairie) May 15. Old River L May 22. Operations in Southeast Missouri and Northeast Arkansas July 18-August 6 (2nd Battalion). Mazzard's Prairie, Ark., July 27. Osceola August 2 and 4. Elkchute August 4. Bayou Letsworth August 11. Operations in Southwest Missouri and Northwest Arkansas August 15-24 (2nd Battalion). Richland Creek, Ark., August 16 (Detachment). Expedition to Clinton, La., August 23-29. Olive Branch, Comite River and Clinton August 25. Near Richwood's, Mo., October 4 (Detachment). Tyler's Mills October 7 (2nd Battalion). Expedition from Baton Rouge to Clinton, Greensburg, Osyke and Camp Moore October 5-9. Expedition from Baton Rouge to Brookhaven, Miss., and skirmishes November 14-21. Davidson's Expedition from Baton Rouge against Mobile & Ohio Railroad November 27-December 3. Expedition from Baton Rouge to Clinton and Comite River March 30-April 2, 1865. Duty in District of Baton Rouge, La., till July and the Dept. of Texas till September. Mustered out September 12, 1865.

Regiment lost during service 2 Officers and 34 Enlisted men killed and mortally wounded and 6 Officers and 273 Enlisted men by disease. Total 315.

6th REGIMENT STATE MILITIA CAVALRY.

Organized at large February 27 to April 23, 1862. Attached to District of Central Missouri to June, 1862. District of Southwest Missouri, Dept. of Missouri, to December, 1862. District of Central Missouri, Dept. of Missouri, to July, 1863. District of Southwest Missouri, Dept. of Missouri, to October, 1864. District of North Missouri, Dept. of Missouri, to February, 1865. District of Southwest Missouri, Dept. of Missouri, to July, 1865.

SERVICE.—Duty at Cameron and in Central Missouri till June, 1862. Scout in Pettis County July 28-31, 1862 (Co. "F"). Arrow Rock July 29 (Detachment). Ordered to Sedalia, Mo., June 3, arriving June 15, and outpost duty there till August 30. Operations in Saline County July 29-August 2. Lone Jack August 15-16 (3 Cos.). Outpost duty at Warrensburg August 30-September 14. Newtonia September 13. At Sedalia till October 28. Camp Cole October 5. Lexington October 17. March to Harrisonville October 28-November 1. Action with Quantrell at Harrisonville November 3 (Co. "G"). Huntsville November 9. At Warrensville November 27, 1862, to March 15, 1863. At Warsaw till May 3. At Booneville till July. Camp Cole June 8. Florence July 10. Duty at Linn Creek, Warsaw and Osceola. Consolidated at Osceola July 20 and march to Springfield July 27-31. Pursuit of Coffee, Garden Hollow, near Pineville, August 9. Pineville August 13. March to Bentonville, Ark.; Fort Gib-

son C. N. and Honey Springs, and join Gen. Blount. Blount's Campaign in Indian Nation and Arkansas August and September. Perryville August 26. Scullyville, Ark., August 30-31. Devil's Back Bone September 1. Capture of Fort Smith September 1. Expedition to Big Lake, Mississippi County September 7-30 (Detachment). Horse Creek September 17. March to Springfield, Mo., arriving September 18. Operations against Shelby and pursuit to Arkansas River September 22-October 26. Carthage October 2. Neosho October 4 (3 Cos.). Humansville October 16-17. Bloomfield October 22 (Cos. "A," "D," "E," "K," "L"). Harrisonville October 24. Buffalo Mountain October 24. Expedition from Springfield to Huntsville and skirmish November 8-18 (Detachment). Expedition from Springfield to Howell, Wright and Oregon Counties November 28-December 13. Duty at Springfield and in District of Southwest Missouri till July, 1865. Scout from Huston December 9-19. Operations in Northeastern Arkansas January 1-30, 1864. Sylamore Creek, Ark., January 23. Sylamore January 24. Scout from Springfield into Northern Arkansas February 23-March 9 (Detachment). Near Buffalo City, Ark., March 1. Bennett's Bayou March 2 (Detachment). Scout from Yellville to Buffalo River March 13-26 (Detachment). Richland Creek April 13-14 (Detachment). Expedition from Patterson to Bloomfield and Pilot Knob May 16-25 (Detachment). Near White Hare June 15 (Co. "E"). Operations in Randolph County July 23-24. Operations in Ray and Carroll Counties August 12-16. Near Roanoke September 10. Moreau Bottom, Jefferson City, October 7. Near Jefferson City October 8. Russellville October 9. Booneville October 9. Dover October 20. Little Blue October 21. Independence, Big Blue and State Line October 22. Westport October 23. Engagement at the Marmiton (or battle of Charlot) October 25. Mine Creek, Little Osage River, Marias des Cygnes, October 25. Newtonia October 28. Duty at Springfield and in Southwest Missouri till July, 1865. Mustered out July 18, 1865.

Regiment lost during service 2 Officers and 48 Enlisted men killed and mortally wounded and 104 Enlisted men by disease. Total 154.

7th REGIMENT CAVALRY.

Organized February 20, 1862, by consolidation of Black Hawk Cavalry and Unattached Companies. Attached to Dept. of Kansas to June, 1862. District of Southwest Missouri, Dept. of Missouri, to October, 1862. 1st Brigade, 2nd Division, Army of the Frontier, Dept. of Missouri, to June, 1863. 1st Brigade, 1st Cavalry Division, District of Southeast Missouri, Dept. of Missouri, to August, 1863. 1st Brigade, 1st Cavalry Division, Arkansas Expedition, to January, 1864. 1st Brigade, 1st Cavalry Division, 7th Army Corps, Dept. of Arkansas, to May, 1864. Clayton's Independent Cavalry Brigade, 7th Army Corps, to September, 1864. 1st Brigade, Cavalry Division, 7th Army Corps, to February, 1865. 2nd Brigade, Cavalry Division, 7th Army Corps, to February, 1865.

SERVICE.—Operations about Miami and Waverly May 25-28, 1862. Scouts to Waverly, Miami, Franklin and Pink Hill June 4-10 (Cos. "H" and "I"). Pink Hill June 11 (Detachment). Haytown June 23 (Co. "B"). Operations about Sibley and Pink Hill June 28-July 1 (Cos. "B," "D," "F" and "K"). Lotspeach Farm, near Wadesburg, July 9. Expeditions in Cass County July 9-11; on Blackwater, near Columbus, July 23. Lone Jack August 16 (5 Cos.). Occupation of Newtonia October 4. Battle of Prairie Grove, Ark., December 7. Van Buren December 21. Expedition over Boston Mountains December 27-29. Moved to Flat Creek February, 1863; thence to Rolla, Mo. Operations against Marmaduke April 17-May 2. At Pilot Knob, Mo., till July. Brownsville, Ark., July 25. Steele's Expedition against Little Rock, Ark., August 1-September 10. Grand Prairie August 17. Brownsville August 25. Bayou Fourche and capture of Little Rock September 10. Pursuit of Price September 11-14. Near Little Rock September 11. Expedition from Benton to Mt. Ida November 10-18. Reconnoissance from Little Rock December 5-13. Princeton December 8. Branchville January 17, 1864. Monticello March 18, 1864. Steele's Expedition to Camden March 23-May 3. Expedition from Pine Bluff to Mt. Elba and Longview March 27-31. Mt. Elba March 30 and pursuit to Big Creek. Mark's Mills April 25 (Detachment). Expedition from Pine Bluff September 9-11. Near Monticello September 10 (Detachment). Brewer's Lane September 11 (Detachment). Reconnoissance from Little Rock toward Monticello and Mt. Elba October 4-11. Expedition from Pine Bluff and skirmish January 7-9, 1865 (Detachment). Near Pine Bluff January 9. Consolidated with 1st Missouri Cavalry February 22, 1865.

Regiment lost during service 4 Officers and 55 Enlisted men killed and mortally wounded and 4 Officers and 228 Enlisted men by disease. Total 291.

7th REGIMENT STATE MILITIA CAVALRY.

Organized at large in Missouri March and April, 1862. Served unattached, Dept. of Missouri, to September, 1862. District of Southwest Missouri, Dept. of Missouri, to October, 1862. Unattached, Army of the Frontier, Dept. of Missouri, to June, 1863. District Central Missouri, Dept. of Missouri, to July, 1865.

SERVICE.—Post Oak Creek, near mouth of Briar, March 26, 1862. Warrensburg April 8. Warrensburg May 17 (Co. "G"). Pursuit of Poindexter August 8-15 (Detachment). Independence August 12. Scout from Fort Leavenworth, Kansas, to Independence August 12-14. Expedition to Hickory Grove August 17-27 (1 Co.). Fayetteville, Ark., October 24. Scout from Linden to White River April 1-5, 1863 (Co. "G"). White River April 17. Scout from Newtonia to French Point and Centre Creek May 13-18 (Detachment). French Point May 15 (Detachment). Carthage May 16 (Detachment). Hartsville May 23. Mountain Store May 26. Carthage June 27-28. Scout from Sedalia August 25-28 (Detachment). Clear Fork August 26 (Detachment). Near Syracuse October 25 (Co. "H"). Warsaw October 7. Near Camp Cole October 9. LaMine Bridge October 10. Booneville October 11-12. Merrill's Crossing and Dug Ford, near Jonesborough, October 12. Blackwater October 12. Marshall, Arrow Rock, Blackwater, October 13. Jonesborough October 14. Warrensburg May 28, 1864. Near Dunksburg June 27-28 (Co. "K"). Wellington July 8. Operations near Wellington July 9-13. Warder's Church July 10 (Detachment). Columbia July 12 (Detachment). Johnson County July 16. Clear Fork, near Warrensburg, July 16 (Detachment). Scout in Johnson County July 26-31 (Detachment). Blackwater River July 27 (Co. "G"). Big Creek July 28 (Co. "C"). Expedition from Warrensburg to Chapel Hill July 29-August 2 (Co. "K"). Near Chapel Hill July 30 (Co. "K"). Operations near Holden August 2-8. Merrick's Creek, near Holden, August 8 (Co. "K"). Operations in Johnson County August 11-19 (Detachment). Near Holden August 12 (Detachment). Scout from Crisp's Mills on Big Creek August 25-30 (Co. "M"). Near Rose Hill August 26 (Co. "M"). Near Lone Jack September 1 (Detachment). Operations in Johnson County September 1-9 (Detachment). Expedition from Sedalia to Scott's Ford on Blackwater September 2-4. Scout in Lafayette County September 20-25 (Detachment). Arrow Rock Road September 23 (Detachment). Prince's Shoals, Osage River, Cole County, October 5-6. Near Jefferson City October 8. California and Booneville October 9. Near Booneville October 11-12. Sedalia October 15. Little Blue October 21. Independence, Big Blue and State Line October 22. Westport October 23. Engagement at the Marmiton or Battle of Charlot October 25. Mine Creek, Osage River, Marias des Cygnes, October 25. Scout from Warrensburg to Greenton Valley November 29-December 3 (Detachment). Scout from Camp Grover to Texas Prairie January 12-15, 1865 (Detachment). Scout from Warrensburg to Miami January 12-17 (Co. "I"). Scout from Warrensburg to Snibar Hills January 18-22 (Detachment). Scout from Warrensburg to Tabo Creek, etc.,

February 1-5 (Detachment). Scout in Lafayette County February 3-8. Scout from Warrensburg to Columbus and skirmish near Greenton March 19-23 (Detachment). Near Booneville May 3. Duty in Central District of Missouri till July. Mustered out July 11, 1865.

Regiment lost during service 4 Officers and 56 Enlisted men killed and mortally wounded and 6 Officers and 152 Enlisted men by disease. Total 218.

8th REGIMENT CAVALRY.

Organized at Springfield, Mo., August 6 to September 15, 1862. Attached to 2nd Brigade, 3rd Division, Army of the Frontier, Dept. of Missouri, to June, 1863. 1st Brigade, 1st Cavalry Division, District of Southeast Missouri, Dept. of Missouri, to August, 1863. 1st Brigade, 1st Cavalry Division, Arkansas Expedition, to December, 1863. 2nd Brigade, 1st Cavalry Division, Army of Arkansas, to January, 1864, and 7th Army Corps, Dept. of Arkansas, to May, 1864. 3rd Brigade, 2nd Division, 7th Army Corps, to September, 1864. 3rd Brigade, Cavalry Division, 7th Army Corps, to February, 1865. 2nd Brigade, Cavalry Division, 7th Army Corps, to March, 1865. 1st Separate Cavalry Brigade, 7th Army Corps, to July, 1865.

SERVICE.—Springfield, Mo., August 9, 1862. Blount's Campaign in Missouri and Arkansas October 17-December 27. Battle of Prairie Grove, Ark., December 7. Expedition from Fayetteville to Huntsville December 21-23. Expedition over Boston Mountains to Van Buren December 27-29. Bloomfield, Mo., May 12, 1863. Join Davidson's Division at Pilot Knob, Mo., June, 1863, and march to Clarendon on White River, Ark. Steele's Expedition against Little Rock, Ark., August 1-September 10. Grand Prairie August 17. Brownsville August 25. Bayou Metoe or Reed's Bridge August 27. Reconnoissance from Brownsville August 29. Ferry's Landing September 7. Bayou Fourche and capture of Little Rock September 10. Pursuit of Price September 11-14. Near Little Rock September 11. Duty at Little Rock till March, 1864. Duvall's Bluff December 1 and December 12, 1863 (Detachments). Indian Bay February 16, 1864. Clarendon March 15. Fitzhugh's Woods, near Augusta, April 1 (Detachment). Cache River Cotton Plant April 21-22. Operations against Shelby north of the Arkansas River May 13-31. Stony Point May 20. Searcy June 3 (Detachment). Bealer's Ferry, Little Red River, June 6 (Detachment). Expedition from Little Rock to Little Red River August 6-16. Jones' Hay Station and Long Prairie August 24. Expedition in pursuit of Shelby August 27-September 6. Expedition from Lewisburg to Strahan Landing November 26-December 2. Expedition from Brownsville to Augusta January 4-27 (Detachment). Duty in the Dept. of Arkansas till July. Mustered out July 20, 1865.

Regiment lost during service 1 Officer and 26 Enlisted men killed and mortally wounded and 3 Officers and 352 Enlisted men by disease. Total 382.

8th REGIMENT STATE MILITIA CAVALRY.

Organized at Jefferson City, Bolivar, Warsaw and Linn Creek December 18, 1861, to May 6, 1862. Unattached, Dept. of Missouri, to September, 1862. District of Southwest Missouri to July, 1865.

SERVICE.—Post and scout duty at Lebanon, Neosho and Springfield, Mo. Gouge's Mill March 26, 1862 (Detachment). Humansville, Polk County, March 26 (Cos. "A," "B," "D" and "E"). Warsaw April 8, 17 and 28. Licking May 4. Cross Timbers July 28. Lone Jack August 16 (2 Cos.). Lamar November 5 (Detachment). Operations in Sugar Creek Hills December 23-31. Operations against Marmaduke in Missouri December 31, 1862, to January 25, 1863. Sarcoxie Prairie, Newton County, February 10, 1863. Scouts in Barton and Jasper Counties February 19-22 (Detachment). Greenville Road on Granby March 3 (Detachment). Scout near Neosho April 19-20 (Cos. "L" and "M"). Scout from Newtonia to French Point and Centre Creek with skirmishes May 3-18 (Detachment). French Point May 15 (Detachment). Jasper County June 10. Scout from

Greenfield to Golden Grove and Carthage August 6-9 (Co. "A"). Capture of Fort Smith, Ark., August 31. Devil's Back Bone, Ark., and Fort Smith September 1. Cotton Gap September 1. Quincy, Mo., September 4 (Co. "A"). Attack on train between Fort Scott and Carthage September 6 (Detachment). Operations against Shelby September 22-October 26. Near Widow Wheeler's October 4 (Cos. "L" and "M"). Jasper County October 5. Humansville October 16-17. Harrisonville October 24. Buffalo Mountain October 24. Near Neosho November 4-6 (Detachment). Shoal and Turkey Creeks, Jasper County, November 18 (Detachment). DeGreen's Farm, near Lawrenceville, Ark., November 19. Scout from Springfield to Howell, Wright and Oregon Counties November 28-December 18. Springfield, Mo., December 16. Scout from Forsyth to Batesville, Ark., December 26, 1863, to January 2, 1864. Operations in Northwest Arkansas January 16-February 15. Clear Creek and Tomahawk, Ark., January 22. Sylamore Creek and near Burrowsville, Ark., January 23. Cowskin Bottom, Newton County, January 23 (Detachment). Rolling Prairie, Ark., February 4. Near California House February 12 (Detachment). Scout from Lebanon into North Alabama and skirmishes March 17-April 1 (Co. "G"). Scout from Springfield toward Fayetteville, Ark., April 28-May 7 (Cos. "A," "B," "C" and "K"). Bee Creek May 2 (Co. "I"). Spavinaw, Ark., May 13. Mill and Honey Creeks May 30-31. Diamond Grove and Neosho June 3. Scout from Forsyth through Ozark and Douglass Counties June 5-12 (Co. "I"). Diamond Grove Prairie August 1 (Detachment). Operations in Southwest Missouri August 1-28. Rutledge August 4 (Detachment). McDonald County August 5. Cowskin August 5-6. Near Enterprise and Buffalo Creek August 7. Diamond Grove August 21. Fayetteville, Ark., August 28. Carthage September 22 (Detachment). Moreau Botttom, Jefferson City, October 7. Little Blue October 21. Independence October 22. Big Blue, State Line, October 22. Westport October 23. Engagement on the Marmiton or battle of Charlot October 25. Mine Creek, Little Osage River, Marias des Cygnes, October 25. Newtonia October 28. Expedition to Quincy October 29-November 8. Cane Creek October 29-30. Newtonia October 30. Quincy November 1. Near Quincy November 1-2. Hermitage November 2. Expedition from Springfield to Fort Smith, Ark., November 5-16 (Detachment). Cane Hill November 6. Duty at Lebanon, Neosho and Springfield till July, 1865. Mustered out July 17, 1865.

Regiment lost during service 3 Officers and 77 Enlisted men killed and mortally wounded and 1 Officer and 131 Enlisted men by disease. Total 212.

9th REGIMENT CAVALRY

Organized originally as Bowen's Cavalry Battalion, which was designated 9th Cavalry October, 1862, by consolidation with other Companies. Attached to District of Rolla, Dept. of Missouri, to December, 1862. Operations in Boone County November 1-10. Expedition from Rolla to Ozark Mountains and skirmish November 30-December 6 (Co. "H"). Discontinued by consolidation with 10th Missouri Cavalry December 4, 1862. Companies "G" and "H" attached to 3rd Missouri Cavalry December 11, 1862.

9th REGIMENT STATE MILITIA CAVALRY.

Organized at large in Missouri February 12, 1862, to September 20, 1863. Attached to District of Rolla, Dept. of Missouri, to February, 1863. District of North Missouri, Dept. of Missouri, to July, 1865.

SERVICE.—Regiment concentrated at Columbia, Mo., May 15, 1862. Ordered to Jefferson City, Mo. Assigned to duty in District of Rolla, Mo., till April, 1863. Action near Memphis, Mo., July 11, 1862. Brown Springs July 27. Moore's Mills, near Fulton, July 28-29. Kirksville August 6 (Detachment). Pursuit of Poindexter and skirmishes at Grand River, Lee's Ford, Chariton River, Walnut Creek, Compton's Ferry, Switzler's Mills and Yellow Creek August 8-15. Near Stock-

ton August 8 and 11 (Detachments). Muscle Shoals August 13. Moved to Jefferson City and duty there and at Glasgow and Fayette till December. Near Cambridge September 26 (Co. "E"). In Scotland and Boone Counties September 30 (Detachment). Near Columbia October 2 (Cos. "B" and "C"). Sim's Cove, Cedar Creek, October 5 (Cos. "F" and "G"). Fayette October 7 (Detachment). Near New Franklin October 7 (Detachment). Ordered to Rolla, Mo., December 12, and duty there till April, 1863. Ordered to North Missouri and duty on Hannibal & St. Jo Railroad from St. Joseph to Hannibal and on North Missouri Railroad from Macon to St. Charles protecting roads and operating against guerrillas till March, 1864. Rocheport, Mo., June 1, 1863 (Cos. "A" and "B"). Black Fork Hills July 4 (Detachment). Switzler's Mills July 12 (Detachment). Macon February 12, 1864. Chariton County April 11 (Detachment). Operations against Anderson's, Quantrell's, Todd's, Stevens' and other bands of guerrillas in North Missouri till April, 1865. Near Fayette July 1, 1864 (Detachment). Platte City July 3. Clay County July 4. Near Camden Point July 22. Union Mills July 22. Near Fayette August 3. Huntsville August 7 (Detachment). Operations against Price September-October. Fayette September 24 (Detachment). Near Centralia September 28. Princess Shoals, Osage River, Cole County, October 5-6. Booneville October 9. Glasgow October 15. Little Blue October 21. Independence October 22. Near Glasgow January 10, 1865 (Cos. "G" and "H"). Near Columbia February 12 (Co. "F"). Near Sturgeon February 27. Skirmish in the Perche Hills May 5. Duty in North Missouri till July. Mustered out July 13, 1865.

Regiment lost during service 2 Officers and 29 Enlisted men killed and mortally wounded and 1 Officer and 76 Enlisted men by disease. Total 108.

10th REGIMENT CAVALRY.

Organized at Jefferson Barracks, Mo., October, 1862, from 28th Missouri Infantry. Bowen's Battalion assigned as Companies "A," "B," "C" and "D," and six Companies organized for 9th Missouri Cavalry assigned December 17, 1862, as Companies "E," "F," "G" and "H." Attached to District of St. Louis, Mo., to January, 1863. District of Memphis, Tenn., 16th Army Corps, Dept. of Tennessee, to March, 1863. Cavalry Brigade, District of Corinth, 16th Army Corps, to June, 1863. 3rd Brigade, 1st Cavalry Division, 16th Army Corps, to August, 1863. Cavalry Brigade, 15th Army Corps, to December, 1863. Winslow's Cavalry Brigade, 17th Army Corps, and District of Vicksburg to April, 1864. 2nd Brigade, 1st Cavalry Division, 16th Army Corps, to June, 1864. 2nd Brigade, Cavalry Division, Sturgis' Expedition, June, 1864. 2nd Brigade, 1st Cavalry Division, District of West Tennessee, to November, 1864. 1st Brigade, 4th Division, Cavalry Corps, Military Division Mississippi, to December, 1864. 2nd Brigade, Cavalry Division, District of West Tennessee, to February, 1865. 1st Brigade, 4th Division, Cavalry Corps, Military Division Mississippi, to May, 1865. 2nd Brigade, 4th Division, Cavalry Corps, Military Division Mississippi, to June, 1865.

SERVICE.—Moved to Memphis, Tenn., December, 1862. Duty in the District of Memphis, Tenn., till February, 1863. Moved to Corinth, Miss., February 7-15. Actions at Glendale and Tuscumbia, Ala., February 22. Duty in that district till June. Courtney's Plantation April 11. Burnsville, Ala., and Glendale, Miss., April 14. Dodge's Expedition into Northern Alabama April 15-May 8. Barton Station April 16-17. Dickson Station, Great Bear Creek, Cherokee Station, and Lundy's Lane April 17. Dickson's Station April 19. Rock Cut near Tuscumbia April 22. Dickson's Station and Tuscumbia April 23. Leighton April 23. Lundy's Lane April 25. Town Creek April 27. Expedition from Burnesville to Tupelo, Miss., May 2-8. Guntown May 4. Tupelo May 5. Near Vicksburg, Miss., May 18 (Co. "C"). Expedition from Corinth to Florence, Ala., May 26-31. Florence, Ala., May 28. Hamburg Landing, Tenn., May

29-30. Iuka, Miss., July 7. Jackson, Miss., July 29. Jacinto August 13. Expedition from Corinth to Henderson, Tenn., September 11-16. Clark's Creek Church September 13 (Detachment). Yazoo City, Miss., September 27. Expedition from Big Black River to Yazoo City September 27-October 1 (Detachment). Brownsville September 28. Canton September 28. Moore's Ford near Benton September 29. Messenger's Ford October 5. Expedition to Canton October 14-22. Brownsville October 15. Canton Road near Brownsville October 15-16. Treadwell's Plantation near Clinton and Vernon Cross Roads October 16. Bogue Chitto Creek October 17. Robinson's Mill near Livingston October 17. Livingston Road near Clinton October 18. Treadwell's Plantation October 20. Brownsville October 22. Near Yazoo City October 31. Operations about Natchez, Miss., December 1-10. Natchez December 10 (Detachment). Meridian Campaign February 3-March 2, 1864. Near Bolton's Depot and Champion's Hill February 4. Jackson February 5. Morton and Brandon February 7. Morton February 8. Meridian February 9-13. Hillsboro February 10. Meridian February 13-14. Lauderdale Springs February 16. Union February 21-22. Canton February 24. Near Canton February 26. Sharon February 27. Canton February 29. Livingston March 27. Near Mechanicsburg April 20. Ordered to Memphis, Tenn., April 29. Bolivar, Tenn., May 2. Sturgis' Expedition to Guntown, Miss., June 1-13. Rienzi, Miss., June 6. Danville, Miss., June 6. Brice's or Tishamingo Creek near Guntown June 10. Guntown June 24. Smith's Expedition to Tupelo, Miss., July 5-21. Tupelo July 14-15. Old Town Creek July 15. Smith's Expedition to Oxford, Miss., August 1-30. Tallahatchie River August 7-9. Hurricane Creek and Oxford August 9. Tallahatchie River August 10. Oxford August 12. Hurricane Creek August 13-14 and 19. Holly Springs August 27-28. Moved to Little Rock September 2-9. Campaign against Price in Arkansas and Missouri September 17-November 30. Actions at Little Blue October 21. Big Blue and State Line October 22. Westport October 23. Engagement at the Marmiton or battle of Charlot October 25. Osage Mine Creek, Marias des Cygnes, October 25. Rolla November 1. Expedition from Memphis to Moscow November 9-13. A detachment on Grierson's Raid on Mobile & Ohio Railroad December 21, 1864, to January 5, 1865. Verona December 25. Egypt Station December 28, 1864. Regiment at Louisville, Ky., till February, 1865. Moved to Gravelly Springs, Ala., February 5-15, 1865. Wilson's Raid from Chickasaw, Ala., to Macon, Ga., March 22-April 24. Near Montevallo, Ala., March 31. Ebenezer Church near Maplesville April 1. Selma April 2. Columbia, Ga., April 16. Capture of Macon, Ga., April 20. Duty at Macon and in Georgia till June. Mustered out June 20, 1865. (Co. "C" in demonstration on Haines' Bluff April 29-May 2, 1863. Siege of Vicksburg May 18-July 4. Advance on Jackson, Miss., July 5-10. Siege of Jackson July 10-17. Jackson July 29. Expedition to Yazoo City September 27-October 1.)

Regiment lost during service 2 Officers and 52 Enlisted men killed and mortally wounded and 3 Officers and 295 Enlisted men by disease. Total 352.

10th REGIMENT STATE MILITIA CAVALRY.

Organized at Louisiana, Mo., May 5, 1862. Attached to District of St. Louis, Mo., and District of North Missouri, Dept. of Missouri, to February, 1863.

SERVICE.—Guard line of North Missouri Railroad, Headquarters at Louisiana, Mo., and duty in North Missouri operating against Porter till November, 1862. Actions at Brown's Springs July 27, 1862 (Cos. "B," "D"). Morris Mills, near Fulton, July 28 (Cos. "B," "D"). Kirksville August 6 (1 Co.). Auxvasse Creek October 16. Moved to Jefferson City, thence to Rolla and to Pilot Knob December 10-26, 1862. Designation changed to 3rd Missouri State Militia Cavalry February 6, 1863, which see for further service.

11th REGIMENT CAVALRY.

Organized at Benton Barracks and St. Joseph, Mo., March 28 to December 11, 1863. Attached to District of St. Louis, Mo., Dept. of Missouri, to December, 1863. District of Southwest Missouri, Dept. of Missouri, to January, 1864. District of Northeast Arkansas, 7th Army Corps, Dept. of Arkansas, to May, 1864. 3rd Brigade, 2nd Division, 7th Army Corps, to September, 1864. 3rd Brigade, Cavalry Division, 7th Army Corps, to February, 1865. 2nd Brigade, Cavalry Division, 7th Corps, to March, 1865. Separate Cavalry Brigade, Cavalry Division, 7th Army Corps, to July, 1865.

SERVICE.—Duty in District of St. Louis, Mo., till December, 1863. At Springfield and Rolla, Mo., till February, 1864. Expedition from Springfield to Huntsville, Carrollton and Berryville, and skirmish, November 10-18, 1863 (Detachment). Operations in Northeast Arkansas January 1-30, 1864. Martin's Creek January 7. Rolling Prairie January 23 (Co. "B"). At Batesville, Ark., February to April. Expedition from Batesville to Searcy Landing January 30-February 3. Morgan's Mill, Spring River, White County, February 9 (Detachment). Independence, Mo., February 19. Waugh's Farm, near Batesville, February 19. Expedition from Rolla to Batesville, Ark., February 29-March 13. Scout from Batesville to West Point, Grand Glaze and Searcy Landing March 15-21 (Detachment). Expedition from Batesville to Coon Creek, Devil's Fork, Red River, March 24-31. Van Buren County March 25. Scout from Batesville to Fairview March 25-26 (Detachment). Near Cross Roads March 27. Spring River, near Smithville, April 13 (Detachment). Jacksonport April 20. Expedition from Jacksonport to Augusta April 23-24. Near Jacksonport April 24. Ordered to Duvall's Bluff May, 1864, and duty there till October. Scout in Craighead and Lawrence Counties June 25-26 (Co. "M"). Clarendon, St. Charles, June 25-26. Clarendon June 27-29. Scout to Searcy and West Point July 26-28 (Detachment). Des Arc July 26 (Detachment). West Point July 28 (Detachment). Hay Station No. 3 July 30 (Detachment). West Point August 5. Expedition from Little Rock to Little Red River August 6-16. Operations in Central Arkansas, with skirmishes August 9-15. Duvall's Bluff August 21 and 24. Long Prairie August 24. Jones' Hay Station August 24. Duvall's Bluff September 6. Searcy September 13. Expedition from Duvall's Bluff toward Clarendon October 16-17 (Detachment). Brownsville October 30. Duty at Brownsville till February, 1865. Expedition from Brownsville to Augusta January 4-27, 1865 (Detachment). Moved to Little Rock February 4, and duty there till June. Moved to New Orleans, La., June 27-July 3. At Greenville till July 27. Mustered out at Greenville July 27 and discharged at St. Louis August 10, 1865.

Regiment lost during service 2 Officers and 28 Enlisted men killed and mortally wounded and 5 Officers and 181 Enlisted men by disease. Total 216.

11th REGIMENT STATE MILITIA CAVALRY.

Organized in Missouri at large January 1 to April 20, 1862. Assigned to duty in District of North Missouri. Actions at Cherry Grove June 26 and July 1. Near Memphis July 18. Newark August 1 (Detachment). Kirksville August 6 (Detachment). Near Stockton August 8 (Detachment). Consolidated with 2nd Regiment Missouri State Militia Cavalry September 2, 1862, which see.

12th REGIMENT CAVALRY.

Organized at St. Louis, Mo., November 3, 1863, to March 23, 1864. Attached to District of St. Louis, Mo., Dept. Missouri, to July, 1864. 1st Brigade, 1st Cavalry Division, District of West Tennessee, Dept. Tennessee, to November, 1864. 1st Brigade, 5th Division, Cavalry Corps, Military Division Mississippi, to May, 1865. Dept. Missouri, Eastern Division, Powder River Expedition, and District of the Plains to April, 1866.

SERVICE.—Duty at St. Louis, Mo., till June 1, 1864. Ordered to Memphis, Tenn., and duty there till August 1. Smith's Expedition to Oxford, Miss., August 1-30. Holly Springs August 1. Elkshute August 4. Tallahatchie

River August 7-9. Hurricane Creek and Oxford August 9. Abbeville August 13. Hurricane Creek August 13-14 and 19. College Hill, Oxford, August 23. At White's Station till September 30. March to Clifton and Lawrenceburg in pursuit of Forest September 30-October 8. At Clifton till October 27. Nashville Campaign November-December. March to Pulaski, Tenn., October 27-November 6. Expedition to Moscow November 9-13. Shoal Creek November 11. Eastport, Miss., November 10-11. On line of Shoal Creek November 16-20. Lawrenceburg November 22. Campbellville and Lynnville November 24. In front of Columbia November 24-27. Crossing of Duck River November 28. Battle of Nashville December 15-16. Pursuit of Hood December 17-28. Richland Creek December 24. King's Gap, near Pulaski, December 25. At Gravelly Springs, Ala., and Eastport, Miss. Scouting in Northern Mississippi and Alabama till May, 1865. Moved to St. Louis, Mo., May 12-17, thence to Fort Leavenworth, Kan., and to Omaha, Neb. Powder River Expedition against Indians in Nebraska July 1-September 20. Actions with Indians on Powder River September 1-4 and 5. March from Fort Connor to Fort Laramie September 25-October 4. Engaged in frontier duty till April, 1866. Mustered out April 9, 1866.

Regiment lost during service 1 Officer and 35 Enlisted men killed and mortally wounded and 1 Officer and 226 Enlisted men by disease. Total 263.

12th REGIMENT STATE MILITIA CAVALRY.

Organized in Missouri at large December 5, 1861, to May 8, 1862. Attached to Dept. of Missouri and participated in the following service: Expedition from Greenville February 23-25, 1862 (Co. "B"). Mingo Creek, near St. Francisville, February 24 (Co. "B"). Cherry Grove July 1. Greenville July 20 (Cos. "B" and "G"). Greenville July 26. Scout in Southeastern Missouri July 26-29 (Detachment). Bolinger's Mills July 28 (Detachment). Dallas August 24. Crooked Creek, near Dallas, August 24 (1st Battalion). Van Buren October 22. Near Pike Creek and Eleven Points October 25. Pittman's Ferry, Ark., October 27 (Detachment). Scouts about Mingo Swamp February 2-14, 1863. Mingo Swamp February 3. Broken up February 4, 1863.

13th REGIMENT CAVALRY.

Organized at St. Louis, Mo., September, 1864, to February, 1865, from Veterans of Missouri State Militia Regiments. Attached to District of Rolla and Dept. of Missouri to July, 1866.
SERVICE.—At St. Louis, Mo., till September, 1864. Operations against Price September to November. Actions at Glasgow, Mo., October 15. Little Blue October 21. Lexington October 21. Independence October 22. Mine Creek, Little Osage River, Marias des Cygnes, October 25. Carthage October 26. Duty at Rolla till May, 1865. Operations about Stephenson's Mill March 22-23, 1865 (Detachment). Scout from Waynesville March 29-April 2 (Detachment). Scout from Rolla April 21-27 (Co. "M"). Skirmish, Spring Valley, April 23 (Co. "M"). Skirmish near Waynesville May 23 (Detachment). Moved to Fort Larned, Kan., and duty in District of the Plains, operating against Indians, till July, 1866. Mustered out July 3, 1866.

Regiment lost during service 11 Enlisted men killed and mortally wounded and 28 Enlisted men by disease. Total 39.

13th REGIMENT STATE MILITIA CAVALRY.

Organized May 19, 1862, and assigned to duty in the District of Rolla, Mo., Dept. of Missouri, Headquarters at Waynesville, Mo., till February, 1863; operating in Pulaski, Miller, Phelps, Texas, Wright and LaClede Counties. Scout from Waynesville to Big Piney July 6-8, 1862 (Cos. "B" and "F"). Pursuit of Poindexter in Missouri and skirmishes at Grand River, Lee's Ford, Chariton River, Walnut Creek, Compton's Ferry, Switzler's Mills and Yellow Creek, August 8-15 (Co. "D"). Expedition from Waynesville August 29. Caledonia House August 29. Expedition from Eureka September 23-24 (Co. "E"). Booneville October 9. California House

October 18 (Detachment). Designation changed to New 5th Regiment State Militia Cavalry February 2, 1863.

14th REGIMENT CAVALRY.

Organized at St. Louis and Springfield, Mo., November 30, 1864, to May 13, 1865. Attached to District of St. Louis, Mo., to June, 1865. District of the Plains, Dept. of Missouri, to November, 1865.
Duty at St. Louis, Mo., till June, 1865. Scout from Waynesville to Coal Camp Creek May 23-26. Moved to Nebraska, and frontier duty on the Plains till November. Mustered out November 17, 1865.
Lost during service 2 killed and 34 by disease. Total 36.

14th REGIMENT STATE MILITIA CAVALRY.

Organized in Missouri at large March to May, 1862. Attached to District of Southwest Missouri, Dept. Missouri, to March, 1863.
SERVICE.—Action at Neosho May 31, 1862. Near Fayetteville, Ark., July 15. Scout in Polk and Dallas Counties July 19-23 (Cos. "B," "C," "E" and "H"). Ozark August 1-2 (Cos. "D," "F," "G" and "H"). White River, near Forsyth, August 4. Scout from Ozark to Forsyth, and skirmish, August 8-9 (2 Cos.). Mt. Vernon from Ozark to Forsyth August 14-17 (2 Cos.). Mt. Vernon September 19 (1 Co.). Expedition from Ozark toward Yellville, Ark., October 12-16 (Detachment). Mountain Home October 17. Operations about Cassville and Keetsville November 17-18. Battle of Prairie Grove, Ark., December 7. Expedition from Ozark into Marion County, Ark., December 9-15 (Cos. "D," "F," "G" and "H"). Expedition over Boston Mountains to Van Buren December 27-29. Operations against Marmaduke in Missouri December 31, 1862, to January 15, 1863. Fort Lawrence, Beaver Station, January 6, 1863 (2nd Battalion). Defence of Springfield January 8. Disbanded March 3, 1863.

15th REGIMENT CAVALRY.

Organized November 1, 1863, from 7th Regiment Enrolled Militia. Attached to District of Southwest Missouri, Dept. Missouri, to April, 1865. District of North Missouri, Dept. Missouri, to July, 1865.
SERVICE.—Scout and patrol duty in District of Southwest Missouri till April, 1865, and in North Missouri till July, 1865. Actions at Mt. Vernon September 30, 1864; Moreau Bottom, Jefferson City, October 7; Booneville October 9-12; Big Blue or State Line October 22. Engagement at the Marmiton, or Battle of Charlot, October 25. Mine Creek, Little Osage River, Marias des Cygnes, October 25. Newtonia October 28. Affair near James Creek April 27, 1865 (Co. "C"). Mustered out July 1, 1865.
Lost during service 1 Officer and 6 Enlisted men killed and mortally wounded and 1 Officer and 35 Enlisted men by disease. Total 43.

16th REGIMENT CAVALRY.

Organized at Springfield, Mo., November 1, 1863, from 6th Regiment Enrolled Militia. Attached to District of Southwest Missouri, Dept. Missouri, to April, 1865, and to District of North Missouri, Dept. Missouri, to July, 1865.
SERVICE.—Scout and patrol duty in District of Southeastern Missouri till April, 1865, and in North Missouri till July. Actions in Wright County July 22, 1864; Dallas County September 19; Booneville October 9-12; Big Blue or State Line October 22. Engagement at the Marmiton, or Battle of Charlot, October 25. Mine Creek, Little Osage River, Marias des Cygnes, October 25. Big Blue October 31. Skirmishes in Texas County January 9-11, 1865. Scout, Ozark County, February 16-20 (Co. "B"). Scouts from Salem and Licking to Spring River, Ark., and skirmishes, February 23-March 2. Operations about Licking March 7-25. Scouts from Licking April 1-30. Skirmish, Big Gravois, April 22. Scout from Lebanon to Warsaw May 18-26. Mustered out July 1, 1865.
Lost during service 1 Officer and 12 Enlisted men killed and mortally wounded and 1 Officer and 31 Enlisted men by disease. Total 45.

BENTON HUSSARS—CAVALRY BATTALION.

Organized at St. Louis, Mo., September 18-December 23, 1861. Served unattached, Army of the West, to January, 1862. 2nd Division, Army Southwest Missouri, Dept. Missouri, to February, 1862, participating in skirmish at Hunter's Farm, near Belmont, Mo., September 26, 1861. At Bird's Point, Mo., October. Operations about Ironton-Fredericktown October 12-25. Engagement at Fredericktown October 21. Expedition from Bird's Point against Thompson's forces November 2-12. Duty in Southeast Missouri till January, 1862, and in District of Southwest Missouri to February, 1862. Assigned to 5th Missouri Cavalry February 14, 1862, which see.

BERRY'S CAVALRY BATTALION.

Organized in Upper Missouri June to August, 1861. Participated in Siege of Lexington, Mo., September 12-20, 1861. Surrender of Lexington September 20. Mustered out February 1, 1862.

Battalion lost during service 3 killed and 2 by disease. Total 5.

BISHOP'S CAVALRY BATTALION ("BLACK HAWK CAVALRY").

Organized at Henderson and LaClede, Mo., November 14-December 31, 1861. Assigned to duty in Northeast Missouri. Action at Spring Hill October 27 (1 Co.). Expedition to Milford December 15-19. Shawnee Mound or Milford, on Blackwater, December 18. Hudson December 21 (Detachment). Assigned to 7th Missouri Cavalry February 20, 1862, which see.

BLACK HAWK CAVALRY BATTALION.

See Bishop's Cavalry Battalion.

BOONEVILLE STATE MILITIA CAVALRY BATTALION ("EPSTEIN'S").

Organized at Booneville March 24, 1862. Assigned to duty at Booneville. Attack on Booneville September 14, 1861. Operating against guerrillas in Cooper, Moniteau, Saline and Cooper Counties till May, 1862. Operations in Saline County March 7-10, 1862. Near Marshall March 16 (Co. "A"). Skirmish on Little Sni April 1. Organized as 13th Missouri State Militia Cavalry May 19, 1862. Changed to 5th Missouri State Militia Cavalry February 12, 1863. See these Regiments.

BOWEN'S CAVALRY BATTALION.

Organized at Rolla, Mo., July 10-October 10, 1861. Attached to Dept. of Missouri to January, 1862. Unattached, Army Southwest Missouri, Dept. Missouri, and District of Southwest Missouri, Dept. Missouri, to October, 1862. 1st Brigade, 3rd Division, Army Frontier, Dept. Missouri, to December, 1862.

SERVICE.—Ordered to join Fremont October 10, 1861. Action at Wet Glaize October 13. Linn Creek October 14. Return to Rolla November 11, and duty there till January 8, 1862. Action at Salem December 3, 1861. Expedition through the Current Hills December 5-9. March to Lebanon, Mo., January 25-29, 1862. Advance on Springfield, Mo., February 10-15. Near Springfield February 12. Springfield February 13-14. Crane Creek February 14. Flat Creek February 15. Keytesville and Sugar Creek, Ark., February 17. Hunnewell and Capture of Bentonville February 19. Battle of Pea Ridge, Ark., March 6-8. Leetown March 7. Elkhorn Tavern March 8. Mountain Grove March 9. Expedition to Huntsville April 6. March to Batesville, thence to Helena, Ark., April 8-July 14. Talbot's Ferry, White River, April 19. Sylamore May 28-29. Reusey's Ferry June 5. Waddell's Farm June 12. Hill's Plantation, Cache River, July 7. Expedition from Helena down Mississippi and up the Yazoo River August 16-27. Tallulah August 18. Greenville August 23. Bolivar August 25. Moved to St. Genevieve, Mo., thence to Rolla, Mo. Assigned to 9th Missouri Cavalry October 1, 1862, and to 10th Missouri Cavalry December 4, 1862.

CASS COUNTY HOME GUARD CAVALRY BATTALION.

Organized in Cass County June-August, 1861, for duty in Cass and adjoining Counties and to protect bridges. Skirmish at Parkersville, Mo., July 17-19, 1861; Harrisonville July 27; Jonesborough August 21-22; Old Randolph September 14; Bush Bridge Road October 14; Butler November 20; Grand River November 30; Dayton December 23; Wadesburg December 24. Mustered out February 28, 1862.

Lost during service 1 Officer and 5 Enlisted men killed and mortally wounded and 10 Enlisted men by disease. Total 16.

COMPANY "A" 1st U. S. RESERVE CORPS CAVALRY.

Organized at St. Louis, Mo., May 16, 1861. Served as mounted orderlies to Gen. Lyon June 11 to August, 1861. Booneville June 17. Carthage July 5. Expedition to Fulton July 14-18. Martinsburg July 18. Battle of Wilson's Creek August 10. Moved to St. Louis, Mo., and mustered out August 18, 1861.

FREMONT'S BODY GUARD.

Organized at Cincinnati, Ohio, and St. Louis, Mo., August, 1861. Attached to Headquarters Western Department, and participated in Fremont's Campaign in Missouri and against Springfield September to November, 1861. Advance on Springfield October 8-25. Wet Glaze October 13. Linn Creek October 14 and 16. Zagony's charge at Springfield October 25, against a force of 2,000 rebels, routing them, and killing and capturing almost as many as the Battalion numbered. Mustered out by order of the Secretary of War November 30, 1861.

Battalion lost during service 16 Enlisted men killed and mortally wounded and 2 Enlisted men by disease. Total 18.

FREMONT HUSSARS.

Organized at St. Louis, Mo., September, 1861. Attached to Fremont's Army of the West to November, 1861. Unattached, Army of Southwest Missouri, Dept. Missouri, to February, 1862.

SERVICE.—Expedition against Green's forces September 6-14, 1861. Fremont's Campaign against Springfield, Mo., September to November. Action at Little Santa Fe November 6. At Rolla, Mo., to December 29. Black Walnut Creek, Sedalia, November 29. Advance to Springfield and the Southwest December 29, 1861, to February 14, 1862. Assigned to 2nd Missouri Cavalry January 9, 1862, and to 4th Missouri Cavalry February 14, 1862.

FREMONT RANGERS.

Organized at Cape Girardeau, Mo., August, 1861. Mustered out January 25, 1862.

HAWKINS' CAVALRY COMPANY.

Organized September, 1861. Operations about Ironton and Fredericktown, Mo., October 12-25, 1861. Skirmish near Fredericktown October 17. Action at Fredericktown October 21. Duty at Pilot Knob, Mo., till February, 1862. Assigned to 6th Missouri Cavalry February 14, 1862.

HOLLAN HORSE U. S. RESERVE CORPS.

Organized at St. Louis and Warrenton, Mo., October 14, 1861, to February 1, 1862. Duty at Warrenton and St. Louis till February, 1862. Assigned to 4th and 5th Regiments, Missouri Cavalry, February, 1862.

IRISH DRAGOONS—NAUGHTON'S CAVALRY COMPANY.

Organized at Jefferson City by authority of Gen Fremont September 11, 1861, to be attached to 23rd Illinois Irish Brigade. Expedition to Lexington October 5-16. Lexington October 16. Johnstown October 24. Assigned to 3rd Missouri Cavalry as Company "L" and to 5th Iowa Cavalry, "Curtis Horse," as Company "L," November, 1861.

LORING'S CAVALRY COMPANY.

Operations in Northeast Missouri August 30-September 7, 1861. Action at Shelbina September 4. Expedition to Paris, Palmyra and Hannibal.

McFADDEN'S STATE MILITIA CAVALRY COMPANY.

Duty at Warrenton, Mo.

MOUNTAIN RANGERS.

Reconnoissance from Springfield to Pea Ridge February 23-24, 1862. (See 14th Missouri State Militia Cavalry.)

OSAGE RIFLES.

Organized at St. Louis, Mo., November 1, 1861. Assigned to "Curtis Horse," 5th Iowa Cavalry, as Company "M," December, 1861.

SCHOFIELD'S HUSSARS.

See 13th Missouri State Militia Cavalry, Company "I."

SOBOLESKI'S INDEPENDENT COMPANY RANGERS.

Organized at Benton Barracks, Mo., November and December, 1861. Mustered out January 24, 1862.

STEWART'S CAVALRY BATTALION.

Organized at St. Louis, Mo., September to November, 1861. Duty in District of Southeast Missouri till February, 1862. Mustered out February 2, 1862.

WHITE'S CAVALRY BATTALION.

Organized September, 1861. Fremont's Campaign in Missouri September to November, 1861. Action at Springfield, Mo., October 25. (See 2nd Missouri State Militia Cavalry.)

BACKOFF'S BATTALION LIGHT ARTILLERY.

Organized at St. Louis, Mo., April 22 to May 18, 1861. Attached to 2nd Brigade, Lyon's Army of the West. Moved to Springfield, Mo., June 16-27. Engagement at Carthage July 5. Dug Springs August 2. Expedition toward Fayette, Ark., August 3-5. Battle of Wilson's Creek August 10. Retreat to Rolla, thence to St. Louis August 11-21. Mustered out September 4, 1861.

Battery lost during service 10 Enlisted men killed and mortally wounded and 2 Enlisted men by disease. Total 12.

CAVENDER'S BATTALION LIGHT ARTILLERY

(See Batteries "D," "H" and "K," 1st Missouri Light Artillery.)

1st BATTERY STATE MILITIA LIGHT ARTILLERY ("WASCHMAN'S").

Organized at Independence, Mo., May 6, 1862. Attached to District of Central Missouri, Dept. of Missouri. Duty at Independence and Sedalia, Mo., till July, 1862. Campaign against Porter's and Poindexter's guerrillas July 20-September 10. Pursuit of Poindexter with skirmishes at Switzler's Mills, Little Compton or Compton's Ferry on Grand River and on Yellow Creek on the Mussel Fork of Chariton River August 8-15. Expedition to Eureka, Boone County, September 23-24. At Independence and Sedalia till January, 1864. Operations against Marmaduke April 17-May 2, 1863. Merrill's Crossing and Dug Fork near Jonesboro September 12. Marshall, Arrow Rock, Blackwater, October 13. Operations against Shelby September 27-October 26. Disbanded January 17, 1864.

Battery lost during service 4 Enlisted men killed and mortally wounded and 1 Officer and 6 Enlisted men by disease. Total 11.

1st REGIMENT LIGHT ARTILLERY.

Organized at St. Louis, Mo., from 1st Missouri Infantry, September 1, 1861.

BATTERY "A," 1st REGIMENT LIGHT ARTILLERY.

Attached to Dept. of Missouri, to January, 1862. 2nd Brigade, Army of Southeast Missouri, to March, 1862. Steele's Comand, Army of Southeast Missouri, to May, 1862. Artillery, 1st Division, Army of Southwest Missouri, to July, 1862. District of Eastern Arkansas, Dept. of Missouri, to October, 1862. District of Southeast Missouri, Dept. of Missouri, to January, 1863. Artillery, 13th Division, 13th Army Corps, Dept. of the Tennessee, to March, 1863. Artillery, 12th Division, 13th Army Corps, to July, 1863. Artillery, 3rd Division, 13th Army Corps, Dept. of the Tennessee, to August, 1863, and Dept. of the Gulf to July, 1864. Defences of New Orleans, La., Dept. of the Gulf, to August, 1864. Reserve Artillery, Dept. of the Gulf, to April, 1865. Hawkins' Colored Division, Military Division West Mississippi, to June, 1865. Dept. of Alabama to August, 1865.

SERVICE.—Operations about Ironton and Fredericktown, Mo., October 12-21, 1861. Engagement at Fredericktown-Ironton February 21. Duty in Southeast Missouri till March, 1862. Ordered to Pilot Knob, thence march to Reeve's Station March 23-27. Moved to Pocohontas, Ark., April 5-11, thence to Jacksonport May 3, and to Batesville March 24. March to Augusta June 20-July 4, thence to Clarksville and Helena, Ark., July 5-14. Action at Hill's Plantation, Cache River, July 7. Duty at Helena, Ark., to October 3. Moved to Pilot Knob, Mo., October 3. Operations in Southeast Missouri till December. Moved to St. Louis, Mo., thence to Columbus, Ky., December 19-25, and to Helena, Ark., January 5-7, 1863. Expedition to Duvall's Bluff, Ark., January 16-20. Expedition to Yazoo Pass, and operations against Fort Pemberton and Greenwood February 24-April 8. Moved to Milliken's Bend, La., April 14. Movement on Bruinsburg and turning Grand Gulf April 25-30. Battle of Thompson's Hill, Port Gibson, Miss., May 1. Fourteen Mile Creek May 12. Battle of Champion's Hill May 16. Big Black River May 17. Siege of Vicksburg, Miss., May 18-July 4. Assaults on Vicksburg May 19 and 22. Advance on Jackson, Miss., July 5-10. Siege of Jackson July 10-17. Ordered to New Orleans, La., August 6, thence to Carrollton, and duty there till October. Western Louisiana Campaign October 3-November 30. Bayou Cortableaux October 21. Carrion Crow Bayou November 3. At New Iberia till December 17. Moved to New Orleans, thence to Madisonville January 7, 1864. Red River Campaign May 2-20. Moved to Alexandria, La., May 2.

Attached to Army of the West and Dept. of Missouri, Retreat to Morganza May 13-20. Expedition from Morganza to the Atchafalaya River May 30-June 6. Moved to Carrollton June. Duty there and in the Defences of New Orleans till April, 1865. Ordered from Greenville, La., to Mobile, Ala., April 19. Duty there and in Dept. of Alabama till August. Mustered out August 23, 1865.

BATTERY "B," 1st REGIMENT LIGHT ARTILLERY.

Organized at St. Louis, Mo., September 1, 1861. Attached to Dept. of Missouri to January, 1862. 2nd Brigade, Army Southwest Missouri, January, 1862. Disbanded January, 1862.

Battery reorganized from Welfley's Battery Missouri Light Artillery December, 1862. Attached to Artillery, 2nd Division, Army of Southeast Missouri, Dept. of Missouri, to March, 1863. Artillery, District of Southeast Missouri, to June, 1863. Artillery, 2nd Brigade, Herron's Division, 13th Army Corps, Army of the Tennessee, to July, 1863. Artillery, 2nd Division, 13th Army Corps, Army of the Tennessee, to August, 1863, and Army of the Gulf to June, 1864. Artillery, U. S. Forces, Texas, to July, 1864. Defences of New Orleans, La., to August, 1864. Reserve Artillery, Dept. of the Gulf, to September, 1864.

SERVICE.—Duty in Southeast Missouri till June, 1863. Operations against Marmaduke April 17-May 2. Cape Girardeau April 26. Castor River, near Bloomfield, April 29. Bloomfield April 30. Chalk Bluffs, St. Francis River, April 30-May 1. Moved to Vicksburg, Miss., June 2-10. Siege of Vicksburg, Miss., June 11-July 4. Expedition to Yazoo City July 12-21. Capture of Yazoo City July 14. Moved to Port Hudson, La., July 23, thence to Carrollton, La., August 12-13, and duty there till September 5. Expedition to Morganza September 5-October 11. Atchafalaya River September 7. Sterling's Plantation September 29. At Morganza till October 11. Moved to New Orleans, La., October 11. Expedition to Brazos Santiago, Texas., October 27-December 2. Expedition to Brownsville November 4-9. Occupation of Brownsville November 6. Duty at Brownsville till July, 1864. Moved to New Orleans, La., July 24-August 7. Reserve Artillery

43

at New Orleans till September, 1864. Consolidated with Batteries "A," "F" and "G," 1st Missouri Light Artillery, September 13, 1864.

BATTERY "C," 1st REGIMENT LIGHT ARTILLERY.

Original Battery "C" disbanded September, 1861. Reorganized from Mann's Independent Battery Missouri Light Artillery August, 1862. Attached to Artillery, District of Memphis, Tenn., Dept. Tennessee, to September, 1862. Artillery, 4th Division, District of Jackson, Tenn., to November, 1862. Artillery, 4th Division, Left Wing 10th Army Corps (Old), Dept. of the Tennessee, to December, 1862. 2nd Brigade, 6th Division, 16th Army Corps, to January, 1863. 2nd Brigade, 6th Division, 17th Army Corps, to September, 1863. Artillery, 1st Division, 17th Army Corps, to April, 1864. Artillery, 4th Division, 17th Army Corps, to November, 1864. Artillery Reserve, Nashville, Tenn., Dept. Cumberland, to July, 1865.

SERVICE.—Duty at Memphis, Tenn., till September 6, 1862. March to Bolivar, Tenn., September 6-14, and duty there till October 4. Expedition from Bolivar to Grand Junction and LaGrange, and skirmishes, September 20-22. Battle of Metamora, Hatchie River, October 5. Grant's Central Mississippi Campaign October 31, 1862, to January 10, 1863. Moved to Memphis, Tenn., thence to Lake Providence, La., January 18, 1863, and duty there till April. Movement on Bruinsburg and turning Grand Gulf April 25-30. Battle of Port Gibson May 1 (Reserve). Battle of Raymond May 12. Jackson May 14. Champion's Hill May 16. Big Black River May 17. Siege of Vicksburg, Miss., May 18-July 4. Assaults on Vicksburg May 19 and 22. Expedition to Mechanicsburg May 26-June 4. Surrender of Vicksburg July 4. Advance on Jackson, Miss., July 5-10. At Vicksburg till April, 1864. Expedition to Monroe, La., August 20-September 2, 1863. Expedition to Canton October 14-20. Meridian Campaign February 3-March 2, 1864. Moved to Clifton, Tenn., thence march to Ackworth, Ga., via Huntsville and Decatur, Ala., and Rome, Ga., April 21-June 8. Atlanta (Ga.) Campaign June 8-September 8. Assigned to duty at Allatoona, Marietta and Kenesaw Mountain till October. Operations against Hood till November. Ordered to Nashville, Tenn., and duty there till July, 1865. Mustered out July 11, 1865.

BATTERY "D," 1st REGIMENT LIGHT ARTILLERY.

Attached to 3rd Brigade, 2nd Division, District of Cairo, February, 1862. 3rd Brigade, 2nd Division, District of West Tennessee, Army of the Tennessee, to April, 1862. Artillery, 2nd Division, Army Tennessee, to July, 1862. Artillery, 2nd Division, District of Corinth, Miss., to November, 1862. Artillery, District of Corinth, Miss., 13th Army Corps (Old), Dept. of the Tennessee, to December, 1862. Artillery, District of Corinth, Miss., 17th Army Corps, to January, 1863. Artillery, District of Corinth, 16th Army Corps, to March, 1863. Artillery, 2nd Division, 16th Army Corps, to September, 1863. Artillery, 4th Division, 15th Army Corps, to April, 1864. Artillery Reserve, Huntsville, Ala., Dept. of the Cumberland, to May, 1864. Artillery, 3rd Division, 15th Army Corps, to September, 1864. Artillery, Huntsville, Ala., Dept. of the Cumberland, to April, 1865.

SERVICE.—Duty in the Dept. of Missouri till February, 1862. Operations against Fort Henry, Tenn., February 2-6. Investment and capture of Fort Donelson, Tenn., February 12-16. Expedition to Clarksville, Tenn., February 19-March 6. Moved to Pittsburg Landing, Tenn., March 6-7. Battle of Shiloh, Tenn., April 6-7. Advance on and siege of Corinth, Miss., April 29-May 30. Duty at Corinth till October. Battle of Corinth October 3-4. Pursuit to Hatchie River October 5-12. Duty at Corinth till April, 1863. Dodge's Expedition to Northern Alabama April 15-May 8. Rock Cut, near Tuscumbia, April 22. Tuscumbia April 23. Town Creek April 28. Duty at Corinth till September. March with 15th Army Corps to Chattanooga, Tenn., October-November. Operations on Memphis & Charleston Railroad in Alabama October 20-29. Battles of Chattanooga November 23-25;

Tunnel Hill November 23-24; Mission Ridge November 25. March to relief of Knoxville November 28-December 8. Moved to Huntsville, Ala., and duty there till October, 1864. Decatur, Ala., October 27-29. Garrison duty at Huntsville, Ala., till April, 1865. Consolidated with Battery "C" April 11, 1865.

BATTERY "E," 1st REGIMENT LIGHT ARTILLERY ("COLE'S").

Left St. Louis, Mo., for Jefferson City, Mo., September 29, 1861. Attached to Army of the West and Dept. of Missouri, to January, 1862. District of Central Missouri, Dept. Missouri, to June, 1862. District of Southwest Missouri, Dept. Missouri, to October, 1862. 2nd Brigade, 3rd Division, Army Frontier, Dept. Missouri, to June, 1863. 1st Brigade, Herron's Division, 13th Army Corps, Army Tennessee, to July, 1863. Artillery, 2nd Division, 13th Army Corps, Army Tennessee, to August, 1863, and Dept. of the Gulf, to June, 1864.

SERVICE.—Fremont's advance on Springfield, Mo., October and November, 1861. Moved to Sedalia November 28. March to Otterville, thence to Lexington, Mo., and duty there February 11 to June 3, 1862. Operations about Miami and Waverly May 25-28. Near Waverly May 26. Moved to Sedalia June 3, and duty there till July 29. Moved to Rolla July 29, and return to Sedalia August 18. Moved to Springfield, Mo., August 29-September 4. Battle of Prairie Grove, Ark., December 7. Expedition over Boston Mountains to Van Buren December 27-29. Moved to Springfield, Mo., arriving there February 15, 1863. Duty there and at Rolla till April. Operations against Marmaduke April 17-May 2. Cape Girardeau April 26. Castor River near Bloomfield April 29. Bloomfield April 30. Chalk Bluffs, St. Francis River, April 30-May 1. Moved to St. Louis, May 9, thence to Vicksburg, Miss., June 4-16. Siege of Vicksburg June 16-July 4. Expedition to Yazoo City July 12-22. Capture of Yazoo City July 14. Moved to Port Hudson, La., July 24, thence to Carrollton, La., August 16. Expedition to Morganza September 5-12. Atchafalaya River September 9-10. Sterling's Farm September 12 and September 29. Moved to New Orleans, La., October 11. Expedition to Rio Grande, Texas, October 27-December 2. Duty at Du Crow's Point and Brownsville till June, 1864. Mustered out June, 1864.

BATTERY "E," 1st ARTILLERY REORGANIZED.

Reorganized September 14, 1864, from Segebarth's Battery "C," Pennsylvania Artillery, Mississippi Marine Brigade. Attached to Artillery Post and District of Vicksburg, Miss., to November, 1864. Reserve Artillery, District of Vicksburg, Miss., to January, 1865. Duty at Vicksburg and Natchez, Miss., till January, 1865. Mustered out January 1, 1865.

BATTERY "F," 1st REGIMENT LIGHT ARTILLERY, ("MURPHEY'S").

to January, 1862. District of Central Missouri to June, 1862. District of Southwest Missouri, Dept. Missouri, to October, 1862. 2nd Brigade, 2nd Division, Army of the Frontier, Dept. Missouri, to June, 1863. 1st Brigade, Herron's Division, 13th Army Corps, Army Tennessee, to July, 1863. Artillery, 2nd Division, 13th Army Corps, to August, 1863. 1st Brigade, 2nd Division, 13th Army Corps, Dept. of the Gulf, to September, 1863. Artillery, 2nd Division, 13th Army Corps, Dept. Gulf, to February, 1864. Artillery, 4th Division, 13th Army Corps, to June, 1864. Defences New Orleans, La., to August, 1864. Reserve Artillery, Dept. Gulf, to December, 1864. Distrist Southern Alabama, to February, 1865. 1st Brigade, 3rd Division, 13th Army Corps, Military Division West Mississippi, to August, 1865.

SERVICE.—Duty at St. Louis and Clinton, Mo., till March, 1862, and in Central District of Missouri till June. Expedition to Milford, Mo., December 15-18, 1861. Shawnee Mound, Milford, December 18. Ordered to Springfield, Mo., June 3, 1862. Moved to Jefferson City August 16, to Sedalia August 18, and to Springfield August 26. Action at Lone Jack August 16. Schofield's

Campaign in Southwest Missouri October, 1862, to January, 1863. Occupation of Newtonia October 4, 1862. Battle of Prairie Grove, Ark., December 7. Expedition over Boston Mountains to Van Buren, Ark., December 27-29. Duty at Springfield, Rolla, and other points in Southwest Missouri till April, 1863. Moved to St. Louis, Mo., and duty there till June. Moved to Vicksburg, Miss., June 3-16. Siege of Vicksburg, Miss., June 16-July 4. Expedition to Yazoo City July 12-22. Capture of Yazoo City July 14. Moved to Port Hudson, La., July 24, thence to Carrollton August 16. Expedition to the Rio Grande, Texas, October 24-December 2. Capture of Mustang Island November 17. Fort Esperanza November 27-30. Reconnoissance on Mattagorda Island January 21, 1864. Duty at Mattagorda Island till June, 1864. Moved to New Orleans, La., and duty there till December. Duty in District of Southern Alabama till March, 1865. Campaign against Mobile and its defences March 17-April 12. Siege of Spanish Fort and Fort Blakely March 26-April 8. Fort Blakely April 9. Capture of Mobile April 12. Duty at Mobile and in District of Alabama till August. Mustered out August 11, 1865.

BATTERY "G," 1st REGIMENT LIGHT ARTILLERY ("HESCOCK'S").

Attached to Army of the West and Dept. of Missouri, to March, 1862. Artillery, 3rd Division, Army of Mississippi, to April, 1862. Artillery, 1st Division, Army Mississippi, to June, 1862. Artillery, 5th Division, Army Mississippi, to September, 1862. Artillery, 11th Division, Army Ohio, September, 1862. Artillery, 11th Division, 3rd Corps, Army Ohio, to November, 1862. 2nd Brigade, 3rd Division, Right Wing 14th Army Corps, Dept. of the Cumberland, to January, 1863. Artillery, 3rd Division, 20th Army Corps, Army Cumberland, to October, 1863. Artillery, 2nd Division, 4th Army Corps, Army Cumberland, to April, 1864. Artillery Chattanooga, Tenn., Dept. Cumberland, to November, 1864. 1st Brigade, 1st Separate Division, District of the Etowah, Dept. Cumberland, to July, 1865.

SERVICE.—Fremont's Campaign in Missouri October-November, 1861. Ordered to Commerce, Mo., February, 1862. Operations against New Madrid, Mo., and Island No. 10, Mississippi River, February 28-April 8. Expedition to Fort Pillow, Tenn., April 13-17. Moved to Hamburg Landing, Tenn., April 18-22. Advance on and siege of Corinth, Miss., April 29-May 30. Actions at Farmington, Miss., May 3 and 9. Occupation of Corinth and pursuit to Booneville May 30-June 12. Moved to Cincinnati, Ohio, August 26-September 4, thence to Louisville, Ky., September 12-19. Pursuit of Bragg into Kentucky October 1-16. Battle of Perryville, Ky., October 8. March to Nashville, Tenn., October 16-November 7, and duty there till December 26. Advance on Murfreesboro December 26-30. Battle of Stone's River December 30-31, 1862, and January 1-3, 1863. Duty at Murfreesboro till June. Expedition toward Columbia March 4-14. Middle Tennessee or Tullahoma Campaign June 23-July 7. Occupation of Middle Tennessee till August 16. Passage of Cumberland Mountains and Tennessee River and Chickamauga (Ga.) Campaign August 16-September 22. Battle of Chickamauga, Ga., September 19-20. Siege of Chattanooga, Tenn., September 24-November 23. Battles of Chattanooga November 23-25. Post and garrison duty at Chattanooga, Tenn., till July, 1865. Mustered out July 28, 1865.

BATTERY "H," 1st REGIMENT LIGHT ARTILLERY.

Attached to Dept. Missouri, to February, 1862. 3rd Brigade, 2nd Division, Dist. Cairo, to March, 1862. 3rd Brigade, 2nd Division, District of West Tennessee, and Army of the Tennessee, to April, 1862. Artillery, 2nd Division, Army Tennessee, to July, 1862. Artillery, 2nd Division, District of Corinth Miss., to November, 1862. Artillery, District of Corinth, 13th Army Corps (Old), Dept. Tennessee, to December, 1862. Artillery, District of Corinth, 17th Army Corps, to January, 1863. Artillery, District of Corinth, 16th Army Corps, to March, 1863. Artillery, 2nd Division, 16th Army Corps, to Sep-

tember, 1864. Artillery Brigade, 15th Army Corps, to June, 1865.

SERVICE.—Duty in Dept. of Missouri till February, 1862. Reconnoissance toward Fort Henry, Tenn., January 31-February 2. Capture of Fort Henry February 6. Investment and capture of Fort Donelson, Tenn., February 12-16. Expedition to Clarksville and Nashville, Tenn., February 22-March 6. Move to Pittsburg Landing, Tenn. Battle of Shiloh, Tenn., April 6-7. Advance on and siege of Corinth, Miss., April 29-May 30. Occupation of Corinth May 30, and pursuit to Booneville May 31-June 6. Duty at Corinth till October. Battle of Corinth October 3-4. Pursuit to Hatchie River October 5-12. Duty at Corinth till April, 1863. Dodge's Expedition to Northern Alabama April 15-May 8. Rock Cut, near Tuscumbia, April 22. Tuscumbia April 23. Town Creek April 28. Expedition to Tupelo, Miss., May 2-8. King's Creek, near Tupelo, May 5. At Corinth, Moscow and Lagrange till October. March to Pulaski, Tenn., October 30-November 11, and duty there till March, 1864. At Prospect, Tenn., till April. Atlanta (Ga.) Campaign May 1-September 8. Sugar Valley May 9. Battle of Resaca May 13-14. Ley's Ferry, Oostenaula River May 15. Rome Cross Roads May 16. Battles about Dallas May 25-June 5. Operations about Marietta and against Kenesaw Mountain June 10-July 2. Assault on Kenesaw June 27. Ruff's Mill July 3-4. Chattahoochie River July 5-7. Battle of Atlanta July 22. Siege of Atlanta July 22-August 25. Flank movement on Jonesboro August 25-30. Battle of Jonesboro August 31-September 1. Lovejoy Station September 2-6. Operations against Hood in North Georgia and North Alabama September 29-November 3. Reconnoissance on Cave Springs Road near Rome October 12-13. March to the sea November 15-December 10. Ogeechee Canal December 9. Siege of Savannah December 10-21. Campaign of the Carolinas January to April, 1865. Salkehatchie Swamps, S. C., February 2-5. South Edisto River February 9. North Edisto River February 12-13. Columbia February 15-17. Little Cohora Creek, N. C., March 16. Battle of Bentonville, N. C., March 19-21. Mill Creek March 22. Occupation of Goldsboro March 24. Advance on Raleigh April 10-14. Occupation of Raleigh April 14. Bennett's House April 26. Surrender of Johnston and his army. March to Washington, D. C., via Richmond, Va., April 29-May 20. Grand Review May 24. Moved to Louisville, Ky., Mustered out June 16, 1865.

BATTERY "I," 1st REGIMENT LIGHT ARTILLERY.

Original Battery disbanded January, 1862, having served at St. Louis, Mo. Battery reorganized August, 1862, from Buell's Independent Battery Light Artillery. Attached to Artillery, District of Corinth, Miss., Dept. Tennessee, to November, 1862. Artillery, District of Corinth, Miss., 13th Army Corps (Old), Dept. Tennessee, to December, 1862. Artillery, District of Corinth, 17th Army Corps, to January, 1863. Artillery, District of Corinth, 16th Army Corps, to March, 1863. Artillery, 2nd Division, 16th Army Corps, to May, 1864. District of Nashville, Tenn., Dept. of the Cumberland, to June, 1865.

SERVICE.—Duty at Corinth, Miss., till October, 1862. Battle of Corinth October 3-4. Pursuit to Ripley October 5-12. Duty at Corinth till April, 1863. Bear Creek December 9, 1862. Raid from Corinth to Tupelo December 13-19. Tallahatchie River January 17, 1863. Dodge's Expedition to Northern Alabama April 15-May 8. Dickson's Station, Lundy's Lane and Great Bear Creek April 17. Rock Cut, near Tuscumbia, April 22. Tuscumbia April 23. Town Creek April 28. Expedition from Pocahontas to New Albany and Ripley, Miss., June 12-14. Operations in Northeast Mississippi June 12-22 (Section). Operations in North Mississippi and West Tennessee against Chalmers October 4-17. Salem October 8. Ingraham's Mills near Byhalia October 12. Wyatt's, Tallahatchie River, October 13. Moved to Pulaski, Tenn., October 30-November 12, and duty along Nashville & Decatur Railroad, and at Decatur till April,

1864. Atlanta (Ga.) Campaign May 1-22. Demonstrations on Resaca May 5-13. Sugar Valley May 9. Battle of Resaca May 13-14. Ley's Ferry, Oostenaula River, May 14-15. Rome Cross Roads May 16. Relieved May 22, and ordered to Nashville, Tenn. Garrison duty there till June, 1865. Battle of Nashville December 15-16, 1864 (Reserve). Mustered out June 30, 1865.

BATTERY "K," 1st REGIMENT LIGHT ARTILLERY.

Attached to Dept. of Missouri, to February, 1862. 3rd Brigade, 2nd Division, District of Cairo, Ill., February, 1862. 3rd Brigade, 2nd Division, District of West Tennessee, Army of the Tennessee, to April, 1862. Artillery, 2nd Division, Army Tennessee, to July, 1862. Artillery, District of Corinth, Miss., to November, 1862. Artillery, District of Corinth, 13th Army Corps (Old), Dept. of the Tennessee, to December, 1862. Artillery, District of Corinth, Miss., 17th Army Corps, to January, 1863. Artillery, District of Jackson, Tenn., 16th Army Corps, to March, 1863. Artillery, 1st Division, 16th Army Corps, to July, 1863. Artillery, 13th Division, 16th Army Corps, District of Eastern Arkansas, to August, 1863. Artillery, 3rd Division, Arkansas Expedition, to January, 1864. Artillery, 3rd Division, 7th Army Corps, Dept. of Arkansas, to May, 1864. Artillery, 2nd Division, 7th Army Corps, to February, 1865. Artillery, 1st Division, 7th Army Corps, to August, 1865.

SERVICE.—Duty in the Dept. of Missouri till February, 1862. Reconnoissance toward Fort Henry, Tenn., January 31-February 2. Capture of Fort Henry February 6. Investment and capture of Fort Donelson, Tenn., February 12-16. Expedition to Clarksville and Nashville, Tenn., February 22-March 6. Moved to Pittsburg Landing, Tenn. Battle of Shiloh, Tenn., April 6-7. Advance on and siege of Corinth, Miss., April 29-May 30. Occupation of Corinth May 30 and pursuit to Booneville May 30-June 6. Duty at Corinth till October. Battle of Corinth October 3-4. Pursuit to Ripley October 5-12. Duty at Corinth till January, 1863, and in the District of Jackson, Tenn., till June, 1863. Ordered to Helena, Ark. Repulse of Holmes' attack on Helena July 4. Steele's Expedition against Little Rock, Ark., August 1-September 10. Bayou Fourche and capture of Little Rock September 10. Garrison duty at Little Rock till August, 1865. Operations against Shelby north of the Arkansas River May 13-31, 1864. Mustered out August 4, 1865.

BATTERY "L," 1st REGIMENT LIGHT ARTILLERY.

Original Battery on duty at St. Louis, Mo., till January, 1862, when disbanded. Battery reorganized October, 1862, by assignment of Battery "A," Schofield's Light Artillery. Attached to 1st Brigade, 3rd Division, Army of the Frontier, Dept. of Missouri, to June, 1863. District of St. Louis, Mo., Dept. Missouri, June, 1863. District of Rolla, Dept. of Missouri, to December, 1863. District of Southwest Missouri, Dept. Missouri, to January, 1864. District of Central Missouri, Dept. Missouri, to April, 1865. District North Missouri, Dept. Missouri, to July, 1865.

SERVICE.—Ordered to join Gen. Herron October 11, 1862. March to Cassville October 11-14. Expedition to Cross Hollows, Ark., over Boston Mountains October 17-24. March to Wilson's Creek November 4-22. Forced march to relief of Gen. Blount December 3-6. Battle of Prairie Grove, Ark., December 7. Expedition over Boston Mountains to Van Buren December 27-29. At various points in Missouri till March, 1863. At Lake Springs and Rolla, Mo., till July. Moved to Houston July 14. Scout from Houston to Spring River Mills and skirmish August 6-11. Duty in District of Rolla till December, 1863, and at Springfield, Mo., District of Southwest Missouri, till January, 1864. Operations in Northwest Arkansas January 16-February 15. Duty at Springfield, Mo., till June, and at Warrensburg, Mo., till August. At Springfield till June, 1865. Ordered to St. Louis, Mo., and mustered out July 20, 1865.

BATTERY "M," 1st REGIMENT LIGHT ARTILLERY.

Attached to Dept. Missouri to March, 1862. Artillery,

5th Division, Army of Mississippi, to April, 1862. Artillery Division, Army Mississippi, to June, 1862. Artillery, 1st Division, Army Mississippi, to September, 1862. Artillery, 3rd Division, Army Mississippi, to November, 1862. Artillery, 7th Division, Left Wing 13th Army Corps (Old), Dept. of the Tennessee, to December, 1862. Artillery, 7th Division, 16th Army Corps, to January, 1863. Artillery, 7th Division, 17th Army Corps, to September, 1863. Artillery, 1st Division, 17th Army Corps, to March, 1864. Artillery, Provisional Division, 17th Army Corps, Dept. Gulf, to June, 1864. 4th Brigade, 1st Division, 16th Army Corps, Army Tennessee, to September, 1864. Artillery Reserve, District of West Tennessee, to July, 1865.

SERVICE.—Fremont's Campaign against Springfield, Mo., September 27-November 2, 1861. Duty at Tipton till December and at Otterville till February 7, 1862. Moved to Jefferson City February 7-10, thence to Commerce, Mo. Operations against New Madrid, Mo., February 28-March 15. Point Pleasant March 7. Operations against Island No. 10, Mississippi River, March 15-April 8. Expedition to Fort Pillow, Tenn., April 13-17. Moved to Hamburg Landing, Tenn., April 18-22. Advance on and siege of Corinth, Miss., April 29-May 30. Reconnoissance before Farmington May 13. Tuscumbia Creek May 31-June 1. Osborn's Creek June 4. Expedition to Rienzi June 30-July 1. At Camp Clear Creek till August. March to Tuscumbia, Ala., August 18-22. March to Iuka, Miss., September 8-12. Action near Iuka September 13-14. Battle of Iuka September 19. Battle of Corinth October 3-4. Pursuit to Ripley October 5-12. Tuscumbia River October 5. Chewalla and Big Hill near Ruckersville and Ripley October 7. Grant's Central Mississippi Campaign November 2, 1862-January 10, 1863. Duty at Memphis till March, 1863. Moved to Helena, Ark., March 1-3. Yazoo Pass Expedition and operations against Fort Pemberton and Greenwood March 13-April 5. Moved to Lake Providence, La., April 17-20. Movement on Bruinsburg and turning Grand Gulf April 25-30. Battle of Port Gibson, Miss., May 1 (Reserve). Big Black River May 3. Raymond May 12. Jackson May 14. Champion's Hill May 16. Big Black River Crossing May 17. Siege of Vicksburg May 18-July 4. Assaults on Vicksburg May 19 and 22. Duty at Vicksburg till February, 1864. Meridian Campaign February 3-March 2. Baker's Creek February 5. Red River Campaign March 10-May 22. Fort De Russy March 14. Pleasant Hill Landing April 2. Battle of Pleasant Hill April 9. Pleasant Hill Landing April 13. About Cloutiersville April 22-23. Alexandria May 2-9. Well's and Boyce's Plantations May 6. Bayou Boeuf May 7. Yellow Bayou May 10. Retreat to Morganza May 13-20. Mansura May 16. Bayou de Glaze May 18. Moved to Vicksburg, Miss., thence to Memphis, Tenn., May 20-June 10. Smith's Expedition to Tupelo, Miss., July 5-21. Tupelo July 14-15. Old Town Creek July 15. Smith's Expedition to Oxford, Miss., August 1-30. Duty at Memphis and in District of West Tennessee till July, 1865. Mustered out July 25, 1865.

2nd REGIMENT LIGHT ARTILLERY.

Organized at St. Louis, Mo., as 1st Regiment, Missouri Artillery, U. S. Reserve Corps, September 16 to November 6, 1861. Designation changed to 2nd Missouri Artillery November 20, 1861, and assigned to duty in forts about St. Louis till September, 1863. Consolidated to a Battalion of 5 Companies September 29, 1863. Landgraeber's Battery, Horse Artillery, assigned as Company "F," September 30, 1863. Companies "C" and "D" form new Company "A." Company "B" retained its organization. Companies "I" and "H" form new Company "C." Companies "A," "F," "G" and "K" form new Company "D." Companies "E," "L" and "M" form new Company "E." Six new Batteries organized as follows: "G" at St. Louis November 15, 1863. "H" at Springfield, Mo., December 4, 1863. "I" at Springfield, Mo., December 29, 1863. "K" at Springfield, Mo., January 14, 1864. "L" at Sedalia, Mo., January 20,

1864 (formerly 1st Battery, Missouri State Militia). "M" at St. Louis February 15, 1864. (See the several Batteries for history.)

BATTERY "A," 2nd REGIMENT LIGHT ARTILLERY.

Organized at St. Louis, Mo., January, 1862. Attached to District of St. Louis, Dept. Missouri, to November, 1862. District of Rolla, Dept. Missouri, to February, 1863. District of St. Louis, Mo., Dept. Missouri, to September, 1863. Battery reorganized from Batteries "C" and "D" September 29, 1863. District of St. Louis, Mo., Dept. Missouri, to December, 1864. Artillery, 3rd Division, Detachment, Army Tennessee, Dept. of the Cumberland, to March, 1865. 3rd Sub-District, Middle Tennessee, Dept. Cumberland, to June, 1865. District of St. Louis to August, 1865.

SERVICE.—Garrison duty at Cape Girardeau, Mo., till June 11, 1864. Ordered to St. Louis, and duty there till September. Moved to Franklin, Mo., during Price's Raid. Moved to St. Louis, October 12, thence to Paducah, Ky., November 6, and to Nashville, Tenn. Garrison duty at Johnsonville, Tenn., January to June, 1865. Ordered to St. Louis, Mo., and duty there till August. Mustered out August 24, 1865.

BATTERY "B," 2nd REGIMENT LIGHT ARTILLERY.

Organized at St. Louis, Mo., January, 1862. Attached to District of St. Louis, Mo., Dept. Missouri, to June, 1864. District of Rolla, Mo., Dept. Missouri, to October, 1864. District of St. Louis, Mo., Dept. Missouri, to July, 1865. District of the Plains, Dept. Missouri, to December, 1865.

SERVICE.—Duty in Forts about St. Louis, Mo., till February, 1863. Garrison duty at New Madrid, Mo., till April 24, 1864. At Cape Girardeau till May. Moved to Springfield, Mo., via St. Louis and Sedalia, thence to Rolla, Mo., June 20, and duty there till October. March from Rolla to Jefferson City October 4-6 (Detachment). Moreau Creek October 7. Jefferson City October 7-8. Expedition to Rocheport October 11-29. At Rocheport till November 13, then rejoined Battery at Rolla. Moved to Franklin November 19-21, and duty there till June 1, 1865. Ordered to St. Louis June 1 and equipped as Cavalry. Moved to Omaha, Neb., June 11-20. Powder River Exposition. March to Powder River and Fort Connor July 11-September 20. Actions on Powder River September 2-8. Mustered out December 20, 1865.

BATTERY "C," 2nd REGIMENT LIGHT ARTILLERY.

Organized at St. Louis January, 1862. Attached to District of St. Louis, Mo., Dept. Missouri, to September, 1862. District Rolla, Dept. Missouri, to February, 1863. District St. Louis, Mo., Dept. Missouri, to September, 1863. Reorganized from Batteries "H" and "I" September 29, 1863. District St. Louis, Mo., Dept. Missouri, to August, 1864. District North Missouri, Dept. Missouri, to June, 1865. District Plains, Dept. Missouri, to December, 1865.

SERVICE.—Duty at Hartsville, Cape Girardeau and in District of St. Louis, till May 8, 1864. Ordered to St. Louis May 8. One section returned to Cape Girardeau May 23, 1864. One section at St. Joseph, Mo., and one section at Warrensburg, Mo., till October, 1864. Ordered to Jefferson City, Mo., October. Defence of Jefferson City against Price's attack October 7-8. Moved to Booneville, thence to Glasgow and to Macon City, arriving November 5 (1 Section). Duty at Macon City and Cape Girardeau till June, 1865. Ordered to St. Louis June 1. Equipped as Cavalry. Moved to Omaha, Neb., June 11-20. Powder River Expedition. March to Powder River and Fort Connor July 11-September 20. Actions on Powder River September 2-8. Mustered out December 20, 1865.

BATTERY "D," 2nd REGIMENT LIGHT ARTILLERY.

Organized at St. Louis, Mo., January, 1862. Attached to District of St. Louis, Mo., Dept. Missouri, to March, 1863. District of Southeast Missouri, Dept. Missouri, to August, 1863. District of St. Louis, Mo., to Septem-

ber, 1863. Battery reorganized from Batteries "A," "F," "G" and "K" September 29, 1863. District of St. Louis, Mo., to December, 1863. Artillery, 1st Cavalry Division, Army Arkansas, and 7th Army Corps, Dept. of Arkansas, to May, 1864. Artillery, 2nd Division, 7th Army Corps, to February, 1865. Mouth of White River, Ark., to August, 1865. Dept. of Arkansas, to November, 1865.

SERVICE.—Duty at Cape Girardeau, Mo., till July, 1863. Operations against Marmaduke April 17-May 2. Cape Girardeau April 26. Moved to St. Louis, Mo., July, and duty there till September, 1863. At Bloomfield till December. Moved to Rolla via Pilot Knob December 1, 1863, thence march with 1st Nebraska Cavalry to Batesville, Ark. Duty at Batesville and Duvall's Bluff, Ark., till January, 1865. Near Batesville February 20, 1864. Pikeville May 25, 1864. Operations on White River June 20-29. Near Clarendon and St. Charles June 25-26, and pursuit to Bayou DeView June 26-28. Augusta September 2. Duty at Post of St. Charles January, 1865, to June, 1865, and at mouth of White River till August. Ordered to St. Louis, Mo. Duty in District of the Plains till November. Mustered out November 21, 1865.

BATTERY "E," 2nd REGIMENT LIGHT ARTILLERY.

Organized at St. Louis, Mo., January, 1862. Attached to District of St. Louis to September, 1863. Reorganized September 29, 1863, from Batteries "E," "L," "M." District of St. Louis, Mo., to December, 1863. Artillery, 1st Cavalry Division, Army Arkansas, and 7th Army Corps, Dept. of Arkansas, to April, 1864. Artillery, 3rd Division, 7th Army Corps, to May, 1864. Artillery, 1st Division, 7th Army Corps, to June, 1865. District of the Plains, Dept. Missouri, to November, 1865.

SERVICE.—Duty in District of St. Louis, Mo., till December, 1863. Actions at Bloomfield, Mo., September 11 and October 22, 1862. Cape Girardeau April 26, 1863. Ordered to Little Rock, Ark. December, 1863, and duty there till March, 1864. Steele's Expedition to Camden April 23-May 3. Elkins' Ferry, Little Missouri River, April 3-4, 1864. Prairie D'Ann April 9-12. Camden April 15-18. Mark's Mills April 25. Duty at Little Rock till June, 1865. Ordered to St. Louis, Mo., and equipped as Cavalry. Moved to Omaha, Neb. Powder River Expedition, march to Powder River and Fort Connor July 11-September 20. Actions on Powder River September 2-8. Mustered out November 22, 1865.

BATTERY "F," 2nd REGIMENT LIGHT ARTILLERY.

Organized at St. Louis, Mo., January, 1862. Attached to District of St. Louis, Mo., to September, 1862. District of Rolla, Mo., Dept. Missouri, to February, 1863. District of St. Louis, Mo., Dept. Missouri, to September, 1863. Transferred to new Battery "D" September 29, 1863. Reorganized September 30, 1863, by assignment of Landgraeber's Battery, Horse Artillery. Attached to 1st Division, 15th Army Corps, to November, 1864. Artillery Reserve, Nashville, Tenn., Dept. of the Cumberland, to March, 1865. 3rd Sub-District, District Middle Tennessee, Dept. Cumberland, to June, 1865. District St. Louis, Mo., to August, 1865.

SERVICE.—March to Chattanooga, Tenn., October-November, 1863. Operations on Memphis & Charleston Railroad in Alabama October 20-29. Barton Station, Cane Creek and Dickson's Station, Ala., October 20. Cherokee Station October 21. Cane Creek October 26. Bear Creek, Tuscumbia, October 27. Cherokee Station October 29. Chattanooga-Ringgold Campaign November 23-27. Lookout Mountain November 23-24. Mission Ridge November 25. Ringgold Gap, Taylor's Ridge, November 27. March to relief of Knoxville November 28-December 8. Garrison duty in Alabama till April, 1864. Atlanta (Ga.) Campaign May 1-September 8. Demonstrations on Resaca May 5-13. Near Resaca May 13. Battle of Resaca May 14-15. Advance on Dallas May 18-25. Battles about Dallas, New Hope Church and Allatoona Hills May 25-June 5. Operations about Marietta and against Kenesaw Mountain June 10-July 2. Assault on Kenesaw June 27. Nickajack Creek July 2-5. Chattahoochie River July 5-17. Battle of Atlanta July 22. Siege of Atlanta July 22-August 25. Ezra Chapel, July 28. Flank movement on Jonesboro August 25-30. Battle of Jonesboro August 31-September 1. Lovejoy Station September 2-6. Pursuit of Hood into Alabama October 1-26. Ordered to Chattanooga, Tenn., October 29. Duty at Chattanooga and Nashville, Tenn., with Reserve Artillery, till June, 1865. Moved to St. Louis, Mo., and duty there till August. Mustered out August 25, 1865.

BATTERY "G," 2nd REGIMENT LIGHT ARTILLERY.

Organized at St. Louis, Mo., January, 1862. Attached to District of St. Louis, Mo., Dept. Missouri, to November, 1862. District of Rolla, Mo., Dept. Missouri, to February, 1863. District of St. Louis, Mo., Dept. Missouri, to September, 1863. Transferred to New Battery "D" September 29, 1863. Reorganized at St. Louis, Mo., November 15, 1863. Attached to District of St. Louis, Mo., Dept. Missouri, to August, 1864. 1st Brigade, District of Memphis, Tenn., District of West Tennessee, to December, 1864. Artillery Reserve, District of West Tennessee, to August, 1865.

SERVICE.—Duty at St. Louis and Rolla, Mo., till February, 1864. Ordered to Pilot Knob February 20, 1864, and duty there till April. Ordered to Cape Girardeau April 12, and duty there till August 9. Moved to Memphis, Tenn., August 9-12. Repulse of Forest's attack on Memphis August 21. Expedition to Clifton, Tenn., and Eastport, Miss., in pursuit of Forest September 30. Near Eastport October 10. Duty at Memphis, Tenn., and in District of West Tennessee till August, 1865. Mustered out August 22, 1865.

BATTERY "H," 2nd REGIMENT LIGHT ARTILLERY.

Organized at St. Louis, Mo., January, 1862. Attached to District of St. Louis, Mo., Dept. Missouri, to September, 1863. Transferred to New Battery "C" September 29, 1863. Reorganized at Springfield, Mo., December 4, 1863. Attached to District of Southwest Missouri, Dept. Missouri, to June, 1865. District of the Plains, Dept. Missouri, to November, 1865.

SERVICE.—Duty in the District of St. Louis, Mo., till April, 1864. Expedition from New Madrid and skirmishes in swamps of Little River near Osceola and on Pemiscott Bayou April 5-9. Ordered to Cape Girardeau April 28. Actions at Ironton, Shutin Gap and Arcadia Valley September 26. Fort Davidson, Pilot Knob, September 26-27. Leesburg or Harrison September 28-29. March from Rolla to Jefferson City October 4-6. Defence of Jefferson City against Price's attack October 7-8. California, Booneville and Russellville October 9. Booneville October 9-12. Little Blue October 21. Big Blue, State Line, October 22. Westport October 23. Engagement at the Marmiton or Battle of Charlott October 25. Mine Creek, Little Osage River, Marias des Cygnes, October 25. Newtonia October 28. At Franklin till June, 1865. Moved to Omaha, Neb., June 11-20. Powder River Expedition. March to Powder River and Fort Connor July 11-September 20. Actions on Powder River September 2-3. Mustered out November 20, 1865.

BATTERY "I," 2nd REGIMENT LIGHT ARTILLERY.

Organized at St. Louis, Mo., January, 1862. Attached to District of St. Louis, Mo., Dept. Missouri, to September, 1863. Transferred to New Battery "C" September 29, 1863. Reorganized at Springfield, Mo., December 28, 1863. Attached to District Southwest Missouri, Dept. Missouri, to December, 1864. 3rd Brigade, 1st Division (Detachment), Army Tennessee, Dept. of the Cumberland, to March, 1865. 3rd Sub-District, District Middle Tennessee, Dept. Cumberland, to June, 1865. District of St. Louis, Mo., Dept. Missouri, to August, 1865.

SERVICE.—Duty in the District of St. Louis till April, 1864. Expedition from New Madrid, Mo., and skirmishes in swamps of Little River near Osceola and on Pemiscott Bayou April 5-9, 1864. Duty in Southwest Missouri till October. Ordered to Paducah, Ky., November 10, thence to Nashville, Tenn. Battle of Nashville Decem-

ber 15-16. Duty in District of Nashville till March, 1865, and in District of Middle Tennessee till June. Ordered to St. Louis, Mo., and duty there till August. Mustered out August 23, 1865.

BATTERY "K" 2nd REGIMENT LIGHT ARTILLERY.

Organized at St. Louis, Mo., January, 1862. Attached to District of St. Louis, Mo., Dept. of Missouri, to June, 1863. Artillery, 1st Cavalry Division, Army of Southeast Missouri, Dept. of Missouri, to July, 1863. Reserve Brigade, 1st Cavalry Division, District of Southeast Missouri, Dept. of Missouri, to August, 1863. Artillery, 1st Cavalry Division, Arkansas Expedition, to September, 1863.

SERVICE.—Duty in District of St. Louis till July, 1863. Operations against Marmaduke April 16-May 2, 1863. Castor River, near Bloomfield, April 29. Bloomfield April 30. Join Davidson's Cavalry Division at Pilot Knob June, 1863. Davidson's march to join Steele and Steele's Expedition to Little Rock, Ark., July 1-September 10. Bayou Metoe or Reed's Bridge August 27. Bayou Fourche and capture of Little Rock September 10. Pursuit of Price September 11-13. Near Little Rock September 11. Transferred to New Battery "D" September 29, 1863. Reorganized at Springfield, Mo., January 14, 1864. Attached to District of St. Louis, Mo., Dept. of Missouri, to June, 1865. District of the Plains, Dept. of Missouri, to November, 1865.

SERVICE.—Duty in the District of St. Louis, Mo., till June, 1865. Expedition from New Madrid, Mo., and skirmishes in swamps of Little River, near Oceola and on Pemiscott Bayou, April 5-9, 1864. Leesburg and Harrison September 28-29. Little Blue October 21. Big Blue and State Line October 22. At Franklin, Mo., till June, 1865. Moved to Omaha, Neb., June 11-20. Powder River Expedition. March to Powder River and Fort Connor July 11-September 20. Skirmishes on Powder River September 2-8. Mustered out November 25, 1865.

BATTERY "L" 2nd REGIMENT LIGHT ARTILLERY.

Organized at St. Louis, Mo., January, 1862. Attached to District of St. Louis, Mo., Dept. of Missouri, to September, 1862. District of Rolla, Dept. of Missouri, to February, 1863. District of St. Louis, Mo., Dept. of Missouri, to September, 1863.

SERVICE.—Duty in District of St. Louis till September, 1862. At Houston July, 1862. Action at Mountain Store, Big Piney, July 25, 1862. At Hartsville, District of Rolla, Mo., till July, 1863, and at St. Louis, Mo., till September, 1863. Scout in Wayne, Stoddard and Dunklin Counties August 20-27, 1862. Little River Bridge August 31, 1862 (Detachment). Hartsville, Wood's Fork, January 11, 1863. Transferred to new Battery "E" September 29, 1863. Reorganized at Sedalia, Mo., January 20, 1864. Attached to District of St. Louis, Mo., and Central District of Missouri, Dept. of Missouri, to April, 1865. District of North Missouri, Dept. of Missouri, to June, 1865. District of the Plains, Dept. of Missouri, to November, 1865.

SERVICE.—Duty at St. Louis and Warrenton, Mo., District of Central Missouri. Action at Moreau Bottom October 7. Defence of Jefferson City against Price's attack October 7-8. California October 9. Battle of Westport October 23. Engagement at the Marmiton or Battle of Charlot October 25. Mine Creek, Little Osage River, Marias des Cygnes, October 25. Duty in District of Central Missouri till April, 1865, and in North Missouri till June. Ordered to St. Louis, Mo. Moved to Omaha, Neb., June 11-20. Powder River Expedition. March to Powder River and Fort Connor July 11-September 20. Actions on Powder River September 2-8. Mustered out November 25, 1865.

BATTERY "M," 2nd REGIMENT LIGHT ARTILLERY.

Organized at St. Louis, Mo., January, 1862. Attached to District of St. Louis, Mo., Dept. of Missouri, to November, 1862. 2nd Division, Army of Southeast Missouri, Dept. of Missouri, to March, 1863. District of

Southeast Missouri, Dept. of Missouri, to June, 1863. Artillery, 1st Cavalry Division, District of Southeast Missouri, to July, 1863. Artillery Reserve, Cavalry Division, Army of Southeast Missouri, Dept. of Missouri, to August, 1863. Artillery 1st Cavalry Division, Arkansas Expedition, to September, 1863.

SERVICE.—Duty in District of St. Louis till November, 1862. Pitman's Ferry, Ark., October 27, 1862. At St. Louis till June, 1863. Joined Division at Pilot Knob, Mo., June, 1863. Davidson's march to join Steele and Steele's Expedition to Little Rock, Ark., July 1-September 10. March to Clarendon, on White River, July 1-August 8. Shallow Ford Bayou, Metoe, August 30. Bayou Fourche and capture of Little Rock September 10. Pursuit of Price September 11-14. Near Little Rock September 11. Transferred to new Battery "E" September 29, 1863. Reorganized at St. Louis, Mo., February 15, 1864. Attached to District of St. Louis, Mo., to June, 1865. Duty at St. Louis till August, 1864. Ordered to Springfield, Mo.,· August 15, and duty there till November. Moved to Paducah, Ky., November 10, to Rolla November 26, thence to Franklin,·Mo., and duty there till June, 1865. Moved to Omaha, Neb., June 11-20. Powder River Expedition. March to Powder River and Fort Connor July 11-September 20. Actions on Powder River September 2-8. Mustered out December 20, 1865.

BUELL'S INDPT. BATTERY LIGHT ARTILLERY.

Organized at St. Louis, Mo., July 12, 1861. Attached to Dept. of Missouri to February, 1862. 1st Brigade, 3rd Division, District of West Tennessee, to March, 1862. Artillery 3rd Division, Army of the Tennessee, to April, 1862. Artillery 2nd Division, Army of the Tennessee, to June, 1862. Artillery 2nd Brigade, 3rd Division, Army of the Mississippi, to August, 1862.

SERVICE.—Dug Springs, Mo., August 2, 1861. At Sulphur Springs, Mo., August. Ordered to Cape Girardeau, Mo., August 25. Duty there and in Missouri to February, 1862. Ordered to join Army of the Tennessee. Expedition to Purdy and operations about Crump's Landing, Tenn., March 14-17. Paris March 11. Battle of Shiloh April 6-7. Advance on and siege of Corinth, Miss., April 29-May 30. Expedition to Ripley June 27-July 1. At Camp Clear Creek till August 15. Assigned to 1st Missouri Light Artillery as Battery "I," August, 1862. For further service see that Battery.

GRAESSELE'S BATTERY INDPT. LT. ARTILLERY.

See Knispel's Battery.

JOHNSON'S STATE MILITIA BATTERY LIGHT ARTILLERY.

Attached to 1st Missouri State Militia Cavalry.

JOYCE'S BATTERY LIGHT ARTILLERY.

Attached to 10th Missouri Cavalry.

KNISPEL'S BATTERY LIGHT ARTILLERY.

Attached to 4th Missouri Cavalry.

KOWALD'S BATTERY LIGHT ARTILLERY.

Organized August, 1861, but failed to complete organization. Mustered out December 14, 1861. Battery lost 1 killed and 2 by disease. Total 3.

LANDGRAEBER'S BATTERY HORSE ARTILLERY.

Organized at St. Louis, Mo., October 8, 1861. Attached to Dept. of Missouri to January, 1862. 5th Brigade, Army of Southwest Missouri, Dept. of Missouri, to March, 1862. Artillery 2nd Division, Army of Southwest Missouri, Dept. of Missouri, to July, 1862. District of Eastern Arkansas, Dept. of Missouri, to December, 1862. 2nd Brigade, 11th Division, Dept. of the Tennessee, to December, 1862. 2nd Brigade, 4th Division, Sherman's Yazoo Expedition, to January, 1863. Artillery 1st Division, 15th Army Corps, Army of the Tennessee, to September, 1863.

SERVICE.—Duty in Southwest Missouri till January, 1862. Curtis' advance on Springfield, Mo., January 23-February 12. Pursuit of Price to Cassville, Ark., February 13-16. Sugar Creek February 17. Battles of Pea Ridge, Ark., March 6-8. March to Batesville April 5-May 3, thence to Helena, Ark., May 25-July 14. Duty at Helena, Ark., till December. Sherman's Yazoo Expedition December 22, 1862, to January 3, 1863. Chickasaw Bayou December 26-28. Chickasaw Bluff December 29. Expedition to Arkansas Post, Ark., January 3-10, 1863. Assault and capture of Fort Hindman, Arkansas Post, January 10-11. Moved to Young's Point, La., January 17-23, and duty there till April. Expedition to Greenville, Black Bayou and Deer Creek April 4-14. Demonstrations on Haines' and Snyder's Bluffs April 29-May 2. Moved to join army in rear of Vicksburg, Miss., May 2-14. Jackson, Miss., May 14. Siege of Vicksburg May 18-July 4. Assaults on Vicksburg May 19 and 22. Advance on Jackson, Miss., July 4-10. Siege of Jackson July 10-17. Bolton's Depot July 16. Briar Creek, near Canton, July 17. Canton July 18. At Big Black till September 22. Moved to Memphis, Tenn., September 22. Assigned to 2nd Missouri Light Artillery as Battery "F," September 30, 1863, and for further history see that Battery.

LINDSAY'S BATTERY LIGHT ARTILLERY.

Attached to 68th Missouri Enrolled Militia Infantry.

LOVEJOY'S BATTERY LIGHT ARTILLERY.

Attached to 2nd Missouri Cavalry.

McCLANAHAN'S BATTERY LIGHT ARTILLERY.

Attached to 2nd Missouri State Militia Cavalry.

MANN'S INDPT. BATTERY LIGHT ARTILLERY.

Organized at St. Louis, Mo., November 4, 1861, to February 14, 1862. Attached to 2nd Brigade, 4th Division, District of West Tennessee, to March, 1862. Artillery 4th Division, Army of the Tennessee, to July, 1862. 2nd Brigade, 4th Division, District of Memphis, Tenn., Dept. of the Tennessee, to August, 1862.

SERVICE.—Ordered to join Army of the Tennessee February, 1862. Battle of Shiloh, Tenn., April 6-7. Advance on and siege of Corinth, Miss., April 29-May 30. March to Memphis, Tenn., via Grand Junction, June 1-July 21, and duty there till August. Assigned to 1st Missouri Light Artillery as Battery "C" August, 1862, and for further service see that Battery.

PFENNINGHAUSSEN'S BATTERY LIGHT ARTY.

See Landgraeber's Battery Light Artillery.

SCHOFIELD'S BATTERY "A," LIGHT ARTILLERY.

Organized at St. Louis, Mo., July 25, 1862. Attached to Dept. of Missouri to October, 1862. At St. Louis, Mo., till August, 1862. Ordered to Jefferson City, Mo., August 17; thence moved to Rolla, Mo., and duty there till October. Assigned to 1st Missouri Light Artillery as Battery "L," October, 1862, and for further history see that Battery.

SCHWARTZ'S BATTERY LIGHT ARTILLERY.

Organized at St. Louis, Mo., and mustered in August 20, 1861. Duty in North Missouri (1st Section) September 6 to December 29, 1861. Battery ordered to Cairo, Ill., September 14, 1861. Duty at Cairo, Fort Holt, Ky., and Jefferson, Ky., till February, 1862. Assigned to 2nd Illinois Light Artillery as Battery "E" February 1, 1862, and for further history see that Battery.

WALLING'S BATTERY, MISSISSIPPI MARINE BRIGADE.

Organized at Philadelphia, Pa., as Battery "C," Segebarth's Pennsylvania Artillery, September 22 to December 27, 1862. Duty on the Mississippi River and other Western waters and at Vicksburg, Miss., participating in the following Duck River Island April 26, 1863. Beaver Dam Lake, near Austin, May 24; and near Austin May 28. Expedition from Young's Point, La., to Richmond, La., June 14-16. Richmond June 15. Grand Lake June 16. Expedition from Snyder's Bluff to Greenville June 29-30. Goodrich Landing June 30. Bayou Tensas June 30. Expedition from Goodrich Landing to Griffin's Landing, Catfish Point, Miss., October 24-November 10. Fayette November 22. Operations about Natchez, Miss.,

December 1-10. Rodney December 24. Port Gibson December 26. Grand Gulf January 16, 17, 18, 1864. Lake Village, Ark., February 10. Expedition to Grand Gulf February 15-March 6. Lima Landing February 22. Rodney March 4. Coleman's March 5. Red River Campaign March 10-May 22. Fort DeRussy March 14. Ashton May 1. Endorah Church May 9. Greenville May 20 and 27. Leland's Point May 27. Columbia June 2. Worthington's and Sunnyside Landings, Fish Bayou, June 5. Old River Lake (or Lake Chicot) June 6. Sunnyside Landing June 7. Duty at Vicksburg till September. Transferred to 1st Missouri Light Artillery as Battery "E" September 14, 1864 (which see).

The Mississippi Marine Brigade lost during its service 11 Enlisted men killed and mortally wounded and 1 Officer and 161 Enlisted men by disease. Total 173.

WASCHMAN'S BATTERY LIGHT ARTILLERY.

See 1st Missouri State Militia Battery.

WELFLEY'S INDPT. BATTERY LIGHT ARTILLERY.

Organized at St. Louis, Mo., September 25, 1861. Attached to Dept. of Missouri to January, 1862. Army of Southwest Missouri, Dept. of Missouri, to March, 1862. Artillery 1st Division, Army of Southwest Missouri, to May, 1862. Artillery 3rd Division, Army of Southwest Missouri, to July, 1862. Artillery District of Eastern Arkansas, Dept. of Missouri, to October, 1862. District of Southeast Missouri, Dept. of Missouri, to December.

SERVICE.—Duty at St. Louis and Rolla, Mo., till January, 1862. Curtis' Campaign against Price in Missouri and Arkansas January to March, 1862. Advance on Springfield February 2-12. Pursuit of Price into Arkansas February 14-24. Battles of Pea Ridge, Ark., March 6-8. March to Batesville April 5-May 3. Searcy Landing, Little Red River, May 19. March to Helena, Ark., May 25-July 14, and duty there till October. Expedition from Helena to mouth of White River August 5-8. Moved to Ironton and Pilot Knob, Mo., October 1, and duty in Southeastern Missouri till December. Assigned to 1st Missouri Light Artillery as Battery "B" December, 1862, which see.

BISSELL'S ENGINEER REGIMENT OF THE WEST.

Organized at St. Louis, Mo. Company "A" mustered in July 10, 1861. Company "B" organized at Paris, Edgar County, Ill., and mustered in at St. Louis August 5, 1861. Company "C" organized at Prairie City, Ill., and mustered in at St. Louis August 19. Company "D" organized at St. Louis and mustered in October 31, 1861. Company "E" organized at Adrian, Mich., and mustered in at St. Louis August 23, 1861. Company "F" organized at Dubuque, Iowa, and mustered in October 31, 1861. Company "G" organized at Cape Girardeau, Mo., and mustered in September 17, 1861. Company "H" organized at Paris, Ill., and mustered in October 31, 1861. Company "I" organized in Iowa and mustered in October 31, 1861, at St. Louis, Mo. Company "K" organized at Burlington, Iowa, and mustered in at St. Louis, Mo., October 31, 1861. Attached to Dept. of Missouri to March, 1862. Unattached, Army of the Mississippi, to June, 1862. Engineer Brigade, District of West Tennessee, Dept. of the Tennessee, to July, 1862. District of Columbus, Ky., to December, 1862. District of Columbus, Ky., 13th Army Corps (Old), Dept. of the Tennessee, to January, 1863. Unattached, Engineers' Dept. of the Tennessee, to February, 1864.

SERVICE.—Companies "A" and "B" ordered to East St. Louis, Mo., August 6, 1861; thence to Cape Girardeau, Mo., August 6-7, and fatigue duty there till March, 1862, when rejoined Regiment at New Madrid, Mo. Built Forts "A," "B," "C" and "D," Defences of Cape Girardeau. Company "G" also at Cape Girardeau and Bird's Point, Mo., till March, 1862, rejoining Regiment March 8. Regiment moved from St. Louis, Mo., to Lamine Bridge, on Missouri Pacific Railroad, September 19, 1861, and duty there till October 26. Moved to Sedalia, Mo., and duty there till December 11. Moved to Georgetown, thence to Otterville, Mo., December 11-19, and duty there till March, 1862. (Co. "I" at Sedalia till January, 1862,

rejoining Regiment January 29. Co. "F" near Sedalia till February, 1862, rejoining Regiment February 7.) Moved to St. Louis, Mo., thence to Commerce, Mo., March 1-5. Siege operations against New Madrid March 8-15. Engaged near Mt. Pleasant March 3 (Cos. "A" and "B"). Operations against Island No. 10 March 15-April 8. (Constructed New Madrid Canal, allowing passage of Gunboats through swamps of New Madrid to rear of Island No. 10.) Expedition to Fort Pillow, Tenn., April 12-14. Moved to Hamburg, Tenn., April 14-22. Cos. "A" and "I" detached at New Madrid till May 4, rejoining before Corinth, Miss., May 8. Advance on and siege of Corinth, Miss., April 26-May 30. Occupation of Corinth and pursuit to Tiptonville May 30-June 6. Tuscumbia Creek May 31-June 1. Repair Mobile & Ohio Railroad to Columbia. Headquarters at Jackson till October, 1862. Wrecking Expedition on Mississippi River about Mt. Pleasant, Island No. 10 and New Madrid July 21-October 20 (Detached). Battle of Corinth, Miss., October 3-4 (Detachment of Co. "E"). Regiment moved to defence of Corinth October 3. Pursuit to Ripley, Miss., October 5-12 (Detachment). Regiment return to Jackson and duty there till November 6. Grant's Central Mississippi Campaign November, 1862, to January, 1863. Duty on Memphis & Charleston Railroad at Lagrange, Obion River and at Memphis, Tenn., till February, 1863. Moved to Young's Point, La., February 11-14, thence to Lake Providence, La. Operations against Vicksburg, Miss., February to July. Engineer operations at Baxter's Bayou and Bayou Macon constructing Batteries at Young's Point, and various expeditions to explore and open Bayous till April, 1863. 6 Companies ordered to Memphis, Tenn., April 1-6. Engaged in opening Memphis & Charleston Railroad to Corinth, Miss., then at Pocahontas May 11 to October 3. Repairing Memphis & Charleston Railroad east of Corinth, Miss., October 3-28. At Iuka and Corinth constructing works till December 26. Moved to Memphis, thence to Nashville, Tenn., December 26, 1863, to January 4, 1864. Cos. "A," "D," "F" and "I" at Duckport, La. Engaged in fatigue duty in that vicinity till April 30. Building drain at Richmond, La., till May 9. Moved to Milliken's Bend May 9; duty there and at Young's Point and Chickasaw Bayou till May 25. Moved to Haines' Bluff and building fortifications till July 1. Surrender of Vicksburg July 4. Duty at Vicksburg till January 15, 1864. Ordered to Nashville, Tenn., and rejoin Regiment February 2, 1864. Consolidated with 25th Missouri Infantry to form 1st Missouri Engineers February 17, 1864, which see.

Regiment lost during service 16 Enlisted men killed and mortally wounded and 1 Officer and 146 Enlisted men by disease. Total 163.

1st REGIMENT ENGINEERS.

Organized February 17, 1864, by consolidation of Bissell's Engineer Regiment of the West and 25th Regiment Missouri Infantry. Attached to Defences of Nashville & Northwestern Railroad, Dept. of the Cumberland, to August, 1864. Engineers Sherman's Army to July, 1865.

SERVICE.—Assigned to duty on line of Nashville & Western Railroad rebuilding road from Nashville to the Tennessee River February 18 to May 10, 1864; then on line of Nashville & Northwestern Railroad building Blockhouses, repairing and protecting road till August 15. Ordered to join Army in the field and march to the Chattahoochie River, Georgia, August 15-25. Flank movement on Jonesboro August 25-30. Battle of Jonesboro August 31-September 1. Lovejoy Station September 2-6. At Atlanta till November 15. March to the sea November 15-December 10. In charge of Pontoons, Army of the Tennessee. Siege of Savannah December 10-21. Campaign of the Carolinas January to April, 1865. Salkehatchie Swamps, S. C., February 2-5. South Edisto River February 9. North Edisto River February 12-13. Columbia February 15-17. Lynch's Creek February 26-27. Battle of Bentonville, N. C., March 19-21. Occupation of Goldsboro March 24-April 10. Advance on Raleigh April 10-14. Bennett's House April 26. Surrender of Johnston and his army. March to Washington, D. C., via Richmond, Va., April 29-May 20. Grand Review May 24. Moved to Louisville, Ky., June 3-7. Mustered out July 22, 1865.

Regiment lost during service 16 Enlisted men killed and mortally wounded and 1 Officer and 146 Enlisted men by disease. Total 163.

BALZ'S COMPANY SAPPERS AND MINERS.

Organized at St. Louis, Mo., September and October, 1861. Mustered out February 19, 1862.

GERSTER'S INDEPENDENT COMPANY PIONEERS.

Organized at St. Louis, Mo., August, 1861, by authority of Gen. Fremont. Attached to Army of the West and Unattached District of Southwest Missouri, Dept. of Missouri, to September, 1862. Fremont's Campaign against Springfield, Mo., September to November, 1861. Duty at Jefferson City, Rolla and Springfield, Mo., till December 29, 1861. Advance to Springfield, Mo., and the Southwest December 29, 1861, to February 14, 1862. Duty in District of Southwest Missouri till September, 1862. Mustered out September, 1862.

SMITH'S INDEPENDENT COMPANY TELEGRAPH CORPS.

Organized at St. Louis September 1, 1861. Mustered out December 10, 1861.

WOLSTER'S INDEPENDENT COMPANY SAPPERS AND MINERS.

Organized at St. Louis, Mo., May 10, 1861, by authority of General Lyon. Duty at St. Louis and repairing road from Rolla to Springfield, Mo. Mustered out September 1, 1861.

BIRGE'S REGIMENT WESTERN SHARPSHOOTERS.

Organized at Benton Barracks, Mo., under authority of General Fremont September and October, 1861. Mustered in as 14th Regiment Missouri Infantry November 23, 1861 (which see).

1st BATTALION STATE MILITIA INFANTRY.—("ALBINS'.")

Organized and mustered in at St. Joseph, Mo., September 19, 1861. Guard and scout duty in Gentry, Worth, DeKalb, Buchanan and Andrew Counties, with many skirmishes. Mustered out February, 1862.

1st BATTALION PROVISIONAL ENROLLED MILITIA INFANTRY.

Duty in 1st Military District of Missouri. Affair at Tuscumbia December 8, 1864 (Detachment).

MISSISSIPPI MARINE BRIGADE INFANTRY.—1st BATTALION.

Organized at St. Louis, Mo., January 3 to April 4, 1863. Organized for duty in Western Waters. Attached to District of Northeast Louisiana, Dept. of the Tennessee, October, 1863, to April, 1864. District of Vicksburg to February, 1865.

SERVICE.—Action at Duck River Island April 26, 1863. Beaver Dam Lake, near Austin, May 24. Near Austin May 28. Expedition from Young's Point, La., to Richmond, La., June 14-16. Richmond June 15. Grand Lake June 16. Expedition from Snyder's Bluff to Greenville June 29-30. Goodrich Landing June 30. Bayou Tensas June 30. Expedition from Goodrich Landing to Griffin's Landing, Catfish Point, Miss., October 24 to November 10. Fayette November 22. Operations about Natchez, Miss., December 1-10. Rodney December 24. Port Gibson December 26. Grand Gulf January 16-17, 1864. Lake Village, Ark., February 10. Expedition to Grand Gulf February 15-March 6. Lima Landing, Ark., February 22. Rodney March 4. Coleman's March 5. Red River Campaign March 10-May 22. Fort DeRussy March 14. Ashton May 1. Endorah Church May 9. Greenville May 20-27. Leland's Point May 27. Columbia June 2. Worthington's and Sunnyside Landings, Fish Bayou, June 5. Old River Lake or Lake Chicot June 6. Sunnyside Landing June 7. Indian Bayou June 8. Coleman's Plantation, Port Gibson, July 4. Port Gibson July 7. Duty in District of

Vicksburg till February, 1865. Mustered out February 1, 1865.

Battalion lost during service 11 Enlisted men killed and mortally wounded and 1 Officer and 161 Enlisted men by disease. Total 173.

1st BATTALION ST. LOUIS CITY GUARD INFANTRY.

Organized September 25, 1864, for the Defence of St. Louis, Mo., during Price's invasion of Missouri. Relieved from active service October 31, 1864.

1st REGIMENT INFANTRY.—(3 MONTHS.)

Organized at St. Louis, Mo., for three months April 22, 1861. Attached to 3rd Brigade, Lyon's Army of the West.

SERVICE.—Removal of arms from St. Louis to Springfield, Ill. (Detachment). Capture of Camp Jackson, St. Louis, May 10. Expedition to Potosi, Mo., May 15-16 (Co. "A" Rifle Battalion). Regiment reorganized for three years June 10, 1861. Capture of Jefferson City June 14. Expedition to Booneville June 17. Dug Springs July 25 (Co. "E"). McCullough's Store July 26 and August 3. Battle of Wilson's Creek August 10. March to Rolla, thence to St. Louis August 11-21. Rifle Battalion mustered out. Company "A" August 2, 1861. Company "B" July 31, 1861. Designation of Regiment changed to 1st Missouri Light Artillery September 1, 1861. (See several Batteries 1st Missouri Light Artillery.)

1st REGIMENT UNITED STATES RESERVE CORPS INFANTRY.—(3 MONTHS.)

Organized for three months at St. Louis, Mo., May 7, 1861. Attached to Lyon's Army of the West. Capture of Camp Jackson, St. Louis, May 10. Provost duty in St. Louis and at the Arsenal till June 20. (Co. "I" at Jaques Garden and Urich's Cave entire service.) Moved to Jefferson City June 20-24. Duty at St. Louis till July 29. (Cos. "A," "F" and "L" moved to Rolla July 30, thence to Cuba August 4, and duty there till August 10.) March to Bird's Point, Mo., July 29-30, and duty there till August 13. Moved to St. Louis, Mo., August 13-14. Mustered out August 20, 1861.

Regiment lost during service 1 Officer and 3 Enlisted men killed and mortally wounded and 4 Officers and 25 Enlisted men by disease. Total 33.

1st REGIMENT UNITED STATES RESERVE CORPS INFANTRY.—(3 YEARS.)

Organized at St. Louis, Mo., September 3, 1861. Attached to 4th Division, Army of the West, to February, 1862. District of Rolla and District of St. Louis, Mo., Dept. of Missouri, to October, 1862. Campaign in Missouri September, 1861, to February, 1862. Duty guarding railroad beyond Rolla and in Southwest Missouri February to October, 1862. Mustered out October 6, 1862.

1st NORTHEAST REGIMENT INFANTRY.

Organized at Athens, Mo., October 25, 1861. Operating in Northeast Missouri till February, 1862. Action at Shelbina, Mo., September 4, 1861. Expedition against Green's guerrillas September 8-9, 1861. Consolidated with 2nd Northeast Regiment to form 21st Missouri Infantry December 31, 1861.

1st REGIMENT STATE MILITIA INFANTRY.

Organized at St. Louis, Mo., May 13, 1862, by consolidation of various Companies State Militia Infantry raised at St. Louis. Served as prison guard and Provost guard at St. Louis till September 28, 1862. Moved to Pilot Knob, Mo., and duty as bridge guard on Iron Mountain Railroad till September, 1863. (Cos. "F" and "I" at Patterson, Mo., till December, 1862; then return to St. Louis.) Ordered to St. Louis, Mo., September, 1863, and return to Pilot Knob, Mo., October 21, 1863. Duty at various points till October, 1864. Company "E" at New Madrid, Mo.; Company "D" at Cape Girardeau, Mo.; Company "H" at Pilot Knob, Mo., and in line of Southwest branch Pacific Railroad and on Iron Mountain Railroad guarding bridges. Company "H" at Defence of Pilot Knob and Fort Davidson September 27-28, 1864. Retreat to Rolla and duty there till October 24. Return to Pilot Knob and duty there till May, 1865. Mustered out May, 1865.

Regiment lost during service 14 Enlisted men killed and mortally wounded and 1 Officer and 52 Enlisted men by disease. Total 67.

1st REGIMENT ENROLLED MILITIA INFANTRY.

Called into service September 25, 1864, to repel Price's invasion of Missouri. Relieved from active service October 31, 1864. Action at Middle or Mill Creek Bridge July 24, 1864.

1st REGIMENT PROVISIONAL ENROLLED MILITIA INFANTRY.

Called into service February 3, 1863. Served in 8th Military District of Missouri. Headquarters at Mexico, Mo., operating against guerrillas and protecting State from invasion. Operations against Shelby September 22-October 26, 1863.

1st REGIMENT COLORED INFANTRY.

Organized at Benton Barracks, Mo., December 7-14, 1863. Attached to District of St. Louis, Mo., to January, 1864. Ordered to Port Hudson, La. Designation changed to 62nd Regiment United States Colored Troops March 11, 1864 (which see).

1st REGIMENT ST. LOUIS CITY GUARD INFANTRY.

Organized September 25, 1864, for the Defence of the city of St. Louis during Price's invasion of Missouri. Relieved from active service October 31, 1864.

2nd BATTALION STATE MILITIA INFANTRY. ("COX'S.")

Organized and mustered in at Cameron for six months September 11, 1861. Duty scouting in Clinton, DeKalb, Caldwell and Davis Counties till March, 1862. Mustered out March 14, 1862.

2nd BATTALION ST. LOUIS CITY GUARD INFANTRY.

Organized September 25, 1864, for the Defence of the city of St. Louis during Price's invasion of Missouri. Relieved from active service October 31, 1864.

2nd BATTALION ST. LOUIS CITY GUARD COLORED INFANTRY.

Organized September 25, 1864, for the Defence of the city of St. Louis during Price's invasion of Missouri. Relieved from active service October 31, 1864.

2nd REGIMENT INFANTRY.—(3 MONTHS.)

Organized at St. Louis, Mo., April 22, 1861. Attached to 3rd Brigade, Lyon's Army of the West. Capture of Camp Jackson, St. Louis, Mo., May 10. Capture of Jefferson City June 14. Booneville June 17 (Co. "B"). Mexico July 15. Battle of Wilson's Creek August 10. Retreat to Rolla, thence to St. Louis, Mo. Mustered out August 31, 1861.

2nd REGIMENT INFANTRY.—(3 YEARS.)

Organized at St. Louis, Mo., September 10, 1861. Attached to 5th Brigade, Army of Southwest Missouri, Dept. of Missouri, November, 1861, to February, 1862. 1st Brigade, 2nd Division, Army of Southwest Missouri, to May, 1862. 2nd Brigade, 5th Division, Army of Mississippi, to September, 1862. 35th Brigade, 11th Division, Army of Ohio, to October, 1862. 35th Brigade, 11th Division, 4th Corps, Army of the Ohio, to November, 1862. 2nd Brigade, 3rd Division, Right Wing 14th Army Corps, Army of the Cumberland, to January, 1863. 2nd Brigade, 3rd Division, 20th Army Corps, to October, 1863. 1st Brigade, 2nd Division, 4th Army Corps, to October, 1864.

SERVICE.—Moved to Jefferson City, Mo., September, 1861. Fremont's Campaign against Springfield, Mo., October 4-November 8. Moved to Rolla, Mo., November 8, and duty there till February, 1862. Curtis' Campaign against Price in Missouri and Arkansas Febru-

ary and March. Advance on Springfield, Mo., February 2-11. Pursuit of Price into Arkansas February 14-29. Battles of Pea Ridge, Ark., March 6, 7 and 8. March to Batesville April 5-May 3. Moved to Cape Girardeau, Mo., May 11-22; thence to Pittsburg Landing, Tenn., May 23-26. Advance on and siege of Corinth, Miss., May 27-30. Pursuit to Booneville May 31-June 6. At Rienzi till August 26. Moved to Cincinnati, Ohio, August 26-September 4; thence to Louisville September 17-19. Pursuit of Bragg into Kentucky October 1-16. Battle of Perryville, Ky., October 8. March to Nashville, Tenn., October 16-November 7, and duty there till December 26. Reconnoissance to Mill Creek November 27. Advance on Murfreesboro, Tenn., December 26-30. Battle of Stone's River December 30-31, 1862, and January 1-3, 1863. At Murfreesboro till June. Expedition toward Columbia March 4-14. Middle Tennessee (or Tullahoma) Campaign June 23-July 7. Fairfield June 27 and 29. Estill Springs July 2. Occupation of Middle Tennessee till August 16. Reconnoissance from Cowan to Anderson July 11-14. Passage of Cumberland Mountains and Tennessee River and Chickamauga (Ga.) Campaign August 16-September 22. Battle of Chickamauga September 19-20. Siege of Chattanooga September 24-November 23. Chattanooga-Ringgold Campaign November 23-27. Orchard Knob November 23-24. Mission Ridge November 25. Pursuit to Graysville November 26-27. March to relief of Knoxville November 28-December 8. Campaign in East Tennessee December, 1863, to February, 1864. Charlestown, Tenn., December 28, 1863. About Dandridge January 16-17, 1864. Moved to Chattanooga, thence to Cleveland, Tenn., and duty there till May. Demonstrations on Rocky Faced Ridge and Dalton, Ga., May 8-13. Buzzard's Roost Gap May 8-9. Assigned to garrison duty at Dalton, Ga., May 14 to September. Action at Dalton August 14-15. Mustered out October 1, 1864.

Regiment lost during service 6 Officers and 85 Enlisted men killed and mortally wounded and 3 Officers and 94 Enlisted men by disease. Total 188.

2nd REGIMENT UNITED STATES RESERVE CORPS INFANTRY.—(3 MONTHS.)

Organized at St. Louis, Mo., May 7, 1861. Attached to Lyon's Army of the West. Capture of Camp Jackson, St. Louis, May 10. Duty at St. Louis till July 23. (Co. "A" detached guarding bridge on Northern Missouri Railroad June 16-August 14.) A Detachment moved to Bird's Point, Mo., July 23, and duty there till August 14. Moved to St. Louis. A Detachment guard bridges on St. Louis & Iron Mountain Railroad. Mustered out August 16, 1861.

2nd REGIMENT UNITED STATES RESERVE CORPS INFANTRY.—(3 YEARS.)

Reorganized at St. Louis August 23 to September 20, 1861. Attached to District of St. Louis to October, 1861. 4th Division, Army of the Southwest, to May, 1862. 2nd Division, Army of the Mississippi, to June, 1862. 5th Division, Army of the Mississippi, to August.

SERVICE.—Campaign in Missouri October, 1861, to February, 1862. Guard railroad beyond Rolla, Mo., till May, 1862. Ordered to Pittsburg Landing, Tenn., May 6. Siege of Corinth, Miss., May 22-30. Duty at Corinth, Miss., till August. Ordered to St. Louis, Mo., August 12, 1862. Mustered out September 3, 1862.

Regiment lost during service 1 Enlisted man killed and 9 Enlisted men by disease.

2nd REGIMENT NORTHEAST INFANTRY.

Organized in Northern Missouri July, 1861. Consolidated with 1st Northeast Infantry and designated 21st Missouri Infantry December 31, 1861.

2nd REGIMENT ENROLLED MILITIA INFANTRY.

Called into service September 25, 1864, to repel Price's invasion of Missouri. Relieved from active service October 31, 1864.

2nd REGIMENT PROVISIONAL ENROLLED MILITIA INFANTRY.

Called into service February 3, 1863. Served in 8th Military District, Headquarters at Hannibal, Mo., and duty in Southwest Missouri operating against guerrillas. Skirmish in Stone County May 9, 1863 (Detachment).

2nd REGIMENT COLORED INFANTRY.

.Organized at Benton Barracks December 18, 1863, to January 16, 1864. Duty there till March, 1864. Designation changed to 65th Regiment United States Colored Troops March 11, 1864 (which see).

2nd REGIMENT ST. LOUIS CITY GUARD INFANTRY.

Organized September 25, 1864, for the Defence of the city of St. Louis during Price's invasion of Missouri. Relieved from active service October 31, 1864.

3rd BATTALION STATE MILITIA INFANTRY.

Organized at St. Joseph, Mo., for six months October 25, 1861. Scout and guard duty in Northwest Missouri till February, 1862. Mustered out February 11, 1862.

3rd BATTALION ST. LOUIS CITY GUARD INFANTRY.

Organized September 25, 1864, for the Defence of the city of St. Louis during Price's invasion. Relieved from active service October 31, 1864.

3rd REGIMENT INFANTRY.—(3 MONTHS.)

Organized at St. Louis, Mo., April 22, 1861. Attached to Lyons' Army of the West. Capture of Camp Jackson, St. Louis, May 10. March to Rolla, thence to Springfield, Mo., June 13-24. March to Neosho June 26-30. Retreat to Mt. Vernon, thence to Springfield, Mo., July 5-11. Action at Carthage July 5. Battle of Wilson's Creek August 10. Retreat to Rolla, thence to St. Louis August 11-21. Mustered out September 4, 1861.

3rd REGIMENT INFANTRY.—(3 YEARS.)

Organized at St. Louis, Mo., September 3, 1861, to January 18, 1862. Attached to 2nd Brigade, Army of Southwest Missouri, to February, 1862. Unassigned, Army of Southwest Missouri, to May, 1862. 3rd Division, Army of Southwest Missouri, to July, 1862. District of Eastern Arkansas, Dept. of Missouri, to November, 1862. 1st Brigade, 1st Division, District of Eastern Arkansas, to December, 1862. 1st Brigade, 11th Division, Right Wing 13th Army Corps (Old), Dept. of the Tennessee, to December, 1862. 2nd Brigade, 4th Division, Sherman's Yazoo Expedition, to January, 1863. 2nd Brigade, 1st Division, 15th Army Corps, Army of the Tennessee, to September, 1863. 1st Brigade, 1st Division, 15th Army Corps, to December, 1863. 3rd Brigade, 1st Division, 15th Army Corps, to November, 1864.

SERVICE.—Four Companies moved to Rolla, Mo., January, 1862, and join Curtis. Two Companies at Alton, Ill., till March, 1862; then join four Companies at Benton Barracks; then join Regiment at Cassville, Mo. Curtis' Campaign against Price in Missouri and Arkansas January to March, 1862. Advance on Springfield, Mo., February 2-11. Pursuit of Price into Arkansas February 14-29. Battles of Pea Ridge, Ark., March 6, 7 and 8. March to Batesville, Ark., April 5-May 3. Searcy Landing, Little Red River, May 19 (Co. "B"). March to Helena, Ark., May 25-July 14. Expedition from Searcy Landing to West Point, Searcy and Bayou des Arc May 27. Expedition from Helena to north of White River August 5-8. Moved to Ironton and Pilot Knob, Mo., September 1. To St. Genevieve November 12, and return to Helena November 23. Duty there till December 22. Sherman's Yazoo Expedition December 22, 1862, to January 3, 1863. Chickasaw Bayou December 26-28. Chickasaw Bluff December 29. Expedition to Arkansas Post, Ark., January 3-10, 1863. Assault and capture of Fort Hindman, Arkansas Post, January 10-11. Moved to Young's Point, La., January 17-23, and duty there till March. At Milliken's Bend till April. Expedition to Greenville, Black Bayou and Deer Creek April 2-14. Demonstration on Haines and Drumgould's Bluffs April 29-May 2. Moved to join army in rear of Vicksburg, Miss., via Richmond and Grand Gulf May 2-14. Mississippi Springs May 12-13. Battle of Jackson, Miss., May 14. Siege of Vicksburg May 18-July 4. Assaults on Vicksburg May 19 and 22. Surrender of Vicksburg July 4. Advance on Jackson, Miss., July 5-10. Siege of Jackson July 10-17. Bolton Depot July 16. Briar Creek, near Canton, July 17. Canton July 18. Camp at Big Black till September 27. Moved to Memphis, Tenn., thence march to Chattanooga, Tenn., September 27-November 21. Operations on Memphis & Charleston Railroad in Alabama October 20-29. Cherokee Station October 21 and 29. Cane Creek October 26. Tuscumbia October 26-27. Battles of Chattanooga November 23-27; Lookout Mountain November 23-24; Mission Ridge November 25; Ringgold Gap, Taylor's Ridge, November 27. Garrison duty at Woodville and Scottsboro, Ala., and Cleveland, Tenn., till May, 1864. Atlanta (Ga.) Campaign May 1-September 8. Demonstration on Resaca May 8-13. Battle of Resaca May 14-15. Advance on Dallas May 18-25. Battles about Dallas, New Hope Church and Allatoona Hills May 25-June 5. Operations about Marietta and against Kenesaw Mountain June 10-July 2. Brushy Mountain June 15-17. Assault on Kenesaw June 27. Nickajack Creek July 2-5. Chattahoochie River July 6-17. Battle of Atlanta July 22. Siege of Atlanta July 22-August 25. Ezra Chapel, Hood's 2nd Sortie, July 28. Flank movement on Jonesboro August 25-30. Battle of Jonesboro August 31-September 1. Lovejoy Station September 2-6. Operations against Hood in North Alabama and North Georgia October 1-26. Mustered out by Companies. Company "B" September 5, Company "K" September 5, Company "C" September 28, Companies "E" and "F" October 17, Company "H" November 2, Company "G" November 3, Company "I" November 16 and Company "D" November 23, 1864. Veterans and Recruits transferred to 15th Missouri Infantry.

Regiment lost during service 3 Officers and 89 Enlisted men killed and mortally wounded and 3 Officers and 145 Enlisted men by disease. Total 240.

3rd REGIMENT UNITED STATES RESERVE CORPS INFANTRY.—(3 MONTHS.)

Organized at Turner Hall, St. Louis, Mo., May 8, 1861. Attached to Lyons' Army of the West. Capture of Camp Jackson May 10. Provost duty at St. Louis till July 1. Three Companies sent to Southwest Missouri July 1. Expedition to Northern Missouri against Harris July 16 (7 Cos.). Action at Fulton July 17. Duty at Fulton and St. Louis till August 18. Mustered out August 18, 1861.

Regiment lost during service 1 Enlisted man killed and 8 Enlisted men by disease.

3rd REGIMENT UNITED STATES RESERVE CORPS INFANTRY.—(3 YEARS.)

Organized at St. Louis, Mo., August and September, 1861. Attached to 2nd Brigade, Sigel's Division, Fremont's Army of the West. Fremont's Campaign in Missouri September to November. At Rolla, Mo., till January, 1862. Consolidated with Gasconade Battalion to form 4th Missouri Infantry January 18, 1862.

3rd REGIMENT ENROLLED MILITIA INFANTRY.

Called into service September 25, 1864, to resist Price's invasion of Missouri. Relieved from active service October 31, 1864.

3rd REGIMENT PROVISIONAL ENROLLED MILITIA INFANTRY.

Duty in District of Northwest Missouri at St. Joseph and in Henry and St. Clair Counties operating against guerrillas.

3rd REGIMENT COLORED INFANTRY.

Organized at Benton Barracks, Mo. Designation changed to 67th United States Colored Troops March 11, 1864 (which see).

3rd REGIMENT ST. LOUIS CITY GUARD INFANTRY.

Organized September 25, 1864, for the Defence of the city of St. Louis during Price's invasion of Missouri. Relieved from active service October 31, 1864.

4th BATTALION STATE MILITIA INFANTRY. ("THOMPSON'S.")

Organized for six months at Rockfort, Mo., and mustered in November 9, 1861. Engaged in scouting and guard duty in Holt and Atchison Counties till February, 1862. Mustered out February 11, 1862.

4th REGIMENT INFANTRY.—(3 MONTHS.)

Organized at St. Louis, Mo., April 22, 1861. Capture of Camp Jackson, St. Louis, May 10. Moved to Bird's Point, Mo., May 21; thence to Cairo, Ill. Guard duty along Pacific Railroad. Moved to Cairo, Ill., thence to St. Louis, Mo., and to Fulton, Mo. Mustered out July 30, 1861.

4th REGIMENT INFANTRY.—(3 YEARS.)

Organized at St. Louis, Mo., by consolidation of Gasconade Battalion and 3rd Regiment United States Reserve Corps January, 1862. On duty in Districts of Southwest Missouri and St. Louis at Pacific City and St. Louis till February, 1863. Mustered out February 1, 1863.

4th REGIMENT UNITED STATES RESERVE CORPS INFANTRY.—(3 MONTHS.)

Organized at St. Louis, Mo., May 8, 1861. Attached to Lyons' Command, Army of the West. Capture of Camp Jackson, St. Louis, May 10. Ordered to Rolla, Mo., May 16, and duty there till June 30. (Cos. "A" and "B" at garrison, Waynesville, till June 30.) March to Springfield, Mo., July 1-5 (except Co. "C" at Waynesville and Co. "L" at Lebanon). March to Mt. Vernon to reinforce General Sigel July 7. Return to Springfield July 9. Moved to St. Louis July 17. To Bird's Point, Mo., July 18, and duty there till August. Mustered out August 18, 1861.

Regiment lost during service 4 Enlisted men killed and 6 Enlisted men by disease.

4th REGIMENT UNITED STATES RESERVE CORPS INFANTRY.—(3 YEARS.)

Organized at St. Louis, Mo., September, 1861. Duty in District of St. Louis till January, 1862. Mustered out January 13, 1862.

4th REGIMENT ENROLLED MILITIA INFANTRY.

Called into service September 25, 1864, to repel Price's invasion of Missouri. Relieved from active service October 31, 1864.

4th REGIMENT PROVISIONAL ENROLLED MILITIA INFANTRY.

Placed on duty April 23, 1863. Placed on duty in District of North Missouri operating against guerrillas in Henry, St. Clair, Ray and Carroll Counties at St. Joseph. Chillicothe, Carrollton, Lisbon and Richmond operations in Ray and Carroll Counties August 12-16, 1864. Skirmish at Fredericksburg August 12. Action at Glasgow October 15 (Detachment).

4th REGIMENT COLORED INFANTRY.

Organized at Benton Barracks, Mo. Designation changed to 68th United States Colored Troops March 11, 1864 (which see).

4th REGIMENT ST. LOUIS CITY GUARD INFANTRY.

Organized September 25, 1861, for the Defence of the city of St. Louis during Price's invasion of Missouri. Relieved from active service October 31, 1864.

5th REGIMENT INFANTRY.—(3 MONTHS.)

Organized at St. Louis, Mo., May 18, 1861. Attached to Lyons' Army of the West. Expedition from St. Louis to Potosi May 15 (Co. "A"). Moved to Springfield, Mo., June 16-17. Action at Dry Forks July 5. Expedition toward Fayette, Ark., August 3-5. Battle of Wilson's Creek August 10. March to Rolla, thence to St. Louis August 11-21. Mustered out August 27, 1861.

Regiment lost during service 1 Officer and 24 Enlisted men killed and mortally wounded and 1 Officer and 32 Enlisted men by disease. Total 58.

5th REGIMENT INFANTRY.—(3 YEARS.)

Organized at St. Louis March 18, 1862, by consolidation of 5th United States Reserve Corps, Voerster's Company Sappers and Miners, Giester's Company Pioneers and Winkelman's Company Pontooneers. Guard bridges on Iron Mountain Railroad and duty in Southeast Missouri till July. At Cape Girardeau, Mo., till November, 1862. Company "F" in District of Mississippi July, 1862. Companies "A" and "I" transferred to 25th Missouri Infantry, and Companies "H" and "K" to 27th Missouri Infantry. Companies "B," "C," "D," "E," "F" and "G" mustered out November 22, 1862.

5th REGIMENT STATE MILITIA INFANTRY. ("FAGG'S.")

Organized at Louisiana, Mo., for six months September, 1861. Guard bridges in Franklin County September, 1861. Duty at Troy, Louisiana, Ashley, Wellsville and Bowling Green till February, 1862. Mustered out February 5, 1862.

5th REGIMENT UNITED STATES RESERVE CORPS INFANTRY.—(3 MONTHS.)

Organized at St. Louis, Mo., May 11, 1861. Attached to Lyons' Army of the West. Riot at Fifth and Market streets, St. Louis, May 11. Duty at St. Louis till June 15. Companies "A," "D" and "K" moved to Jefferson City, Mo., June 15. Regiment moved to Booneville, thence to Lexington July 5-9. Lexington July 9. Moved to St. Louis July 16-19. Between Glasgow and Booneville July 17-18. Blue Mills July 24. Brunswick August 17. Mustered out August 31, 1861.

Regiment lost during service 6 Enlisted men killed and mortally wounded and 11 Enlisted men by disease. Total 17.

5th UNITED STATES RESERVE CORPS INFANTRY. (3 YEARS.)

Organized at St. Louis September, 1861. Consolidated with Captain Voerster's Company Sappers and Miners, Captain Geister's Company Pioneers and Captain Winkleman's Company Pontooneers to form 5th Missouri Infantry March 18, 1862 (which see).

5th REGIMENT ENROLLED MILITIA INFANTRY.

Called into service September 25, 1864, to repel Price's invasion of Missouri. Relieved from active service October 31, 1864.

5th REGIMENT PROVISIONAL ENROLLED MILITIA INFANTRY.

Duty at Sedalia, Mo. Scout from Salem to Sinking Creek, Salem River, April 18-21, 1863. Operations against Quantrell in his raid into Kansas August 20-28, 1863. Big Creek, near Pleasant Hill, August 22. Near Hopewell August 25-26. Operations against Shelby September 22-October 26. Tipton and Syracuse October 10 (Cos. "D" and "E"). Booneville October 10-11 (Cos. "D" and "E"). Merrill's Crossing and Dug Ford, near Jonesborough, October 12 (Cos. "D" and "E"). Marshall October 13 (Cos. "D" and "E"). Johnston October 16. Cedar County October 17. About Honey Creek October 19 (Detachment).

5th REGIMENT ST. LOUIS CITY GUARD INFANTRY.

Organized September 25, 1864, to protect the city of St. Louis during Price's invasion of Missouri. Relieved from active service October 31, 1864.

6th BATTALION STATE MILITIA INFANTRY. ("BURRIS.")

Organized at Bethany, Mo., for six months October 14, 1861. Mustered out at Gallatin March, 1862.

6th REGIMENT INFANTRY.

Organized at St. Louis, Mo., June 15-July 9, 1861. Attached to Pilot Knob, Mo., to September, 1861. Fremont's Army of the West to January, 1862. Dept. of Missouri to April, 1862. 1st Brigade, 5th Division, Army of the Tennessee, to July, 1862. 1st Brigade, 5th Division, District of Memphis, Tenn., to November, 1862. 1st Brigade, 5th Division, Right Wing 13th Army Corps (Old), Dept. of the Tennessee, to November, 1862. 1st Brigade, 2nd Division, Right Wing 13th Army Corps, to December, 1862. 1st Brigade, 2nd Division, Sherman's Yazoo Expedition, to January, 1863. 1st Brigade, 2nd Division, 15th Army Corps, Army of the Tennessee, to July, 1865.

SERVICE.—Ordered to Pilot Knob, Mo., July 19, 1861, and duty there till September. Moore's Mills August 29. Moved to Jefferson City, thence to Tipton, Mo. Fremont's Campaign against Springfield, Mo., October and November. Moved to Tipton and Lamine and guard Pacific Railroad from Syracuse to Jefferson City till April, 1862. Action at Sink Pole Woods March 23, 1862 (Co. "A"). Expedition in Moniteau County and skirmish March 25-28 (Cos. "A" and "C"). Sink Pole Woods April 20. Moved to Pittsburg Landing April, 1862. Advance on and siege of Corinth, Miss., April 29-May 30. Coldwater, Miss., May 11. March to Memphis, Tenn., via Lagrange, Holly Springs and Moscow June 3-July 21. Duty at Memphis till November. Expedition to Coldwater and Hernando, Miss., September 9-13. Grant's Central Mississippi Campaign November-December. "Tallahatchie March" November 26-December 12. Sherman's Yazoo Expedition December 20, 1862, to January 3, 1863. Chickasaw Bayou December 26-28. Chickasaw Bluff December 29. Expedition to Arkansas Post, Ark., January 3-10, 1863. Assault and capture of Fort Hindman, Arkansas Post, January 10-11. Moved to Young's Point, La., January 13-22, and duty there till March. Expedition to Rolling Fork via Muddy Steele's and Black Bayous and Deer Creek March 4-27. Demonstration on Haines and Drumgould's Bluffs April 29-May 2. Haines Bluff May 1. Moved to join army in rear of Vicksburg, Miss., via Richmond and Grand Gulf May 2-16. Battle of Champion's Hill May 16. Siege of Vicksburg May 18-July 4. Assaults on Vicksburg May 19 and 22. Advance on Jackson, Miss., July 4-10. Siege of Jackson July 10-17. Brandin Station July 19. At Big Black till September 25. Moved to Memphis, thence march to Chattanooga, Tenn., September 25 November 21. Operations on Memphis & Charleston Railroad in Alabama October 20-29. Bear Creek, Tuscumbia, October 27. Chattanooga-Ringgold Campaign November 23-27. Brown's Ferry November 23. Foot of Missionary Ridge November 24. Tunnel Hill, Missionary Ridge, November 24-25. Pursuit to Graysville November 26-27. March to relief of Knoxville, Tenn., November 28-December 5. Expedition to Tellico Plains December 6-13. March to Chattanooga, Tenn., December 13-17; thence to Bridgeport, Ala., December 19. Garrison duty in Alabama till May, 1864. Atlanta (Ga.) Campaign May 1 to September 8. Demonstrations on Resaca May 8-13. Battle of Resaca May 14-15. Advance on Dallas May 18-25. Battles about Dallas, New Hope Church and Allatoona Hills May 25-June 5. Operations about Marietta and against Kenesaw Mountain June 10-July 2. Bushy Mountain June 15-17. Assault on Kenesaw June 27. Nickajack Creek July 2-5. Chattahoochie River July 6-17. Battle of Atlanta July 22. Siege of Atlanta July 22-August 25. Ezra Chapel July 28. Hood's 2nd sortie. Flank movement on Jonesboro August 25-30. Battle of Jonesboro August 31-September 1. Lovejoy Station September 2-6. Operations in North Georgia and North Alabama against Hood September 29-November 3. March to the sea November 15-December 10. Near Clinton November 21-23. Oconee River November 25. Statesboro December 3. Siege of Savannah December 10-21. Fort McAllister December 13. Campaign of the Carolinas January to April. Duck Branch, near Loper's Cross Roads, S. C., February 2. Salkehatchie Swamps February 3-5. South Edisto River February 9. North Edisto River February 12-13. Columbia February 16-17. Battle of Bentonville, N. C., March 20-21. Occupation of Goldsboro March 24. Advance on Raleigh April 10-14. Occupation of Raleigh April 14. Bennett's House April 26. Surrender of Johnston and his army. March to Washington, D. C., via Richmond, Va., April 29-May 19. Grand Review May 24. Moved to Louisville, Ky., June —. Duty there and at Little Rock, Ark., till August. Mustered out August 17, 1865.

Regiment lost during service 4 Officers and 80 Enlisted men killed and mortally wounded and 3 Officers and 182 Enlisted men by disease. Total 269.

6th REGIMENT ENROLLED MILITIA INFANTRY.

Called into service September 25, 1864, to repel Price's invasion of Missouri. Relieved from active service October 31, 1864.

6th REGIMENT PROVISIONAL ENROLLED MILITIA INFANTRY.

Duty at Springfield, Mo., and in the District of Southwest Missouri, operating against guerrillas. Bloomfield, Mo., January 27, 1863. Scout on Bennett's Bayou and skirmishes August 23, 1863 (Co. "H"). Operations against Shelby September 22-October 26. Scout from Houston to Jack's Fork November 4-9, 1863 (Detachment). Scouts from Houston December 9-19. Ordered from Springfield to Rolling Prairie February 6, 1864. Duty in Christian, Douglass, Wright, Dade and Stone Counties till July, 1864. Scout from Yellville to Buffalo River March 13-26. Operations in Southwest Missouri July 18-23 and August 1-28. Skirmish Polk County August 28. Operations against Price's invasion of Missouri September to November. Attached to 3rd Brigade, Cavalry Division, Dept. of Missouri. Moreau Creek October 7. Russellville October 9. California October 9. Near Booneville October 11-12. Little Blue October 21. Independence, Big Blue and State Line October 22. Big Blue and Westport October 23. Little Osage, Mine Creek and Marias des Cygnes October 25. Battle of the Marmiton (or Charlot) October 25. Newtonia October 28. Designation changed to 16th Missouri Cavalry November 1, 1864 (which see).

7th BATTALION STATE MILITIA INFANTRY.

Organized and mustered in at Gallatin, Mo., for 6 months October 5, 1861. Mustered out March 4, 1862.

7th REGIMENT INFANTRY.

Organized at St. Louis, Mo., June, 1861. Attached to Booneville, Mo., to September, 1861. Fremont's Army of the West to February, 1862. Lexington, Mo., Dept. of the Missouri, to July, 1862. Unattached, Pittsburg Landing, Tenn., Army of the Tennessee, to September, 1862. 4th Brigade, 1st Division, District of Jackson, Tenn., to November, 1862. 4th Brigade, 3rd Division, Left Wing 13th Army Corps (Old), Dept. of the Tennessee, to December, 1862. 3rd Brigade, 3rd Division, 17th Army Corps, to April, 1864. Maltby's Brigade, District of Vicksburg, Miss., to June, 1864. 1st Brigade, District of Memphis, Tenn., 16th Army Corps, to August, 1864 (Veterans). 1st Brigade, 2nd Division, 19th Army Corps, Dept. of the Gulf, to December, 1864.

SERVICE.—Moved to Booneville, Mo., July 1-4, 1861, thence to Rolla August 30 and to Syracuse, Mo., October 5-10. Fremont's Campaign against Springfield October 21-November 2. Moved to Sedalia November 10-14, thence to Otterville December and duty there till February, 1862. Expedition to Blue Springs January 20-February 3, 1862 (Cos. "B," "F" and "H" detached from Regiment November 21, 1861, and ordered to Kansas City. Rejoined Regiment at Lexington, Mo., February, 1862.) Moved to Lexington, Mo., February 3-10, 1862, and duty there till May 9. Reconnoissance from Greenville February 23-24 (Co. "H"). Skirmish at Mingo Creek, near St. Francisville, February 24 (Co. "H"). Moved to Pittsburg Landing, Tenn., May 9-14, and guard and fatigue duty there till August 15. Moved to Jackson, Tenn., August 15-29, and duty there till October.

Medon Station, Mississippi Central Railroad, August 31. Chewalla and Big Hill October 5. Medon Station October 10. Moved to Corinth with McPherson and to Jackson October 14. To Lagrange November 2. Grant's Central Mississippi Campaign November 2, 1862, to January 10, 1863. At Memphis, Tenn., January 17-February 21. Moved to Lake Providence, La., February 21, and duty there till April. Moved to Milliken's Bend, La., April 12. Passage of Vicksburg batteries April 22 (Detachment). Movement on Bruinsburg and turning Grand Gulf April 25-39. Battle of Port Gibson May 1. Bayou Pierrie May 2. Battles of Raymond May 12. Champion's Hill May 16. Big Black River Bridge May 17. Siege of Vicksburg, Miss., May 18-July 4. Assaults on Vicksburg May 19 and 22. Surrender of Vicksburg July 4. Provost duty there till June, 1864. Stevenson's Expedition from Vicksburg to Monroe, La., August 20-September 2, 1863. Expedition toward Canton October 14-22. Bogue Chitto Creek October 17. Expedition from Vicksburg to Sunnyside Landing, Ark., January 10-16, 1864. Meridian Campaign February 3-March 2. Clinton February 5. Veterans on furlough March to May. Non-Veterans mustered out June 14, 1864. Veterans at Memphis, Tenn., and Vicksburg, Miss., till July 29. Moved to Morganza, La., July 29 and duty there till September 3. Moved to mouth of White River, Ark., September 3-8 and duty there till October 18. Movement to Memphis and return October 18-30. Moved to Duvall's Bluff, Ark., November 9, thence to Memphis, Tenn., November 28. Consolidated with 11th Regiment Missouri Infantry December 17, 1864.

Regiment lost during service 4 Officers and 52 Enlisted men killed and mortally wounded and 2 Officers and 128 Enlisted men by disease. Total 186.

7th REGIMENT ENROLLED MILITIA INFANTRY.

Called into service to repel Price's invasion of Missouri September 25, 1864. Relieved from active service October 31, 1864.

7th REGIMENT PROVISIONAL ENROLLED MILITIA INFANTRY.

Duty at Springfield, Mo., and other points in District of Southwest Missouri. Action at Bloomfield, Mo., January 17, 1863. Dade County July 24, 1863 (Co. "E"). Scout from Greenfield September 15-18. Operations against Shelby September 22-October 16. Oregon (or Bowers' Mill) October 4. Greenfield October 5. Stockton October 5 (Detachment). Operations in Northern Arkansas December, 1863, to February, 1864. Duty in Christian, Douglass and Stone Counties till July. Scouts near Neosho and Carthage May 18-23. At Mt. Vernon May. Skirmish near White Hare June 15. Scout from Mt. Vernon June 19-25. Operations in Southwest Missouri July 18-23 and August 1-28. Skirmish Polk County August 28. Operations against Price's invasion of Missouri September to November. Attached to 3rd Brigade, Cavalry Division, Dept. of Missouri. Moreau Creek October 7. Russellville October 9. California October 9. Near Booneville October 11-12. Little Blue October 21. Independence, Big Blue and State Line October 22. Big Blue and Westport October 23. Little Osage and Mine Creek, Marias des Cygnes, October 25. Engagement on the Marmiton (or Battle of Charlot) October 25. Newtonia October 28. Designated 15th Missouri Cavalry November 1, 1864, which see.

8th REGIMENT INFANTRY.

Organized at St. Louis, Mo., June 12 to August 14, 1861. Attached to Cape Girardeau, Mo., to September, 1861. District of Paducah, Ky., to February, 1862. 5th Brigade, 2nd Division, District of Cairo, February, 1862. 1st Brigade, 3rd Division, Army of the Tennessee, to May, 1862. 1st Brigade, 5th Division, Army of the Tennessee, to July, 1862. 1st Brigade, 5th Division, District of Memphis, Tenn., to November, 1862. 1st Brigade, 5th Division, District of Memphis, 13th Army Corps (Old), Dept. of the Tennessee, to December, 1862. 1st Brigade, 2nd Division, Right Wing 13th Army Corps, December, 1862. 1st Brigade, 2nd Division, Sherman's Yazoo Expedition, to January, 1863. 1st Brigade, 2nd Division. 15th Army Corps, Army of the Tennessee, to August, 1865.

SERVICE.—Expedition against guerrillas on line of Northern Missouri Railroad July 1-24, 1861 (Cos. "B," "C"). Mexico, Mo., July 15. Wentzville July 15-17. Millville July 16. Moved to Cape Girardeau, Mo., July 29, and duty there till September 7. Expedition to Price's Landing, Commerce, Benton and Hamburg August 7-10 (Co. "F"). Expedition to St. Genevieve August 15-16. Moved to Paducah, Ky., September 7-8, and duty there till February 5, 1862. Expedition to Caseyville, Ky., November 30, 1861 (3 Cos.). Moved to Fort Henry, Tenn., February 5, 1862. Investment and capture of Fort Donelson, Tenn., February 12-16. Expedition to Clarksville February 19-21. Moved to Savannah, Tenn. Expedition toward Purdy and operations about Crump's Landing March 9-14. Battle of Shiloh, Tenn., April 6-7. Lick Creek April 24. Corinth Road April 25. Advance on and siege of Corinth, Miss., April 29-May 30. Russell House, near Corinth, May 17. March to Memphis, Tenn., June 3-21, via Lagrange, Holly Springs and Moscow. Duty at Memphis till November. Expedition to Coldwater and Hernando, Miss., September 9-13. Grant's Central Mississippi Campaign November-December. "Tallahatchie March" November 26-December 12. Sherman's Yazoo Expedition December 20, 1862, to January 3, 1863. Chickasaw Bayou December 26-28. Chickasaw Bluff December 29. Expedition to Arkansas Post, Ark., January 3-10, 1863. Assault and capture of Fort Hindman, Arkansas Post, January 10-11. Moved to Young's Point, La., January 13-22, and duty there till March. Expedition to Rolling Fork, via Muddy, Steele's and Black Bayous and Deer Creek March 4-27. Demonstrations on Haines' and Drumgould's Bluffs April 29-May 2. March to join army in rear of Vicksburg, via Richmond and Grand Gulf, May 2-16. Battle of Champion's Hill May 16. Siege of Vicksburg, Miss., May 18-July 4. Assaults on Vicksburg May 19 and 22. Advance on Jackson, Miss., July 4-10. Siege of Jackson July 10-17. Canton July 17-18. Brandon July 20. At Big Black River till October 3. Moved to Memphis, Tenn.; thence march to Chattanooga, Tenn., October 3-November 21. Operations on Memphis & Charleston Railroad in Alabama October 20-29. Bear Creek, Tuscumbia, October 27. Chattanooga-Ringgold Campaign November 23-27. Brown's Ferry November 23. Foot of Missionary Ridge November 24. Tunnel Hill, Missionary Ridge, November 24-25. Pursuit to Graysville November 26-27. March to relief of Knoxville November 28-December 5. Expedition to Tellico Plains December 6-13. March to Chattanooga December 13-17. Garrison duty in Alabama till May, 1864. Expedition from Larkins' Landing to Guntersville March 2-3. Atlanta (Ga.) Campaign May 1-September 8. Demonstration on Resaca May 8-13. Battle of Resaca May 14-15. Advance on Dallas May 18-25. Battles about Dallas, New Hope Church and Allatoona Hills May 25-June 5. Guard duty at Big Shanty. Non-Veterans ordered home for muster out June 5. Mustered out July 7, 1864. Veterans and Recruits consolidated to a Battalion of 2 Companies. Operations about Marietta and against Kenesaw Mountain June 10-July 2. Bushy Mountain June 15-17. Assault on Kenesaw June 27. Nickajack Creek July 2-5. Chattahoochie River July 6-17. Battle of Atlanta July 22. Siege of Atlanta July 22-August 25. Ezra Chapel, Hood's 2nd Sortie, July 28. Flank movement on Jonesboro August 25-30. Battle of Jonesboro August 31-September 1. Lovejoy Station September 2-6. Operations against Hood in North Georgia and North Alabama September 29-November 3. March to the sea November 15-December 10. Near Clinton November 21-23. Oconee River November 25. Statesboro December 4. Siege of Savannah December 10-21. Fort McAllister December 13. Campaign of the Carolinas January to April, 1865. Duck Branch, near Loper's Cross Roads, S. C., February 2. Salkehatchie Swamps February 3-5. South Edisto River February 9. North Edisto River February 12-13. Columbia February 16-17. Battle of Bentonville, N. C.,

March 20-21. Occupation of Goldsboro March 24. Advance on Raleigh April 10-14. Occupation of Raleigh April 14. Bennett's House April 26. Surrender of Johnston and his army. March to Washington, D. C., via Richmond, Va., April 29-May 19. Grand Review May 24. Moved to Louisville, Ky., June. Duty there and at Little Rock, Ark., till August. Mustered out August 14, 1865.

Regiment lost during service 3 Officers and 78 Enlisted men killed and mortally wounded and 1 Officer and 124 Enlisted men by disease. Total 206.

8th REGIMENT ENROLLED MILITIA INFANTRY.

No details.

8th REGIMENT PROVISIONAL ENROLLED MILITIA INFANTRY.

Duty at Cape Girardeau and in District of Southeast Missouri. Expedition from Cape Girardeau and Pilot Knob to Pocahontas, Ark., August 17-26, 1863. Expedition to Big Lake, Mississippi County, September 7-30, 1863. Ordered to Pilot Knob October 1. Mustered out October 26, 1863.

9th REGIMENT INFANTRY.

Organized at St. Louis, Mo., July 6 to September 6, 1861. Attached to Fremont's Army of the West to February, 1862. 2nd Brigade, 3rd Division, Army of Southwest Missouri, February, 1862.

SERVICE.—Companies "A," "B" and "C" at Cape Girardeau, Mo., from August 16, 1861. Regiment moved to Jefferson City, Mo., September 21, 1861; thence to Booneville, Mo. Fremont's advance on Springfield, Mo., October 13-November 3. March to Syracuse, Mo., November 9-17; thence to Lamine River December 7, and to Georgetown December 15. To Lamine Bridge December 23, and duty there till January 25, 1862. Advance to Springfield, Mo., January 25-February 11. Regiment transferred to Illinois and designated 59th Regiment Infantry February 12, 1862. See 59th Illinois Infantry.

9th REGIMENT ENROLLED MILITIA INFANTRY.

No details.

9th REGIMENT PROVISIONAL ENROLLED MILITIA INFANTRY.

Operations against Shelby September 22-October 26, 1863. Booneville October 11-12. Merrill's Crossing, Dug Ford, near Julesborough October 12. Marshall October 13. Mustered out November, 1863.

10th REGIMENT INFANTRY.

Organized at St. Louis, Mo., August, 1861. Attached to Dept. of Missouri to May, 1862. 2nd Brigade, 3rd Division, Army of the Mississippi, to November, 1862. 2nd Brigade, 7th Division, Left Wing 13th Army Corps (Old), Dept. of the Tennessee, to December, 1862. 2nd Brigade, 7th Division, 16th Army Corps, to January, 1863. 2nd Brigade, 7th Division, 17th Army Corps, to September, 1863. 2nd Brigade, 2nd Division, 17th Army Corps, to December, 1863. 2nd Brigade, 3rd Division, 15th Army Corps, to October, 1864.

SERVICE.—Guarding Pacific Railroad till November, 1861. Expedition through Jefferson County September 1-3. Fulton, Mo., October 28. At Hermann, Mo., December 1-23. Expedition through Warren, Callaway, Boone and Audrain Counties December, 1861. At Warrenton, Mo., till February, 1862. At High Bridge till April. At Cape Girardeau, Mo., till April 30. Moved to Pittsburg Landing, Tenn., April 30. Coffey's Landing, Tenn., May 2. Siege of Corinth, Miss., May 5-30. Action at Farmington May 9 (Reserve). Skirmish on Booneville Road May 29. Pursuit to Booneville May 31-June 12. At Corinth till August. At Jacinto till September 18. Battle of Iuka September 19. Battle of Corinth October 3-4. Grant's Central Mississippi Campaign November, 1862, to January, 1863. Escort train to Memphis, Tenn., December 20-30, 1862. Guard duty on Memphis & Charleston Railroad at Germantown and near Memphis till March, 1863. Expedition to Yazoo Pass and operations against Fort Pemberton and Greenwood March 13-

April 5. Moved to Milliken's Bend, La., and duty there till April 25. Movement on Bruinsburg and turning Grand Gulf April 25-30. Battle of Port Gibson May 1. (In support). Big Black River May 3. Battles of Raymond May 12. Jackson May 14. Champion's Hill May 16. Siege of Vicksburg, Miss., May 18-July 4. Assaults on Vicksburg May 19 and 22. Surrender of Vicksburg July 4. Garrison duty at Vicksburg till September 12. At Helena, Ark., till October 1. Moved to Memphis, thence march to Chattanooga, Tenn., October 1-November 22. Operations on Memphis & Charleston Railroad in Alabama October 20-29. Chattanooga-Ringgold Campaign November 23-27. Tunnel Hill November 23-24. Mission Ridge November 25. At Bridgeport, Ala., till January 1, 1864. At Royd's Station and Brownsboro, Ala., along Memphis & Charleston Railroad till June 15. (Constructed bridge across Flint River at Brownsboro.) Moved to Kingston, Ga., via Huntsville and Stevenson, Ala., June 15-20. Moved to Resaca July 2, and duty there till August 17. (Cos. "I" and "K" till October.) Defence of Resaca October 12-13 (Cos. "I" and "K"). Companies "A," "B," "C," "D," "E," "F" and "G" left for muster out August 17, and mustered out August 24, 1864. Company "H" attached to Company "E," 24th Missouri Infantry. Companies "I" and "K" mustered out October 31, 1864.

Regiment lost during service 3 Officers and 98 Enlisted men killed and mortally wounded and 2 Officers and 228 Enlisted men by disease. Total 331.

10th REGIMENT ENROLLED MILITIA INFANTRY.

Called into service September 25, 1864, to repel Price's invasion of Missouri. Relieved from active service October 31, 1864.

10th REGIMENT PROVISIONAL ENROLLED MILITIA INFANTRY.

Called into service against Price, 1863.

11th REGIMENT INFANTRY.

Organized at St. Louis, Mo., August, 1861. Moved to Cape Girardeau, Mo., August 16, 1861. Attached to Military District of Cairo, Ill., Dept. of Missouri, to February, 1862. 2nd Brigade, 1st Division, Army of Mississippi, to March, 1862. 2nd Brigade, 5th Division, Army of Mississippi, to April, 1862. 1st Brigade, 3rd Division, Army of Mississippi, to April, 1862. 2nd Brigade, 2nd Division, Army of Mississippi, to November, 1862. 2nd Brigade, 8th Division, Left Wing 13th Army Corps (Old), Dept. of the Tennessee, to December, 1862. 2nd Brigade, 8th Division, 16th Army Corps, to April, 1863. 2nd Brigade, 3rd Division, 15th Army Corps, Army of the Tennessee, to December, 1863. 2nd Brigade, 1st Division, 16th Army Corps, to December, 1864. 2nd Brigade, 1st Division (Detachment), Army of the Tennessee, Dept. of the Cumberland, to February, 1865. 2nd Brigade, 1st Division, 16th Army Corps (New), Military Division West Mississippi, to August, 1865. District of Alabama to December, 1865.

SERVICE.—Duty at Cape Girardeau, Mo., till February, 1862. Expedition to Perryville August 27-September 2, 1861. Dallas September 2. Expedition against Thompson's Forces and operations about Ironton and Fredericktown October 12-25. Action at Fredericktown October 21. Expedition beyond Whitewater River November 30-December 5. Moved from Cape Girardeau to Commerce, Mo., February 26, 1862. Operations against New Madrid, Mo., February 28-March 14, and against Island No. 10, Mississippi River, March 15-April 8. Pleasant Point March 7. At New Madrid, Mo., till April 13. Expedition to Fort Pillow, Tenn., April 13-17. Moved to Hamburg Landing April 18-22. Advance on and siege of Corinth, Miss., April 29-May 30. Action at Farmington, Miss., May 9. Near Corinth May 24. Pursuit to Booneville May 31-June 12. At Clear Creek, near Corinth, till August 18. Expedition to Rienzi June 30-July 1. March to Tuscumbia, Ala., August 18-23. March to Iuka, Miss., September 2-5, and to Clear Creek September 12-13. Reconnoissance to Iuka and skirmish September 14-16. March to Jacinto September 18. Battle of Iuka September 19. Pursuit of Price September 20-25. At Rienzi till September 30. March to Corinth September 30-October 3. Battle of Corinth October 3-4. Pursuit to Ripley October 5-12. At Corinth till November 2. March to Grand Junction November 2-4. Grant's Central Mississippi Campaign November 4, 1862, to January 10, 1863. Moved from Corinth to Germantown, Tenn., January 20-21, 1863. To Memphis, Tenn., February 10; thence to Helena, Ark., and Young's Point, La., and Ducksport, La., February 13-20, and duty there till May, 1863. Moved to join army in rear of Vicksburg, Miss., via Richmond and Grand Gulf May 2-14. Mississippi Springs May 12. Jackson May 14. Siege of Vicksburg May 18-July 4. Assaults on Vicksburg May 19 and 22. Expedition to Mechanicsburg and Satartia June 2-8. Mechanicsburg June 4. Satartia June 7. Moved to Young's Point, La., June. Expedition to Richmond, La., June 14-16. Action at Richmond June 15. Moved to Big Black River Bridge July 5. Outpost there till October. McPherson's Expedition to Canton October 14-20. Bogue Chitto Creek October 17. Moved to Memphis, thence to LaGrange, Tenn., November 8-13. Scout after Forest December 1-3. Expedition after Forest December 21-24. At LaGrange till January 26, 1864. Moved to Memphis, Tenn., thence to Vicksburg, Miss., February 2-5. Camp at Big Black till February 27. March to Canton February 27-29, thence to Vicksburg March 1-4. Veterans moved to St. Louis March 10-16. Moved to Memphis, Tenn., May 2-5. Expedition to Madison, St. Francis County, Ark., June 3-7. Guard working party Memphis to LaGrange June 16-27. Smith's Expedition to Tupelo, Miss., July 5-21. Pontotoc July 11. Camargo's Cross Roads, near Harrisburg, July 13. Tupelo July 14-15. Old Town Creek July 15. Expedition to Oxford, Miss., August 1-30. Near Abbeville August 12. Hurricane Creek, College Hill, August 21. Abbeville August 23. Moved from Memphis to Duvall's Bluff, Ark., September 2-8. Moved to Brownsville September 10-11. March through Arkansas and Missouri in pursuit of Price September 17-November 13. Moved to Nashville, Tenn., November 24-December 1. Battle of Nashville December 15-16. Pursuit of Hood to the Tennessee River December 17-28. At Clifton, Tenn., and Eastport, Miss., till February 7, 1865. Moved to New Orleans, La., February 7-22; thence to Dauphin Island, Ala., March 5. Campaign against Mobile and its Defences March 19-April 12. Siege of Spanish Fort and Fort Blakely March 26-April 8. Assault and capture of Fort Blakely April 9. Occupation of Mobile April 12. March to Montgomery April 13-25, thence to Selma May 10-14, and to Demopolis May 18-19. Duty there till July 15. Duty by Detachments at Tuscaloosa, Marion, Greensboro and Uniontown till October. At Demopolis till December 24. Moved to Memphis, Tenn., December 24-25. Mustered out January 15, 1866.

Regiment lost during service 6 Officers and 98 Enlisted men killed and mortally wounded and 2 Officers and 179 Enlisted men by disease. Total 285.

11th REGIMENT ENROLLED MILITIA INFANTRY.

Duty in Southwest Missouri at Jefferson City, California, Tipton, Syracuse, Sedalia, LaMine, Booneville, etc. Called into service September 25, 1864, to repel Price's invasion of Missouri. Relieved from active service October 31, 1864.

11th REGIMENT PROVISIONAL ENROLLED MILITIA INFANTRY.

Duty at St. Louis. 1st Military District.

12th REGIMENT INFANTRY.

Organized at St. Louis, Mo., August, 1861. Attached to Fremont's Army of the West to January, 1862. 2nd Brigade, Army of Southwest Missouri, to February, 1862. 2nd Brigade, 1st Division, Army of Southwest Missouri, to May, 1862. 3rd Division, Army of Southwest Missouri, to July, 1862. District of Eastern Arkansas, Dept. of Missouri, to December, 1862. 1st Brigade, 11th Division, Right Wing 13th Army Corps (Old),

Dept. of the Tennessee, to December, 1862. 2nd Brigade, 4th Division, Sherman's Yazoo Expedition, to January, 1863. 2nd Brigade, 1st Division, to September, 1863. 1st Brigade, 1st Division, 15th Army Corps, to December, 1863. 3rd Brigade, 1st Division, 15th Army Corps, to November, 1864.

SERVICE.—Fremont's advance on Springfield, Mo., September to November, 1861. Moved to Jefferson City, thence to Sedalia and Springfield. To Wilson's Creek October 6-8. Duty at Rolla till January, 1862. Expedition to Danville December 26, 1861. Curtis' Campaign in Missouri and Arkansas against Price January to March, 1862. Advance on Springfield February 2-16. Pursuit of Price into Arkansas February 14-29. Battles of Pea Ridge, Ark., March 6-8. March to Batesville April 5-May 3; thence to Helena, Ark., May 25-July 14. Expedition from Helena to mouth of White River August 5-8. Moved to Ironton-Pilot Knob, Mo., September 1. To St. Genevieve November 12, and return to Helena November 23. Sherman's Yazoo Expedition December 22, 1862, to January 3, 1863. Chickasaw Bayou December 26-28. Chickasaw Bluff December 29. Expedition to Arkansas Post, Ark., January 3-10, 1863. Assault and capture of Fort Hindman, Arkansas Post, January 10-11. Moved to Young's Point, La., January 17-23. Duty there till March and at Milliken's Bend till April. Expedition to Greenville, Black Bayou and Deer Creek April 2-14. Demonstration on Haines and Drumgould's Bluffs April 29-May 2. Moved to join army in rear of Vicksburg, Miss., via Richmond and Grand Gulf May 2-14. Mississippi Springs May 12-13. Jackson May 14. Siege of Vicksburg, Miss., May 18-July 4. Assaults on Vicksburg May 19 and 22. Advance on Jackson, Miss., July 4-10. Siege of Jackson July 10-17. Bolton's Depot July 16. Brier Creek, near Canton, July 17. Clinton July 18. Camp at Big Black till September 27. Moved to Memphis, Tenn., thence march to Chattanooga, Tenn., September 27-November 21. Operations on Memphis & Charleston Railroad in Alabama October 20-29. Cherokee Station October 21 and 29. Cane Creek October 26. Tuscumbia October 26-27. Battles of Chattanooga November 23-27. Lookout Mountain November 23-24. Mission Ridge November 25. Ringgold Gap, Taylor's Ridge, November 27. March to relief of Knoxville November 28-December 8. Garrison duty in Alabama at Woodville and Scottsboro, Ala., and at Cleveland, Tenn., to May, 1864. Atlanta (Ga.) Campaign May 1 to September 8. Demonstration on Resaca May 8-13. Battle of Resaca May 13-15. Advance on Dallas May 18-25. Battles about Dallas, New Hope Church and Allatoona Hills May 25-June 5. Operations about Marietta and against Kenesaw Mountain June 10-July 2. Bushy Mountain June 15-17. Assault on Kenesaw June 27. Nickajack Creek July 2-5. Chattahoochie River July 6-17. Battle of Atlanta July 22. Siege of Atlanta July 22-August 25. Ezra Chapel, Hood's 2nd Sortie, July 28. Flank movement on Jonesboro August 25-30. Lovejoy Station September 2-6. Pursuit of Hood into Alabama October 1-21. Mustered out by Companies from August 12 to November 14, 1864. Consolidated with Detachments from 3rd and 17th Missouri Volunteer Infantry and subsequently transferred to 15th Missouri Infantry.

Regiment lost during service 10 Officers and 102 Enlisted men killed and mortally wounded and 2 Officers and 94 Enlisted men by disease. Total 208.

13th REGIMENT INFANTRY.

Organized at St. Louis, Mo., August 9 to November 5, 1861. Attached to Dept. of Missouri to February, 1862. 3rd Brigade, 2nd Division, District of Cairo, to February, 1862. 2nd Brigade, 2nd Division, Army of the Tennessee, to May, 1862.

SERVICE.—Ordered to Cairo, Ill., January 26, 1862. Reconnoissance from Smithland, Ky., toward Fort Henry, Tenn., January 31-February 2. Capture of Fort Henry, Tenn., February 6. Investment and capture of Fort Donelson, Tenn., February 11-16. Expedition to Clarksville and Nashville, Tenn., February 22-March 6.

Moved to Pittsburg Landing, Tenn., March 14-17. Battle of Shiloh, Tenn., April 6-7. Advance on and siege of Corinth, Miss., April 29-May 30. Transferred to Ohio as the 22nd Ohio Volunteer Infantry May 29, 1862 (which see).

13th REGIMENT ENROLLED MILITIA INFANTRY.

Called into service September 25, 1864, to repel invasion of Missouri by Price. Relieved from active service October 31, 1864.

14th REGIMENT MISSOURI INFANTRY.

Organized as "Birge's Western Sharpshooters" at St. Louis, Mo. Mustered in as 14th Infantry November 23, 1861. Attached to Dept. of Missouri to February, 1862. 4th Brigade, 2nd Division, Military District of Cairo, February, 1862. 2nd Brigade, 2nd Division, Army of the Tennessee, to July, 1862. 2nd Brigade, 2nd Division, District of Corinth, Miss., to November, 1862.

SERVICE.—Moved to Centralia, Mo., December 12-14, 1861. Skirmishes with Bushwhackers December 14-28. Capture of Columbia December 26. Battle of Mt. Zion December 28. Moved to Sturgeon December 29. Scouting about Renick, Macon and Centralia till February 4, 1862. Moved to St. Louis, Mo., thence to Cairo, Ill., Paducah, Ky., and Fort Henry, Tenn., February 4-9. Investment and capture of Fort Donelson February 12-16. Duty at Fort Donelson till March 5. Moved to Metal Landing, Tennessee River, thence to Savannah and Pittsburg Landing, Tenn., March 5-17. Battle of Shiloh, Tenn., April 6-7. Advance on and siege of Corinth, Miss., April 29-May 30. Occupation of Corinth May 30 and pursuit to Booneville June 1-3. Duty at Headquarters of General Grant till August 25, and Provost duty at Corinth. Scout to Bethel August 28-30. Expedition to Glendale and Iuka September 18-21. Battle of Iuka September 19. Battle of White House and Corinth October 3-4. Pursuit to the Hatchie River October 5-12. Hatchie River October 9. Scout to Hatchie River November 2-5. Regiment transferred to Illinois as 66th Illinois Infantry November 20, 1862. (See 66th Illinois Infantry.)

Regiment lost during service 4 Enlisted men killed and mortally wounded and 2 Enlisted men by disease. Total 6.

14th REGIMENT HOME GUARD INFANTRY.

Organized at Lexington, Mo., August, 1861. Siege of Lexington September 11-21. Captured and paroled. Mustered out October 19, 1861.

15th REGIMENT INFANTRY.

Organized at St. Louis, Mo., August and September, 1861. Moved to Jefferson City, Mo., September, 1861. Attached to Fremont's Army of the West to January, 1862. 5th Brigade, Army of Southwest Missouri, to March, 1862. 1st Brigade, 2nd Division, Army of Southwest Missouri, to May, 1862. 1st Brigade, 5th Division, Army of Mississippi, to September, 1862. 35th Brigade, 11th Division, Army of Ohio, to October, 1862. 35th Brigade, 11th Division, 3rd Army Corps, Army of Ohio, to November, 1862. 2nd Brigade, 3rd Division, Right Wing 14th Army Corps, Army of the Cumberland, to January, 1863. 2nd Brigade, 3rd Division, 20th Army Corps, Army of the Cumberland, to October, 1863. 1st Brigade, 2nd Division, 4th Army Corps, to April, 1864. 3rd Brigade, 2nd Division, 4th Army Corps, to June, 1865. 2nd Brigade, 2nd Division, 4th Army Corps, to August, 1865. Dept. of Texas to December, 1865.

SERVICE.—Fremont's Campaign against Springfield, Mo., October 4-November 8, 1861. Moved to Rolla, Mo., and duty there till February, 1862. Curtis' Campaign in Missouri and Arkansas against Price February and March. Advance on Springfield February 2-11. Pursuit of Price into Arkansas February 14-29. Battles of Pea Ridge, Ark., March 6-8. March to Batesville April 5-May 3. Moved to Cape Girardeau, Mo., May 11-22; thence to Pittsburg Landing, Tenn., May 23-26. Siege of Corinth May 27-30. Pursuit to Booneville May 31-June 6. At Rienzi till August 26. Moved to Cincin-

nati, Ohio, August 26-September 14; thence to Louisville, Ky., September 17-19. Pursuit of Bragg into Kentucky October 1-16. Battle of Perryville, Ky., October 8. March to Nashville, Tenn., October 16-November 7. Duty at Nashville till December 26. Advance on Murfreesboro December 26-30. Battle of Stone's River December 30-31, 1862, and January 1-3, 1863. Duty near Murfreesboro till June. Expedition toward Columbia March 4-14. Middle Tennessee (or Tullahoma) Campaign June 23-July 7. Fairfield June 27-29. Estill Springs July 2. Reconnoissance to Anderson July 11-14. Occupation of Middle Tennessee till August 16. Passage of Cumberland Mountains and Tennessee River and Chickamauga (Ga.) Campaign August 16-September 22. Battle of Chickamauga September 19-20. Siege of Chattanooga September 24-November 23. Chattanooga-Ringgold Campaign November 23-27. Orchard Knob November 23-24. Mission Ridge November 25. Pursuit to Graysville November 26-27. March to relief of Knoxville, Tenn., November 28-December 8. Operations in East Tennessee December, 1863, to February, 1864. Dandridge January 16-17, 1864. Moved to Chattanooga, thence to Cleveland, Tenn., and duty there till May, 1864. Atlanta (Ga.) Campaign May 1-September 8. Demonstration on Rocky Faced Ridge and Dalton May 8-13. Buzzard's Roost Gap May 8-9. Battle of Resaca May 14-15. Adairsville May 17. Near Kingston May 18-19. Near Cassville May 19. Advance on Dallas May 22-25. Operations on line of Pumpkin Vine Creek and battles about Dallas, New Hope Church and Allatoona Hills May 25-June 5. Operations about Marietta and against Kenesaw Mountain June 10-July 2. Pine Hill June 11-14. Lost Mountain June 15-17. Assault on Kenesaw June 27. Ruff's Station July 4. Chattahoochie River July 5-17. Buckhead, Nancy's Creek, July 18. Peach Tree Creek July 19-20. Siege of Atlanta July 22-August 25. Flank movement on Jonesboro August 25-30. Battle of Jonesboro August 31-September 1. Lovejoy Station September 2-6. Operations against Hood and Forest in North Georgia and North Alabama September 29-November 3. Nashville Campaign November and December. Columbia, Duck River, November 24-27. Spring Hill November 29. Battle of Franklin November 30. Battle of Nashville December 15-16. Pursuit of Hood to the Tennessee River December 17-28. Columbia December 19. Pulaski December 25. March from Pulaski to Decatur, Ala., and duty there till April, 1865. Moved to Blue Springs April 1-5, thence to Nashville, Tenn., April 19, and duty there till June. Moved to New Orleans June 15-23, and to Port Lavaca, Texas, July 18-24. Duty there till October. Moved to Victoria October 27 and duty there till December. Mustered out December 25, 1865.

Regiment lost during service 8 Officers and 107 Enlisted men killed and mortally wounded and 1 Officer and 106 Enlisted men by disease. Total 222.

15th REGIMENT HOME GUARD INFANTRY.

Organized in Polk County, Mo., by authority of General Lyon June, 1861. Duty at Jefferson City and on railroad till December. Mustered out December, 1861.

16th REGIMENT INFANTRY.

Failed to complete organization.

17th REGIMENT INFANTRY.

Organized at St. Louis, Mo., August, 1861. Attached to Army of the West to January, 1862. 2nd Brigade, Army of Southwest Missouri, to March, 1862. 1st Brigade, 1st Division, Army of Southwest Missouri, to May, 1862. 3rd Division, Army of Southwest Missouri, to July, 1862. District of Eastern Arkansas, Dept. of Missouri, to November, 1862. 1st Brigade, 1st Division, District of Eastern Arkansas to December, 1862. 1st Brigade, 11th Division, Right Wing 13th Army Corps (Old), Dept. of the Tennessee, to December, 1862. 2nd Brigade, 4th Division, Sherman's Yazoo Expedition, to January, 1863. 2nd Brigade, 1st Division, 15th Army Corps, Army of the Tennessee, to September, 1863. 1st Brigade, 1st Division, 15th Army Corps, to December,

1863. 3rd Brigade, 1st Division, 15th Army Corps, to December, 1864.

SERVICE.—Fremont's Campaign against Springfield, Mo., October-November, 1861. Duty at Rolla, Mo., till January, 1862. Curtis' Campaign against Price in Missouri and Arkansas January to March. Advance on Springfield February 2-14. Pursuit of Price into Arkansas February 14-29. Battles of Pea Ridge, Ark., March 6-8. March to Batesville, Ark., April 5-May 3. Searcy Landing May 19. March to Helena, Ark., May 25-July 14. Expedition from Helena to mouth of White River August 5-8. Moved to Ironton and Pilot Knob, Mo., September 1. To St. Genevieve November 12 and return to Helena November 23. Sherman's Yazoo Expedition December 22, 1862, to January 3, 1863. Chickasaw Bayou December 26-28. Chickasaw Bluff December 29. Expedition to Arkansas Post, Ark., January 3-10, 1863. Assault and capture of Fort Hindman, Arkansas Post, January 10-11. Moved to Young's Point, La., January 17-23, and duty there till March, and at Milliken's Bend till April. Expedition to Greenville, Black Bayou and Deer Creek April 2-14. Demonstration on Haines' and Drumgould's Bluffs April 29-May 2. Moved to join army in rear of Vicksburg, Miss., via Richmond and Grand Gulf May 2-14. Mississippi Springs May 12-13. Jackson May 14. Siege of Vicksburg May 18-July 4. Assaults on Vicksburg May 19 and 22. Advance on Jackson, Miss., July 4-10. Siege of Jackson July 10-17. Bolton's Depot July 16. Brier Creek, near Canton, July 17. Canton July 18. At Big Black till September 27. Moved to Memphis, Tenn.; thence march to Chattanooga, Tenn., September 27-November 21. Operations on Memphis & Charleston Railroad in Alabama October 20-29. Cherokee Station October 21 and 29. Cane Creek October 26. Tuscumbia October 26-27. Chattanooga-Ringgold Campaign November 23-27. Battles of Lookout Mountain November 23-24. Mission Ridge November 25. Ringgold Gap, Taylor's Ridge, November 27. March to relief of Knoxville, Tenn., November 28-December 8. Garrison duty in Alabama till May, 1864. Atlanta (Ga.) Campaign May 1 to September 8. Demonstration on Resaca May 8-13. Battle of Resaca May 13-15. Advance on Dallas May 18-25. Battles about Dallas, New Hope Church and Allatoona Hills May 25-June 5. Operations about Marietta and against Kenesaw Mountain June 10-July 2. Nickajack Creek July 2-5. Chattahoochie River July 6-17. Battle of Atlanta July 22. Siege of Atlanta July 22-August 25. Ezra Chapel, Hood's 2nd Sortie, July 28. Flank movement on Jonesboro August 25-30. Lovejoy Station September 2-6. Operations against Hood in North Georgia and North Alabama October 1-21. March to the sea November 15-December 10. Non-Veterans mustered out September and October, 1864. Veterans and Recruits transferred to 15th Missouri Infantry December, 1864.

Regiment lost during service 6 Officers and 62 Enlisted men killed and mortally wounded and 3 Officers and 148 Enlisted men by disease. Total 219.

18th REGIMENT INFANTRY.

Organized at Laclede, Mo., July to November, 1861. Attached to District of St. Louis, Dept. of Missouri, to March, 1862. 2nd Brigade, 6th Division, Army of the Tennessee, to July, 1862. 2nd Brigade, 6th Division, District of Corinth, Miss., to November, 1862. 2nd Brigade, 6th Division, District of Corinth, 13th Army Corps (Old), Dept. of the Tennessee, November, 1862. 3rd Brigade, District of Corinth, 13th Army Corps, to December, 1862. 3rd Brigade, District of Corinth, 17th Army Corps, to January, 1863. 3rd Brigade, District of Corinth, 16th Army Corps, to March, 1863. 3rd Brigade, 2nd Division, 16th Army Corps, to November, 1863. Fuller's Brigade, 2nd Division, 16th Army Corps, to January, 1864. 3rd Brigade, 2nd Division, 16th Army Corps, to March, 1864. 1st Brigade, 4th Division, 16th Army Corps, to September, 1864. 1st Brigade, 1st Division, 17th Army Corps, to July, 1865.

SERVICE.—Duty on Hannibal & St. Joseph Railroad during summer and fall of 1861. At Weston, Mo., till December. Ordered from St. Louis to Cairo, Ill., December 22. At Bird's Point, Mo., till March, 1862. Ordered to Pittsburg Landing, Tenn. Battle of Shiloh, Tenn., April 6-7. Advance on and siege of Corinth, Miss., April 29-May 30. At Corinth and Bolivar till December. Battle of Corinth October 3-4 (Cos. "A," "B," "C" and "E"). Pursuit to Ripley October 5-12 (Cos. "A," "B," "C" and "E"). On duty in District of Corinth guarding Railroad toward Bethel till June, 1863. Affairs at Camp Sheldon February 8 and 10, 1863. Operations in Northeast Mississippi June 13-22. Skirmishes at New Albany June 19. Mud Creek June 20. At Corinth till November. March to Pulaski, Tenn., November 2-12. Duty there and guard duty on Railroad till April, 1864. Veterans on furlough January and February, 1864. Atlanta (Ga.) Campaign May 1-September 8. Demonstrations on Resaca May 8-13. Sugar Valley May 9. Near Resaca May 13. Battle of Resaca May 14-15. Advance on Dallas May 18-25. Operations on line of Pumpkin Vine Creek and battles about Dallas, New Hope Church and Allatoona Hills May 25-June 5. Operations about Marietta and against Kenesaw Mountain June 10-July 2. Assault on Kenesaw June 27. Nickajack Creek July 2-5. Ruff's Mills July 3-4. Chattahoochie River July 6-17. Battle of Atlanta July 22. Siege of Atlanta July 22-August 25. Flank movement on Jonesboro August 25-30. Battle of Jonesboro August 31-September 1. Lovejoy Station September 2-6. Operations against Hood in North Georgia and North Alabama September 29-November 3. March to the sea November 15-December 10. Monteith Swamp December 9. Siege of Savannah December 10-21. Campaign of the Carolinas January to April, 1865. Pocotaligo, S. C., January 14-16. Reconnoissance to Salkehatchie River January 25. Skirmishes Rivers' and Broxton's Bridges, Salkehatchie River, February 2. Rivers' Bridge, Salkehatchie River, February 3. Binnaker's Bridge, South Edisto River, February 9. North Edisto River February 12-13. Columbia February 15-17. Juniper Creek, near Cheraw, March 3. Fayetteville, N. C., March 11. Battle of Bentonville March 20-21. Occupation of Goldsboro March 24. Advance on Raleigh April 10-14. Occupation of Raleigh April 14. Bennett's House April 26. Surrender of Johnston and his army. March to Washington, D. C., via Richmond, Va., April 29-May 20. Grand Review May 24. Moved to Louisville, Ky., June, and duty there till July. Mustered out July 18, 1865.

Regiment lost during service 6 Officers and 75 Enlisted men killed and mortally wounded and 164 Enlisted men by disease. Total 245.

19th REGIMENT INFANTRY.
Failed to complete organization.

20th REGIMENT INFANTRY.
Failed to complete organization.

21st REGIMENT INFANTRY.

Organized February 1, 1862, from 1st and 2nd Northeast Regiments Missouri Infantry. Attached to Dept. of Missouri to March, 1862. 1st Brigade, 6th Division, Army of the Tennessee, to July, 1862. 1st Brigade, 6th Division, District of Corinth, Miss., to November, 1862. 1st Brigade, 6th Division, Left Wing 13th Army Corps (Old), Dept. of the Tennessee, to December, 1862. District of Columbus, Ky., 16th Army Corps, Dept. of the Tennessee, to May, 1863. 4th Brigade, District of Memphis, Tenn., 5th Division, 16th Army Corps, to January, 1864. 1st Brigade, 3rd Division, 16th Army Corps, to December, 1864. 1st Brigade, 2nd Division, Detachment Army of the Tennessee, Dept. of the Cumberland, to February, 1865. 1st Brigade, 2nd Division, 16th Army Corps (New), Military Division West Mississippi, to August, 1865. Dept. of Alabama to April, 1866.

SERVICE.—Ordered to Pittsburg Landing, Tenn., March, 1862. Battle of Shiloh, Tenn., April 6-7. Advance on and siege of Corinth, Miss., April 29-May 30. Occupation of Corinth and pursuit to Booneville May 31-June 12. Duty at Corinth till September. Battle of Iuka September 19. Battle of Corinth October 3-4. Pursuit to Ripley October 5-12. Grant's Central Mississippi Campaign November, 1862, to January, 1863. On post and garrison duty at Columbus, Ky.; Union City, Tenn.; Clinton, Ky., and Memphis, Tenn., till January, 1864. Ordered to Vicksburg, Miss., January 26. Actions with guerrillas at Islands Nos. 70 and 71, Mississippi River, while en route, January 29, on steamer "William Wallace," Meridian Campaign February 3-March 2. Queen Hill February 4. Red River Campaign March 10-May 22. Fort DeRussy March 14. Occupation of Alexandria, La., March 16. Battle of Pleasant Hill April 9. About Cloutiersville April 22-24. At Alexandria April 26-May 13. Retreat to Morganza May 13-20. Mansura May 16. Yellow Bayou May 18. Moved to Vicksburg, Miss., thence to Memphis, Tenn., May 22-June 10. Action at Old River Lake or Lake Chicot June 5-6. Smith's Expedition to Tupelo, Miss., July 5-21. Camargo's Cross Roads, near Harrisburg, July 13. Tupelo July 14-15. Old Town Creek July 15. Smith's Expedition to Oxford, Miss., August 1-30. Tallahatchie River August 7-9. Abbeville August 23. Moved to Duvall's Bluff, Ark., September 1-6. March through Arkansas and Missouri in pursuit of Price September 17-November 16. Lone Jack November 1. Moved to Nashville, Tenn., November 25 December 1. Battle of Nashville December 15-16. Pursuit of Hood to the Tennessee River December 17-28. Moved to Clifton, Tenn., thence to Eastport, Miss., January 2-7, 1865, and duty there till February 9. Moved to Vicksburg, Miss., thence to New Orleans, La., February 9-21. Campaign against Mobile and its Defences March 17-April 12. Siege of Spanish Fort and Fort Blakely March 26-April 8. Assault and capture of Fort Blakely April 9. Occupation of Mobile April 12. March to Montgomery April 13-25, and duty there till June. Moved to Mobile June 1. Duty at Mobile and other points in Alabama till April, 1866. Mustered out April 19, 1866.

Regiment lost during service 2 Officers and 68 Enlisted men killed and mortally wounded and 5 Officers and 234 Enlisted men by disease. Total 309.

22nd REGIMENT INFANTRY.

Organized in Missouri at large August to December, 1861. Served unassigned, Dept. of Missouri, to March, 1862. Unassigned, Army of Mississippi, to July, 1862.

SERVICE.—Duty in District of Northeast Missouri to March, 1862. At Commerce and Bird's Point, Mo., March, 1862. Companies "A" and "B" transferred to 7th Missouri Cavalry February 20, 1862. Companies "C," "D" and "E" transferred to 10th Missouri Infantry, and Company "F" to 24th Missouri Infantry, April 21, 1862. Regiment mustered out July 22, 1862.

23rd REGIMENT INFANTRY.

Organized in Missouri at large September, 1861. Moved to Macon City, Mo., October 15, 1881, thence to Chillicothe, Mo., November 1. Attached to Dept. of Missouri to March, 1862. St. Louis, Mo., Dept. of Missouri, to April, 1862. Unattached, 6th Division, Army of the Tennessee, to April, 1862. District of St. Louis, Mo., Dept. of Missouri, to June, 1863. District of Rolla, Dept. of Missouri, to December, 1863. Unattached, District of Nashville, Tenn., Dept. of the Cumberland, to January, 1864. 2nd Brigade, Rousseau's Division, 12th Army Corps, Dept. of the Cumberland, to April, 1864. Unassigned, 4th Division, 20th Army Corps, Dept. of the Cumberland, to July, 1864. 1st Brigade, 3rd Division, 14th Army Corps, to July, 1865.

SERVICE.—Duty at Chillicothe, Mo., November, 1861, to March, 1862, and St. Louis, Mo., till April. Moved to Pittsburg Landing, Tenn., April 1-4. Battle of Shiloh, Tenn., April 6. Regiment captured April 6. Duty at St. Louis, Mo., till August, 1862; at Macon till November, 1862; at Hudson, Mo., till December, 1862, and in Central District of Missouri. Company "A" at Gasconade, Company "D" at Osage City, Company "I" at St. Auberts; rest at Prairie City, District of St. Louis, December, 1862, to July, 1863. Operations against Marmaduke April 14-May 2, 1863. Cape Girardeau April 26. Ordered to Rolla July 5, 1863. Duty in District of Rolla till December, 1863. (Co. "G" ordered to Cape Girardeau July 5, 1863.) Operations against Shelby October 7-22.

Ordered to Nashville, Tenn., December, 1863. Duty at Nashville and McMinnville and guarding Nashville & Chattanooga Railroad till July, 1864. White County January 16, 1864. Joined 1st Brigade, 3rd Division, 14th Army Corps, July 10, 1864. Atlanta (Ga.) Campaign July 10 to September 8. Chattahoochie River July 10-17. Peach Tree Creek July 19-20. Siege of Atlanta July 22-August 25. Flank movement on Jonesboro August 25-30. Battle of Jonesboro August 31-September 1. Operations in North Georgia and North Alabama against Forest and Hood September 29-November 3. March to the sea November 15-December 10. Near Milledgeville November 23. Siege of Savannah December 10-21. Campaign of the Carolinas January to April, 1865. Fayette, N. C., March 11. Battle of Bentonville March 19-21. Occupation of Goldsboro March 24. Advance on Raleigh April 10-14. Occupation of Raleigh April 14. Bennett's House April 26. Surrender of Johnston and his army. March to Washington, D. C., via Richmond, Va., April 29-May 17. Grand Review May 24. Moved to Louisville, Ky., June, and duty there till July. Mustered out July 18, 1865.

Regiment lost during service 2 Officers and 57 Enlisted men killed and mortally wounded and 4 Officers and 173 Enlisted men by disease. Total 236.

24th REGIMENT INFANTRY.

Organized in Missouri at large October 24 to December 28, 1861. Attached to 1st Brigade, Army of Southwest Missouri, to February, 1862. Unassigned, Army of Southwest Missouri, to July, 1862. District of Eastern Arkansas, Dept. of Missouri, to October, 1862. 2nd Brigade, 2nd Division, Army of Southeast Missouri, Dept. of Missouri, to February, 1863. 1st Brigade, 2nd Division, Army of Southeast Missouri, to March, 1863. District of Southeast Missouri to June, 1863. District of Columbus, Ky., 6th Division, 16th Army Corps, Dept. of the Tennessee, to January, 1864. 2nd Brigade, 3rd Division, 16th Army Corps, Dept. of the Tennessee, to March, 1864. 2nd Brigade, 3rd Division, 16th Army Corps, Dept. of the Gulf, to June, and Dept. of the Tennessee to October, 1864.

SERVICE.—Join Curtis at Rolla, Mo., January, 1862. Curtis' Campaign in Missouri and Arkansas against Price, January to March, 1862. Advance on Springfield, Mo., February 2-11. Pursuit of Price into Arkansas February 14-29. Battles of Pea Ridge, Ark., March 6-8. March to Batesville April 5-May 13, thence march to Helena, Ark., May 25-July 14. Duty at Helena till October. Moved to Sulphur Springs, Mo., October 5-11. Pittman's Ferry, Ark., October 27 (3 Cos.). Moved to Pilot Knob, Mo., October 28-30. March to Patterson November 2-4, to Reeve's Station December 9-10. Return to Patterson December 18. Moved to Van Buren December 21-24, and toward Doniphan January 9-10, 1863. To Alton January 14-18, and to West Plains and Salem, Ark., January 28-February 2. To Pilot Knob and Ironton February 2-27. Moved to St. Genevieve and to Cape Girardeau March 8-12. Operations against Marmaduke April 17-May 2 (Co. "G"). Mill Creek Bridge April 24 (Detachment). Duty in Southeast Missouri till June. Richfield, Clay County, May 19 (Detachment). Ordered to New Madrid, Mo., June, and duty in District of Columbus, Ky., till January, 1864. New Madrid, Mo., August 7, 1863 (1 Co.). Expedition from Union City, Tenn., to Conyersville September 1-10 (Detachment). Conyersville September 10. Ordered to Vicksburg, Miss., January, 1864. Meridian Campaign February 3-March 5. Meridian February 14-15. Marion February 15-17. Canton February 28. Red River Campaign March 10-May 22. Fort De Russy March 14. Occupation of Alexandria March 16. Henderson's Hill March 21. Battle of Pleasant Hill April 9. Cloutiersville and Cane River Crossing April 22-24. At Alexandria April 27-May 13. Moore's Plantation May 5-7. Bayou Boeuf May 7. Bayou LaMourie May 12. Retreat to Morganza May 13-20. Mansura May 16. Yellow Bayou May 18-19. Moved to Vicksburg, Miss.; thence to Memphis, Tenn., May 22-June 10. Lake

Chicot, Ark., June 6-7. Smith's Expedition to Tupelo, Miss., July 5-21. Pontotoc July 11. Camargo's Cross Roads, near Harrisburg, July 13. Tupelo July 14-15. Old Town Creek July 15. Smith's Expedition to Oxford, Miss., August 1-30. Tallahatchie River August 7-9. Abbeville and Oxford August 12. Moved to Duvall's Bluff, Ark., September 1-6. Pursuit of Price through Arkansas and Missouri September 7 to October 6. Mineral Point, Mo., September 27. Ordered to St. Louis, Mo., October 6. A detachment of Veterans and Recruits at Franklin, Mo., till November. Ordered to Paducah, Ky., November 7; thence moved to Nashville, Tenn., and Columbia, Tenn., November 22-26. Temporarily attacked to 2nd Brigade, 2nd Division, 23rd Army Corps. Columbia November 26-27. Battle of Franklin November 30. Battles of Nashville, Tenn., December 15-16. Pursuit of Hood to the Tennessee River December 17-28. At Clifton, Tenn., and Eastport, Miss., till February, 1865. Regiment mustered out October, 1864, to February 1, 1865.

Company "E" served detached from May, 1862. Attached to 2nd Brigade, 3rd Division, Army of the Mississippi, May, 1862, to November, 1862. 2nd Brigade, 7th Division, Left Wing 13th Army Corps, Dept. of the Tennessee, to December, 1862. 2nd Brigade, 7th Division, 16th Army Corps, to January, 1863. 2nd Brigade, 7th Division, 17th Army Corps, to September, 1863. 2nd Brigade, 2nd Division, 17th Army Corps, to December, 1863. 2nd Brigade, 3rd Division, 15th Army Corps, to October, 1864, participating in battles of Iuka, Miss., September 19, 1862. Corinth, Miss., October 3-4. Grant's Central Mississippi Campaign November, 1862, to January, 1863. Expedition to Yazoo Pass and operations against Fort Pemberton and Greenwood March 13-April 5, 1863. At Milliken's Bend, La., till April 25. Movement on Bruinsburg and turning Grand Gulf April 25-30. Battles of Port Gibson May 1, Raymond May 12, Jackson May 14, Champion's Hill May 16. Siege of Vicksburg, Miss., May 18-July 4. Surrender of Vicksburg July 4. Garrison duty at Vicksburg till September. Movement to Helena, Ark.; Memphis, Tenn., and march to Chattanooga, Tenn., September 12-November 22. Operations on Memphis & Charleston Railroad in Alabama October 20-29. Chattanooga-Ringgold Campaign November 23-27. Tunnel Hill November 23-24. Mission Ridge November 25. At Bridgeport, Ala., till January, 1864. Duty along Memphis & Charleston Railroad till June, 1864. Moved to Kingston, Ga., June 15-20, thence to Resaca July 2, and duty there till October. Defence of Resaca October 12. Company captured.

Companies "F" and "K" detached and on duty in District of Southeast Missouri to July, 1863. Reserve Brigade, 1st Cavalry Division, Army of Southeast Missouri, to August, 1863. Unattached, Cavalry Division, Arkansas Expedition, to January, 1864. Unattached, 1st Division, 7th Army Corps, Army of Arkansas, to February, 1864. Participating in actions at Licking, Mo., May 4, 1862. Crow's Station, near Licking, May 26, 1862. Scout in Wayne, Stoddard and Dunklin Counties, Mo., August 20-27, 1862. Duty in District of Southeast Missouri till July, 1863. Steele's operations against Litttle Rock, Ark., July 1-September 10. Capture of Little Rock September 10 and duty there till February, 1864. Rejoined Regiment at Vicksburg, Miss., February, 1864.

Regiment lost during service 3 Officers and 40 Enlisted men killed and mortally wounded and 1 Officer and 220 Enlisted men by disease. Total 264.

25th REGIMENT INFANTRY.

Organized as 13th Missouri Infantry June, 1861. Designation changed to 25th Missouri September, 1861. Attached to Dept. of Missouri to March, 1862. 1st Brigade, 6th Division, Army of the Tennessee, to July, 1862. 1st Brigade, 6th Division, District of Corinth, Miss., to September, 1862. 1st Brigade, 2nd Division, District of Southeast Missouri, Dept. of Missouri, to March, 1863. District of Northwest Missouri to June, 1863. New Madrid, Mo., District of Columbus, Ky.,

6th Division, 16th Army Corps, Dept. of the Tennessee, to February, 1864.

SERVICE.—Duty in Missouri till March, 1862. Ordered to Pittsburg Landing, Tenn. Battle of Shiloh, Tenn., April 6-7. Advance on and siege of Corinth, Miss., April 29-May 30. Duty at Corinth, Miss., building fortifications till September. Ordered to St. Louis, Mo., thence to Pilot Knob and Patterson, Mo. Duty in Southeast Missouri till March, 1863. Moved to Iron Mountain, thence to St. Joseph, Mo., and operating against guerrillas in Northwest Missouri till June. Ordered to New Madrid, Mo., and garrison duty there and reconstructing fortifications till February, 1864. Consolidated with Bissell's Engineer Regiment of the West to form 1st Missouri Engineers February 17, 1864. (See 1st Engineers.)

Regiment lost during service 6 Officers and 51 Enlisted men killed and mortally wounded and 3 Officers and 112 Enlisted men by disease. Total 172.

25th REGIMENT ENROLLED MILITIA INFANTRY.

Duty in Northwestern Missouri.

26th REGIMENT INFANTRY.

Organized in Missouri at large September to December, 1861. Attached to Dept. of Missouri to February, 1862. 2nd Brigade, 2nd Division, Army of Mississippi, to April, 1862. 1st Brigade, 3rd Division, Army of Mississippi, to November, 1862. 3rd Brigade, 7th Division, Left Wing 13th Army Corps (Old), Dept. of the Tennessee, to December, 1862. 3rd Brigade, 7th Division, 16th Army Corps, to January, 1863. 3rd Brigade, 7th Division, 17th Army Corps, to September, 1863. 3rd Brigade, 2nd Division, 17th Army Corps, to December, 1863. 3rd Brigade, 3rd Division, 15th Army Corps, to August, 1864. 2nd Brigade, 3rd Division, 15th Army Corps, to April, 1865. 3rd Brigade, 2nd Division, 15th Army Corps, to August, 1865.

SERVICE.—Duty in Missouri till February, 1862. Operations against New Madrid, Mo., February 28-March 15, and against Island No. 10, Mississippi River, March 15-April 8. Pursuit and capture at Tiptonville April 8. Expedition to Fort Pillow, Tenn., April 13-17. Moved to Hamburg Landing, Tenn., April 18-22. Advance on and siege of Corinth, Miss., April 29-May 30. Pursuit to Booneville May 31-June 12. At Clear Creek till August. Moved to Jacinto August 5. March to Iuka, Miss., September 18-19. Battle of Iuka September 19. Battle of Corinth October 3-4. Pursuit to Ripley October 5-12. Grant's Central Mississippi Campaign November, 1862, to January, 1863. At Memphis, Tenn., till March, 1863. Expedition to Yazoo Pass and operations against Fort Pemberton and Greenwood March 13-April 5. Moved to Milliken's Bend, La., April 13. Movement on Bruinsburg and turning Grand Gulf April 25-30. Battle of Port Gibson, Miss., May 1 (Reserve). Raymond May 12. Near Raymond May 13. Jackson May 14. Champion's Hill May 16. Big Black Crossing May 17. Siege of Vicksburg, Miss., May 18-July 4. Assaults on Vicksburg May 19 and 22. Surrender of Vicksburg July 4. Moved to Jackson July 13-15. Siege of Jackson July 15-17. At Vicksburg till September 12. Moved to Helena, Ark., September 12; to Memphis, Tenn., September 30, and march to Chattanooga, Tenn., October 3-November 19. Operations on Memphis & Charleston Railroad in Alabama October 20-29. Chattanooga-Ringgold Campaign November 23-27. Tunnel Hill November 23-24. Mission Ridge November 25. Pursuit to Graysville November 26-27. Moved to Bridgeport, Ala., December 3; to Larkinsville, Ala., December 22, and to Huntsville, Ala., January 17, 1864. Duty there till June, 1864. Demonstration on Dalton February 22-27. Tunnel Hill, Buzzard's Roost Gap and Rocky Faced Ridge February 23-25. Railroad guard duty between Chattanooga and Allatoona, Ga., till November. March to the sea November 15-December 10. Ogeechee River December 7-9. Siege of Savannah December 10-21. Campaign of the Carolinas January to April, 1865. Salkehatchie Swamps, S. C., February 2-5. South Edisto River February 9. North Edisto River

February 11-12. Columbia February 15-17. Cox's Bridge, Neuse River, N. C., March 19-20. Battle of Bentonville March 20-21. Occupation of Goldsboro March 24. Advance on Raleigh April 10-14. Occupation of Raleigh April 14. Bennett's House April 26. Surrender of Johnston and his army. March to Washington, D. C., via Richmond, Va., April 29-May 20. Grand Review May 24. Moved to Louisville, Ky., June. Duty there and at Little Rock, Ark., till August. Mustered out Companies "A," "B," "C," "D," "E," "F" and "G" November 4, 1864, to January 9, 1865. Regiment mustered out August 13, 1865.

Regiment lost during service 6 Officers and 112 Enlisted men killed and mortally wounded and 2 Officers and 183 Enlisted men by disease. Total 303.

26th REGIMENT ENROLLED MILITIA INFANTRY.

Duty in District of Southwest Missouri. Operations against Marmaduke December 31, 1862, to January 25, 1863. Marmaduke's attack on Springfield, Mo., January 8, 1863. Skirmish at Stockton, Mo., July 11, 1863. Scout from Cassville to Huntsville and Berryville, Ark., July 18-26, 1863 (Detachment). Raid on Melville, Mo., June 14, 1864.

27th REGIMENT INFANTRY.

Organized at St. Louis, Mo., September 2, 1862, to January 8, 1863. On duty at Chillicothe, Mo., and as Provost Guard at St. Louis during organization of Regiment. Ordered to Rolla, Mo., January 10, 1863. Attached to District of Rolla, Dept. of Missouri, to March, 1863. 1st Brigade, 1st Division, 15th Army Corps, Army of the Tennessee, to June, 1865.

SERVICE.—Duty at Rolla, Mo., till March 1, 1863. Ordered to join Army of the Tennessee before Vicksburg, Miss., arriving there March 20. At Milliken's Bend, La., till April. Expedition to Greenville, Black Bayou and Deer Creek April 2-14. Deer Creek April 8 and 12. Demonstration on Haines and Drumgould's Bluffs April 29-May 2. Moved to join army in rear of Vicksburg, Miss., via Richmond and Grand Gulf May 2-14. Jackson, Miss., May 14. Siege of Vicksburg, Miss., May 18-July 4. Assaults on Vicksburg May 19 and 22. Advance on Jackson, Miss., July 4-10. Siege of Jackson July 10-17. At Big Black till September 27. Moved to Memphis, thence march to Chattanooga, Tenn., September 27-November 21. Operations on Memphis & Charleston Railroad in Alabama October 20-29. Cherokee Station October 21 and 29. Cane Creek October 26. Tuscumbia October 26-27. Chattanooga-Ringgold Campaign November 23-27. Lookout Mountain November 23-24. Mission Ridge November 25. Ringgold Gap, Taylor's Ridge, November 27. March to relief of Knoxville, Tenn., November 28-December 8. Garrison duty at Woodville and Scottsboro, Ala., till May, 1864. Atlanta (Ga.) Campaign May 1 to September 8. Demonstration on Resaca May 8-13. Battle of Resaca May 13-15. Advance on Dallas May 18-25. Battles about Dallas, New Hope Church and Allatoona Hills May 25-June 5. Operations about Marietta and against Kenesaw Mountain June 10-July 2. Brush Mountain June 15-17. Assault on Kenesaw June 27. Nickajack Creek July 2-5. Chattahoochie River July 6-17. Battle of Atlanta July 22. Siege of Atlanta July 22-August 25. Ezra Chapel, Hood's 2nd Sortie, July 28. Movement on Jonesboro August 25-30. Battle of Jonesboro August 31-September 1. Lovejoy Station September 2-6. Operations against Hood in North Georgia and North Alabama September 29-November 3. Ship's Gap, Taylor's Ridge, October 16. March to the sea November 15-December 10. Clinton November 22. Statesboro December 4. Ogeechee River December 7-9. Siege of Savannah December 10-21. Fort McAllister December 13. Campaign of the Carolinas January to April, 1865. Reconnoissance to Salkehatchie River, S. C., January 25. Hickory Hill, S. C., February 1. Salkehatchie Swamps February 2-5. South Edisto River February 9. North Edisto River February 11-12. Columbia February 15-17. Battle of Bentonville, N. C., March 20-21. Occupation of Goldsboro March 24. Advance on

Raleigh April 10-14. Occupation of Raleigh April 14. Bennett's House April 26. Surrender of Johnston and his army. March to Washington, D. C., via Richmond, Va., April 29-May 20. Grand Review May 24. Moved to Louisville, Ky., June. Mustered out June 13, 1865. Companies "F," "G" and "I" transferred to Consolidated Battalion, 31st and 32nd Missouri Infantry.

Regiment lost during service 2 Officers and 35 Enlisted men killed and mortally wounded and 139 Enlisted men by disease. Total 176.

27th REGIMENT MOUNTED INFANTRY.

Organized in Missouri at large May to November, 1861. Companies "G," "H" and "I" organized for three months. Lookout Station, Mo., August 20, 1861. Siege and surrender of Lexington, Mo., September 11-20. Recapture of Lexington October 16. Duty in Missouri till February, 1862. Mustered out January 27 to February 28, 1862.

Regiment lost during service 1 Officer and 3 Enlisted men killed and mortally wounded and 34 Enlisted men by disease. Total 38.

27th REGIMENT ENROLLED MILITIA INFANTRY.

Duty in North Missouri guarding bridges on North Missouri Railroad.

28th REGIMENT INFANTRY.

Failed to complete organization.

28th REGIMENT ENROLLED MILITIA INFANTRY.

Called into active service September 25, 1864, to repel Price's invasion of Missouri. Skirmishes on Osage River October 5-6. Jefferson City October 7. Relieved from active service October 31, 1864.

29th REGIMENT INFANTRY.

Organized at Benton Barracks, Mo., and St. Louis, Mo., July to October, 1862. Moved to Cape Girardeau, Mo. Companies "A," "B," "C," "D" and "E" September 12; Companies "F," "G" and "H" September 22; Company "I" September 25, and Company "K" October 22, 1862. Attached to Cape Girardeau, Dept. of Missouri, to December, 1862. 1st Brigade, 11th Division, Right Wing 13th Army Corps (Old), Dept. of the Tennessee, to December, 1862. 1st Brigade, 4th Division, Sherman's Yazoo Expedition, December 22, 1862, to January 3, 1863. 1st Brigade, 1st Division, 15th Army Corps, Army of the Tennessee, to December, 1863. 2nd Brigade, 1st Division, 15th Army Corps, to April, 1864. 3rd Brigade, 1st Division, 15th Army Corps, to September, 1864. 1st Brigade, 1st Division, 15th Army Corps, to November, 1864. Unattached, 15th Army Corps, to June, 1865.

SERVICE.—Duty at Cape Girardeau, Mo., till November 10, 1862. Moved to Patterson, Mo., November 10-17. Return to Cape Girardeau November 25-29. Moved to Helena, Ark., December 8-16. Sherman's Yazoo Expedition December 22, 1862, to January 3, 1863. Chickasaw Bayou December 26-28. Chickasaw Bluff December 29. Expedition to Arkansas Post, Ark., January 3-10, 1863. Assault and capture of Fort Hindman, Arkansas Post, January 10-11. Moved to Young's Point, La., January 17-22, and duty there till March. At Milliken's Bend till April. Expedition to Greenville, Black Bayou and Deer Creek April 2-14. Demonstration on Haines and Drumgould's Bluffs April 29-May 2. Moved to join army in rear of Vicksburg via Richmond and Grand Gulf May 2-14. Jackson, Miss., May 14. Siege of Vicksburg May 18-July 4. Assaults on Vicksburg May 19 and 22. Advance on Jackson, Miss., July 4-10. Siege of Jackson July 10-17. Bolton's Depot July 16. Briar Creek, near Clinton, July 17. Clinton July 18. At Big Black till September 27. Moved to Memphis, thence march to Chattanooga, Tenn., September 27-November 21. Operations on Memphis & Charleston Railroad October 20-29. Cherokee Station October 21 and 29. Cane Creek October 26. Tuscumbia October 26-27. Chattanooga-Ringgold Campaign November 23-27. Lookout Mountain November 23-24. Mission Ridge November 25. Ringgold Gap, Taylor's Ridge, November

27. Moved to Bridgeport, Ala., December 2; thence to Woodville, Ala., December 23, and duty there till March 20, 1864. At Cottonville till April 30. Atlanta (Ga.) Campaign May 1 to September 8. Demonstration on Resaca May 8-13. Battle of Resaca May 13-15. Advance on Dallas May 18-25. Battles about Dallas, New Hope Church and Allatoona Hills May 25-June 5. Operations about Marietta and against Kenesaw Mountain June 10-July 2. Brush Mountain June 15-17. Assault on Kenesaw June 27. Nickajack Creek July 2-5. Chattahoochie River July 6-17. Battle of Atlanta July 22. Siege of Atlanta July 22-August 25. Ezra Chapel, Hood's 2nd Sortie, July 28. Flank movement on Jonesboro August 25-30. Battle of Jonesboro August 31-September 1. Lovejoy Station September 2-6. Operations in North Georgia and North Alabama against Hood September 29-November 3. Ship's Gap, Taylor's Ridge, October 16. Regiment led advance of the 15th Army Corps on march to the sea November 15-December 10. Near Stockbridge November 15. Clinton November 22. Station 5, Georgia Central Railroad, December 4. Little Ogeechee River December 5. Siege of Savannah December 10-21. Campaign of the Carolinas January to April, 1865. Hickory Hill, S. C., February 1. Angley's Postoffice and Buford's Bridge February 4. Duncanville February 5. Fishburn's Plantation, near Lane's Bridge, Salkehatchie River, February 6. Cowpen's Ford, Little Salkehatchie River, February 6. Binnaker's Bridge, South Edisto River, February 9. Orangeburg February 11-12. Wolf's Plantation February 14. Congaree Creek February 15. Columbia February 16-17. Lynch's Creek February 26. Expedition to Florence and skirmishes March 4-6. Battle of Bentonville, N. C., March 20-21. Occupation of Goldsboro March 24. Advance on Raleigh April 10-14. Near Nahunta Station April 10. Beulah April 11. Occupation of Raleigh April 14. Bennett's House April 26. Surrender of Johnston and his army. March to Washington, D. C., via Richmond, Va., April 29-May 20. Grand Review May 24. Moved to Louisville, Ky., June. Mustered out June 12, 1865.

Regiment lost during service 7 Officers and 68 Enlisted men killed and mortally wounded and 3 Officers and 291 Enlisted men by disease. Total 369.

29th REGIMENT ENROLLED MILITIA INFANTRY.

Duty at Lancaster, Mo. Skirmishes in Scotland and Boone Counties September, 1862. Skirmish near Uniontown October 18, 1862.

30th REGIMENT INFANTRY.

Organized at St. Louis, Mo., September and October, 1862. Attached to Cape Girardeau, Mo., Dept. of Missouri, to December, 1862. 1st Brigade, 11th Division, Right Wing 13th Army Corps (Old), Dept. of the Tennessee, December, 1862. 1st Brigade, 4th Division, Sherman's Yazoo Expedition, to January, 1863. 1st Brigade, 1st Division, 15th Army Corps, Army of the Tennessee, to August, 1863. Post of Vidalia, District of Natchez, Miss., Dept. of Tennessee, to April, 1864. 1st Brigade, 1st Division, 17th Army Corps, Dept. of Tennessee, to August, 1864. 1st Brigade, 2nd Division, 19th Army Corps, Dept. of the Gulf, to December, 1864. 2nd Brigade, Reserve Division, Military Division West Mississippi, to February, 1865. 3rd Brigade, 1st Division, Reserve Corps, Military Division West Mississippi, to February, 1865. 3rd Brigade, 1st Division, 13th Army Corps (New), Military Division West Mississippi, to July, 1865. Dept. of Texas to August, 1865.
SERVICE.—Duty at Cape Girardeau, Mo., till November 10, 1862. Moved to Patterson, Mo., November 10-17, and return to Cape Girardeau November 25-29. Moved to Helena, Ark., December 8-16. Sherman's Yazoo Expedition December 22, 1862, to January 3, 1863. Chickasaw Bayou December 26-28. Chickasaw Bluff December 29. Expedition to Arkansas Post, Ark., January 3-10, 1863. Assault and capture of Fort Hindman, Arkansas Post, January 10-11. Moved to Young's Point, La., January 17-23, and duty there till March. At Milliken's Bend, La., till April. Expedition to Greenville,

SEE CORRECTION SHEET, PG. 1750

Black Bayou and Deer Creek April 2-14. Demonstration on Haines' and Drumgould's Bluffs April 29-May 2. Moved to join army in rear of Vicksburg, Miss., via Richmond and Grand Gulf, May 2-14. Jackson, Miss., May 14. Siege of Vicksburg, Miss., May 18-July 4. Assaults on Vicksburg May 19 and 22. Advance on Jackson, Miss., July 4-10. Siege of Jackson July 10-17. Ordered to District of Natchez, Miss., August 15. Assigned to garrison duty at post of Vidalia till April, 1864. Action at Vidalia September 14, 1863. Expedition to Trinity November 15-16. Expedition to Tensas River February 2-3, 1864. Repulse of Gen. Polignac's threatened attack on Vidalia February 17, 1864. Expedition to Tensas River March 10-11. Moved to Vicksburg, Miss., April 3-5, and duty there till May 9. Expedition to Big Black River Bridge May 9-16. Camp at Vicksburg till July 1. Pearl River Expedition July 1-10. Guard pontoon train at Big Black River July 3-9. Moved to Morganza July 28-30, thence to Port Hudson, La., August 23-24. Expedition to Clinton August 24-27. Moved to Morganza August 28, and to mouth of White River, Ark., September 3-8. Duty there till October 18. Moved to Memphis, Tenn., October 18-19. At Fort Pickering, Memphis, till October 28. Moved to mouth of White River, Ark., October 28-29, thence to Duvall's Bluff, Ark., November 7-10, and to Memphis, Tenn., November 27-December 1. Consolidated to a Battalion of 4 Companies November 30. Moved to Kenner, La., January 2-8, 1865; thence to Dauphin Island February 11-18. Campaign against Mobile, Ala., and its Defences March 17-April 12. Siege of Spanish Fort and Fort Blakely March 26-April 8. Assault and capture of Fort Blakely April 9. Occupation of Mobile April 12, and camp there till May 10, and at Fort Blakely and Fort Tracy till June 8. At Mobile till June 28. Moved to Galveston, Texas, June 28-July 1, thence to Columbus July 9-11. Post duty at Allayton till August 21. Mustered out at Columbus, Texas, August 21, and discharged at St. Louis, Mo., September 9, 1865.

Regiment lost during service 2 Officers and 10 Enlisted men killed and mortally wounded and 1 Officer and 280 Enlisted men by disease. Total 293.

30th REGIMENT ENROLLED MILITIA INFANTRY.

At Trenton, Grundy County, Mo.

30th REGIMENT PROVISIONAL ENROLLED MILITIA INFANTRY.

Duty in 7th Military District, North Missouri.

31st REGIMENT INFANTRY.

Organized at St. Louis, Carondelet and Ironton, Mo., August 11 to October 7, 1862. Attached to Cape Girardeau, District of Missouri, Dept. of Missouri, to December, 1862. 1st Brigade, 11th Division, Right Wing 13th Army Corps (Old), Dept. of the Tennessee, December, 1862. 1st Brigade, 4th Division, Sherman's Yazoo Expedition, to January, 1863. 1st Brigade, 1st Division, 15th Army Corps, Army of the Tennessee, to December, 1863. 2nd Brigade, 1st Division, 15th Army Corps, to April, 1864. 3rd Brigade, 1st Division, 15th Army Corps, to September, 1864. 1st Brigade, 1st Division, to November, 1864.
SERVICE.—March to Patterson, Mo., October 21, 1862, and duty there till November 24. March to St. Genevieve, Mo., November 24, thence moved to Helena, Ark., December 1. Sherman's Yazoo Expedition December 22, 1862, to January 3, 1863. Chickasaw Bayou December 26-28. Chickasaw Bluff December 29. Expedition to Arkansas Post, Ark., January 3-10, 1863. Assault and capture of Fort Hindman, Arkansas Post, January 10-11. Moved to Young's Point, La., January 17-23, and duty there till March, and at Milliken's Bend till April. Expedition to Greenville, Black Bayou and Deer Creek April 2-14. Demonstrations on Haines' and Drumgould's Bluffs April 29-May 2. Moved to join army in rear of Vicksburg, Miss., via Richmond and Grand Gulf, May 2-14. Mississippi Springs May 12. Jackson, Miss., May 14. Siege of Vicksburg May 18-July 4. Assaults on Vicksburg May 19 and 22. Advance on Jackson, Miss., July

4-10. Siege of Jackson July 10-17. Bolton's Depot July 16. Briar Creek, near Canton, July 17. Canton July 18. At Big Black to September 27. Moved to Memphis, Tenn.; thence march to Chattanooga, Tenn., September 27-November 21. Operations on Memphis & Charleston Railroad in Alabama October 20-29. Cherokee Station October 21 and 29. Cane Creek October 26. Tuscumbia October 26-27. Chattanooga-Ringgold Campaign November 23-27. Battles of Lookout Mountain November 23-24. Mission Ridge November 25. Ringgold Gap, Taylor's Ridge, November 27. Garrison duty in Alabama till May, 1864. Clayton, Ala., March 14, 1864. Atlanta Campaign May 1-September 8. Demonstrations on Resaca May 8-13. Battle of Resaca May 13-15. Advance on Dallas May 18-25. Battles about Dallas, New Hope Church and Allatoona Hills May 25-June 5. Operations about Marietta and against Kenesaw Mountain June 10-July 2. Bushy Mountain June 15-17. Assault on Kenesaw June 27. Nickajack Creek July 2-5. Chattahoochie River July 6-17. Battle of Atlanta July 22. Siege of Atlanta July 22-August 25. Ezra Chapel, Hood's 2nd Sortie, July 28. Flank movement on Jonesboro August 25-30. Battle of Jonesboro August 31-September 1. Lovejoy Station September 2-6. Operations in North Georgia and North Alabama against Hood September 29-November 3. Ship's Gap, Taylor's Ridge, October 16. Consolidated with 32nd Missouri Infantry November 12, 1864, as Consolidated Battalion 31st and 32nd Missouri Infantry. March to the sea November 15-December 10. Clinton November 23. Statesboro December 4. Ogeechee River December 7-9. Siege of Savannah Decembr 10-21. Campaign of the Carolinas January-April, 1865. Reconnoissance to Salkehatchie River January 25. Hickory Hill February 1. Salkehatchie Swamps, S. C., February 2-5. South Edisto River February 9. North Edisto River February 12-13. Columbia February 15-17. Lynch's Creek February 25-26. Battle of Bentonville, N. C., March 20-21. Occupation of Goldsboro March 24. Advance on Raleigh April 10-14. Occupation of Raleigh April 14. Bennett's House April 26. Surrender of Johnson and his army. March to Washington, D. C., via Richmond, Va., April 29-May 20. Grand Review May 24. Moved to Louisville June. Battalion mustered out July 18, 1865.

Regiment lost during service 4 Officers and 51 Enlisted men killed and mortally wounded and 228 Enlisted men by disease. Total 283.

31st REGIMENT ENROLLED MILITIA INFANTRY.

Duty in 7th Military District, North Missouri.

31st REGIMENT PROVISIONAL ENROLLED MILITIA INFANTRY.

Duty at Albany, Mo.

32nd REGIMENT INFANTRY.

Organized at Benton Barracks, Mo., October 18-December 8, 1862. Attached to District of Cape Girardeau, Mo., Dept. of Missouri, to December, 1862. 1st Brigade, 11th Division, Right Wing 13th Army Corps, Dept. of the Tennessee, December, 1862. 1st Brigade, 4th Division, Sherman's Yazoo Expedition, to January, 1863. 1st Brigade, 1st Division, 15th Army Corps, Army of the Tennessee, to December, 1863. 3rd Brigade, 1st Division, 15th Army Corps, to September, 1864. 1st Brigade, 1st Division, 15th Army Corps, to July, 1865.

SERVICE.—Moved to Helena, Ark., December, 1862. Sherman's Yazoo Expedition December 22, 1862, to January 3, 1863. Chickasaw Bayou December 26-28. Chickasaw Bluff December 29. Expedition to Arkansas Post, Ark., January 3-10, 1863. Assault and capture of Fort Hindman, Arkansas Post, January 10-11. Moved to Young's Point, La., January 17-23, and duty there till March. At Milliken's Bend, La., till April. Expedition to Greenville, Black Bayou and Deer Creek April 2-14. Demonstrations against Haines and Drumgould's Bluffs April 29-May 2. Moved to join army in rear of Vicksburg, Miss., May 2-14. Mississippi Springs May 12. Jackson, Miss., May 14. Siege of Vicksburg May 18-July 4. Assaults on Vicksburg May 19 and 22. Ad-

vance on Jackson, Miss., July 4-10. Siege of Jackson July 10-17. Bolton's Depot July 16. Briar Creek, near Clinton, July 17. Clinton July 18. At Big Black till September 27. Moved to Memphis, Tenn., thence march to Chattanooga, Tenn., September 27-November 21. Operations on Memphis & Charleston Railroad in Alabama October 20-29. Cherokee Station October 21 and 29. Cane Creek October 26. Tuscumbia October 26-27. Chattanooga-Ringgold Campaign November 23-27. Battles of Lookout Mountain November 23-24; Mission Ridge November 25. Ringgold Gap, Taylor's Ridge, November 27. Garrison duty in Alabama till May, 1864. Atlanta (Ga.) Campaign May 1-September 8. Demonstration on Resaca May 8-13. Battle of Resaca May 13-15. Advance on Dallas May 18-25. Battles about Dallas, New Hope Church and Allatoona Hills May 25-June 5. Operations about Marietta and against Kenesaw Mountain June 10-July 2. Bushy Mountain June 15-17. Assault on Kenesaw June 27. Nickajack Creek July 2-5. Chattahoochie River July 6-17. Battle of Atlanta July 22. Siege of Atlanta July 22-August 25. Ezra Chapel, Hood's 2nd Sortie, July 28. Flank movement on Jonesboro August 25-30. Battle of Jonesboro August 31-September 1. Lovejoy Station September 2-6. Operations against Hood in North Georgia and North Alabama September 29-November 3. Ship's Gap, Taylor's Ridge, October 16. Consolidated to a Battalion of 3 Companies November 11, 1864, and consolidated with 3 Companies 31st Missouri Infantry as Consolidated Battalion, 31st and 32nd Missouri Infantry. March to the sea November 15-December 10. Clinton November 23. Statesboro December 4. Ogeechee River December 7-9. Siege of Savannah December 10-21. Campaign of the Carolinas January to April, 1865. Reconnoissance to Salkehatchie River January 25. Hickory Hill February 1. Salkehatchie Swamps, S. C., February 2-5. South Edisto River February 9. North Edisto River February 12-13. Columbia February 15-17. Lynch's Creek February 25-26. Battle of Bentonville, N. C., March 20-21. Occupation of Goldsboro March 24. Advance on Raleigh April 10-14. Occupation of Raleigh April 14. Bennett's House April 26. Surrender of Johnston and his army. March to Washington, D. C., via Richmond, Va., April 29-May 20. Grand Review May 24. Moved to Louisville, Ky., June. Redesignated 32nd Regiment Missouri Infantry June 20. Mustered out July 18, 1865.

Regiment lost during service 20 Enlisted men killed and mortally wounded and 6 Officers and 408 Enlisted men by disease. Total 434.

32nd REGIMENT ENROLLED MILITIA INFANTRY.

At Hannibal, Mo. Scout in Halls County September 15-20, 1862.

33rd REGIMENT INFANTRY.

Organized at Benton Barracks, Mo., August 29-September 5, 1862. Attached to District of St. Louis, Mo., Dept. of Missouri, to December, 1862. 1st Brigade, 13th Division, 13th Army Corps, Dept. of the Tennessee, to February, 1863. 2nd Brigade, 13th Division, 13th Army Corps, to July, 1863. 2nd Brigade, 13th Division, 16th Army Corps, to August, 1863. Garrison, Helena, Ark., Army of Arkansas, to January, 1864. 1st Brigade, 4th Division, 16th Army Corps, Army of the Tennessee, January, 1864. 3rd Brigade, 1st Division, 16th Army Corps, to March, 1864. 3rd Brigade, 1st Division, 16th Army Corps, Dept. of the Gulf, to June, 1864, and Dept. of the Tennessee, to December, 1864. 3rd Brigade, 1st Division (Detachment), Army Tennessee, Dept. of the Cumberland, to February, 1865. 3rd Brigade, 1st Division, 16th Army Corps (New), Military Division West Mississippi, to August, 1865.

SERVICE.—Ordered to the field in Missouri September 22, 1862, and operations in Phelps, Dent, Texas and Wright Counties till December 19. Moved to St. Louis, thence to Columbus, Ky., December 19-25, thence to Helena, Ark., January 5, 1863. Expedition to Duvall's Bluff, Ark., January 16-20. Expedition to Yazoo Pass, and operations against Fort Pemberton and Greenwood

February 24-April 8. Garrison duty at Helena, Ark., till January 28, 1864. Repulse of Holmes' attack on Helena July 4, 1863. Ordered to Vicksburg, Miss., January 28, 1864. Meridian Campaign February 3-March 2. Red River Campaign March 10-May 22. Fort DeRussy March 14. Occupation of Alexandria March 16. Henderson's Hill March 21. Battle of Pleasant Hill April 9. About Cloutiersville and Cane River Crossing April 22-24. At Alexandria, La., April 30-May 13. Bayou La Mouri May 7. Retreat to Morganza May 13-20. Mansura May 16. Yellow Bayou May 18. Moved to Vicksburg, Miss., thence to Memphis, Tenn., May 22-June 10. Old River Lake June 6. Smith's Expedition to Tupelo, Miss., July 5-21. Near Camargo's Cross Roads, Harrisburg, July 13. Tupelo July 14-15. Old Town Creek July 15. Smith's Expedition to Oxford August 1-30. Tallahatchie River August 7-9. Moved to Duvall's Bluff, Ark., September 3, thence to Brownsville, Ark. March in pursuit of Price through Arkansas and Missouri to Cape Girardeau, Mo., September 17-October 9. Garrison at Tipton and California, Mo., October 19-November 17. Moved to St. Louis, Mo., thence to Nashville, Tenn., November 24-December 1. Battle of Nashville, Tenn., December 15-16. Pursuit of Hood to the Tennessee River December 17-28. At Clifton, Tenn., and Eastport, Miss., till February, 1865. Moved to New Orleans, La., February 6-19. Campaign against Mobile, Ala., and its defences March 17-April 12. Siege of Spanish Fort and Fort Blakely March 26-April 8. Assault and capture of Fort Blakely April 9. Occupation of Mobile April 12. March to Montgomery April 13-25, thence to Selma May 1, and duty there till July 20. Moved to St. Louis July 20-August 3. Mustered out August 10, 1865.

Regiment lost during service 4 Officers and 52 Enlisted men killed and mortally wounded and 2 Officers and 229 Enlisted men by disease. Total 287.

33rd REGIMENT ENROLLED MILITIA INFANTRY.

Duty in the 7th Military District. Skirmishes near Cravensville, Panther Creek, Walnut Creek and Sear's Ford on the Chariton August 5-9, 1862. Operations in Western Missouri July 6-30, 1864. Skirmishes near Camden Point and Union Mills July 22. Operations against Price September and October. Albany October 26.

33rd REGIMENT PROVISIONAL ENROLLED MILITIA INFANTRY.

Duty in North Missouri, 7th Military District.

34th REGIMENT INFANTRY.

Failed to complete organization.

34th REGIMENT ENROLLED MILITIA INFANTRY.

Called into service September 25, 1864, to repel Price's invasion of Missouri. Skirmishes on the Osage River October 5-6. Jefferson City October 7. Relieved from active services October 30, 1864. Skirmish on Big Piney November 1, 1864.

35th REGIMENT INFANTRY.

Organized at Benton Barracks, Mo., December 3, 1862. Ordered to Helena, Ark., January, 1863, arriving there January 10, 1863. Attached to 2nd Brigade, 12th Division, 13th Army Corps, Dept. of the Tennessee, to February, 1863. 2nd Brigade, 13th Division, 13th Army Corps, to March, 1863. 1st Brigade, 13th Division, 13th Army Corps, to July, 1863. 2nd Brigade, 13th Division, 16th Army Corps, to August, 1863. Garrison, Helena, Ark., District of Eastern Arkansas, to January, 1864. Helena, Ark., District of Eastern Arkansas, 7th Army Corps, Dept. of Arkansas, to February, 1865. 1st Brigade, 1st Division, 7th Army Corps, to June, 1865.

SERVICE.—Garrison duty at Helena, Ark., January, 1863,, to April, 1865. Repulse of Holmes' attack on Helena, Ark., July 4, 1863. Expedition from Helena to Arkansas Post January 24-26, 1864. Moved to Little Rock, Ark., April 3-6, 1865, and garrison duty there till June, 1865. Mustered out June 28, 1865. Moved to Benton Barracks, Mo., July 3-12, and discharged from service,

Regiment lost during service 2 Officers and 8 Enlisted men killed and mortally wounded and 2 Officers and 234 Enlisted men by disease. Total 246.

35th REGIMENT ENROLLED MILITIA INFANTRY.

Operations against Shelby September 22-October 26, 1863. At California, Moniteau County, October, 1863. Placed on duty in Northern Missouri June, 1864. Scout in Chariton County July 27-30. Chariton Road near Keytesville and Union Church July 30. Affair near Brunswick September 6 (Detachment). Surrender of Keytesville September 20 (Co. "I").

35th REGIMENT PROVISIONAL ENROLLED MILITIA INFANTRY.

Duty in 8th Military District, Dept. of Missouri.

36th REGIMENT INFANTRY.

Failed to complete organization.

36th REGIMENT ENROLLED MILITIA INFANTRY.
No details.

37th REGIMENT INFANTRY.

Failed to complete organization.

37th REGIMENT ENROLLED MILITIA INFANTRY.

Duty in 8th Military District, Dept. of Missouri.

38th REGIMENT INFANTRY.

Failed to complete organization.

38th REGIMENT ENROLLED MILITIA INFANTRY.

Scouts in Ralls County September 15-20, 1862. Placed on duty in Linn County June 4, 1864.

39th REGIMENT INFANTRY.

Organized at Hannibal, Mo., August 18 to September 30, 1864. Attached to District of St. Louis, Dept. of Missouri, to November, 1864. Nashville, Tenn., Dept. of the Cumberland, to December, 1864. District of Kentucky, Dept. Ohio, to January, 1865. District of Nashville, Tenn., Dept. of the Cumberland, January, 1865. District of St. Louis, Mo., to July, 1865.

SERVICE.—Scout duty and operating against guerrillas in Macon, Ralls, Pike, Monroe, Audrain, Callaway, Boone, Howard and Chariton Counties, Mo., September. Actions about Sidney, Ralls County, September 11-16 (Co. "D"). Companies "A" and "G" ordered to Paris September 14. Company "E" to Ralls County September 20. Companies "C" and "H" to Paris September 22. Company "D" to Macon September 23. Companies "B" and "I" to Macon September 24, and Company "F" to Macon September 25, 1864. Action with Anderson's guerrillas and massacre on North Missouri Railroad near Centralia September 27 (Cos. "A," "G" and "H"). March from Macon to Jefferson City, Mo., October 1-7. Defence of Jefferson City October 7-8. Moved to LaMine Bridge October 19-20, thence to Glasgow November 1-3, and duty there till December 13. Ordered to Nashville, Tenn., December 13, arriving there January 1, 1865. Return to St. Louis, Mo., January 4-9, 1865. Duty at Benton Barracks and in District of St. Louis, Mo., till July. Companies "A," "G" and "K" provost duty at Cape Girardeau, Mo., April 24 to July 6. Companies "D" and "E" at Glasgow and Company "B" at St. Genevieve. Scout from Glasgow to Perche Hills March 7-15, 1865 (Co. "D"). Company "H" provost duty at Benton Barracks. Companies "C," "E," "F" and "I" mustered out March 20, 1865. Regiment mustered out July 19, 1865.

Regiment lost during service 2 Officers and 130 Enlisted men killed and mortally wounded and 64 Enlisted men by disease. Total 196.

39th REGIMENT ENROLLED MILITIA INFANTRY.

Duty in Platte County, Mo.

40th REGIMENT INFANTRY.

Organized at Benton Barracks, Mo., August 11 to September 8, 1864. Attached to District of St. Louis, Mo., Dept. of Missouri, to November, 1864. Paducah,

Ky., November, 1864. 3rd Brigade, 3rd Division, 4th Army Corps, Army of the Cumberland, to December 14, 1864. 1st Brigade, 3rd Division (Detachment), Army Tennessee, Dept. of the Cumberland, to February, 1865. 1st Brigade, 3rd Division, 16th Army Corps (New), Military Division West Mississippi, to March, 1865. 2nd Brigade, 3rd Division, 16th Army Corps, to August, 1865.

SERVICE.—Moved to Mexico, Mo., October 20, 1864. Expedition against Paris, Mo., October 23-30. Moved to Paducah, Ky., November 7-10, thence to Nashville, Tenn., November 22-26. To Columbia November 26. Battle of Franklin, Tenn., November 30. Battle of Nashville, Tenn., December 15-16. Pursuit of Hood to the Tennessee River December 17-28. Moved to Eastport, Miss., and duty there till February 3, 1865. Moved to Vicksburg, Miss., thence to New Orleans, La., February 3-21. Moved to Lakeport, Mobile Bay, Ala., thence to Dauphin Island, arriving there March 3. Campaign against Mobile and its defences March 17-April 12. Siege of Spanish Fort and Fort Blakely March 26-April 8. Assault and capture of Fort Blakely April 9. March to Montgomery, Ala., April 12-25, and duty there till August. Mustered out August 8, 1865.

Regiment lost during service 10 Enlisted men killed and mortally wounded and 58 Enlisted men by disease. Total 68.

40th REGIMENT ENROLLED MILITIA INFANTRY.

Duty in District of Central Missouri. Skirmish on Clear Fork near Warrensburg September, 1862. Beach Creek, Johnson County, February 5, 1863. Operations against Price September and October, 1864. Defence of Jefferson City September 30-October 7, 1864.

41st REGIMENT INFANTRY.

Organized at Benton Barracks, Mo., August and September, 1864. Mustered in September 16, 1864. On garrison duty at St. Louis, Mo., till July, 1865. Mustered out July 11, 1865.

Regiment lost during service 1 Enlisted man killed and 2 Officers and 34 Enlisted men by disease. Total 37.

41st REGIMENT ENROLLED MILITIA INFANTRY.

Skirmish at Barry, Mo., August 14, 1862.

42nd REGIMENT INFANTRY.

Organized at Macon, Mo., September, 1864. Attached to District of Northern Missouri, Dept. of Missouri, to December, 1864. Tullahoma, Tenn., Dept. of the Cumberland, to February, 1865. Unattached, 4th Division, 20th Army Corps, Dept. of the Cumberland, to March, 1865. 2nd Brigade, Defences Nashville & Chattanooga Railroad, Dept. Cumberland, to April, 1865. 2nd Brigade, 1st Sub-District, District of Middle Tennessee, to June, 1865.

SERVICE.—Companies "A," "C" and "H" moved to Sturgeon, Mo., September 23, 1864. Garrison duty there and at Columbia till November. Regiment assigned to guard duty on line of the Northern Missouri and Hannibal & St. Joseph Railroad, till November 10. Moved to St. Louis, Mo., November 12-13, thence to Paducah, Ky., November 29-December 2. To Clarksville and Fort Donelson, Tenn., December 3-6, and duty there till December 30. Moved to Nashville, Tenn., December 30-31, thence to Tullahoma, Tenn., January 2-3, 1865, and duty there till March, operating against guerrillas in Southern Tennessee and Northern Alabama. Action at Corn's Farm, Franklin County, Tenn., February 6. Garrison duty at Shelbyville, Tenn., till June 23. Moved to Nashville, Tenn., June 23. Mustered out Companies "H," "I" and "K" March 22, 1865; Regiment June 28, 1865.

Regiment lost during service 6 Enlisted men killed and mortally wounded and 124 Enlisted men by disease. Total 134.

42nd REGIMENT ENROLLED MILITIA INFANTRY.

Skirmish near Iberia August 29, 1862. Expeditions from Waynesville August 29-September 2, 1862.

42nd REGIMENT PROVISIONAL ENROLLED MILITIA INFANTRY.

Duty in Central District of Missouri. Skirmish at Iberia, Mo., August 29, 1862.

43rd REGIMENT INFANTRY.

Organized at St. Joseph, Mo., August 22 to September 7, 1864. Attached to District of Northern Missouri, Dept. of Missouri, to April, 1865. District of Central Missouri, to June, 1865.

Duty in District of Northern Missouri till April, 1865. Action at Booneville, Mo., October 9 and 12, 1864. Brunswick October 11. Battle of Glasgow October 15, 1864 (6 Cos.). Operating against guerrillas in District of Central Missouri till June, 1865. Affair Little Blue River March 11, 1865 (Detachment). Skirmish Star House, near Lexington, May 4 (Detachment). Mustered out June 30, 1865.

Regiment lost during service 11 Enlisted men killed and mortally wounded and 53 Enlisted men by disease. Total 64.

43rd REGIMENT ENROLLED MILITIA INFANTRY.

Operations against Shelby September 22-October 26, 1863.

44th REGIMENT INFANTRY.

Organized at St. Joseph, Mo., August 22-September 7, 1864. Attached to District of Rolla, Dept. of Missouri, to November, 1864. Paducah, Ky., Dept. of Ohio, November, 1864. Unattached, 23rd Army Corps, Army Ohio, to December, 1864. 2nd Brigade, 3rd Division (Detachment), Army of the Tennessee, Dept. of the Cumberland, to February, 1865. 1st Brigade, 3rd Division, 16th Army Corps (New), Military Division West Mississippi, to August, 1865.

SERVICE.—Moved to Rolla, Mo., September 14-18, 1864, and duty there till November 5. Expedition from Rolla to Licking November 5-9. Near Licking November 9. Moved to Paducah, Ky., November 12-16, thence to Nashville, Tenn., November 24-27, and to Columbia, Tenn., November 28. Spring Hill November 29. Battle of Franklin November 30. Battle of Nashville December 15-16. Pursuit of Hood to Columbia and Pulaski December 17-28. Moved to Clifton, Tenn., December 29-January 2, 1865, thence to Eastport, Miss., January 9-11, and duty there till February 6, 1865. Near McMinnville, Tenn., February 5 (Detachment). Moved to Vicksburg, Miss., thence to New Orleans, La., February 6-21. Campaign against Mobile, Ala., and its defences March 11-April 12. Expedition from Dauphin Island to Fowl River Narrows March 18-22. Siege of Spanish Fort and Fort Blakely March 26-April 8. Assault and capture of Fort Blakely April 9. Occupation of Mobile April 12. March to Montgomery April 13-25, thence to Tuskegee, and duty there till July 19. Moved to Vicksburg, Miss., thence to St. Louis, Mo., July 19-August 4. Mustered out August 15, 1865.

Regiment lost during service 4 Officers and 61 Enlisted men killed and mortally wounded and 5 Officers and 168 Enlisted men by disease. Total 238.

44th REGIMENT ENROLLED MILITIA INFANTRY.

No details.

44th REGIMENT PROVISIONAL ENROLLED MILITIA INFANTRY.

Duty in North Missouri, 7th Military District, Dept. of Missouri.

45th REGIMENT INFANTRY.

Organized at Sedalia, Warrensburg and Otterville August 10 to September 17, 1864. Attached to District of St. Louis, Mo., Dept. of Missouri, to December, 1864. Unattached, 4th Division, 23rd Army Corps, Army Ohio, to March, 1865.

SERVICE.—Moved from Warrensburg, Mo., to Jefferson City, Mo., October 1, 1864. Price's attack on Jefferson City October 7. Duty at Jefferson City till December. Moved to Nashville, Tenn. Battle of Nashville December 15-16. Garrison and guard duty at Spring Hill, Tenn., till January 5, 1865. Moved to Johnsonville,

Tenn., January 5-13, and duty there till February 20. Moved to St. Louis, Mo. Mustered out March 6, 1865. Companies "C" and "D" transferred to 50th Missouri Infantry and Companies "G" and "H" to 48th Missouri Infantry.

Regiment lost during service 4 Enlisted men killed and mortally wounded and 82 Enlisted men by disease. Total 86.

45th REGIMENT ENROLLED MILITIA INFANTRY.

Duty in North Missouri. Affair near Sugar Loaf Prairie, Ark., January 11, 1865.

46th REGIMENT INFANTRY.

Organized at Springfield, Mo., August to November, 1864, for six months. Attached to District of Southwest Missouri, Dept. of Missouri, to March, 1865. 2nd Brigade, 1st Sub-District, District of Middle Tennessee, Dept. of the Cumberland, to May, 1865.

SERVICE.—Duty at Springfield, Mo., and by detachments in Douglas County, Taney County, at Stockton, Hartsville, Neosho, Cassville, Newtonia and Buffalo till March, 1865, and in District of Middle Tennessee till May, 1865. Surrender of Paris, Mo., October 15, 1864 (Detachment). Operations in Ozark County February 12, 1865 (Co. "H"). Operations about Bennett's Bayou and Tolbert's Mill, Ark., February 16-18, 1865 (Co. "H"). Mustered out March 6 to May 24, 1865.

Regiment lost during service 8 Enlisted men killed and mortally wounded and 18 Enlisted men by disease. Total 26.

46th REGIMENT ENROLLED MILITIA INFANTRY.

Duty in 8th Military District, Dept. of Missouri. Skirmish near Huntsville August 7, 1864. Operations against Price's invasion of Missouri September to November. Skirmish near Glasgow, Mo., January 10, 1865 (Co. "F"). Operations about Bennett's Bayou and Tolbert's Mill February 16-18, 1865 (Co. "H"). Skirmish Switzler's Mill, Chariton County, May 27, 1865.

47th REGIMENT INFANTRY.

Organized at Pilot Knob, Mo., August 22 to September 11, 1864. Attached to District of St. Louis, Mo., Dept. of Missouri, to December, 1864. Nashville, Tenn., Dept. of the Cumberland, December, 1864. Pulaski, Tenn., Dept. Cumberland, to March, 1865.

SERVICE.—Assigned to duty in Southeast Missouri by Companies—"A," "G" and "H" in Wayne County, "B" in Jefferson County, "C" in Perry County, "K" at St. Genevieve, "I" at Fredericktown, "D" guarding bridges on Iron Mountain Railroad, "E" Ironton. Companies retired before Price: Company "C" to Cape Girardeau, "A," "G" and "H" to Pilot Knob. Action at Ironton September 26 (Co. "E"). Retreat to Pilot Knob. Shut-in Gap and Arcadia Valley September 26. Fort Davidson September 26-27. Retreat to Leesburg. Companies returned to above stations; "B" at Franklin. Moved to Nashville, Tenn., December 12-19. Assigned to guard duty at Spring Hill, Columbia and Pulaski, Tenn., till March 15, 1865. Mustered out March 28-30, 1865.

Regiment lost during service 10 Enlisted men killed and mortally wounded and 1 Officer and 82 Enlisted men by disease. Total 93.

47th REGIMENT ENROLLED MILITIA INFANTRY.

Duty in North Missouri, 8th Military District of Missouri.

48th REGIMENT INFANTRY.

Organized at St. Louis, Jefferson City and Rolla, Mo., August 3-November 22, 1864. Attached to District of Rolla, Dept. of Missouri, to December, 1864. Railroad Guard, Tennessee & Alabama Railroad, Dept. of the Cumberland, to February, 1865. Camp Douglas, Chicago, Ill., to June, 1865.

SERVICE.—Duty at Rolla, Mo., till December 9, 1864. Defence of Rolla against Price. Moved to Nashville, Tenn., December 9-19. Assigned to post duty at Columbia, Tenn., and garrison block houses on Tennessee & Alabama Railroad from Franklin to Talioka till February, 1865. Moved to Chicago, Ill., February 18-22. Guard duty at Camp Douglas and escort Confederate prisoners to City Point, Va., for exchange till June 16. Ordered to Benton Barracks, Mo., June 16. Mustered out June 22, 1865.

Regiment lost during service by disease 120.

48th REGIMENT ENROLLED MILITIA INFANTRY.

Duty in Platte and Clinton Counties, Mo.

49th REGIMENT INFANTRY.

Organized at Warrenton, Mexico, Macon and St. Louis, Mo., August 31, 1864, to February 5, 1865. Attached to District of North Missouri, Dept. of Missouri, to February, 1865. 2nd Brigade, 3rd Division, 16th Army Corps (New), Military District of West Mississippi, to August, 1865. Dept. of Alabama to December, 1865.

SERVICE.—Duty in Northern Missouri on line of Northern Missouri Railroad, till January 30, 1865. Moved to St. Louis, Mo., January 30-February 1, thence to New Orleans, La., February 10-21. Campaign against Mobile, Ala., and its defences March 17-April 12. Siege of Spanish Fort and Fort Blakely March 26-April 8. Assault and capture of Fort Blakely April 9. Occupation of Mobile April 12. March to Montgomery April 13-25, and duty there till July 14. Companies "A," "B," "C," "D," "E," "F," "G" and "I" ordered to St. Louis, Mo., and mustered out August 2, 1865. Companies "H" and "K" on duty at Eufaula, Ala., till December, 1865. Mustered out December 20, 1865.

Regiment lost during service 4 Enlisted men killed and mortally wounded and 96 Enlisted men by disease. Total 100.

49th REGIMENT ENROLLED MILITIA INFANTRY.

Duty in North Missouri, 8th Military District of Missouri. Skirmish at Ashley August 28, 1862.

50th REGIMENT INFANTRY.

Organized in Missouri at large September 11, 1864, to April 27, 1865. Attached to District of St. Louis, Mo., Dept. of Missouri. (Co. "F" not mustered, was at Pilot Knob, Mo., and engaged October 26-27, 1864, and on retreat to Leesburg. Co. "E" in action at Potosi, Mo. Not mustered.) Regiment on duty in District of St. Louis and in Missouri till August, 1865. Mustered out July 1 to August 11, 1865.

Regiment lost during service by disease 65.

50th REGIMENT ENROLLED MILITIA INFANTRY.

Skirmish near Uniontown August 28, 1862. On duty in 8th Military District, North Missouri. Relieved January 5, 1865.

51st REGIMENT INFANTRY.

Organized at St. Joseph, Mo., March 1 to April 14, 1865. Stationed at St. Louis, and in the Dept. of Missouri. Mustered out August 31, 1865.

Regiment lost during service 2 Enlisted men killed and 47 Enlisted men by disease. Total 49.

51st REGIMENT ENROLLED MILITIA INFANTRY.

Operations in Carroll, Ray and Livingston Counties July 27-August 4, 1862. Duty in Lafayette County. Affairs in Jackson and Lafayette Counties November 26-29, 1862. Duty in 7th Military District, Dept. of Missouri, August, 1864. At Albany, Ray County, June 7, 1864.

51st REGIMENT PROVISIONAL ENROLLED MILITIA INFANTRY.

Operations in Ray and Carroll Counties August 12-16, 1864. Skirmish Fredericksburg August 12. Albany, Ray County, October 26, 1864.

52nd REGIMENT INFANTRY.

Failed to complete organization.

52nd REGIMENT ENROLLED MILITIA INFANTRY.

Called into service September 25, 1864, to repel Price's invasion of Missouri. Relieved from active service October 31, 1864.

53rd REGIMENT INFANTRY.
Failed to complete organization.

53rd REGIMENT ENROLLED MILITIA INFANTRY.
Scout in Ralls County September 15-20, 1862. Placed on duty in 8th Military District, North Missouri, Dept. of Missouri, June, 1864.

53rd REGIMENT PROVISIONAL ENROLLED MILITIA INFANTRY.
Duty in North Missouri, 8th Military District, Dept. of Missouri.

54th REGIMENT INFANTRY.
Failed to complete organization.

54th REGIMENT ENROLLED MILITIA INFANTRY.
Duty in Franklin County. Operations against Price September and October, 1864.

55th REGIMENT INFANTRY.
Failed to complete organization.

55th REGIMENT ENROLLED MILITIA INFANTRY.
Duty in Franklin County. Operations against Price September and October, 1864.

56th REGIMENT INFANTRY.
Failed to complete organization.

56th REGIMENT ENROLLED MILITIA INFANTRY.
Operations against Marmaduke's Expedition into Missouri April 17-May 3, 1863. Chalk Bluff, St. Francis River, April 30-May 1. Price's invasion of Missouri September and October, 1864. Expedition from Cape Girardeau to Patterson, Wayne County, November 11-16. Skirmishes Reeve's Mountain November 19; Buckskull, Randolph County, Ark., November 20.

57th REGIMENT INFANTRY.
Failed to complete organization.

57th PROVISIONAL ENROLLED MILITIA INFANTRY.
Duty in 7th Military District, North Missouri.

58th REGIMENT INFANTRY.
Failed to complete organization.

59th REGIMENT ENROLLED MILITIA INFANTRY.
Duty in District of North Missouri, 8th Military District. Relieved January 5, 1865.

60th REGIMENT ENROLLED MILITIA INFANTRY.
Duty in District of Central Missouri.

61st REGIMENT ENROLLED MILITIA INFANTRY.
Duty in 8th Military District, North Missouri. Skirmish near Columbia January 21, 1863.

61st PROVISIONAL ENROLLED MILITIA INFANTRY REGIMENT.
Duty in 8th Military District, North Missouri.

62nd REGIMENT ENROLLED MILITIA INFANTRY.
Placed on duty in Linn County June 4, 1862. Expedition from Brookfield to Brunswick, Keytesville and Salisbury November 16-23, 1864.

63rd REGIMENT ENROLLED MILITIA INFANTRY.
Duty in 7th Military District, North Missouri.

64th REGIMENT ENROLLED MILITIA INFANTRY.
Duty in 1st Military District.

65th REGIMENT ENROLLED MILITIA INFANTRY.
Affair near Breckenridge June 9, 1864. Operations against Price September and October, 1864. Surrender of Carrollton October 17, 1864. Duty in District of North Missouri.

66th REGIMENT ENROLLED MILITIA INFANTRY.
Duty in 8th Military District, Dept. Missouri. At Milan, Mo., June 10, 1864.

66th REGIMENT PROVISIONAL ENROLLED MILITIA INFANTRY.
Duty in 8th Military District, North Missouri.

67th REGIMENT ENROLLED MILITIA INFANTRY.
Placed on duty in 8th Military District, North Missouri, June, 1864.

67th REGIMENT PROVISIONAL ENROLLED MILITIA INFANTRY.
At Danville, Mo.

68th REGIMENT ENROLLED MILITIA INFANTRY.
No details.

68th PROVISIONAL ENROLLED MILITIA INFANTRY.
Duty in 1st Military District, Dept. of Missouri, August, 1864. Affair at Bloomfield, Mo., January 27, 1863.

69th REGIMENT ENROLLED MILITIA INFANTRY.
Placed on duty in District of North Missouri June, 1864. Relieved January 17, 1865.

69th PROVISIONAL ENROLLED MILITIA INFANTRY.
Duty in District of North Missouri.

70th REGIMENT ENROLLED MILITIA INFANTRY.
Duty in District of North Missouri. Scout in Monroe County October 31, 1862. Operations against Price September and October, 1864. Surrender of Paris October 15, 1864.

71st REGIMENT ENROLLED MILITIA INFANTRY.
Duty in Ray County. Affairs in Jackson and Lafayette Counties November 26-29, 1862.

72nd REGIMENT ENROLLED MILITIA INFANTRY.
Duty in 4th Military District, Southwest Missouri. Operations against Marmaduke December 31, 1862, to January 25, 1863. Marmaduke's attack on Springfield January 8, 1863.

72nd REGIMENT PROVISIONAL ENROLLED MILITIA INFANTRY.
Duty at Springfield, Mo.

73rd REGIMENT ENROLLED MILITIA INFANTRY.
Duty in District of Southwest Missouri. Expedition from Ozark, Mo., into Marion County, Ark., December 9-15, 1862. Operations against Marmaduke's Expedition into Missouri December 31, 1862, to January 25, 1863.

74th REGIMENT ENROLLED MILITIA INFANTRY.
Duty in Southwest Missouri. Operations against Marmaduke December 31, 1862, to January 25, 1863. Marmaduke's attack on Springfield January 8, 1863.

74th REGIMENT PROVISIONAL ENROLLED MILITIA INFANTRY.
Duty at Sand Springs, Mo.

75th REGIMENT ENROLLED MILITIA INFANTRY.
Duty in 8th Military District of Missouri.

76th REGIMENT ENROLLED MILITIA INFANTRY.
Duty in Southwest Missouri. Relieved February 28, 1865.

77th REGIMENT ENROLLED MILITIA INFANTRY.
No details.

78th REGIMENT ENROLLED MILITIA INFANTRY.
Duty at Perryville, 1st Military District.

79th REGIMENT ENROLLED MILITIA INFANTRY.
Duty in 1st Military District.

80th REGIMENT ENROLLED MILITIA INFANTRY.
Called into service September 25, 1864, to repel Price's Raid into Missouri. Relieved from active service October 31, 1864.

80th REGIMENT PROVISIONAL ENROLLED MILITIA INFANTRY.

Called into service September 25, 1864, to repel Price's invasion of Missouri. Relieved from active service October 31, 1864.

81st PROVISIONAL ENROLLED MILITIA INFANTRY REGIMENT.

Duty in 7th Military District, Dept. of Missouri. At Arnoldsville, DeKalb, Maysville, Plattsburg and St. Joseph, Mo.

82nd REGIMENT ENROLLED MILITIA INFANTRY.

Placed on duty in District of Northern Missouri at Weston and Parksville October, 1863.

82nd PROVISIONAL ENROLLED MILITIA INFANTRY.

Placed on duty in District of Northern Missouri at Weston, Liberty and Parksville.

85th REGIMENT ENROLLED MILITIA INFANTRY.

Called into active service September 25, 1864, to repel Price's invasion of Missouri. Relieved from active service October 30, 1864.

86th REGIMENT ENROLLED MILITIA INFANTRY.

Duty in 8th Military District, North Missouri.

87th PROVISIONAL ENROLLED MILITIA INFANTRY.

Duty in 7th Military District, Northern Missouri. Scout to Taos July 19, 1864 (Detachment).

88th REGIMENT ENROLLED MILITIA INFANTRY.

Duty in 7th Military District, Northern Missouri.

89th REGIMENT ENROLLED MILITIA INFANTRY.

Duty in 8th Military District, Northern Missouri. Skirmish Plattsburg July 21, 1864.

BAYLES' INDEPENDENT COMPANY INFANTRY.

Organized at St. Louis, Mo., May 11, 1861. Guard lines of communication between Rolla and Springfield. Mustered out August 11, 1861.

BENTON CADETS—INDEPENDENT COMPANY INFANTRY.

Organized at St. Louis, Mo., September and October, 1861. Fremont's Campaign in Missouri September to November, 1861. At Rolla till January, 1862. Mustered out January 8, 1862.

DIETRICH'S INDEPENDENT COMPANY INFANTRY.

Organized at Manchester, Mo., August 15, 1861. Guard and patrol duty in Missouri till February, 1862. Mustered out February 3, 1862.

GASCONADE COUNTY BATTALION RESERVE CORPS INFANTRY.

Organized June, 1861, by authority of Gen. Lyon. Guard bridges and trains on Northern Missouri Railroad from Herman to Montgomery City till January, 1862. Transferred to 4th Missouri Infantry January 18, 1862.

KREKEL'S INDEPENDENT COMPANY RESERVE CORPS INFANTRY.

Organized at St. Charles August, 1861. Guard railroad and duty at St. Charles till January, 1862. Mustered out January 10, 1862.

NAGLE'S INDEPENDENT COMPANY RESERVE CORPS INFANTRY.

Organized at St. Louis, Mo., June 6, 1861. Mustered out October 7, 1861.

OSTERHAUS' BATTALION INFANTRY.

Organized at St. Louis, Mo., April 23 to May 1, 1861. Attached to Lyon's Army of the West. Mustered out August 31, 1861. (See 2nd Missouri Infantry, 3 months.)

PEABODY'S INDEPENDENT BATTALION RESERVE CORPS INFANTRY.

Organized at St. Joseph, Mo., by authority of Gen. Lyon, May, 1861. Guard Hannibal & St. Joseph Railroad till August. Ordered to Lexington, Mo., August 29. Siege of Lexington September 12-21. Surrendered September 21. Consolidated with Van Horn's Battalion to form 25th Missouri Infantry December, 1861.

PHELPS' INDEPENDENT REGIMENT INFANTRY.

Organized at Rolla, Mo., September 22 to December 27, 1861. Served unattached, Army of Southwest Missouri, to February, 1862. 2nd Brigade, 4th Division, Army of Southwest Missouri, to May, 1862.

SERVICE.—Duty at Rolla, Mo., till February, 1862. Curtis' Campaign against Price in Missouri and Arkansas February and March. Actions at Sugar Creek and Bentonville February 17. Battles of Pea Ridge, Ark., March 6-8. Mountain Grove March 9. Mustered out May 13, 1862.

Lost 2 Officers and 23 Enlisted men killed and 3 Officers and 91 Enlisted men by disease. Total 119.

VAN HORN'S BATTALION RESERVE CORPS INFANTRY.

Organized at St. Louis, Mo., by authority of Gen. Lyon May 1, 1861, and mustered into service at Kansas City, Mo., May 24. Expedition from Kansas City to relief of Col. Nugent at Austin, Cass County, Mo., July 18-25. Action at Harrisonville July 19. Capture of Harrisonville July 20. March to relief of Lexington, Mo., September 6. Siege of Lexington September 11-21. Surrendered to Price September 21. Mostly mustered out October 29, 1861. Balance transferred to 25th Missouri Infantry December, 1861.

Battalion lost 4 Enlisted men killed and 2 Enlisted men by disease. Total 6.

ALBREE'S BATTALION STATE MILITIA INFANTRY.

(See 1st Battalion S. M. Infantry.)

BURNS' BATTALION STATE MILITIA INFANTRY.

(See 6th Battalion S. M. Infantry.)

COXS' BATTALION STATE MILITIA INFANTRY.

(See 2nd Battalion S. M. Infantry.)

CRAYNOR'S REGIMENT STATE MILITIA INFANTRY.

Organized in Gentry County for six months October 1, 1861. Engaged in scout duty in Northwest Missouri till February, 1862. Mustered out February, 1862.

DALLMEYER'S REGIMENT STATE MILITIA INFANTRY.

Organized for six months and mustered in at Camp Matthews, Gasconade County, September 14, 1861. Guard and scout duty at Chamois till December, 1861, and duty at Franklin till February, 1862. Mustered out February, 1862.

FAGG'S REGIMENT STATE MILITIA INFANTRY.

(See 5th Regiment State Militia Infantry.)

GRUNDY COUNTY BATTALION STATE MILITIA INFANTRY.

Organized at Trenton, Grundy County, for six months, October 20, 1861. Scouting and duty at Chillicothe, Mo., till March, 1862. Mustered out March 4, 1862.

HARRISON COUNTY BATTALION STATE MILITIA INFANTRY.

(See 7th Battalion State Militia Infantry.)

JAMES' BATTALION STATE MILITIA INFANTRY.

Organized for six months and mustered in at Cameron, Mo., October 2, 1861. Duty in Clinton, Caldwell and Davies Counties. Mustered out March 13, 1862.

JOSEPH'S BATTALION STATE MILITIA INFANTRY.

(See 3rd Battalion State Militia Infantry.)

KIMBALL'S REGIMENT STATE MILITIA INFANTRY.

Organized for six months and mustered in at St. Joseph October 2, 1861. Duty at St. Joseph, and scout duty in the District of Northwest Missouri till April, 1862. Mustered out April 2, 1862.

(CLARK'S) MERCER COUNTY BATTALION STATE MILITIA INFANTRY.

Organized at Utica for six months September 19, 1861. Mustered out at Princeton, Mo., March 19, 1862.

RICHARDSON'S REGIMENT STATE MILITIA INFANTRY.

Organized October 1, 1861. Guard Pacific Railroad bridges till December. Mustered out December 18, 1861.

SIMPSON'S REGIMENT STATE MILITIA INFANTRY.

Organized at Perryville for six months October 10, 1861. Duty at Pilot Knob, Ironton, and in District of Southeast Missouri, till February, 1862. Mustered out February 25, 1862.

THOMPSON'S BATTALION STATE MILITIA INFANTRY.

(See 4th Battalion State Militia Infantry.)

WARD'S COMPANY STATE MILITIA INFANTRY.

Duty at Jefferson City and in District of Central Missouri.

WASHINGTON COUNTY BATTALION STATE MILITIA INFANTRY.

Organized at Potosi for six months and mustered in September 19, 1861. Scout and guard duty in District of Southeast Missouri till January, 1862. Mustered out January 8, 1862.

MISSOURI HOME GUARD AUTHORIZED BY GEN. LYON TO ORGANIZE FOR THE PROTECTION AND PRESERVATION OF PEACE IN THEIR RESPECTIVE NEIGHBORHOODS.

ADAIR COUNTY HOME GUARD COMPANY INFANTRY (MOUNTED).

Formed May, 1861. Duty in Adair, Shelby, Monroe, Mercer, Marion, Linn, Livingstone, Caldwell, Clinton and Clay Counties, till October. With 3rd Iowa Infantry in pursuit of Green's forces August 15-21. Action at Blue Mills September 17. Mustered out October, 1861.

ADAIR COUNTY HOME GUARD COMPANY INFANTRY.

Organized August, 1861. Guard fords of the Chariton River and duty at Hartford, Putnam County, Mo. Mustered out October, 1861.

ALLEN'S CITIZENS CORPS HOME GUARD.

Organized by authority of Gen. Lyon June, 1861. Duty at Calhoun, Mo., and guarding lines of communications till September. Mustered out September, 1861.

BENTON COUNTY HOME GUARD REGIMENT INFANTRY.

Organized June 13, 1861, by authority of Gen. Fremont. Action at Cole Camp June 19. Mustered out September 13, 1861.

BOONEVILLE BATTALION HOME GUARD INFANTRY.

Organized by authority of Gen. Lyon, June, 1861. Guard duty at Booneville, Mo., till August, 1861. Mustered out August, 1861.

BROOKFIELD COMPANY HOME GUARD INFANTRY.

Organized at Brookfield, Mo., by authority of Gen. Lyon. Duty at Brookfield, Mo., till August. Mustered out August, 1861.

CALDWELL COUNTY COMPANY HOME GUARD INFANTRY.

Organized June, 1861, by authority of Col. Peabody, 25th Missouri, afterwards recognized by Gen. Hurlbut and Gen. Pope. Guard Hannibal & St. Joseph Railroad. Action at Blue Mills September 17. Mustered into six months Militia September 24, 1861.

CAPE GIRARDEAU BATTALION HOME GUARD INFANTRY.

Organized by authority of Gen. Lyon and Gen. Fremont June, 1861. Duty at Cape Girardeau, Mo., till September. Mustered out September, 1861.

CARONDELET COUNTY COMPANY HOME GUARD INFANTRY.

Organized under authority of Gen. Lyon June, 1861, for the protection and preservation of peace in Carondelet County. Mustered out August, 1861.

CASS COUNTY REGIMENT HOME GUARD INFANTRY.

Organized by authority of Gen Fremont, June, 1861. Duty escorting trains from Kansas City to Springfield, Mo., and duty at Springfield and Kansas City, till September. Mustered out September, 1861.

CLINTON COUNTY COMPANY HOME GUARD INFANTRY.

Organized by authority of Col. Tuttle, Colonel 2nd Iowa Infantry, June 14, 1861. Services recognized by Gen. Pope September 14, 1861. Mustered out November, 1861.

CLINTON COUNTY COMPANY HOME GUARD INFANTRY.

Organized by authority of Gen. Lyon June, 1861. Scouting and guarding bridges on the Hannibal & St. Joseph Railroad till September. Mustered out September, 1861.

COLE COUNTY REGIMENT HOME GUARD INFANTRY.

Organized in Missouri at large June 11 to July 1, 1861, by authority of Gen. Lyon. Company "L" organized August 25, 1861. Post duty at Jefferson City and guard and scout duty in Cole, Callaway, Miller, Moniteau and Osage Counties. At Osage Bridge September 3 to October 1. Disband October 1, 1861.

DALLAS COUNTY REGIMENT HOME GUARD INFANTRY.

Organized June, 1861. Duty at Springfield and in Dallas, Polk, Green, La Clede, Phelps and Hickory Counties. Mustered out August, 1861.

DE KALB COUNTY REGIMENT HOME GUARD INFANTRY.

Organized June, 1861, under authority Gen. Lyon. Mustered out September, 1861.

DE SOTO COUNTY COMPANY HOME GUARD INFANTRY.

Organized in Jefferson County by authority of Gen. Lyon June, 1861. Guard bridges of the Iron Mountain Railroad, and duty in Washington County. Disbanded September, 1861.

DOUGLAS COUNTY COMPANY HOME GUARD INFANTRY.

Organized at Springfield July, 1861. Duty at Springfield, and in Douglas County till October. Joined Phelps' Regiment October 13, 1861.

FRANKLIN COUNTY REGIMENT HOME GUARD INFANTRY.

Organized June, 1861, by authority of Gen. Lyon. Guard bridges in Franklin County till September. Mustered out September, 1861.

FREMONT RANGERS HOME GUARD INFANTRY (5 COMPANIES).

Organized August, 1861, by authority of Gen Fremont. Duty at Cape Girardeau, Rolla and Springfield, to December. Battle of Wilson's Creek August 10 (Switzler's Company). Mustered out December 18, 1861.

GASCONADE COUNTY BATTALION HOME GUARD INFANTRY (2nd).

Organized by authority of Gen. Lyon June, 1861. Guard bridges Pacific Railroad. Disbanded September, 1861.

GREEN COUNTY COMPANY HOME GUARD IN-
FANTRY.

Organized by authority of Gen. Lyon June, 1861.
Scout duty till September. Mustered out September,
1861.

GENTRY COUNTY REGIMENT HOME GUARD IN-
FANTRY.

Organized by authority of Gen. Lyon June, 1861. Guard
duty on line of Hannibal & St. Joseph Railroad. Duty
in DeKalb, Clinton, Caldwell, Buchanan, Gentry, Worth,
Clay, Andrew and Platte Counties. Action at Blue
Mills September 17. Mustered out October, 1861.

GREEN AND CHRISTIAN COUNTIES COMPANY
HOME GUARD INFANTRY.

Organized June, 1861. Duty in Green and Christian
Counties. Ordered to Springfield, Mo. A detachment
in battle of Wilson's Creek August 10. Disbanded August 17, 1861.

HARRISON COUNTY REGIMENT HOME GUARD IN-
FANTRY.

Organized September 3, 1861. Duty in Harrison, Gentry, Andrew and Buchanan Counties. Mustered out
September 23, 1861.

JEFFERSON CITY BATTALION HOME GUARD IN-
FANTRY.

Organized June, 1861, by authority of Gen. Lyon.
Duty at Jefferson City and in adjacent country till
August. Mustered out August, 1861.

JOHNSON COUNTY REGIMENT HOME GUARD IN-
FANTRY.

Organized June, 1861, by authority of Gen. Lyon.
At Lexington, and duty in Johnson, Pettis, Lafayette
and adjoining counties till September. Mustered out
September, 1861.

KING'S COMPANY RAILROAD GUARD.

Organized at Franklin September and October, 1861.
Duty guarding railroad till January, 1862. Mustered out
January 23, 1862.

KNOX COUNTY REGIMENT HOME GUARD IN-
FANTRY.

Organized July, 1861, by authority of Gen. Lyon.
Duty in Marion, Lewis, Clark, Scotland, Knox, Shelby,
Monroe, Macon, Adair and Schuyler Counties. Action
at Clapp's Ford August 14. Mustered out October, 1861.

LAWRENCE COUNTY REGIMENT HOME GUARD IN-
FANTRY.

Organized May 25, 1861. Accepted by Gen. Sigel June
16, 1861. Scouting and guarding trains and posts till
August. Mustered out August 10, 1861.

LEWIS COUNTY COMPANY HOME GUARD IN-
FANTRY.

Organized June, 1861, by authority of Gen. Hardin.
At St. Catherine and guarding bridges on Hannibal
& St. Joseph Railroad. Mustered out July 16, 1861.

LEXINGTON COUNTY COMPANY HOME GUARD IN-
FANTRY.

Organized at Lexington, Mo., August 12, 1861, by authority of Gen. Lyon. Siege and surrender of Lexington September 11-21. Mustered out at St. Louis, Mo.,
October 22, 1861.

LIVINGSTON COUNTY COMPANY HOME GUARD IN-
FANTRY.

Organized June, 1861, by authority of Gen. Lyon.
Scouting in Livingston, Carroll, Ray and Davies Counties. Mustered out September, 1861.

MARION COUNTY BATTALION HOME GUARD IN-
FANTRY.

Organized June and July, 1861, by authority of Gen.
Lyon. Guarding railroad and stores at Hannibal till
September. Disbanded September, 1861.

MONITEAU COUNTY COMPANY HOME GUARD IN-
FANTRY.

Organized at Jefferson City, Mo., June, 1861, by authority of Gen. Lyon. Duty at Jefferson City, California
and Tipton, to August. Disbanded August, 1861.

NODAWAY COUNTY REGIMENT HOME GUARD IN-
FANTRY.

Organized July, 1861, and accepted by Gen. Pope.
Scouting in Nodaway, Audrian, Worth, Gentry and Buchanan Counties. Mustered out August, 1861.

OSAGE COUNTY BATTALION HOME GUARD IN-
FANTRY.

Organized May 27, 1861, by authority of Gen. Lyon.
Guard Pacific Railroad and guard and picket Jefferson
City during session of State Convention. Mustered out
July 21, 1861.

OSAGE COUNTY REGIMENT AND HICKORY COUN-
TY BATTALION HOME GUARD INFANTRY.

Organized by authority of Gen. Fremont June and
July, 1861. Duty in Camden, Miller, Hickory, Benton
and Cole Counties, and at Jefferson City till December.
Disbanded December, 1861.

OZARK COUNTY REGIMENT HOME GUARD IN-
FANTRY.

Organized June, 1861, by authority of Gen. Lyon.
Duty in Ozark and adjacent counties, and scouting on
State Road from Springfield, Mo., to Jacksonport, Ark.,
till October. Mustered out October, 1861.

PACIFIC BATTALION (INK'S) HOME GUARD IN-
FANTRY.

Organized June, 1861, by authority of Gen. Lyon.
Guard bridges Pacific Railroad in St. Louis and Franklin Counties. Mustered out September 17, 1861.

PETTIS COUNTY REGIMENT HOME GUARD IN-
FANTRY.

Organized June, 1861, by authority of Gen. Lyon.
Duty in Pettis and adjacent counties. Mustered out
August, 1861.

PHELPS COUNTY COMPANY HOME GUARD IN-
FANTRY (MARIES CO. INDPT. COMPANY).

Organized at Rolla June, 1861, by authority of Col.
Wyman, and duty there till September. Mustered out
September, 1861.

PHELPS COUNTY COMPANY HOME GUARD IN-
FANTRY (BENNIGHT'S).

Organized at Rolla July, 1861, by authority of Col.
Wyman. Scouting in Phelps and adjacent counties.
Skirmish at Bennight's Mills September 1. Mustered
out September 20, 1861.

PIKE COUNTY REGIMENT HOME GUARD IN-
FANTRY.

Organized July, 1861, by authority of Gen. Lyon.
Duty in Pike, Lincoln and Montgomery Counties. At
Bowling Green, Ashley and Louisiana. Mustered out
September, 1861.

PILOT KNOB COMPANY HOME GUARD INFANTRY.

Organized June, 1861, by authority of Gen. Lyon.
Guard bridges of the Iron Mountain Railroad till October. Mustered out October, 1861.

POLK COUNTY REGIMENT HOME GUARD IN-
FANTRY.

Organized in Polk County June, 1861, and duty in
Polk County till December. Mustered out December,
1861.

POTOSI COUNTY REGIMENT HOME GUARD IN-
FANTRY.

Organized July, 1861, by authority of Gen. Lyon.
Guard bridges of the Iron Mountain Railroad. Action
at Potosi August 10. Mustered out September, 1861.

PUTNAM COUNTY HOME GUARD INFANTRY (2 COMPANIES).

Organized August, 1861. Duty in Putnam, Sullivan, Adair and Schuyler Counties. Mustered out October, 1861.

ST. CHARLES COUNTY BATTALION HOME GUARD INFANTRY (KREKEL'S).

Organized July, 1861, by authority of Gen. Lyon. Duty in St. Charles County. Mustered out August, 1861.

SCOTT COUNTY BATTALION HOME GUARD INFANTRY.

Organized May, 1861. Duty in Scott and adjacent counties. Mustered out August, 1861.

SIBLEY POINT HOME GUARD COMPANY (ADAIR COUNTY).

Organized by authority of Gen. Lyon, June, 1861. Duty in Adair, Schuyler and adjacent counties. Disbanded September, 1861.

STONAS INDEPENDENT COMPANY OZARK COUNTY HOME GUARD INFANTRY.

Organized by authority of Gen. Sweeny July, 1861. Scouting on road from Springfield, Mo., to Jacksonport, Ark. Mustered out at Rolla, Mo., October, 1861.

STONE PRAIRIE (BARRY COUNTY) COMPANY HOME GUARD INFANTRY.

Organized June, 1861, in Barry County by authority of Col. Phelps. Approved by Gen. Sigel August, 1861. Duty in Barry County till August. Mustered out August, 1861.

STONE COUNTY REGIMENT HOME GUARD INFANTRY.

Organized May, 1861. Accepted by Gen. Lyon June 5, 1861. Duty in Stone and Barry Counties. Mustered out July 19, 1861.

SHAWNEETOWN (PUTNAM COUNTY) HOME GUARD COMPANY INFANTRY.

Organized July, 1861. Scouting in Schuyler County, and duty at Kirksville. Mustered out September, 1861.

SULLIVAN COUNTY HOME GUARD INFANTRY (2 COMPANIES).

Organized June, 1861, by authority of Gen. Lyon. Duty in Sullivan, Adair and Macon Counties. Mustered out September, 1861.

SHELBY COUNTY COMPANY HOME GUARD INFANTRY.

Organized July 23, 1861, by authority of Gen. Hurlbut. Duty at Hannibal, Mo., and on Hannibal & St. Joseph Railroad. Mustered out September, 1861.

WEBSTER COUNTY REGIMENT HOME GUARD INFANTRY.

Organized July, 1861. Duty at Springfield, Mo. Mustered out August 18, 1861.

MILITIA ORGANIZATIONS.

ANDREW COUNTY MILITIA.
AUDRIAN COUNTY MILITA.
BATES COUNTY MILITIA.
BOGARD CITIZENS GUARD.
BOLLINGER COUNTY MILITIA.
BOONE COUNTY MILITIA.
BRIDGES' NORTH MISSOURI RAILROAD MILITIA.—Duty in North Missouri.
BUCHANAN COUNTY ENROLLED MILITIA.—Called into service in Buchanan County May-June, 1864.
BUCHANAN COUNTY UNION GUARD.—Organized August, 1864, for duty in Buchanan County.
CALHOUN CITIZENS CORPS.—Duty at Calhoun, Mo.
CALLOWAY COUNTY MILITIA.
CALLOWAY COUNTY ENROLLED MILITIA.—Called into service in Calloway County June 18, 1864.
CAMDEN COUNTY MILITIA.

CAPE GIRARDEAU COUNTY MILITIA.
CARROLL COUNTY MILITIA.—Duty in Carroll County. Scout and skirmishes in Carroll and Ray Counties, May 26-27, 1865.
CHARITON COUNTY MILITIA.—Duty in Chariton County.
CLAY COUNTY MILITIA.—At Liberty April, 1864.
CLAY COUNTY ENROLLED MILITIA.
CLINTON COUNTY ENROLLED MILITIA.—Called into service May 30, 1864. At Plattsburg, Mo.
COOPER AND MONITEAU COUNTY MILITIA.
COOPER COUNTY MILITIA.
DALLAS COUNTY MILITIA.
DE KALB COUNTY MILITIA.—Called into service April 19, 1864.
HOWARD COUNTY MILITIA.
JACKSON COUNTY MILITIA.
JASPER COUNTY MILITIA.
JOHNSON COUNTY MILITIA.
LAFAYETTE COUNTY MILITIA.
LAWRENCE COUNTY MILITIA.
LINN COUNTY MILITIA.—Called into service June, 1864. Descent on LaClede June 18-19.
LIVINGSTON COUNTY MILITIA.
MARIES COUNTY MILITIA.
MISSISSIPPI COUNTY ENROLLED MILITIA.
MISSISSIPPI COUNTY MILITIA.
MORGAN COUNTY MILITIA.
NEWMAN'S PROVISIONAL ENROLLED MILITIA.—Duty on the Pacific Railroad.
OSAGE AND MARIAS COUNTIES MILITIA.
OSAGE COUNTY MILITIA.
PACIFIC RAILROAD MILITIA.
PERRY COUNTY MILITIA.
PETTIS COUNTY MILITIA.
PIKE COUNTY ENROLLED MILITIA.—Called into service June 17, 1864.
RAY COUNTY MILITIA.
ROLLA BATTALION CITIZENS GUARD.—Duty in District of Rolla.
ST. CLAIR COUNTY MILITIA.
SALINE COUNTY MILITIA.
SCOTT COUNTY ENROLLED MILITA.—Called into service June, 1864. Duty at Commerce and St. Louis.
SOUTHWEST BRANCH PACIFIC RAILROAD MILITIA.
STONE COUNTY MILITIA.
TANNEY COUNTY MILITIA.
WARREN COUNTY MILITIA.
WASHINGTON COUNTY MILITIA.
WRIGHT COUNTY MILITA.

MISSISSIPPI VOLUNTEERS.

1st REGIMENT CAVALRY (COLORED).

Organized at Vicksburg, Miss., October 9, 1863. Attached to post of Goodrich Landing, District of Northeast, La., to January, 1864. 1st Brigade, United States Colored Troops, District of Vicksburg, Miss., to March, 1864.

SERVICE.—Duty at Skipwith Landing till January, 1864. Expedition to Tallulah C. H. November 10-13, 1863. Merriwether's Ferry, Bayou Boeuf, Ark., December 13. At Vicksburg till February, 1864. Expedition up Yazoo River February 1-March 8, 1864. Satartia February 7. Occupation of Yazoo City February 9-March 6. Near Yazoo City February 28. Yazoo City March 5. Designation of Regiment changed to 3rd U. S. Colored Cavalry March 11, 1864, which see.

1st REGIMENT MOUNTED RIFLES.

Organized at Memphis, Tenn., March, 1864. Attached to District of Memphis, Tenn., 16th Army Corps, Dept. Tennessee, to June, 1864. 1st Brigade, Cavalry Division, District of West Tennessee, to July, 1864. 1st Brigade, 2nd Cavalry Division, District West Tennessee, to December, 1864. 1st Brigade, Cavalry Division, District West Tennessee, to June, 1865.

SERVICE.—Duty in the Defences of Memphis, Tenn., till August, 1864. Expedition from Memphis to Grand

Gulf, Miss., July 7-24. Near Bolivar July 6. Port Gibson July 14. Grand Gulf July 16. Smith's Expedition to Oxford, Miss., August 1-31. Tallahatchie River August 7-9. Hurricane Creek August 9. Oxford August 9 and 11. Hurricane Creek August 13-14 and 19. At Memphis and in District of West Tennessee, till December. Grierson's Expedition from Memphis against Mobile & Ohio Railroad December 21, 1864, to January 5, 1865. Verona December 25, 1864. Okolona December 27. Egypt Station December 28. Franklin and Lexington January 2, 1865. Mechanicsburg January 3. The Ponds January 4. Moved from Vicksburg to Memphis and duty there till June, 1865. Expedition from Memphis into Southeast Arkansas and Northeast Louisiana January 26-February 11. Mustered out June 26, 1865.

1st REGIMENT HEAVY ARTILLERY (AFRICAN DESCENT).

Organized at Vicksburg, Miss., September 26, 1863. Attached to post of Vicksburg, District of Vicksburg, Miss., to March, 1864. Unassigned, 1st Division, U. S. Colored Troops, District of Vicksburg, to April, 1864.

SERVICE.—Post and garrison duty at Vicksburg, Miss., till April, 1864. Designation changed to 4th U. S. Colored Heavy Artillery, March 11, 1864, and to 5th U. S. Colored Heavy Artillery April 26, 1864 (which see).

2nd REGIMENT HEAVY ARTILLERY (AFRICAN DESCENT).

Organized at Natchez, Miss., September 12, 1863. Attached to post of Natchez, Miss., District of Northeast Louisiana, to January, 1864. Post of Vicksburg, District of Vicksburg, Miss., to March, 1864. District of Natchez, Miss., to April, 1864.

SERVICE.—Garrison duty at Natchez and Vicksburg, Miss., till April, 1864. Skirmish at Vidalia February 7, 1864. Designation changed to 5th U. S. Colored Heavy Artillery March 11, 1864, and to 6th U. S. Colored Heavy Artillery, April 26, 1864 (which see).

1st REGIMENT INFANTRY (AFRICAN DESCENT).

Organized at Milliken's Bend, La., and Vicksburg, Miss., May 16, 1863. Attached to African Brigade, District of Northeast Louisiana, to July, 1863. Post of Vicksburg, District of Vicksburg, Miss., till March, 1864.

SERVICE.—Duty at Milliken's Bend, La., till July, 1863. Action at Milliken's Bend June 7, 1863. At Vicksburg, Miss., till March, 1864. Action at Ross' Landing, Grand Lake, February 14, 1864. Designation of Regiment changed to 51st U. S. Colored Troops March 11, 1864, (which see).

2nd REGIMENT INFANTRY (AFRICAN DESCENT).

Organized at Vicksburg, Miss., July 27, 1863. Attached to post of Vicksburg, District of Vicksburg, Miss., to March, 1864.

SERVICE.—Post and garrison duty at Vicksburg, Miss., till March, 1864. Expedition to Trinity November 15-16, 1863 (Detachment). Designation of Regiment changed to 52nd U. S. Colored Troops March 11, 1864, (which see).

3rd REGIMENT INFANTRY (AFRICAN DESCENT).

Organized at Warrenton, Miss., May 19, 1863. Attached to African Brigade, District of Northeast Louisiana, to July, 1863. Post Goodrich Landing, District of Vicksburg, Miss., to January, 1864. 1st Brigade, U. S. Colored Troops, District of Vicksburg, Miss., to March, 1864.

SERVICE.—Duty at Milliken's Bend and Goodrich Landing till March, 1864. Haines' Bluff February 3, 1864. Designation of Regiment changed to 53rd U. S. Colored Troops, March 11, 1864 (which see).

4th REGIMENT INFANTRY (AFRICAN DESCENT).

Organized at Vicksburg, Miss., December 11, 1863. Attached to post and District of Vicksburg, Miss., to March, 1864. Post Goodrich Landing, District of Vicksburg March, 1864.

SERVICE.—Post duty at Vicksburg and at Goodrich Landing, till March, 1864. Skirmish at Columbia February 4, 1864. Designation of Regiment changed to 66th U. S. Colored Troops March 11, 1864 (which see).

5th REGIMENT INFANTRY (AFRICAN DESCENT).

Organization not completed.

6th REGIMENT INFANTRY (AFRICAN DESCENT).

Organized at Natchez, Miss., August 27, 1863. Attached to Post of Natchez, District of Vicksburg, Miss., to January, 1864. Post of Vicksburg, Miss., to March, 1864.

SERVICE.—Post duty at Natchez and Vicksburg, Miss., till March, 1864. Skirmish near Natchez November 11, 1863 (Detachment). Designation of Regiment changed to 58th U. S. Colored Troops March 11, 1864, (which see).

NEBRASKA VOLUNTEERS.

1st REGIMENT CAVALRY.

Organized from 1st Nebraska Infantry October 11, 1863. Attached to District of Southeast Missouri, Dept. of Missouri, to November, 1864. District of Northeast Arkansas, Dept. Missouri, to January, 1864. District Northeast Arkansas, 7th Army Corps, to May, 1864. 3rd Brigade, 2nd Division, 7th Army Corps, Dept. of Arkansas, to October, 1864. 4th Brigade, Cavalry Division, 7th Army Corps, to October, 1864. District of Nebraska and District of the Plains, to July, 1866. Designated 1st Nebraska Veteran Cavalry from July 10, 1865.

SERVICE.—Duty at St. Louis, Mo., till November 30, 1863. Moved to Batesville, Ark., November 30-December 25. Operations in Northeastern Arkansas January 1-30, 1864. Action at Black River January 18. Jacksonport January 19. Expedition after Freeman's forces January 23-30. Sylamore Creek January 23 (Detachment). Sylamore January 24. Scout to Pocohontas February 9-20. Morgan's Mills, Spring River, February 9. Pocohontas February 10. Expedition from Batesville after Freeman's forces February 12-20. Spring River, near Smithfield, February 13. Expedition to Wild Haws, Strawberry Creek, etc., March 10-12. Scout from Batesville to Fairview March 25-26. Spring River, near Smithville, April 13 (Detachment). Moved to Jacksonport, Ark., April 17-19. Attack on Jacksonport April 20. Expedition to Augusta April 22-24. Near Jacksonport April 24. Moved to Duvall's Bluff May 25-30. Veterans on furlough June 10 to August 13. Left Omaha for Fort Kearney, Neb., August 15, arriving there August 23. Operations against Indians in Nebraska and Colorado till July, 1866, participating in numerous affairs with hostile Indians at Plum Creek, Spring Ranch, Julesburg, Mud Springs, Elm Creek and Smith's Ranch. Also engaged in scout and escort duty. Operations on Overland Stage route between Denver and Julesburg, Colo., January 14-25, 1865. Operations on North Platte River, Colo., February 2-18. Scout from Dakota City April 12-16 and April 22-27 (Detachments). Scout from Fort Laramie to Wind River, Neb., May 3-21 (Detachment). Scout from Plum Creek to Medway Station, Wind River, Neb., May 8-20 (Detachment). Scout from Fort Kearney to Little Blue River, Neb., May 9-June 2 (Detachment). Scout from Cottonwood May 12-14 (1st Battalion). Scout from Plum Creek, Neb., May 26-27 (Detachment). Expedition to Platt and Mojave Rivers, Neb., June 12-July 5 (Detachment). Mustered out July 1, 1866.

1st BATTALION CAVALRY.

Organized at Omaha January to August, 1864. Attached to District of Nebraska and operating against Indians in Nebraska and Colorado and guarding Overland Mail routes. At Fort Cottonwood, Neb., October and November, 1864; at Gillman's Station till January, 1865; at Cottonwood Springs till February, 1865, and at Gillman's Station till July, 1865. Company "B" at Dakota City till July, 1865. Scout from Dakota City April 12-16, 1865. Scout to Middle Bow River April 22-27.

Company "C" at Fort Cottonwood, Neb., till July, 1865. Scout from Cottonwood May 12-14, 1865. Company "D" at Omaha till February, 1865. Moved to Fort Kearney February 25 and duty there till April, and at Fort Laramie till July. Consolidated with 1st Nebraska Veteran Cavalry July 10, 1865.

2nd REGIMENT CAVALRY.

Organized at Omaha October 23, 1862, and assigned to duty at Fort Kearney, Neb., guarding frontier of Nebraska, protecting emigrants, stage and telegraph lines and operating against Indians till April, 1863. Ordered to Sioux City. Attack on Pawnee Agency June 23, 1863 (Co. "D"). Sully's Expedition against Indians in Dakota Territory August 13-September 11. Action at White Stone Hill, Dakota Territory, September 3. Skirmish at White Stone Hill September 5 (Co. "F"). Company "D" on duty at Omaha and at Fort Kearney, Neb. Mustered out December 23, 1863.

1st REGIMENT INFANTRY.

Organized at Omaha June 11 to July 21, 1861. Attached to Dept. of Missouri to February, 1862. District of Cairo, Ill., February, 1862. 2nd Brigade, 3rd Division, Army of the Tennessee, to July, 1862. Helena (Ark.) District of Eastern Arkansas to October, 1862. 2nd Brigade, 2nd Division, Army of Southeast Missouri, Dept. of Missouri, to March, 1863. District of Southeast Missouri to November, 1863.

SERVICE.—Left State for St. Joseph, Mo., July 30, 1861; thence moved to Independence, Mo., August 3-5, and to St. Louis, Mo., August 8-11. Moved to Pilot Knob, Mo., August 13-14, and to Syracuse, Mo., August 19. Duty there till October 21. Fremont's Campaign against Springfield, Mo., October 21-November 2. March to Sedalia and Georgetown November 9-16. Campaign against Bushwhackers December 8-15. Pope's Expedition to Warrensburg and Milford December 15-27. Action at Shawnee Mound, Milford, on the Blackwater, December 18. (Capture of 1,300 prisoners.) Duty at Georgetown till February 2, 1862. Moved to Fort Donelson, Tenn., February 2-13. Investment and capture of Fort Donelson February 13-16. At Fort Henry February 17-March 6. Moved to Pittsburg Landing, Tenn., March 6-13. Battle of Shiloh, Tenn., April 6-7. Advance on and siege of Corinth, Miss., April 29-May 30. March to Memphis, Tenn., June 2-17; thence moved to Helena, Ark., July 24, and duty there till October. Expedition from Helena and capture of Steamer "Fair Play" August 4-19. Milliken's Bend August 18. Expedition up the Yazoo August 20-27. Haines Bluff August 20. Bolivar August 22. Greenville August 23. Moved to Sulphur Springs, Mo., October 5-11; thence to Pilot Knob October 28-30, and to Patterson November 2-4. Moved to Reeves Station December 9-10, and return to Patterson December 19. Moved to Van Buren December 21-24, and toward Doniphan January 9-10, 1863. Moved to Alton January 14-18; to West Plains and Salem, Ark., January 28-February 2. Moved to Pilot Knob and Ironton February 2-27. Moved to St. Genevieve and to Cape Girardeau March 8-12. Operations against Marmaduke April 21-May 2. Action at Cape Girardeau April 26. Pursuit of Marmaduke to St. Francis River April 29-May 5. Castor River, near Bloomfield, April 29. Bloomfield April 30. Chalk Bluffs, St. Francis River, April 30-May 1. Moved to Pilot Knob May 26-29 and duty there till August 28. At St. Louis, Mo., till November. Regiment ordered mounted October 11, 1863, and designation changed to 1st Nebraska Cavalry November 6, 1863 (which see).

INDEPENDENT COMPANY OMAHA SCOUTS.

Organized at Omaha May 3, 1865. Attached to District of Nebraska. Scout from Fort Kearney, Neb., May 19-26, 1865. Powder River Expedition June 20-October 7. Actions on the Powder River September 1, 2, 4, 5, 7 and 8. Operating against Indians on the Plains and protecting lines of communications and emigrants till July, 1866. Mustered out July 16, 1866.

44

INDEPENDENT COMPANY "A" PAWNEE SCOUTS.

Organized at Columbus, Neb., January 13, 1865. Attached to District of Nebraska. At Fort Kearney, Neb., February, 1865. At Fort Rankin April, 1865. Powder River Expedition June 20-October 7, 1865. Action at Tongue River August 28. Actions on Powder River September 1-8. Operations on the Plains against Indians and protecting lines of communications and emigrants till April, 1866. Mustered out April 1, 1866.

NEVADA VOLUNTEERS.

1st BATTALION CAVALRY.

Organized at Fort Churchill, California, June 22, 1863. Attached to District of Utah and District of California, Dept. of the Pacific.

Companies "A" and "B" moved to Camp Douglass, near Salt Lake City, Utah, September 29, 1863. Duty there and at Camp Connor, Utah, till June, 1864. Company "B" moved to Unitah Valley, Utah, May 2, 1864; thence to Fort Bridger, Utah, August 1, 1864. Company "A" moved to Fort Bridger, Utah, June, 1864, and engaged in scouting and protecting emigrants and prospectors.

Companies "C," "D," "E" and "F" at Fort Churchill, Cal., till July, 1864. Expedition from Fort Churchill to Humboldt River, Nevada, June 8-August 9, 1864. Duty scouting in the Smoke Creek District (Co. "D"). Companies "C" and "F" ordered to Camp Douglass, near Salt Lake City, Utah, July 28, 1864. Companies "D" and "E" remained at Fort Churchill, operating in Humboldt District till muster out. Expedition to Pyramid Lake and Walker's Lake March 12-19, 1865 (Cos. "D," "E"). Skirmish at Mud Lake March 14, 1865 (Cos. "D," "E"). Mustered out July 21, 1866.

1st BATTALION INFANTRY.

Organized at Fort Churchill, California, December 24, 1863. Attached to District of California, Dept. of the Pacific.

Company "A" on duty at Fort Churchill till July 28, 1864. Moved to Smoky Creek Region July 28, returning to Fort Churchill October 23, 1864, and duty there till December, 1865. Expedition from Fort Churchill to Pyramid Lake and Walker's Lake March 12-19, 1865.

Company "B" at Fort Churchill till July 28, 1864. Ordered to Fort Ruby, Nevada, July 28, 1864, and duty there till December, 1865. Expedition from Fort Ruby to Humboldt Valley, Nevada, May 25-June 15, 1865. Skirmish at Austin May 29.

Company "C" at Fort Churchill till December 7, 1864. Ordered to Camp Independence, California, and duty there till muster out. Battalion mustered out December 23, 1865.

NEW HAMPSHIRE VOLUNTEERS.

1st REGIMENT CAVALRY.

First organized at Concord, N. H., as a Battalion of four Companies October 24 to December 21, 1861, and attached to 1st New England Cavalry, afterward designated 1st Rhode Island Cavalry, as Companies "I," "K," "L," "M." Moved from Concord, N. H., to Pawtucket, R. I., December 22, 1861, and join Regiment. (For history to January, 1864, see 1st Rhode Island Cavalry.)

Battalion detached from 1st Rhode Island Cavalry January 7, 1864, to form 1st New Hampshire Volunteer Cavalry. Moved to New Hampshire and on Veteran furlough and organizing Regiment, February to April, 1864. 7 Companies organized and ordered to Washington, D. C., April 23, 1864. Attached to 2nd Brigade, 3rd Division, Cavalry Corps, Army of the Potomac and Army of the Shenandoah, Middle Military Division, to February, 1865. Cavalry, Dept. of the Shenandoah, to July, 1865.

SERVICE.—At Camp Stoneman, D. C., till May 17, 1864. Moved to Belle Plains, Va. Guard Aquia Creek and Fredericksburg S. R., and at Belle Plains till June 6, then moved to White House. (A part of Regiment at Hanover Court House and Cold Harbor June 1-12.) Long Bridge June 12. Riddle's Shop and White Oak Swamp June 13. Smith's Store June 15. Wilson's Raid on Southside & Danville Railroad June 22-30. Ream's Station June 22. Nottaway Court House and Black and White Station June 23. Staunton Bridge (or Roanoke Station) June 25. Sappony Church (or Stony Creek) June 28-29. Ream's Station June 29. On picket duty at Light House Point and City Point June 30-August 8. Sheridan's Shenandoah Valley Campaign August to December. Winchester August 17. Summit Station August 20-21. Berryville August 21. Kearneysville August 25. Darkesville September 3. Near Brucetown and Winchester September 7. Abram's Creek September 13. Battle of Opequan, Winchester, September 19. Near Cedarville September 20. Front Royal September 21. Fisher's Hill September 22. Milford September 22. Waynesboro September 29 and October 2. Mt. Crawford October 2. Near Columbia Furnace October 7. Tom's Brook ("Woodstock Races") October 8-9. Battle of Cedar Creek October 19. Near Kernstown November 10. Newtown and Cedar Creek November 12. Rude's Hill, near Mt. Jackson, November 22. Expedition from Kernstown to Lacy Springs December 19-22. Lacy Springs December 20-21. Duty at Winchester till February, 1865. Sheridan's Raid into Virginia February 27-March 3. Waynesboro March 2. Regiment led charge on enemy's works, capturing with the sabre 1,500 prisoners, all their Artillery and the flag of every Regiment engaged. Detached from Division, to guard prisoners back to Winchester, Mt. Jackson March 4. Mt. Sidney March 5. Lacy Springs March 5. New Market March 6. Duty at and in the vicinity of Winchester, and in the Dept. of the Shenandoah, also at Poolesville, Md., till July, 1865.

Five Companies complete organization July, 1864, and ordered to Washington, D. C. Guard and patrol duty and operations against Mosby's guerrillas in the Defences of Washington till March, 1865. Joined Regiment in the Shenandoah Valley.

Regiment lost during service 5 Officers and 28 Enlisted men killed and mortally wounded and 2 Officers and 112 Enlisted men by disease. Total 147.

2nd REGIMENT CAVALRY.

Organized as 8th New Hampshire Volunteer Infantry December 23, 1861. (For history to December, 1863, see 8th New Hampshire Infantry.) Designation changed to 2nd Cavalry December, 1863. Attached to 4th Brigade, Cavalry Division, Dept. of the Gulf, to June, 1864. Defences of New Orleans, Dept. of the Gulf, to September, 1864. District of Natchez, Dept. of Mississippi, to January, 1865. District of Vidalia, Dept. of Mississippi, to March, 1865. Post of Natchez, Dept. of Mississippi, to June, 1865.

SERVICE.—Duty at Franklin, La., till January, 1864. Re-enlisted January 4, 1864. Ordered to New Orleans, La., and duty there till March. Red River Campaign March 10-May 22. Advance from Franklin to Alexandria March 14-26. Action at Natchitoches March 31. Crump's Hill April 2. Wilson's Farm April 7. Bayou de Paul Carroll's Mill April 8. Battle of Pleasant Hill April 9. Natchitoches April 19 and 22. Monett's Bluff and Cane River Crossing April 23. Retreat to Alexandria April 24-30. Alexandria May 1-8. Retreat to Morganza May 10-20. Mansura May 16. Near Moreauville May 17. Yellow Bayou May 18. Expedition from Morganza to the Atchafalaya May 30-June 6. Ordered to New Orleans, La., July 11. Veterans absent on furlough July 11 to August 31. Non-Veterans on duty at Camp Parapet. Regiment ordered to Natchez, Miss., September, and duty there till January 9, 1865. Operating against guerrillas, picket and garrison duty. Non-Veterans ordered home December 23, 1864, and mustered out January 18, 1865. Veterans consolidated to a Battalion of 3 Companies and ordered to Vidalia. Garrison, guard and patrol duty there till March 6, 1865.

Provost duty at Natchez till October. Ordered to Vicksburg, Miss., and there mustered out October 29, 1865. Moved to Concord, N. H., October 29-November 6, and discharged November 9, 1865.

For losses see 8th New Hampshire Infantry.

1st REGIMENT HEAVY ARTILLERY.

Company "A" organized as 1st Company New Hampshire Heavy Artillery and mustered in July 22, 1863. Stationed at Fort Constitution till May 6, 1864. Company "B" organized as 2nd Company New Hampshire Heavy Artillery and mustered in September 17, 1863. Stationed at Fort McClary, Kittery Point, till May 6, 1864. These 2 Companies ordered to Washington, D. C., May 6, 1864. Attached to Augur's Command, Defences of Washington, 22nd Corps, and assigned to duty in the Defences of Washington, D. C. Company "A" at Forts Slocum, Stevens, Totten, Sumner and Batteries Cameron, Parrott, Kendall and Vermont till November, 1864. Ordered to Portsmouth Harbor November 25, 1864. Company "B" at Forts Bunker Hill, Saratoga, Lincoln, Bayard, Gaines and Foote till February, 1865, when ordered to Portsmouth Harbor, N. H. Repulse of Early's attack on Washington July 11-12, 1864 (Cos. "A" and "B"). Companies "C," "D," "E," "F," "G," "H," "I," "K" and "L" organized from September 2 to October 17, 1864. Company "M" formed by assignment of 1st New Hampshire Battery, Volunteer Light Artillery, November 5, 1864, but remained detached as a Light Battery. Each Company ordered to Washington, D. C., as fast as organized, and duty in the Defences of that city till June, 1865. Regiment mustered out June 15, 1865. Recruits consolidated to 2 Companies and mustered out September 11, 1865.

1st BATTERY LIGHT ARTILLERY.

Organized at Manchester and mustered in September 21, 1861. Left State for Washington, D. C., November 1. Attached to McDowell's Division, Army of the Potomac, to March, 1862. 3rd Division, 1st Army Corps, Army of the Potomac, to April, 1862. Artillery, King's Division, Dept. of the Rappahannock, to June, 1862. Artillery, 1st Division, 3rd Corps, Army of Virginia, to September, 1862. Artillery, 1st Division, 1st Army Corps, Army of the Potomac, to May, 1863. 3rd Volunteer Brigade, Artillery Reserve, Army of the Potomac, to October, 1863. Artillery Brigade, 3rd Army Corps, Army of the Potomac, to March, 1864. Artillery Brigade, 2nd Army Corps, Army of the Potomac, to June, 1865.

SERVICE.—Duty at Munson's Hill, Defences of Washington, D. C., till March, 1862. Advance on Manassas, Va., March 10-15. Camp at Upton's Hill till April 9. Advance on Falmouth, Va., April 9-18. Occupation of Fredericksburg April 18 and duty there till May 25. McDowell's advance on Richmond May 25-29. Operations against Jackson June 1-21. Duty at Falmouth till July 28, and at Fredericksburg till August 5. Expedition to Fredericks Hall and Spottsylvania Court House August 5-8. Thornburg Mills August 5-6. Pope's Campaign in Northern Virginia August 16-September 2. Fords of the Rappahannock August 21-23. Rappahannock Station August 22. Sulphur Springs August 26. Battle of Groveton August 29. Battle of Bull Run August 30. Maryland Campaign September-October. Battle of Antietam, Md., September 16-17. Movement to Falmouth, Va., October 30-November 19. Union November 2-3. Battle of Fredericksburg, Va., December 11-15. "Mud March" January 20-24, 1863. At Belle Plains till April. Chancellorsville Campaign April 27-May 6. Operations at Pollock's Mill Creek April 29-May 2. Fitzhugh's Crossing April 29-30. Battle of Chancellorsville May 1-5. Battle of Gettysburg, Pa., July 2-4. Funkstown, Md., July 12-18. Bristoe Campaign October 9-22. Advance to line of the Rappahannock November 7-8. Kelly's Ford November 7. Brandy Station November 8. Mine Run Campaign November 26-December 2. Payne's Farm November 27. At Brandy Station till April, 1864. Demonstration on the Rapidan February 6-7. Campaign from the Rapidan to the

James River May 3-June 12. Battles of the Wilderness May 5-7; Spottsylvania May 8-12; Po River May 10; Spottsylvania Court House May 12-21. Assault on the Salient, "Bloody Angle," May 12. North Anna River May 23-26. Totopotomoy May 28-31. Cold Harbor June 1-12. Before Petersburg June 16-19. Siege of Petersburg June 16, 1864, to April 2, 1865. Jerusalem Plank Road June 22-23. Deep Bottom July 27-28. Mine Explosion, Petersburg, July 30 (Reserve). Demonstration north of the James August 13-20. Strawberry Plains, Deep Bottom, August 14-18. Duty in the trenches before Petersburg August 20-30. At Fort Hill till September 7. At Battery 18 till October 22. Non-Veterans mustered out September 28, 1864. Battery attached to 1st New Hampshire Heavy Artillery as Company "M" November 5, 1864, but remained detached as a Light Battery in the field. Duty in the trenches before Petersburg till March, 1865. Appomattox Campaign March 28-April 9. White Oak Road March 30-31. Sutherland Station and fall of Petersburg April 2. Sailor's Creek April 6. Farmville and High Bridge April 7. Appomattox Court House April 9. Surrender of Lee and his army. Moved to Washington, D. C., May 1-12. Grand Review May 23. Mustered out June 9, 1865.

Battery lost during service 6 Enlisted men killed and mortally wounded and 6 Enlisted men by disease. Total 12.

1st COMPANY SHARPSHOOTERS.

Mustered into United States service September 9, 1861. Left State for Weehawken, N. J., September 11, and there assigned to 1st Regiment Berdan's United States Sharpshooters as Company "E." (See 1st United States Sharpshooters.)

2nd COMPANY SHARPSHOOTERS.

Mustered in November 28, 1861. Left State for Washington, D. C., November 28, 1861, and assigned to 2nd Regiment Berdan's United States Sharpshooters as Company "F." (See 2nd United States Sharpshooters.)

3rd COMPANY SHARPSHOOTERS.

Mustered in December 10, 1861. Left State for Washington, D. C., December 10, 1861, and assigned to 2nd Regiment Berdan's United States Sharpshooters as Company "G". (See 2nd United States Sharpshooters.)

1st REGIMENT INFANTRY.

Organized at Concord and mustered in for three months' service May 1, 1861. Moved to Washington, D. C., May 25-28. Camp at Kalorama Heights till June 10. Assigned to Stone's Brigade, Patterson's Army of the Shenandoah. Rockville Expedition June 10-July 7. Action at Conrad's Ferry June 17. At Poolesville till July 3. Moved to Williamsport, Md., July 3-7; thence to Martinsburg, Va., July 8. Advance toward Winchester July 15-17. Moved to Charlestown July 18; to Harper's Ferry July 21, and to Sandy Hook July 28. Ordered to New Hampshire August 2, and mustered out August 9, 1861, expiration of term.

2nd REGIMENT INFANTRY.

Organized at Portsmouth May 31 to June 8, 1861. Moved to Washington, D. C., June 20-23, and duty there till July 16. Attached to Burnside's Brigade, Hunter's Division, McDowell's Army of Northeastern Virginia, to August, 1861. Hooker's Brigade, Division of the Potomac, to October, 1861. 1st Brigade, Hooker's Division, Army of the Potomac, to March, 1862. 1st Brigade, 2nd Division, 3rd Army Corps, Army of the Potomac, to February, 1863. New Hampshire, Dept. of the East, to June, 1863. 3rd Brigade, 2nd Division, 3rd Army Corps, Army of the Potomac, to July, 1863. Marston's Command, Point Lookout, Md., District of Saint Marys, to April, 1864. 2nd Brigade, 2nd Division, 18th Army Corps, Army of the James, Dept. of Virginia and North Carolina, to June, 1864. Provost Guard, 18th Army Corps, to August, 1864. 1st Brigade, 1st Division, 18th Army Corps, to October, 1864. 3rd Brigade, 1st Division, 18th Army Corps, to December,

1864. 3rd Brigade, 3rd Division, 24th Army Corps, to June, 1865.

SERVICE.—Advance on Manassas, Va., July 16-21, 1861. Battle of Bull Run, Va., July 21. Duty in the Defences of Washington, D. C., at Bladensburg and Budd's Ferry, Md., till April, 1861. Moved to the Peninsula, Va., April 4-8. Siege of Yorktown April 10-May 4. Battle of Williamsburg May 5. Occupation of Williamsburg till May 24. Battle of Fair Oaks, Seven Pines, May 31-June 1. Picket affair June 23-24. Seven days before Richmond June 25-July 1. Oak Grove June 25. Savage Station June 29. White Oak Swamp, Charles City Cross Roads and Glendale June 30. Malvern Hill July 1. At Harrison's Landing till August 16. Malvern Hill August 5. Movement to Centreville August 16-26. Pope's Campaign in Northern Virginia August 26-September 2. Bristoe Station or Kettle Run August 27. Battle of Groveton August 29. Battle of Bull Run August 30. Chantilly September 1. Duty in the Defences of Washington till November. Operations on the Orange & Alexandria Railroad October 10-12. Movement to Falmouth, Va., November 18-28. Battle of Fredericksburg December 12-15. "Mud March" January 20-24, 1863. Operations at Rappahannock Bridge and Grove Church February 5-7. Ordered to Concord, N. H., February 26. Duty there and at Fort Constitution, Portsmouth, till May 25. Moved to Washington, D. C., May 25-28, and duty there till June 11. Moved to Hartwood Church, Va., June 11, and rejoin Army of the Potomac. Battle of Gettysburg, Pa., July 2-4. Williamsport July 11-12. Manassas Gap, Va., July 22-23. Ordered to Point Lookout, Md., July 25, and duty there guarding prisoners till April, 1864. Ordered to Yorktown, Va., April 7; thence to Williamsburg April 22. Butler's operations on south side of James River and against Petersburg and Richmond May 4-28. Capture of City Point and Bermuda Hundred May 5. Chester Station May 6-7. Swift Creek or Arrowfield Church May 9-10. Operations against Fort Darling May 12-16. Drury's Bluff May 14-16. Bermuda Hundred May 16-27. Port Walthal May 26. Moved to White House, thence to Cold Harbor May 27-June 1. Battles about Cold Harbor June 1-12. Non-Veterans left front June 8, and mustered out June 21, 1864. Regiment detached from Brigade June 9, and assigned to duty at Corps Headquarters till August 13. Assaults on Petersburg June 15-19. Siege of Petersburg June 16, 1864, to April 2, 1865. Duty in trenches before Petersburg August 18 to September 1. Ordered to Wilson's Landing September 1 and duty there till October 1. Expedition to Barnett's Ferry September 27-28. Moved to Aikens Landing October 1. Duty in trenches before Richmond till March 3, 1865. Battle of Fair Oaks October 27-28, 1864. Moved to Fort Monroe, Va., March 4-5; thence to White House Landing March 18 to establish a depot for General Sheridan's Cavalry, and duty there till March 24. March to lines north of the James March 24-28. Occupation of Richmond April 3. Duty there and at Manchester till July. Provost duty in District of Northern Neck, Dept. of Virginia, till December. Mustered out December 19, 1865.

Regiment lost during service 15 Officers and 163 Enlisted men killed and mortally wounded and 6 Officers and 166 Enlisted men by disease. Total 350.

3rd REGIMENT INFANTRY.

Organized at Concord and mustered in August 23, 1861. Moved to Camp Scott, Long Island, N. Y., September 3, thence to Washington, D. C., September 18, and to Annapolis, Md., October 4. Attached to Viele's Brigade, Sherman's South Carolina Expeditionary Corps, to April, 1862. 3rd Brigade, 1st Division, Dept. of the South, to July, 1862. District of Hilton Head, S. C., 10th Corps, Dept. of the South, to April, 1863. Guss' Brigade, Seabrook Island, S. C., 10th Corps, to June, 1863. St. Helena Island, S. C., June, 1863. 2nd Brigade, Folly Island, S. C., 10th Corps, to July, 1863. 2nd Brigade, 2nd Division, Morris Island, S. C., 10th Corps, to August, 1863. 1st Brigade, Morris Island, S. C., 10th

Corps, to January, 1864. Light Brigade, District of Florida. Dept. of the South, to April, 1864. 3rd Brigade, 1st Division, 10th Corps, Army of the James, Dept. of Virginia and North Carolina, May, 1864. 2nd Brigade, 1st Division, 10th Corps, to December, 1864. 2nd Brigade, 1st Division, 24th Corps, to March, 1865. 2nd Brigade, 1st Division, 10th Corps, Dept. of North Carolina, to April, 1865. Abbott's Detached Brigade, 10th Corps, to July, 1865.

SERVICE.—Expedition to Port Royal, S. C., October 21-November 7, 1861. Capture of Forts Walker and Beauregard, Port Royal Harbor, S. C., November 7. Duty at Hilton Head, S. C., till April, 1862. Affair Hunting Island, March, 1862. Reconnoissance up Savannah River to Elba Island March 7-11. Expedition to Bluffton March 20-24. Occupation of Edisto Island April 5. Affair at Watts' Court April 10. Reconnoissance of Seabrook Island April 14. Advance on Jehossie Island April 17. Skirmish Edisto Island April 18. Duty at Edisto Island till June 1. Operations on James Island June 1-28. Picket Affair June 8. Battle of Secessionville June 16. Evacuation of James Island and movement to Hilton Head June 28-July 7. Duty at Hilton Head till April, 1863. Affair at Pinckney Island August 21, 1862. Expedition up Broad River to Pocotaligo October 21-23. Action at Caston's and Frampton's Plantations, Pocotaligo, October 22. Movements against Charleston February 16-April 9, 1863. Moved to Seabrook Island April 23, thence to Folly Island, S. C., July 3. Assault on and capture of water batteries on Morris Island July 10. Assaults on Fort Wagner, Morris Island, July 11 and 18. Siege operations on Morris Island against Forts Wagner and Gregg and against Fort Sumpter and Charleston till April 1, 1864. Occupation of Forts Wagner and Gregg September 7, 1863. Ordered to Florida April 1, 1864, and Regiment mounted. Palatka April 3. Moved to Gloucester Point, Va., April 25-29. (Veterans absent on furlough March and April, rejoining at Gloucester Point, Va.) Butler's operations on south side of James River and against Petersburg and Richmond May 4-28. Capture of City Point and Bermuda Hundred May 5. Chester Station May 6-7. Swift Creek May 9-10. Chester Station May 10. Operations against Fort Darling May 12-16. Drury's Bluff May 14-16. Bermuda Hundred May 16-31. Action at Bermuda Hundred June 2 and 14. Petersburg June 9. Port Walthal June 16-17. Siege operations against Petersburg and Richmond June 16, 1864, to January 7, 1865. Deep Bottom July 21, 1864. Demonstration north of the James August 13-20. Strawberry Plains August 14-18. Duty in trenches before Petersburg August 24-September 27. Chaffin's Farm September 28-30. Charles City Cross Roads October 1. Darbytown and New Market Roads October 7. Darbytown Road October 13. Fair Oaks October 27-28. Front of Richmond October 31-November 2. Detached for duty at New York during Presidential Election November 2-17. Duty in front of Richmond November 17 to January 3, 1865. 2nd Expedition to Fort Fisher, N. C., January 3-15. Assault and capture of Fort Fisher January 15. Half Moon Battery January 19. Sugar Loaf Battery February 11. Fort Anderson February 18. Capture of Wilmington February 22. Smith's Creek and North East Ferry February 22. Duty at Wilmington till June 3, and at Goldsboro till July. (Non-Veterans mustered out August 23, 1864.) Mustered out July 25, 1865.

Regiment lost during service 12 Officers and 186 Enlisted men killed and mortally wounded and 2 Officers and 152 Enlisted men by disease. Total 352.

4th REGIMENT INFANTRY.

Organized at Manchester and mustered in September 18, 1861. Moved to Washington, D. C., September 27-30; thence to Annapolis, Md., October 9. Attached to Casey's Provisional Brigade, Army of the Potomac, October, 1861. Wright's 3rd Brigade, Sherman's South Carolina Expeditionary Corps to March, 1862. District of Florida, Dept. of the South, to September, 1862. Brannan's Brigade, District of Beaufort, S. C., 10th Corps, Dept. of the South, to April, 1863. United States

Forces, Folly Island, S. C., 10th Corps to June, 1863. 1st Brigade, United States Forces, Folly Island, S. C., to July, 1863. 1st Brigade, 1st Division, Morris Island, S. C., 10th Corps, July, 1863. 1st Brigade, Morris Island, S. C., to January, 1864. District of Beaufort, S. C., to February, 1864. Foster's Brigade, Dodge's Division, District of Florida, February, 1864. District of Beaufort, S. C., to April, 1864. 1st Brigade, 3rd Division, 10th Corps, Army of the James, Dept. of Virginia and North Carolina, to May, 1864. 3rd Brigade, 3rd Division, 18th Corps, Army of the Potomac, to June, 1864. 3rd Brigade, 2nd Division, 10th Corps, to December, 1864. 3rd Brigade, 2nd Division, 24th Corps, to March, 1865. 3rd Brigade, 2nd Division, 10th Corps, Dept. of North Carolina, to August, 1865.

SERVICE.—Expedition to Port Royal, S. C., October 21-November 7, 1861. Capture of Forts Walker and Beauregard, Port Royal Harbor, November 7. Duty at Hilton Head, S. C., till January 21, 1862. Expedition to Florida January 21-March 2. Occupation of Fernandina, Fla., March 5. Occupation of Jacksonville, Fla., March 12 to April 8 (Cos. "E" and "F," Provost duty at Fernandina till April.) Regiment moved from Jacksonville to St. Augustine, Fla., April 9, and garrison duty there till September 6. (Cos. "B," "H" and "K" moved to James Island, S. C., June 8. Action on James Island June 10. Moved to Beaufort, S. C., June 12, and duty there till April, 1863.) Regiment moved from St. Augustine, Fla., to Beaufort, S. C., September 6, 1862, and duty there till April, 1863. Expedition to Pocotaligo, S. C., October 21-23, 1862. Action at Caston and Frampton's Plantations, Pocotaligo, October 22. Expedition against Charleston April 4-11, 1863. Expedition to North Edisto River April 17-28. Moved to Folly Island, S. C., April 29, and siege operations against Morris Island till July. Expedition to James Island July 9-16. Secessionville July 16. Siege operations against Forts Wagner and Gregg, Morris Island, S. C., and against Fort Sumpter and Charleston till January, 1864. Capture of Forts Wagner and Gregg September 7, 1863. Moved to Beaufort, S. C., January 17. Expedition to Whitmarsh Island February 20-22, 1864. Moved to Jacksonville, Fla., February 23, and return to Beaufort, S. C., February 26. Veterans on furlough March-April. Non-Veterans at Beaufort till April 12, then ordered to Gloucester Point, Va. Butler's operations on south side of James River and against Petersburg and Richmond May 4-27. Capture of Bermuda Hundred and City Point May 5. Chester Station May 6-7. Swift Creek (or Arrowfield Church) May 9-10. Operations against Fort Darling May 12-16. Drury's Bluff May 14-16. Bermuda Hundred May 16-27. Moved to White House Landing, thence to Cold Harbor May 27-June 1. Battles of Cold Harbor June 1-12. Before Petersburg June 15-19. Siege of Petersburg June 16 to December 7. Duty in trenches before Petersburg June 23 to July 30. Mine Explosion July 30. Demonstration north of James River August 13-20. Strawberry Plains August 14-18. Bermuda Hundred August 24-25. Duty in trenches before Petersburg till September 25. (Non-Veterans mustered out September 18, 1864.) New Market Heights, Chaffin's Farm, September 28-30. Duty on north side of the James, operating against Richmond, till December 7. Fair Oaks October 27-28. Expedition to Fort Fisher, N. C., December 7-27. 2nd Expedition to Fort Fisher January 7-15, 1865. Assault and capture of Fort Fisher January 15. Sugar Loaf Battery February 11. Fort Anderson February 18. Capture of Wilmington February 22. Advance on Kinston and Goldsboro March 6-21. Guard Railroad from Little Washington to Goldsboro till August. Mustered out August 23, 1865.

Regiment lost during service 3 Officers and 82 Enlisted men killed and mortally wounded and 5 Officers and 194 Enlisted men by disease. Total 234.

5th REGIMENT INFANTRY.

Organized at Concord, N. H., and mustered in October 22, 1861. Left State for Washington, D. C., October 29, 1861. Attached to Howard's Brigade, Sumner's Division, Army of the Potomac, to March, 1862. 1st Brigade, 1st Division, 2nd Army Corps, Army of the Potomac, to July, 1863. Concord, N. H., Dept. of the East, to November, 1863. Marston's Command, Point Lookout, Md., to May, 1864. 1st Brigade, 1st Division, 2nd Army Corps, Army of the Potomac, to June, 1865.

SERVICE.—Camp at Bladensburg, Defences of Washington, D. C., till November 27, 1861. Expedition to Lower Maryland November 3-11. At Camp California, near Alexandria, Va., till March 10, 1862. Scout to Burke's Station January 17, 1862 (Co. "A"). Advance on Manassas, Va., March 10-15. Reconnoissance to Gainesville March 20, and to Rappahannock Station March 28-29. Warrenton Junction March 28. Moved to the Virginia Peninsula April 4. Siege of Yorktown, Va., April 5-May 4. Temporarily attached to Woodbury's Engineer Brigade. Construct Grapevine Bridge over Chickahominy May 28-30. Battle of Fair Oaks or Seven Pines May 31-June 1. Seven days before Richmond June 25-July 1. Orchard Station June 28. Peach Orchard, Allen's Farm and Savage Station June 29. White Oak Swamp and Glendale June 30. Malvern Hill July 1. At Harrison's Landing till August 16. Movement to Fortress Monroe, thence to Alexandria and to Centreville, Va., August 16-30. Cover Pope's retreat from Bull Run. Maryland Campaign September-October. Battle of South Mountain, Md., September 14 (Reserve). Antietam Creek, near Keadysville, September 15. Battle of Antietam, Md., September 16-17. Duty at Harper's Ferry, W. Va., September 21 to October 29. Reconnoissance to Charlestown October 16-17. Advance up Loudon Valley and movement to Falmouth, Va., October 29-November 17. Battle of Fredericksburg, Va., December 12-15. Burnside's Second Campaign, "Mud March," January 20-24, 1863. Duty at Falmouth till April. Chancellorsville Campaign April 27-May 6. Battle of Chancellorsville May 1-5. Reconnoissance to Rappahannock June 9. Gettysburg (Pa.) Campaign June 13-July 24. Battle of Gettysburg, Pa., July 1-3. Moved to Concord, N. H., July 26-August 3. Duty at Draft Rendezvous, Concord, N. H., till November. Moved to Point Lookout, Md., November 8-13, and duty there guarding prisoners till May 27, 1864. Moved to Cold Harbor, Va., May 27-June 1, and join Army of the Potomac. Battles about Cold Harbor June 1-12. Before Petersburg, Va., June 16-19. Siege of Petersburg June 16, 1864, to April 2, 1865. Jerusalem Plank Road June 22-23, 1865. Deep Bottom, north of James River, July 27-28. Mine Explosion, Petersburg, July 30 (Reserve). Demonstration north of James River August 13-20. Strawberry Plains August 14-18. Ream's Station August 25. Non-Veterans mustered out October 12, 1864. Reconnoissance to Hatcher's Run December 9-10. Dabney's Mills, Hatcher's Run, February 5-7, 1865. Watkins' House March 25. Appomattox Campaign March 28-April 9. On line of Hatcher's and Gravelly Runs March 29-30. Hatcher's Run or Boydton Road March 31. White Oak Road March 31. Sutherland Station April 2. Fall of Petersburg April 2. Sailor's Creek April 6. High Bridge and Farmville April 7. Appomattox Court House April 9. Surrender of Lee and his army. Moved to Washington, D. C., May 2-12. Grand Review May 23. Mustered out July 28, and discharged July 8, 1865.

This Regiment sustained the greatest loss in battle of any Infantry or Cavalry Regiment in the Union Army. Total killed and wounded 1,051.

Death losses during service 18 Officers and 277 Enlisted men killed and mortally wounded and 2 Officers and 176 Enlisted men by disease. Total 473.

6th REGIMENT INFANTRY.

Organized at Keene and mustered in November 27, 1861. Left State for Washington, D. C., December 25, 1861. Attached to Williams' 4th Brigade, North Carolina Expedition, to April, 1862. Hawkins' Brigade, Dept. of North Carolina, to July, 1862. 1st Brigade, 2nd Division, 9th Army Corps, Army of the Potomac, to March, 1863. 1st Brigade, 2nd Division, 9th Army Corps,

Dept. of the Ohio, to June, 1863. 1st Brigade, 2nd Division, 9th Army Corps, Army of the Tennessee, to September, 1863. Bixby's Brigade, District of North Central Kentucky, 1st Division, 23rd Army Corps, Dept. of Ohio, to February, 1864. 1st Brigade, 2nd Division, 9th Army Corps, Army of the Potomac, to April, 1864. 2nd Brigade, 2nd Division, 9th Army Corps, Army of the Potomac, to July, 1865.

SERVICE.—Expedition to Hatteras Inlet, N. C., January 6-13, 1862, and duty there till March 2. Moved to Roanoke Island March 2 and duty there till June 18. Expedition to Elizabeth City April 7-8. Battle of Camden, South Mills, April 19. Expedition to New Berne June 18-July 2. Moved to Newport News, Va., July 2-10, and duty there till August 2. Moved to Aquia Creek and Fredericksburg, Va., August 2-7. Pope's Campaign in Northern Virginia August 16-September 2. Battles of Groveton August 29; Second Bull Run August 30; Chantilly September 1. Maryland Campaign September-October. Battle of South Mountain, Md., September 14. Battle of Antietam, Md., September 16-17. Duty in Pleasant Valley, Md., till October 27. Movement to Falmouth, Va., October 27-November 19. Corbin's Cross Roads, near Amissville, November 10. Sulphur Springs November 14. Battle of Fredericksburg, Va., December 12-15. Burnside's Second Campaign, "Mud March," January 20-24, 1863. Moved to Newport News, Va., February 11; thence to Lexington, Ky., March 26-April 1. To Winchester, thence to Richmond, Ky., April 18. To Paint Lick Creek May 3, and to Lancaster May 10. Movement to Vicksburg, Miss., June 3-14. Siege of Vicksburg June 14-July 4. Advance on Jackson, Miss., July 4-10. Siege of Jackson July 10-17. At Milldale till August 5. Moved to Cincinnati, Ohio, August 5-20; thence to Nicholasville, Ky. Provost duty at Nicholasville, Frankfort and Russellville till October 25. Moved to Camp Nelson, Ky., and Provost duty there till January 16, 1864. Regiment veteranize January, 1864, and on furlough January 16 to March 10, when ordered to Annapolis, Md. Non-Veterans at Camp Nelson, Ky., till March. Campaign from the Rapidan to the James May 3-June 15. Battles of the Wilderness, Va., May 5-7; Spottsylvania May 8-12; Spottsylvania Court House May 12-21. Assault on the Salient at Spottsylvania Court House May 12. North Anna River May 23-26. On line of the Pamunkey May 26-28. Totopotomoy May 28-31. Cold Harbor June 1-12. Bethesda Church June 1-3. Before Petersburg June 16-19. Siege of Petersburg June 16, 1864, to April 2, 1865. Mine Explosion, Petersburg, July 30, 1864. Weldon Railroad August 18-21. Poplar Springs Church September 29-October 2. Hatcher's Run October 27-28. Garrison of Fort Alexander Hays till April, 1865. Appomattox Campaign March 28-April 9. Assaults on and fall of Petersburg April 2. Occupation of Petersburg April 3. Pursuit of Lee to Burkesville April 3-9. Moved to Washington, D. C., April 20-27. Duty at Alexandria till July. Grand Review May 23. Mustered out July 17, 1865.

Regiment lost during service 10 Officers and 177 Enlisted men killed and mortally wounded and 3 Officers and 228 Enlisted men by disease. Total 418.

7th REGIMENT INFANTRY.

Organized at Manchester and mustered in December 13, 1861. Left State for New York January 14, 1862 At White Street Barracks till February 13. Ordered to Dry Tortugas, Fla., February 12. Attached to Brannan's Command, District of Florida, to June, 1862. District of Beaufort, S. C., Dept. of the South, to September, 1862. St. Augustine, Fla., Dept. of the South, to May, 1863. Fernandina, Fla., Dept. of the South, to June, 1863. 1st Brigade, Folly Island, S. C., 10th Corps, Dept. of the South, to July, 1863. 1st Brigade, 2nd Division, Morris Island, S. C., 10th Corps, Dept. of the South, to July, 1863. 3rd Brigade, Morris Island, S. C., 10th Corps, Dept. of the South, to November, 1863. 1st Brigade, Morris Island, S. C., 10th Corps, Dept. of the South, to December, 1863. St. Helena Island, S. C., 10th Corps, Dept. of the South, to February, 1864.

Hawley's Brigade, Ames' Division, District of Florida, Dept. of the South, to April, 1864. 3rd Brigade, 1st Division, 10th Army Corps, Dept. of Virginia and North Carolina, to May, 1864. 2nd Brigade, 1st Division, 10th Army Corps, Army of the James, to December, 1864. 2nd Brigade, 1st Division, 24th Army Corps, Army of the James, to January, 1865. Abbott's Brigade, Terry's Provisional Corps, North Carolina, to March, 1865. Abbott's Detached Brigade, 10th Army Corps, North Carolina, to July, 1865.

SERVICE.—Duty at Dry Tortugas, Fla., till June 16, 1862. Moved to Beaufort, S. C., June 16, and duty there till September 15. Moved to St. Augustine, Fla., September 15, and duty there till May 10, 1863. Skirmish near St. Augustine March 9 (Detachment). At Fernandina, Fla., till June 15. Moved to Hilton Head, S. C.; thence to Folly Island, S. C., June 15-19. Siege operations against Morris Island till July 10. Assault on Water Batteries on Morris Island July 10. Assaults on Fort Wagner, Morris Island, S. C., July 11 and 18. Siege of Fort Wagner July 18-September 7. Capture of Forts Wagner and Gregg September 7. Siege operations against Fort Sumpter and Charleston, S. C., till December 20. Moved to St. Helena Island, S. C., December 20, and duty there till February, 1864. Expedition to Jacksonville, Fla., February 5-6, and from Jacksonville to Lake City, Fla., February 7-22. Battle of Olustee, Fla., February 20. Duty at Jacksonville till April. Ordered to Gloucester Point, Va., April 4. Butler's operations on south side of the James River and against Petersburg and Richmond May 4-28. Occupation of City Point and Bermuda Hundred May 5. Swift Creek or Arrowfield Church May 9-10. Chester Station May 10. Operations against Fort Darling May 12-16. Battle of Drury's Bluff May 14-16. Bermuda Hundred May 16-August 13. Action at Petersburg June 9. Port Walthal June 16-17. Siege operations against Petersburg and Richmond June 16, 1864, to January 3, 1865. Demonstration north of James River August 13-20. Battle of Strawberry Plains, Deep Bottom, August 14-18. In trenches before Petersburg till September 25. Battle of Chaffin's Farm, New Market Heights, September 28-30. Darbytown and New Market Roads October 7. Darbytown and Charles City Cross Roads October 13. Battle of Fair Oaks October 27-28. Front of Richmond October 31-November 2. Detachment for duty at New York City and Staten Island, New York Harbor, during Presidential election November 2-17. Duty in front of Richmond north of the James River November 17, 1864, to January 3, 1865. Second Expedition to Fort Fisher, N. C., January 3-15, 1865. Assault and capture of Fort Fisher January 15. Half Moon Battery January 19. Sugar Loaf Battery February 11. Fort Anderson February 18. Capture of Wilmington February 22. North East Ferry February 22. Duty at Wilmington till June, and at Goldsborough, N. C., till July. Mustered out July 17, 1865.

Regiment lost during service 15 Officers and 169 Enlisted men killed and mortally wounded and 1 Officer and 241 Enlisted men by disease. Total 426.

8th REGIMENT INFANTRY.

Organized at Manchester and mustered in December 23, 1861. Left State for Boston, Mass., January 24, 1862; thence sailed for Ship Island, Miss., February 15, arriving there March 15. Attached to Butler's New Orleans Expedition to March, 1862. 1st Brigade, Dept. of the Gulf, to November, 1862. Independent Command, Dept. of the Gulf, to January, 1863. 2nd Brigade, 3rd Division, 19th Army Corps, Dept. of the Gulf, to September, 1863.

SERVICE.—Duty at Ship Island till April, 1862. Occupation of Forts Wood and Pike, Lake Pontchartrain, May 5. Moved to New Orleans and duty at Camp Parapet till October. Expedition to Lake Pontchartrain July 23-August 2. Operations in District of LaFourche October 24-November 6. Occupation of Donaldsonville October 25. Action at Georgia Landing, near Labadieville, October 27, and at Thibodeauxville October 27. Duty in the District of LaFourche till March, 1863. Ex-

pedition to Bayou Teche January 12-14, 1863. Steamer "Cotton" January 14. Operations on Bayou Plaquemine and the Black and Atchafalaya Rivers February 12-28. Operations against Port Hudson March 7-27. Teche Campaign April 11-20. Fort Bisland, near Centreville, April 12-13. Irish Bend April 14. Expedition from Opelousas to Chicotsville and Bayou Boeuff May 1. Expedition to Alexandria on Red River May 5-17. Movement from Alexandria to Port Hudson May 17-24. Siege of Port Hudson May 24-July 8. Assault on Port Hudson June 14. Expedition to Nibletts Bluff May 26-29. Surrender of Port Hudson July 9. Moved to Baton Rouge, La., August 22. Sabine Pass Expedition September 4-11. Moved to Camp Bisland September 15 and duty there till October. Moved to Opelousas, thence to Franklin December —. Designation of Regiment changed to 2nd New Hampshire Cavalry December, 1863. (See 2nd New Hampshire Cavalry.)

Regiment lost during service 8 Officers and 94 Enlisted men killed and mortally wounded and 2 Officers and 256 Enlisted men by disease. Total 360.

9th REGIMENT INFANTRY.

Organized at Concord and mustered in August 15, 1862. Left State for Washington, D. C., August 25, 1862. At Arlington Heights, Va., till September 6. March to Monocacy River to join army September 6-13. Attached to 1st Brigade, 2nd Division, 9th Army Corps, Army of the Potomac, to March, 1863. 1st Brigade, 2nd Division, 9th Army Corps, Dept. of the Ohio, to June, 1863. 1st Brigade, 2nd Division, 9th Army Corps, Army of the Tennessee, to September, 1863. District of North Central Kentucky, 1st Division, 23rd Army Corps, Dept. of the Ohio, to February, 1864. 1st Brigade, 2nd Division, 9th Army Corps, Army of Ohio, to April, 1864. 2nd Brigade, 2nd Division, 9th Army Corps, Army of the Potomac, to June, 1865.

SERVICE.—Battle of South Mountain, Md., September 14, 1862. Battle of Antietam, Md., September 16-17. Duty in Pleasant Valley, Md., till October 27, 1862. Movement to Falmouth, Va., October 27-November 19. Waterloo Bridge November 9-10. Battle of Fredericksburg, Va., December 12-15. Burnside's Second Campaign, "Mud March," January 20-24, 1863. Moved to Newport News, Va., February 11; thence to Lexington, Ky., March 25-31. Duty in the Blue Grass Region of Kentucky till June. Moved to Vicksburg, Miss., June 3-14. Siege of Vicksburg, Miss., June 14-July 4. Advance on Jackson, Miss., July 4-10. Siege of Jackson, Miss., July 10-17. At Milldale, Miss., till August 10. Moved to Covington, Ky., August 10-21; thence to Camp Nelson, Ky., August 25. Duty guarding railroad between Cincinnati, Ohio, and Camp Nelson, Ky., till January, 1864. Moved to Camp Burnside January 15. March to Knoxville, Tenn., February 19-March 17. March across Cumberland Mountains to Camp Burnside and Nicholasville, Ky., March 21-31. Moved to Annapolis, Md., April 2-5. Campaign from the Rapidan to the James River, Va., May 3-June 15. Battles of the Wilderness May 5-7; Spottsylvania May 8-12; Spottsylvania Court House May 12-21. Assault on the Salient at Spottsylvania Court House May 12. North Anna River May 23-26. On line of the Pamunkey May 26-28. Totopotomoy May 28-31. Cold Harbor June 1-12. Bethesda Church June 1-3. Before Petersburg June 16-19. Siege of Petersburg June 16, 1864, to April 2, 1865. Mine Explosion, Petersburg, July 30, 1864. Weldon Railroad August 18-21. Poplar Springs Church September 29-October 2. Boydton Plank Road, Hatcher's Run, October 27-28. Garrison, Fort Alexander Hays, till April, 1865. Appomattox Campaign March 28-April 9. Assault on and fall of Petersburg April 2. Occupation of Petersburg April 3. Pursuit of Lee April 3-6. Detached to guard Ewell's Army April 6. Moved to Alexandria April 20-27 and duty there till June. Grand Review May 23. Mustered out June 10, 1865. Recruits transferred to 6th New Hampshire Infantry.

Regiment lost during service 10 Officers and 145 Enlisted men killed and mortally wounded and 3 Officers and 251 Enlisted men by disease. Total 409.

10th REGIMENT INFANTRY.

Regiment organized at Manchester and mustered in September 4, 1862. Left State and moved to Washington, D. C., September 22-25; thence to Frederick, Md., September 30; to Sandy Hook, Md., October 4, and to Pleasant Valley October 6. Attached to 1st Brigade, 3rd Division, 9th Army Corps, Army of the Potomac, to April, 1863. 1st Brigade, 2nd Division, 7th Army Corps, Dept. of Virginia, to July, 1863. 3rd Brigade, Getty's Division, United States Forces, Norfolk and Portsmouth, Dept. of Virginia and North Carolina, to April, 1864. 2nd Brigade, 1st Division, 18th Army Corps, Dept. of Virginia and North Carolina, to December, 1864. 2nd Brigade, 3rd Division, 24th Army Corps, Dept. of Virginia, to June, 1865.

SERVICE.—Duty at Pleasant Valley, Md., till October 27, 1862. Movement to Falmouth, Va., October 27-November 19. Battle of Fredericksburg, Va., December 12-15. Burnside's Second Campaign ("Mud March") January 20-24, 1863. Moved to Newport News, Va., February 9, thence to Norfolk and Suffolk March 14. Siege of Suffolk April 12-May 4. Battery Huger, Hill's Point, April 19. Reconnoissance across Nansemond River May 4. Moved to Portsmouth May 13, thence to Yorktown, Va. Dix's Peninsula Campaign June 24-July 7. Expedition from White House to South Anna River July 1-7. Moved to Portsmouth July 8-14, and to Julien Creek July 30. Duty there till March 19, 1864. Ballahock, on Bear Quarter Road, and Deep Creek, February 29-March 1, 1864. Moved to Great Bridge March 19, thence to Yorktown April 19. Butler's operations on south side of the James River against Petersburg and Richmond May 4-28. Port Walthal Junction May 7. Chester Station May 7. Swift Creek (or Arrowfield Church) May 9-10. Operations against Fort Darling May 12-16. Battle of Drewry's Bluff May 14-16. Bermuda Hundred June 17-27. Moved to White House, thence to Cold Harbor May 27-31. Cold Harbor June 1-12. Before Petersburg June 15-19. Siege of Petersburg and Richmond June 15, 1864, to April 2, 1865. Chaffin's Farm, New Market Heights, September 28-30, 1864. Fort Harrison September 28-29. Battle of Fair Oaks October 27-28. Duty in lines north of James River before Richmond till April, 1865. Occupation of Richmond April 3. Provost duty at Manchester till June 21. Mustered out June 21, 1865. Veterans and Recruits transferred to 2nd New Hampshire Infantry.

Losses, 7 Officers and 54 Enlisted men killed and mortally wounded and 1 Officer and 133 Enlisted men died of disease. Total 195.

11th REGIMENT INFANTRY.

Organized at Concord and mustered in September 2, 1862. Moved to Washington, D. C., September 11-14, 1862. Attached to Brigg's Brigade, Casey's Division, Military District of Washington, to October, 1862. 2nd Brigade, 2nd Division, 9th Army Corps, Army of the Potomac, to March, 1863. 2nd Brigade, 2nd Division, 9th Army Corps, Dept. of Ohio, to June, 1863. 2nd Brigade, 2nd Division, 9th Army Corps, Army of the Tennessee, to August, 1863. 2nd Brigade, 2nd Division, 9th Army Corps, Dept. of the Ohio, to April, 1864. 2nd Brigade, 2nd Division, 9th Army Corps, Army of the Potomac, to June, 1865.

SERVICE.—Moved to Pleasant Valley, Md., October 4, and duty there till October 27, 1862. Movement to Falmouth, Va., October 27-November 19. Battle of Fredericksburg, Va., December 12-15. Burnside's Second Campaign ("Mud March") January 20-24, 1863. Moved to Newport News February 11, thence to Covington, Ky., March 26-April 1. Duty at various points in Kentucky till June. Moved to Vicksburg, Miss., June 4-14. Siege of Vicksburg, Miss., June 14-July 4. Advance on Jackson, Miss., July 4-10. Siege of Jackson, Miss., July 10-17. Destruction of Railroad at Madison Station July 18-22. At Milldale, Miss., till August 6. Moved

to Cincinnati, Ohio, August 6-14. At Covington, Ky., till August 26, and at Nicholasville, Camp Parke, Crab Orchard and Loudon till October. March to Knoxville, Tenn., October 12-29. Knoxville Campaign November 4-December 23. Campbell Station November 16. Siege of Knoxville November 17-December 4. Repulse of Longstreet's assault on Fort Saunders November 29. Duty in East Tennessee till March, 1864. Moved to Annapolis, Md., March 18-April 7. Campaign from the Rapidan to the James River, Va., May 3-June 15. Battles of the Wilderness May 5-7. Spottsylvania May 8-12. Spottsylvania Court House May 12-21. Assault on the Salient, Spottsylvania C. H., May 12. North Anna River May 23-26. On line of the Pamunkey May 26-28. Totopotomoy May 28-31. Cold Harbor June 1-12. Bethesda Church June 1-3. Before Petersburg June 15-19. Siege of Petersburg June 16, 1864, to April 2, 1865. Mine Explosion, Petersburg, July 30, 1864. Weldon Railroad August 18-21. Poplar Springs Church September 29-October 2. Boydton Plank Road, Hatcher's Run, October 27-28. Fort Stedman March 25, 1865. Appomattox Campaign March 28-April 9. Assault on and fall of Petersburg April 2. Occupation of Petersburg April 3. Pursuit of Lee April 3-9. Moved to Washington, D. C., April 20-27, and duty at Alexandria till June. Grand Review May 23. Mustered out June 4, 1865.

Regiment lost during service 5 Officers and 140 Enlisted men killed and mortally wounded and 1 Officer and 151 Enlisted men by disease. Total 297.

12th REGIMENT INFANTRY.

Organized at Concord and mustered in September 10, 1862. Left State for Washington, D. C., September 27, 1862. Attached to Casey's Division, Military District of Washington, to December, 1862. 2nd Brigade, 3rd Division, 3rd Army Corps, Army of the Potomac, to June, 1863. 1st Brigade, 2nd Division, 3rd Army Corps, Army of the Potomac, to July, 1863. Marston's Command, Point Lookout, Md., District of St. Mary's, to April, 1864. 2nd Brigade, 2d Division, 18th Army Corps, Dept. of Virginia and North Carolina, to December, 1864. 2nd Brigade, 3rd Division, 24th Army Corps, Dept. of Virginia, to June, 1865.

SERVICE.—Duty in the Defences of Washington till October, 1862. Moved to Point of Rocks, Md., October 18; thence to Pleasant Valley October 19. Movement to Warrenton, Va., October 24-November 16, and to Falmouth November 18-24. Battle of Fredericksburg December 12-15. Burnside's 2nd Campaign ("Mud March") January 20-24, 1863. Duty at Falmouth till April. Chancellorsville Campaign April 27-May 6. Battle of Chancellorsville May 1-5. Gettysburg (Pa.) Campaign June 11-July 24. Battle of Gettysburg July 1-3. Ordered to Point Lookout, Md., July 26, and duty there guarding prisoners till April 7, 1864. Moved to Yorktown April 7, thence to Williamsburg. Butler's operations on south side of the James River and against Petersburg and Richmond May 4-28. Swift Creek (or Arrowfield Church) May 9-10. Operations against Fort Darling May 12-16. Battle of Drewry's Bluff May 14-16. Bermuda Hundred May 16-27. Moved to White House, thence to Cold Harbor, May 27-31. Battles about Cold Harbor June 1-12. Before Petersburg June 15-19. Siege of Petersburg and Richmond June 16, 1864, to April 2, 1865. Mine Explosion, Petersburg, July 30, 1864 (Reserve). Duty on the Bermuda Front August 26 to December, and in trenches before Richmond till April, 1865. Occupation of Richmond April 3. Guard and Provost duty at Manchester till June. Mustered out June 21, 1865. Regiment lost during service 11 Officers and 170 Enlisted men killed and mortally wounded and 1 Officer and 138 Enlisted men by disease. Total 320.

13th REGIMENT INFANTRY.

Organized at Concord and mustered in September 20, 1862. Left State for Washington, D. C, October 5. Attached to Casey's Division, Military District of Washington, to December, 1862. 1st Brigade, 3rd Division,

9th Army Corps, Army of the Potomac, to January, 1863. 3rd Brigade, 3rd Division, 9th Army Corps, to April, 1863. 3rd Brigade, 2nd Division, 7th Army Corps, Dept. of Virginia, to July, 1863. 3rd Brigade, Getty's Division, United States forces, Norfolk and Portsmouth, Dept. of Virginia and North Carolina, to April, 1864. 2nd Brigade, 1st Division, 18th Army Corps, Army of the James, to July, 1864. 1st Brigade, 1st Division, 18th Army Corps, to December, 1864. 1st Brigade, 3rd Division, 24th Army Corps, Dept. of Virginia, to June, 1865.

SERVICE.—Duty near Fort Albany, Defences of Washington, till December 4, 1862. March to Falmouth, Va., December 5-9. Battle of Fredericksburg December 12-15. Burnside's Second Campaign "Mud March" January 20-24, 1863. Moved to Newport News, Va., February 9, thence to Suffolk March 13. Siege of Suffolk April 12-May 4. **Providence Church Road,** Nansemond River, May 3. Reconnoissance across the Nansemond May 4. Moved to Portsmouth May 13, thence to Yorktown. Dix's Peninsula Campaign June 24-July 7. Expedition from White House to South Anna River July 1-7. Moved to Portsmouth July 8-14; thence to Julian Creek July 30, and duty there till March 19, 1864. Moved to Yorktown March 19. Butler's operations on south side of James River and against Petersburg and Richmond May 4-28. Port Walthal Junction, Chester Station, May 6-7. Swift Creek (or Arrowfield Church) May 9-10. Operations against Fort Darling May 12-16. Battle of Drewry's Bluff May 14-16. Bermuda Hundred May 17-27. Moved to White House, thence to Cold Harbor, May 27-31. Battles about Cold Harbor June 1-12. Before Petersburg June 15-19. Siege of Petersburg and Richmond June 16, 1864, to April 2, 1865. In trenches before Petersburg till August 27, 1864. Mine Explosion Petersburg July 30 (Reserve). Duty on the Berumda Front till September 26. Battle of Chaffin's Farm, New Market Heights, September 28-30. Fort Harrison September 29. Assigned to duty as garrison at Fort Harrison. Battle of Fair Oaks October 27-28. Duty in works before Richmond till April, 1865. Occupation of Richmond April 3. (First Regiment whose Colors were brought into the city.) Provost duty at Manchester till June. Mustered out June 22, 1865. Veterans and Recruits transferred to 2nd New Hampshire.

Regiment lost during service 5 Officers and 84 Enlisted men killed and mortally wounded and 92 Enlisted men by disease. Total 181.

14th REGIMENT INFANTRY.

Organized at Concord and mustered in September 24, 1862. Ordered to Washington, D. C. Attached to Grover's Brigade, Military District of Washington, to February, 1863. Jewett's Brigade, 22nd Corps, Defences of Washington, to June, 1863. Garrison of Washington, D. C., 22nd Corps, to March, 1864. Unattached, Defences of New Orleans, La., Dept. of the Gulf, to June, 1864. 1st Brigade, 2nd Division, 19th Army Corps, Dept. of the Gulf, to July, 1864, and Army of the Shenandoah, Middle Military Division, to January, 1865. 1st Brigade, Grover's Division, District of Savannah, Ga., Dept. of the South, to March, 1865. 1st Brigade, 1st Division, 10th Army Corps, Dept. of North Carolina, to May, 1865. Dept. of the South to July, 1865.

SERVICE.—Picket and patrol duty along Upper Potomac, Defences of Washington, November, 1862, to April, 1863. Provost duty at Washington, D. C., till February, 1864. Ordered to Harper's Ferry, W. Va., February 3, thence moved to Cumberland, Md., and return to Washington February 25. Ordered to New Orleans, La., and sailed from New York March 20. Duty at Camp Parapet, Carrollton, Jefferson City and along Lake Pontchartrain till June. Ordered to Morganza, La., June 7. Movement to Fortress Monroe, Va., thence to Washington, D. C., and to Berryville, Va., July 13-August 19. Sheridan's Shenandoah Valley Campaign August to December. Battle of Winchester September 19. Fisher's Hill September 22. Battle of Cedar Creek October 19. Duty at Kernstown and other points in the Shenandoah Valley till January, 1865. Moved to

Washington, D. C., thence to Savannah, Ga., January 3-20, and Provost duty there till May 6. March to Augusta, Ga., May 6-14. Return to Savannah June and mustered out July 8, 1865.

Regiment lost during service 8 Officers and 63 Enlisted men killed and mortally wounded and 4 Officers and 151 Enlisted men by disease. Total 232.

15th REGIMENT INFANTRY.

Organized at Concord October 6-16, 1862, for nine months' service. Left State for New York November 13, 1862; thence sailed for New Orleans, La., December 19, arriving December 26. Attached to Sherman's Division, Dept. of the Gulf, to January, 1863. 1st Brigade, 2nd Division, 19th Army Corps, Army of the Gulf, to July, 1863. 2nd Brigade, 3rd Division, 19th Army Corps, to August, 1863.

SERVICE.—Moved from Carrollton to Camp Parapet, La., January 28, 1863, and duty there till May. Moved to Springfield Landing May 20-22. Siege of Port Hudson, La., May 27-July 9. Assaults on Port Hudson May 27 and June 14. Surrender of Port Hudson July 9. Moved to Concord, N. H., July 26-August 8, and mustered out August 13, 1863.

Regiment lost during service 27 Enlisted men killed and mortally wounded and 134 Enlisted men by disease. Total 161.

16th REGIMENT INFANTRY.

Organized at Concord and mustered in for nine months October 24, 1862. Moved to New York November and join Banks' Expeditionary Corps. Sailed for New Orleans, La., December 6, arriving December 20. Attached to Sherman's Division, Dept. of the Gulf, to January, 1863. 1st Brigade, 3rd Division, 19th Army Corps, Army of the Gulf, to May, 1863. 1st Brigade, 2nd Division, 19th Army Corps. to August, 1863.

SERVICE.—Duty at Carrollton and in the Defences of New Orleans, La., till April, 1863. Operations on Bayou Plaquemine and the Black and Atchafalaya Rivers February 12-28. Operations against Port Hudson, La., March 7-27. Fort Burton, Butte a la Rose, April 19. At Fort Burton till May 30. Ordered to Port Hudson May 30, and assigned as guard at arsenal of Banks' Army at Springfield Landing June 3 to July 9. Surrender of Port Hudson July 9. Occupation of works till August 1. Moved to Concord, N. H., August 1-14. Mustered out August 20, 1863.

Regiment lost during service 5 Officers and 216 Enlisted men by disease. Total 221.

17th REGIMENT INFANTRY.

Organization commenced November 19, 1862; not completed, and the two Companies formed were transferred to the 2nd New Hampshire Infantry, April 16, 1863.

18th REGIMENT INFANTRY.

Organized at Concord September 13, 1864. First six Companies recruited under call of July 19, 1864. Four Companies under call of December 21, 1864. Companies "G," "H" and "I" join Regiment in February, March and April, 1865. Company "K" was on duty at Galloupe's Island, Boston Harbor, entire term, and mustered out May 6, 1865. Six Companies ordered to City Point, Va., September, 1864. Attached to Benham's Engineer Brigade to December, 1864. Clough's Provisional Brigade, Ferrero's Division, Defences of Berumda Hundred, Va., to March, 1865. 3rd Brigade, 1st Division, 9th Army Corps, Army of the Potomac, to May, 1865. Garrison at Washington, D. C., till July, 1865.

SERVICE.—Duty in Fortifications at City Point, Va., till December 10, 1864. At front near Petersburg December 10-13. Reported to Gen. Ferrero, and duty in the Defences of Bermuda Hundred December 18-30. Duty at City Point till March 19, 1865. Reported to Gen. Parke, Commanding 9th Army Corps, before Petersburg, March 19. Repulse of attack on Fort Stedman March 25. Duty at Fort Stedman till April 2. Appomattox Campaign March 28-April 9. Assault on and fall of Petersburg April 2. Occupation of Petersburg

April 3. Moved to South Side Railroad and duty at Ford's Station till April 20. Moved to Washington, D. C., April 20-26. Camp at Alexandria and Provost duty at Georgetown till July. Guard duty in Washington during trial of President Lincoln's assassins. Six original companies muster out June 10, 1865. Balance of Regiment muster out July 29, 1865.

Regiment lost 1 Officer and 4 Enlisted men killed and mortally wounded and 36 Enlisted men by disease. Total 41.

TARBELL'S COMPANY MILITIA ARTILLERY.

Organized at Lyndeborough August 1, 1864. Mustered out September 23, 1864.

LITTLEFIELD'S COMPANY MILITIA INFANTRY.

Organized at Dover for 60 days May 5, 1864. Mustered out July 25, 1864.

CHANDLER'S COMPANY MILITIA INFANTRY.

Organized at Manchester for 60 days May 9, 1864. Mustered out July 27, 1864.

HOUGHTON'S COMPANY MILITIA INFANTRY.

Organized at Manchester for 90 days July 25, 1864. Mustered out September 16, 1864.

NEW JERSEY VOLUNTEERS.

1st REGIMENT CAVALRY.—("16th VOLUNTEERS.")

Organized at Trenton, N. J., under authority of the War Department August 14, 1861, as Halsted's Cavalry. Left State for Washington, D. C.; four Companies August 24 and six Companies August 31, 1861. Attached to Heintzelman's Division, Army of the Potomac, to March, 1862. Wadsworth's Command, Military District of Washington, to May, 1862. Bayard's Cavalry Brigade, Dept. of the Rappahannock, to June, 1862. Bayard's Cavalry Brigade, 3rd Corps, Pope's Army of Virginia, to September, 1862. Bayard's Cavalry Brigade, Army of the Potomac, to October, 1862. 1st Brigade, Cavalry Division, Army of the Potomac, to February, 1863. 2nd Brigade, 3rd Division, Cavalry Corps, Army of the Potomac, to June, 1863. 1st Brigade, 2nd Division, Cavalry Corps, to May, 1865. 1st Brigade, 1st Division, Cavalry Corps, Dept. of Washington, to July, 1865.

SERVICE.—Duty in the Defences of Washington, D. C., till May, 1862. Reconnoissance to Pohick Church, Va., December 18, 1861 (1 Co.). Lee's House, Occoquan Bridge, January 29, 1862 (Detachment). Transferred to State of New Jersey and designated 1st Cavalry February 19, 1862. Rappahannock River May 13. Staunton and Strasburg Road June 1-2. Woodstock June 2. Harrisonburg June 6. Battle of Cross Keys June 8. Reconnoissance to James City July 22-24. Operations about Orange Court House July 29. Barnett's Ford August 1. Slaughter House August 8. Battle of Cedar Mountain August 9. Pope's Campaign in Northern Virginia August 16-September 2. Rappahannock Station August 19. Brandy Station, Stevensburg and Raccoon Ford August 20. Fords of the Rappahannock August 21-23. Warrenton August 26. Faquier White Sulphur Springs August 27. Thoroughfare Gap August 28. Bull Run August 30. Germantown and Centreville August 31. Chantilly August 31. In Defences of Washington September. Reconnoissance from Upton's Hill to Leesburg September 16-18 (2 Cos.). Expedition from Centreville to Warrenton September 29 (Detachment). Expedition to Thoroughfare Gap October 17-18. Near Upperville October 29 (Detachment). Aldie and Mountsville October 31. Salem, New Baltimore and Thoroughfare Gap November 4. Rappahannock Station November 7, 8 and 9. Snicker's Ferry, Berryville, November 30. Near Dumfries December 11. Battle of Fredericksburg December 12-15. Near Chantilly December 29. Near Fairfax Court House and Middleburg January 26. Chancellorsville Campaign April 27-May 6. Stoneman's Raid April 29-May 8. Brandy Station and Beverly Ford June 9. Aldie June 17. Middleburg June 19. Up-

perville June 21. Dover June 22. Battle of Gettysburg, Pa., July 1-3. Emmettsburg, Md., July 4. Old Antietam Forge, near Leitersburg, July 10. Reconnoissance to Ashby's Gap July 11-14. Ashby's Gap July 12. Near Harper's Ferry July 14. Shephardstown July 14-16. Scout to Goose Creek July 25-27. Rixeyville Ford August 5. Advance from the Rappahannock to the Rapidan September 13-17. Culpeper Court House September 13. Bristoe Campaign October 8-22. Skirmishes at James City October 8-10. Near Warrenton October 11. Warrenton or White Sulphur Springs October 12-13. Brentsville October 14. Auburn and Bristoe October 14. Advance to line of the Rappahannock November 7-8. Near Warrenton November 11. Mine Run Campaign November 26-December 2. New Hope Church November 27. Parker's Store November 29. Reconnoissance from Bealeton and Front Royal January 1-4, 1864. Scout from Warrenton to Piedmont February 17-18. Near Piedmont February 18 (Detachment). Custer's Raid into Albemarle County February 28-March 1. Near Charlottesville February 29. Stannardsville March 1. Campaign from the Rapidan to the James May 3-June 15. Todd's Tavern May 5-6. Wilderness May 6-7. Todd's Tavern May 7-8. Corbin's Bridge May 8. Sheridan's Raid May 9-24. Davenport and Childsburg May 9. North Anna River May 9-10. Ground Squirrel Church and Yellow Tavern May 11. Ashland May 11. Brooks' Church or fortifications of Richmond May 12. Line of the Pamunkey May 26-28. Hawes' Shop May 28. Totopotomoy May 28-31. Cold Harbor May 31-June 1. Sumner's Upper Bridge, Sheridan's Trevillian Raid, June 7-24. Trevillian Station June 11-12. Newark or Mallory's Cross Roads June 12. Black Creek or Tunstall Station June 21. White House of St. Peter's Church June 21. St. Mary's Church June 24. Near Petersburg June 29-July 12. Lee's Mills, Warwick Swamp, July 12. Demonstration north of the James July 27-29. Deep Bottom July 27-28. Malvern Hill July 28. Ream's Station August 8. Demonstration north of the James August 13-20. Strawberry Plains August 14-18. Gravel Hill August 14. Weldon Railroad August 18-21. Dinwiddie Road, near Ream's Station, August 23. Ream's Station August 25. Old members mustered out at Trenton, N. J., September 16, 1864. Belcher's Mills September 17. Poplar Springs Church September 29-October 2. Arthur's Swamp September 30-October 1. Vaughan Road October 1. Boydton Plank Road or Hatcher's Run October 27-28. Reconnoissance to Stony Creek November 7. Warren's Raid on Weldon Railroad December 7-12. Bellefield Station December 9-10. Dabney's Mills, Hatcher's Run, February 5-7, 1865. Appomattox Campaign March 28-April 9. Dinwiddie Court House March 30-31. Five Forks April 1. Payne's Cross Roads and Amelia Springs April 5. Sailor's Creek April 6. Farmville April 7. Appomattox Court House April 9. Surrender of Lee and his army. Expedition from Burkesville to Danville and South Boston April 23-27. Moved to Washington, D. C., May 2-12. Grand Review May 23. Company "F" mustered out at Washington May 25, 1865. Mustered out at Cloud's Hills, Va., July 24, 1865.

Regiment lost during service 12 Officers and 116 Enlisted men killed and mortally wounded and 4 Officers and 185 Enlisted men by disease. Total 317.

2nd REGIMENT CAVALRY.—("32nd NEW JERSEY VOLUNTEERS.")

Organized at Camp Parker, Trenton, N. J., and mustered in August 15, 1863. Left State for Washington, D. C., October 5, 1863. Attached to Stoneman's Cavalry Division, 22nd Army Corps, Dept. of Washington, to December, 1863. District of Columbus, Ky., 6th Division, 16th Army Corps, Dept. of the Tennessee, to December, 1863. Waring's Cavalry Brigade, 16th Army Corps, to January, 1864. 1st Brigade, 1st Cavalry Division, 16th Army Corps, to June, 1864. 1st Brigade, 2nd Division, Cavalry Corps, District of West Tennessee, to November, 1864. 2nd Brigade, 6th Division, Cavalry Corps, Military Division Mississippi, to December, 1864. 1st Brigade, Cavalry Division, District of West

Tennessee, to February, 1865. 1st Brigade, 1st Cavalry Division, Military Division West Mississippi, to April, 1865. 2nd Brigade, Cavalry Division, Dept. of the Gulf, to May, 1865. Dept. of Mississippi to November, 1865.

SERVICE.—In camp near Alexandria, Va., till November 9, 1863. Scout to Annandale October 18 (Cos. "B," "C," "G" and "L"). Moved to Eastport, Miss., November 9-28; thence to Columbus, Ky., December 6. To Union City, Tenn., December 15. Garrison and scout duty at Paris, Tenn., December 23, 1863, to January 16, 1864. Moved to Union City January 16-20. Expedition from Union City to Trenton January 22-27. March from Union City to Memphis and Colliersville, Tenn., January 28-February 8. Smith's Expedition to Okolona, Miss., February 11-26. Aberdeen, Miss., February 19. Prairie Station February 20. West Point February 20-21. Okolona February 21-22. Ivy's Farm February 22. Tallahatchie River February 23. Operations against Forest in West Tennessee and Kentucky March 16-April 14. Near Memphis April 5. Raleigh April 10. Sturgis' Expedition to Ripley, Miss., April 30-May 9. Bolivar, Tenn., May 2. Holly Springs May 23. Sturgis' Expedition to Guntown June 1-13. Brice's Cross Roads or Tishamingo Creek, near Guntown, June 10. Ripley June 11. Duty on Memphis & Charleston Railroad between Moscow and LaGrange June 25-July 5. Expedition from Memphis to Grand Gulf, Miss., July 4-24 (Detachment). Moved to Vicksburg, Miss., July 5-6. Port Gibson July 14. Grand Gulf July 15-16. Smith's Expedition to Oxford, Miss., August 1-30. Hurricane Creek and Oxford August 9. Tallahatchie River August 14. Waterford August 19. Duty at Memphis, Tenn., August 31, 1864, to December 20, 1864. Hernando October 15. Yazoo City December 2. Chickasawba Bridge December 10. Grierson's Raid to destroy Mobile & Ohio Railroad December 20, 1864, to January 15, 1865. Verona December 25. Egypt Station December 28. Moved to Natchez, Miss., January 19, and duty there till March 4. Moved to New Orleans, La., and camp at Carrollton till April 5. Moved to Mobile, Ala., April 5. Spanish Fort April 8. Fort Blakely April. Expedition from Blakely, Ala., to Georgetown, Ga., April 17-30. Moved to Columbus, Miss., and duty there till June 7. Moved to Vicksburg June 7. Duty there and at Natchez, Port Gibson and Brookhaven till November. Mustered out at Vicksburg, Miss., November 1, 1865.

Regiment lost during service 3 Officers and 48 Enlisted men killed and mortally wounded and 190 Enlisted men by disease. Total 241.

3rd REGIMENT CAVALRY.—("39th NEW JERSEY VOLUNTEERS.")

Organized at Camp Bayard, Trenton, N. J., and mustered in by Companies as follows: Company "A" January 26, Company "C" January 22, Company "E" January 4, Company "F" January 12, Companies "G" and "H" January 6, 1864; Company "D" December 2, 1863; Company "B" January 29, and Companies "I," "K," "L" and "M" March 24, 1864. March to Annapolis, Md., April 5-7, 1864. Guard Orange & Alexandria Railroad April 29-May 5. Attached to Cavalry, 9th Army Corps, Army of the Potomac, to May, 1864. 1st Brigade, 3rd Division, Cavalry Corps, Army of the Potomac and Middle Military Division, to June, 1865. Defences of Washington, D. C., to August, 1865.

SERVICE.—Campaign from the Rapidan to the James May 3-June 12, 1864. Wilderness May 5-7. Near Germania Ford May 5. Picket on the Rapidan May 6. Guard pontoons May 7. Expedition to Fredericksburg May 8-9. Spottsylvania May 9-12. Spottsylvania Court House May 12-21. United States Ford May 19. North Anna River May 23-26. On line of the Pamunkey May 26-28. Totopotomoy May 28-31. Mechump's Creek May 31. Ashland Station June 1. Cold Harbor June 1-12. Totopotomoy, Gaines' Mill, Salem Church and Hawes' Shop June 2. Hawes' Shop June 3. Bethesda Church June 11. White Oak Swamp June 13. Smith's Store, near St. Mary's Church, June 15. Weldon Railroad June 20. Jerusalem Plank Road June 22-23. Milford Station

June 27. Picket duty at City Point till July 16. Duty at Light House Point July 16-25. Before Petersburg July 25. Mine Explosion, Petersburg, July 30 (Cos. "A" and "E"). Sheridan's Shenandoah Valley Campaign August 7-November 28. Winchester August 17. Summit Point August 21. Middleway August 21. Near Kearneysville August 25. Abraham's Creek, near Winchester, September 13. Battle of Winchester September 19. Near Cedarville September 20. Front Royal September 21. Milford September 22. Waynesboro September 29. Bridgwater October 2. Tom's Brook ("Woodstock Races") October 8-9. Picket at Cedar Creek till October 13. Cedar Creek October 13. Battle of Cedar Creek October 19. Newtown (or Middletown) November 12. Rude's Hill, near Mt. Jackson, November 22. Expedition from Kernstown to Lacey's Springs December 19-22. Lacey's Springs December 21. Sheridan's Raid from Winchester February 27-March 24, 1865. Occupation of Staunton March 2. Action at Waynesboro March 2. Occupation of Charlottesville March 3. Near Ashland March 15. Appomattox Campaign March 28-April 9. Dinwiddie Court House March 30-31. Five Forks April 1. Fall of Petersburg April 2. Namozine Church April 3. Sailor's Creek April 6. Appomattox Station April 8. Appomattox Court House April 9. Surrender of Lee and his army. Expedition to Danville and South Boston April 23-27. March to Washington, D. C., May. Grand Review May 23. Mustered out at Washington, D. C., August 1, 1865.

Regiment lost during service 3 Officers and 47 Enlisted men killed and mortally wounded and 2 Officers and 105 Enlisted men by disease. Total 157.

1st BATTERY ("A") LIGHT ARTILLERY ("HEXAMER'S").

Organized at Hoboken, N. J., and mustered in August 12, 1861. Left State for Washington, D. C., August 20, 1861. Attached to Kearney's Brigade, Division of the Potomac, to October, 1861. Franklin's Division, Army of the Potomac, to March, 1862. Artillery, 1st Division, 1st Army Corps, Army of the Potomac, to May, 1862. Artillery, 1st Division, 6th Army Corps, to May, 1863. Artillery Brigade, 6th Army Corps, to June, 1863. 4th Volunteer Brigade, Artillery Reserve, Army of the Potomac, to October. 1863. 3rd Volunteer Brigade, Artillery Reserve, to March, 1864. 1st Volunteer Brigade, Artillery Reserve, to May, 1864. Artillery Brigade, 6th Army Corps, to July, 1864. Artillery Reserve, Army of the Potomac, to December, 1864. Artillery Brigade, 6th Army Corps, to June, 1865.

SERVICE.—Duty in the Defences of Washington, D. C., till March, 1862. Advance on Manassas, Va., March 10-15, 1862. Advance from Alexandria to Bristoe Station April 7-11. Embarked for the Virginia Peninsula April 17. Siege of Yorktown, Va., April 19-May 4 (on transports). West Point May 7-8. Battle of Seven Pines (or Fair Oaks) May 31-June 1. Seven days before Richmond June 25-July 1. Battles of Gaines' Mill June 27. Brackett's June 30. Charles City Cross Roads and Glendale June 30. Malvern Hill July 1. At Harrison's Landing till August 16. Movement to Manassas August 16-26. Pope's Campaign in Northern Virginia August 26-September 2. Bull Run Bridge August 27. Chantilly September 1. Maryland Campaign September 6-22. Crampton's Pass, Md., September 14. Antietam September 16-17. Duty in Maryland till October 30. Movement to Falmouth, Va., October 30-November 19. Battle of Fredericksburg, Va., December 12-15. Duty near Falmouth, Va., till April 27, 1863. "Mud March" January 20-24. Chancellorsville Campaign April 27-May 6. Operations at Franklin's Crossing April 29-May 2. Battle of Maryes Heights, Fredericksburg, May 3. Salem Heights May 3-4. Banks' Ford May 4. Gettysburg (Pa.) Campaign June 11-July 24. Battle of Gettysburg July 2-4. Pursuit of Lee to Manassas Gap October 5-24. Duty on line of the Rappahannock and Rapidan till October. Bristoe Campaign October 9-22. Advance to line of the Rappahannock November 7-8. Mine Run Campaign November 26-December 2. Payne's Farm November 27. Duty near Brandy Station, Va., till May, 1864. Campaign from the Rapidan to the James May 3-June 15. Battles of the Wilderness May 5-7. Spottsylvania May 8-21. North Anna River May 23-26. On line of the Pamunkey May 26-28. Totopotomoy May 28-31. Cold Harbor June 1-12. (Temporarily with 18th Army Corps.) Before Petersburg June 16-18. Siege of Petersburg June 16, 1864, to April 2, 1865. Jerusalem Plank Road June 22-23, 1864. At City Point July 9-26. Demonstration north of the James July 27-29. Deep Bottom July 27-28. Fort Fisher, Petersburg, March 25, 1865. Appomattox Campaign March 28-April 9. Fall of Petersburg April 2. Sailor's Creek April 6. High Bridge, Farmville, April 7. Appomattox Court House April 9. Surrender of Lee and his army. March to Danville April 23-27, and duty there till May 18. March to Richmond, thence to Washington, D. C., May 18-June 3. Corps Review June 8. Mustered out June 22, 1865.

Battery lost during service 3 Enlisted men killed and mortally wounded and 12 Enlisted men by disease. Total 15.

2nd BATTERY ("B") LIGHT ARTILLERY.

Organized at Camp Olden, Trenton, N. J., and mustered in September 3, 1861. Left State for Washington, D. C., October 22, 1861. Attached to Hamilton's Division, Defences of Washington, to March, 1862. Artillery, 3rd Division, 3rd Army Corps, Army of the Potomac, to June, 1862. Artillery Reserve, 3rd Army Corps, to August, 1862. Artillery, 2nd Division, 3rd Army Corps, to January, 1863. Artillery, 1st Division, 3rd Army Corps, to May, 1863. Artillery Brigade, 3rd Army Corps, to March, 1864. 2nd Volunteer Brigade, Artillery Reserve, Army of the Potomac, to May, 1864. Artillery Brigade, 2nd Army Corps, to June, 1865.

SERVICE.—Duty in the Defences of Washington, D. C., till March, 1862. Ordered to the Virginia Peninsula March, 1862. Siege of Yorktown, Va., April 5-May 4. Battle of Williamsburg May 5. Battle of Fair Oaks (or Seven Pines) May 31-June 1. Action at Fair Oaks Station June 21. Seven days before Richmond June 25-July 1. Battles of Oak Grove, Seven Pines, June 25. Peach Orchard and Savage Station June 29. White Oak Swamp and Glendale June 30. Malvern Hill July 1. At Harrison's Landing till August 16. Moved to Washington, D. C., and duty in the Defences of that city till November. Operations on Orange and Alexandria Railroad November 10-12. Near Falmouth, Va., November 28-December 11. Battle of Fredericksburg, Va., December 12-15. At Falmouth till April 27, 1863. "Mud March" January 20-24. Operations at Rappahannock Bridge and Grove Church February 5-7. Chancellorsville Campaign April 27-May 6. Battle of Chancellorsville May 1-5. Gettysburg (Pa.) Campaign June 11-July 24. Battle of Gettysburg July 1-3. Pursuit of Lee to Manassas Gap, Va., July 5-24. South Mountain, Md., July 12. Wapping Heights, Manassas Gap, Va., July 23. Near Warrenton, Va., till October. Bristoe Campaign October 9-22. Auburn and Bristoe October 14. Advance to line of the Rappahannock November 7-8. Kelly's Ford November 7. Brandy Station November 8. Mine Run Campaign November 26-December 2. At and near Stevensburg till May, 1864. Campaign from the Rapidan to the James May 3-June 15. Battles of the Wilderness May 5-7. Spottsylvania May 8-12. Spottsylvania Court House May 12-21. Assault on the Salient ("Bloody Angle") May 12. Harris Farm (or Fredericksburg Road) May 19. North Anna River May 23-26. On line of the Pamunkey May 26-28. Totopotomoy May 28-31. Cold Harbor June 1-12. Before Petersburg June 16-18. Siege of Petersburg June 16, 1864, to April 2, 1865. Jerusalem Plank Road June 22-23, 1864. Demonstration north of the James River August 13-20. Strawberry Plains August 14-18. Russell's Mills August 18. Ream's Station August 25. Watkins' House March 25. Appomattox Campaign March 28-April 9. Hatcher's

Run March 29-31. Boydton Road, Fall of Petersburg, April 2. Sutherland Station April 2. Sailor's Creek April 6. Farmville April 6-7. Appomattox Court House April 9. Surrender of Lee and his army. Moved to Washington, D. C., May. Grand Review May 23. Mustered out June 16, 1865.

Battery lost during service 1 Officer and 8 Enlisted men killed and mortally wounded and 23 Enlisted men by disease. Total 32.

3rd BATTERY ("C") LIGHT ARTILLERY.

Organized at Trenton, N. J., and mustered in September 11, 1863. Left State for Washington, D. C., September 25, 1863. Attached to Barry's Artillery Command, 22nd Army Corps, Defences of Washington, to May, 1864. Abercrombie's Command, Army of the Potomac, to June, 1864. Artillery Brigade, 2nd Army Corps, to September, 1864. Artillery Reserve, Army of the Potomac, to June, 1865.

SERVICE.—Duty in the Defences of Washington, D. C., till May, 1864. Moved to Belle Plain, Va., May 11-12. Guard rebel prisoners till May 24. Moved to Port Royal, thence to White House Landing, York River, May 24-June 4. Repulse of attack at White House June 20. Charles City Court House June 22. Joined 2nd Army Corps at Petersburg June 29. Siege of Petersburg June 29, 1864, to April 2, 1865. Demonstration north of the James July 27-29, 1864. Deep Bottom July 27-28. Demonstration north of the James August 13-20. Strawberry Plains August 14-18. Ream's Station August 25. In lines before Petersburg at Fort Hell till October 1. At Battery 16 and Fort Alexander Hays till November 22. At Fort Haskell till January 31, 1865, and at Forts Sedgwick and Hascall till April 2. Actions at Fort Sedgwick September 30, 1864. Battery 16 October 3-12. Fort Hascall November 27 and March 29, 1865. Fort Sedgwick April 1-2. Fort Stedman March 25, 1865. Appomattox Campaign March 28-April 9. Fall of Petersburg April 2. Pursuit of Lee April 5-9. At Ford's Station April 7-14, and at Wilson's Station till April 20. Moved to Washington, D. C., April 20-May 2. Grand Review May 23. Mustered out June 19, 1865.

Battery lost during service 8 Enlisted men killed and mortally wounded and 4 Enlisted men by disease. Total 12.

4th BATTERY ("D") LIGHT ARTILLERY.

Organized at Trenton, N. J., and mustered in September 16, 1863. Left State for Washington, D. C., September 29, 1863. Attached to Barry's Artillery Command, Defences of Washington, 22nd Army Corps, to April, 1864. Artillery, 2nd Division, 10th Army Corps, Army of the James, Dept. of Virginia and North Carolina, to May, 1864. Unattached Artillery, 10th Army Corps, to June, 1864. Artillery, 2nd Division, 10th Army Corps, to August, 1864. Artillery Brigade, 10th Army Corps, to December, 1864. Artillery Brigade, 25th Army Corps, to June, 1865.

SERVICE.—At Artillery Camp of Instruction, Defences of Washington, D. C., till April, 1864. Moved to Fortress Monroe, thence to Gloucester Point, Va., April 23-24. Butler's operations on south side of the James River and against Petersburg and Richmond May 4-June 15. Occupation of City Point and Bermuda Hundred, Va., May 5. Swift Creek or Arrowfield Church May 9-10. Petersburg and Richmond Turnpike May 10. Operations against Fort Darling May 12-16. Battle of Drury's Bluff May 14-16. Operations at Bermuda Hundred May 16-30. Siege operations against Petersburg and Richmond June 16, 1864, to April 2, 1865. Garrison Battery, Marshall, Bermuda Hundred front, till August 16, 1864. Actions June 18 and 30, July 10 and 25, and August 7 and 14. Near Malvern Hill August 15-16. Fussell's Mills August 18. Before Petersburg September 16-27. Battle of Chaffin's Farm, New Market Heights, September 28-30. Varina Road September 29. In trenches before Richmond till April, 1865. Occupation of Richmond April 3. (Battery detached from army for duty in New York during Presidential election of 1864 November 2-17.) Moved to near Petersburg April 14, 1865. At City Point till June, and at Richmond, Va., till June 17. Mustered out June 17, 1865.

Battery lost during service 6 Enlisted men killed and mortally wounded and 26 Enlisted men by disease. Total 32.

5th BATTERY ("E") LIGHT ARTILLERY.

Organized at Trenton, N. J., and mustered in September 8, 1863. Left State for Washington, D. C., September 26, 1863. Attached to Barry's Artillery Command, Defences of Washington, 22nd Army Corps, to April, 1864. Artillery, 1st Division, 10th Army Corps, Army of the James, Dept. of Virginia and North Carolina, to August, 1864. Artillery Brigade, 10th Army Corps, to December, 1864. Artillery Brigade, 25th Army Corps, to June, 1865.

SERVICE.—Duty in the Defences of Washington, D. C., till April 22, 1864. Moved to Gloucester Point, Va., April 22. Butler's operations on south side of the James River and against Petersburg and Richmond May 4-28. Occupation of Bermuda Hundred and City Point, Va., May 5. Action at Swift Creek (or Arrowfield Church) May 9-10. Operations against Fort Darling May 12-16. Battle of Drury's Bluff May 14-16. Clover Hill Station May 14. Operations about Bermuda Hundred May 16-June 15. Petersburg June 9. Bermuda Hundred front June 16-17. Siege operations against Petersburg and Richmond June 16, 1864, to April 2, 1865. Deep Bottom July 27. Dutch Gap August 13. Before Petersburg September 2-10. Battle of Chaffin's Farm September 28-30. Darbytown Road October 7. In trenches before Richmond till April, 1865. Occupation of Richmond April 3. Duty at Petersburg, City Point and Richmond till June. Mustered out June 11, 1865.

Battery lost during service 2 Enlisted men killed and mortally wounded and 26 Enlisted men by disease. Total 28.

1st REGIMENT INFANTRY.—(3 MONTHS.)

Organized at Trenton, N. J., and mustered in April 30, 1861. Left State for Annapolis, Md., May 3. Reported to General Butler May 5, thence moved to Washington, D. C., arriving May 6. Camp at Meridian Hill till May 23. Invasion of Virginia May 23-24. Occupation of Arlington Heights May 24. Duty on line of Alexandria & Loudon Railroad till July 16. Attached to 1st Brigade, Runyon's Reserve Division, McDowell's Army of Northeast Virginia. Advance on Manassas, Va., July 17-21. Battle of Bull Run, Va., July 21 (Reserve). Mustered out at Newark, N. J., July 31, 1861.

Regiment lost 1 by disease during service.

1st REGIMENT INFANTRY.—(3 YEARS.)

Organized at Camp Olden, Trenton, N. J., and mustered in May 21, 1861. Left State for Washington, D. C., June 28, 1861. Attached to 2nd Brigade, Runyon's Reserve Division, McDowell's Army of Northeast Virginia, to August, 1861. Kearney's Brigade, Division of the Potomac, to October, 1861. Kearney's Brigade, Franklin's Division, Army of the Potomac, to March, 1862. 1st Brigade, 1st Division, 1st Army Corps, Army of the Potomac, to April, 1862. 1st Brigade, 1st Division, Dept. of the Rappahannock, to May, 1862. 1st Brigade, 1st Division, 6th Army Corps, to June, 1864.

SERVICE.—Advance on Manassas, Va., July 16-21, 1861. Battle of Bull Run, Va., July 21 (Reserve). Duty in the Defences of Washington, D. C., till March, 1862. Little River Turnpike October 15, 1861 (Co. "A"). Advance on Manassas, Va., March 8-15, 1862. Advance from Alexandria to Bristoe Station April 7-11. Embarked for the Peninsula, Va., April 17. Siege of Yorktown April 19-May 4 (on transports). West Point May 7-8. Seven days before Richmond June 25-July 1. Battles of Gaines Mill June 27; Charles City Cross Roads and Glendale June 30; Malvern Hill July 1. Duty at Harrison's Landing till August 16. Moved to Fortress Monroe, thence to Manassas, Va., August 16-26. Pope's Campaign in Northern Virginia August 26-September

2. Bull Run Bridge, Manassas, August 27. Battle of Bull Run August 30. Cover Pope's retreat to Centreville August 30-31. Maryland Campaign September 6-22. Battle of Crampton's Pass, South Mountain, Md., September 14. Antietam September 16-17. Duty at Sharpsburg till October 29. Movement to Falmouth, Va., October 29-November 19. Battle of Fredericksburg, Va., December 12-15. (Co. "K" transferred to 1st New Jersey Battery October 16, 1862.) Duty near Falmouth, Va., till April 27, 1863. "Mud March" January 20-24. Chancellorsville Campaign April 27-May 6. Operations at Franklin's Crossing April 29-May 2. Battle of Maryes Heights, Fredericksburg, May 3. Salem Heights May 3-4. Banks' Ford May 4. Gettysburg (Pa.) Campaign June 11-July 24. Battle of Gettysburg July 2-4. Pursuit of Lee to Manassas Gap, Va., July 5-24. Fairfield, Pa., July 5. Williamsport July 6. At and near Funkstown July 10-13. Hagerstown July 11. In camp near Warrenton, Va., till September 15, and at Culpeper till October. Bristoe Campaign October 9-22. Advance to line of the Rappahannock November 7-8. Rappahannock Station November 7. Mine Run Campaign November 26-December 2. Duty at Brandy Station till May, 1864. Campaign from the Rapidan to the James May 3-June 15. Battles of the Wilderness May 5-7; Spottsylvania May 8-12; Spottsylvania Court House May 12-21. Assault on the Salient, "Bloody Angle," May 12. North Anna River May 23-26. On line of the Pamunkey May 26-28. Totopotomoy May 28-31. Cold Harbor June 1-12. Before Petersburg June 17-19. Siege of Petersburg till July 9. Jerusalem Plank Road June 22-23. Moved to Washington, D. C., July 9-11. Repulse of Early's attack on Fort Stevens and Northern Defences of Washington July 11-12. Pursuit of Early to Snicker's Gap July 14-23. Sheridan's Shenandoah Valley Campaign August 7-November 28. Strasburg August 14-15. Cedar Creek August 15. Winchester August 17. Charlestown August 21-22. Battle of Winchester September 19. Fisher's Hill September 22. Battle of Cedar Creek October 19. Duty in the Shenandoah Valley till December. Moved to Washington, D. C., thence to Petersburg December, 1864. Siege of Petersburg, Va., December, 1864, to April, 1865. Dabney's Mills, Hatcher's Run, February 5-7, 1865. Appomattox Campaign March 28-April 9. Assault on and fall of Petersburg April 2. Pursuit of Lee April 3-9. Appomattox Court House April 9. Surrender of Lee and his army. March to Danville April 23-27 and duty there till May 18. Moved to Richmond, thence to Washington, D. C., May 18-June 3. Corps Review June 8. Mustered out at Hall's Hill, Va., June 29, 1865.

Regiment lost during service 9 Officers and 144 Enlisted men killed and mortally wounded and 1 Officer and 90 Enlisted men by disease. Total 244.

Note.—Non-Veterans left front June, 1864, and mustered out at Trenton, N. J., June 23, 1864. Veterans and Recruits were attached to other Regiments of the Brigade till December, 1864, when they were organized into 1st New Jersey Veteran Battalion.

2nd REGIMENT INFANTRY.—(3 MONTHS.)

Organized at Trenton, N. J. Enrolled April 26 and mustered in May 1, 1861. Left State for Washington, D. C., May 3. Reported to General Butler at Annapolis, Md., May 5; thence moved to Washington, arriving there May 6. Attached to Runyon's New Jersey Brigade, Defences of Washington, to June, 1861. 1st Brigade, Runyon's Reserve Division, McDowell's Army of Northeast Virginia, to July, 1861. Camp at Meridian Hill May 9-24. Occupation of Arlington Heights, Va., May 24. Construction of Fort Runyon. Duty on line of Alexandria & Loudon Railroad till July 16. Advance on Manassas, Va., July 16-21. Battle of Bull Run July 21 (Reserve). Mustered out at Trenton, N. J., July 21, 1861, expiration of term.

2nd REGIMENT INFANTRY.—(3 YEARS.)

Organized at Camp Olden, Trenton, N. J., May 27, 1861. Left State for Washington, D. C., June 28, 1861. Attached to 2nd Brigade, Runyon's Reserve Division,

McDowell's Army of Northeast Virginia, to August, 1861. Kearney's Brigade, Division of the Potomac, to October, 1861. Kearney's Brigade, Franklin's Division, Army of the Potomac, to March, 1862. 1st Brigade, 1st Division, 1st Army Corps, Army of the Potomac, to April, 1862. 1st Brigade, 1st Division, Dept. of the Rappahannock, to May, 1862. 1st Brigade, 1st Division, 6th Army Corps, Army of the Potomac and Army of the Shenandoah, to July, 1865.

SERVICE.—Advance on Manassas, Va., July 16-21, 1861. Battle of Bull Run, Va., July 21 (Reserve). Duty in the Defences of Washington, D. C., till March, 1862. Advance on Manassas, Va., March 8-15. Advance from Alexandria to Bristoe Station April 7-11. Embarked for the Virginia Peninsula April 17. Siege of Yorktown, Va., April 19-May 4 (on transports). West Point May 7-8. Seven days before Richmond June 25-July 1. Battles of Gaines Mill June 27. Garnett's Farm June 27. Golding's Farm June 28. Charles City Cross Roads and Glendale June 30. Malvern Hill July 1. At Harrison's Landing till August 16. Movement to Fortress Monroe and Manassas, Va., June 16-26. Pope's Campaign in Northern Virginia August 26-September 2. Action at Bull Run Bridge, Manassas, August 27. Battle of Bull Run August 30. Cover Pope's retreat to Centreville August 30-31. Maryland Campaign September 6-22. Battles of Crampton's Pass, South Mountain, Md., September 14. Antietam, Md., September 16-17. Duty at Sharpsburg, Md., till October 29. Movement to Falmouth, Va., October 29-November 19. Battle of Fredericksburg, Va., December 12-15. Duty at Falmouth till April 27, 1863. "Mud March" January 20-24. Chancellorsville Campaign April 27-May 6. Operations at Franklin's Crossing April 29-May 2. Battle of Maryes Heights, Fredericksburg, May 3. Salem Heights May 3-4. Banks Ford May 4. Gettysburg (Pa.) Campaign June 11-July 24. Battle of Gettysburg July 2-4. Pursuit of Lee to Manassas Gap, Va. Fairfield, Pa., July 5. At and near Funkstown, Md., July 10-13. Near Warrenton, Va., till September 15, and at Culpeper till October. Bristoe Campaign October 9-22. Advance to line of the Rappahannock November 7-8. Rappahannock Station November 7. Mine Run Campaign November 26-December 2. At Brandy Station till May, 1864. Campaign from the Rapidan to the James May 3-June 15. Battles of the Wilderness May 5-7; Spottsylvania May 8-12; Spottsylvania Court House May 12-21. Assault on the Salient, "Bloody Angle," May 12. North Anna River May 23-26. On line of the Pamunkey May 26-28. Totopotomoy May 28-31. Non-Veterans relieved for muster out. Veterans and Recruits temporarily attached to 15th New Jersey Infantry under orders of May 29, 1864, till December 17, 1864, when reorganized as a Battalion. Non-Veterans mustered out at Newark, N. J., June 21, 1864. Battles about Cold Harbor June 1-12, 1864. Before Petersburg June 17-19. Siege of Petersburg till July 9. Jerusalem Plank Road June 22-23. Moved to Washington, D. C., July 9-11. Repulse of Early's attack on Fort Stevens and the Northern Defences of Washington July 11-12. Pursuit of Early to Snicker's Gap, Va., July 14-23. Sheridan's Shenandoah Valley Campaign August 7-November 28. Strasburg August 14-15. Cedar Creek August 15. Winchester August 17. Charlestown August 21-22. Battle of Winchester September 19. Fisher's Hill September 22. Battle of Cedar Creek October 19. Duty in the Shenandoah Valley till December. Moved to Washington, D. C., thence to Petersburg, Va. Siege of Petersburg December, 1864, to April 2, 1865. Dabney's Mills, Hatcher's Run, February 5-7, 1865. Appomattox Campaign March 28-April 9. Fall of Petersburg April 2. Pursuit of Lee April 3-9. Appomattox Court House April 9. Surrender of Lee and his army. March to Danville April 23-27 and duty there till May 18. March to Richmond, Va., thence to Washington, D. C., May 18-June 3. Corps Review June 8. Mustered out at Hall's Hill, Va., July 11, 1865.

Regiment lost during service 7 Officers and 89 Enlisted men killed and mortally wounded and 2 Officers and 67 Enlisted men by disease. Total 165.

3rd REGIMENT INFANTRY.—(3 MONTHS.)

Regiment organized at Trenton, N. J., and mustered in April 27, 1861. Left State for Annapolis, Md., May 3, 1861. Reported to General Butler May 5, thence moved to Washington, D. C., arriving May 6. At Meridian Hill till May 24. Occupation of Arlington Heights May 24. Attached to Runyon's New Jersey Brigade, Defences of Washington, to June, 1861. 1st Brigade, Runyon's Reserve Division, McDowell's Army of Northeast Virginia, to July, 1861.

SERVICE.—Duty on line of Alexandria & Loudon Railroad till July 16. Advance on Manassas, Va., July 16-21. Battle of Bull Run July 21 (Reserve). Mustered out July 31, 1861.

3rd REGIMENT INFANTRY.—(3 YEARS.)

Organized at Camp Olden, Trenton, N. J., and mustered in June 4, 1861. Left State for Washington, D. C., June 28, 1861. Attached to 2nd Brigade, Runyon's Reserve Division, McDowell's Army of Northeast Virginia, to August, 1861. Kearney's Brigade, Division of the Potomac, to October, 1861. Kearney's Brigade, Franklin's Division, Army of the Potomac, to March, 1862. 1st Brigade, 1st Division, 1st Army Corps, Army of the Potomac, to April, 1862. 1st Brigade, 1st Division, Dept. of the Rappahannock, to May, 1862. 1st Brigade, 1st Division, 6th Army Corps, Army of the Potomac and Army of the Shenandoah, to June, 1865.

SERVICE.—Advance on Manassas, Va., July 16-21, 1861. Battle of Bull Run July 21 (Reserve). Duty in the Defences of Washingtos, D. C., till March, 1862. Munson's Hill or Little River Turnpike August 31, 1861 (Cos. "I" and "K"). Springfield Station October 2 (Detachment). Burke's Station December 4 (Detachment). Advance on Manassas, Va., March 8-15. Advance from Alexandria to Bristoe Station April 7-11. Embarked for the Peninsula, Va., April 17. Siege of Yorktown, Va., April 19-May 5 (on transports). West Point May 7-8. Seven days before Richmond June 25-July 1. Battles of Gaines Mill June 27; Charles City Cross Roads and Glendale June 30; Malvern Hill July 1. At Harrison's Landing till August 16. Movement to Fortress Monroe, thence to Manassas, Va., August 16-26. Pope's Campaign in Northern Virginia August 26-September 2. Bull Run Bridge August 27. Battle of Bull Run August 30. Cover Pope's retreat to Centreville August 30-31. Maryland Campaign September 6-22. Battles of Crampton's Gap, South Mountain, September 14. Antietam September 16-17. Duty at Sharpsburg till October 29. Movement to Falmouth, Va., October 29-November 19. Battle of Fredericksburg, Va., December 12-15. At Falmouth till April 27, 1863. "Mud March" January 20-24. Chancellorsville Campaign April 27-May 6. Operations at Franklin's Crossing April 29-May 2. Battle of Maryes Heights, Fredericksburg, May 3. Salem Heights May 3-4. Banks Ford May 4. Gettysburg (Pa.) Campaign June 11-July 24. Battle of Gettysburg July 2-4. Pursuit of Lee July 5-24. Fairfield, Pa., July 5. At and near Funkstown, Md., July 10-13. Camp near Warrenton, Va., till September 15, and at Culpeper Court House till October. Bristoe Campaign October 9-22. Advance to line of the Rappahannock November 7-8. Rappahannock Station November 7. Mine Run Campaign November 26-December 2. At Brandy Station till May, 1864. Campaign from the Rapidan to the James May 3-June 15. Battles of the Wilderness May 5-7; Spottsylvania May 8-12; Spottsylvania Court House May 12-21. Assault on the Salient, "Bloody Angle," May 12. North Anna River May 23-26. On line of the Pamunkey May 26-28. Totopotomoy May 28-31. Non-Veterans relieved for muster out. Veterans and Recruits temporarily attached to 15th New Jersey Infantry under order of May 29, 1864, till December 17, 1864, when reorganized as a Veteran Battalion at Burke's Station, near Petersburg, Va. Non-Veterans mustered out at Trenton, N. J., June 23, 1864. Battles about Cold Harbor June 1-12. Before Petersburg June 17-19. Siege of Petersburg till July 9. Jerusalem Plank Road June 22-23. Moved to Washington, D. C., July 9-11. Repulse of Early's attack on Fort

Stevens and Northern Defences of Washington July 11-12. Pursuit of Early to Snicker's Gap, Va., July 14-23. Sheridan's Shenandoah Valley Campaign August 7-November 28. Strasburg August 14-15. Cedar Creek August 15. Winchester August 17. Charlestown August 21-22. Battle of Winchester September 19. Fisher's Hill September 22. Battle of Cedar Creek October 19. Duty in the Shenandoah Valley till December. Siege of Petersburg, Va., December, 1864, to April 2, 1865. Dabney's Mills, Hatcher's Run, February 5-7. Appomattox Campaign March 28-April 9. Assault and fall of Petersburg April 2. Pursuit of Lee April 3-9. Appomattox Court House April 9. Surrender of Lee and his army. March to Danville April 23-27 and duty there till May 18. March to Richmond, Va., thence to Washington, D. C., May 18-June 3. Corps Review June 8. Mustered out at Hall's Hill, Va., June 29, 1865.

Regiment lost during service 9 Officers and 148 Enlisted men killed and mortally wounded and 1 Officer and 80 Enlisted men by disease. Total 238.

4th REGIMENT INFANTRY.—(3 MONTHS.)

Organized at Trenton, N. J., and mustered in April 27, 1861. Left State for Annapolis, Md., May 3. Reported to General Butler May 5, then moved to Washington, D. C., arriving there May 6. Attached to Runyon's New Jersey Brigade, Defences of Washington, to June, 1861. 1st Brigade, Runyon's Reserve Division, McDowell's Army of Northeast Virginia, to July, 1861.

SERVICE.—At Meridian Hill till May 24. Occupation of Arlington Heights, Va., May 24. Construction of Fort Runyon. Duty on line of Alexandria & Loudon Railroad till July 16. Advance on Manassas, Va., July 16-21. Battle of Bull Run July 21 (Reserve). Mustered out July 31, 1861. Expiration of term.

4th REGIMENT INFANTRY.—(3 YEARS.)

Organized at Camp Olden, Trenton, N. J., and mustered in August 19, 1861. Left State for Washington, D. C., August 20, 1861. Attached to Kearney's Brigade, Division of the Potomac, to October, 1861. Kearney's Brigade, Franklin's Division, Army of the Potomac, to March, 1862. 1st Brigade, 1st Division, 1st Army Corps, Army of the Potomac, to April, 1862. 1st Brigade, 1st Division, Dept. of the Rappahannock, to May, 1862. 1st Brigade, 1st Division, 6th Army Corps, Army of the Potomac and Army of the Shenandoah, to July, 1865.

SERVICE.—Duty in the Defences of Washington, D. C., till March, 1862. Advance on Manassas, Va., March 8-15, 1862. Advance from Alexandria to Bristoe Station April 7-11. Embarked for the Virginia Peninsula April 17. Siege of Yorktown April 19-May 5 (on transports). West Point May 7-8. Reconnoissance to East Branch Chickahominy June 7 (Cos. "D," "F" and "I"). Seven days before Richmond June 25-July 1. Battles of Gaines Mill June 27; Charles City Cross Roads and Glendale June 30; Malvern Hill July 1. At Harrison's Landing till August 16. Movement to Fortress Monroe, thence to Manassas, Va., August 16-26. Pope's Campaign in Northern Virginia August 26-September 2. Bull Run Bridge, Manassas, August 27. Battle of Bull Run August 30. Cover Pope's retreat to Centreville August 30-31. Maryland Campaign September 6-22. Battles of Crampton's Pass, South Mountain, September 14; Antietam September 16-17. At Sharpsburg, Md., till October 29. Movement to Falmouth, Va., October 29-November 19. Battle of Fredericksburg, Va., December 12-15. At Falmouth till April 27, 1863. "Mud March" January 20-24. Chancellorsville Campaign April 27-May 6. Operations at Franklin's Crossing April 29-May 2. Battle of Maryes Heights, Fredericksburg, May 3. Salem Heights May 3-4. Banks Ford May 4. Gettysburg (Pa.) Campaign June 11-July 24. Battle of Gettysburg July 2-4. Guarding ammunition train July. In camp near Warrenton, Va., till September 15, and at Culpeper Court House till October. Bristoe Campaign October 9-22. Advance to line of the Rappahannock November 7-8. Rappahannock Station November 7. Mine Run Campaign November 26-December 2. At Brandy Station to May, 1864. Campaign from the

Rapidan to the James May 3-June 15. Battles of the Wilderness May 5-7; Spottsylvania May 8-12; Spottsylvania Court House May 12-21. Assault on the Salient, "Bloody Angle," May 12. North Anna River May 23-26. On line of the Pamunkey May 26-28. Totopotomoy May 28-31. Cold Harbor June 1-12. Before Petersburg June 17-18. Siege of Petersburg till July 9. Jerusalem Plank Road June 22-23. Moved to Washington, D. C., June 9-11. Repulse of Early's attack on Fort Stevens and the Northern Defences of Washington July 11-12. Pursuit of Early to Snicker's Gap July 14-23. Sheridan's Shenandoah Valley Campaign August 7-November 28. Strasburg August 14-15. Cedar Creek August 15. Winchester August 17. Charlestown August 21-22. Battle of Winchester September 19. Fisher's Hill September 22. Battle of Cedar Creek October 19. Duty in the Shenandoah Valley till December. Moved to Washington, D. C., thence to Petersburg, Va. Siege of Petersburg December, 1864, to April 2, 1865. Dabney's Mills, Hatcher's Run, February 5-7, 1865. Appomattox Campaign March 28-April 9. Fall of Petersburg April 2. Pursuit of Lee April 3-9. Appomattox Court House April 9. Surrender of Lee and his army. March to Danville April 23-27 and duty there till May 18. Moved to Richmond, Va., thence to Washington, D. C., May 18-June 3. Corps Review June 8. Mustered out at Hall's Hill, Va., July 9, 1865.

Regiment lost during service 5 Officers and 156 Enlisted men killed and mortally wounded and 2 Officers and 103 Enlisted men by disease. Total 266.

5th REGIMENT INFANTRY.

Organized at Camp Olden, Trenton, N. J., and mustered in August 22, 1861. Left State for Washington, D. C., August 29, 1861. Attached to Casey's Provisional Division, Army of the Potomac, to October, 1861. 3rd Brigade, Hooker's Division, Army of the Potomac, to March, 1862. 3rd Brigade, 2nd Division, 3rd Army Corps, Army of the Potomac, to March, 1864. 3rd Brigade, 3rd Division, 2nd Army Corps, to November, 1864.

SERVICE.—Duty in the Defences of Washington, D. C., till March, 1862. Expedition to Lower Maryland November 3-11, 1861. At Meridian Hill till December, and near Budd's Ferry, Md., till April, 1862. Seizure of Cockpit Point March 10. Moved to the Virginia Peninsula April 5-8. Siege of Yorktown April 10-May 5. Battle of Williamsburg May 5. Battle of Fair Oaks or Seven Pines May 31-June 1. Duty near Seven Pines till June 25. Seven days before Richmond June 25-July 1. Action at Oak Grove, near Seven Pines, June 25. Savage Station June 29. Glendale June 30. Malvern Hill July 1. At Harrison's Landing till August 15. Movement to Centreville August 15-26. Pope's Campaign in Northern Virginia August 26-September 2. Action at Bristoe Station or Kettle Run August 27. Battles of Groveton August 29; Bull Run August 30; Chantilly September 1. Duty in the Defences of Washington, near Alexandria, till November 1. Movement to Falmouth, Va., November 1-28. Duty at Falmouth November 28-December 11. Battle of Fredericksburg, Va., December 12-15. At Falmouth till April 27, 1863. "Mud March" January 20-24. Operations at Rappahannock Bridge and Grove Church February 5-7. Chancellorsville Campaign April 27-May 6. Battle of Chancellorsville May 1-5. Gettysburg (Pa.) Campaign June 11-July 24. Battle of Gettysburg July 1-3. Pursuit of Lee to Manassas Gap July 5-24. Wapping Heights, Manassas Gap, Va., July 23. Duty near Warrenton till October. Bristoe Campaign October 9-22. McLean's Ford October 15. Advance to line of the Rappahannock November 7-8. Kelly's Ford November 7. Mine Run Campaign November 26-December 2. Payne's Farm November 27. Duty near Brandy Station till May, 1864. Demonstration on the Rapidan February 6-7. Campaign from the Rapidan to the James May 3-June 15. Battles of the Wilderness May 5-7; Spottsylvania May 8-12; Spottsylvania Court House May 12-21. Assault on the Salient, "Bloody Angle," May 12. Harris Farm, Fredericksburg Road, May 19. North Anna River May 23-26. Ox Ford May 23-24. On line of the Pamunkey May

26-28. Totopotomoy May 28-31. Cold Harbor June 1-12. Before Petersburg June 16-18. Siege of Petersburg June 16 to November 6, 1864. Jerusalem Plank Road June 22-23. In trenches before Petersburg till July 12. In Reserve Camp July 12-26. Demonstration north of the James July 27-29. Deep Bottom July 27-28. Demonstration north of the James August 13-20. Strawberry Plains, Deep Bottom, August 14-18. Non-Veterans mustered out at Trenton, N. J., September 7, 1864. Ream's Station August 25. Fort Sedgwick September 10. Duty in trenches before Petersburg in lines from Fort Morton to Fort Alexander Hays September 10 to October 1. Poplar Springs Church October 1. Yellow House October 2-5. Boydton Plank Road, Hatcher's Run, October 27-28. Fort Morton November 5. Consolidated with 7th New Jersey Infantry November 6, 1864.

Regiment lost during service 12 Officers and 126 Enlisted men killed and mortally wounded and 85 Enlisted men by disease. Total 223.

6th REGIMENT INFANTRY.

Organized at Camp Olden, Trenton, N. J., and mustered in August 19, 1861. Left State for Washington, D. C., September 10, 1861. Attached to Casey's Provisional Brigade, Division of the Potomac, to October, 1861. 3rd Brigade, Hooker's Division, Army of the Potomac, to March, 1862. 3rd Brigade, 2nd Division, 3rd Army Corps, Army of the Potomac, to March, 1864. 1st Brigade, 4th Division, 2nd Army Corps, to May, 1864. 3rd Brigade, 3rd Division, 2nd Army Corps, to October, 1864.

SERVICE.—Expedition to Lower Maryland November 3-11, 1861. At Meridian Hill till December, 1861, and near Budd's Ferry, Md., till April, 1862. Moved to the Virginia Peninsula April 5-8. Siege of Yorktown April 10-May 4. Battle of Williamsburg May 5. Battle of Fair Oaks (or Seven Pines) May 31-June 1. Duty near Seven Pines till June 25. Seven days before Richmond June 25-July 1. Battles of Oak Grove, near Seven Pines, June 25. Savage Station June 29. Glendale June 30. Malvern Hill July 1. At Harrison's Landing till August 15. Movement to Centreville August 15-26. Pope's Campaign in Northern Virginia August 26-September 2. Action at Bristoe Station (or Kettle Run) August 27. Battles of Groveton August 29. Bull Run August 30. Chantilly September 1. Duty in the Defences of Washington till November 1. Movement to Falmouth, Va., November 1-28. Duty near Falmouth November 28-December 11. Battle of Fredericksburg, Va., December 12-15. At Falmouth till April 27, 1863. "Mud March" January 20-24. Operations at Rappahannock Bridge and Grove Church February 5-7. Chancellorsville Campaign April 27-May 6. Battle of Chancellorsville May 1-5. Gettysburg (Pa.) Campaign June 11-July 24. Battle of Gettysburg July 1-3. Pursuit of Lee to Manassas Gap, Va., July 5-24. Wapping Heights July 23. Duty near Warrenton till October. Bristoe Campaign October 9-22. McLean's Ford October 15. Advance to line of the Rappahannock November 7-8. Kelly's Ford November 7. Mine Run Campaign November 26-December 2. Payne's Farm November 27. Duty near Brandy Station till May, 1864. Demonstration on the Rapidan February 6-7. Campaign from the Rapidan to the James May 3-June 15. Battles of the Wilderness May 5-7; Spottsylvania May 8-12; Spottsylvania Court House May 12-21. Assault on the Salient ("Bloody Angle") May 12. Harris Farm (or Fredericksburg Road) May 19. North Anna River May 23-26. Ox Ford May 23-24. On line of the Pamunkey May 26-28. Totopotomoy May 28-31. Cold Harbor June 1-12. Before Petersburg June 16-18. Siege of Petersburg June 16 to October 12, 1864. Jerusalem Plank Road June 22-23. In trenches before Petersburg till July 12. In Reserve Camp till July 26. Demonstration on north side of the James July 27-29. Deep Bottom July 27-28. In trenches till August 12. Demonstration north of the James August 13-20. Strawberry Plains, Deep Bottom, August 14-18. Ream's Station August 25. Before Petersburg till October 12. Non-Veterans mustered out at Trenton,

N. J., September 7, 1864. Veteran Battalion consolidated with 8th New Jersey Infantry October 12, 1864.

Regiment lost during service 3 Officers and 124 Enlisted men killed and mortally wounded and 1 Officer and 71 Enlisted men by disease. Total 199.

7th REGIMENT INFANTRY.

Organized at Camp Olden, Trenton, N. J., and mustered in September 3, 1861. 7 Companies left State for Washington, D. C., September 19, 1861, and 3 Companies October 2, 1861. Attached to Casey's Provisional Brigade, Division of the Potomac, to October, 1861. 3rd Brigade, Hooker's Division, Army of the Potomac, to March, 1862. 3rd Brigade, 2nd Division, 3rd Army Corps, Army of the Potomac, to March, 1864. 1st Brigade, 4th Division, 2nd Army Corps, to May, 1864. 3rd Brigade, 3rd Division, 2nd Army Corps, to July, 1865.

SERVICE.—At Meridian Hill till December 6, 1861. Expedition to Lower Maryland November 3-11. Duty at Budd's Ferry, Md., till April, 1862. Moved to the Virginia Peninsula April 5-8. Siege of Yorktown, Va., April 10-May 4. Battle of Williamsburg May 5. Battle of Fair Oaks (or Seven Pines) May 31-June 1. Duty near Seven Pines till June 25. Seven days before Richmond June 25-July 1. Action at Oak Grove (near Seven Pines) June 25. Battles of Savage Station June 29. Glendale June 30. Malvern Hill July 1. At Harrison's Landing till August 15. Movement to Centreville, Va., August 15-26. Pope's Campaign in Northern Virginia August 26-September 2. Action at Bristoe Station (or Kettle Run) August 27. Battles of Groveton August 29; Bull Run August 30; Chantilly September 1. Duty in the Defences of Washington till November 1. Movement to Falmouth, Va., November 1-28. Duty near Falmouth November 28-December 11. Battle of Fredericksburg, Va., December 12-15. Duty near Falmouth till April 27, 1863. "Mud March" January 20-24. Operations at Rappahannock Bridge and Grove Church February 5-7. Chancellorsville Campaign April 27-May 6. Battle of Chancellorsville May 1-6. Gettysburg (Pa.) Campaign June 11-July 24. Battle of Gettysburg July 1-3. Pursuit of Lee to Manassas Gap, Va., July 5-24. Wapping Heights July 23. Duty near Warrenton till October. Bristoe Campaign October 9-22. McLean's Ford October 15. Advance to line of the Rappahannock November 7-8. Kelly's Ford November 7. Mine Run Campaign November 26-December 2. Payne's Farm November 27. Duty near Brandy Station till May, 1864. Demonstration on the Rapidan February 6-7. Campaign from the Rapidan to the James May 3-June 15. Battles of the Wilderness May 5-7; Spottsylvania May 8-12; Spottsylvania Court House May 12-21. Assault on the Salient ("Bloody Angle") May 12. Harris Farm, Fredericksburg Road, May 19. North Anna River May 23-26. Ox Ford May 23-24. On line of the Pamunkey May 26-28. Totopotomoy May 28-31. Cold Harbor June 1-12. Before Petersburg June 16-18. Siege of Petersburg June 16, 1864, to April 2, 1865. Jerusalem Plank Road June 22-23, 1864. Demonstration north of the James July 27-29. Deep Bottom July 27-28. Demonstration north of the James August 13-20. Strawberry Plains, Deep Bottom, August 14-18. Ream's Station August 25. Fort Sedgwick September 10. Poplar Springs Church September 29-October 2. Yellow House October 2-5. Boydton Plank Road, Hatcher's Run, October 27-28. Warren's Raid on Weldon Railroad December 7-12. Dabney's Mills, Hatcher's Run, February 5-7, 1865. Watkins' House March 25. Appomattox Campaign March 28-April 9. Boydton and White Oak Road March 30-31. Crow's House March 31. Fall of Petersburg April 2. Pursuit of Lee April 3-9. Sailor's Creek April 6. High Bridge, Farmville, April 7. Appomattox Court House April 9. Surrender of Lee and his army. March to Washington, D. C., May 2-12. Grand Review May 23. Duty at Washington, D. C., till July. Mustered out July 17, 1865. Non-Veterans mustered out at Trenton October 7, 1864.

Regiment lost during service 11 Officers and 126 Enlisted men killed and mortally wounded and 2 Officers and 121 Enlisted men by disease. Total 260.

8th REGIMENT INFANTRY.

Organized at Camp Olden, Trenton, N. J., and mustered in September 14, 1861. Left State for Washington, D. C., October 1, 1861. Attached to Casey's Provisional Brigade, Division of the Potomac, October, 1861. 3rd Brigade, Hooker's Division, Army of the Potomac, to March, 1862. 3rd Brigade, 2nd Division, 3rd Army Corps, Army of the Potomac, to March, 1864. 1st Brigade, 4th Division, 2nd Army Corps, to May, 1864. 3rd Brigade, 3rd Division, 2nd Army Corps, to July, 1865.

SERVICE.—At Meridian Hill till December 6, 1861. Expedition to lower Maryland November 3-11. Duty at Budd's Ferry, Md., till April, 1862. Moved to the Virginia Peninsula April 5-8. Siege of Yorktown, Va., April 10-May 4. Battle of Williamsburg May 5. Battle of Fair Oaks (or Seven Pines) May 31-June 1. Duty near Seven Pines till June 25. Seven days before Richmond June 25-July 1. Action at Oak Grove, near Seven Pines, June 25. Battles of Savage Station June 29; Glendale June 30; Malvern Hill July 1. At Harrison's Landing till August 15. Movement to Centreville August 15-26. Pope's Campaign in Northern Virginia August 26-September 2. Action at Bristoe Station (or Kettle Run) August 27. Battles of Groveton August 29; Bull Run August 30; Chantilly September 1. Duty in the Defences of Washington, D. C., till November 1. Movement to Falmouth, Va., November 1-28. Duty near Falmouth, Va., November 28-December 11. Battle of Fredericksburg, Va., December 12-15. At Falmouth till April 27, 1863. "Mud March" January 20-24. Operations at Rappahannock Bridge and Grove Church February 5-7. Chancellorsville Campaign April 27-May 6. Battle of Chancellorsville May 1-5. Gettysburg (Pa.) Campaign June 11-July 24. Battle of Gettysburg July 1-3. Pursuit of Lee to Manassas Gap, Va., July 5-24. Wapping Heights, Va., July 23. Duty near Warrenton, Va., till October. Bristoe Campaign October 9-22. Mc-Lean's Ford October 15. Advance to line of the Rappahannock November 7-8. Kelly's Ford November 7. Mine Run Campaign November 26-December 2. Payne's Farm November 27. Duty near Brandy Station till May, 1864. Demonstration on the Rapidan February 6-7. Campaign from the Rapidan to the James May 3-June 15. Battles of the Wilderness May 5-7; Spottsylvania May 8-12; Spottsylvania Court House May 12-21. Assault on the Salient ("Bloody Angle") May 12. Harris Farm, or Fredericksburg Road, May 19. North Anna River May 23-26. Ox Ford May 23-24. On line of the Pamunkey May 26-28. Totopotomoy May 28-31. Cold Harbor June 1-12. Before Petersburg June 16-18. Siege of Petersburg June 16, 1864, to April 2, 1865. Jerusalem Plank Road June 22-23, 1864. Demonstration north of the James July 27-29. Deep Bottom July 27-28. Demonstration north of the James August 13-20. Strawberry Plains, Deep Bottom, August 14-18. Ream's Station August 25. Fort Sedgwick September 10. Poplar Springs Church September 29-October 2. Yellow House October 2-5. Boydton Plank Road, Hatcher's Run, October 27-28. Warren's Raid on Weldon Railroad December 7-12. Dabney's Mills, Hatcher's Run, February 5-7, 1865. Watkins' House March 25. Appomattox Campaign March 28-April 9. Boydton and White Oak Roads March 30-31. Crow's House March 31. Fall of Petersburg April 2. Pursuit of Lee April 3-9. Sailor's Creek April 6. High Bridge, Farmville, April 7. Appomattox Court House April 9. Surrender of Lee and his army. March to Washington, D. C., May 2-12. Grand Review May 23. Duty at Washington till July. Mustered out July 17, 1865.

Regiment lost during service 9 Officers and 167 Enlisted men killed and mortally wounded and 1 Officer and 109 Enlisted men by disease. Total 286.

9th REGIMENT INFANTRY.

Organized at Camp Olden, Trenton, N. J., September 13 to October 15, 1861. Left State for Washington, D. C., December 4, 1861. Attached to 3rd Brigade, Casey's Division, Army of the Potomac, to January, 1862. 2nd Brigade, Burnside's North Carolina Expeditionary Corps, to April, 1862. 1st Brigade, 3rd Division, Dept. of North Carolina, to July, 1862. 2nd Brigade, 1st Division, Dept. of North Carolina, to December, 1862. Heckman's Brigade, Dept. of North Carolina, to January, 1863. 1st Brigade, 2nd Division, 18th Army Corps, Dept. of North Carolina, to February, 1863. 1st Brigade, 1st Division, 18th Army Corps, Dept. of the South, to April, 1863. District of Beaufort, N. C., Dept. of North Carolina, to June, 1863. Jourdan's Independent Brigade, Dept. of North Carolina, to July, 1863. District of Beaufort, N. C., Dept. of Virginia and North Carolina, to October, 1863. Heckman's Command, Newport News, Va., Dept. of Virginia and North Carolina, to January, 1864. 3rd Brigade, Heckman's Division, Portsmouth, Va., Dept. of Virginia and North Carolina, to April, 1864. 2nd Brigade, Portsmouth, Va., April, 1864. 1st Brigade, 2nd Division, 18th Army Corps, Army of the James, to September, 1864. District of Beaufort, N. C., Dept. of Virginia and North Carolina, to January, 1865. Sub-District of Beaufort, N. C., Dept. of North Carolina, to February, 1865. 1st Brigade, 1st Division, District of Beaufort, N. C., to March, 1865. 2nd Brigade, District of Beaufort, N. C., to April, 1865. 2nd Brigade, 3rd Division, 23rd Army Corps, Dept. of North Carolina, to July, 1865.

SERVICE.—Camp on Bladensburg Pike December 4-14, 1861, and on Meridian Hill, Defences of Washington, D. C., till January 4, 1862. Moved to Annapolis, Md., January 4, 1862. Burnside's Expedition to Roanoke Island and Hatteras Inlet January 5-February 8. Battle of Roanoke Island February 8. Duty at Roanoke Island till March 11. Expedition to Winton February 18-20. Skirmish at Winton February 19. Expedition to New Berne, N. C., March 11-14. Battle of New Berne March 14. At Newport Barracks and siege operations against Fort Macon April 1-26. Newport, N. C., April 7. Bombardment and capture of Fort Macon April 25-26. Expedition to Young's Cross Roads July 26-29 (6 Companies). Young's Cross Roads July 27. Reconnoissance from Newberne to Swansborough August 14-15 (Detachment). Duty at New Berne till December. Expedition to Tarboro November 1-12. Action at Rawle's Mills November 2. Demonstration on New Berne November 11. Foster's Expedition to Goldsboro December 11-20. Southwest Creek December 13-14. Kinston December 14. Whitehall December 16. Goldsboro December 17. Expedition to Port Royal, S. C., January 28-31, 1863. At St. Helena Island, S. C., February 9-April 4. Expedition against Charleston, S. C., April 4-10. Moved from Hilton Head, S. C., to New Berne, N. C., April 12-16. Expedition to relief of Little Washington, N. C., April 17-23. Moved to Carolina City April 25 and duty there till June. Expedition to Trenton July 4-8. Free Bridge Comfort (or Quaker Bridge) July 6. Expedition from Newport Barracks to Cedar Point and White Oak River June 13-16. At New Berne July 26-August 26, and at Carolina City till October 18. Moved to Newport News, Va., October 18-20, and duty there till January 31, 1864. Regiment Veteranize January 21, 1864, and Veterans on furlough January 31-March 17. Skirmishes on Ballahock or Bear Quarter Road and at Deep Creek February 29-March 1. Ballahock Station, near Dismal Swamp, March 1. Deep Creek March 2. At Portsmouth and Getty's Station till April 26. Expedition to Isle of Wight County April 13-15. Smithfield, Cherry Grove, April 14. Moved to Yorktown April 26. Butler's operations on south side of James River and against Petersburg and Richmond May 4-28. Occupation of Bermuda Hundred May 5. Port Walthal Junction May 6-7. Swift Creek May 9-10. Operations against Fort Darling May 12-16. Battle of Drury's Bluff May 14-16. Bermuda Hundred May 16-28. Moved to White House, thence to Cold Harbor May 28-June 1. Battles about Cold Harbor June 1-12. Before Petersburg June 15-18. Siege of Petersburg June 16-September 17. Mine Explosion, Petersburg, July 30 (Reserve). Embarked for North Carolina September 17, arriving at Morehead City and Carolina City September 21, and duty there till December 5. Non-Veterans left front October 21, and mustered out at Trenton, N. J., December 7, 1864. Moved to Newberne, N. C., December 5, thence to Plymouth, N. C. Expedition to Williamston December 9-14. Expedition up the Roanoke December 22-24. At Plymouth, N. C., till January 7. Expedition to Hard's Island February 1-5 (Cos. "B," "E," "H" and "I"). Moved to Carolina City January 7, and duty there till March 4. Campaign of the Carolinas March 1-April 26. Advance on Kinston March 4-14. Battle of Wise's Forks March 8-10. Occupation of Kinston March 14, and garrison there till March 19. Occupation of Goldsboro March 21. Provost duty at Goldsboro till April 10. Advance on Raleigh April 10-14. Occupation of Raleigh April 14. Bennett's House April 26. Surrender of Johnston and his army. At Raleigh till May 2, and at Greensboro till July. (Co. "G" at Charlotte and Co. "I" guard duty at Salisbury.) Mustered out at Greensboro, N. C., July 12, 1865.

Regiment lost during service 7 Officers and 89 Enlisted men killed and mortally wounded and 3 Officers and 163 Enlisted men by disease. Total 262.

10th REGIMENT INFANTRY.

Organized at Beverly, N. J., October 9, 1861, under authority of the War Department, as the "Olden Legion," Left State for Washington, D. C., December 26, 1861. Transferred to State of New Jersey, reorganized and designated 10th Infantry January 29, 1862. Attached to Wadsworth's Command, Military District of Washington, D. C., to February, 1863. District of Washington, D. C., 22nd Army Corps, to April, 1863. 3rd Brigade, 1st Division, 7th Army Corps, Dept. of Virginia, to July, 1863. Philadelphia, Pa., Dept. of the Susquehanna, to September, 1863. Pottsville, Pa., Dept. of the Susquehanna, to November, 1863. Sub-District of Carbon, Dept. of the Susquehanna, to April, 1864. 1st Brigade, 1st Division, 6th Army Corps, Army of the Potomac and Army of the Shenandoah, to July, 1865.

SERVICE.—Provost duty at Washington, D. C., till April, 1863. Ordered to Suffolk, Va., April 12. Siege of Suffolk, Va., April 16-May 4. Edenton Road April 24. Siege of Suffolk raised May 4. Ordered to Washington, D. C., thence to Philadelphia, Pa., and duty there till September, 1863. On provost duty at Pottsville, Pa., till October, and guard fords of the Potomac at and near Shepherdstown till November. At Mauch Chunk, Pa., Sub-District of Carbon, November, 1863, to April, 1864. Ordered to join Army of the Potomac in the field. Campaign from the Rapidan to the James May 3-June 15. Battles of the Wilderness, Va., May 5-7; Spottsylvania May 8-12; Spottsylvania Court House May 12-21. Assault on the Salient, "Bloody Angle," May 12. North Anna River May 23-26. On line of the Pamunkey May 26-28. Totopotomoy May 28-31. Cold Harbor June 1-12. Before Petersburg June 17-July 9. Jerusalem Plank Road June 22-23. Moved to Washington, D. C., July 9-11. Repulse of Early's attack on Fort Stevens and the Northern Defences of Washington July 11-12. Pursuit of Early to Snicker's Gap, Va., July 14-23. Action at Snicker's Ferry July 17-18. Sheridan's Shenandoah Valley Campaign August 7-November 28. Strasburg August 14-16. Winchester August 17. Point Pleasant August 21. Battle of Winchester September 19. Fisher's Hill September 22. Battle of Cedar Creek October 19. Duty in the Shenandoah Valley till December. Moved to Washington, D. C., thence to Petersburg, Va. Siege of Petersburg December, 1864, to April 2, 1865. Dabney's Mills, Hatcher's Run, February 5-7, 1865. Appomattox Campaign March 28-April 9. Assault on and fall of Petersburg April 2. Pursuit of Lee April 3-9. Appomattox Court House April 9. Surrender of Lee and his army. March to Danville April 23-27, and duty there till March 18. March to Richmond, Va., thence to Washington, D. C., May 18-June 3. Corps Review June 8. Mustered out at Hall's Hill, Va., June 22, 1865.

Regiment lost during service 2 Officers and 91 Enlisted men killed and mortally wounded and 3 Officers and 187 Enlisted men by disease. Total 283.

11th REGIMENT INFANTRY.

Organized at Camp Olden, Trenton, N. J., and mustered in August 15, 1862. Left State for Washington, D. C., August 25, 1862. Attached to Whipple's Command, Defences of Washington, D. C., to November, 1862. 1st Brigade, 2nd Division, 3rd Army Corps, Army of the Potomac, to March, 1864. 1st Brigade, 4th Division, 2nd Army Corps, to May, 1864. 3rd Brigade, 3rd Division, 2nd Army Corps, to July, 1865.

SERVICE.—Duty in the Defences of Washington, D. C., till November 16, 1862. March to Falmouth, Va., November 16-27. Duty near Falmouth, Va., November 28-December 11. Battle of Fredericksburg, Va., December 12-15. At Falmouth, Va., till April 27, 1863. "Mud March" January 20-24. Chancellorsville Campaign April 27-May 6. Battle of Chancellorsville May 1-5. Gettysburg (Pa.) Campaign June 11-July 24. Battle of Gettysburg July 1-3. Pursuit of Lee July 5-24. Wapping Heights, Va., July 23. Duty near Warrenton till October. Bristoe Campaign October 9-22. McLean's Ford October 15. Advance to line of the Rappahannock November 7-8. Kelly's Ford November 7. Mine Run Campaign November 26-December 2. Payne's Farm November 27. Duty near Brandy Station to May, 1864. Demonstration on the Rapidan February 6-7. Campaign from the Rapidan to the James May 3-June 15. Battles of the Wilderness May 5-7; Spottsylvania May 8-12; Spottsylvania Court House May 12-21. Assault on the Salient, "Bloody Angle," May 12. Harris Farm, Fredericksburg Road, May 19. North Anna River May 23-26. Ox Ford May 23-24. On line of the Pamunkey May 26-28. Totopotomoy May 28-31. Cold Harbor June 1-12. Before Petersburg June 16-18. Siege of Petersburg June 16, 1864, to April 2, 1865. Jerusalem Plank Road June 22-23, 1864. Demonstration north of the James July 27-29. Deep Bottom July 27-28. Demonstration north of the James August 13-20. Strawberry Plains, Deep Bottom, August 14-18. Ream's Station August 25. Poplar Springs Church September 29-October 2. Yellow House October 2-5. Boydton Plank Road, Hatcher's Run, October 27-28. Forts Hascall and Morton November 5. Expedition to Weldon Railroad December 7-12. Dabney's Mills, Hatcher's Run, February 5-7, 1865. Watkins House March 25. Appomattox Campaign March 28-April 9. Boydton and White Oak Roads March 30-31. Crow's House March 31. Fall of Petersburg April 2. Pursuit of Lee April 3-9. Sailor's Creek April 6. High Bridge, Farmville, April 7. Appomattox Court House April 9. Surrender of Lee and his army. March to Washington, D. C., May 2-12. Grand Review May 23. Mustered out near Washington, D. C., June 6, 1865. Veterans and recruits transferred to 12th New Jersey Infantry.

Regiment lost during service 11 Officers and 131 Enlisted men killed and mortally wounded and 107 Enlisted men by disease. Total 249.

12th REGIMENT INFANTRY.

Organized at Camp Stockton, Woodbury, N. J., and mustered in September 4, 1862. Left State for Baltimore, Md., September 7, 1862. Attached to Defences of Baltimore, Md. Unattached, 8th Army Corps, Middle Dept., to December, 1862. 2nd Brigade, 3rd Division, 2nd Army Corps, Army of the Potomac, to March, 1864. 3rd Brigade, 2nd Division, 2nd Army Corps, to July, 1865.

SERVICE.—Guard duty at Ellicott's Mills, Md., September 8-December 10, 1862. Moved to Washington, D. C., December 10, thence to join Army of the Potomac December 13-17, reporting at Falmouth, Va., December 20. Duty there till April 27, 1863. Chancellorsville Campaign April 27-May 6. Battle of Chancellorsville May 1-5. Gettysburg (Pa.) Campaign June 11-July 24 Battle of Gettysburg July 1-3. Pursuit of Lee to Manassas Gap July 5-24. Duty on Orange & Alexandria

Railroad till September 12. Advance from the Rappahannock to the Rapidan September 13-17. Picket duty on the Rapidan till October. Bristoe Campaign October 9-22. Auburn and Bristoe October 14. Advance to line of the Rappahannock November 7-8. Mine Run Campaign November 26-December 2. Mine Run November 28-30. At Stevensburg till May, 1864. Demonstration on the Rapidan February 6-7. Morton's Ford February 6-7. Campaign from the Rapidan to the James May 3-June 15. Battles of the Wilderness May 5-7; Laurel Hill May 8; Spottsylvania May 8-12; Po River May 10; Spottsylvania Court House May 12-21. Assault on the Salient, "Bloody Angle," May 12. North Anna River May 23-26. On line of the Pamunkey May 26-28. Totopotomoy May 28-31. Cold Harbor June 1-12. Before Petersburg June 16-18. Siege of Petersburg June 16, 1864, to April 2, 1865. Jerusalem Plank Road June 22-23, 1864. Demonstration north of the James July 27-29. Deep Bottom July 27-28. Demonstration north of the James August 13-20. Strawberry Plains, Deep Bottom, August 14-18. Ream's Station August 25. Boydton Plank Road, Hatcher's Run, October 27-28. Dabney's Mills, Hatcher's Run, February 5-7, 1865. Watkins House March 25. Appomattox Campaign March 28-April 9. Boydton and White Oak Roads March 30-31. Fall of Petersburg April 2. Pursuit of Lee April 3-9. Sailor's Creek April 6. High Bridge, Farmville, April 7. Appomattox Court House April 9. Surrender of Lee and his army. March to Washington, D. C., May 2-12. Grand Review May 23. Duty at Washington, D. C., till July. Mustered out at Washington, D. C., July 15, 1865.

Regiment lost during service 9 Officers and 168 Enlisted men killed and mortally wounded and 99 Enlisted men by disease. Total 276.

13th REGIMENT INFANTRY.

Organized at Camp Frelinghuysen, Newark, N. J., and mustered in August 25, 1862. Left State for Washington, D. C., August 31, 1862. Attached to 3rd Brigade, 2nd Division, 2nd Corps, Pope's Army of Virginia, September, 1862. 3rd Brigade, 1st Division, 12th Army Corps, Army of the Potomac, to October, 1863, and Army of the Cumberland, to April, 1864. 2nd Brigade, 1st Division, 20th Army Corps, Army of the Cumberland and Army of Georgia, to June, 1865.

SERVICE.—Camp near Fort Richardson, on Arlington Heights, Va., September 2, 1862. Expedition beyond Rockville, Md., September 6-9. Battle of Antietam, Md., September 16-17. At Maryland Heights September 23-October 30. Picket duty near Sharpsburg, Md., October 30-December 10. March to Fairfax Station, Va., December 10-16, and duty there till December 26. Picket duty on the Occoquan January 4-20. "Mud March" January 20-24. At Fairfax Station till April 27. Chancellorsville Campaign April 27-May 6. Battle of Chancellorsville May 1-5. Gettysburg (Pa.) Campaign June 11-July 24. Battle of Gettysburg July 1-3. Pursuit of Lee to Manassas Gap, Va., July 5-24. Picket duty at Kelly's Ford July 31-August 15, and at Raccoon Ford to September 24. Movement to Stevenson, Ala., September 24-October 4. Guard Nashville & Chattanooga Railroad till April, 1864. Atlanta (Ga.) Campaign May 1-September 8, 1864. Demonstration against Rocky Faced Ridge May 8-11. Battle of Resaca May 14-15. Near Cassville May 19. Advance on Dallas May 22-25. New Hope Church May 25. Battles about Dallas, New Hope Church and Allatoona Hills May 26-June 5. Operations about Marietta and against Kenesaw Mountain June 10-July 2. Pine Hill June 11-14. Lost Mountain June 15-17. Gilgal or Golgotha Church June 15. Muddy Creek June 17. Noyes Creek June 19. Kolb's Farm June 22. Assault on Kenesaw June 27. Ruff's Station, Smyrna Camp Ground, July 4. Chattahoochie River July 5-17. Peach Tree Creek July 19-21. Siege of Atlanta July 22-August 25. Operations at Chattahoochie River Bridge August 26-September 2. Occupation of Atlanta September 2-November 15. March to the sea November 15-December 10. Sandersville November 26. Montieth

Swamp December 9. Siege of Savannah December 10-21. Campaign of the Carolinas January to April, 1865. Brigade train guard January 17-27. Division train guard to February 10. Occupation of Columbia February 16-17. Occupation of Fayetteville, N. C., March 11. Averysboro March 16. Battle of Bentonville March 19-21. Occupation of Goldsboro March 24. Advance on Raleigh April 10-14. Occupation of Raleigh April 14. Bennett's House April 26. Surrender of Johnston and his army. March to Washington, D. C., via Richmond, Va., April 29-May 19. Grand Review May 24. Mustered out near Washington, D. C., June 8, 1865.

Regiment lost during service 3 Officers and 71 Enlisted men killed and mortally wounded and 44 Enlisted men by disease. Total 118.

14th REGIMENT INFANTRY.

Organized at Camp Vredenburg near Freehold, N. J., and mustered in August 26, 1862. Left State for Baltimore, Md., September 2, 1862. Attached to Defences of Baltimore, Md., 8th Army Corps, Middle Department, to January, 1863. 3rd Separate Brigade, 8th Army Corps, to June, 1863. 3rd Provisional Brigade, French's Division, 8th Army Corps, to July, 1863. 1st Brigade, 3rd Division, 3rd Army Corps, Army of the Potomac, to March, 1864. 1st Brigade, 3rd Division, 6th Army Corps, Army of the Potomac and Army of the Shenandoah, to June, 1865.

SERVICE.—Duty near Monocacy, Md., guarding railroad bridges and other points on the Upper Potomac, till June, 1863. Moved to Harper's Ferry, W. Va., and duty there and at Maryland Heights till June 30. Moved to Frederick, Md., June 30, and to Monocacy July 2. Pursuit of Lee July 6-24. Manassas Gap, Va., July 20. Wapping Heights July 23. Duty on line of the Rappahannock and Rapidan till October. Bristoe Campaign October 9-22. Advance to line of the Rappahannock November 7-8. Kelly's Ford November 7. Brandy Station November 8. Mine Run Campaign November 26-December 2. Payne's Farm November 27. Mine Run November 28-30. Demonstration on the Rapidan February 6-7, 1864. Campaign from the Rapidan to the James May 3-June 15. Battles of the Wilderness May 5-7; Spottsylvania May 8-12; Spottsylvania Court House May 12-21. Assault on the Salient, "Bloody Angle," May 12. North Anna River May 23-26. On line of the Pamunkey May 26-28. Totopotomoy May 28-31. Hanovertown May 30-31. Cold Harbor June 1-12. Before Petersburg June 17-July 9. Jerusalem Plank Road June 22-23. Moved to Baltimore, thence to Frederick, Md., July 6-8. Battle of Monocacy July 9. Expedition to Snicker's Gap July 14-23. Sheridan's Shenandoah Valley Campaign August 7-November 28. Battle of Winchester September 19. Fisher's Hill September 22. Battle of Cedar Creek October 19. Duty in the Shenandoah Valley till December. Moved to Washington, D. C., thence to Petersburg, Va., December 3-6. Siege of Petersburg December 6, 1864, to April 2, 1865. Dabney's Mills, Hatcher's Run, February 5-7, 1865. Fort Fisher, Petersburg, March 25. Appomattox Campaign March 28-April 9. Assault on and capture of Petersburg April 2. Pursuit of Lee April 3-9. Appomattox Court House April 9. Surrender of Lee and his army. March to Danville April 23-27, and duty there till May 18. Moved to Richmond, Va., thence to Washington, D. C., May 18-June 2. Corps Review June 8. Mustered out near Washington, D. C., June 18, 1865.

Regiment lost during service 8 Officers and 139 Enlisted men killed and mortally wounded and 110 Enlisted men by disease. Total 257.

15th REGIMENT INFANTRY.

Organized at Camp Fair Oaks, near Flemmington, N. J., and mustered in August 25, 1862. Left State for Washington, D. C., August 27, 1862. At Tennallytown, D. C., till September 30, constructing Fort Kearney. Attached to 1st Brigade, 1st Division, 6th Army Corps, Army of the Potomac, and Army of the Shenandoah, to June, 1865,

SERVICE.—Moved to Frederick, Md., September 30, 1862, thence to Bakerville and joined Army of the Potomac. Duty in Maryland till October 29. Movement to Falmouth, Va., October 29-November 19. Battle of Fredericksburg, Va., December 12-15. Duty near Falmouth, Va., till April 27, 1863. "Mud March" January 20-24. Chancellorsville Campaign April 27-May 6. Operations at Franklin's Crossing April 29-May 2. Battle of Maryes Heights, Fredericksburg, May 3. Salem Heights May 3-4. Banks' Ford May 4. Gettysburg (Pa.) Campaign June 11-July 24. Battle of Gettysburg, Pa., July 2-4. Pursuit of Lee to Manassas Gap, Va., July 5-24. Fairfield, Pa., July 5. At and near Funkstown, Md., July 10-13. In camp near Warrenton till September 15, and at Culpeper till October. Bristoe Campaign October 9-22. Advance to line of the Rappahannock November 7-8. Rappahannock Station November 7. Mine Run Campaign November 26-December 2. Duty at Brandy Station till May, 1864. Campaign from the Rapidan to the James May 3-June 15. Battles of the Wilderness May 5-7; Spottsylvania May 8-12; Spottsylvania Court House May 12-21. Assault on the Salient, "Bloody Angle," May 12. North Anna River May 23-26. On line of the Pamunkey May 26-28. Totopotomoy May 28-31. Cold Harbor June 1-12. Before Petersburg June 17-19. Siege of Petersburg till July 9. Jerusalem Plank Road June 22-23. Moved to Washington, D. C., July 9-11. Repulse of Early's attack on Fort Stevens and the northern defences of Washington, D. C., July 11-12. Pursuit of Early to Snicker's Gap July 14-23. Snicker's Ferry July 17-18. Sheridan's Shenandoah Valley Campaign August 7-November 28. Strasburg August 14-15. Cedar Creek August 15. Winchester August 17. Charlestown August 21-22. Battle of Winchester September 19. Fisher's Hill September 22. Battle of Cedar Creek October 19. Duty in the Shenandoah Valley till December. Moved to Washington, D. C., thence to Petersburg, Va., December. Siege of Petersburg December, 1864, to April 2, 1865. Dabney's Mills, Hatcher's Run, February 5-7, 1865. Appomattox Campaign March 28-April 9. Assault and capture of Petersburg April 2. Pursuit of Lee April 3-9. Appomattox Court House April 9. Surrender of Lee and his army. March to Danville April 23-27, and duty there till May 18. March to Richmond, Va., thence to Washington, D. C., May 18-June 3. Corps Review June 8. Mustered out at Hall's Hill, Va., June 22, 1865.

Regiment lost during service 8 Officers and 232 Enlisted men killed and mortally wounded and 1 Officer and 131 Enlisted men by disease. Total 372.

16th REGIMENT VOLUNTEERS.

See 1st Regiment Cavalry.

17th REGIMENT INFANTRY.

Failed to complete organization.

18th REGIMENT INFANTRY.

Failed to complete organization.

19th REGIMENT INFANTRY.

Failed to complete organization.

20th REGIMENT INFANTRY.

Failed to complete organization.

21st REGIMENT INFANTRY.

Organized at Trenton, N. J., and mustered in September 15, 1862. Left State for Washington, D. C., September 16, 1862, thence moved to Frederick, Md., September 19, and joined Army of the Potomac on battlefield of Antietam, Md. Attached to 3rd Brigade, 2nd Division, 6th Army Corps, Army of the Potomac, to June, 1863.

SERVICE.—Duty at Hagerstown, Md., and guard duty at Dam No. 5 till October 29. Movement to Falmouth, Va., October 29-November 19. Battle of Fredericksburg December 11-15. Cover laying of pontoons December 11. Bowling Green Road December 11 in support of Weirs' Maryland Battery. Duty near White Oak Church and constructing corduroy road below Fredericksburg till

April, 1863. "Mud March" January 20-24. Chancellorsville Campaign April 27-May 6. Operations at Franklin's Crossing April 29-May 2. Battle of Maryes Heights, Fredericksburg, May 3. Salem Heights May 3-4. Banks' Ford May 4. Mustered out at Trenton, N. J., June 19, 1863.

Regiment lost during service 1 Officer and 20 Enlisted men killed and mortally wounded and 1 Officer and 30 Enlisted men by disease. Total 52.

22nd REGIMENT INFANTRY.

Organized at Trenton, N. J., and mustered in September 22, 1862. Left State for Washington, D. C., September 29, 1862. Attached to Abercrombie's Provisional Brigade, Casey's Division, Defences of Washington, to December, 1862. Patrick's Command, Provost Guard, Army of the Potomac, to January, 1863. 3rd Brigade, 1st Division, 1st Army Corps, Army of the Potomac, to June, 1863.

SERVICE.—Duty in the Defences of Washington till November, 1862. Moved to Aquia Creek, Va., and duty there guarding railroad till January, 1863. Moved to Belle Plains and joined Army of the Potomac January 10, 1863. "Mud March" January 20-24. Duty at Belle Plains till April 27. Chancellorsville Campaign April 27-May 6. Operations at Pollock's Mill Creek April 29-May 2. Battle of Chancellorsville May 2-5. Ordered home for muster out June, reaching Trenton June 22. Mustered out June 22, 1863.

Regiment lost during service 1 Officer and 40 Enlisted men by disease. Total 41.

23rd REGIMENT INFANTRY.

Organized at Beverly, N. J., and mustered in September 13, 1862. Left State for Washington, D. C., September 26, thence moved to Frederick, Md. Attached to 1st Brigade, 1st Division, 6th Army Corps, Army of the Potomac, to June, 1863.

SERVICE.—March to Bakersville, Md., October 8, 1862, and join 1st New Jersey Brigade. At Bakersville, Md., till October 30. At New Baltimore November 9-16. Battle of Fredericksburg, Va., December 12-15. Duty near Falmouth, Va., till April 27, 1863. "Mud March" January 20-24. Chancellorsville Campaign April 27-May 6. Operations at Franklin's Crossing April 29-May 2. Battle of Maryes Heights, Fredericksburg, May 3. Salem Heights May 3-4. Banks' Ford May 4. Regiment volunteered for service before muster out during the Gettysburg (Pa.) Campaign, and moved to Harrisburg, Pa. Mustered out June 27, 1863.

Regiment lost during service 4 Officers and 31 Enlisted men killed and mortally wounded and 1 Officer and 54 Enlisted men by disease. Total 90.

24th REGIMENT INFANTRY.

Organized at Camp Cadwallader, Beverly, N. J., and mustered in September 16, 1862. Left State for Washington, D. C., September 30, 1862. Attached to District of Washington October, 1862. Provisional Brigade, Casey's Division, Defences of Washington, to December, 1862. 1st Brigade, 3rd Division, 2nd Army Corps, Army of the Potomac, to June, 1863.

SERVICE.—At Camp Ingham on East Capital Hill till October 14. At Camp Nixon near Chain Bridge till October 18. Picketing Leesburg Road and fatigue duty at Forts Ethan Allen and Marcy till October 25. At Camp Cumberland till December 1. March to Falmouth, Va., December 1-9. Battle of Fredericksburg, Va., December 12-15. At Camp Knight till January, 1863. At Camp Robertson till April 27. Chancellorsville Campaign April 27-May 6. Battle of Chancellorsville May 1-5. Mustered out at Beverly, N. J., June 29, 1863.

Regiment lost during service 3 Officers and 46 Enlisted men killed and mortally wounded and 53 Enlisted men by disease. Total 102.

25th REGIMENT INFANTRY.

Organized at Beverly, N. J., and mustered in Companies "A," "C," "E," "H" and "K" September 18, and Companies "B," "D," "F," "G" and "I" September 26, 1862. Left State for Washington, D. C., October 10,

1862. Attached to 2nd Brigade, Casey's Division, Defences of Washington, to December, 1862. 1st Brigade, 3rd Division, 9th Army Corps, Army of the Potomac, to February, 1863. 3rd Brigade, 3rd Division, 9th Army Corps, to April, 1863. 3rd Brigade, 2nd Division, 7th Army Corps, Dept. of Virginia, to June, 1863.

SERVICE.—Camp on East Capital Hill and picket at Fairfax Seminary till November 30. March to Aquia Creek, Va., November 30-December 8, thence to Falmouth, Va. Battle of Fredericksburg, Va., December 12-15. Camp near Falmouth till February 11, 1863. "Mud March" January 20-24. Moved to Newport News, Va., February 11, and duty there till March 13. Picket at Fort Jericho near Dismal Swamp till April 10. Siege of Suffolk April 11-May 4. Near Suffolk, Reed's Ferry, Nansemond Church Road May 3. Siege of Suffolk raised May 4. Constructing Fort New Jersey near Norfolk, Va., May 10 to June 4. Moved to Portsmouth June 4. At Camp Cadwallader, Beverly, N. J., June 8-20. Mustered out at Beverly, N. J., June 20, 1863.

Regiment lost during service 1 Officer and 19 Enlisted men killed and mortally wounded and 37 Enlisted men by disease. Total 57.

26th REGIMENT INFANTRY.

Organized at Camp Frelinghuysen, Newark, N. J., and mustered in September 18, 1862. Left State for Washington, D. C., September 26. Camp on Capital Hill till October 1. Moved to Frederick, Md., October 1, thence to Hagerstown, Md., October 11. Attached to 2nd Brigade, 2nd Division, 6th Army Corps, Army of the Potomac. At Hagerstown, Md., till October 31. Movement to Falmouth, Va., October 31-November 19. Battle of Fredericksburg, Va., December 12-15. At Falmouth, Va., till April 27. "Mud March" January 20-24. Chancellorsville Campaign April 27-May 6. Operations at Franklin's Crossing April 29-May 2. Battle of Maryes Heights, Fredericksburg, May 3. Salem Heights May 3-4. Banks' Ford May 4. Franklin's Crossing June 5-13. Reached Washington, D. C., June 17. Mustered out at Newark, N. J., June 27, 1863.

Regiment lost during service 1 Officer and 14 Enlisted men killed and mortally wounded and 21 Enlisted men by disease. Total 36.

27th REGIMENT INFANTRY.

Organized at Camp Frelinghuysen, Newark, N. J., and mustered in September 3, 1862. Left State for Washington, D. C., October 9, 1862. At East Capital Hill till October 29 and near Alexandria, Va., till December 1. Attached to 2nd Brigade, Casey's Division, Defences of Washington, D. C., to December, 1862. 2nd Brigade, 1st Division, 9th Army Corps, Army of the Potomac, to March, 1863, and Army of the Ohio, to June, 1863.

SERVICE.—Moved to Fredericksburg December 1-10. Battle of Fredericksburg, Va., December 12-15. "Mud March" January 20-24, 1863. Moved to Newport News, Va., February 11-13, thence to Suffolk, Va., March 18, and to Lexington and Nicholasville, Ky., March 19-28. Operations against Pegram's forces till May. Expedition to Monticello April 25-May 8. Monticello May 1. Camp near Somerset till June 3. Moved to Hickman's Bridge, thence to Cincinnati, Ohio, June 15. Volunteered services in Pennsylvania during Lee's invasion of that state, after term had expired. On duty at Wheeling, W. Va., and at Pittsburg, Pa., and vicinity till June 26. Moved to Harrisburg, Pa., June 26, thence to New Jersey and mustered out July 2, 1863.

Regiment lost during service 1 Officer and 93 Enlisted men by disease. Total 94.

28th REGIMENT INFANTRY.

Organized at Freehold and mustered in September 15, 1862. Left State for Washington, D. C., October 2, 1862. Attached to Provisional Brigade, Casey's Division, Defences of Washington, October to December, 1862. 1st Brigade, 3rd Division, 2nd Army Corps, Army of the Potomac, to June, 1863. Duty in the Defences of Washington, D. C., October 3 to December 1, 1862. March

to Falmouth, Va., December 1-9. Battle of Fredericksburg, Va., December 12-15. At Falmouth, Va., till April 27, 1863. Chancellorsville Campaign April 27-May 6. Battle of Chancellorsville May 1-5. Mustered out July 6, 1863.

Regiment lost during service 51 Enlisted men killed and mortally wounded and 1 Officer and 31 Enlisted men by disease. Total 84.

29th REGIMENT INFANTRY.

Organized at Freehold, N. J., and mustered in September 20, 1862. Left State for Washington, D. C., September 28, 1862. Attached to Abercrombie's Provisional Brigade, Casey's Division, Defences of Washington, to December, 1862. Patrick's Command, Provost Guard, Army of the Potomac, to January, 1863. 3rd Brigade, 1st Division, 1st Army Corps, Army of the Potomac, to June, 1863.

SERVICE.—Duty in the Defences of Washington, D. C., till November, 1862. Moved to Aquia Creek, Va., and duty there guarding railroad till January, 1863. Moved to Belle Plain, Va., and joined Army of the Potomac January 10, 1863. "Mud March" January 20-24. Duty at Belle Plain till April 27. Chancellorsville Campaign April 27-May 6. Operations at Pollock's Mill Creek April 29-May 2. Battle of Chancellorsville May 2-5. Ordered home for muster out June. Mustered out July 6, 1863.

Regiment lost during service 1 Enlisted man killed and 39 Enlisted men by disease. Total 40.

30th REGIMENT INFANTRY.

Organized at Flemmington, N. J., and mustered in September 17, 1862. Left State for Washington, D. C., September 30, 1862. Attached to Abercrombie's Provisional Brigade, Casey's Division, Defences of Washington, to December, 1862. Patrick's Command, Provost Guard, Army of the Potomac, to January, 1863. 3rd Brigade, 1st Division, 1st Army Corps, Army of the Potomac, to June, 1863.

SERVICE.—Duty in the Defences of Washington, D. C., till November, 1862. Moved to Aquia Creek, Va., and duty there guarding railroad till January, 1863. Moved to Belle Plain, Va., and joined Army of the Potomac January 10, 1863. "Mud March" January 20-24. Duty at Belle Plain till April 27. Chancellorsville Campaign April 27-May 6. Operations at Pollock's Mill Creek April 29-May 2. Battle of Chancellorsville May 2-5. Ordered home for muster out June. Mustered out June 27, 1863.

Regiment lost during service 2 Officers and 62 Enlisted men by disease. Total 64.

31st REGIMENT INFANTRY.

Organized at Flemmington, N. J., and mustered in September 17, 1862. Left State for Washington, D. C., September 26, 1862. Attached to Abercrombie's Provisional Brigade, Casey's Division, Defences of Washington, to December, 1862. Patrick's Command, Provost Guard, Army of the Potomac, to January, 1863. 3rd Brigade, 1st Division, 1st Army Corps, Army of the Potomac, to June, 1863.

SERVICE.—Duty in the defences of Washington till November, 1862. Moved to Aquia Creek, Va., and duty there guarding railroad till January, 1863. Moved to Belle Plain, Va., and joined Army of the Potomac January 10, 1863. "Mud March" January 20-24. Duty at Belle Plain till April 27. Chancellorsville Campaign April 27-May 6. Operations at Pollock's, Mill Creek, April 29-May 2. Battle of Chancellorsville May 2-5. Ordered home for muster out June. Mustered out June 24, 1863.

Regiment lost during service 39 Enlisted men by disease.

32nd REGIMENT VOLUNTEERS.

See 2nd Cavalry.

33rd REGIMENT INFANTRY.

Organized at Newark, N. J., and mustered in September 3, 1863. Left State for Washington, D. C., September 8, 1863, thence moved to Warrenton, Va., September 13-19. Attached to 1st Brigade, 2nd Division, 11th Army Corps, Army of the Potomac, to October, 1863, and Army of the Cumberland to April, 1864. 2nd Brigade, 2nd Division, 20th Army Corps, Army of the Cumberland and Georgia, to July, 1865.

SERVICE.—Movement to Bridgeport, Ala., September 26-30, 1863, thence moved to mouth of Battle Creek, October 18, and duty there guarding bridges till November 4. Moved to Lookout Valley, Tenn., November 4-6. Chattanooga-Ringgold Campaign November 23-27. Orchard Knob November 23. Tunnel Hill November 24-25. Mission Ridge November 25. March to relief of Knoxville November 28-December 17. Duty in Alabama till May, 1864. Atlanta (Ga.) Campaign May 1-September 8. Demonstration on Rocky Faced Ridge May 8-11. Dug Gap or Mill Creek May 8. Battle of Resaca May 14-15. Near Cassville May 19. Advance on Dallas May 22-25. New Hope Church May 25. Battles about Dallas, New Hope Church and Allatoona Hills May 26-June 5. Operations about Marietta and against Kenesaw Mountain June 10-July 2. Pine Hill June 11-14. Lost Mountain June 15-17. Gilgal or Golgotha Church June 15. Muddy Creek June 17. Noyes Creek June 19. Kolb's Farm June 22. Assault on Kenesaw June 27. Ruff's Station, Smyrna Camp Ground, July 4. Chattahoochie River July 5-17. Peach Tree Creek July 19-20. Siege of Atlanta July 22-August 25. Operations at Chattahoochie River Bridge August 26-September 2. Occupation of Atlanta September 2-November 15. Expedition to Tuckum's Cross Roads October 26-29. Near Atlanta November 9. March to the sea November 15-December 10. Montieth Swamp December 9. Siege of Savannah December 10-21. Campaign of the Carolinas January to April, 1865. Averysboro, N. C., March 16. Battle of Bentonville March 19-21. Occupation of Goldsboro March 24. Advance on Raleigh April 10-14. Smithfield, N. C., April 11. Occupation of Raleigh April 14. Bennett's House April 26. Surrender of Johnston and his army. March to Washington, D. C., via Richmond, Va., April 29-May 19. Grand Review May 23-24. Mustered out at Washington, D. C., July 17, 1865.

Regiment lost during service 6 Officers and 72 Enlisted men killed and mortally wounded and 85 Enlisted men by disease. Total 163.

34th REGIMENT INFANTRY.

Organization commenced at Beverly, N. J. Company "A" mustered in September 3; Company "C" September 21, and Company "G" September 23, 1863. Transferred to Trenton, N. J., October 3, 1863, and Company "B" organized October 15; Company "D" October 6; Company "E" October 26; Company "F" October 8; Company "H" October 6; Company "I" October 20, and Company "K" November 9, 1863. Left State for Eastport, Miss., November 16, 1863. Attached to District of Columbus, Ky., 6th Division, 16th Army Corps, Dept. of the Tennessee, to August, 1864. District of Paducah, Ky., Dept. of the Ohio, to February, 1865. 3rd Brigade, 2nd Division, 16th Army Corps (New), Military Division West Mississippi, to August, 1865. District of Alabama, Dept. of the Gulf, to April, 1866.

SERVICE.—Moved from Eastport, Miss., to Columbus, Ky., December 12-20, 1863, thence to Union City, Tenn., December 20. Expedition to Huntington, Tenn., in pursuit of Forest December 22, 1863, to January 21, 1864. Garrison duty at Columbus, Ky., January 21 to August 28. Expedition to Riley's Landing February 17. Near Island No. 10 March 6. Scout from Island No. 10 to New Madrid March 18 (Co. "C"). Skirmishes at Columbus, Ky., March 27 and April 11-13. Hickman June 10. Expedition into the interior July 9-12. (Co. "C" on duty at Island No. 10 July and August.) Clinton July 10. Expedition to Uniontown, Ky., against Johnston and Adams August 15-25. Moved to Mayfield, Ky., August 28. Duty there and at Paducah, Ky., till December. Moved to Nashville, Tenn., December 25, thence to Eastport, Miss., January 11, 1865, and duty there till February 7. Moved to New Orleans, La., February 7-22.

Campaign against Mobile, Ala., and its defences March 17-April 12. Siege of Spanish Fort and Fort Blakely March 26-April 8. Assault and capture of Fort Blakely April 9. Occupation of Mobile April 12. March to Montgomery April 13-25, and provost duty there, at Montevallo, Talladega, Gainesville, Tuscaloosa and other points in Alabama till April, 1866. Mustered out April 10, 1866. Discharged at Trenton, N. J., April 30, 1866.

Regiment lost during service 3 Enlisted men killed and mortally wounded and 3 Officers and 164 Enlisted men by disease. Total 170.

35th REGIMENT INFANTRY.

Organized at Flemmington, N. J., and mustered in by Companies as follows: Company "A" August 28; Company "B" September 25; Company "C" September 15; Company "D" October 13; Companies "E" and "F" September 18; Company "G" September 21 at Freehold; Company "I" September 18, and Company "K" September 15, 1863. Left State for Washington, D. C., October 19, 1863. Attached to Provisional Brigade, Casey's Division, 22nd Army Corps, to November, 1863. District of Columbus, Ky., 6th Division, 16th Army Corps, Dept. of the Tennessee, to January, 1864. 1st Brigade, 4th Division, 16th Army Corps, to March, 1864. 2nd Brigade, 4th Division, 16th Army Corps, to September, 1864. 2nd Brigade, 1st Division, 17th Army Corps, to July, 1865.

SERVICE.—Duty in the Defences of Washington, D. C., till November, 1863. Moved to Eastport, Miss., November 9-28, thence to Columbus, Ky., and Union City, Tenn., December 12-20, and duty there till January 16, 1864. Moved to Columbus, Ky., thence to Vicksburg, Miss. Meridian Campaign February 3-March 2. Meridian February 9-13. Marion February 15-17. Meridian February 16. Operations in West Tennessee against Forest March 16-April 14. Atlanta (Ga.) Campaign May 1-September 8. Demonstrations on Resaca May 5-13. Sugar Valley, near Resaca, May 9. Near Resaca May 13. Battle of Resaca May 14-15. Advance on Dallas May 22-25. Operations on line of Pumpkin Vine Creek and battles about Dallas, New Hope Church and Allatoona Hills May 25-June 5. Operations about Marietta and against Kenesaw Mountain June 10-July 2. Assault on Kenesaw June 27. On line of Nickajack Creek July 2-5. Ruff's Mills July 3-4. Chattahoochie River July 5-17. Decatur July 19-22. Battle of Atlanta July 22. Siege of Atlanta July 22-August 25. Flank movement on Jonesboro August 25-30. Battle of Jonesboro August 31-September 1. Lovejoy Station September 2-6. At Eastpoint till October 4. Pursuit of Hood into Alabama October 4-26. March to the sea November 15-December 10. Siege of Savannah December 10-21. Campaign of the Carolinas January to April, 1865. Reconnoissance to Salkehatchie River January 20, 1865. River's and Broxton Bridges, Salkehatchie River, S. C., February 2. River's Bridge February 3. South Edisto River February 9. North Edisto River, Orangeburg, February 11-12. Columbia February 15-17. Cheraw March 3-4. Battle of Bentonville, N. C., March 20-21. Occupation of Goldsboro March 24. Advance on Raleigh April 10-14. Occupation of Raleigh April 14. Bennett's House April 26. Surrender of Johnston and his army. March to Washington, D. C., via Richmond, Va., April 29-May 19. Grand Review May 23. Moved to Louisville, Ky., June 5, and duty there till July. Mustered out July 20, 1865.

Regiment lost during service 1 Officer and 24 Enlisted men killed and mortally wounded and 2 Officers and 132 Enlisted men by disease. Total 159.

36th REGIMENT VOLUNTEERS.

See 3rd Cavalry.

37th REGIMENT INFANTRY.

Organized at Camp Delaware, Trenton, N. J., and mustered in June 23, 1864. Left State for City Point, Va., June 28. Siege operations against Petersburg and Richmond, Va., July 1 to September 26, 1864. Attached to 10th Army Corps, Unassigned, Army of the James, Dept. of Virginia, and North Carolina.

SERVICE.—Fatigue duty at Point of Rocks, Va., and at Redoubt Converse on Spring Hill, near Appomattox River, till August 28. Assigned to duty by detachments, at Broadway Landing, unloading vessels, at Corps Headquarters, with the Ambulance Corps. At Point of Rocks in charge of Commissary Department. Duty in trenches before Petersburg, Va., in rear of Hare House Battery August 28-September 25. Ordered to Trenton, N. J., September 26. Mustered out at Trenton, N. J., October 1, 1864.

Regiment lost during service 5 Enlisted men killed and mortally wounded and 1 Officer and 13 Enlisted men by disease. Total 19.

38th REGIMENT INFANTRY.

Organized at Trenton, N. J., and mustered in by Companies as follows: Company "A" September 22, Company "B" September 9, Company "C" September 10, Company "D" September 24, Company "E" October 1, Company "F" September 22, Company "G" September 27, Company "H" September 30, Company "I" September 12, and Company "K" September 15, 1864. Left State by detachments, Companies "B," "C," "I" and "K" September 20, 1864; Companies "A," "D" and "F" September 29, 1864, and Companies "E," "G" and "H" October 4, 1864, for City Point, Va. Attached to Separate Brigade, Army of the James, Dept. of Virginia and North Carolina, and assigned to garrison duty at Fort Powhatan, James River, till April, 1865. Moved to City Point and mustered out June 30, 1865.

Regiment lost 14 by disease during service.

39th REGIMENT INFANTRY.

Organized at Newark, N. J., October 3, 1864. Left State for City Point, Va., by detachments October 4-10, 1864. Attached to Benham's Engineer Brigade, City Point, Va., temporarily, October, 1864. 1st Brigade, 2nd Division, 9th Army Corps, Army of the Potomac, to June, 1865.

SERVICE.—Duty on breastworks at City Point, Va., October, 1864, then moved to Poplar Grove Church. Battle of Boydton Plank Road, Hatcher's Run, Va., October 27-28, 1864. Siege of Petersburg till April 2, 1865. Appomattox Campaign March 28-April 2, 1865. Assault on and capture of Petersburg April 2. Pursuit of Lee April 3-9. Appomattox Court House April 9. Surrender of Lee and his army. Moved to City Point, thence to Washington and Alexandria April 20-27. Grand Review May 23. Mustered out June 17, 1865.

Regiment lost during service 3 Officers and 29 Enlisted men killed and mortally wounded and 10 Enlisted men by disease. Total 42.

40th REGIMENT INFANTRY.

Organized at Trenton, N. J., February 2, 1865. Left State for Petersburg, Va., by Companies as follows: Company "A" mustered in October 24, 1864, left State October 24, 1864. Company "B" mustered in December 24, 1864, and January 12, 1865, left State December 24, 1864, and January 12, 1865. Company "C" mustered in January 21, 1865, and left State January 21, 1865. Company "D" mustered in January 27, and left State January 31, 1865. Company "E" mustered in February 2, and left State February 6, 1865. Company "F" mustered in February 9, and left State February 10, 1865. Company "G" mustered in February 16, and left State February 17, 1865. Company "H" mustered in February 22, and left State February 24, 1865. Company "I" mustered in March 2, and left State March 4, 1865. Company "K" mustered in March 10, and left State March 12, 1865. Each Company attached to 4th New Jersey Infantry, on arrival, till 6th Company, then assumed Regimental organization, and attached to 1st Brigade, 1st Division, 6th Army Corps. Siege operations against Petersburg December, 1864, to April, 1865. Dabney's Mills, Hatcher's Run, February 5-7, 1865. Appomattox Campaign March 28-April 9. Assault on and capture of Petersburg April 2. Pursuit of Lee April

3-9. Appomattox Court House April 9. Surrender of Lee and his army. March to Danville April 23-27, and duty there till May 18. March to Richmond, Va., thence to Washington, D. C., May 18-June 3. Corps Review June 8. Mustered out July 13, 1865.

Regiment lost during service 2 Enlisted men killed and 17 Enlisted men by disease. Total 19.

NEW MEXICO VOLUNTEERS.

1st REGIMENT CAVALRY.

Organized May 31, 1862, by consolidation of the 1st, 2nd, 4th and 5th Regiments of New Mexico Infantry. Attached to Dept. of New Mexico, and engaged in operations against Indians in New Mexico and Arizona, and on garrison duty by detachments, at Forts Stanton, Goodwin, McRae, Wingate, Craig, Canby, Sumner, Marcy, Bascom, Union, and other points in that Department, during entire term of service. Skirmishes at Jornado del Muerta June 16, 1863. Warm Springs, Fort McRae, June 20. Operations against Navajo Indians July 7-August 19. Rio Hondo July 18. Concha's Springs July 29 (1 Co.). Pueblo, Colorado, August 18 (3 Cos.). Scout from Fort Wingate to Jacob's Wells, Ojo Redondo, September 15-October 5. Riconde Mascaras December 11. Expedition against Navajo Indians January 6-21, 1864. Operations in New Mexico and Arizona February 1-March 7. Expedition from Fort Wingate to Gila and St. Francis Rivers May 27-July 13 (Cos. "B," "F"). Skirmishes on San Carlos River June 7 and 8 (Cos. "B," "F"). Scouts from Fort Sumner August 3-November 4 (Co. "L"). Skirmish Sacramento Mountains August 25 (Co. "L"). Expedition from Fort Craig to Fort Goodwin, Arizona, October 1-November 27 (Detachment). Scout in the Sacramento Mountains October 13-21 (Cos. "A," "L"). Expedition from Fort Wingate against Indians November 23-December 20. Engagement at St. Vrain's Old Fort, Adobe Fort on Canadian River, November 25. Skirmish Red River December 1. Hassayampa Creek December 15 (Co. "K"). Expedition against Indians in Central Arizona and skirmish at Sycamore Springs, Arizona, December 26, 1864-January 1, 1865. Expedition from Fort Wingate to Sierra del Datil January 2-10, 1865. Scout from Fort Wingate to Sierra del Datil January 11-21 (Detachment). Scout from Fort Sumner March 15-21. Scout from Fort Stanton April 12-25 (Cos. "A," "H"). Regiment mustered out September 30, 1866.

1st BATTALION CAVALRY AND INFANTRY.

Organized from 1st Cavalry August 31, 1866. Duty in the Department of New Mexico and Arizona till November, 1867. Mustered out November 23, 1867.

MINK'S INDEPENDENT CAVALRY COMPANY.

Organized at Santa Fe, N. M., July 20, 1861. Duty at Fort Craig, N. M., till October. Skirmish at Canada Alamosa September 25, 1861, and at Alamosa near Fort Craig October 4. Mustered out October 29, 1861.

GRAYDON'S INDEPENDENT CAVALRY COMPANY.

Organized at Fort Craig, N. M., and duty there till January, 1862. Mustered out January 29, 1862.

GRAYDON'S INDEPENDENT CAVALRY COMPANY— REORGANIZED.

Organized at Fort Craig, N. M., February 9, 1862. Action at Valverde, N. M., February 21. Duty at Fort Craig till April. Pursuit of Confederate forces April 13-22. Action at Albuqurque April 8. Mustered out April 29, 1862.

HASPELL'S INDEPENDENT CAVALRY COMPANY.

Organized at Albuqurque, N. M., July 23, 1861. Duty about Fort Craig till October. Skirmishes at Fort Craig August 23 and September 26. Mustered out October 30, 1861.

VIDAL'S INDEPENDENT CAVALRY COMPANY.

Organized at Santa Fe, N. M., July 12, 1861. Duty at Fort Craig, N. M., till October. Mustered out October 12, 1861.

1st REGIMENT INFANTRY.

Organized at Fort Union and Santa Fe, N. M., July 1 to August 13, 1861. Duty at Fort Union till February, 1862. Action at Valverde, N. M., February 21. Pursuit of Confederate forces April 13-22. Duty in Central Northern and Santa Fe Districts till May, 1862. Consolidated with 2nd Infantry, to form 1st New Mexico Cavalry May 31, 1862.

1st REGIMENT INFANTRY—REORGANIZED.

Organized October 1, 1863. Attached to Department of New Mexico and on garrison duty by detachments at Forts Union, Selden, Craig, Bowie, Cummings, McRae, Goodwin and other points in that Department during entire term of service. (Co. "K" at Fort Lyon, Colo., September, 1864, to February, 1865.) Expedition from Fort Craig, N. M., to Fort Goodwin, Ariz., May 16 to August 2, 1864 (Co. "I"). Expedition to Pinal Mountains July 18-August 17, 1864 (Detachment Co. "I"). Expedition to Pinal Creek August 1-5, 1864. Expedition from Fort Craig to Fort Goodwin, Ariz., October 1-November 27, 1864. Mustered out November 7, 1866.

1st REGIMENT MILITIA INFANTRY.

Organized in New Mexico at large November, 1861. Mustered out February, 1862.

2nd REGIMENT INFANTRY.

Organized at Santa Fe., N. M., July and August, 1861. Attached to Dept. of Mexico. Duty at Fort Craig, N. M., till February, 1862. Action at Valverde, N. M., February 21, 1862. Pursuit of Confederate forces April 13-22. Action at Peralta April 15, and at Socorro April 25. Duty in Central, Northern and Santa Fe Districts till May. Consolidated with 1st New Mexico Infantry to form 1st New Mexico Cavalry May 31, 1862.

3rd REGIMENT INFANTRY (MOUNTED).

Organized at Fort Union and Albuquerque, N. M., August 30-October 10, 1861. Duty at Fort Union till February, 1862. Action at Valverde, N. M., February 21. Pursuit of Confederate forces April 13-22. Duty in Central, Northern and Santa Fe Districts till May. Mustered out May 31, 1862.

4th REGIMENT INFANTRY.

Organized at Fort Union, N. M., September, 1861. Duty at Fort Union till February, 1862. Action at Valverde February 21. Engagement at Glorietta or Pigeon Ranch March 28. Pursuit of Confederate forces April 13-22. Duty in Central, Northern and Santa Fe Districts till May. Mustered out May 31, 1862.

5th REGIMENT INFANTRY.

Organized at Albuquerque, N. M., November, 1861. Duty at Albuquerque till February, 1862. Action at Valverde February 21. Engagement at Glorietta or Pigeon Ranch March 28. Duty in Central, Northern and Santa Fe Districts till May, 1862. Mustered out May 31, 1862.

PEREA'S BATTALION MILITIA.

Organized at large November and December, 1861, for the defence of New Mexico. Mustered out February 28, 1862.

ALARID'S INDEPENDENT COMPANY MILITIA.

Organized at Santa Fe, N. M., December 10, 1861, for the defence of New Mexico. Mustered out February 28, 1862.

GONZALES' INDEPENDENT COMPANY MILITIA.

Organized at Fort Craig, N. M., November 23, 1861, for the defence of New Mexico. Mustered out February 28, 1862.

MORA INDEPENDENT COMPANY MILITIA.

Organized at Mora, N. M., November 14, 1861, for the defence of New Mexico. Mustered out February 28, 1862.

TAFOLLA'S INDEPENDENT COMPANY MILITIA.

Organized at Fort Craig, N. M., November 20, 1861, for the defence of New Mexico. Mustered out February 28, 1862.

NEW YORK VOLUNTEERS.

1st REGIMENT ("LINCOLN") CAVALRY.

"Carbine Rangers," "1st U. S. Vol. Cavalry," "Sabre Regiment." Organized at New York City July 16-August 31, 1861. Left State for Washington, D. C., by Detachments, July 31-September 7, 1861. Attached to Defences of Washington and Alexandria to October 4, 1861. Franklin's and Heintzelman's Divisions, Army of the Potomac, to March 24, 1862. Cavalry, 1st Division, 1st Army Corps, Army of the Potomac, to April, 1862. 1st Division, Dept. of the Rappahannock, to May, 1862. Cavalry, 6th Army Corps, Army of the Potomac, to July 8, 1862. 1st Cavalry Brigade, Army of the Potomac, to September, 1862. 4th Brigade, Cavalry Division, Army of the Potomac, to October, 1862. Averill's Cavalry Command, 8th Army Corps, Middle Dept., to November, 1862. Defences Upper Potomac, 8th Army Corps, Middle Dept., to January, 1863. Milroy's Command, Winchester, Va., 8th Army Corps, to February, 1863. 1st Brigade, 2nd Division, 8th Army Corps, February, 1863. 3rd Brigade, 2nd Division, 8th Army Corps, to June, 1863. Pierce's Brigade, Dept. of the Susquehanna, to August, 1863. McReynolds' Cavalry Brigade, Dept. of West Virginia, to November, 1863. Cavalry Brigade, 1st Division, Army of West Virginia, to April, 1864. 1st Brigade, 1st Cavalry Division, Army of West Virginia, to June, 1864. 2nd Brigade, 1st Cavalry Division, Army of West Virginia, to July, 1864. 1st Brigade, 1st Cavalry Division, Army of West Virginia, to August, 1864. 2nd Brigade, 2nd Cavalry Division, Army of West Virginia, to December, 1864. 3rd Brigade, 3rd Division, Cavalry Corps, Middle Military Division and Army Potomac, to March, 1865. 3rd Brigade, 3rd Division, to June, 1865.

SERVICE.—Duty in the Defences of Washington, D. C., till March, 1862. Scout to Accotink August 18, 1861. Skirmish at Pohick Church August 18 (Co. "C"). Reconnoissance to Pohick Church and Accotink River November 12 (Cos. "B," "C" and "G"). Occoquan November 12 (Co. "G"). Fairfax Court House November 27. Annandale Church December 2. Sangster's Station March 9, 1862. Burke Station March 10. Moved to the Virginia Peninsula. (Co. "E" detached as escort to wagon trains on the Peninsula.) Siege of Yorktown April 5-May 4. West Point May 7. Mechanicsville May 22. Hanover C. H. May 27. Fair Oaks May 31-June 1. Hanover C. H. June 13. Oak Grove June 25. Seven days before Richmond June 25-July 1. Mechanicsville June 26. Gaines Mill and Garnett's Farm June 27. Garnett's and Golding's Farms June 28. Savage Station and Willis Church June 29. White Oak Swamp June 30. Glendale June 30. Malvern Cliff June 30. Malvern Hill July 1. Cold Harbor July 1. Crew's Farm, Carter's Hill, July 2. Gum Run Swamp July 3. Long Bridge Road July 9. Harrison's Landing July 31. Stevensburg, Raccoon Ford and Brandy Station August 20. Cacapon Bridge, Md., September 6. Seneca Creek September 6. Hyattstown September 9-10. Frederick City September 12. Emmettsburg September 13-15. Antietam September 16-17. Williamsport September 19. Near Shepherdstown September 20. Blue's Gap, W. Va., October 2 and 4. Hanging Rock October 2. Cacapon Bridge October 4. Hanging Rock October 4. North River Mills, South Branch, October 6. Cacapon Bridge October 6. White's Ford October 10. Hanging Rock October 17. South Branch October 18. Springfield October 27. North River Mills October 29. French's Store October 29. Occoquan Ferry November 4. Pughstown November 5. Lockhart's Gap November 6. Paw Paw Tunnel November 6. Moorefield, South Fork Potomac, November 9 (Detachment). Romney Bridge November 10. Near Springfield November 15. Near Winchester November 22 and December 4. Darkesville December

11. Bunker Hill December 12. Charlestown December 25. Woodstock January 7, 1863. Newtown and Strasburg January 17. Devil's Hole January 26. Millwood February 6. Near Winchester February 9. Woodstock February 15. Kernstown and Strasburg February 26. Snicker's Ferry April 13. Berry's Ferry and Front Royal April 13. Paris April 14. Mansfield April 17. Millwood April 21. Moorefield April 27. Scout in Hampshire County, W. Va., May 4-9. Scout from Snicker's Ferry May 12-14. Upperville May 13. Middleburg May 13. Berry's Ferry May 16. Upperville May 28. Berryville June 5. Piedmont June 8. Goose Creek June 9. Near White Post and Millwood June 13. Berryville and Bunker Hill June 13. Opequan Creek, near Winchester, June 13. Martinsburg June 14. Winchester June 14-15. Milroy's retreat June 15-July 1. Williamsport, Md., June 15. Hancock June 16. Greencastle, Pa., June 20 and 22. Shippensburg June 23. Near Harper's Ferry June 23. Cashtown June 25. Carlisle June 25-26. Harper's Ferry June 26-27. Near Kingston June 27. McConnellsburg, Pa., June 29. Hancock, Md., June 29. Keedysville June 29. Near Kingston June 29. Near Arendtsville June 30. Near Fayette and near Carlisle July 1. Near McConnellsburg July 2. Near Bendersville, Quaker Vale and Falling Water July 3. Cranstown and Frederick City July 4. Cunningham Cross Roads July 5. Near Greencastle, Pa., July 5 (Detachment). Waynesboro July 6. Waterloo July 6. Antietam Creek July 8. Williamsport July 10. Sharpsburg July 12. Bendersville July 14. Pine Grove Furnace July 16. Shepherdstown July 17 and 23. Mount Rock July 22. Martinsburg July 23. Bull Run Mountain and near Winchester August 14. Smithfield August 21. Berryville August 22. Leesburg September 1. Expedition from Martinsburg September 2-23. Bloomer's Gap September 2. Middletown September 5. Near Winchester September 9. Smithfield September 15-16 and 19. Strasburg September 19. Back Creek Valley October 14. Hedgesville October 15. Berryville October 17. Charlestown October 18. Summit Point October 27. Winchester October 31. Newtown November 6. Expedition to New Market November 15-18. Woodstock and Edenburg November 16. Mt. Jackson November 16. Middletown November 17. Edenburg November 18. Wells' Demonstration from Kanawha Valley December 10-24. Mt. Jackson December 12. Near Strasburg December 13. Harrisonburg December 15. Mt. Jackson December 20. Regiment re-enlisted January 1, 1864. Scout to Woodstock, Va., January 23-25. Newtown and Woodstock January 23. Mechanicsburg Gap February 2. Moorefield February 4. Front Royal February 8. Charlestown February 10. Moorefield February 11. Upperville February 20. Custer's Raid into Albemarle County February 28-March 1 (Detachment). Near Charlottesville February 29. Stannardsville March 1. Cablestown March 10. Winchester April 19-20. Near Middletown and New Market April 24 (Detachment). Sigel's Expedition from Martinsburg to New Market April 30-May 16. Upperville May 1. Near Berryville May 6. Upperville May 7. Millwood May 9. Brock's Gap May 10. Woodstock, Luray Gap and near New Market May 13. Rude's Hill May 14. New Market May 14-15. Burnt Bridge May 15. Paris May 16. Salem May 17. Hunter's Raid to Lynchburg May 26-July 1. New Market May 26. Woodstock May 31. Harrisonburg June 2. Piedmont June 5. Occupation of Staunton June 6. Near Staunton June 8. Waynesboro June 10. Lexington June 13. Buchanan June 14. New London June 17. Diamond Hill June 17. Lynchburg June 17-18. Liberty June 19. Buford's Gap June 20. Catawba Mountains June 21. Salem June 21. Leetown June 26. Charlestown and Big Sewell Mountain June 27. Leetown July 3. Martinsburg July 3. Williamsport July 5. Frederick City July 8. Ashby's Gap July 9. White's Ford July 14. Harper's Ferry July 15. Lovettsville and Hillsboro July 15. Purcellville July 16. White's Ford and Snicker's Ferry July 17-18. Ashby's Gap July 18-19. Near Kernstown July 23. Kernstown, Winchester, July 24. Bunker Hill and Martinsburg July 25. Bloomer's Gap July 27.

Sheridan's Shenandoah Valley Campaign August 7-November 28. Moorefield August 7. Strasburg August 15. Leetown and Berryville August 16. Martinsburg August 19. Charlestown August 21. Bolivar Heights August 23. Falling Waters August 24. Halltown August 26. Williamsport August 26. Martinsburg August 31. Stephenson's Depot September 1. Buckletown September 1-3. Darkesville, near Bunker Hill, and Martinsburg, September 2. Bunker Hill September 2-3. Darkesville September 3. Stephenson's Depot September 5. Darkesville September 10. Bunker Hill September 13. Near Berryville September 14. Burnt Factory September 17. Martinsburg September 18. Opequan, Winchester, September 19. Strasburg September 21. Fisher's Hill September 22. Woodstock September 23. Mt. Jackson September 23-24. Forest Hill or Timberville September 24. Harrisonburg September 25. Brown's Gap September 26. Weyer's Cave September 26-27. Luray Valley October 2-3. Rapidan River October 5. Big Springs October 7. Milford October 9. White Post October 14. Cedar Creek October 19. Dry Run October 23. Milford October 25-26. Rood's Hill November 1. Newtown and Nineveh November 12. Rood's Hill November 22. Dicksville December 9. Raid to Gordonsville December 19-28. Liberty Mills December 21. Jack's Shop, near Gordonsville, December 23. Near Ashby's Gap December 27. Sheridan's Raid from Winchester February 27-March 25, 1865. Mt. Crawford February 28. Occupation of Staunton March 2. Waynesboro March 2. Haydensville March 12. Beaver Dam Station March 15. White House March 23. Appomattox Campaign March 28-April 9. Dinwiddie Court House March 29-31. Five Forks April 1. Namozine Church April 3. Jettersville April 4. Amelia Court House April 5. Farmville April 5-6. Sailor's Creek April 6. Stony Point April 7. Appomattox Station April 8. Appomattox Court House April 9. Surrender of Lee and his army. Movement to North Carolina April 23-29. March to Washington, D. C., May. Grand Review May 23. Mustered out June 27, 1865, and honorably discharged from service.

Regiment lost during service 5 Officers and 43 Enlisted men killed and mortally wounded and 1 Officer and 119 Enlisted men by disease, etc. Total 168.

1st REGIMENT VETERAN CAVALRY.

Organized at Geneva, N. Y., and mustered in: Company "A" July 31, 1863; Company "B" September 8, 1863; Companies "C" to "K" at Elmira, N. Y., October 10, 1863; Company "L" November 7, 1863, and Company "M" November 19, 1863. Moved to Washington, D. C., as fast as mustered, and duty in the defences of that city to February, 1864. Attached to Cavalry Division, 22nd Army Corps, Dept. of Washington, to February, 1864. Cavalry Brigade, 1st Division, Army of West Virginia, to April, 1864. 1st Brigade, 1st Cavalry Division, Army of West Virginia, to July, 1864. 2nd Brigade, 1st Cavalry Division, Army of West Virginia, to August, 1864. Remount Camp at Cumberland, Md., to October, 1864. 1st Separate Brigade, District of the Kanawha, Dept. of West Virginia, to March, 1865. Cavalry, Dept. of West Virginia, to July, 1865.

SERVICE.—Action near Upperville, Va., February 20, 1864. Snickersville March 6. Kablestown March 10. Sigel's Expedition from Martinsburg to New Market April 30-May 16. Near Paris and Salem May 10. Mt. Jackson May 13. New Market May 15. Hunter's Raid on Lynchburg May 26-July 1. Woodstock May 28. Newtown May 29-30. Woodstock May 31. New Market June 1. Harrisonburg June 3-4. Piedmont June 5. Occupation of Staunton June 6. Waynesboro June 10. Cheat Mountain June 11. Lexington June 13. Buchanan June 14. Diamond Hill June 17. Lynchburg June 17-18. Liberty June 19. Buford's Gap June 20. Catawba Mountains and Salem June 21. White Sulphur Springs June 25. Bunker Hill June 28 and July 2. Near Martinsburg July 2. Leetown and Martinsburg July 3. Sharpsburg, Md., July 4. Sandy Hook July 6. Near Hillsboro July 15-16. Snicker's Ferry July 17-18.

Ashby's Gap and Berry's Ford July 19. Charlestown July 22. Near Kernstown July 23. Kernstown, Winchester, July 24. Bunker Hill and Martinsburg July 25. Duffield Station August 3. Cedar Creek August 12. Berryville August 16. Near Charlestown August 21-22. Falling Waters August 24. Duty at Remount Camp, Cumberland, Md., till November. Operations in Kanawha Valley against Witcher November 5-12. Newtown and Nineveh November 12. Rude's Hill, near Mt. Jackson, November 22. Duty in District of the Kanawha and in the Shenandoah Valley till July, 1865. Mustered out July 20, 1865, and honorably discharged from service.

Regiment lost during service 4 Officers and 56 Enlisted men killed and mortally wounded and 1 Officer and 89 Enlisted men by disease, etc. Total 150.

1st REGIMENT MOUNTED RIFLES.

(Sometimes designated 7th New York Cavalry.) First organized at New York City as a Squadron of two Companies, "A" and "B," for duty in the Dept. of Virginia, and mustered in at Fortress Monroe, Va., July 30, 1861. Companies "C" and "D" organized at Newburg, N. Y., and mustered in September 18 and October 16, 1861. Companies "E," "F," "G" and "H" organized at New York City and mustered in June to August, 1862. Companies "I," "K," "L" and "M" organized August and September, 1862. Companies "A" and "B" left State for Fortress Monroe, Va., July, 1861; "C" and "D" December 6, 1861; "E," "F," "G" and "H" August, 1862, and "I," "K," "L" and "M" September 19, 1862. Attached to District of Fortress Monroe, Dept. of Virginia, to May, 1862. Unattached, Dept. of Virginia, to July, 1862. Unattached, Division at Suffolk, Va., 7th Army Corps, Dept. of Virginia, to April, 1863. Cavalry, 7th Army Corps, Dept. of Virginia, to July, 1863. Cavalry Brigade, U. S. Forces, Portsmouth, Va., Dept. of Virginia and North Carolina, to October, 1863. U. S. Forces, Yorktown, Va., Dept. of Virginia and North Carolina, to January, 1864. Cavalry Brigade and Wistar's Division, 18th Army Corps, Dept. of Virginia and North Carolina, to April, 1864. Unattached Cavalry, Army of the James, to July, 1864. Cavalry Brigade, Dept. of Virginia and North Carolina, to October, 1864. 3rd Brigade, Kautz's Cavalry Division, Dept. of Virginia and North Carolina, to March, 1865. Headquarters, Dept. of Virginia, to April, 1865. District of Eastern Virginia, Dept. of Virginia, to July, 1865.

SERVICE.—Duty at Fortress Monroe and at Camp Hamilton, Va., till May, 1862. Action in Hampton Roads, Newport News, March 8-9, 1862, between "Monitor" and "Merrimac." Howard's Bridge April 4 (Cos. "A" and "B"). Near Lee's Mills April 5 (Cos. "A" and "B"). Tranter's Creek, Norfolk, Va., May 10. Suffolk, Va., May 14. Reconnoissance to Edenton, N. C., May 27-31. Hertford, N. C., June 30. Duty at Suffolk, Va., till June, 1863. Smithfield July 10, 1862. South Mills September 4. Zuni September 15. Blackwater September 28. Blackwater near Zuni October 4. Zuni October 20 and 25. Near Franklin October 31. Zuni November 3. Providence Church November 12. Blackwater Bridge and Zuni November 14. Zuni Bridge November 15. Near Carrsville November 17. Franklin November 18. Zuni November 25. South Quay December 7. Zuni near Blackwater December 8 and 11-13. Joyner's Ford December 12. Isle of Wight Court House December 22. Providence Church Road December 28. Ely's House near Providence Church January 9, 1863. Burnt Ordinary January 11. Jacksonville, N. C., January 20. Deserted House January 30. Edenton, N. C., February 7. Reconnoissance from Suffolk March 7-9. Chuckatuck March 7. Near Windsor March 9. Blackwater Bridge March 31. Siege of Suffolk April 11-May 4. South Quay Road April 11. Edenton, Providence Church and Somerton Roads April 12-13. Edenton Road April 15. Providence Church Road, Chuckatuck and Reed's Ferry May 3. Lake Drummond May 4. Blackwater Bridge May 12. Near Suffolk and Carrsville May 16. Scott's Mills May 17. Near Blackwater,

Windsor Road, May 18. Antioch and Barber's Cross Roads May 23. Blackwater Bridge May 31. South Mills June 8. South Quay Road June 12. Camden, N. C., July 5. Currituck July 12 and 22. Raid to destroy railroad at Weldon July 25-August 2. Jackson July 28. Expedition from Portsmouth to Edenton, N. C., August 11-19. Edenton August 15. Pasquotank August 18. Expedition from Williamsburg to Bottom's Bridge August 26-29. Barhamsville, Slatersville, New Kent Court House, Crump's Cross Roads and Bottom's Bridge August 29. Expedition to Matthews County October 4-9. Near Williamsburg November 8. Charles City Cross Roads November 16. Expedition to Charles City Court House December 12-14. Charles City Court House December 13. New Kent Court House January 19, 1864. Scouting from Williamsburg January 19-24. Wistar's Expedition toward Richmond February 6-8. Bottom's Bridge February 7. Expedition from Yorktown to New Kent Court House in aid of Kilpatrick March 1-4. White House March 2. Expedition into King and Queen County March 9-12. Belleroy March 9. Carlton's Store March 10. Matthews County Court House March 25. Expedition from Williamsburg April 27-29. Twelve Mile Ordinary April 27. Twelve Mile Ordinary April 28. Butler's operations on south side of James River and against Richmond and Petersburg May 4-28. Chester Station, Port Walthall Junction, May 7. Swift Creek or Arrowfield Church May 8-10. Proctor's Creek May 11. Operations against Fort Darling May 12-16. Wier Bottom Church May 12. Clover Hill Junction May 14. Drury's Bluff May 14-16. Petersburg & Richmond Railroad May 16. Bottom's Church May 17. Bermuda Hundred May 18-26. Walthall Junction June 2. West Point June 5. Petersburg June 8-10. Assaults on Petersburg June 15-18. Siege operations against Petersburg and Richmond June 16, 1864, to March 27, 1865. Deep Bottom June 23, 1864. Surrey Court House July 11. Richmond & Petersburg Railroad July 21. Deep Bottom July 27-29. Strawberry Plains August 14-18. Cox's Mills September 16. Chaffin's Farm September 29-October 1. Darbytown Road October 13 and 16. Fair Oaks October 27-28. Cone's Creek December 21. White Oak Swamp February 5, 1865. Expedition from Fort Monroe to Fredericksburg March 5-8. Expedition from Fort Monroe into Westmoreland County March 11-13. Williamsburg March 11. Near Windsor March 12. Near New Kent Court House March 17. Seven Pines March 18. White House March 19. Expedition from Deep Bottom to near Weldon, N. C., March 28-April 11. Weldon Railroad April 4. Murfreesboro, N. C., April 5. Somerton April 7. Near Jackson April 17. Duty at Fredericksburg, Va., Dept. of Va., till July. Mustered out by consolidation with 3rd New York Cavalry, July 21, 1865, to form 4th Provisional Cavalry.

Regiment lost during service 2 Officers and 30 Enlisted men killed and mortally wounded and 3 Officers and 124 Enlisted men by disease, etc. Total 159.

1st REGIMENT DRAGOONS—19th CAVALRY.

Organized at Portage, N. Y., as 130th Infantry and mustered in September 2, 1862. Left State for Suffolk, Va., September 6, 1862. Attached to Provisional Brigade, Peck's Division at Suffolk, 7th Army Corps, Dept. of Virginia, to October, 1862. Spinola's Brigade, Peck's Division at Suffolk, 7th Army Corps, to December, 1862. Gibbs' Brigade, Peck's Division at Suffolk, 7th Army Corps, to January, 1863. Terry's Brigade, Peck's Division at Suffolk, 7th Army Corps, to April, 1863. Terry's Brigade, Corcoran's 1st Division, 7th Army Corps, to June, 1863. 1st Brigade, 1st Division, 7th Army Corps, to July, 1863. Provost Marshal General's Command, Army of the Potomac, to August, 1863. Designation of Regiment changed to 19th Cavalry August 11, 1863, and to 1st Dragoons September 10, 1863. Reserve Cavalry Brigade, 1st Division, Cavalry Corps, Army of the Potomac, to March, 1864. 3rd (Reserve) Brigade, 1st Division, Cavalry Corps, Army of the Potomac, and Army of the Shenandoah, to September, 1864. 2nd Brigade, 1st Division, Cavalry Corps, Army of the Shenandoah and Army Potomac, to June, 1865.

SERVICE.—Duty at Suffolk, Va., till May, 1863. Expedition from Suffolk December 1-3, 1862. Action on the Blackwater near Franklin December 2. Reconnoissances from Suffolk to Blackwater December 23 and 28. Near Suffolk and at Providence Church December 28. Expedition toward Blackwater January 8-10, 1863. Deserted House January 30. Siege of Suffolk April 12-May 4. South Quay Road, Suffolk, April 17. Suffolk April 19. Nansemond River May 3. Siege of Suffolk raised May 4. South Quay Road June 12. Franklin June 14. Blackwater June 16-17. Dix's Peninsula Campaign June 24-July 7. Expedition from White House to South Anna River July 1-7. Baltimore Cross Roads July 4. Ordered to Washington, D. C. Ashby's Gap July 19. Advance from the Rappahannock to the Rapidan September 13-17. Between Centreville and Warrenton September 22. Manassas Junction October 17. Bristoe Station October 18. Buckland Mills October 18-19. Advance to line of the Rappahannock November 7-8. Culpeper Court House November 20. Mine Run Campaign November 26-December 2. Demonstration on the Rapidan February 6-7, 1864. Barnett's Ford February 6-7. Rapidan Campaign May-June, 1864. Wilderness May 5-7. Todd's Tavern May 7-8. Spottsylvania May 8. Sheridan's Raid to James River May 9-24. Davenport Bridge, North Anna River, May 10. Yellow Tavern and Ground Squirrel Bridge May 11. Fortifications of Richmond, and Meadow Bridge May 12. On line of the Pamunkey May 26-28. Hanovertown May 27. Haw's Shop May 28. Totopotomoy May 28-31. Old Church and Mattadequi Creek May 30. Cold Harbor May 31-June 6. Sheridan's Travillian Raid June 7-24. Trevillian Station June 11-12. Newark or Mallory's Ford Cross Roads June 12. White House or St. Peter's Church June 21. Black Creek or Tunstall's Station June 21. Jones' Bridge June 23. Charles City Court House June 24. Before Petersburg and Richmond June 27-July 30. Demonstration north of the James River July 27-29. Deep Bottom July 27-28. Malvern Hill July 28. Sheridan's Shenandoah Valley Campaign August 7-November 28. Shephardstown August 8. Near Stone Chapel, Berryville Pike, August 10. Toll Gate near White Post and Newtown August 11. Cedar Creek August 12. Cedarville August 13 and 16. Summit Point August 21. Near Kearneysville and Shephardstown August 25. Leetown and Smithfield August 28. Smithfield Crossing, Opequan Creek, August 29. Bunker Hill September 13. Sevier's Ford, Opequan Creek, September 15. Battle of Opequan, Winchester, September 19. Middletown and Strasburg September 20. Fisher's Hill September 21. Near Edenburg September 23. Front Royal, Mt. Jackson, September 23-24. New Market September 24. Port Republic September 26-27. McGaugheysville September 28. Mt. Crawford October 2. Tom's Brook, "Woodstock Races," October 8-9. Hupp's Hill near Strasburg October 14. Battle of Cedar Creek October 19. Fisher's Hill October 20. Liberty Mills October 22. Berryville October 28. Near White Post November 1. Near Kernstown November 11. Newtown November 12. Cedar Creek November 19. Expedition from Winchester into Fauquier and Loudoun Counties November 28-December 3. Bloomfield November 29. Expedition to Gordonsville December 19-28. Liberty Mills December 21. Jack's Shop December 22. Near Gordonsville December 23. Sheridan's Raid from Winchester February 27-March 25, 1865. Occupation of Staunton March 2. Action at Waynesboro March 2. Near Charlottesville March 3. Goochland Court House March 11. Appomattox Campaign March 28-April 9. Dinwiddie Court House March 30-31. Five Forks April 1. Scott's Cross Roads April 2. Deep Creek April 3. Tabernacle Church or Beaver Pond Creek April 4. Sailor's Creek April 6. Appomattox Station April 8. Appomattox Court House April 9. Surrender of Lee and his army. Expedition to Danville April 23-29. March to Washington, D. C., May. Grand Review May 23. Mustered out June 30, 1865, and honorably discharged from service.

Regiment lost during service 4 Officers and 126 Enlisted men killed and mortally wounded and 1 Officer and 130 Enlisted men by disease, etc. Total 261.

1st REGIMENT PROVISIONAL CAVALRY.

Organized June 17, 1865, by consolidation of 10th and 24th Regiments New York Cavalry. Mustered out July 19, 1865.

2nd REGIMENT CAVALRY—"HARRIS LIGHT."

Organized August 9 to October 8, 1861, by order of War Department. Regiment designated 7th United States Cavalry October 26, 1861. This being in excess of number provided for by Act of Congress, Regiment was designated 2nd New York Volunteer Cavalry or "Harris Light Cavalry."

Left New York for Washington, D. C., September 18, 1861. Attached to McDowell's Division, Army of the Potomac, to March, 1862. King's 3rd Division, 1st Army Corps, Army of the Potomac, and Department of the Rappahannock, to June, 1862. Bayard's Cavalry Brigade, 3rd Corps, Army of Virginia, to September, 1862. Bayard's Cavalry Brigade, Army of the Potomac, to December 15, 1862. (Cos. "A," "B," "I" and "K" with 3rd Division, 1st Army Corps, Army of the Potomac, September and October, 1862.) Gregg's Cavalry Brigade, Army of the Potomac, to February 11, 1863. 1st Brigade, 3rd Division, Cavalry Corps, Army of the Potomac, to June 14, 1863. (A Battalion at Yorktown, Va., Unattached, 4th Army Corps, Dept. of Virginia, June, 1863. 1st Brigade, 1st Division, 4th Army Corps, Dept. of Virginia, to July, 1863. King's Division, 22nd Army Corps, to August, 1863.) 2nd Brigade, 2nd Division, Cavalry Corps, Army of the Potomac, to August 12, 1863. 1st Brigade, 3rd Division, Cavalry Corps, to August, 1864. 1st Brigade, 3rd Division, Cavalry Corps, Army of the Shenandoah, Middle Military Division, to March, 1865, and Army of the Potomac, to June, 1865.

SERVICE.—Duty in the Defences of Washington, D. C., till March, 1862. Advance on Manassas, Va., March 10-16. Advance on Falmouth, Va., April 3-18. Falmouth April 17 and 19. Near Fredericksburg May 5. Bowling Green Road May 11. Flipper's Orchard July 4. Expedition from Fredericksburg to Hanover Junction July 19-20. Beaver Dam Station July 20. Reconnoissance to James City July 22-24. Mt. Carmel Church July 23. Expedition to Frederick's Hall Station August 5-8. Thornburg or Massaponax Church August 5-6. Orange Court House August 8. Battle of Cedar Mountain August 9. Pope's Campaign in Northern Virginia August 16-September 2. Near Rapidan Station August 18. Brandy Station August 20. Fords of the Rappahannock August 21-23. Kelly's Ford August 21. Catlett's Station August 22. Culpeper August 23. Waterloo Bridge August 23. Sulphur Springs August 24. Manassas Junction August 26. Thoroughfare Gap August 28. Groveton August 29. Bull Run August 30. Germantown August 31. Centreville and Chantilly August 31. Little River Turnpike September 1. South Mountain, Md., September 14. Goose Creek September 17. Reconnoissance to Leesburg September 16-19 (6 Cos.). Action at Leesburg September 17. Warrenton September 29. Dumfries October 5. Hazel River October 7. Aldie and Mountsville October 31. Sudley Church November 3. New Baltimore, Salem, Warrenton and Upperville November 4. Rappahannock Station November 8-9. Aldie November 25. Stafford Court House December 7. Fredericksburg December 12-15. Rappahannock Station April 14, 1863. Warrenton April 16. Rappahannock Station April 19. Stoneman's Raid April 27-May 8. Louisa Court House May 2. Ashland and Hanover Station May 3. Glen Allen May 4. Aylett's May 5. King and Queen Court House May 6. Centreville May 6. Morrisville May 10. Expedition from Gloucester into Matthews County May 19-20 (Detachment). Falmouth June 1. Brandy Station June 3. Beverly Ford and Brandy Station June 9. Aldie June 17. Middleburg June 19. Upperville June 21. Rockville, Md., June 28. (Dix's Peninsula Campaign June 24-July 7, Battalion.) Cooksville June 29. Battle of

Gettysburg, Pa., July 1-3. Monterey Gap July 4. Smithburg July 5. Emmettsburg July 5. Hagerstown and Williamsport July 6. Boonsborough July 8. Funkstown July 9. Jones' Cross Roads July 10-13. Hagerstown July 11-13. Williamsport July 14. Falling Waters July 14. Berryville July 16. Bristerburg July 27. Fairfax August 3. Thoroughfare Gap August 5. Near Aldie August 12-14. U. S. Ford August 22. Expedition to Port Conway September 1-3. Lamb's Creek September 1. Advance from the Rappahannock to the Rapidan September 13-17. Culpeper Court House September 13. Somerville Ford September 14. Robertson's Ford September 16. U. S. Ford September 17. Culpeper September 19. Madison Court House September 21. White's Ford and Liberty Mills September 21-22. Scout to Hazel River September 27-28. Hazel Run October 2. Hazel River October 6. Culpeper October 7. Bristoe Campaign October 9-22. James City, Robertson's River and Bethesda Church October 10. Near Culpeper October 11. Brandy Station October 11-12. Gainesville October 14. Groveton October 17-18. Haymarket, Buckland's Mills and New Baltimore October 19. Catlett's Station November 4. Advance to line of the Rappahannock November 7-8. Stevensburg November 7. Hartwood Church November 15. Germania Ford November 18. Mine Run Campaign November 26-December 2. Morton's Ford November 26. New Hope Church November 27. Robertson's Tavern November 29. Germania Ford December 2. Raccoon Ford December 5. Somerville December 18. Kelly's Ford January 12, 1864. Ellis Ford January 17. Stevensburg January 19. Ely's Ford January 19. Kilpatrick's Raid to Richmond February 28-March 3. Beaver Dam and Frederick's Hall Station and South Anna Bridge February 29. Defences of Richmond March 1. Old Church and King and Queen March 2. Near Walkertown March 2 (Detachment. Dahlgren killed). Near Tunstall Station March 3 (Detachment). New Kent Court House and Stevensville March 3. Carrollton's Store March 11. Rapidan Campaign May-June. Craig's Meeting House May 5. Todd's Tavern May 5-6. Wilderness May 6-7. Alsop's Farm, Spottsylvania, May 8. Sheridan's Raid to James River May 9-24. North Anna River May 9-10. Ground Squirrel Church and Yellow Tavern May 11. Brooks' Church or fortifications of Richmond May 12. Strawberry Hill May 12. Polecat Station May 23. Demonstration on Little River May 26. Totopotomoy May 28-31. Hanover Court House May 29-30. Mechump's Creek May 31. Cold Harbor June 1-12. Totopotomoy and Gaines' Mill June 2. Haw's Shop June 3. Via's House June 3. Old Church June 10-11. Bethesda June 11. Riddell's Shop and Long Bridge June 12. Malvern Hill June 14. Smith's Store near St. Mary's Church June 15. Wilson's Raid to south side and Danville Railroad June 22-30. Black and White Station and Nottoway Court House June 23. Sapponay Church or Stony Creek June 28. Ream's Station June 29-30 and July 3. Sheridan's Shenandoah Valley Campaign August 7-November 28. Near Winchester August 17. Summit Point, Charlestown, August 21. Near Kearneysville August 25. Waynesboro September 2. Berryville September 4. Near Winchester September 9. Abram's Creek September 13. Battle of Opequan, Winchester, September 19. Near Cedarville September 20. Fisher's Hill September 21. Front Royal Pike September 21. Milford September 22. Staunton September 26. Waynesboro September 29. Mt. Crawford September 30. Bridgewater and Woodstock October 2. Brock's Gap October 6. New Market October 7. Fisher's Hill October 8. Tom's Brook, "Woodstock Races," October 8-9. Cedar Run October 13. Battle of Cedar Creek October 19 and November 7. Nineveh November 12. Mt. Jackson November 22. Hood's Hill November 23. Expedition from Kernstown to Moorefield November 28-December 2. Moorefield December 3. Expedition to Lacy Springs December 19-22. Lacy Springs December 21. Mt. Jackson December 21. Sheridan's Raid from Winchester February 27-March 25, 1865. Occupation of Staunton March 2. Action at Waynesboro March 2. Charlottesville March 3. Ashland March 15. Appomattox

Campaign March 28-April 9. Dinwiddie Court House March 30-31. Five Forks April 1. Fall of Petersburg April 2. Namozine Church April 3. Sailor's Creek April 6. Appomattox Station April 8. Appomattox Court House April 9. Surrender of Lee and his army. Expedition to Danville April 23-29. March to Washington, D. C., May. Grand Review May 23. Mustered out June 5 and honorably discharged from service June 23, 1865.

Regiment lost during service 9 Officers and 112 Enlisted men killed and mortally wounded and 1 Officer and 235 Enlisted men by disease. Total 357.

2nd REGIMENT VETERAN CAVALRY—"EMPIRE LIGHT CAVALRY."

Organized at Saratoga Springs, N. Y., and mustered in by Companies as follows: "A" August 15, "B" and "F" August 25, "C" September 9, "D" and "E" September 8, "G" October 10, "H" October 16, "I" and "K" November 10, "L" December 3, and "M" at Cavalry Depot, Washington, D. C., December 30, 1863. Left State by detachments for Washington, D. C., August to December, 1863. Attached to Cavalry Division, 22nd Army Corps. to February, 1864. 5th Brigade, Cavalry Division, 19th Army Corps, Department of the Gulf, February 15 to June, 1864. 4th Brigade, Cavalry Division, Dept. of the Gulf, to August, 1864. Separate Cavalry Brigade, Dept. of the Gulf, to December, 1864. Separate Cavalry Brigade, Reserve Division, Military Division West Mississippi, to February, 1865. Separate Cavalry Brigade, District of West Florida, to March, 1865. 1st Brigade, Lucas' Cavalry Division, Military Division West Mississippi, to April, 1865. 3rd Brgade, 1st Cavalry Division, Dept. of the Gulf, to July, 1865. District of Alabama, Dept. of the Gulf, to November, 1865.

SERVICE.—Duty in the Defences of Washington, D. C., till February, 1864. Ordered to Dept. of the Gulf February, 1864. Red River Campaign March 10-May 22. Advance from Franklin to Alexandria March 14-26. Monett's Ferry and Cloutiersville March 29-30. Natchitoches March 31. Campti April 4. Sabine Cross Roads April 8. Pleasant Hill April 9. Bayou Saline April 14. Natchitoches April 19. About Cloutiersville April 22-24. Cane River Crossing April 23. Bayou Roberts May 3. Near Wilson's Landing May 4-5. Well's and Moore's Plantations May 6. Retreat to Morganza May 13-20. Mansura May 16. Near Moreauville May 17. Bayou de Glaze May 18. Simsport May 18. Expedition from Morganza to the Atchafalaya River May 29-June 6. Bayou Fordyce Road May 29. Livonia May 30. Bayou Grosse Tete June 1-3. Near Morganza June 24. Franklin July 18. Atchafalaya River July 27. Morgan's Ferry Road and Atchafalaya River July 28. Marinquin Bayou August 9. Rosedale August 10. Expedition to Clinton August 23-29. Morgan's Ferry, on Atchafalaya River, August 28 (Detachment). Expedition from Morganza to Fausse River September 13-17. Bayou Maringowen September 13 and 16. Rosedale September 15. Bayou Alabama and Morgan's Ferry September 20. St. Francisville October 4. Bayou Rara October 5. Fausse River October 16. McLeod's Mills November 10. Clinton and Liberty Creek, Miss., November 15. Davidson's Expedition from Baton Rouge against Mobile & Ohio Railroad November 27-December 13. State Line, Pascagoula River, Miss., November 27. Expedition to Morgan's Ferry December 13-14. Expedition from Atchafalaya River December 16-19. Expedition from Morganza to New Roads January 31, 1865. Scouts to Fausse River and Grosse Tete Bayou February 7-10 (Detachment). Moved to Barrancas, Fla., February, 1865. March to Fort Blakely, Ala., March 20-April 1. College Hill, Fla., March 21. Pine Barren Creek March 23. Canoe Creek or Bluff Springs March 25. Bluff Springs March 25. Pollard, Ala., March 26. Siege operations against Fort Blakely April 1-9. Expedition from Blakely to Claiborne April 9-17. Near Mt. Pleasant April 11. Grierson's Raid through Alabama and Georgia April 17-30. Duty in District of Alabama till November. Mustered out at Talladega, Ala., November 8, 1865.

Regiment lost during service 5 Officers and 29 Enlisted men killed and mortally wounded and 3 Officers and 212 Enlisted men by disease. Total 249.

2nd REGIMENT MOUNTED RIFLES.

Organized at Lockport and Buffalo, N. Y., and mustered in by Companies as follows "A" October 31, "I" November 2, 1863; "B" January 12, "C" January 26, "D" January 27, "E" January 29, "L" January 29, "F" and "G" February 5, "H" February 4, "K" February 6 and "M" February 13, 1864. Moved to Washington, D. C., March 4, 1864, thence to Belle Plains, Va. Attached to 22nd Army Corps, Dept. of Washington, D. C., to May 15, 1864. Provisional Brigade, 1st Division, 9th Army Corps, Army of the Potomac, to June 1, 1864. 3rd Brigade, 1st Division, 9th Army Corps, June, 1864. 1st Brigade, 2nd Division, 9th Army Corps, to September, 1864. 2nd Brigade, 2nd Division, 9th Army Corps, to November 16, 1864. 3rd Brigade, 2nd Division, Cavalry Corps, Army of the Potomac, to May, 1865. Dept. of Virginia to August, 1865.

SERVICE.—Rapidan Campaign May 15-June 12, 1864. Spottsylvania Court House May 15-21. North Anna River May 23-26. On line of the Pamunkey May 26-28. Totopotomoy May 28-31. Hanover Court House May 31. Cold Harbor June 1-12. Bethesda Church June 3. Before Petersburg June 16-18. Siege of Petersburg June 16, 1864, to April 2, 1865. Mine Explosion, Petersburg, July 30, 1864. Weldon Railroad August 18-21. Poplar Springs Church September 29-October 2. Pegram's Farm October 4. Boydton Plank Road, Hatcher's Run, October 27-28. Regiment mounted November 16, 1864. Stony Creek Station December 1. Raid on Weldon Railroad, known as Warren's Hicksford Raid, December 7-12. Bellefield, Hatcher's Run, December 9-10. Dabney's Mills, Hatcher's Run, February 5-7, 1865. Appomattox Campaign March 28-April 9. Dinwiddie Court House March 30-31. Five Forks April 1. Namozine Church April 3. Jettersville April 4. Amelia Springs and Jarrett's Station April 5. Sailor's Creek, Harper's Farm, Gravelly Run and Deatonville Road April 6. Farmville April 7. Pamplin Station April 8. Appomattox Court House April 9. Surrender of Lee and his army. Expedition to Danville to co-operate with Gen. Sherman April 23-29. Provost duty in Sub-District of the Appomattox, District of the Nottaway, Dept. of Virginia, till August. Mustered out August 10, 1865.

Regiment lost during service 8 Officers and 94 Enlisted men killed and mortally wounded and 1 Officer and 112 Enlisted men by disease. Total 215.

2nd REGIMENT PROVISIONAL CAVALRY.

Organized by consolidation of the 6th and 15th Regiments New York Cavalry June 17, 1865. Mustered out at Louisville, Ky., August 9, 1865.

3rd REGIMENT ("VAN ALLEN") CAVALRY.

Regiment organized by Companies as follows: "A" at Rochester July 17, "E" at Syracuse July 30, "C" at Rochester August 4, "D" at Albany August 12, "E" at Elmira August 22, "F" at Rochester August 20, "G" at Boonville August 21, "H" at Rochester August 27, "I" at Syracuse August 27, "K" organized as Company "G," 13th New York Infantry, at Elmira, N. Y., May 14 (attached August 23); "L" at Cincinnati, Ohio, September 13, 1861, and "M" at Albany September 10, 1862. Regiment organized at Meridian Hill, Washington, D. C., September 9, 1861. Attached to Banks' Division, Army of the Potomac (5 Cos.), and Stone's Division, Army of the Potomac (6 Cos.), to December, 1861. Stone's Corps of Observation to March, 1862. Defences of Washington, D. C., to April, 1862. Unattached, Dept. of North Carolina, to December, 1862. Unattached, 18th Army Corps, Dept. of North Carolina, to May, 1863. Cavalry Brigade, 18th Corps, to July, 1863. Defences of New Berne, N. C., Dept. of Virginia and North Carolina, to October, 1863. Heckman's Command, Newport News, Va., Dept. of Virginia and North Carolina, to December, 1863. Heckman's Command, Portsmouth,

Va., Dept. of Virginia and North Carolina, to April, 1864. 1st Brigade, Kautz's Cavalry Division, Army of the James, Dept. of Virginia and North Carolina, to December, 1864. Norfolk, Va., to January, 1865. Portsmouth, Va., to March, 1865. Suffolk, Va., to June, 1865. Norfolk, Va., to July, 1865.

SERVICE.—Duty in the Defences of Washington, D. C., and on the Upper Potomac till April, 1862. Operations on the Potomac October 21-24, 1861. Near Goose Creek and on Leesburg Road October 21. Ball's Bluff October 21. Near Edward's Ferry October 22. Bunker Hill, W. Va., March 5, 1862. Winchester March 10. Ordered to Dept. of North Carolina April 6. Haughton's Mills April 27. Near Burnt Church May 7. Reconnoissance toward Trenton May 15-16. Trenton Bridge May 15. Young's Cross Roads and Pollocksville May 15-16. Tranter's Creek May 30 (Co. "I"). Greenville Road May 31. Tranter's Creek June 2, 5 and 24 (Co. "I"). Swift Creek Bridge June 28 (Detachment). Tranter's Creek July 10. Expedition to Trenton and Pollocksville July 24-28. Trenton and Pollocksville July 25. Mill Creek July 26 (Co. "K"). Pollocksville July 26 (Co. "K"). Reconnoissance to Young's Cross Roads July 26-29 (Detachment). Near Young's Cross Roads July 27. Trenton and Kinston Road August 6. Reconnoissance to Swansboro August 14-15. Washington, N. C., September 6 (Cos. "D," "G," "H," "I" and "L"). Tranter's Creek September 9. Washington October 5. Pingo Creek October 29. Expedition from Newberne October 30-November 12. Rawle's Mills November 2. Near Tarboro November 5. Demonstration on Newberne November 11. Core Creek November 18. Foster's Expedition to Goldsboro December 11-20. Kinston Road December 11-12. Southwest Creek December 13-14. Kinston December 14. Whitehall Bridge December 15. Olive Station, Goshen Swamp and Whitehall December 16. Dudley Station, Thompson's Bridge and Goldsboro December 17. Core Creek January 8, 1863. Reconnoissance to Pollocksville, Tranter's, Young's Cross Roads and Onslow January 17-21. Pollocksville and Northeast River January 17. Near Tranter's January 18. Young's Cross Roads January 18-19. White Oak Creek January 19. Near Jacksonville January 20. Sandy Ridge and near Washington February 13. Near Newberne February 27. Expedition to Swann's Quarter March 1-6 (Co. "F"). Near Fairfield March 3 (Co. "F"). Skeet March 3. Near Fairfield and Swann's Quarter March 3-4 (Co. "F"). Demonstration on Kinston March 6-8 (Cos. "A," "E" and "H"). Core Creek March 7 (Cos. "A," "E" and "H"). Dover March 7 (Co. "H"). Expedition to Mattamuskeet Lake March 7-14 (Co. "F"). Deep Gully, New Berne, March 13-14 (Detachment). Siege of Washington March 30-April 20 (1 Co.). White Forks April 3. Gum Swamp April 4. Swann's Quarter April 4. Rodman's Point April 4-5 (1 Co.). Near Dover, Core Creek and Young's Cross Roads April 7. Little Swift Creek April 8. Blount's and Swift Creek April 9. Expedition to Swift Creek Village April 13-21 (Detachment). Trent Road April 13-14. Near Newberne April 15. Peletier's Mills April 16. Expedition toward Kinston April 16-21 (Co. "H"). Expedition to Little Washington April 17-19 (Detachment). Railroad Crossing, Core Creek, April 17-18. Big Swift Creek April 19. Sandy Ridge April 20 (Co. "H"). Expedition toward Kinston April 27-May 1 (Detachment). Wise's Cross Roads and Dover Road April 28. Near Core Creek April 29. Core Creek April 30. Evans' Mills May 5. Peletier's Mills May 5 (4 Cos.). Stony Creek May 7 (4 Cos.). Demonstration on Kinston May 20-23 (4 Cos.). Gum Swamp May 22 (4 Cos.). Bachelor's Creek May 23. Washington May 24. Tranter's Creek, Jacksonville. May 31-June 2. Plymouth June 16. Scout to Core Creek June 17-18. Raid on Wilmington & Weldon Railroad July 3-7 (Detachment). Trenton July 3. Hallsville July 4. Warsaw and Kenensville July 5. Tar River Expedition July 18-24. Swift Creek July 18. Near Greenville July 19. Tarboro and Rocky Mount Station July 20. Sparta July 20. Hookerstown July 21. Swift Creek and Street's Ferry July 22. Scupperton July 22. Pollocksville July 26.

Near New Berne October 7. Camden Court House and Dismal Swamp November 3. Operations about New Berne against Whiting January 18-February 4, 1864. Wistar's Expedition toward Richmond February 6-8, 1864. Bottom's Bridge and Baltimore Cross Roads February 7. Kautz's Raid against Petersburg & Weldon Railroad May 5-11. Wall's Bridge May 5. Stony Creek Station, Weldon Railroad, May 7. Nottaway Railroad Bridge May 8. White's Bridge, Nottaway River, May 8-9. Kautz's Raid on Richmond & Danville Railroad May 12-17. Flat Creek Bridge, near Chula Depot, May 14. Belcher's Mills May 16. Bermuda Hundred May 17-30. Near Hatcher's Run June 2. Near Petersburg June 9. Baylor's Farm June 15. Assaults on Petersburg June 15-18. Siege operations against Petersburg and Richmond June 16-December 1, 1864. Wilson's Raid on South Side & Danville Railroad June 22-30. Roanoke Bridge June 25. Sappony Church or Stony Creek June 28. Ream's Station June 29. Deep Bottom July 27-29. Malvern Hill August 1. Yellow Tavern August 19-21. Ream's Station August 23-25. Lee's Mills August 31. Reconnoissance to Sycamore Church September 5-6. Prince George Court House September 15. Jerusalem Plank Road and Sycamore Church September 16. Prince George Court House September 22. Chaffin's Farm September 28-30. Charles City Cross Roads October 1. Darbytown Road October 7 and 13. Johnson's Farm and New Market Road October 7. Chaffin's Farm October 8. Charles City Cross Roads October 20. Fair Oaks October 27-28. Charles City Cross Roads November 1. Darbytown Road November 15. Moved to Norfolk, Va., December, and duty there till January, 1865. Operations about Broadwater Ferry, Chowan River, December 11-19. Duty at Suffolk, Portsmouth and Norfolk till July. Scout to South Quay January 2, 1865 (Cos. "A," "B," "C," "H" and "L"). Expedition to Murfree's Depot, N. C., March 10-11. South Quay March 11. Consolidated with 1st New York Mounted Rifles July 21, 1865, to form 4th Regiment Provisional Cavalry.

Regiment lost during service 3 Officers and 45 Enlisted men killed and mortally wounded and 1 Officer and 150 Enlisted men by disease. Total 199.

3rd REGIMENT PROVISIONAL CAVALRY.

Organized June 23, 1865, by consolidation of the 13th and 16th Regiments New York Cavalry. Mustered out September 21, 1865.

4th REGIMENT CAVALRY ("DICKEL'S MOUNTED RIFLES").

Organized at New York City August 10-November 15, 1861. (Co. "K" mustered in November 15, 1862; Co. "L" December, 1862, and Co. "M" February 13, 1863.) Left State for Washington, D. C., August 29, 1861. Attached to Blenker's Brigade and Division, Army of the Potomac, to March, 1862. Blenker's Division, 2nd Army Corps, Army of the Potomac, to April, 1862. Blenker's Division, Mountain Dept., to May, 1862. Advance Brigade, Mountain Dept., to June, 1862. Buford's Cavalry Brigade, 1st Corps, Army of Virginia, to September, 1862. Cavalry Brigade, 11th Army Corps, Army of the Potomac, to February, 1863. 1st Brigade, 2nd Division, Cavalry Corps, Army of the Potomac, to June, 1863. 1st Brigade, 3rd Division, Cavalry Corps, to June 14, 1863. 2nd Brigade, 2nd Division, Cavalry Corps, to August, 1863. 2nd Brigade, 1st Division, Cavalry Corps, Army of the Potomac and Army of the Shenandoah, to February, 1865.

SERVICE.—Duty in the Defences of Washington, D. C., till April, 1862. Moved to Winchester, Va., April, 1862, and operations in the Shenandoah Valley till August. Strasburg and Staunton Road June 1-2. Woodstock June 2. Edenburg and Mt. Jackson June 3. Harrisonburg June 6. Cross Keys June 8. Near Port Republic June 9. New Market June 13. Near Middletown July 8. White House Ford July 22. Near Luray July 29. Cedar Mountain August 9. Pope's Campaign in Northern Virginia August 16-September 2. Fords of the Rappahannock August 20-23. Waterloo Bridge August 24-25. Groveton August 29. Bull Run August

30. Duty in the Defences of Washington till December. Ashby's Gap September 22. Near New Baltimore November 16. Reconnoissance from Chantilly to Snicker's Gap and Berryville November 28-30. Berryville November 29. Snicker's Ferry November 30. Reconnoissance to Kellysville December 21-23. Scouts in Faquier County January 24-26, 1863. Grove Church, near Morrisville, January 26. Somerville February 9. Hartwood Church February 25. Kelly's Ford March 17. Stoneman's Raid April 29-May 8. Aldie June 17. Middleburg June 19. Upperville June 21. Gettysburg, Pa., July 1-3. Monterey Gap July 4. Smithburg July 5. Hagerstown and Williamsport July 6. Boonsboro July 8. Jones' Cross Roads and Hagerstown July 10-13. Falling Waters July 14. Expedition from Leesburg August 30-September 2. Advance from the Rappahannock to the Rapidan September 13-17. Culpeper Court House September 13. Raccoon Ford September 14-16. Reconnoissance across the Rapidan September 21-23. Jack's Shop, Madison Court House, September 22. Bristoe Campaign October 9-22. Raccoon and Morton's Fords October 10. Stevensburg and Kelly's Ford October 11. Brandy Station, Culpeper and Stevensburg October 12. Oak Hill October 15. Bealton Station October 24-25. Advance to line of the Rappahannock November 7-8. Mine Run Campaign November 26-December 2. Robertson's Tavern November 27. Parker's Store November 29. Mine Run November 30. Ely's Ford December 1. Near Culpeper Court House December 23. Barnett's Ford January 29 and February 6-7, 1864. Kilpatrick's Raid on Richmond February 28-March 4. Beaver Dam Station February 29. Defences of Richmond March 1. Aylett's March 2. New Kent Court House March 3. Culpeper March 28. Rapidan Campaign May-June. Todd's Tavern May 5-6. Brock Road and the Furnaces May 6. Wilderness May 6-7. Todd's Tavern May 7-8. Piney Grove Church May 8. Spottsylvania Court House May 8-21. North Anna River May 23-26. Pamunkey River May 26-28. Crump's Creek May 27. Haw's Shop May 28. Totopotomoy May 28-31. Old Church and Mattadequin Creek May 30. Cold Harbor May 31-June 1. Gaines Mills June 2. Sheridan's Trevillian Raid June 7-24. Trevillian Station June 11-12. White House June 21. Jones' Bridge, Chickahominy River, June 23. Prince George Court House June 25. Before Petersburg June 26-July 30. Lee's Mills July 18. Deep Bottom July 28-29. Charles City Cross Roads July 29. Sheridan's Shenandoah Valley Campaign August 6-November 28. Millwood August 10. White Post August 11. Crooked Run August 13. Front Royal August 16. Charlestown August 21. Halltown August 24. Near Kearneysville August 25. Smithfield and Leetown August 28. Bunker Hill September 13. Sevier's Ford September 15. Battle of Winchester September 19. Middletown September 20. Strasburg September 20. Fisher's Hill September 21. Mt. Jackson September 23-24. Fort Republic September 26-27. Mt. Crawford October 1. Newtown October 2. Tom's Brook October 9. Near Strasburg October 14. Cedar Creek October 17 and 19. Woodstock October 20. Nineveh November 12. Rood's Hill November 22. Expedition from Winchester November 28-December 3. Expedition to Gordonsville December 19-28. Liberty Mills December 21. Jack's Shop, near Gordonsville, December 22. Consolidated with 9th New York Cavalry as Companies "B," "E" and "L" February 27, 1865, which see.

Regiment lost during service 5 Officers and 39 Enlisted men killed and mortally wounded and 3 Officers and 54 Enlisted men by disease. Total 101.

4th REGIMENT PROVISIONAL CAVALRY.

Organized July 21, 1865, by consolidation of 1st New York Cavalry and 2nd New York Mounted Rifles. Duty in Dept. of Virginia till November. Mustered out November 29, 1865.

5th REGIMENT CAVALRY—"1st IRA HARRIS GUARD."

Regiment recruited at New York City as Ira Harris Cavalry. Designated Ira Harris Guard October 16,

1861, and 5th New York Cavalry November 14, 1861. Companies mustered in as follows: "A" August 15, "B" August 21, "C" September 3, "D" October 1, "E" October 7, "F" September 21, "G" October 9, "H" October 28, "I," "K," "L" and "M" October 31, 1861. Left State for Baltimore, Md., November 18, 1861. Attached to Dix's Command to March, 1862. Banks' 5th Corps March and April, 1862. Hatch's Cavalry Brigade, Department of the Shenandoah, to June, 1862. Cavalry Brigade, 2nd Corps, Army of Virginia, to September, 1862. Wyndham's Cavalry Brigade, Defences of Washington, to February, 1863. Price's Independent Cavalry Brigade, 22nd Army Corps, Dept. of Washington, to April, 1863. 3rd Brigade, Stahel's Cavalry Division, 22nd Army Corps, to June 28, 1863. 1st Brigade, 3rd Division, Cavalry Corps, Army of the Potomac, and Army of the Shenandoah, Middle Military Division, to March, 1865. Cavalry, Army of the Shenandoah, to July, 1865.

SERVICE.—Duty at Camp Harris, Baltimore, Md., November 18, 1861, to March 31, 1862. Ordered to join Banks in the field March 31. South Fork, Shenandoah River, April 19. New Market April 29. Port Republic May 2. Conrad's Store May 2 and 6. Report to Gen. Hatch May 3. Rockingham Furnace May 4. Near Harrisonburg May 6. New Market May 7. Columbia River Bridge May 8. Bowling Green Road near Fredericksburg May 11. Operations in the Shenandoah Valley May 15-June 17. Woodstock May 18. Front Royal May 23 (Cos. "B" and "D"). Strasburg, Middletown and Newtown May 24. Winchester May 25. Defence of Harper's Ferry May 28-30 (4 Cos.). Reconnoissance to New Market June 15. Near Culpeper Court House July 12. Liberty Mills July 17. Near Orange Court House August 2. Cedar Mountain August 9-10. Pope's Campaign in Northern Virginia August 16-September 2. Louisa Court House August 17. Kelly's Ford August 20. Warrenton Springs August 23-24. Waterloo Bridge August 24. Centreville August 28. Groveton August 29. Lewis Ford and Bull Run August 30. Chantilly September 1. Antietam, Md., September 17-19. Ashby's Gap September 22. Leesburg October 16. Upperville October 17. Thoroughfare Gap and Haymarket October 18. New Baltimore November 5. Cedar Hill November 5. Hopewell Gap November 8. Thoroughfare Gap November 11. Middleburg November 12. Upperville November 16. Aldie November 29. Snicker's Gap and Berryville November 30. Aldie December 18. Cub Run December 31. Frying Pan January 5, 1863. Cub Run January 5. Middleburg January 26. New Baltimore February 9. Warrenton February 10. Aldie March 4. Fairfax Court House March 9. Little River Turnpike and Chantilly March 23. Broad Run April 1. White Plains April 28. Warrenton Junction May 3. Flemming and Shannon Cross Roads May 4. Near Fairfax Court House May 8. Marsteller's Place May 14. Greenwich May 30. Snicker's Gap June 1. Middleburg June 10. Warrenton June 19. Hanover, Pa., June 30. Hunterstown July 2. Gettysburg, Pa., July 3. Monterey Pass July 4. Smithsburg July 5. Hagerstown and Williamsport July 6. Boonsboro July 8. Hagerstown July 11-13. Falling Waters July 14. Hagerstown July 15. Ashby's Gap July 26. Expedition to Port Conway September 1-3. Lamb's Creek September 1. Advance from the Rappahannock to the Rapidan September 13-17. Culpeper Court House September 13. Rapidan Station September 13-14. Somerville Ford September 14. Raccoon Ford September 14-16. Kelly's Ford September 18. Madison Court House September 21. Reconnoissance across the Rapidan September 21-23. White's Ford September 21-22. Brookin's Ford September 22. Hazel River Bridge September 25. Creigerville October 8. Bristoe Campaign October 9-22. Russell's Ford, James City and Bethesda Church October 10. Sperryville Pike, Brandy Station and near Culpeper October 11. Gainesville October 14. New Market October 16. Groveton October 17-18. Haymarket, Gainesville and Buckland's Mills October 19. Advance to line of the Rappahannock November 7-8. Stevensburg November

8. Germania Ford November 18. Mine Run Campaign November 26-December 2. Morton's Ford November 26. Raccoon Ford November 26-27. Ely's Ford January 19 and 22, 1864. Demonstration on the Rapidan February 6-7. Kilpatrick's Raid to Richmond February 28-March 4. Ely's Ford February 28. Beaver Dam Station and South Anna Bridge February 29. Defences of Richmond March 1. Hanovertown March 2. Aylett's and Stevensville March 2. King's and Queen's Court House March 3. Ely's Ford March 4. Field's Ford March 8. Southard's Cross Roads March 11. Rapidan Campaign May-June. Parker's Store May 5. Todd's Tavern May 5-6. Wilderness May 6-7. Germania Ford, Brock Road and the Furnaces May 7. Todd's Tavern May 7-8. Spottsylvania May 8-18. Downer's Bridge and Milford Station May 20. Mattapony River and Bowling Green May 21. North Anna River May 24. Mt. Carmel Church May 25. On line of the Pamunkey May 26-28. Totopotomoy May 28-31. Hanover Court House May 29. Mechump's Creek May 30. Signal Hill May 31. Ashland Station June 1. Cold Harbor June 1-12. Gaines' Mill, Totopotomoy and Salem Church June 2. Haw's Shop June 3. Old Church June 10. Shady Grove and Bethesda Church June 11. Riddell's Shop and Long Bridge June 12. White Oak Swamp June 13. Malvern Hill June 14. Smith's Store near St. Mary's Church June 15. White House Landing June 19. Wilson's Raid on South Side & Danville Railroad. June 22-30. Black and white and Nottaway Court House June 23. Staunton Bridge June 24. Roanoke Bridge June 25. Sappony Church or Stony Creek June 28. Ream's Station June 29. Before Petersburg till July 30. (A detachment of Regiment left at Dismounted Camp, participated in actions at Maryland Heights July 6-7. Rockville, Md., July 10. Toll Gate July 12. Poolesville July 15. Snicker's Ferry July 18, and Kernstown July 24.) Sheridan's Shenandoah Valley Campaign August 7-November 28. Winchester and Halltown August 17. Opequan August 19. Summit Point August 21. Charlestown August 22. Duffield Station August 23. Near Kearneysville August 25. Berryville September 2-4. Duffield Station September 3. Darkesville September 3. Opequan September 7-13-15 and 17. Abraham's Creek near Winchester September 13. Battle of Winchester September 19. Near Cedarville and Crooked Run September 20. Front Royal Pike and Fisher's Hill September 21. Milford September 22. New Market September 23-24. Mt. Crawford September 24. Waynesboro September 26. Port Republic September 26-27. Mt. Meridian September 27. Waynesboro and Railroad Bridge September 29. Bridgewater October 2. Brock's Gap October 6. Forestville October 7. Near Columbia Furnace October 7. Tom's Brook, "Woodstock Races," October 8-9. Back Road Cedar Creek October 13. Lebanon Church October 14. Cedar Run October 18. Battle of Cedar Creek October 19. Newtown and Ninevah November 12. Mt. Jackson November 22. Expedition to Lacy Springs December 19-22. Lacy Springs December 21. Woodstock January 10, 1865. Edenburg January 22. Sheridan's Raid February 27-March 3. Waynesboro March 2. Capture of Gen. Early's Command. Detached from Division to guard prisoners from Waynesboro to Winchester. Mt. Sidney and Lacy Springs March 5. New Market March 6. Rood's Hill March 7. (A portion of Regiment at Dinwiddie Court House March 30-31. Five Forks April 1. Fall of Petersburg April 2. Sweet House Creek April 3. Harper's Farm April 6. Appomattox Station April 8. Appomattox Court House April 9. Surrender of Lee and his army.) Regiment on duty at Headquarters Middle Military Division and in vicinity of Winchester till July. Mustered out July 19, 1865, and honorably discharged from service.

Regiment lost during service 8 Officers and 93 Enlisted men killed and mortally wounded and 3 Officers and 222 Enlisted men by disease. Total 326.

6th REGIMENT CAVALRY "2nd IRA HARRIS GUARD."

Regiment organized at New York City September 12 to December 19, 1861, under special authority of the

War Department, as the Ira Harris Guard. Turned over to State of New York as 6th Cavalry November 20, 1861. Companies were mustered in as follows: "A" September 12, "B" September 27, "D" September 28, "C" September 29, "E" October 3, "F" and "G" October 24, "H" October 28, "I" November 2, "L" November 6, "K" and "M" December 19, 1861. Left State for York, Pa., December 23, 1861, and duty there till March, 1862. Ordered to Washington, D. C., March, 1862, and duty in the Defences of that city (8 Cos.) till July 23, 1862. (Cos. "D" and "K" served detached with 2nd Army Corps, Army of the Potomac, March, 1862, to July, 1863, and Cos. "F" and "H" served detached with 4th Army Corps March, 1862, to August, 1863, and in the Defences of Washington, D. C., 22nd Army Corps, to October, 1863.) Regiment attached to Military District of Washington, D. C., March to July, 1862. 9th Army Corps, Army of the Potomac, August to December, 1862. 2nd Brigade, Pleasanton's Cavalry Division, Army of the Potomac, to February, 1863. 2nd Brigade, 1st Division, Cavalry Corps, Army of the Potomac and Army of the Shenandoah, Middle Military Division, to July, 1865. (Co. "A" detached with 6th Army Corps, September, 1862. Cos. "B" and "C" with 9th Army Corps, January and February, 1863. Co. "A" with 22nd Army Corps July and August, 1863.

SERVICE.—Duty in the Defences of Washington (8 Cos.) till July 23, 1862. Siege of Yorktown, Va., April 5-May 4 (Cos. "D" and "K"). Battle of Williamsburg May 5 (Cos. "D" and "K"). Seven Pines or Fair Oaks May 31-June 1 (Co. "K"). Seven days before Richmond June 25-July 1 (Cos. "D," "F," "H," "K"). Peach Orchard and Savage Station June 29. Glendale June 30. Malvern Hill July 1. Regiment moved to Warrenton, Va., July 23-26. Scout and outpost duty on the Rapidan and Rappahannock Rivers at Barnett's Ford, Va., July and August. Orange Court House August 14. Culpeper Road August 19. Barnett's Ford August 26. Kelly's Ford August 30. Williamsburg September 9. Near Hyattstown September 9-10. Frederick City September 12. South Mountain September 14. Antietam September 16-17. Lovettsville October 3. Reconnoissance to Smithville, W. Va., October 16-17. Kearneysville October 16. Charlestown October 16-17. Near Lovettsville October 21. Near Wheatland October 21. Snickersville October 22. Union and Bloomfield November 2-3. Ashby's Gap November 3. Upperville November 3. Waterloo Bridge November 7. Ellis Ford December 1. Fredericksburg December 12-15. Reconnoissance from Yorktown December 11-15 (Detachment). Matthews County Court House December 12. Buena Vista December 13. Wood's Cross Roads December 14. Expedition from Yorktown to West Point and White House January 7-9, 1863 (Detachment). Pamunkey River January 8. Expedition to Gloucester Court House April 7 (Detachment). Fort Magruder April 11 (Detachment). Chancellorsville Campaign April 27-May 6. Germania and Richard's Fords April 29. Crook's Run April 29. Spottsylvania Court House April 30. Battle of Chancellorsville May 1-5. West Point May 7 (Detachment). Warwick River June 5. Brandy Station and Beverly Ford June 9. Upperville June 21. Middleburg June 22. Haymarket June 24-25. Dix's Peninsula Campaign June 24-July 7 (3rd Battalion). Expedition from White House to Bottom's Bridge July 1-7 (3rd Battalion). Crump's or Baltimore Cross Roads July 2 (3rd Battalion). Battle of Gettysburg, Pa., July 1-3. Williamsport July 6. Boonsboro July 8. Benevola or Beaver Creek, Md., July 9. Funkstown July 10-13. Falling Waters July 14. Manassas Gap July 21-22. Wapping Heights July 23. Barber's Cross Roads July 25. Kelly's Ford July 31-August 1. Brandy Station August 1-3. Advance from the Rappahannock to the Rapidan September 13-17. Culpeper Court House September 13. Raccoon Ford September 14-15 and 19. Reconnoissance across the Rapidan September 21-23. Jack's Shop, Madison Court House, September 22. Bristoe Campaign October 9-22. Raccoon and Morton's Fords October 10. Kelly's Ford and Stevensburg Octo-

ber 11. Brandy Station or Fleetwood October 12. Near Bristoe Station October 14. Oak Hill October 15. Culpeper October 17-18. Bealeton October 24-26. Advance to line of the Rappahannock November 7-8. Muddy Run November 8. Mine Run Campaign November 26-December 2. Parker's Store November 29. Demonstration on the Rapidan February 6-7, 1864. Barnett's Ford February 6-7. Kilpatrick's Raid on Richmond February 28-March 4. Near Taylorstown, Beaver Dam Station, Frederick's Hall and South Anna Bridge February 29. Defences of Richmond March 1. Aylett's March 2. Kings and Queens Court House March 3. Carrollton's Store March 11. Rapidan Campaign May-June. Wilderness May 5-7. Brock Road and the Furnaces May 6. Todd's Tavern May 7-8. Spottsylvania May 8. Sheridan's Raid to James River May 9-24. North Anna May 9-10. Ground Squirrel Church and Yellow Tavern May 11. Fortifications of Richmond and Meadow Bridge May 12. Jones' Bridge May 17. On line of the Pamunkey May 26-28. Crump's Creek and Hanovertown May 27. Totopotomoy May 28-31. Haw's Shop May 28. Old Church and Mattadequin Creek May 30. Cold Harbor May 31-June 6. Bethesda Church May 31-June 1. Sheridan's Trevilian Raid June 7-24. Trevillian Station June 11-12. Newark or Mallory's Cross Roads June 12. White House or St. Peter's Church June 21. Black Creek or Tunstall's Station June 21. Jones' Bridge June 23. Charles City Court House June 23. Before Petersburg June 26-July 30. Deep Bottom July 27-28. Sheridan's Shenandoah Valley Campaign August 7-November 28. Berryville August 10 and 13. Toll Gate near White Post and Newtown August 11. Front Royal August 11. Cedar Creek August 12. Cedarville, Guard Hill or Front Royal and Crooked Run August 16. Charlestown August 21. Kearneyville and near Shephardstown August 25. Leetown and Smithfield August 28. Smithfield Crossing Opequan August 29. Berryville September 3. Bunker Hill September 13. Sevier's Ford, Opequan Creek, September 15. Battle of Winchester September 19. Middletown and Strasburg September 20. Fisher's Hill September 21. Near Edenburg September 23. Mt. Jackson September 23-24. New Market September 24. Port Republic September 26-27. Waynesboro September 29. Mt. Crawford October 2. Tom's Brook, "Woodstock Races" October 8-9. Hupp's Hill near Strasburg October 14. Battle of Cedar Creek October 19. Woodstock October 20. Near Kernstown November 11. Newtown November 12. Hood's Hill November 22. Expedition from Winchester into Faquier and Loudoun Counties November 28-December 3. Expedition to Gordonsville December 19-28. Jack's Shop near Gordonsville December 23. Lovettsville January 18, 1865. Sheridan's Raid from Winchester February 27-March 25. Waynesboro March 2. Occupation of Staunton March 2. Charlottesville March 3. Goochland Court House March 11. Appomattox Campaign March 28-April 9. Dinwiddie Court House March 30-31. Five Forks April 1. Fall of Petersburg April 2. Scott's Cross Roads April 2. Deep Creek April 3. Tabernacle Church or Beaver Pond Creek April 4. Sailor's Creek April 6. Appomattox Station April 8. Appomattox Court House April 9. Surrender of Lee and his army. Expedition to Danville April 23-29. Moved to Washington, D. C., May. Grand Review May 23. Consolidated with 15th New York Cavalry June 17, 1865, to form 2nd Regiment Provisional Cavalry.

Regiment lost during service 9 Officers and 72 Enlisted men killed and mortally wounded and 133 Enlisted men by disease. Total 214.

7th REGIMENT "BLACK HORSE" CAVALRY.

Organized at Troy, N. Y. (7 Cos.), and mustered in November 6, 1861. Designated 2nd Regiment Cavalry, by State authorities November 18, 1861, but designation changed by the War Department to 7th New York Cavalry. Left State for Washington, D. C., November 23, 1861, and duty there till March, 1862. Mustered out March 31, 1862, and honorably discharged from service.

8th REGIMENT CAVALRY "ROCHESTER REGIMENT."

Organized at Rochester, N. Y., and mustered in November 23, 1861. Moved to Washington, D. C., November 28-30, 1861. Attached to Cavalry Brigade, Army of the Potomac, to March, 1862. Cavalry Brigade, Banks' 5th Corps, to April, 1862. Hatch's Cavalry Brigade, Department of the Shenandoah, to May, 1862. Railroad Brigade, 8th Corps, Middle Department, to September, 1862. 4th Brigade, Pleasanton's Cavalry Division, Army of the Potomac, to November, 1862. 1st Cavalry Brigade, Right Grand Division, Army of the Potomac, to February, 1863. 1st Brigade, 1st Division, Cavalry Corps, Army of the Potomac, to March, 1864. 2nd Brigade, 3rd Division, Cavalry Corps, Army of the Potomac, and Army of the Shenandoah, Middle Military Division, to June, 1865.

Duty in the Defences of Washington, D. C., till March, 1862, and at various points in Maryland by detachments, till May. Operations in the Shenandoah Valley May 15-June 17. Berryville May 24. Retreat to Williamsport May 24-25. Battle of Winchester May 25. Stevenson's Station May 25. Harper's Ferry May 28-30. Near Charlestown September 4. Summit Point September 8. Siege of Harper's Ferry September 12-15. Near Williamsport and Greencastle September 15. Antietam, Md., September 16-17. Near Shephardstown September 20. Snicker's Gap October 27. Philomont November 1-2. Union and Bloomfield November 2-3. Barbee's Cross Roads, Chester Gap and Markham November 5-6. Waterloo Bridge November 7. Corbin's Cross Roads near Amissville November 10. Jefferson November 14. Uniontown November 20. Fredericksburg December 12-15. Near Warrenton December 30-31. Warrenton January 4, 1863. Somerville February 9. Belle Plains February 11. Near Dumfries March 2. Independence Hill, Prince William County, March 4. Near Dumfries March 29. Beverly Ford April 1. Beverly Ford, Freeman's Ford and Hazel Run April 15. Stoneman's Raid April 27-May 8. Kelly's Ford April 29. Culpeper April 30. Rapidan Station May 1. Ely's Ford May 2. Rapidan Bridge May 4. Brandy Station and Beverly Ford June 9. Aldie June 17. Ashby's Gap June 20. Upperville June 21. Aldie June 23. Near Middleburg and Upperville June 27. Fairfield, Pa., June 30. Gettysburg, Pa., July 1-3. Williamsport July 6. Funkstown July 6. Boonsboro July 8. Benevola or Beaver Creek July 9. Funkstown July 10-13. Falling Waters July 14. Chester Gap July 21-22. Wapping Heights July 23. Barber's Cross Roads July 25. Kelly's Ford July 31-August 1. Brandy Station August 1, 4 and 10. Advance from the Rappahannock to the Rapidan September 13-17. Culpeper Court House September 13. Rapidan Station September 14-15. Raccoon Ford September 19. Reconnoissance across the Rapidan September 21-23. Jack's Shop, Madison Court House, September 22. Germania Ford October 1. Bristoe Campaign October 9-22. Germania, Raccoon and Morton's Fords October 10. Stevensburg and near Kelly's Station October 11. Brandy Station October 12. Oak Hill October 15. Hunter's Ford October 17-18. Bealeton October 24-26. Snicker's Gap October 27. Advance to line of the Rappahannock November 7-8. Muddy Run November 8. Mine Run Campaign November 26-December 2. Locust Grove November 27. Parker's Store November 29. Demonstration on the Rapidan February 6-7, 1864. Morton's Ford February 6-7. James City March 4. Rapidan Campaign May-June. Craig's Meeting House May 5. Wilderness May 5-7. The Furnaces May 7. Alsop's Farm, Spottsylvania, May 8. Sheridan's Raid to James River May 9-24. North Anna River May 9-10. Ground Squirrel Church and Yellow Tavern May 11. Fortifications of Richmond and Meadow Bridge May 12. On line of the Pamunkey May 26-28. Demonstration on Little Creek May 26. Totopotomoy May 28-31. Mechump's Creek May 30. Hanover Court House May 31. Cold Harbor June 1-12. Gaines Mill, Totopotomoy and Salem Church June 2. Sumner's Upper Bridge June 2. Haw's Shop June 3. Old Church June 10-11. Riddell's Shop and Long Bridge June 12. White Oak Swamp June 13. Near Harrison's Landing June 14. St. Mary's Church and Malvern Hill June 15. Before Petersburg June 17-July 30. Wilson's Raid on South Side & Danville Railroad June 22-30. Ream's Station June 22. Black and White Station and Nottaway Court House June 23. Staunton Bridge and Roanoke Station June 25. Columbia Grove June 27. Sappony Church or Stony Creek June 28. Ream's Station June 29. Sheridan's Shenandoah Valley Campaign August 7-November 28. Winchester August 17. Charlestown Summit Point August 21. Halltown August 23. Kearneysville August 25. Berryville September 3. Near Brucetown and near Winchester September 7. Locke's Ford September 13. Snicker's Gap September 16. Battle of Opequan, Winchester, September 19. Near Cedarville September 20. Front Royal Pike September 21. Milford September 22. Luray September 25. Staunton September 26. Waynesboro September 29. Mt. Crawford September 30. Columbia Furnace October 7. Tom's Brook, "Woodstock Races," October 8-9. Mt. Olive October 9. Battle of Cedar Creek October 19. Near Kernstown November 10. Newtown and Middle Road, Cedar Creek, November 12. Rude's Hill, near Mt. Jackson, November 22. Expedition to Lacy Springs December 19-22. Lacy Springs December 21. Expedition from Winchester to Moorefield, W. Va., February 4-6, 1865. Sheridan's Raid from Winchester February 27-March 25, 1865. Waynesboro March 2. Occupation of Charlottesville March 3. Beaver Dam Station March 13. Appomattox Campaign March 28-April 9. Dinwiddie Court House March 30-31. Five Forks April 1. Fall of Petersburg April 2. Namozine Church April 3. Jettersville April 4. Sailor's Creek April 6. Appomattox Station April 8. Appomattox Court House April 9. Surrender of Lee and his army. Expedition to Danville April 23-29. March to Washington, D. C., May —. Grand Review May 23. Mustered out June 27, 1865, and honorably discharged from service.

Regiment lost during service 14 Officers and 91 Enlisted men killed and mortally wounded and 5 Officers and 200 Enlisted men by disease. Total 310.

9th REGIMENT "STONEMAN" CAVALRY.

Organized at Westfield and Albany, N. Y., September 9 to November 19, 1861. Left State for Washington, D. C., November 26, 1861. Attached to Wadsworth's Command, Military District of Washington, to March, 1862. Artillery Reserve, Army of the Potomac, to May, 1862. Defences of Washington, D. C., to June, 1862. Cavalry Brigade, 1st Corps, Army of Virginia, to September, 1862. Cavalry Brigade, 11th Army Corps, Army of the Potomac, to October, 1862. 3rd Brigade, Cavalry Division, Army of the Potomac, to January, 1863. 1st Brigade, 1st Division, Cavalry Corps, Army of the Potomac, to June, 1863. 2nd Brigade, 1st Division, Cavalry Corps, Army of the Potomac and Army of the Shenandoah, Middle Military Division, to July, 1865.

SERVICE.—Duty in the Defences of Washington, D. C., till March, 1862. Companies "C," "F" and "K" detached for duty with Artillery Reserve. Other Companies on duty as train guard, Army of the Potomac, to May 22, 1862. Siege of Yorktown April 5-May 4. Before Williamsburg May 4-5. West Point May 7. Near Slatersville May 9. Ordered to Washington, D. C., May 22, and duty there till June, when mounted. Action near Cedar Mountain August 12. Pope's Campaign in Northern Virginia August 16-September 2. Freeman's Ford August 22. Fants Ford and Great Run August 23. Sulphur Springs and Jones Ford August 24. Deep Creek August 25. Salem and White Plains August 27. Groveton August 29. Bull Run August 30. Near Centreville August 31. Fairfax Court House September 2. Berryville September 29. Aldie October 1. Snickersville and Middleburg October 12. Paris and Salem October 17. Thoroughfare Gap October 17. Haymarket October 18. Warrenton October 19. Reconnoissance to Snicker's Ferry and Berryville November 28-30. Upperville November 28. Berryville November 29.

Snicker's Ferry, Berryville, November 30. Reconnoissance to Kelleysville December 21-23. Alcock's January 21, 1863. Grove Church, near Morrisville, January 26. Rappahannock Fords and Station Febuary 2. Morrisville February 5. Summerville February 9. Freeman's Ford April 15. Near Warrenton April 28. Stoneman's Raid April 29-May 8. Kelley's Ford April 29. Culpeper April 30. Rapidan Station May 1. Operations on Northern Neck May 20-26. Brandy Station and Beverly Ford June 9. Ashby's Gap June 20. Upperville and Middleburg June 21. Philomont June 22. Haymarket and Thoroughfare Gap June 24-25. Hunterstown, Pa., June 30. Gettysburg, Pa., July 1-3. Williamsport July 6. Downsville July 7. Boonsboro July 8. Benevola or Beaver Creek July 9. Falling Waters July 10. Funkstown July 10-13. Falling Waters July 14. Emmettsburg July 18. Manassas Gap July 21-22. Wapping Heights July 23. Barbee's Cross Roads July 25. Rixey's Ford July 29. Kelly's Ford July 31-August 1. Brandy Station August 1-3. Stafford Court House August 22. Expedition from Leesburg August 30-September 2. Advance from the Rappahannock to the Rapidan September 13-17. Culpeper Court House September 13. Rapidan Station September 14-15. Reconnoissance across the Rapidan September 21-23. Jack's Shop, Madison Court House, September 22. Bristoe Campaign October 9-22. Raccoon and Morton's Fords October 10. Stevensburg and near Kelly's Ford October 11. Brandy Station October 12. Broad Run October 15. Oak Hill October 16. Hunter's Ford, Rapidan River, October 17-18. Bealeton Station October 24. Rappahannock Station October 26. Advance to line of the Rappahannock November 7-8. Muddy Run November 8. Mine Run Campaign November 26-December 2. Parker's Store November 29. Reconnoissance to Woodville December 6. Demonstration on the Rapidan February 6-7, 1864. Barnett's Ford February 6-7. Rapidan Campaign. Battles of the Wilderness May 5-7; Todd's Tavern May 7-8; Spottsylvania May 8. Sheridan's Raid to James River May 9-24. North Anna May 9-10. Ground Squirrel Church and Yellow Tavern May 11. Fortifications of Richmond and Meadow Bridge May 12. Jones Bridge May 17. On line of the Pamunkey May 26-28. Hanovertown and Crump's Creek May 27. Totopotomoy May 28-31. Haw's Shop May 28. Old Church and Mettadequin Creek May 30. Bethesda Church May 31-June 1. Cold Harbor May 31-June 6. Sheridan's Trevillian Raid June 7-24. Trevillian Station June 11-12. Newark or Mallory's Cross Roads June 12. Black Creek or Tunstall Station and White House or St. Peter's Church June 21. Jones Bridge June 23. Before Petersburg June 29-July 31. Demonstration north of the James July 27-29. Deep Bottom July 28-29. Sheridan's Shenandoah Valley Campaign August 7-November 28. Toll Gate, near White Post and Newtown, August 11. Berryville August 12. Near Strasburg August 14. Crooked Run August 13. Cedarville, Guard Hill or Front Royal August 16. Front Royal August 18. Kearneysville August 19. Near Charlestown August 21-22. Near Kearneysville August 25. Near Shephardstown August 25. Leetown and Smithfield August 28. Smithfield Crossing, Opequan, August 29. Berryville September 3-4. Port Republic September 6. Bunker Hill and Opequan September 13. Sevier's Ford, Opequan Creek, September 15. Battle of Winchester September 19. Strasburg and Middletown September 20. Fisher's Hill September 21-22. Near Edenburg September 23. Mt. Jackson September 23-24. New Market September 24. Brown's Gap September 26. Port Republic September 26-27. New Market September 28. Waynesboro September 29 and October 2. Columbia Furnace October 8. Tom's Brook, "Woodstock Races," October 8-9. Hupp's Hill, near Strasburg, October 14. Battle of Cedar Creek October 19. Fisher's Hill October 20. Near Kernstown November 11. Near Winchester November 15. Rude's Hill November 22. Expedition from Winchester into Fauquier and Loudoun Counties November 28-December 3. Expedition to Gordonsville December 19-28. Near Gordonsville December 23. Sheridan's Raid from Winchester February 27-March 25, 1865.

45

Waynesboro March 2. Charlottesville March 3. (A Detachment guard prisoners from Waynesboro to Winchester March 3-8. Near Rude's Hill and Mt. Jackson March 7. Woodstock March 14.) Goochland Court House March 11. Appomattox Campaign March 28-April 9. Dinwiddie Court House March 30-31. Five Forks April 1. Scott's Cross Roads April 2. Fall of Petersburg April 2. Tabernacle Church or Beaver Pond Station April 8. Appomattox Court House April 9. Surrender of Lee and his army. Expedition to Danville April 23-29. March to Washington, D. C., May —. Grand Review May 23. Mustered out July 17, 1865, and honorably discharged from service.

Regiment lost during service 6 Officers and 84 Enlisted men killed and mortally wounded and 7 Officers and 126 Enlisted men by disease. Total 223.

10th REGIMENT CAVALRY.—("PORTER GUARD.")

Organized at Elmira, N. Y., September 27, 1861. Moved to Gettysburg, Pa., December 24, and duty there till March, 1862. Duty at Havre de Grace and Baltimore, Md., Middle Department and in the Defences of Washington, D. C., till August, 1862. Attached to Bayard's Cavalry Brigade, Army of Virginia. August-September, 1862. Bayard's Brigade, Cavalry Division, Army of the Potomac, to January, 1863. 1st Brigade, 3rd Division, Cavalry Corps, Army of the Potomac, to June, 1863. 2nd Brigade, 2nd Division, Cavalry Corps, June, 1863. 3rd Brigade, 2nd Division, Cavalry Corps, to August, 1863. 2nd Brigade, 2nd Division, Cavalry Corps, to May, 1864. 1st Brigade, 2nd Division, Cavalry Corps, to June, 1865.

SERVICE.—Sulphur Springs, Va., August 27, 1862. Near Frying Pan August 27. Reconnoissance to Dranesville, Herndon Station and Frying Pan August 31. Near Centreville September 3. Reconnoissance to Leesburg October 16-17. Aldie and Mountsville October 31. Rappahannock Station November 1. New Baltimore November 4. Rappahannock Station November 7, 8 and 9. United States Ford November 16 (Co. "H"). Battle of Fredericksburg December 12-15. Occoquan, Dumfries, December 19. "Mud March" January 20-24, 1863. Hartwood Church February 25. Rappahannock Railroad Bridge April 14. Stoneman's Raid toward Richmond April 27-May 8. Kelly's Ford April 30. Rapidan Station May 1. Louisa Court House May 2. South Anna Bridge May 3. Ashland Church May 4. Thompson's Cross Roads May 4. Brandy Station and Beverly Ford June 9. Aldie June 17. Middleburg June 18, 19 and 20. Upperville June 21. Aldie June 22. Gettysburg, Pa., July 1-3. Fairfield, Pa., July 5. Hagerstown, Md., July 11. Boonsboro July 11-12. Near Harper's Ferry July 14. Shephardstown July 14 and 16. Halltown July 15. Near Amissville August 4. Little Washington August 5. Advance from the Rappahannock to the Rapidan September 13-17. Culpeper Court House September 13. Bristoe Campaign October 9-22. Near Warrenton October 11. Warrenton or White Sulphur Springs October 12-13. Auburn and St. Stephen's Church October 14. Catlett's Station October 15-16. Rappahannock Station October 24. Philomont November 1. Advance to line of the Rappahannock November 7-8. Mine Run Campaign November 26-December 2. New Hope Church November 27. Parker's Store November 29. Expedition to Luray December 21-23. Rapidan Campaign May-June, 1864. Near Chancellorsville May 4. Todd's Tavern May 5-6. Wilderness May 6-7. Todd's Tavern May 7-8. Spottsylvania May 8. Sheridan's Raid to the James River May 9-24. North Anna River May 9-10. Ground Squirrel Church and Yellow Tavern May 11. Glen Allen May 11. Fortifications of Richmond May 12. Jones Bridge May 17. Haxall's Landing May 18. On line of the Pamunkey May 26-28. Totopotomoy May 28-31. Hanovertown and Haw's Shop May 28. Old Church Tavern May 30. Cold Harbor May 31-June 1. Barker's and Gaine's Mills June 2. Bottom's Bridge June 3. Sheridan's Trevillian Raid June 7-24. Trevillian Station June 11-12. Malvern Hill June 16. Kings and Queens Court House June 18. White House or St. Peter's Church and Black Creek or Tunstall Station June 21. Samaria Church June 24. Before Petersburg June 26, 1864, to April 2, 1865. Ream's Station June 30, 1864. Light House Point July 1. Gaines Hill July 2. Prince George Court House July 10 and 16. Lee's Mills July 12. Deep Bottom July 27-28. Malvern Hill July 28. Lee's Mills July 30. Demonstration north of the James August 13-20. Gravel Hill August 14. Strawberry Plains August 14-18. Weldon Railroad August 19-21. Dinwiddie Road, near Ream's Station, August 23. Ream's Station August 25. Arthur's Swamp August 29-30. Yellow Tavern September 2. Stony Creek Station September 16. Belcher's Mills September 17. Poplar Springs Church, Peeble's Farm, September 29-October 2. Vaughan Road September 30-October 1. Duncan Road October 1. Boydton Plank Road, Hatcher's Run, October 27-28. Near Prince George Court House November 2. Reconnoissance to Stony Creek November 7. Blackwater Creek November 18. Stony Creek December 1. Hicksford Raid December 6-12. Bellefield December 9-10. Jarrett's Station December 10. Dabney's Mills, Hatcher's Run, February 5-7, 1865. Appomattox Campaign March 28-April 9. Dinwiddie Court House March 30-31. Five Forks April 1. Fall of Petersburg April 2. Payne's Cross Roads and Amelia Springs April 5. Deatonville Road and Sailor's Creek April 6. Farmville April 7. Appomattox Station April 8. Appomattox Court House April 9. Surrender of Lee and his army. Expedition to Danville April 23-29. Moved to Washington, D. C., May. Grand Review May 23. Consolidated with 24th New York Cavalry June 17, 1865, to form 1st Regiment Provisional Cavalry.

Regiment lost during service 9 Officers and 93 Enlisted men killed and mortally wounded and 1 Officer and 148 Enlisted men by disease. Total 251.

11th REGIMENT CAVALRY.—("SCOTT'S 900.")

Organized at New York City December, 1861, to May, 1862. Left State for Washington, D. C., May 5, 1862. Attached to Military District of Washington and 22nd Army Corps, Dept. of Washington, May, 1862, to March, 1864. (A Detachment in 8th Army Corps, Middle Department.) District of LaFourche, Dept. of the Gulf, to June, 1864. District of Baton Rouge, La., Dept. of the Gulf, to August, 1864. 2nd Brigade, Cavalry Division, Dept. of the Gulf, to February, 1865. 2nd Brigade, Cavalry Division, District of West Tennessee, to July, 1865. Consolidated to a Battalion July 21, 1865. District of Memphis, Tenn., to September, 1865.

SERVICE.—Duty in the Defences of Washington, D. C., till March, 1864. Action at Blue Ridge Mountain, Va., June 18, 1862. Poolesville, Md., December 14. Near Fairfax Court House, Va., June 27, 1863 (Cos. "B" and "C"). Bolivar Heights June 30. Harper's Ferry July 7. Near Harper's Ferry July 14. Halltown July 15. Edwards' Ferry, Md., August 27 (Detachment). Expedition from Leesburg August 30-September 2 (Co. "F"). Rockville, Md., September 22. Ordered to Dept. of the Gulf March, 1864, and duty in the District of LaFourche, La., till June, and in the District of Baton Rouge, La., till August. Action at New River, La., May 15. Manning's Plantation June 10 and July 20. Orange Grove, near Donaldsonville, July 31. Doyall's Plantation and Donaldsonville August 5. Expedition from Baton Rouge, La., to Clinton, Greensburg, Osyka and Camp Moore October 5-9. Bayou Sara October 5. Lee's Expedition from Baton Rouge to Brookhaven, Miss., and skirmishes, November 14-21. Brookhaven, Miss., November 18. Near Jackson November 21. Clinton November 23. Liberty, Miss., November 24. Davidson's Expedition from Baton Rouge, La., against Mobile & Ohio Railroad November 27-December 13. Franklinsville November 27. Ocean Springs December 27. Ordered to Memphis, Tenn., February, 1865. Expedition from Memphis, Tenn., into Northern Mississippi March 3-11. Germantown March 28 and April 18. Duty at Memphis, Tenn., and in District of West Tennessee till September. Mustered out at Memphis, Tenn., September 30, 1865, and honorably discharged from service.

Regiment lost during service 1 Officer and 22 Enlisted men killed and mortally wounded and 2 Officers and 319 Enlisted men by disease. Total 344.

12th REGIMENT CAVALRY ("3rd IRA HARRIS GUARD").

Organized at New York City November, 1862, to September, 1863. Left State by Detachments for Dept. of North Carolina May to December, 1863. Attached to Cavalry Brigade, 18th Army Corps, Dept. of North Carolina, to July, 1863. Defences of Newberne, N. C., Dept. of Virginia and North Carolina, to October, 1863. Heckman's Command, Newport News, Va., Dept. of Virginia and North Carolina, to January, 1864. District of the Albemarle, N. C., Dept. of Virginia and North Carolina, to February, 1864. Palmer's Brigade, Peck's Division, District of North Carolina, Dept. of Virginia and North Carolina, to February, 1865. Cavalry, District of Beaufort, N. C., Dept. of North Carolina, to April, 1865. Kilpatrick's Cavalry Division, Dept. of North Carolina, to July, 1865.

SERVICE.—Duty in the Dept. of North Carolina May, 1863, to July, 1865. Near Kinston, N. C., June 20, 1863. Succade Ferry June 22. Reconnoissance from Plymouth to Nichol's Mills June 28 (Detachment). Free Bridge July 6. Expedition from Newport Barracks to Cedar Point and White Oak River July 13-16 (1 Co.). Smith's Mill Bridge July 15. Swift Creek July 18. Raid to Tarboro July 18-24. Tarboro July 20. Hookerstown July 21. Swift Creek, Street's Ferry and Scupperton July 22. Expedition from Plymouth to Foster's Mills July 26-29 (Detachment). Williamston July 27. Foster's Mills July 27. Sparta July 20. Chowan July 28. Near Washington August 14. Near Rocky Run November 4. Near Janesville November 20. Near Greenville November 25. Greenville November 30. Near Kinston December 5. Free Bridge. Chincapin Creek, December 16 (Cos. "A," "B" and "E"). Scout from Rocky Run toward Trenton December 21-24 (Detachment). Near Washington December 21. Expedition from Newport Barracks to Young's Cross Roads, Swansboro and Jackson December 27-29. Swansboro Road December 28. Greenville December 30. Operations about New Berne against Whiting January 18-February 16, 1864. Expedition to Onslow County January 27. New Berne February 1-4. Batchelor's Creek February 1. Brice's Creek February 1-2. Beach Grove February 1-3. Near Plymouth February 12. Greenville February 18-19. Near Plymouth April 2. Beaver Creek April 17. Plymouth April 17-20 (Cos. "A," "F"). Tom Mack's Fork April 21. Before New Berne May 4-6. Expedition from Batchelor's Creek to near Kinston June 20-23 (Cos. "B," "D"). Expedition against Wilmington and Weldon Railroad June 20-25 (Co. "E"). Onslow County June 20. North East June 20-21. Southwest Creek June 22. Sneed's Ferry June 22. Jackson's Mills June 22. Swansboro June 23. Near Kinston June 28. Deep Gully September 19. Scout to Gum Swamp October 11-13. Gardiner's Bridge December 4 and 9. Scout to Southwest Creek December 10-25. Foster's Mills December 10. Mosely Ford December 10. Southwest Creek Bridge December 11-12. Jamestown December 29. Greenwich December 30. Plymouth February 2, 1865. Colerain February 2. Plymouth February 12. Greenville February 18-19. Campaign of the Carolinas March 1-April 26. Southwest Creek March 6-7. Wise's Forks March 7-10. Cove Creek, Trent Road, March 11. Kinston March 14. Best's Station March 19. Mosely Hall March 20. Near Goldsboro March 21-22. Hookerstown March 31 (Co. "L"). April 3-4 and 7. Near Faisson's Station April 4. Faisson's Station April 11. Best's Station April 12-13. Bennett's House April 26. Surrender of Johnston and his army. Duty in the Department of North Carolina till July. Mustered out at Raleigh, N. C., July 19, 1865, and honorably discharged from service.

Regiment lost during service 3 Officers and 31 Enlisted men killed and mortally wounded and 5 Officers and 170 Enlisted men by disease. Total 209.

13th REGIMENT CAVALRY ("SEYMOUR LIGHT").

Regiment organized at Staten Island, N. Y., by consolidation of several incomplete Cavalry organizations June 20, 1863. 6 Companies ("A," "B," "C," "D," "E" and "F") left State for Washington, D. C., June 23, 1863. Companies "G" and "H" August 14, 1863, and "I," "K," "L" and "M" in winter of 1863-1864. Attached to Cavalry Brigade, 22nd Army Corps, Dept. of Washington, June to December, 1863. Tyler's Division, 22nd Army Corps, to January, 1864. 3rd Brigade, Tyler's Division, 22nd Army Corps, to May, 1864. Cavalry Brigade, 22nd Army Corps, to November, 1864. 1st Separate Brigade, 22nd Army Corps, to June, 1865.

SERVICE.—Patrol duty in rear of Army of the Potomac, during Gettysburg (Pa.) Campaign, June-July, 1863. New York Riots July 15, 1863 (Cos. "G," "H"). Duty in and covering the Defences of Washington, D. C., till June, 1865. Action at Fairfax, Va., August 24, 1863. Operating against Moseby till October, 1863. Near Bristoe Station October 14. Chantilly October 16. Near Lewinsville December 9. Near Vienna December 16. Fairfax Court House December 22. Scout from Vienna to Leesburg December 25-27. Scout from Vienna to Hopewell Gap December 28-31. Front Royal February 20, 1864. Scout from Vienna to Farmwell February 25-26. Scout from Vienna toward Upperville April 28-May 1. Carter's Farm May 1. Near Aldie June 11 and July 9. Mt. Zion Church, near Aldie, July 6. Scout from Falls Church July 13-21 (Detachment). Fairfax Station August 8. Blue Ridge Mountains August 10. Annandale September 3. Culpeper September 4. Near Centreville September 13. Fairfax Station September 17. Culpeper September 22. Salem and White Plains October 5-7. Moseby's Camp October 14. Union Mills October 16. Piedmont October 19. Near Fall's Church October 22. Rectorstown December 21. Lewinsville January 1, 1865. Near Broad Run February 3. Near Leesburg February 6. Near Peach Grove March 12 (Detachment). Near Dranesville March 18 (Detachment). Consolidated with 16th New York Cavalry June 23, 1865, to form 3rd Regiment Provisional Cavalry.

Regiment lost during service 31 Enlisted men killed and mortally wounded and 1 Officer and 97 Enlisted men by disease. Total 129.

14th REGIMENT CAVALRY ("1st METROPOLITAN CAVALRY").

Organized at New York City and mustered in by Companies as follows: "A" November 24. "B" November 25. "C" December 22. "D" December 4, 1862. "E" February 3. "F" February 26. "G" March 14. "H" March 18. "I" April 25. "K" July 8. "L" June 6, and "M" July 18, 1863. Companies "A" to "E" left State for Department of the Gulf February 8, 1863. 4 Companies left State for Dept. of the Gulf April, 1863, and remaining 3 Companies left State for Dept. of the Gulf October, 1863. Attached to Defences of New Orleans, La., Dept. of the Gulf, to June, 1863. Grierson's Cavalry Division, Dept. of the Gulf, to July, 1863. Defences of New Orleans, La., to October, 1863. 1st Brigade, Cavalry Division, 19th Army Corps, Dept. of the Gulf, to November, 1863. 3rd Brigade, Cavalry Division, Dept. of the Gulf, to January, 1864. 1st Brigade, Cavalry Division, Dept. of the Gulf, to June, 1864. District of Baton Rouge, La., Dept. of the Gulf, to December, 1864. Separate Cavalry Brigade, District of Baton Rouge, La., to February, 1865. District of Morganza, Dept. of the Gulf, to April, 1865. Defences of New Orleans, La., Dept. of the Gulf, to May, 1865. 1st Brigade, Cavalry Division, Dept. of the Gulf, to June, 1865 (Co. "M" detached at Fort Barrancas, Fla., District of West Florida, September, 1863, to February, 1865.)

SERVICE.—Siege of Port Hudson, La., May 24-July 9, 1863. Clinton June 3-4. Near Port Hudson June 11. New York Riots July 13-15 (Detachment). Opposite Donaldsonville September 23 (1 Company). Western Louisiana Campaign October 3-November 30. Washington October 24 and 31. Bayou Bourbeaux November 3. Grand Coteau, Carrion Crow Bayou, November 3. Ver-

million Bayou November 12. Near New Iberia November 19. Camp Pratt November 20. Red River Campaign March 10-May 22, 1864. Advance from Franklin to Alexandria March 14-26. Bayou Rapides March 20. Henderson's Hill March 21. Monett's Ferry and Cloutiersville March 29-30. Natchitoches March 31. Crump's Hill April 2. Wilson's Farm April 7. Bayou de Paul, Carroll's Mill and Sabine Cross Roads, Mansfield, April 8. Pleasant Hill April 9. Natchitoches April 22. About Cloutiersville April 22-24. Bayou Rapides April 26. McNutt's Hill, Alexandria, April 26. About Alexandria April 26-May 13. Retreat to Morganza May 13-20. Wilson's Landing May 14. Avoyelle's Prairie May 15. Mansura and Marksville May 16. Morganza May 23-24. Moved to Baton Rouge, La., and duty there till January, 1865. Highland Stockade, near Baton Rouge July 29, 1864. Bayou Letsworth August 11. Expedition to Clinton August 23-29. Olive Branch, Comite River and Clinton August 25. Near Baton Rouge September 17. Greenville Springs Road September 24. Expedition from Baton Rouge to Clinton, Greensburg, Osyka and Camp Moore October 5-9. Expedition from Baton Rouge to Brookhaven, Miss., and skirmishes November 14-21. Clinton and Liberty Creek November 15. Summit, Miss., November 19. Clinton and Liberty November 23. Davidson's Expedition from Baton Rouge against Mobile & Ohio Railroad November 27-December 13. Jackson November 27. Franklin Creek December 22. Davis Creek, near Mobile, December 22. Five Mile Creek, near East Pascagoula, December 26. Griffin's Mills, near East Pascagoula, January 3, 1865. At Morganza till June, 1865. Raid to Clinton and Jackson March 1-10, 1865. McCullom's Point, Morganza Bend, March 12. Near Morganza April 3.

Company "M" at Jackson's Bridge, Grand Bayou, Fla., January 25, 1864. Cow Ford Creek, near Pensacola, Fla., April 2. Jackson Bridge May 25. Near Barrancas May 26. Expedition from Barrancas toward Pollard, Ala., July 21-25. Fifteen Mile House July 21. Pollard, Ala., July 22. Camp Gonzales July 22. Expedition from Barrancas August 13-14. Little Escanabia River, Ala., December 15. Pollard, Ala., December 16. Pine Barren Creek December 17.

Regiment consolidated with 18th New York Cavalry June 12, 1865.

Regiment lost during service 2 Officers and 16 Enlisted men killed and mortally wounded and 3 Officers and 137 Enlisted men by disease. Total 158.

15th REGIMENT CAVALRY.

Organized at Syracuse, N. Y., and mustered in as follows: Companies "A," "B," "C" August 8; "D," "F," "G," August 26; "E" August 15; "H" September 5; "K" October 15; "I" November 30, 1863; "L" January 20, and "M" January 24, 1864. Left State for Washington, D. C. Companies "A" to "G" September, 1863. "H" and "K" October, 1863. "I" November, 1863, and "L" and "M" January, 1864. Attached to 22nd Army Corps, Dept. of Washington, D. C., to January, 1864. Cavalry Brigade, 1st Division, Army of West Virginia, to April, 1864. 2nd Brigade, 1st Cavalry Division, Army of West Virginia, to August, 1864. Remount Camp Cumberland, Md., to October, 1864. 2nd Brigade, 3rd Division, Cavalry Corps, Army of the Shenandoah, and Army of the Potomac to June, 1865.

SERVICE.—Duty at Camp Stoneman, Defences of Washington, till January, 1864. Action at Hillsboro, Va., January 22. Operations in Hampshire and Hardy Counties, West Virginia, January 27-February 7. Upperville February 20. Expedition to Petersburg and destruction of Salt Works near Franklin, West Va., February 29-March 5. Sigel's Expedition from Martinsburg to New Market April 30-May 16. Moorefield May 12. Luray Gap, Mt. Jackson, and near New Market May 13. New Market May 14-15. Front Royal May 22. Newtown May 25. Hunter's Raid to Lynchburg, Va., May 26-July 1. Woodstock May 27. Newtown May 29-30. Mt. Jackson June 4. Piedmont June 5. Occupation of Staunton June 6. Waynesboro June 10. Lexington June 11. New London June 16. Diamond Hills June 17. Lynchburg June 17-18. Liberty June 19-20. Catawba Mountains and Salem June 21. Newtown June 28. Bunker Hill July 2. Bolivar Heights July 2. Leetown and Martinsburg July 3. Near Hillsboro July 15-16. Snicker's Ferry July 17-18. Ashby's Gap and Berry's Ford July 19. Near Kernstown July 23. Kernstown, Winchester, July 24. Bunker Hill and Martinsburg July 25. Strasburg August 11. Near Charlestown August 21-22. Ordered to Cumberland, Md., August 24, and duty at Remount Camp till October. Green Springs Run November 1 (Detachment). Expedition to Lacy Springs December 19-21. Lacy Springs December 21. Near Harrisonburg December 31. Sheridan's Raid from Winchester February 27-March 25, 1865. Waynesboro March 2. Occupation of Staunton March 2. Charlottesville March 3. Ashland March 15. Appomattox Campaign March 28-April 9. Dinwiddie Court House March 30-31. Five Forks April 1. Fall of Petersburg April 2. Namozine Church April 3. Jettersville April 4. Sailor's Creek April 6. Appomattox Station April 8. Appomattox Court House April 9. Surrender of Lee and his army. Expedition to Danville April 23-29. March to Washington, D. C., May. Grand Review May 23. Consolidated with 6th New York Cavalry June 17, 1865, to form 2nd Regiment Provisional Cavalry.

Regiment lost during service 2 Officers and 35 Enlisted men killed and mortally wounded and 5 Officers and 126 Enlisted men by disease. Total 168.

16th REGIMENT CAVALRY ("SPRAGUE LIGHT CAVALRY").

Organized at Plattsburg, N. Y., and mustered in by Companies as follows "A," "B," "C," "D" June 19, 1863. "F" August 1, 1863. "G" and "H" August 13, 1863. "I" September 2, 1863. "K" September 22, 1863. "L" October 18, 1863, and "M" September 5, 1863. Companies "A," "B," "C," "D" left State for Washington, D. C., June 19, 1863. Companies "E," "F," "G," "H" August 19, 1863, and "I," "K," "L" September, and "M" October 23, 1863. Attached to Cavalry Brigade, 22nd Army Corps, Dept. of Washington, to October, 1863. DeRussy's Division, 22nd Army Corps, Defences of Washington, south of the Potomac, to December, 1863. 4th Brigade, DeRussy's Division, 22nd Army Corps, to March, 1864. Cavalry Brigade, 22nd Army Corps, to November, 1864. 1st Separate Brigade, 22nd Army Corps, to June, 1865.

SERVICE.—Patrol duty in rear of Army of the Potomac during Gettysburg (Pa.) Campaign June and July, 1863. Duty in and covering the Defences of Washington, D. C., and operating against guerrillas till June, 1865. Lewinsville, Va., October 1, 1863 (Co. "B"). Bristoe Station October 14. Near Blue Ridge Mountains November 18. Near Circlesville February 21, 1864. Dranesville February 22. Scout from Vienna to Farmwell February 25-26. Leesburg April 10. Hunter's Point April 23. Expedition from Vienna toward Upperville April 28-May 1. Near Middleburg April 29. Blue Ridge Mountains April 30. Carter's Farm May 1. Middleburg May 29. Fall's Church June 23 (Detachment). Centreville June 24. Annandale June 26. Aldie July 6. Scout to Rapidan Station July 26 (Detachment). Burke's Station July 29. Fairfax Station August 4. Near Fairfax Station August 7. Fairfax Station and near Fall's Church August 8. Annandale August 14. Fort Buffalo August 22. Annandale August 24. Fall's Church September 13. Fairfax Station and Culpeper September 17. Culpeper September 19. Wolf Run Shoal September 20. Culpeper September 22. Near Lewinsville October 1. Salem and White Plains October 5-7. Fall's Church October 18. Piedmont October 10. Flint Hill November 27. Vienna December 3. Operations about Salem, Warrenton, Bealeton Station, Centreville and Sulphur Springs March 3-8. Warrenton March 5, 1865. Near Flint Hill March 7. Vienna March 8. Scout in Loudoun County March 12-14. Scout from Vienna into Loudoun County April 8-10. Garrett's Farm, near Port

Royal, April 26 (Detachment). Capture of J. Wilkes Booth and Daniel E. Harold. Consolidated with 13th New York Cavalry June 23, 1865, to form 3rd Regiment Provisional Cavalry.

Regiment lost during service 1 Officer and 20 Enlisted men killed and mortally wounded and 120 Enlisted men by disease. Total 141.

17th REGIMENT CAVALRY.

Failed to complete organization. Enlisted men transferred to 1st Veteran Cavalry September 17, 1863.

18th REGIMENT CAVALRY.—("CORNISH LIGHT CAVALRY.")

Organized at New York and mustered in by Companies as follows: "A" July 18, "B" July 19, "C" August 12, "D" August 25, "E" August 15, "F" August 31, "G" October 13, "H" October 31, "I" December 2, 1863; "K," "L" and "M" January, 1864. Companies "A" to "F" left State for Washington, D. C., September 26, 1863; Companies "G" and "H" October 23; "I" and "K" December 13, 1863, and "L" and "M" January, 1864. Attached to Defences of Washington, 22nd Army Corps, to December, 1863. Cavalry Division, 22nd Army Corps, to February, 1864. 5th Brigade, Cavalry Division, Dept. of the Gulf, to June, 1864. District of LaFourche, La., Dept. of the Gulf, to January, 1865. Southern Division of Louisiana, Dept. of the Gulf, to April, 1865. 1st Brigade, 2nd Cavalry Division, Military Division of West Mississippi, to June, 1865. Dept. of Louisiana to September, 1865. Dept. of Texas to May, 1866.

SERVICE.—New York Riots July 13-16, 1863. Duty in the Defences of Washington, D. C., till February, 1864. Ordered to the Dept. of the Gulf February 16. Red River Campaign March 10-May 22. Advance from Franklin to Alexandria March 14-26. Monett's Ferry and Cloutiersville March 29-30. Natchitoches March 31. Campti April 4. Pleasant Hill April 7. Sabine Cross Roads April 8. Pleasant Hill April 9. Grand Ecore April 10. Bayou Salina April 14. Campti April 15. Grand Ecore April 16. Bayou Salina April 17-18. Natchitoches April 19. About Cloutiersville April 22-24. Monett's Ferry, Cane River Crossing, April 23. Grand Ecore April 29. Near Alexandria May 1. Bayou Roberts May 3. Moore's Plantation May 4-5. Well's Plantation May 5-6. Near Alexandria May 8. Bayou Rapides May 10. Near Alexandria May 11-12. Retreat to Morganza May 13-20. Mansura May 15-16. Near Moreauville May 17. Yellow Bayou May 17-18. Morganza May 24. Duty in the Defences of New Orleans till January, 1865. Patersonville July 12, 1864. Centreville July 14. Franklin July 18. At LaFourche till November, 1864. At Bonnet Carre till March, 1865. Expedition from Brashear City to Amite River March 26-29, 1865 (Detachment). Duty in District of Louisiana till November, and at various points in Texas till May, 1866. Mustered out at Victoria, Texas, May 31, 1866, and honorably discharged from service. (Cos. "A" and "F" detached in Texas June to November, 1864.) Parish Vico, Texas, June 25. Brownsville and Rancho San Pedro July 25. Clarksville August 14.

Regiment lost during service 1 Officer and 10 Enlisted men killed and mortally wounded and 2 Officers and 203 Enlisted men by disease. Total 216.

19th REGIMENT CAVALRY.

(See 1st Dragoons.)

20th REGIMENT CAVALRY.—("M'CLELLAN.")

Organized at Sackett's Harbor, N. Y., and mustered in Companies "A" to "G" September 3, 1863; Company "H" September 4, 1863; Companies "I" and "K" September 17; "L" September 22, 1863, and Company "M" September 23, 1863. Left State for Washington, D. C., September 30; thence moved to Portsmouth, Va., by Detachments October and November, 1863. Attached to United States Forces, Portsmouth, Va., Dept. of Virginia and North Carolina, to January, 1864. Heckman's Division, 18th Army Corps, Dept. of Virginia and North Carolina, to April, 1864. Defences of Portsmouth, Va.,

Dept. of Virginia and North Carolina, to May, 1864. District of Eastern Virginia, Dept. of Virginia and North Carolina, to December, 1864. 1st Brigade, Kautz's Cavalry Division, Dept. of Virginia and North Carolina, to April, 1865. Cavalry Brigade, Dept. of Virginia, to July, 1865. Company "D" attached to Separate Brigade, Defences of Bermuda Hundred, Va., Army of the James, December, 1864, to June, 1865. Company "F" at Port Powhattan, Separate Brigade, Defences of Bermuda Hundred, Va., December, 1864, to June, 1865. Company "G" attached to 1st Brigade, McKenzie's Cavalry Division, Army of the James, March to June, 1865. Company "I" with Provisional Division, Army of the James, March to June, 1865.

SERVICE.—Duty in the Defences of Portsmouth, Va., November, 1863, to December, 1864. Action at Smithfield, Va., February 1, 1864. Suffolk February 20. Chuckatuck June 6. Wood's Mills Hill June 24. South Quay July 3. Expedition from Suffolk into North Carolina July 27-August 4. Winston, N. C., July 29. Guiam's Ford, N. C., August 12. Jamestown Island September 3. Expedition from Bermuda Mills to Murfrees Depot, N. C., October 15-17 (Cos. "D," "I" and "K"). Blackwater October 16. Before Petersburg and Richmond December, 1864, to April, 1865. Expedition from Portsmouth to Hertford, N. C., December 6-10, 1864 (Detachment). Operations about Broadwater River and Chowan River December 11-19. Darbytown Road January 13, 1865. Appomattox Campaign April 1-9 (Cos. "G" and "I"). Five Forks April 1. Fall of Petersburg April 2. Deep Creek April 3-4. Rice's Station April 6. Burke's Station April 7. Appomattox Court House April 9. Surrender of Lee and his army. Duty in the Dept. of Virginia till July. (Co. "D" at Fort Pocohontas December, 1864, to June, 1865; Co. "F" at Fort Powhatan December, 1864, to June, 1865.) Mustered out July 31, 1865, and honorably discharged from service.

Regiment lost during service 5 Enlisted men killed and mortally wounded and 2 Officers and 125 Enlisted men by disease. Total 132.

21st REGIMENT CAVALRY.—("GRISWOLD LIGHT CAVALRY.")

Organized at Troy, N. Y., and mustered in by Companies as follows: "A," "B," "C" and "D" August 28, 1863; "E" September 1, 1863; "F" September 18, 1863; "G" October 14, 1863; "H" October 15, 1863; "I" October 16, 1863; "K" November, and "L" December, 1863; "M" January, 1864. Companies "A," "B," "C," "D" and "E" left State for Washington, D. C., September 4, 1863. Company "F" September 19; "G," "H" and "I" October 19; "K" November, 1863, and "L" and "M" February, 1864. Attached to 22nd Army Corps, Dept. of Washington, D. C., to January, 1864. Cavalry Brigade, 1st Division, Army of West Virginia, to April, 1864. 1st Cavalry Division, Army of West Virginia, to August, 1864. 2nd Brigade, 1st Cavalry Division, Army of West Virginia, to September, 1864. Remount Camp Cumberland, Md., Dept. of West Virginia, to November, 1864. 1st Brigade, 2nd Division, Cavalry Corps, Army of the Shenandoah, Middle Military Division, to March, 1865. Tibbitt's Brigade, District of Harper's Ferry, Dept. of West Virginia, to May, 1865. 22nd Army Corps, Dept. of Washington, to June, 1865. Dept. of Missouri to June, 1866.

SERVICE.—Duty at Camp Stoneman, Defences of Washington, D. C., till February, 1864. Attempt to capture Lieutenant Washington by Company "H" January 4. Company ambushed near Smithfield, Va. Berryville Ford January 22. Newtown and Woodstock January 23. Operations in Hampshire and Hardy Counties, W. Va., January 27-February 7. Mechanicsburg Gap February 2. Moorefield February 4. Moved to Harper's Ferry, thence to Halltown, Va. Charlestown February 6-7. Near Smithfield February 14. Paris February 20. Near Kablestown April 10. Near Middletown April 24 (Detachment). Sigel's Expedition from Martinsburg to New Market April 30-May 16. Brock's Gap May 10. Battle of New Market May 15. Newtown

May 21, 29 and 30 and June 3. Hunter's Raid on Lynchburg May 26-July 1. Piedmont June 5. Occupation of Staunton June 6. Lexington June 14. Otter Creek June 16. Diamond Hill June 17. Lynchburg June 17-18. Liberty June 19. Catawba Mountains June 21. Salem June 21-22. Bushy Ridge, Charlestown, June 27. Winchester July 1. Bunker Hill July 2. Buckton July 3. Pleasant Valley July 4. Solomon's Gap July 7. Brownsville July 7. Frederick City July 11. Near Hillsboro July 15-16. Purcellsville and near Wood's Grove July 16. Snicker's Gap and Snicker's Ferry July 17-18. Ashby's Gap and Berry's Ford July 19. Salem July 20. Stevenson's Depot July 20. Near Kernstown July 23. Kernstown, Winchester, July 24. Bunker Hill and Martinsburg July 25. Near Charlestown August 21-22. Falling Waters August 24. Duty at Remount Camp, Cumberland, Md., till November. Milford October 25-26. Ninevah November 12. Stony Creek, Hawkinsville, and Rude's Hill, near Front Royal, November 22. Near Kernstown November 24. Near Winchester November 29. Near Millwood December 4. White Post December 6. Raid on Gordonsville December 19-28. Liberty Mills December 21. Gordonsville December 22-23. Warrenton December 26. Ashby's Gap December 27. Near Paris January 19, 1865. Expedition from Winchester into Loudoun County February 18-19. Ashby's Gap February 19. White Post March 22. Near Berryville April 9. Duty at Washington, D. C., till June, and at Fort Leavenworth, Kansas, till September. At Denver, Colo., till June, 1866. Mustered out at Denver, Colo. Company "B" June 23, Company "F" June 26, Company "G" June 29, Company "C" July 3, Company "E" July 5, Company "D" July 7 and Company "A" at Fort Leavenworth, Kansas, August 31, 1866.

Regiment lost during service 3 Officers and 63 Enlisted men killed and mortally wounded and 1 Officer and 76 Enlisted men by disease. Total 143.

22nd REGIMENT CAVALRY.

Organized at Rochester, N. Y., and mustered in by Companies as follows: Company "A" December 20, 1863; Companies "B" 'and "C" January 5; Companies "D," "E" and "F" January 10; Companies "G," "H" and "I" February 2; Company "K" February 6; Company "L" February 12, and Company "M" February 23, 1864. Left State for Washington, D. C., March 4, 1864. Attached to 9th Army Corps, Army of the Potomac, March and April, 1864. 4th Division, 9th Army Corps, to May, 1864. 2nd Brigade, 3rd Division, Cavalry Corps, Army of the Potomac, to August, 1864; and Army of the Shenandoah, Middle Military Division, to March, 1865. Cavalry Brigade, Army of the Shenandoah, to July, 1865.

SERVICE.—Duty at Alexandria, Va., to April, 1864. Rapidan Campaign May-June. Battle of the Wilderness May 5-7. Spottsylvania Court House May 8-21 (Battalion). Escort ambulance trains to Fredericksburg May 9, and picket duty there till May 28. Moved to White House Landing, thence to Cold Harbor. Cold Harbor June 1-12. Long Bridge June 12. Riddell's Shop June 13. White Oak Swamp June 13. Malvern Hill June 15. Wilson's Raid on South Side & Danville Railroad June 22-30. Ream's Station June 22. Jerusalem Plank Road June 22-23 (Detachment). Dinwiddie Court House June 22. Black and White Station June 23. Nottaway Court House June 23. Stony Creek Station June 23. Staunton River Bridge (or Roanoke Station) June 25. Sappony Church (or Stony Creek) June 28. Ream's Station June 29-30. Before Petersburg till July 30. Sheridan's Shenandoah Valley Campaign August 7-November 28. Winchester August 17. Near Charlestown August 21-22. Kearneysville August 25. Near Brucetown and near Winchester September 7. Locke's Ford September 13. Battle of Winchester September 19. Near Cedarville September 20. Front Royal Pike September 21. Fisher's Hill, Luray Valley and Milford, September 22. Waynesboro September 29 and October 2. Tom's Brook ("Woodstock Races") October 8-9. Battle of Cedar Creek October 19. Near Kernstown November 10. Newtown and Cedar Creek November 12. Rude's Hill, near Mt. Jackson, November 22. Moorefield Pike November 30. Expedition to Lacy's Springs December 19-22. Lacy's Springs December 21. Expedition from Winchester to Moorefield, W. Va., February 4-6, 1865. Sheridan's Raid, Waynesboro, March 2. Occupation of Staunton March 2. Detached from Division to guard prisoners from Waynesboro to Winchester March 3-8. Harrisonburg March 5. Mt. Jackson and Rude's Hill March 7. Duty at and in the vicinity of Winchester till July. Scout from Winchester to Edenburg March 17-19 (Detachment). Operations in the Shenandoah Valley April 26-May 5. Mustered out August 1, 1865, and honorably discharged from service.

Regiment lost during service 3 Officers and 20 Enlisted men killed and mortally wounded and 1 Officer and 183 Enlisted men by disease. Total 207.

23rd REGIMENT CAVALRY ("MIX'S BATTALION").

Only two Companies organized, January to May, 1863. Left State for Dept. of North Carolina May, 1863. (Mostly attached to 12th New York Cavalry, which see.) Attached to Cavalry Brigade, 18th Army Corps, Dept. of North Carolina, to July, 1863. Defences of New Berne, N. C., Dept. of Virginia and North Carolina, to October, 1863. Sub-District of Beaufort, N. C., Dept. of Virginia and North Carolina, to January, 1865. Sub-District of New Berne, N. C., Dept. of North Carolina, to July, 1865.

SERVICE.—Raid on Wilmington & Weldon Railroad July 3-7, 1863. Kenansville and Warsaw July 5. Swift Creek July 18. Expedition to Tarboro and Rocky Mount July 18-24. Tarboro July 20. Swift Creek and Street's Ferry July 21. Scupperton July 22. Expedition from Newport Barracks to Young's Cross Roads, Swansboro and Jackson December 27-29. Expedition to Onslow County January 27, 1864. New Berne February 1-3. Gale's Creek and Newport Barracks February 2. Raid on Wilmington & Weldon Railroad June 20-25. (See 12th New York Cavalry.) Mustered out at Raleigh, N. C., July 22, 1865.

Battalion lost 14 Enlisted men by disease during service.

24th REGIMENT CAVALRY.

Organized at Auburn, N. Y., and mustered in Companies "A," "C," "D" and "E" December 28, 1863. "B," "F," "G," "H" and "I" January 7, 1864. "K" and "L" January 19, 1864; and "M," January 26, 1864. Left State for Washington, D. C., February 23, 1864. Attached to Marshall's Provisional Brigade as Infantry, 9th Army Corps, Army of the Potomac, April to June, 1864. 3rd Brigade, 1st Division, 9th Army Corps, June, 1864. 2nd Brigade, 3rd Division, 9th Army Corps, to September, 1864. 2nd Brigade, 1st Division, 9th Army Corps, to October, 1864. 1st Brigade, 2nd Division, Cavalry Corps, Army of the Potomac, to May, 1865. 1st Brigade, 1st Division, Cavalry Corps, to June, 1865.

SERVICE.—Duty in the Defences of Washington, D. C., till April, 1864. Rapidan Campaign May-June. Battles of the Wilderness May 5-7. Spottsylvania May 8-12. Spottsylvania Court House May 12-21. North Anna River May 23-26. On line of the Pamunkey May 26-28. Totopotomoy May 28-31. Cold Harbor June 1-12. Bethesda Church June 3. Before Petersburg June 16-18. Siege of Petersburg June 16, 1864, to April 2, 1865. Mine Explosion, Petersburg, July 30, 1864. Weldon Railroad August 18-21. Ream's Station August 25. Poplar Springs Church September 29-October 2. Vaughan Road October 1. Peeble's Farm October 2. Reconnoissance on Vaughan and Squirrel Level Road October 8. Regiment mounted October 20, 1864. Boydton Plank Road, Hatcher's Run, October 27-28. Prince George Court House November 24. Stony Creek Station December 1. Hicksford Raid December 6-12. Bellefield and Three Creeks December 9. Halifax Road December 10-11. Dabney's Mills, Hatcher's Run, February 5-7, 1865. Appomattox Campaign March 28-April 9. Dinwiddie Court House March 30-31. Five Forks April

1. Fall of Petersburg April 2. Payne's Cross Roads April 5. Amelia Springs April 5. Deatonville Road and Sailor's Creek April 6. Farmville April 7. Appomattox Court House April 9. Surrender of Lee and his army. Expedition to Danville April 23-29. March to Washington, D. C., May. Grand Review May 23. Consolidated with 10th New York Cavalry June 17, 1865, to form 1st Regiment Provisional Cavalry.

Regiment lost during service 7 Officers and 107 Enlisted men killed and mortally wounded and 1 Officer and 133 Enlisted men by disease. Total 248.

25th REGIMENT CAVALRY.

Regiment organized at Saratoga Springs, N. Y., and at Hart's Island, N. Y. Harbor, and mustered in by Companies as follows: Companies "A" and "B" February 20, Companies "C" and "D" March 19, Company "E" April 14, Company "F" April 23, Company "G" April 20, Company "H" July 29, Company "I" September 18, Company "K" May 16, Company "L" October 15 and Company "M" October 20, 1864. Moved to Washington, D. C., by detachments March to October, 1864. Attached to Defences of Washington, D. C., 22nd Army Corps, April to June, 1864. Provost Guard Army of the Potomac, to July, 1864. Defences of Washington, D. C., 22nd Corps, to August, 1864. 3rd Brigade, 1st Division, Cavalry Corps, Army of the Shenandoah, Middle Military Division, to September, 1864. 1st Brigade, 1st Division, Cavalry Corps, Army of the Shenandoah, to January, 1865. Unattached, 2nd Infantry Division, Army of West Virginia, to June, 1865.

SERVICE.—Duty in the Defences of Washington, D. C., till June, 1864. Ordered to the field and Provost duty with Army of the Potomac to July, 1864. Fort Stevens and repulse of Early's attack on Washington, July 11-12. Duty in the Defences of Washington till August. Sheridan's Shenandoah Valley Campaign August 7-November 28. Toll Gate, near White Post, August 11. Cedarville, Guard Hill, or Front Royal, August 16. Winchester August 17. Opequan Creek August 18. Near Kearneysville August 25. Halltown August 26. Duffield Station August 27. Berryville September 3. Opequan Creek September 13. Sevier's Ford, Opequan Creek, September 15. Battle of Winchester September 19. Fisher's Hill September 22. Front Royal September 23-24. Luray Valley September 24. Luray September 25. Port Republic September 26-27. Mt. Crawford October 2. Tom's Brook ("Woodstock Races") October 8-9. Near Conrad's Ferry October 22. Newtown November 12. Rude's Hill, near Mt. Jackson, November 22. White Plains November 27-28. Expedition into Faquier and Loudoun Counties November 28-December 3. Upperville November 29. Snicker's Gap November 30. Expedition to Gordonsville December 19-28. Flint Hill December 20. Jack's Shop, near Gordonsville, December 22-23. Columbia Furnace January 19 and 29, 1865. Duty in the Shenandoah Valley till June. Mustered out at Hart's Island, N. Y., June 27, 1865, and honorably discharged from service.

Regiment lost during service 1 Officer and 16 Enlisted men killed and mortally wounded and 49 Enlisted men by disease. Total 66.

26th REGIMENT CAVALRY.—("FRONTIER CAVALRY.")

Organized for one year's service on the Northern Frontier of New York. Company "G" organized at Plattsburg, N. Y., and mustered in February 11, 1865. Mustered out at Plattsburg, N. Y., July 6, 1865. Company "H" organized at Watertown, N. Y., and mustered in February 22, 1865. Mustered out at Sackett's Harbor, N. Y., July 7, 1865. Company "I" organized at Malone, N. Y., and mustered in February 22, 1865. Mustered out at Ogdensburg, N. Y., July 3, 1865. Company "K" organized at Buffalo, N. Y., and mustered in February 24, 1865. Mustered out at Fort Porter, N. Y., June 29, 1865. Company "L" organized at Malone, N. Y., and mustered in February 24, 1865. Mustered out at Ogdensburg, N. Y., July 1, 1865. Lost 3 by disease.

DEVIN'S COMPANY 1st CAVALRY NEW YORK MILITIA.—("JACKSON HORSE GUARD.")

Volunteered for three months United States service and left State for Washington, D. C., July 3, 1861. Mustered in at Washington July 14, and Provost duty in the Defences of that city till October. Participated in skirmishes at Fall's Church, Vienna and Lewinsville, Va. Mustered out at New York City October 23, 1861.

ONEIDA INDEPENDENT COMPANY CAVALRY.

Organized at Oneida, N. Y., and mustered in September 4, 1861. Moved to Washington, D. C., September, 1861. Attached to Stoneman's Cavalry Command, Army of the Potomac, to April, 1862. At Headquarters, Army of the Potomac, as escort till June, 1865. History Army of the Potomac. Mustered out June 13, 1865, and honorably discharged from service.

Company lost during service 10 by disease.

SAUER'S COMPANY "C" HUSSARS 3rd CAVALRY NEW YORK MILITIA.

Volunteered for three months' United States service and left State July 23, 1861. Mustered out at New York City November 2, 1861.

2nd REGIMENT HEAVY ARTILLERY.

Organized at Staten Island, N. Y., and mustered in by Companies as follows: Companies "C" and "D" September 18, Company "B" August 23, Companies "A" and "E" October 2, Companies "F," "G" and "H" October 15, Company "L" November 18, Companies "I" and "K" December 11 and Company "M" December 12, 1861. Eight Companies left State for Washington, D. C., November 7, 1861. Company "L" left December 2, and Companies "I," "K" and "M" December 12, 1861. Attached to Military District of Washington, D. C., December, 1861, to May, 1862. Sturgis' Command, Military District of Washington, to January, 1863. Artillery, District of Alexandria, Va., to February, 1863. Artillery, District of Alexandria, 22nd Army Corps, Dept. of Washington, to April, 1863. 1st Brigade, DeRussy's Division, 22nd Army Corps, to April, 1864. 2nd Brigade, DeRussy's Division, 22nd Army Corps, to May, 1864. Tyler's Heavy Artillery Division, 2nd Army Corps, Army of the Potomac, May 16-29, 1864. 1st Brigade, 1st Division, 2nd Army Corps, to June, 1865. 1st Brigade, DeRussy's Division, 22nd Army Corps, to September, 1865. (Battery "L" detached March, 1862, and designated 34th New York Independent Battery November, 1863. See 34th Battery for history.)

SERVICE.—Duty in the Defences of Washington till May, 1864. Pope's Campaign in Northern Virginia August, 1862. Action at Bull Run Bridge, Va., August 27. Battle of Bull Run, Va., August 29-30. Ordered to join Army of the Potomac in the field May 15, 1864. Rapidan Campaign May-June. Spottsylvania Court House, Va., May 18-21. Harris Farm or Fredericksburg Road May 19. North Anna River May 23-26. On line of the Pamunkey May 26-28. Totopotomoy May 28-31. Cold Harbor June 1-12. Assault at Cold Harbor June 3. Before Petersburg June 16-18. Siege of Petersburg June 16, 1864, to April 2, 1865. Jerusalem Plank Road June 22-23, 1864. Deep Bottom July 27-28. Mine Explosion, Petersburg, July 30 (Reserve). Deep Bottom, Strawberry Plains, August 14-18. Ream's Station August 25. Boydton Plank Road, Hatcher's Run, October 27-28. Reconnoissance to Hatcher's Run December 9-10. Hatcher's Run December 9. Dabney's Mills, Hatcher's Run, February 5-7, 1865. Watkins' House March 25. Appomattox Campaign March 28-April 9. On line of Hatcher's and Gravelly Runs March 29-30. Hatcher's Run or Boydton Road March 31. White Oak Road March 31. Sutherland Station and fall of Petersburg April 2. Amelia Springs April 5. Sailor's Creek April 6. High Bridge and Farmville April 7. Appomattox Court House April 9. Surrender of Lee and his army. March to Washington, D. C., May 2-12. Grand Review May 23. Duty at Washington, D. C., till September. Mustered out at Washington, D. C., September 29, 1865, and honorably discharged from service.

Regiment lost during service 10 Officers and 204 Enlisted men killed and mortally wounded and 247 Enlisted men by disease. Total 461.

3rd BATTALION GERMAN HEAVY ARTILLERY.

Organized at New York City. Left State for Washington, D. C., December 19, 1861. Attached to Military District of Washington to February, 1863. 1st Brigade, DeRussy's Division, 22nd Army Corps, Dept. of Washington, to June, 1863. 2nd Brigade, DeRussy's Division, 22nd Army Corps, to September, 1863.

SERVICE.—Duty in the Defences of Washington, D. C., south of the Potomac till September, 1863. Consolidated with 15th New York Heavy Artillery September 30, 1863, as Companies "A," "B," "C," "D" and "E." (See 15th Heavy Artillery.)

4th REGIMENT HEAVY ARTILLERY.

Organized at New York November, 1861, to February, 1862. Left State for Washington, D. C., February 10, 1862. Attached to Military District of Washington to May, 1862. Whipple's Command, Military District of Washington, to October, 1862. Abercrombie's Division, Defences of Washington, to February, 1863. Abercrombie's Division, 22nd Army Corps, Dept. of Washington, to April, 1863. 1st Brigade, DeRussy's Division, 22nd Army Corps, to May, 1863. 4th Brigade, DeRussy's Division, 22nd Army Corps, to December, 1863. (4 Cos. 11th New York Heavy Artillery assigned July 25, 1863, as Cos. "I," "K," "L" and "M.") 3rd Brigade, DeRussy's Division, 22nd Army Corps, to March, 1864. Artillery Brigade, 6th Army Corps, Army of the Potomac, to May, 1864 (Cos. "C," "D," "L" and "M" 1st Battalion). Artillery Brigade, 5th Army Corps, to May, 1864 (Cos. "E," "F," "H" and "K" 2nd Battalion). Artillery Brigade, 2nd Army Corps, to May, 1864 (Cos. "A," "B," "G" and "I" 3rd Battalion). Artillery Brigade, 2nd Army Corps, May 31 to June 25, 1864. 1st Brigade, 3rd Division, 2nd Army Corps (1st Battalion). 2nd Brigade, 3rd Division, 2nd Army Corps (2nd Battalion), June 25 to July 13, 1864. Artillery Reserve to August, 1864. Unattached, 1st Division, 2nd Army Corps, to September, 1864. 4th Brigade, 1st Division, 2nd Army Corps, to March, 1865. 2nd Brigade, 1st Division, 2nd Army Corps, to June, 1865. 3rd Brigade, DeRussy's Division, 22nd Army Corps, to August, 1865. 2nd Brigade, Dept. of Washington, to September, 1865. (Co. "D" with Artillery Brigade, 2nd Army Corps, July to December, 1864. Co. "L" with Artillery Brigade, 2nd Army Corps, July, 1864, to March, 1865. Co. "C" with Artillery Brigade, 2nd Army Corps, October, 1864, to May, 1865.)

SERVICE.—Duty in the Defences of Washington, D. C., till March, 1864. Action at Lewinsville, Va., July 6, 1862, and October 1, 1863 (Detachment). Rapidan Campaign May-June, 1864. Battles of the Wilderness May 5-7; Spottsylvania May 8-12; Piney Branch Church May 8 (2nd Battalion); Laurel Hill May 10 (3rd Battalion); Spottsylvania Court House May 12-21; Landron's Farm May 18 (1st Battalion); North Anna River May 23-26. On line of the Totopotomoy May 28-31. Cold Harbor June 1-12. Before Petersburg June 16-18. Siege of Petersburg June 16, 1864, to April 2, 1865. Jerusalem Plank Road, Weldon Railroad, June 22-23, 1864. Deep Bottom July 27-28. Mine Explosion, Petersburg, July 30 (Reserve). Strawberry Plains, Deep Bottom, August 14-18. Ream's Station August 25. Poplar Springs Church, Peeble's Farm, September 29-October 2. Boydton Plank Road, Hatcher's Run, October 27-28. Reconnoissance to Hatcher's Run December 9-10. Dabney's Mills, Hatcher's Run, February 5-7, 1865. Watkin's House March 25. Appomattox Campaign March 28-April 9. Hatcher's Run or Boydton Road and White Oak Road March 31. Sutherland Station and fall of Petersburg April 2. Pursuit of Lee April 3-9. Amelia Springs April 5. Sailor's Creek April 6. Farmville April 7. Appomattox Court House April 9. Surrender of Lee and his army. March to Washington, D. C., May 2-12. Grand Review May 23. Duty in the Defences of Washington till September. Mustered out

September 26, 1865, and honorably discharged from service.

Regiment lost during service 8 Officers and 108 Enlisted men killed and mortally wounded and 4 Officers and 334 Enlisted men by disease. Total 454.

4th REGIMENT NATIONAL GUARD HEAVY ARTILLERY.

Organized at Harrisburg, Pa., June 20, 1863. Gettysburg (Pa.) Campaign June-July. Mustered out July 24, 1863.

4th BATTALION HEAVY ARTILLERY ("1st BATTALION BLACK RIVER ARTILLERY").

Organized at Sackett's Harbor, N. Y., and mustered in September 11, 1862. Duty at Fort Richmond, N. Y., till December, 1862. Transferred to 10th New York Heavy Artillery as Companies "B," "D," "E" and "M," December 31, 1862. (See 10th Heavy Artillery.)

5th REGIMENT HEAVY ARTILLERY ("2nd REGIMENT JACKSON HEAVY").

Organized by consolidation of Jackson Heavy as Companies "E," "F," "G" and "H" and 2nd Jackson Heavy as Companies "A," "B," "C" and "D" March 6, 1862. 6th Battalion Heavy Artillery (3rd Battalion Black River Heavy Artillery) assigned as Companies "I," "K," "L" and "M" December 31, 1862. First 8 Companies served as garrison in New York Harbor at Forts Hamilton, LaFayette, Wood, Gibson, Richmond and Schuyler, March 11 to May 27, 1862. Moved to Baltimore, Md., May 27 and duty there till April 19, 1864. Companies "A" and "F" detached at Harper's Ferry, W. Va., June 19 to September 15, 1862, participating in actions at Point of Rocks and Berlin September 4-5 (Company "A"). Point of Rocks September 7 (Co. "A"). Defence of Harper's Ferry September 12-15. Maryland Heights, September 12-13. Bolivar Heights September 14. Surrendered September 15. Paroled September 16, and rejoind Regiment at Baltimore. Regiment attached to Defences of Baltimore, Md. 8th Army Corps, Middle Department, May, 1862, to February, 1863. Morris' Brigade, 8th Army Corps, to March, 1863. 2nd Separate Brigade, 8th Army Corps, to April, 1864. 3rd Battalion (Cos. "I," "K," "L" and "M" on duty in the Defences of Washington, D. C., north and south of the Potomac, 22nd Army Corps, December 31, 1862, to November 24, 1863; then at Harper's Ferry, Reserve Division, Dept. of West Virginia, to October, 1864. 1st Battalion, attached to 1st Brigade, 1st Infantry Division, Army of West Virginia, April 19 to July 29, 1864, participating in Sigel's Expedition from Martinsburg to New Market April 29-May 16. Battle of New Market May 15. Hunter's Raid on Lynchburg, Va., May 26-July 1. Piedmont June 5. Occupation of Staunton June 6. Diamond Hill June 17. Lynchburg June 17-18. Liberty June 19. Salem June 21. Operations about Harper's Ferry July 4-7. Snicker's Ferry July 17-18. Kernstown, Winchester, July 24. Martinsburg July 25. Duty at Harper's Ferry till October. 2nd Battalion attached to 1st Brigade, 1st Infantry Division, Army of West Virginia, July 29 to October 28, 1864, participating in Sheridan's Campaign in the Shenandoah Valley, August to October. Cedar Creek August 12. Charlestown August 21. Halltown August 23. Berryville September 3. Battle of Winchester September 19. Fisher's Hill September 22. Cedar Creek October 13. Battle of Cedar Creek October 19. At Harper's Ferry till October 29. Regiment on duty in the Shenandoah Valley and in District of Harper's Ferry, W. Va., October, 1864, to July, 1865. Attached to 3rd Brigade, 3rd Division, Army of West Virginia, January to April, 1865. 2nd Brigade, 2nd Infantry Division, West Virginia, to June, 1865. District of Harper's Ferry to July, 1865. 3rd Battalion mustered out July 24, 1865. Regiment mustered out July 19, 1865.

Regiment lost during service 90 Enlisted men killed and mortally wounded and 1 Officer and 295 Enlisted men by disease. Total 386.

5th BATTALION HEAVY ARTILLERY ("2nd BATTALION BLACK RIVER ARTILLERY").

Organized at Sackett's Harbor, N. Y., and mustered in September 11, 1862. Left State for Washington, D. C., September 18, 1862. Transferred to 10th New York Heavy Artillery as Companies "A," "C," "F" and "G" December 31, 1862.

6th REGIMENT HEAVY ARTILLERY ("ANTHONY WAYNE GUARD").

Organized at Yonkers, N. Y., as the 135th Regiment Infantry, and mustered in September 2, 1862. Designation changed October 3, 1862. Left State for Baltimore, Md., September 5, 1862. Attached to Defences of Baltimore, Md., 8th Army Corps, Middle Department, to January, 1863. Defences. Upper Potomac, to March, 1863. 2nd Brigade, 1st Division, 8th Army Corps, to June, 1863. 3rd Provisional Brigade, French's Division, 8th Army Corps, to July, 1863. 1st Brigade, 3rd Division, 3rd Army Corps, to August, 1863. Artillery Reserve and Headquarters and ammunition train guard, Army of the Potomac, to April, 1864. 1st Brigade, Artillery Reserve, Army of the Potomac, to May 13, 1864. Kitching's Heavy Artillery Brigade, 5th Army Corps, Army of the Potomac, to May 30, 1864. 1st Brigade, 3rd Division, 5th Army Corps, to June 2, 1864. 3rd Brigade, 2nd Division, 5th Army Corps, to August, 1864. 1st Brigade, Hardin's Division, 22nd Army Corps, Dept. of Washington, to September, 1864. 1st Brigade, Kitching's Provisional Division, Middle Military Division, September 27 to December 3, 1864. 2nd Brigade, Provisional Division, Army of the James, and 2nd Brigade, Infantry Division, Defences of Bermuda Hundred, Army of the James, to March, 1865. 2nd Brigade, Ferrero's Division, Dept. of Virginia, to May, 1865. Sub-District of Roanoke, District of the Nottaway, Dept. of Virginia, to August, 1865.

SERVICE.—Duty at Fort McHenry, Baltimore, Md., to December, 1862. Companies "B," "E," "F," "I," "L" and "M"). Companies "A," "C," "D," "G," "H" and "K" at Harper's Ferry, W. Va., December, 1862. Duty on the Upper Potomac till July, 1863. Pursuit of Lee July. Wapping Heights, Va., July 23. Ammunition train guard for Army of the Potomac till April, 1864. Bristoe Campaign October 9-22, 1863. Advance to line of the Rappahannock November 7-8. Mine Run Campaign November 26-December 2. Rapidan Campaign May-June, 1864. Battles of the Wilderness May 5-7. Spottsylvania May 8-12. Spottsylvania Court House May 12-21. Harris Farm (or Fredericksburg Road) May 19. North Anna River May 23-26. On line of the Pamunkey May 26-28. Totopotomoy May 28-31. Cold Harbor June 1-12. Bethesda Church June 3. Before Petersburg June 16-18. Siege of Petersburg June 16-July 9. Ordered to Washington, D. C., and duty in the Defences of that city till September. Sheridan's Shenandoah Valley Campaign September to December. Battle of Cedar Creek October 19. Duty in the Shenandoah Valley till December. Moved to Bermuda Hundred, Va., and duty in the Defences at that point till March, 1865. Fort Brady January 24, 1865. Appomattox Campaign March 28-April 9. Fall of Petersburg April 2. Duty in the Sub-District of Roanoke, District of the Nottaway, Dept. of Virginia, till June, and at Petersburg, Va., till August. Mustered out near Washington, D. C., August 24, 1865.

Regiment lost during service 5 Officers and 130 Enlisted men killed and mortally wounded and 6 Officers and 275 Enlisted men by disease. Total 417.

6th BATTALION HEAVY ARTILLERY ("3rd BATTALION BLACK RIVER ARTILLERY").

Organized at Sackett's Harbor, N. Y., and mustered in September 11, 1862. Left State for Washington, D. C., September 20, 1862. Duty in the Defences of that city till December, 1862. Transferred to 5th New York Heavy Artillery December 31, 1862, as Companies "I," "K," "L" and "M." (See 5th New York Heavy Artillery.)

7th REGIMENT HEAVY ARTILLERY—"ALBANY COUNTY REGIMENT," "SEYMOUR GUARD."

Organized at Albany, N. Y., as the 113th Regiment, N. Y. Infantry, and mustered in August 18, 1862. Left State for Washington, D. C., August 18, 1862. Attached to Defences north of the Potomac September, 1862, to February, 1863. 2nd Brigade, Haskin's Division, 22nd Army Corps, Dept. of Washington, to May, 1864. Tyler's Heavy Artillery Division, 2nd Army Corps, Army of the Potomac, May 18-29, 1864. 4th Brigade, 1st Division, 2nd Army Corps, to November 23, 1864. 2nd Brigade, 1st Division, 2nd Army Corps, to February 22, 1865. Defences of Baltimore, Md., 8th Army Corps, Middle Department, to August, 1865.

SERVICE.—Garrison duty in the Defences of Washington, D. C., till May 15, 1864. Ordered to join Army of the Potomac in the field May 15, 1864. Rapidan Campaign May-June. Spottsylvania Court House May 17-21. Harris Farm or Fredericksburg Road May 19. North Anna River May 23-26. On line of the Pamunkey May 26-28. Totopotomoy May 28-31. Cold Harbor June 1-12. Before Petersburg June 16-18. Siege of Petersburg June 16, 1864, to February 22, 1865. Weldon Railroad June 22-23, 1864. Demonstration north of the James July 27-29. Deep Bottom July 27-28. Mine Explosion, Petersburg, July 30 (Reserve). Demonstration north of the James August 13-20. Strawberry Plains, Deep Bottom, August 14-18. Ream's Station August 25. Hatcher's Run October 27-28. Reconnoissance to Hatcher's Run December 9-10. Dabney's Mills, Hatcher's Run, February 5-7, 1865. Ordered to Baltimore, Md., February 22, and garrison duty there till August. Mustered out August 1, 1865, and honorably discharged from service.

Regiment lost during service 14 Officers and 277 Enlisted men killed and mortally wounded and 4 Officers and 374 Enlisted men by disease. Total 669.

7th BATTALION HEAVY ARTILLERY.—("4th BATTALION BLACK RIVER ARTILLERY.")

Organized at Sackett's Harbor, N. Y., and mustered in Companies "A" and "B" September 12, 1862; Company "C" November 12, 1862, and Company "D" December 27, 1862. Companies "A," "B" and "D" moved to Washington, D. C., September 20, 1862, and garrison duty there till December. Company "D" on duty at Fort Schuyler, New York Harbor. Battalion transferred to 10th New York Heavy Artillery December 31, 1862, as Companies "H," "I," "K" and "L." (See 10th New York Heavy Artillery.)

8th REGIMENT HEAVY ARTILLERY.

Organized at Lockport, N. Y., as the 129th Regiment Infantry, and mustered in August 22, 1862. Left State for Baltimore, Md., August 23, 1862. Designation changed October 19, 1862. Attached to Defences of Baltimore, Md., 8th Army Corps, Middle Department, to January, 1863. 2nd Separate Brigade, 8th Army Corps, to July, 1863. 2nd Brigade, Maryland Heights Division, Army of West Virginia, to August, 1863. 2nd Separate Brigade, 8th Army Corps, to May, 1864. Tyler's Heavy Artillery Division, 2nd Army Corps, Army of the Potomac, May 15-29, 1864. 4th Brigade, 2nd Division, 2nd Army Corps, to June 26, 1864. 2nd Brigade, 2nd Division, 2nd Army Corps, to June, 1865.

SERVICE.—Garrison duty at Forts Federal Hill, Marshall and McHenry, Defences of Baltimore, Md. (except from July 10 to August 3, 1863, at Maryland Heights, and a few days in February, 1864, at Green Springs Run and Romney), till May 12, 1864. Ordered to join Army of the Potomac in the field May 12, 1864. (Cos. "L" and "M" join Regiment at Baltimore February, 1864.) Rapidan Campaign May-June, 1864. Spottsylvania Court House May 17-21. Harris Farm or Fredericksburg Road May 19. North Anna River May 23-26. On line of the Pamunkey May 26-28. Totopotomoy May 28-31. Cold Harbor June 1-12. Before Petersburg June 16-18. Siege of Petersburg June 16, 1864, to April 2, 1865. Jerusalem Plank Road June 22-23, 1864. Demonstration north of the James July 27-29. Deep Bottom July 27-28. Mine Explosion, Petersburg, July 30 (Reserve). Demonstration north of the James August 13-20. Strawberry Plains, Deep Bottom, August 14-18. Ream's Station August 25. Boydton Plank Road, Hatcher's Run, October 27-28. Watkin's House March 25, 1865. Appomattox Campaign March 28-April 9. Crow's House March 31. Fall of Petersburg April 2. Sailor's Creek April 6. High Bridge and Farmville April 7. Appomattox Court House April 9. Surrender of Lee and his army. March to Washington, D. C., May 2-12. Grand Review May 23. Mustered out June 5, 1865. Veterans and Recruits of Companies "G," "H," "I" and "K" transferred to 4th New York Heavy Artillery; those of Companies "A," "B," "C," "D," "E" and "F" to 10th New York Heavy Artillery.

Regiment lost during service 19 Officers and 342 Enlisted men killed and mortally wounded and 4 Officers and 298 Enlisted men by disease. Total 663.

9th REGIMENT HEAVY ARTILLERY.—("2nd AUBURN REGIMENT," "CAYUGA AND WAYNE COUNTY REGIMENT.")

Organized at Auburn, N. Y., as the 138th Regiment New York Infantry and mustered in September 8, 1862. Left State for Washington, D. C., September 12, 1862. Designation changed to 9th Heavy Artillery December 9, 1862. 22nd New York Battery assigned to Regiment as Company "M" February 5, 1863. Company "L" organized at Albany, N. Y., and mustered in December 4, 1863. Regiment attached to 1st Brigade, Defences of Washington, D. C., north of the Potomac to December, 1862. 2nd Brigade, Defences North of the Potomac, to February, 1863. 2nd Brigade, Haskins' Division, 22nd Army Corps, Dept. of Washington, to April, 1864. 3rd Brigade, Haskins' Division, 22nd Army Corps, to May, 1864. 2nd Brigade, 3rd Division, 6th Army Corps, Army of the Potomac and Army of the Shenandoah, Middle Military Division, to June, 1865. (2nd Battalion detached with Artillery Brigade, 6th Army Corps, May 31 to July 10, 1864. 1st Brigade, Hardin's Division, 22nd Army Corps, to September 23, 1864. Keim's Provisional Brigade to October 3, 1864; then rejoined Regiment.) 1st Brigade, Hardin's Division, 22nd Army Corps, to June, 1865.

SERVICE.—Garrison duty in the Defences of Washington, D. C., till May, 1864, during which time built and garrisoned Forts Mansfield, Bayard, Gaines and Foote. Relieved from garrison duty and ordered to join Army of the Potomac in the field May 18, 1864. Rapidan Campaign May-June. North Anna River May 26. On line of the Pamunkey May 26-28. Totopotomoy May 28-31. Cold Harbor June 1-12. Bethesda Church June 1-3. Before Petersburg June 18-19. Siege of Petersburg June 18-July 6. Jerusalem Plank Road, Weldon Railroad, June 22-23. Moved to Baltimore, Md., July 6-8. Battle of Monocacy, Md., July 9. Sheridan's Shenandoah Valley Campaign August 7-November 28. Near Charlestown August 21-22. Charlestown August 29. Battle of Winchester September 19. Fisher's Hill September 22. Battle of Cedar Creek October 19. Duty at Kernstown till December. Moved to Washington, D. C., December 3; thence to Petersburg, Va. Siege of Petersburg, Va., December, 1864, to April, 1865. Fort Fisher, Petersburg, March 25, 1865. Appomattox Campaign March 28-April 9. Assault on and fall of Petersburg April 2. Amelia Springs April 5. Sailor's Creek April 6. Appomattox Court House April 9. Surrender of Lee and his army. Expedition to Danville April 17-27. Duty there and at Richmond till June. Moved to Washington, D. C. Corps Review June 8. Consolidated to four Companies June 27, 1865, and transferred to 2nd New York Heavy Artillery.

Regiment lost during service 6 Officers and 198 Enlisted men killed and mortally wounded and 3 Officers and 254 Enlisted men by disease. Total 461.

10th REGIMENT HEAVY ARTILLERY.—("BLACK RIVER ARTILLERY." "JEFFERSON COUNTY REGIMENT.")

Organized by consolidation of 4th, 5th and 7th Battalions of Black River Artillery December 31, 1862. Companies "A," "B," "C," "D," "E," "F," "G" and "M" were originally organized at Sackett's Harbor, N. Y., and mustered in September 11, 1862. Companies "H" and "I" organized at same place and mustered in September 12, 1862. Company "K" organized at Staten Island, N. Y., November 12, 1862. Company "L" at Fort Schuyler, N. Y., December 27, 1862. Companies "A," "C," "F," "G," "H," "I," "K" and "L" left State for Washington, D. C., September 18, 1862. Companies "B," "D," "E" and "M" on duty at Fort Richmond and Sandy Hook, New York Harbor, September, 1862, to June, 1863; then joined Regiment at Washington, D. C. Regiment attached to 3rd Brigade, Haskins' Division, Defences of Washington, D. C., to February, 1863. 3rd Brigade, Haskins' Division, 22nd Army Corps, Dept. of Washington, to March, 1864. 3rd Brigade, DeRussy's Division, 22nd Army Corps, to May, 1864. 3rd Brigade, 2nd Division, 18th Army Corps, Army of the James, June 5-24, 1864. 1st Brigade, 2nd Division, 18th Army Corps, to August, 1864. 1st Brigade, DeRussy's Division, 22nd Army Corps, to September, 1864. 2nd Brigade, Kitching's Provisional Division, Middle Military Division, to December, 1864. 2nd Brigade, Provisional Division, Defences of Bermuda Hundred, Va., Dept. of Virginia and North Carolina, to January, 1865. 2nd Brigade, Ferrero's Division, Army of the James, to March, 1865. 2nd Brigade, Ferrero's Division, Dept. of Virginia, to June, 1865. District of the Nottaway, Dept. of Virginia, to June, 1865.

SERVICE.—Garrison duty in the Defences of Washington, D. C., till May, 1864. Ordered to join Army of the Potomac in the field May 27. Cold Harbor, Va., June 5-12. Before Petersburg June 15-19. Siege of Petersburg June 16 to August 15. Mine Explosion, Petersburg, July 30 (Reserve). Moved to Washington, D. C., August 15, and duty there till September 27. Ordered to the Shenandoah Valley September 27. Battle of Cedar Creek October 19. Duty in the Shenandoah Valley till December. Moved to Washington, D. C., thence to Bermuda Hundred, Va., and duty in the Defences at that point till March, 1865. Appomattox Campaign March 28-April 9. Assault on and fall of Petersburg April 2. Duty in the Dept. of Virginia till June. Mustered out at Petersburg, Va., June 23, 1865. Recruits transferred to 6th New York Heavy Artillery.

Regiment lost during service 47 Enlisted men killed and mortally wounded and 2 Officers and 218 Enlisted men by disease. Total 267.

11th REGIMENT HEAVY ARTILLERY.

Only four Companies organized. Left State for Harrisburg, Pa., June 24, 1863. Duty in the Dept. of the Susquehanna to July 10. Carlisle, Pa., July 1. New York Riots July 13-16. Stationed at Forts Richmond, Hamilton and at Sandy Hook, Dept. of the East, till July 25. Transferred to 4th New York Heavy Artillery as 3rd Battalion (Cos. "I," "K," "L" and "M") July 25, 1863.

12th REGIMENT HEAVY ARTILLERY.

Failed to complete organization. Men enlisted were transferred to the 15th New York Heavy Artillery.

13th REGIMENT HEAVY ARTILLERY.

Organized at New York and mustered in at Elmira, N. Y., by Companies as follows: "A" August 12, 1863. "B" August 29. "C" September 11. "D" at Staten Island, N. Y., August 4, 1863. "E" at Fort Schuyler March 10, 1864. "F" February, 1864. "G" March 14. "H" February 18. "I" at Ricker's Island November 10, 1863. "K" at Norfolk, Va., February 21, 1864. "L" June 11, 1864. "M" December, 1863. Companies "A," "B," "C," "D" left State for Norfolk, Va., October 5, 1863. Attached to Defences of Norfolk and Portsmouth, Va., and Defences of New Berne, N. C., Dept. of Vir-

ginia and North Carolina (1st and 2nd Battalions). 3rd Battalion (Cos. "I," "K," "L," "M") attached to Naval Brigade as guard on board vessels of war along Atlantic Coast and with James River fleet as Naval Brigade, Army of the James, Companies "A" and "H" attached to 3rd Division, 18th Army Corps, May, 1864, to January, 1865, and to Defences of Bermuda Hundred, Va., to June, 1865, participating in Butler's operations on south side of the James River and against Petersburg and Richmond May 4-28, 1864. Before Petersburg June 15-18. Siege operations against Petersburg and Richmond June 16, 1864, to April 2, 1865. Fall of Petersburg April 2, 1865. (Co. "D" at Fort Fisher, N. C., January 15, 1865.) Expedition from Suffolk to Murfree's Depot, N. C., March 10-11, 1865 (Detachment). South Quay March 10. Expedition from Deep Bottom to near Weldon, N. C., March 28-April 11, 1865 (Detachment). Old members and Companies "I," "K," "L" and "M" mustered out June 28, 1865. Balance transferred to 6th New York Heavy Artillery July 18, 1865.

Regiment lost during service 1 Officer and 4 Enlisted men killed and mortally wounded and 2 Officers and 144 Enlisted men by disease. Total 151.

13th NEW YORK STATE MILITIA HEAVY ARTY.

Organized at Suffolk, Va., for three months, May 28, 1862. Mustered out September 28, 1862.

14th REGIMENT HEAVY ARTILLERY.

Organized at Rochester, N. Y., and mustered in by Companies as follows: Companies "A" and "B" August 29, Company "C" September 11, Company "D" September 12, Company "E" October 18, Company "F" October 20, Companies "G" and "H" December 7, Companies "I" and "K" December 21, 1863; Company "L" January 8, and Company "M" at Elmira, N. Y., January 17, 1864. Companies "A," "B," "C," "D," "E" and "F" ordered to New York October 13, 1863, and assigned to garrison duty in New York Harbor till April 23, 1864. Companies "G" and "H" ordered to Fort Hamilton, New York Harbor, December 8, 1863. Companies "I" and "K" to Fort Richmond, New York Harbor, December 24, 1863. Companies "L" and "M" to Fort Richmond January, 1864, and duty at these points till April 23, 1864. Ordered to join Army of the Potomac in the field April 23, 1864. Attached to Provisional Brigade, 1st Division, 9th Army Corps, Army of the Potomac, to June, 1864. 3rd Brigade, 1st Division, 9th Army Corps, to June 1, 1864. 2nd Brigade, 1st Division, 9th Army Corps, to September, 1864. 3rd Brigade, 1st Division, 9th Army Corps, to June, 1865. 1st Brigade, Hardin's Division, 22nd Army Corps, Dept. of Washington, D. C., to August, 1865.

SERVICE.—Rapidan Campaign May-June, 1864. Battles of the Wilderness May 5-7. Spottsylvania May 8-12. Spottsylvania Court House May 12-21. North Anna River May 23-26. Line of the Pamunkey May 26-28. Totopotomoy May 28-31. Cold Harbor June 1-12. Bethesda Church June 1-3. Before Petersburg June 16-18. Siege of Petersburg June 16, 1864, to April 2, 1865. Mine Explosion, Petersburg, July 30, 1864. Weldon Railroad August 18-21. Poplar Springs Church September 29-October 2. Reconnoissance on Vaughan and Squirrel Level Roads October 8. Boydton Plank Road, Hatcher's Run, October 27-28. Fort Stedman March 25, 1865. Appomattox Campaign March 28-April 9. Assault on and fall of Petersburg April 2. Occupation of Petersburg April 3. Moved to South Side Railroad and duty at Ford's Station till April 20. Moved to Washington, D. C., April 20-27, and duty there till August. Grand Review May 23. Mustered out August 26, 1865.

Regiment lost during service 6 Officers and 220 Enlisted men killed and mortally wounded and 2 Officers and 299 Enlisted men by disease. Total 527.

15th REGIMENT HEAVY ARTILLERY.

Originally organized as 3rd Battalion German Heavy Artillery at New York City October to December, 1861. Left State for Washington, D. C., December 19, 1861. Attached to Defences of Washington to March, 1862. Artillery Brigade, Military District of Washington, to

May, 1862. Whipple's Command, Military District of Washington, to July, 1862. Fort Lyon, Defences of Washington, to February, 1863. Tyler's Command, De Russy's Division, 22nd Army Corps, Dept. of Washington, to June, 1863. 2nd Brigade, DeRussy's Division, 22nd Army Corps, to October, 1863. Designation of Regiment changed to 15th New York Heavy Artillery September 30, 1863, and 3rd Battalion assigned as Companies "A," "B," "C," "D" and "E." 4th Brigade, De Russy's Division, 22nd Army Corps, to February, 1864. Artillery Reserve, Army of the Potomac, to March, 1864. 1st Brigade, Artillery Reserve, Army of the Potomac, to May, 1864. Kitching's Independent Brigade, 5th Army Corps, May, 1864. 1st Brigade, 3rd Division, 5th Army Corps, May 30-June 2, 1864. 3rd Brigade, 2nd Division, 5th Army Corps, to August, 1865. 1st Brigade, 2nd Division, 5th Army Corps, to May, 1865. 4th Brigade, DeRussy's Division, 22nd Army Corps, to June, 1865. 1st Brigade, DeRussy's Division, 22nd Army Corps, to August, 1865. (Co. "F" attached to Artillery Reserve, Army of the Potomac, June to December, 1864. Company "M" to Artillery Brigade, 5th Army Corps, January to June, 1865.)

SERVICE.—Duty in the Defences of Washington, D. C., till April, 1864. Campaign from the Rapidan to the James May-June. Battle of the Wilderness May 5-7. Spottsylvania May 8-12. Spottsylvania Court House May 12-21. Harris Farm (or Fredericksburg Road) May 19. North Anna River May 23-26. Jericho Mills May 23. On line of the Pamunkey May 26-28. Totopotomoy May 28-31. Cold Harbor June 1-12. Bethesda Church June 1-3. Before Petersburg June 16-18. Siege of Petersburg June 16, 1864, to April 2, 1865. Weldon Railroad June 22-23, 1864. Mine Explosion, Petersburg, July 30 (Reserve). Six-Mile House, Weldon Railroad, August 18-21. Poplar Springs Church, Peeble's Farm, September 29-October 2. Boydton Plank Road, Hatcher's Run October 27-28. Dabney's Mills, Hatcher's Run, February 5-7, 1865. Appomattox Campaign March 28-April 9. Gravelly Run March 29. Boydton Road and White Oak Road March 31. Five Forks April 1. Fall of Petersburg April 2. Pursuit of Lee April 3-9. Appomattox Court House April 9. Surrender of Lee and his army. March to Washington, D. C., May. Grand Review May 23. Duty at Washington till August. Mustered out August 22, 1865.

Regiment lost during service 8 Officers and 142 Enlisted men killed and mortally wounded and 5 Officers and 225 Enlisted men by disease. Total 380.

16th REGIMENT HEAVY ARTILLERY.

Companies organized and mustered in as follows: Companies "A" and "B" at Albany, N. Y., September 28, 1863. Left State for Fortress Monroe, Va., October 14, 1863. Company "C" October 21, and left State for Fortress Monroe, October 22, 1863. Company "D" December 7, and left State for Fortress Monroe, Va., October 8, 1863. Company "E" at Riker's Island, N. Y., December 16, 1863, and left State for Fortress Monroe, Va., December 16, 1863. Company "G" at Riker's Island January 9, and left State for Fortress Monroe, Va., January 13, 1864. Company "F" at Elmira January 19. Company "H" February 8, 1864. Company "I" January 28. Company "K" February 2. Companies "L" and "M" at Auburn January 26, 1864. All moved to Fortress Monroe, Va. Regiment on duty at Fortress Monroe, Yorktown and Gloucester Point, Va., till June, 1864, as Heavy Artillery and Infantry. Companies "E" and "H" attached to 1st Brigade, 3rd Division, 10th Army Corps, Army of the James, July to December, 1864; then to Separate Brigade at Fort Pocahontas till June, 1865. Companies "A," "B." "C," "F," "G," "K" and "M" attached to 2nd Brigade, 1st Division, 10th Army Corps, Army of the James, July 27 to December 3, 1864. 2nd Brigade, 1st Division, 24th Army Corps, to March, 1865. 2nd Brigade, 1st Division, 10th Army Corps, Dept. of North Carolina, to July, 1865. Company "L" attached to 2nd Brigade, 1st Division, 10th Army Corps, to December, 1864; thence to Artillery Brigade, 24th Army Corps, to July, 1865. 3rd Brigade, DeRussy's Division, 22nd Army Corps, to August, 1865.

SERVICE.—Engagement between White House and Army of the James while laying Army telegraph lines May 29, 1864. Action at West Point, Va., June 20 (Cos. "D," "E," "H," "I," "L" and "M"). Gloucester Point June 23. Siege operations against Petersburg and Richmond July 27, 1864, to January 3, 1865. Dutch Gap Canal August 8-19. Signal Hill August 13. Action at Dutch Gap Canal August 16 (Detachment). Strawberry Plains August 14-18. Chaffin's Farm, New Market Heights, September 28-30. Charles City Cross Roads October 1. Darbytown and New Market Roads October 7. Darbytown Road October 13. Fair Oaks October 27-28. In trenches north of the James River till January, 1865. 2nd Expedition to Fort Fisher, N. C., January 4-15, 1865. Assault and capture of Fort Fisher January 15. Cape Fear Intrenchments February 11-13. Fort Anderson February 18-20. Capture of Wilmington February 22. Near Wilmington February 22-23. Duty at Wilmington, Smithville and Goldsburg, N. C., till July. Regiment concentrated at Washington, D. C., July, and duty there till August. Mustered out August 21, 1865.

Regiment lost during service 42 Enlisted men killed and mortally wounded and 2 Officers and 284 Enlisted men by disease. Total 328.

ANTHON'S BATTALION LIGHT ARTILLERY.

Organization not completed. The several Companies serving at Fort Columbus, New York Harbor, consolidated to two and designated the 20th and 28th New York Independent Batteries Light Artillery November 20, 1862.

BARRY'S ROCKET BATTALION LIGHT ARTILLERY.

Organized at Albany, N. Y., and mustered in Company "A" December 6 and Company "B" December 7, 1861. Left State for Washington, D. C., December 9, 1861. Duty in the Defences of that city till April, 1862. Moved to New Berne, N. C., April 26, and duty there till November, 1862. Attached to 2nd Brigade, 2nd Division, Dept. of North Carolina, to July, 1862. New Berne, N. C., Dept. of North Carolina, to October, 1862. Morehead City, N. C., to November, 1862.

SERVICE.—Garrison duty at New Berne and Morehead City, N. C., till December, 1862. Reconnoissance from New Berne to Young's Cross Roads July 26-29. Action at Young's Cross Roads July 27. Battalion discontinued February 11, 1863, and Company "A" designated 23rd New York Independent Battery Light Artillery. Company "B" designated 24th New York Independent Battery Light Artillery, having served provisionally as such since November 1, 1862. (See 23rd and 24th New York Batteries.)

BRICKEL'S 1st BATTALION GERMAN LIGHT ARTILLERY.

Organized at New York City and mustered in Company "A" August 26, Company "B" August 12, Company "C" September 11 and Company "D" September 20, 1861. Left State for Washington, D. C., October 12, 1861. Attached to Artillery Reserve, Army of the Potomac, to May, 1862. 3rd Brigade, Artillery Reserve, 5th Army Corps, Army of the Potomac, to September, 1862. Artillery Reserve, 5th Army Corps, to December, 1862. Artillery Reserve, Army of the Potomac, to March, 1863.

SERVICE.—Duty in the Defences of Washington, D. C., till March, 1862. Moved to the Virginia Peninsula March —. Siege of Yorktown, Va., April 5-May 4. Near New Bridge June 20. Seven days before Richmond June 25-July 1. Battles of Mechanicsville June 26. Gaines Mill June 27. Garnett's Farm June 28. Turkey Bridge or Malvern Cliff June 30. Malvern Hill July 1. At Harrison's Landing till August 16. Movement to Alexandria August 16-28. Maryland Campaign September-October. Battle of Antietam September 16-17. Movement to Falmouth October-November. Battle of Fredericksburg December 12-15. "Mud March" January 20-24, 1863. Battalion organization discontinued March 5,

1863, and Company "A" designated 29th New York Independent Battery Light Artillery. Company "B" designated 30th New York Independent Battery Light Artillery. Company "C" designated 31st New York Independent Battery Light Artillery, and Company "D" designated 32nd New York Independent Battery Light Artillery (which see).

1st BATTALION NATIONAL GUARD LIGHT ARTILLERY.

Entered service for 100 days August 2, 1864. Duty at Elmira, N. Y., till November. Mustered out November 22, 1864.

1st MARINE ARTILLERY NAVAL BRIGADE.

Organized at New York City and mustered in November 12, 1861, to August 18, 1862. Left State for Annapolis, Md., by Detachments. Companies "A" to "G" moved to New Berne, N. C., April, 1862; Companies "H" and "I" June, 1862; Company "K" August, 1862. Duty in the Dept. of North Carolina, 18th and 10th Army Corps, to March, 1863.

SERVICE.—Burnside's Expedition to Roanoke Island, N. C., January 6-February 7, 1862 (Detachment). Battle of Roanoke Island February 8 (Detachment). Siege of Fort Macon April 12-26. Action at South Mills April 19. Tranter's Creek June 2 and 5. Reconnoissance from Washington, N. C., to Tranter's Creek June 24 (Detachment). Swift's Creek Bridge June 27. Swift Creek and Neuse River August 6. Washington August 6. Near Shiloh September 20. Rawle's Mills November 3. Foster's Expedition to Goldsboro December 11-20. Southwest Creek December 13. Kinston December 14. Whitehall December 16. Goldsboro December 17. Duty at New Berne till January, 1863. Moved to Dept. of the South January, 1863. Regiment disbanded March 31, 1863.

Regiment lost during service 1 Officer and 7 Enlisted men killed and mortally wounded and 1 Officer and 81 Enlisted men by disease. Total 90.

2nd BATTALION LIGHT ARTILLERY.—("IRISH BRIGADE BATTERIES.")

Four Companies organized at New York City and mustered in December 9, 1861. Left State for Washington, D. C., December 16, 1861. Companies consolidated December 21, 1861. "B" and "D" forming new Battery "A," and "A" and "C" forming new Battery "B." Duty in Defences of Washington to March, 1862. Battery "A" attached to Richardson's 1st Division, 2nd Army Corps, Army of the Potomac, March to May, 1862; then Sections detached as follows: 1st Section attached to Battery "C" 4th United States Artillery; 2nd Section to Battery "B" 1st New York Light Artillery, serving with 1st Division, 2nd Army Corps, and 3rd Section to Battery "G" 1st New York Light Artillery, serving with 3rd Division, 2nd Army Corps, to October, 1862.

SERVICE.—Siege of Yorktown, Va., April 5-May 4, 1862. Battle of Fair Oaks, Seven Pines, May 31-June 1. Seven days before Richmond June 25-July 1. Battles of Gaines Mill June 27. Peach Orchard and Savage Station June 29. White Oak Swamp and Glendale June 30. Malvern Hill July 1. Duty at Harrison's Landing till August 16. Movement to Fortress Monroe, thence to Alexandria and Centreville August 16-30. Bull Run August 30. Centreville September 1. Germantown Road September 2. Battle of Antietam September 16-17. Duty at Harper's Ferry, W. Va., till October. Near Charlestown October 16-17. Designated 14th New York Independent Battery Light Artillery October, 1862 (which see).

Battery "B" attached to Williams' Division, Banks' 5th Corps, to April, 1862. Doubleday's Brigade, Dept. of the Rappahannock, to June, 1862. Reserve Artillery, Army of Virginia, to September, 1862. At Relay House, Md., 8th Army Corps, Middle Department, to October, 1862. Designated 15th New York Independent Battery Light Artillery October, 1862 (which see).

1st REGIMENT LIGHT ARTILLERY.
BATTERY "A," 1st REGIMENT LIGHT ARTILLERY.

Organized at Utica, N. Y., and mustered in September 12, 1861. Left State for Washington, D. C., October 31, 1861, and duty at Camp Barry till March, 1862. Attached to 3rd Division, 4th Army Corps, Army of the Potomac, to June, 1862. Moved to the Peninsula, Va., March, 1862. Siege of Yorktown, Va., April 5-May 4. Battle of Williamsburg May 5. Bottom's and Turkey Island Bridge May 23. Chickahominy May 24. Bottom's Bridge May 30. Battle of Seven Pines or Fair Oaks May 31-June 1. Guns captured May 31. Men transferred to Batteries "D" and "H" 1st New York Light Artillery and 7th and 8th Independent Batteries New York Light Artillery June 15, 1862. BATTERY reorganized at Utica, N. Y. Duty at Camp Barry, Washington, D. C., January to June, 1863. Whipple's Brigade, Sigel's Division, Dept. of the Susquehanna, to January, 1864. Actions at Chambersburg, Pa., July 4 and 30, 1863. Lehigh District, Dept. of the Susquehanna, to May, 1864. Harrisburg, Pa., Dept. of the Susquehanna, to August, 1864. District of the Monongahela, Dept. of the Susquehanna, to October, 1864. Chambersburg, Pa., Dept. of the Susquehanna, to November, 1864. District of Philadelphia, Dept. of Pennsylvania, to June, 1865. Duty at Philadelphia, Harrisburg, Chambersburg and Allegheny City, Pa., June, 1863, to June, 1865. Mercersburg, Pa., July 29, 1864 (Section). Mustered out June 28, 1865.

Battery lost during service 4 Enlisted men killed and mortally wounded and 9 Enlisted men by disease. Total 13.

BATTERY "B" 1st REGIMENT LIGHT ARTILLERY. ("EMPIRE BATTERY.")

Organized at Elmira, N. Y., and mustered in August 30, 1861. Left State for Washington, D. C., October 31, 1861, and duty in the Defences of that city till March, 1862. Attached to Artillery Reserve, Army of the Potomac, November, 1861, to March, 1862. Artillery, 1st Division, 2nd Army Corps, Army of the Potomac, to May, 1862. Artillery Brigade, 2nd Army Corps, to May, 1863. 1st Volunteer Brigade, Artillery Reserve, Army of the Potomac, to July, 1863. Artillery Brigade, 2nd Army Corps, to July, 1863. 2nd Volunteer Brigade, Artillery Brigade, Army of the Potomac, to December, 1863. Artillery Reserve, Army of the Potomac, to January, 1864. 1st Brigade, Artillery Reserve, Army of the Potomac, to March, 1864. 2nd Brigade, Artillery Reserve, Army of the Potomac, to May 16, 1864. Artillery Brigade, 5th Army Corps, Army of the Potomac, to June, 1865.

SERVICE.—Advance on Manassas, Va., March 10-15, 1862. Moved to the Peninsula, Va., March. Siege of Yorktown April 5-May 4. Battle of Seven Pines (or Fair Oaks) May 31-June 1. Oak Grove, near Fair Oaks, June 25. Seven days before Richmond June 25-July 1. Battles of Gaines' Mills June 27, Peach Orchard and Savage Station June 29, White Oak Swamp Bridge and Glendale June 30, Malvern Hill July 1. At Harrison's Landing till August 16. Movement to Alexandria, thence to Centreville August 16-30. Near Centreville September 1. Germantown Road September 2. Battle of Antietam, Md., September 16-17. Duty at Harper's Ferry September 22 to October 29. Reconnoissance to Charlestown October 16-17. Advance up Loudoun Valley and movement to Falmouth, Va., October 29-November 17. Snicker's Gap November 2. Falmouth November 17. Battle of Fredericksburg December 12-15. Duty at Falmouth till April 27, 1863. "Mud March" January 20-24, 1863. Chancellorsville Campaign April 27-May 6. Battle of Chancellorsville May 1-5. Battle of Gettysburg, Pa., July 1-3. Bristoe Campaign October 9-22. Advance to line of the Rappahannock November 7-8. Mine Run Campaign November 26-December 2. Campaign from the Rapidan to the James May 3-June 15, 1864. Battles of the Wilderness May 5-7; Laurel Hill May 8; Spottsylvania May 8-12; Spottsylvania Court House May 12-21; Jericho Mills May 23. On line of the Pamunkey May 26-28. Totopotomoy May 28-31. Cold Harbor June 1-12. Bethesda Church June 1-3. Before Petersburg June 16-18. Siege of Petersburg June 16, 1864, to April 2, 1865. Mine Explosion, Petersburg, July 30, 1864 (Reserve). Weldon Railroad August 18-21. Poplar Grove Church, Peeble's Farm, September 29-October 2. Boydton Plank Road, Hatcher's Run, October 27-28. Appomattox Campaign March 28-April 9, 1865. White Oak Road March 31. Five Forks April 1. Fall of Petersburg April 2. Pursuit of Lee April 3-9. Appomattox Court House April 9. Surrender of Lee and his army. Moved to Washington, D. C., May. Grand Review May 23. Mustered out June 18, 1865.

Battery lost during service 16 Enlisted men killed and mortally wouonded and 10 Enlisted men by disease. Total 26.

BATTERY "C," 1st REGIMENT LIGHT ARTILLERY.

Organized at Elmira, N. Y., and mustered in September 6, 1861. Left State for Washington, D. C., October 31, 1861. Attached to Wadsworth's Command, Military District of Washington, November, 1861, to September, 1862. 3rd Division, 5th Army Corps, Army of the Potomac, to May, 1863. Artillery Brigade, 5th Army Corps, to April, 1864. 3rd Brigade, Artillery Reserve, Army of the Potomac, to May 16, 1864. Artillery Brigade, 5th Army Corps, to March, 1865. Artillery Reserve, attached to 9th Army Corps, to June, 1865.

SERVICE.—Duty in the Defences of Washington, D. C., to August, 1862. Action at Manassas Junction August 26. Bull Run Bridge August 27. March to Antietam, Md., September 14-18. Duty near Sharpsburg till October 30. March to Falmouth, Va., October 30-November 19. Battle of Fredericksburg December 12-15. "Mud March" January 20-24, 1863. Duty near Falmouth till April 27. Rappahannock Station March 6. Chancellorsville Campaign April 27-May 6. Battle of Chancellorsville May 1-5. Battle of Gettysburg, Pa., July 1-3. Bristoe Campaign October 9-22. Advance to line of the Rappahannock November 7-8. Rappahannock Station November 7. Mine Run Campaign November 26-December 2. Robertson's Tavern November 27. Mine Run November 28-30. Camp near Rappahannock Station till April, 1864. Campaign from the Rapidan to the James May 3-June 15. Battles of the Wilderness May 5-7. Laurel Hill May 8. Spottsylvania May 8-12. Spottsylvania Court House May 12-21. North Anna River May 23-26. Jericho Mills May 23. On line of the Pamunkey May 26-28. Totopotomoy May 28-31. Cold Harbor June 1-12. Bethesda Church June 1-3. Before Petersburg June 16-18. Siege of Petersburg June 16, 1864, to April 2, 1865. Weldon Railroad August 18-21, 1864. Appomattox Campaign March 28-April 9. Assault and capture of Petersburg April 2. Moved to Washington, D. C., May. Grand Review May 23. Mustered out June 17, 1865.

Battery lost during service 4 Enlisted men killed and mortally wounded and 18 Enlisted men by disease. Total 22.

BATTERY "D," 1st REGIMENT LIGHT ARTILLERY.

Organized at Elmira, N. Y., and mustered in September 6, 1861. Left State for Washington, D. C., October 31, 1861. Attached to Artillery Reserve, Army of the Potomac, to March, 1862. Hooker's 2nd Division, 3rd Army Corps, Army of the Potomac, to July, 1862. Artillery Brigade, 3rd Army Corps, to December, 1862. Artillery, 1st Division, 9th Army Corps, to February, 1863. Artillery, 2nd Division, 3rd Army Corps, to May, 1863. Artillery Brigade, 3rd Army Corps, to March, 1864. Artillery Brigade, 5th Army Corps, to June, 1865.

SERVICE.—Duty at Camp Barry, Defences of Washington, D. C., to March, 1862. Ordered to the Peninsula, Va., March, 1862. Siege of Yorktown April 5-May 4. Battle of Williamsburg May 5. Bottom's Bridge May 24. Battle of Seven Pines (or Fair Oaks) May 31-June 1. Seven days before Richmond June 25-July 1. Oak Grove June 25. Savage Station and Peach Orchard June 29. Turkey Bridge (or Malvern Cliff) June 30.

Malvern Hill July 1. Duty at Harrison's Landing till August 16, and in the Defences of Washington, D. C., near Fairfax Seminary, Munson's Hill and at Fairfax Station till November 25. Rappahannock Campaign December, 1862, to June, 1863. Battle of Fredericksburg, Va., December 12-15. "Mud March" January 20-24, 1863. At Falmouth till April 27. Chancellorsville Campaign April 27-May 6. Battle of Chancellorsville May 1-5. Gettysburg (Pa.) Campaign June 13 to August 1. Battle of Gettysburg, Pa., July 1-3. Wapping Heights July 23. Bristoe Campaign October 9-22. Advance to line of the Rappahannock November 7-8. Kelly's Ford November 7. Brandy Station November 8. Mine Run Campaign November 26-December 2. Payne's Grove November 27. Mine Run November 28-30. Duty near Brandy Station till May, 1864. Campaign from the Rapidan to the James May 3-June 15. Battles of the Wilderness May 5-7. Laurel Hill May 8. Spottsylvania May 8-12. Spottsylvania Court House May 12-21. "Bloody Angle" (Assault on the Salient) May 12. North Anna River May 23-26. Jericho Ford May 23. On line of the Pamunkey May 26-28. Totopotomoy May 28-31. Cold Harbor June 1-12. Bethesda Church June 1-3. Before Petersburg June 16-18. Siege of Petersburg June 16, 1864, to April 2, 1865. Weldon Railroad June 21-23, 1864. Six Mile House, Weldon Railroad, August 18-21. Varuna Road September 29. Poplar Grove Church September 30-October 1. Dabney's Mills, Hatcher's Run, February 5-7, 1865. Appomattox Campaign March 28-April 9. Boydton and White Oak Roads March 29-31. Five Forks April 1. Fall of Petersburg April 2. Pursuit of Lee April 3-9. Appomattox Court House April 9. Surrender of Lee and his army. Moved to Washington, D. C., May. Grand Review May 23. Mustered out June 16, 1865.

Battery lost during service 1 Officer and 12 Enlisted men killed and mortally wounded and 14 Enlisted men by disease. Total 27.

BATTERY "E," 1st REGIMENT LIGHT ARTILLERY.

Organized at Elmira, N. Y., and mustered in September 13, 1861. Left State for Washington, D. C., October 31, 1861. Attached to Defences of Washington and W. F. Smith's Division, Army of the Potomac, to March, 1862. Artillery, Smith's 2nd Division, 4th Army Corps, Army of the Potomac, to May, 1862. Artillery, 2nd Division, 6th Army Corps, Army of the Potomac, to June, 1863. (Attached to 1st New York Independent Battery Light Artillery, August, 1862, to June 20, 1863.) Artillery Brigade, 1st Army Corps, June, 1863, to March, 1864. (Attached to Battery "L," 1st New York Light Artillery, June 20 to October, 1863.) Artillery Brigade, 5th Army Corps, to June, 1864. Artillery Reserve, Army of the Potomac, to April, 1865. Artillery Brigade, 5th Army Corps, to June, 1865.

SERVICE.—Duty at Camp Barry, Defences of Washington, D. C., November, 1861, to March, 1862. Moved to the Peninsula March 22. Action at Lee's Mills April 5. Siege of Yorktown April 5-May 4. Lee's Mills April 16. Battle of Williamsburg May 5. Mechanicsville May 23-24. Seven days before Richmond June 25-July 1. Battle of Mechanicsville June 26. Garnett's Farm and Golding's Farm June 27-28. Savage Station June 29. White Oak Swamp Bridge June 30. Malvern Hill July 1. Duty at Harrison's Landing till August 16. Movement to Fortress Monroe, thence to Centreville August 16-27. In works at Centreville August 28-31. Assist in checking Pope's rout at Bull Run August 30, and cover retreat to Fairfax Court House September 1. Maryland Campaign September 6-22. South Mountain September 14. Lee's Mills September 16. Antietam September 17. Duty at Hagerstown, Md., till October 29. Movement to Falmouth, Va., October 29-November 19. Battle of Fredericksburg, Va., December 12-15. "Mud March" January 20-24, 1863. Chancellorsville Campaign April 27-May 6. Operations at Franklin's Crossing April 29-May 2. Maryes Heights, Fredericksburg, May 3. Salem Heights May 3-4. Battle of Gettysburg, Pa., July 2-4. On line of the Rappahannock and Rapidan till October. Bristoe Campaign October 9-22. Advance to line of the Rappahannock November 7-8. Mine Run Campaign November 26-December 2. Demonstration on the Rapidan February 6-7, 1864. Campaign from the Rapidan to the James River May 3-June 15. Battles of the Wilderness May 5-7; Laurel Hill May 8; Spottsylvania May 8-12; Spottsylvania Court House May 12-21. Assault on the Salient, "Bloody Angle," May 12. North Anna River May 23-26. Jericho Ford May 23. On line of the Pamunkey May 26-28. Totopotomoy May 28-31. Cold Harbor June 1-12. Bethesda Church June 1-3. Before Petersburg June 16-18. Siege of Petersburg June 16, 1864, to April 2, 1865. In the trenches as a Mortar Battery June, 1864, to January, 1865. Appomattox Campaign March 28-April 9. Assault and capture of Petersburg April 2. Moved to Washington, D. C., May. Grand Review May 23. Mustered out June 6, 1865.

Battery lost during service 1 Officer and 4 Enlisted men killed and mortally wounded and 1 Officer and 12 Enlisted men by disease. Total 18.

BATTERY "F" 1st REGIMENT LIGHT ARTILLERY.

Organized at Elmira, N. Y., and mustered in September 14, 1861. Left State for Washington, D. C., October 31, 1861. Attached to Franklin's Division, Army of the Potomac, to March, 1862. Franklin's 1st Division, 1st Army Corps, Army of the Potomac, to April, 1862. Artillery, 1st Division, Dept. of the Rappahannock, to May, 1862. Artillery, 1st Division, 6th Army Corps, Army of the Potomac, to June, 1862. Artillery Reserve, Yorktown, Va., 4th Army Corps, Dept. of Virginia, to July, 1863. Camp Barry, Washington, D. C., 22nd Army Corps, to May, 1864. 2nd Brigade, DeRussy's Division, 22nd Army Corps, to July, 1864. 3rd Brigade, DeRussy's Division, 22nd Army Corps, to December, 1864. 1st Brigade, DeRussy's Division, 22nd Army Corps, to June, 1865.

SERVICE.—Duty at Camp Barry, Washington, D. C., November, 1861, to March, 1862. Advance on Manassas, Va., March 10-15, 1862. McDowell's advance on Fredericksburg, Va., April 4-12. Ordered to the Peninsula April 22. Siege of Yorktown April 24-May 4 (on transports). West Point May 7-8. Near Slatersville May 9. Mechanicsville May 24. Operations about White House Landing May 26-July 2. Duty at White House till July. Garrison duty at Yorktown, Va., till July, 1863, and in the Defences of Washington, D. C., till June, 1865. Mustered out June 17, 1865.

Battery lost during service 14 Enlisted men by disease.

BATTERY "G" 1st REGIMENT LIGHT ARTILLERY.

Organized at Elmira, N. Y., and mustered in September 24, 1861. Left State for Washington, D. C., October 31, 1861. Attached to Sumner's Division, Army of the Potomac, November, 1861, to March, 1862. Richardson's 1st Division, 2nd Army Corps, Army of the Potomac, to May, 1862. Unattached, Artillery Reserve, 5th Army Corps, to June, 1862. Reserve Artillery, 2nd Army Corps, to November, 1862. Artillery, 3rd Division, 2nd Army Corps, to May, 1863. 1st Volunteer Brigade, Artillery Reserve, Army of the Potomac, to June, 1863. 4th Volunteer Brigade, Artillery Reserve, Army of the Potomac, to August, 1863. Artillery Brigade, 2nd Army Corps, to September, 1864. Artillery Reserve, attached to 2nd Army Corps, to January, 1865. Artillery Reserve, attached to 9th Army Corps, to June, 1865.

SERVICE.—Duty at Camp Barry, Defences of Washington, D. C., November, 1861, to March, 1862. Advance on Manassas, Va., March 10-15, 1862. Operations on Orange & Alexandria Railroad March 28-31. Bealeton Station March 28. Warrenton Junction March 29. Rappahannock Station March 29. Moved to the Virginia Peninsula April 3. Siege of Yorktown April 5-May 4. Battle of Seven Pines or Fair Oaks May 31-June 1. Seven days before Richmond June 25-July 1. Fair Oaks June 27. Savage Station June 29. White Oak Swamp and Glendale June 30. Malvern Hill July 1. At Harrison's Landing till August 16. Movement to

Fortress Monroe, thence to Centreville August 15-30. Maryland Campaign September 6-22. Battle of Antietam September 16-17. Duty at Harper's Ferry, W. Va., September 22-October 29. Reconnoissance to Leesburg October 1-2. Leesburg October 1. Reconnoissance to Charlestown October 16-17. Advance up Loudoun Valley and movement to Falmouth, Va., October 29-November 19. Snicker's Gap November 2. Falmouth November 17. Battle of Fredericksburg December 12-15. "Mud March" January 20-24, 1863. At Falmouth till April. Chancellorsville Campaign April 27-May 6. Battle of Chancellorsville May 1-5. Battle of Gettysburg, Pa., July 1-3. On line of the Rappahannock and Rapidan till October. Bristoe Campaign October 9-22. Auburn and Bristoe Station October 14. Advance to line of the Rappahannock November 7-8. Mine Run Campaign November 26-December 2. At Stevensburg till May, 1864. Campaign from the Rapidan to the James May 3-June 15. Battles of the Wilderness May 5-7; Spottsylvania May 8-12; Po River May 10; Spottsylvania Court House May 12-21. "Bloody Angle," Assault on the Salient, May 12. North Anna River May 23-26. On line of the Pamunkey May 26-28. Totopotomoy May 28-31. Hanover Court House May 30. Cold Harbor June 1-12. Before Petersburg June 16-18. Siege of Petersburg June 16, 1864, to April 2, 1865. Jerusalem Plank Road, Weldon Railroad, June 22-23, 1864. Deep Bottom July 27-28. Mine Explosion, Petersburg, July 30 (Reserve). Demonstration north of the James August 13-20. Deep Bottom, Strawberry Plains, August 14-18. Fort Steadman March 25, 1865. Appomattox Campaign March 28-April 9. Assault on and fall of Petersburg April 2. Moved to Washington May. Grand Review May 23. Mustered out June 19, 1865.

Battery lost during service 1 Officer and 11 Enlisted men killed and mortally wounded and 2 Officers and 16 Enlisted men by disease. Total 30.

BATTERY "H" 1st REGIMENT LIGHT ARTILLERY.

Organized at Elmira, N. Y., and mustered in October 10, 1861. Left State for Washington, D. C., October 31, 1861. Attached to Casey's Division, Army of the Potomac, November, 1861, to March, 1862. Casey's 3rd Division, 4th Army Corps, Army of the Potomac, to June, 1862. Reserve Artillery, 4th Army Corps, Yorktown, Va., to July, 1863. Defences of Washington, 22nd Army Corps, to October, 1863. Artillery Brigade, 1st Army Corps, Army of the Potomac, to March, 1864. Artillery Brigade, 5th Army Corps, to June, 1865.

SERVICE.—Duty at Camp Barry, Defences of Washington, D. C., till March, 1862. Advance on Manassas, Va., March 10-15. Moved to Newport News, Va., March 28. Siege of Yorktown April 5-May 4. Battle of Williamsburg May 5. Reconnoissance to Seven Pines May 24-27. Chickahominy May 24. Seven Pines May 24. Battle of Seven Pines or Fair Oaks May 31-June 1. Seven days before Richmond June 25-July 1. Long Bridge June 28-29. Malvern Cliff June 30. Malvern Hill July 1. At Harrison's Landing till August 16. Moved to Yorktown, Va., and garrison duty there till July, 1863. Expedition to Gloucester, King and Queen and Middlesex Counties December 11-15, 1862. Expedition to Matthews County May 19, 1863. Dix's Peninsula Campaign June 24 to July 7. Action at Baltimore or Crump's Cross Roads July 2. Moved to Washington, D. C., July 8, and duty in the Defences of that city till September, 1863. Joined Army of the Potomac in the field. Bristoe Campaign October 9-22. Advance to line of the Rappahannock November 7-8. Mine Run Campaign November 26-December 2. Demonstration on the Rapidan February 6-7, 1864. Campaign from the Rapidan to the James May 3-June 15. Battles of the Wilderness May 5-7; Spottsylvania May 8-12; Laurel Hill May 8; Spottsylvania Court House May 12-21. "Bloody Ankle," Assault on the Salient, May 12. North Anna River May 23-26. Jericho Ford May 23. On line of the Pamunkey May 26-28. Totopotomoy May 28-31. Cold Harbor June 1-12. Bethesda Church June 1-3. Before Petersburg June 16-18. Siege of Petersburg June 16, 1864, to April 2, 1865. Six-Mile House, Weldon

Railroad, August 18-21, 1864. Poplar Grove Church September 29-October 1. Boydton Plank Road, Hatcher's Run, October 27-28. Warren's Raid on Weldon Railroad. "Hicksford Raid" December 7-12. Appomattox Campaign March 28-April 9, 1865. White Oak Road March 29-31. Five Forks April 1. Fall of Petersburg April 2. Pursuit of Lee April 3-9. Appomattox Court House April 9. Surrender of Lee and his army. Moved to Washington, D. C., May. Grand Review May 23. Mustered out June 19, 1865.

Battery lost during service 7 Enlisted men killed and mortally wounded and 10 Enlisted men by disease. Total 17.

BATTERY "I," 1st REGIMENT LIGHT ARTILLERY.

Organized at Buffalo, N. Y. Left Buffalo for Washington, D. C., October 16, 1861. Attached to Blenker's Division, Army of the Potomac, to March, 1862. 3rd Brigade, Blenker's Division, 2nd Army Corps, Army of the Potomac, to April, 1862. 3rd Brigade, Blenker's Division, Mountain Department, to June, 1862. Reserve Artillery, 1st Corps, Army of Virginia, to September, 1862. Artillery, 3rd Division, 11th Army Corps, Army of the Potomac, to October, 1862. Artillery, 2nd Division, 11th Army Corps, to May, 1863. Artillery Brigade, 11th Army Corps, to October, 1863. Artillery Brigade, 11th Army Corps, Dept. of the Cumberland, to January, 1864. Artillery, 2nd Division, 11th Army Corps, to April, 1864. Artillery, 1st Division, 20th Army Corps, Army of the Cumberland, to July, 1864. Artillery Brigade, 20th Army Corps, to June, 1865.

SERVICE.—Duty in the Defences of Washington, D. C., till March, 1862. Advance on Manassas, Va., March 10. At Fairfax Court House till March 24. Ordered to join Fremont in West Virginia, and pursuit of Jackson up the Valley April and May. Near Strasburg June 1. Union Church June 5. Battle of Cross Keys June 8. Near Port Republic June 9. At Sperryville till August. Pope's Campaign in Northern Virginia August 16-September 2. Fords of the Rappahannock August 20-23. Sulphur Springs August 23-24. Plains of Manassas August 27-29. Battle of Bull August 30. Duty in the Defences of Washington till December. March to Fredericksburg, Va., December 10-16. Duty at Falmouth and Brook's Station till April, 1863. "Mud March" January 20-24. Chancellorsville Campaign April 27-May 6. Battle of Chancellorsville May 1-5. Battle of Gettysburg, Pa., July 1-3. Pursuit of Lee July 5-24. Near Bristoe Station till September. Movement to Bridgeport, Ala., September 24-October 3. Reopening Tennessee River October 26-29. Battle of Wauhatchie, Lookout Valley, Tenn., October 28-29. Chattanooga-Ringgold Campaign November 23-27. Battle of Lookout Mountain November 23-24. Mission Ridge November 25. March to relief of Knoxville November 28-December 17. At Bridgeport, Ala., till April, 1864. Atlanta (Ga.) Campaign May 1 to September 8. Operations about Rocky Faced Ridge, Tunnel Hill, and Buzzard's Roost Gap May 8-11. Battle of Resaca May 14-15. Adairsville May 17-18. Cassville May 19. Advance on Dallas May 23-25. New Hope Church May 25. Operations on line of Pumpkin Vine Creek and battles about Dallas, New Hope Church and Allatoona Hills May 25-June 5. Operations about Marietta and against Kenesaw Mountain June 10-July 2. Pine Mountain June 11-14. Lost Mountain June 15-17. Gilgal (or Golgotha Church) June 15. Muddy Creek June 17. Noyes' Creek June 19. Kolb's Farm June 22. Assault on Kenesaw June 27. Ruff's Station, Smyrna Camp Ground, July 4. Chattahoochie River July 5-17. Peach Tree Creek July 19-20. Siege of Atlanta July 22-August 25. Operations at Chattahoochie River Bridge August 26-September 2. Occupation of Atlanta September 2-November 15. March to the sea November 15-December 10. Siege of Savannah December 10-21. Campaign of the Carolinas January to April, 1865. Lawtonville, S. C., February 2. Averysboro, N. C., March 16. Battle of Bentonville March 19-21. Occupation of Goldsboro March 24, and of Raleigh April 14. Bennett's House April 26. Surrender of Johnston

aand his army. March to Washington, D. C., via Richmond, Va., April 29-May 20. Grand Review May 24. Mustered out June 23, 1865.

Battery lost during service 1 Officer and 12 Enlisted men killed and mortally wounded and 1 Officer and 15 Enlisted men by disease. Total 29.

BATTERY "K," 1st REGIMENT LIGHT ARTILLERY.

Organized at Elmira, N. Y., and mustered in November 20, 1861. Left State for Washington, D. C., November 21, 1861. Attached to Defences of Washington, D. C., till April, 1862. Railroad Brigade, Middle Department, Harper's Ferry, W. Va., to May 25, 1862. 2nd Brigade, Sigel's Division, Dept. of the Shenandoah, to June 28, 1862. 2nd Division, 2nd Corps, Army of Virginia, to September, 1862. 2nd Division, 12th Army Corps, Army of the Potomac, to October, 1862. 1st Division, 12th Army Corps, to February, 1863. Dept. of Washington, 22nd Army Corps, to April, 1863. 1st Division, 12th Army Corps, Army of the Potomac, to May 12, 1863. 4th Volunteer Brigade, Artillery Reserve, Army of the Potomac, to July, 1863. 3rd Volunteer Brigade, Artillery Reserve, to March, 1864. 1st Volunteer Brigade, Artillery Reserve, to April, 1864. Camp Barry, 22nd Army Corps, to July, 1864. 2nd Brigade, DeRussy's Division, 22nd Army Corps, to October, 1864. 1st Brigade, DeRussy's Division, 22nd Army Corps, to June, 1865.

SERVICE.—Duty at Camp Barry, Defences of Washington, D. C., till April, 1862. Moved to Harper's Ferry, W. Va., and duty there and in the Shenandoah Valley till August. Charlestown May 28. Defence of Harper's Ferry May 28-30. Battle of Cedar Mountain August 9. Pope's Campaign in Northern Virginia August 16-September 2. Fords of the Rappahannock August 21-23. Beverly Ford August 22-24. Battle of Bull Run August 30. Battle of Antietam, Md., September 16-17. At Maryland Heights till December. March to Fredericksburg, Va., December 12-16. "Mud March" January 20-24, 1863. Chancellorsville Campaign April 27-May 6. Battle of Chancellorsville May 1-5. Battle of Gettysburg, Pa., July 1-3. Bristoe Campaign October 9-22. Advance to line of the Rappahannock November 7-8. Mine Run Campaign November 26-December 2. Duty in the Defences of Washington, D. C., March, 1864, to June, 1865. Mustered out June 20, 1865.

Battery lost during service 2 Enlisted men killed and mortally wounded and 15 Enlisted men by disease. Total 17.

BATTERY "L," 1st REGIMENT LIGHT ARTILLERY ("ROCHESTER UNION GRAYS").

Organized at Rochester, N. Y., September, 1861. Moved to Elmira, N. Y., and mustered in November 17, 1861. Left State for Washington, D. C., November 21, 1861. Attached to Defences of Washington, D. C., to February, 1862. Baltimore, Md., Dix's Command, to May, 1862. 1st Brigade, Sigel's Division, Dept. of the Shenandoah, to June, 1862. 1st Division, 3rd Army Corps, Army of Virginia, to September, 1862. 1st Division, 1st Army Corps, Army of the Potomac, to May, 1863. Artillery Brigade, 1st Army Corps, to March, 1864. Artillery Brigade, 5th Army Corps, to March, 1865. Artillery Reserve, Army of the Potomac, attached to 9th Army Corps, to April, 1865. Artillery Brigade, 5th Army Corps, to June, 1865.

SERVICE.—Duty at Camp Barry, Defences of Washington, till February, 1862, and at Baltimore, Md., till May, 1862. Moved to Winchester, Va. Skirmish at Charlestown May 28. Defence of Harper's Ferry, W. Va., May 28-30. Battle of Cedar Mountain, Va., August 9. Pope's Campaign in Northern Virginia August 16-September 2. Fords of the Rappahannock August 21-23. Sulphur Springs August 26. Battles of Gainesville August 28, Groveton August 29, Bull Run August 30, Chantilly September 1. Maryland Campaign September 6-22. Battles of South Mountain September 14, Antietam September 16-17. Movement to Falmouth, Va., October 29-November 19. Battle of Fredericksburg, Va., December 12-15. "Mud March" January 20-24, 1863. Duty at Falmouth and Belle Plains till April. Chancellorsville Campaign April 27-May 6. Operations at Pollock's Mill Creek April 29-May 2. Fitzhugh's Crossing April 29-30. Battle of Chancellorsville May 1-5. Gettysburg (Pa.) Campaign June 11-July 24. Battle of Gettysburg, Pa., July 1-3. On line of the Rappahannock and Rapidan till October. Bristoe Campaign October 9-22. Advance to line of the Rappahannock November 7-8. Mine Run Campaign November 26-December 2. Demonstration on the Rapidan February 6-7, 1864. Campaign from the Rapidan to the James May 3-June 15. Battles of the Wilderness May 5-7; Laurel Hill May 8; Spottsylvania May 8-12; Spottsylvania Court House May 12-21. Assault on the Salient May 12. North Anna River May 23-26. Jericho Ford May 23. On line of the Pamunkey May 26-28. Totopotomoy May 28-31. Cold Harbor June 1-12. Bethesda Church June 1-3. Before Petersburg June 16-18. Siege of Petersburg June 16, 1864, to April 2, 1865. Weldon Railroad August 18-21, 1864. Dabney's Mills, Hatcher's Run, February 5-7, 1865. Appomattox Campaign March 28-April 9. Assault on and fall of Petersburg April 2. Pursuit of Lee April 3-9. Moved to Washington, D. C. Grand Review May 23. Mustered out June 17, 1865.

Battery lost during service 11 Enlisted men killed and mortally wounded and 12 Enlisted men by disease. Total 23.

BATTERY "M" 1st REGIMENT LIGHT ARTILLERY.

Organized at Lockport, N. Y., and mustered in at Rochester November 15, 1861. Left State for Washington, D. C., November 21, 1861. Attached to Banks' Division, Army of the Potomac, to March, 1862. Artillery, Williams' Division, Banks' 5th Army Corps, to April, 1862, and Dept. of the Shenandoah to June, 1862. Artillery, 1st Division, 2nd Army Corps, Army of Virginia, to September, 1862. Artillery, 1st Division, 12th Army Corps, Army of the Potomac, to May, 1863. Artillery Brigade, 12th Army Corps, Army of the Potomac, to October, 1863. Artillery, 1st Division, 12th Army Corps, Army of the Cumberland, to April, 1864. Artillery, 1st Division, 20th Army Corps, to July, 1864. Artillery Brigade, 20th Army Corps, to June, 1865.

SERVICE.—Duty in the Defences of Washington, D. C., till March, 1862. Advance on Winchester March, 1862. Occupation of Winchester March 12. Advance from Strasburg to Woodstock and Edenburg April 1-2. Woodstock April 1. Edenburg April 1-2. Near Edenburg April 7-11 and 14. South Fork of the Shenandoah April 19. McGaheysville April 27. Operations in the Shenandoah Valley to June 17. Middletown and Newtown May 24. Winchester May 25. Retreat to Williamsport May 25-26. Battle of Cedar Mountain August 9. Pope's Campaign in Northern Virginia August 16-September 2. Beverly Ford August 20. Rappahannock River August 21. Plains of Manassas August 27-29. Battle of Bull Run August 30 (Reserve). Battle of Antietam September 16-17. At Maryland Heights till December. March to Fairfax Station December 10-14 and duty there till January 20, 1863. "Mud March" January 20-24, 1863. Duty at Stafford Court House till April 27. Chancellorsville Campaign April 27-May 6. Battle of Chancellorsville May 1-5. Gettysburg (Pa.) Campaign June 11-July 24. Battle of Gettysburg, Pa., October 4. Guard Nashville & Chattanooga Railroad till April, 1864. Reopening Tennessee River October 26-29. Atlanta (Ga.) Campaign May 1 to September 8. Operations about Rocky Faced Ridge, Tunnel Hill and Buzzard's Roost Gap May 8-13. Battle of Resaca May 14-15. Cassville May 19. New Hope Church May 25. Operations on line of Pumpkin Vine Creek and battles about Dallas, New Hope Church and Allatoona Hills May 26-June 5. Operations about Marietta and against Kenesaw Mountain June 10-July 2. Pine Hill June 11-14. Lost Mountain June 15-17. Gilgal or Golgotha Church June 15. Muddy Creek June 17. Noyes Creek June 19. Kolb's Farm June 22. Assault on Kenesaw June 27. Ruff's Station, Smyrna Camp Ground,

July 4. Chattahoochie River July 5-17. Peach Tree Creek July 19-20. Siege of Atlanta July 22-August 25. Operations at Chattahoochie River Bridge August 26-September 2. Occupation of Atlanta September 2-November 15. March to the sea November 15-December 10. Siege of Savannah December 10-21. Campaign of the Carolinas January to April, 1865. Robertsville, S. C., January 29, 1865. Averysboro, N. C., March 16. Battle of Bentonville March 19-21. Occupation of Goldsboro March 24 and of Raleigh April 14. Bennett's House April 26. Surrender of Johnston and his army. March to Washington, D. C., via Richmond April 29-May 20. Grand Review May 24. Mustered out June 23, 1865.

Battery lost during service 13 Enlisted men killed and mortally wounded and 1 Officer and 11 Enlisted men by disease. Total 25.

3rd REGIMENT LIGHT ARTILLERY.

Organized at Washington, D. C., from 19th Regiment Infantry December 11, 1861.

BATTERY "A" 3rd REGIMENT LIGHT ARTILLERY.

Attached to Porter's Division, Army of the Potomac, to March, 1862. Unattached, Dept. of North Carolina, to December, 1862. Artillery Brigade, Dept. of North Carolina, to January, 1863. Artillery Brigade, 18th Army Corps, Dept. of North Carolina, to April, 1863. Defences of New Berne, N. C., to June, 1863.

SERVICE.—Duty in the Defences of Washington, D. C., December, 1861, to March, 1862. Sailed for New Berne, N. C., March 27, arriving there April 2, and duty there till January, 1863. Foster's Expedition to Port Royal, S. C., January 30-February 2, 1863. At St. Helena Island, S. C., till April. Expedition against Charleston, S. C., April 3-11. Moved to New Berne, N. C., April 14-16. Three years' men transferred to Batteries "E," "I" and "K" May 22. Ordered to New York and mustered out at Syracuse, N. Y., June 2, 1863, expiration of term.

A new Battery "A" organized and mustered in September 23, 1864. Ordered to North Carolina. Attached to District of New Berne, N. C., Dept. of Virginia and North Carolina, to January, 1865. District of Beaufort, N. C., Dept. of North Carolina, to April, 1865. Carter's Division, Provisional Corps, Dept. of North Carolina, to July, 1865.

SERVICE.—Duty at Carolina City and New Berne, N. C., till March, 1865. Demonstration against Kinston, N. C., December 9-15, 1864. Gardner's Bridge December 9. Foster's Mills December 10. Butler's Bridge December 11-12 and January 10, 1865. Campaign of the Carolinas March 1-April 26. Wise's Forks March 7-10. Duty in the Dept. of North Carolina till June. Ordered to New York and mustered out at Syracuse, N. Y., July 3, 1865.

BATTERY "B" 3rd REGIMENT LIGHT ARTILLERY.

First organized from Company "B" 19th Regiment Infantry, but consolidated with Batteries "C" and "D." A new Battery "B" organized at New York City and mustered in December 19, 1861. Joined Regiment at Washington, D. C. Attached to Defences of Washington, D. C., to March, 1862. Unattached, Dept. of North Carolina, to December, 1862. Artillery Brigade, Dept. of North Carolina, to January, 1863. Artillery Brigade, 18th Army Corps, Dept. of North Carolina, and Dept. of the South to April, 1863. Guss' Brigade, Seabrook Island, S. C., 10th Army Corps, Dept. of the South, to June, 1863. St. Helena Island, S. C., 10th Army Corps, to July, 1863. Artillery, 1st Division, 10th Army Corps, Morris Island, S. C., to April, 1864. Morris Island, S. C., Northern District, Dept. of the South, to November, 1864. Artillery, Coast Division, Dept. of the South, to January, 1865. 1st Separate Brigade, Northern District, Dept. of the South, to March, 1865. 1st Separate Brigade, District of Charleston, S. C., to July, 1865. Duty in the Defences of Washington, D. C., till March, 1862. Sailed for Newberne March 27, arriving there April 3.

SERVICE.—Duty at New Berne, N. C., till January, 1863. Reconnoissance toward Trenton, N. C., May 15-

16, 1862. Trenton Bridge May 15. Expedition to Trenton and Pollocksville July 25-29. Expedition to Tarboro November 2-12. Action at Rawle's Mills November 2. Foster's Expedition to Goldsboro December 11-20. Southwest Creek December 13-14. Kinston December 14. Whitehall December 16. Goldsboro December 17. Moved to Port Royal, S. C., January 30-February 2, 1863. At St. Helena Island till April. Expedition against Charleston, S. C., April 3-11. At Seabrook Island, S. C., till June. Edisto Island June 19. At St. Helena Island, S. C., till July. Attack on Morris Island July 10. Assaults on Fort Wagner, Morris Island, S. C., July 11 and 18. Siege of Forts Wagner and Gregg, Morris Island, S. C., and operations against Fort Sumpter and Charleston July 18-September 7. Bombardment of Fort Sumpter and Charleston August 17-23. Capture of Forts Wagner and Gregg September 7. Operations against Charleston from Morris and Folly Islands and duty at Hilton Head, S. C., till November, 1864. Expedition to Johns and James Islands July 2-10, 1864. Operations against Battery Pringle July 4-9. Johns Island July 7. James Island July 10. Hatch's Expedition up Broad River November 28-30. Battle of Honey Hill November 30. Demonstration on Charleston & Savannah Railroad December 6-9. Deveaux's Neck December 6. Tillifinny Station December 9. Occupation of Deveaux's Neck till January 19, 1865. Moved to Morris Island January 19. Cole's Island February 7. Ashepoo February 8. Occupation of Charleston February 18. Duty in Dept. of the South till July. Ordered to New York and mustered out July 13, 1865.

BATTERY "C" 3rd REGIMENT LIGHT ARTILLERY.

Organized from Company "C" 19th Regiment Infantry December 11, 1861. Attached to Defences of Washington to March, 1862. Unattached, Dept. of North Carolina, to December, 1862. Artillery Brigade, Dept. of North Carolina, to January, 1863. Artillery Brigade, 18th Army Corps, Dept. of North Carolina and Dept. of the South, to April, 1863. Dept. of the South to May, 1863. Duty in the Defences of Washington, D. C., till March, 1862. Sailed for New Berne, N. C., March 27, arriving there April 2.

SERVICE.—Duty at New Berne, N. C., till January, 1863. Expedition from New Berne on Neuse River Road July 28, 1862. French's Farm July 28. Moved to Port Royal, S. C., January 30-February 2, 1863. At St. Helena Island, S. C., till April. Expedition against Charleston April 3-11. Moved to New Berne April 14-16. Three years men transferred to Batteries "I" and "K" May 22, 1863. Battery mustered out June 2, 1863, at Syracuse, N. Y.

A new Battery "C" organized and mustered in August 31, 1863. Ordered to North Carolina and attached to Defences of New Berne, Dept. of Virginia, and North Carolina, to January, 1865. District of Beaufort, N. C., Dept. of North Carolina, to February, 1865. Carter's Provisional Division, Provisional Corps, Dept. of North Carolina, to April, 1865. Reserve Artillery, 23rd Army Corps, Dept. of North Carolina, to July, 1865.

SERVICE.—Duty at New Berne and other points in North Carolina till March, 1865. Operations about New Berne against Whiting January 18-February 10, 1864. Beech Grove and Batchelor's Creek February 1-3. Expedition toward Kinston June 20-23. Expedition against Wilmington & Weldon Railroad June 20-25 (Detachment). Campaign of the Carolinas March 1-April 26, 1865. Southwest Creek March 7. Battle of Kinston or Wise's Forks March 8-10. Occupation of Goldsboro March 21. Bennett's House April 26. Surrender of Johnston and his army. Duty in the Dept. of North Carolina till July. Mustered out July 14, 1865.

BATTERY "D," 3rd REGIMENT LIGHT ARTILLERY.

Organized from Company "D," 19th Regiment Infantry, December 11, 1861. Attached to Defences of Washington, D. C., to March, 1862. Unattached, Dept. of North Carolina, to December, 1862. Artillery Brigade, Dept. of North Carolina, to January, 1863. Artillery Brigade, 18th Army Corps, Dept. of North Carolina, to April, 1863. Defences of New Berne, N. C., Dept. of North Carolina, to May, 1863.

SERVICE.—Duty in the Defences of Washington, D. C., till March, 1862. Sailed for New Berne, N. C., March 27, arriving there April 2, and duty there till May, 1863. Three years men transferred to Batteries "E," "I" and "K" May 22, 1863. Mustered out at Elmira, N. Y., June 2, 1863.

A new Battery "D" organized at Syracuse, N. Y., and mustered in February, 1864. Ordered to Dept. of North Carolina and attached to District of Beaufort, N. C., Dept. of Virginia and North Carolina, to January 1865. District of Beaufort, N. C., Dept. of North Carolina, to February, 1865. Carter's Provisional Division, Provisional Corps, Dept. of North Carolina, to April, 1865. Reserve Artillery, 23rd Army Corps, Dept. of North Carolina, to July, 1865.

SERVICE.—Duty at New Berne and other points in North Carolina till March, 1865. Campaign of the Carolinas March 1-April 26, 1865. Southwest Creek March 7. Battle of Kinston or Wise's Forks March 8-10. Occupation of Goldsboro March 21. Bennett's House April 26. Surrender of Johnston and his army. Duty in the Dept. of North Carolina till July. Mustered out at Syracuse, N. Y., July 5, 1865.

BATTERY "E," 3rd REGIMENT LIGHT ARTILLERY.

Organized from Company "E," 19th Regiment Infantry, December 11, 1861. Attached to Defences of Washington, D. C., to March, 1862. Unattached, Dept. of North Carolina, to December, 1862. Artillery Brigade, Dept. of North Carolina, to January, 1863. Artillery Brigade, 18th Army Corps, Dept. of North Carolina, to April, 1863. Defences of New Berne, 18th Army Corps, to July, 1863. Defences of New Berne, N. C., Dept. of Virginia and North Carolina, to April, 1864. Yorktown, Va., 18th Army Corps, Army of the James, to May, 1864. Artillery, 2nd Division, 18th Army Corps, to July, 1864. Artillery Brigade, 18th Army Corps, to December, 1864. Artillery Brigade, 24th Army Corps, to June, 1865.

SERVICE.—Duty in the Defences of Washington, D. C., till March, 1862. Sailed for New Berne, N. C., March 27, arriving there April 2, and duty there till April, 1864. Foster's Expedition to Goldsboro December 11-20, 1862. Actions at Kinston December 14. Whitehall December 16. Goldsboro December 17. Deep Gully, N. C., March 13-14, 1863. New Berne March 14. Moved to Yorktown, Va., April, 1864. Butler's operations on south side of the James and against Petersburg and Richmond May 4-28. Port Walthall May 6-7. Swift Creek May 8-10. Operations against Fort Darling May 12-16. Proctor's Creek May 12-13. Drury's Bluff May 14-16. Bermuda Hundred May 16-June 15. Before Petersburg June 15-18. Siege operations against Petersburg and Richmond June 16, 1864, to April 3, 1865. Chaffin's Farm, New Market Heights, September 28-30. Before Richmond till April 2, 1865. Occupation of Richmond April 3. Pursuit of Lee April 3-9. Surrender of Lee at Appomattox Court House April 9. Mustered out at Richmond, Va., June 23, 1865.

BATTERY "F," 3rd REGIMENT LIGHT ARTILLERY.

Originally organized at Syracuse, N. Y., as 10th Battery Light Artillery and mustered in December 18, 1861. Assigned to Regiment as Battery "F," and joined at Washington, D. C. Attached to Defences of Washington, D. C., to March, 1862. Unattached, Dept. of North Carolina, to December, 1862. Artillery Brigade, 18th Army Corps, Dept. of North Carolina and Dept. of the South, to April, 1863. U. S. Forces, Folly Island, S. C., 10th Army Corps, Dept. of the South, to July, 1863. Artillery, Morris Island, S. C., 10th Army Corps, to November, 1863. Folly Island, S. C., 10th Corps, to March, 1864. District of Beaufort, S. C., Dept. of the South, to September, 1864. District of Florida, Dept. of the South, to November, 1864. Artillery Brigade, Coast Division, Dept. of the South, to January, 1865. 1st Separate Brigade, Northern District, Dept. of the South, to March, 1865. 1st Separate Brigade, District of Charleston, S. C., Dept. of the South, to July, 1865.

SERVICE.—Duty in the Defences of Washington, D. C., till March, 1862. Sailed for New Berne, N. C., March 27, arriving there April 2. Duty at New Berne till January, 1863. Foster's Expedition to Goldsboro December 11-20, 1862. Actions at Kinston December 14. Whitehall December 16. Goldsboro December 17. Moved to Port Royal, S. C., January 30-February 2, 1863. At St. Helena Island, S. C., till April. Expedition against Charleston, S. C., April 3-11. Duty on Folly Island, S. C., operating against Morris Island and Charleston till July. Attack on Morris Island July 10. Assaults on Fort Wagner July 11 and 18. Siege of Forts Wagner and Gregg, Morris Island, and operations against Fort Sumpter and Charleston July 18-September 7. Bombardment of Fort Sumpter and Charleston August 17-23. Capture of Forts Wagner and Gregg September 7. Operations against Charleston from Morris and Folly Islands till September, 1864. Expedition to Johns and James Islands July 2-10, 1864. Operations against Battery Pringle July 4-9. Burden's Causeway, John's Island, July 9. Ordered to Florida September 13, and duty there till November. Hatch's Expedition up Broad River November 28-30. Battle of Honey Hill November 30. Demonstration on Charleston & Savannah Railroad December 6-9. Deveaux's Neck December 6. Tillifinny Station December 9. Occupation of Deveaux's Neck till January 19, 1865. Moved to Morris Island January 19, and duty there till March. Occupation of Charleston till April. Potter's Expedition to Camden, S. C., April 5-25. Dingle's Mills April 9. Statesburg April 15. Occupation of Camden April 17. Boykin's Mills April 18. Denkin's Mills and Beech Creek near Statesburg April 19. Duty in Dept. of the South till July. Mustered out at Syracuse, N. Y., July 24, 1865.

BATTERY "G," 3rd REGIMENT LIGHT ARTILLERY.

Organized from Company "G," 19th Regiment Infantry, December 11, 1861. Attached to Defences of Washington, D. C., to March, 1862. Unattached, Dept. of North Carolina, to December, 1862. Artillery Brigade, Dept. of North Carolina, to January, 1863. Artillery Brigade, 18th Army Corps, Dept. of North Carolina, to April, 1863. Defences of New Berne, N. C., Dept. of North Carolina, to May, 1863.

SERVICE.—Duty in the Defences of Washington, D. C., till March, 1862. Sailed for New Berne, N. C., March 27, arriving there April 2, and duty there and at Washington, N. C., till May, 1863. Action at Washington, N. C., September 6, 1862. Siege of Washington March 30-April 20, 1863. Three years men transferred to Battery "K" May 22, 1863. Mustered out at Elmira, N. Y., June 2, 1863.

A new Battery "G" organized February, 1864. Attached to Defences of New Berne, N. C., Dept. of Virginia and North Carolina, to February, 1865. Artillery Division, District of Beaufort, N. C., Dept. of North Carolina, to April, 1865. Artillery Reserve, 23rd Army Corps, Dept. of North Carolina, to July, 1865.

SERVICE.—Duty at New Berne and other points in North Carolina till March, 1865. Campaign of the Carolinas March 1-April 26. Southwest Creek March 7. Battle of Kinston or Wise's Forks March 8-10. Occupation of Goldsboro March 21. Bennett's House April 26. Surrender of Johnston and his army. Duty in the Dept. of North Carolina till June. Mustered out at Syracuse, N. Y., July 7, 1865.

BATTERY "H," 3rd REGIMENT LIGHT ARTILLERY.

Organized at Rome, N. Y., February 22, 1862. Joined Regiment in the Defences of Washington. Attached to Defences of Washington to March, 1862. Unattached, Dept. of North Carolina, to December, 1862. Artillery Brigade, Dept. of North Carolina, to January, 1863. Artillery Brigade, 18th Army Corps, Dept. of North Carolina, to May, 1863. Artillery Brigade, Defences of New Berne, N. C., 18th Army Corps, to October, 1863. Heckman's Command, Newport News, Va., Dept. of Virginia

and North Carolina, to January, 1864. U. S. Forces, Portsmouth, Va., Dept. of Virginia and North Carolina, to June, 1864. Artillery Brigade, 18th Army Corps, Army of the James, to December, 1864. Artillery Brigade, 24th Army Corps, to June, 1865.

SERVICE.—Duty in the Defences of Washington, D. C., till March, 1862. Sailed for New Berne, N. C., March 27, arriving there April 2. Expedition to Swift Creek Village April 13-21 (Section). Duty at New Berne till October, 1863. Skirmish at Washington, N. C., September 6, 1862. Foster's Expedition to Goldsboro, N. C., December 11-20. Action at Kinston December 14. Whitehall December 16. Goldsboro December 17. Expedition to relief of Washington April 7-10, 1863. Action at Blount's Mills April 9. Expedition to Swift Creek Village April 13-21 (Detachment). Expeditions toward Kinston April 16-21 and April 27-May 1. Wise's Cross Roads April 28. Expedition toward Kinston May 20-23. Gum Swamp May 22. Raid on Wilmington & Weldon Railroad July 3-7. Warsaw and Kenansville July 5. Moved to Newport News, Va., October 16-18. Duty there and in the Defences of Portsmouth, Va., till June, 1864. Ordered to report to Gen. Butler June 13. Siege operations against Petersburg and Richmond June 16, 1864, to April 2, 1865. Mine Explosion, Petersburg, July 30, 1864 (Reserve). Bermuda Hundred August 24-25. Chaffin's Farm, New Market Heights, September 28-30. Darbytown and New Market Road October 7. Fair Oaks October 27-28. In trenches before Richmond till March, 1865. Appomattox Campaign March 28-April 9. Fall of Petersburg April 2. Pursuit of Lee April 3-9. Appomattox Court House April 9. Surrender of Lee and his army. Duty in the Department of Virginia till June. Mustered out at Richmond, Va., June 24, 1865.

BATTERY "I," 3rd REGIMENT LIGHT ARTILLERY.

Organized from Company "I," 19th Regiment Infantry, December 11, 1861. Attached to Defences of Washington, D. C., to March, 1862. Unattached, Dept. of North Carolina, to December, 1862. Artillery Brigade, Dept. of North Carolina, to January, 1863. Artillery Brigade, 18th Army Corps, Dept. of North Carolina, to May, 1863. Defences of New Berne, N. C., 18th Army Corps, Dept. of North Carolina, to July, 1863. Defences of New Berne, N. C., Dept. of Virginia and North Carolina, to February, 1865. Reserve Artillery Division, District of Beaufort, N. C., Dept. of North Carolina, to April, 1865. Reserve Artillery, 23rd Army Corps, Dept. of North Carolina, to June, 1865.

SERVICE.—Duty in the Defences of Washington till March 27, 1862. Sailed for New Berne, N. C., March 27, arriving April 2. Siege of Fort Macon April 12-26. Bombardment and capture of Fort Macon April 25-26. Duty at New Berne till January, 1863. Foster's Expedition to Goldsboro December 11-20, 1862. Actions at Kinston December 14. Whitehall December 16. Goldsboro December 17. Duty at New Berne, N. C., till March, 1865. Expedition from Plymouth to Cedar Point and White Oak River July 13-16, 1863. (Old members mustered out June 2, 1863.) Operations about New Berne against Whiting January 18-February 10, 1864. Beech Grove and Batchelor's Creek February 1-3. Campaign of the Carolinas March 1-April 26, 1865. Southwest Creek March 7. Battle of Wise's Forks March 8-10. Occupation of Goldsboro March 21. Bennett's House April 26. Surrender of Johnston and army. Duty in the Dept. of North Carolina till June. Mustered out at Syracuse, N. Y., July 7, 1865.

BATTERY "K," 3rd REGIMENT LIGHT ARTILLERY.

Organized at Auburn and mustered in December 20, 1861. Attached to Defences of Washington to March, 1862. Unattached, Department of North Carolina, to December, 1862. Artillery Brigade, Dept. of North Carolina, to January, 1863. Artillery Brigade, 18th Army Corps, Dept. of North Carolina, to May, 1863. Defences of Newberne, N. C., 18th Corps, to April, 1864. U. S. Forces, Yorktown, Va., Dept. of Virginia and North Carolina, April, 1864. Artillery, 1st Division, 18th Army

Corps, Army of the James, to May, 1864. Artillery, 3rd Division, 18th Army Corps, to June, 1864. Artillery Brigade, 18th Army Corps, to December, 1864. Artillery Brigade, 24th Army Corps, to June, 1865.

SERVICE.—Duty in the Defences of Washington, D. C., till March, 1862. Sailed for New Berne, N. C., March 27, arriving there April 2. Duty at New Berne till April, 1864. Expedition from New Berne to Tarboro November 1-12. Action at Rawle's Mills November 2. Foster's Expedition to Goldsboro December 11-20. Actions at Kinston December 14. Whitehall December 16. Goldsboro December 17. Expedition to Trenton July 4-8, 1863. Quaker Bridge July 6. Expedition to Swift Creek July 17-20. and to Winton July 25-31. About New Berne February 1-4, 1864. Moved to Yorktown, Va., April, 1864. Butler's operations on south side of the James River and against Petersburg and Richmond May 4-28. Port Walthall May 6-7. Swift Creek May 9-10. Proctor's Creek May 12-13. Operations against Fort Darling May 12-16. Battle of Drury's Bluff May 14-16. Bermuda Hundred May 17. Before Petersburg June 15-18. Siege operations against Petersburg and Richmond June 16, 1864, to April 2, 1865. Battle of Chaffin's Farm, New Market Heights, September 28-30, 1864. Before Richmond till March, 1865. Appomattox Campaign March 28-April 9, 1865. Fall of Petersburg and Richmond April 2-3. Pursuit of Lee April 3-9. Appomattox Court House April 9. Surrender of Lee and his army. Mustered out at Richmond, Va., June 30, 1865.

BATTERY "L," 3rd REGIMENT LIGHT ARTILLERY.

Twenty-fourth New York Battery Light Artillery assigned as Battery "L" March 8, 1865. Joined Regiment May 28, 1865. Duty in the Dept. of North Carolina till July, 1865. Mustered out July 7, 1865.

BATTERY "M," 3rd REGIMENT LIGHT ARTILLERY.

Originally organized as Company "I," 75th New York Infantry. Transferred to 3rd Light Artillery January 24, 1862. Joined Regiment at Washington, D. C., February 22, 1862. Attached to Defences of Washington to March, 1862. Unattached, Dept. of North Carolina, to December, 1862. Artillery Brigade, Dept. of North Carolina, to January, 1863. Artillery Brigade, 18th Army Corps, Dept. of North Carolina, to May, 1863. Defences of New Berne, N. C., to October, 1863. Heckman's Command, Newport News, Va., to December, 1863. U. S. Forces, Portsmouth, Va., Dept. of Virginia and North Carolina, to April, 1864. 1st Division, 18th Army Corps, Army of the James, to May, 1864. 3rd Division, 18th Army Corps, to June, 1864. Artillery Brigade, 18th Army Corps, to December, 1864. Artillery Brigade, 24th Army Corps, to June, 1865.

SERVICE.—Duty in the Defences of Washington, D. C., till March, 1862. Sailed for New Berne, N. C., March 27, arriving there April 2. Duty at New Berne till October, 1863. Moved to Newport News, Va., October 16-18. Duty there and in the Defences of Portsmouth, Va., till May, 1864. Butler's operations on south side of the James River and against Petersburg and Richmond May 4-28. Capture of Fort Powhatan, James River, May 5. Fort Clifton May 9. Harrison's Church May 11. Harrison's Plantation May 15. Bermuda Hundred May 16. Spring Hill May 18. Fort Powhatan May 21. Wilson's Wharf Landing May 24. Before Petersburg June 15-18. Siege operations against Petersburg and Richmond June 16, 1864, to April 2, 1865. Chaffin's Farm, New Market Heights, September 28-30, 1864. At Battery Anderson, Bermuda Hundred front, to December, and at Spring Hill to April, 1865. Fall of Petersburg and Richmond April 2-3, 1865. Duty at Richmond till June. Mustered out at Richmond, Va., June 26, 1865.

1st INDEPENDENT BATTERY LIGHT ARTILLERY.

Organized at Auburn, N. Y., and mustered in November 23, 1861. Left State for Washington, D. C., December 4, 1861. Attached to W. F. Smith's Division, Army of the Potomac, to March, 1862. W. F. Smith's 2nd Division, 4th Army Corps, Army of the Potomac, to May, 1862. Artillery, 2nd Division, 6th Army Corps, to May, 1863. Artillery Brigade, 6th Army Corps, Army of the Potomac and Army of the Shenandoah, to June, 1865.

SERVICE.—Duty in the Defences of Washington, D. C., till March, 1862. Moved to Fortress Monroe, Va., March 23-24. Action at Lee's Mills April 5. Siege of Yorktown April 5-May 4. Lee's Mills April 16. Battle of Williamsburg May 5. Seven days before Richmond June 25-July 1. Gaines' Mill June 27. Golding's Farm June 28. Savage Station June 29. White Oak Swamp and Glendale June 30. Malvern Hill July 1. At Harrison's Landing till August 16. Moved to Fortress Monroe, thence to Alexandria August 16-24. Maryland Campaign September 6-22. Crampton's Pass, South Mountain, September 14. Battle of Antietam September 16-17. At Hagerstown, Md., September 26-October 29. Movement to Falmouth, Va., October 29-November 19. Battle of Fredericksburg, Va., December 12-15. "Mud March" January 20-24, 1863. At Falmouth, Va., till April. Chancellorsville Campaign April 27-May 6. Operations at Franklin's Crossing April 29-May 2. Maryes Heights, Fredericksburg, May 3. Salem Heights May 3-4. Deep Run Ravine June 5-13. Battle of Gettysburg, Pa., July 2-4. Near Fairfield, Pa., July 5. Bristoe Campaign October 9-22. Advance to line of the Rappahannock November 7-8. Rappahannock Station November 7. Mine Run Campaign November 26-December 2. Reconnoissance to Madison Court House February 27-March 2, 1864. Campaign from the Rapidan to the James May 3-June 15. Battles of the Wilderness May 5-7. Spottsylvania May 8-12. Spottsylvania Court House May 12-21. Assault on the Salient, "Bloody Angle," May 12. North Anna River May 23-26. On line of the Pamunkey May 26-28. Totopotomoy May 28-31. Cold Harbor June 1-12. Before Petersburg June 17-19. Siege of Petersburg June 18-July 9. Jerusalem Plank Road, Weldon Railroad, June 22-23. Moved to Washington, D. C., July 9-11. Repulse of Early's attack on Washington July 12-13. Sheridan's Shenandoah Valley Campaign August 7-November 28. Cedar Creek August 12. Charlestown August 21. Leetown August 28-29. Opequan Creek September 13. Battle of Winchester September 19. Fisher's Hill September 22. Battle of Cedar Creek October 19. Duty at Kernstown till December. Moved to Petersburg, Va., December 9-12. Siege of Petersburg December, 1864, to April, 1865. Fort Fisher, Petersburg, March 25, 1865. Appomattox Campaign March 28-April 9. Assault and capture of Petersburg April 2. Pursuit of Lee April 3-9. Sailor's Creek April 6. High Bridge April 7. Appomattox Court House April 9. Surrender of Lee and his army. At Farmville and Burkesville till April 23. March to Danville April 23-27, and duty there till May 18. March to Richmond, thence to Washington, D. C., May 18-June 3. Corps Review June 8. Mustered out June 23, 1865.

Battery lost during service 2 Officers and 16 Enlisted men killed and mortally wounded and 38 Enlisted men by disease. Total 56.

2nd INDEPENDENT BATTERY LIGHT ARTILLERY, "BLENKER'S BATTERY."

Organized by transfer of detachments from 8th and 29th Regiments New York Infantry, who were detached to serve guns of Varian's Battery during Bull Run Campaign of 1861. Battery reorganized at Washington, D. C., and mustered in August 16, 1861, being designated 2nd N. Y. Independent Battery, December 7, 1861. Attached to Blenker's Brigade, Division of the Potomac, to October, 1861. Blenker's Brigade, Hooker's Division, Army of the Potomac, to November, 1861. Blenker's Division, Army of the Potomac, to March, 1862. 1st Brigade, Blenker's 2nd Division, 2nd Army Corps, Army of the Potomac, to April, 1862. 1st Brigade, Blenker's Division, Dept. of the Mountains, to June, 1862. 1st Brigade, 1st Division, 1st Corps, Pope's Army of Virginia, to September, 1862. Artillery, 1st Division, 11th Army Corps, Army of the Potomac, to March, 1863. Reserve Artillery, 11th Army Corps, to May, 1863. Artillery Brigade, 11th Army Corps, to June, 1863.

SERVICE.—Duty in the Defences of Washington, D. C., August, 1861, to April, 1862. Operations in the Shenandoah Valley, Va., May to August, 1862. Strasburg June 1. Woodstock June 2. Near Woodstock, Edenburg and Mt. Jackson June 3. Near Harrisonburg June 6. Battle of Cross Keys June 8. Pope's Campaign in Northern Virginia August 16-September 2. Fords of the Rappahannock August 21-23. Waterloo Bridge August 24-25. Sulphur Springs August 26. Battles of Gainesville August 28; Groveton August 29; 2nd Bull Run August 30. Duty in the Defences of Washington, D. C., till December. March to Fredericksburg, Va., December 10-16. Duty at Falmouth and Brook's Station till April, 1863. "Mud March" January 20-24, 1863. Chancellorsville Campaign April 27-May 6. Battle of Chancellorsville May 1-5. Three years men transferred to Battery "I," 1st New York Light Artillery, June 6, 1863. Battery mustered out June 13, 1863.

Battery lost during service 1 Officer and 4 Enlisted men killed and mortally wounded and 5 Enlisted men by disease. Total 10.

2nd BATTERY REORGANIZED.

Organization not completed and men enlisted transferred to 15th New York Heavy Artillery.

3rd INDEPENDENT BATTERY LIGHT ARTILLERY.

Originally organized as Company "D," 2nd Regiment New York State Militia, later known as 82nd Regiment Infantry. Detached from Regiment and known as Battery "B," New York Artillery, till December, 1861. Designated 3rd New York Battery December 7, 1861. Organized at New York City, and left State for Washington, D. C., May 18, 1861. Mustered in at Washington June 17, and shortly after detached and converted into a Light Battery. Attached to Schenck's Brigade, Tyler's Division, McDowell's Army of Northeast Virginia, June to August, 1861. W. F. Smith's Brigade, Division of the Potomac, to October, 1861. Hancock's Brigade, Smith's Division, Army of the Potomac, to March, 1862. Smith's 2nd Division, 4th Army Corps, Army of the Potomac, to May, 1862. Artillery, 2nd Division, 6th Army Corps, to September, 1862. Artillery, 3rd Division, 6th Army Corps, to November, 1862. Artillery, 2nd Division, 6th Army Corps, to January, 1863. Artillery, Light Division, 6th Army Corps, to May, 1863. Artillery, 2nd Division, 6th Army Corps, to June, 1863. Artillery Brigade, 6th Army Corps, to July 10, 1864. Artillery Reserve, Army of the Potomac, to December, 1864. Artillery Brigade, 6th Army Corps, to June, 1865.

SERVICE.—Duty in the Defences of Washington, D. C., till July, 1861. Advance on Manassas, Va., July 16-21. Battle of Bull Run July 21. Duty in the Defences of Washington till March, 1862. Reconnoissances to Lewinsville September 11 and September 25, 1861. Ordered to Fortress Monroe, Va., March 23, 1862. Siege of Yorktown April 5-May 4. Lee's Mills April 16. Battle of Williamsburg May 5. Seven days before Richmond June 25-July 1. Garnett's and Golding's Farms June 27-28. Savage Station June 29. White Oak Swamp and Glendale June 30. Malvern Hill July 1. At Harrison's Landing till August 16. Moved to Fortress Monroe, thence to Alexandria August 16-24. Maryland Campaign September 6-22. Crampton's Pass, South Mountain, September 14. Lee's Mills September 16. Antietam September 16-17. At Hagerstown, Md., till October 29. Movement to Falmouth, Va., October 29-November 19. Battle of Fredericksburg, Va., December 12-15. "Mud March" January 20-24, 1863. At Falmouth till April, 1863. Chancellorsville Campaign April 27-May 6. Operations at Franklin's Crossing April 29-May 2. Maryes Heights, Fredericksburg, May 8. Salem Heights May 3-4. Deep Run Crossing June 5-13. Battle of Gettysburg, Pa., July 2-4. Fairfield, Pa., July 5. Funkstown, Md., July 10-13. On line of the Rappahannock and Rapidan till October. Bristoe Campaign October 9-22. Advance to line of the Rappahannock November 7-8. Rappahannock Station November 7. Mine Run Campaign November 26-December 2. Campaign

from the Rapidan to the James May 3-June 15, 1864. Battles of the Wilderness May 5-7; Spottsylvania May 8-12; Spottsylvania Court House May 12-21. Assault on the Salient, "Bloody Angle," May 12. North Anna River May 23-26. On line of the Pamunkey May 26-28. Totopotomoy May 28-31. Cold Harbor June 1-12. Before Petersburg June 18-19. Siege of Petersburg June 18, 1864, to April 2, 1865. Jerusalem Plank Road, Weldon Railroad, June 22-23, 1864. Fort Fisher, Petersburg, March 25, 1865. Appomattox Campaign March 28-April 9. Assault and capture of Petersburg April 2. Sailor's Creek April 6. High Bridge May 7. Appomattox Court House April 9. Surrender of Lee and his army. Moved to Danville April 23-27. Duty there till May 18. Moved to Richmond, thence to Washington, D. C., May 18-June 2. Corps Review June 8. Mustered out June 24, 1865.

Battery lost during service 14 Enlisted men killed and mortally wounded and 4 Enlisted men by disease. Total 18.

4th INDEPENDENT BATTERY LIGHT ARTILLERY.

Organized at New York as Company "L," Artillery Company, Serrell's New York Engineer Regiment, and mustered in at Staten Island, N. Y., October 25, 1861. Left State for Washington, D. C., October 25, 1861. Designated Battery "C" and later Battery "D," New York Light Artillery, and 4th New York Battery, December 7, 1861. Attached to Hooker's Division, Army of the Potomac, January to March, 1862. Artillery, 2nd Division, 3rd Army Corps, Army of the Potomac, to May, 1863. Artillery Brigade, 3rd Army Corps, to July, 1863. 1st Volunteer Brigade, Artillery Reserve, Army of the Potomac, to December, 1863.

SERVICE.—Duty in the Defences of Washington, D. C., till March, 1862. Ordered to the Peninsula, Va., March. Siege of Yorktown April 5-May 4. Battle of Williamsburg May 5. Battle of Seven Pines or Fair Oaks May 31-June 1. Seven days before Richmond June 25-July 1. Battles of Oak Grove near Seven Pines June 25; Peach Orchard and Savage Station June 29; White Oak Swamp and Glendale June 30; Malvern Hill July 1. At Harrison's Landing till August 16. Movement to Fortress Monroe, thence to Centreville, August 16-26. Pope's Campaign in Northern Virginia August 26-September 2. Bristoe Station August 27. Battles of Groveton August 29; Bull Run August 30. Duty in the Defences of Washington till November. At Fairfax Station, Va., till November 25. Operations on the Orange & Alexandria Railroad November 10-12. Rappahannock Campaign December, 1862, to June, 1863. Battle of Fredericksburg, Va., December 12-15. "Mud March" January 20-24, 1863. Operations at Rappahannock Bridge and Grove Church February 5-7. At Falmouth till April. Chancellorsville Campaign April 27-May 6. Battle of Chancellorsville May 1-5. Gettysburg, (Pa.) Campaign June 3-August 1. Battle of Gettysburg, Pa., July 1-3. On line of the Rappahannock and Rapidan till October. Bristoe Campaign October 9-22. Advance to line of the Rappahannock November 7-8. Mine Run Campaign November 26 December 2. Battery broken up December 4, 1863, Special Orders No. 538. "A," "G," "O" and men transferred to 1st New York Engineers, 5th and 15th New York Independent Batteries, and Battery "B" to 1st New York Light Artillery.

Battery lost during service 5 Enlisted men killed and mortally wounded and 1 Officer and 11 Enlistd men by disease. Total 17.

5th INDEPENDENT BATTERY LIGHT ARTILLERY, "1st EXCELSIOR LIGHT ARTILLERY."

Organized at New York City and mustered in November 8, 1861. Left State for Washington, D. C., November 8, 1861. Attached to Artillery Reserve, Army of the Potomac, to May, 1862. Unattached, Artillery Reserve, 5th Army Corps, Army of the Potomac, to September, 1862. Reserve Artillery, 5th Army Corps, to December, 1862. Artillery Reserve, Army of the Potomac, to May, 1863. 2nd Volunteer Brigade, Artillery Reserve, Army of the Potomac, to November, 1863.

1st Volunteer Brigade, Artillery Reserve, to March, 1864. 2nd Brigade, Artillery Reserve, to May, 1864. Artillery Brigade, 5th Army Corps, May 15-19. DeRussy's Division, 22nd Army Corps, Dept. of Washington, to July, 1864. Artillery Brigade, 6th Army Corps, to August, 1864. Artillery, 1st Division, 19th Army Corps, Army of the Shenandoah, Middle Military Division, to December, 1864. Artillery Brigade, 19th Army Corps, to February, 1865. Artillery Reserve, Army of the Shenandoah, and Dept. of West Virginia, to July, 1865.

SERVICE.—Duty in the Defences of Washington, D. C., till March, 1862. Peninsula Campaign March to August, 1862. Siege of Yorktown April 5-May 4. Battle of Seven Pines or Fair Oaks May 31-June 1. Seven days before Richmond June 25-July 1. Battle of Mechanicsville June 26. Savage Station June 29. White Oak Swamp and Glendale June 30. Malvern Hill July 1. At Harrison's Landing till August 16. Moved to Alexandria August 16-24. Maryland Campaign September 6-22. Battle of Antietam September 16-17. Duty in Maryland till October 29. Movement to Falmouth, Va., October 29-November 19. Battle of Fredericksburg, Va., December 12-15. "Mud March" January 20-24, 1863. At Falmouth till April. Chancellorsville Campaign April 27-May 6. Battle of Chancellorsville May 1-5. Gettysburg (Pa.) Campaign June 3-July 31. Battle of Gettysburg, Pa., July 1-3. On line of the Rappahannock till October. Bristoe Campaign October 9-22. Advance to line of the Rappahannock November 7-8. Rappahannock Station November 7. Mine Run Campaign November 26-December 2. Campaign of the Rapidan May 3-19, 1864. Battle of the Wilderness May 5-7. Laurel Hill May 8. Spottsylvania May 8-12. Spottsylvania Court House May 12-19. Ordered to Washington May 19, and duty in the Defences of that city till July. Repulse of Early's attack on Washington July 11-12. Sheridan's Shenandoah Valley Campaign August 7-November 28. Battle of Winchester September 19. Fisher's Hill September 22. Battle of Cedar Creek October 19. Duty in the Shenandoah Valley and in the Dept. of West Virginia till July, 1865. Mustered out July 6, 1865.

Battery lost during service 4 Enlisted men killed and mortally wounded and 13 Enlisted men by disease. Total 17.

6th INDEPENDENT BATTERY LIGHT ARTILLERY.

Organized at New York City as Artillery Company "K," 9th Regiment State Militia Infantry, later known as 83rd Regiment Infantry, and mustered in June 15, 1861. Left State June 16, 1861. Served with its Regiment till September 25, 1861, then detached and designated 6th Battery December 7, 1861. Attached to Stone's Division, Army of the Potomac, to December, 1861. Hooker's Division, Army of the Potomac, to March, 1862. Artillery, 2nd Division, 3rd Army Corps, Army of the Potomac, to June, 1862. Artillery Reserve, 3rd Army Corps, to December, 1862. Artillery Reserve, Army of the Potomac, to February, 1863. 1st Brigade, Horse Artillery, Army of the Potomac, serving with Pleasanton's 1st Division, Cavalry Corps, to May, 1863, and with 2nd Division, Cavalry Corps, Army of the Potomac, to June, 1864. Defences of Washington, D. C., 22nd Army Corps, to September, 1864. Horse Artillery, 1st Division, Cavalry Corps, Middle Military Division, to December, 1864. 1st Brigade, Horse Artillery, Army of the Shenandoah, to April, 1865. Horse Artillery Brigade, Defences of Washington, D. C., 22nd Army Corps, to July, 1865.

SERVICE.—Duty in the Defences of Washington and on the Upper Potomac, till March, 1862. Pritchard's Mills, Md., September 15, 1861. Point of Rocks September 24. Operations on the Potomac October 21-24. Ball's Bluff October 21. Moved to the Virginia Peninsula March, 1862. Siege of Yorktown April 5-May 4. Battle of Williamsburg May 5. Battle of Seven Pines or Fair Oaks May 31-June 1. Fair Oaks June 18. Seven days before Richmond June 25-July 1. Malvern Hill July 1 and August 5. At Harrison's Landing till August 16. Movement to Alexandria August 16-24, and duty in the Defences of Washington till January, 1863. Action at Kelly's Ford, Va., March 17. Chancellorsville Campaign April 27-May 6. Battle of Chancellorsville May 1-5. Brandy Station and Beverly Ford June 9. Upperville June 21. Battle of Gettysburg, Pa., July 1-3. Scout to Middleburg September 10-11. Advance from the Rappahannock to the Rapidan September 13-17. Culpeper Court House September 13. Bristoe Campaign October 9-22. Warrenton or White Sulphur Springs October 12-13. St Stephen's Church, Auburn and Bristoe October 14. Advance to line of the Rappahannock November 7-8. Mine Run Campaign November 26-December 2. New Hope Church November 27. Rapidan Campaign May-June, 1864. Battles of the Wilderness May 5-7; Todd's Tavern May 7-8. Sheridan's Raid to James River May 9-24. North Anna River May 9-10. Ground Squirrel Church and Yellow Tavern May 11. Ashland Station May 11. Richmond Fortifications May 12. On line of the Pamunkey May 26-28. Hanovertown May 27. Hawe's Shop and Aenon Church May 28. Totopotomoy May 28-31. Cold Harbor May 31-June 3. In Defences of Washington, D. C., June 6 to September. Sheridan's Shenandoah Valley Campaign September to November. Tom's Brook October 8-9. Battle of Cedar Creek October 19. Duty in the Shenandoah Valley till April, 1865. Expedition from Winchester into Fauquier and Loudoun Counties November 28-December 3, 1864. Expedition to Gordonsville December 19-28. Moved to Washington, D. C., April, 1865, and duty in the defences of that city till July. Mustered out July 8, 1865.

Battery lost during service 8 Enlisted men killed and mortally wounded and 9 Enlisted men by disease. Total 17.

7th INDEPENDENT BATTERY LIGHT ARTILLERY.

Organized at Windsor as an Artillery Company for the 56th Regiment Infantry, and mustered in October 30, 1861. Left State for Washington, D. C., November 7, 1861. Designated 7th Independent Battery December 7, 1861. Attached to Casey's Division, Army of the Potomac, to March, 1862. Artillery, 3rd Division, 4th Army Corps, Army of the Potomac, to June, 1862. Artillery, 2nd Division, 4th Army Corps, to September, 1862. Norfolk and Portsmouth, Va., 7th Army Corps, Dept. of Virginia, to July, 1863. Norfolk, Va., Dept. of Virginia and North Carolina, to March, 1864. U. S. Forces, Yorktown, Va., 18th Army Corps, Dept. of Virginia and North Carolina, to April, 1864. Artillery, 2nd Division, 18th Army Corps, Army of the James, to June, 1864. Artillery Brigade, 18th Army Corps, to December, 1864. Artillery Brigade, 24th Army Corps, to January, 1865. Ferrero's Infantry Division, Defences of Bermuda Hundred, Va., to April, 1865. Dept. of Virginia to July, 1865.

SERVICE.—Duty in the Defences of Washington, D. C., till March, 1862. Ordered to the Virginia Peninsula March. Siege of Yorktown, Va., April 5-May 4. Battle of Williamsburg May 5. Operations about Bottom's Bridge May 20-23. Seven Pines and Savage Station May 24. Chickahominy May 24. Battle of Seven Pines or Fair Oaks May 31-June 1. Seven days before Richmond June 25-July 1. White Oak Swamp June 29-30. Malvern Hill July 1. Moved to Camp Hamilton, Va., and duty there till August. At Norfolk, Va., till October and at Portsmouth, Va., till July, 1863. At Norfolk till March, 1864. Expedition from Norfolk to South Mills and Camden Court House, N. C., December 5-24, 1863. At Yorktown, Va., March to May, 1864. Butler's operations on south side of the James River and against Petersburg and Richmond May 4-28. Operations against Fort Darling May 12-16. Drury's Bluff May 14-16. Bermuda Hundred 16-30. Before Petersburg June 15-18. Siege operations against Petersburg and Richmond June 16, 1864, to April 2, 1865. Battle of Chaffin's Farm, New Market Heights, September 28-30, 1864. Appomattox Campaign March 28-April 9, 1865. Fall of Petersburg April 2. Pursuit of Lee April 3-9. Surrender of Lee at Appomattox Court House April 9. Duty in the Dept. of Virginia till July. Mustered out July 22, 1865.

Battery lost during service 4 Enlisted men killed and mortally wounded and 27 Enlisted men by disease. Total 31.

8th INDEPENDENT BATTERY LIGHT ARTILLERY.

Organized at Newburg, N. Y., as a part of the 10th Legion, 56th Regiment Infantry, and mustered in October 30, 1861. Designated 8th Battery December 7, 1861. Left State for Washington, D. C., December 7, 1861. Attached to Casey's Division, Army of the Potomac, to March, 1862. 3rd Division, 4th Army Corps, Army of the Potomac, to June, 1862. Artillery Reserve, 4th Army Corps, Yorktown, Va., to June, 1863. 1st Brigade, King's Division, 4th Army Corps, Dept. of Virginia, to July, 1863. Artillery Reserve, Yorktown, Va., Dept. of Virginia and North Carolina, to January, 1864. Portsmouth, Va., Dept. of Virginia and North Carolina, to June, 1865. (1 Section with Cavalry Division, Army of the James, May to June, 1864.)

SERVICE.—Duty in the Defences of Washington, D. C., till March, 1862. Ordered to the Virginia Peninsula March. Siege of Yorktown April 5-May 4. Battle of Williamsburg May 5. Operations about Bottom's Bridge May 20-24. Battle of Seven Pines or Fair Oaks May 31-June 1. Seven days before Richmond June 25-July 1. Malvern Hill July 1. At Harrison's Landing till August 16. Moved to Yorktown, Va., and duty there and at Gloucester Point till January, 1864. Dix's Peninsula Campaign June 24-July 7, 1863. Expedition to Gloucester Court House July 25. Expedition to Matthews County October 4-9. Garrison duty at Portsmouth, Va., till June, 1865. (1 Section with Kautz's Cavalry Division May-June, 1864, participating in Butler's operations on south side of the James River and against Petersburg and Richmond May 3-28. Kautz's Raid from Suffolk against Petersburg & Weldon Railroad May 5-11. Wall's Bridge May 5. Stony Creek Station May 7. Nottaway Railroad Bridge May 8. Jarrett's Station and Nottaway River May 8-9. Kautz's Raid on Richmond & Danville Railroad May 12-17. Flat Creek Bridge near Chula Depot May 14. Belcher's Mills May 16. Bermuda Hundred May 18. Petersburg June 9.) Expedition from Suffolk into North Carolina July 27-August 4. Expedition from Bernard's Mills to Murfree's, N. C., October 15-17 (Section). Blackwater October 16 (Section). Expedition from Suffolk to Murfree's Depot, N. C., March 10-11, 1865 (Detachment). South Quay March 10 (Detachment). Mustered out at Norfolk, Va., June 30, 1865.

Battery lost during service 36 Enlisted men by disease.

9th INDEPENDENT BATTERY LIGHT ARTILLERY.

Organized at New York City as Company "F," 41st New York Infantry, and mustered in June 6, 1861. Left State for Washington, D. C., July 8, 1861. Detached from Regiment and designated 9th Battery December 7, 1861. Attached to Defences of Washington, D. C., to February, 1863. 3rd Brigade, Haskins' Division, 22nd Army Corps, Dept. of Washington, to March, 1863. 2nd Brigade, Haskins' Division, 22nd Army Corps, to April, 1864. 3rd Brigade, Haskins' Division, 22nd Army Corps, to June, 1864.

SERVICE.—Duty in the Defences of Washington north of the Potomac, at Fort Washington, till June, 1864. No engagements. Mustered out June 13, 1864.

Battery lost 4 Enlisted men by disease during service.

10th INDEPENDENT BATTERY LIGHT ARTILLERY.

First organized at Syracuse, N. Y., and mustered in December 18, 1861. Assigned to 3rd New York Light Artillery as Battery "F" January 21, 1862. Again organized at New York City as "2nd Excelsior Battery," and mustered in April 9, 1862. Left State for Washington, D. C., April 10. Attached to Wadsworth's Command, Defences of Washington, D. C., to June, 1862. Artillery 2nd Corps, Pope's Army of Virginia, to September, 1862. Artillery, 2nd Division, 12th Army Corps, Army of the Potomac, to November, 1862. Artillery, 3rd Division, 3rd Army Corps, Army of the Potomac, to May, 1863. Artillery Brigade, 3rd Army Corps, to May 12, 1863.

1st Volunteer Brigade, Artillery Reserve, Army of the Potomac, to July, 1863. (Served by detachments with 1st New Hampshire Battery, 5th Massachusetts Battery, and Batteries "C" and "G," 1st Rhode Island Light Artillery, to July.) Defences of Washington, 22nd Army Corps, Camp Barry, Dept. of Washington, to June, 1864.

SERVICE.—Duty in the Defences of Washington to June, 1862. Moved to Harper's Ferry, W. Va., June 28. Pope's Campaign in Northern Virginia July to September, 1862. Battle of Cedar Mountain August 9. Rappahannock Station August 19. Fords of the Rappahannock August 21-23. Sulphur Springs August 23-24. Battles of Groveton August 29; Bull Run August 30. Duty in the Defences of Washington till November. Rappahannock Campaign December, 1862, to June, 1863. Battle of Fredericksburg, Va., December 12-15. "Mud March" January 20-24, 1863. At Falmouth, Va., till April. Chancellorsville Campaign April 27-May 6. Battle of Chancellorsville May 1-5. Battles of Gettysburg, Pa., July 1-3. Ordered to Washington, D. C., July, 1863, and duty at Camp Barry, defences of that city, till June, 1864. Transferred to 6th New York Battery Light Artillery June 21, 1864.

Battery lost during service 2 Enlisted men killed and mortally wounded and 9 Enlisted men by disease. Total 11.

11th INDEPENDENT BATTERY LIGHT ARTILLERY, "HAVELOCK BATTERY."

Organized at Albany, N. Y., and mustered in January 8, 1862. Moved to Washington, D. C., January 17, 1862. Attached to Wadsworth's Command, Military District of Washington, to August, 1862. Whipple's Brigade, Defences of Washington, to November, 1862. Artillery Brigade, 3rd Division, 3rd Army Corps, Army of the Potomac, to May, 1863. Artillery Brigade, 3rd Army Corps, to May 12, 1863. 4th Volunteer Brigade, Artillery Reserve, Army of the Potomac, to June, 1863. 3rd Volunteer Brigade, Artillery Reserve, to July, 1863. Attached to Battery "K," 1st New York Light Artillery, to December, 1863. 2nd Brigade, Artillery Reserve, Army Potomac, to April, 1864. 3rd Brigade, Artillery Reserve, to May, 1864. Artillery Brigade, 2nd Army Corps, May 16 to August, 1864. 1st Division, 2nd Army Corps, August, 1864. Artillery Brigade, 2nd Army Corps, to May, 1865. Artillery Reserve to June, 1865.

SERVICE.—Duty in the Defences of Washington, building Fort Ellsworth, and duty there till August 25, 1862. Pope's Campaign in Northern Virginia August 25-September 2. Bull Run Bridge August 27. Plains of Manassas August 28-29. Battle of Bull Run August 30. Duty in the Defences of Washington till November. Movement to Falmouth, Va., November. Battle of Fredericksburg, Va., December 12-15. "Mud March" January 20-24, 1863. At Falmouth till April. Chancellorsville Campaign April 27-May 6. Battle of Chancellorsville May 1-5. Battle of Gettysburg, Pa., July 1-3. On line of the Rappahannock till October. Bristoe Campaign October 9-22. Bristoe Station October 14. Advance to line of the Rappahannock November 7-8. Kelly's Ford November 7. Mine Run Campaign November 26-December 2. Campaign from the Rapidan to the James May 3-June 15. Battles of the Wilderness May 5-7; Spottsylvania May 8-12; Spottsylvania Court House May 12-21; North Anna River May 23-26. On line of the Pamunkey May 26-28. Totopotomoy May 28-31. Cold Harbor June 1-12. Before Petersburg June 16-18. Siege of Petersburg June 16, 1864, to April 2, 1865. Jerusalem Plank Road June 22-23, 1864. Demonstration on north side of the James July 27-29. Deep Bottom July 27-28. Demonstration north of the James August 13-20. Strawberry Plains, New Market Heights, August 14-18. Appomattox Campaign March 28-April 9, 1865. Sailor's Creek April 6. High Bridge April 7. Appomattox Court House April 9. Surrender of Lee and his army. Moved to Washington, D. C., May. Grand Review May 23. Mustered out June 13, 1865.

Battery lost during service 8 Enlisted men killed and mortally wounded and 13 Enlisted men by disease. Total 21.

12th INDEPENDENT BATTERY LIGHT ARTILLERY.

Organized at Albany, N. Y., and mustered in January 14, 1862. Left State for Washington, D. C., January 17. Attached to Whipple's Brigade, Wadsworth's Command, Military District of Washington, to February, 1863. 22nd Army Corps, Dept. of Washington, to July, 1863. Artillery Brigade, 3rd Army Corps, Army of the Potomac, to March, 1864. 2nd Brigade, Artillery Reserve, Army Potomac, to May 18, 1864. Artillery Brigade, 2nd Army Corps, to September, 1864. Artillery Reserve, Army of the Potomac, to June, 1865.

SERVICE.—Duty at Artillery Camp, Defences of Washington, D. C., to February, 1863, and in the Defences of Washington, till July. Pursuit of Lee July 6-24. Wapping Heights, Va., July 23. On line of the Rappahannock till October. Bristoe Campaign October 9-22. Auburn and Bristoe October 14. Advance to line of the Rappahannock November 7-8. Kelly's Ford November 7. Mine Run Campaign November 26-December 2. Payne's Farm November 27. Mine Run November 28-30. Rapidan Campaign May 3-June 15, 1864. Battle of the Wilderness May 5-7. Spottsylvania May 8-12. Spottsylvania Court House May 12-21. Harris Farm or Fredericksburg Road May 19. North Anna River May 23-26. On line of the Pamunkey May 26-28. Totopotomoy May 28-31. Cold Harbor June 1-12. Before Petersburg June 16-18. Siege of Petersburg June 16, 1864, to April 2, 1865. Jerusalem Plank Road, Weldon Railroad, June 22-23, 1864. Demonstration on north side of the James July 27-29. Deep Bottom July 27-28. Ream's Station August 25. Appomattox Campaign March 28-April 9, 1865. Assault and capture of Petersburg April 2. Moved to Washington, May. Grand Review May 23. Mustered out June 14, 1865.

Battery lost during service 1 Officer and 4 Enlisted men killed and mortally wounded and 14 Enlisted men by disease. Total 19.

13th INDEPENDENT BATTERY LIGHT ARTILLERY.

Organized at New York City and mustered in October 15, 1861. Left State for Washington, D. C., October 17. Attached to Baker's Brigade, Stone's Division, Army of the Potomac, to December, 1861. Blenker's Division, Army of the Potomac, to March, 1862. Blenker's 2nd Division, 2nd Army Corps, Army of the Potomac, to April, 1862. Blenker's Division, Dept. of the Mountains, to June, 1862. Reserve Artillery, 1st Corps, Pope's Army of Virginia, to September, 1862. Artillery, 1st Division, 11th Army Corps, Army of the Potomac, to May, 1863. Artillery Brigade, 11th Army Corps, to October, 1863. Artillery Brigade, 11th Army Corps, Dept. of the Cumberland, to January, 1864. Artillery, 3rd Division, 11th Army Corps, to April, 1864. Artillery, 2nd Division, 20th Army Corps, Army of the Cumberland, to September, 1864. Unattached Artillery, Post of Murfreesboro, Tenn., Dept. of the Cumberland, to December, 1864. Defences Nashville & Chattanooga Railroad, Dept. of the Cumberland, to March, 1865. 2nd Brigade, 1st Sub-District, Middle Tennessee, Dept. of the Cumberland, to July, 1865.

SERVICE.—Duty on the Upper Potomac to December, 1861, and in the Defences of Washington, D. C., till April, 1862. Operations in the Shenandoah Valley till July. Reconnoissance to Rappahannock River and action at Rappahannock Crossing April 18. Battle of Cross Keys June 8. Occupation of Luray July 22. Pope's Campaign in Northern Virginia August 16-September 2. Fords of the Rappahannock August 21-23. Battles of Groveton August 29; Bull Run August 30. Duty in the Defences of Washington, D. C., till December. March to Fredericksburg, Va., December 10-16. "Mud March" January 20-24, 1863. At Brook's Station till April. Chancellorsville Campaign April 27-May 6. Battle of Chancellorsville May 1-5. Battle of Gettysburg, Pa., July 1-3. Pursuit of Lee July 5-24. Near Bristoe Station till September. Movement to Bridgeport, Ala., September 24-October 4. Reopening Tennessee River October 26-29. Chattanooga-Ringgold Campaign November 23-27. Orchard Knob November 23-24. Mission Ridge November 24-25. March to relief of Knoxville November 28-December 8. Duty in Lookout Valley till April, 1864. Atlanta (Ga.) Campaign May 1-September 8. Demonstration on Rocky Faced Ridge, Tunnel Hill and Buzzard's Roost Gap May 8-11. Dug Gap or Mill Creek May 8. Battle of Resaca May 14-15. Near Cassville May 19. New Hope Church May 25. Operations on line of Pumpkin Vine Creek and battles about Dallas, New Hope Church and Allatoona Hills May 26-June 5. Operations about Marietta and against Kenesaw Mountain June 10-July 2. Pine Hill June 11-14. Lost Mountain June 15-17. Gilgal or Golgotha Church June 15. Muddy Creek June 17. Noyes Creek June 19. Kolb's Farm June 22. Assault on Kenesaw June 27. Ruff's Station, Smyrna Camp Ground, July 4. Chattahoochie River July 5-17. Peach Tree Creek July 19-20. Siege of Atlanta July 22-August 25. Operations at Chattahoochie River Bridge August 26-September 2. Occupation of Atlanta September 2. Ordered to Murfreesboro, Tenn., and duty in that District till July, 1865. Overall's Creek December 4, 1864. Hood's attack on Murfreesboro December 5-12, 1864. Wilkinson's Pike, Murfreesboro, December 7. Mustered out July 28, 1865.

Battery lost during service 1 Officer and 11 Enlisted men killed and mortally wounded and 16 Enlisted men by disease. Total 28.

14th INDEPENDENT BATTERY LIGHT ARTILLERY.

Organized October, 1862, from Battery "A," 2nd Battalion, New York Light Artillery. Served by detachments as follows: First Section attached to Battery "C," 4th U. S. Artillery, October, 1862, to January 16, 1863, then to Battery "G," 1st New York Light Artillery, till September 7, 1863. Second Section attached to Battery "G," 1st New York Light Artillery, October, 1862, to September 7, 1863. Third Section attached to Battery "B," 1st New York Light Artillery, October, 1862, to September 7, 1863. These detachments transferred to above named Batteries permanently September 7, 1863. (See histories of each Battery.)

Battery lost during service 2 Officers and 3 Enlisted men killed and mortally wounded and 4 Enlisted men by disease. Total 9.

15th INDEPENDENT BATTERY LIGHT ARTILLERY.

Organized October, 1862, from Battery "B," 2nd Battalion, New York Light Artillery. Attached to 8th Army Corps, Middle Department, October, 1862, to January, 1863. Artillery Reserve, Army of the Potomac, to May, 1863. 1st Volunteer Brigade, Artillery Reserve, Army of the Potomac, to August, 1863. 4th Volunteer Brigade, Artillery Reserve, to August, 1863. 3rd Volunteer Brigade, Artillery Reserve, to December, 1863. 2nd Brigade, Artillery Reserve, Army of the Potomac, to May 16, 1864. Artillery Brigade, 5th Army Corps, to December, 1864. 22nd Army Corps, December, 1864. Reserve Division, Dept. of West Virginia, to February, 1865.

SERVICE.—Duty at Relay House, Md., October, 1862, to January, 1863. Chancellorsville Campaign April 27-May 6. Battle of Chancellorsville May 1-5. Battle of Gettysburg, Pa., July 1-3. On line of the Rappahannock till October. Bristoe Campaign October 9-22. Advance to line of the Rappahannock November 7-8. Rappahannock Station November 7. Mine Run Campaign November 26-December 2. Rapidan Campaign May 3-June 15, 1864. Battle of the Wilderness May 5-7. Spottsylvania May 8-12. Spottsylvania Court House May 12-21. North Anna River May 23-26. Jericho Ford May 23. On line of the Pamunkey May 26-28. Totopotomoy May 28-31. Cold Harbor June 1-12. Bethesda Church June 1-3. Before Petersburg June 16-18. Siege of Petersburg June 16 to December, 1864. Weldon Railroad August 18-21. Poplar Springs Church September 29-October 2. Duty in the Defences of Washington, D. C., December, 1864, and in the Dept. of West Virginia till February, 1865. Transferred to 32nd New York Independent Battery Light Artillery February 4, 1865.

Battery lost during service 8 Enlisted men killed and mortally wounded and 3 Enlisted men by disease. Total 11.

16th INDEPENDENT BATTERY LIGHT ARTILLERY ("DICKINSON LIGHT ARTILLERY").

Organized at Binghampton, N. Y. Left State for Washington, D. C., March 10, 1862. Mustered in at Washington March 27, to date from December 10, 1861. Attached to Artillery Camp, Military District of Washington, and 22nd Army Corps, Dept. of Washington, to April, 1863. Unattached, Suffolk, Va., 7th Army Corps, Dept. of Virginia, April, 1863. Reserve Brigade, 3rd Division, 7th Army Corps, to June, 1863. Wistar's Brigade, 3rd Division, 7th Army Corps, to July, 1863. U. S. Forces, Yorktown, Va., Dept. of Virginia and North Carolina, to October, 1863. Newport News, Va., Dept. of Virginia and North Carolina, to June, 1864. Artillery Brigade, 18th Army Corps, Army of the James, to August, 1864. Artillery Brigade, 10th Army Corps, to September, 1864. Artillery Brigade, 18th Army Corps, to December, 1864. Artillery Brigade, 24th Army Corps, to March, 1865. Attached to 2nd Division, 24th Army Corps, and 2nd Division, Terry's Provisional Corps, Dept. of North Carolina, to March, 1865. Artillery, 2nd Division, 10th Army Corps, and 10th Army Corps, Dept. of North Carolina, to July, 1865.

SERVICE.—Duty in Artillery Camp of Instruction and Defences of Washington, D. C., till April, 1863. Ordered to Suffolk, Va., April, 1863. Siege of Suffolk April 19-May 4. South Quay Bridge May 1. Siege of Suffolk raised May 4. Moved to Yorktown, Va., and duty there till November. Dix's Peninsula Campaign June 24-July 7. Duty at Newport News, Va., November, 1863, to June, 1864. Before Petersburg June 15-18. Siege operations against Petersburg and Richmond June 16 to December 7, 1864. Battle of Chaffin's Farm, New Market Heights, September 28-30. Duty before Richmond north of the James till December. Expedition to Fort Fisher, N. C., December 6-27. Second Expedition to Fort Fisher, N. C., January 3-15, 1865. Assault and capture of Fort Fisher January 15. Cape Fear Intrenchments February 11-12. Fort Anderson February 18-20. Capture of Wilmington February 22. Campaign of the Carolinas March 1-April 26. Advance on Kinston and Goldsboro March 6-21. Occupation of Goldsboro and Raleigh, N. C. Bennett's House April 26. Surrender of Johnston and his army. Duty in the Dept. of North Carolina till July. Mustered out July 6, 1865.

Battery lost during service 44 Enlisted men by disease.

17th INDEPENDENT BATTERY LIGHT ARTILLERY ("ORLEANS BATTERY").

Organized at Lockport, N. Y., and mustered in August 26, 1862. Left State for Washington, D. C., August 28. Attached to Military District of Washington to October, 1862. Abercrombie's Division, Defences of Washington, to February, 1863. Abercrombie's Division, 22nd Army Corps, Dept. of Washington, to April, 1863. Camp Barry, 22nd Army Corps, to July, 1863. Artillery, King's Division, 22nd Army Corps, to March, 1864. Camp Barry, 22nd Army Corps, to May, 1864. 2nd Brigade, DeRussy's Division, 22nd Army Corps, to July, 1864. Artillery Brigade, 18th Army Corps, Army of the James, to December, 1864. Artillery Brigade, 24th Army Corps, to June, 1865.

SERVICE.—Duty at Artillery Camp of Instruction and in the Defences of Washington, D. C., September, 1862, to July, 1864. Ordered to join Army of the James in the field at Petersburg, Va. Siege operations against Petersburg and Richmond July 6, 1864, to April 2, 1865. Battle of Chaffin's Farm, New Market Heights, September 28-30, 1864. Duty on north side of the James River before Richmond till March, 1865. Appomattox Campaign March 28-April 9. Fall of Petersburg April 2. Pursuit of Lee April 3-9. Rice's Station April 6. Appomattox Court House April 9. Surrender of Lee and his army. Duty in the Dept. of Virginia till June. Mustered out June 12, 1865.

Battery lost during service 1 Enlisted man killed and 16 Enlisted men by disease. Total 17.

18th INDEPENDENT BATTERY LIGHT ARTILLERY ("BLACK HORSE ARTILLERY," "BILLINGHURST BATTERY").

Organized at Rochester, N. Y., and mustered in September 13, 1862. Left Rochester for New York City November 18. Attached to Banks' New Orleans Expedition November-December, 1862. Sherman's Division, Dept. of the Gulf, to January, 1863. 2nd Division, 19th Army Corps, Dept. of the Gulf, to May, 1863. 1st Division, 19th Army Corps, to August, 1863. Reserve Artillery, 19th Army Corps, Defences of New Orleans, La. to December, 1863. District of Baton Rouge, La., Dept. of the Gulf, to February, 1865. Siege Artillery, Canby's Forces, Military Division West Mississippi, to July, 1865.

SERVICE.—Sailed for New Orleans, La., December 2, 1862, arriving there December 13, and duty there till February, 1863. Moved to Baton Rouge, La., February 3. Reconnoissance to Port Hudson, La., March 13-20. Operations in Western Louisiana April 9-May 14. Teche Campaign April 11-20. Fort Bisland, near Centreville, April 12-13. Irish Bend April 14. Vermillion Bayou April 17. Opelousas April 20. Amite River May 3. Action at Plain's Store 21. Siege of Port Hudson May 24-July 9. Assaults on Port Hudson May 27 and June 14. Surrender of Port Hudson July 9. Bayou LaFourche July 13. Duty in the Defences of New Orleans and in the District of Baton Rouge till February, 1865. Action at Comite Bridge May 3, 1864. Clinton and Liberty Creek November 15. Campaign against Mobile, Ala., and its defences March 17-April 12, 1865. Siege of Spanish Fort and Fort Blakely March 26-April 8. Fort Blakely April 9. March to Montgomery April 13-25. Duty in District of Alabama till July. Mustered out July 20, 1865.

Battery lost during service 3 Enlisted men killed and mortally wounded and 23 Enlisted men by disease. Total 26.

19th INDEPENDENT BATTERY LIGHT ARTILLERY ("STAHL'S BATTERY").

Organized at Lockport, N. Y., and mustered in at Elmira, N. Y., October 27, 1862. Left State for Washington, D. C., October 29, 1862. Attached to Defences of Washington, D. C., and 22nd Army Corps, Dept. of Washington, to April, 1863. Unattached, Suffolk, Va., 7th Army Corps, Dept. of Virginia, to June, 1863. Artillery, 1st Division, 7th Army Corps, to July, 1863. Camp Barry, Defences of Washington, 22nd Army Corps, to March, 1864. Artillery, 2nd Division, 9th Army Corps, Army of the Potomac, to July, 1864. Artillery Brigade, 9th Army Corps, to June, 1865.

SERVICE.—Duty in the Defences of Washington, D. C., till April 16, 1863. Ordered to Suffolk, Va. Siege of Suffolk April 17-May 4. Action at Suffolk April 17. Siege of Suffolk raised May 4. Duty at Suffolk and in the Dept. of Virginia till July. Ordered to Washington, D. C., and duty in the defences of that city till March, 1864. Campaign from the Rapidan to the James May 3-June 15. Battles of the Wilderness May 5-7; Spottsylvania May 8-12; Spottsylvania Court House May 12-21. Assault on the Salient May 12. North Anna River May 23-26. On line of the Pamunkey May 26-28. Totopotomoy May 28-31. Cold Harbor June 1-12. Bethesda Church June 1-3. Before Petersburg June 16-18. Siege of Petersburg June 16, 1864, to April 2, 1865. Mine Explosion, Petersburg, July 30, 1864. Weldon Railroad August 18-21. Poplar Springs Church September 29-October 2. Boydton Plank Road, Hatcher's Run, October 27-28. Fort Stedman March 25, 1865. Appomattox Campaign March 28-April 9. Assault and capture of Petersburg April 2. Pursuit to Appomattox. Moved to Washington, D. C., April 21-27. Grand Review May 23. Mustered out June 13, 1865.

Battery lost during service 14 Enlisted men killed and mortally wounded and 1 Officer and 16 Enlisted men by disease. Total 31.

20th INDEPENDENT BATTERY LIGHT ARTILLERY.

Organized at New York City December 27, 1862. Assigned to duty at Fort Schuyler, New York Harbor, Dept. of the East, as garrison till March, 1864. Duty at Hart's Island, New York Harbor, till May, 1864. At Fort Columbus, New York Harbor, Dept. of the East, till April, 1865, and at Battery Barracks, New York, till July, 1865. Mustered out July 31, 1865.

Battery lost during service 6 by disease.

21st INDEPENDENT BATTERY LIGHT ARTILLERY.

Organized at Oswego, N. Y., and mustered in at New York City December 12, 1862. Left State for New Orleans, La., December 12, 1862. Attached to Defences of New Orleans, Dept. of the Gulf, January to May, 1863. Artillery, 2nd Division, 19th Army Corps, Dept. of the Gulf, to July, 1863. District of Port Hudson, La., Dept. of the Gulf, to July, 1864. Reserve Artillery, Dept. of the Gulf, to February, 1865. Artillery, 3rd Division, Reserve Corps, Military Division West Mississippi, February, 1865. Artillery, 3rd Division, 13th Army Corps, to July, 1865. Dept. of Alabama to September, 1865.

SERVICE.—Duty in the Defences of New Orleans, La., till May, 1863. Expedition to Amite River May 7-19. Action at Civique's Ferry May 10. Moved to Baton Rouge, thence to Port Hudon May 20-22. Siege of Port Hudson May 22-July 9. Surrender of Port Hudson July 9. Garrison duty at Port Hudson till July, 1864. Action at Plain's Store April 7, 1864. Moved to Morganza July, 1864, and duty there till February, 1865. Campaign against Mobile, Ala., and its defences March 17-April 12. Siege of Spanish Fort and Fort Blakely March 26-April 12. Fort Blakely April 9. Capture of Mobile April 12. Duty in the District of Alabama till September. Mustered out September 8, 1865.

Battery lost during service 2 Enlisted men killed and mortally wounded and 1 Officer and 30 Enlisted men by disease. Total 33.

22nd INDEPENDENT BATTERY LIGHT ARTILLERY.

Organized at Lockport, N. Y., and mustered in at Elmira, N. Y., October 28, 1862. Left State for Washington, D. C., November 23, 1862. Duty in the defences of that city till February, 1863. Assigned to 9th New York Heavy Artillery as Company "M" February 5, 1863.

23rd INDEPENDENT BATTERY LIGHT ARTILLERY.

Organized as Battery "A," New York Rocket Battalion, and designated 23rd New York Battery February 11, 1863, having served as such provisionally from November 1, 1862. Attached to Artillery Brigade, 18th Army Corps, Dept. of North Carolina, to May, 1863. District of Pamlico, Dept. of North Carolina, and District of North Carolina, Dept. of Virginia and North Carolina, to February, 1864. Sub-District Defences of New Berne, N. C., Dept. of Virginia and North Carolina, to February, 1865. District of Beaufort, N. C., Dept. of North Carolina, to April, 1865. Artillery, Kilpatrick's 3rd Cavalry Division, Army of Georgia, to July, 1865.

SERVICE.—Expedition from New Berne, N. C., to Tarboro November 2-12, 1862. Action at Rawle's Mills November 2. Demonstration on New Berne November 11. Foster's Expedition to Goldsboro, N. C., December 11-20. Actions at Kinston December 14; Whitehall December 16; Thompson's Bridge and Goldsboro December 17. Reconnoissance to Diascund Bridge December 17. Duty in the District of the Pamlico, N. C., till March, 1865. Operations on the Pamlico April 4-6, 1863. Expedition to Swift Creek Village April 13-21 (Section). Action at Washington, N. C., April 27-28, 1864. Near Greenville November 25. Greenville December 30. Campaign of the Carolinas March 1-April 26. Bennett's House April 26. Surrender of Johnston and his army. Duty in the Dept. of North Carolina till July. Mustered out July 14, 1865.

Battery lost during service 47 Enlisted men by disease.

24th INDEPENDENT BATTERY LIGHT ARTILLERY.

Organized as Battery "B," New York Rocket Battalion, and designated 24th Battery February 11, 1863, having served as such provisionally from October 19, 1862. Attached to Artillery Brigade, Dept. of North Carolina, to January, 1863. Artillery Brigade, 18th Army Corps, Dept. of North Carolina, to May, 1863. District of the Albemarle, Dept. of North Carolina, to July, 1863, and Dept. of Virginia and North Carolina to February, 1864. District of Plymouth, N. C., to April, 1864.

SERVICE.—Expedition from New Berne, N. C., November 2-12, 1862. Action at Rawle's Hill November 2. Demonstration on New Berne November 11. Foster's Expedition to Goldsboro December 11-20. Actions at Kinston December 14. Whitehall December 16. Goldsboro December 17. Duty at New Berne, N. C., till March, 1863. Expedition from Newberne to Trenton, Pollocksville, Young's Cross Roads and Swansborough March 6-10. Expedition to Plymouth, N. C., March 27-April 1, and duty there till April, 1864. Expedition from Plymouth to Foster's Mills July 26-29, 1863. Expedition to Lake Phelps January 27, 1864. Siege of Plymouth, N. C., April 17-20. Captured April 20. Transferred to 3rd New York Light Artillery as Battery "L" March 8, 1865. Joined Regiment in Dept. of North Carolina May 28, 1865.

Battery lost during service 4 Enlisted men killed and mortally wounded and 77 Enlisted men by disease. Total 81.

25th INDEPENDENT BATTERY LIGHT ARTILLERY.

Organized at Lockport, N. Y., and mustered in December 12, 1862. Left State for New Orleans, La., December 18, 1862. Wrecked enroute on transport "Sparkling Sea" January 9, 1863, arriving at New Orleans, La., February 4, 1863. Attached to Defences of New Orleans, La., Dept. of the Gulf, to June, 1863. Artillery Reserve, Dept. of the Gulf, to August, 1863. 4th Division, 19th Army Corps, Dept. of the Gulf, to December, 1863. Reserve Artillery, 19th Army Corps, to February, 1864. 1st Division, 19th Army Corps, to May, 1864. Defences of New Orleans to June, 1864. District of LaFourche, La., to December, 1864. Southern District of Louisiana, Dept. of the Gulf, to August, 1865.

SERVICE.—Duty in the Defences of New Orleans, La., till June, 1863. Action at LaFourche Crossing June 20-21. Duty in District of LaFourche till October. Western Louisiana ("Teche") Campaign October 3-November 30. At New Iberia till January 7, 1864. Moved to New Orleans, thence to Franklin, and duty there till March, 1864. Red River Campaign March 10-May 22. Advance from Franklin to Alexandria March 14-26. Battle of Sabine Cross Roads April 8. Pleasant Hill April 9. Monett's Ferry (or Cane River Crossing) April 23. Alexandria April 30-May 13. Retreat to Morganza May 13-20. Mansura May 16. Ordered to New Orleans and duty there till June. Duty in District of LaFourche till December and in Southern District of Louisiana till July, 1865. Mustered out at Rochester, N. Y., August 1, 1865.

Battery lost during service 3 Enlisted men killed and mortally wounded and 27 Enlisted men by disease. Total 30.

26th INDEPENDENT BATTERY LIGHT ARTILLERY,
"BARNES' RIFLE BATTERY."

Organized at Rochester, N. Y. Left State for New Orleans, La., December 4, 1862. Wrecked twice en route, and arrived at New Orleans, La., January 24, 1863. Attached to Defences of New Orleans, Dept. of the Gulf, to June, 1863. 4th Division, 19th Army Corps, Army of the Gulf, to October, 1863. District of LaFourche, Dept. of the Gulf, to February, 1864. Artillery, 2nd Division, 19th Army Corps, to December, 1864. Artillery Reserve Division, Military Division West Mississippi, to February, 1865. Artillery, 3rd Division, Reserve Corps, February, 1865. Artillery, 3rd Division,

13th Army Corps, to July, 1865. District of Alabama, to September, 1865.

SERVICE.—Duty in the Defences of New Orleans, La., and in the District of LaFourche, La., till February, 1864. Red River Campaign March 10-May 22. At Alexandria till May 13. Retreat to Morganza May 13-20. Mansura May 16. Moved to Baton Rouge, La., and duty there till February, 1865. Expedition to Clinton, La., August 23-29, 1864. Campaign against Mobile and its Defences March 17-April 12. Siege of Spanish Fort and Fort Blakely March 26-April 9. Capture of Mobile April 12. Duty in the Dept. of Alabama till September. Mustered out at New Orleans, La., September 12, 1865.

Battery lost during service 33 Enlisted men by disease.

27th INDEPENDENT BATTERY LIGHT ARTILLERY. ("BUFFALO LIGHT ARTILLERY." "EATON'S BATTERY.")

Organized at Buffalo, N. Y., and mustered in December 17, 1862. Left State for Washington, D. C., December 22, 1862. Attached to Defences of Washington, D. C., and 22nd Army Corps, Dept. of Washington, to July, 1863. Philadelphia, Pa., Dept. of the Susquehanna, to January, 1864. Camp Barry, 22nd Army Corps, Dept. of Washington, D. C., to April, 1864. Artillery Reserve, 9th Army Corps, Army of the Potomac, to May 16, 1864. Defences of Washington, D. C., 22nd Army Corps, to June 5, 1864. Artillery, 1st Division, 9th Army Corps, Army of the Potomac, to July, 1864. Artillery Brigade, 9th Army Corps, to June, 1865.

SERVICE.—Duty at Artillery Camp of Instruction and in the Defences of Washington, D. C., till July, 1863. At Philadelphia, Pa., till January, 1864. At Washington, D. C., till April, 1864. Rapidan Campaign May, 1864. Battles of the Wilderness May 5-7; Spottsylvania May 8-12; Spottsylvania Court House May 12-16. At Washington, D. C., till June 5. Before Petersburg, Va., June 16-18. Siege of Petersburg, Va., June 16, 1864, to April 2, 1865. Mine Explosion, Petersburg, July 30, 1864. Fort Stedman March 25, 1865. Appomattox Campaign March 28-April 9. Assault and fall of Petersburg April 2. Pursuit of Lee April 3-9. Moved to Washington, D. C., April 21-27. Grand Review May 23. Mustered out June 22, 1865.

Battery lost during service 2 Enlisted men killed and mortally wounded and 17 Enlisted men by disease. Total 19.

28th INDEPENDENT BATTERY LIGHT ARTILLERY.

Organized at Fort Schuyler, N. Y., and mustered in December 27, 1862. Assigned to duty as garrison at Fort Schuyler, New York Harbor, and at Sandy Hook, N. Y., Dept. of the East, till July, 1865. Mustered out July 31, 1865.

Battery lost during service 8 Enlisted men by disease.

29th INDEPENDENT BATTERY LIGHT ARTILLERY.

Organized from Battery "A" 1st Independent Battalion Light Artillery March 16, 1863. Attached to Artillery Reserve, Army of the Potomac, to May, 1863. 2nd Volunteer Brigade, Artillery Reserve, Army of the Potomac, to July, 1863. Attached to 32nd New York Battery July, 1863, to August, 1864. Old members mustered out August 15, 1864. Veterans and Recruits transferred to 32nd New York Battery. Participated in the Chancellorsville Campaign April 27-May 6, 1863. Operations at Pollock's Mill Creek April 29-May 2. Battle of Chancellorsville May 2-5. Duty at and near Harper's Ferry, W. Va., till August, 1864.

Battery lost during service 2 Enlisted men killed and mortally wounded and 1 Enlisted man by disease. Total 3.

30th INDEPENDENT BATTERY LIGHT ARTILLERY.

Organized from Battery "B" 1st Independent Battalion New York Light Artillery March 16, 1863. Attached to Artillery Reserve, Army of the Potomac, to May, 1863. 2nd Volunteer Brigade, Artillery Reserve, Army of the Potomac, to July, 1863. 1st Division, Dept. of the Susquehanna, to August, 1863. Artillery, Martinsburg, W. Va., to December, 1863. 2nd Brigade, 1st Division, Army of West Virginia, to January, 1864. Artillery, 1st Division, West Virginia, to May, 1864. Artillery Brigade, West Virginia, to July, 1864. Reserve Division, Harper's Ferry, West Virginia, to January, 1865. Camp Barry, Washington, D. C., 22nd Army Corps, to June, 1865.

SERVICE.—Chancellorsville Campaign April 27-May 6, 1863. Duty at Harper's Ferry and Martinsburg, W. Va., till April, 1864. Sigel's Expedition from Martinsburg to New Market April 30-May 16, 1864. Battle of New Market May 15. Hunter's Raid to Lynchburg May 24-July 1. Advance to Staunton May 24-June 5. Piedmont June 5. Occupation of Staunton June 6. Lexington June 12. Lynchburg June 17-18. Catawba Mountains and Salem June 21. Charlestown July 19. Kernstown, Winchester, July 24. Bunker Hill and Martinsburg July 25. Duty at Harper's Ferry and vicinity till January, 1865, and in the Defences of Washington, D. C., till June, 1865. Mustered out June 23, 1865.

Battery lost during service 7 Enlisted men killed and mortally wounded and 11 Enlisted men by disease. Total 18.

31st INDEPENDENT BATTERY LIGHT ARTILLERY.

Organized from Battery "C" 1st Independent Battalion New York Light Artillery March 16, 1863. Attached to Artillery Reserve, Army of the Potomac, to May, 1863. 2nd Volunteer Brigade, Artillery Reserve, Army of the Potomac, to July, 1863. Harper's Ferry, W. Va., Dept. of West Virginia, to January, 1864.

SERVICE.—Chancellorsville Campaign April 27-May 6. 1863. Duty at Harper's Ferry, W. Va., July, 1863, to January, 1864. Attached to 30th New York Battery January to October, 1864. Old members mustered out October 25, 1864. Veterans and Recruits transferred to 30th New York Battery.

Battery lost during service 5 Enlisted men by disease.

32nd INDEPENDENT BATTERY LIGHT ARTILLERY.

Organized from Battery "D" 1st Independent Battalion New York Light Artillery March 16, 1863. Attached to Artillery Reserve, Army of the Potomac, to May, 1863. 2nd Volunteer Brigade, Artillery Reserve, Army of the Potomac, to June, 1863. Barry's Command, Washington, D. C., 22nd Army Corps, to July, 1863. 2nd Brigade, Maryland Heights Division, Dept. of West Virginia, to September, 1863. 2nd Brigade, 1st Division, West Virginia, to December, 1863. Artillery, 1st Division, West Virginia, to April, 1864. Reserve Division, Dept. of West Virginia, to December, 1864. 3nd Infantry Division, West Virginia, to January, 1865. 1st Brigade, 2nd Infantry Division, West Virginia, to March, 1865. 1st Brigade, 1st Infantry Division, West Virginia, to July, 1865.

SERVICE.—Chancellorsville Campaign April 27-May 6, 1863. Moved to Washington, D. C., June, and duty in the Defences of that city till July, and at Maryland Heights and Harper's Ferry, W. Va., till July, 1865. Mustered out July 14, 1865.

Battery lost during service 2 Enlisted men killed and mortally wounded and 3 by disease. Total 5.

33rd INDEPENDENT BATTERY LIGHT ARTILLERY.

Organized at Buffalo, N. Y., and mustered in at Elmira, N. Y., September 4, 1863. Left State for Washington, D. C., September 4, 1863. Attached to Camp Barry, Defences of Washington, 22nd Army Corps, to February, 1864. United States Forces, Yorktown, Va., Dept. of Virginia and North Carolina, to April, 1864. Artillery, 3rd Division, 10th Army Corps, Army of the James, to May, 1864. Unattached Artillery, 10th Army Corps, to June, 1864. Artillery, 3rd Division, 10th Army Corps, to August, 1864. Artillery Brigade, 10th Army Corps, to October, 1864. Separate Brigade, Dept. of Virginia and North Carolina. Garrison at Fort Pocohontas on James River to January, 1865. Ferrero's Division, Defences of Bermuda Hundred, Va., to April, 1865. Dept. of Virginia to June, 1865.

SERVICE.—Duty at Camp Barry, Defences of Washington, 22nd Army Corps, till February, 1864, and at Yorktown and Gloucester Point, Va., till May, 1864. Butler's operations on south side of the James River and against Petersburg and Richmond May 4-28. Occupation of City Point and Bermuda Hundred, Va., May 5. Swift Creek May 8-10. Operations against Fort Darling May 12-16. Battle of Drury's Bluff May 14-16. Bermuda Hundred May 16-June 15. Action at Bermuda Hundred June 2. Siege operations against Petersburg and Richmond June 15, 1864, to April 2, 1865. Assaults on Petersburg June 15-18, 1864. Assigned to duty as Garrison Artillery at Fort Pocohontas on James River till January, 1865. Duty in the Defences of Bermuda Hundred, Va., till April. Operations resulting in the fall of Petersburg and Richmond March 28-April 2. Duty at Petersburg till June. Mustered out June 25, 1865.

Battery lost during service 1 Officer and 12 Enlisted men by disease.

34th INDEPENDENT BATTERY LIGHT ARTILLERY ("HAMILTON ARTILLERY," "FLUSHING BATTERY")

Originally organized as Battery "L," 2nd New York Heavy Artillery, and mustered in November 18, 1861. Left State for Washington, D. C., December 2, 1861. Detached from Regiment March, 1862. Attached to Sturgis' Brigade, Military District of Washington, to June, 1862. Artillery, 2nd Army Corps, Pope's Army of Virginia, to August, 1862. 2nd Brigade, 3rd Division, 1st Army Corps, Army of Virginia, to September, 1862. Artillery, 1st Division, 9th Army Corps, Army of the Potomac, to October, 1862. Artillery, 2nd Division, 9th Army Corps, to December, 1862. Artillery, 3rd Division, 9th Army Corps, to February, 1863. Artillery, 2nd Division, 9th Army Corps, Army of the Potomac, to April, 1863, and Army of the Ohio to June, 1863. Artillery, 2nd Division, 9th Army Corps, Army of the Tennessee, to August, 1863. Artillery, 2nd Division, 9th Army Corps, Army of the Ohio, to September, 1863. Artillery, 1st Division, 9th Army Corps, Army of the Ohio, to April, 1864. Artillery, 3rd Division, 9th Army Corps, Army of the Potomac, to July, 1864. Artillery Brigade, 9th Army Corps, to June, 1865. Designated 34th Independent Battery November 19, 1863.

SERVICE.—Duty in the Defences of Washington, D. C., till June, 1862. Battle of Cedar Mountain, Va., August 9. Pope's Campaign in Northern Virginia August 16-September 2. Fords of the Rappahannock August 20-23. Sulphur Springs August 23-24. Buckland's Bridge, Broad Run, August 27. Battles of Groveton August 29. Bull Run August 30. Duty in the Defences of Washington and in Pleasant Valley, Md., till October 27. Movement to Falmouth, Va., October 27-November 19. Action at Jefferson November 11. Sulphur Springs November 13 and 15. Battle of Fredericksburg, Va., December 12-15. "Mud March" January 20-24, 1863. At Falmouth till February 19. Moved to Newport News, Va., February 19; thence to Paris, Ky., March 26-April 2. Duty at various points in Kentucky till June. Movement to Vicksburg, Miss., June 3-14. Siege of Vicksburg, Miss., June 14-July 4. Advance on Jackson, Miss., July 5-10. Siege of Jackson, Miss., July 10-17. At Milldale till August 6. Moved to Cincinnati, Ohio, August 6-14. March to Nicholasville, Ky., August 18-25, and to Crab Orchard September 9-11. March over Cumberland Mountains to Knoxville, thence to Lenoir Station October 2-29. Action at Blue Springs October 10. Knoxville Campaign November 4-December 23. At Lenoir Station till November 14. Action at Lenoir Station November 14-15. Campbell's Station November 16. Siege of Knoxville November 17-December 4. Pursuit of Longstreet December 5-19. Operations in East Tennessee till March 20, 1864. Movement to Annapolis, Md., March 20-April 7. Campaign from the Rapidan to the James May 3-June 15. Battles of the Wilderness May 5-7; Spottsylvania May 8-12;

Ny River May 10; Spottsylvania Court House May 12-21. Assault on the Salient (or "Bloody Angle") May 12. North Anna River May 23-26. Ox Ford May 23-24. On line of the Pamunkey May 26-28. Totopotomoy May 28-31. Cold Harbor June 1-12. Bethesda Church June 1-3. Before Petersburg June 16-18. Siege of Petersburg June 16, 1864, to April 2, 1865. Mine Explosion, Petersburg, July 30, 1864. Weldon Railroad August 18-21. Poplar Springs Church September 29-October 2. Boydton Plank Road, Hatcher's Run, October 27-28. Fort Stedman March 25, 1865. Assault and fall of Petersburg April 2. Pursuit of Lee April 3-9. Moved to Washington, D. C., April 21-27. Grand Review May 23. Mustered out June 21, 1865.

Battery lost during service 7 Enlisted men killed and mortally wounded and 14 Enlisted men by disease. Total 21.

35th INDEPENDENT BATTERY LIGHT ARTILLERY.

Failed to complete organization. Men enlisted transferred to 16th Regiment New York Heavy Artillery September 25, 1863.

36th INDEPENDENT BATTERY LIGHT ARTILLERY.

Failed to complete organization. Men enlisted transferred to 13th Regiment New York Heavy Artillery October 14, 1863.

ALLEE'S HOWITZER BATTERY.

Attached to 3rd New York Cavalry (which see).

BOOKWOOD'S INDEPENDENT BATTERY LIGHT ARTILLERY.

Organized June, 1861, from detachments of 8th and 29th Regiments New York Infantry. Attached to Blenker's Brigade, Miles' Division, McDowell's Army of Northeast Virginia. Advance on Manassas, Va., July 16-21. Battle of Bull Run July 21. Battery reorganized at Washington and mustered in August 16, 1861. (See 2nd New York Independent Battery.)

FISH'S HOWITZER BATTERY.

Attached to 12th New York Cavalry (which see).

GOODWIN'S STATE MILITIA BATTERY LIGHT ARTILLERY.

Organized for duty during the Gettysburg (Pa.) Campaign June, 1863. Attached to 2nd Brigade, Dana's Division, Dept. of the Susquehanna, and stationed at Harrisburg, Bridgeport, Chambersburg, Shippensburg and Pottsville, Pa., till August. Mustered out August, 1863.

VARIAN'S STATE MILITIA BATTERY LIGHT ARTILLERY ("1st TROOP WASHINGTON GRAYS").

Entered service of the United States for three months and left State for Annapolis, Md., April 19, 1861. Duty at Annapolis till May. Near Light House at Smith's Point, Chesapeake Bay, Md., May 18. Ordered to Washington, D. C., and outpost duty at Fall's Church, Va., till June. Fairfax Court House June 17. Attached to Keyes' Brigade, Tyler's Division, McDowell's Army of Northeast Virginia. to July. Mustered out July 20, 1861.

Again entered service as a part of the 8th Regiment, New York National Guard, for 30 days' service as Artillery and Cavalry. Left State for Harrisburg, Pa., June 17, 1863. Attached to 1st Brigade, 1st Division, Dept. of the Susquehanna. Shippensburg, Pa., June 23. Kingston June 26. Oyster Point June 28. Near Fort Washington June 29. Sporting Hill June 30. Carlisle July 1. Mustered out at New York City July 23, 1863.

1st REGIMENT ENGINEERS ("SERRELL'S ENGRS").

Organized at New York City and mustered in by Companies as follows: Companies "A," "B," "C," "D" and "E" October 11, 1861. Company "G" December 2, 1861. Company "K" December 3, 1861. Company "I" December 13, 1861. Company "F" January, 1862. Company "H" February 19, 1862. Companies "L" and "M" in the field April, 1864. Companies "A" to "E" left

State for Annapolis, Md., October 2, 1861. Companies "G," "I" and "K" left State for Port Royal, S. C., December 14, 1861. Companies "F" and "H" left State for Port Royal, S. C., February, 1862. Served unattached, Sherman's South Carolina Expeditionary Corps, to April, 1862. District of Hilton Head, Dept. of the South, to September, 1862. District of Hilton Head, S. C., 10th Army Corps, Dept. of the South, to April, 1864. Engineer Brigade, 10th Army Corps, Army of the James, to May, 1864. Engineer Brigade, Headquarters Army of the James, Dept. of Virginia and North Carolina, to June, 1864. (4 Cos., "A," "C," "G" and "I," remained in the Dept. of the South April, 1864, to June, 1865.)

SERVICE.—Sherman's Expedition to Port Royal, S. C., October 21-November 7, 1861. Capture of Forts Walker and Beauregard, Port Royal Harbor, and Hilton Head, S. C., November 7. Port Royal Ferry, S. C., January 1, 1862. Action with Commodore Tatnall's Flotilla January 28. Battery Vulcan February 4. Siege operations against Fort Pulaski, Ga., February to April. Bombardment and capture of Fort Pulaski April 10-11. Operations on James Island June 1-28. Actions on James Island June 10 and 13. Battle of Secessionville June 16. Evacuation of James Island and movement to Hilton Head June 28-July 7. Expedition from Hilton Head to Pocotaligo, S. C., October 21-23 (Cos. "F" and "G"). Coosawhatchie October 22. Colton's and Frampton's Plantation October 22. Duty at Hilton Head, S. C., till April, 1863. Operations on Folly Island, S. C., against Morris Island and Charleston till July. Attack on Morris Island July 10. Assaults on Fort Wagner, Morris Island, July 11 and 18. Siege of Forts Wagner and Gregg, Morris Island, and against Fort Sumpter and Charleston July 18-September 7. Bombardment of Fort Sumpter and Charleston August 17-23. Vinegar Hill August 26. (Co. "K" built Fort Duane at Beaufort, S. C., summer 1863.) Capture of Forts Wagner and Gregg September 7. Bombardment of Fort Sumpter October 26-November 9. Before Charleston till December. At Hilton Head, S. C., till April, 1864. 8 Companies ordered to Gloucester Point, Va., April, 1864. Butler's operations on south side of the James River and against Petersburg and Richmond May 4-28. Swift Creek May 6-10. Operations against Drury's Bluff May 12-16. Bermuda Hundred May 16-June 15. Assaults on Petersburg June 15-18. Siege operations against Petersburg and Richmond June 16, 1864, to April 2, 1865. Mine Explosion, Petersburg, July 30, 1864. Construction of Fort Hell before Petersburg September and October. Construction of Dutch Gap Canal October to December. Chaffin's Farm, New Market Heights, September 28-30. Fair Oaks October 27-28. Fall of Petersburg and Richmond April 2-3. Occupation of Richmond April 3. Rebuilt Mayo's Bridge June.

Detachment in Dept. of the South participated in skirmish at King's Creek July 3, 1864. The Hatch Expedition up Broad River, S. C., November 28-30, 1864. Battle of Honey Hill November 30. Deveaux's Neck December 6. Regiment mustered out June 30, 1865.

Regiment lost during service 2 Officers and 25 Enlisted men killed and mortally wounded and 5 Officers and 116 Enlisted men by disease. Total 148.

2nd REGIMENT ENGINEERS.

Failed to complete organization. Men enlisted transferred to 15th Regiment Engineers October 9, 1863.

15th REGIMENT ENGINEERS.

Organized at Washington, D. C., October 25, 1861, from 15th Regiment New York Infantry. Attached to Engineer Brigade, Army of the Potomac.

SERVICE.—Duty at Washington and Alexandria till March, 1862. Moved to the Virginia Peninsula March. Siege of Yorktown April 5-May 4. Advance up the Peninsula and constructing bridges on the Chickahominy River May. Seven days before Richmond June 25-July 1. Seven Pines June 27. White Oak Swamp and Charles City Cross Roads June 30. Malvern Hill July

1. At Harrison's Landing till August 16. Moved to Washington, D. C., August 16-22. Maryland Campaign September-October. Rappahannock Campaign November, 1862, to June, 1863. Battle of Fredericksburg, Va., December 12-15. "Mud March" January 20-24, 1863. Chancellorsville Campaign April 27-May 6. Operations about Franklin's Crossing April 29-May 2. Maryes Heights, Fredericksburg, May 3. Salem Heights May 3-4. Banks' Ford May 4. Deep Run Ravine June 5-13. Mustered out June 25, 1863. Three years men consolidated to a Battalion of three Companies, "A," "B" and "C." Company "D" assigned December 9, 1863; Company "E" assigned March, 1864, and other seven Companies November, 1864. Gettysburg (Pa.) Campaign June-July, 1863. Battle of Gettysburg July 1-3. Bristoe Campaign October 9-22. Advance to line of the Rappahannock November 7-8. Mine Run Campaign November 26-December 2. Rapidan Campaign May-June, 1864. Battles of the Wilderness May 5-7; Spottsylvania Court House May 8-21; North Anna River May 23-26. On line of the Pamunkey May 26-28. Totopotomoy May 28-31. Cold Harbor June 1-12. Crossing of James River June 15. Before Petersburg June 16-18. Siege operations against Petersburg and Richmond June 16, 1864, to April 2, 1865. Deep Bottom July 27-28, 1864. Hatcher's Run February 5-7, 1865. Appomattox Campaign March 28-April 9. Fall of Petersburg and Richmond April 2-3. Pursuit of Lee April 3-9. Appomattox Court House April 9. Surrender of Lee and his army. Expedition to reinforce General Sherman April 23-29. Moved to Washington, D. C., May 2-15. Grand Review May 23. (Cos. "A," "B" and "H" with Terry's Expedition to Fort Fisher, N. C., January 3-15, 1865. Capture of Fort Fisher January 15. Capture of Wilmington, N. C., February 22. Campaign of the Carolinas March 1-April 26. Occupation of Goldsboro and Raleigh. Bennett's House April 26. Surrender of Johnston and his army. Duty in Dept. of North Carolina till June.) Mustered out Companies "E," "F," "G," "H," "I," "K," "L" and "M" at Washington, D. C., June 13, 1865; Companies "C" June 14, 1865, and Companies "A," "B" and "D" July 2, 1865.

Regiment lost during service 7 Enlisted men killed and mortally wounded and 3 Officers and 119 Enlisted men by disease. Total 129.

50th REGIMENT ENGINEERS.

Organized at Washington, D. C., from 50th New York Infantry October 22, 1861. Attached to Woodbury's Brigade, Army of the Potomac, to April, 1862, and to Engineer Brigade, Army of the Potomac, to June, 1865.

SERVICE.—Duty at Alexandria, Va., till March, 1862, and at Washington, D. C., till March 18. Moved with Army of the Potomac to the Virginia Peninsula. Siege of Yorktown April 5-May 4. Advance up the Peninsula and constructing bridges on the Chickahominy River May. Battle of Fair Oaks, Seven Pines, May 31-June 1. Seven days before Richmond June 25-July 1. Battle of Seven Pines June 27. White Oak Swamp and Charles City Cross Roads June 30. Malvern Hill July 1. At Harrison's Landing till August 16. Moved to Washington, D. C., August 16-22. Maryland Campaign September-October. Operating at and about Harper's Ferry, W. Va., and Berlin, Md., during and after the battle of Antietam. Threw two pontoon bridges over the Potomac River at Berlin, Md., for the crossing of the Army of the Potomac in their pursuit of Lee from Antietam. Rappahannock Campaign November, 1862, to June, 1863. Battle of Fredericksburg, Va., December 12-15. "Mud March" January 20-24, 1863. Chancellorsville Campaign April 27-May 6. Operations at Franklin's Crossing April 29-May 2. Maryes Heights, Fredericksburg, May 3. Salem Heights May 3-4. Banks' Ford May 4. Operations at Deep Run Ravine June 5-13. Gettysburg (Pa.) Campaign June 13-July 24. Battle of Gettysburg, Pa., July 1-4. Bristoe Campaign October 9-22. Advance to line of the Rappahannock November 7-8. Mine Run Campaign November 26-December 2. Campaign from the Rapidan to the James River

May 3-June 15, 1864. Laid all bridges for Army of the Potomac during the Campaign. Battles of the Wilderness May 5-7; Spottsylvania Court House May 8-21. To expedite the transportation of wounded three Companies made a forced march to Fredericksburg on May 10, starting at 11:30 a. m. Built bridge over the Rappahannock at Fredericksburg Lower Crossing, having it completed and ready for use at 4:30 p. m., having marched 8 miles and built bridge 420 feet long in 5 hours. North Anna River May 23-26. On line of the Pamunkey May 26-28. On line of the Totopotomoy May 28-31. About Cold Harbor June 1-12. Crossing of James River June 15. Before Petersburg June 16-18. Siege operations against Petersburg and Richmond June, 1864, to April, 1865. Jerusalem Plank Road June 22-23, 1864. Demonstration on north side of James River July 27-29. Deep Bottom July 27-28. Hatcher's Run February 5-7, 1865. Appomattox Campaign March 28-April 9. Fall of Petersburg April 2. Appomattox Court House April 9. Surrender of Lee and his army. (Co. "I" march to Danville with 6th Army Corps April 23-27.) Mustered out at Washington, D. C., June 13, 1865.

Regiment lost during service 1 Officer and 19 Enlisted men killed and mortally wounded and 1 Officer and 206 Enlisted men by disease. Total 227.

1st BATTALION SHARPSHOOTERS.

Organized by consolidation of 6th Company Sharpshooters. Organized at Rochester, N. Y., September 13, 1862. 7th Company Sharpshooters organized at Jamestown September 12, 1862. 8th Company Sharpshooters organized at Staten Island January, 1863, and 9th Company Sharpshooters organized at Staten Island for nine months' service January, 1863. Ordered to Suffolk, Va., February 3, 1863. Attached to Gibb's Provisional Brigade, Division at Suffolk, 7th Army Corps, Dept. of Virginia, to April, 1863. 1st Brigade, 1st Division, 7th Army Corps, to July, 1863. 1st Brigade, 1st Division, 1st Army Corps, Army of the Potomac to March, 1864. 1st Brigade, 4th Division, 5th Army Corps, to August, 1864. 3rd Brigade, 3rd Division, 5th Army Corps, to September, 1864. 1st Brigade, 3rd Division, 5th Army Corps, to July, 1865.

SERVICE.—Siege of Suffolk, Va., April 12-May 4, 1863. Action at Suffolk April 17. Dix's Peninsula Campaign June 24-July 7. Expedition from White House to Bottom's Bridge July 1-7. Baltimore Cross Roads July 2. Ordered to Washington, D. C., July 8; thence to join Army of the Potomac in the field. Joined 1st Army Corps July 15. Pursuit of Lee July 15-24. Duty on line of the Rappahannock till October. Bristoe Campaign October 9-22. Haymarket October 19. Advanced to line of the Rappahannock November 7-8. Mine Run Campaign November 26-December 2. Demonstration on the Rapidan February 5-7, 1864. Campaign from the Rapidan to the James May 3-June 15. Battles of the Wilderness May 5-7; Laurel Hill May 8; Spottsylvania May 8-12; Spottsylvania Court House May 12-21. Assault on the Salient, "Bloody Angle," May 12. North Anna River May 23-26. Jericho Ford May 23. On line of the Pamunkey May 26-28. Totopotomoy May 28-31. About Cold Harbor June 1-12. Bethesda Church June 1-3. Before Petersburg June 16-18. Siege of Petersburg June 16, 1864, to April 2, 1865. Weldon Railroad August 18-21, 1864. Reconnoissance to Boydton Road October 8. Boydton Plank Road, Hatcher's Run, October 27-28. Warren's Raid on Weldon Railroad, Hicksford Raid, December 7-12. Dabney's Mills February 5-7, 1865. Appomattox Campaign March 28-April 9. White Oak Road March 31. Five Forks April 1. Fall of Petersburg April 2. Pursuit of Lee April 3-9. Appomattox Court House April 9. Surrender of Lee and his army. Moved to Washington, D. C., May. Grand Review May 23. Mustered out 6th, 7th and 8th Companies July 10, 1865. 9th Company August 5, 1863.

Battalion lost during service 23 Enlisted men killed and mortally wounded and 1 Officer and 38 Enlisted men by disease. Total 62.

1st UNITED STATES SHARPSHOOTERS.—("BERDAN'S.")

Companies "A," "D" and "H" organized at New York City, and Company "B" at Albany, N. Y. Mustered in at Washington, D. C., November 29, 1861. (See 1st United States Sharpshooters for service.) Company "A" mustered out August 19, 1864. Company "D" mustered out August 28, 1864. Veterans and Recruits to Companies "I" and "K" November 22, 1864. Veterans of Company "H" to Company "D" September 16, 1864. Regiment consolidated with 2nd United States Sharpshooters December 31, 1864. Veterans and Recruits of these Companies transferred to 124th New York Infantry February 28, 1865.

1st REGIMENT INFANTRY.

Organized at New York City and mustered in April 22, 1861. Left State for Fortress Monroe, Va., May 20, 1861, and duty there till July 3. Attached to Fort Monroe, Camp Hamilton and Newport News, Va., Dept. of Virginia, May, 1861, to May, 1862. 1st Brigade, 1st Division, Dept. of Virginia, to June, 1862. 3rd Brigade, 3rd Division, 3rd Army Corps, Army of the Potomac, to August, 1862. 2nd Brigade, 1st Division, 3rd Army Corps, to September, 1862. 3rd Brigade, 1st Division, 3rd Army Corps, to May, 1863.

SERVICE.—Occupation of Newport News May 29, 1861. Action at Big Bethel, Va., June 10. Duty at Camp Hamilton and Newport News, Va., till June, 1862. Action between Monitor and Merrimac in Hampton Roads March 8, 1862. Joined Army of the Potomac on the Peninsula June 5. Actions near Fair Oaks June 20, 23 and 24. Oak Grove, near Fair Oaks, June 25. Seven days before Richmond June 25-July 1. About Fair Oaks June 26-29. Peach Orchard and Savage Station June 29. White Oak Swamp and Glendale June 30. Malvern Hill July 1. Duty at Harrison's Landing till August 16. Movement to Fortress Monroe, thence to Centreville, Va., August 16-27. Pope's Campaign in Northern Virginia August 28-September 2. Battle of Groveton August 29. Bull Run August 30. Duty in the Defences of Washington, D. C., till October 11. March up the Potomac to Leesburg, thence movement to Falmouth, Va., October 11-November 23. Battle of Fredericksburg December 12-15. "Mud March" January 20-24, 1863. At Falmouth till April 27. Chancellorsville Campaign April 27-May 6. Battle of Chancellorsville May 1-5. Mustered out May 25, 1863, expiration of term.

Regiment lost during service 79 Enlisted men killed and mortally wounded and 3 Officers and 31 Enlisted men by disease. Total 113.

2nd REGIMENT INFANTRY.—("TROY REGIMENT.")

Organized at Troy, N. Y., and mustered in May 14, 1861, for two years. Left State for Fortress Monroe, Va., May 18, 1861. Attached to Fortress Monroe, Camp Hamilton and Newport News, Va., Dept. of Virginia, to May, 1862. 1st Brigade, 1st Division, Dept. of Virginia, to June, 1862. 3rd Brigade, 2nd Division, 3rd Army Corps, Army of the Potomac, to May, 1863.

SERVICE.—Occupation of Newport News, Va., May 29, 1861. Action at Big Bethel June 10. Duty at Camp Hamilton and Newport News, Va., till June, 1862. Expedition up James River January 17, 1862. Action between Monitor and Merrimac in Hampton Roads March 8. Joined Army of the Potomac on the Peninsula June 5. Near Fair Oaks June 16, 18 and 21. Battle of Oak Grove June 25. Seven days before Richmond June 25-July 1. About Fair Oaks June 26-29. Peach Orchard and Savage Station June 29. White Oak Swamp and Glendale June 30. Malvern Hill July 1. Duty at Harrison's Landing till August 16. Malvern Hill August 5. Movement to Fortress Monroe, thence to Centreville August 16-26. Pope's Campaign in Northern Virginia, Bristoe Station or Kettle Run August 27. Battles of Groveton August 29; Bull Run August 30. Duty in the Defences of Washington, D. C., near Fort Lyon, Fairfax Seminary and at Munson's Hill till November, and at Fairfax Station, Va., November 2-25. Operations on Orange & Alexandria Railroad November 10-12. Near Falmouth, Va., November 28-December 11. Battle of Fredericksburg December 12-15. "Mud March" January 20-24, 1863. Operations at Rappahannock Bridge and Grove Church February 5-7. At Falmouth till April 27. Chancellorsville Campaign April 27-May 6. Battle of Chancellorsville May 1-5. Mustered out May 26, 1863, expiration of term.

Regiment lost during service 1 Officer and 25 Enlisted men killed and mortally wounded and 22 Enlisted men by disease. Total 48.

2nd REGIMENT STATE MILITIA INFANTRY.

(See 82nd Regiment Infantry.)

3rd REGIMENT INFANTRY.

Organized at Albany, N. Y., and mustered in May 14, 1861, for two years' service. Reorganized May, 1863. Left State for Fortress Monroe, Va., May 31, 1861, and duty there till July 30. Moved to Baltimore, Md., July 30, and duty there till June 6, 1862. Attached to Fort Monroe and Camp Hamilton, Va., Dept. of Virginia, to July, 1861. Dix's Command, Baltimore, Md., to June, 1862. Mansfield's Division, Newport News, Va., Dept. of Virginia, to July, 1862. Weber's Brigade, Division at Suffolk, 7th Army Corps, Dept. of Virginia, to September, 1862. Fortress Monroe, Va., Dept. of Virginia, to April, 1863. Suffolk, Va., 1st Division, 7th Army Corps, Dept of Virginia, to July, 1863. Alvord's Brigade, Vodges' Division, Folly Island, S. C., 10th Army Corps, Dept. of the South, to February, 1864. 2nd Brigade, Vodges' Division, Northern District Folly Island, 10th Army Corps, to April, 1864. 3rd Brigade, 2nd Division, 10th Army Corps, Army of the James, to May, 1864. 1st Brigade, 2nd Division, 10th Army Corps, to May, 1864. 3rd Brigade, 3rd Division, 18th Army Corps, to June, 1864. 1st Brigade, 2nd Division, 10th Army Corps, to December, 1864. 1st Brigade, 2nd Division, 24th Army Corps, to January, 1865. 1st Brigade, 2nd Division, Terry's Provisional Corps, to March, 1865. 1st Brigade, 2nd Division, 10th Army Corps, Army of the Ohio, to August, 1865.

SERVICE.—Action at Big Bethel, Va., June 10, 1861. Moved to Baltimore, Md., July 30, and duty there till June 6, 1862. Moved to Suffolk, Va., June 6, and duty there till September. Moved to Fortress Monroe, Va., and duty there till April, 1863. Moved to Suffolk April 19. Siege of Suffolk April 19-May 4. Siege of Suffolk raised May 4. (2 years' men mustered out May 21, 1863.) Dix's Peninsula Campaign June 24-July 7. Expedition from White House to South Anna River July 1-7. Ordered to Folly Island, S. C. Action at Morris Island, S. C., August 3. Siege operations against Forts Wagner and Gregg, Morris Island, S. C., and against Fort Sumpter and Charleston August 9-September 7. Bombardment of Fort Sumpter August 17-23. Capture of Forts Wagner and Gregg September 7. Operations in Charleston Harbor against Forts Sumpter and Charleston September 8 to December 21. Bombardment of Fort Sumpter October 27-November 9. Duty on Folly Island, S. C., till April, 1864. Moved to Gloucester Point, Va. Butler's operations on south side of James River and against Petersburg and Richmond May 4-28. Port Walthall May 7. Swift Creek or Arrowfield Church May 9-10. Operations against Fort Darling May 12-16. Battle of Drury's Bluff May 14-16. Bermuda Hundred May 16-28. Moved to White House, thence to Cold Harbor May 28-31. Cold Harbor June 1-12. Before Petersburg June 15-18. Siege operations against Petersburg and Richmond June 16 to December 12, 1864. Mine Explosion, Petersburg, July 30. Duty in the trenches before Petersburg and on the Bermuda front till September 27. Chaffin's Farm, New Market Heights, September 28-30. Battle of Fair Oaks October 27-28. In trenches before Richmond till December 7. Expedition to Fort Fisher, N. C., December 7-27. 2nd Expedition to Fort Fisher, N. C., January 3-15, 1865. Assault on and capture of Fort Fisher, N. C., January 15. Sugar Loaf Battery February 11. Fort Anderson February

18-20. Capture of Wilmington February 22. Advance on Kinston and Goldsboro March 6-21. Duty in the Dept. of North Carolina till August. Mustered out August 28, 1865.

Regiment lost during service 1 Officer and 36 Enlisted men killed and mortally wounded and 2 Officers and 83 Enlisted men by disease. Total 122.

4th REGIMENT INFANTRY.—("1st SCOTT LIFE GUARDS.")

Organized at New York City and mustered in as follows: Companies "C," "D," "E," "F," "H" and "K" May 2; Companies "A" and "G" May 7; Companies "B" and "I" May 9, 1861. Left State for Newport News, Va., June 3. Attached to Newport News, Va., Dept. of Virginia, to July, 1861. Dix's Command, Baltimore, Md., to June, 1862. Webber's Brigade, Division at Suffolk, 7th Army Corps, Dept. of Virginia, to September, 1862. 3rd Brigade, 3rd Division, 2nd Army Corps, Army of the Potomac, to May, 1863.

SERVICE.—Duty at Newport News, Va., June 7 to July 25, 1861. Moved to Baltimore, Md., July 25, and duty there and at Havre de Grace till June 5, 1862. Moved to Suffolk, Va., June 5, and duty there till September. Ordered to join Army of the Potomac September 8. Maryland Campaign. Battle of Antietam September 16-17. Moved to Harper's Ferry, W. Va., September 22, and duty there till October 30. Reconnoissance to Charlestown October 16-17. Advance up Loudoun Valley and movement to Falmouth, Va., October 30-November 17. Battle of Fredericksburg December 12-15. "Mud March" January 20-24, 1863. At Falmouth till April 27. Chancellorsville Campaign April 27-May 6. Battle of Chancellorsville May 1-5. Mustered out May 25, 1863.

Regiment lost during service 2 Officers and 62 Enlisted men killed and mortally wounded and 1 Officer and 23 Enlisted men by disease. Total 88.

4th REGIMENT NATIONAL GUARD INFANTRY.

Organized at Harrisburg, Pa., June 18, 1863, for thirty days' United States service. On duty in the Dept. of the Susquehanna during the Gettysburg (Pa.) Campaign. Mustered out July 24, 1863.

5th REGIMENT INFANTRY.—(3 MONTHS.)

Tendered service to State April 19, 1861. Sailed from New York for Fortress Monroe, Va., April 27; thence to Annapolis, Md., April 30. Guard duty along railroad from Annapolis to Annapolis Junction till May 12. Moved to Washington, D. C., May 12, and quartered in the United States Capital till May 23. Mustered in for three months' United States service May 16. Advance into Virginia and occupation of Arlington Heights May 24. Guard and picket duty till June 3. Camp on Meridian Hill till July 7. Moved to Baltimore, thence to Hagerstown, Md., July 7, and to Martinsburg, Va., July 9-10. Attached to Butterfield's Brigade, Sandford's Division, Patterson's Army. Advance to Bunker Hill July 15. To Smithfield July 17, thence to Charlestown. Moved to Harper's Ferry, W. Va., July 21, and duty at Bolivar Heights till July 28. Moved to Knoxville, Md., July 28; thence to Baltimore July 30; then to New York City. Mustered out August 7, 1861.

5th REGIMENT INFANTRY.—("DURYEA'S ZOUAVES.")

Organized at New York City and mustered in for two years' service May 9, 1861. Left State for Fortress Monroe, Va., May 23. Attached to Pierce's Brigade, Newport News, Va., Dept. of Virginia, to July, 1861. Dix's Division, Baltimore, Md., to March, 1862. Sykes' Infantry (Reserve), Army of the Potomac, to May, 1862. 3rd Brigade, Sykes' 2nd Division, 5th Army Corps, Army of the Potomac, to May, 1863.

SERVICE.—Duty at Newport News, Va., May 25 to July 26, 1861. Action at Big Bethel June 10. Moved to Baltimore, Md., July 26, and duty there till April 11, 1862. Expedition through Accomac and Northampton Counties, Va., November 14-22, 1861. Moved to the Peninsula, Va., April 11, 1862. Siege of Yorktown, Va., April 15-May 4. Reconnoissance to near Hanover Court House May 26. Hanover Court House May 27. Operations about Hanover Court House May 27-29. New Bridge June 5. Operations against Stuart June 13-15. Old Church June 13. Seven days before Richmond June 25-July 1. Battle of Mechanicsville June 26. Battle of Gaines Mill June 27. (Note.—At Gaines Mill, under command of Lieut.-Col. Hiram Duryea, it faced a musketry fire which cut down one-third of its men and won praises from all who witnessed its remarkable efficiency and drill while in the thickest of that fight. It was in that battle that after having received several deadly volleys it paused at one time, while still under fire, to count off anew so that its movements might not be deranged by the absence of the fallen men. At Manassas it took into action 490 men of whom 117 were killed or mortally wounded.) White Oak Swamp and Turkey Bend June 30. Malvern Hill July 1. Duty at Harrison's Landing till August 15. Movement to Fortress Monroe, thence to Centreville August 15-28. Pope's Campaign in Northern Virginia August 28-September 2. Battle of Bull Run August 30. Maryland Campaign September 6-22. Battle of Antietam September 16-17. Shephardstown Ford September 20. Duty in Maryland to October 29. Movement to Falmouth, Va., October 29-November 19. Battle of Fredericksburg December 12-15. "Mud March" January 20-24, 1863. At Falmouth till April. Chancellorsville Campaign April 27-May 6. Battle of Chancellorsville May 1-5. Mustered out May 14, 1863, expiration of term. Recruits assigned to 146th New York Infantry.

Regiment lost during service 6 Officers and 171 Enlisted men killed and mortally wounded and 34 Enlisted men by disease. Total 211.

5th REGIMENT NATIONAL GUARD INFANTRY.

Entered service of the United States for thirty days June, 1863. Left State for Harrisburg, Pa., June 18. Guard duty at Harrisburg, Marysville, Carlisle and Chambersburg, Pa., till July 17. Attached to Yates' 1st Brigade, Dana's Division, Dept. of the Susquehanna. Mustered out July 22, 1863.

5th REGIMENT VETERAN INFANTRY.

Organized into a Battalion of four Companies by consolidation of the Veterans and Recruits of the 5th New York Infantry, with those recruited for the reorganized 31st and 37th New York Infantry October 14, 1863. A Battalion of the 12th New York Infantry assigned as Companies "E" and "F," and the Veterans and Recruits of the 94th New York Infantry assigned June 2, 1864, as Companies "G," "H," "I" and "K." Left State for Washington, D. C., October 27, 1863. Attached to Garrison of Alexandria, 22nd Army Corps, Dept. of Washington, to May, 1864. 1st Brigade, 1st Division, 5th Army Corps, Army of the Potomac, to June, 1864. 1st Brigade, 2nd Division, 5th Army Corps, to June, 1865. Hart's Island, N. Y., to August, 1865.

SERVICE.—Duty in the Defences of Washington, D. C., till May, 1864. Ordered to join Army of the Potomac in the field May, 1864. Battles about Cold Harbor May 31-June 12; Bethesda Church June 1-3. Before Petersburg June 16-18. Siege of Petersburg June 16, 1864, to April 2, 1865. Weldon Railroad June 22-23, 1864. Mine Explosion, Petersburg, July 30 (Reserve). Weldon Railroad August 18-21. Poplar Springs Church September 29-October 2. Boydton Plank Road, Hatcher's Run, October 27-28. Warren's Raid on Weldon Railroad, "Hicksford Raid," December 7-12. Dabney's Mills, Hatcher's Run, February 5-7, 1865. Appomattox Campaign March 28-April 9. White Oak Road March 29-31. Five Forks April 1. Fall of Petersburg April 2. Pursuit of Lee April 3-9. Appomattox Court House April 9. Surrender of Lee and his army. March to Washington, D. C., May. Grand Review May 23.

Moved to Hart's Island, N. Y., and duty there till August, 1865. Mustered out August 21, 1865.

Regiment lost during service 8 Officers and 91 Enlisted men killed and mortally wounded and 90 Enlisted men by disease. Total 189.

6th REGIMENT INFANTRY.—(3 MONTHS.)—("GOVERNOR'S GUARD.")

Organized for three months' United States service April 19, 1861. Left State for Annapolis, Md., April 21. On duty at Annapolis and at Washington, D. C., till July. Mustered out July 31, 1861.

6th REGIMENT INFANTRY.—("WILSON'S ZOUAVES.")

Organized at New York City as follows: Companies "A," "B," "C," "D" and "E" April 30, and Companies "F," "G," "H," "I" and "K" May 25, 1861. Left State and moved to Santa Rosa Island, Fla., June 15-23, 1861. Attached to Santa Rosa Island, District of Florida, Dept. of the South, to May, 1862. Arnold's Brigade, District of Pensacola, Fla., Dept. of the South, to September, 1862. Wilson's Brigade, District of West Florida, Dept. of the Gulf, to November, 1862. Grover's Division, Dept. of the Gulf, to January, 1863. 1st Brigade, 4th Division, 19th Army Corps, Dept. of the Gulf, to June, 1863.

SERVICE.—Duty at Santa Rosa Island, Fla., June 23, 1861, to May 9, 1862. (3 Cos. at Fort Jefferson, Fla., January to March, 1862.) Action at Santa Rosa Island October 9, 1861. Engagement with Confederate works at Pensacola November 22-23. Bombardment of Forts McRae and Barrancas January 1, 1862. Reconnoissance on Santa Rosa Island March 27-31 (Co. "K"). Duty at Pensacola, Fla., May 9 to November, 1862. Expedition to Milton, Fla., June 14-15 (Cos. "B," "C," "E" and "H"). Reconnoissance from Pensacola to Bagdad and Milton, Fla., August 7-10 (Cos. "A" and "E"). Ordered to New Orleans, La., November, 1862. Occupation of Baton Rouge December 17 and duty there till March 13, 1863. Operations against Port Hudson March 13-27. Moved to Donaldsonville March 28. Operations in Western Louisiana April 9-May 14. Teche Campaign April 11-20. Fort Bisland April 12-13. Porter's and McWilliams' Plantations at Indian Bend April 13. Irish Bend April 14. Bayou Vermillion April 17. Opelousas April 20. Moved to Barre Landing May 11, thence with trains to Berwick May 21-26. Action at Franklin and Centreville May 25. Ordered home for muster out. Mustered out at New York City June 25, 1863, expiration of term.

Regiment lost during service 14 Enlisted men killed and mortally wounded and 32 Enlisted men by disease. Total 46.

6th REGIMENT NATIONAL GUARD INFANTRY.

Organized June 22, 1863, for thirty days' United States service. Left State for Baltimore, Md., June 22. Duty in the Defences of that city, attached to 2nd and 3rd Separate Brigade, 8th Army Corps, Middle Department, till July. Mustered out at New York City July 22, 1863.

7th REGIMENT INFANTRY.

Organized at New York City and mustered in April 23, 1861. Left State for Newport News, Va., May 24, 1861. Attached to Newport News, Va., Dept. of Virginia, to May, 1862. 1st Brigade, 1st Division, 2nd Army Corps, Army of the Potomac, to May, 1863.

SERVICE.—Occupation of Newport News, Va., May 27, and duty there till March, 1862. Action at Big Bethel, Va., June 10, 1861. Baker Lee's Farm, Newport News, July 12. Battle between Monitor and Merrimac in Hampton Roads March 8-9, 1862. Joined Army of the Potomac on the Virginia Peninsula May, 1862. Seven days before Richmond June 25-July 1. About Fair Oaks June 26-29. Peach Orchard and Savage Station June 29. White Oak Swamp and Glendale June 30. Malvern Hill July 1. At Harrison's Landing till August 16. Movement to Fortress Monroe, thence to

Centreville August 16-30. Maryland Campaign September 6-22. Battle of South Mountain September 14. Antietam September 16-17. Moved to Harper's Ferry, W. Va., September 22, and duty there till October 30. Reconnoissance to Charlestown October 16-17. Advance up Loudoun Valley and movement to Falmouth October 30-November 17. Battle of Fredericksburg December 12-15. "Mud March" January 20-24, 1863. At Falmouth till April 27. Chancellorsville Campaign April 27-May 6. Battle of Chancellorsville May 1-5. Mustered out May 8, 1863, expiration of term. Three years' men attached to 52nd New York Infantry to July 22, 1864, then assigned to 7th Veteran Infantry.

Regiment lost during service 14 Officers and 88 Enlisted men killed and mortally wounded and 1 Officer and 46 Enlisted men by disease. Total 149.

7th REGIMENT STATE MILITIA INFANTRY.

Left New York City for Washington, D. C., on special call of President Lincoln April 19, 1861. Occupation of Annapolis Junction, Md., and opening communications with Washington April 24-25. In Capital Buildings at Washington April 25-May 2. Mustered into United States service April 26. Duty at Camp Cameron, Meridian Hill, May 2-23. Occupation of Arlington Heights, Va., May 24-26. Assist in building Fort Runyon. Return to Camp Cameron May 26. Mustered out at New York City June 3, 1861.

Again mustered in for three months' service May 25, 1862. Left New York City for Baltimore, Md., May 26. Attached to Dix's Command, Middle Department, to July, 1862. 8th Army Corps, Middle Department, to September, 1862. Camp at Stewart's Hill, Baltimore, Md., May 28 to June 5, and duty at Fort Federal Hill June 6 to August 28. Mustered out at New York City September 5, 1862.

Again mustered in for thirty days' service June 16, 1863. Left State for Baltimore, Md., June 17. Attached to Morris' Brigade, 8th Army Corps, Middle Department, to July 7. 3rd Division, 3rd Army Corps, Army of the Potomac, to July 15. Duty at Fort Federal Hill and provost duty in Baltimore, Md., June 18 to July 5. Ordered to Frederick, Md., July 5, and picket and outpost duty there till July 14. Reached New York July 16. On duty during Draft Riots July 16-21. Mustered out July 21, 1863.

7th REGIMENT VETERAN INFANTRY.

Organized at Hart's Island, N. Y., and mustered in by Companies as follows: Company "A" March 29, Company "B" May 1, Company "C" June 4, Company "D" July 15, Company "E" August 9, 1864. Companies "A," "B," "C" and "D" left State for Army of the Potomac as organized, and were attached to 52nd New York Infantry to July 22, 1864. (See 52nd Infantry.) Attached to Consolidated Brigade, 1st Division, 2nd Army Corps, Army of the Potomac, to November, 1864. 3rd Brigade, 1st Division, 2nd Army Corps, to June, 1865. Hart's Island, N. Y., to August, 1865.

SERVICE.—Siege of Petersburg, Va., July 22, 1864, to April 2, 1865. Demonstration north of the James River July 27-29, 1864. Deep Bottom July 27-28. Mine Explosion, Petersburg, July 30 (Reserve). Demonstration north of James River August 13-20. Strawberry Plains, Deep Bottom, August 14-18. Ream's Station August 25. Reconnoissance to Hatcher's Run December 9-10. Dabney's Mills, Hatcher's Run, February 5-7, 1865. Watkins House March 25. Appomattox Court House March 28-April 9. Hatcher's Run or Boydton Road March 29-30. White Oak Road March 31. Sutherland Station and fall of Petersburg April 2. Sailor's Creek April 6. High Bridge, Farmville, April 7. Appomattox Court House April 9. Surrender of Lee and his army. March to Washington, D. C., May. Grand Review May 23. Moved to Hart's Island, N. Y., and duty there till August. Mustered out August 4, 1865.

Regiment lost during service 3 Officers and 52 Enlisted men killed and mortally wounded and 73 Enlisted men by disease. Total 128.

8th REGIMENT STATE MILITIA INFANTRY. ("WASHINGTON GRAYS.")

Organized for three months' United States service April, 1861. Left State for Washington, D. C., April 20, 1861. Mustered in April 26. Duty in the Defences of Washington till July. Attached to Porter's 1st Brigade, Hunter's 2nd Division, McDowell's Army of Northeast Virginia. Advance on Manassas, Va., July 16-21. Battle of Bull Run July 21. Mustered out at New York City August 2, 1861, expiration of term.

8th REGIMENT INFANTRY.—("1st GERMAN RIFLES.")

Organized at New York City and mustered in April 23, 1861. Left State for Washington, D. C., May 26. Attached to Blenker's Brigade, Miles' Division, McDowell's Army of Northeast Virginia, June to August, 1861. Blenker's Brigade, Division of the Potomac, to October, 1861. Blenker's Brigade, Hooker's Division, Army of the Potomac, to January, 1862. Stahl's Brigade, Blenker's Division, Army of the Potomac, to March, 1862. 1st Brigade, Blenker's Division, 2nd Army Corps, Army of the Potomac, to April, 1862. 1st Brigade, Blenker's Division, Dept. of the Mountains, to June, 1862. 1st Brigade, 1st Division, 1st Corps, Pope's Army of Virginia, to September, 1862. 1st Brigade, 1st Division, 11th Army Corps, Army of the Potomac, to April, 1863.

SERVICE.—Duty in the Defences of Washington, D. C., till July 16, 1861. Advance on Manassas, Va., July 16-21. Battle of Bull Run July 21. Duty in the Defences of Washington till April, 1862. Operations in the Shenandoah Valley May to August. Battle of Cross Keys June 8. Duty at Sperryville and Centreville till August. Pope's Campaign in Northern Virginia August 16-September 2. Fords of the Rappahannock August 21-23. Gainesville August 28. Groveton August 29. 2nd Bull Run August 30. Duty in the Defences of Washington, D. C., till December. Reconnoissance to Snicker's Ferry and Berryville November 28-30. March to Fredericksburg, Va., December 10-16. "Mud March" January 20-24, 1863. Duty at Brook's Station till April. Mustered out April 23, 1863, expiration of term. Three years' men consolidated to a Company April 22, 1863, and transferred to 68th Regiment New York Infantry May 5, 1863.

Regiment lost during service 90 Enlisted men killed and mortally wounded and 1 Officer and 42 Enlisted men by disease. Total 133.

8th REGIMENT NATIONAL GUARD INFANTRY.

Organized for three months' United States service May 29, 1862. Left State for Washington, D. C., May 29, 1862, and duty in the Defences of that city till September. Mustered out September 9, 1862.

Again entered service for thirty days June, 1863. Left State for Harrisburg, Pa., June 18, and duty there till July. Attached to 1st Brigade, 1st Division, Dept. of the Susquehanna. Mustered out at New York City July 23, 1863.

9th REGIMENT INFANTRY.—("HAWKIN'S ZOUAVES.")

(The nucleus of this Regiment was old Company of New York Zouaves.) Organized at New York City and mustered into State service April 23, 1861. Mustered into United States service May 4, 1861. At Castle Garden till May 15, and Riker's Island, N. Y., till June 5. Left State for Newport News, Va., June 6, 1861. Attached to Newport News, Va., Dept. of Virginia, to January, 1862. Parke's 3rd Brigade, Burnside's North Carolina Expeditionary Corps, to April, 1862. Hawkins' 4th Brigade, Roanoke Island, N. C., Dept. of North Carolina, to July, 1862. 1st Brigade, 3rd Division, 9th Army Corps, Army of the Potomac, to April, 1863. 1st Brigade, 2nd Division, 7th Army Corps, Dept. of Virginia, to May, 1863.

SERVICE.—Duty at Newport News, Va., till September 10, 1861. Forced march to Big Bethel June 10. Baker Lee's, Va., June 29 (Co. "A"). James River, near Newport News, July 5 (Co. "F"). Near Bethel July 8 (Co. "A"). Expedition to Hatteras Inlet August 26-29 (Cos. "C," "G" and "H"). Bombardment and capture of Forts Hatteras and Clark August 28-29 (Cos. "C," "G" and "H"). Companies "A," "D," "E," "F" and "I" moved to Fort Clark September 10 and duty there till February 5, 1862. (Cos. "B" and "K" at Newport News till October 5, 1861, then rejoin Regiment.) Relief of 20th Indiana at Chickamicomoco October 5-6, 1861. Burnside's Expedition to Roanoke Island February 5-8, 1862. Battle of Roanoke Island February 8. Reconnoissance to Nag's Head February 10-11 (Cos. "A" and "H"). Expedition up Chowan River to Winton February 18-20. Expedition to Elizabeth City, N. C., April 7-8 (Cos. "H" and "I"). Battle of Camden, South Mills, April 19. Duty at Roanoke Island till July 10. Expedition up Chowan River May 7-9 (Co. "C"). Moved to Norfolk, thence to Newport News, Va., July 10-24. (Co. "F" detached at Plymouth, N. C., June to November, 1862. Capture of Hamilton July 9. Plymouth September 2. Expedition to Tarboro October 30-November 12. Rawle's Mills November 2. Rejoined Regiment at Fredericksburg.) Moved to Aquia Creek and Fredericksburg August 3-5 and duty there till August 30. Expedition to Port Royal August 15-16 (Co. "H"). Rappahannock River August 15 (Co. "H"). Moved to Brooks' Station, thence to Washington, D. C., August 31-September 5. Maryland Campaign. Near Jefferson September 13. South Mountain September 14. Battle of Antietam September 16-17. Duty in Pleasant Valley till October 28. Movement to Falmouth, Va., October 28-November 19. Battle of Fredericksburg, Va., December 12-15. (Co. "G" at Burnside's Headquarters October 31, 1862, to January, 1863.) "Mud March" January 20-24, 1863. Moved to Newport News, Va., February 6; thence to Suffolk March 10. Siege of Suffolk April 12-May 4. Moved to New York May 3-5. Three years' men assigned to 3rd New York Infantry May 6, 1863. Regiment mustered out May 20, 1863, expiration of term.

Regiment lost during service 2 Officers and 69 Enlisted men killed and mortally wounded and 2 Officers and 23 Enlisted men by disease. Total 96.

9th REGIMENT VETERAN INFANTRY.

Organization not completed. Men enlisted transferred October 14, 1863, to 17th New York Veteran Infantry.

10th REGIMENT INFANTRY.—("NATIONAL GUARD ZOUAVES.")

Organized at New York City April 27 to May 2, 1861. Left State for Fortress Monroe, Va., June 6, 1861. Attached to Fortress Monroe and Camp Hamilton, Va., Dept. of Virginia, to May, 1862. 1st Brigade, 1st Division, Dept. of Virginia, to May, 1862. 3rd Brigade, 2nd Division, 5th Army Corps, Army of the Potomac, to September, 1862. 3rd Brigade, 3rd Division, 2nd Army Corps, to May, 1863. 2nd Brigade, 3rd Division, 2nd Army Corps, to March, 1864. 3rd Brigade, 2nd Division, 2nd Army Corps, to June, 1865.

SERVICE.—Duty at Camp Hamilton, Va., till May, 1862. Occupation of Norfolk and Portsmouth May 10 and duty there till June 7. Joined Army of the Potomac on the Peninsula, Va. Operations against Stuart June 13-15. Old Church June 13. Seven days before Richmond, Va., June 25-July 1. Gaines Mill June 27. White Oak Swamp and Turkey Bend June 30. Malvern Hill July 1. At Harrison's Landing till August 16. Movement to Fortress Monroe, thence to Centreville August 16-28. Battle of Bull Run August 30. Battle of Antietam, Md., September 16-17. Shepherdstown Ford and Shepherdstown September 19-20. Movement to Falmouth, Va., October 29-November 19. Provost guard for Sumner's Grand Division December 7-24. Battle of Fredericksburg December 12-15. Burnside's 2nd Campaign, "Mud March," January 20-24, 1863. At Falmouth till April 27. Chancellorsville Campaign April 27-May 6. Provost Guard, 3rd Division, 2nd Army Corps, April

27 to June 14. Battle of Chancellorsville May 1-5. Battle of Gettysburg, Pa., July 2-4. Advance from the Rappahannock to the Rapidan September 13-17. Bristoe Campaign October 9-22. Auburn and Bristoe October 14. Blackburn's Ford October 15. Advance to line of the Rappahannock November 7-8. Mine Run Campaign November 26-December 2. Demonstration on the Rapidan February 6-7, 1864. Morton's Ford February 6-7. Campaign from the Rapidan to the James May 3-June 15. Battles of the Wilderness May 5-7; Spottsylvania May 8-12; Laurel Hill May 8; Po River May 10; Spottsylvania Court House May 12-21. Assault on the Salient, "Bloody Angle," May 12. North Anna River May 23-26. On line of the Pamunkey May 26-28. Totopotomoy May 28-31. Cold Harbor June 1-12. Before Petersburg June 16-18. Siege of Petersburg June 16, 1864, to April 2, 1865. Jerusalem Plank Road June 22-23, 1864. Demonstration north of the James July 27-29. Deep Bottom July 27-28. Mine Explosion July 30 (Reserve). Demonstration north of the James August 13-20. Strawberry Plains, Deep Bottom, August 14-18. Ream's Station August 25. Boydton Plank Road, Hatcher's Run, October 27-28. Dabney's Mills, Hatcher's Run, February 5-7, 1865. Watkins' House March 25. Appomattox Campaign March 28-April 9. Crow's House March 31. Fall of Petersburg April 2. Sailor's Creek April 6. High Bridge, Farmville, April 7. Appomattox Court House April 9. Surrender of Lee and his army. At Burkesville till May 2. March to Washington, D. C., May 2-12. Grand Review May 23. Mustered out June 30, 1865.

Regiment lost during service 6 Officers and 106 Enlisted men killed and mortally wounded and 3 Officers and 86 Enlisted men by disease. Total 201.

10th REGIMENT NATIONAL GUARD INFANTRY.

(See 177th Regiment Infantry.)

11th REGIMENT INFANTRY.—("1st NEW YORK FIRE ZOUAVES." "ELLSWORTH'S ZOUAVES.")

Organized at New York City and mustered in May 7, 1861. Left State for Washington, D. C., April 29, 1861. Duty at Washington May 2-23. Occupation of Arlington Heights and Alexandria, Va., May 24 (Ellsworth killed). Duty near Alexandria till July 16. Attached to Willcox's Brigade, Heintzelman's Division, McDowell's Army of Northeast Virginia. Advance on Manassas, Va., July 16-21. Occupation of Fairfax Court House July 17. Battle of Bull Run July 21. Duty in New York Harbor and in Westchester County, N. Y., September-October, 1861, and at Newport News, Va., Dept. of Virginia, to May, 1862. Action between Monitor and Merrimac in Hampton Roads March 8, 1862. Duty at New York May 7 to June 2. Mustered out June 2, 1862. Efforts failed to effect a new organization of this Regiment, known as the J. T. Brady Light Infantry, in summer of 1863, and the men enlisted were transferred to the 17th New York Veteran Infantry October 1, 1863.

Regiment lost during service 3 Officers and 48 Enlisted men killed and mortally wounded and 3 Officers and 12 Enlisted men by disease. Total 66.

11th REGIMENT NATIONAL GUARD INFANTRY.

Left State for Harper's Ferry, W. Va., May 28, 1862. Attached to 2nd Brigade, Sigel's Division, Dept. of the Shenandoah, and duty at Harper's Ferry till September. Mustered out September 16, 1862.

Again left State for Harrisburg, Pa., June 18, 1863. Attached to 4th Brigade, 1st Division, Dept. of the Susquehanna. Skirmish at Oyster Point, Pa., June 28. Mustered out July 20, 1863.

12th REGIMENT INFANTRY.—(3 MONTHS.)

Sailed from New York for Fortress Monroe, Va., April 21, 1861; arrived April 23; thence moved to Annapolis and Washington, D. C. Assigned to Mansfield's Command. Mustered in May 2, 1861. Advance into Virginia May 23. Occupation of Arlington Heights, Va., May 24. Ordered to join Patterson's Army July 6. Skirmish near Martinsburg July 12. Near Bunker Hill July 15. Mustered out at New York City August 5, 1861, expiration of term.

12th REGIMENT INFANTRY.—("ONONDAGA REGIMENT." "INDEPENDENCE GUARD.")

Organized at Elmira, N. Y., and mustered in for two years' State service May 8, 1861. Mustered in for three months' United States service May 13, and remustered for full term of State service August 2, 1861. Moved to Washington, D. C., May 29, 1861. Attached to Richardson's Brigade, Tyler's Division, McDowell's Army of Northeast Virginia, June to August, 1861. Richardson's Brigade, Division of the Potomac, to October, 1861. Wadsworth's Brigade, McDowell's Division, Army of the Potomac, to March, 1862. Butterfield's 3rd Brigade, Porter's 1st Division, 3rd Army Corps, Army of the Potomac, to May, 1862. 3rd Brigade, 1st Division, 5th Army Corps, to May, 1863. Headquarters, 5th Army Corps, to June, 1864.

SERVICE.—Duty in the Defences of Washington, D. C., till July 16, 1861. Advance on Manassas, Va., July 16-21. Battle of Bull Run July 21. Upton's Hill August 27. Duty in the Defences of Washington, D. C., till March 10, 1862. Advance on Manassas, Va., March 10. Moved to the Virginia Peninsula March 22-24. Warwick Road April 5. Siege of Yorktown April 5-May 4. Before Yorktown April 11. Reconnoissance up the Pamunkey May 10. Reconnoissance to Hanover Court House May 26. Battle of Hanover Court House May 27. Operations about Hanover Court House May 27-29. Seven days before Richmond June 25-July 1. Battle of Gaines Mill July 27. White Oak Swamp and Turkey Bend June 30. Malvern Hill July 1. Duty at Harrison's Landing till August 16. Movement to Fortress Monroe, thence to Centreville August 16-28. Pope's Campaign in Northern Virginia August 28-September 2. Battle of Bull Run August 30. Maryland Campaign September 6-22. Battle of Antietam September 16-17. Shepherdstown September 19. At Sharpsburg, Md., till October 30. Movement to Falmouth, Va., October 30-November 19. Battle of Fredericksburg, Va., December 12-15. Expedition to Richard's and Ellis' Fords December 29-30. "Mud March" January 20-24, 1863. At Falmouth till April. Chancellorsville Campaign April 27-May 6. Battle of Chancellorsville May 1-5. Mustered out May 17, 1863, expiration of term. Three years men consolidated to a Battalion of two Companies and assigned to duty as Provost Guard at Headquarters, 5th Army Corps, to June, 1864. Participating in the Gettysburg (Pa.) Campaign June 11-July 24, 1863. Battle of Gettysburg July 1-3. Bristoe Campaign October 9-22. Advance to line of the Rappahannock November 7-8. Mine Run Campaign November 26-December 2. Campaign from the Rapidan to the James May 3-June 2. Battles of the Wilderness May 5-7; Spottsylvania May 8-12; Spottsylvania Court House May 12-21; North Anna River May 23-26. On line of the Pamunkey May 26-28. Totopotomoy May 28-31. Transferred to 5th New York Infantry June 2, 1864, as Companies "E" and "F."

Regiment lost during service 3 Officers and 61 Enlisted men killed and mortally wounded and 1 Officer and 59 Enlisted men by disease. Total 124.

12th REGIMENT NATIONAL GUARD INFANTRY.

Left State for Washington, D. C., May 27, 1862. Mustered in for three months May 31, 1862. Attached to Railroad Brigade, Middle Department, 8th Army Corps. (Co. "A" detached at Fort McHenry, Baltimore, Md.) Assigned to duty at Harper's Ferry, W. Va., June to September. Defence of Harper's Ferry September 12-15. Maryland Heights September 12-13. Surrender of Harper's Ferry September 15. Paroled as prisoners of war September 16. Mustered out October 12, 1862. Declared exchanged January 11, 1863.

Again entered service for thirty days June 18, 1863. Moved to Harrisburg, Pa., and attached to 1st Brigade, Dana's Division, Dept. of the Susquehanna. Duty at Fenwick, Pa. Mustered out at New York City July 20, 1863.

13th REGIMENT INFANTRY.—(3 MONTHS.)

Organized at Brooklyn, N. Y. Moved to Annapolis, Md., April 21, 1861. Mustered into United States service for three months April 23. Guard railroad at Annapolis, Md., till June, and duty at Baltimore, Md., till August. Affair at Smith's Point, Md., May 18. Mustered out August 6, 1861.

13th REGIMENT INFANTRY.—("ROCHESTER REGIMENT.")

Organized at Rochester, N. Y., and mustered in for two years' service April 25, 1861. Moved to Elmira, N. Y., May 4. Mustered into United States service for three months May 14. Left State for Washington, D. C., May 30. Attached to Sherman's Brigade, Tyler's Division, McDowell's Army of Northeast Virginia, June to August, 1861. Fort Corcoran, Defences of Washington, to October, 1861. Martindale's Brigade, Porter's Division, Army of the Potomac, to March, 1862. 1st Brigade, 1st Division, 3rd Army Corps, Army of the Potomac, to May, 1862. 1st Brigade, 1st Division, 5th Army Corps, to May, 1863.

SERVICE.—Camp on Meridian Hill, Defences of Washington, till June 3, 1861, and at Fort Corcoran till July 16. Advance on Manassas, Va., July 16-21. Occupation of Fairfax Court House July 17. Blackburn's Ford July 18. Battle of Bull Run July 21. Transferred to United States service for balance of term by order of Governor Morgan August 2, 1861. Duty in the Defences of Washington till March, 1862. Moved to the Virginia Peninsula March 16. Warwick Road April 5. Siege of Yorktown April 5-May 4. Reconnoissance from Yorktown April 11-13. New Bridge May 24. Battle of Hanover Court House May 27. Operations about Hanover Court House May 27-29. Seven days before Richmond June 25-July 1. Mechanicsville June 26. Gaines Mill June 27. White Oak Swamp and Turkey Bend June 30. Malvern Hill July 1. At Harrison's Landing till August 16. Retreat from the Peninsula and movement to Centreville August 16-28. Pope's Campaign in Northern Virginia August 28-September 2. Battle of Bull Run August 30. Maryland Campaign September 6-22. Battle of Antietam, Md., September 16-17. Shepherdstown September 19. At Sharpsburg, Md., to October 30. Movement to Falmouth, Va., October 30-November 19. Battle of Fredericksburg, Va., December 12-15. Expedition to Richards' and Ellis' Fords December 29-30. "Mud March" January 20-24, 1863. At Falmouth till April 26. Ordered home April 26, and mustered out May 14, 1863, expiration of term. Three years' men consolidated to two Companies and duty as Provost Guard, 1st Division, 5th Army Corps, April 27 to June 23. Chancellorsville Campaign April 27-May 6. Battle of Chancellorsville May 1-5. Transferred to 140th New York Infantry June 23, 1863.

Regiment lost during service 4 Officers and 67 Enlisted men killed and mortally wounded and 29 Enlisted men by disease. Total 100.

13th REGIMENT NATIONAL GUARD INFANTRY.

Left State for Washington, D. C., May 30, 1862; thence moved to Suffolk, Va., and duty there attached to Division at Suffolk, 7th Army Corps, Dept. of Virginia, till September, 1862. Mustered out at Brooklyn, N. Y., September 28, 1862.

Again left State for Harrisburg, Pa., June 20, 1863. Attached to 2nd Brigade, 1st Division, Dept. of the Susquehanna. Action near Fort Washington, Pa., July 2. Mustered out July 20, 1863.

14th REGIMENT INFANTRY.—("1st ONEIDA COUNTY REGIMENT.")

Organized at Albany, N. Y., and mustered in for two years' service May 24, 1861. Left State for Washington, D. C., June 12, 1861. Attached to Porter's Brigade, Hunter's Division, McDowell's Army of Northeast Virginia, to August, 1861. W. T. Sherman's Brigade, Division of the Potomac, to October, 1861. Morell's Brigade, Porter's Division, Army of the Potomac, to March, 1862. 2nd Brigade, 1st Division, 3rd Army Corps, Army of the Potomac, to May, 1862. 2nd Brigade, 1st Division, 5th Army Corps, to May, 1863.

SERVICE.—Duty in the Defences of Washington, D. C., till July 16, 1861. Advance on Manassas, Va., July 16-21. Battle of Bull Run July 21. Duty in the Defences of Washington till March, 1862. Little River Turnpike October 14, 1861. Fall's Church Road November 18. Moved to the Peninsula, Va., March 16. Howard's Mills, near Cockleton, April 4. Warwick Road April 5. Siege of Yorktown April 5-May 4. Battle of Hanover Court House May 27. Operations about Hanover Court House May 27-29. Seven days before Richmond June 25-July 1. Battle of Mechanicsville June 26. Gaines Mill June 27. White Oak Swamp and Turkey Bend June 30. Malvern Hill July 1. At Harrison's Landing till August 16. Movement to Fortress Monroe, thence to Centreville August 16-28. Pope's Campaign in Northern Virginia August 28-September 2. Maryland Campaign September 6-22. Battle of Antietam September 16-17. Shepherdstown September 19. At Sharpsburg, Md., till October 30. Reconnoissance to Smithville, W. Va., October 16-17. Movement to Falmouth, Va., October 30-November 19. Battle of Fredericksburg, Va., December 12-15. Expedition to Richards' and Ellis' Fords December 29-30. "Mud March" January 20-24. At Falmouth till April 27. Chancellorsville Campaign April 27-May 6. Battle of Chancellorsville May 1-5. Mustered out May 24, 1863, expiration of term. Three years' men and Recruits transferred to 44th and 140th New York Infantry.

Regiment lost during service 4 Officers and 56 Enlisted men killed and mortally wounded and 43 Enlisted men by disease. Total 103.

14th REGIMENT STATE MILITIA INFANTRY.—("14th BROOKLYN.")

(See 84th Regiment Infantry.)

15th REGIMENT INFANTRY.

Organized at New York City and mustered in for two years' service June 17, 1861. Left State for Washington, D. C., June 29. Duty as Infantry in the Defences of that city till October, 1861. Attached to McCune's Brigade July 30 to August 4, 1861. Franklin's Brigade, Division of the Potomac, to September 26, and to Newton's Brigade to November, 1861. Designation of Regiment changed to 15th New York Engineers October 25, 1861. (See 15th Engineers.)

15th REGIMENT NATIONAL GUARD INFANTRY.

Mustered in for thirty days' United States service June 6, 1864. Duty at various posts in New York Harbor. Mustered out July 7, 1864.

16th REGIMENT INFANTRY.

Organized at Albany, N. Y., and mustered in for two years May 15, 1861. Left State for Washington, D. C., June 27. Attached to Davies' Brigade, Miles' Division, McDowell's Army of Northeast Virginia, to August, 1861. Heintzelman's Brigade, Division of the Potomac, to October, 1861. Slocum's Brigade, Franklin's Division, Army of the Potomac, to March, 1862. 2nd Brigade, 1st Division, 1st Army Corps, Army of the Potomac, to May, 1862. 2nd Brigade, 1st Division, 6th Army Corps, to May, 1863.

SERVICE.—Reconnoissance from Alexandria on Fairfax Road July 14, 1861. Advance on Manassas, Va., July 16-21. Fairfax Court House July 17. Battle of Bull Run July 21. Duty in the Defences of Washington till March, 1862. Expedition to Pohick Church October 3, 1861. Advance on Manassas, Va., March 10-15, 1862. McDowell's advance on Fredericksburg, Va., April 4-12. Ordered to the Virginia Peninsula April 22. Siege of

Yorktown April 24-May 4 (on transports). West Point May 7-8. Near Mechanicsville May 22. Seven days before Richmond June 25-July 1. Gaines Mill June 27. Savage Station June 29. White Oak Swamp and Glendale June 30. Malvern Hill July 1. At Harrison's Landing till August 16. Movement to Fortress Monroe, thence to Centreville August 16-28. In works at Centreville August 28-31, and cover Pope's retreat from Bull Run to Fairfax Court House September 1. Maryland Campaign September 6-22. Crampton's Gap, South Mountain, September 14. Battle of Antietam September 16-17. Duty in Maryland till October 29. Movement to Falmouth, Va., October 29-November 19. Battle of Fredericksburg, Va., December 12-15. "Mud March" January 20-24, 1863. At Falmouth till April. Chancellorsville Campaign April 27-May 6. Operations about Franklin's Crossing April 29-May 2. Maryes Heights, Fredericksburg, May 3. Salem Heights May 3-4. Banks' Ford May 4. Mustered out May 22, 1863, expiration of term. Three years' men transferred to 121st New York Infantry.

Regiment lost during service 5 Officers and 106 Enlisted men killed and mortally wounded and 1 Officer and 85 Enlisted men by disease. Total 197.

17th REGIMENT INFANTRY.—("WESTCHESTER CHASSEURS.")

Organized at New York City and mustered in for two years' service May 28, 1861. Left State for Washington, D. C., June 21. Attached to Mansfield's Command, Dept. of Washington, June to August, 1861. Garrison, Fort Ellsworth, Defences of Washington, to October, 1861. Butterfield's Brigade, Porter's Division, Army of the Potomac, to March, 1862. 3rd Brigade, 1st Division, 3rd Army Corps, Army of the Potomac, to May, 1862. 3rd Brigade, 1st Division, 5th Army Corps, to June, 1863.

SERVICE.—Duty in the Defences of Washington, D. C., till March, 1862. Advance on Manassas, Va., March 10-15, 1862. Moved to the Peninsula, Va., March 22-24. Peninsula Campaign March to August. Warwick Road April 5. Siege of Yorktown April 5-May 4. Reconnoissance up the Pamunkey May 10. Battle of Hanover Court House May 27. Operations about Hanover Court House May 27-29. Seven days before Richmond June 25-July 1. Operations about White House Landing June 26-July 2. White House June 28. Duty at Harrison's Landing till August 16. Movement to Fortress Monroe, thence to Centreville August 16-28. Pope's Campaign in Northern Virginia August 28-September 2. Battle of Bull Run August 30. Maryland Campaign September 6-22. Battle of Antietam September 16-17. Shepherdstown September 19. Duty at Sharpsburg, Md., till October 30. Movement to Falmouth, Va., October 30-November 17. Battle of Fredericksburg, Va., December 12-15. Expedition to Richards' and Ellis' Fords, Rappahannock River, December 29-30. "Mud March" January 20-24, 1863. At Falmouth till April 27. Chancellorsville Campaign April 27-May 6. Battle of Chancellorsville May 1-5. Three years' men detached May 13, 1863; assigned to a Battalion of New York Volunteers and on June 23, 1863, transferred to 146th Regiment New York Infantry. Regiment mustered out June 2, 1863.

Regiment lost during service 5 Officers and 32 Enlisted men killed and mortally wounded and 3 Officers and 37 Enlisted men by disease. Total 77.

17th REGIMENT VETERAN INFANTRY.

Organized at Staten Island, N. Y., June 13 to October 17, 1863. Two Companies under Captain Horner. Moved to Fort Hamilton, N. Y., September 2, 1863. Left State for Washington, D. C., October 18, 1863. Moved to Louisville, Ky., thence to Eastport, Miss., and Columbus, Ky., October 28-November 8, 1863. Attached to District of Columbus, Ky., 6th Division, 16th Army Corps, Dept. of the Tennessee, to January, 1864. 2nd Brigade, 4th Division, 16th Army Corps, to April, 1864. 3rd Brigade, 4th Division, 16th Army Corps, to August,

1864. 1st Brigade, 2nd Division, 14th Army Corps, Army of the Cumberland, to June, 1865.

SERVICE.—Duty at Union City, Tenn., December 11, 1863, to January 24, 1864. Moved to Vicksburg, Miss., January 24. Meridian Campaign February 3-March 2. Operations in Alabama and duty at Decatur, Ala., April 10 to August 4. Pond Springs, near Courtland, May 27. Pond Springs June 29. Courtland July 25. Ordered to Atlanta, Ga., August 4. Siege of Atlanta August 8-25. Flank movement on Jonesboro August 25-30. Battle of Jonesboro August 31-September 1. Lovejoy Station September 2-6. Pursuit of Hood into Alabama October 3-26. March to the sea November 15-December 10. Sandersville November 26. Siege of Savannah December 10-21. Campaign of the Carolinas January to April, 1865. Averysboro, N. C., March 16. Battle of Bentonville March 19-21. Occupation of Goldsboro March 24. Advance on Raleigh April 9-13. Occupation of Raleigh April 14. Bennett's House April 26. Surrender of Johnston and his army. March to Washington, D. C., via Richmond, Va., April 29-May 20. Grand Review May 24. Duty in Dept. of Washington, attached to 1st Brigade, Bartlett's Division, 22nd Army Corps, to July. Mustered out July 13, 1865.

Regiment lost during service 2 Officers and 51 Enlisted men killed and mortally wounded and 56 Enlisted men by disease. Total 109.

17th REGIMENT NATIONAL GUARD INFANTRY.

Organized for thirty days' United States service July, 1863. Left State for Baltimore, Md., July 3, and duty in the Defences of that city till August. Attached to 2nd Separate Brigade, 8th Army Corps, Middle Department. Mustered out August 13, 1863.

18th REGIMENT INFANTRY.

Organized at Albany, N. Y., and mustered in May 17, 1861. Left State for Washington, D. C., June 19. Attached to Davies' Brigade, Miles' Division, McDowell's Army of Northeast Virginia, June to August, 1861. Franklin's Brigade, Division of the Potomac, to October, 1861. Newton's Brigade, Franklin's Division, Army of the Potomac, to March, 1862. 3rd Brigade, 1st Division, 1st Army Corps, Army of the Potomac, to May, 1862. 3rd Brigade, 1st Division, 6th Army Corps, to May, 1863.

SERVICE.—Reconnoissance on Fairfax Road July 14, 1861. Advance on Manassas, Va., July 16-21. Fairfax Court House July 17. Battle of Bull Run July 21. Duty in the Defences of Washington, D. C., till March, 1862. Skirmish at Springfield Station October 3, 1861. Advance on Manassas, Va., March 10-15, 1862. McDowell's advance on Fredericksburg, Va., April 4-12. Ordered to the Virginia Peninsula April 22. Siege of Yorktown April 24-May 4 (on transports). West Point May 7-8. Seven days before Richmond June 25-July 1. Gaines Mill June 27. White Oak Swamp and Glendale June 30. Malvern Hill July 1. At Harrison's Landing till August 16. Movement to Fortress Monroe, thence to Centreville August 16-28. In works at Centreville August 29-31. Cover Pope's retreat to Fairfax Court House September 1. Maryland Campaign September 6-22. Crampton's Pass, South Mountain, September 14. Battle of Antietam September 16-17. Duty in Maryland till October 30. Movement to Falmouth, Va., October 30-November 19. Battle of Fredericksburg, Va., December 12-15. "Mud March" January 20-24, 1863. At Falmouth till April. Chancellorsville Campaign April 27-May 6. Operations at Franklin's Crossing April 29-May 2. Maryes Heights, Fredericksburg, May 3. Salem Heights May 3-4. Banks' Ford May 4. Three years men transferred to 121st Regiment New York Infantry May 11. Regiment moved to New York May 16, and mustered out May 28, 1863, expiration of term.

Regiment lost during service 4 Officers and 34 Enlisted men killed and mortally wounded and 1 Officer and 32 Enlisted men by disease. Total 71.

18th REGIMENT NATIONAL GUARD INFANTRY.

Organized for thirty days' United States service and left State for Baltimore, Md., July 3, 1863. Duty at Baltimore and at Frederick, Md. Attached to 2nd Separate Brigade, 8th Army Corps, Middle Department, to August. Mustered out August 15, 1863.

19th REGIMENT INFANTRY.—("SEWARD INFANTRY.")

Organized at Elmira, N. Y., and mustered in for two years May 22, 1861. Left State for Washington, D. C., June 5, and duty in the Defences of that city till July. Attached to Sandford's Division, Patterson's Army, July. Butterfield's Brigade, Patterson's Army, July 11-29, 1861. 1st Brigade, Banks' Division, Army of the Potomac, to September 15, 1861. 3rd Brigade, Banks' Division, Army of the Potomac, to December, 1861.

SERVICE.—Joined Patterson's Army July 6, 1861. Occupation of Martinsburg, Va., July 10. Skirmish at Bunker Hill July 17. Picket duty at Bolivar Heights July 25. Occupation of Maryland Heights July 28. Lovettsville August 8 (Detachment). Moved to Hyattstown August 16. Duty near Darnestown till September 24. Duty on Upper Potomac till December. Designation of Regiment changed to 3rd Regiment New York Light Artillery December 11, 1862 (which see).

19th REGIMENT NATIONAL GUARD INFANTRY.

Organized for three months' United States service May 26, 1862. Left State for Baltimore, Md., June 4. Duty at Baltimore and along line of railroad from Baltimore to Havre de Grace till September. Mustered out September 6, 1862.

20th REGIMENT INFANTRY.—(3 MONTHS.) ("ULSTER GUARD.")

Organized for three months' service April 23, 1861. Left State for Annapolis, Md., May 7. Mustered in May 11. Duty at Annapolis and Baltimore, Md., till August. Mustered out August 2, 1861.

20th REGIMENT INFANTRY.—("UNITED TURNER REGIMENT.")

Organized at New York City May 6, 1861. Left State for Fortress Monroe, Va., June 13. Attached to Fortress Monroe and Camp Hamilton, Dept. of Virginia, to May, 1862. 2nd Brigade, 1st Division, Dept. of Virginia, to June, 1862. 3rd Brigade, 2nd Division, 6th Army Corps, to May, 1863.

SERVICE.—Duty at Fortress Monroe and Camp Hamilton June 15 to August 26, 1861. Hampton, Va., August 7. Bombardment and capture of Forts Hatteras and Clarke, N. C., August 28-29. Duty at Fortress Monroe and Camp Hamilton September 13, 1861, to May 10, 1862. New Market Bridge, near Newport News, December 22, 1861. Reconnoissance to Big Bethel January 3, 1862. Tranter's Creek and occupation of Norfolk and Portsmouth May 10. Duty at Norfolk till June 9. Ordered to join Army of the Potomac in the field June 9. Seven days before Richmond June 25-July 1. Savage Station June 29. White Oak Swamp and Glendale June 30. Malvern Hill July 1. At Harrison's Landing till August 16. Movement to Fortress Monroe, thence to Centreville August 16-28. In works at Centreville August 29-31, and cover Pope's retreat to Fairfax Court House September 1. Maryland Campaign September 6-22. Crampton's Pass, South Mountain, September 14. Battle of Antietam September 16-17. At Hagerstown, Md., till October 29. Movement to Falmouth, Va., October 29-November 19. Battle of Fredericksburg, Va., December 12-15. "Mud March" January 20-24, 1863. At White Oak Church till April 27. Chancellorsville Campaign April 27-May 6. Operations at Franklin's Crossing April 29-May 2. Maryes Heights, Fredericksburg, May 3. Salem Heights May 3-4. Banks' Ford May 4. Three years men transferred to 3rd New York Battery and to Battery "F" 5th United States Artillery May 6. Regiment mustered out June 1, 1863, expiration of term.

Regiment lost during service 8 Officers and 53 Enlisted men killed and mortally wounded and 1 Officer and 58 Enlisted men by disease. Total 120.

20th REGIMENT STATE MILITIA INFANTRY.

(See 80th Regiment Infantry.)

20th REGIMENT VETERAN INFANTRY.

Organization not completed. Men enlisted transferred to 16th Regiment New York Cavalry October 14, 1863.

21st REGIMENT INFANTRY.—("1st BUFFALO REGIMENT.")

Organized at Buffalo, N. Y., and mustered in for two years' State service May 8, 1861. Remustered at Elmira, N. Y., for three months' United States service May 20, 1861. Left Elmira, N. Y., for Washington, D. C., June 18. Attached to Mansfield's Command, Dept. of Washington, to August, 1861. Division of the Potomac to October, 1861. Wadsworth's Brigade, McDowell's Division, Army of the Potomac, to March, 1862. Patrick's 2nd Brigade, King's 3rd Division, 1st Army Corps, Army of the Potomac, to April, 1862. 2nd Brigade, King's Division, Dept. of the Rappahannock, to June, 1862. 3rd Brigade, 1st Division, 3rd Corps, Pope's Army of Virginia, to September, 1862. 3rd Brigade, 1st Division, 1st Army Corps, Army of the Potomac, to January, 1863. Provost Marshal, General Patrick's Command, Army of the Potomac, to May, 1863.

SERVICE.—Camp at Kalorama Heights, Washington, D. C., till July 14, 1861. Garrison at Fort Runyon till August 20. Transferred to United States service for balance of State enlistment by order of Governor E. D. Morgan August 2, 1861. Moved to Rip Raps with mutineers August 20-30. Camp at Arlington Heights, Va., till September 28, and at Upton's Hill, Va., till March, 1862. Advance on Manassas, Va., March 10-15. Camp at Upton's Hill till April 9. McDowell's advance on Falmouth, Va., April 9-19. Duty at Fredericksburg till May 25. McDowell's advance on Richmond May 25-29. Operations against Jackson June 1-21. At Falmouth till July 28, and at Fredericksburg till August 6. Pope's Campaign in Northern Virginia August 16-September 2. Fords of the Rappahannock August 21-23. Sulphur Springs August 26. Gainesville August 28. Groveton August 29. 2nd Bull Run August 30. Maryland Campaign September 6-22. Battles of South Mountain September 14; Antietam September 16-17. Duty in Maryland till October 29. Movement to Falmouth, Va., October 29-November 19. Battle of Fredericksburg, Va., December 12-15. Assigned to provost duty at Aquia Creek January to May, 1863. Chancellorsville Campaign April 27-May 6. Mustered out May 18, 1863, expiration of term.

Regiment lost during service 2 Officers and 74 Enlisted men killed and mortally wounded and 2 Officers and 40 Enlisted men by disease. Total 118.

21st REGIMENT NATIONAL GUARD INFANTRY.

Organized for thirty days' service June 22, 1863. Left State for Baltimore, Md., June 27, and duty there till August. Attached to 2nd Separate Brigade, 8th Army Corps, Middle Department. Mustered out August 6, 1863.

22nd REGIMENT INFANTRY.—("2nd NORTHERN NEW YORK REGIMENT.")

Organized at Troy, N. Y., and mustered in June 6, 1861. Left State for Washington, D. C., June 28. Attached to Key's Brigade, Division of the Potomac, to October, 1861. Key's Brigade, McDowell's Division, Army of the Potomac, to March, 1862. Augur's 1st Brigade, King's 3rd Division, McDowell's 1st Army Corps, Army of the Potomac, to April, 1862. 1st Brigade, King's Division, Dept. of the Rappahannock, to June, 1862. 1st Brigade, 1st Division, 3rd Corps, Pope's Army of Virginia, to September, 1862. 1st Brigade, 1st Division, 1st Army Corps, Army of the Potomac, to June, 1863.

SERVICE.—Duty in the Defences of Washington, D. C., till March, 1862. Advance on Manassas, Va., March 10-15. Camp at Upton's Hill till April 9. McDowell's advance on Falmouth, Va., April 9-19. Duty at Fredericksburg, Va., till May 25. McDowell's advance on Richmond May 25-29. Operations against Jackson June 1-21. At Falmouth and Fredericksburg till August 6. Pope's Campaign in Northern Virginia August 16-September 2. Fords of the Rappahannock August 21-23. Battles of Gainesville August 28. Groveton August 29, and 2nd Bull Run August 30. Maryland Campaign September 6-22. Battles of South Mountain September 14; Antietam September 16-17. Duty in Maryland till October 29. Advance on Falmouth, Va., October 29-November 19. Battle of Fredericksburg, Va., December 12-15. "Mud March" January 20-24, 1863. At Belle Plains till April 27. Chancellorsville Campaign April 27-May 6. Operations at Pollock's Mill Creek April 29-May 2. Fitzhugh's Crossing April 29-30. Battle of Chancellorsville May 1-5. Three years men transferred to 76th and 93rd New York Regiments Infantry. Mustered out June 19, 1863, expiration of term.

Regiment lost during service 11 Officers and 62 Enlisted men killed and mortally wounded and 1 Officer and 28 Enlisted men by disease. Total 102.

22nd REGIMENT NATIONAL GUARD INFANTRY.

Organized for three months' service May 28, 1862. Left State for Baltimore, Md., May 28, and duty there till September. Mustered out September 5, 1862.

Again organized for thirty days' service June 18, 1863. Left State for Harrisburg, Pa., June 19. Attached to 4th Brigade, 1st Division, Dept. of the Susquehanna, to July 8, and to 3rd Brigade, 2nd Division, 6th Army Corps, Army of the Potomac, to July 20, 1863. Action at Sporting Hill, Pa., June 30. Carlisle, Pa., July 1. Mustered out July 24, 1863.

23rd REGIMENT INFANTRY.—("SOUTHERN TIER REGIMENT.")

Organized at Elmira, N. Y., May 10, 1861. Mustered in July 2, 1861. Left State for Washington, D. C., July 5. Attached to Hunter's Brigade, Division of the Potomac, to October, 1861. Wadsworth's Brigade, McDowell's Division, Army of the Potomac, to March, 1862. 2nd Brigade, King's 3rd Division, McDowell's 1st Army Corps, Army of the Potomac, to April, 1862. 2nd Brigade, King's Division, Dept. of the Rappahannock, to June, 1862. 3rd Brigade, 1st Division, 3rd Corps, Pope's Army of Virginia, to September, 1862. 3rd Brigade, 1st Division, 1st Army Corps, Army of the Potomac, to January, 1863. Provost Marshal, General Patrick's Command, Army of the Potomac, to May, 1863.

SERVICE.—Duty in the Defences of Washington, D. C., till March, 1862. Action at Ball's Cross Roads, Va., August 27-28, 1861 (Cos. "I" and "K"). Munson's Hill August 31 (Cos. "I" and "K"). Advance on Manassas, Va., March 10-15. At Upton's Hill till April 9. McDowell's advance on Falmouth, Va., April 9-19. Duty at Fredericksburg till May 25. McDowell's advance on Richmond May 25-29. Operations against Jackson June 1-21. At Falmouth till July 24. Reconnoissance to Orange Court House July 24-27. Pope's Campaign in Northern Virginia August 16-September 2. Fords of the Rappahannock August 21-23. Sulphur Springs August 23-24. Battles of Gainesville August 28; Groveton August 29; 2nd Bull Run August 30. Maryland Campaign September 6-22. Battles of South Mountain September 14; Antietam September 16-17. Duty in Maryland till October 29. Movement to Falmouth October 29-November 19. Battle of Fredericksburg, Va., December 12-15. Assigned to provost duty at Aquia Creek January to May, 1863. Chancellorsville Campaign April 27-May 6. Mustered out May 22, 1863, expiration of term. Three years men transferred to 80th Regiment New York Infantry.

Regiment lost during service 17 Enlisted men killed and mortally wounded and 2 Officers and 53 Enlisted men by disease. Total 72.

23rd REGIMENT NATIONAL GUARD INFANTRY.

Organized for thirty days' service June 16, 1863. Left State for Harrisburg, Pa., June 18. Attached to 3rd Brigade, 1st Division, Dept. of the Susquehanna. Action at Oyster Point, Pa., June 28. Carlisle, Pa., July 1. Mustered out July 22, 1863.

24th REGIMENT INFANTRY.—("OSWEGO COUNTY REGIMENT.")

Organized at Elmira, N. Y., and mustered in July 2, 1861, to date from May 17, 1861. Left State for Washington, D. C., July 2, 1861. Attached to Keyes' Brigade, Division of the Potomac, to October, 1861. Keyes' Brigade, McDowell's Division, Army of the Potomac, to January, 1862. Augur's Brigade, McDowell's Division, Army of the Potomac, to March, 1862. 1st Brigade, King's 3rd Division, McDowell's 1st Army Corps, Army of the Potomac, to April, 1862. 1st Brigade, King's Division, Dept. of the Rappahannock, to June, 1862. 1st Brigade, 1st Division, 3rd Corps, Pope's Army of Virginia, to September, 1862. 1st Brigade, 1st Division, 1st Army Corps, Army of the Potomac, to May, 1863.

SERVICE.—Duty in the Defences of Washington, D. C., till March, 1862. Advance on Manassas, Va., March 10-15, 1862. At Upton's Hill till April 9. McDowell's advance on Falmouth, Va., April 9-19. Duty at Fredericksburg, Va., till May 25. McDowell's advance on Richmond May 25-29. Operations against Jackson June 1-21. Duty at Falmouth till August. Pope's Campaign in Northern Virginia August 16-September 2. Fords of the Rappahannock August 21-23. Sulphur Springs August 24. Battles of Gainesville August 28; Groveton August 29; 2nd Bull Run August 30. Maryland Campaign September 6-22. Battles of South Mountain September 14; Antietam September 16-17. Duty in Maryland till October 29. Movement on Falmouth, Va., October 29-November 19. Battle of Fredericksburg, Va., December 12-15. "Mud March" January 20-24, 1863. At Belle Plains till April 27. Chancellorsville Campaign April 27-May 6. Operations at Pollock's Mill Creek April 29-May 2. Battle of Chancellorsville May 1-5. Mustered out May 29, 1863, expiration of term. Three years men transferred to 76th New York Infantry.

Regiment lost during service 6 Officers and 82 Enlisted men killed and mortally wounded and 1 Officer and 30 Enlisted men by disease. Total 119.

25th REGIMENT INFANTRY.—(3 MONTHS.)

Moved to Washington, D. C., April 22, 1861. Attached to Mansfield's Command, Dept. of Washington, D. C. Advance into Virginia May 23. Occupation of Arlington Heights, Va., May 24. Engaged in fatigue duty at Arlington Heights building, Fort Albany, till July. Mustered out August 4, 1861.

25th REGIMENT INFANTRY.—("UNION RANGERS.")

Organized at New York City May 11, 1861. Mustered in June 28, 1861, and left State for Washington, D. C., July 3, 1861. Attached to Garrison at Fort Albany, Defences of Washington, till July 21. McCunn's Brigade, Army of Northeast Virginia, to August 4, 1861. Hunter's Brigade, Division of the Potomac, to October, 1861. Butterfield's Brigade, Porter's Division, Army of the Potomac, to March, 1862. Martindale's 1st Brigade, Porter's 1st Division, 3rd Army Corps, Army of the Potomac, to May, 1862. 1st Brigade, 1st Division, 5th Army Corps, to June, 1863.

SERVICE.—Duty in the Defences of Washington, D. C., till March, 1862. Moved to the Virginia Peninsula March 16. Warwick Road April 5. Siege of Yorktown April 5-May 4. Battle of Hanover Court House May 27. Operations about Hanover Court House May 27-29. Seven days before Richmond June 25-July 1. Battles of Mechanicsville June 26; Gaines Mill June 27; White Oak Swamp and Turkey Bend June 30; Malvern Hill July 1. At Harrison's Landing till August 16. Retreat from the Peninsula and movement to Centreville August 16-28. Pope's Campaign in Northern Virginia August 28-September 2. Battle of 2nd Bull Run August

30. Maryland Campaign September 6-22. Battle of Antietam September 16-17. Shepherdstown September 19. At Sharpsburg, Md., till October 30. Movement to Falmouth, Va., October 30-November 19. Battle of Fredericksburg, Va., December 12-15. Expedition to Richards' and Ellis' Fords, Rappahannock River, December 29-30. "Mud March" January 20-24, 1863. At Falmouth, Va., till April 27. Chancellorsville Campaign April 27-May 6. Battle of Chancellorsville May 1-5. Mustered out June 26, 1863, and honorably discharged from service July 10, 1865. Three years men transferred to 44th New York Infantry.

Regiment lost during service 7 Officers and 54 Enlisted men killed and mortally wounded and 4 Officers and 25 Enlisted men by disease. Total 90.

25th REGIMENT NATIONAL GUARD INFANTRY.

Mustered in for three months' service May 31, 1862. Left State for Suffolk, Va., June 4. Duty at Suffolk, Va., attached to 7th Army Corps, Dept. of Virginia, till September. Mustered out September 8, 1862.

26th REGIMENT INFANTRY.—("2nd ONEIDA REGIMENT.")

Organized at Elmira, N. Y., and mustered in May 21, 1861. Left State for Washington, D. C., June 19. Attached to McCunn's Brigade, Army of Northeast Virginia, to August, 1861. Heintzelman's Brigade, Division of the Potomac, to October, 1861. Slocum's Brigade, Franklin's Division, Army of the Potomac, to November, 1861. Wadsworth's Command, Defences of Washington, to May, 1862. 1st Brigade, 2nd Division, Dept. of the Rappahannock, to June, 1862. 2nd Brigade, 2nd Division, 3rd Corps, Pope's Army of Virginia, to September, 1862. 2nd Brigade, 2nd Division, 1st Army Corps, Army of the Potomac, to May, 1863.

SERVICE.—Duty in the Defences of Washington, D. C., and at Fort Lyon till May, 1862. Expedition to Pohick Church, Va., October 3, 1861. Duty near Fredericksburg, Va., till May 25. Expedition to Front Royal May 25-June 18. Duty at Manassas, Warrenton and Culpeper till August. Battle of Cedar Mountain August 9. Pope's Campaign in Northern Virginia August 16-September 2. Fords of the Rappahannock August 21-23. Thoroughfare Gap August 28. Battles of Groveton August 29; 2nd Bull Run August 30; Chantilly September 1. Maryland Campaign September 6-22. Battles of South Mountain September 14; Antietam September 16-17. At Sharpsburg, Md., till October 30. Movement to Falmouth, Va., October 30-November 19. At Brook's Station till December 10. Battle of Fredericksburg December 12-15. "Mud March" January 20-24, 1863. At Falmouth and Belle Plains till April 27. Chancellorsville Campaign April 27-May 6. Operations at Pollock's Mill Creek April 29-May 2. Battle of Chancellorsville May 1-5. Mustered out May 28, 1863. Three years men transferred to 97th Regiment New York Infantry.

Regiment lost during service 5 Officers and 101 Enlisted men killed and mortally wounded and 42 Enlisted men by disease. Total 148.

27th REGIMENT INFANTRY ("UNION REGIMENT").

Organized at Elmira, N. Y., May 21, 1861. Mustered in June 15, 1861, and left State for Washington, D. C., July 10. Attached to Porter's Brigade, Hunter's Division, McDowell's Army of Northeast Virginia, to August, 1861. Heintzelman's Brigade, Division of the Potomac, to October, 1861. Slocum's Brigade, Franklin's Division, Army of the Potomac, to March, 1862. Slocum's 2nd Brigade, Franklin's 1st Division, 1st Army Corps, Army of the Potomac, to May, 1862. 2nd Brigade, 1st Division, 6th Army Corps, to May, 1863.

SERVICE.—Advance on Manassas, Va., July 16-21, 1861. Battle of Bull Run, Va., July 21. Duty in the Defences of Washington, D. C., till March, 1862. Expedition to Pohick Church October 3, 1861. Advance on Manassas, Va., March 10-15, 1862. McDowell's advance on Fredricksburg April 4-12. Orderd to the Peninsula, Virginia, April 22. Siege of Yorktown, Va., April 24-

May 4, on transports. West Point May 7-8. Near Mechanicsville May 20. Seven days before Richmond June 25-July 1. Gaines' Mill and Chickahominy June 27. White Oak Swamp and Glendale June 30. Malvern Hill July 1. At Harrison's Landing till August 16. Movement to Fortress Monroe, thence to Centreville August 16-28. In works at Centreville August 28-31, and cover Pope's retreat to Fairfax Court House September 1. Maryland Campaign September 6-22. Crampton's Gap, South Mountain, September 14. Battle of Antietam September 16-17. Duty in Maryland till October 29. Movement to Falmouth, Va., October 29-November 19. Battle of Fredericksburg, Va., December 12-15. "Mud March" January 20-24, 1863. At Falmouth till April. Chancellorsville Campaign April 27-May 6. Operations about Franklin's Crossing April 29-May 2. Maryes Heights, Fredericksburg, May 3. Salem Heights May 3-4. Banks' Ford May 4. Mustered out May 31, 1863, expiration of term. Three years' men transferred to 121st Regiment New York Infantry.

Regiment lost during service 2 Officers and 72 Enlisted men killed and mortally wounded and 2 Officers and 70 Enlisted men by disease. Total 146.

28th REGIMENT INFANTRY (3 MONTHS).

Embarked on transport "Star of the South" April 23, 1861. Arrived at Washington, D. C., April 29. Mustered in May 10, 1861. Advance into Virginia and occupation of Arlington Heights May 24. Skirmish near Chain Bridge June 2. Engaged in picket and fatigue duty, constructing Fort Bennett, and a redoubt near Aqueduct Bridge; also guarding bridge at Georgetown during battle of Bull Run. Mustered out August 5, 1861.

28th REGIMENT INFANTRY ("SCOTT LIFE GUARD")

Organized at Albany, N. Y., and mustered in May 22, 1861. Left State for Washington, D. C., June 25, 1861. Attached to Mansfield's Command to July, 1861. Butterfield's Brigade, Sandford's Division, Patterson's Army of the Shenandoah, to October, 1861. Gordon's Brigade, Banks' Division, Army of the Potomac, to March, 1862. 1st Brigade, 1st Division, Banks' 5th Army Corps, to April, 1862. 1st Brigade, 1st Division, Dept. of the Shenandoah, to June, 1862. 1st Brigade, 1st Division, 2nd Army Corps, Pope's Army of Virginia, to September, 1862. 1st Brigade, 1st Division, 12th Army Corps, Army of the Potomac, to June, 1863.

SERVICE.—Near Martinsburg, Va., July 11, 1861. Expedition to Point of Rocks, Md., August 5. Guard and outpost duty on the Upper Potomac till February, 1862. Operations near Edwards' Ferry October 20-24, 1861. Advance on Winchester, Va., March 1-12, 1862. Occupation of Winchester March 12. Ordered to Manassas, Va., March 18, and back to Winchester March 19. Pursuit of Jackson March 24-April 27. Columbia Furnace April 16. Near Harrisonburg April 24. Gordonsville April 26. Operations in the Shenandoah Valley May 15-June 17. At Strasburg till May 20. Retreat to Winchester May 20-25. Front Royal May 23. Battle of Winchester May 24-25. Retreat to Williamsport May 25-26. Bunker Hill May 25. At Williamsport till June 10. Moved to Front Royal June 10-18. Reconnoissance to Luray June 29-30. Battle of Cedar Mountain August 9. Pope's Campaign in Northern Virginia August 16-September 2. Fords of the Rappahannock August 20-23. White Sulphur Springs August 23-25. Plains of Manassas August 26-28. Battles of Groveton August 29; Bull Run August 30. Battle of Antietam, Md., September 16-17. At Sandy Hook and Maryland Heights September 22 to December 10. March to Fairfax Station December 10-14, and duty there till January 19. Moved to Stafford Court House January 19-23, and duty there till April 27. Chancellorsville Campaign April 27-May 6. Battle of Chancellorsville May 1-5. Mustered out June 2, 1863, expiration of term. Three years' men transferred to 60th Regiment New York Infantry.

Regiment lost during service 2 Officers and 46 Enlisted men killed and mortally wounded and 50 Enlisted men by disease. Total 98.

28th REGIMENT NATIONAL GUARD INFANTRY.

Organized for 30 days' service June 20, 1863. Left State for Harrisburg, Pa., June 20. Duty at Marysville, Md., Carlisle and Gettysburg, Pa. Attached to 2nd Brigade, 1st Division, Dept. of the Susquehanna, Carlisle July 1. Duty at Arsenal, New York, during Draft Riots. Mustered out July 23, 1863.

Again entered service for 100 days September 2, 1864. Mustered out November 13, 1864.

29th REGIMENT INFANTRY ("ASTOR RIFLES," "1st GERMAN INFANTRY").

Organized at New York City and mustered in June 6, 1861. Left State for Washington, D. C., June 21, 1861. Attached to Blenker's Brigade, Miles' Division, McDowell's Army of Northeast Virginia, to August, 1861. Blenker's Brigade, Division of the Potomac, to October, 1861. Blenker's Brigade, Hooker's Division, Army of the Potomac, to January, 1862. 2nd Brigade, Blenker's Division, Army of the Potomac, to March, 1862. 2nd Brigade, Blenker's 2nd Division, 2nd Army Corps, Army of the Potomac, to April, 1862. 2nd Brigade, Blenker's Division, Dept. of the Mountains, to June, 1862. 1st Brigade, 2nd Division, 1st Army Corps, Pope's Army of Virginia, to September, 1862. 1st Brigade, 2nd Division, 11th Army Corps, Army of the Potomac, to June, 1863.

SERVICE.—Advance on Manassas, Va., July 16-21, 1861. Battle of Bull Run July 21. Duty in the Defences of Washington, D. C., till April, 1862. Movement to Winchester, Va., April 5-18. Operations in the Shenandoah Valley till June. Battle of Cross Keys June 8. At Sperryville July 7 to August 8. Pope's Campaign in Northern Virginia August 16-September 2. Fords of the Rappahannock August 20-23. Sulphur Springs August 24. Battle of Groveton August 29. Bull Run August 30. Duty in the Defences of Washington, D. C., till November. Moved to Centreville, Va., November 1-19. Moved to support of Burnside at Fredericksburg, Va., December 9-16. "Mud March" January 20-24, 1863. At Stafford Court House till April 27. Chancellorsville Campaign April 27-May 6. Battle of Chancellorsville May 1-5. Mustered out June 20, 1863, expiration of term. Three years' men consolidated into a Company known as Independent Company 29th New York Infantry, and provost duty at Headquarters 11th Army Corps, Army of the Potomac, and Army of the Cumberland to April 19, 1864, when transferred to 68th Regiment New York Infantry.

Regiment lost during service 2 Officers and 40 Enlisted men killed and mortally wounded and 1 Officer and 21 Enlisted men by disease. Total 64.

29th REGIMENT VETERAN INFANTRY.

Failed to complete organization. Men enlisted transferred to 13th Regiment New York Heavy Artillery, October 14, 1863.

30th REGIMENT INFANTRY.

Organized at Troy, N. Y., and mustered in June 1, 1861. Left State for Washington, D. C., June 28, 1861. Attached to Defences of Washington to August, 1861. Keyes' Brigade, Division of the Potomac, to October, 1861. Keyes' Brigade, McDowell's Division, Army of the Potomac, to March, 1862. Augur's Brigade, King's 3rd Division, 1st Army Corps, Army of the Potomac, to April, 1862. 1st Brigade, King's Division, Dept. of the Rappahannock, to June, 1862. 1st Brigade, 1st Division, 3rd Corps, Pope's Army of Northern Virginia, to September, 1862. 1st Brigade, 1st Division, 1st Army Corps, Army of the Potomac, to June, 1863.

SERVICE.—Duty in the Defences of Washington, D. C., till March, 1862. Doolan's Farm November 16, 1861 (Detachment). Advance on Manassas, Va., March 10-16, 1862. McDowell's Advance on Falmouth, Va., April 9-19. Duty at Fredericksburg, Va., till May 25. McDowell's advance on Richmond May 25-29. Operations against Jackson June 1-21. At Falmouth till August. Pope's Campaign in Northern Virginia August 16-September 2. Fords of the Rappahannock August 20-23. Thoroughfare Gap August 28. Battles of Groveton

August 29; Bull Run August 30. Maryland Campaign September 6-22. Battles of South Mountain September 14; Antietam September 16-17. Duty in Maryland till October 29. Movement to Falmouth, Va., October 29-November 19. Battle of Fredericksburg, Va., December 12-15. "Mud March" January 20-24, 1863. At Falmouth till April 27. Chancellorsville Campaign April 27-May 6. Operations at Pollock's Mill Creek April 29-May 2. Battle of Chancellorsville May 2-5. Three years' men transferred to 76th Regiment New York Infantry May 24. Mustered out June 18, 1863, expiration of term.

Regiment lost during service 6 Officers and 72 Enlisted men killed and mortally wounded and 2 Officers and 31 Enlisted men by disease. Total 111.

31st REGIMENT INFANTRY ("BAXTER'S LIGHT GUARD," "MONTEZUMA REGIMENT").

Organized at New York City and mustered in May 14, 1861. Left State for Washington, D. C., June 24, 1861. Attached to Davies' Brigade, Miles' Division, McDowell's Army of Northeast Virginia, to August, 1861. Franklin's Brigade, Division of the Potomac, to October, 1861. Newton's Brigade, Franklin's Division, Army of the Potomac, to March, 1862. 3rd Brigade, 1st Division, 1st Army Corps, Army of the Potomac, and Dept. of the Rappahannock, to May, 1862. 3rd Brigade, 1st Division, 6th Army Corps, Army of the Potomac, to February, 1863. Light Division, 6th Army Corps, to May, 1863. 2nd Brigade, 1st Division, 6th Army Corps, to June, 1863.

SERVICE.—Reconnoissance from Alexandria on Fairfax Road July 14, 1861. Advance on Manassas, Va., July 16-21. Battle of Bull Run July 21. Duty in the Defences of Washington, D. C., till March, 1862. Skirmish at Springfield Station October 3, 1861. Scout to Fairfax Court House December 24-25, 1861 (Co. "E"). Advance on Manassas, Va., March 10-15, 1862. McDowell's advance on Falmouth, Va., April 4-12. Ordered to the Peninsula, Va., April 22. Siege of Yorktown April 24-May 4, on transports. West Point May 7-8. Seven days before Richmond June 25-July 1. Gaines' Mill June 27. White Oak Swamp, Charles City Cross Roads, and Glendale June 30. Malvern Hill July 1. At Harrison's Landing till August 16. Movement to Fortress Monroe, thence to Centreville August 16-28. In works at Centreville August 28-31, and cover Pope's retreat to Fairfax Court House September 1. Maryland Campaign September 6-22. Crampton's Gap, South Mountain, September 14. Battle of Antietam, Md., September 16-17. Duty in Maryland till October 29. Movement to Falmouth, Va., October 29-November 19. Battle of Fredericksburg, Va., December 12-15. "Mud March" January 20-24, 1863. At Falmouth till April 27. Chancellorsville Campaign April 27-May 6. Operations about Franklin's Crossing April 29-May 2. Maryes Heights, Fredericksburg, May 3. Salem Heights May 3-4. Banks' Ford May 4. Mustered out June 4, 1863, expiration of term. Three years' men transferred to 121st Regiment New York Infantry.

Regiment lost during service 6 Officers and 62 Enlisted men killed and mortally wounded and 1 Officer and 29 Enlisted men by disease. Total 98.

31st REGIMENT VETERAN INFANTRY.

Failed to complete organization. Men enlisted transferred to 5th Regiment New York Veteran Infantry, October 14, 1863.

32nd REGIMENT INFANTRY ("1st CALIFORNIA REGIMENT").

Organized at Staten Island, N. Y., and mustered in May 31, 1861. Left State for Washington, D. C., June 29, 1861. Attached to Davies' Brigade, Miles' Division, McDowell's Army of Northeast Virginia, to August, 1861. Franklin's Brigade, Division of the Potomac, to October, 1861. Newton's Brigade, Franklin's Division, Army of the Potomac, to March, 1862. 3rd Brigade, 1st Division, 1st Army Corps, Army of the Potomac, and Dept. of the Rappahannock, to May, 1862. 3rd Brigade, 1st Division, 6th Army Corps, Army of the Potomac, to June, 1863.

SERVICE.—Reconnoissance from Alexandria on Fairfax Road July 14, 1861. Advance on Manassas, Va., July 16-21. Near Fairfax Court House July 17. Battle of Bull Run July 21. Duty in the Defences of Washington till March, 1862. Skirmish at Springfield Station October 3, 1861. Advance on Manassas, Va., March 10-15. McDowell's advance on Falmouth, Va., April 4-12. Ordered to the Peninsula, Va., April 22. Siege of Yorktown, Va., April 24-May 4, on transports. West Point May 7-8. Seven days before Richmond June 25-July 1. Gaines' Mill June 27. White Oak Swamp, Charles City Cross Roads and Glendale June 30. Malvern Hill July 1. At Harrison's Landing till August 16. Movement to Fortress Monroe, thence to Centreville August 16-28. In works at Centreville August 28-31, and cover Pope's retreat to Fairfax Court House September 1. Maryland Campaign September 6-22. Crampton's Gap, South Mountain, September 14. Battle of Antietam September 16-17. Duty in Maryland till October 29. Movement to Falmouth, Va., October 29-November 19. Battle of Fredericksburg, Va., December 12-15. "Mud March" January 20-24, 1863. At Falmouth till April 27. Chancellorsville Campaign April 27-May 6. Operations about Franklin's Crossing April 29-May 2. Maryes Heights, Fredericksburg, May 3. Salem Heights May 3-4. Banks' Ford May 4. Mustered out June 9, 1863, expiration of term. Three years men transferred to 121st Regiment New York Infantry.

Regiment lost during service 8 Officers and 37 Enlisted men killed and mortally wounded and 1 Officer and 53 Enlisted men by disease. Total 99.

33rd REGIMENT INFANTRY—"ONTARIO REGIMENT."

Organized at Elmira, N. Y., and mustered in July 3, 1861, to date May 22, 1861. Moved to Washington, D. C., July 8. Attached to W. F. Smith's Brigade, Division of the Potomac, to October, 1861. 2nd Brigade, W. F. Smith's Division, Army of the Potomac, to March, 1862. 3rd Brigade, 2nd Division, 4th Army Corps, Army of the Potomac, to May, 1862. 3rd Brigade, 2nd Division, 6th Army Corps, to June, 1863.

SERVICE.—Duty in the Defences of Washington, D. C., till March, 1862. Advance on Manassas, Va., March 10-15, 1862. Embarked for the Peninsula, Va., March 23. Near Lee's Mills April 5. Siege of Yorktown April 5-May 4. Lee's Mills near Burnt Chimneys April 16. Battle of Williamsburg May 5. Storming of Fort Magruder. Mechanicsville May 23-24. Seven days before Richmond June 25-July 1. Gaines' Mill, Garnett's Farm, June 27. Garnett's and Golding's Farms June 28. Savage Station June 29. White Oak Swamp and Glendale June 30. Malvern Hill July 1. At Harrison's Landing till August 16. Movement to Fortress Monroe, thence to Centreville August 16-28. In works at Centreville August 28-31, and cover Pope's retreat to Fairfax Court House September 1. Maryland Campaign September 6-22. Crampton's Pass, South Mountain, September 14. Battle of Antietam September 16-17. Duty in Maryland till October 29. Movement to Falmouth, Va., October 29-November 19. Battle of Fredericksburg, Va., December 12-15. "Mud March" January 20-24, 1863. At Falmouth till April 27. Chancellorsville Campaign April 27-May 6. Operations about Franklin's Crossing April 29-May 2. Maryes Heights, Fredericksburg, May 3. Salem Heights May 3-4. Banks' Ford May 4. Three years men transferred to 49th Regiment New York Infantry May 14. Mustered out June 2, 1863, expiration of term.

Regiment lost during service 3 Officers and 44 Enlisted men killed and mortally wounded and 105 Enlisted men by disease. Total 152.

34th REGIMENT INFANTRY.—("HERKIMER REGIMENT.")

Organized at Albany, N. Y., and mustered in June 15, 1861. Left State for Washington, D. C., July 3, 1861. Attached to Stone's Brigade, Division of the Potomac, to October, 1861. Gorman's 2nd Brigade, Stone's (Sedgwick's) Division, Army of the Potomac, to March, 1862.

1st Brigade, 2nd Division, 2nd Army Corps, Army of the Potomac, to June, 1863.

SERVICE.—Outpost duty on the Upper Potomac till March, 1862. Reneca Mills, Md., September 1 and 16, 1861. Operations on the Potomac October 21-24. Near Edwards Ferry October 22. Moved to Harper's Ferry February, 1862; thence to Charlestown and Berryville, Va., March 12-15. Moved to Fortress Monroe, Va., March 22-April 1. Siege of Yorktown April 5-May 4. Battle of Seven Pines, Fair Oaks, May 31-June 1. Seven days before Richmond June 25-July 1. Peach Orchard and Savage Station June 29. White Oak Swamp and Glendale June 30. Malvern Hill July 1. Duty at Harrison's Landing till August 16. Movement to Newport News, thence to Centreville August 16-29. Cover Pope's retreat from Bull Run August 31-September 1. Maryland Campaign September 6-22. Battle of Antietam September 16-17. Moved to Harper's Ferry September 22, and duty there till October 30. Movement to Falmouth, Va., October 30-November 20. Battle of Fredericksburg, Va., December 12-15. "Mud March" January 20-24, 1863. At Falmouth till April. Chancellorsville Campaign April 27-May 6. Operations at Franklin's Crossing April 29-May 2. Maryes Heights, Fredericksburg, May 3. Salem Heights May 3-4. Banks' Ford May 4. Three years men transferred to 82nd New York Infantry June 8, 1863. Mustered out June 30, 1863, expiration of term.

Regiment lost during service 3 Officers and 90 Enlisted men killed and mortally wounded and 1 Officer and 68 Enlisted men by disease. Total 162.

35th REGIMENT INFANTRY.—("JEFFERSON COUNTY REGIMENT.")

Organized at Elmira, N. Y., and mustered in June 11, 1861. Moved to Washington, D. C., attached to Hunter's Brigade, Division of the Potomac, to October, 1861. Wadsworth's Brigade, McDowell's Division, Army of the Potomac, to March, 1862. 2nd Brigade, King's 3rd Division, 1st Army Corps, Army of the Potomac, to April, 1862. 2nd Brigade, King's Division, Dept. of the Rappahannock, to June, 1862. 3rd Brigade, 1st Division, 3rd Corps, Pope's Army of Virginia, to September, 1862. 3rd Brigade, 1st Division, 1st Army Corps, Army of the Potomac, to January, 1863. Provost Marshal General Patrick's Command, Army of the Potomac, to June, 1863.

SERVICE.—Duty in the Defences of Washington, D. C., till March, 1862. Advance on Manassas, Va., March 10-15. At Upton's Hill till April 9. McDowell's advance on Falmouth, Va., April 9-19. Duty at Falmouth till May 25. McDowell's advance on Richmond May 25-29. Operations against Jackson June 1-21. Duty at Falmouth till July 24. Reconnoissance to Orange Court House July 24-27. Battle of Cedar Mountain August 9. Pope's Campaign in Northern Virginia August 16-September 2. Fords of the Rappahannock August 21-23. Battles of Gainesville August 28; Groveton August 29; Bull Run August 30. Maryland Campaign September 6-22. South Mountain September 14. Antietam September 16-17. Duty at Sharpsburg till October 30. Movement to Falmouth, Va., October 30-November 19. Battle of Fredericksburg, Va., December 12-15. "Mud March" January 20-24, 1863. Provost duty at Aquia Creek till June. Chancellorsville Campaign April 27-May 6. Mustered out June 5, 1863, expiration of term. Three years men transferred to 80th New York Infantry.

Regiment lost during service 1 Officer and 40 Enlisted men killed and mortally wounded and 53 Enlisted men by disease. Total 94.

36th REGIMENT INFANTRY.—("WASHINGTON VOLUNTEERS.")

Organized at New York City and mustered in June 17, 1861. Left State for Washington, D. C., July 12. Attached to Couch's Brigade, Division of the Potomac, to October, 1861. Couch's Brigade, Buell's Division, Army of the Potomac, to March, 1862. 1st Brigade, 1st Division, 4th Army Corps, Army of the Potomac, to September, 1862. 2nd Brigade, 3rd Division, 6th Army Corps, to June, 1863.

SERVICE.—Duty at Kalorma Heights and Camp Brightwood, Defences of Washington, D. C., till March, 1862. March to Prospect Hill, Va., March 11-15. Moved to the Peninsula, Va., March 28. Siege of Yorktown April 5-May 4. Battle of Williamsburg May 5. Reconnoissance to Bottom's Bridge May 20-23, and to White Oak Swamp May 25-28. Battle of Fair Oaks or Seven Pines May 31-June 1. Seven days before Richmond June 25-July 1. Battles of Oak Grove, near Seven Pines, June 25; Savage Station June 29; White Oak Swamp June 30; Malvern Hill July 1. At Harrison's Landing till August 16. Movement to Fortress Monroe, thence to Centreville August 16-29. Maryland Campaign September 6-22. Battle of Antietam September 16-17. Duty in Maryland till October 29. Movement to Falmouth, Va., October 29-November 19. Battle of Fredericksburg, Va., December 12-15. "Mud March" January 20-24, 1863. At Falmouth till April 27. Chancellorsville Campaign April 27-May 6. Operations about Franklin's Crossing April 29-May 2. Maryes Heights, Fredericksburg, May 3. Salem Heights May 3-4. Banks' Ford May 4. Deep Run Ravine June 5-13. Ordered home for muster out. Three years men transferred to 65th Regiment, New York Infantry. Duty in New York during draft riots July 13-15. Mustered out July 15, 1863, expiration of term.

Regiment lost during service 1 Officer and 36 Enlisted men killed and mortally wounded and 4 Officers and 26 Enlisted men by disease. Total 67.

37th REGIMENT INFANTRY—"IRISH RIFLES."

Organized at New York City and mustered in June 7, 1861. Left State for Washington, D. C., June 23. Attached to Hunter's Brigade, Division of the Potomac, August to October, 1861. Richardson's Brigade, Heintzelman's Division, Army of the Potomac, to March, 1862. 3rd Brigade, 3rd Division, 3rd Army Corps, Army of the Potomac, to July, 1862. 3rd Brigade, 1st Division, 3rd Army Corps, to June, 1863.

SERVICE.—Duty in the Defences of Washington, D. C., till March, 1862. (Cos. "H" and "I" detached as garrison at Fort Washington August, 1861, to March, 1862.) Reconnoissance to Pohick Church and Occoquan October 18, 1861, and November 11, 1861. Lee's House, Occoquan Bridge, January 29, 1862. Mason's Creek February 24. Moved to the Peninsula, Va., March 17. Siege of Yorktown April 5-May 4. Battle of Williamsburg May 5. Battle of Seven Pines or Fair Oaks May 31-June 1. Seven days before Richmond June 25-July 1. Oak Grove near Seven Pines June 25. Charles City Cross Roads and Glendale June 30. Malvern Hill July 1. At Harrison's Landing till August 16. Moved to Fortress Monroe, thence to Centreville August 16-27. Pope's Campaign in Northern Virginia August 28-September 2. Battles of Groveton August 29; Bull Run August 30; Chantilly September 1. Duty in the Defences of Washington till October. Movement to Falmouth October and November. Battle of Fredericksburg, Va., December 12-15. "Mud March" January 20-24, 1863. At Falmouth till April. Chancellorsville Campaign April 27-May 6. Operations at Franklin's Crossing April 29-May 1. Battle of Chancellorsville May 1-5. Mustered out June 22, 1863, expiration of term. Three years men transferred to 40th Regiment New York Infantry.

Regiment lost during service 5 Officers and 69 Enlisted men killed and mortally wounded and 1 Officer and 37 Enlisted men by disease. Total 112.

37th REGIMENT VETERAN INFANTRY.

Failed to complete organization. Men enlisted transferred to 5th Regiment New York Veteran Infantry October 14, 1863.

37th REGIMENT NATIONAL GUARD INFANTRY.

Organized for three months' service May 29, 1862. Left State for Middle Department May 29, and duty there till September. Mustered out September 2, 1862.

Again mustered in for 30 days' service June 18, 1863. Left State for Harrisburg, Pa., June 19. Attached to 4th Brigade, 1st Division, Dept. of the Susquehanna. Action at Sporting Hill June 30. Carlisle July 1. Mustered out July 22, 1863.

Again mustered in for 30 days' service May 6, 1864. Duty in New York Harbor. Mustered out June 6, 1864.

38th REGIMENT INFANTRY—"2nd REGIMENT SCOTT LIFE GUARD."

Organized at New York City and mustered in June 3, 1861. Left State for Washington, D. C., June 19. Attached to Willcox's Brigade, Heintzelman's Division, McDowell's Army of Northeast Virginia, to August, 1861. Howard's Brigade, Division of the Potomac, to October, 1861. Sedgwick's Brigade, Heintzelman's Division, Army of the Potomac, to March, 1862. 2nd Brigade, 3rd Division, 3rd Army Corps, Army of the Potomac, to July, 1862. 2nd Brigade, 1st Division, 3rd Army Corps, to June, 1863.

SERVICE.—Duty in the Defences of Washington, D. C., till July 16. Advance on Manassas, Va., July 16-21. Battle of Bull Run, Va., July 21. Duty in the Defences of Washington, D. C., till March, 1862. Advance on Manassas, Va., March 10-15, 1862. Ordered to the Peninsula, Va., March 17. Peninsula Campaign April to August. Siege of Yorktown April 5-May 4. Battle of Williamsburg May 5. Battle of Seven Pines or Fair Oaks May 31-June 1. Seven days before Richmond June 25-July 1. Battles of Oak Grove near Seven Pines June 25. White Oak Swamp and Glendale June 30. Malvern Hill July 1. At Harrison's Landing till August 16. Movement to Fortress Monroe, thence to Centreville August 16-26. Pope's Campaign in Northern Virginia August 27-September 2. Battles of Groveton August 29; Bull Run August 30; Chantilly September 1. Duty in the Defences of Washington, D. C., till October. Movement to Falmouth, Va., October and November. Battle of Fredericksburg, Va., December 12-15. "Mud March" January 20-24, 1863. At Falmouth till April. Chancellorsville Campaign April 27-May 6. Battle of Chancellorsville May 1-5. Three years men transferred to 40th Regiment New York Infantry June 3. Mustered out June 22, 1863, expiration of term.

Regiment lost during service 3 Officers and 72 Enlisted men killed and mortally wounded and 3 Officers and 39 Enlisted men by disease. Total 117.

38th REGIMENT VETERAN INFANTRY.

Failed to complete organization. Men enlisted transferred to 5th Regiment New York Veteran Infantry October 14, 1862.

39th REGIMENT INFANTRY—"GARIBALDI GUARD."

Organized at New York City and left State for Washington, D. C., May 28, 1861. Mustered in June 6 to date from May 28. Attached to Blenker's Brigade, Miles' Division, McDowell's Army of Northeast Virginia, to August, 1861. Blenker's Brigade, Division of the Potomac, to October, 1861. Blenker's Brigade, Hooker's Division, Army of the Potomac, to January, 1862. Stahl's 1st Brigade, Blenker's Division, Army of the Potomac, to March, 1862. 1st Brigade, Blenker's 2nd Division, 2nd Army Corps, Army of the Potomac, to April, 1862. 1st Brigade, Blenker's Division, Mountain Department, to June, 1862. 3rd Brigade, 1st Division, 1st Army Corps, Pope's Army of Virginia, to July, 1862. White's Brigade, Army of Virginia, at Winchester, Va., to September, 1862. Miles' Command, Harper's Ferry, W. Va., September, 1862. Camp Douglas, Chicago, Ill., to December, 1862. Casey's Division, Defences of Washington, D. C., to February, 1863. 3rd Brigade, Abercrombie's Division, 22nd Army Corps, Dept. of Washington, to June, 1863. 3rd Brigade, 3rd Division, 2nd Army Corps, Army of the Potomac, to March, 1864. 3rd Brigade, 1st Division, 2nd Army Corps, to June, 1864. Colsolidated Brigade, 1st Division, 2nd Army Corps, to November, 1864. 3rd Brigade, 1st Division, 2nd Army Corps, to July, 1865.

SERVICE.—Duty in the Defences of Washington, D. C., till July 16, 1861. Advance on Manassas, Va., July 16-21. Battle of Bull Run July 21. Duty in the Defences of Washington till April, 1862. Operations in the Shenandoah Valley May to July. Near Strasburg June 1. Strasburg and Woodstock June 2. Near Harrisonburg June 6. Battle of Cross Keys June 8. Near Middletown July 15. Duty at Winchester July to September. Solomon's Gap September 12. Defence of Harper's Ferry September 12-15. Maryland Heights September 12-13. Bolivar Heights September 14. Surrendered September 15. Paroled September 16, and sent to Annapolis, Md., thence to Camp Douglas, Chicago, Ill., and duty there till December. Exchanged November 22. Moved to Washington, D. C., November 22-25. Duty at Arlington Heights and Centreville, Va., Defences of Washington, till June, 1863. Ordered to join Army of the Potomac in the field and joined 2nd Army Corps June 25. Battle of Gettysburg July 1-4. Pursuit of Lee July 5-24. On line of the Rappahannock till October. Advance from the Rappahannock to the Rapidan September 13-17. Bristoe Campaign October 9-22. Auburn and Bristoe October 14. Mitchell's Ford October 15. Advance to line of the Rappahannock November 7-8. Mine Run Campaign November 26-December 2. Demonstration on the Rapidan February 6-7, 1864. Morton's Ford February 6-7. At Stevensburg, Va., till April, 1864. Campaign from the Rapidan to the James River May 3-June 15. Battles of the Wilderness May 5-7; Spottsylvania May 8-12; Po River May 10; Spottsylvania Court House May 12-21. Assault on the Salient or "Bloody Angle" May 12. North Anna River May 23-26. On line of the Pamunkey May 26-28. Totopotomoy May 28-31. Cold Harbor June 1-12. Before Petersburg June 16-18. Siege of Petersburg June 16, 1864, to April 2, 1865. Jerusalem Plank Road June 22-23, 1864. Demonstration on north side of the James July 27-29. Deep Bottom July 27-28. Demonstration north of the James August 13-20. Strawberry Plains, Deep Bottom, August 14-18. Ream's Station August 25. Boydton Plank Road, Hatcher's Run, October 27-28. Reconnoissance to Hatcher's Run December 9-10. Dabney's Mills, Hatcher's Run, February 5-7, 1865. Watkins' House March 25. Appomattox Campaign March 28-April 9. Hatcher's Run or Boydton and White Oak Roads March 30-31. Sutherland Station and fall of Petersburg April 2. Sailor's Creek April 6. High Bridge and Farmville April 7. Appomattox Court House April 9. Surrender of Lee and his army. At Burkesville till May 2. Moved to Washington, D. C., May 2-12. Grand Review May 23. Mustered out July 1, 1865. Veterans and Recruits transferred to 185th N. Y. Infantry.

Regiment lost during service 8 Officers and 107 Enlisted men killed and mortally wounded and 1 Officer and 158 Enlisted men by disease. Total 274.

40th REGIMENT INFANTRY—"MOZART REGIMENT," "CONSTITUTION GUARD."

Organized at Yonkers, N. Y., June 27, 1861. Left State for Washington, D. C., July 4, 1861. Duty near Alexandria till August 4. Attached to Howard's Brigade, Division of the Potomac, to October, 1861. Sedgwick's Brigade, Heintzelman's Division, Army of the Potomac, to March, 1862. 2nd Brigade, 3rd Division, 3rd Army Corps, Army of the Potomac, to July, 1862. 2nd Brigade, 1st Division, 3rd Army Corps, to May, 1863. 3rd Brigade, 1st Division, 3rd Army Corps, to March, 1864. 1st Brigade, 3rd Division, 2nd Army Corps, to June, 1865.

SERVICE.—Duty in the Defences of Washington, and on the Upper Potomac, till March, 1862. Operations on the Potomac October 21-24, 1861. Action at Ball's Bluff October 21. Advance on Manassas, Va., March 10-15, 1862. Ordered to the Peninsula, Va., March 17. Siege of Yorktown, Va., April 5-May 4. Battle of Williamsburg May 5. Battle of Seven Pines or Fair Oaks May 31-June 1. Seven days before Richmond June 25-July 1. Battles of Oak Grove near Seven Pines June 25; Jordan's Ford June 29; Savage Station June 29;

White Oak Swamp and Glendale June 30; Malvern Hill July 1; Turkey Bend July 3. At Harrison's Landing till August 16. Movement to Fortress Monroe, thence to Centreville August 16-26. Pope's Campaign in Northern Virginia August 26-September 2. Battles of Groveton August 29; Bull Run August 30; Chantilly September 1. Picket duty at Conrad's Ferry till October. Movement up the Potomac to Leesburg, thence to Falmouth, Va., October 11-November 19. Battle of Fredericksburg, Va., December 12-15. "Mud March" January 20-24, 1863. At Falmouth till April 27. Chancellorsville Campaign April 27-May 6. Battle of Chancellorsville May 1-5. Gettysburg (Pa.) Campaign June 11-July 24. Battle of Gettysburg, Pa., July 1-4. Pursuit of Lee July 5-24. Wapping Heights, Va., July 23. Duty on line of the Rappahannock till October. Bristoe Campaign October 9-22. Auburn and Bristoe October 13-14. Advance to line of the Rappahannock November 7-8. Kelly's Ford November 7. Mine Run Campaign November 26-December 2. Payne's Farm November 27. Mine Run November 28-30. Demonstration on the Rapidan February 6, 1864. Near Brandy Station till May. Campaign from the Rapidan to the James River May 3-June 15. Battles of the Wilderness May 5-7; Spottsylvania May 8-12; Laurel Hill May 8; Po River May 10; Spottsylvania Court House May 12-21. Assault on the Salient or "Bloody Angle" May 12. Harris Farm or Fredericksburg Road May 19. North Anna River May 23-26. On line of the Pamunkey May 26-28. Totopotomoy May 28-31. Cold Harbor June 1-12. Before Petersburg June 16-18. Siege of Petersburg June 16, 1864, to April 2, 1865. Jerusalem Plank Road June 21-23, 1864. Demonstration north of the James July 27-29. Deep Bottom July 27-28. Demonstration north of the James August 13-20. Strawberry Plains, Deep Bottom, August 14-18. Poplar Springs Church September 29-October 2. Boydton Plank Road, Hatcher's Run, October 27-28. Raid on Weldon Railroad December 7-12. Dabney's Mill, Hatcher's Run, February 5-7, 1865. Watkins' House March 25. Appomattox Campaign March 28-April 9. White Oak Road March 29-30. Crow's House March 31. Fall of Petersburg April 2. Sailor's Creek April 6. High Bridge and Farmville April 7. Appomattox Court House April 9. Surrender of Lee and his army. At Burkesville till May 2. March to Washington, D. C., May 2-15. Grand Review May 23. Mustered out June 27, 1865.

Regiment lost during service 10 Officers and 228 Enlisted men killed and mortally wounded and 2 Officers and 170 Enlisted men by disease. Total 410.

41st REGIMENT INFANTRY—"DE KALB REGIMENT," "2nd YAGER REGIMENT."

Organized at Yorkville, N. Y., and mustered in June 6, 1861. Left State for Washington, D. C., July 8. Attached to 2nd Brigade, Runyon's Reserve Division, McDowell's Army of Northeast Virginia, to August, 1861. W. T. Sherman's Brigade, Division of the Potomac, to September, 1861. Martindale's Brigade, Porter's Division, Army of the Potomac, to November, 1861. Unassigned, Blenker's Division, Army of the Potomac, to March, 1862. Unassigned, Blenker's 2nd Division, 2nd Army Corps, Army of the Potomac, to April, 1862. 1st Brigade, Blenker's Division, Dept. of the Mountains, to June, 1862. 1st Brigade, 1st Division, 1st Corps, Pope's Army of Virginia, to September, 1862. 1st Brigade, 1st Division, 11th Army Corps, Army of the Potomac, to August, 1863. 1st Brigade, Gordon's Division, Folly Island, S. C., 10th Corps, Dept. of the South, to April, 1864. Folly Island, S. C., Northern District, Dept. of the South, to August, 1864. 1st Brigade, Hardin's Division, 22nd Army Corps, Dept. of Washington, to September, 1864. 2nd Brigade, Kitching's Provisional Division, Army of the Shenandoah, to December, 1864. Ferrero's Division, Defences of Bermuda Hundred, Va., Army of the James, to August, 1865. Dept. of Virginia to December, 1865.

SERVICE.—Duty in the Defences of Washington, D. C., till April, 1862. Operations in the Shenandoah Valley May to August. Battle of Cross Keys June 8. Duty at Sperryville and Centreville till August. Pope's Campaign in Northern Virginia August 16-September 2. Fords of the Rappahannock August 20-23. Sulphur Springs August 24. Battles of Groveton August 29; Bull Run August 30. Duty in the Defences of Washington till December. Reconnoissance to Snicker's Ferry and Berryville November 28-30. March to Fredericksburg, Va., December 10-16. Duty at Falmouth and Brook's Station till April 27, 1863. "Mud March" January 20-24. Chancellorsville Campaign April 27-May 6. Battle of Chancellorsville May 1-5. Gettysburg (Pa.) Campaign June 11-August 1. Battle of Gettysburg, Pa., July 1-3. Ordered to Folly Island, S. C., August 1. Siege operations against Forts Wagner and Gregg, Morris Island, and against Fort Sumpter and Charleston, S. C., August 8-September 7. Operations against Charleston and duty on Folly Island, S. C., September, 1863, to August, 1864. Expedition to Johns and James Islands February 6-14, 1864. Action at Bugbee's Bridge February 9 and 11. Demonstrations on James Island May 21-22 and July 1-10. Ordered to Washington, D. C., August, 1864, and duty there till September 27. Ordered to Shenandoah Valley September 27, and duty there till November 22. Battle of Cedar Creek October 19. Moved to Washington, D. C., thence to Bermuda Hundred, Va., and duty in the defences at that point till March, 1865. Siege operations against Petersburg and Richmond, Va., December, 1864, to April, 1865. Fall of Petersburg April 2. Duty in the Dept. of Virginia till December. Mustered out December 9, 1865.

Regiment lost during service 1 Officer and 69 Enlisted men killed and mortally wounded and 4 Officers and 69 Enlisted men by disease. Total 143.

42nd REGIMENT INFANTRY—"TAMMANY REGIMENT," "JACKSON GUARD."

Organized at Great Neck and mustered in June 22, 1861. Left State for Washington, D. C., July 18. Attached to Stone's Brigade, Division of the Potomac, October, 1861. Gorman's Brigade, Stone's Division, Army of the Potomac, to January, 1862. Burns' Brigade, Sedgwick's Division, Army of the Potomac, to March, 1862. 3rd Brigade, 2nd Division, 2nd Army Corps, Army of the Potomac, to March, 1864. 1st Brigade, 2nd Division, 2nd Army Corps, to July, 1864.

SERVICE.—Duty in the Defences of Washington, D. C., till October, and on Upper Potomac to March, 1862. Operations on the Upper Potomac October 21-24, 1861. Action at Ball's Bluff October 21. Moved to Harper's Ferry, W. Va., thence to Charlestown and Berryville, Va., March 7-13, 1862. Movement toward Winchester and return to Bolivar Heights March 13-15. Moved to Fortress Monroe March 22-April 1. Siege of Yorktown April 5-May 4. Battle of Seven Pines or Fair Oaks May 31-June 1. Tunstall Station June 14. Seven days before Richmond June 25-July 1. Battles of Peach Orchard and Savage Station June 29; White Oak Swamp and Glendale June 30; Malvern Hill July 1. At Harrison's Landing till August 16. Movement to Alexandria August 16-28, thence march to Fairfax Court House August 28-31, and cover retreat of Pope's army to Washington August 31-September 2. Maryland Campaign September 6-22. Battle of Antietam September 16-17. Moved to Harper's Ferry, W. Va., September 22, and duty there till October 30. Reconnoissance to Charlestown October 16-17. Advance up Loudoun Valley and movement to Falmouth, Va., October 30-November 17. Battle of Fredericksburg, Va., December 12-15. "Mud March" January 20-24, 1863. At Falmouth till April. Chancellorsville Campaign April 27-May 6. Battle of Maryes Heights, Fredericksburg, May 3. Salem Heights May 3-4. Banks' Ford May 4. Gettysburg (Pa.) Campaign June 11-July 24. Battle of Gettysburg, Pa., July 1-4. Pursuit of Lee July 5-24. Duty on line of the Rappahannock till October. Advance from the Rappahannock to the Rapidan September 13-17. Bristoe Campaign October 9-22. Bristoe Station October 14. Advance to line of the Rappahannock November 7-8. Mine Run Campaign November 26-December 2. Demonstration on the Rapidan February 6-7, 1864. At Stevensburg till May. Campaign from the Rapidan to the James May 3-June 15. Battles of the Wilderness May 5-7; Laurel Hill May 8; Spottsylvania May 8-12; Po River May 10; Spottsylvania Court House May 12-21. Assault on the Salient or "Bloody Angle" May 12. North Anna River May 23-26. On line of the Pamunkey May 26-28. Totopotomoy May 28-31. Cold Harbor June 1-12. Before Petersburg June 16-18. Siege of Petersburg June 16 to July 13. Jerusalem Plank Road June 22-23. Mustered out July 13, 1865. Veterans and Recruits transferred to 82nd Regiment New York Infantry.

Regiment lost during service 11 Officers and 141 Enlisted men killed and mortally wounded and 1 Officer and 103 Enlisted men by disease. Total 256.

43rd REGIMENT INFANTRY—"ALBANY AND YATES' RIFLES."

Organized at Albany, N. Y., August and September, 1861. Left State for Washington, D. C., September 21, 1861. Attached to Hancock's Brigade, W. F. Smith's Division, Army of the Potomac, to March, 1862. 1st Brigade, 2nd Division, 4th Army Corps, Army of the Potomac, to May, 1862. 1st Brigade, 2nd Division, 6th Army Corps, to February, 1863. Light Division, 6th Army Corps, to May, 1863. 3rd Brigade, 2nd Division, 6th Army Corps, Army of the Potomac, to July, 1864, Army of the Shenandoah to December, 1864, and Army of the Potomac to June, 1865.

SERVICE.—Duty in the Defences of Washington, D. C., till March, 1862. Expedition to Vienna and Flint Hill February 22, 1862. Advance on Manassas, Va., March 10-15. Moved to Alexandria March 16, thence to Fortress Monroe, Va. Advance on Yorktown April 4-5. Siege of Yorktown April 5-May 4. Lee's Mills April 16. Reconnoissance toward Lee's Mills April 28. Battle of Williamsburg May 5. Duty at White House till May 18. Picket duty near Richmond till June. Seven days before Richmond June 25-July 1. Garnett's Farm June 27. Garnett's and Golding's Farms June 28. White Oak Swamp June 30. Malvern Hill July 1. At Harrison's Landing till August 16. Movement to Fortress Monroe, thence to Centreville August 16-28. In works at Centreville August 28-31, and cover Pope's retreat to Fairfax Court House September 1. Maryland Campaign September 6-22. Sugar Loaf Mountain September 10-11. Crampton's Gap, South Mountain, September 14. Battle of Antietam September 16-17. Duty at Hagerstown, Md., till October 30. Movement to Falmouth, Va., October 30-November 19. Battle of Fredericksburg, Va., December 12-15. "Mud March" January 20-24, 1863. At Falmouth till April. Chancellorsville Campaign April 27-May 6. Operations about Franklin's Crossing April 29-May 2. Battle of Maryes Heights, Fredericksburg, May 3. Salem Heights May 3-4. Banks' Ford May 4. Operation at Franklin's Crossing June 5-13. Battle of Gettysburg, Pa., July 2-4. Pursuit of Lee July 5-24. Duty on line of the Rappahannock till October. Bristoe Campaign October 9-22. Advance to line of the Rappahannock November 7-8. Rappahannock Station November 7. Mine Run Campaign November 26-December 2. Duty near Brandy Station till May, 1864. Campaign from the Rapidan to the James May 3-June 15. Battles of the Wilderness May 5-7; Spottsylvania May 8-12; Spottsylvania Court House May 12-21. Assault on the Salient or "Bloody Angle" May 12. North Anna River May 23-26. On line of the Pamunkey May 26-28. Totopotomoy May 28-31. Cold Harbor June 1-12. Before Petersburg June 17-18. Siege of Petersburg June 17 to July 6. Jerusalem Plank Road, Weldon Railroad, June 22-23. Moved to Washington, D. C., June 6-9. Repulse of Early's attack on Fort Stevens and Northern Defences of Washington July 11-12. Pursuit of Early July 14-22. Sheridan's Shenandoah Valley Campaign August 7-November 28. Gilbert's Ford, Opequan Creek, September 13. Battle of Winchester Sep-

tember 19. Fisher's Hill September 22. Battle of Cedar Creek October 19. Duty in the Shenandoah Valley till December. Moved to Petersburg December 13-16. Siege of Petersburg December 16, 1864, to April 2, 1865. Fort Fisher, Petersburg, March 25, 1865. Appomattox Campaign March 28-April 9. Assault on and fall of Petersburg April 2. Pursuit of Lee April 3-9. Sailor's Creek April 6. Appomattox Court House April 9. Surrender of Lee and his army. Moved to Danville, Va., April 23-27, and duty there till May 18. Moved to Richmond, thence to Washington, D. C., May 18-June 2. Corps Review June 8. Mustered out June 27, 1865.

Regiment lost during service 13 Officers and 110 Enlisted men killed and mortally wounded and 1 Officer and 120 Enlisted men by disease. Total 244.

44th REGIMENT INFANTRY—"PEOPLE'S ELLSWORTH REGIMENT."

Organized at Albany, N. Y., and mustered in August 30, 1861. Moved to Washington, D. C., October 21, 1861. Attached to Butterfield's Brigade, Fitz-John Porter's Division, Army of the Potomac, to March, 1862. Butterfield's 3rd Brigade, Porter's 1st Division, 3rd Army Corps, Army of the Potomac, to May, 1862. 3rd Brigade, 1st Division, 5th Army Corps, to October, 1864.

SERVICE.—Duty in the Defences of Washington, D. C., till March, 1862. Advance on Manassas, Va., March 10-15. Moved to the Peninsula, Va., March 22-24. Reconnoissance to Big Bethel March 30. Warwick Road April 5. Siege of Yorktown April 5-May 4. Reconnoissance up the Pamunkey May 10. New Bridge May 24. Battle of Hanover Court House May 27. Operations near Hanover Court House May 27-29. Seven days before Richmond June 25-July 1. Battles of Mechanicsville June 26. Gaines' Mill June 27. White Oak Swamp and Turkey Bend June 30. Malvern Hill July 1. At Harrison's Landing till August 16. Movement to Fortress Monroe, thence to Centreville August 16-28. Pope's Campaign in Northern Virginia August 28-September 2. Battle of Bull Run August 30. Maryland Campaign September 6-22. Battle of Antietam September 16-17. Shepherdstown September 19. At Sharpsburg, Md., till October 30. Movement to Falmouth, Va., October 30-November 19. Battle of Fredericksburg, Va., December 12-15. Expedition to Richards and Ellis Fords, Rappahannock River, December 29-30. "Mud March" January 20-24, 1863. At Falmouth till April 27. Chancellorsville Campaign April 27-May 6. Battle of Chancellorsville May 1-5. Aldie June 11. Middleburg and Upperville June 21. Battle of Gettysburg, Pa., July 1-4. Pursuit of Lee July 5-24. Duty at Warrenton, Beverly Ford and Culpeper till October. Bristoe Campaign October 9-22. Advance to line of the Rappahannock November 7-8. Rappahannock Station November 7. Mine Run Campaign November 26-December 2. At Beverly Ford till May, 1864. Campaign from the Rapidan to the James May 3-June 15. Battles of the Wilderness May 5-7; Laurel Hill May 8; Spottsylvania May 8-12; Spottsylvania Court House May 12-21. Assault on the Salient May 12. North Anna River May 23-26. Jericho Ford May 23. On line of the Pamunkey May 26-28. Totopotomoy May 28-31. Cold Harbor June 1-12. Bethesda Church June 1-3. Before Petersburg June 16-18. Siege of Petersburg June 16 to October 11, 1864. Six Mile House, Weldon Railroad, August 18-21. Poplar Springs Church, Peeble's Farm, September 29-October 2. Mustered out October 11, 1864. Recruits transferred to 140th and 146th Regiments New York Infantry.

Regiment lost during service 4 Officers and 178 Enlisted men killed and mortally wounded and 2 Officers and 145 Enlisted men by disease. Total 329.

45th REGIMENT INFANTRY—"5th GERMAN RIFLES."

Organized at New York City and mustered in September 9, 1861. Left State for Washington, D. C., October 9. Attached to Stahl's Brigade, Blenker's Division, Army of the Potomac, to March, 1862. Stahl's Brigade, Blenker's Division, 2nd Army Corps, Army of the Potomac, to April, 1862. Stahl's 1st Brigade, Blenker's Division, Dept. of the Mountains, to June, 1862. 1st Brigade, 1st Division, 1st Corps, Pope's Army of Virginia, to September, 1862. 1st Brigade, 1st Division, 11th Army Corps, Army of the Potomac, to June, 1863. 1st Brigade, 3rd Division, 11th Army Corps, Army of the Potomac, to October, 1863, and Army of the Cumberland, to April, 1864. 3rd Brigade, 1st Division, 20th Army Corps, Army of the Cumberland, to July, 1864. Unassigned, 4th Division, 20th Army Corps, to November, 1864. 2nd Brigade, 4th Division, 20th Army Corps, Dept. of the Cumberland, to March, 1865. 1st Brigade, 1st Division, District of Nashville, Tenn., Dept. of the Cumberland, to June, 1865.

SERVICE.—Duty in the Defences of Washington, D. C., till April, 1862. Annandale Church, Va., December 2, 1861. Operations in the Shenandoah Valley May to August, 1862. Battle of Cross Keys June 8. At Sperryville and Centreville till August. Outpost duty at Madison Court House July 28. Pope's Campaign in Northern Virginia August 16-September 2. Fords of the Rappahannock August 20-23. Battles of Groveton August 29; Bull Run August 30. Duty in the Defences of Washington, D. C., till December. Reconnoissance to Snicker's Ferry and Berryville November 28-30. March to Fredericksburg, Va., December 10-15. Duty at Falmouth and Brooks' Station till April, 1863. "Mud March" January 20-24. Chancellorsville Campaign April 27-May 6. Battle of Chancellorsville May 1-5. Gettysburg (Pa.) Campaign June 11-July 24. Battle of Gettysburg, Pa., July 1-3. Duty near Bristoe Station till September. Movement to Bridgeport, Ala., September 24-October 3. Reconnoissance from Bridgeport to Trenton October 20. March along Nashville & Chattanooga Railroad to Lookout Valley, Tenn., October 25-28. Reopening Tennessee River October 26-29. Battle of Wauhatchie, Tenn., October 28-29. Chattanooga-Ringgold Campaign November 23-27. Orchard Knob November 23. Tunnel Hill November 24-25. Mission Ridge November 25. March to relief of Knoxville November 28-December 17. Duty in Lookout Valley till May, 1864. Atlanta (Ga.) Campaign May 1-July 6. Demonstrations on Rocky Faced Ridge and Dalton May 5-13. Battle of Resaca May 14-15. Near Cassville May 19. Advance on Dallas May 22-25. Battle of New Hope Church May 25. Battles about Dallas, New Hope Church and Allatoona Hills May 26-June 4. Operations about Marietta and against Kenesaw Mountain June 10-July 2. Pine Mountain June 11-14. Lost Mountain June 15-17. Gilgal or Golgotha Church June 15. Muddy Creek June 17. Noyes Creek June 19. Kolb's Farm June 22. Assault on Kenesaw June 27. Ruff's Station, Smyrna Camp Ground, July 4. Ordered to Nashville, Tenn., July 6, and duty there till June, 1865. Battles of Nashville December 15-16, 1864. Consolidated with 58th Regiment New York Infantry June 30, 1865.

Regiment lost during service 5 Officers and 42 Enlisted men killed and mortally wounded and 1 Officer and 106 Enlisted men by disease. Total 154.

46th REGIMENT INFANTRY—"FREMONT RIFLE REGIMENT."

Organized at New York City and mustered in by Companies as follows: Company "A" July 29, Company "B" August 5, Company "C" August 14, Company "D" August 22, Company "E" August 27, Company "F" August 30, Company "G" September 3, Company "H" September 6, and Companies "I" and "K" September 16, 1861. Left State for Washington, D. C. September 16, 1861, thence moved to Annapolis, Md. Attached to Viele's 1st Brigade, Sherman's South Carolina Expeditionary Corps, October, 1861, to April, 1862. 2nd Brigade, 2nd Division, Dept. of the South, to July, 1862. 2nd Brigade, 1st Division, 9th Army Corps, Army of the Potomac, to April, 1863. 2nd Brigade, 1st Division, 9th Army Corps, Army of the Ohio, to June, 1863. 3rd Brigade, 2nd Division, 9th Army Corps, Army of the Tennessee, to August, 1863. 2nd Brigade, 1st Division, 9th Army Corps, Army of the Ohio, to April, 1864. 2nd Brigade, 1st Division, 9th Army Corps, Army of the Potomac, to May, 1864. 2nd Brigade, 4th Division, 5th Army Corps, to June 11, 1864. 2nd Brigade, 3rd Division, 9th Army Corps, to September, 1864. 2nd Brigade, 1st Division, 9th Army Corps, to July, 1865.

SERVICE.—Expedition to Port Royal, S. C., October 21-November 7, 1861. Capture of Forts Walker and Beauregard, Port Royal Harbor and Hilton Head, S. C., November 7. Duty at Hilton Head, S. C., till March, 1862. Occupation of Edisto Island, S. C., February 11. Wilmington and Whitmarsh Islands March 30-31. Bombardment and capture of Fort Pulaski, Ga., April 10-11. Expedition to James Island June 1-28. Action at James Island June 8. Battle of Secessionville June 16. Evacuation of James Island and movement to Hilton Head June 28-July 7. Moved to Newport News July 12-17, thence to Fredericksburg, Va., August 2-6. Operations on the Rapidan and Rappahannock Rivers August 13-27. Pope's Campaign in Northern Virginia August 16-September 2. Battle of Groveton August 29. Bull Run August 30. Chantilly September 1. Maryland Campaign September 6-22. Battles of South Mountain September 14; Antietam September 16-17. Duty in Maryland till October 11. March up the Potomac to Leesburg, thence to Falmouth, Va., October 11-November 18. Battle of Fredericksburg, Va., December 12-15. "Mud March" January 20-24, 1863. Moved to Newport News, Va., February 13, thence to Kentucky March 21-26. Duty at Paris, Nicholasville, Lancaster, Stanford and Somerset, Ky., till June. Movement through Kentucky to Cairo, Ill., June 4-10, thence to Vicksburg, Miss., June 10-14. Siege of Vicksburg June 14-July 4. Advance on Jackson, Miss., July 5-10. Siege of Jackson July 10-17. Destruction of Mississippi Central Railroad at Madison Station July 18-22. At Milldale till August 12. Moved to Covington, Ky., August 12-22. Burnside's Campaign in East Tennessee August 16-October 17. March over Cumberland Mountains into East Tennessee August 27-September 26. Action at Blue Springs October 10. At Lenoir till November 14. Campbell's Station November 16. Siege of Knoxville November 17-December 4. Pursuit of Longstreet December 5-24. Operations in East Tennessee till March, 1864. Moved to Annapolis, Md., March-April. Campaign from the Rapidan to the James May 3-June 15. Battles of the Wilderness May 5-7; Spottsylvania May 8-12; Spottsylvania Court House May 12-21. Assault on the Salient or "Bloody Angle" May 12. North Anna River May 23-26. Jericho Ford May 23. On line of the Pamunkey May 26-28. Totopotomoy May 28-31. Cold Harbor June 1-12. Bethesda Church June 1-3. Before Petersburg June 16-18. Siege of Petersburg June 16, 1864, to April 2, 1865. Mine Explosion, Petersburg, July 30, 1864. Weldon Railroad August 18-21. Poplar Springs Church September 29-October 2. Reconnoissance on Vaughan and Squirrel Level Road October 8. Boydton Plank Road, Hatcher's Run, October 27-28. Fort Stedman March 25, 1865. Appomattox Campaign March 28-April 9. Fall of Petersburg April 2. Occupation of Petersburg April 3. Pursuit of Lee April 3-7. Moved to Washington, D. C., April 21-27, and duty there till July. Grand Review May 23. Mustered out July 28, 1865.

Regiment lost during service 8 Officers and 96 Enlisted men killed and mortally wounded and 2 Officers and 89 Enlisted men by disease. Total 195.

47th REGIMENT INFANTRY—"WASHINGTON GRAYS."

Organized at New York and mustered in September 14, 1861. Moved to Washington, D. C., thence to Annapolis, Md., September, 1861. Attached to Viele's 1st Brigade, Sherman's South Carolina Expeditionary Corps, to April, 1862. 2nd Brigade, 2nd Division, Dept. of the South, to July, 1862. District of Hilton Head, S. C., 10th Corps, Dept. of the South, to April, 1863. Ossabaw Sound and Folly Island, S. C., to July, 1863. Folly Island, S. C., 10th Corps, to August, 1863. 5th Brigade, Morris Island, S. C., 10th Army Corps, to October, 1863. Unattached, Folly Island, S. C., to November,

1863. District of Hilton Head, S. C., to December, 1863. Barton's Brigade, District of Hilton Head, S. C., to February, 1864. Barton's Brigade, District of Florida, February, 1864. Barton's Brigade, Ames' Division, District of Florida, to April, 1864. 2nd Brigade, 2nd Division, 10th Army Corps, Army of the James, Dept. of Virginia and North Carolina, to May, 1864. 1st Brigade, 3rd Division, 18th Army Corps, to June, 1864. 2nd Brigade, 2nd Division, 10th Army Corps, to December, 1864. 2nd Brigade, 2nd Division, 24th Army Corps, to January, 1865. 2nd Brigade, 2nd Division, Terry's Provisional Corps, Dept. of North Carolina, to March, 1865. 2nd Brigade, 2nd Division, 10th Army Corps, Dept. of North Carolina, to July, 1865. Dept. of North Carolina to August, 1865.

SERVICE.—Expedition to Port Royal, S. C., October 21-November 7, 1861. Capture of Forts Wagner and Beauregard, Port Royal Harbor, S. C., November 7. Hilton Head, S. C., November 7-8. Port Royal Ferry, Coosaw River, January 1, 1862. Reconnoissance to Wright River February 6. Siege operations against Fort Pulaski Ga., February 11-April 11. Bombardment and capture of Fort Pulaski April 10-11. Expedition to James Island, S. C., June 1-28. Action on James Island June 10. Battle of Secessionville June 16. Evacuation of James Island and movement to Hilton Head, S. C., June 28-July 7. Hilton Head, S. C., till April, 1863. Duty at Ossabaw Island and Folly Island, S. C., till July. Siege operations against Forts Wagner and Gregg, Morris Island, S. C., July 18-September 7. Bombardment of Fort Sumpter and Charleston August 17-23. Operations against Charleston and duty on Folly Island, S. C., till December, and at Hilton Head, S. C., till February, 1864. Expedition to Jacksonville, Fla., February 5-7. Occupation of Jacksonville February 7. Expedition into Central Florida February 7-22. Battle of Olustee February 20. Occupation of Palatka March 10. Duty at Jacksonville till April. Moved to Gloucester Point, Va., April 22-28. Butler's operations on south side of the James and against Petersburg and Richmond May 4-28. Port Walthall Junction, Chester Station, May 7. Operations against Fort Darling May 12-14. Battle of Drury's Bluff May 14-16. Bermuda Hundred May 16-28. Moved to White House, thence to Cold Harbor May 28-June 1. Battles about Cold Harbor June 1-12. Before Petersburg June 15-18. Siege operations against Petersburg and Richmond June 16 to December 7, 1864. Demonstration on north side of the James August 13-20. Strawberry Plains, Deep Bottom, August 14-18. Chaffin's Farm, New Market Heights, September 28-30. Fair Oaks October 27-28. Expedition to Fort Fisher, N. C., December 7-25. 2nd Expedition to Fort Fisher, N. C., January 3-15, 1865. Assault and capture of Fort Fisher January 15. Cape Fear entrenchments February 11-12. Sugar Loaf Battery February 11. Fort Anderson February 18-20. Capture of Wilmington February 22. Campaign of the Carolinas March 1-April 26. Advance on Kinston and Goldsboro March 6-21. Advance on Raleigh April 9-14. Bennett's House April 26. Surrender of Johnston and his army. Duty at Raleigh and in the Dept. of North Carolina till August. Mustered out August 30, 1865.

Regiment lost during service 7 Officers and 70 Enlisted men killed and mortally wounded and 160 Enlisted men by disease. Total 237.

47th REGIMENT NATIONAL GUARD INFANTRY.

Mustered in for three months' United States service May 27, 1862. Left State for Baltimore, Md., May 30, and duty at Fort McHenry till September. Mustered out September 1, 1862.

Again mustered in for 30 days' United States service June 17, 1863. Left State for Washington, D. C., June 18, 1863. Duty in the defences of that city. Attached to 3rd Brigade, defences south of the Potomac, 22nd Army Corps, till July. Mustered out July 23, 1863.

48th REGIMENT INFANTRY—"CONTINENTAL GUARD," "PERRY'S SAINTS."

Organized at Brooklyn, N. Y., September 10, 1861. Left State for Annapolis, Md., September 17, 1861. Attached to Viele's 1st Brigade, Sherman's South Carolina Expeditionary Corps, to April, 1862. Fort Pulaski, Ga., 10th Army Corps, Dept. of the South, to May, 1863. St. Helena Island, S. C., 10th Army Corps, to June, 1863. 2nd Brigade, Folly Island, S. C., to July, 1863. 2nd Brigade, 2nd Division, Morris Island, S. C., to August, 1863. St. Augustine, Fla., to October, 1863. District of Hilton Head, S. C., to January, 1864. Barton's Brigade, District of Hilton Head, S. C., to February, 1864. Barton's Brigade, District of Florida, February, 1864. Barton's Brigade, Ames' Division, District of Florida, to April, 1864. 2nd Brigade, 2nd Division, 10th Army Corps, Army of the James, Dept. of Virginia and North Carolina, to May, 1864. 1st Brigade, 3rd Division, 18th Army Corps, to June, 1864. 2nd Brigade, 2nd Division, 10th Army Corps, to December, 1864. 2nd Brigade, 2nd Division, 24th Army Corps, to January, 1865. 2nd Brigade, 2nd Division, Terry's Provisional Corps, Dept. of North Carolina, to March, 1865. 2nd Brigade, 2nd Division, 10th Army Corps, Dept. of North Carolina, to July, 1865. Dept. of North Carolina to August, 1865.

SERVICE.—Expedition to Port Royal, S. C., October 21-November 7, 1861. Capture of Forts Walker and Beauregard, Port Royal Harbor, S. C., November 7. Hilton Head, S. C., November 7-8. Port Royal Ferry, Coosaw River, S. C., January 1, 1862. Siege operations against Fort Pulaski, Ga., January 28-April 11. Bombardment and capture of Fort Pulaski April 10-11. Garrison duty at Fort Pulaski till May, 1863. Tybee Island August 5, 1862. Skull Creek September 24. Reconnoissance on May and Savannah Rivers September 30-October 13. Kirk's Bluff, Coosawhatchie River, October 18. Expedition from Hilton Head to Pocotaligo October 21-23. Pocotaligo, Coosawhatchie, October 22. Expedition on U. S. Steamers Potomski and Darlington up Sapelo River, and destruction of salt works November 7. Moved to Hilton Head, S. C., thence to St. Helena Island, S. C., May, 1863. (Cos. "G" and "I" remained at Hilton Head.) Moved to Folly Island, S. C., June, 1863. Attack on Morris Island, S. C., July 10. Assaults on Fort Wagner, Morris Island, July 11 and 18. Siege of Forts Wagner and Gregg, Morris Island July 18 to August. At St. Augustine, Fla., August to October. (Cos. "G" and "I" at Fort Pulaski.) Duty at Hilton Head and Beaufort, S. C., October, 1863, to February, 1864. Expedition to Jacksonville, Fla., February 5-7. Expedition into Central Florida February 8-22. Battle of Olustee February 20. Occupation of Palatka March 10. Moved to Gloucester Point, Va., April 22-28. Butler's operations on south side of the James and against Petersburg and Richmond May 4-28. Port Walthall, Chester Station, May 7. Operations against Fort Darling May 12-16. Battle of Drury's Bluffs May 14-16. Bermuda Hundred May 16-28. Moved to White House, thence to Cold Harbor June 1-12. Battles about Cold Harbor June 1-12. Before Petersburg June 15-18. Siege operations against Petersburg and Richmond June 16 to December 7, 1864. Bermuda Hundred June 25. Mine Explosion, Petersburg, July 30. Demonstration on north side of the James August 13-20. Strawberry Plains, Deep Bottom, August 14-18. Bermuda Hundred August 24-25. Chaffin's Farm, New Market Heights, September 28-30. Fair Oaks October 27-28. Expedition to Fort Fisher, N. C., December 7-25. 2nd Expedition to Fort Fisher, N. C., January 3-15, 1865. Assault and capture of Fort Fisher January 15. Cape Fear Intrenchments February 11-12. Sugar Loaf Battery February 11. Fort Anderson February 18-20. Fort Strong February 21. Capture of Wilmington February 22. Campaign of the Carolinas March 1-April 26. Advance on Kinston and Goldsboro March 6-21. Advance on Raleigh April 9-14. Bennett's House April 26. Surrender of Johnston and his army. Duty at Raleigh and in the Dept. of North Carolina till August. Mustered out August 16, 1865.

Regiment lost during service 18 Officers and 218 Enlisted men killed and mortally wounded and 2 Officers and 131 Enlisted men by disease. Total 369.

49th REGIMENT INFANTRY.

Organized at Buffalo, N. Y., and mustered in September 18, 1861. Left State for Washington, D. C., September 20, 1861. Attached to Stevens' 3rd Brigade, W. F. Smith's Division, Army of the Potomac, to March, 1862. 3rd Brigade, 2nd Division, 4th Army Corps, Army of the Potomac, to May, 1862. 3rd Brigade, 2nd Division, 6th Army Corps, Army of the Potomac, and Army of the Shenandoah, to June, 1865.

SERVICE.—Camp near Lewinsville, Defences of Washington, D. C., till March, 1862. Skirmish at Lewinsville, Va., October 13, 1861. Advance on Manassas, Va., March 10-15, 1862. Ordered to the Peninsula, Va., March 22. Action at Lee's Mills April 5. Siege of Yorktown April 5-May 4. Lee's Mills April 16. Battle of Williamsburg May 5. Mechanicsville May 23-24. Seven days before Richmond June 25-July 1. Garnett's Farm June 27. Garnett's and Golding's Farm June 28. Savage Station June 29. White Oak Swamp June 30. Malvern Hill July 1. At Harrison's Landing till August 16. Movement to Fortress Monroe, thence to Centreville August 16-27. In works at Centreville August 28-31, and cover Pope's retreat to Fairfax Court House September 1. Maryland Campaign September 6-22. Battles of Crampton's Pass, South Mountain September 14. Antietam September 16-17. Duty in Maryland till October 29. Movement to Falmouth, Va., October 29-November 19. Battle of Fredericksburg, Va., December 12-15. "Mud March" January 20-24, 1863. At Falmouth till April 27. Chancellorsville Campaign April 27-May 6. Operations about Franklin's Crossing April 29-May 2. Battle of Maryes Heights, Fredericksburg, May 3. Salem Heights May 3-4. Banks' Ford May 4. Deep Run Ravine June 5-13. Battle of Gettysburg, Pa., July 2-4. Pursuit of Lee July 5-24. Fairfield, Pa., July 7. Duty on line of the Rappahannock till October. Bristoe Campaign October 9-22. Advance to line of the Rappahannock November 7-8. Rappahannock Station November 7. Mine Run Campaign November 26-December 2. Duty near Brandy Station till May, 1864. Campaign from the Rapidan to the James May 3-June 15. Battles of the Wilderness May 5-7; Spottsylvania May 8-12; Spottsylvania Court House May 12-21. Assault on the Salient or "Bloody Angle" May 12. North Anna River May 23-26. On line of the Pamunkey May 26-28. Totopotomoy May 28-31. Cold Harbor June 1-12. Before Petersburg June 17-18. Siege of Petersburg June 17-July 9. Jerusalem Plank Road June 22-23. Moved to Washington, D. C., July 9-11. Repulse of Early's attack on Fort Stevens and the Northern Defences of Washington July 11-12. Pursuit of Early July 14-22. Sheridan's Shenandoah Valley Campaign August 7-November 28. Near Charlestown August 21-22. Gilbert's Ford, Opequan Creek, September 13. Battle of Winchester September 19. Fisher's Hill September 22. Battle of Cedar Creek October 19. Duty in the Shenandoah Valley till December. Moved to Washington, thence to Petersburg December 13-16. Siege of Petersburg December 16, 1864, to April 2, 1865. Fort Fisher, Petersburg, March 25, 1865. Appomattox Campaign March 28-April 9. Assault on and fall of Petersburg April 2. Pursuit of Lee April 3-9. Sailor's Creek April 6. Appomattox Court House April 9. Surrender of Lee and his army. March to Danville, Va., April 23-27. Duty there till May 18. Moved to Richmond, thence to Washington May 18-June 2. Corps Review June 8. (Old members mustered out September 17, 1864.) Mustered out June 27, 1865.

Regiment lost during service 15 Officers and 126 Enlisted men killed and mortally wounded and 5 Officers and 174 Enlisted men by disease. Total 320.

50th REGIMENT INFANTRY.

Organized at Elmira, N. Y., September 18, 1861. Left State for Washington, D. C., September 20, 1861. Attached to 3rd Brigade, Porter's Division, Army of the Potomac, September 22-30. Duty at Hall's Hill, Va., and near Navy Yard, Washington, till October. Detailed as sappers, miners and pontooners, and designated 50th New York Engineers October 22, 1861. (See 50th Regiment N. Y. Engineers.)

50th REGIMENT NATIONAL GUARD INFANTRY.

Companies "A" and "B" mustered in for 3 months' service at Elmira, N. Y., August 27, 1864. Duty at Elmira, N. Y., as Companies "L" and "M," 58th Regiment New York National Guard Infantry, till December, 1864. Mustered out December 3, 1864.

51st REGIMENT INFANTRY—"SHEPARD RIFLES."

Organized at New York City July 27 to October 23, 1861. Left State for Annapolis, Md., October 29. Attached to Reno's 2nd Brigade, Burnside's North Carolina Expeditionary Corps, to April, 1862. 2nd Brigade, 2nd Division, Dept. of North Carolina, to July, 1862. 2nd Brigade, 2nd Division, 9th Army Corps, Army of the Potomac, to April, 1863, Army of the Ohio to June, 1863, Army of the Tennessee to August, 1863, and Army of the Ohio, to September, 1863. District of North Central Kentucky, 1st Division, 23rd Army Corps, Army of the Ohio, to February, 1864. 2nd Brigade, 2nd Division, 9th Army Corps, Army of the Potomac, to April, 1864. 1st Brigade, 2nd Division, 9th Army Corps, Army of the Potomac, to May 26, 1864. Engineers, 2nd Division, 9th Army Corps, to July 2, 1864. 1st Brigade, 2nd Division, 9th Army Corps, to July, 1865.

SERVICE.—Duty at Annapolis, Md., till January 6, 1862. Burnside's Expedition to Hatteras Inlet and Roanoke, Island, N. C., January 6-February 7, 1862. Battle of Roanoke Island February 8. Duty at Roanoke Island till March 11. Movement to New Berne, N. C., March 11-13. Battle of New Berne March 14. Expedition to Elizabeth City April 17-19. Duty at New Berne till July. Moved to Newport News, Va., July 6-9, thence to Fredericksburg August 2-4. March to relief of Pope, August 12-15. Pope's Campaign in Northern Virginia August 16-September 2. Kelly's Ford August 21. Sulphur Springs August 23-24. Plains of Manassas August 27-29. Battles of Groveton August 29; Bull Run August 30; Chantilly September 1. Maryland Campaign September 6-22. Battles of Frederick City September 12; South Mountain September 14; Antietam September 16-17. At Pleasant Valley till October 27. March to Falmouth, Va., October 27-November 17. Jefferson November 11. Sulphur Springs November 13. Warrenton November 15. Battle of Fredericksburg December 12-15. "Mud March" January 20-24, 1863. Moved to Newport News, Va., February 19, thence to Covington and Paris, Ky., March 26-April 1. Moved to Mt. Sterling, Ky., April 3, to Lancaster May 6-7, and to Crab Orchard May 23. Movement to Vicksburg, Miss., June 3-17. Siege of Vicksburg June 17-July 4. Advance on Jackson, Miss., July 5-10. Siege of Jackson July 10-17. Destruction of railroad at Madison Station July 19-22. At Milldale till August 6. Moved to Cincinnati, Ohio, August 6-20, thence to Nicholasville, Ky. Provost duty in District of Kentucky, Dept. of the Ohio, to February, 1864. Veterans on furlough March-April. Moved to Annapolis, Md., and rejoined corps. Campaign from the Rapidan to the James May 3-June 15. Battles of the Wilderness May 5-7; Spottsylvania May 8-12; Po River May 10; Ny River May 12; Spottsylvania Court House May 12-21. Assault on the Salient May 22. North Anna River May 23-26. On line of the Pamunkey May 26-28. Totopotomoy May 28-31. Cold Harbor June 1-12. Bethesda Church June 1-3. Before Petersburg June 16-18. Siege of Petersburg June 16, 1864, to April 2, 1865. Mine Explosion, Petersburg, July 30, 1864. Weldon Railroad August 18-21. Poplar Grove Church, Peeble's Farm September 29-October 2. Boydton Plank Road, Hatcher's Run, October 27-28. Fort Stedman, Petersburg, March

25, 1865. Appomattox Campaign March 28-April 9. Assault on and fall of Petersburg April 2. Pursuit of Lee to Farmville April 3-9. Moved to Petersburg, thence to City Point and Washington, D. C., April 20-28. Grand Review May 23. Duty at Washington, D. C., and Alexandria, Va., till July. Mustered out July 25, 1865.

Regiment lost during service 9 Officers and 193 Enlisted men killed and mortally wounded and 2 Officers and 174 Enlisted men by disease. Total 378.

52nd REGIMENT INFANTRY—"GERMAN RANGERS," "SIGEL RIFLES."

Organized at New York City October 11, 1861. Left State for Washington, D. C., November 11, 1861. Attached to French's 3rd Brigade, Sumner's Division, Army of the Potomac, to March, 1862. 3rd Brigade, Richardson's 1st Division, 2nd Army Corps, Army of the Potomac, to August, 1862. 1st Brigade, 1st Division, 2nd Army Corps, to September, 1862. 3rd Brigade, 1st Division, 2nd Army Corps, to June, 1864. Consolidated Brigade, 1st Division, 2nd Army Corps, to November, 1862. 3rd Brigade, 1st Division, 2nd Army Corps, to July, 1865.

SERVICE.—Duty in the Defences of Washington, D. C., till March, 1862. Advance on Manassas, Va., March 10-15. Moved to the Peninsula, Va., April 3. Siege of Yorktown April 5-May 4. Battle of Fair Oaks or Seven Pines May 31-June 1. Seven days before Richmond June 25-July 1. Battles of Gaines Mill June 27. Peach Orchard and Savage Station June 29. White Oak Swamp and Glendale June 30. Malvern Hill July 1. At Harrison's Landing till August 16. Movement to Fortress Monroe, thence to Alexandria and Centreville August 16-30. Cover Pope's retreat to Fairfax Court House September 1. Maryland Campaign September 6-22. Battles of Antietam Creek September 15-16. Antietam September 17. Duty at Harper's Ferry, W. Va., September 22-October 29. Reconnoissance to Charlestown October 16-17. Advance up Loudoun Valley and movement to Falmouth, Va., October 29-November 17. Battle of Fredericksburg December 12-15. "Mud March" January 20-24, 1863. At Falmouth, Va., till April 27. Chancellorsville Campaign April 27-May 6. Battle of Chancellorsville May 1-5. Gettysburg (Pa.) Campaign June 11-July 24. Battle of Gettysburg, Pa., July 1-3. Pursuit of Lee July 5-24. Duty on line of the Rappahannock till October. Advance from the Rappahannock to the Rapidan September 13-17. Bristoe Campaign October 9-22. Auburn and Bristoe October 14. Advance to line of the Rappahannock November 7-8. Mine Run Campaign November 26-December 2. At Stevensburg till May, 1864. Demonstration on the Rapidan February 6-7, 1864. Campaign from the Rapidan to the James May 3-June 15. Battles of the Wilderness May 5-7; Spottsylvania May 8-12; Po River May 10; Spottsylvania Court House May 12-21. Assault on the Salient or "Blood Angle" May 12. North Anna River May 23-26. On line of the Pamunkey May 26-28. Totopotomoy May 28-31. Cold Harbor June 1-12. Before Petersburg June 16-18. Siege of Petersburg June 16, 1864, to April 2, 1865. Jerusalem Plank Road, Weldon Railroad, June 22-23, 1864. Demonstration north of the James July 27-29. Deep Bottom July 27-28. Demonstration north of the James August 13-20. Strawberry Plains, Deep Bottom, August 14-18. Ream's Station August 25. Reconnoissance to Hatcher's Run December 9-10. Dabney's Mills, Hatcher's Run, February 5-7, 1865. Watkins' House March 25. Appomattox Campaign March 28-April 9. Hatcher's Run or Boydton Road March 31. White Oak Road March 31. Sutherland Station and fall of Petersburg April 2. Sailor's Creek April 6. High Bridge and Farmville April 7. Appomattox Court House April 9. Surrender of Lee and his army. At Burkesville till May 2. March to Washington, D. C., May 2-15. Grand Review May 23. Duty at Washington, D. C., till July. Mustered out July 25, 1865.

Regiment lost during service 14 Officers and 139 Enlisted men killed and mortally wounded and 197 Enlisted men by disease. Total 350.

52nd REGIMENT NATIONAL GUARD INFANTRY.

Organized for thirty days' service June 19, 1863. Left State for Harrisburg, Pa., June 22. Attached to 3rd Brigade, 1st Division, Dept. of the Susquehanna. Skirmish at Oyster Point, Pa., June 28. Mustered out July 25, 1863.

53rd REGIMENT INFANTRY.—("D'EPINEUIL'S ZOUAVES.")

Organized at New York City August 27 to November 15, 1861. Left State for Washington, D. C., November 18; thence moved to Annapolis, Md. Attached to Parke's 3rd Brigade, Burnside's North Carolina Expeditionary Corps.

SERVICE.—Duty at Annapolis, Md., till January 3, 1862. Burnside's Expedition to Hatteras Inlet and Roanoke Island, N. C., January 7-February 8. Vessel wrecked at Roanoke Island. A Detachment at battle of Roanoke Island, N. C., February 8. Duty at Fort Monroe, Va., Suffolk, Va., Annapolis, Md., and Washington, D. C., till March. Mustered out March 21, 1862, except Company "A," which was transferred to 17th New York Infantry as Company "G."

Regiment lost during service 1 Officer and 3 Enlisted men killed and mortally wounded and 7 Enlisted men by disease. Total 11.

53rd REGIMENT INFANTRY REORGANIZED.

Failed to complete organization. Men enlisted transferred to 132nd and 162nd Regiments New York Infantry September 10, 1862.

54th REGIMENT INFANTRY.

Organized at Hudson, N. Y., and mustered in September 5 to October 16, 1861. Left State for Washington, D. C., October 29, 1861. Attached to Provisional Brigade, Casey's Division, Army of the Potomac, to December, 1861. Steinwehr's Brigade, Blenker's Division, Army of the Potomac, to March, 1862. Steinwehr's 2nd Brigade, Blenker's 2nd Division, 2nd Army Corps, Army of the Potomac, to April, 1862. 2nd Brigade, Blenker's Division, Dept. of the Mountains, to June, 1862. 2nd Brigade, 3rd Division, 1st Corps, Pope's Army of Virginia, to September, 1862. 2nd Brigade, 3rd Division, 11th Army Corps, Army of the Potomac, to November, 1862. 1st Brigade, 1st Division, 11th Army Corps, to August, 1863. 1st Brigade, Gordon's Division, Folly Island, S. C., 10th Army Corps, Dept. of the South, to April, 1864. Folly Island, S. C., Northern District, Dept. of the South, to October, 1864. 1st Separate Brigade, Morris Island, S. C., Dept. of the South, to July, 1865. 3rd Sub-District, Dept. of the South, to August, 1865. 1st Brigade, Dept. of the South, to April, 1865.

SERVICE.—Duty in the Defences of Washington, D. C., till April, 1862. Movement to Winchester, Va., April 5-18. Operations in the Shenandoah Valley till June. Battle of Cross Keys June 8. At Sperryville July 7 to August 8. Battle of Cedar Mountain August 9. Pope's Campaign in Northern Virginia August 16-September 2. Fords of the Rappahannock August 20-23. Sulphur Springs August 26-27. Battles of Groveton August 29. Bull Run August 30. Duty in the Defences of Washington, D. C., till November. Movement to Centreville November 1-19. Waterloo Bridge November 7. Reconnoissance to Snicker's Ferry and Berryville November 28-30. Movement to Fredericksburg December 9-15. "Mud March" January 20-24, 1863. At Stafford Court House till April 27. Chancellorsville Campaign April 27-May 6. Battle of Chancellorsville May 1-5. Gettysburg (Pa.) Campaign June 11-July 24. Battle of Gettysburg, Pa., July 1-3. Ordered to Dept. of the South August 1. Siege of Forts Wagner and Gregg, Morris Island, and operations against Fort Sumpter and Charleston August 9-September 7. Operations against Charleston and duty on Folly and Morris Islands, S. C., till June, 1865. Expedition to John's and James Islands February 6-14, 1864. James Island February 6 and October 24, 1864. Santee River February 27, 1865. Duty in District of South Carolina, Dept. of the South, till April, 1866. Mustered out April 14, 1866.

Regiment lost during service 2 Officers and 38 Enlisted men killed and mortally wounded and 1 Officer and 101 Enlisted men by disease. Total 142.

54th REGIMENT, NATIONAL GUARD INFANTRY.

Organized at Rochester, N. Y., for 3 months' service July 24, 1864. On duty in the State of New York. Mustered out November 10, 1864.

55th REGIMENT INFANTRY ("GARDE DE LAFAYETTE").

Organized at New York City and mustered in August 28, 1861. Left State for Washington, D. C., August 31, 1861. Duty at Fort Gaines, Md., September and October, 1861. Attached to Peck's Brigade, Buell's Division, Army of the Potomac, to March, 1862. 2nd Brigade, 1st Division, 4th Army Corps, Army of the Potomac, to September, 1862. 3rd Brigade, 1st Division, 3rd Army Corps, to November, 1862. 2nd Brigade, 1st Division, 3rd Army Corps, to December, 1862.

SERVICE.—Duty in the Defences of Washington, D. C., till March, 1862. March to Prospect Hill, Va., March 11-15. Moved to the Peninsula, Virginia, March 28. Siege of Yorktown April 5-May 4. Battle of Williamsburg May 5. Operations about Bottom's Bridge May 20-23. Battle of Seven Pines (or Fair Oaks) May 31-June 1. Seven days before Richmond June 25-July 1. Malvern Hill July 1. At Harrison's Landing till August 16. Movement to Fortress Monroe, thence to Centreville August 16-29. Duty in the Defences of Washington till October. Movement to Falmouth, Va., October-November. Battle of Fredericksburg, Va., December 12-15. Consolidated with 38th New York Infantry as Companies "G," "H," "I" and "K" December 21, 1862.

Regiment lost during service 33 Enlisted men killed and mortally wounded and 29 Enlisted men by disease. Total 62.

55th REGIMENT NATIONAL GUARD INFANTRY.

Entered service for 30 days June 24, 1863. Attached to 2nd Separate Brigade, 8th Army Corps, Middle Department. Mustered out July 27, 1863.

56th REGIMENT INFANTRY ("10th LEGION").

Organized at Newburg, N. Y., and mustered in October 28, 1861. Left State for Washington, D. C., November 7, 1861. Attached to 1st Brigade, Casey's Division, Army of the Potomac, to March, 1862. 1st Brigade, 3rd Division, 4th Army Corps, Army of the Potomac, to June, 1862. 1st Brigade, 2nd Division, 4th Army Corps, to December, 1862. Naglee's Brigade, Dept. of North Carolina, to January, 1863. 2nd Brigade, 3rd Division, 18th Army Corps, Dept. of North Carolina, January, 1863. 2nd Brigade, 2nd Division, 18th Army Corps, Dept. of the South, to April, 1863. Stephenson's Brigade, Seabrook Island, S. C., 10th Army Corps, Dept. of the South, to July, 1863. 2nd Brigade, 1st Division, Morris Island, S. C., 10th Army Corps, July, 1863. Davis' Brigade, Folly Island, S. C., 10th Army Corps, to August, 1863. Saxton's Division, District of Beaufort, S. C., 10th Army Corps, to April, 1864. District of Beaufort, S. C., Dept. of the South, Northern District, Dept. of the South, to November, 1864. 1st Brigade, Coast Division, Dept. of the South, to January, 1865. 1st Separate Brigade, Morris Island, S. C., Dept. of the South, to March, 1865. 4th Separate Brigade, Dept. of the South, to July, 1865. 2nd Sub-District, District of Western South Carolina, to September, 1865.

SERVICE.—Duty in the Defences of Washington, D. C., till March, 1862. Advance on Manassas, Va., March 10-15. Moved to Newport News, Va., March 28. Siege of Yorktown April 5-May 4. Battle of Williamsburg May 5. Operations about Bottom's Bridge May 20-23. Battle of Seven Pines (or Fair Oaks) May 31-June 1. Seven days before Richmond June 25-July 1. Battle of Gaines Mill June 27. Bottom's Bridge June 28-29. White Oak Swamp June 30. Malvern Hill July 1. At Harrison's Landing till August 16. Moved to Fortress Monroe, Va., August 16-22, thence to Yorktown, Va. Duty there and at Gloucester Point till December 26. Action at Lee's Mills September 16. Reconnoissance to Gloucester and Matthews Counties December 11-15. Moved to Morehead City, N. C., December 26-January 1, 1863; thence to Port Royal, S. C., January 28-31. At St. Helena Island, S. C., till March 27, and at Seabrook Island till July 6. Expedition to James Island July 9-16. Grimball's Landing, Secessionville, July 16. Siege of Fort Wagner, Morris Island, S. C., and operations against Fort Sumpter and Charleston till August. Duty in District of Beaufort, S. C., till September, 1864. Expedition to James Island, S. C., June 30-July 10, 1864. James Island July 4. John's Island July 9. Duty on Morris and Folly Islands, S. C., till November. Hatch's Expedition up Broad River November 28-30. Battle of Honey Hill November 30. Demonstration on Charleston and Savannah Railroad December 6-9. Deveaux's Neck December 6. Coosawhatchie December 9. Ordered to Morris Island January 18, 1865, and duty there till March 25. Potter's Expedition to Camden, S. C., April 5-25. Dingle's Mills April 9. Statesburg April 15. Occupation of Camden April 17. Boykin's Mills April 18. Denkin's Mills and Beech Creek, near Statesburg, April 19. Duty in Northern and Western Districts of South Carolina till September. Mustered out October 17, 1865.

Regiment lost during service 1 Officer and 63 Enlisted men killed and mortally wounded and 3 Officers and 213 Enlisted men by disease. Total 280.

56th REGIMENT NATIONAL GUARD INFANTRY.

Mustered in for 30 days United States service June 18, 1863. Left State for Harrisburg, Pa., June 20. Attached to 3rd Brigade, 1st Division, Dept. of the Susquehanna. Mustered out July 24, 1863.

Mustered in for 100 days' service August 2, 1864. Duty at Elmira, N. Y., till November. Mustered out November 6, 1864.

57th REGIMENT INFANTRY ("NATIONAL GUARD RIFLES").

Organized at New York City August 12 to November 19, 1861. Left State for Washington, D. C., November 19, 1861. Attached to French's 3rd Brigade, Sumner's Division, Army of the Potomac, to March, 1862. 3rd Brigade, 1st Division, 2nd Army Corps, Army of the Potomac, to June, 1864. Consolidated Brigade, 1st Division, 2nd Army Corps, to November, 1864.

SERVICE.—Duty in the Defences of Washington, D. C., till March, 1862. Advance on Manassas, Va., March 10. Reconnoissance to Cedar Run March 14-16. Ordered to the Peninsula, Va. Siege of Yorktown, Va., April 5-May 4. Battle of Seven Pines or Fair Oaks May 31-June 1. Seven days before Richmond June 25-July 1. Battles of Gaines Mill June 27; Peach Orchard and Savage Station June 29; White Oak Swamp and Glendale June 30; Malvern Hill July 1. At Harrison's Landing till August 16. Movement to Fortress Monroe, thence to Alexandria and Centreville August 16-30. Cover Pope's retreat to Washington August 31-September 1. Maryland Campaign September 6-22. Sharpsburg, Md., September 15. Battle of Antietam, Md., September 16-17. Duty at Harper's Ferry, W. Va., September 22-October 29. Reconnoissance to Charlestown October 16-17. Advance up Loudoun Valley and movement to Falmouth, Va., October 29-November 17. Battle of Fredericksburg, Va., December 12-15. "Mud March" January 20-24, 1863. At Falmouth till April 27. Chancellorsville Campaign April 27-May 6. Battle of Chancellorsville May 1-5. Gettysburg (Pa.) Campaign June 11-July 24. Battle of Gettysburg, Pa., July 1-4. Duty on line of the Rappahannock till October. Advance from the Rappahannock to the Rapidan September 13-17. Bristoe Campaign October 9-22. Auburn and Bristoe October 14. Advance to line of the Rappahannock November 7-8. Mine Run Campaign November 26-December 2. Demonstration on the Rapidan February 6-7, 1864. At and near Stevensburg, Va., till May. Campaign from the Rapidan to the James May 3-June 15. Battles of the Wilderness May 5-7; Spottsylvania May 8-12; Spottsylvania Court House May 12-21. Assault on the Salient or "Bloody Angle" May 12. North Anna River May 23-26. On line of the Pamunkey May 26-28. Totopotomoy May 28-31. Cold Harbor June 1-12. Before Petersburg June 16-18. Siege of Petersburg June 16 to December 6, 1864. Jerusalem Plank Road June 22-23. Demonstration north of the James July 27-29. Deep Bottom July 27-28. Demonstration north of the James August 13-20. Strawberry Plains, Deep Bottom, August 14-18. Ream's Station August 25. Mustered out by Companies as follows: Company "C" July 14, Company "F" August 11, Company "D" August 14, Company "I" August 13, Company "K" September 3, Company "A" September 10, Company "B" September 23 and Company "H" October 15, 1864. Veterans and Recruits transferred to 61st Regiment New York Infantry December 6, 1864.

Regiment lost during service 8 Officers and 95 Enlisted men killed and mortally wounded and 1 Officer and 90 Enlisted men by disease. Total 194.

58th REGIMENT INFANTRY.—("POLISH LEGION.")

Organized at New York City August to November, 1861. Left State for Washington, D. C., November 7, 1861. Attached to Bohlen's Brigade, Blenker's Division, Army of the Potomac, to March, 1862. 2nd Brigade, Blenker's 2nd Division, 2nd Army Corps, Army of the Potomac, to April, 1862. 2nd Brigade, Blenker's Division, Dept. of the Mountains, to June, 1862. 2nd Brigade, 3rd Division, 1st Army Corps, Pope's Army of Virginia, to September, 1862. 2nd Brigade, 3rd Division, 11th Army Corps, Army of the Potomac, to October, 1863, and Army of the Cumberland to April, 1864. Unattached, 4th Division, 20th Army Corps, Dept. of the Cumberland, to July, 1864. 3rd Brigade, Defences of Nashville & Chattanooga Railroad, Dept. of the Cumberland, to February, 1865. Stevenson, Ala., District of North Alabama, Dept. of the Cumberland, to July, 1865. District of Nashville, Tenn., Dept. of the Cumberland, to October, 1865.

SERVICE.—Duty in the Defences of Washington, D. C., till April, 1862. Advance on Manassas, Va., March 10. Movement to Winchester, Va., April 5-18. Operations in the Shenandoah Valley till June. Battle of Cross Keys June 8. Duty at Sperryville July 7 to August 8. Pope's Campaign in Northern Virginia August 16-September 2. Fords of the Rappahannock August 20-23. Battles of Groveton August 29; Bull Run August 30. Duty in the Defences of Washington, D. C., till November 1. Movement to Centreville, Va., November 1-18. March to Fredericksburg, Va., December 9-16. "Mud March" January 20-24, 1863. At Stafford Court House, Va., till April 27. Chancellorsville Campaign April 27-May 6. Battle of Chancellorsville May 1-5. Gettysburg (Pa.) Campaign June 11-July 24. Battle of Gettysburg, Pa., July 1-3. Duty along Orange & Alexandria Railroad till September. Movement to Bridgeport, Ala., September 24-October 3. Operations in Lookout Valley, Tenn., October 19-27. Reopening Tennessee River October 26-29. Battle of Wauhatchie, Tenn., October 28-29. Chattanooga-Ringgold Campaign November 23-27. Orchard Knob November 23. Tunnel Hill November 24-25. Mission Ridge November 25. March to relief of Knoxville November 28-December 17. Garrison duty at Bridgeport, Ala., and guard duty along Nashville & Chattanooga Railroad till February, 1865. Garrison and guard duty at Stevenson, Ala., and Nashville, Tenn., till October, 1865. Mustered out October 1, 1865.

Regiment lost during service 4 Officers and 28 Enlisted men killed and mortally wounded and 3 Officers and 60 Enlisted men by disease. Total 95.

58th REGIMENT NATIONAL GUARD INFANTRY.

Mustered in for 100 days' United States service August 27, 1864. Duty at Elmira, N. Y., till December. Mustered out December 3, 1864.

59th REGIMENT INFANTRY.

Organized at New York City July to November, 1861. Left State for Washington, D. C., November 23, 1861. Attached to Wadsworth's Command, Defences of Washington, to January, 1862. 2nd Brigade, Casey's Division, Army of the Potomac, to March, 1862. Military District of Washington to May, 1862. Sturgis' Brigade, Military District of Washington, to July, 1862. 3rd Brigade, 2nd Division, 2nd Army Corps, Army of the Potomac, to March, 1864. 1st Brigade, 2nd Division, 2nd Army Corps, to June, 1865.

SERVICE.—Duty in the Defences of Washington, D. C., till May, 1862. At Fort Pennsylvania till June. Ordered to the Peninsula, Va., and join Army of the Potomac at Harrison's Landing, Va., and duty there till August 16. Movement from Harrison's Landing to Fortress Monroe, thence to Alexandria and Centreville August 16-28; thence to Fairfax Court House August 28-31. Cover Pope's retreat to Washington August 31-September 2. Maryland Campaign September 6-22. Battles of South Mountain September 14. Antietam September 16-17. Moved to Harper's Ferry, W. Va., September 22, and duty there till October 29. Reconnoissance to Charlestown October 16-17. Advance up Loudoun Valley and movement to Falmouth, Va., October 30-November 19. Battle of Fredericksburg, Va., December 12-15. "Mud March" January 20-24, 1863. At Falmouth till April 27. Chancellorsville Campaign April 27-May 6. Operations at Franklin's Crossing April 29-May 2. Battle of Maryes Heights, Fredericksburg, May 3. Salem Heights May 3-4. Banks' Ford May 4. Gettysburg (Pa.) Campaign June 11-July 24. Battle of Gettysburg, Pa., July 1-4. Pursuit of Lee July 5-24. Duty on line of the Rappahannock till October. Advance from the Rappahannock to the Rapidan September 13-17. Bristoe Campaign October 9-22. Auburn and Bristoe October 14. Blackburn's Ford October 15. Advance to line of the Rappahannock November 7-8. Mine Run Campaign November 26-December 2. At Stevensburg till May, 1864. Campaign from the Rapidan to the James May 3-June 15. Battles of the Wilderness May 5-7; Laurel Hill May 8; Spottsylvania May 8-12; Po River May 10; Spottsylvania Court House May 12-21. Assault on the Salient or "Blood Angle" May 12. North Anna River May 23-26. On line of the Pamunkey May 26-28. Totopotomoy May 28-31. Cold Harbor June 1-12. Before Petersburg June 16-18. Siege of Petersburg June 16, 1864, to April 2, 1865. Jerusalem Plank Road June 22-23, 1864. Demonstration north of the James July 27-29. Deep Bottom July 27-28. Demonstration north of the James August 13-20. Strawberry Plains, Deep Bottom, August 14-18. Ream's Station August 25. Boydton Plank Road, Hatcher's Run, October 27-28. Dabney's Mills, Hatcher's Run, February 5-7, 1865. Watkins' House March 25. Appomattox Campaign March 28-April 9. On line of Gravelly and Hatcher's Run March 29. Boydton and White Oak Road March 30-31. Crow's House March 31. Fall of Petersburg April 2. Sailor's Creek April 6. High Bridge and Farmville April 7. Appomattox Court House April 9. Surrender of Lee and his army. At Burkesville till May 2. March to Washington, D. C., May 2-16. Grand Review May 23. Mustered out June 30, 1865.

Regiment lost during service 14 Officers and 129 Enlisted men killed and mortally wounded and 127 Enlisted men by disease. Total 270.

60th REGIMENT INFANTRY.—("ST. LAWRENCE REGIMENT.")

Organized at Ogdensburg, N. Y., and mustered in October 30, 1861. Left State for Baltimore, Md., November 4, 1861. Attached to Dix's Division to March, 1862. Railroad Brigade, Army of the Potomac, to June, 1862. 2nd Brigade, Sigel's Division, Dept. of the Shenandoah, to June 26, 1862. 2nd Brigade, 2nd Division, 2nd Corps, Pope's Army of Virginia, to August, 1862. 3rd Brigade, 2nd Division, 2nd Corps, Army of Virginia, to September, 1862. 3rd Brigade, 2nd Division, 12th Army Corps, Army of the Potomac, to October, 1862. 2nd Brigade, 2nd Division, 12th Army Corps, to May, 1863. 3rd Brigade, 2nd Division, 12th Army Corps, Army of the Potomac, to October, 1863, and Army of the Cumberland to April, 1864. 3rd Brigade, 2nd Division. 20th Army Corps, Army of the Cumberland, to July, 1865.

SERVICE.—Duty at Baltimore, Md., and between there and Washington, D. C.; also at Relay House, Md., and Harper's Ferry, W. Va., till June, 1862. Defence of Harper's Ferry May 28-30. Operations in the Shenandoah Valley till August. Pope's Campaign in Northern Virginia August 16-September 2. Sulphur Springs August 24. Battle of Groveton August 29. Bull Run August 30. Maryland Campaign September 6-22. Battle of Antietam, Md., September 16-17. Duty at Bolivar Heights till December. Reconnoissance to Rippon, W. Va., November 9. Expedition to Winchester December 2-6. March to Fredericksburg, Va., December 9-16. Duty at Fairfax till January 20, 1863. "Mud March" January 20-24. Chancellorsville Campaign April 27-May 6. Battle of Chancellorsville May 1-5. Gettysburg (Pa.) Campaign June 11-July 24. Battle of Gettysburg, Pa., July 1-3. Pursuit of Lee to Manassas Gap, Va., July 5-24. Duty on line of the Rappahannock till September 24. Movement to Bridgeport, Ala., September 24-October 3. Duty in Lookout Valley till November. Reopening Tennessee River October 26-29. Chattanooga-Ringgold Campaign November 23-27. Battles of Lookout Mountain November 23-24. Mission Ridge November 25. Ringgold Gap, Taylor's Ridge, November 27. Duty at Bridgeport, Ala., till May, 1864. Scout from Stevenson to Caperton's Ferry April 11 (Detachment). Veterans on furlough December, 1863-January, 1864. Atlanta (Ga.) Campaign May 1-September 8. Operations about Rocky Faced Ridge, Tunnel Hill and Buzzard's Roost May 8-11. Battle of Resaca May 14-15. Near Cassville May 19. New Hope Church May 25. Battles about Dallas, New Hope Church and Allatoona Hills May 26-June 5. Operations about Marietta and against Kenesaw Mountain June 10-July 2. Pine Mountain June 11-14. Ackworth June 12. Lost Mountain June 15-17. Gilgal or Golgotha Church June 15. Muddy Creek June 17. Noyes Creek June 19. Kolb's Farm June 22. Assault on Kenesaw June 27. Ruff's Station, Smyrna Camp Ground, July 4. Chattahoochie River July 6-17. Peach Tree Creek July 19-20. Siege of Atlanta July 22-August 25. Operations at Chattahoochie River Bridge August 26-September 2. Occupation of Atlanta September 2 to November 15. Expedition from Atlanta to Tuckum's Cross Roads October 26-29. Near Atlanta November 9. March to the sea November 15-December 10. Near Davisboro November 28. Siege of Savannah December 10-21. Campaign of the Carolinas January to April, 1865. North Edisto River, S. C., February 12-13. Battle of Bentonville, N. C., March 19-21. Occupation of Goldsboro March 24. Advance on Raleigh April 9-13. Occupation of Raleigh April 14. Bennett's House April 26. Surrender of Johnston and his army. March to Washington, D. C., via Richmond, Va., April 29-May 20. Grand Review May 24. Mustered out July 17, 1865.

Regiment lost during service 3 Officers and 64 Enlisted men killed and mortally wounded and 5 Officers and 96 Enlisted men by disease. Total 168.

61st REGIMENT INFANTRY.—("ASTOR REGIMENT." "1st REGIMENT CLINTON GUARD.")

Organized at New York City October 25, 1861. Left State for Washington, D. C., November 9, 1861. Attached to Howard's Brigade, Sumner's Division, Army of the Potomac, to March, 1862. Howard's 1st Brigade, Richardson's 1st Division, 2nd Army Corps, Army of the Potomac, to July, 1862. 1st Brigade, 1st Division, 2nd Army Corps, to July, 1865.

SERVICE.—Duty at Bladensburg, Defences of Washington, D. C., till November 27, 1861. Expedition to Lower Maryland November 3-11. At Camp California, near Alexandria, Va., till March 10, 1862. Advance on Manassas, Va., March 10-15. Reconnoissance to Gainesville March 20. Operations on Orange & Alexandria Railroad March 28-31. Ordered to the Peninsula, Va. Siege of Yorktown April 16-May 4. Battle of Seven Pines or Fair Oaks May 31-June 1. Seven days before Richmond June 25-July 1. Battles of Peach Orchard, Allen's Farm and Savage Station June 29; White Oak Swamp and Glendale June 30; Malvern Hill July 1. At Harrison's Landing till August 16. Movement to Fortress Monroe, thence to Alexandria and Centreville August 16-30. Cover Pope's retreat to Washington August 31-September 2. Maryland Campaign September 6-22. Battle of Antietam September-16-17. Duty at Harper's Ferry, W. Va., September 22 to October 29. Reconnoissance to Charlestown October 16-17. Advance up Loudoun Valley and movement to Falmouth October 29-November 17. Battle of Fredericksburg, Va., December 12-15. Duty at Falmouth till April, 1863. "Mud March" January 20-24. Chancellorsville Campaign April 27-May 6. Battle of Chancellorsville May 1-5. Gettysburg (Pa.) Campaign June 11-July 24. Battle of Gettysburg, Pa., July 1-4. Pursuit of Lee to Manassas, Va., July 5-24. Duty on line of the Rappahannock till October. Advance from the Rappahannock to the Rapidan September 13-17. Bristoe Campaign October 9-22. Auburn and Bristoe October 14. Advance to line of the Rappahannock November 7-8. Mine Run Campaign November 26-December 2. Duty at Stevensburg till May, 1864. Demonstration on the Rapidan February 6-7. Campaign from the Rapidan to the James May 3-June 15. Battles of the Wilderness May 5-7; Corbin's Bridge May 8; Spottsylvania May 8-12; Po River May 10; Spottsylvania Court House May 12-21. Assault on the Salient or "Bloody Angle" May 12. North Anna River May 23-26. On line of the Pamunkey May 26-28. Totopotomoy May 28-31. Cold Harbor June 1-12. Before Petersburg June 16-18. Siege of Petersburg June 16, 1864, to April 2, 1865. Jerusalem Plank Road June 22-23, 1864. Demonstration on north side of the James July 27-29. Deep Bottom July 27-29. Demonstration north of the James August 13-20. Strawberry Plains, Deep Bottom, August 14-18. Ream's Station August 25. Reconnoissance to Hatcher's Run December 9-10. Hatcher's Run December 9. Dabney's Mills, Hatcher's Run, February 5-7, 1865. Watkins' House March 25. Appomattox Campaign March 28-April 9. On line of Hatcher's and Gravelly Runs March 29-30. Hatcher's Run or Boydton Road March 31. White Oak Road March 31. Sutherland Station and Fall of Petersburg April 2. Sailor's Creek April 6. High Bridge and Farmville April 7. Appomattox Court House April 9. Surrender of Lee and his army. At Burkesville till May 2. March to Washington, D. C., May 2-12. Grand Review May 23. Mustered out July 14, 1865.

Regiment lost during service 16 Officers and 177 Enlisted men killed and mortally wounded and 2 Officers and 121 Enlisted men by disease. Total 316.

62nd REGIMENT INFANTRY.—("ANDERSON ZOUAVES.")

Organized at New York City and mustered in June 30, 1861. Left State for Washington, D. C., August 21, 1861. Attached to Defences of Washington, D. C., to October, 1861. Pack's Brigade, Buell's Division, Army of the Potomac, to March, 1862. 3rd Brigade, 1st Division, 4th Army Corps, Army of the Potomac, to July, 1862. 2nd Brigade, 1st Division, 4th Army Corps, to September, 1862. 2nd Brigade, 3rd Division, 6th Army Corps, to October, 1862. 3rd Brigade, 3rd Division, 6th Army Corps, to January, 1864. Wheaton's Brigade, Dept. of West Virginia, to March, 1864. 1st Brigade, 2nd Division, 6th Army Corps, Army of the Potomac, and Army of the Shenandoah to July, 1865. Fort Schuyler, N. Y., to August, 1865.

SERVICE.—Duty in the Defences of Washington, D. C., till March, 1862. March to Prospect Hill, Va., March 11-15. Ordered to the Peninsula, Virginia, March 25. Siege of Yorktown, Va., April 5-May 4. Battle of Williamsburg May 5. Operations about Bottom's Bridge May 20-23. Battle of Seven Pines or Fair Oaks May 31-June 1. Seven days before Richmond June 25-July 1. Battle of Malvern Hill July 1. At Harrison's Landing till August 16. Movement to Alexandria August 16-September 1. Maryland Campaign September 6-22. Battle of Antietam, Md., September 16-17. At Downsville, Md., September 23 to October 20. Movement to Stafford Court House, Va., October 20-November 19, and to Belle Plains December 5. Battle of Fredericksburg, Va., December 12-15. "Mud March" January 20-24, 1863. At Falmouth till April 27, 1863. Chancellorsville Campaign April 27-May 6. Operations about Franklin's Crossing April 29-May 2. Battle of Maryes Heights, Fredericksburg, May 3. Salem Heights May 3-4. Banks' Ford May 4. Franklin's Crossing June 5-7. Battle of Gettysburg, Pa., July 2-4. Pursuit of Lee July 5-24. Funkstown, Md., July 10-13. Duty on line of the Rappahannock till October. Bristoe Campaign October 9-22. Advance to line of the Rappahannock November 7-8. Rappahannock Station November 7. Mine Run Campaign November 26-December 2. Duty at Brandy Station and vicinity till May, 1864. Campaign from the Rapidan to the James May 3-June 15. Battles of the Wilderness May 5-7. Spottsylvania May 8-12. Spottsylvania Court House May 12-21. Assault on the Salient or "Bloody Angle" May 12. North Anna River May 23-26. On line of the Pamunkey May 26-28. Totopotomoy May 28-31. Cold Harbor June 1-12. Before Petersburg June 17-18. Siege of Petersburg June 17-July 9. Jerusalem Plank Road June 22-23. Moved to Washington, D. C., July 9-11. Repulse of Early's attack on Fort Stevens and the Northern defences of Washington July 11-12. Pursuit of Early July 14-21. Sheridan's Shenandoah Valley Campaign August 7-November 28. Gilbert's Ford, Opequan Creek, September 13. Battle of Winchester September 19. Strasburg September 21. Fisher's Hill September 22. Battle of Cedar Creek October 19. Duty in the Shenandoah Valley till December. Moved to Petersburg, Va., December 9-12. Siege of Petersburg December 12, 1864, to April 2, 1865. Fort Fisher, Petersburg, March 25, 1865. Appomattox Campaign March 28-April 9. Assault on and fall of Petersburg April 2. Pursuit of Lee April 3-9. Sailor's Creek April 6. Appomattox Court House April 9. Surrender of Lee and his army. March to Danville, Va., April 23-27, and duty there till May 24. March to Richmond, Va., thence to Washington, D. C., May 24-June 3. Corps Review June 8. Duty in the Defences of Washington, D. C., till July, and Fort Schuyler, N. Y., till August 30. Mustered out August 30, 1865.

Regiment lost during service 3 Officers and 85 Enlisted men killed and mortally wounded and 2 Officers and 82 Enlisted men by disease. Total 172.

63rd REGIMENT INFANTRY ("INDEPENDENT IRISH REGT.," "3rd REGT. IRISH BRIGADE").

Organized at New York City August 7 to November 4, 1861. Left State for Washington, D. C., November 28, 1861. Attached to Meagher's Brigade, Sumner's Division, Army of the Potomac, to March, 1862. 2nd Brigade, 1st Division, 2nd Army Corps, Army of the Potomac, to June, 1864. Consolidated Brigade, 1st Division, 2nd Army Corps, to November, 1864. 2nd Brigade, 1st Division, 2nd Army Corps, to June, 1865.

SERVICE.—Duty in the Defences of Washington, D. C., November 30, 1861, to March 10, 1862. Advance on Manassas, Va., March 10-15. Ordered to the Virginia Peninsula. Siege of Yorktown, Va., April 16-May 4. Battle of Seven Pines or Fair Oaks May 31-June 1. Fair Oaks June 24. Seven days before Richmond June 25-July 1. Battles of Gaines' Mill June 27. About Fair Oaks June 28-29. Peach Orchard and Savage Station June 29. White Oak Swamp Bridge and Glendale June 30. Malvern Hill July 1. At Harrison's Landing till August 16. Moved to Fortress Monroe, thence to Alexandria and Centreville August 16-30. Cover retreat of Pope's Army to Washington, D. C., August 31-September 2. Maryland Campaign September 6-22. Battle of Antietam September 16-17. Duty at Harper's Ferry, W. Va., September 22-October 29. Reconnoissance to Charlestown October 16-17. Advance up Loudoun Valley and movement to Falmouth, Va., October 29-November 17. Battle of Fredericksburg, Va., December 12-15. At Falmouth till April 27, 1863. "Mud March" January 20-24. Chancellorsville Campaign April 27-May 6. Battle of Chancellorsville May 1-5. Gettysburg (Pa.) Campaign June 11-July 24. Battle of Gettysburg, Pa., July 1-4. Duty on line of the Rappahannock till October. Advance from the Rappahannock to the Rapidan September 13-17. Bristoe Campaign October 9-22. Auburn and Bristoe October 14. Advance to line of the Rappahannock November 7-8. Mine Run Campaign November 26-December 2. Duty at and near Stevensburg, Va., till May, 1864. Demonstration on the Rapidan February 6-7. Campaign from the Rapidan to the James May 3-June 15. Battles of the Wilderness May 5-7. Spottsylvania May 8-12. Po River May 10. Spottsylvania Court House May 12-21. Assault on the Salient or "Bloody Angle" May 12. North Anna River May 23-26. On line of the Pamunkey May 26-28. Totopotomoy May 28-31. Cold Harbor June 1-12. Before Petersburg June 16-18. Siege of Petersburg June 16, 1864, to April 2, 1865. Jerusalem Plank Road June 22-23, 1864. Demonstration north of the James July 27-29. Deep Bottom July 27-28. Demonstration north of the James August 13-20. Strawberry Plains, Deep Bottom, August 14-18. Ream's Station August 25. Reconnoissance to Hatcher's Run December 9-10. Dabney's Mills, Hatcher's Run, February 5-7, 1865. Watkins' House March 25. Appomattox Campaign March 28-April 9. Hatcher's Run or Boydton Road March 29-31. White Oak Road March 31. Sutherland Station and fall of Petersburg April 2. Sailor's Creek April 6. High Bridge, Farmville, April 7. Appomattox Court House April 9. Surrender of Lee and his army. Moved to Washington, D. C., May 2-12. Grand Review May 23. Mustered out June 30, 1865.

Regiment lost during service 15 Officers and 141 Enlisted men killed and mortally wounded and 1 Officer and 92 Enlisted men by disease. Total 249.

64th REGIMENT INFANTRY ("CATTARAUGAS REGIMENT").

Organized at Elmira, N. Y., September 10 to December 10, 1861. Left State for Washington, D. C., December 10, 1861. Attached to Casey's Provisional Division, Army of the Potomac, to January, 1862. Howard's Brigade, Sumner's Division, Army of the Potomac, to March, 1862. 1st Brigade, 1st Division, 2nd Army Corps, Army of the Potomac, to June, 1862. 3rd Brigade, 1st Division, 2nd Army Corps, to August, 1862. 1st Brigade, 1st Division, 2nd Army Corps, to April, 1863. 4th Brigade, 1st Division, 2nd Army Corps, to July, 1865.

SERVICE.—Duty in the Defences of Washington, D. C., till March, 1865. Advance on Manassas, Va., March 10-15. Ordered to the Peninsula, Virginia, March. Siege of Yorktown April 16-May 4. Battle of Fair Oaks or Seven Pines May 31-June 1. Seven days before Richmond June 25-July 1. Battles of Gaines' Mill June 27. Peach Orchard and Savage Station June 29. White Oak Swamp Bridge and Glendale June 30. Malvern Hill July 1. At Harrison's Landing till August 16. Moved to Fort Monroe, thence to Alexandria and Centreville August 16-30. Cover retreat of Pope's army to Washington, D. C., August 31-September 2. Maryland Campaign September 6-22. Battle of Antietam September 16-17. At Harper's Ferry, W. Va., September 22 to October 29. Reconnoissance to Charlestown October 16-17. Advance up Loudoun Valley and movement to Falmouth, Va., October 29-November 17. Battle of Fredericksburg, Va., December 12-15. Duty at Falmouth till April 27, 1863. "Mud March" January

20-24. Chancellorsville Campaign April 27-May 6. Battle of Chancellorsville May 1-5. Gettysburg (Pa.) Campaign June 11-July 24. Battle of Gettysburg, Pa., July 1-4. Pursuit of Lee July 5-24. Duty on line of the Rappahannock till October. Advance from the Rappahannock to the Rapidan September 13-17. Bristoe Campaign October 9-22. Auburn and Bristoe October 14. Advance to line of the Rappahannock November 7-8. Mine Run Campaign November 26-December 2. At and near Stevensburg, Va., till May, 1864. Demonstration on the Rapidan February 6-7. Campaign from the Rapidan to the James May 3-June 15. Battles of the Wilderness May 5-7. Spottsylvania May 8-12. Po River May 10. Spottsylvania Court House May 12-21. Assault on the Salient, or "Bloody Angle," May 12. North Anna River May 23-26. On line of the Pamunkey May 26-28. Totopotomoy May 28-31. Cold Harbor June 1-12. Before Petersburg June 16-18. Siege of Petersburg June 16, 1864, to April 2, 1865. Jerusalem Plank Road June 22-23, 1864. Demonstration north of the James July 27-29. Deep Bottom July 27-28. Demonstration north of the James August 13-20. Strawberry Plains, Deep Bottom, August 14-18. Ream's Station August 25. Reconnoissance to Hatcher's Run December 9-10. Dabney's Mills, Hatcher's Run, February 5-7, 1865. Watkins' House March 25. Appomattox Campaign March 28-April 9. Hatcher's Run or Boydton Road March 29-31. White Oak Road March 31. Sutherland Station and fall of Petersburg April 2. Sailor's Creek April 6. High Bridge and Farmville April 7. Appomattox Court House April 9. Surrender of Lee and his army. Moved to Washington, D. C., May 2-12. Grand Review May 23. Mustered out July 14, 1865.

Regiment lost during service 13 Officers and 160 Enlisted men killed and mortally wounded and 5 Officers and 114 Enlisted men by disease. Total 292.

65th REGIMENT INFANTRY ("1st UNITED STATES CHASSEURS").

Organized at Willett's Point, N. Y., and left State for Washington, D. C., August 27, 1861. Attached to Defences of Washington to October, 1861. Graham's Brigade, Buell's Division, Army of the Potomac, to March, 1862. 2nd Brigade, 1st Division, 4th Army Corps, Army of the Potomac, to July, 1862. 3rd Brigade, 1st Division, 4th Army Corps, to September, 1862. 2nd Brigade, 3rd Division, 6th Army Corps, to October, 1862. 1st Brigade, 3rd Division, 6th Army Corps, to April, 1864. 4th Brigade, 1st Division, 6th Army Corps, to June, 1864. 2nd Brigade, 1st Division, 6th Army Corps, Army of the Potomac, and Army of the Shenandoah, to July, 1865.

SERVICE.—Duty in the Defences of Washington, D. C., till March, 1862. Reconnoissance to Lewinsville October 10-11, 1861. March to Prospect Hill, Va., March 10-15, 1862. Ordered to the Peninsula March 25. Siege of Yorktown April 5-May 4. Battle of Williamsburg May 5. Chickahominy River May 21-22. Battle of Seven Pines or Fair Oaks June 31-July 1. Seven days before Richmond June 25-July 1. Malvern Hill July 1. Duty at Harrison's Landing till August 16. Movement to Alexandria August 16-September 1. Maryland Campaign September 6-22. Battle of Antietam, Md., September 16-17. Duty in Maryland till October 20. Movement to Stafford Court House, Va., October 20-November 18, and to Belle Plains December 5. Battle of Fredericksburg, Va., December 12-15. At Falmouth till April 27. "Mud March" January 20-24, 1863. Chancellorsville Campaign April 27-May 6. Operations about Franklin's Crossing April 29-May 2. Battle of Maryes Heights, Fredericksburg, May 3. Salem Heights May 3-4. Banks' Ford May 4. Battle of Gettysburg, Pa., July 2-4. Pursuit of Lee to Manassas Gap, Va., July 5-24. Duty on line of the Rappahannock till October. Bristoe Campaign October 9-22. Advance to line of the Rappahannock November 7-8. Rappahannock Station November 7. Mine Run Campaign November 26-December 2. Duty at Brandy Station till January, 1864, and at Johnson's Island, Lake Erie, Ohio, till March.

Campaign from the Rapidan to the James May 3-June 15. Battles of the Wilderness May 5-7. Spottsylvania May 8-12. Spottsylvania Court House May 12-21. "Bloody Angle" May 12. North Anna River May 23-26. On line of the Pamunkey May 26-28. Totopotomoy May 28-31. Cold Harbor June 1-12. Before Petersburg June 17-18. Siege of Petersburg June 17-July 9. Jerusalem Plank Road, Hatcher's Run, June 22-23. Moved to Washington, D. C., July 9-11. Repulse of Early's attack on Fort Stevens and the Northern defences of Washington July 11-12. Sheridan's Shenandoah Valley Campaign August 6-November 28. Battle of Opequan, Winchester, September 19. Fisher's Hill September 22. Battle of Cedar Creek October 19. Duty in the Shenandoah Valley till December. Moved to Petersburg, Va., December 9-12. Siege of Petersburg December 12, 1864, to April 2, 1865. Dabney's Mills, Hatcher's Run, February 5-7, 1865. Appomattox Campaign March 28-April 9. Assault on and fall of Petersburg April 2. Pursuit of Lee April 3-9. Sailor's Creek April 6. Appomattox Court House April 9. Surrender of Lee and his army. At Farmville and Burkesville till April 23. March to Danville April 23-27, and duty there till May 24. March to Richmond, Va., thence to Washington, D. C., May 24-June 3. Corps Review June 8. Mustered out July 17, 1865.

Regiment lost during service 5 Officers and 112 Enlisted men killed and mortally wounded and 1 Officer and 88 Enlisted men by disease. Total 206.

65th REGIMENT NATIONAL GUARD INFANTRY.

Left State for Harrisburg, Pa., June 19, 1863. Duty at Mt. Union, Pa. Mustered out July 30, 1863.

66th REGIMENT INFANTRY ("GOVERNOR'S GUARD").

Organized at New York City and mustered in November 4, 1861. Left State for Washington, D. C., November 16, 1861. Attached to Graham's Brigade, Buell's Division, Army of the Potomac, to January, 1862. French's Brigade, Sumner's Division, Army of the Potomac, to March, 1862. 3rd Brigade, 1st Division, 2nd Army Corps, to March, 1864. 4th Brigade, 1st Division, 2nd Army Corps, to May, 1865. Fort Richardson, N. Y., to August, 1865.

SERVICE.—Duty in the Defences of Washington, D. C., till March, 1862. Advance on Manassas, Va., March 10. Ordered to the Virginia Peninsula, March, 1862. Siege of Yorktown April 16-May 4. Battle of Seven Pines or Fair Oaks May 31-June 1. Seven days before Richmond June 25-July 1. Battles of Gaines' Mill June 27. Peach Orchard and Savage Station June 29. White Oak Swamp and Glendale June 30. Malvern Hill July 1. At Harrison's Landing till August 16. Movement to Fortress Monroe, thence to Alexandria and Centreville August 16-30. Cover retreat of Pope's army to Washington, D. C., August 31-September 1. Battle of Antietam, Md., September 16-17. Duty at Harper's Ferry, W. Va., September 22 to October 29. Reconnoissance to Charlestown October 16-17. Movement up Loudoun Valley and to Falmouth, Va., October 29-November 19. Battle of Fredericksburg, Va., December 12-15. Duty at Falmouth, Va., till April 27, 1863. "Mud March" January 20-24. Chancellorsville Campaign April 27-May 6. Battle of Chancellorsville May 1-5. Gettysburg (Pa.) Campaign June 11-July 24. Battle of Gettysburg, Pa., July 1-4. Pursuit of Lee July 5-24. Duty on line of the Rappahannock till October. Advance from the Rappahannock to the Rapidan September 13-17. Bristoe Campaign October 9-22. Auburn and Bristoe October 14. Advance to line of the Rappahannock November 7-8. Mine Run Campaign November 26-December 2. Duty at and near Stevensburg, Va., till May, 1864. Demonstration on the Rapidan February 6-7. Campaign from the Rapidan to the James May 3-June 15. Battles of the Wilderness May 5-7. Spottsylvania May 8-12. Po River May 10. Spottsylvania Court House May 12-21. Assault on the Salient or "Bloody Angle" May 12. North Anna River May 23-26. On line of the

Pamunkey May 26-28. Totopotomoy May 28-31. Cold Harbor June 1-12. Before Petersburg June 16-18. Siege of Petersburg June 16, 1864, to April 2, 1865. Jerusalem Plank Road, Weldon Railroad, June 22-23, 1864. Demonstration on the north side of the James July 27-29. Deep Bottom July 27-28. Demonstration on north side of the James August 13-20. Strawberry Plains, Deep Bottom, August 14-18. Ream's Station August 25. Reconnoissance to Hatcher's Run December 9-10. Dabney's Mills, Hatcher's Run, February 5-7, 1865. Watkins' House March 25. Appomattox Campaign March 28-April 9. Boydton and White Oak Roads March 29-31. Sutherland Station and fall of Petersburg April 2. Sailor's Creek April 6. High Bridge and Farmville April 7. Appomattox Court House April 9. Surrender of Lee and his army. Moved to Washington, D. C., May 2-12. Grand Review May 23. Moved to New York and duty at Fort Richmond, New York harbor, till August. Mustered out August 30, 1865.

Regiment lost during service 9 Officers and 88 Enlisted men killed and mortally wounded and 4 Officers and 120 Enlisted men by disease. Total 221.

67th REGIMENT INFANTRY ("1st LONG ISLAND REGIMENT").

Organized at Brooklyn, N. Y., June 24, 1861. Left State for Washington, D. C., August 21, 1861. Attached to Graham's Brigade, Division of the Potomac, to October, 1861. Graham's Brigade, Buell's Division, Army of the Potomac, to March, 1862. 2nd Brigade, 1st Division, 4th Army Corps, Army of the Potomac, to July, 1862. 3rd Brigade, 1st Division, 4th Army Corps, to September, 1862. 2nd Brigade, 3rd Division, 6th Army Corps, to October, 1862. 1st Brigade, 3rd Division, 6th Army Corps, to April, 1863. 4th Brigade, 1st Division, 6th Army Corps, to July, 1864. 2nd Brigade, 1st Division, 6th Army Corps, Army of the Shenandoah, and Army of the Potomac, to September, 1864.

SERVICE.—Duty in the Defences of Washington, D. C., till March, 1862. March to Prospect Hill, Va., March 11-15. Ordered to the Peninsula, Va., March 25. Siege of Yorktown, Va., April 5-May 4. Battle of Williamsburg May 5. Battle of Seven Pines or Fair Oaks May 31-June 1. Seven days before Richmond June 25-July 1. Malvern Hill July 1. At Harrison's Landing till August 16. Movement to Alexandria August 16-September 1. Maryland Campaign September 6-22. Battle of Antietam September 16-17. Duty in Maryland till October 20. Movement to Stafford Court House, Va., October 20-November 19, and to Belle Plains December 5. Battle of Fredericksburg, Va., December 12-15. "Mud March" January 20-24, 1863. Chancellorsville Campaign April 27-May 6. Operations about Franklin's Crossing April 29-May 2. Battle of Maryes Heights, Fredericksburg, May 3. Salem Heights May 3-4. Banks' Ford May 4. Battle of Gettysburg, Pa., July 2-4. Pursuit of Lee July 5-24. Duty on line of the Rappahannock till October. Bristoe Campaign October 9-22. Advance to line of the Rappahannock November 7-8. Rappahannock Station November 7. Mine Run Campaign November 26-December 2. Duty at Johnson's Island, Lake Erie, Ohio, January to March, 1864. Campaign from the Rapidan to the James May 3-June 15. Battles of the Wilderness May 5-7; Spottsylvania May 8-12; Spottsylvania Court House May 12-21. Assault on the Salient or "Bloody Angle" May 12. North Anna River May 23-26. On line of the Pamunkey May 26-28. Totopotomoy May 28-31. Cold Harbor June 1-12. Before Petersburg June 17-18. Siege of Petersburg June 17 to July 9. (Non-Veterans mustered out July 4, 1864.) Moved to Washington, D. C., July 9-11. Repulse of Early's attack on Fort Stevens and the Northern Defences of Washington July 11-12. Sheridan's Shenandoah Valley Campaign August 7-September 1. Battalion consolidated with 65th Regiment New York Infantry September 1, 1864.

Regiment lost during service 5 Officers and 96 Enlisted men killed and mortally wounded and 2 Officers and 75 Enlisted men by disease. Total 178.

67th REGIMENT NATIONAL GUARD INFANTRY.

Organized for thirty days' United States service June 25, 1863. Left State for Harrisburg, Pa., June 25. Duty at Camp Curtin, Pa., till August. Mustered out August 3, 1863.

68th REGIMENT INFANTRY.—("CAMERON RIFLES." "2nd GERMAN RIFLE REGIMENT.")

Organized at New York City August 1-20, 1861. Left State for Washington, D. C., August 24, 1861. Attached to Blenker's Brigade, Division of the Potomac, to October, 1861. Blenker's Brigade, Hooker's Division, Army of the Potomac, to November, 1861. Steinwehr's 2nd Brigade, Blenker's Division, Army of the Potomac, to March, 1862. 2nd Brigade, Blenker's 2nd Division, 2nd Army Corps, Army of the Potomac, to April, 1862. 2nd Brigade, Blenker's Division, Mountain Department, to June, 1862. 1st Brigade, 2nd Division, 1st Corps, Pope's Army of Virginia, to July, 1862. 2nd Brigade, 3rd Division, 1st Army Corps, Army of Virginia, to September, 1862. 2nd Brigade, 3rd Division, 11th Army Corps, Army of the Potomac, to October, 1862. 1st Brigade, 3rd Division, 11th Army Corps, to May, 1863. 1st Brigade, 1st Division, 11th Army Corps, to July, 1863. 2nd Brigade, 2nd Division, 11th Army Corps, to October, 1863. 3rd Brigade, 3rd Division, 11th Army Corps, Army of the Cumberland, to April, 1864. Unattached, 4th Division, 20th Army Corps, to July, 1864. 3rd Brigade, Defences of Nashville & Chattanooga Railroad, to December, 1864. Unattached, District of the Etowah, to March, 1865. 2nd Brigade, 2nd Separate Division, District of the Etowah, to July, 1865. District of Allatoona, Ga., to November, 1865. District of Savannah, Ga., to November, 1865.

SERVICE.—Duty in the Defences of Washington, D. C., till April, 1862. Advance on Manassas, Va., March 10-15. Movement to Winchester, Va., April 5-18. Operations in the Shenandoah Valley till June. Battle of Cross Keys June 8. Duty at Sperryville July 7 to August 8. Pope's Campaign in Northern Virginia August 16-September 2. Battles of Groveton August 29; Bull Run August 30. Duty in the Defences of Washington till November 1. Movement to Centreville November 1-18. Advance to Fredericksburg, Va., December 9-16. At Stafford Court House till April 27, 1863. "Mud March" January 20-24. Chancellorsville Campaign April 27-May 6. Battle of Chancellorsville May 1-5. Gettysburg (Pa.) Campaign June 11-July 24. Battle of Gettysburg, Pa., July 1-3. Guard duty along Orange & Alexandria Railroad till September. Movement to Bridgeport, Ala., September 24-October 3. Operations in Lookout Valley, Tenn., October 19-26. Reopening Tennessee River October 26-29. Battle of Wauhatchie, Tenn., October 28-29. Chattanooga-Ringgold Campaign November 23-27. Orchard Knob November 23. Tunnel Hill November 24-25. Mission Ridge November 25. March to relief of Knoxville, Tenn., November 28-December 17. Assigned to Railroad Guard and garrison duty in the District of Nashville, Tenn., Dept. of the Cumberland, till July, 1865. Elrod's Tan Yard January 27, 1865 (Detachment). Skirmish at Ladd's House, Hog Jaw Valley, February 3-4 (Detachment). Skirmish at Johnson's Crook February 10. Duty in District of Allatoona, Ga., till November, 1865, and at Savannah, Ga., November, 1865. Mustered out November 30, 1865.

Regiment lost during service 5 Officers and 38 Enlisted men killed and mortally wounded and 1 Officer and 74 Enlisted men by disease. Total 118.

68th REGIMENT NATIONAL GUARD INFANTRY.

Organized for thirty days' United States service June 22, 1863. Left State for Harrisburg, Pa., June 24. Attached to 5th Brigade, 1st Division, Dept. of the Susquehanna. Mustered out July 25, 1863.

69th REGIMENT INFANTRY.—("1st REGIMENT IRISH BRIGADE.")

Organized at New York and mustered in November 18, 1861. Left State for Washington, D. C., November

18. Attached to Meagher's Brigade, Sumner's Division, Army of the Potomac, to March, 1862. 2nd Brigade, 1st Division, 2nd Army Corps, Army of the Potomac, to June, 1864. Consolidated Brigade, 1st Division, 2nd Army Corps, to November, 1864. 2nd Brigade, 1st Division, 2nd Army Corps, to June, 1865.

SERVICE.—Duty in the Defences of Washington, D. C., till March, 1862. Advance on Manassas, Va., March 10. Ordered to the Peninsula, Va., March 28. Siege of Yorktown April 16-May 4. Battle of Seven Pines or Fair Oaks May 31-June 1. Seven days before Richmond June 25-July 1. Battles of Gaines Mill June 27; Peach Orchard and Savage Station June 29; White Oak Swamp and Glendale June 30; Malvern Hill July 1. At Harrison's Landing till August 16. Movement to Fortress Monroe, thence to Alexandria and Centreville August 16-30. Cover retreat of Pope's Army to Washington August 31-September 2. Maryland Campaign September 6-22. Battle of Antietam September 16-17. At Harper's Ferry, W. Va., September 22-October 29. Reconnoissance to Charlestown October 16-17. Advance up Loudoun Valley and movement to Falmouth, Va., October 29-November 17. Battle of Fredericksburg, Va., December 12-15. At Falmouth, Va., till April 27, 1863. "Mud March" January 20-24. Chancellorsville Campaign April 27-May 6. Battle of Chancellorsville May 1-5. Gettysburg (Pa.) Campaign June 11-July 24. Battle of Gettysburg, Pa., July 1-4. Pursuit of Lee to Manassas Gap July 5-24. Duty on line of the Rappahannock till October. Advance from the Rappahannock to the Rapidan September 13-17. Bristoe Campaign October 9-22. Auburn and Bristoe October 14. Advance to line of the Rappahannock November 7-8. Mine Run Campaign November 26-December 2. Duty at and near Stevensburg, Va., till May, 1864. Demonstration on the Rapidan February 6-7. Campaign from the Rapidan to the James May 3-June 15. Battles of the Wilderness May 5-7; Spottsylvania May 8-12; Po River May 10; Spottsylvania Court House May 12-21. Assault on the Salient or "Bloody Angle" May 12. North Anna River May 23-26. On line of the Pamunkey May 26-28. Totopotomoy May 28-31. Cold Harbor June 1-12. Before Petersburg June 16-18. Siege of Petersburg June 16, 1864, to April 2, 1865. Jerusalem Plank Road, Weldon Railroad, June 22-23, 1864. Demonstration north of James River July 27-29. Deep Bottom July 27-28. Demonstration north of James River August 13-20. Strawberry Plains, Deep Bottom, August 14-18. Ream's Station August 25. Reconnoissance to Hatcher's Run December 9-10. Dabney's Mills, Hatcher's Run, February 5-7, 1865. Watkins' House March 25. Appomattox Campaign March 28-April 9. Hatcher's Run or Boydton Road March 29-31. White Oak Road March 31. Sutherland Station and fall of Petersburg April 2. Sailor's Creek April 6. High Bridge and Farmville April 7. Appomattox Court House April 9. Surrender of Lee and his army. Moved to Washington, D. C., May 2-12. Grand Review May 23. Mustered out June 30, 1865.

Regiment lost during service 13 Officers and 246 Enlisted men killed and mortally wounded and 142 Enlisted men by disease. Total 401.

69th REGIMENT STATE MILITIA INFANTRY.

Left State for Washington, D. C., April 23, 1861. Duty at Annapolis, Md., April 27-May 2. Moved to Washington, D. C., and duty in the defences of that city till July 16. Mustered in for three months May 9. Advance into Virginia and occupation of Arlington Heights May 24. Attached to Sherman's Brigade, Tyler's Division, McDowell's Army of Northeast Virginia, June and July. Advance on Manassas, Va., July 16-21. Battle of Bull Run, Va., July 21. Mustered out at New York City August 3, 1861.

Regiment lost during service 1 Officer and 44 Enlisted men killed and mortally wounded and 6 Enlisted men by disease. Total 51.

69th REGIMENT NATIONAL GUARD INFANTRY.

Mustered for three months' United States service May 26, 1862. Left State for Washington, D. C., May 30, 1862, and duty in the defences of that city till September. Mustered out September 3, 1862.

Again entered United States service for thirty days and left State for Baltimore, Md., June 22, 1863. Duty at Baltimore, Md. Attached to 2nd Separate Brigade, 8th Army Corps, Middle Department. Mustered out July 25, 1863.

Again mustered in for three months' United States service July 6, 1864. Duty in New York Harbor till October. Mustered out October 6, 1864.

70th REGIMENT INFANTRY.—("1st EXCELSIOR.")

Organized under authority of the War Department as 1st Regiment, Sickles' Brigade, at Camp Scott, Staten Island, N. Y., and mustered in June 20, 1861. Left State for Washington, D. C., July 23, 1861. Attached to Sickles' Brigade, Division of the Potomac, to October, 1861. Sickles' Brigade, Hooker's Division, Army of the Potomac, to March, 1862. (Designated 70th Regiment New York Infantry December 11, 1861.) 2nd Brigade, 2nd Division, 3rd Army Corps, Army of the Potomac, to March, 1864. 2nd Brigade, 4th Division, 2nd Army Corps, to May, 1864. 4th Brigade, 3rd Division, 2nd Army Corps, to July, 1864.

SERVICE.—Duty in the Defences of Washington, D. C., till March, 1862. Expedition to Lower Maryland September 15-October 2, 1861. Advance on Manassas, Va., March 10, 1862. Expedition from Dumfries to Fredericksburg and capture of stores March 18. Reconnoissance from Liverpool Point to Stafford Court House, Va., and action at Stafford Court House April 4. Ordered to the Peninsula, Va. Siege of Yorktown April 10-May 4. Battle of Williamsburg May 5. Battle of Seven Pines or Fair Oaks May 31-June 1. Seven days before Richmond June 25-July 1. Battles of Oak Grove June 25; Peach Orchard and Savage Station, White Oak Swamp and Glendale June 30; Malvern Hill July 1 and August 5. At Harrison's Landing till August 16. Movement to Fortress Monroe, thence to Centreville August 16-28. Pope's Campaign in Northern Virginia August 26-September 2. Action at Bristoe Station or Kettle Run August 27. Battles of Groveton August 29; Bull Run August 30; Chantilly September 1. Duty in the Defences of Washington, D. C., till November. At Fairfax Station, Va., till November 25. Operations on the Orange & Alexandria Railroad November 10-12. Battle of Fredericksburg, Va., December 12-15. Duty at Falmouth till April 27, 1863. "Mud March" January 20-24. Operations about Rappahannock Bridge and Grove Church February 5-7. Chancellorsville Campaign April 27-May 6. Battle of Chancellorsville May 1-5. Gettysburg (Pa.) Campaign June 11-July 24. Battle of Gettysburg, Pa., July 1-3. Pursuit of Lee July 5-24. Wapping Heights, Va., July 23. Duty on line of the Rappahannock till October. Bristoe Campaign October 9-22. Advance to line of the Rappahannock November 7-8. Kelly's Ford November 7. Mine Run Campaign November 26-December 2. Payne's Farm November 27. Duty near Brandy Station till May, 1864. Demonstration on the Rapidan February 6-7. Campaign from the Rapidan to the James River May 3-June 15. Battles of the Wilderness May 5-7; Spottsylvania May 8-12; Po River May 10; Spottsylvania Court House May 12-21. Assault on the Salient or "Bloody Angle" May 12. Harris Farm or Fredericksburg Road May 19. North Anna River May 23-26. On line of the Pamunkey May 26-28. Totopotomoy May 28-31. Cold Harbor June 1-12. Before Petersburg June 16-18. Ordered to New York for muster out June 22. Veterans and Recruits transferred to 86th Regiment New York Infantry. Mustered out July 7, 1864, to date from July 1, 1864, expiration of term.

Regiment lost during service 9 Officers and 181 Enlisted men killed and mortally wounded and 2 Officers and 62 Enlisted men by disease. Total 254.

71st REGIMENT INFANTRY.—("2nd EXCELSIOR.")

Organized under authority of the War Department at Camp Scott, Staten Island, N. Y., as 2nd Regiment, Sickles' Brigade, June, 1861. Left State for Washington, D. C., July 23, 1861. Attached to Sickles' Brigade, Division of the Potomac, to October, 1861. Sickles' Brigade, Hooker's Division, Army of the Potomac, to March, 1862. 2nd Brigade, 2nd Division, 3rd Army Corps, Army of the Potomac, to March, 1864. 2nd Brigade, 4th Division, 2nd Army Corps, to May, 1864. 4th Brigade, 3rd Division, 2nd Army Corps, to July, 1864.

SERVICE.—Duty in the Defences of Washington, D. C., till March, 1862. Expedition to Lower Maryland September 15-October 2, 1861. Expedition to Matthias Point November 9. Advance on Manassas, Va., March 10, 1862. Expedition from Dumfries to Fredericksburg, Va., and capture of stores March 18. Reconnoissance from Liverpool Point to Stafford Court House and action at Stafford Court House April 4. Ordered to the Peninsula, Va., April. Siege of Yorktown April 10-May 4. Battle of Williamsburg May 5. Battle of Seven Pines or Fair Oaks May 31-June 1. Seven days before Richmond June 25-July 1. Battles of Oak Grove June 25; Peach Orchard and Savage Station June 29; White Oak Swamp and Glendale June 30; Malvern Hill July 1 and August 5. At Harrison's Landing till August 16. Movement to Fortress Monroe, thence to Centreville August 16-26. Pope's Campaign in Northern Virginia August 26-September 2. Action at Bristoe Station or Kettle Run August 27. Battles of Groveton August 29; Bull Run August 30. Duty in the Defences of Washington, D. C., till November. At Fairfax Station to November 25. Operations on the Orange & Alexandria Railroad November 10-12. Battle of Fredericksburg, Va., December 12-15. At Falmouth till April 27, 1863. "Mud March" January 20-24. Operations at Rappahannock Bridge and Grove Church February 5-7. Chancellorsville Campaign April 27-May 6. Battle of Chancellorsville May 1-5. Gettysburg (Pa.) Campaign June 11-July 24. Battle of Gettysburg, Pa., July 1-3. Pursuit of Lee to Manassas Gap, Va., July 5-24. Wapping Heights July 23. Duty on line of the Rappahannock till October. Bristoe Campaign October 9-22. Advance to line of the Rappahannock November 7-8. Kelly's Ford November 7. Mine Run Campaign November 26-December 2. Payne's Farm November 27. Duty near Brandy Station, Va., till May, 1864. Demonstration on the Rapidan February 6-7. Campaign from the Rapidan to the James River May 3-June 15. Battles of the Wilderness May 5-7; Spottsylvania May 8-12; Po River May 10; Spottsylvania Court House May 12-21. Assault on the Salient or "Bloody Angle" May 12. Harris Farm or Fredericksburg Road May 19. North Anna River May 23-26. On line of the Pamunkey May 26-28. Totopotomoy May 28-31. Cold Harbor June 1-12. Before Petersburg June 16-18. Siege of Petersburg June 16-July 7. Jerusalem Plank Road, Weldon Railroad, June 22-23. Veterans and Recruits transferred to 120th Regiment, New York Infantry, July 7. Regiment mustered out at New York City July 30, 1864, expiration of term.

Regiment lost during service 5 Officers and 83 Enlisted men killed and mortally wounded and 2 Officers and 73 Enlisted men by disease. Total 163.

71st REGIMENT STATE MILITIA INFANTRY.

Organized for three months' United States service April 10, 1861. Left New York for Annapolis, Md., April 21, 1861, arriving there April 24; thence marched to Washington, D. C., April 25 and assigned to duty at the Navy Yard. Mustered into United States service April 30. Attached to Mansfield's Command till June. Burnside's Brigade, Hunter's Division, McDowell's Army of Northeast Virginia, to July.

SERVICE.—Occupation of Alexandria, Va., May 24. Attack on Batteries at Aquia Creek May 31 and June 1. Attack on Matthias Point June 27. Performed escort duty at the funerals of Colonel Elmer E. Ells-

worth and Captain Ward, United States Navy. Advance on Manassas, Va., July 16-21. Action at Sudley Springs July 21. Battle of Bull Run July 21. Volunteered to build and man Batteries beyond Alexandria. Mustered out July 30, 1861.

Regiment lost during service 1 Officer and 14 Enlisted men killed and mortally wounded and 1 Officer and 4 Enlisted men by disease. Total 20.

71st REGIMENT NATIONAL GUARD INFANTRY.

Mustered in for three months' United States service May 12, 1862. Left State for Washington, D. C., May 28. Attached to Sturgis' Command, Military District of Washington, and duty in the defences of that city till September. Mustered out September 2, 1862.

Again mustered for 30 days' United States service June 17, 1863. Left State for Harrisburg, Pa., June 18. Attached to 1st Brigade, 1st Division, Dept. of the Susquehanna. Skirmish at Kingston June 25. Oyster Point June 28-29, near Harrisburg, June 29. Mustered out June 22, 1863.

72nd REGIMENT INFANTRY ("3rd EXCELSIOR").

Organized under authority of the War Department at Camp Scott, Staten Island, N. Y., as 3rd Regiment, Sickles' Brigade. Left State for Washington, D. C., July 24, 1861. Attached to Sickles' Brigade, Division of the Potomac, to October, 1861. Sickles' Brigade, Hooker's Division, Army of the Potomac, to March, 1862. 2nd Brigade, 2nd Division, 3rd Army Corps, Army of the Potomac, to March, 1864. 2nd Brigade, 4th Division, 2nd Army Corps, to May, 1864. 4th Brigade, 3rd Division, 2nd Army Corps, to July, 1864.

SERVICE.—Duty in the Defences of Washington, D. C., till March, 1862. Expedition to Lower Maryland September 15-October 2, 1861. Advance on Manassas, Va., March 10, 1862. Expedition from Dumfries to Fredericksburg, Va., and capture of stores March 18. Reconnoissance from Liverpool Point to Stafford Court House and action at Stafford Court House April 4. Ordered to the Peninsula April. Siege of Yorktown April 10-May 4. Battle of Williamsburg May 5. Battle of Seven Pines or Fair Oaks May 31-June 1. Seven days before Richmond June 25-July 1. Battles of Oak Grove June 25. Peach Orchard and Savage Station June 29. White Oak Swamp and Glendale June 30. Malvern Hill July 1 and August 5. At Harrison's Landing till August 16. Movement to Fortress Monroe, thence to Centreville, August 16-26. Pope's Campaign in Northern Virginia August 26-September 2. Action at Bristoe Station or Kettle Run August 27. Battles of Groveton August 29. Bull Run August 30. Duty in the Defences of Washington till November. At Fairfax Station till November 25. Operations on the Orange & Alexandria Railroad November 10-12. Battle of Fredericksburg, Va., December 12-15. At Falmouth till April 27. "Mud March" January 20-24. Operations at Rappahannock Bridge and Grove Church February 5-7. Chancellorsville Campaign April 27-May 6. Battle of Chancellorsville May 1-5. Gettysburg (Pa.) Campaign June 11-July 24. Battle of Gettysburg July 1-3. Pursuit of Lee to Manassas Gap July 5-24. Wapping Heights, Va., July 23. Duty on line of the Rappahannock till October. Bristoe Campaign October 9-22. Advance to line of the Rappahannock November 7-8. Kelly's Ford November 7. Mine Run Campaign November 26-December 2. Payne's Farm November 27. Duty near Brandy Station till May, 1864. Demonstration on the Rapidan February 6-7. Campaign from the Rapidan to the James River May 3-June 15. Battles of the Wilderness May 5-7. Spottsylvania May 8-12. Po River May 10. Spottsylvania Court House May 12-21. Assault on the Salient or "Bloody Angle" May 12. Harris Farm, or Fredericksburg Road, May 19. North Anna River May 23-26. On line of the Pamunkey May 26-28. Totopotomoy May 28-31. Cold Harbor June 1-12. Before Petersburg June 16-18. Eight Companies mustered out June 20, 1864 (Cos. "A," "B," "D," "E," "F," "I" and "K"). Companies "C," "G" and "H" attached to 120th Regiment, New York Infantry. Company "C" mustered out July 20, Company "G" July 2 and Company "H" October 31, 1864. Veterans and Recruits transferred to 120th Regiment New York Infantry.

Regiment lost during service 11 Officers and 150 Enlisted men killed and mortally wounded and 1 Officer and 88 Enlisted men by disease. Total 250.

73rd REGIMENT INFANTRY ("4th EXCELSIOR").

Organized under authority of the War Department, at Camp Scott, Staten Island, N. Y., as 4th Regiment, Sickles' Brigade, July to October, 1861. Left State for Washington, D. C., October 8, 1861. Attached to Sickles' Brigade, Division of the Potomac, October, 1861. Sickles' Brigade, Hooker's Division, Army of the Potomac, to March, 1862. 2nd Brigade, 2nd Division, 3rd Army Corps, Army of the Potomac, to March, 1864. 2nd Brigade, 4th Division, 2nd Army Corps, to May, 1864. 4th Brigade, 3rd Division, 2nd Army Corps, to July, 1864. 1st Brigade, 3rd Division, 2nd Army Corps, to June, 1865.

SERVICE.—Duty in the Defences of Washington, D. C., till March, 1862. Expedition to Matthias Point November 9, 1861. Advance on Manassas, Va., March 10, 1862. Expedition from Dumfries to Fredericksburg and capture of stores March 18. Reconnoissance from Liverpool Point to Stafford Court House and action at Stafford Court House April 4. Ordered to the Peninsula April. Siege of Yorktown April 10-May 4. Battle of Williamsburg May 5. Battle of Seven Pines or Fair Oaks May 31-June 1. Seven days before Richmond June 25-July 1. Battles of Oak Grove June 25; Peach Orchard and Savage Station June 29; White Oak Swamp and Glendale June 30; Malvern Hill July 1 and August 5. At Harrison's Landing till August 16. Movement to Fortress Monroe, thence to Centreville, August 16-26. Pope's Campaign in Northern Virginia August 26-September 2. Action at Bristoe Station or Kettle Run August 27. Battles of Groveton August 29; Bull Run August 30. Duty in the Defences of Washington till November. At Fairfax Station Va., till November 25. Operations on Orange & Alexandria Railroad November 10-12. Battle of Fredericksburg, Va., December 12-15. At Falmouth till April 27, 1863. "Mud March" January 20-24. Operations at Rappahannock Bridge and Grove Church February 5-7. Chancellorsville Campaign April 27-May 6. Battle of Chancellorsville May 1-5. Gettysburg (Pa.) Campaign June 11-July 24. Battle of Gettysburg, Pa., July 1-3. Pursuit of Lee to Manassas Gap, Va., July 5-24. Wapping Heights, Va., July 23. Duty on line of the Rappahannock till October. Bristoe Campaign October 9-22. Advance to line of the Rappahannock November 7-8. Kelly's Ford November 7. Mine Run Campaign November 26-December 2. Payne's Farm November 27. Duty near Brandy Station, Va., till May, 1864. Demonstration on the Rapidan February 6-7. Campaign from the Rapidan to the James River May 3-June 15. Battles of the Wilderness May 5-7. Spottsylvania May 8-12. Po River May 10. Spottsylvania Court House May 12-21. Assault on the Salient or "Bloody Angle" May 12. Harris Farm or Fredericksburg Road May 19. North Anna River May 23-26. On line of the Pamunkey May 26-28. Totopotomoy May 28-31. Cold Harbor June 1-12. Before Petersburg June 16-18. Siege of Petersburg June 16, 1864, to April 2, 1865. Jerusalem Plank Road, Weldon Railroad, June 22-23, 1864. Demonstration on North side of the James July 27-29. Deep Bottom July 27-28. Demonstration on North side of the James August 13-20. Strawberry Plains, Deep Bottom, August 14-18. Ream's Station August 25. Poplar Springs Church September 29-October 2. Boydton Plank Road, Hatcher's Run, October 27-28. Reconnoissance to Hatcher's Run December 9-10. Dabney's Mills, Hatcher's Run, February 5-7, 1865. Watkins' House March 25. Appomattox Campaign March 28-April 9. Boydton Road and White Oak Ridge March 29-31. Crow's House March 31. Fall of Petersburg April 2. Sailor's Creek April 6. High Bridge and Farmville April 7. Appomattox Court House

April 9. Surrender of Lee and his army. Moved to Washington, D. C., May 2-12. Grand Review May 23. Mustered out at Washington, D. C., June 29, 1865.

Regiment lost during service 18 Officers and 138 Enlisted men killed and mortally wounded and 1 Officer and 76 Enlisted men by disease. Total 233.

74th REGIMENT INFANTRY ("5th EXCELSIOR").

Organized under authority of the War Department at Camp Scott, Staten Island, N. Y., as 5th Regiment, Sickles' Brigade. Left State for Washington, D. C., August 20, 1861. Attached to Sickles' Brigade, Division of the Potomac, to October, 1861. Sickles' Brigade, Hooker's Division. Army of the Potomac, to March, 1862. Designated 74th New York Infantry December 11, 1861. 2nd Brigade, 2nd Division, 3rd Army Corps, Army of the Potomac. to March, 1864. 2nd Brigade, 4th Division, 2nd Army Corps, to May, 1864. 4th Brigade, 3rd Division, 2nd Army Corps, to July, 1864. 1st Brigade, 3rd Division, 2nd Army Corps, to August, 1864.

SERVICE.—Duty in the Defences of Washington, D. C., till March, 1862. Expedition to Lower Maryland September 15-October 2, 1861. Expedition to Matthias Point November 9. Advance on Manassas, Va., March 10, 1862. Expedition from Dumfries to Fredericksburg, Va., and capture of stores March 18. Reconnoissance from Liverpool Point to Stafford Court House and action at Stafford Court House April 4. Ordered to the Virginia Peninsula April. Siege of Yorktown April 10-May 4. Battle of Williamsburg May 5. Battle of Seven Pines or Fair Oaks May 31-June 1. Seven days before Richmond June 25-July 1. Battles of Oak Grove June 25; Peach Orchard and Savage Station June 29; White Oak Swamp and Glendale June 30; Malvern Hill July 1 and August 5. At Harrison's Landing till August 16. Movement to Fortress Monroe, thence to Centreville August 16-26. Pope's Campaign in Northern Virginia August 26-September 2. Action at Bristoe Station or Kettle Run August 27. Battles of Groveton August 29; Bull Run August 30. Duty in the Defences of Washington, D. C., till November. At Fairfax Station till November 25. Operations on Orange & Alexandria Railroad November 10-12. Battle of Fredericksburg, Va., December 12-15. At Falmouth till April 27, 1863. "Mud March" January 20-24. Operations at Rappahannock Bridge and Grove Church February 5-7. Chancellorsville Campaign April 27-May 6. Battle of Chancellorsville May 1-5. Gettysburg (Pa.) Campaign June 11-July 24. Battle of Gettysburg July 1-3. Pursuit of Lee to Manassas Gap, Va., July 5-24. Wapping Heights July 23. Duty on the Rappahannock till October. Bristoe Campaign October 9-22. Advance to line of the Rappahannock November 7-8. Kelly's Ford November 7. Mine Run Campaign November 26-December 2. Payne's Farm November 27. Duty near Brandy Station till May, 1864. Demonstration on the Rapidan February 6-7. Campaign from the Rapidan to the James River May 3-June 15. Battles of the Wilderness May 5-7; Spottsylvania May 8-12; Po River May 10; Spottsylvania Court House May 12-21. Assault on the Salient or "Bloody Angle" May 12. Harris Farm or Fredericksburg Road May 19. North Anna River May 23-26. On line of the Pamunkey May 26-28. Totopotomoy May 28-31. Cold Harbor June 1-12. Before Petersburg June 16-19. Siege of Petersburg June 16 to August 3. Jerusalem Plank Road, Weldon Railroad, June 22-23. Demonstration north of the James July 27-29. Deep Bottom July 27-28. Regiment mustered out before Petersburg, Va., by Companies as follows: Company "D" June 19, Company "A" June 21, Company "B" June 26, Company "G" June 28, Company "C" July 6, Companies "E," "F," "H," "I" and "K" August 3, 1864. Veterans and Recruits transferred to 40th Regiment New York Infantry August 3 as Companies "G" and "H."

Regiment lost during service 8 Officers and 122 Enlisted men killed and mortally wounded and 2 Officers and 67 Enlisted men by disease. Total 199.

74th REGIMENT NATIONAL GUARD INFANTRY.

Ordered to Harrisburg, Pa., for thirty days' United States service June 18, 1863. Duty at Mt. Union, Pa. Skirmish near Clear Springs, Md., July 10. Mustered out August 3, 1863.

Again mustered for thirty days' service at Buffalo, N. Y., November 16, 1863. Mustered out December 16, 1863.

75th REGIMENT INFANTRY.—("2nd AUBURN REGIMENT.")

Organized at Auburn, N. Y., and mustered in November 26, 1861. Left State for Florida December 6, 1861, arriving at Santa Rosa Island, Fla., December 15. Duty there and at Fort Pickens, Fla., till May, 1862. Attached to District of Santa Rosa Island, Dept. of Florida, to February, 1862. District of Santa Rosa Island, Fla., Dept. of the Gulf, to March, 1862. Western District of Florida, Dept. of the South, to August, 1862. Pensacola, Fla., Division of West Florida, Dept. of the Gulf, to September, 1862. Weitzel's Reserve Brigade, Dept. of the Gulf, to January, 1863. 2nd Brigade, 1st Division, 19th Army Corps, Dept. of the Gulf, to July, 1863. 3rd Brigade, 1st Division, 19th Army Corps, to October, 1863. Unassigned, Cavalry Division, Dept. of the Gulf, to December, 1863. 1st Brigade, Cavalry Division, Dept. of the Gulf, to June, 1864. 1st Brigade, 2nd Division, 19th Army Corps, to July, 1864. 1st Brigade, 2nd Division, 19th Army Corps, Army of the Shenandoah, Middle Military Division, to January, 1865. 1st Brigade, Grover's Division, District of Savannah, Ga., Dept. of the South, to March, 1865. 1st Brigade, 1st Division, 10th Army Corps, to May, 1865. District of Savannah, Ga., Dept. of the South, to August, 1865.

SERVICE.—Bombardment of Forts McRae and Barrancas, Pensacola Harbor, Fla., January 1, 1862. Occupation of Pensacola, Fla., May 10, and duty there till August. Fair Oaks, Fla., May 28. Moved to New Orleans, La., August, arriving there August 9. Duty at Carrollton till October. Operations in District of LaFourche October 24-November 6. Occupation of Donaldsonville October 25. Action at Georgia Landing, near Labadieville, and at Thibodeauxville October 28. Duty in the District of LaFourche till February, 1863. Expedition to Bayou Teche January 12-15. Bayou Teche January 13. Steamer "Cotton" January 14. Operations against Port Hudson March 7-27. Duty at Brashear City till April. Operations in Western Louisiana April 9-May 14. Expedition from Brashear City to Opelousas April 11-20. Fort Bisland April 12-13. Jeanerette, Irish Bend, April 14. Bayou Vermillion April 17. Opelousas April 20. Expedition to Alexandria and Simsport May 5-18. Boyce's Bridge, Cotile Bayou, May 14 (Detachment). Siege of Port Hudson May 25-July 9. Assaults on Port Hudson May 27 and June 14. Surrender of Port Hudson July 9. Donaldsonville, Bayou LaFourche, July 12-13. At Baton Rouge August 1-September 3. Sabine Pass Expedition September 4-11. Sabine Pass September 8. Moved from Algiers to Brashear City September 17. Regiment changed to Mounted Infantry October. Western Louisiana Campaign October 3-November 30. Vermillion Bayou October 9-10. Near New Iberia November 19. Camp Pratt November 20. Camp Lewis December 3. Regiment veteranize January 1, 1864. Veterans on furlough January to April, then at Washington, D. C., 22nd Army Corps, as Infantry, April 2 to May 20; then moved to Dept. of the Gulf and rejoin Regiment June 28. Non-Veterans attached to 14th New York Cavalry till June 28, 1864, participating in the Red River Campaign March 10-May 22. Advance from Franklin to Alexandria March 14-26. Bayou Rapides March 20. Henderson's Hill March 21. Monett's Ferry and Cloutiersville March 29-30. Natchitoches March 31. Crump's Hill April 2. Wilson's Farm April 7. Bayou de Paul, Carroll's Mill, April 8. Pleasant Hill April 9. Natchitoches April 20. About Cloutiersville April 21-22. Monett's Ferry, Cane River Crossing, April 23. Above Alexandria April 28. Hudnot's Planta-

tion May 1. Alexandria May 4-8. Retreat to Morganza May 13-20. Choctaw Bayou May 13-14. Avoyelle's Prairie May 15. Mansura May 16. Yellow Bayou May 17-18. Sailed for Fortress Monroe, Va., July 13. Before Richmond July 21-30. Deep Bottom July 27-29. Moved to Washington, D. C., July 31. Sheridan's Shenandoah Valley Campaign August 7-November 28. Halltown August 23-24. Berryville September 3-4. Battle of Winchester September 19. Fisher's Hill September 22. Battle of Cedar Creek October 19. Duty in the Shenandoah Valley till January, 1865. Ordered to Savannah, Ga., January 11, 1865, and provost duty there till August. Mustered out August 23, 1865.

Regiment lost during service 4 Officers and 91 Enlisted men killed and mortally wounded and 103 Enlisted men by disease. Total 198.

76th REGIMENT INFANTRY.—("COURTLAND COUNTY REGIMENT.")

Organized at Courtland and Albany, N. Y., and mustered in January 16, 1862. Left State for Washington, D. C., January 17, 1862. Attached to 3rd Brigade, Casey's Division, Army of the Potomac, to March, 1862. Wadsworth's Command, Military District of Washington, to May, 1862. Doubleday's Brigade, Dept. of the Rappahannock, to June, 1862. 2nd Brigade, 1st Division, 3rd Corps, Pope's Army of Virginia, to September, 1862. 2nd Brigade, 1st Division, 1st Army Corps, Army of the Potomac, to January, 1864. 1st Brigade, 1st Division, 1st Army Corps, to March, 1864. 2nd Brigade, 1st Division, 1st Army Corps, to March, 1864. 2nd Brigade, 4th Division, 5th Army Corps, to August, 1864. 3rd Brigade, 2nd Division, 5th Army Corps, to September, 1864. 3rd Brigade, 3rd Division, 5th Army Corps, to January, 1865.

SERVICE.—Duty in the Defences of Washington, D. C., till May, 1862. Duty at and near Fredericksburg, Va., till August. Pope's Campaign in Northern Virginia August 16-September 2. Fords of the Rappahannock August 20-23. Battles of Gainesville August 28; Groveton August 29, Bull Run August 30. Maryland Campaign September 6-22. Battles of South Mountain September 14; Antietam September 16-17. At Sharpsburg, Md., till October 29. Advance to Falmouth, Va., October 29-November 19. Battle of Fredericksburg, Va., December 12-15. "Mud March" January 20-24, 1863. At Falmouth and Belle Plains till April 27. Chancellorsville Campaign April 27-May 6. Operations at Pollock's Mill Creek April 29-May 2. Battle of Chancellorsville May 2-5. Gettysburg (Pa.) Campaign June 11-July 24. Battle of Gettysburg, Pa., July 1-3. Pursuit of Lee to Manassas Gap, Va., July 5-24. Duty on line of the Rappahannock till October. Bristoe Campaign October 9-22. Advance to line of the Rappahannock November 7-8. Mine Run Campaign November 26-December 2. Demonstration on the Rapidan February 6-7, 1864. Campaign from the Rapidan to the James River May 3-June 15. Battles of the Wilderness May 5-7; Laurel Hill May 8; Spottsylvania May 8-12; Spottsylvania Court House May 12-21. Assault on the Salient May 12. North Anna River May 23-26. Jericho Ford May 23. On line of the Pamunkey May 26-28. Totopotomoy May 28-31. Cold Harbor June 1-12. Bethesda Church June 1-3. Before Petersburg June 16-18. Siege of Petersburg June 16, 1864, to January 28, 1865. Weldon Railroad August 18-21, 1864. Poplar Springs Church September 29-October 2. Boydton Plank Road, Hatcher's Run, October 27-28. Hicksford Raid December 7-11. Companies mustered out as follows: Companies "B," "F" and "K" July 1, 1864; Company "A" October 11; Company "G" October 20; Company "C" November 8; Company "E" November 18; Company "I" December 1, 1864; Company "H" January 1, 1865; Company "D" and Veterans and Recruits transferred to 147th Regiment, New York Infantry, January 28, 1865.

Regiment lost during service 12 Officers and 161 Enlisted men killed and mortally wounded and 1 Officer and 156 Enlisted men by disease. Total 330.

77th REGIMENT INFANTRY ("BEMIS HEIGHTS REGIMENT").

Organized at Saratoga, N. Y. and mustered in November 22, 1861. Left State for Washington, D. C., November 28, 1861. Attached to 3rd Brigade, Casey's Division, Army of the Potomac, to March, 1862. 3rd Brigade, 2nd Division, 4th Army Corps, Army of the Potomac, to May, 1862. 3rd Brigade, 2nd Division, 6th Army Corps, Army of the Potomac, and Army of the Shenandoah, to June, 1865.

SERVICE.—Duty in the Defences of Washington, D. C., till March, 1862. Advance on Manassas, Va., March 10. Ordered to the Virginia Peninsula March 22. Near Lee's Mills April 5. Siege of Yorktown April 5-May 4. Lee's Mills April 16. Battle of Williamsburg May 5. Mechanicsville May 23-24 and June 24. Seven days before Richmond June 25-July 1. Garnett's Farm June 27. Garnett's and Golding's Farms June 28. Savage Station June 29. White Oak Swamp and Glendale June 30. Malvern Hill July 1. At Harrison's Landing till August 16. Movement to Fortress Monroe, thence to Centreville, August 16-28. In works at Centreville August 28-31. Assist in checking Pope's rout at Bull Run August 30, and cover retreat to Fairfax Court House September 1. Maryland Campaign September 6-22. Crampton's Pass, South Mountain, September 14. Battle of Antietam September 16-17. Duty in Maryland till October 29. Movement to Falmouth, Va., October 29-November 19. Union November 2-3. Battle of Fredericksburg, Va., December 12-15. At Falmouth till April 27, 1863. "Mud March" January 20-24. Chancellorsville Campaign April 27-May 6. Operations about Franklin's Crossing April 29-May 2. Battle of Maryes Heights, Fredericksburg, May 3. Salem Heights May 3-4. Banks' Ford May 4. Deep Run Ravine June 5-13. Battle of Gettysburg, Pa., July 2-4. Pursuit of Lee July 5-24. Duty on line of the Rappahannock till October. Bristoe Campaign October 9-22. Advance to line of the Rappahannock November 7-8. Rappahannock Station November 7. Mine Run Campaign November 26-December 2. Duty near Brandy Station till May, 1864. Demonstration on the Rapidan February 6-7. Campaign from the Rapidan to the James River May 3-June 15. Battles of the Wilderness May 5-7; Spottsylvania May 8-12; Spottsylvania Court House May 12-21. Assault on the Salient or "Bloody Angle" May 12. North Anna River May 23-26. On line of the Pamunkey May 26-28. Totopotomoy May 28-31. Cold Harbor June 1-12. Before Petersburg June 17-18. Siege of Petersburg June 17 to July 9. Jerusalem Plank Road, Weldon Railroad, June 22-23. Moved to Washington, D. C., July 9-11. Repulse of Early's attack on Fort Stevens and the northern defences of Washington July 11-12. Sheridan's Shenandoah Valley Campaign August 7-November 28. Gilbert's Ford, Opequan Creek, September 13. Battle of Winchester September 19. Fisher's Hill September 22. Battle of Cedar Creek October 19. Duty in the Shenandoah Valley till December. Moved to Washington, D. C., thence to Petersburg, Va., December 13-16. Siege of Petersburg December 16, 1864, to April 2, 1865. Fort Fisher, Petersburg, March 25, 1865. Appomattox Campaign March 28-April 9. Assault on and fall of Petersburg April 2. Sailor's Creek April 6. Appomattox Court House April 9. Surrender of Lee and his army. March to Danville April 23-27, and duty there till May 24. March to Richmond, Va., thence to Washington, D. C., May 24-June 3. Corps Review June 8. Mustered out June 27, 1865.

Regiment lost during service 9 Officers and 87 Enlisted men killed and mortally wounded and 2 Officers and 175 Enlisted men by disease. Total 273.

77th REGIMENT NATIONAL GUARD INFANTRY.

Organized for 100 days August 2, 1864. Duty at Elmira, N. Y., till November 2. Mustered out November 19, 1864.

78th REGIMENT INFANTRY ("1st REGIMENT EAGLE BRIGADE," "CAMERON HIGHLANDERS").

Organized at New York City January to April, 1862. Left State for Washington, D. C., April 29, 1862. Attached to Defences of Washington, D. C., to May, 1862. 2nd Brigade, Sigel's Division, Dept. of the Shenandoah, to June, 1862. 2nd Brigade, 2nd Division, 2nd Corps, Pope's Army of Virginia, to August, 1862. 3rd Brigade, 2nd Division, 2nd Corps, Army of Virginia, to September, 1862. 3rd Brigade, 2nd Division, 12th Army Corps, Army of the Potomac, to October, 1863. 3rd Brigade, 2nd Division, 12th Army Corps, Army of the Cumberland, to April, 1864. 3rd Brigade, 2nd Division, 20th Army Corps, Army of the Cumberland, to July, 1864.

SERVICE.—Duty in the Defences of Washington till May 24, 1862. Moved to Harper's Ferry, W. Va., May 24. Defence of Harper's Ferry May 28-30. Operations in the Shenandoah Valley till August. Battle of Cedar Mountain August 9. Pope's Campaign in Northern Virginia August 16-September 2. Battles of Sulphur Springs August 23-24; Groveton August 29; Bull Run August 30. Maryland Campaign September 6-12. South Mountain, Md., September 14. Battle of Antietam, Md., September 16-17. Duty at Bolivar Heights till December. Reconnoissance to Rippon, West Va., November 9. Reconnoissance from Bolivar Heights to Winchester December 2-6. March to Fredericksburg, Va., December 9-16. Duty at Fairfax till January 20, 1863. "Mud March" January 20-24. Chancellorsville Campaign April 27-May 6. Battle of Chancellorsville May 1-5. Gettysburg (Pa.) Campaign June 11-July 24. Battle of Gettysburg, Pa., July 1-3. Pursuit of Lee to Manassas Gap, Va., July 5-24. Duty on line of the Rappahannock till September 24. Movement to Bridgeport, Ala., September 24-October 3. Reopening Tennessee River October 26-29. Battle of Wauhatchie, Tenn., October 28-29. Chattanooga-Ringgold Campaign November 23-27. Battles of Lookout Mountain November 23-24; Mission Ridge November 25; Ringgold Gap, Taylor's Ridge, November 27. Duty at Bridgeport, Ala., till May, 1864. Atlanta (Ga.) Campaign May 1 to July 12, 1864. Operations about Rocky Faced Ridge, Tunnel Hill and Buzzard's Roost Gap May 8-11. Battle of Resaca May 14-15. Near Cassville May 19. New Hope Church May 25. Battles about Dallas, New Hope Church and Allatoona Hills May 26-June 5. Operations about Marietta and against Kenesaw Mountain June 10-July 2. Pine Hill June 11-14. Lost Mountain June 15-17. Gilgal or Golgotha Church June 15. Muddy Creek June 17. Noyes' Creek June 19. Kolb's Farm June 22. Assault on Kenesaw June 27. Ruff's Station, Smyrna Camp Ground, July 4. Chattahoochie River July 5-12. Consolidated with 102nd Regiment New York Infantry July 12, 1864.

Regiment lost during service 3 Officers and 55 Enlisted men killed and mortally wounded and 73 Enlisted men by disease. Total 131.

79th REGIMENT INFANTRY.—("HIGHLANDERS.")

Organized at New York City and mustered in May 29, 1861. Left State for Washington, D. C., June 2, 1861. Attached to Mansfield's Command, Dept. of Washington, to June, 1861. Sherman's Brigade, Tyler's Division, McDowell's Army of Northeast Virginia, to August, 1861. W. F. Smith's Brigade, Division of the Potomac, to October. Stevens' Brigade, Smith's Division, Army of the Potomac, to October, 1861. Stevens' 2nd Brigade, Sherman's South Carolina Expeditionary Corps, to April, 1862. 2nd Brigade, 2nd Division, Dept. of the South, to July, 1862. 2nd Brigade, 1st Division, 9th Army Corps, Army of the Potomac, to September, 1862. 1st Brigade, 1st Division, 9th Army Corps, to April, 1863. 1st Brigade, 1st Division, 9th Army Corps, Army of the Ohio, to June, 1863. 3rd Brigade, 1st Division, 9th Army Corps, Army of the Tennessee, to August, 1863. 1st Brigade, 1st Division, 9th Army Corps, Army of the Ohio, to April, 1864. 2nd Brigade, 3rd Division, 9th Army Corps, Army of the Potomac, to September, 1864. 1st Brigade, 1st Division,

9th Army Corps, to October, 1864. Provost Guard, 9th Army Corps, to July, 1865.

SERVICE.—Duty in the Defences of Washington, D. C., till July 16, 1861. Advance on Manassas, Va., July 16-21. Occupation of Fairfax Court House July 17. Battle of Bull Run, Va., July 21. Duty in the Defences of Washington till October. Reconnoissance to Lewinsville, Va., September 25. Reconnoissance to Lewinsville, Va., October 10-11. Little River Turnpike, near Lewinsville, October 10. Bailey's Cross Roads October 12. Sherman's Expedition to Port Royal, S. C., October 21-November 7. Capture of Forts Walker and Beauregard, Port Royal Harbor, S. C., November 7. Occupation of Bay Point November 8 to December 11. Duty at Beaufort, S. C., and vicinity till June 1, 1862. Expedition to Port Royal Ferry January 1. Port Royal Ferry January 1. Action at Pocotaligo, S. C., May 29. Expedition to James Island, S. C., June 1-28. Battle of Secessionville June 16. Evacuation of James Island and movement to Hilton Head, S. C., June 28-July 7. Moved to Newport News, Va., July 12-16; thence to Fredericksburg, Va., August 4-6. Pope's Campaign in Northern Virginia August 13-September 2. Operations on the Rappahannock and Rapidan Rivers August 13-27. Battle of Bull Run August 30. Chantilly September 1. Maryland Campaign September 6-22. Battles of South Mountain September 14; Antietam September 16-17. Duty in Maryland till October 11. March up the Potomac to Leesburg, thence to Falmouth, Va., October 11-November 18. Battle of Fredericksburg December 12-15. "Mud March" January 20-24. Moved to Newport News, Va., March 13; thence to Kentucky March 20-28. Duty at Paris, Nicholasville, Lancaster, Stanford and Somerset till June. Movement through Kentucky to Cairo, Ill., June 4-10; thence to Vicksburg, Miss., June 14-17. Siege of Vicksburg June 17-July 4. Advance on Jackson, Miss., July 5-10. Siege of Jackson July 10-17. Destruction of Mississippi Central Railroad at Madison Station July 18-22. At Milldale till August 6. Moved to Crab Orchard, Ky., August 6-12. Burnside's Campaign in East Tennessee August 16-October 17. Action at Blue Springs October 10. At Lenoir till November 15. Knoxville Campaign November 4-December 23. Action at Campbell's Station November 16. Siege of Knoxville November 17-December 4. Repulse of Longstreet's assault on Fort Sanders November 29. Operations in East Tennessee till March, 1864. Action at Holston River January 20. Strawberry Plains January 21-22. Moved to Annapolis, Md., March, 1864. Campaign from the Rapidan to the James May 3-June 15. Battles of the Wilderness May 5-7; Spottsylvania May 8-12; Ny River May 10; Spottsylvania Court House May 12-21. Assault on the Salient May 12. (Non-Veterans left front May 13. Guard prisoners to Alexandria, Va., May 13-15; thence moved to New York and mustered out May 31, 1864.) North Anna River May 23-27. Totopotomoy May 28-31. Cold Harbor June 1-12. Bethesda Church June 1-3. Before Petersburg June 16-18. Siege of Petersburg June 16, 1864, to April 2, 1865. Mine Explosion, Petersburg, July 30, 1864. Weldon Railroad August 18-21. Poplar Springs Church September 29-October 2. Boydton Plank Road, Hatcher's Run, October 27-28. Fort Stedman March 25, 1865. Appomattox Campaign March 28-April 9. Assault on and fall of Petersburg April 2. Occupation of Petersburg April 3. Pursuit of Lee April 3-9. Surrender of Lee and his army April 9. Moved to Washington, D. C., April 21-28. Grand Review May 23. Duty at Washington, D. C., till July. Mustered out July 14, 1865.

Regiment lost during service 3 Officers and 116 Enlisted men killed and mortally wounded and 1 Officer and 78 Enlisted men by disease. Total 198.

80th REGIMENT INFANTRY.—("ULSTER GUARD." "20th REGIMENT STATE MILITIA INFANTRY.")

Tendered services to Government February, 1861. Organized at Kingston, N. Y., from 20th Regiment State Militia Infantry and mustered in September 20 to Oc-

tober 20, 1861. Left State for Washington, D. C., October 26. Designated 80th New York Infantry December 7, 1861. Attached to Wadsworth's Brigade, McDowell's Division, Army of the Potomac, to March, 1862. Patrick's 2nd Brigade, 3rd Division, 1st Army Corps, Army of the Potomac, to April, 1862. 2nd Brigade, King's Division, Dept. of the Rappahannock, to June, 1862. 3rd Brigade, 1st Division, 3rd Corps, Pope's Army of Virginia, to September, 1862. 3rd Brigade, 1st Division, 1st Army Corps, Army of the Potomac, to January, 1863. Patrick's Command, Provost Guard, Army of the Potomac, to June, 1863. 1st Brigade, 3rd Division, 1st Army Corps, to July, 1863. Provost Guard, Army of the Potomac, to June, 1864. City Point, Va., Provost Guard Headquarters, Army of the Potomac, to March, 1865. Independent Brigade, 9th Army Corps, to April, 1865. Richmond, Va., Dept. of Virginia, to November, 1865. Norfolk and Portsmouth, Va., Dept. of Virginia, to January, 1866.

SERVICE.—Duty at Upton's Hill, Defences of Washington, D. C., till March, 1862. Advance on Manassas, Va., March 10-15. McDowell's advance on Falmouth, Va., April 4-19. Occupation of Fredericksburg till May 25. McDowell's advance on Richmond May 26-29. Duty at Fredericksburg till August. Pope's Campaign in Northern Virginia August 16-September 2. Fords of the Rappahannock August 20-23. Beverly Ford August 20. Sulphur Springs August 26. Battles of Gainesville August 28; Groveton August 29; Bull Run August 30; Chantilly September 1. Maryland Campaign September 6-22. Battles of South Mountain September 14; Antietam September 16-17. At Sharpsburg, Md., till October 20. Movement to Falmouth, Va., October 20-November 19. Battle of Fredericksburg, Va., December 12-15. Duty at Hall's Landing December 20, 1862, to January 7, 1863. Provost Guard duty at Aquia Creek and along Richmond and Fredericksburg & Potomac Railroad till June 27. Relieved and ordered to join 1st Army Corps June 27. Battle of Gettysburg, Pa., July 1-3. Provost Guard duty, Army of the Potomac, July 16, 1863, to June 18, 1864. Participating in the Bristoe Campaign October 9-22, 1863. Advance to line of the Rappahannock November 7-8. Mine Run Campaign November 26-December 2. Campaign from the Rapidan to the James May 3-June 15, 1864. Battles of the Wilderness May 5-7; Spottsylvania May 8-12; Spottsylvania Court House May 12-21; North Anna River May 23-26. On line of the Pamunkey May 26-28. Totopotomoy May 28-31. Cold Harbor June 1-12. Before Petersburg June 16-18. Siege operations against Petersburg and Richmond June 16, 1864, to April 2, 1865. Assigned to garrison and guard duty at City Point, Va., Headquarters of the Army, June 18, 1864, to April 14, 1865. Assault on and fall of Petersburg April 2. Occupation of Petersburg April 3. Provost duty at Richmond April 14 to November 27, 1865, and at Norfolk and Portsmouth, Va., till January 29, 1866. Mustered out January 29, 1866.

Regiment lost during service 8 Officers and 120 Enlisted men killed and mortally wounded and 157 Enlisted men by disease. Total 285.

81st REGIMENT INFANTRY.—("2nd OSWEGO REGIMENT." "MOHAWK RANGERS.")

Organized at Albany, N. Y., December 20, 1861, to February 20, 1862. Left State for Washington, D. C., March 5, 1862. Attached to 3rd Brigade, 3rd Division, 4th Army Corps, Army of the Potomac, to June, 1862. 2nd Brigade, 2nd Division, 4th Army Corps, to June, 1862. 1st Brigade, 2nd Division, 4th Army Corps, to December, 1862. Naglee's Brigade, Dept. of North Carolina, to January, 1863. 1st Brigade, 2nd Division, 18th Army Corps, Dept. of North Carolina, to February, 1863. 1st Brigade, 1st Division, 18th Army Corps, Dept. of the South, to April, 1863. District of Beaufort, N. C., 18th Army Corps, to October, 1863. Newport News, Va., Dept. of Virginia and North Carolina, to January, 1864. District of the Currituck, Dept. of Virginia and North Carolina, to March, 1864. 1st Brigade, Heckman's Division, Dept. of Virginia and North Carolina, to April, 1864. 1st Brigade, 1st Division, 18th Army Corps, Army of the James, to December, 1864. 1st Brigade, 3rd Division, 24th Army Corps, to July, 1865. 1st Independent Brigade, 24th Army Corps, to August, 1865.

SERVICE.—Duty at Kalorama Heights, Defences of Washington, D. C. March 7-13, 1862. Moved to the Peninsula, Va., March 28. Siege of Yorktown April 5-May 4. Reconnoissance toward Lee's Mills April 29. Battle of Williamsburg May 5. Battle of Seven Pines or Fair Oaks May 31-June 1. Seven days before Richmond June 25-July 1. White Oak Swamp June 30. Malvern Hill July 1. At Harrison's Landing till August 16. Movement to Fortress Monroe August 16-22, and duty there till September 18. Duty at Yorktown, Norfolk and Portsmouth till December. Moved to Morehead City, N. C., December 28, 1862-January 1, 1863; thence to Port Royal, S. C., January 28-31, 1863. At St. Helena Island, S. C., till April. Expedition against Charleston, S. C., April 3-11. Moved to New Berne, N. C., April 12-15. Expedition to relief of Little Washington April 17-21. Expedition to Trenton July 4-8. Action at Quaker Bridge July 6. Duty in District of Beaufort, N. C., till October. Moved to Newport News, Va., October 16-18, and duty there till January, 1864. Moved to Portsmouth, Va., January 22, and duty there and in the District of the Currituck till April, 1864. Moved to Yorktown, Va., April 26. Butler's operations on south side of the James River and against Petersburg and Richmond May 4-28. Occupation of Bermuda Hundred and City Point May 5. Swift Creek or Arrowfield Church May 9-10. Operations against Fort Darling May 12-16. Battle of Drury's Bluff May 14-16. Bermuda Hundred May 16-28. Moved to White House Landing, thence to Cold Harbor May 27-31. Battles about Cold Harbor June 1-12. Before Petersburg June 15-18. Siege operations against Petersburg and Richmond June 16, 1864, to April 2, 1865. Mine Explosion, Petersburg, July 30, 1864 (Reserve). Battle of Chaffin's Farm, New Market Heights, September 28-30. Battle of Fair Oaks October 27-28. Duty in trenches before Richmond till April, 1865. Occupation of Richmond April 3. Pursuit of Lee April 4-9. Appomattox Court House April 9. Surrender of Lee and his army. Duty in the Department of Virginia till August. Mustered out August 31, 1865.

Regiment lost during service 13 Officers and 129 Enlisted men killed and mortally wounded and 1 Officer and 98 Enlisted men by disease. Total 239.

82nd REGIMENT INFANTRY ("2nd REGIMENT STATE MILITIA INFANTRY").

Left State for Washington, D. C., May 18, 1861. Mustered into United States service May 28, 1861. Attached to Schenck's Brigade, Tyler's Division, McDowell's Army of Northeast Virginia, to August, 1861. Stone's Brigade, Division of the Potomac, to October, 1861. Gorman's Brigade, Stone's (Sedgwick's) Division, Army of the Potomac, to March, 1862. 1st Brigade, 2nd Division, 2nd Army Corps, Army of the Potomac, to June, 1864.

SERVICE.—Duty in the Defences of Washington, D. C., and at Ball's Cross Roads, Va., till July 16, 1861. Advance on Manassas, Va., July 16-21. Occupation of Fairfax Court House July 17. Battle of Bull Run July 21. Moved to Poolesville, Md., August 5. Picket and outpost duty on the Upper Potomac till February, 1862. Operations on the Potomac October 21-24, 1861. Battle of Ball's Bluff October 21. Edwards' Ferry October 22. Moved to Harper's Ferry, W. Va., February 23, 1862, and duty there till March 7. Movement in support of General Shields at Winchester, Va., March 7-15. Moved to Washington, D. C., thence to Fortress Monroe, Va., March 22-April 1. Siege of Yorktown April 5-May 4. West Point May 7-8. Battle of Seven Pines or Fair Oaks May 31-June 1. Skirmishing before Richmond till June 25. Seven days before Richmond June 25-July 1. Gaines' Mill, Garnett's Farm, June 27. Peach Or-

chard and Savage Station June 29. White Oak Swamp and Glendale June 30. Malvern Hill July 1. At Harrison's Landing till August 16. Movement to Fortress Monroe, thence to Centreville August 16-30. Battle of Bull Run August 30. Maryland Campaign September 6-22. Battles of South Mountain September 14; Antietam September 16-17. Moved to Harper's Ferry, W. Va., September 22, and duty there till October 30. Movement to Falmouth, Va., October 30-November 20. Battle of Fredericksburg, Va., December 12-15. At Falmouth till April 27, 1863. "Mud March" January 20-24. Chancellorsville Campaign April 27-May 6. Operations about Franklin's Crossing April 29-May 2. Battle of Maryes Heights, Fredericksburg, May 3. Salem Heights May 3-4. Banks' Ford May 4. Battle of Gettysburg, Pa., July 2-4. Pursuit of Lee July 5-24. Duty on line of the Rappahannock to October. Advance from the Rappahannock to the Rapidan September 13-17. Bristoe Campaign October 9-22. Bristoe Station October 14. Advance to line of the Rappahannock November 7-8. Mine Run Campaign November 26-December 2. Mine Run November 28-30. At and near Stevensburg till May, 1864. Demonstration on the Rapidan February 6-7. Morton's Ford February 6-7. Campaign from the Rapidan to the James May 3-June 15. Battles of the Wilderness May 5-7; Spottsylvania May 8-12; Po River May 10; Spottsylvania Court House May 12-21. Assault on the Salient or "Bloody Angle" May 12. North Anna River May 23-26. On line of the Pamunkey May 26-28. Totopotomoy May 28-31. Cold Harbor June 1-12. Before Petersburg June 16-18. Siege of Petersburg June 16-25. Jerusalem Plank Road, Weldon Railroad, June 22-23. Mustered out June 25, 1864, expiration of term. Veterans and Recruits transferred to 59th Regiment New York Infantry July 10, 1864.

Regiment lost during service 10 Officers and 171 Enlisted men killed and mortally wounded and 5 Officers and 83 Enlisted men by disease. Total 269.

83rd REGIMENT INFANTRY ("9th REGIMENT STATE MILITIA INFANTRY," "CITY GUARD").

Volunteered for three years' service. Left New York City for Washington, D. C., May 27, 1861. Mustered in at Washington June 8, 1861. Attached to Stone's Command, June 10 to July 7, 1861. Stone's Brigade, Patterson's Army, to August 17, 1861. Stile's Brigade, Banks' Division, Army of the Potomac, to March, 1862. Abercrombie's 2nd Brigade, Williams' 1st Division, Banks' 5th Corps, to April, 1862. 2nd Brigade, 1st Division, Dept. of the Shenandoah, to May, 1862. 3rd Brigade, 2nd Division, Dept. of the Rappahannock, to June, 1862. 3rd Brigade, 2nd Division, 3rd Corps, Pope's Army of Virginia, to September, 1862. 3rd Brigade, 2nd Division, 1st Army Corps, Army of the Potomac, to May, 1863. 2nd Brigade, 2nd Division, 1st Army Corps, to March, 1864. 2nd Brigade, 2nd Division, 5th Army Corps, to May 9, 1864. 2nd Brigade, 3rd Division, 5th Army Corps, to May 30, 1864. 2nd Brigade, 2nd Division, 5th Army Corps, to June 7, 1864.

SERVICE.—Rockville Expedition June 10-July 7, 1861. Duty on the Upper Potomac till March, 1862. Harper's Ferry, W. Va., July 4, 1861. Operations in the Shenandoah Valley March and April, 1862. Occupation of Winchester March 12. Pursuit of and operations against Jackson March 24-April 27. Near Warrenton Junction April 6 and 16. Reconnoissance to Rappahannock River and North Fork April 18. Rappahannock Crossing April 18. Pope's Campaign in Northern Virginia June to September. Battle of Cedar Mountain August 9. Fords of the Rappahannock August 20-23. Thoroughfare Gap August 28. Battles of Groveton August 29; Bull Run August 30; Chantilly September 1. Maryland Campaign September 6-22. Battles of South Mountain, Md., September 14. Antietam September 16-17. At Sharpsburg till October 30. Movement to Falmouth, Va., October 30-November 19. Battle of Fredericksburg, Va., December 12-15. At Falmouth till April 27, 1863. "Mud March" January 20-24. Chancellorsville Campaign April 27-May 6. Operations about Fitzhugh's Crossing April 29-May 3. Battle of Chancellorsville May 3-5. Gettysburg (Pa.) Campaign June 11-July 24. Battle of Gettysburg July 1-3. Pursuit of Lee to Manassas Gap, Va., July 5-24. Duty on line of the Rappahannock and Rapidan till October. Bristoe Campaign October 9-22. Advance to line of the Rappahannock November 7-8. Mine Run Campaign November 26-December 2. Duty on the Orange & Alexandria Railroad till April, 1864. Demonstration on the Rapidan February 6-7. Campaign from the Rapidan May 3-June 7. Battles of the Wilderness May 5-7; Laurel Hill May 8; Spottsylvania May 8-12; Spottsylvania Court House May 12-21. Assault on the Salient May 12. North Anna River May 23-26. Jericho Ford May 25. On line of the Pamunkey May 26-28. Totopotomoy May 28-31. Cold Harbor June 1-7. Bethesda Church June 1-3. Relieved June 7 and ordered to the rear for muster out. Veterans and Recruits transferred to 97th New York Infantry June 7, 1864. Regiment mustered out at New York City June 23, 1864, expiration of term.

Regiment lost during service 9 Officers and 147 Enlisted men killed and mortally wounded and 2 Officers and 86 Enlisted men by disease. Total 244.

84th REGIMENT INFANTRY.—("14th BROOKLYN STATE MILITIA INFANTRY.")

Tendered services to Government and left Brooklyn for Washington, D. C., May 18, 1861. Mustered into United States service at Washington May 25, 1861. Attached to Mansfield's Command, Defences of Washington, to June, 1861. Porter's Brigade, Hunter's Division, McDowell's Army of Northeast Virginia, to August, 1861. Keyes' Brigade, Division of the Potomac, to October, 1861. Keyes' Brigade, McDowell's Division, Army of the Potomac, to March, 1862. 1st Brigade, 3rd Division, 1st Army Corps, Army of the Potomac, to April, 1862. 1st Brigade, King's Division, Dept. of the Rappahannock, to June, 1862. 1st Brigade, 1st Division, 3rd Corps, Pope's Army of Virginia, to September, 1862. 1st Brigade, 1st Division, 1st Army Corps, Army of the Potomac, to June, 1863. 2nd Brigade, 1st Division, 1st Army Corps, to March, 1864. 2nd Brigade, 4th Division, 5th Army Corps, to June, 1864.

SERVICE.—Camp at Meridian Hill, Defences of Washington, D. C., till July 2, 1861. Advance into Virginia and occupation of Arlington Heights May 23-24. Camp near Arlington House July 2-16. Advance on Manassas, Va., July 16-21. Battle of Bull Run July 21. Duty at Arlington Heights till September 28. Advance on Munson's and Hall's Hills September 28. At Upton's Hill till March, 1862. Skirmish, Fall's Church Road, near Fairfax Court House, November 18, 1861. Advance on Manassas, Va., March 10-15, 1862. McDowell's advance on Falmouth, Va., April 4-19. Camp at Falmouth till May 25. McDowell's advance on Richmond, Va., May 25-29. Operations against Jackson May 29-June 21. Duty at Falmouth till August 5. Expedition to Po River July 23-25 (Cos. "B" and "E"). Mt. Carmel Church July 23. Reconnoissance to Spottsylvania Court House August 5-8. March to Cedar Mountain March 10-11. Pope's Campaign in Northern Virginia August 16-September 2. Fords of the Rappahannock August 20-23. Battles of Gainesville August 28; Groveton August 29; Bull Run August 30; Chantilly September 2. Maryland Campaign September 6-22. Battles of South Mountain September 14; Antietam September 16-17. At Sharpsburg, Md., till October 20. March to Falmouth, Va., October 26-November 22. At Brooks' Station November 22-December 8. Battle of Fredericksburg, Va., December 12-15. At Falmouth and Belle Plain till April 27, 1863. "Mud March" January 20-24. Expedition to Port Conway April 22-24. Chancellorsville Campaign April 27-May 6. Operations at Pollock's Mill Creek April 29-May 2. Fitzhugh's Crossing April 29-30. Battle of Chancellorsville May 2-5. Gettysburg (Pa.) Campaign June 11-July 24. Battle of Gettysburg, Pa., July 1-3. Pursuit of Lee to Manassas Gap, Va., July 5-24. At Manassas Junction till August 1. At

Rappahannock Station till August 14. Duty on line of the Rappahannock till October. Bristoe Campaign October 9-22. Advance to line of the Rappahannock November 7-8. Mine Run Campaign November 26-December 2. Provost duty at Culpeper, Va., December 28, 1863, to May 4, 1864. Demonstration on the Rapidan February 6-7. Rapidan Campaign May 4-22. Battles of the Wilderness May 5-7; Laurel Hill May 8; Spottsylvania May 8-12; Spottsylvania Court House May 12-21. Assault on the Salient May 12. Left front May 22 and arrived at Brooklyn May 24. Veterans and Recruits attached to 12th New York Battalion May 21, then transferred to 5th New York Veteran Infantry June 2, 1864. Regiment mustered out June 14 to date June 6, 1864.

Regiment lost during service 8 Officers and 154 Enlisted men killed and mortally wounded and 69 Enlisted men by disease. Total 231.

84th REGIMENT NATIONAL GUARD INFANTRY.

Organized July 3, 1863, for thirty days' United States service. Moved to Baltimore, Md., and duty in the Defences of that city till August. Attached to 8th Army Corps, Middle Department. Mustered out August 4, 1863.

Again mustered in for 100 days' United States service July 12, 1864. Duty at and near Washington, D. C., Great Falls, Md., and at Winchester, Va., till October. Skirmish near Muddy Branch, Md., September 29. Mustered out October 29, 1864.

85th REGIMENT INFANTRY.

Organized at Elmira, N. Y., and mustered in December 2, 1861. Left State for Washington, D. C., December 3, 1861. Attached to 3rd Brigade, Casey's Division, Army of the Potomac, to March, 1862. 3rd Brigade, 3rd Division, 4th Army Corps, Army of the Potomac, to June, 1862. 2nd Brigade, 2nd Division, 4th Army Corps, to September, 1862. Wessell's Brigade, Division at Suffolk, 7th Army Corps, Dept. of Virginia, to December, 1862. 1st Brigade, 1st Division, Dept. of North Carolina, to January, 1863. 1st Brigade, 4th Division, 18th Army Corps, Dept. of North Carolina, to May, 1863. District of the Albemarle, Dept. of North Carolina, to August, 1863. Sub-District of the Albemarle, District of North Carolina, Dept. of Virginia and North Carolina, to April, 1864. Plymouth, N. C., District of North Carolina, January to March, 1865. 2nd Brigade, Division District of Beaufort, N. C., Dept. of North Carolina, to April, 1865. Unattached, 23rd Army Corps, Dept. of North Carolina, to June, 1865.

SERVICE.—Duty in the Defences of Washington, D. C., till March, 1862. Advance on Manassas, Va., March 10-15. Moved to the Peninsula, Va., March 28. Siege of Yorktown April 5-May 4. Reconnoissance toward Lee's Mills April 29. Battle of Williamsburg May 5. Reconnoissance to Bottom's Bridge May 20-23. Seven Pines, Savage Station and Chickahominy May 24. Reconnoissance to Seven Pines May 24-27. Battle of Seven Pines or Fair Oaks May 31-June 1. New Market Road June 8. Seven days before Richmond June 25-July 1. Bottom's Bridge June 27-28. White Oak Swamp June 30. Malvern Hill July 1. At Harrison's Landing till August 16. Moved to Fortress Monroe August 16-23, thence to Suffolk, Va., September 18, and duty there till December. Reconnoissance to Franklin October 3. Blackwater October 9, 26, 29 and 30. Franklin October 31. Zuni November 18. Ordered to New Berne, N. C., December 4. Foster's Expedition to Goldsboro, N. C., December 11-20. Actions at Kinston December 14. Whitehall December 16. Goldsboro December 17. Duty at New Berne, N. C., till April, 1863. Expedition to relief of Little Washington April 7-10. Moved to Plymouth, N. C., May 2, and duty there till July. Expedition to Williamston and Gardiner's Bridge July 5-7 (Detachment). Expedition from Plymouth to Foster's Mills July 26-29. Expedition to Roanoke Island August 6-13, and to Columbia August 26-27. Duty at Albemarle Sound and Chowan River till November. Expedition to Winton November 6-9. Regiment veteranize January 1, 1864. Expedition up the Chowan January 6-21. Harrellsville January 20 (Detachment). Siege of Plymouth, N. C., April 17-20. Surrendered at Plymouth April 20. Regiment reorganized January, 1865, and duty in the Dept. of North Carolina till June. Campaign of the Carolinas March 1-April 26. Advance on Kinston and Goldsboro March 6-21. Battle of Wise's Forks March 8-10. Occupation of Kinston March 14, and of Goldsboro March 21. Occupation of Raleigh April 14. Bennett's House April 26. Surrender of Johnston and his army. Duty in the Dept. of North Carolina till June. Mustered out June 27, 1865.

Regiment lost during service 1 Officer and 34 Enlisted men killed and mortally wounded and 2 Officers and 324 Enlisted men by disease. Total 361.

86th REGIMENT INFANTRY.—("STEUBEN RANGERS.")

Organized at Elmira and mustered in November 20, 1861. Left State for Washington, D. C., November 23, 1861. Attached to 2nd Brigade, Casey's Division, Army of the Potomac, to March, 1862. Wadsworth's Command, Military District of Washington, to August, 1862. Piatt's Brigade, Whipple's Division, to September, 1862. 1st Brigade, 3rd Division, 3rd Army Corps, Army of the Potomac, to June, 1863. 2nd Brigade, 1st Division, 3rd Army Corps, to March, 1864. 1st Brigade, 3rd Division, 2nd Army Corps, to June, 1865.

SERVICE.—Duty in the Defences of Washington, D. C., till August, 1862. Pope's Campaign in Northern Virginia August 16-September 2. Duty in the Defences of Washington till October. Moved to Point of Rocks, thence to Pleasant Valley, Md., October 18-19. Movement toward Warrenton, Va., October 24-November 16. Reconnoissance to Manassas Gap, Va., and skirmish November 5-6. Movement to Falmouth, Va., November 18-24. Battle of Fredericksburg, Va., December 12-15. Duty near Falmouth till April 27, 1863. "Mud March" January 20-24. Chancellorsville Campaign April 27-May 6. Battle of Chancellorsville May 1-5. Brandy Station and Beverly Ford June 9. Gettysburg (Pa.) Campaign June 11-July 24. Battle of Gettysburg July 1-3. Pursuit of Lee July 5-24. Wapping Heights, Va., July 23. Duty on line of the Rappahannock till October. Bristoe Campaign October 9-22. Advance to line of the Rappahannock November 7-8. Kelly's Ford November 7. Mine Run Campaign November 26-December 2. Duty near Brandy Station till May, 1864. Demonstration on the Rapidan February 6-7. Campaign from the Rapidan to the James May 3-June 15. Battles of the Wilderness May 5-7; Spottsylvania May 8-12; Po River May 10; Spottsylvania Court House May 12-21. Assault on the Salient, "Bloody Angle," May 12. North Anna River May 23-26. On line of the Pamunkey May 26-28. Totopotomoy May 28-31. Cold Harbor June 1-12. Before Petersburg June 16-18. Siege of Petersburg June 16, 1864, to April 2, 1865. Jerusalem Plank Road, Weldon Railroad, June 22-23, 1864. Demonstration north of the James July 27-29. Deep Bottom July 27-28. Demonstration north of the James August 13-20. Strawberry Plains, Deep Bottom, August 14-18. Poplar Springs Church September 29-October 2. Boydton Plank Road, Hatcher's Run, October 27-28. Reconnoissance to Weldon Railroad December 9-10. Dabney's Mills, Hatcher's Run, February 5-7, 1865. Watkins' House March 25. Appomattox Campaign March 28-April 9. Boydton and White Oak Roads March 29-31. Crow's House March 31. Fall of Petersburg April 2. Sailor's Creek April 6. High Bridge and Farmville April 7. Appomattox Court House April 9. Surrender of Lee and his army. At Burkesville till May 2. Moved to Washington, D. C., May 2-12. Grand Review May 23. Mustered out June 27, 1865.

Regiment lost during service 13 Officers and 159 Enlisted men killed and mortally wounded and 2 Officers and 129 Enlisted men by disease. Total 303.

87th REGIMENT INFANTRY.—("13th BROOKLYN.")

Organized at Brooklyn, N. Y., and mustered in November 20, 1861. Left State for Washington, D. C., December 2, 1861. Attached to 3rd Brigade, Casey's Division, Army of the Potomac, to March, 1862. 1st Brigade, 3rd Division, 3rd Army Corps, Army of the Potomac, to August, 1862. 1st Brigade, 1st Division, 3rd Army Corps, to September, 1862.

SERVICE.—Duty in the Dept. of Washington till March, 1862. Advance on Manassas, Va., March 10-15. Ordered to the Peninsula, Va., March 17. Siege of Yorktown April 5-May 4. Skirmish at Yorktown April 11. Battle of Williamsburg May 5. Battle of Seven Pines or Fair Oaks May 31-June 1. Seven days before Richmond June 25-July 1. Battle of Oak Grove June 25. Malvern Hill July 1. At Harrison's Landing till August 16. Movement to Fortress Monroe, thence to Centreville August 16-26. Pope's Campaign in Northern Virginia August 26-September 2. Action at Bristoe Station or Kettle Run August 27. Buckland's Bridge, Broad Run, August 27. Battles of Groveton August 29; Bull Run August 30; Chantilly September 1. Consolidated with 40th Regiment New York Infantry September 6, 1862. Company "B" transferred to 173rd New York Infantry September 11, 1862.

Regiment lost during service 1 Officer and 22 Enlisted men killed and mortally wounded and 26 Enlisted men by disease. Total 49.

88th REGIMENT INFANTRY.—("MEAGHER'S OWN." "5th REGIMENT IRISH BRIGADE.")

Organized at Fort Schuyler, N. Y., and left State for Washington, D. C., December 16, 1861. Attached to Meagher's Brigade, Sumner's Division, Army of the Potomac, to March, 1862. Meagher's 2nd Brigade, Richardson's 1st Division, 2nd Army Corps, Army of the Potomac, to May, 1862. 2nd Brigade, 1st Division, 2nd Army Corps, to June, 1864. Consolidated Brigade, 1st Division, 2nd Army Corps, to November, 1864. 2nd Brigade, 1st Division, 2nd Army Corps, to June, 1865.

SERVICE.—Duty in the Defences of Washington, D. C., till March, 1862. Advance on Manassas, Va., March 10-15. Ordered to the Peninsula, Va., April. Siege of Yorktown April 16-May 4. Battle of Fair Oaks or Seven Pines May 31-June 1. Seven days before Richmond June 25-July 1. Battles of Gaines Mill June 27; Peach Orchard and Savage Station June 29; White Oak Swamp Bridge and Glendale June 30; Malvern Hill July 1. At Harrison's Landing till August 16. Movement to Fortress Monroe, thence to Alexandria and Centreville August 16-30. Maryland Campaign September 6-22. Battle of Antietam, Md., September 16-17. Moved to Harper's Ferry, W. Va., September 22, and duty there till October 29. Reconnoissance to Charlestown October 16-17. Advance up Loudoun Valley and movement to Falmouth October 29-November 17. Battle of Fredericksburg, Va., December 12-15. At Falmouth till April 27, 1863. "Mud March" January 20-24. Chancellorsville Campaign April 27-May 6. Battle of Chancellorsville May 1-5. Gettysburg (Pa.) Campaign June 11-July 24. Battle of Gettysburg, Pa., July 1-3. Pursuit of Lee to Manassas Gap, Va., July 5-24. Duty on line of the Rappahannock till October. Advance from the Rappahannock to the Rapidan September 13-17. Bristoe Campaign October 9-22. Auburn and Bristoe October 14. Advance to line of the Rappahannock November 7-8. Mine Run Campaign November 26-December 2. Mine Run November 28-30. Duty at and near Stevensburg till May, 1864. Demonstration on the Rapidan February 6-7. Campaign from the Rapidan to the James May 3-June 15. Battles of the Wilderness May 5-7; Spottsylvania May 8-12; Po River May 10; Spottsylvania Court House May 12-21. Assault on the Salient or "Bloody Angle" May 12. North Anna River May 23-26. On line of the Pamunkey May 26-28. Totopotomoy May 28-31. Cold Harbor June 1-12. Before Petersburg June 16-18. Siege of Petersburg June 16, 1864, to April 2, 1865. Jerusalem Plank Road June 22-23, 1864. Demonstration north of the James July 27-29.

Deep Bottom July 27-28. Demonstration north of the James August 13-20. Strawberry Plains, Deep Bottom, August 14-18. Ream's Station August 25. Boydton Plank Road, Hatcher's Run, October 27-28. Front of Forts Morton and Sedgwick October 27. Reconnoissance to Hatcher's Run December 9-10. Dabney's Mills, Hatcher's Run, February 5-7, 1865. Watkins' House March 25. Appomattox Campaign March 28-April 9. Hatcher's Run or Boydton Road March 30-31. White Oak Road March 31. Sutherland Station and fall of Petersburg April 2. Sailor's Creek April 6. Farmville April 7. Appomattox Court House April 9. Surrender of Lee and his army. At Burkesville till May 2. Moved to Washington, D. C., May 2-12. Grand Review May 23. Mustered out June 30, 1865.

Regiment lost during service 15 Officers and 136 Enlisted men killed and mortally wounded and 3 Officers and 69 Enlisted men by disease. Total 223.

89th REGIMENT INFANTRY.—("DICKINSON GUARD.")

Organized at Elmira, N. Y., and mustered in December 4, 1861. Left State for Washington, D. C., December 6, 1861. Attached to Provisional Brigade, Casey's Division, Army of the Potomac, to December, 1861. Williams' Brigade, Burnside's North Carolina Expeditionary Corps, to April, 1862. 4th Brigade, Dept. of North Carolina, to July, 1862. 1st Brigade, 3rd Division, 9th Army Corps, Army of the Potomac, to April, 1863. 1st Brigade, 2nd Division, 7th Army Corps, Dept. of Virginia, to July, 1863. Alvord's Brigade, Vodges' Division, Folly Island, S. C., 10th Army Corps, Dept. of the South, to January, 1864. 2nd Brigade, Folly Island, S. C., Northern District, Dept. of the South, to February, 1864. 2nd Brigade, Gordon's Division, Northern District, Dept. of the South, to April, 1864. 1st Brigade, 2nd Division, 10th Army Corps, Army of the James, Dept. of Virginia and North Carolina, to May, 1864. 1st Brigade, 2nd Division, 18th Army Corps, to June, 1864. 3rd Brigade, 2nd Division, 18th Army Corps, to December, 1864. 4th Brigade, 1st Division, 24th Army Corps, to May, 1865. 3rd Brigade, 1st Division, 24th Army Corps, to June, 1865. 2nd Brigade, 1st Division, 24th Army Corps, to August, 1865.

SERVICE.—Duty in the Defences of Washington, D. C., till January, 1862. Expedition to Hatteras Inlet, N. C., January 6-13, and duty there till March 2. Moved to Roanoke Island, N. C., March 2, and duty there till June 18. Battle of Camden, South Mills, April 19. Expedition to New Berne June 18-July 2. Moved to Newport News, Va., July 4-6; thence to Aquia Creek and Fredericksburg, Va., August 2-7, and duty there till August 30. Moved to Brooks' Station, thence to Washington, D. C., August 31-September 5. Maryland Campaign September 6-22. Battles of South Mountain September 14; Antietam, Md., September 16-17. Duty in Pleasant Valley till October 27. Movement to Falmouth, Va., October 27-November 19. Battle of Fredericksburg, Va., December 12-15. "Mud March" January 20-24, 1863. Moved to Newport News, Va., February 9; thence to Norfolk and Suffolk March 14. Siege of Suffolk April 12-May 4. Battery Huger, Hill's Point, April 18-19. Near Suffolk April 19. Providence Church Road May 3. Reconnoissance across the Nansemond May 4. Dix's Peninsula Campaign June 24-July 7. Expedition from White House to South Anna River July 1-7. Ordered to Folly Island, S. C., July. Siege operations against Forts Wagner and Gregg, Morris Island, S. C., and against Fort Sumpter and Charleston August 14-September 7. Bombardment of Fort Sumpter August 17-23. Capture of Forts Wagner and Gregg September 7. Operations against Charleston and duty on Morris and Folly Islands, S. C., till April, 1864. Moved to Gloucester Point, Va., April, 1864. Butler's operations on south side of the James and against Petersburg and Richmond May 4-28. Occupation of Bermuda Hundred and City Point May 5. Port Walthall May 7. Swift Creek or Arrowfield Church May 9-10. Operations against Fort Darling May 12-16. Battle of Drury's Bluff May 14-16. Bermuda Hundred May 16-27. Moved to White House, thence to Cold Harbor May 27-31. Battles about Cold Harbor June 1-12. Before Petersburg June 15-18. Siege operations against Petersburg and Richmond June 16, 1864, to April 2, 1865. Mine Explosion, Petersburg, July 30, 1864 (Reserve). Duty in trenches before Petersburg and on the Bermuda front till September 27. Battle of Chaffin's Farm, New Market Heights, September 28-30. Battle of Fair Oaks October 27-28. Duty in trenches before Richmond on north side of the James till March, 1865. Moved to Hatcher's Run March 27-28. Appomattox Campaign March 28-April 9. Assault and capture of Forts Gregg and Baldwin and fall of Petersburg April 2. Rice's Station April 6. Appomattox Court House April 9. Surrender of Lee and his army. Duty in the Department of Virginia till August. Mustered out August 3, 1865.

Regiment lost during service 6 Officers and 89 Enlisted men killed and mortally wounded and 159 Enlisted men by disease. Total 254.

90th REGIMENT INFANTRY.

Organized by consolidation of McClellan Chasseurs and McClellan Rifles at New York City November and December, 1861. Left State for Key West, Fla., January 5, 1862. Attached to Brannan's Florida Expedition to March, 1862. District of Key West, Dept. of the South, to August, 1862. District of Key West, Fla., Dept. of the Gulf, to November, 1862. District of Beaufort, S. C., 10th Army Corps, Dept. of the South, to March, 1863. District of Key West, Fla., Dept. of the Gulf, to April, 1863. 1st Brigade, 4th Division, 19th Army Corps, Dept. of the Gulf, to February, 1864. 2nd Brigade, 2nd Division, 19th Army Corps, Dept. of the Gulf, to July, 1864. 1st Brigade, 1st Division, 19th Army Corps, Army of the Shenandoah, Middle Military Division, to February, 1865. 1st Brigade, 1st Division (Provisional), Army of the Shenandoah, to April, 1865. 1st Brigade, Dwight's Division, Dept. of Washington, D. C., to June, 1865. 1st Brigade, Dwight's Division, District of Savannah, Ga., Dept. of the South, to July, 1865. District of Georgia, Dept. of the South, to February, 1866.

SERVICE.—Duty at Key West, Fla., till November, 1862; then in District of Beaufort, S. C. Ordered to New Orleans, La., April, 1863. Expedition from Barrie's Landing toward Berwick City May 21-26. Action at Franklin May 25. Moved to Algiers, thence to Port Hudson May 26-June 3. Siege of Port Hudson June 3-July 9. Assault on Port Hudson June 14. Surrender of Port Hudson July 9. Kock's Plantation, Donaldsonville, Bayou LaFourche, July 12-13. Duty in the Defences of New Orleans, La., till April, 1864. Moved to Alexandria, La. Red River Campaign April 30-May 22. Construction of dam at Alexandria April 30-May 10. Retreat to Morganza May 13-20. Mansura May 16. At Morganza till July. Moved to New Orleans, thence to Fortress Monroe, Va., and Washington, D. C., July 3-28. Sheridan's Shenandoah Valley Campaign August 7-November 28. Battle of Winchester September 19. Fisher's Hill September 22. Battle of Cedar Creek October 19. At Winchester, Stephenson's Depot and Kernstown till April, 1865. Moved to Washington, D. C., April 21-22, and duty there till June 1. Grand Review May 23-24. Moved to Savannah, Ga., June 2-6. Duty there and at Hawkinsville, Ga., till February, 1866. Mustered out February 9, 1866.

Regiment lost during service 2 Officers and 58 Enlisted men killed and mortally wounded and 7 Officers and 181 Enlisted men by disease. Total 248.

91st REGIMENT INFANTRY ("ALBANY REGT").

Organized at Albany, N. Y., September to December, 1861. Left State for Washington, D. C., January 9, 1862; thence moved to Pensacola, Fla. Attached to Brannan's Command, District of Florida, to March, 1862. District of Key West, Fla., Dept. of the South, to August, 1862. District of West Florida, Dept. of the Gulf, to December, 1862. Grover's Division, Dept. of the Gulf, to January, 1863. 1st Brigade, 3rd Division, 19th Army Corps, Dept. of the Gulf, to January, 1863. 2nd Brigade, 4th Division, 19th Army Corps, to March, 1863. 1st Brigade, 4th Division, 19th Army Corps, to July, 1863. Garrison at Fort Jackson, Defences of New Orleans, Dept. of the Gulf, to October, 1864. Defences of Baltimore, Md., 8th Army Corps, Middle Department, to February, 1865. 1st Brigade, 3rd Division, 5th Army Corps, Army of the Potomac, to June, 1865. 3rd Brigade, 3rd Division, 5th Army Corps, to July, 1865.

SERVICE.—Duty at Key West, Fort Pickens and Pensacola, Fla., till December, 1862. Expedition from Pensacola to Bagdad and Milton, Fla., August 7-10 (Cos. "I" and "K"). Action at Gonzales, Fla., October 27. Ordered to New Orleans, La., December; thence to Baton Rouge, La., and occupation of that city December 17. Duty at Baton Rouge, La., till March, 1863. Operations against Port Hudson March 7-27. Moved to Donaldsonville March 26, thence to Brashear City. Operations in Western Louisiana April 9-May 14. Teche Campaign April 11-20. Madam Porter's and McWilliams' Plantations at Indian Bend April 13. Irish Bend April 14. Vermillion Bayou April 17. Opelousas April 20. Siege of Port Hudson May 24-July 9. Assaults on Port Hudson May 27 and June 14. Surrender of Port Hudson July 9. Kock's Plantation, Donaldsonville, Bayou LaFourche, July 12-13. Duty at Fort Jackson, Defences of New Orleans, as garrison from July, 1863, to August, 1864. On Veteran furlough till October. Duty at Baltimore, Md., Middle Department, till February, 1865. Ordered to join Army of the Potomac before Petersburg, Va. Siege of Petersburg March 1-April 2. Appomattox Campaign March 28-April 9. Lewis Farm, near Gravelly Run, March 29. Boydton and White Oak Roads March 30-31. Five Forks April 1. Fall of Petersburg April 2. Pursuit of Lee April 3-9. Appomattox Court House April 9. Surrender of Lee and his army. March to Washington, D. C., May 1-12. Grand Review May 23. Duty at Washington till July. (Co. "E" detached at Baltimore, Md., October, 1864, to July, 1865.) Mustered out July 3, 1865.

Regiment lost during service 3 Officers and 110 Enlisted men killed and mortally wounded and 1 Officer and 184 Enlisted men by disease. Total 298.

92nd REGIMENT INFANTRY.

Organized at Potsdam, N. Y., and mustered in January 1, 1862. Left State for Washington, D. C., March 5, 1862. Attached to 3rd Brigade, 3rd Division, 4th Army Corps, Army of the Potomac, to June, 1862. 2nd Brigade, 2nd Division, 4th Army Corps, to September, 1862. Wessell's Brigade, Division of Suffolk, Va., 7th Army Corps, Dept. of Virginia, to December, 1862. 1st Brigade, 1st Division, Dept. of North Carolina, to January, 1863. 1st Brigade, 4th Division, 18th Army Corps, Dept. of North Carolina, to May, 1863. Lee's Brigade, Defences of New Berne, N. C., Dept. of North Carolina, to August, 1863. Sub-District of the Albemarle District of North Carolina, Dept. of Virginia and North Carolina, to April, 1864. Palmer's Brigade, Peck's Division, 18th Army Corps, April, 1864. 3rd Brigade, 1st Division, 18th Army Corps, to October, 1864. 2nd Brigade, 1st Division, 18th Army Corps, to December, 1864.

SERVICE.—Advance on Manassas, Va., March 10-15, 1862. Ordered to the Peninsula, Virginia, March 28. Siege of Yorktown April 5-May 4. Reconnoissance toward Lee's Mills April 29. Battle of Williamsburg May 5. Operations about Bottom's Bridge May 21-23. Near Seven Pines May 29-30. Battle of Seven Pines or Fair Oaks May 31-June 1. New Market Road June 8. Seven days before Richmond June 25-July 1. Bottom's Bridge June 27-28. White Oak Swamp June 30. Malvern Hill July 1. At Harrison's Landing till August 16. Moved to Fortress Monroe August 16-23. Duty there till September 18. Moved to Suffolk, Va., September 18, and duty there till December. Reconnoissance to Franklin October 3. Affairs on the Blackwater October 9, 26, 29 and 30. Franklin October 31. Ordered to New Berne, N. C., December 4. Foster's Expedition

47

to Goldsboro, N. C., December 11-20. Actions at Kinston March 14; Whitehall December 16; Goldsboro December 17. Duty at and near New Berne till April, 1864. Operations against Whiting January 18-February 10. Fort Anderson March 14, 1863. Expedition to relief of Little Washington April 7-10. Beech Grove and Batchelor's Creek, near New Berne, February 1-3, 1864. Ordered to Yorktown, Va., April 28, 1864. Butler's operations on south side of the James River and against Petersburg and Richmond May 4-28. Occupation of City Point and Bermuda Hundred May 5. Swift Creek or Arrowfield Church May 8-10. Operations against Fort Darling May 12-16. Battle of Drury's Bluff May 14-16. Bermuda Hundred May 16-27. Moved to White House, thence to Cold Harbor, May 27-31. Battles about Cold Harbor June 1-12. Before Petersburg June 15-18. Wier Bottom Church June 20. Siege operations against Petersburg and Richmond June 16 to December 1, 1864. Hare's House June 24 and 28. Mine Explosion, Petersburg, July 30 (Reserve). Duty in the trenches before Petersburg and on the Bermuda front till September 26. Battle of Chaffin's Farm, New Market Heights, September 28-30. Battle of Fair Oaks October 27-28. Duty in trenches before Richmond north of the James River till December. Consolidated with 96th Regiment New York Infantry December 1, 1864. Old members mustered out January 7, 1865.

Regiment lost during service 1 Officer and 67 Enlisted men killed and mortally wounded and 2 Officers and 115 Enlisted men by disease. Total 185.

93rd REGIMENT INFANTRY ("MORGAN RIFLES").

Organized at Albany, N. Y., October, 1861, to January, 1862. Moved to New York City February 17, thence to Washington, D. C., March 7, 1862. Attached to 3rd Brigade, 3rd Division, 4th Army Corps, Army of the Potomac, to May 18, 1862. Provost Guard, Army of the Potomac, to April, 1864. 2nd Brigade, 3rd Division, 2nd Army Corps, Army of the Potomac, to June, 1865.

SERVICE.—Embarked at Alexandria, Va., for the Virginia Peninsula March 30, 1862. Siege of Yorktown, Va., April 5-May 4. Reconnoissance toward Lee's Mills April 29. Battle of Williamsburg, Va., May 5. Operations about Bottom's Bridge May 20-23 (Cos. "A," "F," "H" and "K"). Duty at White House Landing May 19-June 25 (Cos. "B," "C," "D," "E," "G" and "I"). Seven days before Richmond June 25-July 1. Operations about White House Landing June 26-July 2. Maryland Campaign September 6-22. Battle of South Mountain September 14. Antietam September 16-17. Battle of Fredericksburg, Va., December 12-15. "Mud March" January 20-24, 1863. Chancellorsville Campaign April 27-May 6. Battle of Chancellorsville May 1-5. Gettysburg (Pa.) Campaign June 11-July 24. Battle of Gettysburg, Pa., July 1-4. Duty on line of the Rappahannock till October. Bristoe Campaign October 9-22. Advance to line of the Rappahannock November 7-8. Mine Run Campaign November 26-December 2. Campaign from the Rapidan to the James River May 3-June 15, 1864. Battles of the Wilderness May 5-7; Laurel Hill May 8; Spottsylvania May 8-12; Po River May 10; Spottsylvania Court House May 12-21. Assault on the Salient or "Bloody Angle" May 12. Harris Farm or Fredericksburg Road May 19. North Anna River May 23-26. On line of the Pamunkey May 26-28. Totopotomoy May 28-31. Cold Harbor June 1-12. Before Petersburg June 16-18. Siege of Petersburg June 16, 1864, to April 2, 1865. Jerusalem Plank Road, Weldon Railroad, June 22-23, 1864. Demonstration north of the James July 27-29. Deep Bottom July 27-28. Demonstration north of the James River August 13-20. Strawberry Plains, Deep Bottom, August 14-18. Poplar Springs Church September 29-October 2. Boydton Plank Road, Hatcher's Run, October 27-28. Reconnoissance to Weldon Railroad December 9-10. Dabney's Mills, Hatcher's Run, February 5-7, 1865. Watkins' House March 25. Appomattox Campaign March 28-April 9. Vaughan Road, near Hatcher's Run, March 29. Crow's House March 31. Fall of Petersburg April 2. Pursuit of Lee April 3-9.

Sailor's Creek April 6. High Bridge and Farmville April 7. Appomattox Court House April 9. Surrender of Lee and his army. March to Burkesville April 11-13, thence to Washington, D. C., May 2-15. Grand Review May 23. Mustered out June 29, 1865.

Regiment lost during service 6 Officers and 120 Enlisted men killed and mortally wounded and 2 Officers and 130 Enlisted men by disease. Total 258.

93rd REGIMENT NATIONAL GUARD INFANTRY.

Mustered in for 100 days' United States service July 20, 1864. Mustered out November 1, 1864. Served in State of New York.

94th REGIMENT INFANTRY ("BELLE JEFFERSON RIFLES").

Organized at Sackett's Harbor, N. Y., and mustered in March 10, 1862. Left State for Washington, D. C., March 18, 1862. Attached to Wadsworth's Command, Military District of Washington, D. C., to May, 1862. 1st Brigade, 2nd Division, Dept. of the Rappahannock, to June, 1862. 2nd Brigade, 2nd Division, 3rd Army Corps, Pope's Army of Virginia, to September, 1862. 2nd Brigade, 2nd Division, 1st Army Corps, Army of the Potomac, to December, 1862. 1st Brigade, 2nd Division, 1st Army Corps, to May, 1863. Provost Guard, Army of the Potomac, to June, 1863. 1st Brigade, 2nd Division, 1st Army Corps, to December, 1863. District of Annapolis, Md., 8th Army Corps, Middle Dept., to May, 1864. 2nd Brigade, 2nd Division, 5th Army Corps, Army of the Potomac, to May 30, 1864. 1st Brigade, 2nd Division, 5th Army Corps, to June 6, 1864. 1st Brigade, 3rd Division, 5th Army Corps, to June 11. 2nd Brigade, 3rd Division, 5th Army Corps, to September. 3rd Brigade, 3rd Division, 5th Army Corps, to October, 1864. 2nd Brigade, 3rd Division, 5th Army Corps, to November, 1864. 3rd Brigade, 3rd Division, 5th Army Corps, to July, 1865.

SERVICE.—Duty in the Defences of Washington, D. C., till May, 1862. Moved to Fredericksburg, Va., and duty there till May 25. Expedition to Front Royal May 25-June 18. Duty at Manassas, Warrenton and Culpeper, Va., till August. Battle of Cedar Mountain August 9. Pope's Campaign in Northern Virginia August 16-September 2. Fords of the Rappahannock August 20-23. Thoroughfare Gap August 28. Battles of Groveton August 29; Bull Run August 30; Chantilly September 1. Maryland Campaign September 6-22. Battles of South Mountain September 14; Antietam September 16-17. Duty at Sharpsburg, Md., till October 30. Movement to Falmouth, Va., October 30-November 19. Battle of Fredericksburg, Va., December 12-15. At Falmouth and Belle Plains till April 27, 1863. "Mud March" January 20-24. Chancellorsville Campaign April 27-May 6. Operations at Fitzhugh's Crossing April 29-May 2. Battle of Chancellorsville May 2-5. Gettysburg (Pa.) Campaign June 11-July 24. Battle of Gettysburg, Pa., July 1-3. Pursuit of Lee to Manassas Gap, Va., July 5-24. Duty on line of the Rappahannock and Rapidan till October. Bristoe Campaign October 9-22. Advance to line of the Rappahannock November 7-8. Mine Run Campaign November 26-December 2. Duty in the District of Annapolis, Md., till May, 1864. Rapidan Campaign May 26-June 15. Totopotomoy May 28-31. Cold Harbor June 1-12. Bethesda Church June 1-3. White Oak Swamp June 13. Before Petersburg June 16-18. Siege of Petersburg June 16, 1864, to April 2, 1865. Mine Explosion, Petersburg, July 30, 1864 (Reserve). Weldon Railroad August 18-21. Reconnoissance toward Dinwiddie Court House September 15. Warren's Raid on Weldon Railroad December 7-12. Dabney's Mills, Hatcher's Run, February 5-7, 1865. Appomattox Campaign March 28-April 9. Lewis Farm, near Gravelly Run, March 29. White Oak Road March 31. Five Forks April 1. Fall of Petersburg April 2. Pursuit of Lee April 3-9. Appomattox Court House April 9. Surrender of Lee and his army. Moved to Washington, D. C., May 1-12. Grand Review May 23. Duty in the Defences of Washington till July. Mustered out July 18, 1865.

Regiment lost during service 5 Officers and 105 Enlisted men killed and mortally wounded and 137 Enlisted men by disease. Total 247.

95th REGIMENT INFANTRY ("WARREN RIFLES").

Organized at New York City November, 1861, to March, 1862. Left State for Washington, D. C., March 18, 1862. Attached to Wadsworth's Command, Military District of Washington, D. C., to May, 1862. Doubleday's Brigade, Dept. of the Rappahannock, to June, 1862. 2nd Brigade, 1st Division, 3rd Corps, Pope's Army of Virginia, to September, 1862. 2nd Brigade, 1st Division, 1st Army Corps, Army of the Potomac, to March, 1864. 2nd Brigade, 4th Division, 5th Army Corps, to August, 1864. 3rd Brigade, 2nd Division, 5th Army Corps, to September, 1864. 3rd Brigade, 3rd Division, 5th Army Corps, to July, 1865.

SERVICE.—Duty in the Defences of Washington, D. C., till May, 1862, and at Aquia Creek, Va., till June. Duty at and near Fredericksburg till August. Pope's Campaign in Northern Virginia August 16-September 2. Fords of the Rappahannock August 21-23. Sulphur Springs August 26. Battles of Gainesville August 28; Groveton August 29; Bull Run August 30. Maryland Campaign September 6-22. Battles of South Mountain September 14; Antietam September 16-17. Duty at Sharpsburg, Md., till October 30. Movement to Falmouth, Va., October 30-November 19. Union November 2-3. Battle of Fredericksburg, Va., December 12-15. At Falmouth and Belle Plains till April 27, 1863. "Mud March" January 20-24. Chancellorsville Campaign April 27-May 6. Operations at Fitzhugh's Crossing April 29-May 2. Battle of Chancellorsville May 1-5. Gettysburg (Pa.) Campaign June 11-July 24. Battle of Gettysburg, Pa., July 1-3. Pursuit of Lee to Manassas Gap, Va., July 5-24. Duty on line of the Rappahannock and Rapidan to October. Bristoe Campaign October 9-22. Advance to line of the Rappahannock November 7-8. Mine Run Campaign November 26-December 2. Demonstration on the Rapidan February 6-7, 1864. Campaign from the Rapidan to the James May 3-June 15. Battles of the Wilderness May 5-7; Laurel Hill May 8; Spottsylvania May 8-12; Spottsylvania Court House May 12-21. Assault on the Salient May 12. North Anna River May 23-26. Jericho Ford May 23. On line of the Pamunkey May 26-28. Totopotomoy May 28-31. Cold Harbor June 1-12. Bethesda Church June 1-3. Before Petersburg June 16-18. Siege of Petersburg June 16, 1864, to April 2, 1865. Mine Explosion, Petersburg, July 30, 1864 (Reserve). Weldon Railroad August 18-21. Poplar Springs Church September 29-October 2. Boydton Plank Road, Hatcher's Run, October 27-28. Warren's Raid on Weldon Railroad December 7-12. Dabney's Mills, Hatcher's Run, February 5-7, 1865. Appomattox Campaign March 28-April 9. Lewis Farm, near Gravelly Run, March 29. White Oak Road March 31. Five Forks April 1. Fall of Petersburg April 2. Pursuit of Lee April 3-9. Appomattox Court House April 9. Surrender of Lee and his army. Moved to Washington, D. C., May 1-12. Grand Review May 23. Duty at Washington till July. Mustered out July 16, 1865.

Regiment lost during service 5 Officers and 114 Enlisted men killed and mortally wounded and 1 Officer and 136 Enlisted men by disease. Total 256.

96th REGIMENT INFANTRY ("McCOMB'S PLATTSBURG REGIMENT").

Organized at Plattsburg, N. Y., February 20-March 7, 1862. Left State for Washington, D. C., March 11, 1862. Attached to 3rd Brigade, 3rd Division, 4th Army Corps, Army of the Potomac, to June, 1862. 2nd Brigade, 2nd Division, 4th Army Corps, to September, 1862. Wessell's Brigade, Division at Suffolk, 7th Army Corps, Dept. of Virginia, to December, 1862. 1st Brigade, 1st Division, Dept. of North Carolina, to January, 1863. 1st Brigade, 4th Division, 18th Army Corps, Dept. of North Carolina, to May, 1863. District of the Albemarle, Dept. of North Carolina, to October, 1863. Newport News, Va., Dept. of Virginia and North Carolina, to December, 1863. District of the Currituck, Dept. of Virginia and North Carolina, to March, 1864. 1st Brigade, Heckman's Division, 18th Army Corps, to April, 1864. 1st Brigade, 1st Division, 18th Army Corps, Army of the James, to July, 1864. 2nd Brigade, 1st Division, 18th Army Corps, to December, 1864. 2nd Brigade, 3rd Division, 24th Army Corps, to June, 1865. 1st Brigade, 3rd Division, 24th Army Corps, to July, 1865. 1st Independent Brigade, 24th Army Corps, to August, 1865. Dept. of Virginia to February, 1866.

SERVICE.—Ordered to the Virginia Peninsula March 28, 1862. Siege of Yorktown, Va., April 5-May 4. Battle of Williamsburg May 5. Seven Pines May 29. Fair Oaks May 30. Battle of Seven Pines or Fair Oaks May 31-June 1. Seven days before Richmond June 25-July 1. Bottom's Bridge June 27-29. White Oak Swamp June 30. Malvern Hill July 1. At Harrison's Landing till August 16. Moved to Fortress Monroe August 16-23, thence to Suffolk September 18, and duty there till December. Reconnoissance to Franklin on the Blackwater October 3. Ordered to New Berne, N. C., December 4. Foster's Expedition to Goldsboro December 11-20. Actions at Kinston December 14; Whitehall December 16; Goldsboro December 17. Duty at and in the vicinity of New Berne, N. C., till May, 1863. At Plymouth, N. C., and in the District of the Albemarle till October, 1863. Expedition to relief of Little Washington April 7-10. Expedition from Plymouth to Gardiner's Bridge and Williamston July 5-7 (Detachment). Expedition from Plymouth to Foster's Mills July 26-29. Moved to Newport News, Va., October, and duty there till December. Scout from Great Bridge to Indiantown, N. C., October 13. Duty in District of the Currituck till April, 1864. Ordered to Yorktown, Va., April 28. Butler's operations on south side of the James River and against Petersburg and Richmond May 4-28. Occupation of Bermuda Hundred and City Point, Va., May 5. Swift Creek or Arrowfield Church May 8-10. Operations against Fort Darling May 12-16. Battle of Drury's Bluff May 14-16. Bermuda Hundred May 16-27. Moved to White House, thence to Cold Harbor May 27-31. Battles about Cold Harbor June 1-12. Before Petersburg June 15-18. Siege operations against Petersburg and Richmond June 16, 1864, to April 2, 1865. Mine Explosion, Petersburg, July 30, 1864 (Reserve). In trenches before Petersburg and on the Bermuda front till September 26. Battle of Chaffin's Farm, New Market Heights, September 28-30. Battle of Fair Oaks October 27-28. Duty in trenches before Richmond till April, 1865. Occupation of Richmond April 3. Duty in the Dept. of Virginia till February, 1866. Mustered out at City Point, Va., February 6, 1866.

Regiment lost during service 9 Officers and 59 Enlisted men killed and mortally wounded and 2 Officers and 158 Enlisted men by disease. Total 228.

97th REGIMENT INFANTRY ("CONKLIN RIFLES").

Organized at Boonville, N. Y., and mustered in February 18, 1862. Left State for Washington, D. C., March 12, 1862. Attached to Wadsworth's Command, Military District of Washington, to May, 1862. 2nd Brigade, 2nd Division, Dept. of the Rappahannock, to June, 1862. 1st Brigade, 2nd Division, 3rd Corps, Pope's Army of Virginia, to September, 1862. 1st Brigade, 2nd Division, 1st Army Corps, Army of the Potomac, to December, 1862. 3rd Brigade, 2nd Division, 1st Army Corps, to May, 1863. 2nd Brigade, 2nd Division, 1st Army Corps, to March, 1864. 2nd Brigade, 2nd Division, 5th Army Corps, to May, 1864. 2nd Brigade, 3rd Division, 5th Army Corps, May 9-30, 1864. 2nd Brigade, 2nd Division, 5th Army Corps, to June 6, 1864. 2nd Brigade, 3rd Division, 5th Army Corps, to July, 1865.

SERVICE.—Duty in the Defences of Washington, D. C., till May, 1862. Expedition to Front Royal, Va., to intercept Jackson, May 28-June 1. Picket duty on the Shenandoah and at Front Royal to June 10. Duty at Catlett's Station, Warrenton and Waterloo, Va., till August. Battle of Cedar Mountain August 9. Pope's Campaign in Northern Virginia August 16-September 2. Fords of the Rappahannock August 21-23. Thorough-

fare Gap August 28. Battles of Groveton August 29; Bull Run August 30. Maryland Campaign September 6-22. Battles of South Mountain September 14; Antietam September 16-17. Duty near Sharpsburg, Md., till October 30. Movement to Falmouth, Va., October 30-November 19. At Brooks' Station till December 10. Battle of Fredericksburg, Va., December 12-15. At Falmouth and Belle Plains till April 27, 1863. "Mud March" January 20-24. Chancellorsville Campaign April 27-May 6. Operations about Fitzhugh's Crossing April 29-May 2. Battle of Chancellorsville May 2-5. Gettysburg (Pa.) Campaign June 11-July 24. Battle of Gettysburg July 1-3. Pursuit of Lee to Manassas Gap, Va., July 5-24. Duty on line of the Rappahannock and Rapidan till October. Bristoe Campaign October 9-22. Advance to line of the Rappahannock November 7-8. Mine Run Campaign November 26-December 2. Demonstration on the Rapidan February 6-7, 1864. Campaign from the Rapidan to the James May 3-June 15. Battles of the Wilderness May 5-7; Laurel Hill May 8; Spottsylvania May 8-12; Spottsylvania Court House May 12-21. Assault on the Salient May 12. North Anna River May 23-26. Jericho Ford May 23. On line of the Pamunkey May 26-28. Totopotomoy May 28-31. Cold Harbor June 1-12. Bethesda Church June 1-3. White Oak Swamp June 13. Before Petersburg June 16-18. Siege of Petersburg June 16, 1864, to April 2, 1865. Mine Explosion, Petersburg, July 30, 1864 (Reserve). Weldon Railroad August 18-21. Reconnoissance toward Dinwiddie Court House September 15. Warren's Raid on Weldon Railroad December 7-12. Sussex Court House December 10. Dabney's Mills, Hatcher's Run, February 5-7, 1865. Appomattox Campaign March 28-April 9. Lewis Farm, near Gravelly Run, March 29. White Oak Road March 31. Five Forks April 1. Fall of Petersburg April 2. Pursuit of Lee April 3-9. Appomattox Court House April 9. Surrender of Lee and his army. Moved to Washington, D. C., May 1-12. Grand Review May 23. Duty at Washington till July. Mustered out July 18, 1865.

Regiment lost during service 12 Officers and 169 Enlisted men killed and mortally wounded and 1 Officer and 156 Enlisted men by disease. Total 338.

98th REGIMENT INFANTRY ("MALONE AND LYONS REGIMENT").

Organized (Cos. "A," "B," "C," "D," "E," "G" and "H") at Malone, N. Y., and (Cos. "F," "I" and "K") at Lyons, N. Y., January 25-February 8, 1862. Organization completed at Albany, N. Y. Left State for Washington, D. C., March 8, 1862. Attached to 3rd Brigade, 3rd Division, 4th Army Corps, Army of the Potomac, to June, 1862. 2nd Brigade, 2nd Division, 4th Army Corps, to July, 1862. 1st Brigade, 2nd Division, 4th Army Corps, to December, 1862. Naglee's Brigade, Dept. of North Carolina, to January, 1863. 1st Brigade, 2nd Division, 18th Army Corps, Dept. of North Carolina, to February, 1863. 1st Brigade, 1st Division, 18th Army Corps, Dept. of the South, to April, 1863. District of Beaufort, N. C., Dept. of North Carolina, to October, 1863. Newport News, Va., Dept. of Virginia and North Carolina, to January, 1864. District of the Currituck, Dept. of Virginia and North Carolina, to March, 1864. 1st Brigade, Heckman's Division, 18th Army Corps, to April, 1864. 1st Brigade, 1st Division, 18th Army Corps, Army of the James, to December, 1864. 1st Brigade, 3rd Division, 24th Army Corps, to June, 1865. 2nd Brigade, 3rd Division, 24th Army Corps, to July, 1865. 2nd Independent Brigade, 24th Army Corps, to August, 1865.

SERVICE.—Moved to the Virginia Peninsula March 28, 1862. Siege of Yorktown, Va., April 5-May 4. Reconnoissance toward Lee's Mills April 29. Battle of Williamsburg May 5. Operations about Bottom's Bridge May 21-23. Reconnoissance to Seven Pines May 24-27. Chickahominy, near Savage Station, and Seven Pines May 24. Battle of Seven Pines or Fair Oaks May 31-June 1. Seven days before Richmond June 25-July 1. White Oak Swamp June 30. Malvern Hill July 1. At

Harrison's Landing till August 16. Moved to Fortress Monroe August 16-23, and duty there till September 18. Duty at Yorktown till December. Moved to Morehead City, N. C., December 25-January 1, 1863. At Carolina City till January 21. Moved to Port Royal Harbor, S. C., January 28-31. At St. Helena Island, S. C., February 10-April 3. Expedition against Charleston, S. C., April 3-11. Moved to New Berne, N. C., April 12-15. Expedition to relief of Little Washington April 17-21. Duty in the District of Beaufort, N. C., till October. Moved to Newport News, Va., October 16-18, and duty there till December. At Portsmouth, Va., and in the District of the Currituck till February, 1864. Veterans on furlough March-April. Moved to Yorktown, Va., April 26. Butler's operations on south side of the James River and against Petersburg and Richmond May 3-28. Occupation of City Point and Bermuda Hundred May 5. Swift Creek or Arrowfield Church May 8-10. Operations against Fort Darling May 12-16. Battle of Drury's Bluff May 14-16. Bermuda Hundred May 16-28. Moved to White House, thence to Cold Harbor May 27-31. Battles about Cold Harbor June 1-12. Before Petersburg June 15-18. Siege operations against Petersburg and Richmond June 16, 1864, to April 2, 1865. Mine Explosion, Petersburg, July 30, 1864 (Reserve). Duty in the trenches before Petersburg and on the Bermuda Hundred front till September 27. Battle of Chaffin's Farm, New Market Heights, September 28-30. Battle of Fair Oaks October 27-28. Detached for duty in New York during Presidential election of 1864, November 2-17. Duty in trenches north of James and before Richmond till April, 1865. Occupation of Richmond April 3. Provost duty in Richmond and in the Dept. of Virginia till August. Mustered out at Richmond, Va., August 31, 1865.

Regiment lost during service 4 Officers and 95 Enlisted men killed and mortally wounded and 4 Officers and 132 Enlisted men by disease. Total 235.

98th REGIMENT NATIONAL GUARD INFANTRY.

Organized for 100 days' United States service August 10, 1864. Duty at Elmira, N. Y., till December. Mustered out December 22, 1864.

99th REGIMENT INFANTRY ("UNION COAST GUARD").

Organized at New York City under authority of War Department as Naval Brigade, to be provided with Gunboats to cruise along Atlantic coast, May 28, 1861. Left State for Fortress Monroe, Va., May 28, 1861. Attached to Fortress Monroe and Camp Hamilton, Dept. of Virginia, to May, 1862. 3rd Brigade, 1st Division, Dept. of Virginia, May, 1862. Camp Hamilton, Va., Dept. of Virginia, to July, 1862. Viele's Command, Norfolk, Va., 7th Army Corps, Dept. of Virginia, to February, 1863. Terry's Provisional Brigade, Division at Suffolk, Va., 7th Army Corps, to April, 1863. Reserve Brigade, Gurney's 3rd Division, 7th Army Corps, to July, 1863. Wistar's Brigade, Yorktown, Va., Dept. of Virginia and North Carolina, to October, 1863. New Berne, N. C., Dept. of Virginia and North Carolina, to January, 1865. Sub-District of New Berne, N. C., Dept. of North Carolina, to July, 1865.

SERVICE.—Regiment reorganized as Infantry August 21, 1861. Duty at Fortress Monroe, Va., till May, 1862. Designated 99th New York Infantry January, 1862. Fletcher's Wharf, Pocomoco, July 30, 1861. Cherrystone Inlet July 31. Company "B" detached on Steamers "Southfield" and "Hunchback" with Burnside's Expedition to Roanoke Island, N. C., January 7-February 8, 1862. Battle of Roanoke Island February 8. Battle of New Berne, N. C., March 14. Siege of Fort Macon April 12-26. Regiment—Bombardment and capture of Forts Hatteras and Clarke August 28-29, 1861. Beacon Island September 16. Newport News, Va., and destruction of "Congress" and "Cumberland" in Hampton Roads March 8-9, 1862. Tranter's Creek and occupation of Norfolk and Portsmouth May 10. At Camp Hamilton, Va., May to August, 1862. Expedition from Fortress Monroe June 28-July 4 (Detachment). Near Windsor Shade June 30. James River July 4. Duty by detachments at Fortress Monroe, Norfolk, Fort Wood and Sewell's Point August to October, 1862. Company "I" detached on Gunboats "West End" and "Smith Briggs" August, 1862, to March, 1863. Duty at Norfolk and Suffolk, Va., till May, 1863. Siege of Suffolk April 12-May 4. South Quay Road April 17. Suffolk April 28-30. South Quay Bridge May 1. Providence Church Road, Suffolk, May 3. Operations on Norfolk & Petersburg Railroad May 15-28. Near Providence Church May 17. Antioch Church and Paker's Cross Roads May 23. Walkerton June 5. Blackwater June 16. Dix's Peninsula Campaign June 24-July 7. Expedition from White House to South Anna River July 1-7. South Anna Bridge July 4. Duty at White House, Yorktown and Gloucester till October, 1863. Expedition from Norfolk to Isle of Wight County January 29-February 1, 1864 (Detachment). Smithfield, N. C., January 31 and February 1 (Detachment). Duty in the Defences of New Berne, N. C., October, 1863, to July, 1865. Operations about New Berne against Whiting January 18-February 10. Actions at New Berne February 1-4, 1864. Batchelor's Creek February 1. Beech Grove February 2. Old members mustered out June 14, 1864. Regiment consolidated to 4 Companies and again to 3 Companies September 15, 1864, and to 2 Companies February, 1865. Mustered out at Salisbury, N. C., July 15, 1865.

Regiment lost during service 2 Officers and 37 Enlisted men killed and mortally wounded and 3 Officers and 161 Enlisted men by disease. Total 203.

99th REGIMENT NATIONAL GUARD INFANTRY.

Organized for 100 days' United States service August 2, 1864. Duty at Elmira, N. Y., till November. Mustered out November 9, 1864.

100th REGIMENT INFANTRY ("2nd REGIMENT, EAGLE BRIGADE").

Organized at Buffalo, N. Y., January, 1862. Moved to New York City March 7, thence to Washington, D. C., March 10, 1862. Attached to 1st Brigade, 3rd Division, 4th Army Corps, Army of the Potomac, to June, 1862. 1st Brigade, 2nd Division, 4th Army Corps, to December, 1862. Naglee's Brigade, Dept. of North Carolina, to January, 1863. 2nd Brigade, 2nd Division, 18th Army Corps, Dept. of North Carolina, to February, 1863. 1st Brigade, 2nd Division, 18th Army Corps, Dept. of the South, to April, 1863. Folly Island, S. C., 10th Army Corps, Dept. of the South, to June, 1863. 2nd Brigade, Folly Island, S. C., 10th Army Corps, to July, 1863. 1st Brigade, Folly Island, S. C., 10th Army Corps, July, 1863. 2nd Brigade, 1st Division, Morris Island, S. C., 10th Army Corps, July, 1863. 3rd Brigade, Morris Island, S. C., 10th Corps, to November, 1863. 2nd Brigade, Morris Island, S. C., 10th Army Corps, to January, 1864. 2nd Brigade, Morris Island, S. C., Northern District, Dept. South, to April, 1864. 2nd Brigade, 1st Division, 10th Army Corps, Army of the James, Dept. of Virginia and North Carolina, to May, 1864. 3rd Brigade, 1st Division, 10th Army Corps, to December, 1864. 3rd Brigade, 1st Division, 24th Army Corps, to July, 1865. 2nd Brigade, 1st Division, 24th Army Corps, to August, 1865.

SERVICE.—Ordered to the Virginia Peninsula March 28, 1862. Siege of Yorktown, Va., April 5-May 4. Battle of Williamsburg May 5. Operations about Bottom's Bridge May 20-23. Reconnoissance to Seven Pines May 24-27. Battle of Seven Pines or Fair Oaks May 31-June 1. Seven days before Richmond June 25-July 1. Bottom's Bridge June 27-29. White Oak Swamp June 30. Malvern Hill July 1. At Harrison's Landing till August 16. Moved to Fortress Monroe August 16-22, thence to Yorktown, Va., September 18. Duty at Yorktown and Gloucester Point till December 26. Reconnoissance to Gloucester and Matthews Counties December 11-15. Skirmish at Wood's Cross Roads, Gloucester Court House, December 14. Moved to Beaufort, N. C., December 26, thence to Port Royal, S. C., January 28-31. Camp at St. Helena Island, S. C., February 12-March

23. Capture of Forts Wagner and Gregg September 7. till April 3. Action at Cole's Island March 31. Occupation of Folly Island, S. C., April 5-July 10. Action at Folly Island April 10. Attack on Morris Island July 10. Assaults on Fort Wagner, Morris Island, S. C., July 11 and 18. Siege of Forts Wagner and Gregg, and operations against Fort Sumpter and Charleston, July 18-September 7. Boat Expedition against Fort Gregg August 17. Bombardment of Fort Sumpter August 17-23. Capture of Forts Wagner and Gregg September 7. Duty on Morris Island and operations against Charleston till April, 1864. Affair, Vincent's Creek, August 4, 1863. Moved to Gloucester Point, Va., April. Butler's operations on south side of the James River and against Petersburg and Richmond May 4-28. Occupation of Bermuda Hundred May 5. Port Walthall Junction, Chester Station, May 7. Swift Creek May 8-10. Operations against Fort Darling May 12-16. Battle of Drury's Bluff May 14-16. Bermuda Hundred May 16-June 20. Attacks on picket line May 21 and June 2 and 14. Port Walthall June 16-17. Siege operations against Petersburg and Richmond June 16, 1864, to April 2, 1865. Action at Deep Bottom June 23. Grover House, Deep Bottom, July 21. Deep Bottom July 27-28. Strawberry Plains, New Market Heights, August 14-18. Moved to Petersburg front August 26, and duty there in trenches till September 27. Battle of Chaffin's Farm September 28-30. Darbytown Road October 7. Reconnoissance to Darbytown Road October 13. Battle of Fair Oaks October 27-28. Johnson's Farm October 29. Duty in trenches before Richmond till March, 1865. Appomattox Campaign March 28-April 9. On line of Hatcher's and Gravelly Runs March 29-30. Assault on Fort Gregg and fall of Petersburg April 2. Pursuit of Lee April 3-9. Rice's Station April 6. Appomattox Court House April 9. Surrender of Lee and his army. Duty in the Dept. of Virginia till August. Mustered out August 28, 1865.

Regiment lost during service 12 Officers and 182 Enlisted men killed and mortally wounded and 1 Officer and 202 Enlisted men by disease. Total 397.

101st REGIMENT INFANTRY ("UNION REGIMENT").

Organized at Hancock, N. Y., September 2, 1861. Left State for Washington, D. C., March 9, 1862. Attached to Wadsworth's Command, Military District of Washington, to May, 1862. Whipple's Brigade, Defences of Washington, to June, 1862. 2nd Brigade, 3rd Division, 3rd Army Corps, Army of the Potomac, to August, 1862. 2nd Brigade, 1st Division, 3rd Army Corps, to December, 1862.

SERVICE.—Duty in the Defences of Washington, D. C., till June, 1862. Ordered to join Army of the Potomac on the Virginia Peninsula June, 1862. Seven days before Richmond June 25-July 1. Battles of Oak Grove June 25; Jordan's Ford June 27; White Oak Swamp Bridge and Glendale June 30; Malvern Hill July 1. At Harrison's Landing till August 16. Movement to Fortress Monroe, thence to Centreville August 16-26. Pope's Campaign in Northern Virginia August 26-September 2. Battles of Groveton August 29; Bull Run August 30; Chantilly September 1. Guard fords of the Monocacy till October 11. Movement up the Potomac and to Falmouth, Va., October 11-November 19. Battle of Fredericksburg, Va., December 12-15. Transferred to 37th New York Infantry December 24, 1862.

Regiment lost during service 1 Officer and 24 Enlisted men killed and mortally wounded and 1 Officer and 48 Enlisted men by disease. Total 74.

102nd REGIMENT INFANTRY ("VAN BUREN LIGHT INFANTRY").

Organized at New York City. Left State for Washington, D. C., March 10, 1862. Attached to Wadsworth's Command, Military District of Washington, to May, 1862. Cooper's 1st Brigade, Sigel's Division, Dept. of the Shenandoah, to June, 1862. 1st Brigade, 2nd Division, 2nd Army Corps, Pope's Army of Virginia, to

August, 1862. 2nd Brigade, 2nd Division, 2nd Army Corps, Army of Virginia, to September, 1862. 2nd Brigade, 2nd Division, 12th Army Corps, Army of the Potomac, to October, 1862. 3rd Brigade, 2nd Division, 12th Army Corps, Army Potomac, to October, 1863, and Army of the Cumberland to April, 1864. 3rd Brigade, 2nd Division, 20th Army Corps, Army of the Cumberland, to June, 1865. 1st Brigade, Bartlett's Division, 22nd Army Corps, Dept. of Washington, to July, 1865.

SERVICE.—Duty in the Defences of Washington, D. C., till May, 1862. Moved to Harper's Ferry, W. Va., May. Defence of Harper's Ferry against Jackson's attack May 28-30. Operations in the Shenandoah Valley till August. Battle of Cedar Mountain August 9. Pope's Campaign in Northern Virginia August 16-September 2. Guard trains during the campaign. Maryland Campaign September 6-22. Battle of Antietam September 16-17. Duty at Bolivar Heights till December. Reconnoissance to Rippon, W. Va., November 9. Expedition to Winchester December 2-6. March to Fredericksburg, Va., December 9-16. At Fairfax Station till January 20, 1863. "Mud March" January 20-24. Regiment detached in New York on special duty March 10-April 4. Chancellorsville Campaign April 27-May 6. Battle of Chancellorsville May 1-5. Gettysburg (Pa.) Campaign June 11-July 24. Battle of Gettysburg July 1-3. Pursuit of Lee to Manassas Gap, Va., July 5-24. Duty on line of the Rappahannock till September. Movement to Bridgeport, Ala., September 24-October 3. Reopening Tennessee River October 26-29. Guarding railroad till November. Chattanooga-Ringgold Campaign November 23-27. Battles of Lookout Mountain November 23-24; Mission Ridge November 25; Ringgold Gap, Taylor's Ridge, November 27. Duty in Lookout Valley till May, 1864. Atlanta (Ga.) Campaign May 1-September 8. Demonstrations on Rocky Faced Ridge May 8-11. Battle of Resaca May 14-15. Near Cassville May 19. Advance on Dallas May 22-25. New Hope Church May 25. Battles about Dallas, New Hope Church and Allatoona Hills May 26-June 5. Operations about Marietta and against Kenesaw Mountain June 10-July 2. Pine Hill June 11-14. Lost Mountain June 15-17. Gilgal or Golgotha Church June 15. Muddy Creek June 17. Noyes Creek June 19. Kolb's Farm June 22. Assault on Kenesaw June 27. Ruff's Station, Smyrna Camp Ground, July 4. Chattahoochie River July 5-17. Peach Tree Creek July 19-20. Siege of Atlanta July 22-August 25. Operations at Chattahoochie River Bridge August 26-September 2. Occupation of Atlanta September 2-November 15. Expedition from Atlanta to Tuckum's Cross Roads October 26-29. Near Atlanta November 9. March to the sea November 15-December 10. Near Davidsboro November 28. Siege of Savannah December 10-21. Campaign of the Carolinas January to April, 1865. Battle of Bentonville, N. C., March 19-21. Occupation of Goldsboro March 24. Advance on Raleigh April 9-13. Occupation of Raleigh April 14. Bennett's House April 26. Surrender of Johnston and his army. March to Washington, D. C., via Richmond, Va., April 29-May 20. Grand Review May 24. Duty at Washington, D. C., till July. Mustered out July 21, 1865.

Regiment lost during service 7 Officers and 66 Enlisted men killed and mortally wounded and 82 Enlisted men by disease. Total 155.

102nd REGIMENT NATIONAL GUARD INFANTRY.

Mustered in for 100 days' United States service August 6, 1864. Duty at Elmira, N. Y., till November. Mustered out November 13, 1864.

103rd REGIMENT INFANTRY ("SEWARD INFANTRY").

Organized at New York City November, 1861, to March, 1862. Left State for Washington, D. C., March 5, 1862, thence moved to Norfolk, Va., March 21, and to New Berne, N. C., April. Attached to Norfolk, Va., Dept. of Virginia, to April, 1862. 1st Brigade, 2nd Division, Dept. of North Carolina, to July, 1862. 1st Brigade, 3rd Division, 9th Army Corps, Army of the Potomac, to April, 1863. 1st Brigade, 2nd Division, 7th Army Corps, Dept. of Virginia, to July, 1863. Alvord's Brigade, Vodges' Division, Folly Island, S. C., 10th Army Corps, Dept. of the South, to February, 1864. 2nd Brigade, Gordon's Division, Folly Island, S. C., Northern District, to April, 1864. Folly Island, S. C., Northern District, Dept. of the South, to August, 1864. 3rd Brigade, DeRussy's Division, 22nd Army Corps, Dept. of Washington, to September, 1864. 1st Brigade, Kitching's Division. (Provisional), Army of the Shenandoah, to December, 1864. 1st Brigade, Provisional Division, Dept. of Virginia and North Carolina, to March, 1865. 1st Brigade, Infantry Division, Defences of Bermuda Hundred, Va., to May, 1865. Dept. of Virginia to December, 1865.

SERVICE.—Duty in the Defences of Washington, D. C., till March 21, 1862, and at Norfolk, Va., till April, 1862. Ordered to New Berne, N. C., and duty there till July. Action at Gillett's Farm, Pebbly Run, April 13. Haughton's Mills April 27. Moved to Newport News, Va., July 2-6, thence to Aquia Creek and Fredericksburg, Va., August 2-6. Duty there till August 31. Moved to Washington, D. C., August 31-September 3. Maryland Campaign September 6-22. Battles of South Mountain September 14; Antietam September 16-17. Duty at Pleasant Valley, Md., till October 27. Movement to Falmouth, Va., October 27-November 19. Battle of Fredericksburg, Va., December 12-15. "Mud March" January 20-24, 1863. Moved to Newport News, Va., February 6-9, thence to Suffolk March 13, and duty there till June. Siege of Suffolk April 12-May 4. Edenton Road April 24. Suffolk May 2-4. Providence Church Road May 3. Dix's Peninsula Campaign June 24-July 7. Expedition from White House to South Anna River July 1-7. Ordered to Folly Island, S. C., July 28. Siege operations against Forts Wagner and Gregg on Morris Island and against Fort Sumpter and Charleston, S. C., August 14-September 7. Bombardment of Fort Sumpter August 17-23. Capture of Forts Wagner and Gregg September 7. Operations against Charleston and duty on Folly Island, S. C., September, 1863, to August, 1864. Demonstrations on James Island May 21-22 and July 1-10, 1864. Ordered to Washington, D. C., August, 1864, and duty there till September 27. Ordered to the Shenandoah Valley, Va., September 27, and duty there till November 22. Battle of Cedar Creek October 19. Ordered to Bermuda Hundred, Va., November 22, and duty in the defences at that point to March, 1865. Siege operations against Petersburg and Richmond December, 1864, to April, 1865. Fall of Petersburg and Richmond April 2-3. Duty in the Dept. of Virginia till December, 1865. Mustered out December 7, 1865.

Regiment lost during service 5 Officers and 61 Enlisted men killed and mortally wounded and 2 Officers and 100 Enlisted men by disease. Total 168.

104th REGIMENT INFANTRY ("WADSWORTH GUARDS," "LIVINGSTON COUNTY REGIMENT").

Organized at Geneseo, N. Y., October, 1861, to March, 1862. Left State for Washington, D. C., March 22, 1862. Attached to Wadsworth's Command, Military District of Washington, to May, 1862. 2nd Brigade, 2nd Division, Dept. of the Rappahannock, to June, 1862. 1st Brigade, 2nd Division, 3rd Corps, Pope's Army of Virginia, to September, 1862. 1st Brigade, 2nd Division, 1st Army Corps, Army of the Potomac, to March, 1864. 1st Brigade, 2nd Division, 5th Army Corps, to June, 1864. 1st Brigade, 3rd Division, 5th Army Corps, to August, 1864. 2nd Brigade, 3rd Division, 5th Army Corps, to September, 1864. Provost Guard, 5th Army Corps, to May, 1865. 2nd Brigade, 3rd Division, 5th Army Corps, to July, 1865.

SERVICE.—Duty in the Defences of Washington, D. C., till May, 1862. Expedition to Front Royal, Va., to intercept Jackson, May 28-June 1. Picket duty on the Shenandoah and at Front Royal till June 10. Duty at Catlett's Station, Warrenton and Waterloo, Va., till August. Battle of Cedar Creek August 9. Pope's Cam-

paign in Northern Virginia August 16-September 2. Fords of the Rappahannock August 21-23. Thoroughfare Gap August 28. Groveton August 29. Bull Run August 30. Chantilly September 1. Maryland Campaign September 6-22. Battles of South Mountain September 14; Antietam September 16-17. Duty near Sharpsburg till October 30. Movement to Falmouth, Va., October 30-November 19. Battle of Fredericksburg, Va., December 12-15. At Falmouth and Belle Plains till April 27, 1863. "Mud March" January 20-24. Chancellorsville Campaign April 27-May 6. Operations at Fitzhugh's Crossing April 29-May 2. Battle of Chancellorsville May 2-5. Gettysburg (Pa.) Campaign June 11-July 24. Battle of Gettysburg, Pa., July 1-3. Pursuit of Lee July 5-24. Duty on line of the Rappahannock and Rapidan till October. Bristoe Campaign October 9-22. Advance to line of the Rappahannock November 7-8. Mine Run Campaign November 26-December 2. Demonstration on the Rapidan February 6-7, 1864. Campaign from the Rapidan to the James May 3-June 15. Battles of the Wilderness May 5-7; Laurel Hill May 8; Spottsylvania May 8-12; Spottsylvania Court House May 12-21. Assault on the Salient May 12. North Anna River May 23-26. Jericho Ford May 23. On line of the Pamunkey May 26-28. Totopotomoy May 28-31. Cold Harbor June 1-12. Bethesda Church June 1-3. White Oak Swamp June 13. Before Petersburg June 16-18. Siege of Petersburg June 16, 1864, to April 2, 1865. Mine Explosion, Petersburg, July 30, 1864 (Reserve). Weldon Railroad August 18-21. Reconnoissance toward Dinwiddie Court House September 15. Warren's Raid on Weldon Railroad December 7-12. Dabney's Mills, Hatcher's Run, February 5-7, 1865. Appomattox Campaign March 28-April 9. Lewis Farm, near Gravelly Run, March 29. White Oak Road March 31. Five Forks April 1. Fall of Petersburg April 2. Pursuit of Lee April 3-9. Appomattox Court House April 9. Surrender of Lee and his army. Moved to Washington, D. C., May 1-12. Grand Review May 23. Duty at Washington till July. Mustered out July 17, 1865.

Regiment lost during service 5 Officers and 81 Enlisted men killed and mortally wounded and 2 Officers and 145 Enlisted men by disease. Total 233.

105th REGIMENT INFANTRY ("LEROY REGIMENT").

Organized at Leroy, N. Y., March 28, 1862. Left State for Washington, D. C., April 4, 1862. Attached to Duryea's Brigade, Military District of Washington, to May, 1862. 2nd Brigade, 2nd Division, Dept. of the Rappahannock, to June, 1862. 1st Brigade, 2nd Division, 3rd Corps, Pope's Army of Virginia, to September, 1862. 1st Brigade, 2nd Division, 1st Army Corps, Army of the Potomac, to March, 1863.

SERVICE.—Duty in the Defences of Washington, D. C., till May 11, 1862. Guard Orange & Alexandria Railroad to May 28. Expedition to Front Royal, Va., to intercept Jackson, May 28-June 1. Picket duty on the Shenandoah and at Front Royal, Va., till June 10. Duty at Catlett's Station, Warrenton and Waterloo till August. Battle of Cedar Mountain August 9. Pope's Campaign in Northern Virginia August 16-September 2. Fords of the Rappahannock August 21-23. Thoroughfare Gap August 28. Groveton August 29. Bull Run August 30. Chantilly September 1. Maryland Campaign September 6-22. Battles of South Mountain September 14; Antietam September 16-17. Duty at Sharpsburg, Md., till October 30. Movement to Falmouth, Va., October 30-November 19. Battle of Fredericksburg, Va., December 12-15. At Falmouth and Belle Plains till March, 1863. "Mud March" January 20-24. Consolidated with 97th Regiment New York Infantry March 17, 1863, as Companies "F," "G" and "I."

Regiment lost during service 2 Officers and 43 Enlisted men killed and mortally wounded and 45 Enlisted men by disease. Total 90.

106th REGIMENT INFANTRY ("ST. LAWRENCE COUNTY REGIMENT").

Organized at Ogdensburg, N. Y., and mustered in August 27, 1862. Left State for Baltimore, Md., August 28, 1862, thence ordered to New Creek, Va. Attached to Railroad District, 8th Corps, Middle Dept., to September, 1862. Railroad District, West Virginia, to January, 1863. Martinsburg, W. Va., Milroy's Command, 8th Corps, Middle Dept., to March, 1863. 3rd Brigade, 1st Division, 8th Army Corps, to June, 1863. Elliott's Command, 8th Army Corps, to July, 1863. 3rd Brigade, 3rd Division, 3rd Army Corps, Army of the Potomac, to March, 1864. 1st Brigade, 3rd Division, 6th Army Corps, Army of the Potomac and Army of the Shenandoah, to June, 1865.

SERVICE.—Guard and provost duty in Defences of the Upper Potomac, with Headquarters at New Creek, Va., till June, 1863. Expedition to Greenland Gap April 15-22, 1863. Fairmount April 29. Martinsburg, W. Va., June 14. Battle of Winchester, Va., and retreat to Harper's Ferry June 14-15. Guard stores to Washington, D. C., July 1-4. Join Army of the Potomac at Frederick, Md., July 5. Pursuit of Lee to Manassas Gap, Va., July 5-24. Action at Wapping Heights, Va., July 23. Duty on line of the Rappahannock and Rapidan till October. Bristoe Campaign October 9-22. Advance to line of the Rappahannock November 7-8. Kelly's Ford November 7. Brandy Station November 8. Mine Run Campaign November 26-December 2. Demonstration on the Rapidan February 6-7, 1864. Campaign from the Rapidan to the James May 3-June 15. Battles of the Wilderness May 5-7; Spottsylvania May 8-12; Spottsylvania Court House May 12-21. Assault on the Salient, "Bloody Angle," May 12. North Anna River May 23-26. On line of the Pamunkey May 26-28. Totopotomoy May 28-31. Cold Harbor June 1-12. Before Petersburg June 17-18. Siege of Petersburg June 17-July 6. Jerusalem Plank Road, Weldon Railroad, June 22-23. Ordered to Baltimore, Md., July 6. Battle of Monocacy, Md., July 9. Expedition to Snicker's Gap, Va., July 14-24. Sheridan's Shenandoah Valley Campaign August 7-November 28. Near Charlestown August 21-22. Battle of Winchester September 19. Fisher's Hill September 22. Battle of Cedar Creek October 19. Duty at Kernstown till December. Moved to Washington, D. C., thence to Petersburg, Va., December 3-6. Siege of Petersburg December, 1864, to April, 1865. Fort Fisher, Petersburg, March 25, 1865. Appomattox Campaign March 28-April 9. Assault on and fall of Petersburg April 2. Pursuit of Lee April 3-9. Sailor's Creek April 6. Appomattox Court House April 9. Surrender of Lee and his army. March to Danville, Va., April 23-27, and duty there till May 16. Moved to Richmond, Va., thence to Washington, D. C., May 16-June 2. Corps Review June 8. Mustered out June 27, 1865.

Regiment lost during service 10 Officers and 127 Enlisted men killed and mortally wounded and 4 Officers and 166 Enlisted men by disease. Total 307.

107th REGIMENT INFANTRY—"CAMPBELL GUARDS."

Organized at Elmira, N. Y., and mustered in August 13, 1862. Left State for Washington, D. C., August 13, 1862. Attached to Whipple's Command, Defences of Washington, D. C., to September, 1862. 3rd Brigade, 1st Division, 12th Army Corps, Army of the Potomac, to October, 1863, and Army of the Cumberland, to April, 1864. 2nd Brigade, 1st Division, 20th Army Corps, Army of the Cumberland, to June, 1865.

SERVICE.—Maryland Campaign September 6-22, 1862. Battle of Antietam, Md., September 16-17. Duty at Maryland Heights September 22-October 29. Picket duty at Blackford's Ford and Sharpsburg till December. March to Fredericksburg, Va., December 12-16. "Mud March" January 20-24, 1863. At Stafford Court House till April 27. Chancellorsville Campaign April 27-May 6. Battle of Chancellorsville May 1-5. Gettysburg (Pa.) Campaign June 11-July 24. Battle of Gettysburg, Pa., July 1-3. Pursuit of Lee to Warrenton Junction

July 5-26. Duty on line of the Rappahannock till September. Movement to Bridgeport, Ala., September 24-October 3. Guarding Nashville & Chattanooga Railroad till April, 1864. Atlanta (Ga.) Campaign May 1-September 8. Operations about Rocky Faced Ridge, Tunnel Hill and Buzzard's Roost Gap May 8-11. Battle of Resaca May 14-15. Near Cassville May 19. New Hope Church May 25. Battles about Dallas, New Hope Church and Allatoona Hills May 26-June 5. Operations about Marietta and against Kenesaw Mountain June 10-July 2. Pine Hill June 11-14. Lost Mountain June 15-17. Gilgal or Golgotha Church June 15. Muddy Creek June 17. Noyes Creek June 19. Kolb's Farm June 22. Assault on Kenesaw June 27. Ruff's Station, Smyrna Camp Ground, July 4. Chattahoochie River July 5-17. Peach Tree Creek July 19-20. Siege of Atlanta July 22-August 25. Operations at Chattahoochie River Bridge August 26-September 2. Occupation of Atlanta September 2-November 15. Expedition from Atlanta to Tuckum's Cross Roads October 26-29. Near Atlanta November 9. March to the sea November 15-December 10. Montieth Swamp December 9. Siege of Savannah December 10-21. Campaign of the Carolinas January to April, 1865. Robertsville, S. C., January 29. Averysboro, N. C., March 16. Battle of Bentonville March 19-21. Occupation of Goldsboro March 24, and of Raleigh April 14. Moccasin Swamp April 10. Bennett's House April 26. Surrender of Johnston and his army. March to Washington, D. C., via Richmond, Va., April 29-May 19. Grand Review May 24. Mustered out June 5, 1865. Veterans and Recruits transferred to 60th New York Infantry.

Regiment lost during service 4 Officers and 87 Enlisted men killed and mortally wounded and 131 Enlisted men by disease. Total 222.

108th REGIMENT INFANTRY—"ROCHESTER REGIMENT."

Organized at Rochester and mustered in August 18, 1862. Moved to New York August 19, thence to Washington, D. C., August 22, 1862. Attached to Whipple's Command, Defences of Washington, D. C., to September, 1862. 2nd Brigade, 3rd Division, 2nd Army Corps, Army of the Potomac, to March, 1864. 3rd Brigade, 2nd Division, 2nd Army Corps, to May, 1865.

SERVICE.—Maryland Campaign September 6-22, 1862. Battle of Antietam, Md., September 16-17. (Regiment lost 196 killed and wounded in this its first battle.) Duty at Harper's Ferry, W. Va., September 22 to October 30. Reconnoissance to Charleston October 16-17. Advance up Loudoun Valley and movement to Falmouth, Va., October 30-November 17. Battle of Fredericksburg, Va., December 12-15. At Falmouth till April 27, 1863. "Mud March" January 20-24. Chancellorsville Campaign April 27-May 6. Battle of Chancellorsville May 1-5. Gettysburg (Pa.) Campaign June 11-July 24. Battle of Gettysburg July 1-3. Pursuit of Lee to Manassas Gap, Va., July 5-24. Duty along Orange & Alexandria Railroad till September 12. Advance from the Rappahannock to the Rapidan September 13-17. Picket duty on the Rapidan till October 8. Bristoe Campaign October 8-22. Auburn and Bristoe October 14. Advance to line of the Rappahannock November 7-8. Mine Run Campaign November 26-December 2. At Stevensburg till May, 1864. Demonstration on the Rapidan February 6-7. Morton's Ford February 6-7. Campaign from the Rapidan to the James May 3-June 15. Battles of the Wilderness May 5-7; Laurel Hill May 8; Spottsylvania May 8-12; Po River May 10; Spottsylvania Court House May 12-21. Assault on the Salient or "Bloody Angle" May 12. North Anna River May 23-26. On line of the Pamunkey May 26-28. Totopotomoy May 28-31. Cold Harbor June 1-12. Before Petersburg June 16-18. Siege of Petersburg June 16, 1864, to April 2, 1865. Jerusalem Plank Road June 22-23, 1864. Demonstration north of the James July 27-29. Deep Bottom July 27-28. Demonstration north of the James August 13-20. Strawberry Plains, Deep Bottom, August 14-18. Ream's Station August 25. Boydton Plank Road, Hatcher's Run, October 27-28. Dabney's Mills, Hatcher's Run, February 5-7, 1865. Appomattox Campaign March 28-April 9. Boydton and White Oak Roads March 29-31. Crow's House March 31. Fall of Petersburg April 2. Sailor's Creek April 6. High Bridge and Farmville April 7. Appomattox Court House April 9. Surrender of Lee and his army. At Burkesville till May 2. March to Washington, D. C., May 2-12. Grand Review May 23. Mustered out May 28, 1865. Veterans and Recruits transferred to 59th New York Infantry.

Regiment lost during service 9 Officers and 95 Enlisted men killed and mortally wounded and 87 Enlisted men by disease. Total 191.

109th REGIMENT INFANTRY.

Organized at Binghampton and mustered in August 27, 1862. Left State for Annapolis, Md., August 30, 1862. Attached to 8th Army Corps, Middle Department, to October, 1862. Railroad Guard, 22nd Army Corps, Dept. of Washington, to April, 1864. 1st Brigade, 3rd Division, 9th Army Corps, Army of the Potomac, to September, 1864. 1st Brigade, 1st Division, 9th Army Corps, to June, 1865.

SERVICE.—Guard railroad from Annapolis Junction, Md., to Washington, D. C., and garrison duty in the Defences of Washington till April, 1864. Campaign from the Rapidan to the James May 3-June 15, 1864. Battles of the Wilderness May 5-7; Spottsylvania May 8-12; Spottsylvania Court House May 12-21. Assault on the Salient May 12. North Anna River May 23-26. Ox Ford May 23-24. On line of the Pamunkey May 26-28. Totopotomoy May 28-31. Cold Harbor June 1-12. Bethesda Church June 1-3. Before Petersburg June 16-18. Siege of Petersburg June 16, 1864, to April 2, 1865. Mine Explosion, Petersburg, July 30, 1864. Weldon Railroad August 18-21. Ream's Station August 25. Poplar Springs Church, Peeble's Farm, September 29-October 2. Reconnoissance on Vaughan and Squirrel Level Roads October 8. Boydton Plank Road, Hatcher's Run, October 27-28. Fort Stedman March 25, 1865. Appomattox Campaign March 28-April 9. Assault on and fall of Petersburg April 2. Occupation of Petersburg April 2. Pursuit of Lee April 3-9. Surrender of Lee and his army at Appomattox Court House April 9. Moved to Washington, D. C., April 22-27, and duty there till June. Grand Review May 23. Mustered out June 4, 1865. Veterans and Recruits transferred to 51st New York Infantry.

Regiment lost during service 5 Officers and 160 Enlisted men killed and mortally wounded and 164 Enlisted men by disease. Total 329.

110th REGIMENT INFANTRY.

Organized at Oswego, N. Y., and mustered in August 27, 1862. Left State for Baltimore, Md., August 29, 1862. Attached to the Defences of Baltimore, Md., 8th Army Corps, Middle Department, to October, 1862. Emery's Brigade, 8th Army Corps, to November, 1862. Emery's Brigade, Louisiana Expedition, to December, 1862. Sherman's Division, Dept. of the Gulf, to January, 1863. 3rd Brigade, 3rd Division, 19th Army Corps, Dept. of the Gulf, to February, 1863. 1st Brigade, 3rd Division, 19th Army Corps, to February, 1864. Key West, Fla., District of West Florida, Dept. Gulf, to August, 1865.

SERVICE.—Duty at Baltimore, Md., till November 6, 1862. Moved to Fortress Monroe, Va., November 6, thence sailed for New Orleans, La., December 4, arriving at Carrollton December 26, and duty there till March, 1863. Operations on Bayou Plaquemine February 12-28. Moved to Baton Rouge, La., March 7. Operations against Port Hudson, La., March 7-27. Moved to Algiers April 3, thence to Brashear City April 8. Expedition to Franklin April 11-17. Fort Bisland April 12-13. Franklin April 14. Expedition from Opelousas to Barre Landing April 21. Expedition from Barre Landing to Berwick City May 21-26. Franklin and Centreville May 25. Moved to Port Hudson, La., May 30. Siege of Port Hudson June 3-July 9. Assault on Port

Hudson June 14. Surrender of Port Hudson July 9. Duty at Baton Rouge, Donaldsonville, Brashear City and Berwick till October. Western Louisiana (Teche) Campaign October 3-November 30. Vermillionville November 11. Duty at New Iberia till January 7, 1864. Moved to Franklin January 7, thence to Key West, Fla., February, 1864, and garrison duty at Fort Jefferson till August, 1865. Attack on Fort Myers, Fla., February 20, 1865 (Detachment). Mustered out August 28, 1865.

Regiment lost during service 2 Officers and 14 Enlisted men killed and mortally wounded and 3 Officers and 191 Enlisted men by disease. Total 210.

111th REGIMENT INFANTRY.

Organized at Auburn, N. Y., and mustered in August 20, 1862. Left State for Harper's Ferry, W. Va., August 21, 1862. Attached to Miles' Command, Harper's Ferry, to September, 1862. Camp Douglass, Chicago, Ill., to December, 1862. Wadsworth's Command, Military District of Washington, to February, 1863. 3rd Brigade, Casey's Division, 22nd Army Corps, Dept. of Washington, to April, 1863. 3rd Brigade, Abercrombie's Division, 22nd Army Corps, to June, 1863. 3rd Brigade, 3rd Division, 2nd Army Corps, Army of the Potomac, to March, 1864. 3rd Brigade, 1st Division, 2nd Army Corps, to June, 1864. Consolidated Brigade, 1st Division, 2nd Army Corps, to November, 1864. 3rd Brigade, 1st Division, 2nd Army Corps, to June, 1865.

SERVICE.—Defence of Harper's Ferry, W. Va., September 12-15, 1862. Regiment surrendered September 15. Paroled September 16 and sent to Annapolis, Md., thence to Camp Douglass, Chicago, Ill., and duty there guarding prisoners till December, 1862. Exchanged November 23, 1862. Ordered to Washington, D. C., and duty in the defences of that city and at Centreville, Va., till June, 1863. Ordered to join Army of the Potomac in the field and joined 2nd Army Corps June 25. Gettysburg (Pa.) Campaign June 25-July 24. Battle of Gettysburg July 2-4. Pursuit of Lee to Manassas Gap, Va., July 5-24. Duty on line of the Rappahannock and Rapidan till October. Advance from the Rappahannock to the Rapidan September 13-17. Lewinsville October 3. Bristoe Campaign October 9-22. Auburn and Bristoe October 14. Blackburn's and Mitchell's Fords October 15. Advance to line of the Rappahannock November 7-8. Mine Run Campaign November 26-December 2. At and near Stevensburg, Va., till May, 1864. Demonstration on the Rapidan February 6-7. Morton's Ford February 6-7. Campaign from the Rapidan to the James May 3-June 15. Battles of the Wilderness May 5-7; Spottsylvania May 8-12; Po River May 10; Spottsylvania Court House May 12-21. Assault on the Salient, or "Bloody Angle," May 12. North Anna River May 23-26. On line of the Pamunkey May 26-28. Totopotomoy May 28-31. Cold Harbor June 1-12. Before Petersburg June 16-18. Siege of Petersburg June 16, 1864, to April 2, 1865. Jerusalem Plank Road, Weldon Railroad, June 22-23. Demonstration north of the James July 27-29. Deep Bottom July 27-28. Demonstration north of the James August 13-20. Strawberry Plains, Deep Bottom, August 14-18. Ream's Station August 25. Reconnoissance to Hatcher's Run December 9-10. Dabney's Mills, Hatcher's Run, February 5-7, 1865. Watkins' House March 25. Appomattox Campaign March 28-April 9. On line of Hatcher's and Gravelly Runs March 29-30. Hatcher's Run or Boydton Road March 31. White Oak Road March 31. Sutherland Station and fall of Petersburg April 2. Pursuit of Lee April 3-9. Sailor's Creek April 6. High Bridge and Farmville April 7. Appomattox Court House April 9. Surrender of Lee and his army. At Burkesville till May 2. Moved to Washington, D. C., May 2-12. Grand Review May 23. Mustered out June 3, 1865. Veterans and recruits transferred to 4th New York Heavy Artillery.

Regiment lost during service 10 Officers and 210 Enlisted men killed and mortally wounded and 2 Officers and 178 Enlisted men by disease. Total 400.

112th REGIMENT INFANTRY ("CHAUTAUQUA REGIMENT").

Organized at Jamestown, N. Y., September 11, 1862. Left State for Fortress Monroe, Va., September 12, thence moved to Suffolk September 16, 1862. Attached to Foster's Provisional Brigade, Division at Suffolk, 7th Army Corps, Dept. of Virginia, to December, 1862. Gibbs' Provisional Brigade, Division at Suffolk, 7th Army Corps, to April, 1863. 2nd Brigade, 1st Division, 7th Army Corps, to July, 1863. Foster's Brigade, Vodges' Division, Folly Island, S. C., 10th Army Corps, Dept. of the South, to February, 1864. 1st Brigade, Vodges' Division, District of Florida, to April, 1864. 2nd Brigade, 3rd Division, 10th Army Corps, Army of the James, Dept. of Virginia and North Carolina, to May, 1864. 2nd Brigade, 3rd Division, 18th Army Corps, to July, 1864. 1st Brigade, 2nd Division, 10th Army Corps, to December, 1864. 1st Brigade, 2nd Division, 24th Army Corps, to January, 1865. 1st Brigade, 2nd Division, Terry's Provisional Corps, Dept. of North Carolina, to March, 1865. 1st Brigade, 2nd Division, 10th Army Corps, Army of the Ohio, Dept. of North Carolina, to June, 1865.

SERVICE.—Duty at Suffolk, Va., September, 1862, to June, 1863. Expedition toward Blackwater January 7-9, 1863. Action at Deserted House, Va., January 30, 1863. Leesville April 4. Siege of Suffolk, Va., April 12-May 4. Edenton, Providence Church and Somerton Roads April 12-13. Edenton Road April 15 and 24. Nansemond River May 3. Siege of Suffolk raised May 4. Dix's Peninsula Campaign June 24-July 7. Expedition from White House to South Anna Bridge July 1-7. South Anna Bridge July 4. Near Portsmouth July 10-28. Ordered to Dept. of the South, arriving at Folly Island, S. C., August 12. Duty at Folly and Black Islands and operations against Charleston till February, 1864. Expedition to John's and James Islands February 6-14. Ordered to Jacksonville, Fla., February 20, and duty there till April 21. Ordered to Yorktown, Va., April 21. Butler's operations on south side of James River and against Petersburg and Richmond May 4-28. Occupation of City Point and Bermuda Hundred May 5. Port Walthal Junction, Chester Station, May 6-7. Operations against Fort Darling May 12-16. Battle of Drury's Bluff May 14-16. Bermuda Hundred May 16-27. Moved to White House, thence to Cold Harbor May 27-31. Battles about Cold Harbor June 1-12. Before Petersburg June 15-18. Siege operations against Petersburg and Richmond June 16-December 7, 1864. Duty in trenches before Petersburg and on the Bermuda Hundred front till September 27. Action at Bermuda Hundred June 25 and August 24-25. Mine Explosion, Petersburg, July 30. Battle of Chaffin's Farm, New Market Heights, September 28-30. Battle of Fair Oaks October 27-28. Duty at Staten Island and New York City during Presidential election of 1864, November 3-17, and in trenches before Richmond till December 7. Expedition to Fort Fisher, N. C., December 7-27. Second Expedition to Fort Fisher, N. C., January 3-15, 1865. Assault on and capture of Fort Fisher January 15. Sugar Loaf Battery February 11. Fort Anderson February 18. Capture of Wilmington February 22. Campaign of the Carolinas March 1-April 26. Advance on Kinston and Goldsboro March 6-21. Occupation of Goldsboro March 21. Occupation of Raleigh April 14. Bennett's House April 26. Surrender of Johnston and his army. Duty at Raleigh till June. Mustered out June 13, 1865. Veterans and Recruits transferred to 3rd New York Infantry.

Regiment lost during service 9 Officers and 122 Enlisted men killed and mortally wounded and 3 Officers and 190 Enlisted men by disease. Total 324.

113th REGIMENT INFANTRY ("ALBANY COUNTY REGIMENT," "SEYMOUR GUARD").

Organized at Albany, N. Y., and mustered in August 18, 1862. Moved to Washington, D. C., August 19, 1862, and duty in the defences of that city till December 19, 1862. Designation of Regiment changed to 7th Regiment Heavy Artillery December 19, 1862 (which see).

114th REGIMENT INFANTRY.

Organized at Norwich, N. Y., and mustered in September 3, 1862. Moved to Baltimore, Md., September 6-9. Attached to Emery's Brigade, Defences of Baltimore, 8th Army Corps, Middle Department, to November, 1862. Emery's Brigade, Louisiana Expedition, to December, 1862. Sherman's Division, Dept. of the Gulf, to January, 1863. 1st Brigade, 3rd Division, 19th Army Corps, Dept. of the Gulf, January, 1863. 1st Brigade, 2nd Division, 19th Army Corps, to July, 1863. 3rd Brigade, 1st Division, 19th Army Corps, to February, 1864. 1st Brigade, 1st Division, 19th Army Corps, to July, 1864. 1st Brigade, 1st Division, 19th Army Corps, Army of the Shenandoah, Middle Military Division, to March, 1865. 1st Brigade, Dwight's 1st Provisional Division, Army of the Shenandoah, to April, 1865. 1st Brigade, Dwight's Division, Dept. of Washington, to June, 1865.

SERVICE.—Duty at Baltimore, Md., till November 6, 1862. Movement into Pennsylvania against Stuart, October 12-16. Moved to Fortress Monroe, Va., November 6, thence sailed for Ship Island, Miss., December 4, arriving at Carrollton December 26 and January 4, 1863. Moved to Algiers January 7, 1863, and guard duty along Opelousas and Great Western Railroad till February. Duty at Brashear City till March 20. At Bayou Boeuff and Pattersonville till April 2. Moved to Brashear City April 2, thence to Berwick City April 9. Operations in Western Louisiana April 9-May 14. Teche Campaign April 11-20. Fort Bisland April 12-13. Jeanerette April 14. Guard live stock to Brashear City April 20-28. At Newtown May 4. Opelousas May 9. Expedition from Berne's Landing to Brashear City May 21-26. Franklin May 25. Moved to Algiers May 29 and to Port Hudson May 30. Siege of Port Hudson May 31-July 9. Assault on Port Hudson June 14. Brashear City June 21. Surrender of Port Hudson July 9. Expedition to Donaldsonville July 10-30. Kock's Plantation July 13. Duty near Thibodeaux till August 19, and at Brashear City till September 2. Sabine Pass Expedition September 4-12. Moved to Algiers, thence to Berwick September 17. Western Louisiana Campaign October 3-November 30. At New Iberia November 17, 1863, to January 8, 1864. Moved to Franklin January 8-10, and duty there till March 15. Red River Campaign March 15-May 22. Advance from Franklin to Alexandria April 15-26. Battle of Sabine Cross Roads April 8. Pleasant Hill April 9. Monett's Ferry or Cane River Crossing April 23. Construction of dam at Alexandria April 30-May 10. Retreat to Morganza May 13-22. Mansura May 16. At Morganza till July 1. Moved to Fortress Monroe, Va., thence to Washington, D. C., July 1-12. Repulse of Early's attack on Washington July 12-13. Snicker's Gap Expedition July 14-23. Sheridan's Shenandoah Valley Campaign August 7-November 28. Battle of Winchester September 19. Fisher's Hill September 22. Battle of Cedar Creek October 19. Duty near Middletown till November 9, and near Newtown till January 1, 1865. Near Stephenson's Depot till April 5. Moved to Washington, D. C., April 5, and duty there till May 23. Grand Review May 23-24. Camp near Bladensburg May 28 to June 5. Mustered out June 8 and discharged at Elmira, N. Y., June 17, 1865. Veterans and Recruits transferred to 90th New York Infantry.

Regiment lost during service 9 Officers and 112 Enlisted men killed and mortally wounded and 2 Officers and 192 Enlisted men by disease. Total 315.

115th REGIMENT INFANTRY—"IRON HEARTED REGIMENT."

Organized at Fonda and mustered in August 26, 1862. Left State for Middle Department August 30, 1862. Attached to Miles' Command, Harper's Ferry, W. Va., September, 1862. Camp Douglas, Chicago, Ill., to December, 1862. 3rd Brigade, Casey's Division, 22nd Army Corps, Dept. of Washington, December, 1862.

Busteed's Independent Brigade, 7th Army Corps, Dept. of Virginia, to January, 1863. District of Hilton Head, S. C., 10th Army Corps, Dept. of the South, to June, 1863. District of Beaufort, S. C., 10th Army Corps, to December, 1863. District of Hilton Head, S. C., 10th Army Corps, to January, 1864. Barton's Brigade, District of Hilton Head, S. C., to February, 1864. Barton's Brigade, District of Florida, February, 1864. Barton's Brigade, Ames' Division, District of Florida, to April, 1864. 2nd Brigade, 2nd Division, 10th Army Corps, Army of the James, Dept. of Virginia and North Carolina, to May, 1864. 1st Brigade, 3rd Division, 18th Army Corps, to June, 1864. 2nd Brigade, 2nd Division, 10th Army Corps, to July, 1864. 3rd Brigade, 2nd Division, 10th Army Corps, to December, 1864. 3rd Brigade, 2nd Division, 24th Army Corps, to January, 1865. 3rd Brigade, 2nd Division, Terry's Provisional Corps, Dept. of North Carolina, to March, 1865. 3rd Brigade, 2nd Division, 10th Army Corps, Army of the Ohio, to June, 1865.

SERVICE.—Defence of Harper's Ferry, W. Va., September 12-15, 1862. Maryland Heights September 12-13. Regiment surrendered September 15. Paroled September 16 and sent to Annapolis, Md., thence to Camp Douglas, Chicago, Ill., and duty there till November 22. Moved to Washington, D. C., November 22, and duty in the defences of that city till December 28. Moved to Yorktown, Va., December 28. Duty there and at Gloucester Point, Va., till January, 1863. Expedition to West Point and White House January 7-9 (Detachment). Ordered to Hilton Head, S. C., January, and duty there till June, 1863. At Beaufort, S. C., till December, 1863, and at Hilton Head, S. C., till February, 1864. Expedition to Jacksonville, Fla., February 5-7. Occupation of Jacksonville February 7. Expedition into Central Florida February 7-28. Camp Finnegan February 9. Sanderson February 12. Battle of Olustee February 20. Occupation of Palatka March 10. Moved to Gloucester Point, Va., April 22-28. Butler's operations on south side of the James River and against Petersburg and Richmond May 4-28. Port Walthall Junction, Chester Station, May 6-7. Operations against Fort Darling May 12-16. Battle of Drury's Bluff May 14-16. Bermuda Hundred May 16-28. Moved to White House, thence to Cold Harbor May 28-June 1. Battles about Cold Harbor June 1-12. Before Petersburg June 15-18. Siege operations against Petersburg and Richmond June 16 to December 7, 1864. Duty in trenches before Petersburg and on the Bermuda Hundred front till August. Mine Explosion, Petersburg, July 30. Demonstration on north side of the James August 13-20. Strawberry Plains, Deep Bottom, August 14-18. Battle of Chaffin's Farm, New Market Heights, September 28-30. Battle of Fair Oaks October 27-28. Duty in trenches before Richmond till December. Expedition to Fort Fisher, N. C., December 7-27. 2nd Expedition to Fort Fisher, N. C., January 3-15, 1865. Assault and capture of Fort Fisher January 15. Cape Fear intrenchments February 11-12. Sugar Loaf Battery February 11. Fort Anderson February 18-19. Capture of Wilmington February 22. Campaign of the Carolinas March 1-April 26. Advance on Goldsboro March 6-21. Advance on Raleigh April 9-13. Occupation of Raleigh April 14. Bennett's House April 26. Surrender of Johnston and his army. Duty at Raleigh till June. Mustered out June 17, 1865. Veterans and Recruits transferred to 47th New York Infantry.

Regiment lost during service 7 Officers and 128 Enlisted men killed and mortally wounded and 188 Enlisted men by disease. Total 323.

116th REGIMENT INFANTRY.

Organized at Camp Morgan, Buffalo, N. Y., August 10 to September 3, 1862. Left Buffalo for Baltimore, Md., September 5. Attached to Emery's Brigade, 8th Army Corps, Baltimore, Md., Middle Department, to November, 1862. Emery's Brigade, Banks' Louisiana Expedition, to December, 1862. Sherman's Division, Dept. of the Gulf, to January, 1863. 1st Brigade, 3rd Division, 19th Army Corps, Dept. of the Gulf, to February, 1863. 1st Brigade, 1st Division, 19th Army Corps, to July, 1864. 1st Brigade, 1st Division, 19th Army Corps, Army of the Shenandoah, Middle Military Division, to March, 1865. 1st Brigade, Dwight's 1st Division (Provisional), Army of the Shenandoah, to April, 1865. 1st Brigade, Dwight's Division, Dept. of Washington, to June, 1865.

SERVICE.—Camp at Druid's Hill Park, Baltimore, till November 5, 1862. Movement into Pennsylvania against Stuart October 12-15. Reach Gettysburg, Pa., October 15. Ordered to join Banks' Expedition and embarked on Steamer "Atlantic" for Fortress Monroe, Va., November 6. Sailed for Ship Island, Miss., December 4. Moved to Carrollton December 30, thence to Baton Rouge, La., February 3, 1863. Operations against Port Hudson, La., March 7-27. Moved to Winter's Plantation March 16-22. Duty at Baton Rouge till May 19. Advance on Port Hudson May 19-24. Action at Plain's Store May 21. Siege of Port Hudson May 24-July 9. Assaults on Port Hudson May 27 and June 14. Surrender of Port Hudson July 9. Expedition to Donaldsville July 9-30. Action at Kock's Plantation, Bayou LaFourche, July 12-13. Moved to Baton Rouge August 1, thence to New Orleans August 28. Sabine Pass Expedition September 4-12. Moved to Brashear City September 17. Western Louisiana Campaign October 3-November 30. Camp at New Iberia November 17, 1863, to January 8, 1864. Moved to Franklin January 8, and duty there till March 15. Red River Campaign March 15-May 22. Advance from Franklin to Alexandria March 15-26. Battle of Sabine Cross Roads April 8. Pleasant Hill April 9. Monett's Ferry, Cane River Crossing, April 23. Construction of dam at Alexandria April 30-May 10. Retreat to Morganza May 13-20. Mansura May 16. Camp at Morganza till July. Ordered to Fortress Monroe, Va., July 2, thence to Washington July 12. Snicker's Gap Expedition July 14-23. Sheridan's Shenandoah Valley Campaign August 7-November 28. Battle of Winchester September 19. Fisher's Hill September 22. Battle of Cedar Creek October 19. Duty near Middletown till November 9, and near Newtown till December 30. At Stephenson's Depot April 5, 1865. Moved to Washington, D. C., and duty there till June. Grand Review May 23-24. Mustered out June 8, 1865, and discharged at Buffalo, N. Y., June 26, 1865. Veterans and Recruits transferred to 90th New York Infantry.

Regiment lost during service 5 Officers and 91 Enlisted men killed and mortally wounded and 2 Officers and 124 Enlisted men by disease. Total 222.

117th REGIMENT INFANTRY—"4th ONEIDA REGIMENT."

Organized at Oneida and mustered in August 8, 1862. Left State for Washington, D. C., August 22, 1862. Attached to Defences of Washington north of the Potomac, to October, 1862. 2nd and 3rd Brigade, Haskins' Division, north of the Potomac, to March, 1863. 2nd and 3rd Brigades, Haskins' Division, north of the Potomac, 22nd Army Corps, to April, 1863. 1st Brigade, 2nd Division, 7th Army Corps, Dept. of Virginia, to July, 1863. Alvord's Brigade, Vodge's Division, Folly Island, S. C., 10th Army Corps, Dept. of the South, to February, 1864. 2nd Brigade, Folly Island, Northern District, Dept. of the South, to April, 1864. 1st Brigade, 2nd Division, 10th Army Corps, Army of the James, Dept. of Virginia and North Carolina, to May, 1864. 3rd Brigade, 3rd Division, 18th Army Corps, to June, 1864. 1st Brigade, 2nd Division, 10th Army Corps, to December, 1864. 1st Brigade, 2nd Division, 24th Army Corps, to January, 1865. 1st Brigade, 2nd Division, Terry's Provisional Corps, Dept. of North Carolina, to March, 1865. 1st Brigade, 2nd Division, 10th Army Corps, Army of the Ohio, Dept. of North Carolina, to June, 1865.

SERVICE.—Duty in the Defences of Washington, D. C., and at Tennallytown till April, 1863. Ordered to Suffolk, Va., April 16. Siege of Suffolk April 20-May 4. Providence Church Road, Nansemond River, May 3. Dix's Peninsula Campaign June 24-July 7. Expedition from White House to South Anna River July 1-7. Ordered to Folly Island, S. C., July 12. Siege operations against Forts Wagner and Gregg, Morris Island, S. C., and against Charleston and Fort Sumpter August 17-September 7. Bombardment of Fort Sumpter and Charleston August 17-23. Operations against Charleston, S. C., and duty on Folly Island, S. C., till April, 1864. Moved to Gloucester Point, Va., April. Butler's operations on south side of the James River and against Petersburg and Richmond May 4-28. Occupation of City Point and Bermuda Hundred May 5. Swift Creek or Arrowfield Church May 9-10. Operations against Fort Darling May 12-16. Battle of Drury's Bluff May 14-16. Bermuda Hundred May 16-28. Moved to White House, thence to Cold Harbor May 28-31. Battles about Cold Harbor June 1-12. Before Petersburg June 15-18. Siege operations against Petersburg and Richmond June 16 to December 7, 1864. Duty in trenches before Petersburg and on the Bermuda Hundred front till September 27. Battle of Chaffin's Farm, New Market Heights, September 28-30. Battle of Fair Oaks October 27-28. Duty in trenches before Richmond till December 7. Expedition to Fort Fisher, N. C., December 7-27. 2nd Expedition to Fort Fisher, N. C., January 3-15. Assault and capture of Fort Fisher January 15. Cape Fear Intrenchments February 11-13. Sugar Loaf Battery February 11. Fort Anderson February 18-19. Capture of Wilmington February 22. Campaign of the Carolinas March 1-April 26. Advance on Goldsboro March 6-21. Occupation of Raleigh April 14. Bennett's House April 26. Surrender of Johnston and his army. Duty in North Carolina till June. Mustered out at Raleigh June 8, 1865. Veterans and Recruits transferred to 48th New York Infantry.

Regiment lost during service 7 Officers and 123 Enlisted men killed and mortally wounded and 1 Officer and 135 Enlisted men by disease. Total 266.

118th REGIMENT INFANTRY—"ADIRONDACK REGIMENT."

Organized at Plattsburg, N. Y., and mustered in August 27, 1862. Left State for Washington, D. C., September 3, 1862. Attached to Provisional Brigade, Abercrombie's Division, Defences of Washington, D. C., to February, 1863. District of Washington, 22nd Army Corps, Dept. of Washington, to April, 1863. Reserve Brigade, 3rd Division, 7th Army Corps, Dept. of Virginia, to June, 1863. Wardrop's Independent Brigade, 7th Army Corps, to July, 1863. U. S. Forces, Yorktown, Va., Dept. of Virginia and North Carolina, to October, 1863. Heckman's Command, Newport News, Va., to January, 1864. 1st Brigade, U. S. Forces, Yorktown, Va., Dept. of Virginia and North Carolina, to February, 1864. Unattached, Yorktown, Pa., Dept. Virginia and North Carolina, to April, 1864. 2nd Brigade, 1st Division, 18th Army Corps, Army of the James, to December, 1864. 2nd Brigade, 3rd Division, 24th Army Corps, to June, 1865.

SERVICE.—Guard and provost duty at Washington, D. C., till April, 1863. Ordered to Suffolk, Va., April 16. Siege of Suffolk April 20-May 4. Moved to Portsmouth, Va., May 13. Operations on Norfolk & Petersburg Railroad May 15-28. Antioch Church and Barber's Cross Roads May 23. Reconnoissance to the Chickahominy June 9-16. Dix's Peninsula Campaign June 24-July 7. Expedition from White House to South Anna Bridge July 1-7. Action at South Anna Bridge July 4. Expedition to Gloucester Court House July 25. Duty at Yorktown and vicinity till October, and at Portsmouth and vicinity till March, 1864. Wistar's Expedition against Richmond February 6-8, 1864. Ballahoe or Bear Quarter Road and Deep Creek February 29-March 1. Demonstration against Portsmouth March 4-5. Moved to Yorktown March 17. Expedition to Isle of Wight County April 13-15. Smithfield, Cherry Grove, April 14. Butler's operations on south side of the James River and against Petersburg and Richmond May 4-28. Occupation of Bermuda Hundred and City Point May 5. Port Walthall Junction, Chester Station, May 7. Swift Creek or Arrowfield Church May 9-10. Operations against Fort Darling May 12-16. Battle of Drury's Bluff May 14-16. Bermuda Hundred May 16-28. Moved to White House, thence to Cold Harbor May 27-31. Battles about Cold Harbor June 1-12. Before Petersburg June 15-18. Siege operations against Petersburg and Richmond June 16, 1864, to April 2, 1865. Mine Explosion, Petersburg, July 30, 1864. In trenches before Petersburg and on the Bermuda Hundred front till September 27. Battle of Chaffin's Farm, New Market Heights, September 28-30. Battle of Fair Oaks October 27-28. Duty in the trenches before Richmond till March, 1865. Fall of Petersburg and Richmond April 2-3. Pursuit of Lee April 3-9. Appomattox Court House April 9. Surrender of Lee and his army. Provost duty at Richmond and Manchester till June. Mustered out June 13, 1865. Veterans and Recruits transferred to 96th New York Infantry.

Regiment lost during service 6 Officers and 93 Enlisted men killed and mortally wounded and 188 Enlisted men by disease. Total 287.

119th REGIMENT INFANTRY.

Organized at New York City and mustered in September 4, 1862. Left State for Washington, D. C., September 6, 1862. Attached to 2nd Brigade, 3rd Division, 11th Army Corps, Army of the Potomac, to October, 1863, and Army of the Cumberland to April, 1864. 2nd Brigade, 2nd Division, 20th Army Corps, Army of the Cumberland, to June, 1865.

SERVICE.—Duty in the Defences of Washington, D. C., till November, 1862. Movement to Gainesville, Va., November 1-9, thence to Centreville November 18, and to Falmouth December 9-16. At Stafford Court House till January 20, 1863. "Mud March" January 20-24. At Stafford Court House till April 27. Chancellorsville Campaign April 27-May 6. Battle of Chancellorsville May 1-5. Gettysburg (Pa.) Campaign June 11-July 24. Battle of Gettysburg July 1-3. Pursuit of Lee to Manassas Gap, Va., July 5-24. Guard duty on Orange & Alexandria Railroad till September. Movement to Bridgeport, Ala., September 24-October 3. Duty there and in Lookout Valley till November 22. Reopening Tennessee River October 26-29. Battle of Wauhatchie, Tenn., October 28-29. Chattanooga-Ringgold Campaign November 23-27. Orchard Knob November 23. Tunnel Hill November 24-25. Mission Ridge November 25. March to relief of Knoxville November 28-December 17. Duty in Alabama till April, 1864. Atlanta (Ga.) Campaign May 1-September 8. Operations against Rocky Faced Ridge May 8-11. Mill Creek or Dug Gap May 8. Battle of Resaca May 14-15. Near Cassville May 19. New Hope Church May 25. Battles about Dallas, New Hope Church and Allatoona Hills May 26-June 5. Operations about Marietta and against Kenesaw Mountain June 10-July 2. Pine Hill June 11-14. Lost Mountain June 15-17. Gilgal or Golgotha Church June 15. Muddy Creek June 17. Noyes Creek June 19. Kolk's Farm June 22. Assault on Kenesaw June 27. Ruff's Station, Smyrna Camp Ground, July 4. Chattahoochie River July 5-17. Peach Tree Creek July 19-20. Siege of Atlanta July 22-August 25. Operations at Chattahoochie River Bridge August 26-September 2. Occupation of Atlanta September 2 to November 15. Expedition from Atlanta to Tuckum's Cross Roads October 26-29. Near Atlanta November 9. March to the sea November 15-December 10. Between Eden and Pooler's Stations December 9. Siege of Savannah December 10-21. Campaign of the Carolinas January to April, 1865. Battle of Bentonville, N. C., March 19-21. Occupation of Goldsboro March 24. Advance on Raleigh April 9-13. Smithfield, N. C., April 11. Occupation of Raleigh April 14. Bennett's House April 26. Surrender of Johnston and his army. March to Washington, D. C., via Richmond, Va., April 30-May 19. Grand Review May 24. Mustered out June 7, 1865. Veterans and Recruits transferred to 102nd New York Infantry.

Regiment lost during service 6 Officers and 66 Enlisted men killed and mortally wounded and 2 Officers and 92 Enlisted men by disease. Total 166.

120th REGIMENT INFANTRY.—("ULSTER REGIMENT." "WASHINGTON GUARD.")

Organized at Kingston, N. Y., and mustered in August 22, 1862. Left State for Washington, D. C., August 24, 1862. Attached to Whipple's Brigade, Defences of Washington, D. C., to October, 1862. 1st Brigade, 2nd Division, 3rd Army Corps, Army of the Potomac, to December, 1862. 2nd Brigade, 2nd Division, 3rd Army Corps, to March, 1864. 2nd Brigade, 4th Division, 2nd Army Corps, to May, 1864. 4th Brigade, 3rd Division, 2nd Army Corps, to July, 1864. 3rd Brigade, 3rd Division, 2nd Army Corps, to June, 1865.

SERVICE.—Duty in the Defences of Washington, D. C., till November, 1862. At Fairfax Station, Va., till November 25. Operations on Orange & Alexandria Railroad November 10-12. Rappahannock Campaign December, 1862, to June, 1863. Battle of Fredericksburg, Va., December 12-15, 1862. At Falmouth, Va., till April, 1863. "Mud March" January 20-24. Operations at Rappahannock Bridge and Grove Church February 5-7. Chancellorsville Campaign April 27-May 6. Battle of Chancellorsville May 1-5. Gettysburg (Pa.) Campaign June 11-July 24. Battle of Gettysburg July 1-3. Pursuit of Lee to Manassas Gap, Va., July 5-24. Wapping Heights July 23. Duty on line of the Rappahannock and Rapidan till October. Advance from the Rappahannock to the Rapidan September 13-17. Bristoe Campaign October 8-22. James City October 8, 9 and 10. Russell's Ford, Robertson's River, and Bethesda Church October 10. Advance to line of the Rappahannock November 7-8. Kelly's Ford November 7. Mine Run Campaign November 26-December 2. Payne's Farm November 27. Mine Run November 28-30. Duty near Brandy Station till May, 1864. Demonstration on the Rapidan February 6-7. Campaign from the Rapidan to the James May 3-June 15. Battles of the Wilderness May 5-7; Laurel Hill May 8; Spottsylvania May 8-12; Spottsylvania Court House May 12-21. Assault on the Salient or "Bloody Angle" May 12. Harris Farm or Fredericksburg Road May 19. North Anna River May 23-26. On line of the Pamunkey May 26-28. Totopotomoy May 28-31. Cold Harbor June 1-12. Before Petersburg June 16-18. Siege of Petersburg June 16, 1864, to April 2, 1865. Jerusalem Plank Road, Weldon Railroad, June 22-23, 1864. Demonstration north of the James July 27-29. Deep Bottom July 27-28. Mine Explosion, Petersburg, July 30 (Reserve). Demonstration north of the James August 13-20. Strawberry Plains, Deep Bottom, August 14-18. Poplar Springs Church September 29-October 2. Boydton Plank Road, Hatcher's Run, October 27-28. Front of Forts Hascall and Morton November 5. Reconnoissance to Hatcher's Run December 9-10. Dabney's Mills, Hatcher's Run, February 5-7, 1865. Watkins' House March 25. Appomattox Campaign March 28-April 9. Boydton and White Oak Roads March 29-31. Fall of Petersburg April 2. Pursuit of Lee April 3-9. Sailor's Creek April 6. High Bridge, Farmville, April 7. Appomattox Court House April 9. Surrender of Lee and his army. At Burkesville till May 2. Moved to Washington, D. C., May 2-12. Grand Review May 23. Mustered out June 3, 1865. Veterans and Recruits transferred to 73rd New York Infantry.

Regiment lost during service 11 Officers and 140 Enlisted men killed and mortally wounded and 3 Officers and 179 Enlisted men by disease. Total 333.

121st REGIMENT INFANTRY.—("ORANGE AND HERKIMER REGIMENT.")

Organized at Herkimer and mustered in August 13, 1862. Left State for Washington, D. C., September 2, 1862. Attached to 2nd Brigade, 1st Division, 6th Army Corps, Army of the Potomac and Army of the Shenandoah, to June, 1865.

SERVICE.—Maryland Campaign September 6-22, 1862. Duty at Sharpsburg, Md., till October 30. Movement to Falmouth, Va., October 30-November 19. Battle of Fredericksburg, Va., December 12-15. At Falmouth till April, 1863. "Mud March" January 20-24. Chancellorsville Campaign April 27-May 6. Operations at Franklin's Crossing April 29-May 2. Battle of Maryes Heights, Fredericksburg, May 3. Salem Heights May 3-4. Banks' Ford May 4. Gettysburg (Pa.) Campaign June 14-July 24. Battle of Gettysburg July 2-4. Pursuit of Lee to Manassas Gap, Va., July 5-24. Duty on line of the Rappahannock and Rapidan till October. Bristoe Campaign October 9-22. Advance to line of the Rappahannock November 7-8. Rappahannock Station November 7. Mine Run Campaign November 26-December 2. Campaign from the Rapidan to the James May 3-June 15, 1864. Battles of the Wilderness May 5-7; Spottsylvania May 8-12; Spottsylvania Court House May 12-21. Assault on the Salient, "Bloody Angle," May 12. North Anna River May 23-26. On line of the Pamunkey May 26-28. Totopotomoy May 28-31. Cold Harbor June 1-12. Before Petersburg June 17-18. Siege of Petersburg to July 9. Jerusalem Plank Road June 22-23. Moved to Washington, D. C., July 9-11. Repulse of Early's attack on Fort Stevens and the Northern Defences of Washington July 11-12. Expedition to Snicker's Gap July 14-23. Sheridan's Shenandoah Valley Campaign August 7-November 28. Near Charleston August 21-22. Battle of Winchester September 19. Fisher's Hill September 22. Mt. Jackson September 23-24. Battle of Cedar Creek October 19. Duty in the Shenandoah Valley till December. Moved to Petersburg, Va., December 9-12. Siege of Petersburg December 12, 1864, to April 2, 1865. Dabney's Mills, Hatcher's Run, February 5-7, 1865. Appomattox Campaign March 28-April 9. Assault on and fall of Petersburg April 2. Sailor's Creek April 6. Appomattox Court House April 9. Surrender of Lee and his army. At Farmville and Burkesville till April 23. March to Danville April 23-27 and duty there till May 24. March to Richmond, thence to Washington, D. C., May 24-June 3. Corps Review June 8. Mustered out June 25, 1865. Veterans and Recruits transferred to 65th New York Infantry.

Regiment lost during service 14 Officers and 212 Enlisted men killed and mortally wounded and 4 Officers and 117 Enlisted men by disease. Total 347.

122nd REGIMENT INFANTRY.—("ONONDAGAS.")

Organized at Syracuse, N. Y., and mustered in August 28, 1862. Left State for Washington, D. C., August 31, 1862. Attached to 3rd Brigade, 1st Division, 4th Army Corps, Army of the Potomac, to September, 1862. 2nd Brigade, 3rd Division, 6th Army Corps, to October, 1862. 1st Brigade, 3rd Division, 6th Army Corps, to January, 1864. Johnson's Island, Ohio, to March, 1864. 4th Brigade, 1st Division, 6th Army Corps, to July, 1864. 3rd Brigade, 2nd Division, 6th Army Corps, Army of the Potomac and Army of the Shenandoah, to June, 1865.

SERVICE.—Maryland Campaign September 6-22, 1862. Battle of Antietam, Md., September 16-17. Duty in Maryland till October 20. Moved to Stafford Court House, Va., October 20-November 18, and to Belle Plains December 5. Battle of Fredericksburg, Va., December 12-15. At Falmouth, Va., till April, 1863. "Mud March" January 20-24. Chancellorsville Campaign April 27-May 6. Operations at Franklin's Crossing April 29-May 2. Battle of Maryes Heights, Fredericksburg, May 3. Salem Heights May 3-4. Banks' Ford May 4. Gettysburg (Pa.) Campaign June 11-July 24. Battle of Gettysburg July 2-4. Pursuit of Lee to Manassas Gap, Va., July 5-24. Duty on line of the Rappahannock and Rapidan till October. Bristoe Campaign October 9-22. Advance to line of the Rappahannock November 7-8. Rappahannock Station November 7. Mine Run Campaign November 26-December 2. Duty at and near Brandy Station till January, 1864. On detached duty at Johnson's Island, Lake Erie, till March. Campaign from the Rapidan to the James May 3-June 15.

Battles of the Wilderness May 5-7; Spottsylvania May 8-12; Spottsylvania Court House May 12-21. Assault on the Salient, "Bloody Angle," May 12. North Anna River May 23-26. On line of the Pamunkey May 26-28. Totopotomoy May 28-31. Cold Harbor June 1-12. Before Petersburg June 17-18. Jerusalem Plank Road, Weldon Railroad, June 22-23. Siege of Petersburg till July 9. Moved to Washington, D. C., July 9-11. Repulse of Early's attack on Fort Stevens and the Northern Defences of Washington July 11-12. Expedition to Snicker's Gap, Va., July 14-23. Sheridan's Shenandoah Valley Campaign August 7-November 28. Gilbert's Ford, Opequan Creek, September 13. Battle of Winchester September 19. Fisher's Hill September 22. Battle of Cedar Creek October 19. Duty in the Shenandoah Valley till December. Moved to Petersburg, Va., December 9-12. Siege of Petersburg December 12, 1864, to April 2, 1865. Fort Fisher, Petersburg, March 25. Appomattox Campaign March 28-April 9. Assault on and fall of Petersburg April 2. Sailor's Creek April 6. Appomattox Court House April 9. Surrender of Lee and his army. At Farmville and Burkesville till April 23. March to Danville, Va., April 23-27, and duty there till May 24. March to Richmond, thence to Washington, D. C., May 24-June 3. Corps Review June 8. Mustered out June 28, 1865.

Regiment lost during service 6 Officers and 85 Enlisted men killed and mortally wounded and 3 Officers and 85 Enlisted men by disease. Total 179.

123rd REGIMENT INFANTRY ("WASHINGTON COUNTY REGIMENT").

Organized at Salem, N. Y., and mustered in September 4, 1862. Left State for Washington, D. C., September 5, 1862. Attached to 2nd Brigade, 1st Division, 12th Army Corps, Army of the Potomac, to May, 1863. 1st Brigade, 1st Division, 12th Army Corps, Army of the Potomac, to October, 1863, and Army of the Cumberland to April, 1864. 1st Brigade, 1st Division, 20th Army Corps, Army of the Cumberland, to June, 1865.

SERVICE.—Duty in the Defences of Washington, D. C., till September 29, 1862, and at Frederick, Md., and Sandy Hook till December 13, 1862. Moved to support of Burnside at Fredericksburg, Va., December 10-14. At Stafford Court House till April 27, 1863. "Mud March" January 20-24. Chancellorsville Campaign April 27-May 6. Battle of Chancellorsville May 1-5. Gettysburg (Pa.) Campaign June 11-July 24. Battle of Gettysburg July 1-3. Pursuit of Lee to Manassas Gap, Va., July 5-24. Duty on line of the Rappahannock till September. Moved to Bealeton Station, Va., thence to Stevenson, Ala., September 24-October 4. Guard duty along Nashville & Chattanooga Railroad till April, 1864. Action near Tullahoma, Tenn., March 16, 1864. Atlanta (Ga.) Campaign May 1-September 8. Operations against Rocky Faced Ridge May 8-11. Battle of Resaca May 14-15. Near Cassville May 19. Advance on Dallas May 22-25. New Hope Church May 25. Battles about Dallas, New Hope Church and Allatoona Hills May 26-June 5. Operations about Marietta and against Kenesaw Mountain June 10-July 2.: Pine Hill June 11-14. Lost Mountain June 15-17. Gilgal or Golgotha Church June 15. Muddy Creek June 17. Noyes' Creek June 19. Kolb's Farm June 22. Assault on Kenesaw Mountain June 27. Ruff's Station, Smyrna Camp Ground, July 4. Chattahoochie River July 5-17. Peach Tree Creek July 19-20. Siege of Atlanta July 22-August 25. Operations at Chattahoochie River Bridge August 26-September 2. Occupation of Atlanta September 2-November 15. March to the sea November 15-December 10. Siege of Savannah December 10-21. Campaign of the Carolinas January to April, 1865. Thompson's Creek, near Chesterfield Court House, S. C., and near Cheraw March 2. Averysboro, N. C., March 16. Battle of Bentonville March 19-21. Occupation of Goldsboro March 24, and of Raleigh April 14. Bennett's House April 26. Surrender of Johnston and his army. March to Washington, D. C., via Richmond, Va., April 29-May 20. Grand

Review May 24. Mustered out June 8, 1865. Veterans and Recruits transferred to 60th New York Infantry.

Regiment lost during service 6 Officers and 66 Enlisted men killed and mortally wounded and 95 Enlisted men by disease. Total 167.

124th REGIMENT INFANTRY ("AMERICAN GUARD," "ORANGE BLOSSOMS").

Organized at Goshen and mustered in September 5, 1862. Left State for Washington, D. C., September 6. Attached to Piatt's Brigade, Whipple's Division, 3rd Army Corps, to October, 1862. 1st Brigade, 3rd Division, 3rd Army Corps, Army of the Potomac, to June, 1863. 2nd Brigade, 1st Division, 3rd Army Corps, to March, 1864. 1st Brigade, 3rd Division, 2nd Army Corps, to June, 1865.

SERVICE.—Duty in the Defences of Washington, D. C., till October, 1862. Moved to Point of Rocks, thence to Pleasant Valley, Md., October 18-19. Movement toward Warrenton, Va., October 24-November 16. Reconnoissance to Manassas Gap November 5-6. Movement to Falmouth, Va., November 18-24. Battle of Fredericksburg, Va., December 12-15. Duty near Falmouth till April 27, 1863. "Mud March" January 20-24. Chancellorsville Campaign April 27-May 6. Battle of Chancellorsville May 1-5. Beverly Ford and Brandy Station June 9. Gettysburg (Pa.) Campaign June 11-July 24. Battle of Gettysburg, Pa., July 1-3. Pursuit of Lee to Manassas Gap, Va., July 5-24. Wapping Heights, Va., July 23. Duty on line of the Rappahannock and the Rapidan till October. Bristoe Campaign October 9-22. Advance to line of the Rappahannock November 7-8. Kelly's Ford November 7. Mine Run Campaign November 26-December 2. Payne's Farm November 27. Mine Run November 28-30. Duty near Brandy Station till May, 1864. Demonstration on the Rapidan February 6-7. Campaign from the Rapidan to the James May 3-June 15. Battles of the Wilderness May 5-7. Laurel Hill May 8. Spottsylvania May 8-12. Po River May 10. Spottsylvania Court House May 12-21. Assault on the Salient "Bloody Angle" May 12. Harris Farm, or Fredericksburg Road, May 19. North Anna River May 23-26. On line of the Pamunkey May 26-28. Totopotomoy May 28-31. Cold Harbor June 1-12. Before Petersburg June 16-18. Siege of Petersburg June 16, 1864, to April 2, 1865. Jerusalem Plank Road, Weldon Railroad, June 22-23, 1864. Demonstration north of the James July 27-29. Deep Bottom July 27-28. Demonstration on north side of the James August 13-20. Strawberry Plains, Deep Bottom, August 14-18. Poplar Springs Church September 29-October 2. Boydton Plank Road, Hatcher's Run, October 27-28. Raid on Weldon Railroad December 9-10. Dabney's Mills, Hatcher's Run, February 5-7, 1865. Watkins' House March 25. Appomattox Campaign March 28-April 9. Boydton and White Oak Roads March 29-31. Crow's House March 31. Fall of Petersburg April 2. Sailor's Creek April 6. High Bridge and Farmville April 7. Appomattox Court House April 9. Surrender of Lee and his army. At Burkesville till May 2. Moved to Washington, D. C., May 2-12. Grand Review May 23. Mustered out June 3, 1865. Veterans and Recruits transferred to 93rd New York Infantry.

Regiment lost during service 11 Officers and 137 Enlisted men killed and mortally wounded and 1 Officer and 92 Enlisted men by disease. Total 241.

125th REGIMENT INFANTRY.

Organized at Troy, N. Y., and mustered in August 29, 1862. Left State for Baltimore, Md., August 31; thence moved to Martinsburg, Va., September 2, 1862. Retreat to Harper's Ferry, W. Va., September 11-12. Attached to Miles' Command, Harper's Ferry, W. Va., September, 1862. Camp Douglas, Chicago, Ill., to December, 1862. 3rd Brigade, Casey's Division, Defences of Washington, D. C., to February, 1863. 3rd Brigade, Abercrombie's Division, 22nd Army Corps, Dept. of Washington, to June, 1863. 3rd Brigade, 3rd Division, 2nd Army Corps, Army of the Potomac, to March, 1864. 3rd Brigade, 1st Division, 2nd Army Corps, to June,

1864. Consolidated Brigade, 1st Division, 2nd Army Corps, to November, 1864. 3rd Brigade, 1st Division, 2nd Army Corps, to June, 1865.

SERVICE.—Defense of Harper's Ferry, West Va., September 12-15, 1862. Maryland Heights September 12-13. Bolivar Heights September 14-15. Surrendered September 15. Paroled September 16 and sent to Annapolis, Md., thence to Camp Douglas, Chicago, Ill., and duty there guarding prisoners till November, 1862. Declared exchanged November 22, 1862. Moved to Washington, D. C., November 23-25. Camp at Arlington Heights, Va., till December 3, and at Centreville, Va., till June, 1863. Ordered to join Army of the Potomac in the field and joined 2nd Army Corps June 25, 1863. Gettysburg (Pa.) Campaign June 25-July 24. Battle of Gettysburg, Pa., July 2-4. Pursuit of Lee to Manassas Gap, Va., July 5-24. Duty on lines of the Rappahannock and Rapidan till October. Advance from the Rappahannock to the Rapidan September 13-17. Bristoe Campaign October 9-22. Auburn and Bristoe October 14. Advance to line of the Rappahannock November 7-8. Mine Run Campaign November 26-December 2. Duty near Brandy Station till May, 1864. Demonstration on the Rapidan February 6-7. Campaign from the Rapidan to the James May 3-June 15. Battles of the Wilderness May 5-7. Spottsylvania May 8-12. Po River May 10. Spottsylvania Court House May 12-21. Assault on the Salient "Bloody Angle" May 12. North Anna River May 23-26. On line of the Pamunkey May 26-28. Totopotomoy May 28-31. Cold Harbor June 1-12. Before Petersburg June 16, 1864, to April 2, 1865. Jerusalem Plank Road, Weldon Railroad, June 22-23, 1864. Demonstration on north side of the James July 27-29. Deep Bottom July 27-28. Demonstration north side of the James August 13-20. Strawberry Plains, Deep Bottom, August 14-18. Ream's Station August 25. Reconnoissance to Hatcher's Run December 9-10. Dabney's Mills, Hatcher's Run, February 5-7, 1865. Watkins' House March 25. Appomattox Campaign March 28-April 9. On line of Hatcher's and Gravelly Runs March 29-30. White Oak Road March 31. Sutherland Station and fall of Petersburg April 2. Pursuit of Lee April 3-9. Sailor's Creek April 6. High Bridge and Farmville April 7. Appomattox Court House April 9. Surrender of Lee and his army. Moved to Washington, D. C., May 2-12. Grand Review May 23. Mustered out at Alexandria, Va., June 5, 1865. Veterans and Recruits transferred to 4th New York Heavy Artillery.

Regiment lost during service 15 Officers and 112 Enlisted men killed and mortally wounded and 1 Officer and 112 Enlisted men by disease. Total 240.

126th REGIMENT INFANTRY.

Organized at Geneva, N. Y., and mustered in August 22, 1862. Left State for Baltimore, Md., thence moved to Martinsburg, Va., September 2, 1862. Retreat to Harper's Ferry, W. Va., September 11-12. Attached to Miles' Command, Harper's Ferry, W. Va., September, 1862. Camp Douglas, Chicago, Ill., to December, 1862. 3rd Brigade, Casey's Division, Defences of Washington, D. C., to February, 1863. 3rd Brigade, Casey's Division, 22nd Army Corps, to April, 1863. 3rd Brigade, Abercrombie's Division, 22nd Army Corps, to June, 1863. 3rd Brigade, 3rd Division, 2nd Army Corps, Army of the Potomac, to March, 1864. 3rd Brigade, 1st Division, 2nd Army Corps, to June, 1864. Consolidated Brigade, 1st Division, 2nd Army Corps, to November, 1864. 3rd Brigade, 1st Division, 2nd Army Corps, to June, 1865.

SERVICE.—Defence of Harper's Ferry, W. Va., September 12-15, 1862. Maryland Heights September 12-13. Bolivar Heights September 14-15. Regiment surrendered September 15. Paroled September 16 and sent to Annapolis, Md.; thence to Camp Douglas, Chicago, Ill., and duty there guarding prisoners till November. Declared exchanged November 22, 1862. Moved to Washington, D. C., November 23-25. Camp at Arlington Heights, Va., Defences of Washington, to December 3, 1862, and at Centreville, Va., till June, 1863. Or-

dered to join Army of the Potomac in the field and joined 2nd Army Corps June 25. Gettysburg (Pa.) Campaign June 25-July 24. Battle of Gettysburg July 1-3. Pursuit of Lee to Manassas Gap, Va., July 5-24. Duty on line of the Rappahannock and Rapidan till October. Advance from the Rappahannock to the Rapidan September 13-17. Bristoe Campaign October 9-22. Auburn and Bristoe October 14. Advance to line of the Rappahannock November 7-8. Brandy Station November 8. Mine Run Campaign November 26-December 2. Duty near Brandy Station, Va., till May, 1864. Demonstration on the Rapidan February 6-7. Morton's Ford February 6-7. Campaign from the Rapidan to the James May 3-June 15. Battles of the Wilderness May 5-7; Spottsylvania May 8-12; Po River May 10; Spottsylvania Court House May 12-21. Assault on the Salient, "Bloody Angle," May 12. North Anna River May 23-26. On line of the Pamunkey May 26-28. Totopotomoy May 28-31. Cold Harbor June 1-12. Before Petersburg June 16-18. Siege of Petersburg June 16, 1864, to April 2, 1865. Jerusalem Plank Road, Weldon Railroad, June 22-23, 1864. Demonstration north of James River July 27-29. Deep Bottom July 27-28. Demonstration north of James River August 13-20. Strawberry Plains, Deep Bottom, August 14-18. Ream's Station August 25. Reconnoissance to Hatcher's Run December 9-10. Dabney's Mills February 5-7, 1865. Watkins' House March 25. Appomattox Campaign March 28-April 9. On line of Hatcher's and Gravelly Runs March 29-30. White Oak Road March 31. Sutherland Station and fall of Petersburg April 2. Pursuit of Lee April 3-9. Deatonville Road, Sailor's Creek, April 6. High Bridge and Farmville April 7. Appomattox Court House April 9. Surrender of Lee and his army. At Burkesville till May 2. Moved to Washington, D. C., May 2-12. Grand Review May 23. Mustered out June 3, 1865. Veterans and Recruits transferred to 4th New York Heavy Artillery.

Regiment lost during service 16 Officers and 137 Enlisted men killed and mortally wounded and 1 Officer and 122 Enlisted men by disease. Total 276.

127th REGIMENT INFANTRY.—("NATIONAL VOLUNTEERS.")

Organized at Staten Island, N. Y., and mustered in September 8, 1862. Left State for Washington, D. C., September 10, 1862. Attached to Abercrombie's Brigade, Defences of Washington, D. C., to October. 2nd Brigade, 1st Division, and 4th Brigade, 1st Division, 12th Army Corps, to October, 1862. 3rd Brigade, Abercrombie's Division, Defences of Washington, to February, 1863. 3rd Brigade, Abercrombie's Division, 22nd Army Corps, Dept. of Washington, to April, 1863. 2nd Brigade, 3rd Division, 7th Army Corps, Dept. of Virginia, to July, 1863. 1st Brigade, 1st Division, 11th Army Corps, Army of the Potomac, to August, 1863. 1st Brigade, Gordon's Division, Folly Island, S. C., 10th Army Corps, Dept. of the South, to January, 1864. 1st Brigade, Folly Island, S. C., Northern District, Dept. of the South, to April, 1864. Morris Island, S. C., Northern District, Dept. of the South, to October, 1864. District of Beaufort, S. C., 2nd Separate Brigade, Dept. of the South, to November, 1864. 1st Brigade, Coast Division, Dept. of the South, to January, 1865. 1st Separate Brigade, Northern District, Dept. of the South, to March, 1865. 1st Separate Brigade, District of Charleston, S. C., Dept. of the South, to June, 1865.

SERVICE.—Duty in the Defences of Washington, D. C., till April, 1863. Moved to Suffolk, Va., April 18. Siege of Suffolk April 20-May 4. Dix's Peninsula Campaign June 24-July 7. Ordered to Washington, D. C., July 10. Pursuit of Lee to Berlin, Md., July 13-22. Moved to Folly Island, S. C., August 1-8. Siege operations against Forts Wagner and Gregg on Morris Island and against Fort Sumpter and Charleston, S. C., August 9-September 7. Bombardment of Fort Sumpter August 17-23. Operations against Charleston and duty on Folly and Morris Islands, S. C., till October, 1864. Assault on Fort Johnson and Battery Simpkins, James

Island, S. C., July 3, 1864. Duty at Beaufort, S. C., till November, 1864. Hatch's Expedition up Broad River November 28-30. Battle of Honey Hill November 30. Demonstration on Charleston & Savannah Railroad December 6-9. Deveaux's Neck, Tullifinney River, December 6. Tullifinney River December 9. Charleston & Savannah Railroad December 19 and 29. Duty in Northern District and at Charleston, S. C., Dept. of the South, till June, 1865. Mustered out June 30, 1865.

Regiment lost during service 35 Enlisted men killed and mortally wounded and 1 Officer and 94 Enlisted men by disease. Total 130.

128th REGIMENT INFANTRY.

Organized at Hudson, N. Y., and mustered in September 4, 1862. Left State for Washington, D. C., September 5, 1862. Attached to Defences of Washington and Baltimore, Md., till December, 1862. 1st Brigade, Sherman's Division, Dept. of the Gulf, to January, 1864. 1st Brigade, 2nd Division, 19th Army Corps, Dept. of the Gulf, to July, 1863. 2nd Brigade, 1st Division, 19th Army Corps, to February, 1864. 3rd Brigade, 2nd Division, 19th Army Corps, Dept. of the Gulf, to July, 1864, and Army of the Shenandoah, Middle Military Division, to January, 1865. 3rd Brigade, Grover's Division, District of Savannah, Ga., Dept. of the South, to March, 1865. 3rd Brigade, 1st Division, 10th Army Corps, Army of the Ohio, to April, 1865. District of Savannah, Ga., Dept. of the South, to July, 1865.

SERVICE.—At Washington and Baltimore till December, 1862. Moved to New Orleans, La., and duty at Camps Parrapet and Kenner till March, 1863. Expedition to Ponchatoula March 20-May 15. Ponchatoula March 24-26. Barratara April 7. Gainesville April 18. Ponchatoula May 13. Camp Moore May 15. Moved to New Orleans, thence to Port Hudson, La., May 21-23. Siege of Port Hudson May 24-July 9. Assaults on Port Hudson May 27 and June 14. Surrender of Port Hudson July 9. Moved to Baton Rouge July 11, thence to Donaldsonville July 15. Duty there and at Baton Rouge till March, 1864. Red River Campaign March 23-May 22. Duty at Alexandria March 25-April 12. Grand Ecore April 13. Retreat to Alexandria April 21-26. Monett's Ferry, Cane River Crossing, April 23. Construction of dam at Alexandria April 30-May 10. Retreat to Morganza May 13-20. Mansura May 16. Expedition from Morganza to the Atchafalaya May 30-June 6. At Morganza till July 3. Moved to New Orleans, thence to Fortress Monroe, Va., and Washington, D. C., July 3-29. Sheridan's Shenandoah Valley Campaign August 7-November 28. Battle of Winchester September 19. Fisher's Hill September 22. Battle of Cedar Creek October 19. Duty at Kernstown and Winchester till January, 1865. Moved to Savannah, Ga., January 5-22, and duty there till March 5. Moved to Wilmington, N. C., March 5; thence to Morehead City, N. C., March 10. Moved to Goldsboro April 8, thence to Savannah May 2, and duty there till July. Mustered out at Savannah, Ga., July 12, 1865.

Regiment lost during service 2 Officers and 58 Enlisted men killed and mortally wounded and 3 Officers and 203 Enlisted men by disease. Total 266.

129th REGIMENT INFANTRY.

Organized at Lockport, N. Y., and mustered in August 22, 1862. Left State for Baltimore, Md., August 23, 1862. Attached to Defences of Baltimore, Md., 8th Army Corps, Middle Department. Designation of Regiment changed to 8th New York Heavy Artillery October 3, 1862 (which see).

130th REGIMENT INFANTRY.

Organized at Portage, N. Y., and mustered in September 2, 1862. Left State for Suffolk, Va., September 6, 1862. Attached to Foster's Provisional Brigade, Division at Suffolk, Va., 7th Army Corps, Dept. of Virginia, to December, 1862. Gibbs' Provisional Brigade, Division at Suffolk, to April, 1863. 1st Brigade, 1st Division, 7th Army Corps, Dept. of Virginia, to July, 1863. Defences of Washington, D. C., to August, 1863.

SERVICE.—Duty at Suffolk, Va., till May, 1863. Expedition from Suffolk December 1-3, 1862. Action on the Blackwater, near Franklin, December 2. Reconnoissances from Suffolk to Blackwater December 22 and 28. Near Suffolk and at Providence Church December 28. Expedition toward Blackwater January 8-10, 1863. Deserted House January 30. Siege of Suffolk April 12-May 4. South Quay Road, Suffolk, April 17. Suffolk April 19. Nansemond River May 3. Siege of Suffolk raised May 4. South Quay Road June 12. Franklin June 14. Blackwater June 16-17. Dix's Peninsula Campaign June 24-July 7. Expedition from White House to South Anna River July 1-7. Baltimore Cross Roads July 4. Ordered to Washington, D. C., July 8. Designation of Regiment changed to 19th New York Cavalry August 11, 1863, and to 1st New York Dragoons September 10, 1863 (which see).

131st REGIMENT INFANTRY.—("1st REGIMENT METROPOLITAN GUARD.")

Organized at New York City and mustered in September 6, 1862. Left State for Annapolis, Md., September 14, 1862. Attached to District of Annapolis, Md., 8th Army Corps, Middle Department, to December, 1862. Grover's Division, Dept. of the Gulf, to January, 1863. 1st Brigade, 4th Division, 19th Army Corps, Dept. of the Gulf, to February, 1864. 2nd Brigade, 2nd Division, 19th Army Corps, Dept. of the Gulf, to July, 1864, and Army of the Shenandoah, Middle Military Division, to January, 1865. 2nd Brigade, Grover's Division, District of Savannah, Dept. of the South, to March, 1865. 1st Brigade, 1st Division, 10th Army Corps, Army of the Ohio, Dept. of North Carolina, to April, 1865. District of Savannah, Dept. of the South, to July, 1865.

SERVICE.—Duty at Annapolis, Md., till November 18, 1862. Ordered to New Orleans, La., November 18; thence moved to Baton Rouge, La., December, and duty there till March, 1863. Operations against Port Hudson March 7-27. Moved to Donaldsonville March 27, thence to Brashear City, La. Operations in Western Louisiana April 9-May 14. Teche Campaign April 11-20. Fort Bisland April 12-13. Madam Porter's Plantation, Indian Bend, April 13. Irish Bend April 14. Bayou Vermillion April 17. March to Opelousas April 19-20. Moved to New Iberia April 25. Siege of Port Hudson May 24-July 9. Assaults on Port Hudson May 27 and June 14. Action at Plaquemine June 18 (Detachment). Surrender of Port Hudson July 9. Kock's Plantation, Bayou LaFourche, July 12-13. Duty at Thibodeauxville till March, 1864. Expedition from Brashear City February 3-6, 1864 (Detachment). Red River Campaign March 25-May 22. Alexandria May 1. Construction of dam at Alexandria April 30-May 10. Retreat to Mansura May 13-20. Mansura May 16. Duty at Morganza till July 3. Moved to New Orleans, La., thence to Fortress Monroe, Va., and to Bermuda Hundred, Va., July 3-22. In trenches at Bermuda Hundred, Va., till July 28. Deep Bottom July 28-29. Moved to Washington, D. C., thence to Tennallytown July 31-August 2. Sheridan's Shenandoah Valley Campaign August 7-November 28. Battle of Winchester September 19. Fisher's Hill September 22. Battle of Cedar Creek October 19. Duty at Kernstown and Winchester till January, 1865. Moved to Savannah, Ga., January 5-22, and duty there till March. At Morehead City and Newberne, N. C., till April. At Savannah, Ga., till July. Mustered out at Savannah, Ga., July 26, 1865.

Regiment lost during service 2 Officers and 82 Enlisted men killed and mortally wounded and 3 Officers and 107 Enlisted men by disease. Total 194.

132nd REGIMENT INFANTRY.—("2nd REGIMENT EMPIRE BRIGADE.")

Organized at New York City and mustered in at Washington, D. C., October 4, 1862. Left State for Washington September 27, 1862. Attached to Spinola's Brigade, Division at Suffolk, Va., 7th Army Corps, Dept. of Virginia, to January, 1863. 1st Brigade, 5th

Division, 18th Army Corps, Dept. of North Carolina, to March, 1863. 2nd Brigade, 5th Division, 18th Army Corps, to July, 1863. Unattached, Defences of New Berne, N. C., Dept. of Virginia and North Carolina, to January, 1864. Palmer's Brigade, Peck's Division, Dept. of Virginia and North Carolina, to April, 1864. Sub-District New Berne, N. C., District of North Carolina, Dept. of Virginia and North Carolina, to March, 1865. 2nd Brigade, 1st Division, District of Beaufort, N. C., Dept. of North Carolina, to March, 1865. 1st Brigade, Division District of Beaufort, N. C., Dept. of North Carolina, to April, 1865. 1st Brigade, 2nd Division, 23rd Army Corps, Dept. of North Carolina, to June, 1865.

SERVICE.—Moved from Washington, D. C., to Norfolk; thence to Suffolk, Va., October, 1862, and duty there till December, 1862. Ordered to New Berne, N. C., December 17, and duty there till March, 1865. Expedition from New Berne to Trenton, Pollocksville, Young's Cross Roads and Swansborough March 6-10, 1863. Expedition from New Berne for relief of Little Washington April 7-10. Expedition from New Berne toward Kinston April 16-21. Operations about New Berne against Whiting January 18-February 10, 1864. Newberne February 1-4, 1864. Batchelor's Creek February 1. Beech Grove February 1-3. Batchelor's Creek May 26. Scout to Dover and Core Creek June 17-18. Expedition toward Kinston June 20-23. Jackson's Mills, Southwest Creek, June 22. Campaign of the Carolinas March 1-April 26, 1865. Southwest Creek March 7. Battle of Wise's Forks March 8-10. Kinston March 14. Occupation of Goldsboro March 21. Advance on Raleigh April 9-13. Occupation of Raleigh April 14. Bennett's House April 26. Surrender of Johnston and his army. Duty at Salsbury, N. C., till June. Mustered out June 29, 1865. Recruits transferred to 99th New York Infantry.

Regiment lost during service 1 Officer and 13 Enlisted men killed and mortally wounded and 1 Officer and 159 Enlisted men by disease. Total 174.

133rd REGIMENT INFANTRY.—("2nd REGIMENT METROPOLITAN GUARD.")

Organized at New York City and mustered in September 24, 1862. Left State for Washington, D. C., October 8, 1862. Attached to Abercrombie's Division, Defences of Washington, D. C., to November, 1862. Grover's Brigade, Banks' New Orleans Expedition, to December, 1862. Grover's Division, Dept. of the Gulf, to January, 1863. 2nd Brigade, 3rd Division, 19th Army Corps, Dept. of the Gulf, to October, 1863. Defences of New Orleans, La., to April, 1864. 1st Brigade, 2nd Division, 19th Army Corps, to June, 1864. 3rd Brigade, 1st Division, 19th Army Corps, Dept. of the Gulf, to July, 1864, and Army of the Shenandoah, Middle Military Division, to February, 1865. 3rd Brigade, 1st Provisional Division, Army of the Shenandoah, to April, 1865. 3rd Brigade, Dwight's Division, Defences of Washington, D. C., 22nd Corps, to June, 1865.

SERVICE.—Duty in the Defences of Washington, D. C., till November, 1862. Moved to New Orleans, La., November, 1862. Occupation of Baton Rouge, La., December 17, and duty there till March, 1863. Operations on Bayou Plaquemine February 12-28. Operations against Port Hudson, La., March 7-27. Moved to Algiers April 3, thence to Brashear City April 8. Operations in Western Louisiana April 9-May 14. Teche Campaign April 11-20. Fort Bisland, near Centreville, April 12-13. Pursuit to Opelousas April 15-20. Expedition from Opelousas to Chicotsville and Bayou Boeuf April 26-29. Expedition to Alexandria May 4-12. March to Port Hudson May 19-26. Siege of Port Hudson May 26-July 9. Expedition to Niblitt's Bluff May 26-29. Assault on Port Hudson June 14. Surrender of Port Hudson July 9. Moved to New Orleans July 15 and duty there till August 28. Sabine Pass Expedition September 4-12. Moved to Brashear City September 16, thence to Berwick City. Western Louisiana "Teche" Campaign October 3-November 30. Duty in the Defences of New

Orleans till April, 1864. Red River Campaign April 26-May 22. Construction of dam at Alexandria April 30-May 10. Retreat to Mansura May 13-20. Mansura May 16. At Morganza till July 2. Moved to New Orleans, La., thence to Fortress Monroe and Deep Bottom, Va., July 2-18. Moved to Washington, D. C., July 31. Sheridan's Shenandoah Valley Campaign August 7-November 28. Detached from army August 14, and duty as Train Guard for Sheridan's army till October 27. Duty at Middletown, Newtown, Stephenson's Depot and Winchester and in the Shenandoah Valley till April, 1865. Moved to Washington, D. C., April 20, and duty there till June. Grand Review May 23-24. Recruits transferred to 90th New York Infantry May 31. Regiment mustered out June 6, 1865.

Regiment lost during service 2 Officers and 41 Enlisted men killed and mortally wounded and 1 Officer and 78 Enlisted men by disease. Total 122.

134th REGIMENT INFANTRY.

Organized at Schoharie, N. Y., and mustered in September 22, 1862. Left State for Washington, D. C., September 25, 1862. Attached to 2nd Brigade, 2nd Division, 11th Army Corps, Army of the Potomac, to October, 1863, and Army of the Cumberland to April, 1864. 2nd Brigade, 2nd Division, 20th Army Corps, Army of the Cumberland, to June, 1865.

SERVICE.—Joined Corps at Fairfax Court House, Va., October 2, 1862, and duty there till November 1. Movement to Warrenton, thence to Germantown November 1-20. March to Fredericksburg, Va., December 10-15. At Falmouth till April 27, 1863. "Mud March" January 20-24. Chancellorsville Campaign April 27-May 6. Battle of Chancellorsville May 1-5. Gettysburg (Pa.) Campaign June 11-July 24. Battle of Gettysburg July 1-3. Pursuit of Lee July 5-24. At Bristoe Station to September 24. Movement to Bridgeport, Ala., September 24-October 3. March along line of Nashville & Chattanooga Railroad to Lookout Valley October 25-29. Reopening Tennessee River October 26-29. Battle of Wauhatchie, Tenn., October 28-29. Chattanooga-Ringgold Campaign November 23-27. Orchard Knob November 23. Tunnel Hill November 24-25. Mission Ridge November 25. March to relief of Knoxville November 27-December 17. Duty in Lookout Valley till May, 1864. Atlanta (Ga.) Campaign May 1-September 8. Demonstration on Rocky Faced Ridge May 8-11. Dug Gap or Mill Creek May 8. Battle of Resaca May 14-15. Near Cassville May 19. New Hope Church May 25. Battles about Dallas, New Hope Church and Allatoona Hills May 26-June 5. Operations about Marietta and against Kenesaw Mountain June 10-July 2. Pine Hill June 11-14. Lost Mountain June 15-17. Gilgal or Golgotha Church June 15. Muddy Creek June 17. Noyes' Creek June 19. Kolb's Farm June 22. Assault on Kenesaw June 27. Ruff's Station, Smyrna Camp Ground, July 4. Chattahoochie River July 6-17. Peach Tree Creek July 19-20. Siege of Atlanta July 22-August 25. Operations at Chattahoochie River Bridge August 26-September 2. Occupation of Atlanta September 2-November 15. Expedition from Atlanta to Tuckum's Cross Roads October 26-29. Near Atlanta November 9. March to the sea November 15-December 10. Siege of Savannah December 10-21. Campaign of the Carolinas January to April, 1865. Averysboro, N. C., March 16. Battle of Bentonville March 19-21. Occupation of Goldsboro March 24. Advance on Raleigh April 9-14. Occupation of Raleigh April 14. Bennett's House April 26. Surrender of Johnston and his army. March to Washington, D. C., via Richmond, Va., April 29-May 20. Grand Review May 24. Mustered out June 10, 1865. Recruits transferred to 102nd New York Infantry.

Regiment lost during service 2 Officers and 41 Enlisted men killed and mortally wounded and 1 Officer and 78 Enlisted men by disease. Total 122.

135th REGIMENT INFANTRY ("ANTHONY WAYNE GUARD").

Organized at Yonkers, N. Y., and mustered in September 2, 1862. Left State for Baltimore, Md., September 5, 1862. Designation of Regiment changed to 6th New York Heavy Artillery October 3, 1862.

136th REGIMENT INFANTRY ("IRON CLADS").

Organized at Portage, N. Y., and mustered in September 25, 1862. Left State for Washington, D. C., October 3, 1862. Attached to 1st Brigade, 3rd Division, 11th Army Corps, Army of the Potomac, to November, 1862. 2nd Brigade, 2nd Division, 11th Army Corps, Army of the Potomac, to October, 1863, and Army of the Cumberland to April, 1864. 3rd Brigade, 3rd Division, 20th Army Corps, Army of the Cumberland, to June, 1865.

SERVICE.—Moved to Fairfax Station, Va., October 10, 1862; thence to Fairfax Court House, and duty there till November 1. Movement to Warrenton, thence to Germantown, Va., November 1-20. March to Fredericksburg December 10-15. At Falmouth, Va., till April 27, 1863. "Mud March" January 20-24. Chancellorsville Campaign April 27-May 6. Battle of Chancellorsville May 1-5. Gettysburg (Pa.) Campaign June 11-July 24. Battle of Gettysburg, Pa., July 1-3. Pursuit of Lee July 5-24. Camp at Bristoe Station August 1 to September 24. Movement to Bridgeport, Ala., September 24-October 3. March along line of Nashville & Chattanooga Railroad to Lookout Valley, Tenn., October 25-28. Reopening Tennessee River October 26-29. Battle of Wauhatchie, Tenn., October 28-29. Ringgold-Chattanooga Campaign November 23-27. Orchard Knob November 23. Tunnel Hill November 24-25. Mission Ridge November 25. March to relief of Knoxville, Tenn., November 28-December 17. Duty in Lookout Valley till May, 1864. Atlanta (Ga.) Campaign May 1 to September 8. Demonstration on Rocky Faced Ridge May 8-11. Buzzard's Roost Gap May 8-9. Battle of Resaca May 14-15. Near Cassville May 19. Advance on Dallas May 22-25. New Hope Church May 25. Battles about Dallas, New Hope Church and Allatoona Hills May 26-June 5. Operations about Marietta and against Kenesaw Mountain June 10-July 2. Pine Hill June 11-14. Lost Mountain June 15-17. Gilgal or Golgotha Church June 15. Muddy Creek June 17. Noyes' Creek June 19. Kolb's Farm June 22. Assault on Kenesaw June 27. Ruff's Station, Smyrna Camp Ground, July 4. Chattahoochie River July 6-17. Peach Tree Creek July 11-20. Siege of Atlanta July 22-August 25. Operations at Chattahoochie River Bridge August 26-September 2. Occupation of Atlanta September 2-November 15. March to the sea November 15-December 10. Campaign of the Carolinas January to April, 1865. Lawtonville, S. C., February 2. Skirmish of Goldsboro Road, near Fayetteville, N. C., March 14. Averysboro March 16. Battle of Bentonville March 19-21. Occupation of Goldsboro March 24. Advance on Raleigh April 9-13. Occupation of Raleigh April 14. Bennett's House April 26. Surrender of Johnston and his army. March to Washington, D. C., via Richmond, Va., April 29-May 30. Grand Review May 24. Mustered out June 13, 1865. Veterans and Recruits transferred to 60th New York Infantry.

Regiment lost during service 2 Officers and 71 Enlisted men killed and mortally wounded and 1 Officer and 91 Enlisted men by disease. Total 165.

137th REGIMENT INFANTRY.

Organized at Binghampton, N. Y., and mustered in September 25, 1862. Left State for Washington, D. C., September 25, 1862. Attached to 2nd Brigade, 1st Division, 12th Army Corps, Army of the Potomac, to October, 1862. 4th Brigade, 1st Division, 12th Army Corps, October, 1862. 3rd Brigade, 2nd Division, 12th Army Corps, Army of the Potomac, to October, 1863, and Army of the Cumberland to April, 1864. 3rd Brigade, 2nd Division, 20th Army Corps, Army of the Cumberland, to June, 1865.

SERVICE.—Moved to Harper's Ferry, Va., September 27-30, 1862. Duty at Bolivar Heights till December. Reconnoissance to Rippon, W. Va., November 9. Charlestown November 9. Reconnoissance to Winches-

ter December 2-6. Charlestown and Berryville December 2. March to Fredericksburg, Va., December 9-16. At Fairfax Station till April 27, 1863. "Mud March" January 20-24. Chancellorsville Campaign April 27-May 6. Battle of Chancellorsville May 1-5. Gettysburg (Pa.) Campaign June 11-July 24. Battle of Gettysburg July 1-3. Pursuit of Lee to Manassas Gap, Va., July 5-24. Duty on line of the Rappahannock till September. Movement to Bridgeport, Ala., September 24-October 4. Reopening Tennessee River October 26-29. Battle of Wauhatchie, Tenn., October 28-29. Chattanooga-Ringgold Campaign November 23-27. Lookout Mountain November 23-24. Mission Ridge November 25. Ringgold Gap, Taylor's Ridge, November 27. Duty at Bridgeport till May, 1864. Atlanta (Ga.) Campaign May 1-September 8. Demonstration on Rocky Faced Ridge May 8-11. Battle of Resaca May 14-15. Near Cassville May 19. Advance on Dallas May 25. Battles about Dallas, New Hope Church and Allatoona Hills May 26-June 5. Operations about Marietta and against Kenesaw Mountain June 10-July 2. Pine Hill June 11-14. Lost Mountain June 15-17. Gilgal or Golgotha Church June 15. Muddy Creek June 17. Noyes' Creek June 19. Kolb's Farm June 22. Assault on Kenesaw June 27. Ruff's Station, Smyrna Camp Ground, July 4. Chattahoochie River July 5-17. Peach Tree Creek July 19-20. Siege of Atlanta July 22-August 25. Operations at Chattahoochie River Bridge August 26-September 2. Occupation of Atlanta September 2-November 15. Expedition to Tuckum's Cross Roads October 26-29. Near Atlanta November 9. March to the sea November 15-December 10. Near Davisboro November 28. Siege of Savannah December 10-21. Campaign of the Carolinas January to April, 1865. Averysboro, N. C., March 16. Battle of Bentonville March 19-21. Occupation of Goldsboro March 24. Advance on Raleigh April 9-13. Occupation of Raleigh April 14. Bennett's House April 26. Surrender of Johnston and his army. March to Washington, D. C., via Richmond, Va., April 29-May 19. Grand Review May 24. Veterans and Recruits transferred to 102d New York Infantry June 1. Regiment mustered out June 9, 1865.

Regiment lost during service 6 Officers and 121 Enlisted men killed and mortally wounded and 4 Officers and 163 Enlisted men by disease. Total 294.

138th REGIMENT INFANTRY ("2nd AUBURN, CAYUGA AND WAYNE COUNTY REGIMENT").

Organized at Auburn, N. Y., and mustered in September 8, 1862. Left State for Washington, D. C., September 12, 1862. Attached to 2nd Brigade, 1st Division, 12th Army Corps, Army of the Potomac, to October, 1862. 4th Brigade, 1st Division, 12th Army Corps, October, 1862. 2nd Brigade, Defences north of the Potomac, Defences of Washington, to December, 1862. Designation of Regiment changed to 9th New York Heavy Artillery December 9, 1862 (which see).

139th REGIMENT INFANTRY.

Organized at Brooklyn, N. Y., and mustered in September 9, 1862. Left State for Fortress Monroe, Va., September 11, 1862. Attached to Camp Hamilton, Va., Dept. of Virginia, to December, 1862. Busteed's Independent Brigade, Yorktown, Va., 7th Army Corps, Dept. of Virginia, to April, 1863. West's Brigade, 7th Army Corps, to May, 1863. West's Advance Brigade, 4th Army Corps, to July, 1863. Wistar's Brigade, United States forces, Yorktown, Va., Dept. of Virginia and North Carolina, to January, 1864. 1st Brigade, United States forces, Yorktown, Va., to February, 1864. District of the Currituck, Dept. of Virginia and North Carolina, to March, 1864. Heckman's Division, Portsmouth, Va., to April, 1864. 1st Brigade, 1st Division, 18th Army Corps, Army of the James, to December, 1864. 1st Brigade, 3rd Division, 24th Corps, to June, 1865.

SERVICE.—Duty at Camp Hamilton, Va., September 20, 1862, to April, 1863. Action at Whittaker's Mills, Williamsburg and Fort Magruder April 11, 1863. Moved to Yorktown, Va., April, and duty there, at Williamsburg and in the District of the Currituck till April,

1864. Dix's Peninsula Campaign June 24-July 7, 1863. Expedition from White House to Bottom's Bridge July 1-7. Baltimore Cross Roads July 2. Crump's Cross Roads, Bottom's Bridge, July 2-3. Expedition from Williamsburg to Charles City Court House December 12-14. Near Chickahominy River December 11. Forge Bridge December 12. Charles City Court House December 13. Scouts from Williamsburg January 19 and 24, 1864. Wistar's Expedition against Richmond February 6-8. Butler's operations on south side of the James River and against Petersburg and Richmond May 4-28. Occupation of City Point and Bermuda Hundred May 5. Swift Creek or Arrowfield Church May 9-10. Operations against Fort Darling May 12-16. Battle of Drury's Bluff May 14-16. Bermuda Hundred May 16-27. Moved to White House, thence to Cold Harbor May 28-31. Battles about Cold Harbor June 1-12. Before Petersburg June 15-18. Siege operations against Petersburg and Richmond June 16, 1864, to April 2, 1865. In trenches before Petersburg and on the Bermuda Hundred front till September 27, 1864. Mine Explosion, Petersburg, July 30 (Reserve). Battle of Chaffin's Farm, New Market Heights, September 28-30. Assault and capture of Fort Harrison September 29. Battle of Fair Oaks October 27-28. Duty in lines before Richmond till April, 1865. Occupation of Richmond April 3. Provost duty at Richmond and Manchester, Va., till June. Mustered out June 19, 1865. Veterans and Recruits transferred to 98th New York Infantry.

Regiment lost during service 5 Officers and 66 Enlisted men killed and mortally wounded and 1 Officer and 79 Enlisted men by disease. Total 151.

140th REGIMENT INFANTRY ("MONROE COUNTY REGIMENT," "ROCHESTER RACE HORSES").

Organized at Rochester, N. Y., and mustered in September 13, 1862. Left State for Washington, D. C., September 19, 1862. Attached to 2nd Brigade, 1st Division, 12th Army Corps, Army of the Potomac, to October, 1862. 2nd Brigade, 2nd Division, 12th Army Corps, to November, 1862. 3rd Brigade, 2nd Division, 5th Army Corps, to March, 1864. 4th Brigade, 1st Division, 5th Army Corps, to April, 1864. 1st Brigade, 1st Division, 5th Army Corps, to June, 1864. 1st Brigade, 2nd Division, 5th Army Corps, to June, 1865.

SERVICE.—Camp at Arlington Heights, Va., till September 23, 1862. Duty at Bolivar Heights till November. Battle of Fredericksburg, Va., December 12-15. At Falmouth, Va., till April 27, 1862. "Mud March" January 20-24. Chancellorsville Campaign April 27-May 6. Battle of Chancellorsville May 1-5. Gettysburg (Pa.) Campaign June 11-July 24. Battle of Gettysburg, Pa., July 1-3. Pursuit of Lee July 5-24. Duty at Warrenton, Beverly Ford and Culpeper till October. Bristoe Campaign October 9-22. Advance to line of the Rappahannock November 7-8. Rappahannock Station November 7. Mine Run Campaign November 26-December 2. At Beverly Ford till May, 1864. Campaign from the Rapidan to the James May 3-June 15. Battles of the Wilderness May 5-7. Laurel Hill May 8. Spottsylvania May 8-12. Spottsylvania Court House May 12-21. Assault on the Salient May 12. North Anna River May 23-26. On line of the Pamunkey May 26-28. Totopotomoy May 28-31. Cold Harbor June 1-12. Bethesda Church June 1-3. Before Petersburg June 16-18. Siege of Petersburg June 16, 1864, to April 2, 1865. Weldon Railroad June 21-23, 1864. Mine Explosion, Petersburg, July 30 (Reserve). Poplar Springs Church, Peeble's Farm, September 29-October 2. Warren's Raid on Weldon Railroad December 7-12. Dabney's Mills, Hatcher's Run, February 5-7, 1865. Appomattox Campaign March 28-April 9. Lewis' Farm, near Gravelly Run, March 29. White Oak Road March 31. Five Forks April 1. Fall of Petersburg April 2. Pursuit of Lee April 3-9. Appomattox Court House April 9. Surrender of Lee and his army. March to Washington, D. C., May 1-12. Grand Review May 23. Mustered out June 3, 1865. Veterans and Recruits transferred to 5th New York Veteran Infantry.

Regiment lost during service 8 Officers and 141 Enlisted men killed and mortally wounded and 2 Officers and 168 Enlisted men by disease. Total 319.

141st REGIMENT INFANTRY.

Organized at Elmira and mustered in September 11, 1862. Left State for Middle Department September 15, 1862. Attached to 8th Army Corps, Middle Department, to October, 1862. 2nd Brigade, Abercrombie's Division, Defences of Washington, to February, 1863. 2nd Brigade, Abercrombie's Division, 22nd Army Corps, to April, 1863. 1st Brigade, 3rd Division, 7th Army Corps, Dept. of Virginia, to May, 1863. 2nd Brigade, 2nd Division, 4th Army Corps, to July, 1863. 2nd Brigade, 3rd Division, 11th Army Corps, Army of the Potomac, to October, 1863, and Army of the Cumberland to April, 1864. 1st Brigade, 1st Division, 20th Army Corps, Army of the Cumberland, to June, 1865.

SERVICE.—Duty in the Defences of Washington, D. C., till April, 1863. Moved to Norfolk, thence to Suffolk, Va., April 15-17. Siege of Suffolk April 17-May 4. Siege of Suffolk raised May 4. Moved to West Point May 5, thence to Yorktown May 31. Dix's Peninsula Campaign June 24-July 7. Expedition to Bottom's Bridge July 1-7. Moved to Washington, D. C., July 10-11. March in pursuit of Lee to Berlin, Md., July 13-24. Duty along Orange & Alexandria Railroad till September. Movement to Bridgeport, Ala., September 24-October 3. Duty there and in Lookout Valley till November. Reopening Tennessee River October 26-29. Battle of Wauhatchie, Tenn., October 28-29. Chattanooga-Ringgold Campaign November 23-27. Orchard Knob November 23. Tunnel Hill November 24-25. Mission Ridge November 25. March to relief of Knoxville, Tenn., November 27-December 17. Loudoun December 4-5. Duty in Lookout Valley till May, 1864. Atlanta (Ga.) Campaign May 1 to September 8. Demonstrations on Rocky Faced Ridge May 8-11. Battle of Resaca May 14-15. Near Cassville May 19. Advance on Dallas May 22-25. New Hope Church May 25. Battles about Dallas, New Hope Church and Allatoona Hills May 26-June 5. Ackworth June 5. Operations about Marietta and against Kenesaw Mountain June 10-July 2. Pine Hill June 11-14. Lost Mountain June 15-17. Gilgal or Golgotha Church June 15. Muddy Creek June 17. Noyes' Creek June 19. Kolb's Farm June 22. Assault on Kenesaw June 27. Ruff's Station, Smyrna Camp Ground, July 4. Chattahoochie River July 5-17. Peach Tree Creek July 19-20. Siege of Atlanta July 22-August 25. Operations at Chattahoochie River Bridge August 26-September 2. Occupation of Atlanta September 2-November 15. March to the sea November 15-December 10. Siege of Savannah December 10-21. Campaign of the Carolinas January to April, 1865. Thompson's Creek, near Chesterfield, S. C., March 2. Thompson's Creek, near Cheraw, S. C., March 3. Averysboro, N. C., March 16. Battle of Bentonville March 19-21. Occupation of Goldsboro March 24. Advance on Raleigh April 9-13. Moccasin Swamp April 10. Occupation of Raleigh April 14. Bennett's House April 26. Surrender of Johnston and his army. March to Washington, D. C., via Richmond, Va., April 29-May 20. Grand Review May 24. Mustered out June 8, 1865. Veterans and Recruits transferred to 60th New York Infantry.

Regiment lost during service 4 Officers and 71 Enlisted men killed and mortally wounded and 2 Officers and 172 Enlisted men by disease. Total 249.

142nd REGIMENT INFANTRY.—("ST. LAWRENCE COUNTY REGIMENT.")

Organized at Ogdensburg, N. Y., and mustered in September 29, 1862. Left State for Washington, D. C., October 6, 1862. Attached to 3rd Brigade, Abercrombie's Division, Defences of Washington, D. C., to February, 1863. 3rd Brigade, Abercrombie's Division, 22nd Army Corps, Dept. of Washington, to April, 1863. 2nd Brigade, 3rd Division, 7th Army Corps, Dept. of Virginia, to May, 1863. 1st Brigade, 2nd Division, 4th

Army Corps, to July, 1863. 1st Brigade, 1st Division, 11th Army Corps, Army of the Potomac, to August, 1863. 1st Brigade, Gordon's Division, Folly Island, S. C., 10th Army Corps, Dept. of the South, to January, 1864. 1st Brigade, Gordon's Division, Northern District, Dept. of the South, to April, 1864. 1st Brigade, 2nd Division, 10th Army Corps, Army of the James, Dept. of Virginia and North Carolina, to May, 1864. 3rd Brigade, 3rd Division, 18th Army Corps, to June, 1864. 1st Brigade, 2nd Division, 10th Army Corps, to December, 1864. 1st Brigade, 2nd Division, 24th Army Corps, to January, 1865. 1st Brigade, 2nd Division, Terry's Provisional Corps, Dept. of North Carolina, to March, 1865. 1st Brigade, 2nd Division, 10th Army Corps, Army of the Ohio, Dept. of North Carolina, to June, 1865.

SERVICE.—Duty in the Defences of Washington, D. C., till April, 1862. Moved to Suffolk, Va., April 19. Siege of Suffolk, Va., April 20-May 4. Siege of Suffolk raised May 4. Expedition to Kings and Queens County May 15 (1 Co.). Dix's Peninsula Campaign June 24-July 7. Ordered to Washington, D. C., July 10. Pursuit of Lee to Berlin, Md., July 13-22. Moved to Folly Island, S. C., August 1-8. Siege operations against Forts Wagner and Gregg, Morris Island, S. C., and against Fort Sumpter and Charleston, S. C., August 9-September 7. Operations against Charleston and duty at Folly Island, Johns Island and Hilton Head, S. C., till April, 1864. Expedition to Johns and James Islands February 6-14, 1864. Skirmishes at Bugbee's Bridge February 9 and 11. Ordered to Yorktown, Va., April, 1864. Butler's Campaign on south side of the James and operations against Petersburg and Richmond May 4-28. Occupation of City Point and Bermuda Hundred May 5. Swift Creek or Arrowfield Church May 9-10. Operations against Fort Darling May 12-16. Battle of Drury's Bluff May 14-16. Bermuda Hundred May 16-28. Moved to White House, thence to Cold Harbor May 28-31. Battles about Cold Harbor June 1-12. Before Petersburg June 15-18. Siege operations against Petersburg and Richmond June 16, 1864, to December 7, 1864. Mine Explosion, Petersburg, July 30. Duty in trenches before Petersburg and on the Bermuda Hundred front till September 27. Battle of Chaffin's Farm, New Market Heights, September 28-30. Battle of Fair Oaks October 27-28. Duty in trenches before Richmond till December. Expedition to Fort Fisher, N. C., December 7-27. 2nd Expedition to Fort Fisher, N. C., January 3-15, 1865. Assault and capture of Fort Fisher January 15. Cape Fear Intrenchments February 11-13. Fort Anderson February 18-19. Capture of Wilmington February 22. Campaign of the Carolinas March 1-April 26. Advance on Goldsboro March 6-21. Advance on Raleigh April 9-13. Occupation of Raleigh April 14. Bennett's House April 26. Surrender of Johnston and his army. Duty at Raleigh till June. Mustered out June 7, 1865. Veterans and Recruits transferred to 169th New York Infantry.

Regiment lost during service 3 Officers and 126 Enlisted men killed and mortally wounded and 2 Officers and 161 Enlisted men by disease. Total 292.

143rd REGIMENT INFANTRY.—("SULLIVAN COUNTY REGIMENT.")

Organized at Monticello, N. Y., and mustered in October 8, 1862. Left State for Washington, D. C., October 14, 1862. Attached to 3rd Brigade, Abercrombie's Division, Defences of Washington, D. C., to February, 1863. 3rd Brigade, Abercrombie's Division, 22nd Army Corps, Dept. of Washington, to April, 1863. 2nd Brigade, 3rd Division, 7th Army Corps, Dept. of Virginia, to May, 1863. 1st Brigade, 2nd Division, 4th Army Corps, to July, 1863. 1st Brigade, 3rd Division, 11th Army Corps, Army of the Potomac, to October, 1863, and Army of the Cumberland to April, 1864. 3rd Brigade, 1st Division, 20th Army Corps, Army of the Cumberland, to July, 1865.

SERVICE.—Duty in the Defences of Washington, D. C., till April, 1863. Moved to Suffolk, Va., April 18.

Siege of Suffolk April 20-May 4. Providence Church Road May 3. Siege of Suffolk raised May 4. Dix's Campaign on the Peninsula June 24-July 7. Moved to Washington, D. C., July 10. Pursuit of Lee to Berlin, Md., July 13-22. Near Bristoe Station, Va., till September. Movement to Bridgeport, Ala., September 24-October 3. Reconnoissance from Bridgeport to Trenton October 20 (Detachment). March along line of Nashville & Chattanooga Railroad to Lookout Valley, Tenn., October 25-29. Reopening Tennessee River October 26-29. Battle of Wauhatchie, Tenn., October 28-29. Chattanooga-Ringgold Campaign November 23-27. Orchard Knob November 23. Tunnel Hill November 24-25. Mission Ridge November 25. March to relief of Knoxville November 28-December 17. Duty in Lookout Valley till May, 1864. Atlanta (Ga.) Campaign May 1-September 8. Demonstration on Rocky Faced Ridge May 8-11. Battle of Resaca May 14-15. Near Cassville May 19. Advance on Dallas May 22-25. New Hope Church May 25. Battles about Dallas, New Hope Church and Allatoona Hills May 26-June 5. Ackworth June 4. Operations about Marietta and against Kenesaw Mountain June 10-July 2. Pine Hill June 11-14. Lost Mountain June 15-17. Gilgal or Golgotha Church June 15. Muddy Creek June 17. Noyes Creek June 19. Kolb's Farm June 22. Assault on Kenesaw June 27. Ruff's Station or Smyrna Camp Ground July 4. Chattahoochie River July 5-17. Peach Tree Creek July 19-20. Siege of Atlanta July 22-August 25. Operations at Chattahoochie River Bridge August 26-September 2. Occupation of Atlanta September 2-November 15. Expedition from Atlanta to Tuckum's Cross Roads October 26-29. March to the sea November 15-December 10. Montieth Swamp December 9. Siege of Savannah December 10-21. Campaign of the Carolinas January to April. Averysboro, N. C., March 16. Battle of Bentonville March 19-21. Occupation of Goldsboro March 24. Advance on Raleigh April 7-13. Occupation of Raleigh April 14. Bennett's House April 26. Surrender of Johnston and his army. March to Washington, D. C., via Richmond, Va., April 29-May 20. Grand Review May 24. Duty at Washington, D. C., till July. Mustered out July 20, 1865.

Regiment lost during service 5 Officers and 37 Enlisted men killed and mortally wounded and 1 Officer and 177 Enlisted men by disease. Total 220.

144th REGIMENT INFANTRY.

Organized at Delhi, N. Y., and mustered in September 27, 1862. Left State for Washington, D. C., October 11, 1862. Attached to 3rd Brigade, Abercrombie's Division, Defences of Washington, to February, 1863. 3rd Brigade, Abercrombie's Division, 22nd Army Corps, Dept. of Washington, to April, 1863. 2nd Brigade, 3rd Division, 7th Army Corps, Dept. of Virginia, to May, 1863. 1st Brigade, 2nd Division, 4th Army Corps, to July, 1863. 2nd Brigade, 1st Division, 11th Army Corps, Army of the Potomac, to August, 1863. 2nd Brigade, Gordon's Division, Folly Island, S. C., 10th Army Corps, Dept. of the South, to February, 1864. 1st Brigade, Ames' Division, District of Florida, to April, 1864. District of Florida, Dept. of the South, to June, 1864. District of Hilton Head, S. C., Dept. of the South, to October, 1864. 3rd Separate Brigade, Dept. of the South, to November, 1864. 1st Brigade, Coast Division, Dept. of the South, to January, 1865. 3rd Separate Brigade, District of Hilton Head, S. C., Dept. of the South, to May, 1865. Port Royal, Dept. of the South, to June, 1865.

SERVICE.—Duty in the Defences of Washington, D. C., till April, 1863. Ordered to Suffolk, Va., April 18. Siege of Suffolk April 20-May 4. Providence Church Road May 3. Siege of Suffolk raised May 4. Dix's Peninsula Campaign June 24-July 7. Ordered to Washington, D. C., July 10. Pursuit of Lee to Berlin, Md., July 13-22. Moved to Folly Island, S. C., August 1-10. Siege of Forts Wagner and Gregg, Morris Island, S. C., and operations against Fort Sumpter and Charleston August 11-September 7. Bombardment of Fort Sumpter and Charleston August 17-23. Capture of Forts Wagner and Gregg September 7. Operations against Charleston and duty on Folly Island, S. C., till December 31. Bombardment of Fort Sumpter October 27-November 9. Moved to Hilton Head, S. C., January, 1864. Ordered to Jacksonville, Fla., February, and duty there till June. Expedition from Jacksonville to Camp Milton May 31-June 3. Moved to Hilton Head, S. C., June. Expedition to Johns and James Islands against Charleston July 2-10. Operations against Battery Pringle, Johns Island, July 9. Duty in District of Hilton Head, S. C., till November. Hatch's Expedition up Broad River November 28-30. Battle of Honey Hill, S. C., November 30. Demonstration on Charleston & Savannah Railroad December 6-9. Deveaux's Neck December 6. Tullifinney River December 9. Moved to Hilton Head, S. C., and duty in that district till June, 1865. Mustered out June 25, 1864. Veterans and Recruits transferred to 1st New York Engineers.

Regiment lost during service 2 Officers and 37 Enlisted men killed and mortally wounded and 4 Officers and 174 Enlisted men by disease. Total 217.

145th NEW YORK INFANTRY ("STANTON LEGION").

Organized at Staten Island, N. Y., and mustered in September 11, 1862. Left State for Washington, D. C., and Harper's Ferry, W. Va., September 27, 1862. Attached to 2nd Brigade, 1st Division, 12th Army Corps, Army of the Potomac, to October, 1862. 2nd Brigade, 2nd Division, 12th Army Corps, to May, 1863. 2nd Brigade, 1st Division, 12th Army Corps, May, 1863. 1st Brigade, 1st Division, 12th Army Corps, Army of the Potomac, to October, 1863, and Army of the Cumberland, to December, 1863.

SERVICE.—Duty at Bolivar Heights, Md., till December, 1862. Reconnoissance to Rippon, W. Va., November 9. Expedition to Winchester and Skirmishes at Charlestown and Berryville December 2-6. March to Fairfax Station, Va., December 10-14, and duty there till January 19, 1863. Burnside's 2nd Campaign, "Mud March," January 20-24. At Stafford Court House till April 27. Chancellorsville Campaign April 27-May 6. Battle of Chancellorsville May 1-5. Gettysburg (Pa.) Campaign June 11-July 24. Battle of Gettysburg July 1-3. Pursuit of Lee July 5-24. At Raccoon Ford, Va., till September. Movement to Stevenson, Ala., September 24-October 4. Duty along Nashville & Chattanooga Railroad till December. Regiment disbanded December 9, 1863, and men transferred to 107th, 123rd and 150th New York Infantry.

Regiment lost during service 1 Officer and 14 Enlisted men killed and mortally wounded and 35 Enlisted men by disease. Total 50.

146th REGIMENT INFANTRY ("5th ONEIDA," "HALLECK INFANTRY," "GARRARD'S TIGERS").

Organized at Rome, N. Y., and mustered in October 10, 1862. Left State for Washington, D. C., October 11, 1862. Attached to Casey's Division, Defences of Washington, to November, 1862. 3rd Brigade, 2nd Division, 5th Army Corps, Army of the Potomac, to March, 1864. 4th Brigade, 1st Division, 5th Army Corps, to April, 1864. 1st Brigade, 1st Division, 5th Army Corps, to June, 1864. 1st Brigade, 2nd Division, 5th Army Corps, to July, 1865.

SERVICE.—Duty in the Defences of Washington, D. C., till November, 1862. Joined Army of the Potomac at Snicker's Gap, Va., November 2. Rappahannock Campaign November, 1862, to June, 1863. Battle of Fredericksburg, Va., December 12-15, 1862. At Falmouth to April 27, 1863. "Mud March" January 20-24. Chancellorsville Campaign April 27-May 6. Battle of Chancellorsville May 1-5. Gettysburg (Pa.) Campaign June 11-July 24. Battle of Gettysburg July 1-3. Pursuit of Lee July 5-24. At Warrenton, Beverly Ford and Culpeper till October. Bristoe Campaign October 9-22. Advance to line of the Rappahannock November 7-8. Rappahannock Station November 7. Mine Run Campaign November 26-December 2. At Beverly Ford, Va.,

till May, 1864. Campaign from the Rapidan to the James May 3-June 15. Battles of the Wilderness May 5-7. Spottsylvania May 8-12. Laurel Hill May 8. Spottsylvania Court House May 12-21. Assault on the Salient May 12. North Anna River May 23-26. On line of the Pamunkey May 26-28. Totopotomoy May 28-31. Cold Harbor June 1-12. Bethesda Church June 1-3. Before Petersburg June 16-18. Siege of Petersburg June 16, 1864, to April 2, 1865. Mine Explosion, Petersburg, July 30, 1864 (Reserve). Weldon Railroad August 18-21. Poplar Springs Church, Peeble's Farm, September 29-October 2. Boydton Plank Road, Hatcher's Run, October 27-28. Warren's Raid on Weldon Railroad December 7-12. Dabney's Mills, Hatcher's Run, February 5-7, 1865. Appomattox Campaign March 28-April 9. Lewis Farm, near Gravelly Run, March 29. White Oak Road March 31. Five Forks April 1. Fall of Petersburg April 2. Pursuit of Lee April 3-9. Appomattox Court House April 9. Surrender of Lee and his army. March to Washington, D. C., May 1-12. Grand Review May 23. Mustered out at Washington, D. C., July 16, 1865.

Regiment lost during service 7 Officers and 126 Enlisted men killed and mortally wounded and 2 Officers and 179 Enlisted men by disease. Total 314.

147th REGIMENT INFANTRY ("OSWEGO REGIMENT").

Organized at Oswego, N. Y., and mustered in September 22, 1862. Left State for Washington, D. C., September 25, 1862. Attached to Defences of Washington, D. C., to December, 1862. Provost Guard, Army of the Potomac, to January, 1863. 3rd Brigade, 1st Division, 1st Army Corps, Army of the Potomac, to March, 1863. 2nd Brigade, 1st Division, 1st Army Corps, to March, 1864. 2nd Brigade, 4th Division, 5th Army Corps, to August, 1864. 3rd Brigade, 2nd Division, 5th Army Corps, to September, 1864. 3rd Brigade, 3rd Division, 5th Army Corps, to June, 1865.

SERVICE.—Duty in the Defences of Washington north of the Potomac to December, 1862. Duty at Belle Plains, Va., till April 27, 1863. Chancellorsville Campaign April 27-May 6. Operations at Pollock's Mill Creek April 29-May 2. Fitzhugh's Crossing April 29-30. Battle of Chancellorsville May 2-5. Gettysburg (Pa.) Campaign June 11-July 24. Battle of Gettysburg July 1-3. Pursuit of Lee July 5-24. Duty on line of the Rappahannock and Rapidan till October. Bristoe Campaign October 9-22. Advance to line of the Rappahannock November 7-8. Mine Run Campaign November 26-December 2. Duty near Culpeper, Va., till May, 1864. Demonstration on the Rapidan February 6-7. Campaign from the Rapidan to the James May 3-June 15. Battles of the Wilderness May 5-7. Laurel Hill May 8. Spottsylvania May 8-12. Spottsylvania Court House May 12-21. Assault on the Salient May 12. North Anna River May 23-26. Jericho Ford May 23. On line of the Pamunkey May 26-28. Totopotomoy May 28-31. Cold Harbor June 1-12. Bethesda Church June 1-3. Before Petersburg June 16-18. Siege of Petersburg June 16, 1864, to April 2, 1865. Mine Explosion, Petersburg, July 30, 1864 (Reserve). Weldon Railroad August 18-21. Poplar Springs Church, Peeble's Farm, September 29-October 2. Boydton Plank Road, Hatcher's Run, October 27-28. Warren's Raid on Weldon Railroad December 7-12. Dabney's Mills, Hatcher's Run, February 5-7, 1865. Appomattox Campaign March 28-April 9. Lewis Farm, near Gravelly Run, March 29. White Oak Road March 31. Five Forks April 1. Fall of Petersburg April 2. Pursuit of Lee April 3-9. Appomattox Court House April 9. Surrender of Lee and his army. March to Washington, D. C., May 1-12. Grand Review May 23. Mustered out June 7, 1865. Veterans and Recruits transferred to 91st New York Infantry.

Regiment lost during service 9 Officers and 154 Enlisted men killed and mortally wounded and 2 Officers and 175 Enlisted men by disease. Total 340.

148th REGIMENT INFANTRY.

Organized at Geneva, N. Y., and mustered in September 14, 1862. Left State for Suffolk, Va., September 22, 1862. Attached to Viele's Command, Norfolk, Va., 7th Army Corps, Dept. of Virginia, to July, 1863. Norfolk, Va., Dept. of Virginia and North Carolina, to October, 1863. Wistar's Brigade, United States forces, Yorktown, Va.; Dept. of Virginia and North Carolina, to April, 1864. 2nd Brigade, 2nd Division, 18th Army Corps, Army of the James, to September, 1864. 1st Brigade, 2nd Division, 18th Army Corps, to December, 1864. 4th Brigade, 1st Division, 24th Army Corps, to May, 1865. 2nd Brigade, 1st Division, 24th Army Corps, to June, 1865.

SERVICE.—Garrison and guard duty at Norfolk, Va., till October, 1863, and at Yorktown, Va., till April, 1864. Wistar's Expedition against Richmond February 6-8, 1864. Butler's operations on south side of the James and against Petersburg and Richmond May 4-28. Occupation of City Point and Bermuda Hundred, Va., May 5. Swift Creek or Arrowfield Church May 9-10. Operations against Fort Darling May 12-16. Battle of Drury's Bluff May 14-16. Bermuda Hundred May 16-27. Moved to White House, thence to Cold Harbor, May 28-31. Battles about Cold Harbor June 1-12. Before Petersburg June 15-18. Siege operations against Petersburg and Richmond June 16, 1864, to April 2, 1865. Duty in the trenches before Petersburg and on the Bermuda Hundred front till September 27. Mine Explosion, Petersburg (Reserve). Battle of Chaffin's Farm, New Market Heights, September 28-30. Battle of Fair Oaks October 27-28. Duty in trenches before Richmond till March, 1865. Appomattox Campaign March 28-April 9. On line of Hatcher's and Gravelly Runs March 29-30. Fall of Petersburg April 2. Pursuit of Lee April 3-9. Rice's Station April 6. Appomattox Court House April 9. Surrender of Lee and his army. Duty in the Department of Virginia till June. Mustered out June 22, 1865. Veterans and Recruits transferred to 100th New York Infantry.

Regiment lost during service 4 Officers and 112 Enlisted men killed and mortally wounded and 2 Officers and 149 Enlisted men by disease. Total 267.

149th REGIMENT INFANTRY ("4th ONONDAGAS").

Organized at Syracuse, N. Y., and mustered in September 18, 1862. Left State for Washington, D. C., September 23, 1862. Attached to 2nd Brigade, 1st Division, 12th Army Corps, Army of the Potomac, to October, 1862. 4th Brigade, 1st Division, 12th Army Corps, October, 1862. 3rd Brigade, 2nd Division, 12th Army Corps, Army of the Potomac, to October, and Army of the Cumberland to April, 1864. 3rd Brigade, 2nd Division, 20th Army Corps, Army of the Cumberland, and Georgia to June, 1865.

SERVICE.—Duty in the Defences of Washington, D. C., till September 30, 1862, and at Bolivar Heights, Va., till December 10. Reconnoissance to Rippon, W. Va., November 9. Expedition to Winchester December 2-6. March to Fredericksburg, Va., December 10-15. At Falmouth, Va., till April 27, 1863. "Mud March" January 20-24. Chancellorsville Campaign April 27-May 6. Battle of Chancellorsville May 1-5. Gettysburg (Pa.) Campaign June 11-July 24. Battle of Gettysburg July 1-3. Pursuit of Lee to Manassas Gap, Va., July 5-24. Duty on line of the Rappahannock till September 24. Movement to Bridgeport, Ala., September 24-October 3. March along line of the Nashville & Chattanooga Railroad to Lookout Valley, Tenn., October 25-28. Reopening Tennessee River October 26-29. Battle of Wauhatchie, Tenn., October 28-29. Chattanooga-Ringgold Campaign November 23-27. Battles of Lookout Mountain November 23-24; Mission Ridge November 25; Taylor's Ridge, Ringgold Gap, November 27. Duty at Bridgeport, Ala., till May, 1864. Atlanta (Ga.) Campaign May 3-September 8. Demonstration on Rocky Faced Ridge May 8-11. Battle of Resaca May 14-15. Near Cassville May 19. Advance on Dallas May 22-25. New Hope Church May 25. Battles about Dallas, New

Hope Church and Allatoona Hills May 26-June 5. Operations about Marietta and against Kenesaw Mountain June 10-July 2. Pine Hill June 11-14. Lost Mountain June 15-17. Gilgal or Golgotha Church June 15. Muddy Creek June 17. Noyes Creek June 19. Kolb's Farm June 22. Assault on Kenesaw June 27. Ruff's Station, Smyrna Camp Ground, July 4. Chattahoochie River July 5-17. Peach Tree Creek July 19-20. Siege of Atlanta July 22-August 25. Operations at Chattahoochie River Bridge August 26-September 2. Occupation of Atlanta September 2-November 15. Expedition from Atlanta to Tuckum's Cross Roads October 26-29. Near Atlanta November 9. March to the sea November 15-December 10. Near Davidsboro November 28. Siege of Savannah December 10-21. Campaign of the Carolinas January to April, 1865. Averysboro, N. C., March 16. Battle of Bentonville March 19-21. Occupation of Goldsboro March 24. Advance on Raleigh April 9-13. Occupation of Raleigh April 14. Bennett's House April 26. Surrender of Johnston and his army. March to Washington, D. C., via Richmond April 29-May 19. Grand Review May 24. Mustered out June 12, 1865. Veterans and Recruits transferred to 102nd New York Infantry.

Regiment lost during service 4 Officers and 129 Enlisted men killed and mortally wounded and 78 Enlisted men by disease. Total 211.

150th REGIMENT INFANTRY.—("DUCHESS COUNTY REGIMENT.")

Organized at Poughkeepsie, N. Y., and mustered in October 10, 1862. Left State for Baltimore, Md., October 11, 1862. Attached to Defences of Baltimore, Md., 8th Army Corps, Middle Department, to January, 1863. 2nd Separate Brigade, 8th Army Corps, to February, 1863. 3rd Separate Brigade, 8th Army Corps, to July, 1863. 2nd Brigade, 1st Division, 12th Army Corps, Army of the Potomac, to July, 1863. 3rd Brigade, 1st Division, 12th Army Corps, Army of the Potomac, to October, 1863, and Army of the Cumberland to April, 1864. 2nd Brigade, 1st Division, 20th Army Corps, Army of the Cumberland and Georgia, to June, 1865.

SERVICE.—Duty at Baltimore, Md., till February, 1863, and in the Middle Department till July, 1863. Joined Army of the Potomac in the field. Gettysburg (Pa.) Campaign July. Battle of Gettysburg, Pa., July 1-3. Pursuit of Lee July 5-24. Duty on line of the Rappahannock till September, 1863. Movement to Stevenson, Ala., September 24-October 3. Guard duty on line of the Nashville & Chattanooga Railroad till April, 1864. Atlanta (Ga.) Campaign May 1-September 8. Demonstration on Rocky Faced Ridge May 8-11. Battle of Resaca May 14-15. Near Cassville May 19. Advance on Dallas May 22-25. New Hope Church May 25. Battles about Dallas, New Hope Church and Allatoona Hills May 26-June 5. Operations about Marietta and against Kenesaw Mountain June 10-July 2. Pine Hill June 11-14. Lost Mountain June 15-17. Gilgal or Golgotha Church June 15. Muddy Creek June 17. Noyes Creek June 19. Kolb's Farm June 22. Assault on Kenesaw June 27. Ruff's Station, Smyrna Camp Ground, July 4. Chattahoochie River July 5-17. Peach Tree Creek July 19-20. Siege of Atlanta July 22-August 25. Operations at Chattahoochie River Bridge August 26-September 2. Occupation of Atlanta September 2-November 15. March to the sea November 15-December 10. Montieth Swamp December 9. Siege of Savannah December 10-21. Campaign of the Carolinas January to April, 1865. Averysboro, N. C., March 16. Battle of Bentonville March 19-21. Occupation of Goldsboro March 24. Advance on Raleigh April 9-13. Occupation of Raleigh April 14. Bennett's House April 26. Surrender of Johnston and his army. March to Washington, D. C., via Richmond, Va., April 29-May 19. Grand Review May 24. Mustered out at Washington, D. C., June 8, 1865. Veterans and Recruits transferred to 60th New York Infantry.

Regiment lost during service 2 Officers and 49 Enlisted men killed and mortally wounded and 3 Officers and 78 Enlisted men by disease. Total 132.

151st REGIMENT INFANTRY.

Organized at Lockport, N. Y., and mustered in October 22, 1862. Left State for Baltimore, Md., October 23, 1862. Attached to Defences of Baltimore, Md., 8th Army Corps, Middle Department, to January, 1863. 3rd Separate Brigade, 8th Army Corps, to June, 1863. 3rd Provisional Brigade, French's Division, 8th Army Corps, to July, 1863. 1st Brigade, 3rd Division, 3rd Army Corps, Army of the Potomac, to April, 1864. 1st Brigade, 3rd Division, 6th Army Corps, Army of the Potomac and Army of the Shenandoah, to June, 1865.

SERVICE.—Duty at Baltimore, Md., till April 22, 1863, and in the Middle Department till June. At South Mountain, Md., till July. Gettysburg (Pa.) Campaign. Pursuit of Lee to Manassas Gap, Va., July 5-24. Wapping Heights July 23. Duty on line of the Rappahannock and Rapidan to October. Bristoe Campaign October 9-22. McLean's Ford October 15. Advance to line of the Rappahannock November 7-8. Kelly's Ford November 7. Mine Run Campaign November 26-December 2. Payne's Farm November 27. Mine Run November 28-30. Demonstration on the Rapidan February 6-7, 1864. Campaign from the Rapidan to the James May 3-June 15. Battles of the Wilderness May 5-7; Spottsylvania May 8-12; Spottsylvania Court House May 12-21. Assault on the Salient, "Bloody Angle," May 12. North Anna River May 23-26. On line of the Pamunkey May 26-28. Totopotomoy May 28-31. Hanover Court House May 31. Cold Harbor June 1-12. Before Petersburg June 17-18. Siege of Petersburg June 17 to July 6. Jerusalem Plank Road, Weldon Railroad, June 22-23. Moved to Baltimore, Md., thence to Frederick, Md., July 6-8. Battle of Monocacy July 9. Sheridan's Shenandoah Valley Campaign August 7-November 28. Battle of Winchester September 19. Fisher's Hill September 22. Battle of Cedar Creek October 19. Duty at Kernstown and Winchester till December. Moved to Washington, D. C., thence to Petersburg, Va., December 3-6. Siege of Petersburg December 12, 1864, to April 2, 1865. Fort Fisher, Petersburg, March 25, 1865. Appomattox Campaign March 28-April 9. Fall of Petersburg April 2. Pursuit of Lee April 3-9. Sailor's Creek April 6. Appomattox Court House April 9. Surrender of Lee and his army. March to Danville April 23-27. Moved to Richmond, Va., May 16; thence to Washington, D. C., May 24-June 2. Corps Review June 8. Mustered out at Washington, D. C., June 26, 1865.

Regiment lost during service 5 Officers and 101 Enlisted men killed and mortally wounded and 1 Officer and 99 Enlisted men by disease. Total 206.

152nd REGIMENT INFANTRY.

Organized at Mohawk, N. Y., and mustered in October 14, 1862. Left State for Washington, D. C., October 25, 1862. Attached to Provisional Brigade, Abercrombie's Division, Defences of Washington, to February, 1863. District of Washington, 22nd Army Corps, to April, 1863. 1st Brigade, 1st Division, 7th Army Corps, Dept. of Virginia, to July, 1863. Dept. of the East to October, 1863. 1st Brigade, 2nd Division, 2nd Army Corps, Army of the Potomac, to March, 1864. 2nd Brigade, 2nd Division, 2nd Army Corps, to June, 1864. 1st Brigade, 2nd Division, 2nd Army Corps, to June, 1865.

SERVICE.—Duty in the Defences of Washington, D. C., till April, 1863. Ordered to Suffolk, Va., April 18. Siege of Suffolk April 20-May 4. Dix's Peninsula Campaign June 24-July 7. Expedition from White House to Bottom's Bridge July 1-7. Ordered to New York July 12. Duty at New York City July 16 to October 18. Rejoined Army of the Potomac in the field October 24. Advance to line of the Rappahannock November 7-8. Mine Run Campaign November 26-December 2. Demonstration on the Rapidan February 6-7, 1864. Mor-

ton's Ford February 6-7. At and near Stevensburg till May. Campaign from the Rapidan to the James May 3-June 15. Battles of the Wilderness May 5-7; Laurel Hill May 8; Spottsylvania May 8-12; Po River May 10; Spottsylvania Court House May 12-21. Assault on the Salient, "Bloody Angle," May 12. North Anna River May 23-26. On line of the Pamunkey May 26-28. Totopotomoy May 28-31. Cold Harbor June 1-12. Before Petersburg June 16-18. Siege of Petersburg June 16, 1864, to April 2, 1865. Jerusalem Plank Road, Weldon Railroad, June 22-23, 1864. Demonstration north of the James July 27-29. Deep Bottom July 27-28. Demonstration north of the James August 13-20. Strawberry Plains, Deep Bottom, August 14-18. Ream's Station August 25. Boydton Plank Road, Hatcher's Run, October 27-28. Dabney's Mills, Hatcher's Run, February 5-7, 1865. Watkins' House March 25. Appomattox Campaign March 28-April 9. Boydton Road and White Oak Ridge March 29-31. Crow's House March 31. Fall of Petersburg April 2. Pursuit of Lee April 3-9. Sailor's Creek April 6. High Bridge, Farmville, April 7. Appomattox Court House April 9. Surrender of Lee and his army. At Burkesville till May 2. March to Washington, D. C., May 2-12. Grand Review May 23. Mustered out at Washington, D. C., June 13, 1865.

Regiment lost during service 3 Officers and 66 Enlisted men killed and mortally wounded and 1 Officer and 91 Enlisted men by disease. Total 161.

153rd REGIMENT INFANTRY.

Organized at Fonda, N. Y., and mustered in October 17, 1862. Left State for Washington, D. C., October 18, 1862. Attached to Provisional Brigade, Abercrombie's Division, Defences of Washington, to October, 1862. District of Alexandria, Defences of Washington and 22nd Army Corps, Dept. of Washington, to August, 1863. Martindale's Command, Garrison of Washington, D. C., 22nd Army Corps, to February, 1864. 1st Brigade, 1st Division, 19th Army Corps, Dept. of the Gulf, to July, 1864, and Army of the Shenandoah, Middle Military Division, to February, 1865. 2nd Brigade, 1st Provisional Division, Army of the Shenandoah, to April, 1865. 2nd Brigade, Dwight's Division, Dept. of Washington, to July, 1865. Dept. of Georgia to October, 1865.

SERVICE.—Guard and police duty at Alexandria, Va., and at Washington, D. C., till February, 1864. Ordered to Dept. of the Gulf February, 1864. Red River Campaign March 10-May 22. Advance from Franklin to Alexandria March 14-26. Battle of Sabine Cross Roads April 8. Pleasant Hill April 9. Monett's Ferry, Cane River Crossing, April 23. At Alexandria April 26-May 13. Retreat to Morganza May 13-20. Mansura May 16. Avoyelle's Prairie May 16. Duty at Morganza till July 1. Moved to Fortress Monroe, Va., thence to Washington, D. C., July 1-12. Repulse of Early's attack on Washington July 12-13. Snicker's Gap Expedition July 14-23. Sheridan's Shenandoah Valley Campaign August 7-November 28. Battle of Winchester September 19. Fisher's Hill September 22. Battle of Cedar Creek October 19. Duty at Middletown, Newtown and Stephenson's Depot till April 5, 1865. Moved to Washington, D. C., April 5, and duty there till July. Grand Review May 23-24. Ordered to Savannah, Ga., July, and duty in the Dept. of Georgia till October. Mustered out at Savannah, Ga., October 2, 1865.

Regiment lost during service 1 Officer and 38 Enlisted men killed and mortally wounded and 1 Officer and 160 Enlisted men by disease. Total 200.

154th REGIMENT INFANTRY.

Organized at Jamestown, N. Y., and mustered in September 24, 1862. Left State for Washington, D. C., September 30, 1862. Attached to 1st Brigade, 2nd Division, 11th Army Corps, Army of the Potomac, to October, 1863, and Army of the Cumberland to April, 1864. 2nd Brigade, 2nd Division, 20th Army Corps, Army of the Cumberland and Army of Georgia, to June, 1865.

SERVICE.—Joined Corps at Fairfax, Va., October 2, 1862, and duty there till November 1. Movement to Warrenton, thence to Germantown November 1-20. March to Fredericksburg, Va., December 10-15. At Falmouth, Va., till April 27, 1863. "Mud March" January 20-24. Chancellorsville Campaign April 27-May 6. Battle of Chancellorsville May 1-5. Gettysburg (Pa.) Campaign June 11-July 24. Battle of Gettysburg July 1-3. Pursuit of Lee July 5-24. At Bristoe Station till September 24. Movement to Bridgeport, Ala., September 24-October 3. March along line of Nashville & Chattanooga Railroad to Lookout Valley, Tenn., October 25-28. Reopening Tennessee River October 26-29. Battle of Wauhatchie, Tenn., October 28-29. Chattanooga-Ringgold Campaign November 23-27. Orchard Knob November 23. Tunnel Hill November 24-25. Mission Ridge November 25. March to relief of Knoxville November 28-December 17. Duty in Lookout Valley till May, 1864. Atlanta (Ga.) Campaign May 1-September 8. Demonstration on Rocky Faced Ridge May 8-11. Dug Gap or Mill Creek May 8. Battle of Resaca May 14-15. Near Cassville May 19. Advance on Dallas May 22-25. New Hope Church May 25. Battles about Dallas, New Hope Church and Allatoona Hills May 26-June 5. Operations about Marietta and against Kenesaw Mountain June 10-July 2. Pine Hill June 11-14. Lost Mountain June 15-17. Gilgal or Golgotha Church June 15. Muddy Creek June 17. Noyes Creek June 19. Kolb's Farm June 22. Assault on Kenesaw June 27. Ruff's Station, Smyrna Camp Ground, July 4. Chattahoochie River July 5-17. Peach Tree Creek July 19-20. Siege of Atlanta July 22-August 25. Operations at Chattahoochie River Bridge August 26-September 2. Occupation of Atlanta September 2-November 15. Expedition from Atlanta to Tuckum's Cross Roads October 26-29. Near Atlanta November 9. March to the sea November 15-December 10. Siege of Savannah December 10-21. Campaign of the Carolinas January to April, 1865. Averysboro, N. C., March 16. Battle of Bentonville March 19-21. Occupation of Goldsboro March 24. Advance on Raleigh April 9-13. Occupation of Raleigh April 14. Bennett's House April 26. Surrender of Johnston and his army. March to Washington, D. C., via Richmond, Va., April 29-May 19. Grand Review May 24. Mustered out June 11, 1865. Veterans and Recruits transferred to 102nd New York Infantry.

Regiment lost during service 2 Officers and 81 Enlisted men killed and mortally wounded and 2 Officers and 193 Enlisted men by disease. Total 278.

155th REGIMENT INFANTRY.

Organized at New York City and mustered in November 18, 1862, at Newport News, Va. Left State for Newport News, Va., November 10, 1862. Attached to Newport News, Va., Dept. of Virginia, to December, 1862. Corcoran's Brigade, Division at Suffolk, Va., 7th Army Corps, Dept. of Virginia, to April, 1863. 3rd Brigade, 1st Division, 7th Army Corps, to July, 1863. Corcoran's Brigade, King's Division, 22nd Army Corps, Defences of Washington, to November, 1863. 1st Brigade, Corcoran's Division, 22nd Army Corps, to December, 1863. 2nd Brigade, Tyler's Division, 22nd Army Corps, to May, 1864. 4th Brigade, 2nd Division, 2nd Army Corps, Army of the Potomac, to June, 1864. 2nd Brigade, 2nd Division, 2nd Army Corps, to July, 1865.

SERVICE.—Duty at Newport News, Va., till December, 1862, and at Suffolk, Va., till June, 1863. Expedition toward Blackwater January 8-10, 1863. Action at Deserted House January 30. Siege of Suffolk April 12-May 4. Edenton Road and Nansemond April 15. Edenton Road April 24. Providence Church Road, Nansemond River, May 3. Siege of Suffolk raised May 4. Expedition to Blackwater June 12-18. Carrsville June 16. Blackwater June 17. Dix's Peninsula Campaign June 24-July 7. Moved to Washington, D. C., July 10, and duty in the Defences of that city and guard duty on Orange & Alexandria Railroad till May, 1864. Actions at Sangster's Station December 15 and 17, 1863. Ordered to join Army of the Potomac in the field May,

1864. Rapidan Campaign May 17-June 15. Spottsylvania Court House May 17-21. North Anna River May 23-26. On line of the Pamunkey May 26-28. Totopotomoy May 28-31. Cold Harbor June 1-12. Before Petersburg June 16-18. Siege of Petersburg June 16, 1864, to April 2, 1865. Jerusalem Plank Road, Weldon Railroad, June 22-23, 1864. Demonstration north of the James July 27-29. Deep Bottom July 27-28. Demonstration north of the James August 13-20. Strawberry Plains, Deep Bottom, August 14-18. Ream's Station August 25. Boydton Plank Road, Hatcher's Run, October 27-28. Dabney's Mills, Hatcher's Run, February 5-7, 1865. Watkins' House March 25. Appomattox Campaign March 28-April 9. Boydton Road and White Oak Ridge March 29-31. Crow's House March 31. Fall of Petersburg April 2. Pursuit of Lee April 3-9. Sailor's Creek April 6. High Bridge, Farmville, April 7. Appomattox Court House April 9. Surrender of Lee and his army. At Burkesville till May 2. March to Washington May 2-12. Grand Review May 23. Duty at Washington till July. Mustered out July 15, 1865.

Regiment lost during service 9 Officers and 105 Enlisted men killed and mortally wounded and 2 Officers and 71 Enlisted men by disease. Total 187.

156th REGIMENT INFANTRY ("THE MOUNTAIN LEGION").

Organized at Kingston, N. Y., and mustered in November 17, 1862. Left State for New Orleans, La., December 4, 1862. Attached to Sherman's Division, Dept. of the Gulf, to January, 1863. 1st Brigade, 3rd Division, 19th Army Corps, Dept. of the Gulf, January, 1863. 3rd Brigade, 3rd Division, 19th Army Corps, to July, 1863. 2nd Brigade, 1st Division, 19th Army Corps, to February, 1864. 3rd Brigade, 2nd Division, 19th Army Corps, Dept. of the Gulf, to July, 1864, and Army of the Shenandoah, Middle Military Division, to January, 1865. 3rd Brigade, Grover's Division, District of Savannah, Ga., Dept. of the South, to March, 1865. 3rd Brigade, 1st Division, 10th Army Corps, Army of the Ohio, to May, 1865. District of Savannah, Ga., Dept. of Georgia, to July, 1865.

SERVICE.—Camp at Carrollton, La., till February 11, 1863. Expedition to Plaquemines February 11-19. At Carrollton till March 6. Moved to Baton Rouge, La., March 6. Operations against Port Hudson March 7-27. Moved to Algiers April 1, thence to Berwick City April 9. Operations in Western Louisiana April 9-May 14. Teche Campaign April 11-20. Fort Bisland near Centreville, April 12-13. Vermillion Bayou April 17. Opelousas April 20. Expedition from Opelousas to Alexandria and Simsport May 5-18. Moved to Port Hudson May 22-25. Siege of Port Hudson May 25-July 9. Assaults on Port Hudson May 27 and June 14. Expedition to Clinton June 3-8. Surrender of Port Hudson July 9. Moved to Baton Rouge, thence to Donaldsonville, July 11-15, and duty there till August 15. At Baton Rouge till March, 1864. Red River Campaign March 23-May 22. At Alexandria March 25-April 12. Cane River April 23-24. Construction of dam at Alexandria April 30-May 10. Actions at Alexandria May 2 and 9. Retreat to Morganza May 13-20. Mansura May 16. At Morganza till July. Expedition from Morganza to the Atchafalaya May 30-June 5. Atchafalaya River June 1. Moved to Fortress Monroe, Va., thence to Washington, D. C., July 5-29. Sheridan's Shenandoah Valley Campaign August 5-November 28. Battle of Winchester September 19. Fisher's Hill September 22. Battle of Cedar Creek October 19. Duty at Kernstown and Winchester till January, 1865. Moved to Savannah, Ga., January 5-22, and duty there till March 5. Moved to Wilmington, N. C., March 5, thence to Morehead City March 10, and duty there till April 8. Moved to Goldsboro April 8, thence to Savannah May 2. Duty at Savannah, Ga., and in the Dept. of Georgia till October. Mustered out at Augusta, Ga., October 23, 1865.

Regiment lost during service 4 Officers and 56 Enlisted men killed and mortally wounded and 3 Officers and 164 Enlisted men by disease. Total 227.

157th REGIMENT INFANTRY.

Organized at Hamilton, N. Y., and mustered in September 19, 1862. Left State for Washington, D. C., September 25, 1862. Attached to 1st Brigade, 3rd Division, 11th Army Corps, Army of the Potomac, to July, 1863. 2nd Brigade, 1st Division, 11th Army Corps, to August, 1863. 2nd Brigade, Gordon's Division, Folly Island, S. C., 10th Army Corps, Dept. of the South, to February, 1864. 1st Brigade, Ames' Division, District of Florida, to April, 1864. District of Florida, Dept. of the South, to June, 1864. District of Hilton Head, S. C., Dept. of the South, to October, 1864. 3rd Separate Brigade, Dept. of the South, to November, 1864. 1st Brigade, Coast Division, Dept. of the South, to February, 1865 (Detachment). Regiment garrison at Fort Pulaski, Ga., October, 1864, to February, 1865. 1st Separate Brigade, Northern District, Dept. of the South, to March, 1865. 1st Separate Brigade, District of Charleston, S. C., Dept. of the South, to July, 1865.

SERVICE.—Duty in the Defences of Washington, D. C., till November 1, 1862. Movement to Centreville, Va., November 1-19. Advance to Fredericksburg, Va., December 8-17. At Stafford Court House till April 27, 1863. "Mud March" January 20-24. Chancellorsville Campaign April 27-May 6. Battle of Chancellorsville May 1-5. Gettysburg, Pa., Campaign June 11-July 24. Battle of Gettysburg July 1-3. Pursuit of Lee July 5-24. Movement to Morris Island, S. C., August 6-17. Siege operations against Forts Wagner and Gregg, Morris Island, and against Fort Sumpter and Charleston August 17-September 7. Capture of Forts Wagner and Gregg September 7. Picket and outpost duty on Folly Island, S. C., and operating against Charleston till February, 1864. Expedition to Johns and James Islands February 6-14. Ordered to Jacksonville, Fla., February 23 and duty there till June. Moved to Hilton Head, S. C. Expedition to Johns and James Islands June 30-July 10. Operations against Battery Pringle July 4-9. Boudren's Causeway July 9. Duty at Morris Island till October. Moved to Fort Pulaski, Ga., October, 1864, and duty there as garrison till February, 1865. A detachment with Hatch's Expedition up Broad River November 28-30, 1864. Battle of Honey Hill November 30. Partridge Hill December 3. Demonstration on Charleston & Savannah Railroad December 6-9. Deveaux's Neck December 6. Tullifinney Station December 9. Expedition to destroy Charleston & Savannah Railroad January 14-16, 1865. Duty at Morris Island till March, 1865, and in District of Charleston till April. Potter's Expedition from Georgetown to Camden, S. C., April 5-25. Dingle's Mills April 9. Operations about Sumpter and Statesburg April 9-15. Statesburg April 15. Occupation of Camden April 17. Boykins' Mills April 18. Denkins' Mills and Beech Creek, near Statesburg, April 19. Duty at Georgetown and Charleston, S. C., till July. Mustered out July 10, 1865. Veterans and Recruits transferred to 54th New York Infantry.

Regiment lost during service 7 Officers and 87 Enlisted men killed and mortally wounded and 2 Officers and 104 Enlisted men by disease. Total 200.

158th REGIMENT INFANTRY ("1st EMPIRE BRIGADE").

Organized at Brooklyn, N. Y., and mustered in November 10, 1862, at Norfolk, Va. Left State for Norfolk, Va., September 18, 1862. Attached to Viele's Brigade, Norfolk, Va., Dept. of Virginia, to December, 1862. Spinola's Brigade, Division at Suffolk, 7th Army Corps, Dept. of Virginia, to January, 1863. 2nd Brigade, 5th Division, 18th Army Corps, Dept. of North Carolina, to April, 1863. Jourdan's Independent Brigade, Dept. of North Carolina, to July, 1863. Defences of New Berne, N. C., Dept. of Virginia and North Carolina, to December, 1863. Sub-District of Beaufort, N. C., Dept. of Virginia and North Carolina, to August, 1864. 1st Brigade, 2nd Division, 18th Army Corps, Army of the James, to December, 1864. 4th Brigade, 1st Division, 24th Army Corps, to May, 1865. 2nd Brigade, 1st Division, 24th Army Corps, to June, 1865.

SERVICE.—Duty at Norfolk and Suffolk, Va., till January, 1863. Moved to New Berne, N. C., and duty there till December, 1863. Expedition from New Berne to Trenton, Pollocksville, Young's Cross Roads and Swansborough March 6-10, 1863. Action at Deep Gully March 30. Expedition for relief of Little Washington April 7-10. Expedition toward Kinston April 16-21. Expedition to Trenton July 3-7. Quaker Bridge July 6. Expedition to Swift Creek July 17-20. Big Swift Creek July 18. Expedition to Winton July 25-31. Bear Inlet December 25. Destruction of Salt Works. Duty at Newport Barracks and in the District of Beaufort, N. C., till August, 1864. Expedition from Newport Barracks to Young's Cross Roads, Swansborough and Jackson December 27-29. Operations about New Berne against Whiting January 18-February 10, 1864. Reconnoissance toward Swansboro February 9. Expedition to Bogue and Bear Inlet March 25-26. Batchelor's Creek March 26. Expedition from Newport Barracks to Swansborough April 29-30. Expedition against Wilmington and Weldon Railroad June 20-25. Ordered to Petersburg, Va., August, 1864. Siege operations against Petersburg and Richmond, Va., August, 1864, to April, 1865. In trenches before Petersburg and on the Bermuda Hundred front till September 27. Battle of Chaffin's Farm, New Market Heights, September 28-30. Duty in trenches before Richmond till March, 1865. Appomattox Campaign March 28-April 9. Fall of Petersburg April 2. Pursuit of Lee April 3-9. Rice's Station April 6. Appomattox Court House April 9. Surrender of Lee and his army. Duty in the Department of Virginia till June. Mustered out at Richmond, Va., June 30, 1865. Veterans and Recruits transferred to 100th New York Infantry.

Regiment lost during service 2 Officers and 45 Enlisted men killed and mortally wounded and 83 Enlisted men by disease. Total 130.

159th REGIMENT INFANTRY.—("2nd DUCHESS AND COLUMBIA REGIMENT.")

Organized at New York City and mustered in November 1, 1862. Left State for New Orleans, La., December 4, 1862. Attached to Grover's Division, Dept. of the Gulf, to January, 1863. 3rd Brigade, 4th Division, 19th Army Corps, Dept. of the Gulf, to August, 1863. 1st Brigade, 4th Division, 19th Army Corps, to February, 1864. 2nd Brigade, 2nd Division, 19th Army Corps, Dept. of the Gulf, to July, 1864, and Army of the Shenandoah, Middle Military Division, to January, 1865. 2nd Brigade, Grover's Division, District of Savannah, Ga., Dept. of the South, to March, 1865. 3rd Brigade, 1st Division, 10th Army Corps, Army of the Ohio, to May, 1865. District of Savannah, Ga., Dept. of the South, to July, 1865. District of Augusta, Ga., Dept. of Georgia, to October, 1865.

SERVICE.—Occupation of Baton Rouge, La., December 17, 1862, and duty there till March, 1863. Operations against Port Hudson, La., March 7-27. Moved to Donaldsonville March 28, thence to Berwick April 9. Operations in Western Louisiana April 9-May 14. Expedition to Franklin and Opelousas, Teche Campaign, April 11-20. Irish Bend April 14. Bayou Vermillion April 17. Opelousas April 20. Expedition to Alexandria and Simsport May 5-18. Moved to Port Hudson May 22-25. Siege of Port Hudson May 25-July 9. Assaults on Port Hudson May 27 and June 14. Surrender of Port Hudson July 9. Duty at Thibodeauxville till March, 1864. Red River Campaign March 25-May 22. Cane River Crossing April 23. Construction of dam at Alexandria April 30-May 10. Retreat to Morganza May 13-20. Mansura May 16. Duty at Morganza till July. Moved to New Orleans, La., thence to Fortress Monroe and Bermuda Hundred, Va., July 17-25. Duty in trenches at Bermuda Hundred till July 31. Moved to Washington, D. C., July 31-August 2. Sheridan's Shenandoah Valley Campaign August 7-November 28. Near Charlestown August 21-22. Battle of Winchester September 19. Fisher's Hill September 22. Battle of Cedar Creek October 19. Duty at Kernstown and Winchester till January, 1865. Moved to Savannah, Ga., January 5-22, and duty there till March 5. Moved to Wilmington, N. C., March 5; thence to Morehead City, N. C., March 10, and duty there till April 8. Moved to Goldsboro, N. C., April 8; thence to Savannah, Ga., May 2. Duty there and in the Dept. of Georgia till October. Mustered out at Augusta, Ga., October 23, 1865.

Regiment lost during service 10 Officers and 74 Enlisted men killed and mortally wounded and 1 Officer and 130 Enlisted men by disease. Total 215.

160th REGIMENT INFANTRY.

Organized at Auburn, N. Y., and mustered in November 21, 1862. Left State for New Orleans, La., December 4, 1862. Attached to Sherman's Division, Dept. of the Gulf, to January, 1863. 2nd Brigade, 1st Division, 19th Army Corps, Dept. of the Gulf, to July, 1863. 3rd Brigade, 1st Division, 19th Army Corps, to February, 1864. 2nd Brigade, 1st Division, 19th Army Corps, to June, 1864. 3rd Brigade, 1st Division, 19th Army Corps, Army of the Gulf, to July, 1864, and Army of the Shenandoah, Middle Military Division, to February, 1865. 3rd Brigade, 1st Provisional Division, Army of the Shenandoah, to April, 1865. 3rd Brigade, Dwight's Division, Dept. of Washington, to June, 1865. 3rd Brigade, Dwight's Division, Dept. of the South, to November, 1865.

SERVICE.—Expedition to Bayou Teche January 12-15, 1863. Steamer "Cotton" January 14. Operations on Bayou Plaquemine February 12-28. Duty at Brashear City till March 20. Berwick City March 13. Duty at Bayou Boeuf and Patersonville till April 2. Patersonville March 28 (Detachment). Operations in Western Louisiana April 9-May 14. Teche Campaign April 11-20. Fort Bisland, near Centreville, April 12-13. Jeanerette April 14. Bayou Vermillion April 17. Opelousas April 20. Expedition to Alexandria and Simsport May 5-18. Moved to Port Hudson May 18-25. Siege of Port Hudson May 25-July 9. Assaults on Port Hudson May 27 and June 14. Springfield Landing July 2. Surrender of Port Hudson July 9. Expedition to Donaldsonville July 10-30. Kock's Plantation, Donaldsonville, on Bayou Fourche, July 13-14. Duty near Thibodeaux and at Brashear City till September 2. Sabine Pass Expedition September 4-12. Sabine Pass September 8. Moved to Algiers, thence to Berwick September 17. Western Louisiana Campaign October 3-November 30. Vermillion Bayou October 9-10. Carrion Crow Bayou October 11. At New Iberia till January 7, 1864. Moved to Franklin January 7, and duty there till March. Red River Campaign March 10-May 22. Advance from Franklin to Alexandria March 14-26. Battle of Sabine Cross Roads April 8. Pleasant Hill April 9. Monett's Ferry or Cane River Crossing April 23. At Alexandria April 26-May 13. Construction of dam at Alexandria April 30-May 10. Retreat to Mansura May 13-20. Avoyelle's Prairie, Mansura, May 16. At Morganza till July. Moved to Fortress Monroe, Va., thence to Washington, D. C. July 1-12. Repulse of Early's attack on Washington July 12-13. Pursuit of Early to Snicker's Gap, Va., July 14-23. Snicker's Ferry July 20. Sheridan's Shenandoah Valley Campaign August 7-November 28. Served detached as Train Guard for the army from August 14 to October 27. Duty at Middletown and Newtown till December, and at Stephenson's Depot and Winchester till April, 1865. Moved to Washington, D. C., and duty there till June. Grand Review May 23-24. Moved to Savannah, Ga., June 30-July 7. Duty there and at various points in the Dept. of Georgia till November. Mustered out November 1, 1865.

Regiment lost during service 6 Officers and 53 Enlisted men killed and mortally wounded and 1 Officer and 159 Enlisted men by disease. Total 219.

161st REGIMENT INFANTRY.

Organized at Elmira, N. Y., August to October, 1862. Left State for New Orleans, La., December 4, 1862. Attached to Grover's Division, Dept. of the Gulf, to January, 1863. 3rd Brigade, 1st Division, 19th Army Corps, Dept. of the Gulf, to August, 1863. 1st Brigade, 1st Division, 19th Army Corps, to June, 1864. Bailey's Engineer Brigade, Dept. of the Gulf, to August, 1864. 3rd Brigade, 2nd Division, 19th Army Corps, Dept. of the Gulf, August, 1864. Guppey's Brigade, United States Forces, Mobile Bay, to December, 1864. United States Forces, mouth of White River, Military Division West Mississippi, to February, 1865. 3rd Brigade, 1st Division, Reserve Corps, Military Division West Mississippi, to February, 1865. 3rd Brigade, 1st Division, 13th Army Corps (New), Military Division West Mississippi, to May, 1865. District of West Florida, Dept. of Florida, to July, 1865. Sub-District of Key West, District of Middle Florida, Dept. of Florida, to November, 1865.

SERVICE.—Occupation of Baton Rouge, La., December 17, 1862, and duty there till March, 1863. Operations against Port Hudson March 7-27. At Baton Rouge till May. Reconnoissance from Baton Rouge May 13. Advance on Port Hudson May 14-24. Action at Plain's Store May 21. Siege of Port Hudson May 24-July 9. Assaults on Port Hudson May 27 and June 14. Surrender of Port Hudson July 9. Kock's Plantation, Donaldsonville, July 12-13. At Baton Rouge till September 2. Sabine Pass Expedition September 4-11. Sabine Pass, Texas, September 8. Moved from Algiers to Brashear City September 16, thence to Berwick and Camp Bisland September 26. Western Louisiana Campaign October 3-November 30. At New Iberia till January 7, 1864. Moved to Franklin January 7 and duty there till March. Red River Campaign March 10-May 22. Advance from Franklin to Alexandria March 14-26. Battle of Sabine Cross Roads April 8. Pleasant Hill April 9. Monett's Crossing, Cane River, April 23. At Alexandria April 26-May 13. Construction of dam at Alexandria April 30-May 10. Retreat to Morganza May 13-20. Mansura May 16. At Morganza till July. Expedition to Mobile Bay August 18-September 2. Moved to Morganza September 2 and duty there till November 1. Operations near Morganza September 16-25. Expedition from Morganza to Bayou Sara October 3-6. Bayou Sara October 4. Moved to mouth of White River, Ark., November 1, and duty there till February, 1865. Campaign against Mobile and its Defences March and April. Siege of Spanish Fort and Fort Blakely March 26-April 8. Assault and capture of Fort Blakely April 9. Occupation of Mobile April 12. Duty at and near Mobile till May. Ordered to Barrancas, Fla. Expedition from Barrancas to Appalachicola, Fla., May 31-June 6. Duty in District of West Florida and in Sub-District of Key West, District of Middle Florida, till November. Mustered out November 12, 1865.

Regiment lost during service 1 Officer and 55 Enlisted men killed and mortally wounded and 250 Enlisted men by disease. Total 306.

162nd REGIMENT INFANTRY ("3rd METROPOLITAN GUARD").

Organized at New York August 22 to October 18, 1862. Left State for Washington, D. C., October 24, 1862; thence moved to New Orleans, La., November. Attached to Abercrombie's Division, Defences of Washington, D. C., to November, 1862. Sherman's Division, Dept. of the Gulf, to January, 1863. 3rd Brigade, 3rd Division, 19th Army Corps, Dept. of the Gulf, to March, 1863. 1st Brigade, 3rd Division, 19th Army Corps, to May, 1863. 1st Brigade, 2nd Division, 19th Army Corps, to August, 1863. 1st Brigade, 3rd Division, 19th Army Corps, to February, 1864. 3rd Brigade, 1st Division, 19th Army Corps, Dept. of the Gulf, to July, 1864, and Army of the Shenandoah, Middle Military Division, to February, 1865. 3rd Brigade, 1st Provisional Division, Army of the Shenandoah, to April, 1865. 3rd Brigade, Dwight's Division, Dept. of Washington, to June, 1865. District of Savannah, Ga., Dept. of Georgia, to October, 1865.

SERVICE.—Duty at Carrollton, La., till March, 1863. Plaquemine December 31, 1862, and January 3, 1863. Moved to Baton Rouge, La., March 7 (3 Cos.). Operations against Port Hudson till March 27. Moved to Algiers April 3, thence to Brashear City April 9. Operations in Western Louisiana April 9-May 14. Teche Campaign April 11-20. Fort Bisland, near Centreville, April 12-13. Franklin April 14. Expedition from Opelousas to Barre Landing April 21. Advance on Port Hudson, La., May 17-24. Siege of Port Hudson May 24-July 9. Assaults on Port Hudson May 27 and June 14. Surrender of Port Hudson July 9. Moved to Baton Rouge, La., and duty there till September. Sabine Pass Expedition September 4-11. Moved from Algiers to Brashear City September 16, thence to Berwick September 26. Western Louisiana Campaign October 3-November 30. At New Iberia till January 7, 1864. Moved to Franklin January 7, and duty there till March. Red River Campaign March 10-May 22. Advance from Franklin to Alexandria March 14-26. Battle of Sabine Cross Roads April 8. Pleasant Hill April 9. Monett's Ferry, Cane River Crossing, April 23. At Alexandria April 26-May 13. Retreat to Morganza May 13-20. Mansura May 16. Duty at Morganza till July. Moved to New Orleans, thence to Fortress Monroe, Va., and Washington, D. C., July 1-13. Snicker's Gap Expedition July 14-23. Sheridan's Shenandoah Valley Expedition August 7-November 28. Detached with Brigade as Train Guard for the army August 14 to October 27. Duty near Middletown and Newtown till December, and at Stephenson's Depot and Winchester till April, 1865. Moved to Washington, D. C., and duty there till June. Grand Review May 23-24. Moved to Savannah, Ga., June 30-July 7. Duty there and at various points in Dept. of the South till October. Mustered out October 12, 1865.

Regiment lost during service 8 Officers and 58 Enlisted men killed and mortally wounded and 3 Officers and 152 Enlisted men by disease. Total 221.

163rd REGIMENT INFANTRY ("3rd REGIMENT EMPIRE BRIGADE").

Organized at New York City and mustered in October 10, 1862, at Washington, D. C. Left State for Washington October 5, 1862. Attached to Carroll's Brigade, Whipple's Division, Defences of Washington, to November, 1862. 2nd Brigade, 3rd Division, 3rd Army Corps, Army of the Potomac, to January, 1863.

SERVICE.—Moved to Pleasant Valley, Md., October 18-19, 1862. Movement toward Warrenton, Va., October 24-November 16. Movement to Falmouth November 18-24. Battle of Fredericksburg, Va., December 12-15. Duty at Falmouth, till January 20, 1863. Transferred to 73rd New York Infantry January 20, 1863.

Regiment lost during service 3 Officers and 15 Enlisted men killed and mortally wounded and 8 Enlisted men by disease. Total 26.

164th REGIMENT INFANTRY ("CORCORAN GUARD").

Organized at New York City September and October, 1862. Left State for Newport News, Va., November 6, 1862. Reorganized at Newport News, Va., and mustered in November 19, 1862. Attached to District of Newport News, Va., Dept. of Virginia, to December, 1862. Corcoran's Brigade, Division of Suffolk, 7th Army Corps, Dept. of Virginia, to April, 1863. 3rd Brigade, 1st Division, 7th Army Corps, to July, 1863. Corcoran's Brigade, King's Division, 22nd Army Corps, Dept. of Washington, to November, 1863. 1st Brigade, Corcoran's Division, 22nd Army Corps, to December, 1863. 2nd Brigade, Tyler's Division, 22nd Army Corps, to May, 1864. 4th Brigade, 2nd Division, 2nd Army Corps, Army of the Potomac, to June, 1864. 2nd Brigade, 2nd Division, 2nd Army Corps, to July, 1865.

SERVICE.—At Newport News, Va., till December, 1862, and at Suffolk, Va., till May, 1863. Action at Deserted House, Va., January 30, 1863. Siege of Suffolk April 12-May 4. Edenton Road April 15 and 24. Providence Church Road, Nansemond River, May 3. Siege of Suffolk raised May 4. Blackwater May 12 and June 17. Dix's Peninsula Campaign June 24-July 7. Moved to Washington, D. C., July 12. Provost duty in the

Defences of that city, and at Alexandria, Va., and guard duty on the Orange & Alexandria Railroad till May, 1864. Ordered to join Army of the Potomac in the field May, 1864. Rapidan Campaign May 17 to June 15. Spottsylvania Court House, Va., May 17-21. North Anna River May 23-26. On line of the Pamunkey May 26-28. Totopotomoy May 28-31. Cold Harbor June 1-12. Before Petersburg June 16-18. Siege of Petersburg June 16, 1864, to April 2, 1865. Jerusalem Plank Road, Weldon Railroad, June 22-23, 1864. Demonstration on north side of James River July 27-29. Deep Bottom July 27-28. Demonstration north of James River August 13-20. Strawberry Plains, Deep Bottom, August 14-18. Ream's Station August 25. Boydton Plank Road, Hatcher's Run, October 27-28. Dabney's Mills, Hatcher's Run, February 5-7, 1865. Watkins' House March 25. Appomattox Campaign March 28-April 9. Boydton Road March 30-31. Crow's House March 31. Fall of Petersburg April 2. Pursuit of Lee April 3-9. Sailor's Creek April 6. High Bridge, Farmville, April 7. Appomattox Court House April 9. Surrender of Lee and his army. At Burkesville till May 2. March to Washington, D. C., May 2-12. Grand Review May 23. Duty at Washington till July. Mustered out July 15, 1865.

Regiment lost during service 10 Officers and 106 Enlisted men killed and mortally wounded and 3 Officers and 126 Enlisted men by disease. Total 245.

165th REGIMENT INFANTRY ("2nd DURYEA'S ZOUAVES").

Organized at New York City November, 1862. Left State for New Orleans, La., December 2, 1862. Attached to Independent Command, Dept. of the Gulf, to January, 1863. 3rd Brigade, 2nd Division, 19th Army Corps, Dept. of the Gulf, to July, 1863. 1st Brigade, 3rd Division, 19th Army Corps, to February, 1864. 3rd Brigade, 1st Division, 19th Army Corps, Dept. of the Gulf, to July, 1864, and Army of the Shenandoah, Middle Military Division, to February, 1865. 3rd Brigade, 1st Provisional Division, Army of the Shenandoah, to April, 1865. 3rd Brigade, Dwight's Division, Dept. of Washington, to June, 1865. Dwight's Division, Dept. of the South, to September, 1865.

SERVICE.—Expedition from New Orleans, La., to Ponchatoula March 21-30, 1863. Action at North Pass March 23. Capture of Ponchatoula March 24. Berwick Bay March 26. Expedition to Amite River May 7-19. Moved to Baton Rouge May 20-24. Siege of Port Hudson May 24-July 9. Assaults on Port Hudson May 27 and June 14. Surrender of Port Hudson July 9. Moved to Baton Rouge July 22 and duty there till September. Sabine Pass (Texas) Expedition September 4-11. Sabine Pass September 8. Moved from Algiers to Brashear City, thence to Berwick. Western Louisiana Campaign October 3-November 30. Bayou Vermillion October 9-10. Carrion Crow Bayou October 11. Bayou Vermillion November 11. At New Iberia till January 7, 1864. Moved to Franklin January 7, and duty there till March. Red River Campaign March 10-May 22. Advance from Franklin to Alexandria March 14-26. Battle of Sabine Cross Roads April 8. Pleasant Hill April 9. Monett's Ferry, Cane River Crossing, April 23. At Alexandria April 26-May 13. Construction of dam at Alexandria April 30-May 10. Retreat to Morganza May 13-20. Mansura May 16. Duty at Morganza till July. Movement to New Orleans, thence to Fortress Monroe, Va., and Washington, D. C., July. Sheridan's Shenandoah Valley Campaign August 7-November 28. Detached with Brigade as Train Guard for the army August 14 to October 27. Duty near Middletown and Newtown till December, 1864, and at Stevenson's Depot and Winchester till April, 1865. Moved to Washington, D. C., and duty there till June. Grand Review May 23-24. Moved to Savannah, Ga., June 30-July 7. Duty at Savannah, Ga., and at Charleston, S. C., till September. Mustered out September 1, 1865.

Regiment lost during service 2 Officers and 41 Enlisted men killed and mortally wounded and 2 Officers and 79 Enlisted men by disease. Total 124.

166th REGIMENT INFANTRY.

Failed to complete organization. Men enlisted transferred to 176th New York Infantry November 13, 1862.

167th REGIMENT INFANTRY.

Failed to complete organization. Men enlisted were transferred to 159th New York Infantry October 12, 1862.

168th REGIMENT INFANTRY.—("19th STATE MILITIA INFANTRY.")

Organized at Newburg, N. Y., and mustered in February 11, 1863. Left State for Baltimore, Md., February 12, 1863; thence moved to Norfolk, Va. Attached to Busteed's Independent Brigade, 4th Army Corps, Dept. of Virginia, to April, 1863. King's Independent Brigade, 4th Army Corps, to June, 1863. 3rd Brigade, 1st Division, 4th Army Corps, to July, 1863. 2nd Brigade, 2nd Division, 11th Army Corps, Army of the Potomac, to October, 1863.

SERVICE.—Garrison duty at Yorktown, Va., till June, 1863. Dix's Peninsula Campaign June 24-July 7. Ordered to Washington, D. C., July 9; thence to Funkstown, Md. Join Army of the Potomac at Hagerstown, Md., July 14. Pursuit of Lee to Manassas Gap, Va., July 14-24. Guard duty along Orange & Alexandria Railroad till October. Mustered out October 31, 1863.

Lost during service 1 Enlisted man killed and 1 Officer and 36 Enlisted men by disease. Total 38.

169th REGIMENT INFANTRY.—("TROY REGIMENT.")

Organized at Troy and Staten Island, N. Y., and mustered in Companies "A" to "E" at Troy September 25, 1862; Companies "F" to "K" at Staten Island October 6, 1862. Left State for Washington, D. C., October 9, 1862. Attached to Provisional Brigade, Abercrombie's Division, Defences of Washington, to February, 1863. Military District of Washington, 22nd Army Corps, Dept. of Washington, to April, 1863. Foster's Brigade, Division at Suffolk, 7th Army Corps, Dept. of Virginia, to April, 1863. 2nd Brigade, 1st Division, 7th Army Corps, to July, 1863. Foster's Brigade, Vodges' Division, Folly Island, S. C., 10th Army Corps, Dept. of the South, to January, 1864. 1st Brigade, Folly Island, Northern District, Dept. of the South, to February, 1864. 1st Brigade, Vodges' Division, District of Florida, to April, 1864. 2nd Brigade, 3rd Division, 10th Army Corps, Army of the James, Dept. of Virginia and North Carolina, to May, 1864. 2nd Brigade, 3rd Division, 18th Army Corps, to June, 1864. 3rd Brigade, 2nd Division, 10th Army Corps, to December, 1864. 3rd Brigade, 2nd Division, 24th Army Corps, to January, 1865. 3rd Brigade, 2nd Division, Terry's Provisional Corps, Dept. of North Carolina, to March, 1865. 3rd Brigade, 2nd Division, 10th Army Corps, Army of the Ohio, Dept. of North Carolina, to July, 1865.

SERVICE.—Duty in the Defences of Washington, D. C., till April 18, 1863. Ordered to Suffolk, Va., April 18. Siege of Suffolk April 20-May 4. Edenton Road April 24. Siege of Suffolk raised May 4. Expedition into Matthews County May 19-22. Expedition to Walkerton and Aylett's June 4-5. Walkerton June 5. Dix's Peninsula Campaign June 24-July 7. Expedition from White House to South Anna River July 1-7. South Anna Bridge July 4. Ordered to Dept. of the South, arriving at Folly Island, S. C., July 12. Siege of Forts Wagner and Gregg, Morris Island, S. C., and operations against Fort Sumpter and Charleston August 12-September 7. Bombardment of Fort Sumpter and Charleston August 17-23. Capture of Forts Wagner and Gregg September 7. Operations against Charleston and picket duty on Folly and Black Islands, S. C., till February, 1864. Expedition to Johns and James Islands February 6-14. Ordered to Jacksonville, Fla., February 20, and duty there till April. Expedition to Cedar Creek March 2. Ordered to Yorktown, Va., April 21. Butler's operations on south side of the James River and against Petersburg and Richmond May 4-28.

Port Walthall Junction, Chester Station, May 6-7. Chester Station May 10. Operations against Fort Darling May 12-16. Battle of Drury's Bluff May 14-16. Port Walthall Junction May 16. Bermuda Hundred May 16-27. Moved to White House, thence to Cold Harbor May 28-31. Battles about Cold Harbor June 1-12. Before Petersburg June 15-18. Siege operations against Petersburg and Richmond June 16 to December 7. In trenches before Petersburg and on the Bermuda Hundred front till August. Demonstration north of the James August 13-20. Dutch Gap August 13. Strawberry Plains August 14-18. Battle of Chaffin's Farm, New Market Heights, September 28-30. Battle of Fair Oaks October 27-28. In trenches before Richmond till December 7. Expedition to Fort Fisher, N. C., December 7-27. 2nd Expedition to Fort Fisher, N. C., January 3-15, 1865. Assault and capture of Fort Fisher January 15. Cape Fear Intrenchments February 11-13. Sugar Loaf Battery February 11. Fort Anderson February 18-19. Capture of Wilmington February 22. Campaign of the Carolinas March 1-April 26. Advance on Goldsboro March 6-21. Advance on Raleigh April 9-13. Occupation of Raleigh April 14. Bennett's House April 26. Surrender of Johnston and his army. Duty in North Carolina till July. Mustered out at Raleigh, N. C., July 19, 1865.

Regiment lost during service 10 Officers and 147 Enlisted men killed and mortally wounded and 3 Officers and 125 Enlisted men by disease. Total 285.

170th REGIMENT INFANTRY.—("4th CORCORAN LEGION.")

Organized at New York City and mustered in at Staten Island, N. Y., October 7, 1862. Left State for Washington, D. C., October 16, 1862; thence moved to Newport News, Va. Attached to Newport News, Va., Dept. of Virginia, to December, 1862. Corcoran's Brigade, Division at Suffolk, Va., 7th Army Corps, Dept. of Virginia, to April, 1863. 3rd Brigade, 1st Division, 7th Army Corps, to July, 1863. Corcoran's Brigade, King's Division, 22nd Army Corps, Dept. of Washington, to November, 1863. 1st Brigade, Corcoran's Division, 22nd Army Corps, to December, 1863. 2nd Brigade, Tyler's Division, 22nd Army Corps, to May, 1864. 4th Brigade, 2nd Division, 2nd Army Corps, Army of the Potomac, to June, 1864. 2nd Brigade, 2nd Division, 2nd Army Corps, to July, 1865.

SERVICE.—Duty at Newport News, Va., till December, 1862, and at Suffolk, Va., till May, 1863. Action at Deserted House January 30, 1863. Siege of Suffolk April 12-May 4. Edenton Road April 15. Attack on Suffolk April 24. Providence Church Road, Nansemond River, May 3. Siege of Suffolk raised May 4. Operations on Seaboard & Roanoke Railroad May 12-26. Blackwater May 12. Holland House, Carrsville, May 15-16. Carrsville May 18. Dix's Peninsula Campaign June 24-July 7. Moved to Washington, D. C., July 12. Duty at and about that city and guard duty on the Orange & Alexandria Railroad till May, 1864. Ordered to join Army of the Potomac in the field. Rapidan Campaign May 17-June 15. Spottsylvania Court House May 17-21. North Anna River May 23-26. On line of the Pamunkey May 26-28. Totopotomoy May 28-31. Cold Harbor June 1-12. Before Petersburg June 16-18. Siege of Petersburg June 16, 1864, to April 2, 1865. Jerusalem Plank Road, Weldon Railroad, June 22-23, 1864. Demonstration on north side of the James July 27-29. Deep Bottom July 27-28. Demonstration north of the James August 13-20. Strawberry Plains, Deep Bottom, August 14-18. Ream's Station August 25. Boydton Plank Road, Hatcher's Run, October 27-28. Dabney's Mills, Hatcher's Run, February 5-7, 1865. Watkins' House March 25. Appomattox Campaign March 28-April 9. Boydton and White Oak Roads March 30-31. Crow's House March 31. Fall of Petersburg April 2. Pursuit of Lee April 3-9. Sailor's Creek April 6. High Bridge, Farmville, April 7. Appomattox Court House April 9. Surrender of Lee and his army. At Burkesville till May 2. March to Washington, D. C.,

May 2-12. Grand Review May 23. Duty at Washington, D. C., till July. Mustered out July 15, 1865.

Regiment lost during service 10 Officers and 119 Enlisted men killed and mortally wounded and 2 Officers and 96 Enlisted men by disease. Total 227.

171st REGIMENT INFANTRY.

Failed to complete organization. Men enlisted transferred to 175th New York Infantry.

172nd REGIMENT INFANTRY.

Failed to complete organization. Men enlisted transferred to 6th New York Heavy Artillery.

173rd REGIMENT INFANTRY ("4th NATIONAL GUARD").

Organized at Brooklyn, N. Y., October and November, 1862. Left State for New Orleans, La., December 9, 1862. Attached to Grover's Division, Dept. of the Gulf, to January, 1863. 2nd Brigade, 3rd Division, 19th Army Corps, Dept. of the Gulf, to September, 1863. 1st Brigade, 3rd Division, 19th Army Corps, to February, 1864. 3rd Brigade, 1st Division, 19th Army Corps, Dept. of the Gulf, to July, 1864, and Army of the Shenandoah, Middle Military Division, to February, 1865. 3rd Brigade, 1st Provisional Division, Army of the Shenandoah, to April, 1865. 3rd Brigade, Dwight's Division, Dept. of Washington, to June, 1865. District of Savannah, Ga., Dept. of the South, to October, 1865.

SERVICE.—Occupation of Baton Rouge, La., December 17, 1862, and duty there till March, 1863. Operations on Bayou Plaquemine and the Black and Atchafalaya Rivers February 18-28. Operations against Port Hudson, La., March 7-27. Moved to Algiers April 3, thence to Brashear April 8. Operations in Western Louisiana April 9-May 14. Teche Campaign April 11-20. Fort Bisland, near Centreville, April 12-13. Expedition from St. Martinsville to Breaux Bridge April 17-21. Expedition from Opelousas to Chicotsville and Bayou Boeuf April 26-29. Expedition to Alexandria, on Red River, May 4-12. March to Port Hudson May 19-26. Siege of Port Hudson May 26-July 9. Assaults on Port Hudson May 27 and June 14. Surrender of Port Hudson July 9. Moved to New Orleans July 15, and duty there till August 28. Sabine Pass (Texas) Expedition September 4-11. Moved to Brashear City September 16, thence to Berwick. Western Louisiana Campaign October 3-November 30. Vermillionville November 11. At New Iberia till January 7, 1864. Moved to Franklin January 7, and duty there till March. Red River Campaign May 10-May 22. Advance from Franklin to Alexandria March 14-26. Battle of Sabine Cross Roads April 8. Pleasant Hill April 9. Monett's Bluff, Cane River Crossing, April 23. At Alexandria April 26-May 13. Construction of dam at Alexandria April 30-May 10. Retreat to Morganza May 13-20. Mansura May 16. Duty at Morganza till July. Moved to Fortress Monroe, Va., thence to Washington, D. C., July 2-31. Sheridan's Shenandoah Valley Campaign August 7-November 28. Served with Brigade, detached as train guard for the army, from August 14 to October 27. Duty near Middletown and Newtown till December, and at Stevenson's Depot and Winchester till April, 1865. Moved to Washington, D. C., and duty there till June. Grand Review May 23-24. Moved to Savannah, Ga., June 30-July 7. Duty there and in the Sub-District of Ogeechee, District of Savannah, till October. Mustered out October 18, 1865.

Regiment lost during service 6 Officers and 38 Enlisted men killed and mortally wounded and 2 Officers and 129 Enlisted men by disease. Total 175.

174th REGIMENT INFANTRY ("5th METROPOLITAN GUARD").

Organized at New York City and mustered in November 13, 1862. Left State for New Orleans, La., December 7, 1862. Attached to Grover's Division, Dept. of the Gulf, to January, 1863. 2nd Brigade, 1st Division, 19th Army Corps, Dept. of the Gulf, January, 1863. 3rd Brigade, 1st Division, 19th Army Corps, to August, 1863. 1st Brigade, 1st Division, 19th Army Corps, to February, 1864.

SERVICE.—Moved to Baton Rouge, La., January 13-14, 1863, and duty there till May, 1863. Operations against Port Hudson March 7-27. Advance on Port Hudson May 12-24. Operations about Monett's Plantation and on Bayou Sara Road May 18-19. Reconnoissance to False River March 19. Action at Plain's Store May 21. Siege of Port Hudson May 24-July 9. Assaults on Port Hudson May 27 and June 14. Surrender of Port Hudson July 9. Kock's Plantation, Donaldsonville, July 12-13. Duty at Baton Rouge August 1 to September 2. Sabine Pass (Texas) Expedition September 4-11. Moved from Algiers to Brashear City September 16, thence to Berwick. Western Louisiana Campaign October 3-November 30. At New Iberia till January 7, 1864. Moved to Franklin January 7. Consolidated with 162nd New York Infantry February 17, 1864.

Regiment lost during service 1 Officer and 22 Enlisted men killed and mortally wounded and 1 Officer and 59 Enlisted men by disease. Total 83.

175th REGIMENT INFANTRY.

Organized in New York at large September and October, 1862. Left State for Suffolk, Va., November 21, 1862. Attached to Division at Suffolk, Va., 7th Army Corps, Dept. of Virginia, to December, 1862. 1st Brigade, Augur's Division, Dept. of the Gulf, to March, 1863. 3rd Brigade, 3rd Division, 19th Army Corps, Dept. of the Gulf, to May, 1863. 3rd Brigade, 2nd Division, 19th Army Corps, to August, 1863. 2nd Brigade, 1st Division, 19th Army Corps, to February, 1864. 3rd Brigade, 2nd Division, 19th Army Corps, Dept. of the Gulf, to July, 1864, and Army of the Shenandoah, Middle Military Division, to January, 1865. 3rd Brigade, Grover's Division, District of Savannah, Ga., Dept. of the South, to March, 1865. 3rd Brigade, 1st Division, 10th Army Corps, Army of the Ohio, Dept. of North Carolina, to May, 1865. District of Savannah, Ga., Dept. of the South, to July, 1865. Dept. of Georgia to November, 1865.

SERVICE.—Duty at Suffolk, Va., till December, 1862. Moved to New Orleans, La., and duty at Carrollton till March 6, 1863. Moved to Baton Rouge March 6. Operations against Port Hudson March 7-27. Moved to Algiers April 1, thence to Berwick April 9. Operations in Western Louisiana April 9-May 14. Teche Campaign April 11-20. Fort Bisland, near Centreville, April 12-13. Vermillion Bayou April 17. Expedition from Opelousas to Alexandria and Simsport May 5-18. Expedition from Berne's Landing to Berwick May 21-26. Franklin May 25. Moved to Port Hudson May 26-30. Siege of Port Hudson May 30-July 9. Assault on Port Hudson June 14. Surrender of Port Hudson July 9. Moved to Baton Rouge July 22, and duty there till March, 1864. Operations about St. Martinsville November 12, 1863. Red River Campaign March 23-May 22. At Alexandria March 25-April 12. Cane River April 23-24. At Alexandria April 26-May 13. Retreat to Morganza May 13-20. Mansura May 16. At Morganza till July. Expedition from Morganza to the Atchafalaya May 30-June 5. Atchafalaya River June 1. Moved to Fortress Monroe, Va., thence to Washington, D. C., July 5-29. Sheridan's Shenandoah Valley Campaign August 7-November 28. Battle of Winchester September 19. Fisher's Hill September 22. Battle of Cedar Creek October 19. Duty at Kernstown and Winchester till January, 1865. Moved to Savannah, Ga., January 5-22, and duty there till March. Moved to Wilmington, N. C., March 5, thence to Morehead City March 10, and duty there till April 8. Moved to Goldsboro April 8, thence to Savannah, Ga., May 2. Duty at Savannah and at other points in the Dept. of Georgia till November, 1865. Mustered out November 29, 1865.

Regiment lost during service 2 Officers and 12 Enlisted men killed and mortally wounded and 3 Officers and 117 Enlisted men by disease. Total 134.

176th REGIMENT INFANTRY ("IRONSIDES").

Organized at New York November 20, 1862, to January 10, 1863. Mustered in December 22, 1862. Company "K" mustered in January 10, 1863. Left State for New Orleans, La., January 11, 1863. Attached to Defences of New Orleans, La., Dept. of the Gulf, to February, 1864. 1st Brigade, 2nd Division, 19th Army Corps, Dept. of the Gulf, to June, 1864. 3rd Brigade, 2nd Division, 19th Army Corps, Dept. of the Gulf, to July, 1864, and Army of the Shenandoah, Middle Military Division, to January, 1865. 3rd Brigade, Grover's Division, District of Savannah, Dept. of the South, to March, 1865. 3rd Brigade, 1st Division, 10th Army Corps, Army of the Ohio, Dept. of North Carolina, to May, 1865. District of Savannah, Ga., Dept. of the South, to July, 1865. Districts of Augusta and Columbus, Ga., Dept. of Georgia, to April, 1866.

SERVICE.—Duty in the District of LaFourche, Defences of New Orleans, La., guarding lines of New Orleans & Opelousas Railroad at Brashear City, LaFourche Crossing, Tigerville, Bonnet Carre, and other points till January, 1864. Actions at Pattersonville June 17 and 19, 1863. LaFourche Crossing June 19-21. Thibodeaux June 20 (Co. "D"). Fort Buchanan and Bayou Boeuf June 23. Brashear City June 23. Ordered to Franklin, La., January 4, 1864, and duty there till April. Red River Campaign April 15-May 22. Moved from Carrollton to Alexandria April 15-18. At Alexandria till May 13. Gov. Moore's Plantation May 3. Wilson's Farm May 5. Retreat to Morganza May 13-20. Mansura May 16. At Morganza till May 3. Moved to New Orleans, thence to Fortress Monroe, Va., and Washington, D. C., July 3-29. Sheridan's Shenandoah Valley Campaign August 7-November 28. Berryville September 8. Battle of Winchester September 19. Fisher's Hill September 22. Battle of Cedar Creek October 19. At Kernstown and Winchester till January 5, 1865. Moved to Savannah, Ga., January 5-22, and duty there till March. Moved to Wilmington, N. C., March 5, thence to Morehead City March 10, and duty there till April 8. Moved to Goldsboro, N. C., April 8, and duty there till May 2. Moved to Savannah May 2-7. Duty there and the Districts of Augusta, Columbus and Macon, Ga., Dept. of Georgia, till April, 1866. Mustered out at Savannah, Ga., April 27, 1866.

Regiment lost during service 2 Officers and 30 Enlisted men killed and mortally wounded and 2 Officers and 146 Enlisted men by disease. Total 180.

177th REGIMENT INFANTRY—"10th NEW YORK NATIONAL GUARD."

Organized at Albany, N. Y., and mustered in November 21, 1862. Ordered to Dept. of the Gulf, and left State for New Orleans, La., December 16, 1862. Attached to 3rd Brigade, 2nd Division, 19th Army Corps, Dept. of the Gulf, to July, 1863. 1st Brigade, 3rd Division, 19th Army Corps, to September, 1863.

SERVICE.—Duty at New Orleans and Carrollton, La., till March, 1863. Scout to Pass Manchac, February 8-11 (Detachment). Advance on Ponchatoula March 21-24. Expedition to Amite River March 24-30. Duty at Bonnet Carre till May 7. Expedition to Amite River May 7-19. Action at Civique's Ferry May 10. Moved to Baton Rouge May 20, thence to Port Hudson, La. Siege of Port Hudson May 24-July 9. Assaults on Port Hudson May 27-June 14. Surrender of Port Hudson July 9. Duty at and near Port Hudson till August 22. March to Baton Rouge, thence ordered home for muster out. Mustered out September 10 and discharged September 24, 1863, expiration of term.

Regiment lost during service 2 Officers and 7 Enlisted men killed and mortally wounded and 3 Officers and 149 Enlisted men by disease. Total 161.

178th REGIMENT INFANTRY.

Regiment organized at Staten Island, N. Y., June 18, 1863. Companies "A" to "E" left State for Washington, D. C., June 21, 1863. Company "F" joined Regiment September 1, 1863, and Companies "G" to "K"

October 24, 1863. Attached to 3rd Brigade, DeRussy's Division, 22nd Army Corps, Dept. of Washington, D. C., to July, 1863. Provost guard Washington, D. C., 22nd Army Corps, to November, 1863. District of Columbus, Ky., 6th Division, 16th Army Corps, Dept. of the Tennessee, to January, 1864. 3rd Brigade, 3rd Division, 16th Army Corps, Army of the Tennessee, to March, 1864. 3rd Brigade, 3rd Division, 16th Army Corps (Detachment), Army of the Tennessee, Dept. of the Gulf, to June, 1864. 3rd Brigade, 3rd Division, 16th Army Corps, Dept. of the Tennessee, to December, 1864. 3rd Brigade, 2nd Division (Detachment), Army of the Tennessee, Dept. of the Cumberland, to February, 1865. 2nd Brigade, 3rd Division, 16th Army Corps (New), Military Division West Mississippi, to August, 1865. District of Alabama, Dept. of the Gulf, to April, 1866.

SERVICE.—Duty at Fairfax Seminary and Washington, D. C., till October 31, 1863. Little River Turnpike, Va., June 28-29. Moved to Eastport, Miss., October 31. Duty at Eastport, Miss., Columbus, Ky., Fort Pillow, Tenn., and Vicksburg, Miss., till February, 1864. Meridian Campaign February 3 to March 2, 1864. Red River Campaign March 10-May 22. Fort DeRussy March 14. Occupation of Alexandria March 16. Battle of Pleasant Hill April 9. Retreat to Alexandria April 22-26. About Cloutiersville, Cane River, April 22-23. Luciaville April 23-25. Construction of dam at Alexandria April 30-May 10. Retreat to Morganza May 13-20. Mansura May 16. Yellow Bayou May 18-19. Moved to Vicksburg, Miss., thence to Memphis, Tenn., May 20-June 9. Old River Lake or Lake Chicot, Ark., June 6-7. Colliersville, Tenn., June 23. Near Lafayette June 23. Smith's Expedition to Tupelo, Miss., July 5-21. Near Tupelo July 14-15. Old Town or Tishamingo Creek July 15. Smith's Expedition to Oxford August 1-30. Hurricane Creek August 13-14. Moved to Duvall's Bluff, Ark., September 1-7. March through Arkansas and Missouri in pursuit of Price September 17-November 19. Moved to Nashville, Tenn., November 21-December 1. Battles of Nashville December 15-16. Pursuit of Hood to the Tennessee River December 17-28. At Clifton, Tenn., and Eastport, Miss., till February, 1865. Movement to New Orleans, La., February 6-22. Campaign against Mobile and its defences March 17-April 12. Siege of Spanish Fort and Fort Blakely March 26-April 8. Assault and capture of Fort Blakely April 9. Occupation of Mobile April 12. March to Montgomery April 13-25, and duty there and at Greenville, Ala., till April, 1866. Mustered out April 20, 1866.

Regiment lost during service 18 Enlisted men killed and mortally wounded and 2 Officers and 190 Enlisted men by disease. Total 210.

179th REGIMENT INFANTRY.

Organized at Elmira, N. Y., and mustered in by Companies as follows: Company "A" April 5, "B" April 13, "C" April 23, "D" May 11, "E" May 16, "F" May 25, "G" July 20, "H" September 13, and "K" September 15, 1864. Left State for Washington, D. C., by detachments. Companies "A" to "F" attached to Defences of Washington, D. C., May to June 11, 1864. 2nd Brigade, 1st Division, 9th Army Corps, Army of the Potomac, to June 18, 1864. 1st Brigade, 1st Division, 9th Army Corps, to July 1, 1864. 2nd Brigade, 1st Division, 9th Army Corps, to September, 1864. 2nd Brigade, 2nd Division, 9th Army Corps, to June, 1865.

SERVICE.—Rapidan Campaign, Cold Harbor, June 11-12, 1864. Before Petersburg June 16-18. Siege of Petersburg June 16, 1864, to April 2, 1865. Mine Explosion, Petersburg, July 30, 1864. Weldon Railroad August 18-21. Poplar Grove Church September 29-October 2. Jerusalem Plank Road, Hatcher's Run, October 27-28. Fort Stedman March 25, 1865. Appomattox Campaign March 28-April 9. Assault on and fall of Petersburg April 2. Occupation of Petersburg April 3. Pursuit of Lee April 3-9. Appomattox Court House April 9. Surrender of Lee and his army. Moved to Washington, D C., April 20-27, and duty at Alexandria till June

8. Grand Review May 23. Mustered out at Alexandria, Va., June 8, 1865.

Regiment lost during service 7 Officers and 61 Enlisted men killed and mortally wounded and 118 Enlisted men by disease. Total 186.

180th REGIMENT INFANTRY.

Failed to complete organization. Men enlisted transferred to 179th New York Infantry February 21, 1865, as Company "G."

181st REGIMENT INFANTRY.

Failed to complete organization.

182nd REGIMENT INFANTRY—"69th NEW YORK NATIONAL GUARD."

Organized at New York City November, 1862. Left State for Newport News, Va., November 10, 1862. Attached to Newport News, Va., Dept. of Virginia, to December, 1862. Corcoran's Brigade, Division at Suffolk, 7th Army Corps, Dept. of Virginia, to April, 1863. 3rd Brigade, 1st Division, 7th Army Corps, to July, 1863. Corcoran's Brigade, King's Division, 22nd Army Corps, Dept. of Washington, to November, 1863. 1st Brigade, Corcoran's Division, 22nd Army Corps, to December, 1863. 2nd Brigade, Tyler's Division, 22nd Army Corps, to May, 1864. 4th Brigade, 2nd Division, 2nd Army Corps, Army of the Potomac, to June, 1864. 2nd Brigade, 2nd Division, 2nd Army Corps, to July, 1865.

SERVICE.—Duty at Newport News, Va., till December, 1862, and at Suffolk till May, 1863. Action at Deserted House, Va., January 30, 1863. Siege of Suffolk April 12-May 4. Attack on Suffolk April 24. Nansemond River May 3. Siege of Suffolk raised May 4. Operations on Seaboard & Roanoke Railroad May 12-26. Holland House, Carrsville, May 15-16. Dix's Peninsula Campaign June 24-July 7. Moved to Washington, D. C., July 12, and duty in and about the defences of that city and guard duty along Orange & Alexandria Railroad till May, 1864. Ordered to join Army of the Potomac in the field May, 1864. Rapidan Campaign May 17-June 15. Spottsylvania Court House May 17-21. North Anna River May 23-26. On line of the Pamunkey May 26-28. Totopotomoy May 28-31. Cold Harbor June 1-12. Before Petersburg June 16-18. Siege of Petersburg June 16, 1864, to April 2, 1865. Jerusalem Plank Road, Weldon Railroad, June 22-23, 1864. Demonstration north of the James July 27-29. Deep Bottom July 27-28. Demonstration north of the James August 13-20. Strawberry Plains, Deep Bottom, August 14-18. Ream's Station August 25. Boydton Plank Road, Hatcher's Run, October 27-28. Dabney's Mills, Hatcher's Run, February 5-7, 1865. Watkins' House March 25. Appomattox Campaign March 28-April 9. Boydton and White Oak Road March 29-31. Crow's House March 31. Fall of Petersburg April 2. Pursuit of Lee April 3-9. Sailor's Creek April 6. High Bridge, Farmville, April 7. Appomattox Court House April 9. Surrender of Lee and his army. At Burkesville till May 2. March to Washington, D. C., May 2-12. Grand Review May 23. Duty at Washington till July. Mustered out July 15, 1865.

Regiment lost during service 8 Officers and 65 Enlisted men killed and mortally wounded and 53 Enlisted men by disease. Total 126.

183rd REGIMENT INFANTRY.

Failed to complete organization. Men enlisted transferred to 188th New York Infantry August 3, 1864, as Company "A."

184th REGIMENT INFANTRY.

Organized at Oswego, N. Y., and mustered in at Elmira, N. Y., September 12, 1864. Companies "A," "B," "D" and "F" left State for the Shenandoah Valley, Va., September 12, 1864. Attached to 1st Brigade, 3rd Division, 6th Army Corps, September to December, 1864. Battle of Cedar Creek, Va., October 19. Duty at Kernstown till December. Moved to Washington, D. C., thence to Petersburg, Va., December 3-6, and joined Regiment. Companies "C," "E," "G," "H," "I" and "K"

left State for Bermuda Hundred, Va., September 16, 1864. Attached to Defences of Bermuda Hundred, Va., Dept. of Virginia and North Carolina, to December, 1864. Separate Brigade, Army of the James, at Harrison's Landing, Va., December, 1864, to June, 1865. Operations against Petersburg and Richmond September, 1864, to April, 1865. Duty in the Defences of Bermuda Hundred, Va., till December, 1864, and at Harrison's Landing, Va., till June, 1865. (Co. "I" detached at Fort Pocahontas December, 1864, to June, 1865.) Mustered out at City Point, Va., June 29, 1865. Recruits transferred to 96th New York Infantry.

Regiment lost during service 1 Officer and 10 Enlisted men killed and mortally wounded and 27 Enlisted men by disease. Total 38.

185th REGIMENT INFANTRY.

Organized at Syracuse, N. Y., and mustered in September 19, 1864. Company "K" mustered in September 21, 1864, and Company "F" September 25, 1864. Left State for Petersburg, Va., September 27, 1864. Attached to 1st Brigade, 1st Division, 5th Army Corps, Army of the Potomac, to May, 1865.

SERVICE.—Siege of Petersburg, Va., October 1, 1864, to April 2, 1865. Boydton Plank Road, Hatcher's Run, October 27-28, 1864. Warren's Raid on Weldon Railroad December 7-12. Dabney's Mills, Hatcher's Run, February 5-7, 1865. Appomattox Campaign March 28-April 9. Lewis Farm, near Gravelly Run, March 29. Junction of Boydton and Quaker Roads March 29. White Oak Road March 31. Five Forks April 1. Pursuit of Lee April 3-9. Appomattox Court House April 9. Surrender of Lee and his army. March to Washington, D. C., May 1-12. Grand Review May 23. Mustered out at Washington, D. C., May 30, 1865. Veterans and recruits transferred to 5th New York Veteran Infantry.

Regiment lost during service 3 Officers and 53 Enlisted men killed and mortally wounded and 3 Officers and 39 Enlisted men by disease. Total 98.

186th REGIMENT INFANTRY.

Organized at Sackett's Harbor, N. Y., and mustered in by Companies as follows: Companies "A" and "B," September 5, 1864; Companies "C" and "D," September 7, 1864; Companies "E" and "F," September 8, 1864; Company "H," September 10, 1864; Company "I," September 21, 1864, and Company "K," September 29, 1864. (Co. "G" mustered in at Hart's Island, N. Y., September 26, 1864.) Left State for Petersburg, Va., September 28, 1864. Attached to 2nd Brigade, 2nd Division, 9th Army Corps, Army of the Potomac, to June, 1865.

SERVICE.—Siege of Petersburg, Va., October 1, 1864, to April 2, 1865. Boydton Plank Road, Hatcher's Run, October 27-28, 1864. Fort Stedman, Petersburg, March 25, 1865. Appomattox Campaign March 28-April 9, 1865. Assault on and fall of Petersburg April 2. Occupation of Petersburg April 3. Moved to Washington, D. C., April 20-27, and duty at Alexandria, Va., till June. Grand Review May 23. Mustered out June 2, 1865. Recruits transferred to 79th New York Infantry.

Regiment lost during service 48 Enlisted men killed and mortally wounded and 1 Officer and 39 Enlisted men by disease. Total 88.

187th REGIMENT INFANTRY.

Organized at Buffalo, N. Y., and mustered in October 13, 1864. Left State for Petersburg, Va., October 15, 1864. Attached to 2nd Brigade, 1st Division, 5th Army Corps, Army of the Potomac, to July, 1865.

SERVICE.—Siege of Petersburg, Va., October 20, 1864, to April 2, 1865. Boydton Plank Road, Hatcher's Run, October 27-28, 1864. Warren's Raid on Weldon Railroad December 7-12. Dabney's Mills, Hatcher's Run, February 5-6, 1865. Appomattox Campaign March 28-April 9. Lewis Farm, near Gravelly Run, March 29. Junction of Quaker and Boydton Roads March 29. White Oak Road March 31. Five Forks April 1. Fall of Petersburg April 2. Pursuit of Lee April 3-9. Appomattox Court House April 9. Surrender of Lee and his army. March to Washington, D. C., May 1-12.

Grand Review May 23. Duty at Washington, D. C., till July. Mustered out July 1, 1865.

Regiment lost during service 15 Enlisted men killed and mortally wounded and 32 Enlisted men by disease. Total 47.

188th REGIMENT INFANTRY.

Organized at Rochester, N. Y., and mustered in October 4-22, 1864. (Co. "A" organized as Co. "E," 183rd New York Infantry, and mustered in at Elmira, N. Y., September 24, 1864.) Left State under orders to join Army of the Potomac in the field October 13, 1864. Attached to 2nd Brigade, 1st Division, 5th Army Corps, Army of the Potomac, October, 1864, to July, 1865.

SERVICE.—Siege of Petersburg, Va., October 20, 1864, to April 2, 1865. Boydton Plank Road, Hatcher's Run, October 27-28, 1864. Warren's Raid on Weldon Railroad December 7-12. Dabney's Mills, Hatcher's Run, February 5-7, 1865. Hatcher's Run March 25. Appomattox Campaign March 28-April 9. Lewis Farm, near Gravelly Run, March 29. Junction of Boydton and Quaker Roads March 29. White Oak Road March 31. Five Forks April 1. Fall of Petersburg April 2. Pursuit of Lee April 3-9. Appomattox Court House April 9. Surrender of Lee and his army. March to Washington, D. C., May 1-12. Grand Review May 23. Duty at Washington till July. Mustered out July 1, 1865.

Regiment lost during service 9 Officers and 36 Enlisted men killed and mortally wounded and 53 Enlisted men by disease. Total 90

189th REGIMENT INFANTRY.

Regiment organized at Elmira, N. Y., October 3, 1864. Companies "D," "E," "G" and "K" left State under orders to join Army of the Potomac before Petersburg September 18, 1864. Companies "A," "B," "C," "F," "H" and "I" left State for Petersburg, Va., October 23, 1864. (Co. "K" transferred to 15th New York Engineers and a new Co. "K" assigned December 15, 1864.) Attached to 2nd Brigade, 1st Division, 5th Army Corps, Army of the Potomac, to June, 1865.

SERVICE.—Siege of Petersburg, Va., October, 1864, to April 2, 1865. Boydton Plank Road, Hatcher's Run, October 27-28, 1864 (Cos. "D," "E," "G" and "K"). Warren's Raid on Weldon Railroad December 7-12. Dabney's Mills, Hatcher's Run, February 5-7, 1865. Hatcher's Run March 25. Appomattox Campaign March 28-April 9. Lewis Farm near Gravelly Run March 29. Junction of Quaker and Boydton Roads March 29. White Oak Road March 31. Five Forks April 1. Fall of Petersburg April 2. Pursuit of Lee April 3-9. Appomattox Court House April 9. Surrender of Lee and his army. March to Washington, D. C., May 2-12. Grand Review May 23. Duty at Washington, D. C., till June. Mustered out June 1, 1865. Recruits transferred to 5th N. Y. Veteran Infantry.

Regiment lost during service 1 Officer and 8 Enlisted men killed and mortally wounded and 1 Officer and 70 Enlisted men by disease. Total 80.

190th REGIMENT INFANTRY.

Failed to complete organization.

191st REGIMENT INFANTRY.

Failed to complete organization.

192nd REGIMENT INFANTRY.

Organized at Albany, N. Y., and mustered in by Companies as follows: "A," "B," "C" and "D" March 13, "E," "F," "G" and "H" March 28, "I" April 3, and "K" April 8, 1865. Left State for the Shenandoah Valley, Va., by detachments March and April, 1865. Attached to 3rd Brigade, 3rd Provisional Division, Army of the Shenandoah, to August, 1865, and duty in the Shenandoah Valley and Dept. of West Virginia. Mustered out August 28, 1865.

Regiment lost 26 by disease during service.

193rd REGIMENT INFANTRY.

Organized at Albany, N. Y., and mustered in by Companies as follows: "A" March 6, "E" March 28, "K" April 7, "C" March 14, "D" March 28, "G" April 9, "H" April 3, "I" April 9, "B" March 16, and "F" March 28, 1865. Left State for Shenandoah Valley, Va., by detachments March and April, 1865. Attached to 3rd Brigade, 3rd Division, Army of the Shenandoah, to July, 1865, and District of West Virginia to January, 1866. Duty in the Shenandoah and Dept. of West Virginia. Mustered out at Harper's Ferry, W. Va., January 28, 1866.

Regiment lost 25 by disease during service.

194th REGIMENT INFANTRY.

Organized at Elmira, N. Y., and mustered in Companies "A" and "B" March 29, Company "C" April 7, "D" April 16, "E" April 22, "F" April 26, "G" at Hart's Island, N. Y., April 27, 1865. Mustered out May 3 to 10, 1865.

INDEPENDENT BATTALION INFANTRY—"ENFANS PERDU," "LOST CHILDREN," "GERMAN LEGION."

Organized at New York City and Companies "A" to "G" mustered in April 18, 1862. Left State for Gloucester, Va., April 18, 1862. Attached to Yorktown, Va., 4th Army Corps, Unattached, to July, 1862. 1st Brigade, 2nd Division, 4th Army Corps, to December, 1862. Naglee's Brigade, Dept. of North Carolina, to January, 1863. 2nd Brigade, 2nd Division, 18th Army Corps, Dept. of North Carolina, January, 1863. 1st Brigade, 2nd Division, 18th Army Corps, Dept. of the South, to April, 1863. District of Beaufort, S. C., 10th Army Corps, Dept. of the South, to June, 1863. St. Helena Island, S. C., 10th Army Corps, to July, 1863. 1st Brigade, Folly Island, S. C., 10th Army Corps, to July, 1863. 1st Brigade, 2nd Division, Morris Island, S. C., 10th Army Corps, July, 1863. 2nd Brigade, Morris Island, S. C., 10th Army Corps, July, 1863. Davis Brigade, Folly Island, S. C., 10th Army Corps, to August, 1863. 5th Brigade, Morris Island, S. C., 10th Army Corps, to November, 1863. 2nd Brigade, Morris Island, S. C., 10th Army Corps, to December, 1863. District of Hilton Head, S. C., 10th Army Corps, to January, 1864.

SERVICE.—Garrison duty at Gloucester Point and Yorktown, Va., April to December, 1862. Action at Williamsburg September 9. Moved to Beaufort, N. C., December 26, thence to Port Royal, S. C., January 26. Duty at Port Royal, St. Helena Island and Beaufort, S. C., till June, 1863, and on Folly Island, S. C., till July. Attack on Morris Island, S. C., July 10. Duty on Folly Island, S. C., till August. Siege operations against Forts Wagner and Gregg, Morris Island, and against Fort Sumpter and Charleston August 2 to September 7. Bombardment of Fort Sumpter and Charleston August 17-23. Capture of Fort Wagner September 7. Action at Morris Island September 1. Operations against Fort Sumpter and Charleston on Morris Island, S. C., September 8 to December 31. Port Gregg September 23 and October 21. Bombardment of Fort Sumpter and Charleston October 26-November 9. Moved to Hilton Head, S. C., December 31, and duty there till January 30, 1864. Transferred to 47th New York Infantry January 30, 1864.

Battalion lost during service 9 Enlisted men killed and mortally wounded and 52 Enlisted men by disease. Total 61.

NORTH CAROLINA VOLUNTEERS.

1st REGIMENT HEAVY ARTILLERY (AFRICAN DESCENT).

Organized at New Berne and Morehead City, N. C., March, 1864. Attached to District of New Berne, N. C., Dept. Virginia and North Carolina, to February, 1865. District of New Berne, N. C., Dept. of North Carolina, to March, 1865.

SERVICE.—Garrison duty at New Berne, N. C., and other points in District and Dept. of North Carolina, till March, 1865. Designation of Regiment changed to 14th U. S. Colored Heavy Artillery, March 17, 1865 (which see).

1st REGIMENT INFANTRY.

Authorized by Gen. Burnside May, 1862. Organized June 27, 1862. Attached to Dept. of North Carolina, Unassigned, to December, 1862. Unattached, 18th Army Corps, Dept, of North Carolina, to January, 1863. Unattached, 5th Division, 18th Army Corps, to July, 1863. District of the Pamlico, Dept. Virginia and North Carolina, to April, 1864. Sub-District Beaufort, N, C., Dept. Virginia and North Carolina, to January, 1865. Sub-District, Beaufort, N. C., Dept. North Carolina, to June, 1865.

SERVICE.—Attack on Washington, N. C., September 6, 1862. Operations at and about Shiloh September 17-20. Attack on Plymouth, N. C., December 10 (Co. "C"). Expedition from New Berne to Swan Quarters March 1, 1863 (Co. "G"). Fairfield March 3. Swan Quarter March 4. Winfield March 23. Siege of Washington March 30-April 20 (Co. "B"). Rodman Point March 30. Nixonton April 6 (Co. "D"). Raid from New Berne on Wilmington & Weldon Railroad July 3-7. Expedition from New Berne to Tarboro and Rocky Mount July 18-24. Tarboro and Sparta July 20. Street's Ferry July 21. Scupperton July 22. Reconnoissance on Greenville Road November 10. Near Greenville November 25 and December 30. Evacuation of Washington, N. C., April 26, 1864. At New Berne, Beaufort and Morehead City till July, 1865. Advance on Kinston and Goldsboro March 1-21 (Co. "L"). Battle of Wise's Forks March 8-10. Kinston March 14. Occupation of Goldsboro March 21. Mustered out June 27, 1865.

1st REGIMENT INFANTRY (AFRICAN DESCENT).

Organized at New Berne, N. C., and Portsmouth, Va., June 30, 1863. Attached to Wild's African Brigade, U. S. Forces, Folly Island, S. C., 10th Army Corps, Dept. of the South, to December, 1863. 3rd Brigade, Vodge's Division, Folly Island, S. C., to February, 1864.

SERVICE.—Transferred from Dept. of Virginia and North Carolina to Folly Island, S. C., July 29-August 9. Operations on Folly and Morris Islands against Fort Sumpter and Charleston, S. C., till February, 1864. Moved to Jacksonville, Fla., February 13-16. (A detachment at New Berne, N. C., and participated in raid on Wilmington & Weldon Railroad July 3-7, 1863. Ford's Mill near New Berne October 30. Near Greenville November 25 and December 30.) (A detachment at Portsmouth, Va., and participated in Expedition from Portsmouth to South Mills, Camden, etc., December 5-24, 1863.) Designation of Regiment changed to 35th U. S. Colored Troops February 8, 1864 (which see).

2nd REGIMENT INFANTRY.

Organized at New Berne, N. C., November, 1863. Attached to District of New Berne, N. C., Dept. of Virginia and North Carolina, to April, 1864. Sub-District of Beaufort, N. C., Dept. Virginia and North Carolina, to February, 1865.

SERVICE.—Duty in the Defences of New Berne, N. C., till April, 1864. Scout from Rocky Run toward Trenton December 21-24, 1863. Windsor January 30, 1864 (Detachment). Demonstration on New Berne January 28-February 10. Batchelor's Creek February 1 (Co. "F"). Bogue Island Block House April 2 (Detachment). Siege of Plymouth, N. C., April 17-20 (2 Cos.). Surrender of Plymouth, N. C., April 20 (2 Cos.). At New Berne and in the Sub-District of the Albemarle till April, 1864, and at Beaufort and Morehead City till February, 1865. Consolidated with 1st North Carolina Infantry February 27, 1865.

2nd REGIMENT MOUNTED INFANTRY.

Organized at Knoxville, Tenn., October, 1863. Attached to 1st Brigade, Willcox's Division, 9th Army Corps, Left Wing Forces, Dept. Ohio, to April, 1864. 1st Brigade, 4th Division, 23rd Army Corps, Dept. Ohio, to February, 1865. 1st Brigade, 4th Division, District of East Tennessee, Dept. of the Cumberland, to August, 1865.

SERVICE.—Ordered to Greenville, Tenn., October 16, 1863, and duty there till November 6. Moved to Bull's Gap November 6, and duty there till December. March across Clinch Mountains to Clinch River. Action at Walker's Ford December 2. Gibson's and Wyerman's, Miss., February 22, 1864. Duty at Cumberland Gap and patrol duty in East Tennessee till April, 1865. Scout from Cumberland Gap January 23-27, 1865. Expedition from East Tennessee into Western North Carolina March 21-April 25, 1865. Moved to Boone, N. C., April 6, and to Asheville, N. C., April 27-30. Duty in North Carolina and East Tennessee till August. Mustered out August 16, 1865.

2nd REGIMENT INFANTRY (AFRICAN DESCENT).

Organized at Portsmouth, Va., October 28, 1863. Attached to Wild's African Brigade, U. S. Forces, Norfolk and Portsmouth, Dept. Virginia and North Carolina, to February, 1864. (A Detachment, with African Brigade, to Folly Island, S. C., 10th Army Corps, Dept. of the South, July 29-August 9, 1863, and in operations on Morris Island and Folly Island against Fort Sumpter and Charleston till December, 1863.) (A Detachment at New Berne, N. C., and participated in scout from Rocky Run toward Trenton, N. C., December 21-24, 1863.) Regiment on Expedition from Norfolk, Va., to South Mills, Camden, etc., N. C., December 5-24, 1863. Designation of Regiment changed to 36th United States Colored Troops February 8, 1864, which see.

3rd REGIMENT MOUNTED INFANTRY.

Organized at Knoxville, Tenn., June, 1864. Attached to 2nd Brigade, 4th Division, 23rd Army Corps, Dept. of Ohio, to February, 1865. 2nd Brigade, 4th Division, District East Tennessee, Dept. of the Cumberland, to August, 1865.

SERVICE.—Scout and patrol duty about Knoxville, Tenn., and in East Tennessee till December, 1864. Scout from Morristown, Tenn., into North Carolina June 13-July 15, 1864. Camp Vance June 28. Russellville, Tenn., October 28. Big Pigeon River November 5-6. Moved to Paint Rock December 7. Expedition into Western North Carolina March 21-April 25, 1865. Moved to Boone, N. C., April 6, and to Asheville, N. C., April 27-30. Duty in North Carolina and East Tennessee till August, 1865. Mustered out August 8, 1865.

3rd REGIMENT INFANTRY (AFRICAN DESCENT).

Organized at Norfolk, Va., January 30, 1864. Attached to District of Norfolk and Portsmouth, Va., Dept. of Virginia and North Carolina, to February, 1864. (A Detachment transferred with African Brigade from Dept. of Virginia and North Carolina to Folly Island, S. C., 10th Army Corps, Dept. of the South, July 29-August 9, 1863, and engaged in operations on Folly and Morris Islands against Fort Sumpter and Charleston, S. C., till December, 1863. Designation of Regiment changed to 37th United States Colored Troops February 8, 1864, which see.

OHIO VOLUNTEERS.

1st REGIMENT CAVALRY.

Organized at Camp Chase, Ohio, August 17-October 30, 1861. Left State for Louisville, Ky., December 9, 1861. Attached to 1st Division, Army Ohio, to October, 1862. (Cos. "F," "I," "K," "L" and "M" attached to 5th Division, Army Ohio, May to October, 1862.) Zahm's 2nd Brigade, Cavalry Division, Army Ohio, to November, 1862. (Cos. "F," "I," "K," "L" and "M" attached to 2nd Corps, Army Ohio, to November, 1862.) 2nd Brigade, Cavalry Division, Army of the Cumberland, to January, 1863. 2nd Brigade, 1st Cavalry Division, Army of the Cumberland, to March, 1863. 2nd Brigade, 2nd Cavalry Division, Army of the Cumberland, to October, 1864. 2nd Brigade, 2nd Division, Wilson's Cavalry Corps, Military Division Mississippi, to February, 1865. 2nd Brigade, 4th Division, Wilson's Cavalry Corps, to May, 1865. 1st Brigade, 4th Division, Wilson's Cavalry Corps, and Dept. of Georgia, to September, 1865.

SERVICE.—Company "B" was at Headquarters of Gen. Mitchel in Kentucky October to December, 1861.

Action at West Liberty, Ky., October 23. Rejoined Regiment at Louisville, Ky., December, 1861. Operations near Greensburg and Lebanon, Ky., January 28-February 2, 1862. Moved to Louisville, Ky., February 14, thence to Nashville, Tenn., February 28-March 3. Advance on Columbia March 14-15. Near Columbia March 15. March to Savannah, Tenn., March 28-April 7, thence moved to Pittsburg Landing, Tenn. Advance on and siege of Corinth, Miss., April 29-May 30. Pursuit to Booneville May 30-June 12. Reconnoissance toward Carrollville and Baldwyn June 3. Skirmish at Blackland June 3. Osborn's and Wolf Creeks, near Blackland, June 4 (Cos. "E," "I" and "M"). Guard duty along Memphis & Charleston Railroad till August. Near Russellville July 3 (Cos. "B" and "G"). Expedition to Decatur, Ala., July 12-16 (Detachment). Near Davis Gap July 12 (Detachment). Near Decatur July 15 (Co. "I"). Pond Springs July 24. Courtland and Trinity July 25 (Detachment). Moved to Dechard, Tenn., August 1. Salem August 6. Scout to Fayetteville August 17-20. March to Louisville, Ky., in pursuit of Bragg August 21-September 25. Pursuit of Bragg into Kentucky October 1-22. Cedar Church, near Shepherdstown, October 3. Bardstown October 4. Battle of Perryville October 8 (Detachment). Pursuit of Bragg to Loudon October 10-22. Harrodsburg October 13. Stanford October 14. March to Nashville, Tenn., October 22-November 7. Duty there till December 26. Franklin December 12 and 26. Reconnoissance from Rural Hill December 20. Advance on Murfreesboro December 26-30. Nolinsville December 26. Near Murfreesboro December 29-30. Battle of Stone's River December 30-31, 1862, and January 1-3, 1863. Overall's Creek December 31, 1862. Shelbyville Pike January 5. Duty at Lavergne till June. Reconnoissance from Lavergne May 12. Middle Tennessee or Tullahoma Campaign June 23-July 7. Moore's Ford, Elk River, July 2. Occupation of Middle Tennessee till August 16. Expedition to Huntsville July 13-22. Passage of Cumberland Mountains and Tennessee River, and Chickamauga (Ga.) Campaign August 16-September 22. Reconnoissance from Stevenson to Trenton, Ga., August 28-31. Reconnoissance from Winston's Gap to Broomtown Valley September 5. Alpine, Ga., September 3 and 8. Reconnoissance from Alpine toward Lafayette, Ga., September 10. Alpine September 11. Battle of Chickamauga, Ga., September 19-21. Cotton Port Ford, Tennessee River, September 30. Operations against Wheeler and Roddy September 30-October 17. Greenville October 2. McMinnville October 4. Farmington October 7. Sim's Farm, near Shelbyville, October 7. At Paint Rock till November 18. Chattanooga-Ringgold Campaign November 23-27. Raid on East Tennessee & Georgia Railroad November 24-27. Charleston November 26. Cleveland November 27. March to relief of Knoxville, Tenn., November 28-December 8. Near Loudoun December 2. Expedition to Murphey, N. C., December 6-11. Charleston and Calhoun December 28. Regiment re-enlisted January 4, 1864. Demonstration on Dalton, Ga., February 22-27, 1864 (Non-Veterans). Near Dalton February 23. Tunnel Hill, Buzzard's Roost Gap and Rocky Faced Ridge February 23-25. Tunnel Hill February 25. Buzzard's Roost February 27. Atlanta (Ga.) Campaign May 1-September 8, 1864. Decatur, Ala., May 26. Courtland Road, Ala., May 26. Pond Springs, near Courtland, May 27. Moulton May 28-29. Operations about Marietta and against Kenesaw Mountain June 10-July 2. McAffee's Cross Roads June 11. Noonday Creek June 15-19 and 27. Kenesaw Mountain June 21. Near Marietta June 23. Assault on Kenesaw June 27. Nickajack Creek July 2-5. Rottenwood Creek July 4. Chattahoochie River July 5-17. Raid to Covington July 22-24. Siege of Atlanta July 24-August 15. Garrard's Raid to South River July 27-31. Flat Rock Bridge and Lithonia July 28. Kilpatrick's Raid around Atlanta August 18-22. Flint River and Red Oak August 19. Jonesborough August 19. Lovejoy Station August 20. Operations at Chattahoochoe River Bridge August 26-September 2. Occupation of Atlanta September 2. Operations against Hood and Forest in North

48

Georgia and North Alabama September 29-November 3. Near Lost Mountain October 4-7. New Hope Church October 5. Dallas October 7. Rome October 10-11. Narrows November 11. Coosaville Road, near Rome, November 13. Near Summerville October 18. Little River October 20. Blue Pond and Leesburg October 21. Coosa River October 25. Ladiga, Terrapin Creek, October 28. Ordered to Louisville, Ky., and duty there till December. Ordered to Gravelly Springs, Ala., December 28, and duty there till March, 1865. Wilson's Raid to Macon, Ga., March 22-April 24. Near Montevallo March 31. Ebenezer Church April 1. Selma April 2. Montgomery April 12-13. Crawford and Girard April. Columbus and West Point April 16. Capture of Macon April 20. Irwinsville, Ga., May 10. Capture of Jeff Davis. Duty in Georgia and South Carolina till September. Mustered out September 13, 1865.

Companies "A" and "C" ordered to West Virginia September 17, 1861. Attached to Army of Occupation, West Virginia, to October, 1861. Cheat Mountain District, West Virginia, to January, 1862. Landers' Division, Army Potomac, to March, 1862. Shields' 2nd Division, Banks' 5th Army Corps, and Dept. of the Shanandoah, to May, 1862. Cavalry, Shields' Division, Dept. of the Rappahannock, to June, 1862. Headquarters 2nd Corps, Army of Virginia, to September, 1862. Price's Cavalry Brigade, Military District of Washington, D. C., to March, 1863. 2nd Brigade, Stahel's Cavalry Division, 22nd Army Corps, Dept. of Washington, to June, 1863. Headquarters 3rd Division, Cavalry Corps, Army of the Potomac, to December, 1863. Defences of Washington, D. C., to January, 1864.

Participating in skirmish at Bloomery Gap, Va., February 4, 1862. Advance on Winchester March 7-15. Battle of Winchester March 23. Occupation of Mt. Jackson April 17. Battle of Cedar Mountain August 9. Pope's Campaign in Northern Virginia August 16-September 2. Catlett's Station August 22. Centreville August 27-28. Groveton August 29. Bull Run August 30. Chantilly September 1. Duty in Defences of Washington till June, 1863. Battle of Gettysburg, Pa., July 1-3, 1863. Monterey Gap July 4. Emmettsburg July 5. Hagerstown July 6-12. Falling Waters July 14. Hartwood Church August 28. Advance from the Rappahannock to the Rapidan September 13-17. Bristoe Campaign October 9-22. Hartwood Church November 5. Mine Run Campaign November 26-December 2. In Defences of Washington, D. C., till January, 1864, when rejoined Regiment.

Regiment lost during service 6 Officers and 45 Enlisted men killed and mortally wounded and 3 Officers and 150 Enlisted men by disease. Total 204.

2nd REGIMENT CAVALRY.

Organized at Cleveland and Camp Dennison, Ohio, August to October, 1861. Duty at Camp Dennison, Ohio, November 1, 1861, to January 27, 1862. Scout duty on the Missouri Border January 27-February 18, 1862. Attached to Doubleday's Brigade, Dept. of Missouri, February to June, 1862. Fort Scott, Kan., to August, 1862. Solomon's Brigade, Dept. of Kansas, to October, 1862. 1st Brigade, 1st Division, Army of the Frontier, to December, 1862. Columbus, Ohio, to April, 1863. Kautz's 1st Cavalry Brigade, District of Central Kentucky, Dept. Ohio, to June, 1863. 3rd Brigade, 1st Division, 23rd Army Corps, Army Ohio, to August, 1863. 3rd Brigade, 4th Division, 23rd Army Corps, to November, 1863. 1st Brigade, 2nd Division Cavalry, 23rd Army Corps, to February, 1864. Columbus, Ohio, to April, 1864. Cavalry, 9th Army Corps, Army of the Potomac, to May 24, 1864. 1st Brigade, 3rd Division, Cavalry Corps, Army of the Potomac, and Middle Military Division, to May, 1865. Dept. of Missouri to October, 1865.

SERVICE.—Expedition to Fort Scott, Kan., February 18-March 2, 1862. Action at Independence, Mo., February 22. Expedition to Diamond Grove, Kan., April 15-May 7. Action at Horse Creek May 7. Expedition into Indian Territory May 25-July 8. Action at Grand River June 6. Capture of Fort Gibson July 18. Bayou Bernard July 27. Montevallo August 5. Lone Jack, Mo., August 11. Blount's Campaign in Missouri and Arkansas September 17-December 3. Expedition to Sarcoxie September 28-30. Newtonia September 30. Occupation of Newtonia October 4. Skirmishes at Carthage, Cow Hill, Cow Skin Prairie, Wolf Creek, Maysville and White River. Ordered to Columbus, Ohio, December, 1862, and duty there till March, 1863. Moved to Somerset, Ky., and duty there till June 27. Mt. Sterling, Ky., March 19 (3rd Battalion). Owensville March 31. Expedition to Monticello and operations in Southeastern Kentucky April 26-May 12. Action at Monticello May 1. Near Mill Springs May 29. Monticello, Rocky Gap and Steubenville June 9. Sanders' Raid in East Tennessee June 14-24 (3rd Battalion). Knoxville June 19-20. Strawberry Plains and Rogers' Gap June 20. Powder Springs Gap June 21. Pursuit of Morgan July 1-25. Columbia, Ky., July 3. Buffington Island, Ohio, July 18-19. Operations in Eastern Kentucky against Scott July 25-August 6. Near Rogersville July 27. Richmond July 28. Lancaster and Paint Lick Bridge July 31. Lancaster August 1. Burnside's Campaign in East Tennessee August 16-October 17. Winter's Gap August 31. Expedition to Cumberland Gap September 4-7. Operations about Cumberland Gap September 7-10. Capture of Cumberland Gap September 9. Greenville September 11. Carter's Depot September 22. Zollicoffer September 24. Jonesboro September 28. Greenville October 2. Blue Springs October 5 and 10. Sweetwater October 10-11. Knoxville Campaign November 4-December 23. Lenoir Station November 14-15. Stock Creek November 15. Siege of Knoxville November 17-December 5. Morristown and Long's Ford December 10. Cheek's Cross Roads December 12. Russellville December 12-13. Bean's Station December 14. Blain's Cross Roads December 16-19. Rutledge December 16. Stone's Mill December 19. Dandridge December 24. Mossy Creek Station December 26. Regiment re-enlisted January 1, 1864. On Veteran furlough till March. Ordered to Annapolis, Md., March 20. Campaign from the Rapidan to the James May 4-June 15. Battles of the Wilderness May 5-7; Piney Branch Ford May 8; Spottsylvania May 8-21; Piney Branch Ford May 15; U. S. Ford May 21 (Detachment); North Anna River May 23-26. On line of the Pamunkey May 26-28. Totopotomoy May 28-31. Mechump's Creek and Hanover Court House May 31. Ashland June 1. Cold Harbor June 1-12. Gaines' Mill, Salem Church, Haw's Shop and Totopotomoy June 2. Haw's Shop June 3-5. Long Bridge and White House Landing June 12. Smith's Store, near Samaria Church, June 15. Wilson's Raid on Southside & Danville Railroad June 22-30. Black and White Station June 23. Staunton River Bridge, or Roanoke Station, June 25. Sappony Church, or Stony Creek, June 28-29. Ream's Station June 29. Sheridan's Shenandoah Valley Campaign August 7-November 28. Winchester August 17. Summit Point August 21. Charlestown August 21-22. Smithfield and Kearneysville August 25. White Post September 3. Abram's Creek, near Winchester, September 13. Battle of Opequan, Winchester, September 19. Near Cedarville September 20. Front Royal Pike September 21. Milford and Fisher's Hill September 22. Waynesboro September 29. Bridgewater October 4. Near Columbia Furnace October 7. Tom's Brook October 8-9. Cedar Creek October 13. Battle of Cedar Creek October 19. New Market November 6. Kearneysville November 10. Newtown and Cedar Creek November 12. Rude's Hill, near Mt. Jackson, November 22. Raid to Lacey's Springs December 19-22. Lacey's Springs December 21. Expedition from Winchester to Moorefield, W. Va., February 4-6, 1865. Sheridan's Raid from Winchester to Petersburg February 27-March 25. Occupation of Staunton March 2. Waynesboro March 2. Occupation of Charlottesville March 3. Ashland March 15. Appomattox Campaign March 28-April 9. Dinwiddie Court House March 30-31. Five Forks April 1. Namozine Church April 3. Sailor's Creek April 6. Appomattox Station April 8. Appomattox Court House

April 9. Surrender of Lee and his army. Expedition to Danville April 23-29. March to Washington, D. C., May. Grand Review May 23. Ordered to St. Louis, Mo., May 27. Duty in Dept. of Missouri till October. Mustered out October 12, 1865.

Regiment lost during service 7 Officers and 76 Enlisted men killed and mortally wounded and 5 Officers and 179 Enlisted men by disease. Total 267.

3rd REGIMENT CAVALRY.

Organized at Camp Worcester September 4-December 11, 1861. Moved to Camp Dennison, near Cincinnati, Ohio, January 14, 1862, and to Jeffersonville, Ind., February 21. Moved to Nashville, Tenn., March 2. Attached to 6th Division, Army Ohio, to June, 1862. Cavalry Brigade, Army Ohio, to September, 1862. 2nd Brigade, Cavalry Division, Army Ohio, to November, 1862. 2nd Brigade, Cavalry Division, Army of the Cumberland, to January, 1863. 2nd Brigade, 1st Cavalry Division, Army Cumberland, to March, 1863. 2nd Brigade, 2nd Cavalry Division, Army of the Cumberland, to October, 1864. 2nd Brigade, 2nd Division, Wilson's Cavalry Corps, Military Division Mississippi, to August, 1865.

SERVICE.—March with 6th Division, Army Ohio, from Nashville to Savannah, Tenn., March 29-April 6, 1862. Action at Lawrenceburg April 4 (1st Battalion). Advance on and siege of Corinth, Miss., April 29-May 30. Guard duty along Memphis & Charleston Railroad June to August. Near Woodville, Ala., August 4. Expedition from Woodville to Guntersville, Ala. (3rd Battalion). Guntersville and Law's Landing August 28 (3rd Battalion). Expedition to Dunlap August 29-31. Old Deposit Ferry August 29 (3rd Battalion). March to Louisville, Ky., in pursuit of Bragg September 3-25. Glasgow, Ky., September 18. Munfordsville September 20-21 (1st Battalion). Pursuit of Bragg into Kentucky October 1-15. Bardstown Pike October 1. Near Bardstown October 4. Battle of Perryville October 8. Lexington October 17-18. Pursuit of Morgan to Gallatin, Tenn. March to Nashville, Tenn., and duty there till December 26. Tunnel Hill November 19. Advance on Murfreesboro December 26-30. Franklin December 26-27. Battle of Stone's River December 30-31, 1862, and January 1-3, 1863. Overall's Creek December 31. Stewart's Creek and Lavergne January 1, 1863. Conduct trains to Nashville and return. Insane Asylum January 3. Shelbyville Pike January 5. Near Woodbury January 19 (Cos. "A," "D," "E" and "F"). Bradysville Pike, near Murfreesboro, January 23. Expedition to Liberty, Auburn and Alexandria February 3-5. Vaught's Hill, Milton, February 18. Bradysville March 1. Expedition toward Columbia March 4-14. Chapel Hill March 5. Rutherford Creek March 10-11. Woodbury Pike March 27 (2nd Battalion). Expedition from Readyville to Woodbury April 2 (2nd Battalion). Smith's Ford April 2. Expedition from Murfreesboro to Auburn, Snow Hill, Liberty, etc., April 2-6. Snow Hill, Woodbury, April 3. Liberty April 3. Franklin April 9-10. Schoeppe House May 9. Reconnoissance from Lavergne May 12. Middleton May 21-22. Scout to Smithville June 4-5. Snow Hill June 4. Smithville June 5. Middle Tennessee or Tullahoma Campaign June 23-July 7. Morris Ford, Elk River, July 2. Occupation of Middle Tennessee till August 16. Expedition to Huntsville July 13-22. Passage of Cumberland Mountains and Tennessee River, and Chickamauga (Ga.) Campaign August 16-September 22. Reconnoissance from Stevenson to Trenton, Ga., August 28-31. Reconnoissance from Winston's Gap to Broomtown Valley September 5. Alpine September 3 and 8. Reconnoissance from Alpine to Lafayette September 10. Battle of Chickamauga, Ga., September 19-21. Operations against Wheeler and Roddy September 30-October 17. McMinnville October 4. Garrison's Creek, near Fosterville, October 6 (1st Battalion). Wartrace October 6 (1st Battalion). Farmington October 7. Sim's Farm, near Shelbyville, October 7. Chattanooga-Ringgold Campaign November 23-27. Raid on East Tennessee & Georgia Railroad November

24-27. Charleston November 26. Cleveland November 27. March to relief of Knoxville November 28-December 8. Near Loudoun December 2. Philadelphia December 3. Expedition to Murphey, N. C., December 6-11. Regiment re-enlisted January, 1864. Demonstration on Dalton, Ga., February 22-27. Near Dalton February 23. Tunnel Hill, Buzzard's Roost Gap and Rocky Faced Ridge February 23-25. Atlanta (Ga.) Campaign May 1-September 8. Courtland Road, Ala., May 26. Pond Springs, near Courtland, May 27. Moulton May 28-29. Operations about Marietta and against Kenesaw Mountain June 10-July 1. Rosswell June 10. McAffee's Cross Roads June 11. Noonday Creek June 15-19 and 27. Powder Springs June 20. Near Marietta June 23. Assault on Kenesaw June 27. Nickajack Creek July 2-5. Big Shanty June 3. Rottenwood Creek July 4. On line of the Chattahoochie River July 5-17. Garrard's Raid to Covington July 22-24. Covington July 22. Siege of Atlanta July 24-August 15. Garrard's Raid to South River July 27-31. Flat Rock Bridge July 28. Peach Tree Road August 15. Kilpatrick's Raid around Atlanta August 18-22. Red Oak, Flint River and Jonesborough August 19. Lovejoy Station August 20. Jonesborough August 22. Operations at Chattahoochie River Bridge August 26-September 2. Occupation of Atlanta September 2. Florence September 17. Operations against Hood and Forest in North Georgia and North Alabama September 29-November 3. Near Lost Mountain October bed 4-7. New Hope Church October 5. Dallas October 7. Rome October 10-11. Narrows October 11. Coosaville Road, near Rome, October 13. Near Summerville October 18. Little River, Ala., October 20. Leesburg and Blue Pond October 21. King's Hill, near Gadsden, Ala., October 23. Ladiga, Terrapin Creek, October 28. Ordered to Louisville, Ky., and duty there till December. Ordered to Gravelly Springs, Ala., December 28, and duty there till March, 1865. Wilson's Raid to Macon, Ga., March 22-April 24. Selma April 2. Montgomery April 12. Pleasant Hill April 18. Double Bridges, Flint River, April 18. Macon, Ga., April 20. Duty at Macon and in Dept. of Georgia till August. Mustered out August 14, 1865.

Regiment lost during service 1 Officer and 58 Enlisted men killed and mortally wounded and 6 Officers and 229 Enlisted men by disease. Total 294.

4th REGIMENT CAVALRY.

Organized at Cincinnati, Lima, St. Maryes and Camp Dennison, Ohio, August to November, 1861. Moved to Camp Dennison, Ohio, November 23, thence to Jeffersonville, Ind., December 5, and to Bacon Creek, Ky., December 27. Attached to 3rd Division, Army Ohio, to October, 1862. 2nd Brigade, Cavalry Division, Army Ohio, to November, 1862. 2nd Brigade, Cavalry Division, Army of the Cumberland, to January, 1863. 2nd Brigade, 1st Cavalry Division, Army of the Cumberland, to March, 1863. 2nd Brigade, 2nd Cavalry Division, Army of the Cumberland, to October, 1864. 2nd Brigade, 2nd Division, Cavalry Corps, Military Division Mississippi, to August, 1865.

SERVICE.—Action at Roan's Tan Yard, Silver Creek, Mo., January 8, 1862. Advance on Bowling Green, Ky., February 10-15, 1862. Occupation of Bowling Green February 15. Occupation of Nashville, Tenn., February 23. Action near Nashville March 8-9. Camp Jackson March 24. Reconnoissance to Shelbyville, Tullahoma and McMinnville March 25-28. Capture of Huntsville, Ala., April 11. Bridgeport, Ala., April 23. West Bridge, near Bridgeport, April 29. Shelbyville Road April 24. Tuscumbia April 25. Bolivar April 28. Pulaski May 11. Watkins' Ferry May 2. Athens May 8. Fayetteville May 14. Elk River May 20. Fayetteville May 26. Whitesburg, Ala., May 29. Huntsville June 4-5. Winchester, Tenn., June 10. Battle Creek June 21. Huntsville July 2. Stevenson, Ala., July 28. Bridgeport August 27 (Detachment). Fort McCook, Battle Creek, August 27 (Detachment). March to Louisville in pursuit of Bragg August 28-September 26. Huntsville September 1. Tyree Springs September 13. Glas-

gow, Ky., September 18. Pursuit of Bragg into Kentucky October 1-10. Bardstown Pike, near Mt. Washington, October 1. Frankford October 9. Pursuit of Bragg from Perryville to Loudon October 10-22. Lexington October 17-18. Bardstown and Pittman's Cross Roads October 19. Lawrenceburg October 25. Sandersville, Tenn., November 6. Reconnoissance from Rural Hill December 20. Near Nashville, Tenn., December 24. Advance on Murfreesboro December 26-30. Franklin December 26. Wilkinson's Cross Roads December 29. Near Murfreesboro December 29-30. Battle of Stone's River December 30-31, 1862, and January 1-3, 1863. Overall's Creek December 31, 1862. Insane Asylum January 3, 1863. Shelbyville Pike January 5. Expedition to Auburn, Liberty and Alexandria February 3-5. Bradysville March 1. Expedition toward Columbia March 4-14. Rutherford Creek March 10-11. Expedition from Murfreesboro to Auburn, Liberty, Snow Hill, etc., April 2-6. Smith's Ford April 2. Snow Hill, Woodbury and Liberty April 3. Franklin April 10. Expedition to McMinnville April 20-30. Reconnoissance to Lavergne May 12. Expedition to Middleton and skirmishes May 21-22. Near Murfreesboro June 3. Expedition to Smithville June 4-5. Snow Hill June 4. Smithville June 5. Middle Tennessee or Tullahoma Campaign June 23-July 7. Morris Ford, Elk River, July 2. Kelly's Ford July 2. Expedition to Huntsville July 13-22. Occupation of Middle Tennessee till August 16. Passage of Cumberland Mountains and Tennessee River, and Chickamauga (Ga.) Campaign August 16-September 22. Reconnoissance from Stevenson, Ala., to Trenton, Ga., August 28-31. Alpine, Ga., September 3 and 8. Reconnoissance from Alpine toward Lafayette September 10. Battle of Chickamauga, Ga., September 19-21. Operations against Wheeler and Roddy September 30-October 17. McMinnville October 4. Farmington October 7. Sim's Farm, near Shelbyville, October 7. Farmington October 9. Maysville, Ala., November 4. Winchester November 22. Chattanooga-Ringgold Campaign November 23-27. Raid on East Tennessee & Georgia Railroad November 24-27. Charleston November 26. Cleveland November 27. March to relief of Knoxville, Tenn., November 28-December 8. Charleston, Tenn., December 28 (Detachment). Expedition to Murphey, N. C., December 6-11. Expedition from Scottsboro, Ala., toward Rome, Ga., January 25-February 5, 1864. Ringgold, Ga., February 8. Demonstration on Dalton, Ga., February 22-27. Near Dalton February 23-24. Tunnel Hill, Buzzard's Roost Gap and Rocky Faced Ridge February 24-25. Scout to Dedmon's Trace April 10. Atlanta (Ga.) Campaign May 1-September 8, 1864. Courtland Road, Ala., May 26. Pond Springs, near Courtland, May 27. Moulton May 28-29. Operations about Marietta and against Kenesaw Mountain June 10-July 2. McAffee's Cross Roads June 11. Noonday Creek June 15-19 and 27. Near Marietta June 23. Assault on Kenesaw June 27. Nickajack Creek July 2-5. Rottenwood Creek July 4. Chattahoochie River July 5-17. Alpharetta July 10. Garrard's Raid to Covington July 22-24. Siege of Atlanta July 24-August 15. Garrard's Raid to South River July 27-31. Flat Rock Bridge and Lithonia July 28. Kilpatrick's Raid around Atlanta August 18-22. Red Oak and Flint River August 19. Jonesborough August 19. Lovejoy Station August 20. Operations at Chattahoochie River Bridge August 26-September 2. Sandtown September 1. Ordered to Nashville, Tenn., September 21, thence to Louisville November 8, and duty there till January, 1865. Moved to Gravelly Springs, Ala., January 12, and duty there till March. Wilson's Raid to Macon, Ga., March 22-April 24. Selma April 2. Montgomery April 12. Macon April 20. Duty at Macon till May 23, and at Nashville, Tenn., till July. Mustered out July 15, 1865.

Regiment lost during service 5 Officers and 50 Enlisted men killed and mortally wounded and 1 Officer and 169 Enlisted men by disease. Total 225.

5th REGIMENT CAVALRY.

Regiment originally organized at Camp Dick Corwin, near Cincinnati, Ohio, October 23-November 14, 1861, as 2nd Ohio Cavalry. Designation changed by Gov. Dennison November, 1861. Duty at Camp Dick Corwin till November 5, 1861, and at Camp Dennison, Ohio, till March, 1862. Ordered to Paducah, Ky. 2nd Battalion left Cincinnati, Ohio, February 28, and 1st and 3rd Battalions on March 1, 1862. Attached to District of Paducah, Ky., March, 1862. Sherman's 5th Division, Army of the Tennessee, to April, 1862. 1st and 2nd Battalions attached to 4th Division, Army of the Tennessee, to July, 1862. District of Memphis, Tenn., to September, 1862. District of Jackson, Tenn., to November, 1862. Lee's 2nd Brigade, Cavalry Division, 13th Army Corps (Old), Dept. of the Tennessee, to December, 1862. Lee's 2nd Brigade, Cavalry Division, 16th Army Corps, to March, 1863. 2nd Brigade, 1st Cavalry Division, 16th Army Corps, to April, 1863. 4th Brigade, 5th Division, District of Memphis, Tenn., 16th Army Corps, to August, 1863. 2nd Brigade, 1st Cavalry Division, 16th Army Corps, to October, 1863. 3rd Battalion (Cos. "E," "H," "I" and "K") attached to 3rd Division, Army Tennessee, April, 1862. 2nd Division, Army Tennessee, to July, 1862. 2nd Division, District of Corinth, Miss., to November, 1862. Unattached Cavalry, District of Corinth, Miss., 13th Army Corps (Old), Dept. Tennessee, to December, 1862. District of Corinth, Miss., 16th Army Corps, to March, 1863. Cavalry Brigade, 2nd Division, District of Corinth, 16th Army Corps, to May, 1863. 3rd Brigade, 1st Cavalry Division, 16th Army Corps, to August, 1863. 2nd Brigade, 1st Cavalry Division, 16th Army Corps, to October, 1863. Regiment attached to Headquarters 15th Army Corps October, 1863, to April, 1864. Cavalry, 3rd Division, 15th Army Corps, to October, 1864. 2nd Brigade, Kilpatrick's 3rd Division, Cavalry Corps, Military Division Mississippi, to January, 1865. 3rd Brigade, 3rd Cavalry Division, to June, 1865. Dept. of North Carolina to October, 1865.

SERVICE.—March from Danville to Savannah, Tenn., March 10-11, 1862. Expedition to Mobile & Ohio Railroad to destroy bridges March 14-15. Beach Creek Bridge, Tenn., March 13. Near Eastport, Miss., March 14. Burnsville March 14-15. Reach Pittsburg Landing March 15. Skirmish Pittsburg Landing March 16. Reconnoissance toward Corinth March 16. Black Jack Forest March 16 (Detachment). Near Shiloh Church March 24 (1st and 2nd Battalions). Purdy Road near Adamsville March 31 (Co. "I"). Expedition to Chickasaw, Ala., and Eastport, Miss., April 1. Near Monterey, Tenn., April 3. Crump's Landing April 4 (Detachment). Battle of Shiloh April 6-7. Corinth Road April 8. Beech Creek Bridge April 13 (3rd Battalion). Affair with Cavalry April 14. Advance on and siege of Corinth, Miss., April 29-May 30. Pursuit to Tuscumbia River June 1-6. March to Memphis, Tenn., via LaGrange and Grand Junction June 10-July 27 (1st and 2nd Battalions), and duty there till September. Horn Lake Creek August 16 (Cos. "A," "C"). 3rd Battalion at Corinth, Miss., till August, 1863. 1st and 2nd Battalion moved from Memphis to Jackson, Tenn., September 6-12, 1862. Battle of Corinth, Miss., October 3-4 (3rd Battalion). Pursuit to Ripley October 5-12 (3rd Battalion). Battle of the Hatchie, Metamora, October 5, 1862 (1st and 2nd Battalions). Chewalla October 5 (3rd Battalion). Ruckersville and near Ripley October 7 (3rd Battalion). Guard Mobile & Ohio Railroad at Glendale October 15 to November 8, 1862 (3rd Battalion). Grant's Central Mississippi Campaign November, 1862, to January, 1863. About Oxford, Miss., December 1-3, 1862. Free Bridge December 3. Water Valley Station December 4. Coffeeville December 5. Raid from Corinth to Tupelo December 13-19 (3rd Battalion). Operations against Forest December 18, 1862, to January 3, 1863 (1st and 2nd Battalions). Lexington December 18, 1862. Salem Cemetery near Jackson December 19. Davis Mills, Wolf River, December 21 (Cos. "B," "M"). Guard Memphis & Charleston Railroad till March, 1863 (1st and 2nd Battalions), and duty at and about Memphis, Tenn., till August, 1863 (1st and 2nd Battalions). Expedition from Memphis, Tenn., to Coldwater, Miss., April 18-24, 1863. Tuscumbia, Ala., February 22 (3rd Battalion).

Hernando April 18. Perry's Ferry, Coldwater River, April 19. Expedition from Memphis toward Hernando, Miss., May 23-24 (Detachment). Scouts from Memphis toward Hernando, Miss., May 26 and 28 (Detachments). Operations in Northeast Mississippi June 13-22 (3rd Battalion). Operations in Northeastern Mississippi June 15-25 (1st and 2nd Battalions). New Albany and Coldwater June 19 (3rd Battalion). Hernando June 20 (3rd Battalion). Adkin's Plantation, Mud Creek Bottom, Rocky Crossing, Tallahatchie River and Hernando, June 20 (3rd Battalion). Near Memphis July 16 and 18. At Camp Davies till October. Wartrace September 6. Joined Gen. Sherman at Chickasaw, Ala., and march to Chattanooga, Tenn., leading advance. Operations on Memphis & Charleston Railroad in Alabama October 10-30. Cane Creek and Barton's Station October 20. Dickson's Station October 20. Cherokee Station October 21. Cane Creek and Barton's Station October 26. Bear Creek, Tuscumbia, October 27. Cherokee Station October 29. Barton's Station October 31. Guarding trains, escort and courier duty during battles of Chattanooga, Tenn., November 23-25. Pursuit to Ringgold, Ga., November 26-27. March to relief of Knoxville, Tenn., November 28-December 8. Near Loudon December 2. (3rd Battalion joined Long's Brigade in Knoxville.) Expedition to Tellico Plains after Longstreet's trains December 6-11. Report to Gen. Howard at Athens, Tenn. Picket Hiawassee River and courier duty between Grant and Burnside. Regiment veteranize at Larkinsville, Ala., January, 1864. Near Kelly's Plantation, Sulphur Springs, April 11 (Detachment). Atlanta (Ga.) Campaign May 1 to September 8. Advance guard of 3rd Division, 15th Army Corps, to near Rome, Ga. Operations on line of Pumpkin Vine Creek and battles about Dallas, New Hope Church and Allatoona Hills May 25-June 5. Old Church June 13. March to Kingston June 22. Duty there and at Cartersville guarding railroad till November 7. Cartersville July 24. Canton August 22. Shadow Church and Westbrooks near Fairburn October 2 (Detachment). Marietta October 4. March to the sea November 15-December 10. Bear Creek Station November 16. East Macon, Walnut Creek, November 20. Waynesboro November 27-28. Buckhead Creek or Reynolds' Plantation November 28. Rocky Creek Church December 2. Ebenezer Creek December 8. Siege of Savannah December 10-21. Altamaha Bridge December 17. Campaign of the Carolinas January to April, 1865. Williston, S. C., February 8. North Edisto February 12-13. Monroe's Cross Roads March 16. Taylor's Hole Creek, Averysboro, N. C., March 16. Battle of Bentonville March 19-21. Goldsboro March 23. Advance on Raleigh April 10-13. Raleigh April 13. Morrisville April 14. Bennett's House April 26. Surrender of Johnston and his army. Picket near Raleigh till April 30. Duty in Sub-District of Morgantown, District of Western North Carolina, Dept. of North Carolina, to October, 1865. Mustered out October 30, 1865.

Regiment lost during service 1 Officer and 26 Enlisted men killed and mortally wounded and 3 Officers and 140 Enlisted men by disease. Total 170.

6th REGIMENT CAVALRY.

Organized at Warren, Ohio, October 7, 1861. Duty at Warren till January, 1862, and at Camps Chase and Dennison, Ohio, to May, 1862. Moved to Wheeling, W. Va., May 13, thence to Strasburg, Va., and join Fremont's army. Attached to Mountain Department to June, 1862. 2nd Brigade, 2nd Division, 1st Corps, Pope's Army of Virginia, to July, 1862. Cavalry Brigade, 1st Corps, Army of Virginia, to September, 1862. Cavalry Brigade, 11th Army Corps, Army of the Potomac, to February, 1863. 1st Brigade, 2nd Division, Cavalry Corps, Army Potomac, to June, 1863. 2nd Brigade, 2nd Division, Cavalry Corps, Army Potomac, to August, 1863. 1st Brigade, 2nd Division, Cavalry Corps, Army Potomac, to October, 1864. 3rd Brigade, 2nd Division, Cavalry Corps, Army Potomac, to May, 1865. Dept. of Virginia to August, 1865.

SERVICE.—Strasburg, Va., June 1, 1862. Woodstock June 2. Mt. Jackson June 4. New Market June 5. Harrisonburg June 6. Battle of Cross Keys June 8. Near Mt. Jackson June 16. Rapidan River August 3-4 and 12. Pope's Campaign in Northern Virginia August 16-September 2. Fords of the Rappahannock August 16-23. Kelly's Ford August 21. Catlett's Station August 21-22. Fant's Ford, Great Run, August 22. Thoroughfare Gap and Haymarket August 28. Battle of Bull Run August 29-30. Expedition from Centreville to Bristoe and Warrenton Stations September 25-28. Reconnoissance to near Warrenton October 12. Thoroughfare Gap October 17-18. Haymarket October 19 (Detachment). Operations on Orange & Alexandria Railroad November 10-12. Reconnoissance from Chantilly to Snicker's Ferry and Berryville November 28-30. Berryville November 30. Battle of Fredericksburg, Va., December 12-15 (Detachment). Scout to Luray Valley December 22. Kelly's Ford March 17, 1863. Stoneman's Raid April 27-May 8. Brandy Station, Stevensburg, Beverly Ford, June 9. Aldie June 17. Middleburg June 19. Upperville June 21. Battle of Gettysburg, Pa., July 1-3. Monterey July 4. Smithburg July 6. Williamsport and Hagerstown July 6-7. Boonsboro July 8. Jones' Cross Roads near Williamsport July 10 and 13. Hagerstown July 11-13. Falling Waters July 14. Jones' Cross Roads July 15. Barber's Cross Roads September 1. Scout to Middleburg September 10-11. Advance from the Rapidan to the Rappahannock September 13-17. Culpeper Court House September 13. Rapidan Station September 15. Bristoe Campaign October 9-22. Warrenton or White Sulphur Springs October 12-13. Auburn Bristoe and Bristoe October 14. Advance to line of the Rappahannock November 7-8. Mine Run Campaign November 26-December 2. New Hope Church November 27. Reconnoissance to Front Royal January 1-4, 1864. Custer's Raid into Albemarle County February 28-March 1. Near Charlottesville February 29. Stannardsville March 1. Burton's Ford, Rapidan River, March 1 (Detachment). Rapidan Campaign May 3-June 15. Todd's Tavern May 5-6. Wilderness May 6-7. Todd's Tavern May 7-8. Corbin's Bridge May 8. Sheridan's Raid to the James River May 9-24. Childsburg and Davenport May 9. North Anna May 9-10. Ashland, Ground Squirrel Church and Yellow Tavern May 11. Brook's Church or fortifications of Richmond May 12. On line of the Pamunkey May 26-28. Haw's Shop May 28. Totopotomoy May 28-31. Cold Harbor May 31-June 7. Sumner's Upper Bridge June 2. Sheridan's Trevillian Raid June 7-24. Trevillian Station June 11-12. Mallory's Cross Roads June 12. Black Creek or Tunstall Station and St. Peter's Church, White House, June 21. St. Mary's Church June 24. Siege operations against Petersburg and Richmond June 24, 1864, to April 2, 1865. Warwick Swamp July 12, 1864. (Poolesville, Md., July 12, Detachment.) Demonstration north of the James July 27-29. Deep Bottom and Malvern Hill July 27-28. Lee's Mills July 30. Demonstration north of the James August 13-20. Strawberry Plains, Deep Bottom, August 14-18. Six Mile House, Weldon Railroad, August 20-21. Dinwiddie Road near Ream's Station August 23. Ream's Station August 25. Arthur's Swamp and Poplar Grove Church September 29-October 2. Expedition into Surrey County October 16-19. Boydton Plank Road, Hatcher's Run, October 27-28. Stony Creek Station December 1. Reconnoissance to Hatcher's Run and skirmishes December 8-10. Dabney's Mills, Hatcher's Run, February 5-7, 1865. Appomattox Campaign March 28-April 9. Dinwiddie Court House March 30-31. Five Forks April 1. Amelia Springs and Jettersville April 5. Sailor's Creek April 6. Farmville April 7. Appomattox Court House April 9. Surrender of Lee and his army. Expedition to Danville April 23-29. Duty in Sub-District of the Appomattox, Dept. of Virginia, till August. Mustered out August 7, 1865.

Regiment lost during service 5 Officers and 52 Enlisted men killed and mortally wounded and 4 Officers and 177 Enlisted men by disease. Total 238.

7th REGIMENT CAVALRY—"RIVER REGIMENT."

Regiment organized at Ripley, Ohio, October, 1862, and duty there till December, 1862. First Battalion (Cos. "A," "B," "C," "D"), ordered to Lexington, Ky., November 22, 1862, and duty there till December 21. 2nd Battalion ordered to Lexington, Ky., December 20, 1862, and 3rd Battalion to same point December 31, 1862. Attached to District of Central Kentucky, Dept. Ohio, to January, 1863. 2nd Brigade, District of Central Kentucky, to April, 1863. 1st Provisional Cavalry Brigade, 23rd Army Corps, Army Ohio, to June, 1863. 3rd Brigade, 1st Division, 23rd Army Corps, to August, 1863. 3rd Brigade, 4th Division, 23rd Army Corps, to November, 1863. 1st Brigade, 2nd Division, Cavalry Corps, Dept. Ohio, to May, 1864. 1st Brigade, Cavalry Division, District of Kentucky, 5th Division, 23rd Army Corps, to July, 1864. 1st Brigade, Cavalry Division, 23rd Army Corps, to August, 1864. Mounted Brigade, Cavalry Division, 23rd Army Corps, to September, 1864. 2nd Brigade, Cavalry Division, 23rd Army Corps, to November, 1864. 2nd Brigade, 6th Division, Wilson's Cavalry Corps, Military Division Mississippi, to December, 1864. 1st Brigade, 6th Division, Cavalry Corps, to February, 1865. 2nd Brigade, 4th Division, Cavalry Corps, to July, 1865.

SERVICE.—1st Battalion participated in Carter's Raid into East Tennessee and Southwest Virginia December 21, 1862, to January 5, 1863. Passage of Moccasin Gap December 29, 1862. Actions at Zollicoffer Station December 30. Watauga Bridge, Carter's Station, December 30 (Cos. "A," "D"). Regiment participated in operations in Central Kentucky against Cluke's forces February 18-March 5, 1863. Slate Creek near Mt. Sterling February 24 and March 2. Operations against Pegram March 22-April 1. Dutton's Hill March 30. Expedition to Monticello and operations in Southeast Kentucky April 26-May 12. Monticello May 1. Rocky Gap, Monticello, June 9. Carter's Raid in East Tennessee June 16-24. Knoxville June 19-20. Roger's Gap June 20. Powder Springs Gap June 21. Scout to Creelsborough June 28-30. Pursuit of Morgan July 1-25. Buffington Island, Ohio, July 19. Operations against Scott in Eastern Kentucky July 26-August 6. Near Rogersville July 27. Richmond July 28. Lancaster July 31. Paint Lick Bridge July 31. Lancaster August 1. Burnside's Campaign in East Tennessee August 16-October 19. Winter's Gap August 31. Expedition to Cumberland Gap September 4-9. Capture of Cumberland Gap September 9. Carter's Station September 22. Zollicoffer September 24. Jonesboro September 28. Blue Springs October 5 and 10. Sweetwater October 10-11. Pursuit to Bristol October 11-17. Blountsville October 13-14. Moved to Rogersville October 17-19. Knoxville Campaign November 4-December 23. Action at Rogersville November 6. Stock Creek November 14. Defence of Cumberland Gap during siege of Knoxville November 17-December 5. Morristown December 10. Cheek's Cross Roads December 12. Russellville December 12-13. Bean's Station December 14. Rutledge December 16. Blain's Cross Roads December 16-19. Rutledge December 18. Stone's Mill December 19. New Market December 23. Dandridge December 24. Mossy Creek December 26. Operations about Dandridge January 16-17, 1864. Kimbrough's Cross Roads January 16. Dandridge January 17. Operations about Dandridge January 26-28. Fair Garden January 27. Ordered to Nicholasville, Ky., February. Operations against Morgan in Kentucky May 31-June 20 (Detachment). Cynthiana June 12. March to Atlanta, Ga., July 4-26. Siege of Atlanta July 26-September 2. Stoneman's Raid to Macon July 27-August 6 (Co. "D"). Clinton and Macon July 30 (Co. "D"). Hillsborough July 30-31 (Co. "D"). Sandtown and Fairburn August 15. At Decatur till October 4. At Atlanta till November 6. Moved to Nashville, Tenn. Nashville Campaign November-December. Henryville November 23. Columbia, Duck River, November 24-27. Duck River Crossing November 28. Columbia Ford November 29. Franklin November 30.

Nashville December 15-16. Pursuit of Hood to the Tennessee River December 17-28. West Harpeth River and Franklin December 17. Spring Hill December 18. Richland Creek December 24. Pulaski December 25-26. Moved to Gravelly Springs, Ala., and duty there till March, 1865. Wilson's Raid from Chickasaw, Ala., to Macon, Ga., March 22-April 24. Montevallo March 31. Ebenezer Creek near Mapleville April 1. Selma April 2. Montgomery April 12. Columbia, Ga., April 16. Capture of Macon April 20. Scout duty in Northern Georgia till May 15. Moved to Nashville, Tenn., and duty there till July. Mustered out July 4, 1865.

Regiment lost during service 2 Officers and 26 Enlisted men killed and mortally wounded and 4 Officers and 197 Enlisted men by disease. Total 229.

8th REGIMENT CAVALRY.

Organized from 44th Ohio Infantry January 4, 1864. Regiment organizing at Camp Dennison, Ohio, January to May, 1864. Six Companies moved to Charleston, W. Va., April 26 and balance of Regiment to same place May 8, 1864. Attached to 1st Brigade, 2nd Cavalry Division, Army of West Virginia (a detachment at Beverly, W. Va., July to December, 1864), to December, 1864. Reserve Division, West Virginia, Beverly and Clarksburg, W. Va., to April, 1865. 1st Brigade, 1st Division, West Virginia, to July, 1865.

SERVICE.—March to Lewisburg May 29. Hunter's Raid to Lynchburg May 29-July 1, 1864. Action at Lexington June 11. Buchanan June 13. New London June 16. Diamond Hill June 17. Lynchburg June 17-18. Retreat to White Sulphur Springs June 18-25. Liberty June 19. Buford's Gap June 20. About Salem June 21. Moved from White Sulphur Springs to Beverly, W. Va., and duty there till January, 1865. Action near Huttonsville August 5, 1864. Action near Moorefield August 7, 1864. Moorefield and Huttonsville August 24 (Cos. "A," "C," "H" and "K" captured). Action at Beverly October 29. A detachment participated in actions at Stephenson's Depot or Newtown July 22, 1864. Battle of Winchester, Kernstown, July 24. Martinsburg July 25. Hagerstown, Md., July 29. Hancock, Md., July 31. McConnellsburg, Pa., July 31. Williamsport August 26. Martinsburg, W. Va., August 31. Bunker Hill September 2-3. Darkesville September 10. Bunker Hill September 13. Near Berryville September 14. Near Martinsburg September 18. Battle of Opequan, Winchester, September 19. Fisher's Hill September 22. Mt. Jackson September 23-24. Forest Hill or Timberville September 24. Port Republic September 28. North Shenandoah October 6. Luray Valley October 7. Battle of Cedar Creek October 19. Dry Run October 20. Milford October 25-26. Ninevah November 12. Rude's Hill near Mt. Jackson November 22. Detachment rejoined Regiment at Beverly, W. Va., December 1, 1864. Action at Beverly January 11, 1865. Mostly captured January 11. Paroled February 15 and mustered out as prisoners of war June, 1865, except the four Mounted Companies which were stationed at Clarksburg, W. Va., till July. Scout to Carrick's Ford March 14-16. Expedition through Pocohontas and Pendleton Counties June 1-13. Mustered out July 30, 1865.

Regiment lost during its service (both as 44th Ohio Infantry and 8th Ohio Cavalry) 3 Officers and 53 Enlisted men killed and mortally wounded and 1 Officer and 113 Enlisted men by disease. Total 210.

9th REGIMENT CAVALRY.

Regiment authorized October 3, 1862. Four Companies organized at Zanesville, Ohio, and designated 1st Battalion. Moved to Camp Dennison, Ohio, December 1, 1862, and duty there till April, 1863. Moved to Lexington, Ky., April 23, 1863, thence to Manchester, Ky., and duty there till June 15. Attached to 2nd Brigade, 1st Division, 23rd Army Corps, Army Ohio, to July, 1863 (1st Battalion). 2nd Brigade, 4th Division, 23rd Army Corps, to October, 1863 (1st Battalion). 4th Brigade, 4th Division, 23rd Army Corps, to November, 1863 (1st Battalion). 2nd Brigade, 2nd Division, Cavalry Corps, Army Ohio, to March, 1864 (1st Battalion). Athens, Florence and Decatur, Ala., District of North Alabama, Dept. of the Cumberland, to August, 1864 (Regiment). Mounted Brigade, Garrard's Cavalry Division, 23rd Army Corps, Army Ohio, to October, 1864. 2nd Brigade, Kilpatrick's 3rd Division, Cavalry Corps, Military Division Mississippi, to June, 1865. Dept. of North Carolina to August, 1865.

SERVICE.—Expedition into East Tennessee June 15-28, 1863. Pine Mountain Gap June 16. Big Creek Gap June 17. Wartzburg June 18. Knoxville June 19-20. Moved to Loudon, Ky., thence to Stanford July 5, and to Danville July 7. Pursuit of Morgan and Scott July 10-26. Moved to Glasgow, Ky., August 1. Burnside's Campaign in East Tennessee August 16-October 17. Occupation of Knoxville September 2. Kingsport September 18. Bristol September 19. Zollicoffer September 20-21. Hall's Ford, Watauga River September 22. Carter's Depot and Blountsville September 22. Blue Springs October 10. Rheatown October 11. Blountsville October 14. Bristol October 15. Knoxville Campaign November 4-December 23. Siege of Knoxville November 17-December 6. Kimbrough's Cross Roads January 16. Operations about Dandridge January 16-17. Dandridge January 17. Operations about Dandridge January 26-28. Fair Garden January 27. Duty at Knoxville, Tenn., till March. 2nd Battalion of Regiment organized at Camp Dennison, Ohio, November 6, 1863. 3rd Battalion organized at Camp Dennison, Ohio, December 16, 1863. Left State under orders for Nashville, Tenn., February 6, 1864, thence moved to Athens, Ala., where 1st Batalion joined. Patrol duty along the Tennessee River at Athens and Florence, Ala., till May. Moved to Decatur, Ala., May 1-5. Repulse of attack on Decatur May 8. Centre Star May 15. Duty at Decatur till July 10. Expedition to Pulaski June 1-12. Operations in District of North Alabama July 24-August 20. Curtis Wells June 24. Pond Springs June 29. Rousseau's Raid to Atlanta & West Point Railroad July 10-22. Ten Island Ford, Coosa River, July 13. Courtland, Ala., July 25. Near Auburn and Chehaw Station July 18. Siege of Atlanta July 25-August 25. McCook's Raid on Atlanta and West Point and Macon & Western Railroad July 27-31 (Detachment). Lovejoy Station July 29. Near Newnan's July 30. Near East Point August 30. Big Shanty September 2. Ordered to Nashville, Tenn., thence to Louisville, Ky., to refit. March to the sea November 15-December 10. Bear Creek Station November 16. Walnut Creek and East Macon November 20. Waynesboro November 27-28. Buckhead Creek or Reynolds' Plantation November 28. Rocky Creek Church December 2. Waynesboro December 4. Buck Creek December 7. Cypress Swamp near Sister's Ferry December 7. Ebenezer Creek December 8. Siege of Savannah December 10-21. Campaign of the Carolinas January to April, 1865. Barnwell, S. C., February 6. Aiken and Blackville February 11. Phillips' Cross Roads March 4. Taylor's Hole Creek, Averysboro March 16. Battle of Bentonville, N. C., March 19-21. Occupation of Goldsboro March 23. Raleigh April 13. Morristown April 13. Bennett's House April 26. Surrender of Johnston and his army. Duty at Concord, N. C., till July 20. Mustered out August 2, 1865.

Regiment lost during service 1 Officer and 16 Enlisted men killed and mortally wounded and 2 Officers and 186 Enlisted men by disease. Total 205.

10th REGIMENT CAVALRY.

Organized at Camp Taylor, Cleveland, Ohio, October, 1862. Left State for Nashville, Tenn., February 27, 1863. Attached to 2nd Brigade, 2nd Cavalry Division, Army of the Cumberland, to August, 1863. 3rd Brigade, 2nd Division, Cavalry Corps, Army Cumberland, to November, 1863. 2nd Brigade, 2nd Division, Cavalry Corps, Army Cumberland, to April, 1864. 2nd Brigade, Kilpatrick's 3rd Division, Cavalry Corps, Army of the Cumberland, to October, 1864. 2nd Brigade, 3rd Division, Cavalry Corps, Military Division Mississippi, to June, 1865. Dept. of North Carolina to July, 1865.

SERVICE.—Duty at Murfreesboro till June, 1863. Expedition to Auburn, Snow Hill, Liberty, etc., April 2-6. Smith's Ford April 2. Snow Hill, Woodbury, April 3. Scout to Smithville June 4-5. Snow Hill June 4. Smithville June 5. Scout on Salem Pike June 12. Middle Tennessee or Tullahoma Campaign June 23-July 7. Occupation of Middle Tennessee till August 16. Passage of Cumberland Mountains and Tennessee River and Chickamauga (Ga.) Campaign August 16-September 22. Battle of Chickamauga September 19-21. Operations against Wheeler and Roddy September 30-October 17. McMinnville October 4. Farmington October 7. March to relief of Knoxville November 27-December 8. Near Loudon December 2. Expedition to Murphey, N. C., December 6-11. Near Dandridge December 22-23 (Detachment). Dandridge December 24 (Detachment). Mossy Creek, Talbot Station, December 29. Schulz's Mill, Cosby Creek, January 14, 1864 (Detachment). Near Wilsonville January 22, 1864. Expedition to Quallatown, N. C., January 31-February 7 (Detachment). Quallatown February 5. Scout from Ringgold, Ga., to Lafayette April 24-25. Atlanta (Ga.) Campaign May 1 to September 8. Stone Church May 1. Lee's Cross Roads and Ringgold Gap May 2. Demonstrations on Resaca May 8-13. Sugar Valley May 11. Near Resaca May 13. Battle of Resaca May 14-15. Rome May 17-18. Battles about Dallas, New Hope Church and Allatoona Hills May 25-June 5. Near Stilesboro June 9 (Detachment). Operations about Marietta and against Kenesaw Mountain June 10-July 2. On line of the Chattahoochie River July 3-17. Siege of Atlanta July 22-August 25. Frogtown August 3. Lovejoy Station August 10. Sandtown and Fairburn August 15. Kilpatrick's Raid around Atlanta July 18-22. Camp Creek August 18. Red Oak and Jonesboro August 19. Lovejoy Station August 20. Claiborne August 24. Flank movement on Jonesborough August 25-30. Fairburn August 27-28. Red Oak August 28. Flint River Station and Jonesborough August 30. Battle of Jonesboro August 31-September 1. Lovejoy Station September 2-6. Campbellton September 10. Operations against Hood in North Georgia and North Alabama September 30-November 3. Camp Creek September 30. Sweetwater and Noyes Creek near Powder Springs October 2-3. Van Wert October 9-10. Dallas October 21. March to the sea November 10-December 15. Bear Creek Station November 16. Walnut Creek and East Macon November 20. Waynesboro November 27-28. Buckhead Creek or Reynolds' Plantation November 28. Louisville November 30. Waynesboro December 4. Ebenezer Creek December 8. Siege of Savannah December 10-21. Campaign of the Carolinas January to April, 1865. Aiken and Blackville, S. C., February 11. North Edisto River February 12-13. Guenter's Bridge February 14. Phillips' Cross Roads, N. C., March 4. Rockingham March 7-8. Monroe's Cross Roads March 10. Taylor's Hole Creek, Averysboro, March 16. Battle of Bentonville March 19-21. Raleigh April 12-13. Morrisville April 13. Bennett's House April 26. Surrender of Johnston and his army. Duty in the Dept. of North Carolina till July. Mustered out July 24, 1865.

Regiment lost during service 3 Officers and 34 Enlisted men killed and mortally wounded and 1 Officer and 158 Enlisted men by disease. Total 201.

11th REGIMENT CAVALRY.

Organization commenced as 7th Ohio Cavalry October, 1861. Consolidated with 6th Cavalry as a Battalion of four complete Companies December 1, 1861. Duty at Camp Dennison, Ohio, till February, 1862. Ordered to St. Louis, Mo. Battalion permanently detached from 6th Cavalry, and designated 1st Independent Battalion Ohio Cavalry. Ordered to Fort Leavenworth, Kans., April 4, 1862. March to Fort Laramie April 26-May 30. Assigned to duty along the North Platte and Sweetwater Rivers with headquarters at Pacific Springs, N. T., and the South Pass. Engaged in guarding Overland Mail routes across the plains from Julesburg to Green

River, June, 1862, to July, 1866. Action at Upper Crossing, Sweetwater, N. T., November 24, 1862. Another Battalion organized at Camp Dennison and Camp Chase, Ohio, June 26 to July 31, 1863, assigned and designation changed to 11th Regiment Cavalry, July, 1863. Action at Platte River, N. T., April 17, 1863. Cheyenne Fork July 19, 1863, and July 19, 1864. Deer Creek, Telegraph Station July 26. Operations against Indians in Nebraska August 11 to November 28, 1864. La Bonte Creek, I. T., August 14, 1864. Operations on North Platte February 2-18, 1865. Mud Springs, N. T., February 5 to 9, 1865. Rush Creek February 8-9. La Prelle, I. T., February 12. Poison Creek, I. T., March 8. LaBonte Creek, I. T., March 28. Sage Creek Station, D. T., April 6. LaPrelle Creek, I. T., April 21. Marshall Camp, I. T., April 23. Scout from Fort Laramie to Wind River, N. T., May 3-21. Skirmish at Sweetwater Station May 26. Operations on Platte and Sweetwater Rivers May 26-June 9 (Detachment). Skirmish St. Mary's Station May 27 (Detachment). Skirmishes at Sweetwater Station, N. T., May 28 and June 1. Dry Creek, I. T., June 3. Skirmish at Sage Creek, D. T., June 8 (Detachment). Platte Bridge, D. T., July 26. Tongue River, D. T., August 29. North Platte, D. T., September 15. 1st Battalion mustered out April 1, 1865. Regiment mustered out July 14, 1866.

Regiment lost during service 3 Officers and 20 Enlisted men killed and mortally wounded and 1 Officer and 60 Enlisted men by disease. Total 84.

12th REGIMENT CAVALRY.

Organized at Cleveland, Ohio, and mustered in November 24, 1863. Duty at Camp Chase, Ohio, till February, 1864, and at Camp Dennison till March. Ordered to Nashville, Tenn., March 31, 1862. Attached to 2nd Brigade, 5th Division, 23rd Army Corps, District of Kentucky, Dept. to July, 1864. 4th Brigade, 1st Division, District of Kentucky, Dept. Ohio, to February, 1865. 1st Brigade, Cavalry Division, District of East Tennessee, Dept. of the Cumberland, to July, 1865. Cavalry Brigade, District East Tennessee, to November, 1865.

SERVICE.—Operations against Morgan's Invasion of Kentucky May 31-June 20, 1864. Action at Mt. Sterling, Ky., June 9. Cynthiana June 12. Skirmish at Lebanon, Ky., July 30 (1 Co.). Burbridge's Expedition into Southwest Virginia September 20-October 17. McCormack's Farm September 23. Laurel Mountain September 29. Action at Saltsville, Va., October 2. Stoneman's Raid from Bean's Station, Tenn., into Southwest Virginia, December 10-29. Bristol December 14. Marion December 17-18. Saltsville December 20-21. Stoneman's Raid into Southwest Virginia and Western North Carolina March 21-April 25, 1865. Wilkesborough March 29. Wilkinsville N. C., April 8. Danbury April 9. Statesville and Salem April 11. Salisbury April 12. Dallas and Catawba River April 17. Swannanoah Gap April 20. Howard's Gap, Blue Ridge Mountains, April 22. Asheville April 25. Duty in Middle and East Tennessee, Dept. of the Cumberland, and in North Carolina, till November, 1865. Mustered out November 14, 1865.

Regiment lost during service 50 Enlisted men killed and mortally wounded and 112 Enlisted men by disease. Total 164.

13th REGIMENT CAVALRY.

Organized by a consolidation of 4th and 5th Battalions Cavalry, and mustered in May 5, 1864. Left State for Annapolis, Md., May 11, thence moved to White House Landing, Va., May 18. Attached to 1st Brigade, 3rd Division, 9th Army Corps, Army Potomac, June 8 to August 10, 1864. 1st Brigade, 1st Division, 9th Army Corps, to December 10. 3rd Brigade, 2nd Division, Cavalry Corps, Army of the Potomac, to May, 1865. Sub-District of the Appomattox, District of the Nottaway, Dept. of Virginia, to August, 1865.

SERVICE.—At Washington, D. C., May 14-18, 1864. March to White House Landing May 18, and duty there till June. Moved to Cold Harbor, Va. Operations about

Cold Harbor June 6-12. Before Petersburg June 16-19. Siege operations against Petersburg and Richmond, Va., June 16, 1864, to April 2, 1865. Mine Explosion July 30, 1864. Weldon Railroad August 18-21. Poplar Springs Church September 29-October 2. Vaughan and Squirrel Level Road October 8. Boydton Plank Road, Hatcher's Run, October 27-28. Equipped for Cavalry services December 12. Dabney's Mills, Hatcher's Run, February 5-7, 1865. Appomattox Campaign March 28-April 9. Dinwiddie Court House March 30-31. Five Forks April 1. Fall of Petersburg April 2. Amelia Springs April 5. Sailor's Creek and Harper's Farm April 6. Farmville April 7. Appomattox Court House April 9. Surrender of Lee and his army. Expedition to Danville to co-operate with Gen. Sherman April 23-29. Assigned to provost duty in Amelia and Powhatan Counties till August 10. Mustered out August 10, 1865.

Regiment lost during service 4 Officers and 61 Enlisted men killed and mortally wounded and 1 Officer and 51 Enlisted men by disease. Total 117.

1st INDEPENDENT BATTALION CAVALRY.

Organization commenced as 7th Ohio Cavalry October, 1861. Consolidated with 6th Cavalry as a Battalion of four complete Companies December 1, 1861. Duty at Camp Dennison, Ohio, till February, 1862. Ordered to St. Louis, Mo. Battalion permanently detached from 6th Cavalry and designated 1st Independent Battalion Cavalry February, 1862. Ordered to Fort Leavenworth, Kan., April 4, 1862. March to Fort Laramie April 26-May 30. Assigned to duty along the North Platte and Sweetwater Rivers with Headquarters at Pacific Springs, N. T., and the South Pass. Engaged in guarding Overland Mail routes across the plains from Julesburg to Green River. Action at Upper Crossing, Sweetwater, N. T., November 24, 1862. Action at Platte River, N. T., April 17, 1863. Cheyenne Fork July 19, 1863. Designation changed to 11th Ohio Cavalry July, 1863 (which see).

2nd INDEPENDENT BATTALION CAVALRY.

Organized at Columbus, Ohio, for guard duty. 1st Company August 16, 1864; 2nd Company October 18, 1864. Mustered out 1st Company October 15, 1864; 2nd Company December 16, 1864.

Battalion lost during service 3 by disease.

4th INDEPENDENT BATTALION CAVALRY.

Organized at Cincinnati, Ohio, for 6 months August 3 to September 21, 1863. Mustered out February 15 to March 14, 1864.

Battalion lost during service 16 by disease.

5th INDEPENDENT BATTALION CAVALRY.

Organized at Columbus, Ohio, for six months July 9-September 2, 1863. Duty on southern border of Ohio till August. Moved to Camp Chase, Ohio, and Battalion organization there completed. Ordered to Cincinnati, Ohio, September 8, thence moved into District of Eastern Kentucky, Headquarters at Flemingsburg. Engaged in scouting and raiding guerrillas in that District till February, 1864. Skirmish in Morgan County, Ky., October 6, 1863, and at Liberty, Ky., October 12, 1863. Mustered out February 15, 1864.

Battalion lost during service 1 Enlisted man killed and 2 Enlisted men by disease. Total 3.

McLAUGHLIN'S INDEPENDENT SQUADRON CAVALRY.

Organized at Mansfield, Ohio, October and November, 1861. Left State for Kentucky November 29, 1861. Attached to 18th Brigade, Army Ohio, to March, 1862. District of Eastern Kentucky, Dept. Ohio, to July, 1862. 3rd Brigade, Kanawha Division, West Virginia, to November, 1862. District of Eastern Kentucky, Dept. Ohio, to June, 1863. 1st Brigade, 4th Division, 23rd Army Corps, Dept. Ohio, to September, 1863. Headquarters 23rd Army Corps, Dept. Ohio, to April, 1864. 3rd Brigade, 2nd Division, District of Kentucky, 5th Division, 23rd Army Corps, to June, 1864. 3rd Brigade,

Cavalry Division, 23rd Army Corps, to August, 1864. Mounted Brigade, Cavalry Division, 23rd Army Corps, to September, 1864. 2nd Brigade, Cavalry Division, 23rd Army Corps, to October, 1864. 2nd Brigade, Kilpatrick's 3rd Division, Cavalry Corps, Military Division Mississippi, to July, 1865.

SERVICE.—Garfield's Campaign in Eastern Kentucky against Humphrey Marshall December 23, 1861, to January 30, 1862. Garfield's Expedition to the Big Sandy September 23-30, 1861. Advance on Paintsville December 31, 1861, to January 8, 1862. Action at Jennies January 7, 1862. Occupation of Paintsville January 8. Abbott's Hill January 9. Middle Creek January 10. Prestonburg January 11. Expedition to the Little Sandy January 24-30. Expedition to Pound Gap, Cumberland Mountains, March 14-17. Action at Pound Gap March 16. Duty at Piketown till June. Moved to Prestonburg, thence to Louisa, Ky., July 15. Duty at Louisa till December. Operations in District of Eastern Kentucky, Dept. of the Ohio, to August, 1863. Skirmishes near Louisa March 25-26, 1863. Expedition from Beaver Creek into Southwest Virginia July 3-11. Capture of Abingdon, Va., July 5. Action at Gladesville, Va., July 7. Burnside's Campaign in East Tennessee August 16-October 17. Escort and picket duty at Knoxville till January 10, 1864. Near Loudoun November 14. Siege of Knoxville, Tenn., November 17-December 5. Moved to Nicholasville, Ky. Duty there and in Kentucky till June. Moved to join Stoneman June 13-19. Join Sherman's Army near Big Shanty, Ga., June 26. Atlanta (Ga.) Campaign June 26-September 8. Assault on Kenesaw June 27. On line of the Chattahoochie River July 5-17. Stoneman's Raid to Macon July 27-August 6. Macon and Clinton July 30. Hillsborough July 30-31. Sunshine Church August 3. Jug Tavern and Mulberry Creek August 3. Siege of Atlanta August 11-September 3. March to the sea November 15-December 10. Bear Creek Station November 16. Walnut Creek and East Macon November 20. Waynesboro November 27-28. Buckhead Creek, or Reynolds' Plantation, November 28. Rocky Creek Church December 2. Waynesboro December 4. Ebenezer Creek December 8. Siege of Savannah December 10-21. Campaign of the Carolinas January to April, 1865. Aiken and Blackville, S. C., February 11. North Edisto River February 12-13. Phillips Cross Roads, N. C., March 4. Taylor's Hole Creek, Averysboro, March 16. Bentonville March 19-21. Raleigh April 12-13. Morrisville April 13. Bennett's House April 26. Surrender of Johnston and his army. Duty at Concord, N. C., till July. Moved to Raleigh and consolidated with 5th Ohio Cavalry July 28, 1865.

Squadron lost during service 1 Enlisted man killed and 49 Enlisted men by disease. Total 50.

BURDSELL'S INDEPENDENT COMPANY CAVALRY.

Organized at Cincinnati, Ohio, June 5, 1861. Ordered to West Virginia. Attached to Rosecrans' Brigade, Army of West Virginia, to July, 1861. 1st Brigade, Army of Occupation, West Virginia, to August. West Virginia Campaign July 6-17, 1861. Actions at Rich Mountain July 11 and August 5. Scarytown July 17. Mustered out August 23, 1861.

GEORGE'S INDEPENDENT COMPANY CAVALRY.

Organized for three months at Gallipolis, Ohio, July 2, 1861. Attached to Cox's Kanawha Brigade, and duty in Kanawha District, West Virginia, till September. Mustered out September 10, 1861.

HARLAN'S LIGHT CAVALRY.

Organized at Camp Chase, Ohio, August 31, 1861. Moved to Philadelphia and attached to 11th Pennsylvania Cavalry as Company "M." (See 11th Pennsylvania Cavalry.)

IRONTON INDEPENDENT COMPANY CAVALRY.

No details.

UNION LIGHT GUARD.

Organized at Columbus, Ohio, December 17, 1863, for duty as body guard to President Lincoln. Left State for Washington, D. C., September 22, 1863. Duty as guard at the White House and at the War Department and other public buildings till September, 1865. Mustered out September 9, 1865.

3rd INDEPENDENT COMPANY CAVALRY.

Organized at Cincinnati, Ohio, July 4, 1861. Ordered to the Kanawha Valley, W. Va. Attached to Cox's Kanawha Brigade to October, 1861. District of the Kanawha, W. Va., to March, 1862. Kanawha Division, West Virginia, to August, 1862. Kanawha Division, 9th Army Corps, Army of the Potomac, to October, 1862. Kanawha Division, District West Virginia, Dept. Ohio, to March, 1863. Averill's 4th Separate Brigade, 8th Corps, Middle Dept., to June, 1863. Averill's 4th Separate Brigade, Dept. of West Virginia, to December, 1863. 2nd Brigade, 4th Division, West Virginia, to April, 1864. Kelly's Command, Reserve Division, West Virginia, to April, 1865. 2nd Brigade, 1st Infantry Division, West Virginia, to May, 1865.

SERVICE.—Duty in the Kanawha Valley, W. Va., till August, 1862. Action at Princeton September 16, 1861. Greenbrier River October 3. Operations in the Kanawha Valley and New River Region October 19-November 16, 1861. New River October 19-21. Moved to Gauley and duty there till May, 1862. Advance on Virginia & Tennessee Railroad May 10. At Flat Top Mountain till August, 1862. Moved to Washington, D. C., August 15-24. Maryland Campaign September 6-24. Frederick City, Md., September 12. South Mountain September 14. Battle of Antietam September 16-17. March to Clear Springs October 8, thence to Hancock and to the Kanawha Valley October 9-November 17. Duty in the Kanawha Valley till April, 1863. Operations against Imboden's Raid in West Virginia April 20-May 14. At Buckhannon, Bulltown, Clarksburg, Parkersburg and Weston May to July. Moved to Beverly July 2-7. Beverly July 2-3. Duty at Beverly till November. Shanghai July 16. Martinsburg July 18-19. Averill's Raid through Hardy, Pendleton, Highland, Bath, Greenbrier and Pocohontas Counties August 5-31. Rocky Gap, near White Sulphur Springs, August 25-26. Averill's Raid from Beverly to Lewisburg and the Virginia & Tennessee Railroad November 1-17. Droop Mountain November 6. Averill's Raid from New Creek to Salem and the Virginia & Tennessee Railroad December 8-25. Descent on Salem December 16. Jackson River, near Covington, December 19. Duty at Beverly till April, 1864, and at Harper's Ferry and on the Baltimore & Ohio Railroad till May, 1865. Mustered out May 22, 1865.

Company lost during service 5 Enlisted men killed and mortally wounded and 10 Enlisted men by disease. Total 15.

4th INDEPENDENT CAVALRY COMPANY.

Organized at Georgetown, Ohio, July 9, 1861. Moved to Camp Chase, Ohio, July 10, thence to St. Louis, Mo., August 19-21. Provost duty there till September, and at Syracuse, Mo., till October. Attached to Gen. Pope's Command, Army of the West. Fremont's advance on Springfield, Mo., October 21-November 7. Scouting and skirmishing in Western and Northern Missouri till February, 1862. Skirmish at Roan's Tan Yard, Silver Creek, January 8, 1862. Moved to Benton Barracks, Mo., February, 1862; thence to St. Louis, and duty at Headquarters of Gen. Halleck till April 9. Moved to Pittsburg Landing, Tenn., as escort to Gen. Halleck, and duty at Dept. Headquarters till August. Advance on and siege of Corinth, Miss., April 29-May 30. Pursuit to Booneville May 31-June 12. Scout duty in Western Tennessee, attached to the Commands of Gen. McClernand, Logan and Lawler, till November. Actions at Bolivar, Tenn., August 22; Greenville August 23; Bolivar August 25; Britton's Lane, near Denmark September 1. Grant's Central Mississippi Campaign Novem-

ber-December. Assigned to duty as escort to Gen. J. B. McPherson, Commanding 17th Army Corps, Army of the Tennessee, December, 1862, to April, 1864, and as escort to Gen. McPherson, Commanding Army of the Tennessee, to July, 1864, then as escort to Headquarters 17th Army Corps to May, 1865, participating in the movement to Young's Point and Milliken's Bend, La., and operations against Vicksburg, Miss., February to July, 1863. Movement on Bruinsburg and turning Grand Gulf April 25-30. Battles of Port Gibson May 1; North Fork, Bayou Pierrie, May 3; Willow Springs May 3; Utica May 9-10; Raymond May 12; Jackson May 14; Champion's Hill May 16. Siege of Vicksburg May 18-July 4. Meridian Campaign February 3-March 2, 1864. Champion's Hill February 4. Atlanta (Ga.) Campaign May to September. Demonstrations on Resaca May 8-13. Battle of Resaca. Battles about Dallas May 25-June 5. Operations about Marietta and against Kenesaw Mountain June 10-July 2. Assault on Kenesaw June 27. Nickajack Creek July 2-5. Chattahoochie River July 5-17. Battle of Atlanta July 22. Siege of Atlanta July 22-August 25. Operations against Hood in North Georgia and North Alabama September 29-November 3. March to the sea November 15-December 10. Siege of Savannah December 10-21. Campaign of the Carolinas January to April, 1865. Mt. Elon, S. C., February 27. Battle of Bentonville, N. C., March 20-21. Occupation of Goldsboro and Raleigh. Bennett's House April 26. Surrender of Johnston and his army. March to Washington, D. C., via Richmond, Va., April 29-May 20. Grand Review May 24. Old members mustered out July 16, 1864. Company mustered out May 28, 1865.

Company lost during service 5 Enlisted men killed and mortally wounded and 16 Enlisted men by disease. Total 21.

5th INDEPENDENT COMPANY CAVALRY.

No details.

6th INDEPENDENT COMPANY CAVALRY.

Organized at Camp Dennison, Ohio, August and September, 1861. Moved to Washington, D. C., September 23, 1861. Duty at Park House and near Old Soldiers' Home till December. Assigned to 3rd New York Cavalry as Company "I" and joined Regiment at Poolesville, Md., December 9, 1861. (See 3rd New York Cavalry.)

1st REGIMENT HEAVY ARTILLERY.

Regiment organized at Portsmouth, Ohio, as the 117th Ohio Volunteer Infantry September 15, 1862. Ordered to Kentucky October 2. Attached to District of Eastern Kentucky, Dept. of the Ohio, October, 1862, to February, 1863. Covington, Ky., District Kentucky, Dept. Ohio, to August, 1863. Designation of Regiment changed to 1st Heavy Artillery May 2, 1863. District of North Central Kentucky, Dept. Ohio, to April, 1864. 2nd Brigade, 4th Division, 23rd Army Corps, Dept. of Ohio, to February, 1865. 1st Brigade, 4th Division, District of East Tennessee, Dept. of the Cumberland, to July, 1865.

SERVICE.—Ordered to Kentucky, October 2, 1862. Camp at Ashland, Ky., till January, 1863. Moved to Paintsville, Ky., thence to Covington, Ky., via Peach Orchard, Louisa and Catlettsburg, February, 1863. Constructing fortifications around Coverington and Newport, Ky., till August. Guard duty in Kentucky by detachments, Company "D" at Paris, Companies "F" and "I" at Lexington, "H," "K," "L," and "M" at Camp Nelson, till January, 1864. At Camp Burnside January 14 to February 19. March over mountains to Knoxville, Tenn., February 19-March 9 and duty there till June. On railroad guard duty in Tennessee till September. Murphy, N. C., June 28 (Cos. "C," "H," "L," "M"). Repulse of Wheeler's attacks on the Chattanooga, Knoxville & Virginia Railroad, August. Athens August 1 (Detachment). Pursuit of Confederates from Athens into North Carolina August 1-3. Murphy, N. C., August 2 (Cos. "C," "H," "L" and "M"). Detachments from Companies "C," "H," "L" and "M". Sweetwater and Philadelphia August 20 (Detachments).

Strawberry Plains, August 24. Gillem's Expedition from East Tennessee toward Southwestern Virginia September 20-October 17 (Cos. "B," "F," "G," "I" and "K"). Moved to Cleveland, Tenn., October 7, thence to Chattanooga October 11 and return to Cleveland October 19. Duty at Cleveland and Charleston till December. Foraging Expeditions on the French Broad and Chucky River in East Tennessee and North Carolina December, 1864, to January, 1865. Stoneman's Campaign in Southwest Virginia and Western North Carolina February to April, 1865. Duty in District of East Tennessee, Dept. of the Cumberland, to July. Mustered out July 25, 1865.

Regiment lost during service 6 Enlisted men killed and mortally wounded and 1 Officer and 164 Enlisted men by disease. Total 171.

2nd REGIMENT HEAVY ARTILLERY.

Organized at Camp Dennison, Ohio, and Covington, Ky., and mustered in Company "A" July 20, Company "B" August 5, Company "C" August 26, Companies "D," "H," "I," "K" and "L" September 7, Companies "E" and "M" September 9, Company "G" September 19 and Company "F" September 23, 1863. Regiment served by Detachments till May, 1864. Attached to District of Kentucky, Dept. of the Ohio, to May, 1864. Cleveland, Tenn., Dept. of the Ohio, to October, 1864. 2nd Brigade, 4th Division, 23rd Army Corps, Dept. of the Ohio, to February, 1864. 2nd Brigade, 4th Division, District of East Tennessee, Dept. of the Cumberland, to March, 1865. 1st Brigade, 4th Division, District East Tennessee, to August, 1865.

SERVICE.—Company "A" moved to Covington August 19, 1863, thence to Fort Jones Muldraugh's Hill October 11, and duty there till January 10, 1864. At Fort DeWolf, near Shepherdsville, till May. Moved to Cleveland, Tenn., May 24. Company "B" moved to Covington Barracks August 19, thence to Bowling Green, Ky., September 5, and duty there till May 26, 1864. Moved to Charleston, Tenn., May 26. Company "D" moved to Muldraugh's Hill, Ky., and duty at Fort Saunders till May 26, 1864. Garrison at Tyner's Station till October 9, 1864, then joined Regiment at Loudoun, Tenn. Company "E" moved to Muldraugh's Hill and garrison Fort Boyle till May 26, 1864. Moved to Cleveland, Tenn., May 26, 1864. Company "F" moved to Bowling Green, Ky., and duty there till May 26, 1864. Moved to Charleston, Tenn., May 26. Company "G" duty at Bowling Green till May 26, 1864. Moved to Charleston, Tenn., May 26. Company "H" moved to Munfordsville October 11, 1863, and garrison duty at Battery McConnell till May 26, 1864. Moved to Cleveland, Tenn., May 26. Company "I" moved to Shepherdsville and duty at Fort DeWolf till January 10, 1864, and at Fort Nelson till May 26. Moved to Cleveland May 26, 1864. Company "K" moved to Munfordsville October 11 and duty there till May 26, 1864. Moved to Charleston, Tenn., May 26. Company "L" moved to Frankfort, Ky., October 11, 1863, and duty at Fort Boone till December. At Battery Simons, Munfordsville, till May 26 1864. Moved to Cleveland, Tenn., May 26. Company "M" moved to Munfordsville, Ky., September 18, 1863, and garrison duty at Fort Willich till January 10, 1864, and at Fort Taylor, Camp Nelson, till May 26. Moved to Cleveland, Tenn., May 26. Duty at Cleveland, Tenn., till October, 1864 (Cos. "A," "E," "H," "I," "L" and "M"). At Charleston, Tenn., till August, 1864 (Cos. "B," "C," "F," "G" and "K"); then at Cleveland till October. Action with Wheeler near Cleveland August 17. Charleston August 19. Pursuit of Wheeler August 22-28. Moved to Loudoun, Tenn., October 9, and duty there till November 18. Morristown November 13. Russellsville November 14. Tillson's movement to Strawberry Plains, Tenn., November 16-17. Flat Creek November 17. At Knoxville till December 7. Ammon's Expedition to Bean's Station December 7-29 (Co. "A" duty at Knoxville till January 9, 1865). At Camp Rothrock and Fort Saunders till August. Company "B" duty at Knoxville, Camp

Rothrock and Fort Saunders till August. Cos. "C," "D," "E" and "F" at Knoxville, Camp Rothrock and Loudoun till August. Co. "G" at Nashville till February 1, 1865, and at Athens till August. Skirmish at Athens February 16, 1865 (Detachment). Sweetwater February 16 (Detachment). Company "H" at Strawberry Plains till August. Company "I" at Fort Gilpin, Knoxville, till August. Company "K" at Clinch Gap till December 21, 1864, at Fort Lee Knoxville, and at Greenville till August. Company "L" at Knoxville till August, 1865. Company "M" at Athens till August, 1865. Regiment mustered out August 23, 1865.

Regiment lost during service 1 Officer and 2 Enlisted men killed and mortally wounded and 3 Officers and 170 Enlisted men by disease. Total 176.

BARNETT'S 1st LIGHT ARTILLERY

Six Companies organized at Cleveland, Ohio. Moved to Columbus, Ohio, and mustered in April 22, 1861. Moved to Marietta, Ohio, and duty there till May 30. Batteries "D" and "F" moved from Camp Putnam, Marietta to Parkersburg, W. Va., May 29, thence to Clarksburg, Webster and Phillippi May 29-June 3. Action at Phillippi June 3. Other four Companies left Marietta May 30. Moved to Benwood, thence to Grafton and Phillippi, W. Va. West Virginia Campaign July 6-17. Action at Bealington July 7. Laurel Hill July 8. Carrick's Ford July 14. Ordered to Columbus, Ohio, and mustered out July 27, 1861.

COTTER'S INDEPENDENT BATTERY LIGHT ARTILLERY.

Organized at Cleveland, Ohio, April 25, 1861. Moved to Camp Chase, Ohio, and mustered in July 1, 1861. Moved to Gallipolis, Ohio, thence with Cox, into West Virginia. Action at Scarrytown July 17. At Gauley Bridge till August. Mustered out at Columbus, Ohio, September 3, 1861.

PAULSON'S INDEPENDENT BATTERY LIGHT ARTILLERY.

Organized at Columbus, Ohio, September 2, 1862. Mustered out September 22, 1862.

WILLIAMS' INDEPENDENT BATTERY LIGHT ARTILLERY.

Organized at Canton, Ohio, June 25, 1861, and mustered in at Camp Chase June 28. Attached to Cox's Kanawha Brigade, Army of West Virginia. Operations on the Gauley and Kanawha Rivers, W. Va., to October, 1861. Affair at Scarry Creek July 17. Captured a gun and became a two gun Battery. Charlestown, W. Va, July 21. Gauley Bridge July 29. Hawk's Nest or Devil's Elbow, Little Sewell Mountain, August 18. Served three months and re-enlisted for three months. Mustered out at Columbus, Ohio, November 6, 1861.

1st REGIMENT LIGHT ARTILLERY.
BATTERY "A," 1st REGIMENT LIGHT ARTILLERY.

Organized at Camp Chase, Ohio, and mustered in September 6, 1861. Moved to Louisville, Ky., September 25, thence to Camp Nevin, Ky., October 22. Attached to Thomas' Command, Camp Nevin, Ky., to November, 1861. Negley's Brigade, McCook's Command, at Nolin, Ky., to December, 1861. 6th Brigade, 2nd Division, Army Ohio, to September, 1862. Artillery, 2nd Division, 1st Corps, Army Ohio, to November, 1862. 1st Brigade, 2nd Division, Right Wing, 14th Army Corps, Army of the Cumberland, to January, 1863. Artillery, 2nd Division, 20th Army Corps, Army of the Cumberland, to October, 1863. 1st Division, Artillery Reserve, Dept. of the Cumberland, to March, 1864. 2nd Division, Artillery Reserve, Dept. of the Cumberland, to April, 1864. Artillery, 2nd Division, 4th Army Corps, Dept. of the Cumberland, to July, 1864. Artillery Brigade, 4th Army Corps, to November, 1864. District of Nashville, Tenn., Dept. Cumberland, to March, 1865. 4th Sub-District, Middle Tennessee, Dept. of the Cumberland, to July, 1865.

SERVICE.—Duty on Green River, Ky., December 10, 1861, to February 13, 1862. Advance on Bowling Green and Nashville, Tenn., February 13-March 3. March to Duck River March 16-21, and to Savannah, Tenn., March 31-April 6. Battle of Shiloh April 7. Advance on and siege of Corinth, Miss., April 29-May 30. March to Battle Creek, Ala., June 10-July 18, and duty there till August 20. March to Louisville, Ky., in pursuit of Bragg August 20-September 26. Siege of Munfordsville, Ky., September 14-17. Pursuit of Bragg into Kentucky October 1-16: Lawrenceburg October 8. Dog Walk October 9. March to Nashville, Tenn., October 19-November 7, and duty there till December 26. Advance on Murfreesboro December 26-30. Battle of Stone's River December 30-31, 1862, and January 1 3, 1863. At Murfreesboro till June. Reconnoissance from Murfreesboro March 6-7. Duck River Island April 26. Middle Tennessee or Tullahoma Campaign June 23-July 7. Liberty Gap June 24-27. Manchester July 1. Occupation of Middle Tennessee till August 16. Passage of Cumberland Mountains and Tennessee River and Chickamauga (Ga.) Campaign August 16-September 22. Battle of Chickamauga September 19-20. Siege of Chattanooga, Tenn., September 24-October 18. Joined Gen. Spear at Sale Creek October 18. Action at Blythe's Ferry November 13. March through East Tennessee to Strawberry Plains November 28, 1863, to January 30, 1864. Duty in East Tennessee till April, 1864. Atlanta (Ga.) Campaign May to September. Demonstration on Rocky Faced Ridge May 8-11. Buzzard's Roost Gap May 8-9. Battle of Resaca May 14-15. Adairsville May 17. Near Kingston May 18-19. Near Cassville May 19. Advance on Dallas May 22-25. Operations on line of Pumpkin Vine Creek and battles about Dallas, New Hope Church and Allatoona Hills May 25-June 5. Operations about Marietta and against Kenesaw Mountain June 10-July 2. Pine Hill June 11-14. Lost Mountain June 15-17. Assault on Kenesaw June 27. Ruff's Station, Smyrna Camp Ground, July 4. Chattahoochie River July 5-17. Buckhead, Nancy's Creek, July 18. Peach Tree Creek July 19-20. Siege of Atlanta July 22-August 25. Flank movement on Jonesboro August 25-30. Battle of Jonesboro August 31-September 1. Lovejoy Station September 2-6. Operations against Hood in North Georgia and North Alabama September 29-November 3. Nashville, Tenn., Campaign November-December. In front of Columbia, Duck River, November 24-27. Spring Hill November 29. Battle of Franklin November 30. Battle of Nashville December 15-16. Moved captured cannon off the field December 17. Duty at Nashville and Gallatin, Tenn., and in District of Middle Tennessee till July. Mustered out July 31, 1865.

Battery lost during service 15 Enlisted men killed and mortally wounded and 33 Enlisted men by disease. Total 48.

BATTERY "B" 1st REGIMENT LIGHT ARTILLERY.

Battery organized at Camp Dennison, Ohio, and mustered in October 8, 1861. Ordered to Camp Dick Robinson, Ky. Attached to 1st Division, Army of Ohio, to March, 1862. 7th Independent Brigade, Army of Ohio, to July, 1862. Artillery, 4th Division, Army of Ohio, to September, 1862. Artillery, 4th Division, 2nd Corps, Army of Ohio, to November, 1862. Artillery, 2nd Division, Left Wing 14th Army Corps, Army of the Cumberland, to January, 1863. Artillery, 2nd Division, 21st Army Corps, Army of the Cumberland, to October, 1863. 1st Division, Artillery Reserve, Dept. of the Cumberland, to March, 1864. Artillery, 2nd Division, 12th Army Corps, Army of the Cumberland, to April, 1864. Garrison Artillery, Bridgeport, Ala., Dept. of the Cumberland, to July, 1865.

SERVICE.—Action at Rockcastle Hills or Camp Wildcat, Ky., October 21, 1861. Duty at Fishing Creek November 5, 1861, to January 17, 1862. Action at Logan's Cross Roads, Ky., January 19. Battle of Mill Springs January 20. At Somerset, Ky., till February 10. Movement to Nashville, Tenn., February 10-March 4. Expedition to Rodgersville May 13-14. Lambs Ferry, Ala.,

May 14. Action at Chattanooga June 7. Engaged by sections in Expeditions through Middle Tennessee till July 10. Moved to Murfreesboro, Tenn., July 18. March in pursuit of Bragg to Louisville, Ky., September 3-22. Pursuit of Bragg into Kentucky October 1-10. Battle of Perryville, Ky, October 8 (Reserve). Pursuit of Bragg to Loudon October 10-22. Wild Cat October 17. Nelson's Cross Roads October 18. March to Nashville, Tenn., October 22-November 7, and duty there till December 26. Advance on Murfreesboro, Tenn., December 26-30. Lavergne December 26-27. Battle of Stone's River December 30-31, 1862, and January 1-3, 1863. Outpost duty at Cripple Creek January 7 to June 24. Expedition to Woodbury April 2. Middle Tennessee or Tullahoma Campaign June 24-July 7. Occupation of Middle Tennessee till August 16. Passage of Cumberland Mountains and Tennessee River and Chickamauga (Ga.) Campaign August 16-September 22. Lee and Gordon's Mills September 11-13. Battle of Chickamauga September 19-21. Siege of Chattanooga, Tenn., September 24-November 23. Chattanooga-Ringgold Campaign November 23-27. Battles of Mission Ridge November 24-25. Moved to Nashville, Tenn., December 4, and duty there till March, 1864. Moved to Bridgeport, Ala., March 26, and garrison duty there till July, 1865. Elrod's Tan Yard January 27, 1865 (Detachment). Mustered out July 22, 1865.

Battery lost during service 11 Enlisted men killed and mortally wounded and 1 Officer and 28 Enlisted men by disease. Total 40.

BATTERY "C" 1st REGIMENT LIGHT ARTILLERY.

Organized at Camp Dennison, near Cincinnati, Ohio, and mustered in September 9, 1861. Left State for Camp Dick Robinson, Ky., October 1. Attached to Schoepf's Brigade, Army of Ohio, to December, 1861. Artillery, 1st Division, Army of Ohio, to September, 1862. Artillery, 1st Division, 3rd Army Corps, Army of the Ohio, to November, 1862. Artillery 3rd Division (Centre), 14th Army Corps, Army of the Cumberland, to January, 1863. Artillery, 3rd Division, 14th Army Corps, to October, 1863. 1st Division, Artillery Reserve, Dept. of the Cumberland, to March, 1864. Artillery, 2nd Division, 11th Army Corps, Army of the Cumberland, to April, 1864. Artillery, 3rd Division, 20th Army Corps, Army of the Cumberland, to July, 1864. Artillery Brigade, 20th Army Corps, to June, 1865.

SERVICE.—Advance on Camp Hamilton, Ky., January 1-17, 1862. Battle of Mill Springs January 19-20. Moved to Louisville, Ky., thence to Nashville, Tenn., February 11-March 3. Moved to Savannah, Tenn., March 20-April 8. Advance on and siege of Corinth, Miss., April 29-May 30. Pursuit to Booneville May 31-June 12. March to Iuka, Miss., and Tuscombia, Ala., June 17-29; thence to Winchester July 29-August 7; thence to Dechard and Pelham Gap August 19-31. Moved to Nashville, Tenn., September 1-7; thence march to Louisville, Ky., in pursuit of Bragg September 14-26. Pursuit of Bragg into Kentucky October 1-15. Battle of Perryville, Ky., October 8 (Reserve). March to Gallatin, Tenn., October 20-November 7, and duty there till December 25. Expedition through Kentucky to intercept Morgan December 25, 1862, to January 2, 1863. Boston December 29, 1862. Action at Rolling Fork December 29-30. Duty at Lavergne till June, 1863. Expedition toward Columbia March 4-14. Middle Tennessee (or Tullahoma) Campaign June 24-July 7. Hoover's Gap June 24-26. Occupation of Middle Tennessee till August 16. Passage of the Cumberland Mountains and Tennessee River and Chickamauga (Ga.) Campaign August 16-September 22. Battle of Chickamauga, Ga., September 19-21. Siege of Chattanooga, Tenn., September 24-November 23. Chattanooga-Ringgold Campaign November 23-27. Battles of Mission Ridge November 24-25. Re-enlisted January 4, 1864. Atlanta (Ga.) Campaign May to September, 1864. Demonstrations against Rocky Faced Ridge and Dalton May 5-13. Battle of Resaca May 14-15. Near Cassville May 19.

New Hope Church May 25. Battles about Dallas, New Hope Church and Allatoona Hills May 25-June 5. Big Shanty June 4. Operations about Marietta and against Kenesaw Mountain June 10-July 2. Pine Hill June 11-14. Lost Mountain June 15-17. Golgotha or Gilgal Church June 15. Muddy Creek June 17. Noyes Church June 19. Kolb's Farm June 22. Assault on Kenesaw June 27. Ruff's Station July 4. Chattahoochie River July 5-17. Peach Tree Creek July 19-20. Siege of Atlanta July 22-August 25. Operations at Chattahoochie River Bridge August 26-September 2. Occupation of Atlanta September 2-November 15. March to the sea November 15-December 10. Siege of Savannah December 10-21. Campaign of the Carolinas January to April, 1865. Chesterfield, S. C., and Thompson's Creek, near Chesterfield, March 2. Taylor's Hole Creek, Averysboro, N. C., March 16. Battle of Bentonville March 19-21. Occupation of Goldsboro and Raleigh, N. C. Near Smithfield April 11. Bennett's House April 26. Surrender of Johnston and his army. March to Washington, D. C., via Richmond, Va., April 29-May 20. Grand Review May 24. Mustered out June 15, 1865.

Battery lost during service 7 Enlisted men killed and mortally wounded and 29 Enlisted men by disease. Total 36.

BATTERY "D" 1st REGIMENT LIGHT ARTILLERY.

Organized at Camp Dennison, near Cincinnati, Ohio, September, 1861. Moved to Mt. Sterling, Ky., October 1-10. Attached to Nelson's Command, Mt. Sterling, Ky., to December, 1861. Artillery, 2nd Division, Army of Ohio, to February, 1862. Artillery, 4th Division, Army of Ohio, to September, 1862. Captured at Munfordsville, Ky. 33rd Brigade, 10th Division, 1st Corps, Army of Ohio, to November, 1862 (1 Section). 2nd Brigade, Cavalry Division, Army of the Cumberland, to December, 1862 (Section). Artillery, 1st Cavalry Division, Army of the Cumberland, to March, 1863. Artillery, 2nd Cavalry Division, Army of the Cumberland, to December, 1863 (Section). Battery at Columbus, Ohio, January to April, 1863. 2nd Brigade, 1st Division, 23rd Army Corps, Army of Ohio, to July, 1863. 1st Brigade, 4th Division, 23rd Army Corps, to August, 1863. 1st Brigade, 3rd Division, 23rd Army Corps, to April, 1864. Artillery, 3rd Division, 23rd Army Corps, to February, 1865. Artillery, 3rd Division, 23rd Army Corps, Dept. of North Carolina, to July, 1865.

SERVICE.—Skirmish at West Liberty, Ky., October 23, 1861. Nelson's Expedition up the Big Sandy October 23-November 17. Ivy Creek November 7. Ivy Mountain November 8. Moved to Louisville, Ky., November 17-25; thence to Munfordsville, Ky., November 28-29. Moved to Nashville, Tenn., February 13-25, 1862. Occupation of Nashville February 25. Moved to Pittsburg Landing, Tenn., March 18-April 6. Battle of Shiloh, Tenn., April 7. Advance on and siege of Corinth, Miss., April 29-May 30. Occupation of Corinth May 30. Pursuit to Booneville October 31-June 12. Buell's Campaign in Northern Alabama and Middle Tennessee till August. March to Lebanon, thence to Munfordsville, Ky., August 23-September 6. Siege of Munfordsville September 14-17. Battery captured September 17, except Newell's Section, which participated in the pursuit of Bragg into Kentucky October 1-15. Battle of Perryville, Ky., October 8. Assigned to duty with Minty's Cavalry Brigade November, 1862. Gallatin, Tenn., November 8. Lebanon November 9. Rural Hill November 15. Hollow Tree Gap December 4. Wilson's Creek Road December 11. Franklin December 12. Advance on Murfreesboro December 26-30. Lavergne December 26. Battle of Stone's River December 30-31, 1862, and January 1-3, 1863. Stewart's Creek January 1, 1863. Lavergne January 1. Expedition against Forest January 9-19. Expedition to Franklin January 31-February 10. Unionville and Rover January 31. Rover February 13. Bradysville February 16. Expedition toward Columbia March 4-14. Rover March 4. Expedition from Franklin to Columbia March 8-12. Thompson's Station March 9. Rutherford Creek March 10-11.

Expedition to Auburn, Liberty, Snow Hill, etc., April 2-6. Snow Hill, Woodbury, April 3. Franklin April 10. Expedition to McMinnville April 20-30. Near Murfreesboro June 3. Shelbyville Pike and operations on Edgefield Pike, near Murfreesboro, June 4. Marshall's Pass June 4. Scout on Middleton and Eagleville Pike June 10. Middle Tennessee (or Tullahoma) Campaign June 23-July 7. Eagleville and Rover June 23. Middleton June 24. Fosterville, Guy's Gap and Shelbyville June 27. Occupation of Middle Tennessee till August 16. Expedition to Huntsville July 13-22. Chickamauga (Ga.) Campaign August 16-September 22. Reconnoissance toward Rome, Ga., September 11. Alpine and Dirt Town, Lafayette Road, Chattanooga River, September 12. Reconnoissance toward Lafayette and skirmish September 13. Near Stevens' Gap September 18. Battle of Chickamauga September 19-21. Cotton's Ferry September 30. Anderson's Cross Roads October 2. Farmington October 7. Rejoined Battery at Knoxville, Tenn., December. Battery reorganized at Columbus, Ohio, January, 1863. Ordered to Lexington, Ky., thence to Mt. Vernon, Ky., April 4-18. Saunder's Raid into East Tennessee June 14-24. Knoxville June 19-20. Strawberry Plains June 20. Powder Springs, Ga., June 21. Burnside's Campaign in East Tennessee August 16-October 17. Expedition to Cumberland Gap September 3-7. Operations about Cumberland Gap September 7-10. Knoxville Campaign November 4-December 23. Siege of Knoxville November 17-December 4. Re-enlisted January, 1864. Atlanta (Ga.) Campaign May to September, 1864. Movements on Dalton May 5-8. Demonstration on Rocky Faced Ridge May 8-11. Battle of Resaca May 13-15. Cartersville May 20. Kingston May 24. Operations on line of Pumpkin Vine Creek and battles about Dallas, New Hope Church and Allatoona Hills May 25-June 5. Operations about Marietta and against Kenesaw Mountain June 10-July 2. Muddy Creek June 17. Noyes Creek June 19. Cheyney's Farm June 22. Olley's Farm June 26-27. Assault on Kenesaw June 27. Nickajack Creek July 2-5. Chattahoochie River July 6-17. Battle of Atlanta July 22. Siege of Atlanta July 22-August 25. Utoy Creek August 5-7. Flank movement on Jonesboro August 25-30. Battle of Jonesboro August 31-September 1. Lovejoy Station September 2-6. Pursuit of Hood into Alabama October 3-26. Nashville Campaign November-December. Columbia, Duck River, November 24-27. Columbia Ford November 28-29. Franklin November 30. Battle of Nashville December 15-16. Pursuit of Hood to the Tennessee River December 17-28. Movement to North Carolina January 15-February 9, 1865. Fort Anderson February 18-19. Town Creek February 19-20. Capture of Wilmington February 22. Campaign of the Carolinas March 1-April 26. Advance on Goldsboro March 6-21. Occupation of Goldsboro March 21. Gulleys March 31. Advance on Raleigh April 10-14. Occupation of Raleigh April 14. Bennett's House April 26. Surrender of Johnston and his army. Duty at Raleigh and Greensboro, N. C., till July. Mustered out July 15, 1865.

Battery lost during service 8 Enlisted men killed and mortally wounded and 28 Enlisted men by disease. Total 36.

BATTERY "E" 1st REGIMENT LIGHT ARTILLERY.

Organized at Camp Dennison, near Cincinnati, Ohio, and mustered in October 7, 1861. Action at West Liberty, Ky., October 23. Expedition into Eastern Ohio and West Virginia after Jenkins' Cavalry November 23-29. Moved to Louisville, Ky., December 2, 1861; thence to Bacon Creek, Ky., and duty there till February, 1862. Attached to 3rd Division, Army of Ohio, December, 1861, to September, 1862. Artillery, 2nd Division, 1st Army Corps, Army of Ohio, to November, 1862. 2nd Brigade, 2nd Division, Right Wing 14th Army Corps, Army of the Cumberland, to January, 1863. Post of Nashville, Tenn., Dept. of the Cumberland, to June, 1863. Artillery, 2nd Division, Reserve Corps, Army of the Cumberland, to October, 1863. Unassigned, Dept.

of the Cumberland, to November, 1863. 1st Division, Artillery Reserve, Dept. of the Cumberland, to December, 1863. Garrison Artillery at Bridgeport, Ala., Dept. of the Cumberland, to July, 1864. 1st Division, Artillery Reserve, Dept. of the Cumberland, to November, 1864. Garrison Artillery, Nashville, Tenn., Dept. of the Cumberland, to July, 1865.

SERVICE.—Advance on Bowling Green, Ky., and Nashville, Tenn., February 10-25. Occupation of Nashville February 25. Reconnoissance to Shelbyville and McMinnville March 25-29. Advance on Fayetteville April 4-7, and on Huntsville April 10-11. Capture of Huntsville April 11. Advance on and capture of Decatur, Florence and Tuscumbia April 11-14. Action at West Bridge, near Bridgeport, April 29. Destruction of railroad bridge across the Tennessee River. Relief of 18th Ohio at Athens May 1 and dispersement of Scott's Forces. Negley's Chattanooga Campaign May 27-June 14. Duty at Battle Creek June-July. Action at Battle Creek June 21. Occupy Fort McCook August 20-25. March to Louisville, Ky., in pursuit of Bragg August 25-September 26. Pursuit of Bragg into Kentucky October 1-15. Lawrenceburg October 6. Dog Walk October 9. March to Nashville, Tenn., October 20-November 7, and duty there till December 26. Reconnoissance from Lavergne November 19. Advance on Murfreesboro December 26-30. Battle of Stone's River December 30-31, 1862, and January 1-3, 1863. Battery captured December 31. Ordered to Nashville, Tenn., January 20, 1863, and duty there till September. Moved to Stevenson, Ala., September 6; thence to Battle Creek, Anderson's Cross Roads and Chattanooga. Chattanooga-Ringgold Campaign November 23-27. Battles of Chattanooga November 23-25. Garrison duty at Bridgeport, Ala., till July, 1864, and at Nashville, Tenn., till July, 1865. Battle of Nashville December 15-16, 1864. Mustered out July 10, 1865.

Battery lost during service 3 Enlisted men killed and mortally wounded and 29 Enlisted men by disease. Total 32.

BATTERY "F" 1st REGIMENT LIGHT ARTILLERY.

Organized at Camp Lucas, Ohio, August, 1861. Moved to Camp Dennison, Ohio, September 1, and mustered in December 2, 1861. Left State for Louisville, Ky., December 3. Attached to 4th Division, Army of Ohio, to February, 1862. Artillery, 6th Division, Army of Ohio, to July, 1862. Artillery, 4th Division, Army of Ohio, to September, 1862. 19th Brigade, 4th Division, 2nd Corps, Army of Ohio, to November, 1862. Artillery, 2nd Division, Left Wing 14th Army Corps, Army of the Cumberland, to January, 1863. Artillery, 2nd Division, 21st Army Corps, Army of the Cumberland, to October, 1863. Artillery, 1st Division, Artillery Reserve, Dept. of the Cumberland, to March, 1864. 2nd Division, Artillery Reserve, Dept. of the Cumberland, to March, 1864. Garrison Artillery, Decatur, Ala., District of Northern Alabama, Dept. of the Cumberland, to July, 1865.

SERVICE.—Moved to Nashville, Tenn., February 10-25, 1862. March to Savannah, Tenn., March 18-April 6. Battle of Shiloh April 7. Advance on and siege of Corinth, Miss., April 29-May 30. Pursuit to Booneville May 31-June 12. Buell's Campaign in North Alabama and Middle Tennessee June to August. March to Louisville, Ky., in pursuit of Bragg August 21-September 26. Pursuit of Bragg to London, Ky., October 1-22. Battle of Perryville, Ky., October 8 (Reserve). Danville October 11. Wild Cat Mountain October 16. Big Rockcastle River October 16. Near Mt. Vernon October 16. Near Crab Orchard October 16. March to Nashville, Tenn., October 23-November 7. Duty at Nashville till December 26. Advance on Murfreesboro December 26-30. Battle of Stone's River December 30-31, 1862, and January 1-3, 1863. Woodbury, Tenn., January 24. At Readyville till June. Middle Tennessee (or Tullahoma) Campaign June 23-July 7. At Manchester till August 16. Passage of Cumberland Mountains and Tennessee River and Chickamauga (Ga.) Campaign August 16-

September 22. Battle of Chickamauga, Ga., September 19-20. Siege of Chattanooga, Tenn., September 24-November 23. Battles of Chattanooga November 23-27. Moved to Nashville, Tenn., and duty there till March, 1864. Moved to Decatur, Ala., and duty there till July, 1865. Expedition from Decatur to Moulton, Ala., July 25-28, 1864. Action at Courtland, Ala., July 25. Siege of Decatur October 26-29, 1864. Mustered out July 22, 1865.

Battery lost during service 1 Officer and 7 Enlisted men killed and mortally wounded and 28 Enlisted men by disease. Total 36.

BATTERY "G" 1st REGIMENT LIGHT ARTILLERY.

Organized at Camp Dennison, near Cincinnati, Ohio, and mustered in December 17, 1861. Moved to Louisville, Ky., February 10, 1862; thence to Nashville, Tenn., February 27. Attached to 5th Division, Army of Ohio, to June, 1862. Artillery Reserve, Army of Ohio, to September, 1862. Artillery, 8th Division, Army of Ohio, to November, 1862. Artillery, 2nd Division (Centre), 14th Army Corps, Army of the Cumberland, to January, 1863. Artillery, 2nd Division, 14th Army Corps, to October, 1863. 1st Division, Artillery Reserve, Army of the Cumberland, to March, 1864. 2nd Division, Artillery Reserve, Dept. of the Cumberland, to August, 1864. Unattached Artillery, Dept. of the Cumberland, to October, 1864. Artillery Post of Chattanooga, Tenn., Dept. of the Cumberland, to November, 1864. Artillery Brigade, 4th Army Corps, Army of the Cumberland, to August, 1865.

SERVICE.—March to Savannah, Tenn., March 18-April 6, 1862. Battle of Shiloh April 6-7. Advance on and siege of Corinth, Miss., April 29-May 30. Pursuit to Booneville May 31-June 10. Movement to Athens, Ala., June 10-30, and duty there till August. Moved to Nashville, Tenn., August 19. Siege of Nashville September to November. Repulse of Forest's attack on Edgefield November 5. Advance on Murfreesboro, Tenn., December 26-30. Battle of Stone's River December 30-31, 1862, and January 1-3, 1863. Duty at Murfreesboro till June. Middle Tennessee (or Tullahoma) Campaign June 23-July 7. Hoover's Gap June 24-26. Occupation of Middle Tennessee till August 16. Passage of Cumberland Mountains and Tennessee River and Chickamauga (Ga.) Campaign August 16-September 22. Davis Cross Roads or Dug Gap September 11. Battle of Chickamauga September 19-21. Siege of Chattanooga September 24-November 23. Battles of Chattanooga November 23-25; Mission Ridge November 24-25. Moved to Nashville, Tenn., December 2, and duty there till August, 1864. Battery veteranize January 4, 1864. March to relief of Fort Donelson, Tenn., March 3-12. Spring Hill March 9. Rutherford Creek March 10. Duck River March 11. Ordered to join army in the field August, 1864. Rousseau's pursuit of Wheeler September 1-8. Lavergne September 1. Franklin September 2. Campbellsville September 5. Expedition after Forest. Pulaski September 26-27. Nashville Campaign November-December. Columbia, Duck River, November 24-27. Spring Hill November 29. Battle of Franklin November 30. Battle of Nashville December 15-16. Pursuit of Hood to the Tennessee River December 17-28. Rutherford Creek December 19. At Huntsville, Ala., till March, 1865. Expedition to Bull's Gap and operations in East Tennessee March 20-April 5. Duty at Nashville till June. Moved to New Orleans, La., June 16. Ordered home for muster out August 31, 1865.

Battery lost during service 6 Enlisted men killed and mortally wounded and 1 Officer and 26 Enlisted men by disease. Total 33.

BATTERY "H" 1st REGIMENT LIGHT ARTILLERY.

Organized at Camp Dennison, near Cincinnati, Ohio, and mustered in November 7, 1861. Left State for Parkersburg, W. Va., January 20, 1862. Attached to Landers' Division, Army of the Potomac, to March, 1862. Artillery, Shields' 2nd Division, Banks' 5th Army

Corps, and Dept. of the Shenandoah to May, 1862. Artillery, Shields' Division, Dept. of the Shenandoah, to June, 1862. Alexandria, Va., Military District of Washington, D. C., to October, 1862. Artillery, 3rd Division, 3rd Army Corps, Army of the Potomac, to May, 1863. 1st Volunteer Brigade, Artillery Reserve, Army of the Potomac, to June, 1863. 3rd Volunteer Brigade, Artillery Reserve, Army of the Potomac, to August, 1863. 4th Volunteer Brigade, Artillery Reserve, Army of the Potomac, to October, 1863. Artillery Brigade, 2nd Army Corps, Army of the Potomac, to December, 1863. Artillery Reserve, Army of the Potomac, to February, 1864. 2nd Volunteer Brigade, Artillery Reserve, Army of the Potomac, to April, 1864. 3rd Volunteer Brigade, Artillery Reserve, Army of the Potomac, to May, 1864. Artillery Brigade, 6th Army Corps, Army of the Potomac, to July, 1864. Artillery Reserve, Army of the Potomac, to December, 1864. Artillery Brigade, 6th Army Corps, Army of the Potomac, to March, 1865. Artillery Reserve, Army of the Potomac, to June, 1865.

SERVICE.—Moved from Parkersburg, W. Va., to Paw Paw Tunnel January, 1862, and duty there till March. Advance on Winchester March 7-15. Action at Strasburg March 19. Battle of Winchester March 23. Occupation of Mt. Jackson April 17. March to Fredericksburg, Va., May 12-21, and return to Front Royal May 25-30. Battle of Port Republic June 9. Moved to Alexandria June 29 and duty in the Defences of Washington, D. C., till October 17. Moved to Harper's Ferry, W. Va., October 17. Advance up Loudoun Valley and movement to Falmouth, Va., October 30-November 17. Battle of Fredericksburg, Va., December 12-15. At Falmouth till April, 1863. "Mad March" January 20-24. Chancellorsville Campaign April 27-May 6. Battle of Chancellorsville May 1-5. Gettysburg (Pa.), Campaign June 11-July 24. Battle of Gettysburg July 1-3. Advance from the Rappahannock to the Rapidan September 13-17. Bristoe Campaign October 9-22. Bristoe Station October 14. Advance to line of the Rappahannock November 7-8. Mine Run Campaign November 26-December 2. Campaign from the Rapidan to the James May 3-June 15, 1864. Battles of the Wilderness May 5-7; Spottsylvania May 8-21; North Anna River May 23-27. Line of the Pamunkey May 26-28. Totopotomoy May 28-31. Cold Harbor June 1-12. Before Petersburg June 16-18. Siege of Petersburg June 16, 1864, to April 2, 1865. Jerusalem Plank Road, Weldon Railroad, June 22-23, 1864. Fall of Petersburg April 2, 1865. Ordered to Cleveland, Ohio, for muster out June 5. Mustered out June 17, 1865.

Battery lost during service 10 Enlisted men killed and mortally wounded and 22 Enlisted men by disease. Total 32.

BATTERY "I" 1st REGIMENT LIGHT ARTILLERY.

Organized at Cincinnati, Ohio, as a Company of Light Artillery, and engaged in guarding the fortifications and approaches to that city, back of Newport, Ky., Mt. Adams and Price's Hill October to December, 1861. Organized and mustered in as Battery "I" December 3, 1861. Left Cincinnati, Ohio, for Parkersburg, W. Va., January 26, 1862, thence moved to New Creek February 3. Attached to Milroy's Command, Cheat Mountain District, W. Va., to April, 1862. Milroy's Independent Brigade, Dept. of the Mountains, to June, 1862. Unattached, 3rd Division, 1st Corps, Pope's Army of Virginia, to September, 1862. Artillery, 3rd Division, 11th Army Corps, Army of the Potomac, to May, 1863. Artillery Brigade, 11th Army Corps, Army of the Potomac, to September, 1863, and Army of the Cumberland to November, 1863. Artillery, 2nd Division, 4th Army Corps, Army of the Cumberland, to December, 1863. Garrison Artillery, Chattanooga, Tenn., Dept. of the Cumberland, to April, 1864. Artillery, 1st Division, 14th Army Corps, Army of the Cumberland, to July, 1864. Artillery Brigade, 14th Army Corps, to September, 1864. Garrison Artillery, Chattanooga, Tenn.,

to March, 1865. 2nd Separate Division, District of the Etowah, Dept. of the Cumberland, to July, 1865.

SERVICE.—Expedition to Moorefield, W. Va., February 11-16, 1862. Action at Moorefield February 12. Moved to Clarksburg, W. Va., thence to Beverly March 26. Joined Milrow at Monterey, Dinwiddie Gap, April 25. Shenandoah Mountain May 7. McDowell May 8. Franklin May 26. Strasburg June 1. Harrisonburg June 6. Cross Keys June 8. Port Republic June 9. Luray June 10. At Middletown till July 7, and at Luray till August. Pope's Campaign in Northern Virginia August 16-September 2. Fords of the Rappahannock August 21-23. Freeman's Ford and Hazel Run August 22. Battles of Gainesville August 28. Groveton August 29. Bull Run August 30. Duty in the Defences of Washington and at Fairfax Court House till December. Manassas Gap November 5-6. March to Fredericksburg, Va., December 10-16. Burnside's 2nd Campaign "Mud March" January 20-24, 1863. Chancellorsville Campaign April 27-May 6. Battle of Chancellorsville May 1-5. Gettysburg (Pa.) Campaign June 11-July 24. Battle of Gettysburg July 1-3. On line of the Rappahannock till September. Movement to Bridgeport, Ala., September 24-October 3. Re-opening Tennessee River October 26-29. Battle of Wauhatchie, Tenn., October 28-29. Chattanooga-Ringgold Campaign November 23-27. Orchard Knob November 23. Mission Ridge November 24-25. Garrison duty at Chattanooga till April 23, 1864. Atlanta (Ga.) Campaign May 1 to September 8, 1864. Demonstrations on Rocky Faced Ridge May 8-11. Buzzard's Roost Gap May 8-9. Battle of Resaca May 14-15. Advance on Dallas May 18-25. Operations on line of Pumpkin Vine Creek and battles about Dallas, New Hope Church and Allatoona Hills May 25-June 5. Pickett's Mills May 27. Operations about Marietta and against Kenesaw Mountain June 10-July 2. Pine Hill June 11-14. Lost Mountain June 15-17. Assault on Kenesaw June 27; Ruff's Station, Smyrna Camp Ground, July 4; Chattanooga River July 5-17; Peach Tree Creek July 19-20. Siege of Atlanta July 22-August 25. Utoy Creek August 5-7. Flank movement on Jonesboro August 25-30. Battle of Jonesboro August 31-September 1. Ordered to Chattanooga, Tenn., September, and garrison duty there till June, 1865. Mustered out June 13, 1865.

Battery lost during service 1 Officer and 13 Enlisted men killed and mortally wounded and 15 Enlisted men by disease. Total 29.

BATTERY "K" 1st REGIMENT LIGHT ARTILLERY.

Organized at Cleveland, Marietta and Camp Dennison, Ohio, and mustered in October 22, 1861. Left State for West Virginia February, 1862. Attached to Cheat Mountain District, West Virginia, to March, 1862. Cheat Mountain District, Dept. of the Mountains, to June, 1862. 2nd Brigade, 1st Division, 1st Army Corps, Pope's Army of Virginia, to September, 1862. Artillery, 1st Division, 11th Army Corps, Army of the Potomac, to March, 1863. Reserve Artillery, 11th Army Corps, Army of the Potomac, to March, 1863. Artillery Brigade, 11th Army Corps, Army of the Potomac, to September, 1863, and Army of the Cumberland to December, 1863. Garrison Artillery, Bridgeport, Ala., Dept. of the Cumberland, to April, 1864. Unattached Artillery, Dept. of the Cumberland, to May, 1864. Stevenson, Ala., District of North Alabama, Dept. of the Cumberland, to October, 1864. 3rd Brigade, Defences Nashville & Chattanooga Railroad, Dept. of the Cumberland, to March, 1865. Post of Stevenson, Ala., Dept. of the Cumberland, to July, 1865.

SERVICE.—Battle of McDowell May 8, 1862; Franklin May 28. Pursuit of Jackson up the Shenandoah Valley, Strasburg and Staunton Road June 1-2. Harrisonburg June 6; Cross Keys June 8; Port Republic June 9; at Middletown till July, and at Sperryville till August. Pope's Campaign in Northern Virginia August 16-September 2. Fords of the Rappahannock August 21-23. Freeman's Ford, Hazel River and Leary's Ford August 22. Waterloo Bridge August 23-25. Battle of

Groveton August 29; Bull Run August 30. Duty in the Defences of Washington, D. C., till December. Expedition from Centreville to Warrenton Junction and Bristoe Station September 25-28. March to Fredericksburg, Va., December 10-16. Burnside's 2nd Campaign, "Mud March," January 20-24. Chancellorsville Campaign April 27-May 6. Battle of Chancellorsville May 1-5. Gettysburg (Pa.) Campaign June 11-July 24. Battle of Gettysburg July 1-3. Duty on line of the Rappahannock till September. Moved to Bridgeport, Ala., September 24-October 3. Reopening Tennessee River October 26-29. Battle of Wauhatchie October 28-29. Chattanooga-Ringgold Campaign November 23-27. Lookout Mountain November 23-24. Mission Ridge November 25. Assigned to Reserve Artillery and Garrison duty at Bridgeport and Stevenson, Ala., December, 1863, to July, 1865. Ordered home July 3. Mustered out July 17, 1865.

Battery lost during service 1 Officer and 5 Enlisted men killed and mortally wounded and 14 Enlisted men by disease. Total 20.

BATTERY "L" 1st REGIMENT LIGHT ARTILLERY.

Organized at Portsmouth, Ohio, and mustered in at Camp Dennison, Ohio, October 8, 1861, to January 20, 1862. Moved to Patterson's Creek, Va., January 20-27, 1862. Attached to Landers' Division, Army of the Potomac, to March, 1862. Artillery, Shields' 2nd Division, Banks' 5th Army Corps and Dept. of the Shenandoah to May, 1862. Artillery, Shields' Division, Dept. of the Rappahannock, to June, 1862. Alexandria, Va., Military District of Washington, D. C., to September, 1862. Artillery, 3rd Division, 5th Army Corps, Army of the Potomac, to October, 1862. Artillery, 2nd Division, 5th Army Corps, to May, 1863. Artillery Brigade, 5th Army Corps, to April, 1864. Camp Barry, Defences of Washington, D. C., 22nd Army Corps, to May, 1864. 2nd Brigade, Hardin's Division, 22nd Army Corps, to July, 1864. Artillery, 1st Division, 19th Army Corps, Middle Military Division, to August, 1864. Reserve Division, Dept. of West Virginia, to September, 1864. Artillery Brigade, Dept. of West Virginia, to January, 1865. 1st Separate Brigade, 3rd Division, West Virginia, to April, 1865. Artillery, 2nd Division, Dept. of West Virginia, to July, 1865.

SERVICE.—Advance on Winchester, Va., March 7-15, 1862. Reconnoissance to Strasburg March 19-20. Battle of Winchester March 23. Occupation of Mt. Jackson April 17. March to Fredericksburg May 12-21, and return to Front Royal May 25-30. Moved to Alexandria June 29, and duty in the Defences of Washington till September. Movement to Falmouth, Va., October-November. Battle of Fredericksburg December 12-15. At Falmouth till April, 1863. Chancellorsville Campaign April 27-May 6. Battle of Chancellorsville May 1-5. Gettysburg (Pa.) Campaign June 11-July 24. Battle of Gettysburg July 1-3. Duty on line of the Rappahannock and Rapidan till October. Bristoe Campaign October 9-22. Advance to line of the Rappahannock November 7-8. Rappahannock Station November 7. Mine Run Campaign November 26-December 2. Duty at Camp Barry and at Forts Sumner and Kearney, Defences of Washington, till July, 1864. Repulse of Early's attack on Washington July 11-12. Expedition to Snicker's Gap July 14-23. Sheridan's Shenandoah Valley Campaign. Berryville September 3. Battle of Opequan, Winchester, September 19. Fisher's Hill September 22. Battle of Cedar Creek October 19. Duty at Winchester till December 28, and at New Creek till June 30, 1865. Ordered to Columbus, Ohio, June 30. Mustered out July 4, 1865.

Battery lost during service 1 Officer and 7 Enlisted men killed and mortally wounded and 1 Officer and 15 Enlisted men by disease. Total 24.

BATTERY "M" 1st REGIMENT LIGHT ARTILLERY.

Organized at Camp Dennison, Ohio, and mustered in December 3, 1861. Ordered to Louisville, Ky., December 3; thence moved to Bacon Creek, Ky., and duty

there till February, 1862. Attached to Artillery Reserve, Army of Ohio, to September, 1862. 8th Division, Army of Ohio, to November, 1862. Artillery, 2nd Division (Centre), 14th Army Corps, Army of the Cumberland, to January, 1863. Artillery, 2nd Division, 14th Army Corps, to October, 1863. 1st Division, Artillery Reserve, Dept. of the Cumberland, to March, 1864. 2nd Division, Artillery Reserve, Dept. of the Cumberland, to July, 1864. Artillery Brigade, 4th Army Corps, Army of the Cumberland, to October, 1864. Garrison Artillery, Chattanooga, Tenn., Dept. of the Cumberland, to April, 1865.

SERVICE.—March to Nashville, Tenn., February 10-March 3, 1862, and to Savannah, Tenn., March 17-April 6. Battle of Shiloh, Tenn., April 7. Advance on and siege of Corinth, Miss., April 29-May 30. Buell's Campaign in North Alabama and Middle Tennessee June to August. Garrison duty at Nashville, Tenn., August to December, 1862. Advance on Murfreesboro, Tenn., December 26-30. Battle of Stone's River December 30-31, 1862, and January 1-3, 1863. Duty at Murfreesboro till June. Middle Tennessee (or Tullahoma) Campaign June 23-July 7. Occupation of Middle Tennessee till August 16. Passage of Cumberland Mountains and Tennessee River and Chickamauga (Ga.) Campaign August 16-September 22. Davis Cross Roads or Dug Gap September 11. Near Blue Bird Gap September 11. Battle of Chickamauga September 19-21. Siege of Chattanooga, Tenn., September 24-November 23. Chattanooga-Ringgold Campaign November 23-27. Mission Ridge November 24-25. Ordered to Nashville, Tenn., December, 1863, and duty there till June, 1864. Joined Sherman's army at Kenesaw Mountain, Ga., June 25. Operations against Kenesaw Mountain June 25-July 2. Assault on Kenesaw June 27. Chattahoochie River July 3-17. Peach Tree Creek July 19-20. Siege of Atlanta July 22-August 25. Flank movement on Jonesboro August 25-30. Battle of Jonesboro August 31-September 1. Ordered to Chattanooga, Tenn., September, and duty there till December. Mustered out (Non-Veterans) at Camp Dennison, Ohio, December 17, 1864. Veterans and Recruits garrison at Chattanooga, Tenn., till April, 1865. Consolidated with Battery "I," 1st Ohio Light Artillery, April 11, 1865.

Battery lost during service 2 Enlisted men killed and mortally wounded and 17 Enlisted men by disease. Total 19.

1st INDEPENDENT BATTERY LIGHT ARTILLERY.

Organized at Camp Chase, Columbus, Ohio, and mustered in August 6, 1861. Ordered to the Kanawha Valley, W. Va. Attached to Cox's Brigade, District of the Kenawha, W. Va., to September, 1861. Benham's Brigade, District of the Kanawha, W. Va., to October, 1861. 1st Brigade, District of the Kanawha, W. Va., to March, 1862. 1st Brigade, Kanawha Division, W. Va., to August, 1862. 1st Brigade, Kanawha Division, 9th Army Corps, Army of the Potomac, to October, 1862. 3rd Brigade, Kanawha Division, W. Va., Dept. of Ohio, to March, 1863. 2nd Brigade, 3rd Division, 8th Army Corps, Middle Department, to June, 1863. 2nd Brigade, Scammon's Division, Army of West Virginia, to December, 1863. 2nd Brigade, 3rd Division, West Virginia, to April, 1864. Artillery, 2nd Infantry Division, West Virginia, to July, 1864. Artillery Brigade, West Virginia, to August, 1864. Artillery Reserve Division, Harper's Ferry, W. Va., to April, 1865. 3rd Brigade, Hardins' Division, 22nd Army Corps, Defences of Washington, to June, 1865.

SERVICE.—Action at Carnifex Ferry, W. Va., September 10, 1861. Moved to Camp Anderson and Big Sewell Mountain September 15-23, thence to Camp Anderson October 6-9. Operations in the Kanawha Valley and New River Region October 19-November 16. Moved to Gauley and duty there till May, 1862. Advance on Virginia & Tennessee Railroad April 22-May 1. Princeton May 11, 16 and 17. At Flat Top Mountain till August. Movement to Washington, D. C., August 15-24. Maryland Campaign September 6-22. Battles of South Mountain September 14; Antietam September 16-17. Moved to Clear Springs October 8, thence to Hancock and march to the Kanawha Valley, W. Va., October 9-November 17, via Clarksburg, Summerville, Gauley Bridge and Kanawha Falls. Duty at Kanawha Falls (Falls of the Great Kanawha) till March, 1863, and at Charleston till April, 1864. Fayetteville May 17-20, 1863 (Section). Operations against Morgan's Raid in Ohio July 2-26, 1863. Scammon's Demonstration from Kanawha Valley December 8-25. Lewisburg and Greenbrier River December 12, 1863. Crook's Raid on Virginia & Tennessee Railroad May 3-19, 1864. Battle of Cloyd's Mountain May 9. New River Bridge May 10. Salt Pond Gap, Pond Mountain Gap, May 13. Hunter's Expedition to Lynchburg May 26-July 1. Lexington June 11. Diamond Hill June 17. Lynchburg June 17-18. Buford's Gap June 20. Salem June 21. Moved to Shenandoah Valley July 12-15. Action at Bunker Hill July 19. Stephenson's Depot, Carter's Farm, July 20. Battle of Winchester July 24. Retreat to Williamsport, Md.; thence ordered to Martinsburg, W. Va., and duty there guarding stores till March, 1865. Moved to Harper's Ferry, thence to Washington, D, C., and duty in the Defences of that city till June. Mustered out June 26, 1865.

Battery lost during service 1 Officer and 6 Enlisted men killed and mortally wounded and 15 Enlisted men by disease. Total 22.

2nd INDEPENDENT BATTERY LIGHT ARTILLERY.

Organized at Camp Chase and mustered in August 7, 1861. Ordered to St. Louis, Mo., August 15; thence to Jefferson City, Mo., and duty there till October 4. Attached to Army of the West and Dept. of Missouri to January, 1862. 5th Brigade, Army of Southwest Missouri, to March, 1862. Artillery, 2nd Division, Army of Southwest Missouri, to May, 1862. Artillery, 3rd Division, Army of Southwest Missouri, to July, 1862. District of Eastern Arkansas, Dept. of Missouri, to January, 1863. Artillery, 12th Division, 13th Army Corps, Dept. of the Tennessee, to July, 1863. Artillery, 3rd Division, 13th Army Corps, Dept. of the Tennessee, to August, 1863, and Dept. of the Gulf to November, 1863. Plaquemine, La., District of Baton Rouge, La., Dept. of the Gulf, to March, 1864. Artillery, 3rd Division, 13th Army Corps, to June, 1864. Defences of New Orleans, La., Dept. of the Gulf, to August, 1864. Reserve Artillery, Dept. of the Gulf, to February, 1865. Post of Ship Island, Dept. of the Gulf, to August, 1865.

SERVICE.—Fremont's advance on Springfield, Mo., October 4-27, 1861. Duty at Springfield till November 8. Moved to Rolla, Mo., and duty there till February 24, 1862. Curtis' Campaign against Price in Missouri and Arkansas February-March. Battles of Pea Ridge, Ark., March 6-8. March to Batesville over Ozark Mountains April 5-May 8, thence to Helena, Ark., May 25-July 13. Duty at Helena, Ark., till March, 1863. Expedition from Helena to St. Francis and Little Rivers March 5-12. Madison March 9. Ordered to Milliken's Bend, La., March 20, and duty there till April. Movements on Bruinsburg and turning Grand Gulf April 25-30. Battle of Port Gibson May 1. Fourteen-Mile Creek May 12-13. Battle of Champion's Hill May 16. Siege of Vicksburg, Miss., May 18-July 4. Assaults on Vicksburg May 19 and 22. Advance on Jackson, Miss., July 5-10. Siege of Jackson July 10-17. At Big Black till August. Ordered to New Orleans, La., August 13; duty there and at Plaquemine, La., till March, 1864. Western Louisiana Campaign October 3-November 30, 1863. Red River Campaign March 10-May 22, 1864. Advance from Franklin to Alexandria, La., March 14-26. Middle Bayou May 8. Retreat to Morganza May 13-20. Duty at Plaquemine till February, 1865, and at Ship Island, Miss., till July. Mustered out July 21, 1865.

Battery lost during service 2 Enlisted men killed and 45 Enlisted men by disease. Total 47.

2nd BATTERY LIGHT ARTILLERY—(NATIONAL GUARD.)

Organized at Camp Cleveland, Ohio, for sixty days' service October 17, 1864. Guard duty at Johnson's Island, Sandusky, Ohio, till December. Mustered out December 22, 1864.

3rd INDEPENDENT BATTERY LIGHT ARTILLERY.

Organized at Canton, Minerva and Massillon, Ohio, November 9, 1861, to March 15, 1862. Ordered to Pittsburg Landing, Tenn., March 15, 1862. Attached to 6th Division, Army of the Tennessee, to July, 1862. Artillery, 6th Division, District of Corinth, Miss., to November, 1862. 3rd Division, Left Wing 13th Army Corps, Dept. of the Tennessee, to December, 1862. Artillery, 3rd Division, 17th Army Corps, Army of the Tennessee, to November, 1864. Artillery Reserve, Nashville, Tenn., Dept. of the Cumberland, to March, 1865. Garrison Fort Donelson, Tenn., 5th Sub-District, District of Middle Tennessee, to July, 1865.

SERVICE—Battle of Shiloh, Tenn., April 6-7, 1862. Advance on and siege of Corinth, Miss., April 29-May 30. Duty at Corinth till November. Battle of Corinth October 3-4. Grant's Central Mississippi Campaign November, 1862, to January, 1863. Reconnoissance to LaGrange November 8-9. Moved to Memphis, Tenn., January, 1863, and duty there till February 21. Moved to Lake Providence, La., February 21, thence to Milliken's Bend, La. Movement on Bruinsburg and turning Grand Gulf April 25-30. Battle of Port Gibson May 1. (Reserve). Forty Hills, Hankinson's Ferry, May 3-4. Battle of Raymond May 12. Jackson May 14. Champion's Hill May 16. Siege of Vicksburg May 18-July 4. Assaults on Vicksburg May 19 and 22. Surrender of Vicksburg July 4. Duty at Vicksburg till February, 1864. Expedition to Canton and Brownsville October 14-20, 1863. Bogue Chitto Creek October 17. Meridian Campaign February 3-March 2, 1864. Clinton, Miss., March 26. At Vicksburg till April 4. March to Huntsville, Ala., thence to Ackworth, Ga., April 4-June 8. Atlanta (Ga.) Campaign June 8-September 8. Operations about Marietta and against Kenesaw Mountain June 10-July 2. Bushy Mountain June 15-17. Assault on Kenesaw June 27. Nickajack Creek July 2-5. Chattahoochie River July 5-17. Howell's Ferry July 5. Leggett's or Bald Hill July 20-21. Battle of Atlanta July 22. Siege of Atlanta July 22-August 25. Flank movement on Jonesboro August 25-30. Battle of Jonesboro August 31-September 1. Lovejoy Station September 2-6. Operations in North Georgia and North Alabama against Hood September 29-November 3. Ordered to Nashville, Tenn., and duty there and at Fort Donelson, Tenn., and vicinity as mounted Infantry till June, 1865. Ordered to Camp Taylor, Ohio, for muster out. Mustered out August 1, 1865.

Battery lost during service 1 Enlisted man killed and 57 Enlisted men by disease. Total 58.

4th INDEPENDENT BATTERY LIGHT ARTILLERY.

Organized at Cincinnati, Ohio, and mustered in August 17, 1861. Moved to St. Louis, Mo., August 21, 1861, thence to Jefferson City and to Sedalia, Mo., September 30. Attached to Army of the West and Dept. of Missouri to February, 1862. 1st Division Army of Southwest Missouri to May, 1862. Artillery, 3rd Division, Army of Southwest Missouri to July, 1862. District of Eastern Arkansas, Dept. of Missouri, to November, 1862. 2nd Brigade, 11th Division, Right Wing 13th Army Corps, Dept. of the Tennessee, to December, 1862. 2nd Brigade, 4th Division, Sherman's Yazoo Expedition, to January, 1863. Artillery, 1st Division, 15th Army Corps, Army of the Tennessee, August, 1864.

SERVICE.—Fremont's Campaign against Springfield, Mo., October 13-27. Duty at Springfield till November 8. Moved to Rolla, Mo., November 8, and duty there till February, 1862. Curtis' advance on Springfield, Mo., February 2-13. Campaign against Price in Missouri and Arkansas February and March. Battles of Pea Ridge March 6-8. March to Batesville, Ark., April 5-

May 8, and to Helena, Ark., May 25-July 14. Duty there till October. Expedition up Yazoo August 16-27. Capture of Steamer "Fair Play" August 17. Milliken's Bend August 18. Haines Bluff August 21. Bolivar Landing August 22. Greenville August 23. Ordered to St. Genevieve, Mo., October 7, thence to Pilot Knob, Mo., and duty there till November 11. Moved to St. Genevieve, thence to Camp Steele, and duty there till December 22. Sherman's Yazoo Expedition December 22, 1862, to January 3, 1863. Chickasaw Bayou December 26-28. Chickasaw Bluff December 29. Expedition to Arkansas Post, Ark., January 3-10, 1863. Assault and capture of Fort Hindman, Arkansas Post, January 10-11. Moved to Young's Point, La., January 17-23. Duty at Perkins' Plantation and Ballard's Farm till April 2. Expedition to Greenville, Black Bayou and Deer Creek April 2-14. Demonstrations on Haines and Snyder's Bluff April 26-May 2. Movement to join army in rear of Vicksburg, Miss., via Richmond and Grand Gulf May 2-14. Battle of Jackson, Miss., May 14. Siege of Vicksburg May 18-July 4. Assaults on Vicksburg May 19 and 22. Expedition to Greenville June 25-July 1. Gaines' Landing June 28. Surrender of Vicksburg July 4. Advance on Jackson, Miss., July 5-10. Siege of Jackson July 10-17. Duty at Big Black till September. Moved to Memphis, Tenn., thence march to Chattanooga, Tenn., September 22-November 21. Operations on Memphis & Charleston Railroad in Alabama October 20-29. Cherokee Station October 21. Cane Creek October 26. Bear Creek (Tuscumbia) October 27. Chattanooga-Ringgold Campaign November 23-27. Battles of Lookout Mountain November 23-24. Mission Ridge November 25. At Larkinsville and Woodville, Ala., till May, 1864. Atlanta (Ga.) Campaign May 1 to August 14. Demonstrations on Resaca May 8-13. Near Resaca May 13. Battle of Resaca May 14-15. Advance on Dallas May 18-25. Operations on line of Pumpkin Vine Creek and battles about Dallas, New Hope Church and Allatoona Hills May 25-June 5. Operations about Marietta and against Kenesaw Mountain June 10-July 2. Assault on Kenesaw June 27. Nickajack Creek July 2-5. Chattahoochie River July 5-17. Battle of Atlanta July 22. Siege of Atlanta July 22-August 14. Ezra Chapel, Hood's 2nd sortie, July 28. Ordered to rear August 14, and Non-Veterans mustered out August 29, 1864. Veterans and Recruits attached to Artillery Reserve, Nashville, Tenn., attached to 10th Ohio Battery till March, 1865. Transferred to 10th Ohio Battery March 19, 1865.

Battery lost during service 1 Officer and 5 Enlisted men killed and mortally wounded and 1 Officer and 27 Enlisted men by disease. Total 34.

5th INDEPENDENT BATTERY LIGHT ARTILLERY.

Organized at St. Louis, Mo., under authority of General Fremont August 31, 1861, and mustered in at St. Louis, Mo., as 5th Ohio Battery September 22, 1861. Moved to Jefferson City, Mo., October 11, and duty there till March 7, 1862. Attached to Dept. of Missouri till March, 1862. Artillery, 6th Division, Army of the Tennessee, to July, 1862. Artillery, 6th Division, District of Corinth, Miss., to November, 1862. Artillery, 6th Division, Left Wing 13th Army Corps (Old), Dept. of the Tennessee, to December, 1862. Artillery, 4th Division, 17th Army Corps, to January, 1863. Artillery, 4th Division, 16th Army Corps, to July, 1863. Artillery, 13th Division, 16th Army Corps, to August, 1863. Artillery, 3rd Division, Arkansas Expedition, to November, 1863. 3rd Brigade, 2nd Division, Army of Arkansas, to January, 1864. 3rd Brigade, 2nd Division, 7th Army Corps, Dept. of Arkansas, to May, 1864. Artillery, 2nd Division, 7th Army Corps, to October, 1864. Artillery, 1st Division, 7th Army Corps, to July, 1865.

SERVICE.—Ordered to Pittsburg Landing, Tenn., March 7, 1862. Battle of Shiloh, Tenn., April 6-7. Advance on and siege of Corinth, Miss., April 29-May 30. Duty at Corinth, Miss., till November. Battle of Corinth October 3-4. Moved to Grand Junction November 2. Grant's Central Mississippi Campaign. Operations on the Mississippi Central Railroad November 2, 1862, to January 10, 1863. Moved to Moscow, Tenn., and duty there till March 8. Moved to Memphis, Tenn., and duty there till May. Ordered to Vicksburg, Miss., May 17. Siege of Vicksburg, Miss., May 25-July 4. Advance on Jackson, Miss., July 5-10. Siege of Jackson July 10-17. Assault on Jackson July 12. Ordered to Helena, Ark., July 25. Steele's Expedition to Little Rock, Ark., August 3-September 10. Bayou Fourche and capture of Little Rock September 10. Duty at Little Rock as Garrison Artillery till July, 1865. Expedition from Little Rock to Little Red River August 6-16, 1864. Expedition from Little Rock in pursuit of Shelby August 27-September 6, 1864. Non-Veterans mustered out September 20, 1864. Veterans and Recruits at Little Rock till July, 1865. Mustered out July 31, 1865.

Battery lost during service 5 Enlisted men killed and mortally wounded and 36 Enlisted men by disease. Total 41.

6th INDEPENDENT BATTERY LIGHT ARTILLERY.

Organized at Camp Buckingham, Mansfield, Ohio, November 20, 1861. Mustered in December 10, 1861. Ordered to Louisville, Ky., December 15; thence to Nolin River, Ky., and duty at Camp Dick Robinson till January 12, 1862. Attached to 5th Division, Army of Ohio, December, 1861, to March, 1862. Artillery Reserve, Army of Ohio, to June, 1862. Artillery, 6th Division, Army of Ohio, to September, 1862. 20th Brigade, 6th Division, 2nd Corps, Army of Ohio, to November, 1862. 3rd Brigade, 1st Division, Left Wing 14th Army Corps, Army of the Cumberland, to January, 1863. Artillery, 1st Division, 21st Army Corps, Army of the Cumberland, to October, 1863. Artillery, 3rd Division, 4th Army Corps, Army of the Cumberland, to July, 1864. Artillery Brigade, 4th Army Corps, to June, 1865. Dept. of Louisiana to August, 1865.

SERVICE.—Moved to Columbia, Ky., January 12, 1862; thence to Jimtown and Camp Green and duty blockading Cumberland River till March 14. Moved to Nashville, Tenn., March 15-19. March to Savannah, Tenn., March 25-April 10. Advance on and siege of Corinth, Miss., April 29-May 30. Buell's Campaign in North Alabama and Middle Tennessee June to August. At Stevenson, Ala., June 18-August 21. March to Louisville, Ky., in pursuit of Bragg August 21-September 26. Pursuit of Bragg into Kentucky October 1-17. Harrodsburg, Ky., October 11. Danville October 14. March to Nashville, Tenn., October 17-November 6, and duty there till December 26. Advance on Murfreesboro December 26-30. Lavergne December 26-27. Battle of Stone's River December 30-31, 1862, and January 1-3, 1863. Duty at Murfreesboro till June. Reconnoissance to Nolensville and Versailles January 13-15. Middle Tennessee (or Tullahoma) Campaign June 23-July 7. Occupation of Middle Tennessee till August 16. Passage of the Cumberland Mountains and Tennessee River and Chickamauga (Ga.) Campaign August 16-September 22. Lookout Valley September 7-8. Occupation of Chattanooga September 9. Lee and Gordon's Mills September 11-13. Battle of Chickamauga September 19-20. Rossville Gap September 21. Siege of Chattanooga September 24-November 23. Chattanooga-Ringgold Campaign November 23-27. Battles of Chattanooga November 23-25. Garrison, Fort Wood, and in Reserve. Re-enlisted December 12, 1863. Veterans on furlough January, 1864. Non-Veterans attached to 20th Ohio Battery. Reconnoissance of Dalton February 22-27, 1864. Rocky Faced Ridge and Buzzard's Roost Gap February 23-25. Atlanta (Ga.) Campaign May 1 to September 8. Demonstrations on Rocky Faced Ridge and Dalton May 8-13. Buzzard's Roost Gap May 8-9. Battle of Resaca May 14-15. Adairsville May 17. Near Kingston May 18-19. Near Cassville May 19. Advance on Dallas May 22-25. Operations on line of Pumpkin Vine Creek and battles about Dallas, New Hope Church and Allatoona Hills May 25-June 5. Pickett's Mills May 27. Operations about Marietta and against Kenesaw Mountain June 10-July 2. Pine Hill June 11-14. Lost

Mountain June 15-17. Assault on Kenesaw June 27. Ruff's Station, Smyrna Camp Ground, July 4. Chattahoochie River July 5-17. Peach Tree Creek July 19-20. Siege of Atlanta July 22-August 25. Flank movement on Jonesboro August 25-30. Battle of Jonesboro August 31-September 1. Lovejoy Station September 2-6. Pursuit of Hood into Alabama October 3-23. Ordered to Nashville, Tenn., October 23. Temporarily attached to 23rd Army Corps. Nashville Campaign November-December. In front of Columbia November 24-27. Spring Hill November 29. Battle of Franklin November 30. Battle of Nashville December 15-16. Pursuit of Hood December 17-28. Moved to Huntsville, Ala., and duty there till February 1. Expedition to Eastport, Miss., February 1-9. Operations in East Tennessee March-April. At Nashville till June. Moved to New Orleans, La., June 19, and duty in the Dept. of Louisiana till August. Mustered out at Camp Chase, Ohio, September 1, 1865.

Battery lost during service 1 Officer and 8 Enlisted men killed and mortally wounded and 34 Enlisted men by disease. Total 43.

7th INDEPENDENT BATTERY LIGHT ARTILLERY.

Organized at Camp Dennison, Ohio, and mustered in January 1, 1862. Moved to St. Louis, Mo., March 18; thence to Pittsburg Landing, Tenn., April 6. Attached to 6th Division, Army of the Tennessee, to June, 1862. Artillery, 4th Division, Army of the Tennessee and District of Memphis, Tenn., to September, 1862. Artillery, 4th Division, District of Jackson, Tenn., to November, 1862. Artillery, 4th Division, Right Wing 13th Army Corps (Old), Dept. of the Tennessee, to December, 1862. Artillery, 4th Division, 17th Army Corps, to January, 1863. Artillery, 4th Division, 16th Army Corps, to July, 1863. Artillery, 4th Division, 13th Army Corps, to August, 1863. Artillery, 4th Division, 17th Army Corps, to April, 1864. Artillery, 1st Division, 17th Army Corps, to September, 1864. Artillery, Post of Vicksburg, Miss., District of Vicksburg, Miss., to November, 1864. Artillery Reserve, District of Vicksburg, Miss., to August, 1865.

SERVICE.—Advance on and siege of Corinth, Miss., April 29-May 30, 1862. March to Memphis, Tenn., via Grand Junction, Lagrange and Holly Springs June 1-July 21. At Memphis till September 6. March to Bolivar, Tenn., September 6-16. Battle of Hatchie River, Metamora, October 5. Grant's Central Mississippi Campaign November-December. Moved to Memphis, Tenn., and duty there till May, 1863. Ordered to Vicksburg, Miss., May 13. Siege of Vicksburg, Miss., May 18-July 4. Assaults on Vicksburg May 19 and 22. Advance on Jackson, Miss., July 5-10. Siege of Jackson July 10-17. Assault on Jackson July 12. Ordered to Natchez, Miss., August 12, and duty there till November 11. Expedition to Harrisonburg, La., September 1-8. Moved to Vicksburg November 11 and camp at Big Black till February, 1864. Meridian Campaign February 3-March 2. Champion's Hill February 4. Duty at Vicksburg till May. Expedition to Yazoo City May 4-22. Benton May 7 and 9. Duty at Vicksburg till January 3, 1865. At Jackson and Hazelhurst as Infantry till July. Mustered out August 11, 1865.

Battery lost during service 1 Enlisted man killed and 1 Officer and 31 Enlisted men by disease. Total 33.

8th INDEPENDENT BATTERY LIGHT ARTILLERY.

Organized at Camp Dennison, Ohio, and mustered in March 11, 1862. Moved to Benton Barracks, Mo.; thence to Savannah, Tenn., March 22-28, 1862. Served Unattached, Army of the Tennessee, to April, 1862. Artillery, 5th Division, Army of the Tennessee, to April, 1862. Artillery, 3rd Division, Army of the Tennessee, to July, 1862. Artillery, 5th Division, District of Memphis, Tenn., to November, 1862. Artillery, 2nd Division, District of Memphis, Right Wing 13th Army Corps (Old), Dept. of the Tennessee, to December, 1862. Artillery, 2nd Division, Sherman's Yazoo Expedition, to January, 1863. Artillery, 2nd Division, 15th

Army Corps, Army of the Tennessee, to September, 1863. Artillery, 1st Division, 17th Army Corps, to April, 1864. Maltby's Brigade, District of Vicksburg, to November, 1864. Artillery Reserve, District of Vicksburg, to August, 1865.

SERVICE.—Battle of Shiloh, Tenn., April 6-7, 1862. Advance on and sieze of Corinth, Miss., April 29-May 30. March to Memphis, Tenn., June 1-17, and duty there till November, 1862. Grant's Central Mississippi Campaign November-December. "Tallahatchie March" November 26-December 12. Sherman's Yazoo Expedition December 20, 1862, to January 3, 1863. Chickasaw Bayou December 26-28. Chickasaw Bluff December 29. Expedition to Arkansas Post, Ark., January 3-10, 1863. Assault on and capture of Fort Hindman, Arkansas Post, January 10-11. Moved to Young's Point, La., January 17, and duty there till March. Expedition to Rolling Fork via Muddy, Steele's and Black Bayous and Deer Creek March 14-27. Moved to Milliken's Bend and duty there till April. Demonstrations on Haines and Drumgould's Bluffs April 29-May 2. Moved to join army in rear of Vicksburg via Richmond and Grand Gulf May 2-14. Jackson, Miss., May 14. Siege of Vicksburg May 18-July 4. Assaults on Vicksburg May 19 and 22. Advance Jackson, Miss., May 5-10. Siege of Jackson July 10-17. Duty at Vicksburg till February, 1864. Expedition from Vicksburg to Sunnyside Landing, Ark., January 10-16, 1864. Duty in the Defences of Vicksburg till May 20, 1865. Expedition to Central Mississippi Railroad November 28-December 2, 1864. Moved to Natchez, Miss., May 20, 1865, and duty there till June 28. At Vicksburg till July 20. Mustered out August 7, 1865.

Battery lost during service 1 Enlisted man killed and 22 Enlisted men by disease. Total 23.

8th BATTERY LIGHT ARTILLERY—(NATIONAL GUARD.)

Organized at Johnson's Island, Ohio, for sixty days' service August 15, 1864. Guard duty at Johnson's Island, Sandusky Bay, Ohio. Mustered out October 17, 1864. Reorganized for four months' service December 19, 1864. Guard duty at Johnson's Island, Sandusky Bay, Ohio. Mustered out April 19, 1865.

9th INDEPENDENT BATTERY LIGHT ARTILLERY.

Organized at Camp Wood, Cleveland, Ohio, and mustered in October 11, 1861. Moved to Louisville, Ky., December 17-20, and duty at Camp Gilbert, Louisville, till January 11, 1862. Attached to 12th Brigade, 1st Division, Army of the Ohio, to March, 1862. 24th Brigade, 7th Division, Army of the Ohio, to October, 1862. Unattached, Army of Kentucky, Dept. of Ohio, to December, 1862. Artillery, 3rd Division, Army of Kentucky, Dept. of Ohio, to February, 1863. Coburn's Brigade, Baird's Division, Army of Kentucky, Dept. of the Cumberland, to June, 1863. Artillery, 1st Division, Reserve Corps, Dept. of the Cumberland, to October, 1863. Coburn's Unattached Brigade, Dept. of the Cumberland, to December, 1863. Artillery, 1st Division, 12th Army Corps, Army of the Cumberland, to April, 1864. Unassigned, 4th Division, 20th Army Corps, Dept. of the Cumberland, to July, 1864. 3rd Brigade, Defence Nashville & Chattanooga Railroad, Dept. of the Cumberland, to December, 1864. Garrison Artillery, Bridgeport, Ala., Dept. of the Cumberland, to July, 1865.

SERVICE.—March to Somerset, Ky., January 11-17, 1862. March from Somerset to Loudon, thence to Cumberland Ford, January 30-February 16. Reconnoissance in force under General Carter to Cumberland Gap March 21-23. At Cumberland Ford March 23 to June 7. March to Powell Valley June 7-14. Occupation of Cumberland Gap June 17, and operations in vicinity till September. Evacuation of Cumberland Gap and retreat to the Ohio River September 17-October 3 (in charge of ammunition trains). March to Lexington, Ky., October 27-31. March from Nicholasville to Danville December 10-11. Movement to intercept Morgan December 20-27. Moved to Nashville,

Tenn., January 31, 1863, and duty there till March 6. Moved to Franklin March 6. Pursuit of Van Dorn to Columbia March 9-12. Return to Franklin April 8. Repulse of attack on Franklin April 10. Duty at Franklin till June 2. Moved to Triune June 2. Tullahoma Campaign June 23-July 7. Moved to Salem, thence to Guy's Gap, June 23-29. Moved to Murfreesboro July 17, and duty there till September 5. At Tullahoma till April, 1864. March to Bridgeport April 23-27, and garrison duty there till July, 1865. Mustered out July 25, 1865.

Battery lost during service 1 Enlisted man killed and 22 Enlisted men by disease. Total 23.

10th INDEPENDENT BATTERY LIGHT ARTILLERY.

Organized at Xenia, Ohio, January 9, 1862. Moved to Camp Dennison, Ohio, and mustered in March 3, 1862. Ordered to St. Louis, Mo., thence moved to Pittsburg Landing, Tenn., April 4-9. Attached to 6th Division, Army of the Tennessee, to July, 1862. Artillery, 6th Division, District of Corinth, Miss., to November, 1862. Artillery, 6th Division, Left Wing 13th Army Corps (Old), Dept. of the Tennessee, to December, 1862. 3rd Brigade, 6th Division, 16th Army Corps, to January, 1863. 3rd Brigade, 6th Division, 17th Army Corps, to September, 1863. Artillery, 1st Division, 17th Army Corps, to April, 1864. Artillery, 4th Division, 17th Army Corps, April, 1864. Artillery, 3rd Division, 17th Army Corps, to November, 1864. Artillery Reserve, Nashville, Tenn., Dept. of the Cumberland, to February, 1865. 2nd Brigade, 4th Division, District of East Tennessee, Dept. of the Cumberland, to July, 1865.

SERVICE.—Advance on and siege of Corinth, Miss., April 29-May 30, 1862. Duty at Corinth, Miss., till September 15. Moved to Iuka, Miss., and duty there till October 1. Battle of Iuka Setpember 19 and 27. Moved to Corinth October 1-2. Battle of Corinth October 3-4. Pursuit to Ripley October 5-12. Grant's Central Mississippi Campaign November, 1862, to January, 1863. Moved to Memphis, Tenn., January 10, 1863, thence to Lake Providence, La., January 21, and duty there till April. Movement on Bruinsburg and turning Grand Gulf April 25-30. Duty at Grand Gulf till June. Siege of Vicksburg June 13-July 4. Messenger's Ferry, Big Black River, June 29-30 and July 3. Advance on Jackson, Miss., July 4-10. Bolton's Ferry, Big Black River, July 4-6. Siege of Jackson, Miss., July 10-17. Duty at Vicksburg till April, 1864. Moved to Clifton, Tenn., thence march via Huntsville and Decatur, Ala., to Ackworth, Ga., April to June 9. Atlanta Campaign June 9 to September 8. Operations about Marietta and against Kenesaw Mountain June 10-July 2. Assault on Kenesaw June 27. Nickajack Creek July 2-5. Chattahoochie River July 5-12. Turner's Ferry July 5. Moved to Marietta, Ga., July 12, and duty there till November. Moved to Nashville, Tenn., November 2, and duty there till April, 1865. Battles of Nashville December 15-16, 1864 (Reserve). Moved to Sweetwater, Tenn., April 1, 1865, thence to Loudon, Tenn., and duty there till July. Mustered out July 17, 1865.

Battery lost during service 18 Enlisted men by disease.

11th INDEPENDENT BATTERY LIGHT ARTILLERY.

Battery organized at St. Louis, Mo., and mustered in October 27, 1861. Attached to Army of the West and Dept. of Missouri to March, 1862. Artillery, 2nd Division, Army of Mississippi, to April, 1862. Artillery, 3rd Division, Army of Mississippi, to November, 1862. 7th Division, Left Wing 13th Army Corps, Dept. of the Tennessee, to December, 1862. Artillery, 7th Division, 16th Army Corps, to January, 1863. Artillery, 7th Division, 17th Army Corps, to July, 1863. Kimball's Division, Arkansas Expedition, to August, 1863. 2nd Brigade, 2nd Division, Arkansas Expedition, to January, 1864. Artillery, 2nd Division, 7th Army Corps, Dept. of Arkansas, to May, 1864. Garrison Pine Bluff, Ark., 2nd Division, 7th Army Corps, to November, 1864.

SERVICE.—Moved to South Point, Mo., October 28, 1861. March to Syracuse, Mo., November 22, thence to

Tipton, Mo., November, 29, and duty there till December 15. Moved to Otterville, Mo., December 15, and duty there till February 2, 1862. March to Booneville, thence to St. Charles, February 2-17. Siege of New Madrid, Mo., March 3-14. Siege and capture of Island No. 10, Mississippi River, March 15-April 8. Expedition to Fort Pillow, Tenn., April 13-17. Moved to Pittsburg Landing, Tenn., April 17-23. Advance on and siege of Corinth, Miss., April 29-May 30. Pursuit to Booneville May 30-June 13. Duty at Corinth till June 23. Expedition to Ripley June 27-July 2. At Corinth till August 4. At Jacinto till September 18. Battle of Iuka, Miss., September 19. Battle of Corinth October 3-4. Pursuit to Ripley October 5-12. Grant's Central Mississippi Campaign November-December. At Germantown, Tenn., till January 15, 1863. At Mmphis, Tenn., till March. Yazoo Pass Expedition and operations against Fort Pemberton and Greenwood, March 11-April 5. Moved to Milliken's Bend, La. Movement on Bruinsburg and turning Grand Gulf April 25-30. Battle of Thompson's Hill, Port Gibson, May 1 (Reserve). Battle of Raymond May 12. Jackson May 14. Battle of Champion's Hill May 16. Siege of Vicksburg, Miss., May 18-July 4. Assaults on Vicksburg May 19 and 22. Ordered to Helena, Ark., July 28. Steele's Expedition to Little Rock, Ark., August 10-September 10. Bayou Fourche and capture of Little Rock September 10. Duty at Little Rock till April, 1864, and at Pine Bluff till October. Ordered home for muster out. Mustered out at Columbus, Ohio, November 5, 1864, expiration of term.

Battery lost during service 20 Enlisted men killed and mortally wounded and 30 Enlisted men by disease. Total 50.

12th INDEPENDENT BATTERY LIGHT ARTILLERY.

Entered service as Company "G," 25th Ohio Volunteer Infantry, July 27, 1861. Ordered to West Virginia July 29. Attached to 1st Brigade, Army of Occupation West Virginia, to November, 1861. Milroy's Cheat Mountain District, West Virginia, to March, 1862. Company permanently detached from 25th Ohio Infantry as 12th Ohio Battery, March 17, 1862. Milroy's Independent Brigade, Dept. of the Mountains, to June, 1862. Milroy's Independent Brigade, 1st Army Corps, Army of Virginia, to September, 1862. Artillery, 2nd Division, 11th Army Corps, Army of the Potomac, to January, 1863. Provost Guard, Army of the Potomac, to May, 1863. Unattached, Artillery Reserve, Army of the Potomac, to June, 1863. Camp Barry, Defences of Washington, D. C., 22nd Army Corps, to September, 1863. Artillery Brigade, 11th Army Corps, Army of the Cumberland, to December, 1863. 2nd Division, Artillery Reserve, Dept. of the Cumberland, to April, 1864. Garrison Artillery, Murfreesboro, Tenn., Dept. of the Cumberland, to July, 1864. 1st Brigade, Defences Nashville & Chattanooga Railroad, Dept. of the Cumberland, to July, 1865.

SERVICE.—Duty along the Baltimore & Ohio Railroad from Grafton to the Ohio River till August 21, 1861. Moved to Cheat Mountain Summit August 21. Action at Cheat Mountain September 12-17. Cheat Mountain Pass September 14-15. Greenbrier October 3-4. Moved to Huttonsville November 25, and duty there till February 27, 1862. Expedition to Camp Baldwin December 11-13, 1861. Buffalo Mountain December 12-13. Raid to Huntersville December 31-January 5, 1862. At Elkwater till March. Expedition on the Seneca April 1-12. At Staunton to May 7. Battle of McDowell May 8. Franklin May 10-12. Battle of Cross Keys June 8. Pope's Campaign in Northern Virginia August 16-September 2. Fords of the Rappahannock August 21-23. Freeman's Ford and Hazel Run August 22. Battle of Groveton August 29. Battle of Bull Run August 30. Duty in the Defences of Washington, D. C., till December. Moved to Fredericksburg, Va., December 12-16. "Mud March" January 20-24, 1863. Chancellorsville Campaign April 27-May 6. Duty in the Defences of Washington, D. C., till September. Moved to Bridgeport, Ala., September 25-October 6. Garrison duty at

Nashville, Tenn., till April, 1864; and at Murfreesboro, Tenn., till July, 1865. Defence of Murfreesboro December 5-12, 1864. Wilkinson's Pike December 7. Mustered out July 12, 1865.

Battery lost during service 3 Enlisted men killed and mortally wounded and 17 by disease. Total 20.

13th INDEPENDENT BATTERY LIGHT ARTILLERY.

Battery never fully organized. One Section mustered in February 15, 1862. Attached to 4th Division, Army of the Tennessee. At Shiloh, Tenn., April 6-7, 1862. Lost guns and organization discontinued April 20, 1862, the men being transferred to 7th, 10th and 14th Ohio Batteries.

14th INDEPENDENT BATTERY LIGHT ARTILLERY.

Organized at Cleveland, Ohio, and mustered in September 10, 1861. Moved to Camp Dennison, Ohio, January 1, 1862, and to St. Louis, Mo., February 9; thence to Cairo, Ill., and to Paducah, Ky., February 13. Attached to 1st Brigade, 4th Division, Army of the Tennessee to April, 1862. Artillery, 1st Division, Army of the Tennessee, to July, 1862. Artillery, 1st Division, District of Jackson, Tenn., to November, 1862. Artillery, District of Jackson, Tenn., 13th Army Corps (Old), Dept. of the Tennessee, to December, 1862. Artillery, District of Jackson, Tenn., 16th Army Corps, to March, 1863. Artillery, 3rd Division, 16th Army Corps, to June, 1863. District of Corinth, Miss., 2nd Division, 16th Army Corps, to January, 1864. Artillery, 4th Division, 16th Army Corps, to September, 1864. Artillery, 1st Division, 17th Army Corps, to November, 1864. Artillery Post, Nashville, Tenn., to November, 1864. Artillery, 7th Division, Wilson's Cavalry Corps, Military Division Mississippi, to February, 1865. Artillery, 1st Cavalry Division, Dept. of the Gulf, to June, 1865. Dept. of Mississippi to July, 1865.

SERVICE.—Battle of Shiloh, Tenn., April 6-7, 1862. Advance on and siege of Corinth, Miss., April 29-May 30. March to Jackson, Tenn., and duty there till June 2, 1863. Moved to Corinth, Miss., and duty there till November 2, 1863. Moved to Lynnville, Tenn., and duty there till March 13, 1864. Re-enlisted January 1, 1864. Atlanta (Ga.) Campaign May 1-September 8, 1864. Demonstrations on Resaca May 8-13. Sugar Valley, near Resaca, May 9. Near Resaca May 13. Battle of Resaca May 14-15. Advance on Dallas May 18-25. Operations on line of Pumpkin Vine Creek and battles about Dallas, New Hope Church and Allatoona Hills May 25-June 5. Operations about Marietta and against Kenesaw Mountain June 10-July 2. Assault on Kenesaw Mountain June 27. Nickajack Creek July 2-5. Ruff's Mills July 3-4. Chattahoochie River July 6-17. Battle of Atlanta July 22. Siege of Atlanta July 22-August 25. Flank movement on Jonesboro August 25-30. Battle of Jonesboro August 31-September 1. Lovejoy Station September 2-6. Pursuit of Hood into Alabama October 3-26. Ordered to Nashville, Tenn., October 24. Battle of Nashville December 15-16. Pursuit of Hood to the Tennessee River December 17-28. Hollow Tree Gap and Franklin December 17. West Harpeth River December 17. Richland Creek December 24. Sugar Creek, Pulaski, December 25-26. Moved to Huntsville, Ala., thence to Eastport, Miss., and duty there till February 6. Ordered to New Orleans, La., and duty there till April. Moved to Mobile Bay April 3-7. March to Greenville, Ala., April 18-22; thence to Eufala April 24-27, and to Montgomery May 5. March to Columbus, Miss., May 11-21, and duty there till July 27. Mustered out August 11, 1865.

Battery lost during service 11 Enlisted men killed and mortally wounded and 1 Officer and 37 Enlisted men by disease. Total 49.

15th INDEPENDENT BATTERY LIGHT ARTILLERY.

Organized at Camp Dennison, Ohio, and mustered in February 1, 1862. Ordered to Cincinnati, Ohio, thence to Fort Leavenworth, Kansas, February 16. While en route disembarked at Paducah, Ky., and duty

there till April 15. Ordered to Pittsburg Landing, Tenn., April 15. Whitehall Landing April 17. Attached to Artillery, 4th Division, Army of the Tennessee, to July, 1862. 4th Division, District of Memphis, Tenn., to September, 1862. 4th Division, District of Jackson, Tenn., to November, 1862. 4th Division, Right Wing 13th Army Corps (Old), Dept. of the Tennessee, to December, 1862. Artillery, 4th Division, 17th Army Corps, to January, 1863. Artillery, 4th Division, 16th Army Corps, to July, 1863. Artillery, 4th Division, 13th Army Corps, to August, 1863. Artillery, 4th Division, 17th Army Corps, to November, 1864. Artillery Brigade, 17th Army Corps, to June, 1865.

SERVICE.—Advance on and siege of Corinth, Miss., April 29-May 30. March to Memphis, Tenn., via Grand Junction, LaGrange and Holly Springs June 1-July 21. Duty at Memphis till September 6. March to Bolivar and Hatchie River September 6-14. Expedition to Grand Junction September 20. Skirmish with Price and Van Dorn September 21. Battle of Metamora or Hatchie River October 5. Bolivar October 7. Expedition from LaGrange toward Lamar, Miss., November 5. Grant's Central Mississippi Campaign. Operations on the Mississippi Central Railroad November, 1862, to January, 1863. Action at Worsham's Creek November 6. At Calersville, Tenn., January to March, 1863. Moved to Memphis, Tenn., March 9, and duty there till May. Expedition to the Coldwater April 18-24. Hernando April 18. Perry's Ferry, Coldwater River, April 19. Ordered to Vicksburg, Miss., May 11. Siege of Vicksburg May 18-July 4. Assaults on Vicksburg May 19 and 22. Advance on Jackson, Miss., July 5-10. Siege of Jackson July 10-17. At Vicksburg till August 2. Ordered to Natchez, Miss., August 15. Expedition to Harrisonburg September 1-8. Near Harrisonburg and capture of Fort Beauregard September 4. At Natchez till December. Ordered to Vicksburg and camp at Clear Creek till February, 1864. Meridian Campaign February 3-March 2. Veterans on furlough March-April. Moved to Clifton, Tenn., thence march via Huntsville and Decatur, Ala., to Kingston, Ga., and Ackworth, Ga., April 28-June 8. Atlanta (Ga.) Campaign June 8 to September 8. Operations about Marietta and against Kenesaw Mountain June 10-July 5. Assault on Kenesaw June 27. Nickajack Creek July 2-5. Chattahoochie River July 5-17. Turner's Ferry July 5. Leggett's or Bald Hill July 20-21. Battle of Atlanta July 22. Siege of Atlanta July 22-August 25. Flank movement on Jonesboro August 25-30. Battle of Jonesboro August 31-September 1. Lovejoy Station September 2-6. Operations against Hood in North Georgia and North Alabama September 29-November 3. March to the sea November 15-December 10. Siege of Savannah December 10-21. Campaign of the Carolinas January to April, 1865. Pocotaligo, S. C., January 14. Barker's Mills, Whippy Swamp, February 2. Salkehatchie Swamp February 2-5. Binnaker's Bridge February 9. Orangeburg February 12-13. Columbia February 15-17. Taylor's Hole Creek, Averysboro, N. C., March 16. Battle of Bentonville March 20-21. Occupation of Goldsboro March 24, and of Raleigh April 14. Bennett's House April 26. Surrender of Johnston and his army. March to Washington, D. C., via Richmond, Va., April 29-May 20. Grand Review May 24. Moved to Columbus, Ohio, and mustered out June 20, 1865.

Battery lost during service 8 Enlisted men killed and mortally wounded and 30 Enlisted men by disease. Total 38.

16th INDEPENDENT BATTERY LIGHT ARTILLERY.

Organized at Springfield, Ohio, August 20, 1861; the 3rd Battery organized in Ohio. Ordered to St. Louis, Mo., September 5. Mustered in September 6, 1861. Moved from St. Louis to Jefferson City, Mo., October 13, and duty there till February 14, 1862. Moved to St. Louis, Mo., thence to Pilot Knob, Mo., March 6. Attached to 1st Division, District of Southeast Missouri, Dept. of Missouri, to May, 1862. Artillery, 1st Division, Army of Southwest Missouri, to July, 1862. District of Eastern Arkansas, Dept. of Missouri, to January, 1863. Artillery, 12th Division, 13th Army Corps, Army of the Tennessee, to July, 1863. Artillery, 3rd Division, 13th Army Corps, Dept. of the Tennessee, to August, 1863, and Dept. of the Gulf to January, 1864. Artillery, 1st Division, 13th Army Corps, Dept. of the Gulf, to June, 1864. Defences of New Orleans, La., Dept. of the Gulf, to August, 1864. Artillery Reserve, Dept. of the Gulf, to August, 1865.

SERVICE.—March to Doniphan March 21-31, 1862. Action at Pitman's Ferry April 1. Moved to Pocahontas, Ark., April 5-11; thence to Jacksonport May 3. To Batesville May 14, thence march to Augusta, Ark., June 20-July 4. March to Clarendon, thence to Helena, Ark., July 5-14. Duty at Helena and at Old Town Landing till April, 1863. Ordered to Milliken's Bend, La., April 8. Movement on Bruinsburg and turning Grand Gulf April 25-30. Battle of Port Gibson May 1. Fourteen-Mile Creek May 12-13. Battle of Champion's Hill May 16. Siege of Vicksburg, Miss., May 18-July 4. Assaults on Vicksburg May 19 and 22. Advance on Jackson, Miss., July 5-10. Siege of Jackson July 10-17. Ordered to New Orleans, La., August 21, and duty there till September 20. Moved to Berwick Bay and duty there till December 27. Ordered to New Orleans, thence to Texas January 1, 1864. Duty at Matagardo Peninsula, Indianola, Powder Horn and Matagorda Island till June, 1864. Ordered to New Orleans, La., and garrison duty there till July 13, 1865. Ordered home July 13, and mustered out at Camp Chase, Ohio, August 2, 1865.

Battery lost during service 1 Officer and 1 Enlisted man killed and 45 Enlisted men by disease. Total 47.

17th INDEPENDENT BATTERY LIGHT ARTILLERY.

Organized at Dayton, Ohio, and mustered in August 21, 1862. Ordered to Covington, Ky., September 3. Attached to Artillery, 1st Division, Army of Kentucky, Dept. of Ohio, to October, 1862. Unattached, Army of Kentucky, Dept. of Ohio, Lexington, Ky., to November, 1862. Artillery, 10th Division, 13th Army Corps, Dept. of the Tennessee, to December, 1862. Artillery, 1st Division, Sherman's Yazoo Expedition, to January, 1863. Artillery, 10th Division, 13th Army Corps, Army of the Tennessee, to August, 1863. 2nd Brigade, 4th Division, 13th Army Corps, Dept. of the Gulf, to June, 1864. Defences of New Orleans, La., to August, 1864. United States Forces, Mobile Bay, Dept. of the Gulf, to September, 1864. Unattached Artillery, 19th Army Corps, Dept. of the Gulf, to December, 1864. Unattached, Artillery Reserve Corps, Military Division West Mississippi, to February, 1865. Artillery Brigade, 16th Army Corps (New), Military Division West Mississippi, to July, 1865.

SERVICE.—Duty at Covington, Ky., during threatened attack on Cincinnati by Kirby Smith. March to Lexington, Ky., thence to Louisville, Ky., and duty there till December 1. Ordered to Memphis, Tenn., December 1. Sherman's Yazoo Expedition December 20, 1862, to January 3, 1863. Expedition from Milliken's Bend to Dallas Station and Delhi December 25-26. Chickasaw Bayou December 26-28. Chickasaw Bluff December 29. Expedition to Arkansas Post, Ark., January 3-10, 1863. Assault on and capture of Fort Hindman, Arkansas Post, January 10-11. Moved to Young's Point, La., January 15. Expedition to Greenville, Miss., and Cypress Bend, Ark., February 14-26. Action at Cypress Bend February 19. Moved to Milliken's Bend March 8. Movement on Bruinsburg and turning Grand Gulf April 25-30. Battle of Port Gibson May 1. Battle of Champion's Hill May 16. Siege of Vicksburg, Miss., May 18-July 4. Assaults on Vicksburg May 19 and 22. Advance on Jackson July 5-10. Siege of Jackson, Miss., July 10-17. Assault on Jackson July 12. Duty at Vicksburg till August 20. Ordered to New Orleans, La., and duty there till September 5. At Brashear City till October 3. Expedition to New and Amite Rivers September 24-29. Western Louisiana ("Teche") Campaign October 3-November 30.

Grand Coteau November 3. Moved to New Orleans, La., and duty there till August, 1864. Operations in Mobile Bay against Forts Gaines and Morgan August 2-23. Siege and capture of Fort Gaines August 3-8. Siege and capture of Fort Morgan August 10-23. Duty at New Orleans till March, 1865. Campaign against Mobile, Ala., and its defences March 17-April 12. Siege of Spanish Fort and Fort Blakely March 26-April 8. Assault and capture of Fort Blakely April 9. Occupation of Mobile April 12. March to Montgomery April 13-25. Duty at Montgomery and Selma, Ala., till July. Ordered home for muster out. Mustered out August 16, 1865.

Battery lost during service 1 Enlisted man killed and 1 Officer and 42 Enlisted men by disease. Total 44.

18th INDEPENDENT BATTERY LIGHT ARTILLERY.

Organized at Camp Portsmouth, Ohio, and mustered in September 13, 1862. Left State for Covington, Ky., October 9, 1862. Attached to 2nd Division, Army of Kentucky, Dept. of Ohio, to February, 1863. 2nd Brigade, Baird's Division, Army of Kentucky, Dept. of the Cumberland, to June, 1863. Artillery, 1st Division, Reserve Corps, Army of the Cumberland, to October, 1863. 1st Division, Artillery Reserve, Dept. of the Cumberland, to March, 1864. 2nd Division, Artillery Reserve, Dept. of the Cumberland, to December, 1864. Unassigned, District of the Etowah, Dept. of the Cumberland, to January, 1865. Post of Chattanooga, Tenn., Dept. of the Cumberland, to June, 1865.

SERVICE.—March to Lexington, Ky., October 23-29, 1862, and duty there till December 26. Moved to Louisville, Ky., December 26; thence to Nashville, Tenn., arriving there February 7, 1863. Moved to Brentwood, Tenn., February 21. Expedition to Franklin and Spring Hill March 2-5. Action at Franklin March 4. Thompson's Station, Spring Hill, March 4-5. Duty at Franklin till June. Repulse of Van Dorn's attack on Franklin April 10. Moved to Triune June 2. Action at Triune June 11. Middle Tennessee (or Tullahoma) Campaign June 23-July 7. Action at Fosterville, Guy's Gap and Shelbyville June 27. Moved to Watrace July 3, and duty there till August 12. Chickamauga (Ga.) Campaign August 16-September 22. Reconnoissance from Rossville September 17. Ringgold, Ga., September 17. Spring Creek September 18. Battle of Chickamauga September 19-20. Siege of Chattanooga September 24-November 23. Battles of Chattanooga November 23-25; Lookout Mountain November 23-24; Mission Ridge November 25. Pursuit to Graysville November 26-28. Ordered to Nashville, Tenn., December 1, and garrison duty there till October, 1864. March to Chattanooga October 6-21. Moved to Nashville November 27. Battles of Nashville December 15-16. Pursuit of Hood to the Tennessee River December 17-28. Duty at Chattanooga, Tenn., till May 1, 1865, and at Resaca, Ga., till June 20. Mustered out June 29, 1865.

Battery lost during service 2 Enlisted men killed and 21 Enlisted men by disease. Total 23.

19th INDEPENDENT BATTERY LIGHT ARTILLERY.

Organized at Cleveland, Ohio, September 10, 1862. Moved to Covington, Ky., October 6; thence march to Lexington, Ky., October 23-28. Attached to Army of Kentucky, Dept. of Ohio, to December, 1862. Artillery, 2nd Division, Army of Kentucky, Dept. of Ohio, to January, 1863. District of Central Kentucky, Dept. of Ohio, to June, 1863. 2nd Brigade, 4th Division, 23rd Army Corps, Army of Ohio, to July, 1863. 2nd Brigade, 1st Division, 23rd Army Corps, to August, 1863. Reserve Artillery, 23rd Army Corps, to January, 1864. 1st Brigade, 3rd Division, 23rd Army Corps, to April, 1864. Artillery, 2nd Division, 23rd Army Corps, to February, 1865. Artillery, 2nd Division, 23rd Army Corps, Dept. of North Carolina, to June, 1865.

SERVICE.—Camp at Ashland, Ky., till December, 1862. Moved to Richmond, Ky., December 10; thence to Danville, Ky., December 31, and to Frankfort January 5, 1863. Return to Lexington, Ky., February 22, and duty there till June 6. March to Somerset June 6-10. Pursuit of Morgan from Somerset, Ky., to Steubenville, Ohio, July 5-29. Burnside's Campaign in East Tennessee August 16-October 17. Expedition to Cumberland Gap September 3-7. Operations about Cumberland Gap September 7-10. Duty at Knoxville, Tenn., till December. Knoxville Campaign November 4 to December 23. Campbell's Station November 16. Siege of Knoxville November 17-December 5. Camp at College Hill till March, 1864. Moved to Morristown March 15, thence to Mossy Creek. Moved to Knoxville April 20, thence march to Cleveland, Tenn., April 27-May 3. Atlanta (Ga.) Campaign May to September. Demonstrations on Dalton May 9-13. Rocky Faced Ridge May 9-11. Battle of Resaca May 14-15. Advance on Dallas May 18-25. Operations on line of Pumpkin Vine Creek and battles about Dallas, New Hope Church and Allatoona Hills May 25-June 5. Operations about Marietta and against Kenesaw Mountain June 10-July 2. Pine Hill June 11-14. Lost Mountain June 15-17. Muddy Creek June 17. Noyes Creek June 19. Kolb's Farm June 22. Assault on Kenesaw June 27. Nickajack Creek July 2-5. Chattahoochie River July 5-17. Capture of Decatur July 19. Howard House July 20. Siege of Atlanta July 22-August 25. Utoy Creek August 5-7. Flank movement on Jonesboro August 25-30. Battle of Jonesboro August 31-September 1. Lovejoy Station September 2-6. Duty at Decatur till October, and at Atlanta till November 1. Moved to Nashville, Tenn., November 1. Nashville Campaign November-December. In front of Columbia, Tenn., November 24-27. Battle of Franklin November 30. Battle of Nashville December 15-16. Pursuit of Hood to the Tennessee River December 17-28. At Clifton, Tenn., till January 15, 1865. Movement to North Carolina via Washington, D. C., January 15-22. Occupation of Wilmington February 22; duty there till March 6. Advance on Goldsboro March 6-21. Occupation of Goldsboro March 21. Advance on Raleigh April 10-13. Occupation of Raleigh April 14. Bennett's House April 26. Surrender of Johnston and his army. Duty at Raleigh and Salisbury, N. C., till June. Mustered out at Salisbury, N. C., June 28, 1865.

Battery lost during service 2 Enlisted men killed and 7 Enlisted men by disease. Total 9.

20th INDEPENDENT BATTERY LIGHT ARTILLERY.

Organized at Camp Taylor, Cleveland, Ohio, and mustered in October 29, 1862. Moved to Murfreesboro, Tenn., December 31, 1862, arriving there February 8, 1863. Attached to 2nd Division, 20th Army Corps, Army of the Cumberland, to October, 1863. 1st Division, Artillery Reserve, Dept. of the Cumberland, to November, 1863. Artillery, 3rd Division, 4th Army Corps, Army of the Cumberland, to December, 1863. Garrison Artillery, Chattanooga, Tenn., Dept. of the Cumberland, to November, 1864. Garrison Artillery, at Nashville, Tenn., Dept. of the Cumberland, to February, 1865. Garrison Artillery, at Chattanooga, Tenn., till July, 1865.

SERVICE.—Duty at Murfreesboro, Tenn., till June, 1863. Middle Tennessee (or Tullahoma) Campaign June 23-July 7. Liberty Gap June 24-27. Chickamauga (Ga.) Campaign August 16-September 22. Battle of Chickamauga September 19-20. Siege of Chattanooga, Tenn., September 24-November 23. Attached to Garrison Artillery at Chattanooga till June, 1864. Chattanooga-Ringgold Campaign November 23-27, 1863. Engaged in repelling attacks of Rebel Cavalry under Forest and Wheeler on the flanks of Sherman's army during the Atlanta (Ga.) Campaign. Action at Dalton, Ga., August 14-16. March to Alpine, Ga., September 4-20, thence march to Pulaski, Tenn. Surrender of Dalton October 13 (Section). Nashville Campaign November-December. In front of Columbia, Duck River, November 24-27. Spring Hill and Thompson's Station November 29. Battle of Franklin November 30. Battle of Nashville December 15-16. Pursuit of Hood to the Tennessee River December 17-28. Moved to Chattanooga,

Tenn., and garrison duty there till July 2, 1865. Mustered out July 19, 1865.

Battery lost during service 1 Officer and 5 Enlisted men killed and mortally wounded and 1 Officer and 17 Enlisted men by disease. Total 24.

21st INDEPENDENT BATTERY LIGHT ARTILLERY.

Organized at Camp Dennison, Ohio, April 29, 1863. Ordered to West Virginia May 5. Return to Camp Dennison May 20, and duty there till September. Pursuit of Morgan through Indiana and Ohio July 5-28. Moved to Camp Nelson, Ky., September 22. Attached to Willcox's Left Wing forces, 9th Army Corps, Dept. of Ohio, to October, 1863. 2nd Brigade, Left Wing forces, Dept. of Ohio, to January, 1864. District of the Clinch, Dept. of Ohio, to April, 1864. 2nd Brigade, 23rd Army Corps, Dept. of the Ohio, to February, 1865. 2nd Brigade, 4th Division, District of East Tennessee, Dept. of the Cumberland, to July, 1865.

SERVICE.—Moved from Camp Nelson, Ky., to Greenville, Tenn., October 1. Action at Blue Springs October 10. Walker's Ford December 2. Duty at various points in Tennessee and Alabama till July, 1865. Mustered out July 21, 1865.

Battery lost during service 1 Officer and 8 Enlisted men by disease. Total 9.

22nd INDEPENDENT BATTERY LIGHT ARTILLERY.

One section organized April 1, 1863. Moved to Wheeling, W. Va., April 1. Duty there and in Holmes county, Ohio, till June. Moved to Camp Chase, Ohio, June 19. Battery organization completed at Camp Chase and mustered in July 14, 1863. Moved to Parkersburg, W. Va., thence to Wheeling, W. Va., and to Hancock, Md., to support Kelly's operations against General Lee in his retreat from Gettysburg, Pa. Sent to operate against Morgan, July. Moved to Camp Nelson, Ky., August 12, 1863. Attached to Willcox's Left Wing forces, 9th Army Corps, Dept. of the Ohio, to October, 1863. DeCourcy's Brigade, Cumberland Gap, Willcox's Left Wing forces, 9th Army Corps, to January, 1864. District of the Clinch, Dept. of the Ohio, to April, 1864. 1st Brigade, 4th Division, 23rd Army Corps, Dept. of the Ohio, to August, 1864. 2nd Brigade, 4th Division, 23rd Army Corps, to February, 1865. 2nd Brigade, 4th Division, District of East Tennessee, Dept. of the Cumberland, to July, 1865.

SERVICE.—Expedition to Cumberland Gap August 17-September 7. Operations about Cumberland Gap September 7-10. Capture of Cumberland Gap September 9. Duty there till June 27, 1864. Action at Crab Gap December 5, 1863. Reconnoissance from Cumberland Gap January 3, 1864. Near Cumberland Gap June 21. Moved to Knoxville, Tenn., June 27, 1864, and garrison duty there till July 5, 1865. Ordered to Camp Chase, Ohio, July 5. Mustered out July 13, 1865.

Battery lost during service 1 Officer and 2 Enlisted men killed and mortally wounded and 1 Officer and 16 Enlisted men by disease. Total 20.

23rd INDEPENDENT BATTERY LIGHT ARTILLERY.

Detached from 2nd Kentucky Infantry 1861. No record in Ohio troops. See Simmons' 1st Kentucky Battery.

24th INDEPENDENT BATTERY LIGHT ARTILLERY.

Organized at Camp Dennison, Ohio, and mustered in August 4, 1863. Ordered to Cincinnati, Ohio, September 22, thence moved to Johnson's Island, Sandusky Bay, Ohio, November 10, and duty there guarding Rebel prisoners till August 6, 1864. Moved to Camp Chase August 6, thence to Camp Douglas, Chicago, Ill., August 27, and duty there guarding Rebel prisoners till June 10, 1865. Mustered out June 24, 1865.

Battery lost during service 6 by disease.

25th INDEPENDENT BATTERY LIGHT ARTILLERY.

Organized by detachment from 2nd Ohio Cavalry at Fort Scott, Kansas, August 27, 1862. First designated

3rd Kansas Independent Battery. Organized as 25th Ohio Battery February 17, 1863. Attached to 1st Brigade, 1st Division, Army of the Frontier, October, 1862, to June, 1863. Artillery, Cavalry Division, District Southeast Missouri, Dept. of Missouri, to August, 1863. Artillery, 1st Cavalry Division, Arkansas Expedition, to January, 1864. Columbus, Ohio, to April, 1864. Artillery, 3rd Division, 7th Army Corps, Dept. of Arkansas, to May, 1864. Artillery, 1st Division, 7th Army Corps, to February, 1865. Artillery, Cavalry Division, 7th Army Corps, to July, 1865. Garrison Artillery, Little Rock, Ark., Dept. of Arkansas, to December, 1865.

SERVICE.—Blount's Campaign in Missouri and Arkansas September 17-December 10, 1862. Expedition to Sarcoxie September 17-25. Reconnoissance to Newtonia September 29-31. Action at Newtonia September 30. Occupation of Newtonia October 4. Cane Hill November 29. Battle of Prairie Grove, Ark., December 7. Expedition to Van Buren, Ark., December 27-29. March over Ozark and Boston Mountains to Cane Creek, Mo., January 1-10, 1863. Moved to Camp Solomon February 27. Campaign against Marmaduke March and April. Ordered to Rolla, Mo., May 22 and refitting till June 26. Moved to Pilot Knob, Mo., June 26, and reported to General Davidson. Expedition against Price and Marmaduke in Arkansas. March to Clarendon, Ark., on White River July 1-August 8. Grand Prairie August 17. Steele's Expedition against Little Rock August 18-September 10. Bayou Metoe or Reed's Bridge August 27. Bayou Fourche and capture of Little Rock September 10. Duty at Little Rock till November. Ferry's Ford October 7. Duty at Benton, Pine Bluff, and Little Rock till January, 1864. Reconnoissance from Little Rock December 5-13, 1863. Re-enlisted January 3, 1864. Moved to Columbus, Ohio, January 21-29. Return to Little Rock, Ark., March 17, and garrison duty there at Fort Steele till December, 1865. Mustered out December 12, 1865.

Battery lost during service 23 Enlisted men by disease. Total 23.

26th INDEPENDENT BATTERY LIGHT ARTILLERY.

Organized at Camp Dennison, Ohio, as Company "F" 32nd Ohio Infantry, August, 1861. Left State for West Virginia September 15. At Grafton, W. Va., September 18, and at Beverly September 22. Attached to Kimball's Brigade, Reynolds' Command, West Virginia, to October, 1861. Cheat Mountain District, West Virginia, to November, 1861. Milroy's Brigade, Cheat Mountain District, to March, 1862. Milroy's Brigade, Mountain Department, to May, 1862. Schenck's Brigade, Mountain Department, to June, 1862. 2nd Brigade, 1st Division, 1st Army Corps, Army of Virginia, to July, 1862. Garrison at Winchester, Va., to September, 1862. Miles' Command, Harper's Ferry, W. Va., September, 1862.

SERVICE.—Stationed at Cheat Mountain Summit, W. Va., October, 1861. Action at Greenbrier October 3. Duty at Greenbrier till December 13. Camp Allegheny December 13. Ordered to Beverly and duty there till April, 1862. Expedition on the Seneca April 1-12. Action at Monterey April 12. At Staunton till May 7. Battle of McDowell May 8. March to Franklin and duty there till May 25. Pursuit of Jackson up the Shenandoah Valley. Battle of Cross Keys June 8. Duty at Strasburg and Winchester till July. Detached from 32nd Infantry for Artillery duty July 20, 1862, and stationed at Winchester till September 11. Retreat to Harper's Ferry September 11-12. Defence of Harper's Ferry September 12-15. Battery surrendered September 15. Paroled and sent to Annapolis, Md., thence to Chicago, Ill., and to Camp Taylor, Cleveland, Ohio. Exchanged January 12, 1863. Again attached to 32nd Infantry and moved to Memphis, Tenn., January 20-25, 1863. Attached to 3rd Brigade, 3rd Division, 17th Army Corps, to December, 1863. Moved to Lake Providence, La., February 20, and to Milliken's Bend, La., April 17. Movement on Bruinsburg and turning Grand Gulf April 25-30. Battle of Port Gibson, Miss., May 1. Raymond

May 12. Jackson May 14. Champion's Hill May 16. Capture a Battery of six guns and assigned to duty as Artillery till August 3, 1863. Siege of Vicksburg, Miss., May 18-July 4. Assaults on Vicksburg May 19 and 22. Attached to Battery "D" 1st Illinois Artillery and to 3rd Ohio Battery August 3 to December 22, 1863, and garrison duty at Vicksburg, Miss. Served with Artillery, 3rd Division, 17th Army Corps. Expedition to Monroe, La., August 20-September 2, 1863. Expedition to Canton and Brownsville October 14-20. Permanently detached from 32nd Ohio as 26th Ohio Battery December 22, 1864. On Veteran furlough January 1 to February 3, 1864. Meridian Campaign February 3-March 2. Duty at Vicksburg till November, 1864, attached to Maltby's Brigade, District of Vicksburg. Expedition to Rodney and Fayette September 29-October 3. Expedition to Woodville October 4-11. Woodville October 5-6. Moved to Natchez, Miss., and garrison duty there till April, 1865. Ordered to Texas April, 1865, and duty on the Rio Grande, Texas, till August. Ordered home for muster out. Mustered out at Todd's Barracks, Columbus, Ohio, September 2, 1865.

Battery lost during service 22 Enlisted men by disease.

1st INDEPENDENT COMPANY SHARPSHOOTERS.

Organized at Dayton, Ohio, September-October, 1861. Attached to Birge's Western Sharpshooters, 14th Missouri Infantry, and later 66th Illinois Infantry as Company "G."

2nd INDEPENDENT COMPANY SHARPSHOOTERS.

Organized at Findlay, Ohio, September-October, 1861. Attached to Birge's Western Sharpshooters, 14th Missouri Infantry, and later 66th Illinois Infantry as Company "H."

3rd INDEPENDENT COMPANY SHARPSHOOTERS.

Organized at Lima, Ohio, March and April, 1862. Attached to Birge's Western Sharpshooters, 14th Missouri Infantry, and later 66th Illinois Infantry as Company "K."

4th INDEPENDENT COMPANY SHARPSHOOTERS.

Organized at Goshen and Camp Dennison, Ohio, and mustered in September 29, 1862. Attached to 79th Ohio Infantry as Company "K."

5th INDEPENDENT COMPANY SHARPSHOOTERS.

Organized at Camp Cleveland, Ohio, and mustered in February 25, 1863. At Headquarters Generals Rosecrans and Thomas, Commanding Army and Dept. of the Cumberland, March, 1863, to July, 1865. Mustered out July 19, 1865.

6th INDEPENDENT COMPANY SHARPSHOOTERS.

Organized at Camp Cleveland, Ohio, and mustered in December 30, 1862. At Headquarters of Generals Rosecrans and Thomas, Commanding Army and Dept. of the Cumberland, March, 1863, to July, 1865. Mustered out July 19, 1865.

7th INDEPENDENT COMPANY SHARPSHOOTERS.

Organized at Camp Cleveland, Ohio, and mustered in January 27, 1863. At Headquarters of Generals Rosecrans and Thomas, Commanding Army and Dept. of the Cumberland, March, 1863, to May, 1864, and at Headquarters of General Sherman, Commanding Military Division Mississippi, May 20, 1864, to July 17, 1865. Mustered out July 28, 1865.

8th INDEPENDENT COMPANY SHARPSHOOTERS.

Organized at Camp Dennison, Ohio, March 9, 1863. At Headquarters of Generals Rosecrans and Thomas, Commanding Army and Dept. of the Cumberland, March, 1863, to July, 1865. Mustered out July 19, 1865.

9th INDEPENDENT COMPANY SHARPSHOOTERS.

Organized February 26, 1864. Attached to 60th Ohio Infantry as Company "G."

10th INDEPENDENT COMPANY SHARPSHOOTERS.

Organized April 1, 1864. Attached to 60th Ohio Infantry as Company "H."

1st REGIMENT INFANTRY.—(3 MONTHS.)

Organized at large April 14 to April 29, 1861. Mustered in April 17, 1861. Moved to Washington, D. C., April 19, and duty in the Defences of that city till July. Attached to Schenck's Brigade, Tyler's Division, McDowell's Army of Northeast Virginia. Actions at Vienna, Va., June 17 and July 9. McDowell's advance on Manassas, Va., July 16-21. Occupation of Fairfax Court House, Va., July 17. Battle of Bull Run, Va., July 21. Cover retreat to Washington. Ordered to Ohio and mustered out August 2, 1861, expiration of term.

1st REGIMENT INFANTRY.—(3 YEARS.)

Organized at Camp Corwin, Dayton, Ohio, August 5 to October 30, 1861. Moved to Cincinnati, Ohio, October 31; thence to Louisville, Ky., November 5, and to West Point, Ky., November 8. Moved to Elizabethtown and Camp Nevin, Ky., November 15-16. Camp at Bacon Creek and Green River, Ky., till February, 1862. Attached to 4th Brigade, 2nd Division, Army of Ohio, to September, 1862. 4th Brigade, 2nd Division, 1st Army Corps, Army of Ohio, to November, 1862. 3rd Brigade, 2nd Division, Right Wing 14th Army Corps, Army of the Cumberland, to January, 1863. 3rd Brigade, 2nd Division, 20th Army Corps, Army of the Cumberland, to October, 1863. 2nd Brigade, 3rd Division, 4th Army Corps, Army of the Cumberland, to September, 1864.

SERVICE.—March to Nashville, Tenn., February 14-25, 1862. Occupation of Nashville February 25 to March 16. March to Duck River March 16-21, and to Savannah, Tenn., March 31-April 6. Battle of Shiloh, Tenn., April 6-7. Advance on and siege of Corinth, Miss., April 29-May 30. Duty at Corinth till June 10. Moved to Iuka, Miss., thence to Tuscumbia, Florence and Huntsville, Ala., June 10-July 5. Duty at Boulay Fork till August 30. Expedition to Tullahoma July 14-18. March to Pelham August 24, thence to Altamont August 28. Reconnoissance toward Sequatchie Valley August 29-30. March to Louisville, Ky., in pursuit of Bragg August 30-September 26. Pursuit of Bragg into Kentucky October 1-17. Lawrenceburg October 8. Dog Walk, Perryville, October 9. March to Nashville, Tenn., October 17-November 7, and duty there till December 26. Kimbrough's Mills, Mill Creek, December 6. Advance on Murfreesboro December 26-30. Battle of Stone's River December 30-31, 1862, and January 1-3, 1863. Duty at Murfreesboro till June. Middle Tennessee (or Tullahoma) Campaign June 23-July 7. Liberty Gap June 24-27. Occupation of Middle Tennessee till August 16. Passage of the Cumberland Mountains and Tennessee River and Chickamauga (Ga.) Campaign August 16-September 22. Battle of Chickamauga September 19-20. Siege of Chattanooga, Tenn., September 24-October 27. Reopening Tennessee River October 26-29. Brown's Ferry October 27. Chattanooga-Ringgold Campaign November 23-27. Orchard Knob November 23. Mission Ridge November 24-25. March to relief of Knoxville November 28-December 8. East Tennessee Campaign December, 1863-January, 1864. Operations about Dandridge January 16-17, 1864. Operations in East Tennessee till April. Atlanta (Ga.) Campaign May 1 to July 25. Demonstration on Rocky Faced Ridge and Dalton May 8-13. Battle of Resaca May 14-15. Adairsville May 17. Near Kingston May 18-19. Near Cassville May 19. Advance on Dallas May 22-25. Operations on line of Pumpkin Vine Creek and battles about Dallas, New Hope Church and Allatoona Hills May 25-June 5. Operations about Marietta and against Kenesaw Mountain June 10-July 2. Pine Hill June 11-14. Lost Mountain June 15-17. Assault on Kenesaw June 27. Ruff's Station July 4. Chattahoochie River July 5-17. Peach Tree Creek July 19-20. Siege of Atlanta July 22-26. Ordered to the reach for

muster out. Scout from Whitesides, Tenn., to Sulphur Springs September 2-5 (Detachment). Mustered out September 24 to October 14, 1864. Recruits transferred to 18th Ohio Volunteers Infantry October 31, 1864.

Regiment lost during service 5 Officers and 116 Enlisted men killed and mortally wounded and 130 Enlisted men by disease. Total 251.

2nd REGIMENT INFANTRY—(3 MONTHS.)

Organized at Columbus, Ohio, and mustered in April 18, 1861. Ordered to Washington, D. C., April 19, and duty in the defences of that city till July. Attached to Schenck's Brigade, Tyler's Division, McDowell's Army of Northeast Virginia, June-July. Advance on Manassas, Va., July 16-21. Occupation of Fairfax Court House July 17. Battle of Bull Run July 21. Mustered out July 31, 1861.

2nd REGIMENT INFANTRY.—(3 YEARS.)

Organized at Camp Dennison, Ohio, July 17 to September 20, 1861. Left State for Kentucky September 4. Operations in vicinity of Olympian Springs, Ky., till November. Action at West Liberty October 23. Olympian Springs November 4. Ivy Mountain November 8. Piketown November 8-9. Moved to Louisville, Ky., thence to Bacon Creek, Ky., and duty there till February, 1862. Attached to 9th Brigade, Army of the Ohio, October to December, 1861. 9th Brigade, 3rd Division, Army of the Ohio, to September, 1862. 9th Brigade, 3rd Division, 1st Army Corps, Army of the Ohio, to November, 1862. 1st Brigade, 1st Division, Centre 14th Army Corps, Army of the Cumberland, to January 1863. 1st Brigade, 1st Division, 14th Army Corps, to June, 1864. Headquarters 14th Army Corps to August, 1864.

SERVICE—Advance on Bowling Green, Ky., and Nashville, Tenn., February 10-25, 1862. Occupation of Nashville, Tenn., February 25 to March 17. Advance on Murfreesboro, Tenn., March 17-19. Advance on Huntsville, Ala., April 4-11. Pittenger's Raid on Georgia State Railroad April 7-12 (Detachment). Capture of Huntsville, Ala., April 11. Action at West Bridge and occupation of Bridgeport, Ala., April 29. Near Pulaski May 1. Duty along Memphis & Charleston Railroad till August. Actions at Battle Creek June 21 and July 20. March to Louisville, Ky., in pursuit of Bragg August 21-September 26. Pursuit of Bragg to Crab Orchard, Ky., October 1-15. Battle of Perryville October 8. March to Nashville, Tenn., October 16-November 7 and duty there till December 26. Advance on Murfreesboro December 26-30. Battle of Stone's River December 30-31, 1862, and January 1-3, 1863. Duty at Murfreesboro till June. Middle Tennessee (or Tullahoma) Campaign June 23-July 7. Hoover's Gap June 24-26. Occupation of Middle Tennessee till August 16. Passage of Cumberland Mountains and Tennessee River and Chickamauga (Ga.) Campaign August 16-September 24. Battle of Chickamauga, Ga., September 19-20. Rossville Gap September 21. Siege of Chattanooga, Tenn., September 24-November 23. Chattanooga-Ringgold Campaign November 23-27. Orchard Knob November 23. Lookout Mountain November 24. Mission Ridge November 24-25. Pea Vine Valley November 26. Graysville, Ga., November 26. Ringgold, Ga., November 27. Reconnoissance of Dalton, Ga., February 22-27, 1864. Tunnel Hill, Buzzard's Roost Gap and Rocky Faced Ridge February 23-25. Atlanta (Ga.) Campaign May 1 to August 1, 1864. Demonstration on Rocky Faced Ridge May 8-11. Buzzard's Roost Gap May 8-9. Battle of Resaca May 14-15. Advance on Dallas May 18-25. Operations on Pumpkin Vine Creek and battles about Dallas, New Hope Church and Allatoona Hills May 25-June 5. Pickett's Mills May 27. Kingston June 1. Operations about Marietta and against Kenesaw Mountain June 10-July 2. Pine Hill June 11-14. Lost Mountain June 15-17. Assault on Kenesaw June 27. Ruff's Station July 4. Chattahoochie River July 5-17. Buckhead, Nancy's Creek, July 18. Peach Tree Creek July 19-20. Siege of Atlanta July 22-August 1. Ordered to Chattanooga. Tenn., August 1. Mustered out October 10, 1864, expiration of term. Recruits transferred to 18th Ohio Infantry.

Regiment lost during service 9 Officers and 96 Enlisted men killed and mortally wounded and 138 Enlisted men by disease. Total 243.

3rd REGIMENT INFANTRY.—(3 MONTHS.)

Organized at Camp Jackson, Columbus, Ohio, April 25, 1861. Moved to Camp Dennison, Ohio, April 28, and duty there till June 12. Reorganized for three years' service June 12, 1861. Three-months men. mustered out July 24, 1861.

3rd REGIMENT INFANTRY.—(3 YEARS.)

Organized at Camp Dennison, near Cincinnati, Ohio, June 4, 1861. Moved to Grafton, W. Va., thence to Clarksburg, W. Va., June 20-25, 1861. Attached to 1st Brigade, Army of Occupation, West Virginia, to September, 1861. Reynolds' Command, Cheat Mountain, W. Va., to November, 1861. 17th Brigade, Army of the Ohio, to December, 1861. 17th Brigade, 3rd Division, Army of the Ohio, to September, 1862. 17th Brigade, 3rd Division, 1st Corps, Army of the Ohio, to November, 1862. 2nd Brigade, 1st Division, Centre 14th Army Corps, Army of the Cumberland, to January, 1863. 2nd Brigade, 1st Division, 14th Army Corps, to April, 1863. Streight's Provisional Brigade, 14th Army Corps, to May, 1863. Unattached, Dept. of the Cumberland, August to November, 1863. 2nd Brigade, 2nd Division, 14th Army Corps, to April, 1865. Garrison at Chattanooga, Tenn., to June, 1864.

SERVICE.—West Virginia Campaign July 6-17, 1861. Action at Middle Fork Bridge, W. Va., July 6-7. Rich Mountain July 10-11. Pursuit to Cheat Mountain Summit July 11-16. Moved to Elkwater Creek August 4. Operations on Cheat Mountain September 11-17. Action at Elkwater September 11. Cheat Mountain Pass September 12. Scout to Marshall October 3. Reconnoissance to Big Springs October 6. Moved to Louisville, Ky., November 26-28. Duty at Elizabethtown and Bacon Creek, Ky., till Febuary, 1862. Advance on Nashville, Tenn., February 10-25. Occupation of Nashville February 25-March 17. Advance on Murfreesboro, Tenn., March 17-19. Reconnoissance to Shelbyville, Tullahoma and McMinnville March 25-28. Moved to Fayetteville April 7. Advance on Huntsville, Ala., April 10-11. Capture of Huntsville April 11. Pursuit to Decatur April 11-14. Action at Bridgeport April 27. West Bridge, near Bridgeport, April 29. Duty at Huntsville till August 23. March to Louisville, Ky., in pursuit of Bragg August 23-September 25. Pursuit of Bragg into Kentucky October 1-15. Battle of Perryville October 8. March to Nashville, Tenn., October 16-November 7, and duty there till December 26. Advance on Murfreesboro December 26-30. Battle of Stone's River December 30-31, 1862, and January 1-3, 1863. At Murfreesboro till April, 1863. Streight's Raid to Rome, Ga., April 26-May 3. Day's Gap, Sand Mountain and Crooked Creek and Hog Mountain, April 30. East Branch Black Warrior Creek May 1. Blount's Farm Gadsden, May 2. Near Centre May 2. Cedar Creek. near Rome, May 3. Regiment captured. Exchanged May, 1863. At Camp Chase, Ohio, reorganizing till August. Quelling Holmes County Rebellion June 13-18. Pursuit of Morgan July 15-26. Moved to Nashville, Tenn., August 1, thence moved to Bridgeport, Ala., and guard duty there till October. Expedition against Wheeler October 1-8. Duty at Battle Creek, Looney Creek and Kelly's Ford till November 27. Garrison duty at Chattanooga, Tenn., till June, 1864. Ordered to Camp Dennison, Ohio, June 9. Mustered out June 23, 1864.

Regiment lost during service 4 Officers and 87 Enlisted men killed and mortally wounded, and 3 Officers and 78 Enlisted men by disease. Total 172.

4th REGIMENT INFANTRY.—(3 MONTHS.)

Organized at Camp Jackson, Columbus, Ohio, April 25, 1861. Moved to Camp Dennison, Ohio, May 2, and duty there till June 4. Reorganized for three years' service June 4, 1861. Three months men mustered out July 24, 1861.

4th REGIMENT INFANTRY.—(3 YEARS.)

Organized at Camp Dennison, Ohio, June 4, 1861. Moved to Grafton, W. Va., June 20-23. Attached to McCook's Advance Brigade, West Virginia, to July, 1861. 3rd Brigade, Army of Occupation, West Virginia, to November, 1861. Kelly's Command, West Virginia, to January, 1862. 2nd Brigade, Landers' Division, Army of the Potomac, to March, 1862. 1st Brigade, Shields' 2nd Division, Banks' 5th Army Corps and Dept. of the Shenandoah, to May, 1862. Kimball's Independent Brigade, Dept. of the Rappahannock, to July, 1862. Kimball's Independent Brigade, 2nd Army Corps, Army of the Potomac, to September, 1862. 1st Brigade, 3rd Division, 2nd Army Corps, to March, 1864. 3rd Brigade, 2nd Division, 2nd Army Corps, to June, 1865.

SERVICE.—West Virginia Campaign July 6-17, 1861. Capture of Beverly July 12. Expedition to Huttonsville July 13-16. At Beverly till July 23; thence moved to New Creek. At Pendleton August 7 to October 25. Action at Petersburg September 7 and 12. Hanging Rock, Romney, September 23. Romney September 23-25. Mill Creek Mills, Romney, October 26. Duty at Romney till January, 1862. Expedition to Blue's Gap January 6-7. Blue's Gap January 7. Evacuation of Romney January 10. At Paw Paw Tunnel February 9 to March 7. Advance on Winchester March 7-15. Martinsburg March 9. Cedar Creek March 18. Strasburg March 19. Battle of Winchester March 23. Cedar Creek March 25. Woodstock April 1. Edenburg April 2. Mt. Jackson April 16. March to Fredericksburg May 12-21, and return to Front Royal May 25-30. Front Royal May 30. Battle of Port Republic June 9. Moved to Alexandria, thence to Harrison's Landing June 29-30. Haxell's, Herring Creek, July 3-4. At Harrison's Landing till August 16. Movement to Fortress Monroe, thence to Centreville August 16-28. Cover Pope's retreat from Bull Run to Fairfax Court House September 1. Maryland Campaign September 6-22. Battle of Antietam September 16-17. Moved to Harper's Ferry, W. Va., September 22, and duty there till October 30. Reconnoissance to Leesburg October 1-2. March to Falmouth, Va., October 30-November 19. Battle of Fredericksburg, Va., December 12-15. At Falmouth, Va., till April 27, 1863. "Mud March" January 20-24. Chancellorsville Campaign April 27-May 6. Battle of Chancellorsville May 1-5. Pursuit of Lee to Manassas Gap, Va., July 5-24. On detached duty at New York City August 15 to September 16. Bristoe Campaign October 9-22. Auburn and Bristoe October 14. Advance to line of the Rappahannock November 7-8. Mine Run Campaign November 26-December 2. Robertson's Tavern or Locust Grove November 27. Mine Run November 28-30. Demonstration on the Rapidan February 6-7, 1864. Morton's Ford February 6-7. Campaign from the Rapidan to the James May 3 to June 15. Battles of the Wilderness May 5-7; Laurel Hill May 8; Spottsylvania May 8-12; Po River May 10; Spottsylvania Court House May 12-21; "Bloody Angle" May 12; North Anna River May 23-26. On line of the Pamunkey May 26-28. Totopotomoy May 28-31. Cold Harbor June 1-12. Before Petersburg June 16-18. Siege of Petersburg June 16, 1864, to April 2, 1865. Old members mustered out June 21, 1864. Consolidated to a Battalion June 26, 1864. Jerusalem Plank Road, Weldon Railroad, June 22-23, 1864. Demonstration north of James River July 27-29. Deep Bottom July 27-28. Demonstration north of James River August 13-20. Strawberry Plains, Deep Bottom, August 14-18. Ream's Station August 25. Boydton Plank Road, Hatcher's Run, October 27-28. Dabney's Mills, Hatcher's Run, February 5-7, 1865. Watkins' House March 25. Appomattox Campaign March 28-April 9. Boydton and White Oak Road March 29-31. Crow's House March 31. Fall of Petersburg April 2. Sailor's Creek April 6. High Bridge and Farmville

April 7. Appomattox Court House April 9. Surrender of Lee and his army. March to Washington, D. C., May 1-12. Grand Review May 23. Mustered out July 12, 1865.

Regiment lost during service 8 Officers and 95 Enlisted men killed and mortally wounded and 3 Officers and 155 Enlisted men by disease. Total 261.

5th REGIMENT INFANTRY.—(3 MONTHS.)

Organized at Camp Harrison, near Cincinnati, Ohio, April 20, 1861. Mustered in May 8, 1861. Moved to Camp Dennison May 23, and duty there till June 20, 1861. Reorganized for three years' service at Camp Dennison, Ohio, June 20, 1861. Three months men mustered out July 24, 1861.

5th REGIMENT INFANTRY.—(3 YEARS.)

Organized at Camp Dennison, Ohio, June 20, 1861. Left State for West Virginia July 10, 1861, and duty at Grafton, Clarksburg, Oakland and Parkersburg, W. Va., till August 5. Attached to Kelly's Command, West Virginia, to January, 1862. 2nd Brigade, Landers' Division, Army of the Potomac, to March, 1862. 2nd Brigade, Shields' 2nd Division, Banks' 5th Army Corps, and Dept. of the Shenandoah to May, 1862. 2nd Brigade, Shields' Division, Dept. of the Rappahannock, to June, 1862. 2nd Brigade, 1st Division, 2nd Corps, Pope's Army of Virginia, to August, 1862. 1st Brigade, 2nd Division, 2nd Corps, Army of Virginia, to September, 1862. 1st Brigade, 2nd Division, 12th Army Corps, Army of the Potomac, to October, 1863, and Army of the Cumberland to April, 1864. 1st Brigade, 2nd Division, 20th Army Corps, Army of the Cumberland and Georgia, to July, 1865.

SERVICE.—Duty at Buckhannon, W. Va., till November 3, 1861. Action at French Creek November 3 (Cos. "A," "B" and "C"). Picket duty near Romney till January, 1862. Action near Romney December 8, 1861. Expedition to Blue's Gap January 6-7, 1862. Blue's Gap January 7. At Paw Paw Tunnel till March. Advance on Winchester March 7-15. Reconnoissance to Strasburg March 18-21. Battle of Winchester March 22-23. Strasburg and Staunton Road April 1-2. Mt. Jackson April 16. March to Fredericksburg, Va., May 12-21, and return to Front Royal May 25-30. Battle of Port Republic June 9. Battles of Cedar Mountain August 9. Pope's Campaign in Northern Virginia August 16-September 2. Guard trains during the Battles of Bull Run August 28-30. Maryland Campaign September 6-22. Battle of Antietam, Md., September 16-17. Moved to Harper's Ferry, W. Va., September 22, and duty at Bolivar Heights till December. Reconnoissance to Rippon, W. Va., November 9. Reconnoissance to Winchester December 2-6. March to Stafford Court House, Va., December 10-14, and duty there till January 20, 1863. Dumfries, Va., December 27, 1862. "Mud March" January 20-24, 1863. At Stafford Court House till April 27. Chancellorsville Campaign April 27-May 6. Battle of Chancellorsville May 1-5. Gettysburg (Pa.) Campaign June 11-July 24. Battle of Gettysburg, Pa., July 1-3. Pursuit of Lee to Manassas Gap, Va., July 5-24. Duty at New York during draft disturbances August 15-September 8. Moved to Bridgeport, Ala., September 24-October 3. Reopening Tennessee River October 26-29. Battle of Wauhatchie October 28-29. Chattanooga-Ringgold Campaign November 23-27. Lookout Mountain November 23-24. Mission Ridge November 25. Ringgold Gap, Taylor's Ridge, November 27. Scout to Caperton's Ferry March 31-April 2, 1864. Atlanta (Ga.) Campaign May 1-September 8. Demonstrations on Rocky Faced Ridge May 8-11. Dug Gap or Mill Creek May 8. Battle of Resaca May 14-15. Cassville May 19. New Hope Church May 25. Operations on line of Pumpkin Vine Creek and battles about Dallas, New Hope Church and Allatoona Hills May 26-June 5. Operations about Marietta and against Kenesaw Mountain June 10-July 2. Pine Hill June 11-14. Lost Mountain June 15-17. Gilgal or Golgotha Church June 15. Muddy Creek June 17. Noyes Creek June 19. Kolb's

Farm June 22. Assault on Kenesaw June 27. Ruff's Station or Smyrna Camp Ground July 4. Chattahoochie River July 5-17. Peach Tree Creek July 19-20. Siege of Atlanta July 22-August 25. Operations at Chattahoochie River Bridge August 26-September 2. Occupation of Atlanta September 2-November 15. Near Atlanta November 9. March to the sea November 15-December 10. Siege of Savannah December 10-21. Campaign of the Carolinas January to April, 1865. North Edisto River February 12-13. Battle of Bentonville, N. C., March 19-21. Occupation of Goldsboro March 24. Advance on Raleigh April 10-14. Occupation of Raleigh April 14. Bennett's House April 26. Surrender of Johnston and his army. March to Washington, D. C., via Richmond, Va., April 29-May 20. Grand Review May 24. Moved to Louisville, Ky., June 6. Mustered out July 26, 1865.

Regiment lost during service 9 Officers and 137 Enlisted men killed and mortally wounded and 2 Officers and 55 Enlisted men by disease. Total 203.

6th REGIMENT INFANTRY ("GUTHRIE GRAYS") (3 MONTHS).

Organized at Camp Harrison, near Cincinnati, and mustered in April 27, 1861. Duty at Camp Harrison till May 17. Moved to Camp Dennison, Ohio, May 17, and duty there till June 18. Reorganized for three years' service June 18, 1861. Three-months men mustered out July 24, 1861.

6th REGIMENT INFANTRY (3 YEARS).

Organized at Camp Dennison, Ohio, June 18, 1861. Moved to Fetterman, W. Va., June 29-July 2. Attached to 1st Brigade, Army of Occupation, West Virginia, to September, 1861. Reynolds' Command, Cheat Mountain, W. Va., to November, 1861. 10th Brigade, Army Ohio, to December, 1861. 10th Brigade, 4th Division, Army Ohio, to September, 1862. 10th Brigade, 4th Division, 2nd Corps, Army Ohio, to November, 1862. 3rd Brigade, 2nd Division, Left Wing 14th Army Corps, Army of the Cumberland, to January, 1863. 3rd Brigade, 2nd Division, 21st Army Corps, Army of the Cumberland, to October, 1863. 2nd Brigade, 3rd Division, 4th Army Corps, to June, 1864.

SERVICE.—At Grafton, W. Va., July 2, 1861. March to Philippi July 4. West Virginia Campaign July 6-21. Laurel Hill July 8. Carrick's Ford July 13. Pursuit of Garnett's forces July 15-16. Duty at Beverly till August 6. Camp at Elkwater, foot of Cheat Mountain, August 6-November 19. Operations on Cheat Mountain against Lee September 11-17. Cheat Mountain Pass September 12. Reconnoissance up Tygart Valley September 26-29. Moved to Louisville November 19-30. Duty at Camp Buell till December 9, and at Camp Wickliffe, Ky., till February 14, 1862. Expedition down Ohio River to reinforce Gen. Grant at Fort Donelson, thence to Nashville, Tenn., February 14-25. Occupation of Nashville February 25, the first Regiment to enter city. Camp on Murfreesboro Pike till March 17. March to Savannah, Tenn., March 17-April 6. Battle of Shiloh, Tenn., April 6-7. Duty at Pittsburg Landing till May 24. Siege of Corinth, Miss., May 24-30. Occupation of Corinth May 30. Pursuit to Booneville May 30-July 12. Moved to Athens, Ala., and duty there till July 17. Ordered to Murfreesboro July 17, thence to McMinnville and duty there till August 17. March to Louisville, Ky., in pursuit of Bragg August 17-September 26. Pursuit of Bragg into Kentucky October 1-22. Battle of Perryville October 8. March to Nashville, Tenn., October 22-November 7, and duty there till December 26. Advance on Murfreesboro, Tenn., December 26-30. Battle of Stone's River December 30-31, 1862, and January 1-3, 1863. Duty at and near Murfreesboro till June. Actions at Woodbury, Tenn., January 24 and April 4. Middle Tennessee or Tullahoma Campaign June 23-July 7. At Manchester till August 16. Passage of Cumberland Mountains and Tennessee River, and Chickamauga (Ga.) Campaign August 16-September 22. Battle of Chickamauga September 19-20. Siege of Chattanooga,

Tenn., September 24-November 23. Reopening Tennessee River October 26-29. Brown's Ferry October 27. Chattanooga-Ringgold Campaign November 23-27. Orchard Knob November 23-24. Mission Ridge November 25. March to relief of Knoxville, Tenn., November 28-December 8. Operations in East Tennessee till April, 1864. About Dandridge January 16-17. Garrison at Cleveland, Tenn., April 12-May 17, and at Resaca, Ga., guarding railroad bridge over the Oostenaula River, till June 6. Ordered to the rear for muster out June 6. Mustered out at Camp Dennison, Ohio, June 23, 1864, expiration of term.

Regiment lost during service 4 Officers and 82 Enlisted men killed and mortally wounded and 2 Officers and 56 Enlisted men by disease. Total 144.

7th REGIMENT INFANTRY (3 MONTHS).

Organized at Cleveland, Ohio, April 22-25, 1861. Moved to Camp Dennison, Ohio, May 2, and duty there till June 16. Reorganized for three years' service June 16, 1861. Three-months men mustered out July 24, 1861.

7th REGIMENT INFANTRY (3 YEARS).

Organized at Camp Dennison, Ohio, June 16, 1861. Left State for Clarksburg, W. Va., June 26, 1861, arriving there June 29. Attached to Railroad District, West Virginia, to January, 1862. 3rd Brigade, Landers' Division, Army Potomac, to March, 1862. 3rd Brigade, Shields' 2nd Division, Banks' 5th Army Corps, and Dept. of the Shenandoah, to May, 1862. 3rd Brigade, Shields' Division, Dept. of the Rappahannock, to June, 1862. 2nd Brigade, 1st Division, 2nd Corps, Pope's Army of Virginia, to August, 1862. 1st Brigade, 2nd Division, 2nd Corps, Army of Virginia, to September, 1862. 1st Brigade, 2nd Division, 12th Army Corps, Army Potomac, to October, 1863, and Army of the Cumberland, to April, 1864. 1st Brigade, 2nd Division, 20th Army Corps, Army of the Cumberland, to June, 1864.

SERVICE.—Expedition to Weston, W. Va., June 29-30. Relief of Glenville July 5. Advance to Sutton and Cross Lanes July 7-August 15. Moved to Gauley Bridge August 21-22. Cross Lanes, near Summerville, August 26. At Charleston till November. Operations in the Kanawha Valley October 19-November 16. Expedition to Loop Creek and Fayetteville November 1-15. McCoy's Mills November 15. Expedition to Blue's Gap January 6-7, 1862. Blue's Gap January 7. Duty at Hampton Heights and Paw Paw Tunnel till March 7. Advance on Winchester March 7-15. Reconnoissance to Strasburg March 18-21. Battle of Winchester March 22-23. Monterey April 12. March to Fredericksburg May 12-21, and return to Front Royal May 25-30. Battle of Port Republic June 9. Battle of Cedar Mountain August 9. Pope's Campaign in Northern Virginia August 16-September 2. Guard trains during battles of Bull Run August 28-30. Maryland Campaign September 6-22. Battle of Antietam September 16-17. Moved to Harper's Ferry, W. Va., and duty at Bolivar Heights till December. Reconnoissance to Rippon, W. Va., November 8. Reconnoissance to Charleston December 1-6. Berryville December 1. March to Stafford Court House December 10-14, and duty there till January 20, 1863. Dumfries December 29. "Mud March" January 20-24. At Stafford Court House till April 27. Chancellorsville Campaign April 27-May 6. Battle of Chancellorsville May 1-5. Gettysburg (Pa.) Campaign June 11-July 24. Battle of Gettysburg, Pa., July 1-3. Pursuit of Lee to Manassas Gap, Va., July 5-24. Duty at New York during draft disturbances August 29-September 8. Movement to Bridgeport, Ala., September 24-October 3. Garrison's Creek, near Fosterville, October 6 (Detachment). Reopening Tennessee River October 26-29. Chattanooga-Ringgold Campaign November 23-27. Lookout Mountain November 23-24. Mission Ridge November 25. Ringgold Gap, Taylor's Ridge, November 27. At Bridgeport, Ala., till May. Atlanta (Ga.) Campaign May 1-June 11. Demonstration on Rocky Faced Ridge May 8-11. Dug Gap, or Mill Creek, May 8. Battle of Resaca May 14-15. Near Cassville May 19. New Hope Church

May 25. Operations on line of Pumpkin Vine Creek and battles about Dallas, New Hope Church and Allatoona Hills May 26-June 5. Left front for muster out June 11. Veterans and Recruits transferred to 5th Ohio Infantry. Mustered out July 6, 1864, expiration of term.

Regiment lost during service 10 Officers and 174 Enlisted men killed and mortally wounded and 2 Officers and 87 Enlisted men by disease. Total 273.

8th REGIMENT INFANTRY (3 MONTHS).

Organized at Cleveland, Ohio, April 18-May 4, 1861. Moved to Camp Dennison, Ohio, and duty there till June 22. Reorganized for three years June 22, 1861. Three-months men mustered out July 24, 1861.

8th REGIMENT INFANTRY (3 YEARS).

Organized at Camp Dennison, Ohio, June 22, 1861, and duty there till July 8. Moved to Grafton, W. Va., July 8. At West Union, Preston County, till July 13. Pursuit of Garnett's forces July 13-18. Guard duty on Baltimore & Ohio Railroad to September. Attached to Hill's Brigade, Army of Occupation, West Virginia, to August, 1861. 3rd Brigade, Army of Occupation, to January, 1862. Landers' Division, Army Potomac, to March, 1862. 1st Brigade, Shields' 2nd Division, Banks' 5th Army Corps, and Dept. of the Shenandoah, to May, 1862. Kimball's Independent Brigade, Dept. of the Rappahannock, to July, 1862. Kimball's Independent Brigade, 2nd Army Corps, Army of the Potomac, to September, 1862. 1st Brigade, 3rd Division, 2nd Army Corps, to March, 1864. 3rd Brigade, 2nd Division, 2nd Army Corps, to June, 1864.

SERVICE.—Action at Worthington, W. Va., September 2, 1861. Hanging Rock, Romney, September 23. Romney September 23-25. Mill Creek Mills, Romney, October 26. Duty at Romney till January, 1862. Expedition to Blue's Gap January 6-7. Blue's Gap January 7. Evacuation of Romney January 10. Bloomery Gap February 9 and 13. Duty at Paw Paw Tunnel till March 7. Advance on Winchester, Va., March 7-15. Strasburg March 19. Battle of Kernstown March 22. Winchester March 23. Cedar Creek March 25. Woodstock April 1. Edenburg April 2. Mt. Jackson April 16. March to Fredericksburg, Va., May 12-21, and return to Front Royal May 25-30. Front Royal May 30. Expedition to Luray June 3-7. Port Republic Bridge June 8. Port Republic June 9. Moved to Alexandria, thence to Harrison's Landing June 29-30. Haxall's, Herring Creek, Harrison's Landing, July 3-4. At Harrison's Landing till August 16. Movement to Fortress Monroe, thence to Centreville August 16-28. Cover Pope's retreat from Bull Run to Fairfax Court House September 1. Maryland Campaign September 6-22. Battle of Antietam September 16-17. Moved to Harper's Ferry September 22, and duty there till October 30. Reconnoissance to Leesburg October 1-2. March to Falmouth October 30-November 19. Battle of Fredericksburg, Va., December 12-15. At Falmouth, Va., till April 27, 1863. "Mud March" January 20-24. Chancellorsville Campaign April 27-May 6. Battle of Chancellorsville May 1-5. Gettysburg (Pa.) Campaign June 11-July 24. Battle of Gettysburg July 1-3. Pursuit of Lee to Manassas Gap, Va., July 5-24. On detached duty at New York during draft disturbances August 15-September 16. Bristoe Campaign October 9-22. Auburn and Bristoe October 14. Advance to line of the Rappahannock November 7-8. Mine Run Campaign November 26-December 2. Robertson's Tavern, or Locust Grove, November 27. Mine Run November 28-30. Demonstration on the Rapidan February 5-7, 1864. Morton's Ford February 6-7. Rapidan Campaign May 3-June 15. Battles of the Wilderness May 5-7; Laurel Hill May 8; Spottsylvania May 8-12; Po River May 10; Spottsylvania Court House May 12-21; "Bloody Angle" May 12; North Anna River May 23-26. On line of the Pamunkey May 26-28. Totopotomoy May 8-31. Cold Harbor June 1-12. Before Petersburg June 16-18. Siege of Petersburg June 16-25. Jerusalem Plank Road, Weldon Railroad, June 22-23. Left trenches June 24. Veterans and Recruits formed into two Companies and transferred to 4th Ohio Infantry

Battalion June 25, 1864. Regiment mustered out at Cleveland, Ohio, July 13, 1865.

Regiment lost during service 8 Officers and 124 Enlisted men killed and mortally wounded and 1 Officer and 72 Enlisted men by disease. Total 205.

9th REGIMENT INFANTRY (3 MONTHS).

Organized at Camp Harrison near Cincinnati, Ohio, April 22, 1861. Moved to Camp Dennison, Ohio, and duty there till May 27. Reorganized at Camp Dennison for three years May 27 to June 13, 1861, the first three-years Regiment from the State. Three months' men mustered out August 4, 1861.

9th REGIMENT INFANTRY (3 YEARS).

Organized at Camp Dennison, Ohio, May 27 to June 13, 1861. Ordered to West Virginia June 16. Attached to 3rd Brigade, Army of Occupation, W. Va., to August, 1861. 2nd Brigade, Kanawha Division West Virginia, to November, 1861. 3rd Brigade, Army Ohio, to December, 1861. 3rd Brigade, 1st Division, Army Ohio, to September, 1862. 3rd Brigade, 1st Division, 3rd Corps, Army Ohio, to November, 1862. 3rd Brigade, 3rd Division, Center 14th Army Corps, Army of the Cumberland, to January, 1863. 3rd Brigade, 3rd Division, 14th Army Corps, to October, 1863. 2nd Brigade, 3rd Division, 14th Army Corps, to May, 1864.

SERVICE.—West Virginia Campaign July 6-17, 1861. Battle of Rich Mountain July 10. Capture of Beverly July 12. Duty at New Creek till August 27. At New River till November 24. Moved to Louisville, Ky., November 24-December 2, thence to Lebanon, Ky., and duty there till January, 1862. Advance to Camp Hamilton January 1-17. Battle of Mill Springs January 19-20. March to Louisville, Ky., thence moved to Nashville, Tenn., via Ohio and Cumberland Rivers February 10-March 2. March to Pittsburg Landing, Tenn., March 20-April 7. (Presented by ladies of Louisville with a National flag for gallantry at Mill Springs.) Advance on and siege of Corinth, Miss., April 29-May 30. Ordered to Tuscumbia, Ala., June 22, and duty there till July 27. Moved to Decherd, Tenn., July 27, thence march to Louisville, Ky., in pursuit of Bragg August 21-September 26. Pursuit of Hood into Kentucky October 1-15. Battle of Perryville, Ky., October 8. March to Nashville, Tenn., via Bowling Green, Lancaster, Danville and Lebanon October 16-November 7. Duty at South Tunnel opening communications with Nashville November 8-26. Guard fords of the Cumberland till January 14, 1863. Duty at Nashville, Tenn., January 15-March 6. Expedition toward Columbia March 6-14. Moved to Triune and duty there till June. Franklin June 4-5. Middle Tennessee or Tullahoma Campaign June 23-July 27. Occupation of Middle Tennessee till August 16. Passage of the Cumberland Mountains and Tennessee River and Chickamauga (Ga.) Campaign August 16-September 22. Battle of Chickamauga, Ga., September 19-21. Siege of Chattanooga, Tenn., September 24-November 23. Reopening Tennessee River October 26-29. Brown's Ferry October 27. Chattanooga-Ringgold Campaign November 23-27. Battles of Orchard Knob November 23. Mission Ridge November 24-25. Demonstration on Dalton, Ga., February 22-27, 1864. Tunnel Hill, Buzzard's Roost Gap and Rocky Faced Ridge February 23-25. Reconnoissance from Ringgold toward Tunnel Hill April 29. Atlanta (Ga.) Campaign May 1-25. Demonstration on Rocky Faced Ridge May 8-11. Battle of Resaca May 14-15. Advance on Dallas May 18-25. Left front May 25. Mustered out at Camp Dennison, Ohio, June 7, 1864, expiration of term.

Regiment lost during service 6 Officers and 85 Enlisted men killed and mortally wounded and 2 Officers and 60 Enlisted men by disease. Total 153.

10th REGIMENT INFANTRY (3 MONTHS).

Organized at Camp Harrison near Cincinnati, Ohio, and mustered in May 7, 1861. Moved to Camp Dennison, Ohio, May 12, and duty there till June 3. Reorganized for three years' service June 3, 1861. Three months' men mustered out August 21, 1861.

10th REGIMENT INFANTRY (3 YEARS).

Organized at Camp Dennison, Ohio, June 3, 1861. Left State for West Virginia June 24, and duty at Grafton, Clarksburg and Buckhannon till August. Attached to 2nd Brigade, Army of Occupation, W. Va., to September, 1861. Benham's Brigade, Kanawha Division, West Virginia, to October, 1861. 1st Brigade, Kanawha Division West Virginia, to November, 1861. 17th Brigade, Army Ohio, to December, 1861. 17th Brigade, 3rd Division, Army Ohio, to September, 1862. 17th Brigade, 3rd Division, 1st Corps, Army Ohio, to November, 1862. 2nd Brigade, 1st Division, Center 14th Army Corps, Army of the Cumberland, to January, 1863. 2nd Brigade, 1st Division, 14th Army Corps, January, 1863. Headquarters Provost Guard, Dept. of the Cumberland, to May, 1864.

SERVICE.—West Virginia Campaign July to September, 1861. Battle of Carnifex Ferry September 10. Operations in the Kanawha Valley and New River Region October 19-November 24. Pursuit of Floyd November 10-15. Gauley Bridge November 10. Cotton Mountain November 10-11. Moved to Louisville, Ky., November 24-December 2, thence to Elizabethtown, and to Bacon Creek December 26. Duty there till February, 1862. Movement to Bowling Green, Ky., February 10-15. Occupation of Bowling Green February 15-22. Advance on Nashville, Tenn., February 22-March 2. Advance on Murfreesboro March 17-19. Occupation of Shelbyville, Fayetteville, and advance on Huntsville, Ala., March 28-April 11. Capture of Huntsville April 11. Advance on Decatur April 11-14. Action at West Bridge near Bridgeport April 29. Duty at Huntsville till August. March to Louisville, Ky., in pursuit of Bragg August 27-September 26. Pursuit of Bragg into Kentucky October 1-15. Battle of Perryville October 8. March to Nashville, Tenn., October 16-November 7. Provost duty at Headquarters of Gen. Rosecrans, Commanding Army of the Cumberland, till December, 1863, and at Headquarters, Gen. Thomas Commanding, Army and Dept. of the Cumberland, till May, 1864. Advance on Murfreesboro, Tenn., December 26-30, 1862. Battle of Stone's River December 30-31, 1862, and January 1-3, 1863. Stewart's Creek January 1. Duty at Murfreesboro till June. Middle Tennessee or Tullahoma Campaign June 23-July 7. Occupation of Middle Tennessee till August 16. Passage of the Cumberland Mountains and Tennessee River and Chickamauga (Ga.) Campaign August 16-September 22. Battle of Chickamauga September 19-21. Siege of Chattanooga September 24-November 23. Battles of Chattanooga November 23-25. Mission Ridge November 24-25. Reconnoissance of Dalton, Ga., February 22-27, 1864. Atlanta (Ga.) Campaign May 1-27. Demonstration on Rocky Faced Ridge May 8-11. Battle of Resaca May 14-15. Ordered to rear for muster out May 27. Mustered out June 3, 1864, expiration of term. Seventy-five Enlisted men unassigned, Army of the Cumberland, till September, then assigned to 18th Ohio Battalion Infantry.

Regiment lost during service 3 Officers and 86 Enlisted men killed and mortally wounded and 2 Officers and 77 Enlisted men by disease. Total 168.

11th REGIMENT INFANTRY (3 MONTHS).

Organized at Camp Dennison, Ohio, April 18-26, 1861. Duty at Camp Dennison, Ohio, till June 20. Reorganized for three years' service June 20, 1861. Three months' men mustered out July 20, 1861.

11th REGIMENT INFANTRY (3 YEARS).

Organized at Camp Dennison, Ohio, June 20, 1861. Ordered to the Kanawha Valley, W. Va., July 7, 1861. Attached to Cox's Kanawha Brigade, West Virginia, to September, 1861. Benham's Brigade, District of the Kanawha, West Virginia, to October, 1861. 1st Brigade, District of the Kanawha, to March, 1862. 1st Brigade, Kanawha Division West Virginia, Dept. of the Mountains, to September, 1862. 1st Brigade, Kanawha Division, 9th Army Corps, Army of the Potomac, to October, 1862. 1st Brigade, Kanawha Division, District of West Virginia, Dept. of the Ohio, to February, 1863. Crook's Brigade, Baird's Division, Army of Kentucky, Dept. of the Cumberland, to June, 1863. 3rd Brigade, 4th Division, 14th Army Corps, Army of the Cumberland, to October, 1863. 1st Brigade, 3rd Division, 14th Army Corps, to June, 1865.

SERVICE.—Action at Hawk's Nest, W. Va., August 20, 1861. Near Piggott's Mills, Big Run, August 25. Operations in the Kanawha Valley and New River Region October 19-November 16. Gauley Bridge November 10. Blake's Farm, Cotton Mountain, November 10-11. Moved to Point Pleasant December 11, and duty there till April 16, 1862. Operations in the Kanawha Valley April to August. Moved to Washington, D. C., August 18-24. Pope's Campaign in Northern Virginia August 25-September 2. Bull Run Bridge August 27. Maryland Campaign September 6-22. Frederick City, Md., September 12. Battle of South Mountain September 14. Battle of Antietam September 16-17. Moved to Hagerstown, Md., October 8, thence to Clarksburg and Summerville, W. Va., and duty at Summerville till January 24, 1863. Expedition to Cold Knob Mountain November 24-30, 1862. Lewis Mill on Sinking Creek November 26. Ordered to Nashville, Tenn., January 24, 1863, thence to Carthage February 22, and duty there till June. Near Carthage March 8 (2 Cos.). Scout to Rome March 24-25. Reconnoissance to McMinnville April 13. Middle Tennessee or Tullahoma Campaign June 23-July 7. Hoover's Gap June 24-26. Occupation of Middle Tennessee till August 16. Passage of Cumberland Mountains and Tennessee River and Chickamauga (Ga.) Campaign August 16-September 22. Catlett's Gap, Pigeon Mountain, September 15-18. Battle of Chickamauga September 19-21. Rossville Gap September 21. Siege of Chattanooga September 24-November 23. Reopening Tennessee River October 26-29. Brown's Ferry October 27. Chattanooga-Ringgold Campaign November 23-27. Orchard Knob November 23-24. Mission Ridge November 25. Demonstration on Dalton, Ga., February 22-27, 1864. Tunnel Hill, Buzzard's Roost Gap and Rocky Faced Ridge February 23-25. Veterans absent on furlough March and April. Atlanta (Ga.) Campaign May to September. Demonstrations on Rocky Faced Ridge May 8-11. Battle of Resaca May 14-15. Detached for duty as garrison at Resaca May 14 to June 10. Non-Veterans relieved for muster out June 10 and ordered to Cincinnati, Ohio. Mustered out June 21, 1864. Veterans and Recruits organized as a Battalion and attached to 92nd Ohio Infantry till January, 1865, participating in operations about Marietta, Ga., and against Kenesaw Mountain June 10-July 2, 1864. Pine Hill June 11-14. Lost Mountain June 15-17. Assault on Kenesaw June 27. Smyrna Camp Ground July 4. Chattahoochie River July 5-17. Peach Tree Creek July 19-20. Siege of Atlanta July 22-August 25. Utoy Creek August 5-7. Flank movement on Jonesboro August 25-30. Battle of Jonesboro August 31-September 1. Lovejoy Station September 2-6. Operations against Hood in North Georgia and North Alabama September 29-November 3. March to the sea November 15-December 10. Siege of Savannah December 10-21. Campaign of the Carolinas January to April, 1865. Fayetteville, N. C., March 11. Battle of Bentonville March 19-21. Occupation of Goldsboro March 24. Advance on Raleigh April 10-14. Occupation of Raleigh April 14. Bennett's House April 26. Surrender of Johnston and his army. March to Washington, D. C., via Richmond, Va., April 29-May 20. Grand Review May 24. Mustered out June 11, 1865.

Regiment lost during service 4 Officers and 50 Enlisted men killed and mortally wounded and 98 Enlisted men by disease. Total 152.

12th REGIMENT INFANTRY (3 MONTHS).

Organized at Camp Jackson, Columbus, Ohio, April and May, 1861. Moved to Camp Dennison, Ohio, May 6, and duty there till June 28. Reorganized for three years June 28, 1861. Three months' men mustered out July 25, 1861.

12th REGIMENT INFANTRY (3 YEARS).

Organized at Camp Dennison, Ohio, June 28, 1861. Left State for the Kanawha Valley, W. Va., July 6. Attached to Cox's Kanawha Brigade, W. Va., to September, 1861. Benham's Brigade, Dist. of the Kanawha, W. Va., to October, 1861. 1st Brigade, District of the Kanawha, to March, 1862. 1st Brigade, Kanawha Division West Virginia, Dept. of the Mountains, to September, 1862. 1st Brigade, Kanawha Division, 9th Army Corps, Army of the Potomac, to October, 1862. 1st Brigade, Kanawha Division, District of West Virginia, Dept. of the Ohio, to March, 1863. 1st Brigade, 3rd Division, 8th Army Corps, Middle Department, to June, 1863. 2nd Brigade, Scammon's Division, Dept. of West Virginia, to December, 1863. 2nd Brigade, 3rd Division, Army of West Virginia, to April, 1864. 2nd Brigade, 2nd Infantry, Division West Virginia, to July, 1864.

SERVICE.—Action at Scary Creek, W. Va., July 17, 1861. Battle of Carnifex Ferry September 10. Operations in the Kanawha Valley, W. Va., and New River Region September to November. Gauley River September 12. Wilderness Ferry September 14. Hough's Ferry September 16. Advance to Sewell Mountain September 24. Sewell Mountain September 25. At Hawk's Nest October 10 to November 1. Movement on Cotton Mountain and pursuit of Floyd November 1-18. Laurel Creek November 12 (Co. "H"). Duty at Charleston till April, 1862. Advance on Princeton April 22-May 1. Narrows of New River May 4. Operations on Flat Top Mountain May 20 to August 14. Scout in Wayne County July 24-26 (Detachment). Moved to Washington August 24-September 2. Action at Bull Run Bridge August 27. Maryland Campaign September 6-22. Battle of South Mountain, Md., September 14. Battle of Antietam September 16-17. March to Clear Springs October 8, thence to Hancock and to the Kanawha Valley, W. Va., October 14-November 17. Moved to Fayette Court House December 4, and duty there till May, 1864. Action at Blake's Farm May 9, 1863. Repulse of McCausland's attack on Fayetteville May 17-20, 1863. Fayette Court House May 19. Pursuit of Morgan's forces and patrol on the Ohio River July 17-26. Expedition from Charlestown to Lewisburg November 3-13. Action at Meadow Bluff December 4, 1863. Scammon's demonstration from the Kanawha Valley December 8-25, 1863. Action at Big Sewell Mountain and Meadow Bluff December 11. Lewisburg and Greenbrier River December 12. Near Meadow Bluff December 14. Crook's Raid on Virginia & Tennessee Railroad May 2-19. Princeton May 6 (Cos. "B," "D"). Battle of Cloyd's Mountain May 9. New River Bridge May 10. Hunter's Raid to Lynchburg May 26-July 1. Diamond Hill June 17. Lynchburg June 17-18. Retreat to Charleston June 19-July 1. Ordered to Columbus, Ohio, July 2. Veterans and Recruits transferred to 23rd Ohio Infantry. Mustered out July 11, 1864, expiration of term.

Regiment lost during service 3 Officers and 93 Enlisted men killed and mortally wounded and 2 Officers and 77 Enlisted men by disease. Total 175.

13th REGIMENT INFANTRY (3 MONTHS).

Organized at Columbus, Ohio, April 20 to May 7, 1861. Moved to Camp Dennison, Ohio, May 9, and duty there till June 22. Reorganized for three years' service June 22, 1861. Three months' men mustered out August 14-25, 1861.

13th REGIMENT INFANTRY (3 YEARS).

Organized at Camp Dennison, Ohio, June 22, 1861. Left State for Parkersburg, W. Va., June 30, 1861. Attached to 2nd Brigade, Army of Occupation, W. Va., to September, 1861. Benham's Brigade, District of the Kanawha, W. Va., to October, 1861. 1st Brigade, Kanawha Division West Virginia, to November, 1861. 17th Brigade, Army Ohio, to December, 1861. 17th Brigade, 3rd Division, Army Ohio, to April, 1862. 14th Brigade, 5th Division, Army Ohio, to September, 1862. 14th Brigade, 5th Division, 2nd Corps, Army Ohio, to November,

1862. 2nd Brigade, 3rd Division, Left Wing 14th Army Corps, Army of the Cumberland, to January, 1863. 2nd Brigade, 3rd Division, 21st Army Corps, Army of the Cumberland, to October, 1863. 3rd Brigade, 3rd Division, 4th Army Corps, to June, 1865. 2nd Brigade, 3rd Division, 4th Army Corps, to August, 1865. Central District of Texas to October, 1865. Sub-District of San Antonio, Central District of Texas, to December, 1865.

SERVICE.—West Virginia Campaign July 6-17, 1861. Moved to Oakland, W. Va., July 14. Expedition to Greenland Gap July 15-16. Duty at Sutton till September. Battle of Carnifex Ferry September 10. At Gauley Bridge till November. Operations in the Kanawha Valley and New River Region October 19-November 16. Gauley Bridge November 3. Pursuit of Floyd November 12-16. Cotton Hill and Laurel Creek November 12. McCoy's Mills November 15. Ordered to Louisville, Ky., and camp at Jeffersonville, Ind., till December 11. Near Elizabethtown, Ky., till December 26, and at Bacon Creek till February 10, 1862. Advance on Bowling Green, Ky., and Nashville, Tenn., February 10-25. Occupation of Nashville till March 17. March to Savannah, Tenn., March 17-April 6. Battle of Shiloh April 6-7. Advance on and siege of Corinth, Miss., April 29-May 30. Buell's Campaign in Northern Alabama and Middle Tennessee June to August. March to Louisville, Ky., in pursuit of Bragg August 21-September 26. Pursuit of Bragg into Kentucky October 1-16. Battle of Perryville October 8 (Reserve). March to Nashville, Tenn., October 16-November 7. Duty there till December 26. Action at Rural Hill November 18. Advance on Murfreesboro, Tenn., December 26-30. Battle of Stone's River December 30-31, 1862, and January 1-3, 1863. Duty at Murfreesboro till June. Stone's River Ford, McMinnville, June 4. Middle Tennessee or Tullahoma Campaign June 22-July 7. Liberty Gap June 22-24. Occupation of Middle Tennessee till August 16. Passage of Cumberland Mountains and Tennessee River, and Chickamauga (Ga.) Campaign August 16-September 22. Battle of Chickamauga, Ga., September 19-20. Mission Ridge September 22. Siege of Chattanooga September 24-November 23. Chattanooga-Ringgold Campaign November 23-27. Orchard Knob November 23. Mission Ridge November 24-25. Pursuit to Graysville November 26-27. March to relief of Knoxville, Tenn., November 28-December 3. Operations in East Tennessee till April, 1864. Atlanta (Ga.) Campaign May 1-September 8. Demonstrations on Rocky Faced Ridge and Dalton, Ga., May 8-13. Battle of Resaca May 14-15. Adairsville May 17. Near Kingston May 18-19. Near Cassville May 19. Advance on Dallas May 22-25. Operations on Pumpkin Vine Creek and battles about Dallas, New Hope Church and Allatoona Hills May 25-June 5. Pickett's Mills May 27. Operations about Marietta and against Kenesaw Mountain June 10-July 2. Pine Hill June 10-14. Lost Mountain June 15-17. Non-Veterans mustered out June 21, 1864. Veterans and Recruits consolidated to a Battalion. Assault on Kenesaw June 27. Ruff's Station, Smyrna Camp Ground, July 4. Chattahoochie River July 5-17. Peach Tree Creek July 19-20. Siege of Atlanta July 22-August 25. Flank movement on Jonesboro August 25-30. Battle of Jonesboro August 31-September 1. Lovejoy Station September 2-6. Operations against Hood in North Georgia and North Alabama September 29-November 3. Nashville Campaign November-December. Columbia, Duck River, November 24-27. Battle of Franklin November 30. Battle of Nashville December 15-16. Pursuit of Hood to the Tennessee River December 17-28. Moved to Huntsville and duty there till March, 1865. Operations in East Tennessee March 16-April 22. Duty at Nashville till June. Moved to New Orleans, La., June 16, thence to Texas. Duty at Green Lake till September 4, and at San Antonio, Texas, till December. Mustered out December 5, 1865.

Regiment lost during service 8 Officers and 109 Enlisted men killed and mortally wounded and 2 Officers and 102 Enlisted men by disease. Total 221.

14th REGIMENT INFANTRY (3 MONTHS).

Organized at Toledo, Ohio, April 25, 1861. Moved to Cleveland, Ohio, April 25, thence to Columbus, Ohio, May 22. Left State for West Virginia May 27. Moved to Clarksburg May 29, and to Phillippi June 2. Action at Philippi June 3. West Virginia Campaign June 6-17. Laurel Hill July 7. Belington July 8. Pursuit of Garnett July 13-17. Carrick's Ford July 13-14. Ordered to Toledo July 22, and mustered out August 13, 1861, expiration of term.

14th REGIMENT INFANTRY (3 YEARS).

Organized at Toledo, Ohio, August 14-September 5, 1861. Moved to Cincinnati, Ohio, August 23, thence to Frankfort, Ky., August 25, and to Nicholasville August 28. At Camp Dick Robinson and Lebanon, Ky., October 2, 1861, to January 1, 1862. Action at Camp Wild Cat, Rockcastle Hills, October 21, 1861. Attached to Thomas' Command, Camp Dick Robinson, Ky., to November, 1861. 2nd Brigade, Army Ohio, to December, 1861. 2nd Brigade, 1st Division, Army Ohio, to September, 1862. 2nd Brigade, 1st Division, 3rd Corps, Army Ohio, to November, 1862. 2nd Brigade, 3rd Division, Centre 14th Army Corps, Army of the Cumberland, to January, 1863. 2nd Brigade, 3rd Division, 14th Army Corps, to October, 1863. 3rd Brigade, 3rd Division, 14th Army Corps, to July, 1865.

SERVICE.—Advance on Camp Hamilton January 1-15, 1862. Action at Logan's Cross Roads or Fishing Creek January 19-20 (Co. "C"). Battle of Mill Springs January 19-20. Duty at Mill Springs till February 11. Moved to Louisville, Ky., thence to Nashville, Tenn., February 11-March 2. March to Savannah, Tenn., March 20-April 7. Bear Creek, Ala., April 12-13. Advance on and siege of Corinth, Miss., April 29-May 30. Duty at Iuka, Miss., and Tuscumbia, Ala., June to August. Action at Decatur, Ala., August 7. March to Nashville, Tenn., thence to Louisville, Ky., August 20-September 26. Pursuit of Bragg into Kentucky October 1-16. Battle of Perryville, Ky., October 8 (Headquarters Guard). March to Gallatin, Tenn., and duty there till January 13, 1863. Operations against Morgan December 22, 1862, to January 2, 1863. Boston December 29, 1862. Rolling Fork September 29-30. Moved to Nashville January 13, thence to Murfreesboro, Tenn., and duty there till June. Expedition toward Columbia March 4-14. Middle Tennessee or Tullahoma Campaign June 23-July 7. Hoover's Gap June 24-26. Tullahoma July 1. Occupation of Middle Tennessee till August 16. Passage of the Cumberland Mountains and Tennessee River, and Chickamauga (Ga.) Campaign August 16-September 22. Battle of Chickamauga September 19-21. Siege of Chattanooga, Tenn., September 24-November 23. Chattanooga-Ringgold Campaign November 23-27. Orchard Knob November 23-24. Mission Ridge November 25. Re-enlisted December 17, 1863. Atlanta (Ga.) Campaign May 1-September 8, 1864. Demonstrations on Rocky Faced Ridge May 8-11. Battle of Resaca May 14-15. Advance on Dallas May 18-25. Operations on line of Pumpkin Vine Creek and battles about Dallas, New Hope Church and Allatoona Hills May 25-June 5. Operations about Marietta and against Kenesaw Mountain June 10-July 2. Pine Hill June 11-14. Lost Mountain June 15-17. Pine Knob, near Marietta, June 19. Assault on Kenesaw June 27. Ruff's Station July 4. Chattahoochie River July 5-17. Peach Tree Creek July 19-20. Siege of Atlanta July 22-August 25. Utoy Creek August 5-7. Flank movement on Jonesboro August 25-30. Battle of Jonesboro August 31-September 1. Operations against Hood in North Georgia and North Alabama September 29-November 3. March to the sea November 15-December 10. Siege of Savannah December 10-21. Campaign of the Carolinas January to April, 1865. Fayetteville, N. C., March 11. Battle of Bentonville March 19-21. Occupation of Goldsboro March 24. Advance on Raleigh April 10-14. Occupation of Raleigh April 14. Bennett's House April 26. Surrender of Johnston and his army. March to Washington, D. C., via Richmond, Va., April 29-May 19. Grand Review May 24. Moved to Louisville,

Ky., June 15. Mustered out at Louisville, Ky., July 11, 1865.

Regiment lost during service 5 Officers and 141 Enlisted men killed and mortally wounded and 1 Officer and 185 Enlisted men by disease. Total 332.

15th REGIMENT INFANTRY (3 MONTHS).

Organized at Columbus, Ohio, April 27, 1861. Moved to Zanesville, Ohio, May 8, thence to West Virginia. Duty on the Baltimore & Ohio Railroad and operations in the vicinity of Philippi, Laurel Hill and Carrick's Ford June 3-July 16. Action at Bowman's Place June 29. Ordered to Columbus, Ohio, and mustered out August 27-31, 1861.

15th REGIMENT INFANTRY (3 YEARS).

Organized at Mansfield, Ohio, September, 1861. Moved to Camp Dennison, Ohio, September 26, thence to Lexington, Ky., October 4. Duty at Camp Nevin, Ky., October 14-December 9, 1861. Attached to McCook's Command at Nolin October to November, 1861. 6th Brigade, Army of the Ohio, to December, 1861. 6th Brigade, 2nd Division, Army Ohio, to September, 1862. 6th Brigade, 2nd Division, 1st Army Corps, Army Ohio, to November, 1862. 1st Brigade, 2nd Division, Right Wing 14th Army Corps, Army of the Cumberland, to January, 1863. 1st Brigade, 2nd Division, 20th Army Corps, Army of the Cumberland, to October, 1863. 1st Brigade, 3rd Division, 4th Army Corps, to August, 1865. Dept. of Texas to November, 1865.

SERVICE.—Occupation of Munfordsville, Ky., December 10, 1861. Duty at Bacon Creek, Ky., till February 14, 1862. Advance to Bowling Green, Ky., and Nashville, Tenn., February 14-March 2. March to Savannah, Tenn., March 16-April 6. Battle of Shiloh April 6-7. Advance on and siege of Corinth, Miss., April 29-May 30. March to Battle Creek, Ala., June 10-July 18, and duty there till August 20. March to Louisville, Ky., in pursuit of Bragg, August 20-September 26. Pursuit of Bragg into Kentucky October 1-15. March to Nashville, Tenn., October 16-November 7, and duty there till December 26. Advance on Murfreesboro, Tenn., December 26-30. Battle of Stone's River December 30-31, 1862, and January 1-3, 1863. Duty at Murfreesboro till June. Reconnoissance from Murfreesboro March 6-7. Middle Tennessee or Tullahoma Campaign June 22-July 7. Liberty Gap June 22-27. Occupation of Middle Tennessee till August 16. Passage of the Cumberland Mountains and Tennessee River, and Chickamauga (Ga.) Campaign August 16-September 22. Battle of Chickamauga September 19-20. Siege of Chattanooga, Tenn., September 24-November 23. Chattanooga-Ringgold Campaign November 23-27. Orchard Knob November 23-24. Mission Ridge November 25. Pursuit to Graysville November 26-27. March to relief of Knoxville, Tenn., November 28-December 8. Operations in East Tennessee till February, 1864. At Cleveland, Tenn., till April. Atlanta (Ga.) Campaign May 1-September 8. Demonstrations on Rocky Faced Ridge and Dalton May 8-13. Battle of Resaca May 14-15. Adairsville May 17. Near Kingston May 18-19. Near Cassville May 19. Advance on Dallas May 22-25. Operations on line of Pumpkin Vine Creek and battles about Dallas, New Hope Church and Allatoona Hills May 25-June 5. Pickett's Mills May 27. Operations about Marietta and against Kenesaw Mountain June 10-July 2. Pine Hill June 11-14. Lost Mountain June 15-17. Assault on Kenesaw June 27. Ruff's Station July 4. Chattahoochie River July 5-17. Peach Tree Creek July 19-20. Siege of Atlanta July 22-August 25. Flank movement on Jonesboro August 25-30. Battle of Jonesboro August 31-September 1. Lovejoy Station September 2-6. Operations against Hood in North Georgia and North Alabama September 29-November 3. Nashville Campaign November-December. Columbia, Duck River, November 24-27. Battle of Franklin November 30. Battle of Nashville December 15-16. Pursuit of Hood to the Tennessee River December 17-28. Camp at Bird Springs, Ala., till March, 1865. Operations in East Tennessee March 15-April 22. At Nashville, Tenn., till June. Moved to New Orleans,

La., June 16, thence to Texas. Duty at Green Lake till August 10, and at San Antonio till November. Mustered out November 21, 1865. Reach Columbus, Ohio, December 25, and discharged from service December 27, 1865.

Regiment lost during service 7 Officers and 172 Enlisted men killed and mortally wounded and 1 Officer and 135 Enlisted men by disease. Total 315.

16th REGIMENT INFANTRY (3 MONTHS).

Organized at Columbus, Ohio, May 3, 1861. Left State for West Virginia May 25. Attached to Gen. Kelly's Command May 28. Occupation of Grafton, W. Va., May 30. West Virginia Campaign June 1-July 17. Action at Phillippi June 3. Bowman's Place June 29. Pursuit of Garnett July 7-12. Ordered to Columbus, Ohio, and mustered out August 18, 1861.

16th REGIMENT INFANTRY (3 YEARS).

Organized at Camp Tiffin, Wooster, Camp Chase and Zanesville, Ohio, September 23-December 2, 1861. Moved to Camp Dennison, Ohio, November 28, thence to Lexington, Ky., December 19. Moved to Somerset, Ky., January 12, 1862. Attached to 12th Brigade, Army Ohio, to March, 1862. 26th Brigade, 7th Division, Army Ohio, to October, 1862. 4th Brigade, Cumberland Gap Division, District of West Virginia, Dept. Ohio, to November, 1862. 3rd Brigade, 9th Division, Right Wing, 13th Army Corps (Old), Dept. of the Tennessee, to December, 1862. 3rd Brigade, 3rd Division, Sherman's Yazoo Expedition, to January, 1863. 3rd Brigade, 9th Division, 13th Army Corps, Army of the Tennessee, to February, 1863. 2nd Brigade, 9th Division, 13th Army Corps, to July, 1863. 4th Brigade, 1st Division, 13th Army Corps, Dept. Tennessee, to August, 1863, and Dept. of the Gulf to September, 1863. 3rd Brigade, 1st Division, 13th Army Corps, Dept. of the Gulf, to March, 1864. 2nd Brigade, 1st Division, 13th Army Corps, to June, 1864. 2nd Brigade, 3rd Division, 19th Army Corps, to October, 1864.

SERVICE.—March to support of Gen. Thomas at battle of Mill Springs, Ky., January 18-20, 1862. Duty at Somerset till January 31. March to London, thence to Cumberland Ford January 31-February 12, repairing and rebuilding roads. Reconnoissance toward Cumberland Gap March 21-23. Skirmish at Elrod's Ridge March 22. Cumberland Gap Campaign March 28-June 18. Cumberland Mountain April 28. Cumberland Gap April 29. Occupation of Cumberland Gap June 18-September 15. Action at Wilson's Gap June 18. Tazewell July 26 and August 6. Operations about Cumberland Gap September 2-6. Evacuation of Cumberland Gap and retreat to the Ohio River September 17-October 3. Action at West Liberty September 26. Expedition to Charleston, W. Va., October 21-November 10. Ordered to Memphis, Tenn., November 10. Sherman's Yazoo Expedition December 20, 1862, to January 3, 1863. Chickasaw Bayou December 26-28, 1862. Chickasaw Bluffs December 29. Expedition to Arkansas Post, Ark., January 3-10, 1863. Assault and capture of Fort Hindman, Arkansas Post, January 10-11. Moved to Young's Point, La., January 15, thence to Milliken's Bend March 8. Operations from Milliken's Bend to New Carthage March 31-April 17. Movement on Bruinsburg and turning Grand Gulf April 25-30. Battle of Thompson's Hill, Grand Gulf, May 1. Battle of Champion's Hill May 16. Big Black River May 17. Siege of Vicksburg, Miss., May 18-July 4. Assaults on Vicksburg May 19 and 22. Advance on Jackson, Miss., July 5-10. Near Clinton July 8. Siege of Jackson July 10-17. Ordered to New Orleans, La., August 13, and duty there till September 6. At Brashear City till October 3. Western Louisiana Campaign October 3-November 18. Moved to DeCrow Point, Matagorda Bay, Texas, November 18-28, and duty there till January, 1864, and at Matagorda Island till April. Moved to New Orleans, La., April 18, thence to Alexandria, La., April 23. Red River Campaign April 26-May 22. Construction of dam at Alexandria April 30-May 10. Graham's Plantation April 5. Retreat to Morganza May 13-20. Mansura May 16. Expedition to the Atchafalaya

May 30-June 6. Duty at Morganza till October. Ordered to Columbus, Ohio, October 6. Recruits transferred to 114th Ohio Infantry. Regiment mustered out October 31, 1864, expiration of term.

Regiment lost during service 2 Officers and 63 Enlisted men killed and mortally wounded and 4 Officers and 217 Enlisted men by disease. Total 286.

17th REGIMENT INFANTRY (3 MONTHS).

Organized at Lancaster, Ohio, April 20, 1861. Moved to Benwood, Ohio, thence to Parkersburg, W. Va., April 20-23. Attached to Rosecrans' Brigade, W. Va., to July, 1861. 2nd Brigade, Army of Occupation, West Virginia, to August, 1861.

SERVICE.—Railroad guard duty and operating against guerrillas in Jackson County till July. (2 Companies garrison Ravenswood till July 10.) Skirmish at Glenville July 7. West Virginia Campaign July 7-17. Regiment concentrated at Buckhannon. Expedition to Sutton July 15-20. Duty at Sutton till August 3. Left front for Zanesville, Ohio, August 3. Mustered out August 15, 1861.

17th REGIMENT INFANTRY (3 YEARS).

Organized at Camp Dennison, Ohio, August 30, 1861. Ordered to Camp Dick Robinson, Ky., September 30, and duty there till October 19. March to Wild Cat October 19-21. Action at Camp Wild Cat, Rockcastle Hills, October 21. Attached to 1st Brigade, Army of the Ohio, November to December, 1861. 1st Brigade, 1st Division, Army of the Ohio, to September, 1862. 1st Brigade, 1st Division, 3rd Army Corps, Army of the Ohio, to November, 1862. 1st Brigade, 3rd Division, Center 14th Army Corps, Army of the Cumberland, to January, 1863. 1st Brigade, 3rd Division, 14th Army Corps, Army of the Cumberland and Army of Georgia, to July, 1865.

SERVICE.—Operations about Mill Springs and Somerset, Ky., December 1-13, 1861. Advance on Camp Hamilton January 1-17, 1862. Battle of Mill Springs January 19-20. Moved from Mill Springs to Louisville, Ky., February 10-16, thence to Nashville, Tenn., February 18-March 2, and duty there till March 20. March to Savannah, Tenn., March 20-April 8. Advance on and siege of Corinth, Miss., April 29-May 30. Pursuit to Booneville May 31-June 6. Buell's Campaign in North Alabama and Middle Tennessee June to August. Duty at Iuka, Miss., and Tuscumbia, Ala. March to Louisville, Ky., in pursuit of Bragg August 20-September 26. Pursuit of Bragg into Kentucky October 1-15. Battle of Perryville, Ky., October 8. March to Nashville, Tenn., October 16-November 7, and duty there till December 26. Advance on Murfreesboro December 26-30. Battle of Stone's River December 30-31, 1862, and January 1-3, 1863. Duty at Murfreesboro till June. Expedition toward Columbia March 4-14. Middle Tennessee or Tullahoma Campaign June 23-July 7. Hoover's Gap June 24-26. Occupation of Middle Tennessee till August 16. Passage of Cumberland Mountains and Tennessee River and Chickamauga (Ga.) Campaign August 16-September 22. Battle of Chickamauga September 19-21. Siege of Chattanooga, Tenn., September 24-November 23. Near Chattanooga October 8. Re-opening Tennessee River October 25-29. Brown's Ferry October 27. Chattanooga-Ringgold Campaign November 23-27. Orchard Knob November 23-24. Mission Ridge November 25. Regiment re-enlisted January 1, 1864. Veterans on furlough January 22, to March 7, 1864. Reconnoissance to Dalton, Ga., February 22-27, 1864. Tunnel Hill, Buzzard's Roost Gap and Rocky Faced Ridge February 23-25. Atlanta (Ga.) Campaign May 1 to September 8. Demonstrations on Rocky Faced Ridge May 8-11. Battle of Resaca May 14-15. Advance on Dallas May 18-25. Operations on line. of Pumpkin Vine Creek and battles about Dallas, New Hope Church and Allatoona Hills May 25-June 5. Operations about Marietta and against Kenesaw Mountain June 10-July 2. Pine Mountain June 11-14. Lost Mountain June 15-17. Assault on Kenesaw June 27. Ruff's Station, Smyrna Camp

Ground, July 4. Chattahoochie River July 5-17. Peach Tree Creek July 19-20. Siege of Atlanta July 22-August 25. Utoy Creek August 5-7. Flank movement on Jonesboro August 25-30. Battle of Jonesboro August 31-September 1. Operations against Hood in North Georgia and North Alabama September 29-November 3. March to the sea November 15-December 10. Siege of Savannah December 10-21. Campaign of the Carolinas January to April, 1865. Fayetteville, N. C., March 11. Battle of Bentonville March 19-21. Occupation of Goldsboro March 24. Advance on Raleigh April 10-14. Occupation of Raleigh April 14. Bennett's House April 26. Surrender of Johnston and his army. March to Washington, D. C., via Richmond, Va., April 29-May 20. Grand Review May 24. Moved to Louisville, Ky., June, and duty there till July. Mustered out July 16, 1865.

Regiment lost during service 6 Officers and 71 Enlisted men killed and mortally wounded and 1 Officer and 154 Enlisted men by disease. Total 232.

18th REGIMENT INFANTRY (3 MONTHS).

Companies "A," "C" and "E" enrolled at Ironton, Ohio, April 22, 1861; Company "B" at Marietta April 27; Company "D" at McArthur April 18; Company "F" at Gallipolis April 22; Company "I" at Jackson April 24; Company "K" at Beverly April 23, 1861. Regiment organized at Parkersburg and organization perfected May 29, 1861. Companies sent to different points on the Baltimore & Ohio Railroad and guard railroad and trains between Parkersburg and Clarksburg, W. Va., till August. Mustered out at Columbus, Ohio, August 28, 1861, expiration of term.

18th REGIMENT INFANTRY (3 YEARS).

Organized at Athens, Ohio, August 16 to September 28, 1861. Moved to Camp Dennison, Ohio, and organization there completed November 4, 1861. Moved to Louisville, Ky., November 6, thence to Elizabethtown, Ky., November 15. Attached to 8th Brigade, Army of the Ohio to December, 1861. 8th Brigade, 3rd Division, Army of the Ohio, to July, 1862. Unattached, Railroad Guard, Army Ohio, to September, 1862. 29th Brigade, 8th Division, Army Ohio, to November, 1862. 2nd Brigade, 2nd Division, Center 14th Army Corps, Army of the Cumberland, to January, 1863. 2nd Brigade, 2nd Division, 14th Army Corps, to October, 1863. 2nd Brigade, 1st Division, 14th Army Corps, to November, 1863. Engineer Brigade, Dept. of the Cumberland, to November, 1864.

SERVICE.—Duty at Elizabethtown and Bacon Creek, Ky., November, 1861, to February, 1862. Advance on Bowling Green, Ky., February 10-15, and on Nashville, Tenn., February 18-25. Occupation of Nashville, Tenn., February 25-March 18. Reconnoissance to Shelbyville, Tullahoma and McMinnville March 25-28. To Fayetteville April 7. Expedition to Huntsville, Ala., April 10-11. Capture of Huntsville April 11. Advance on and capture of Decatur April 11-14. Operations near Athens, Limestone Bridge, Mooresville and Elk River May 1-2. Near Pulaski and near Bridgeport May 1. Moved to Fayetteville May 31. Negley's Expedition to Chattanooga June 1-15. At Battle Creek till July 11. Guard duty along Tennessee & Alabama Railroad from Tullahoma to McMinnville till September. Short Mountain Road and McMinnville August 29 (Cos. "A" and "I"). Retreat to Nashville, Tenn. Siege of Nashville September 12-November 7. Near Lavergne October 7. Duty at Nashville till December 26. Advance on Murfreesboro December 26-30. Battle of Stone's River December 30-31, 1862, and January 1-3, 1863. Duty at Murfreesboro till June. Middle Tennessee or Tullahoma Campaign June 23-July 7. Occupation of Middle Tennessee till August 16. Passage of Cumberland Mountains and Tennessee River and Chickamauga (Ga.) Campaign August 16-September 22. Davis Cross Roads or Dug Gap September 11. Battle of Chickamauga September 19-21. Rossville Gap September 21. Siege of Chattanooga, Tenn., September 24-November 23. Re-opening Tennessee River October 26-29. Brown's Ferry October

27. Chattanooga-Ringgold Campaign November 23-27. Orchard Knob November 23-24. Mission Ridge November 25. Engaged in Engineer duty at Chattanooga till October 20, 1864. Mustered out November 9, 1864.

Regiment lost during service 4 Officers and 72 Enlisted men killed and mortally wounded and 1 Officer and 107 Enlisted men by disease. Total 184.

18th REGIMENT VETERAN INFANTRY.

Organized at Chattanooga, Tenn., by consolidation of the Veteran detachments of the 1st, 2nd, 18th, 24th and 35th Ohio Infantry October 31, 1864. Attached to Post of Chattanooga, Dept. of the Cumberland, to November, 1864. 2nd Brigade, 1st Separate Division, District of the Etowah, Dept. of the Cumberland, to July, 1865. District of Augusta, Ga., to October, 1865.

SERVICE.—Occupation of Nashville, Tenn., during Hood's investment December 1-15. Battles of Nashville December 15-16. Pursuit of Hood to the Tennessee River December 17-28. Duty at Chattanooga January 10 to April, 1865, and at Fort Phelps till July. Guard and provost duty at Augusta, Ga., till October. Mustered out at Augusta, Ga., October 9, and discharged at Columbus, Ohio, October 22, 1865.

Regiment lost during service 2 Officers and 19 Enlisted men killed and mortally wounded and 53 Enlisted men by disease. Total 74.

19th REGIMENT INFANTRY (3 MONTHS).

Organized at Cleveland, Ohio, April and May, 1861. Moved to Columbus, Ohio, May 27 and mustered in May 29, to date from April 27, 1861. Companies "A" and "B" moved to Bellaire, Ohio, May 27, and guard duty there till June 3, and at Glover's Gap and Manington till June 20. Regiment at Zainesville till June 20. Moved to Parkersburg, W. Va., June 20-23. Attached to Rosecran's Brigade, Army of West Virginia. Moved to Clarksburg June 25. March to Buckhannon June 29-30. Occupation of Buckhannon June 30. Campaign in West Virginia July 6-17. Battle of Rich Mountain July 11. Moved to Columbus, Ohio, July 23-27. Mustered out by Companies: "A" August 27, "B" and "C" August 29, "D" August 30, "E" August 28, "F" August 30, "G" August 31, "H" August 18, "I" August 30, "K" August 31, 1861.

19th REGIMENT INFANTRY (3 YEARS).

Organized at Alliance, Ohio, September 25, 1861. Moved to Camp Dennison, Ohio, November 6, thence to Louisville, Ky., November 16. Attached to 11th Brigade, Army of the Ohio, to December, 1861. 11th Brigade, 1st Division, Army of the Ohio, to March, 1862. 11th Brigade, 5th Division, Army of the Ohio, to September, 1862. 11th Brigade, 5th Division, 2nd Corps, Army of the Ohio, to November, 1862. 1st Brigade, 3rd Division, Left Wing 14th Army Corps, Army of the Cumberland, to January, 1863. 1st Brigade, 3rd Division, 21st Army Corps, Army of the Cumberland, to October, 1863. 3rd Brigade, 3rd Division, 4th Army Corps, to June, 1865. 2nd Brigade, 3rd Division, 4th Army Corps, to August, 1865. Dept. of Texas, to October, 1865.

SERVICE.—Duty at Camp Jenkins, Louisville, Lebanon, Renick's Creek, Jamestown and Greasy Creek till February, 1862. March to Nashville, Tenn., February 15-March 8, and to Savannah, Tenn., March 18-April 6. Battle of Shiloh, Tenn., April 6-7. Advance on and siege of Corinth, Miss., April 29-May 30. Pursuit to Booneville May 31-June 6. Buell's Campaign in North Alabama and Middle Tennessee June to August. March to Battle Creek, Ala., and duty there till August 21. March to Louisville, Ky., in pursuit of Bragg August 21-September 26. Pursuit of Bragg into Kentucky October 1-15. Battle of Perryville, Ky., October 8 (Reserve). March to Nashville, Tenn., October 16-November 7, and duty there till December 26. Advance on Murfreesboro, Tenn., December 26-30. Battle of Stone's River December 30-31, and January 1-3, 1863. Duty at Murfreesboro till June. Middle Tennessee or Tullaho-

ma Campaign June 22-July 7. Liberty Gap June 22-24. At McMinnville till August 16. Passage of the Cumberland Mountains and Tennessee River and Chickamauga (Ga.) Campaign August 16-September 22. Battle of Chickamauga September 19-20. Siege of Chattanooga, Tenn., September 24-November 23. Chattanooga-Ringgold Campaign November 23-27. Orchard Knob November 23-24. Mission Ridge November 25. Pursuit to Graysville November 26-27. March to relief of Knoxville November 28-December 8. Operations in East Tennessee December, 1863, to April, 1864. Regiment re-enlisted January 1, 1864. Atlanta (Ga.) Campaign May 1-September 8. Duty at Parker's Gap May 6-18. Advance to the Etowah May 18-23. Cassville May 19. Advance on Dallas May 22-25. Operations on Pumpkin Vine Creek and battles about Dallas, New Hope Church and Allatoona Hills May 25-June 5. Pickett's Mills May 27. Operations about Marietta and against Kenesaw Mountain June 10-July 2. Pine Mountain June 11-14. Lost Mountain June 15-17. Assault on Kenesaw June 27. Ruff's Station July 4. Chattahoochie River July 5-17. Peach Tree Creek July 19-20. Siege of Atlanta July 22-August 25. Flank movement on Jonesboro August 25-30. Battle of Jonesboro August 31-September 1. Lovejoy Station September 2-6. Operations against Hood, in North Georgia and North Alabama September 29-November 3. Nashville Campaign November-December. Columbia, Duck River, November 24-27. Battle of Franklin November 30. Battle of Nashville December 15-16. Pursuit of Hood to the Tennessee River December 17-28. Moved to Huntsville, Ala., and duty there till March, 1865. Expedition from Whitesburg February 17. Operations in East Tennessee March 15-April 22. Duty at Nashville till June. Moved to New Orleans, La., June 16, thence to Texas. Duty at Green Lake till September 11, and at San Antonio till October 21. Mustered out October 24, 1865.

Regiment lost during service 7 Officers and 104 Enlisted men killed and mortally wounded and 6 Officers and 162 Enlisted men by disease. Total 279.

20th REGIMENT INFANTRY (3 MONTHS).

Organized at Columbus, Ohio, April and May, 1861. Mustered in May 23, 1861. Ordered to West Virginia, and attached to Kelly's Command. Action at Richter June 23. Pursuit of Garnett July 15-16. Duty along Baltimore & Ohio Railroad till August. Mustered out August 23, 1861.

20th REGIMENT INFANTRY (3 YEARS).

Organized at Columbus, Ohio, August 19 to September 21, 1861. Moved to Camp King near Covington, Ky., and mustered in October 21. Duty at Covington and Newport, Ky., till February 11, 1862. Attached to 3rd Brigade, 3rd Division, Army of the Tennessee, February to May, 1862. 2nd Brigade, 3rd Division, Army Tennessee, to July, 1862. Unattached, District of Jackson, Tenn., to November, 1862. 2nd Brigade, 3rd Division, Right Wing 13th Army Corps (Old), Dept. of the Tennessee, to December, 1862. 2nd Brigade, 3rd Division, 17th Army Corps, Army of the Tennessee and Army of Georgia, to July, 1865.

SERVICE.—Investment and capture of Fort Donelson, Tenn., February 14-16, 1862. Expedition toward Purdy and operations about Crump's Landing, Tenn., March 9-14. Battle of Shiloh, Tenn., April 6-7. Advance on and siege of Corinth, Miss., April 29-May 30. Guard duty at Pittsburg Landing till June, and at Bolivar, Tenn., till September. Action at Bolivar August 30. Duty in the District of Jackson till November. Grant's Central Mississippi Campaign November 2, 1862, to January 10, 1863. Action at Holly Springs, Miss., December 21, 1862. Lafayette, Tenn., January 14, 1863. Moved to Memphis, Tenn., January 26, thence to Lake Providence, La., February 22, and duty there till April. Movement on Bruinsburg and turning Grand Gulf April 25-30. Battle of Port Gibson, Miss., May 1. Forty Hills and Hankinson's Ferry May 3-4. Battle of Raymond May 12. Jackson May 14. Champion's Hill May 16. Siege of Vicksburg May 18 to July 4. Assaults on Vicksburg May 19-22. Surrender of Vicksburg July 4. Duty at Vicksburg till February, 1864. Stevenson's Expedition to Monroe, La., August 20-September 2, 1863. Expedition to Canton October 14-20. Bogue Chitto Creek October 17. Regiment re-enlisted January 1, 1864. Meridian Campaign February 3-March 2. Canton February 26. Veterans on furlough March and April. Moved to Clifton, Tenn., thence march to Ackworth, Ga., April 29-June 9. Atlanta (Ga.) Campaign June 9 to September 8. Operations about Marietta and against Kenesaw Mountain June 10-July 2. Assault on Kenesaw June 27. Nickajack Creek July 2-5. Howell's Ferry July 5. Chattahoochie River July 6-17. Leggett's or Bald Hill July 20-21. Battle of Atlanta July 22. Siege of Atlanta July 22-August 25. Flank movement on Jonesboro August 25-30. Sandtown August 28. Battle of Jonesboro August 31-September 2. Lovejoy Station September 2-6. Operations against Hood in North Georgia and North Alabama September 29-November 3. March to the sea November 15-December 10. Siege of Savannah December 10-21. Campaign of the Carolinas January to April, 1865. Pocotaligo, S. C., January 14. Barker's Mills, Whippy Swamp, February 2. Salkehatchie Swamp February 3-5. South Edisto River February 9. North Edisto River February 11-13. Columbia February 16-17. Battle of Bentonville, N. C., March 20-21. Occupation of Goldsboro March 24. Advance on Raleigh April 10-14. Occupation of Raleigh April 14. Bennett's House April 26. Surrender of Johnston and his army. March to Washington, D. C., via Richmond, Va., April 29-May 20. Grand Review May 24. Moved to Louisville, Ky., June. Mustered out at Louisville, Ky., July 18, 1865. (A detachment participated in the Battle of Nashville, Tenn., December 15-16, 1864.)

Regiment lost during service 2 Officers and 87 Enlisted men killed and mortally wounded and 4 Officers and 267 Enlisted men by disease. Total 360.

21st REGIMENT INFANTRY (3 MONTHS).

Organized at Camp Taylor, Cleveland, Tenn., and mustered in April 27, 1861. Moved to Gallipolis, Ohio, May 23, and duty there till July. Attached to Cox's Kanawha Brigade, West Virginia, to August. Reconnoissance up the Kanawha River July 7. Expedition to Guyandotte July 9 (Co. "F"). Scarey Creek July 14-17. Mustered out August 12, 1861.

21st REGIMENT INFANTRY (3 YEARS).

Organized at Findlay, Ohio, and mustered in September 19, 1861. Left State for Nicholasville, Ky., October 2. Attached to Thomas' Command, Army of the Ohio, to November, 1861. 9th Brigade, Army of the Ohio, to December, 1861. 9th Brigade, 3rd Division, Army of the Ohio, to July, 1862. 7th Independent Brigade, Army of the Ohio, to September, 1862. 7th Brigade, 8th Division, Army of the Ohio, to November, 1862. 3rd Brigade, 2nd Division, Center 14th Army Corps, Army of the Cumberland, to January, 1863. 3rd Brigade, 2nd Division, 14th Army Corps, to October, 1863. 3rd Brigade, 1st Division, 14th Army Corps, to June, 1865. 1st Brigade, 1st Division, 14th Army Corps, to July, 1865.

SERVICE.—Action at Ivy's Mountain, Ky., November 8, 1861. Try Mountain and Piketown November 8-9. Duty at Bacon Creek and Green River, Ky., till February, 1862. Advance on Bowling Green, Ky., February 10-15, and on Nashville, Tenn., February 22-25. Occupation of Nashville February 25-March 17. Advance on Murfreesboro, Tenn., March 17-19. Advance on Huntsville, Ala., April 4-11. Capture of Huntsville April 11. (Pittinger's Raid on Georgia State Railroad April 7-12, Detachment.) Near Pulaski May 1. At Athens May 28 to August 28. Action on Richland Creek near Pulaski August 27. March to Nashville August 29-September 2. Siege of Nashville September 12-November 7. Murfreesboro Road November 8. Advance on Murfreesboro December 26-30. Battle of Stone's River December 30-31, 1862, and January 1-3, 1863. Duty at Murfreesboro till June. Middle Tennessee or Tullaho-

ma Campaign June 23-July 7. Occupation of Middle Tennessee till August 16. Passage of Cumberland Mountains and Tennessee River and Chickamauga (Ga.) Campaign August 16-September 22. Davis Cross Roads or Dug Gap September 11. Battle of Chickamauga, Ga., September 19-21. Siege of Chattanooga, Tenn., September 24-November 23. Chattanooga-Ringgold Campaign November 23-27. Orchard Knob November 23-24. Mission Ridge November 25. Pursuit to Graysville November 26-27. Rossville Gap November 26. Regiment re-enlisted January 1, 1864. Reconnoissance of Dalton, Ga., February 22-27, 1864 (Non-Veterans). Rocky Faced Ridge and Buzzard's Roost Gap February 23-25 (Non-Veterans). Atlanta (Ga.) Campaign May 1 to September 8. Demonstrations on Rocky Faced Ridge May 8-11. Buzzard's Roost Gap May 8-9. Battle of Resaca May 14-15. Advance on Dallas May 18-25. Operations on line of Pumpkin Vine Creek and battles about Dallas, New Hope Church and Allatoona Hills May 25-June 5. Operations about Marietta and against Kenesaw Mountain June 10-July 2. Pine Hill June 11-14. Lost Mountain June 15-17. Assault on Kenesaw June 27. Ruff's Station July 4. Chattahoochie River July 5-17. Vining Station July 9-11. Peach Tree Creek July 19-20. Siege of Atlanta July 22-August 25. Utoy Creek August 5-7. Flank movement on Jonesboro August 25-30. Operations against Hood in North Georgia and North Alabama April 29-November 3. Near Atlanta October 2. March to the sea November 15-December 10. Jacksonboro December 11. Siege of Savannah December 10-21. Campaign of the Carolinas January to April, 1865. Taylor's Hole Creek, Averysboro, N. C., March 16. Battle of Bentonville, N. C., March 19-21. Occupation of Goldsboro March 24. Advance on Raleigh April 10-14. Occupation of Raleigh April 14. Bennett's House April 26. Surrender of Johnston and his army. March to Washington, D. C., via Richmond, Va., April 29-May 19. Grand Review May 24. Moved to Louisville, Ky., June, and duty there till July. Mustered out July 25, 1865.

Regiment lost during service 6 Officers and 166 Enlisted men killed and mortally wounded and 2 Officers and 218 Enlisted men by disease. Total 392.

22nd REGIMENT INFANTRY (3 MONTHS).

Organized at Camp Jackson, Columbus, Ohio, April and May, 1861. Moved to Parkersburg, W. Va., May 30, thence to Burning Springs and Elizabethtown, and to Three Forks. Attached to Cox's Brigade, District of the Kanawha, W. Va. Operations against guerrillas in Gilmer, Calhoun and Braxton Counties and railroad guard duty till August. Mustered out August 19, 1861.

22nd REGIMENT INFANTRY (3 YEARS).

Organized at Benton Barracks, Mo., as the 13th Missouri Infantry and mustered in November 5, 1861. Ordered to Cairo, Ill., January 26, 1862. Attached to 2nd Brigade, 2nd Division, District of West Tennessee and Army of the Tennessee, to July, 1862. Designation of Regiment changed to 22nd Ohio Infantry July 7, 1862. 2nd Brigade, 2nd Division, District of Corinth, Miss., to September, 1862. 1st Brigade, 2nd Division, District of Corinth, Miss., to October, 1862. 2nd Brigade, 2nd Division, District of Corinth, Miss., to November, 1862. 2nd Brigade, District of Corinth, Miss., 13th Army Corps (Old), Dept. of the Tennessee, to December, 1862. 2nd Brigade, District of Corinth, 17th Army Corps, to January, 1863. 4th Brigade, District of Jackson, 16th Army Corps, Army of the Tennessee, to March, 1863. 2nd Brigade, 3rd Division, 16th Army Corps, to May, 1863. Kimball's Provisional Division, 16th Army Corps, to July, 1863. 2nd Brigade, Kimball's Division, District of Eastern Arkansas, to August, 1863. 2nd Brigade, 2nd Division, Arkansas Expedition, to January, 1864. 2nd Brigade, 2nd Division, 7th Army Corps, Dept. of Arkansas, to March, 1864. 3rd Brigade, 3rd Division, 7th Army Corps, Dept. of Arkansas, to May, 1864. 2nd Brigade, 2nd Division, 7th Army Corps, to February,

1865. 1st Brigade, 3rd Division, 7th Army Corps, to August, 1865.

SERVICE.—Reconnoissance from Smithland, Ky., toward Fort Henry, Tenn., January 31-February 2. Operations against Fort Henry, Tenn., February 2-6. Capture of Fort Henry February 6. Investment and capture of Fort Donelson, Tenn., February 12-16. Expedition to Clarksville and Nashville, Tenn., February 22-March 5. Moved to Pittsburg Landing, Tenn., March 14-17. Battle of Shiloh April 6-7. Advance on and siege of Corinth, Miss., April 29-May 30. Pursuit to Booneville June 1-6. Duty at Corinth, Miss., till October. Expedition to Iuka, Miss., September 17-19. Battle of Corinth October 3-4. Pursuit to Ripley October 5-12. Box Ford, Hatchie River October 7 (3 Cos.). Near Ruckersville October 7 (Detachment). Near Ripley October 7 (Detachment). Garrison at Trenton and duty along line of the Mobile & Ohio Railroad till March, 1863. Near Yorkville January 28, 1863. Dyersburg January 30. Moved to Jackson, Tenn., March 11, thence to Corinth, Miss., April 29, and return to Jackson, Tenn., May 3. Ordered to Memphis, Tenn., May 20, thence to Vicksburg, Miss., June 1. Siege of Vicksburg June 3-July 4. Surrender of Vicksburg July 4. Ordered to Helena, Ark., July 16. Steele's Expedition to Little Rock, Ark., August 13-September 10. Bayou Fourche and capture of Little Rock September 10. Duty at Little Rock till October 28. Ordered to Brownsville October 28, and duty there till October 24, 1864. Near Searcy May 18, 1864. Near Brownsville July 13. Near Searcy August 13. Ordered to Camp Dennison, Ohio, October 24. Mustered out November 18, 1864. Veterans and Recruits consolidated to two Companies and mustered out August 28, 1865.

Regiment lost during service 2 Officers and 36 Enlisted men killed and mortally wounded and 2 Officers and 167 Enlisted men by disease. Total 207.

23rd REGIMENT INFANTRY.

Organized at Camp Chase, Columbus, Ohio, and mustered in June 11, 1861. Left State for Benwood, W. Va., July 25. Moved to Weston July 28. Duty at Weston, Suttonville, Summerville and Glenville till September 1. Attached to Cox's Kanawha Brigade, West Virginia, to September, 1861. Scammon's Brigade, District of the Kanawha, W. Va., to October, 1861. 3rd Brigade, Kanawha Division, to March, 1862. 1st Brigade, Kanawha Division, Dept. of the Mountains, to September, 1862. 1st Brigade, Kanawha Division, 9th Army Corps, Army of the Potomac, to October, 1862. 1st Brigade, Kanawha Division, District of West Virginia, Dept. of the Ohio, to March, 1863. 1st Brigade, 3rd Division, 8th Army Corps, Middle Department, to June, 1863. 1st Brigade, Scammon's Division, Dept. of West Virginia, to December, 1863. 1st Brigade, 3rd Division, Dept. of West Virginia, to April, 1864. 1st Brigade, 2nd Infantry, Division West Virginia, to January, 1865. 1st Brigade, 1st Infantry, Division West Virginia, to April, 1865. 4th Provisional Division West Virginia to July, 1865.

SERVICE.—Action at Cross Lanes, W. Va., August 26, 1861. Action at Carnifex Ferry September 10. Moved to Little Sewell Mountain September 15. Retreat to New River October. Operations in Kanawha Valley and New River Region October 19-November 16. Cotton Mountain November 11-12. At Fayette Court House till April, 1862. Occupation of Raleigh Court House December 28, 1861, to April, 1862 (Cos. "A," "B," "F," "G"). Action at mouth of Blue Stone February 8. Advance on Princeton April 23-May 1. Camp Creek May 1 (Co. "C"). Princeton May 5. Giles Court House May 7-10. Flat Top Mountain July 4. Pack's Ferry, New River, August 6. Movement to Washington, D. C., August 15-24. Maryland Campaign September 6-22. Battles of South Mountain September 14. Antietam September 16-17. Moved to Chambersburg October 8. Expedition after Stuart October 13-14. Moved to Clarksburg, Suttonville, Summerville, Gauley Bridge and Kana-

wha Falls, October 26-November 14. Duty at Falls of the Great Kanawha November 18, 1862, to March 15, 1863, and at Charleston till July. Expedition to Piney in pursuit of Loring July 5-14, thence moved in pursuit of Morgan July 2-26. Action at Pomeroy, Ohio, July 18. Little Hocking River July 19. Return to Charleston, W. Va., and duty there till April, 1864. Morris Mills July 31, 1863. Expedition to Wayne Court House November 24-28, 1863. Crook's Raid on Virginia & Tennessee Railroad May 2-19. Battle of Cloyd's Mountain May 9. New River Bridge and Doublin Depot May 10. Meadow Bluff May 24. Hunter's Raid to Lynchburg May 26-July 1. Covington June 2. Piedmont June 5. Buffalo Gap June 6. Lexington June 11-12. Diamond Hill June 17. Lynchburg June 17-18. Buford's Gap June 19. About Salem June 21. Moved to Shenandoah Valley July 12-15. Battle of Winchester July 24. Martinsburg July 25. Sheridan's Shenandoah Valley Campaign August 7-November 28. Strasburg and Fisher's Hill August 15. Summit Point August 24. Halltown August 26. Berryville September 3. Battle of Opequan, Winchester, September 19. Fisher's Hill September 22. Battle of Cedar Creek October 19. Duty at Kernstown till December 20. Kablestown November 20 and 30. Moved to Stephenson's Depot December 20, thence to Martinsburg, W. Va., December 29, and to Cumberland, Md., January 1, 1865. Duty at Cumberland till July. Mustered out July 26, 1865.

Regiment lost during service 5 Officers and 154 Enlisted men killed and mortally wounded and 1 Officer and 130 Enlisted men by disease. Total 290.

24th REGIMENT INFANTRY.

Organized at Camps Chase and Jackson, Ohio, May 29, to June 17, 1861. Left State for West Virginia July 26, reaching Cheat Mountain Summit August 14. Attached to Cheat Mountain Brigade, West Virginia, to November, 1861. 10th Brigade, Army of the Ohio, to December, 1861. 10th Brigade, 4th Division, Army of the Ohio, to September, 1862. 10th Brigade, 4th Division, 2nd Corps, Army of the Ohio, to November, 1862. 3rd Brigade, 2nd Division, Left Wing 14th Army Corps, Army of the Cumberland, to January, 1863. 3rd Brigade, 2nd Division, 21st Army Corps, Army of the Cumberland, to October, 1863. 3rd Brigade, 1st Division, 4th Army Corps, Army of the Cumberland, to April, 1864. 1st Separate Brigade, Post of Chattanooga, Tenn., Dept. of the Cumberland, to June, 1864.

SERVICE.—Operations on Cheat Mountain, W. Va., September 11-17, 1861. Action at Cheat Mountain September 12. Greenbrier River October 3-4 and October 31. Moved to Louisville, Ky., November 18, thence to Camp Wickliffe and duty there till February, 1862. Advance on Nashville, Tenn., February 14-25. Occupation of Nashville February 25-March 18. March to Savannah, Tenn., March 18-April 6. Battle of Shiloh, Tenn., April 6-7. Advance on and siege of Corinth, Miss., April 29-May 30. Occupation of Corinth May 30. Pursuit to Booneville May 30-June 12. Buell's Campaign in North Alabama and Middle Tennessee June to August. At Athens, Ala., till July 17. At Murfreesboro and McMinnville, Tenn., till August 17. March to Louisville, Ky., in pursuit of Bragg August 17-September 26. Pursuit of Bragg to Loudon, Ky., October 1-22. Battle of Perryville, Ky., October 8. Nelson's Cross Roads October 18. March to Nashville, Tenn., October 22-November 7, and duty there till December 26. Advance on Murfreesboro December 26-30. Battle of Stone's River December 30-31, 1862, and January 1-3, 1863. Action at Woodbury January 24, 1863. Duty at Readyville till June. Middle Tennessee or Tullahoma Campaign June 23-July 7. At Manchester till August 16. Passage of Cumberland Mountains and Tennessee River and Chickamauga (Ga.) Campaign August 16-September 7. Battle of Chickamauga September 19-20. Siege of Chattanooga, Tenn., September 24-November 23. Re-opening Tennessee River October 26-29. Chattanooga-Ringgold Campaign November 23-27. Battles of Lookout Mountain November 23-24. Mission Ridge November 25.

Ringgold Gap, Taylor's Ridge, November 27. Duty at Shellmound till February, 1864. Demonstration on Dalton, Ga., February 22-27, 1864. Near Dalton February 23. Buzzard's Roost Gap and Rocky Faced Ridge February 23-25. Garrison duty at Chattanooga, Tenn., till June. Mustered out June 17-24, 1864, expiration of term.

Regiment lost during service 6 Officers and 62 Enlisted men killed and mortally wounded and 2 Officers and 106 Enlisted men by disease. Total 176.

25th REGIMENT INFANTRY.

Organized at Camp Chase, Columbus, Ohio, and mustered in June 28, 1861. Ordered to West Virginia July 29, and duty along the Baltimore & Ohio Railroad from Grafton to the Ohio River, till August 21. Attached to Cheat Mountain, District West Virginia, to November, 1861. Milroy's Command, Cheat Mountain, District West Virginia, to April, 1862. Milroy's Brigade, Dept. of the Mountains, to June, 1862. 2nd Brigade, 1st Division, 1st Corps, Army of Virginia, to September, 1862. 2nd Brigade, 1st Division, 11th Army Corps, Army of the Potomac, to August, 1863. 2nd Brigade, Gordon's Division, Folly Island, S. C., 10th Army Corps, Dept. of the South, to January, 1864. District of Hilton Head, S. C., 10th Army Corps, Dept. of the South, to April, 1864. District of Hilton Head, S. C., Dept. of the South, to October, 1864. 3rd Separate Brigade, Dept. of the South, to November, 1864. 1st Brigade, Coast Division, Dept. of the South, to February, 1865. 3rd Separate Brigade, Hilton Head, S. C., Dept. of the South, to March, 1865. 1st Separate Brigade, District of Charleston, S. C., Dept. of the South, to August, 1865. 4th Separate Brigade, District of Western South Carolina, Dept. of the South, to January, 1866. Dept. of the South to June, 1866.

SERVICE.—Moved to Cheat Mountain Summit, W. Va., August 21, 1861, and duty there August 25-November 25. Operations on Cheat Mountain September 11-17. Action at Cheat Mountain September 12. Greenbrier River October 3-4. Duty at Huttonsville November 25, 1861, to February 27, 1862. Expedition to Camp Baldwin December 11-13, 1861. Action at Camp Allegheny, Buffalo Mountain, December 12. Expedition to Huntersville December 31, 1861, to January 6, 1862. Duty at Beverly, Cheat Mountain, March. Expedition on the Seneca April 1-12. Action at Monterey April 12. At Staunton till May 7. Battle of McDowell May 8. March from Franklin to Strasburg May 26-June 10, pursuing Jackson up the Shenandoah Valley. Battle of Cross Keys June 8. Duty at Sperryville and Centreville, Va., till August. Battle of Cedar Mountain August 9. Pope's Campaign in Northern Virginia August 16-September 2. Freeman's Ford August 22. Battle of Bull Run August 29-30. Duty in the Defences of Washington, D. C., till December. Expedition from Centreville to Bristoe September 25-28. March to Fredericksburg, Va., December 10-16. "Mud March" January 20-24, 1863. At Brook's Station till April 27. Chancellorsville Campaign April 27-May 6. Battle of Chancellorsville May 1-5. Gettysburg (Pa.) Campaign June 11-July 22. Battle of Gettysburg, Pa., July 1-3. Pursuit of Lee, to Manassas Gap, Va., July 5-24. At Warrenton Junction July 25-August 6. Moved to Folly Island, S. C., Dept. of the South, August 6-12. Duty at Folly and Morris Islands, S. C., operating against Fort Sumpter and Charleston till January, 1864. Duty at Hilton Head, S. C., till November 23, 1864. (Veterans absent on furlough January to March, 1864. Cos. "A," "G" and "I" at Fort Pulaski, Ga., September 25 to October 23.) Expedition against Charleston & Savannah Railroad November 28-30. Battle of Honey Hill November 30. Coosaw River December 4. Demonstration on Charleston & Savannah Railroad December 6-9. Deveaux's Neck December 6. Occupation of Charleston February 26, 1865. Expedition toward Santee River February 28-March 10. Camp at Mt. Pleasant March 12-April 3. Potter's Expedition to Camden, S. C., April 5-25. Dingle's Mills April 9. Statesburg April 15. Occupation of Camden April 17. Boykins' Mills April 18. Denkins'

Mills and Beach Creek near Statesburg April 19. Return to Mt. Pleasant April 28, thence moved to Charleston May 6 and to Columbia May 7, and garrison duty there till May 25. Duty in Fairfield, Newberry, Edgefield, Lexington and Richland Counties till April, 1866. At Summerville till May and duty on the Sea Islands till June. Ordered to Todd's Barracks, Ohio, June 6. Mustered out June 18, 1866.

Regiment lost during service 7 Officers and 151 Enlisted men killed and mortally wounded and 3 Officers and 119 Enlisted men by disease. Total 280.

26th REGIMENT INFANTRY.

Organized at Camp Chase, Columbus, Ohio, June 8-July 24, 1861. Ordered to the Kanawha Valley, W. Va., July 25. Attached to Cox's Kanawha Brigade, West Virginia, to October, 1861. District of the Kanawha, West Virginia, to January, 1862. 15th Brigade, 4th Division, Army of the Ohio, to March, 1862. 15th Brigade, 6th Division, Army of the Ohio, to September, 1862. 15th Brigade, 6th Division, 2nd Corps, Army of the Ohio, to November, 1862. 1st Brigade, 1st Division, Left Wing 14th Army Corps, Army of the Cumberland, to January, 1863. 1st Brigade, 1st Division, 21st Army Corps, Army of the Cumberland, to October, 1863. 2nd Brigade, 2nd Division, 4th Army Corps, Army of the Cumberland, to June, 1865. 1st Brigade, 2nd Division, 4th Army Corps, to August, 1865. Dept. of Texas to October, 1865.

SERVICE.—Duty in the Kanawha Valley, W. Va., August, 1861, to January, 1862. Action at Boone Court House, W. Va., September 1, 1861. Operations in the Kanawha Valley and New River Region October 19-November 16, 1861. Ordered to Kentucky January 1, 1862. Advance on Nashville, Tenn., February 14-25. Occupation of Nashville February 25-March 18. March to Savannah, Tenn., March 18-April 6. Lawrenceburg April 4. Battle of Shiloh, Tenn., April 6-7. Advance on and siege of Corinth, Miss., April 29-May 30. Pursuit to Booneville May 31-June 6. Buell's Campaign in North Alabama and Middle Tennessee June to August. Little Pond, near McMinnville, August 20. March to Louisville, Ky., in pursuit of Bragg August 30-September 26. Pursuit of Bragg into Kentucky October 1-15. Battle of Perryville October 8. March to Nashville, Tenn., October 16-November 7, and duty there till December 26. Advance on Murfreesboro December 26-30. Lavergne December 26-27. Battle of Stone's River December 30-31, 1862, and January 1-3, 1863. Duty at Murfreesboro till June. Middle Tennessee or Tullahoma Campaign June 23-July 7. Passage of Cumberland Mountains and Tennessee River, and Chickamauga (Ga.) Campaign August 16-September 22. Expedition from Tracy City to Tennessee River August 22-24 (Detachment). Reconnoissance toward Chattanooga November 7. Lookout Valley November 7-8. Occupation of Chattanooga September 9. Lee and Gordon's Mills September 17-18. Battle of Chickamauga September 19-20. Siege of Chattanooga September 24-November 23. Chattanooga-Ringgold Campaign November 23-27. Orchard Knob November 23-24. Mission Ridge November 25. Pursuit to Graysville November 26-27. March to relief of Knoxville November 28-December 8. Regiment re-enlisted January 1, 1864. Atlanta (Ga.) Campaign May 1-September 8, 1864. Demonstrations on Rocky Faced Ridge and Dalton May 8-13. Buzzard's Roost Gap or Mill Creek May 8. Battle of Resaca May 14-15. Adairsville May 17. Near Kingston May 18-19. Cassville May 19. Advance on Dallas May 22-25. Operations on line of Pumpkin Vine Creek and battles about Dallas, New Hope Church and Allatoona Hills May 25-June 5. Operations about Marietta and against Kenesaw Mountain June 10-July 2. Pine Hill June 11-14. Lost Mountain June 15-17. Assault on Kenesaw June 27. Ruff's Station July 4. Chattahoochie River July 6-17. Buckhead, Nancy's Creek, July 18. Peach Tree Creek July 19-20. Siege of Atlanta July 22-August 25. Flank movement on Jonesboro August 25-30. Battle of Jonesboro August 31-September 1. Lovejoy Station September 2-6.

Operations against Hood in North Georgia and North Alabama September 29-November 3. Nashville Campaign November-December. Columbia, Duck River, November 24-27. Battle of Franklin November 30. Battle of Nashville December 15-16. Pursuit of Hood to the Tennessee River December 17-28. Moved to Huntsville, Ala., and duty there till March, 1865. Operations in East Tennessee March 15-April 22. Duty at Nashville till June. Moved to New Orleans June 16, thence to Texas. Duty at San Antonio and Victoria till October. Mustered out October 21, 1865.

Regiment lost during service 6 Officers and 116 Enlisted men killed and mortally wounded and 116 Enlisted men by disease. Total 238.

27th REGIMENT INFANTRY.

Organized at Camp Chase, Columbus, Ohio, July 15-August 18, 1861. Left State for St. Louis, Mo., August 20, thence moved to Mexico, Mo., and duty on the St. Joseph Railroad till September 12. March to relief of Col. Mulligan at Lexington, Mo., September 12-20. Attached to Army of the West and Dept. of Missouri to February, 1862. 1st Brigade, 1st Division, Army of Mississippi, to April, 1862. 1st Brigade, 2nd Division, Army of Mississippi, to November, 1862. 1st Brigade, 8th Division, Left Wing, 13th Army Corps (Old), Dept. of the Tennessee, to December, 1862. 1st Brigade, 8th Division, 16th Army Corps, to March, 1863. 4th Brigade, District of Corinth, Miss., 2nd Division, 16th Army Corps, to May, 1863. 3rd Brigade, District of Memphis, Tenn., 5th Division, 16th Army Corps, to November, 1863. Fuller's 4th Brigade, 2nd Division, 16th Army Corps, to March, 1864. 1st Brigade, 4th Division, 16th Army Corps, to September, 1864. 1st Brigade, 1st Division, 17th Army Corps, to July, 1865.

SERVICE.—Fremont's advance on Springfield, Mo., October 15-November 2, 1861. March to Sedalia, Mo., November 9-17. Duty there and at Syracuse till February, 1862. Expedition to Milford December 15-19, 1861. Blackwater, Mo., December 18. Moved to St. Louis, Mo., February 2, 1862, thence to Commerce, Mo. Siege operations against New Madrid, Mo., March 3-14. Picket affair March 12. Siege and capture of Island No. 10, Mississippi River, and pursuit to Tiptonville March 15-April 8. Expedition to Fort Pillow, Tenn., April 13-17. Moved to Hamburn Landing, Tenn., April 18-22. Action at Monterey April 29. Advance on and siege of Corinth, Miss., April 29-May 30. Reconnoissance toward Corinth May 8. Occupation of Corinth and pursuit to Booneville May 30-June 12. Duty at Corinth till August. Battle of Iuka September 19. Reconnoissance from Rienzi to Hatchie River September 30. Battle of Corinth October 3-4. Pursuit to Ripley October 5-12. Grant's Central Mississippi Campaign November 2, 1862, to January 12, 1863. Expedition to Jackson December 18, 1862. Action at Parker's Cross Roads December 30. Red Mound or Parker's Cross Roads December 31. Duty at Corinth till April, 1863. Dodge's Expedition to Northern Alabama April 15-May 8. Rock Cut, near Tuscumbia, April 22. Tuscumbia April 23. Town Creek April 28. Duty at Memphis, Tenn., till October, and at Prospect, Tenn., till February, 1864. Atlanta (Ga.) Campaign May 1-September 8. Demonstrations on Resaca May 8-13. Sugar Valley, near Resaca, May 9. Near Resaca May 13. Battle of Resaca May 14-15. Advance on Dallas May 18-25. Operations on line of Pumpkin Vine Creek and battles about Dallas, New Hope Church and Allatoona Hills May 25-June 5. Operations against Marietta and against Kenesaw Mountain June 10-July 2. Assault on Kenesaw June 27. Nickajack Creek July 2-5. Ruff's Mills July 3-4. Chattahoochie River July 6-17. Battle of Atlanta July 22. Siege of Atlanta July 22-August 25. Flank movement on Jonesboro August 25-30. Battle of Jonesboro August 31-September 1. Lovejoy Station September 2-6. Duty at Marietta till October. Pursuit of Hood into Alabama October 3-26. March to the sea November 10. Montieth Swamp December 9. Siege of Savannah December 10-21. Campaign of the Carolinas January to April,

1865. Reconnoissance to Salkehatchie River, S. C., January 20. Salkehatchie Swamp February 3-5. River's Bridge, Salkehatchie River, February 3. Binnaker's Bridge February 9. Orangeburg February 11-13. Columbia February 16-17. Juniper Creek, near Cheraw, March 3. Battle of Bentonville, N. C., March 20-21. Occupation of Goldsboro and Raleigh. Bennett's House April 26. Surrender of Johnston and his army. March to Washington, D. C., via Richmond, Va., April 29-May 20. Grand Review May 24. Moved to Louisville, Ky., June, and duty there till July. Mustered out July 11, 1865.

Regiment lost during service 6 Officers and 80 Enlisted men killed and mortally wounded and 6 Officers and 122 Enlisted men by disease. Total 214.

28th REGIMENT INFANTRY.

Organized at Camp Dennison, Ohio, June 10 and mustered in July 6, 1861. Moved to Point Pleasant, W. Va., July 31. Attached to 2nd Brigade, Army of Occupation, W. Va., to October, 1861. McCook's 2nd Brigade, District of the Kanawha, W. Va., to March, 1862. 2nd Brigade, Kanawha Division, Dept. of the Mountains, to September, 1862. 2nd Brigade, Kanawha Division, 9th Army Corps, Army of the Potomac, to October, 1862. 2nd Brigade, Kanawha Division, District of West Virginia, Dept. of the Ohio, to March, 1863. Averill's 4th Separate Brigade, 8th Army Corps, Middle Department, to June, 1863. Averill's 4th Separate Brigade, Dept. of West Virginia, to December, 1863. 1st Brigade, 4th Division, West Virginia, to April, 1864. 1st Brigade, 1st Infantry, Division West Virginia, to June, 1864.

SERVICE.—Moved from Point Pleasant, Va., to Clarksburg, August 11-12, 1861, thence to Buckhannon, August 17-19, to Bulltown August 28-29, to Sutton September 1 and to Summerville September 7-9. Battle of Carnifex Ferry, W. Va., September 10. March to Camp Lookout and Big Sewell Mountain September 15-23. Retreat to Camp Anderson October 6-9. Operations in the Kanawha Valley and New River Region October 19-November 17. New River October 19-21. Moved to Gauley December 6, and duty there till May, 1862. Advance on Virginia & Tennessee Railroad May 10. Princeton May 11-15-16 and 17. Wolf Creek May 15. At Flat Top Mountain till August. Blue Stone August 13-14. Movement to Washington, D. C., August 15-24. Maryland Campaign September 6-22. Battles of Frederick City, Md., September 12. South Mountain September 14. Antietam September 16-17. March to Clear Springs October 8, thence to Hancock October 9. March to the Kanawha Valley, West Va., October 14-November 17. Duty at Brownstown November 17, 1862, to January 8, 1863. Scout to Boone, Wyoming and Logan Counties December 1-10, 1862. Moved to Buckhannon January 8, 1863, thence to Clarksburg April 26-27, and to Weston May 9-12. Moved to New Creek June 17, thence to Beverly July 2-7, and duty there till November 1. Averill's Raid from Beverly against Lewisburg and the Virginia & Tennessee Railroad November 1-17. Mill Point November 5. Droop Mountain November 6. Elk Mountain near Hillsborough November 10. March through Elk Mountain Pass to Beverly December 13-17, and duty at Beverly till April 23, 1864. Moved to join Army of the Shenandoah at Bunker Hill April 23-29. Sigel's Expedition to New Market April 30-May 16. Near Strasburg May 15. Battle of New Market May 16. Hunter's Expedition to Lynchburg, Va., May 26-June 8. Piedmont June 5. Occupation of Staunton June 6. March to Webster on the Baltimore & Ohio Railroad with 1,000 prisoners, wounded and refugees, June 8-18. Guard prisoners to Camp Morton, Ind., thence moved to Cincinnati, Ohio. Mustered out June 23, 1864.

Reorganized as a Veteran Battalion September, 1864, and ordered to Wheeling, W. Va. Duty there and in the Reserve Division of West Virginia, till July, 1865. Mustered out at Wheeling, W. Va., July 13, 1865.

Regiment lost during service 2 Officers and 66 Enlisted men killed and mortally wounded and 66 Enlisted men by disease. Total 134.

29th REGIMENT INFANTRY.

Organized at Camp Giddings, Jefferson, Ohio, August 26, 1861. Moved to Camp Chase, Ohio, December 25, 1861, thence to Cumberland, Md., January 17, 1862. Attached to 3rd Brigade, Landers' Division, Army of the Potomac, to March, 1862. 3rd Brigade, Shields' 2nd Division, Banks' 5th Army Corps, and Dept. of the Shenandoah, to May, 1862. 3rd Brigade, Shields' Division, Dept. of the Rappahannock, to June, 1862. 2nd Brigade, 1st Division, 2nd Army Corps, Pope's Army of Virginia, to August, 1862. 1st Brigade, 2nd Division, 2nd Corps, Army Virginia, to September, 1862. 1st Brigade, 2nd Division, 12th Army Corps, Army of the Potomac, to October, 1863, and Army of the Cumberland, to April, 1864. 1st Brigade, 2nd Division, 20th Army Corps, Army of the Cumberland and Army of Georgia, to July, 1865.

SERVICE.—Duty at Hampton Heights and Paw Paw Tunnel till March, 1862. Advance on Winchester, Va., March 7-15. Reconnoissance to Strasburg March 18-19. Battle of Winchester, Va., March 22-23. March to Fredericksburg, Va., May 12-21, and return to Front Royal May 25-30. Battle of Port Republic June 9. Battle of Cedar Mountain August 9. Pope's Campaign in Northern Virginia August 16-September 2. Guard trains during battles of Bull Run August 28-30. Maryland Campaign September 6-22. Battle of Antietam September 16-17 (Reserve). Moved to Harper's Ferry, W. Va., September 22, and duty at Bolivar Heights till December. Reconnoissance to Rippon, W. Va., November 9. Reconnoissance to Winchester December 2-6. March to Stafford Court House December 10-14, and duty there till January 20, 1863. Burnside's second Campaign, "Mud March," January 20-24. At Stafford Court House till April 27. Chancellorsville Campaign April 27-May 6. Battle of Chancellorsville May 1-5. Gettysburg (Pa.) Campaign June 11-July 24. Battle of Gettysburg July 1-3. Pursuit of Lee to Manassas Gap, Va., July 5-24. Detached for duty at New York during draft disturbances August 29-September 8. Movement to Bridgeport, Ala., September 24-October 3. Re-opening Tennessee River October 26-29. Chattanooga-Ringgold Campaign November 23-27. Battles of Lookout Mountain November 23-24. Mission Ridge November 25. Ringgold Gap, Taylor's Ridge, November 27. Duty at Bridgeport, Ala., till May, 1864. Atlanta (Ga.) Campaign May 1-September 8. Demonstrations on Rocky Faced Ridge May 8-11. Dug Gap or Mill Creek May 8. Battle of Resaca May 14-15. Near Cassville May 19. New Hope Church May 25. Operations on line of Pumpkin Vine Creek and battles about Dallas, New Hope Church and Allatoona Hills May 25-June 5. Operations about Marietta and against Kenesaw Mountain June 10-July 2. Pine Hill June 11-14. Lost Mountain June 15-17. Gilgal or Golgotha Church June 15. Muddy Creek June 17. Noyes Creek June 19. Kolb's Farm June 22. Assault on Kenesaw June 27. Ruff's Station July 4. Chattahoochie River July 5-17. Peach Tree Creek July 19-20. Siege of Atlanta July 22-August 25. Operations at Chattahoochie River Bridge August 26-September 2. Occupation of Atlanta September 2-November 15. Near Atlanta November 9. March to the sea November 15-December 10. Buckhead Church December 2. Siege of Savannah December 10-21. Campaign of the Carolinas January to April, 1865. North Edisto River, S. C., February 12-13. Battle of Bentonville, N. C., March 19-21. Occupation of Goldsboro March 24. Advance on Raleigh April 10-14. Occupation of Raleigh April 14. Bennett's House April 26. Surrender of Johnston and his army. March to Washington, D. C., via Richmond, Va., April 29-May 20. Grand Review May 24. Moved to Louisville, Ky., June. Mustered out at Louisville, Ky., July 13, 1865.

Regiment lost during service 6 Officers and 114 Enlisted men killed and mortally wounded and 1 Officer and 150 Enlisted men by disease. Total 271.

30th REGIMENT INFANTRY.

Organized at Camp Chase, Columbus, Ohio, August 28, 1861. Moved to Clarksburg, W. Va., August 30-September 2, thence moved to Weston and to Suttonville September 3-6. Attached to Scammon's Brigade, District of the Kanawha, W. Va., to October, 1861. 3rd Brigade, District of the Kanawha, W. Va., to March, 1862. 1st Brigade, Kanawha Division West Virginia, Dept. of the Mountains, to September, 1862. 1st Brigade, Kanawha Division, 9th Army Corps, Army of the Potomac, to October, 1862. 1st Brigade, Kanawha Division, District of West Virginia, Dept. of the Ohio, to January, 1863. 3rd Brigade, 2nd Division, 15th Army Corps, Army of the Tennessee, to October, 1863. 2nd Brigade, 2nd Division, 15th Army Corps, to August, 1864. 1st Brigade, 2nd Division, 15th Army Corps, to July, 1865. Dept. of Arkansas to August, 1865.

SERVICE.—Action at Carnifex Ferry, W. Va., September 10, 1861. Advance to Sewell Mountain September 24, thence to Falls of the Gauley. Operations in the Kanawha Valley and New River Region October 19-November 16. Moved to Fayetteville November 14, and duty there till April 17, 1862. (Cos. "D," "F," "G" and "I" served detached at Sutton September 6-December 23, 1861, then rejoined Regiment at Fayetteville.) Advance on Princeton April 22-May 5. About Princeton May 15-18. Moved to Flat Top Mountain May 19, and duty there till August. Moved to Washington, D. C., August 16-22. Pope's Campaign in Northern Virginia. Right Wing at Gen. Pope's Headquarters till September 3. Left Wing in Robertson's Brigade till August 31. Battles of Bull Run August 28-30. Maryland Campaign September 6-22. Battles of South Mountain September 14; Antietam September 16-17. March to Clear Springs October 8, thence to Hancock October 9. March to the Kanawha Valley October 12-November 13. Camp at Cannelton November 13-December 1. Expedition toward Logan Court House December 1-10. Ordered to Louisville, Ky., December, thence to Helena, Ark., and to Young's Point, La., January 21, 1863. Duty there till March. Expedition to Rolling Fork via Muddy, Steele's and Black Bayous and Deer Creek March 14-27. Demonstrations against Haines and Drumgould's Bluffs April 27-May 1. Movement to join Army in rear of Vicksburg, Miss., via Richmond and Grand Gulf May 2-14. Siege of Vicksburg May 18-July 4. Assaults on Vicksburg May 19 and 22. Advance on Jackson, Miss., July 5-10. Siege of Jackson July 10-17. Camp at Big Black till September 26. Moved to Memphis, Tenn., thence marched to Chattanooga, Tenn., September 26-November 20. Sequatchie Valley October 5. Operations on Memphis & Charleston Railroad in Alabama October 20-29. Bear Creek, Tuscumbia, October 27. Chattanooga-Ringgold Campaign November 23-27. Tunnel Hill November 24-25. Mission Ridge November 25. March to relief of Knoxville November 27-December 8. Moved to Bridgeport, Ala., December 19, thence to Bellefonte Station December 26, and to Larkin's Ferry January 26, 1864. Moved to Cleveland, Tenn., Veterans absent on furlough April and May. Rejoined Regiment at Kingston, Ga. Atlanta (Ga.) Campaign May 1-September 8, 1864. Demonstrations on Resaca May 8-13. Near Resaca May 13. Battle of Resaca May 14-15. Advance on Dallas May 18-25. Operations on line of Pumpkin Vine Creek and battles about Dallas, New Hope Church and Allatoona Hills May 25-June 5. Operations about Marietta and against Kenesaw Mountain June 10-July 2. Assault on Kenesaw June 27. Nickajack Creek July 2-5. Ruff's Mills July 3-4. Chattahoochie River July 5-17. Battle of Atlanta July 22. Siege of Atlanta July 22-August 25. Ezra Chapel, Hood's second sortie, July 28. Flank movement on Jonesboro August 25-30. Battle of Jonesboro August 31-September 1. Lovejoy Station September 2-6. Operations against Hood in North Georgia and North Alabama September 29-November 3. March to the sea November 15-December 10. Clinton November 21-23. Siege of Savannah December 10-21. Fort McAllister December 13. Campaign of the Carolinas January to April, 1865. Duck Branch, near Loper's

Cross Roads, S. C., February 2. South Edisto River February 9. North Edisto River February 11-13. Columbia February 16-17. Battle of Bentonville, N. C., March 20-21. Occupation of Goldsboro March 24. Advance on Raleigh April 10-14. Occupation of Raleigh April 14. Bennett's House April 26. Surrender of Johnston and his army. March to Washington, D. C., via Richmond, Va., April 29-May 20. Grand Review May 24. Moved to Louisville, Ky., June 2, thence to Little Rock, Ark., June 25, and duty there till August. Mustered out August 13, 1865.

Regiment lost during service 9 Officers and 119 Enlisted men killed and mortally wounded and 149 Enlisted men by disease. Total 277.

31st REGIMENT INFANTRY.

Organized at Camp Chase, Columbus, Ohio, August 4, 1861. Left State for Louisville, Ky., September 27, thence moved to Camp Dick Robinson, Ky., October 2, and duty there till December 12. Attached to Thomas' Command, Camp Dick Robinson, Ky., to November, 1861. 12th Brigade, Army of the Ohio, to December, 1861. 12th Brigade, 1st Division, Army of the Ohio, to January, 1862. 1st Brigade, 1st Division, Army of the Ohio, to September, 1862. 1st Brigade, 1st Division, 3rd Corps, Army of the Ohio, to November, 1862. 1st Brigade, 3rd Division, Centre 14th Army Corps, Army of the Cumberland, to January, 1863. 1st Brigade, 3rd Division, 14th Army Corps, to July, 1865.

SERVICE.—March to Somerset, Ky., December 12, 1861, and to relief of Gen. Thomas at Mill Springs, Ky., January 19-21, 1862. Moved to Louisville, Ky., February 10-16, thence to Nashville, Tenn., February 18-March 2. March to Savannah, Tenn., March 20-April 8. Advance on and siege of Corinth, Miss., April 29-May 30. Pursuit to Booneville May 31-June 6. March to Iuka, Miss., with skirmishing June 22, thence to Tuscumbia, Ala., June 26-28, and to Huntsville, Ala., July 18-22. Action at Trinity, Ala., July 24 (Co. "E"). Courtland Bridge July 25. Moved to Dechard, Tenn., July 27. March to Louisville, Ky., in pursuit of Bragg August 21-September 26. Pursuit of Bragg into Kentucky October 1-15. Battle of Perryville, Ky., October 8. March to Nashville, Tenn., October 22-November 6, and duty there till December 26. Advance on Murfreesboro December 26-30. Battle of Stone's River December 30-31, 1862, and January 1-3, 1863. Duty at Murfreesboro till March 13, and at Triune till June. Middle Tennessee or Tullahoma Campaign June 23-July 7. Hoover's Gap June 24-26. Occupation of Middle Tennessee till August 16. Passage of Cumberland Mountains and Tennessee River, and Chickamauga (Ga.) Campaign August 16-September 22. Battle of Chickamauga September 19-21. Siege of Chattanooga, Tenn., September 24-November 23. Sequatchie Valley October 5. Reopening Tennessee River October 26-29. Brown's Ferry October 27. Chattanooga-Ringgold Campaign November 23-27. Orchard Knob November 23. Mission Ridge November 24-25. Duty at Chattanooga till February, 1864, and at Graysville till May. Atlanta (Ga.) Campaign May 1-September 8. Demonstrations on Rocky Faced Ridge May 8-11. Battle of Resaca May 14-15. Advance on Dallas May 18-25. Operations on line of Pumpkin Vine Creek and battles about Dallas, New Hope Church and Allatoona Hills May 25-June 5. Operations about Marietta and against Kenesaw Mountain June 10-July 2. Pine Mountain June 11-14. Lost Mountain June 15-17. Assault on Kenesaw June 27. Ruff's Station, Smyrna Camp Ground, July 4. Chattahoochie River July 5-17. Peach Tree Creek July 19-20. Siege of Atlanta July 22-August 25. Utoy Creek August 5-7. Flank movement on Jonesboro August 25-30. Battle of Jonesboro August 31-September 1. Operations against Hood in North Georgia and North Alabama September 29-November 3. March to the sea November 15-December 10. Near Milledgeville November 23. Siege of Savannah December 10-21. Campaign of the Carolinas January to April, 1865. Fayetteville, N. C., March 11. Battle of Bentonville March 19-21. Occupation of Goldsboro March 24.

Advance on Raleigh April 10-14. Occupation of Raleigh April 14. Bennett's House April 26. Surrender of Johnston and his army. March to Washington, D. C., via Richmond, Va., April 29-May 20. Grand Review May 24. Moved to Louisville, Ky., June 5, and duty there till July. Mustered out July 20, 1865.

Regiment lost during service 2 Officers and 77 Enlisted men killed and mortally wounded and 1 Officer and 153 Enlisted men by disease. Total 233.

32nd REGIMENT INFANTRY.

Organized at Mansfield, Ohio, August 20 to September 7, 1861. Left State for Grafton, W. Va., September 15, thence moved to Cheat Mountain Summit. Attached to Kimball's Brigade, Cheat Mountain, District West Virginia, to November, 1861. Milroy's Brigade, Reynolds' Command, Cheat Mountain, District West Virginia, to March, 1862. Milroy's Brigade, Dept. of the Mountains, to June, 1862. Piatt's 2nd Brigade, 1st Division, 1st Corps, Pope's Army of Virginia, to July, 1862. Piatt's Brigade, White's Division, Winchester, Va., to September, 1862. Miles' Command, Harper's Ferry, W. Va., September, 1862. Captured September 15, 1862. 3rd Brigade, 3rd Division, 17th Army Corps, Army of the Tennessee, January to December, 1863. 2nd Brigade, 3rd Division, 17th Army Corps, to July, 1864. 1st Brigade, 4th Division, 17th Army Corps, to April, 1865. 2nd Brigade, 4th Division, 17th Army Corps, to July, 1865.

SERVICE.—Action at Greenbrier River, W. Va., October 3-4, 1861. Duty at Greenbrier till December. Action at Camp Allegheny December 13. Duty at Beverly December, 1861, to April, 1862. Expedition on the Seneca April 1-12. Action at Monterey April 12. At Staunton till May 7. Battle of McDowell May 8. Battle of Cross Keys June 8. Duty at Strasburg and Winchester till September. Evacuation of Winchester September 2. Defence of Harper's Ferry, W. Va., September 12-15. Maryland Heights September 12-13. Regiment surrendered September 15. Paroled September 16 and sent to Annapolis, Md., thence to Chicago, Ill., and to Cleveland, Ohio. Exchanged January 12, 1863. Moved to Memphis, Tenn., January 20-25, 1863, thence to Lake Providence, La., February 20, and to Milliken's Bend, La., April 17. Movement on Bruinsburg and turning Grand Gulf April 25-30. Battle of Port Gibson May 1. Raymond May 12. Jackson May 14. Champion's Hill May 16. Siege of Vicksburg, Miss., May 18-July 4. Assaults on Vicksburg May 19 and 22. Surrender of Vicksburg July 4, and garrison duty there till February, 1864. Expedition to Monroe, La., August 20-September 2, 1863. Expedition to Canton October 14-20. Bogue Chitto Creek October 17. Meridian Campaign February 3-March 2. Baker's Creek February 5. Moved to Clifton, Tenn., thence march to Ackworth, Ga., April 21-June 8. Atlanta (Ga.) Campaign, June 8-September 8. Operations about Marietta and against Kenesaw Mountain June 10-July 2. Assault on Kenesaw June 27. Nickajack Creek July 2-5. Howell's Ferry July 5. Chattahoochie River July 6-17. Leggett's or Bald Hill July 20-21. Battle of Atlanta July 22. Siege of Atlanta July 22-August 25. Flank movement on Jonesboro August 25-30. Battle of Jonesboro August 31-September 1. Lovejoy Station September 2-6. Operations against Hood in North Georgia and North Alabama September 29-November 3. Shadow Church and Westbrook's near Fairburn October 2. March to the sea November 15-December 10. Louisville November 30. Siege of Savannah December 10-21. Campaign of the Carolinas January to April, 1865. Salkehatchie Swamp, S. C., February 2-5. River's Bridge, Salkehatchie River, February 3. South Edisto River February 9. Orangeburg February 11-12. Columbia February 15-17. Fayetteville, N. C., March 11. Battle of Bentonville March 20-21. Occupation of Goldsboro March 24. Advance on Raleigh April 10-14. Occupation of Raleigh April 14. Bennett's House April 26. Surrender of Johnston and his army. March to Washington, D. C., via Richmond,

Va., April 29-May 20. Grand Review May 24. Moved to Louisville, Ky., June 8. Mustered out July 20, 1865.

Regiment lost during service 5 Officers and 99 Enlisted men killed and mortally wounded and 2 Officers and 143 Enlisted men by disease. Total 240.

33rd REGIMENT INFANTRY.

Organized at Portsmouth, Ohio, August 5 to September 13, 1861. Left State for Kentucky September 13 and joined Gen. Nelson at Maysville, Ky. Attached to 9th Brigade, Army of the Ohio, October to December, 1861. 9th Brigade, 3rd Division, Army of the Ohio, to September, 1862. 9th Brigade, 3rd Division, 1st Corps, Army of the Ohio, to November, 1862. 1st Brigade, 1st Division, Center 14th Army Corps, Army of the Cumberland, to January, 1863. 1st Brigade, 1st Division, 14th Army Corps, to July, 1865.

SERVICE.—Capture of Hazel Green, Ky., October 23, 1861. Operations against Williams' invasion of the Blue Grass Region, Ky., November-December. Action at Ivy Mountain November 8. Piketon, Ky., November 8-9. Duty at Bacon Creek till February, 1862. Advance on Bowling Green, Ky., February 10-15, and on Nashville, Tenn., February 22-25. Occupation of Nashville February 25 to March 17. Advance on Murfreesboro, Tenn., March 17-19. Occupation of Shelbyville and Fayetteville and advance on Huntsville, Ala., March 29-April 11. Capture of Huntsville April 11. (Pittinger's Raid on Georgia Central Railroad April 7-12, Detachment.) Advance to Decatur, Ala., April 11-14. Duty along Memphis & Charleston Railroad till August. Action at Battle Creek June 21. Moved to Bridgeport and occupy Fort McCook at mouth of Battle Creek. Action at Battle Creek August 27 (6 Cos.), and at Bridgeport August 27 (4 Cos.). March to Louisville, Ky., in pursuit of Bragg, August 28-September 26. Pursuit of Bragg into Kentucky October 1-15. Battle of Perryville, Ky., October 8. March to Nashville, Tenn., October 16-November 7, and duty there till December 26. Advance on Murfreesboro, Tenn., December 26-30. Battle of Stone's River December 30-31, 1862, and January 1-3, 1863. Duty at Murfreesboro till June. Middle Tennessee or Tullahoma Campaign June 23-July 7. Hoover's Gap June 24-26. Occupation of Middle Tennessee till August 16. Passage of the Cumberland Mountains and Tennessee River and Chickamauga (Ga.) Campaign August 16-September 22. Davis Cross Roads or Dug Gap September 11. Battle of Chickamauga September 19-21. Rossville Gap September 21. Siege of Chattanooga, Tenn., September 24-November 23. Re-opening Tennessee River October 26-29. Brown's Ferry October 27 (Detachment). Chattanooga-Ringgold Campaign November 23-27. Orchard Knob November 23. Lookout Mountain November 23-24. Mission Ridge November 25. Ringgold Gap, Taylor's Ridge, November 27. Demonstration on Dalton, Ga., February 22-27, 1864. Tunnel Hill, Buzzard's Roost Gap and Rocky Faced Ridge February 23-25. Atlanta (Ga.) Campaign May 1 to September 8. Demonstrations on Rocky Faced Ridge May 8-11. Buzzard's Roost Gap or Mill Creek May 9. Battle of Resaca May 14-15. Advance on Dallas May 18-25. Operations on line of Pumpkin Vine Creek and battles about Dallas, New Hope Church and Allatoona Hills May 25-June 5. Pickett's Mill May 27. Operations about Marietta and against Kenesaw Mountain June 10-July 2. Pine Hill June 11-14. Lost Mountain June 15-17. Assault on Kenesaw June 27. Ruff's Station July 4. Chattahoochie River July 5-17. Buckhead, Nancy's Creek, July 18. Peach Tree Creek July 19-20. Siege of Atlanta July 22-August 25. Utoy Creek August 5-7. Flank movement on Jonesboro August 25-30. Red Oak August 29. Battle of Jonesboro August 31-September 1. Operations against Hood in North Georgia and North Alabama September 29-November 3. Cassville November 7. March to the sea November 15-December 10. Siege of Savannah December 10-21. Campaign of the Carolinas January to April, 1865. Taylor's Hole Creek, Averysboro, N. C., March 16. Battle of Bentonville

March 19-21. Occupation of Goldsboro March 24. Advance on Raleigh April 10-14. Occupation of Raleigh April 14. Bennett's House April 26. Surrender of Johnston and his army. March to Washington, D. C., via Richmond, Va., April 20-May 19. Grand Review May 24. Moved to Louisville, Ky., June 6. Mustered out at Louisville, Ky., July 12, 1865.

Regiment lost during service 7 Officers and 130 Enlisted men killed and mortally wounded and 3 Officers and 192 Enlisted men by disease. Total 332.

34th REGIMENT INFANTRY.

Organized at Camp Lucas, Ohio. Moved to Camp Dennison, Ohio, September 1, 1861; thence to West Virginia September 15. Arrived at Camp Enyart, Kanawha River, September 20. Attached to Cox's Kanawha Brigade, West Virginia, to October, 1861. Unattached, District of the Kanawha, West Virginia, to March, 1862. 2nd Brigade, Kanawha Division, West Virginia, Dept. of the Mountains, to September, 1862. Point Pleasant, District of the Kanawha, West Virginia, Dept. of the Ohio, to March, 1863. 2nd Brigade, 3rd Division, 8th Army Corps, Middle Department, to June, 1863. 2nd Brigade, Scammon's Division, West Virginia, to July, 1863. 3rd Brigade, Scammon's Division, West Virginia, to December, 1863. 3rd Brigade, 3rd Division, West Virginia, to April, 1864. 1st Brigade, 2nd Cavalry Division, West Virginia, to June, 1864. 3rd Brigade, 2nd Cavalry Division, West Virginia, to July, 1864. 2nd Brigade, 2nd Infantry Division, West Virginia, to January, 1865. Unassigned, 1st Infantry Division, West Virginia, to February, 1865.

SERVICE.—Action at Chapmansville, W. Va., September 25, 1861. Duty at Camp Red House October, and at Barboursville November. Guard and scout duty and operating against guerrillas in Cabell, Putnam, Mason, Wayne and Logan Counties till March, 1862. Moved to Gauley Bridge March, and at Fayetteville April. Cox's demonstrations on the Virginia & Tennessee Railroad May 10-18. Princeton May 15-17. Retreat to Flat Top Mountain May 18, and duty there till August. At Fayetteville till September. Campaign in the Kanawha Valley September 6-16. Loring's attack on Fayetteville September 10. Cotton Mountain September 11. Charleston September 12-13. At Point Pleasant till October 15. At Fayetteville till May, 1863. Regiment mounted May, 1863. Expedition to Virginia & Tennessee Railroad July 13-25. Wytheville July 18-19 and 27. Scouts from Camp Piatt September 11-13. Elk River September 12. Scouts from Charleston to Boone Court House October 21-26. Expedition from Charleston to Lewisburg November 3-13. Little Sewell Mountain November 6. Muddy Creek and capture of Lewisburg November 7. Second Creek, near Union, November 8. Scammon's demonstration from the Kanawha Valley December 8-25. Regiment re-enlisted December 23, 1863, and mustered as a Veteran organization January 19, 1864. Crook's Expedition against Virginia & Tennessee Railroad May 2-19, 1864 (Detachment). Averill's Raid on Virginia & Tennessee Railroad May 5-19. Callahan Station May 4. Jeffersonville May 8. Abb's Valley, Wytheville, May 9. Cloyd's Mountain May 9. New River Bridge May 10. Grassy Lick, Cove Mountain, near Wytheville, May 10. Hunter's Raid to Lynchburg May 26-July 1. Buffalo Gap June 6. Lexington June 11. Buchanan June 14. New London June 16. Diamond Hill June 17. Lynchburg June 17-18. Liberty June 19. Buford's Gap June 20. Catawba Mountains and near Salem June 21. Moved to the Shenandoah Valley July 12-15. Stephenson's Depot July 20. Battle of Winchester July 24. Martinsburg July 25. Sheridan's Shenandoah Valley Campaign August 6-November 28. Bolivar Heights August 24. Halltown August 26. Berryville September 3. Battle of Opequan, Winchester, September 19. Fisher's Hill September 22. Battle of Cedar Creek October 19. Duty near Kernstown till December. Moved to Webster December 22, thence to Beverly, and garrison duty there till January, 1865. Rosser's attack on Beverly January

11. Many of Regiment captured. Regiment consolidated with 36th Ohio Infantry February 22, 1865.

Regiment lost during service 10 Officers and 120 Enlisted men killed and mortally wounded and 130 Enlisted men by disease. Total 260.

35th REGIMENT INFANTRY.

Organized at Hamilton, Ohio, and mustered in September 20, 1861. Moved to Covington, Ky., September 26. Assigned to guard duty along the Kentucky Central Railroad. Headquarters at Cynthiana, till November. At Paris, Ky., till December. Attached to 3rd Brigade, Army of the Ohio, November-December, 1861. 3rd Brigade, 1st Division, Army of the Ohio, to September, 1862. 3rd Brigade, 1st Division, 3rd Corps, Army of the Ohio, to November, 1862. 3rd Brigade, 3rd Division, Centre 14th Army Corps, Army of the Cumberland, to January, 1863. 3rd Brigade, 3rd Division, 14th Army Corps, Army of the Cumberland, to October, 1863. 2nd Brigade, 3rd Division, 14th Army Corps, to August, 1864.

SERVICE.—Operations about Mill Springs and Somerset, Ky., December 1-13, 1861. Action at Fishing Creek, near Somerset, December 8. Advance to Camp Hamilton January 1-17, 1862. Battle of Mill Springs January 19-20. March to Louisville, Ky., thence moved to Nashville, Tenn., via Ohio and Cumberland Rivers February 10-March 2. March to Savannah, Tenn., March 20-April 8. Advance on and siege of Corinth, Miss., April 29-May 30. Pursuit to Booneville May 31-June 14. Moved to Tuscumbia, Ala., June 22, and duty there till July 27. Moved to Dechard, Tenn., July 27. March to Louisville, Ky., in pursuit of Bragg August 21-September 26. Pursuit of Bragg into Kentucky October 1-15. Battle of Perryville, Ky., October 8 (Reserve). March to Nashville, Tenn., October 16-November 7. Duty at South Tunnel, opening railroad communications with Nashville, November 8-26. Guarding fords of the Cumberland till January 14, 1863. Duty at Nashville, Tenn., January 15-March 6. Moved to Triune March 6, and duty there till June. Expedition toward Columbia March 6-14. Franklin June 4-5. Middle Tennessee or Tullahoma Campaign June 23-July 7. Hoover's Gap June 24-26. Occupation of Middle Tennessee till August 16. Passage of the Cumberland Mountains and Tennessee River, and Chickamauga (Ga.) Campaign August 16-September 22. Battle of Chickamauga September 19-21. Siege of Chattanooga, Tenn., September 24-November 23. Demonstration on Dalton, Ga., February 22-27, 1864. Tunnel Hill, Buzzard's Roost Gap and Rocky Faced Ridge February 23-25. Reconnoissance from Ringgold toward Tunnel Hill April 29. Atlanta (Ga.) Campaign May 1-August 3. Demonstration on Rocky Faced Ridge May 8-11. Battle of Resaca May 14-15. Advance on Dallas May 18-25. Operations on Pumpkin Vine Creek and battles about Dallas, New Hope Church and Allatoona Hills May 25-June 5. Operations about Marietta and against Kenesaw Mountain June 10-July 2. Pine Hill June 11-14. Lost Mountain June 15-17. Assault on Kenesaw June 27. Ruff's Station July 4. Chattahoochie River July 5-17. Peach Tree Creek July 19-20. Siege of Atlanta July 22-August 3. Ordered to Chattanooga, Tenn., August 3. Mustered out August 26-September 28, 1864, expiration of term. Veterans and Recruits transferred to 18th Ohio Infantry (Reorganized).

Regiment lost during service 5 Officers and 75 Enlisted men killed and mortally wounded and 2 Officers and 126 Enlisted men by disease. Total 208.

36th REGIMENT INFANTRY.

Organized at Marietta, Ohio, July 30-August 31, 1861. Left State for West Virginia September 10, 1861. Moved to Summerville, and duty there till May, 1862. Attached to Cox's Kanawha Brigade, West Virginia, to October, 1861. District of the Kanawha, West Virginia, to March, 1862. 3rd Brigade, Kanawha Division, West Virginia, to September, 1862. 2nd Brigade, Kanawha Division, 9th Army Corps, Army of the Potomac, to October, 1862. 2nd Brigade, Kanawha Division, District

of West Virginia, Dept. of the Ohio, to February, 1863. Crook's Brigade, Baird's Division, Army of Kentucky, Dept. of the Cumberland, to June, 1863. 3rd Brigade, 4th Division, 14th Army Corps, Army of the Cumberland, to October, 1863. 1st Brigade, 3rd Division, 14th Army Corps, to April, 1864. 1st Brigade, 2nd Infantry Division, West Virginia, to January, 1865. 1st Brigade, 1st Infantry Division, West Virginia, to July, 1865.

SERVICE.—Expedition to Meadow Bluff December 15-21, 1861. Expedition from Summerville to Addison April 17-21, 1862 (Cos. "E," "G," "I" and "K"). Expedition to Lewisburg, W. Va., May 12-23. Jackson River Depot May 20. Action at Lewisburg May 23. Moved to Meadow Bluff May 29. Expedition to Salt Sulphur Springs June 22-25. Operations in Kanawha Valley till August. Movement to Washington, D. C., August 14-22. Joined Gen. Pope, and on duty at his Headquarters till September 3, during battles of Bull Run August 28-30. Maryland Campaign September 6-22. Frederick City, Md., September 12. Battles of South Mountain September 14 and Antietam September 16-17. March to Hagerstown, thence to Hancock, Md., Clarksburg and the Kanawha Valley October 6-November 16. Duty at Charleston, W. Va., till January 25, 1863. Ordered to Nashville, Tenn., January 25, thence to Carthage February 22, and duty there till June. Middle Tennessee or Tullahoma Campaign June 23-July 7. Hoover's Gap June 24-26. Occupation of Middle Tennessee till August 16. Passage of the Cumberland Mountains and the Tennessee River, and Chickamauga (Ga.) Campaign August 16-September 22. Catlett's Gap September 15-18. Battle of Chickamauga, Ga., September 19-21. Siege of Chattanooga September 24-November 23. Reopening Tennessee River October 26-29. Brown's Ferry October 27. Chattanooga-Ringgold Campaign November 23-27. Orchard Knob November 23-24. Mission Ridge November 25. Regiment re-enlisted January, 1864, and Veterans on furlough March and April. Ordered to Charleston, W. Va. Crook's Raid to Dublin Depot, Virginia & Tennessee Railroad, May 2-19. Battle of Cloyd's Mountain May 9. New River Bridge May 10. Hunter's Raid on Lynchburg May 26-July 1. Lexington June 11-12. Diamond Hill June 17. Lynchburg June 17-18. Buford's Gap June 20. Salem June 21. Moved to the Shenandoah Valley July 12-15. Cablestown July 19. Battle of Winchester July 23-24. Martinsburg July 25. Sheridan's Shenandoah Valley Campaign August 6-November 28. Cedar Creek, Strasburg, August 15. Summit Point August 24. Halltown August 26. Berryville September 3. Battle of Opequan, Winchester, September 19. Fisher's Hill September 22. Battle of Cedar Creek October 19. Kablestown November 18. Duty at Kernstown till December. Ordered to Cumberland, Md., and duty there till April, 1865. Moved to Winchester, and duty there till June, and at Wheeling, W. Va., till July. Mustered out July 27, 1865.

Regiment lost during service 4 Officers and 136 Enlisted men killed and mortally wounded and 163 Enlisted men by disease. Total 303.

37th REGIMENT INFANTRY.

Organized at Camp Dennison, Ohio, and mustered in October 2, 1861. Ordered to the Kanawha Valley, West Virginia. Attached to Benham's Brigade, District of the Kanawha, West Virginia, to October, 1861. District of the Kanawha, West Virginia, to March, 1862. 2nd Brigade, Kanawha Division, Dept. of the Mountains, to May, 1862. 2nd Brigade, Kanawha Division, West Virginia, to August, 1862. District of the Kanawha, West Virginia, Dept. of the Ohio, to December, 1862. Ewing's Brigade, Kanawha Division, West Virginia, to January, 1863. 3rd Brigade, 2nd Division, 15th Army Corps, Army of the Tennessee, to October, 1863. 2nd Brigade, 2nd Division, 15th Army Corps, to June, 1865. Dept. of Arkansas to August, 1865.

SERVICE.—Operations in the Kanawha District and New River Regiment, West Virginia, October 19-November 16, 1861. Duty at Clifton till March, 1862. Expedition to Logan Court House and Guyandotte Valley

1514 COMPENDIUM OF THE WAR OF THE REBELLION

January 12-23. Demonstrations against Virginia & Tennessee Railroad May 10-18. Actions at Princeton May 15, 16 and 17. Charleston May 17. Moved to Flat Top Mountain and duty there till August. Moved to Raleigh Court House August 1. Operations about Wyoming Court House August 2-8. Wyoming Court House August 5. Operations in the Kanawha Valley August 29-September 18. Repulse of Loring's attack on Fayetteville September 10. Cotton Hill September 11. Charleston September 12-13. Duty at Point Pleasant till October 15, and at Gauley Bridge till December 20. Ordered to Napoleon, Ark., December 20; thence to Young's Point, La., January 21, 1863, and duty there till March. Expedition to Rolling Fork via Muddy, Steele's and Black Bayous and Deer Creek March 14-27. Demonstrations on Haines and Drumgould's Bluffs April 27-May 1. Movement to join army in rear of Vicksburg, Miss., via Richmond and Grand Gulf May 2-14. Siege of Vicksburg, Miss., May 18-July 4. Assaults on Vicksburg May 19 and 22. Advance on Jackson, Miss., July 5-10. Siege of Jackson July 10-17. Camp at Big Black till September 26. Moved to Memphis, thence march to Chattanooga, Tenn., September 26-November 21. Operations on the Memphis & Charleston Railroad in Alabama October 20-29. Bear Creek, Tuscumbia, October 27. Chattanooga-Ringgold Campaign November 23-27. Tunnel Hill November 24-25. Mission Ridge November 25. March to relief of Knoxville November 29-December 8. Re-enlisted at Larkinsville, Ala., February 9, 1864. Atlanta (Ga.) Campaign May 1 to September 8. Demonstrations on Resaca May 8-13. Near Resaca May 13. Battle of Resaca May 14-15. Advance on Dallas May 18-25. Operations on line of Pumpkin Vine Creek and battles about Dallas, New Hope Church and Allatoona Hills May 25-June 5. Operations about Marietta and against Kenesaw Mountain June 10-July 2. Assault on Kenesaw June 27. Nickajack Creek July 2-5. Ruff's Mills July 3-4. Chattahoochie River July 6-17. Battle of Atlanta July 22. Siege of Atlanta July 22-August 25. Ezra Chapel, Hood's 2nd Sortie, July 28. Flank movement on Jonesboro August 25-30. Battle of Jonesboro August 31-September 1. Lovejoy Station September 2-6. Operations against Hood in North Georgia and North Alabama September 29-November 3. Turkeytown and Gadsden Road October 25. March to the sea November 15-December 10. Siege of Savannah December 10-21. Fort McAllister December 13. Campaign of the Carolinas January to April, 1865. Salkehatchie Swamp, S. C., February 2-5. Cannon's Bridge, South Edisto River, February 8. North Edisto River February 12-13. Columbia February 16-17. Battle of Bentonville, N. C., March 20-21. Mill Creek March 22. Occupation of Goldsboro March 24. Advance on Raleigh April 10-14. Occupation of Raleigh April 14. Bennett's House April 26. Surrender of Johnston and his army. March to Washington, D. C., via Richmond, Va., April 29-May 20. Grand Review May 24. Moved to Louisville, Ky., June; thence to Little Rock, Ark., and duty there till August. Mustered out August 7, 1865.

Regiment lost during service 9 Officers and 102 Enlisted men killed and mortally wounded and 1 Officer and 94 Enlisted men by disease. Total 206.

38th REGIMENT INFANTRY.

Organized at Defiance, Ohio, September 1, 1861. Ordered to Nicholasville, Ky., September 1. At Camp Dick Robinson, Ky., till October 19. March to relief of Wild Cat October 19-21. March to Somerset, Ky., and duty there till January, 1862. Attached to 1st Brigade, Army of the Ohio, October-November, 1861. 1st Brigade, 1st Division, Army of the Ohio, to September, 1862. 1st Brigade, 1st Division, 3rd Army Corps, Army of the Ohio, to November, 1862. 1st Brigade, 3rd Division (Centre), 14th Army Corps, Army of the Cumberland, to January, 1863. 1st Brigade, 3rd Division, 14th Army Corps, to October, 1863. 3rd Brigade, 3rd Division, 14th Army Corps, to July, 1865.

SERVICE.—Advance on Camp Hamilton, Ky., January 1-17, 1862. Battle of Mill Springs, Ky., January 19-20. Moved to Louisville, Ky., February 10-16; thence to Nashville, Tenn., via Ohio and Cumberland Rivers February 18-March 2. March to Savannah, Tenn., March 20-April 8. Advance on and siege of Corinth, Miss., April 29-May 30. Pursuit to Booneville June 1-6. March to Iuka, Miss., June 22; thence to Tuscumbia, Ala., June 26. Moved to Huntsville, Ala., July 19-22; thence to Deckard, Tenn., July 27. Decatur, Ala., August 7 (Detachment). March to Louisville, Ky., in pursuit of Bragg August 21-September 26. Pursuit of Bragg into Kentucky October 1-15. Battle of Perryville, Ky., October 8. March to Nashville, Tenn., October 16-November 7, and duty there till December 26. Advance on Murfreesboro December 26-30. Battle of Stone's River December 30-31, 1862, and January 1-3, 1863. Duty at Murfreesboro till March, and at Triune till June. Expedition toward Columbia March 4-14. Middle Tennessee (or Tullahoma) Campaign June 23-July 7. Hoover's Gap June 24-26. Occupation of Middle Tennessee till August 16. Passage of the Cumberland Mountains and Tennessee River and Chickamauga (Ga.) Campaign August 16-September 22. Conducting trains of the army from the Cumberland to Chattanooga during battle of Chickamauga, Ga., Chattanooga, Tenn., September 25-26. Siege of Chattanooga September 26-November 23. Chattanooga-Ringgold Campaign November 23-27. Orchard Knob November 23-24. Mission Ridge November 25. Regiment re-enlisted December, 1863. Atlanta (Ga.) Campaign May 1 to September 8, 1864. Demonstrations on Rocky Faced Ridge May 8-11. Buzzard's Roost Gap May 8-9. Battle of Resaca May 14-15. Advance on Dallas May 18-25. Operations on line of Pumpkin Vine Creek and battles about Dallas, New Hope Church and Allatoona Hills May 25-June 5. Ackworth June 4. Operations about Marietta and against Kenesaw Mountain June 10-July 2. Pine Hill June 11-14. Lost Mountain June 15-17. Assault on Kenesaw June 27. Ruff's Station July 4. Chattahoochie River July 5-17. Peach Tree Creek July 19-20. Siege of Atlanta July 22-August 25. Utoy Creek August 5-7. Flank movement on Jonesboro August 25-30. Battle of Jonesboro August 31-September 1. Operations against Hood in North Georgia and North Alabama September 29-November 3. March to the sea November 15-December 10. Siege of Savannah December 10-21. Campaign of the Carolinas January to April, 1865. Fayetteville, N. C. Battle of Bentonville March 19-21. Occupation of Goldsboro March 24. Advance on Raleigh April 10-14. Occupation of Raleigh April 14. Bennett's House April 26. Surrender of Johnston and his army. March to Washington, D. C., via Richmond, Va., April 29-May 19. Grand Review May 24. Moved to Louisville, Ky., June 12. Mustered out July 12, 1865.

Regiment lost during service 8 Officers and 132 Enlisted men killed and mortally wounded and 2 Officers and 227 Enlisted men by disease. Total 369.

39th REGIMENT INFANTRY.

Organized at Camp Colerain and Camp Dennison, Ohio, July 31 to August 13, 1861. Left State for St. Louis, Mo., August 18; thence moved to Medon September 6 (9 Cos.). (Co. "K" served detached at St. Louis, Mo., September, 1861, to February, 1862.) Companies "A," "B," "E" and "I" on duty at St. Joseph, Mo., guarding Northern Missouri Railroad September, 1861, to February, 1862. Companies "C," "D," "F," "G" and "H" march to relief of Lexington, Mo., September 12-20; thence to Kansas City September 21-22. Attached to Army of the West and Dept. of Missouri to February, 1862. 1st Brigade, 1st Division, Army of Mississippi, to April, 1862. 1st Brigade, 2nd Division, Army of Mississippi, to November, 1862. 1st Brigade, 8th Division, Left Wing 13th Army Corps (Old), Dept. of the Tennessee, to December, 1862. 1st Brigade, 8th Division, 16th Army Corps, to March, 1863. 4th Brigade, District of Corinth, Miss., 2nd Division, 16th

Army Corps, to May, 1863. 3rd Brigade, District of Memphis, Tenn., 5th Division, 16th Army Corps, to November, 1863. Fuller's Brigade, 2nd Division, 26th Army Corps, to January, 1864. 1st Brigade, 4th Division, 16th Army Corps, to September, 1864. 1st Brigade, 1st Division, 17th Army Corps, to July, 1865.

SERVICE.—Fremont's advance on Springfield, Mo., October 15-November 2, 1861. March to Sedalia November 9-17. Duty at Sedalia and Syracuse, Mo., till February, 1862. Action at Shanghai December 1, 1861. Moved to St. Louis, Mo., February 2, 1862, thence to Commerce, Mo., February 22-24. Siege operations against New Madrid, Mo., March 3-14. Siege and capture of Island No. 10, Mississippi River, and pursuit to Tiptonville March 15-April 8. Expedition to Fort Pillow, Tenn., April 13-17. Moved to Hamburg Landing, Tenn., April 18-22. Action at Monterey April 29. Advance on and siege of Corinth, Miss., April 29-May 30. Reconnoissance toward Corinth May 8. Near Corinth May 24. Occupation of Corinth and pursuit to Booneville May 30-June 12. Duty at Clear Creek till August 29. Battle of Iuka, Miss., September 19. Battle of Corinth, Miss., October 3-4. Pursuit to Ripley October 5-12. Grant's Central Mississippi Campaign November 2, 1862, to January 12, 1863. Expedition to Jackson December 18. Action at Parker's Cross Roads December 30. Red Mound or Parker's Cross Roads December 31. Duty at Corinth till April, 1863. Dodge's Expedition to Northern Alabama April 15-May 8. Rock Cut, near Tuscumbia, April 22. Tuscumbia April 23. Town Creek April 28. Duty at Memphis, Tenn., till October, and at Prospect, Tenn., till February, 1864. Re-enlisted at Prospect December 26, 1863. Atlanta (Ga.) Campaign May 1 to September 8, 1864. Demonstrations on Resaca May 8-13. Sugar Valley, near Resaca, May 9. Near Resaca May 13. Battle of Resaca May 14-15. Advance on Dallas May 18-25. Operations on line of Pumpkin Vine Creek and battles about Dallas, New Hope Church and Allatoona Hills May 25-June 5. Operations about Marietta and against Kenesaw Mountain June 10-July 2. Assault on Kenesaw June 27. Nickajack Creek July 2-5. Ruff's Mills July 3-4. Chattahoochie River July 5-17. Battle of Atlanta July 22. Siege of Atlanta July 22-August 25. Flank movement on Jonesboro August 25-30. Battle of Jonesboro August 31-September 1. Lovejoy Station September 2-6. Operations against Hood in North Georgia and North Alabama September 29-November 3. March to the sea November 15-December 10. Monteith Swamp December 9. Siege of Savannah December 10-21. Campaign of the Carolinas January to April, 1865. Reconnoissance to the Salkehatchie River, S. C., January 20. Skirmishes at Rivers and Broxton Bridges, Salkehatchie River, February 2. Action at Rivers Bridge, Salkehatchie River, February 3. Binnaker's Bridge, South Edisto River, February 9. Orangeburg, North Edisto River, February 12-13. Columbia February 16-17. Juniper Creek, near Cheraw, March 3. Battle of Bentonville, N. C., March 20-21. Occupation of Goldsboro and Raleigh, Bennett's House, April 26. Surrender of Johnston and his army. March to Washington, D. C., via Richmond, Va., April 29-May 20. Grand Review May 24. Moved to Louisville, Ky., June. Mustered out July 9, 1865.

Regiment lost during service •2 Officers and 62 Enlisted men killed and mortally wounded and 3 Officers and 129 Enlisted men by disease. Total 196.

40th REGIMENT INFANTRY.

Organized at Camp Chase, Columbus, Ohio, September to November, and mustered in December 7, 1861. Ordered to Eastern Kentucky December 11, 1861. Attached to 18th Brigade, Army of the Ohio, to March, 1862. Unattached, Army of the Ohio to August, 1862. District of Eastern Kentucky, Dept. of the Ohio, to October, 1862. District of the Kanawha, West Virginia, Dept. of the Ohio, to February, 1863. 2nd Brigade, Baird's Division, Army of Kentucky, Dept. of the Cumberland, to June, 1863. 1st Brigade, 1st Division, Reserve Corps, Army of the Cumberland, to October, 1863.

1st Brigade, 2nd Division, 4th Army Corps, Army of the Cumberland, October, 1863. 2nd Brigade, 1st Division, 4th Army Corps, to December, 1864.

SERVICE.—Garfield's Campaign against Humphrey Marshall December 23, 1861, to January 30, 1862. Advance on Paintsville, Ky., December 31, 1861, to January 7, 1862. Occupation of Paintsville January 8 to February 1. Middle Creek, near Prestonburg January 10. Expedition to Pound Gap, Cumberland Mountains, March 14-17. Pound Gap March 16. Moved to Piketon, Ky., and duty there till June 13. Moved to Prestonburg June 12, thence to Louisa July 16, and duty there till September 13. Moved to Gallipolis, Ohio, September 13, thence to Guyandotte, Va., October 4. Moved to Eastern Kentucky November 14, and duty there till February 20, 1863. Ordered to Nashville, Tenn., February 20, thence to Franklin, Tenn. Repulse of Van Dorn's attack on Franklin April 10. Harpeth River, near Franklin, April 10. Duty at Franklin till June 2. Moved to Triune June 2. Middle Tennessee (or Tullahoma) Campaign June 23-July 7. At Wartrace and Tullahoma till September 7. Chickamauga (Ga.) Campaign September 7-22. Reconnoissance from Rossville September 17. Ringgold, Ga., September 17. Battle of Chickamauga September 19-21. Siege of Chattanooga, Tenn., September 24-November 23. Reopening Tennessee River October 26-29. Chattanooga-Ringgold Campaign November 23-27. Lookout Mountain November 23-24. Mission Ridge November 25. Ringgold Gap, Taylor's Ridge, November 27. Duty at Whiteside, Ala., till February, 1864. Demonstration on Dalton, Ga., February 22-27. Tunnel Hill, Buzzard's Roost Gap and Rocky Faced Ridge February 23-25. Atlanta (Ga.) Campaign May 1 to September 8. Tunnel Hill May 6-7. Demonstration on Rocky Faced Ridge and Dalton May 8-13. Buzzard's Roost Gap May 8-9. Battle of Resaca May 14-15. Adairsville May 17. Near Kingston May 18-19. Near Cassville May 19. Advance on Dallas May 22-25. Operations on line of Pumpkin Vine Creek and battles about Dallas, New Hope Church and Allatoona Hills May 25-June 5. Allatoona Pass June 1-2. Operations about Marietta and against Kenesaw Mountain June 10-July 2. Pine Hill June 11-14. Lost Mountain June 15-17. Assault on Kenesaw June 27. Ruff's Station, Smyrna Camp Ground, July 4. Chattahoochie River July 5-17. Peach Tree Creek July 19-20. Siege of Atlanta July 22-August 25. Flank movement on Jonesboro August 25-30. Red Oak Station August 29. Battle of Jonesboro August 31-September 1. Lovejoy Station September 2-6. Companies "A," "B," "C" and "D" mustered out at Pilot Knob, Ga., October 7, 1864. Operations against Hood in North Georgia and North Alabama September 29-November 3. Moved to Pulaski, Tenn., and duty there till November 22. Battle of Franklin November 30. Veterans and Recruits consolidated with 51st Ohio Infantry December 10, 1864.

Regiment lost during service 6 Officers and 96 Enlisted men killed and mortally wounded and 1 Officer and 134 Enlisted men by disease. Total 237.

41st REGIMENT INFANTRY.

Organized at Camp Wood, Cleveland, Ohio, August 26 to October 29, 1861. Mustered in October 31, 1861. Moved to Camp Dennison, Ohio, November 6, thence to Gallipolis, Ohio, November 16, thence to Louisville, Ky. Duty at Camp Wickliffe, Ky., till February, 1862. Attached to 15th Brigade, Army of the Ohio, December, 1861, to January, 1862. 15th Brigade, 4th Division, Army of the Ohio, to February, 1862. 19th Brigade, 4th Division, Army of the Ohio, to September, 1862. 19th Brigade, 4th Division, 2nd Corps, Army of the Ohio, to November, 1862. 2nd Brigade, 2nd Division, Left Wing 14th Army Corps, Army of the Cumberland, to January, 1863. 2nd Brigade, 2nd Division, 21st Army Corps, Army of the Cumberland, to October, 1863. 2nd Brigade, 3rd Division, 4th Army Corps, Army of the Cumberland, to August, 1865. Dept. of Texas to November, 1865.

SERVICE.—Advance on Nashville, Tenn., February 14-25, 1862. Occupation of Nashville February 25 to March 18. March to Savannah, Tenn., March 18-April 6. Battle of Shiloh, Tenn., April 6-7. Advance on and siege of Corinth, Miss., April 29-May 30. Occupation of Corinth and pursuit to Booneville May 30-June 12. March to Athens, Ala., and duty there till July 17, and at Murfreesboro till August 17. March to Louisville, Ky., in pursuit of Bragg August 17-September 26. Pursuit of Bragg into Kentucky October 1-22. Battle of Perryville, Ky., October 8. Danville October 11. Rockcastle River October 18. Nelson's Cross Roads October 18. Pittman's Cross Roads October 19. March to Nashville, Tenn., October 23-November 6, and duty there till December 26. Advance on Murfreesboro December 26-30. Battle of Stone's River December 30-31, 1862, and January 1-3, 1863. Woodbury January 24. Duty at Murfreesboro till June. Expedition from Readyville to Woodbury April 2. Snow Hill, Woodbury, April 3. Middle Tennessee (or Tullahoma) Campaign June 22-July 7. Liberty Gap June 22-23. Occupation of Middle Tennessee till August 16. Passage of the Cumberland Mountains and Tennessee River and Chickamauga (Ga.) Campaign August 16-September 22. Lee and Gordon's Mills September 11-13. Battle of Chickamauga, Ga., September 19-20. Siege of Chattanooga, Tenn., September 24-November 23. Reopening Tennessee River October 26-29. Brown's Ferry October 27. Chattanooga-Ringgold Campaign November 23-27. Orchard Knob November 23-24. Mission Ridge November 25. March to relief of Knoxville November 28-December 8. Operations in East Tennessee till April, 1864. Atlanta (Ga.) Campaign May 1 to September 8. Demonstrations on Rocky Faced Ridge and Dalton, Ga., May 8-13. Battle of Resaca May 14-15. Adairsville May 17. Near Kingston May 18-19. Near Cassville May 19 and May 24. Operations on line of Pumpkin Vine Creek and battles about Dallas, New Hope Church and Allatoona Hills May 25-June 5. Pickett's Mills May 27. Operations about Marietta and against Kenesaw Mountain June 10-July 2. Pine Hill June 10-14. Lost Mountain June 15-17. Assault on Kenesaw Mountain June 27. Ruff's Station, Smyrna Camp Ground, July 4. Chattahoochie River July 5-17. Pace's Ferry July 5. Peach Tree Creek July 19-20. Siege of Atlanta July 22-August 25. Flank movement on Jonesboro August 25-30. Battle of Jonesboro August 31-September 1. Lovejoy Station September 2-6. Operations against Hood in North Georgia and North Alabama September 29-November 3. Nashville Campaign November-December. Columbia, Duck River, November 24-27. Battle of Franklin November 30. Battle of Nashville December 15-16. Pursuit of Hood to the Tennessee River December 17-28. Moved to Huntsville, Ala., and duty there till March, 1865. Operations in East Tennessee March 15-April 22. Duty at Nashville till June. Moved to New Orleans, La., June 16; thence to Texas. Duty at San Antonio till November. Mustered out November 27, 1865.

Regiment lost during service 8 Officers and 168 Enlisted men killed and mortally wounded and 1 Officer and 153 Enlisted men by disease. Total 330.

42nd REGIMENT INFANTRY.

Organized at Camp Chase, Columbus, Ohio, September to November, 1861. Moved to Catlettsburg, Ky., December 14, 1861; thence to Louisa, Ky. Attached to 18th Brigade, Army of the Ohio, to March, 1862. 26th Brigade, 7th Division, Army of the Ohio, to October, 1862. 4th Brigade, Cumberland Division, District of West Virginia, Dept. of the Ohio, to November, 1862. 3rd Brigade, 9th Division, Right Wing 13th Army Corps (Old), Dept. of the Tennessee, to December, 1862. 3rd Brigade, 3rd Division, Sherman's Yazoo Expedition, to January, 1863. 3rd Brigade, 9th Division, 13th Army Corps, Army of the Tennessee, to February, 1863. 2nd Brigade, 9th Division, 13th Army Corps, to July, 1863. 4th Brigade, 1st Division, 13th Army Corps, Dept. of the Tennessee, to August, 1863, and Dept. of the Gulf to September, 1863. 3rd Brigade, 1st Division,

13th Army Corps, Dept. of the Gulf, to November, 1863. Plaquemine, District of Baton Rouge, La., Dept. of the Gulf, to March, 1864. 2nd Brigade, 1st Division, 13th Army Corps, Dept. of the Gulf, to June, 1864. 1st Brigade, 3rd Division, 19th Army Corps, to December, 1864.

SERVICE.—Garfield's Campaign against Humphrey Marshall December 23, 1861, to January 30, 1862. Advance on Paintsville, Ky., December 31, 1861, to January 7, 1862. Jennies Creek January 7. Occupation of Paintsville January 8. Middle Creek, near Prestonburg, January 10. Occupation of Prestonburg January 11. Expedition to Pound Gap, Cumberland Mountains, March 14-17. Pound Gap March 16. Cumberland Gap Campaign March 28-June 18. Cumberland Mountain April 28. Occupation of Cumberland Gap June 18 to September 16. Tazewell July 26. Operations about Cumberland Gap August 2-6. Big Springs August 3. Tazewell August 6. Evacuation of Cumberland Gap and retreat to the Ohio River September 17-October 3. Expedition to Charleston October 21-November 10. Ordered to Memphis, Tenn., November 10, and duty there till December 20. Sherman's Yazoo Expedition December 20, 1862, to January 3, 1863. Chickasaw Bayou December 26-28. Chickasaw Bluff December 29. Expedition to Arkansas Post, Ark., January 3-10, 1863. Assault and capture of Fort Hindman, Arkansas Post, January 10-11. Moved to Young's Point, La., January 17. Duty there and at Milliken's Bend, La., till April 25. Operations from Milliken's Bend to New Carthage March 31-April 17. Movement on Bruinsburg and turning Grand Gulf April 25-30. Battle of Port Gibson May 1. Skirmish near Edwards Station May 15. Battle of Champion's Hill May 16. Big Black River May 17. Siege of Vicksburg, Miss., May 18-July 4. Assaults on Vicksburg May 19 and 22. Advance on Jackson, Miss., July 5-10. Near Clinton July 8. Siege of Jackson July 10-17. Moved to New Orleans, La., August 13. Duty at Carrollton, Berwick and Brashear City till October. Western Louisiana Campaign October 3-November 20. Duty at Plaquemine November 21, 1863, to March 24, 1864. Provost duty at Baton Rouge till May 1. Expedition to Clinton May 1-3. Comite River May 1. Moved to Simsport May 18, thence to Morganza and duty there till September 6. Expeditions up White River July 15 and September 6-15. Moved to Duvall's Bluff, Ark., September 15, and duty there till November. Companies "A," "B," "C" and "D" mustered out September 30, 1864. Companies "E" and "F" mustered out November 25, 1864, and Companies "G," "H," "I" and "K" mustered out December 2, 1864.

Regiment lost during service 1 Officer and 58 Enlisted men killed and mortally wounded and 3 Officers and 178 Enlisted men by disease. Total 240.

43rd REGIMENT INFANTRY.

Organized at Mount Vernon, Ohio, September 28, 1861, to February 1, 1862. Left State for Commerce, Mo., February 21, 1862. Attached to 1st Brigade, 1st Division, Army of Mississippi, to March, 1862. 2nd Brigade, 1st Division, Army of Mississippi, to April, 1862. 1st Brigade, 2nd Division, Army of Mississippi, to November, 1862. 1st Brigade, 8th Division, Left Wing 13th Army Corps (Old), Dept. of the Tennessee, to December, 1862. 1st Brigade, 8th Division, 16th Army Corps, to March, 1863. 4th Brigade, District of Corinth, Miss., 2nd Division, 16th Army Corps, to May, 1863. 3rd Brigade, District of Memphis, Tenn., 5th Division, 16th Army Corps, to November, 1863. Fuller's Brigade, 2nd Division, 16th Army Corps, to March, 1864. 2nd Brigade, 4th Division, 16th Army Corps, to September, 1864. 2nd Brigade, 1st Division, 17th Army Corps, to July, 1865.

SERVICE.—Siege operations against New Madrid, Mo., March 3-14, 1862. Siege and capture of Island No. 10, Mississippi River, and capture of McCall's forces at Tiptonville, Mo., March 15-April 8. Expedition to Fort Pillow, Tenn., April 13-17. Moved to Hamburg Landing, Tenn., April 18-22. Action at Monterey

April 29. Advance on and siege of Corinth, Miss., April 29-May 30. Reconnoissance toward Corinth May 8. Occupation of Corinth and pursuit to Booneville May 30-June 12. Duty at Clear Creek till August 20, and at Bear Creek till September 11. Battle of Iuka, Miss., September 19. Battle of Corinth October 3-4. Pursuit to Ripley October 5-12. Grant's Central Mississippi Campaign November 2, 1862, to January 12, 1863. Duty at Corinth till April, 1863. Dodge's Expedition to Northern Alabama April 15-May 8. Rock Cut, near Tuscumbia, April 22. Tuscumbia April 23. Town Creek April 28. Duty at Memphis, Tenn., till October, and at Prospect, Tenn., till February, 1864. Atlanta (Ga.) Campaign May 1 to September, 1864. Demonstrations on Resaca May 8-13. Sugar Valley, near Resaca, May 9. Near Resaca May 13. Battle of Resaca May 14-15. Advance on Dallas May 18-25. Operations on line of Pumpkin Vine Creek and battles about Dallas, New Hope Church and Allatoona Hills May 25-June 5. Operations about Marietta and against Kenesaw Mountain June 10-July 2. Assault on Kenesaw June 27. Nickajack Creek July 2-5. Ruff's Mills July 3-4. Chattahoochie River July 6-17. Battle of Atlanta July 22. Siege of Atlanta July 22-August 25. Flank movement on Jonesboro August 25-30. Battle of Jonesboro August 31-September 1. Lovejoy Station September 2-6. Operations against Hood in North Georgia and North Alabama September 29-November 3. March to the sea November 15-December 10. Montieth Swamp December 9. Siege of Savannah December 10-21. Campaign of the Carolinas January to April, 1865. Reconnoissance to the Salkehatchie River, S. C., January 20. Skirmishes at Rivers and Broxton Bridges, Salkehatchie River, February 2. Actions at Rivers Bridge, Salkehatchie River, February 3. Binnaker's Bridge, South Edisto River, February 9. Orangeburg, North Edisto River, February 12-13. Columbia February 16-17. Juniper Creek, near Cheraw, March 3. Battle of Bentonville, N. C., March 19-20. Occupation of Goldsboro March 24. Advance on Raleigh April 10-14. Occupation of Raleigh April 14. Bennett's House April 26. Surrender of Johnston and his army. March to Washington, D. C., via Richmond, Va., April 29-May 30. Grand Review May 24. Moved to Louisville, Ky., June. Mustered out July 13, 1865.

Regiment lost during service 4 Officers and 61 Enlisted men killed and mortally wounded and 2 Officers and 189 Enlisted men by disease. Total 256.

44th REGIMENT INFANTRY.

Organized at Springfield, Ohio, September 12 to October 14, 1861. Ordered to Camp Piatt, W. Va., October 14. Attached to Benham's Brigade, District of the Kanawha, West Virginia, October, 1861. 1st Brigade, District of the Kanawha, West Virginia, to March, 1862. 3rd Brigade, Kanawha Division, West Virginia, to September, 1862. 2nd Brigade, 2nd Division, Army of Kentucky, Dept. of the Ohio, to January, 1863. 1st Brigade, District of Central Kentucky, Dept. of the Ohio, to June, 1863. 2nd Brigade, 1st Division, 23rd Army Corps, Dept. of the Ohio, to July, 1863. 2nd Brigade, 4th Division, 23rd Army Corps, to August, 1863. 1st Brigade, 3rd Division, 23rd Army Corps, to January, 1864.

SERVICE.—Operations in the Kanawha Valley and New River Region, West Virginia, October 19-November 16, 1861. Duty at Camp Piatt, W. Va., till May, 1862. Action at Chapmansville April 18. Moved to Gauley Bridge May 1. Expedition to Lewisburg and Jackson River Depot May 12-23. Jackson River Depot May 20. Action at Lewisburg May 23. Moved to Meadow Bluffs May 29, and duty there till August. Expedition to Salt Sulphur Springs June 22-25. Scout from Meadow Bluffs to Greenbrier River August 2-5 (Cos. "F," "G" and "K"). Greenbrier River August 3. Near Cannelton September 1. Campaign in the Kanawha Valley September 6-16. Camp Tompkins September 9. Miller's Ferry and Gauley Bridge September 11. Near Cannellton September 12. Charleston September 13. Point

Pleasant September 20. Ordered to Covington, Ky., September 27. Brookville September 28. Moved to Lexington, Ky., October 6. To Richmond December 1, thence to Danville, Ky., December 20. Regiment mounted at Frankfort, Ky. Operations in Central Kentucky against Cluke's forces February 18-March 5, 1863. Action at Slate Creek, near Mt. Sterling, February 24. Stoner's Bridge February 24. Hazel Green March 9 and 19. Operations against Pegram March 22-April 1. Hickman's Bridge March 28. Dutton's Hill, Somerset, March 30. Expedition to Monticello and operations in Southeastern Kentucky April 26-May 12. Barboursville April 27. Monticello May 1. Saunder's Raid into East Tennessee June 14-24. Pine Mountain June 16. Big Creek Gap June 17. Knoxville June 19-20. Strawberry Plains, Rogers' Gap and Powder Springs Gap, June 20. Williams' Gap and Powell Valley June 22. Rogers' Gap June 26. Operations against Scott July 22-27. Williamsburg July 25 (Detachment). Loudoun July 26. Richmond and Manchester Cross Roads July 27. Burnside's Campaign in East Tennessee August 16-October 17. Expedition to Cumberland Gap September 4-7. Operations about Cumberland Gap September 7-10. Cumberland Iron Works September 23. Blue Springs October 10. Knoxville Campaign November 4-December 23. Siege of Knoxville November 17-December 5. Bean's Station December 14. Designation of Regiment changed to 8th Ohio Cavalry January 4, 1864.

(For losses, etc., see 8th Ohio Cavalry.)

45th REGIMENT INFANTRY.

Organized at Camp Chase, Columbus, Ohio, August 19, 1862. Ordered to Cynthiana, Ky., August 19; thence moved to Covington, Ky., and Defence of Cincinnati, Ohio, against threatened attack by Kirby Smith. Attached to 3rd Division, Army of Kentucky, Dept. of the Ohio, September and October, 1862. 1st Brigade, 2nd Division, Army of Kentucky, to January, 1863. District of Central Kentucky, Dept. of the Ohio, to June, 1863. 2nd Brigade, 1st Division, 23rd Army Corps, Dept. of the Ohio, to July, 1863. 2nd Brigade, 4th Division, 23rd Army Corps, to August, 1863. 1st Brigade, 4th Division, 23rd Army Corps, to October, 1863. 2nd Brigade, 4th Division, 23rd Army Corps, to December, 1863. 3rd Brigade, 1st Division Cavalry Corps, Dept. of the Ohio, to April, 1864. 2nd Brigade, 2nd Division, 23rd Army Corps, to June, 1864. 1st Brigade, 2nd Division, 23rd Army Corps, June, 1864. 2nd Brigade, 1st Division, 4th Army Corps, Army of the Cumberland, to June, 1865.

SERVICE.—Duty at Lexington, Ky., October, 1862, to January, 1863. Moved to Danville, Ky., January 25, and duty there till March. Operations in Central Kentucky against Cluke's forces February 18-March 5. Regiment mounted at Danville and Brigaded with 7th Ohio and 10th Kentucky Cavalry. Operations against Pegram March 22-April 1. Action at Dutton's Hill, near Somerset, March 30. Expedition to Monticello and operations in Southeastern Kentucky April 26-May 12. Monticello May 1. Skirmishes about Monticello April 28-May 2. Waitsborough June 6. Monticello and Rocky Gap June 9. West Farm June 9. Operations against Morgan July 2-26. Columbia July 3. Buffington Island, Ohio, July 19. Cheshire and Coal Hill July 20. Operations in Eastern Kentucky against Scott's forces July 25-August 6. Burnside's Campaign in East Tennessee August 16-October 17. Winter's Gap August 31. Near Sweetwater September 6. Athens, Calhoun and Charleston September 25. Near Philadelphia October 15. Philadelphia October 20. Jones' Hill October 26-27. Knoxville Campaign November 4-December 23. Marysville November 14. Rockford November 14. Stock Creek November 15. Holston River November 15. Near Knoxville November 16. Skirmishes about Kingston November 16-23. Siege of Knoxville November 17-December 5. Skirmishes at and near Bean's Station December 9-15. Russellsville December 10. Bean's Station December 10-14-15. Rutledge December 16. Blain's Cross Roads December 16-19. Operations about Dandridge January 26-28, 1864. Near Fair Garden January 27. At Cumberland Gap till February 8. At Mt. Sterling, Ky., till April 6, when dismounted. March to Knoxville, thence moved to Cleveland, Tenn., April 6-May 5. Atlanta (Ga.) Campaign May to September. Demonstrations on Dalton May 9-13. Battle of Resaca May 14-15. Advance on Dallas May 18-25. Operations on line of Pumpkin Vine Creek and battles about Dallas, New Hope Church and Allatoona Hills May 25-June 5. Operations about Marietta and against Kenesaw Mountains June 10-July 2. Pine Hill June 11-14. Lost Mountain June 15-17. Muddy Creek June 17. Noyes' Creek June 19. Kolb's Farm June 22. Assault on Kenesaw June 27. Ruff's Station July 4. Chattahoochie River July 5-17. Peach Tree Creek July 19-20. Siege of Atlanta July 22-August 25. Flank movement on Jonesboro August 25-30. Battle of Jonesboro August 31-September 1. Lovejoy Station September 2-6. Operations against Hood in North Georgia and North Alabama September 29-November 3. Moved to Pulaski, Tenn., Nashville Campaign, November-December. Columbia, Duck River, November 24-27. Battle of Franklin November 30. Battle of Nashville December 15-16. Pursuit of Hood to the Tennessee River December 17-28. Moved to Huntsville, Ala., and duty there till March, 1865. Operations in East Tennessee March 15-April 22. At Nashville, Tenn., till June. Mustered out June 12, 1865. Recruits transferred to 51st Ohio Infantry.

Regiment lost during service 5 Officers and 58 Enlisted men killed and mortally wounded and 1 Officer and 275 Enlisted men by disease. Total 339.

46th REGIMENT INFANTRY.

Organized at Worthington, Ohio, October 16, 1861, to January 28, 1862. At Camp Chase, Ohio, till February 18, 1862. Ordered to Paducah, Ky., February 18. Attached to District of Paducah, Ky., to March, 1862. 1st Brigade, 5th Division, Army of the Tennessee, to May, 1862. 2nd Brigade, 5th Division, Army Tennessee, to July, 1862. 2nd Brigade, 5th Division, District of Memphis, Tenn., to November, 1862. 2nd Brigade, 5th Division, Right Wing 13th Army Corps (Old), Dept. of the Tennessee, November, 1862. 1st Brigade, 1st Division, District of Memphis, Tenn., 13th Army Corps, to December, 1862. 1st Brigade, 1st Division, 17th Army Corps, to January, 1863. 1st Brigade, 1st Division, 16th Army Corps, to March, 1863. 2nd Brigade, 1st Division, 16th Army Corps, to July, 1863. 2nd Brigade, 4th Division, 16th Army Corps, to September, 1864. 2nd Brigade, 1st Division, 15th Army Corps, to July, 1865.

SERVICE.—Moved to Savannah, Tenn., March 6-10, 1862. Expedition to Yellow Creek, Miss., and occupation of Pittsburg Landing, Tenn., March 14-17. Battle of Shiloh, Tenn., April 6-7. Duty at Pittsburg Landing till April 27. Advance on and siege of Corinth, Miss., April 29-May 30. March to Memphis, Tenn., via LaGrange, Grand Junction and Holly Springs June 1-July 2. Guard duty along Memphis & Charleston Railroad and provost duty at Memphis, Tenn., till November. Affair at Randolph September 25. Grant's Central Mississippi Campaign. Operations on the Mississippi Central Railroad November, 1862, to January 10, 1863. Guard duty along Memphis & Charleston Railroad, and scout duty in Northern Mississippi till June 8. Ordered to Vicksburg, Miss., June 8. Siege of Vicksburg, Miss., June 11-July 4. Advance on Jackson, Miss., July 4-10. Bolton's Ferry July 4-6. Siege of Jackson July 10-17. Camp at Big Black till September 26. Moved to Memphis, thence march to Chattanooga, Tenn., September 25-November 20. Operations on Memphis & Charleston Railroad in Alabama October 20-29. Paint Rock, Ala., November 20. Chattanooga-Ringgold Campaign November 23-27. Tunnel Hill November 23-24. Mission Ridge November 25. Pursuit to Graysville November 26-27. March to relief of Knoxville, Tenn., November 28-December 8. Duty at Scottsboro, Ala., December 31, 1863, to May 1, 1864. Atlanta (Ga.) Campaign May 1-September 8. Demonstrations on Resaca

May 8-13. Near Resaca May 13. Battle of Resaca May 14-15. Advance on Dallas May 18-25. Operations on line of Pumpkin Vine Creek and battles about Dallas, New Hope Church and Allatoona Hills May 25-June 5. Operations about Marietta and against Kenesaw Mountain June 10-July 2. Assault on Kenesaw June 27. Nickajack Creek July 2-5. Chattahoochie River July 6-17. Battle of Atlanta July 22. Siege of Atlanta July 22-August 25. Ezra Chapel, Hood's 2nd Sortie, July 28. Flank movement on Jonesboro August 25-30. Battle of Jonesboro August 31-September 1. Lovejoy Station September 2-6. Operations against Hood in North Georgia and North Alabama September 29-November 3. Rome October 17. March to the sea November 15-December 10. Griswoldsville November 22. Siege of Savannah December 10-21. Campaign of the Carolinas January to April, 1865. Reconnoissance to Salkehatchie River, S. C., January 25. Salkehatchie Swamp February 2-5. South Edisto River February 9. North Edisto River February 11-12. Congaree and Savannah Creeks February 15. Columbia February 16-17. Battle of Bentonville, N. C., March 20-21. Mill Creek March 22. Occupation of Goldsboro March 24. Advance on Raleigh April 10-14. Occupation of Raleigh April 14. Bennett's House April 26. Surrender of Johnston and his army. March to Washington, D. C., via Richmond, Va., April 29-May 20. Grand Review May 24. Moved to Louisville, Ky., June, and duty there till July. Mustered out July 22, 1865.

Regiment lost during service 10 Officers and 124 Enlisted men killed and mortally wounded and 7 Officers and 149 Enlisted men by disease. Total 290.

47th REGIMENT INFANTRY.

Organized at Camp Dennison, Ohio, and mustered in August 13, 1861. Ordered to Clarksburg, W. Va., August 27; thence moved to Weston August 29. Attached to McCook's Brigade, Kanawha District, West Virginia, to October, 1861. 1st Brigade, Kanawha Division, West Virginia, to March, 1862. 2nd Brigade, Kanawha Division, West Virginia, to May, 1862. 3rd Brigade, Kanawha Division, West Virginia, to August, 1862. District of the Kanawha, West Virginia, Dept. of the Ohio, to December, 1862. Ewing's Brigade, Kanawha Division, West Virginia, to January, 1863. 3rd Brigade, 2nd Division, 15th Army Corps, Army of the Tennessee, to October, 1863. 2nd Brigade, 2nd Division, 15th Army Corps, to June, 1865. Dept. of Arkansas to August, 1865.

SERVICE.—Battle of Carnifex Ferry, W. Va., September 10, 1861. Advance to Camp Lookout and Big Sewell Mountain September 24-26. Retreat to Camp Anderson October 6-9. Operations in the Kanawha Valley and New River Region October 19-November 16. Moved to Gauley Bridge December 6, and duty there till April 23, 1862. Expedition to Lewisburg April 23-May 10. Moved to Meadow Bluff May 29. Expedition to Salt Sulphur Springs June 22-25. Duty there till August. Moved to Gauley Bridge, thence to Summerville September 3. Campaign in the Kanawha Valley September 6-16. Retreat to Gauley Bridge September 10. Cotton Hill, Loop Creek and Armstrong's Creek September 11. Charleston September 11. Duty at Point Pleasant and in the Kanawha Valley till December. Ordered to Louisville, Ky., December 30; thence to Memphis, Tenn., and to Young's Point, La., January 21, 1863. Expedition to Rolling Fork via Muddy, Steele's and Black Bayous and Deer Creek March 14-27. Demonstrations on Haines and Drumgould's Bluffs April 29-May 2. Moved to join army in rear of Vicksburg, Miss., May 2-14 via Richmond and Grand Gulf. Siege of Vicksburg May 18-July 4. Assaults on Vicksburg May 19 and 22. Advance on Jackson, Miss., July 4-10. Siege of Jackson, Miss., July 10-17. At Camp Sherman, Big Black, till September 26. Moved to Memphis, Tenn., thence march to Chattanooga September 26-November 21. Operations on Memphis & Charleston Railroad in Alabama October 20-29. Bear Creek, Tuscumbia, October 27. Chattanooga-Ringgold Campaign November

23-27. Tunnel Hill November 23-24. Mission Ridge November 25. Pursuit to Graysville November 26-27. March to relief of Knoxville November 28-December 8. Return to Bellefonte, Ala., thence moved to Larkins' Landing, Ala. Reconnoissance to Rome January 25-February 5, 1864. Re-enlisted March 8. Veterans on furlough March 18-May 3. Atlanta (Ga.) Campaign May to September. Demonstrations on Resaca May 8-13. Near Resaca May 13. Battle of Resaca May 14-15. Advance on Dallas May 18-25. Operations on line of Pumpkin Vine Creek and battles about Dallas, New Hope Church and Allatoona Hills May 25-June 5. Operations about Marietta and against Kenesaw Mountain June 10-July 2. Assault on Kenesaw June 27. Nickajack Creek July 2-5. Ruff's Mills July 3-4. Chattahoochie River July 5-17. Battle of Atlanta July 22. Siege of Atlanta July 22-August 25. Flank movement on Jonesboro August 25-30. Battle of Jonesboro August 31-September 1. Lovejoy Station September 2-6. Operations against Hood in North Georgia and North Alabama September 29-November 3. Turkeytown and Gadsden Road October 25. March to the sea November 15-December 10. Siege of Savannah December 10-21. Fort McAllister December 13. Campaign of the Carolinas January to April, 1865. Cannon's Bridge, South Edisto River, S. C., February 8. North Edisto River February 12-13. Columbia February 15-17. Battle of Bentonville, N. C., March 20-21. Occupation of Goldsboro March 24. Advance on Raleigh April 10-14. Bennett's House April 26. Surrender of Johnston and his army. March to Washington, D. C., via Richmond, Va., April 29-May 30. Grand Review May 24. Moved to Louisville, Ky., June; thence to Little Rock, Ark., and duty there till August. Mustered out August 11, 1865.

Regiment lost during service 2 Officers and 80 Enlisted men killed and mortally wounded and 1 Officer and 136 Enlisted men by disease. Total 219.

48th REGIMENT INFANTRY.

Organized at Camp Dennison, Ohio, September to December, 1861, and mustered in February 17, 1862. Ordered to Paducah, Ky., and duty there till March 6. Attached to District of Paducah, Ky., to March, 1862. 4th Brigade, 5th Division, Army of the Tennessee, to May, 1862. 3rd Brigade, 5th Division, Army of the Tennessee, to July, 1862. 3rd Brigade, 5th Division, District of Memphis, Tenn., to November, 1862. 3rd Brigade, 5th Division, Right Wing 13th Army Corps (Old), Dept. of the Tennessee, to November, 1862. 2nd Brigade, 1st Division, Right Wing 13th Army Corps, to December, 1862. 2nd Brigade, 1st Division, Sherman's Yazoo Expedition, to January, 1863. 2nd Brigade, 10th Division, 13th Army Corps, Army of the Tennessee, to August, 1863. 2nd Brigade, 4th Division, 13th Army Corps, Dept. of the Tennessee and Dept. of the Gulf, to April, 1864. Captured at Sabine Cross Roads, La., April 8, 1864. Attached to Defences of New Orleans, La., Dept. of the Gulf, November, 1864, to January, 1865.

SERVICE.—Moved from Paducah, Ky., to Savannah, Tenn., March 6-10, 1862. Expedition from Savannah to Yellow Creek, Miss., and occupation of Pittsburg Landing, Tenn., March 14-17. Battle of Shiloh, Tenn., April 6-7. Advance on and siege of Corinth, Miss., April 29-May 30. March to Memphis, Tenn., via LaGrange, Grand Junction and Holly Springs June 1-July 21. Near Holly Springs July 1. Duty at Memphis and along Memphis & Charleston Railroad till November. Grant's Central Mississippi Campaign. Operations on the Mississippi Central Railroad. "Tallahatchie March" November 26-December 12. Sherman's Yazoo Expedition December 20, 1862, to January 2, 1863. Chickasaw Bayou December 26-28, 1862. Chickasaw Bluff December 29. Expedition to Arkansas Post, Ark., January 3-10, 1863. Assault and capture of Fort Hindman, Arkansas Post, Ark., January 10-11. Moved to Young's Point, La., January 15, and duty there till March 8. At Milliken's Bend, La., till April 25. Movement on

Bruinsburg and turning Grand Gulf April 25-30. Battle of Port Gibson May 1. Battle of Champion's Hill May 16. Siege of Vicksburg, Miss., May 18-July 4. Assaults on Vicksburg May 19 and 22. Advance on Jackson, Miss., July 4-10. Siege of Jackson July 10-17. Camp at Big Black till August 13. Ordered to New Orleans, La., August 13. Western Louisiana ("Teche") Campaign October 3-November 30. At New Iberia till December 13. Moved to New Orleans, La., December 13; thence to Pass Cavallo, Texas, and duty there and at Du Crow's Point till March 1, 1864. Moved to New Orleans, La., March 1. Red River Campaign March 10 to April 23. Advance from Franklin to Alexandria March 14-26. Bayou De Paul, Carroll's Mill, April 8. Battle of Sabine Cross Roads April 8. Regiment captured and prisoners of war till October, 1864, when exchanged. Duty at New Orleans till January, 1865. Consolidated with 83rd Ohio Infantry January 17, 1865. Moved to Kennersville January 28, thence to Barrancas, Fla. March from Pensacola, Fla., to Fort Blakely, Ala., March 20-April 2. Siege of Fort Blakely April 2-9. Assault and capture of Fort Blakely April 9. Occupation of Mobile April 12. March to Montgomery and Selma April 13-21. Duty at Selma till May 12. Moved to Mobile May 12, thence to Galveston, Texas, June 13, and duty there till July 24.

48th OHIO BATTALION INFANTRY.

Organized July 24, 1865, by consolidation of the 48th, 83rd and 114th Ohio Infantry. Duty at Galveston and Houston, Texas, till May, 1866. Mustered out May 9, 1866.

Regiment lost during service 3 Officers and 54 Enlisted men killed and mortally wounded and 3 Officers and 120 Enlisted men by disease. Total 180.

49th REGIMENT INFANTRY.

Organized at Tiffin, Ohio, August and September, 1861. Moved to Camp Dennison, Ohio, September 10, 1861; thence to Louisville, Ky., September 21. (1st organized Regiment to enter Kentucky.) Moved to Camp Nevin, Ky., October 10. Attached to Johnson's Brigade, McCook's Command, at Nolin, Ky., to November, 1861. 6th Brigade, Army of the Ohio, to December, 1861. 6th Brigade, 2nd Division, Army of the Ohio, to September, 1862. 6th Brigade, 2nd Division, 1st Army Corps, Army of the Ohio, to November, 1862. 1st Brigade, 2nd Division, Right Wing 14th Army Corps, Army of the Cumberland, to January, 1863. 1st Brigade, 2nd Division, 20th Army Corps, Army of the Cumberland, to October, 1863. 1st Brigade, 3rd Division, 4th Army Corps, to August, 1865. Dept. of Texas to November 1865.

SERVICE.—Occupation of Munfordsville December 10, 1861. Duty at Munfordsville till February, 1862. Advance to Bowling Green, Ky., and Nashville, Tenn., February 14-March 3. March to Savannah, Tenn., March 16-April 6. Battle of Shiloh, Tenn., April 6-7. Advance on and siege of Corinth, Miss., April 29-May 30. March to Battle Creek, Ala., June 10-July 18, and duty there till August 20. March to Louisville, Ky., in pursuit of Bragg August 20-September 26. Pursuit of Bragg into Kentucky October 1-15. Lawrenceburg, Ky., October 8. Dog Walk October 9. March to Nashville, Tenn., October 16-November 7, and duty there till December 26. Advance on Murfreesboro December 26-30. Battle of Stone's River December 30-31, 1862, and January 1-3, 1863. Duty at Murfreesboro till June. Christiana and Middleton March 6. Middle Tennessee (or Tullahoma) Campaign June 22-July 7. Liberty Gap June 22-27. Occupation of Middle Tennessee till August 16. Passage of the Cumberland Mountains and Tennessee River and Chickamauga (Ga.) Campaign August 16-September 22. Battle of Chickamauga September 19-20. Siege of Chattanooga, Tenn., September 24-November 23. Chattanooga-Ringgold Campaign November 23-27. Orchard Knob November 23-24. Mission Ridge November 25. Pursuit to Graysville November 26-27. March to relief of Knoxville, Tenn., November

28-December 8. Operations in East Tennessee till February, 1864. At Cleveland, Tenn., till April. Atlanta (Ga.) Campaign May 1 to September 8. Demonstrations on Rocky Faced Ridge and Dalton May 8-13. Battle of Resaca May 14-15. Adairsville May 17. Near Kingston May 18-19. Near Cassville May 19. Advance on Dallas May 22-25. Operations on line of Pumpkin Vine Creek and battles about Dallas, New Hope Church and Allatoona Hills May 25-June 5. Pickett's Mills May 27. Operations about Marietta and against Kenesaw Mountain June 10-July 2. Pine Hill June 11-14. Lost Mountain June 15-17. Assault on Kenesaw June 27. Ruff's Station July 4. Chattahoochie River July 5-17. Peach Tree Creek July 19-20. Siege of Atlanta July 22-August 25. Flank movement on Jonesboro August 25-30. Battle of Jonesboro August 25-30. Battle of Jonesboro August 31-September 1. Lovejoy Station September 2-6. Operations against Hood in North Georgia and North Alabama September 29-November 3. Nashville Campaign November-December. Columbia, Duck River, November 24-27. Battle of Franklin November 30. Battle of Nashville December 15-16. Pursuit of Hood to the Tennessee River December 17-28. Moved to Huntsville, Ala., and duty there till March, 1865. Operations in East Tennessee March 15-April 22. Duty at Nashville, Tenn., till June. Moved to New Orleans, La., June 16; thence to Texas. Duty at Green Lake, San Antonio and Victoria till November. Mustered out November 30, 1865.

Regiment lost during service 14 Officers and 188 Enlisted men killed and mortally wounded and 1 Officer and 160 Enlisted men by disease. Total 363.

50th REGIMENT INFANTRY.

Organized at Camp Dennison, Ohio, and mustered in August 27, 1862. Ordered to Covington, Ky., September 1. Defence of Cincinnati, Ohio, against Kirby Smith's threatened attack. Moved to Louisville, Ky., September 20. Attached to 34th Brigade, 10th Division, Army of the Ohio, September, 1862. 34th Brigade, 10th Division, 1st Army Corps, Army of the Ohio, to November, 1862. District of West Kentucky, Dept. of the Ohio, to May, 1863. Unattached, 2nd Division, 23rd Army Corps, Dept. of the Ohio, to August, 1863. Unattached, 1st Division, 23rd Army Corps, to September, 1863. District of South Central Kentucky, 1st Division, 23rd Army Corps, to April, 1864. 3rd Brigade, 4th Division, 23rd Army Corps, to June, 1864. 3rd Brigade, 2nd Division, 23rd Army Corps, Army of the Ohio, to February, 1865, and Dept. of North Carolina to June, 1865.

SERVICE.—Pursuit of Bragg into Kentucky October 1-15. Battle of Perryville, Ky., October 8. Moved to Lebanon, Ky., and duty there till February, 1863. At Muldraugh's Hill, Ky., building fortifications and bridges over Sulphur and Rolling Forks of Green River till September. Also built Forts Boyle, Sands and McAllister. Ordered to Nashville, Tenn., September 18; thence to Gallatin, Tenn., and to Glasgow, Ky., and to Knoxville, Tenn., December 25. March across mountains to Jacksboro December 26, 1863, to January 7, 1864. Duty there till February 22. At Knoxville and Loudoun till May. Moved to Cleveland, Tenn., thence march to Kingston, Ga., and join Sherman's army May 23, 1864. Atlanta (Ga.) Campaign May 23-September 8. Kingston May 24. Operations on line of Pumpkin Vine Creek and battles about Dallas, New Hope Church and Allatoona Hills May 25-June 5. Operations about Marietta and against Kenesaw Mountain June 10-July 2. Pine Hill June 11-14. Lost Mountain June 15-17. Muddy Creek June 17. Noyes Creek June 19. Kolb's Farm June 22. Assault on Kenesaw June 27. Nickajack Creek July 2-5. Chattahoochie River July 6-17. Decatur July 19. Howard House, Atlanta, July 20. Siege of Atlanta July 22-August 25. Utoy Creek August 5-7. Flank movement on Jonesboro August 25-30. Battle of Jonesboro August 31-September 1. Lovejoy Station September 2-6. Camp at Decatur till October 4. Pursuit of Hood into Alabama October 4-26. Nashville

Campaign November-December. Columbia, Duck River, November 24-27. Columbia Ford November 28-29. Battle of Franklin November 30. Battle of Nashville December 15-16. Pursuit of Hood to the Tennessee River December 17-28. Moved to Clifton, Tenn., and duty there till January 16, 1865. Movement to Washington, D. C., thence to Smithville, N. C., January 16-February 10. Operations against Hoke February 12-14. Fort Anderson February 18-19. Town Creek February 19-20. Capture of Wilmington February 22. Campaign of the Carolinas March 1-April 26. Advance on Goldsboro, N. C., March 6-21. Occupation of Goldsboro and Raleigh. Bennett's House April 26. Surrender of Johnston and his army. Duty at Raleigh till May 5, and Greensboro and Salisbury till June. Mustered out June 26, 1865.

Regiment lost during service 6 Officers and 70 Enlisted men killed and mortally wounded and 134 Enlisted men by disease. Total 210.

51st REGIMENT INFANTRY.

Organized at Camp Dover, Ohio, September 17 to October 26, 1861. Moved to Wellsville November 3, thence to Louisville, Ky., and duty there till December 10. Attached to 15th Brigade, Army of the Ohio, to December, 1861. 15th Brigade, 4th Division, Army of the Ohio, to March, 1862. Unattached, Nashville, Tenn., to June, 1862. 10th Brigade, 4th Division, Army of the Ohio, to July, 1862. 23rd Independent Brigade, Army of the Ohio, to August, 1862. 23rd Brigade, 5th Division, Army of the Ohio, to September, 1862. 23rd Brigade, 5th Division, 2nd Army Corps, Army of the Ohio, to November, 1862. 3rd Brigade, 3rd Division, Left Wing 14th Army Corps, Army of the Cumberland, to January, 1863. 3rd Brigade, 3rd Division, 21st Army Corps, Army of the Cumberland, to October, 1863. 2nd Brigade, 1st Division, 4th Army Corps, to June, 1865. 1st Brigade, 1st Division, 4th Army Corps, to August, 1865. Dept. of Texas to October, 1865.

SERVICE.—Duty at Camp Wickliffe, Ky., till February, 1862. Expedition down the Ohio River to reinforce General Grant, thence to Nashville, Tenn., February 14-25. Occupation of Nashville February 25. Provost duty there till July 9. Moved to Tullahoma, Tenn., and joined Nelson's Division. March to Louisville, Ky., in pursuit of Bragg August 21-September 26. Pursuit of Bragg into Kentucky October 1-22. Battle of Perryville, Ky., October 8. March to Nashville, Tenn., October 22-November 7, and duty there till December 26. Dobbins' Ferry, near Lawrence, December 9. Advance on Murfreesboro December 26-30. Battle of Stone's River December 30-31, 1862, and January 1-3, 1863. Duty at Murfreesboro till June. Middle Tennessee (or Tullahoma) Campaign June 23-July 7. At McMinnville till August 16. Passage of Cumberland Mountain and Tennessee River and Chickamauga (Ga.) Campaign August 16-September 22. Battle of Chickamauga September 19-20. Siege of Chattanooga, Tenn., September 24-November 23. Reopening Tennessee River October 26-29. Chattanooga-Ringgold Campaign November 23-27. Lookout Mountain November 23-24. Mission Ridge November 25. Ringgold Gap, Taylor's Ridge, November 27. Duty at Whiteside till January, 1864. Re-enlisted January 1, 1864. At Blue Springs, near Cleveland, till May. Atlanta (Ga.) Campaign May to September. Tunnel Hill May 6-7. Demonstration on Rocky Faced Ridge and Dalton May 8-13. Buzzard's Roost Gap May 8-9. Battle of Resaca May 14-15. Near Kingston May 18-19. Near Cassville May 19. Advance on Dallas May 22-25. Operations on line of Pumpkin Vine Creek and battles about Dallas, New Hope Church and Allatoona Hills May 25-June 5. Operations about Marietta and against Kenesaw Mountain June 10-July 2. Pine Hill June 11-14. Lost Mountain June 15-17. Assault on Kenesaw June 27. Ruff's Station, Smyrna Camp Ground, July 4. Chattahoochie River July 5-17. Peach Tree Creek July 19-20. Siege of Atlanta July 22-August 25. Flank movement on Jonesboro August 25-30. Battle of Jonesboro August 31-September 1. Lovejoy Station September 2-6. Operations against Hood in North Georgia and North Alabama September 29-November 3. Moved to Pulaski, Tenn. Nashville Campaign November-December. Columbia, Duck River, November 24-27. Battle of Franklin November 30. Battle of Nashville December 15-16. Pursuit of Hood to the Tennessee River December 17-28. Moved to Huntsville, Ala., and duty there till March, 1865. Operations in East Tennessee March 15-April 22. Duty at Nashville, Tenn., till June. Ordered to New Orleans, La., June 16, thence to Texas. Duty at Indianola, Green Lake and Victoria, Texas, to October. Mustered out at Victoria October 3, 1865. Discharged at Columbus, Ohio, November 3, 1865.

Regiment lost during service 4 Officers and 108 Enlisted men killed and mortally wounded and 1 Officer and 233 Enlisted men by disease. Total 346.

52nd REGIMENT INFANTRY.

Organized at Camp Dennison, Ohio, August, 1862. Left State for Lexington, Ky., August 25. Attached to 36th Brigade, 11th Division, Army of the Ohio, to October, 1862. 36th Brigade, 11th Division, 3rd Army Corps, Army of the Ohio, to November, 1862. 2nd Brigade, 4th Division, Centre 14th Army Corps, Army of the Cumberland, to January, 1863. 2nd Brigade, 4th Division, 14th Army Corps, to June, 1863. 2nd Brigade, 2nd Division, Reserve Corps, Dept. of the Cumberland, to October, 1863. 3rd Brigade, 2nd Division, 14th Army Corps, to June, 1865.
SERVICE.—March to relief of General Nelson August 29-September 1. Action at Richmond August 30. Kentucky River August 31. Lexington September 2. Pursuit of Bragg to Crab Orchard, Ky., October 3-15. Battle of Perryville, Ky., October 8. March to Nashville, Tenn., October 16-November 7. Action at Mitchellsville November 5. Duty at Nashville, Tenn., till March, 1863. Escort ammunition trains to Stone's River December 28-30, 1862. Moved to Brentwood, Tenn., March, 1863, and duty there till June 5. Moved to Murfreesboro, Tenn., and duty there till July 16. Garrison duty at Nashville, Tenn., till August 20. March to Bridgeport, Ala., via Franklin, Columbia, Athens and Huntsville, August 20-September 14. Battle of Chickamauga, Ga., September 19-21. Duty in Lookout Valley till November 6. (Temporarily attached to 3rd Brigade, 2nd Division, 11th Army Corps.) At Chickamauga Creek till November 24. Chattanooga-Ringgold Campaign November 24-27. Tunnel Hill November 24-25. Mission Ridge November 25. Pursuit to Graysville November 26-27. March to relief of Knoxville, Tenn., November 28-December 18. At North Chickamauga and McAffee's Church, Ga., till May, 1864. Demonstration on Dalton February 22-27. Tunnel Hill, Buzzard's Roost Gap and Rocky Faced Ridge February 23-25. Atlanta (Ga.) Campaign May to September. Tunnel Hill May 6-7. Demonstration on Rocky Faced Ridge May 8-11. Buzzard's Roost Gap May 8-9. Battle of Resaca May 14-15. Rome May 17-18. Operations on line of Pumpkin Vine Creek and battles about Dallas, New Hope Church and Allatoona Hills May 25-June 5. Operations about Marietta and against Kenesaw Mountain June 10-July 2. Pine Hill June 11-14. Lost Mountain June 15-17. Assault on Kenesaw June 27. Ruff's Station, Smyrna Camp Ground, July 4. Chattahoochie River July 5-17. Peach Tree Creek July 19-20. Siege of Atlanta July 22-August 25. Utoy Creek August 5-7. Flank movement on Jonesboro August 25-30. Battle of Jonesboro August 31-September 1. Lovejoy Station September 2-6. Operations against Hood in North Georgia and North Alabama September 29-November 3. March to the sea November 15-December 10. Louisville November 30. Siege of Savannah December 10-21. Campaign of the Carolinas January to April, 1865. Taylor's Hole Creek, Averysboro, N. C., March 16. Battle of Bentonville March 19-21. Occupation of Goldsboro March 24. Advance on Raleigh April 10-14. Bennett's House April 26. Surrender of Johnston and his army. March to Washington, D. C., via Richmond, Va., April 29-May 20. Grand review May 24. Mustered out June 3, 1865.

Regiment lost during service 7 Officers and 94 Enlisted men killed and mortally wounded and 1 Officer and 168 Enlisted men by disease. Total 270.

53rd REGIMENT INFANTRY.

Organized at Jackson, Ohio, September 3, 1861, to February 11, 1862. Ordered to Paducah, Ky., February 16. Attached to District of Paducah, Ky., to March, 1862. 3rd Brigade, 5th Division, Army of the Tennessee, to July, 1862. 3rd Brigade, 5th Division, District of Memphis, Tenn., to November, 1862. 3rd Brigade, 5th Division, Right Wing 13th Army Corps (Old), Dept. of the Tennessee, November, 1862. 2nd Brigade, 1st Division, District of Memphis, 13th Army Corps, to December, 1862. 2nd Brigade, 1st Division, 17th Army Corps, to January, 1863. 2nd Brigade, 1st Division, 16th Army Corps, to July, 1863. 3rd Brigade, 4th Division, 15th Army Corps, to May, 1864. 2nd Brigade, 2nd Division, 15th Army Corps, to July, 1865. Dept. of Arkansas to August, 1865.
SERVICE.—Moved from Paducah, Ky., to Savannah, Tenn., March 6-10, 1862. Expedition to Yellow Creek, Miss., and occupation of Pittsburg Landing, Tenn., March 14-17. Expedition toward Eastport, Miss., April 1-2. Battle of Shiloh, Tenn., April 6-7. Corinth Road, Monterey, April 8. Advance on and siege of Corinth, Miss., April 29-May 30. March to Memphis, Tenn., via Moscow, Lafayette, Grand Junction and Holly Springs, June 1-July 21. Duty at Memphis and along Memphis & Charleston Railroad till November. Grant's Central Mississippi Campaign. Operations on the Mississippi Central Railroad to the Yockna River November, 1862, to January, 1863. Moved to LaGrange, Tenn., January, 1863, and duty there till June. Moved to Memphis, thence to Young's Point, La., June 9-12. Siege of Vicksburg, Miss., June 12-July 4. Advance on Jackson, Miss., July 4-10. Bolton's Ferry July 4-6. Siege of Jackson July 10-17. Camp at Big Black till September 26. Moved to Memphis, thence march to Chattanooga, Tenn., September 26-November 20. Operations on Memphis & Charleston Railroad in Alabama October 20-29. Chattanooga-Ringgold Campaign November 23-27. Tunnel Hill November 23-24. Mission Ridge November 25. March to relief of Knoxville, Tenn., November 28-December 28. Duty at Scottsboro, Ala., till March, 1864. Veterans on furlough till April. Atlanta (Ga.) Campaign May to September. Demonstrations on Resaca May 8-13. Near Resaca May 13. Battle of Resaca May 14-15. Advance on Dallas May 18-25. Operations on line of Pumpkin Vine Creek and battles about Dallas, New Hope Church and Allatoona Hills May 25-June 5. Operations about Marietta and against Kenesaw Mountain June 10-July 2. Bush Mountain June 15. Assault on Kenesaw June 27. Nickajack Creek July 2-5. Ruff's Mills July 3-4. Chattahoochie River July 6-17. Battle of Atlanta July 22. Siege of Atlanta July 22-August 25. Ezra Chapel, Hood's 2nd sortie. July 28. Flank movement on Jonesboro August 25-30. Near Jonesboro August 30. Battle of Jonesboro August 31-September 1. Lovejoy Station September 2-6. Operations against Hood in North Georgia and North Alabama September 29-November 3. Turkeytown and Gadsden Road, Ala., October 25. March to the sea November 15-December 10. Siege of Savannah December 10-21. Fort McAllister December 13. Campaign of the Carolinas January to April, 1865. Salkehatchie Swamps, S. C., February 2-5. Cannon's Bridge, South Edisto River, February 8. North Edisto River February 11-13. Columbia February 16-17. Battle of Bentonville, N. C., March 20-21. Occupation of Goldsboro March 24. Advance on Raleigh April 10-14. Occupation of Raleigh April 14. Bennett's House April 26. Surrender of Johnston and his army. March to Washington, D. C., via Richmond, Va., April 29-May 20. Grand Review May 24. Moved to Louisville, Ky., June, thence to Little Rock, Ark., and duty there till August. Mustered out August 11, 1865.

Regiment lost during service 4 Officers and 76 Enlisted men killed and mortally wounded and 6 Officers and 190 Enlisted men by disease. Total 276.

54th REGIMENT INFANTRY.

Organized at Camp Dennison, Ohio, October, 1861. Left State for Paducah, Ky., February 17, 1862. Attached to District of Paducah, Ky., to March, 1862. 2nd Brigade, 5th Division, Army of the Tennessee, to May, 1862. 1st Brigade, 5th Division, Army of the Tennessee, to July, 1862. 1st Brigade, 5th Division, District of Memphis, Tenn., to November, 1862. 1st Brigade, 5th Division, District of Memphis, Tenn., Right Wing 13th Army Corps (Old), Dept. of the Tennessee, November, 1862. 1st Brigade, 2nd Division, Right Wing 13th Army Corps, to December, 1862. 2nd Brigade, 2nd Division, Sherman's Yazoo Expedition, to January, 1863. 2nd Brigade, 2nd Division, 15th Army Corps, Army of the Tennessee, to July, 1865. Dept. of Arkansas to August, 1865.

SERVICE.—Moved from Paducah, Ky., to Savannah, Tenn., March 6-12, 1862. Expedition to Yellow Creek, Miss., and occupation of Pittsburg Landing, Tenn., March 14-17. Battle of Shiloh, Tenn., April 6-7. Advance on and siege of Corinth, Miss., April 29-May 30. Russell's House, near Corinth, May 17. March to Memphis, Tenn., via LaGrange, Grand Junction and Holly Springs, June 1-July 21. Duty at Memphis till November. Expedition from Memphis to Coldwater and Hermando, Miss., September 8-13. Grant's Central Mississippi Campaign, "Tallahatchie March," November 26-December 13. Sherman's Yazoo Expedition December 20, 1862, to January 3, 1863. Chickasaw Bayou December 26-28, 1862. Chickasaw Bluff December 29. Expedition to Arkansas Post, Ark., January 3-10, 1863. Assault and capture of Fort Hindman, Arkansas Post, January 10-11. Moved to Young's Point, La., January 17-21, and duty there till March. Expedition up Rolling Fork via Muddy, Steele's and Black Bayous and Deer Creek, March 14-27. Demonstrations on Haines and Drumgould's Bluffs April 29-May 2. Moved to join army in rear of Vicksburg, Miss., May 2-14, via Richmond and Grand Gulf. Battle of Champion's Hill May 16. Siege of Vicksburg, Miss., May 18-July 4. Assaults on Vicksburg May 19 and 22. Advance on Jackson, Miss., July 4-10. Siege of Jackson, Miss., July 10-17. Camp at Big Black till September 26. Moved to Memphis, Tenn., thence march to Chattanooga, Tenn., September 26-November 21. Operations on Memphis & Charleston Railroad in Alabama October 20-29. Bear Creek, Tuscumbia, October 27. Chattanooga-Ringgold Campaign November 23-27. Tunnel Hill November 23-24. Mission Ridge November 25. Pursuit to Graysville November 26-27. March to relief of Knoxville November 28-December 8. March to Chattanooga, Tenn., thence to Bridgeport, Ala., Bellefonte, Ala., and Larkinsville, Ala., December 13-31. Duty at Larkinsville, Ala., to May 1, 1864. Expedition toward Rome, Ga., January 25-February 5. Atlanta (Ga.) Campaign May 1 to September 8. Demonstration on Resaca May 8-13. Near Resaca May 13. Battle of Resaca May 14-15. Movements on Dallas May 18-25. Operations on line of Pumpkin Vine Creek and battles about Dallas, New Hope Church and Allatoona Hills May 25-June 5. Operations about Marietta and against Kenesaw Mountain June 10-July 2. Assault on Kenesaw June 27. Nickajack Creek July 2-5. Chattahoochie River July 6-17. Battle of Atlanta July 22. Siege of Atlanta July 22-August 25. Ezra Chapel, Hood's 2nd sortie, July 28. Flank movement on Jonesboro August 25-30. Battle of Jonesboro August 31-September 1. Lovejoy Station September 2-6. Operations in North Georgia and North Alabama against Hood September 29-November 3. March to the sea November 15-December 10. Siege of Savannah December 10-21. Fort McAllister December 13. Campaign of the Carolinas January to April, 1865. Salkehatchie Swamps, S. C., February 2-5. Cannon's Bridge, South Edisto River, February 9. North Edisto River, February 11-13. Columbia February 16-17. Battle of Bentonville, N. C., March 20-21. Occupation of Goldsboro March 24. Advance on Raleigh April 10-14. Bennett's House April 26. Surrender of Johnston and his army. March to Washington, D. C., via Richmond, Va., April 29-May 19. Grand Review May 24. Moved to Louisville, Ky., June 2, thence to Little Rock, Ark., and duty there till August. Mustered out August 15, 1865.

Regiment lost during service 4 Officers and 83 Enlisted men killed and mortally wounded and 3 Officers and 143 Enlisted men by disease. Total 233.

55th REGIMENT INFANTRY.

Organized at Norwalk, Ohio, September to December, 1861. Mustered in January 25, 1862. Ordered to Grafton, W. Va., January 25. Attached to Schenck's Brigade, Railroad District, West Virginia, to March, 1862. Railroad District, Dept. of the Mountains, to April, 1862. Schenck's Brigade, Dept. of the Mountains, to June, 1862. 2nd Brigade, 1st Division, 1st Corps, Pope's Army of Virginia, to September, 1862. 2nd Brigade, 1st Division, 11th Army Corps, Army of the Potomac, to May, 1863. 2nd Brigade, 2nd Division, 11th Army Corps, Army of the Potomac, to October, 1863, and Army of the Cumberland, to April, 1864. 3rd Brigade, 3rd Division, 20th Army Corps, Army of the Cumberland and Army of Georgia, to July, 1865.

SERVICE.—Moved from Grafton to New Creek, W. Va., February 3, 1862. Expedition to Romney February 6. Expedition to Moorefield February 12-16. Action at Moorefield February 12. Moved to Grafton February 19, and duty there till March 31. Moved to Green Spring River March 31, thence to Romney April 10. Ordered to join Milroy at Monterey. Battle of McDowell May 8. March to the Shenandoah Valley May 26-29. Near Franklin May 26. Harrisonburg June 6. Battle of Cross Keys June 8. At Middletown till July 7, and at Sperryville till August 8. Reconnoissance to Madison Court House July 16-19. Battle of Cedar Mountain August 9 (Reserve). Slaughter Mountain August 10. Pope's Campaign in Northern Virginia August 16-September 2. Catlett's Station August 22. Battles of Bull Run August 28-30. Duty in the Defences of Washington, D. C., till December. Reconnoissance to Bristoe Station and Warrenton Junction September 25-28. Moved to Fredericksburg December 12-16. "Mud March" January 20-24, 1863. At Falmouth till April. Chancellorsville Campaign April 27-May 6. Battle of Chancellorsville May 1-5. Gettysburg (Pa.) Campaign June 11-July 24. Battle of Gettysburg July 1-3. Pursuit of Lee July 5-24. At Catlett's Station, Va., July 25 to September 24. Movement to Bridgeport, Ala., September 24-October 3. Reopening Tennessee River October 26-29. Battle of Wauhatchie, Tenn., October 28-29. Chattanooga-Ringgold Campaign November 23-27. Orchard Knob November 23. Tunnel Hill November 24-25. Mission Ridge November 25. March to relief of Knoxville, Tenn., November 28-December 17. Duty in Lookout Valley till May, 1864. Atlanta (Ga.) Campaign May 1 to September 8. Demonstrations on Rocky Faced Ridge May 8-11. Buzzard's Roost Gap May 8-9. Battle of Resaca May 14-15. Cassville May 19. Advance on Dallas May 22-25. Action at New Hope Church May 25. Operations on line of Pumpkin Vine Creek and battles about Dallas, New Hope Church and Allatoona Hills May 26-June 5. Operations about Marietta and against Kenesaw Mountain June 10-July 2. Pine Hill June 11-14. Lost Mountain June 15-17. Gilgal or Golgotha Church June 15. Muddy Creek June 17. Noyes Creek June 19. Cassville June 20. Kolb's Farm June 22. Assault on Kenesaw June 27. Ruffs Station July 4. Chattahoochie River July 5-17. Peach Tree Creek July 19-20. Siege of Atlanta July 22-August 25. Operations at Chattahoochie River Bridge August 26-September 2. Farmer's Ferry August 27. Occupation of Atlanta September 2 to November 15. March to the sea November 15-December 10. Siege of Savannah December 10-21. Campaign of the Carolinas January to April, 1865. Lawtonville, S. C., February 2. North Edisto River February 12-13. Reconnoissance on Goldsboro Road, near Fayetteville, N. C., March 14. Taylor's Hole Creek, Aversyboro, March 16. Battle of Bentonville March 19-21. Occupation of Goldsboro March 24. Advance on Raleigh April 10-14. Occupation of Raleigh April 14. Bennett's House April 26. Surrender of Johnston and his army. March to Washington, D. C., via Richmond, Va., April 29-May 19. Grand Review May 24. Moved to Louisville, Ky., June 10, and duty there till July. Mustered out July 11, 1865.

Regiment lost during service 7 Officers and 136 Enlisted men killed and mortally wounded and 119 Enlisted men by disease. Total 262.

56th REGIMENT INFANTRY.

Organized at Camp Morrow, Portsmouth, Ohio, and mustered in December 12, 1861. Moved to Paducah, Ky., thence to Fort Donelson, Tenn., February 12-15, 1862. Fort Donelson February 15-16. Attached to 3rd Brigade, 3rd Division, Army of the Tennessee, to July, 1862. Helena, Ark., District of Eastern Arkansas, to November, 1862. 2nd Brigade, 12th Division, District of Eastern Arkansas, Dept. of the Tennessee, to January, 1863. 2nd Brigade, 12th Division, 13th Army Corps, Army of the Tennessee, to July, 1863. 2nd Brigade, 3rd Division, 13th Army Corps, Dept. of the Tennessee, to August, 1863, and Dept. of the Gulf, to June, 1864. Defences of New Orleans, La., Dept. of the Gulf, to April, 1866.

SERVICE.—Expedition toward Purdy and operations about Crump's Landing March 9-14, 1862. Battle of Shiloh, Tenn., April 6-7. Advance on and siege of Corinth, Miss., April 29-May 30. March to Memphis, Tenn., June 1-13, and duty there till July 24. Germantown and Lafayette Station June 25. Ordered to Helena, Ark., June 24, and duty there till April, 1863. Gorman's Expedition from Helena to Eunice August 28-September 5, 1862. Expedition against Arkansas Post November 16-21. Ordered to Milliken's Bend, La., April 11, 1863. Movement on Bruinsburg and turning Grand Gulf April 25-30. Battle of Port Gibson May 1. Fourteen-Mile Creek May 12. Battle of Champion's Hill May 16. Siege of Vicksburg, Miss., May 18-July 4. Assaults on Vicksburg May 19 and 22. Advance on Jackson, Miss., July 4-10. Siege of Jackson July 10-17. Ordered to New Orleans, La., August 13. Duty there till September 13, and at Berwick Bay till October. Western Louisiana ("Teche") Campaign October 3-November 30. Grand Coteau November 3. At New Iberia till December 17. Moved to New Orleans December 17, thence to Madisonville January 22, 1864, and duty there till March 1. Moved to New Orleans March 1. Red River Campaign March 10-May 5. Advance from Franklin to Alexandria March 14-26. Battle of Sabine Cross Roads April 8. Pleasant Hill April 9. Monett's Ferry, Cane River, April 23. At Alexandria April 26-May 4. Davidson's Ferry, Red River, May 4-5. Natchitoches May 5. Dunn's Bayou, destruction of Transport "Warner," May 5. Veterans absent on furlough May to July. Return to New Orleans, La., and duty in the Defences of that city till April, 1866. Expedition from New Orleans to Mandeville January 15-17, 1865 (Detachment). Non-Veterans mustered out November, 1864. Regiment mustered out April 25, 1866.

Regiment lost during service 3 Officers and 55 Enlisted men killed and mortally wounded and 2 Officers and 156 Enlisted men by disease. Total 216.

57th REGIMENT INFANTRY.

Organized at Camp Vance, Findlay, Ohio, September 16, 1861. Moved to Camp Chase, Ohio, January 22, 1862. Ordered to Paducah, Ky., February 18. Attached to District of Paducah, Ky., to March, 1862. 3rd Brigade, 5th Division, Army of the Tennessee, to May, 1862. 1st Brigade, 5th Division, Army of the Tennessee, to July, 1862. 1st Brigade, 5th Division, District of Memphis, Tenn., to November, 1862. 4th Brigade, 5th Division, Right Wing 13th Army Corps (Old), Dept. of the Tennessee, to November, 1862. 2nd Brigade, 2nd

Division, District of Memphis, 13th Army Corps, to December, 1862. 2nd Brigade, 2nd Division, Sherman's Yazoo Expedition, to January, 1863. 2nd Brigade, 2nd Division, 15th Army Corps, Army of the Tennessee, to September, 1863. 1st Brigade, 2nd Division, 15th Army Corps, to July, 1865. Dept. of Arkansas to August, 1865.

SERVICE.—Duty at Paducah, Ky., till March 6, 1862. Moved to Savannah, Tenn., March 6-10. Expedition to Yellow Creek and occupation of Pittsburg Landing, Tenn., March 14-17. Expedition to Eastport, Miss., and Chickasaw, Ala., April 1-2. Battle of Shiloh, Tenn., April 6-7. Corinth Road April 8. Advance on and siege of Corinth, Miss., April 29-May 30. Russell House, near Corinth, May 17. March to Memphis, Tenn., via La-Grange, Grand Junction and Holly Springs June 1-July 18. Rising Sun, Tenn., June 30. Duty at Memphis till November. Expedition from Memphis to Coldwater and Herando, Miss., September 8-13. Skirmish at Wolf Creek Bridge September 23. Grant's Central Mississippi Campaign. "Tallahatchie March" November 26-December 13. Sherman's Yazoo Expedition December 20, 1862, to January 3, 1863. Chickasaw Bayou December 26-28, 1862. Chickasaw Bluff December 29. Expedition to Arkansas Post, Ark., January 3-10, 1863. Assault and capture of Fort Hindman, Arkansas Post, January 10-11. Expedition to South Bend, Arkansas River, January 14-15. Moved to Young's Point, La., January 17-21, and duty there till March. Expedition to Rolling Fork, Miss., via Muddy, Steele's and Black Bayous and Deer Creek March 14-27. Demonstration on Haines and Drumgould's Bluffs April 29-May 2. Movement to join army in rear of Vicksburg, Miss., via Richmond and Grand Gulf May 2-14. Battle of Champion's Hill May 16. Siege of Vicksburg May 18-July 4. Assaults on Vicksburg May 19 and 22. Advance on Jackson, Miss., July 4-10. Siege of Jackson July 10-17. Duty at Big Black till September 27. Moved to Memphis, thence march to Chattanooga, Tenn., September 27-November 20. Operations on Memphis & Chattanooga Railroad in Alabama October 26-29. Bear Creek, Tuscumbia, October 27. Chattanooga-Ringgold Campaign November 23-27. Tunnel Hill November 23-25. Foot of Missionary Ridge November 24. Mission Ridge November 25. Pursuit to Graysville November 26-27. March to relief of Knoxville, Tenn., November 28-December 8. Re-enlisted January 1, 1864. Veterans on furlough February-March. Atlanta (Ga.) Campaign May 1-September 8. Demonstrations on Resaca May 8-13. Near Resaca May 13. Battle of Resaca May 14-15. Advance on Dallas May 18-25. Operations on line of Pumpkin Vine Creek and battles about Dallas, New Hope Church and Allatoona Hills May 25-June 5. Operations about Marietta and against Kenesaw Mountain June 10-July 5. Assault on Kenesaw June 27. Nickajack Creek July 2-5. Chattahoochie River July 6-17. Battle of Atlanta July 22. Siege of Atlanta July 22-August 25. Ezra Chapel, Hood's 2nd Sortie, July 28. Flank movement on Jonesboro August 25-30. Battle of Jonesboro August 31-September 1. Lovejoy Station September 2-6. Operations against Hood in North Georgia and North Alabama September 29-November 3. March to the sea November 15-December 10. Clinton November 21-23. Ball's Ferry and Georgia Central Railroad Bridge November 23-25. Siege of Savannah December 10-21. Fort McAllister December 13. Campaign of the Carolinas January to April, 1865. Salkehatchie Swamps, S. C., February 2-5. Holman's Bridge, South Edisto River, February 9. North Edisto River February 12-13. Columbia February 16-17. Battle of Bentonville, N. C., March 20-21. Occupation of Goldsboro March 24. Advance on Raleigh April 10-14. Occupation of Raleigh April 14. Bennett's House April 26. Surrender of Johnston and his army. March to Washington, D. C., via Richmond, Va., April 29-May 30. Grand Review May 24. Moved to Louisville, Ky., June 2; thence to Little Rock, Ark., and duty there till August. Mustered out August 14, 1865.

Regiment lost during service 4 Officers and 77 Enlisted men killed and mortally wounded and 4 Officers and 234 Enlisted men by disease. Total 319.

58th REGIMENT INFANTRY.

Organized at Camp Chase, Ohio, October 1, 1861, to January 28, 1862. Moved to Cincinnati, Ohio, February 10, 1862; thence to Fort Donelson, Tenn. Attached to 2nd Brigade, 3rd Division, Army of the Tennessee, to July, 1862. Helena, Ark., District of Eastern Arkansas, to November, 1862. 1st Brigade, 1st Division, District of Eastern Arkansas, Dept. of the Tennessee, to December, 1862. 1st Brigade, 11th Division, Right Wing 13th Army Corps (Old), Dept. of the Tennessee, to December, 1862. 1st Brigade, 4th Division, Sherman's Yazoo Expedition, to January, 1863. 1st Brigade, 1st Division, 15th Army Corps, Army of the Tennessee, to February, 1863. Detached duty on ironclads Mississippi Squadron to September, 1863. 1st Brigade, 1st Division, 17th Army Corps, to September, 1864. Post and Defences of Vicksburg, Miss., to September, 1865.

SERVICE.—Investment and capture of Fort Donelson, Tenn., February 14-16, 1862. Expedition toward Purdy and operations about Crump's Landing, Tenn., March 9-14. Battle of Shiloh April 6-7. Advance on and siege of Corinth, Miss., April 29-May 30. March to Memphis, Tenn., June 1-17, and duty there till July 24. Moved to Helena, Ark., July 24, and duty there till October 5. Expedition to Milliken's Bend, La., August 16-27. Capture of Steamer "Fair Play" August 17. Milliken's Bend August 18. Haines Bluff August 20. Bolivar August 22 and 25. Greenville August 23. Moved to St. Genevieve, Mo., October 5. Expedition to Pilot Knob October 22-November 12. Moved to Helena, Ark., and Expedition against Arkansas Post, Ark., November 16-21. At Camp Steele, Helena, Ark., till December 22. Sherman's Yazoo Expedition December 22, 1862, to January 3, 1863. Chickasaw Bayou December 26-28. Chickasaw Bluff December 29. Expedition to Arkansas Post, Ark., January 3-10, 1863. Assault and capture of Fort Hindman, Arkansas Post, January 10-11. Moved to Young's Point, La., January 17-21. Assigned to duty by Companies on the ironclads of the Mississippi Squadron February 8, and participated in the following service: Attack on Fort Pemberton March 13. Expedition up Steele's Bayou March 16-22. Deer Creek, "Long Taw," March 21. Running Vicksburg Batteries April 15. Grand Gulf April 29. Haines Bluff April 30-May 1 and 6. Expedition up Wachita to Trinity May 8-12. Fort Beauregard May 10-12. Siege of Vicksburg May 18-July 4. Yazoo City May 23. Lake Providence June 10. Patrol duty on the Mississippi River from mouth of Red River till July 26. Expedition to Grand Gulf July 10-17. Grand Gulf July 16. Relieved from duty with the fleet and ordered to Vicksburg, Miss. Provost duty at Vicksburg July, 1863, to September, 1865. Old members ordered to Columbus, Ohio, December 24, 1864. Mustered out January 14, 1865. Veterans and Recruits consolidated to a Battalion of five Companies and mustered out September 16, 1865.

Regiment lost during service 3 Officers and 85 Enlisted men killed and mortally wounded and 2 Officers and 215 Enlisted men by disease. Total 305.

59th REGIMENT INFANTRY.

Organized at Ripley, Ohio, September 12, 1861. Moved to Maysville, Ky., October 1. Nelson's Campaign in Kentucky October-November. Action at West Liberty October 21. Olympian Springs November 4. Ivy Mountain November 8. Piketown November 8-9. Moved to Louisa, thence to Louisville and to Columbia, Ky., December 11. Attached to 11th Brigade, Army of the Ohio, to December, 1861. 11th Brigade, 1st Division, Army of the Ohio, to March, 1862. 11th Brigade, 5th Division, Army of the Ohio, to September, 1862. 11th Brigade, 5th Division, 2nd Corps, Army of the Ohio, to November, 1862. 2nd Brigade, 3rd Division, Left Wing 14th Army Corps, Army of the Cumberland, to January, 1863. 2nd Brigade, 3rd Division, 21st Army Corps, Army of the Cumberland, to October, 1863. 3rd Brigade, 3rd Division, 4th Army Corps, Army of the Cumberland, to September, 1864. Unattached, 4th Division, 20th Army Corps, Dept. of the Cumberland, to October, 1864. Tullahoma, Tenn., Defences of Nashville & Chattanooga Railroad, Dept. of the Cumberland, to October, 1864.

SERVICE.—Duty at Columbia, Ky., December 11, 1861, to February 15, 1862. March to Bowling Green, Ky., thence to Nashville, Tenn., February 15-March 8. March to Savannah, Tenn., March 18-April 6. Battle of Shiloh, Tenn., April 6-7. Advance on and siege of Corinth, Miss., April 29-May 30. Occupation of Corinth May 30, and pursuit to Booneville May 31-June 12. March to Stevenson, Ala., via Iuka, Miss., Tuscumbia, Florence, Huntsville and Athens, Ala., June 12-July 24; thence to Battle Creek and duty there till August 20. March to Louisville, Ky., in pursuit of Bragg August 20-September 26. Pursuit of Bragg into Kentucky October 1-22. Battle of Perryville October 8 (Reserve). Nelson's Cross Roads October 18. March to Nashville, Tenn., October 22-November 7, and duty there till December 26. Advance on Murfreesboro December 26-30. Battle of Stone's River December 30-31, 1862, and January 1-3, 1863. At Murfreesboro till June. Middle Tennessee (or Tullahoma) Campaign June 23-July 7. Occupation of Middle Tennessee till August 16. Passage of the Cumberland Mountains and Tennessee River and Chickamauga (Ga.) Campaign August 16-September 22. Battle of Chickamauga September 19-20. Siege of Chattanooga September 24-November 23. Chattanooga-Ringgold Campaign November 23-26. Orchard Knob November 23. Tunnel Hill November 24-25. Mission Ridge November 25. Pursuit to Graysville November 26-27. March to relief of Knoxville November 28-December 8. Operations in East Tennessee till April, 1864. Action at Charleston December 28, 1863 (Detachment). Atlanta (Ga.) Campaign May 1-September 8. Demonstrations on Rocky Faced Ridge and Dalton May 8-13. Battle of Resaca May 14-15. Adairsville May 17. Near Kingston May 18-19. Near Cassville May 19. Advance on Dallas May 22-25. Operations on line of Pumpkin Vine Creek and battles about Dallas, New Hope Church and Allatoona Hills May 25-June 5. Pickett's Mills May 27. Operations about Marietta and against Kenesaw Mountain June 10-July 2. Pine Hill June 10-14. Lost Mountain June 15-17. Assault on Kenesaw June 27. Ruff's Station July 4. Chattahoochie River July 5-17. Peach Tree Creek July 19-20. Siege of Atlanta July 22-August 25. Flank movement on Jonesboro August 25-30. Battle of Jonesboro August 31-September 1. Lovejoy Station September 2-6. Transferred to 23rd Army Corps and ordered to Tullahoma, Tenn., thence to Nashville, Tenn., October 24. Mustered out October 31, 1864.

Regiment lost during service 2 Officers and 45 Enlisted men killed and mortally wounded and 1 Officer and 109 Enlisted men by disease. Total 157.

60th REGIMENT INFANTRY.

Organized at Gallipolis, Ohio, and mustered in February 25, 1862. Moved to New Creek, Va., April 27-30. Served Unattached, Kanawha District, West Virginia, to April, 1862. Cluserett's Advance Brigade, Dept. of the Mountains, to June, 1862. Piatt's Brigade, 1st Division, 1st Corps, Army of Virginia, to September, 1862. Miles' Command, Harper's Ferry, W. Va., September, 1862.

SERVICE.—Duty at Franklin May 25, 1862. Pursuit of Jackson up the Shenandoah Valley June. Mt. Carmel Road, near Strasburg, June 1. Strasburg and Staunton Road June 1-2. Harrisonburg June 6. Battle of Cross Keys June 9. Moved to Strasburg June 19-22, thence to Middletown June 24, and duty there till July. At Winchester, Va., till September 2. Evacuation of Winchester September 2, and retreat to Harper's Ferry. Defence of Harper's Ferry September 11-15. Bolivar Heights September 14. Surrendered September 15.

Paroled as prisoners of war September 16 and sent to Annapolis, Md.; thence to Camp Douglas, Chicago, Ill. Mustered out November 10, 1862.

Regiment lost during service 1 Officer and 9 Enlisted men killed and mortally wounded and 2 Officers and 30 Enlisted men by disease. Total 42.

60th REGIMENT INFANTRY REORGANIZED.

Organized at Cleveland and Columbus, Ohio, February to April, 1864. Left State for Alexandria, Va., April 21, 1864. Attached to 2nd Brigade, 3rd Division, 9th Army Corps, Army of the Potomac, to September, 1864. 2nd Brigade, 1st Division, 9th Army Corps, to July, 1865.

SERVICE.—Campaign from the Rapidan to the James River, Va., May 3-June 15, 1864. Battles of the Wilderness May 5-7. Spottsylvania May 8-12. Ny River May 10. Spottsylvania Court House May 12-21. Assault on the Salient May 12. North Anna River May 23-26. Ox Ford May 23-24. On line of the Pamunkey May 26-28. Totopotomoy May 28-31. Cold Harbor June 1-12. Bethesda Church June 1-3. Before Petersburg June 16-18. Siege of Petersburg June 16, 1864, to April 2, 1865. Mine Explosion July 30, 1864. Six-Mile House, Weldon Railroad, August 18-21. Poplar Springs Church September 29-October 2. Reconnoissance on Vaughan and Squirrel Level Road October 8. Boydton Plank Road, Ratcher's Run, October 27-28. (Co. "K" organized November and December, 1864); 9th and 10th Independent Companies Sharpshooters as Companies "G" and "H," February 25, 1865.) Fort Stedman March 25, 1865. Appomattox Campaign March 28-April 9. Assault on and fall of Petersburg April 2. Occupation of Petersburg April 3. Pursuit of Lee April 3-9. Surrender of Lee and his army at Appomattox Court House April 9. Moved to Alexandria, Va., April 21-28. Duty there and at Washington, D. C., till July. Grand Review at Washington May 23. Mustered out July 28, 1865.

Regiment lost during service 3 Officers and 110 Enlisted men killed and mortally wounded and 130 Enlisted men by disease. Total 243.

61st REGIMENT INFANTRY.

Organized at Camp Chase, Columbus, Ohio, April 23, 1862. Ordered to West Virginia May 27, and joined Fremont's army at Strasburg, Va., June 23, 1862. Attached to 1st Brigade, 3rd Division, 1st Corps, Army of Virginia, June to September, 1862. 1st Brigade, 3rd Division, 11th Army Corps, Army of the Potomac, to October, 1862. 2nd Brigade, 2nd Division, 11th Army Corps, to November, 1862. 1st Brigade, 3rd Division, 11th Army Corps, Army of the Potomac, to October, 1863. Army of the Cumberland to April, 1864. 3rd Brigade, 1st Division, 20th Army Corps, Army of the Cumberland, to March, 1865.

SERVICE.—March to Sperryville and duty there till August 8, 1862. Pope's Campaign in Northern Virginia August 16-September 2. Freeman's Ford August 22. Sulphur Springs August 23-24. Battles of Groveton August 29, and Bull Run August 30. Duty in the Defences of Washington, D. C., till December. March to Fredericksburg, Va., December 10-15. "Mud March" January 20-24, 1863. Duty at Stafford Court House till April 27. Chancellorsville Campaign April 27-May 6. Battle of Chancellorsville May 1-5. Gettysburg (Pa.) Campaign June 11-July 24. Battle of Gettysburg, Pa., July 1-3. Pursuit of Lee to Manassas Gap, Va., July 5-24. Duty along Orange & Alexandria Railroad July 26 to September 26. Movement to Bridgeport, Ala., September 26-October 3. Reopening Tennessee River October 26-29. Battle of Wauhatchie, Tenn., October 28-29. Chattanooga-Ringgold Campaign November 23-27. Orchard Knob November 23. Mission Lodge November 24-25. March to relief of Knoxville, Tenn., November 28-December 8. Moved to Bridgeport, Ala., and duty there till March, 1864. Veterans on furlough March and April. Atlanta (Ga.) Campaign May 1-September 8. Demonstration on Rocky Faced Ridge May 8-11. Battle of Resaca May 14-15. Cassville May 19.

New Hope Church May 25. Battles about Dallas, New Hope Church and Allatoona Hills, May 25-June 5. Lost Mountain June 8. Operations about Marietta and against Kenesaw Mountain June 10-July 2. Pine Hill June 11-14. Lost Mountain June 15-17. Gilgal, or Golgotha Church, June 15. Muddy Creek June 17. Noyes' Creek June 19. Kolb's Farm June 22. Assault on Kenesaw June 27. Ruff's Station July 4. Chattahoochie River June 5-17. Peach Tree Creek July 19-20. Siege of Atlanta July 22-August 25. Operations at Chattahoochie River Bridge May 26-September 2. Occupation of Atlanta September 2-November 15. Expedition from Atlanta to Tuckum's Cross Roads October 26-29. March to the sea November 15-December 10. Montieth Swamp December 9. Siege of Savannah December 10-21. Campaign of the Carolinas January to March, 1865. Taylor's Hole Creek, Averysboro, N. C., March 16. Battle of Bentonville March 19-21. Occupation of Goldsboro March 24. Consolidated with 82nd Ohio Infantry March 31. 1865.

Regiment lost during service 7 Officers and 68 Enlisted men killed and mortally wounded and 90 Enlisted men by disease. Total 165.

62nd REGIMENT INFANTRY.

Organized at Zanesville, McConnellsville and Somerton, Ohio, September 17 to December 24, 1861. Left State for Cumberland, Md., January 17, 1862, thence moved to Paw Paw Tunnel February 3. Attached to 2nd Brigade, Landers' Division, Army of the Potomac, to March, 1862. 2nd Brigade, Shields' Division, Banks' 5th Army Corps, and Dept. of the Shenandoah, to May, 1862. 2nd Brigade, Shields' Division, Dept. of the Rappahannock, to July, 1862. 3rd Brigade, 2nd Division, 4th Army Corps, Army of the Potomac, to September, 1862. Ferry's Brigade, Division at Suffolk, Va., 7th Army Corps, Dept. of Virginia, to January, 1863. 1st Brigade, 3rd Division, 18th Army Corps, Dept. of North Carolina, to February, 1863. 3rd Brigade, 2nd Division, 18th Army Corps, Dept. of the South, to April, 1863. United States forces, Folly Island, S. C., 10th Army Corps, Dept. of the South, to June, 1863. 1st Brigade, Folly Island, S. C., 10th Army Corps, to July, 1863. 1st Brigade, 2nd Division, 10th Army Corps, Morris Island, S. C., July, 1863. 2nd Brigade, Morris Island, S. C., 10th Army Corps, to October, 1863. Howell's Brigade, Gordon's Division, Folly Island, S. C., 10th Army Corps, to December, 1863. District Hilton Head, S. C., 10th Army Corps, to April, 1864. 1st Brigade, 1st Division, 10th Army Corps, Army of the James, Dept. of Virginia and North Carolina, to December, 1864. 1st Brigade, 1st Division, 24th Army Corps, to September, 1865.

SERVICE.—Duty at Paw Paw Tunnel and Great Cacapon Creek till March 10, 1862. Advance on Winchester, Va., March 10-15. Reconnoissance to Strasburg March 18-21. Battle of Winchester March 22-23. Mt. Jackson March 25. Strasburg March 27. Woodstock April 1. Edenburg April 2. Expedition to Harrisonburg May 2-4. March to Fredericksburg, Va., May 12-22. Great Cross Roads May 11. March to Front Royal May 25-30. Port Republic June 5. Battle of Port Republic June 9 (cover retreat). Ordered to the Peninsula, Va., June 29. Harrison's Landing July 3-4. At Harrison's Landing till August 16. Movement to Fortress Monroe August 16-23, thence moved to Suffolk, Va., and duty there till December 31. Action on the Blackwater October 25. Expedition from Suffolk December 1-3. Action near Franklin on Blackwater December 2. Zuni December 12. Moved to Norfolk, Va., December 31, thence to Beaufort and New Berne, N. C., January 4, 1863. Moved to Port Royal, S. C., January 25. At St. Helena Island, S. C., till April. Occupation of Folly Island, S. C., April 3 to July 10. Skirmish at Folly Island April 7. Attack on Morris Island, S. C., July 10. Assaults on Fort Wagner, Morris Island, July 11 and 18. Siege operations against Fort Wagner, Morris Island, and against Fort Sumter and Charleston, July 10-September 7. Capture of

Forts Wagner and Gregg, Morris Island, September 7. Operations against Charleston till October 31. Moved to Hilton Head, S. C., November 7, and duty there till April, 1864. Regiment re-enlisted January 3, 1864. Moved to Yorktown, Va., April. Butler's operations on south side of the James River against Petersburg and Richmond May 4-28. Capture of Bermuda Hundred and City Point May 5. Swift Creek May 9-10. Operations against Fort Darling May 12-16. Battle of Drury's Bluff May 14-16. Bermuda Hundred front May 16-30. Ware Bottom Church May 20. Port Walthal and on the Bermuda Hundred front June 16-17. Siege operations against Petersburg and Richmond June 16, 1864, to April 2, 1865. Demonstration north of the James at Deep Bottom, August 13-20, 1864. Strawberry Plains August 14-18. New Market Heights, Chaffin's Farm, September 29-October 1. Darbytown Road October 7 and 13. Battle of Fair Oaks October 27-28. Duty in trenches north of the James before Richmond Hill March, 1865. Moved to Hatcher's Run March 27-28. Appomattox Campaign March 28-April 9. Fall of Petersburg April 2. Pursuit of Lee April 3-9. Rice's Station April 6. Appomattox Court House April 9. Surrender of Lee and his army. Garrison and guard duty in District of South Anna, Dept. of Virginia, till September. Consolidated with 67th Ohio Infantry September 1, 1865. Mustered out December 7, 1865.

Regiment lost during service 11 Officers and 102 Enlisted men killed and mortally wounded and 2 Officers and 129 Enlisted men by disease. Total 244.

63rd REGIMENT INFANTRY.

Organized at Marietta, Ohio, by consolidation of Battalions of the 22nd and 63rd Ohio Infantry January 25, 1862. Moved to Paducah, Ky., February 18-23, thence to Commerce, Mo. Attached to 2nd Brigade, 1st Division, Army of the Mississippi, to April, 1862. 1st Brigade. 2nd Division, Army of the Mississippi, to November, 1862. 1st Brigade, 8th Division, Left Wing 13th Army Corps (Old), Dept. of the Tennessee, to December, 1862. 1st Brigade, 8th Division, 16th Army of the Tennessee, to March, 1863. 4th Brigade, District of Corinth, Miss., 2nd Division, 16th Army Corps, to May, 1863. 3rd Brigade, District of Memphis, 5th Division, 16th Army Corps, to November, 1863. Fuller's Brigade, 2nd Division, 16th Army Corps, to March, 1864. 2nd Brigade, 4th Division, 16th Army Corps, to September, 1864. 2nd Brigade, 1st Division, 17th Army Corps, to July, 1865.

SERVICE.—Operations against New Madrid, Mo., March 3-14, 1862. Siege and capture of Island Number 10, Mississippi River, and pursuit to Tiptonville, March 15-April 8. Tiptonville April 8. Expedition to Fort Pillow, Tenn., April 13-17. Moved to Hamburg Landing, Tenn., April 18-23. Action at Monterey April 29. Advance on and siege of Corinth, Miss., April 29-May 30. Skirmish at Farmington May 1. Reconnoissance toward Corinth May 8. Occupation of Corinth May 30, and pursuit to Booneville May 30-June 12. Duty at Clear Creek till August 29. Battle of Iuka, Miss., September 19. Reconnoissance from Rienzi to Hatchie River September 30. Battle of Corinth October 3-4. Pursuit to Ripley October 5-12. Grant's Central Mississippi Campaign, operations on the Mississippi Central Railroad November 2, 1862, to January 12, 1863. Expedition to Jackson after Forest December 18, 1862, to January 3, 1863. Action at Parker's Cross Roads December 31, 1862. Red Mound, or Parker's Cross Roads, December 31. Lexington, Tenn., January 3, 1863. Moved to Corinth, Miss., January 9, and duty there till April. Dodge's Expedition into Northern Alabama April 15-May 8. Rock Cut, near Tuscumbia, April 22. Tuscumbia April 23. Town Creek April 28. Duty at Memphis, Tenn., till October 18. Movement to Prospect, Tenn., October 18-November 30, and duty there till January, 1864. Veterans absent on furlough January 2 to February 28, 1864. Decatur, Ala., March 8. Duty at Decatur till May. Atlanta Campaign May 1-September 8. Demonstrations on Resaca May 8-13.

Sugar Valley near Resaca May 9. Battle of Resaca May 14-15. Advance on Dallas May 18-25. Operations on line of Pumpkin Vine Creek and battles about Dallas, New Hope Church and Allatoona Hills May 25-June 5. Operations about Marietta and against Kenesaw Mountain June 10-July 2. Assault on Kenesaw June 27. Nickajack Creek July 2-5. Ruff's Mills July 3-4. Chattahoochie River July 5-17. Decatur and Battle of Atlanta July 22. Siege of Atlanta July 22-August 25. Ezra Chapel July 28. Flank movement on Jonesboro August 25-30. Battle of Jonesboro August 31-September 1. Lovejoy Station September 2-6. At East Point till October 4. Pursuit of Hood into Alabama October 4-26. March to the sea November 15-December 10. Montieth Swamp December 9. Siege of Savannah December 10-21. Campaign of the Carolinas January to April, 1865. Reconnoissance to the Salkehatchie River, S. C., January 20. Salkehatchie Swamps February 2-5. Skirmishes at Rivers and Broxton Bridges February 2. Action at Rivers Bridge February 3. Binnaker's Bridge, South Edisto River, February 9. Orangeburg February 12-13. Columbia February 16-17. Battle of Bentonville, N. C., March 20-21. Occupation of Goldsboro March 24. Advance on Raleigh April 10-14. Occupation of Raleigh April 14. Bennett's House April 26. Surrender of Johnston and his army. March to Washington, D. C., via Richmond, Va., April 29-May 20. Grand Review May 24. Moved to Louisville, Ky., June 5, and duty there till July. Mustered out July 8, 1865.

Regiment lost during service 2 Officers and 91 Enlisted men killed and mortally wounded and 5 Officers and 259 Enlisted men by disease. Total 357.

64th REGIMENT INFANTRY.

Organized at Camp Buckingham, Mansfield, Ohio, and mustered in November 9, 1861. Moved to Louisville, Ky., December 14; thence to Bardstown, Ky., December 25. Attached to 20th Brigade, Army of the Ohio, to January, 1862. 20th Brigade, 6th Division, Army of the Ohio, to September, 1862. 20th Brigade, 6th Division, 2nd Corps, Army of the Ohio, to November, 1862. 3rd Brigade, 1st Division, Left Wing 14th Army Corps, Army of the Cumberland, to January, 1863. 3rd Brigade, 1st Division, 21st Army Corps, Army of the Cumberland, to October, 1863. 3rd Brigade, 2nd Division, 4th Army Corps, Army of the Cumberland, to June, 1865. 2nd Brigade, 2nd Division, 4th Army Corps, to August, 1865. Dept. of Texas to November, 1865.

SERVICE.—Duty at Danville and Ball's Gap, Ky., January and February, 1862. March to Munfordsville, thence to Nashville, Tenn., February 7-March 13, and to Savannah, Tenn., March 29-April 6. Battle of Shiloh, Tenn., April 6-7. Advance on and siege of Corinth, Miss., April 29-May 30. Pursuit to Booneville June 1-12. Duty along Memphis & Charleston Railroad till August. March to Louisville, Ky., in pursuit of Bragg, August 21-September 26. Pursuit of Bragg into Kentucky October 1-15. Bardstown, Ky., October 3. Battle of Perryville October 8. March to Nashville, Tenn., October 16-November 7, and duty there till December 26. Advance on Murfreesboro December 26-30. Nolensville December 27. Battle of Stone's River December 30-31, 1862, and January 1-3, 1863. Duty at Murfreesboro till June. Reconnoissance to Nolensville and Versailles January 13-15. Middle Tennessee (or Tullahoma) Campaign June 23-July 7. Occupation of Middle Tennessee till August 16. Passage of the Cumberland Mountains and Tennessee River, and Chickamauga (Ga.) Campaign August 16-September 22. Reconnoissance toward Chattanooga September 7. Lookout Valley September 7-8. Occupation of Chattanooga September 9. Lee and Gordon's Mills September 11-13. Near Lafayette September 14. Battle of Chickamauga September 19-20. Siege of Chattanooga, Tenn., September 24-November 23. Chattanooga-Ringgold Campaign November 23-27. Orchard Knob November 23-24. Mission Ridge November 25. Pursuit to Graysville September 26-27. March to relief of Knoxville, Tenn., November

28-December 8. Operations in East Tennessee till April, 1864. Atlanta (Ga.) Campaign May 1-September 8. Demonstrations on Rocky Faced Ridge and Dalton May 8-13. Buzzard's Roost Gap or Mill Springs May 8-9. Battle of Resaca May 14-15. Near Calhoun May 16. Adairsville May 17. Near Kingston May 18-19. Near Cassville May 19. Advance on Dallas May 22-25. Operations on line of Pumpkin Vine Creek and battles about Dallas, New Hope Church and Allatoona Hills May 25-June 5. Operations about Marietta and against Kenesaw Mountain June 10-July 2. Pine Hill June 11-14. Lost Mountain June 15-17. Assault on Kenesaw June 27. Ruff's Station or Smyrna Camp Ground July 4. Chattahoochie River July 5-17. Buckhead, Nancy's Creek, July 18. Peach Tree Creek July 19-20. Siege of Atlanta July 22 August 25. Flank movement on Jonesboro August 25-30. Battle of Jonesboro August 31-September 1. Lovejoy Station September 2-6. Operations in North Georgia and North Alabama against Hood September 29-November 3. Nashville Campaign November-December. Near Edenton November 21. Columbia, Duck River, November 24-27. Spring Hill November 29. Battle of Franklin November 30. Battle of Nashville December 15-16. Pursuit of Hood to the Tennessee River December 17-28. Moved to Huntsville, Ala., and duty there till March, 1865. Operations in East Tennessee March 15-April 22. At Nashville, Tenn., till June. Moved to New Orleans, La., June 16, thence to Texas, and duty there till December. Mustered out December 3, 1865.

Regiment lost during service 6 Officers and 108 Enlisted men killed and mortally wounded and 1 Officer and 159 Enlisted men by disease. Total 274.

65th REGIMENT INFANTRY.

Organized at Mansfield, Ohio, October 3 to November 14, 1861. Moved to Louisville, Ky., December 18; thence to Bardstown and to Hall's Gap, Ky., January 13, 1862. Attached to 20th Brigade, Army of the Ohio, to January, 1862. 20th Brigade, 6th Division, Army of the Ohio, to September, 1862. 20th Brigade, 6th Division, 2nd Corps, Army of the Ohio, to November, 1862. 3rd Brigade, 1st Division, Left Wing 14th Army Corps, Army of the Cumberland, to January, 1863. 3rd Brigade, 1st Division, 21st Army Corps, Army of the Cumberland, to October, 1863. 3rd Brigade, 2nd Division, 4th Army Corps, Army of the Cumberland, to June, 1865. 2nd Brigade, 2nd Division, 4th Army Corps, to August, 1865. Dept. of Texas to December, 1865.

SERVICE.—March to Munfordsville, Ky., thence to Nashville, Tenn., February 7-March 13, and to Savannah, Tenn., March 29-April 6. Battle of Shiloh, Tenn., April 6-7. Advance on and siege of Corinth, Miss., April 29-May 30. Pursuit to Booneville June 1-12. Duty along Memphis & Charleston Railroad in Alabama and at Bridgeport, Ala., till August 21. March to Louisville, Ky., in pursuit of Bragg August 21-September 26. Pursuit of Bragg into Kentucky October 1-15. Battle of Perryville, Ky., October 8 (Reserve). March to Nashville, Tenn., October 15-November 7, and duty there till December 26. Advance on Murfreesboro, Tenn., December 26-30. Battle of Stone's River December 30-31, 1862, and January 1-3, 1863. Duty at Murfreesboro till June. Reconnoissance to Nolensville and Versailles January 13-15. Middle Tennessee (or Tullahoma) Campaign June 23-July 7. Occupation of Middle Tennessee till August 16. Passage of the Cumberland Mountains and Tennessee River and Chickamauga (Ga.) Campaign August 16-September 22. Reconnoissance toward Chattanooga September 7. Lookout Valley September 7-8. Occupation of Chattanooga September 9. Lee and Gordon's Mills September 11-13. Battle of Chickamauga September 19-20. Siege of Chattanooga, Tenn., September 24-November 23. Chattanooga-Ringgold Campaign November 23-27. Orchard Knob November 23-24. Mission Ridge November 25. Pursuit to Graysville November 26-27. March to relief of Knoxville, Tenn., November 28-December 8. Operations in East Tennessee till April, 1864. Atlanta (Ga.) Campaign May 1 to Sep-

tember 8. Demonstrations on Rocky Faced Ridge and Dalton May 8-13. Buzzard's Roost Gap or Mill Springs May 8-9. Battle of Resaca May 14-15. Near Calhoun May 16. Adairsville May 17. Near Kingston May 18-19. Near Cassville May 19. Advance on Dallas May 22-25. Operations on line of Pumpkin Vine Creek and battles about Dallas, New Hope Church and Allatoona Hills May 25-June 5. Operations about Marietta and against Kenesaw Mountain June 10-July 2. Pine Hill June 11-14. Lost Mountain June 15-17. Assault on Kenesaw June 27. Ruff's Station, Smyrna Camp Ground, July 4. Chattahoochie River July 5-17. Buckhead, Nancy's Creek, July 18. Peach Tree Creek July 19-20. Siege of Atlanta July 22-August 25. Flank movement on Jonesboro August 25-30. Battle of Jonesboro August 31-September 1. Lovejoy Station September 2-6. Operations in North Georgia and North Alabama against Hood October 4-26. Nashville Campaign November-December. Columbia, Duck River, November 24-27. Spring Hill November 29. Battle of Franklin November 30. Battle of Nashville December 15-16. Pursuit of Hood to the Tennessee River December 17-28. Moved to Huntsville, Ala., and duty there till March, 1865. Operations in East Tennessee March 15-April 22. At Nashville, Tenn., till June. Moved to New Orleans, La., June 16; thence to Texas and duty at San Antonio till December. Mustered out November 30, 1865, and honorably discharged from service January 2, 1866.

Regiment lost during service 8 Officers and 114 Enlisted men killed and mortally wounded and 6 Officers and 129 Enlisted men by disease. Total 257.

66th REGIMENT INFANTRY.

Organized at Camp McArthur, Urbana, Ohio, and mustered in December 17, 1861. Ordered to New Creek, W. Va., January 17, 1862. Attached to 3rd Brigade, Landers' Division, Army of the Potomac, to March, 1862. 2nd Brigade, Shields' 2nd Division, Banks' 5th Army Corps and Dept. of the Shenandoah, to May, 1862. 2nd Brigade, Shields' Division, Dept. of the Rappahannock, to June, 1862. 2nd Brigade, 1st Division, 2nd Corps, Army of Virginia, to August, 1862. 1st Brigade, 2nd Division, 2nd Corps, Army of Virginia, to September, 1862. 1st Brigade, 2nd Division, 12th Army Corps, Army of the Potomac, to October, 1863, and Army of the Cumberland to April, 1864. 1st Brigade, 2nd Division, 20th Army Corps, Army of the Cumberland, to July, 1865.

SERVICE. Advance toward Winchester, Va., March 7-15, 1862. Provost duty at Martinsburg, Winchester and Strasburg till May. March to Fredericksburg, Va., May 12-21, and to Port Republic May 25-June 7. Battle of Port Republic June 9. Ordered to Alexandria and duty there till August. Operations near Cedar Mountain August 10-18. Pope's Campaign in Northern Virginia August 18-September 2. Guarding trains of the army during the battles of Bull Run August 28-30. Maryland Campaign September 6-22. Battle of Antietam September 16-17. Duty at Bolivar Heights till December. Reconnoissance to Rippon, W. Va., November 9. Reconnoissance to Winchester December 2-6. Berryville December 1. Dumfries December 27. "Mud March" January 20-24, 1863. At Stafford Court House till April 27. Chancellorsville Campaign April 27-May 6. Battle of Chancellorsville May 1-5. Gettysburg (Pa.) Campaign June 11-July 24. Battle of Gettysburg July 1-3. Pursuit of Lee to Manassas Gap, Va., July 5-24. Duty at New York during draft disturbances August 15-September 8. Movement to Bridgeport, Ala., September 24-October 3. Skirmish at Garrison's Creek near Fosterville October 6 (Detachment). Re-opening Tennessee River October 26-29. Chattanooga-Ringgold Campaign November 23-27. Lookout Mountain November 23-24. Mission Ridge November 25. Ringgold Gap, Taylor's Ridge, November 27. Regiment re-enlisted December 15, 1863. Duty at Bridgeport and in Alabama till May, 1864. Scout to Caperton's Ferry March 29-April 2. Expedition from Bridgeport down Tennessee River to Triana April 12-16. Atlanta (Ga.) Campaign

May 1-September 8. Demonstrations on Rocky Faced Ridge May 8-11. Dug Gap or Mill Creek May 8. Battle of Resaca May 14-15. Cassville May 19. New Hope Church May 25. Operations on line of Pumpkin Vine Creek and battles about Dallas, New Hope Church and Allatoona Hills May 25-June 5. Operations about Marietta and against Kenesaw Mountain June 10-July 2. Pine Hill June 11-14. Lost Mountain June 15-17. Gilgal or Golgotha Church June 15. Muddy Creek June 17. Noyes Creek June 19. Kolb's Farm June 22. Assault on Kenesaw June 27. Ruff's Station July 4. Chattahoochie River July 5-17. Peach Tree Creek July 19-20. Siege of Atlanta July 22-August 25. Operations at Chattahoochie River Bridge August 26-September 2. Occupation of Atlanta September 2-November 15. Near Atlanta November 9. March to the sea November 15-December 10. Siege of Savannah December 10-21. Campaign of the Carolinas January to April, 1865. Little Cohora Creek, N. C., March 16. Battle of Bentonville March 19-21. Occupation of Goldsboro March 24. Advance on Raleigh April 10-14. Occupation of Raleigh April 14. Bennett's House April 26. Surrender of Johnston and his army. March to Washington, D. C., via Richmond, Va., April 29-May 20. Grand Review May 24. Moved to Louisville, Ky., June, and there mustered out July 15, 1865.

Regiment lost during service 5 Officers and 96 Enlisted men killed and mortally wounded and 1 Officer and 143 Enlisted men by disease. Total 245.

67th REGIMENT INFANTRY.

Organized in Ohio at large October, 1861, to January, 1862. Left State for West Virginia January 19, 1862. Attached to 1st Brigade, Landers' Division, Army of the Potomac, to March, 1862. 1st Brigade, Shields' 2nd Division, Banks' 5th Army Corps, and Dept. of the Shenandoah, to May, 1862. 1st Brigade, Shields' Division, Dept. of the Rappahannock May, 1862. 2nd Brigade, Shields' Division, Dept. of the Rappahannock, to July, 1862. 3rd Brigade, 2nd Division, 4th Army Corps, Army of the Potomac, to September, 1862. Ferry's Brigade, Division at Suffolk, Va., 7th Army Corps, Dept. of Virginia, to January, 1863. 1st Brigade, 3rd Division, 18th Army Corps, Dept of North Carolina, to February, 1863. 3rd Brigade, 2nd Division, 18th Army Corps, Dept. of the South, to April, 1863. U. S. Forces, Folly Island, S. C., 10th Army Corps, Dept. of the South, to June, 1863. 1st Brigade, Folly Island, S. C., 10th Army Corps, to July, 1863. 1st Brigade, 2nd Division, Morris Island, S. C., 10th Army Corps, July, 1863. 2nd Brigade, Morris Island, S. C., 10th Army Corps, to October, 1863. Howell's Brigade, Gordon's Division, Folly Island, S. C., 10th Army Corps, to December, 1863. District Hilton Head, S. C., 10th Army Corps, to April, 1864. 1st Brigade, 1st Division, 10th Army Corps, Army of the James, Dept. of Virginia and North Carolina, to December, 1864. 1st Brigade, 1st Division, 24th Army Corps, to August, 1865. Dept. of Virginia to December, 1865.

SERVICE.—Duty at Paw Paw Tunnel and Great Cacapon Creek till March 10, 1862. Advance on Winchester, Va., March 10-15. Reconnoissance to Strasburg March 18-21. Battle of Winchester March 22-23. Strasburg March 27. Woodstock April 1. Edenburg April 2. March to Fredericksburg, Va., May 12-21, thence to Front Royal May 25-30. Battle of Port Republic June 9 (cover retreat). Ordered to the Virginia Peninsula June 29. Harrison's Landing July 3-4. Westover July 3. At Harrison's Landing till August 16. Movement to Fortress Monroe August 16-23, thence moved to Suffolk, Va., and duty there till December 31. Moved to Norfolk, Va., December 31, thence to Beaufort and New Berne, N. C., January 4, 1863. Moved to Port Royal, S. C., January 25. At Hilton Head February 9, and at St. Helena Island, S. C., till April. Occupation of Folly Island, S. C., April 3-July 10. Attack on Morris Island July 10. Assaults on Fort Wagner, Morris Island, S. C., July 11 and 18. Siege of Fort Wagner, Morris Island, and operations against Fort Sumpter and Charleston July 18-September 7. Capture of Forts Wag-

ner and Gregg, Morris Island, September 7. Operations against Charleston till October 31. Moved to Hilton Head, S. C., and duty there till April, 1864. Regiment re-enlisted January, 1864. Whitmarsh Island, Ga., February 22. Moved to Yorktown, Va., April. Butler's operations on south side of the James River and against Petersburg and Richmond May 4-28. Occupation of Bermuda Hundred and City Point, Va., May 5. Ware Bottom Church May 9. Swift Creek May 9-10. Operations against Fort Darling May 12-16. Battle of Drury's Bluff May 14-16. Bermuda Hundred front May 17-30. Ware Bottom Church May 20. Petersburg June 9. Port Walthal and on the Bermuda Hundred front June 16-17. Siege operations against Petersburg and Richmond June 16, 1864, to April 2, 1865. Wier Bottom Church June 20, 1864. Demonstration north of the James at Deep Bottom August 13-20. Strawberry Plains August 14-18. New Market Heights, Chaffin's Farm, September 29-October 2. Darbytown Road October 7 and 13. Fair Oaks October 27-28. Duty in trenches north of James before Richmond till March, 1865. Moved to Hatcher's Run March 27-28. Appomattox Campaign March 28-April 9. Fall of Petersburg April 2. Pursuit of Lee April 3-9. Rice's Station April 6. Appomattox Court House April 9. Surrender of Lee and his army. Garrison and guard duty in District of South Anna, Dept. of Virginia, till December. Mustered out December 12, 1865.

Regiment lost during service 11 Officers and 131 Enlisted men killed and mortally wounded and 1 Officer and 150 Enlisted men by disease. Total 293.

68th REGIMENT INFANTRY.

Organized at Camp Latta, Napoleon, October to December, 1861. Moved to Camp Chase, Ohio, January 21, 1862, thence ordered to Fort Donelson, Tenn., February 7. Attached to 3rd Brigade, 3rd Division, Military District of Cairo, February, 1862. 2nd Brigade, 3rd Division, Army of the Tennessee, to May, 1862. 3rd Brigade, 3rd Division, Army of the Tennessee, to July, 1863. Unattached, District of Jackson, Tenn., to November, 1862. 2nd Brigade, 3rd Division, Right Wing 13th Army Corps, Dept. of the Tennessee, to December, 1862. 2nd Brigade, 3rd Division, 17th Army Corps, Army of the Tennessee, to July, 1865.

SERVICE.—Investment and capture of Fort Donelson, Tenn., February 12-16, 1862. Expedition toward Purdy and operations about Crump's Landing March 9-14. Battle of Shiloh April 6-7. Advance on and siege of Corinth, Miss., April 29-May 30. March to Purdy, thence to Bolivar, and duty there till September. March to Iuka, Miss., September 1-19. Battle of the Hatchie or Metamora October 5. Grant's Central Mississippi Campaign, operations on the Mississippi Central Railroad, November 2, 1862, to January 10, 1863. Reconnoissance from LaGrange November 8-9, 1862. Moved to Memphis, Tenn., January 20, 1863, thence to Lake Providence, La., February 22. Moved to Milliken's Bend April 10. Movement on Bruinsburg and turning Grand Gulf April 25-30. Battle of Port Gibson May 1. Forty Hills and Hankinson's Ferry May 3-4. Battle of Raymond May 12. Jackson May 14. Battle of Champion's Hill May 16. Siege of Vicksburg May 18-July 4. Surrender of Vicksburg July 4, and duty there till February, 1864. Expedition to Monroe, La., August 20-September 2, 1863. Expedition to Canton October 14-20. Bogue Chitto Creek October 17. Meridian Campaign February 3-March 2, 1864. Morton February 10. Veterans absent on furlough February 20-May 8. Moved to Cairo, Ill., May 7-8, thence to Clifton, Tenn., and march via Pulaski, Huntsville and Decatur, Ala., to Rome and Ackworth, Ga., May 12-June 9. Atlanta (Ga.) Campaign June 9-September 8. Operations about Marietta and against Kenesaw Mountain June 10-July 2. Assault on Kenesaw June 27. Nickajack Creek July 2-5. Chattahoochie River July 5-17. Howell's Ferry July 5. Leggett's or Bald Hill July 20-21. Battle of Atlanta July 22. Siege of Atlanta July 22-August 25. Flank movement on Jonesboro August 25-30. Battle of Jonesboro August 31-September 1. Lovejoy Station September 2-6. Jonesboro September 5. Operaticns in North Georgia and North Alabama against Hood September 29-November 3. March to the sea November 15-December 10. Siege of Savannah December 10-21. Campaign of the Carolinas January to April, 1865. Pocotaligo, S. C., January 14. Salkehatchie Swamps February 2-5. Barker's Mills, Whippy Swamp, February 2. Binnaker's Bridge, South Edisto River, February 9. Orangeburg, North Edisto River, February 12-13. Columbia February 16-17. Battle of Bentonville, N. C., March 20-21. Occupation of Goldsboro March 24. Advance on Raleigh April 10-14. Occupation of Raleigh April 14. Bennett's House April 26. Surrender of Johnston and his army. March to Washington, D. C., via Richmond, Va., April 29-May 20. Grand Review May 24. Moved to Louisville, Ky., June 1, and duty there till July. Mustered out July 10, 1865.

Regiment lost during service 2 Officers and 48 Enlisted men killed and mortally wounded and 1 Officer and 249 Enlisted men by disease. Total 300.

69th REGIMENT INFANTRY.

Organized at Hamilton, Ohio, and Camp Chase, Ohio, November, 1861, to April, 1862. Moved to Camp Chase, Ohio, February 19, 1862, and duty there till April, 1862. Moved to Nashville, Tenn., April 19-22, thence to Franklin, Tenn., May 1, and duty there till June 8. Attached to District of Nashville and Franklin, Unattached, Army of the Ohio, to September, 1862. 29th Brigade, 8th Division, Army of the Ohio, to November, 1862. 2nd Brigade, 2nd Division, Centre 14th Army Corps, Army of the Cumberland, to January, 1863. 2nd Brigade, 2nd Division, 14th Army Corps, to October, 1863. 2nd Brigade, 1st Division, 14th Army Corps, to September, 1864. 3rd Brigade, 1st Division, 14th Army Corps, to November, 1864. 2nd Brigade, 1st Division, 14th Army Corps, to July, 1865.

SERVICE.—Moved to Nashville, Tenn., June 8, 1862, thence to Murfreesboro, Tenn. Expedition to McMinnville and Pikesville June 12-20. Provost duty at Nashville till December. Expedition to Gallatin and action with Morgan August 13. Siege of Nashville September 12-November 7. Near Nashville November 5. Nashville and Franklin Pike December 14. Advance on Murfreesboro December 26-30. Battle of Stone's River December 30-31, 1862, and January 1-3, 1863. Duty at Murfreesboro till June. Middle Tennessee or Tullahoma Campaign June 23-July 7. Occupation of Middle Tennessee till August 16. Passage of the Cumberland Mountains and Tennessee River, and Chickamauga (Ga.) Campaign August 16-September 22. Battle of Chickamauga September 19-21 (train guard during battle). Rossville Gap September 21. Siege of Chattanooga, Tenn., September 24-November 23. Orchard Knob November 23-24. Mission Ridge November 25. Graysville November 26. Duty at Rossville, Ga., till March, 1864. Veterans absent on furlough March 16-May 11, rejoin at Buzzard's Roost, Ga. Atlanta Campaign May to September. Demonstration on Rocky Faced Ridge May 8-11. Battle of Resaca May 14-15. Advance on Dallas May 18-25. Operations on line of Pumpkin Vine Creek and battles about Dallas, New Hope Church and Allatoona Hills May 25-June 5. Pickett's Mills May 27. Operations about Marietta and against Kenesaw Mountain June 10-July 2. Pine Hill June 11-14. Lost Mountain June 15-17. Assault on Kenesaw June 27. Ruff's Station, Smyrna Camp Ground, July 4. Chattahoochie River July 5-17. Peach Tree Creek June 19-20. Siege of Atlanta July 22-August 25. Utoy Creek August 5-7. Flank movement on Jonesboro August 25-30. Battle of Jonesboro August 31-September 1. Lovejoy Station September 2-6. Operations against Hood in North Georgia and North Alabama September 29-November 3. March to the sea November 15-December 10. Siege of Savannah December 10-21. Campaign of the Carolinas January to April, 1865. Near Cheraw, S. C., February 28. Taylor's Hole Creek, Averysboro, N. C., March 16. Battle of Bentonville March 19-21. Occupation of Goldsboro March 24. Advance on Raleigh April 10-14. Occupation of Raleigh April 14. Bennett's House April

26. Surrender of Johnston and his army. March to Washington, D. C., via Richmond, Va., April 29-May 19. Grand Review May 24. Moved to Louisville, Ky., June, and duty there till July. Mustered out July 17, 1865.

Regiment lost during service 5 Officers and 84 Enlisted men killed and mortally wounded and 98 Enlisted men by disease. Total 187.

70th REGIMENT INFANTRY.

Organized at West Union, Ohio, October 14, 1861. Moved to Ripley, Ohio, December 25, thence to Paducah, Ky., February 17, 1862. Attached to District of Paducah, Ky., to March, 1862. 3rd Brigade, 5th Division, Army of the Tennessee, to July, 1862. 3rd Brigade, 5th Division, District of Memphis, Tenn., to November, 1862. 3rd Brigade, 5th Division, District of Memphis, Right Wing 13th Army Corps (Old), Dept. of the Tennessee, November, 1862. 2nd Brigade, 1st Division, District of Memphis, 13th Army Corps, to December, 1862. 2nd Brigade, 1st Division, 17th Army Corps, to January, 1863. 2nd Brigade, 1st Division, 16th Army Corps, to March, 1863. 3rd Brigade, 1st Division, 16th Army Corps, to July, 1863. 3rd Brigade, 4th Division, 15th Army Corps, to August, 1864. 1st Brigade, 4th Division, 15th Army Corps, to September, 1864. 3rd Brigade, 2nd Division, 15th Army Corps, to July, 1865. Dept. of Arkansas to August, 1865.

SERVICE.—Moved from Paducah, Ky., to Savannah, Tenn., March 6-10, 1862. Expedition to Yellow Creek and occupation of Pittsburg Landing, Tenn., March 14-17. Crump's Landing April 4. Battle of Shiloh, Tenn., April 6-7. Advance on and siege of Corinth, Miss., April 29-May 30. Russell House, near Corinth, May 17. Occupation of Corinth May 30. March to Memphis, Tenn., via LaGrange, Grand Junction and Holly Springs June 1-July 21. Duty at Memphis till November. Grant's Central Mississippi Campaign, operations on the Mississippi Central Railroad, November, 1862, to January, 1863. Moved to LaGrange, Tenn., and duty there till March 7, and at Moscow till June 9. Ordered to Vicksburg, Miss., June 9. Siege of Vicksburg June 14-July 4. Advance on Jackson, Miss., July 4-10. Bolton's Ferry, Black River, July 4-6. Siege of Jackson July 10-17. Camp at Big Black till September 26. Moved to Memphis, Tenn., thence march to Chattanooga, Tenn., September 26-November 20. Chattanooga-Ringgold Campaign November 23-27. Tunnel Hill November 23-25. Mission Ridge November 25. March to relief of Knoxville, Tenn., November 28-December 28. Regiment re-enlisted January 1, 1864. Veterans on furlough February. Duty at Scottsboro, Ala., till May. Atlanta (Ga.) Campaign May 1-September 8. Demonstrations on Resaca May 8-13. Near Resaca May 13. Battle of Resaca May 14-15. Advance on Dallas May 18-25. Operations on line of Pumpkin Vine Creek and battles about Dallas, New Hope Church and Allatoona Hills May 25-June 5. Operations about Marietta and against Kenesaw Mountain June 10-July 2. Brush Mountain June 15. Assault on Kenesaw June 27. Nickajack Creek July 2-5. Ruff's Mills July 3-4. Chattahoochie River July 5-17. Battle of Atlanta July 22. Siege of Atlanta July 22-August 25. Ezra Chapel July 28 (Hood's second sortie). Flank movement on Jonesboro August 25-30. Battle of Jonesboro August 31-September 1. Lovejoy Station September 2-6. Operations against Hood in North Georgia and North Alabama September 29-November 3. Reconnoissance from Rome on Cave Springs Road and skirmishes October 12-13. March to the sea November 15-December 10. Statesboro December 4. Near Bryan Court House December 8. Siege of Savannah December 10-21. Fort McAllister December 13. Campaign of the Carolinas January to April, 1865. Columbia, S. C., February 16-17. Battle of Bentonville, N. C., March 20-21. Occupation of Goldsboro March 24. Advance on Raleigh April 10-14. Occupation of Raleigh April 14. Bennett's House April 26. Surrender of Johnston and his army. March to Washington, D. C., via Richmond, Va., April 29-May 30. Grand Review May 24. Moved to Louisville, Ky., June, thence to Little Rock, Ark., and duty there till August. Mustered out August 14, 1865.

Regiment lost during service 5 Officers and 70 Enlisted men killed and mortally wounded and 2 Officers and 188 Enlisted men by disease. Total 265.

71st REGIMENT INFANTRY.

Organized at Camp Todd, Troy, Ohio, September, 1861, to January, 1862. Mustered in February 1, 1862. Ordered to Paducah, Ky., February 10. Attached to District of Paducah, Ky., to March, 1862. 2nd Brigade, 5th Division, Army of the Tennessee, to April, 1862. Garrison at Fort Donelson, Tenn., to June, 1863. 1st Brigade, 3rd Division, Reserve Corps, Dept. of the Cumberland, to September, 1863. Post of Gallatin, Tenn., Dept. of the Cumberland, to April, 1864. Unassigned, 4th Division, 20th Army Corps, Dept. of the Cumberland, to August, 1864. 2nd Brigade, 3rd Division, 4th Army Corps, Army of the Cumberland, to June, 1865. 1st Brigade, 3rd Division, 4th Army Corps, to August, 1865. Dept. of Texas to November, 1865.

SERVICE.—Reconnoissance toward Columbus, Ky., February 25-March 3, 1862. Action at and occupation of Columbus March 3. Moved from Paducah, Ky., to Savannah, Tenn., March 6-10. Expedition to Yellow Creek, Miss., and occupation of Pittsburg Landing, Tenn., March 14-17. Battle of Shiloh, Tenn., April 6-7. Ordered to Fort Donelson, Tenn., April 16. Garrison duty at Fort Donelson and Clarksville, Tenn., and operations in Northern and Middle Tennessee till August. Action at Clarksville August 18. Post surrendered by Col. Mason. Fort Donelson August 25 (Cos. "A," "B," "G" and "H"). Cumberland Iron Works August 26 (Cos. "A," "B," "G" and "H"). Expedition to Clarksville September 5-10. Pickett's Hill, Clarksville, September 7. Garrison duty at Forts Donelson and Henry, Tenn., till August, 1863. Guard duty along Louisville & Nashville Railroad (Headquarters at Gallatin, Tenn.) till July, 1864. Expedition from Gallatin to Carthage October 10-14, 1863 (Detachment). Near Hartsville October 10 (Detachment). Expedition from Gallatin to Cumberland Mountains January 28-February 8. Winchester May 10 (Detachment). Relieved from garrison duty July, 1864, and ordered to join Sherman's Army before Atlanta, Ga. Atlanta (Ga.) Campaign July 31-September 8. Siege of Atlanta July 31-August 25. Flank movement on Jonesboro August 25-30. Battle of Jonesboro August 31-September 1. Operations against Hood in North Georgia and North Alabama September 29-November 3. At Athens, Ga., October 31-November 23. March to Columbia, Tenn., November 23-24. Nashville Campaign November-December. Columbia, Duck River, November 24-27. Battle of Franklin November 30. Battle of Nashville December 15-16. Pursuit of Hood to the Tennessee River December 17-28. Moved to Huntsville, Ala., and duty there till March, 1865. Operations in East Tennessee March 15-April 22. Duty at Strawberry Plains and Nashville till June. Ordered to New Orleans, La., June 16, thence moved to Texas. Duty at San Antonio till November. Mustered out November 30, 1865.

Regiment lost during service 3 Officers and 66 Enlisted men killed and mortally wounded and 5 Officers and 132 Enlisted men by disease. Total 206.

72nd REGIMENT INFANTRY.

Organized at Fremont, Ohio, October, 1861, to February, 1862. Moved to Camp Chase, Ohio, January 24, thence to Paducah, Ky. Attached to District of Paducah, Ky., to March, 1862. 4th Brigade, 5th Division, Army of the Tennessee, to May, 1862. 3rd Brigade, 5th Division, Army of the Tennessee, to July, 1862. 3rd Brigade, 5th Division, District of Memphis, Tenn., to November, 1862. 5th Brigade, 5th Division, District of Memphis, Right Wing 13th Army Corps (Old), Dept. of the Tennessee, November, 1862. 3rd Brigade, 1st Division, District of Memphis, 13th Army Corps, to December, 1862. 3rd Brigade, 8th Division, 16th Army Corps, to April, 1863. 1st Brigade, 3rd Division, 15th Army Corps, Army of the Tennessee, to December, 1863. 1st Brigade, 1st Division, 16th Army Corps, to December,

1864. 1st Brigade, 1st Division, Detachment Army Tennessee, Dept. of the Cumberland, to February, 1865. 1st Brigade, 1st Division, 16th Army Corps (New), Military Division West Mississippi, to July, 1865. Dept. of Mississippi to September, 1865.

SERVICE.—Moved from Paducah, Ky., to Savannah, Tenn., March 6-10, 1862. Expedition from Savannah to Yellow Creek, Miss., and occupation of Pittsburg Landing, Tenn., March 14-17. Crump's Landing April 4. Battle of Shiloh April 6-7. Advance on and siege of Corinth, Miss., April 29-May 30. Russell House, near Corinth, May 17. March to Memphis, Tenn., via LaGrange, Grand Junction and Holly Springs June 1-July 21. Duty at Memphis, Tenn., till November. Grant's Central Mississippi Campaign, operations on the Mississippi Central Railroad, November 2, 1862, to January 12, 1863. Duty at White's Station till March 13. Ordered to Memphis, Tenn., thence to Young's Point, La. Operations against Vicksburg, Miss., April 2-July 4. Moved to join army in rear of Vicksburg, Miss., May 2-14. Mississippi Springs May 13. Jackson, Miss., May 14. Siege of Vicksburg May 18-July 4. Assaults on Vicksburg May 19 and 22. Expedition to Mechanicsburg May 26-June 4. Advance on Jackson, Miss., July 5-10. Siege of Jackson July 10-17. Brandon Station July 19. Camp at Big Black till November. Expedition to Canton October 13-20. Bogue Chitto Creek October 17. Ordered to Memphis, Tenn. and guard Memphis & Charleston Railroad at Germantown till January, 1864. Expedition to Wyatt's, Miss., February 6-18. Coldwater Ferry February 8. Near Senatobia February 8-9. Wyatt's February. Operations against Forest in West Tennessee and Kentucky March 16-April 14. Defence of Paducah, Ky., April 14 (Veterans). Sturgis' Expedition to Ripley, Miss., April 30-May 2. Sturgis' Expedition to Guntown, Miss., June 1-13. Brice's Cross Roads, near Guntown, June 10. Salem June 11. Smith's Expedition to Tupelo, Miss., July 5-21. Camargo's Cross Roads, Harrisburg, July 13. Harrisburg, near Tupelo, July 14-15. Old Town or Tishamingo Creek July 15. Smith's Expedition to Oxford, Miss., August 1-30. Abbeville August 23. Moved to Duvall's Bluff, Ark., September 1. March through Arkansas and Missouri in pursuit of Price September 17-November 16. Moved to Nashville, Tenn., November 21-December 1. Reconnoissance from Nashville December 6. Battles of Nashville December 15-16. Pursuit of Hood to the Tennessee River December 17-28. At Eastport, Miss., till February, 1865. Moved to New Orleans, La., February 9-22. Campaign against Mobile, Ala., and its defences March 17-April 12. Siege of Spanish Fort and Fort Blakely March 26-April 8. Assault and capture of Fort Blakely April 9. Occupation of Mobile April 12. March to Montgomery April 13-25, and duty there till May 10. Moved to Meridian, Miss., and duty there till September. Mustered out at Vicksburg, Miss., September 11, 1865.

Regiment lost during service 4 Officers and 56 Enlisted men killed and mortally wounded and 2 Officers and 236 Enlisted men by disease. Total 298.

73rd REGIMENT INFANTRY.

Organized at Chillicothe, Ohio, and mustered in December 30, 1861. Duty at Camp Logan till January 24, 1862. Moved to Grafton, W. Va., thence to Fetterman January 24-26, and to New Creek February 3. Attached to Cheat Mountain, District Western Virginia, to March, 1862. Schenck's Brigade, Dept. of the Mountains, to June, 1862. 2nd Brigade, 1st Division, 1st Corps, Army of Virginia, to September, 1862. 2nd Brigade, 1st Division, 11th Army Corps, Army of the Potomac, to October, 1862. 2nd Brigade, 2nd Division, 11th Army Corps, Army of the Potomac, to October, 1863, and Army of the Cumberland, to April, 1864. 3rd Brigade, 3rd Division, 20th Army Corps, Army of the Cumberland, to July, 1865.

SERVICE.—Expedition to Romney, W. Va., February 6-7, 1862, and to Moorefield February 12-16. Moved to Clarksburg February 18, and duty there till March 20. Moved to Weston, W. Va., March 20, and duty there till April 10. Moved to join Milroy at Monterey. Battle of McDowell May 8. Woodstock June 2. Mt. Jackson June 3. New Market June 4. Harrisonburg June 6. Battle of Cross Keys June 8. At Middletown till July 7, and at Sperryville till August 8. Expedition to Madison Court House July 16-19. Pope's Campaign in Northern Virginia August 16 to September 2. Freeman's Ford August 22. Battles of Bull Run August 29-30. Duty in the Defences of Washington, D. C., till December. Reconnoissance to Bristoe Station and Warrenton Junction September 25-28. March to Fredericksburg, Va., December 12-16. "Mud March" January 20-24, 1863. At Falmouth till April 27. Chancellorsville Campaign April 27-May 6. Battle of Chancellorsville May 1-5. Gettysburg (Pa.) Campaign June 11-July 24. Battle of Gettysburg July 1-3. Pursuit of Lee to Manassas Gap, Va., July 5-24. Camp at Bristoe till September 24. Moved to Bridgeport, Ala., September 24-October 3. Duty at Bridgeport and Stevenson, Ala., till October 24. Re-opening Tennessee River October 24-29. Battle of Wauhatchie, Tenn., October 28-29. Chattanooga-Ringgold Campaign November 23-27. Orchard Knob November 23. Tunnel Hill November 24-25. Mission Ridge November 25. March to relief of Knoxville, Tenn., November 28-December 17. Regiment re-enlisted January 1, 1864, and Veterans on furlough till March. Atlanta (Ga.) Campaign May 1-September 8. Demonstrations on Rocky Faced Ridge May 8-11. Buzzard's Roost Gap May 8-9. Battle of Resaca May 14-15. Cassville May 19. New Hope Church May 25. Operations on line of Pumpkin Vine Creek and battles about Dallas, New Hope Church and Allatoona Hills May 25-June 5. Operations about Marietta and against Kenesaw Mountain June 10-July 2. Pine Hill June 11-14. Lost Mountain June 15-17. Gilgal or Golgotha Church June 15. Muddy Creek June 17. Noyes Creek June 19. Kolb's Farm June 22. Assault on Kenesaw June 27. Ruff's Station July 4. Chattahoochie River July 5-17. Peach Tree Creek July 19-20. Siege of Atlanta July 22-August 25. Operations at Chattahoochie River Bridge August 26-September 2. Occupation of Atlanta September 2-November 15. March to the sea November 15. Siege of Savannah December 10-21. Campaign of the Carolinas January to April, 1865. Lawtonville, S. C., February 2. Reconnoissance on Goldsboro Road, N. C., March 14. Taylor's Hole Creek, Averysboro, March 16. Battle of Bentonville March 19-21. Occupation of Goldsboro March 24. Advance on Raleigh April 10-14. Occupation of Raleigh April 14. Bennett's House April 26. Surrender of Johnston and his army. March to Washington, D. C., via Richmond, Va., April 29-May 20. Grand Review May 24. Moved to Louisville, Ky., June and duty there till July. Mustered out July 20, 1865.

Regiment lost during service 4 Officers and 167 Enlisted men killed and mortally wounded and 1 Officer and 149 Enlisted men by disease. Total 321.

74th REGIMENT INFANTRY.

Organized at Xenia, Ohio, October 5, 1861, to March 27, 1862. Ordered to Camp Chase, Ohio, February 24, 1862, and duty there till April 20. Moved to Nashville, Tenn., April 20-24. Attached to Dumont's Independent Brigade, Army of the Ohio, to June, 1862. Unattached, Army of the Ohio, to September, 1862. 7th Brigade, 8th Division, Army of the Ohio, to November, 1862. 3rd Brigade, 2nd Division, Center 14th Army Corps, Army of the Cumberland, to January, 1863. 3rd Brigade, 2nd Division, 14th Army Corps, Army of the Cumberland, to October, 1863. 3rd Brigade, 1st Division, 14th Army Corps, to June, 1865. 2nd Brigade, 1st Division, 14th Army Corps, to July, 1865.

SERVICE.—Dumont's Expedition over the Cumberland Mountains, Tenn., June, 1862. Guard duty along railroad between Nashville and Columbia, Tenn., till September 3. Siege of Nashville September 12-November 7. Fort Riley near Nashville October 5. Gallatin Pike near Nashville October 20. Duty at Nashville till December 26. Advance on Murfreesboro December 26-30. Battle of Stone's River December 30-31, 1862, and January 1-3, 1863. Duty at Murfreesboro till June. Middle Tennessee or Tullahoma Campaign June 23-July 7. Occupation of Middle Tennessee till August 16. Passage of the Cumberland Mountains and Tennessee River and Chickamauga (Ga.) Campaign August 16-September 22. Davis Cross Roads or Dug Gap September 11. Battle of Chickamauga September 19-21. Rossville Gap September 21. Siege of Chattanooga, Tenn., September 24-November 23. Chattanooga-Ringgold Campaign November 23-27. Orchard Knob November 23-24. Mission Ridge November 25. Regiment re-enlisted January 1, 1864. Veterans on furlough January 25-April 12. Atlanta (Ga.) Campaign May 1-September 8. Demonstration on Rocky Faced Ridge May 8-11. Buzzard's Roost Gap May 8-9. Battle of Resaca May 14-15. Mill Springs Gap May 19. Operations on line of Pumpkin Vine Creek and battles about Dallas, New Hope Church and Allatoona Hills May 25-June 5. Pickett's Mills May 27. Operations about Marietta and against Kenesaw Mountain June 10-July 2. Pine Hill June 11-14. Lost Mountain June 15-17. Assault on Kenesaw June 27. Ruff's Station July 4. Chattahoochie River July 5-17. Peach Tree Creek July 19-20. Siege of Atlanta July 22-August 25. Utoy Creek August 5-7. Flank movement on Jonesboro August 25-30. Battle of Jonesboro August 31-September 1. Operations against Hood in North Georgia and North Alabama September 29-November 3. March to the sea November 15-December 10. Siege of Savannah December 10-21. Campaign of the Carolinas January to April, 1865. Taylor's Hole Creek, Averysboro, N. C., March 16. Battle of Bentonville March 19-21. Occupation of Goldsboro March 24. Advance on Raleigh April 10-14. Occupation of Raleigh April 14. Bennett's House April 26. Surrender of Johnston and his army. March to Washington, D. C., via Richmond, Va., April 29-May 20. Grand Review May 24. Moved to Louisville, Ky., June, and duty there till July. Mustered out July 11, 1865.

Regiment lost during service 2 Officers and 51 Enlisted men killed and mortally wounded and 2 Officers and 105 Enlisted men by disease. Total 164.

75th REGIMENT INFANTRY.

Organized at Camp McLain, Cincinnati, Ohio, November 7, 1861, to January 8, 1862. Left State for Grafton, W. Va., January 28, 1862. Attached to Milroy's Command, Cheat Mountain, District West Virginia, to March, 1862. Milroy's Brigade, Dept. of the Mountains, to April, 1862. Schenck's Brigade, Dept. of the Mountains, to June, 1862. 2nd Brigade, 1st Division, 1st Corps, Army of Virginia, to September, 1862. 2nd Brigade, 1st Division, 11th Army Corps, Army of the Potomac, to July, 1863. 2nd Brigade, Gordon's Division, Folly Island, S. C., 10th Army Corps, Dept. of the South, to February, 1864. 1st Brigade, Ames' Division, District of Florida, to April, 1864. District of Florida, Dept. of the South, to October, 1864. 4th Separate Brigade, Dept. of the South, to December, 1864. 1st Brigade, Coast Division, Dept. of the South, to January, 1865. 4th Separate Brigade, Dept. of the South, to July, 1865.

SERVICE.—March to Huttonville February 17-March 1, 1862. Expedition to Lost River Region April 1-12. Action at Monterey April 12. Battle of McDowell May 8. Retreat to Franklin May 10-12. Franklin May 29. Pursuit of Jackson to Shenandoah Valley. Strasburg and Staunton Road June 1-2. Mt. Jackson June 3. New Market June 4. Harrisonburg June 6. Battle of Cross Keys June 8. At Middletown till July 7, and at Sperryville till August 8. Reconnoissance to Madison Court House July 16-19. Battle of Cedar Mountain August 9. Pope's Campaign in Northern Virginia August 16-September 2. Freeman's Ford August 22. Battle of Bull Run August 29-30. Duty in the Defences of Washington, D. C., till December. Expedition from Centreville to Bristoe Station and Warrenton Junction September 25-28. March to Fredericksburg, Va., December 10-15. "Mud March" January 20-24, 1863. At Falmouth till April 27. Woodstock and Cedar Run February 26. Chancellorsville Campaign April 27-May 6. Battle of Chancellorsville May 1-5. Gettysburg (Pa.) Campaign June 11-July 24. Battle of Gettysburg July 1-3. Pursuit of Lee July 5-24. Moved to Morris Island, S. C., August 6-12. Siege operations against Fort Wagner, Morris Island, S. C., and against Fort Sumpter and Charleston August 18-September 7. Capture of Fort Wagner and Gregg, Morris Island, September 7. Moved to Folly Island, S. C., and duty there till February 22, 1864. Expedition to John's and James' Islands February 6-14. Ordered to Jacksonville, Fla., February 22, 1864. Regiment mounted and duty in the District of Florida till December 8. Expedition from Jacksonville to Cedar Creek April 2. Cedar Run April 2. Expedition to Headwaters of the St. Johns and Kissinee Rivers April 25-May 10, destroying and capturing a large amount of stores and property. Action near Jacksonville April 28. Near Camp Finnegan May 25. Expedition from Jacksonville to Camp Milton May 31-June 3. King's Creek, S. C., July 3 (Detachment). Raid from Jacksonville to Baldwin July 23-28. Near Trail Ridge July 25. Action at St. Mary's Trestle July 26. Camp Baldwin August 12. Raid on Florida Railroad August 15-19. Gainesville August 17. Expedition to Enterprise September 28. Companies "A," "B," "C," "D," "F" and "G" mustered out October and November, 1864. Balance moved to Hilton Head, S. C., December 8-10. Pocotaligo Bridge, S. C., December 29. Returned to Florida January, 1865, and duty at District Headquarters, Jacksonville, and at Tallahatchie, Fla., till July. Mustered out July 15, 1865.

Regiment lost during service 4 Officers and 110 Enlisted men killed and mortally wounded and 2 Officers and 101 Enlisted men by disease. Total 217.

76th REGIMENT INFANTRY.

Organized at Camp Sherman, Newark, Ohio, October 5, 1861, to February 3, 1862. Moved to Paducah, Ky., February 9, thence to Fort Donelson, Tenn. Attached to 3rd Brigade, 3rd Division, District of West Tennessee and Army of the Tennessee, to July, 1862. Helena, Ark., District of Eastern Arkansas, to December, 1862. 1st Brigade, 1st Division, District of Eastern Arkansas, Dept. of the Tennessee, December, 1862. 2nd Brigade, 11th Division, 13th Army Corps (Old), Dept. of the Tennessee, December, 1862. 1st Brigade, 4th Division, Sherman's Yazoo Expedition, to January, 1863. 2nd Brigade, 1st Division, 15th Army Corps, Army of the Tennessee, to September, 1863. 1st Brigade, 1st Division, 15th Army Corps, to July, 1865.

SERVICE.—Investment and capture of Fort Donelson, Tenn., February 13-16, 1862. Expedition toward Purdy and operations about Crump's Landing, Tenn., March 9-14. Battle of Shiloh, Tenn., April 6-7. Advance on and siege of Corinth, Miss., April 29-May 30. March to Memphis, Tenn., June 1-17, and duty there till July 24. Moved to Helena, Ark., July 24, and duty there till October. Expedition to Milliken's Bend, La., August 16-27. Capture of Steamer "Fair Play" August 17. Milliken's Bend August 16 and 18. Expedition up the Yazoo August 20-27. Bolivar August 22 and 25. Greenville August 23. Expedition to Pilot Knob, Mo., October 22-November 12. Expedition from Helena against Arkansas Post, Ark., November 16-21. At Helena till December 22. Sherman's Yazoo Expedition December 22, 1862, to January 3, 1863. Chickasaw Bayou December 26-28. Chickasaw Bluff December 29. Expedition to Arkansas Post, Ark., January 3-10, 1863. Assault and capture of Fort Hindman, Arkansas Post, January 10-11. Moved to Young's Point January 17-23, and duty there till April. Expedition to Greenville, Black Bayou and Deer Creek April 2-14. Deer Creek April 7. Black Bayou April 10. Demonstrations on Haines and Drumgould's Bluffs April 29-May 2. Moved to join army in rear of Vicksburg, Miss., via Richmond and Grand Gulf, May 2-14. Fourteen Mile Creek May 12-13. Jackson May 14. Siege of Vicksburg May 18-July 4. Assaults on Vicksburg May 19 and 22. Advance on Jackson, Miss., July 4-10. Siege of Jackson July 10-17. Bolton's

Depot July 16. Briar Creek near Canton July 17. Canton July 18. Camp at Big Black till September 23. Moved to Memphis, Tenn., thence march to Chattanooga, Tenn., September 23-November 20. Operations on Memphis & Charleston Railroad in Alabama October 20-29. Cherokee Station October 21 and 29. Cane Creek October 26. Bear Creek, Tuscumbia, October 27. Chattanooga-Ringgold Campaign November 23-27. Battles of Lookout Mountain November 23-24. Mission Ridge November 25. Ringgold Gap, Taylor's Ridge, November 27. March to relief of Knoxville, Tenn., November 28-December 8. Moved to Alabama and duty at Paint Rock till May, 1864. Regiment re-enlisted January 4, 1864. Atlanta (Ga.) Campaign May 1-September 8. Demonstrations on Resaca May 8-13. Near Resaca May 13. Battle of Resaca May 14-15. Advance on Dallas May 18-25. Operations on line of Pumpkin Vine Creek and battles about Dallas, New Hope Church and Allatoona Hills May 25-June 5. Operations about Marietta and against Kenesaw Mountain June 10-July 2. Assault on Kenesaw June 27. Nickajack Creek July 2-5. Chattahoochie River July 5-17. Battle of Atlanta July 22. Siege of Atlanta July 22-August 25. Ezra Chapel, Hood's second sortie, July 28. Flank movement on Jonesboro August 25-30. Battle of Jonesboro August 31-September 1. Lovejoy Station September 2-6. Operations against Hood in North Georgia and North Alabama September 29-November 3. Ship's Gap, Taylor's Ridge, October 16. March to the sea November 15-December 10. Siege of Savannah December 10-21. Campaign of the Carolinas January to April, 1865. Reconnoissance to Salkehatchie River, S. C., January 20. Salkehatchie Swamp February 2-5. South Edisto River February 9. North Edisto River February 12-13. Congaree Creek February 15. Columbia February 16-17. Battle of Bentonville, N. C., March 19-21. Occupation of Goldsboro March 24. Advance on Raleigh April 10-24. Occupation of Raleigh April 14. Bennett's House April 26. Surrender of Johnston and his army. March to Washington, D. C., via Richmond, Va., April 29-May 21. Grand Review May 24. Moved to Louisville, Ky., June, and there mustered out July 15, 1865.

Regiment lost during service 9 Officers and 82 Enlisted men killed and mortally wounded and 5 Officers and 265 Enlisted men by disease. Total 361.

77th REGIMENT INFANTRY.

Organized at Marietta, Ohio, September 28, 1861, to January 5, 1862. Left State for Paducah, Ky., February 17, 1862. Attached to District of Paducah, Ky., to March, 1862. 3rd Brigade, 5th Division, Army of the Tennessee, to May, 1862. 2nd Brigade, 5th Division, Army Tennessee, to July, 1862. 2nd Brigade, 5th Division, District of Memphis, Tenn., to August, 1862. Alton, Ill., to August, 1863. 1st Brigade, 3rd Division, Arkansas Expedition, to January, 1864. 1st Brigade, 3rd Division, 7th Army Corps, Dept. of Arkansas, to April, 1864. 2nd Brigade, 3rd Division, 7th Army Corps, to May, 1864. 3rd Brigade, 1st Division, 7th Army Corps, to February, 1865. 3rd Brigade, 3rd Division, 13th Army Corps (New), Military Division West Mississippi, to June, 1865. Dept. of Texas, to March, 1866.

SERVICE.—Moved from Paducah, Ky., to Savannah, Tenn., March 6-10, 1862. Expedition to Yellow Creek, Miss., and occupation of Pittsburg Landing, Tenn., March 14-17. Expedition to Eastport, Miss., and Chickasaw, Ala., April 1. Battle of Shiloh, Tenn., April 6-7. Corinth Road April 8. Advance on and siege of Corinth, Miss., April 29-May 30. March to Memphis, Tenn., via LaGrange, Grand Junction and Holly Springs June 1-July 21. Duty there till August 27. Ordered to Alton, Ill., and duty there as guard of Military Prisons till July 31, 1863. Moved to Helena, Ark., July 31, thence to Duvall's Bluff August 22. Steele's Expedition to Little Rock, Ark., September 1-10. Bayou Fourche and capture of Little Rock September 10. Duty at Little Rock till September 23. Regiment re-enlisted December 20, 1863, and mustered in as Veterans January 22, 1864, and moved to Columbus, Ohio. Returned to Little Rock

March 1-17. Steele's Expedition to Camden March 23-May 3. Okalona April 2-3. Prairie D'Ann April 9-12. Camden April 15-18. Mark's Mills April 25, most of Regiment captured. Evacuation of Camden April 27. Jenkins' Ferry April 30. Duty in the Dept. of Arkansas till February, 1865. Regiment exchanged February, 1865, and ordered to New Orleans, La., February 9. Moved to Mobile Point, Ala., February 20. Campaign against Mobile and its defences March 17-April 12. Siege of Spanish Fort and Fort Blakely March 26-April 9. Occupation of Mobile April 12. Advance to Mt. Vernon April 13-22. Moved to Mobile May 12, thence to Texas June 1-9. Duty at Brazos Santiago and Brownsville and in the Dept. of Texas, till March, 1866. Mustered out March 8, 1866.

Regiment lost during service 2 Officers and 68 Enlisted men killed and mortally wounded and 2 Officers and 208 Enlisted men by disease. Total 280.

78th REGIMENT INFANTRY.

Organized at Zanesville, Ohio, October, 1861, to January, 1862, and mustered in January 11, 1862. Moved to Cincinnati, Ohio, thence to Fort Donelson, Tenn., February 11-16. Attached to 2nd Brigade, 3rd Division, District of West Tennessee, to March, 1862. 3rd Brigade, 3rd Division, Army of the Tennessee, to July, 1862. Unattached, District of Jackson, Tenn., to November, 1862. 2nd Brigade, 3rd Division, Right Wing 13th Army Corps (Old), Dept. of the Tennessee, to December, 1862. 2nd Brigade, 3rd Division, 17th Army Corps, Army of the Tennessee, to July, 1865.

SERVICE.—Capture of Fort Donelson, Tenn., February 16, 1862. Expedition toward Purdy and operations about Crump's Landing, Tenn., March 9-14. Battle of Shiloh, Tenn., April 6-7. Advance on and siege of Corinth, Miss., April 29-May 30. Capture of Jackson June 7. Duty at Bethel and Grand Junction till August. Bolivar August 30. March to Iuka, Miss., September 1-19. Battle of Iuka September 19 (Reserve). Duty at Bolivar till November. Grant's Central Mississippi Campaign, operations on the Mississippi Central Railroad, November 2, 1862, to January 20, 1863. Reconnoissances from LaGrange toward Colliersville November 5 and November 8-9. Moved to Memphis, Tenn., January 20, thence to Lake Providence, La., February 22, and to Milliken's Bend, La., April 17. Movement on Bruinsburg and turning Grand Gulf April 25-30. Battle of Port Gibson May 1. Forty Hills and Hankinson's Ferry May 3-4. Battles of Raymond May 12; Jackson May 14; Champion's Hill May 16. Siege of Vicksburg, Miss., May 18-July 4. Assaults on Vicksburg May 19 and 22. Surrender of Vicksburg July 4, and duty there till February, 1864. Clinton July 16. Expedition to Monroe, La., August 20-September 2, 1863. Expedition to Canton October 14-20. Bogue Chitto Creek October 17. Regiment re-enlisted January 5, 1864. Meridian Campaign February 3-March 2, 1864. Baker's Creek February 5. Wyatt's February 13. Meridian February 14-15. Canton February 26. Veterans on furlough March and April. Moved to Clifton, Tenn., thence marched to Ackworth, Ga., May 5-June 8. Atlanta (Ga.) Campaign June 8-September 8. Operations about Marietta and against Kenesaw Mountain June 10-July 2. Assault on Kenesaw June 27. Nickajack Creek July 2-5. Howell's Ferry July 5. Chattahoochie River July 5-17. Leggett's or Bald Hill July 20-21. Battle of Atlanta July 22. Siege of Atlanta July 22-August 25. Flank movement on Jonesboro August 25-30. Battle of Jonesboro August 31-September 1. Lovejoy Station September 2-6. Duty near Atlanta till October 15. Moved to Chattanooga, Tenn., and duty guarding railroad near Chattanooga till November 13. Little River, Ala., October 27. March to the sea November 15-December 10. Siege of Savannah December 10-21. Campaign of the Carolinas January to April, 1865. Pocotaligo, S. C., January 14. Barker's Mills, Whippy Swamp, February 3. Orangeburg February 12-13. Columbia February 16-17. Battle of Bentonville, N. C., March 20-21. Occupation of Goldsboro March 24. Advance on Raleigh April 10-

14. Occupation of Raleigh April 14. Bennett's House April 26. Surrender of Johnston and his army. March to Washington, D. C., via Richmond, Va., April 29-May 20. Grand Review May 24. Moved to Louisville, Ky., June, and there mustered out July 11, 1865.

Regiment lost during service 2 Officers and 71 Enlisted men killed and mortally wounded and 2 Officers and 280 Enlisted men by disease. Total 355.

79th REGIMENT INFANTRY.

Organized at Camp Dennison, Ohio, August, 1862. Ordered to Kentucky September 3, 1862. Advance to Crittenden, Ky., September 7, thence moved to Louisville, Ky. Attached to Ward's Brigade, 12th Division, Army of the Ohio, to November, 1862. Ward's Brigade, Post of Gallatin, Tenn., Dept. of the Cumberland, to June, 1863. 2nd Brigade, 3rd Division, Reserve Corps, Army of the Cumberland, to August, 1863. Ward's Brigade, Nashville, Tenn., Dept. of the Cumberland, to January, 1864. 1st Brigade, 1st Division, 11th Army Corps, Army of the Cumberland, to April, 1864. 1st Brigade, 3rd Division, 20th Army Corps, Army of the Cumberland, to June, 1865.

SERVICE.—March to Frankfort, Ky., October 3-9, 1862. Occupation of Frankfort October 9, and duty there till October 26. Expedition to Lawrenceburg in pursuit of Morgan October 10-13. March to Bowling Green, Ky., October 26-November 4, thence to Scottsville and to Gallatin November 25, and duty there till December 11. Moved to South Tunnel December 11, and duty there till February 1, 1863. Duty at Gallatin till June 1. Moved to Lavergne June 1, thence to Murfreesboro, Tenn., July 2, and to Lavergne July 29. To Nashville, Tenn., August 19, and duty there till February 24, 1864. March to Wauhatchie Valley, Tenn., February 24-March 10, and duty there till May 2. Atlanta (Ga.) Campaign May 2-September 8. Demonstration on Rocky Faced Ridge May 8-11. Battle of Resaca May 14-15. Cassville May 19. Advance on Dallas May 22-25. New Hope Church May 25. Operations on line of Pumpkin Vine Creek and battles about Dallas, New Hope Church and Allatoona Hills May 25-June 5. Operations about Marietta and against Kenesaw Mountain June 10-July 2. Pine Hill June 11-14. Lost Mountain June 15-17. Golgotha or Gilgal Church June 15. Muddy Creek June 17. Noyes Creek June 19. Kolb's Farm June 22. Assault on Kenesaw June 27. Ruff's Station July 4. Chattahoochee River July 5-17. Peach Tree Creek July 19-20. Siege of Atlanta July 22-August 25. Operations at Chattahoochie River Bridge August 26-September 2. Occupation of Atlanta September 2-November 15. March to the sea November 15-December 10. Siege of Savannah December 10-21. Campaign of the Carolinas January to April, 1865. Occupation of Robertsville, S. C., January 30. Lawtonville February 2. Taylor's Hole Creek, Averysboro, N. C., March 16. Battle of Bentonville March 19-21. Occupation of Goldsboro March 24. Advance on Raleigh April 10-14. Occupation of Raleigh April 14. Bennett's House April 26. Surrender of Johnston and his army. March to Washington, D. C., via Richmond, Va., April 29-May 20. Grand Review May 24. Mustered out June 9, 1865.

Regiment lost during service 54 Enlisted men killed and mortally wounded and 1 Officer and 91 Enlisted men by disease. Total 146.

80th REGIMENT INFANTRY.

Organized at Canal Dover, Ohio, October, 1861, to January, 1862. Left State for Paducah, Ky., February 10, 1862. Attached to District of Paducah, Ky., to April, 1862. 2nd Brigade, 3rd Division, Army of the Mississippi, to November, 1862. 2nd Brigade, 7th Division, Left Wing 13th Army Corps (Old), Dept. of the Tennessee, to December, 1862. 2nd Brigade, 7th Division, 16th Army Corps, Army of the Tennessee, to January, 1863. 2nd Brigade, 7th Division, 17th Army Corps, to September, 1863. 2nd Brigade, 2nd Division, 17th Army Corps, to December, 1863. 2nd Brigade, 3rd Division, 15th Army Corps, to April, 1865. 1st Brigade, 2nd Division, 15th Army Corps, to July, 1865. Dept. of Arkansas to August, 1865.

SERVICE.—Duty at Paducah, Ky., February to April, 1862. Moved to Hamburg Landing, Tenn., April 20. Advance on and siege of Corinth, Miss., April 29-May 30. Pursuit to Booneville May 31-June 12. Expedition to Ripley June 22-23, and duty at Ripley till September. Battle of Iuka, Miss., September 16. Battle of Corinth, Miss., October 3-4. Pursuit to Hatchie River October 5-12. Grant's Central Mississippi Campaign, operations on the Mississippi Central Railroad, November 2, 1862, to January 4, 1863. Reconnoissance from LaGrange November 8-9, 1862. Reconnoissance from Davis Mills to Coldwater November 12-13. Guard trains to Memphis, Tenn., January 4-8, 1863. Duty at Forest Hill till February 16, and at Memphis till March 1. Moved to Helena, Ark., March 1. Yazoo Pass Expedition and operations against Fort Pemberton and Greenwood March 10-April 5. Moved to Milliken's Bend, La., April 13. Movement on Bruinsburg and turning Grand Gulf April 25-30. Battle of Port Gibson, Miss., May 1 (Reserve). Battles of Raymond May 12; Jackson May 14; Champion's Hill May 16. Escort prisoners to Memphis, Tenn., May 17-June 4. Siege of Vicksburg June 6-July 4. Moved to Helena, Ark., August 20, thence to Memphis, Tenn., September 20. March to Chattanooga, Tenn., October 10-November 22. Operations on the Memphis & Charleston Railroad in Alabama October 20-29. Chattanooga-Ringgold Campaign November 23-27. Tunnel Hill November 24-25. Mission Ridge November 25. Pursuit to Graysville November 26-27. Guard duty on the Memphis & Charleston Railroad till June 6, 1864. Duty at Allatoona June 7-25, and at Resaca till November 10. Repulse of attack on Resaca October 12-13. March to the sea November 15-December 10. Siege of Savannah December 10-21. Campaign of the Carolinas January to April, 1865. Fishburn's Plantation, near Lane's Bridge, Salkehatchie River, S. C., February 6. South Edisto River February 9. North Edisto River February 12-13. Columbia February 16-17. Cox's Bridge, N. C., March 19-20. Battle of Bentonville March 20-21. Occupation of Goldsboro March 24. Advance on Raleigh April 10-14. Occupation of Raleigh April 10. Bennett's House April 26. Surrender of Johnston and his army. March to Washington, D. C., via Richmond, Va., April 29-May 20. Grand Review May 24. Moved to Louisville, Ky., June, thence to Little Rock, Ark., and duty there till August. Mustered out August 15, 1865.

Regiment lost during service 4 Officers and 48 Enlisted men killed and mortally wounded and 2 Officers and 170 Enlisted men by disease. Total 224.

81st REGIMENT INFANTRY.

Organized in Ohio at large, under authority granted by Gen. Fremont, as Morton's Independent Rifle Regiment. Accepted by State September, 1861. Duty at Benton Barracks, Mo., till September 24, 1861. Moved to Franklin, Mo., September 24, thence to Harman, Mo., September 27, and duty there till December 20. Attached to Dept. of Missouri to March, 1862. 2nd Brigade, 2nd Division, Army of the Tennessee, to July, 1862. 2nd Brigade, 2nd Division, District of Corinth, Miss., to September, 1862. 1st Brigade, 2nd Division, District of Corinth, Miss., to November, 1862. 2nd Brigade, District of Corinth, Miss., 13th Army Corps (Old), Dept. of the Tennessee, to December, 1862. 2nd Brigade, District of Corinth, 17th Army Corps, to January, 1863. 2nd Brigade, District of Corinth, 16th Army Corps, to March, 1863. 2nd Brigade, 2nd Division, 16th Army Corps, to September, 1864. 2nd Brigade, 4th Division, 15th Army Corps, to July, 1865.

SERVICE.—Expedition to Fulton, Calloway County, Mo., November, 1861. Expedition after guerrillas in Northern Missouri December 20, 1861, to January 4, 1862. Duty along Northern Missouri Railroad at Wellsville, Montgomery City and Danville (Headquarters at Danville) till March 1, 1862. Moved to St. Louis, Mo., thence to Pittsburg Landing, Tenn., March 1-15, 1862. Battle of Shiloh, Tenn., April 6-7. Advance on and

siege of Corinth, Miss., April 29-May 30. Pursuit to Booneville June 1-14. Duty at Corinth till August. Guard stores at Hamburg till September 17. Movements on Iuka, Miss., September 17-20. Battle of Corinth October 3-4. Pursuit to Ripley October 5-12. 5 Companies join October 19. Duty at Corinth till April, 1863. Raid to Tupelo, Miss., December 13-19, 1862, and January 3-19, 1863. Raid to intercept Forest January 2-3. Cornersville Pike January 28 (Detachment). Dodge's Expedition to Northern Alabama April 15-May 8. Great Bear Creek April 17. Rock Cut, near Tuscumbia, April 22. Tuscumbia April 23. Town Creek April 28. Moved to Pocahontas June 3, and duty there till October 29. March to Pulaski October 29-November 10. Duty at Pulaski, Wales, Sam's Mills and Nancy's Mills (Headquarters at Pulaski) till March, 1864. Moved to Lynnville March 5, and to Pulaski April 19. March to Chattanooga, Tenn., April 29-May 4. Atlanta (Ga.) Campaign May to September. Demonstrations on Resaca May 8-12. Snake Creek Gap and Sugar Valley, near Resaca, May 9. Near Resaca May 13. Battle of Resaca May 14. Lay's Ferry, Oostenaula River, May 14-15. Rome Cross Roads May 16. Advance on Dallas May 18-25. Operations on line of Pumpkin Vine Creek and battles about Dallas, New Hope Church and Allatoona Hills May 25-June 5. Operations about Marietta and against Kenesaw Mountain June 10-July 2. Assault on Kenesaw June 27. Nickajack Creek July 2-5. Ruff's Mills July 3-4. Chattahoochie River July 6-17. Battle of Atlanta July 22. Siege of Atlanta July 22-August 25. Ezra Chapel July 28. Flank movement on Jonesboro August 25-30. Battle of Jonesboro August 31-September 1. Lovejoy Station September 2-6. Non-Veterans mustered out September 26, 1864. Garrison duty at Rome till November. Reconnoissance from Rome on Cave Springs Road and skirmishes October 12-13. March to the sea November 15-December 10. Ogeechee Canal December 8. Siege of Savannah December 10-21. Campaign of the Carolinas January to April, 1865. Salkehatchie Swamps, S. C., February 2-5. South Edisto River February 9. North Edisto River February 12-13. Columbia February 16-17. Lynch's Creek February 26. Battle of Bentonville, N. C., March 19-21. Occupation of Goldsboro March 24. Advance on Raleigh April 10-14. Occupation of Raleigh April 14. Bennett's House April 26. Surrender of Johnston and his army. March to Washington, D. C., via Richmond, Va., April 29-May 20. Grand Review May 24. Moved to Louisville, Ky., June, and there mustered out July 13, 1865.

Regiment lost during service 4 Officers and 58 Enlisted men killed and mortally wounded and 160 Enlisted men by disease. Total 222.

82nd REGIMENT INFANTRY.

Organized at Kenton, Ohio, October to December, 1861. Mustered in December 31, 1861. Left State for Grafton, W. Va., January 25, 1862. Attached to District of Cumberland, Md., Dept. of Western Virginia, to March, 1862. Cumberland, Md., Dept. of the Mountains, to April, 1862. Schenck's Brigade, Dept. of the Mountains, to June, 1862. Milroy's Independent Brigade, 1st Army Corps, Army of Virginia, to September, 1862. Headquarters 3rd Division, 11th Army Corps, Army of the Potomac, to December, 1862. Headquarters 11th Army Corps to May, 1863. 2nd Brigade, 3rd Division, 11th Army Corps, to July, 1863. 1st Brigade, 3rd Division, 11th Army Corps, Army of the Potomac, to October, 1863, and Army of the Cumberland to April, 1864. 3rd Brigade, 1st Division, 20th Army Corps, Army of the Potomac, to July, 1865.

SERVICE.—Expedition to Lost River Region, W. Va., April 1-12, 1862. Battle of McDowell May 8. Franklin May 10-12. Operations in the Shenandoah Valley May to August. Battle of Cross Keys June 8. Battle of Cedar Mountain August 9. Pope's Campaign in Northern Virginia August 16-September 2. Fords of the Rappahannock August 21-23. Freeman's Ford August 22. Waterloo Bridge August 23-25. Battles of Groveton August 29, and Bull Run August 30. Duty in the Defences of Washington, D. C., till November. Detached at Headquarters 3rd Division and 11th Corps Headquarters as provost guard till May, 1863. Movement to Gainesville November 1-9, 1862, thence to Centreville November 18, and to Falmouth, Va., December 9-16. At Stafford Court House till January 20, 1863. "Mud March" January 20-24. At Stafford Court House till April 27. Chancellorsville Campaign April 27-May 6. Battle of Chancellorsville May 1-5. Gettysburg (Pa.) Campaign June 11-July 24. Battle of Gettysburg, Pa., July 1-3. Pursuit of Lee to Manassas Gap, Va., July 5-24. Guard duty along Orange & Alexandria Railroad till September. Movement to Bridgeport, Ala., September 24-October 3. Duty at Bridgeport and in Lookout Valley till November. Reopening Tennessee River October 26-29. Battle of Wauhatchie, Tenn., October 28-29. Chattanooga-Ringgold Campaign November 23-27. Orchard Knob November 23. Tunnel Hill November 24-25. Mission Ridge November 25. Chickamauga Station November 26. March to relief of Knoxville November 28-December 17. Regiment re-enlisted January 1, 1864. Atlanta (Ga.) Campaign May 1-September 8, 1864. Demonstrations on Rocky Faced Ridge May 8-11. Battle of Resaca May 14-15. Cassville May 19. Advance on Dallas May 22-25. New Hope Church May 25. Operations on line of Pumpkin Vine Creek and battles about Dallas, New Hope Church and Allatoona Hills May 25-June 5. Operations about Marietta and against Kenesaw Mountain June 10-July 2. Pine Hill June 11-14. Lost Mountain June 15-17. Gilgal or Golgatha Church June 15. Muddy Creek June 17. Noyes Creek June 19. Kolb's Farm June 22. Assault on Kenesaw Mountain June 27. Ruff's Station July 4. Chattahoochie River July 5-17. Peach Tree Creek July 19-20. Siege of Atlanta July 22-August 25. Operations at ·Chattahoochie River Bridge August 26-September 2. Occupation of Atlanta September 2-November 15. Expedition from Atlanta to Tuckum's Cross Roads October 26-29. March to the sea November 15-December 10. Montieth Swamp December 9. Siege of Savannah December 10-21. Campaign of the Carolinas January to April, 1865. Taylor's Hole Creek, Averysboro, N. C., March 16. Battle of Bentonville March 19-21. Occupation of Goldsboro March 24. Advance on Raleigh April 10-14. Occupation of Raleigh April 14. Bennett's House April 26. Surrender of Johnston and his army. March to Washington, D. C., via Richmond, Va., April 29-May 19. Grand Review May 24. Moved to Louisville, Ky., June, and mustered out July 29, 1865.

Regiment lost during service 16 Officers and 122 Enlisted men killed and mortally wounded and 1 Officer and 118 Enlisted men by disease. Total 257.

83rd REGIMENT INFANTRY.

Organized at Camp Dennison, Ohio, August and September, 1862. Moved to Covington September 3, 1862, to repel Kirby Smith's threatened attack on Cincinnati, Ohio. Attached to 1st Brigade, 2nd Division, Army of Kentucky, Dept. of the Ohio, to December, 1862. 1st Brigade, 10th Division, 13th Army Corps (Old), Dept. of the Tennessee, December, 1862. 1st Brigade, 1st Division, Sherman's Yazoo Expedition, to January, 1863. 1st Brigade, 10th Division, 13th Army Corps, Army of the Tennessee, to August, 1863. 1st Brigade, 4th Division, 13th Army Corps, Army of the Tennessee, August, 1863, and Dept. of the Gulf to January, 1864. 2nd Brigade, 3rd Division, 13th Army Corps, Army of the Gulf, to March, 1864. 1st Brigade, 4th Division, 13th Army Corps, to June, 1864. 3rd Brigade, 3rd Division, 19th Army Corps, Dept. of the Gulf, to December, 1864. Post of Natchez, Miss., District of Vicksburg, Miss., to January, 1864. 3rd Brigade, Reserve Corps, Military Division West Mississippi, to February, 1865. 3rd Brigade, 2nd Division, Reserve Corps, February, 1865. 3rd Brigade, 2nd Division, 13th Army Corps (New), to July, 1865.

SERVICE.—Expedition to Cynthiana, Ky., September 18, 1862. Moved to Camp Shaler September 25, thence to Paris, Ky., October 15. To Louisville, Ky., October

28, and to Memphis, Tenn., November 23. Sherman's Yazoo Expedition December 20, 1862, to January 3, 1863. Expedition from Milliken's Bend to Dallas Station and Delhi, December 25-26. Chickasaw Bayou December 26-28. Chickasaw Bluff December 29. Expedition to Arkansas Post, Ark., January 3-10, 1863. Assault and capture of Fort Hindman, Arkansas Post, January 10-11. Moved to Young's Point, La., January 15, and duty there till March 10. Expedition to Greenville, Miss., and Cypress Bend, Ark., February 14-26. Deer Creek near Greenville February 23. At Milliken's Bend, La., till April 15. Movement on Bruinsburg and turning Grand Gulf April 25-30. Battle of Port Gibson May 1. Battle of Champion's Hill May 16. Big Black River May 17. Siege of Vicksburg, Miss., May 18-July 4. Assaults on Vicksburg May 19 and 22. Advance on Jackson, Miss., July 4-10. Siege of Jackson July 10-17. Camp at Vicksburg till August 24. Ordered to New Orleans, La., August 24. Expedition from Carrollton to New and Amite Rivers September 24-29. Moved to Brashear City. Western Louisiana Campaign October 3-November 30. Grand Coteau November 3. At New Iberia till December 19. Moved to New Orleans, La., thence to Madisonville January 19, 1864, and duty there till March. Red River Campaign March 10-May 22. Advance from Franklin to Alexandria March 14-26. Bayou de Paul and battle of Sabine Cross Roads April 8, 1864. Monett's Ferry, Cane River Crossing, April 23. Construction of dam at Alexandria April 30-May 10. Gov. Moore's Plantation May 2. Alexandria May 2-9. Retreat to Morganza May 13-20. Mansura May 16. Moved to Baton Rouge, La., May 28, and duty there till July 21. Moved to Morganza July 21, and duty there till November. Expedition to Morgan's Ferry October 1-9, and to the Atchafalaya October 18-29. At mouth of White River November 1-December 6. Moved to Natchez December 6 and duty there till January 28, 1865. Consolidated with 48th Ohio Infantry January 17, 1865. Moved to Kennersville, La., January 28, thence to New Orleans and to Barrancas, Fla. Campaign against Mobile, Ala., and its defences March-April. March from Pensacola, Fla., to Blakely, Ala., March 20-April 2. Occupation of Canoe Station March 27. Siege of Fort Blakely April 2-9. Assault and capture of Fort Blakely April 9. Capture of Mobile April 12. March to Montgomery and Selma April 13-25. Duty at Selma till May 12. Moved to Mobile May 12, thence to Galveston, Texas, June 13, and duty there till July 24. Veterans and Recruits transferred to 48th Ohio Infantry Battalion. Mustered out July 24, and discharged at Camp Dennison, Ohio, August 10, 1865.

Regiment lost during service 4 Officers and 52 Enlisted men killed and mortally wounded and 2 Officers and 161 Enlisted men by disease. Total 219.

84th REGIMENT INFANTRY.

Organized at Camp Chase, Ohio, for three months' service May-June, 1862. Ordered to Cumberland, Md., June 11, and provost duty there till September. Attached to Railroad District, Dept. of the Mountains, to July, 1862, and 8th Army Corps, Middle Department, to September. Moved to New Creek September 13 to repel attack on that point by Jenkins and Imboden. Moved to Camp Chase, thence to Camp Delaware, and mustered out October 14, 1862.

Lost by disease during service 14 Enlisted men.

85th REGIMENT INFANTRY.

Organized at Camp Chase for three months' service May-June, 1862. Zinn's Battalion moved to Kentucky and participated in operations against Morgan July, 1862. Prison guard at Camp Chase, Ohio, till September. Zinn's Battalion moved to Cincinnati, Ohio, and participated in the operations for the defence of that city against Kirby Smith's threatened attack August-September. Mustered out September 23 and September 27, 1862.

Lost during service by disease 10 Enlisted men.

86th REGIMENT INFANTRY.

Organized at Camp Chase, Ohio, for three months' service, June 10, 1862. Moved to Clarksburg, W. Va., June 16-17, and assigned to Kelly's Railroad Command, June 19. Railroad guard duty at Clarksburg June 17 to August 21. Companies "A," "C," "H" and "I" on duty at Parkersburg July 27 to August 21. Expedition from Clarksburg to Huttonville to intercept raid by Jenkins August 21-25. Garrison duty at Clarksburg, also constructing fortifications and guarding stores August 25 to September 17. Ordered to Camp Delaware, Ohio, September 17, and mustered out September 25.

86th REGIMENT INFANTRY REORGANIZED.

Organized at Camp Cleveland, Ohio, and mustered in for six months' service July 17, 1863. Moved to Zanesville, Ohio, July 19. Expedition from Zanesville to Eagleport, Ohio, to intercept Morgan July 20-24. Skirmish at Eagleport July 20. Expedition from Zanesville to Cambridge, Ohio, in pursuit of Morgan July 19-25. Skirmish near New Lisbon July 26. Capture of Gen. Morgan's Command near Salineville July 26. Moved to Camp Nelson, Ky., August 8-11. Attached to DeCourcy's Brigade, Willcox's Left Wing forces, 23rd Army Corps, Dept. of Ohio, to October, 1863. 3rd Brigade, 2nd Division, 9th Army Corps, Dept. Ohio, to February, 1864.
SERVICE.—Expedition under DeCourcy to Cumberland Gap August 17-September 7, 1863. Operations about Cumberland Gap September 7-10. Capture of Cumberland Gap September 9. Occupation of Rocky Fort September 9. Garrison at Cumberland Gap September 9, 1863, to January 16, 1864. March to Nicholasville, Ky., January 16-23, thence moved to Cleveland, Ohio, January 23-26. Mustered out February 10, 1864.
Regiment lost during service by disease 37 Enlisted men.

87th REGIMENT INFANTRY.

Organized at Columbus, Ohio (Camp Chase), for three months' service June 10, 1862. Left State for Baltimore, Md., June 12, and duty in the defences of that city till July 28. Attached to Railroad Brigade, 8th Army Corps, Middle Department. Ordered to Harper's Ferry, W. Va., July 28, and attached to Miles' Command. Garrison duty in the Defences of Bolivar Heights till September. Skirmishes at Berlin and Point of Hooks, Md., September 4-5 (Detachment). Defence of Harper's Ferry September 12-15. Surrender of Harper's Ferry September 15. Paroled September 16 and sent to Annapolis, Md. Mustered out at Camp Chase, Columbus, Ohio, September 20, 1862.
Regiment lost during service 1 Enlisted man killed and 5 Enlisted men by disease.

88th REGIMENT INFANTRY—"1st BATTALION GOVERNOR'S GUARD."

Organized at Camp Chase, Ohio, and mustered in October 27, 1862. Duty at Camp Chase till October, 1863, and at Cincinnati till December 20, 1863. Duty at Camp Chase till July, 1865. Mustered out July 3, 1865.
Lost by disease 80 men.

89th REGIMENT INFANTRY.

Organized at Camp Dennison, Ohio, and mustered in August 26, 1862. Ordered to Covington, Ky., September 3, 1862, and duty there till October 5, during the threatened attack on Cincinnati, Ohio, by Kirby Smith. Ordered to Point Pleasant, W. Va., October 5. Attached to Army of Kentucky, Dept. of the Ohio, September-October, 1862. 2nd Brigade, Kanawha Division, District of West Virginia, Dept. of the Ohio, to February, 1863. Crook's Brigade, Baird's Division, Army of Kentucky, Dept. of the Cumberland, to June, 1863. 3rd Brigade, 4th Division, 14th Army Corps, Army of the Cumberland, to September, 1863. 1st Brigade, 1st Division, Reserve Corps, Army of the Cumberland, to October, 1863. 1st Brigade, 3rd Division, 14th Army Corps, Army of the Cumberland, to June, 1865.

SERVICE.—Advance to Falls of the Kanawha, Va., October 10-November 3, 1862, thence moved to Fayetteville Court House November 17, and duty there till January 6, 1863. Moved to Nashville, Tenn., January 25-February 7. Relief of 83rd Illinois Infantry, at Dover, from attack by Forest's Cavalry February 3. Expedition to Carthage, Tenn., February 22-25. Duty at Carthage till June 5. Ordered to Murfreesboro, Tenn., June 5. Middle Tennessee or Tullahoma Campaign June 23-July 7. Hoover's Gap June 24-26. Tullahoma June 29-30. Occupation of Middle Tennessee till August 16. Chickamauga (Ga.) Campaign August 16-September 22. Expedition to Tracy City and destruction of Salt Petre Works at Nickajack Cove August 20-September 10. Reconnoissance from Rossville September 17. Near Ringgold, Ga., September 17. Battle of Chickamauga September 19-21 (most of Regiment captured). Siege of Chattanooga, Tenn., September 24-November 22. Reopening Tennessee River October 26-29. Brown's Ferry October 27. Near Chattanooga November 6. Chattanooga-Ringgold Campaign November 23-27. Orchard Knob November 23-24. Mission Ridge November 25. Pursuit to Graysville November 26-27. Duty at Chattanooga till February 22, 1864. Demonstration on Dalton, Ga., February 22-27. Tunnel Hill, Buzzard's Roost Gap and Rocky Faced Ridge February 23-25. Atlanta (Ga.) Campaign May 1-September 8. Demonstrations on Rocky Faced Ridge May 8-11. Battle of Resaca May 14-15. Advance on Dallas May 18-25. Operations on line of Pumpkin Vine Creek and battles about Dallas, New Hope Church and Allatoona Hills May 25-June 5. Operations about Marietta and against Kenesaw Mountain June 10-July 2. Pine Hill June 11-14. Lost Mountain June 15-17. Assault on Kenesaw June 27. Ruff's Station, Smyrna Camp Ground, July 4. Chattahoochie River July 5-17. Peach Tree Creek July 19-20. Siege of Atlanta July 22-August 25. Utoy Creek August 5-7. Flank movement on Jonesboro August 25-30. Battle of Jonesboro August 31-September 1. Operations against Hood in North Georgia and North Alabama September 29-November 3. March to the sea November 15-December 10. Siege of Savannah December 10-21. Campaign of the Carolinas January to April, 1865. Fayetteville, N. C., March 11. Battle of Bentonville March 19-21. Occupation of Goldsboro March 24. Advance on Raleigh April 10-14. Occupation of Raleigh April 14. Bennett's House April 26. Surrender of Johnston and his army. March to Washington, D. C., via Richmond, Va., April 29-May 20. Grand Review May 24. Mustered out June 14, 1865.
Regiment lost during service 3 Officers and 47 Enlisted men killed and mortally wounded and 5 Officers and 245 Enlisted men by disease. Total 300.

90th REGIMENT INFANTRY.

Organized at Camp Circleville, Lancaster, Ohio, and mustered in August 29, 1862. Ordered to Covington, Ky., August 30, thence to relief of Lexington September 1. Retreat to Louisville, Ky., September 2-15. Attached to 22nd Brigade, 4th Division, Army of the Ohio, September, 1862. 22nd Brigade, 4th Division, 2nd Army Corps, Army of the Ohio, to November, 1862. 1st Brigade, 2nd Division, Left Wing 14th Army Corps, Army of the Cumberland, to January, 1863. 1st Brigade, 2nd Division, 21st Army Corps, Army of the Cumberland, to October, 1863. 1st Brigade, 1st Division, 4th Army Corps, Army of the Cumberland, to June, 1865.

SERVICE.—Pursuit of Bragg to London, Ky., October 1-22, 1862. Battle of Perryville, Ky., October 8. At Glasgow, Ky., till November 8. March to Nashville, Tenn., and duty there till December 26. Advance on Murfreesboro, Tenn., December 26-30. Lavergne December 26-27. Battle of Stone's River December 30-31, 1862, and January 1-3, 1863. Duty at Murfreesboro till June. Expedition to Woodbury April 2. Middle Tennessee or Tullahoma Campaign June 23-July 7. Occupation of Middle Tennessee till August 18. Passage of Cumberland Mountains and Tennessee River, and Chickamauga (Ga.) Campaign August 16-September 22. Lee and Gordon's Mills September 11-13. Battle of Chickamauga September 19-20. Siege of Chattanooga, Tenn., September 24-October 26. Moved to Bridgeport, Ala., October 26, and duty there till January 24, 1864. At Coltewah, Tenn., till May. Atlanta (Ga.) Campaign May 1-September 8. Tunnel Hill May 6-7. Demonstrations on Rocky Faced Ridge and Dalton May 8-13. Buzzard's Roost Gap May 8-9. Battle of Resaca May 14-15. Near Kingston May 18-19. Near Cassville May 19. Advance on Dallas May 22-25. Operations on line of Pumpkin Vine Creek and battles about Dallas, New Hope Church and Allatoona Hills May 25-June 5. Operations about Marietta and against Kenesaw Mountain June 10-July 2. Pine Hill June 11-14. Lost Mountain June 15-17. Assault on Kenesaw June 27. Ruff's Station, Smyrna Camp Ground, July 4. Chattahoochie River July 5-17. Peach Tree Creek July 19-20. Siege of Atlanta July 22-August 25. Flank movement on Jonesboro August 25-30. Battle of Jonesboro August 31-September 1. Lovejoy Station September 2-6. Duty at Atlanta till October 3. Operations against Hood in North Georgia and North Alabama October 3-November 3. Moved to Pulaski, Tenn. Nashville Campaign November-December. Columbia, Duck River, November 24-27. Battle of Franklin November 30. Battle of Nashville December 15-16. Pursuit of Hood to the Tennessee River December 17-28. Moved to Huntsville, Ala., and duty there till March, 1865. Operations in East Tennessee March 15-April 22. Moved to Nashville, Tenn., and duty there till June. Mustered out June 13, and discharged at Camp Dennison, Ohio, June 21, 1865.

Regiment lost during service 5 Officers and 77 Enlisted men killed and mortally wounded and 170 Enlisted men by disease. Total 252.

91st REGIMENT INFANTRY.

Organized at Camp Ironton, Ohio, August 26, 1862. Moved to Ironton, Ohio, August 26-September 3, thence to Guyandotte, Va., September 4. Mustered into United States service September 5. Ordered to Maysville, Ky., September 15. Orders changed to Point Pleasant, W. Va. Attached to District of the Kanawha, W. Va., Dept. of the Ohio, to March. 1863. 2nd Brigade, 3rd Division, 8th Army Corps, Middle Dept., to June, 1863. 2nd Brigade, Scammon's Division, Dept. of West Virginia, to December, 1863. 2nd Brigade, 3rd Division, Dept. West Virginia, to April, 1864. 2nd Brigade, 2nd Infantry Division, West Virginia, to January, 1865. 1st Brigade, 3rd Division, West Virginia, to April, 1865. 1st Brigade, 4th Provisional Division, West Virginia, to June, 1865.

SERVICE.—Duty at Point Pleasant, Va., till September 26, 1862. Raid up the Kanawha to Buffalo September 26-28. Action at Buffalo September 27. Advance to Gauley Bridge, Falls of the Great Kanawha, October 20-November 3, thence moved to Fayetteville November 8, and duty there till April, 1863. Advance to Summerville April. Duty at Summerville and Fayetteville till May, 1864. Pursuit of Morgan July 20-31, 1863. Expedition from Charleston to Lewisburg November 3-13. Scammon's demonstration from the Kanawha Valley December 8-21. Big Sewell and Meadow Bluff December 11. Lewisburg and Greenbrier River December 12. Crook's Expedition to Dublin Depot and New River Bridge, Virginia & Tennessee Railroad, May 2-19, 1864. Cloyd's Mountain May 9. New River Bridge and Newbern Bridge May 10. March to join Hunter at Staunton May 31-June 4. Piedmont June 5. Hunter's Raid to Lynchburg June 10-July 1. Diamond Hill June 17. Lynchburg June 17-18. Buford's Gap June 20. Salem June 21. Moved to the Shenandoah Valley July 8, and reach Martinsburg July 15. Stevenson's Depot July 20. Battle of Winchester, Kernstown, July 24. Martinsburg July 25. Sheridan's Shenandoah Valley Campaign August 7-November 28. Near Charlestown August 24. Halltown August 24. Near Charlestown August 26. Halltown August 26. Wormley's Gap August 29. Berryville September 3. Battle of Opequan, Winchester, September 19. Fisher's Hill September 22. Battle of Cedar Creek October 19. Kablestown November 18.

Guarding Railroad Bridge at Opequan till December 20. Ordered to Martinsburg December 30, and duty there till March 17, 1865. Moved to Cumberland, Md., March 17, thence to Winchester April 5, and duty there till June 2. At Cumberland, Md., till June 24. Mustered out June 24, 1865.

Regiment lost during service 3 Officers and 60 Enlisted men killed and mortally wounded and 3 Officers and 87 Enlisted men by disease. Total 153.

92nd REGIMENT INFANTRY.

Organized at Camp Marietta and at Gallipolis, Ohio, August-September, 1862. (Cos. "A," "B" and "C" garrison duty at Gallipolis, Ohio, September.) Ordered to Point Pleasant, Va., October 7, 1862. Attached to District of the Kanawha, W. Va., Dept. of the Ohio, to December, 1862. 2nd Brigade, Kanawha Division, W. Va., Dept. Ohio, to February, 1863. Crook's Brigade, Baird's Division, Army of Kentucky, Dept. of the Cumberland, to June, 1863. 3rd Brigade, 4th Division, 14th Army Corps, Army of the Cumberland, to October, 1863. 1st Brigade, 3rd Division, 14th Army Corps, to June, 1865.

SERVICE.—March to Charleston, W. Va., October 14-November 16, 1862. Duty at Camp Vinton till January 1, 1863. Moved to Tompkin's Farm and Colesworth January 1-3. Moved to Nashville, Tenn., January 7-22, and duty there till February 17. Moved to Carthage, Tenn., February 17, and duty there till June 5. Moved to Murfreesboro, Tenn., June 5. Middle Tennessee or Tullahoma Campaign June 23-July 7. Hoover's Gap June 24-26. Tullahoma June 29-30. Occupation of Middle Tennessee till August 16. Passage of the Cumberland Mountains and Tennessee River and Chickamauga (Ga.) Campaign August 16-September 22. Near Graysville September 10. Catlett's Gap September 15-18. Battle of Chickamauga September 19-21. Siege of Chattanooga, Tenn., September 24-November 23. Re-opening Tennessee River October 26-29. Brown's Ferry October 27. Chattanooga-Ringgold Campaign November 23-27. Orchard Knob November 23-24. Mission Ridge November 25. Pursuit to Graysville November 26-27. At Chattanooga till February 22, 1864. Demonstration on Dalton, Ga., February 22-27. Tunnel Hill, Buzzard's Roost Gap and Rocky Faced Ridge February 23-25. Atlanta (Ga.) Campaign May 1 to September 8. Demonstrations on Rocky Faced Ridge May 8-11. Buzzard's Roost Gap May 8-9. Battle of Resaca May 14-15. Advance on Dallas May 18-25. Operations on line of Pumpkin Vine Creek and battles about Dallas, New Hope Church and Allatoona Hills May 25-June 5. Operations about Marietta and against Kenesaw Mountain June 10-July 2. Pine Hill June 11-14. Lost Mountain June 15-17. Assault on Kenesaw June 27. Ruff's Station, Smyrna Camp Ground, July 4. Chattahoochie River July 5-17. Peach Tree Creek July 19-20. Siege of Atlanta July 22-August 25. Utoy Creek August 5-7. Flank movement on Jonesboro August 25-30. Battle of Jonesboro August 31-September 1. Operations against Hood in North Georgia and North Alabama September 29-November 3. March to the sea November 15-December 10. Siege of Savannah December 10-21. Campaign of the Carolinas January to April, 1865. Fayetteville, N. C., March 11. Battle of Bentonville March 19-21. Occupation of Goldsboro March 24. Advance on Raleigh April 10-14. Occupation of Raleigh April 14. Bennett's House April 26. Surrender of Johnston and his army. March to Washington, D. C., via Richmond, Va., April 29-May 20. Grand Review May 24. Mustered out June 19, 1865.

Regiment lost during service 4 Officers and 47 Enlisted men killed and mortally wounded and 1 Officer and 192 Enlisted men by disease. Total 244.

93rd REGIMENT INFANTRY.

Organized at Dayton, Ohio, and mustered in August 20, 1862. Left State for Lexington, Ky., August 23. March to relief of Nelson August 29-September 1. Retreat from Lexington to Louisville, Ky., September 1-4. Attached to Ward's Brigade, 12th Division, Army of the

Ohio, September, 1862. 4th Brigade, 2nd Division, 1st Corps, Army of the Ohio, to November, 1862. 3rd Brigade, 2nd Division, Right Wing 14th Army Corps, Army of the Cumberland, to January, 1863. 3rd Brigade, 2nd Division, 20th Army Corps, Army of the Cumberland, to October, 1863. 2nd Brigade, 3rd Division, 4th Army Corps, Army of the Cumberland, to June, 1865.

SERVICE.—Pursuit of Bragg into Kentucky October 1-15, 1862. Battle of Perryville, Ky., October 8. March to Nashville, Tenn., October 16-November 7. Action at Kimbrough's Mills, Mill Creek and Lebanon (Antioch Church), December 6. Duty at Nashville till December 26. Advance on Murfreesboro December 26-30. Battle of Stone's River December 30-31, 1862, and January 1-3, 1863. Duty at Murfreesboro till June. Middle Tennessee or Tullahoma Campaign June 23-July 7. Liberty Gap June 24-27. Occupation of Middle Tennessee till August 16. Passage of the Cumberland Mountains and Tennessee River and Chickamauga (Ga.) Campaign August 16-September 22. Battle of Chickamauga, Ga., September 19-20. Siege of Chattanooga, Tenn., September 24-November 23. Re-opening Tennessee River October 26-29. Brown's Ferry October 27. Chattanooga-Ringgold Campaign November 23-27. Orchard Knob November 23-24. Mission Ridge November 25. March to relief of Knoxville November 28-December 8. Operations in East Tennessee till April, 1864. Charleston, Tenn., December 28, 1863 (Detachment). Operations about Dandridge January 16-17, 1864. Dandridge January 17. Atlanta (Ga.) Campaign May 1 to September 8, 1864. Demonstrations on Rocky Faced Ridge and Dalton, Ga., May 8-13. Buzzard's Roost Gap May 8-9. Battle of Resaca May 14-15. Adairsville May 17. Near Kingston May 18-19. Near Cassville May 19. Advance on Dallas May 22-25. Operations on line of Pumpkin Vine Creek and battles about Dallas, New Hope Church and Allatoona Hills May 25-June 5. Pickett's Mills May 27. Operations about Marietta and against Kenesaw Mountain June 10-July 2. Pine Hill June 11-14. Lost Mountain June 15-17. Assault on Kenesaw June 27. Ruff's Station, Smyrna Camp Ground, July 4. Chattahoochie River July 5-17. Pace's Ferry July 5. Peach Tree Creek July 19-20. Siege of Atlanta July 22-August 25. Flank movement on Jonesboro August 25-30. Battle of Jonesboro August 31-September 1. Lovejoy Station September 2-6. Operations against Hood in North Georgia and North Alabama September 29-November 3. Nashville Campaign November-December. Columbia, Duck River, November 24-27. Battle of Franklin November 30. Battle of Nashville December 15-16. Pursuit of Hood to the Tennessee River December 17-23. Moved to Huntsville, Ala., and duty there till March, 1865. Operations in East Tennessee March 15-April 22. Moved to Nashville, Tenn., and duty there till June. Mustered out June 8, 1865.

Regiment lost during service 4 Officers and 106 Enlisted men killed and mortally wounded and 107 Enlisted men by disease. Total 217.

94th REGIMENT INFANTRY.

Organized at Camp Piqua, Ohio, and mustered in August 22, 1862. Ordered to Lexington, Ky., August 28. Expedition to Yates' Ford, Kentucky River, August 30-September 3. Yates' Ford August 31. Tait's Ferry, Kentucky River, September 1. Retreat to Louisville, Ky., September 2-3. Attached to 9th Brigade, 3rd Division, Army of the Ohio, September, 1862. 9th Brigade, 3rd Division, 1st Corps, Army of the Ohio, to November, 1862. 1st Brigade, 1st Division, Center 14th Army Corps, Army of the Cumberland, to January, 1863. 1st Brigade, 1st Division, 14th Army Corps, to June, 1865.

SERVICE.—Pursuit of Bragg into Kentucky October 1-15, 1862. Battle of Perryville, Ky., October 8. March to Nashville, Tenn., October 16-November 7, and duty there till December 26. Advance on Murfreesboro December 26-30. Battle of Stone's River December 30-31, 1862, and January 1-3, 1863. Duty at Murfreesboro till June. Middle Tennessee or Tullahoma Campaign June

23-July 7. Hoover's Gap June 24-26. Occupation of Middle Tennessee till August 16. Passage of the Cumberland Mountains and Tennessee River, and Chickamauga (Ga.) Campaign August 16-September 22. Davis Cross Roads or Dug Gap September 11. Battle of Chickamauga September 19-21. Rossville Gap September 21. Siege of Chattanooga, Tenn., September 24-November 23. Chattanooga-Ringgold Campaign November 23-27. Lookout Mountain November 24-25. Mission Ridge November 25. Pea Vine Valley and Graysville November 26. Ringgold Gap, Taylor's Ridge, November 27. Demonstrations on Dalton, Ga., February 22-27, 1864. Tunnel Hill, Buzzard's Roost Gap and Rocky Faced Ridge February 23-25. Atlanta (Ga.) Campaign May 1-September 8. Demonstrations on Rocky Faced Ridge May 8-11. Buzzard's Roost Gap May 8-9. Battle of Resaca May 14-15. Advance on Dallas May 18-25. Operations on line of Pumpkin Vine Creek and battles about Dallas, New Hope Church and Allatoona Hills May 25-June 5. Pickett's Mills May 27. Operations about Marietta and against Kenesaw Mountain June 10-July 2. Pine Hill June 11-14. Lost Mountain June 15-17. Assault on Kenesaw June 27. Ruff's Station, Smyrna Camp Ground, July 4. Chattahoochie River May 5-17. Buckhead, Nancy's Creek, July 18. Peach Tree Creek July 19-20. Siege of Atlanta July 22-August 25. Utoy Creek August 5-7. Flank movement on Jonesboro August 25-30. Near Red Oak August 29. Battle of Jonesboro August 31-September 1. Operations against Hood in North Georgia and North Alabama September 29-November 3. March to the sea November 15-December 10. Siege of Savannah December 10-21. Campaign of the Carolinas January to April, 1865. Near Rocky Mount, S. C., February 28. Taylor's Hole Creek, Averysboro, N. C., March 16. Battle of Bentonville March 19-21. Occupation of Goldsboro March 24. Advance on Raleigh April 10-14. Occupation of Raleigh April 14. Bennett's House April 26. Surrender of Johnston and his army. March to Washington, D. C., via Richmond, Va., April 29-May 20. Grand Review May 24. Mustered out June 6, 1865.

Regiment lost during service 2 Officers and 52 Enlisted men killed and mortally wounded and 1 Officer and 144 Enlisted men by disease. Total 199.

95th REGIMENT INFANTRY.

Organized at Camp Chase, Columbus, Ohio, and mustered in August 19, 1862. Moved to Lexington, Ky., August 20. Attached to Cruft's Brigade, Army of Kentucky, Dept. of the Ohio. Battle of Richmond, Ky., August 29-30. Regiment mostly captured. Exchanged November 20, 1862. Reorganizing at Camp Chase, Ohio, till, March, 1863. Left State for Memphis, Tenn., March 25. Moved from Memphis, Tenn., to Young's Point, La., and Ducksport Landing March 29-April 1. Attached to 1st Brigade, 3rd Division, 15th Army Corps, Army of the Tennessee, to December, 1863. 1st Brigade, 1st Division, 16th Army Corps, to December, 1864. 1st Brigade, 1st Division, Detachment Army of the Tennessee, Dept. of the Cumberland, to February, 1865. 1st Brigade, 1st Division, 16th Army Corps (New), Military Division West Mississippi, to August, 1865.

SERVICE.—Operations against Vicksburg, Miss., April 2-July 4. Moved to join army in rear of Vicksburg, Miss., May 2-14. Mississippi Springs May 13. Baldwyn's Ferry May 13. Jackson May 14. Siege of Vicksburg May 18-July 4. Assaults on Vicksburg May 19 and 22. Expedition to Mechanicsburg May 26-June 4. Advance on Jackson, Miss., July 4-10. Siege of Jackson July 10-17. Camp at Big Black till November. Expedition to Canton October 14-20. Bogue Chitto Creek October 17. Ordered to Memphis, Tenn., November 12, and guard Memphis & Charleston Railroad near that city till February, 1864. Lafayette, Tenn., December 27, 1863 (Detachment). Expedition to Wyatt's, Miss., February 6-18. Coldwater Ferry February 8. Near Senatobia February 8-9. Hickahala Creek February 10. Duty at Memphis till June. Sturgis' Expedition from Memphis to Ripley April 30-May 9. Sturgis' Expedition to Guntown, Miss., June 1-13. Brice's or

Tishamingo Creek, near Guntown, June 10. Davis Mills June 12. Smith's Expedition to Tupelo, Miss., July 5-21. Camargo's Cross Roads, near Harrisburg, July 13. Harrisburg, near Tupelo, July 14-15. Old Town or Tishamingo Creek July 15. Smith's Expedition to Oxford, Miss., August 1-30. Abbeville August 23. Moved to Duvall's Bluff, Ark., September 1. March through Arkansas and Missouri in pursuit of Price September 17-November 16. Moved to Nashville, Tenn., November 21-December 1. Little Harpeth December 6. Battle of Nashville December 15-16. Pursuit of Hood to the Tennessee River December 17-28. At Eastport, Miss., till February, 1865. Moved to New Orleans, La., February 9-22, thence to Mobile Point, Ala. Campaign against Mobile, Ala., and its defences March 17-April 12. Siege of Spanish Fort and Fort Blakely March 26-April 8. Assault and capture of Fort Blakely April 9. Occupation of Mobile April 12. March to Montgomery April 13-26. Duty there and in the Depts. of Alabama and Mississippi till August. Mustered out August 19, 1865.

Regiment lost during service 1 Officer and 58 Enlisted men killed and mortally wounded and 2 Officers and 215 Enlisted men by disease. Total 276.

96th REGIMENT INFANTRY.

Organized at Camp Delaware, Ohio, and mustered in August 29, 1862. Ordered to Cincinnati, Ohio, September 1, thence to Covington and Newport, Ky., September 3, and duty there during threatened attack on Cincinnati by Kirby Smith. Attached to 2nd Brigade, 2nd Division, Army of Kentucky, Dept. of Ohio, to October, 1862. 1st Brigade, 1st Division, Army of Kentucky, to November, 1862. 1st Brigade, Right Wing 13th Army Corps (Old), Dept. of the Tennessee, to December, 1862. 1st Brigade, 1st Division, Sherman's Yazoo Expedition, to January, 1862. 1st Brigade, 10th Division, 13th Army Corps, Army of the Tennessee, to August, 1863. 1st Brigade, 4th Division, 13th Army Corps, Army of the Tennessee and Army of the Gulf, to March, 1864. 2nd Brigade, 4th Division, 13th Army Corps, to June, 1864. 3rd Brigade, 3rd Division, 19th Army Corps, Dept. of the Gulf, to December, 1864. U. S. forces, mouth of White River, Reserve Corps, Military Division West Mississippi, to February, 1865. 1st Brigade, 3rd Division, Reserve Corps, February, 1865. 1st Brigade, 3rd Division, 13th Army Corps, Military Division West Mississippi, to July, 1865.

SERVICE.—Moved to Falmouth, Ky., October 8, 1862, thence to Nicholasville October 23. Moved to Louisville, Ky., thence to Memphis, Tenn., November 13-22. Sherman's Yazoo Expedition December 20, 1862, to January 3, 1863. Landed at Milliken's Bend, La., and Expedition to Dallas Station, on Vicksburg & Shreveport Railroad, and destruction of railroad and stores December 25-26, 1862. Chickasaw Bayou December 26-28. Chickasaw Bluff December 29. Expedition to Arkansas Post, Ark., January 3-10, 1863. Assault and capture of Fort Hindman, Arkansas Post, January 10-11. Moved to Young's Point January 17, and duty there till March 10. Expedition to Greenville, Miss., and Cypress Bend, Ark., February 14-26. Moved to Milliken's Bend, La., March 10, and duty there till April 25. Movement on Bruinsburg and turning Grand Gulf April 25-30. Battle of Magnolia Hills, Port Gibson, Miss., May 1. Battle of Champion's Hill May 16. Siege of Vicksburg, Miss., May 18-July 4. Assaults on Vicksburg May 19 and 22. Advance on Jackson, Miss., July 4-10. Siege of Jackson July 10-17. Camp at Vicksburg till August 26. Ordered to New Orleans, La., August 26. Expedition from Carrollton to New and Amite Rivers September 24-29. At Brashear City October 3. Western Louisiana Campaign October 3-November 30. Grand Coteau November 3. Moved to Algiers December 13, thence embark for Texas December 18. Duty at Du Crow's Point, Texas, till March, 1864. Moved to Algiers, La., March 1-6. Red River Campaign March 10-May 22. Advance from Franklin to Alexandria March 14-26. Skirmish at Bayou de Paul, Carroll's Mills, April 8. Battle of Sabine Cross Roads April 8. Monett's Bluff, Cane River Crossing, April 23.

Operations about Alexandria April 26-May 13. Construction of dam at Alexandria April 30-May 10. Retreat to Morganza May 13-20. Mansura May 16. Moved to Baton Rouge May 28, and duty there till July 20. Moved to Algiers July 20, thence to Dauphin Island, Ala. Operations in Mobile Bay against Forts Gaines and Morgan August 2-23. Siege and capture of Fort Gaines August 3-8. Siege of capture of Fort Morgan August 9-23. Moved to Morganza September 1. Raid to Greenville Farms September 4. Moved to mouth of White River November 1, and duty there till February 4, 1865. Consolidated to 4 Companies November 18, 1864. Moved to Kennersville, La., February 4, 1865, thence to Mobile Point February 16. Campaign against Mobile and its defences March 17-April 13. Siege of Spanish Fort and Fort Blakely March 26-April 8. Assault and capture of Fort Blakely April 9. Occupation of Mobile April 12. Expedition to Tombigbee River and McIntosh Bluffs April 13-May 9. Duty at Mobile till July. Mustered out July 7, 1865.

Regiment lost during service 2 Officers and 46 Enlisted men killed and mortally wounded and 5 Officers and 286 Enlisted men by disease. Total 339.

97th REGIMENT INFANTRY.

Organized at Zanesville, Ohio, September 1, 1862. Moved to Covington, Ky., September 7, thence to Louisville, Ky., September 20. Attached to 21st Brigade, 6th Division, Army of the Ohio, September, 1862. 21st Brigade, 6th Division, 2nd Corps, Army Ohio, to November, 1862. 2nd Brigade, 1st Division, Left Wing 14th Army Corps, Army of the Cumberland, to January, 1863. 2nd Brigade, 1st Division, 21st Army Corps, Army of the Cumberland, to October, 1863. 2nd Brigade, 2nd Division, 4th Army Corps, Army of the Cumberland, to June, 1865.

SERVICE.—Pursuit of Bragg into Kentucky October 1-15, 1862. Battle of Perryville, Ky., October 8 (Reserve). March to Nashville, Tenn., October 16-November 21, and duty there till December 26. Action at Kimbrough's Mill, Mill Creek, December 6. Advance on Murfreesboro December 26-30. Battle of Stone's River December 30-31, 1862, and January 1-3, 1863. Duty at Murfreesboro till June. Reconnoissance to Nolensville and Versailles January 13-15. Expedition to McMinnville April 20-30. Middle Tennessee or Tullahoma Campaign June 23-July 7. Passage of the Cumberland Mountains and Tennessee River and Chickamauga (Ga.) Campaign August 16-September 22. Occupation of Chattanooga, Tenn., September 9. First Regiment to enter city and assigned to duty as its garrison. Siege of Chattanooga September 24-November 23. Chattanooga-Ringgold Campaign November 23-27. Orchard Knob November 23-24. Mission Ridge November 25. Pursuit to Graysville November 26-27. March to relief of Knoxville, Tenn., November 28-December 8. Operations in East Tennessee till April, 1864. Atlanta (Ga.) Campaign May 1 to September 8. Demonstrations on Rocky Faced Ridge and Dalton, Ga., May 8-13. Buzzard's Roost Gap May 8-9. Battle of Resaca May 14-15. Adairsville May 17. Near Kingston May 18-19. Near Cassville May 19. Advance on Dallas May 22-25. Operations on line of Pumpkin Vine Creek and battles about Dallas, New Hope Church and Allatoona Hills May 25-June 5. Operations about Marietta and against Kenesaw Mountain June 10-July 2. Pine Hill June 11-14. Lost Mountain June 15-17. Ackworth June 18. Assault on Kenesaw June 27. Ruff's Station, Smyrna Camp Ground, July 4. Chattahoochie River July 5-17. Buckhead, Nancy's Creek, July 18. Peach Tree Creek July 19-20. Siege of Atlanta July 22-August 25. Flank movement on Jonesboro August 25-30. Battle of Jonesboro August 31-September 1. Lovejoy Station September 2-6. Operations against Hood in North Georgia and North Alabama September 29-November 3. Nashville Campaign November-December. Columbia, Duck River, November 24-27. Battle of Franklin November 30. Battle of Nashville December 15-16. Pursuit of Hood to the Tennessee River December 17-28. Moved to Huntsville, Ala., and duty there till March, 1865. Operations in East Tennessee March 15-April 22. Moved to Nashville, Tenn., and duty there till June. Mustered out June 10, 1865.

Regiment lost during service 1 Officer and 92 Enlisted men killed and mortally wounded and 1 Officer and 160 Enlisted men by disease. Total 254.

98th REGIMENT INFANTRY.

Organized at Steubenville, Ohio, August 20, 1862. Ordered to Covington, Ky., August 23, thence to Lexington, Ky., August 27. Retreat to Louisville August 30-September 5. Attached to 34th Brigade, 10th Division, Army of the Ohio, September, 1862. 34th Brigade, 10th Division, 1st Army Corps, Army Ohio, to November, 1862. District of West Kentucky, Dept. of the Ohio, to February, 1863. Reed's Brigade, Baird's Division, Army of Kentucky, Dept. of the Cumberland, to June, 1863. 2nd Brigade, 1st Division, Reserve Corps, Army of the Cumberland, to October, 1863. 2nd Brigade, 2nd Division, 14th Army Corps, Army of the Cumberland, to June, 1865.

SERVICE.—Pursuit of Bragg into Kentucky October 1-15, 1862. Battle of Perryville October 8. Moved to Lebanon, Ky., and duty there till December. Operations against Morgan, December 23, 1862, to January 3, 1863. Moved to Louisville, Ky., thence to Nashville, Tenn., February 9. Occupation of Franklin, Tenn., February 12, and duty there till June. Middle Tennessee or Tullahoma Campaign June 23-July 7. At Wartrace till August 25. Passage of Cumberland Mountains and Tennessee River and Chickamauga (Ga.) Campaign August 25-September 22. Battle of Chickamauga September 19-21. Siege of Chattanooga, Tenn., September 24-November 23. Chattanooga-Ringgold Campaign November 23-27. Orchard Knob November 23. Tunnel Hill November 24-25. Mission Ridge November 25. March to relief of Knoxville, Tenn., November 28-December 24. Duty at Rossville, Ga., till May, 1864. Demonstration on Dalton, Ga., February 22-27, 1864. Atlanta (Ga.) Campaign Tunnel Hill May 6-7. Demonstration on Rocky Faced Ridge May 8-11. Buzzard's Roost Gap May 8-9. Battle of Resaca May 14-15. Advance on Dallas May 18-25. Operations on line of Pumpkin Vine Creek and battles about Dallas, New Hope Church and Allatoona Hills May 25-June 5. Operations about Marietta and against Kenesaw Mountain June 10-July 2. Pine Hill June 11-14. Lost Mountain June 15-17. Assault on Kenesaw June 27. Ruff's Station, Smyrna Camp Ground, July 4. Chattahoochie River July 5-17. Peach Tree Creek July 19-20. Siege of Atlanta July 22-August 25. Utoy Creek August 5-7. Flank movement on Jonesboro August 25-30. Battle of Jonesboro August 31-September 1. Operations against Forest and Hood in North Georgia and North Alabama September 29-November 3. March to the sea November 15-December 10. Siege of Savannah December 10-21. Campaign of the Carolinas January to April, 1865. Taylor's Hole Creek, Averysboro, N. C., March 16. Battle of Bentonville March 19-21. Occupation of Goldsboro March 24. Advance on Raleigh April 10-14. Occupation of Raleigh April 14. Bennett's House April 26. Surrender of Johnston and his army. March to Washington, D. C., via Richmond, Va., April 29-May 19. Grand Review May 24. Mustered out June 1, 1865.

Regiment lost during service 10 Officers and 110 Enlisted men killed and mortally wounded and 2 Officers and 125 Enlisted men by disease. Total 247.

99th REGIMENT INFANTRY.

Organized at Camp Lima, Allen County, Ohio, and mustered in August 26, 1862. Ordered to Lexington, Ky., August 31, thence moved to Cynthiana, Ky., September 3, thence to Covington, Ky., and to Louisville, Ky., September 17. Attached to 23rd Brigade, 5th Division, Army of the Ohio, September, 1862. 23rd Brigade, 5th Division, 2nd Corps, Army Ohio, to November, 1862. 3rd Brigade, 3rd Division, Left Wing 14th Army Corps, Army of the Cumberland, to January, 1863. 3rd

Brigade, 3rd Division, 21st Army Corps, Army of the Cumberland, to October, 1863. 2nd Brigade, 1st Division, 4th Army Corps, Army of the Cumberland, to June, 1864. 2nd Brigade, 1st Division, 23rd Army Corps, Army Ohio, June, 1864. 4th Brigade, 2nd Division, 23rd Army Corps, to August, 1864. 1st Brigade, 2nd Division, 23rd Army Corps, to December, 1864.

SERVICE.—Pursuit of Bragg into Kentucky October 1-15. Battle of Perryville, Ky., October 8 (Reserve). March to Nashville, Tenn., October 16-November 7, and duty there till December 26. Advance on Murfreesboro, Tenn., December 26-30. Battle of Stone's River December 30-31, 1862, and January 1-3, 1863. Duty at Murfreesboro till June. Middle Tennessee or Tullahoma Campaign June 23-July 7. March to McMinnville, and duty there till August 16. Passage of the Cumberland Mountains and Tennessee River and Chickamauga (Ga.) Campaign August 16-September 22. Battle of Chickamauga September 19-20. Siege of Chattanooga September 24-November 23. Re-opening Tennessee River October 26-29. Chattanooga-Ringgold Campaign November 23-27. Orchard Knob November 23. Lookout Mountain November 23-24. Mission Ridge November 25. Pigeon Hills November 26. Ringgold Gap, Taylor's Ridge, November 27. Camp at Shellmound till February, 1864. Demonstration on Dalton, Ga., February 22-27. Tunnel Hill, Buzzard's Roost Gap, and Rocky Faced Ridge February 23-25. At Cleveland till May. Atlanta (Ga.) Campaign May 1-September 8. Tunnel Hill May 6-7. Demonstration on Rocky Raced Ridge May 8-11. Buzzard's Roost Gap May 8-9. Demonstrations on Dalton May 9-13. Battle of Resaca May 14-15. Near Kingston May 18-19. Near Cassville May 19. Advance on Dallas May 22-25. Operations on line of Pumpkin Vine Creek and battles about Dallas, New Hope Church and Allatoona Hills May 25-June 5. Operations about Marietta and against Kenesaw Mountain June 10-July 2. Pine Hill June 11-14. Lost Mountain June 15-17. Muddy Creek June 17. Noyes Creek June 19. Kolb's Farm June 22. Assault on Kenesaw June 27. Nickajack Creek July 2-5. Ruff's Mills July 3-4. Chattahoochie River July 5-17. Decatur July 19. Siege of Atlanta July 22-August 25. Utoy Creek August 5-7. Flank movement on Jonesboro August 25-30. Battle of Jonesboro August 31-September 1. Lovejoy Station September 2-6. Pursuit of Hood into Alabama October 3-26. Nashville Campaign November-December. Columbia, Duck River, November 24-27. Battle of Franklin November 30. Battle of Nashville December 15-16. Pursuit of Hood to the Tennessee River December 17-28. Consolidated with 50th Ohio Infantry December 31, 1864.

Regiment lost during service 4 Officers and 80 Enlisted men killed and mortally wounded and 2 Officers and 256 Enlisted men by disease. Total 342.

100th REGIMENT INFANTRY.

Organized at Toledo, Ohio, July to September, 1862. Ordered to Cincinnati, Ohio, September 8, thence to Covington, Ky., and duty there till October 8. Attached to 2nd Brigade, 1st Division, Army of Kentucky, Dept. of the Ohio, to October, 1862. 2nd Brigade, 2nd Division, Army of Kentucky, to January, 1863. District of Central Kentucky, Dept. Ohio, to June, 1863. 2nd Brigade, 1st Division, 23rd Army Corps, Army Ohio, to July, 1863. 2nd Brigade, 4th Division, 23rd Army Corps, to August, 1863. 1st Brigade, 3rd Division, 23rd Army Corps, to February, 1865. 1st Brigade, 3rd Division, 23rd Army Corps, Dept. of North Carolina, to June, 1865.

SERVICE.—Ordered to Lexington, Ky., October 8, 1862, thence to Richmond, Ky., December 1, and to Danville, Ky., December 26. To Frankfort, Ky., January 3, 1863. Duty at various points in Central Kentucky till August. Expedition to Monticello and operations in Southeastern Kentucky April 26-May 12. Burnside's Campaign in East Tennessee August 16-October 17. Telford Station and Limestone September 8. (240 men captured at Telford Station while guarding railroad.) Knoxville Campaign November 4-December 23.

Siege of Knoxville November 17-December 5. Pursuit to Blain's Cross Roads. Duty at Blain's Cross Roads till April, 1864. Atlanta (Ga.) Campaign May 1-September 8. Demonstrations on Rocky Faced Ridge May 8-11. Battle of Resaca May 14-15. Cartersville May 20. Operations on line of Pumpkin Vine Creek and battles about Dallas, New Hope Church and Allatoona Hills May 25-June 5. Operations about Marietta and against Kenesaw Mountain June 10-July 2. Lost Mountain June 15-17. Muddy Creek June 17. Noyes Creek June 19. Cheyney's Farm June 22. Near Marietta June 23. Assault on Kenesaw June 27. Nickajack Creek July 2-5. Chattahoochie River July 5-17. Peach Tree Creek July 19-20. Siege of Atlanta July 22-August 25. Utoy Creek August 5-7. Flank movement on Jonesboro August 25-30. Battle of Jonesboro August 31-September 1. Lovejoy Station September 2-6. Duty at Decatur till October 4. Pursuit of Hood into Northern Alabama October 4-26. Nashville Campaign November-December. Columbia, Duck River, November 24-27. Battle of Franklin November 30. Battle of Nashville December 15-16. Pursuit of Hood to the Tennessee River December 17-28. At Clifton, Tenn., till January 16, 1865. Movement to Washington, D. C., thence to Federal Point, N. C., January 16-February 9. Fort Anderson February 18-19. Town Creek February 19-20. Capture of Wilmington February 22. Campaign of the Carolinas March-April. Advance on Goldsboro, N. C., March 6-21. Occupation of Goldsboro March 21. Advance on Raleigh April 10-14. Near Raleigh April 13. Bennett's House April 26. Surrender of Johnston and his army. Duty at Greensboro, N. C. till June. Mustered out June 20, and discharged at Cleveland, Ohio, July 1, 1865.

Regiment lost during service 3 Officers and 90 Enlisted men killed and mortally wounded and 6 Officers and 268 Enlisted men by disease. Total 317.

101st REGIMENT INFANTRY.

Organized at Monroeville, Ohio, August 30, 1862. Left State for Covington, Ky., September 4, thence moved to Louisville, Ky., September 24. Attached to 31st Brigade, 9th Division, Army of the Ohio, September, 1862. 31st Brigade, 9th Division, 3rd Corps, Army Ohio, to November, 1862. 2nd Brigade, 1st Division, Right Wing 14th Army Corps, Army of the Cumberland, to January, 1863. 2nd Brigade, 1st Division, 20th Army Corps, Army of the Cumberland, to October, 1863. 1st Brigade, 1st Division, 4th Army Corps, Army of the Cumberland, to June, 1865.

SERVICE.—Pursuit of Bragg into Kentucky October 1-15. Battle of Perryville, Ky., October 8. March to Nashville, Tenn., October 16-November 7, and duty there till December 26. Advance on Murfreesboro, Tenn., December 26-30. Nolensville December 26. Battle of Stone's River December 30-31, 1862, and January 1-3, 1863. Duty at Murfreesboro till June. Reconnoissance from Murfreesboro March 6-7. Reconnoissance to Versailles March 9-14. Operations on Edgefield Pike, near Murfreesboro, June 4. Middle Tennessee or Tullahoma Campaign June 23-July 7. Liberty Gap June 24-27. Occupation of Middle Tennessee till August 16. Passage of the Cumberland Mountains and Tennessee River, and Chickamauga (Ga.) Campaign August 16-September 22. Battle of Chickamauga September 19-20. Siege of Chattanooga, Tenn., September 24-October 26. Reopening Tennessee River October 26-28. Moved to Bridgeport, Ala., October 28, and duty there till January 16, 1864, and at Ooltewah till May. Atlanta (Ga.) Campaign May to September. Tunnel Hill May 6-7. Demonstrations on Rocky Faced Ridge and Dalton May 8-13. Buzzard's Roost Gap May 8-9. Battle of Resaca May 14-15. Near Kingston May 18-19. Near Cassville May 19. Advance on Dallas May 22-25. Operations on line of Pumpkin Vine Creek and battles about Dallas, New Hope Church and Allatoona Hills May 25-June 5. Operations about Marietta and against Kenesaw Mountain June 10-July 2. Pine Hill June 11-14. Lost Mountain June 15-17. Assault on Kenesaw June 27. Ruff's Station, Smyrna Camp Ground, July 4. Chattahoochie River July 5-17.

Peach Tree Creek July 19-20. Siege of Atlanta July 22-August 25. Flank movement on Jonesboro August 25-30. Battle of Jonesboro August 31-September 1. Lovejoy Station September 2-6. Operations against Hood in North Georgia and North Alabama October 3-26. Nashville Campaign November-December. Columbia, Duck River, November 24-27. Battle of Franklin November 30. Battle of Nashville December 15-16. Pursuit of Hood to the Tennessee River December 17-28. Moved to Huntsville, Ala., and duty there till March, 1865. Operations in East Tennessee March 15-April 22. Moved to Nashville, Tenn., and duty there till June. Mustered out June 12, 1865.

Regiment lost during service 9 Officers and 86 Enlisted men killed and mortally wounded and 1 Officer and 140 Enlisted men by disease. Total 236.

102nd REGIMENT INFANTRY.

Organized at Mansfield, Ohio, and mustered in August 18, 1862. Moved to Covington, Ky., September 4. Attached to 38th Brigade, 12th Division, Army of the Ohio, to November, 1862. District of Western Kentucky, Dept. of the Ohio, to December, 1862. Clarksville, Tenn., Dept. of the Cumberland, to June, 1862. 1st Brigade, 3rd Division, Reserve Corps, Dept. of the Cumberland, to October, 1863. Unattached, District of Nashville, Tenn., Dept. of the Cumberland, to January, 1864. 1st Brigade, 3rd Division, 12th Army Corps, Army of the Cumberland, to April, 1864. 1st Brigade, 4th Division, 20th Army Corps, Dept. of the Cumberland, to April, 1865. District of North Alabama, Dept. of the Cumberland, to June, 1865.

SERVICE.—Regiment mustered in at Covington, Ky., September 6, 1862. Duty in the Defences of Cincinnati, Ohio, till September 22. Moved to Louisville, Ky., September 22, and duty there till October 5. Train guard to Shelbyville October 5-6. Pursuit of Bragg into Kentucky October 6-15. March to Bowling Green, Ky., and duty there guarding railroad to Nashville, Tenn., till December 19. Moved to Russellville December 19, thence to Clarksville, Tenn. Duty there and in vicinity, building bridges, forwarding supplies, etc., till September 23, 1863. Movements to repel Wheeler's Raid September 26-October 30. Moved to Nashville, Tenn., and duty there till April 26, 1864. Guard duty on Nashville & Chattanooga Railroad from Normandy to Dechard till June 6. Engaged in the defence of the line of the Tennessee River from Stevenson to Seven Mile Island June 10-September 1. Duty on cars protecting Tennessee & Alabama Railroad from Decatur, Ala., to Columbia, Tenn., September 1-15. Action at Athens September 23-24. Operations on the Tennessee River in rear of Hood's army October to December. Siege of Decatur October 26-29. Evacuation of Decatur November 25. March to Stevenson, Ala., November 25-December 2, and duty there till May, 1865. Moved to Decatur, Ala., May 23, and duty there till June 30. Mustered out June 30, 1865.

Regiment lost during service 2 Officers and 11 Enlisted men killed and mortally wounded and 2 Officers and 247 Enlisted men by disease. Total 262.

103rd REGIMENT INFANTRY.

Organized at Cleveland, Ohio, August, 1862. Ordered to Kentucky September 3, 1862. Attached to 2nd Brigade, 1st Division, Army of Kentucky, Dept. of the Ohio, to October, 1862. 2nd Brigade, 2nd Division, Army of Kentucky, Dept. Ohio, January, 1863. 1st Brigade, District of Central Kentucky, Dept. Ohio, to June, 1863. 1st Brigade, 1st Division, 23rd Army Corps, Army of Ohio, to August, 1863. 2nd Brigade, 3rd Division, 23rd Army Corps, Army of Ohio, to February, 1865, and Dept. of North Carolina, to June, 1865.

SERVICE.—Pursuit of Kirby Smith to Lexington, Ky., September 18-22, 1862. Duty at Snow's Pond till October 6, and at Frankfort till May, 1863. Expedition to Monticello and operations in Southeastern Kentucky April 26-May 12, 1863. Action at Monticello May 1. Duty in Central Kentucky till August. Burnside's Campaign in East Tennessee August 16-October 17. At Greenville till September 19. Carter's Depot September 20-21. Jonesboro September 21. Knoxville Campaign November 4-December 23. Siege of Knoxville November 17-December 5. Operations about Dandridge January 16-17, 1864. Duty at Blain's Cross Roads till April, 1864. Atlanta (Ga.) Campaign May 1 to September 8. Demonstrations on Rocky Faced Ridge and Dalton, Ga., May 8-13. Battle of Resaca May 14-15. Cartersville May 20. Operations on line of Pumpkin Vine Creek and battles about Dallas, New Hope Church and Allatoona Hills May 25-June 5. Near Marietta June 1-9. Operations about Marietta and against Kenesaw Mountain June 10-July 2. Lost Mountain June 15-17. Muddy Creek June 17. Noyes Creek June 19. Cheyney's Farm June 22. Olley's Farm June 26-27. Assault on Kenesaw June 27. Nickajack Creek July 2-5. Chattahoochie River July 5-17. Isham's Ford, Chattahoochie River, July 8 (1st Regiment to cross). Decatur July 18-19. Siege of Atlanta July 22-August 25. Utoy Creek August 5-7. Flank movement on Jonesboro August 25-30. Near Rough and Ready August 31. Battle of Jonesboro August 31-September 1. Lovejoy Station September 2-6. Operations against Hood in Northern Georgia and Northern Alabama October. At Decatur till October 20. Nashville Campaign November-December. Columbia, Duck River, November 24-27. Battle of Franklin November 30. Battle of Nashville December 15-16. Pursuit of Hood to the Tennessee River December 17-28. At Clifton, Tenn., till January 16, 1865. Movement to Washington, D. C., thence to North Carolina January 16-February 9. Operations against Hoke, near Fort Fisher, N. C., February 11-14. Near Sugar Loaf Battery February 11. Fort Anderson, Cape Fear River, February 18-19. Town Creek February 19-20. Capture of Wilmington February 22. Campaign of the Carolinas March 1-April 26. Advance on Goldsboro March 6-21. Occupation of Goldsboro March 21. Advance on Raleigh April 10-14. Occupation of Raleigh April 14. Bennett's House April 26. Surrender of Johnston and his army. Duty at Raleigh, N. C., and in the Dept. of North Carolina till June. Mustered out June 12, 1865.

Regiment lost during service 2 Officers and 137 Enlisted men killed and mortally wounded and 3 Officers and 106 Enlisted men by disease. Total 248.

104th REGIMENT INFANTRY.

Organized at Camp Massillon, Ohio, and mustered in August 30, 1862. Moved to Covington, Ky., September 1, 1862. Attached to 2nd Brigade, 1st Division, Army of Kentucky, Dept. of the Ohio, to November, 1862. 2nd Brigade, 2nd Division, Army of Kentucky, to January, 1863. 1st Brigade, District of Central Kentucky, Dept. of Ohio, to June, 1863. 2nd Brigade, 1st Division, 23rd Army Corps, Dept. of Ohio, to July, 1863. 2nd Brigade, 4th Division, 23rd Army Corps, to August, 1863. 1st Brigade, 3rd Division, 23rd Army Corps, Army Ohio, to· February, 1865, and Dept. of North Carolina, to June, 1865.

SERVICE.—Defence of Cincinnati, Ohio, against Kirby Smith's threatened attack September 2-12, 1862. Skirmish at Fort Mitchell, Covington, Ky., September 10. Pursuit to Lexington, Ky., September 12-15. Duty at Lexington till December 6. Moved to Richmond and Danville, Ky., in pursuit of Morgan December 6-26. At Frankfort, Ky., till February, 1863. Operations in Central Kentucky till August. Expedition to Monticello and operations in Southeastern Kentucky April 26-May 12. Burnside's Campaign in East Tennessee, Campaign August 16-October 17. Expedition to Cumberland Gap September 4-7. Operations about Cumberland Gap September 7-10. Knoxville Campaign November 4-December 23. Siege of Knoxville November 17-December 5. Duty in East Tennessee till April, 1864. Atlanta (Ga.) Campaign May 1 to September 8. Demonstration on Rocky Faced Ridge and Dalton, Ga., May 8-13. Battle of Resaca May 14-15. Cartersville May 20. Operations on line of Pumpkin Vine Creek and battles about Dallas, New Hope Church and Allatoona Hills May 25-

June 5. Operations about Marietta and against Kenesaw Mountain June 10-July 2. Skirmishes about Lost Mountain June 11-14. Combats about Lost Mountain June 15-17. Noyes Creek June 19. Cheyney's Farm June 22. Ulley's Farm June 26-27. Assault on Kenesaw June 27. Nickajack Creek July 2-5. Chattahoochie River July 5-17. Buckhead, Nancy's Creek, July 18. Peach Tree Creek July 19-20. Siege of Atlanta July 22-August 25. Utoy Creek August 5-7. Flank movement on Jonesboro August 25-30. Battle of Jonesboro August 31-September 1. Lovejoy Station September 2-6. Operations against Hood in North Georgia and North Alabama September 29-November 3. Nashville Campaign November-December. Columbia, Duck River, November 24-27. Columbia Ford November 28-29. Battle of Franklin November 30. Battle of Franklin December 15-16. Pursuit of Hood to the Tennessee River December 17-28. At Clifton, Tenn., till January 15, 1865. Movement to Washington, D. C., thence to Federal Point, N. C., January 15-February 9. Operations against Hoke near Fort Fisher February 11-14. Orton's Pond February 18. Fort Anderson February 18-19. Town Creek February 19-20. Capture of Wilmington February 22. Campaign of the Carolinas March 1-April 26. Advance on Goldsboro March 6-21. Occupation of Goldsboro March 21. Advance on Raleigh April 10-14. Occupation of Raleigh April 14. Bennett's House April 26. Surrender of Johnston and his army. Duty at Raleigh till May 2, and at Greensboro till June. Mustered out June 17, 1865.

Regiment lost during service 3 Officers and 46 Enlisted men killed and mortally wounded and 4 Officers and 130 Enlisted men by disease. Total 183.

105th REGIMENT INFANTRY.

Organized at Cleveland, Ohio, and mustered in August 20, 1862. Ordered to Covington, Ky., August 21, 1862; thence to Lexington, Ky., August 25. March to relief of Nelson August 30. Retreat to Louisville, Ky., September 1-15. Attached to 33rd Brigade, 10th Division, Army of the Ohio, to September, 1862. 33rd Brigade, 10th Division, 2nd Corps, Army of the Ohio, to November, 1862. 1st Brigade, 5th Division (Centre), 14th Army Corps, Army of the Cumberland, to January, 1863. 1st Brigade, 5th Division, 14th Army Corps, Army of the Cumberland, to June, 1863. 2nd Brigade, 4th Division, 14th Army Corps, to October, 1863. 2nd Brigade, 3rd Division, 14th Army Corps, to July, 1865.

SERVICE.—Pursuit of Bragg into Kentucky October 1-12. Battle of Perryville, Ky., October 8. March to Munfordsville, Ky., October 12, and duty there till November 30. Expedition to Cave City October 31 and November 26. Moved to Bledsoe Creek November 30. Operations against Morgan December 22, 1862, to January 2, 1863. March to Nashville, Tenn., thence to Murfreesboro January 3-11, and duty there till June. Expedition to Auburn, Liberty and Alexandria February 3-5. Expedition to Woodbury March 3-8. Vaught's Hill, near Milton, March 20. Expedition to McMinnville April 20-30. Middle Tennessee (or Tullahoma) Campaign June 23-July 7. Hoover's Gap June 24-26. Occupation of Middle Tennessee till August 16. Passage of the Cumberland Mountains and Tennessee River and Chickamauga (Ga.) Campaign August 16-September 22. Shellmound August 21. Reconnoissance toward Chattanooga August 30-31. Battle of Chickamauga September 19-21. Siege of Chattanooga, Tenn., September 24-November 23. Chattanooga-Ringgold Campaign November 23-27. Orchard Knob November 23-24. Mission Ridge November 25. Demonstrations on Dalton, Ga., February 22-27, 1864. Tunnel Hill, Buzzard's Roost Gap and Rocky Faced Ridge February 23-25. Reconnoissance from Ringgold toward Tunnel Hill April 29. Atlanta (Ga.) Campaign May 1 to September 8. Demonstrations on Rocky Faced Ridge May 8-11. Battle of Resaca May 14-15. Advance on Dallas May 18-25. Operations on line of Pumpkin Vine Creek and battles about Dallas, New Hope Church and Allatoona Hills

May 25-June 5. Operations about Marietta and against Kenesaw June 10-July 2. Pine Hill June 11-14. Lost Mountain June 15-17. Assault on Kenesaw June 27. Ruff's Station July 4. Chattahoochie River July 5-17. Peach Tree Creek July 19-20. Siege of Atlanta July 22-August 25. Utoy Creek August 5-7. Flank movement on Jonesboro August 25-30. Battle of Jonesboro August 31-September 1. Operations against Hood in North Georgia and North Alabama September 29-November 3. March to the sea November 15-December 10. Siege of Savannah December 10-15. Campaign of the Carolinas January to April, 1865. Fayetteville, N. C., March 11. Battle of Bentonville March 19-21. Occupation of Goldsboro March 24. Advance on Raleigh April 10-14. Occupation of Raleigh April 14. Bennett's House April 26. Surrender of Johnston and his army. March to Washington, D. C., via Richmond, Va., April 29-May 20. Grand Review May 24. Mustered out June 3, 1865.

Regiment lost during service 3 Officers and 104 Enlisted men killed and mortally wounded and 7 Officers and 126 Enlisted men by disease. Total 240.

106th REGIMENT INFANTRY.

Organized at Camp Dennison, Ohio, and mustered in August 26, 1862. Ordered to Covington. Ky., September 4. Defence of Covington, Ky., and Cincinnati, Ohio, against Kirby Smith's threatened attack September 4-12. Ordered to Louisville, Ky., September 18. Attached to 39th Brigade, 12th Division, Army of the Ohio, to November, 1862. District of Western Kentucky, Dept. of Ohio, to December, 1862. Prisoners of war to March, 1863. District of Western Kentucky, Dept. Ohio, to June, 1863. Post of Gallatin, Tenn., Dept. of the Cumberland, to May, 1864. Unassigned, 4th Division, 20th Army Corps, Dept. of the Cumberland, Garrison of Bridgeport, Ala., to July, 1864. 3rd Brigade, Defences of Nashville & Chattanooga Railroad, Dept. of the Cumberland, to February, 1865. Stevenson, Ala., District of North Alabama, Dept. of the Cumberland, to June, 1865.

SERVICE.—March to Frankfort, Ky., October 3-9, 1862, and duty there till October 24. March to Bowling Green, Ky., October 24-November 4, thence to Glasgow, Ky., November 19. Action near Tompkinsville November 10. Moved to Hartsville, Tenn., November 28. Battle of Hartsville December 7. Regiment captured and paroled. Exchanged January 12, 1863. At Camp Parole, Columbus, Ohio, till March. Ordered to Lexington, Ky., March 24, thence to Frankfort, and duty there till May, operating against guerrillas. Moved to Nashville, Tenn., May 1-4, thence to Gallatin, Tenn., June, and guard duty along Louisville & Nashville Railroad from Nashville to borders of Kentucky till May, 1864. Butler's Mill, near Buck Lodge, June 30 (Detachment). Moved to Bridgeport, Ala., May 4. and garrison duty there till January, 1865. Skirmish at Cane Creek, Ala., June 10, 1864. At Stevenson, Ala., January to June, 1865. Mustered out June 29, 1865.

Regiment lost during service 3 Officers and 27 Enlisted men killed and mortally wounded and 1 Officer and 21 Enlisted men by disease. Total 52.

107th REGIMENT INFANTRY.

Organized at Camp Taylor, Cleveland, Ohio, and mustered in September 9, 1862. Moved to Covington, Ky., September 28, and duty in the Defences of Cincinnati, Ohio, till October 5, 1862. At Delaware, Ohio, October 5-12. Ordered to Washington, D. C., October 12. Attached to 2nd Brigade, 3rd Division, 11th Army Corps, Army of the Potomac, to December, 1862. 2nd Brigade, 1st Division, 11th Army Corps, to July, 1863. 1st Brigade, 1st Division, 11th Army Corps, to August, 1863. 1st Brigade, Gordon's Division, Folly Island, S. C., 10th Army Corps, Dept. of the South. to January, 1864. 2nd Brigade, Gordon's Division, Folly Island, S. C., Northern District, Dept. of the South, to February, 1864. 1st Brigade, Ames' Division, District of Florida, Dept. of the South, to April, 1864. District of Florida, Dept. of

the South. to October, 1864. 4th Separate Brigade, District of Florida, Dept. of the South, to November, 1864. 1st Brigade, Coast Division, Dept. of the South, to December, 1864. 3rd Separate Brigade, Dept. of the South, to January, 1865. 1st Separate Brigade, Northern District, Dept. of the South, to March, 1865. 1st Separate Brigade, District of Charleston, Dept. of the South, to July, 1865.

SERVICE.—Duty in the Defences of Washington, D. C., till December, 1862. March to Fredericksburg, Va., to support of Burnside December 8-15. Burnside's 2nd Campaign, "Mud March," January 20-24, 1863. At Stafford Court House till April. Chancellorsville Campaign April 27-May 6. Battle of Chancellorsville May 1-5. Gettysburg (Pa.) Campaign June 11-July 24. Battle of Gettysburg July 1-3. Pursuit of Lee July 5-24. Hagerstown, Md., July 11-13. Ordered to Dept. of the South and sailed for Folly Island, S. C., August 1. Siege operations against Fort Wagner, Morris Island, S. C., August 9-September 7. Picket and fatigue duty on Folly Island, S. C., and operating against Charleston, S. C., till February, 1864. Expedition to Johns and James Islands February 6-14. Moved to Jacksonville, Fla., February 23. Duty there and in the District of Florida till December. Skirmishing near Jacksonville May 1 and 28. Expedition from Jacksonville to Camp Milton May 31-June 3. At Fernandina, Fla., July-August. Return to Jacksonville and duty there till December. Moved to South Carolina December 8. Pocotaligo Bridge December 29. Expedition to destroy Charleston & Savannah Railroad January 14-16, 1865. Occupation of Charleston March 10. Potter's Expedition to Camden, S. C., April 5-25. Operations about Sumpter and Statesburg April 9-15. Statesburg April 15. Occupation of Camden April 17. Boykin's Mills April 18. Denkin's Mills and Beech Creek, near Statesburg, April 19. Provost duty at Georgetown and at Charleston till July. Mustered out July 10, 1865. Recruits transferred to 25th Ohio Infantry.

Regiment lost during service 3 Officers and 54 Enlisted men killed and mortally wounded and 2 Officers and 74 Enlisted men by disease. Total 133.

108th REGIMENT INFANTRY.

Organized at Camp Dennison, Ohio, August, 1862. Ordered to Covington, Ky., August 21; thence moved to Louisville, Ky. Attached to 39th Brigade, 12th Division, Army of the Ohio, September to November, 1862. District of Western Kentucky, Dept. of the Ohio, to December, 1862. Prisoners of war to March, 1863. District of Central Kentucky, Dept. of the Ohio, to June, 1863. 3rd Brigade, 2nd Division, Reserve Corps, Dept. of the Cumberland, to October, 1863. Unassigned, Dept. of the Cumberland, to December, 1863. 2nd Brigade, 2nd Division, 14th Army Corps, Army of the Cumberland, to July, 1865.

SERVICE.—March to Frankfort, Ky., October 3-9, 1862; thence to Bowling Green, Ky., October 24-November 4. Moved to Glasgow November 10, and to Tompkinsville November 22. To Hartsville, Tenn., November 28. Battle of Hartsville (Morgan's attack) December 7. Regiment surrendered by Colonel Moore. Paroled December 8 and Exchanged January 12, 1863. Regiment reorganized at Camp Dennison, Ohio, till March, 1863. Ordered to Lexington, Ky., March 24; thence to Frankfort, Ky., and duty there till May. Moved to Nashville, Tenn., May 1-4, and duty guarding Railroad to Chattanooga, Tenn., till September. Moved to Stevenson, Ala., September 6; thence march to Battle Creek and Anderson's Cross Roads, repairing road to Waldron's Ridge; thence march to Chattanooga, Tenn. Chattanooga-Ringgold Campaign November 23-27. Orchard Knob November 23. Tunnel Hill November 24-25. Mission Ridge November 25. Chickamauga Station November 26. March to relief of Knoxville November 28-December 8. Return to Chattanooga and duty at Rossville, Ga., till February, 1864. Demonstration on Dalton, Ga., February 22-27. Tunnel Hill, Buzzard's Roost Gap and Rocky Faced Ridge February

23-25. Atlanta (Ga.) Campaign May 1 to September 8.
Tunnel Hill May 6-7. Demonstration on Rocky Faced
Ridge May 8-11. Buzzard's Roost Gap May 8-9. Battle
of Resaca May 14-15. Rome May 17-18. Advance on
Dallas May 18-25. Operation on line of Pumpkin Vine
Creek and battles about Dallas, New Hope Church and
Allatoona Hills, May 25-June 5. Operations about Mari-
etta and against Kenesaw Mountain June 10-July 2.
Assault on Kenesaw June 27. Assigned to Train Guard
duty on Railroad till November. Dalton August 14-16.
March to the sea November 15-December 10. Sanders-
ville November 26. Siege of Savannah December 10-21.
Campaign of the Carolinas January to April, 1865.
Taylor's Hole Creek Averysboro, N. C., March 16. Bat-
tle of Bentonville March 19-21. Occupation of Goldsboro March 24. Advance on Raleigh April 10-14. Occupation of Raleigh April 14. Bennett's House April 26.
Surrender of Johnston and his army. March to Washington, D. C., April 29-May 19. Grand Review May 24.
Mustered out June 9, 1865.

Regiment lost during service 3 Officers and 22 Enlisted men killed and mortally wounded and 42 Enlisted men by disease. Total 67.

109th REGIMENT INFANTRY.

Organization of Regiment not completed.

110th REGIMENT INFANTRY.

Organized at Camp Piqua, Ohio, October 3, 1862.
Moved to Zanesville, Ohio, October 19; thence to Parkersburg, W. Va. Attached to Railroad Division, Clarksburg, W. Va., Middle Department, to January, 1863.
Milroy's Command, Winchester, Va., 8th Army Corps,
Middle Department, to March, 1863. 1st Brigade, 2nd
Division, 8th Army Corps, Middle Department, to June,
1863. 1st Brigade, Elliott's Command, 8th Army Corps,
to July, 1863. 2nd Brigade, 3rd Division, 3rd Army
Corps, Army of the Potomac, to March, 1864. 2nd Brigade, 3rd Division, 6th Army Corps, Army of the Potomac and Army of the Shenandoah, Middle Military
Division, to June, 1865.

SERVICE.—Moved to Clarksburg, W. Va., November
3, 1862; thence moved to New Creek November 25, and
to Moorefield December 13. Expedition to Winchester
December 28, 1862, to January 1, 1863, and duty there
till June. Reconnoissance toward Wardensville and
Strasburg April 20. Battle of Winchester June 13-15.
Retreat to Harper's Ferry June 15-16, thence to Washington, D. C., July 1-4. Moved to Frederick City, Md.,
and join Army of the Potomac July 5. Pursuit of Lee
to Manassas Gap, Va., July 1-24. Wapping Heights
July 23. Duty on line of the Rappahannock till August
15, and at New York during draft disturbances August
16-September 6. Bristoe Campaign October 9-22. Advance to line of the Rappahannock November 7-8.
Kelly's Ford November 7. Mine Run Campaign November 26-December 2. Payne's Farm November 27.
Demonstration on the Rapidan February 6-7, 1864. Campaign from the Rapidan to the James River May 3-June
15. Battles of the Wilderness May 5-7; Spottsylvania
May 8-12; Spottsylvania Court House May 12-21. Assault on the Salient, "Bloody Angle," May 12. North
Anna River May 23-26. On line of the Pamunkey May
26-28. Totopotomoy May 28-31. Cold Harbor June 1-
12. Before Petersburg June 18-July 6. Jerusalem Plank
Road June 22-23. Moved to Baltimore, Md., July 6-8.
Battle of Monocacy Junction, Md., July 9. Sheridan's
Shenandoah Valley Campaign August 7-November 28.
Charlestown August 29. Battle of Opequan, Winchester, September 19. Fisher's Hill September 22. Battle of Cedar Creek October 19. Duty at Kernstown
till December. Moved to Washington, D. C., thence
to Petersburg, Va., December 3-6. Siege of Petersburg
December 6, 1864, to April 2, 1865. Appomattox Campaign March 28-April 9, 1865. Fall of Petersburg April
2. Pursuit of Lee April 3-9. Sailor's Creek April 6.
Appomattox Court House April 9. Surrender of Lee
and his army. March to Danville, Va., April 17-27, and
duty there till May. Moved to Richmond, Va., May 16;

thence to Washington, D. C., May 24-June 2. Corps Review June 9. Mustered out June 25, 1865.

Regiment lost during service 10 Officers and 107 Enlisted men killed and mortally wounded and 2 Officers
and 111 Enlisted men by disease. Total 230.

111th REGIMENT INFANTRY.

Organized at Toledo, Ohio, and mustered in Septem-
ber 5, 1862. Moved to Covington, Ky., September 12.
Attached to 38th Brigade, 12th Division, Army of the
Ohio, September to November, 1862. District of West-
ern Kentucky, Dept. of the Ohio, to May, 1863. 1st
Brigade, 3rd Division, 23rd Army Corps, Army of the
Ohio, to August, 1863. 2nd Brigade, 2nd Division, 23rd
Army Corps, Army of the Ohio, to February, 1865, and
Dept. of North Carolina to June, 1865.

SERVICE.—Duty at Covington, Ky., September 13-25,
1862. Reconnoissance to Crittenden September 18-20.
Moved to Louisville, Ky., September 25. Pursuit of
Bragg to Crab Orchard, Ky., October 1-15. Moved to
Bowling Green, Ky., October 16, and duty there guarding railroad to Nashville, Tenn., till May 29, 1863. Skirmish at Negro Head Cut, near Woodburn's, April 27.
Moved to Glasgow, Ky., May 29, and duty there till
June 18. Pursuit of Morgan June 18-July 26. Burnside's Campaign in East Tennessee August 16-October
17. At Loudoun, Tenn., September 4 to November 14.
Knoxville Campaign November 4-December 23. Action
at Ruff's Ferry November 14. Near Loudon and Lenoir November 15. Campbell's Station November 16.
Siege of Knoxville November 17-December 5. Pursuit
of Longstreet to Blain's Cross Roads December 5-16. Operations about Dandridge January 16-17, 1864. Expedition to Flat Creek February 1. Near Knoxville February 13. At Mossy Creek till April 26. Atlanta (Ga.)
Campaign May 1 to September 8. Demonstrations on
Rocky Faced Ridge and Dalton May 8-13. Battle of
Resaca May 14-15. Advance on Dallas May 18-25. Operations on line of Pumpkin Vine Creek and battles
about Dallas, New Hope Church and Allatoona Hills
May 25-June 5. Ackworth June 2. Operations about
Marietta and against Kenesaw Mountain June 10-July
2. Lost Mountain June 15-17. Muddy Creek June 17.
Noyes Creek June 19. Kolb's Farm June 22. Assault
on Kenesaw June 27. Nickajack Creek July 2-5. Chat-
tahoochie River July 5-17. Decatur July 19. Howard
House July 20. Siege of Atlanta July 22-August 25.
Utoy Creek August 5-7. Flank movement on Jonesboro
August 25-30. Battle of Jonesboro August 31-Septem-
ber 1. Lovejoy Station September 2-6. At Decatur
September 8 to October 4. Operations against Hood
in North Georgia and North Alabama October 4-26. At
Johnsonville till November 20. Nashville Campaign
November-December. Columbia, Duck River, Novem-
ber 24-27. Columbia Ford November 28-29. Battle of
Franklin November 30. Battle of Nashville December
15-16. Pursuit of Hood to the Tennessee River De-
cember 17-28. At Clifton, Tenn., till January 7, 1865.
Movement to Washington, D. C., thence to Fort Fisher,
N. C., January 7-February 9. Operations against Hoke
February 11-14. Fort Anderson February 18-19. Town
Creek February 19-20. Capture of Wilmington Febru-
ary 22. Campaign of the Carolinas March 1-April 26.
Advance on Goldsboro March 6-21. Occupation of
Goldsboro March 21. Advance on Raleigh April 10-14.
Occupation of Raleigh April 14. Bennett's House April
26. Surrender of Johnston and his army. Duty at
Salisbury, N. C., till June. Mustered out June 27, 1865.

Regiment lost during service 2 Officers and 52 Enlisted men killed and mortally wounded and 3 Officers
and 158 Enlisted men by disease. Total 215.

112th REGIMENT INFANTRY.

Regiment failed to complete organization.

113th REGIMENT INFANTRY.

Organized at Camp Chase, Zanesville, and Camp Dennison, Ohio, October 10 to December 12, 1862. Moved
to Louisville, Ky., December 27; thence to Muldraugh's

Hiil, Ky., January 3, 1863, and to Nashville, Tenn., January 28. Attached to District of Western Kentucky, Dept. of the Ohio, to February, 1863. Reed's Brigade, Baird's Division, Army of Kentucky, Dept. of the Cumberland, to June, 1863. 2nd Brigade, 1st Division, Reserve Corps, Dept. of the Cumberland, to October, 1863. 2nd Brigade, 2nd Division, 14th Army Corps, Army of the Cumberland, to July, 1865.

SERVICE.—Moved from Nashville to Franklin, Tenn., February 12, 1863, and duty there till June. Middle Tennessee (or Tullahoma) Campaign June 23-July 7. Duty at Wartrace till August 25. Chickamauga (Ga.) Campaign August 25-September 22. Battle of Chickamauga September 19-21. Siege of Chattanooga, Tenn., September 24-November 23. Chattanooga-Ringgold Campaign November 23-27. Orchard Knob November 23. Tunnel Hill November 24-25. Mission Ridge November 25. Chickamauga Station November 26. March to relief of Knoxville November 28-December 8. Return to Chattanooga and duty in that vicinity till May, 1864. Demonstration on Dalton, Ga., February 22-27, 1864. Tunnel Hill, Buzzard's Roost Gap and Rocky Faced Ridge February 23-25. Atlanta (Ga.) Campaign May 1 to September 8. Tunnel Hill May 6-7. Demonstration on Rocky Faced Ridge May 8-11. Buzzard's Roost Gap May 8-9. Battle of Resaca May 14-15. Advance on Dallas May 18-25. Operations on line of Pumpkin Vine Creek and battles about Dallas, New Hope Church and Allatoona Hills May 25-June 5. Operations about Marietta and against Kenesaw Mountain June 10-July 2. Pine Hill June 11-14. Lost Mountain June 15-17. Assault on Kenesaw June 27. Ruff's Station July 4. Chattahoochie River July 5-17. Peach Tree Creek July 19-20. Siege of Atlanta July 22-August 25. Utoy Creek August 5-7. Flank movement on Jonesboro August 25-30. Battle of Jonesboro August 31-September 1. Operations against Forest and Hood in North Georgia and North Alabama September 29-November 3. March to the sea November 15-December 10. Sandersville November 26. Siege of Savannah December 10-21. Campaign of the Carolinas January to April, 1865. Two League Cross Roads, near Lexington, S. C., February 15. Taylor's Hole Creek, Averysboro, N. C., March 16. Battle of Bentonville March 19-21. Occupation of Goldsboro March 24. Advance on Raleigh April 10-14. Occupation of Raleigh April 14. Bennett's House April 26. Surrender of Johnston and his army. March to Washington, D. C., via Richmond, D. C., April 29-May 19. Grand Review May 24. Moved to Louisville, Ky., June, and there mustered out July 6, 1865.

Regiment lost during service 9 Officers and 110 Enlisted men killed and mortally wounded and 1 Officer and 149 Enlisted men by disease. Total 269.

114th REGIMENT INFANTRY.

Organized at Camp Circleville, Ohio, and mustered in September 11, 1862. Ordered to Marietta, Ohio, September 12; thence to Memphis, Tenn., December 1. Attached to 2nd Brigade, 9th Division, Right Wing 13th Army Corps (Old), Dept. of the Tennessee, to December, 1862. 2nd Brigade, 3rd Division, Sherman's Yazoo Expedition, to January, 1863. 2nd Brigade, 9th Division, 13th Army Corps, Army of the Tennessee, to July, 1863. 4th Brigade, 1st Division, 13th Army Corps, Dept. of the Tennessee, to August, 1863, and Dept. of the Gulf to September, 1863. 3rd Brigade, 1st Division, 13th Army Corps, Dept. of the Gulf, to March, 1864. 2nd Brigade, 1st Division, 13th Army Corps, to June, 1864. 2nd Brigade, 3rd Division, 19th Army Corps, Dept. of the Gulf, to December, 1864. 3rd Brigade, 2nd Division, Reserve Corps, Military Division West Mississippi, to February, 1865. 3rd Brigade, 2nd Division, 13th Army Corps (New), Military Division West Mississippi, to July, 1865.

SERVICE.—Sherman's Yazoo Expedition December 20, 1862, to January 3, 1863. Chickasaw Bayou December 26-28, 1862. Chickasaw Bluff December 29. Expedition to Arkansas Post, Ark., January 3-10, 1863. Assault and capture of Fort Hindman, Arkansas Post, January 10-11. Moved to Young's Point, La., January 17-23, and duty there till March 8. Moved to Milliken's Bend, La., and duty there till April. Operations from Milliken's Bend to New Carthage March 31-April 17. Expedition from Perkins' Plantation to Hard Times Landing April 25-29. Phelps' and Clark's Bayous April 26. Choctaw Bayou, or Lake Bruin, April 28. Battle of Port Gibson May 1. Battle of Champion's Hill May 16. Big Black River May 17. Siege of Vicksburg, Miss., May 18-July 4. Assaults on Vicksburg May 19 and 22. Duty at Warrenton May 25 to July 14, and at Vicksburg till August 13. Ordered to New Orleans, La., August 13, and duty there till September 8. At Brashear City till October 3. Western Louisiana Campaign October 3-November 18. Moved to DeCrow's Point, Matagorda Bay, Texas, November 18-28, and duty there till January 14, 1864. At Matagorda Island till April 18. Moved to Alexandria, La., April 18-26. Red River Campaign April 26-May 22. Graham's Plantation May 5. Retreat to Morganza May 13-20. Mansura, or Marksville Prairie, May 16. Expedition to Atchafalaya May 30-June 6. Duty at Morganza till November 21. Moved to mouth of White River, Ark., November 21-26. Return to Morganza December 6. Expedition to Morgan's Ferry, Atchafalaya River, December 13-14. Moved to Kenner, La., January 8, 1865; thence to Barrancas, Fla., January 24. Campaign against Mobile, Ala., and its Defences, March 20-April 12. March from Pensacola, Fla., to Blakely, Ala., March 20-April 2. Occupation of Canoe Station March 27. Siege of Spanish Fort and Fort Blakely April 2-8. Assault and capture of Fort Blakely April 9. Occupation of Mobile April 12. March to Montgomery and Selma April 13-25. Duty at Selma till May 12, and at Mobile till June 13. Moved to Galveston, Texas, June 13, and duty there till July. Veterans and Recruits transferred to 48th Ohio Veteran Battalion July 24. Mustered out July 31, 1865.

Regiment lost during service 3 Officers and 36 Enlisted men killed and mortally wounded and 2 Officers and 270 Enlisted men by disease. Total 311.

115th REGIMENT INFANTRY.

Organized at Camp Massillon, Ohio, and mustered in September 18, 1862. Moved to Cincinnati, Ohio, September 27. Assigned to duty by detachments as Provost Guard and guarding Forts, Arsenals, Store Houses and Magazines at Camps Chase, Dennison, Ohio, Maysville, Covington and Newport, Ky., and Cincinnati, Ohio, till October, 1863. Ordered to Chattanooga, Tenn., October 23, 1863; thence to Murfreesboro, Tenn. Attached to Post of Murfreesboro, Tenn., Dept. of the Cumberland, to January, 1864. 2nd Brigade, 3rd Division, 12th Army Corps, Army of the Cumberland, to April, 1864. Unassigned, 4th Division, 20th Army Corps, Army of the Cumberland, to July, 1864. 1st Brigade, Defences of Nashville & Chattanooga Railroad, Dept. of the Cumberland, to March, 1865. 1st Brigade, 1st Sub-District, District of Middle Tennessee, Dept. of the Cumberland, to June, 1865.

SERVICE.—Duty at Murfreesboro, Tenn., and along line of the Nashville & Chattanooga Railroad, in Block Houses and at Bridges till June, 1865. Regiment was specially selected for this arduous duty because of the great number of skilled mechanics and artisans in its ranks. Skirmishes at Cripple Creek, Woodbury Pike, May 25, 1864 (Detachment). Smyrna August 31, 1864. Block House No. 4 August 31, 1864. Company "B" captured by Wheeler. Block House No. 5 (Co. "B"). Block House No. 2, on Mill Creek, Nashville & Chattanooga Railroad, December 2-3. Block House No. 1 December 3 (Detachment). Block House No. 3 December 3 (Detachment). Block House No. 4 December 4 (Detachment). Block House No. 7 December 4 (Detachment). Siege of Murfreesboro December 5-12. "The Cedars" December 5-7. Lavergne December 8. Duty along Nashville & Chattanooga Railroad from Nashville to Tullahoma, Tenn., till June, 1865. Mustered out June 23, 1865.

Regiment lost during service 1 Officer and 8 Enlisted men killed and mortally wounded and 4 Officers and 138 Enlisted men by disease. Total 151.

116th REGIMENT INFANTRY.

Organized at Marietta and Gallipolis, Ohio, and mustered in September 18, 1862 (Cos. "F" and "K" mustered in October 28, 1861, and joined Regiment at Buckhannon, W. Va.). Left State for Parkersburg, W. Va., October 16; thence moved to Clarksburg and Buckhannon. Moved to New Creek November 9, and to Moorefield December 12. Attached to Railroad Division, West Virginia, to January, 1863. Romney, W. Va., Defenses of the Upper Potomac, 8th Army Corps, Middle Department, to March, 1863. 1st Brigade, 2nd Division, 8th Army Corps, Middle Department, to June, 1863. 1st Brigade, Elliott's Command, 8th Army Corps, to July, 1863. 1st Brigade, 1st Division, Dept. of the Susquehanna, July, 1863. McReynolds' Command, Martinsburg, W. Va., Dept. of West Virginia, to December, 1863. 1st Brigade, 1st Division, West Virginia, to April, 1864. 1st Infantry Division, West Virginia, to December, 1864. 1st Brigade, Independent Division, 24th Army Corps, Army of the James, to June, 1865.

SERVICE.—Duty at Moorefield, W. Va., December 15, 1862, to January 10, 1863. Moorefield January 3. At Romney till March 17. Near Romney February 16. At Winchester, Va., till June. Operations in Shenandoah Valley April 20-29. Scout toward Wardensville and Strasburg April 20. Scout to Strasburg April 25-29. Bunker Hill June 13 (Cos. "A" and "I"). Battle of Winchester June 13-15. Retreat to Harper's Ferry, W. Va., June 15-16; thence to Washington, D. C., July 1-4, and join Army of the Potomac at Frederick, Md., July 5. Pursuit of Lee to Manassas Gap, Va., July 5-24. Wapping Heights, Va., July 23. At Martinsburg, W. Va., August 4, 1863, to April 29, 1864. Skirmish at Hedgesville October 16, 1863 (Detachment). Sigel's Expedition from Martinsburg to New Market April 29-May 16, 1864. Battle of New Market May 15. Advance on Staunton May 24-June 6. Piedmont June 5. Occupation of Staunton June 6. Hunter's raid on Lynchburg June 10-July 1. Lynchburg June 17-18. Ordered to the Shenandoah Valley July. Battle of Kernstown-Winchester, July 24. Sheridan's Shenandoah Valley Campaign August 7-November 28. Charlestown August 21, 22 and 29. Berryville September 3. Battle of Winchester, Opaquan Creek September 19. Fisher's Hill September 22. Cedar Creek October 13. Battle of Cedar Creek October 19. Duty at Opequan Crossing November 18 to December 19. Moved to Washington, D. C., December 19; thence to Aiken's Landing, Va. Siege of Petersburg and Richmond December 27, 1864, to April 2, 1865. Appomattox Campaign March 28-April 9. Hatcher's Run March 29-April 1. Fall of Petersburg April 2. Pursuit of Lee April 3-9. Rice's Station April 6. Appomattox Court House April 9. Surrender of Lee and his army. Duty at Richmond, Va., till June. Mustered out June 14, 1865. Companies "F" and "K" consolidated with 62nd Ohio Infantry.

Regiment lost during service 4 Officers and 90 Enlisted men killed and mortally wounded and 3 Officers and 88 Enlisted men by disease. Total 185.

117th REGIMENT INFANTRY.

Organized at Portsmouth, Ohio, September 15, 1862. Ordered to Kentucky October 2. Camp at Ashland, Ky., till January, 1863. Attached to District of Eastern Kentucky, Dept. of the Ohio. Moved to Paintsville, Ky., January, 1863; thence to Covington via Peach Orchard, Louisa and Catlettsburg, February. Duty at Covington till May. Designation of Regiment changed to 1st Ohio Heavy Artillery May 2, 1863 (which see).

118th REGIMENT INFANTRY.

Organized at Lima, Cincinnati and Camp Mansfield, Ohio, August and September, 1862. Ordered to Kentucky and assigned to duty as guard along Kentucky Central Railroad from Buston's Station to Paris, Ky.; September, 1862, to August, 1863. Attached to 2nd Brigade, 2nd Division, Army of Kentucky, Dept. of the Ohio, September to November, 1862. 1st Brigade, 1st Division, Army of Kentucky, November, 1862. District of Central Kentucky, Dept. of the Ohio, to June, 1863. 2nd Brigade, 4th Division, 23rd Army Corps, Dept. of the Ohio, to July, 1863. 2nd Brigade, 1st Division, 23rd Army Corps, to August, 1863. 1st Brigade, 2nd Division, 23rd Army Corps, to April, 1864. 2nd Brigade, 2nd Division, 23rd Army Corps, Army of the Ohio, to February, 1865, and Dept. of North Carolina to June, 1865.

SERVICE.—Skirmish at Paris, Ky., July 29, 1863 (Detachment). Burnside's Campaign in East Tennessee August 16-October 17, 1863. Duty at Kingston till December 6. Action at Kingston November 24, and near Kingston December 4. Moved to Nashville December 5; thence march to Blain's Cross Roads and Mossy Creek. Action at Mossy Creek December 29. Operations in East Tennessee December, 1863, to April, 1864. Atlanta (Ga.) Campaign May 1 to September 8. Demonstrations on Dalton May 9-13. Battle of Resaca May 14-15. Advance on Dallas May 18-25. Operations on line of Pumpkin Vine Creek and battles about Dallas, New Hope Church and Allatoona Hills May 25-June 5. Operations about Marietta and against Kenesaw Mountain June 10-July 2. Lost Mountain June 15-17. Muddy Creek June 19. Noyes Creek June 19. Kolb's Farm June 22. Assault on Kenesaw June 27. Nickajack Creek July 2-5. Chattahoochie River July 5-17. Decatur July 19. Howard House July 20. Siege of Atlanta July 22-August 25. Utoy Creek August 5-7. Flank movement on Jonesboro August 25-30. Battle of Jonesboro August 31-September 1 (Reserve). Lovejoy Station September 2-6. Operations against Hood in North Georgia and North Alabama September 29-November 3. Nashville Campaign November-December. Columbia, Duck River, November 24-27. Battle of Franklin November 30. Battle of Nashville December 15-16. Pursuit of Hood to the Tennessee River December 17-28. At Clifton, Tenn., till January 16, 1865. Movement to Washington, D. C., thence to Fort Fisher, N. C., January 16-February 9. Operations against Hoke February 11-14. Fort Anderson February 18-19. Town Creek February 19-20. Capture of Wilmington February 22. Campaign of the Carolinas March 1-April 26. Advance on Goldsboro March 21. Advance on Raleigh April 10-14. Occupation of Raleigh April 14. Bennett's House April 26. Surrender of Johnston and his army. Duty at Raleigh, Greensboro and Salisbury till June. Mustered out June 24, 1865.

Regiment lost during service 1 Officer and 55 Enlisted men killed and mortally wounded and 1 Officer and 127 Enlisted men by disease. Total 184.

119th REGIMENT INFANTRY.

Organization of Regiment commenced but not completed.

120th REGIMENT INFANTRY.

Organized at Mansfield, Ohio, August 29, 1862. Moved to Cincinnati, Ohio, October 25; thence to Covington, Ky., and duty there till November 24. Served Unattached, Army of Kentucky, Dept. of the Ohio, to November, 1862. 1st Brigade, 9th Division, Right Wing 13th Army Corps (Old), Dept. of the Tennessee, to December, 1862. 1st Brigade, 3rd Division, Sherman's Yazoo Expedition, to January, 1863. 1st Brigade, 9th Division, 13th Army Corps, Army of the Tennessee, to July, 1863. 3rd Brigade, 1st Division, 13th Army Corps, Dept. of the Tennessee, to August, 1863, and Dept. of the Gulf to November, 1863. Plaquemine, La., District of Baton Rouge, La., Dept. of the Gulf, to March, 1864. 2nd Brigade, 1st Division, 13th Army Corps, to June, 1864. 2nd Brigade, 3rd Division, 19th Army Corps, Dept. of the Gulf, to August, 1864. 2nd Brigade, 2nd Division, 19th Army Corps, to November, 1864.

SERVICE.—Moved to Memphis, Tenn., November 24-December 7, 1862. Sherman's Yazoo Expedition December 20, 1862, to January 3, 1863. Chickasaw Bayou December 26-28, 1862. Chickasaw Bluff December 29. Expedition to Arkansas Post, Ark., January 3-10, 1863. Assault and capture of Fort Hindman, Arkansas Post, January 10-11. Moved to Young's Point, La., January 17, and duty there till March 8. Moved to Milliken's Bend March 8. Operations from Milliken's Bend to New Carthage March 31-April 17. James' Plantation, near New Carthage, April 8. Dunbar's Plantation, Bayou Vidal, April 15. Movement on Bruinsburg and turning Grand Gulf April 25-30. Battle of Port Gibson May 1. Duty at Raymond till May 18. Siege of Vicksburg, Miss., May 18-July 4. Assaults on Vicksburg May 19 and 22. Advance on Jackson, Miss., July 4-10. Near Jackson July 9. Siege of Jackson, Miss., July 10-17. Camp at Vicksburg till August. Moved to New Orleans August 18. Duty at Carrollton till September 3, and at Brashear City till October 3. Western Louisiana Campaign October 3-November 30. Duty at Plaquemine, La., till March 23, 1864. Moved to Baton Rouge March 23, and duty there till May 1. Ordered to join Banks at Alexandria on Red River Expedition May 1. Embarked on Steamer "City Belle." Action en route at Snaggy Point May 3. Most of Regiment captured. Those who escaped formed into a Battalion of three Companies and marched to Alexandria. Retreat from Alexandria to Morganza May 13-20. Mansura or Marksville Prairie May 16. Duty at Morganza till September. Expedition to mouth of White River and St. Charles September 13-20. Expedition to Duvall's Bluff, Ark., October 21-27. Consolidated with 114th Ohio Infantry November 25, 1864.

Regiment lost during service 2 Officers and 17 Enlisted men killed and mortally wounded and 6 Officers and 275 Enlisted men by disease. Total 300.

121st REGIMENT INFANTRY.

Organized at Delaware, Ohio, September 11, 1862. Ordered to Cincinnati, Ohio, September 11; thence to Covington, Ky., September 15, and to Louisville, Ky., September 20. Attached to 34th Brigade, 10th Division, Army of the Ohio, September, 1862. 34th Brigade, 10th Division, 1st Army Corps, Army of the Ohio, to November, 1862. District of West Kentucky, Dept. of the Ohio, to February, 1863. Reed's Brigade, Baird's Division, Army of Kentucky, Dept. of the Cumberland, to June, 1863. 2nd Brigade, 1st Division, Reserve Corps, Army of the Cumberland, to October, 1863. 2nd Brigade, 2nd Division, 14th Army Corps, Army of the Cumberland, to June, 1865.

SERVICE.—Pursuit of Bragg into Kentucky October 1-15, 1862. Battle of Perryville, Ky., October 8. Moved to Lebanon, Ky., and duty there till November, and at Columbia till December. Operations against Morgan December 22, 1862, to January 3, 1863. Ordered to Louisville, thence moved to Nashville, Tenn., February 9; thence to Franklin, Tenn., February 12, and duty there till June. Middle Tennessee (or Tullahoma) Campaign June 23-July 7. Duty at Fayetteville August 25-September 5. Chickamauga (Ga.) Campaign. Battle of Chickamauga September 19-21. Siege of Chattanooga, Tenn., September 24-November 23. Chattanooga-Ringgold Campaign November 23-27. Orchard Knob November 23. Tunnel Hill November 24-25. Mission Ridge November 25. Chickamauga Station November 26. March to relief of Knoxville, Tenn., November 28-December 17. Duty at Rossville, Ga., till May, 1864. Atlanta (Ga.) Campaign May 1 to September 8. Tunnel Hill May 6-7. Demonstration on Rocky Faced Ridge May 8-11. Buzzard's Roost Gap May 8-9. Battle of Resaca May 14-15. Advance on Dallas May 18-25. Operations on line of Pumpkin Vine Creek and battles about Dallas, New Hope Church and Allatoona Hills May 25-June 5. Operations about Marietta and against Kenesaw Mountain June 10-July 2. Pine Hill June 11-14. Lost Mountain June 15-17. Assault on Kenesaw June 27. Ruff's Station July 4. Chattahoochie River July 5-17. Peach Tree Creek July 19-20. Siege of Atlanta July 22-August 25. Utoy Creek August 5-7. Flank

movement on Jonesboro August 25-30. Battle of Jonesboro August 31-September 1. Operations against Forest and Hood in North Georgia and North Alabama September 29-November 3. March to the sea November 15-December 10. Sandersville November 26. Siege of Savannah December 10-21. Campaign of the Carolinas January to April, 1865. Taylor's Hole Creek, Averysboro, N. C., March 16. Battle of Bentonville March 19-21. Occupation of Goldsboro March 24. Advance on Raleigh April 10-14. Occupation of Raleigh April 14. Bennett's House April 26. Surrender of Johnston and his army. March to Washington, D. C., via Richmond, Va., April 29-May 19. Grand Review May 24. Mustered out June 8, 1865.

Regiment lost during service 9 Officers and 92 Enlisted men killed and mortally wounded and 2 Officers and 246 Enlisted men by disease. Total 349.

122nd REGIMENT INFANTRY.

Organized at Zanesville, Ohio, September 30, 1862. Company "C" October 3, Company "G" October 5, Company "F" October 6 and Companies "I" and "K" October 8, 1862. Left State for Parkersburg, W. Va., October 23; thence moved to Clarksburg and to New Creek November 15. Attached to Railroad Division, West Virginia, to January, 1863. Milroy's Command, Winchester, Va., 8th Army Corps, Middle Department, to February, 1863. 1st Brigade, 2nd Division, 8th Army Corps. to June, 1863. Elliott's Command, 8th Army Corps, to July, 1863. 2nd Brigade, 3rd Division, 3rd Army Corps, Army of the Potomac, to March, 1864. 2nd Brigade, 3rd Division, 6th Army Corps, Army of the Potomac, and Army of the Shenandoah, Middle Military Division, to June, 1865.

SERVICE.—Duty at New Creek, Va., November 15 to December 28, 1862. Expedition up the south branch of Potomac River December 28, 1862, to January 1, 1863. Moved to Romney, W. Va., and duty there till March 17, 1863. Skirmish near Romney February 16. Moved to Winchester March 17, and duty in that vicinity till June. Reconnoissance toward Wardensville and Strasburg April 20. Battle of Winchester June 13-15. Retreat to Harper's Ferry June 15-17. Garrison, Maryland Heights, till July 1. Guard stores to Georgetown, thence moved to Frederick, Md., July 1-5. Pursuit of Lee to Manassas Gap, Va., July 5-24. Action at Wapping Heights, Va., July 23. Duty at New York City during draft disturbances August 17-September 5. Bristoe Campaign October 9-22. Advance to line of the Rappahannock November 7-8. Kelly's Ford November 7. Brandy Station November 8. Mine Run Campaign November 26-December 2. Payne's Farm November 27. Demonstrations on the Rapidan February 6-7, 1864. Campaign from the Rapidan to the James River May 3-June 15. Battles of the Wilderness May 5-7; Spottsylvania May 8-12; Spottsylvania Court House May 12-21. Assault on the Salient, "Bloody Angle," May 12. North Anna River May 23-26. On line of the Pamunkey May 26-28. Totopotomoy May 28-31. Cold Harbor June 1-12. Before Petersburg June 17-July 6. Jerusalem Plank Road June 22-23. Moved to Baltimore, Md., July 6; thence to Monocacy July 8. Battle of Monocacy Junction, Md., July 9. (Cover retreat.) Sheridan's Shenandoah Valley Campaign August 7-November 29. Charlestown August 21, 22 and 29. Battle of Opequan, Winchester, September 19. Fisher's Hill September 22. Battle of Cedar Creek October 19. Duty at Kernstown till December. Skirmish at Kernstown November 10. Moved to Washington, D. C., December 3; thence to Petersburg, Va. Siege of Petersburg, Va., December 6, 1864, to April 2, 1865. Appomattox Campaign March 28-April 9, 1865. Assault on and fall of Petersburg April 2. Pursuit of Lee April 3-9. Sailor's Creek April 6. Appomattox Court House April 9. Surrender of Lee and his army. March to Danville April 17-27, and duty there till May. Moved to Richmond, Va., May 16; thence to Washington, D. C., May 24-June 1. Corps Review June 9. Mustered out June 26, 1865.

Regiment lost during service 7 Officers and 86 Enlisted men killed and mortally wounded and 137 Enlisted men by disease. Total 230.

123rd REGIMENT INFANTRY.

Organized at Monroeville, Ohio, and mustered in September 24, 1862. Left State for Parkersburg, W. Va., October 16, 1862; thence moved to Clarksburg October 20. Attached to Railroad Division, West Virginia, to January, 1863. Defences of the Upper Potomac, 8th Army Corps, Middle Department, to March, 1863. 1st Brigade, 2nd Division, 8th Army Corps, to July, 1863. 1st Brigade, 1st Division, Dept. of the Susquehanna, to July, 1863. McReynolds' Command, Martinsburg, W. Va., to December, 1863. 3rd Brigade, 1st Division, Dept. of West Virginia, to April, 1864. 1st Brigade, 1st Infantry Division, West Virginia, to December, 1864. 1st Brigade, Independent Division, 24th Army Corps, Army of the James, to June, 1865.

SERVICE.—March from Clarksburg to Buckhannon, W. Va., October 27-30, 1862, and to Beverly November 3. Moved to Huttonville November 8; to Webster November 16, and to New Creek November 18. Duty at New Creek till December 12. Moved to Petersburg December 12. March to relief of Moorefield January 3, 1863. Duty at Romney January 10 to March 4, and at Winchester, Va., till June. Reconnoissance toward Wardensville and Strasburg April 20. Operations in Shenandoah Valley April 22-29. Scout to Strasburg April 25-30. Battle of Winchester June 13-15. Regiment surrendered by Colonel Ely, Commanding Brigade, June 15, 1863. Exchanged August, 1863. Provost duty at Martinsburg, W. Va., October, 1863, to March, 1864. Duty along Baltimore & Ohio Railroad from Harper's Ferry to Monocacy Junction till April. Sigel's Expedition from Martinsburg to New Market April 30-May 16. Battle of New Market May 16. Advance to Staunton May 24-June 5. Action at Piedmont June 5. Occupation of Staunton June 6. Hunter's Raid on Lynchburg June 10-July 1. Lynchburg June 17-18. Moved to Shenandoah Valley July 12-15. Snicker's Ferry July 15. Battle of Winchester, Kernstown, July 24. Sheridan's Shenandoah Valley Campaign August 7-November 28. Berryville September 3. Battle of Opequan, Winchester, September 19. Fisher's Hill September 22. Cedar Creek October 13. Battle of Cedar Creek October 19. Duty at Kernstown till December. Moved to Washington, D. C., December 19; thence to Aikens' Landing, Va. Siege operations against Richmond and Petersburg December, 1864, to April, 1865. Appomattox Campaign March 28-April 9. Hatcher's Run March 29-31. Fall of Petersburg April 2. Pursuit of Lee April 3-9. Rice's Station April 6. Appomattox Court House April 9. Surrender of Lee and his army. Duty in the Dept. of Virginia till June. Mustered out June 12, 1865.

Regiment lost during service 1 Officer and 90 Enlisted men killed and mortally wounded and 4 Officers and 92 Enlisted men by disease. Total 187.

124th REGIMENT INFANTRY.

Organized at Cleveland, Ohio, and mustered in January 1, 1863. Left State for Louisville, Ky., January 1; thence moved to Elizabethtown, Ky., and duty there till February 10, 1863. Attached to District of Western Kentucky, Dept. of the Ohio, to February, 1863. Franklin, Tenn., Army of Kentucky, Dept. of the Cumberland, to June, 1863. 2nd Brigade, 2nd Division, 21st Army Corps, Army of the Cumberland, to October, 1863. 2nd Brigade, 3rd Division, 4th Army Corps, Army of the Cumberland, to June, 1865.

SERVICE.—Moved to Nashville, Tenn., February 10, 1863; thence to Franklin February 21, and duty there till June. Action at Thompson's Station, Spring Hill, March 4-5. Thompson's Station June 2. Middle Tennessee (or Tullahoma) Campaign June 23-July 7. Camp at Manchester till August 16. Passage of the Cumberland Mountains and Tennessee River and Chickamauga (Ga.) Campaign August 16-September 22. At Poe's Tavern August 20-September 9. Passage of the Ten-

nessee River September 10. Lee and Gordon's Mills September 11-13. Battle of Chickamauga September 19-20. Siege of Chattanooga, Tenn., September 24-November 23. Reopening Tennessee River October 26-29. Brown's Ferry October 27. Chattanooga-Ringgold Campaign November 23-27. Orchard Knob November 23-24. Mission Ridge November 25. March to relief of Knoxville, Tenn., November 28-December 8. Operations in East Tennessee till April, 1864. Operations about Dandridge January 16-17. Atlanta (Ga.) Campaign May 1 to September 8. Demonstrations on Rocky Faced Ridge and Dalton, Ga., May 8-13. Battle of Resaca May 14-16. Adairsville May 17. Near Kingston May 18-19. Near Cassville May 19. Advance on Dallas May 22-25. Operations on line of Pumpkin Vine Creek and battles about Dallas, New Hope Church and Allatoona Hills May 25-June 5. Pickett's Mills May 27. Operations about Marietta and against Kenesaw Mountain June 10-July 2. Pine Hill June 11-14. Lost Mountain June 15-17. Assault on Kenesaw June 27. Ruff's Station July 4. Chattahoochie River July 5-17. Peach Tree Creek July 19-20. Siege of Atlanta July 22-August 25. Flank movement on Jonesboro August 25-30. Battle of Jonesboro August 31-September 1. Lovejoy Station September 2-6. Pursuit of Hood into Alabama October 3-26. At Athens, Ga., October 31 to November 23. March to Columbia, Tenn., November 23-24. Columbia, Duck River, November 24-27. Battle of Franklin November 30. Battle of Nashville December 15-16. Pursuit of Hood to the Tennessee River December 17-28. Moved to Huntsville, Ala., and duty there till March, 1865. Operations in East Tennessee March 15-April 22. Duty at Strawberry Plains and Nashville till June. Mustered out June 16, 1865.

Regiment lost during service 7 Officers and 78 Enlisted men killed and mortally wounded and 1 Officer and 124 Enlisted men by disease. Total 210.

125th REGIMENT INFANTRY.

Organized at Camp Taylor, Cleveland, Ohio, October 6, 1862. Moved to Cincinnati, Ohio, January 3, 1863; thence moved to Louisville, Ky., and duty there till January 28. Attached to District of Western Kentucky, Dept. of the Ohio, to February, 1863. Franklin, Tenn., Army of Kentucky, Dept. of the Cumberland, to June, 1863. 3rd Brigade, 1st Division, 21st Army Corps, Army of the Cumberland, to October, 1863. 3rd Brigade, 2nd Division, 4th Army Corps, Army of the Cumberland, to October, 1864. 1st Brigade, 2nd Division, 4th Army Corps and Dept. of Texas, to September, 1865.

SERVICE.—Moved from Louisville, Ky., to Nashville, Tenn., January 28, 1863; thence to Franklin, Tenn., March 5, and duty there till June. Repulse of attack on Franklin March 9. Moved to Triune June 2, thence to Murfreesboro, Tenn. Middle Tennessee (or Tullahoma) Campaign June 23-July 7. At Hillsboro July 3-August 5. Passage of the Cumberland Mountains and Tennessee River and Chickamauga (Ga.) Campaign August 16-September 22. Occupation of Chattanooga September 9. Lee and Gordon's Mills September 11-13. Near Lafayette September 14. Battle of Chickamauga September 19-20. Siege of Chattanooga, Tenn., September 24-November 23. Colwell's Ford November 19. Chattanooga-Ringgold Campaign November 23-27. Orchard Knob November 23-24. Mission Ridge November 25. Pursuit to Graysville November 26-27. March to relief of Knoxville, Tenn., November 28-December 8. Operations in East Tennessee till April, 1864. Charlestown December 28, 1863. Operations about Dandridge January 16-17, 1864. Atlanta (Ga.) Campaign May 1 to September 8. Demonstrations on Rocky Faced Ridge and Dalton May 8-13. Buzzard's Roost Gap May 8-9. Battle of Resaca May 14-15. Adairsville May 17. Near Kingston May 18-19. Near Cassville May 19. Advance on Dallas May 22-25. Operations on line of Pumpkin Vine Creek and battles about Dallas, New Hope Church and Allatoona Hills May 25-June 5. Operations about Marietta and against Kenesaw Mountain June 10-July 2. Pine Hill June 11-14.

Lost Mountain June 15-17. Assault on Kenesaw June 27. Ruff's Mills July 4. Chattahoochie River July 5-17. Buckhead, Nancy's Creek, June 18. Peach Tree Creek July 19-20. Siege of Atlanta July 22-August 25. Flank movement on Jonesboro August 25-30. Battle of Jonesboro August 31-September 1. Lovejoy Station September 2-6. Operations against Hood in North Georgia and North Alabama October 3-November 3. Nashville Campaign November-December. Columbia, Duck River, November 24-27. Spring Hill November 29. Battle of Franklin November 30. Battle of Nashville December 15-16. Pursuit of Hood to the Tennessee River December 17-28. Moved to Huntsville, Ala., and duty there till March, 1865. At Knoxville, Blue Springs and Nashville till June. Moved to New Orleans, La., June 16; thence to Texas and duty there till September. Mustered out September 25, 1865.

Regiment lost during service 7 Officers and 104 Enlisted men killed and mortally wounded and 114 Enlisted men by disease. Total 225.

126th REGIMENT INFANTRY.

Organized at Camp Steubenville, Ohio, and mustered in September 4, 1862. Moved to Parkersburg, W. Va., September 16, 1862. Attached to Railroad Division, West Virginia, to January, 1863. Martinsburg, W. Va., 8th Army Corps, Middle Department, to March, 1863. 2nd Brigade, 1st Division, 8th Army Corps, to June, 1863. 3rd Brigade, French's Command, 8th Army Corps, to July, 1863. 3rd Brigade, 3rd Division, 3rd Army Corps, Army of the Potomac, to March, 1864. 2nd Brigade, 3rd Division, 6th Army Corps, Army of the Potomac and Army of the Shenandoah, Middle Military Division, to June, 1865.

SERVICE.—Moved to Cumberland, Md., October 17, 1862, and to North Mountain December 12. Guard duty on Baltimore & Ohio Railroad from North Mountain to Martinsburg December 12-20, and duty at Martinsburg till June 14, 1863. Expedition to Greenland Gap April 15-22. Action at Martinsburg June 14 (Co. "B"). Retreat to Harper's Ferry June 15-17. Guard stores to Washington, D. C.; thence to Frederick, Md., July 1-5. Pursuit of Lee to Manassas Gap, Va., July 5-24. Action at Wapping Heights, Va., July 23. Duty in New York City during draft disturbances August 18-September 5. Bristoe Campaign October 9-22. Advance to line of the Rappahannock November 7-8. Kelly's Ford November 7. Brandy Station November 8. Mine Run Campaign November 26-December 2. Demonstration on the Rapidan February 6-7, 1864. Campaign from the Rapidan to the James River May 3-June 15. Battles of the Wilderness May 5-7. Spottsylvania May 8-12; Spottsylvania Court House May 12-21. Assault on the Salient "Bloody Angle" May 12. North Anna River May 23-26. On line of the Pamunkey May 26-28. Totopotomoy May 28-31. Cold Harbor June 1-12. Before Petersburg June 18-July 6. Jerusalem Plank Road June 22-23. Ordered to Baltimore, Md., July 6. Battle of Monocacy Junction, Md., July 9. Sheridan's Shenandoah Valley Campaign August 7-November 28. Battle of Opequan, Winchester, September 19. Fisher's Hill September 22. Battle of Cedar Creek October 19. Duty at Kernstown till December. Moved to Washington, D. C., December 3; thence to Petersburg, Va. Siege of Petersburg December 9, 1864, to April 2, 1865. Appomattox Campaign March 28-April 9. Assault on and fall of Petersburg April 2. Pursuit of Lee April 3-9. Sailor's Creek April 6. Guard prisoners at Burkesville April 6-15. March to Danville April 15-27, and duty there till May 16. Moved to Richmond, Va., May 16; thence to Washington, D. C., May 24-June 2. Corps Review June 9. Mustered out June 25, 1865.

Regiment lost during service 9 Officers and 148 Enlisted men killed and mortally wounded and 2 Officers and 142 Enlisted men by disease. Total 296.

127th REGIMENT INFANTRY.—(COLORED.)

Organized at Camp Delaware, Ohio, August to November, 1863. Designated 5th United States Colored Troops (which see).

128th REGIMENT INFANTRY.

Organized at Columbus and Johnson's Island, Ohio, December, 1863, to January, 1864. Moved from Columbus to Sandusky, Ohio, January, 1864. Guard duty at Sandusky and at Johnson's Island, Sandusky Bay, till July, 1865. Moved to Camp Chase, Ohio, July 10, and mustered out July 17, 1865.

Regiment lost during service 1 Officer and 63 Enlisted men by disease. Total 64.

129th REGIMENT INFANTRY.

Organized at Camp Taylor, near Cleveland, Ohio, August 10, 1863. Moved to Camp Nelson, Ky., August 10. Attached to DeCourcy's Brigade, Willcox's Left Wing Forces, Dept. of the Ohio, to October, 1863. 3rd Brigade, 2nd Division, 9th Army Corps, Army of the Ohio, to January, 1864. District of the Clinch, Dept. of the Ohio, to March, 1864.

SERVICE.—Expedition under DeCourcy to Cumberland Gap, Tenn., August 20-September 8, 1863. Capture of Cumberland Gap September 9. Duty at Cumberland Gap picketing and foraging till December 1. March toward Clinch River December 1-2. Patrol duty along Clinch River till December 29. Moved to Tazewell, thence to Cumberland Gap, and duty there till January 11, 1864. Ordered to Camp Nelson, Ky. Skirmish at Barboursville, Ky., February 8. Ordered to Cleveland, Ohio, March and mustered out March 10, 1864.

Regiment lost during service 25 Enlisted men by disease.

130th REGIMENT INFANTRY.

Organized at Sandusky, Ohio, and mustered in May 13, 1864. Guard duty at Johnson's Island, Sandusky Bay, till June 4. Moved to Washington, D. C., June 4; thence to Bermuda Hundred, Va., June 8. Attached to 2nd Brigade, 3rd Division, 10th Army Corps, Army of the James. Picket duty at Bermuda Hundred and at Point of Rocks till June 21. March to Deep Bottom June 21, and duty there till August 11. Duty in lines at Bermuda Hundred and at Fort Powhatan August 11 to September 16. Mustered out September 22, 1864.

Regiment lost during service by disease 1 Officer and 22 Enlisted men. Total 23.

131st REGIMENT INFANTRY.

Organized at Camp Chase, Ohio, and mustered in May 14, 1864. Left State for Baltimore, Md., May 15. Attached to 2nd Separate Brigade, 8th Army Corps, Middle Department. Assigned to garrison duty at Forts McHenry, Marshall and Federal Hill till August 19. Detachments at Washington, Harper's Ferry, W. Va., Fortress Monroe and City Point, Va. Ordered home for muster out August 19. Mustered out August 25, 1864.

Regiment lost during service 2 by disease.

132nd REGIMENT INFANTRY.

Organized at Camp Chase, Ohio, and mustered in May 15, 1864. Left State for Washington, D. C., May 22. Camp near Fort Albany till May 30. Embarked at Alexandria, Va., for White House, Va., May 30. Fatigue duty at White House till June 11. Moved to Bermuda Hundred, Va., June 11. Attached to 2nd Brigade, 3rd Division, 10th Army Corps, Army of the James. Fatigue and picket duty at Bermuda Hundred till August 12. Moved to Norfolk, Va., August 12; thence to Washington, D. C., August 27, and arrived at Columbus, Ohio, August 30. Mustered out September 10, 1864.

Regiment lost during service 2 Enlisted men killed and 45 Enlisted men by disease. Total 47.

133rd REGIMENT INFANTRY.

Organized by consolidation of 58th and 76th Battalions and 3rd Regiment Ohio National Guard, and mustered in May 6, 1864. Moved to Parkersburg, W. Va., May 6; thence to New Creek May 8. Duty at New Creek till June 7. Moved to Washington, D. C., June 7; thence to Bermuda Hundred, Va., arriving June 12.

Attached to 1st Brigade, 3rd Division, 10th Army Corps, Army of the James. Bermuda front June 16-17. Duty in trenches at Bermuda Hundred till July 17. Moved to Fort Powhatan, on James River, July 17, and duty there repairing telegraph lines from Fort to Swan's Point, and in the fortifications to August. Built a Magazine, also a Signal tower 80 feet high. Moved to Washington, D. C., August 10; thence to Camp Chase, Ohio. Mustered out August 20, 1864.

Regiment lost during service 1 Enlisted man killed and 1 Officer and 29 Enlisted men by disease. Total 31.

134th REGIMENT INFANTRY.

Organized at Camp Chase, Ohio, and mustered in May 5, 1864. Left State for Cumberland, Md., May 7, and duty there till June 6. Moved to Washington, D. C., June 6; thence to White House and City Point, Va. Duty at City Point pontooning the James River and building roads till June 17. Picket duty at Bermuda Hundred till June 22. Attached to 2nd Brigade, 3rd Division, 10th Army Corps, Army of the James. Marched to Deep Bottom June 22, and engaged in building works. Picket duty and operations against Richmond on north side of the James River till August. Mustered out August 31, 1864.

Regiment lost during service 1 Enlisted man killed and 30 Enlisted men by disease. Total 31.

135th REGIMENT INFANTRY.

Organized at Camp Chase, Ohio, and mustered in May 11, 1864. Left State for Cumberland, Md., May 11. Assigned to duty as railroad guard on Baltimore Railroad at North Mountain, Opequan Station and Martinsburg till July 3. Operations about Harper's Ferry July 4-7. Guard duty at Maryland Heights till September. Actions at Maryland Heights July 3-7. Mustered out September 1, 1864.

Regiment lost during service 7 Enlisted men killed and mortally wounded and 66 Enlisted men by disease. Total 73.

136th REGIMENT INFANTRY.

Organized at Camp Chase, Ohio, and mustered in May 18, 1864. Left State for Washington, D. C., May 13. Attached to 2nd Brigade, DeRussy's Division, 22nd Army Corps, to July, 1864. 3rd Brigade, DeRussy's Division, 22nd Corps, to August, 1864. Assigned to garrison duty at Forts Ellsworth, Williams and in the Northern Defences of Washington till August. Repulse of Early's attack on Washington July 11-12. Mustered out August 30, 1864.

Regiment lost during service 2 Officers and 23 Enlisted men by disease. Total 25.

137th REGIMENT INFANTRY.

Organized at Camp Dennison, Ohio, and mustered in May 6, 1864. Left State for Baltimore, Md., May 12. Assigned to duty as garrison at Forts McHenry, Federal Hill, Marshall and Carroll. Defences of Baltimore, 8th Army Corps, Middle Department, till August. Mustered out August 21, 1864.

Regiment lost during service 5 Enlisted men by disease.

138th REGIMENT INFANTRY.

Organized at Camp Dennison, Ohio, and mustered in May 14, 1864. Left State for Washington, D. C., May 14. Picket duty at Harper's Ferry, W. Va., May 16-22. Reached Washington May 22. Attached to 1st Brigade, DeRussy's Division, 22nd Army Corps. Assigned to duty as garrison at Forts Albany, Craig and Tillinghast, Defences of Washington, south of the Potomac, till June 5. Moved to White House Landing, Va., June 5. Picket and guard duty there till June 16. Moved to Bermuda Hundred, Va., June 16. Assigned to 2nd Brigade, 3rd Division, 10th Army Corps, Army of the James. Picket and fatigue duty at Bermuda Hundred, Point of Rocks, Broadway Landing and Cherrystone Inlet till August. Mustered out September 1, 1864.

Regiment lost during service 8 Enlisted men by disease.

139th REGIMENT INFANTRY.

Organized at Camp Chase, Ohio, and mustered in May 11, 1864. Left State for Washington, D. C., May 20; thence moved to Point Lookout, Md., June 1, and assigned to duty there as Prison Guard till August 22. Mustered out August 26, 1864.

Regiment lost during service 14 Enlisted men by disease.

140th REGIMENT INFANTRY.

Organized at Gallipolis, Ohio, and mustered in May 10, 1864. Left State for Charleston, W. Va., May 10. Assigned to duty as garrison at Charleston and on guard duty along Kenewha and Gauley Rivers till September. Mustered out September 3, 1864.

Lost 2 by disease.

141st REGIMENT INFANTRY.

Organized at Gallipolis, Ohio, and mustered in May 14, 1864. Left State for Charleston, W. Va., May 21. Garrison duty at Charleston. Attached to Reserve Division, Dept. of West Virginia, till August 25. Mustered out September 3, 1864.

Lost during service 4 Enlisted men by disease. Total 4.

142nd REGIMENT INFANTRY.

Organized at Camp Chase, Ohio, and mustered in September 13, 1864. Moved to Martinsburg, W. Va., May 14; thence to Washington, D. C., May 19. Duty at Fort Lyons till June 3. Attached to 2nd Brigade, DeRussy's Division, 22nd Army Corps. Embarked at Alexandria, Va., for White House, Va., June 7. Duty guarding supply trains through the Wilderness near Cold Harbor June 9-14. Moved to Point of Rocks, Va., and duty there till August 19. Ordered home and mustered out September 2, 1864.

Regiment lost during service 1 Officer and 42 Enlisted men by disease. Total 43.

143rd REGIMENT INFANTRY.

Organized at Camp Chase, Ohio, and mustered in May 12, 1864. Left State for Washington, D. C., May 15. Guard duty at Forts Slemmer, Totten, Slocum and Stevens, attached to 1st Brigade, Haskins' Division, 22nd Army Corps, till June 8. Moved to White House Landing June 8, thence to Bermuda Hundred. Assigned to 1st Brigade, 3rd Division, 10th Army Corps, Army of the James. Duty in the trenches at Bermuda Hundred, City Point and Fort Pocohontas till August 29. Ordered to Camp Chase, Ohio, and mustered out September 13, 1864.

Regiment lost during service 32 Enlisted men by disease. Total 32.

144th REGIMENT INFANTRY.

Organized at Camp Chase, Ohio, and mustered in May 11, 1864. Left State for Baltimore, Md., May 11. Companies assigned to duty as follows: "G" and "K" in the Defences of Baltimore; "B" at Camp Parole, Annapolis, Md.; "E" at Wilmington, Del.; "I" 'at Fort Dix, Relay House. Balance of Regiment at Fort McHenry. Attached to 1st Separate Brigade, 8th Army Corps, Middle Department. Regiment relieved from duty at Baltimore and moved to Relay House. Battle of Monocacy Junction, Md., July 9. Moved to Washington, D. C., July 13. Advance to Winchester and Snicker's Gap July 14-20. Attached to Kenley's Independent Brigade, 8th Army Corps. Operations in Shenandoah Valley July 20 to August 13. Repulse of attack by Moseby at Berryville August 13. Guard duty near Berryville till August 20. Ordered home and mustered out August 31, 1864.

Regiment lost during service 10 Enlisted men killed and mortally wounded and 53 Enlisted men by disease. Total 63.

145th REGIMENT INFANTRY.

Organized at Camp Chase, Ohio, and mustered in May 12, 1864. Left State for Washington, D. C., May 12. Attached to 1st Brigade, DeRussy's Division, 22nd Army Corps, and assigned to garrison duty at Forts Whipple,

Woodbury, Chase, Tillinghast and Albany, Defences of Washington, south of Potomac, till August. Repulse of Early's attack on Washington July 11-12. Mustered out August 20, 1864.

Lost during service 10 Enlisted men by disease.

146th REGIMENT INFANTRY.

Organized at Camp Dennison, Ohio, and mustered in May 12, 1864. Left State for Charleston, W. Va., May 17; thence moved to Fayetteville, W. Va., and garrison duty there till August 27. (Cos. "A" and "H" detached at Camp Chase, Ohio, to guard prisoners.) Moved to Camp Piatt, W. Va., August 27; thence to Camp Dennison, Ohio, and mustered out September 7, 1864.

Lost during service 8 Enlisted men by disease.

147th REGIMENT INFANTRY.

Organized at Camp Dennison, Ohio, and mustered in May 16, 1864. Left State for Washington, D. C., May 20. Attached to 1st Brigade, DeRussy's Division, 22nd Army Corps, to July, 1864. 2nd Brigade, DeRussy's Division, 22nd Army Corps, to August. Assigned to duty as garrison at Forts Ethan Allen, Marcy, Reno and Stevens, Defences of Washington, till August 23. Repulse of Early's attack on Washington July 11-12. Mustered out August 30, 1864.

Lost during service 22 Enlisted men by disease.

148th REGIMENT INFANTRY.

Organized at Marietta, Ohio, and mustered in May 17, 1864. Left State for Harper's Ferry, W. Va., May 23; thence moved to Washington, D. C., June 1, and to White House Landing, Va., June 9. Moved to Bermuda Hundred, Va., June 11, and to City Point June 15. Attached to 1st Brigade, 3rd Division, 10th Army Corps, Army of the James. Duty at City Point till August 29. Moved to Marietta September 5, and mustered out September 14, 1864.

Lost during service 2 Officers and 37 Enlisted men by disease. Total 39.

149th REGIMENT INFANTRY.

Organized at Camp Dennison, Ohio, May 8, 1864. Left State for Baltimore, Md., May 11. Attached to Defences of Baltimore, 8th Army Corps, Middle Department, to July, 1864. 1st Separate Brigade, 8th Army Corps, to July, 1864. Kenly's Independent Brigade, 8th Army Corps, to August, 1864.

SERVICE.—Duty in the Defences of Baltimore, Md., and at different points on the eastern shore of Maryland till July 4. Moved to Monocacy Junction July 4. Battle of Monocacy Junction July 9. Moved to Washington, D. C., July 13. Advance to Snicker's Gap, Va., July 13-20. Operations in the Shenandoah Valley July 20-August 23. Action with Moseby at Berryville August 13. Mustered out August 30, 1864.

Regiment lost during service 4 Enlisted men killed and mortally wounded and 38 Enlisted men by disease. Total 42.

150th REGIMENT INFANTRY.

Organized at Cleveland, Ohio, and mustered in May 5, 1864. Moved to Washington, D. C., May 7, and assigned to duty as garrison at Forts Lincoln, Saratoga, Thayer, Bunker Hill, Slocum, Totten and Stevens, Defences of Washington, till August. Attached to 1st Brigade, Haskins' Division, 22nd Army Corps, to July, 1864. 2nd Brigade, Haskins' Division, 22nd Army Corps, to August. Repulse of Early's attack on Washington, D. C., July 11-12. Mustered out August 23, 1864.

Regiment lost during service 2 Enlisted men killed and 10 Enlisted men by disease. Total 12.

151st REGIMENT INFANTRY.

Organized at Camp Dennison, Ohio, and mustered in May 18, 1864. Left State for Washington, D. C., May 14. Attached to 2nd Brigade, Haskins' Division, 22nd Army Corps, to July, 1864. 1st Brigade, Haskins' Division, 22nd Army Corps, to August, 1864. Assigned to duty as garrison at Forts Sumner, Mansfield and Simmons till August 23. Companies "C" and "G" at Fort Stevens, Company "I" at Fort Smeade, Company "K" at Fort Kearney. Repulse of Early's attack on Washington, D. C., July 11-12. Regiment concentrated at Fort Simmons August 17. Moved to Camp Chase, Ohio, August 23, and mustered out August 27, 1864.

Lost during service 10 Enlisted men by disease.

152nd REGIMENT INFANTRY.

Organized at Camp Dennison, Ohio, May 11, 1864. Left State for New Creek, W. Va., May 15; thence moved to Martinsburg and duty there till June. March with train from Martinsburg to Beverly (430 miles) June 4-27. Action at Greenbrier Gap June 22. Sweet White Sulphur June 23. Moved to Cumberland, Md., June 29. Duty along Baltimore & Ohio Railroad and at Cumberland till August 25. Attached to Reserve Division, Dept. of West Virginia. Ordered to Camp Dennison, Ohio, August 25, and mustered out September 2.

Regiment lost during service 1 Enlisted man killed and 20 Enlisted men by disease. Total 21.

153rd REGIMENT INFANTRY.

Organized at Camp Dennison, Ohio, and mustered in May 10, 1864. Left State for Harper's Ferry, W. Va., May 10. Attached to Railroad Guard, Reserve Division, Dept. of West Virginia. Guard duty at Harper's Ferry and along line of the Baltimore & Ohio Railroad till June 29. Action at Hammack's Mills, Oldtown, July 3. North Mountain July 3. South Branch Bridge and Patterson's Creek Bridge July 4. Sir John's Run July 6. Green Springs Run August 2. Moved to Camp Chase, Ohio, August 30. Mustered out September 9, 1864.

Regiment lost during service 1 Officer and 2 Enlisted men killed and mortally wounded and 26 Enlisted men by disease. Total 29.

154th REGIMENT INFANTRY.

Organized at Camp Dennison, Ohio, and mustered in May 8, 1864. Left State for New Creek, W. Va., May 12. Guard and picket duty at New Creek till May 29. (Co. "F" detached at Piedmont May 22 to August 22.) Moved to Greenland Gap May 29. Skirmish near Moorefield June 4. (1 Co. detached at Youghiogheny Bridge till July 25.) Engaged in numerous scouting expeditions till July 25. Moved to New Creek July 25. Action at New Creek August 4. Moved to Camp Chase, Ohio, August 10 in charge of prisoners; thence to Camp Dennison August 22, and there mustered out September 1, 1864.

Regiment lost during service 1 Enlisted man killed and 3 Enlisted men by disease. Total 4.

155th REGIMENT INFANTRY.

Organized at Camp Dennison, Ohio, and mustered in May 8, 1864. Left State for New Creek, W. Va., May 9; thence moved to Martinsburg. Attached to Reserve Division, West Virginia, to June. Moved to Washington, D. C., June 3; thence to Bermuda Hundred and City Point, Va. Ordered to Norfolk, Va., June 29, and duty there till August 19. Expedition to Elizabeth City, N. C., July 27-August 4. Ordered home for muster out August 19. Mustered out August 27.

Regiment lost during service 20 Enlisted men by disease.

156th REGIMENT INFANTRY.

Organized at Camp Dennison, Ohio, and mustered in May 15, 1864. Companies "A," "B," "C," "D," "E," "F" and "H" moved to Cincinnati, Ohio, May 20 and engaged in guard and patrol duty in and about that city till July 18. Companies "G," "I" and "K" on guard and patrol duty at Camp Dennison till July; moved to Falmouth, Ky., thence to Covington and rejoin Regiment July 18. Moved to Cumberland, Md., July 28 and assigned to General Kelly's Command, Dept. of West Virginia. Duty at Cumberland till August 28. Action near Folck's Mills, Cumberland, August 1. Mustered out September 1, 1864.

Regiment lost during service 1 Officer and 22 Enlisted men by disease. Total 23.

157th REGIMENT INFANTRY.

Organized at Camp Chase, Ohio, and mustered in May 15, 1864. Left State for Baltimore, Md., May 17. Assigned to Tyler's Command, 8th Army Corps, Middle Department. Duty in the Defences of Baltimore and at Fort Delaware guarding Confederate prisoners till September. Mustered out September 2, 1864.

Regiment lost during service 10 Enlisted men by disease.

158th REGIMENT INFANTRY.

Organization of this Regiment was commenced but not completed.

159th REGIMENT INFANTRY.

Organized at Zanesville, Ohio, and mustered in May 9, 1864. Left State for Harper's Ferry, W. Va., May 9. Assigned to 3rd Separate Brigade, 8th Army Corps, Middle Department. At Maryland Heights till May 17. Guard duty in the Defences of Baltimore, Md., and guarding bridges along Philadelphia, Wilmington & Baltimore Railroad by Detachments till July. Battle of Monocacy Junction, Md., July 9. Expedition to Parkesville July 12. Companies "B," "E," "G" and "I" guard railroad at Havre de Grace July 28 to August 13. Ordered home August 13, and mustered out August 24, 1864.

Regiment lost 10 Enlisted men by disease during service.

160th REGIMENT INFANTRY.

Organized at Zanesville and mustered in May 12, 1864. Left State for Harper's Ferry, W. Va., May 12. Detached for duty guarding supply train at Martinsburg. Assigned to Reserve Division, Dept. of West Virginia, May 25. Moved to Woodstock, W. Va. Detached and moved to Martinsburg in charge of supply trains. Newtown May 29-30. Skirmish at Middletown June 7. Operations in the Shenandoah Valley in charge of wagon trains till July. Operations about Harper's Ferry July 4-7. Maryland Heights July 6-7. Duty in the trenches about Harper's Ferry till August 25. Ordered home and mustered out September 7, 1864.

Regiment lost during service 1 Enlisted man killed and 1 Officer and 14 Enlisted men by disease. Total 16.

161st REGIMENT INFANTRY.

Organized at Camp Chase, Ohio, and mustered in May 9, 1864. Left State for Cumberland, Md., May 9, and duty there till May 28. Attached to Reserve Division, Dept. of West Virginia. Moved to Martinsburg, W. Va., May 28, and assigned to 1st Brigade, 1st Division, West Virginia. Detached June 4 and assigned to duty in charge of supply trains for Hunter's Army. Hunter's Raid on Lynchburg June 6-25. Retreat to Martinsburg June 19-25. Moved to Beverly June 28, thence to Webster June 30, and to Martinsburg July 2. Operations about Harper's Ferry July 4-7. Defence of Maryland Heights July 6-7. Duty in the Defences of Maryland Heights till August 25. Ordered home and mustered out September 2, 1864.

Regiment lost during service 1 Enlisted man killed and 1 Officer and 12 Enlisted men by disease. Total 14.

162nd REGIMENT INFANTRY.

Organized at Camp Chase, Ohio, and mustered in May 20, 1864. Companies "A," "C," "F" and "K" on duty at Tod Barracks, Columbus, Ohio, till September 4. Companies "B," "D," "E," "G," "H" and "I" moved to Covington, Ky., June 11. Expedition to Carrollton, Ky., in search of Moses Webster's men. Duty at Carrollton and Covington, Ky., recruiting for the 117th United States Colored Troops and arresting prominent Rebels till September. Mustered out at Camp Chase, Ohio, September 4, 1864.

Regiment lost during service 20 Enlisted men by disease.

163rd REGIMENT INFANTRY.

Regiment organized at Camp Chase, Ohio, and mustered in May 12, 1864. Moved to Washington, D. C., May 13. Assigned to 1st Brigade, Haskins' Division, 22nd Army Corps, to June, 1864. Duty in the Defences of Washington, D. C., Headquarters at Fort Reno, till June 8. Moved to Bermuda Hundred, Va., June 8-12. Attached to 1st Brigade, 3rd Division, 10th Army Corps, Army of the James. Reconnoissance on the Petersburg & Richmond Railroad June 14-15. Skirmish on Petersburg and Richmond Turnpike June 15-16. Moved to Wilson's Landing June 16. Fatigue duty building Fort Pocahontas and scouting on west side of the James River till August. Ordered to Columbus, Ohio, August 29, and mustered out September 10, 1864.

Regiment lost during service 29 Enlisted men by disease.

164th REGIMENT INFANTRY.

Organized at Camp Taylor, Cleveland, Ohio, and mustered in May 11, 1864. Left State for Washington, D. C., May 14. Attached to 1st Brigade, DeRussy's Division, 22nd Army Corps, and assigned to duty on south side of the Potomac as garrison at Forts Smith, Strong, Bennett, Hagerty and other Forts and Batteries till August. Repulse of Early's attack on Washington July 11-12. Mustered out August 27, 1864.

Regiment lost during service 18 Enlisted men by disease.

165th REGIMENT INFANTRY.

Organized at Camp Dennison, Ohio, and mustered in May 14, 1864. Duty at Camp Dennison till May 20. Moved to Johnson's Island, Sandusky Bay, Ohio, May 20, and duty there till June 25. Moved to Kentucky June 25, and duty there till August. Moved to Cumberland, Md., August 8, and duty in Maryland and Virginia till August 27. Mustered out August 31, 1864.

Lost 2 Enlisted men by disease during service.

166th REGIMENT INFANTRY.

Organized at Camp Cleveland, Ohio, and mustered in May 13, 1864. Left State for Washington, D. C., May 15. Attached to 2nd Brigade, DeRussy's Division, 22nd Army Corps, to July, 1864. 3rd Brigade, DeRussy's Division, 22nd Army Corps, to August, 1864. Assigned to duty as garrison at Forts Richardson, Barnard, Raynalds, Ward and Worth (Headquarters at Fort Richardson), Defences of Washington south of the Potomac, till September. Repulse of Early's attack on Washington July 11-12. Mustered out September 9, 1864.

Regiment lost during service 39 Enlisted men by disease.

167th REGIMENT INFANTRY.

Organized at Hamilton, Ohio, and mustered in May 14, 1864. Left State for Charleston, W. Va., May 18. Six Companies moved to Camp Piatt May 22, and four Companies to Gauley Bridge. Duty at these points guarding supply trains and stores till September. Mustered out September 8, 1864.

Regiment lost during service 5 Enlisted men by disease.

168th REGIMENT INFANTRY.

Organized at Camp Dennison, Ohio, and mustered in May 19, 1864. Moved to Covington, Ky., May 19. Detachments stationed at Falmouth and Cynthiana guarding railroad and bridges. Operations against Morgan May 31-June 20. Action at Cynthiana June 9 (Detachment captured). Keller's Bridge, near Cynthiana, June 11. Duty in Kentucky till July 10. Moved to Camp Dennison July 11. Guard duty there and at Cincinnati, Ohio, till September 8. Mustered out September 8, 1864.

Regiment lost during service 11 Enlisted men killed and mortally wounded and 8 Enlisted men by disease. Total 19.

169th REGIMENT INFANTRY.

Organized at Camp Taylor, Cleveland, Ohio, and mustered in May 13, 1864. Left State for Washington, D. C., May 19. Attached to 1st Brigade, DeRussy's Division, 22nd Army Corps, to July, 1864. 2nd Brigade, DeRussy's Division, 22nd Army Corps, to August, 1864. Assigned to duty in the Defences of Washington south of the Potomac as garrison at Fort Ethan Allen and in fortifications south of the Potomac till September. Repulse of Early's attack on Washington July 11-12. Mustered out September 4, 1864.

Regiment lost during service 41 Enlisted men by disease.

170th REGIMENT INFANTRY.

Organized at Bellaire, Ohio, and mustered in May 13, 1864. Left State for Washington, D. C., May 17. Attached to 2nd Brigade, Haskins' Division, 22nd Army Corps, to July, 1864, and assigned to duty as garrison at Forts Simmons, Bayard, Mansfield, Gaines and Battery Vermont, Defences of Washington, till July 4. Moved to Sandy Hook, Md., July 4, and duty in the Defences of Maryland Heights till July 15. Attached to Reserve Division, Dept. of West Virginia. Operations in the Shenandoah Valley July 15-August 24. Expedition to Snicker's Ford July 17-18. Rocky Ford July 18. Battle of Kernstown, Winchester, July 24. Martinsburg July 25. Moved to Frederick, Md., July 30; thence guard supply trains to Harper's Ferry and duty there till August 24. Mustered out September 10, 1864.

Regiment lost during service 4 Enlisted men killed and mortally wounded and 1 Officer and 19 Enlisted men by disease. Total 24.

171st REGIMENT INFANTRY.

Organized at Sandusky, Ohio, and mustered in May 7, 1864. On guard and fatigue duty at Johnson's Island till June 8. Moved to Covington, Ky., thence to Cynthiana, Ky. Attached to General Hobson's Command, District of Kentucky, Dept. of the Ohio. Action at Kellar's Bridge, Ky., near Cynthiana, Ky., June 11. Cynthiana, Ky., June 12. Regiment captured. Paroled June 13 and ordered to Camp Dennison, Ohio. Duty there and at Johnson's Island, Ohio, till August. Mustered out August 20, 1864.

Regiment lost during service 17 Enlisted men killed and mortally wounded and 15 Enlisted men by disease. Total 32.

172nd REGIMENT INFANTRY.

Organized at Gallipolis, Ohio, and mustered in May 14, 1864. Guard duty at Gallipolis till September. Mustered out September 3, 1864.

Lost 12 Enlisted men by disease during service.

173rd REGIMENT INFANTRY.

Organized at Gallipolis, Ohio, and mustered in September 18, 1864. Left State for Nashville, Tenn., September 18, arriving there October 1. Attached to Post and Defences of Nashville, Tenn., Dept. of the Cumberland, to March, 1865. 3rd Sub-District, District of Middle Tennessee, Dept. of the Cumberland, to June, 1865.

SERVICE.—Assigned to guard duty at Nashville, Tenn., till February, 1865. Occupation of Nashville during Hood's investment December 1-15, 1864. Battle of Nashville December 15-16. Guarding prisoners at Nashville till February, 1865. Moved to Columbia, Tenn., February 15. Duty there and at Johnsonville till June 20. Moved to Nashville June 20, and there mustered out June 26. Disbanded at Camp Dennison, Ohio, July 5, 1865.

Regiment lost during service 108 Enlisted men by disease.

174th REGIMENT INFANTRY.

Organized at Camp Chase, Ohio, August 16 to September 21, 1864. Mustered in September 21, 1864. Left State for Nashville, Tenn., September 23, arriving there September 26. Moved to Murfreesboro, Tenn., and duty in the Defences of that city till October 27. Attached to Post of Murfreesboro, Tenn., Dept. of the Cumberland, to October, 1864. District of North Alabama, Dept. of the Cumberland, to December, 1864. 3rd Brigade, 1st Division, 23rd Army Corps, Army of the Ohio, to February, 1865, and Dept. of North Carolina to June, 1865.

SERVICE.—Moved from Murfreesboro to Decatur, Ala., October 27. Defence of Decatur October 27-29. Moved to Elk River October 29. (4 Cos. Detached at Athens, Ala.). Returned to Decatur November 1 and duty there till November 25. Moved to Murfreesboro November 25. Action at Overall's Creek December 4. Siege of Murfreesboro December 5-12. Wilkinson's Pike, near Murfreesboro, December 7. Ordered to Clifton, Tenn., and duty there till January 17, 1865. Movement to Washington, D. C., January 17-29, and duty there till February 21. Moved to Fort Fisher, N. C., February 21-23, to Morehead City February 24, and to New Berne February 25. Advance on Kinston and Goldsboro March 6-21. Battle of Wise's Forks March 8-10. Occupation of Kinston March 14, and of Goldsboro March 21. Advance on Raleigh April 10-14. Occupation of Raleigh April 14. Bennett's House April 26. Surrender of Johnston and his army. Duty at Raleigh and Charlotte, N. C., till June. Mustered out at Charlotte, N. C., June 28, 1865.

Regiment lost during service 1 Officer and 21 Enlisted men killed and mortally wounded and 1 Officer and 94 Enlisted men by disease. Total 117.

175th REGIMENT INFANTRY.

Organized at Camp Dennison, Ohio, and mustered in October 11, 1864. Left State for Nashville, Tenn., October 11; thence moved to Columbia, Tenn., October 20, and assigned to post and garrison duty there, also guarding Tennessee & Alabama Railroad till November 24. Attached to 3rd Brigade, 3rd Division, 23rd Army Corps, Army of the Ohio, to December, 1864. Post of Columbia, Tenn., Dept. of the Cumberland, to March, 1865. 2nd Sub-District, District of Middle Tennessee, to June, 1865.

SERVICE.—Nashville Campaign November 24-December 28. Columbia, Duck River, November 24-27. Battle of Franklin November 30. Occupation of Nashville during Hood's investment December 1-15. Battle of Nashville December 15-16. Occupation of Fort Negley till December 25. Ordered to Columbia, Tenn., December 25, and garrison duty there till June, 1865. Moved to Nashville, Tenn., June 23. Mustered out June 27, 1865.

Regiment lost during service 1 Officer and 15 Enlisted men killed and mortally wounded and 2 Officers and 106 Enlisted men by disease. Total 124.

176th REGIMENT INFANTRY.

Organized at Camp Chase, Ohio, August 10 to September 21, 1864. Mustered in September 21, 1864. Left State for Nashville, Tenn., September 21. Attached to Post and Defences of Nashville, Dept. of the Cumberland, to December, 1864. 2nd Brigade, 4th Division, 20th Army Corps, Dept. of the Cumberland, to March, 1865. District of Nashville, Tenn., Dept. of the Cumberland, to June, 1865.

SERVICE.—Provost and guard duty at Nashville, Tenn., September, 1864, to June, 1865. Battle of Nashville December 15-16, 1864. Mustered out June 18, 1865.

Regiment lost during service 102 Enlisted men by disease.

177th REGIMENT INFANTRY.

Organized at Camp Cleveland, Ohio, and mustered in October 9, 1864. Ordered to Nashville, Tenn.; thence to Tullahoma, Tenn., and garrison duty there under General Milroy till November 30. Ordered to Murfreesboro, Tenn., November 30, arriving there December 2. Attached to Defences Nashville & Chattanooga Railroad, Dept. of the Cumberland, to January, 1865. 2nd Brigade, 3rd Division, 23rd Army Corps, Army of the Ohio, and Dept. of North Carolina, to June, 1865.

SERVICE.—Siege of Murfreesboro December 5-12, 1864. Wilkinson's Pike, near Murfreesboro, December 7. Near Murfreesboro December 13-14. Ordered to Clifton, Tenn., and duty there till January 16, 1865. Movement to Washington, D. C., thence to Fort Fisher, N. C., January 16-February 7. Operations against Hoke February 11-14. Near Sugar Loaf Battery February 11. Fort Anderson February 18-19. Town Creek February 19-20. Capture of Wilmington February 22. Campaign of the Carolinas March 1-April 26. Advance on Goldsboro March 6-21. Occupation of Goldsboro March 21. Advance on Raleigh April 10-14. Occupation of Raleigh April 14. Bennett's House April 26. Surrender of Johnston and his army. Duty at Raleigh and Greensboro till June. Mustered out at Greensboro, N. C., June 24 and discharged July 7, 1865.

Regiment lost during service 2 Enlisted men killed and 82 Enlisted men by disease. Total 84.

178th REGIMENT INFANTRY.

Organized at Camp Chase, Ohio, and mustered in September 26, 1864. Left State for Nashville, Tenn., October 8. Attached to Defences Nashville & Chattanooga Railroad, Dept. of the Cumberland, to January, 1865. 3rd Brigade, 1st Division, 23rd Army Corps, Army of the Ohio, and Dept. of North Carolina, to June, 1865.

SERVICE.—Duty at Nashville, Tenn., till October 22, 1864. and at Tullahoma, Tenn., till November 30. Moved to Murfreesboro, Tenn., November 30-December 2. Siege of Murfreesboro December 5-12. Wilkinson's Cross Roads, near Murfreesboro, "The Cedars," December 7. Wilkinson's Pike, near Murfreesboro, December 13-14. Ordered to Clifton, Tenn., and duty there till January 16, 1865. Movement to Washington, D. C., January 16-29, and to Fort Fisher, N. C., February 21-23; to Morehead City February 24, thence to New Berne February 25. Campaign of the Carolinas March 1-April 26. Advance on Kinston and Goldsboro March 6-21. Battle of Wise's Forks March 8-10. Occupation of Kinston March 14. Occupation of Goldsboro March 21. Advance on Raleigh April 10-14. Occupation of Raleigh April 14. Bennett's House April 26. Surrender of Johnston and his army. Duty at Raleigh and Charlotte, N. C., till June. Mustered out June 29, 1865.

Regiment lost during service 2 Enlisted men killed and 66 Enlisted men by disease. Total 68.

179th REGIMENT INFANTRY.

Organized at Camp Chase, Ohio, and mustered in September 29, 1864. Ordered to Nashville, Tenn., arriving there October 8. Attached to Post of Nashville, Tenn., Dept. of the Cumberland, to December, 1864. 2nd Brigade, 4th Division, 20th Army Corps, Dept. of the Cumberland, to March, 1865. Post of Nashville to June, 1865.

SERVICE.—Engaged in post and garrison duty at Nashville, Tenn., October, 1864, to June, 1865. Battle of Nashville December 15-16, 1864. Mustered out June 18, 1865.

Regiment lost during service 80 Enlisted men by disease.

180th REGIMENT INFANTRY.

Organized at Camp Chase September-October, 1864. Left State for Nashville, Tenn., October 15. Attached to 3rd Brigade, Defences of Nashville & Chattanooga Railroad, Dept. of the Cumberland, to January, 1865. 1st Brigade, 1st Division, 23rd Army Corps, Army of the Ohio, and Dept. of North Carolina, to July, 1865.

SERVICE.—Moved from Nashville to Decherd, Tenn., October, 1864, and guard duty on line of the Nashville & Chattanooga Railroad, Right Wing at Decherd, Left Wing at Elk River Bridge, till January, 1863. Moved to Nashville, Tenn., January 6; thence moved as Train Guard to Columbia, Tenn., January 10. Return to Nashville and movement to Washington, D. C.; thence to North Carolina January 16-February 25. Campaign of the Carolinas March 1-April 26. Advance on Kinston and Goldsboro March 6-21. Battle of Wise's Forks March 8-10. Occupation of Kinston March 14. Occu-

pation of Goldsboro March 21. Advance on Raleigh April 10-14. Occupation of Raleigh April 14. Bennett's House April 26. Surrender of Johnston and his army. Duty at Raleigh, Greensboro and Charlotte, N. C., till July. Mustered out July 12, 1865.

Regiment lost during service 1 Officer and 5 Enlisted men killed and mortally wounded and 1 Officer and 84 Enlisted men by disease. Total 91.

181st REGIMENT INFANTRY.

Organized at Camp Dennison, Ohio, and mustered in October 10, 1864. Left State for Huntsville, Ala., October 24. Attached to District of Northern Alabama October, 1864. 1st Brigade, Defences Nashville & Chattanooga Railroad, to January, 1865. 3rd Brigade, 2nd Division, 23rd Army Corps, Army of the Ohio and Dept. of North Carolina, to July, 1865.

SERVICE.—Duty at Huntsville and Decatur, Ala., till November, 1864. Moved to Murfreesboro, Tenn., November 30. Siege of Murfreesboro December 5-12. Wilkinson's Pike, near Murfreesboro, December 7 and December 13-14. Duty at Murfreesboro till December 24. Moved to Columbia, Tenn., December 24. Movement to Washington, D. C., thence to Fort Fisher, N. C., January 15 to February 9, 1865. Operations against Hoke February 11-14. Capture of Wilmington February 22. Campaign of the Carolinas March 1-April 26. Advance on Goldsboro March 6-21. Occupation of Goldsboro March 21. Advance on Raleigh April 10-14. Occupation of Raleigh April 14. Bennett's House April 26. Surrender of Johnston and his army. Duty at Raleigh, Greensboro and Salisbury till July. Mustered out July 29, 1865.

Regiment lost during service 5 Enlisted men killed and mortally wounded and 1 Officer and 27 Enlisted men by disease. Total 33.

182nd REGIMENT INFANTRY.

Organized at Camp Chase, Ohio, August 4 to October 13, 1864. Mustered in October 27, 1864. Left State for Nashville, Tenn., November 1. Attached to Post and Defences of Nashville, Dept. of the Cumberland, to December, 1864. 2nd Brigade, 4th Division, 20th Army Corps, Dept. of the Cumberland, to March, 1865. Garrison at Nashville, Tenn., Dept. of the Cumberland, to July, 1865.

SERVICE.—Post and garrison duty at Nashville, Tenn., November, 1864, to July, 1865. Battle of Nashville December 15-16, 1864. Mustered out July 7, 1865.

Regiment lost during service 61 Enlisted men by disease.

183rd REGIMENT INFANTRY.

Organized at Cincinnati and Sandusky, Ohio, September-October, 1864. Mustered in at Camp Dennison, Ohio, October 12, 1864. Left State for Columbia, Tenn., November 19, arriving there November 28. Attached to 3rd Brigade, 2nd Division, 23rd Army Corps, Army of the Ohio, and Dept. of North Carolina, to July, 1865.

SERVICE.—Battle of Franklin, Tenn., November 30, 1864. Battle of Nashville December 15-16. Pursuit of Hood to the Tennessee River December 17-28. Duty at Clifton, Tenn., till January 16, 1865. Movement to Washington, D. C., thence to Fort Fisher, N. C., January 16-February 9. Operations against Hoke February 11-14. Capture of Wilmington February 22. Campaign of the Carolinas March 1-April 26. Advance on Goldsboro March 6-21. Occupation of Goldsboro March 21. Advance on Raleigh April 10-14. Occupation of Raleigh April 14. Bennett's House April 26. Surrender of Johnston and his army. Duty at Raleigh and Salisbury, N. C., till July. Mustered out July 17, 1865.

Regiment lost during service 2 Officers and 22 Enlisted men killed and mortally wounded and 2 Officers and 57 Enlisted men by disease. Total 83.

184th REGIMENT INFANTRY.

Organized at Camp Chase, Ohio, and mustered in February 21, 1865. Left State for Nashville, Tenn., February 21; thence moved to Chattanooga and to Bridgeport, Ala., March 21. Guard railroad bridge over Tennessee River at Bridgeport, Ala., also railroad between Bridgeport, Ala., and Chattanooga, Tenn., with frequent skirmishing with Rebel Cavalry and guerrillas, March 21 to July 25. Garrison duty at Edgefield, Tenn., July 25 to September 20, 1865. Mustered out September 20, and discharged at Camp Chase, Ohio, September 27, 1865.

Regiment lost during service 1 Enlisted man killed and 1 Officer and 58 Enlisted men by disease. Total 60.

185th REGIMENT INFANTRY.

Organized at Camp Chase, Ohio, and mustered in February 25, 1865. Left State under orders for Nashville, Tenn.. February 27. Detained at Louisville, Ky., and assigned to guard duty at various points in Kentucky from Owensboro to Cumberland Gap, with Headquarters at Eminence, till September, 1865. Skirmish in Bath County, Ky., March 26. Garrisoned Mt. Sterling, Shelbyville, LaGrange, Greensboro, Cumberland Gap, etc. Mustered out at Lexington, Ky., September 26, 1865.

Regiment lost during service 35 Enlisted men by disease.

186th REGIMENT INFANTRY.

Organized at Camp Chase February, 1865. Left State for Nashville, Tenn., March 2. Attached to 2nd Brigade, 2nd Separate Division, Dept. of the Cumberland, to May, 1865. 2nd Brigade, 1st Separate Division, District of the Etowah, Dept. of the Cumberland, to July, 1865. 2nd Brigade, 4th Division, District East Tennessee, Dept. of the Cumberland, to September, 1865.

SERVICE.—Moved to Murfreesboro, Tenn., March 8, 1865; thence to Cleveland, Tenn., and duty there till May. Moved to Dalton, Ga., May 2; thence to Chattanooga, Tenn., May 10, and duty there till July 20, Moved to Nashville, Tenn., July 20, and duty there till September 19. Ordered to Columbus, Ohio, September 19, and mustered out September 25, 1865.

Regiment lost during service 1 Enlisted man killed and 49 Enlisted men by disease. Total 50.

187th REGIMENT INFANTRY.

Organized at Camp Chase, Ohio, and mustered in March 2, 1865. Left State for Nashville, Tenn., March 3, 1865. Provost duty at Nashville, Tenn., Dalton and Macon, Ga., till January, 1866. Attached to 1st Brigade, 2nd Separate Division, District of the Etowah, and Dept. of Georgia. Mustered out January 20, 1866.

Regiment lost during service 1 Enlisted man killed and 1 Officer and 52 Enlisted men by disease. Total 54.

188th REGIMENT INFANTRY.

Organized at Camp Chase, Ohio, and mustered in March 4, 1865. Left State for Nashville, Tenn., March 4. Attached to 1st Brigade, Defences Nashville & Chattanooga Railroad, Dept. of the Cumberland, to April, 1865. 1st Brigade, 1st Sub-District, District of Middle Tennessee, to September, 1865.

SERVICE.—Provost duty at Murfreesboro, Tenn., till May, 1865. At Tullahoma, Tenn., till July, and at Nashville, Tenn., till September, 1865. Mustered out at Nashville, Tenn., September 21, 1865.

Regiment lost during service 45 Enlisted men by disease.

189th REGIMENT INFANTRY.

Organized at Camp Chase, Ohio, and mustered in March 5, 1865. Left State for Huntsville, Ala., March 7. Attached to District of North Alabama, Dept. of the Tennessee, to September.

SERVICE.—Arrived at Huntsville, Ala., March 17, 1865. Assigned to duty along Memphis & Charleston Railroad guarding bridges and building stockades till June. Regiment concentrated June 20 and assigned to post duty at Huntsville till September 25. Mustered out September 28, 1865.

Regiment lost during service 1 Enlisted man killed and 48 Enlisted men by disease. Total 49.

190th REGIMENT INFANTRY.

Failed to complete organization.

191st REGIMENT INFANTRY.

Organized at Camp Chase, Ohio, January and February, 1865. Moved to Harper's Ferry, W. Va., March 10, 1865. Attached to 2nd Brigade, 1st Provisional Division, Army of the Shenandoah, March 20. March to Charleston March 21. Transferred to 2nd (Ohio) Brigade, 2nd Provisional Division, March 27. Duty near Charleston till April 4. Operations in the Shenandoah Valley in vicinity of Winchester, Stevenson's Depot and Jordan's Springs, April to August. Mustered out August 27, and discharged September 5, 1865.

Regiment lost during service 29 Enlisted men by disease.

192nd REGIMENT INFANTRY.

Organized at Camp Chase, Ohio, and mustered in March 9, 1865. Left State for Harper's Ferry, W. Va., March 10. Attached to 2nd Brigade, 1st Provisional Division, Army of the Shenandoah, March 20. March to Charleston March 21. Duty there till April 4. Transferred to 2nd (Ohio) Brigade, 2nd Provisional Division, March 27. March to Winchester April 4. Duty in the Shenandoah Valley in the vicinity of Winchester, Stevenson's Depot, Reed's Hill and Harrisonburg till August 25. Mustered out at Winchester September 1, 1865.

Regiment lost during service 1 Enlisted man killed and 26 Enlisted men by disease. Total 27.

193rd REGIMENT INFANTRY.

Organized at Camp Chase, Ohio, March, 1865. Ordered to Harper's Ferry, W. Va. Assigned to 2nd Brigade, 1st Provisional Division, Army of the Shenandoah, March 20. March to Charleston March 21, and duty there till April 4. Transferred to 2nd Brigade, 2nd Provisional Division, March 27. Moved to Winchester April 4, and duty there till August. Mustered out August 4, 1865.

Regiment lost during service 29 Enlisted men by disease.

194th REGIMENT INFANTRY.

Organized at Camp Chase March, 1865. Left State for Charleston, W. Va., March 14. Assigned to General Egan's Provisional Division, Army of the Shenandoah. Operation in the Shenandoah Valley till April. Ordered to Washington, D. C., and garrison duty there till October. Mustered out October 24, 1865.

Regiment lost during service 38 Enlisted men by disease.

195th REGIMENT INFANTRY.

Organized at Camp Chase, Ohio, and mustered in March 14 to March 20, 1865. Moved to Harper's Ferry, W. Va., March 22-25; thence to Winchester, Va., and assigned to Brooks' Provisional Division, Army of the Shenandoah. Ordered to Alexandria, Va., April 28 and provost duty there till December. Mustered out December 18, 1865.

Regiment lost during service 32 Enlisted men by disease.

196th REGIMENT INFANTRY.

Organized at Camp Chase, Ohio, and mustered in March 25, 1865. Left State for Winchester, Va., March 26. Assigned to 2nd Brigade, 2nd Provisional Division, Army of the Shenandoah. Duty at Winchester till July. Moved to Baltimore, Md., and garrison duty there and at Fort Delaware till September. Mustered out September 11, 1865.

Regiment lost during service 25 Enlisted men by disease.

197th REGIMENT INFANTRY.

Organized at Camp Chase, Ohio, and mustered in March 28, 1865. Left State for Washington, D. C., April 25. Assigned to a Provisional Brigade, 9th Army Corps. Duty at Washington and Alexandria till May 11. Moved to Dover, Del., and duty at Camp Harrington till May 31. Attached to 3rd Separate Brigade,

8th Army Corps, Middle Department, to May, 1865. Moved to Havre de Grace May 31, and assigned to duty as guard on line of the Philadelphia, Wilmington & Baltimore Railroad by Detachments till July. Moved to Baltimore, Md., July 3, and duty as guards at camps and hospitals around that city till July 31. Mustered out July 31, 1865.

Regiment lost during service 18 Enlisted men by disease.

HOFFMAN'S BATTALION INFANTRY.

Organized December, 1861, for prison guard duty at Johnson's Island, near Sandusky, Ohio. Transferred to 128th Ohio Infantry January 5, 1864.

BARD'S INDEPENDENT COMPANY INFANTRY.

Organized at Cincinnati, Ohio, for thirty days' service September 2, 1862. Duty in Defences of Cincinnati. Mustered out October 3, 1862.

DENNISON GUARD.

Organized at Camp Dennison, Ohio, May 19, 1862. Mustered out January 24, 1863.

DEPARTMENTAL CORPS.

Arrick's, Beard's and Eaton's Companies. Organized at Barnesville, Somerton and Hendrysburg July 12 to 27, 1863, for service in the Dept. of the Monongahela during the pleasure of the President. Mustered out November 1, 1864.

TRUMBULL GUARD.

Organized at Gallipolis, Ohio, November 9, 1862, for River Guard. Mustered out July 1, 1865.

Lost 6 Enlisted men by disease.

WALLACE GUARD.

Organized at Cincinnati, Ohio, for thirty days' service September 2, 1862. Duty in the Defences of Cincinnati. Mustered out October 4, 1862.

OREGON VOLUNTEERS.

1st REGIMENT CAVALRY.

Organized at large in Oregon February to April, 1862. Regiment concentrated in Williamette Valley and ordered May, 1862, to Walla Walla Country and Mining Districts of Nez Perce and Salmon River Countries to protect emigrants and miners. Headquarters at Fort Walla Walla, Washington Territory.

Company "A" moved from near Oregon City to Fort Dallas; thence to Fort Walla Walla, Washington Territory, June 24-July 12, 1862. Left Fort Walla Walla July 25, 1862, for Salmon Falls on Snake River Expedition against Snake Indians in Idaho August 19-October 11, 1862, and protecting emigrant roads till November. At Fort Dalles till April, 1863. Ordered to Fort Walla Walla April 20. Expedition against Snake Indians in Idaho May 4-October 26, 1863. Expedition from Fort Walla Walla to Snake River, Washington Territory, February 16-23, 1864, and to Southeastern Oregon April 30-October 6, 1864. Expedition from Fort Boies to Salmon Falls, Idaho Territory, and skirmishes August 27-October 5, 1864. At Fort Vancouver and other stations in Oregon and Idaho till muster out. Expedition from Camp Lyon, Idaho Territory, to Malheur River, Ore., and skirmish July 2-13, 1865.

Company "B" moved from Salem, Ore., to Fort Vancouver; thence to Fort Walla Walla via Fort Dalles May 14-June 2, 1862. Left Fort Walla Walla July 25, 1862, for Salmon Falls on Snake River. Expedition against Snake Indians in Idaho August 19-October 11, 1862, and protect emigrant roads till November 1, 1862. At Fort Walla Walla till April, 1863. Moved to Fort Lapwai June 13, 1863; thence to Canyon City July 10. Ordered to Fort Vancouver September 29, 1863, and duty there till April, 1864. Expedition to Southeastern Oregon and skirmishes April 20-October 6, 1864. Duty at Forts Vancouver, Walla Walla, Boies and other points in District of Oregon till muster out. Expedi-

tion from Camp Lyon, Idaho Territory, to Malheur River, Ore., and skirmish July 2-13, 1865.

Company "C" moved from near Oregon City to Fort Vancouver June 24, 1862. (A Detachment ordered to Jacksonville, Ore., July 2, 1862.) Duty there and at Klamath operating against Indians in Rogue River District till June, 1865. At Fort Steilacoom and other points in District of Oregon till muster out.

Company "D" moved from near Oregon City to Fort Dalles; thence to Fort Walla Walla June 24-July 12, 1862. Left Fort Walla Walla July 25 for Salmon Falls on Snake River. Expedition against Snake Indians in Idaho and protecting emigrant roads August 19 to October 11, 1862. At Fort Walla Walla November, 1862, to April, 1863. Expedition from Fort Walla Walla against Snake Indians in Idaho May 4-October 20, 1863. Ordered to Fort Dalles October 29, and duty there till April, 1864. Expedition to Southeastern Oregon and skirmishes April 20-October 6, 1864. Ordered to Fort Vancouver October 6, 1864. Duty at Fort Vancouver, Fort Walla Walla and other points in the District of Oregon till muster out. Expedition from Camp Lyon, Idaho Territory, to Malheur River, Ore., and skirmish July 2-13, 1865.

Company "E" moved from Salem to Fort Vancouver; thence to Fort Walla Walla via Fort Dalles May 14-June 3, 1862. Duty at Fort Walla Walla till April, 1863. Expedition to Grand Ronde Prairie August 10-22, 1862. Expedition against Snake Indians in Idaho May 4-October 20, 1863. At Fort Walla Walla till April, 1864. Expedition from Fort Walla Walla to Snake River, Washington Territory, February 16-23, 1864. Expedition from Fort Walla Walla to Southeastern Oregon and skirmishes April 20-October 6, 1864. At Forts Dalles, Colville and other points in District of Oregon till muster out.

Company "F" moved from near Oregon City to Fort Dalles; thence to Fort Walla Walla June 24-July 12, 1862. Duty near Lewiston, Nez Perce Reservation, July 25 to November 1, 1862. Garrison at Fort Lapwai till May, 1865. Expedition from Fort Lapwai to the Meadows August 22 to September 20, 1863. At Fort Walla Walla and other points in District of Oregon May, 1865, to muster out.

Companies "G," "H," "I," "K," "L" and "M" authorized January, 1863. Companies "G" and "H" at Camp Watson on Rock Creek, Ore.; Company "I" at Fort Klamath, Company "K" at Fort Dalles and Companies "L" and "M" at Fort Boies. Expedition from Camp Lincoln, near Canyon City, to Harney Lake Valley March 24-April 16, 1864 (Detachment). Skirmish, Harney Lake Valley April 7 (Detachment). Expedition from Siletz Block House to Coos Bay, Crooked River, April 21-May 12, 1864 (Co. "D"). Skirmish, Crooked River May 18 (Detachment). Skirmish near Fort Klamath June 24, 1864 (Detachment). Expedition from Fort Boies to Booneville July 20-August 17, 1864 (Detachment). Expedition from Fort Boies to Salmon Falls, Idaho, August 27-October 5, 1864 (Detachment). Skirmish, Harney Lake Valley September 23, 1864 (Cos. "F" and "H"). Operations on Canyon City Road January 1 to November 30. Skirmish on Owyhee River July 17, 1865 (Detachment). Regiment mustered out November 20, 1866.

1st REGIMENT INFANTRY.

Organized at large November 11, 1864, to January 2, 1865. Ordered to Fort Vancouver, Washington Territory, December 19, 1864. Duty in District of Oregon by Detachments at Fort Vancouver, Fort Klamath, Fort Yamhill, Fort Steilacoom, Fort Dalles, Fort Walla Walla, Colville, Fort Hoskins and Fort Boies, Idaho Territory, covering Boies and Snake River Country and the Owyhee Mines from Indian Raids. Mustered out July 19, 1867.

PENNSYLVANIA VOLUNTEERS.

1st REGIMENT CAVALRY.—(44th VOLUNTEERS.)

Companies "A," "B," "C," "D," "E," "F" and "G" organized at Camp Curtin, Pa., and mustered into State service July and August, 1861. Moved to Camp Jones, near Washington, D. C., August. Companies "H," "I" and "K" organized at Camp Wilkins, Pittsburg, August, 1861. Joined Regiment at Washington. Company "L" organized as an Independent Company July 30, 1861. On duty at Baltimore till January, 1862; then joined Regiment. Company "M" organized as an Independent Company August 5, 1861. At Baltimore, Md., till October 3, 1861; then on eastern shore of Maryland under Lockwood picketing and scouting till January, 1862; then joined Regiment. Regiment attached to McCall's Division. Army of the Potomac, to March, 1862. Cavalry, McDowell's 1st Army Corps, Army of the Potomac, to April, 1862. Bayard's Cavalry Brigade, Dept. of the Rappahannock, to June, 1862. Bayard's Cavalry Brigade, 3rd Army Corps, Army of Virginia, to September, 1862. Bayard's Brigade, Cavalry Division, Army of the Potomac, to January, 1863. 2nd Brigade, 3rd Division, Cavalry Corps, Army of the Potomac, to June, 1863. 1st Brigade, 2nd Division, Cavalry Corps, Army of the Potomac, to June, 1865.

SERVICE.—Reconnoissance to Leesburg, Va., October 20, 1861. Reconnoissance to Hunter's Mills October 20 (Detachment). Expedition to Dranesville November 26-27. Action at Dranesville November 27. Expedition to Gunnell's Farm December 6. Action at Dranesville December 20 (Cos. "C," "D," "E," "H" and "I"). At Camp Pierpont till March, 1862. Companies "L" and "M" join Regiment January 7. Advance on Manassas, Va., March 10-15. McDowell's advance to Falmouth April 9-17. Reconnoissance to Falmouth April 17-19. Falmouth April 19. Rappahannock River May 13 (Cos. "F," "G," "H," "L" and "M"). Strasburg and Staunton Road June 1-2. Mount Jackson June 3. New Market June 5. Harrisonburg June 6. Battle of Cross Keys June 8. Harrisonburg June 9. Scouting on the Rappahannock June-July. Reconnoissance to James City July 22-24. Skirmish at Madison Court House July 23. Slaughter House August 8. Battle of Cedar Mountain August 9. Pope's Campaign in Northern Virginia August 16-September 2. Stevensburg, Raccoon Ford and Brandy Station August 20. Fords of the Rappahannock August 21-23. Special duty at General Pope's Headquarters August 22-30. Thoroughfare Gap August 28 (Cos. "I" and "M"). Gainesville August 28. Battle of Bull Run August 29-30. Germantown August 31. Centreville and Chantilly August 31. Chantilly September 1. Fairfax Court House September 2. Battle of Antietam, Md., September 16-17. Scout to Warrenton September 29. Aldie and Mountsville October 31. Salem, New Baltimore and Thoroughfare Gap November 4. Warrenton November 6. Rappahannock Station November 7, 8 and 9. Battle of Fredericksburg, Va., December 12-15. Picket near King George Court House till January, 1863. "Mud March" January 20-24. (Co. "H" at Headquarters of 6th Corps February 22 to August 15.) Picket duty from Falmouth to Port Conway till April 26. Chancellorsville Campaign April 26-May 8. Oak Grove April 26. Rapidan Station May 1. (Co. "H" at Chancellorsville May 1-5.) Stoneman's Raid May 27-April 8. Brandy Station or Fleetwood and Beverly Ford June 9. Aldie June 17. Special duty at Corps Headquarters June 28. Battle of Gettysburg, Pa., July 1-3. Emmettsburg, Md., July 4. Guarding Reserve Artillery July 5-10. Companies "A" and "B" advance for 6th Army Corps from Gettysburg to Hagerstown, Md., July 5-10. Old Antietam Forge, near Leitersburg, July 10. Near Harper's Ferry, W. Va., July 14. Shepherdstown July 15-16. Picket near Warrenton July-August. Rixeyville and Muddy Run August 5. Wilford's Ford August 9 (Detachment). Carter's Run September 6. Scout to Middleburg September 10-11. Advance from the Rappahannock to the Rapidan September 13-17. Culpeper Court House September 13. Near Auburn October 1 (Detachment). Bristoe Campaign October 9-22. Warrenton or White Sulphur Springs October 12-13. Auburn and Bristoe October 14. Brentsville October 14. Advance to line of the Rappahannock November 7-8. Rappahannock Bridge November 7-8. Mine Run Campaign November 26-December 2. New Hope Church November 27. Expedition to Turkey Run Station January 1-4, 1864. Scout to Piedmont February 17-18. Campaign from the Rapidan to the James May 4-June 12. Todd's Tavern May 5, 6, 7 and 8. Corbin's Bridge May 8. Sheridan's Raid May 9-24. New Castle and Davenport May 9. North Anna River May 9-10. Ashland May 11. Ground Squirrel Church and Yellow Tavern May 11. Brook's Church, Richmond Fortifications, May 12. Milford Station May 21. On line of the Pamunkey May 26-28. Haw's Shop May 28. Totopotomoy May 28-31. Cold Harbor May 28-31. Sumner's Upper Bridge June 2. Sheridan's Trevillian Raid June 7-24. Trevillian Station June 11-12. Newark or Mallory's Cross Roads June 12. White House or St. Peter's Church June 21. Black Creek or Tunstall's Station June 21. St. Mary's Church June 24. Hope Church June 24. Bellefield July. Warwick Swamp July 12. Demonstration north of the James July 27-29. Malvern Hill and Gaines Hill July 28. Lee's Mills July 30. Demonstration north of James River August 13-20. Gravel Hill August 14. Malvern Hill August 16. Strawberry Plains August 16-18. Dinwiddie Road, near Ream's Station, August 23. Ream's Station August 25. Old members mustered out September 9. Consolidated to a Battalion of five Companies September 9. Belcher's Mills September 17. Poplar Springs Church September 29-October 2. Arthur's Swamp September 30-October 1. Charles City Cross Roads October 1. Hatcher's Run October 27-28. Reconnoissance toward Stony Creek November 7. Stony Creek Station December 1. Hicksford Raid December 7-12. Bellefield December 9-10. Dabney's Mills, Hatcher's Run, February 5-7, 1865. Appomattox Campaign March 28-April 9. Dinwiddie Court House March 30-31. Five Forks April 1. Amelia Springs April 5. Sailor's Creek April 6. Farmville April 7. Appomattox Court House April 9. Surrender of Lee and his army. Expedition to Danville April 23-29. Moved to Washington, D. C. Grand Review May 23. Consolidated with 6th and 17th Pennsylvania Cavalry to form 2nd Provisional Cavalry June 17, 1865.

Regiment lost during service 9 Officers and 87 Enlisted men killed and mortally wounded and 1 Officer and 104 Enlisted men by disease. Total 201.

1st REGIMENT PROVISIONAL CAVALRY.

Organized at Cloud's Mills, Va., June 17, 1865, by consolidation of 2nd and 20th Pennsylvania Cavalry. Duty at Cloud's Mills till July. Mustered out July 13, 1865.

1st BATTALION MILITIA CAVALRY.

Organized at Harrisburg, Pa., July 13, 1863. Attached to Dept. of the Susquehanna. Mustered out August 21, 1863.

2nd REGIMENT CAVALRY.—(59th VOLUNTEERS.)

Organized at Philadelphia and Harrisburg, Pa., September, 1861, to April, 1862. Seven Companies dismounted, left State for Baltimore, Md., April 1, 1862. Five Companies joined at Baltimore April 14, 1862. Moved to Washington, D. C., April 25, and camp on Capital Hill till June 27. Attached to Sturgis' Command, Military District of Washington, to August, 1862. Buford's Cavalry Brigade, 2nd Army Corps, Army of Virginia, to September, 1862. Price's Cavalry Brigade, Defences of Washington, to March, 1863. 2nd Brigade, Stahel's Cavalry Division, 22nd Army Corps, to June, 1863. Provost Guard, Army of the Potomac, to December, 1863. 2nd Brigade, 2nd Division, Cavalry Corps, Army of the Potomac, to February, 1865. Provost Guard, Army of the Potomac, to June, 1865.

SERVICE.—Duty in Defences of Washington, D. C., till July 27, 1862. Moved to Warrenton, thence to Madison Court House, Va., July 27-August 5. Action at Wolftown August 5. Battle of Cedar Mountain August 9. Pope's Campaign in Northern Virginia August 16-September 2. Chantilly September 1. Reconnoissance to Thoroughfare Gap and Aldie September 16. Antietam September 16-17. Ashby's Gap September 22. Duty in the Defences of Washington, D. C., till June, 1863. Reconnoissance to Snicker's Ferry and Berryville November 28-30. Berryville November 30. Frying Pan, near Chantilly, December 27-28. Occoquan December 29. Mrs. Violet's and Seleman's Ford, near Occoquan, March 22, 1863 (Detachment). Expedition from Gainesville June 7-8 (Detachment). Headquarter Guard for General Meade June 29. Battle of Gettysburg, Pa., July 1-3. Provost duty at Gettysburg July 5-7. Old Antietam Forge, South Mountain, Md., July 10. Provost Guard duty with Army of the Potomac till December. Bristoe Campaign October 9-22. Near Bealeton October 22. Fayetteville October 23. Advance to line of the Rappahannock November 7-8. Mine Run Campaign November 26-December 2. New Hope Church November 27. Parker's Store November 29. Expedition to Luray December 21-23. Luray December 23. Campaign from the Rapidan to the James May-June, 1864. Todd's Tavern May 5, 6, 7 and 8. Sheridan's Raid to James River May 9-24. North Anna River May 9-10. Ground Squirrel Church and Yellow Tavern May 11. Brook's Church, Fortifications of Richmond, May 12. Line of the Pamunkey May 26-28. Totopotomoy May 28-31. Haw's Church May 28. Cold Harbor May 31-June 1. Sheridan's Trevillian Raid June 7-24. Louisa Court House June 10. Trevillian Station June 11-12. White House or St. Peter's Church June 21. Black Creek or Tunstall's Station June 21. Germantown June 22. St. Mary's Church June 24. Charles City Cross Roads June 29. Warwick Swamp and Jerusalem Plank Road July 12. Demonstration on north side of the James at Deep Bottom July 27-29. Malvern Hill July 28. Warwick Swamp July 30. Demonstration north of James River at Deep Bottom August 13-20. Gravel Hill August 14. Strawberry Plains August 16-18. Deep Bottom and Malvern Hill August 18. Dinwiddie Road, near Ream's Station, August 23. Ream's Station August 25. Belcher's Mills September 17. Poplar Springs Church September 29-October 2. Arthur's Swamp September 30-October 1. Boydton Plank Road, Hatcher's Run, October 27-28. Reconnoissance toward Stony Creek November 7. Stony Creek Station December 1. Expedition to Hicksford December 7-11. Bellefield December 8. Dabney's Mills, Hatcher's Run, February 5-7, 1865. On provost duty, Army of the Potomac, till June, 1865. Fall of Petersburg April 2. Pursuit of Lee April 3-9. Appomattox Court House April 9. Surrender of Lee and his army. March to Washington, D. C., May. Grand Review May 23. Consolidated with 20th Pennsylvania Cavalry June 17, 1865, to form 1st Provisional Cavalry.

Regiment lost during service 6 Officers and 52 Enlisted men killed and mortally wounded and 2 Officers and 193 Enlisted men by disease. Total 253.

2nd REGIMENT PROVISIONAL CAVALRY.

Organized at Cloud's Mills, Va., June 17, 1865, by consolidation of 1st, 6th and 17th Pennsylvania Cavalry. Mustered out at Lebanon, Ky., August 7, 1865.

3rd REGIMENT CAVALRY.—(60th VOLUNTEERS.) ("YOUNG'S KENTUCKY LIGHT CAVALRY.")

Organized at Philadelphia July and August, 1861. Moved to Washington, D. C., August, 1861. Attached to Porter's Division, Army of the Potomac, to March, 1862. Cavalry, 3rd Army Corps, Army of the Potomac, to July, 1862. 1st Brigade, Cavalry Division, Army of the Potomac, to August, 1862. 5th Brigade, Pleasanton's Cavalry Division, to November, 1862. Averill's Cavalry Brigade, Centre Grand Division, Army of the Potomac, to February, 1863. 2nd Brigade, 2nd Division, Cavalry Corps, Army of the Potomac, to June, 1863. 3rd Brigade, 2nd Division, Cavalry Corps, Army of the Potomac, to March, 1864. Headquarters, Army of the Potomac, Provost Marshal General's Command, to May, 1865.

SERVICE.—Duty in the Defences of Washington, D. C., till March, 1862. Skirmish at Magruder's Ferry September 16, 1861. Springfield Station September 27. Hunter's Mills or Vienna November 26 (Co. "C"). Vienna December 3 (Cos. "F" and "M"). Advance on Manassas, Va., March 10-15, 1862. Reconnoissance to Cedar Run March 14-16. Moved to the Virginia Peninsula March 22-30. Howard's Mills April 4. Near Cockletown April 4 (Co. "A"). Warwick Road April 5. Siege of Yorktown April 5-May 4. Cheese Cake Church May 4. Near Williamsburg May 4. Battle of Williamsburg May 5. Expedition to James River May 25-26 (Detachment Co. "I"). Battle of Seven Pines, Fair Oaks, May 31-June 1. New Market Road June 8 (Cos. "D," "K"). Seven days before Richmond June 25-July 1. Savage Station June 29. James River Road near Fair Oaks June 29-30 (Detachment). Jones' Bridge and Jordan's Ford June 30. White Oak Church July 1. Malvern Hill July 2. Reconnoissance toward White Oak Church July 10. Reconnoissance to Jones' Ford July 31, and to Malvern Hill August 2-8. Sycamore Church August 3. White Oak Swamp Bridge August 4. Malvern Hill August 5. Warrenton August 26. Battle of Antietam, Md., September 16-17. Sharpsburg September 19. Shepherdstown Ford September 19. Harper's Ferry September 27. Four Locks, Md., October 9. Reconnoissance to Smithfield October 16-17. Bloomfield November 2-3. Markham Station November 4. Manassas Gap November 5-6. Newby's Cross Roads November 9. Newby's Cross Roads near Amissville November 10. Near Hartwood Church November 28. Reconnoissance to Grove Church December 1. Battle of Fredericksburg December 12-15. Expedition to Richard's and Ellis' Fords, Rappahannock River, December 29-31. Operations at Rappahannock Bridge and Grove Church February 5-7, 1863. Hartwood Church February 25. Kelly's Ford March 17. Chancellorsville Campaign, Stoneman's Raid, April 27-May 8. Near Dumfries May 17 (Detachment). Brandy Station or Fleetwood, Stevensburg and Beverly Ford June 9. Aldie June 17. Upperville June 21. Aldie June 22. Lisbon or Poplar Springs June 29. Westminster June 30. Battle of Gettysburg, Pa., July 1-3. Emmettsburg July 4. Old Antietam Forge near Leitersburg July 10. Near Harper's Ferry July 14. Shepherdstown September 15-16. Scouting and picketing Upper Rappahannock July to September. Scout to Middleburg September 10-11. Advance from the Rappahannock to the Rapidan September 13-17. Culpeper Court House September 13. Near Catlett's Station October 6 (Detachment). Bristoe Campaign October 9-22. Warrenton or White Sulphur Springs October 12-13. Auburn and Bristoe October 14. Brentsville October 14. Advance to line of the Rappahannock November 7-8. Vine Run Campaign November 26-December 2. New Hope Church November 27. Ellis Ford December 3. Scout to Piedmont February 17-18, 1864. Sprigg's Ford February 28 (Co. "L"). Campaign from the Rapidan to the James May-June, 1864. Battles of the Wilderness May 5-7; Spottsylvania May 8-12; Spottsylvania C. H. May 12-21; Guinea Station May 21; North Anna River May 23-26. On line of the Pamunkey May 26-28. Totopotomoy May 28-31. Cold Harbor June 1-12. Before Petersburg June 16, 1864, to April 2, 1865. Assaults on Petersburg June 16-18, 1864. Charles City Cross Roads June 29. Consolidated to a Battalion of three Companies July 27, 1864. Non-Veterans on duty in Cumberland Valley till mustered out August 24, 1864. Reconnoissance to Hatcher's Run December 9-10. Hatcher's Run December 9. Dabney's Mills, Hatcher's Run, February 5-7, 1865. Fall of Petersburg April 2. Pursuit of Lee to Appomattox C. H. April 3-9. Provost duty at Richmond May 4-8. Transferred to 5th Pennsylvania Cavalry May 8, 1865.

Regiment lost during service 1 Officer and 41 Enlisted men killed and mortally wounded and 2 Officers and 125 Enlisted men by disease. Total 169.

3rd REGIMENT PROVISIONAL CAVALRY.

Organized at Cumberland, Md., June 24, 1865, by consolidation of 18th and 22nd Pennsylvania Cavalry. Duty at Clarksburg, W. Va., till October, 1865. Mustered out October 31, 1865.

4th REGIMENT CAVALRY (64th VOLUNTEERS).

Organized at Harrisburg, Philadelphia and Pittsburg August to October, 1861. Ordered to Washington, D. C. Attached to Defences of Washington, D. C., till May, 1862. McCall's Division, Dept. of the Rappahannock, to June, 1862. McCall's Division, 5th Army Corps, Army of the Potomac, to July, 1862. 1st Brigade, Cavalry Division, Army Potomac, to September, 1862. 3rd Brigade, Pleasanton's Cavalry Division, Army Potomac, to November, 1862. Averill's Cavalry Brigade, Center Grand Division, Army Potomac, to February, 1863. 2nd Brigade, 2nd Division, Cavalry Corps, Army Potomac, to June, 1863. 3rd Brigade, 2nd Division, Cavalry Corps, Army Potomac, to August, 1863. 2nd Brigade, 2nd Division, Cavalry Corps, Army Potomac, to July, 1865.

SERVICE.—Provost duty at Washington, D. C., till May 10, 1862. (Cos. "A," "B" escort to Gen. Keys December 28, 1861, to February 25, 1862.) Joined McDowell at Fredericksburg May, 1862, and scouting on the Rappahannock till June 14. Moved to the Virginia Peninsula, arriving at White House June 24. Companies "A," "G," "H" and "K" ordered to Yorktown, Va., June 25. Seven days before Richmond June 25-July 1. Meadow Bridge near Mechanicsville June 26. Mechanicsville June 26. Gaines' Mill, Cold Harbor, June 27. Reconnoissance to Bottom's Bridge June 28. Rear guard to Army Potomac June 29. Glendale or Nelson's Farm June 30. Malvern Hill July 1. Reconnoissance to Charles City C. H. July 2-3. At Harrison's Landing till August 16. Reconnoissance from Harrison's Landing July 11 and July 29 (Co. "F"). Rear Guard to Yorktown August 16-18. Duty at Yorktown till August 25. Reached Washington, D. C., September 4. Maryland Campaign September-October. Battles of South Mountain September 14, and Antietam September 16-17. Sharpsburg September 19. Shepherdstown Ford September 19. Kearneysville and Shepherdstown, W. Va., October 15-16 (Detachment). Scout to Smithfield October 16-17 (Detachment). Hedgesville October 20 and 22. Hillsboro and Lovettsville Road October 21. Bloomfield, Union and Upperville November 2-3. Ashby's Gap November 3. Markham Station November 4. Manassas Gap November 5-6. Jefferson November 7. Little Washington November 8. Duty near Hartwood Church till December. Gaines' Cross Roads November 10. Waterloo November 14. Battle of Fredericksburg December 12-15. Scout to Catlett's Station and Brentsville December 21-23 (Detachment). Expedition to Richard's and Ellis' Fords, Rappahannock River, December 29-30. "Mud March" January 20-24, 1863. Operations at Rappahannock Bridge and Grove Church February 5-7. Hartwood Church February 25. Kelly's Ford March 17 and 29. Chancellorsville Campaign, Stoneman's Raid, April 29-May 8. Passage of Kelly's Ford April 29. Raccoon Ford April 30. Ely's Ford May 2. Stevensburg, Brandy Station and Beverly Ford June 9. Aldie June 17. Middleburg June 18-19. Upperville June 21. Hanover, Pa., June 30. Battle of Gettysburg, Pa., July 1-3. Green Oak July 5. Near Harper's Ferry July 14. Shepherdstown July 15-16. Scouting till September. Corbin's Cross Roads September 1. Advance from the Rappahannock to the Rapidan September 13-17. Culpeper C. H. September 13. Near Culpeper C. H. October 1. Bristoe Campaign October 9-22. James City October 10-11. Near Warrenton October 11. Warrenton or White Sulphur Springs October 12-13. Jeffersonton October 12. Auburn and Bristoe Station October 14. St. Stephen's Church October 14. Advance to line of the Rappahannock November 7-8.

Mine Run Campaign November 26-December 2. Brentsville November 26. New Hope Church and Catlett's Station November 27. Brentsville November 29. (Cos. "A," "F" at Bull Run Bridge November, 1863, to January 20, 1864.) Scout to Middleburg January 22-24, 1864 (Detachment). Kilpatrick's Raid on Richmond February 28-May 4. Beaver Dam Station February 29. Brook's Turnpike March 1 (Veterans on furlough March 25-April 25. At Camp Stoneman till May 12, and joined Army Potomac May 19.) Campaign from the Rapidan to the James May-June, 1864. Sumner's Bridge May 3. Todd's Tavern May 5-8. Sheridan's Raid to James River May 9-24. North Anna River May 9-10. Ground Squirrel Church and Yellow Tavern May 11. Glen Allen Station May 11. Brook Church or Richmond Fortifications May 12. Line of the Pamunkey May 26-28. Haw's Shop May 28. Totopotomoy May 28-31. Cold Harbor May 31-June 1. Sumner's Upper Bridge June 2. Sheridan's Trevillian Raid June 7-24. Elliott's Mills June 8. Trevillian Station June 11-12. White House or St. Peter's Church June 21. Black Creek or Tunstall Station June 21. St. Mary's Church June 24. Siege of Petersburg June, 1864, to April, 1865. Charles' Cross Roads June 29. Warwick Swamp July 12. Demonstration on north side of the James July 27-29. Malvern Hill July 28. Warwick Swamp July 30. Demonstration north of the James at Deep Bottom August 13-20. Gravel Hill August 14. Strawberry Plains August 16-18. White Oak Swamp August 18. Weldon Railroad August 18-21 (Detachment). Dinwiddie Road near Ream's Station August 23. Ream's Station August 25. Reconnoissance to Poplar Springs Church September 13. Reconnoissance toward Dinwiddie C. H. September 15. Belcher's Mills September 17. Ream's Station September 29. Poplar Springs Church September 29-October 2. Arthur's Swamp September 30-October 1. Boydton Plank Road, Hatcher's Run, October 27-28. Reconnoissance to Stony Creek November 7. Stony Creek Station December 1. Hicksford Expedition December 7-12. Bellefield December 8. High Hill December 10. Rowanty Creek February 5, 1865. Dabney's Mills, Hatcher's Run, February 5-7. Appomattox Campaign March 28-April 9. Lewis Farm near Gravelly Run March 29 (Co. "C"). Dinwiddie C. H. March 30-31. White Oak Road March 31 (Co. "C"). Five Forks April 1. Paine's Cross Roads and Amelia Springs April 5. Sailor's Creek April 6. Farmville April 7. Appomattox Court House April 9. Surrender of Lee and his army. Expedition to Danville April 23-29. Expedition after Extra Billy Smith May 20-22. At Lynchburg till June 10. Mustered out July 1, 1865.

Regiment lost during service 9 Officers and 89 Enlisted men killed and mortally wounded and 3 Officers and 257 Enlisted men by disease. Total 358.

5th REGIMENT CAVALRY (65th VOLUNTEERS) "CAMERON DRAGOONS."

Organized at Philadelphia July to September, 1861. Moved to Washington, D. C., August 22, 1861. Attached to Smith's Division, Army Potomac, to March, 1862. Unattached, 4th Army Corps, Army Potomac, to December, 1862. West's Advance Brigade, 4th Corps, Dept. Virginia, to June, 1863. 2nd Brigade, 1st Division, 4th Army Corps, Dept. of Virginia, to July, 1863. Wistar's Brigade, Yorktown, Va., Dept. Virginia and North Carolina, to August, 1863. U. S. Forces, Portsmouth, Va., Dept. Virginia and North Carolina, to December, 1863. District Currituck, Dept. Virginia and North Carolina, to January, 1864. Heckman's Division, 18th Army Corps, Dept. Virginia and North Carolina, to April, 1864. 2nd Brigade, Cavalry Division, Dept. of Virginia and North Carolina, Army of the James, to May, 1864. 1st Brigade, Kautz's Cavalry Division, Dept. Virginia and North Carolina, to April, 1865. Cavalry Brigade, Dept. of Virginia, to July, 1865. Richmond, Va., District Henrico, Dept. Virginia, to August, 1865.

SERVICE.—Duty in the Dept. of Washington, D. C., till May 8, 1862. Reconnoissance to Pohick Church,

Va., December 18, 1861 (Cos. "C," "F," "H"). Flint Hill and Hunter's Mill February 7, 1862. Fairfax C. H. February 6. Expedition to Vienna and Flint Hill February 22. Duty near Alexandria till May. Ordered to Yorktown, Va., May 8. Scouting about Gloucester Point May 10 (Cos. "A," "B," "E" and "L"). Scouting about Williamsburg May 12. Skirmishes at Mechanicsville May 23-24. Seven days before Richmond June 25-July 1 (Cos. "I," "K"). Savage Station June 29. White Oak Swamp Bridge June 30. Malvern Hill July 1. Reconnoissance from Yorktown to Gloucester, Matthews and King and Queen Counties July 7-9 (Cos. "B," "E," "L," "M"). Duty at Yorktown and Williamsburg till September 8, 1863. Williamsburg and Fort Magruder September 9, 1862. Reconnoissance from Yorktown to Gloucester, Matthews, King and Queen and Middlesex Counties December 11-15. Reconnoissance to Burnt Ordinary December 17. Expedition to West Point and White House January 7-9, 1863 (Detachment). Burnt Ordinary January 19. Near Olive Creek Church February 5 (Cos. "L," "M"). Williamsburg and Olive Branch Church February 7. Williamsburg March 23 and 29. Whittaker's Mills April 11. Reconnoissance through Gates County and down Chowan River June 5-13. Nine Mile Ordinary June 14. Diascund Bridge June 20. Dix's Peninsula Campaign June 24-July 8. Barnesville June 28. Baltimore Cross Roads June 29. Expedition from White House to Bottom's Bridge July 1-7. Baltimore Cross Roads July 1. Bottom's Bridge July 2. Expedition to Bottom's Bridge August 26-29. New Kent C. H. August 28. Bottom's Bridge August 29. Ordered to Norfolk, Va., September 8, and duty about Norfolk and Portsmouth, Va., till December. Companies "C," "D," "F," "H" and "I" at South Mills, N. C., September 13. Companies "A," "B," "E," "G," "K," "L" and "M" at Great Bridge. Expedition to Indiantown, N. C., September 15-20 (Co. "D"). Near Kempsville September 15. Indiantown September 20. (Cos. "F" and "H" at Drummond Lake September 15.) Companies "C," "F," "H" and "I" advance to Raleigh September 22; Companies "A," "B," "L" and "M" to Currituck C. H. September 23. Affair on Back Bay September 30 (Detachment). Scout from Great Bridge to Indiantown, N. C., October 13 (Detachment). Bingo Landing October 16-17 (Detachment). Camden C. H. October 17. Regiment assembled at Great Bridge October 20. Expedition from Norfolk to South Mills, Camden, etc., N. C., December 5-24. Duty at Yorktown and in District of the Currituck till May, 1864. Wistar's Expedition toward Richmond February 6-8. Bottom's Bridge February 4. Ballahock on Bear Quarter Road and Deep Creek February 29-March 1. Ballahock Station near Dismal Swamp Canal March 1. Deep Creek March 2. Reconnoissance from Portsmouth to the Blackwater April 13-15 (Detachment). Kautz's Raid on Petersburg & Weldon Railroad May 5-11. Birch Island Bridges May 5. Stony Creek Station and Jarrett's Station May 7. White's Bridge, Nottaway Creek, May 8. Nottaway Railroad Bridge May 8. Jarrett's Station May 8-9. Kautz's Raid on Richmond & Danville Railroad May 12-17. Coalfield Station May 13. Powhatan Station May 14. Belcher's Mills May 16. Petersburg June 9. Before Petersburg June 15-18. Siege operations against Petersburg and Richmond June, 1864, to April, 1865. Roanoke Station June 20, 1864. Wilson's Raid on South Side & Danville Railroad June 22-July 2. Staunton River Bridge or Roanoke Station June 25. Sappony Church, Stony Creek, June 28-29. Ream's Station June 29. Demonstration north of the James at Deep Bottom July 27-29. Malvern Hill July 30. Chaffin's Farm, New Market Heights, September 29-30. Darbytown Road October 7-13 and December 10. Charles City Cross Roads October 20. Battle of Fair Oaks October 27-28. Appomattox Campaign March 28-April 9, 1865. Dinwiddie C. H. March 31. Five Forks April 1. Gravelly Ford on Hatcher's Run April 2. Near Amelia C. H. April 4-5. Burkesville and Sailor's Creek April 6. Prince Edward's C. H. April 7. Appomattox Court House April 9. Surrender

of Lee and his army. Duty at Richmond, Va., and in District of Henrico, Dept. of Virginia, to August. Mustered out August 7, 1865, and discharged at Philadelphia, Pa., August 16, 1865.

Regiment lost during service 1 Officer and 76 Enlisted men killed and mortally wounded and 6 Officers and 210 Enlisted men by disease. Total 293.

6th REGIMENT CAVALRY (70th VOLUNTEERS), "RUSH'S LANCERS."

Organized at Philadelphia August to October, 1861. Moved to Washington, D. C., December 10 to December 16, 1861. Attached to Emory's Brigade, Cooke's Cavalry Brigade, Cavalry Reserve, Army Potomac, to July, 1862. Cavalry Command, Army Potomac, to April, 1862. Emory's 2nd Brigade, Cavalry Division, Army Potomac, to August, 1862. 3rd Brigade, Pleasanton's Cavalry Division, Army Potomac, to November, 1862. Headquarters Left Grand Division, Army Potomac, to February, 1863. Reserve Brigade, Cavalry Corps, Army of the Potomac, to June, 1863. Reserve Brigade, 1st Division, Cavalry Corps, Army Potomac, to August, 1864. 3rd (Reserve) Brigade, 1st Cavalry Division, Cavalry Corps, Army Shenandoah and Army Potomac, to June, 1865.

SERVICE.—Provost duty in the Defences of Washington, D. C., till May, 1862. Scout to Hunter's Mills March 19. Moved to Fortress Monroe, thence to Yorktown, Va., May 3-5. Reconnoissance to Mulberry Point, Va., May 7-8 (Detachment). Reconnoissance to New Castle and Hanovertown Ferry May 22. Reconnoissance to Hanover C. H. May 24. Charge on picket line with lances May 25 (Co. "C"). Hanover C. H. May 27 (Co. "A"). Operations near Hanover C. H. May 27-29. Occupation of Ashland May 30. Reconnoissance to Hanover C. H. June 10-12. Operations about White House against Stuart June 13-15. Garlick's Landing, Pamunkey River, June 13. Seven days before Richmond June 25-July 1. Beaver Dam Station June 26 (Cos. "B," "C," "G," "H"). Companies "A," "D," "I," "K" with Stoneman on retreat to White House and Williamsburg. Gaines' Mill June 27. Savage Station June 29 (Co. "F"). Glendale June 30. White Oak Swamp June 30. Company "F" Malvern Hill July 1. (Cos. "C" and "H" at Headquarters, 5th Corps.) Company "F" escort Heavy Artillery from Malvern Hill to Harrison's Landing. Fall's Church September 2-4 (Cos. "C," "H"). South Mountain and near Jefferson, Md., September 13. Crampton's Pass, South Mountain, September 14 (Cos. "B," "G," "I"). Antietam September 16-17 (Cos. "B," "G," "I"). Sharpsburg September 19. Shepherdstown Ford September 19. (Co. "K" at Headquarters, 6th Corps, November, 1862, to February 24, 1863.) Bloomfield and Upperville November 2-3. Battle of Fredericksburg December 12-15. Occoquan River December 19-20 (Cos. "B," "G"). "Mud March" January 20-24, 1863 (Cos. "A," "D," "E"). Chancellorsville Campaign April 27-May 6. Stoneman's Raid April 29-May 8 (Co. "L"). Raccoon Ford April 30 (Detachment). Brandy Station and Beverly Ford June 9. Reconnoissance to Ashby's Gap June 14 (Co. "A"). Greencastle, Pa., June 20. Upperville June 21. Battle of Gettysburg, Pa., July 1-3. Williamsport, Md., July 6. Boonsborough July 8. Funkstown July 10-13. Aldie July 11. Kelly's Ford July 31-August 1. Brandy Station August 1. Advance from the Rappahannock to the Rapidan September 13-17. Bristoe Campaign October 9-22. Manassas Junction October 17. Bristoe Station October 18. Advance to line of the Rappahannock November 7-8. Mine Run Campaign November 26-December 2. Demonstration on the Rapidan February 6-7, 1864. Custer's Raid in Albemarle County February 28-March 1. Near Charlottesville February 29. Burton's Ford, Stannardsville, March 1. Rapidan Campaign May and June. Todd's Tavern May 7-8. Sheridan's Raid to James River May 9-24. Ground Squirrel Church and Yellow Tavern May 11. Meadow Bridge, Richmond, May 12. Mechanicsville May 12. Line of the Pamunkey May 26-28. Hanovertown Ferry and Hanovertown May 27. Totopotomoy May 28-31.

Old Church May 30. Mattadequin Creek May 30. Bethesda Church, Cold Harbor, May 31-June 1. McClellan's Bridge June 2. Haw's Shop June 4-5. Sheridan's Trevillian Raid June 7-24. Trevillian Station June 11-12. Newark or Mallory's Cross Roads June 12. White House or St. Peter's Church June 21. Black Creek or Tunstall Station June 21. Jones' Bridge June 23. Siege of Petersburg July 3-30. Demonstration north of James at Deep Bottom July 27-29. Charles City Cross Roads July 27-28. Malvern Hill July 28. Shenandoah Valley Campaign August to November. Near Stone Chapel August 10. Toll Gate near White Post August 11. Near Newtown August 11. Near Strasburg August 14. Summit Point August 21. Kearneysville August 25. Leetown and Smithfield August 28. Smithfield Crossing, Opequan, August 29. Ordered to Pleasant Valley, Md., September 8, and to Hagerstown, November. Sheridan's Raid from Winchester February 27-March 25, 1865. Waynesboro March 2. Appomattox Campaign March 28-April 9. Gravelly Run near Five Forks March 30. Dinwiddie C. H. March 30-31. Five Forks April 1. Scott's Cross Roads April 2. Tabernacle Church or Beaver Pond Creek April 4. Sailor's Creek April 6. Appomattox Station April 8. Appomattox C. H. April 9. Surrender of Lee and his army. Expedition to Danville April 23-29. March to Washington, D. C., May. Grand Review May 23. Consolidated with 1st and 17th Pennsylvania Cavalry June 17, 1865, to form 2nd Provisional Cavalry.

Regiment lost during service 7 Officers and 71 Enlisted men killed and mortally wounded and 3 Officers and 86 Enlisted men by disease. Total 167.

7th REGIMENT CAVALRY (80th VOLUNTEERS).

Organized at Harrisburg September to December, 1861. At Camp Cameron, Harrisburg, till December 19, 1861. Moved to Louisville, Ky., December 19, and ordered to Jeffersonville, Ind. Duty there till February, 1862. Served unattached, Army Ohio, to March, 1862. Negley's 7th Independent Brigade, Army Ohio (1st Battalion). Post of Nashville, Tenn., Dept. Ohio (2nd Battalion). 23rd Independent Brigade, Army Ohio (3rd Battalion), to September, 1862. Cavalry, 8th Division, Army Ohio (1st and 2nd Battalions), Unattached, Army Ohio (3rd Battalion), to November, 1862. 1st Brigade, Cavalry Division, Army Ohio, to January, 1863. 1st Brigade, 2nd Division, Cavalry Corps, Army Cumberland, to November, 1864. 2nd Brigade, 2nd Division, Cavalry Corps, Military Division Mississippi, to July, 1865.

SERVICE.—1st Battalion (Cos. "A," "D," "H" and "I") sent to Columbia, Tenn. Expedition to Rodgersville May 13-14. Lamb's Ferry, Ala., May 14. Advance on Chattanooga June 1. Sweeden's Cove June 4. Chattanooga June 7-8. Occupation of Manchester July 1. Paris July 19. Raid on Louisville & Nashville Railroad August 19-23. Huntsville Road, near Gallatin, August 21. Brentwood September 19-20. Near Perryville October 6-7. Chaplin Hills October 8. Expedition from Crab Orchard to Big Hill and Richmond October 21. 2nd Battalion (Cos. "C," "E," "F" and "K"), under Gen. Dumont, in garrison at Nashville, Tenn., and scouting in that vicinity till November. 3rd Battalion (Cos. "B," "G," "L" and "M"), in Duffield's Command, scouting in West and Middle Tennessee. Lebanon and pursuit to Carthage May 5. Readyville June 7. Murfreesboro July 13. Sparta August 4-5 and 7. Regiment reunited in November, 1862. Nashville November 5. Reconnoissance from Nashville to Franklin December 11-12. Wilson's Creek Pike December 11. Franklin December 12. Near Nashville December 24. Advance on Murfreesboro December 26-30. Lavergne December 26-27. Battle of Stone's River December 30-31, 1862, and January 1-3, 1863. Overall's Creek December 31. Manchester Pike and Lytle's Creek January 5, 1863. Expedition to Franklin January 31-February 13. Unionville and Rover January 31. Murfreesboro February 7. Rover February 13. Expedition toward Columbia March 4-14. Unionville and Rover March 4. Chapel Hill March 5. Thomp-

son's Station March 9. Rutherford Creek March 10-11. Snow Hill, Woodbury, April 3. Franklin April 10. Expedition to McMinnville April 20-30. Middletown May 21-22. Near Murfreesboro June 3. Operations on Edgeville Pike June 4. Marshall Knob June 4. Shelbyville Pike June 4. Scout on Middleton and Eagleville Pike June 10. Scout on Manchester Pike June 13. Expedition to Lebanon June 15-17. Lebanon June 16. Middle Tennessee or Tullahoma Campaign June 23-July 7. Guy's Gap or Fosterville and capture of Shelbyville June 27. Expedition to Huntsville July 13-22. Reconnoissance to Rock Island Ferry August 4-5. Sparta August 9. Passage of Cumberland Mountains and Tennessee River, and Chickamauga (Ga.) Campaign August 16-September 22. Calfkiller River, Sparta, August 17. Battle of Chickamauga September 19-20. Rossville, Ga., September 21. Re-enlisted at Huntsville, Ala., November 28, 1863. Atlanta Campaign May to September, 1864. Demonstration on Rocky Faced Ridge May 8-11. Battle of Resaca May 14-15. Tanner's Bridge and Rome May 15. Near Dallas May 24. Operations on line of Pumpkin Vine Creek and battles about Dallas, New Hope Church and Allatoona Hills May 25-June 5. Near Big Shanty June 9. Operations about Marietta and against Kenesaw Mountain June 10-July 2. McAffee's Cross Roads June 11. Powder Springs June 20. Noonday Creek June 27. Line of Nickajack Creek July 2-5. Rottenwood Creek July 4. Rossville Ferry July 5. Line of the Chattahoochie July 6-17. Garrard's Raid on Covington July 22-24. Siege of Atlanta July 22-August 25. Garrard's Raid to South River July 27-31. Flat Rock Bridge July 28. Kilpatrick's Raid around Atlanta August 18-22. Flint River and Jonesborough August 19. Red Oak August 19. Lovejoy Station August 20. Operations at Chattahoochie River Bridge August 26-September 2. Operations in North Georgia and North Alabama against Hood September 29-November 3. Carter Creek Station October 1. Near Columbia October 2. Near Lost Mountain October 4-7. New Hope Church October 5. Dallas October 7. Rome October 10-11. Narrows October 11. Coosaville Road, near Rome, October 13. Near Summerville October 18. Little River, Ala., October 20. Leesburg October 21. Ladiga, Terrapin Creek, October 28. Ordered to Louisville, Ky., to refit; duty there till December 28. March to Nashville, Tenn., December 28-January 8, 1865, thence to Gravelly Springs, Ala., January 25, and duty there till March. Wilson's Raid to Selma, Ala., and Macon, Ga., March 22-April 24. Selma April 2. Occupation of Montgomery April 12. Occupation of Macon April 20. Duty in Georgia and at Nashville, Tenn., till August. Mustered out August 13, 1865.

Regiment lost during service 8 Officers and 94 Enlisted men killed and mortally wounded and 5 Officers and 185 Enlisted men by disease. Total 292.

8th REGIMENT CAVALRY (89th VOLUNTEERS).

Organized at Philadelphia August to October, 1861. Left State for Washington, D. C., October 4, 1861. Attached to Porter's Division, Army Potomac, to March, 1862. Unattached, 4th Army Corps, Army Potomac, to April, 1862. Blake's Brigade, Cavalry Reserve, Army Potomac, to July, 1862. 2nd Brigade, Stoneman's Cavalry Division, Army Potomac, to September, 1862. 2nd Brigade, Pleasanton's Cavalry Division, Army Potomac, to February, 1863. 2nd Brigade, 1st Division, Cavalry Corps, Army Potomac, to June, 1863. 2nd Brigade, 2nd Division, Cavalry Corps, Army Potomac, to July, 1865.

SERVICE.—Duty at Arlington Heights, Va., Defences of Washington, D. C., till March, 1862. Advance on Manassas, Va., March 10-15. Moved to the Virginia Peninsula April. Siege of Yorktown April 11-May 4. Baltimore Cross Roads, near New Kent Court House, May 13. Operations about Bottom's Bridge May 20-23. Reconnoissance toward Richmond and to Turkey Island Creek Bridge May 23. Savage Station May 24. Reconnoissance to Seven Pines May 24-27. Chickahominy May 24. Garnett's Farm and White Oak May 27. Battle of Fair Oaks (Seven Pines) May 31-June 1. Reconnoissance to White Oak Swamp June 22-23. Seven days before Richmond June 25-July 1. Bottom's Bridge June

28-29. Savage Station June 29. Malvern Hill July 1. At Harrison's Landing till August 16. (Co. "A" at Headquarters of Gen. Porter; Co. "B" at Headquarters of Gen. McClellan; Co. "D" at Headquarters of Gen. P. St. G. Cooke.) Turkey Island Bridge July 20. Reconnoissance to Malvern Hill July 23. Retreat from the Peninsula and movement to Alexandria. Maryland Campaign September. Falls Church September 3-4. Sugar Loaf Mountain September 10-11. Frederick September 12. Middletown September 13. Antietam September 16-17. Boteler's Ford, Sharpsburg, Md., September 19. Shepherdstown Ford September 19. Amissville September 30. Reconnoissance from Sharpsburg to Shepherdstown and Martinsburg, W. Va., October 1 (3 Cos.). Philomont November 1-2. Castleman's Ferry, Upperville, Union and Bloomfield November 2-3. Aldie and Ashby's Gap November 3. Markham Station November 4. Barbee's Cross Roads November 5. Waterloo Bridge November 7. Hazel River November 8. Newby's Cross Roads, near Amissville, November 10. Philomont November 19. Leed's Ferry and King George Court House December 2. Battle of Fredericksburg December 12-15. Chancellorsville Campaign April 27-May 6, 1863. Richard's Ford and Barnett's Ford April 29. Ely's Ford Road April 30. Chancellorsville May 1-2. Salem Heights and Banks' Ford May 4. Aldie June 17. Middleburg June 19. Upperville June 21. Thoroughfare Gap June 25. Westminster, Md., June 30. Battle of Gettysburg, Pa., July 1-3. Monterey Gap July 4. Smithsburg July 5. Williamsport and Hagerstown, Md., July 6. Boonsboro July 8. Jones' Cross Roads, near Williamsport, July 10 and 13. Hagerstown July 10-13. St. James College July 11-12. Williamsport Road July 14. Shepherdstown July 16. Rixey's Ford September 2. Advance from the Rappahannock to the Rapidan September 13-17. Culpeper Court House September 13. Rapidan Station September 15-16. Robertson's River September 22. Bristoe Campaign October 9-22. Near Warrenton October 11. Warrenton or White Sulphur Springs October 12. Auburn and Bristoe October 14. St. Stephen's Church October 14. Advance to line of the Rappahannock November 7-8. Mine Run Campaign November 26-December 2. New Hope Church November 27. Blind Ferry December 5. Raid to Luray Valley December 21-23. Regiment re-enlisted December 31, 1863. Raid through Chester Gap January 1-4, 1864. Rapidan Campaign May-June, 1864. Todd's Tavern May 5-8. Spottsylvania Court House May 8-21 (Co. "A"). Sheridan's Raid to James River May 9-24. Matapony Church May 9. North Anna River May 9-10. Ground Squirrel Church and Yellow Tavern May 11. Brook Church or Fortifications of Richmond May 12. Haxall's Landing May 18. Line of the Pamunkey May 26-28. Totopotomoy May 28-31. Haw's Shop May 28. Cold Harbor May 31-June 1. Sumner's Upper Bridge June 2. Sheridan's Trevillian Raid June 7-24. Trevillian Station June 11-12. White House or St. Peter's Church June 21. Black Creek or Tunstall Station June 21. St. Mary's Church June 24. Siege of Petersburg and Richmond June, 1864, to April, 1865. Warwick Swamp July 12. Charles City Cross Roads July 15-16. Demonstration north of the James at Deep Bottom July 27-29. Malvern Hill July 28. Warwick Swamp July 30. Demonstration north of the James at Deep Bottom August 13-20. Gravel Hill August 14. Strawberry Plains and Deep Run August 14-18. Charles City Cross Roads August 16. Dinwiddie Road, near Ream's Station, August 23. Ream's Station August 25. Belcher's Mills September 17. Poplar Springs Church September 29-October 2. Arthur's Swamp September 30-October 1. Boydton Plank Road, Hatcher's Run, October 27-28. Reconnoissance to Stony Creek November 7. Stony Creek Station December 1. Bellefield Raid December 7-12. Dabney's Mills, Hatcher's Run, February 5-7, 1865. Appomattox Campaign March 28-April 9. Dinwiddie C. H. March 30-31. Five Forks April 1. Paine's Cross Roads and Amelia Springs April 5. Deatonville Road and Sailor's Creek April 6. Farmville April 7. Appomattox C. H. April 9. Surrender of Lee and his army. Expedition to Danville April 23-29. Duty at

Lynchburg and in the Dept. of Virginia till July. Mustered out by consolidation with 16th Pennsylvania Cavalry July 24, 1865.

Regiment lost during service 5 Officers and 55 Enlisted men killed and mortally wounded and 2 Officers and 126 Enlisted men by disease. Total 188.

9th REGIMENT CAVALRY (92nd VOLUNTEERS) ("LOCHIEL CAVALRY").

Organized at Harrisburg October and November, 1861. Left State for Louisville, Ky., November 20, 1861, thence moved to Jeffersonville, Ind., and duty there till January 10, 1862. 1st Battalion at Grayson Springs, Ky.; 2nd Battalion at Calhoun, Ky., and 3rd Battalion at Bacon Creek, Ky., till March 5, 1862. Ordered to Tennessee, and 1st Battalion at Springfield, 2nd Battalion at Clarksville and 3rd Battalion at Gallatin till August, 1862. Served unattached, Army Ohio, to September, 1862. 3rd Brigade, 1st Cavalry Division, Army Ohio, to November, 1862. District of Louisville, Ky., Dept. Ohio, to December, 1862. District Central Kentucky, Dept. Ohio, to March, 1863. 1st Brigade, 1st Division, Cavalry Corps, Dept. Cumberland, to May, 1864. District of Kentucky, Dept. Ohio, to September, 1864. District of Middle Tennessee, Dept. Cumberland, to October, 1864. 1st Brigade, 3rd Division, Cavalry Corps, Army Cumberland, to November, 1864. 1st Brigade, 3rd Division, Cavalry Corps, Military Division Mississippi, to July, 1865.

SERVICE.—Lebanon, Ky., May 4-5, 1862 (3rd Battalion). Spring Creek May 14 (3rd Battalion). Tompkinsville June 6 (3rd Battalion). Operations against Morgan July 4-28. Tompkinsville July 9 (3rd Battalion). Glasgow July 10. Paris July 19. Regiment assembled at Lebanon, Ky., August. Crab Orchard, Ky., August 22. Frankfort September 2. Near Perryville October 6-7. Doctor's Fork October 7. Perryville October 8. Carter's Raid from Winchester, Ky., to East Tennessee and Southwest Kentucky December 20, 1862, to January 5, 1863. Passage of Moccasin Gap December 29. Watauga Bridge, Carter's Station and Union December 30. Carter's Depot December 31. Watauga River January 1, 1863. Jonesville, Va., January 2. Union January 15. Reconnoissance from Franklin February 21. Thompson's Station, Spring Hill, March 4-5 (Detachment). Expedition from Franklin to Columbia March 8-12. Thompson's Station March 9. Rutherford Creek March 10-11. Spring Hill March 19. Near Thompson's Station March 23. Little Harpeth River March 25. Near Franklin March 31. Davis Mills April 5 (Detachment). Thompson's Station May 2. Franklin June 4-5. Triune June 9 and 11. Middle Tennessee or Tullahoma Campaign June 23-July 7. Eaglesville and Rover June 23. Middleton June 24. Guy's Gap and Fosterville June 27. Capture of Shelbyville June 27. Bethpage Bridge, Elk River, July 2. Expedition to Huntsville July 13-22. Jonesboro July 12. Chickamauga (Ga.) Campaign August 16-September 22. Rawlingsville September 5. Stevenson, Ala., September 7. Reconnoissance from Alpine, Ga., toward Rome September 10-11. Alpine September 12. Dirt Town, Lafayette Road, September 12. Chattooga River September 12. Reconnoissance from Lee and Gordon's Mills toward Lafayette and skirmish September 13. Battle of Chickamauga, Ga., September 19-20. Buck Town Tavern, near New Market, October 12. Sparta November 24-26 and December 9. On road to Coosaville, Cumberland Mountain, December 9. Operations about Dandridge and Mossy Creek December 24-28. Dandridge, Tenn., December 24. Talbot Station December 28. Mossy Creek, Talbot Station, December 29. Bend of Chucky Road, near Dandridge, January 16, 1864. Operations about Dandridge January 16-17. Dandridge January 17. Fair Garden January 27. McNutt's Bridge January 27. Veterans on furlough April-May. Operations against Morgan May 31-June 20. Defence of Frankfort June 10. Duty in District of Kentucky till September. Lawrenceburg September 6. Readyville, Tenn., September 6. Woodbury September 10. Operations against Hood in North Georgia and North Alabama September 29-November 3. Camp Creek September 30. Sweetwater and Noyes Creek, near Powder Springs, October 1-3. Lafayette, Ga., October 12. March to the sea November 15-December 10. Lovejoy Station November 16. East Macon November 20. Gordon November 21. Clinton November 21-23. Griswoldsville November 22. Sylvan Grove November 27. Waynesboro November 27-28. Near Louisville November 29. Millen or Shady Grove November 30. Waynesboro December 4. Briar Creek December 7. Siege of Savannah December 10-21. Campaign of the Carolinas January to April, 1865. Johnson's Station February 10-11. Phillips Cross Roads March 4. Rockingham March 7. Averysboro, N. C., March 16. Bentonville March 19-21. Morrisville and occupation of Raleigh April 13. Bennett's House April 26. Surrender of Johnston and his army. Duty at Lexington, N. C., till July. Mustered out July 18, 1865.

Regiment lost during service 6 Officers and 66 Enlisted men killed and mortally wounded and 2 Officers and 155 Enlisted men by disease. Total 229.

10th REGIMENT CAVALRY.

Organization not completed.

11th REGIMENT CAVALRY (108th VOLUNTEERS).

Organized at Philadelphia as an independent Regiment, "Harlan's Light Cavalry," under authority of the Secretary of War, August to October, 1861. Moved to Washington, D. C., October 14, 1861. At Camp Palmer, near Ball's Cross Roads, October 16-November 17. Designation of Regiment changed to 11th Cavalry November 13, 1861. Ordered to Fortress Monroe, Va., November 17. Attached to Dept. of Virginia to July, 1862. Unattached, Division at Suffolk, 7th Army Corps, Dept. of Virginia, to July, 1863. U. S. Forces, Norfolk and Portsmouth, Va., Dept. Virginia and North Carolina, to October, 1863. Cavalry Brigade, Portsmouth, Va., Dept. Virginia and North Carolina, to April, 1864. 2nd Brigade, Cavalry Division, Dept. Virginia and North Carolina, to January, 1865. 2nd Brigade, Cavalry Division, Dept. of Virginia, to August, 1865.

SERVICE.—Duty at Camp Hamilton, Va., till May, 1862. Reconnoissance to Big Bethel January 3. Moved to Portsmouth May 15. (Cos. "C" and "M" at Newport News March to May.) Action at Blackwater, near Zuni, May 30, 1862. Companies "A," "E," "G," "H" and "L" ordered to Suffolk, Va., June, 1862, and picket and outpost duty there and toward the Blackwater till June, 1863. Company "M" to Portsmouth, Va., and duty there till March 20, 1863. Companies "B," "C," "D," "F," "I" and "K" ordered to join Army Potomac at White House, participating in operations against Stuart June 13-15, and picket duty at White House and in rear of army till July 2. Operations about New Kent C. H. June 23, and about White House June 26-July 2. Evacuation of White House July 2, and moved to Williamsburg, rejoining other Companies at Suffolk August 20, 1862. Action at Franklin August 31. Reconnoissance from Franklin to Blackwater October 3. Suffolk October 15. Reconnoissance from Suffolk December 1-3. Beaver Dam Creek December 1. Near Franklin and Blackwater December 2. Suffolk December 12. Expedition toward Blackwater January 8-10, 1863. Action at Deserted House January 30. Norfolk February 10 (Co. "M"). Franklin and Blackwater March 17. Siege of Suffolk April 12-May 4. Somerton Road April 15. Edenton Road April 24. Reconnoissance through Gates County, N. C., and down Chowan River June 5-7. Near Suffolk June 11 (Detachment). Expedition to South Anna Bridge June 23-28 (Detachment). Dix's Peninsula Campaign June 24-July 8. South Anna Bridge June 26. Hanover C. H. June 26. Capture of Gen. W. H. F. Lee. Expedition from White House to South Anna River July 1-7. South Anna Bridge July 4. Moved to Portsmouth, Va., and duty there till January, 1864. Expedition from Portsmouth to Jackson, N. C., July 25-August 3, 1864. Jackson July 28. Expedition to Camden and Currituck Counties, N. C., August 5-12. Expedition to Edenton, N. C., August 11-19 (Cos. "G,"

"I" and "K"). Near Pasquotank August 18. South Mills September 12. Reconnoissance to Blackwater River September 14-17. Expedition from Yorktown to Matthews County October 4-9 (Detachment). Expedition to South Mills and Camden, N. C., December 5-24. Moved to Williamsburg, Va., January 23, 1864, and duty there till April. Wistar's Expedition against Richmond February 6-8. Scout in Gloucester County February 28. Expedition in support of Kilpatrick March 1-4. Expedition into King and Queen County March 9-12. Carlton's Store March 10. Expedition into Matthews and Middlesex Counties March 17-21. Reconnoissance to Blackwater April 13-15. Butler's operations on south side of the James and against Petersburg and Richmond May 4-28. Kautz's Raid on Petersburg & Weldon Railroad and to City Point, Va., May 5-11. Birch Island Bridges May 5. Bird Island Bridges, Blackwater River, May 6. Stony Creek Station, Weldon Railroad, May 7. White's Bridge, Nottaway Creek, May 8. Jarrett's Station and White's Bridge May 9. (Cos. "B" and "H" to Headquarters 18th Corps May 4; Co. "H" there till September 28.) Kautz's Raid on Richmond & Danville Railroad May 12-17. Flat Creek Bridge, near Chula Depot, May 14. Belcher's Mills May 16. Bermuda Hundred June 2 (Detachment). Petersburg June 9. Before Petersburg June 15-18. Siege operations against Petersburg and Richmond June 16, 1864, to April 2, 1865. (Co. "B" rejoined Regiment June 20.) Wilson's Raid on South Side & Danville Railroad June 22-30, 1864. Staunton River Bridge and Roanoke Station June 25. Sappony Church or Stony Creek June 28-29. Ream's Station June 29. Demonstration on north side of the James at Deep Bottom July 27-29. Deep Bottom July 27-28. Ream's Station August 18-21. Vaughan Road August 22. Dinwiddie Road, near Ream's Station, August 23. Near Ream's Station August 24. Ream's Station August 25. Jerusalem Plank Road September 15. Sycamore Church September 16. Chaffin's Farm, New Market Heights, September 28-30. Darbytown Road October 7 and 13. Fair Oaks October 27-28. Johnson's Farm October 29. Darbytown Road December 10. Expedition to Fearnsville and Smithfield February 11-15, 1865. Appomattox Campaign March 28-April 9. Five Forks April 1. Gravelly Ford, Hatcher's Run, April 2. Deep Creek April 4. Amelia C. H. April 4-5. Prince Edward C. H. April 7. Appomattox Station April 8. Appomattox C. H. April 9. Surrender of Lee and his army. March to Lynchburg, Va., April 12-16, thence to Richmond April 16-24. Expedition to Staunton May 5-11. Duty in the Sub-District of Albemarle till July. Mustered out at Richmond August 13, 1865. (Co. "L" detached on eastern shore of Virginia from 1863.)

12th REGIMENT CAVALRY (113th VOLUNTEERS).

Organized at Philadelphia December, 1861, to April, 1862. Ordered to Washington, D. C., April, 1862. Attached to Military District of Washington, to September, 1862. 4th Brigade, Pleasanton's Cavalry Division, Army Potomac, to October, 1862. Averill's Cavalry Command, 8th Army Corps, Middle Department, to November, 1862. Defences Upper Potomac, 8th Corps, to February, 1863. 1st Brigade, 2nd Division, 8th Corps, to June, 1863. Pierce's Brigade, Dept. of the Susquehanna, to July, 1863. McReynold's Command, Dept. Susquehanna, to August, 1863. Martinsburg, W. Va., Dept. West Virginia, to October, 1863. 3rd Brigade, 1st Division, Dept. West Virginia, to February, 1864. Reserve Division, Dept. West Virginia, to July, 1864. 1st Brigade, 1st Cavalry Division, West Virginia, to August, 1864. Reserve Division, Dept. West Virginia, to January, 1865. 3rd Infantry Division, West Virginia, to April, 1865. Cavalry, Army Shenandoah, to July, 1865.

SERVICE.—Duty at Washington, D. C., till June 20, 1862. Moved to Manassas Junction, Va., and guard Orange & Alexandria Railroad till August. Moved to Bristoe, thence to Alexandria, and picket north bank Potomac from Chain Bridge to Edward's Ferry till September. Maryland Campaign September-October.

Frederick, Md., September 12. Battle of Antietam, Md., September 16-17. Assigned to duty on line of the Baltimore & Ohio Railroad, Headquarters at Sir John's Run and Bath. Martinsburg, W. Va., November 6. Moorefield November 9. Newtown November 24. Kearneysville December 26. Bunker Hill January 1, 1863. Near Smithfield and Charlestown February 12. Millwood Road near Winchester April 8. Reconnoissance from Winchester to Wardensville and Strasburg April 20. Operations in Shenandoah Valley April 22-29. Strasburg Road, Fisher's Hill, April 22. Scout to Strasburg April 25-30. Cedarville and Winchester June 12. Winchester June 13-15. McConnellsburg, Pa., June 24 Cunningham's Cross Roads July 5. Greencastle, Pa., July 5 (Detachment). Near Clear Springs, Md., July 10. Moved to Sharpsburg, Md., thence to Martinsburg August 3, and duty there till July, 1864. Jeffersonton, Va., October 10, 1863. Near Winchester February 5, 1864. Middletown February 6. Winchester April 26. Affair in Loudoun County June 9 (Detachment). Charlestown and Duffield Station June 29. Bolivar Heights July 2. Near Hillsboro July 15-16. Charlestown July 17. Snicker's Ferry July 17-18. Ashby's Gap and Berry's Ford July 19. Near Kernstown July 23. Winchester July 24. Bunker Hill and Martinsburg July 25. Cherry Run July 28. Winchester July 29. Guard and garrison duty at Charlestown, covering railroad from Harper's Ferry to Winchester till March, 1865. Charlestown September 27, 1864. Halltown November 12. Mount Zion Church November 12. Newtown November 24. Charlestown November 29 (Detachment). Affair at Harper's Ferry February 3, 1865 (Detachment). Scout from Harper's Ferry into Loudoun County March 20-23. Near Hamilton March 21. Goose Creek March 23. Duty at Winchester and in the Shenandoah Valley till July. Mustered out July 20, 1865.

Regiment lost during service 2 Officers and 32 Enlisted men killed and mortally wounded and 1 Officer and 107 Enlisted men by disease. Total 142.

13th REGIMENT CAVALRY (117th VOLUNTEERS).

Organized at Philadelphia and Harrisburg December, 1861, to April, 1862. Ordered to Baltimore, Md., April, 1862. Attached to Defences of Baltimore, 8th Corps, Middle Department, to September, 1862. Defences Upper Potomac, 8th Corps, to February, 1863. Elliott's Brigade, Milroy's Command, Winchester, Va., 8th Corps, February, 1863. 1st Brigade, 2nd Division, 8th Corps, to July, 1863. 3rd Brigade, 2nd Division, Cavalry Corps, Army Potomac, to August, 1863. 2nd Brigade, 2nd Division, Cavalry Corps, Army Potomac, to February, 1865. (Served attached to 9th Army Corps, Army Potomac, May 3-26, 1864.) Terry's Provisional Corps, Dept. North Carolina, to March, 1865. 3rd Brigade, Kilpatrick's 3rd Division, Cavalry Corps, Military Division Mississippi, to July, 1865.

SERVICE.—Duty in the Defences of Baltimore, Md., till September 24, 1862. Moved to Point of Rocks, Md., September 24, and guard duty on line of the Potomac between Berlin and Edward's Ferry, and scouting in Loudoun and Jefferson Counties, Va., till February, 1863. Ordered to join Milroy at Winchester, Va., February 3. Woodstock February 25. Strasburg Road and Woodstock February 26 (Cos. "G," "L"). Cedar Creek April 13. Reconnoissance toward Wardensville and Strasburg April 20. Operations in the Shenandoah Valley April 22-29. Fisher's Hill, Strasburg Road, April 22 and 26. Scout to Strasburg April 25-30. Strasburg April 28. Fairmont April 29. Scout in Hampshire County May 4-9. Operations about Front Royal Ford and Buck's Ford May 12-26. Piedmont Station May 16 (Detachment). Middletown and Newtown June 12. Battle of Winchester June 13-15. Retreat to Harper's Ferry June 15, and duty there till June 30. Moved to Frederick, Md., thence to Boonsboro July 8, and joined Cavalry Corps, Army Potomac. Scouting in Virginia till September. Oak Shade September 2. Hazel River September 4. Advance to the Rapidan September 13-17. Culpeper C. H. September 13. Bristoe Campaign Oc-

tober 9-22. James City October 10. Near Warrenton October 11. Jeffersonton October 12. Warrenton or White Sulphur Springs October 12-13. Auburn and Bristoe October 14. St. Stephen's Church October 14. Advance to line of the Rappahannock November 7-8. Rappahannock Station November 7. Catlett's Station November 15. Mine Run Campaign November 26-December 2. New Hope Church November 27. Mine Run November 28-30. Scout from Vienna to White Plains December 28-31. Brentsville February 14, 1864. Near Sprigg's Ford February 28 (Co. "L"). Near Greenwich March 6. Scout to Brentsville March 8. Scout to Greenwich March 9. Near Greenwich March 9. Scout to Greenwich March 11. Bristoe Station March 16. Scout to Aldie and Middleburg March 28-29. Bristoe Station April 9. Near Nokesville April 13. Near Milford April 15. Near Middletown April 24. Rapidan Campaign May-June. Battles of the Wilderness May 5-7; Spottsylvania C. H. May 8-21; Strasburg May 12 (Detachment). North Anna River May 23-26. Rejoined Brigade May 26. Haw's Shop May 28. Old Church May 30. Cold Harbor May 31-June 1. Sumner's Upper Bridge June 2. About Cold Harbor June 2-7. Sheridan's Trevillian Raid June 7-24. Trevillian Station June 11-12. White House and St. Peter's Church June 21. Black Creek or Tunstall Station June 21. St. Mary's Church June 24. Charles City Cross Roads June 30. Proctor's Hill July 1. Warwick Swamp July 12. Demonstration north of James River at Deep Bottom July 27-29. Malvern Hill July 28. Warwick Swamp July 30. Demonstration north of James River at Deep Bottom August 13-20. Gravel Hill August 14. White Oak Swamp August 14-15. Charles City Cross Roads August 16. Strawberry Plains August 16-18. Dinwiddie Road near Ream's Station August 23. Ream's Station August 25. Coggin's Point and Fort Powhatan September 16. Poplar Grove Church September 29-October 2. Wyatt's Farm September 29. Arthur's Swamp September 30-October 1. Stony Creek October 11-12. Boydton Plank Road October 27-28. Reconnoissances toward Stony Creek November 7 and November 28. Stony Creek Station December 1. Reconnoissance to Hatcher's Run December 8-10. Hatcher's Run December 8-9. Dabney's Mills, Hatcher's Run, February 5-7, 1865. Rowanty Creek February 5. Ordered to Wilmington, N. C., February 17, arriving there March 6. Advance on Goldsboro March 6-21. Reported to Sherman at Fayetteville, N. C. Occupation of Goldsboro March 21. Advance on Raleigh April 10-13. Near Raleigh April 12. Occupation of Raleigh April 13. Received surrender of Artillery. Surrender of Johnston and his army at Bennett's House April 26. Duty at Fayetteville and in Dept. of North Carolina till July. Mustered out July 14, 1865, and discharged at Philadelphia, Pa., July 27, 1865.

Regiment lost during service 3 Officers and 67 Enlisted men killed and mortally wounded and 220 Enlisted men by disease. Total 290.

14th REGIMENT CAVALRY (159th VOLUNTEERS).

Organized at Pittsburg, Philadelphia and Erie October and November, 1862. Moved to Hagerstown, Md., November 24, 1862, thence to Harper's Ferry, W. Va., December 28. Attached to Defences Upper Potomac, 8th Army Corps, Middle Department, to March, 1863. 1st Brigade, 1st Division, 8th Corps, March, 1863. 4th Separate Brigade, 8th Corps, to June, 1863. Averill's 4th Separate Brigade, Dept. West Virginia, to December, 1863. 2nd Brigade, 4th Division, Dept. West Virginia, to April, 1864. 2nd Brigade, 2nd Cavalry Division, West Virginia, to June, 1864. 1st Brigade, 2nd Cavalry Division, West Virginia, to August, 1864. 3rd Brigade, 1st Division, Cavalry Corps, Army Shenandoah, Middle Military Division, August, 1864. 1st Brigade, 2nd Cavalry Division, West Virginia, to April, 1865. 1st Separate Brigade, 22nd Corps, Dept. of Washington, to June, 1865. Dept. of Missouri to August, 1865.

SERVICE.—Picket and outpost duty in the vicinity of Harper's Ferry, W. Va., till May, 1863. Scout to Leesburg March 15 and April 21-24, 1863. Ordered to Grafton, W. Va., May, 1863, and duty protecting Phillippi, Beverly and Webster till July. Forced march to relief of Beverly July 2-3. Huttonsville July 4. Moved to Webster, thence to Cumberland, Md., and to Williamsport, Md., July 5-14, and join Army of the Potomac. Advance to Martinsburg July 15. Martinsburg and Hedgesville July 18-19. McConnellsburg, Pa., July 30. Averill's Raid from Winchester through Hardy, Pendleton, Highland, Bath, Greenbrier and Pocahontas Counties, W. Va., August 1-31. Newtown August 2. Moorefield and Cacapon Mountain August 6 (Detachment). Salt Works, near Franklin, August 19. Jackson River August 25. Rocky Gap, near White Sulphur Springs, August 26-27. Hedgesville October 15 (Detachment). Averill's Raid against Lewisburg and the Virginia & Tennessee Railroad November 1-17. Cackletown November 4. Mill Point November 5. Droop Mountain November 6. Averill's Raid from New Creek to Salem, on Virginia & Tennessee Railroad, December 8-25. Marling's Bottom Bridge December 11. Gatewood's December 12. Descent upon Salem December 16. Scott's or Barber's Creek December 19. Jackson River, near Covington, December 19. Winchester March 22 and April 8, 1864. Sigel's Expedition from Martinsburg to New Market April 23-May 16 (Detachment). Averill's Raid on Virginia & Tennessee Railroad May 5-19. Grassy Lick, Cove Mountain, near Wytheville, May 10. New River Bridge May 10. New Market May 15 (Detachment). Hunter's Expedition to Lynchburg May 26-July 1. Piedmont, Mount Crawford, June 5. Occupation of Staunton June 6. (Detachment with Sigel rejoined Regiment at Staunton.) Lexington June 11. Scout around Lynchburg June 13-15. Near Buchanan June 13. New London June 16. Diamond Hill June 17. Lynchburg June 17-18. Liberty June 19. Buford's Gap June 20. Catawba Mountains and about Salem June 21. Liberty June 22. Moved to the Shenandoah Valley July. Buckton July 17. Stephenson's Depot July 20. Newtown July 22. Kernstown, Winchester, July 24. Near Martinsburg July 25. Hagerstown July 29. Hancock, Md., July 31. Antietam Ford August 4. Sheridan's Shenandoah Valley Campaign August to November. Near Moorefield August 7. Williamsport, Md., August 26. Martinsburg August 31. Bunker Hill September 2-3. Winchester September 5. Darkesville September 10. Bunker Hill September 13. Near Berryville September 14. Opequan, Winchester, September 19. Fisher's Hill September 22. Mount Jackson September 23-24. Forest Hill or Timberville September 24. Brown's Gap September 26. Weyer's Cave September 26-27. Mount Jackson October 3 (Detachment). Battle of Cedar Creek October 19. Dry Run October 23 (Detachment). Milford October 25-26. Cedar Creek November 8. Nineveh November 12. Rude's Hill November 23. Snicker's Gap November 30. Millwood December 17 (Detachment). Expedition from Winchester to Gordonsville December 19-28. Madison C. H. December 21. Liberty Mills December 22. Near Gordonsville December 23. At Winchester till April, 1865. Expedition into Loudoun County February 18-19 (Detachment). Expedition to Ashby's Gap February 19. Operations in the valley till April 20. Ordered to Washington, D. C., April 20, and duty there till June. Grand Review May 23-24. Moved to Fort Leavenworth, Kan., June, and duty in the District of the Plains till August. Mustered out August 24, 1865.

Regiment lost during service 2 Officers and 97 Enlisted men killed and mortally wounded and 296 Enlisted men by disease. Total 395.

15th REGIMENT CAVALRY (160th VOLUNTEERS).

Organized at Carlisle, Pa., July to October, 1862. Engaged in scout and picket duty near Chambersburg, Pa., during Maryland Campaign, September 6-24, 1862. Attached to Cavalry Division, Army Potomac, unassigned, September, 1862. A Detachment moved to Greencastle, thence to Hagerstown, Md., September 6-15. Skirmish near Hagerstown September 12-13. Hagerstown September 15. Advance to Jones' Cross Roads September 16, and scouting during battle of Antietam, Md., September 17. Led advance of Pennsylvania Militia to Williamsport September 20-21. Regiment left State for Louisville, Ky., November 7, 1862, thence moved to Nashville, Tenn., December 8. Served unattached, Army Cumberland, to December, 1862. Reserve, Cavalry Brigade, Army Cumberland, to March, 1863. Unattached, Cavalry Corps, Army Cumberland, to June, 1863. Headquarters Army Cumberland to October, 1863. Unattached Cavalry, Dept. Cumberland, to May, 1864. Post and District of Nashville, Dept. Cumberland, to August, 1864. Unattached, Dept. Cumberland, to November, 1864. 3rd Brigade, 6th Division, Cavalry Corps, Military Division Mississippi, to March, 1865. 1st Brigade, Cavalry Division, District East Tennessee, Dept. Cumberland, to June, 1865.

SERVICE.—Skirmish on Hillsboro Pike, near Nashville, Tenn., December 25, 1862. Advance on Murfreesboro December 26-30. Nolensville December 26-27. Triune December 27. Wilkinson's Cross Roads December 29. Battle of Stone's River December 30-31, 1862, and January 1-3, 1863. Lavergne December 30, 1862. Scout to Woodbury January 4, 1863. Lytle's Creek January 5. At Murfreesboro till June. Scout to Woodbury April 4. Near Woodbury April 5-6. The Barrens April 7. (Cos. "B," "H" and "K" at Dept. Headquarters.) Middle Tennessee or Tullahoma Campaign June 22-July 7. Near Rover June 24. Winchester August 1. Passage of Cumberland Mountains and Tennessee River, and Chickamauga (Ga.) Campaign August 16-September 22. Battle of Chickamauga September 19-21. Duty in Sequatchie Valley till November. Near Dunlap October 2. Sequatchie Valley October 26. March to relief of Knoxville November 28-December 8. Gatlinsburg December 10. Near Dandridge Mills December 13. Near Morristown December 14. Near Dandridge December 22-23. Dandridge December 24. Mossy Creek, Talbot Station, December 29. Scout from Dandridge to Clark's Ferry January 10-11, 1864. Schultz's Mill, Cosby Creek, January 14 (Detachment). Near Wilsonville January 22 (Detachment). Indian Creek January 28. Fair Garden January 28-29. Fain's Island January 28. Expedition from Marysville to Quallatown, N. C., January 31-February 7. Quallatown February 5. Moved to Chattanooga, Tenn., arriving February 12. Demonstration on Dalton, Ga., February 22-27. Tunnel Hill, Buzzard's Roost Gap and Rocky Faced Ridge February 23-25. Scouting till May. Ordered to Nashville, Tenn., May 4, and duty there till September. Gillem's Expedition from East Tennessee toward Southwest Virginia September 20-October 17. Jonesboro and Watauga River September 29. Kingsport October 7. Rogersville October 8. Scouting about Chattanooga till December. Dalton December 13. Pursuit of Hood's forces and trains December 20, 1864, to January 6, 1865. Near Decatur, Ala., December 28. Pond Springs December 29. Near Leighton December 30. Russellville December 31. Nauvoo, Ala., January 2. Thorn Hill January 3. Near Mt. Hope January 5. Pursuit of Lyon January 13-16. Red Hill January 14. Warrenton January 15. Paint Rock January 26. Stoneman's Raid into Southwest Virginia and Western North Carolina March 21-April 25. Demonstration on Virginia & Tennessee Railroad to near Lynchburg, Va., March 26-April 6 (Detachment under Major Wagner). Yadkin River March 29. Boone, N. C., April 1. Hillsville and Wytheville, Va., April 3. New London, Va., April 8. Martinsville April 8. Near Greensboro April 11. Capture of Saulsbury April 12. Jamestown, N. C., April 19. Howard's Gap, Blue Ridge Mountains, April 22. Pursuit of Jeff Davis May. (A Detachment of Regiment was on duty at Headquarters Army Cumberland June 24, 1863, to December, 1864; participated in the Atlanta Campaign and Nashville Campaign.) Mustered out at Nashville, Tenn., June 21, 1865. Company "A" retained in service till July 18, 1865.

Regiment lost during service 3 Officers and 22 Enlisted men killed and mortally wounded and 103 Enlisted men by disease. Total 128.

16th REGIMENT CAVALRY (161st VOLUNTEERS).

Organized at Harrisburg September to November, 1862. Left State for Washington, D. C., November 23, 1862. Attached to Defences of Washington to January, 1863. Averill's Cavalry Brigade, Army of the Potomac, to February, 1863. 2nd Brigade, 2nd Division, Cavalry Corps, Army Potomac, to June, 1863. 3rd Brigade, 2nd Division, Cavalry Corps, Army Potomac, to August, 1863. 2nd Brigade, 2nd Division, Cavalry Corps, Army Potomac, to May, 1865. Dept. of Virginia to August, 1865.

SERVICE.—At Camp Casey, near Bladensburg, Md., till January 3, 1863. Moved to Falmouth, Va., January 3, and duty on line of the Rappahannock till April, 1863. Operations at Rappahannock Bridge and Grove Church February 5-7. Hartwood Church February 25. Kelly's Ford March 17. Operations about Bealeton Station April 13-27. Elk Run April 13. Chancellorsville Campaign April 26-May 8. Stoneman's Raid April 29-May 8. Kelly's Ford April 29. Ely's Ford May 2. Brandy Station, Stevensburg and Beverly Ford June 9. Aldie June 17. Near Middleburg June 18. Middleburg June 19. Battle of Gettysburg, Pa., July 1-3. Steven's Furnace July 5. Shepherdstown, W. Va., July 14-16. Little Washington August 27. Advance to the Rapidan September 13-17. Culpeper C. H. September 13. Crooked Run September 18. Bristoe Campaign October 9-22. Warrenton or White Sulphur Springs October 12-13. Auburn and Bristoe October 14. St. Stephen's Church October 14. Catlett's Station October 14. Mine Run Campaign November 26-December 2. New Hope Church November 27. Parker's Store November 29. Expedition to Luray December 21-23. Amissville, Gaines Cross Roads and Sperryville December 22. Kilpatrick's Raid on Richmond February 28-March 4, 1864. Beaver Dam Station February 29. Fortifications of Richmond March 1. Rapidan Campaign May-June. Todd's Tavern, Wilderness, May 5-8. Sheridan's Raid to James River May 9-24. North Anna River May 9-10. Ground Squirrel Church and Yellow Tavern May 11. Brook Church, Fortifications of Richmond, May 12. Milford Station May 21. Line of the Pamunkey May 26-28. Haw's Shop May 28. Totopotomoy May 28-31. Cold Harbor May 31-June 1. Sumner's Upper Bridge June 2. Sheridan's Trevillian Raid June 7-24. Trevillian Station June 11-12. White House or St. Peter's Church June 21. Black Creek or Tunstall Station June 21. St. Mary's Church June 24. Siege operations against Petersburg and Richmond July, 1864, to April, 1865. Warwick Swamp July 12, 1864. Demonstration on north side of the James at Deep Bottom July 27-29. Deep Bottom July 28-29. Malvern Hill July 28. Warwick Swamp July 30. Demonstration on north side of James River at Deep Bottom August 13-20. Gravel Hill August 14. Strawberry Plains, Deep Bottom, August 14-18. Charles City Cross Roads August 16. Dinwiddie Road, near Ream's Station, August 23. Ream's Station August 25. Reconnoissance to Poplar Springs Church September 13. Reconnoissance toward Dinwiddie C. H. September 15. Poplar Springs Church September 29-October 2. Arthur's Swamp September 30-October 1. Boydton Plank Road, Hatcher's Run, October 27-28. Reconnoissance to Stony Creek November 7. Near Lee's Mills November 16 (Detachment). Stony Creek Station December 1. Hicksford Raid December 7-12. Bellefield December 8. Disputantia Station January 9, 1865. Dabney's Mills, Hatcher's Run, February 5-7. Appomattox Campaign March 28-April 9. Dinwiddie C. H. March 30-31. Five Forks April 1. Paine's Cross Roads and Amelia Springs April 5. Sailor's Creek April 6. Farmville April 7. Appomattox C. H. April 9. Surrender of Lee and his army. Expedition to Danville April 23-29. Moved to Lynchburg, Va., and duty there and in the Dept. of Virginia till August. Mustered out August 11, 1865.

Regiment lost during service 5 Officers and 100 Enlisted men killed and mortally wounded and 3 Officers and 194 Enlisted men by disease. Total 302.

17th REGIMENT CAVALRY (162nd VOLUNTEERS).

Organized at Harrisburg September to November, 1862. Left State for Washington, D. C., November 25, 1862. Attached to Cavalry Brigade, 11th Corps, Army Potomac, to February, 1863. 2nd Brigade, 1st Division, Cavalry Corps, Army Potomac, to August, 1864, and Army Shenandoah to March, 1865. 2nd Brigade, 1st Division, Cavalry Corps, Army Potomac, to June, 1865.

SERVICE.—Camp at East Capital Hill, Defences of Washington, till December, 1862. Skirmish at Occoquan, Dumfries, Va., December 19. Occoquan December 19-20 and 27-28. Frying Pan, near Chantilly, December 29. Wiggenton's Mills February 6, 1863. Kelly's Ford April 28. Chnacellorsville Campaign April 26-May 8. Rapidan River April 29. Chancellorsville April 30-May 6. Brandy Station and Beverly Ford June 9. Upperville June 21. Battle of Gettysburg, Pa., July 1-3. Williamsport, Md., July 6. Boonsboro July 8. Benevola or Beaver Creek July 9. Funkstown July 10-13. Falling Water July 14. Kelly's Ford July 30-August 1. Brandy Station August 1. Expedition from Leesburg August 30-September 2. Advance to the Rapidan September 13-17. Brandy Station and Culpeper C. H. September 13. Raccoon Ford September 14-16. Reconnoissance across the Rapidan September 21-23. Jack's Shop, Madison C. H., September 22. Bristoe Campaign October 9-22. Raccoon Ford and Morton's Ford October 10. Stevensburg October 11. Near Kelly's Ford October 11. Brandy Station or Fleetwood October 12. Oak Hill October 15. Advance to line of the Rappahannock November 7-8. Mine Run Campaign November 26-December 2. Parker's Store November 29. Demonstration on the Rapidan February 6-7, 1864. Kilpatrick's Raid on Richmond February 28-March 4. Fortifications of Richmond March 1. Ashland March 1. Reconnoissance to Madison C. H. April 28. Rapidan Campaign May-June. Wilderness May 5-7. Brock Road and the Furnaces May 6. Todd's Tavern May 7-8. Sheridan's Raid to the James River May 9-24. North Anna River May 9-10. Ground Squirrel Church and Yellow Tavern May 11. Meadow Bridge May 12. Line of the Pamunkey May 26-28. Hanovertown May 26. Hanovertown Ferry and Hanovertown May 27. Crump's Creek May 28. Haw's Shop May 28. Totopotomoy May 28-31. Old Church and Mattadequin Creek May 30. Bethesda Church, Cold Harbor, May 31-June 1. Bottom's Bridge June 1. Sheridan's Trevillian Raid June 7-24. Trevillian Station June 11-12. Newark or Mallory's Cross Roads June 12. White House or St. Peter's Church June 21. Black Creek or Tunstall Station June 21. Baltimore Cross Roads June 22. Jones' Bridge June 23. Demonstration on north side of the James at Deep Bottom July 27-29. Sheridan's Shenandoah Valley Campaign August 7-November 28. Toll Gate, near White Post, August 11. Near Newtown August 11. Cedarville, Guard Hill or Front Royal, August 16. Summit Point August 21. Kearneysville and Shepherdstown August 25. Leetown and Smithfield August 28. Smithfield Crossing of the Opequan August 29. Berryville September 6. Sevier's Ford, Opequan Creek, September 15. Battle of Opequan, Winchester, September 19. Middletown and Strasburg September 20. Near Winchester and Smithfield September 24. Fisher's Hill September 29 and October 1. Newtonia October 11. Winchester November 16. Expedition from Winchester into Fauquier and Loudoun Counties November 28-December 3. Expedition to Gordonsville December 19-28. Madison C. H. December 21. Liberty Mills December 22. Near Gordonsville December 23. Sheridan's Expedition from Winchester February 27-March 25, 1865. Occupation of Staunton March 2. Waynesboro March 2. Appomattox Campaign March 28-April 9. Dinwiddie C. H. March 30-31. Five Forks April 1. Scott's Cross Roads April 2. Tabernacle Church or Beaver Pond Creek April 4. Sailor's Creek April 6. Appomattox Station April 8. Appomattox C. H. April 9. Surrender of Lee and his army. Expedition to Danville April 23-29. March to Washington, D. C., May. Grand Review May 23. Consolidated with 1st and 6th Pennsylvania Cavalry to form 2nd Provisional Cavalry June 17, 1865.

Regiment lost during service 6 Officers and 98 Enlisted men killed and mortally wounded and 128 Enlisted men by disease. Total 232.

18th REGIMENT CAVALRY (163rd VOLUNTEERS).

Organized at Pittsburg and Harrisburg October to December, 1862. Left State for Washington, D. C., December 8, 1862. Attached to Wyndham's Cavalry Brigade, Defences of Washington, to February, 1863. Price's Independent Cavalry Brigade, 22nd Corps, Dept. of Washington, to April, 1863. 3rd Brigade, Stahel's Cavalry Division, 22nd Corps, to June, 1863. 1st Brigade, 3rd Division, Cavalry Corps, Army Potomac, to August, 1864, and Army Shenandoah to February, 1865. Cavalry Brigade, Army Shenandoah, to June, 1865.

SERVICE.—Duty at Bladensburg and Germantown and in the Defences of Washington till June, 1863. Skirmishes at Chantilly, Va., February 10 and 26, 1863. Scout from Centreville to Falmouth, Va., February 27-28. Left Fairfax C. H. with Stahel's Division to join Army Potomac, June 25, 1863. Hanover, Pa., June 30. Battle of Gettysburg, Pa., July 1-3. Hunterstown July 2. Monterey Gap July 4. Smithburg, Md., July 5. Williamsport July 6. Hagerstown July 6. Boonsboro July 8. Hagerstown July 11-13. Falling Water July 14. Battle Mountain near Newby's Cross Roads July 24. Expedition to Port Conway September 1-3. Lamb's Creek September 1. Advance to the Rapidan September 13-17. Culpeper C. H. and Brandy Station September 13. Rapidan Station September 13-14. Reconnoissance across the Rapidan September 21-23. Bristoe Campaign October 9-22. James City and Bethesda Church October 10. Near Culpeper October 11. Near Warrenton and Brandy Station October 11. Gainesville October 14. Groveton October 17-18. Gainesville, New Baltimore, Buckland's Mills and Haymarket October 19. Advance to line of the Rappahannock November 7-8. (Cos. "B," "H" at Headquarters, 5th Corps, and at Rappahannock Station November 7. Rejoined Regiment November 19.) Germania Ford November 18. Mine Run Campaign November 26-December 2. Morton's Ford November 26. Near Ely's Ford January 13, 1864. Demonstration on the Rapidan February 6-7. Kilpatrick's Raid on Richmond February 28-March 4. Fortifications of Richmond March 1. Rapidan Campaign May-June. Wilderness May 5-7. Craig's Meeting House May 5. Todd's Tavern May 5-6. Alsop's Farm May 8. Sheridan's Raid to James River May 9-24. North Anna River May 9-10. Ground Squirrel Church and Yellow Tavern May 11. Brook's Church or Richmond fortifications May 12. Strawberry Hills May 12. Line of the Pamunkey May 26-28. Demonstration on Little River May 27. Totopotomoy May 28-31. Hanover C. H. May 30. Mechump's Creek May 31. Cold Harbor May 31-June 1. Totopotomoy and Gaines' Mill June 2. Salem Church and Haw's Shop June 2. Haw's Shop June 3. Old Church June 10. Bethesda Church June 11. Long Bridge June 12. Smith's Store near St. Mary's Church June 15. Siege of Petersburg June to August. Jerusalem Plank Road June 22-23. (Co. "B" at Headquarters, 6th Corps, June 25-July 16.) White Oak Swamp July 14. Sheridan's Shenandoah Valley Campaign August 7-November 28. Winchester August 15 and 17. Near Charlestown August 21-22. Limestone Ridge September 1. Abraham's Creek near Winchester September 13. Battle of Opequan, Winchester, September 19. Near Cedarville September 20. Front Royal September 21. Milford September 22. Waynesboro September 29. Near Brock's Gap October 6. Tom's Brook October 8-9. Cedar Creek October 13. Battle of Cedar Creek October 19. Cedar Creek November 11. Newtown or Middletown November 12. Rude's Hill near Mt. Jackson November 22. Expedition to Lacy Springs December 19-22. Duty at and near Winchester till May, 1865. Scout to Edenburg March 17-19. At Cumberland, Md., to June. Consoli-dated with 22nd Pennsylvania Cavalry June 24, 1865, to form 3rd Provisional Cavalry.

Regiment lost during service 5 Officers and 55 Enlisted men killed and mortally wounded and 2 Officers and 232 Enlisted men by disease. Total 294.

19th REGIMENT CAVALRY (180th VOLUNTEERS).

Organized at Philadelphia June to October, 1863. Moved to Washington, D. C., November 5 and 8, 1863, thence to Eastport, Miss., November 13 and joined Gen. A. J. Smith at Columbus, Ky., December 3. Attached to District of Columbus, 6th Division, 16th Army Corps, Dept. Tennessee, December, 1863. Waring's Cavalry Brigade, 16th Corps, to January, 1864. 1st Brigade, 1st Cavalry Division, 16th Corps, to June, 1864. 1st Brigade, 2nd Cavalry Division, District of West Tennessee, to November, 1864. 1st Brigade, 7th Division, Cavalry Corps, Military Division, Mississippi, to February, 1865. 2nd Brigade, 7th Division, Cavalry Corps, Military Division Mississippi, to March, 1865. Cavalry Brigade, District of Baton Rouge, La., Dept. Gulf, to August, 1865. Dept. Louisiana, to December, 1865. Dept. of Texas to May, 1866.

SERVICE.—Moved to Union City, Tenn., December 6, 1863. Expedition from Union City to Trenton January 22-24, 1864. Moved to Colliersville January 28-February 5. Smith's Expedition from Colliersville to Okolona, Miss., February 11-26. Egypt Station February 19. West Point February 20. Ivy Farm, Okolona, February 22. Tallahatchie River February 23. Operations against Forest in West Tennessee March 16-April 14. Cypress Creek and near Raleigh April 3. Near Raleigh April 9. Sturgis' Expedition from Memphis to Ripley, Miss., April 30-May 9. Sturgis' Expedition to Guntown, Miss., June 1-13. Corinth June 6. Ripley June 7. Brice's or Tishamingo Creek near Guntown June 10. Waldron Bridge June 11. Davis' Mills June 12. Expedition from Memphis to Grand Gulf, Miss., July 4-24. Near Bolivar July 6. Blackwater July 10. Port Gibson July 14. Grand Gulf July 16-17. Smith's Expedition to Oxford, Miss., August 1-30. Hurricane Creek August 9. A detachment moved to Little Rock, Ark., and on expedition against Price, Nonconah Creek, November 20 (Co. "F"). Moved to Nashville, Tenn., November 26-December 3. Owen's Cross Roads December 1. Battle of Nashville December 15-16. Hollow Tree Gap, Franklin and West Harpeth River December 17. King's Hill near Pulaski December 25. Sugar Creek December 26. At Gravelly Springs, Ala., till February 8, 1865. Moved to Vicksburg, Miss., thence to New Orleans, La., February 8-March 9, and to Baton Rouge, La., March 20. Duty there till August 12. Moved to Alexandria August 12. (Consolidated to 6 Companies February 4, 1865, and to 4 Companies June 13.) Company "A" duty at Shreveport till December 15, then at Marshall, Texas, till April, 1866. Company "B" at Alexandria till March, 1866. Company "C" at Monroe till December 15, 1865, then at Jefferson, Texas, till April, 1866. Company "D" at Natchitoches till March, 1866. Companies "A" and "C" to New Orleans April, 1866. Companies "B" and "D" to New Orleans March, 1866. Provost duty there till May. Mustered out May 14, 1866.

Regiment lost during service 15 Enlisted men killed and mortally wounded and 3 Officers and 109 Enlisted men by disease. Total 124.

20th REGIMENT CAVALRY (181st VOLUNTEERS)
SIX MONTHS.

Organized at Harrisburg June to August, 1863, for six months. March to Greencastle July 7, 1863. Scouting into Maryland and pursuit of Lee July 8-24. Moved to Falling Water and picket shores of the Potomac till August. Ordered to Sir John's Run, W. Va., and assigned to guard duty on Baltimore & Ohio Railroad. Companies "F" and "I" at Berkeley Springs. Companies "D" and "E" at Bloomery Gap. Skirmish at Bloomery Gap September 1. Companies "A" and "H" at Great Cacapon Bridge. Skirmish at Bath September 1. Company "C" at Hancock. The five Emergency

Companies on duty at Philadelphia, Reading and Pottsville, Pa. Regiment concentrated at Sir John's Run, W. Va., September, 1863. Duty there and at Springfield till December. Scout in Hampshire, Hardy, Frederick and Shenandoah Counties December 7-11 (Detachment). Regiment moved to Harrisburg, Pa., December 24 and mustered out January 7, 1864.

20th REGIMENT CAVALRY (3 YEARS).

Organized at Harrisburg and Philadelphia February, 1864. Reported to Sigel at Martinsburg, W. Va., March, 1864. Attached to 2nd Brigade, 1st Cavalry Division, Dept. West Virginia, to August, 1864. 1st Brigade, 1st Cavalry Division, West Virginia, to November, 1864. 2nd Brigade, 1st Division, Cavalry Corps, Army of the Shenandoah, to February, 1865, and Army Potomac to June, 1865.

SERVICE.—Sigel's Expedition to New Market, Va., April 30-May 16, 1864. Rude's Hill and New Market May 14. Battle of New Market May 15. Hunter's Expedition to Lynchburg May 26-July 1. Harrisonburg June 4. Piedmont, Mt. Crawford, June 5. Occupation of Staunton June 6. Staunton June 10. Midway June 11. Cedar Creek June 12. Piney River near Amherst C. H. June 12. Near Glasgow June 14. Lynchburg June 17-18. Retreat to Kanawha Valley, thence to Parkersburg and Martinsburg June 19-July 15. Catawba Mountains and about Salem June 21. Martinsburg July 17. Snicker's Ferry July 17-18. Ashby's Gap and Berry's Ford July 19. Ashby's Gap July 21. Near Kernstown July 23. Kernstown, Winchester, July 24. Bunker Hill and Martinsburg July 25. Ordered to Harper's Ferry July 30. Duty at Halltown, Pleasant Valley and Cumberland, Md., till December. Expedition from Winchester to Gordonsville December 19-28. Madison C. H. December 21. Liberty Mills December 22. Near Gordonsville December 23. Sheridan's Expedition from Winchester February 27-March 25. Swoope's Depot and Staunton March 2. Waynesboro March 2. Goochland C. H. March 11. Appomattox Campaign March 28-April 9. Dinwiddie C. H. March 30-31. Five Forks April 1. Scott's Cross Roads April 2. Tabernacle Church or Beaver Pond Creek April 4. Sailor's Creek April 6. Appomattox Station April 8. Appomattox C. H. April 9. Surrender of Lee and his army. Expedition to Danville April 23-29. March to Washington, D. C., May. Grand Review May 23. Consolidated with 2nd Pennsylvania Cavalry June 17, 1865, to form 1st Provisional Cavalry.

Regiment lost during service 3 Officers and 22 Enlisted men killed and mortally wounded and 3 Officers and 100 Enlisted men by disease. Total 128.

21st REGIMENT CAVALRY (182nd VOLUNTEERS) SIX MONTHS.

Organized at Harrisburg and Chambersburg June 28-August 1, 1863, for six months. Companies "C," "E," "H," "K," "L," "M," duty at Pottsville, Pa., and Scranton, Pa., and Company "B" at Gettysburg, Pa. Companies "A," "D," "F," "G" and "I" ordered to Harper's Ferry, W. Va., August 23, 1863. Attached to Cavalry Brigade, 1st Division, Dept. West Virginia, to February, 1864. Duty about Harper's Ferry, W. Va. Expedition from Charlestown to New Market November 15-18 (Detachment). Mount Jackson November 16. Wells' demonstration from Harper's Ferry December 10-21. Skirmish at Winchester January 3, 1864. Mustered out February 20, 1864.

21st REGIMENT CAVALRY (3 YEARS).

Organized at Harrisburg February, 1864. (Co. "D" detached April 1, 1864, and duty at Scranton, Pa., entire term.) Regiment moved to Washington, D. C., May 15, 1864, thence to join Army Potomac in the field, arriving at Cold Harbor, Va., June 1. Attached to 2nd Brigade, 1st Division, 5th Army Corps, Army Potomac, to September, 1864. 1st Brigade, 1st Division, 5th Corps, to October, 1864. 3rd Brigade, 2nd Division, Cavalry Corps, Army Potomac, to March, 1865. 2nd Brigade, 2nd Division, Cavalry Corps, to July, 1865.

SERVICE.—Battles about Cold Harbor, Va., June 1-12, 1864. Before Petersburg June 16-18. Siege operations against Petersburg and Richmond June 16, 1864, to April 2, 1865. Weldon Railroad August 18-21. Poplar Springs Church September 29-October 2. Sent to City Point October 5 and mounted. Boydton Plank Road, Hatcher's Run, October 27-28. Warren's Expedition to Hicksford December 7-12. Bellefield December 9-10. Dabney's Mills, Hatcher's Run, February 5-7, 1865. Appomattox Campaign March 28-April 9. Dinwiddie C. H. March 30-31. Five Forks April 1. Paine's Cross Road April 5. Sailor's Creek April 6. Appomattox C. H. April 9. Surrender of Lee and his army. Expedition to Danville April 23-29. Moved to Lynchburg, Va., and duty there and in Dept. of Virginia till July. Mustered out July 8, 1865.

Regiment lost during service 4 Officers and 80 Enlisted men killed and mortally wounded and 2 Officers and 116 Enlisted men by disease. Total 202.

22nd REGIMENT CAVALRY (185th VOLUNTEERS) SIX MONTHS.

Organized at Harrisburg for six months June and July, 1863. Engaged in guarding fords of the Susquehanna above and below Harrisburg, and picketing roads into Cumberland Valley during Gettysburg Campaign and battle. Pursuit of Lee July 6-24, 1863. Moved to Harper's Ferry, W. Va., August. Attached to Cavalry Brigade, 1st Division, Dept. West Virginia, and duty at Harper's Ferry and in the Shenandoah Valley till February, 1864. Action at Burlington, W. Va., October 13, 1863. Mt. Jackson and Upperville November 16. Mustered out February 5, 1864.

22nd REGIMENT CAVALRY (3 YEARS).

Organized at Chambersburg February, 1864, by consolidation of a Battalion of six months Cavalry and the Ringgold Battalion of five Companies, Washington County Cavalry Company and LaFayette Cavalry Company, assigned February 22, 1864. Moved to Martinsburg, W. Va., March 1, 1864, thence to Cumberland, Md. Attached to Reserve Division, Dept. of West Virginia, to April, 1864. 2nd Brigade, 1st Cavalry Division, West Virginia, to August, 1864. (Dismounted men attached to Reserve Division, Pleasant Valley, Md., Dept. West Virginia, to June, 1864. Kelly's Command, West Virginia, to August, 1864.) 3rd Brigade, Cavalry Corps, Army Shenandoah, August, 1864 (dismounted men). 1st Brigade, 2nd Cavalry Division, West Virginia, to December, 1864. Reserve Division, Dept. West Virginia, to April, 1865. 2nd Brigade, 1st Infantry Division, West Virginia, to June, 1865.

SERVICE.—Sigel's Expedition from Martinsburg to New Market April 30-May 16, 1864. Lost River Gap May 10. Lynchburg May 12. New Market May 15. Hunter's Expedition to Lynchburg May 26-July 1. Piedmont, Mt. Crawford, June 5. Occupation of Staunton June 6. Lynchburg May 17-18. Newtown June 19. Salem June 20. Catawba Mountains June 21. (Dismounted men moved to Pleasant Valley April, 1864, and duty there till May 15. At Camp Stoneman till June. Moved to Martinsburg June 16. Leetown and Darkesville July 3. Operations about Harper's Ferry July 4-7. Hagerstown, Md., July 6. Maryland Heights July 6-7. Antietam Bridge July 7. Ordered to Pleasant Valley July 22. Joined Torbert August 8.) Moved to Shenandoah Valley July 5-15. Snicker's Ferry July 17-18. Ashby's Gap and Berry's Ford July 19. Near Kernstown July 23. Kernstown, Winchester, July 24. Bunker Hill and Martinsburg July 25. Near Moorefield August 7. Regiment reunite at Hagerstown August. Sheridan's Shenandoah Valley Campaign August to November. Near Opequan Creek August 19. Opequan Creek August 20. Near Berryville August 21. Summit Point August 21. Charlestown August 21-22. Williamsport August 26. Martinsburg August 31. Darkesville September 2. Bunker Hill September 2-3. Darkesville September 10. Bunker Hill September 13. Near Berryville September 14. Near

Martinsburg September 18. Battle of Opequan, Winchester, September 19. Fisher's Hill September 22. Mt. Jackson September 23-24. Forest Hill or Timberville September 24. Brown's Gap September 26. Weyer's Cave September 26-27. Port Republic September 28. Battle of Cedar Creek October 19. Dry Run October 23. Moved to Martinsburg, and duty there till December 20. At New Creek and duty in Hardy, Hampshire and Pendleton Counties till June, 1865. Scout to Greenland Gap and Franklin January 11-15, 1865. Scout to Moorefield March 14-17, 1865. Consolidated with 18th Pennsylvania Cavalry June 24, 1865, to form 3rd Provisional Cavalry.

Regiment lost during service 33 Enlisted men killed and mortally wounded and 1 Officer and 96 Enlisted men by disease. Total 130.

INDEPENDENT BATTALION CAVALRY.

Organized at Pittsburg, Pa., June and July, 1863. Mustered out December 29, 1863.

RINGGOLD BATTALION CAVALRY.

Organized in the field September, 1862, by consolidation of Keys' Washington (Pa.) Cavalry Company, organized at Washington, Pa., June 29, 1861; Work's Washington County Company, organized September 6, 1862; Young's Cavalry, organized September 6, 1862; Barr's Cavalry Company, organized October 13, 1862, and Chessrown's Cavalry Company, organized October 14, 1862. Attached to Railroad District, 8th Corps, Middle Dept., to January, 1863. Romney, W. Va., Defences Upper Potomac, 8th Corps, Middle Dept., to March, 1863. 4th Brigade, 1st Division, 8th Corps, to June, 1863. Campbell's Brigade, Scammon's Division, Dept. West Virginia, to December, 1863. 2nd Brigade, 2nd Division, West Virginia, to February, 1864.

SERVICE.—Guard and scout duty in the Railroad District and on Upper Potomac, West Virginia, till February, 1864. Actions: Ridgeville Road, near Petersburg, W. Va., October 29, 1862; Moorefield, South Fork Potomac, November 9; Moorefield December 3; near Romney February 16, 1863; near Burlington April 6-7; Purgetsville and Going's Ford April 6-7; Burlington April 26; Moorefield September 4 and 11. Descent upon Salem, Va., December 16. Jackson River, near Covington, December 19. Operations in Hampshire and Hardy Counties, W. Va., December 31, 1863-January 5, 1864, and January 27-February 5. Medley, Williamsport, January 29-30. Evacuation of Petersburg January 30. Moorefield February 4. Expedition to Petersburg February 29-March 5. Petersburg March 3. Transferred to 22nd Pennsylvania Cavalry February 22, 1864, which see.

Lost during service 3 Enlisted men killed and mortally wounded and 1 Officer and 18 Enlisted men by disease. Total 22.

ANDERSON TROOP CAVALRY.

Organized at Carlisle, Pa., November 30, 1861, for Headquarters and escort duty with Gen. Anderson in Kentucky. Retained at Headquarters of Gens. Sherman, Buell and Rosecrans, Commanding Army and Dept. of the Ohio and Cumberland, till March, 1863.

SERVICE.—Moved to Louisville, Ky., December 2-7, 1861. Duty there till February, 1862. Moved with Headquarters Army Ohio to Nashville, Tenn., February 24. March to Savannah, Tenn., to reinforce Army Tennessee March-April. Battle of Shiloh April 7. Advance on and siege of Corinth, Miss., April 29-May 30. Pursuit to Booneville May 31-June 12. Buell's Campaign in North Alabama and Middle Tennessee June to August. March to Louisville, Ky., in pursuit of Bragg August 21-September 26. Pursuit of Bragg into Kentucky October 1-22. Springfield October 6. Battle of Perryville October 8. March to Nashville, Tenn., October 22-November 7, and duty there till December 26. Advance on Murfreesboro December 26-30. Lavergne December 26-27. Wilkinson's Cross Roads December 29. Battle of Stone's River December 30-31, 1862, and January 1-3, 1863. Overall's Creek December 31, 1862. Lavergne January 1, 1863. Lytle's Creek January 5. At Murfreesboro till March, 1863. Mustered out March 24, 1863.

Lost during service 1 killed and 5 by disease. Total 6.

BELL'S INDEPENDENT COMPANY MILITIA CAVALRY.

Organized at Altoona June 30, 1863. Mustered out August 9, 1863.

BROWN'S INDEPENDENT COMPANY MILITIA CAVALRY.

Organized at Harrisburg June 19, 1863. Mustered out August 1, 1863.

COMLEY'S INDEPENDENT COMPANY MILITIA CAVALRY.

Organized at Harrisburg July 19, 1863. Mustered out July 30, 1863.

DICK'S INDEPENDENT COMPANY MILITIA CAVALRY.

Organized at Pittsburg July 9, 1863. Mustered out October 5, 1863.

HAMMILL'S INDEPENDENT COMPANY MILITIA CAVALRY.

Organized at Philadelphia July 2, 1863. Mustered out September 16, 1863.

HEBBLE'S INDEPENDENT COMPANY CAVALRY.

Organized at Lancaster July 19, 1864. Mustered out October 29, 1864.

JONES' INDEPENDENT COMPANY MILITIA CAVALRY.

Organized at Harrisburg June 21, 1863. Mustered out August 12, 1863.

LAFAYETTE COMPANY CAVALRY.

Organized at Wheeling, W. Va., November 6, 1862. Attached to Railroad District, 8th Corps, Middle Dept., to March, 1863. 4th Brigade, 1st Division, 8th Corps, to June, 1863. Campbell's Brigade, Scammon's Division, West Virginia, to December, 1863. 2nd Brigade, 2nd Division, West Virginia, to February, 1864.

SERVICE.—Scout and guard duty in Railroad District, Middle Dept., and on Upper Potomac till February, 1864. Action near Moorefield, W. Va., April 6, 1863. Williamsport, Md., August 4. Burlington October 13. Descent upon Salem December 16. Jackson River, near Covington, December 19. Operations in Hampshire and Hardy Counties December 31, 1863-January 5, 1864. Medley January 29-30. Evacuation of Petersburg January 30. Burlington February 1. Consolidated with Ringgold Battalion February 9, 1864.

LAMBERT'S INDEPENDENT CAVALRY COMPANY.

Organized at Harrisburg August 12, 1864. Mustered out November 25, 1864.

MOREHEAD CAVALRY COMPANY.

Organized at Allegheny City August 19, 1861. Attached to 1st Virginia Union Cavalry and transferred to 1st Maryland Cavalry as Company "L" January, 1862.

MURRAY'S INDEPENDENT COMPANY MILITIA CAVALRY.

Organized at Harrisburg June 18, 1863. Mustered out August 11, 1863.

MYERS' INDEPENDENT COMPANY MILITIA CAVALRY.

Organized at Harrisburg June 20, 1863. Mustered out July 31, 1863.

NEGLEY'S BODY GUARD.

Organized at Philadelphia January 21, 1862. Mustered out January 26, 1862.

PHILADELPHIA CITY TROOP.

Tendered services to the Government April 15, 1861. Not at first accepted, but finally mustered in May 13,

51

1861. Moved to Carlisle, Pa., May 29-30. Attached to Geo. H. Thomas' Command. Moved to Chambersburg May 31, and to Greencastle June 7. To Williamsport June 12. Advance to Falling Waters June 17. Action at Falling Waters July 2. Bunker Hill July 2. Occupation of Martinsburg July 3. Advance to Bunker Hill July 6. Bunker Hill July 15. Occupation of Charlestown July 17. Moved to Harper's Ferry July 21. To Sandy Hook August 3. Guard Kelly's and Antietam Fords and Charlestown Road. Mustered out August 17, 1861.

Again tendered services May, 1862, and August, 1862. Not accepted.

Tendered services June 16, 1863. Accepted June 18. Moved to Gettysburg, Pa., to observe enemy. Driven from South Mountain and Gettysburg June 26, and from York to Wrightsville June 27. Retreat to Columbia and duty there till July 4. Moved to Harrisburg. Relieved from duty July 31, 1863.

READING CITY TROOP.

Organized at Reading July 30, 1861. Transferred to 1st Pennsylvania Cavalry as Company "L" November, 1861.

RINGGOLD CAVALRY COMPANY.

Organized at Washington, Pa., June 29, 1861. Ordered to West Virginia and attached to Army of Occupation, West Virginia, July to October, 1861. Cheat Mountain District to January, 1862. Lander's Division to March, 1862. Hatch's Cavalry Command, Banks' 5th Corps, to April, 1862. Railroad District, Mountain Dept., to July, 1862. Railroad District, 8th Corps, Middle Dept., to September, 1862.

SERVICE.—Campagin in West Virginia July 6-17. Rich Mountain July 11. Carrick's Ford July 13-14. Burlington September 2. Operations on Cheat Mountain September 11-17. Petersburg September 12. Romney, Hanging Rock, September 23. Romney September 23-25. Mill Creek Mills, Romney, October 26. Near Romney November 13. At Romney till January, 1862. Expedition to Blue's Gap January 6-7. Hanging Rock Pass January 7. Bloomery Furnace February 14. Advance on Winchester March 7-15. Strasburg March 18. Kernstown March 22. Battle of Winchester March 23. Columbia Furnace April 15. Two Churches and Rood's Hill April 17. Duty in Railroad District, West Virginia, till September. North River Mills August 15. Huttonsville August 18. Transferred to Ringgold Battalion September, 1862, which see.

SANNO'S INDEPENDENT COMPANY CAVALRY.

Organized at Harrisburg July 15, 1864. Mustered out October 29, 1864.

STROUD'S INDEPENDENT COMPANY CAVALRY.

Railroad troops. Organized at Philadelphia July 15, 1864. Mustered out October 31, 1864.

UNION CAVALRY COMPANY.

Organized at Allegheny City April 5, 1861. Entered 1st Virginia Union Cavalry and transferred to 1st Maryland Cavalry as Company "G" January, 1862.

WARREN'S INDEPENDENT COMPANY CAVALRY.

Organized at Harrisburg August 17, 1864. Mustered out November 30, 1864.

WASHINGTON COUNTY CAVALRY COMPANY.

Organized at Wheeling, W. Va., August 19, 1861. Attached to Army of Occupation, West Virginia, to November, 1861. Railroad District, Mountain Dept., West Virginia, to January, 1862. Lander's Division, West Virginia, to March, 1862. Hatch's Cavalry Command, Banks' 5th Corps, to April, 1862. Railroad District, Mountain Dept., to July, 1862. Railroad District, 8th Corps, Middle Dept., to January, 1863. Romney, Defences Upper Potomac, 8th Corps, to March, 1863. 4th Brigade, 1st Division, 8th Corps, to June, 1863. Campbell's Brigade, Scammon's Division, Dept. West Virginia, to December, 1863. 2nd Brigade, 2nd Division, Dept. West Virginia, to February, 1864.

SERVICE.—Greenbrier River October 3-4, 1861. Expedition to Blue's Gap January 6-7, 1862. Hanging Rock Pass, Blue's Gap, January 7. Advance on Winchester March 7-15. Strasburg March 18. Battle of Winchester March 23. Columbia Furnace April 16. Two Churches and Rood's Hill April 17. Guard and scout duty in Railroad District of West Virginia and Defences of the Upper Potomac till February, 1864. Actions at North River Mills August 15, 1862. Wire Bridge August 16. Moorefield August 23. Glenville September 30. South Branch Potomac, Moorefield, November 9. Romney December 1. Green Springs Run March 7, 1863. Williamsport, Md., July 8. Fairview July 9. Hedgesville and Martinsburg July 18-19. Whitehall July 22. Burlington August 4. Descent upon Salem December 16. Jackson River, near Covington, December 19. Petersburg January 10, 1864. Operations in Hampshire and Hardy Counties January 27-February 7. Moorefield February 4. Consolidated with Ringgold Battalion February 9, 1864, which see.

WEAVER'S INDEPENDENT COMPANY CAVALRY.

Organized at Chambersburg September, 1864. Mustered out August 4, 1865.

2nd REGIMENT HEAVY ARTILLERY (112th VOLUNTEERS).

Organized at Philadelphia January 8, 1862. (Cos. "D," "G" and "H" ordered to Fort Delaware January 9, and duty there till March 19, 1862, when rejoined Regiment in Defences of Washington.) Companies "A," "B," "C," "E," "F," "I" and "K" moved to Washington, D. C., February 25, 1862. Attached to Artillery Brigade, Military District of Washington, to August, 1862. Defences of Washington north of the Potomac to October, 1862. 1st Brigade, Haskins' Division, Defences north of the Potomac, to February, 1863. 1st Brigade, Haskins' Division, 22nd Army Corps, Dept. Washington, to March, 1864. 1st Brigade, DeRussy's Division, 22nd Corps, to May, 1864. 3rd Brigade, 2nd Division, 18th Army Corps, Dept. of Virginia and North Carolina, to December, 1864. Provisional Brigade, Defences of Bermuda Hundred, Va., Dept. of Virginia and North Carolina, to April, 1865. 1st Brigade, Ferrero's Division, Dept. of Virginia, to May, 1865. Sub-District of the Blackwater, Dept. of Virginia, to January, 1866.

SERVICE.—Garrison duty in the Defences of Washing north of the Potomac till May 27, 1864. (2 Independent Cos. Heavy Artillery assigned as Cos. "L" and "M" November 24, 1862.) Moved to Port Royal, Va., May 27-28, 1864, thence marched to Cold Harbor May 28-June 4. Battles about Cold Harbor June 4-12. Before Petersburg June 15-19. Siege operations against Petersburg and Richmond June 16, 1864, to April 2, 1865. In trenches before Petersburg till August 23, 1864. Mine Explosion, Petersburg, July 30. Duty on the Bermuda Hundred front till September. Weldon Railroad August 18-21. Chaffin's Farm, New Market Heights, September 28-30. Fair Oaks October 27-28 (Co. "G"). Ordered to Bermuda front December 2, and duty there till April, 1865. Fall of Petersburg April 2. Duty at Petersburg till May, and in counties of lower Virginia, Sub-District of the Blackwater, District of the Nottaway, till January, 1866. Mustered out at City Point, Va., January 29, 1866, and discharged at Philadelphia, Pa., February 16, 1866.

Regiment lost during service 5 Officers and 221 Enlisted men killed and mortally wounded and 5 Officers and 385 Enlisted men by disease. Total 616.

2nd REGIMENT PROVISIONAL HEAVY ARTILLERY.

Organized April 20, 1864, from surplus men of the 2nd Regiment Heavy Artillery. Attached to Provisional Brigade, 1st Division, 9th Army Corps, Army Potomac, to June, 1864. 3rd Brigade, 1st Division, 9th Corps, June, 1864. 2nd Brigade, 1st Division, 9th Corps, to August, 1864.

SERVICE.—Campaign from the Rapidan to the James May 4-June 12. Battles of the Wilderness, Va., May 5-7; Spottsylvania May 8-21; North Anna River May 23-26.

Line of the Pamunkey May 26-28. Totopotomoy May 28-31. Cold Harbor June 1-12. Before Petersburg June 15-18. Siege of Petersburg till August 20. Mine Explosion, Petersburg, July 30. Regiment disbanded August 20, 1864, and rejoined original Regiment September 5, 1864.

3rd REGIMENT HEAVY ARTILLERY (152nd VOLUNTEERS).

Organized at Philadelphia by consolidation of Robert's Battalion Pennsylvania Heavy Artillery, assigned as Companies "C," "D" and "F"; Segebarth's Battalion Marine Artillery, assigned as Companies "A," "B," "G," "H," "K" and "L," and 1st Battalion Pennsylvania Heavy Artillery, assigned as Company "E." Two more Companies organized at Philadelphia as Companies "I" and "M." Regiment organized February 17, 1863, and ordered to Fortress Monroe, Va. Attached to Camp Hamilton, 7th Corps, Dept. of Virginia, to May, 1863. Fortress Monroe, Va., 7th Corps, to July, 1863. Fortress Monroe, Va., Dept. of Virginia and North Carolina, to May, 1864. District of Eastern Virginia to June, 1865. Fortress Monroe, Va., Dept. of Virginia, to November, 1865.

SERVICE.—Duty in the Dept. of Virginia entire term, with Headquarters at Fortress Monroe, Va. Detachments of all Companies but "H" served at times in Graham's Naval Brigade and participated in several engagements on the James, Chickahominy and Nansemond Rivers. Defence of Suffolk, Va., April 12-May 4, 1863 (Cos. "A," "B," "F" and "G"). A Detachment of Company "A" in action at Smithfield, N. C., February 1, 1864, and at siege of Plymouth, N. C., April 17-20, 1864, on Gunboat "Bombshell." Companies "D," "E" and "G" in Butler's operations on south side of James River against Petersburg and Richmond May, 1864, then at various redoubts and forts on the Bermuda Hundred front till May, 1865. Company "F" was in charge of Prison Camp at Camp Hamilton, near Fortress Monroe, September, 1863, to end of war. Company "I" served at Headquarters Army of the James in Appomattox Campaign and was present at Appomattox C. H. April 9, 1865; surrender of Lee and his army. Company "M" served as Siege Artillery, Army James, in siege operations against Petersburg and Richmond May, 1864, to May, 1865. Posted principally on the Bermuda Hundred front. Detachments of Companies "F" and "G" were in attack on and capture of Fort Fisher, N. C., January 15, 1865.

Company "H" served detached at Baltimore, Md., entire term; was at Gettysburg, Pa., July 2-3, 1863. Companies "A" and "B" mustered out July 11, 1865; Company "H" July 25, 1865, and Regiment November 9, 1865.

Regiment lost during service 19 Enlisted men killed and mortally wounded and 1 Officer and 214 Enlisted men by disease. Total 234.

5th REGIMENT HEAVY ARTILLERY (204th VOLUNTEERS).

Organized at Pittsburg August and September, 1864. Ordered to Washington, D. C., September, 1864. Attached to District of Alexandria, 22nd Corps, to November, 1864. 1st Separate Brigade, 22nd Corps, to June, 1865.

SERVICE.—Duty in Northern Defences of Washington, D. C., and along Manassas Gap Railroad, protecting supplies for Sheridan, and constantly engaged with Mosby. Action at Salem October 4, 1864. Rectortown October 7. White Plains October 11. Destruction of Manassas Gap Railroad October and November. Duty in the Northern Defences of Washington; 1st Battalion at Prospect Hill, 2nd Battalion at Vienna and 3rd Battalion at Fairfax C. H. Duty on Bull Run battlefield in spring of 1865, burying nearly 2,000 dead. Ordered to Pittsburg for muster out. Mustered out June 30, 1865.

Regiment lost during service 3 Enlisted men killed and 46 by disease. Total 49.

6th REGIMENT HEAVY ARTILLERY (212th VOLUNTEERS).

Organized at Pittsburg, Pa., September 15, 1864. Moved to Washington, D. C., September 17. Attached to 2nd Brigade, DeRussy's Division, 22nd Corps, to December, 1864. 1st Brigade, DeRussy's Division, 22nd Corps, to June, 1865.

SERVICE.—Guard Orange & Alexandria Railroad between Alexandria and Manassas, Va., September 29-November 17, 1864. Garrison Forts Marcy, Ward, Craig, Aeno, Albany and Lyon, Defences of Washington, south of the Potomac, till June, 1865. Mustered out June 13, 1865.

Lost during service 2 Enlisted men killed and 44 by disease. Total 46.

ROBERTS' BATTALION HEAVY ARTILLERY.

Organized at Harrisburg and Philadelphia October 8 to November 14, 1862. Transferred to 3rd Pennsylvania Heavy Artillery February 17, 1863, as Companies "C," "D," "F" (which see).

SEGEBARTH'S BATTALION MARINE ARTILLERY.

Organized at Philadelphia January 5, 1862, to January 31, 1863. Companies "A" and "B" duty at Fort Delaware till December, 1862. Transferred to 3rd Pennsylvania Heavy Artillery February 17, 1863, as Companies "A," "B," "G," "H," "K" and "L" (which see).

COMMONWEALTH INDEPENDENT COMPANY HEAVY ARTILLERY.

Organized at Philadelphia April 24, 1861. Duty at Fort Delaware. Mustered out August 5, 1861.

ERMENTROUT'S COMPANY MILITIA HEAVY ARTILLERY.

Organized at Reading July 3, 1863. Mustered out August 26, 1863.

GUSS' BATTERY MILITIA LIGHT ARTILLERY.

Organized at West Chester July 1, 1863. Mustered out August 24, 1863.

JONES' INDEPENDENT COMPANY HEAVY ARTILLERY.

SCHOOLEY'S INDEPENDENT COMPANY HEAVY ARTILLERY.

TYLER'S INDEPENDENT BATTERY HEAVY ARTILLERY.

Organized at Pittsburg June 16, 1863. On duty at Harper's Ferry and other points in the Department of West Virginia. Mustered out January 28, 1864.

WOODWARD'S INDEPENDENT COMPANY HEAVY ARTILLERY.

Organized at Philadelphia July 9, 1863. Mustered out February 1, 1864.

PENNSYLVANIA VOLUNTEERS.

BATTERY "A," 1st REGIMENT LIGHT ARTILLERY (43rd VOLUNTEERS).

Organized at Philadelphia August 5, 1861. Ordered to Washington, D. C., August, 1861. Attached to McCall's Pennsylvania Reserve Division, Army Potomac, to March, 1862. Artillery, 2nd Division, 1st Army Corps, Army Potomac, to April, 1862. Artillery, McCall's Division, Dept. of the Rappahannock, to June, 1862. Artillery, 3rd Division, 5th Army Corps, Army Potomac, to August, 1862. Artillery, 3rd Division, 3rd Corps, Army of Virginia, to September, 1862. Artillery, 3rd Division, 1st Army Corps, Army Potomac, to February, 1863. Artillery, 3rd Division, 9th Army Corps, Army Potomac, to April, 1863. Artillery, 2nd Division, 7th Corps, Dept. of Virginia, to July, 1863. U. S. Forces, Norfolk and Portsmouth, Va., Dept. Virginia and North Carolina, to January, 1864. Artillery, Heckman's Division, 18th Army Corps, Dept. Virginia and North Carolina, to April, 1864. Defences of Portsmouth, Va., Dept. Virginia and North Carolina, to May, 1864. District

Eastern Virginia, Dept. Virginia and North Carolina, to July, 1864. Artillery Brigade, 10th Army Corps, to October, 1864. Artillery Brigade, 18th Army Corps, to December, 1864. Artillery Brigade, 24th Army Corps, Dept. of Virginia, to July, 1865.

SERVICE.—Camp at Tennallytown, Md., till October, 1861, and at Camp Pierpont near Langley, Va., till March, 1862. Expedition to Grinnell's Farm December 6, 1861. Action at Dranesville, Va., December 20. Advance on Manassas, Va., March 10-15. McDowell's advance on Falmouth April 9-19. Duty at Falmouth and Fredericksburg till June. Ordered to the Virginia Peninsula. Seven days before Richmond, Va., June 25-July 1. Beaver Dam Creek or Mechanicsville June 26. Gaines' Mill June 27. Charles City Cross Roads and Glendale June 30. Malvern Hill July 1. At Harrison's Landing till August 15. Movement to join Pope August 15-26. Battles of Gainesville August 28. Groveton August 29. Bull Run August 30. Maryland Campaign September. South Mountain September 14. Battle of Antietam, Md., September 16-17. Movement to Falmouth, Va., October-November. Battle of Fredericksburg, Va., December 12-15. "Mud March" January 20-24, 1863. Ordered to Newport News February 9, thence to Suffolk, March. Siege of Suffolk April 12-May 4. Dix's Peninsula Campaign June 26-July 8. Expedition from White House to South Anna River July 1-7. Duty at Portsmouth, Va., till July, 1864. Siege operations against Petersburg and Richmond July, 1864, to April, 1865. Chaffin's Farm, New Market Heights, September 28-30, 1864. Fair Oaks October 27-28. Before Richmond till April, 1865. Occupation of Richmond April 3. Engaged in demolishing defences and removing Ordnance till July. Mustered out July 25, 1865.

Battery lost during service 1 Officer and 16 Enlisted men killed and mortally wounded and 21 Enlisted men by disease. Total 38.

BATTERY "B," 1st REGIMENT LIGHT ARTILLERY (43rd VOLUNTEERS).

Organized at Philadelphia August 5, 1861. Moved to Washington, D. C., August, 1861. Attached to McCall's Division, Army Potomac, to March, 1862. Artillery, 2nd Division, 1st Army Corps, Army of the Potomac, to April, 1862. Artillery, McCall's Division, Dept. of the Rappahannock, to June, 1862. Artillery, 3rd Division, 5th Army Corps, Army Potomac, to August, 1862. Artillery, 3rd Division, 3rd Corps, Army of Virginia, to September, 1862. Artillery, 3rd Division, 1st Army Corps, Army Potomac, to May, 1863. Artillery Brigade, 1st Army Corps, to March, 1864. Artillery Brigade, 5th Army Corps, to March, 1865. Artillery Reserve, Army Potomac, to June, 1865.

SERVICE.—At Camp Berry, Washington, D. C., till August 14, 1861, and at Tennallytown, Md., till September. At Great Falls, Md., September to December, temporarily transferred to Banks' Division, December 25. Duty at Seneca Falls and Edward's Ferry till January 9, 1862, when rejoined McCall's Division, and at Camp Pierpont near Langley till March, 1862. Advance on Manassas March 10-15. McDowell's advance on Falmouth April 9-19. Duty at Falmouth and Fredericksburg till June. Moved to the Peninsula June 13, and joined Division at Mechanicsville June 30. Seven days before Richmond June 25-July 1. Beaver Dam Creek or Mechanicsville June 26. Gaines' Mill June 27. Charles City Cross Roads and Glendale June 30. Malvern Hill July 1. At Harrison's Landing till August 15. Movement to join Pope August 15-26. Battles of Gainesville August 28. Groveton August 29. Bull Run August 30. Chantilly September 1 (Reserve). Maryland Campaign September. Battles of South Mountain September 14 and Antietam September 16-17. Movement to Falmouth, Va., October-November. Battle of Fredericksburg December 12-15. "Mud March" January 20-24, 1863. At Belle Plains till April. Chancellorsville Campaign April 27-May 6. Operations at Pollock's Mill Creek April 29-May 2. Fitzhugh's Crossing April 29-30. Chancellorsville May 2-5. Gettysburg (Pa.) Cam-

paign June 11-July 24. Battle of Gettysburg, Pa., July 1-3. Duty on the Rappahannock till September 10. Bristoe Campaign October 9-22. Advance to line of the Rappahannock November 7-8. Mine Run Campaign November 26-December 2. Near Kelly's Ford till April, 1864. Rapidan Campaign May 4-June 12. Battles of the Wilderness May 5-7; Laurel Hill May 8; Spottsylvania C. H. May 8-21; North Anna River May 23-26. Line of the Pamunkey May 26-28. Cold Harbor June 1-12. Before Petersburg June 16-18. Siege of Petersburg June 16, 1864, to April 2, 1865. Weldon Railroad August 18-21, 1864. In trenches before Petersburg till April, 1865. Fort Stedman March 25, 1865. Fall of Petersburg April 2. Ordered to City Point April 3. Moved to Washington, D. C., May. Grand Review May 23. Mustered out June 9, 1865.

Battery lost during service 2 Officers and 19 Enlisted men killed and mortally wounded and 17 Enlisted men by disease. Total 38.

BATTERY "C," 1st REGIMENT LIGHT ARTILLERY (43rd VOLUNTEERS).

Organized at Philadelphia August 5, 1861, and moved to Washington, D. C. Attached to W. F. Smith's Division, Army Potomac, October, 1861, to March, 1862. Artillery, 1st Division, 4th Army Corps, Army Potomac, to September, 1862. Artillery, 3rd Division, 6th Army Corps, Army Potomac, to May, 1863. Artillery Brigade, 6th Corps, to June, 1863. Camp Barry, Defences of Washington, D. C., 22nd Corps, to July, 1863. 1st Brigade, Lockwood's Division, Dept. Susquehanna, to August, 1863. Maryland Heights Division, Dept. West Virginia, to October, 1863.

SERVICE.—Duty at Camp Barry and in the Defences of Washington till March, 1862. Ordered to the Virginia Peninsula March. Siege of Yorktown April 5-May 4. Battle of Williamsburg May 5. Battle of Fair Oaks or Seven Pines May 31-June 1. Seven days before Richmond June 25-July 1. James River Road near Fair Oaks June 29. Savage Station June 29. Charles City Cross Roads and Glendale June 30. Malvern Hill July 1. At Harrison's Landing till August 16. Movement to Fortress Monroe, thence to Alexandria August 16-24. Maryland Campaign September. Battle of Antietam, Md., September 16-17. Duty in Maryland till October 29. Movement to Falmouth, Va., October 29-November 19. Battle of Fredericksburg December 12-15. "Mud March" January 20-24, 1863. Chancellorsville Campaign April 27-May 6. Operations at Franklin's Crossing April 29-May 2. Maryes Heights, Fredericksburg, May 3. Salem Heights May 3-4. Banks' Ford May 4. Ordered to Washington, D. C., June, and duty there till July. Moved to Maryland Heights July 9. Duty at Harper's Ferry. W. Va., till October. Consolidated with Battery "D," 1st Pennsylvania Artillery, October 23, 1863 (which see).

SECOND BATTERY "C," 1st REGIMENT LIGHT ARTILLERY.

Organized December, 1864. Attached to 3rd Infantry Division, West Virginia, to April, 1865. 2nd Infantry Division, West Virginia, to June, 1865. Duty at Harper's Ferry, Martinsburg and in the Shenandoah Valley till June, 1865. Mustered out June 30, 1865.

Battery "C" lost during service 2 Enlisted men killed and 12 by disease.

BATTERY "D," 1st REGIMENT LIGHT ARTILLERY (43rd VOLUNTEERS).

Organized at Philadelphia August 5, 1861. Moved to Washington, D. C., August, 1861. Attached to Buell's Division, Army Potomac, October, 1861, to March, 1862. Artillery, 1st Division, 4th Army Corps, Army Potomac, to September, 1862. Artillery, 3rd Division, 6th Army Corps, Army Potomac, to May, 1863. Artillery Brigade, 6th Army Corps, to June, 1863. Camp Barry, Defences of Washington, D. C., to August, 1863. Unattached, Artillery, Dept. West Virginia, to December, 1863. 1st Brigade, 1st Division, West Virginia, to January, 1864. Wheaton's Brigade, Dept. West Virginia, to April, 1864.

Artillery Brigade, Dept. West Virginia, to January, 1865. 1st Separate Brigade, Dept. West Virginia, to May, 1865. 2nd Infantry Division, West Virginia, to June, 1865.

SERVICE.—Duty in the Defences of Washington, D. C., till March, 1862. Ordered to the Virginia Peninsula March. Siege of Yorktown April 5-May 4. Battle of Williamsburg May 5. Battle of Fair Oaks, Seven Pines, May 31-June 1. Seven days before Richmond June 25-July 1. James River Road near Fair Oaks June 29. Charles City Cross Roads June 29. Malvern Hill July 1. At Harrison's Landing till August 16. Movement to join Pope August 16-26. Sulphur Springs August 26. Maryland Campaign September. Battle of Antietam, Md., September 16-17 (Reserve). Duty in Maryland till October 29. Movement to Falmouth, Va., October 29-November 19. Battle of Fredericksburg December 12-15. "Mud March" January 20-24, 1863. At Falmouth till April. Chancellorsville Campaign April 27-May 6. Operations at Franklin's Crossing April 29-May 2. Maryes Heights, Fredericksburg, May 3. Salem Heights May 3-4. Banks' Ford May 4. Ordered to Washington, D. C., June, and duty at Camp Barry till August. Ordered to Harper's Ferry, W. Va., and duty there till August, 1864. Sheridan's Shenandoah Valley Campaign August to November. Berryville September 3. Battle of Opequan, Winchester, September 19. Fisher's Hill September 22. Battle of Cedar Creek October 19. Duty at Maryland Heights and in Dept. of West Virginia till June, 1865. Mustered out June 30, 1865.

Lost during service 11 Enlisted men killed and mortally wounded and 1 Officer and 18 Enlisted men by disease. Total 30.

BATTERY "E" 1st REGIMENT LIGHT ARTILLERY.
(43rd VOLUNTEERS.)

Organized at Philadelphia August 5, 1861, and ordered to Washington, D. C. Attached to W. F. Smith's Division, Army of the Potomac, October-November, 1861. Buell's Division, Army of the Potomac, to March, 1862. Artillery, 1st Division, 4th Army Corps, Army of the Potomac, to June, 1862. Reserve Artillery, 4th Army Corps, to June, 1863. 2nd Brigade, 1st Division, 4th Army Corps, to July, 1863. United States Forces, Yorktown, Va., Dept. of Virginia and North Carolina, to June, 1864. Unattached, Dept. of Virginia and North Carolina, to July, 1864. Artillery Brigade, 18th Army Corps, to August, 1864. Artillery Brigade, 10th Army Corps, to December, 1864. Artillery Brigade, 25th Army Corps, Dept. of Virginia, to July, 1865.

SERVICE.—Duty at Camp Barry and in the Defences of Washington, D. C., till March, 1862. Advance on Manassas, Va., March 10-15. Moved to the Virginia Peninsula March. Siege of Yorktown April 5-May 4. Battle of Williamsburg May 5. Battle of Fair Oaks, Seven Pines, May 31-June 1. Seven days before Richmond June 25-July 1. Defence of Bottom's Bridge June 25-29. Malvern Hill July 1. At Harrison's Landing till August 16. Retreat from the Peninsula August 16-24. Garrison duty at Yorktown and Gloucester till April, 1864. Dix's Peninsula Campaign June 26-July 8, 1863. Expedition to Matthews County October 4-9, 1863, and to Gloucester Court House December 11-15, 1863. At Williamsburg, Va., April, 1864, and in Defences of Yorktown till July. Ordered to join 18th Army Corps in the field July 5. Siege operations against Petersburg and Richmond July, 1864, to April, 1865. Chaffin's Farm, New Market Heights, and Fort Harrison September 28-30. Near Richmond September 30. In trenches before Richmond till April, 1865. Duty dismantling forts and removing Ordnance till July. Mustered out July 20, 1865.

Lost 2 Enlisted men killed and mortally wounded and 21 Enlisted men by disease.

BATTERY "F" 1st REGIMENT LIGHT ARTILLERY.
(43rd VOLUNTEERS.)

Organized at Philadelphia August 5, 1861, and ordered to Washington, D. C. Attached to Banks' Division, Army of the Potomac, October, 1861, to March, 1862. 1st Division, Banks' 5th Army Corps and 1st Division, Dept. of the Shenandoah, to May, 1862. Artillery, 2nd Division, Dept. of the Rappahannock, to June, 1862. Artillery, 2nd Division, 3rd Corps, Army of Virginia, to September, 1862. Artillery, 2nd Division, 1st Army Corps, Army of the Potomac, to January, 1863. Artillery, 3rd Division, 1st Army Corps, to May, 1863. 3rd Volunteer Brigade, Artillery Reserve, Army of the Potomac, to July, 1863. Artillery Brigade, 2nd Army Corps, Army of the Potomac, to September, 1864. Artillery Reserve, Army of the Potomac, to June, 1865.

SERVICE.—Duty in the Defences of Washington till October, 1861, and on the Upper Potomac, between Edward's Ferry and Hancock, Md., till February, 1862. Advance on Winchester March 1-12. Reconnoissance toward Strasburg and action near Winchester March 7. Ordered to join Abercrombie's Brigade March 21, and moved to Warrenton Junction. Pursuit of Jackson up the Valley March 24-April 27. Rappahannock Crossing April 18. Pope's Campaign in Northern Virginia August 1-September 2. Battle of Cedar Mountain August 9. Fords of the Rappahannock August 21-23. Thoroughfare Gap August 28. Battles of Groveton August 29. Bull Run August 30. Chantilly September 1. Maryland Campaign September 6-24. Battle of Antietam, Md., September 16-17. Duty at Sharpsburg, Md., till October 30. Movement to Falmouth, Va., October 30-November 19. Battle of Fredericksburg December 12-15. "Mud March" January 20-24, 1863. At Falmouth and Belle Plain till April. Chancellorsville Campaign April 27-May 6. Operations at Pollock's Mill Creek April 29-May 2. Fitzhugh's Crossing April 29-30. Chancellorsville May 2-5. Gettysburg (Pa.) Campaign June 11-July 24. Battle of Gettysburg, Pa., July 2-4. Advance to line of the Rapidan September 13-17. Bristoe Campaign October 9-22. Auburn and Bristoe October 14. Advance to line of the Rappahannock November 7-8. Mine Run Campaign November 26-December 2. Demonstration on the Rapidan February 6-7, 1864. Morton's Ford February 6-7. Camp near Stevensburg, Va., till May. Rapidan Campaign May 4-June 12. Battles of the Wilderness May 5-7; Spottsylvania May 8-12; Spottsylvania Court House May 12-21. Assault on the Salient May 12. North Anna River May 23-26. Line of the Pamunkey May 26-28. Totopotomoy May 28-31. Cold Harbor June 1-12. Before Petersburg June 16-18. Siege of Petersburg June 16, 1864, to April 2, 1865. Jerusalem Plank Road June 21-22, 1864. Demonstration north of the James River at Deep Bottom July 27-29. Deep Bottom July 27-29. Demonstration north of the James at Deep Bottom August 13-20. Strawberry Plains August 14-18. Fall of Petersburg April 2, 1865. Moved to Washington, D. C., May. Grand Review May 23. Mustered out July 9, 1865.

Lost 1 Officer and 17 Enlisted men killed and 13 Enlisted men by disease. Total 31.

BATTERY "G" 1st REGIMENT LIGHT ARTILLERY.
(43rd VOLUNTEERS.)

Organized at Philadelphia August 5, 1861, and ordered to Washington, D. C. Attached to McCall's Pennsylvania Reserve Division, Army of the Potomac, to March, 1862. Artillery, 2nd Division, 1st Army Corps, Army of the Potomac, to April, 1862. Artillery, McCall's Division, Dept. of the Rappahannock, to June, 1862. Artillery Brigade, 3rd Division, 5th Army Corps, Army of the Potomac, to August, 1862. Artillery, 3rd Division, 3rd Corps, Army of Virginia, to September, 1862. Artillery, 3rd Division, 1st Army Corps, Army of the Potomac, to May, 1863. 3rd Volunteer Brigade, Artillery Reserve, Army of the Potomac, to July, 1863. Artillery Brigade, 2nd Army Corps, Army of the Potomac, to April, 1864. Camp Barry, 22nd Corps, to May, 1864. 1st Brigade, DeRussy's Division, 22nd Corps, to July, 1864. Reserve Division, Dept. of West Virginia, to January, 1865. 1st Infantry Division, West Virginia, to April, 1865. 3rd Brigade, Hardins' Division, 22nd Army Corps, to June, 1865.

SERVICE.—Duty at Camp Barry and Tennallytown, Md., Defences of Washington, D. C., till October, 1861, and at Camp Pierpont, near Langley, Va., till March, 1862. Expedition to Grinnell's Farm December 6, 1861. Advance on Manassas, Va., March 10-15. McDowell's advance on Falmouth April 9-19. Duty at Falmouth and Fredericksburg till June. Ordered to the Virginia Peninsula. Seven days before Richmond June 25-July 1. Battles of Mechanicsville June 26; Gaines Mill June 27; Charles City Cross Roads and Glendale June 30; Malvern Hill July 1. Duty at Harrison's Landing till August 16. Movement to join Pope August 16-26. Duty at Washington, D. C., till October 9. Rejoined Division at Sharpsburg, Md. Movement to Falmouth, Va., October-November. Battle of Fredericksburg December 12-15. "Mud March" January 20-24, 1863. At Falmouth and Belle Plains till April. Chancellorsville Campaign April 27-May 6. Operations at Pollock's Mill Creek April 29-May 2. Fitzhugh's Crossing April 29-30. Chancellorsville May 2-5. Battery attached to Battery "F" 1st Pennsylvania Light Artillery May 12, 1863, to April 3, 1864. Gettysburg (Pa.) Campaign June 11-July 24. Battle of Gettysburg, Pa., July 1-3. Advance to line of the Rapidan September 13-17. Bristoe Campaign October 9-22. Auburn and Bristoe October 14. Advance to line of the Rappahannock November 7-8. Mine Run Campaign November 26-December 2. Demonstration on the Rapidan February 6-7, 1864. Morton's Ford February 6-7. At Stevensburg till April. At Camp Berry, Defences of Washington, D. C., April. At Arlington Heights, Va., as garrison of Forts Bennett, Cochran and Haggerty till July. Ordered to Frederick, Md., July 3. Infantry duty at Point of Rocks, Md., July 6 to December 12. At Maryland Heights till April 16, 1865. At Fort Lincoln, near Washington, D. C., till April 27, and at Fort Foote till June. Mustered out at Camp Cadwalader June 29, 1865.

Battery lost during service 1 Officer and 16 Enlisted men killed and mortally wounded and 14 Enlisted men by disease. Total 31.

BATTERY "H," 1st REGIMENT LIGHT ARTILLERY (43rd VOLUNTEERS).

Organized at Philadelphia August 5, 1861, and ordered to Washington, D. C. Attached to Defences of Washington to October, 1861. Buell's Division, Army Potomac, March, 1862. Artillery, 1st Division, 4th Army Corps, Army Potomac, to July, 1862. Reserve Artillery, 4th Army Corps, Yorktown, Va., to June, 1863. Camp Barry, Washington, D. C., 22nd Army Corps, to May, 1864. 1st Brigade, DeRussy's Division, 22nd Corps, to June, 1865.

SERVICE.—Duty in the Defences of Washington, D. C., till March, 1862. Advance on Manassas, Va., March 10-15. Ordered to the Virginia Peninsula. Siege of Yorktown April 5-May 4. Battle of Williamsburg May 5. Battle of Fair Oaks (Seven Pines) May 31-June 1. Seven days before Richmond June 25-July 1. Bottom's Bridge June 28-29. Glendale June 30. Malvern Hill July 1. At Harrison's Landing till August 16. Moved to Yorktown, Va., and duty there till June, 1863. Ordered to Washington, D. C., arriving July 1, and march to Gettysburg July 1-4. Return to Washington, and duty at Camp Barry till May, 1864. Garrison duty at Fort Whipple till December, and at Fort Marcy till February, 1865. Outpost duty at Edward's Ferry, Md., till June. Mustered out June 27, 1865.

Lost during service 1 Enlisted man killed and 1 Officer and 18 Enlisted men by disease. Total 20.

BATTERY "I," 1st REGIMENT LIGHT ARTILLERY. —(43rd VOLUNTEERS.)

Organized March 2, 1865. Duty in the Defences of Washington, D. C. Attached to DeRussy's Division, Defences south of the Potomac, till July. Mustered out July 1, 1865.

Lost 2 by disease.

INDEPENDENT BATTERY "A," LIGHT ARTILLERY.

Organized at Philadelphia September 19, 1861. Garrison at Fort Delaware entire term. Mustered out June 30, 1865.

Lost during service 1 Officer and 16 Enlisted men by disease. Total 17.

INDEPENDENT BATTERY "B," LIGHT ARTILLERY.

Organized at Erie and Chambersburg August, 1861. Moved, with 77th Pennsylvania, to Louisville, Ky., October 18, 1861; thence to Camp Nevin, Ky. Attached to Negley's Brigade, McCook's Command, Army of the Ohio, to December, 1861. Artillery, 2nd Division, Army of the Ohio, to June, 1862. Artillery, 5th Division, Army of the Ohio, to September, 1862. Artillery, 5th Division, 2nd Army Corps, Army of the Ohio, to November, 1862. Artillery, 3rd Division, Left Wing, 14th Army Corps, Army of the Cumberland, to January, 1863. Artillery, 3rd Division, 21st Corps, Army of the Cumberland, to October, 1863. Artillery, 3rd Division, 4th Army Corps, Army of the Cumberland, to April, 1864. Artillery, 1st Division, 4th Corps, to July, 1864. Artillery Brigade, 4th Corps, to August, 1865. Dept. of Texas to October, 1865.

SERVICE.—Camp at Nolin River, Ky., till February, 1862. March to Bowling Green, Ky.; thence to Nashville, Tenn., February 14-March 3. March to Savannah, Tenn., March 16-April 6. Battle of Shiloh, Tenn., April 6-7 (Reserve). Advance on and Siege of Corinth, Miss., April 29-May 30. Pursuit to Booneville May 31-June 6. Buell's Campaign in Northern Alabama and Middle Tennessee June to August. March to Louisville, Ky., in pursuit of Bragg, August 20-September 26. Pursuit of Bragg into Kentucky October 1-22. Battle of Perryville, Ky., October 8. Logan's Cross Roads October 18. March to Nashville, Tenn., October 22-November 6 and duty there till December 26. Advance on Murfreesboro December 26-30. Battle of Stone's River December 30-31, 1862, and January 1-3, 1863. Duty at Murfreesboro till June. Middle Tennessee (or Tullahoma) Campaign June 23-July 7. Occupation of Middle Tennessee till August 16. Passage of Cumberland Mountains and Tennessee River, and Chickamauga (Ga.) Campaign, August 16-September 22. Battle of Chickamauga September 19-20. Siege of Chattanooga September 24-October 27. Battles of Chattanooga November 23-25; Mission Ridge November 24-25; Atlanta (Ga.) Campaign May to September, 1864. Demonstration on Rocky Faced Ridge May 8-11. Buzzard's Roost Gap May 8-9. Demonstration on Dalton May 9-13. Battle of Resaca May 14-15. Near Kingston May 18-19. Near Cassville May 19. Kingston May 21. Cassville May 24. New Hope Church May 25. Operations on line of Pumpkin Vine Creek and battles about Dallas, New Hope Church and Allatoona Hills, May 26-June 5. Operations about Marietta and against Kenesaw Mountain June 10-July 2. Pine Hill June 11-14. Lost Mountain June 15-17. Assault on Kenesaw June 27. Ruff's Station, or Smyrna Camp Ground, July 4. Chattahoochee River July 5-17. Peach Tree Creek July 19-20. Siege of Atlanta July 22-August 25. Flank movement on Jonesboro August 25-30. Battle of Jonesboro August 31-September 1. Operations in North Georgia and North Alabama against Hood September 29-November 3. Nashville Campaign November-December. Spring Hill November 23 and November 29. Battle of Franklin November 30. Near Nashville December 6. Battle of Nashville December 15-16. Pursuit of Hood to the Tennessee River December 17-28. Moved to Huntsville, Ala., and duty there till March, 1865. Operations in North Georgia and East Tennessee January 31-April 24. Duty at Nashville, Tenn., till June. Moved to New Orleans, La., thence to Texas, and duty there till October, 1865. Mustered out October 12, 1865.

Battery lost during service 2 Officers and 8 Enlisted men killed and mortally wounded and 25 Enlisted men by disease. Total 35.

INDEPENDENT BATTERY "C" LIGHT ARTILLERY.

Organized at Pittsburg November 6, 1861. Moved to Washington, D. C., November. Attached to Military District of Washington till May, 1862. Ord's Division, Dept. of the Rappahannock, to June, 1862. 2nd Division, 3rd Army Corps, Army of Virginia, to September, 1862. 2nd Division, 1st Army Corps, Army of the Potomac, to June, 1863. 1st Volunteer Brigade, Artillery Reserve, Army of the Potomac, to November, 1863. Artillery Brigade, 2nd Army Corps, Army of the Potomac, to March, 1864. Camp Barry, Defences of Washington, 22nd Army Corps, to June, 1865.

SERVICE.—Duty in the Defences of Washington, D. C., till May, 1862. Duty at Front Royal, Catlett's Station, Warrenton and Waterloo, till August. Battle of Cedar Mountain August 9. Pope's Campaign in Northern Virginia August 10-September 2. Crooked Run August 12. Fords of the Rappahannock August 21-23. Thoroughfare Gap August 28. Bull Run August 29-30. Chantilly September 1. Maryland Campaign September 6-24. Battle of Antietam, Md., September 16-17. Duty at Sharpsburg, Md., till October 30. Movement to Falmouth, Va., October 30-November 19. Battle of Fredericksburg December 12-15. "Mud March" January 20-24, 1863. At Falmouth and Belle Plains till April. Chancellorsville Campaign April 27-May 6. Operations at Pollock's Mill Creek April 29-May 2. Fitzhugh's Crossing April 29-30. Chancellorsville May 2-5. Gettysburg (Pa.) Campaign June 11-July 24. Advance to line of the Rapidan September 13-17. Bristoe Campaign October 9-22. Advance to line of the Rappahannock November 7-8. Mine Run Campaign November 26-December 2. Demonstration on the Rapidan February 6-7, 1864. Morton's Ford February 6-7. Ordered to Defences of Washington and duty at Camp Barry and in Defences south of the Potomac till June, 1865. Mustered out June 30, 1865.

Battery lost during service 1 Officer and 2 Enlisted men killed and 21 Enlisted men by disease. Total 24.

INDEPENDENT BATTERY "D" LIGHT ARTILLERY. ("DURRELL'S.")

Organized at Doylestown and mustered in September 24, 1861. Left State for Washington, D. C., November 5, 1861. Attached to McDowell's Division, Army of the Potomac, to March, 1862. King's 1st Division, 1st Army Corps, Army of the Potomac, to April, 1862. King's Division, Dept. of the Rappahannock, to June, 1862. Artillery, 1st Division, 3rd Army Corps, Army of Virginia, to August, 1862. Artillery, 2nd Division, 9th Army Corps, Army of the Potomac, to April, 1863. Army of the Ohio to June, 1863, and Army of the Tennessee to August, 1863. Covington, Ky., Dept. of the Ohio, to March, 1864. Artillery, 4th Division, 9th Army Corps, Army of the Potomac, to June, 1865.

SERVICE.—Duty at Kalorama Heights, Defences of Washington, D. C., till November 14, 1861. At East Capital Hill till December 18, and at Munson's Hill till March 10, 1862. Advance on Manassas, Va., March 10-15. McDowell's advance to Falmouth April 9-19. Capture of Fredericksburg April 18. Expedition to Thoroughfare Gap and operations against Jackson May 29-June 21. At Falmouth till August. Pope's Campaign in Northern Virginia August 16-September 2. Kelly's Ford August 21. Near Warrenton August 22-23 supporting Buford's Cavalry. Kettle Run or Bristoe Station August 27. Battle of Bull Run August 29-30. Chantilly September 1. Maryland Campaign September 6-24. Battles of South Mountain September 14, and Antietam September 16-17. At Pleasant Valley till October 25. Movement to Falmouth, Va., October 25-November 19. Warrenton or Sulphur Springs November 15. Berryville December 2. Battle of Fredericksburg, Va., December 12-15. "Mud March" January 20-24, 1863. Moved to Newport News February 7, thence to Cynthiana, Ky., March 23-April 1. At Paris, Mt. Sterling, Richmond, Lancaster, Crab Orchard and Stanford, Ky., till June. Movement to Vicksburg, Miss., June 3-14. Siege of Vicksburg June 15-July 4. Advance on Jackson, Miss., July 5-10. Siege of Jackson July 10-17. At Milldale till August 6. Moved to Covington, Ky., August 6-22, and duty there till March 21, 1864. Moved to Johnson's Island, Lake Erie, Ohio, November 12-16 to repel threatened raid to release prisoners. Moved to Annapolis, Md., March 21-26. Rap-

idan Campaign May-June. Guarding supply trains through the Wilderness and to James River May 4-June 16. Siege of Petersburg June 16-18 to April 2, 1865. Mine Explosion, Petersburg, July 30, 1864. Ream's Station, Weldon Railroad, August 25. Peeble's Farm, Poplar Grove Church, September 30-October 1. Old members mustered out September 23, 1864. Fort Stedman March 25, 1865. Assault on and fall of Petersburg April 2. Moved to City Point April 20; thence to Alexandria April 25-27. Grand Review May 23. Mustered out June 13, 1865.

Battery lost during service 1 Officer and 2 Enlisted men killed and mortally wounded and 21 Enlisted men by disease. Total 24.

INDEPENDENT BATTERY "E" LIGHT ARTILLERY. ("KNAP'S.")

Organized at Point of Rocks, Md., from a Company formed for 63rd Pennsylvania and surplus men of the 28th Pennsylvania Infantry September, 1861. Attached to W. F. Smith's Division, Army of the Potomac, to November, 1861. Banks' Division, Army of the Potomac, to March, 1862. Geary's Separate Brigade, Banks' 5th Army Corps, to April, 1862. Geary's Separate Brigade, Dept. of the Shenandoah, to May, 1862. Geary's Separate Brigade, Dept. of the Rappahannock, to June, 1862. Artillery, 2nd Corps, Army of Virginia, to September, 1862. Artillery, 2nd Division, 12th Army Corps, Army of the Potomac, to May, 1863. Artillery Brigade, 12th Army Corps, to December, 1863. Artillery, 2nd Division, 12th Corps, Army of the Cumberland, to April, 1864. Artillery, 2nd Division, 20th Army Corps, to July, 1864. Artillery Brigade, 20th Army Corps, to June, 1865.

SERVICE.—Camp at East Capital Hill, Defences of Washington, till November 24, 1861. Moved to Point of Rocks November 24. Duty there and near Harper's Ferry till February 28, 1862. Action at Point of Rocks December 19. Occupation of Loudon Heights February 28. Operations on line of Manassas Gap Railroad March 1-April 14. Capture of Lovettsville March 1. March to Wheetland and Leesburg March 7-8. Capture of Leesburg March 8. Advance to Snickersville March 12. Upperville March 14. Ashby's Gap March 15. Middleburg March 27. Operations about Middleburg and White Plains March 27-28. Salem April 1. Thoroughfare Gap April 2. Piedmont April 14. Guarding Railroad at Salem till May 23. Front Royal May 23. Retreat to Manassas May 24-25. Guard Railroad and operations in the Valley till August. Reconnoissance to Orange and Culpeper Court House July 12-17. Battle of Cedar Mountain August 9. Pope's Campaign in Northern Virginia August 16-September 2. Rappahannock Bridge August 21. Sulphur Springs August 23-25. Maryland Campaign September 2-23. Battle of Antietam September 16-17. Moved to Harper's Ferry September 19-23. Duty at Sandy Hook till December. Reconnoissance to Rippon November 9. Reconnoissance to Winchester December 2-6. Berryville December 2. Winchester December 4. March to Fairfax Station December 9-17, and duty there till January 20, 1863. "Mud March" January 20-24. At Aquia Creek till April 27. Chancellorsville Campaign April 27-May 6. Battle of Chancellorsville May 1-5. Gettysburg (Pa.) Campaign June 11-July 24. Battle of Gettysburg July 1-3. Movement to Bridgeport, Ala., September 24-October 3. Wauhatchie, Tenn., October 28-29. Battles of Chattanooga November 23-25; Lookout Mountain November 23-24; Mission Ridge November 25; Ringgold Gap, Taylor's Ridge, November 27. Re-enlisted January, 1864, and on furlough January and February. Expedition down Tennessee River to Triana April 12-16. Atlanta (Ga.) Campaign May to September. Demonstration on Rocky Faced Ridge May 8-11. Dug Gap or Mill Springs May 8. Battle of Resaca May 14-15. Near Cassville May 19. New Hope Church May 25. Operations on line of Pumpkin Vine Creek and battles about Dallas, New Hope Church and Allatoona Hills May 26-June 5. Operations about Marietta and against

Kenesaw Mountain June 10-July 2. Pine Mountain June 11-14. Gilgal or Golgotha Church June 15. Lost Mountain June 15-17. Muddy Creek June 17. Noyes Creek June 19. Kolb's Farm June 22. Assault on Kenesaw June 27. Ruff's Station or Smyrna Camp Ground July 4. Chattahoochie River July 5-17. Peach Tree Creek July 19-20. Siege of Atlanta July 22-August 25. Operations at Chattahoochie River Bridge August 26-September 2. Occupation of Atlanta September 2-November 15. Near Atlanta November 9. March to the sea November 15-December 10. Siege of Savannah December 10-21. Campaign of the Carolinas January to April, 1865. Averysboro, N. C., March 16. Battle of Bentonville March 19-21. Occupation of Goldsboro March 24. Advance on Raleigh April 9-13. Neuse River April 10. Occupation of Raleigh April 14. Bennett's House April 26. Surrender of Johnston and his army. March to Washington, D. C., via Richmond, Va., April 29-May 20. Grand Review May 24. Mustered out at Pittsburg June 14, 1865.

Battery lost during service 2 Officers and 12 Enlisted men killed and mortally wounded and 11 Enlisted men by disease. Total 25.

INDEPENDENT BATTERY "F" LIGHT ARTILLERY. ("HAMPTON'S.")

Organized at Williamsport December 7, 1861. Joined Banks on Upper Potomac December 15, 1861. Attached to Banks' Division, Army of the Potomac, to March, 1862. Artillery, 1st Division, Banks' 5th Army Corps, and Dept. of the Shenandoah to June, 1862. Artillery, 2nd Army Corps, Army of Virginia, to September, 1862. Artillery, 2nd Division, 12th Army Corps, Army of the Potomac, to May, 1863. 4th Volunteer Brigade, Artillery Reserve, Army of the Potomac, to October, 1863. Artillery Brigade, 2nd Army Corps, to March, 1864. Camp Barry, Defences of Washington, 22nd Corps, to May, 1864. 2nd Brigade, DeRussy's Division, 22nd Corps, to July, 1864. Reserve Division, Dept. of West Virginia, to January, 1865. 1st Separate Brigade, 3rd Division, West Virginia, to March, 1865. Artillery Reserve, Army of the Shenandoah, to April, 1865. 3rd Brigade, Hardins' Division, 22nd Corps, Dept. of Washington, to June, 1865.

SERVICE.—Duty on the Upper Potomac till February, 1862. Advance on Winchester March 1-12. Occupation of Winchester March 12. Pursuit of Jackson up the Valley March 24-April 27. Operations in the Shenandoah Valley May 15-June 17. Action at Newtown and Middletown May 24. Retreat to Williamsport May 24-26. Battle of Winchester May 25. Reconnoissance to Front Royal June 29-30. Luray June 30. At Front Royal till August. Pope's Campaign in Northern Virginia August 16-September 2. Sulphur Springs August 24. Bull Run August 30. Chantilly September 1. Maryland Campaign September. Battle of Antietam September 16-17. Moved to Harper's Ferry September 19, and duty there till December. Near Snickersville November 8. Reconnoissance to Rippon November 9. Reconnoissance to Winchester December 2-6. March to Fredericksburg December 12-16. "Mud March" January 20-24, 1863. At Stafford Court House till April 27. Chancellorsville Campaign April 27-May 6. Battle of Chancellorsville May 1-5. Gettysburg (Pa.) Campaign June 11-July 24. Battle of Gettysburg, Pa., July 1-3. Advance from the Rappahannock to the Rapidan September 13-17. Bristoe Campaign November 9-22. Auburn and Bristoe October 14. Advance to line of the Rappahannock November 7-8. Mine Run Campaign November 26-December 2. Demonstration on the Rapidan February 6-7, 1864. Morton's Ford February 6-7. Duty at Camp Barry, Washington, D. C., and in the Defences of Washington south of the Potomac till July. Duty at Harper's Ferry, W. Va., till April, 1865, and in the Defences of Washington till June, 1865. Mustered out June 26, 1865.

Battery lost during service 2 Officers and 8 Enlisted men killed and mortally wounded and 14 Enlisted men by disease. Total 24.

INDEPENDENT BATTERY "G" LIGHT ARTILLERY.

Organized at Harrisburg August 22, 1862. Garrison duty at Fort Delaware entire term. Mustered out June 15, 1865.

Lost 9 by disease.

INDEPENDENT BATTERY "H" LIGHT ARTILLERY.

Organized at Pittsburg October 21, 1862. Attached to Defences of Washington, D. C., to December, 1862. Camp Barry Defences of Washington, D. C., to March, 1863. Slough's Command, Garrison of Alexandria, 22nd Corps, Dept. of Washington, to January, 1865. Camp Barry, 22nd Corps, to June, 1865.

SERVICE.—Garrison duty in the Defences of Washington entire term. Mustered out June, 1865.

Lost 7 by disease.

INDEPENDENT BATTERY "I" LIGHT ARTILLERY. ("NEVINS.")

Organized at Philadelphia and Harrisburg December 31, 1863, to January 7, 1864. Attached to Camp Barry, 22nd Corps, Dept. of Washington, to May, 1864. 2nd Brigade, DeRussy's Division, 22nd Corps, to July, 1864. 3rd Brigade, DeRussy's Division, to December, 1864. 1st Brigade, DeRussy's Division, to June, 1865. Garrison duty in Defences of Washington south of the Potomac entire term. Mustered out June 23, 1865.

KNAP'S INDEPENDENT BATTALION LIGHT ARTILLERY.

Organized at Pittsburg May and June, 1864. Ordered to Washington, D. C. Attached to 3rd Brigade, Hardin's Division, 22nd Corps, Dept. of Washington, June, 1864. 1st Brigade, Hardin's Division, 22nd Corps, to September, 1864. Garrison duty in the Defences of Washington north of the Potomac, entire term. Mustered out September 6, 1864.

HASTINGS' INDEPENDENT BATTERY LIGHT ARTILLERY.

Organized at Philadelphia July 12, 1864. Mustered out October 25, 1864.

KEYSTONE INDEPENDENT BATTERY LIGHT ARTILLERY.

Organized at Philadelphia August 13, 1862. Ordered to Washington, D. C. Attached to Casey's Provisional Brigade, Military District of Washington, to October, 1862. Casey's Division, Military District of Washington, to February, 1863. Casey's Division, 22nd Corps, Dept. of Washington, to April, 1863. Abercrombie's Division, 22nd Corps, to June, 1863. Camp Barry, 22nd Corps, to July, 1863. Artillery Brigade, 3rd Army Corps, Army Potomac, July, 1863. Maryland Heights Division, Dept. of West Virginia, to August, 1863. Garrison duty in the Defences of Washington, D. C., till July, 1863. Joined Army Potomac and pursuit of Lee July. Action at Wapping Heights, Va., July 23. Moved to Harper's Ferry, W. Va., and duty there till August. Mustered out August 20, 1863.

KEYSTONE INDEPENDENT MILITIA BATTERY NO. 2.—(LIGHT ARTILLERY.)

Organized at Philadelphia July 6, 1863. Mustered out August 24, 1863.

KNAP'S INDEPENDENT MILITIA BATTERY LIGHT ARTILLERY.

Organized at Pittsburg for the Pennsylvania Emergency June 27, 1863. Mustered out July 15, 1863.

LANDIS' INDEPENDENT MILITIA BATTERY LIGHT ARTILLERY.

Organized at Philadelphia for the Pennsylvania Emergency June 27, 1863. Mustered out July 30, 1863.

MILLER'S INDEPENDENT MILITIA BATTERY LIGHT ARTILLERY.

Organized at Harrisburg June 19, 1863. Mustered out July 25, 1863.

NEVIN'S INDEPENDENT BATTERY LIGHT ARTILLERY.

Organized at Harrisburg June and July, 1863. Ordered to Philadelphia July, 1863, and duty there till November, 1863. Ordered to Harper's Ferry, W. Va., and duty there till January, 1864. Ordered to Harrisburg and mustered out January 7, 1864.

ULMAN'S INDEPENDENT BATTERY LIGHT ARTILLERY.

Organized at Harrisburg February 14, 1862. Mustered out March 7, 1862.

WRIGLEY'S INDEPENDENT COMPANY ENGINEERS.

Organized at Philadelphia August 9, 1862. Ordered to Washington, D. C. Attached to Whipple's Command, Military District of Washington, to November, 1862. Harper's Ferry, W. Va., to March, 1862. 2nd Brigade, 3rd Division, 8th Army Corps, Middle Department, to June, 1863. Unattached, Dept. of West Virginia, to December, 1863. Unattached, 1st Division, Dept. of West Virginia, to April, 1864. Reserve Division, Dept. of West Virginia, to June, 1865. Engaged in Engineer operations in the Defences of Washington to November, 1862, and at Harper's Ferry, W. Va., till muster out, June 20, 1865.

INDEPENDENT COMPANY SHARPSHOOTERS.

Organized June, 1861. Assigned to 2nd United States Sharpshooters as Company "C" (which see).

M'LANE'S ERIE REGIMENT INFANTRY.

Companies "A," "B," "C," Wayne Guard; Company "D," Conneautville Rifles; Company "F," Titusville Guards: Company "G," Girard Guards; Company "H," Parson Guards; Company "I," German Rifles; Company "K," Reed Guard. Mustered in April 28, 1861, by Lieutenant-Colonel Grant at Camp Wayne, Erie, Pa. Ordered to Camp Wilkins, near Pittsburg, April 28, and duty there till June. Moved to Camp Wright, near Pittsburg, and duty there till July. Mustered out at Erie, Pa., July 25, 1861.

"FIRST DEFENDERS."—(5 COMPANIES.)

Ringgold Light Artillery of Reading, Logan Guard of Lewiston, Washington Artillery of Pottsville, National Light Infantry of Pottsville, and Allen Rifles of Allentown tendered services April 13, 1861. Moved to Harrisburg April 16-17. Mustered in April 18, and moved to Washington, D. C., via Baltimore, Md., April 18. Quartered in the Capitol, guard Arsenal and Navy Yard. Logan Guard and Washington Artillery on duty at Fort Washington. Assigned to 25th Pennsylvania as Companies "A," "D," "E," "G" and "H" (which see).

1st REGIMENT INFANTRY.--(3 MONTHS.)

Organized at Harrisburg April 20, 1861. Moved to Cockeysville on Northern Central Railroad April 20; thence to Camp Scott, near York, Pa., and duty there till May 14. Guard Northern Central Railroad, near Baltimore, May 14-25, and Harper's Ferry Road May 25-June 3. Moved to Catonsville, Md., May 25; to Franklintown May 29, and to Chambersburg, Pa., June 3. Expedition to Rockville, Md., June 10-July 7. Attached to Wyocoop's 2nd Brigade, Keim's 2nd Division, Patterson's Army. Duty at Hagerstown and Funkstown, Goose Creek, Edward's Ferry, June 18. At Frederick June 22, and at Martinsburg, Va., July 8-21. Moved to Harper's Ferry July 21. Mustered out July 27, 1861.

1st REGIMENT RESERVES INFANTRY.—(30th VOLUNTEERS.)

Organized at West Chester June 9, 1861. Moved to Harrisburg, Pa., July 20; thence reported to General Dix at Baltimore, Md., July 22, 1861. Mustered into United States service at Camp Carroll, near Baltimore, July 26. Moved to Annapolis, Md., July 27. Attached to Dix's Command to September, 1861. 1st Brigade, McCall's Pennsylvania Reserves Division, Army of the Potomac, to March, 1862. 1st Brigade, 2nd Division,

1st Army Corps, Army of the Potomac, to April, 1862. 1st Brigade, McCall's Division, Dept. of the Rappahannock, to June, 1862. 1st Brigade, 3rd Division, 5th Army Corps, Army of the Potomac, to August, 1862. 1st Brigade, 3rd Division, 3rd Corps, Army of Virginia, to September, 1862. 1st Brigade, 3rd Division, 1st Army Corps, Army of the Potomac, to February, 1863. 1st Brigade, Pennsylvania Reserves Division, 22nd Army Corps, to June, 1863. 1st Brigade, 3rd Division, 5th Army Corps, Army of the Potomac, to June, 1864.

SERVICE.—Duty at Annapolis, Md., July 27 to August 30, 1861. Moved to Washington, D. C., thence to Tennallytown, Md., August 30-31. March to Langley October 10, and duty at Camp Pierpont till March, 1862. Reconnoissance to Dranesville December 6, 1861. Action at Dranesville December 20 (Co. "A"). Advance on Manassas, Va., March 10-15. McDowell's advance on Fredericksburg, Va., April 9-19. Duty at Fredericksburg till May 31. Ordered to the Virginia Peninsula June. Seven days before Richmond June 25-July 1. Battles of Mechanicsville June 26; Gaines Mill June 27; Charles City Cross Roads and Glendale June 30; Malvern Hill July 1. At Harrison's Landing till August 16. Movement to join Pope August 16-26. Battles of Groveton August 29; Bull Run August 30. Maryland Campaign September 6-24. Battles of South Mountain September 14, and Antietam September 16-17. Duty in Maryland till October 30. Movement to Falmouth October 30-November 19. Battle of Fredericksburg, Va., December 12-15. "Mud March" January 20-24, 1863. Ordered to Washington, D. C., and duty in the Defences there till June 25. Rejoined Army of the Potomac. Battle of Gettysburg, Pa., July 1-3. Pursuit of Lee July 5-24. Williamsport July 13. Bristoe Campaign October 9-22. Advance to line of the Rappahannock November 7-8. Rappahannock Station November 7. Mine Run Campaign November 26-December 2. Mine Run November 26-30. Rapidan Campaign May and June, 1864. Battles of the Wilderness May 5-7; Laurel Hill May 8; Spottsylvania May 8-12; Spottsylvania Court House May 12-21. Assault on the Salient May 12. Harris Farm May 19. North Anna River May 23-26. Jericho Ford May 25. Line of the Pamunkey May 26-28. Totopotomoy May 28-31. Left front June 1. Mustered out June 10, 1864.

Regiment lost during service 6 Officers and 102 Enlisted men killed and mortally wounded and 2 Officers and 64 Enlisted men by disease. Total 174.

1st REGIMENT MILITIA INFANTRY.

Called September 4, 1862, to resist Lee's invasion of Maryland. Disbanded September 24, 1862.

1st BATTALION INFANTRY.—(6 MONTHS.)

Organized at Harrisburg June and July, 1863. Mustered out January 9, 1864.

1st BATTALION INFANTRY.—(100 DAYS.)

Organized at Philadelphia, Pittsburg and Harrisburg July, 1864. Mustered out November 14, 1864.

2nd REGIMENT INFANTRY.—(3 MONTHS.)

Organized at Harrisburg April 20, 1861. Moved to Cockeysville, Md., April 21. Return to York, Pa., and duty there till June 1. Moved to Chambersburg June 1. Attached to Wyncoop's 2nd Brigade, Keim's 2nd Division, Patterson's Army. Moved to Hagerstown June 16. At Funkstown till June 23. Falling Waters July 2 (Support). Occupation of Martinsburg July 3. Advance on Bunker Hill July 15. Moved to Charlestown July 17, and to Harper's Ferry July 23. Mustered out July 26, 1861.

2nd REGIMENT RESERVES INFANTRY.—(31st VOLUNTEERS.)

Organized at Philadelphia. Moved to Easton, Pa., May 29, 1861; thence to Harrisburg, Pa., July 24. Moved to Baltimore, thence to Sandy Hook, near Harper's Ferry, Va. Ordered to Darnestown, Md., August 28; thence to Tennallytown, Md., September 25 and join

McCall. Attached to 1st Brigade, McCall's Pennsylvania Reserves Division, Army of the Potomac, to March, 1862. 1st Brigade, 2nd Division, 1st Army Corps, Army of the Potomac, to April, 1862. 1st Brigade, McCall's Division, Dept. of the Rappahannock, to June, 1862. 1st Brigade, 3rd Division, 5th Army Corps, Army of the Potomac, to August, 1862. 1st Brigade, 3rd Division, 3rd Corps, Army of Virginia, to September, 1862. 1st Brigade, 3rd Division, 1st Army Corps, Army of the Potomac, to February, 1863. 1st Brigade, Pennsylvania Reserves Division, 22nd Corps, Dept. of Washington, to June, 1863. 1st Brigade, 3rd Division, 5th Army Corps, Army of the Potomac, to June, 1864.

SERVICE.—Moved to Langley, Va., October 10, 1861, and duty at Camp Pierpont till March, 1862. Reconnoissance toward Dranesville October 18-21, 1861. Expedition to Grinnell's Farm December 6. Advance on Manassas, Va., March 10-15. McDowell's advance on Falmouth April 9-19. Duty at Fredericksburg till June. Moved to White House June 9-11. Seven days before Richmond June 25-July 1. Battles of Mechanicsville June 26. Gaines Mill June 27. Savage Station June 29. Charles City Cross Roads and Glendale June 30. Malvern Hill July 1. At Harrison's Landing till August 16. Movement to join Pope August 16-26. Battles of Groveton August 29; Bull Run August 30. Maryland Campaign September 6-24. Battles of South Mountain September 14, and Antietam, Md., September 16-17. Duty in Maryland till October 30. Movement to Falmouth, Va., October 30-November 19. Battle of Fredericksburg, Va., December 12-15. "Mud March" January 20-24, 1863. Ordered to Washington, D. C., and duty in the Defences there till June 25. Rejoined Army of the Potomac. Battle of Gettysburg, Pa., July 1-3. Pursuit of Lee July 5-24. Bristoe Campaign October 9-22. Advance to line of the Rappahannock November 7-8. Rappahannock Station November 7. Mine Run Campaign November 26-December 2. Rapidan Campaign May, 1864. Battles of the Wilderness May 5-7; Laurel Hill May 8; Spottsylvania May 8-12; Spottsylvania Court House May 12-21. Assault on the Salient May 12. Harris Farm May 19. North Anna River May 23-26. Jericho Ford May 25. On line of the Pamunkey May 26-28. Totopotomoy May 28-31. Left front June 1. Mustered out June 16, 1864.

Regiment lost during service 4 Officers and 73 Enlisted men killed and mortally wounded and 3 Officers and 71 Enlisted men by disease. Total 151.

2nd REGIMENT MILITIA INFANTRY.

Called September 4, 1862, to resist Lee's invasion of Maryland. Disbanded September 24, 1862.

2nd BATTALION INFANTRY.

Organized at Pittsburg June and July, 1863, for six months. Mustered out January 21, 1864.

3rd REGIMENT INFANTRY.—(3 MONTHS.)

Organized at Harrisburg April 20, 1861. (Co. "G" the first Company to enter Camp Curtin on April 18.) Moved to Cockeysville, Md., April 20; thence to York, Pa., April 22, and duty there till May 27. At Chambersburg till June 7, and at Funkstown till July 1. Attached to 2nd Brigade, 2nd Division, Patterson's Army. Occupation of Martinsburg, Va., July 3. Detached from Brigade and on duty at Williamsport till July 26. Moved to Harrisburg and mustered out July 29, 1861.

3rd REGIMENT RESERVES INFANTRY.—(32nd VOLUNTEERS.)

Organized at Philadelphia and moved to Easton, Pa., May 20, 1861. Camp there till July 22. Moved to Harrisburg, Pa., July 22, and mustered into United States service July 28. Moved to Washington, D. C., thence to Tennallytown, Md. Attached to 2nd Brigade, McCall's Pennsylvania Reserves Division, Army of the Potomac, to March, 1862. 2nd Brigade, 2nd Division, 1st Army Corps, Army of the Potomac, to April, 1862. 2nd Brigade, McCall's Division, Dept. of the Rappahannock,

to June, 1862. 2nd Brigade, 3rd Division, 5th Army Corps, Army Potomac, to August, 1862. 2nd Brigade, 3rd Division, 3rd Corps, Army of Virginia, to September, 1862. 2nd Brigade, 3rd Division, 1st Army Corps, Army of the Potomac, to February, 1863. 2nd Brigade, Pennsylvania Reserves Division, 22nd Corps, Dept. of Washington, D. C., to April, 1864. 2nd Brigade, Pennsylvania Reserves Division, District of Alexandria, 22nd Corps, to January, 1864. Dept. of West Virginia to April, 1864. 3rd Brigade, 2nd Infantry Division, Dept. of West Virginia, to June, 1864.

SERVICE.—Duty at Tennallytown, Md., till Oct. 9, 1861, and at Camp Pierpont, near Langley, Va., till March, 1862. Expedition to Grinnell's Farm December 6, 1861. Advance on Manassas, Va., March 10-15, 1862. McDowell's advance on Falmouth April 9-19. Duty at Fredericksburg, Va., till June. Moved to White House June 9-11. Seven days before Richmond June 25-July 1. Battles of Mechanicsville June 26. Gaines' Mill June 27. Charles City Cross Roads and Glendale June 30. Malvern Hill July 1. At Harrison's Landing till August 16. Movement to join Pope August 16-26. Battles of Gainesville August 28. Groveton August 29. Bull Run August 30. Maryland Campaign September 6-24. Battles of South Mountain September 14; Antietam September 16-17. Duty in Maryland till October 30. Movement to Falmouth, Va., October 30-November 19. Battle of Fredericksburg December 12-15. "Mud March" January 20-24, 1863. Ordered to Washington, D. C., February 6, and duty there and in District of Alexandria till January 6, 1864. Duty near Martinsburg, W. Va., till January 27. Operations in Hampshire and Hardy counties, W. Va., January 27-February 7. Duty near Kearneysville, W. Va., till March 27, and near Harper's Ferry till April 3. Moved to Webster, thence to the Kanawha Valley, W. Va., April 22. Crook's Expedition to Virginia & Tennessee Railroad May 2-19. Battle of Cloyd's Mountain May 9. New River Bridge May 10. Expedition to Meadow Bluff, Fayette county, May 10-19. Near Newport May 12-13. Left front for Pittsburg, Pa., June 4. Mustered out June 17, 1864. Veterans and Recruits transferred to 54th Pennsylvania June 8, 1864.

Regiment lost during service 3 Officers and 69 Enlisted men killed and mortally wounded and 1 Officer and 54 Enlisted men by disease. Total 127.

3rd REGIMENT MILITIA INFANTRY.

Called September 4, 1862, to resist Lee's invasion of Maryland. Disbanded September 24, 1862.

3rd BATTALION INFANTRY.

Organized at Philadelphia June and July, 1863, for six months. Mustered out January 29, 1864.

4th REGIMENT INFANTRY.—(3 MONTHS.)

Organized at Harrisburg April 20, 1861. Moved to Philadelphia April 21. Occupation of Perryville, Md., April 22. Right Wing moved by boat to Annapolis, Md., April 23. Regiment moved to Washington, D. C., May 8, and camp near Bladensburg. Moved to Shutter's Hill, near Alexandria, June 24. Picket attack on Shutter's Hill July 1 (Co. "E"). Attached to 1st Brigade, Franklin's Heintzelman's Division, McDowell's Army of Northeast Virginia. Advance on Manassas, Va. July 16-21. Battle of Bull Run July 21. Mustered out July 27, 1861.

4th REGIMENT RESERVES INFANTRY.—(33rd VOLUNTEERS.)

Organized at Harrisburg July 17, 1861. Moved to Washington, D. C., thence to Tennallytown, Md. Attached to 2nd Brigade, McCall's Pennsylvania Reserves Division, Army of the Potomac, to March, 1862. 2nd Brigade, 2nd Division, 1st Army Corps, Army of the Potomac, to April, 1862. 2nd Brigade, McCall's Division, Dept. of the Rappahannock, to June, 1862. 2nd Brigade, 3rd Division, 5th Army Corps, Army of the Potomac, to August, 1862. 2nd Brigade, 3rd Division, 3rd Corps, Army of Virginia, to September, 1862. 2nd

Brigade, 3rd Division, 1st Army Corps, Army of the Potomac, to February, 1863. 2nd Brigade, Pennsylvania Reserves Division, 22nd Corps, Dept. of Washington, to January, 1864. Dept. of West Virginia to April, 1864. 3rd Brigade, 2nd Infantry Division, Dept. of West Virginia, to June, 1864.

SERVICE.—Duty at Tennallytown, Md., till October 10, and at Camp Pierpont, near Langley, Va., till March, 1862. Expedition to Grinnell's Farm December 6, 1861. Advance on Manassas, Va., March 10-15, 1862. McDowell's advance on Falmouth, Va., April 9-19. Duty at Fredericksburg till June. Moved to White House June 9-11. Seven days before Richmond June 25-July 1. Battles of Mechanicsville June 26; Gaines' Mill June 27; Charles City Cross Roads and Glendale June 30; Malvern Hill July 1. At Harrison's Landing till August 16. Movement to join Pope August 16-26. Battles of Gainesville August 28. Groveton August 29. Bull Run August 30. Maryland Campaign September 6-24. Battles of South Mountain September 14; Antietam September 16-17. Duty in Maryland till October. Movement to Falmouth, Va., October 30-November 19. Battle of Fredericksburg December 12-15. "Mud March" January 20-24, 1863. Ordered to Washington, D. C., February 6, and duty there and in the District of Alexandria till January 6, 1864. Duty near Martinsburg, W. Va., till January 27. Operations in Hampshire and Hardy counties January 27-February 7. Duty near Kearneysville till March 27. Moved to Webster, thence to the Kanawha Valley April 22. Crook's Expedition to Virginia & Tennessee Railroad May 2-19. Battle of Cloyd's Mountain May 9. New River Bridge May 10. Expedition to Meadow Bluff May 10-19. Near Newport May 12-13. Left front for Philadelphia via Pittsburg, Pa., June 4. Mustered out June 17, 1864. Veterans and Recruits transferred to 54th Pennsylvania June 8, 1864.

Regiment lost during service 2 Officers and 76 Enlisted men killed and mortally wounded and 1 Officer and 60 Enlisted men by disease. Total 139.

4th REGIMENT MILITIA INFANTRY.

Called September 4, 1862, to resist Lee's invasion of Maryland. Disbanded September 24, 1862.

5th REGIMENT INFANTRY.—(3 MONTHS.)

Organized at Camp Curtin, Harrisburg, April 20, 1861. Moved to Philadelphia April 22, then to Perryville and Annapolis, Md., April 23, and to Washington, D. C., April 27. At Alexandria, Va., May 28. Moved to Shutter's Hill June 3. Attached to McDowell's Army of Northeast Virginia. Duty at Alexandria till muster out. Mustered out July 25, 1861.

5th REGIMENT RESERVES INFANTRY.—(34th VOLUNTEERS.)

Organized at Harrisburg June, 1861. Ordered to point on State line opposite Cumberland, Md., June 22; thence moved into West Virginia in support of Lew Wallace. Moved to Washington, D. C., August 8. Attached to 1st Brigade, McCall's Pennsylvania Reserves Division, Army of the Potomac, to March, 1862. 1st Brigade, 2nd Division, 1st Army Corps, Army of the Potomac, to April, 1862. 1st Brigade, McCall's Division, Dept. of the Rappahannock, to June, 1862. 1st Brigade, 3rd Division, 5th Army Corps, Army Potomac, to August, 1862. 1st Brigade, 3rd Division, 3rd Corps, Army of Virginia, to September, 1862. 1st Brigade, 3rd Division, 1st Army Corps, Army of the Potomac, to November, 1862. 3rd Brigade, 3rd Division, 1st Army Corps, Army of the Potomac, to February, 1863. 3rd Brigade, Pennsylvania Reserves Division, 22nd Army Corps, Dept. of Washington, to June 26, 1863. 3rd Brigade, 3rd Division, 5th Army Corps, Army of the Potomac, to June, 1864.

SERVICE.—Duty at Tennallytown, Md., till October 10, 1861, and at Camp Pierpont, near Langley, Va., till March, 1862. Expedition to Grinnell's Farm December 6, 1861. Advance on Manassas, Va., March 10-15, 1862. McDowell's advance on Falmouth April 9-19. Duty at Fredericksburg till June. Moved to White House June

11-13. Seven days before Richmond June 25-July 1. Battles of Mechanicsville June 26; Gaines' Mill June 27; Charles City Cross Roads and Glendale June 30; Malvern Hill July 1. At Harrison's Landing till August 16. Movement to join Pope August 16-26. Battles of Groveton August 29; Bull Run August 30. Maryland Campaign September 6-24. Battles of South Mountain September 14. Antietam September 16-17. Duty in Maryland till October 30. Movement to Falmouth, Va., October 30-November 19. Battle of Fredericksburg December 12-15. "Mud March" January 20-24, 1863. Ordered to Washington, D. C., February 6. Duty in the Defences of Washington and Alexandria till June 25. Joined Army of Potomac in the field. Battle of Gettysburg, Pa., July 1-3. Pursuit of Lee July 5-24. Bristoe Campaign October 9-22. Advance to line of the Rappahannock November 7-8. Rappahannock Station November 7. Mine Run Campaign November 26-December 2. Duty at Alexandria till May, 1864. Rapidan Campaign May, 1864. Battles of the Wilderness May 5-7. Laurel Hill May 8. Spottsylvania May 8-12. Spottsylvania Court House May 12-21. Assault on the Salient May 12. Harris Farm May 19. North Anna River May 23-26. Jericho Ford May 25. Line of the Pamunkey May 26-28. Totopotomoy May 28-31. Left front May 31. Mustered out June 13, 1864.

Regiment lost during service 14 Officers and 127 Enlisted men killed and mortally wounded and 68 Enlisted men by disease. Total 209.

5th REGIMENT MILITIA INFANTRY.

Called September 4, 1862, to resist Lee's invasion of Maryland. Disbanded September 24, 1862.

6th REGIMENT INFANTRY.—(3 MONTHS.)

Organized at Harrisburg April 22, 1861. Moved to Philadelphia April 22, and duty there till May 7. Duty along Pittsburg, Wilmington & Baltimore Railroad May 7-28. One Company at Newark, one Company at Chesapeake City, one Company at North East, one Company at Charleston, three Companies at Elkton and three Companies at Perryville. Moved to Chambersburg May 28. Attached to George H. Thomas' Brigade, 1st Division, Patterson's Army. March to Greencastle June 6. Cross Potomac and advance on Martinsburg Road June 15. At Williamsport June 16-24. At Downsville till July 1. Falling Waters July 2. Occupation of Martinsburg July 3. Advance on Bunker Hill July 15. Moved to Charleston July 17. Mustered out July 27, 1861.

6th REGIMENT RESERVES INFANTRY.—(35th VOLUNTEERS.)

Organized at Harrisburg June, 1861. At Camp Biddle, Greencastle, Pa., July 12-22, 1861. Moved to Washington, D. C., July 22. Mustered into United States service July 27, 1861. Attached to 3rd Brigade, McCall's Pennsylvania Reserves Division, Army of the Potomac, to March, 1862. 3rd Brigade, 2nd Division, 1st Army Corps, Army of the Potomac, to April, 1862. 3rd Brigade, McCall's Division, Dept. of the Rappahannock, to June, 1862. 3rd Brigade, 3rd Division, 5th Army Corps, Army of the Potomac, to July, 1862. 1st Brigade, 3rd Division, 5th Army Corps, to August, 1862. 1st Brigade, 3rd Division, 3rd Army Corps, Army of Virginia, to September, 1862. 1st Brigade, 3rd Division, 1st Army Corps, Army of the Potomac, to February, 1863. 1st Brigade, Pennsylvania Reserve Division, 22nd Corps, Dept. of Washington, to June, 1863. 1st Brigade, 3rd Division, 5th Army Corps, Army of the Potomac, to June, 1864.

SERVICE.—Duty at Tennallytown, Md., July 27 to October 10, 1861, and at Camp Pierpont, near Langley, Va., till March, 1862. Expedition to Grinnell's Farm December 6, 1861. Action at Dranesville December 20. Advance on Manassas, Va., March 10-15, 1862. McDowell's advance on Falmouth, Va., April 9-19. Duty at Fredericksburg, Va., till June. Moved to White House June 11-13. Seven days before Richmond June 25-July 1. Guarding supplies at Tunstall's Station and White

House June 26-July 2. At Harrison's Landing till August 16. Movement to join Pope August 16-26. Battles of Gainesville August 28; Groveton August 29; Bull Run August 30. Maryland Campaign September 6-24. Battles of South Mountain September 14; Antietam September 16-17. Near Sharpsburg till September 26. Movement to Falmouth, Va., September 26-November 19. Battle of Fredericksburg December 12-15. "Mud March" January 20-24, 1863. Ordered to Washington, D. C., February 6, and duty there and at Alexandria till June 25, 1863. Rejoined Army of the Potomac in the field. Battle of Gettysburg, Pa., July 1-3. Pursuit of Lee July 5-24. Bristoe Campaign October 9-22. Advance to line of the Rappahannock November 7-8. Rappahannock Station November 7. Mine Run Campaign November 26-December 2. Bristoe Station February 1, 1864. Rapidan Campaign May. Battles of the Wilderness May 5-7; Laurel Hill May 8; Spottsylvania May 8-12; Spottsylvania Court House May 12-21. Assault on the Salient May 12. Harris Farm May 19. North Anna River May 23-26. Jericho Ford May 25. Line of the Pamunkey May 26-28. Totopotomoy May 28-31. Mustered out June 11, 1864.

Regiment lost during service 3 Officers and 107 Enlisted men killed and mortally wounded and 73 Enlisted men by disease. Total 183.

6th REGIMENT MILITIA INFANTRY.

Called September 4, 1862, to repel Lee's invasion of Maryland. Disbanded September 24, 1862.

7th REGIMENT INFANTRY.—(3 MONTHS.)

Organized at Harrisburg April 23, 1861. Moved to Chambersburg April 23, and duty there till June 8. At Camp Williams June 8-14. Attached to Williams' 3rd Brigade, Cadwalader's 1st Division, Patterson's Army. Advance to Williamsport June 14-16. Skirmish with Cavalry June 25. Occupation of Martinsburg July 3. Advance on Bunker Hill July 15. At Keyes Ford July 20. Mustered out July 29, 1861.

7th REGIMENT RESERVES INFANTRY.—(36th VOLUNTEERS.)

Organized at Camp Curtin, Harrisburg, July, 1861. Ordered to Washington, D. C., July 21, and mustered into United States service July 27, 1861. Attached to 2nd Brigade, McCall's Pennsylvania Reserves Division, Army of the Potomac, to March, 1862. 2nd Brigade, 2nd Division, 1st Army Corps, Army of the Potomac, to April, 1862. 2nd Brigade, McCall's Division, Dept. of the Rappahannock, to June, 1862. 2nd Brigade, 3rd Division, 5th Army Corps, Army of the Potomac, to August, 1862. 2nd Brigade, 3rd Division, 3rd Corps, Army of Virginia, to September, 1862. 2nd Brigade, 3rd Division, 1st Army Corps, Army of the Potomac, to February, 1863. 2nd Brigade, Pennsylvania Reserves Division, 22nd Army Corps, Dept. of Washington, to April, 1864. 1st Brigade, 3rd Division, 5th Army Corps, Army of the Potomac, to June, 1864.

SERVICE.—Duty at Tennallytown, Md., August 2 to October 10, 1861, and at Camp Pierpont, near Langley, till March, 1862. Skirmish at Great Falls September 4, 1861. Expedition to Grinnell's Farm December 6. Advance on Manassas, Va., March 10-15. At Fairfax Station till April 9. At Manassas Junction till April 17. At Catlett's Station till May 11, and at Falmouth till June 9. Moved to the Virginia Peninsula June 9-11. Seven days before Richmond June 25-July 1. Battles of Mechanicsville June 26; Gaines Mill June 27; Charles City Cross Roads and Glendale June 30; Malvern Hill July 1. At Harrison's Landing till August 16. Movement to join Pope August 16-26. Battles of Groveton August 29; Bull Run August 30. Maryland Campaign September 6-24. Battles of South Mountain, Md., September 14; Antietam September 16-17. Duty in Maryland till October 30. Movement to Falmouth, Va., October 30-November 19. Battle of Fredericksburg December 12-15. "Mud March" January 20-24, 1863. Ordered to Washington, D. C., February 6, and duty there and at Alexandria till April, 1864.

Rapidan Campaign May. Battle of the Wilderness May 5-7. Regiment captured except Company "B." Spottsylvania May 8-12. Laurel Hill May 8. Spottsylvania Court House May 12-21. Assault on the Salient May 12. Harris Farm May 19. North Anna River May 23-26. Jericho Ford May 25. Line of the Pamunkey May 26-28. Totopotomoy May 28-31. Left front May 31. Mustered out June 16, 1864.

Regiment lost during service 3 Officers and 80 Enlisted men killed and mortally wounded and 135 Enlisted men by disease. Total 218.

7th REGIMENT MILITIA INFANTRY.

Called September 4, 1862, to resist Lee's invasion of Maryland. Disbanded September 24, 1862.

8th REGIMENT INFANTRY.—(3 MONTHS.)

Organized at Camp Curtin, Harrisburg, April 23, 1861. Duty at Chambersburg till June 7. Attached to Williams' 3rd Brigade, Cadwalader's 1st Division, Patterson's Army. Moved to Greencastle June 7. Guard duty along the Potomac. Guard of stores and fords at Williamsport July 2. Falling Waters July 2. Ordered to join Brigade at Martinsburg July 6. Advance on Bunker Hill July 15. Guard at Keyes Ford July 20. Mustered out July 29, 1861.

8th REGIMENT RESERVES INFANTRY.—(37th VOLUNTEERS.)

Organized at Pittsburg July, 1861. Ordered to Washington, D. C., July 30. Attached to 1st Brigade, McCall's Pennsylvania Reserves Division, Army of the Potomac, to March, 1862. 1st Brigade, 2nd Division, 1st Army Corps, Army of the Potomac, to April, 1862. 1st Brigade, McCall's Division, Dept. of the Rappahannock, to June, 1862. 2nd Brigade, 2nd Division, Dept. of the Rappahannock, to June, 1862. 2nd Brigade, 3rd Division, 5th Army Corps, Army of the Potomac, to August, 1862. 2nd Brigade, 3rd Division, 3rd Corps, Army of Virginia, to September, 1862. 2nd Brigade, 3rd Division, 1st Army Corps, Army of the Potomac, to February, 1863. 2nd Brigade, Pennsylvania Reserves Corps, 22nd Corps, Dept. of Washington, to April, 1863. District of Alexandria, 22nd Corps, to April, 1864. 3rd Brigade, 3rd Division, 5th Army Corps, Army of the Potomac, to May, 1864.

SERVICE.—Duty at Tennallytown, Md., August 2 to October 10, 1861, and at Camp Pierpont, near Langley, Va., till March, 1862. Skirmish at Great Falls September 4, 1861. Advance on Manassas, Va., March 10-15, 1862. McDowell's advance on Falmouth April 9-19. Duty at Fredericksburg till June. Moved to White House June 9-11. Seven days before Richmond June 25-July 1. Battles of Mechanicsville June 26; Gaines Mill June 27; Charles City Cross Roads and Glendale June 30; Malvern Hill July 1. At Harrison's Landing till August 16. Movement to join Pope August 16-26. Battles of Gainesville August 28; Groveton August 29; Bull Run August 30. Maryland Campaign September 6-24. Battles of South Mountain, Md., September 14; Antietam September 16-17. Duty in Maryland till October 30. Movement to Falmouth, Va., October 30-November 19. Battles of Fredericksburg, Va., December 12-15. "Mud March" January 20-24, 1863. Ordered to Washington, D. C., February 6, and duty there and at Alexandria till April, 1864. Rapidan Campaign. Battles of the Wilderness, Va., May 5-7; Laurel Hill May 8; Spottsylvania May 8-17. Assault on the Salient May 12. Left the front May 17. Mustered out May 24, 1864.

Regiment lost during service 5 Officers and 153 Enlisted men killed and mortally wounded and 68 Enlisted men by disease. Total 226.

8th REGIMENT MILITIA INFANTRY.

Called September 4, 1862, to repel Lee's invasion of Maryland. Disbanded September 24, 1862.

9th REGIMENT INFANTRY.—(3 MONTHS.)

Organized at Camp Curtin, Harrisburg, April 24, 1861. Moved to Camp Wayne, West Chester, May 4; thence to Hare's Corners, Delaware, May 26, and duty there till June 6. Moved to Chambersburg, Pa., June 6. Attached to 4th Brigade, 1st Division, Patterson's Army. Duty at Chambersburg till June 13. Advance to the Potomac June 13-16. Near Williamsport till July 1. Failing Waters July 2. Occupation of Martinsburg July 3. Advance to Bunker Hill July 15. At Charlestown July 17-21, thence moved to Harrisburg via Hagerstown. Mustered out July 29, 1861.

9th REGIMENT RESERVES INFANTRY.—(38th VOLUNTEERS.)

Organized at Pittsburg July, 1861. Ordered to Washington, D. C., July 22. Mustered into United States service July 27, 1861. Attached to 3rd Brigade, McCall's Pennsylvania Reserves Division, Army of the Potomac, to March, 1862. 3rd Brigade, 2nd Division, 1st Army Corps, Army of the Potomac, to April, 1862. 3rd Brigade, McCall's Division, Dept. of the Rappahannock, to June, 1862. 3rd Brigade, 3rd Division, 5th Army Corps, Army of the Potomac, to August, 1862. 3rd Brigade, 3rd Division, 3rd Army Corps, Army of Virginia, to September, 1862. 3rd Brigade, 3rd Division, 1st Army Corps, Army of the Potomac, to February, 1863. 3rd Brigade, Pennsylvania Reserves Division, 22nd Army Corps, Dept. of Washington, to June, 1863. 3rd Brigade, 3rd Division, 5th Army Corps, Army of the Potomac, to May, 1864.

SERVICE.—Camp at Capital Hill, Washington, till August 5, and at Tennallytown, Md., till October 10. Picket at Great Falls September 9-16. Moved to Camp Pierpont, near Langley, Va., October 10, 1861, and duty there till March 10, 1862. Companies "A," "B," "D," "F" and "G" on reconnoissance to Hunter's Mills November 19. Expedition to Gunnell's Farm December 6, and action at Dranesville December 20, 1861. Advance on Manassas, Va., March 10-15, 1862. McDowell's advance on Falmouth April 9-19. Duty at Fredericksburg till June. Moved to White House, Va., June 9-12. Seven days before Richmond June 25-July 1. Battles of Mechanicsville June 26. Gaines Mill June 27. Charles City Cross Roads or Glendale June 30. Malvern Hill July 1. At Harrison's Landing till August 16. Movement to join Pope August 16-26. Battles of Groveton August 29; Bull Run August 30. Maryland Campaign September 6-24. Battles of South Mountain, Md., September 14; Antietam September 16-17. Duty in Maryland till October 30. Movement to Falmouth, Va., October 30-November 19. Battle of Fredericksburg December 12-15. "Mud March" January 20-24, 1863. Ordered to Washington, D. C., February 6. Duty there and at Alexandria till June 25. Ordered to rejoin Army of the Potomac in the field. Battle of Gettysburg, Pa., July 1-3. Pursuit of Lee July 5-24. Bristoe Campaign October 9-22. Advance to line of the Rappahannock November 7-8. Rappahannock Station November 7. Mine Run Campaign November 26-December 2. Rapidan Campaign. Battle of the Wilderness May 5, 1864. Ordered home while in line of battle. Mustered out May 12, 1864.

Regiment lost during service 6 Officers and 131 Enlisted men killed and mortally wounded and 1 Officer and 49 Enlisted men by disease. Total 187.

9th REGIMENT MILITIA INFANTRY.

Called September 4, 1862, to repel Lee's invasion of Maryland. Disbanded September 24, 1862.

10th REGIMENT INFANTRY.—(3 MONTHS.)

Organized at Camp Curtin, Harrisburg, April 26, 1861. Moved to Chambersburg May 1, and duty there till June 8. At Newcastle till June 16. Attached to 3rd Brigade, 1st Division, Patterson's Army. March to Williamsport June 16. Occupation of Martinsburg July 3. Advance on Bunker Hill July 15. Moved to Harper's Ferry July 23. Mustered out July 31, 1861.

10th REGIMENT RESERVES INFANTRY.—(39th VOLUNTEERS.)

Organized at Camp Wilkins, near Pittsburg, June and July, 1861. Ordered to Harrisburg, Pa., July 18, and

mustered in July 21, 1861. Moved to Baltimore, Md., July 22; thence to Washington, D. C., July 24. Attached to 3rd Brigade, McCall's Pennsylvania Reserves Division, Army of the Potomac, to March, 1862. 3rd Brigade, 2nd Division, 1st Army Corps, Army of the Potomac, to April, 1862. 3rd Brigade, McCall's Division, Dept. of the Rappahannock, to June, 1862. 3rd Brigade, 3rd Division, 5th Army Corps, Army of the Potomac, to August, 1862. 3rd Brigade, 3rd Division, 3rd Corps, Army of Virginia, to September, 1862. 3rd Brigade, 3rd Division, 1st Army Corps, Army of the Potomac, to February, 1863. 3rd Brigade, Pennsylvania Reserves Division, 22nd Corps, Dept. of Washington, to June, 1863. 3rd Brigade, 3rd Division, 5th Army Corps, Army of the Potomac, to June, 1864.

SERVICE.—At Tennallytown, Md., August 1 to October 10, 1861, and at Camp Pierpont, near Langley, Va., till March, 1862. Expedition to Gunnell's Mills December 6, 1861. Action at Dranesville December 20. Advance on Manassas, Va., March 10-15, 1862. McDowell's advance on Falmouth April 9-19. Duty at Fredericksburg till June. Moved to White House June 9-12. Seven days before Richmond June 25-July 1. Battles of Mechanicsville June 26; Gaines Mill June 27; Charles City Cross Roads and Glendale June 30; Malvern Hill July 1. At Harrison's Landing till August 16. Movement to join Pope August 16-26. Battles of Gainesville August 28; Groveton August 29; Bull Run August 30. Maryland Campaign September 6-24. Battles of South Mountain, Md., September 14; Antietam September 16-17. Duty in Maryland till October 30. Movement to Falmouth, Va., October 30-November 19. Battle of Fredericksburg December 12-15. "Mud March" January 20-24, 1863. Ordered to Washington, D. C., February 6, and duty there and at Alexandria till June 25. Ordered to join Army of the Potomac in the field. Battle of Gettysburg, Pa., July 1-3. Pursuit of Lee July 5-24. Bristoe Campaign October 9-22. Advance to line of the Rappahannock November 7-8. Rappahannock Station November 7. Mine Run Campaign November 26-December 2. Bristoe Station April 15, 1864 (Detachment). Rapidan Campaign May 4-31. Battles of the Wilderness May 5-7; Laurel Hill May 8; Spottsylvania May 8-12; Spottsylvania Court House May 12-21. Assault on the Salient May 12. Harris Farm May 19. North Anna River May 23-26. Jericho Ford May 25. On line of the Totopotomoy May 28-31. Left front May 31. Mustered out June 11, 1864.

Regiment lost during service 7 Officers and 153 Enlisted men killed and mortally wounded and 47 Enlisted men by disease. Total 207.

10th REGIMENT MILITIA INFANTRY.

Called September 4, 1862, to repel Lee's invasion of Maryland. Disbanded September 24, 1862.

11th REGIMENT INFANTRY.—(3 MONTHS.)

Organized at Camp Curtin, Harrisburg, April 26, 1861. Ordered to Camp Wayne, West Chester, Pa., and duty there and guarding Pittsburg, Wilmington & Baltimore Railroad till June 18. Ordered to Chambersburg June 18. Attached to Negley's 5th Brigade, Abercrombie's 2nd Division, Patterson's Army. Transferred to 6th Brigade June 20. Moved to Williamsport, Md., June 29. Falling Waters July 2. Occupation of Martinsburg July 3. Advance on Bunker Hill July 15. Moved to Harper's Ferry July 25. Mustered out August 1, 1861.

11th REGIMENT INFANTRY.—(3 YEARS.)

Organized at Harrisburg and in Westmoreland County August, 1861. At Camp Curtin till November 27. Moved to Baltimore, Md., November 27; thence to Annapolis, Md. Attached to Annapolis, Md., Middle Department, to April, 1862. Wadsworth's Command, Military District of Washington, to May, 1862. 3rd Brigade, Ord's Division, Dept. of the Rappahannock, to June, 1862. 3rd Brigade, 2nd Division, 3rd Corps, Army of Virginia, to September, 1862. 3rd Brigade, 2nd Division, 1st Army Corps, Army of the Potomac, to May, 1863. 2nd

Brigade, 2nd Division, 1st Army Corps, to July, 1863. 1st Brigade, 2nd Division, 1st Army Corps, July, 1863. 2nd Brigade, 2nd Division, 1st Army Corps, to March, 1864. 2nd Brigade, 2nd Division, 5th Army Corps, to May, 1864. 2nd Brigade, 3rd Division, 5th Army Corps, to March, 1865. 3rd Brigade, 3rd Division, 5th Army Corps, to July, 1865.

SERVICE.—Duty at Annapolis, Md., till April 9, 1862. Moved to Washington, D. C., April 9-10; thence to Manassas Junction April 17, and guard Manassas Gap Railroad till May 12. Moved to Catlett's Station May 12 and to Falmouth May 14. Expedition to Front Royal June. Battle of Cedar Mountain August 9. Pope's Campaign in Northern Virginia August 16-September 2. Fords of the Rappahannock August 21-23. Warrenton August 26. Thoroughfare Gap August 28. Bull Run August 30. Chantilly September 1. Maryland Campaign September 6-24. Battles of South Mountain September 14. Antietam September 16-17. Duty at Sharpsburg till October 30. Movement to Falmouth, Va., October 30-November 19. Battle of Fredericksburg, Va., December 12-15. "Mud March" January 20-24, 1863. At Falmouth and Belle Plain till April 27. Chancellorsville Campaign April 27-May 6. Operations at Pollock's Mill Creek April 29-May 2. Fitzhugh's Crossing April 29-30. Chancellorsville May 2-5. Gettysburg (Pa.) Campaign June 11-July 24. Battle of Gettysburg July 1-3 (served with 1st Brigade July 1 to 18). Duty on the Rapidan till October. Bristoe Campaign October 9-22. Advance to line of the Rappahannock November 7-8. Mine Run Campaign November 26-December 2. Demonstration on the Rapidan February 6-7, 1864. Regiment re-enlisted January 5, 1864. Veterans on furlough February 5 to March 28. Rapidan Campaign May-June. Battles of the Wilderness May 5-7. Laurel Hill May 8; Spottsylvania May 8-12; Spottsylvania Court House May 12-21. Assault on the Salient May 12. North Anna River May 23-26. Jericho Ford May 25. On line of the Pamunkey May 26-28. Totopotomoy May 28-31. Cold Harbor June 1-12. Bethesda Church June 1-3. White Oak Swamp June 13. Before Petersburg June 16-18. Siege of Petersburg June 16, 1864, to April 2, 1865. Mine Explosion Petersburg July 30, 1864 (Reserve). Weldon Railroad August 18-21. Reconnoissance toward Dinwiddie Court House September 15. Warren's Raid to Weldon Railroad December 7-12. Dabney's Mills, Hatcher's Run, February 5-7, 1865. Appomattox Campaign March 28-April 9. Lewis Farm, Gravelly Run, March 29. White Oak Road March 31. Five Forks April 1. Appomattox Court House April 9. Surrender of Lee and his army. Moved to Washington May. Grand Review May 23. Mustered out July 1, 1865.

Regiment lost during service 12 Officers and 224 Enlisted men killed and mortally wounded and 4 Officers and 177 Enlisted men by disease. Total 417.

11th REGIMENT RESERVES INFANTRY.—(40th VOLUNTEERS.)

Organized at Camp Wright, near Pittsburg, June, 1861. Moved to Harrisburg, Pa., June 24; thence to Baltimore, Md., June 25, and to Washington, D. C., June 26. Mustered into United States service June 29, 1861. Attached to 2nd Brigade, McCall's Pennsylvania Reserves Division, Army of the Potomac, to March, 1862. 2nd Brigade, 2nd Division, 1st Army Corps, Army of the Potomac, to April, 1862. 2nd Brigade, McCall's Division, Dept. of the Rappahannock, to June, 1862. 2nd Brigade, 3rd Division, 5th Army Corps, to August, 1862. 3rd Brigade, 3rd Division, 3rd Corps, Army of Virginia, to September, 1862. 3rd Brigade, 3rd Division, 1st Corps, Army of the Potomac, to February, 1863. 3rd Brigade, Pennsylvania Reserves Division, 22nd Corps, Dept. of Washington, to June, 1863. 3rd Brigade, 3rd Division, 5th Army Corps, Army of the Potomac, to November, 1863. 1st Brigade, 3rd Division, 5th Corps, to June, 1864.

SERVICE.—Duty at Tennallytown, Md., and picket at Great Falls August 2 to October 10, 1861. At Camp Pierpont, near Langley, Va., till March, 1862. Expedition to Grinnell's Farm December 6, 1861. Advance on Manassas, Va., March 10-15, 1862. McDowell's advance on Falmouth April 9-19. Duty at Manassas Junction, Catlett's Station, and Falmouth, till June. Moved to White House June 9-12. Seven days before Richmond June 25-July 1. Battles of Mechanicsville June 26; Gaines' Mill June 27 (most of Regiment captured, exchanged August 5, 1862); Charles City Cross Roads, Glendale, June 30; Malvern Hill July 1. At Harrison's Landing till August 16. Movement to join Pope August 16-26. Battles of Groveton August 29; Bull Run August 30. Maryland Campaign September 6-24. Battles of South Mountain, Md., September 14; Antietam September 16-17. Duty in Maryland till October 30. Movement to Falmouth, Va., October 30-November 19. Battle of Fredericksburg, Va., December 12-15. "Mud March" January 20-24, 1863. Moved to Washington, D. C., February 6. Duty there and at Alexandria till June 25. Ordered to rejoin Army of the Potomac in the field. Battle of Gettysburg, Pa., July 1-3. Pursuit of Lee July 5-24. Duty on the Rapidan till October. Bristoe Campaign October 9-22. Advance to line of the Rappahannock November 7-8. Rappahannock Station November 7. Mine Run Campaign November 26-December 2. Duty at Alexandria till April, 1864. Rapidan Campaign May 4-30. Battles of the Wilderness May 5-7; Laurel Hill May 8; Spottsylvania May 8-12; Spottsylvania Court House May 12-21. Assault on the Salient May 12. Harris Farm May 19. North Anna River May 23-26. Jericho Ford May 25. On line of the Pamunkey May 26-28. Totopotomoy May 28-30. Left front May 30. Mustered out June 13, 1864.

Regiment lost during service 11 Officers and 185 Enlisted men killed and mortally wounded and 1 Officer and 112 Enlisted men by disease. Total 309.

11th REGIMENT MILITIA INFANTRY.

Called September 4, 1862, to repel Lee's invasion of Maryland. Disbanded September 24, 1862.

12th REGIMENT INFANTRY.—(3 MONTHS.)

Organized at Pittsburg April 22, 1861. Moved to Harrisburg, Pa., April 24; thence to York, Pa., April 25 and duty there till May 25. Attached to 3rd Brigade, 1st Division, Patterson's Army. Guard duty on Northern Central Railroad from State line to Baltimore Md. Headquarters at Cockeyville, Md., till August. Mustered out August 5, 1861.

12th REGIMENT RESERVES INFANTRY.—(41st VOLUNTEERS.)

Organized at Harrisburg August, 1861. At Camp Curtin till August 10. Moved to Washington, D. C.; thence to Tennallytown, Md., August 10-13. Attached to 3rd Brigade, McCall's Pennsylvania Reserves Division, Army of the Potomac, to March, 1862. 3rd Brigade, 2nd Division, 1st Army Corps, Army of the Potomac, to April, 1862. 3rd Brigade, McCall's Division, Dept. of the Rappahannock, to June, 1862. 3rd Brigade, 3rd Division, 5th Army Corps, Army of the Potomac, to August, 1862. 3rd Brigade, 3rd Division, 3rd Corps, Army of Virginia, to September, 1862. 3rd Brigade, 3rd Division, 1st Army Corps, Army of the Potomac, to February, 1863. 3rd Brigade, Pennsylvania Reserves Division, 22nd Corps, Dept. of Washington, to June, 1863. 3rd Brigade, 3rd Division, 5th Army Corps, Army of the Potomac, to June, 1864.

SERVICE.—Duty at Tennallytown, Md., August 13 to October 10, 1861, and at Camp Pierpont, near Langley, Va., to March, 1862. Expedition to Grinnell's Farm December 6, 1861. Action at Dranesville December 20, 1861. Advance on Manassas, Va., March 10-15, 1862. McDowell's advance on Falmouth April 9-19. Duty at Fredericksburg till June. Moved to White House June 9-12. Seven days before Richmond June 25-July 1. Battles of Mechanicsville June 26; Gaines' Mill June 27; Charles City Cross Roads, Glendale June 30; Malvern Hill July 1. At Harrison's Landing till August 16. Movement to join Pope August 16-26. Battles of

Gainesville August 28; Groveton August 30; Bull Run August 30. Maryland Campaign September 6-24. Battles of South Mountain September 14; Antietam September 16-17. Duty in Maryland till October 30. Movement to Falmouth, Va., October 30-November 19. Battle of Fredericksburg, Va., December 12-15. "Mud March" January 20-24, 1863. Ordered to Washington, D. C., February 6, and duty there and at Alexandria till June 25. Ordered to rejoin Army of the Potomac in the field. Battle of Gettysburg, Pa., July 1-3. Pursuit of Lee July 5-24. Duty on the Rapidan till October. Bristoe Campaign October 9-22. Advance to line of the Rappahannock November 7-8. Rappahannock Station November 7. Mine Run Campaign November 26-December 2. Guard Orange & Alexander Railroad till April, 1864. Rapidan Campaign May 4-31. Battles of the Wilderness May 5-7; Laurel Hill May 8; Spottsylvania May 8-12; Spottsylvania Court House May 12-21. Assault on the Salient May 12. Harris Farm May 19. North Anna River May 23-26. Jericho Mills, or Ford, May 25. Line of the Pamunkey May 26-28. Totopotomoy May 28-31. Mustered out June 11, 1864.

Regiment lost during service 1 Officer and 110 Enlisted men killed and mortally wounded and 1 Officer and 69 Enlisted men by disease. Total 181.

12th REGIMENT MILITIA INFANTRY.

Called September 4, 1862, to repel Lee's invasion of Maryland. Disbanded September 24, 1862.

13th REGIMENT INFANTRY.—(3 MONTHS.)

Organized at Camp Curtin, Harrisburg, and mustered in April 25, 1861. Moved to York, Pa., April 26, and duty there till June 4. Moved to Chambersburg June 4. Attached to 4th Brigade, 1st Division, Patterson's Army. Moved to Greencastle June 14, thence advance on Williamsport June 15-16. Goose Creek, Edward's Ferry, June 18. At Williamsport till July 4. Escort Rhode Island Battery to Martinsburg. Moved to Bunker Hill July 16, and to Charlestown July 17. To Harper's Ferry July 21. Moved to Harrisburg, Pa., and mustered out August 6, 1861.

13th REGIMENT RESERVES INFANTRY.—1st RIFLES.
(42nd VOLUNTEERS. "BUCKTAILS.")

Organized at Harrisburg June 21, 1861. Moved to a point opposite Cumberland, Md., June 22; thence into West Virginia in support of Lew Wallace. Duty on State line till July 27. Ordered to Harper's Ferry August 1. Assigned to George H. Thomas' Brigade, Banks' Division, and duty at Harper's Ferry till October. Moved to Tennallytown, Md., October 1. Attached to 2nd Brigade, McCall's Pennsylvania Reserves Division, Army of the Potomac, to March, 1862. 1st Brigade, 2nd Division, 1st Army Corps, Army of the Potomac, to April, 1862. 3rd Brigade, McCall's Division, Dept. of the Rappahannock, to June, 1862. (Cos. "C," "G," "H" and "I" detached May 12, 1862, and attached to Bayard's Cavalry Brigade, Dept. of the Rappahannock, to June, 1862. 1st Corps, Army of Virginia, to August, 1862.) 3rd Brigade, 3rd Division, 5th Army Corps, Army of the Potomac, to August, 1862. 3rd Brigade, 3rd Division, 3rd Corps, Army of Virginia, to September, 1862. 1st Brigade, 3rd Division, 1st Army Corps, Army of the Potomac, to February, 1863. 1st Brigade, Pennsylvania Reserve Division, 22nd Corps, Dept. of Washington, to June, 1863. 1st Brigade, 3rd Division, 5th Army Corps, Army of the Potomac, to June, 1864.

SERVICE.—Moved from Tennallytown, Md., to Camp Pierpont, near Langley, Va., October 10, 1861, and duty there till March, 1862. Expedition to Hunter's Mills October 20, 1861 (Cos. "A," "G," "H," "I" and "K"). Expedition to Grinnell's Farm December 6. Action at Dranesville December 20. Advance on Manassas, Va., March 10-15. McDowell's advance on Falmouth April 9-19. Duty at Fredericksburg till June. (Cos. "C," "G," "H" and "I" reported to Colonel Bayard May 15, 1862. Pursuit of Jackson up the Shenandoah Valley May 25-June 6. Harrisonburg June 1. Strasburg June 2.

Strasburg and Staunton Road June 2. Woodstock June 3. Mount Jackson June 3. Harrisonburg June 6-7. Cross Keys June 8. Pope's Campaign in Northern Virginia August 16-September 2. Catlett's Station August 22. Bull Run Bridge August 30-31. Rejoined Regiment September 7, 1862.) Regiment moved to White House June 9-12. Seven days before Richmond June 25-July 1. Battles of Mechanicsville June 26; Meadow Bridge, near Mechanicsville, June 26; Gaines Mill June 27; Savage Station June 29; Charles City Cross Roads or Glendale June 30; Malvern Hill July 1. At Harrison's Landing till August 16. Movement to join Pope August 16-26. Battles of Gainesville August 28; Groveton August 29; Bull Run August 30. Maryland Campaign September 6-24. Battles of South Mountain September 14; Antietam September 16-17. Duty in Maryland till October 30. Movement to Falmouth, Va., October 30-November 19. Battle of Fredericksburg December 12-15. "Mud March" January 20-24, 1863. Ordered to Washington, D. C., February 6, and duty there and at Alexandria till June 25. Ordered to join Army of the Potomac in the field. Battle of Gettysburg, Pa., July 1-3. Pursuit of Lee July 5-24. Duty on the Rapidan till October. Bristoe Campaign October 9-22. Advance to line of the Rappahannock November 7-8. Rappahannock Station November 7. Mine Run Campaign November 26-December 2. Guard Orange & Alexandria Railroad till April, 1864. Rapidan Campaign May 4-31. Battles of the Wilderness May 5-7; Laurel Hill May 8; Spottsylvania May 8-12; Spottsylvania Court House May 12-21. Assault on the Salient May 12. Harris Farm May 19. North Anna River May 23-26. Jericho Ford May 25. On line of the Pamunkey May 26-28. Totopotomoy May 28-31. Veterans and Recruits transferred to 190th Pennsylvania June 1. Mustered out June 11, 1864.

Regiment lost during service 11 Officers and 151 Enlisted men killed and mortally wounded and 2 Officers and 88 Enlisted men by disease. Total 252.

13th REGIMENT MILITIA INFANTRY.

Called September 4, 1862, to repel Lee's invasion of Maryland. Disbanded September 24, 1862.

14th REGIMENT INFANTRY.—(3 MONTHS.)

Organized at Harrisburg April 30, 1861. Moved to Lancaster May 9, and duty there till June 3. At Chambersburg June 3-16. Attached to Negley's 5th Brigade, Keim's 2nd Division, Patterson's Army. At Hagerstown, Md., June 16-20. Duty near Sharpsburg till July 2. Falling Waters July 2. Company "A" captured by Ashby's Cavalry and sent to Richmond, Va. Occupation of Martinsburg July 3. Advance to Bunker Hill July 15. Moved to Charlestown July 18. Skirmish at Charlestown July 21. Moved to Harper's Ferry July 21, thence to Carlisle, Pa., and mustered out August 7, 1861.

14th REGIMENT RESERVES.—(43rd VOLUNTEERS.)
(See 1st Cavalry.)

14th REGIMENT MILITIA INFANTRY.

Called September 4, 1862, to repel Lee's invasion of Maryland. Disbanded September 24.

15th REGIMENT INFANTRY.—(3 MONTHS.)

Organized at Camp Curtin, Harrisburg, April 26, and duty there till May 9. At Lancaster, Pa., till June 3, and at Chambersburg, Pa., till June 16. Attached to Negley's 5th Brigade, Keim's 2nd Division, Patterson's Army. Moved to Hagerstown June 16, and to Williamsport June 18. Affair with Ashby's Cavalry July 2 (Co. "I" captured). Occupation of Martinsburg, Va., July 3. Advance on Bunker Hill July 15. At Charlestown July 17-25. At Carlisle, Pa., July 27-August 8. Mustered out August 8, 1861.

15th REGIMENT RESERVES.—(44th VOLUNTEERS.)
(See 1st Light Artillery.)

15th REGIMENT MILITIA INFANTRY.

Called September 4, 1862, to repel Lee's invasion of Maryland. Disbanded September 24, 1862.

16th REGIMENT INFANTRY.—(3 MONTHS.)

Organized at Camp Curtin, Harrisburg, May 3, 1861. (Co. "C" mustered for three years April 20, 1861, the first Company of Pennsylvania to so volunteer.) Moved to York, Pa., May 9, and duty there till June 3. Moved to Chambersburg June 3, thence to Williamsport June 16. Attached to Miles' 4th Brigade, Cadwalader's 1st Division, Patterson's Army. At Williamsport June 16-July 2. Occupation of Martinsburg July 3. Advance on Bunker Hill July 15. At Charlestown July 17. Mustered out July 30, 1861.

16th REGIMENT MILITIA INFANTRY.

Called September 4, 1862, to repel Lee's invasion of Maryland. Disbanded September 24, 1862.

17th REGIMENT INFANTRY.—(3 MONTHS.)

Organized at Philadelphia and mustered in April 25, 1861. Designated 17th May 15, 1861. Moved to Perryville, thence to Baltimore, Md., May 8, and to Washington, D. C., May 10. Camp on Kalorama Heights till June 10. Attached to Stone's Command, Rockville Expedition, June 10-July 1. Edward's Ferry June 18. Join Patterson at Martinsburg, Va., July 7. Attached to 7th Brigade, 3rd Division, Patterson's Army. Advance on Bunker Hill July 15. March to Charleston July 17, thence to Harper's Ferry July 21. Moved to Philadelphia and mustered out August 2, 1861.

17th REGIMENT MILITIA INFANTRY.

Called September 4, 1862, to repel Lee's invasion of Maryland. Disbanded September 24, 1862.

18th REGIMENT INFANTRY.—(3 MONTHS.)

Organized at Philadelphia and mustered in April 24, 1861. At Washington Square, Philadelphia, Pa., till May 14. Moved to Baltimore, Md., and duty near Fort McHenry till May 22, and at Federal Hill till August. (Cos. "B" and "K" at Pikesville Arsenal removing stores to Fort McHenry June 12 to July 23.) Companies "B," "C," "D," "E," "G," "H" and "K" and part of "I" re-enlisted for ten days at the request of General Banks. Mustered out August 6, 1861.

18th REGIMENT MILITIA INFANTRY.

Called September 4, 1862, to repel Lee's invasion of Maryland. Disbanded September 24, 1862.

19th REGIMENT INFANTRY.—(3 MONTHS.)

Organized at Philadelphia and mustered April 27, 1861. Moved to Baltimore, Md., May 10, and provost duty near Fort McHenry till August. Mustered out August 29, 1861.

19th REGIMENT MILITIA INFANTRY.

Called September 4, 1862, to repel Lee's invasion of Maryland. Disbanded September 24, 1862.

20th REGIMENT INFANTRY.—(3 MONTHS.)

Organized at Philadelphia and mustered in April 30, 1861. Duty at Philadelphia till June. Moved to Chambersburg, Pa., and joined Patterson. Attached to 3rd Brigade, 1st Division, Patterson's Army. March to Williamsport, Md., June 16. Occupation of Martinsburg July 3. Advance on Bunker Hill July 15. Moved to Harper's Ferry July 23. Mustered out August 6, 1861.

20th REGIMENT MILITIA INFANTRY.

Called September 4, 1862, to repel Lee's invasion of Maryland. Disbanded September 24, 1862.

20th REGIMENT EMERGENCY INFANTRY.

Organized at Harrisburg June 17, 1863, to repel Lee's invasion of Pennsylvania. Duty in Dept. of the Susquehanna during Gettysburg Campaign. Mustered out August 10, 1863.

21st REGIMENT INFANTRY.—(3 MONTHS.)

Organized at Philadelphia and mustered in April 20, 1861. Moved to Chambersburg May 28. Attached to Geo. H. Thomas' Brigade, 1st Division, Patterson's Army. March to Greencastle June 6. Cross Potomac and advance on Martinsburg Road June 15. At Williamsport June 16-24. At Downsville till July 1. Falling Waters July 2. Occupation of Martinsburg July 3. Advance on Bunker Hill July 15. Moved to Charlestown July 17; thence to Harper's Ferry. Mustered out August 9, 1861.

21st REGIMENT MILITIA INFANTRY.

Called September 4, 1862, to repel Lee's invasion of Maryland. Disbanded September 24, 1862.

22nd REGIMENT INFANTRY.—(3 MONTHS.)

Organized at Philadelphia and mustered in April 23, 1861. Moved to Baltimore, Md., May 17. Duty near Fort McHenry, Locust Point, Patterson's Park and Mt. Clair till August. Mustered out August 7, 1861.

22nd REGIMENT MILITIA INFANTRY.

Called September 4, 1862, to repel Lee's invasion of Maryland. Disbanded September 24, 1862.

23rd REGIMENT INFANTRY.—(3 MONTHS.)

Organized at Philadelphia and mustered in April 21, 1861. Moved to Perryville April 21, and duty by detachments along Philadelphia, Wilmington & Baltimore Railroad till May 11. Moved to Chambersburg, Pa., May 11. Attached to Geo. H. Thomas' Brigade, 1st Division, Patterson's Army. March to Greensburg June 6. Cross Potomac and advance on Martinsburg Road June 15. At Williamsport June 16-24. At Downsville till July 1. Falling Waters July 2. Occupation of Martinsburg July 3. Advance on Bunker Hill July 15. Moved to Charlestown July 17, thence to Harper's Ferry. Mustered out July 31, 1861.

23rd REGIMENT INFANTRY.—(3 YEARS.)

Organized at Philadelphia August 31, 1861. Ordered to Washington, D. C., September. Attached to Buell's (Couch's) Division, Army of the Potomac, to March, 1862. 2nd Brigade, 1st Division, 4th Army Corps, Army of the Potomac, to July, 1862. 3rd Brigade, 1st Division, 4th Army Corps, to September, 1862. 3rd Brigade, 3rd Division, 6th Army Corps, Army of the Potomac, to October, 1862. 1st Brigade, 3rd Division, 6th Army Corps, to January, 1864. Johnson's Island, Sandusky, Ohio, to May 1864. 4th Brigade, 1st Division, 6th Army Corps, Army of the Potomac, to July, 1864. 3rd Brigade, 1st Division, 6th Corps, Army of the Shenandoah, to September, 1864.

SERVICE.—Duty in the Defences of Washington till March, 1862. Advance on Manassas, Va., March 10-15. Moved to the Virginia Peninsula March 26. Warwick River April 4. Siege of Yorktown April 5-May 4. Battle of Williamsburg May 5. Operations about Bottom's Bridge May 20-23. Reconnoissance toward Richmond May 23. Battle of Fair Oaks, Seven Pines, May 31-June 1. Seven days before Richmond June 25-July 1. White Oak Swamp and Charles City Cross Roads June 30. Malvern Hill July 1. At Harrison's Landing till August 16. Reconnoissance to Malvern Hill August 5-7. Movement to Alexandria, thence to Chantilly August 16-30. Chantilly September 1. Maryland Campaign September-October. Guard Potomac from White's Ford to Nolan's Ferry September 11-24 during battles of South Mountain and Antietam. White's Ford September 15. (Company "B" captured at Nolin's Ford September 15 by Colonel White's Command.) Moved to Downsville September 24 and picket duty on the Potomac till November 1. Movement to Falmouth, Va., November 1-19. Battle of Fredericksburg December 12-15. "Mud March" January 20-24, 1863. At Falmouth till April. Chancellorsville Campaign April 27-May 6. Operations at Franklin's Crossing April 29-May 2. Fredericksburg, Maryes Heights, May 3. Salem Heights May 3-4. Banks' Ford May 4. Operations about Depp

Run Ravine June 6-13. Battle of Gettysburg, Pa., July 2-4. At Warrenton and Culpeper to October. Bristoe Campaign October 9-22. Advance to line of the Rappahannock November 7-8. Rappahannock Station November 7 (Reserve). Mine Run Campaign November 26-December 2. Regiment re-enlisted December 30, 1863. Veterans on furlough till February 11, 1864. Moved to Johnson's Island, Lake Erie, Ohio, January 6, 1864, and guard Rebel Prisoners at that place till May 6. Moved to Washington, D. C., May 9-13; thence to Belle Plains and guard Rebel Prisoners and escort trains to the front till May 23. Rapidan Campaign May 23-June 12. North Anna River May 23-26. On line of the Pamunkey November 26-28. Totopotomoy May 28-31. Cold Harbor June 1-12. Before Petersburg June 17-19. Ream's Station, Weldon Railroad, June 22-23. Siege of Petersburg till July 9. Moved to Washington July 9-11. Repulse Early's attack on Washington July 11-12. Snicker's Gap Expedition July 14-18. Operations in Shenandoah Valley till September. Charlestown August 21. Ordered home for muster out. Mustered out September 8, 1864. Veterans and Recruits transferred to 82nd Pennsylvania September 8, 1864.

Regiment lost during service 5 Officers and 110 Enlisted men killed and mortally wounded and 3 Officers and 70 Enlisted men by disease. Total 188.

23rd REGIMENT MILITIA INFANTRY.

Called September 4, 1862, to repel Lee's invasion of Maryland. Disbanded September 24, 1862.

24th REGIMENT INFANTRY.—(3 MONTHS.)

Organized at Philadelphia and mustered in May 1, 1861. Moved to Chambersburg, Pa., June 3. Attached to Negley's 5th Brigade, Keim's 2nd Division, Patterson's Army. Moved to Hagerstown, Md., June 16; thence to Williamsport June 18. Occupation of Martinsburg July 3. Advance on Bunker Hill July 15. At Charlestown July 17. Moved to Harper's Ferry; thence to Philadelphia and mustered out August 10, 1861.

24th REGIMENT MILITIA INFANTRY.

Called September 4, 1862, to repel Lee's invasion of Maryland. Disbanded September 24, 1862.

25th REGIMENT INFANTRY.—(3 MONTHS.)

Organized by consolidation of First Defenders (5 Cos. and 5 new Cos.). Organized at Harrisburg, Pa., April 18, 1861. Moved to Washington, D. C. (see First Defenders), rest of Regiment camp near Arsenal till June 28. (Cos. "B," "E" and "H" Garrison Fort Washington till mustered out, and Cos. "A," "C" at Washington Arsenal till mustered out.) Companies "D," "F," "G," "I" and "K" march to Rockville, Md., to join Stone, June 29-30. Reported at Poolesville July 1, and moved to Sandy Hook, opposite Harper's Ferry, W. Va. Attached to Stone's 7th Brigade, Sanford's 3rd Division, Patterson's Army. March to Martinsburg July 6-8. Advance to Bunker Hill July 15. Camp at Harper's Ferry July 17-23. Mustered out August 1, 1861.

25th REGIMENT MILITIA INFANTRY.

Called September 4, 1862, for service during Lee's invasion of Maryland. Sent to Wilmington, Del., and guard Dupont Powder Works. Mustered out September 24, 1862.

26th REGIMENT INFANTRY.

Organized at Philadelphia April 20, 1861. Mustered in May 27, 1861 (a detachment attacked in streets of Baltimore April 19, 1861). Moved to Washington, D. C., June 15, 1861. Attached to Defences of Washington to August, 1861. Hooker's Brigade, Division of the Potomac, to October, 1861. Grover's Brigade, Hooker's Division, Army of the Potomac, to March, 1862. 1st Brigade, 2nd Division, 3rd Army Corps, Army of the Potomac, to March, 1864. 1st Brigade, 4th Division, 2nd Army Corps, to June, 1864.

SERVICE.—Duty in the Defences of Washington, D. C., till October, 1861, and at Budd's Ferry, Md., October 20, 1861, to April 1, 1862. Moved to the Virginia Peninsula, Siege of Yorktown, April 5-May 4. Battle of Williamsburg May 5. Battle of Fair Oaks, Seven Pines. May 31-June 1. Seven days before Richmond June 25-July 1. Oak Grove June 25. Savage Station June 29. White Oak Swamp and Glendale June 30. Malvern Hill July 1. Duty at Harrison's Landing till August 16. Action at Malvern Hill August 5. Movement to Centreville August 16-26. Pope's Campaign in Northern Virginia August 26-September 2. Bristoe Station, Kettle Run, August 27. Battles of Groveton August 29; Bull Run August 30; Chantilly September 1. Duty in the Defences of Washington, D. C., till November. Operations on Orange & Alexandria Railroad October 10-12. Movement to Falmouth, Va., November 18-28. Battle of Fredericksburg, Va., December 12-15. "Mud March" January 20-24, 1863. Operations at Rappahannock Bridge and Grove Church February 5-7. At Falmouth till April. Chancellorsville Campaign April 27-May 6. Battle of Chancellorsville May 1-5. Gettysburg (Pa.) Campaign June 11-July 24. Battle of Gettysburg (Pa.) July 1-3. Wapping Heights, Va., July 23. Duty on line of the Rapidan till October. Bristoe Campaign October 9-22. Advance to line of the Rappahannock November 7-8. Kelly's Ford November 7. Mine Run Campaign November 26-December 2. Payne's Farm November 27. Demonstration on the Rapidan February 6-7, 1864. Near Brandy Station till May. Rapidan Campaign May 4-28. Battles of the Wilderness May 5-7; Spottsylvania May 8-12; Spottsylvania Court House May 12-21. Assault on the Salient May 12. Harris Farm, on Fredericksburg Road, May 19. North Anna River May 23-26. Ox Ford May 24. Line of the Pamunkey May 26-28. Left front May 28. Mustered out June 18, 1864. Veterans and Recruits transferred to 99th Pennsylvania.

Regiment lost during service 6 Officers and 143 Enlisted men killed and mortally wounded and 2 Officers and 71 Enlisted men by disease. Total 222.

26th REGIMENT EMERGENCY MILITIA INFANTRY.

Organized at Harrisburg June 22, 1863, for the protection of Pennsylvania against Lee's invasion. Duty in Dept. of the Susquehanna, near Gettysburg, Pa., June 26. Mustered out July 31, 1863.

27th REGIMENT INFANTRY.—("WASHINGTON BRIGADE.")

Organized at Philadelphia January, 1861. Moved to Baltimore, Md., April 18. Attacked in streets of Baltimore April 19. Returned to Philadelphia and reorganized for three years. Mustered in May 31 to date from May 5, 1861. Moved to Washington, D. C., June 17-18. Attached to 1st Brigade, Miles' Division, McDowell's Army of Northeast Virginia, to August, 1861. Blenker's Brigade, Division of the Potomac, to October, 1861. Stahel's Brigade, Blenker's Division, Army of the Potomac, to March, 1862. 1st Brigade, Blenker's 2nd Division, 2nd Army Corps, Army of the Potomac, March, 1862. 1st Brigade, Blenker's Division, Dept. of the Mountains, to June, 1862. 1st Brigade, 1st Division, Army of Virginia, to September, 1862. 1st Brigade, 1st Division, 11th Army Corps, Army of the Potomac, to October, 1862. 1st Brigade, 2nd Division, 11th Corps, Army of the Potomac, to October, 1863, and Army of the Cumberland to April, 1864. 2nd Brigade, 2nd Division, 20th Army Corps, Army of the Cumberland, to May, 1864.

SERVICE.—Advance on Manassas, Va., July 16-21, 1861. Battle of Bull Run July 21. Duty in the Defences of Washington, D. C., till April, 1862. Operations in the Shenandoah Valley May to August. Battle of Cross Keys June 8. At Sperryville and Centreville till August. Pope's Campaign in Northern Virginia August 16-September 2. Battles of Groveton August 29; Bull Run August 30. Duty in the Defences of Washington, D. C., till December. Reconnoissance to Snicker's Ferry and Berryville November 28-30. March to Fredericksburg, Va., December 10-15. Duty at Falmouth and Brooks' Station till April, 1863. Operations at Welford's, Kelly's and Beverly Fords April 14-15.

Chancellorsville Campaign April 27-May 6. Battle of Chancellorsville May 1-5. Gettysburg (Pa.) Campaign June 11-July 24. Battle of Gettysburg July 1-3. Pursuit of Lee July 5-24. Duty on line of the Rapidan, near Bristoe Station, till September. Movement to Bridgeport, Ala., September 24-October 3. March along Nashville & Chattanooga Railroad to Lookout Valley, Tenn., October 25-28. Reopening Tennessee River October 26-29. Battle of Wauhatchie October 28-29. Battles of Chattanooga November 23-27; Orchard Knob November 23; Tunnel Hill November 23-24; Mission Ridge November 25. March to relief of Knoxville November 27-December 17. Duty in Lookout Valley till May, 1864. Atlanta Campaign May 1-25. Demonstration on Rocky Faced Ridge May 8-11. Dug Gap, or Mill Creek, May 8. Battle of Resaca May 14-15. Near Cassville May 19. Advance on Dallas May 22-25. Left front May 25. Mustered out June 11, 1864. Veterans and Recruits transferred to 109th Pennsylvania.

Regiment lost during service 5 Officers and 67 Enlisted men killed and mortally wounded and 62 Enlisted men by disease. Total 134.

27th REGIMENT EMERGENCY MILITIA INFANTRY.

Organized at Harrisburg June 22, 1863, for the protection of Pennsylvania against Lee's invasion. Duty in the Dept. of the Susquehanna. Duty at Columbia and Wrightsville. Defence and destruction of railroad bridge June 28. Gettysburg Campaign. Mustered out July 31, 1863.

28th REGIMENT INFANTRY.—("GOLDSTREAM REGIMENT.")

Organized at Philadelphia and mustered in June 28, 1861. Moved to Baltimore, Md., and Harper's Ferry, W. Va., July 27. Attached to Geo. H. Thomas' Brigade, Dept. of the Shenandoah, to August, 1861. 1st Brigade, Banks' Division, Dept. of the Shenandoah, to October, 1861. Geary's Independent Brigade, Banks' Division, Army of the Potomac, to March, 1862. 1st Brigade, 1st Division, Banks' 5th Army Corps, to April, 1862. Geary's Independent Brigade, Dept. of the Shenandoah, to June, 1862. 2nd Brigade, 1st Division, 2nd Corps, Army of Virginia, to August, 1862. 1st Brigade, 2nd Division, 2nd Corps, Army of Virginia, to September, 1862. 1st Brigade, 2nd Division, 12th Army Corps, Army of the Potomac, to October, 1863, and Army of the Cumberland, to April, 1864. 1st Brigade, 2nd Division, 20th Army Corps, Army of the Cumberland, to June, 1865. 3rd Brigade, Bartlett's Division, 22nd Corps, Dept. of Washington, to July, 1865.

SERVICE.—Duty at Sandy Hook, opposite Harper's Ferry, till August 13, 1861. Moved to Point of Rocks, Md., and guard frontier from Nolan's Ferry to Antietam Aqueduct. Pritchard's Mills, Va., September 15 (Cos. "B," "D," "I"). Point of Rocks September 24. Knoxville October 2. Bolivar Heights October 16 (Cos. "A," "D," "F," "G"). Nolan's Ferry October 30. Berlin November 10. Point of Rocks December 19. Crossed Potomac February 24-25. Operations in Loudoun County, Va., February 25-May 6. Occupation of Bolivar Heights February 26. Lovettsville March 1. Wheatland March 7. Occupation of Leesburg March 8. Upperville March 14. Ashby's Gap March 15. Capture of Rectortown, Piedmont, Markham, Linden and Front Royal March 15-20. Operations about Middleburg and White Plains March 27-28. Thoroughfare Gap April 2. Warrenton April 6. Near Piedmont April 14. Linden May 15 (Co. "O"). Reconnoissance from Front Royal to Browntown May 24. Guard railroad from White Plains to Manassas till May 24, and railroad and gaps of the Blue Ridge till June 23. Joined Banks at Middletown June 29. Reconnoissance to Thoroughfare Mountain August 9. Pope's Campaign in Northern Virginia August 16-September 2. White Sulphur Springs August 24. Bull Run August 30. Maryland Campaign September 6-24. Battle of Antietam September 16-17. Duty at Bolivar Heights till December. Reconnoissance to Lovettsville October 21. Reconnoissance to Rippon, W. Va., November 9. Reconnoissance to Winches-

ter December 2-6. Moved to Fredericksburg, Va., December 10-14. At Stafford Court House till April 27, 1863. "Mud March" January 20-24, 1863. Chancellorsville Campaign April 27-May 6. Old Wilderness Tavern April 30. Battle of Chancellorsville May 1-5. Gettysburg (Pa.) Campaign June 11-July 24. Battle of Gettysburg, Pa., July 1-3. Fair Play, Md., July 13. Duty on line of the Rapidan till September. Movement to Bridgeport, Ala., September 24-October 3. Reopening Tennessee River October 26-29. Companies "L," "M," "N" and "O" transferred to 147th Pennsylvania October 28. Battle of Wauhatchie, Tenn., October 28-29. Chattanooga-Ringgold Campaign November 23-27. Battles of Lookout Mountain November 23-24; Mission Ridge November 25; Ringgold Gap, Taylor's Ridge, November 27. Guard duty on Nashville & Chattanooga Railroad till April, 1864. Regiment re-enlisted December 24, 1863. Veterans on furlough January and February, 1864. Expedition down the Tennessee River to Triana April 12-16. Atlanta (Ga.) Campaign May 1-September 8. Demonstration on Rocky Faced Ridge and Dalton May 5-13. Dug Gap, or Mill Springs, May 8. Battle of Resaca May 14-15. Near Cassville May 19. Advance on Dallas May 22-25. New Hope Church May 25. Operations on line of Pumpkin Vine Creek and battles about Dallas, New Hope Church and Allatoona Hills, May 25-June 5. Operations about Marietta and against Kenesaw Mountain June 10-July 2. Pine Hill June 11-14. Lost Mountain June 15-17. Gilgal, or Golgotha Church, June 15. Muddy Creek June 17. Noyes Creek June 19. Kolb's Farm June 22. Assault on Kenesaw June 27. Ruff's Station or Smyrna Camp Ground July 4. Chattahoochie River July 5-17. Peach Tree Creek July 19-20. Siege of Atlanta July 22-August 25. Operations at Chattahoochie River Bridge August 26-September 2. Occupation of Atlanta September 2-November 15. Whitehall Road, near Atlanta, November 9. March to the sea November 15-December 10. Siege of Savannah December 10-21. Campaign of the Carolinas January to April, 1865. North Edisto, S. C., February 12-13. Red Bank Creek February 15. Congaree Creek February 15. Averysboro, N. C., March 16. Battle of Bentonville March 19-21. Occupation of Goldsboro March 24. Advance on Raleigh April 9-13. Occupation of Raleigh April 14. Bennett's House April 26. Surrender of Johnston and his army. March to Washington, D. C., via Richmond, Va., April 29-May 20. Grand Review May 24. Duty in the Dept. of Washington till July. Mustered out July 18, 1865.

Regiment lost during service 6 Officers and 151 Enlisted men killed and mortally wounded and 3 Officers and 124 Enlisted men by disease. Total 284.

28th REGIMENT EMERGENCY MILITIA INFANTRY.

Organized at Harrisburg June 24, 1863, for the protection of Pennsylvania against Lee's invasion. Duty in the Dept. of the Susquehanna. Destruction of railroad bridge at Wrightsville June 28. Moved to Carlisle, Pa., thence over South Mountain to Boonsboro, Md. Skirmish near Hagerstown July 11. Mustered out July 28, 1863.

29th REGIMENT INFANTRY.

Organized at Philadelphia July 1, 1861. Left State for Harper's Ferry, W. Va., August 3. Attached to Gordon's Brigade, Dept. of the Susquehanna, August, 1861. 3rd Brigade, Banks' Division, Army of the Potomac, to March, 1862. 3rd Brigade, 1st Division, Banks' 5th Corps, and Dept. of the Shenandoah to June, 1862. 3rd Brigade, 1st Division, 2nd Corps, Army of Virginia, to September, 1862. 3rd Brigade, 1st Division, 12th Army Corps, Army of the Potomac, to March, 1863. 2nd Brigade, 2nd Division, 12th Army Corps, Army of the Potomac, to October, 1863, and Army of the Cumberland to April, 1864. 3rd Brigade, 2nd Division, 20th Army Corps, Army of the Cumberland, to June, 1865. Bartlett's Division, 22nd Army Corps, Dept. of Washington, to July, 1865.

SERVICE.—Duty at Harper's Ferry and on Upper Potomac till February, 1862. Operations about Dams

4 and 5 December 17-20, 1861. Advance on Winchester March 1-12. Occupation of Winchester March 12. Pursuit of Jackson up the Shenandoah Valley March 24-April 27. Woodstock April 1. Edenburg April 1-2. Stony Creek April 2. Operations in Shenandoah Valley May 15-June 17. Front Royal May 23 (Cos. "B" and "G"). Buckton Station May 23. Middletown and Newtown May 24. Retreat to Williamsport May 24-26. Battle of Winchester May 25. At Williamsport till June 10. Moved to Front Royal June 10-18; thence to Warrenton and Little Washington July 11-18. Pope's Campaign in Northern Virginia August 6-September 2. Battle of Cedar Mountain August 9 (Reserve). Guarding trains during Bull Run Battles. Maryland Campaign September 6-24. Battle of Antietam, Md., September 16-17 (Provost and Rear Guard). Chambersburg, Pa., October 11. Duty at Maryland Heights till December. March to Fredericksburg, Va., December 10-16. Fairfax Station December 12. At Stafford Court House till April, 1863. "Mud March" January 20-24, 1863. Chancellorsville Campaign April 27-May 6. Battle of Chancellorsville May 1-5. Gettysburg (Pa.) Campaign June 11-July 24. Battle of Gettysburg, Pa., July 1-3. Pursuit of Lee July 5-24. Duty on line of the Rappahannock till September. Movement to Bridgeport, Ala., September 24-October 3. Reopening Tennessee River October 26-29. Battle of Wauhatchie, Tenn., October 28-29. Chattanooga-Ringgold Campaign November 23-27. Battles of Lookout Mountain November 23-24; Mission Ridge November 25; Ringgold Gap, Taylor's Ridge, November 27. Re-enlisted December 10, 1863. Guard duty on Nashville & Chattanooga Railroad till April, 1864. Atlanta (Ga.) Campaign May 1-September 8. Demonstration on Rocky Faced Ridge and Dalton May 8-13. Battle of Resaca May 14-15. Near Cassville May 19. New Hope Church May 25. Operations on line of Pumpkin Vine Creek and battles about Dallas, New Hope Church and Allatoona Hills May 26-June 5. Operations about Marietta and against Kenesaw Mountain June 10-July 2. Pine Hill June 11-14. Lost Mountain June 15-17. Gilgal or Golgotha Church June 15. Muddy Creek June 17. Noyes Creek June 19. Kolb's Farm June 22. Assault on Kenesaw Mountain June 27. Ruff's Station or Smyrna Camp Ground July 4. Chattahoochie River July 5-17. Peach Tree Creek July 19-20. Siege of Atlanta July 22-August 25. Operations at Chattahoochie River Bridge August 26-September 2. Occupation of Atlanta September 2-November 15. Expedition to Tuckum's Cross Roads October 26-29. Near Atlanta November 9. March to the sea November 15-December 10. Near Davidsboro November 28. Siege of Savannah December 10-21. Campaign of the Carolinas January to April, 1865. Battle of Bentonville, N. C., March 19-21. Occupation of Goldsboro March 24. Advance on Raleigh April 9-13. Occupation of Raleigh April 14. Bennett's House April 26. Surrender of Johnston and his army. March to Washington, D. C., via Richmond, Va., April 29-May 20. Grand Review May 24. Duty in Dept. of Washington, D. C., till July. Mustered out July 11, 1865.

Regiment lost during service 3 Officers and 99 Enlisted men killed and mortally wounded and 1 Officer and 84 Enlisted men by disease. Total 187.

29th REGIMENT EMERGENCY MILITIA INFANTRY.

Organized at Harrisburg June 23, 1863, for the protection of Pennsylvania against Lee's invasion. Duty in the Dept. of the Susquehanna during Gettysburg Campaign. Mustered out July 29, 1863.

30th REGIMENT INFANTRY.

(See 66th Pennsylvania Infantry.)

30th REGIMENT INFANTRY, 1st RESERVES INFANTRY.

(See 1st Reserves Infantry.)

30th REGIMENT EMERGENCY MILITIA INFANTRY.

Organized at Harrisburg June 25, 1863, for the protection of Pennsylvania against Lee's invasion. Duty in the Dept. of the Susquehanna at Chambersburg, Hagerstown, Md., Mercersburg, Pa., Fort Washington, etc. Oyster Point June 28. Carlisle July 1. Mustered out August 1, 1863.

31st REGIMENT INFANTRY.

(See 82nd Pennsylvania Infantry.)

31st REGIMENT INFANTRY, 2nd RESERVES INFANTRY.

(See 2nd Reserves Infantry.)

31st REGIMENT EMERGENCY MILITIA INFANTRY.

Organized at Harrisburg June 30, 1863, for the protection of Pennsylvania against Lee's invasion. Duty in the Dept. of the Susquehanna. Mustered out August 8, 1863.

32nd REGIMENT INFANTRY.

(See 99th Pennsylvania Infantry.)

32nd REGIMENT INFANTRY, 3rd RESERVES INFANTRY.

(See 3rd Reserves Infantry.)

32nd REGIMENT EMERGENCY MILITIA INFANTRY.

Organized at Harrisburg June 26, 1863, for the protection of Pennsylvania against Lee's invasion. Duty in the Dept. of the Susquehanna during Gettysburg (Pa.) Campaign. Mustered out August 1, 1863.

33rd REGIMENT INFANTRY.

(See 62nd Pennsylvania Infantry.)

33rd REGIMENT INFANTRY, 4th RESERVES INFANTRY.

(See 4th Reserves Infantry.)

33rd REGIMENT EMERGENCY MILITIA INFANTRY.

Organized at Harrisburg June 26, 1863, for the protection of Pennsylvania against Lee's invasion. Duty in the Dept. of the Susquehanna during Gettysburg Campaign. Mustered out August 4, 1863.

34th REGIMENT INFANTRY, 5th RESERVES INFANTRY.

(See 5th Reserves Infantry.)

34th REGIMENT MILITIA INFANTRY.

Organized at Reading July 3, 1863, for the protection of Pennsylvania during Lee's invasion. Duty at Reading and Philadelphia. Mustered out August 10, 1863.

35th REGIMENT INFANTRY.

(See 74th Infantry.)

35th REGIMENT INFANTRY, 6th RESERVES INFANTRY.

(See 6th Reserves Infantry.)

35th REGIMENT MILITIA INFANTRY.

Organized at Harrisburg July 4, 1863, for the protection of Pennsylvania during Lee's invasion. Duty in the Dept. of the Susquehanna. Mustered out August 7, 1863.

36th REGIMENT INFANTRY.

(See 81st Infantry.)

36th REGIMENT INFANTRY, 7th RESERVES INFANTRY.

(See 7th Reserves Infantry.)

36th REGIMENT MILITIA INFANTRY.

Organized at Harrisburg July 4, 1863, for the protection of Pennsylvania during Lee's invasion. Duty in the Dept. of the Susquehanna at Greencastle, Chambersburg and Hagerstown, Md. Mustered out August 11, 1863.

37th REGIMENT INFANTRY, 8th RESERVES INFANTRY.

(See 7th Reserves Infantry.)

37th REGIMENT MILITIA INFANTRY.

Organized at Harrisburg July 4, 1863, for the protection of Pennsylvania during Lee's invasion. Guard duty in the Dept. of the Susquehanna. Mustered out August 3, 1863.

38th REGIMENT INFANTRY, 9th RESERVES INFANTRY.

(See 9th Reserves Infantry.)

38th REGIMENT MILITIA INFANTRY.

Organized at Reading July 3, 1863, for the protection of Pennsylvania during Lee's invasion. Duty at Reading till July 10; at Chambersburg till July 20, and at Pottsville, Pa., enforcing the draft till July 31. Moved to Reading and mustered out August 7, 1863.

39th REGIMENT INFANTRY, 10th RESERVES INFANTRY.

(See 10th Reserves Infantry.)

39th REGIMENT MILITIA INFANTRY.

Organized at Reading July 4, 1863, for the protection of Pennsylvania during Lee's invasion. Duty in the Dept. of the Susquehanna. Mustered out August 2, 1863.

40th REGIMENT INFANTRY.

(See 75th Infantry.)

40th REGIMENT INFANTRY, 11th RESERVES INFANTRY.

(See 11th Reserves Infantry.)

40th REGIMENT MILITIA INFANTRY.

Organized at Harrisburg July 2, 1863, for the protection of Pennsylvania during Lee's invasion. Duty in the Dept. of the Susquehanna. Mustered out August 16, 1863.

41st REGIMENT INFANTRY, 12th RESERVES INFANTRY.

(See 12th Reserves Infantry.)

41st REGIMENT MILITIA INFANTRY.

Organized at Reading July 1, 1863, for the protection of Pennsylvania during Lee's invasion. Duty in the Dept. of the Susquehanna. Mustered out August 4, 1863.

42nd REGIMENT INFANTRY, 13th RESERVES INFANTRY.

(See 13th Reserves Infantry, 1st Rifles.)

42nd REGIMENT MILITIA INFANTRY.

Organized at Reading July 6, 1863, for the protection of Pennsylvania during Lee's invasion. Duty in the Dept. of the Susquehanna and guarding railroad in Maryland. Mustered out August 11, 1863.

43rd REGIMENT VOLUNTEERS.—1st RESERVES CAVALRY.

(See 1st Pennsylvania Cavalry.)

43rd REGIMENT MILITIA INFANTRY.

Organized at Reading July 6, 1863, for the protection of Pennsylvania during Lee's invasion. Duty in the Dept. of the Susquehanna. Mustered out August 13, 1863.

44th REGIMENT VOLUNTEERS.—1st RESERVES LIGHT ARTILLERY.

(See 1st Pennsylvania Light Artillery.)

44th REGIMENT MILITIA INFANTRY.

Organized at Harrisburg July 1, 1863, for the protection of Pennsylvania during Lee's invasion. Duty in the Dept. of Susquehanna. Mustered out August 27, 1863.

45th REGIMENT INFANTRY.

Organized at Camp Curtin, Harrisburg, October 21, 1861. Moved to Washington, D. C., October 21-23. Attached to Jameson's Brigade, Heintzelman's Division, Army of the Potomac, to October, 1861. Unattached, Sherman's South Carolina Expeditionary Corps, to April, 1862. 2nd Brigade, 1st Division, Dept. of the South, to July, 1862. 2nd Brigade, 1st Division, 9th Army Corps, Army of the Potomac, to September, 1862. 3rd Brigade, 1st Division, 9th Army Corps, Army of the Potomac, to April, 1863, and Army of the Ohio to June, 1863. 1st Brigade, 1st Division, 9th Army Corps, Army of the Tennessee, to August, 1863, and Army of the Ohio to April, 1864. 1st Brigade, 2nd Division, 9th Army Corps, Army of the Potomac, to July, 1865.

SERVICE.—Expedition into Lower Maryland November 3-11, 1861. Moved to Baltimore, Md., thence to Fortress Monroe, Va., November 19-21. Sailed for Port Royal, S. C., December 6-8. Companies "A," "C," "D," "E" and "I" assigned to duty at Bay Point; Companies "B," "F," "G," "H" and "K" occupy Otter Island, S. C., December 11, and duty there till May, 1862; Companies "F" and "K" occupy Fenwick Island December 20, 1861; Company "F" at Fenwick Island April 4 to May 20, 1862; Companies "B," "F," "G," "H," "I" and "K" moved to North Edisto Island, S. C., May 21, 1862. Operations against James Island, S. C., May 21-June 28. Action on James Island June 10. Battle of Secessionville June 16. Evacuation of James Island and movement to Hilton Head June 28-July 1. Moved to Newport News, Va., July 18-21; thence to Aquia Creek August 4-5. Operations on the Rapidan and Rappahannock Rivers till September. At Brook's Station August 5-29. Destruction of bridges at Potomac Creek and Brook's Station September 4. Destruction of stores at Aquia Creek September 6. Battles of South Mountain September 14; Antietam September 16-17. Duty at Pleasant Valley, Md., till October 26. March to Lovettsville, Va., October 26-29; thence to Warrenton October 29-November 19. Battle of Fredericksburg December 12-15. Burnside's 2nd Campaign January 20-24, 1863. At Falmouth till February 11. Moved to Newport News February 11, thence to Lexington, Ky., March 19-23. Duty at various points in Kentucky till June. Moved to Vicksburg, Miss., June 7-14. Siege of Vicksburg June 14-July 4. Advance on Jackson, Miss., July 5-10. Siege of Jackson July 10-17. At Milldale till August 5. Moved to Covington, Ky., thence to Crab Orchard August 5-18. Burnside's Campaign in East Tennessee August 16-October 17. Blue Springs October 10. Knoxville Campaign November 4-December 23. Lenoir Station November 14-15. Campbell's Station November 16. Siege of Knoxville November 17-December 4. Pursuit of Longstreet December 5-24. Regiment re-enlisted January 1, 1864. Operations in East Tennessee till March, 1864. Strawberry Plains January 21-22. Movement to Annapolis, Md., March 21-April 6. Rapidan Campaign May 4-June 12. Battles of the Wilderness May 5-7; Spottsylvania May 8-12; Spottsylvania Court House May 12-21. Assault on the Salient May 12. Stannard's Mill May 21. North Anna River May 23-26. Line of the Pamunkey May 26-28. Totopotomoy May 28-31. Cold Harbor June 1-12. Bethesda Church June 1-3. Before Petersburg June 16-18. Siege of Petersburg June 16, 1864, to April 2, 1865. Mine Explosion, Petersburg, July 30, 1864. Weldon Railroad August 18-21. Poplar Springs Church September 29-October 2. Peeble's Farm October 1. Boydton Plank Road, Hatcher's Run, October 27-28. At Fort Rice till April, 1865. Fort Stedman March 25, 1865. Assault on and fall of Petersburg April 2. March to Farmville April 3-9. Moved to Petersburg and City Point April 20-24, thence to Alexandria April 26-28. Grand Review May 23. Duty at Washington and Alexandria till July. Mustered out July 17, 1865.

Regiment lost during service 13 Officers and 214 Enlisted men killed and mortally wounded and 252 Enlisted men by disease. Total 479.

45th REGIMENT MILITIA INFANTRY.

Organized at Harrisburg July 1, 1863, for the protection of Pennsylvania during Lee's invasion. Mustered out August 29, 1863.

46th REGIMENT INFANTRY.

Organized at Harrisburg October 31, 1861. Ordered to join Banks November, 1861. Attached to Gordon's Brigade, Banks' Division, to March, 1862. 1st Brigade, 1st Division, Banks' 5th Corps, and Dept. of the Shenandoah to June, 1862. 1st Brigade, 1st Division, 2nd Corps, Army of Virginia, to September, 1862. 1st Brigade, 1st Division, 12th Army Corps, Army of the Potomac, to October, 1863, and Army of the Cumberland to April, 1864. 1st Brigade, 1st Division, 20th Army Corps, Army of the Cumberland, to July, 1865.

SERVICE.—Guard and outpost duty on the Upper Potomac till February, 1862. Advance on Winchester March 1-12, 1862. Near Winchester March 7. Occupation of Winchester March 12. Ordered to Manassas, Va., March 18, and return to Winchester. Pursuit of Jackson up the Valley March 24-April 7. Columbia Furnace April 16: Skirmish at Gordonsville and Keazletown Cross Roads April 26. Operations in the Shenandoah Valley May 15-June 17. At Strasburg till May 20. Retreat to Winchester May 20-25. Front Royal May 23. Kernstown and Middletown May 24. Battle of Winchester May 25. Retreat to Williamsport May 25-26. At Williamsport till June 10. Moved to Front Royal June 10-18. Reconnoissance to Luray June 29-30. Luray June 30. At Warrenton, Gordonsville and Culpeper, July. Battle of Cedar Mountain August 9. Pope's Campaign in Northern Virginia August 16-September 2. Guard trains during the Bull Run battles. Manassas Junction August 28. Maryland Campaign September 6-24. Battle of Antietam September 16-17 (Reserve). Duty in Maryland till December 10. March to Fairfax Station December 10-14, and duty there till January 19, 1863. "Mud March" January 20-24. Moved to Stafford Court House and duty there till April 27. Chancellorsville Campaign April 27-May 6. Battle of Chancellorsville May 1-5. Gettysburg (Pa.) Campaign June 11-July 24. Battle of Gettysburg July 1-3. Pursuit of Lee July 5-24. Duty on line of the Rappahannock till September. Movement to Bridgeport, Ala., September 24-October 3. Guard duty on Nashville & Chattanooga Railroad till April, 1864. Regiment re-enlisted January, 1864. Atlanta Campaign May 1-September 8. Demonstration on Rocky Faced Ridge May 8-11. Battle of Resaca May 14-15. Near Cassville May 19. New Hope Church May 25. Operations on line of Pumpkin Vine Creek and battles about Dallas, New Hope Church and Allatoona Hills May 25-June 5. Operations about Marietta and against Kenesaw Mountain June 10-July 2. Pine Hill June 11-14. Gilgal, or Golgotha Church, June 15. Lost Mountain June 15-17. Muddy Creek June 17. Noyes Creek June 19. Kolb's Farm June 22. Assault on Kenesaw June 27. Ruff's Station or Smyrna Camp Ground July 4. Chattahootchie River July 5-17. Peach Tree Creek July 19-20. Siege of Atlanta July 22-August 25. Operations at Chattahootchie River Bridge August 26-September 2. Occupation of Atlanta September 2-November 15. March to the sea November 15-December 10. Siege of Savannah December 10-21. Campaign of the Carolinas January to April, 1865. Thompson's Creek, near Chesterfield Court House, S. C., March 2. Thompson's Creek, near Cheraw, S. C., March 3. Averysboro, N. C., March 16. Battle of Bentonville March 19-21. Occupation of Goldsboro March 24. Advance on Raleigh April 9-13. Occupation of Raleigh April 14. Bennett's House April 26. Surrender of Johnston and his army. March to Washington, D. C., via Richmond, Va., April 29-May 20. Grand Review May 24. Duty at Washington till July. Mustered out July 16, 1865.

Regiment lost during service 14 Officers and 165 Enlisted men killed and mortally wounded and 2 Officers and 136 Enlisted men by disease. Total 317.

46th REGIMENT MILITIA INFANTRY.

Organized at Huntingdon July 1, 1863, for the protection of Pennsylvania during Lee's invasion. Mustered out August 18, 1863.

47th REGIMENT INFANTRY.

Organized at Harrisburg August and September, 1861. Moved to Washington, D. C., September 20-21. Attached to 3rd Brigade, W. F. Smith's Division, Army Potomac, to January, 1862. District of Key West, Fla., to June, 1862. District of Beaufort, S. C., Dept. South, to November, 1862. District of Key West, Fla., 10th Corps, Dept. of the South, November, 1862, and Dept. of the Gulf to February, 1864. 2nd Brigade, 1st Division, 19th Army Corps, Dept. of the Gulf, to July, 1864, and Army of the Shenandoah, Middle Military Division, to February, 1865. 2nd Brigade, Provisional Division, Army Shenandoah, to April, 1865. 2nd Brigade, Dwight's Division, 22nd Corps, Dept. of Washington, to May, 1865. 3rd Brigade, Dwight's Division, District of Savannah, Ga., Dept. South, to July, 1865. 1st Sub-District, South Carolina, Dept. South Carolina, to December, 1865.

SERVICE.—Duty in the Defences of Washington, D. C., till January, 1862. Moved to Key West, Fla., via Annapolis, Md., and on Steamer "Oriental" January 22-February 4. Duty at Fort Taylor, Key West, Fla., till June 18. Moved to Hilton Head, S. C., June 18-22, thence to Beaufort, S. C., July 2, and duty there till October. Expedition to Florida September 30-October 13. St. John's Bluff October 3. Capture of Jacksonville October 5 (Cos. "E" and "K"). Expedition from Jacksonville to Lake Beresford and capture of Steamer "Gov. Milton" near Hawkinsville October 6 (Cos. "E" and "K"). Expedition to Pocotaligo, S. C., October 21-23. Frampton's Plantation and Pocotaligo Bridge October 22. Ordered to Key West, Fla., November 15. Garrison Fort Taylor (Cos. "A," "B," "C," "E," "G" and "I") and Fort Jefferson (Cos. "D," "F," "H" and "K") till February, 1864. Moved to New Orleans, La., February 25. (Regiment re-enlisted October, 1863, to February, 1864.) At Algiers, La., February 28. Banks' Red River Campaign March 10-May 22. Advance from Franklin to Alexandria March 14-26. Battle of Sabine Cross Roads April 8. Pleasant Hill April 9. Monett's Ferry, Cane River Crossing, April 23. Fatigue duty at Alexandria constructing dam across Red River April 30-May 10. Retreat to Morganza May 13-20. Mansura May 16. At Morganza till June 20. At New Orleans till July 5. Moved to Washington, D. C., July 5-12. Sheridan's Shenandoah Valley Campaign August to November. Battle of Opequan, Winchester, September 19. Fisher's Hill September 22. Battle of Cedar Creek October 19. At Camp Russell, near Winchester, till December 20, and at Camp Fairview, Charlestown, and on outpost duty in West Virginia till April, 1865. Moved to Washington, D. C., April 19-21. Grand Review May 23-24. Moved to Savannah, Ga., May 31-June 4, and to Charleston, S. C., June 17. Duty at Charleston and other points in South Carolina till December. Mustered out December 25, 1865.

Regiment lost during service 5 Officers and 112 Enlisted men killed and mortally wounded and 3 Officers and 170 Enlisted men by disease. Total 290.

47th REGIMENT MILITIA INFANTRY.

Organized at Harrisburg July 9, 1863. Duty in mining regions of Schuylkill County. Mustered out August 13, 1863.

48th REGIMENT INFANTRY.

Organized at Harrisburg September, 1861. Moved to Fortress Monroe, Va., September 24-25, and duty there till November 11, 1861. Duty at Fort Clarke, Hatteras Inlet, till May, 1862. Attached to Williams' Brigade, Burnside's North Carolina Expedition, to April, 1862. 1st Brigade, 2nd Division, Dept. North Carolina, to July, 1862. 1st Brigade, 2nd Division, 9th Army Corps, Army Potomac, to April, 1863, and Army of the Ohio to June, 1863. Unattached, 1st Division, 23rd Army Corps, Army Ohio, to October, 1863. 1st Brigade, 2nd Division, 9th Army Corps, Army Ohio, to April, 1864, and Army Potomac to July, 1865.

SERVICE.—Companies "A," "B," "C," "D," "H" and "I" at New Berne, N. C., March 14, 1862. Regiment re-united at New Berne May 23, and duty there till July 6. Moved to Fortress Monroe July 6-8, thence to Fredericksburg August 2-4. Joined Pope at Culpeper, Va., August 13. Pope's Campaign in Northern Virginia August 16-September 2. Battles of Groveton August 29; Bull Run August 30; Chantilly September 1. Maryland Campaign September 6-24. Battles of South Mountain September 14; Antietam September 16-17. At Pleasant Valley, Md., till October 27. Movement to Falmouth, Va., October 27-November 17. Corbin's Cross Roads, near Amissville, November 10. Battle of Fredericksburg December 12-15. Burnside's second Campaign January 20-24, 1863. Duty at Falmouth till February 19. Moved to Newport News, thence to Covington, Ky., March 26-April 1. Provost and guard duty at Lexington, Ky., till September 10. At Knoxville, Tenn., till October 4. Blue Springs, Tenn., October 10. Knoxville Campaign November 4-December 23. Campbell's Station November 16. Siege of Knoxville November 17-December 5. Pursuit of Longstreet December 5-29. Regiment re-enlisted at Blain's Cross Roads December 7, and on Veteran furlough till March, 1864. Left Pottsville, Pa., March 14. At Annapolis, Md., till April. Rapidan Campaign May 4-June 12. Battles of the Wilderness May 5-7; Spottsylvania May 8-12; Spottsylvania C. H. May 12-21. Assault on the Salient May 12. Stannard's Mills May 21. North Anna River May 23-26. Line of the Pamunkey May 26-28. Totopotomoy May 28-31. Cold Harbor June 1-12. Bethesda Church June 1-3. Before Petersburg June 16-18. Siege of Petersburg June 16, 1864, to April 2, 1865. Jerusalem Plank Road June 22-23, 1864. Mine Explosion, Petersburg, July 30. Weldon Railroad August 18-21. Poplar Springs Church September 29-October 2. Boydton Plank Road, Hatcher's Run, October 27-28. Assault on and fall of Petersburg April 2, 1865. Occupation of Petersburg April 3. March to Farmville April 3-9. Moved to Petersburg and City Point April 20-24, thence to Alexandria April 26-28. Grand Review May 23. Duty at Washington and Alexandria till July. Mustered out July 17, 1865.

Regiment lost during service 11 Officers and 145 Enlisted men killed and mortally wounded and 3 Officers and 142 Enlisted men by disease. Total 301.

48th REGIMENT MILITIA INFANTRY.

Organized at Reading July 2, 1863. Mustered out August 26, 1863.

49th REGIMENT INFANTRY.

Organized at Lewistown and Harrisburg September, 1861. Left State for Washington, D. C., September 22, 1861. Attached to Hancock's Brigade, W. F. Smith's Division, Army Potomac, to March, 1862. 1st Brigade, 2nd Division, 4th Army Corps, Army Potomac, to May, 1862. 1st Brigade, 2nd Division, 6th Army Corps, Army Potomac, to February, 1863. 3rd Brigade, 1st Division, 6th Army Corps, to July, 1864. 3rd Brigade, 1st Division, 6th Army Corps, Army Shenandoah, to August, 1864. Reserve Division, Dept. West Virginia, to September, 1864. 3rd Brigade, 1st Division, 6th Army Corps, Army Shenandoah, to December, 1864, and Army Potomac, to July, 1865.

SERVICE.—Duty near Lewinsville, Va., Defences of Washington, D. C., till March, 1862. Advance on Manassas, Va., March 10-15. Return to Alexandria and embark for the Virginia Peninsula. Siege of Yorktown April 5-May 4. Lee's Mills, Burnt Chimneys, April 16. Battle of Williamsburg May 5. Pursuit to the Chickahominy River and picket duty till June 25. Seven days before Richmond June 25-July 1. Garnett's Farm June 27. Golding's Farm June 28. Savage Station June 29. White Oak Swamp Bridge June 30. Malvern Hill July 1. At Harrison's Landing till August 16. Movement to Centreville August 16-27. In works at Centreville August 27-31. Assist in checking Pope's rout at Bull Run August 30, and cover retreat to Fairfax C. H. August 31-September 1. Maryland Campaign September 6-24. Sugar Loaf Mountain September 10-11.

Crampton's Pass, South Mountain, September 14. Battle of Antietam September 16-17. Duty in Maryland till October 29. Movement to Falmouth, Va., October 29-November 19. Battle of Fredericksburg, Va., December 12-15. Consolidated to four Companies January 9, 1863. "Mud March" January 20-24. At White Oak Church till April 27. Chancellorsville Campaign April 27-May 6. Operations at Franklin's Crossing April 29-May 2. Bernard House April 29. Maryes Heights, Fredericksburg, May 3. Salem Heights May 3-4. Banks' Ford May 4. At White Oak Church till June 6. Deep Run Ravine June 6-13. Battle of Gettysburg, Pa., July 2-4. At and near Funkstown, Md., July 10-13. Duty on line of the Rappahannock till October. Bristoe Campaign October 9-22. Advance to line of the Rappahannock November 7-8. Rappahannock Station November 7. Mine Run Campaign November 26-December 2. Duty at Hazel River till May, 1864. Rapidan Campaign May 4-June 13. Battles of the Wilderness May 5-7; Spottsylvania May 8-12; Spottsylvania C. H. May 12-21. Assault on the Salient May 12. North Anna River May 23-26. On line of the Pamunkey May 26-28. Totopotomoy May 28-31. Cold Harbor May 31-June 12. Before Petersburg June 17-19. Siege of Petersburg June 17-July 9. Jerusalem Plank Road, Weldon Railroad, June 22-23. Moved to Washington, D. C., July 9-11. Repulse of Early's attack on Washington July 12-13. Pursuit of Early July 14-18. Sheridan's Shenandoah Valley Campaign August to December. Battle of Opequan, Winchester, September 19. Guard duty at Winchester till October 29, and in the valley till December 1. Ordered to Petersburg, Va. Siege operations against Petersburg December, 1864, to April, 1865. Dabney's Mills, Hatcher's Run, February 5-7, 1865. Appomattox Campaign March 28-April 9. Assault on and fall of Petersburg April 2. Sailor's Creek April 6. Detached to escort prisoners April 6. March to Danville April 23-29, and duty there till May 23. Moved to Richmond, Va., thence to Washington, D. C. Corps Review June 8. Duty at Hall's Hill till July 15. Mustered out July 15, 1865.

Regiment lost during service 9 Officers and 184 Enlisted men killed and mortally wounded and 168 Enlisted men by disease. Total 361.

49th REGIMENT MILITIA INFANTRY.

Organized at Harrisburg July 2, 1863, for the protection of Pennsylvania during Lee's invasion. Mustered out September 2, 1863.

50th REGIMENT INFANTRY.

Organized at Harrisburg October 1, 1861. Left State for Washington, D. C., October 2, 1861, thence moved to Annapolis, Md., October 9. Attached to Stevens' Brigade, W. T. Sherman's South Carolina Expedition, to April, 1862. District of Beaufort, S. C., Dept. South, to July, 1862. 1st Brigade, 1st Division, 9th Army Corps, Army Potomac, to September, 1862. 2nd Brigade, 1st Division, 9th Army Corps, Army of the Potomac, to April, 1863, and Army of the Ohio to June, 1863. 3rd Brigade, 2nd Division, 9th Army Corps, Army of the Tennessee, to August, 1863. 2nd Brigade, 1st Division, 9th Army Corps, Army Ohio, to April, 1864. 2nd Brigade, 3rd Division, 9th Army Corps, Army Potomac, to September, 1864. 2nd Brigade, 1st Division, Army Potomac, to July, 1865.

SERVICE.—Sherman's Expedition to Port Royal, S. C., October 21-November 7, 1861. Sailed on Steamer "Winfield Scott" and shipwrecked off coast of North Carolina. Occupation of Beaufort, S. C., December 6. Port Royal Ferry, Coosaw River, January 1, 1862. Duty at Port Royal Island, S. C., till July, 1862. Barnwell's Island, S. C., February 10 (Co. "D"). Pocotaligo May 29. Camp Stevens June 7. Moved to Hilton Head, S. C., thence to Newport News, Va., July 14-18, thence to Aquia Creek and Fredericksburg, Va., August 3-6. Operations in support of Pope August 6-16. Pope's Campaign in Northern Virginia August 16-September 2. Sulphur Springs August 24. Battles of Groveton August 29; Bull Run August 30; Chantilly September 1. Maryland Campaign September 6-24. Battles of South Mountain,

Md., September 14; Antietam September 16-17. March to Pleasant Valley September 19-October 2, and duty there till October 25. Movement to Falmouth, Va., October 25-November 19. Battle of Fredericksburg December 12-15. Burnside's 2nd Campaign January 20-24, 1863. At Falmouth till February 12. Moved to Newport News February 12-14, thence to Kentucky March 21-26. Duty at Paris, Ky., till April 27. Moved to Nicholasville, Lancaster and Stanford April 27-29, thence to Somerset May 6-8, thence through Kentucky to Cairo, Ill., June 4-10, and to Vicksburg, Miss., June 14-17. Siege of Vicksburg, Miss., June 17-July 4. Advance on Jackson, Miss., July 5-10. Siege of Jackson July 10-17. At Milldale till August 12. Moved to Covington, Ky., August 12-23. Burnside's Campaign in East Tennessee August to October. Action at Blue Springs, Tenn., October 10. Clinch Mountain October 27. Knoxville Campaign November 4-December 23. Campbell's Station November 16. Siege of Knoxville November 17-December 5. Pursuit of Longstreet's army to Blain's Cross Roads December 5-26. Re-enlisted at Blain's Cross Roads January 1, 1864. Moved to Annapolis, Md., April, 1864. Rapidan Campaign May 4-June 12. Battles of the Wilderness May 5-7; Spottsylvania May 8-12; Ny River May 9; Spottsylvania C. H. May 12-21. Assault on the Salient May 12. North Anna River May 23-26. Ox Ford May 24. Line of the Pamunkey May 26-28. Totopotomoy May 28-31. Cold Harbor June 1-12. Bethesda Church June 1-3. Before Petersburg June 16-18. Siege of Petersburg June 16, 1864, to April 2, 1865. Mine Explosion, Petersburg, July 30, 1864. Weldon Railroad August 18-21. Poplar Springs Church or Peeble's Farm September 29-October 2. Reconnoissance on Vaughan or Squirrel Level Road October 8. Boydton Plank Road, Hatcher's Run, October 27-28. Fort Stedman March 25, 1865. Appomattox Campaign March 28-April 9. Assault on and fall of Petersburg April 2. Pursuit of Lee to Burkesville April 3-9. Moved to City Point, thence to Washington, D. C., April 21-28. Grand Review May 23. Present at the laying of corner stone at Gettysburg July 4. Mustered out July 30, 1865.

Regiment lost during service 8 Officers and 156 Enlisted men killed and mortally wounded and 4 Officers and 180 Enlisted men by disease. Total 348.

50th REGIMENT MILITIA INFANTRY.

Organized at Harrisburg July 1, 1863, for the protection of Pennsylvania during Lee's invasion. Mustered out August 15, 1863.

51st REGIMENT INFANTRY.

Organized at Harrisburg November 16, 1861. Left State for Annapolis, Md., November 16. Attached to Reno's Brigade, Burnside's North Carolina Expeditionary Corps, to April, 1862. 2nd Brigade, 2nd Division, Dept. of North Carolina, to July, 1862. 2nd Brigade, 2nd Division, 9th Army Corps, Army of the Potomac, to April, 1863; Army of the Ohio to June, 1863; Army of the Tennessee to August, 1863, and Army of the Ohio to April, 1864. 1st Brigade, 3rd Division, 9th Army Corps, Army Potomac, to September, 1864. 1st Brigade, 1st Division, 9th Army Corps, to July, 1865.

SERVICE.—Duty at Annapolis till January 9, 1862. Burnside's Expedition to Hatteras Inlet and Roanoke Island, N. C., January 9-February 8. Battle of Roanoke Island February 8. Moved to New Berne March 11-13. Battle of New Berne March 14. Expedition to Pollocksville March 21-22. Expedition to Elizabeth City April 17-19. Camden, South Mills, April 19. Duty at New Berne till July. Moved to Newport News, Va., July 6-9, thence to Fredericksburg August 2-4. March to relief of Pope August 12-15. Pope's Campaign in Northern Virginia August 16-September 2. Battles of Groveton August 29; Bull Run August 30; Chantilly September 1; Maryland Campaign September 6-24. Battle of South Mountain September 14. Antietam September 16-17. Duty at Pleasant Valley till October 27. Movement to Falmouth, Va., October 27-November 19. Battle of Fredericksburg, Va., December 12-15. Burnside's second

Campaign. "Mud March" January 20-24, 1863. Moved to Newport News February 19, thence to Covington and Paris, Ky., March 26-April 1. Moved to Mount Sterling April 3, to Lancaster May 6-7 and to Crab Orchard May 23. Movement to Vicksburg, Miss., June 3-17. Siege of Vicksburg June 17-July 4. Advance on Jackson, Miss., July 5-10. Siege of Jackson July 10-17. At Milldale till August 6. Moved to Cincinnati, Ohio, August 6-20. Duty in Kentucky till October. Operations in East Tennessee till November 14. Knoxville Campaign November 4-December 23. Campbell's Station November 16. Siege of Knoxville November 17-December 4. Pursuit of Longstreet December 5-29. Regiment re-enlisted January 1, 1864, and on Veteran furlough January 11-March 9. At Annapolis, Md., till April 23. Rapidan Campaign May 4-June 12. Battles of the Wilderness May 5-7; Spottsylvania May 8-12; Ny River May 9; Spottsylvania C. H. May 12-21. Assault on the Salient May 12. North Anna River May 23-26. Ox Ford May 24. Line of the Pamunkey May 26-28. Totopotomoy May 28-31. Cold Harbor June 1-12. Bethesda Church June 1-3. Before Petersburg June 16-18. Siege of Petersburg June 16, 1864, to April 2, 1865. Mine Explosion, Petersburg, July 30, 1864. Weldon Railroad August 18-21. Poplar Springs Church, Peeble's Farm, September 29-October 2. Reconnoissance on Vaughan and Squirrel Level Road October 8. Boydton Plank Road, Hatcher's Run, October 27-28. Fort Stedman March 25, 1865. Appomattox Campaign March 28-April 9. Assault on and fall of Petersburg April 2. Pursuit of Lee to Farmville. Moved to City Point, thence to Alexandria April 20-28. Grand Review May 23. Duty at Washington and Alexandria till July. Mustered out July 27, 1865.

Regiment lost during service 12 Officers and 165 Enlisted men killed and mortally wounded and 137 Enlisted men by disease. Total 314.

51st REGIMENT MILITIA INFANTRY.

Organized at Philadelphia July 3, 1863, for the protection of Pennsylvania during Lee's invasion. Mustered out September 2, 1863.

52nd REGIMENT INFANTRY.

Organized at Harrisburg November 5, 1861. Left State for Washington, D. C., November 8. Attached to 1st Brigade, Casey's Division, Army Potomac, to March, 1862. 1st Brigade, 3rd Division, 4th Army Corps, Army Potomac, to June, 1862. 1st Brigade, 2nd Division, 4th Army Corps, to December, 1862. Naglee's Brigade, Dept. of North Carolina, to January, 1863. 2nd Brigade, 2nd Division, 18th Army Corps, Dept. North Carolina, to February, 1863. 2nd Brigade, 1st Division, 18th Army Corps, Dept. of the South, to April, 1863. District of Beaufort, S. C., 10th Corps, Dept. of the South, to July, 1863. 2nd Brigade, 1st Division, Morris Island, S. C., 10th Corps, July, 1863. Davis' Brigade, Folly Island, S. C., 10th Corps, to August, 1863. 5th Brigade, Morris Island, S. C., 10th Corps, to November, 1863. 2nd Brigade, Morris Island, S. C., 10th Corps, to April, 1864. District of Hilton Head, S. C., Dept. South, to June, 1864. Morris Island, S. C., Northern District, Dept. of the South, to October, 1864. 1st Separate Brigade, Morris Island, S. C., Dept. South, to March, 1865. 1st Brigade, 2nd Division, 23rd Army Corps, Dept. North Carolina, to July, 1865.

SERVICE.—Duty in the Defences of Washington, D. C., till March, 1862. Advance on Manassas, Va., March 10-15. Moved to the Virginia Peninsula March 28. Siege of Yorktown April 5-May 4. Battle of Williamsburg May 5. Bottom's Bridge May 19-20. Operations about Bottom's Bridge May 20-23. Reconnoissance to Seven Pines May 24-27. Skirmishes at Seven Pines, Savage Station and Chickahominy May 24. Battle of Fair Oaks (Seven Pines) May 31-June 1. At Bottom's Bridge June 13-26. Seven days before Richmond June 25-July 1. Bottom's Bridge June 28-29. White Oak Swamp Bridge June 30. Malvern Hill July 1. At Harrison's Landing till August 15. Moved to Yorktown August 16-20, and duty there till December

31. Expedition to Gloucester, Matthews, King and Queen and Middlesex Counties December 11-15. Ordered to Beaufort, N. C., December 31. At Carolina City till January 28. Moved to Port Royal, S. C., January 28-31. At St. Helena Island, S. C., February 10-April 4. Operations against Charleston April 4-15. Duty at Beaufort, S. C., till July 6. Moved to Folly Island July 6. Expedition to James Island, S. C., July 9-16. Secessionville July 16. Operations on Morris and Folly Islands, S. C., against Forts Wagner and Gregg, Morris Island, and Fort Sumpter and Charleston July 18-September 7. Capture of Forts Wagner and Gregg September 7. Operations against Charleston till April, 1864. Regiment re-enlisted December 31, 1863. Duty at Hilton Head, S. C., till June, 1864. Reconnoissance to Dafuskie Island May 11. Moved to Morris Island, S. C., and operations against Charleston till February, 1865. Assault on Fort Johnson and Battery Simpkins, James Island, July 3, 1864. Occupation of Charleston February 18. Duty in Charleston Harbor till April 18. Ordered to North Carolina and duty at Salisbury till July. Mustered out July 12, 1865.

Regiment lost during service 1 Officer and 43 Enlisted men killed and mortally wounded and 2 Officers and 173 Enlisted men by disease. Total 219.

52nd REGIMENT MILITIA INFANTRY.

Organized at Philadelphia July 9, 1863. Duty in Pennsylvania during draft disturbances. Mustered out September 1, 1863.

53rd REGIMENT INFANTRY.

Organized at Harrisburg October, 1861. Left State for Washington, D. C., November 7. Attached to French's Brigade, Sumner's Division, Army Potomac, to March, 1862. 3rd Brigade, 1st Division, 2nd Army Corps, Army Potomac, to April, 1863. 4th Brigade, 1st Division, 2nd Army Corps, to June, 1865.

SERVICE.—Duty in the Defences of Washington and Alexandria till March, 1862. Advance on Manassas, Va., March 10-15. Ordered to the Virginia Peninsula. Siege of Yorktown April 5-May 4. Duty near Yorktown till June 12. Construction of Grape Vine Bridge over the Chickahominy May 28-30. Battle of Fair Oaks (Seven Pines) May 31-June 1. Seven days before Richmond June 25-July 1. Gaines Mill June 27. Peach Orchard and Savage Station June 29. White Oak Swamp Bridge and Glendale June 30. Malvern Hill July 1. Turkey Bend July 2. At Harrison's Landing till August 16. Movement to Fortress Monroe, thence to Alexandria and Centreville August 16-30. Assist in checking Pope's rout at Bull Run August 30, and cover retreat to Fairfax C. H. August 31-September 1. Maryland Campaign September 6-24. Battle of Antietam September 16-17. Duty at Bolivar Heights September 22-October 29. Reconnoissance to Charlestown October 16-17. Movement up Loudoun Valley and to Falmouth, Va., October 29-November 17. Snicker's Gap November 2. Manassas November 5-6. Battle of Fredericksburg December 12-15. Duty at Falmouth till April, 1863. Chancellorsville Campaign April 27-May 6. Battle of Chancellorsville May 1-5. Gettysburg (Pa.) Campaign June 13-July 24. Battle of Gettysburg, Pa., July 1-3. Funkstown, Md., July 12-13. Advance from the Rappahannock to the Rapidan September 13-17. Bristoe Campaign October 9-22. Auburn and Bristoe October 14. Advance to line of the Rappahannock November 7-8. Mine Run Campaign November 26-December 2. Payne's Farm November 27. Mine Run November 28-30. New Hope Church November 29. Regiment re-enlisted December 27, 1863. Duty near Stevensburg till April, 1864. Demonstration on the Rapidan February 6-7. Rapidan Campaign May 4-June 12. Battles of the Wilderness May 5-7; Spottsylvania C. H. May 8-21; Po River May 10. Assault on the Salient May 12. North Anna River May 23-26. On line of the Pamunkey May 26-28. Totopotomoy May 28-31. Cold Harbor June 1-12. Before Petersburg June 16-18. Siege of Petersburg June 16, 1864, to April 2, 1865. Weldon Railroad June 22-23, 1864. Demonstration north of the James at Deep Bottom July 27-

29 and August 13-20. Strawberry Plains, Deep Bottom, August 14-18. Ream's Station August 25. Reconnoissance to Hatcher's Run December 9-10. Dabney's Mills, Hatcher's Run, February 5-7, 1865. Watkins' House, Petersburg, March 25. Appomattox Campaign March 28-April 9. Boydton Plank Road, Hatcher's Run, March 31. White Oak Road March 31. Fall of Petersburg April 2. Sutherland Station April 2. Sailor's Creek April 6. High Bridge, Farmville, April 7. Appomattox C. H. April 9. Surrender of Lee and his army. March to Washington, D. C., May 2-12. Grand Review May 23. Mustered out June 30, 1865.

Regiment lost during service 5 Officers and 195 Enlisted men killed and mortally wounded and 1 Officer and 193 Enlisted men by disease. Total 394.

53rd REGIMENT MILITIA INFANTRY.

Organized at Reading July 2, 1863. Duty in Pennsylvania during Lee's invasion and draft disturbances. Mustered out August 20, 1863.

54th REGIMENT INFANTRY.

Organized at Harrisburg August and September, 1861. Duty at Camp Curtin till February, 1862. Left State for Washington, D. C., February 27. Attached to Defences of Washington to April, 1862. Railroad Brigade, Middle Dept., to July, 1862. Railroad Brigade, 8th Corps, Middle Dept., to September, 1862. Defences Upper Potomac, 8th Corps, to March, 1863. 4th Brigade, 1st Division, 8th Corps, to June, 1863. Campbell's Brigade, Dept. West Virginia, to December, 1863. 1st Brigade, 2nd Division, Dept. West Virginia, to April, 1864. 2nd Brigade, 1st Infantry Division, West Virginia, to June, 1864. 3rd Brigade, 2nd Infantry Division, West Virginia, to July, 1864. 2nd Brigade, 3rd Division, West Virginia, July, 1864. 3rd Brigade, 1st Division, West Virginia, to December, 1864. 2nd Brigade, Independent Division, 24th Army Corps, Army of the James, to June, 1865. 1st Brigade, Independent Division, 24th Corps, to July, 1865.

SERVICE.—Duty in the Defences of Washington till March, 1862. Ordered to Harper's Ferry, W. Va., March 29. Assigned to guard duty along line of the Baltimore & Ohio Railroad by Detachments—Company "A" at South Branch Bridge, Company "B" at Paw Paw, Company "C" at Great Cacapon Bridge, Company "D" at Alpine Station, Company "E" at No. 12 Water Station, Company "F" at Sleepy Creek Bridge, Company "G" at Back Creek Bridge, Company "H" at Rockwell's Run, Company "I" at Sir John's Run and Company "K" at Little Cacapon Bridge—till January, 1863. Skirmishes at Back Creek Bridge September 11, 1862 (Co. "G"); North Mountain September 12 (Cos. "D," "I" and "G"); Back Creek Bridge September 21 (Co. "G"); Little Cacapon October 4 (Co. "K"); Paw Paw October 4 (Co. "B"); Hanging Rock, Blue's Gap, October 2. Moved to Romney January 6, 1863. Purgetsville and Going's Ford April 6-7. Duty at Romney till June 30. Moved to New Creek June 30. Pursuit of Lee July 6-19. Skirmishes with enemy July 10 and 19. Return to Romney. March to relief of Mulligan at Petersburg, W. Va., August 1-5, and duty there till November 7. Moved to Springfield, thence to Cumberland, Md., January 4, 1864. Operations in Hampshire and Hardy Counties January 26-February 7. Patterson Creek February 3 (Co. "F"). Fremont's Ford April 1. Little Cacapon April 10 (Co. "K"). Sigel's Expedition from Martinsburg to New Market April 30-May 16. Battle of New Market May 15. Hunter's Expedition to Lynchburg May 26-July 1. Piedmont, Mount Crawford, June 5. Occupation of Staunton June 6. Middlebrook and Brownsburg June 10. Lexington June 11. Otter Creek, near Liberty, June 16. Diamond Hill June 17. Lynchburg June 17-18. Buford's Gap June 20. At and near Salem June 21. Movement to the Valley July 1-14. Reached Martinsburg July 14. Snicker's Gap July 17-18. Winchester and Kernstown July 24. Martinsburg July 25. Sheridan's Shenandoah Valley Campaign August to December. At Halltown till August 28. Berryville September 3. Battle of Opequan, Winchester, September 19. Fisher's Hill September 22. Cedar Creek October 13. Battle of Cedar Creek October 19. Moved to Washington, D. C., December 19-20, thence to City Point, Va., and Bermuda Hundred, Va., December 20-23. Siege operations against Petersburg and Richmond December, 1864, to April, 1865. Appomattox Campaign March 28-April 9, 1865. Hatcher's Run March 29-April 1. Fall of Petersburg April 2. Pursuit of Lee April 3-9. Rice's Station April 9. Regiment captured. Sent to Parole Camp, Annapolis, Md. Mustered out at Harrisburg, Pa., July 15, 1865.

Regiment lost during service 5 Officers and 108 Enlisted men killed and mortally wounded and 2 Officers and 137 Enlisted men by disease. Total 152.

54th REGIMENT MILITIA INFANTRY.

Organized at Pittsburg June 30, 1863. Duty in Pennsylvania during Lee's invasion and draft disturbances. Mustered out August 17, 1863.

55th REGIMENT INFANTRY.

Organized at Harrisburg November, 1861. Left Camp Curtin for Fortress Monroe, Va., November 22. Attached to Sherman's South Carolina Expedition to February, 1862. Edisto Island, S. C., Dept. of the South, to July, 1862. District of Beaufort, S. C., Dept. South, to September, 1862. District Beaufort, S. C., 10th Army Corps, Dept. South, to April, 1864. 1st Brigade, 3rd Division, 10th Army Corps, Dept. of Virginia and North Carolina, to May, 1864. 1st Brigade, 2nd Division, 18th Army Corps, Dept. of Virginia and North Carolina, to December, 1864. 4th Brigade, 1st Division, 24th Army Corps, Dept. of Virginia, to May, 1865. 2nd Brigade, 1st Division, 24th Army Corps, Dept. Virginia, to August, 1865.

SERVICE.—At Fortress Monroe, Va., till December 8, 1861. Moved to Port Royal, S. C., December 8, and duty near Hilton Head, S. C., till February 25, 1862. Duty at Edisto Island, S. C., till October. Companies "E," "F" and "G" attacked on Little Edisto March 29. Edisto Island April 18 (Detachment). Expedition up Broad River to Pocotaligo October 21-23. Caston's and Frampton's Plantations, Pocotaligo, October 22. Duty at Port Royal Ferry near Beaufort, S. C., till January, 1864. Regiment re-enlisted January 1, and on furlough January 22-March 23. Embarked for Virginia April 12. Butler's operations on south side of the James and against Petersburg and Richmond May 5-28. Swift Creek or Arrowfield Church May 9-10. Operations against Fort Darling May 12-16. Battle of Drewry's Bluff May 14-16. Operations on the Bermuda Hundred front May 17-28. Moved to White House, thence to Cold Harbor May 28-June 1. Battle of Cold Harbor June 1-12. Before Petersburg June 15-18. Siege operations against Petersburg and Richmond June 16, 1864, to April 2, 1865. Mine Explosion, Petersburg, July 30, 1864 (Support). Battle of Chaffin's Farm, New Market Heights, north of James River September 28-30. Duty in trenches before Richmond till March, 1865. Signal Hill December 10, 1864. Appomattox Campaign March 26-April 9. Hatcher's and Gravelly Runs March 29-30. Capture of Forts Gregg and Baldwin and fall of Petersburg April 2. Pursuit of Lee April 3-9. Rice's Station April 6. Appomattox C. H. April 9. Surrender of Lee and his army. At Appomattox C. H. till April 17, and at Richmond till July. Duty in Virginia till August. Mustered out at Petersburg, Va., August 30, 1865.

Regiment lost while in service 7 Officers and 201 Enlisted men killed and mortally wounded and 3 Officers and 268 Enlisted men by disease. Total 479.

55th REGIMENT MILITIA INFANTRY.

Organized at Pittsburg June 27, 1863. Duty in Pennsylvania during Lee's invasion and in the Dept. of West Virginia. Attached to Wilkinson's Brigade, Scammon's Division. Mustered out August 26, 1863.

56th REGIMENT INFANTRY.

Organized at Camp Curtin, Harrisburg, March 7, 1862. Left State for Washington, D. C., March 8. Attached to Defences of Washington to May, 1862. Doubleday's Brigade, Dept. of the Rappahannock, to June, 1862. 2nd Brigade, 3rd Division, 3rd Corps, Army of Virginia, to September, 1862. 2nd Brigade, 1st Division, 1st Army Corps, Army of the Potomac, to March, 1864. 3rd Brigade, 2nd Division, 5th Army Corps, Army Potomac, to September, 1864. 3rd Brigade, 3rd Division, 5th Army Corps, to July, 1865.

SERVICE.—Duty at Fort Albany, Defences of Washington, till April 4, 1862, and at Budd's Ferry till April 24. At Aquia Creek Landing till May 10. Guard railroad bridge at Potomac Creek May 21-27. (Five Companies moved to Belle Plains May 10.) Guard duty near Fredericksburg till August 9. Pope's Campaign in Northern Virginia August 16-September 2. Battles of Gainesville August 28; Groveton August 29; Bull Run August 30. Maryland Campaign September 6-24. Battles of South Mountain September 14; Antietam September 16-17. Duty on the battlefield of Antietam till October 20. (Co. "A" at Fairfax October 20-30.) At Bakersville October 20-30. Movement to Falmouth, Va., October 30-November 19. Union, Va., November 2-3. Battle of Fredericksburg December 12-15. Burnside's 2nd Campaign, "Mud March," January 20-24, 1863. At Falmouth and Belle Plains till April 27, 1863. Chancellorsville Campaign April 27-May 6. Operations at Pollock's Mill Creek April 29-May 2. Fitzhugh's Crossing April 29-30.. Chancellorsville May 2-5. Brandy Station and Beverly Ford June 9. Gettysburg (Pa.) Campaign June 11-July 24. Battle of Gettysburg, Pa., July 1-3. Pursuit of Lee July 5-24. Duty on line of the Rappahannock till October. Bristoe Campaign October 9-22. Advance to line of the Rappahannock November 7-8. Mine Run Campaign November 26-December 2. Demonstration on the Rapidan February 6-7, 1864. On Veteran furlough March 10-April 17. Rapidan Campaign May 4-June 12. Battles of the Wilderness May 5-7; Laurel Hill May 8; Spottsylvania May 8-12; Spottsylvania C. H. May 12-21. Assault on the Salient May 12. North Anna River May 23-26. Jericho Ford May 25. Totopotomoy May 28-31. Cold Harbor June 1-12. Bethesda Church June 1-3. Before Petersburg June 16-18. Siege of Petersburg June 16, 1864, to April 2, 1865. Mine Explosion, Petersburg, July 30, 1864 (Reserve). Weldon Railroad August 18-21. Poplar Springs Church September 29-October 2. Boydton Plank Road, Hatcher's Run, October 27-28. Warren's Raid on Weldon Railroad December 7-12. Dabney's Mills, Hatcher's Run, February 5-7, 1865. Appomattox Campaign March 28-April 9. Lewis Farm near Gravelly Run March 29. Boydton and White Oak Road March 31. Five Forks April 1. Fall of Petersburg April 2. Appomattox C. H. April 9. Surrender of Lee and his army. March to Washington, D. C., May 2-12. Grand Review May 23. Mustered out at Philadelphia, Pa., July 1, 1865.

Regiment lost during service 7 Officers and 111 Enlisted men killed and mortally wounded and 1 Officer and 96 Enlisted men by disease. Total 215.

56th REGIMENT MILITIA INFANTRY.

Organized at Pittsburg June 27, 1863. Duty in Pennsylvania during Lee's invasion and draft disturbances. Mustered out August 13, 1863.

57th REGIMENT INFANTRY.

Organized at Harrisburg December 14, 1861. Left State for Washington, D. C., December 14. Attached to Jameson's Brigade, Heintzelman's Division, Army Potomac, to March, 1862. 1st Brigade, 3rd Division, 3rd Army Corps, Army Potomac, to August, 1862. 2nd Brigade, 1st Division, 3rd Army Corps, Army Potomac, to March, 1863. 1st Brigade, 1st Division, 3rd Army Corps, to March, 1864. 2nd Brigade, 3rd Division, 2nd Army Corps, to June, 1865.

SERVICE.—Duty in the Defences of Washington, D. C., till March, 1862. Moved to the Virginia Peninsula March 16-18. Siege of Yorktown April 5-May 4. Skirmish Yorktown April 11. Battle of Williamsburg May 5. Battle of Fair Oaks, Seven Pines, May 31-June 1.

Seven Days before Richmond June 25-July 1. Oak Grove June 25. Peach Orchard and Savage Station June 29. Charles City Cross Roads and Glendale June 30. Malvern Hill July 1. Duty at Harrison's Landing till August 16. Movement to Centreville August 16-26. Skirmish at Bull Run August 20. Pope's Campaign in Northern Virginia. Battles of Gainesville August 28; Groveton August 29; Bull Run August 30; Chantilly September 1. Guard fords from Monocacy River to Conrad's Ferry till October. March up the Potomac to Leesburg, thence to Falmouth, Va., October 11-November 19. Battle of Fredericksburg, Va., December 12-15. Burnside's 2nd Campaign, "Mud March," January 20-24, 1863. At Falmouth, Va., till April 27. Chancellorsville Campaign April 27-May 6. Battle of Chancellorsville May 1-5. Gettysburg (Pa.) Campaign June 11-July 24. Battle of Gettysburg, Pa., July 1-3. Pursuit of Lee July 5-24. Wapping Heights, Va., July 23. Duty on line of the Rappahannock till October. Bristoe Campaign October 9-22. Auburn and Bristoe October 13-14. Advance to line of the Rappahannock November 7-8. Kelly's Ford November 7. Mine Run Campaign November 26-December 2. Payne's Farm November 27. Veterans on furlough January to March, 1864. Rapidan Campaign May 4-June 12. Battles of the Wilderness May 5-7; Laurel Hill May 8; Spottsylvania May 8-12; Po River May 10; Spottsylvania C. H. May 12-21. Assault on the Salient May 12. Harris' Farm May 19. North Anna River May 23-26. Line of the Pamunkey May 26-28. Totopotomoy May 28-31. Cold Harbor June 1-12. Before Petersburg June 16-18. Siege of Petersburg June 16, 1864, to April 2, 1865. Weldon Railroad June 22-23, 1864. Demonstration north of the James at Deep Bottom July 27-29, and August 13-20. Strawberry Plains, Deep Bottom, August 14-18. Ream's Station August 25. Poplar Springs Church September 29-October 2. Boydton Plank Road, Hatcher's Run, October 27-28. Expedition to Weldon Railroad December 7-12. Consolidated to five Companies January 11, 1865. Dabney's Mills, Hatcher's Run, February 5-7. Appomattox Campaign March 28-April 9. Boydton Road March 30-31. Fall of Petersburg April 2. Sailor's Creek April 6. High Bridge, Farmville, April 7. Appomattox C. H. April 9. Surrender of Lee and his army. At Burkesville till May. March to Washington D. C., May 2-12. Grand Review May 23. Duty at Alexandria till June. Mustered out June 29, 1865.

Regiment lost during service 12 Officers and 149 Enlisted men killed and mortally wounded and 217 Enlisted men by disease. Total 378.

57th REGIMENT MILITIA INFANTRY.

Organized at Pittsburg July 3, 1863. Duty in Pennsylvania during Lee's invasion and draft disturbances. Mustered out August 17, 1863.

58th REGIMENT INFANTRY.

Organized at Camp Curtin, Harrisburg, September 21, 1861, to March 1, 1862. Moved to Fortress Monroe, Va., March 8-10. Attached to Camp Hamilton, Va., Dept. Virginia, to May, 1862. 2nd Brigade, 1st Division, Dept. of Virginia, to July, 1862. Viele's Command, Norfolk, Va., Dept. Virginia, to October, 1862. Foster's Provisional Brigade, Peck's Division, at Suffolk, 7th Corps, Dept. of Virginia, to December, 1862. Gibb's Provisional Brigade, Division at Suffolk, 7th Corps, Dept. Virginia, to January, 1863. 2nd Brigade, 3rd Division, 18th Army Corps, Dept. of North Carolina, to April, 1863. Jourdan's Independent Brigade, Defences of New Berne, Dept. North Carolina, to June, 1863. District of Pamlico, 18th Army Corps, Dept. North Carolina, to August, 1863. Sub-District Pamlico, District North Carolina, Dept. of Virginia and North Carolina, to April, 1864. 3rd Brigade, 1st Division, 18th Army Corps, Dept. Virginia and North Carolina, to December, 1864. 3rd Brigade, 3rd Division, 24th Army Corps, Dept. of Virginia, to June, 1865. 2nd Brigade, 3rd Division, 24th Corps, to July, 1865. 2nd Independent Brigade, 24th Army Corps, to August, 1865. District of Southwest Virginia to September, 1865. Sub-District Staunton, District Central

Virginia, Dept. Virginia, to January, 1865. Mustered out January 24, 1866.

SERVICE.—Duty at Camp Hamilton, Va., till May 10, 1862. Occupation of Norfolk and Portsmouth May 10, and duty there till October 11. Ordered to Suffolk, Va., October 11, and duty there till January, 1863. Embarked for Beaufort, N. C., January 5, thence moved to New Berne, and duty there till June. Expedition to Core Creek February 12-13. Sandy Ridge February 13. Demonstration on Kinston March 6-8. Near Dover March 7. Expedition toward Kinston April 16-21. Core Creek April 17-18. Sandy Ridge April 20. Demonstration on Kinston April 27-May 1. Wise's Cross Roads and Dover Road April 28. Demonstration on Kinston May 20-23. Gum Swamp May 22. Batchelor's Creek May 23. Moved to Washington, N. C., June 26, and duty there till April, 1864. Expedition from Washington to Chicora Creek December 17, 1863 (Co. "B"). Regiment re-enlisted January 1, 1864. Reconnoissance on Neuse River Road January 27-28. Near Blount's Creek April 5, 1864 (Detachment). Ordered to Yorktown, Va., April 28. Butler's operations on south side of James River and against Petersburg and Richmond May 4-28. Swift Creek or Arrowfield Church May 9-10. Operations against Fort Darling April 12-16. Battle of Drewry's Bluff May 14-16. Operations at Bermuda Hundred May 17-28. Movement to White House, thence to Cold Harbor May 28-June 1. Battles about Cold Harbor June 1-12. Before Petersburg June 15-18. Siege operations against Petersburg and Richmond June 16, 1864, to April 2, 1865. Hare's Hill June 24 and 28, 1864. Veterans on furlough June 24-August 25. Chaffin's Farm, New Market Heights, September 28-30. Fair Oaks October 27-28. Expedition to Fredericksburg March 5-8, 1865, and into Westmoreland County March 11-13. Moved to White House March 13-18. March to Signal Hill before Richmond March 24-26. Occupation of Richmond April 3, and duty there till August. At Staunton till November and at Charlottesville till January, 1866. Mustered out January 24, 1866.

Regiment lost during service 6 Officers and 68 Enlisted men killed and mortally wounded and 4 Officers and 139 Enlisted men by disease. Total 217.

58th REGIMENT MILITIA INFANTRY.

Organized at Pittsburg July 1, 1863. Duty in Pennsylvania during Lee's invasion and draft disturbances. Mustered out August 15, 1863.

59th VOLUNTEERS.

(See 2nd Cavalry.)

59th REGIMENT MILITIA INFANTRY.

Organized at Philadelphia July 1, 1863. Duty in Pennsylvania during Lee's invasion and draft disturbances. Mustered out September 9, 1863.

60th VOLUNTEERS.

(See 3rd Cavalry.)

60th REGIMENT MILITIA INFANTRY.

Organized at Philadelphia June 19, 1863. Duty in Pennsylvania during Lee's invasion and draft disturbances. Mustered out September 8, 1863.

61st REGIMENT INFANTRY.

Organized at Pittsburg September 7, 1861. Ordered to Washington, D. C. Attached to Jameson's Brigade, Heintzelman's Division, Army Potomac, to February, 1862. Graham's Brigade, Couch's Division, Army Potomac, to March, 1862. 2nd Brigade, 1st Division, 4th Army Corps, Army Potomac, to July, 1862. 3rd Brigade, 1st Division, 4th Army Corps, to September, 1862. 2nd Brigade, 3rd Division, 6th Army Corps, to October, 1862. 1st Brigade, 3rd Division, 6th Army Corps, to February, 1863. Light Brigade, 6th Army Corps, to May, 1863. 3rd Brigade, 2nd Division, 6th Army Corps, Army Potomac, to July, 1864. Army of the Shenandoah to December, 1864, and Army Potomac to June, 1865.

SERVICE.—Duty in the Defences of Washington, D. C., till March, 1862. Reconnoissance to Pohick Church and Occoquan River November 12, 1861. Advance on Manassas, Va., March 10-15, 1862. Reconnoissance to Gainesville March 20. Moved to the Peninsula, Va., March 26. Siege of Yorktown April 5-May 4. Battle of Williamsburg May 5. Operations about Bottom's Bridge May 20-23. Battle of Fair Oaks, Seven Pines, May 31-June 1. Seven days before Richmond June 25-July 1. Seven Pines June 27. White Oak Swamp and Charles City Cross Roads June 30. Malvern Hill July 1. At Harrison's Landing till August 16. Reconnoissance to Malvern Hill August 5-7. Movement to Alexandria, thence to Chantilly August 16-30. Chantilly September 1. Maryland Campaign September 6-24. Battle of Antietam, Md., September 16-17. Williamsport September 19-20. Duty in Maryland and on the Potomac till November. Movement to Falmouth, Va., November 1-19. Battle of Fredericksburg December 12-15. Burnside's 2nd Campaign, "Mud March," January 20-24, 1863. At Falmouth till April. Chancellorsville Campaign April 27-May 6. Operations at Franklin's Crossing April 29-May 2. Maryes Heights, Fredericksburg, May 3. Salem Heights May 3-4. Banks' Ford May 4. Operations about Deep Run Ravine June 6-13. Battle of Gettysburg, Pa., July 2-4. South Mountain, Md., July 6. Duty on line of the Rappahannock and Rapidan till October. Bristoe Campaign October 9-22. Advance to line of the Rappahannock November 7-8. Rappahannock Station November 7. Mine Run Campaign November 26-December 2. At Brandy Station till April, 1864. Rapidan Campaign May 4-June 12. Battles of the Wilderness May 5-7; Parker's Store May 5; Spottsylvania May 8-12; Spottsylvania C. H. May 12-21. Assault on the Salient May 12. North Anna River May 23-26. Line of the Pamunkey May 26-28. Totopotomoy May 28-31. Cold Harbor June 1-12. Before Petersburg June 17-19. Siege of Petersburg till July 9. Jerusalem Plank Road June 22-23. Moved to Washington, D. C., July 9-11. Repulse of Early's attack on Fort Stevens and the Northern Defences of Washington July 11-12. Pursuit of Early to Snicker's Gap July 14-19. Sheridan's Shenandoah Valley Campaign August to December. Charlestown August 21. Gilbert's Ford, Opequan Creek, September 13. Battle of Opequan, Winchester, September 19. Fisher's Hill September 22. Battle of Cedar Creek October 19. Duty in the Shenandoah Valley till December. Ordered to Petersburg, Va., December 1. Siege of Petersburg December, 1864, to April, 1865. Fort Fisher, Petersburg, March 25, 1865. Appomattox Campaign March 28-April 9. Assault on and fall of Petersburg April 2. Pursuit of Lee April 3-9. Appomattox C. H. April 9. Surrender of Lee and his army. March to Danville April 23-29, and duty there till May 23. Moved to Richmond, Va., thence to Washington, D. C. Corps Review June 8. Mustered out June 28, 1865.

Regiment lost during service 19 Officers and 218 Enlisted men killed and mortally wounded and 1 Officer and 100 Enlisted men by disease. Total 338.

62nd REGIMENT INFANTRY.

Organized at Pittsburg as 33rd Regiment August 31, 1861. Left State for Washington, D. C., August 31, 1861. Designation changed to 62nd Pennsylvania Volunteers November 18, 1861. Attached to Morrell's Brigade, Fitz John Porter's Division, Army Potomac, to March, 1862. 2nd Brigade, 1st Division, 3rd Army Corps, Army Potomac, to May, 1862. 2nd Brigade, 1st Division, 5th Army Corps, to July, 1864.

SERVICE.—Camp near Fort Corcoran, Defences of Washington, D. C., till October, 1861, and near Fall's Church, Va., till March, 1862. Moved to the Peninsula March 22-24. Reconnoissance to Big Bethel March 30. Howard's Mills, near Cockletown, April 4. Warwick Road April 5. Siege of Yorktown April 5-May 4. Hanover C. H. May 27. Operations about Hanover C. H. May 27-29. Seven days before Richmond June 25-July 1. Battles of Mechanicsville June 26; Gaines Mill June 27; Savage Station June 29; Turkey Bridge or Malvern Cliff June 30; Malvern Hill July 1. At Harrison's Landing till August 16. Movement to Fortress Monroe,

thence to Centreville August 16-28. Battle of Bull Run August 30. Battle of Antietam, Md., September 16-17. Shepherdstown Ford September 19. Blackford's Ford September 19. Reconnoissance to Smithfield October 16-17. Battle of Fredericksburg, Va., December 12-15. Expedition to Richard's and Ellis' Fords, Rappahannock River, December 30-31. Burnside's second Campaign, "Mud March," January 20-24, 1863. At Falmouth till April. Chancellorsville Campaign April 27-May 6. Battle of Chancellorsville May 1-5. Middleburg June 19. Uppervile June 21. Battle of Gettysburg, Pa., July 1-3. Pursuit of Lee July 5-24. Duty on line of the Rappahannock till October. Bristoe Campaign October 9-22. Advance to line of the Rappahannock November 7-8. Rappahannock Station November 7. Mine Run Campaign November 26-December 2. Duty at Bealeton Station till May, 1864. Rapidan Campaign May 4-June 12. Battles of the Wilderness May 5-7; Laurel Hill May 8; Spottsylvania May 8-12; Spottsylvania C. H. May 12-21. Assault on the Salient May 12. North Anna River May 23-26. Jericho Ford May 25. Line of the Pamunkey May 26-28. Totopotomoy May 28-31. Cold Harbor June 1-12. Bethesda Church June 1-3. Before Petersburg June 16-18. Siege of Petersburg till July 3. Left front July 3. Mustered out July 13, 1864. Companies "L" and "M" transferred to 91st Pennsylvania. Mustered out August 15, 1864. Veterans and Recruits transferred to 155th Pennsylvania.

Regiment lost during service 17 Officers and 152 Enlisted men killed and mortally wounded and 89 Enlisted men by disease. Total 258.

63rd REGIMENT INFANTRY.

Organized at Pittsburg August, 1861. Left State for Washington, D. C., August 26. Attached to Jameson's Brigade, Heintzelman's Division, Army Potomac, to March, 1862. 1st Brigade, 3rd Division, 3rd Army Corps, Army Potomac, to August, 1862. 1st Brigade, 1st Division, 3rd Army Corps, to March, 1864. 2nd Brigade, 3rd Division, 2nd Army Corps, to September, 1864.

SERVICE.—Duty in the Defences of Washington, D. C., till March, 1862. Reconnoissance to Pohick Church and the Occoquan November 12, 1861. Pohick Church and the Occoquan March 5, 1862 (Detachment). Moved to the Peninsula March 16-18. Siege of Yorktown April 5-May 4. Battle of Williamsburg May 5. Battle of Fair Oaks (Seven Pines) May 31-June 1. Seven days before Richmond June 25-July 1. Oak Grove June 25. Glendale June 30. Malvern Hill July 1. Duty at Harrison's Landing till August 16. Movement to Centreville August 16-26. Bristoe Station or Kettle Run August 27. Buckland's Bridge, Broad Run, August 27. Battles of Groveton August 29; Bull Run August 30; Chantilly September 1. Duty in the Defences of Washington and guarding fords in Maryland till October. March up the Potomac to Leesburg, thence to Falmouth, Va., October 11-November 19. Battle of Fredericksburg December 12-15. Burnside's second Campaign, "Mud March," January 20-24, 1863.. At Falmouth till April. Chancellorsville Campaign April 27-May 6. Battle of Chancellorsville May 1-5. Gettysburg (Pa.) Campaign June 11-July 24. Battle of Gettysburg July 1-3. Pursuit of Lee July 5-24. Wapping Heights, Va., July 23. Duty on line of the Rappahannock till October. Bristoe Campaign October 9-22. Auburn and Bristoe October 13-14. Advance to line of the Rappahannock November 7-8. Kelly's Ford November 7. Mine Run Campaign November 26-December 2. Payne's Farm November 27. Demonstration on the Rapidan February 6-7, 1864. Rapidan Campaign May 4-June 12. Battles of the Wilderness May 5-7; Laurel Hill May 8; Spottsylvania May 8-12; Po River May 10; Spottsylvania C. H. May 12-21. Assault on the Salient May 12. Harris' Farm May 19. North Anna River May 23-26. Line of the Pamunkey May 26-28. Totopotomoy May 28-31. Cold Harbor June 1-12. Before Petersburg June 16-18. Siege of Petersburg and Richmond June 16-September 5. Weldon Railroad June 22-23. Demonstration on north side of the

James River at Deep Bottom July 27-29. Deep Bottom July 27-28. Mine Explosion July 30 (Reserve). Demonstration on rforth side of the James August 13-20. Strawberry Plains, Deep Bottom, August 14-18. Veterans and Recruits transferred to 105th Pennsylvania September 5, 1864. Mustered out September 9, 1864.

Regiment lost during service 17 Officers and 169 Enlisted men killed and mortally wounded and 1 Officer and 133 Enlisted men by disease. Total 320.

64th REGIMENT VOLUNTEERS.
(See 4th Cavalry.)

65th REGIMENT VOLUNTEERS.
(See 5th Cavalry.)

66th REGIMENT INFANTRY.
Organized at Philadelphia as 30th Pennsylvania Volunteers July and August, 1861. Designation changed September, 1861. Moved to Washington, D. C., September 20, 1861. Attached to Abercrombie's Brigade, Banks' Division, Army Potomac. Duty on the Upper Potomac at Frederick, Md., till February, 1862. Operations on the Potomac October 21-24, 1861. Ordered to Washington, D. C., February, 1862, and consolidated with 73rd and 99th Pennsylvania Volunteers March 1, 1862.

67th REGIMENT INFANTRY.
Organized at Philadelphia March 31, 1862. Left State for Annapolis, Md., April 3. Attached to District of Annapolis, Defences of Baltimore, Middle Dept., to July, 1862. Annapolis, Md., 8th Corps, Middle Dept., to January, 1863. Defences Upper Potomac, 8th Corps, to March, 1863. 3rd Brigade, 2nd Division, 8th Corps, to June, 1863. Elliott's Command, 8th Corps, to July, 1863. 3rd Brigade, 3rd Division, 3rd Army Corps, Army Potomac, to March, 1864. 2nd Brigade, 3rd Division, 6th Army Corps, Army Potomac, and Army Shenandoah to June, 1865.

SERVICE.—Guard and provost duty in East Maryland and at Camp Parole, Annapolis, Md., till February, 1863. Moved to Harper's Ferry, thence to Berryville. Duty on the Upper Potomac till June. Battle of Winchester, Va., June 13-15. Retreat to Harper's Ferry, W. Va. (Those captured paroled July 7 and declared exchanged October 11, rejoining Regiment October 13, 1862.) Guard stores from Harper's Ferry to Washington July 1-5. Join Army Potomac at Frederick, Md., and pursuit of Lee July 5-24. Wapping Heights, Va., July 23. Duty on line of the Rappahannock till October. Bristoe Campaign October 9-22. Advance to line of the Rappahannock November 7-8. Kelly's Ford November 7. Brandy Station November 8. Mine Run Campaign November 26-December 2. Payne's Farm November 27. Duty at Brandy Station till April, 1864. Demonstration on the Rapidan February 6-7. Veterans on furlough March-April. Non-Veterans temporarily attached to 138th Pennsylvania till June. Veterans return to Washington, D. C., April. Rapidan Campaign May-June. Report to Gen. Abercrombie at Belle Plains, thence ordered to Fredericksburg and reported to Gen. Shriver. Escort trains to Front Royal and White House. Action at White House June 20. Joined Brigade at Yellow Tavern. Non-Veterans participated in battles of the Wilderness May 5-7; Spottsylvania C. H. May 8-21. Assault on the Salient May 12. North Anna May 23-26. On line of the Pamunkey May 26-28. Totopotomoy May 28-31. Cold Harbor June 1-12. Before Petersburg June 17-19. Ream's Station June 22-23. Siege of Petersburg till July 6. Ordered to Baltimore, Md., July 6. Battle of Monocacy, Md., July 9. Sheridan's Shenandoah Valley Campaign August to December. Charlestown August 29. Battle of Opequan, Winchester, September 19. Fisher's Hill September 22. Battle of Cedar Creek October 19. Duty in the Shenandoah Valley till December. Moved to Washington, D. C., thence to Petersburg, Va., December 3-6. Siege of Petersburg December, 1864, to April, 1865. Fort Fisher, Petersburg, March 25, 1865. Assault on and fall of Petersburg April 2. Pursuit of Lee April 3-9. Appomattox C. H. April 9. Surrender of Lee and his army. March to Danville April 23-29, and duty there till May. March to Richmond, thence to Washington, D. C. Corps Review June 8. Mustered out July 17, 1865.

Regiment lost during service 2 Officers and 77 Enlisted men killed and mortally wounded and 3 Officers and 150 Enlisted men by disease. Total 232.

68th REGIMENT INFANTRY.
Organized at Philadelphia August, 1862. Left State for Washington, D. C., September 1, 1862. Camp at Arlington Heights till October. Moved to Poolesville, Md., and attached to 1st Brigade, 1st Division, 3rd Army Corps, Army Potomac, to March, 1864. 1st Brigade, 3rd Division, 2nd Army Corps, Army Potomac, to April, 1864. Provost Guard, Army Potomac, to April, 1865. Collis' Independent Brigade, 9th Army Corps, April, 1865. Hart's Island, N. Y., Harbor, Dept. of the East, to June, 1865.

SERVICE.—March up the Potomac to Leesburg, thence to Falmouth, Va., October 11-November 19, 1862. Battle of Fredericksburg, Va., December 12-15. Burnside's 2nd Campaign, "Mud March," January 20-24, 1863. At Falmouth till April. Chancellorsville Campaign April 27-May 6. Battle of Chancellorsville May 1-5. Gettysburg (Pa.) Campaign June 13-July 24. Battle of Gettysburg July 1-3. Pursuit of Lee July 5-24. Wapping Heights, Va., July 23. Duty on line of the Rappahannock till October. Bristoe Campaign October 9-22. Auburn October 13. Auburn and Bristoe October 14. Advance to line of the Rappahannock November 7-8. Kelly's Ford November 7. Mine Run Campaign November 26-December 2. Payne's Farm November 27. At Brandy Station till April, 1864. Demonstration on the Rapidan February 6-7. Rapidan Campaign May 4-June 12. Assigned to provost duty at Meade's Headquarters April 18. Battles of the Wilderness May 5-7; Spottsylvania C. H. May 8-21; Guinea Station May 21; North Anna River May 23-26. On line of the Pamunkey May 26-28. Totopotomoy May 28-31. Cold Harbor June 1-12. Before Petersburg June 16-18. Siege operations against Petersburg and Richmond June 16, 1864, to April 2, 1865. Garrison and provost duty at City Point, Va., June 18, 1864, to April 1, 1865. Assault on and fall of Petersburg April 2. Occupation of Petersburg April 3. Moved from before Petersburg to Hart's Island, N. Y. Harbor, April, 1865, and duty there guarding prisoners till June. Mustered out June 9, 1865.

Regiment lost during service 10 Officers and 61 Enlisted men killed and mortally wounded and 51 Enlisted men by disease. Total 122.

69th REGIMENT INFANTRY.
Organized at Philadelphia August 18, 1861. Left State for Washington, D. C., September 17. Attached to Baker's Brigade, Stone's (Sedgwick's) Division, Army Potomac, to March, 1862. 2nd Brigade, 2nd Division, 2nd Army Corps, Army Potomac, to June, 1864. 3rd Brigade, 2nd Division, 2nd Army Corps, to June, 1865.

SERVICE.—Duty in the Defences of Washington, D. C., till October. Affair at Vaderburg's House, Munson's Hill, September 29, 1861. Moved to Poolesville, Md., and duty on the Upper Potomac till February, 1862. At Harper's Ferry, W. Va., till March 24. Moved to the Virginia Peninsula March 24-April 1. Siege of Yorktown April 5-May 4. Moved to West Point May 7. Duty at Tyler's Farm till May 31. Battle of Fair Oaks, Seven Pines, May 31-June 1. Duty at Fair Oaks till June 28. Skirmish at Fair Oaks June 18. Seven days before Richmond June 25-July 1. Battles of Peach Orchard and Savage Station June 29. Charles City Cross Roads and Glendale June 30. Malvern Hill July 1. At Harrison's Landing till August 16. Movement to Newport News, thence to Alexandria August 16-28, and to Centreville and Chantilly August 29-30. Cover Pope's retreat August 31-September 1. Chantilly September 1. Maryland Campaign September 6-24. Battle of Antietam September 16-17. Moved to Harper's Ferry September 22, and duty there till October 30. Movement to Falmouth, Va., October 30-November 20. Battle of

Fredericksburg, Va., December 12-15. Burnside's 2nd Campaign, "Mud March," January 20-24, 1863. At Falmouth till April. Hartwood Church February 25. Chancellorsville Campaign April 27-May 6. Banks' Ford May 1 and 4. Gettysburg (Pa.) Campaign June 13-July 24. Battle of Gettysburg, Pa., July 2-4. Pursuit of Lee July 5-24. At Banks' Ford and Culpeper till October. Advance from the Rappahannock to the Rapidan September 13-17. Bristoe Campaign October 9-22. Advance to line of the Rappahannock November 7-8. Mine Run Campaign November 26-December 2. Robertson's Tavern or Locust Grove November 27. Duty on the Rapidan till May, 1864. Demonstration on the Rapidan February 6-7. Veterans on furlough March and April. Rapidan Campaign May 4-June 12. Battles of the Wilderness May 5-7; Laurel Hill May 8; Spottsylvania May 8-12; Po River May 10; Spottsylvania C. H. May 12-21. Assault on the Salient May 12. North Anna River May 23-26. Line of the Pamunkey May 26-28. Totopotomoy May 28-31. Cold Harbor June 1-12. Before Petersburg June 16-18. Siege of Petersburg June 16, 1864, to April 2, 1865. Jerusalem Plank Road June 22-23, 1864. Demonstration north of the James at Deep Bottom July 27-29. Mine Explosion, Petersburg, July 30 (Reserve). Demonstration north of the James at Deep Bottom August 13-20. Strawberry Plains, Deep Bottom, August 14-18. Ream's Station August 25. Boydton Plank Road, Hatcher's Run, October 27-28. Dabney's Mills, Hatcher's Run, February 5-7, 1865. Watkins' House March 25. Appomattox Campaign March 28-April 9. Vaughan Road near Hatcher's Run March 29. Crow's House March 31. Fall of Petersburg April 2. Sailor's Creek April 6. High Bridge and Farmville April 7. Appomattox C. H. April 9. Surrender of Lee and his army. At Burkesville till May 2. March to Washington, D. C., May 2-12. Grand Review May 23. At Ball's Cross Roads till July. Mustered out July 1, 1865.

Regiment lost during service 12 Officers and 166 Enlisted men killed and mortally wounded and 3 Officers and 107 Enlisted men by disease. Total 288.

70th REGIMENT VOLUNTEERS.

(See 6th Cavalry.)

71st REGIMENT INFANTRY, "BAKER'S CALIFORNIA REGIMENT."

At Fort Schuyler, N. Y., till July 1, 1861. Moved to Fortress Monroe, Va., thence to Washington, D. C., July 22. Duty in the Defences of Washington till October. Affair at Vanderburg's House, Munson's Hill, September 29. Ordered to Poolesville, Md. Attached to Baker's Brigade, Stone's (Sedgwick's) Division, Army Potomac, to March, 1864. 2nd Brigade, 2nd Division, 2nd Army Corps, Army Potomac, to June, 1864.

SERVICE.—Operations on the Potomac October 21-24, 1861. Ball's Bluff October 21. Duty on the Upper Potomac till February, 1862. At Harper's Ferry, W. Va., till March 24. Moved to the Virginia Peninsula March 24-April 1. Siege of Yorktown April 5-May 4. At Tyler's Farm till May 31. Battle of Fair Oaks, Seven Pines, May 31-June 1. At Fair Oaks till June 28. Skirmish at Fair Oaks June 18. Seven days before Richmond June 25-July 1. Peach Orchard and Savage Station June 29. Charles City Cross Roads and Glendale June 30. Malvern Hill July 1. At Harrison's Landing till August 16. Movement to Newport News, thence to Alexandria August 16-28, thence to Centreville and Chantilly August 28-30. Cover Pope's retreat August 31-September 1. Maryland Campaign September 6-24. Battle of Antietam September 16-17. Moved to Harper's Ferry September 22, and duty there till October 30. Movement to Falmouth October 30-November 19. Battle of Fredericksburg December 12-15. Burnside's 2nd Campaign, "Mud March," January 20-24, 1863. Hartwood Church February 25. At Falmouth till April. Chancellorsville Campaign April 27-May 6. Banks' Ford May 1 and 4. Gettysburg (Pa.) Campaign June 13-July 24. Battle of Gettysburg July 2-4. Pursuit of

Lee July 5-24. At Banks' Ford and Culpeper till October. Advance from the Rappahannock to the Rapidan September 13-17. Bristoe Campaign October 9-22. Advance to the line of the Rappahannock November 7-8. Mine Run Campaign November 26-December 2. Robertson's Tavern or Locust Grove November 27. Duty on the Rapidan till May. Demonstration on the Rapidan February 6-7. Rapidan Campaign May 4-June 12. Battles of the Wilderness May 5-7; Laurel Hill May 8; Spottsylvania May 8-12; Po River May 10; Spottsylvania C. H. May 12-21. Assault on the Salient May 12. North Anna River May 23-26. On line of the Pamunkey May 26-28. Totopotomoy May 28-31. Cold Harbor June 1-12. Transferred to 69th Pennsylvania Infantry June 12, 1864. Mustered out July 2, 1864.

Regiment lost during service 14 Officers and 147 Enlisted men killed and mortally wounded and 1 Officer and 98 Enlisted men by disease. Total 260.

72nd REGIMENT INFANTRY ("FIRE ZOUAVE REGIMENT").

Organized at Philadelphia August 10, 1861. Moved to Washington, D. C., August, 1861. At Munson's Hill till September 30. Attached to Baker's Brigade, Stone's (Sedgwick's) Division, Army Potomac, to March, 1862. 2nd Brigade, 2nd Division, 2nd Army Corps, Army Potomac, to June, 1864. 3rd Brigade, 2nd Division, 2nd Army Corps, to August, 1864.

SERVICE.—Moved to Poolesville, Md., September 30, 1861, and duty on the Upper Potomac till February, 1862. At Harper's Ferry till March 24. Moved to the Virginia Peninsula March 24-April 1. Siege of Yorktown April 5-May 4. Moved to West Point May 7. At Tyler's Farm till May 31. Battle of Fair Oaks (Seven Pines) May 31-June 1. At Fair Oaks till June 28. Near Fair Oaks June 8. Seven Pines June 15. Fair Oaks June 19. Seven days before Richmond June 25-July 1. Battles of Peach Orchard and Savage Station June 29; Charles City Cross Roads and Glendale June 30; Malvern Hill July 1. At Harrison's Landing till August 16. Movement to Newport News, thence to Alexandria August 16-28, and to Centreville and Chantilly August 28-30. Cover Pope's retreat August 31-September 1. Maryland Campaign September 6-24. Battle of Antietam September 16-17. Moved to Harper's Ferry September 22, and duty there till October 30. Reconnoissance to Charlestown October 16-17. Movement to Falmouth, Va., October 30-November 20. Battle of Fredericksburg December 12-15. Burnside's second Campaign, "Mud March," January 20-24, 1863. At Falmouth till April. Hartwood Church February 25. Chancellorsville Campaign April 27-May 6. Banks Ford May 1 and 4. Gettysburg (Pa.) Campaign June 13-July 24. Battle of Gettysburg July 2-4. Pursuit of Lee July 5-24. At Banks Ford and Culpeper till October. Advance from the Rappahannock to the Rapidan September 13-17. Bristoe Campaign October 9-22. Advance to line of the Rappahannock November 7-8. Mine Run Campaign November 26-December 2. Robertson's Tavern or Locust Grove November 27. Duty on the Rapidan till May, 1864. Demonstration on the Rapidan February 6-7. Rapidan Campaign May 4-June 12. Battles of the Wilderness May 5-7; Laurel Hill May 8; Spottsylvania May 8-12; Po River May 12-21. Assault on the Salient May 12. North Anna River May 23-26. On line of the Pamunkey May 26-28. Totopotomoy May 28-31. Cold Harbor June 1-12. Before Petersburg June 16-18. Siege of Petersburg June 16-August 20. Jerusalem Plank Road June 22-23. Demonstration north of the James at Deep Bottom July 27-29. Deep Bottom July 27-28. Mine Explosion, Petersburg, July 30 (Reserve). Mustered out at Philadelphia August 24, 1864.

Regiment lost during service 11 Officers and 182 Enlisted men killed and mortally wounded and 2 Officers and 69 Enlisted men by disease. Total 264.

73rd REGIMENT INFANTRY.

Organized at Philadelphia September 19, 1861. Left State for Washington, D. C., September 24. Attached to Steinwehr's Brigade, Blenker's Division, Army Potomac, to March, 1862. 2nd Brigade, Blenker's Division, 2nd Army Corps, Army Potomac, to April, 1862. 2nd Brigade, Blenker's Division, Dept. of the Mountains, to June, 1862. 2nd Brigade, 1st Division, 1st Corps, Army of Virginia, to September, 1862. 1st Brigade, 2nd Division, 11th Army Corps, Army of the Potomac, to October, 1863, and Army of the Cumberland to April, 1864. 2nd Brigade, 2nd Division, 20th Army Corps, to July, 1865.

SERVICE.—Duty in the Defences of Washington, D. C., till March, 1862. Advance on Manassas, Va., March 10-15. Near Catlett's Station, Va., till April 6. Moved to Petersburg, W. Va., April 6-May 11. Operations in the Shenandoah Valley till June. Battle of Cross Keys June 8. Duty in the Shenandoah Valley and at Sperryville till August. Occupation of Luray July 22. Battle of Cedar Mountain August 9 (Reserve). Pope's Campaign in Northern Virginia August 16-September 2. Fords of the Rappahannock August 21-23. Sulphur Springs August 24. Gainesville August 28. Groveton August 30. Bull Run August 30. Duty in the Defences of Washington, D. C., till November. Movement to Centreville November 1-19, thence to Fredericksburg December 9-16. "Mud March" January 20-24, 1863. At Stafford C. H. till April 27. Operations at Welford's, Kelly's and Beverly Fords April 14-15. Chancellorsville Campaign April 27-May 6. Battle of Chancellorsville May 1-5. Gettysburg (Pa.) Campaign June 11-July 24. Battle of Gettysburg July 1-3. Pursuit of Lee July 5-24. Guard duty along Orange & Alexandria Railroad till September. Movement to Bridgeport, Ala., September 24-October 3. Operations in Lookout Valley October 19-26. Reopening Tennessee River October 26-29. Battle of Wauhatchie, Tenn., October 28-29. Chattanooga-Ringgold Campaign November 23-27. Battles of Orchard Knob November 23; Tunnel Hill November 24-25. Mostly captured November 25 at Tunnel Hill. Duty in Lookout Valley till May, 1864. Atlanta (Ga.) Campaign May 1-September 8. Demonstration on Rocky Faced Ridge May 8-11. Dug Gap or Mill Creek May 8. Battle of Resaca May 14-15. Near Cassville May 19. New Hope Church May 25. Operations on line of Pumpkin Vine Creek and battles about Dallas, New Hope Church and Allatoona Hills May 26-June 5. Operations about Marietta and against Kenesaw Mountain June 10-July 2. Pine Hill June 11-14. Lost Mountain June 15-17. Gilgal or Golgotha Church June 15. Muddy Creek June 17. Noyes Creek June 19. Kolb's Farm June 22. Assault on Kenesaw June 27. Ruff's Station or Smyrna Camp Ground July 4. Chattahoochie River July 5-17. Peach Tree Creek July 19-20. Siege of Atlanta July 22-August 25. Operations at Chattahoochie River Bridge August 26-September 2. Occupation of Atlanta September 2-November 15. Expedition to Tuckum's Cross Roads October 26-29. Near Atlanta November 9. March to the sea November 15-December 10. Siege of Savannah December 10-21. Campaign of the Carolinas January to April, 1865. Averysboro, N. C., March 16. Battle of Bentonville March 19-21. Occupation of Goldsboro March 24. Advance on Raleigh April 9-13. Occupation of Raleigh April 14. Bennett's House April 26. Surrender of Johnston and his army. March to Washington, D. C., via Richmond, Va., April 29-May 20. Grand Review May 24. Duty in the Defences of Washington till July. Mustered out July 14, 1865.

Regiment lost during service 5 Officers and 98 Enlisted men killed and mortally wounded and 113 Enlisted men by disease. Total 216.

74th REGIMENT INFANTRY.

Organized at Pittsburg as 35th Pennsylvania Volunteers September 14, 1861. Moved to Philadelphia, thence to Washington, D. C., September 23. Attached to Blenker's Brigade, Division of the Potomac, to November, 1861. Bohlen's Brigade, Blenker's Division, Army Potomac, to March, 1862. Bohlen's 3rd Brigade, Blenker's Division, 2nd Army Corps, Army Potomac, to

April, 1862. 3rd Brigade, Blenker's Division, Dept. of the Mountains, to June, 1862. 1st Brigade, 3rd Division, 1st Army Corps, Army of Virginia, to September, 1862. 1st Brigade, 3rd Division, 11th Army Corps, Army Potomac, to November, 1862. 1st Brigade, 2nd Division, 11th Corps, to July, 1863. 1st Brigade, 1st Division, 11th Corps, to August, 1863. 1st Brigade, Gordon's Division, Folly Island, S. C., 10th Corps, Dept. of the South, to April, 1864. Folly Island, S. C., Northern District, Dept. of the South, to August, 1864. 2nd Brigade, DeRussy's Division, 22nd Corps, Dept. of Washington, to October, 1864. Reserve Division, Dept. of West Virginia, to January, 1865. 2nd Brigade, 2nd Infantry Division, West Virginia, to April, 1865. 1st Brigade, 1st Infantry Division, West Virginia, to May, 1865. Sub-District of Clarksburg, W. Va., Dept. West Virginia, to August, 1865.

SERVICE.—Duty in the Defences of Washington, D. C., till March, 1862. At Fairfax C. H., Va., March 10-24. Moved to Petersburg, W. Va., April 6-May 11. Operations in the Shenandoah Valley till June. Cross Keys June 8. At Sperryville July 7-August 8. Pope's Campaign in Northern Virginia August 16-September 2. Freeman's Ford and Hazel Run August 22. Groveton August 29. Bull Run August 30. Duty in the Defences of Washington, D. C., till November. Moved to Centreville November 1-19, thence to Fredericksburg, Va., December 9-16. "Mud March" January 20-24, 1863. At Stafford C. H., Va., till April 27. Chancellorsville Campaign April 27-May 6. Battle of Chancellorsville May 1-5. Gettysburg (Pa.) Campaign June 13-July 24. Battle of Gettysburg July 1-3. Pursuit of Lee July 5-24. Moved to Folly Island, S. C., August 7-14. Duty on Folly Island, S. C., operating against Charleston, S. C., till August, 1864. Demonstration on James Island, S. C., May 21-22, 1864, and June 30-July 10. James Island, near Secessionville, July 2. Ordered to Washington, D. C., August 17. Duty at Forts Ethan Allen and Marcy till October. Ordered to West Virginia, and duty guarding Baltimore & Ohio Railroad till April, 1865. At Beverly April 8-May 12, and at Clarksburg, W. Va., and guarding Parkersburg branch of Baltimore & Ohio Railroad till August. Mustered out August 29, 1865.

Regiment lost during service 2 Officers and 54 Enlisted men killed and mortally wounded and 1 Officer and 88 Enlisted men by disease. Total 145.

75th REGIMENT INFANTRY.

Organized at Philadelphia August and September, 1861, as 40th Pennsylvania Volunteers. Left State for Washington, D. C., September 26, 1861. Attached to Casey's Provisional Division, Army Potomac, to November, 1861. Bohlen's 3rd Brigade, Blenker's Division, Army Potomac, to March, 1862. 3rd Brigade, Blenker's Division, 2nd Army Corps, Army Potomac, to April, 1862. 3rd Brigade, Blenker's Division, Dept. of the Mountains, to June, 1862. 2nd Brigade, 3rd Division, 1st Corps, Army of Virginia, to September, 1862. 2nd Brigade, 3rd Division, 11th Army Corps, Army Potomac, to October, 1863. 3rd Brigade, 3rd Division, 11th Army Corps, Army Cumberland, to April, 1864. Unattached, 4th Division, 20th Army Corps, Dept. Cumberland, to March, 1865. 1st Brigade, 1st Sub-District, Middle Tennessee, to September, 1865.

SERVICE.—Duty in the Defences of Washington, D. C., till March, 1862. Advance on Manassas, Va., March 10-15. Near Catlett's Station till April 6. Moved to Petersburg, W. Va., April 6-May 11. Operations in the Shenandoah Valley till June. Battle of Cross Keys June 8. At Sperryville July 7-August 8. Pope's Campaign in Northern Virginia August 16-September 2. Freeman's Ford August 22. Sulphur Springs August 24. Battles of Gainesville August 28; Groveton August 29; Bull Run August 30. Duty in the Defences of Washington, D. C., till November. Moved to Centreville November 1-19, thence to Fredericksburg December 9-16. "Mud March" January 20-24, 1863. At Stafford C. H. till April 27. Chancellorsville Campaign April 27-May 6. Battle of Chancellorsville May 1-5. Gettysburg (Pa.) Campaign June 13-July 24. Battle of Gettysburg July 1-3. Guard duty along Orange & Alexandria Railroad till September. Movement to Bridgeport, Ala., September 24-October 3. Operations in Lookout Valley October 19-26. Re-opening Tennessee River October 26-29. Battle of Wauhatchie, Tenn., October 28-29. Chattanooga-Ringgold Campaign November 23-27. Orchard Knob November 23. Tunnel Hill November 24-25. Mission Ridge November 25. March to relief of Knoxville November 28-December 17. Duty in Pleasant Valley till January, 1864. Veterans on furlough till March. Moved to Bridgeport, Ala., March 8, and duty there till July. Moved to Nashville, Tenn., July 31, and guard trains on Nashville & Northwestern Railroad till December. Moved to Franklin December 20, and duty there till September, 1865, guarding trains, scouting and provost duty. (Co. "C" was stationed on Tennessee & Alabama Railroad and captured.) Mustered out September 1, 1865.

Regiment lost during service 6 Officers and 46 Enlisted men killed and mortally wounded and 2 Officers and 107 Enlisted men by disease. Total 161.

76th REGIMENT INFANTRY, "KEYSTONE ZOUAVES."

Organized at Harrisburg October 18, 1861. Left State for Fort Monroe, Va., October 19. Attached to Wright's 3rd Brigade, Sherman's South Carolina Expedition, to April, 1862. 2nd Brigade, 1st Division, Dept. of the South, to July, 1862. District of Hilton Head, S. C., 10th Corps, Dept. South, to April, 1863. Guss' Brigade, Seabrook Island, S. C., 10th Corps, to June, 1863. 2nd Brigade, Folly Island, S. C., 10th Corps, to July, 1863. 2nd Brigade, 2nd Division, Morris Island, S. C., 10th Corps, July, 1863. 1st Brigade, Morris Island, S. C., 10th Corps, to August, 1863. District of Hilton Head, S. C., 10th Corps, to April, 1864. 2nd Brigade, 2nd Division, 10th Army Corps, Dept. of Virginia and North Carolina, to May, 1864. 1st Brigade, 3rd Division, 18th Army Corps, to June, 1864. 2nd Brigade, 2nd Division, 10th Army Corps, to December, 1864. 2nd Brigade, 2nd Division, 24th Army Corps, Dept. Virginia, to January, 1864. 2nd Brigade, 2nd Division, Terry's Provisional Corps, Dept. North Carolina, to March, 1865. 2nd Brigade, 2nd Division, 10th Army Corps, Dept. of North Carolina, to July, 1865.

SERVICE.—Sherman's Expedition to Port Royal, S. C., October 21-November 7, 1861. Duty at Hilton Head, S. C., till May 30, 1862. Operations on James Island, S. C., June 1-28. Battle of Secessionville, S. C., June 16. Evacuation of James Island and movement to Hilton Head June 28-July 7. Duty there till October. Expedition to Pocotaligo, S. C., October 21-23. Frampton's Plantation, Pocotaligo, October 22. Duty at Hilton Head, S. C., till April, 1863, and at Seabrook Island till June. Moved to Folly Island, S. C. Attack on Morris Island, S. C., July 10. Assaults on Fort Wagner, Morris Island, July 11 and 18. Siege operations against Fort Wagner till August. Ordered to Hilton Head, S. C., and duty there till April, 1864. Moved to Yorktown, Va., April. Butler's operations on south side of the James River and against Petersburg and Richmond May 4-28. Capture of Bermuda Hundred May 5. Walthal Junction, Chester Station, May 6-7. Proctor's Creek and operations against Fort Darling May 12-13. Battle of Drewry's Bluff May 14-16. On Bermuda Hundred front May 17-28. Moved to White House, thence to Cold Harbor May 28-June 1. Cold Harbor June 1-12. Before Petersburg June 15-18. Siege operations against Petersburg and Richmond June 16 to December 6. Mine Explosion, Petersburg, July 30, 1864 (Reserve). Demonstration on north side of the James at Deep Bottom August 13-20. Strawberry Plains. Deep Bottom, August 14-18. Battle of Chaffin's Farm, New Market Heights, September 28-30. Battle of Fair Oaks October 27-28. In trenches before Richmond till December 6. Expedition to Fort Fisher, N. C., December 6-24. Second Expedition to Fort Fisher January 3-15, 1865. Assault on and capture of Fort Fisher January 15. Sugar Loaf

Battery February 11. Fort Anderson February 18-19. Capture of Wilmington February 22. Advance on Goldsboro March 6-24. Advance on Raleigh April 9-13. Occupation of Raleigh April 14. Bennett's House April 26. Surrender of Johnston and his army. Duty at Raleigh, N. C., till July. Mustered out July 18, 1865.

Regiment lost during service 9 Officers and 161 Enlisted men killed and mortally wounded and 2 Officers and 192 Enlisted men by disease. Total 364.

77th REGIMENT INFANTRY.

Organized at Pittsburg October 15, 1861. Left State for Louisville, Ky., October 18. Attached to Negley's 4th Brigade, McCook's Command, at Nolin, Army Ohio, to November, 1861. 5th Brigade, Army Ohio, to December, 1861. 5th Brigade, 2nd Division, Army Ohio, to September, 1862. 2nd Brigade, 2nd Division, Right Wing Army Cumberland, to January, 1863. 2nd Brigade, 2nd Division, 20th Army Corps, Army Cumberland, to October, 1863. 3rd Brigade, 1st Division, 4th Army Corps, Army Cumberland, to June, 1865. 1st Brigade, 1st Division, 4th Corps, to August, 1865. Dept. of Texas to December, 1865.

SERVICE.—Camp at Nolin River till December, 1861, and at Munfordsville, Ky., till February, 1862. March to Bowling Green, Ky., thence to Nashville, Tenn., February 14-March 3, and to Savannah, Tenn., March 16-April 6. Battle of Shiloh, Tenn., April 6-7. Duty at Pittsburg Landing till May 28. Siege of Corinth, Miss., May 28-30. Skirmish near Corinth May 9. Pursuit to Booneville May 31-June 1. Buell's Campaign in Northern Alabama and Middle Tennessee June to August. March to Louisville, Ky., in pursuit of Bragg August 21-September 26. Pursuit of Bragg into Kentucky October 1-22. Floyd's Fork October 1. Near Clay Village October 4. Dog Walk October 9. March to Nashville, Tenn., October 22-November 7. Reconnoissance toward Lavergne November 19 and November 26-27. Lavergne, Scrougesville November 27. Advance on Murfreesboro December 26-30. Triune, Tenn., December 27. Battle of Stone's River December 30-31 and January 1-3, 1863. Duty near Murfreesboro till June. Middle Tennessee or Tullahoma Campaign June 24-July 7. Liberty Gap June 24-27. Occupation of Middle Tennessee till August 16. Passage of Cumberland Mountains and Tennessee River and Chickamauga (Ga.) Campaign August 16-September 22. Battle of Chickamauga September 19-20. Siege of Chattanooga September 24-October 27. Re-opening Tennessee River October 26-29. Duty at Whitesides, Tyner's Station and Blue Springs, Tenn., till April, 1864. Atlanta (Ga.) Campaign May 1-September 8. Tunnel Hill May 6-7. Demonstration on Rocky Faced Ridge and Dalton May 8-13. Near Dalton May 13. Battle of Resaca May 14-15. Near Kingston May 18-19. Near Cassville May 19. Kingston May 21. Operations on line of Pumpkin Vine Creek and battles about Dallas, New Hope Church and Allatoona Hills May 25-June 5. Operations about Marietta and against Kenesaw Mountain June 10-July 2. Pine Hill June 11-14. Lost Mountain June 15-17. Assault on Kenesaw June 27. Ruff's Station, Smyrna Camp Ground, July 4. Chattahoochie River July 6-17. Peach Tree Creek July 19-20. Siege of Atlanta July 22-August 25. Utoy Creek August 5-7. Flank movement on Jonesboro August 25-30. Battle of Jonesboro August 31-September 1. Lovejoy Station September 2-6. Operations in North Georgia and North Alabama against Hood September 29-October 26. Nashville Campaign November-December. Columbia, Duck River, November 24-28. Battle of Franklin November 30. Battle of Nashville December 15-16. Pursuit of Hood to the Tennessee River December 17-28. At Huntsville, Ala., till March, 1865. Expedition to Bull's Gap and operations in East Tennessee March 13-April 25. Moved to Nashville, Tenn., April 25, and duty there till June. Moved to New Orleans, La., June 17-25, thence to Indianola, Texas, July 13-21. Duty at Indianola and Victoria, Texas, till December. Mustered out December 6, 1865.

Regiment lost during service 5 Officers and 60 Enlisted men killed and mortally wounded and 254 Enlisted men by disease. Total 319.

78th REGIMENT INFANTRY.

Organized at Pittsburg October 15, 1861. Left State for Louisville, Ky., October 18, thence moved to Nolin Station, Ky., October 24, and duty there till December. Attached to Negley's 4th Brigade, McCook's Division, at Nolin, to November, 1861. 7th Brigade, Army Ohio, to December, 1861. 7th Brigade, 2nd Division, Army Ohio, to March, 1862. Negley's Independent Brigade, Army Ohio, to August, 1862. 7th Brigade, 8th Division, Army Ohio, to November, 1862. 3rd Brigade, 2nd Division, Centre Army of the Cumberland, to January, 1863. 3rd Brigade, 2nd Division, 14th Army Corps, Army Cumberland, to October, 1863. 3rd Brigade, 1st Division, 14th Army Corps, to July, 1864. Unassigned, 4th Division, 20th Army Corps, Dept. of the Cumberland, to October, 1864. Garrison Nashville, Tenn., to September, 1865.

SERVICE.—At Munfordsville, Ky., December, 1861, to February, 1862. March to Nashville, Tenn., February 14-March 3. Guard railroad from Nashville to Columbia till May, and at Decatur May. Expedition to Rodgersville May 13-14. Negley's Expedition to Chattanooga May 28-June 17. Chattanooga June 7-8. Garrison at Rodgersville and guarding Lamb's Ferry till July 18. Moved to Nashville, Tenn., and garrison duty there till December. Hermitage Ford October 20. Nashville November 5. Advance on Murfreesboro December 26-30. Battle of Stone's River December 30-31, 1862, and January 1-3, 1863. Duty at Murfreesboro till June. Middle Tennessee or Tullahoma Campaign June 23-July 7. Hoover's Gap June 24-26. At Dechard, Ala., July 8-August 15. Passage of Cumberland Mountains and Tennessee River, and Chickamauga (Ga.) Campaign August 16-September 22. Davis Cross Roads or Dug Gap September 11. Battle of Chickamauga September 19-21. Rossville Gap September 21. Siege of Chattanooga September 24-October 27. Reopening Tennessee River October 26-29. Battles of Chattanooga November 23-25; Mission Ridge November 24-25. Reconnoissance to Lookout Mountain November 29-December 2. Duty on Lookout Mountain till May, 1864. Atlanta (Ga.) Campaign May 1-June 21. Demonstration on Rocky Faced Ridge May 8-11. Battle of Resaca May 14-15. Near Cassville May 19. Operations on line of Pumpkin Vine Creek and battles about Dallas, New Hope Church and Allatoona Hills May 25-June 5. Pickett's Mills May 27. Operations about Marietta and against Kenesaw Mountain June 10-21. Pine Hill June 11-14. Lost Mountain June 15-17. Ordered to Chattanooga, Tenn., June 21. Duty guarding trains to the front July to September. Action at Dalton, Ga., August 14-15. Ordered to Decatur, Ala., September 24, thence to Nashville, Tenn., and to Tullahoma September 29. Returned to Nashville and duty there till September, 1865. Old members ordered home October, 1864, and mustered out at Pittsburg, Pa., November 4, 1864. Battles of Nashville, Tenn., December 16-17, 1864. Mustered out September 11, 1865.

Regiment lost during service 2 Officers and 68 Enlisted men killed and mortally wounded and 3 Officers and 194 Enlisted men by disease. Total 267.

79th REGIMENT INFANTRY.

Organized at Lancaster September 19, 1861. Moved to Pittsburg, thence to Louisville, Ky., October 18, and to Nolin Station, Ky., October 24. Attached to Negley's 4th Brigade, McCook's Command, at Nolin, to November, 1861. 7th Brigade, Army Ohio, to December, 1861. 7th Brigade, 2nd Division, Army Ohio, to March, 1862. Negley's Independent Brigade, Army Ohio, to August, 1862. 28th Brigade, 3rd Division, Army Ohio, to September, 1862. 28th Brigade, 3rd Division, 1st Corps, Army Ohio, to November, 1862. 3rd Brigade, 1st Division, Centre Army of the Cumberland, to January, 1863. 3rd Brigade, 1st Division, 14th Army Corps, Army Cumberland, to April, 1863. 2nd Brigade, 1st

Division, 14th Army Corps, to October, 1863. 3rd Brigade, 1st Division, 14th Army Corps, to July, 1865.

SERVICE.—Duty at Nolin till December, 1861, and at Munfordsville till February, 1862. Moved to Bowling Green, Ky., thence to Nashville, Tenn., February 14-March 3. At Nashville till March 28. Ordered to Columbia, Tenn., and guard Nashville & Decatur Railroad till May. Expedition to Rodgersville, Ala., May 13-14. Lamb's Ferry May 14. Negley's Expedition to Chattanooga May 28-June 17. Jasper, Sweeden's Cove, June 4. Chattanooga June 7-8. Ordered to Tullahoma, Tenn., and duty there till August. Ordered to Nashville, thence march to Louisville, Ky., in pursuit of Bragg August 21-September 26. Pursuit of Bragg into Kentucky October 1-16. Battle of Perryville October 8. Guard Louisville & Nashville Railroad at Mitchellsville November 9-December 7. Advance on Murfreesboro December 26-30. Jefferson December 30. Battle of Stone's River December 30-31, 1862, and January 1-3, 1863. Duty at Murfreesboro till June. Expedition to McMinnville April 20-30. Middle Tennessee or Tullahoma Campaign June 23-July 7. Hoover's Gap June 24-26. Occupation of Middle Tennessee till August 16. Passage of Cumberland Mountains and Tennessee River, and Chickamauga (Ga.) Campaign August 16-September 22. Davis Cross Roads or Dug Gap September 11. Battle of Chickamauga September 19-21. Rossville Gap September 21. Siege of Chattanooga September 24-October 26. Reopening Tennessee River October 26-29. Battle of Chattanooga November 23-25. Re-enlisted February 9, 1864. Veterans on furlough March and April. Atlanta (Ga.) Campaign May 1-September 8. Demonstration on Rocky Faced Ridge May 8-11. Battle of Resaca May 14-15. Operations on line of Pumpkin Vine Creek and battles about Dallas, New Hope Church and Allatoona Hills May 25-June 5. Pickett's Mills May 27. Operations about Marietta and against Kenesaw Mountain June 10-July 2. Pine Hill June 11-14. Lost Mountain June 15-17. Assault on Kenesaw June 27. Ruff's Station, Smyrna Camp Ground, July 4. Chattahoochie River July 5-17. Peach Tree Creek July 19-20. Siege of Atlanta July 22-August 25. Utoy Creek August 5-7. Flank movement on Jonesboro August 25-30. Battle of Jonesboro August 31-September 1. Operations in North Georgia and North Alabama against Hood September 29-November 3. March to the sea November 15-December 10. Siege of Savannah December 10-21. Campaign of the Carolinas January to April, 1865. League Cross Roads, near Lexington, S. C., February 15. Cloud's House February 27. Averysboro, N. C., March 16. Battle of Bentonville March 19-21. Occupation of Goldsboro March 24. Advance on Raleigh April 9-13. Occupation of Raleigh April 14. Bennett's House April 26. Surrender of Johnston and his army. March to Washington, D. C., via Richmond, Va., April 29-May 20. Grand Review May 24. Mustered out July 12, 1865.

Regiment lost during service 4 Officers and 118 Enlisted men killed and mortally wounded and 1 Officer and 145 Enlisted men by disease. Total 268.

80th REGIMENT VOLUNTEERS.

(See 7th Cavalry.)

81st REGIMENT INFANTRY.

Organized at Philadelphia October, 1861. At Easton, Pa., till October 10. Moved to Washington, D. C., October 10. Attached to Howard's Brigade, Richardson's Division, Army Potomac, to March, 1862. 1st Brigade, 1st Division, 2nd Army Corps, Army Potomac, to June, 1865.

SERVICE.—Duty in the Defences of Washington D. C., till March, 1862. Advance on Manassas, Va., March 10-15. Reconnoissance to Gainesville March 20. Operations on Orange & Alexandria Railroad March 28-31. Ordered to the Virginia Peninsula. Siege of Yorktown April 5-May 4. Construction of Grape Vine Bridge on Chickahominy May 28-30. Battle of Fair Oaks (Seven Pines) May 31-June 1. Fair Oaks June 18. Fair Oaks Station June 21. Seven days before Richmond June 25-

July 1. Orchard Station June 28. Peach Orchard, Allen's Farm, June 29. Savage Station June 29. White Oak Swamp Bridge and Glendale June 30. Malvern Hill July 1. At Harrison's Landing till August 16. Movement to Fortress Monroe, thence to Alexandria and Centreville August 16-30. Centreville September 1. Maryland Campaign September 6-24. Battle of Antietam, Md., September 16-17. Moved to Harper's Ferry, W. Va., and duty there till October 29. Reconnoissance to Charlestown October 16-17. Advance up Loudoun Valley and movement to Falmouth, Va., October 29-November 17. Snicker's Gap November 2. Manassas Gap November 5-6. Battle of Fredericksburg, Va., December 12-15. At Falmouth till April, 1863. Chancellorsville Campaign April 27-May 6. Battle of Chancellorsville May 1-5. Reconnoissance to the Rappahannock June 9. Kelly's Ford June 10. Gettysburg (Pa.) Campaign June 13-July 24. Battle of Gettysburg July 1-3. Pursuit of Lee July 5-24. Duty on line of the Rappahannock till September. Advance from the Rappahannock to the Rapidan September 13-17. Bristoe Campaign October 9-22. Auburn and Bristoe October 14. Advance to line of the Rappahannock November 7-8. Mine Run Campaign November 26-December 2. Mine Run November 28-30. At Stevensburg till May, 1864. Demonstration on the Rapidan February 6-7. Rapidan Campaign May 4-June 12. Battles of the Wilderness May 5-7; Corbin's Bridge May 8; Spottsylvania May 8-12; Po River May 10; Spottsylvania C. H. May 12-21. Assault on the Salient May 12. Landron House May 18. North Anna River May 23-26. Line of the Pamunkey May 26-28. Totopotomoy May 28-31. Cold Harbor June 12. Before Petersburg June 16-18. Siege of Petersburg June 16, 1864, to April 2, 1865. Jerusalem Plank Road June 22-23, 1864. Demonstration north of the James at Deep Bottom July 27-29. Deep Bottom July 27-28. Mine Explosion, Petersburg, July 30 (Reserve). Demonstration north of the James at Deep Bottom August 13-20. Strawberry Plains, Deep Bottom, August 14-18. Ream's Station August 25. Reconnoissance to Hatcher's Run December 7-10. Hatcher's Run December 8. Dabney's Mills, Hatcher's Run, February 5-7, 1865. Watkins' House, Petersburg, March 25. Appomattox Campaign March 28-April 9. On line of Hatcher's and Gravelly Runs March 29-30. Hatcher's Run or Boydton Road March 31. White Oak Road March 31. Sutherland Station April 2. Sailor's Creek April 6. High Bridge, Farmville, April 7. Appomattox C. H. April 9. Surrender of Lee and his army. March to Washington, D. C., May 2-12. Grand Review May 23. Mustered out June 29, 1865.

Regiment lost during service 18 Officers and 190 Enlisted men killed and mortally wounded and 2 Officers and 96 Enlisted men by disease. Total 306.

82nd REGIMENT INFANTRY.

Organized at Philadelphia as 31st Regiment Volunteers August, 1861, and ordered to Washington, D. C. Attached to Graham's Brigade, Buell's (Couch's) Division, Army Potomac, October, 1861, to March, 1862. 2nd Brigade, 1st Division, 4th Army Corps, Army Potomac, to July, 1862. 3rd Brigade, 1st Division, 4th Army Corps, to September, 1862. 3rd Brigade, 3rd Division, 6th Army Corps, Army Potomac, to October, 1862. 1st Brigade, 3rd Division, 6th Army Corps, to January, 1864. Johnson's Island, Sandusky, Ohio, to May, 1864. 4th Brigade, 1st Division, 6th Army Corps, Army Potomac, to July, 1864. 3rd Brigade, 1st Division, 6th Army Corps, Army Potomac, and Army Shenandoah, to July, 1865.

SERVICE.—Duty in the Defences of Washington, D. C., till March, 1862. Advance on Manassas, Va., March 10-15. Moved to the Virginia Peninsula March 26. Siege of Yorktown April 5-May 4. Battle of Williamsburg May 5. Operations about Bottom's Bridge May 20-23. Battle of Fair Oaks (Seven Pines) May 31-June 1. Seven days before Richmond June 25-July 1. Savage Station June 29. White Oak Swamp June 30. Malvern Hill July 1. At Harrison's Landing till August 16. Reconnoissance to Malvern Hill August 5-7.

Movement to Alexandria, thence to Chantilly August 16-30. Chantilly September 1. Maryland Campaign September 6-24. Battle of Antietam September 16-17. Williamsport September 19-20. Duty in Maryland and along the Potomac till November 1. Movement to Falmouth, Va., November 1-19. Battle of Fredericksburg December 12-15. Burnside's second Campaign. "Mud March" January 20-24, 1863. At Falmouth till April. Chancellorsville Campaign April 27-May 6. Operations about Franklin's Crossing April 29-May 2. Maryes Heights, Fredericksburg, May 3. Salem Heights May 3-4. Banks' Ford May 4. Operations about Deep Run Ravine June 6-13. Gettysburg (Pa.) Campaign June 13-July 24. Battle of Gettysburg July 2-4. Pursuit of Lee July 5-24. At and near Funkstown, Md., July 10-13. At Warrenton and Culpeper till October. Bristoe Campaign October 9-22. Advance to line of the Rappahannock November 7-8. Rappahannock Station November 7. Mine Run Campaign November 26-December 2. Moved to Johnson's Island, Lake Erie, January 6, 1864, and duty there guarding prisoners till May 6. Moved to Washington, D. C., thence joined Army of the Potomac in the field. Rapidan Campaign May 12-June 12. Spottsylvania C. H. May 12-21. Assault on the Salient May 12. North Anna River May 23-26. On line of the Pamunkey May 26-28. Totopotomoy May 28-31. Cold Harbor June 1-12. Before Petersburg June 17-18. Jerusalem Plank Road June 22-23. Siege of Petersburg till July 9. Moved to Washington, D. C., July 9-11. Repulse of Early's attack on Washington July 11-12. Snicker's Gap Expedition July 14-18. Sheridan's Shenandoah Valley Campaign August to December. (Old members mustered out September 16, 1864.) Battle of Opequan, Winchester, September 19. Fisher's Hill September 22. Battle of Cedar Creek October 19. Duty in the Shenandoah Valley till December. Ordered to Petersburg, Va., December 1. Siege of Petersburg December, 1864, to April, 1865. Dabney's Mills, Hatcher's Run, February 5-7, 1865. Fort Fisher, Petersburg, March 25, 1865. Appomattox Campaign March 28-April 9. Assault on and fall of Petersburg April 2. Pursuit of Lee April 3-9. Sailor's Creek April 6. Appomattox C. H. April 9. Surrender of Lee and his army. At Farmville and Burkesville till April 23. March to Danville April 23-27, and duty there till May 24. Moved to Richmond, Va., thence to Washington, D. C., May 24-June 3. Corps Review June 8. Mustered out July 13, 1865.

Regiment lost during service 5 Officers and 106 Enlisted men killed and mortally wounded and 67 Enlisted men by disease. Total 178.

83rd REGIMENT INFANTRY.

Organized at Erie and mustered into United States service September 8, 1861. Moved to Washington, D. C., September 18-20. Attached to Butterfield's Brigade, Fitz John Porter's Division, Army of the Potomac, to March, 1862. 3rd Brigade, 1st Division, 3rd Army Corps, Army Potomac, to May, 1862. 3rd Brigade, 1st Division, 5th Army Corps, Army Potomac, to June, 1865.

SERVICE.—Duty in the Defences of Washington, D. C., till March, 1862. Advance on Manassas, Va., March 10-15. Moved to the Virginia Peninsula March 22-24. Reconnoissance to Big Bethel March 30. Warwick Road April 5. Siege of Yorktown April 5-May 4. Reconnoissance up the Pamunkey May 10. Action at Hanover C. H. May 27. Operations about Hanover C. H. May 27-29. Seven days before Richmond June 25-July 1. Battle of Mechanicsville June 26. Gaines Mill June 27. Savage Station June 29. Turkey Bridge or Malvern Cliff June 30. Malvern Hill July 1. At Harrison's Landing till August 16. Movement to Fortress Monroe, thence to Centreville August 16-27. Pope's Campaign in Northern Virginia August 27-September 2. Battle of Bull Run August 30. Maryland Campaign September 6-24. Battle of Antietam September 16-17. Sharpsburg and Shepherdstown Ford September 19. Duty at Sharpsburg, Md., till October 30. Movement to Falmouth, Va., October 30-November 19. Battle of Fredericksburg December 12-15. Expedition to Richards and Ellis Fords, Rappahannock River, December 29-30. Burnside's second Campaign, "Mud March," January 20-24. 1863. At Falmouth, Va., till April. Chancellorsville Campaign April 26-May 6. Battle of Chancellorsville May 1-5. Gettysburg (Pa.) Campaign June 13-July 24. Aldie June 17. Middleburg and Upperville June 21. Battle of Gettysburg July 1-3. Pursuit of Lee July 5-24. Duty at Warrenton, Beverly Ford and Culpeper till October. Advance to line of the Rappahannock November 7-8. Rappahannock Station November 7. Mine Run Campaign November 26-December 2. At Beverly Ford till May, 1864. Rapidan Campaign May 4-June 12. Battles of the Wilderness May 5-7; Laurel Hill May 8; Spottsylvania May 8-12; Spottsylvania C. H. May 12-21. Assault on the Salient May 12. North Anna River May 23-26. Jericho Ford May 25. Line of the Pamunkey May 26-28. Tototopotomoy May 28-31. Cold Harbor June 1-12. Bethesda Church June 1-3. Before Petersburg June 16-18. Siege of Petersburg June 16, 1864, to April 2, 1865. Mine Explosion, Petersburg, July 30, 1864. Weldon Railroad August 18-21. Old members mustered out September 7, 1864. Consolidated to 6 Companies. Peeble's Farm, Poplar Springs Church, September 29-October 2. Boydton Plank Road, Hatcher's Run, October 27-28. Warren's Expedition to Weldon Railroad December 7-12. Dabney's Mills, Hatcher's Run, February 5-7, 1865. Appomattox Campaign March 28-April 9. Lewis Farm, near Gravelly Run, March 31. Junction of the Quaker and Boydton Roads March 29. White Oak Road March 31. Five Forks April 1. Appomattox C. H. April 9. Surrender of Lee and his army. March to Washington, D. C., May 2-12. Grand Review May 23. Mustered out June 28, 1865, and disbanded at Harrisburg, Pa., July 4, 1865.

Regiment lost during service 11 Officers and 271 Enlisted men killed and mortally wounded and 2 Officers and 151 Enlisted men by disease. Total 435.

84th REGIMENT INFANTRY.

Organized at Huntingdon and Camp Curtin August to October, 1861. At Camp Curtin, Pa., till December 31, 1861. Moved to Hancock, Md., December 31-January 2, 1862, thence to Bath. Action at Bath January 4, and at Hancock January 5. Attached to 1st Brigade, Lander's Division, Army Potomac, to March, 1862. 1st Brigade, Shield's 2nd Division, Banks' 5th Corps, to April, 1862. 1st Brigade, Shield's Division, Dept. of the Shenandoah, to May, 1862. 4th Brigade, Shield's Division, Dept. of the Rappahannock, to June, 1862. 4th Brigade, 2nd Division, 3rd Corps, Army of Virginia, to September, 1863. 2nd Brigade, 3rd Division, 3rd Army Corps, Army Potomac, to June, 1863. 1st Brigade, 2nd Division, 3rd Army Corps, to March, 1864. 2nd Brigade, 4th Division, 2nd Army Corps, to May, 1864. 4th Brigade, 3rd Division, 2nd Army Corps, to July, 1864. 2nd Brigade, 3rd Division, 2nd Army Corps, to January, 1865.

SERVICE.—Retreat to Cumberland, Md., January 10-12, 1862. Duty guarding North and South Branch Bridges and at Paw Paw Tunnel till March, 1862. Advance on Winchester, Va., March 5-15. Battle of Winchester March 23. Occupation of Mt. Jackson April 17. Provost at Berryville till May 2. March to Fredericksburg May 12-22, and return to Front Royal May 25-29. Action near Front Royal May 31. Port Republic June 8-9. Moved to Alexandria June 29. Duty there till July. Battle of Cedar Mountain August 9. Pope's Campaign in Northern Virginia August 16-September 2. Fords of the Rappahannock August 20-24. Thoroughfare Gap August 28. Battles of Groveton August 29; Bull Run August 30; Chantilly September 1. Duty at Arlington Heights, Defences of Washington, Whipple's Command, till October. Moved to Pleasant Valley, Md., October 18, thence to Warrenton and Falmouth October 24-November 19. Battle of Fredericksburg, Va., December 12-15. Burnside's 2nd Campaign, "Mud March," January 20-24, 1863. At Falmouth, Va., till April. Chancellorsville Campaign April 27-May 6. Battle of Chancellorsville May 1-5. Gettysburg (Pa.) Campaign June 11-July 24. Guarding Corps' trains during battle of Get-

tysburg July 1-3. Pursuit of Lee July 5-24. Wapping Heights, Va., July 23. Duty on line of the Rappahannock till October. Bristoe Campaign October 9-22. Advance to line of the Rappahannock November 7-8. Kelly's Ford November 7. Mine Run Campaign November 26-December 2. Payne's Farm November 27. Regiment re-enlisted January, 1864. Demonstration on the Rapidan February 6-7. Duty near Brandy Station till May. Rapidan Campaign May 4-June 12. Battles of the Wilderness May 5-7; Spottsylvania May 8-12; Spottsylvania C. H. May 12-21. Assault on the Salient May 12. Harris Farm May 19. North Anna River May 23-26. Line of the Pamunkey May 26-28. Totopotomoy May 28-31. Haw's Shop May 31. Cold Harbor June 1-12. Before Petersburg June 16-18. Siege of Petersburg June 16, 1864, to January 6, 1865. Weldon Railroad June 22-23, 1864. Demonstration north of James River at Deep Bottom July 27-29. Deep Bottom July 27-28. Mine Explosion, Petersburg, July 30 (Reserve). Demonstration north of the James at Deep Bottom August 13-20. Strawberry Plains, Deep Bottom, August 14-18. Peeble's Farm, Poplar Grove Church, September 29-October 2. Boydton Plank Road, Hatcher's Run, October 27-28. Consolidated with 57th Pennsylvania Infantry January 13, 1865.

Regiment lost during service 6 Officers and 119 Enlisted men killed and mortally wounded and 1 Officer and 98 Enlisted men by disease. Total 224.

85th REGIMENT INFANTRY.

Organized at Uniontown October 16 to November 12, 1861. Left State for Washington, D. C. Attached to 2nd Brigade, Casey's Division, Army Potomac, to March, 1862. 2nd Brigade, 3rd Division, 4th Army Corps, Army Potomac, to June, 1862. 2nd Brigade, 2nd Division, 4th Army Corps, to September, 1862. Wessell's Brigade, Division at Suffolk, Va., 7th Corps, Dept. of Virginia, to December, 1862. 1st Brigade, 1st Division, Dept. of North Carolina, to January, 1863. 2nd Brigade, 3rd Division, 18th Army Corps, Dept. of North Carolina, to February, 1863. 2nd Brigade, 2nd Division, 18th Corps, Dept. of the South, to April, 1863. Folly Island, S. C., 10th Corps, Dept. South, to June, 1863. 1st Brigade, Folly Island, S. C., 10th Corps, to July, 1863. 1st Brigade, 2nd Division, Morris Island, S. C., 10th Corps, July, 1863. 2nd Brigade, Morris Island, S. C., 10th Corps, to October, 1863. Howell's Brigade, Gordon's Division, Folly Island, S. C., 10th Corps, to December, 1863. District of Hilton Head, S. C., 10th Corps, to April, 1864. 1st Brigade, 1st Division, 10th Army Corps, Dept. of Virginia and North Carolina, to November, 1864.

SERVICE.—Duty in the Defences of Washington, D. C., till March, 1862. Advance on Manassas, Va., March 10-15. Moved to the Peninsula March 28. Siege of Yorktown April 5-May 4. Battle of Williamsburg May 5. Reconnoissance to Seven Pines May 24-27. Skirmishes at Seven Pines, Savage Station and Chickahominy May 24. Seven Pines May 29. Battle of Seven Pines, Fair Oaks, May 31-June 1. Seven days before Richmond June 25-July 1. Brackett's June 30. Malvern Hill July 1. At Harrison's Landing till August 16. Moved to Fortress Monroe August 16-23, thence to Suffolk September 18, and duty there till December. Reconnoissance to Franklin on the Blackwater October 3. Ordered to New Berne, N. C., December 4. Foster's Expedition to Goldsboro December 10-21. Southwest Creek December 13-14. Kinston December 14. Whitehall December 16. Goldsboro December 17. Duty at New Berne, N. C., till January, 1863. Moved to Port Royal, S. C., January 28-31. At St. Helena Island, S. C., till April. At Folly Island, S. C., till July. Attack on Morris Island July 10. Assaults on Fort Wagner, Morris, Island, S. C., July 11 and 18. Siege of Forts Wagner and Gregg, Morris Island, and operations against Fort Sumpter and Charleston July 18-September 7. Duty on Morris and Folly Islands operating against Charleston till December. Moved to Hilton Head, S. C., and duty there till April, 1864. Expedition to Whitmarsh Island, Ga., February 22. Moved to Gloucester

Point, Va., April. Butler's operations on south side of James River and against Petersburg and Richmond May 4-28. Ware Bottom Church May 9. Swift Creek or Arrowfield Church May 9-10. Proctor's Creek and operations against Fort Darling May 12-16. Battle of Drewry's Bluff May 14-16. Operations on Bermuda Hundred front May 17-30. Ware Bottom Church May 20. Port Walthal June 16-17. Siege operations against Petersburg and Richmond June 16 to November 22, 1864. Ware Bottom Church June 20. Demonstration on north side of the James at Deep Bottom August 13-20. Strawberry Plains, Deep Bottom, August 14-18. Chaffin's Farm, New Market Heights, September 28-30. Darbytown Road October 7. Battle of Fair Oaks October 27-28. Mustered out November 22, 1864. Veterans and Recruits transferred to 188th Pennsylvania Infantry.

Regiment lost during service 7 Officers and 90 Enlisted men killed and mortally wounded and 4 Officers and 146 Enlisted men by disease. Total 247.

86th REGIMENT VOLUNTEERS.

(Failed to complete organization.)

87th REGIMENT INFANTRY.

Organized at Yorktown September, 1861. Attached to Railroad Guard, Middle Department, to May, 1862. Baltimore, Md., Middle Department, to June, 1862. Railroad Division, 8th Corps, Middle Department, to March, 1863. 2nd Brigade, 2nd Division, 8th Corps, Middle Department, to June, 1863. 1st Brigade, Elliott's Command, 8th Corps, to July. 3rd Brigade, 3rd Division, 3rd Army Corps, Army Potomac, to March, 1864. 1st Brigade, 3rd Division, 6th Army Corps, Army Potomac and Army Shenandoah, to June, 1865.

SERVICE.—Guard duty on Northern Central Railroad from Pennsylvania line to Baltimore, Md., September 16, 1861, to May 24, 1862. Duty at Baltimore, Md., till June 23. At New Creek, W. Va., till August 20. Expedition under Gen. Kelly across Laurel Hill and Rich Mountain August 27-September 12. Expedition over Cheat and Allegheny Mountains October 31-November 12. March on Petersburg, W. Va., December 6-9. At Winchester till May, 1863. Reconnoissance toward Wardensville and Strasburg April 20. Expedition to Webster May 20. At Winchester till June 15. Reconnoissance toward Strasburg June 10. Middletown June 12. Newtown June 12. Bunker Hill June 13 (Cos. "G," "H"). Battles of Winchester June 13-15. Retreat to Harper's Ferry. Escort stores from Harper's Ferry to Washington, D. C., July 1-3. Joined Army of the Potomac and pursuit of Lee July 5-24. Wapping Heights, Manassas Gap, Va., July 23. Bristoe Campaign October 9-22. Advance to line of the Rappahannock November 7-8. Kelly's Ford November 7. Brandy Station November 8. Mine Run Campaign November 26-December 2. Payne's Farm November 27. Re-enlisted December, 1863. Demonstration on the Rapidan February 6-7, 1864. Rapidan Campaign May 4-June 12, 1864. Battles of the Wilderness May 5-7; Spottsylvania C. H. May 8-21. Assault on the Salient May 12. North Anna River May 23-26. Line of the Pamunkey May 26-28. Totopotomoy May 28-31. Cold Harbor June 1-12. Before Petersburg June 17-18. Siege of Petersburg till July 6. Weldon Railroad June 22-23. Moved to Baltimore, Md., July 6-9. Battle of Monocacy Junction July 9. Sheridan's Shenandoah Valley Campaign August 7-December 1. Charlestown August 21-22. Battle of Opequan, Winchester, September 19. Fisher's Hill September 22. (Old members mustered out October 13, 1864.) Battle of Cedar Creek. Duty at Kernstown till December. Moved to Washington, D. C., thence to Petersburg, Va., December 3-7. Siege of Petersburg December, 1864, to April, 1865. Fort Fisher, Petersburg, March 25, 1865. Appomattox Campaign March 28-April 9. Assault on and fall of Petersburg April 2. Pursuit of Lee April 3-9. Appomattox C. H. April 9. Surrender of Lee and his army. March to Danville April 23-27, and duty there till May 23. March to Richmond, Va., thence to Wash-

ington, D. C., May 23-June 3. Corps Review June 8. Mustered out at Alexandria, Va., June 29, 1865.

Regiment lost during service 10 Officers and 80 Enlisted men killed and mortally wounded and 112 Enlisted men by disease. Total 202.

88th REGIMENT INFANTRY.

Organized at Philadelphia September, 1861. Left State for Washington, D. C., October 1. At Kendall Green, Washington, D. C., till October 12. Provost duty at Alexandria till April 17, 1862. (Cos. "A," "C," "D," "E" and "I" garrison forts on Maryland side of the Potomac River February 18 to April 17.) At Cloud's Mills, Va., April 17-23. Guard Orange & Alexandria Railroad between Bull Run and Fairfax C. H. till May 7. Attached to 1st Brigade, Ord's 2nd Division, Dept. of the Rappahannock, to June, 1862. 2nd Brigade, 2nd Division, 3rd Corps, Army of Virginia, to September, 1862. 2nd Brigade, 2nd Division, 1st Army Corps, Army Potomac, to March, 1863. 3rd Brigade, 2nd Division, 1st Army Corps, to May, 1863. 2nd Brigade, 2nd Division, 1st Army Corps, to March, 1864. 2nd Brigade, 2nd Division, 5th Army Corps, to June, 1864. 2nd Brigade, 3rd Division, 5th Army Corps, to March, 1865. 3rd Brigade, 3rd Division, 5th Army Corps, to June, 1865.

SERVICE.—Duty near Fredericksburg, Va., till May 25. Expedition to Front Royal to intercept Jackson May 25-June 18. Duty at Manassas, Warrenton and Culpeper till August. Battle of Cedar Mountain August 9. Pope's Campaign in Northern Virginia August 16-September 2. Fords of the Rappahannock August 21-23. Thoroughfare Gap August 28. Battle of Bull Run August 30. Chantilly September 1. Maryland Campaign September 6-24. Battles of South Mountain September 14; Antietam September 16-17. Duty near Sharpsburg, Md., till October 30. Movement to Falmouth, Va., October 30-November 19. Battle of Fredericksburg December 12-15. Burnside's 2nd Campaign, "Mud March," January 20-24, 1863. At Falmouth and Belle Plains till April 27. Chancellorsville Campaign April 27-May 6. Operations at Pollock's Mill Creek April 29-May 2. Fitzhugh's Crossing April 29-30. Chancellorsville May 2-5. Gettysburg (Pa.) Campaign June 11-July 24. Battle of Gettysburg July 1-3. Pursuit of Lee July 5-24. Duty on line of the Rappahannock till October. Bristoe Campaign October 9-22. Advance to line of the Rappahannock November 7-8. Mine Run Campaign November 26-December 2. Demonstration on the Rapidan February 6-7, 1864. Regiment re-enlisted February 6, 1864, and on furlough till April 7. Rapidan Campaign May 4-June 12. Battles of the Wilderness May 5-7; Laurel Hill May 8; Spottsylvania May 8-12; Spottsylvania C. H. May 12-21. Assault on the Salient May 12. North Anna River May 23-26. Jericho Ford May 25. On line of the Pamunkey May 26-28. Totopotomoy May 28-31. Cold Harbor June 1-12. Bethesda Church June 1-3. White Oak Swamp June 13. Before Petersburg June 16-18. Siege of Petersburg June 16, 1864, to April 2, 1865. Mine Explosion, Petersburg, July 30, 1864 (Reserve). Weldon Railroad August 18-21. Hatcher's Run October 27-28. Warren's Expedition to Weldon Railroad December 7-12. Dabney's Mills, Hatcher's Run, February 5-7, 1865. Appomattox Campaign March 28-April 9. Lewis Farm near Gravelly Run March 29. White Oak Road March 30-31. Five Forks April 1. Pursuit of Lee April 2-9. Appomattox C. H. April 9. Surrender of Lee and his army. Moved to Washington, D. C., May 1-12. Grand Review May 23. Mustered out June 30, 1865.

Regiment lost during service 8 Officers and 101 Enlisted men killed and mortally wounded and 72 Enlisted men by disease. Total 181.

89th REGIMENT VOLUNTEERS.

(See 8th Cavalry.)

90th REGIMENT INFANTRY.

Organized at Philadelphia October 1, 1861. Moved to Baltimore, Md., March 31, 1862, thence to Washington,

D. C., April 21 and to Aquia Creek Landing, Va., and duty there till May 9. Attached to 1st Brigade, 2nd Division, Dept. of the Rappahannock, to June, 1862. 2nd Brigade, 2nd Division, 3rd Corps, Army of Virginia, to September, 1862. 2nd Brigade, 2nd Division, 1st Army Corps, Army Potomac, to March, 1864. 2nd Brigade, 2nd Division, 5th Army Corps, to May, 1864. 1st Brigade, 2nd Division, 5th Army Corps, to June, 1864. 1st Brigade, 3rd Division, 5th Army Corps, to September, 1864. 2nd Brigade, 3rd Division, 5th Army Corps, to November, 1864.

SERVICE.—Duty near Fredericksburg, Va., till May 25. Expedition to Front Royal to intercept Jackson May 25-June 16. Duty at Manassas, Warrenton and Culpeper till August. Battle of Cedar Mountain August 9. Pope's Campaign in Northern Virginia August 16-September 2. Fords of the Rappahannock August 21-23. Thoroughfare Gap August 28. Battle of Bull Run August 30. Chantilly September 1. Maryland Campaign September 6-24. Battles of South Mountain September 14. Antietam September 16-17. Duty near Sharpsburg, Md., till October 30. Movement to Falmouth, Va., October 30-November 19. Battle of Fredericksburg December 12-15. Burnside's 2nd Campaign, "Mud March," January 20-24, 1863. At Falmouth and Belle Plains till April 27. Chancellorsville Campaign April 27-May 6. Operations at Pollock's Mill Creek April 29-May 2. Fitzhugh's Crossing April 29-30. Chancellorsville May 2-5. Gettysburg (Pa.) Campaign June 11-July 24. Battle of Gettysburg July 1-3. Pursuit of Lee July 5-24. Duty on line of the Rappahannock till October. Bristoe Campaign October 9-22. Advance to line of the Rappahannock November 7-8. Mine Run Campaign November 26-December 2. Demonstration on the Rapidan February 6-7, 1864. Duty on Orange & Alexandria Railroad till May. Rapidan Campaign May 4-June 12. Battles of the Wilderness May 5-7; Laurel Hill May 8; Spottsylvania May 8-12; Spottsylvania C. H. May 12-21. Assault on the Salient May 12. North Anna River May 23-26. Jericho Ford May 25. On line of the Pamunkey May 26-28. Totopotomoy May 28-31. Cold Harbor June 1-12. Bethesda Church June 1-3. White Oak Swamp June 13. Before Petersburg June 16-18. Siege of Petersburg June 16 to November 26, 1864. Mine Explosion, Petersburg, July 30. Weldon Railroad August 18-21. Reconnoissance to Dinwiddie C. H. September 15. Consolidated with 11th Pennsylvania Infantry November 26, 1864.

Regiment lost during service 5 Officers and 98 Enlisted men killed and mortally wounded and 1 Officer and 126 Enlisted men by disease. Total 230.

91st REGIMENT INFANTRY.

Organized at Philadelphia and mustered in December 4, 1861. Left State for Washington, D. C., January 21, 1862. Attached to Defences of Washington, D. C., to August, 1862. 1st Brigade, 3rd Division, 5th Army Corps, Army Potomac, to May, 1863. 3rd Brigade, 2nd Division, 5th Army Corps, to March, 1864. 4th Brigade, 1st Division, 5th Army Corps, to April, 1864. 1st Brigade, 1st Division, 5th Army Corps, to June, 1864. 1st Brigade, 2nd Division, 5th Army Corps, June, 1864. 2nd Brigade, 2nd Division, 5th Army Corps, to July, 1864. 2nd Brigade, 1st Division, 5th Army Corps, to December, 1864. 3rd Brigade, 1st Division, 5th Army Corps, to March, 1865. 1st Brigade, 3rd Division, 5th Army Corps, to July, 1865.

SERVICE.—Duty at Washington, D. C., till April 27, 1862, and at Alexandria, Va., till August 21. Near Fairfax C. H. till September 15. Reached Antietam, Md., September 18. Duty at Sharpsburg, Md., till October 30. Skirmishes at Kearneysville and Shepherdstown October 15-16. Reconnoissance to Leesburg, W. Va., October 16-17. Movement to Falmouth, Va., October 30-November 19. Battle of Fredericksburg, Va., December 12-15. Burnside's second Campaign, "Mud March," January 20-24, 1863. Duty at Falmouth, Va., till April 27. Chancellorsville Campaign April 27-May 6. Battle of Chancellorsville May 1-5. Gettysburg (Pa.) Campaign June 13-July 24. Battle of Gettysburg, Pa.,

July 1-3. Pursuit of Lee July 5-24. Duty on line of the Rappahannock till October. Bristoe Campaign October 9-22. Advance to line of the Rappahannock November 7-8. Rappahannock Station November 7. Mine Run Campaign November 26-December 2. Regiment re-enlisted December 26, 1863. Veterans on furlough January 2-February 16, 1864, and near Chester till March 2. Rapidan Campaign May 4-June 12. Battles of the Wilderness May 5-7; Laurel Hill May 8; Spottsylvania C. H. May 8-21. Assault on the Salient May 12. North Anna River May 23-26. On line of the Pamunkey May 26-28. Totopotomoy May 28-31. Cold Harbor June 1-12. Bethesda Church June 1-3. Before Petersburg June 16-18. Siege of Petersburg June 16, 1864, to April 2, 1865. Mine Explosion, Petersburg, July 30, 1864 (Reserve). Six Mile House, Weldon Railroad, August 18-21. Poplar Grove Church, Peeble's Farm, September 29-October 2. Boydton Plank Road, Hatcher's Run, October 27-28. Warren's Raid to Weldon Railroad December 7-12. Dabney's Mills, Hatcher's Run, February 5-7, 1865. Appomattox Campaign March 28-April 9. Lewis Farm, Gravelly Run, March 29. Junction of Quaker and Boydton Roads March 29. White Oak Road March 30-31. Five Forks April 1. Appomattox C. H. April 9. Surrender of Lee and his army. Moved to Washington, D. C., May 1-12. Grand Review May 23. Mustered out July 10, 1865.

Regiment lost during service 6 Officers and 110 Enlisted men killed and mortally wounded and 2 Officers and 82 Enlisted men by disease. Total 200.

92nd REGIMENT VOLUNTEERS.
(See 9th Cavalry.)

93rd REGIMENT INFANTRY.

Organized at Lebanon September 21 to October 28, 1861. Left State for Washington, D. C., November 21. Attached to Peck's Brigade, Couch's Division, Army Potomac, to March, 1862. 3rd Brigade, 1st Division, 4th Army Corps, Army Potomac, to September, 1862. 2nd Brigade, 3rd Division, 6th Army Corps, Army Potomac, to November, 1862. 3rd Brigade, 3rd Division, 6th Army Corps, to January, 1864. Wheaton's Brigade, Dept. West Virginia, to March, 1864. 1st Brigade, 2nd Division, 6th Army Corps, Army Potomac, and Army Shenandoah, to June, 1865.

SERVICE.—Duty in the Defences of Washington till March, 1862. Advance on Manassas, Va., March 10-15. Moved to the Peninsula March 25. Siege of Yorktown April 5-May 4. Battle of Williamsburg May 5. Reconnoissance to the Chickahominy and Bottom's Bridge May 20-23. Battle of Fair Oaks (Seven Pines) May 31-June 1. Seven days before Richmond June 25-July 1. Seven Pines June 27. Malvern Hill July 1. At Harrison's Landing till August 16. Movement to Alexandria, thence to Centreville August 16-30. Cover Pope's retreat to Fairfax C. H. August 30-September 1. Chantilly September 1. Maryland Campaign September 6-24. Reconnoissance to Harper's Ferry and Sandy Hook September 12-14. Battle of Antietam September 16-17 (Reserve). At Downsville, Md., September 23-October 20. Movement to Stafford C. H. October 20-November 18, and to Belle Plains December 5. Battle of Fredericksburg December 12-15. Burnside's second Campaign, "Mud March," January 20-24, 1863. At Falmouth till April. Chancellorsville Campaign April 27-May 6. Operations at Franklin's Crossing April 29-May 2. Maryes Heights, Fredericksburg, May 3. Salem Heights May 3-4. Banks' Ford May 4. Gettysburg (Pa.) Campaign June 13-July 24. Battle of Gettysburg July 2-4. Pursuit of Lee July 5-24. Duty on the line of the Rappahannock till October. Bristoe Campaign October 9-22. Advance to line of the Rappahannock November 7-8. Rappahannock Station November 7. Mine Run Campaign November 26-December 2. Regiment re-enlisted February 7, 1864. Duty at Brandy Station till May. Rapidan Campaign May 4-June 12. Battles of the Wilderness May 5-7; Spottsylvania May 8-21. Assault on the Salient May 12. North Anna River May 23-26. On line of the Pamunkey May 26-28. Totopotomoy May

28-31. Cold Harbor June 1-12. Before Petersburg June 17-18. Siege of Petersburg till July 9. Jerusalem Plank Road June 22-23. Moved to Washington, D. C., July 9-11. Defence of Washington against Early's attack July 11-12. Pursuit to Snicker's Gap July 14-18. Sheridan's Shenandoah Valley Campaign August to December. Charlestown August 21-22. Demonstration on Gilbert's Ford, Opequan Creek, September 13. Battle of Opequan, Winchester, September 19. Strasburg September 21. Fisher's Hill September 22. Battle of Cedar Creek October 19. Duty in the Shenandoah Valley till December. Moved to Petersburg December 9-12. Siege of Petersburg December, 1864, to April, 1865. Dabney's Mills, Hatcher's Run, February 5-7, 1865. Fort Fisher, Petersburg, March 25. Appomattox Campaign March 28-April 9. Assault on and fall of Petersburg April 2. Pursuit of Lee April 3-9. Appomattox C. H. April 9. Surrender of Lee and his army. March to Danville April 23-27, and duty there till May 23. Moved to Richmond, Va., thence to Washington. D. C., May 23-June 3. Corps Review June 8. Mustered out June 27, 1865.

Regiment lost during service 11 Officers and 161 Enlisted men killed and mortally wounded and 1 Officer and 111 Enlisted men by disease. Total 274.

94th REGIMENT INFANTRY.

(Failed to complete organization.)

95th REGIMENT INFANTRY.

Organized at Philadelphia August to October, 1861. Left State for Washington, D. C., October 12. Attached to Newton's Brigade, Franklin's Division, Army Potomac, to March, 1862. 3rd Brigade, 1st Division, 1st Army Corps, Army Potomac, to April, 1862. 3rd Brigade, 1st Division, Dept. of the Rappahannock, to May, 1862. 3rd Brigade, 1st Division, 6th Army Corps, Army Potomac, to May, 1863. 2nd Brigade, 1st Division, 6th Army Corps, Army Potomac, and Army Shenandoah, to June, 1865.

SERVICE.—Camp at Kendall Green, Defences of Washington, D. C., till October 29, 1861, and at Fairfax Seminary, Va., till March, 1862. Advance on Manassas, Va., March 10-15. McDowell's advance on Falmouth, Va., April 4-17. Moved to Shipping Point, Va., April 17, thence to the Virginia Peninsula April 22. Siege of Yorktown April 24-May 4 (on transports). West Point May 7-8. Seven days before Richmond June 25-July 1. Gaines' Mill June 27. Charles City Cross Roads, and Glendale June 30. Malvern Hill July 1. At Harrison's Landing till August 16. Movement to Fortress Monroe, thence to Centreville August 16-28. In works at Centreville August 28-31. Cover Pope's retreat to Fairfax C. H. September 1. Maryland Campaign September 6-24. Crampton's Pass, South Mountain, September 14. Antietam September 16-17. Duty in Maryland till October 29. Movement to Falmouth, Va., October 29-November 19. Battle of Fredericksburg, Va., December 12-15. Burnside's second Campaign, "Mud March," January 20-24, 1863. At Falmouth till April. Chancellorsville Campaign April 27-May 6. Bernard House April 29. Maryes Heights, Fredericksburg, May 3. Salem Heights May 3-4. Banks' Ford May 4. Gettysburg (Pa.) Campaign June 13-July 24. Battle of Gettysburg July 2-4. Pursuit of Lee July 5-24. At and near Funkstown July 10-13. Hagerstown July 14. Duty on line of the Rappahannock till October. Bristoe Campaign October 9-22. Advance to line of the Rappahannock November 7-8. Rappahannock Station November 7. Mine Run Campaign November 26-December 2. Regiment reenlisted December 26. At Brandy Station till May, 1864. Rapidan Campaign May 4-June 12. Battles of the Wilderness May 5-7; Spottsylvania C. H. May 8-12. Assault on the Salient May 12. North Anna River May 23-26. On line of the Pamunkey May 26-28. Totopotomoy May 28-31. Cold Harbor June 1-12. Before Petersburg June 17-18. Siege of Petersburg till July 9. Jerusalem Plank Road June 22-23. Moved to Washington, D. C., July 9-11. Repulse of Early's attack on Washington July 11-12. Pursuit of Early to Snicker's Gap July 14-18.

Sheridan's Shenandoah Valley Campaign August to December. Summit Point August 21. Battle of Opequan, Winchester, September 19. Fisher's Hill September 22. New Market September 24. Battle of Cedar Creek October 19. Duty in the Shenandoah Valley till December. Moved to Petersburg, Va., December. Siege of Petersburg December, 1864, to April, 1865. Dabney's Mills, Hatcher's Run, February 5-7, 1865. Appomattox Campaign March 28-April 9. Assault on and fall of Petersburg April 2. Pursuit of Lee April 3-9. Appomattox C. H. April 9. Surrender of Lee and his army. Moved to Danville April 23-27, and duty there till May 23. March to Richmond, Va., thence to Washington, D. C., May 23-June 3. Corps Review June 8. Mustered out July 17, 1865.

Regiment lost during service 11 Officers and 171 Enlisted men killed and mortally wounded and 1 Officer and 72 Enlisted men by disease. Total 255.

96th REGIMENT INFANTRY.

Organized at Pottsville September 9 to October 30, 1861. Left State for Washington, D. C., November 18, 1861. Attached to Slocum's Brigade, Franklin's Division. Army Potomac, to March, 1862. 2nd Brigade, 1st Division, 1st Army Corps, Army Potomac, to April, 1862. 2nd Brigade, 1st Division, Dept. of the Rappahannock, to May, 1862. 2nd Brigade, 1st Division, 6th Army Corps, Army Potomac, and Army of the Shenandoah, to October, 1864.

SERVICE.—Duty in the Defences of Washington, D. C., till March. 1862. Advance on Manassas, Va., March 10-15. McDowell's advance on Falmouth April 4-17. Return to Alexandria and embark for the Peninsula. Siege of Yorktown April 24-May 4 (on transports). West Point May 7-8. Seven days before Richmond June 25-July 1. Gaines' Mill June 27. Charles City Cross Roads and Glendale June 30. Malvern Hill July 1. At Harrison's Landing till August 16. Movement to Fortress Monroe, thence to Centreville August 16-28. In works at Centreville August 28-31. Cover Pope's retreat to Fairfax C. H. September 1. Maryland Campaign September 6-24. Crampton's Pass, South Mountain, September 14. Antietam September 16-17. Duty in Maryland till October 30. Movement to Falmouth, Va., October 30-November 19. Battle of Fredericksburg December 12-15. Burnside's second Campaign, "Mud March," January 20-24, 1863. At Falmouth till April. Chancellorsville Campaign April 27-May 6. Operations at Franklin's Crossing April 29-May 2. Maryes Heights, Fredericksburg, May 3. Salem Heights May 3-4. Banks' Ford May 4. Gettysburg Campaign June 13-July 24. Battle of Gettysburg, Pa., July 2-4. Pursuit of Lee July 5-24. At and near Funkstown, Md., July 10-13. Hagerstown July 14. Duty on line of the Rappahannock till October. Bristoe Campaign October 9-22. Advance to line of the Rappahannock November 7-8. Rappahannock Station November 7. Mine Run Campaign November 26-December 2. Duty at Hazel River till May, 1864. Rapidan Campaign May 4-June 12. Battles of the Wilderness May 5-7; Spottsylvania C. H. May 8-21. Assault on the Salient May 12. North Anna River May 23-26. On line of the Pamunkey May 26-28. Totopotomoy May 28-31. Cold Harbor June 1-12. Before Petersburg June 17-18. Jerusalem Plank Road June 22-23. Siege of Petersburg till July 9. Moved to Washington, D. C., July 9-11. Repulse of Early's attack on Washington July 11-12. Pursuit of Early to Snicker's Gap July 14-18. Sheridan's Shenandoah Valley Campaign August to October. Near Charlestown August 21-22. Charlestown August 24. Battle of Opequan, Winchester, September 19. Fisher's Hill September 22. New Market September 24. Battle of Cedar Creek October 19. Mustered out October 21, 1864, expiration of term.

Regiment lost during service 6 Officers and 126 Enlisted men killed and mortally wounded and 1 Officer and 86 Enlisted men by disease. Total 219.

97th REGIMENT INFANTRY.

Organized at West Chester August 22 to October 28, 1861. Moved to Washington, D. C., November 16-17, thence to Fortress Monroe, Va., November 20-22. Attached to Dept. of Virginia to December, 1861. Wright's 3rd Brigade, Sherman's South Carolina Expedition, to April, 1862. 1st Brigade, 1st Division, Dept. of the South, to July, 1862. District of Hilton Head, S. C., Dept. South, to September, 1862. District Hilton Head, S. C., 10th Corps, Dept. South, to April, 1863. Stevenson's Brigade, Seabrook Island, S. C., 10th Corps, to July, 1863. 1st Brigade, 1st Division, Morris Island, S. C., 10th Corps, July, 1863. 3rd Brigade, Morris Island, S. C., 10th Corps, to August, 1863. 1st Brigade, Morris Island, S. C., 10th Corps, to October, 1863. Fernandina, Fla., Dept. South, to April, 1864. 1st Brigade, 3rd Division, 10th Army Corps, Dept. Virginia and North Carolina, to May, 1864. 3rd Brigade, 3rd Division, 18th Corps, to June, 1864. 3rd Brigade, 2nd Division, 10th Corps, to December, 1864. 2nd Brigade, 2nd Division, 24th Army Corps, to January, 1865. 2nd Brigade, 2nd Division, Terry's Provisional Corps, Dept. North Carolina, to March, 1865. 2nd Brigade, 2nd Division, 10th Corps, Dept. North Carolina, to August, 1865.

SERVICE.—Duty at Camp Hamilton, near Fortress Monroe, Va., till December 8, 1861. Moved to Port Royal, S. C., December 8-11. Duty at Hilton Head, S. C., till January 21, 1862. Operations in Warsaw Sound, Ga., against Fort Pulaski, January 21-February 25. Expedition to Florida February 25-March 5. Occupation of Fernandina March 5, and duty there till March 24. Moved to Jacksonville, Fla., March 24, and duty there till April 9. Moved to Hilton Head, S. C., April 9-14. Expedition to Edisto Island, S. C., April 19-20. Expedition to James Island, S. C., June 1-28. Action on James Island June 10. Battle of Secessionville June 16. Evacuation of James Island June 28, and duty at North Edisto Island till July 18. Moved to Hilton Head, S. C., July 18, and duty there till November 20. At St. Helena Island, S. C., till January 15, 1863. At Hilton Head and Seabrook Point till April. At Seabrook Island till July 8. Expedition to James Island July 9-16. Battle of Secessionville July 16. Moved to Folly and Morris Islands July 17-18. Assault on Fort Wagner, Morris Island, July 18. Siege of Fort Wagner, Morris Island, and operations against Fort Sumpter and Charleston July 18-September 7. Capture of Forts Wagner and Gregg, Morris Island, September 7. Duty on Morris Island till October 2. Moved to Fernandina, Fla., October 2-5, and duty there till April 23, 1864. Expedition from Fernandina to Woodstock and King's Ferry Mills February 15-23, 1864. Moved to Hilton Head, S. C., thence to Gloucester Point, Va., April 23-28. Butler's operations on south side of the James and against Petersburg and Richmond May 4-28. Capture of Bermuda Hundred and City Point May 5. Swift Creek or Arrowfield Church May 9-10. Proctor's Creek and operations against Fort Darling May 12-16. Battle of Drewry's Bluff May 14-16. Bermuda Hundred front May 17-28. Chester Station May 18. Green Plains May 20. Movement to White House, thence to Cold Harbor May 28-June 1. Battles about Cold Harbor June 1-12. Before Petersburg June 15-18. Siege operations against Petersburg and Richmond June 16 to December 7, 1864. Mine Explosion, Petersburg, July 30 (Reserve). Demonstration on north side of James River at Deep Bottom August 13-20. Strawberry Plains, Deep Bottom, August 14-18. Bermuda Hundred August 24-25. Battle of Chaffin's Farm, New Market Heights, September 28-30. Charles City Road October 7. Battle of Fair Oaks October 27-28. In trenches before Richmond till December 6. Expedition to Fort Fisher, N. C., December 6-27. Second Expedition to Fort Fisher January 3-15, 1865. Assault and capture of Fort Fisher January 15. Sugar Loaf Battery February 11. Fort Anderson February 18-19. Capture of Wilmington February 22. Advance on Goldsboro March 6-21. Advance on Raleigh April 9-13. Oc-

cupation of Raleigh April 14. Bennett's House April 26. Surrender of Johnston and his army. Duty at Raleigh till July 10, and at Gaston and Weldon, N. C., till August 28. Mustered out August 28, 1865, at Weldon, N. C. Moved to Philadelphia, Pa., and discharged September 4, 1865.

Regiment lost during service 6 Officers and 130 Enlisted men killed and mortally wounded and 2 Officers and 184 Enlisted men by disease. Total 322.

98th REGIMENT INFANTRY.

Organized at Philadelphia August 23 to November 6, 1861. Regiment moved to Washington, D. C., September 30, 1861. Companies "G" and "H" joined in December, 1861. Attached to Peck's Brigade, Couch's Division, Army Potomac, to March, 1862. 3rd Brigade, 1st Division, 4th Army Corps, Army Potomac, to July, 1862. 2nd Brigade, 1st Division, 4th Army Corps, to September, 1862. 2nd Brigade, 3rd Division, 6th Army Corps, Army Potomac, to October, 1862. 3rd Brigade, 3rd Division, 6th Army Corps, to January, 1864. Wheaton's Brigade, Dept. West Virginia, to March, 1864. 1st Brigade, 2nd Division, 6th Army Corps, Army of the Potomac, and Army of the Shenandoah, to June, 1865.

SERVICE.—Duty in the Defences of Washington, D. C., till March, 1862. Advance on Manassas, Va., March 10-15. Moved to the Virginia Peninsula March 25. Siege of Yorktown April 5-May 4. Battle of Williamsburg May 5. Slatersville, New Kent C. H., and Sister's Mills May 9. Battle of Fair Oaks, Seven Pines, May 31-June 1. Seven days before Richmond June 25-July 1. About Fair Oaks June 26-29. Malvern Hill July 1. At Harrison's Landing to August 16. Movement to Alexandria, thence to Centreville August 16-30. Cover Pope's retreat to Fairfax C. H. August 30-September 1. Chantilly September 1 (Reserve). Maryland Campaign September 6-24. Battle of Antietam September 16-17 (Reserve). At Downsville, Md., September 23-October 20. Movement to Stafford C. H. October 20-November 18, and to Belle Plains December 5. Battle of Fredericksburg, Va., December 12-15. Burnside's 2nd Campaign, "Mud March," January 20-24, 1863. At Falmouth till April. Chancellorsville Campaign April 27-May 6. Operations at Franklin's Crossing April 29-May 2. Maryes Heights, Fredericksburg, May 3. Salem Heights May 3-4. Banks' Ford May 4. Gettysburg (Pa.) Campaign June 13-July 24. Battle of Gettysburg July 2-4. Pursuit of Lee July 5-24. Duty on line of the Rappahannock till October. Bristoe Campaign October 9-22. Advance to line of the Rappahannock November 7-8. Rappahannock Station November 7. Mine Run Campaign November 26-December 2. Duty at Brandy Station till May, 1864. Rapidan Campaign May 4-June 12. Battles of the Wilderness May 5-7; Spottsylvania May 8-21. Assault on the Salient May 12. North Anna River May 23-26. On line of the Pamunkey May 26-28. Totopotomoy May 28-31. Cold Harbor June 1-12. Before Petersburg June 17-18. Jerusalem Plank Road June 22-23. Siege of Petersburg till July 9. Moved to Washington D. C., July 9-11. Defence of Washington against Early's attack July 11-12. Pursuit to Snicker's Ferry July 14-18. Sheridan's Shenandoah Valley Campaign August to December. Charlestown August 21-22. Demonstration on Gilbert's Ford, Opequan Creek September 13. Battle of Opequan, Winchester, September 19. Strasburg September 21. Fisher's Hill September 22. Battle of Cedar Creek October 19. Duty in the Shenandoah Valley till December. Ordered to Petersburg December 9-12. Siege of Petersburg December, 1864, to April, 1865. Dabney's Mills, Hatcher's Run, February 5-7, 1865. Fort Fisher, Petersburg, March 25. Appomattox Campaign March 28-April 9. Assault on and fall of Petersburg April 2. Pursuit of Lee April 3-9. Appomattox C. H. April 9. Surrender of Lee and his army. March to Danville April 23-27, and duty there till May 23. Moved to Richmond, thence to Washington May 23-June 3. Corps Review June 8. Mustered out June 29, 1865.

Regiment lost during service 9 Officers and 112 Enlisted men killed and mortally wounded and 1 Officer and 72 Enlisted men by disease. Total 194.

99th REGIMENT INFANTRY.

Organized at Philadelphia as 32nd Pennsylvania Volunteers July 26, 1861, to January 18, 1862. Three Companies moved to Washington, D. C., August 8, 1861. Attached to Defences of Washington, D. C., to October, 1861. Jameson's Brigade, Heintzelman's Division, Army Potomac, to February, 1862. Military District of Washington to June, 1862. 3rd Brigade, 3rd Division, 3rd Army Corps, Army Potomac, to August, 1863. 3rd Brigade, 1st Division, 3rd Army Corps, to December, 1862. 2nd Brigade, 1st Division, 3rd Army Corps, to August, 1863. 3rd Brigade, 1st Division, 3rd Army Corps, to October, 1863. 2nd Brigade, 1st Division, 3rd Army Corps, to March, 1864. 1st Brigade, 3rd Division, 2nd Army Corps, to July, 1865.

SERVICE.—Duty in the Defences of Washington, D. C., till June 29, 1862. Moved to Harrison's Landing June 29-July 4, and duty there till August 16. Movement to Fortress Monroe, thence to Centreville August 16-26. Pope's Campaign in Northern Virginia August 26-September 2. Battles of Groveton August 29; Bull Run August 30; Chantilly September 1. Duty in the Defences of Washington, D. C., and outpost picket duty till October. White's Ford, Md., October 12. Movement up the Potomac to Leesburg, thence to Falmouth, Va., October 11-November 19. Battle of Fredericksburg December 12-15. Burnside's 2nd Campaign, "Mud March," January 20-24, 1863. At Falmouth till April. Chancellorsville Campaign April 27-May 6. Battle of Chancellorsville May 1-5. Gettysburg (Pa.) Campaign June 11-July 24. Battle of Gettysburg, Pa., July 1-3. Pursuit of Lee July 5-24. Wapping Heights, Va., July 23. Duty on line of the Rappahannock till October. Bristoe Campaign October 9-22. Auburn October 13. Advance to line of the Rappahannock November 7-8. Kelly's Ford November 7. Mine Run Campaign November 26-December 2. Payne's Farm November 27. Demonstration on the Rapidan February 6-7, 1864. Duty near Brandy Station till May. Rapidan Campaign May 4-June 12. Battles of the Wilderness May 5-7; Laurel Hill May 8; Spottsylvania May 8-12; Po River May 10; Spottsylvania C. H. May 12-21. Assault on the Salient May 12. Harris Farm, Fredericksburg Road May 19. North Anna River May 23-26. On line of the Pamunkey May 26-28. Totopotomoy May 28-31. Cold Harbor June 1-12. Before Petersburg June 16-18. Siege of Petersburg June 16, 1864, to April 2, 1865. Jerusalem Plank Road June 21-23, 1864. Demonstration on north side of the James at Deep Bottom July 27-29. Deep Bottom July 27-28. Mine Explosion, Petersburg, July 30 (Reserve). Demonstration on north side of the James at Deep Bottom August 13-18. Strawberry Plains, Deep Bottom, August 14-18. Poplar Springs Church September 29-October 2. Boydton Plank Road, Hatcher's Run, October 27-28. Raid on Weldon Railroad December 7-12. Dabney's Mills, Hatcher's Run, February 5-7, 1865. Watkins' House, Petersburg, March 25. Appomattox Campaign March 28-April 9. Crow's House March 31. Fall of Petersburg April 2. Sailor's Creek April 6. High Bridge, Farmville, April 7. Appomattox C. H. April 9. Surrender of Lee and his army. At Burkesville till May 2. March to Washington, D. C., May 2-12. Grand Review May 23. Mustered out July 1, 1865.

Regiment lost during service 9 Officers and 113 Enlisted men killed and mortally wounded and 1 Officer and 112 Enlisted men by disease. Total 235.

100th REGIMENT INFANTRY.

Organized at Pittsburg August 31, 1861. Left State for Washington, D. C., September 2, and duty there till October 9. Moved to Annapolis, Md., October 9. Attached to Stevens' 2nd Brigade, Sherman's South Carolina Expedition, to April, 1862. 2nd Brigade, 2nd Division, Dept. of the South, to July, 1862. 2nd Brigade, 1st Division, 9th Army Corps, Army Potomac, to September, 1862. 3rd Brigade, 1st Division, 9th Army Corps, to April, 1863. 3rd Brigade, 1st Division, 9th Army Corps, Dept. Ohio, to June, 1863. Army of the Tennessee, to August, 1863, and Army Ohio, to March, 1864. 2nd Brigade, 1st Division, 9th Army Corps, Army Potomac, to June, 1864. 1st Brigade, 1st Division, 9th Army Corps, to September, 1864. 3rd Brigade, 1st Division, 9th Army Corps, to July, 1865.

SERVICE.—Sherman's Expedition to Port Royal Harbor, S. C., October 21-November 7, 1861. Capture of Forts Walker and Beauregard, Port Royal Harbor, November 7. Occupation of Beaufort, S. C., December 8, and duty there till June, 1862. Port Royal Ferry, Coosa River, January 1. Operations on James Island, S. C., June 1-28. Legaire's Point, James Island, June 3. Skirmishes on James Island June 3-4. Battle of Secessionville, James Island, June 16. Evacuation of James Island and movement to Hilton Head, S. C., June 28-July 7. Moved to Newport News, Va., July 12-17, thence to Fredericksburg August 4-6. Operations in support of Pope August 6-16. Pope's Campaign in Northern Virginia August 16-September 2. Battles of Groveton August 29; Bull Run August 30; Chantilly September 1. Maryland Campaign September 6-24. Battles of South Mountain September 14 and Antietam September 16-17. March up the Potomac to Leesburg, thence to Falmouth October 11-November 18. Battle of Fredericksburg December 12-15. Burnside's 2nd Campaign, "Mud March," January 20-24, 1863. Moved to Newport News, Va., February 13, thence to Covington, Ky., March 20-28. Duty in District of Kentucky. At Paris, Nicholasville, Lancaster, Stanford and Somerset till June. Movement through Kentucky to Cairo, Ill., June 4-10, thence to Vicksburg, Miss., June 14-17. Siege of Vicksburg June 17-July 4. Advance on Jackson, Miss., July 5-10. Siege of Jackson July 10-17. Duty at Milldale till August 6. Moved to Covington, Ky., thence to Crab Orchard, Ky., August 6-18. March to Knoxville, Tenn., September 10-26, and duty there till October 3. Action at Blue Springs October 10. Knoxville Campaign November 4-December 23. Campbell Station November 16. Siege of Knoxville November 17-December 4. Repulse of Longstreet's assault on Fort Saunders November 29. Pursuit of Longstreet December 5-24. At Blain's Cross Roads till January, 1864. Veterans marched over Cumberland Mountains to Nicholasville, Ky., January, and on furlough till March. Ordered to Annapolis, Md., and duty there till April. Rapidan Campaign May 4-June 12. Battles of the Wilderness May 5-7; Spottsylvania May 8-12; Ny River May 10; Spottsylvania C. H. May 12-21. Assault on the Salient May 12. North Anna River May 12-21. Ox Ford May 24. Line of the Pamunkey May 26-28. Totopotomoy May 28-31. Cold Harbor June 1-12. Bethesda Church June 1-3. Before Petersburg June 16-18. Siege of Petersburg June 16, 1864, to April 2, 1865. Mine Explosion, Petersburg, July 30, 1864. Weldon Railroad August 18-21. Poplar Springs Church September 29-October 2. Reconnoissance on Vaughan and Squirrel Level Road November 8. Boydton Plank Road, Hatcher's Run, October 27-28. Fort Stedman March 25, 1865. Appomattox Campaign March 28-April 9. Assault on and fall of Petersburg April 2. Occupation of Petersburg April 3. Pursuit of Lee April 3-8. Moved to Washington, D. C., April 21-28, and duty there till July. Grand Review May 23. Mustered out July 24, 1865.

Regiment lost during service 16 Officers and 208 Enlisted men killed and mortally wounded and 2 Officers and 183 Enlisted men by disease. Total 409.

101st REGIMENT INFANTRY.

Organized at Harrisburg November 21, 1861, to February 24, 1862. Moved to Washington, D. C., February 27, 1862. Attached to 2nd Brigade, 3rd Division, 4th Army Corps, Army of the Potomac, to June, 1862. 2nd Brigade, 2nd Division, 4th Army Corps, to September, 1862. Wessell's Brigade, Division at Suffolk, Va., 7th Corps, Dept. of Virginia, to December, 1862. 1st Brigade, 1st Division, Dept. of North Carolina, to January, 1863. 1st Brigade, 4th Division, 18th Army Corps, Dept. of North Carolina, to May, 1863. District of Albemarle, Dept. of North Carolina, to August, 1863. Sub-District, Albemarle, District of North Carolina, Dept. of Virginia and North Carolina, to April, 1864. Defences of New Berne, N. C., Dept. of Virginia and North Carolina, to February, 1865. District of New Berne, N. C., Dept. of North Carolina, to June, 1865.

SERVICE.—Advance on Manassas, Va., March 10-15, 1862. Ordered to the Peninsula March 28. Siege of Yorktown April 5-May 4. Battle of Williamsburg May 5. Battles of Fair Oaks, Seven Pines, May 31-June 1. Seven days before Richmond June 25-July 1. Brackett's June 30. Malvern Hill July 1. At Harrison's Landing till August 16. Moved to Fortress Monroe August 16-23, thence to Suffolk September 18, and duty there till December. Ordered to New Berne, N. C., December 4. Foster's Expedition to Goldsboro December 10-21. Kinston December 14. Whitehall December 16. Goldsboro December 17. Duty at New Berne till May, 1863. Expedition from New Berne to Mattamuskeet Lake March 7-14. Operations on the Pamlico April 4-6. Expedition for relief of Little Washington April 7-10. Moved to Plymouth May, 1863, and duty there till March, 1864. Expedition from Plymouth to Nichol's Mills June 28, 1863 (Detachment). Expedition from Plymouth to Gardner's Bridge and Williamston July 5-7. Expedition from Plymouth to Foster's Mills July 26-29. Harrellsville January 20, 1864 (Detachment). Windsor January 30. Fairfield February 16. Moved to New Berne March, 1864; thence to Roanoke Island and to Plymouth April. Siege of Plymouth April 17-20. Regiment mostly captured April 20. Those not captured served as garrison at Roanoke Island till June, 1865. Mustered out at New Berne June 25, 1865.

Regiment lost during service 39 Enlisted men killed and mortally wounded and 1 Officer and 281 Enlisted men by disease. Total 321.

102nd REGIMENT INFANTRY.

Organized at Pittsburg August, 1861. Five Companies left State for Washington, D. C., August 21, 1861. Attached to Peck's Brigade, Couch's Division, Army of the Potomac, October, 1861, to March, 1862. 3rd Brigade, 1st Division, 4th Army Corps, Army of the Potomac, to July, 1862. 2nd Brigade, 1st Division, 4th Corps, to September, 1862. 2nd Brigade, 3rd Division, 6th Army Corps, Army of the Potomac, to October, 1862. 3rd Brigade, 3rd Division, 6th Army Corps, to January, 1864. Wheaton's Brigade, Dept. of West Virginia, to March, 1864. 1st Brigade, 2nd Division, 6th Army Corps, Army of the Potomac and Army of the Shenandoah, to June, 1865.

SERVICE.—Duty in the Defences of Washington, D. C., till March, 1862. Advance on Manassas, Va., March 10-15. Moved to the Peninsula March 28. Siege of Yorktown April 5-May 4. Battle of Williamsburg May 5. Operations about Bottom's Bridge May 20-23. Battle of Fair Oaks, Seven Pines, May 31-June 1. Seven days before Richmond June 25-July 1. Malvern Hill July 1. At Harrison's Landing till August 16. Movement to Alexandria, thence to Centreville August 16-30. Cover Pope's retreat to Fairfax Court House August 30-September 1. Chantilly September 1 (Reserve). Maryland Campaign September 6-27. Battle of Antietam September 16-17. At Downsville, Md., September 23 to October 20. Movement to Stafford Court House October 20-November 18, and to Belle Plains December 5. Battle of Fredericksburg, Va., December 12-15. Burnside's 2nd Campaign, "Mud March," January 20-24, 1863. At Falmouth till April. Chancellorsville Campaign April 27-May 6. Operations at Franklin's Crossing April 29-May 2. Maryes Heights, Fredericksburg, May 3. Salem Heights May 3-4. Banks' Ford May 4. Gettysburg (Pa.) Campaign June 13-July 24. Battle of Gettysburg July 2-4. Pursuit of Lee July 5-24. Duty on line of the Rappahannock till October. Bristoe Campaign October 9-22. Advance to line of the Rappahannock

November 7-8. Rappahannock Station November 7. Mine Run Campaign November 26-December 2. Rapidan Campaign May 4-June 12, 1864. Battles of the Wilderness May 5-7; Spottsylvania May 8-21. Assault on the Salient May 12; North Anna River May 23-26. On line of the Pamunkey May 26-28. Tototopotomoy May 28-31. Cold Harbor June 1-12. Before Petersburg June 17-18. Jerusalem Plank Road June 22-23. Siege of Petersburg till July 9. Moved to Washington, D. C., July 9-11. Repulse of Early's attack on Washington July 11-12. Pursuit of Early to Snicker's Gap July 14-18. Sheridan's Shenandoah Valley Campaign August to December. Charlestown August 21-22. Demonstration on Gilbert's Ford, Opequan Creek, September 13. Strasburg September 21. Battle of Opequan, Winchester, September 19. Fisher's Hill September 22. Battle of Cedar Creek October 19. Duty in the Shenandoah Valley till December. Ordered to Petersburg December 9-12. Siege of Petersburg December, 1864, to April, 1865. Fort Fisher, Petersburg, March 25, 1865. Appomattox Campaign March 28-April 9. Assault on and fall of Petersburg April 2. Pursuit of Lee April 3-9. Appomattox Court House April 9. Surrender of Lee and his army. March to Danville April 23-27, and duty there till May 23. Moved to Richmond, thence to Washington, D. C., May 23-June 3. Corps Review June 8. Mustered out June 28, 1865.

Regiment lost during service 10 Officers and 171 Enlisted men killed and mortally wounded and 1 Officer and 81 Enlisted men by disease. Total 263.

103rd REGIMENT INFANTRY.

Organized at Kittanning September 7, 1861, to February 22, 1862. Moved to Harrisburg, Pa., February 24; thence to Washington, D. C. Attached to 2nd Brigade, 3rd Division, 4th Army Corps, Army of the Potomac, to June, 1862. 2nd Brigade, 2nd Division, 4th Army Corps, to September, 1862. Wessell's Brigade, Division at Suffolk, Va., 7th Corps, Dept. of Virginia, to December, 1862. 1st Brigade, 1st Division, Dept. of North Carolina, to January, 1863. 1st Brigade, 4th Division, 18th Army Corps, Dept. of North Carolina, to May, 1863. District of Albemarle, Dept. of North Carolina, to August, 1863. Sub-District, Albemarle, District of North Carolina, Dept. of Virginia and North Carolina, to January, 1865. District of Albemarle, Dept. of North Carolina, to June, 1865.

SERVICE.—Advance on Manassas, Va., March 10-15, 1862. Ordered to the Peninsula March 28. Siege of Yorktown April 5-May 4. Skirmish at Yorktown April 11. Battle of Williamsport May 5. Skirmish at Fair Oaks May 30. Battle of Fair Oaks, Seven Pines, May 31-June 1. Seven days before Richmond June 25-July 1. Brackett's June 30. Malvern Hill July 1. At Harrison's Landing till August 16. Moved to Fortress Monroe August 16-23; thence to Suffolk September 18. Duty at Suffolk till December. Blackwater October 9. Blackwater, near Zuni, October 25. Blackwater October 29. Expedition from Suffolk December 1-3. Beaver Dam Station December 1. Near Franklin on the Blackwater December 2. Ordered to New Berne, N. C., December 4. Foster's Expedition from New Berne to Goldsboro December 10-21. Southwest Creek December 13-14. Kinston December 14. Whitehall December 16. Goldsboro December 17. Duty at New Berne till May, 1863. Expedition from New Berne to Mattamuskeet Lake February 7-14. Expedition for relief of Little Washington April 7-10. Moved to Plymouth, N. C., May, 1863, and duty there till April, 1864. Expedition from Plymouth to Gardner's Bridge and Williamston July 5-7, 1863. Expedition to Foster's Mills July 26-29. Herford December 10. Harrellsville January 20, 1864 (Detachment). Windsor January 30. Siege of Plymouth April 17-20. Regiment mostly captured April 20. Those not captured on duty in District of the Albemarle as garrison at Roanoke Island till June, 1865. Mustered out June 25, 1865.

Regiment lost during service 3 Officers and 50 Enlisted men killed and mortally wounded and 1 Officer and 352 Enlisted men by disease. Total 406.

104th REGIMENT INFANTRY.

Organized at Doylestown September 20 to October 16, 1861. Left State for Washington, D. C., November 6, 1861. Attached to Casey's Division to March, 1862. 1st Brigade, 3rd Division, 4th Army Corps, Army Potomac, to June, 1862. 1st Brigade, 2nd Division, 4th Army Corps, to December, 1862. Naglee's Brigade, Dept. of North Carolina, to January, 1863. 2nd Brigade, 2nd Division, 18th Army Corps, Dept. of North Carolina, to February, 1863. 2nd Brigade, 1st Division, 18th Army Corps, Dept. of the South, to April, 1863. District of Beaufort, S. C., 10th Army Corps, to July, 1863. 2nd Brigade, 1st Division, 10th Army Corps, Dept. South, July, 1863. Davis' Brigade, Folly Island, S. C., 10th Corps, to August, 1863. 5th Brigade, Morris Island, S. C., 10th Corps, to November, 1863. 2nd Brigade, Morris Island, S. C., 10th Corps, to April, 1864. District of Hilton Head, S. C., Dept. South, to June, 1864. Morris Island, Northern District, Dept. South, to July, 1864. District of Florida, Dept. South, to August, 1864. Defences of Washington, 22nd Corps, South of the Potomac, to September, 1864. Train Guard, Army Shenandoah, Middle Military Division, to November, 1864. 1st Brigade, Defences Bermuda Hundred, Va., Dept. Virginia and North Carolina, to April, 1865. Norfolk and Portsmouth, Va., Dept. Virginia, to August, 1865.

SERVICE.—Duty in the Defences of Washington till March, 1862. Advance on Manassas, Va., March 10-15. Moved to the Peninsula March 28. Siege of Yorktown April 5-May 4. Battle of Williamsburg May 5. Operations about Bottom's Bridge May 20-23. Reconnoissance to Seven Pines May 24-27. Skirmishes at Seven Pines, Savage Station and Chickahominy May 24. Battle of Fair Oaks or Seven Pines May 31-June 1. Seven days before Richmond June 25-July 1. Bottom's Bridge June 28-29. White Oak Swamp June 30. Malvern Hill July 1. At Harrison's Landing till August 15. Moved to Yorktown August 16-23, and duty there till December 28. Gloucester Point November 16. Expedition to Matthews County December 11-15. Moved to Morehead City, N. C., December 28-January 1, 1863, thence to Port Royal Harbor, S. C., January 28-31. Moved to St. Helena Island, S. C., February 10, and duty there till April 4. Expedition against Charleston, S. C., April 4-12. Duty at Beaufort, S. C., till July. Expedition to James Island, S. C., July 9-16. Battle of Secessionville, James Island, July 16. Moved to Folly and Morris Island, S. C., July 16-18. Assault on Fort Wagner, Morris Island, July 18. Siege of Fort Wagner July 18-September 7, and operations against Fort Sumpter and Charleston from Morris and Folly Islands till June, 1864. Reconnoissance to Dafuskie Island May 11, 1864. Expedition to John's Island July 2-10. Operations against Battery Pringle July 4-9. Boudren's Causeway, James Island, July 9. At Hilton Head, S. C., till July and in Florida till August. Ordered to Washington, D. C., and duty in the Defences south of the Potomac to September. Moved to Harper's Ferry, W. Va., and duty escorting trains to Sheridan's army till November. Moved to Bermuda Hundred, Va., November 22. Siege operations against Petersburg and Richmond December, 1864, to April, 1865. Fall of Petersburg April 2. Duty there till April 20. Moved to Norfolk, Va., April 20-24, and duty there till August. Mustered out August 25, 1865.

Regiment lost during service, 2 Officers and 68 Enlisted men killed and mortally wounded and 115 Enlisted men by disease. Total 185.

105th REGIMENT INFANTRY.

Organized at Pittsburg September 9, 1861, and ordered to Washington, D. C. Attached to Jameston's Brigade, Heintzelman's Division, Army of the Potomac, to March, 1862. 1st Brigade, 3rd Division, 3rd Army Corps, Army of the Potomac, to August, 1862. 1st Brigade, 1st Division, 3rd Army Corps, to March, 1864. 2nd Brigade, 3rd Division, 2nd Army Corps, to July, 1865.

SERVICE.—Duty in the Defences of Washington, D. C., till March, 1862. Moved to the Virginia Peninsula

March 16-18. Siege of Yorktown April 5-May 4. Battle of Williamsburg May 5. Battle of Fair Oaks, Seven Pines, May 31-June 1. Seven days before Richmond June 25-July 1. Battles of Oak Grove June 25; Charles City Cross Roads and Glendale June 30; Malvern Hill July 1. At Harrison's Landing till August 16. Movement to Centreville August 16-26. Pope's Campaign in Northern Virginia August 26-September 2. Bristoe Station or Kettle Run August 27. Buckland's Bridge, Broad Run, August 27. Battles of Groveton August 29; Bull Run August 30; Chantilly September 1. Guard fords from Monocacy River to Conrad's Ferry till October. March up the Potomac to Leesburg, thence to Falmouth, Va., October 11-November 19. Battle of Fredericksburg, Va., December 12-15. Burnside's 2nd Campaign, "Mud March," January 20-24, 1863. At Falmouth till April. Chancellorsville Campaign April 27-May 6. Battle of Chancellorsville May 1-5. Gettysburg (Pa.) Campaign June 11-July 24. Battle of Gettysburg July 1-3. Pursuit of Lee July 5-24. Wapping Heights July 23. Duty on line of the Rappahannock till October. Bristoe Campaign October 9-22. Auburn and Bristoe October 13-14. Advance to line of the Rappahannock November 7-8. Kelly's Ford November 7. Mine Run Campaign November 26-December 2. Demonstration on the Rapidan February 6-7, 1864. Rapidan Campaign May 4-June 12. Battles of the Wilderness May 5-7; Laurel Hill May 8; Spottsylvania May 8-12; Po River May 10; Spottsylvania Court House May 12-21. Assault on the Salient May 12. Harris Farm, Fredericksburg Road, May 19. North Anna River May 23-26. On line of the Pamunkey May 26-28. Totopotomey May 28-31. Cold Harbor June 1-12. Before Petersburg June 16-18. Siege of Petersburg June 16, 1864, to April 2, 1865. Jerusalem Plank Road June 22-23, 1864. Demonstration north of the James at Deep Bottom July 27-29. Deep Bottom July 27-28. Mine Explosion, Petersburg, July 30 (Reserve). Demonstration on north side of James at Deep Bottom August 13-20. Strawberry Plains August 14-18. Poplar Springs Church September 29-October 2. Boydton Plank Road, Hatcher's Run, October 27-28. Warren's expedition to Hicksford December 7-12. Dabney's Mills, Hatcher's Run, February 5-7, 1865. Watkins' House, Petersburg, March 25. Appomattox Campaign March 28-April 9. Boydton Road March 30-31. Crow's House March 31. Fall of Petersburg April 2. Sailor's Creek April 6. High Bridge, Farmville, April 7. Appomattox Court House April 9. Surrender of Lee and his army. At Burkesville till May. March to Washington, D. C., May 2-12. Grand Review May 23. Duty at Alexandria till July. Mustered out July 11, 1885.

Regiment lost during service 14 Officers and 231 Enlisted men killed and mortally wounded and 1 Officer and 139 Enlisted men by disease. Total 384.

106th REGIMENT INFANTRY.

Organized at Philadelphia August 14 to October 31, 1861. Moved to Washington, D. C., November. Attached to Baker's Brigade, Stone's (Sedgwick's) Division, Army of the Potomac, to March, 1862. 2nd Brigade, 2nd Division, 2nd Army Corps, Army of the Potomac, to June, 1864. 3rd Brigade, 2nd Division, 2nd Army Corps, to June, 1865.

SERVICE.—Duty on Upper Potomac till March, 1862. Moved to Virginia Peninsula March 24-April 1. Siege of Yorktown April 5-May 4. Moved to West Point May 7. At Tyler's Farm till May 31. Battle of Fair Oaks or Seven Pines, May 31-June 1. Skirmish at Fair Oaks June 8. Seven days before Richmond June 25-July 1. Peach Orchard and Savage Station June 29. Charles City Cross Roads and Glendale June 30. Malvern Hill July 1. At Harrison Landing till August 16. Movement to Newport News, thence to Alexandria August 16-28, and to Centreville August 28-30. Cover Pope's retreat August 31-September 1. Chantilly September 1 (Reserve). Maryland Campaign September 6-22. Battle of Antietam September 16-17. Moved to Harper's Ferry, W. Va., September 22, and duty there till October 30. Movement to Falmouth, Va., October 30-November 20. Battle of Fredericksburg, Va., December 12-15. Burnside's 2nd Campaign, "Mud March," January 20-24, 1863. At Falmouth till April. Hartwood Church February 25. Chancellorsville Campaign April 27-May 6. Operations at Franklin's Crossing April 29-May 2. Maryes Heights, Fredericksburg, May 3. Salem Heights May 3-4. Banks Ford May 4. Gettysburg (Pa.) Campaign June 11-July 24. Haymarket June 21 and 25. Battle of Gettysburg July 1-3. Pursuit of Lee July 5-24. Advance from the Rappahannock to the Rapidan September 13-15. Bristoe Campaign October 9-22. Advance to line of the Rappahannock November 7-8. Mine Run Campaign November 26-December 2. Payne's Farm November 27. Demonstration on the Rapidan February 6-7, 1864. Rapidan Campaign May 4-June 12. Battles of the Wilderness May 5-7. Laurel Hill May 8. Spottsylvania May 8-12. Po River May 10. Spottsylvania Court House May 12-21. Assault on the Salient May 12. North Anna River May 23-26. On line of the Pamunkey May 26-28. Totopotomoy May 28-31. Cold Harbor June 1-12. Before Petersburg June 16-18. Siege of Petersburg June 16, 1864, to April 2, 1865. Jerusalem Plank Road June 22-23, 1864. Demonstration on north side of the James at Deep Bottom July 27-29. Deep Bottom July 27-28. Mine Explosion, Petersburg, July 30. Demonstration on north side of the James at Deep Bottom August 18-20. Strawberry Plains, Deep Bottom, August 14-18. Ream's Station August 25. Boydton Plank Road, Hatcher's Run, October 27-28. Dabney's Mills, Hatcher's Run, February 5-7, 1865. Watkins' House, Petersburg, March 25. Appomattox Campaign March 28-April 9. Vaughan Road, near Hatcher's Run, March 29. Crow's House March 31. Fall of Petersburg April 2. Sailor's Creek April 6. High Bridge and Farmville April 7. Appomattox Court House April 9. Surrender of Lee and his army. At Burkesville May 2. March to Washington May 2-12. Grand Review May 23. Mustered out June 30, 1865.

Regiment lost during service 9 Officers and 95 Enlisted men killed and mortally wounded and 1 Officer and 92 Enlisted men by disease. Total 197.

107th REGIMENT INFANTRY.

Organized at Harrisburg February 20 to March 8, 1862. Left State for Washington, D. C., March 9, 1862. Attached to Defences of Washington, D. C., to April, 1862. 1st Brigade, 2nd Division, Dept. of the Rappahannock, to June, 1862. 1st Brigade, 2nd Division, 3rd Corps, Army of Virginia, to September, 1862. 1st Brigade, 2nd Division, 1st Army Corps, Army of the Potomac, to March, 1864. 1st Brigade, 2nd Division, 5th Army Corps, Army of the Potomac, to June, 1864. 1st Brigade, 3rd Division, 5th Army Corps, to September, 1864. 2nd Brigade, 3rd Division, 5th Army Corps, to February, 1865. 3rd Brigade, 3rd Division, 5th Army Corps, to July, 1865.

SERVICE.—Camp at Kendall Green, Defences of Washington, D. C., till April 2, 1862. Moved to Upton's Hill April 2; thence to Cloud's Mills, Va., April 16, and duty there till May 11. Guard duty on Orange & Alexandria Railroad from Manassas to Catlett's Station. Expedition to Front Royal to intercept Jackson May 28-June 1. At Front Royal till June 10. At Catlett's Station, Weaversville, Warrenton and Waterloo till August 5. Battle of Cedar Mountain August 9. Pope's Campaign in Northern Virginia August 16-September 2. Fords of the Rappahannock August 21-23. Rappahannock Station August 24-25. Thoroughfare Gap August 28. Battle of Bull Run August 30. Chantilly September 1. Maryland Campaign September 6-24. Battles of South Mountain September 14; Antietam September 16-17. Duty near Sharpsburg, Md., till October 28. Moved to Warrenton October 28-November 7, thence to Falmouth, Va., November 11-19. At Brook's Station till December 11. Battle of Fredericksburg December 12-15. Burnside's 2nd Campaign, "Mud March," January 20-24, 1863. At Falmouth and Belle Plains till April. Chancellorsville Campaign April 27-May 6. Operations at Pollock's Mill Creek April 29-May 2. Fitz-

hugh's Crossing April 29-30. Chancellorsville May 2-5. Gettysburg (Pa.) Campaign June 11-July 24. Battle of Gettysburg July 1-3. Pursuit of Lee July 5-24. Duty along the Rappahannock till October. Bristoe Campaign October 9-22. Advance to line of the Rappahannock November 7-8. Mine Run Campaign November 26-December 2. Demonstration on the Rapidan February 6-7, 1864. Re-enlisted February, 1864. (Veterans absent till May 16.) Duty on Orange & Alexandria Railroad till May. Rapidan Campaign May 4-June 12. Battles of the Wilderness May 5-7; Spottsylvania May 8-12; Spottsylvania Court House May 12-21; North Anna River May 23-26; Jericho Ford May 25. On line of the Pamunkey May 26-28. Totopotomoy May 28-31. Cold Harbor June 1-12. Bethesda Church June 1-3. White Oak Swamp June 13. Before Petersburg June 16-18. Siege of Petersburg June 16, 1864, to April 2, 1865. Weldon Railroad August 18-21, 1864. Reconnoissance toward Dinwiddie Court House September 15. Boydton Plank Road, Hatcher's Run, October 27-28. Warren's Raid to Hicksford December 7-12. Dabney's Mills, Hatcher's Run, February 5-7, 1865. Appomattox Campaign March 28-April 9. Lewis Farm, near Gravelly Run, March 29. White Oak Road March 31. Five Forks April 1. Appomattox Court House April 9. Surrender of Lee and his army. Moved to Washington, D. C., May 1-12. Grand Review May 23. Duty at Washington and Alexandria to July. Mustered out July 13, 1865.

Regiment lost during service 2 Officers and 106 Enlisted men killed and mortally wounded and 3 Officers and 140 Enlisted men by disease. Total 251.

108th REGIMENT VOLUNTEERS.

(See 11th Cavalry.)

109th REGIMENT INFANTRY.

Organized at Philadelphia March to May, 1862. Moved to Washington, D. C., May 10; thence to Harper's Ferry May 24, 1862. Attached to 1st Brigade, Sigel's Division, Dept. of the Shenandoah, to June, 1862. 1st Brigade, 2nd Division, 2nd Army Corps, Army of Virginia, to August, 1862. 2nd Brigade, 2nd Division, 2nd Army Corps, Army of Virginia, to September, 1862. 2nd Brigade, 2nd Division, 12th Army Corps, Army of the Potomac, to October, 1862. 3rd Brigade, 2nd Division, 12th Army Corps, to January, 1863. 2nd Brigade, 2nd Division, 12th Army Corps, Army of the Potomac, to October, 1863, and Army of the Cumberland to April, 1864. 2nd Brigade, 2nd Division, 20th Army Corps, Army of the Cumberland, to March, 1865.

SERVICE.—Defence of Harper's Ferry, W. Va., May 24-30, 1862. Operations in the Shenandoah Valley till August. Battle of Cedar Mountain August 9. Pope's Campaign in Northern Virginia August 16-September 2. Guarding trains during Battles of Bull Run. Maryland Campaign September 6-22. Battle of Antietam September 16-17 (Reserve). Duty at Bolivar Heights till December. Reconnoissance to Rippon, W. Va., November 9. Reconnoissance to Winchester December 2-6. March to Fredericksburg December 9-16. Burnside's 2nd Campaign, "Mud March," January 20-24, 1863. At Stafford Court House till April 27. Chancellorsville Campaign April 27-May 6. Battle of Chancellorsville May 1-5. Gettysburg (Pa.) Campaign June 11-July 24. Battle of Gettysburg July 1-3. Pursuit of Lee July 5-24. Duty near Raccoon Ford till September. Movement to Bridgeport, Ala., September 24-October 3. Reopening Tennessee River October 26-29. Battle of Wauhatchie, Tenn., October 28-29. Chattanooga-Ringgold Campaign November 23-27. Lookout Mountain November 23-24. Mission Ridge November 25. Ringgold Gap, Taylor's Ridge, Ga., November 27. Duty on Nashville & Chattanooga Railroad till April, 1864. Atlanta (Ga.) Campaign May 1-September 8. Demonstration on Rocky Faced Ridge May 8-11. Battle of Resaca May 14-15. Near Cassville May 19. New Hope Church May 25. Operations on line of Pumpkin Vine Creek and battles about Dallas, New Hope Church and Allatoona Hills May 25-June 5. Operations about Marietta and against Kenesaw Mountain June 10-July 2. Pine Hill June 11-14. Lost Mountain June 15-17. Gilgal or Golgotha Church June 15. Muddy Creek June 17. Noyes Creek June 19. Kolb's Farm June 22. Assault on Kenesaw June 27. Ruff's Station or Smyrna Camp Ground July 4. Chattahoochie River July 5-17. Peach Tree Creek July 19-20. Siege of Atlanta July 22-August 25. Operations at Chattahoochie River Bridge August 26-September 2. Occupation of Atlanta September 2-November 15. Expedition to Tuckum's Cross Roads October 26-29. Near Atlanta November 9. March to the sea November 15-December 10. Siege of Savannah December 10-21. Campaign of the Carolinas January to March, 1865. Battle of Bentonville, N. C., March 19-21. Consolidated with 111th Pennsylvania Infantry March 31, 1865.

Regiment lost during service 3 Officers and 61 Enlisted men killed and mortally wounded and 71 Enlisted men by disease. Total 135.

110th REGIMENT INFANTRY.

Organized at Harrisburg, Huntingdon and Philadelphia August 19, 1861. Left State for Hancock, Md., January 2, 1862. Defence of Hancock January 5. Attached to Tyler's Brigade, Landers' Division, Army of the Potomac, to March, 1862. 3rd Brigade, Shield's 2nd Division, Banks' 5th Corps and Dept. of the Shenandoah, to May, 1862. 4th Brigade, Shield's Division, Dept. of the Rappahannock, to June, 1862. 4th Brigade, 2nd Division, 3rd Army Corps, Army of Virginia, to September, 1862. 2nd Brigade, 3rd Division, 3rd Army Corps, Army of the Potomac, to June, 1863. 3rd Brigade, 1st Division, 3rd Army Corps, to March, 1864. 1st Brigade, 3rd Division, 2nd Army Corps, to June, 1865.

SERVICE.—At Cumberland and south branch of the Potomac guarding bridges of the Baltimore & Ohio Railroad till February 6. Moved to Paw Paw Tunnel and duty there till March 7, 1862. Advance on Winchester March 7-15. Reconnoissance to Strasburg March 18-21. Battle of Winchester March 23. Pursuit of Jackson up the Valley March 24-April 27. Occupation of Mt. Jackson April 17. March to Fredericksburg May 12-21, and to Front Royal May 25-30. Near Front Royal May 31. Port Republic June 9. Battle of Cedar Mountain August 9. Pope's Campaign in Northern Virginia August 16-September 2. Fords of the Rappahannock August 21-23. Manassas August 23. Thoroughfare Gap August 28. Groveton August 29. Bull Run August 30. Duty at Arlington Heights, Defences of Washington, Whipple's Command, till October. Moved to Pleasant Valley October 18, thence to Warrenton and Falmouth, Va., October 24-November 19. Battle of Fredericksburg December 12-15. Burnside's 2nd Campaign, "Mud March," January 20-24, 1863. At Falmouth till April. Chancellorsville Campaign April 27-May 6. Battle of Chancellorsville May 1-5. Gettysburg (Pa.) Campaign June 11-July 24. Battle of Gettysburg July 1-3. Pursuit of Lee July 5-24. Wapping Heights, Va., July 23. On line of the Rappahannock till October. Bristoe Campaign October 9-22. Auburn and Bristoe October 13-14. Advance to line of the Rappahannock November 7-8. Kelly's Ford November 7. Mine Run Campaign November 26-December 2. Payne's Farm November 27. Demonstration on the Rapidan February 6-7, 1864. Duty near Brandy Station till May. Rapidan Campaign May 4-June 12. Battles of the Wilderness May 5-7; Laurel Hill May 8; Spottsylvania May 8-12; Po River May 10; Spottsylvania Court House May 12-21. Assault on the Salient May 12. Harris Farm May 19. North Anna River May 23-26. On line of the Pamunkey May 26-28. Totopotomoy May 28-31. Cold Harbor June 1-12. Before Petersburg June 16-18. Siege of Petersburg June 16, 1864, to April 2, 1865. Jerusalem Plank Road June 22-23, 1864. Demonstration north of the James at Deep Bottom July 27-29. Deep Bottom July 27-28. Mine Explosion, Petersburg, July 30 (Reserve). Demonstration north of the James at Deep Bottom August 13-20. Strawberry Plains, Deep Bot-

tom, August 14-18. Poplar Springs Church September 29-October 2. Boydton Plank Road, Hatcher's Run, October 27-28. Warren's Raid on Hicksford December 7-12. Dabney's Mills, Hatcher's Run, February 5-7, 1865. Watkins' House March 25. Appomattox Campaign March 28-April 9. White Oak Road March 30-31. Crow's House March 31. Fall of Petersburg April 2. Sailor's Creek April 6. High Bridge, Farmville, April 7. Appomattox Court House April 9. Surrender of Lee and his army. At Burkesville till May 2. March to Washington, D. C., May 2-12. Grand Review May 23. Mustered out June 28, 1865.

Regiment lost during service 7 Officers and 111 Enlisted men killed and mortally wounded and 78 Enlisted men by disease. Total 196.

111th REGIMENT INFANTRY.

Organized at Erie December, 1861, to January, 1862. Moved to Harrisburg, Pa., thence to Baltimore, Md., February 25-March 1, 1862. Duty there till May. Moved to Harper's Ferry, W. Va., May 16. Defence of Harper's Ferry May 24-30. Reconnoissance to Charlestown May 28. Attached to Cooper's 1st Brigade, Sigel's Division, Dept. of the Shenandoah, to June, 1862. 1st Brigade, 1st Division, 2nd Corps, Army of Virginia, to August, 1862. 2nd Brigade, 2nd Division, 2nd Corps, Army of Virginia, to September, 1862. 2nd Brigade, 2nd Division, 12th Army Corps, Army of the Potomac, to October, 1862. 3rd Brigade, 2nd Division, 12th Army Corps, to January, 1863. 2nd Brigade, 2nd Division, 12th Army Corps, Army of the Potomac, to October, 1863, and Army of the Cumberland to April, 1864. 3rd Brigade, 2nd Division, 20th Army Corps, Army of the Cumberland, to July, 1865.

SERVICE.—Operations in the Shenandoah Valley till August, 1862. Battle of Cedar Mountain, Va., August 9. Pope's Campaign in Northern Virginia August 16-September 2. Guard trains during Bull Run Battles. Maryland Campaign September 6-24. Battle of Antietam, Md., September 16-17 (Reserve). Duty at Bolivar Heights till December. Reconnoissance to Rippon, W. Va., November 9. Reconnoissance to Winchester December 2-6. March to Fredericksburg December 9-16. Burnside's 2nd Campaign, "Mud March," January 20-24, 1863. At Stafford Court House till April. Chancellorsville Campaign April 27-May 6. Battle of Chancellorsville May 1-5. Gettysburg (Pa.) Campaign June 11-24. Battle of Gettysburg July 1-3. Pursuit of Lee July 5-24. Duty near Raccoon Ford till September. Movement to Bridgeport, Ala., September 24-October 3. Reopening Tennessee River October 26-29. Battle of Wauhatchie, Tenn., October 28-29. Chattanooga-Ringgold Campaign November 23-27. Battles of Lookout Mountain November 23-24; Mission Ridge November 25; Ringgold Gap, Taylor's Ridge November 27. Duty on Nashville & Chattanooga Railroad till April, 1864. Atlanta (Ga.) Campaign May 1-September 8. Demonstration on Rocky Faced Ridge May 8-11. Battle of Resaca May 14-15. Near Cassville May 19. New Hope Church May 25. Operations on line of Pumpkin Vine Creek and battles about Dallas, New Hope Church and Allatoona Hills May 25-June 5. Operations about Marietta and against Kenesaw Mountain June 10-July 2. Pine Hill June 11-14. Lost Mountain June 15-17. Gilgal or Golgotha Church June 15. Muddy Creek June 17. Noyes Creek June 19. Kolb's Farm June 22. Assault on Kenesaw June 27. Ruff's Station, Smyrna Camp Ground, July 4. Chattahoochee River July 5-17. Peach Tree Creek July 19-20. Siege of Atlanta July 22-August 25. Operations at Chattahoochee River Bridge August 26-September 2. Occupation of Atlanta September 2-November 15. Expedition to Tuckum's Cross Roads October 26-29. Near Atlanta November 9. March to the sea November 15-December 10. Davidsboro November 28. Siege of Savannah December 10-21. Campaign of the Carolinas January to April, 1865. Battle of Bentonville, N. C., March 19-21. Occupation of Goldsboro March 24. Advance on Raleigh April 9-13. Occupation of Raleigh April 14. Bennett's House April

26. Surrender of Johnston and his army. March to Washington, D. C., via Richmond, April 29-May 20. Grand Review May 24. Duty at Washington till July. Mustered out July 19, 1865.

Regiment lost during service 7 Officers and 138 Enlisted men killed and mortally wounded and 4 Officers and 155 Enlisted men by disease. Total 304.

112th REGIMENT VOLUNTEERS.
(See 2nd Heavy Artillery.)

113th REGIMENT VOLUNTEERS.
(See 12th Cavalry.)

114th REGIMENT INFANTRY.

Organized at Philadelphia August, 1862. Left State for Washington, D. C., August 31, 1862. Duty at Fort Slocum, Defences of Washington, September, 1862. Attached to 1st Brigade, 1st Division, 3rd Army Corps, to March, 1864. Provost Guard, Headquarters Army of the Potomac, to March, 1865. Collins' Independent Brigade, 9th Army Corps, to April, 1865. 1st Brigade, 2nd Division, 5th Army Corps, to May, 1865.

SERVICE.—March up the Potomac to Leesburg, thence to Falmouth, Va., October 11-November 19, 1862. Battle of Fredericksburg, Va., December 12-15. Burnside's 2nd Campaign, "Mud March," January 20-24, 1863. At Falmouth till April. Chancellorsville Campaign April 27-May 6. Battle of Chancellorsville May 1-5. Gettysburg (Pa.) Campaign June 11-July 24. Battle of Gettysburg July 1-3. Pursuit of Lee July 5-24. Wapping Heights, Va., July 23. Duty on line of the Rappahannock till October. Bristoe Campaign October 9-22. Auburn October 13. Auburn and Bristoe October 14. Advance to line of the Rappahannock November 7-8. Kelly's Ford November 7. Mine Run Campaign November 26-December 2. Payne's Farm November 27. Demonstration on the Rapidan February 6-7, 1864. At Brandy Station till May, 1864. Assigned to duty as Provost Guard at Headquarters Army of the Potomac April 18. Rapidan Campaign May 4-June 12. Battles of the Wilderness May 5-7. Spottsylvania Court House May 8-21. Guinea Station May 21. North Anna River May 23-26. On line of the Pamunkey May 26-28. Totopotomoy May 28-31. Cold Harbor June 1-12. Before Petersburg June 16-18. Siege operations against Petersburg and Richmond June 16, 1864, to April 2, 1865. Garrison and Provost duty at City Point, Va., June 18, 1864, to March 28, 1865. Assault on and fall of Petersburg April 2. Occupation of Petersburg April 3. Moved to Washington, D. C., May 1-12. Grand Review May 23. Mustered out May 29, 1865.

Regiment lost during service 7 Officers and 66 Enlisted men killed and mortally wounded and 1 Officer and 37 Enlisted men by disease. Total 111.

115th REGIMENT INFANTRY.

Organized at Philadelphia and Harrisburg January 28, 1862. Moved from Camden to Harrisburg, Pa., May 31, 1862, thence to Camp Hamilton, Va., June 25-28, and to Harrison's Landing, Va., July 4. Attached to 3rd Brigade, 2nd Division, 3rd Army Corps, Army of the Potomac, to March, 1864. 1st Brigade, 4th Division, 2nd Army Corps, to May, 1864. 3rd Brigade, 3rd Division, 2nd Army Corps, to June, 1864.

SERVICE.—Duty at Harrison's Landing, Va., till August 16, 1862. Movement to Centreville August 16-26. Action at Bristoe Station or Kettle Run August 27. Battles of Groveton August 29; Bull Run August 30. Duty in the Defences of Washington till November. At Fairfax Station November 2-25. Operations on Orange & Alexandria Railroad November 10-12. Duty near Falmouth, Va., November 28-December 11. Battle of Fredericksburg December 12-15. Burnside's 2nd Campaign, "Mud March," January 20-24, 1863. Operations at Rappahannock Bridge and Grove Church February 5-7. Chancellorsville Campaign April 27-May 6. Battle of Chancellorsville May 1-5. Gettysburg (Pa.) Campaign June 11-July 24. Battle of Gettysburg July 1-3. Pursuit of Lee July 5-24. Wapping Heights,

Va., July 23. Duty near Warrenton, Va., till October. Bristoe Campaign October 9-22. McLean's Ford, Bull Run, October 15. Advance to line of the Rappahannock November 7-8. Kelly's Ford November 7. Mine Run Campaign November 26-December 2. Payne's Farm November 27. Demonstration on the Rapidan February 6-7, 1864. Duty near Brandy Station till May. Rapidan Campaign May 4-June 12. Battles of the Wilderness May 5-7; Spottsylvania May 8-12; Spottsylvania Court House May 12-21. Assault on the Salient May 12. North Anna River May 23-26. On line of the Pamunkey May 26-28. Totopotomoy May 28-31. Cold Harbor June 1-12. Before Petersburg June 16-18. Consolidated with 110th Pennsylvania Infantry June 22, 1864.

Regiment lost during service 6 Officers and 32 Enlisted men killed and mortally wounded and 2 Officers and 40 Enlisted men by disease. Total 80.

116th REGIMENT INFANTRY.

Organized at Philadelphia June 11 to September 4, 1862. Left State for Washington, D. C., August 31, thence moved to Rockville, Md., September 7. Moved to Fairfax Court House September 21 and duty there till October 6. Moved to Harper's Ferry, W. Va., October 6. Attached to 2nd Brigade, 1st Division, 2nd Army Corps, Army of the Potomac, to June, 1864. 4th Brigade, 1st Division, 2nd Army Corps, to July, 1865.

SERVICE.—Duty at Harper's Ferry till October 29. Advance up Loudoun Valley and movement to Falmouth, Va., October 29-November 17. Battle of Fredericksburg, Va., December 12-15. Burnside's 2nd Campaign, "Mud March," January 20-24, 1863. At Falmouth till April. Chancellorsville Campaign April 27-May 6. Battle of Chancellorsville May 1-5. Gettysburg (Pa.) Campaign June 11-July 24. Battle of Gettysburg July 1-3. Pursuit of Lee July 5-24. Advance from Rappahannock to the Rapidan September 13-17. Bristoe Campaign October 9-22. Auburn and Bristoe October 14. Advance to line of the Rappahannock November 7-8. Mine Run Campaign November 26-December 2. Demonstration on the Rapidan February 6-7, 1864. Duty at Stevensburg till May. Rapidan Campaign May 4-June 12. Battles of the Wilderness May 5-7; Spottsylvania May 8-12; Po River May 10; Spottsylvania Court House May 12-21. Assault on the Salient May 12. North Anna River May 23-26. On line of the Pamunkey May 26-28. Totopotomoy May 28-31. Cold Harbor June 1-12. Before Petersburg June 16-18. Siege of Petersburg June 16, 1864, to April 2, 1865. Jerusalem Plank Road June 22-23, 1864. Demonstration on north side of the James River July 27-29. Deep Bottom July 27-28. Mine Explosion, Petersburg, July 30 (Reserve). Demonstration on north side of James River at Deep Bottom August 13-20. Strawberry Plains, Deep Bottom, August 14-18. Ream's Station August 25. Front of Forts Morton and Sedgwick October 27. Reconnoissance to Hatcher's Run December 9-10. Dabney's Mills February 5-7, 1865. Watkins' House, Petersburg, March 25. Appomattox Campaign March 28-April 9. Hatcher's Run or Boydton Road March 31. White Oak Road March 31. Sutherland Station April 2. Fall of Petersburg April 2. Sailor's Creek April 6. High Bridge, Farmville, April 7. Appomattox Court House April 9. Surrender of Lee and his army. At Burkesville till May 2. March to Washington, D. C., May 2-12. Grand Review May 23. Companies "A," "B," "C" and "D" mustered out June 3, 1865. Companies "E," "F," "G," "H," "I" and "K" mustered out July 14, 1865.

Regiment lost during service 8 Officers and 137 Enlisted men killed and mortally wounded and 1 Officer and 88 Enlisted men by disease. Total 234.

117th REGIMENT VOLUNTEERS.
(See 13th Cavalry.)

118th REGIMENT INFANTRY.

Organized at Philadelphia May 15-30, 1862. Moved to Baltimore, Md., August 31; thence to Washington, D. C. Attached to 1st Brigade, 1st Division, 5th Army

Corps, Army of the Potomac, to April, 1864. 3rd Brigade, 1st Division, 5th Army Corps, to June, 1865.

SERVICE.—Maryland Campaign September 6-24, 1862. Battle of Antietam, Md., September 16-17. Shepherdstown Ford September 19. At Sharpsburg till October 30. Movement to Falmouth, Va., October 30-November 19. Battle of Fredericksburg, Va., December 12-15. Reconnoissance to Richard's and Ellis' Fords, Rappahannock River, December 29-30. Burnside's 2nd Campaign, "Mud March," January 20-24, 1863. At Falmouth till April. Chancellorsville Campaign April 27-May 6. Battle of Chancellorsville May 1-5. Gettysburg (Pa.) Campaign June 11-July 24. Battle of Gettysburg July 1-3. Pursuit of Lee July 5-24. Wapping Heights, Va., July 23. At Warrenton and Beverly Ford to September 17, and at Culpeper till October 11. Bristoe Campaign October 9-22. Advance to line of the Rappahannock November 7-8. Rappahannock Station November 7. Mine Run Campaign November 26-December 2. At Beverly Ford till May, 1864. Rapidan Campaign May 4-June 12. Battles of the Wilderness May 5-7; Laurel Hill May 8; Spottsylvania May 8-21. Assault on the Salient May 12. North Anna River May 23-26. Jericho Ford May 25. On line of the Pamunkey May 26-28. Totopotomoy May 28-31. Cold Harbor June 1-12. Before Petersburg June 16-18. Siege of Petersburg June 16, 1864, to April 2, 1865. Jerusalem Plank Road June 22-23, 1864. Weldon Railroad August 18-21. Poplar Springs Church September 29-October 2. Boydton Plank Road, Hatcher's Run, October 27-28. Warren's Expedition to Hicksford December 7-12. Dabney's Mills, Hatcher's Run, February 5-7, 1865. Appomattox Campaign March 28-April 9. Lewis Farm, near Gravelly Run, March 29. Junction of Quaker and Boydton Roads March 29. White Oak Road March 31. Five Forks April 1. Appomattox Court House April 9. Surrender of Lee and his army. March to Washington, D. C., May 1-12. Grand Review May 23. Mustered out June 1, 1865.

Regiment lost during service 9 Officers and 132 Enlisted men killed and mortally wounded and 1 Officer and 111 Enlisted men by disease. Total 253.

119th REGIMENT INFANTRY.

Organized at Philadelphia August 15, 1862. Moved to Washington, D. C., August 31-September 1. Duty in the Defences of Washington till October. Joined Army of the Potomac in the field and attached to 1st Brigade, 2nd Division, 6th Army Corps, Army of the Potomac, to February, 1863. 3rd Brigade, 1st Division, 6th Army Corps, Army of the Potomac, and Army of the Shenandoah to June, 1865.

SERVICE.—Duty at Hagerstown, Md., till October 29, 1862. Movement to Falmouth, Va., October 29-November 19. Battle of Fredericksburg, Va., December 12-15. Burnside's 2nd Campaign, "Mud March," January 20-24, 1863. At White Oak Church till April. Chancellorsville Campaign April 27-May 6. Operations at Franklin's Crossing April 29-May 2. Bernard House April 29. Maryes Heights, Fredericksburg, May 3. Salem Heights May 3-4. Banks' Ford May 4. Gettysburg (Pa.) Campaign June 13-July 24. Battle of Gettysburg July 2-4. Pursuit of Lee July 5-24. At and near Funkstown, Md., July 10-13. Bristoe Campaign October 9-22. Advance to line of the Rappahannock November 7-8. Rappahannock Station November 7. Mine Run Campaign November 26-December 2. Duty near Brandy Station till May, 1864. Rapidan Campaign May 4-June 12. Battles of the Wilderness May 5-7; Spottsylvania May 8-12. Assault on the Salient May 12. North Anna River May 23-26. On line of the Pamunkey May 26-28. Totopotomoy May 28-31. Cold Harbor June 1-12. Before Petersburg June 17-18. Weldon Railroad June 22-23. Siege of Petersburg till July 9. Moved to Washington, D. C., July 9-11. Repulse of Early's attack on Washington July 11-12. Pursuit of Early July 14-22. Sheridan's Shenandoah Valley Campaign August to December. Demonstration on Gilbert's Ford, Opequan, September 13. Battle of Opequan, Winchester, September 19. Duty in the Shenandoah Valley till December. Moved to Petersburg, Va. Siege of Petersburg December, 1864, to April, 1865. Fort Fisher, Petersburg, March 25, 1865. Appomattox Campaign March 28-April 9. Assault on and fall of Petersburg April 2. Appomattox Court House April 9. Surrender of Lee and his army. Moved to Danville April 23-27, and duty there till May 23. Moved to Richmond, thence to Washington May 23-June 3. Corps Review June 8. Mustered out June 19, 1865.

Regiment lost during service 9 Officers and 132 Enlisted men killed and mortally wounded and 1 Officer and 71 Enlisted men by disease. Total 213.

120th REGIMENT VOLUNTEERS.
(Failed to complete organization.)

121st REGIMENT INFANTRY.

Organized at Philadelphia August 22 to September 5, 1862. Moved to Washington, D. C., September. Camp at Arlington Heights, near Washington, till October 1. Moved to Frederick, Md., and join Army of the Potomac. Attached to 1st Brigade, 3rd Division, 1st Army Corps, Army of the Potomac, to March, 1864. 3rd Brigade, 4th Division, 5th Army Corps, to June, 1864. 1st Brigade, 1st Division, 5th Army Corps, to September, 1864. 3rd Brigade, 3rd Division, 5th Army Corps, to June, 1865.

SERVICE.—Duty at Sharpsburg, Md., till October 30. Movement to Falmouth, Va., October 30-November 19. Battle of Fredericksburg, Va., December 12-15. Burnside's 2nd Campaign, "Mud March," January 20-24, 1863. Duty at Belle Plains till April. Chancellorsville Campaign April 27-May 6. Fitzhugh's Crossing April 29-30. Battle of Chancellorsville May 2-5. Gettysburg (Pa.) Campaign June 11-July 24. Battle of Gettysburg July 1-3. Pursuit of Lee July 5-24. Duty on line of the Rappahannock till October. Bristoe Campaign October 9-22. Advance to line of the Rappahannock November 7-8. Mine Run Campaign November 26-December 2. Licking River Bridge November 30. Demonstration on the Rapidan February 6-7, 1864. Duty near Culpeper till April, 1864. Rapidan Campaign May 4-June 12. Battles of the Wilderness May 5-7; Laurel Hill May 8; Spottsylvania May 8-12; Spottsylvania Court House May 12-21. Assault on the Salient May 12. North Anna River May 23-26. Jericho Ford May 25. On line of the Pamunkey May 26-28. Totopotomoy May 28-31. Cold Harbor June 1-12. Bethesda Church June 1-3. Before Petersburg June 16-18. Siege of Petersburg June 16, 1864, to April 2, 1865. Mine Explosion, Petersburg, July 30, 1864 (Reserve). Weldon Railroad August 18-21. Poplar Springs Church, Peeble's Farm, September 29-October 2. Boydton Plank Road, Hatcher's Run, October 27-28. Warren's Raid on Weldon Railroad December 7-12. Dabney's Mills, Hatcher's Run, February 5-7, 1865. Appomattox Campaign March 28-April 9. Lewis Farm, near Gravelly Run, March 29. White Oak Road March 30-31. Five Forks April 1. Appomattox Court House April 9. Surrender of Lee and his army. March to Washington, D. C., May 1-12. Grand Review May 23. Mustered out June 2, 1865.

Regiment lost during service 5 Officers and 104 Enlisted men killed and mortally wounded and 2 Officers and 64 Enlisted men by disease. Total 175.

122nd REGIMENT INFANTRY.

Organized at Harrisburg August 12, 1862. Moved to Washington, D. C., August 15-16. Attached to Casey's Command, Defences of Washington, to September, 1862. Piatt's 1st Brigade, Whipple's 3rd Division, 3rd Army Corps, Army of the Potomac, to May, 1863.

SERVICE.—Duty in the Defences of Washington at Fort Richardson, Cloud's Mills, near Georgetown, and at Fairfax Court House till October. Moved to Point of Rocks, Md., thence to Pleasant Valley October 11-19. Movement toward Warrenton, Va., October 24-November 16. Reconnoissance to and skirmish at Manassas Gap November 5-6. Movement to Falmouth November 18-24. Battle of Fredericksburg December 12-15. Burnside's 2nd Campaign, "Mud March," January 20-24, 1863. Duty near Falmouth till April 27. Chancellorsville Campaign April 27-May 6. Battle of Chancellorsville May 1-5. Moved to Washington and escort to General Whipple's funeral May 8. Mustered out May 16, 1863.

Regiment lost during service 16 Enlisted men killed and mortally wounded and 1 Officer and 42 Enlisted men by disease. Total 59.

123rd REGIMENT INFANTRY.

Organized at Allegheny City August, 1862. Moved to Harrisburg, Pa., thence to Washington, D. C., August 20-23, 1862. Attached to 2nd Brigade, 3rd Division, 5th Army Corps, Army of the Potomac, to May, 1863.

SERVICE.—Maryland Campaign September 6-24, 1862. Duty at Sharpsburg, Md., till October 30. Movement to Falmouth, Va., October 30-November 19. Battle of Fredericksburg, Va., December 12-15. Burnside's 2nd Campaign, "Mud March," January 20-24, 1863. Duty at Falmouth till April 27. Chancellorsville Campaign April 27-May 6. Battle of Chancellorsville May 1-5. Mustered out May 13, 1863.

Regiment lost during service 3 Officers and 27 Enlisted men killed and mortally wounded and 1 Officer and 41 Enlisted men by disease. Total 72.

124th REGIMENT INFANTRY.

Organized at Harrisburg August, 1862. Left State for Washington, D. C., August 12. Camp near Fort Albany, Defences of Washington, till September 7. March to Rockville, Md., and attached to 1st Brigade, 1st Division, 12th Army Corps, Army of the Potomac, to October, 1862. 2nd Brigade, 1st Division, 12th Army Corps, to January, 1863. 2nd Brigade, 2nd Division, 12th Army Corps, to May, 1863.

SERVICE.—Maryland Campaign September 7-24. Battle of Antietam, Md., September 16-17. Burying dead September 18. March to Pleasant Valley, Md., September 19-20. At Maryland Heights till October 30. At Loudon Heights till November 8. Reconnoissance up the Shenandoah Valley November 8-19. Near Harper's Ferry till December 10. March to Fredericksburg, Va., December 10-15; thence to Fairfax Station. Burnside's 2nd Campaign, "Mud March," January 20-24, 1863. At Stafford Court House till April 27. Chancellorsville Campaign April 27-May 6. Battle of Chancellorsville May 1-5. Ordered to Harrisburg, Pa., and there mustered out May 16, 1863.

Regiment lost during service 1 Officer and 17 Enlisted men killed and mortally wounded and 36 Enlisted men by disease. Total 54.

125th REGIMENT INFANTRY.

Organized at Harrisburg August, 1862. Left State for Washington, D. C., August 16, and duty in the Defences of that city till September 6. March to Rockville, Md., September 6, and attached to 1st Brigade, 1st Division, 12th Army Corps, Army of the Potomac, to October, 1862. 2nd Brigade, 1st Division, 12th Army Corps, to January, 1863. 2nd Brigade, 2nd Division, 12th Army Corps, to May, 1863. Maryland Campaign September 6-24, 1862. Battle of Antietam, Md., September 16-17 (Reserve). March to Pleasant Valley September 19-20. At Maryland Heights till October 30. At Loudon Heights till November 8. Reconnoissance up the Shenandoah Valley November 8-19. Near Harper's Ferry till December 10. March to Fredericksburg, Va., December 10-15; thence to Fairfax Station. Burnside's 2nd Campaign, "Mud March," January 20-24, 1863. At Stafford Court House, Va., till April 27. Chancellorsville Campaign April 27-May 6. Battle of Chancellorsville May 1-5. Mustered out May 18, 1863.

Regiment lost during service 2 Officers and 48 Enlisted men killed and mortally wounded and 1 Officer and 39 Enlisted men by disease. Total 90.

126th REGIMENT INFANTRY.

Organized at Harrisburg August, 1862. Left State for Washington, D. C., August 15, and duty there till September 12. Moved to Sharpsburg, Md., and attached to 1st Brigade, 3rd Division, 5th Army Corps, Army of the Potomac. Duty at Sharpsburg, Md., till October 30, 1862. Reconnoissance from Sharpsburg to Smithfield, W. Va., October 16-17. Movement to Falmouth, Va., October 30-November 19. Battle of Fredericksburg, Va., December 12-15. Burnside's 2nd Campaign, "Mud March," January 20-24, 1863. Duty at Falmouth till April 27. Chancellorsville Campaign April 27-May 6. Battle of Chancellorsville May 1-5. Mustered out May 20, 1865.

Regiment lost during service 1 Officer and 30 Enlisted men killed and mortally wounded and 34 Enlisted men by disease. Total 65.

127th REGIMENT INFANTRY.

Organized at Harrisburg August 16, 1862. Moved to Washington, D. C., August 17. (Co. "A" detached at Harrisburg, Pa., on provost duty entire term.) Duty in the Defences of Washington till December. Attached to Jennings' Brigade, Abercrombie's Division, Defences of Washington, to December, 1862. March to Falmouth, Va., December 1-9. Attached to 3rd Brigade, 2nd Division, 2nd Army Corps, Army of the Potomac. Battle of Fredericksburg December 12-15. Duty at Falmouth till April. Chancellorsville Campaign April 27-May 6. Operations at Franklin's Crossing April 29-May 2. Maryes Heights, Fredericksburg, May 3. Salem Heights May 3-4. Banks' Ford May 4. Mustered out May 29, 1863.

Regiment lost during service 4 Officers and 15 Enlisted men killed and mortally wounded and 16 Enlisted men by disease. Total 35.

128th REGIMENT INFANTRY.

Organized at Harrisburg August, 1862. Left State for Washington, D. C., August 16, and duty there till September 6. Moved to Frederick, Md., September 6-14. Attached to 1st Brigade, 1st Division, 12th Army Corps, Army of the Potomac. Battle of Antietam, Md., September 16-17. At Sandy Hook and Maryland Heights September 22 to December 10. Moved to Fairfax Station, Va., December 10-14. Duty there till January 19, 1863. Moved to Stafford Court House January 19-23, and duty there till April 27. Chancellorsville Campaign April 27-May 6. Battle of Chancellorsville May 1-5. Mustered out May 19, 1863.

Regiment lost during service 2 Officers and 31 Enlisted men killed and mortally wounded and 26 Enlisted men by disease. Total 59.

129th REGIMENT INFANTRY.

Organized at Harrisburg August, 1862. Moved to Washington, D. C., August 16, and duty there till September 12. Moved to Sharpsburg, Md., and attached to 1st Brigade, 3rd Division, 5th Army Corps, Army of the Potomac. Duty at Sharpsburg, Md., till October 30. Reconnoissance from Sharpsburg to Smithfield, W. Va., October 16-17. Movement to Falmouth, Va., October 30-November 19. Battle of Fredericksburg, Va., December 12-15. Burnside's 2nd Campaign, "Mud March," January 20-24, 1863. At Falmouth till April. Chancellorsville Campaign April 27-May 6. Battle of Chancellorsville May 1-5. Mustered out May 18, 1863.

Regiment lost during service 3 Officers and 37 Enlisted men killed and mortally wounded and 1 Officer and 42 Enlisted men by disease. Total 83.

130th REGIMENT INFANTRY.

Organized at Harrisburg August, 1862. Moved to Washington, D. C., August 18, and duty there till September 7. March to Rockville, Md., September 7-12. Attached to 2nd Brigade, 3rd Division, 2nd Army Corps, Army of the Potomac. Maryland Campaign. Battle of Antietam September 16-17. Moved to Harper's Ferry, W. Va., September 22, and duty there till October 30. Advance up Loudoun Valley and movement to Falmouth, Va., October 30-November 19. Battle of Fredericksburg, Va., December 12-15. Duty at Falmouth till April, 1863. Chancellorsville Campaign April 27-May 6. Battle of Chancellorsville May 1-5. Mustered out May 21, 1863.

Regiment lost during service 4 Officers and 56 Enlisted men killed and mortally wounded and 32 Enlisted men by disease. Total 92.

131st REGIMENT INFANTRY.

Organized at Harrisburg August, 1862. Moved to Washington, D. C., August 20, and duty there till September 14. Moved to Sharpsburg, Md., and duty there till October 30. Attached to 2nd Brigade, 3rd Division, 5th Army Corps, Army of the Potomac. Movement to Falmouth, Va., October 30-November 19. Battle of Fredericksburg December 12-15. Burnside's 2nd Campaign, "Mud March," January 20-24, 1863. Duty at Falmouth till April. Chancellorsville Campaign April 27-May 6. Battle of Chancellorsville May 1-5. Mustered out May 23, 1863.

Regiment lost during service 2 Officers and 36 Enlisted men killed and mortally wounded and 1 Officer and 44 Enlisted men by disease. Total 83.

132nd REGIMENT INFANTRY.

Organized at Harrisburg August, 1862. Moved to Washington, D. C., August 19, and duty there till September 2. Ordered to Rockville, Md., September 2. Attached to 1st Brigade, 3rd Division, 2nd Army Corps, Army of the Potomac, to November, 1862. 2nd Brigade, 3rd Division, 2nd Army Corps, to May, 1863.

SERVICE.—Maryland Campaign September 6-22, 1862. Battle of Antietam, Md., September 16-17. Moved to Harper's Ferry, W. Va., September 22, and duty there till October 30. Reconnoissance to Leesburg October 1-2. Advance up Loudoun Valley and movement to Falmouth, Va., October 30-November 17. Battle of Fredericksburg December 12-15. Duty at Falmouth till April 27. Chancellorsville Campaign April 27-May 6. Battle of Chancellorsville May 1-5. Mustered out May 24, 1863.

Regiment lost during service 3 Officers and 70 Enlisted men killed and mortally wounded and 40 Enlisted men by disease. Total 113.

133rd REGIMENT INFANTRY.

Organized at Harrisburg August, 1862. Moved to Washington, D. C., August 19, and duty there till September 2. Moved to Rockville, Md., September 2, and attached to 2nd Brigade, 3rd Division, 5th Army Corps, Army of the Potomac. Duty at Sharpsburg, Md., till October 30. Moved to Falmouth, Va., October 30-November 17. Battle of Fredericksburg, Va., December 12-15. Burnside's 2nd Campaign, "Mud March," January 20-24, 1863. At Falmouth till April 27. Chancellorsville Campaign April 27-May 6. Battle of Chancellorsville May 1-5. Mustered out May 26, 1863.

Regiment lost during service 4 Officers and 40 Enlisted men killed and mortally wounded and 33 Enlisted men by disease. Total 77.

134th REGIMENT INFANTRY.

Organized at Harrisburg August, 1862. Moved to Washington, D. C., August 20. Attached to 1st Brigade, 3rd Division, 5th Army Corps, Army of the Potomac. March into Maryland September 1-18. Duty at Sharpsburg, Md., till October 30. Reconnoissance to Smithfield, W. Va., October 16-17. Movement to Falmouth, Va., October 30-November 19. Battle of Fredericksburg, Va., December 12-15. Burnside's 2nd Campaign January 20-24, 1863. Duty at Falmouth, Va., till April 27. Chancellorsville Campaign April 27-May 6. Battle of Chancellorsville May 1-5. Mustered out May 26, 1863.

Regiment lost during service 4 Officers and 38 Enlisted men killed and mortally wounded and 1 Officer and 66 Enlisted men by disease. Total 109.

135th REGIMENT INFANTRY.

Organized at Harrisburg August, 1862. Moved to Washington, D. C., August 19. Attached to Military District of Washington, D. C., till February, 1863. 1st Brigade, 3rd Division, 1st Army Corps, Army of the Potomac, to May, 1863.

SERVICE.—Provost duty at Washington and Georgetown till February, 1863. Joined the Army of the Potomac and duty at Falmouth and Belle Plains, Va., till April 27. Chancellorsville Campaign April 27-May 6. Operations at Pollock's Mill Creek April 29-May 2. Fitzhugh's Crossing April 29-30. Battle of Chancellorsville May 2-5. Mustered out May 24, 1863.

Regiment lost during service 37 Enlisted men by disease.

136th REGIMENT INFANTRY.

Organized at Harrisburg August, 1862. Moved to Washington, D. C., August 29, and duty there till September 29. Moved to Fort Frederick, Md., thence to Sharpsburg. Attached to 2nd Brigade, 2nd Division, 1st Army Corps, Army of the Potomac. Duty at Sharpsburg, Md., till October 30. Movement to Falmouth, Va., October 30-November 19. Battle of Fredericksburg, Va., December 12-15. Burnside's 2nd Campaign, "Mud March," January 20-24, 1863. Duty at Falmouth and Belle Plains till April 27. Chancellorsville Campaign April 27-May 6. Operations at Pollock's Mill Creek April 29-May 2. Fitzhugh's Crossing April 29-30. Battle of Chancellorsville May 2-5. Mustered out May 29, 1863.

Regiment lost during service 3 Officers and 23 Enlisted men killed and mortally wounded and 30 Enlisted men by disease. Total 56.

137th REGIMENT INFANTRY.

Organized at Harrisburg August 25, 1862, and ordered to Washington, D. C. Attached to 1st Brigade, 2nd Division, 6th Army Corps, Army of the Potomac, to December, 1862. Provisional Brigade, Aquia Creek, Va., Patrick's Command, Army of the Potomac, to January, 1863. 3rd Brigade, 1st Division, 1st Army Corps, Army of the Potomac, to May, 1863.

SERVICE.—Maryland Campaign September, 1862. Sugar Loaf Mountain September 10-11. Crampton's Gap September 14. Antietam September 17. Duty in Maryland to November. In Defences of Washington, D. C., till December, and at Aquia Creek, Va., till January, 1863. Burnside's 2nd Campaign, "Mud March," January 20-24, 1863. Duty at Belle Plains till April. Chancellorsville Campaign April 27-May 6. Operations at Pollock's Mill Creek April 29-May 2. Chancellorsville May 2-5. Ordered to Harrisburg, Pa. Mustered out June 1, 1863.

Regiment lost during service 1 Officer and 58 Enlisted men by disease. Total 59.

138th REGIMENT INFANTRY.

Organized at Harrisburg August 16, 1862. Moved to Baltimore, Md., August 30, thence to Relay House. Attached to Relay House, Defences of Baltimore, 8th Corps, Middle Dept., to February, 1863. 3rd Separate Brigade, 8th Corps, to June, 1863. Elliott's Command, 8th Corps, to July, 1863. 2nd Brigade, 3rd Division, 3rd Army Corps, Army of the Potomac, to March, 1864. 2nd Brigade, 3rd Division, 6th Army Corps, Army of the Potomac, and Army of the Shenandoah, to June, 1865.

SERVICE.—Duty at Relay House, Md., till June, 1863. Moved to Harper's Ferry, W. Va., June 16. Escort stores to Washington July 1-5. Join Division at Frederick, Md., July 7. Pursuit of Lee July 7-24. Wapping Heights July 23. Bristoe Campaign October 9-22. Advance to line of the Rappahannock November 7-8. Kelly's Ford November 7. Brandy Station November 8. Mine Run Campaign November 26-December 2. Payne's Farm November 27. Demonstration on the Rapidan February 6-7, 1864. Duty at and near Brandy Station till May. Rapidan Campaign May 4-June 12. Battles of the Wilderness May 5-7; Spottsylvania May

8-12; Spottsylvania Court House May 12-21. Assault on the Salient May 12. North Anna River May 23-26. On line of the Pamunkey May 26-28. Totopotomoy May 28-31. Cold Harbor June 1-12. Before Petersburg June 17-18. Jerusalem Plank Road, Weldon Railroad, June 22-23. Siege of Petersburg till July 6. Moved to Baltimore, Md., July 6-8. Battle of Monocacy July 9. Pursuit of Early to Snicker's Gap July 14-24. Sheridan's Shenandoah Valley Campaign August to December. Charlestown August 21-22. Battle of Opequan, Winchester, September 19. Fisher's Hill, September 22. Battle of Cedar Creek October 19. Duty at Kernstown till December. Moved to Washington, D. C., thence to Petersburg, Va., December. Siege of Petersburg December, 1864, to April, 1865. Fort Fisher, Petersburg, March 25, 1865. Appomattox Campaign March 28-April 9. Assault on and fall of Petersburg April 2. Sailor's Creek April 6. Appomattox Court House April 9. Surrender of Lee and his army. March to Danville April 23-27, and duty there till May 23. March to Richmond, Va., thence to Washington, D. C., May 23-June 3. Corps review June 8. Mustered out June 23, 1865.

Regiment lost during service 6 Officers and 90 Enlisted men killed and mortally wounded and 1 Officer and 70 Enlisted men by disease. Total 167.

139th REGIMENT INFANTRY.

Organized at Pittsburg September 1, 1862. Moved to Washington, D. C., September 1-3. Attached to 2nd Brigade, 1st Division, 4th Army Corps, Army of the Potomac, to September, 1862. 2nd Brigade, 3rd Division, 6th Army Corps, Army of the Potomac, to October, 1862. 3rd Brigade, 3rd Division, 6th Army Corps, to January, 1864. Wheaton's Brigade, Dept. of West Virginia, to March, 1864. 1st Brigade, 2nd Division, 6th Army Corps, Army of the Potomac, and Army of the Shenandoah to June, 1865.

SERVICE.—Bury dead at Bull Run, Va., September 4-7, 1862. Maryland Campaign September 7-24. Battle of Antietam September 16-17 (Reserve). At Downsville September 23-October 20. Movement to Stafford Court House October 20-November 18, and to Belle Plains December 5. Battle of Fredericksburg, Va., December 12-15. Burnside's 2nd Campaign, "Mud March," January 20-24, 1863. At Falmouth till April. Chancellorsville Campaign April 27-May 6. Operations at Franklin's Crossing April 29-May 2. Maryes Heights, Fredericksburg, May 3. Salem Heights May 3-4. Banks' Ford May 4. Gettysburg (Pa.) Campaign June 13-July 24. Battle of Gettysburg July 2-4. Pursuit of Lee July 5-24. Duty on line of the Rappahannock and Rapidan till October. Bristoe Campaign October 9-22. Advance to line of the Rappahannock November 7-8. Rappahannock Station November 7. Mine Run Campaign November 26-December 2. At Harper's Ferry till March, 1864. Rapidan Campaign May 4-June 12. Battles of the Wilderness May 5-7; Spottsylvania May 8-21. Assault on the Salient May 12. North Anna River May 23-26. On line of the Pamunkey May 26-28. Totopotomoy May. 28-31. Cold Harbor June 1-12. Before Petersburg June 17-18. Jerusalem Plank Road, Weldon Railroad, June 22-23. Siege of Petersburg to July 9. Moved to Washington, D. C., July 9-11. Repulse of Early's attack on Washington July 11-12. Pursuit to Snicker's Gap July 14-24. Sheridan's Shenandoah Valley Campaign August to December. Near Strasburg August 13. Near Charlestown August 21-22. Demonstration on Gilbert's Ford, Opequan, September 13. Battle of Opequan, Winchester, September 19. Strasburg September 21. Fisher's Hill September 22. Battle of Cedar Creek October 19. Duty in the Shenandoah Valley till December. Moved to Petersburg, Va., December 9-12. Siege of Petersburg December, 1864, to April, 1865. Dabney's Mills, Hatcher's Run, February 5-7, 1865. Fort Fisher, Petersburg, March 25. Appomattox Campaign March 28-April 9. Assault on and fall of Petersburg April 2. Pursuit of Lee April 3-9. Sailor's Creek April 6. Appomattox Court House April 9. Surrender of Lee and his army. March to Danville April 23-27, and duty there till May 23. March to Richmond, Va., thence to Washington, D. C., May 23-June 3. Corps Review June 8. Mustered out June 21, 1865.

Regiment lost during service 10 Officers and 135 Enlisted men killed and mortally wounded and 5 Officers and 86 Enlisted men by disease. Total 236.

140th REGIMENT INFANTRY.

Organized at Pittsburg and Harrisburg and mustered in September 8, 1862. Ordered to Parkton, Md., September 9, and duty guarding Northern Central Railroad till December. Attached to 8th Corps, Middle Department, to December, 1862. 3rd Brigade, 1st Division, 2nd Army Corps, Army of the Potomac, to September, 1863. 1st Brigade, 1st Division, 2nd Army Corps, to May, 1865.

SERVICE.—Ordered to join Army of the Potomac in the field, and reached Aquia Creek December 15, 1862. Duty near Falmouth, Va., till April, 1863. Chancellorsville Campaign April 27-May 6. Battle of Chancellorsville May 1-5. Gettysburg (Pa.) Campaign June 11-July 24. Battle of Gettysburg July 1-3. Pursuit of Lee July 5-24. Advance from the Rappahannock to the Rapidan September 13-17. Bristoe Campaign October 9-22. Auburn and Bristoe October 14. Advance to line of the Rappahannock November 7-8. Mine Run Campaign November 26-December 2. Demonstration on the Rapidan February 6-7, 1864. At Stevensburg till May. Rapidan Campaign May 4-June 12. Battles of the Wilderness May 5-7; Corbin's Bridge May 8; Spottsylvania May 8-12; Po River May 10; Spottsylvania Court House May 12-21. "Bloody Angle," assault on the Salient, May 12. North Anna River May 23-26. On line of the Pamunkey May 26-28. Totopotomoy May 28-31. Cold Harbor June 1-12. Before Petersburg June 16-18. Siege of Petersburg June 16, 1864, to April 2, 1865. Jerusalem Plank Road June 22-23, 1864. Demonstration north of James River July 27-29. Deep Bottom July 27-28. Mine Explosion, Petersburg, July 30 (Reserve). Demonstration north of James River at Deep Bottom August 13-20. Strawberry Plains, Deep Bottom, August 14-18. Ream's Station August 25. Reconnoissance to Hatcher's Run December 9-10. Hatcher's Run December 9. Dabney's Mills, Hatcher's Run, February 5-7, 1865. Watkins' House March 25. Appomattox Campaign March 28-April 9. Skirmishes on line of Hatcher's and Gravelly Runs March 29-30. Boydton Road and White Oak Road or Hatcher's Run March 31. Sutherland Station April 2. Fall of Petersburg April 2. Flat Creek, near Amelia Court House, April 5. Sailor's Creek April 6. High Bridge, Farmville, April 7. Appomattox Court House April 9. Surrender of Lee and his army. March to Washington, D. C., May 2-12. Grand Review May 24. Mustered out May 31, 1865.

Regiment lost during service 10 Officers and 188 Enlisted men killed and mortally wounded and 1 Officer and 127 Enlisted men by disease. Total 326.

141st REGIMENT INFANTRY.

Organized at Harrisburg August 29, 1862, and moved to Washington. Duty in the Defences of that city till October. Attached to 1st Brigade, 1st Division, 3rd Army Corps, Army of the Potomac, to March, 1864. 1st Brigade, 3rd Division, 2nd Army Corps, to July, 1864. 2nd Brigade, 3rd Division, 2nd Army Corps, to May, 1865.

SERVICE.—March up the Potomac to Leesburg, thence to Falmouth, Va., October 11-November 19. Battle of Fredericksburg, Va., December 12-15. Burnside's 2nd Campaign, "Mud March," January 20-24, 1863. Duty at Falmouth till April. Chancellorsville Campaign April 27-May 6. Battle of Chancellorsville May 1-5. Gettysburg (Pa.) Campaign June 11-July 24. Battle of Gettysburg July 1-3. Pursuit of Lee July 5-24. Wapping Heights, Va., July 23. Duty on line of the Rappahannock and the Rapidan till October. Bristoe Campaign October 9-22. Auburn October 13. Advance to line of the Rappahannock November 7-8. Kelly's Ford

November 7. Mine Run Campaign November 26-December 2. Payne's Farm November 27. Demonstration on the Rapidan February 6-7, 1864. Rapidan Campaign May 4-June 12. Battles of the Wilderness May 5-7; Laurel Hill May 8; Spottsylvania May 8-12; Po River May 10; Spottsylvania Court House May 12-21. Assault on the Salient May 12. Harris Farm May 19. North Anna River May 23-26. On line of the Pamunkey May 26-28. Totopotomoy May 28-31. Cold Harbor June 1-12. Before Petersburg June 16-18. Siege of Petersburg June 16, 1864, to April 2, 1865. Jerusalem Plank Road June 22-23, 1864. Demonstration north of James at Deep Bottom July 27-29. Deep Bottom July 27-28. Mine Explosion, Petersburg, July 30 (Reserve). Demonstration north of the James at Deep Bottom August 13-20. Strawberry Plains, Deep Bottom, August 14-18. Ream's Station August 25. Poplar Springs Church September 29-October 2. Boydton Plank Road, Hatcher's Run, October 27-28. Expedition to Weldon Railroad December 7-12. Dabney's Mills, Hatcher's Run, February 5-7, 1865. Watkins' House March 25. Appomattox Campaign March 28-April 9. Crow's House March 31. Fall of Petersburg April 2. Sailor's Creek April 6. High Bridge April 7. Appomattox Court House April 9. Surrender of Lee and his army. March to Washington, D. C., May 2-12. Grand Review May 23. Mustered out May 28, 1865.

Regiment lost during service 6 Officers and 161 Enlisted men killed and mortally wounded and 3 Officers and 76 Enlisted men by disease. Total 246.

142nd REGIMENT INFANTRY.

Organized at Harrisburg September 1, 1862. Left State for Washington, D. C., September 2, and duty there till September 19. Moved to Frederick, Md., September 19. Attached to 2nd Brigade, 3rd Division, 1st Army Corps, Army of the Potomac, to February, 1863. 1st Brigade, 3rd Division, 1st Corps, to March, 1864. 3rd Brigade, 4th Division, 5th Army Corps, to June, 1864. 1st Brigade, 1st Division, 5th Army Corps, to September, 1864. 3rd Brigade, 3rd Division, 5th Army Corps, to May, 1865.

SERVICE.—Duty at Frederick, Md., till October 30, 1862. Movement to Falmouth, Va., October 30-November 19. Battle of Fredericksburg, Va., December 12-15. Burnside's 2nd Campaign, "Mud March," January 20-24, 1863. Duty at Belle Plains till April. Chancellorsville Campaign April 27-May 6. Operations at Pollock's Mill Creek April 29-May 2. Battle of Chancellorsville May 2-5. Gettysburg (Pa.) Campaign June 11-July 24. Battle of Gettysburg July 1-3. Pursuit of Lee July 5-24. Duty on line of the Rappahannock till October. Bristoe Campaign October 9-22. Advance to line of the Rappahannock November 7-8. Mine Run Campaign November 26-December 2. Demonstration on the Rapidan February 6-7, 1864. Duty near Culpeper till May. Rapidan Campaign May 4-June 12. Battles of the Wilderness May 5-7; Laurel Hill May 8; Spottsylvania May 8-12; Spottsylvania Court House May 12-21. Assault on the Salient May 12. North Anna River May 23-26. Jericho Ford May 25. On line of the Pamunkey May 26-28. Totopotomoy May 28-31. Cold Harbor June 1-12. Bethesda Church June 1-3. Before Petersburg June 16-18. Siege of Petersburg June 16, 1864, to April 2, 1865. Mine Explosion, Petersburg, July 30, 1864. Weldon Railroad August 18-21. Poplar Springs Church, Peeble's Farm, September 29-October 2. Boydton Plank Road, Hatcher's Run, October 27-28. Warren's Expedition to Weldon Railroad December 7-12. Dabney's Mills, Hatcher's Run, February 5-7, 1865. Appomattox Campaign March 28-April 9. Lewis Farm, near Gravelly Run, March 29. White Oak Road March 31. Five Forks April 1. Appomattox Court House April 9. Surrender of Lee and his army. Escort captured stores to Burkesville Station. March to Washington, D. C., May 1-12. Grand Review May 23. Mustered out May 29, 1865.

Regiment lost during service 7 Officers and 148 Enlisted men killed and mortally wounded and 72 Enlisted men by disease. Total 227.

143rd REGIMENT INFANTRY.

Organized at Wilkesbarre October 18, 1862. Left State for Washington, D. C., November 7, and duty in the Defences of that city till January 17, 1863. Attached to 1st Brigade, Defences of Washington, north of the Potomac, to January, 1863. 2nd Brigade, 3rd Division, 1st Army Corps, Army of the Potomac, to December, 1863. 1st Brigade, 3rd Division, 1st Army Corps, to March, 1864. 3rd Brigade, 4th Division, 5th Army Corps, to June, 1864. 1st Brigade, 1st Division, 5th Army Corps, to September, 1864. 1st Brigade, 3rd Division, 5th Army Corps, to February, 1865. Hart's Island, New York Harbor, Dept. of the East, to June, 1865.

SERVICE.—Ordered to join Army of the Potomac in the field January, 1863. Duty at Belle Plains, Va., till April 27. Chancellorsville Campaign April 27-May 6. Operations at Pollock's Mill Creek April 29-May 2. Battle of Chancellorsville May 2-5. Gettysburg (Pa.) Campaign June 11-July 24. Battle of Gettysburg July 1-3. Pursuit of Lee July 5-24. Duty at Bealeton Station till October. Bristoe Campaign October 9-22. Haymarket October 19. Advance to line of the Rappahannock November 7-8. Warrenton November 7. Guard at Manassas Junction November 22-December 5. Demonstration on the Rapidan February 6-7, 1864. Duty near Culpeper till May. Rapidan Campaign May 4-June 12. Battles of the Wilderness May 5-7; Laurel Hill May 8; Spottsylvania May 8-12; Spottsylvania Court House May 12-21. Assault on the Salient May 12. North Anna River May 23-26. Jericho Ford May 25. On line of the Pamunkey May 26-28. Totopotomoy May 28-31. Cold Harbor June 1-12. Bethesda Church June 1-3. Before Petersburg June 16-18. Siege of Petersburg June 16, 1864, to February 10, 1865. Mine Explosion July 30, 1864 (Reserve). Weldon Railroad August 18-21. Boydton Plank Road, Hatcher's Run, October 27-28. Warren's Raid to Weldon Railroad December 7-12. Dabney's Mills, Hatcher's Run, February 5-7, 1865. Ordered to New York February 10. Assigned to duty at Hart's Island, New York Harbor, guarding prison camp, and escorting recruits and convalescents to the front till June. Mustered out June 12, 1865.

Regiment lost during service 8 Officers and 143 Enlisted men killed and mortally wounded and 2 Officers and 150 Enlisted men by disease. Total 303.

144th REGIMENT VOLUNTEERS.

(Failed to complete organization.)

145th REGIMENT INFANTRY.

Organized at Erie September 5, 1862. Moved to Chambersburg, Pa., September 11-12, thence to Hagerstown and Antietam, Md., September 15-17. Attached to 2nd Brigade, 1st Division, 2nd Army Corps, Army of the Potomac, to October, 1862. 1st Brigade, 1st Division, 2nd Army Corps, to April, 1863. 4th Brigade, 1st Division, 2nd Army Corps, to May, 1865.

SERVICE.—Moved to Harper's Ferry, W. Va., September 22, 1862, and duty there till October 29. Reconnoissance to Charlestown October 16-17. Advance up Loudoun Valley and movement to Falmouth, Va., October 29-November 17. Battle of Fredericksburg December 12-15. Duty at Falmouth, Va., till April, 1863. Chancellorsville Campaign April 27-May 6. Battle of Chancellorsville May 1-5. Gettysburg (Pa.) Campaign June 11-July 24. Battle of Gettysburg July 1-3. Pursuit of Lee July 5-24. Duty on line of the Rappahannock till September. Advance from the Rappahannock to the Rapidan September 13-17. Bristoe Campaign October 9-22. Auburn and Bristoe October 14. Advance to line of the Rappahannock November 7-8. Mine Run Campaign November 26-December 2. At Stevensburg till May, 1864. Demonstration on the Rapidan February 6-7. Rapidan Campaign May 4-June 12. Battles of the Wilderness May 5-7; Corbin's Bridge May 8; Spottsylvania May 8-12; Po River May 10; Spottsylvania Court House May 12-21. Assault on the

Salient May 12. North Anna River May 23-26. On line of the Pamunkey May 26-28. Totopotomoy May 28-31. Coid Harbor June 1-12. Before Petersburg June 16-18. Siege of Petersburg June 16, 1864, to April 2, 1865. Jerusalem Plank Road June 22-23, 1864. Demonstration north of the James at Deep Bottom July 27-29. Deep Bottom July 27-28. Mine Explosion, Petersburg, July 30 (Reserve). Demonstration on north side of the James at Deep Bottom August 13-20. Strawberry Plains, Deep Bottom, August 14-18. Ream's Station August 25. Reconnoissance to Hatcher's Run December 7-10. Dabney's Mills, Hatcher's Run, February 5-7, 1865. Watkins' House March 25. Appomattox Campaign March 28-April 9. Skirmishes on line of Hatcher's and Gravelly Runs March 29-30. Hatcher's Run or Boydton Road March 31. Crow's House March 31. Sutherland Station April 2. Sailor's Creek April 6. High Bridge, Farmville, April 7. Appomattox Court House April 9. Surrender of Lee and his army. March to Washington, D. C., May 2-12. Grand Review May 23. Mustered out May 31, 1865.

Regiment lost during service 18 Officers and 187 Enlisted men killed and mortally wounded and 3 Officers and 214 Enlisted men by disease. Total 422.

146th REGIMENT VOLUNTEERS.
(Failed to complete organization.)

147th REGIMENT INFANTRY.

Organized at Loudoun Heights, Va., October 10, 1862, from surplus men of the 28th Regiment, Pennsylvania Infantry, as Companies "A," "B," "C," "D" and "E." Companies "F," "G" and "H" organized at Harrisburg, Pa., September 29 to November 20. Company "I" organized at Philadelphia October 10, 1862, and Company "K" organized at Philadelphia February, 1864. Attached to 1st Brigade, 2nd Division, 12th Army Corps, Army of the Potomac, to October, 1863, and Army of the Cumberland to April, 1864. 1st Brigade, 2nd Division, 20th Army Corps, Army of the Cumberland, to July, 1865.

SERVICE.—Duty at Bolivar Heights, Va., till December, 1862. Reconnoissance to Rippon, W. Va., November 9, and to Winchester, Va., December 2-6. Moved to Fredericksburg December 10-14. At Stafford Court House till April 27, 1863. Burnside's 2nd Campaign, "Mud March," January 20-24. Chancellorsville Campaign April 27-May 6. Battle of Chancellorsville May 1-5. Gettysburg (Pa.) Campaign June 11-July 24. Battle of Gettysburg July 1-3. Pursuit of Lee July 5-24. Movement to Bridgeport, Ala., September 24-October 3. Reopening Tennessee River October 26-29. Wauhatchie, Tenn., October 28-29. Chattanooga Ringgold Campaign November 23-27. Battles of Lookout Mountain November 23-24; Mission Ridge November 25; Ringgold Gap, Taylor's Ridge, November 27. Guard duty on Nashville & Chattanooga Railroad till April, 1864. Expedition down the Tennessee River to Triana, Ala., April 12-16. Atlanta (Ga.) Campaign May 1-September 8. Demonstration on Rocky Faced Ridge May 8-11. Dug Gap or Mill Creek May 8. Battle of Resaca May 14-15. Near Cassville May 19. New Hope Church May 25. Operations on line of Pumpkin Vine Creek and battles about Dallas, New Hope Church and Allatoona Hills May 26-June 5. Operations about Marietta and against Kenesaw Mountain June 10-July 2. Pine Hill June 11-14. Lost Mountain June 15-17. Gilgal or Golgotha Church June 15. Muddy Creek June 17. Noyes Creek June 19. Kolb's Farm June 22. Assault on Kenesaw June 27. Ruff's Station, Smyrna Camp Ground, July 4. Chattahoochie River July 6-17. Peach Tree Creek July 19-20. Siege of Atlanta July 22-August 25. Operations at Chattahoochie River Bridge August 26-September 2. Occupation of Atlanta September 2-November 15. Near Atlanta November 9. March to the sea November 15-December 10. Siege of Savannah December 10-21. Campaign of the Carolinas January to April, 1865. North Edisto River, S. C., February 12-13. Red Bank and Congaree Creek February 15. Averysboro, N. C., March 16. Battle of Bentonville

March 19-21. Occupation of Goldsboro March 24. Advance on Raleigh, N. C., April 9-13. Occupation of Raleigh April 14. Bennett's House April 26. Surrender of Johnston and his army. March to Washington, D. C., via Richmond, Va., April 29-May 20. Grand Review May 24. Duty in the Dept. of Washington till July. Companies "F" and "G" mustered out June 6, 1865. Regiment mustered out July 15, 1865.

Regiment lost during service 7 Officers and 71 Enlisted men killed and mortally wounded and 3 Officers and 61 Enlisted men by disease. Total 142.

148th REGIMENT INFANTRY.

Organized at Camp Curtin, Harrisburg, September 8, 1862. Moved to Cockeyville, Md., September 9-10, 1862, and guard duty on Northern Central Railroad till December 9, 1862. Unattached, Defences of Baltimore, 8th Corps, Middle Department. Moved to Falmouth, Va., December 9-18, 1862. Attached to 1st Brigade, 1st Division, 2nd Army Corps, Army of the Potomac, to September, 1863. 3rd Brigade, 1st Division, 2nd Army Corps, to March, 1864. 4th Brigade, 1st Division, 2nd Army Corps, to June, 1865.

SERVICE.—Duty at Falmouth, Va., till April 27, 1863. Chancellorsville Campaign April 27-May 6. Battle of Chancellorsville May 1-5. Gettysburg (Pa.) Campaign June 14-July 24. Skirmish at Haymarket June 25. Battle of Gettysburg, Pa., July 1-3. Pursuit of Lee July 5-24. Wapping Heights, Va., July 23. Expedition to Port Conway August 31-September 4. Richardson's Ford September 1. Duty on Orange & Alexandria Railroad and the Rappahannock till October. Advance from the Rappahannock to the Rapidan September 13-17. Bristoe Campaign October 9-22. South side of the Rappahannock October 12. Auburn and Bristoe October 14. Advance to line of the Rappahannock November 7-8. Kelly's Ford November 7. Mine Run Campaign November 26-December 2. Demonstration on the Rapidan February 6-7, 1864. Morton's Ford February 6-7. Duty near Stevensburg till May. Rapidan Campaign May 4-June 12. Battles of the Wilderness May 5-7; Spottsylvania May 8-12; Po River May 9-10; Spottsylvania Court House May 12-21. Assault on the Salient May 12. Milford Station May 20. Reconnoissance by Regiment across North Anna River May 22. North Anna River May 23-26. On line of the Pamunkey May 26-28. Totopotomoy May 28-31. Cold Harbor June 1-12. Before Petersburg June 16-18. Siege of Petersburg June 16, 1864, to April 2, 1865. Jerusalem Plank Road June 21-23, 1864. Demonstration on north side of the James at Deep Bottom July 27-29. Deep Bottom July 27-28. Mine Explosion, Petersburg, July 30 (Reserve). Demonstration north of the James at Deep Bottom August 13-20. Strawberry Plains, Deep Bottom, August 14-18. Ream's Station, Weldon Railroad, August 25. Assault on Davidson's Confederate Battery October 27. Front of Forts Morton and Sedgwick October 29. Reconnoissance to Hatcher's Run December 9-10. Dabney's Mills, Hatcher's Run, February 5-7, 1865. Watkins' House March 25. Appomattox Campaign March 28-April 9. Gravelly Run March 29. Boydton Road or Hatcher's Run March 30-31. Crow's House, White Oak Road, March 31. Sutherland Station April 2. Sailor's Creek April 6. High Bridge, Farmville, April 7. Appomattox Court House April 9. Surrender of Lee and his army. March to Washington, D. C., May 2-12. Grand Review May 23. Mustered out near Alexandria June 1, 1865.

Regiment lost during service 12 Officers and 198 Enlisted men killed and mortally wounded and 4 Officers and 183 Enlisted men by disease. Total 397.

149th REGIMENT INFANTRY.—("2nd BUCKTAILS.")

Organized at Harrisburg August, 1862. Ordered to Washington, D. C., September, 1862. Attached to Defences of Washington, D. C., to February, 1863. 2nd Brigade, 3rd Division, 1st Army Corps, Army of the Potomac, to December, 1863. 1st Brigade, 3rd Division, 1st Army Corps, to March, 1864. 3rd Brigade, 4th Division, 5th Army Corps, to June, 1864. 1st Brigade, 1st Division, 5th Army Corps, to September, 1864. 1st Brigade, 3rd Division, 5th Army Corps, to June, 1865.

SERVICE.—Duty in the Defences of Washington, D. C., till February, 1863. Ordered to join 1st Army Corps at Belle Plains, Va., and duty there till April 27, 1863. Chancellorsville Campaign April 27-May 6. Operations about Pollock's Mill Creek April 29-May 2. Battle of Chancellorsville May 2-5. Gettysburg (Pa.) Campaign June 11-July 24. Battle of Gettysburg July 1-3. Pursuit of Lee July 5-24. At Bealeton Station till October. Bristoe Campaign October 9-22. Haymarket October 19. Advance to line of the Rappahannock November 7-8. Mine Run Campaign November 26-December 2. Demonstration on the Rapidan February 6-7, 1864. Duty near Culpeper till May. Rapidan Campaign May 4-June 12. Battles of the Wilderness May 5-7; Laurel Hill May 8; Spottsylvania May 8-12; Spottsylvania Court House May 12-21. Assault on the Salient May 12. North Anna River May 23-26. Jericho Ford May 25. On line of the Pamunkey May 26-28. Totopotomoy May 28-31. Cold Harbor June 1-12. Bethesda Church June 1-3. Before Petersburg June 16-18. Siege of Petersburg June 16, 1864, to April 2, 1865. Mine Explosion, Petersburg, July 30, 1864 (Reserve). Weldon Railroad August 18-21. Poplar Springs Church September 29-October 2. Boydton Plank Road, Hatcher's Run, October 27-28. Warren's Raid on Weldon Railroad December 7-12. Dabney's Mills, Hatcher's Run, February 5-7, 1865. Ordered to Baltimore, Md., February 10; thence to Draft Rendezvous, Elmira, N. Y., and duty there till June. Mustered out June 24, 1865.

Regiment lost during service 4 Officers and 160 Enlisted men killed and mortally wounded and 172 Enlisted men by disease. Total 336.

150th REGIMENT INFANTRY.

Organized at Philadelphia and Harrisburg September 4, 1862. Moved to Washington, D. C., September. Attached to Defences of Washington to February, 1863. 2nd Brigade, 3rd Division, 1st Army Corps, Army of the Potomac, to December, 1863. 1st Brigade, 3rd Division, 1st Army Corps, to March, 1864. 3rd Brigade, 4th Division, 5th Army Corps, to June, 1864. 1st Brigade, 1st Division, 5th Army Corps, to September, 1864. 1st Brigade, 3rd Division, 5th Corps, to June, 1865.

SERVICE.—Guard duty in the Defences of Washington, D. C., till February, 1863. (Co. "K" body guard to President Lincoln till muster out.) Ordered to join Army of the Potomac in the field. Reported to 1st Army Corps at Belle Plains, Va., February, 1863, and duty there till April 27. Chancellorsville Campaign April 27-May 6. Operations at Pollock's Mill Creek April 29-May 2. Battle of Chancellorsville May 2-5. Gettysburg (Pa.) Campaign June 11-July 24. Battle of Gettysburg July 1-3. Pursuit of Lee July 5-24. At Bealeton Station till October. Bristoe Campaign October 9-22. Advance to line of the Rappahannock November 7-8. Mine Run Campaign November 26-December 2. Demonstration on the Rapidan February 6-7, 1864. Duty near Culpeper till May. Rapidan Campaign May 4-June 12. Battles of the Wilderness May 5-7; Laurel Hill May 8; Spottsylvania May 8-12; Spottsylvania Court House May 12-21. Assault on the Salient May 12. North Anna River May 23-26. Jericho Ford May 25. On line of the Pamunkey May 26-28. Totopotomoy May 28-31. Cold Harbor June 1-12. Bethesda Church June 1-3. Before Petersburg June 16-18. Siege of Petersburg June 16, 1864, to April 2, 1865. Mine Explosion, Petersburg, July 30, 1864 (Reserve). Weldon Railroad August 18-21. Poplar Springs Church September 29-October 2. Boydton Plank Road, Hatcher's Run, October 27-28. Warren's Raid on Weldon Railroad December 7-12. Dabney's Mills, Hatcher's Run, February 5-7, 1865. Ordered to Baltimore, Md., February 10; thence to Elmira, N. Y., and duty there till June. Mustered out June 23, 1865.

Regiment lost during service 4 Officers and 108 Enlisted men killed and mortally wounded and 1 Officer and 94 Enlisted men by disease. Total 207.

151st REGIMENT INFANTRY.

Organized at Harrisburg October 18 to November 24, 1862. Moved to Washington, D. C., November 26. Attached to 3rd Brigade, Casey's Division, Defences of Washington, to February, 1863. 1st Brigade, 3rd Division, 1st Army Corps, Army of the Potomac, to July, 1863.

SERVICE.—Duty in the Defences of Washington till February, 1863. Moved to Belle Plains, Va., and joined 1st Army Corps. Duty there till April 27. Chancellorsville Campaign April 27-May 6. Operations about Pollock's Mill Creek April 29-May 2. Battle of Chancellorsville May 2-5. Gettysburg (Pa.) Campaign June 11-July 24. Battle of Gettysburg, Pa., July 1-3. Pursuit of Lee July 5-24. Mustered out July 27, 1863.

Regiment lost during service 2 Officers and 67 Enlisted men killed and mortally wounded and 1 Officer and 53 Enlisted men by disease. Total 123.

152nd REGIMENT VOLUNTEERS.

(See 3rd Regiment Heavy Artillery.)

153rd REGIMENT INFANTRY.

Organized at Easton September, 1862. Moved to Camp Curtin, Harrisburg, October 6; thence to Washington, D. C., October 12, 1862. Attached to 1st Brigade, 1st Division, 11th Army Corps, Army of the Potomac, to July, 1863.

SERVICE.—Duty in the Defences of Washington, D. C., till December, 1862. Reconnoissance from Chantilly to Snicker's Ferry and Berryville, Va., November 28-30. March to Fredericksburg, Va., December 9-16. Duty at Stafford Court House till January 19, 1863. Burnside's 2nd Campaign, "Mud March," January 20-24, 1863. At Stafford Court House till April 27. Chancellorsville Campaign April 27-May 6. Battle of Chancellorsville May 1-5. Gettysburg (Pa.) Campaign June 11-July 24. Battle of Gettysburg July 1-3. Pursuit of Lee July 5-12. Mustered out July 24, 1863.

Regiment lost during service 1 Officer and 48 Enlisted men killed and mortally wounded and 28 Enlisted men by disease. Total 77.

154th REGIMENT INFANTRY.

Organized at Philadelphia October 29, 1862, to January 21, 1862. On provost duty at Philadelphia entire term. Mustered out September 29 to October 21, 1863.

Lost 4 by disease.

155th REGIMENT INFANTRY.

Organized at Pittsburg and Harrisburg September 2-19, 1862. Moved to Washington, D. C., September 4. Attached to 2nd Brigade, 3rd Division, 5th Army Corps, Army Potomac, to May, 1863. 3rd Brigade, 2nd Division, 5th Army Corps, to March, 1864. 4th Brigade, 1st Division, 5th Army Corps, to April, 1864. 1st Brigade, 1st Division, 5th Army Corps, to June, 1864. 1st Brigade, 2nd Division, 5th Army Corps, June, 1864. 2nd Brigade, 2nd Division, 5th Army Corps, to July, 1865. 2nd Brigade, 1st Division, 5th Army Corps, to December, 1864. 3rd Brigade, 1st Division, 5th Army Corps, to June, 1865.

SERVICE.—Moved to Sharpsburg, Md., and duty there till October 30, 1862. Movement to Falmouth, Va., October 30-November 19. Battle of Fredericksburg December 12-15. Burnside's 2nd Campaign, "Mud March," January 20-24, 1863. Duty at Falmouth, Va., till April 27. Chancellorsville Campaign April 27-May 6. Battle of Chancellorsville May 1-5. Gettysburg (Pa.) Campaign June 11-July 24. Battle of Gettysburg July 1-3. Pursuit of Lee July 5-24. Duty on line of the Rappahannock and Rapidan till October. Bristoe Campaign October 9-22. Auburn October 13. Advance to line of the Rappahannock November 7-8. Rappahannock Station November 7. Mine Run Campaign November 26-December 2. Duty on Orange & Alexandria Railroad till April, 1864. Rapidan Campaign May 4-June 12. Battles of the Wilderness May 5-7; Laurel Hill May 8; Spottsylvania May 8-12; Spottsylvania Court House May 12-21. Assault on the Salient May 12.

North Anna River May 23-26. On line of the Pamunkey May 26-28. Totopotomoy May 28-31. Cold Harbor June 1-12. Bethesda Church June 1-3. Before Petersburg June 16-18. Siege of Petersburg June 16, 1864, to April 2, 1865. Mine Explosion, Petersburg, July 30 (Reserve). Six Mile House, Weldon Railroad, August 18-21. Poplar Springs Church, Peeble's Farm, September 29-October 2. Boydton Plank Road, Hatcher's Run, October 27-28. Warren's Raid on Weldon Railroad December 7-12. Dabney's Mills, Hatcher's Run, February 5-7, 1865. Appomattox Campaign March 28-April 9. Junction Boydton and Quaker Roads and Lewis Farm, near Gravelly Run, March 29. White Oak Road March 31. Five Forks April 1. Appomattox Court House April 9. Surrender of Lee and his army. Moved to Washington, D. C., May 1-12. Grand Review May 23. Mustered out June 2, 1865.

Regiment lost during service 5 Officers and 137 Enlisted men killed and mortally wounded and 1 Officer and 111 Enlisted men by disease. Total 254.

156th REGIMENT VOLUNTEERS.

(Failed to complete organization. Transferred to 157th Pennsylvania February 27, 1863.)

157th REGIMENT INFANTRY.

Organized at Philadelphia October, 1862, to February, 1863. Moved to Fort Delaware December, 1862, and duty there till February, 1863. Moved to Washington, D. C., and duty in the Defences of that city till May, 1864. Attached to Tyler's Division, 22nd Corps, to May, 1864. 2nd Brigade, 4th Division, 5th Army Corps, Army of the Potomac, to August, 1864. 3rd Brigade, 2nd Division, 5th Army Corps, to March, 1865.

SERVICE.—Ordered to join Army of the Potomac in the field and joined May 29, 1864. Battles about Cold Harbor June 1-12; Bethesda Church June 1-3. Before Petersburg June 16-18. Siege of Petersburg June 16, 1864, to March 21, 1865. Mine Explosion, Petersburg, July 30, 1864 (Reserve). Weldon Railroad August 18-21. Poplar Springs Church September 29-October 2. Yellow House October 1-3. Boydton Plank Road, Hatcher's Run, October 27-28. Warren's Raid on Weldon Railroad December 7-12. Dabney's Mills, Hatcher's Run, February 5-7, 1865. Appomattox Campaign March 28-April 9. Regiment transferred to 191st Pennsylvania Infantry March 21, 1865.

Regiment lost during service 31 Enlisted men killed and mortally wounded and 34 Enlisted men by disease. Total 65.

158th REGIMENT INFANTRY.

Organized at Chambersburg November 1, 1862, and ordered to Suffolk, Va. Attached to Spinola's Brigade, Division at Suffolk, 7th Corps, Dept. of Virginia, to December, 1862. 1st Brigade, 5th Division, 18th Corps, Dept. of North Carolina, to May, 1863. District of the Pamlico, Dept. of North Carolina, to June, 1863. Spinola's Brigade, 7th Corps, Dept. of Virginia, to July, 1863. Harper's Ferry, W. Va., to August, 1863.

SERVICE.—Duty at Suffolk, Va., till December 28, 1862. Moved to New Berne, N. C., December 28-January 1, 1863, and duty there till June, 1863. Expedition from New Berne to Trenton, Pollocksville, Young's Cross Roads and Swansborough March 6-10. Expedition to relief of Little Washington, N. C., April 7-10. Blount's Creek April 9. Expedition to Swift Creek Village April 13-21. Big Swift Creek April 19. Ordered to Fortress Monroe, Va., June. Dix's Peninsula Campaign July 1-7. Moved to Harper's Ferry July 7-9, thence moved to Boonsboro, Md., and reported to Gen. Meade July 11. Pursuit of Lee July 11-24. Ordered to Harrisburg, Pa., August 3. Mustered out August 12, 1863.

Regiment lost during service 45 by disease.

159th REGIMENT VOLUNTEERS.

(See 14th Regiment Cavalry.)

160th REGIMENT VOLUNTEERS.

(See 15th Regiment Cavalry.)

161st REGIMENT VOLUNTEERS.

(See 16th Regiment Cavalry.)

162nd REGIMENT VOLUNTEERS.

(See 17th Regiment Cavalry.)

163rd REGIMENT VOLUNTEERS.

(See 18th Regiment Cavalry.)

164th REGIMENT INFANTRY.

(Failed to complete organization.)

165th REGIMENT INFANTRY.

Organized at Chambersburg and Gettysburg November 25-December 5, 1862. Moved to Washington, D. C., thence to Newport News and Suffolk, Va., December 8-17, 1862. Attached to Foster's Brigade, Division at Suffolk, 7th Corps, Dept. of Virginia, to April, 1863. 2nd Brigade, 1st Division, 7th Corps, Dept. of Virginia.

SERVICE.—Duty at Suffolk till May, 1863. Expedition toward Blackwater, Va., January 8-10, 1863. Deserted House January 30. Leesville April 4. Siege of Suffolk April 11-May 4. Edenton, Providence Church and Somerton Roads April 12-13. Somerton Road April 15 and 20. Edenton Road April 24. Operations on Seaboard & Roanoke Railroad May 12-26. Holland House, Carrsville, May 15-16. Dix's Peninsula Campaign June 27-July 7. Expedition from White House to South Anna River July 1-7. South Anna Bridge July 4. Moved to Washington, D. C., July 8. Mustered out July 28, 1863.

Regiment lost during service 1 killed and 1 Officer and 14 Enlisted men by disease. Total 16.

166th REGIMENT INFANTRY.

Organized at York October 24 to December 8, 1862. Moved to Washington, D. C., thence to Newport News and Suffolk, Va., December 8-17. Attached to Foster's Brigade, Division at Suffolk, Va., 7th Corps, Dept. of Virginia, to April, 1863. 2nd Brigade, 1st Division, 7th Corps, to July 1863.

SERVICE.—Duty at Suffolk till June, 1863. Expedition toward Blackwater January 8-10, 1863. Deserted House January 30. Leesville April 4. Siege of Suffolk April 11-May 4. Edenton, Providence Church and Somerton Roads April 12-13. Somerton Road April 15 and 20. Edenton Road April 24. Operations on Seaboard & Roanoke Railroad May 12-26. Holland House, Carrsville, May 15-16. Dix's Peninsula Campaign June 27-July 7. Expedition from White House to South Anna River July 1-7. South Anna Bridge July 4. Moved to Washington, D. C., July 8. Mustered out July 28, 1863.

Regiment lost during service 6 Enlisted men killed and mortally wounded and 11 Enlisted men by disease. Total 17.

167th REGIMENT INFANTRY.

Organized at Reading November 10 to December 6, 1862. Moved to Washington, D. C., thence to Newport News and Suffolk, Va., December 8-17. Attached to Foster's Brigade, Division at Suffolk, Va., 7th Corps, Dept. of Virginia, to April, 1863. 1st Brigade, 1st Division, 7th Corps, Dept. of Virginia, to July, 1863. 1st Brigade, 1st Division, 1st Army Corps, Army of the Potomac, to August, 1863.

SERVICE.—Duty at Suffolk till May, 1863. Action at Deserted House, Va., January 30. Siege of Suffolk April 11-May 4. Suffolk April 19. Operations on Seaboard & Roanoke Railroad May 12-26. Holland House, Carrsville, May 15-16. Dix's Peninsula Campaign June 27-July 7. Expedition from White House to Bottom's Bridge July 1-7. Baltimore Cross Roads July 2. Moved to Washington, D. C., July 8; thence into Maryland and joined 1st Army Corps, Army of the Potomac, July 15. Pursuit of Lee beyond the Rappahannock July 15-24. Mustered out August 12, 1863.

Regiment lost 1 Officer and 1 Enlisted man killed and 22 Enlisted men by disease.

168th REGIMENT INFANTRY.

Organized at Pittsburg October 16 to December 1, 1862. Moved to Washington, D. C., thence to Newport News and Suffolk, Va., December 6-17, 1862. Attached to Spinola's Brigade, Division at Suffolk, Va., 7th Corps, Dept. of Virginia, to December, 1863. 2nd Brigade, 5th Division, 18th Corps, Dept. of North Carolina, to May, 1863. District of the Pamlico, Dept. of North Carolina, to June, 1863. Spinola's Brigade, 7th Corps, Dept. of Virginia, to July, 1863. Harper's Ferry, W. Va., July, 1863.

SERVICE.—Duty at Suffolk, Va., till December 28, 1862. Moved to New Berne, N. C., December 28-January 1, 1863, and duty there till June, 1863. Expedition from New Berne to Trenton, Pollocksville, Young's Cross Roads and Swansborough March 6-10. Expedition to relief of Little Washington April 7-10. Blount's Creek April 9. Expedition to Swift Creek Village April 13-21. Moved to Fortress Monroe, Va., June. Dix's Campaign on the Peninsula June 27-July 7. Moved to Harper's Ferry, W. Va., July 7-9; thence moved to Boonsborough, Md., and reported to General Meade July 11. Pursuit of Lee July 11-24. Mustered out July 25, 1863.

Regiment lost during service 1 Officer and 24 Enlisted men by disease. Total 25.

169th REGIMENT INFANTRY.

Organized at Pittsburg October 16, 1862. Duty at Camp Howe, Pittsburg, till December 1. Moved to Washington, D. C., thence to Fortress Monroe and Yorktown, Va., December 1-7, and to Gloucester Point, Va., December 8. Attached to Busteed's Independent Brigade, Yorktown, Va., 4th Corps, Dept. of Virginia, to April, 1863. King's Independent Brigade, 4th Corps, Dept. of Virginia, to June, 1863. 1st Division, 4th Corps, Dept. of Virginia, to July, 1863. 1st Brigade, 3rd Division, 11th Army Corps, Army of the Potomac, to muster out.

SERVICE.—Duty at Yorktown and Gloucester Point, Va., till June, 1863. Expedition to Gloucester Court House April 7. Expedition from Yorktown to Walkerton and Aylett's June 4-5. Dix's Peninsula Campaign June 27-July 7. Ordered to Washington, D. C., July 9; thence march to Funkstown, Md. Joined Army of the Potomac at Hagerstown, Md., July 14. Pursuit of Lee to Williamsport, Md. Moved to Harrisburg, Pa., via Baltimore and Philadelphia. Mustered out July 27, 1863.

Regiment lost during service 11 by disease.

170th REGIMENT VOLUNTEERS.
(Failed to complete organization.)

171st REGIMENT INFANTRY.

Organized at Harrisburg October and November, 1862. Moved to Washington, D. C., November 27; thence to Suffolk, Va. Attached to Spinola's Brigade, Division at Suffolk, Va., 7th Corps, Dept. of Virginia, to January, 1863. 1st Brigade, 5th Division, 18th Corps, Dept. of North Carolina, to May, 1863. District of the Pamlico, Dept. of North Carolina, to June, 1863. Spinola's Brigade, 7th Corps, Dept. of Virginia, to July, 1863. Harper's Ferry, W. Va., July, 1863.

SERVICE.—Duty at Suffolk, Va., till December 28. Moved to New Berne, N. C., December 28-January 1, 1863, and duty there till April, 1863. Expedition from New Berne to Trenton, Pollocksville, Young's Cross Roads and Swansborough March 6-10. Expedition to relief of Little Washington April 7-10. Blount's Creek April 9. Expedition to Swift Creek Village April 13-21. Duty at Little Washington till June. Ordered to Fortress Monroe, Va. Dix's Peninsula Campaign July 1-7. Moved to Washington, D. C., thence to Harper's Ferry, W. Va., July 7-9; thence to Boonsboro, Md., and reported to General Meade July 11. Pursuit of Lee July 11-24. Ordered to Harrisburg, Pa., August 3. Mustered out August 8, 1863.

Regiment lost 38 by disease during service.

172nd REGIMENT INFANTRY.

Organized at Harrisburg October 27 to November 29, 1862. Moved to Washington, D. C., December 2; thence to Newport News, Va., December 4, and to Yorktown, Va., December 12. Unassigned, Yorktown, Va., 4th Corps, Dept. of Virginia, to April, 1863. West's Advance Brigade, 4th Corps, Dept. of Virginia, to June, 1863. 3rd Brigade, 1st Division, 4th Corps, to July, 1863. 1st Brigade, 3rd Division, 11th Corps, Army of the Potomac, to August, 1863.

SERVICE.—Garrison duty at Yorktown, Va., till June, 1863. Dix's Peninsula Campaign June 27-July 7. Ordered to Washington, D. C., July 9. Join Army of the Potomac at Hagerstown, Md., July 14. Pursuit of Lee to Williamsport, Md. March to Warrenton Junction, Va., July 19-25, 1863. Ordered to Harrisburg, Pa., and mustered out August 1, 1863.

Regiment lost during service 13 by disease.

173rd REGIMENT INFANTRY.

Organized at Harrisburg October and November, 1862. Left State for Washington, D. C., November 30; thence moved to Suffolk and Norfolk, Va. Attached to District of Norfolk, Va., 7th Corps, Dept. of Virginia, to July, 1863. 1st Brigade, 2nd Division, 11th Army Corps, Army of the Potomac, to August, 1863.

SERVICE.—Guard, outpost and provost duty at Norfolk, Va., till July, 1863. Ordered to Washington, D. C., July 9; thence moved to Frederick, Md. Pursuit of Lee July 12-24. Guard duty on Orange & Alexandria Railroad till August. Mustered out August 18, 1863.

Regiment lost during service 19 by disease.

174th REGIMENT INFANTRY.

Organized at Philadelphia November 19, 1862. Moved to Washington, D. C., November; thence to Suffolk, Va., and duty there till December 28. Attached to Ferry's Brigade, Division at Suffolk, Va., 7th Corps, Dept. of Virginia, to December, 1862. 2nd Brigade, 3rd Division, 18th Corps, Dept. of North Carolina, to February, 1863. 2nd Brigade, 2nd Division, 18th Corps, Dept. of the South, to February, 1863. District of Beaufort, S. C., 10th Corps, Dept. of the South, to June, 1863. District of Hilton Head, S. C., 10th Corps, Dept. of the South, to August, 1863.

SERVICE.—Duty at Suffolk, Va., till December 31, 1862. Moved to New Berne, N. C., December 31-January 6, 1863, and to Port Royal Harbor, S. C., January 27-February 5. At St. Helena Island, S. C., till February 27. At Beaufort, S. C., till June, and at Hilton Head, S. C., till July 28. Moved to Philadelphia and mustered out August 7, 1863.

Regiment lost during service 13 by disease.

175th REGIMENT INFANTRY.

Organized at Philadelphia November 6, 1862. Moved to Washington, D. C., December 1; thence to Fortress Monroe and Suffolk, Va. Attached to Gibbs' Brigade, Division at Suffolk, Va., December, 1862. Spinola's Brigade, Division at Suffolk, 7th Corps, to December, 1862. 1st Brigade, 5th Division, 18th Corps, Dept. of North Carolina, to May, 1863. District of the Pamlico, Dept. of North Carolina, to June, 1863. Well's Brigade, Harper's Ferry, W. Va., 8th Corps, Middle Department, to July, 1863.

SERVICE.—Duty at Suffolk, Va., till December 28, 1862. Moved to New Berne, N. C., December 28-January 1, 1863, and duty there till April, 1863. Expedition from New Berne to Trenton, Pollocksville, Young's Cross Roads and Swansborough March 6-10. Operations on the Pamlico April 4-6. Expedition to relief of Little Washington April 7-10. Expedition to Swift Creek Village April 13-21. Garrison duty at Little Washington till June. Moved to Fortress Monroe, Va., thence to Harper's Ferry, W. Va., and to Frederick, Md. Mustered out August 7, 1863.

Regiment lost during service 21 by disease.

176th REGIMENT INFANTRY.

Organized at Philadelphia November 3-11, 1862. Moved to Washington, D. C., thence to Suffolk, Va. Attached to Foster's Brigade, Division at Suffolk, 7th Corps, Dept. of Virginia, to December, 1862. Ferry's Brigade, Division at Suffolk, 7th Corps, to January, 1863. 1st Brigade, 3rd Division, 18th Corps, Dept. of North Carolina, to February, 1863. 2nd Brigade, 2nd Division, 18th Corps, Dept. of the South, to April, 1863. District of Beaufort, S. C., 10th Corps, Dept. of the South, to June, 1863. District of Hilton Head, S. C., 10th Corps, to July, 1863.

SERVICE.—Duty at Suffolk, Va., till December 31, 1862. Moved to New Berne, N. C., December 31-January 5, 1863; thence to Port Royal Harbor, S. C., January 27-February 3. Duty at St. Helena Island, S. C., Beaufort, S. C., and Hilton Head, S. C., till July, 1863. Ordered home and mustered out August 19, 1863.

Regiment lost during service 44 by disease.

177th REGIMENT INFANTRY.

Organized at Harrisburg November 20, 1862. At Camp Curtin till December 3. Moved to Washington, D. C., thence to Newport News, Va., and duty there till December 17. Moved to Suffolk, Va., December 17. Attached to Gibbs' Brigade, Division at Suffolk, Va., 7th Corps, Dept. of Virginia, to March, 1863. Viele's Brigade, Norfolk, Va., 7th Corps, to July, 1863. 2nd Brigade, 2nd Division, 12th Army Corps, Army of the Potomac, to August, 1863.

SERVICE.—Duty at Suffolk, Va., till March, 1863, and in District of Norfolk, Va. At Deep Creek till July, 1863. Ordered to Washington July 10, thence to Funkstown, Md. Pursuit of Lee till July 24. At Maryland Heights till August 1. Mustered out August 4 and 7, 1863.

Regiment lost during service 24 by disease.

178th REGIMENT INFANTRY.

Organized at Harrisburg October 22-November 27, 1862. Moved to Washington, D. C., December 5; thence to Newport News, Va. Attached to Busteed's Brigade, 4th Corps, Dept. of Virginia, December, 1862, to April, 1863. West's Independent Brigade, 4th Corps, Dept. of Virginia, to May, 1863. West's Advance Brigade, 4th Corps, to July, 1863. 2nd Brigade, King's Division, 22nd Corps, to August, 1863.

SERVICE.—Duty at Newport News, Va., till December 29, 1862, and at Yorktown, Va., and on the Peninsula till July 8, 1863. Reconnoissance to Bottom's Bridge July 1-7. Skirmish at Chickahominy July 2. Moved to Washington, D. C., July 8, and duty there till July 27. Mustered out July 27, 1863.

Regiment lost during service 10 by disease.

179th REGIMENT INFANTRY.

Organized at Philadelphia and Harrisburg October 23 to December 6, 1862. Ordered to Fortress Monroe, Va., December, 1862. Attached to Busteed's Independent Brigade, 4th Corps, Dept. of Virginia, to April, 1863. West's Independent Brigade, 4th Corps, to June, 1863. King's Independent Brigade, 4th Corps, to July, 1863. 2nd Brigade, King's Division, 22nd Corps, to July, 1863.

SERVICE.—Duty at Yorktown, Va., and on the Peninsula, Va., till July, 1863. Dix's Peninsula Campaign June 24-July 7. Expedition from White House to Bottom's Bridge July 1-7. Skirmish at Baltimore Cross Roads July 2. Ordered to Washington, D. C., July 8; thence to Harrisburg, and mustered out July 27, 1863.

Regiment lost during service 6 by disease.

180th REGIMENT VOLUNTEERS.

(See 19th Regiment Cavalry.)

181st REGIMENT VOLUNTEERS.

(See 20th Regiment Cavalry.)

182nd REGIMENT VOLUNTEERS.

(See 21st Regiment Cavalry.)

183rd REGIMENT INFANTRY.

Organized at Philadelphia December 24, 1863, to March 8, 1864. Ordered to join Army of the Potomac on the Rapidan, Va., and attached to 1st Brigade, 1st Division, 2nd Army Corps, Army of the Potomac, to March, 1865. 4th Brigade, 1st Division, 2nd Army Corps, to July, 1865.

SERVICE.—Campaign from the Rapidan to the James River, Va., May 4-June 12, 1864. Battles of the Wilderness May 5-7; Corbin's Bridge May 8; Spottsylvania May 8-12; Po River May 10; Spottsylvania Court House May 12-21. Assault on the Salient May 12. North Anna River May 23-26. On line of the Pamunkey May 26-28. Totopotomoy May 28-31. Cold Harbor June 1-12. Before Petersburg June 16-18. Siege of Petersburg June 16, 1864, to April 2, 1865. Jerusalem Plank Road, Weldon Railroad, June 22-23, 1864. Demonstration north of the James at Deep Bottom July 27-29. Deep Bottom July 27-28. Mine Explosion, Petersburg, July 30 (Reserve). Demonstration north of the James at Deep Bottom August 13-20. Strawberry Plains, Deep Bottom, August 14-18. Ream's Station August 25. Boydton Plank Road, Hatcher's Run, October 27-28. Reconnoissance to Hatcher's Run December 9-10. Dabney's Mills, Hatcher's Run, February 5-7, 1865. Watkins' House March 25. Appomattox Campaign March 28-April 9. Hatcher's Run or Boydton Road March 30-31. White Oak Road March 31. Sutherland Station April 2. Sailor's Creek April 6. High Bridge, Farmville, April 7. Appomattox Court House April 9. Surrender of Lee and his army. March to Washington, D. C., May 2-12. Grand Review May 23. Mustered out July 13, 1865.

Regiment lost during service 4 Officers and 92 Enlisted men killed and mortally wounded and 2 Officers and 89 Enlisted men by disease. Total 187.

184th REGIMENT INFANTRY.

Organized at Harrisburg May, 1864. Ordered to join Army of the Potomac in the field, and reported May 28, 1864. Attached to 1st Brigade, 1st Division, 2nd Army Corps, Army of the Potomac.

SERVICE.—Rapidan (Va.) Campaign May 28-June 12. Totopotomoy May 28-31. Cold Harbor June 1-12. Before Petersburg June 16-18. Siege of Petersburg June 16, 1864, to April 2, 1865. Jerusalem Plank Road, Weldon Railroad, June 22-23, 1864. Demonstration on north side of the James at Deep Bottom July 27-29. Deep Bottom July 27-28. Mine Explosion, Petersburg, July 30 (Reserve). Demonstration north of the James at Deep Bottom August 13-20. Strawberry Plains, Deep Bottom, August 14-18. Ream's Station August 25. Boydton Plank Road, Hatcher's Run, October 27-28. Reconnoissance to Hatcher's Run December 9-10. Dabney's Mills, Hatcher's Run, February 5-7, 1865. Watkins' House March 25. Appomattox Campaign March 28-April 9. Boydton and White Oak Roads March 30-31. Crow's House March 31. Sailor's Creek April 6. High Bridge and Farmville April 7. Appomattox Court House April 9. Surrender of Lee and his army. March to Washington, D. C., May 2-12. Grand Review May 23. Mustered out July 14, 1865.

Regiment lost during service 3 Officers and 110 Enlisted men killed and mortally wounded and 122 Enlisted men by disease. Total 235.

185th REGIMENT VOLUNTEERS.

(See 22nd Regiment Cavalry.)

186th REGIMENT INFANTRY.

Organized at Philadelphia January 29 to May 31, 1864. Duty at Fort Mifflin and on provost duty at Philadelphia entire term. Mustered out August 15, 1865. Lost 17 by disease.

187th REGIMENT INFANTRY.

Organized at Philadelphia March 3 to May 4, 1864, from 1st Battalion Militia Infantry (6 Mos.). Moved to Washington, D. C., May 18, 1864. Moved to join Army of the Potomac May 26, and reported at Cold Harbor, Va., June 6. Cold Harbor June 6-12. Before

Petersburg June 16-18. Siege of Petersburg June 16 to September 22. Attached to 1st Brigade, 1st Division, 5th Army Corps. Jerusalem Plank Road, Weldon Railroad, June 21-23. Mine Explosion, Petersburg, July 30 (Reserve). Weldon Railroad August 18-21. Relieved September 22 and ordered to Philadelphia. Garrison and escort duty at Camp Cadwalader, Philadelphia, Pa., and provost duty at other points in Pennsylvania till August, 1865. Guard of honor over remains of President Lincoln in Independence Hall, Philadelphia, and escort to funeral cortege May, 1865. Mustered out August 3, 1865.

Regiment lost during service 66 Enlisted men killed and mortally wounded and 1 Officer and 69 Enlisted men by disease. Total 136.

188th REGIMENT INFANTRY.

Organized at Fortress Monroe, Va., April 1, 1864, from 3rd Pennsylvania Heavy Artillery. Moved from Camp Hamilton, Va., to Yorktown April 25. Attached to 3rd Brigade, 1st Division, 18th Army Corps, Dept. of Virginia and North Carolina, to December, 1864. 3rd Brigade, 3rd Division, 24th Army Corps, Dept. of Virginia, to July, 1865. 2nd Independent Brigade, 24th Army Corps, to August, 1865. Dept. of Virginia to December, 1865.

SERVICE.—Butler's operations on south side of James River and against Petersburg and Richmond, Va. May 4-28. Swift Creek or Arrowfield Church May 9-10. Proctor's Creek and operations against Fort Darling May 12-16. Battle of Drewry's Bluff May 14-16. On Bermuda Hundred front May 16-28. Moved to White House, thence to Cold Harbor May 28-June 1. Battles of Cold Harbor June 1-12. Before Petersburg June 15-18. Siege operations against Petersburg and Richmond June 16, 1864, to April 2, 1865. Hare's Hill June 24 and 28, 1864. In trenches before Petersburg till September. Mine Explosion, Petersburg, July 30 (Reserve). Battle of Chaffin's Farm, New Market Heights, north of the James, September 28-30. Battle of Fair Oaks, near Richmond, October 27-28. Duty in trenches before Richmond till March, 1865. Expedition up the Rappahannock to Fredericksburg and destruction of large quantities of tobacco and stores March 5-8. Expedition from Fort Monroe into Westmoreland County March 11-13. March to Signal Hill before Richmond. Occupation of Richmond April 3. Guard and provost duty at Lynchburg and in Central Virginia till December, 1865. Mustered out at City Point, Va., December 14, 1865.

Regiment lost during service 10 Officers and 114 Enlisted men killed and mortally wounded and 2 Officers and 66 Enlisted men by disease. Total 192.

189th REGIMENT INFANTRY.
(Failed to complete organization.)

190th REGIMENT INFANTRY.

Organized in the field from Veterans and Recruits of the Pennsylvania Reserve Corps May 31, 1864. Attached to 3rd Brigade, 3rd Division, 5th Army Corps, Army of the Potomac, to August, 1864. 1st Brigade, 3rd Division, 5th Army Corps, to September, 1864. 3rd Brigade, 2nd Division, 5th Army Corps, to June, 1865.

SERVICE.—Battles about Cold Harbor, Va., June 1-12, 1864; Bethesda Church June 1-3; White Oak Swamp Bridge June 13. Before Petersburg June 16-18. Siege of Petersburg June 16, 1864, to April 2, 1865. Weldon Railroad June 21-23, 1864. Mine Explosion, Petersburg, July 30 (Reserve). Weldon Railroad August 18-21. Poplar Springs Church September 29-October 2. Boydton Plank Road, Hatcher's Run, October 27-28. Warren's Expedition to Weldon Railroad December 7-12. Dabney's Mills, Hatcher's Run, February 5-7, 1865. Appomattox Campaign March 28-April 9. Lewis Farm, near Gravelly Run, March 29. White Oak Road March 31. Five Forks April 1. Appomattox Court House April 9. Surrender of Lee and his army. March to Washington, D. C., May 1-12. Grand Review May 23. Mustered out June 28, 1865.

Regiment lost during service 3 Officers and 43 Enlisted men killed and mortally wounded and 168 Enlisted men by disease. Total 214.

191st REGIMENT INFANTRY.

Organized in the field from Veterans and Recruits of the Pennsylvania Reserve Corps May 31, 1864. Attached to 3rd Brigade, 3rd Division, 5th Army Corps, Army of the Potomac, to August, 1864. 1st Brigade, 3rd Division, 5th Army Corps, to September, 1864. 3rd Brigade, 2nd Division, 5th Army Corps, to June, 1865.

SERVICE.—Battles about Cold Harbor, Va., June 1-12, 1864. Bethesda Church June 1-3. White Oak Swamp Bridge June 13. Before Petersburg June 16-18. Siege of Petersburg June 16, 1864, to April 2, 1865. Weldon Railroad June 21-23, 1864. Mine Explosion, Petersburg, July 30 (Reserve). Weldon Railroad August 18-21. Poplar Springs Church September 29-October 2. Boydton Plank Road, Hatcher's Run, October 27-28. Warren's Expedition to Weldon Railroad December 7-12. Dabney's Mills, Hatcher's Run, February 5-7, 1865. Appomattox Campaign March 28-April 9. Lewis Farm, near Gravelly Run, March 29. White Oak Road March 31. Five Forks April 1. Appomattox Court House April 9. Surrender of Lee and his army. March to Washington, D. C., May 1-12. Grand Review May 23. Mustered out June 28, 1865.

Regiment lost during service 1 Officer and 40 Enlisted men killed and mortally wounded and 161 Enlisted men by disease. Total 202.

192nd REGIMENT INFANTRY.

Organized at Philadelphia for 100 days July, 1864. At Camp Cadwalader till July 23. Moved to Baltimore, Md., July 23. Attached to 2nd Separate Brigade, 8th Corps, Middle Department, July, 1864. Gallipolis, Ohio, Northern Department, to November.

SERVICE.—Duty at Baltimore, Md., till August 1 and at Fort McHenry till August 15. Moved to Johnson's Island, Lake Erie, August 15. Company "K." at Ironton, Ohio, August to November. Duty at Gallipolis, Ohio, September to November. Mustered out November 11, 1864. Regiment reorganized for one year February, 1865. Attached to 2nd Brigade, 3rd Division, Army of the Shenandoah, to April, 1865. Sub-District of Harper's Ferry, District of West Virginia, Middle Department, to August, 1865. Duty in the Shenandoah Valley. Mustered out August 24, 1865.

Regiment lost during service 16 by disease.

193rd REGIMENT INFANTRY.

Organized at Camp Knox, Pittsburg, for 100 days, July 19, 1864. Atached to 3rd Separate Brigade, 8th Corps, Middle Department. Moved to Baltimore, Md., and assigned to duty as guard to bridges on Philadelphia, Wilmington & Baltimore Railroad. Company "B" on provost duty at Wilmington, Del., August 10. Mustered out at Pittsburg November 19, 1864.

Regiment lost during service 10 by disease.

194th REGIMENT INFANTRY.

Organized at Harrisburg for 100 days July 22, 1864. Moved to Baltimore, Md., July 22, and provost duty there till November. Attached to 3rd Separate Brigade, 8th Corps, Middle Department. Mustered out November 6, 1864.

Regiment lost 2 by disease.

195th REGIMENT INFANTRY.

Organized at Camp Curtin for 100 days July 24, 1864. Moved to Baltimore, Md., July 24, thence to Monocacy Junction July 28. Attached to 3rd Separate Brigade, 8th Corps, Middle Department, to August, 1864. 1st Separate Brigade, 8th Corps, to October, 1864. Reserve Division, Dept. of West Virginia, to November, 1864.

SERVICE.—Guard bridge and railroad at Monocacy Junction, Md., till October. Guard duty in Berkeley County, W. Va., along B. & O. Railroad till November. Mustered out November 4, 1864.

Regiment reorganized for one year February, 1865. (A Detachment of first Regiment was on duty guarding Baltimore & Ohio Railroad, with Headquarters at North Mountain Station, October, 1864, to March 16, 1865.) Ordered to Charlestown, W. Va., March 31, 1865. Attached to 2nd Brigade, 3rd Division, West Virginia, to July, 1865. Dept. of Washington, D. C., 22nd Corps, to January, 1865.

SERVICE.—Guard fords of the Shenandoah, Headquarters at Kablestown, W. Va., April 1-4, 1865. At Stevenson's Station till April 22. At Berryville till June 6. Expedition to Staunton June 6-26. Duty at Harrisonburg July. Ordered to Washington, D. C., and duty there till January, 1866. Mustered out January 31, 1866.

Regiment lost during service 10 by disease.

196th REGIMENT INFANTRY.

Organized at Philadelphia for 100 days July 20, 1864. Moved to Baltimore, Md., July 27. Attached to 3rd Separate Brigade, 8th Corps, to August, 1864. Moved to Camp Douglas, Chicago, Ill., August, and duty there guarding prisoners till November. Company "H" on provost at Springfield, Ill., August 26 to November. Mustered out November 17, 1864.

Regiment lost during service 10 by disease.

197th REGIMENT INFANTRY.

Organized at Philadelphia for 100 days July 22, 1864. Moved to Baltimore, Md., and duty at Camp Bradford, Mankin's Woods, till August, 1864. Guard prisoners at Rock Island, Ill., till November. Mustered out November 11, 1864. Lost 6 by disease.

198th REGIMENT INFANTRY.

Organized at Philadelphia September 9, 1864. Left State for Petersburg, Va., September 19, 1864. Attached to 1st Brigade, 1st Division, 5th Army Corps.

SERVICE.—Siege of Petersburg September, 1864, to April, 1865. Poplar Springs Church September 29-October 2, 1864. Reconnoissance to Boydton Road October 8. Boydton Plank Road, Hatcher's Run, October 27-28. Warren's Raid to Weldon Railroad December 7-12. Dabney's Mills, Hatcher's Run, February 5-7, 1865. Appomattox Campaign March 28-April 9. Junction, Quaker and Boydton Roads March 29. Lewis Farm near Gravelly Run March 29. White Oak Road March 30-31. Five Forks April 1. Appomattox C. H. April 9. Surrender of Lee and his army. March to Washington, D. C., May 1-12. Grand Review May 23. Mustered out June 4, 1865.

Regiment lost during service 6 Officers and 67 Enlisted men killed and mortally wounded and 44 Enlisted men by disease. Total 117.

199th REGIMENT INFANTRY.

Organized at Philadelphia September and October, 1864. Moved to Deep Bottom Landing, Va., October. Attached to 1st Brigade, 1st Division, 10th Army Corps, Army of the James, to December, 1864. 1st Brigade, 1st Division, 24th Army Corps, to July, 1865.

SERVICE.—Duty in trenches before Richmond, Va., till March, 1865. Appomattox Campaign March 28-April 9. Assaults on Forts Gregg and Alexander April 2. Fall of Petersburg April 2. Pursuit of Lee April 3-9. Rice's Station April 6. Appomattox Court House April 9. Surrender of Lee and his army. Duty at Richmond, Va., till June. Consolidated with 188th Pennsylvania Infantry June 28, 1865.

Regiment lost during service 2 Officers and 30 Enlisted men killed and mortally wounded and 52 Enlisted men by disease. Total 84.

200th REGIMENT INFANTRY.

Organized at Harrisburg September 3, 1864. Left State for Bermuda Hundred, Va., September 9. Attached to Engineer Brigade, Army of the Potomac, to October, 1864. Provisional Brigade, Army of the James, to November, 1864. Provisional Brigade, 9th Army Corps, Army of the Potomac, to December, 1864. 1st Brigade, 3rd Division, 9th Army Corps, to May, 1865.

SERVICE.—Duty near Dutch Gap, Va., with Army of the James September 11 to November 28, 1864. Repulse of attack November 19. Transferred to Army Potomac November 28. Siege of Petersburg December, 1864, to April, 1865. Dabney's Mills, Hatcher's Run, February 5-7, 1865. Fort Stedman March 25. Appomattox Campaign March 28-April 9. Assault on and capture of Petersburg April 2. Occupation of Petersburg April 3. Pursuit of Lee April 3-9. Appomattox C. H. April 9. Surrender of Lee and his army. Duty at Nottaway C. H. till May. Ordered to City Point, thence to Alexandria and duty there till May 30. Mustered out May 30, 1865. Recruits transferred to 51st Pennsylvania.

Regiment lost during service 30 Enlisted men killed and mortally wounded and 24 Enlisted men by disease. Total 54.

201st REGIMENT INFANTRY.

Organized at Harrisburg August 29, 1864. Moved to Chambersburg, Pa., September, and duty there till September 28. Company "H" at York, Pa., September 17. Companies "F" and "G" to Bloody Run September 17. Company "E" to Scranton September 18. Rest of Regiment guard Manassas Gap Railroad till November. At Camp Slough, Alexandria, November 13. Company "G" moved to Pittsburg May 24, 1865. Regiment moved to Fort Delaware May 26. Mustered out June 21, 1865.

Regiment lost during service 1 Enlisted man killed and 15 Enlisted men by disease. Total 16.

202nd REGIMENT INFANTRY.

Organized at Harrisburg September 3, 1864. Moved to Chambersburg, Pa., September 10. Attached to Dept. of the Susquehanna to October, 1864. District of Alexandria, 22nd Corps, to November, 1864. 1st Separate Brigade, 22nd Corps, to May, 1865. Dept. of Pennsylvania to August, 1865.

SERVICE.—At Chambersburg, Pa., till September 29, 1864. Moved to Alexandria, Va., via Washington, D. C., September 29. Guard duty on Manassas Gap Railroad from Thoroughfare Gap to Rectortown. Skirmishes at Salem October 8 and 16, 1864. Guarding Orange & Alexandria Railroad from Bull Run to Alexandria. Duty in the Defences of Washington and Alexandria till May, 1865. Ordered to Pennsylvania May 20. Duty in the Lehigh District coal regions of Pennsylvania till July. Mustered out at Harrisburg August 3, 1865.

Regiment lost during service 3 Enlisted men killed and 33 Enlisted men by disease. Total 36.

203rd REGIMENT INFANTRY.

Organized at Philadelphia September 10, 1864. Moved to Petersburg, Va., September 22-27. Attached to 2nd Brigade, 2nd Division, 10th Army Corps, Army of the James, to December, 1864. 2nd Brigade, 2nd Division, 24th Army Corps, to January, 1865. 2nd Brigade, 2nd Division, Terry's Provisional Corps, Dept. North Carolina, to March, 1865. 2nd Brigade, 2nd Division, 10th Army Corps, Dept. of North Carolina, to June, 1865.

SERVICE.—Detached from Brigade and provost at Deep Bottom, Va., and picket at Malvern Hill September 27-October 5. Rejoined Brigade October 5. Siege operations against Richmond till December 7. Battle of Fair Oaks October 27-28. Expedition to Fort Fisher, N. C., December 7-27. 2nd Expedition to Fort Fisher, N. C., January 3-15, 1865. Assault and capture of Fort Fisher January 15. Advance on Wilmington February 11-22. Sugar Loaf Battery February 11. Fort Anderson February 19. Capture of Wilmington February 22. Advance on Goldsboro March 6-21. Guard railroad at Faison's Depot March 21-April 10. Advance on Raleigh April 10-14. Occupation of Raleigh April 14. Bennett's House April 26. Surrender of Johnston and his army. Duty at Raleigh till June. Mustered out June 22, 1865.

Regiment lost during service 4 Officers and 70 Enlisted men killed and mortally wounded and 72 Enlisted men by disease. Total 146.

204th REGIMENT VOLUNTEERS.

(See 5th Regiment Heavy Artillery.)

205th REGIMENT INFANTRY.

Organized at Harrisburg September 2, 1864. Moved to Washington, D. C., September 5, thence to City Point, Va., in charge of 1,300 Recruits. Attached to Provisional Brigade, Defences of Bermuda Hundred, Va., Army of the James, to October, 1864. Hartranft's Provisional Brigade, 9th Army Corps, Army Potomac, to December, 1864. 2nd Brigade, 3rd Division, 9th Army Corps, to June, 1865.

SERVICE.—Siege operations against Petersburg and Richmond, Va., September, 1864, to April, 1865. Duty at City Point, Va., constructing fortifications, till October 9, 1864. Picket with Army of the James till October 29. Join Army Potomac October 29. Movement in support of Weldon Railroad Expedition December 7-11. Dabney's Mills, Hatcher's Run, February 5-7, 1865. Fort Stedman March 25. Appomattox Campaign March 28-April 9. Assault on and fall of Petersburg April 2. Pursuit of Lee to Burkesville. Moved to City Point, thence to Alexandria April 21-28, and duty there till June. Grand Review May 23. Mustered out June 2, 1865.

Regiment lost during service 3 Officers and 37 Enlisted men killed and mortally wounded and 17 Enlisted men by disease. Total 57.

206th REGIMENT INFANTRY.

Organized at Pittsburg September, 1864. Left State for City Point, Va., September 9. Attached to Provisional Brigade, Defences of Bermuda Hundred, Army of the James, to October, 1864. 3rd Brigade, 1st Division, 10th Corps, Army James, to December, 1864. 3rd Brigade, 1st Division, 24th Army Corps, to June, 1865.

SERVICE.—Duty with Engineer Corps engaged in fatigue duty at Dutch Gap, Va., till October 26, 1864. Duty in trenches before Richmond north of the James till April, 1865. Occupation of Richmond April 3. (Temporarily attached to Devens' 3rd Division, March 27 to April 22.) Provost duty at Richmond till May. At Lynchburg and Richmond till June. Mustered out June 26, 1865.

Regiment lost during service 1 Enlisted man killed and 29 Enlisted men by disease. Total 30.

207th REGIMENT INFANTRY.

Organized at Harrisburg September 8, 1864. Left State for City Point, Va., September 12. Attached to Provisional Brigade, Army of the James, to October, 1864. Provisional Brigade, 9th Army Corps, Army of the Potomac, to December, 1864. 2nd Brigade, 3rd Division, 9th Army Corps, to May, 1865.

SERVICE.—Siege operations against Petersburg and Richmond, Va., September, 1864, to April, 1865. Picketing Bermuda Hundred front from the James to the Appomattox. Joined Army of the Potomac November. Movement in support of Weldon Railroad Expedition December 7-11. Dabney's Mills, Hatcher's Run, February 5-7, 1865. Fort Stedman March 25. Appomattox Campaign March 28-April 9. Assault on and fall of Petersburg April 2. Pursuit of Lee to Burkesville April 3-9. Moved to City Point, thence to Alexandria April 21-28, and duty there till May 31. Grand Review May 23. Mustered out May 31, 1865.

Regiment lost during service 3 Officers and 51 Enlisted men killed and mortally wounded and 1 Officer and 24 Enlisted men by disease. Total 79.

208th REGIMENT INFANTRY.

Organized at Harrisburg August 16-September 12, 1864. Left State for Bermuda Hundred, Va., September 13. Attached to Provisional Brigade, Defences of Bermuda Hundred, Army of the James, to November, 1864. Provisional Brigade, 9th Army Corps, Army Potomac, to December, 1864. 1st Brigade, 3rd Division, 9th Army Corps, to June, 1865.

SERVICE.—Siege operations against Petersburg and Richmond, Va., September, 1864, to April, 1865. Picket and fatigue duty on the Bermuda Hundred front till November 27, 1864. Joined Army Potomac before Petersburg. Movement in support of Weldon Railroad Expedition December 7-11. Dabney's Mills, Hatcher's Run,

February 5-7, 1865. Fort Stedman March 25. Appomattox Campaign March 28-April 9. Assault on and capture of Petersburg April 2. Pursuit of Lee April 3-9. At Nottaway C. H. April 9-20. Moved to City Point, thence to Alexandria April 20-28. Duty at Alexandria till June. Grand Review May 23. Mustered out June 1, 1865.

Regiment lost during service 2 Officers and 19 Enlisted men killed and mortally wounded and 7 Enlisted men by disease. Total 28.

209th REGIMENT INFANTRY.

Organized at Harrisburg September 16, 1864. Left State for Bermuda Hundred, Va., September 17. Attached to Provisional Brigade, Defences of Bermuda Hundred, Army of the James, to November, 1864. Hartranft's Provisional Brigade, 9th Army Corps, Army Potomac, to December, 1864. 1st Brigade, 3rd Division, 9th Army Corps, to May, 1865.

SERVICE.—Siege operations against Petersburg and Richmond, Va., September, 1864, to April, 1865. Duty in the Defences of Bermuda Hundred, Va., till November 27, 1864. Joined Army Potomac before Petersburg. Movement in support of Weldon Railroad Expedition December 7-11. Dabney's Mills, Hatcher's Run, February 5-7, 1865. Fort Stedman March 25. Assault on and fall of Petersburg April 2. Pursuit of Lee April 3-9. At Nottaway C. H. April 9-20. Moved to City Point, thence to Alexandria April 20-28, and duty there till May 31. Grand Review May 23. Mustered out May 31, 1865.

Regiment lost during service 2 Officers and 17 Enlisted men killed and mortally wounded and 20 Enlisted men by disease. Total 39.

210th REGIMENT INFANTRY.

Organized at Harrisburg September 12-24, 1864. Ordered to join Army Potomac before Petersburg, Va. Attached to 3rd Brigade, 2nd Division, 5th Army Corps, Army Potomac.

SERVICE.—Siege of Petersburg, Va., October, 1864, to April, 1865. Boydton Plank Road, Hatcher's Run October 27-28, 1864. Warren's Raid on Weldon Railroad December 7-12. Dabney's Mills, Hatcher's Run, February 5-7, 1865. Appomattox Campaign March 28-April 9. Lewis Farm near Gravelly Run March 29. White Oak Road March 30-31. Five Forks April 1. Appomattox C. H. April 9. Surrender of Lee and his army. March to Washington, D. C., May 1-12. Grand Review May 23. Mustered out May 30, 1865.

Regiment lost during service 3 Officers and 37 Enlisted men killed and mortally wounded and 1 Officer and 44 Enlisted men by disease. Total 85.

211th REGIMENT INFANTRY.

Organized at Pittsburg September 16, 1864. Moved to Bermuda Hundred, Va., September and attached to Provisional Brigade, Defences of Bermuda Hundred, Army James, to November, 1864. Provisional Brigade, 9th Army Corps, Army Potomac, to December, 1864. 2nd Brigade, 3rd Division, 9th Army Corps, to June, 1865.

SERVICE.—Siege operations against Petersburg and Richmond, Va., September, 1864, to April, 1865. Duty in the Defences of Bermuda Hundred, Va., till November, 1864. Joined Army of the Potomac before Petersburg November 28. Movement in support of Weldon Railroad Expedition December 7-11. Dabney's Mills, Hatcher's Run, February 5-7, 1865. Fort Stedman March 25. Appomattox Campaign March 28-April 9. Assault on and fall of Petersburg April 2. Pursuit of Lee April 3-9. At Nottaway C. H. till April 20. Moved to City Point, thence to Alexandria April 20-28, and duty there till June. Grand Review May 23. Mustered out June 2, 1865.

Regiment lost during service 6 Officers and 38 Enlisted men killed and mortally wounded and 53 Enlisted men by disease. Total 97.

212th REGIMENT VOLUNTEERS.

(See 6th Regiment Heavy Artillery.)

213th REGIMENT INFANTRY.

Organized at Philadelphia February 4 to March 2, 1865. Moved to Annapolis, Md., March 4. Guard duty at Camp Parole till April. Duty at Frederick, Md., and on line of Baltimore & Ohio Railroad. Ordered to Washington, D. C., and duty in northern defences till November. Mustered out November 18, 1865.

Regiment lost during service 18 by disease.

214th REGIMENT INFANTRY.

Organized at Philadelphia March, 1865, and ordered to the Shenandoah Valley, Va. Attached to 2nd Brigade, 3rd Division, Army Shenandoah, to July, 1865. Garrison of Washington, 22nd Corps, to March, 1866.

SERVICE.—Guard and provost duty in the Shenandoah Valley till July, 1865, and garrison duty at Washington till March, 1866. Mustered out March 21, 1866.

Regiment lost 24 by disease.

215th REGIMENT INFANTRY.

Organized at Philadelphia April, 1865. Duty in Delaware and at Fort Delaware till July, 1865. Mustered out July 31, 1865.

Lost 11 by disease.

INDEPENDENT BATTALION MILITIA INFANTRY.

Organized at Huntingdon July 18, 1863. Mustered out August 8, 1863.

LETZINGER'S BATTALION MILITIA INFANTRY.

Organized June 23, 1863. Mustered out August 8, 1863.

LININGER'S BATTALION MILITIA INFANTRY.

Organized July 23, 1863. Mustered out January 21, 1864.

McKEAG'S BATTALION MILITIA INFANTRY.

Organized July 3, 1863. Mustered out August 8, 1863.

ZELL'S BATTALION MILITIA INFANTRY.

Organized July 23, 1863. Mustered out January 29, 1864.

BALDWIN'S INDEPENDENT COMPANY MILITIA INFANTRY.

Organized at Garland August 9, 1862. Mustered out June 5, 1863.

BEALE'S INDEPENDENT COMPANY MILITIA INFANTRY.

Organized at Philadelphia November 14, 1862. Mustered out August 15, 1863.

CAMPBELL'S INDEPENDENT COMPANY MILITIA INFANTRY.

Organized at Philadelphia July 2, 1863. Mustered out September 16, 1863.

CARSON'S INDEPENDENT COMPANY MILITIA INFANTRY.

GERMAN'S INDEPENDENT COMPANY MILITIA INFANTRY.

Organized at Philadelphia June 18, 1863. Mustered out July 23, 1863.

GREEN'S INDEPENDENT COMPANY MILITIA INFANTRY.

Organized at West Chester July 6, 1863. Mustered out September 4, 1863.

GUTHRIE'S INDEPENDENT COMPANY MILITIA INFANTRY.

Organized at Pittsburg October 16, 1862. Mustered out July 23, 1863.

COLLIS' INDEPENDENT COMPANY "ZOUAVES DE AFRIQUE."

Organized at Philadelphia and mustered in August 17, 1861. Moved to Fort Delaware August 17, thence to Frederick, Md., September 25, thence to Darnestown. Attached to Banks' Division, Dept. Shenandoah, September, 1861. Banks' Division, Army Potomac, to March, 1862. Banks' 5th Corps, and Dept. of the Shenandoah, March, 1862. Geary's Independent Brigade to April, 1862. 3rd Brigade, 1st Division, Dept. of the Shenandoah, to June, 1862. Unattached, 2nd Corps, Army Virginia, June, 1862. 3rd Brigade, 1st Division, 2nd Corps, to August, 1862.

SERVICE.—Duty on the Upper Potomac till February, 1862. Moved to Edward's Ferry October 21, 1861, thence to Muddy Branch October 26. Duty there till December 2. At Frederick, Md., till February 22, 1862. Advance on Winchester March 1-12. Occupation of Winchester March 12. March to Warrenton Junction with Abercrombie's Brigade, then with Geary at Rectortown. Rejoined Banks at Strasburg May. Operations in the Shenandoah Valley May 15-June 17. Strasburg May 24. Middletown May 24. Retreat to Williamsport May 24-26. Battle of Winchester May 25. At Williamsport till June 10. Moved to Front Royal, thence to Warrenton and Little Washington June 10-18. Battle of Cedar Mountain August 9. Transferred to 114th Pennsylvania Infantry as Company "A" August, 1862. See 114th Pennsylvania Infantry.

DEPARTMENTAL CORPS (FOUR COMPANIES).

Organized in the Dept. of the Monongahela June 24 to October 15, 1863, to serve during the pleasure of the President. Mustered out July 21 to November 1, 1864.

GRIFFITH'S INDEPENDENT COMPANY INFANTRY.

Organized at Pittsburg June and July, 1863. Mustered out January 29, 1864.

JAMES' INDEPENDENT COMPANY INFANTRY ("WARREN COUNTY RIFLES").

Organized at Warren August and September, 1862. Provost duty at Harrisburg, Pa., till March, 1863. Provost duty at Washington and Alexandria, Defences of Washington, 22nd Corps, till July, 1865. Mustered out July 20, 1865.

JONES' INDEPENDENT COMPANY INFANTRY.

Organized at Harrisburg October 2, 1862. Mustered out July 9, 1863.

TANNER'S INDEPENDENT COMPANY INFANTRY.

Organized at Pittsburg August 30, 1864. Mustered out December 10, 1864.

"ZOUAVES DE AFRIQUE," INDEPENDENT COMPANY INFANTRY.

(See Collis' Independent Company Infantry.)

HELMBOLD'S INDEPENDENT COMPANY MILITIA INFANTRY.

Organized at Harrisburg July 18, 1863. Mustered out September 7, 1863.

HUBBELL'S INDEPENDENT COMPANY MILITIA INFANTRY.

Organized at Philadelphia November 14, 1862. Mustered out August 15, 1863.

HUFF'S INDEPENDENT COMPANY MILITIA INFANTRY.

Organized at Altoona July 1, 1863. Mustered out August, 1863.

LUTHER'S INDEPENDENT COMPANY MILITIA INFANTRY.

Organized at Harrisburg October, 1862, and February, 1863. Mustered out July, 1863.

McKNIGHT'S INDEPENDENT COMPANY MILITIA INFANTRY.

Organized at Philadelphia July 11, 1863. Mustered out August, 1863.

MANN'S INDEPENDENT COMPANY MILITIA INFANTRY.

Organized at Philadelphia June 17, 1863. Mustered out July 24, 1863.

MITCHELL'S INDEPENDENT COMPANY MILITIA INFANTRY.

Organized at Harrisburg July 18, 1863. Mustered out September 2, 1863.

RICH'S INDEPENDENT COMPANY MILITIA INFANTRY.

Organized at Philadelphia June 29, 1863. Mustered out July 8, 1863.

ROBERTS' INDEPENDENT COMPANY MILITIA INFANTRY.

Organized at West Chester July 1, 1863. Mustered out July 8, 1863.

SPEAR'S INDEPENDENT COMPANY MILITIA INFANTRY.

Organized at Philadelphia June 17, 1863. Mustered out July 21, 1863.

STEPHENS' INDEPENDENT COMPANY MILITIA INFANTRY.

Organized at Lancaster July 2, 1863. Mustered out July 30, 1863.

RHODE ISLAND VOLUNTEERS.

1st REGIMENT CAVALRY.

Organized at Pawtucket as 1st New England Cavalry, afterwards designated 1st Rhode Island Cavalry, December 14, 1861, to March 3, 1862. Left State for Washington, D. C., March 12 and 14, 1862. Attached to Stoneman's Cavalry Command, Army of the Potomac, March, 1862. Hatch's Cavalry Brigade, Banks' 5th Corps, and Dept. of the Shenandoah. to May, 1862. Shields' Division, Dept. of the Rappahannock (3rd Battalion); Geary's Command, Dept. of the Rappahannock (1st Battalion), to June, 1862. Bayard's Cavalry Brigade, 3rd Corps, Army of Virginia, to September, 1862. Stoneman's Corps of Observation to December, 1862. Averill's Cavalry Brigade, Centre Grand Division, Army of the Potomac, to February, 1863. 1st Brigade, 2nd Division, Cavalry Corps, Army Potomac, to January, 1864. Cavalry Brigade, Camp Stoneman, 22nd Army Corps, to May, 1864. Abercrombie's Command, Belle Plains, Va., to June, 1864. Reserve Brigade, 1st Division, Cavalry Corps, Army Potomac, to August, 1864. Headquarters Cavalry Corps, Army of the Shenandoah, Middle Military Division, to October, 1864. 3rd (Reserve) Brigade, 1st Division, Cavalry Corps, Army Shenandoah, to March, 1865. Cavalry Brigade, Army Shenandoah, to June, 1865. Middle Dept. to August, 1865.

SERVICE.—Duty in the Defences of Washington, D. C., till April. 1862. Moved to Warrenton Junction, Va., April 4. Reconnoissance to Rappahannock River April 16 (3rd Battalion). Warrenton Junction April 16. Reconnoissance to Liberty Church April 16. Occupation of Mt. Jackson April 17 (4 Cos.). Reconnoissance to Rappahannock Crossing April 18 (4 Cos.). Advance to Front Royal May 29. Front Royal May 30 (3rd Battalion). Strasburg June 1. Columbia Bridge April 2. Edenburg June 3. Miller's Bridge June 4. New Market June 5. Harrisonburg June 6. Cross Keys June 8. Port Republic and Mountain Road June 9. Scouting on the Rappahannock till August. Reconnoissance to James City July 22-24. Rapidan River August 3-4. Slaughter River August 7. Robinson's River August 8. Battle of Cedar Mountain August 9. Pope's Campaign in Northern Virginia August 16-September 2. Stevensburg, Raccoon Ford and Brandy Station August 20. Fords of the Rappahannock August 21-23. Catlett's Station August 22. Rappahannock Station August 23. New Baltimore August 27. Gainesville August 28. Bull Run August 30. Centreville, Chantilly and Germantown August 31. Chantilly September 1. White's Ford September 15 and October 12. Advance to Falmouth, Va., October 27. Mountsville October 31 (Cos. "K," "L" and "M"). Hazel Run November 16. Battle of Fredericksburg December 12-15 (Cos. "K" and "M"). Expedition to Richards and Ellis Fords December 29-30.

Hartwood Church February 25, 1863. Kelly's Ford March 17. Chancellorsville Campaign April 27-May 8. Stoneman's Raid April 29-May 8. Kelly's Ford April 29. Rapidan Station May 1. Ellis Ford May 4. Stevensburg, Beverly Ford and Brandy Station June 9. Near Middleburg and Thoroughfare Gap June 17. Aldie June 18 and 27. Battle of Gettysburg, Pa., July 1-3. Scouting and outpost duty on Upper Potomac till September. Advance from Rapidan to the Rappahannock September 13-17. Culpeper Court House September 13. Rapidan Station September 15. Bristoe Campaign October 9-22. Near Warrenton October 12. White Sulphur Springs, Culpeper, October 12-13. Auburn and Bristoe October 14. Brentsville October 14. Mine Run Campaign November 26-December 2. New Hope Church November 27. Duty in the Defences of Washington till May, 1864. (3rd Battalion transferred to 1st New Hampshire Cavalry January 5, 1864.) Regiment reported to Gen. Abercrombie at Belle Plain, Va., May 14. Picket duty at Port Conway and Port Royal May 24-30. Bowling Green May 29. Demonstration north of the James July 27-29. Deep Bottom July 27-28. Malvern Hill July 28. Sheridan's Shenandoah Valley Campaign August 7-November 28. Shepherdstown August 25-26. Kearneysville August 25. Smithfield August 29. Battle of Opequan, Winchester, September 19. Fisher's Hill and Milford September 21-22. Brown's Gap September 24. Waynesboro September 29. Battle of Cedar Creek October 19. Raid to Gordonsville December 8-28. Jack's Shop, near Gordonsville, December 23. Consolidated to a Battalion of 4 Companies January 1, 1865. Sheridan's Raid from Winchester February 27-March 3. Waynesboro March 2. Guard prisoners from Waynesboro to Winchester March 3-8. Duty in the Shenandoah Valley till June 22. At Monrovia Station and Relay House, Md., till August. Mustered out at Baltimore, Md., August 3, 1865.

Regiment lost during service 1 Officer and 16 Enlisted men killed and mortally wounded and 2 Officers and 77 Enlisted men by disease. Total 96.

2nd REGIMENT CAVALRY.

Organized at Providence November 21, 1862. Ordered to New Orleans, La., and duty there till March, 1863. Attached to 1st Division, 19th Army Corps, Dept. of the Gulf, to July, 1863. Cavalry Brigade, 19th Army Corps, to August, 1863.

SERVICE.—Moved to Baton Rouge, La., March 6-7, 1863. Operations against Port Hudson March 7-27. Moved to Algiers, thence to Berwick April 1-9. Operations in Western Louisiana April 9-May 14. Teche Campaign April 11-20. Franklin April 14. Near Washington May 1. Expedition from Opelousas to Alexandria and Simsport May 5-18. Operations about Monett's Plantation and on Bayou Sara Road May 18-19. Moved to Bayou Sara, thence to Port Hudson May 22-25. Siege of Port Hudson May 25-July 9. Jackson Cross Roads June 20. Springfield Landing July 2. Surrender of Port Hudson July 9. Consolidated to a Battalion of 4 Companies August 24, 1863, and transferred to 1st Louisiana Cavalry August 24, 1863. Camp Hubbard, Thibodeaux, August 29-30. Again transferred to 3rd Rhode Island Cavalry January 14, 1864.

Regiment lost during service 4 Enlisted men killed and 31 by disease. Total 35.

3rd REGIMENT CAVALRY.

Organized at Providence September 12, 1863. 1st Battalion moved to New Orleans, La., December 31, 1863, to January 14, 1864. Attached to Defences of New Orleans, Dept. Gulf, to March, 1864. 5th Brigade, Cavalry Division, Dept. of the Gulf, to June, 1864. Defences of New Orleans, La., to October, 1864. District of LaFourche, Dept. Gulf, to November, 1865.

SERVICE.—Red River Campaign March 10-May 22, 1864. Advance to Alexandria March 14-26. Monett's Ferry and Cloutiersville March 29-30. Natchitoches March 31. Campti April 4. Sabine Cross Roads April 8. Pleasant Hill April 9. Natchitoches April 19. (Cos. "E," "F" and "L" moved to join Regiment at Alexandria April 20-22.) Action at Tunica Bend April 21. About Cloutierville April 22-24. Monett's Ferry or Cane River Crossing April 23. Gov. Moore's Plantation May 1-2. Alexandria May 11-12. Retreat from Alexandria to Morganza May 13-20. Natchitoches May 14. Mansura May 16. Near Moreauville May 17. Yellow Bayou May 18. Near Morganza May 24. Reached Fort Banks, opposite New Orleans, June 2. Companies "G" and "H" reported at New Orleans May 8 and joined Regiment at Greenville June 10. Regiment dismounted June 22, and duty as Infantry in the Defences of New Orleans till September. Remounted September 20. Assigned to duty in the District of LaFourche at Donaldsonville, Napoleonville, Thibodeaux, Camp Parapet, Plaquemine, Houma, Hermitage Plantation and other points in Louisiana, scouting and patrol duty and operating against guerrillas, till November, 1865. Action at Napoleonville November 1, 1864, and at Doyall's Plantation November 29, 1864 (Detachment). Expedition from Brashear City to Whiskey Bayou January 16-18, 1865 (Cos. "B," "I" and "K"). Expedition from Napoleonville to Grand River January 18-19 (Detachment). Scout from Donaldsonville January 19-20 (Detachment). Skirmish, Thompson's Plantation, January 23. Scouts from Bayou Goula to Grand River January 29-February 7. Skirmish, Richland Plantation, January 30. Expedition from Thibodeaux to Lake Verret and Bayou Planton January 30-31 (Co. "H"). Near Lake Verret January 30. Skirmish, Kittredge's Sugar House, near Napoleon, February 10. Expedition from Donaldsonville to Grand Bayou and Bayou Goula February 14-18. Skirmish, Martin's Lane, February 15 (Cos. "D," "F" and "K"). Expediton from Plaquemine to the Park February 17-22 (Detachment). Expedition from the Hermitage to the French Settlement April 2-5 (Detachment). Expedition to Lake Verret, Grand Bayou, etc., April 2-10. Expedition from Terre Bonne to Pelton's Plantation and Grand Caillou April 19-25 (Co. "M"). Operations about Brashear City April 30-May 12. Bayou Goula May 9. Expedition from Bayou Boeuf to Bayou de Large May 25-27. Affair, Bayou de Large, May 27. Mustered out November 29, 1865.

Lost during service 8 Enlisted men killed and 4 Officers and 135 Enlisted men by disease. Total 147.

7th SQUADRON CAVALRY.

Organized at Providence and mustered in for three months June 24, 1862. Moved to Washington, D. C., June 28-30. Attached to Military District of Washington, Wadsworth's Command, to July, 1862. Sturgis' Command. Military District of Washington, to August, 1862. Winchester, Va., to September, 1862. Miles' Command, Harper's Ferry, W. Va., September, 1862.

SERVICE.—Duty at Camp Clark and Camp Sprague, Defences of Washington, till July 25, 1862. Moved to Alexandria, Va., July 25, thence to Winchester, Va., August 1. Duty at Camp Sigel, Winchester, till September 3. Retreat to Newtown and Middleburg, thence to Harper's Ferry, W. Va., September 3-4. Maryland Heights September 12-13. Defence of Harper's Ferry September 13-15. Escaped through enemy's lines September 15 and participated in the capture of 100 wagons of Longstreet's train September 16. Mustered out September 26, 1862, expiration of term.

3rd REGIMENT HEAVY ARTILLERY.

Organized at Providence as 3rd Infantry August, 1861, but reorganized at Hilton Head, S. C., as Heavy Artillery December 19, 1861. (See Batteries.)

Regiment lost during service 2 Officers and 39 Enlisted men killed and mortally wounded and 4 Officers and 90 Enlisted men by disease. Total 135.

BATTERY "A."

Attached to Sherman's Expeditionary Corps to April, 1862. 3rd Brigade, 1st Division, Dept. of the South, to July, 1862. U. S. Forces Hilton Head, S. C., Dept. South, to September, 1862. U. S. Forces Hilton Head, S. C., 10th Corps, Dept. South, to January, 1863. District of Beaufort, S. C., 10th Corps, to November, 1863. Morris Island. S. C., 10th Corps, Dept. South, to December, 1863. Folly Island, S. C., 10th Corps, to January, 1864. District of Hilton Head, S. C., 10th Corps, to April, 1864. District of Florida, Dept. South, to October, 1864. District of Beaufort, S. C., 2nd Separate Brigade, Dept. of the South, to November, 1864. Artillery Brigade, Coast Division, Dept. of the South, to January, 1865. District of Beaufort, 2nd Separate Brigade, Dept. of the South, and Dept. of South Carolina, to August, 1865.

SERVICE.—Duty at Hilton Head, S. C., till January, 1863. Action at Whitmarsh and Wilmington Islands April 16, 1862. At Beaufort, S. C., till November, 1863. Moved to Morris Island, S. C., November 14-16, and operations against Charleston, S. C., from Morris and Folly Islands, till December, 1863. Moved to Hilton Head, S. C., and duty there till April, 1864. Moved to Jacksonville, Fla., and duty there till October, 1864. Expedition from Jacksonville to Finnegan's Camp May 25. Cedar Creek May 25. Expedition from Jacksonville to Camp Milton May 31-June 3. Expedition to Baldwin July 23-28. South Fork Black Creek July 24. Near Whitesides July 27. Raid on Florida Railroad August 15-19. Engagement at Gainesville August 17. Moved to Beaufort, S. C., October, and duty there till November 29. Expedition to Boyd's Neck November 29-30. Battle of Honey Hill November 30. Demonstration on Charleston & Savannah Railroad December 6-9. Deveaux Neck December 6 and December 27. Duty at Beaufort, S. C., till May, 1865, and in Dept. of the South till August, 1865. Mustered out August 27, 1865.

BATTERY "B."

Attached to Sherman's Expeditionary Corps to April, 1862. 3rd Brigade, 1st Division, Dept. of the South, to July, 1862. U. S. Forces, Hilton Head, S. C., Dept. South to September, 1862. U. S. Forces, Hilton Head, S. C., 10th Corps, Dept. of the South, to July, 1863. U. S. Forces, Morris Island, S. C., 10th Army Corps, Dept. South, to March, 1864. District of Hilton Head, S. C., Dept. South, to October, 1864. Morris Island, S. C., Northern District, Dept. South, 1st Separate Brigade, to August, 1865.

SERVICE.—Duty at Hilton Head, S. C., till February, 1862. Operations against Fort Pulaski, Ga., February 21-April 10. Bombardment and capture of Fort Pulaski April 9-10. At Hilton Head till May 23. Moved to Edisto Island, S. C., May 23. Operations on James Island, S. C., June 1-28. Action on James Island June 10. Battle of Secessionville June 16. Moved to Hilton Head, S. C., June 28-July 1, and duty there till July, 1863. Assaults on Fort Wagner, Morris Island, July 11 and 18. Siege of Fort Wagner, Morris Island, July 18-September 7. Capture of Forts Wagner and Gregg September 7. Operations against Fort Sumpter and Charleston till March, 1864. Duty at Hilton Head, S. C., till October, 1864. Operations against Charleston from Morris Island, S. C., till February, 1865. Duty at Sullivan's Island, S. C., and in the Dept. of South Carolina till August. Mustered out August 27, 1865.

BATTERY "C."

Attached to Sherman's Expeditionary Corps to April, 1862. 3rd Brigade, 1st Division, Dept. of the South, to July, 1862. U. S. Forces, Hilton Head, S. C., Dept. South, to September, 1862. U. S. Forces, Hilton Head, S. C., 10th Corps, Dept. South, to January, 1863. District of Beaufort, S. C., 10th Corps, to June, 1863. St. Helena Island, S. C., 10th Corps, to July, 1863. U. S. Forces, Morris Island, S. C., 10th Corps, to October, 1863. Artillery, Gordon's Division, Folly Island, S. C., 10th Corps, to December, 1863. District of Hilton Head, S. C., 10th Corps, to February, 1864. Artillery, District of Florida, Dept. South, to April, 1864. Artillery, 3rd Division, 10th Army Corps, Dept. of Virginia and North Carolina, to May, 1864. Unattached Artillery, 10th Corps, Dept. of Virginia and North Carolina, to June, 1864. Artillery, 1st Division, 10th Army Corps, Dept. of Virginia and North Carolina, to August, 1864. Artillery Brigade, 10th Corps, Dept. Virginia and North Carolina, to December, 1864. Artillery Brigade, 25th Army Corps, Dept. of Virginia, to June, 1865.

SERVICE.—Action at Port Royal Ferry, S. C., December 29, 1861. Venus Point February 15, 1862. Moved to Edisto Island, S. C., April 5. Operations on James Island, S. C., June 1-28. Action James Island June 10. Battle of Secessionville June 16. Moved to Hilton Head, S. C., June 28-July 1, and duty there till October. Expedition to Pocotaligo, S. C., October 21-23. Action at Caston and Frampton's Plantation, near Pocotaligo, October 22. Coosawhatchie October 22. At Hilton Head, S. C., till January, 1863, and at Beaufort, S. C., till June, 1863. Broad River April 8. Port Royal Ferry April 9. Combahee River June 1. Combahee Ferry June 2. Expedition to Darien June 5-24. Moved to St. Helena Island, S. C., thence to Folly Island, S. C., July 4-5. Attack on Morris Island, S. C., July 10. Operations against Forts Wagner and Gregg and against Fort Sumpter and Charleston, S. C., till December. Capture of Forts Wagner and Gregg September 7. Moved to Hilton Head, S. C., and duty there till February, 1864. Expedition to Jacksonville, Fla., February 5-7, and to Lake City February 7-22. Battle of Olustee February 20. Occupation of Palatka March 10. Duty at Jacksonville till April 30. Moved to Yorktown, Va., April 30. Butler's operations on south side of James River and against Petersburg and Richmond May 5-June 15. Operations against Fort Darling May 12-16. Battle of Drewry's Bluff May 14-16. On Bermuda Hundred front May 17-June 15. Appomattox River May 28-31 and June 5. Before Petersburg June 15-19. Siege of Petersburg and Richmond June 16, 1864, to April 2, 1865. Demonstration on north side of the James August 13-20, 1864. Strawberry Plains, Deep Bottom, August 14-18. Laurel Hill August 17. Chaffin's Farm September 28-30. Darbytown and New Market Roads October 7. Fort Burnham December 10 and January 24, 1865. Fall of Petersburg and Richmond April 2-3. Duty in the Dept. of Virginia till June. Mustered out June 9, 1865.

BATTERY "D."

Attached to Sherman's Expeditionary Corps, to April, 1862. 3rd Brigade, 1st Division, Dept. of the South, to July, 1862. District of Hilton Head, S. C., Dept. South, to September, 1862. District Hilton Head, S. C., 10th Corps, Dept. South, to April, 1863. U. S. Forces, Folly Island, S. C., 10th Corps, Dept. South, to July, 1863. U. S. Forces, Morris Island, S. C., 10th Corps, Dept. South, to March, 1864. Fort Pulaski, Ga., District Hilton Head, S. C., Dept. of the South, to October, 1864.

SERVICE.—Duty at Hilton Head, S. C., till April, 1863. Expedition to Stono Inlet April 2-11, 1862. Moved to Folly Island, S. C., April, 1863, and duty there till July, 1863. Attack on Morris Island July 10. Assaults on Fort Wagner, Morris Island, S. C., July 11 and 18. Siege operations against Forts Wagner and Gregg, Morris Island, and against Charleston till March, 1864. Capture of Forts Wagner and Gregg September 7, 1863. Moved to Fort Pulaski, Ga., March 18, 1864, and garrison duty there till September. Moved to Hilton Head, S. C., thence to New York and Providence September 26-30. Mustered out October 4, 1864. A new Battery "D" consolidated Battalion, organized by transfers March 10, 1865. Attached to 1st Separate Brigade, Morris Island, S. C., Northern District, Dept. of the South, and duty on Morris Island, and in the Dept. of the South, till August. Mustered out August 27, 1865.

BATTERY "E."

Attached to Sherman's Expeditionary Corps to April, 1862. 3rd Brigade, 1st Division, Dept. of the South, to July, 1862. District of Hilton Head, S. C., Dept. of the South, to September, 1862. District of Hilton Head, S. C., 10th Corps, Dept. of the South, to November, 1863. Morris Island, S. C., 10th Corps, Dept. of the South, to April, 1864. Morris Island, S. C., Northern District, Dept. of the South, to October, 1864.

SERVICE.—Duty at Hilton Head, S. C., till May, 1862. Whitmarsh and Wilmington Islands April 16. Moved to Edisto Island, S. C., May 23. Operations on James Island, S. C., June 1-28. Action on James Island June 10. Battle of Secessionville June 16. Moved to Hilton Head, S. C., June 28-July 1, and duty there till November, 1863. Expedition to Pocotaligo, S. C., October 21-23, 1862. Actions at Caston's and Frampton's Plantations near Pocotaligo and Coosawhatchie River October 22, 1862. Ordered to Morris Island, S. C., November, 1863, and duty there operating against Fort Sumpter and Charleston, S. C., till September, 1864. Actions on James Island, S. C., July 1-2, and Fort Johnson July 3. Moved to Hilton Head, S. C., thence to New York and Providence September 26-30. Mustered out October 4, 1864.

BATTERY "F."

Attached to Sherman's Expeditionary Corps to April, 1862. 3rd Brigade, 1st Division, Dept. of the South, to July, 1862. District of Hilton Head, S. C., Dept. of the South, to September, 1862. District of Hilton Head, S. C., 10th Corps, Dept. of the South, to December, 1863. Tybee Island, S. C., 10th Corps, Dept. of the South, to March, 1864. Morris Island, S. C., Northern District, Dept. of the South, to September, 1864.

SERVICE.—Duty at Hilton Head, S. C., till February, 1862. Operations against Fort Pulaski, Ga., February 21-April 10. Bombardment and capture of Fort Pulaski April 9-10. Moved to Hilton Head, thence to Edisto Island, S. C., May 23. Operations on James Island, S. C., June 1-28. Action on James Island June 10. Battle of Secessionville June 16. Moved to Hilton Head, S. C., June 28-July 1, and duty there till December, 1863. Moved to Tybee Island, S. C., December, 1863, and duty there till March, 1864. Moved to Morris Island, S. C., March 18, and duty there operating against Fort Sumpter and Charleston till September. Actions on James Island July 1-2, and at Fort Johnson July 3. Moved to Hilton Head, S. C., thence to New York and Providence September 26-30. Mustered out October 4, 1864.

BATTERY "G."

Attached to Sherman's Expeditionary Corps to April, 1862. District of Hilton Head, S. C., Dept. of the South, to May, 1862. Garrison Fort Pulaski, Ga., to September, 1862. Fort Pulaski, Ga., District Hilton Head, S. C., 10th Corps, Dept. of the South, to April, 1864. Tybee Island, District of Hilton Head, S. C., Dept. of the South, to September, 1864.

SERVICE.—Duty at Hilton Head, S. C., till May, 1862. Assigned to duty at Fort Pulaski, Ga., as garrison, May, 1862, to March, 1864. Near Bluffton August 29, 1862. Affair on Skull Creek September 24, 1862. Reconnoissance on May and Savannah Rivers September 30-October 3, 1862. Affair Kirk's Bluff October 18. Expedition to Pocotaligo October 21-22, 1862. Actions at Caston and Frampton's Plantations and Coosawhatchie River October 22. Moved to Tybee Island March 18, 1864, and duty there till September. Moved to Hilton Head, thence to New York and Providence September 26-30. Mustered out October 4, 1864.

BATTERY "H."

Attached to Sherman's Expeditionary Corps to April, 1862. 3rd Brigade, 1st Division, Dept. of the South, to July, 1862. District of Hilton Head, S. C., Dept. of the South, to September, 1862. District of Hilton Head, S. C., 10th Corps, Dept. of the South, to July, 1863. Morris Island, S. C., 10th Corps, to April, 1864. Morris Island, S. C., Northern District, Dept. of the South, to September, 1864.

SERVICE.—At Hilton Head, S. C., till February, 1862. Operations against Fort Pulaski, Ga., February 21-April 10. Bombardment and capture of Fort Pulaski April 9-10. Escort captured garrison to Hilton Head, and duty there till May. Moved to Edisto Island May 23. Operations on James Island, S. C., June 1-28. Action James Island June 10. Battle of Secessionville June 16. Moved to Hilton Head, S. C., June 28-July 1, and duty there till July, 1863. Moved to Folly Island, S. C. Attack on Morris Island July 10. Assaults on Fort Wagner, Morris Island, July 11 and 18. Siege of Forts Wagner and Gregg, Morris Island, July 18-September 7. Capture of Forts Wagner and Gregg September 7. Operations against Fort Sumpter and Charleston from Morris and Folly Islands till September, 1864. Actions on James Island July 1-2, and at Fort Johnson July 3. Moved to Hilton Head, thence to New York and Providence September 26-30. Mustered out October 4, 1864.

BATTERY "I."

Attached to Sherman's Expeditionary Corps to April, 1862. 3rd Brigade, 1st Division, Dept. of the South, to July, 1862. District of Hilton Head, S. C., Dept. South, to September, 1862. District of Hilton Head, S. C., 10th Corps, Dept. of the South, to April, 1864. U. S. Forces, Folly Island, S. C., 10th Corps, to July, 1863. Morris Island, 10th Corps, to April, 1864. Morris Island, S. C., Northern District, Dept. of the South, to September, 1864.

SERVICE.—At Hilton Head till December, 1861. Garrison Fort Drayton, Otter Island, S. C., till May, 1862. Duty at Hilton Head till April, 1863. Moved to Folly Island, S. C., and duty there till July, 1863. Attack on Morris Island, S. C., July 10. Assaults on Fort Wagner, Morris Island, July 11 and 18. Siege of Fort Wagner July 18-September 7. Capture of Forts Wagner and Gregg, Morris Island, September 7. Siege operations against Fort Sumpter and Charleston, S. C., from Morris and Folly Islands till September, 1864. Actions on James Island July 1-2, and at Fort Johnson July 3. Moved to Hilton Head, S. C., thence to New York and Providence September 26-30. Mustered out October 4, 1864.

BATTERY "K."

Attached to Sherman's Expeditionary Corps to April, 1862. 3rd Brigade, 1st Division, Dept. of the South, to July, 1862. District of Hilton Head, S. C., Dept. of the South, to September, 1862. District of Hilton Head, S. C., 10th Corps, Dept. of the South, to December, 1863. Fort Pulaski, Ga., District of Hilton Head, S. C., Dept. of the South, to September, 1864.

SERVICE.—Duty at Hilton Head, S. C., till May, 1862. Moved to Edisto Island, S. C., May 23. Operations on James Island, S. C., June 1-30. Action on James Island June 10. Battle of Secessionville June 16. Moved to Hilton Head, S. C., June 28-July 1, and duty there till December, 1863. Expedition to Pocotaligo, S. C., October 21-23, 1862. Actions at Caston's and Frampton's Plantations and Coosawhatchie October 22. Moved to Fort Pulaski, Ga., December 5, 1863, and duty there till September, 1864. Moved to Hilton Head, thence to New York and Providence September 26-30. Mustered out October 4, 1864.

BATTERY "L."

Organized at Providence March 17, 1862. Joined Regiment at Hilton Head, S. C. Attached to 3rd Brigade, 1st Division, Dept. of the South, to July, 1862. District of Hilton Head, S. C., Dept. of the South, to September, 1862. District of Hilton Head, S. C., 10th Corps, Dept. of the South, to December, 1863. Fort Pulaski, Ga., District of Hilton Head, S. C., Dept. of the South, to September, 1864. Morris Island, S. C., 1st Separate Brigade, Dept. of the South, to March, 1865.

SERVICE.—Duty at Hilton Head, S. C., till December, 1863. Expedition to Pocotaligo, S. C., October 21-23, 1862. Actions at Gaston's and Frampton's Plantations and at Coosawhatchie October 22. Moved to Fort Pulaski, Ga., December 5, 1863, and duty there till September, 1864. Moved to Morris Island, S. C., and siege operations against Fort Sumpter and Charleston till March, 1865. Transferred to other Companies March 10, 1865.

BATTERY "M."

Organized at Providence March, 1862, and joined Regiment at Hilton Head, S. C. Attached to 3rd Brigade, 1st Division, Dept. of the South, to July, 1862. District of Hilton Head, S. C., Dept. South, to September, 1862. District of Hilton Head, S. C., 10th Corps, Dept. of the South, to July, 1863. Folly Island, S. C.,

10th Corps, July, 1863. Morris Island, S. C., 10th Corps, to April, 1864. Morris Island, S. C., Northern District, Dept. of the South, to March, 1865.

SERVICE.—Duty at Hilton Head, S. C., till July, 1863. Expedition to Pocotaligo, S. C., October 21-23, 1862. Actions at Caston's and Frampton's Plantations and Coosawhatchie October 22. Moved to Folly Island, S. C., July, 1863. Attack on Morris Island July 10. Assaults on Fort Wagner, Morris Island, S. C., July 11 and 18. Siege of Fort Wagner July 18-September 7. Capture of Forts Wagner and Gregg September 7. Siege operations against Fort Sumpter and Charleston till March, 1865. Actions on James Island, S. C., July 1-2, 1864, and at Fort Johnson July 3, 1864. Consolidated with other Companies of Battalion then organized March 10, 1865.

5th REGIMENT HEAVY ARTILLERY.

Organized at New Berne, N. C., from 5th Rhode Island Infantry, May 27, 1863. Attached to Defences of New Berne, N. C., Dept. of Virginia and North Carolina, to January, 1865. Sub-District of New Berne, Dept. of North Carolina, to June, 1865.

SERVICE.—Served as garrison in Forts and Defences of New Berne, Washington and Roanoke Island, N. C., by Detachments. At Forts Totten, Gaston, Chase, Spinola, Hatteras, Clarke, Foster, Parke, Reno and Washington. Operations about New Berne against Whiting January 18-February 10, 1864. Operations about New Berne and in Albemarle Sound May 4-6. Skirmish, south side of Trent River, May 5, 1864. Mustered out June 26, 1865. (See 5th Infantry.)

14th REGIMENT HEAVY ARTILLERY (COLORED).

Organized at Providence August 28, 1863, to January 25, 1864. 1st Battalion moved to New Orleans, La., December 19-30, 1863, thence to Pass Cavallo, Texas, December 31, 1863-January 8, 1864. Served unattached, 13th Army Corps, Dept. of the Gulf, to May, 1864 (1st Battalion). Defences of New Orleans, Dept. of the Gulf, to October, 1865. Designation of Regiment changed to 8th U. S. Colored Heavy Artillery April 4, 1864, and to 11th U. S. Colored Heavy Artillery May 21, 1864.

SERVICE.—1st Battalion assigned to garrison duty at Fort Esperanza. Matagorda Island, Texas, till May 19, 1864. Moved to Camp Parapet, New Orleans, La., May 19-23; joined 3rd Battalion and duty there till July, 1864. Ordered to Port Hudson, La., and garrison duty there till April, 1865. Duty at Brashear City and New Orleans till October, 1865. 2nd Battalion moved to New Orleans January 8-February 3, 1864. Duty in the Defences of New Orleans at English Turn and at Plaquemine till October, 1865. Expedition from Brashear City to Ratliff's Plantation May 14-16, 1865 (Detachment). Action at Indian Village, Plaquemine, August 6, 1864. 3rd Battalion moved to New Orleans April 3-15, and duty at Camp Parapet till October, 1865. Mustered out at New Orleans October 2, 1865.

1st REGIMENT LIGHT ARTILLERY.
BATTERY "A," 1st REGIMENT LIGHT ARTILLERY.

Organized at Providence and mustered in June 6, 1861. Left State for Washington, D. C., June 19. Attached to Burnside's Brigade, Hunter's Division, McDowell's Army of Northeast Virginia, to August, 1861. Dept. of the Shenandoah to October, 1861. Banks' Division, Army of the Potomac, to March, 1862. Artillery, 2nd Division, 2nd Army Corps, Army of the Potomac, to June, 1863. Artillery Brigade, 2nd Army Corps, Army Potomac, to September, 1864.

SERVICE.—Duty in the Defences of Washington, D. C., till July 16, 1861. Advance on Manassas, Va., July 16-21. Battle of Bull Run July 21. Moved to Sandy Hook, Md., July 28. Duty there and at Berlin and Darnestown till September. Moved to Harper's Ferry September 16. Action at Bolivar Heights October 16. At Muddy Branch and Poolesville, Md., till March, 1862. Moved to Washington, thence to Hampton, Va., March 22-April 1. Virginia Peninsula Campaign April to August. Siege of Yorktown April 5-May 4. Battle of Fair Oaks (Seven Pines) May 31-June 1. Seven days before Richmond June 25-July 1. Peach Orchard and Savage Station June 29. Charles City Cross Roads and Glendale June 30. Malvern Hill July 1. At Harrison's Landing till August 16. Movement to Alexandria August 16-28. March to Fairfax C. H. August 28-31. Cover retreat of Pope's Army from Bull Run to Washington August 31-September 1. Maryland Campaign September. Battles of South Mountain, Md., September 14, and Antietam September 16-17. Moved to Harper's Ferry September 22, and duty there till October 30. Reconnoissance to Charlestown October 16-17. Action at Charlestown October 16. Advance up Loudoun Valley and movement to Falmouth, Va., October 30-November 17. Battle of Fredericksburg December 11-15. Duty at Falmouth till April, 1863. Chancellorsville Campaign April 27-May 6. Maryes Heights, Fredericksburg, May 3. Salem Heights May 3-4. Gettysburg (Pa.) Campaign June 11-July 24. Battle of Gettysburg July 1-4. Advance from the Rappahannock to the Rapidan September 13-17. Bristoe Campaign October 9-22. Bristoe Station October 14. Auburn Heights October 14. Advance to line of the Rappahannock November 7-8. Mine Run Campaign November 26-December 2. At Stevensburg, Va., till May, 1864. Demonstration on the Rapidan February 6-7. Morton's Ford February 6-7. Campaign from the Rapidan to the James May-June. Battles of the Wilderness May 5-7; Spottsylvania May 8-12; Po River May 10; Spottsylvania C. H. May 12-21. Assault on the Salient May 12. North Anna River May 23-26. Line of the Pamunkey May 26-28. Totopotomoy May 28-31. Shallow Creek May 31. Cold Harbor June 1-12. Before Petersburg June 16-18. Non-Veterans mustered out June 18, 1864. Siege of Petersburg June 16-September 30. Jerusalem Plank Road June 21-23. Deep Bottom July 27-28. Mine Explosion, Petersburg, July 30 (Reserve). Strawberry Plains, Deep Bottom, August 14-18. Ream's Station August 25. Transferred to Battery "B," 1st Rhode Island Artillery, September 30, 1864.

Battery lost during service 1 Officer and 12 Enlisted men killed and mortally wounded and 5 Enlisted men by disease. Total 18.

BATTERY "B," 1st REGIMENT LIGHT ARTILLERY.

Organized at Providence and mustered in August 13, 1861. Left State for Washington, D. C., August 23. Attached to Stone's Brigade, Division of the Potomac, to October, 1861. Artillery, Stone's (Sedgwick's) Division, Army of the Potomac, to March, 1862. Artillery, 2nd Division, 2nd Army Corps, Army of the Potomac, to June, 1863. Artillery Brigade, 2nd Army Corps, to June, 1865.

SERVICE.—Duty at Camp Stone and along Upper Potomac till February, 1862. Operations on the Potomac October 21-24, 1861. Battle of Ball's Bluff October 21. March to Harper's Ferry, W. Va., February 25-26, 1862, and duty there till March 7. Moved to Charlestown, thence to Berryville March 7-10. Advance toward Winchester March 13-14. Return to Harper's Ferry, thence moved to Washington, D. C., and Hampton, Va., March 22-April 1. Siege of Yorktown April 5-May 4. Battle of Fair Oaks (Seven Pines) May 31-June 1. Seven days before Richmond June 25-July 1. Peach Orchard and Savage Station June 29. Charles City Cross Roads and Glendale June 30. Malvern Hill July 1. At Harrison's Landing till August 16. Movement to Fortress Monroe, thence to Alexandria and Fairfax C. H. August 16-31. Cover retreat of Pope's Army from Bull Run to Washington August 31-September 2. Maryland Campaign September. Battles of South Mountain September 14, and Antietam September 16-17. Moved to Harper's Ferry September 22, and duty there till October 30. Reconnoissance to Charlestown October 16-17. Advance up Loudoun Valley and movement to Falmouth, Va., October 30-November 17. Battle of Fredericksburg December 11-15. Duty at Falmouth till April 27, 1863. Chancellorsville Campaign April 27-May 6. Maryes Heights, Fredericksburg, May 3. Salem Heights May

3-4. Banks' Ford May 4. Gettysburg (Pa.) Campaign June 11-July 24. Battle of Gettysburg July 1-4. Advance from the Rappahannock to the Rapidan September 13-17. Bristoe Campaign October 9-22. Auburn and Bristoe October 14. Advance to line of the Rappahannock November 7-8. Mine Run Campaign November 26-December 2. At Stevensburg, Va., till May, 1864. Demonstration on the Rapidan February 6-7. Campaign from the Rapidan to the James May-June. Battles of the Wilderness May 5-7; Spottsylvania May 8-12; Spottsylvania C. H. May 12-21. Assault on the Salient May 12. North Anna River May 23-26. Line of the Pamunkey May 26-28. Totopotomoy May 28-31. Cold Harbor June 1-12. Before Petersburg June 16-18. Siege of Petersburg June 16, 1864, to April 2, 1865. Jerusalem Plank Road June 22-23, 1864. Deep Bottom July 27-28. Strawberry Plains, Deep Bottom, August 14-18. Ream's Station August 25. Hatcher's Run October 27-28. Dabney's Mills February 5-7, 1865. Appomattox Campaign March 28-April 9. Fall of Petersburg April 2. Sailor's Creek April 6. High Bridge and Farmville April 7. Appomattox C. H. April 9. Surrender of Lee and his army. Moved to Washington, D. C., May 2-15. Grand Review May 23. Mustered out June 13, 1865.

Battery lost during service 1 Officer and 13 Enlisted men killed and mortally wounded and 15 Enlisted men by disease. Total 29.

BATTERY "C," 1st REGIMENT LIGHT ARTILLERY.

Organized at Providence and mustered in August 25, 1861. Left State for Washington, D. C., August 31. Attached to Porter's Division, Army of the Potomac, to March, 1862. Artillery, 1st Division, 3rd Army Corps, Army of the Potomac, to May, 1862. Artillery, 1st Division, 5th Army Corps, Army Potomac, to May, 1863. 3rd Volunteer Brigade, Artillery Reserve, Army Potomac, to June, 1863. Artillery Brigade, 6th Army Corps, Army Potomac, to August, 1864, and Army Shenandoah to November, 1864. Camp Barry, 22nd Corps, Dept. Washington, to December, 1864.

SERVICE.—Duty at Camp Sprague, Defences of Washington, till October, 1861, and at Hall's and Munson's Hills till March, 1862. Advance on Manassas, Va., March 10-16. Moved to Alexandria, thence to Fortress Monroe, Va., March 16-23. Action at Howard's Bridge April 4. Siege of Yorktown April 5-May 4. Battle of Williamsburg May 5. Hanover C. H. May 27. Operations about Hanover C. H. May 27-29. Seven days before Richmond June 25-July 1. Battles of Mechanicsville June 26; Gaines' Mill June 27; Turkey Bridge and Malvern Cliff June 30; Malvern Hill July 1. At Harrison's Landing till August 16. Movement to Fortress Monroe, thence to Centreville August 16-28. Battle of Bull Run August 30. Battle of Antietam, Md., September 16-17. Shepherdstown September 19. At Sharpsburg till October 30. Movement to Falmouth, Va., October 30-November 19. Battle of Fredericksburg, Va., December 12-15. "Mud March" January 20-24, 1863. At Falmouth, Va., till April 27. Chancellorsville Campaign April 27-May 6. Battle of Chancellorsville May 1-5. Operations at Franklin's Crossing June 5-13. Battle of Gettysburg, Pa., July 2-4. At Warrenton, Va., till September 15. Bristoe Campaign October 9-22. Advance to line of the Rappahannock November 7-8. Rappahannock Station November 7. Mine Run Campaign November 26-December 2. At Brandy Station till May, 1864. Campaign from the Rapidan to the James May-June. Battles of the Wilderness May 5-7; Spottsylvania May 8-12; Spottsylvania C. H. May 12-21; North Anna River May 23-26. Line of the Pamunkey May 26-28. Totopotomoy May 28-31. Cold Harbor June 1-12. Before Petersburg June 16-18. Siege of Petersburg June 16-July 9. Jerusalem Plank Road June 22-23. Moved to Washington, D. C., June 9-11. Repulse of Early's attack on Washington July 11-12. Sheridan's Shenandoah Valley Campaign August to November. Battle of Opequan, Winchester, September 19. Fisher's Hill September 22. Battle of Cedar Creek October 19. Duty at Winchester and Kernstown till November, and at Camp Barry, Defences of Washington, till December. Consolidated with Battery "G," 1st Rhode Island Light Artillery, December 23, 1864.

Battery lost during service 19 Enlisted men killed and mortally wounded and 8 Enlisted men by disease. Total 27.

BATTERY "D," 1st REGIMENT LIGHT ARTILLERY.

Organized at Providence and mustered in September 4, 1861. Left State for Washington, D. C., September 14. Attached to McDowell's Division, Army of the Potomac, to March, 1862. Artillery, 1st Division, 1st Army Corps, Army Potomac, to April, 1862. Artillery, 3rd Division, Dept. of the Rappahannock, to June, 1862. Artillery, 3rd Division, 3rd Army Corps, Army of Virginia, to September, 1862. Artillery, 1st Division, 1st Army Corps, Army Potomac, to October, 1862. Artillery, 1st Division, 9th Army Corps, Army Potomac, to March, 1863. Artillery, 2nd Division, 9th Army Corps, Dept. of Ohio, to June, 1863. Unassigned, 1st Division, 23rd Army Corps, Dept. Ohio, to August, 1863. Artillery Reserve, 23rd Army Corps, Dept. Ohio, to October, 1863. Artillery, 1st Division, 9th Army Corps, Dept. of Ohio, to April, 1864. Reserve Artillery, 9th Army Corps, Army Potomac, to June, 1864. 1st Brigade, Haskins' Division, 22nd Army Corps, Dept. of Washington, to August, 1864. Reserve Artillery, 19th Army Corps, Army Shenandoah, Middle Military Division, to December, 1864. Artillery Brigade, 19th Army Corps, Army Shenandoah, to March, 1865. Artillery Reserve, Army Shenandoah, to July, 1865.

SERVICE.—Duty at Upton's Hill, Va., Defences of Washington, till March 9, 1862. March to Fairfax C. H. March 9-16, thence to Bristoe March 29, thence to Falmouth. Duty at Falmouth and Fredericksburg till June. McDowell's advance on Richmond May 25-29. Pursuit of Jackson June 2-11. Reconnoissance to Orange C. H. July 24-27. Expedition to Virginia Central Railroad August 5-8. Action at Thornburg's Mill or Massaponax Church August 5-6. Pope's Campaign in Northern Virginia August 16-September 2. Battles of Gainesville August 28; Groveton August 29; Bull Run August 30; Chantilly September 1; Antietam, Md., September 16-17. Movement to Falmouth, Va., October 30-November 19. Battle of Fredericksburg, Va., December 12-15. "Mud March" January 20-24, 1863. At Falmouth till February 19. Moved to Newport News February 19, thence to Covington, Ky., March 19-29, and to Lexington, Ky. Moved to Camp Nelson, Ky., May 8, and to Cincinnati, Ohio, July 12. To Camp Nelson August 15. Burnside's Campaign in East Tennessee August 16-October 17. March over Cumberland Mountains to Loudon, Tenn., August 16-September 4. March to Blue Springs October 7-10. Action at Blue Springs October 10. March to Knoxville, Tenn., October 13-17, thence to Loudon October 20-22, and to Lenoir Station October 28. Knoxville Campaign November 4-December 23. Campbell's Station November 16. Siege of Knoxville November 17-December 4. Repulse of Longstreet's assault on Fort Saunders November 29. Pursuit to Rutledge December 5-14. Operations in East Tennessee till March 20, 1864. Veterans on furlough February and March. Movement to Washington, D. C., March 20-April 7. Campaign from the Rapidan to the James May. Battles of the Wilderness May 5-7. Garrison duty at Fort Lincoln, Defences of Washington, D. C., till July. Sheridan's Shenandoah Valley Campaign August to December. Battle of Opequan, Winchester, September 19. Strasburg September 21. Fisher's Hill September 22. Battle of Cedar Creek October 19. Duty in the Shenandoah Valley to July, 1865. Mustered out July 17, 1865.

Battery lost during service 10 Enlisted men killed and mortally wounded and 12 Enlisted men by disease. Total 22.

BATTERY "E," 1st REGIMENT LIGHT ARTILLERY.

Organized at Providence September 23, 1861. Left State for Washington, D. C., October 4. Attached to Heintzelman's Division, Army of the Potomac, to March. Artillery, 3rd Division, 3rd Army Corps, Army Potomac, to August, 1862. Artillery, 1st Division, 3rd Army Corps, Army Potomac, to June, 1863. Artillery Brigade, 3rd Army Corps, to March, 1864. Artillery Brigade, 6th Army Corps, to July, 1864. Artillery Reserve, Army Potomac, to December, 1864. Artillery Brigade, 6th Army Corps, to April, 1865. Artillery Reserve, Army Potomac, to June, 1865.

SERVICE.—Duty at Camp Sprague till November 5, 1861, and at Fort Lyon, near Alexandria, Va., Defences of Washington, till April, 1862. Virginia Peninsula Campaign April to August. Siege of Yorktown April 5-May 4. Warwick Road April 15. Battle of Williamsburg May 5. Battle of Fair Oaks or Seven Pines May 31-June 1. Seven days before Richmond June 25-July 1. Oak Grove, near Seven Pines, June 25. Jordan's Ford June 27. Peach Orchard and Savage Station June 29. Brackett's June 30. Charles City Cross Roads and Glendale June 30. Malvern Hill July 1. At Harrison's Landing till August 15. Movement to Centreville August 15-26. Bristoe Station or Kettle Run August 27. Groveton August 29. Battle of Bull Run August 30. Chantilly September 1. Duty in the Defences of Washington till October 11. March up the Potomac to Leesburg, thence to Falmouth, Va., October 11-November 23. Battle of Fredericksburg December 12-15. "Mud March" January 20-24, 1863. At Falmouth till April 27. Chancellorsville Campaign April 27-May 6. Battle of Chancellorsville May 1-5. Battle of Gettysburg, Pa., July 1-4. Wapping Heights, Va., July 23. Bristoe Campaign October 9-22. Advance to line of the Rappahannock November 7-8. Kelly's Ford November 7. Mine Run Campaign November 26-December 2. Payne's Farm November 27. Rapidan Campaign May-June, 1864. Battles of the Wilderness May 5-7; Spottsylvania May 8-12; Spottsylvania C. H. May 12-21; North Anna River May 23-26. Line of the Pamunkey May 26-28. Totopotomoy May 28-31. Cold Harbor June 1-12. Bethesda Church June 1-3. Before Petersburg June 18-22. Jerusalem Plank Road June 22-23. Moved to Baltimore, Md., July 9-16, thence back to City Point, Va., July 17-19. Operations against Petersburg and Richmond July, 1864, to April, 1865. Fall of Petersburg April 2. Ordered to City Point April 3. Mustered out June 11, 1865.

Battery lost during service 17 Enlisted men killed and mortally wounded and 12 Enlisted men by disease. Total 29.

BATTERY "F," 1st REGIMENT LIGHT ARTILLERY.

Organized at Providence October 29, 1861. Left State for Washington, D. C., November 7. Duty at Camp Sprague and at Camp California, near Alexandria, Defences of Washington, till January, 1862. Moved to Annapolis, Md. Attached to Burnside's Expeditionary Corps to April, 1862. Unattached, Dept. North Carolina, to December, 1862. Artillery Brigade, Dept. North Carolina, to January, 1863. Artillery Brigade, 18th Army Corps, Dept. of North Carolina, to May, 1863. Defences of New Berne, N. C., to November, 1863. District of St. Marys, Dept. Virginia and North Carolina, to January, 1864. U. S. Forces, Yorktown, Va., Dept. Virginia and North Carolina, to April, 1864. Artillery, 2nd Division, 18th Army Corps, Dept. Virginia and North Carolina, to June, 1864. Artillery Brigade, 18th Army Corps, to December, 1864. Artillery Brigade, 24th Army Corps, Dept. of Virginia, to June, 1865.

SERVICE.—Burnside's Expedition to Hatteras Inlet and Roanoke Island, N. C., January 9-February 7, 1862. At Hatteras Inlet till February 26, and at Roanoke Island till March 11. Moved to New Berne, N. C., March 11-14, and duty there till October, 1863. Picket and outpost duty as Cavalry March 20 to May 18, 1862. Action at Deep Gully March 31. Trent Road April 19. Expedition to Trenton and Pollocksville July 24-28. Expedition to Little Washington October 29-30. Expedition from New Berne November 2-12. Action at Rawle's Mills November 2. Demonstration on New Berne November 11. Foster's Expedition to Goldsboro December 11-20. Kinston December 14. Whitehall December 16. Goldsboro December 17. Expedition for relief of Little Washington April 7-10, 1863. Action at Blount's Creek April 9. Expedition to Swift Creek Village April 13-21

(Section). Expedition to Washington April 17-19. Expedition to Trenton July 4-8. Actions at Free Bridge and Quaker Bridge July 6. Expedition to Winston July 25-26. Pattacassy Creek, Mt. Tabor Church, July 26. Expedition to Elizabeth City October 10-16. Moved to Newport News, Va., October 30-November 5, thence to Point Lookout, Md., November 23-24, and duty there till January, 1864. Moved to Yorktown, Va., January 24. Wistar's Expedition toward Richmond February 6-8. Ball's Cross Roads February 7. Bottom's Bridge February 7. Expedition from Yorktown to New Kent C. H. in support of Kilpatrick's Cavalry March 1-4. Expedition into King and Queen County March 9-12. Butler's operations on south side of the James River and against Petersburg and Richmond May 4-28. Swift Creek or Arrowfield Church May 9-10. Operations against Fort Darling May 12-16. Battle of Drewry's Bluff May 14-16. On Bermuda Hundred line May 16-June 15. Before Petersburg June 15-18. Siege operations against Petersburg and Richmond June 16, 1864, to April 2, 1865. Battle of Chaffin's Farm September 28-30, 1864. Duty at Aiken's Landing October 7-November 8, 1864, and at Chaffin's Farm before Richmond till April 7, 1865. Moved to Richmond April 7, and duty there till June 25. Mustered out June 27, 1865.

Battery lost during service 10 Enlisted men killed and mortally wounded and 17 Enlisted men by disease. Total 27.

BATTERY "G," 1st REGIMENT LIGHT ARTILLERY.

Organized at Providence December, 1861. Left State for Washington, D. C., December 7. Attached to Sedgwick's Division, Army of the Potomac, to March, 1862. Reserve Artillery, 2nd Army Corps, Army of the Potomac, to October, 1862. Artillery, 3rd Division, 2nd Army Corps, Army Potomac, to May, 1863. 4th Volunteer Brigade, Artillery Reserve, Army Potomac, to July, 1863. Artillery Brigade, 6th Army Corps, Army Potomac, to August, 1864, and Army of the Shenandoah, Middle Military Division, to November, 1864. Camp Barry, 22nd Army Corps, Dept. of Washington, to December, 1864. Artillery Brigade, 6th Army Corps, Army of the Potomac, to June, 1865.

SERVICE.—Duty at Camp Sprague, Defences of Washington, D. C., till January 3, 1862. Moved to Darnestown January 3 and to Poolesville, Md. Duty there till February and at Edward's Ferry till March. At Bolivar Heights till March 26. Moved to Washington, D. C., thence to the Virginia Peninsula March 26-April 2. Siege of Yorktown April 5-May 4. Battle of Fair Oaks, Seven Pines, May 31-June 1. Seven days before Richmond June 25-July 1. Peach Orchard and Savage Station June 29. Charles City Cross Roads and Glendale June 30. Malvern Hill July 1. At Harrison's Landing till August 16. Movement to Alexandria August 16-28, thence march to Fairfax C. H. August 28-31. Cover retreat of Pope's army from Bull Run to Washington, D. C., August 31-September 2. Battle of Antietam, Md., September 16-17. Moved to Harper's Ferry, W. Va., September 22, and duty there till October 22. Advance up Loudoun Valley and movement to Falmouth, Va., October 30-November 18. Battle of Fredericksburg December 12-15. "Mud March" January 20-24, 1863. At Falmouth till April. Chancellorsville Campaign April 27-May 6. Maryes Heights, Fredericksburg, May 3. Salem Heights May 3-4. Banks' Ford May 4. Franklin's Crossing June 5-13. Battle of Gettysburg, Pa., July 2-4. Near Fairfield July 5. Funkstown, Md., July 10-13. Bristoe Campaign October 9-22. Advance to line of the Rappahannock November 7-8. Rappahannock Station November 7. Mine Run Campaign November 26-December 2. At Brandy Station till May, 1864. Rapidan Campaign May-June. Battles of the Wilderness May 5-7; Spottsylvania May 8-12; Spottsylvania C. H. May 12-21. Assault on the Salient May 12. North Anna River May 23-26. On line of the Pamunkey May 26-28. Totopotomoy May 28-31. Cold Harbor June 1-12. Before Petersburg June 17-18. Siege of Petersburg June 16-July 9. Jerusalem Plank Road June 22-23. Moved

to Washington, D. C., July 9-12. Repulse of Early's attack on Washington July 12. Snicker's Ferry July 17-18. Sheridan's Shenandoah Valley Campaign August to November. Battle of Opequan, Winchester, September 19. Fisher's Hill September 22. Mount Jackson September 23-24. Battle of Cedar Creek October 19. Duty at Winchester and Kernstown till November. Moved to Washington, D. C., and refit, thence moved to Petersburg, Va. Siege of Petersburg December, 1864, to April, 1865. Fort Fisher, Petersburg, March 25, 1865. Appomattox Campaign March 28-April 9. Assault on and fall of Petersburg April 2. Pursuit of Lee April 3-9. Sailor's Creek April 6. High Bridge and Farmville April 7. Appomattox C. H. April 9. Surrender of Lee and his army. Mustered out June 24, 1865.

Battery lost during service 2 Officers and 10 Enlisted men killed and mortally wounded and 18 Enlisted men by disease. Total 30.

BATTERY "H," 1st REGIMENT LIGHT ARTILLERY.

Organized at Providence October 14. 1862. Left State for Washington, D. C., October 23. Attached to Camp Barry, Military District of Washington, October, 1862. Stannard's 2nd Brigade, Casey's Division, Military District Washington, to February, 1863. Artillery, Casey's Division, 22nd Army Corps, Dept. of Washington, to April, 1863. Artillery, Abercrombie's Division, 22nd Army Corps, to May, 1863. 3rd Brigade, DeRussy's Division, 22nd Army Corps, to November, 1863. Camp Barry, 22nd Army Corps, to April, 1864. Artillery, 1st Division, 9th Army Corps, Army Potomac, to May, 1864. Reserve Artillery, 9th Army Corps, to June, 1864. 2nd Brigade, DeRussy's Division, 22nd Army Corps, to July, 1864. 1st Brigade, DeRussy's Division, 22nd Army Corps, to October, 1864. City Point, Va., Dept. Virginia and North Carolina, to December, 1864. Artillery Reserve, Army Potomac, to January, 1865. Artillery Brigade, 6th Army Corps, to June, 1865.

SERVICE.—Duty at Camp Barry, Washington, D. C., till January, 1863. Moved to Fairfax Station January 19-23, and duty there till March 23. Moved to Union Mills March 23, and duty there till May 20. Moved to Chantilly, Va., May 20, and duty there till June 25. Moved to Fairfax C. H. June 25, thence to Arlington Heights, and duty in the Defences of Washington, south of the Potomac, till April, 1864. Rapidan Campaign May 3-10. Battle of the Wilderness May 5-7. Spottsylvania May 8-10. March to Fredericksburg, thence to Aquia Creek May 10-18, thence moved to Washington. Duty at Fort Richardson till July 10, and at Fort Smith till October 16. At Camp Barry till October 25. Moved to City Point, Va., October 25-26, and duty there till January 2, 1865. Ordered to join Army Potomac January 2. Siege of Petersburg January 2-April 2. Fort Fisher, Petersburg, March 25. Appomattox Campaign March 28-April 9. Assault on and fall of Petersburg April 2. Sailor's Creek April 6. High Bridge and Farmville April 7. Appomattox C. H. April 9. Surrender of Lee and his army. March to Danville April 23-27, thence to Burkesville Station May 3-6. Moved to Washington, D. C., via City Point and Richmond May 20-June 7. Corps Review June 8. Ordered to Providence, R. I., June 13, and mustered out June 28, 1865. Discharged July 3, 1865.

Battery lost during service 2 Enlisted men killed and 10 Enlisted men by disease. Total 12.

1st BATTERY LIGHT ARTILLERY, "TOMPKINS' MARINE ARTILLERY."

Organized at Providence for three months' service April, 1861. Left State for Jersey City, N. J., April 18, thence moved to Easton, Pa., April 19, and to Washington, D. C., April 27. Duty in the defences of that city till June 9. Mustered into service May 2. Attached to Hunter's Division, McDowell's Army of Northeast Virginia. Moved to Williamsport, Md., June 9-15, and return to Washington June 17-20, thence march to Williamsport July 9-13, and to Martinsburg, W. Va. Attached to Thomes' Brigade, Patterson's Army. March to Bunker Hill, Va., and action July 15. Moved to

Charlestown July 17, and to Harper's Ferry July 22. Moved to Sandy Hook, thence to Providence, R. I., July 29-31. Mustered out August 2, 1861.

10th BATTERY LIGHT ARTILLERY.

Organized at Providence for three months' service. Moved to Washington, D. C., May 27-29, 1862. Attached to Whipple's Command, Military District of Washington. Duty at Camp Frieze, Tennallytown, till June 23. At Cloud's Mills till June 30, and near Fort Pennsylvania till August. Mustered out August 30, 1862.

1st REGIMENT INFANTRY.

Organized in Rhode Island, April, 1861. Moved to Washington, D. C., April 20 and 24, 1861. Duty at Camp Sprague, Defences of Washington, till July 16. Attached to Burnside's Brigade, Hunter's Division, McDowell's Army of Northeast Virginia, June-July. Advance on Manassas, Va., July 16-21. Battle of Bull Run July 21. Left Washington for home July 25. Mustered out August 2, 1861.

Regiment lost during service 1 Officer and 16 Enlisted men killed and mortally wounded and 8 Enlisted men by disease. Total 25.

2nd REGIMENT INFANTRY.

Organized at Providence June, 1861. Left State for Washington, D. C., June 19. Attached to Burnside's Brigade, Hunter's Division, McDowell's Army of Northeast Virginia, to August, 1861. Couch's Brigade, Division of the Potomac, to October, 1861. Couch's Brigade, Buell's Division, Army Potomac, to March, 1862. 1st Brigade, 1st Division, 4th Army Corps, Army Potomac, to September, 1862. 1st Brigade, 1st Division, 6th Army Corps, Army Potomac, to October, 1862. 2nd Brigade, 3rd Division, 6th Army Corps, to March, 1864. 4th Brigade, 2nd Division, 6th Army Corps, to July, 1864. 3rd Brigade, 1st Division, 6th Army Corps, Army Potomac and Army Shenandoah, Middle Military Division, to December, 1864. 3rd Brigade, 1st Division, 6th Army Corps, Army Potomac, to July, 1865.

SERVICE.—At Camp Sprague, Washington, D. C., till July 16, 1861. Advance on Manassas, Va., July 16-21. Battle of Bull Run July 21. At Camp Sprague and Brightwood, Defences of Washington, till March, 1862. March to Prospect Hill, Va., March 11-15. Embarked at Alexandria, Va., for the Peninsula March 26. Siege of Yorktown April 5-May 4. Battle of Williamsburg May 5. Slatersville, New Kent C. H., May 9. Battle of Fair Oaks, Seven Pines, May 31-June 1. Seven days before Richmond June 25-July 1. Oak Grove near Seven Pines June 25. James River Road near Fair Oaks June 29. White Oak Swamp June 30. Malvern Hill July 1. At Harrison's Landing till August 15. Reconnoissance to Turkey Island August 5-6, and to Haxall's Landing August 8-11. Movement to Alexandria August 15-September 1, thence march into Maryland September 3-18. At Downsville September 23-October 20. Movement to Stafford C. H., Va., October 20-November 18, and to Belle Plains December 5. Battle of Fredericksburg December 12-15. "Mud March" January 20-24, 1863. Chancellorsville Campaign April 27-May 6. Operations about Franklin's Crossing April 29-May 2. Maryes Heights, Fredericksburg, May 3. Salem Heights May 3-4. Banks' Ford May 4. Deep Run Ravine or Franklin's Crossing June 5-13. Battle of Gettysburg, Pa., July 2-4. Funkstown, Md., July 10-13. At Warrenton, Va., till September. Bristoe Campaign October 9-22. Advance to line of the Rappahannock November 7-8. Rappahannock Station November 7. Mine Run Campaign November 26-December 2. At Brandy Station till May, 1864. Rapidan Campaign May-June. Battles of the Wilderness May 5-7; Spottsylvania May 8-12; Spottsylvania C. H. May 12-21. Assault on the Salient May 12. North Anna River May 23-26. On line of the Pamunkey May 26-28. Totopotomoy May 28-31. Cold Harbor June 1-12. Old members left front for muster out June 11. Mustered out June 17, 1864. Before Petersburg June 17-18. Jerusalem Plank Road June 22-23. Siege of Petersburg till July 9. Moved to Washington, D. C., July 9-11. Re-

pulse of Early's attack on Washington July 11-12. Sheridan's Shenandoah Valley Campaign August to December. Battle of Opequan, Winchester, September 19. Garrison duty at Winchester September 22-December 1. Moved to Petersburg, Va., December 2-6. Siege of Petersburg December, 1864, to April, 1865. Dabney's Mills, Hatcher's Run, February 5-7, 1865. Fort Fisher, Petersburg, March 25. Appomattox Campaign March 28-April 9. Assault on and fall of Petersburg April 2. Pursuit of Lee April 3-9. Expedition to Danville April 23-27. Moved to Washington via Richmond May 20-June 7. Corps Review June 8. Mustered out July 13, 1865.

Regiment lost during service 9 Officers and 111 Enlisted men killed and mortally wounded and 2 Officers and 74 Enlisted men by disease. Total 196.

3rd REGIMENT INFANTRY.

Organized at Providence August, 1861. Left State for Fort Hamilton, N. Y. Harbor, September 7, 1861, thence moved to Washington, D. C., September 14-16, returning to Fort Hamilton September 22. Moved to Fortress Monroe, Va., October 12-14. Attached to Sherman's South Carolina Expeditionary Corps. Expedition to Port Royal, S. C., October 28-November 7. Capture of Forts Walker and Beauregard, Port Royal Harbor, November 7. Designation of Regiment changed to 3rd Rhode Island Heavy Artillery December 19, 1861. (See 3rd Heavy Artillery.)

4th REGIMENT INFANTRY.

Organized at Providence, 1861. Left State for Washington, D. C., October 2. At Camp Casey till November 28, and at Camp California till December 14. Mustered in October 30, 1861. Attached to Casey's Provisional Division, Army Potomac, October-November, 1861. Howard's Brigade, Sumner's Division, Army of the Potomac, to December, 1861. Parke's 3rd Brigade, Burnside's Expeditionary Corps, to April, 1862. 1st Brigade, 3rd Division, Dept. of North Carolina, to July, 1862. 2nd Brigade, 3rd Division, 9th Army Corps, Army Potomac, to January, 1863. 3rd Brigade, 3rd Division, 9th Army Corps, to April, 1863. 3rd Brigade, 2nd Division, 7th Army Corps, Dept. of Virginia, to July, 1863. 3rd Brigade, Getty's Division, at Portsmouth, Va., Dept. of Virginia and North Carolina, to January, 1864. 3rd Brigade, Heckman's Division, Portsmouth, Va., to March, 1864. Norfolk, Va., to April, 1864. District of St. Mary's Point, Lookout, Md., to July, 1864. 1st Brigade, 2nd Division, 9th Army Corps, Army Potomac, to October, 1864.

SERVICE.—At Edsall's Hill, Defences of Washington, D. C., December 14, 1861, to January 3, 1862. Moved to Annapolis, Md., January 3, 1862. Burnside's Expedition to Hatteras Inlet and Roanoke Island, N. C., January 7-February 8, 1862. Battle of Roanoke Island February 9. Duty at Roanoke Island till March 11. Advance on New Berne March 11-13. Battle of New Berne March 14. Siege of Fort Macon March 23-April 26. Bombardment and capture of Fort Macon April 25-26. Duty at Beaufort and New Berne till July. Moved to Newport News, Va., July 6-8, thence to Fredericksburg August 3-6, and duty there till August 31. Moved to Brook's Station, thence to Washington, D. C., August 31-September 3. Maryland Campaign September-October. Battles of South Mountain September 14, and Antietam September 16-17. Duty in Pleasant Valley, Md., till October 30. Advance to Falmouth, Va., October 30-November 19. Battle of Fredericksburg, Va., December 12-15. "Mud March" January 20-24, 1863. Moved to Newport News, Va., February 8, thence to Suffolk March 13. Siege of Suffolk April 12-May 4. Nansemond River May 4. Reconnoissance to the Chickahominy June 9-13. Dix's Peninsula Campaign June 24-July 8. Expedition from White House to South Anna River July 1-7. Duty at Portsmouth till March 1, 1864, and at Norfolk till April 1. At Point Lookout, Md., guarding prisoners till July. Ordered to Petersburg, Va., July 16. Siege of Petersburg July to October. Mine Explosion, Petersburg, July 30. Weldon Railroad August 18-21. Poplar Springs

Church September 29-October 2. Old members mustered out October 15, 1864. Veterans and Recruits consolidated with 7th Rhode Island Infantry.

Regiment lost during service 5 Officers and 68 Enlisted men killed and mortally wounded and 67 Enlisted men by disease. Total 140.

5th REGIMENT INFANTRY.

Organized at Providence as a Battalion of 5 Companies and mustered in December 16, 1861. (5 new Cos. organized December 27. 1862.) Moved to Annapolis, Md., December 27-29, 1861. Attached to Parke's 3rd Brigade, Burnside's Expeditionary Corps, to April, 1862. 1st Brigade, 3rd Division, Dept. of North Carolina, to July, 1862. 2nd Brigade, 1st Division, Dept. North Carolina, to January, 1863. 2nd Brigade, 4th Division, 18th Army Corps, Dept. of North Carolina, to May, 1863. Lee's Brigade. Defences of New Berne, N. C., Dept. North Carolina, to July, 1863.

SERVICE.—Burnside's Expedition to Hatteras Inlet and Roanoke Island, N. C., January 7-February 8, 1862. Battle of Roanoke Island February 9. At Roanoke Island till March 11. Expedition up Currituck Sound February 19. Advance to New Berne March 11-13. Battle of New Berne March 14. Operations against Fort Macon March 19-April 26. Moved to Havelock Station, Atlantic & North Carolina Railroad, March 19-20. Companies "A," "B" and "C" to Newport Barracks March 23, thence Battalion moved to Carolina City April 4. At Bogue Banks April 6-30. Camden, South Mills, April 19. At Fort Macon April 30-June 30. At Beaufort, N. C., till August 7, and at New Berne till December. Expedition to Tarboro November 2-12. Rawle's Mills November 2. Demonstration on New Berne November 11. Foster's Expedition to Goldsboro December 11-20. Kinston December 14. Whitehall December 16. Goldsboro December 17. Duty at New Berne till May, 1863. Expedition to relief of Little Washington April 7-10. Duty in the Defences of New Berne till July. Designation of Regiment changed to 5th Rhode Island Heavy Artillery July, 1863. (See 5th Heavy Artillery.)

Regiment lost during service as Infantry and Heavy Artillery 1 Officer and 8 Enlisted men killed and mortally wounded and 4 Officers and 106 Enlisted men by disease. Total 119.

6th REGIMENT INFANTRY.

(Failed to complete organization.)

7th REGIMENT INFANTRY.

Organized at Providence May to September, 1862. Moved to Washington, D. C., September 10-12, 1862. Attached to 2nd Brigade, Casey's Division, Military District of Washington, to October, 1862. 1st Brigade, 2nd Division, 9th Army Corps, Army Potomac, to April, 1863; Dept. Ohio to June, 1863, and Army Tennessee to September, 1863. District of North Central Kentucky, 1st Division, 23rd Army Corps, Dept. Ohio, to April, 1864. 1st Brigade, 2nd Division, 9th Army Corps, Army Potomac, to July, 1865.

SERVICE.—Camp at Capital Hill, Defences of Washington, D. C., till September 16, 1862, and at Arlington Heights, Va., till October 1. Moved to Sandy Hook, Md., October 1. Movement to Falmouth, Va., October 27-November 19. Warrenton, Sulphur Springs, November 15. Battle of Fredericksburg December 12-15. "Mud March" January 20-24, 1863. Moved to Newport News February 9, thence to Lexington, Ky., March 25-31. Moved to Winchester, thence to Richmond, Ky., April 18. To Paint Creek May 3, and to Lancaster May 10. Moved to Vicksburg, Miss., June 4-14. Siege of Vicksburg June 15-July 4. Advance on Jackson, Miss., July 5-10. Siege of Jackson July 10-17. At Milldale till August 8. Moved to Nicholasville, Ky., August 8-18, thence to Lexington September 7, and provost duty there till April, 1864. Moved to Virginia April 2-23. Campaign from the Rapidan to the James May-June. Battles of the Wilderness May 5-7; Spottsylvania May 8-12; Spottsylvania C. H. May 12-21; Stannard's Mill May 21; North Anna River May 23-26. On line of the Pamunkey May 26-28. Totopotomoy May 28-31. Cold Harbor June 1-12. Bethesda Church June 1-3. Before Petersburg June 16-18. Siege of Petersburg June 16, 1864, to April 2, 1865. Mine Explosion, Petersburg, July 30, 1864. Weldon Railroad August 18-21. Poplar Springs Church September 29-October 2. Boydton Plank Road, Hatcher's Run, October 27-28. Garrison of Fort Sedgwick November 1, 1864, to April 2, 1865. Fort Stedman March 25, 1865. Appomattox Campaign March 28-April 9. Assault on and fall of Petersburg April 2. Pursuit of Lee to Farmville April 3-9. Moved to Petersburg and City Point, thence to Washington, D. C., April 20-28. Grand Review May 23. Mustered out June 9, 1865.

Regiment lost during service 5 Officers and 85 Enlisted men killed and mortally wounded and 1 Officer and 108 Enlisted men by disease. Total 199.

8th REGIMENT INFANTRY.

(Failed to complete organization.)

9th REGIMENT INFANTRY.

Organized at Providence May 26, 1862. Moved to Washington, D. C., by Detachments, May 27 and 29. Duty at Camp Frieze, Tennallytown, till July. Moved to Fairfax Seminary, Va., July 1. Garrison duty in the Defences of Washington till September. Company "A" at Fort Greble, "B" at Fort Meigs, "C" at Fort Ricketts, "D" at Fort Snyder, "E" and "K" at Fort Baker, "F" at Fort Carroll, "G" at Fort Dupont, "H" at Fort Wagner, "I" at Fort Stanton and "L" at Fort Davis. Mustered out September 2, 1862.

Regiment lost 4 by disease.

10th REGIMENT INFANTRY.

Organized at Providence May 26, 1862. Moved to Washington, D. C., May 27-29. Attached to Sturgis' Command. Military District of Washington. Duty at Camp Frieze, Tennallytown, till June 26. Assigned to garrison duty in the Defences of Washington. Company "A" at Fort Franklin, "B" and "K" at Fort Pennsylvania, "C" at Fort Cameron, "D" at Fort DeRussy, "E" and "I" at Fort Alexander, "F" at Fort Ripley, "G" at Fort Gaines, "H" at Battery Vermond and Battery Martin Scott and "L" near Fort Pennsylvania. Left for home August 25. Mustered out September 1, 1862.

Regiment lost 3 by disease.

11th REGIMENT INFANTRY.

Organized at Providence and mustered in October 1, 1862. Left State for Washington, D. C., October 6. Attached to Military District of Washington to December, 1862. District of Alexandria, Defences of Washington, and 22nd Army Corps, to April, 1863. 1st Brigade, 1st Division, 7th Army Corps, Dept. of Virginia, to June, 1863. 2nd Brigade, 1st Division, 4th Army Corps, Dept. of Virginia, to July, 1863.

SERVICE.— Duty at East Capital Hill, Fort Ethan Allen and Miner's Hill, Defences of Washington, till January 14, 1863. Guard duty at Convalescent Camp till April 15. Moved to Norfolk, thence to Suffolk April 15-19. Siege of Suffolk April 19-May 4. Siege of Suffolk raised May 4. Expedition to destroy Norfolk & Petersburg Railroad and Seaboard & Roanoke Railroad May 16-27. Expedition to Blackwater June 12-18. Moved to Norfolk June 19, thence to Yorktown, and to Williamsburg June 22. Duty at Williamsburg till June 30. Left Yorktown for home July 2. Mustered out July 13, 1863.

Regiment lost 8 by disease.

12th REGIMENT INFANTRY.

Organized at Providence and mustered in for nine months October 18, 1862. Left State for Washington, D. C., October 21. Attached to 1st Brigade, Casey's Division, Military District of Washington, to December, 1862. 1st Brigade, 2nd Division, 9th Army Corps, Army of the Potomac, to April, 1863. 1st Brigade, 2nd Division, Dept. Ohio, to May, 1863. 1st Brigade, 1st Division, 23rd Army Corps, Dept. Ohio, to July, 1863.

SERVICE.—Camp at Arlington Heights and at Fairfax Seminary, Va., Defences of Washington, D. C., till December 1, 1862. March to Falmouth, Va., December 1-8. Battle of Fredericksburg, Va., December 12-15. Burnside's second Campaign, "Mud March," January 20-24, 1863. Moved to Newport News, Va., February 9, thence to Lexington, Ky., March 25-31. Duty at Lexington, Winchester, Boonsboro, Richmond, Paint Lick and Lancaster, Ky., till April 23. Moved to Crab Orchard April 23, and duty there till June 3. March from Nicholasville to Somerset June 3-9. Duty at Stigall's Ferry, Jamestown and guarding fords of the Cumberland River till July 5. Moved to Somerset July 5, thence to Crab Orchard, and started home July 11. Duty at Cincinnati, Ohio, July 15-19. Moved to Providence July 19-22. Mustered out July 29, 1863.

Regiment lost during service 1 Officer and 11 Enlisted men killed and mortally wounded and 2 Officers and 45 Enlisted men by disease. Total 59.

INDEPENDENT COMPANY HOSPITAL GUARDS.

Organized at Portsmouth Grove December 6, 1862. Mustered out August 26, 1865.

SOUTH CAROLINA VOLUNTEERS.

1st REGIMENT INFANTRY (AFRICAN DESCENT).

Organized at Beaufort, S. C., January 31, 1863. Attached to District of Beaufort, S. C., 10th Army Corps, Dept. of the South, to January, 1864. Barton's Brigade, District of Hilton Head, S. C., 10th Corps, to February, 1864.

SERVICE.—Before muster, 3 Companies on Expedition along coasts of Georgia and Florida November 3-10, 1862. Spalding's, on Sapello River, Ga., November 7 (Co. "A"). Doboy River November 8. Duty at Beaufort, S. C., and Port Royal Island till March, 1863. Expedition from Beaufort up St. Mary's River in Georgia and Florida January 23-February 1. Skirmish at Township January 26. Expedition from Beaufort to Jacksonville, Fla., March 6-10. Occupation of Jacksonville March 10-31. Camp Jackson March 10. Operations near Jacksonville March 23-31. Skirmish near Jacksonville March 29. At Beaufort, S. C., till January, 1864. Expedition up South Edisto River July 9-11, 1863. Action, Williston Bluff, Pon, Pon River, July 10. Expedition to Pocotaligo, S. C., November 23-25 (Cos. "E" and "K"). Skirmish near Cunningham's Bluff November 24. (Cos. "C" and "K" at Hilton Head, S. C., till September, 1863, then moved to Beaufort, S. C.; Cos. "A" and "F" moved to Hilton Head September, 1863, returning to Beaufort, S. C., October 2.) Regiment moved to Hilton Head, S. C., January, 1864. Expedition to Jacksonville, Fla., February 6-8. Designation of Regiment changed to 33rd U. S. Colored Troops February 8, 1864, which see.

2nd REGIMENT INFANTRY (AFRICAN DESCENT).

Organized at Beaufort and Hilton Head, S. C., May 22, 1863. Attached to Districts of Hilton Head and Beaufort, S. C., 10th Army Corps, Dept. of the South, to July, 1863. 3rd Brigade, 1st Division, Morris Island, S. C., 10th Corps, July, 1863. 2nd Brigade, Morris Island, S. C., 10th Corps, to August, 1863. 4th Brigade, Morris Island, S. C., 10th Corps, to November, 1863. 3rd Brigade, Morris Island, S. C., 10th Corps, to January, 1864. Montgomery's Brigade, District Hilton Head, S. C., to February, 1864.

SERVICE.—Duty at Hilton Head, S. C., to March, 1863. Expedition to Jacksonville, Fla., March 6-10. Occupation of Jacksonville March 10-31. Operations about Jacksonville March 23-31. Evacuation of Jacksonville March 31. At Beaufort, S. C., till July. Raid on Combahee River June 2. Expedition to James Island, S. C., July 7-17. Engagement at Grimball's Landing July 16. Operations on Morris Island against Forts Wagner and Gregg July 18-September 7. Capture of Forts Wagner and Gregg September 7. Operations against Fort Sumpter and Charleston, S. C., September 7, 1863, to January 29, 1864. Moved to Hilton Head,

S. C., thence to Jacksonville, Fla., February 5-7. Designation of Regiment changed to 34th U. S. Colored Troops February 8, 1864, which see.

3rd REGIMENT INFANTRY (AFRICAN DESCENT).

Organized at Hilton Head, S. C., June, 1863. Attached to District of Hilton Head, S. C., 10th Army Corps, Dept. South, to January, 1864. Barton's Brigade, District Hilton Head, S. C., to February, 1864. 3rd Brigade, Vodges' Division, District of Florida, to March, 1864.

SERVICE.—Post duty at Hilton, Head, S. C., till February, 1864. Moved to Jacksonville, Fla., February 6-8, and duty there till March. Designation of Regiment changed to 21st U. S. Colored Troops March 14, 1864, which see.

4th REGIMENT INFANTRY (AFRICAN DESCENT).

Organized at Fernandina, Fla., July, 1863. Attached to Post of Fernandina, Fla., Dept. South, to January, 1864. Barton's Brigade, District of Hilton Head, S. C., to February, 1864. 3rd Brigade, Vodges' Division, District of Florida, to March, 1864.

SERVICE.—Duty at Fernandina, Fla., till January, 1864. At Hilton Head, S. C., till February, 1864. Moved to Jacksonville, Fla., February 6-8, and duty there till March. Regiment consolidated with 3rd South Carolina Infantry to form 21st U. S. Colored Troops March 14, 1864.

5th REGIMENT INFANTRY (AFRICAN DESCENT).

Organization of Regiment not completed. Transferred to 3rd and 4th South Carolina Infantry.

TENNESSEE VOLUNTEERS.

1st REGIMENT CAVALRY.

Organized at Camp Dennison, Ohio, November, 1862, from 4th Tennessee Infantry. Attached to Camp Dennison, Ohio, to December, 1862. Reserve Brigade, Cavalry Division, Army of the Cumberland, to January, 1863. 1st Brigade, 1st Cavalry Division, Army of the Cumberland, to November, 1864. 1st Brigade, 1st Division, Cavalry Corps, Military Division Mississippi, to January, 1865. District Middle Tennessee, Dept. of the Cumberland, to June, 1865.

SERVICE.—Duty at Camp Dennison, Ohio, till December 24, 1862. Moved to Cincinnati, Ohio, thence to Louisville, Ky.; to Shepherdsville, Ky., and return to Louisville, Ky., thence moved to Nashville, Tenn., January 9-17, 1863. Reconnoissance to Franklin and Brentwood and occupation of Franklin February 2, 1863. Moved to Concord Church February 2, and duty there till February 28. Expedition from Lexington to Clifton February 17-20 (Detachment). Moved to Triune February 28, and duty there till June. Petersburg March 2. Action at Harpeth River, near Triune, March 8. Franklin April 10. Near Chapel Hill April 13 (Detachment). Rigg's Cross Roads April 16. College Grove April 26 (Detachment). Expedition to Thompson's Station May 2. Rover May 5. Jordan's Store May 30. Franklin June 4. Triune June 9. Middle Tennessee or Tullahoma Campaign June 23-July 7. Eaglesville, Uniontown and Rover June 23. Middletown June 24. Fosterville, Guy's Gap and Shelbyville June 27. Bethpage Bridge, Elk River, July 1-2. Occupation of Middle Tennessee till August 16. At Dechard Station till July 12, then at Huntsville, Ala. Crossing Cumberland Mountains and passage of the Tennessee River, Chickamauga (Ga.) Campaign, August 16-September 22. Lebanon and Rawlinsville, Ala., September 5. Alpine September 9. Reconnoissance toward Rome September 10-11. Dirt Town September 12. Lafayette September 12. Battle of Chickamauga September 19-21. Operations against Wheeler and Roddy September 30-October 17. Anderson's Cross Roads October 2. McMinnville October 2. Shelbyville and Farmington October 4. Bucktown Tavern, Ala., October 12. Sulphur Springs, Tenn., October 21. At Winchester till November 18. Scout to Estill Springs and Tullahoma October 25-27. Moved to Alexandria November 18, and to Sparta November

20. Actions at Sparta November 20, 24, 26 and 27 Yankeetown November 30 (Detachment). March to Knoxville December 7-15, and to Strawberry Plains December 15-16. East Tennessee Campaign December, 1863, to February, 1864. Operations about Dandridge and Mossy Creek December 24-28, 1863. Hay's Ferry, near Dandridge, December 24. Mossy Creek December 25. Talbot Station December 27. Talbot Station, Mossy Creek, December 29. Expedition to Cosby Creek, N. C., January, 1864. Cosby Creek January 17. Near Wilsonville January 22. Operations about Dandridge January 26-28. Fair Garden January 26-27. McNutt's Bridge January 27. Scout from Marysville toward Seviersville February 1-2. Moved to Cleveland, Tenn., February 10-March 11. Atlanta (Ga.) Campaign May to September. Catoosa Springs May 4. Varnell's Station May 7-8. Demonstration on Dalton May 9-13. Tilton May 13. Resaca May 14-15. Pursuit to Cassville May 16-19. Near Cassville May 19. Stilesborough May 23. Huntsville or Burnt Hickory May 24. About Dallas, New Hope Church and Allatoona Hills May 25-June 5. Burned Church May 30 and June 11. Ackworth June 3-4. Big Shanty June 6. Operations about Marietta and against Kenesaw Mountain June 10-July 2. Pine Hill June 11-14. McAffee's Cross Roads June 11-12. Powder Springs and Noonday Creek June 20. Allatoona July 1. Nickajack Creek July 2-6. Kingston July 3. Ruff's Station July 4. Chattahoochie River July 6-17. Cochran's Ford July 9. Siege of Atlanta July 22-August 25. Mason's Church July 23. McCook's Raid on Atlanta & West Point Railroad July 27-31. Campbellton July 28. Lovejoy Station July 29. Clear Creek and Newnan July 31. Ordered to Nashville, Tenn. Rousseau's pursuit of Wheeler September 1-8. Lavergne September 1. Franklin September 2. Union City September 2 (Detachment). Campbellsville September 5. Pursuit of Forest September 25-October 10. Pulaski September 26-27. Franklin September 27. Cypress Creek, Ala., October 6. Florence, Ala., October 6-7. Mussel Shoals, near Florence, October 30. Near Shoal Creek October 31. Near Florence November 5-6 and 9. Nashville Campaign November and December. On line of Shoal Creek November 16-20. Lawrenceburg November 21. Fouche Springs November 23. Campbellsville November 24. Columbia November 24-27. Battle of Franklin November 30. Battle of Nashville December 15-16. Pursuit of Hood to the Tennessee River December 17-28. Lynnville December 24. Richland Creek December 24-25. Pulaski December 25-26. Expedition into Mississippi January 15-21, 1865. Moved from Eastport, Miss., to Nashville, Tenn., February 10-17, and duty there till June. Mustered out June, 1865.

Regiment lost during service 4 Officers and 56 Enlisted men killed and mortally wounded and 3 Officers and 293 Enlisted men by disease. Total 356.

1st MIDDLE TENNESSEE CAVALRY.

See 5th Regiment Tennessee Cavalry.

1st WEST TENNESSEE CAVALRY.

See 6th Regiment Tennessee Cavalry.

2nd REGIMENT CAVALRY.

Organized at Murfreesboro, Tenn., July, 1862. Attached to 7th Division, Army of the Ohio, to October, 1862. District of West Virginia, Dept. of the Ohio, to November. Unattached Cavalry, Cavalry Division, 14th Army Corps, Army of the Cumberland, November, 1862. Reserve Cavalry, Cavalry Division, Dept. of the Cumberland, to March, 1863. 2nd Brigade, 1st Cavalry Division, Army of the Cumberland, to January, 1864. 3rd Brigade, Cavalry Division, 16th Army Corps, Dept. of the Tennessee, to April, 1864. 1st Brigade, 4th Division, Cavalry Corps, Dept. of the Cumberland, to June, 1864. District of North Alabama, Dept. of the Cumberland, to October, 1864. 1st Brigade, 4th Division, Cavalry Corps, Military Division Mississippi, to November, 1864. 1st Brigade, 7th Division, Cavalry Corps, Military Division Mississippi, to March, 1865. Dept.

of Mississippi to May, 1865. Dept. of the Cumberland to July, 1865.

SERVICE.—Operations about Cumberland Gap, Tenn., till September, 1862. Evacuation of Cumberland Gap and retreat to Greenupsburg, Ky., September 17-October 3. Operations in the Kanawha Valley, W. Va., till November. Ordered to Cincinnati, Ohio, thence to Louisville, Ky., and to Nashville, Tenn. Advance on Murfreesboro, Tenn., December 26-30. Nolensville December 27-28. Triune December 28. Wilkinson's Cross Roads December 29. Lizzard's between Triune and Murfreesboro December 29. Overall's Creek December 30. Battle of Stone's River December 30-31, 1862, and January 1-3, 1863. Lytle's Creek January 5. Reconnoissance to Auburn, Liberty and Cainsville January 21-22. Expedition to Franklin January 31-February 13. Unionville, Middletown and Rover January 31. Rover February 13. Near Murfreesboro March 22. Operations against Pegram March 22-April 2. Danville March 24. Engagement at Franklin April 10. Expedition to McMinnville April 20-30. McMinnville April 21. Hickory Creek April 21. Slatersville April 22. Alexandria April 23. Wartrace April 29 and June 3. Triune June 9 and 11. Middle Tennessee or Tullahoma Campaign June 23-July 7. Eaglesville and Rover June 23. Middleton June 24. Fosterville, Guy's Gap and Shelbyville June 27. Bethpage Bridge, Elk River, July 1-2. Cocke County July 10. Expedition to Huntsville, Ala., July 13-22. Sparta August 9. Crossing Cumberland Mountains and Tennessee River and Chickamauga (Ga.) Campaign August 16-September 2. Reconnoissance from Shellmound toward Chattanooga August 30-31. Will's Valley August 31. Winston's Gap, Alpine, September 9. Alpine and Dirt Town September 12. Reconnoissance toward Lafayette September 13. Stevens' Gap September 18. Battle of Chickamauga, Ga., September 19-21. Dry Valley September 21. Operations against Wheeler and Roddy September 30-October 17. Anderson's Cross Roads October 2. Fayetteville October 13-14. Duty on Nashville & Chattanooga Railroad till December. Operations about Dandridge and Mossy Creek December 24-28. Expedition to Memphis, Tenn., December 28-January 4, 1864, thence moved to Colliersville, Tenn., January 14. Skirmish near Mossy Creek, Tenn., January 12, 1864 (Detachment). Smith's Expedition to Okolona, Miss., February 11-26. Near Okolona February 18. Houston February 19. West Point February 20-21. Prairie Station February 21. Okolona February 22. Tallahatchie River February 22. Ordered to Nashville, Tenn., February 27, and duty there till June. Duty on line of Nashville & Chattanooga Railroad, and in District of North Alabama till November. Operations in District of North Alabama June 24-August 20. Pond Springs, Ala., June 29. Operations against Wheeler August-September. Expedition from Decatur to Moulton August 17. Near Antioch Church August 18-19. Courtland and near Pond Springs August 19. Pursuit of Wheeler to Shoal Creek September 8-11. Operations against Forest and Hood September 16-November 3. Athens October 1-2. Defence of Decatur October 26-29. Nashville Campaign November-December. Owens' Cross Roads December 1. Near Paint Rock Bridge December 7. Battle of Nashville December 15-16. Pursuit of Hood to the Tennessee River December 17-28. Hollow Tree Gap, Franklin and West Harpeth River December 17. Rutherford Creek December 19. Lynnville December 23. Anthony's Hill near Pulaski December 25. Sugar Creek December 25-26. Near Decatur December 27-28. Pond Springs and Hillsboro December 29. Near Leighton December 30. Russellville December 31. Duty at Gravelly Springs, Ala., till February 6, 1865. Moved to Vicksburg, Miss., thence to New Orleans, La., February 6-March 10. Return to Vicksburg, Miss., and duty there and at various points in the Dept. of Mississippi till May 27. Ordered to Nashville, Tenn., reporting there June 12. Mustered out July 6, 1865.

Regiment lost during service 2 Officers and 14 Enlisted men killed and mortally wounded and 208 Enlisted men by disease. Total 224.

2nd WEST TENNESSEE CAVALRY.

See 7th Regiment Tennessee Cavalry.

3rd REGIMENT CAVALRY.

Organized at Murfreesboro and Nashville, Tenn., January 27, 1863. Attached to 4th Division, Center 14th Army Corps, Dept. of the Cumberland, November, 1862, to January, 1863. Post of Nashville, Tenn., Dept. of the Cumberland, to June, 1863. 2nd Brigade, 1st Cavalry Division, Army of the Cumberland, to August, 1863. Post of Nashville, Tenn., Dept. of the Cumberland, to January, 1864. 3rd Brigade, Cavalry Division, 16th Army Corps, Dept. of the Tennessee, to April, 1864. 1st Brigade, 4th Division, Cavalry Corps, Army of the Cumberland, to June, 1864. District of North Alabama, Dept. of the Cumberland, to October, 1864. 1st Brigade, 4th Division, Cavalry Corps, Military Division Mississippi, to November, 1864. 2nd Brigade, 6th Division, Cavalry Corps, Military Division Mississippi and District Middle Tennessee, to August, 1865.

SERVICE.—Guard trains from Nashville to Murfreesboro, Tenn., January 2-3, 1863. Battle of Stone's River January 3. Expedition to Franklin January 31-February 13. Middletown and Rover January 31. Rover February 13. At Camp Spear, Nashville, till June. Near Murfreesboro March 22. Middle Tennessee or Tullahoma Campaign June 23-July 7. Duty at Nashville till December, 1863. Operations about Dandridge and Mossy Creek December 24-28. Expedition to Memphis, Tenn., December 28-January 4, 1864. Moved to Colliersville January 14. Smith's Expedition to Okolona, Miss., February 11-26. Pontotoc February 17. Okolona February 18. Egypt Station February 19. West Point February 20-21. Ivy's Hill or Okolona February 22. Near New Albany February 22. Ordered to Nashville, Tenn., February 27, and duty there till June. Duty on line of Nashville & Chattanooga Railroad and in the District of North Alabama about Decatur, Ala., till September. Operations in District of North Alabama June 24-August 20. Scout in Morgan and Lawrence Counties July (Detachment). Expedition from Decatur to Courtland and Moulton and skirmish July 25-28. Courtland July 28. Summerville Road near Decatur August 6 (Detachment). Near Pond Springs August 9. Expedition from Decatur to Moulton August 17-20. Near Antioch Church August 18-19. Florence September 10. Operations against Forest September 16-25. Action at Athens September 23-24 (Detachment), captured. Action at Sulphur Branch Trestle September 25. Most of Regiment captured. Duty on Nashville and Chattanooga Railroad till December. At Decatur, Pulaski and Nashville. Joined Brigade at Nashville, Tenn., December 13. Battle of Nashville December 15-16. On post duty at Nashville till August, 1865. Mustered out August 3, 1865.

Regiment lost during service 2 Officers and 8 Enlisted men killed and mortally wounded and 4 Officers and 532 Enlisted men by disease. Total 546.

4th REGIMENT CAVALRY.

Organized at Nashville, Tenn., February 9, 1863. Attached to post of Nashville, Tenn., Dept. of the Cumberland, to January, 1864. 3rd Brigade, Cavalry Division, 16th Army Corps, Dept. of the Tennessee, to April, 1864. 1st Brigade, 4th Division, Cavalry Corps, Army of the Cumberland, to June, 1864. Districts of Nashville and North Alabama, Dept. of the Cumberland, to October, 1864. 1st Brigade, 4th Division, Cavalry Corps, Military Division Mississippi, to December, 1864. 1st Brigade, 7th Division, Cavalry Corps, Military Division Mississippi, to February, 1865. 2nd Brigade, 7th Division, Cavalry Corps, Military Division Mississippi, February, 1865. 2nd Brigade, 1st Division, Cavalry Corps, Military Division West Mississippi, to May, 1865. 1st Brigade, 2nd Cavalry Division, West Missisipi, to July, 1865.

SERVICE.—Duty at Camp Spear, Nashville, Tenn., till August, 1863. Green Hill June 14. Ordered to Carthage, Tenn., August 30. Duty there, at Murfreesboro and Nashville, Tenn., till December. Action at Friendship

Church September 29. Expedition to Memphis, Tenn., December 28-January 4, 1864. Moved to Colliersville January 14. Smith's Expedition to Okolona, Miss., February 11-26. Coldwater February 11. Holly Springs February 12. Near Okolona February 18. West Point February 20-21. Prairie Station February 21. Okolona and Tallahatchie River February 22. Ordered to Nashville, Tenn., February 27, and duty there till June. Duty on line of the Nashville & Chattanooga Railroad and in District of North Alabama till July. Decatur, Ala., June 1. (A detachment at Decatur, Ala., till October, 1864.) Sand Mountain July —. Rousseau's Raid from Decatur to West Point & Montgomery Railroad July 10-22. Near Coosa River July 13. Greenpoint and Ten Island Ford, Coosa River July 14. Opetika, Chehaw Station, and near Auburn July 18. Siege of Atlanta, Ga., till August 5. Scouts to England Cove, Tenn., July 7-9 and July 12-18 (Detachments). McCook's Raid on Atlanta & West Point Railroad July 27-31. Near Campbellton July 28. Lovejoy Station July 29. Clear Creek and near Newnan July 31. Chattahoochie River July 31. Ordered to Decatur, Ala., August 5. Near Pond Springs, Ala., August 9 (Detachment). Expedition from Decatur to Moulton August 17-20. Near Pond Springs August 18-19 (Detachment). Rousseau's pursuit of Wheeler September 1-8. Operations against Forest in East Tennessee September 16-October 10. Action at Pulaski September 26-27. At Nashville, Tenn., till December. Action at Owen's Cross Roads December 1. Demonstration on Murfreesboro December 5-7. Wilkinson's Cross Roads near Murfreesboro December 7. Battle of Nashville December 15-16. Pursuit of Hood to the Tennessee River December 17-28. Hollow Tree Gap, Franklin and West Harpeth River December 17. Franklin December 18. Rutherford Creek December 19. Lynnville December 23. Anthony's Hill December 25. Sugar Creek December 25-26. Hillsboro December 29. Near Leighton December 30. Narrows January 2, 1865. Thorn Hill January 3. At Gravelly Springs till February. Moved to Vicksburg, Miss., thence to New Orleans, La., and Mobile Bay, Ala., February 11-March 23. Campaign against Mobile and its defences March 26-April 9. Occupation of Mobile April 12. March to Montgomery April 13-25. Ordered to Mobile April 27. Expedition from Spring Hill, Ala., to Baton Rouge May 8-22. Ordered to Nashville, Tenn., May 27. Garrison duty at Johnsonville till July. Mustered out July 12, 1865.

Regiment lost during service 1 Officer and 24 Enlisted men killed and mortally wounded and 4 Officers and 205 Enlisted men by disease. Total 234.

5th REGIMENT CAVALRY (1st MIDDLE TENNESSEE).

Organized at Murfreesboro, Nashville and Carthage, Tenn., July 15, 1862. Attached to Post of Nashville, Tenn., Army of the Ohio, to November, 1862. Reserve Cavalry, Cavalry Division, Army of the Cumberland, to January, 1863. Post of Nashville, Tenn., Dept. of the Cumberland, to June, 1863. Post of Nashville, Tenn., Reserve Corps, Dept. of the Cumberland, June, 1863. 1st Brigade, 2nd Cavalry Division, Army of the Cumberland, to August, 1863. 3rd Brigade, 2nd Division, Cavalry Corps, Dept. of the Cumberland, to November, 1863. 1st Brigade, 2nd Cavalry Division, Army of the Cumberland, to April, 1864. 2nd Brigade, 4th Division, Cavalry Corps, Dept. of the Cumberland, to October, 1864. 2nd Brigade, 4th Division, Cavalry Corps, Military Division Mississippi, to November, 1864. 3rd Brigade, 6th Division, Cavalry Corps, Military Division Mississippi, to February, 1865. 3rd Brigade, 6th Division, Cavalry Corps, Military Division Mississippi, to February, 1865. District Middle Tennessee, to August, 1865.

SERVICE.—Duty at Nashville, Tenn., till December 26, 1862. Affair at Kinderhook August 11, 1862. Skirmish near Nashville September 2. Siege of Nashville September 7-November 7. Goodlettsville September 30. Gallatin October 1. Near Humboldt October 9. Near Nashville November 5. Near Lavergne November 7.

Reconnoissance toward Lavergne November 19. Reconnoissance to Franklin December 11-12. Franklin December 12. Advance on Murfreesboro December 26-30. Nolensville Pike December 27. Wilkinson's Cross Roads December 29. Battle of Stone's River December 30-31, 1862, and January 1-3, 1863. Overall's Creek December 31, 1862. Lytle's Creek January 5. Reconnoissance to Auburn, Liberty and Cainesville January 20-22. Near Cainesville February 15. Manchester Pike February 22. Bradysville March 1. Expedition to Woodbury March 3-8. Near Auburn March 8. Vaught's Hill near Milton March 20 (Co. "E"). Expedition to Auburn, Liberty, Snow Hill, etc., April 2-6. Snow Hill or Smith's Ford and Liberty April 3. Liberty April 7. Expedition to McMinnville April 20-30. Hartsville April 22. Bradyville Pike May 17. (Two Companies on Streight's Raid toward Rome, Ga., April 26-May 3. Day's Gap or Sand Mountain, Crooked Creek and Hog Mountain April 30. Blountsville and East Branch, Big Warrior River, May 1. Blake's Creek near Gadsden May 2. Blount's Farm and near Centre May 2. Near Cedar Bluff May 3.) Bradyville Pike May 17. Expedition to Middleton May 21-22. Scout on Middleton or Eagleville Pike June 10. Expedition to Lebanon June 15-17. Skirmish at Lebanon June 16. Dixon Springs June 20. Middle Tennessee or Tullahoma Campaign June 23-July 7. Shelbyville June 25. Fosterville, Guy's Gap and Shelbyville June 27. Duty at Carthage, McMinnville, Alexandria, Tracy City and Shelbyville, operating against guerrillas on line of the Nashville & Chattanooga Railroad till February, 1864. Pulaski July 15, 1863. Expedition to Huntsville, Ala., July 18-22. Scout in Sequatchie Valley September 21-22. Missionary Ridge and Shallow Ford Gap September 22. Operations against Wheeler and Roddy October 1-17. (Re-opening Tennessee River October 26-29 (Co. "G"). Battle of Wauhatchie, Tenn., October 28-29 (Co. "G"). Centreville October 29 (Co. "G"). Eagleville December 7. McMinnville December 21. Lavergne December 29. Scout to White and Putnam Counties February 1-7, 1864. Operations against guerrillas about Sparta February to April, Johnson's Mills February 22 (Detachment). Sparta and Calf Killer River February 22. White County March 10. Operations about Sparta March 11-28. Calf Killer River March 11. Winchester March 17. Beersheeba Springs March 19. Duty at Nashville, Tenn., and on line of the Nashville & Chattanooga Railroad at McMinnville, Carthage, Tullahoma and other points till November, 1864. Scout in Lincoln County July 12-15. McMinnville August —. Murfreesboro September 4. Operations about Murfreesboro November, 1864, to January, 1865. Siege of Murfreesboro December 4-12, 1864. Overall's Creek December 4 (Detachment). Demonstrations on Murfreesboro December 5-7. Wilkinson's Cross Road near Murfreesboro and the Cedars December 7. Ordered to Fayetteville January, 1865, and duty patroling line of the Nashville & Chattanooga Railroad and duty in District of East Tennessee till August, 1865. Skirmish near McMinnville February 5, 1865. Mustered out August 14, 1865.

Regiment lost during service 1 Officer and 68 Enlisted men killed and mortally wounded and 1 Officer and 175 Enlisted men by disease. Total 245.

5th REGIMENT CAVALRY (5th EAST TENNESSEE).

Organized at Camp Nelson, Ky. (5 Cos), for 10th Tennessee Cavalry, June 30 to August 14, 1863. Attached to District of Central Kentucky, Dept. of the Ohio, to July, 1863. 3rd Brigade, 3rd Division, 23rd Army Corps, Army of the Ohio, July, 1863. 2nd Brigade, 4th Division, 23rd Army Corps, July, 1863. 2nd Brigade, 1st Division, 23rd Army Corps, to August, 1863.

SERVICE.—Duty at Cynthiana, Ky., and along railroad till August, 1863. Pursuit of Morgan July 1-20. Buffington Island, Ohio, July 19. Operations against Scott July 25-August 6. Near Winchester, Ky., July 29. Irvine July 30. Lancaster, Stanford and Paint Lick Bridge July 31. Smith Shoals, Cumberland River, August 1. Assigned to 8th Tennessee Cavalry August, 1863 (which see).

6th REGIMENT CAVALRY (1st WEST TENNESSEE).

Organized at Bethel, LaGrange, Bolivar, Trenton, etc., Tenn., August 11, 1862. Attached to District of Jackson, Dept. of the Tennessee, to November, 1862. District of Jackson, 13th Army Corps, Dept. of the Tennessee, to December, 1862. Cavalry Brigade, District of Jackson, 16th Army Corps, to March, 1863. Cavalry Brigade, 3rd Division, 16th Army Corps, to June, 1863. 2nd Brigade, 1st Cavalry Division, 16th Army Corps, to December, 1863. 1st Brigade, 1st Cavalry Division, 16th Army Corps, to June, 1864. Unassigned, District of West Tennessee, Dept. of the Tennessee, to November, 1864. 2nd Brigade, 4th Division, Cavalry Corps, Military Division Mississippi, to December, 1864. 2nd Brigade, 7th Division, Cavalry Corps, Military Division Mississippi, to February, 1865. 1st Brigade, 6th Division, Cavalry Corps, Military Division Mississippi, and District of Middle Tennessee, to August, 1865.

SERVICE.—Pursuit to Ripley, Miss., October 5-12, 1862. Chewalla and Big Hill October 5. Operations about Bolivar, Tenn., November 3-December 31, 1862. Expedition from Corinth, Miss., against Forest December 18, 1862-January 3, 1863. Action near Jackson December 19, 1862. Near Ripley, Miss., December 23. Near Middleburg December 24-25. Bolivar December 24. Near Clifton, Tenn., January 1, 1863. Scout between Bolivar, Tenn., and Ripley, Miss., January 25-28. Pocahontas March 24. Expedition to Hatchie River and skirmishes April 1-16. Scout from LaGrange into Northern Mississippi April 29-May 5. Linden May 12 (Detachment). Expedition from Jackson across Tennessee River June 2-7. Operations in Northwest Mississippi June 15-25. Skirmishes at Forked Deer Creek and Jackson July 13, and at Forked Deer Creek July 15. Holly Springs September 7. Expedition from LaGrange to Toone Station September 11-16. Montezuma September 16. Locke's Mills, near Moscow, September 26. Operations in North Mississippi and West Tennessee against Chalmers October 4-17. Lockhart's Mills, Coldwater River, October 6. Salem October 8. Ingraham's Mills, near Byhalia, October 12. Wyatt's October 13. Operations on Memphis & Charleston Railroad November 3-5. Holly Springs, Miss., November 5. Operations on Memphis & Charleston Railroad against Lee's attack November 28-December 10. Operations in Northern Mississippi and West Tennessee December 18-31. Ordered to Memphis, Tenn., January 17, 1864, and duty there till November. Scout in Hardin County February 9. Seviersville and Miflin February 18. Operations against Forest in West Tennessee March 16-April 14. Bolivar March 29. Sturgis' Expedition to Ripley April 30-May 9. Tracy City August 4. Florence, Ala., October 6-7. Ordered to Nashville, Tenn., November 24. Battle of Nashville, Tenn., December 15-16. Pursuit of Hood to the Tennessee River December 17-28. Hollow Tree Gap and Franklin December 17. Rutherford Creek December 19. Lynnville December 23. Pulaski December 25-26. Hillsboro December 29. Near Leighton December 30. Narrows January 2, 1865. Thorn Hill January 3. At Gravelly Springs, Ala., till February. At Edgefield and Pulaski and in District of Middle Tennessee till August, 1865. Mustered out July 26, 1865.

Regiment lost during service 2 Officers and 33 Enlisted men killed and mortally wounded and 9 Officers and 352 Enlisted men by disease. Total 396.

7th REGIMENT CAVALRY (2nd WEST TENNESSEE).

Organized at Jackson, Grand Junction and Trenton, Tenn., August 28, 1862. Attached to District of Jackson, Dept. of the Tennessee, to November, 1862. District of Jackson, 13th Army Corps, Dept. of the Tennessee, to December, 1862. Cavalry Brigade, District of Jackson, 16th Army Corps, to April, 1863. Unassigned, 1st Division, 16th Army Corps, to June, 1863. 4th Brigade, 1st Cavalry Division, 16th Army Corps, to August, 1863. District of Columbus, 6th Division, 16th Army Corps, to October, 1863. Detached Cavalry Brigade, 16th Army Corps, to December, 1863. Waring's Cavalry Brigade, 16th Army Corps, to January, 1864. District of Columbus, Ky., to August, 1865.

SERVICE.—Duty in District of Jackson, Tenn., till January, 1863. Actions at Salem Cemetery, near Jackson, December 19, and near Jackson December 29, 1862. Near Middleburg December 24. At LaGrange, Moscow and Germantown till June, 1863. Expedition to Clifton February 17-21, 1863 (Detachment). Scout from La-Grange into Northern Mississippi April 29-May 5. Operations in Northwest Mississippi June 15-25. Jack's Creek, Tenn., June 20. At Grand Junction June, 1863. Skirmishes at and near Union City, Tenn., September 2. At Union City and Colliersville, Tenn., till January, 1864. Expedition to Toone Station September 11-16, 1863. Skirmish at Montezuma September 16. (Co. "A" detached at Paducah, Ky.) Skirmish at Dukedom February 28, 1864 (Detachment). Skirmish near Union City March 12. Operations against Forest in West Tennessee March 16-April 14. Reynoldsburg March 21. Attack on Union City March 24 (most of Regiment captured). Scout from Columbus to Hickman, Ky., July 17-18 (Detachment). Skirmish near Union City September 2. Duty at Paducah, Ky., till June, 1865. Ordered to Rockville, on Tennessee River, June 27. and duty there till August. Mustered out August 9, 1865.

Regiment lost during service 8 Enlisted men killed and mortally wounded and 1 Officer and 328 Enlisted men by disease. Total 337.

8th REGIMENT CAVALRY (5th EAST TENNESSEE).

Organized August, 1863, by consolidation of 5 Companies organized at Camp Nelson, Ky., June 30 to August 14, 1863, for 10th Tennessee Cavalry, and 7 Companies organized in Tennessee at large for 5th East Tennessee Cavalry. Attached to 2nd Brigade, 4th Division, 23rd Army Corps, Army of the Ohio, August to October, 1863. 4th Brigade, 4th Division, 23rd Army Corps, to April, 1864. 3rd Brigade, 4th Division, Cavalry Corps, Army of the Cumberland, to October, 1864. 3rd Brigade, 4th Division, Cavalry Corps, Military Division Mississippi, to November, 1864. District East Tennessee, Dept. of the Cumberland, to March, 1865. 3rd Brigade, Cavalry Division, District of East Tennessee. to July, 1865. Cavalry Brigade, District of East Tennessee, to September, 1865.

SERVICE.—Skirmish, Hawkins County, August 1, 1863. Burnside's Campaign in East Tennessee August 16-October 17, 1863. Occupation of Knoxville September 2. Greenville September 11. Kingsport September 18. Bristol September 19. Carter's Depot September 20-21. Zollicoffer September 20-21. Watauga River Bridge September 21-22. Jonesboro September 21. Hall's Ford, on Watauga River, September 22. Blountsville, Johnson's Depot and Carter's Depot September 22. Blue Springs October 10. Henderson's Mill and Rheatown October 11. Zollicoffer October 12. Blountsville October 14. Bristol October 15. Knoxville Campaign November 4-December 23. Siege of Knoxville November 17-December 5. Duty at Knoxville, Greenville, Nashville and Columbia and patrol duty on line of Nashville & Chattanooga Railroad from Columbia to Nashville till August, 1864. At Bull's Gap till October, 1864. Rheatown September 28. Watauga River September 29. Carter's Station September 30-October 1. Operations in East Tennessee October 10-28. Greenville October 12. Bull's Gap October 16. Clinch Mountain October 18. Clinch Valley, near Sneedsville, October 21. Mossy Creek and Panther Gap October 27. Morristown October 28. Russellville October 28. Operations against Breckenridge in East Tennessee November 4-17. Russellville November 11. Bull's Gap November 11-13. Russellville November 14. Strawberry Plains November 16-17. Flat Creek November 17. Stoneman's Saltsville (Va.) Raid December 10-29. Big Creek. near Rogersville, December 12. Kingsport December 13. Near Glade Springs December 15. Near Marion and capture of Wythevill December 16. Mt. Airey December 17. Near Marion December 17-18.

Capture and destruction of Salt Works at Saltsville December 20-21. Stoneman's Expedition from East Tennessee into Southwest Virginia and Western North Carolina March 21-April 25, 1865. Wytheville March 6. Shallow Ford and near Mocksville April 11. Salisbury April 12. Catawba River April 17. Swannanoa Gap April 22. Near Hendersonville April 23. Duty in District of East Tennessee till September, 1865. Mustered out September 11, 1865.

Regiment lost during service 1 Officer and 37 Enlisted men killed and mortally wounded and 1 Officer and 241 Enlisted men by disease. Total 280.

9th TENNESSEE CAVALRY.

Organized at Knoxville, Tenn., August 13, 1863. Joined DeCourcy at Crab Orchard, Ky., September 24, 1863. Attached to District of North Central Kentucky, Dept. of the Ohio, to April, 1864. 3rd Brigade, 4th Division, Cavalry Corps, Army of the Cumberland, to October, 1864. 3rd Brigade, 4th Division, Cavalry Corps, Military Division Mississippi, to November, 1864. District of East Tennessee. Dept. of the Cumberland, to March, 1865. 3rd Brigade, Cavalry Division, District of East Tennessee, to July, 1865. Cavalry Brigade, District of East Teneseee, to September, 1865.

SERVICE.—Duty at Crab Orchard, Ky., till October, 1863. (A Detachment on march to Cumberland Gap September 24-October 3, 1863, and operations about there.) Duty in District of East Tennessee, at Knoxville, Nashville and on line of the Nashville & Chattanooga Railroad, and at Bull's Gap, Tenn., till October, 1864. Rogersville August 21, 1864. Pursuit to Greenville August 21-23. Blue Springs August 23. Operations in East Tennessee August 29-September 4. Park Gap and Greenville September 4. Death of Gen. J. H. Morgan. Gillem's Expedition from East Tennessee toward Southwest Virginia September 20-October 17. Rheatown September 28. Watauga River September 29. Carter's Station September 29-October 1. Operations in East Tennessee October 10-28. Greenville October 12. Bull's Gap October 16. Clinch Mountain October 18. Clinch Valley, near Sneedsville, October 21. Mossy Creek and Panther Gap October 27. Morristown and Russellville October 28. Operations against Breckenridge's advance into East Tennessee November 4-17. Russellville November 11. Bull's Gap November 11-14. Russellville November 14. Strawberry Plains November 16-17. Flat Creek November 17. Stoneman's Expedition to Saltsville, Va., December 10-29. Big Spring, near Rogersville, December 12. Kingsport December 13. Glade Springs December 15. Marion and capture of Wytheville December 16. Mt. Airy December 17. Engagement near Marion December 17-18. Capture and destruction of Saltsville December 20-21. Duty in East Tennessee till March, 1865. Stoneman's Raid into Southwest Virginia and Western North Carolina March 21-April 25. Wytheville April 6. Shallow Ford and near Mocksville, N. C., April 11. Salisbury April 12. Catawba River April 17. Swannanoa Gap, N. C., April 20. Near Hendersonville April 23. Duty in East Tennessee till September. Mustered out September 11, 1865.

10th REGIMENT CAVALRY.

Organized at Nashville, Tenn., August 25, 1863. Attached to District of North Central Kentucky, Dept. of the Ohio, to January, 1864. Defences of Nashville & Northwestern Railroad, Dept. of the Cumberland, to April, 1864. 2nd Brigade, 4th Division, Cavalry Corps, Dept. of the Cumberland, to October, 1864. 2nd Brigade, 4th Division, Cavalry Corps, Military Division Mississippi, to November, 1864. 1st Brigade, 5th Division, Cavalry Corps, Military Division Mississippi, to February, 1865. 1st Brigade, 7th Division, Cavalry Corps, Military Division Mississippi, to March, 1865. Dept. of Mississippi to May, 1865. District of Nashville, Tenn., Dept. of the Cumberland, to August, 1865.

SERVICE.—Duty in District of North Central Kentucky till January, 1864. At Nashville and Pulaski, Tenn., and on line of the Nashville & Chattanooga

Railroad and Nashville & Northwestern Railroad till November, 1864. Scouts in Hickman and Maury Counties May 2-12, 1864. Long's Mill, near Mulberry Creek, July 28. Clifton August 15-16. Skirmish at Rogersville August 21, 1864. Pursuit to Greenville August 21-23. Blue Springs August 23. Operations against Forest's Raid in Northern Alabama and Middle Tennessee September 16-October 10. Richland Creek, near Pulaski, September 26. Pulaski September 26-27. Guard Tennessee River October. Florence October 30. On line of Shoal Creek November 5-11. Nashville Campaign November-December. On line of Shoal Creek November 16-20. Near Maysville and near New Market November 17. On front of Columbia November 24-27. Crossing of Duck River November 28. Franklin November 30. Battle of Nashville December 15-16. Pursuit of Hood to the Tennessee River December 17-28. Hollow Tree Gap and West Harpeth River December 17. Rutherford Creek December 19. Richland Creek December 24. Pulaski December 25-26. Hillsboro December 29. Leighton December 30. At Gravelly Springs, Ala., till February, 1865. Moved to Vicksburg, Miss., thence to New Orleans, La., February 6-March 10. Ordered to Natchez, Miss., March, and duty there and at Rodney, Miss., till May 25. Ordered to Nashville, Tenn., May 25. Garrison duty at Johnsonville, Tenn., till August. Mustered out August 1, 1865.

Regiment lost during service 1 Officer and 24 Enlisted men killed and mortally wounded and 1 Officer and 181 Enlisted men by disease. Total 207.

11th REGIMENT CAVALRY.

Organized at large May to October, 1863. Attached to Willcox's Division, Left Wing Forces 23rd Army Corps, Dept. of the Ohio, to January, 1864. District of the Clinch to April, 1864. 1st Brigade, 4th Division, 23rd Army Corps, Dept. of the Ohio, to January, 1865.

SERVICE.—Joined DeCourcy at Crab Orchard, Ky., August 24, 1863. March to Cumberland Gap September 24-October 3. Operations about Cumberland Gap till February, 1864. Mulberry Creek January 3. Tazewell January 24. Near Jonesville January 28-29. Skirmishes on Jonesville and Mulberry Roads February 12. Gibson and Wyerman's Mills on Indian Creek, and at Powell's Bridge February 22. Duty at and about Cumberland Gap guarding communications with Knoxville till January, 1865. Action at Johnsonville, Tenn., November 4-5, 1864. Mustered out by consolidation with 9th Tennessee Cavalry January 9, 1865.

12th REGIMENT CAVALRY.

Organized at Nashville, Tenn., August 24, 1863. Attached to District of Nashville, Dept. of the Cumberland, to January, 1864. Defences of Nashville & Northwestern Railroad to April, 1864. 2nd Brigade, 4th Division, Cavalry Corps, Dept. of the Cumberland, to October, 1864. 2nd Brigade, 4th Division, Cavalry Corps, Military Division Mississippi, to December, 1864. 2nd Brigade, 5th Division, Cavalry Corps, Military Division Mississippi, to February, 1865. 1st Brigade, 5th Division, Cavalry Corps, Military Division Mississippi, to May, 1865. Dept. of the Missouri to October, 1865.

SERVICE.—Scout to Florence, Ala., July 20-25, 1863 (Detachment). Duty at Nashville and on Nashville & Northwestern Railroad at Pulaski, Tenn., till November, 1864. Duck River April 22, 1864. Scout in Hickman and Maury Counties May 2-12. Lincoln County June 14. Scout from Pulaski to Florence, Ala., July 20-25 (Detachment). Triune August 3-4. Florence August 10. Operations against Forest in North Alabama and Middle Tennessee September 16-October 10. Richland Creek, near Pulaski, September 26. Pulaski September 26-27. Nashville Campaign November-December. On line of Shoal Creek November 5-20. Campbellsville and Lynnville November 24. In front of Columbia November 24-27. Franklin November 30. Battle of Nashville December 15-16. Pursuit of Hood to the Tennessee River December 17-28. West Harpeth River December 17. Spring Hill December 18. Rutherford Creek December 19. Curtis Creek December 19. Lawrence-

burg December 22. Lynnville and Richland Creek December 24. King's Gap, near Pulaski, December 25. At Gravelly Springs, Ala., till February, 1865. At Eastport, Miss., till May. Moved to St. Louis, Mo., May 15-17, thence to Rolla, Mo., June 20-26, and to Fort Riley, Kan., June 29-July 8. Powder River Expedition July to September. Mustered out October 7, 1865.

Regiment lost during service 5 Officers and 28 Enlisted men killed and mortally wounded and 2 Officers and 191 Enlisted men by disease. Total 226.

13th REGIMENT CAVALRY.

Organized at Strawberry Plains, Nashville and Gallatin, Tenn., October, 1863. Attached to District of Columbus, Ky., 6th Division, 16th Army Corps, Dept. of the Tennessee, to November, 1863. District of North Central Kentucky, Dept. of the Ohio, to January, 1864. District of Nashville, Tenn., Dept. of the Cumberland, to April, 1864. 3rd Brigade, 4th Division, Cavalry Corps, Army of the Cumberland, to October, 1864. 3rd Brigade, 4th Division, Cavalry Corps, Military Division Mississippi, November, 1864. District of East Tennessee to March, 1865. 3rd Brigade, Cavalry Division, District of East Tennessee, Dept. of the Cumberland, to July, 1865. Cavalry Brigade, District of East Tennessee, to September, 1865.

SERVICE.—Duty in District of Columbus, Ky., and at Camp Nelson, Ky., till January, 1864. Duty in District of Nashville and on Nashville & Chattanooga Railroad, and at Bull's Gap, Tenn., till September, 1864. Rogersville August 21, 1864. Pursuit to Greenville August 21-23. Blue Springs August 23. Park's Gap, Greenville, September 4. Morgan killed. Gillem's Expedition from East Tennessee toward Southwest Virginia September 20-October 17. Rheatown September 28. Watauga River September 29. Carter's Station September 30-October 1. Operations in East Tennessee October 10-28. Greenville October 12. Bull's Gap October 16. Clinch Mountain October 18. Clinch Valley near Sneedsville October 21. Near Memphis October 25. Mossy Creek and Panther Gap October 27. Morristown and Russellville October 28. Operations against Breckenridge's advance into East Tennessee November 4-17. Russellville November 11. Bull's Gap November 11-13. Russellville November 14. Strawberry Plains November 16-17. Flat Creek November 17. Stoneman's Saltsville Raid December 10-29. Big Creek near Rogersville December 12. Kingsport December 13. Glade Springs December 15. Marion and capture of Wytheville December 16. Mt. Airy December 17. Engagement near Marion December 17-18. Capture and destruction of Saltsville, Va., December 20-21. Duty in East Tennessee till March, 1865. Stoneman's Expedition from East Tennessee into Southwest Virginia and Western North Carolina March 21-April 25. Wytheville April 6. Shallow Ford and near Mocksville April 11. Salisbury April 12. Catawba River near Morgantown April 17. Swannanoa Gap, N. C., April 20. Near Hendersonville April 23. Duty in District of East Tennessee till September. Mustered out September 5, 1865.

14th REGIMENT CAVALRY.

Failed to complete organization. Those enlisted on duty on Nashville & Northwestern Railroad, Dept. of the Cumberland, to February, 1865. Affair near Triune February 10, 1865. Scout from Nashville on Nolensville Pike February 15-16.

BRADFORD'S BATTALION CAVALRY.

Organized December, 1863. Consolidated to a Company April, 1864, and assigned to 14th Tennessee Cavalry as Company "A," then to 6th Tennessee Cavalry as Company "E."

SERVICE.—Attached to District of Cairo, Dept. of the Tennessee. At Paducah, Ky., January, 1864. Ordered to Fort Pillow, Tenn., February 4, 1864, and garrison duty there till April. Forest's attack on and massacre at Fort Pillow April 12.

1st TENNESSEE AND ALABAMA VIDETTE CAVALRY.

Organized Companies "A," "B," "C," "G" and "H" at Stevenson and Bridgeport, Ala., September 10, 1863, to April 26, 1864. Companies "D," "E" and "F" at Tracy City and Nashville, Tenn., December 9, 1863, to February 24, 1864. Participated in skirmish at Hunt's Mills near Larkinsville, Ala., September 28, 1863. Beersheeba Springs November 26. Expedition to Lebanon December 12-29. Skirmish at Sand Mountain, Ala., December 26. Mustered out June 16, 1864.

1st REGIMENT HEAVY ARTILLERY (AFRICAN DESCENT).

Organized at Memphis, Tenn., June, 1863. Attached to 1st Brigade, 5th Division, District of Memphis, 16th Army Corps, Dept. of the Tennessee, to April, 1864. Post and garrison duty at Memphis, and at Fort Pickering, Defences of Memphis, June, 1863, to April, 1864. Designation changed to 3rd United States Colored Heavy Artillery April 26, 1864 (which see).

2nd REGIMENT HEAVY ARTILLERY (AFRICAN DESCENT).

Organized at Columbus, Ky., June, 1863. Attached to District of Columbus, Ky., 6th Division, 16th Army Corps, Dept. of the Tennessee, to April, 1864. Post and garrison duty at Union City, Tenn., and Columbus, Ky., till April, 1864. Designation of Regiment changed to 4th United States Colored Heavy Artillery April 26, 1864 (which see).

1st BATTALION LIGHT ARTILLERY.

Organized at Memphis, Tenn., Nashville and Knoxville, Tenn., June 13, 1862, to October 16, 1863.

BATTERY "A."

Attached to Post of Nashville, Dept. of the Ohio, August to December, 1862. Post of Clarksville, District of Western Kentucky, Dept. of the Ohio, to April, 1863. Post of Clarksville, Tenn., District of Central Kentucky, Dept. of the Ohio, to June, 1863. 1st Brigade, 1st Division, 23rd Army Corps, Army Ohio, June, 1863. 1st Brigade, 3rd Division, Reserve Corps, Dept. of the Cumberland, to August, 1863. 3rd Brigade, 3rd Division, Reserve Corps, August, 1863. 3rd Brigade, 4th Division, 23rd Army Corps, Dept. of the Ohio, to November, 1862. 2nd Division, Artillery Reserve, Army of the Cumberland, to March, 1864. Garrison Decatur, Ala., District Northern Alabama, Dept. of the Cumberland, to April, 1864. Artillery, 4th Division, Cavalry Corps, Dept. of the Cumberland, to October, 1864. Artillery, 6th Division, Cavalry Corps, Military Division Mississippi, to March, 1865. District Middle Tennessee to July, 1865.

SERVICE.—Duty at Nashville and Clarksville, Tenn., till August, 1863. Siege of Nashville September 7-November 7, 1862. Operations against Scott's Forces in West Kentucky July 25-August 6, 1863. Near Winchester July 29. Irvine July 30. Lancaster, Stanford and Paint Lick Bridge July 30. Smith's Shoals, Cumberland River, August 1. Ordered to Murfreesboro, Tenn., August; thence to McMinnville September 5, and march to Chattanooga September 12-22. Garrison Artillery at Chattanooga till March, 1864. Reopening Tennessee River October 26-29, 1863. Battles of Chattanooga November 23-25. Garrison Artillery at Decatur, Ala., March, 1864, to January, 1865. Skirmishes at Athens, Ala., October 1-2, 1864. Siege of Decatur October 26-29. Ordered to Pulaski, Tenn., January 16, 1865. Duty at Pulaski and in Middle Tennessee on line of railroad till July. Mustered out July, 1865.

BATTERY "B."

Attached to District of Kentucky, Dept. of Ohio, to August, 1863. Willcox's Division, Left Wing Forces, 23rd Army Corps, Dept. of the Ohio, to January, 1864. District of the Clinch, Dept. of the Ohio, to April, 1864. 1st Brigade, 4th Division, 23rd Army Corps, Dept. of the Ohio, to February, 1865. 1st Brigade, 4th Division, District of East Tennessee, to March, 1865. 2nd Brigade, 4th Division, District of East Tennessee, to July, 1865.

SERVICE.—Duty in Kentucky till August, 1863. Action at Tripletts Bridge June 16. Operations against Scott in Eastern Kentucky July 25-August 6. Expedition to Cumberland Gap August 17-September 7. Winter's Gap August 31. Operations about Cumberland Gap September 7-10. Duty at Cumberland Gap till May, 1865, and in District of East Tennessee till July. Mustered out July, 1865.

BATTERY "C."

Attached to Defences of Memphis, Fort Pickering, 16th Army Corps, Dept. of the Tennessee, to March, 1864. Post and District of Nashville, Tenn., Dept. of the Cumberland, to March, 1865. Artillery, 3rd Sub-District, District of Middle Tennessee, to July.

SERVICE.—Garrison duty at Fort Pickering, Defences of Memphis, Tenn., till March, 1864, and Garrison Artillery at Nashville, Tenn., till March, 1865. Battle of Nashville December 15-16, 1864. Ordered to Johnsonville March 22, 1865, and duty there till July. Mustered out July, 1865.

BATTERY "D."

Attached to Post and District of Nashville, Dept. of the Cumberland, to March, 1865. 3rd Brigade, 4th Division, District of East Tennessee, Dept. of the Cumberland, to July, 1865.

SERVICE.—Garrison Artillery at Nashville entire term. Battle of Nashville December 15-16, 1864. Mustered out July, 1865.

BATTERY "E."

Attached to District of North Central Kentucky, Dept. of the Ohio, 1st Division, 23rd Army Corps, October, 1863, to April, 1864. District of Nashville, Tenn., Dept. of the Cumberland, to May, 1865. 1st Brigade, 4th Division, District of East Tennessee, to July, 1865.

SERVICE.—Duty in District of North Central Kentucky, at Booneville, Camp Nelson, Flemmingsburg, Mt. Sterling and Paris, December, 1863, to April, 1864, and at Nashville and Bull's Gap, Tenn., to August, 1864. Pursuit to Greenville, Tenn., August 21-23. Blue Springs August 23. Operations in East Tennessee August 29-September 4. Park's Gap and Greenville September 4. Death of Gen. J. H. Morgan. Blue Springs September 6. Carter's Station September 30-October 1. Operations in East Tennessee October 10-28. Clinch Valley, near Sneedsville, October 21. Mossy Creek and Panther Springs October 27. Morristown and Russellville October 28. Operations against Breckenridge November 4-17. Bull's Gap November 11-13. Morristown November 13. Russellville November 14. Strawberry Plains November 16-17. Duty in East Tennessee till March, 1865. Stoneman's Expedition from East Tennessee into Southwest Virginia and Western North Carolina March 21-April 25, 1865. Wytheville April 6. Martinsville April 8. Shallow Ford and near Mocksville April 11. Saulsbury April 12. Catawba River April 17. Catawba River near Morganstown, April 20. Howard's Gap and Blue Ridge Mountains April 22. Near Hendersonville April 23. Duty in East Tennessee till June. Ordered to Nashville June 25. Mustered out July, 1865.

BATTERY "F."

Attached to 1st Brigade, 4th Division, 23rd Army Corps, Dept. of the Ohio, and duty in District of East Tennessee entire term. Mustered out July, 1865.

BATTERY "G."

Post and garrison duty at Nashville and Bull's Gap, Tenn., entire term. Mustered out July, 1865. Attached to Governor's Guard.

BATTERY "K."

Ordered to Knoxville March 22, 1865, and garrison duty there till July. Mustered out July, 1865.

MEMPHIS LIGHT BATTERY (AFRICAN DESCENT).

Organized at Memphis, Tenn., November 23, 1863. Attached to Garrison of Fort Pickering, District of

Memphis, 5th Division, 16th Army Corps, Dept. of the Tennessee, to January, 1864. 1st Colored Brigade, District of Memphis, Tenn., 16th Army Corps, to April, 1864.

SERVICE.—Post and garrison duty at Memphis, Tenn., till April, 1864. A section sent to Fort Pillow, Tenn., February 15, 1864. Designation of Battery changed to Battery "F," 2nd United States Colored Light Artillery, April 26, 1864 (which see).

1st REGIMENT INFANTRY.

Organized at Camp Dick Robinson, Ky., August and September, 1861. Attached to Thomas' Command, Army of the Ohio, to November, 1861. 12th Brigade, Army of the Ohio, to December, 1861. 12th Brigade, 1st Division, Army of the Ohio, to February, 1862. 24th Brigade, 7th Division, Army of the Ohio, to October, 1862. 3rd Brigade, District of West Virginia, Dept. of the Ohio, to November, 1862. 1st Brigade, 2nd Division, Centre 14th Army Corps, Army of the Cumberland, to January, 1863. 1st Brigade, 2nd Division, 14th Army Corps, to April, 1863. District of Central Kentucky, Dept. of the Ohio, to June, 1863. 1st Brigade, 1st Division, 23rd Army Corps, Army of the Ohio, to August, 1863. 1st Brigade, 4th Division, 23rd Army Corps, to October, 1863. 2nd Brigade, 4th Division, 23rd Army Corps, to November, 1863. 2nd Brigade, 1st Division, Cavalry Corps, Dept. of the Ohio, to April, 1864. 3rd Brigade, 4th Division, 23rd Army Corps, to May, 1864. 3rd Brigade, 3rd Division, 23rd Army Corps, to August, 1864. 2nd Brigade, 4th Division, 23rd Army Corps, to February, 1865. 2nd Brigade, 4th Division, District of East Tennessee, to August, 1865.

SERVICE.—Duty at Camp Dick Robinson and at London, Ky., till January, 1862. Battle of Logan's Cross Roads January 19, 1862. At London and covering Cumberland Gap till March. Skirmishes at Big Creek Gap and at Jacksborough March 14 (Co. "A"). Reconnoissance to Cumberland Gap and skirmishes March 21-23. Cumberland Gap Campaign March 28-June 18. Occupation of Cumberland Gap June 18-September 17. Skirmish near Cumberland Gap August 27. Rogers' Gap August 31. Operations at Rogers' and Big Creek Gaps September 10. Evacuation of Cumberland Gap and retreat to Greenupsburg, Ky., September 17-October 3. Operations at Kanawha Valley, W. Va., till November. Ordered to Louisville, Ky., thence to Nashville, Tenn., and duty there till January, 1863. Escort trains to Murfreesboro, Tenn., January 2-3. Action at Cox's or Blood's Hill January 3, 1863. Reconnoissance to Franklin and Brentwood February 1-2. Ordered to Lexington, Ky., March 11, 1863. Duty in District of Central Kentucky till June. At Camp Dick Robinson till April. Expedition to Monticello and operations in Southeast Kentucky April 25-May 2. At Nicholasville May. Actions at Monticello and Rocky Gap June 9. Sander's Raid on East Tennessee & Virginia Railroad and destruction of Slate Creek, Strawberry Plains and Mossy Creek bridges June 14-24. Kingston June 16. Wartzburg June 17. Lenoir Station June 19. Knoxville June 19-20. Rogers' Gap June 20. Powder Springs Gap June 21. Powell Valley June 22. Pursuit of Morgan July 3-23. At Lebanon and Camp Nelson July. Operations against Scott's forces in Eastern Kentucky July 25-August 6. Near Winchester July 29. Irvine July 30. Lancaster, Stanford and Pain's Lick Bridge July 31. Smith's Shoals, Cumberland River, August 1. Burnside's Campaign in East Tennessee August 16-October 19. Jacksborough August 28. Winter's Gap August 31. Athens September 10 and 25. Calhoun September 18. Calhoun and Charleston September 25. Cleveland October 9. Philadelphia October 20-22. Sweetwater October 24. Leiper's Ferry October 28. Knoxville Campaign November 4-December 23. Marysville November 14. Lenoir Station November 14-15. Near Loudoun and Holston River November 15. Campbell's Station November 16. Siege of Knoxville November 17-December 5. Russellville December 10. At and near Bean's Station December 9-15. Blain's Cross Roads December 16-19. Hay's Ferry, near Dandridge, December

24. Mossy Creek, Talbot Station, December 29. Bend of Chucky and Rutledge January 16, 1864. Operations about Dandridge January 16-17. Seviersville January 26. Near Fair Garden January 27. Fentress County February 13. Sulphur Springs February 26. Atlanta, Ga., Campaign May to August. Demonstration on Dalton May 8-11. Battle of Resaca May 14-15. Cartersville May 20. Operations on line of Pumpkin Vine Creek and battles about Dallas, New Hope Church and Allatoona Hills May 25-June 5. Operations about Marietta and against Kenesaw Mountain June 10-July 2. Lost Mountain June. 15-17. Muddy Creek June 17. Noyes Creek June 19. Cheyney's Farm June 22. Olley's Creek June 26-27. Assault on Kenesaw June 27. Nickajack Creek July 2-5. Chattahoochie River July 6-17. Peach Tree Creek July 19-20. Siege of Atlanta July 22-August 11. Relieved August 11 and ordered to Knoxville, Tenn. Duty there and in East Tennessee till March, 1865. Expedition from Irish Bottom to Evans' Island January 25, 1865. Ordered to Cumberland Gap March 16, 1865, and duty there till August. Mustered out August 8, 1865.

Regiment lost during service 49 Enlisted men killed and mortally wounded and 2 Officers and 334 Enlisted men by disease. Total 385.

1st REGIMENT MOUNTED INFANTRY.

Organized at Nashville and Carthage, Tenn., December, 1863, to November, 1864. Attached to District of Middle Tennessee, Dept. of the Cumberland, to February, 1865. 1st Brigade, 1st Sub-District, District of Middle Tennessee, Dept. of the Cumberland, to July, 1865.

SERVICE.—Duty at Carthage, Granville and on line of the Nashville & Chattanooga Railroad in District of Middle Tennessee till April, 1865. Ordered to Murfreesboro, Tenn., April 18, and duty there till June 26. Ordered to Nashville and mustered out July 22, 1865.

1st REGIMENT INFANTRY (AFRICAN DESCENT).

Organized at LaGrange June 6, 1863. Mustered in June 27, 1863. Attached to District of Corinth, 2nd Division, 16th Army Corps, Army of the Tennessee, to November, 1863. Post of Corinth, 2nd Division, 16th Army Corps, to January, 1864. 1st Colored Brigade, District of Memphis, Tenn., 5th Division, 16th Army Corps, to March, 1864.

SERVICE.—Post duty at LaGrange, Tenn., till September, 1863. Moved to Corinth, Miss., and post and garrison duty there till January, 1864. Moved to Memphis, Tenn., and post and garrison duty there till March. Designation changed to 59th United States Colored Troops March 11, 1865 (which see).

1st REGIMENT ENROLLED MILITIA INFANTRY.

Organized at Memphis, Tenn., for the defence of that city.

2nd REGIMENT INFANTRY.

Organized at Camp Dick Robinson and Somerset, Ky., September 28, 1861. Attached to George H. Thomas' Command, Army of the Ohio, to November, 1861. 12th Brigade, Army of the Ohio, to December, 1861. 12th Brigade, 1st Division, Army of the Ohio, to February, 1862. 24th Brigade, 7th Division, Army of the Ohio, to October, 1862. 3rd Brigade, District of West Virginia, Dept. of the Ohio, to November, 1862. 1st Brigade, 2nd Division (Centre), 14th Army Corps, Army of the Cumberland, to January, 1863. 1st Brigade, 2nd Division, 14th Army Corps, to April, 1863. 2nd Brigade, District of Central Kentucky, Dept. of the Ohio, to June, 1863. 1st Brigade, 1st Division, 23rd Army Corps, Dept. of the Ohio, to August, 1863. 3rd Brigade, 4th Division, 23rd Army Corps, to November, 1863. 1st Brigade, 2nd Division, Cavalry Corps, Dept. of the Ohio, to April, 1864. 2nd Brigade, 4th Division, 23rd Army Corps, to February, 1865. 2nd Brigade, 4th Division, District of East Tennessee, to August, 1865.

SERVICE.—Duty at Camp Dick Robinson, Ky., till January, 1862. Battle of Logan's Cross Roads January 19. At Loudon and covering Cumberland Gap till March. Skirmishes at Big Creek Gap and Jacksborough March

14 (Co. "B"). Reconnoissance to Cumberland Gap and skirmish March 21-23. Cumberland Gap Campaign March 28-June 18. Occupation of Cumberland Gap June 18-September 17. Tazewell July 22. Skirmish near Cumberland Gap August 27. Operations at Rogers and Big Creek Gaps September 10. Evacuation of Cumberland Gap and retreat to Greenupsburg, Ky., September 17-October 3. Operations in Kanawha Valley, W. Va., till November. Ordered to Louisville, Ky., Cincinnati, Ohio, and thence to Nashville, Tenn. Duty there till January, 1863. Guard trains from Nashville to Murfreesboro, Tenn., January 2-3. Cox's or Blood's Hill January 3. Ordered to Lexington, Ky., March 11. Duty in District of Central Kentucky till August. At Somerset, Ky., May. Liberty May 25. Pursuit of Morgan July. Operations in Eastern Kentucky against Scott July 25-August 6. Burnside's Campaign in East Tennessee August, 1863, to February, 1864. Winter's Gap August 31, 1863. Expedition to Cumberland Gap September 4-9. Tazewell September 5. Capture of Cumberland Gap September 9. Carter's Station September 20, 21 and 22. Zollicoffer September 20-21 and September 24. Jonesboro September 21 and 28. Blue Springs October 5-10. Sweetwater October 10-11. Pursuit to Bristol October 11-17. Blountsville October 13-14. Bristol October 15. Knoxville Campaign November 4-December 23. Near Loudon and Stock Creek November 15. Marysville November 15. Lenoir Station November 15. Campbell's Station November 16. Defence of Cumberland Gap during siege of Knoxville November 17-December 5. Walker's Ford, Clinch River, December 5. Rutledge December 7. Clinch Mountain December 9. Moresburg December 10. Morristown December 10. Cheex's Cross Roads December 12. Russellville December 12-13. Bean's Station December 14. Rutledge December 16. Blain's Cross Roads December 16-19. New Market December 25. Operations about Dandridge and Mossy Creek December 24-28. Mossy Creek December 26. Talbot's Station December 29. Shoal Creek, Ala., January 14, 1864. Operations about Dandridge January 16-17. Kimbrough's Cross Roads January 16. Dandridge January 17. Operations about Dandridge January 26. Fair Garden January 27. Duty at Knoxville and Loudon till August, 1864. Operations against Wheeler in East Tennessee August 15-31. Duty at Knoxville and in East Tennessee till March, 1865. Ordered to Cumberland Gap March 16, and duty there till August. Mustered out August 3, 1865.

Regiment lost during service 3 Officers and 24 Enlisted men killed and mortally wounded and 4 Officers and 609 Enlisted men by disease. Total 640.

2nd REGIMENT MOUNTED INFANTRY.

Organized at Nashville, Clifton and Franklin, Tenn., October 2, 1863, to April 10, 1864. Attached to Defences of Nashville & Louisville Railroad, Dept. of the Cumberland, to March, 1865. 2nd Brigade, District of East Tennessee, Dept. of the Cumberland, to June, 1865.

SERVICE.—Duty at Clifton and on line of the Louisville & Nashville Railroad till November, 1864. Stone's Mill December 19, 1863. Skirmish in Berry County April 29, 1864. Decatur County June 21. Centreville July. Blount County July 20. Skirmishes at Clifton July 22, 23, 30 and August 15-16. Marysville August 21. Clinton Road August 27. Clifton August 31 and September 1. Lobelville and Beardstown September 27. Centreville September 29. Moved to Johnsonville, Tenn., November, 1864, and duty on line of Duck River. Ordered to Gallatin December 9. Patrol river from Gallatin to Carthage. Duty at Clifton and on line of Louisville & Nashville Railroad till June. Mustered out June 27, 1865.

Lost during service 3 Officers and 30 Enlisted men killed and mortally wounded and 3 Officers and 78 Enlisted men by disease. Total 114.

2nd REGIMENT INFANTRY (AFRICAN DESCENT).

Organized at LaGrange, Tenn., June 30, 1863. Attached to 1st Brigade, 2nd Division, 16th Army Corps, Dept. of the Tennessee, to November, 1863. Post of Corinth, 2nd Division, 16th Army Corps, to January, 1864. 1st Colored Brigade, District of Memphis, 16th Army Corps, to March, 1864.

SERVICE.—Post and garrison duty at LaGrange and Moscow, Tenn., till January, 1864. Skirmish at Moscow December 3, 1863 (Detachment). Wolf Bridge, near Moscow, December 3-4. Ordered to Memphis, Tenn., January, 1864, and post and garrison duty there till March, 1864. Designation of Regiment changed to 61st United States Colored Troops March 11, 1864 (which see).

2nd REGIMENT ENROLLED MILITIA INFANTRY.

Organized at Memphis, Tenn., for the protection of that city.

3rd REGIMENT INFANTRY.

Organized at Flat Lick, Ky., December, 1861, to February, 1862. Attached to 25th Brigade, 7th Division, Army of the Ohio, to October, 1862. 1st Brigade, District of West Virginia, Dept. of the Ohio, to November, 1862. 1st Brigade, 2nd Division (Centre), 14th Army Corps, Army of the Cumberland, to January, 1863. 1st Brigade, 2nd Division, 14th Army Corps, to April, 1863. District of Central Kentucky, Dept. of the Ohio, to June, 1863. 3rd Brigade, 3rd Division, 23rd Army Corps, Army of the Ohio, to August, 1863. 3rd Brigade, 3rd Division, Reserve Corps, Army of the Cumberland, to October, 1863. 2nd Brigade, 2nd Division, 14th Army Corps, Army of the Cumberland, to November, 1863. Spear's Brigade, Chattanooga, Tenn., to December, 1863. Spear's Tennessee Brigade, 2nd Division, 23rd Army Corps, to January, 1864. 3rd Brigade, Rousseau's 3rd Division, 12th Army Corps, Army of the Cumberland, to April, 1864. 1st Brigade, 2nd Division, 23rd Army Corps, Army of the Ohio, to February, 1865.

SERVICE.—Duty at Somerset and London, Ky., till January, 1862. Battle of Logan's Cross Roads January 19. Duty at London and covering Cumberland Gap till March, 1862. Cumberland Gap Campaign March 28-June 18. Big Creek Gap June 11-12 and 15. Occupation of Cumberland Gap and covering rear at London June 18-September 17. Operations about Cumberland Gap August 16-22. Action at London August 17. Big Hill August 23. (Battle of White's Farm, Richmond, Ky., August 30, Battalion). Expedition to Fine Mountain September 6-10. Big Creek Gap September 7. Evacuation of Cumberland Gap and retreat to Greenupsburg, Ky., September 17-October 3. Near Gallipolis, Ohio, and operations in the Kanawha Valley till November. Ordered to Louisville, thence to Cincinnati, Ohio, and to Nashville, Tenn. Duty at Nashville, Tenn., till April, 1863, and at Carthage, Tenn., till August. Ordered to McMinnville August 31. March to Chattanooga September 12-20. Action near Summerton September 23. At Sale Creek till December. Ordered to Kingston. Action at Kingston December 4. Duty near Knoxville and operations in East Tennessee till April, 1864. Love's Hill, near Knoxville, January 24. Panther Springs March 5. Companies "E," "G," "H" and "L," Atlanta (Ga.) Campaign May to September. Demonstrations on Dalton May 5-13. Rocky Ford Ridge May 8-11. Battle of Resaca May 14-15. Pursuit to Cassville May 16-19. Near Cassville May 18-19. Etowah River May 20. Operations on line of Pumpkin Vine Creek and battles about Dallas, New Hope Church and Allatoona Hills May 26-June 5. Kingston May 27. Allatoona May 26 and 29. Pine Mountain June 3-7. Operations about Marietta and against Kenesaw Mountain June 10-July 2. Lost Mountain June 15-17. Muddy Creek June 17. Noyes Creek June 19. Kolb's Farm June 22. Assault on Kenesaw June 27. Nickajack Creek July 2-5. Vining Station July 4. Chattahootchie River July 5-17. Decatur July 19. Howard House July 20. Siege of Atlanta July 22-August 25. Utoy Creek August 5-7. Flank movement on Jonesboro August 25-31. Battle of Jonesboro August 31-September 1. Lovejoy Station September 2-6. Pursuit of Hood into Alabama October 3-26. Nashville Campaign November and December. Guard fords of

Duck River till November 28. Spring Hill November 29. Battle of Franklin November 30. Battle of Nashville December 15-16. Pursuit of Hood to the Tennessee River December 17-28. At Clifton, Tenn., till February, 1865. Moved to Nashville and mustered out February 23, 1865.

Regiment lost during service 3 Officers and 54 Enlisted men killed and mortally wounded and 168 Enlisted men by disease. Total 225.

3rd REGIMENT MOUNTED INFANTRY.

Organized at Loudon, Strawberry Plains and Knoxville July to September, 1864. Duty in East Tennessee till November. Skirmish at Lee's Ferry September 6. Greenville October 12. Mustered out November 30, 1864.

3rd REGIMENT ENROLLED MILITIA INFANTRY.

Organized at Memphis, Tenn., for the protection of that city.

4th REGIMENT INFANTRY.

Organized at Camp Garber, near Flat Lick, Ky., November, 1861, to March, 1862. Attached to 25th Brigade, 7th Division, Army of the Ohio, to October, 1862. 1st Brigade, District of West Virginia, Dept. of the Ohio, to November, 1862.

SERVICE.—Cumberland Gap Campaign March 28-June 18, 1862. Moved to Cumberland Ford April. Skirmishes at Big Creek Gap June 11-12 and 15. Occupation of Cumberland Gap June 18 to September 17. Expedition to Pine Mountain September 6-10. Big Creek Gap September 7. Evacuation of Cumberland Gap and retreat to Greenupsburg, Ky., September 17-October 3. At Gallipolis, Ohio, and operations in Kanawha Valley, W. Va., till November. Designation of Regiment changed to 1st Tennessee Cavalry November 1, 1862 (which see).

Regiment reorganized at Nashville, Tenn., May, 1863. Ordered to Lebanon May 22. Attached to District of North Central Kentucky, 1st Division, 23rd Army Corps, Dept. of the Ohio, to January, 1864. 2nd Brigade, District of Nashville, Dept. of the Cumberland, January, 1864. 2nd Brigade, 3rd Division, 12th Army Corps, Dept. of the Cumberland, to April, 1864. 3rd Brigade, 4th Division, 23rd Army Corps, Dept. of the Ohio, to October, 1864. 2nd Brigade, 4th Division, 23rd Army Corps, to February, 1865. 2nd Brigade, 4th Division, District of East Tennessee, to March, 1865. 1st Brigade, 4th Division, District of East Tennessee, to August, 1865.

SERVICE.—Duty in District of North Central Kentucky to September, 1863, and in District of Nashville, Tenn., till April, 1864. Ordered to McMinnville September 9, 1863. Action at McMinnville October 3 (Captured). At Nashville and Knoxville, Tenn., till April, 1864. Action at Holston River February 20, 1864. Near Greenville February 21-22. Moved to Loudon April 12. Duty at Loudon, Kingston, Knoxville and Cumberland Gap and in District of East Tennessee till August, 1865. Scouts from Kingston to England Cove July 7-9 and July 12-18, 1864. Mustered out August 2, 1865.

4th REGIMENT MOUNTED INFANTRY.

Organized at large in Tennessee September 1, 1864. Stationed at Alexandria, Tenn., operating against guerrillas. Four companies at La Fayette, Tenn., 4th Sub-District, Middle Tennessee, April, 1865. Action at Wall's Hill September 28, 1864. Polk County November 23, 1864. Operating against guerrillas in White, Overton, Fentress and Montgomery Counties and quieting country till August, 1865. Mustered out August 25, 1865.

4th REGIMENT MILITIA INFANTRY.

Organized at Memphis, Tenn., for the protection of that city.

5th REGIMENT INFANTRY.

Organized at Barboursville, Ky., and Harrison, Tenn., February and March, 1862. Attached to 25th Brigade, 7th Division, Army of the Ohio, to October, 1862. 1st Brigade, District of West Virginia, Dept. of the Ohio, to November, 1862. 1st Brigade, 2nd Division Centre, 14th Army Corps, Army of the Cumberland, to January, 1863. 1st Brigade, 2nd Division, 14th Army Corps, to April,

1863. District of Central Kentucky, Dept. of the Ohio, to June, 1863. 3rd Brigade, 3rd Division, 23rd Army Corps, Dept. of the Ohio, to August, 1863. 3rd Brigade, 3rd Division, Reserve Corps, Army of the Cumberland, to October, 1863. 2nd Brigade, 2nd Division, 14th Army Corps, to November, 1863. Spear's Tennessee Brigade, Chattanooga, Tenn., to December, 1863. Spear's Tennessee Brigade, 2nd Division, 23rd Army Corps, to January, 1864. 3rd Brigade, Rousseau's 3rd Division, 12th Army Corps, Dept. of the Cumberland, to April, 1864. 2nd Brigade, 3rd Division, 23rd Army Corps, Army of the Ohio, to June, 1864. 3rd Brigade, 3rd Division, 23rd Army Corps, to December, 1864. 2nd Brigade, 3rd Division, 23rd Army Corps, to January, 1865. Post of Nashville, Tenn., to February, 1865. 2nd Brigade, 3rd Division, 23rd Army Corps, Dept. of North Carolina, to June, 1865.

SERVICE.—Cumberland Gap Campaign March 28-June 18, 1862. Moved to Cumberland Ford April. Big Creek Gap June 11-12 and 15. Occupation of Cumberland Gap June 18-September 17. Cumberland Gap August 16. Expedition to Pine Mountain September 6-10. Big Creek Gap September 7. Evacuation of Cumberland Gap and retreat to Greenupsburg, Ky., September 17-October 3. Near Gallipolis, Ohio, and operations in the Kanawha Valley, W. Va., till November. Ordered to Louisville, Ky., thence to Cincinnati, Ohio, and Nashville, Tenn. Duty at Nashville till April, 1863, and at Carthage, Tenn., till August. Ordered to McMinnville August 31. March to Chattanooga September 13-20. Sequatchie Valley September 21-23. Missionary Ridge and Shallow Ford Gap September 22. Near Summerville September 23. At Sale Creek till December. Ordered to Kingston, Tenn. Near Kingston December 4. Duty near Knoxville and operations in East Tennessee till April, 1864. Atlanta (Ga.) Campaign May to September. Demonstrations on Dalton May 5-13. Rocky Faced Ridge May 8-11. Battle of Resaca May 14-15. Cartersville May 20. Operations on line of Pumpkin Vine Creek and battles about Dallas, New Hope Church and Allatoona Hills May 25-June 5. Operations about Marietta and against Kenesaw Mountain June 10-July 2. Lost Mountain June 15-17. Muddy Creek June 17. Cheney's Farm June 22. Olley's Farm June 26-27. Assault on Kenesaw June 27. Nickajack Creek July 2-5. Chattahootchie River July 5-17. Decatur July 19. Howard House July 20. Siege of Atlanta July 22-August 25. Utoy Creek August 5-7. Flank movement on Jonesboro August 25-30. Near Rough and Ready August 31. Jonesboro September 1. Lovejoy Station September 2-6. At Decatur till October. Operations against Hood in North Georgia and North Alabama October 3-26. Nashville Campaign November-December. Columbia Duck River November 24-27. Spring Hill November 29. Battle of Franklin November 30. Battle of Nashville December 15-16. Pursuit of Hood to the Tennessee River December 17-28. At Clifton, Tenn., till January 15, 1865. Moved to Washington, D. C., thence to Fort Fisher, N. C., January 16-February 9. Operations against Hoke February 11-14. Fort Anderson February 18. Town Creek February 20. Capture of Wilmington February 22. Campaign of the Carolinas March 1-April 26. Advance on Kinston and Goldsboro March 6-21. Occupation of Goldsboro March 21. Advance on Raleigh April 9-14. Occupation of Raleigh April 14. Bennett's House April 26. Surrender of Johnston and his army. Duty at Raleigh and Greensboro till June. Mustered out June 30, 1865.

Regiment lost during service 1 Officer and 40 Enlisted men killed and mortally wounded and 204 Enlisted men by disease. Total 246.

5th REGIMENT MOUNTED INFANTRY.

Organized at Cleveland, Nashville, Calhoun and Chattanooga, Tenn., September 23, 1864. Attached to District of the Etowah, Dept. of the Cumberland, and garrison duty in that District and at Dalton and Marietta, Ga., till July, 1865. Skirmish at McLemore's Cove, Ga., February 1, 1865. Expedition from Dalton to Coosawattie River and Spring Place, Ga., April 1-4. Mustered out July 17, 1865.

6th REGIMENT INFANTRY.

Organized at Boston and Williamsburg, Ky., April 18, 1862. Attached to 25th Brigade, 7th Division, Army of the Ohio, to October, 1862. 1st Brigade, District of West Virginia, Dept. of the Ohio, to November, 1862. 1st Brigade, 2nd Division (Centre), 14th Army Corps, Army of the Cumberland, to January, 1863. 1st Brigade, 2nd Division, 14th Army Corps, to April, 1863. District of Central Kentucky, Dept. of the Ohio, to June, 1863. 3rd Brigade, 3rd Division, 23rd Army Corps, Army of the Ohio, to August, 1863. 3rd Brigade, 3rd Division, Reserve Corps, Army of the Cumberland, to October, 1863. 2nd Brigade, 2nd Division, 14th Army Corps, to November, 1863. Spear's Tennessee Brigade, Chattanooga, Tenn., to December, 1863. Spear's Tennessee Brigade, 2nd Division, 23rd Army Corps, to January, 1864. 3rd Brigade, Rousseau's 3rd Division, 12th Army Corps, Dept. of the Cumberland, to April, 1864. 1st Brigade, 2nd Division, 23rd Army Corps, Army of the Ohio, to February, 1865. 1st Brigade, 2nd Division, 23rd Army Corps, Dept. of North Carolina, to May, 1865.

SERVICE.—Moved to Cumberland Ford April, 1862. Cumberland Gap Campaign April to June. Big Creek Gap June 11, 12 and 15. Occupation of Cumberland Gap June 18-September 17. Wallace Cross Roads July 15. Big Creek Gap September 4. Expedition to Pine Mountain September 6-10. Pine Mountain September 7 (Co. "B"). Evacuation of Cumberland Gap and retreat to Greenupsburg, Ky., September 17-October 3. Goose Creek Salt Works September 19. Near Gallipolis, Ohio, and operations in the Kenawha Valley, W. Va., till November. Ordered to Louisville, Ky., thence to Cincinnati, Ohio, and Nashville, Tenn. Duty at Nashville till January, 1863. Guard trains from Nashville to Murfreesboro January 2-3. Action at Cox's or Blood's Hill January 3. Manchester Pike January 5. At Nashville till April, and at Carthage, Tenn., till August. Ordered to McMinnville August 31. March to Chattanooga September 12-20. Sequatchie Valley September 21-23. Action at Missionary Ridge and Shallow Ford Gap September 22. Near Summerville September 23. At Sale Creek till December. Ordered to Kingston, Tenn. Action at Kingston December 4. Duty near Knoxville and operations in East Tennessee till April, 1864. Atlanta (Ga.) Campaign May to September. Demonstrations on Dalton May 5-13. Rocky Faced Ridge May 8-11. Battle of Resaca May 14-15. Pursuit to Cassville May 18-19. Etowah River May 20. Operations on Pumpkin Vine Creek and battles about Dallas, New Hope Church and Allatoona Hills May 2-June 5. Kingston May 27. Allatoona May 26-29. Pine Mountain June 3-7. Operations about Marietta and against Kenesaw Mountain June 10-July 2. Lost Mountain June 15-17. Muddy Creek June 17. Noyes Creek June 19-20. Kolb's Farm June 22. Assault on Kenesaw June 27. Nickajack Creek July 2-5. Vining Station July 4. Chattahoochie River July 6-17. Decatur July 19. Howard House July 20. Siege of Atlanta July 22-August 25. Utoy Creek August 5-7. Flank movement on Jonesboro August 25-30. Lovejoy Station September 2-6. Pursuit of Hood into Alabama October 3-26. Nashville Campaign November-December. Guard fords of Duck River till November 28. Spring Hill November 29. Battle of Franklin November 30. Battle of Nashville December 15-16. Pursuit of Hood to the Tennessee River December 17-28. At Clifton, Tenn., till January 15, 1865. Movement to Washington, D. C., thence to Fort Fisher, N. C., January 15-February 15. Fort Anderson February 18. Town Creek February 20. Capture of Wilmington February 22. Campaign of the Carolinas March 1 to April 26. Advance on Kinston and Goldsboro March 6-21. Relieved for muster out March 31, and ordered to Nashville, Tenn. Mustered out April 2 to May 17, 1865.

Regiment lost during service 1 Officer and 43 Enlisted men killed and mortally wounded and 157 Enlisted men by disease. Total 201.

6th REGIMENT MOUNTED INFANTRY.

Organized at Chattanooga, Tenn., August 20, 1864. Attached to District of the Etowah, Dept. of the Cumberland, to February, 1865. 1st Brigade, 2nd Separate Division, District of the Etowah, to June, 1865.

SERVICE.—Duty at Chattanooga, Tenn., and railroad guard duty in District of Georgia. Skirmish at McLemore's Cove February 1, 1865. Mustered out June 30, 1865.

7th REGIMENT INFANTRY.

Organized in Tennessee at large August 10, 1862, to June 1, 1863. Attached to District of Jackson, Dept. of the Tennessee, to November, 1862. District of Jackson, 13th Army Corps (Old), Dept. of the Tennessee, to December, 1862. District of Jackson, 3rd Division, 16th Army Corps, Dept. of the Tennessee, to July, 1863.

SERVICE.—Duty at Jackson and Bolivar, Tenn. Grant's Central Mississippi Campaign November, 1862, to January, 1863. Action at Forked Deer Creek December 20, 1862. Expedition against Forest December 18, 1862, to January 3, 1863. Skirmish at Huntingdon December 30, 1862. Engagement at Parker's Cross Roads December 30. Duty in the District of Jackson till July. Mustered out July 31, 1863.

7th REGIMENT MOUNTED INFANTRY.

Organized at Athens and Nashville, Tenn., August, 1864. Attached to District of East Tennessee to March, 1865. 2nd Brigade, District of East Tennessee, Dept. of the Cumberland, to July, 1865.

SERVICE.—Duty at Nashville and Athens till March, 1865. Action at Athens January 28, 1865. Near Philadelphia March 1. Operations about Athens March 2-4. Guard passes east of Athens till July. Mustered out July 27, 1865.

8th REGIMENT INFANTRY.

Organized at Camp Dick Robinson and Camp Nelson, Ky., November 11, 1862, to August 11, 1863. Attached to District of Central Kentucky, Dept. of the Ohio, to June, 1863. 2nd Brigade, 4th Division, 23rd Army Corps, Army of the Ohio, to July, 1863. 2nd Brigade, 1st Division, 23rd Army Corps, to August, 1863. 2nd Brigade, 3rd Division, 23rd Army Corps, to September, 1863. 2nd Brigade, Left Wing Forces, 23rd Army Corps, to January, 1864. 1st Brigade, 3rd Division, 23rd Army Corps, to February, 1865. 1st Brigade, 3rd Division, 23rd Army Corps, Dept. of North Carolina, to June, 1865.

SERVICE.—Duty at Nicholasville, Ky., Camp Dick Robinson, Camp Nelson and Lexington, Ky., till August, 1863. Burnside's Campaign in East Tennessee August 16-October 17. At Greenville till September 19. Carter's Depot September 20-21. Jonesborough September 21. Watauga River September 25. At Bull's Gap and Jonesborough till December. About Dandridge January 16-17, 1864. Strawberry Plains January 22. Duty in East Tennessee till April. Atlanta (Ga.) Campaign May to September, 1864. Demonstrations on Dalton May 5-13. Rocky Faced Ridge May 8-11. Battle of Resaca May 14-15. Cartersville May 20. Operations on line of Pumpkin Vine Creek and battles about Dallas, New Hope Church and Allatoona Hills May 25-June 5. Operations about Marietta and against Kenesaw Mountain June 10-July 2. Lost Mountain June 15-17. Muddy Creek June 17. Allatoona June 18. Noyes Creek June 19. Cheyney's Farm June 22. Olley's Farm June 26-27. Assault on Kenesaw June 27. Nickajack Creek July 2-5. Chattahoochie River July 6-17. Buckhead, Nancy's Creek, July 18. Peach Tree Creek July 19-30. Siege of Atlanta July 22-August 25. Utoy Creek August 5-7. Flank movement on Jonesboro August 25-30. Battle of Jonesboro August 31-September 1. Lovejoy Station September 2-6. Pursuit of Hood into Alabama October 3-26. Nashville Campaign November and December. Columbia, Duck River, November 24-27. Columbia Ford November 28-29. Battle of Franklin November 30. Battle of Nashville December 15-16. Pursuit of Hood to the Tennessee River December 17-

28. At Clifton, Tenn., till January 15, 1865. Movement to Washington, D. C., thence to North Carolina January 15-February 9. Operations against Hoke February 11-14. Fort Anderson February 18. Town Creek February 20. Capture of Wilmington February 22. Campaign of the Carolinas March 1-April 26. Advance on Goldsboro March 6-21. Occupation of Goldsboro March 21. Advance on Raleigh April 10-14. Occupation of Raleigh April 14. Bennett's House April 26. Surrender of Johnston and his army. Duty at Raleigh and in the Dept. of North Carolina till June. Mustered out June 30, 1865.

Regiment lost during service 2 Officers and 48 Enlisted men killed and mortally wounded and 1 Officer and 226 Enlisted men by disease. Total 277.

8th TENNESSEE MOUNTED INFANTRY.

Organized at Nashville and Carthage, Tenn., November, 1864. Attached to District of Middle Tennessee, Dept. of the Cumberland, to February, 1865. 4th Sub-District, District of Middle Tennessee, to August, 1865.

SERVICE.—Duty at Nashville and Carthage, Tenn., till June, 1865. At Clifton and Savannah, Tenn., and in District of Middle Tennessee till August. Mustered out August 17, 1865.

9th REGIMENT INFANTRY.

(See 6th Regiment Cavalry.)

10th REGIMENT INFANTRY.—(1st MIDDLE TENNESSEE INFANTRY.)

Organized at Nashville, Tenn., May to August, 1862. Attached to Post and District of Nashville, Tenn., Dept. of the Cumberland, to June, 1863. 3rd Brigade, 2nd Division, Reserve Corps, Dept. of the Cumberland, to September, 1863. Defences of Nashville & Northwestern Railroad to January, 1864. 1st Brigade, Defences of Nashville, Tenn., January, 1864. 1st Brigade, 3rd Division, 12th Army Corps, Dept. of the Cumberland, to April, 1864. 1st Brigade, 4th Division, 20th Army Corps, Dept. of the Cumberland, to April, 1865. 1st Brigade, 4th Division, District of East Tennessee, to June, 1865.

SERVICE.—Post and garrison duty at Nashville, Tenn., till September, 1863. Ordered to Bridgeport, Ala., September 24, 1863. Guard duty on Nashville & Northwestern Railroad, and garrison and guard duty at Nashville, Tenn., till April, 1865. Ordered to Greenville April 24, 1865, and duty in District of East Tennessee till June. Mustered out June 23, 1865.

NASHVILLE UNION GUARDS.

Organized at Nashville September, 1862, for post duty at Nashville. No reports on file.

TEXAS VOLUNTEERS.

1st REGIMENT CAVALRY.

Organized at New Orleans, La., November 6, 1862. Attached to Independent Command, Dept. of the Gulf, to January, 1863. Defences of New Orleans to May, 1863. Cavalry, 19th Army Corps, Dept. of the Gulf, to July, 1863. Defences of New Orleans to October, 1863. Unattached Cavalry, 13th Army Corps, Dept. of the Gulf, to June, 1864. Cavalry Brigade, United States Forces, Texas, to July, 1864. District of Morganza, La., Dept. of the Gulf, to August, 1864. Cavalry Brigade, 19th Corps, Dept. of the Gulf, to November, 1864. 2nd Separate Cavalry Brigade, 19th Corps, Dept. of the Gulf, to December, 1864. Separate Cavalry Brigade, Reserve Corps, Dept. of the Gulf, to February, 1865. Cavalry Brigade, District of Baton Rouge, La., to July, 1865. Dept. of Texas to November, 1865.

SERVICE.—Duty in the Defences of New Orleans, La., till September, 1863. Sabine Pass Expedition September 4-11. Western Louisiana ("Teche") Campaign October 3-17. Nelson's Bridge, near New Iberia, October 4. Vermillion Bayou October 9-10. Carrion Crow Bayou October 14-15. Ordered to New Orleans, La., October 17. Expedition to the Rio Grande, Texas, Oc-

tober 23-December 2. Occupation of Brazos Santiago November 2, and of Brownsville November 6. Duty at Brownsville and on line of the Rio Grande till July, 1864. Rancho las Rinas June 26, 1864 (Cos. "A" and "C"). Ordered to New Orleans July, thence to Morganza, La., August 6, and duty there till November. (A Detachment remained in Texas at Brownsville till January, 1865. Participated in skirmish at Palmetto Ranch September 6, 1864. Ordered to join Regiment at Baton Rouge, La., January 27, 1865.) Operations about Morganza September 16-25, 1864. Williamsport September 16. Atchafalaya River September 17. Bayou Alabama and Morgan's Ferry September 20. Ordered to Baton Rouge November 19. Davidson's Expedition against Mobile & Ohio Railroad November 27-December 13. Ordered to Lakeport December 17. United States Forces at mouth of White River and at Baton Rouge, La., till May, 1865. Expedition to Clinton and the Comite River March 30-April 2, 1865. Ordered to Vidalia, District of Natchez, Miss., May 23, 1865, and duty there till June 29. Ordered to Military District of the Southwest and duty in Texas till November. Mustered out November 4, 1864.

2nd REGIMENT CAVALRY.

Organized at Brownsville, Texas, December 15, 1863. Served Unattached, Cavalry, 13th Army Corps, Texas, Dept. of the Gulf, to June, 1864. Cavalry Brigade, United States Forces, Texas, to June, 1864. District of Morganza, Dept. of the Gulf, to August, 1864. Separate Cavalry Brigade, 19th Corps, Dept. of the Gulf, to November, 1864.

SERVICE.—Duty at Brownsville and on the Rio Grande, Texas, till July, 1864. Ordered to New Orleans, La., thence to Morganza August 6, and duty there till November. Consolidated with 1st Texas Cavalry November 1, 1864.

2nd BATTALION CAVALRY.

Organized at Brazos Santiago, Texas, March, 1865. Duty at Brownsville, Brazos Santiago and other points in Texas till November, 1865. Expedition from Brazos Santiago May 11-14. Actions at Palmetto Ranch May 12-13, and White's Ranch May 13. Mustered out November 10, 1865.

INDEPENDENT COMPANY PARTISAN RANGERS.

Organized at Brownsville, Texas, November 10, 1863. Duty at Brownsville and on the Rio Grande till July, 1864. Ordered to New Orleans and mustered out July 31, 1864.

VERMONT VOLUNTEERS.

1st REGIMENT CAVALRY.

Organized at Burlington and mustered in November 19, 1861. Left State for Washington, D. C., December 14; thence moved to Annapolis, Md., December 25, and duty there till March, 1862. Attached to Banks' Division, Army of the Potomac, December, 1861, to March, 1862. Hatch's Cavalry Brigade, Banks' 5th Army Corps, Army of the Potomac, and Dept. of the Shenandoah to June, 1862. Cavalry Brigade, 2nd Army Corps, Army of Virginia, to September, 1862. Price's Cavalry Brigade, Defences of Washington, and 22nd Army Corps to April, 1863. 3rd Brigade, Stahel's Cavalry Division, 22nd Army Corps, to June, 1863. 1st Brigade, 3rd Division, Cavalry Corps, Army of the Potomac, to August, 1863. 2nd Brigade, 3rd Division, Cavalry Corps, Army of the Potomac, to August, 1864, and Army of the Shenandoah, Middle Military Division, to June, 1865.

SERVICE.—Moved to Washington, D. C., March 9-10, 1862; thence to Rockville, Md., and Edward's Ferry March 12-13. Moved to Harper's Ferry, W. Va., March 28; thence to Middletown April 1. Advance up the Valley April 16. Mt. Jackson April 17. McGaheysville April 27 (Cos. "A," "D" and "K"). Somerville Heights May 7 (Co. "B"). Operations in Shenandoah Valley May 15-June 17. Middletown May 24. Winchester May

25. Retreat to Williamsport May 25-26. Near Winchester June 18-19. Reconnoissance from Front Royal to Luray June 29-30. Luray Court House June 30. Culpeper Court House July 12. Gordonsville July 17. Orange Court House August 2 and 13. Pope's Campaign in Northern Virginia August 16-September 2. Fords of the Rappahannock August 21-23. Kelly's Ford August 21. Liberty Bridge September 1. Aquia Creek September 5. Conrad's Ferry September 15. Orange Court House September 21. Ashby's Gap September 22. Duty in the Defences of Washington till March, 1863. Warrenton November 8, 1862. Annandale December 28. Fairfax Court House January 9. Dranesville February 6, 9, 13 and 14. Goose Creek February 16. Leesburg February 19. Aldie March 2. Herndon Station March 17. Broad Run, Dranesville, April 1. Warrenton May 11, 23 and 31. Near Greenwich May 30. Littleton and Hanover, Pa., June 30. Hunterstown July 2. Gettysburg, Pa., July 3. Monterey Gap July 4. Smithburg, Md., July 5. Hagerstown July 6. Boonsboro July 8. Hagerstown July 11-13. Falling Water July 14. King George Court House August 25. Lamb's Creek Church September 1. Expedition to Port Conway September 1-3. Advance from the Rappahannock to the Rapidan September 13-17. Culpeper Court House September 13. Somerville Ford September 14. Reconnoissance across the Rapidan September 21-23. Richard's Ford September 26. Bristoe Campaign October 9-22. James City October 10. Bethesda Church October 10. Brandy Station and near Culpeper October 11. Gainesville October 14 and 19. Groveton October 17-18. Catlett's Station and Buckland's Mills October 19. Falmouth November 4. Advance to the Rappahannock November 7-8. Mine Run Campaign November 26-December 2. Morton's Ford November 26. Raccoon Ford November 26-27. Demonstration on the Rapidan February 6-7, 1864. Kilpatrick's Raid on Richmond February 28-March 4. Fortifications of Richmond and near Atlee's March 1. Old Church March 2. Campaign from the Rapidan to the James May-June. Near Chancellorsville May 4. Craig's Meeting House May 5. Wilderness May 5-7 (Co. "M"). Todd's Tavern May 5-6 and May 7-8. Alsop's Farm, Spottsylvania, May 8. Sheridan's Raid from Todd's Tavern to James River May 9-24. North Anna River May 9. Ground Squirrel Church and Yellow Tavern May 11. Brook Church or Richmond Fortifications May 12. Line of the Pamunkey May 26-28. Demonstration on Little River May 27. Salem Church May 27. On line of the Totopotomoy May 28-31. Ashland May 30. Mechump's Creek May 31. Cold Harbor May 31-June 1. Ashland June 1. Gaines' Mill June 2. Totopotomoy June 2. Haw's Shop June 3. Sumner's Upper Bridge June 3. Salem Church June 4. White Oak Swamp June 12. Riddell's Shop June 13. Malvern Hill June 15. Wilson's Raid on South Side & Danville Railroad June 22-30. Ream's Station June 22. Near Nottaway Court House June 23. Black and White Station June 23. Staunton Bridge or Roanoke Station June 25. Sappony Church or Stony Creek June 28-29. Ream's Station June 29. Siege of Petersburg till August. Sheridan's Shenandoah Valley Campaign August 7-November 28. Winchester August 17. Kearneysville August 25. Near Brucetown and Winchester September 7. Battle of Opequan September 20. Near Cedarville September 20. Front Royal September 21. Milford September 22. Fisher's Hill September 22. Waynesboro September 29. Columbia Furnace and Back Road, near Strasburg, October 7. Tom's Brook, "Woodstock Races," October 8-9. Mount Olive October 9. Battle of Cedar Creek October 19. Near Kernstown November 10. Newtown and Cedar Creek November 12. Rude's Hill, near Mt. Jackson, November 22. Expedition to Lacy Springs December 19-22. Lacy Springs December 21. Sheridan's Raid February 27-March 25, 1865. Waynesboro March 2. Occupation of Staunton March 2. Occupation of Charlottesville March 3. Appomattox Campaign March 28-April 9. Dinwiddie Court House March 30-31. Five Forks April 1. Scott's Corners April 2. Namozine Church April

3. Sailor's Creek April 6. Appomattox Station April 8. Appomattox Court House April 9. Surrender of Lee and his army. Expedition to Danville April 24-29. March to Washington, D. C., May 10-15. Grand Review May 23. Frontier duty at Champlain, N. Y., June to August. Non-Veterans mustered out November 18, 1864. Regiment mustered out August 9, 1865. (Co. "L" was organized at St. Albans September 29, 1862, and Co. "M" at Burlington December 30, 1862.)

Regiment lost during service 10 Officers and 124 Enlisted men killed and mortally wounded and 4 Officers and 200 Enlisted men by disease. Total 438.

1st REGIMENT HEAVY ARTILLERY.

Organized at Brattleboro and mustered in as 11th Vermont Infantry September 1, 1862. Left State for Washington, D. C., September 7, 1862. Designation of Regiment changed to 1st Heavy Artillery December 10, 1862. (Co. "L" organized July 11, 1863, and Co. "M" October 7, 1863.) Attached to 1st Brigade, Haskins' Division, Military District of Washington, to February, 1863. 1st Brigade, Haskins' Division, 22nd Army Corps, Defences of Washington, to May, 1864. 2nd Brigade, 2nd Division, 6th Army Corps, Army of the Potomac, and Army of the Shenandoah, Middle Military Division, to June, 1865. Middle Department, 8th Corps, to August, 1865.

SERVICE.—Duty in the Defences of Washington, D. C., north of the Potomac September, 1862, to May, 1864. Company "A" at Fort Lincoln September 27 to November 17, 1862, then at Fort Totten till March, 1864, and at Fort Lincoln till May, 1864. Company "B" at Forts Massachusetts and Stevens till March, 1864, then at Fort Totten till May, 1864. Companies "C" and "D" at Fort Saratoga till November 17, 1862, then at Fort Massachusetts till March, 1864. Company "C" at Fort Stevens till May, 1864. Company "D" at Fort Saratoga till May, 1864. Company "E" at Fort Totten till November 17, 1862, then at Fort Slocum till May, 1864. Company "F" at Fort Bunker Hill till November 17, 1862, then at Fort Slocum till March, 1864, and at Fort Thayer till May, 1864. Company "G" at Fort Lincoln till November 17, 1862, then at Fort Slocum till May, 1864. Company "H" at Fort Slocum till March, 1864, then at Fort Bunker Hill till May, 1864. Company "I" at Fort Thayer till November 17, 1862, then at Fort Massachusetts till March, 1864, and at Fort Bunker Hill till May, 1864. Company "K" at Fort Totten till May, 1864. Company "L" at Fort Lincoln till May, 1864. Company "M" at Fort Bunker Hill till May, 1864. Ordered to join army in the field May 12, 1864. Moved to Belle Plains, Va., and join 6th Army Corps at Spottsylvania Court House, Va., May 15. Spottsylvania Court House May 15-21. North Anna River May 23-26. Line of the Pamunkey May 26-28. Totopotomoy May 28-31. Cold Harbor June 1-12. Before Petersburg June 17-July 9. Jerusalem Plank Road June 22-23. Moved to Washington, D. C., July 9-11. Repulse of Early's attack on Fort Stevens July 11-12. Snicker's Gap Expedition July 15-23. Sheridan's Shenandoah Valley Campaign August 7-November 28. Near Charlestown August 21-22. Gilbert's Ford, Opequan, September 13. Battle of Opequan, Winchester, September 19. Fisher's Hill September 22. Battle of Cedar Creek October 19. Duty at Strasburg till November 9, and at Kernstown till December 9. Moved to Petersburg, Va., December 9-12. Siege of Petersburg December 13, 1864, to April 2, 1865. Fort Fisher, Petersburg, March 25, 1865. Appomattox Campaign March 28-April 9. Assault on and fall of Petersburg April 2. Pursuit of Lee. Duty at Burkesville till April 23. March to Danville April 23-27, and duty there till May 18. At Manchester May 19-24, and at Munson's Hill, Washington, till June 24. Corps Review June 8. Old members mustered out June 24, 1865. Veterans and Recruits consolidated to a Battalion of four Companies, and duty at Fort Foote, Md., Defences of Washington, till August. Mustered out August 25, 1865.

Regiment lost during service 10 Officers and 154 Enlisted men killed and mortally wounded and 2 Officers and 410 Enlisted men by disease. Total 576.

1st COMPANY HEAVY ARTILLERY.

Organized April, 1865, from surplus Recruits of 2nd Vermont Battery Light Artillery. Duty at Port Hudson, La., till July, 1865. Moved to Vermont July 7-20, and mustered out July 25, 1865.

1st BATTERY LIGHT ARTILLERY.

Organized at Brattleboro and mustered in February 18, 1862. Left State for New York City March 6. Sailed on Steamer "Wallace" for Ship Island March 10, arriving April 5. Attached to Phelps' 1st Brigade, Dept. of the Gulf, to December, 1862. Artillery, 2nd Division, 19th Army Corps, Dept. of the Gulf, to June, 1863. Artillery, 3rd Division, 19th Army Corps, to September, 1863. Artillery, District of LaFourche, Dept. of the Gulf, to January, 1864. Artillery, 2nd Division, 19th Army Corps, Army of the Gulf, to July, 1864. Artillery, 1st Division, 19th Army Corps, to August, 1864.

SERVICE.—Duty at Ship Island till May 16, 1863. Moved to Camp Parapet, Defences of New Orleans, La., May 16, and duty there till January 17, 1863. (Centre Section at Fort Pike May 6 to June 4, 1862.) Duty at New Orleans till May 19, 1863. Expedition to Lake Pontchartrain April 18-21. Moved to Baton Rouge, La., May 19. Advance on Port Hudson, La., May 21-24. Siege of Port Hudson May 24-July 9. Surrender of Port Hudson July 9. March to Baton Rouge July 11-12. Return to Port Hudson July 23, and duty there till September 1. Ordered to New Orleans, La., September 1. Sabine Pass, Texas Expedition, September 3-11. Moved to Brashear City, thence to Berwick City and to Fort Bisland September 16-23. Return to Brashear City September 28, and duty there till March 3, 1864. Moved to Franklin March 3. Red River Campaign March 10-May 22. Advance from Franklin to Alexandria March 14-26. Battle of Sabine Cross Roads April 8. Pleasant Hill April 9. Monett's Bluff, Cane River Crossing, April 23. Alexandria April 30-May 10. Retreat to Morganza May 13-20. Mansura May 16. Yellow Bayou May 18. Duty at Morganza till July. Moved to Baton Rouge July 3, thence ordered home July 28. Mustered out August 10, 1864. Recruits transferred to 2nd Vermont Battery.

Battery lost during service 3 Enlisted men killed and mortally wounded and 51 Enlisted men by disease. Total 54.

2nd BATTERY LIGHT ARTILLERY.

Organized at Brandon and mustered in December 24, 1861. Moved to Lowell, Mass., December 24; thence to Boston February 4, 1862. Embark on Steamer "Idaho" for Ship Island, La., February 6, arriving there March 8. Attached to Phelps' 1st Brigade, Dept. of the Gulf, to December, 1862. Artillery, 3rd Division, 19th Army Corps, Army of the Gulf, to August, 1863. Garrison Artillery, Port Hudson, La., to July, 1865.

SERVICE.—Operations against New Orleans, La., April 11-May 2, 1862. Occupation of New Orleans May 2 (the first Union Battery to enter the city). Duty in New Orleans till May 31, and at Camp Parapet till October 31. Expedition to Pass Manchac July 25-August 2. Duty at New Orleans October 31 to December 26. Expedition to Galveston, Texas, December 26, 1862, to January 3, 1863. Action at Galveston January 1, 1863. Duty at New Orleans till March. Expedition to Port Hudson, La., March 7-20. At Baton Rouge till May. Advance on Port Hudson May 18-24. Action at Plain's Store May 21. Siege of Port Hudson May 24-July 9. Assaults on Port Hudson May 27 and June 14. Surrender of Port Hudson July 9. Jackson, La., August 3. Garrison and guard duty at Port Hudson till July, 1865. Expedition to Clinton July 28, 1864. Non-Veterans mustered out September 30, 1864. Battery moved to Vermont July 7-20, 1865, and mustered out July 31, 1865.

Losses during service 1 Enlisted man killed and 53 Enlisted men by disease. Total 54.

3rd BATTERY LIGHT ARTILLERY.

Organized at Burlington and mustered in January 1, 1864. Moved to Washington, D. C., January 15-18, and duty at Camp Barry till April 5. Attached to Artillery, 4th Division, 9th Army Corps, Army of the Potomac, to July, 1864. Reserve Artillery, 2nd Army Corps, Army of the Potomac, to September, 1864. Reserve Artillery, 6th Army Corps, and Artillery Reserve, Army of the Potomac, to June, 1865.

SERVICE.—Rapidan (Va.) Campaign May-June, 1864. Guard trains of the Army of the Potomac through the Wilderness and to Petersburg, Va. Siege of Petersburg June 16, 1864, to April 2, 1865. Garrison Fort Morton June 20 to August 19, 1864. Mine Explosion, Petersburg, July 30. Weldon Railroad August 18-21. At Aiken House August 27-30. At Fort Sedgwick till September 6. At Avery House till September 19. At Fort Meikel September 19 to October 3. At Battery 27 till October 5. Moved to Poplar Springs Church October 5 and built Fort Urmston October 5-12. At Battery 16 October 12-25. Ordered to City Point October 25, and duty in the Defences there till January, 1865. Joined 6th Army Corps at Weldon Railroad January 15, and stationed at Fort Fisher till April. Fort Fisher March 25. Assault on and fall of Petersburg April 2. Moved to City Point and duty there till May 3. March to Washington, D. C., March 3-18. Grand Review May 23. Mustered out June 15, 1862.

Losses: Died of disease 21.

COMPANY "F" 1st REGIMENT U. S. SHARP-SHOOTERS.

Organized at West Randolph September 13, 1861. Left State for Weehawken, N. J., September 14, thence to Washington, D. C., September 25. (See 1st U. S. Sharpshooters.)

COMPANY "E" 2nd REGIMENT U. S. SHARPSHOOTERS.

Organized at West Randolph and mustered in November 9, 1861 Left State for Washington, D. C., November 25, 1861. (See 2nd U. S. Sharpshooters.)

COMPANY "H" 2nd REGIMENT U. S. SHARPSHOOTERS.

Organized at Brattleboro and mustered in December 31, 1861. Left State for Washington, D. C., December 31, 1861. (See 2nd U. S. Sharpshooters.)

1st REGIMENT INFANTRY.

Organized at Rutland and mustered in for three months May 9, 1861. Left State for Fortress Monroe, Va., May 9, arriving there May 13. Camp at Hygea Hotel till May 25. Demonstration on Hampton May 20. Reconnoissance to Hampton May 23. Occupation of Newport News May 27, and duty there till August. Advance on Big Bethel June 9. Battle of Big Bethel June 10. Moved to Brattleboro, Vt., August 4-7 and mustered out August 15, 1861.

Losses 2 Enlisted men killed and 6 Enlisted men died of disease. Total 8.

2nd REGIMENT INFANTRY.

Organized at Burlington and mustered in June 20, 1861. Left State for Washington, D. C., June 24. Attached to Howard's Brigade, Heintzelman's Division, McDowell's Army of Northeast Virginia, to August, 1861. W. F. Smith's Brigade, Division of the Potomac, to October, 1861. Brook's Brigade, Smith's Division, Army of the Potomac, to March, 1862. 2nd Brigade, 2nd Division, 4th Army Corps, Army of the Potomac, to May, 1862. 2nd Brigade, 2nd Division, 6th Army Corps, Army of the Potomac, and Army of the Shenandoah, Middle Military Division, to July, 1865.

SERVICE.—Advance on Manassas, Va., July 16-21, 1861. Battle of Bull Run, Va., July 21. Scout to Great Falls August 20-25. Skirmish near Lewinsville September 11 (Cos. "A" and "F."). Reconnoissance to Lewinsville September 25 (Cos. "A" and "F"). Expedition to Munson's Hill September 28. Reconnoissance to Vienna October 17. Reconnoissance to Peacock Hill November 9. Duty in the Defences of Washington till March, 1862. Moved to Alexandria March 10, thence to the Virginia Peninsula March 23-24. Young's Mill April 4. Siege of Yorktown April 5-May 4. Lee's Mills April 16. Reconnoissance to Warwick River April 30. Battle of Williamsburg May 5. Seven days before Richmond June 25-July 1. Garnett's Farm June 27. Savage Station June 29. White Oak Swamp Bridge June 30. Malvern Hill July 1. At Harrison's Landing till August 16. Movement to Fortress Monroe, thence to Alexandria August 16-24. Maryland Campaign September-October. Crampton's Pass, Md., September 14. Battle of Antietam, Md., September 16-17. At Hagerstown September 26-October 29. Movement to Falmouth, Va., October 29-November 19. Battle of Fredericksburg, Va., December 12-15. Burnside's Second Campaign, "Mud March," January 20-24, 1863. Chancellorsville Campaign April 27-May 6. Operations at Franklin's Crossing April 29-May 2. Maryes Heights, Fredericksburg, May 3. Salem Heights May 3-4. Banks' Ford May 4. Franklin's Crossing June 5-13. Battle of Gettysburg, Pa., July 2-4. Funkstown, Md., July 10-13. Ordered to New York City August 14. Duty there and at Poughkeepsie, N. Y., till September 13. Moved to Alexandria, thence to Fairfax Court House, Va., September 13-17, and to Culpeper Court House September 22. Bristoe Campaign October 9-22. Advance to the Rappahannock November 7-8. Rappahannock Station November 7. Mine Run Campaign November 26-December 2. Campaign from the Rapidan to the James May-June, 1864. Battles of the Wilderness May 5-7; Spottsylvania May 8-12; Spottsylvania Court House May 12-21. Assault on the Salient at Spottsylvania May 12. North Anna River May 23-26. Line of the Pamunkey May 26-28. Totopotomoy May 28-31. Cold Harbor June 1-12. Before Petersburg June 18-19. Jerusalem Plank Road June 22-23. Moved to Washington, D. C., July 9-11. Repulse of Early's attack on Fort Stevens July 11-12. Sheridan's Shenandoah Valley Campaign August 7-November 28. Charlestown August 21-22. Gilbert's Ford, Opequan River, September 18. Battle of Opequan, Winchester, September 19. Fisher's Hill September 22. Battle of Cedar Creek October 19. At Strasburg till November 9 and at Kernstown till December 9. Moved to Petersburg December 9-12. Siege of Petersburg December 12, 1864, to April 2, 1865. Dabney's Mills February 5-7, 1865. Fort Fisher, before Petersburg, March 25. Appomattox Campaign March 28-April 9. Assault on and fall of Petersburg April 2. Sailor's Creek April 6. Appomattox Court House April 9. Surrender of Lee and his army. At Farmville and Burkesville Junction till April 23. March to Danville April 23-27, and duty there till May 18. At Manchester till May 24. March to Washington May 24-June 3. Corps Review June 8. Non-veterans mustered out June 29, 1864. Regiment mustered out July 15, 1865.

Regiment lost during service 6 Officers and 218 Enlisted men killed and mortally wounded and 175 Enlisted men by disease. Total 399.

3rd REGIMENT INFANTRY.

Organized at St. Johnsbury and mustered in July 16, 1861. Moved to Washington, D. C., July 24-26. Attached to W. F. Smith's Brigade, Division of the Potomac, to October, 1861. Brook's Brigade, Smith's Division, Army of the Potomac, to March, 1862. 2nd Brigade, 2nd Division, 4th Army Corps, Army of the Potomac, to May, 1862. 2nd Brigade, 2nd Division, 6th Army Corps, Army of the Potomac and Army of the Shenandoah, Middle Military Division, to July, 1865.

SERVICE.—Duty at Georgetown Heights and at Camp Griffin, defences of Washington, till March 10, 1862. Skirmish at Lewinsville September 11, 1861. Reconnoissance to Lewinsville September 25. Moved to Alexandria March 10, 1862, thence to Fortress Monroe, Va., March 23-24. Action at Young's Mill April 4. Siege of Yorktown April 5-May 4. Lee's Mills April 16. Battle of Williamsburg May 5. Seven days before Richmond

June 25-July 1. Garnett's Farm June 27. Savage Station June 29. White Oak Swamp Bridge June 30. Malvern Hill July 1. At Harrison's Landing till August 16. Moved to Fortress Monroe, thence to Alexandria August 16-24. Maryland Campaign September-October. Crampton's Pass September 14. Battle of Antietam September 16-17. At Hagerstown, Md., September 26 to October 29. Movement to Falmouth, Va., October 29-November 19. Battle of Fredericksburg December 12-15. Burnside's Second Campaign, "Mud March," January 20-24, 1863. Chancellorsville Campaign April 27-May 6. Operations at Franklin's Crossing April 29-May 2. Maryes Heights, Fredericksburg, May 3. Salem Heights May 3-4. Banks' Ford May 4. Franklin's Crossing June 5-13. Battle of Gettysburg. Pa., July 2-4. Funkstown, Md., July 10-13. Ordered to New York City August 14, and duty there till September 13. Moved to Alexandria, thence to Fairfax Court House September 13-17, and to Culpeper Court House September 22. Bristoe Campaign October 9-22. Advance to the Rappahannock November 7-8. Rappahannock Station November 7. Mine Run Campaign November 26-December 2. Campaign from the Rapidan to the James May-June, 1864. Battles of the Wilderness May 5-7; Spottsylvania May 8-12; Spottsylvania Court House May 12-21. Assault on the Salient, Spottsylvania Court House, May 12. North Anna River May 23-26. Line of the Pamunkey May 26-28. Totopotomoy May 28-31. Cold Harbor June 1-12. Before Petersburg June 18-19. Jerusalem Plank Road June 22-23. Siege of Petersburg till July 9. Moved to Washington, D. C., July 9-11. Repulse of Early's attack on Fort Stevens July 11-12. Non-veterans mustered out July 27, 1864. Sheridan's Shenandoah Valley Campaign August 7-November 28. Near Charlestown August 21-22. Opequan Creek September 1. Gilbert's Ford, Opequan Creek, September 13. Battle of Opequan, Winchester, September 19. Fisher's Hill September 22. Battle of Cedar Creek October 19. At Strasburg to November 9 and at Kernstown till December 9. Moved to Petersburg, Va., December 9-12. Siege of Petersburg December 13, 1864, to April 2, 1865. Fort Fisher, before Petersburg, March 25, 1865. Appomattox Campaign March 28-April 9. Assault on and fall of Petersburg April 2. Sailor's Creek April 6. Appomattox Court House April 9. Surrender of Lee and his army. At Farmville and Burkesville Junction till April 23. March to Danville April 23-27, and duty there till May 18. Moved to Manchester May 18, thence marched to Washington, D. C., May 24-June 2. Corps Review June 8. Mustered out July 11, 1865.

Regiment lost during service 5 Officers and 201 Enlisted men killed and mortally wounded and 1 Officer and 164 Enlisted men by disease. Total 371.

4th REGIMENT INFANTRY.

Organized at Brattleboro and mustered in September 21, 1861. Moved to Washington, D. C., September 21-23. Attached to Brook's Brigade, Smith's Division, Army of the Potomac, to March, 1862. 2nd Brigade, 2nd Division, 4th Army Corps, Army of the Potomac, to May, 1862. 2nd Brigade, 2nd Division, 6th Army Corps, Army of the Potomac, and Army of the Shenandoah, Middle Military Division, to July, 1865.

SERVICE.—Duty at Camp Griffin Defences of Washington till March 10, 1862. Reconnoissance to Vienna, Va., October 19, 1861. Moved to Alexandria March 10, 1862, thence to Fortress Monroe March 23-24. Reconnoissance to Big Bethel March 27-28. Reconnoissance to Warwick March 30. Young's Mills April 4. Siege of Yorktown April 5-May 4. Lee's Mills April 16. Battle of Williamsburg May 5. Seven days before Richmond June 25-July 1. Garnett's Farm June 27. Savage Station June 29. White Oak Swamp Bridge June 30. Malvern Hill July 1. At Harrison's Landing till August 16. Moved to Fortress Monroe, thence to Alexandria August 16-24. Maryland Campaign September-October. Crampton's Pass, Md., September 14. Battle of Antietam September 16-17. At Hagerstown, Md., September 26-October 29. Movement to Falmouth October 29-November 19. Battle of Fredericksburg December 12-15. Burnside's Second Campaign, "Mud March," January 20-24,

1863. Chancellorsville Campaign April 27-May 6. Operations at Franklin's Crossing April 29-May 2. Maryes Heights. Fredericksburg, May 3. Salem Heights May 3-4. Banks' Ford May 4. Franklin's Crossing June 5-13. Battle of Gettysburg, Pa., July 2-4. Funkstown July 10-13. Detached for duty at New York August 14-September 16. Moved to Alexandria, thence to Fairfax Court House, Va., and to Culpeper Court House September 16-23. Bristoe Campaign October 9-22. Advance to the Rappahannock November 7-8. Rappahannock Station November 7. Mine Run Campaign November 26-December 2. Campaign from the Rapidan to the James May-June, 1864. Battles of the Wilderness May 5-7; Spottsylvania May 8-12; Spottsylvania Court House May 12-21. Assault on the Salient, Spottsylvania, May 12. North Anna River May 23-26. On line of the Pamunkey May 26-28. Totopotomoy May 28-31. Cold Harbor June 1-12. Before Petersburg June 18-19. Jerusalem Plank Road June 22-23. Siege of Petersburg till July 9. Moved to Washington, D. C., July 9-11. Repulse of Early's attack on Fort Stevens July 11-12. Sheridan's Shenandoah Valley Campaign August 7-November 28. Near Charlestown August 21-22. Gilbert's Ford, Opequan River, September 13. Battle of Opequan, Winchester, September 19. Fisher's Hill September 22. Battle of Cedar Creek October 19. Non-veterans mustered out September 30, 1864. Duty at Strasburg till November 9 and at Kernstown till December 9. Moved to Petersburg, Va., December 9-12. Siege of Petersburg December 13, 1864, to April 2, 1865. Fort Fisher, before Petersburg, March 25, 1865. Appomattox Campaign March 28-April 9. Assault on and fall of Petersburg April 2. Sailor's Creek April 6. Appomattox Court House April 9. Surrender of Lee and his army. At Farmville and Burkesville Junction till April 28. March to Danville April 23-27, and duty there till May 18. Moved to Manchester May 18, thence march to Washington May 24-June 3. Corps Review June 8. Mustered out July 13, 1865.

Regiment lost during service 12 Officers and 150 Enlisted men killed and mortally wounded and 1 Officer and 279 Enlisted men by disease. Total 442.

5th REGIMENT INFANTRY.

Organized at St. Albans and mustered in September 16, 1861. Moved to Washington, D. C., September 23-25. Attached to Brook's Brigade, Smith's Division, Army of the Potomac, to March, 1862. 2nd Brigade, 2nd Division, 4th Army Corps, Army of the Potomac, to May, 1862. 2nd Brigade, 2nd Division, 6th Army Corps, Army of the Potomac, and Army of the Shenandoah, Middle Military Division, to June, 1865.

SERVICE.—At Camp Griffin Defences of Washington till March 10, 1862. Moved to Alexandria March 10, thence to Fortress Monroe March 23-24. Reconnoissance to Warwick River March 30. Young's Mills April 4. Siege of Yorktown April 5-May 4. Lee's Mills April 16. Battle of Williamsburg May 5. Seven days before Richmond June 25-July 1. Garnett's Farm June 27. Savage Station June 29. White Oak Swamp Bridge June 30. Malvern Hill July 1. At Harrison's Landing till August 16. Moved to Fortress Monroe, thence to Alexandria August 16-24. Maryland Campaign September-October. Crampton's Pass September 14. Battle of Antietam September 16-17. At Hagerstown, Md., September 26-October 29. Movement to Falmouth, Va., October 29-November 19. Battle of Fredericksburg December 12-15. Burnside's Second Campaign, "Mud March," January 20-24, 1863. Chancellorsville Campaign April 27-May 6. Operations at Franklin's Crossing April 29-May 2. Maryes Heights, Fredericksburg, May 3. Salem Heights May 3-4. Banks' Ford May 4. Franklin's Crossing June 5-12. Battle of Gettysburg, Pa., July 2-4. Funkstown, Md., July 10-13. Detached from Army for duty at New York City and Kingston, N. Y., August 14-September 16. Rejoined army at Culpeper Court House, Va., September 23. Bristoe Campaign October 9-22. Advance to line of the Rappahannock November 7-8. Rappahannock Station November 7. Mine Run Campaign November 26-December 2. Campaign from the Rapidan to the James May-June, 1864. Battles of the Wilder-

ness May 5-7; Spottsylvania May 8-12; Spottsylvania Court House May 12-21. Assault on the Salient, Spottsylvania Court House, May 12. North Anna River May 23-26. Line of the Pamunkey May 26-28. Totopotomoy May 28-31. Cold Harbor June 1-12. Before Petersburg June 18-19. Jerusalem Plank Road June 22-23. Siege of Petersburg till July 9. Moved to Washington, D. C., July 9-11. Repulse of Early's attack on Fort Stevens July 11-12. Sheridan's Shenandoah Valley Campaign August 7-November 28. Near Charlestown August 21-22. Gilbert's Ford, Opequan Creek, September 13. Battle of Opequan, Winchester, September 19. Fisher's Hill September 22. Battle of Cedar Creek October 19. At Strasburg till November 9 and at Kernstown till December 9. Moved to Petersburg, Va., December 9-12. Siege of Petersburg December 13, 1864, to April 2, 1865. Fort Fisher, before Petersburg, March 25, 1865. Appomattox Campaign March 28-April 9. Assault on and fall of Petersburg April 2. Sailor's Creek April 6. Appomattox Court House April 9. Surrender of Lee and his army. At Farmville and Burkesville Station till April 23. March to Danville April 23-27, and duty there till May 18. Moved to Manchester, thence march to Washington, D. C., May 24-June 8. Corps Review June 8. Mustered out non-veterans October 14, 1864. Regiment June 29, 1865.

Regiment lost during service 11 Officers and 202 Enlisted men killed and mortally wounded and 1 Officer and 124 Enlisted men by disease. Total 338.

6th REGIMENT INFANTRY.

Organized at Montpelier and mustered in October 15, 1861. Moved to Washington, D. C., October 19-22. Attached to Brook's Brigade, Smith's Division, Army of the Potomac, to March, 1862. 2nd Brigade, 2nd Division, 4th Army Corps, Army of the Potomac, to May, 1862. 2nd Brigade, 2nd Division, 6th Army Corps, Army of the Potomac and Army of the Shenandoah, Middle Military Division, to June, 1865.

SERVICE.—Duty in the Defences of Washington till March 10, 1862. Moved to Alexandria March 10, thence to Fortress Monroe, Va., March 23-24. Reconnoissance to Warwick River March 30. Siege of Yorktown April 5-May 4. Lee's Mills April 16. Battle of Williamsburg May 5. Seven days before Richmond June 25-July 1. Garnett's Farm June 27. Savage Station June 29. White Oak Swamp Bridge June 30. Malvern Hill July 1. At Harrison's Landing till August 16. Moved to Fortress Monroe, thence to Alexandria August 16-24. Maryland Campaign September-October. Crampton's Pass, Md., September 14. Battle of Antietam September 16-17. At Hagerstown, Md., till October 29. Movement to Falmouth, Va., October 29-November 19. Battle of Fredericksburg December 12-15. Burnside's Second Campaign, "Mud March," January 20-24, 1863. Chancellorsville Campaign April 27-May 6. Operations at Franklin's Crossing April 29-May 2. Maryes Heights, Fredericksburg, May 3. Salem Heights May 3-4. Banks' Ford May 4. Franklin's Crossing June 5-13. Battle of Gettysburg, Pa., July 2-4. Funkstown, Md., July 10-13. Detached for duty in New York August 14-September 16. Rejoined Army at Culpeper Court House September 23. Bristoe Campaign October 9-22. Advance to line of the Rappahannock November 7-8. Rappahannock Station November 7. Mine Run Campaign November 26-December 2. Campaign from the Rapidan to the James May-June, 1864. Battles of the Wilderness May 5-7; Spottsylvania May 8-12; Spottsylvania Court House May 12-21. Assault on the Salient, Spottsylvania Court House, May 12. North Anna River May 23-26. Line of the Pamunkey May 26-28. Totopotomoy May 28-31. Cold Harbor June 1-12. Before Petersburg June 18-19. Jerusalem Plank Road June 22-23. Siege of Petersburg till July 9. Moved to Washington, D. C., July 9-11. Repulse of Early's attack on Fort Stevens July 11-12. Sheridan's Shenandoah Valley Campaign August 7-November 28. Near Charlestown August 21-22. Gilbert's Ford, Opequan Creek, September 13. Battle of Opequan, Winchester, September 19. Fisher's Hill September 22.

Battle of Cedar Creek October 19. At Strasburg till November 9, and at Kernstown till December 9. Moved to Petersburg December 9-12. Siege of Petersburg December 13, 1864, to April 2, 1865. Fort Fisher, before Petersburg, March 25, 1865. Appomattox Campaign March 28-April 9. Assault on and fall of Petersburg April 2. Sailor's Creek April 6. Appomattox Court House April 9. Surrender of Lee and his army. At Farmville and Burkesville Station till April 23. March to Danville April 23-27, and duty there till May 18. Moved to Manchester, thence march to Washington, D. C., May 24-June 3. Corps Review June 8. Mustered out June 26, 1865.

Regiment lost during service 12 Officers and 191 Enlisted men killed and mortally wounded and 3 Officers and 212 Enlisted men by disease. Total 418.

7th REGIMENT INFANTRY.

Organized at Brattleboro and mustered in February 12, 1862, to date from June 1, 1861. Left State for New York March 10, 1862. Embarked March 14 for Ship Island, Miss., right wing on Steamer "Premier," and left wing on Steamer "Tamerlaine," arriving at Ship Island April 7 and 10. Attached to Phelps' 1st Brigade, Dept. of the Gulf, to October, 1862. District of West Florida to December, 1863. Defences of New Orleans, Dept. of the Gulf, to November, 1864. 2nd Brigade, Reserve Division, Dept. of the Gulf, to February, 1865. 2nd Brigade, 3rd Division, 13th Army Corps, Dept. of the Gulf, to June, 1865. Dept. of Texas to March, 1866.

SERVICE.—Duty at Ship Island, Miss., till May 13, 1862. (Cos. "B," "C" and "D" detached at Fort Pike May 5 to June 13.) Regiment moved to New Orleans, La., May 13-16. At Carrollton till June 15. Moved to Baton Rouge June 15-16. Expedition from Baton Rouge to Vicksburg, Miss., and operations against Vicksburg June 20-July 26. Hamilton's Plantation, near Grand Gulf, June 24. Battle of Baton Rouge August 5. Evacuation of Baton Rouge August 20. Duty at Carrollton till October 13. Ordered to Pensacola, Fla., October 13, and garrison duty there till February 20, 1863. Reconnoissance to Oakfield December 29, 1862. Garrison, Forts Barrancas and Pickens, till June 19, 1863. Expedition to Oakfield February 17, 1863. Duty at Barrancas and at Santa Rosa Island till August, 1864. Near Point Washington February 9, 1864 (Co. "B"). Expedition from Barrancas toward Pollard, Ala., July 21-25, 1864. Gonzales Station July 22. Old members mustered out August 10, 1864. Veterans absent on furlough August 10 to September 27. Left State for Dept. of the Gulf September 30. Sailed from New York to New Orleans, La., October 4, arriving October 13. Duty at New Orleans till February 19, 1865. Moved to Mobile Point, Ala., February 19. Campaign against Mobile and its Defences March 17-April 12. Siege of Spanish Fort and Fort Blakely March 26-April 8. Fort Blakely April 9. Occupation of Mobile April 12. Action at Whistler's Station April 13. Expedition to McIntosh Bluff on Tombigbee River April 19-May 9. At Mobile till June 2. Moved to Brazos Santiago, Texas, June 2-5; thence to Clarksville June 14, and duty there till August 2, and at Brownsville till March, 1866. Mustered out March 14, 1866.

Regiment lost during service 3 Officers and 10 Enlisted men killed and mortally wounded and 4 Officers and 403 Enlisted men by disease. Total 420.

8th REGIMENT INFANTRY.

Organized at Brattleboro and mustered in February 18, 1862. Left State for New York March 14. Sailed for Ship Island, Miss., March 19, arriving April 6. Attached to Phelps' 1st Brigade, Dept. of the Gulf, to October, 1862. Weitzel's Reserve Brigade, Dept. of the Gulf, to January, 1863. 2nd Brigade, 1st Division, 19th Army Corps, Dept. of the Gulf, to July, 1863. 3rd Brigade, 1st Division, 19th Army Corps, to February, 1864. 1st Brigade, 1st Division, 19th Army Corps, to July, 1864. 2nd Brigade, 1st Division, 19th Army Corps, Army of the Shenandoah, Middle Military Division, to March, 1865. 2nd Brigade, 1st Division, Army of the

Shenandoah, to April, 1865. 2nd Brigade, 1st Provisional Division, Army of the Shenandoah, to April, 1865. 2nd Brigade, 1st Division, Defences of Washington, 22nd Corps, to June, 1865.

SERVICE.—Moved from Ship Island to New Orleans May 7-8, 1862. Duty there and at Algiers and guarding Opelousas Railroad till September. Bayou des Allemands June 20 and 22. Raceland Station June 22. St. Charles Station August 29 (Cos. "A" and "C"). Bote Station September 4 (Co. "K"). Operations in LaFourche District October 24-November 6. Georgia Landing, near Labadieville, October 27. Repair railroad to Brashear City November 1-December 8. At Brashear City till January 13, 1863. Action with Steamer "Cotten" on Bayou Teche January 14. At Camp Stevens, Bayou Boeuf, and at Brashear City till March. Operations on Bayou Plaquemine, Black and Atchafalaya Rivers February 12-28. Operations against Port Hudson March 7-27. Operations in Western Louisiana April 9-May 14. Teche Campaign April 11-20. Fort Bisland, near Centreville, April 12-13. Jeanerette April 14. Expedition to Alexandria on Red River May 5-17. Moved from Alexandria to Port Hudson May 17-25. Siege of Port Hudson May 25-July 9. Assaults on Port Hudson May 27 and June 14. Surrender of Port Hudson July 9. Duty at Thibodeaux July 31-September 1. Sabine Pass Expedition September 3-11. Western Louisiana ("Teche") Campaign October 3-November 30. At New Iberia till January 6, 1864. March to Franklin and duty there till March 8. Moved to Algiers March 8. Veteranize January 28, 1864, and on furlough April 7 to June 3. Non-Veterans at Algiers till May 6, and at Thibodeaux till June 5. Left for home June 5, and mustered out June 22, 1864. Veterans moved from home to Dept. of the Gulf May 25-June 3. Moved to Alexandria June 8-11. Expedition to Tunica Bend June 19-21. Moved to Algiers July 2, thence sailed to Fortress Monroe, Va., July 5-12, and to Washington, D. C., July 12-13. Pursuit of Early to Snicker's Gap July 14-21. Sheridan's Shenandoah Valley Campaign August 7-November 28. Battle of Opequan, Winchester, September 19. Fisher's Hill September 22. Battle of Cedar Creek October 19. At Newtown till December 20, and at Summit Point till April 4, 1865. Hancock's operations in the Valley April 4-15. Moved to Washington April 21, and duty there till June. Grand Review May 23-24. Mustered out June 28, 1865.

Regiment lost during service 4 Officers and 115 Enlisted men killed and mortally wounded and 7 Officers and 241 Enlisted men by disease. Total 367.

9th REGIMENT INFANTRY.

Organized at Brattleboro and mustered in July 9, 1862. Moved to Washington, D. C., July 15-17. Attached to Piatt's Brigade, Winchester, Va., to September, 1862. Miles' Command, Harper's Ferry, W. Va., September, 1862. Camp Douglas, Ill., to April, 1863. Wardrop's Reserve Brigade, 7th Army Corps, Dept. of Virginia, to June, 1863. Wistar's Independent Brigade, 7th Army Corps, to July, 1863. Yorktown, Va., Dept. of Virginia and North Carolina, to October, 1863. District of Beaufort, N. C., Dept. of Virginia and North Carolina, to July, 1864. Defences of New Berne, N. C., Dept. of Virginia and North Carolina, to September, 1864. 2nd Brigade, 2nd Division, 18th Army Corps, Army of the James, to December, 1864. 2nd Brigade, 3rd Division, 24th Army Corps, Dept. of Virginia, to July, 1865. 2nd Independent Brigade, 24th Army Corps, to August, 1865. Dept. of Virginia to December, 1865.

SERVICE.—Moved from Washington, D. C., to Cloud's Mills, Va., July 19, 1862; thence to Winchester, Va., July 23, and duty there till September 2. Retreat to Harper's Ferry, W. Va., September 2. Defence of Harper's Ferry September 13-15. Bolivar Heights September 14. Surrendered September 15. Paroled September 16, and sent to Annapolis, Md.; thence to Chicago, Ill., September 25. Guard Rebel prisoners at Camp Douglas, Chicago, Ill., till March 28, 1863. Declared exchanged January 10, 1863. Guard Rebel prisoners to City Point, Va., March 28-April 7. Moved to Fortress Monroe April 7-9, thence to Suffolk, Va., April 12. Siege of Suffolk April 13-May 4. Edenton Road April 24. Siege of Suffolk raised May 4. Duty at Suffolk till June 17. Operations on Norfolk & Petersburg Railroad May 15-18. Antioch Church and Barber's Cross Roads May 23. Moved to Yorktown June 17, thence to West Point June 25, and outpost duty there till July 7. Duty at Yorktown till October 23. Expedition to Gloucester Court House July 25. Ordered to New Berne, N. C., October 23, and reached Morehead City October 26. Duty at Newport Barracks till July, 1864. Cedar Point December 1, 1863. Destruction of salt works on Bear Inlet, N. C., December 25 (Detachment). Expedition to Onslow County January 27, 1864. Newport Barracks February 2. Bogue Sound Blockhouse February 2 (Cos. "B" and "H"). Gale's Creek, near New Berne, February 2 (Detachment). Ordered to New Berne, N. C., July 11, and duty there till September 17; "A" at Evans Mills, "B" and "C" near Fort Spinola, "D" and "G" at Red House, "E" and "I" at Rocky Run, "F" at Fort Spinola, "H" at Buckwood and "K" on the Trent. Moved to Bermuda Hundred September 13-15. Siege operations against Petersburg and Richmond September 15, 1864, to April 2, 1865. Duty at Bailey's Cross Roads September 20-26, 1864. (A Detachment in Fort Dutton, Bermuda Hundred front, September 27 to November 28, 1864.) Battle of Chaffin's Farm and Fort Harrison September 28-30. Battle of Fair Oaks October 27-28. Detached for duty at New York City November 2-17 duringing presidential election of 1864. Duty in trenches before Richmond till April, 1865. Occupation of Richmond April 3. Provost duty there till August. Non-Veterans mustered out June 13, 1865. Regiment consolidated to a Battalion of four Companies, and provost duty at Norfolk, Drummondsville and Portsmouth till December. Mustered out December 1, 1865.

Regiment lost during service 2 Officers and 22 Enlisted men killed and mortally wounded and 3 Officers and 278 Enlisted men by disease. Total 305.

10th REGIMENT INFANTRY.

Organized at Brattleboro and mustered in September 1, 1862. Moved to Washington, D. C., September 6-8. Attached to Grover's Brigade, Military District of Washington, to February, 1863. Jewett's Brigade, Provisional Division, 22nd Army Corps, Dept. of Washington, to June, 1863. French's Command, 8th Army Corps, Middle Department, to July, 1863. 1st Brigade, 3rd Division, 3rd Army Corps, Army of the Potomac, to March, 1864. 1st Brigade, 3rd Division, 6th Army Corps, Army of the Potomac and Army of the Shenandoah, Middle Military Division, to June, 1865.

SERVICE.—Camp at Arlington Heights till September 14, 1862. March to Seneca Locks, Md., September 14-17, and guard duty along the Potomac from Edward's Ferry to Muddy Branch till October 11 and at Seneca Creek till November 13. At Offutt's Cross Roads till December 21. Moved to Poolesville December 21, and duty at White's Ford (Cos. "C," "E," "H" and "I"); at mouth of the Monocacy (Cos. "A," "F" and "D"); at Conrad's Ferry (Cos. "B," "G" and "K") till April 19, 1863. At Poolesville, Md., to June 24. Moved to Harper's Ferry, W. Va., June 24-26, thence to Frederick, Md., June 30, and to Monocacy July 2. Pursuit of Lee July 6-23. Wapping Heights July 23. At Routt's Hill August 1-September 15. At Culpeper till October 8. Bristoe Campaign October 9-22. Auburn and Bristoe October 14. Advance to the Rappahannock November 7-8. Kelly's Ford November 7. Brandy Station November 8. Mine Run Campaign November 26-December 2. Payne's Farm November 27. Demonstration on the Rapidan February 6-7, 1864. Campaign from the Rapidan to the James May-June. Battles of the Wilderness May 5-7; Spottsylvania May 8-12; Spottsylvania Court House May 12-21. Assault on the Salient, Spottsylvania Court House, May 12. North Anna River May 23-26. Pamunkey River May 26-28. Totopotomoy May 28-31. Cold Harbor June 1-12. Before Petersburg June 18-19. Jeru-

salem Plank Road June 22-23. Siege of Petersburg till July 6. Moved to Baltimore, Md., July 6-8. Battle of Monocacy July 9. Expedition to Snicker's Gap July 14-24. Sheridan's Shenandoah Valley Campaign August 6-November 28. Gilbert's Ford, Opequan, September 13. Battle of Opequan, Winchester, September 19. Fisher's Hill September 22. Battle of Cedar Creek October 19. Camp Russell November 10. Duty at Kernstown till December. Moved to Washington, D. C., thence to Petersburg, Va., December 3-6. Siege of Petersburg December 13, 1864, to April 2, 1865. Fort Fisher, before Petersburg, March 25, 1865. Appomattox Campaign March 28-April 9. Assault on and capture of Petersburg April 2. Sailor's Creek April 6. Appomattox Court House April 9. Surrender of Lee and his army. March to Danville April 23-27 and duty there till May 16. Moved to Richmond, thence march to Washington May 24-June 3. Corps Review June 8. Mustered out June 22, 1865, recruits to 5th Vermont.

Regiment lost during service 9 Officers and 140 Enlisted men killed and mortally wounded and 203 Enlisted men by disease. Total 352.

11th REGIMENT INFANTRY.

Organized at Brattleboro September 1, 1862. Left State for Washington, D. C., September 7. Attached to 1st Brigade, Haskins' Division, Military District of Washington, to December, 1862. Duty in the Defences of Washington north of the Potomac. Designation of Regiment changed to 1st Vermont Heavy Artillery December 10, 1862. (See 1st Heavy Artillery.)

12th REGIMENT INFANTRY.

Organized at Brattleboro October 4, 1862, for nine months. Moved to Washington, D. C., October 7-10, 1862. Attached to 2nd Brigade, Abercrombie's Division, Military District of Washington, to February, 1863. 2nd Brigade, Casey's Division, 22nd Army Corps, to April, 1863. 2nd Brigade, Abercrombie's Division, 22nd Corps, to July, 1863. 3rd Brigade, 3rd Division, 1st Army Corps, Army of the Potomac, to muster out.

SERVICE.—Camp on East Capital Hill, Washington, to October 30, 1862. Moved to Munson's Hill October 30, thence to Hunting Creek October 31. At Camp Vermont, near Hunting Creek, till December 12. Picket duty near Fairfax Court House December 12, 1862, to January 20, 1863. Defence of Fairfax Court House from attack by Stuart's Cavalry December 29, 1862. Duty at Wolf Run Shoals January 20 to May 1. Guard railroad at Warrenton Junction till May 7 and at Rappahannock Station till May 18. At Bristoe and Catlett's till June 1. At Union Mills till June 25. March to Gettysburg, Pa., June 25-July 1. Detached at Westminster as train guard till July 4. Guard prisoners to Baltimore July 4-6. Moved to Brattleboro July 6-9, and there mustered out July 14, 1863.

Lost by disease 2 Officers and 65 Enlisted men. Total 67.

13th REGIMENT INFANTRY.

Organized at Brattleboro October 10, 1862, for nine months. Moved to Washington, D. C., October 11-13. Attached to 2nd Brigade, Abercrombie's Division, Military District of Washington, to February, 1863. 2nd Brigade, Casey's Division, 22nd Army Corps, to April, 1863. 2nd Brigade, Abercrombie's Division, 22nd Army Corps, to July, 1863. 3rd Brigade, 3rd Division, 1st Army Corps, Army of the Potomac, July, 1863.

SERVICE.—At Camp Chase, Arlington, Va., October 25-28, 1862, and at East Capital Hill till October 30. March to Munson's Hill October 30, thence to Hunting Creek November 5. At Camp Vermont, near Hunting Creek, till November 26. Picket duty near Occoquan Creek till December 5. At Camp Vermont till December 12. Picket duty near Fairfax Court House till January 20, 1863. Defence of Fairfax Court House from attack by Stuart's Cavalry December 29, 1862. Duty at Wolf Run Shoals January 20-April 2. Guard duty at Occoquan Creek till June 25. March to Gettysburg, Pa., June 25-July 1. Battle of Gettysburg July 1-3. Pursuit of Lee to Middletown, Md., July 4-8. Left front July 8 and moved to Brattleboro, Vt., July 8-13. Mustered out July 21, 1863.

Regiment lost during service 1 Officer and 16 Enlisted men killed and mortally wounded and 4 Officers and 55 Enlisted men by disease. Total 76.

14th REGIMENT INFANTRY.

Organized at Brattleboro October 21, 1862, for nine months. Moved to Washington, D. C., October 22-25. Attached to 2nd Brigade, Abercrombie's Division, Military District of Washington, to February, 1863. 2nd Brigade, Casey's Division, 22nd Army Corps, to April, 1863. 2nd Brigade, Abercrombie's Division, 22nd Army Corps, to July, 1863. 3rd Brigade, 3rd Division, 1st Army Corps, Army of the Potomac, to muster out.

SERVICE.—At Camp Chase, Arlington, Va., October 25-28 and at East Capital Hill to October 30. March to Munson's Hill October 30 and to Hunting Creek November 5. At Camp Vermont, near Hunting Creek, November 5-26. Picket duty near Occoquan Creek November 26-December 5. At Camp Vermont till December 12. Duty near Fairfax Court House till January 20, 1863. Defence of Fairfax Court House from attack by Stuart's Cavalry December 29, 1862. At Fairfax Station January 20-March 24, 1863. At Wolf Run Shoals, Union Mills and on the Occoquan March 24 to June 25. March to Gettysburg, Pa., June 25-July 1. Battle of Gettysburg, Pa., July 1-3. Pursuit of Lee July 4-18. Moved to Brattleboro, Vt., July 18-21. Mustered out July 30, 1863.

Regiment lost during service 1 Officer and 26 Enlisted men killed and mortally wounded and 43 Enlisted men by disease. Total 70.

15th REGIMENT INFANTRY.

Organized at Brattleboro and mustered in October 22, 1862, for nine months. Moved to Washington, D. C., October 23-26. Attached to 2nd Brigade, Abercrombie's Division, Military District of Washington, to February, 1863. 2nd Brigade, Casey's Division, 22nd Army Corps, to April, 1863. 2nd Brigade, Abercrombie's Division, 22nd Army Corps, to June, 1863. 3rd Brigade, 3rd Division, 1st Army Corps, Army of the Potomac, to muster out.

SERVICE.—At Camp Chase, Arlington, Va., October 26-28, 1862, and at East Capital Hill till October 30. March to Munson's Hill March 30, thence to Hunting Creek November 5. At Camp Vermont, near Hunting Creek, till November 26. Picket duty at Occoquan Creek November 26-December 4. At Camp Vermont till December 12. Picket duty near Fairfax Court House December 12, 1862, to January 20, 1863. At Fairfax Station till March 24. At Union Mills till May 7. At Bealeton till May 18. At Union Mills till June 15. At Bristoe Station, Catlett's Station and Manassas till June 25. March to Gettysburg, Pa., June 25-July 1. Detached at Westminster as train guard till July 4. Pursuit of Lee July 4-18. Moved to Brattleboro, Vt., July 18-21, and mustered out August 5, 1863.

Regiment lost during service by disease 1 Officer and 80 Enlisted men. Total 81.

16th REGIMENT INFANTRY.

Organized at Brattleboro and mustered in October 23, 1862, for nine months. Moved to Washington, D. C., Ocotber 24-27. Attached to 2nd Brigade, Abercrombie's Division, Military District of Washington, to February, 1863. 2nd Brigade, Casey's Division, 22nd Army Corps, to April, 1863. 2nd Brigade, Abercrombie's Division, 22nd Army Corps, to June, 1863. 3rd Brigade, 3rd Division, 1st Army Corps, Army of the Potomac, July, 1863.

SERVICE.—At East Capital Hill, Washington, till October 30, 1862. March to Munson Hill October 30, thence to Hunting Creek November 5. At Camp Vermont, near Hunting Creek, till December 12. Picket duty near Fairfax Court House to January 20, 1863. At Fairfax Station till March 20. Defence of Fairfax Court House from attack by Stuart's Cavalry December 29, 1862. At Union Mills March 24 to June 1. At Bristoe Station, Catlett's Station and Manassas till June 15. At

Union Mills till June 25. March to Gettysburg, Pa., June 25-July 1. Battle of Gettysburg July 1-3. Pursuit of Lee July 4-18. Moved to Brattleboro, Vt., July 18-21. Mustered out August 10, 1863.

Regiment lost during service 1 Officer and 23 Enlisted men killed and mortally wounded and 1 Officer and 48 Enlisted men by disease. Total 73.

17th REGIMENT INFANTRY.

Organized and mustered in: Companies "A" January 5, 1864; "B," "C" and "D" March, 1864; "E," "F" and "G" April 12, 1864. Moved to Alexandria, Va., April 18-22, 1864. Attached to 2nd Brigade, 2nd Division, 9th Army Corps, Army of the Potomac, to July, 1865.

SERVICE.—Campaign from the Rapidan to the James, Va., May-June, 1864. Battles of the Wilderness May 5-7; Spottsylvania May 8-12; Spottsylvania Court House May 12-21. Assault on the Salient, Spottsylvania Court House, May 12. North Anna River May 23-26. Line of the Pamunkey May 26-28. Totopotomoy May 28-31. Cold Harbor June 1-12. Bethesda Church June 1-3. Before Petersburg June 16-19. Siege of Petersburg June 16, 1864, to April 2, 1865. Mine Explosion, Petersburg, July 30, 1864. Weldon Railroad August 18-21. Poplar Springs Church, Peebles Farm, September 29-October 2. Boydton Plank Road, Hatcher's Run, October 27-28. Fort Stedman March 25, 1865. Assaults on Petersburg April 1-2. Fall of Petersburg April 2. Occupation of Petersburg April 3. Moved to Washington April 20-27. Guard and patrol duty at Alexandria till July. Grand Review May 23. Mustered out July 14, 1865.

Regiment lost during service 14 Officers and 133 Enlisted men killed and mortally wounded and 1 Officer and 116 Enlisted men by disease. Total 264.

18th REGIMENT INFANTRY.

Organization not completed.

VIRGINIA VOLUNTEERS.

MEAN'S LOUDOUN RANGERS.

Organized at Waterford, Va., and Point of Rocks, Md. Company "A" June 20, 1862; Company "B" January 26, 1864. Attached to Point of Rocks, Md., Middle Department, June, 1862. Railroad District, Middle Department, 8th Army Corps, to September, 1862. Railroad District, Dept. of West Virginia, to January, 1863. Point of Rocks, Md., 8th Corps, Middle Department, to March, 1863. Unattached, 8th Corps, to May, 1863. 3rd Separate Brigade, 8th Corps, to June, 1863. Lockwood's Command, 8th Corps, to July, 1863. 3rd Separate Brigade, 8th Corps, to August, 1863. 2nd Brigade, Maryland Heights Division, Dept. of West Virginia, to December, 1863. Unattached, 1st Division, Dept. of West Virginia, to April, 1864. Reserve Division, Dept. of West Virginia, to January, 1865. 3rd Brigade, 3rd Division, Dept. of West Virginia, to April, 1865. Unattached, 2nd Division, Dept. of West Virginia, to May, 1865.

SERVICE.—Duty at and about Point of Rocks and guarding fords of the Potomac River from Monocacy River to Brunswick to September, 1862. Action at Upperville August 27. Hillsboro September 1. Leesburg September 2. Edward's Ferry September 4. Siege of Harper's Ferry September 12-14. Capture of Longstreet's ammunition train at Sharpsburg, Md., September 15. Battle of Antietam September 16-17. Duty at Point of Rocks, Md., till February, 1863. Moved to Brunswick February 1, to Bolivar Heights March 1 and to Berryville April. Scouting in the Shenandoah Valley till June 18. Moved to Harper's Ferry, thence to Frederick, Md. Duty there scouting and keeping open communications between Washington, D. C., and Baltimore, Md., during Gettysburg (Pa.) Campaign. At Dripping Springs, near Point of Rocks, July 15-September 12. Scout into Loudoun County September 12-16. Snickersville, Leesburg, Rector's Cross Roads and Bloomfield September 14. Neersville September 14. At Harper's Ferry till December, 1863. Charlestown October 18 (Detachment). Scout to Leesburg and skirmish at Big Springs October 26. At Brunswick till January, 1864, and at Point of Rocks till February. Actions with Mosby at Big Springs and Hillsboro May 16. Waterford May 17. Near Wheatland June 10. Mosby's attack on Point of Rocks July 4. Near Middleton July 7. Solomon's Gap July 7. Frederick July 8. Monocacy July 9. Leesburg August 21. Hamilton August 21. Duty in Military District of Harper's Ferry till March, 1865. Adamstown October 14, 1864. Leesburg November 28. Paxton's Store, Hillsboro, December 1. Expedition into Loudoun County, Va., March 20-25, 1865. Purcellsville and Hamilton March 21. Mustered out at Bolivar, W. Va., May 31, 1865.

WASHINGTON TERRITORY VOLUNTEERS.

1st REGIMENT INFANTRY.

Companies "A," "B," "C" and "D," organized at Alcartraz Island, San Francisco, Cal., January to April, 1862. Other companies organized at San Francisco and in Oregon at various dates.

Companies "A," "B," "C" and "D" ordered to Fort Vancouver, Wash. Ter., April 18, 1862, and sailed April 30, 1862. Company "A" on duty at Fort Vancouver till August 1, 1862, and at Fort Walla Walla till December, 1865.

Companies "B" and "C" at Fort Vancouver till June 26, 1862, and at Fort Colville till muster out. (Co. "C") Expedition to Snake Indian Country May 4-October 26, 1863. Company "B" moved to Fort Walla Walla May 25, 1864, and duty there till muster out.

Company "D" at Fort Vancouver till June 25, 1862. At Fort Hoskins till June, 1863. Moved to Fort Boies June 1-July 4 and duty there till February, 1865. Expedition from Fort Boies to Salmon Falls August 27-October 5, 1864 (Detachment). Ordered to Fort Vancouver February 16, 1865, and duty there till muster out.

Company "E" ordered to Fort Walla Walla August 1, 1862, thence to Fort Steilacoom September 23, 1862, and to Camp Lapwai October 19, 1862. Duty there till April, 1864. At Fort Vancouver till muster out.

Company "F" at Fort Dalles, Ore., till February, 1865, and at Fort Vancouver till muster out.

Company "G" at Fort Steilacoom till April, 1863. Ordered to Fort Vancouver April 8, 1863, thence moved to Fort Boies June 1-July 4, 1863, and duty there till February, 1865. Ordered to Fort Vancouver and duty there till muster out.

Company "H" joined July 13, 1862, at Fort Walla Walla, and duty there till June, 1863. Moved to Fort Boies June 1-July 4. Operations against Snake Indians and protecting Emigrants till October, 1863. At Fort Walla Walla till May, 1864. Ordered to Fort Vancouver May 25, 1864. Duty there and at Fort Dalles till muster out.

Company "I" joined July 13, 1862. At Fort Vancouver till June, 1863. Moved to Fort Boies June 1-July 4. Operating against Snake Indians and protecting Emigrants till October. Duty at Fort Boies till muster out.

Company "K" at Fort Steilacoom December, 1862, to muster out.

Regiment mustered out December 11, 1865.

WEST VIRGINIA VOLUNTEERS.

1st REGIMENT CAVALRY.

Organized at Wheeling, Clarksburg and Morgantown July 10 to November 25, 1861. Attached to Cheat Mountain District, W. Va., to January, 1862. Landers' Division, Army of the Potomac, to March, 1862. Shields' 2nd Division, Banks' 5th Corps, and Dept. of the Shenandoah to May, 1862 (8 Cos.). Milroy's Cheat Mountain District, W. Va., to June, 1862 (4 Cos.). Shields' Division, Dept. of the Rappahannock, to June, 1862 (8 Cos.). Buford's Cavalry Brigade, 2nd Army Corps, Army of Virginia, to September, 1862 (8 Cos.). Milroy's Independent Brigade, 1st Army Corps, Army of Virginia, to September, 1862 (4 Cos.). Unassigned, Defences of Washington, D. C., to February, 1863. Price's Cavalry Brigade, Defences of Washington, D. C., and 22nd Army Corps, to April, 1863. 3rd Brigade,

Stahel's Cavalry Division, 22nd Army Corps, to June, 1863. 1st Brigade, 3rd Division, Cavalry Corps, Army of the Potomac, to December, 1863. Unassigned, Dept. of West Virginia, to March, 1864. 2nd Brigade, 2nd Cavalry Division, W. Va., to May, 1864. 3rd Brigade, 2nd Cavalry Division, W. Va., to June, 1864. 2nd Brigade, 2nd Cavalry Division, W. Va., to November, 1864. 2nd Brigade, 2nd Division, Cavalry Corps, Middle Military Division, to February, 1865. 3rd Brigade, 3rd Division, Cavalry Corps, Army of the Potomac, to July, 1865. (Co. "A" attached to Averill's 4th Separate Brigade, 8th Army Corps, Middle Department, March to June, 1863. Averill's 4th Separate Brigade, W. Va., to December, 1863. 2nd Brigade, 4th Division, W. Va., to April, 1864. Kelly's Command, Reserve Division, W. Va., to April, 1865. 1st Brigade, 1st Infantry Division, W. Va., to July, 1865.)

SERVICE.—Action at Carnifex Ferry, W. Va., September 10, 1861 (Detachment). Romney, W. Va., October 26 (Co. "A"). Guyandotte, W. Va., November 10 (Detachment). Wirt Court House November 19. Capture of Suttonville, Braxton Court House, November 29. In support of Garfield's operations in Eastern Kentucky against Humphrey Marshall December 23, 1861, to January 30, 1862 (Detachment). Skirmishes in Clay, Braxton and Webster Counties December 29-31. Jennies Creek, Ky., January 7, 1862 (Detachment). Regiment engaged in scouting, picket and outpost duty and guarding Baltimore & Ohio Railroad in West Virginia till March, 1862. Expedition to Blue's Gap January 6-7. Hanging Rock Pass, Romney, January 7. Bloomery Gap February 13. Bloomen February 15. Advance on Winchester, Va., March 5-12 (Cos. "C," "E" and "L"). Phillippi March 20 (4 Cos.). Battle of Winchester March 23. Monterey April 12 (Cos. "C," "E" and "L"). Buffalo Gap May 3 (Cos. "C," "E" and "L"). McDowell May 7 (Cos. "C," "E" and "L"). Scouts to Roane and Clay Counties May 8-21. Giles Court House May 10 (Detachment). Strasburg June 1. Cross Keys June 8. Port Republic June 9. White Plains June 10. Expedition to Madison Court House, Culpeper Court House and Orange Court House July 12-17. Near Culpeper July 12. Cedar Mountain August 9 (Cos. "C," "E" and "L"). Orange Court House August 13. Pope's Campaign in Northern Virginia August 16-September 2. Rapidan August 18. Freeman's Ford, Hazel River, August 22 (Cos. "C," "E" and "L"). Kelly's Ford August 22. Sulphur Springs August 23. Waterloo Bridge August 23-25. Buckland Bridge, near Gainesville, August 28 (Cos. "C," "E" and "L"). Groveton August 29 (Cos. "C," "E" and "L"). Bull Run August 30 (Cos. "C," "E" and "L"). Lewis Ford August 30. Chantilly September 1. (2 Cos. at Antietam, Md., September 16-17.) Ashby's Gap September 22. Expedition to Thoroughfare Gap October 17-18. Gainesville October 18. Near Warrenton November 4. Reconnoissance to Snicker's Ferry and Berryville November 28-30. Snicker's Ferry November 30. Moorefield, W. Va., December 3 (1 Co.). Near Moorefield, W. Va., January 5, 1863. Cocklestown, Pocahontas County, W. Va., January 22. Scout from Centreville to Falmouth February 27-28. Beverly April 24 (Co. "A"). Warrenton Junction May 3 (Detachment). Winchester June 13-15 (Cos. "C" and "K"). Hanover, Pa., June 30. Gettysburg, Pa., July 1-3. Hunterstown July 2. Monterey Gap July 4. Smithburg July 5. Hagerstown July 6. Boonsboro July 8. Hagerstown July 11-13. Falling Water July 14. Expedition from Fayetteville, W. Va., to Wytheville July 13-15 (2 Cos.). Shanghai July 16 (Co. "A"). Wytheville July 18-19 (Co. "A"). Near Hedgesville and Martinsburg July 18-19 (Co. "A"). Near Gaines' Cross Roads July 23. McConnellsburg, Pa., July 30. Averill's Raid through Hardy, Pendleton, Highland, Bath, Greenfield and Pocahontas Counties, W. Va., August 25-31 (Co. "A"). Rocky Gap, near White Sulphur Springs, August 26-27 (Co. "A"). Expedition to Port Conway September 1-3. Culpeper Court House September 13. Raccoon Ford September 14-16. Robertson's Station September 16. Raccoon Ford September 17-18. White's Ford September 22-23,

Bristoe Campaign October 9-22. James City and Bethesda Church October 10. Near Culpeper, Brandy Station and Griffinsburg October 11. Gainesville October 14. Groveton October 17-18. Gainesville, New Baltimore, Buckland's Mill and Haymarket October 19. Catlett's Station November 7. Mine Run Campaign November 26-December 2. Raccoon Ford November 26-27. Averill's Raid from Lewisburg to Virginia & Tennessee Railroad November 1-17 (Co. "A"). Droop Mountain November 6 (Co. "A"). Averill's Raid from New Creek to Salem December 8-25 (Co. "A"). Regiment on duty at various points in West Virginia till May, 1864. Averill's Raid on Virginia & Tennessee Railroad May 5-19. Baltimore & Ohio Railroad, between Bloomfield and Piedmont, May 5. Abb's Valley, Jeffersonville, May 8. Grassy Lick, Cove Mountain, near Wytheville, May 10. Doublin Station May 12. Rude's Hill and New Market May 14. Lewisburg May 20 (Detachment). Hunter's Raid on Lynchburg May 26-July 1. Staunton June 8. White Sulphur Springs June 10. Lexington June 11. Scout around Lynchburg June 13-15. Near Buchanan June 13. New London June 16. Diamond Hill June 17. Lynchburg June 17-18. Snicker's Ford June 18. Liberty June 19. Buford's Gap June 20. Catawba Mountains and about Salem June 21. Snicker's Ferry, Va., July 17-18. Carter's Farm, near Stephenson's Depot, July 20. Newtown July 22. Kernstown, Winchester, July 24. Falling Waters July 24. Martinsburg July 25. Hagerstown July 29. Hancock July 31. Williamsport and Hagerstown August 5. Near Moorefield August 7. Williamsport August 26. Martinsburg August 31. Bunker Hill September 3-4. Stephenson's Depot September 5. Darkesville September 10. Bunker Hill September 13. Berryville and near Brentsville September 14. Centreville September 14. Charlestown September 17. Winchester September 19. Fisher's Hill September 22. Mt. Jackson September 23-24. Forest Hill or Timberville September 24. Brown's Gap September 26. Weyer's Cave September 26-27. Battle of Cedar Creek October 19. Dry Run October 23 (Detachment). Milford October 25 (Detachment). Nineveh November 12. Rude's Hill, near Mt. Jackson, November 22. Expedition to Gordonsville December 19-28. Gordonsville December 23. Sheridan's Raid from Winchester February 25-March 25, 1865. Mt. Crawford February 28. Waynesboro March 2. Charlottesville March 3. Augusta Court House March 10. Haydensville March 12. Beaver Dam Station March 15. White House March 26. Appomattox Campaign March 28-April 9. Dinwiddie Court House March 29-31. Five Forks April 1. Namozine Church and Scott's Corners April 2. Jettersville April 4. Amelia Court House April 5. Sailor's Creek April 6. Stony Point April 7. Appomattox Station April 8. Appomattox Court House April 9. Surrender of Lee and his army. Expedition to Danville April 23-29. March to Washington, D. C., May. Grand Review May 23. Mustered out July 8, 1865.

Regiment lost during service 10 Officers and 71 Enlisted men killed and mortally wounded and 126 Enlisted men by disease. Total 207.

2nd REGIMENT CAVALRY.

Organized at Parkersburg, W. Va., September to November, 1861. Attached to District of the Kanawha, W. Va., to March, 1862. Unattached, Kanawha Division, W. Va., to September, 1862. Unattached, District of the Kanawha, Dept. of the Ohio, to January, 1863. Unattached, 3rd Division, 8th Army Corps, Middle Department, to June, 1863. Scammon's Division, W. Va., to December, 1863. 3rd Brigade, 3rd Division, Army of West Virginia, to April, 1864. 1st Brigade, 2nd Cavalry Division, Army of West Virginia, to June, 1864. 3rd Brigade, 2nd Cavalry Division, Army of West Virginia, to July, 1864. 2nd Brigade, 2nd Cavalry Division, W. Va., to November, 1864. 2nd Brigade, 2nd Division, Cavalry Corps, Middle Military Division, to February, 1865. 3rd Brigade, 3rd Division, Cavalry Corps, Army of the Potomac, to June, 1865.

SERVICE.—Ordered to Guyandotte, W. Va., December 15, 1861, and duty there till April, 1862. Co-operate with Garfield against Humphrey Marshall January 7-8, 1862. Dry Fork, Cheat River, February 8. 1st Battalion (Cos. "B," "C," "F," "H" and "I") moved to Meadow Bluff April, 1862. 2nd Battalion (Cos. "A," "D," "E," "G" and "K") moved to Raleigh with General Cox engaged in scouting and operating against bushwhackers in Raleigh, Fayette and Wyoming Counties till August, then rejoined Regiment. Demonstration on Virginia & Tennessee Railroad May 10-18. Lewisburg May 12. Princeton May 15-17. Retreat to Flat Top Mountain May 18. Jackson River Depot May 20. Lewisburg May 23. Raid to Shaver River May 30. Lewisburg May 30. Middle Creek June 8. Alderson's Ferry June 9. Wolf Creek July 10. Lamb's Mill July 15. Blue Sulphur Springs July 20. Alderson's Ferry July 23. Williamsport July 28. At Meadow Bluff till August. Ordered to Kanawha Falls August 14. Shady Springs August 28 (Detachment). Campaign in Kanawha Valley September 6-16. Barboursville September 8. Fayetteville September 10. Cotton Hill September 11. Loop Creek September 11. Hurricane Bridge September 12. Charlestown September 13. At Point Pleasant to October 20. Moved to Charlestown October 20, thence to Camp Piatt. Expedition from Summerville to Cold Knob Mountain November 24-30. Lewis Mill on Sinking Creek November 26. Peters Mountain Raid January 5-20, 1863. Scout into Wyoming County February 5-8. Expedition into Pocahontas County February 10-12. Scout through Boone, Wyoming and Logan Counties March 12-16. Expedition through Logan and Cabell Counties April 3-6. Mud River April 5. Lewisburg May 2. West Union May 6. Summerville May 12 Fayetteville May 18-20. Scout on Big and Little Coal Rivers June 18-19. Loup Creek June 26 (Cos. "B" and "I"). Raleigh July 4. Expedition from Fayetteville to Wytheville July 13-25. Shady Springs July 14. Wytheville July 18-19. Fayetteville July 28. Cold Springs Gap August 5 (Detachment). Scouts from Camp Piatt September 11-13. Smythe County September 14. Scout to Boone Court House October 21-22. Expedition from Charlestown to Lewisburg November 3-13. Little Sewell Mountain November 6. Capture of Lewisburg November 7. Muddy Creek November 7. Near Union November 8. Scammon's Demonstration from the Kanawha Valley December 8-25. Meadow Bluff December 11. Lewisburg and Greenbrier River December 12. Scout in Cabell and Wayne Counties March 16-18, 1864. Averill's Raid on Virginia & Tennessee Railroad May 5-19. Princeton, Grassy Lick Cove, near Wytheville, Wytheville, Ingle and Cove Gap May 10. Salt Pond and Pond Mountain Gap May 13. Hunter's Raid on Lynchburg, Va., May 26-July 1. Staunton June 8. Newport June 10. Lexington June 11. Near Buchanan June 13. New London June 16. Otter Creek June 16. Diamond Hill June 17. Lynchburg June 17-18. Liberty June 19. Buford's Gap June 20. Catawba Mountains and near Salem June 21. Cove Gap June 23. Snicker's Ferry July 17-18. Carter's Farm July 20. Newtown July 22. Kernstown, Winchester, July 24. Martinsburg July 25. Hagerstown July 29. McConnellsburg, Pa., July 30. Hancock, Md., July 31. Near Moorefield August 7. Williamsport August 26. Martinsburg August 31. Bunker Hill September 2-3. Near Bunker Hill September 5. Near Stephenson's Depot September 5. Darkesville September 10. Bunker Hill September 13. Near Berryville September 14. Battle of Winchester September 19. Fisher's Hill September 22. Mt. Jackson September 23-24. Forest Hill or Timberville September 24. Piedmont September 25. Brown's Gap September 26. Weyer's Cave September 26-27. Battle of Cedar Creek October 19. Dry Run October 23. Nineveh November 12. Rude's Hill, Front Royal, November 22. Expedition to Gordonsville December 19-28. Liberty Mills December 22. Jack's Shop, near Gordonsville, December 23. Near Ashby's Gap December 27. Sheridan's Raid from Winchester February 25-March 25, 1865. Mt. Crawford February 28. Waynesboro March 2. Charlottesville March 3. Augusta Court House March 10. Haydensville March 12. Beaver Dam

Station March 15. White House March 26. Appomattox Campaign March 28-April 9. Dinwiddie Court House March 29-31. Five Forks April 1. Namozine Church and Scott's Corners April 2. Jettersville April 4. Sailor's Creek April 6. Stony Point April 7. Appomattox Station April 8. Appomattox Court House April 9. Surrender of Lee and his army. Expedition to North Carolina April 23-29. March to Washington, D. C., May. Grand Review May 23. Mustered out June 30, 1865.

Regiment lost during service 4 Officers and 77 Enlisted men killed and mortally wounded and 115 Enlisted men by disease. Total 196.

3rd REGIMENT CAVALRY.

Organized December, 1861. Attached to Railroad District, West Virginia, to March, 1862. Railroad District, Mountain Department, to May, 1862. Unattached, Mountain Department, to June, 1862. 2nd Brigade, 2nd Division, 1st Army Corps, Army of Virginia, to September, 1862 (Cos. "A" and "C"). District of West Virginia, Dept. of the Ohio and Dept. of West Virginia. Unassigned, to March, 1864 (Regiment). Milroy's Command, Winchester, Va., 8th Army Corps, Middle Department, to February, 1863 (Cos. "D" and "E"). 2nd Brigade, 2nd Division, 8th Army Corps, to June, 1863 (Cos. "D" and "E"). 4th Separate Brigade, 8th Army Corps, to June, 1864 (Cos. "F," "H" and "I"). 4th Separate Brigade, Dept. of West Virginia, to December, 1863 (Cos. "F," "H" and "I"). Bloody Run, Pa., Dept. of the Susquehanna, and Scammon's Division, Dept. of West Virginia, to July, 1863 (Cos. "D" and "E"). McReynolds' Command, Martinsburg, W. Va., Dept. of West Virginia, to December, 1863 (Cos. "D" and "E"). 1st Brigade, 3rd Division, West Virginia (1 Co.). 2nd Brigade, 4th Division, West Virginia (3 Cos.). 3rd Brigade, 3rd Division, West Virginia (2 Cos.), to March, 1864. 3rd Brigade, 2nd Cavalry Division, West Virginia, to May, 1864. 2nd Brigade, 2nd Cavalry Division, West Virginia, to November, 1864. 2nd Brigade, 2nd Cavalry Corps, Middle Military Division, to February, 1865. 3rd Brigade, 3rd Division, Cavalry Corps, Army of the Potomac, to June, 1865. Companies "A" and "C" attached to Headquarters, 11th Army Corps, Army of the Potomac, September, 1862, to December, 1862. Headquarters, Grand Reserve Division, Army of the Potomac, to February, 1863. 3rd Brigade, Cavalry Division, 22nd Army Corps, to June, 1863. 2nd Brigade, 1st Division, Cavalry Corps, Army of the Potomac, to November, 1863. Ordered to Dept. of West Virginia November, 1863.

SERVICE.—Duty in Railroad District, Mountain Department, to May, 1862. Monterey April 12. Skirmish at Grass Lick, W. Va., April 23. Franklin May 5. Raid to Shaver River May 30 (Detachment). Strasburg and Staunton Road June 1-2. Harrisonburg June 6. Cross Keys June 8. Near Mt. Jackson June 13. Pope's Virginia Campaign August 16-September 2. Groveton August 29. Bull Run August 30. Aldie October 9. Near Bristoe Station October 24. Chester Gap November 16. Dumfries December 12. Wardensville December 22 and 25. Petersburg, W. Va., January 3, 1863 (Detachment). Williamsport, Md., February 9. Truce Fork, Mud River, W. Va., February 20. Winchester March 19. Reconnoissance toward Wardensville and Strasburg April 20. Fisher's Hill, Strasburg Road, April 22. Lambert's Run April 22. Near Simpson's Creek April 30. Grove Church May 4. Janelew May 5 (Co. "E"). Strasburg May 6. Operations about Front Royal, Road Ford and Buck's Ford, May 12-16. Piedmont Station May 16. Brandy Station and Beverly Ford June 9. Winchester June 13-15 (Cos. "D" and "E"). Upperville June 21. Battle of Gettysburg, Pa., July 1-3. Boonesborough, Md., July 8. Benevola or Beaver Creek July 9. Funkstown July 10-13. Falling Waters July 14. Shanghai, W. Va., July 16. Near Hedgesville and Martinsburg July 18-19 (Co. "C"). Hagerstown July 29. Hancock July 31. Kelly's Ford July 31-August 1. Brandy Station August 1. Averill's Raid

through Hardy, Pendleton, Highland, Greenbrier, Bath and Pocahontas Counties, W. Va., August 5-25 (Cos. "E," "H" and "I"). Affair near Franklin August 19. Jackson River August 25. Williamsport, Md., August 26. Expedition to Leesburg August 30-September 2. Advance to the Rapidan September 13-17 (Cos. "A" and "C"). Culpeper Court House September 13 (Cos. "A" and "C"). Fisher's Hill September 21. Bristoe Campaign October 9-22 (Cos. "A" and "C"). Morton's Ford October 10 (Cos. "A" and "C"). Stevensburg and near Kelly's Ford October 11 (Cos. "A" and "C"). Brandy Station October 11 (Cos. "A" and "C"). Brandy Station and Fleetwood October 12 (Cos. "A" and "C"). Auburn and Bristoe October 14 (Cos. "A" and "C"). Oak Hill October 15 (Cos. "A" and "C"). Averill's Raid against Lewisburg and the Virginia & Tennessee Railroad November 1-17 (Cos. "E," "H" and "I"). Cackletown November 4 (Cos. "E," "H" and "I"). Droop Mountain November 6 (Cos. "E," "H" and "I"). Advance to line of the Rappahannock November 7-8 (Cos. "A" and "C"). Near Little Boston November 24 (Detachment). Mine Run Campaign November 26-December 2 (Cos. "A" and "C"). Averill's Raid from New Creek to Salem and Virginia & Tennessee Railroad December 8-25 (Cos. "E," "F" and "H"). Scammon's Demonstration from Kanawha Valley December 8-25 (Detachment). Near Wayne Court House, W. Va., January 27, 1864 (Co. "G"). Near Hurricane Bridge February 20. Averill's Raid on Virginia & Tennessee Railroad May 5-19. Grassy Lick, Cove Mountain, near Wytheville May 10. Wytheville May 10. Hunter's Raid to Lynchburg May 26-July 1. Hamlin May 29. Lexington June 11. Near Buchanan June 13. Otter Creek, near Liberty, June 16. Diamond Hill June 17. Lynchburg June 17-18. Liberty June 19. Buford's Gap June 20. Catawba Mountains and about Salem June 21. Snicker's Ferry July 17-18. Bunker Hill July 19. Stephenson's Depot July 21. Winchester July 21-22. Newtown July 22. Kernstown, Winchester, July 24. Martinsburg July 26. McConnellsburg, Pa., July 30. Sheridan's Shenandoah Valley Campaign August 7-November 28. Near Moorefield August 7. Franklin August 19. Martinsburg August 25. Williamsport August 26. Big Springs August 29. Martinsburg August 31. Bunker Hill September 2-3. Martinsburg September 4. Stephenson's Depot September 5. Darkesville September 10. Bunker Hill September 13. Near Berryville September 14. Battle of Winchester September 19. Fisher's Hill September 22. Mt. Jackson September 23-24. Forest Hill or Timberville September 24. Browns Gap and Mt. Sidney September 26. Weyer's Cave September 26-27. Charlestown September 27. Mt. Jackson September 28. Nineveh November 12. Rude's Hill November 20. Near Mt. Jackson November 22. Raid to Gordonsville December 19-28. Liberty Mills December 22. Jack's Shop, near Gordonsville, December 23. Sheridan's Expedition from Winchester February 25-March 25, 1865. Mt. Crawford March 1. Occupation of Staunton March 2. Waynesboro March 2. Charlottesville March 3. Augusta Court House March 10. Haydensville March 12. Beaver Dam Station March 15. Appomattox Campaign March 28-April 9. Dinwiddie Court House March 29-31. Five Forks April 1. Namozine Church April 3. Sailor's Creek April 6. Appomattox Station April 8. Appomattox Court House April 9. Surrender of Lee and his army. Expedition to Danville April 23-29. March to Washington, D. C., May. Grand Review May 23. Mustered out June 23, 1865.

Regiment lost during service 6 Officers and 40 Enlisted men killed and mortally wounded and 136 Enlisted men by disease. Total 182.

4th REGIMENT CAVALRY.

Organized at Parkersburg and Wheeling, W. Va., July and August, 1863, for one year. Attached to Wilkinson's Brigade, Army of West Virginia, to December, 1863. 3rd Brigade, 2nd Division, West Virginia, to

April, 1864. Kelly's Command, Reserve Division, West Virginia, to June, 1864.

SERVICE.—Duty at Parkersburg, Clarksburg, Grafton, New Creek and other points on the Baltimore & Ohio Railroad till June, 1864, guarding railroad and operating against guerrillas. Actions at Salt Lick Bridge October 11 and 14, 1863. Operations in Hampshire and Hardy Counties January 27 to February 7, 1864. Action at Medley, Williamsport, January 29-30. Mustered out June 23, 1864.

Regiment lost during service 30 by disease.

5th REGIMENT CAVALRY.

Organized from 2nd Regiment West Virginia Mounted Infantry January 26, 1864. Attached to Martinsburg, W. Va., to March, 1864. 3rd Brigade, 4th Division, West Virginia, to April, 1864. 3rd Brigade, Cavalry Division, West Virginia, to June, 1864. 2nd Brigade, 2nd Cavalry Division, West Virginia, to July, 1865. Kelly's Command, Reserve Division, West Virginia, to December, 1864.

SERVICE.—Duty at Martinsburg, W. Va., till March 19, 1864. Operations in Hampshire and Hardy Counties January 27-February 7. Springfield February 2. Moved to Cumberland, Md., and duty there and at Patterson's Creek till April 27. Moved to Charleston April 27-30. Crook's Expedition to Virginia & Tennessee Railroad May 2-19. Cloyd's Mountain or Farm May 9. New River Bridge May 10. Hunter's Expedition to Lynchburg May 26-July 1. Lexington June 11. Near Buchanan June 13. New London June 16. Diamond Hill June 17. Lynchburg June 17-18. Liberty June 19. Buford's Gap June 20. Catawba Mountains and about Salem June 21. At Camp Piatt, Charleston and New Creek guarding railroad in district west of Sleepy Hollow till December. Consolidated to a Battalion at Charleston September. Expedition from New Creek to Moorefield November 6-8 (Detachment). New Creek November 28. Transferred to 6th West Virginia Cavalry December 14, 1864.

Regiment lost during service 3 Officers and 68 Enlisted men killed and mortally wounded and 118 Enlisted men by disease. Total 189.

6th REGIMENT CAVALRY.

Organized from 3rd West Virginia Mounted Infantry January 26, 1864. Attached to 3rd Brigade, 4th Division, Army West Virginia, to April, 1864. 3rd Brigade, 2nd Cavalry Division, West Virginia, to June, 1864. 2nd Brigade, 2nd Cavalry Division, West Virginia, to July, 1864. Reserve Division, Harper's Ferry, W. Va., to January, 1865. Remount Camp Pleasant Valley, Md., to April, 1865. Dept. of Washington, D. C., 22nd Army Corps, to June, 1865. District of the Plains, Dept. of Missouri, to May, 1866.

SERVICE.—Duty at Martinsburg, W. Va., till March, 1864. Operations in Hampshire and Hardy Counties January 27-February 7. Springfield February 2. Moved to Beverly, March, and duty there till May. Winchester April 8 (Detachment). Kablestown June 10 (Detachment). White Post June 13 (Detachment). Wire Bridge and Springfield June 26 (Detachment). Frankfort July 4. Back Creek Bridge July 26. Regiment reorganized at Cumberland, Md., July 7. Remounted at North Bridge August 22, and ordered to New Creek. Duty there till January 12, 1865. Expedition to Moorefield November 6-8, 1864 (Detachment). Moorefield November 27-28. New Creek November 28. Moved to Remount Camp, Md., January 12, 1865, and duty there till April 4. Duty at Washington, D. C., till June 12. Moved to Leavenworth, Kan., June 12-29, and duty there till July 16. A detachment moved to Fort Kearney, Neb., and duty under Major Squires. Regiment moved to Julesburg and duty escorting Overland mails and operating against hostile Indians at Julesburg and Cottonwood Springs till April, 1866. Moved to Fort Leavenworth, Kan., and mustered out May 22, 1866.

Regiment lost during service 5 Officers and 28 Enlisted men killed and mortally wounded and 2 Officers and 201 Enlisted men by disease. Total 236.

7th REGIMENT CAVALRY.

Organized from 8th West Virginia Mounted Infantry January 26, 1864. Attached to 3rd Brigade, 4th Division, West Virginia, to April, 1864. 3rd Brigade, 2nd Cavalry Division, West Virginia, to June, 1864. 2nd Brigade, 2nd Cavalry Division, West Virginia, to July, 1864. 1st Separate Brigade, Kanawha Valley, W. Va., to August, 1865.

SERVICE.—Duty at Martinsburg and Charleston, W. Va., to April, 1864. Crook's Raid on Virginia & Tennessee Railroad May 2-19. Rocky Gap May 6. Cloyd's Mountain May 9. New River Bridge May 10. Cove Gap May 10. Blacksburg May 11. Union and Pond Mountain Gap May 12. Meadow Bluff May 24. Hunter's Raid to Lynchburg May 26-July 1. Buffalo Gap June 6. Lexington June 11. Buchanan June 13. New London June 16. Diamond Hill June 17. Lynchburg June 17-18. Liberty June 19. Buford's Gap June 20. About Salem June 21. At Loup Creek June 29. Ordered to the Kanawha Valley and duty at Charleston, Coalsmouth, Winfield, Point Pleasant and Guyandotte till August, 1865. Coalsmouth September 30, 1864. Skirmish at Winfield October 26, 1864 (1 Co.). Operations in the Kanawha Valley November 5-12. Mustered out August 1, 1865.

Regiment lost during service 5 Officers and 28 Enlisted men killed and mortally wounded and 2 Officers and 201 Enlisted men by disease. Total 236.

BATTERY "A" LIGHT ARTILLERY ("DAUM'S").

Organized at Wheeling, W. Va., and mustered in June 28, 1861. Attached to Army of Occupation, W. Va., to September, 1861. Cheat Mountain, District West Virginia, to January, 1862. Landers' Division, Army Potofac, to March, 1862. Shields' 2nd Division, Banks' 5th Army Corps, and Dept. of the Shenandoah, to May, 1862. Shields' Division, Dept. of the Rappahannock, to June, 1862. Slough's Command, Defences of Washington, D. C., to February, 1863. Camp Barry, Defences of Washington, 22nd Army Corps, to July, 1863. Maryland Heights, 2nd Division, Dept. of West Virginia, to December, 1863. 1st Brigade, 1st Division, Army of West Virginia, to April, 1864. Reserve Division, Harper's Ferry, W. Va., to October, 1864. 1st Separate Brigade, Dept. of West Virginia, to July, 1865.

SERVICE.—At Elkwater till October, 1861. Operations on Cheat Mountain September 11-17. Action at Cheat Mountain September 11. Cheat Mountain Pass September 12. Point Mountain Turnpike and Elkwater September 12. Greenbrier River October 3-4. At Romney till January, 1862. Expedition to Blue's Gap January 6. Hanging Rock, Blue's Gap, January 7. At Paw Paw Tunnel till March. Advance on Winchester March 7-12. Battle of Kernstown, Winchester, March 22-23. Cedar Mountain March 25. Woodstock April 1. Edenburg April 2. Occupation of Mt. Jackson April 17. March to Fredericksburg May 12-22, and to Front Royal May 25-30. Front Royal May 30. Duty in the Defences of Washington, D. C., till July, 1863. Ordered to Harper's Ferry, W. Va., thence to Charlestown. Expedition to near New Market November 15-18. Mt. Jackson November 16. Wells' demonstration up the Shenandoah Valley December 10-25. Duty at Harper's Ferry, Charlestown and Martinsburg till May, 1864. At Maryland Heights till October 17. Moved to Parkersburg October 17. Duty at Parkersburg, Charlestown and in the Kanawha Valley till July, 1865. Mustered out July 27, 1865.

BATTERY "B" LIGHT ARTILLERY ("KEEPER'S").

Organized at Ceredo October 1, 1861. Attached to Reynolds' Cheat Mountain District, W. Va., to January, 1862. Landers' Division, Army of the Potomac, to March, 1862. Artillery, Shields' 2nd Division, Banks' 5th Army Corps, and Dept. of the Shenandoah to May, 1862. Shields' Division, Dept. of the Rappahannock, to June, 1862. Military District of Washington, D. C., to January, 1863. Milroy's Command, Winchester, Va., 8th Army Corps, Middle Department, to February, 1863. 2nd

Brigade, 2nd Division, 8th Army Corps, to May, 1863. 4th Separate Brigade, 8th Army Corps, to June, 1863. Averill's 4th Separate Brigade, Dept. of West Virginia, to December, 1863. 1st Brigade, 4th Division, Army of West Virginia, to April, 1864. Artillery, 1st Cavalry, Division of West Virginia, to February, 1865.

SERVICE.—At Romney till January, 1862, and at Paw Paw Tunnel till March. Advance on Winchester, Va., March 7-12. Battle of Kernstown-Winchester, March 22-23. Occupation of Mount Jackson and New Market April 17. March to Fredericksburg May 12-22, and to Front Royal May 25-30. Front Royal May 30. Ordered to Camp Barry, Washington, D. C., and duty in the Defences of that city and in Railroad District, 8th Corps, Middle Department, till January, 1863. Action at Faquier, White Sulphur Springs, Va., August 27, 1862. Duty at Winchester, Va., January to May, 1863. Ordered to Grafton, W. Va., May 10. Moved to Beverly, Buckhannon, Clarksburg, Parkersburg and Weston, arriving at Grafton June 17. Moved to New Creek and Phillippi July 1 and to Cumberland, Md., July 7; to Fairview July 12. Averill's Raid through Hardy, Pendleton, Highland, Bath, Greenbrier and Pocahontas Counties August 5-31. Jackson River August 25. Rocky Gap, near White Sulphur Springs, August 26-27. Averill's Raid from Beverly against Lewisburg and the Virginia & Tennessee Railroad November 1-17. Mill Point, Pocahontas County, November 5. Engagement at Droop Mountain November 6. At Beverly and Martinsburg till May, 1864. Hunter's Raid to Lynchburg May 26-July 1. Piedmont, Mount Crawford, June 5. Buffalo Gap June 6. Occupation of Staunton June 6. Diamond Hill June 17. Lynchburg June 17-18. Catawba Mountains June 21. Leetown July 3. About Harper's Ferry July 4-7. Near Hillsborough July 15-16. Snicker's Ferry July 17-18. Ashby's Gap and Berry's Ford July 19. Ashby's Gap July 23. Battle of Kernstown, Winchester, July 24. Bunker Hill and Martinsburg July 25. Duty in District of Harper's Ferry till December. Consolidated with Battery "E," West Virginia Light Artillery, December 31, 1864.

BATTERY "C" LIGHT ARTILLERY.

Organized at Wheeling, W. Va., January 25 to March 30, 1862. Served unattached, Railroad District, Dept. of the Mountains, to May, 1862. 1st Brigade, Blenker's Division, Dept. of the Mountains, to June, 1862. Reserve Artillery, 1st Corps, Pope's Army of Virginia, to September, 1862. Artillery, 3rd Division, 11th Army Corps, Army of the Potomac, to March, 1863. Reserve Artillery, 11th Army Corps, to May, 1863. 3rd Volunteer Brigade, Artillery Reserve, Army of the Potomac, to August, 1863. 4th Volunteer Brigade, Artillery Reserve, Army of the Potomac, to October, 1863. 2nd Brigade, Artillery Reserve, to November, 1863. 1st Volunteer Brigade, Artillery Reserve, Army of the Potomac, to March, 1864. Camp Barry, Washington, D. C., 22nd Corps, to May, 1864. 2nd Brigade, De Russy's Division, 22nd Army Corps, to July, 1864. 4th Brigade, De Russy's Division, 22nd Army Corps, to October, 1864. 3rd Brigade, De Russy's Division, 22nd Army Corps, to December, 1864. 1st Brigade, De Russy's Division, 22nd Army Corps, to June, 1865.

SERVICE.—Duty at Franklin, Va., till May 25, 1862. Pursuit of Jackson up the Shenandoah Valley May 25-June 14. Mount Carmel Road, near Strasburg, June 1. Strasburg June 2. Tom's Brook June 3. Mount Jackson June 6. Battle of Cross Keys June 8. Port Republic June 9. At Sperryville till August. Pope's Campaign in Northern Virginia August 8-September 2. Battle of Cedar Mountain August 9 (Reserve). Rappahannock Station August 20-21. Freeman's Ford August 22. Sulphur Springs August 24. Waterloo Bridge August 24-25. Plains of Manassas August 27. Gainesville August 28. Groveton August 29. Bull Run August 30. Duty in the Defences of Washington, D. C., till December. Reconnoissance to Leesburg and skirmish September 16-19. March to Fredericksburg, Va., December 10-16. Raid on Dumfries and Fairfax Station December 27-29. At Falmouth, Va., till April, 1863. "Mud March"

January 20-24. Chancellorsville Campaign April 27-May 6. Battle of Chancellorsville May 1-5. Gettysburg (Pa.) Campaign June 12-July 24. Battle of Gettysburg, Pa., July 1-3. Bristoe Campaign October 9-22. Advance to line of the Rappahannock November 7-8. Mine Run Campaign November 26-December 2. Ordered to Washington, D. C., and duty in the Defences of that city south of the Potomac till June, 1865. Repulse of Early's attack on Washington July 11-12, 1864. Mustered out June 28, 1865.

BATTERY "D" LIGHT ARTILLERY.

Organized at Wheeling, W. Va., August 20, 1862. Attached to Railroad District, District of West Virginia, Dept. of Ohio, to January, 1863. Milroy's Command, Winchester, Va., 8th Army Corps, Middle Department, to February, 1863. 1st Brigade, 2nd Division, 8th Army Corps, to June, 1863. 2nd Brigade, 2nd Division, 8th Army Corps, June, 1863. Mulligan's Brigade, Dept. of West Virginia, to December, 1863. 2nd Brigade, 2nd Division, West Virginia, to March, 1864. 2nd Infantry Division, West Virginia, to May, 1864. Artillery Brigade, West Virginia, to August, 1864. Wheeling, W. Va., to September, 1864. Parkersburg, W. Va., to April, 1865. 1st Brigade, 1st Division, West Virginia, to June, 1865.

SERVICE.—Duty at Parkersburg, W. Va., till January, 1863. Moved to Winchester, Va., and duty there till June. Scouts to Strasburg April 20 and April 25-29. Operations in Shenandoah Valley April 22-29. Scout to Moorefield and into Hampshire County May 4-9. Battle of Winchester June 13-15. At Bloody Run, Pa., till July. At Wheeling, W. Va., till August 31. At New Creek till April, 1864. Operations in Hampshire and Hardy Counties against Rosser January 27-February 7, 1864. Ordered to Burlington April 3, thence to Martinsburg. Sigel's Expedition from Martinsburg to New Market April 30-May 16. Battle of New Market May 15. Advance to Staunton May 24-June 6. Piedmont June 5. Occupation of Staunton June 6. Hunter's Raid on Lynchburg June 6-July 1. Near Lynchburg June 14. Diamond Hill June 17. Lynchburg June 17-18. Liberty June 19. Buford's Gap June 20. Salem June 21. At Wheeling, W. Va., August 8 to September 13 and at Parkersburg, W. Va., to June, 1865. Mustered out June 27, 1865.

BATTERY "E" LIGHT ARTILLERY.

Organized at Buckhannon, W. Va., September 18, 1862. Attached to Railroad District, District of West Virginia, Dept. of Ohio, to January, 1863. Romney, W. Va., 8th Army Corps, Middle Department, to March, 1863. 4th Brigade, 1st Division, 8th Army Corps, to June, 1863. Campbell's Brigade, Dept. of West Virginia, to December, 1863. 1st Brigade, 2nd Division, Army of West Virginia, to April, 1864. Kelly's Command, Reserve Division, West Virginia, to July, 1864. Artillery Brigade, West Virginia, July, 1864. Artillery, 1st Cavalry Division, West Virginia, to October, 1864. District of Harper's Ferry, W. Va., to January, 1865. Camp Barry and Defences of Washington, D. C., to June, 1865.

SERVICE.—Ordered to Clarksburg, W. Va., thence to New Creek and Romney. Railroad guard duty at Romney, Clarksburg, New Creek, Moorefield and Petersburg till January, 1864. Action near Moorefield April 6, 1863. Near Burlington and at Purgitsville and Going's Ford April 6-7. Moved to Cumberland, Md., January 4-5, 1864, and duty in South Branch Valley till July. Action at Snicker's Ferry July 17-18. Stephenson's Depot July 20. Near Berryville July 22. Battle of Kernstown-Winchester July 23-24. Bunker Hill July 25. At Harper's Ferry and with Reserve Division till January, 1865. Action at New Creek November 28, 1864. Ordered to Washington, D. C., January, 1865, and duty at Camp Barry, Defences of Washington, till June. Mustered out June 28, 1865.

BATTERY "F" LIGHT ARTILLERY.

Organized as Company "C," 6th West Virginia Infantry. Detached as an Independent Battery April 8, 1863. Attached to 3rd Brigade, 1st Division, 8th Army

Corps, Middle Dept., to June, 1863. Artillery, French's Command, 8th Army Corps, to July, 1863. Camp Barry, Washington, D. C., 22nd Army Corps, to December, 1863. 3rd Brigade, 2nd Division, West Virginia, to April, 1864. Kelly's Command, Reserve Division, West Virginia, to July, 1864. Artillery Brigade, West Virginia, to September, 1864.

SERVICE.—Duty at Clarksburg, Cumberland, Md., and Martinsburg, W. Va., till April, 1863. Moved from Martinsburg to New Creek April 26, 1863, and to Berryville May 31. Return to Martinsburg May 31. Action at Martinsburg June 14. Retreat to Harper's Ferry, thence guard stores to Washington, D. C., July 1-4. Duty at Camp Barry, Defences of Washington, July to December. Ordered to Clarksburg, W. Va., thence to New Creek January 30, 1864, and duty there till May 31. At Clarksburg till July, and at Maryland Heights till September. Battle of Kernstown July 24. Transferred to Battery "A," West Virginia Light Artillery, September 14, 1864.

BATTERY "G" LIGHT ARTILLERY.

Organized May 26, 1863, from Company "G," 2nd West Virginia Infantry. Duty at Beverly, Buckhannon, Bulltown, Clarksburg, Parkersburg, Weston and Martinsburg till May, 1864. Operations against Imboden in West Virginia April 20-May 14, 1863. Scout to Beverly June 16. Engagement at Beverly July 2-3. Huttonsville July 4. Hedgesville and Martinsburg July 18-19. Averill's Raid through Hardy, Pendleton, Highland, Bath, Greenbrier and Pocahontas Counties, W. Va., August 5-31. Jackson River August 25. Rocky Gap, near White Sulphur Springs, August 26-27. Averill's Raid against Lewisburg and the Virginia & Tennessee Railroad November 1-17. Droop Mountain November 6. Averill's Salem Raid December 8-25. Salem December 16. Scott's or Barber's Creek and Jackson River, near Covington, December 19. Operations in Hampshire and Hardy Counties against Rosser January 27-February 7, 1864. Springfield February 2. Sigel's Expedition from Martinsburg to New Market April 30-May 16. New Market May 15. Advance to Staunton May 17-June 6. Piedmont June 5. Occupation of Staunton June 6. Ordered to Wheeling, W. Va., via Cheat Mountain, Beverly and Weston. Mustered out June 22, 1864.

BATTERY "H" LIGHT ARTILLERY.

Organized at Maryland Heights, Md., January 4, 1864. Attached to 1st Division, Army of West Virginia, to April, 1864. Kelly's Command, Reserve Division, West Virginia, to July, 1865.

SERVICE.—Garrison and guard duty at Harper's Ferry, New Creek, Cumberland, Md., Moorefield, W. Va., and at various points on the Baltimore & Ohio Railroad west of Sleepy Hollow till July, 1865. Action at New Creek August 4, 1864. Affair at Moorefield November 27-28, 1864. Mustered out July 11, 1865.

1st REGIMENT INFANTRY.

Organized and mustered in for three months as follows: Company "A" at Wheeling May 10; Company "B" at Wheeling May 11; Company "C" at Wheeling May 15; Company "D" at Steubenville, Ohio, May 15; Company "E" at Wheeling May 16; Company "F" at Wellsburg May 17; Company "G" at Wellsburg May 18; Company "H" in Marshall County May 21; Company "I" in Hancock County May 21, and Company "K" at Wheeling May 23, 1861. Left Wheeling May 27. Occupation of Grafton May 30. Action at Philippi June 3. Duty at Rowlesburg, Grafton and Philippi till July. Bowman's Place June 29. Occupation of Beverly and Sutton and guarding Baltimore & Ohio Railroad till August 19. Moved to Wheeling August 19-21. Mustered out August 27, 1861.

1st REGIMENT INFANTRY (3 YEARS).

Organized at Wheeling, W. Va., October 30, 1861. Companies "A," "B," "D" and "E" moved from Wheeling to Little Kanawha, Wirt County, W. Va., October 13, and duty there till November 2, when rejoined Regiment at Romney. Regiment left Wheeling for Romney, W. Va., November 9, 1861, and duty there till January 10,

1862. Attached to Railroad District, West Virginia, to January, 1862. 3rd Brigade, Landers' Division, Army Potomac, to March, 1862. 3rd Brigade, Shields' Division, Banks' 5th Army Corps, and Dept. of the Shenandoah, to May, 1862. 4th Brigade, Shields' Division, Dept. of the Rappahannock, to June, 1862. 4th Brigade, 2nd Division, 3rd Army Corps, Pope's Army of Virginia, to September, 1862. 2nd Brigade, Whipple's Division, Military District of Washington, D. C., to October, 1862. Wheeling, W. Va., to December, 1862. Cumberland, Md., September, 1862. North Mountain, Defences of Upper Potomac, 8th Army Corps, Middle Dept., to March, 1863. 4th Brigade, 1st Division, 8th Army Corps, to June, 1863. Campbell's Brigade, Scammon's Division, West Virginia, to December, 1863. 2nd Brigade, 2nd Division, West Virginia, to April, 1864. 2nd Brigade, 1st Infantry Division, West Virginia, to October, 1864. Cumberland, Md., to December, 1864.

SERVICE.—Expedition to Blue's Gap January 6-7, 1862. Hanging Rock Pass, Blue's Gap, January 7. Moved to Patterson Creek January 10, and duty there till February 5. Moved to Paw Paw Tunnel February 5-13. Advance on Winchester March 1-15. Reconnoissance to Strasburg March 18-21. Battle of Winchester March 22-23. Pursuit of Jackson March 24-April 4. Edenburg March 27. Occupation of Mt. Jackson April 1. New Market April 17. Columbia Bridge May 5. March to Falmouth, Va., May 12-21, and to Port Republic May 25-June 7. Gaines' Cross Roads, near Front Royal, May 31. White Plains June 1. Front Royal June 3. Port Republic June 9. March to Cloud's Mills, near Alexandria, June 10-27. Camp there till July 24. Battle of Cedar Mountain August 9. Pope's Campaign in Northern Virginia August 16-September 2. Rappahannock Station August 20-23. Sulphur Springs August 26. Thoroughfare Gap August 28. Groveton August 29. Bull Run August 30. In the Defences of Washington till October 11. Moved to Wheeling, W. Va., October 11-13, and duty there to November 27. Moved to Cumberland, Md., November 27-28, thence to Romney December 8. Moved to North Mountain, and duty there till March 6, 1863. At Mechanicsville Gap till June 14. Moved to New Creek Station, thence to Cumberland, Md., June 14-20. Moved to Hancock, thence to Williamsport July 13. At Back Creek July 28. To Winchester August 3, thence to Romney and to Petersburg August 15. Operating against guerrillas and Imboden's and McNeil's forces till January 10, 1864. Moorefield September 5 and 11, 1863 (Cos. "B," "D," "E," "F" and "H"); mostly captured by McNeil. Descent on Salem December 16, 1863. Guard train from Petersburg to McDowell December 10-23. Retreat from Petersburg to New Creek January 10-12, 1864. Operations in Hampshire and Hardy Counties against Rosser January 27-February 7. Veterans on furlough February and March. Moved to Grafton April 18, thence to Martinsburg April 19-22. Sigel's Expedition to New Market April 30-May 16. Mt. Jackson May 14. New Market May 15. At Cedar Creek May 16-June 1. Advance to Staunton June 1-6. Piedmont, Mt. Crawford, June 5. Occupation of Staunton June 6. Hunter's Raid on Lynchburg June 10-July 1. Lexington June 11. Lynchburg June 17-18. Retreat to Gauley Bridge June 18-29. Moved to the Shenandoah Valley July 5-17. Snicker's Ferry July 17-18. Battle of Winchester July 23-24. Sheridan's Shenandoah Valley Campaign August to November. Cedar Creek August 12. Charlestown August 22-24. Halltown August 26. Berryville September 3-4. Battle of Opequan, Winchester, September 19. Fisher's Hill September 22. Battle of Cedar Creek October 19. Ordered to Cumberland, Md., October 29, and duty there till December. Consolidated with 4th West Virginia Infantry to form 2nd West Virginia Veteran Infantry December 10, 1864.

Regiment lost during service 3 Officers and 51 Enlisted men killed and mortally wounded and 2 Officers and 136 Enlisted men by disease. Total 192.

1st REGIMENT VETERAN INFANTRY.

Organized November 9, 1864, by consolidation of 5th and 9th West Virginia Infantry. Attached to 1st Brigade, 2nd Infantry Division, West Virginia, to January, 1865. 1st Brigade, 1st Infantry Division, West Virginia, to April, 1865. 1st Brigade, 4th Provisional Division, West Virginia, to July, 1865.

SERVICE.—Duty at Beverly, W. Va., Cumberland, Md., and other points in the Dept. of West Virginia till July, 1865. Mustered out July 21, 1865.

2nd REGIMENT INFANTRY.

Company "A" organized at Pittsburg, Pa., April, 1861. Not accepted by Pennsylvania. Moved to Wheeling, W. Va., May 9, 1861, and mustered in May 21, 1861. Moved with 1st West Virginia Infantry May 25 along line of Baltimore & Ohio Railroad. Guard Glover's Gap till May 28. Action with Capt. Roberts' Command May 27. Moved to Grafton May 28. Detached as Body Guard to Gen. Geo. B. McClellan on his assuming command of the Army of West Virginia. Participated in the West Virginia Campaign July 6-17. Assigned to 2nd Regiment as Company "A." Company "B," Grafton Guards, organized May 20, 1861. Moved to Wheeling, W. Va., and mustered in May 25. Moved to Mannington June 28, thence to Grafton July 1, and to Phillippi July 4. West Virginia Campaign July 6-17. Laurel Hill July 7. Carrick's Ford July 13. Moved to Beverly and assigned to 2nd Regiment as Company "B." (A detachment of Company at Bealington till January 25, 1862, guarding supply trains between Webster and Beverly and scouting. Company "C" organized at Wheeling and mustered in June 1, 1861. Moved to Beverly, W. Va., July 1, and joined Regiment. Company "D" organized at Pittsburg, Pa., and mustered in at Wheeling, W. Va., June 14, 1861. Moved to Clarksburg, W. Va. Guard supply train to Rich Mountain (Cos. "C," "D," "E") July 5-6, thence march to Beverly. Company "E" organized at Wheeling, W. Va., and mustered in June 16, 1861. Moved to Clarksburg, W. mustered in June 16, 1861. Moved to Clarksburg, W. Va. Guard supply train to Rich Mountain July 5-6, thence march to Beverly. Company "F" organized at Pittsburg, Pa., and mustered in at Wheeling, W. Va., June 24, 1861. Company "G" organized at Pittsburg, Pa., and mustered in at Wheeling, W. Va., June 13, 1861. Companies "F" and "G" left Wheeling July 5, and joined Regiment at Beverly. Company "H" organized at Ironton, Ohio, and mustered in at Wheeling, W. Va., June 28, 1861. Company "I" organized in Washington County, Pa. Moved to Wheeling, W. Va., July 9-10, and mustered in July 10. Moved to Grafton, Webster and Beverly July 22-27. Company "K" organized at Parkersburg, W. Va., and mustered in July 21, 1861. Regiment attached to Army of Occupation, W. Va., to September, 1861. Cheat Mountain, District West Virginia, to March, 1862. Cheat Mountain District, Dept. of the Mountains, to April, 1862. Milroy's Brigade, Dept. of the Mountains, to June, 1862. Milroy's Independent Brigade, 1st Army Corps, Pope's Army of Virginia, to September, 1862. Defences of Washington, D. C., to October, 1862. Beverly, W. Va., District of West Virginia, Dept. of Ohio, to March, 1863. 4th Separate Brigade, 8th Army Corps, Middle Department, to June, 1863. Averill's 4th Separate Brigade, West Virginia, to December, 1863. 3rd Brigade, 4th Division, West Virginia, to January, 1864.

SERVICE.—Duty at Beverly, W. Va., till September 11, 1861. Laurel Fork Creek August 20. Ordered to Elkwater September 11. Operations on Cheat Mountain September 11-17. Cheat Mountain Pass September 12. Camp Allegheny September 13. Expedition to Huntersville December 31, 1861, to January 6, 1862. Huntersville January 3, 1862. At Cheat Mountain Summit till April 5. Dry Fork, Cheat River, January 8 (Co. "B"), and February 8. Advance on Staunton April 5-May 8. Monterey April 12. Battle of McDowell May 8. Near Franklin May 26. Battle of Cross Keys June 8. At Strasburg June 20-July 5. Advance to Luray July 5-11. Moved to Sperryville July 11, thence to Woodville July 22, and duty there till August 9. Battle of Cedar Mountain August 9. Pope's Campaign in Northern Virginia August 16-September 2. Fords of the

Rappahannock August 21-23. Freeman's Ford, Hazel River, August 22. Waterloo Bridge August 23-25. Gainesville August 28. Groveton August 29. Bull Run August 30. Duty in the Defences of Washington till September 29. Moved to Beverly, W. Va., September 29-October 9. Duty there till April 24, 1863. Cockletown January 22, 1863. Expedition into Pocahontas County February 10-12 (Detachment). Scout to Franklin April 11-18. Beverly April 24. Regiment mounted at Grafton. West Union May 6. Averill's Raid through Hardy, Pendleton, Highland, Bath, Greenbrier and Pocahontas Counties August 5-31. Jackson River August 25. Rocky Gap near White Sulphur Springs August 26-27. Seneca Trace Crossing, Cheat River, September 25 (Detachment). Averill's Raid on Lewisburg and the Virginia & Tennessee Railroad November 1-17. Mill Point November 5. Droop Mountain November 6. Averill's Raid from New Creek to Salem on Virginia & Tennessee Railroad December 8-25. Gatewood's December 12. Salem December 16. Scott's or Barber's Creek December 19 (Detachment). Covington December 30. At Martinsburg till January 26, 1864. Designation changed to 5th West Virginia Cavalry January 26, 1864 (which see).

2nd REGIMENT VETERAN INFANTRY.

Organized December 10, 1864, by consolidation of 1st and 4th West Virginia Infantry. Attached to Reserve Division, Dept. of West Virginia, to April, 1865. 2nd Brigade, 1st Infantry Division, West Virginia, to July, 1865. On duty at Cumberland, Md., and at Bulltown, Braxton County, W. Va. Mustered out July 16, 1865.

Regiment lost during service 1 Enlisted man killed and 16 Enlisted men by disease. Total 17.

3rd REGIMENT INFANTRY.

Organized at Wheeling, Clarksburg and Newburg, W. Va., June-July, 1861. Served unattached, Army of West Virginia, to September, 1861. Cheat Mountain, District West Virginia, to March, 1862. Cheat Mountain District, Dept. of the Mountains, to April, 1862. Milroy's Independent Brigade, Dept. of the Mountains, to June, 1862. Milroy's Independent Brigade, 1st Army Corps, Pope's Army of Virginia, to September, 1862. Defences of Washington, D. C., to October, 1862. Unattached, District of West Virginia, Dept. of the Ohio, to March, 1863. Averill's 4th Separate Brigade, 8th Army Corps, Middle Department, to June, 1863. Averill's 4th Separate Brigade, Dept. of West Virginia, to December, 1863. 3rd Brigade, 4th Division, Army of West Virginia, to January, 1864.

SERVICE.—Protecting border counties against guerrillas from Phillippi to Suttonville, W. Va., till September, 1861. Rowell's Run September 6. Moved to Beverly September 10, thence to Elkwater, and duty there till April, 1862. Romney, Hanging Rock, September 23, 1861. Romney September 23-25. Mill Creek Mills October 26. Skirmishes in Clay, Braxton and Webster Counties December 29-31. Elk Mountain March 19, 1862. Advance on Staunton April 5-May 8. Cow Pasture May 7. Battle of McDowell May 8. Bull Pasture Mountain May 8. Reconnoissance to Franklin May 9-11. Franklin May 11-13. Strasburg and Staunton Road June 1-2. Battle of Cross Keys June 8. At Strasburg June 20-July 5. Advance to Luray July 5-11. Moved to Sperryville July 11, thence to Woodville July 22, and duty there till August 9. Battle of Cedar Mountain August 9. Crooked Creek August 12. Pope's Campaign in Northern Virginia August 16-September 2. Fords of the Rappahannock August 21-23. Freeman's Ford and Hazel Run August 22. Waterloo Bridge August 23-25. Gainesville August 28. Groveton August 29. Bull Run August 30. Duty in the Defences of Washington till September 30. Moved to Clarksburg, W. Va., September 30-October 1. Duty at Clarksburg, Mt. Pleasant, and outpost duty at Buckhannon, Centreville, Bulltown, Sutton and Glenville till April, 1863. Regiment mounted, Janelew, May 5. Huttonsville July 4. Near Hedgeville and Martinsburg July 18-19. Averill's Raid through Hardy, Pendleton, Highland, Bath, Greenbrier and Pocahontas Counties August 5-31. Huntersville August 22 (Detachment). Jackson River August 25. Rocky Gap near White Sulphur Springs August 26-27. Averill's Raid against Lewisburg and the Virginia & Tennessee Railroad November 1-11. Cockletown November 4. Mill Point November 5. Droop Mountain November 6. Averill's Raid to Salem on Virginia & Tennessee Railroad December 8-25. Gatewood's December 12. Salem December 16. Scott's or Barber's Creek December 19. Moorefield December 28. Designation changed to 6th West Virginia Cavalry January 26, 1864 (which see).

4th REGIMENT INFANTRY.

Organized at Macon City, Point Pleasant and Grafton, W. Va., June 17 to August 22, 1861. Served unattached, District of the Kanawha, W. Va., to March, 1862. 4th Brigade, Kanawha Division, West Virginia, to September, 1862. Point Pleasant, W. Va., District of the Kanawha, W. Va., Dept. of the Ohio, to January, 1863. 3rd Brigade, 2nd Division, 15th Army Corps, Army of the Tennessee, to October, 1863. 2nd Brigade, 2nd Division, 15th Army Corps, to May, 1864. 2nd Brigade, 1st Infantry Division, West Virginia, to December, 1864.

SERVICE.—Skirmish at Grafton, W. Va., August 13, 1861 (Co. "A"). Moved up the Kanawha Valley August 22. Operations in the Kanawha Valley and New River Region October 19-November 16. Mill Creek Mills October 26. At Ceredo till January, 1862. March to Louisa Court House and operating with Garfield in operations against Humphrey Marshall in Eastern Kentucky January, 1862. March up the Kanawha Valley to join Gen. Cox April 3. At Flat Top Mountain till August. Operations about Wyoming Court House August 2-8. Wyoming Court House August 5 (Cos. "H" and "I"). Beech Creek August 6. Campaign in the Kanawha Valley September 2-16. Repulse of Loring's attack on Fayetteville September 10. Cotton Hill and Charlestown September 11. Gauley Ferry September 11. Gauley Bridge September 12. Charlestown September 12-13. At Point Pleasant till October 19. Bulltown, Braxton County, October 3. Salt Lick Bridge October 14. Expedition up the Kanawha Valley to Charlestown October 21-November 10. At Fayetteville till December 30. Ordered to Napoleon, Ark., thence to Young's Point, La., January 21, 1863, and duty there till March. Expedition to Rolling Fork via Muddy, Steele's and Black Bayous and Deer Creek March 14-27. At Milliken's Bend till April. Expedition to Black Bayou April 5-10. Demonstration against Haines and Drumgould's Bluffs April 29-May 2. Moved to join army in rear of Vicksburg, Miss., via Richmond and Grand Gulf May 2-14. Siege of Vicksburg, Miss., May 18-July 4. Assaults on Vicksburg May 19 and 22. Surrender of Vicksburg July 4. Advance on Jackson, Miss., July 5-10. Siege of Jackson July 10-17. At Big Black River till September 26. Moved to Memphis, Tenn., thence march to Chattanooga, Tenn., September 26-November 20. Operations on Memphis & Charleston Railroad in Alabama October 20-29. Brier Creek, Tuscumbia, October 27. Chattanooga-Ringgold Campaign November 23-27. Tunnel Hill November 23-24. Mission Ridge November 25. Pursuit to Graysville November 26-27. March to relief of Knoxville, Tenn., November 28-December 8. Regiment re-enlisted February 3, 1864, and Veterans on furlough March 15 to May 3. Joined Hunter at Cedar Creek, W. Va., May. Hunter's Expedition to Lynchburg, Va., May 26-July 1. Piedmont, Mt. Crawford, June 5. Occupation of Staunton June 6. Lynchburg June 17-18. Retreat to Martinsburg June 18-July 1. Moved to the Shenandoah Valley, Snicker's Gap, July 17-18. Kernstown or Winchester July 24. Shenandoah Valley Campaign August-September. Berryville September 3. At Stephenson's Depot till December. Moved to Cumberland, Md. Consolidated with 1st West Virginia Infantry December 21, 1864, to form 2nd West Virginia Veteran Infantry (which see).

Regiment lost during service 3 Officers and 80 Enlisted men killed and mortally wounded and 2 Officers and 156 Enlisted men by disease. Total 241.

5th REGIMENT INFANTRY.

Organized at Ceredo, W. Va., September 2, 1861, and mustered in October 18, 1861. Served Unattached, District of the Kanawha, West Virginia, to March, 1862. District of Cumberland, Md., Mountain Department, to April, 1862. Milroy's Independent Brigade, Mountain Department, to June, 1862. Milroy's Independent Brigade, 1st Army Corps, Army of Virginia, to September, 1862. Defences of Washington, D. C., to October, 1862. District of the Kanawha, West Virginia, Dept. Ohio, to January, 1863. Unattached, District of the Kanawha, West Virginia, to March, 1863. 1st Brigade, 3rd Division, 8th Army Corps, Middle Department, to June, 1863. 1st Brigade, Scammon's Division, Dept. of West Virginia, to December, 1863. 1st Brigade, 3rd Division, West Virginia, to April, 1864. 1st Brigade, 2nd Infantry Division, West Virginia, to November, 1864.

SERVICE.—Duty at Ceredo and in the Kanawha Valley, W. Va., to December 10, 1861. Moved to Parkersburg, W. Va., December 10, thence to New Creek, W. Va., February, 1862. Linn Creek, Logan County, February 8. Duty at New Creek till May. Joined Milroy's Brigade May 2. Battle of McDowell May 8. Near Franklin May 10-12 and May 26. Battle of Cross Keys June 8. At Strasburg June 20-July 5. Advance to Luray July 5-11. Moved to Sperryville July 11, thence to Woodville July 22, and duty there till August 9. Battle of Cedar Mountain August 9. Cedar Run August 10. Pope's Campaign in Northern Virginia August 16-September 2. Fords of the Rappahannock August 20-23. Freeman's Ford, Hazel River, August 22. Johnson's Ford August 22. Waterloo Bridge August 24-25. Gainesville August 28. Groveton August 29. Bull Run August 30. Duty in the Defences of Washington, D. C., till September 29. Moved to Beverly, W. Va., September 29-October 9. Parkersburg October 10. Duty at Ceredo till March, 1863. Scouting Little Kanawha and east side of Big Sandy Rivers. Ordered to Wayne Court House March. Hurricane Creek March 28. At Charlestown, Barboursville, Hurricane Bridge and other points in the Kanawha Valley till April, 1864. Scammon's demonstration from the Kanawha Valley December 8-25, 1863. Crook's Raid on the Virginia & Tennessee Railroad May 2-19, 1864. Rocky Gap May 6. Battle of Cloyd's Mountain May 9. New River Bridge May 10. Blacksburg May 10. Union May 12. Meadow Bluff May 24. Hunter's Expedition to Lynchburg May 26-July 1. Lexington June 11-12. Buchanan June 14. Otter Creek June 16. Diamond Hill June 17. Lynchburg June 17-18. Buford's Gap June 19. Salem June 21. Moved to the Shenandoah Valley July 13-15. Kablestown July 19. Battle of Kernstown, Winchester, July 23-24 Martinsburg July 25. Sheridan's Shenandoah Valley Campaign August 6-November 1. Strasburg August 15. Summit Point August 24. Halltown August 2. Berryville September 3. Battle of Opequan, Winchester, September 19. Fisher's Hill September 22. Battle of Cedar Creek October 19. Consolidated with 9th West Virginia Infantry November 9, 1864, to form 1st West Virginia Veteran Infantry (which see).

Regiment lost during service 4 Officers and 57 Enlisted men killed and mortally wounded and 2 Officers and 88 Enlisted men by disease. Total 151.

6th REGIMENT INFANTRY.

Organized at Grafton, Mannington, Cairo, Parkersburg and Wheeling, W. Va., August 13 to December 26, 1861. Attached to Railroad District, West Virginia, to March, 1862. Railroad District, Mountain Department, to July, 1862. Railroad District, 8th Army Corps, Middle Department, to September, 1862. Railroad District, West Virginia, to January, 1863. Clarksburg, W. Va., 8th Army Corps, to March, 1863. 6th Brigade, 1st Division, 8th Army Corps, to June, 1863. Wilkinson's Brigade, Scammon's Division, Dept. of West Virginia, to December, 1863. 3rd Brigade, 2nd Division, West Virginia, to April, 1864. Kelly's Command, Reserve Division, West Virginia, to April, 1865. 1st Brigade, 1st Infantry Division, West Virginia, to June, 1865.

SERVICE.—Regiment organized for railroad guard duty and served on line of the Baltimore & Ohio Railroad by detachments, at various points west of Sleepy Hollow entire term. Raid from Fairmont to Valley River and Bootheville April 12, 1862 (Co. "A"). Skirmish at Valley River April 12 (Co. "A"). Skirmish at Big Bend June 7. Skirmish at Weston August 31 (2 Cos.). Skirmish at Weston September 3 (Detachment). Skirmish at Standing Stone September 28. Capture of St. George November 9 (Co. "B"). Skirmish at Johnstown April 18, 1863 (Detachment). Skirmish at Rowlesburg April 23. Rowlesburg and Portland April 26. Oakland, Md., April 26 (1 Co.). Skirmish at Bridgeport April 29 (Detachment). Fairmont April 29 (Detachment). Bridgeport April 30. Sutton August 26 (Cos. "G" and "I"). Ball's Mills and on Elk River August 27 (Detachment). Bulltown, Braxton County, October 13, 1863 (Detachment). Bulltown May 3, 1864 (Detachment). South Branch Bridge July 4 (Detachment). Patterson's Creek Bridge July 4 (Detachment). Back Creek Bridge July 27 (Detachment). Cumberland, Md., August 1 (1 Co.). New Creek August 4 (2 Cos.). Bulltown August 20 (Detachment). Sutton August 24 (Detachment). Nutter Hill August 27 (Detachment). New Creek November 28 (Detachment). Mustered out June 10, 1865.

Regiment lost during service 8 Enlisted men killed and mortally wounded and 2 Officers and 167 Enlisted men by disease. Total 177.

7th REGIMENT INFANTRY.

Organized at Portland, Cameron, Grafton, Wheeling, Morgantown and Greenland, W. Va., July 16 to December 3, 1861. Attached to Railroad District, West Virginia, to January, 1862. 1st Brigade, Landers' Division, Army Potomac, to March, 1862. 1st Brigade, Shields' 2nd Division, Banks' 5th Army Corps and Dept. of the Shenandoah, to May, 1862. 1st Brigade, Shields' Division, Dept. of the Rappahannock, to June, 1862. Kimball's Independent Brigade, 2nd Army Corps, Army of the Potomac, to September, 1862. 1st Brigade, 3rd Division, 2nd Army Corps, Army Potomac, to March, 1864. 3rd Brigade, 2nd Division, 2nd Army Corps, to June, 1865.

SERVICE.—Moved to Romney, W. Va., and duty there till January 10, 1862. Skirmish at Romney, Mill Creek Mills, October 26, 1861. Expedition to Blue's Gap January 6-7, 1862. Hanging Rock, Blue's Gap, January 7. At Paw Paw Tunnel till March 4. Advance on Winchester March 4-15. Battle of Winchester March 23. Cedar Creek March 25. Woodstock April 1. Edenburg April 2. Columbia Furnace April 16. Occupation of Mt. Jackson April 17. March to Fredericksburg, Va., May 12-22. Ravenswood May 15. March to Front Royal May 25-30. Front Royal May 30. Expedition to Luray June 3-7. Forced march to Port Republic June 8-9. Battle of Port Republic June 9 (Reserve). Moved to Alexandria June 29, thence to Harrison's Landing June 30-July 2. Haxall's, Herring Creek, Chickahominy Swamp, July 3-5. Moved to Alexandria, thence to Centreville August 16-29. Plains of Manassas August 29-30. Germantown September 1. Maryland Campaign September 6-22. Battles of South Mountain, Md., September 14; Antietam September 16-17. Moved to Harper's Ferry, W. Va., September 22, and duty there till October 30. Reconnoissance to Leesburg October 1-2. Advance up Loudoun Valley and march to Falmouth, Va., October 30-November 18. Battle of Fredericksburg, Va., December 12-15. Duty at Falmouth till April. "Mud March" January 20-24. Chancellorsville Campaign April 27-May 6. Battle of Chancellorsville May 1-5. Gettysburg (Pa.) Campaign June 11-July 24. Battle of Gettysburg, Pa., July 1-3. Pursuit of Lee to Manassas Gap, Va., July 5-24. Duty on line of the Rappahannock till September. Advance from line of the Rappahannock to the Rapidan September 13-17. Bristoe Campaign October 9-22. Auburn and Bristoe October 14. Advance to line of the Rappahannock November 7-8. Kelly's Ford November 7. Mine Run Campaign November 26-December 2. Robertson's Tavern November 27. Mine Run November 28-30. Demonstration on the Rapidan February 6-7, 1864. Morton's Ford February 6-7. Campaign from the Rapidan to the James May 3-June 15. Battles of the Wilderness May 5-7; Laurel Hill May 8; Spottsylvania May 8-12; Po River May 10; Spottsylvania Court House May 12-21. Assault on the Salient or "Bloody Angle" May 12. North Anna River May 23-26. On line of the Pamunkey May 26-28. Totopotomoy May 28-31. Cold Harbor June 1-12. Before Petersburg June 16-18. Siege of Petersburg June 16, 1864, to April 2, 1865. Jerusalem Plank Road June 22-23, 1864. Demonstration north of the James July 27-29. Deep Bottom July 27-28. Demonstration north of the James August 13-20. Strawberry Plains, Deep Bottom, August 14-18. Ream's Station August 25. Poplar Springs Church September 29-October 1. Yellow House October 1-3. Hatcher's Run October 27-28. Raid on Weldon Railroad December 7-12. Dabney's Mills, Hatcher's Run, February 5-7, 1865. Watkins' House March 25. Appomattox Campaign March 28-April 9. Boydton and White Oak Roads March 30-31. Crow's House March 31. Fall of Petersburg April 2. Sailor's Creek April 6. Farmville and High Bridge April 7. Clover Hill, Appomattox Court House, April 9. Surrender of Lee and his army. March to Washington, D. C., May 1-12. Grand Review May 23. Moved to Louisville, Ky., June. Mustered out July 1, 1865.

Regiment lost during service 9 Officers and 133 Enlisted men killed and mortally wounded and 4 Officers and 154 Enlisted men by disease. Total 300.

8th REGIMENT INFANTRY.

Organized at Buffalo, W. Va., November, 1861. Attached to District of the Kanawha, W. Va. Unassigned to May, 1862. Cluserett's Advance Brigade, Dept. of the Mountains, to June, 1862. Bohlen's Brigade, 3rd Division, 1st Corps, Pope's Army of Virginia, to September, 1862. Milroy's Independent Brigade, Defences of Washington, D. C., to October, 1862. Point Pleasant, W. Va., District of the Kanawha, W. Va., Dept. of the Ohio, to March, 1863. Averill's 4th Separate Brigade, 8th Army Corps, Middle Department, to June, 1863. Averill's 4th Separate Brigade, Dept. of West Virginia, to December, 1863. 3rd Brigade, 4th Division, Army of West Virginia, to January, 1864.

SERVICE.—Post duty at Buffalo, W. Va., till April, 1862. Ordered to New Creek, W. Va. At Franklin till May 25. Pursuit of Jackson up the Shenandoah Valley May 26-June 19. Mt. Carmel Road near Strasburg June 1. Strasburg and Staunton Road June 1-2. Harrisonburg June 6. Battle of Cross Keys June 8. Port Republic June 9. Moved to Strasburg June 19-22, thence to Middletown June 24, and duty there till July. Middletown July 7. At Winchester till August 2. Pope's Campaign in Northern Virginia August 2-September 22. Fords of the Rappahannock August 20-23. Freeman's Ford August 22. Sulphur Springs August 23-24. Waterloo Bridge August 25. Gainesville August 28. Groveton August 29. Bull Run August 30. In the Defences of Washington, D. C., till September 29. Moved to Mt. Pleasant, W. Va., September 29-October 9. Outpost duty at various points in District of West Virginia, till June, 1863. Skirmish, Gilmer County, W. Va., April 24, 1863. Regiment mounted at Bridgeport June, 1863. Moved to Grafton June 17. Beverly July 2-3. Huttonsville July 4. Moved to Cumberland, Md., July 7. Hedgesville and Martinsburg July 18-19. Averill's Raid through Hardy, Pendleton, Highland, Bath, Greenbrier and Pocahontas Counties, W. Va., August 5-31. Huntersville August 22. Warm Springs August 24. Jackson River August 25. Rocky Gap near White Sulphur Springs August 26-27. At Martinsburg till November. Averill's Raid against Lewisburg and the Virginia & Tennessee Railroad November 1-17. Mill Point November 5. Droop Mountain November 6. Covington November 9. Averill's Raid to Salem on Virginia & Tennessee Railroad December 8-25. Gatewood's December

12. Covington, Jackson River and Scott's or Barber's Creek December 19. At Martinsburg till January, 1864. Designation changed to 7th West Virginia Cavalry January 26, 1864 (which see).

9th REGIMENT INFANTRY.

Organized at Guyandotte November 28, 1861, to April 30, 1862. Attached to District of the Kanawha, West Virginia, to May, 1862. 4th Brigade, Kanawha Division, West Virginia, to September, 1862. District of the Kanawha, West Virginia, Dept. of the Ohio, to January, 1863. Milroy's Command, Winchester, Va., 8th Army Corps, Middle Department, to February, 1863. 2nd Brigade, 2nd Division, 8th Army Corps, to June, 1863. 1st Brigade, Scammon's Division, West Virginia, to August, 1863. 2nd Brigade, Scammon's Division, West Virginia, to December, 1863. 2nd Brigade, 3rd Division, West Virginia, to April, 1864. 2nd Brigade, 2nd Infantry Division, West Virginia, to November, 1864.

SERVICE.—Duty at Guyandotte, W. Va., till April, 1862. Affair at Guyandotte November 10, 1861. Assigned to garrison duty in the Kanawha Valley by detachments at Fayette, Gauley Bridge, Summerville, Point Pleasant, Coalsmouth and Calhoun till July, 1862. Scout in Roane and Clay Counties May 8-21. Affair at Summerville July 25 (Cos. "A," "F"). Moved to Flat Top Mountain July 28. To Summerville and Gauley August 14. Campaign in the Kanawha Valley September 1-16. Repulse of Loring's attack on Fayetteville September 10. Cotton Hill, Charleston and Gauley Ferry September 11. Charleston September 13. At Point Pleasant to January, 1863. Expedition up the Kanawha Valley October 21-November 10, 1862. At Winchester and Beverly January to June, 1863. Scout to Wardensville, Strasburg, etc., April 25-30. Winchester May 4. West Creek May 23. Winchester June 18. Duty in the Kanawha Valley till May, 1864. Crook's Expedition against Virginia & Tennessee Railroad May 2-19. Action at Cloyd's Mountain May 9. New River Bridge May 10. Cove Mountain or Grassy Lick near Wytheville May 10. Salt Pond Mountain and Gap Mountain May 12-13. Hunter's Expedition against Lynchburg May 26-July 1. Lexington June 11. Diamond Hill June 17. Lynchburg June 17-18. Retreat to Charleston June 19-July 1. Buford's Gap June 20. About Salem June 21. Moved to Shenandoah Valley July 12-15. Stephenson's Depot July 20. Battle of Kernstown, Winchester, July 23-24. Martinsburg July 25. Sheridan's Shenandoah Valley Campaign August 6-November 1. Halltown August 24 and 26. Berryville September 3. Battle of Opequan, Winchester, September 19. Fisher's Hill September 22. Battle of Cedar Creek October 19. At Camp Russell till November. Consolidated with 5th West Virginia Infantry November 9, 1864, to form 1st West Virginia Veteran Infantry (which see).

Regiment lost during service 3 Officers and 96 Enlisted men killed and mortally wounded and 1 Officer and 107 Enlisted men by disease. Total 207.

10th REGIMENT INFANTRY.

Organized at Camp Pickens, Canaan, Glenville, Clarksville, Sutton, Phillippi and Piedmont March 12 to May 18, 1862. Attached to Cheat Mountain District, Mountain Department, to May, 1862. Railroad District, Mountain Department, to July, 1862. Railroad District, 8th Corps, Middle Department, to September, 1862. Railroad Division, West Virginia, to January, 1863. Milroy's Command, Winchester, Va., 8th Army Corps, to February, 1863. 2nd Brigade, 2nd Division, 8th Army Corps, to March, 1863. Averill's 4th Separate Brigade, 8th Army Corps, Middle Department, to June, 1863. Averill's 4th Separate Brigade, Dept. West Virginia, to December, 1863. 1st Brigade, 4th Division, West Virginia, to April, 1864. Kelly's Command, Reserve Division, West Virginia, to July, 1864. 3rd Brigade, 1st Division, West Virginia, July, 1864. 1st Brigade, 1st Infantry Division, West Virginia, to December, 1864. 3rd Brigade, Independent Division, 24th Army Corps, Army of the James, to June, 1865. 2nd Brigade, Independent Division, 24th Army Corps, to August, 1865.

SERVICE.—At Monterey April, 1862. Assigned to railroad guard duty in Railroad District, District of West Virginia, till January, 1863; at Beverly, Bulltown, Martinsburg, etc. Expedition from Summerville to Addison April 17-21, 1862. Skirmish at Holly River, W. Va., April 17. Mung's Flats June 25. Buckhannon August 30. Sutton September 23. Big Birch October 6. Wardensville December 22. At Winchester, Va., January, 1863. At Beverly May, 1863. Scout to Beverly June 16. Action at Beverly July 2-3. At Martinsburg August, 1863. Averill's Raid through Hardy, Pendleton, Bath, Highland, Greenbrier and Pocahontas Counties August 5-31. Rocky Gap near White Sulphur Springs August 26-27. Sutton August 26 (Cos. "G," "I"). Bell's Mills and on Elk River August 27 (Detachment). Bulltown, Braxton County, October 13. Averill's Raid against Lewisburg and the Virginia & Tennessee Railroad November 1-17. Mill Point November 5. Droop Mountain November 6. Hillsboro November 10. At Beverly till May, 1864; scouting Counties of Randolph, Tucker, Pocahontas, Greenbrier, Braxton, Highland, Pendleton and Webster. Cheat River December 6, 1863. Moorefield Junction January 3, 1864. Scout from Beverly through Pocahontas, Webster and Braxton Counties May 15-30. Leetown July 3. Maryland Heights, Md., July 6-7. Operations about Harper's Ferry July 10. Snicker's Ferry July 17-18. Kernstown, Winchester, July 23-24. Sheridan's Shenandoah Valley Campaign August 6 to November 28. Strasburg and Massametton Mountain August 16. Winchester August 17. Battle of Opequan, Winchester, September 19. Fisher's Hill September 22. Cedar Creek October 13. Battle of Cedar Creek October 19. Duty in Shenandoah Valley till December. Moved to Washington, D. C., December 19-20, thence to Bermuda Hundred December 20-23. Duty in the trenches north of James River till March, 1865. Appomattox Campaign March 28-April 9. Moved to front of Petersburg March 28-29. Hatcher's Run March 30-31, and April 1. Assault on and fall of Petersburg April 2. Pursuit of Lee April 3-9. Rice's Station April 6. Appomattox Court House April 9. Surrender of Lee and his army. March to Lynchburg April 12-15. March to Farmville and Burkesville April 15-19, thence to Richmond April 22-25. Duty near Richmond till August. Mustered out August 9, 1865.

Regiment lost during service 2 Officers and 93 Enlisted men killed and mortally wounded and 2 Officers and 144 Enlisted men by disease. Total 241.

11th REGIMENT INFANTRY.

Organized at Wheeling, Elizabeth, Burning Springs, Parkersburg, Ravenswood, Kanawha Station and Point Pleasant, W. Va., October 29, 1861, to October 8, 1862. At Ceredo and Parkersburg, W. Va., till October, 1862. Attached to Railroad District, West Virginia, Dept. of the Mountains and Middle Department, to January, 1863. Parkersburg, W. Va., to March, 1863. 6th Brigade, 1st Division, 8th Army Corps, Middle Department, to June, 1863. Wilkinson's Brigade, Scammon's Division, Dept. West Virginia, to December, 1863. 3rd Brigade, 2nd Division, West Virginia, to April, 1864. 3rd Brigade, 2nd Infantry Division, West Virginia, to July, 1864. 2nd Brigade, 3rd Infantry Division, West Virginia, July, 1864. 3rd Brigade, 1st Infantry Division, West Virginia, to December, 1864. 3rd Brigade, Independent Division, 24th Army Corps, Army of the James, to June, 1865.

SERVICE.—Duty at Parkersburg and guarding Baltimore & Ohio Railroad through counties south of line from Jackson County to Lewis County till June, 1863. Skirmishes at Arnoldsburg and Camp McDonald, W. Va., May 6, 1862. Scout to Roane and Clay Counties May 8-21. Big Bend June 4. Mouth West Fork June 10. Glenville September 1. Spencer Roane Court House September 2. Operations against Jones' Raid on Baltimore & Ohio Railroad April 21-May 21, 1863. Duty on the Upper Potomac till August. West Union May 6, 1863 (1 Co.). Elizabeth Court House May 16. At Parkersburg, Clarksburg, Grafton, Sutton, Bulltown and Beverly guarding Baltimore & Ohio Railroad till April,

1864. Operations against Morgan July 2-26, 1863. Glenville August 21, 1863 (Cos. "C," "H"). Near Glenville August 27, 1863 (Cos. "C," "H"). Skirmish at Beech Fork, Calhoun County, September 8, 1863. Roane County September 12. Bulltown, Braxton County, October 13. Salt Lick Bridge October 14. Ravenswood October 26. Sandy River near Elizabeth October 27. Hurricane Creek December 3 (Detachment). Crook's Raid on Virginia & Tennessee Railroad May 2-19, 1864. Princeton May 6. Battle of Cloyd's Mountain May 9. Cove Mountain or Grassy Lick near Wytheville and New River Bridge May 10. Salt Pond Mountain and Gap Mountain May 12-13. Hunter's Expedition to Lynchburg May 26-July 1. Panther Gap June 4. Middlebrook and Brownsville June 10. Lexington June 11. Otter Creek near Liberty June 16. Spencer June 16. Diamond Hill June 17. Lynchburg June 17-18. Retreat to Charleston, W. Va., June 19-July 1. Buford's Gap June 19. About Salem June 21. Moved to Shenandoah Valley July. Sandy Hook, Md., July 8. Snicker's Ferry or Gap July 17-18. Battle of Kernstown, Winchester, July 24. Flintstone Creek, Md., August 1. Cumberland, Md., August 1 (4 Cos.). Sheridan's Shenandoah Valley Campaign August 7-November 28. Berryville September 3. Battle of Opequan, Winchester, September 19. Fisher's Hill September 22. Skirmishes at Cedar Creek October 1 and 13. Battle of Cedar Creek October 19. Duty in Shenandoah Valley at Camp Russell till December 19. Moved to Washington, D. C., thence to Bermuda Hundred, Va., December 19-23. Duty in the trenches before Richmond till March, 1865. Appomattox Campaign March 28-April 9. Moved to front of Petersburg March 28-29. Hatcher's Run March 30-31 and April 1. Fall of Petersburg April 2. Pursuit of Lee April 3-9. Rice's Station April 6. Appomattox Court House April 9. Surrender of Lee and his army. March to Lynchburg April 12-15, thence to Farmville and Burkesville Junction April 15-19, and to Richmond April 22-25. Duty near Richmond till June. Mustered out June 17, 1865.

Regiment lost during service 4 Officers and 63 Enlisted men killed and mortally wounded and 148 Enlisted men by disease. Total 215.

12th REGIMENT INFANTRY.

Organized at Wheeling, W. Va., August 30, 1862. Attached to Railroad District, 8th Army Corps, Middle Dept., to January, 1863. Milroy's Command, Winchester, Va., 8th Army Corps, to February, 1863. 2nd Brigade, 2nd Division, 8th Army Corps, to June, 1863. 1st Brigade, 1st Division, Dept. of the Susquehanna, to July, 1863. McReynolds' Command, Martinsburg, W. Va., to December, 1863. 1st Brigade, 1st Division, West Virginia, to January, 1864. 1st Brigade, 2nd Division, West Virginia, to April, 1864. 2nd Brigade, 1st Infantry Division, West Virginia, to December, 1864. 2nd Brigade, Independent Division, 24th Army Corps, Army of the James, to June, 1865.

SERVICE.—At Buckhannon October, 1862. Wardensville October 16. Moved to Winchester, Va., January, 1863, and duty there till May. At Beverly May. Battle of Winchester June 13-15. Retreat to Harper's Ferry June 15-17. At Bloody Run, Pa., June 30. At Martinsburg, W. Va., July 14-December 10, 1863. Wells' demonstration up the Shenandoah Valley December 10-25. At Harper's Ferry till February 1, 1864. At New Creek till April. At Cumberland, Md., Webster and Beverly April. Sigel's Expedition from Martinsburg to New Market, Va., April 30-May 16. Rude's Hill May 14. Battle of New Market May 15. Advance to Staunton May 24-June 6. Piedmont, Mt. Crawford, June 5. Occupation of Staunton June 6. Hunter's Expedition to Lynchburg June 10-July 1. Near Lynchburg June 14. Diamond Hill June 17. Lynchburg June 17-18. Retreat to Charleston, W. Va., June 18-July 1. Moved to Shenandoah Valley July 12-15. Snicker's Ferry July 17-18. Battle of Kernstown-Winchester July 23-24. Sheridan's Shenandoah Valley Campaign August 6-November 28. Cedar Creek August 12. Strasburg August 15. Berryville September 3. Battle of Opequan, Winchester, September 19 (guarding

trains). Fisher's Hill September 22 (guarding trains). Duty at Winchester and in the Shenandoah Valley till December. Moved to Washington, D. C., thence to Bermuda Hundred, Va., December 19-23. Duty in trenches before Richmond till March, 1865. Appomattox Campaign March 28-April 9. Moved to front of Petersburg March 28-29. Hatcher's Run March 30-31 and April 1. Fall of Petersburg April 2. Pursuit of Lee April 3-9. Rice's Station April 6. Appomattox Court House April 9. Surrender of Lee and his army. March to Lynchburg, Va., April 12-15, thence to Farmville and Burkesville Junction April 15-19, and to Richmond April 22-25. Duty near Richmond till June. Mustered out June 16, 1865.

Regiment lost during service 3 Officers and 56 Enlisted men killed and mortally wounded and 131 Enlisted men by disease. Total 190.

13th REGIMENT INFANTRY.

Organized at Mt. Pleasant and Barboursville October, 1862. Attached to District of the Kanawha, West Virginia, Dept. of the Ohio, to March, 1863. 1st Brigade, 3rd Division, 8th Army Corps, Middle Dept., to June, 1863. 1st Brigade, Scammon's Division, Dept. of West Virginia, to December, 1863. 1st Brigade, 3rd Division, West Virginia, to January, 1864. 1st Brigade, 2nd Division, West Virginia, to April, 1864. 1st Brigade, 2nd Infantry Division, West Virginia, to January, 1865. 1st Brigade, 1st Infantry Division, West Virginia, to April, 1865. 1st Brigade, 4th Provisional Division, West Virginia, to June, 1865.

SERVICE.—Duty at Point Pleasant and Coalsmouth, W. Va., till April, 1863. Hurricane Bridge March 28. Skirmish at Point Pleasant March 30. Hurricane and Coal River till July. Fayetteville May 20. Expedition to Piney in pursuit of Loring July 5-14, and in pursuit of Morgan July 17-26. Duty at Charleston and other points in the Kanawha Valley till May, 1864. Crook's Raid on Virginia & Tennessee Railroad May 2-19. Battle of Cloyd's Mountain May 9. New River Bridge and Cove Mountain May 10. Salt Pond Mountain and Gap Mountain May 12-13. Hunter's Expedition to Lynchburg May 26-July 1. Lexington June 11. Diamond Hill June 17. Lynchburg June 17-18. Retreat to Charleston June 18-July 1. Buford's Gap June 19. About Salem June 21. Moved to the Shenandoah Valley July 12-15. Battle of Kernstown-Winchester July 23-24. Martinsburg July 25. Sheridan's Shenandoah Valley Campaign August 6-November 28. Near Charlestown, W. Va., August 21-22. Halltown August 26. Berryville September 3. Battle of Opequan, Winchester, September 19. Fisher's Hill September 22. Battle of Cedar Creek October 19. At Camp Russell and in the Shenandoah Valley till December. Kablestown November 18. At Cumberland, Md., till April, 1865. At Winchester and Staunton till June. Mustered out June 22, 1865.

Regiment lost during service 4 Officers and 57 Enlisted men killed and mortally wounded and 1 Officer and 108 Enlisted men by disease. Total 170.

14th REGIMENT INFANTRY.

Organized at Wheeling, W. Va., August 25, 1862. Attached to Railroad Division, West Virginia, to January, 1863. New Creek, W. Va., Defences Upper Potomac, 8th Army Corps, Middle Dept., to March, 1863. 5th Brigade, 1st Division, 8th Army Corps, to June, 1863. Mulligan's Brigade, Scammon's Division, West Virginia, to December, 1863. 2nd Brigade, 2nd Division, West Virginia, to April, 1864. 2nd Brigade, 2nd Infantry Division, West Virginia, to January, 1865. 1st Brigade, 2nd Infantry Division, West Virginia, to June, 1865.

SERVICE.—Ordered to Clarksburg, W. Va., and guard duty on the Upper Potomac, Headquarters at New Creek, till June, 1863. Expedition to Greenland Gap April 13-22, 1863. Action at Greenland Gap April 25 (Co. "A"). Duty at New Creek, Petersburg and Romney till April, 1864. Skirmish near Burlington November 16, 1863. Burlington and Petersburg Turnpike November 19. Salem December 16. Jackson River, near Covington, December 19. Operations in Hampshire and Hardy Counties Decem-

54

ber 31, 1863-January 5, 1864. Operations in Hampshire and Hardy Counties against Rosser January 27-February 7, 1864. Evacuation of Petersburg January 30. Crook's Expedition against Virginia & Tennessee Railroad May 2-19. Battle of Cloyd's Mountain May 9. New River Bridge May 10. Cove Mountain or Grassy Lick, near Wytheville, May 10. Salt Pond Mountain and Gap Mountain May 12-13. Hunter's Expedition against Lynchburg May 26-July 1. Diamond Hill June 17. Lynchburg June 17-18. Retreat to Charleston June 18-July 1. Buford's Gap June 20. About Salem June 21. Moved to the Shenandoah Valley July 12-15. Snicker's Ferry July 17-18. Stephenson's Depot July 20. Battle of Kernstown-Winchester July 23-24. Martinsburg July 25. Sheridan's Shenandoah Valley Campaign August 6-November 28. Strasburg August 15. Halltown August 24 and 26. Berryville September 3. Battle of Opequan, Winchester, September 19. Fisher's Hill September 22. Battle of Cedar Creek October 19. Duty at Camp Russell and in Shenandoah Valley till December. Myerstown November 28. Duty at Martinsburg, Cumberland, Md., and Winchester, Va., till June, 1865. Near Patterson Creek Station March 22, 1865 (Co. "H"). Mustered out June 28, 1865.

Regiment lost during service 7 Officers and 81 Enlisted men killed and mortally wounded and 1 Officer and 157 Enlisted men by disease. Total 246.

15th REGIMENT INFANTRY.

Organized at Wheeling, W. Va., August-October, 1862. Attached to Railroad Division, West Virginia, to January, 1863. Sir John's Run, Defences Upper Potomac, 8th Army Corps, Middle Dept., to March, 1863. 3rd Brigade, 1st Division, 8th Army Corps, to June, 1863. Unattached, New Creek, W. Va., Dept. of West Virginia, to August, 1863. Campbell's Brigade, Scammon's Division, Dept. West Virginia, to December, 1863. 1st Brigade, 2nd Division, West Virginia, to April, 1864. 3rd Brigade, 2nd Division, West Virginia, April, 1864. 2nd Brigade, 3rd Division, West Virginia, to July, 1864. 3rd Brigade, 1st Infantry Division, West Virginia, to December, 1864. 3rd Brigade, Independent Division, 24th Army Corps, Army of the James, to June, 1865.

SERVICE.—At New Creek Station October 18-December 22. 1862. Moved to Sir John's Run December 22, and duty there guarding Baltimore & Ohio Railroad till June 16, 1863. Moved to New Creek June 16, thence to Cumberland, Md., and to Hancock, Md., July 4. To Fairview July 11, and to Williamsport, Md., July 14. Operations against Lee till July 28. At Mechanicsburg Gap, near Romney, August 5-November 5, and at Alpine till April, 1864. Bath March 19. Crook's Expedition against Virginia & Tennessee Railroad May 2-19. Battle of Cloyd's Mountain May 9. New River Bridge May 10. Cove Mountain or Grassy Lick, near Wytheville, May 10. Salt Pond Mountain and Gap Mountain May 12-13. Meadow Bluff May 19. Hunter's Expedition to Lynchburg May 26-July 1. Middlebrook and Brownsville June 10. Lexington June 11-12. Otter Creek, near Liberty, June 16. Diamond Hill June 17. Lynchburg June 17-18. Retreat to Charleston June 18-July 1. Buford's Gap June 20. About Salem June 21. Moved to Shenandoah Valley July 12-15. Snicker's Ferry or Gap July 17-18. Battle of Kernstown-Winchester July 23-24. Sheridan's Shenandoah Valley Campaign August 6-November 28. Berryville September 3. Battle of Opequan, Winchester, September 19. Fisher's Hill September 22. Skirmish at Cedar Creek October 13. Battle of Cedar Creek October 19. Duty at Camp Russell and in the Shenandoah Valley till December. Moved to Washington, D. C., thence to Bermuda Hundred, Va., December 19-23. Duty in the trenches before Richmond, Va., till March, 1865. Appomattox Campaign March 28-April 9. Moved to front of Petersburg March 28-29. Hatcher's Run March 30-31 and April 1. Fall of Petersburg April 2. Pursuit of Lee April 3-9. Rice's Station April 6. Appomattox Court House April 9. Surrender of Lee and his army. March to Lynchburg April 12-15, thence to Farmville and Burkesville Junction April 15-19, and to Richmond, Va.,

April 22-25. Duty near Richmond till June. Mustered out June 14, 1865.

Regiment lost during service 3 Officers and 50 Enlisted men killed and mortally wounded and 1 Officer and 99 Enlisted men by disease. Total 153.

16th REGIMENT INFANTRY.

Organized at Washington, D. C., August and September, 1862. Attached to Abercrombie's Division, Defences of Washington, D. C., to February, 1863. 2nd Brigade, Abercrombie's Division, 22nd Army Corps, to April, 1863. 2nd Brigade, DeRussy's Division, 22nd Army Corps, Defences South of the Potomac, to June, 1863.

SERVICE.—On duty in the Defences of Washington, D. C., north and south of the Potomac, during entire term. Mustered out June 10, 1863.

Regiment lost during service 7 by disease.

17th REGIMENT INFANTRY.

Organized at Wheeling, W. Va., September 26, 1864, to February 25, 1865. Attached to Reserve Division, District of Harper's Ferry, W. Va., west of Sleepy Hollow, to March, 1865. 1st Brigade, 1st Infantry Division, West Virginia, to June, 1865.

SERVICE.—Moved to Clarksburg, W. Va., September 27, 1864, and guarding railroad and on garrison duty till mustered out. Mustered out June 30, 1865.

Regiment lost during service 1 killed and 24 by disease. Total 25.

INDEPENDENT BATTALION INFANTRY.

Organized at Wheeling, W. Va., October 1, 1862, to January 9, 1863. On duty at Wheeling, W. Va., entire term. Mustered out: Company "B" April 23, 1864; Company "A" May 31, 1865.

1st INDEPENDENT COMPANY LOYAL VIRGINIANS.

Organized at Cobb's Island June 30, 1864. Mustered out December 1, 1865.

WISCONSIN VOLUNTEERS.

1st REGIMENT CAVALRY.

Organized at Rippon and Kenosha, Wis., September 1, 1861, to February 2, 1862. Mustered in March 10, 1862. Left State for St. Louis, Mo., March 17, 1862, and duty at Benton Barracks, Mo., till April 28. Moved to Camp Girardeau, Mo., April 28. Attached to Vandever's Brigade, District of Southeast Missouri, Dept. of Missouri, to October, 1862. Cavalry Brigade, District of Southeast Missouri, Dept. of Missouri, to June, 1863. 2nd Brigade, 1st Cavalry Division, Army of the Cumberland, to October, 1864. 2nd Brigade, 1st Division, Wilson's Cavalry Corps, Military Division Mississippi, to July, 1865.

SERVICE.—Scout and patrol duty in Southeast Missouri till October, 1862. Expedition to Bloomfield, Mo., May 10-11. Action at Bloomfield May 10. Chalk Bluffs May 15. Operations in Dunklin County May 16-20. Expedition to Madison, Ark., July 9-22. Scatterville July 10. Guerrilla Campaign against Porter's and Poindexter's forces July 20-September 10. West Prairie July 23. Bloomfield July 29. Jonesboro, Ark., August 2-3 (2nd Battalion). Jackson, Languelle's Ferry and Scatterville August 3. At Cape Girardeau till October 3. Scout to Wayne, Stoddard and Dunklin Counties August 20-27 (Detachment). Bloomfield August 29 and September 11. Moved to Greenville October 3, thence to Patterson October 19. Expedition after Greene's guerrillas October 20-November 3. Duty at Patterson till January, 1863. Moved to Alton and West Plains January. At West Plains, Pilot Knob and St. Genevieve till March. Batesville February 4. Moved to Cape Girardeau March 10. Scout from Bloomfield to Scatterville March 24-April 1. Operations against Marmaduke April 17-May 2. Whitewater River April 24 (Co. "E"). Cape Girardeau April 26. Near Whitewater Bridge April 27. Castor River, near Bloomfield, April 29. Bloomfield April 29-30. Chalk Bluff, St. Francis River, April 30-May 1. Moved to Nashville, Tenn., May 31-June 13. Triune June 19. Middle

Tennessee or Tullahoma Campaign June 23-July 7. Eaglesville and Rover June 23. Middleton June 24. Fosterville, Guy's Gap and Shelbyville June 27. Bethpage Bridge, Elk River, July 2. Expedition to Huntsville July 13-22. At Huntsville and Fayetteville, Ala., till August 15. At Larkinsville till August 31. Chickamauga (Ga.) Campaign. Reconnoissance toward Rome, Ga., September 11. Apine and Dirt Town September 12. Near Stevens' Gap September 18. Battle of Chickamauga September 19-20. Boy Valley and Lookout Church September 22. Missionary Ridge and Shallow Ford Gap September 22. Operations against Wheeler and Roddy September 30-October 17. Anderson's Cross Roads October 2. Maysville, Ala., October 13. Camp at Winchester till November 20. Movement to Murfreesboro, thence into East Tennessee November 20-December 14. Operations about Dandridge and Mossy Creek November 24-28. Mossy Creek Station December 24. Pack's House, near New Market, December 24. Mossy Creek December 26. Talbot Station December 28. Mossy Creek, Talbot Station, December 29. Near Mossy Creek January 11-12, 1864. Operations about Dandridge January 16-17. Bend of Chucky Road, near Dandridge, January 16. Dandridge January 17. Operations about Dandridge January 26-28. Fair Garden January 27. Swann's Island January 28. Expedition from Motley's Ford to Murphey, N. C., February 17-22. Cleveland April 2. Mink Springs, near Cleveland, April 13. Atlanta (Ga.) Campaign May 1-September 8. Catoosa Springs May 3. Varnell's Station May 7 and 9. Demonstrations on Dalton May 9-13. Tilton May 13. Battle of Resaca May 14-15. Cassville May 19. Stilesboro May 23. Burnt Hickory May 24. About Dallas May 25-June 5. Burned Church May 26 and May 30-June 1. Ackworth June 3-4. Big Shanty June 6. Operations about Marietta and against Kenesaw Mountain June 10-July 2. Lost Mountain June 15-17. Assault on Kenesaw June 27. Howell's Ferry July 1. Nickajack Creek July 2-5. Chattahoochie River July 6-17. Beachtown July 22. Siege of Atlanta July 22-August 25. McCook's Raid on Atlanta & West Point Railroad July 27-31. Campbellton July 28. Newnan July 30-31. Expedition to Jasper August 11-15. At Cartersville August 18-October 17. Rousseau's pursuit of Wheeler September 1-8. At Calhoun till November 14. Ordered to Louisville, Ky., November 14, and duty there till December 4. Pursuit of Lyon from Paris to Hopkinsville, Ky., thence march to Nashville, Tenn., December 6, 1864, to January 8, 1865. Action at Hopkinsville, Ky., December 16. At Chickasaw, Ala., till March, 1865. Wilson's Raid from Chickasaw, Ala., to Macon, Ga., March 22-April 24. Centreville April 1. Selma April 2. Lowndesborough April 10 (Cos. "A" and "B"). Montgomery April 12. Columbus Road, near Tuskegee, April 14. Fort Tyler, West Point, Ga., April 16. Macon April 20. Irwinsville, Ga., May 10. Capture of Jeff Davis. At Macon and Nashville, Tenn., till July. Mustered out at Edgefield, Tenn., July 19, 1865.

Regiment lost during service 6 Officers and 67 Enlisted men killed and mortally wounded and 7 Officers and 321 Enlisted men by disease. Total 401.

2nd REGIMENT CAVALRY.

Organized at Milwaukee, Wis., December 30, 1861, to March 10, 1862. Left State for St. Louis, Mo., March 24, 1862. Duty at Benton Barracks, Mo., till May 15. Moved to Jefferson City, thence to Springfield, Mo., and duty there till June 14. Attached to Steele's Command, Army of Southwest Missouri, Dept. of Missouri, to July, 1862. District of Eastern Arkansas, Dept. of Missouri, to November, 1862. 2nd Brigade, Cavalry Division, District of Eastern Arkansas, Dept. of the Tennessee, to January, 1863. 2nd Brigade, 2nd Cavalry Division, 13th Army Corps, Dept. of the Tennessee, to February, 1863. 3rd Brigade, District of Memphis, Tenn., 5th Division, 16th Army Corps, Dept. of the Tennessee, to June, 1863. Bussey's Cavalry Brigade, Herron's Division, 13th Army Corps, to August, 1863. Cavalry Division, 17th Army Corps, to September, 1863. 1st Division, 17th Army Corps, to January, 1864. Winslow's Cavalry Brigade, District of Vicksburg, Miss., to December, 1864. 3rd

Brigade, Cavalry Division, District of West Tennessee, to July, 1865. 2nd Brigade, 2nd Cavalry Division, Military Division Gulf, to August, 1865. Dept. of Texas to November, 1865.

SERVICE.—March to Batesville, Jacksonport and Helena, Ark., June 14-July 12, 1862, and duty there till January, 1863. Action at Yellville, Ark., June 25, 1862. Near Fayetteville July 15. Expedition from Helena to Moro August 5-8 (Detachment). Near Helena August 11. Near Helena September 19-20. Expedition against Arkansas Post November 16-21. Expedition to Yellville November 25-29. Expedition from Helena to Grenada, Miss., November 27-December 5. Oakland, Miss., December 3. LaGrange, Ark., December 30. Lick Creek, Ark., January 12, 1863. Clarendon Road, near Helena, January 15. Ordered to Memphis, Tenn., February 4, and duty there till May. Nonconah Creek, near Memphis, April 4. Expedition to Coldwater April 17-20. Horn Lake Creek May 18 (Co. "L"). Expeditions to Hernando, Miss., May 23-24, 26 and 28 (Detachments). Moved to Vicksburg, Miss., June 10-13. Siege of Vicksburg, Miss., June 13-July 4. Advance on Jackson, Miss., July 4-10. Clinton July 8. Siege of Jackson July 10-17. Canton July 12. Expedition to Yazoo City July 12-21, 1863 (Detachment). Bolton's Depot July 16. Grant's Ferry, Pearl River, July 16. Briar Creek, near Canton, July 17. Duty at Red Bone Church till April 27, 1864. Action at Red Bone Church September 25, 1863. Ingraham's Plantation, near Port Gibson, October 10. Red Bone April 21, 1864. Moved to Vicksburg April 27, and duty there till December. Salem May 29 (Detachment). Worthington's and Sunnyside Landings, Fish Bayou, June 5. Old River Lake or Lake Chicot June 6. Expedition from Vicksburg to Pearl River July 2-10. Clinton July 4. Jackson July 5-6. Clinton July 7. Expedition from Vicksburg to Rodney and Fayette September 29-October 3. Port Gibson October 1. Fayette and Cole Creek October 3. Expedition from Natchez to Woodville October 4-11. Woodville October 5-6. Fort Adams, La., October 5 and 7. Operations in Issaqueena and Washington Counties October 24-31. Expedition from Vicksburg to Gaines' Landing and Bayou Macon, La., November 6-8. Expedition from Vicksburg to Yazoo City November 23-December 4. Concord Church December 1. Moved to Memphis, Tenn., December 8. Grierson's Expedition to destroy Mobile & Ohio Railroad December 21, 1864, to January 15, 1865. Franklin Creek December 21-22, 1864. Egypt Station December 28. Expedition from Memphis to Marion, Ark., January 19-22, 1865 (Detachment). Duty at Memphis, Tenn., till June. Expedition into Northern Mississippi March 3-11. (Part of Regiment ordered to Grenada, Miss., May 9, and duty there till June 24, when rejoined Regiment at Alexandria, La.) Ordered to Alexandria, La., June. March from Alexandria to Hempstead, Texas, August 8-26, and duty there till October. March to Austin, Texas, and there mustered out November 15, 1865.

1st Battalion (Cos. "A," "D," "G" and "K") served detached June 13. 1862, to September, 1864. Ordered to Cassville, Mo., June 13, 1862, and duty there till October, 1862. Pineville June 23. Attached to 1st Brigade, 3rd Division, Army of the Frontier, Dept. of Missouri, to June, 1863. District of Rolla, Dept. of Missouri, to August, 1864. District of North Missouri to September, 1864. Duty at Osage Springs, Mo., October, 1862, to December, 1862. Battle of Prairie Grove, Ark., December 7. Expedition over Boston Mountains to Van Buren, Ark., December 27-29. At Forsythe, Mo., till March, 1863. At Lake Springs till June, 1863. At Rolla till September, 1864. Lane's Prairie, Mo., May 26, 1864. Scout in Phelps and Marias Counties August 1 (Co. "A"). Rejoined Regiment at Vicksburg, Miss., September, 1864.

Regiment lost during service 24 Enlisted men killed and mortally wounded and 4 Officers and 284 Enlisted men by disease. Total 312.

3rd REGIMENT CAVALRY.

Organized at Janesville, Wis., November 30, 1861, to January 31, 1862. Mustered in January 28, 1862. Moved to St. Louis, Mo., March 26-28, 1862, and duty at Benton Barracks, Mo., till May 23. Moved to Fort Leavenworth, Kan., May 23-27. Assigned to frontier and provost duty in Kansas till September, 1862. Company "D" at Atchison; Company "G" at Shawnee; Company "L" at Aubrey; Companies "B" and "H" at Fort Leavenworth; Companies "A," "E" and "K" at Leavenworth City. Companies "C," "F," "I" and "M" moved to Fort Scott, Kan., June 12-17. Company "C" stationed at Trading Post till August; Company "I" at Carthage till August. Action at Monticello August 5. Rocky Bluff August 7. Taberville August 11. Expedition to Montevallo August 14-24. Hickory Grove August 23. Regiment assembled at Fort Scott September. Attached to Solomon's 1st Brigade, Herron's 1st Division, Army of the Frontier, Dept. of Missouri, to November, 1862. Cavalry Command, Herron's Division, Army of the Frontier, to June, 1863. District of the Frontier, Dept. of Missouri, to December, 1863. 3rd Brigade, District of the Frontier, to January, 1864. Unassigned, District of the Frontier, 7th Army Corps, Dept. of Arkansas, to April, 1864. Unassigned, Little Rock, Ark., 7th Army Corps, to September, 1864. 4th Brigade, Cavalry Division, 7th Army Corps, to February, 1865. Cavalry Brigade, Post of Little Rock, 7th Army Corps, to April, 1865. Unassigned, 1st Division, 7th Army Corps, to June, 1865. District of South Kansas, to September, 1865.

SERVICE.—Expedition from Fort Leavenworth to Independence August 12-14, 1862. (Cos. "I" and "M" at Fort Scott till May, 1863: also "C" and "G," December, 1862, to July, 1863; Co. "G" relieved and ordered to Regiment.) 1st and 3rd Battalions in Blount's Campaign in Missouri and Arkansas against Raines and Parsons September to December, 1862. Cross Hollows September 27-28. Newtonia September 30. Occupation of Newtonia October 4. Cane Hill November 28. Battle of Prairie Grove, Ark., December 7. Expedition over Boston Mountains to Van Buren, Ark., December 27-29. Dripping Springs December 28. Carthage, Mo., January 13, 1863. Moved to Forsythe, thence to Springfield, Mo. Duty there and at Drywood till June. Scouting in Southwest Counties of Missouri and Northwest Arkansas, and operating against Patty's, Livingston's and Quantrell's guerrillas, with numerous skirmishes in Barton, Jasper and Newton Counties. Action at Carrollton March 2. Yellville March 4. The Island March 30. Clapper's Saw Mill, near Crooked Creek, I. T., March 31 (Detachment). Jackson County April 2. Companies "B," "G," "H," "I" and "M" march to Fort Blount, C. N., as escort to train, May 14-30. Near Fort Gibson May 20 and 25, and near Fort Blount May 30. Regiment moved to Fort Blount June 20-July 5. Action at Cabin Creek July 1-2 (Co. "B"). Honey Springs July 17 and August 22. Perryville August 26. Marias des Cygnes August 31. At Schuyleyville. C. N., till October. Expedition through Jackson, Cass, Johnson and Lafayette Counties September 8-23 (Cos. "B" and "L"). Choctaw Nation October 2. Baxter Springs October 6 (Cos. "C" and "I"). Fort Blair, Waldron, October 7. Choctaw Nation October 7. Waldron October 16. Clarksville October 28. Raid from Van Buren to Dallas November 12-22. Duty at Van Buren November, 1863, to March, 1864. Moved to Little Rock March 30-April 16. Veterans on furlough March 30-June 16, then moved to Little Rock via St. Louis, Memphis and Devall's Bluff June 16-July 27. Clarendon July 14 (Non-Veterans). Expedition from Little Rock to Little Red River August 6-16. Hickory Plains and Bull's Bayou August 7. Bull's Bayou and Jacksonport August 26. Pursuit of Shelby's forces August 28-September 7. Expedition from Little Rock to Fort Smith September 25-October 13 (Detachment). Clarksville September 28 and October 19. Expedition from Lewisburg to Benton November 2-3. Duty at Little Rock till April, 1865 (Cos. "B," "E," "G," "H," "I," "K" and "L"). Expedition up White River to Devall's Bluff December 13-15, 1864. Regiment reorganized into 5 Companies April 16, 1865. Moved to Duvall's Bluff April 21, and duty there till June 3. Moved to St. Louis, Mo., June 3, thence to Rolla and Springfield, Mo., and marched to

Fort Leavenworth, Kan., July 18-August 3. Mustered out at Fort Leavenworth September 8, 1865.

Companies "A," "C," "D," "F" and "M" served detached in District of the Border October, 1863, to January, 1864. In District of Kansas to September, 1864. District of South Kansas to April, 1865, and District of North Kansas to September, 1865, serving at different posts in Missouri and Kansas, Sub-District of Fort Scott, at Forts Insley, Mo., Hamer, Mo., Curtis, Mo., McKean, Mo., Pawnee Creek, Kan., etc. Arkansas Creek near Fort Larned November 13, 1863 (Detachment). Dogwood Creek May 16 (Co. "C"). Lane's Prairie, Marian County, May 26. Actions at Montevallo, Mo., June 12, 1864 (Detachment). Big North Fork Creek Mo., June 16 (Co. "C"). Near Dogwood July 7. Osage Mission, Kan., September 26. Operations against Price in Missouri and Arkansas September to November, 1864. Lexington October 19 (Detachment). Near Montevallo October 19. Little Blue October 21. Big Blue and State Line October 22. Westport October 23. Engagement at the Marmiton or Battle of Charlot October 25. Mine Creek, Little Osage River, October 25. Newtonia October 28. Drywood October 29. Company "A" changed to Company "K," Company "C" to Company "H," Company "D" to Company "I," and Company "M" to Company G," April 16, 1865. Companies "F" and "H" on expedition to explore country from Fort Riley, Kan., to Denver, Colo., Smoky Hill Route, March to July, 1865. Mustered out at Fort Leavenworth, Kan., September 29, 1865. Companies "G" and "L" mustered out October 26, 1865.

Regiment lost during service 3 Officers and 61 Enlisted men killed and mortally wounded and 6 Officers and 147 Enlisted men by disease. Total 217.

4th REGIMENT CAVALRY.

Organized at Racine, Wis., as 4th Wisconsin Infantry and mustered in July 2, 1861. Moved to Baltimore, Md., July 15-22. Attached to Dix's Division, Baltimore, Md., to February, 1862. Williams' Brigade, Butler's New Orleans Expedition, to April, 1862. 2nd Brigade, Dept. of the Gulf, to December, 1862. Grover's Division, Dept. of the Gulf, to January, 1863. 2nd Brigade, 3rd Division, 19th Army Corps, Dept. of the Gulf, to July, 1863. Cavalry Brigade, 19th Army Corps, July, 1863. District of Baton Rouge, La., Dept. of the Gulf, to October, 1863. (Designation changed to 4th Cavalry August 22, 1863.) Unattached, Cavalry Division, Dept. of the Gulf, to January, 1864. District Baton Rouge, La., Dept. Gulf, to June, 1864. 4th Brigade, Cavalry Division, Dept. Gulf, to August, 1864. 2nd Brigade, Cavalry Division, Dept. Gulf, to February, 1865. Cavalry Brigade, District of Baton Rouge, to March, 1865. 1st Brigade, 1st Cavalry Division, Military Division West Mississippi to April, 1865. 2nd Brigade, 1st Division, Cavalry Corps, Dept. of the Gulf, to May, 1865. 3rd Brigade, 1st Cavalry Division, Dept. of the Gulf, to July, 1865. Dept. of Texas, to May, 1866.

SERVICE.—Guard railroad near Baltimore, Md., till November, 1861. Expedition to eastern shore of Maryland November 14-22. Duty at Baltimore till February, 1862. Moved to Fortress Monroe, Va., February 19, thence sailed on Steamer "Constitution" for Ship Island, Miss., March 5, arriving there March 13, and duty there till April 16. Operations against Forts St. Phillip and Jackson April 16-29. Surrender of Fort St. Phillip April 29. Occupation of New Orleans May 2. Expedition to New Orleans and Jackson Railroad May 8-10. Occupation of Baton Rouge May 12. Reconnoissance to Warrenton May 14-29. At Baton Rouge till June 17. Expedition from Baton Rouge June 7-9 (2 Cos.). Williams' Expedition to Vicksburg, Miss., and operations in that vicinity June 20-July 26. Grand Gulf June 23-24. Battle of Baton Rouge, La., August 5. Evacuation of Baton Rouge August 20. At Carrollton till September 29 and at Camp Parapet till December 19. Bayou Des Allemands September 4-5. Expedition from Carrollton to St. Charles' Court House September 7-8. Bonnet Carre near St. Charles' Court House September 8. Moved to

Baton Rouge December 19, and duty there till February, 1863. (Co. "G" detached for Heavy Artillery service in the Defences of New Orleans November 13, 1862, to August 14, 1863.) Moved to Bayou Plaquemine February 6, 1863. Expedition to Indian Village February 13. To New Orleans February 23, thence to Baton Rouge March 6. Demonstration on Port Hudson March 7-27. Operations in Western Louisiana April 9-May 14. Teche Campaign April 11-20. Fort Bisland April 12-13. Pursuit to Opelousas April 15-20. Expedition to Bayou Plaquemine April 22-23. Expedition from Opelouses to Chicotsville and Bayou Boeuf April 26-29. Near Washington May 1. Boyce's Bridge, Cotile Bayou, May 14. Cheyneyville May 18. March to Port Hudson May 19-25. Siege of Port Hudson May 25-June 9. Expedition to Niblitt's Bluff May 26-29. Assault on Port Hudson June 14. Grierson's Expedition to Clinton June 1-6. Clinton June 3-4. Surrender of Port Hudson July 9. Moved to Baton Rouge, La., July 25, and duty there till September. Designation of Regiment changed to 4th Wisconsin Cavalry August 22, 1863. Duty at Baton Rouge engaged in scouting, picketing and operating against guerrillas in that section of country lying between the Comite, Amite and Mississippi Rivers till June, 1864. Near Baton Rouge September 8, 1863 (Detachment). Greenwell Springs Road September 19 (Detachment), and October 5. Donaldsville February 8, 1864. New River February 9. Expedition to Rosedale February 14-22. Baton Rouge March 8. Black Bayou March 19. Reconnoissance to Clinton May 1. Olive Branch Church near Baton Rouge May 3. Baton Rouge June 16. Plaquemine June 28. Ordered to Morganza June 29, and duty there till August 9. Plaquemine August 6. Moved to Baton Rouge August 9. Near Bayou Letsworth August 11. Expedition to Clinton August 25-29. Olive Branch, Comite River and Clinton August 25. Expedition to Clinton, Greensburg and Camp Moore October 5-9. Expedition from Baton Rouge to Brookhaven, Miss., and skirmishes November 14-21. Liberty Creek November 15. Jackson November 21. Davidson Expedition to Mobile & Ohio Railroad and Pascagoula Bay November 27-December 13. At Baton Rouge till April, 1865. Mobile Campaign April. Capture of Mobile April 12. March through Alabama to Georgia and to Vicksburg, Miss., April 18-June 5. Moved to Shreveport, La., June 26-July 2. March to San Antonio, Texas July 8-August 3, and duty there till October. Expedition to Fort Inge and to Fort Clark and Eagle Pass September. Guard and patrol duty along the Rio Grande from Brownsville to Laredo till May, 1866. Mustered out at Brownsville May 28, 1866. Moved to Madison, Wis., June 3-18, and discharged June 19, 1866.

Regiment lost during service 11 Officers and 106 Enlisted men killed and mortally wounded and 3 Officers and 311 Enlisted men by disease. Total 431.

1st REGIMENT HEAVY ARTILLERY.

Battery "A" organized as Company "K," 2nd Wisconsin Infantry. Detached from Regiment August, 1861, and assigned to duty as Heavy Artillery at Forts Corcoran, Marcy and Ethan Allen, Defences of Washington, D. C., till October, 1861. Rejoined Regiment October 10. Permanently detached as Battery "A," 1st Wisconsin Heavy Artillery, December 9, 1861. Attached to Military District of Washington, to May, 1862. Whipple's Command, Military District of Washington, to February, 1863. Defences of Alexandria, 22nd Army Corps, to April, 1863. 1st Brigade, DeRussy's Division, 22nd Army Corps, to May, 1863. 3rd Brigade, DeRussy's Division, 22nd Army Corps, to December, 1863. 4th Brigade, DeRussy's Division, 22nd Army Corps, to March, 1864. 3rd Brigade, DeRussy's Division, 22nd Army Corps, to May, 1864. 2nd Brigade, DeRussy's Division, 22nd Army Corps, to August, 1865. Assigned to duty in the Defences of Washington, D. C., at Forts Cass, Buffalo, Ellsworth, Worth, Rodgers and Willard till August, 1865. Defence of Washington against Early's attack July 11-12, 1864. Mustered out August 18, 1865.

Battery "B" organized at Milwaukee, Wis., and left State for Murfreesboro, Tenn., September, 1863. Duty at Fort Terrell, Murfreesboro, Tenn., till January, 1864. Moved to Lexington, Ky., January 4, 1864, and duty at Fort Clay, Lexington, Ky., till August, 1865. Mustered out August 30, 1865.

Battery "C" left State October 30, 1863, for Chattanooga, Tenn. Attached to 2nd Division, Artillery Reserve, Dept. of the Cumberland, to December, 1863. Garrison Artillery, Chattanooga, Tenn., to April, 1865. 3rd Brigade, 4th Division, District of East Tennessee, Dept. of the Cumberland, to July, 1865. 1st Brigade, 4th Division, District of East Tennessee, to August, 1865.

Duty at Chattanooga, Tenn., till March 29, 1865. At Athens, Mouse Creek and Strawberry Plains, Tenn., till September. Mustered out September 21, 1865.

Battery "D" mustered in November 7, 1863. Ordered to New Orleans, La., February 9, 1864. Attached to the Defences of New Orleans, La., Dept. of the Gulf, to July, 1864. District of LaFourche, La., Dept. of the Gulf, to June, 1865. Defences of Washington, D. C., 22nd Army Corps, to August, 1865. Garrison at Fort Jackson till July 23, 1864, thence moved to Fort Berwick near Brashear City and duty there till June, 1865. Ordered to Washington, D. C., and there mustered out August 18, 1865.

Batteries "E," "F," "G," "H," "I," "K," "L" and "M" organized September and October, 1864. Ordered to Washington, D. C. Attached to 3rd Brigade, DeRussy's Division, 22nd Army Corps, to December, 1864. 4th Brigade, DeRussy's Division, 22nd Army Corps, to June, 1865.

Assigned to duty in the Defences of Washington, D. C. Company "E" at Fort O'Rourke, "F" at Fort Ellsworth, "G" and "H" at Fort Lyon ("G" also at Fort Ellsworth), "I" at Fort Farnsworth, "K" at Fort Lyon, "L" at Fort Willard, "M" at Forts Lyon, Weed and Farnsworth. Batteries "E" to "M" mustered out June 26, 1865.

Regiment lost during service 4 Enlisted men killed and mortally wounded and 2 Officers and 77 Enlisted men by disease. Total 83.

1st INDEPENDENT BATTERY LIGHT ARTILLERY.

Organized at LaCrosse, Wis., and mustered in October 10, 1861. Moved to Camp Utley, Racine, Wis., and duty there till January 23, 1862. Ordered to Louisville, Ky., January 23, and duty there till April 3. Attached to Artillery, 7th Division, Army of the Ohio, to October, 1862. Cumberland Division, District of West Virginia, Dept. of the Ohio, to November, 1862. Artillery, 9th Division, Right Wing 13th Army Corps (Old), Dept. of the Tennessee, to December, 1862. Artillery, 3rd Division, Sherman's Yazoo Expedition, to January, 1863. Artillery, 9th Division, 13th Army Corps, Army of the Tennessee, to July, 1863. 4th Brigade, 1st Division, 13th Army Corps, Army of the Tennessee, to August, 1863, and Dept. of the Gulf to August, 1863. Defences of New Orleans, La., Dept. of the Gulf, to January, 1864. Artillery, 1st Division, 13th Army Corps, to June, 1864. District of Morganza, Dept. of the Gulf, to August, 1864. Artillery, Cavalry Division, Dept. of the Gulf, to February, 1865. Cavalry Brigade, District of Baton Rouge, La., to July, 1865.

SERVICE.—Cumberland Gap Campaign April 3-June 18, 1862. Occupation of Cumberland Gap June 18 to September 17. Evacuation of Cumberland Gap and retreat to Greenupsburg, Ky., and to the Ohio River September 17-October 3. Expedition to Charleston, W. Va., October 21-November 10. Ordered to Cincinnati, Ohio, November 20; thence to Memphis, Tenn., November 26. Sherman's Yazoo Expedition December 20, 1862, to January 3, 1863. Chickasaw Bayou December 26-28. Chickasaw Bluff December 29. Expedition to Arkansas Post, Ark., January 3-10, 1863. Assault and capture of Fort Hindman, Arkansas Post, January 10-11. Moved to Young's Point, La., January 14-23, and duty there till March 8. Moved to Milliken's Bend, La., March 8.

Operations from Milliken's Bend to New Carthage March 31-April 17. Movement on Bruinsburg and turning Grand Gulf April 25-30. Battle of Port Gibson May 1. Battle of Champion's Hill May 16. Big Black River May 17. Siege of Vicksburg, Miss., May 18-July 4. Assaults on Vicksburg May 19 and 22. Advance on Jackson, Miss., July 4-10. Near Clinton July 8. Siege of Jackson July 10-17. Battery refitted with 30-lb. Parrott's and ordered to the Dept. of the Gulf August 13. Duty at Carrollton till September 3. Moved to Brashear City September 3-4, and to Berwick City September 24. Western Louisiana Campaign October 3-November 30. Duty at Brashear City till December. Moved to New Orleans and duty there till April 22, 1864. Red River Campaign April-May. Moved to Alexandria April 22-28, and duty there till May 13. Retreat to Morganza May 13-20. At Morganza and New Orleans till August, then moved to Baton Rouge, La. Bayou Letsworth August 11. Expedition to Clinton August 23-29. Olive Branch, Comite River and Clinton August 25. Expedition to Clinton, Greensburg and Camp Moore October 5-9. Expedition to Brookhaven, Miss., November 14-21. Liberty Creek November 15. Jackson November 21. Davidson's Expedition to Mobile & Ohio Railroad November 26-December 13. Duty at New Orleans and Baton Rouge till July, 1865. Mustered out July 18, 1865.

Battery lost during service 5 Enlisted men killed and mortally wounded and 1 Officer and 22 Enlisted men by disease. Total 28.

2nd INDEPENDENT BATTERY LIGHT ARTILLERY.

Organized at LaCrosse and mustered in at Racine, Wis., October 10, 1861. Moved to Baltimore, Md., thence to Fortress Monroe, Va., January 21-27, 1862, and garrison duty there till September. Attached to Fortress Monroe, Va., Dept. of Virginia, to July, 1862. Fortress Monroe, Va., 7th Army Corps, Dept. of Virginia, to September, 1862. Camp Hamilton, Va., 7th Army Corps, Dept. of Virginia, to January, 1863. Artillery Division at Suffolk, Va., 7th Army Corps, to April, 1863. Artillery, 1st Division, 7th Army Corps, to June, 1863. 2nd Brigade, 1st Division, 4th Army Corps, Dept. of Virginia, to August, 1863. Artillery, Yorktown, Va., Dept. of Virginia and North Carolina, to January, 1864. Point Lookout, Md., to July, 1865.

SERVICE.—Moved to Camp Hamilton, Hampton, Va., September, 1862, and duty there till January 10, 1863. Moved to Suffolk, Va., January 10. Action at Deserted House January 30. Siege of Suffolk, Va., April 11-May 4. Norfleet House April 15. Moved to Portsmouth, Va., May 6; thence to West Point. Dix's Peninsula Campaign June 24-July 7. Moved to Yorktown, Va., July 20, and duty there till January 20, 1864. Moved to Point Lookout, Md., January 20, and duty there guarding prisoners till July, 1865. Mustered out July 10, 1865.

Battery lost during service 12 by disease.

3rd INDEPENDENT BATTERY LIGHT ARTILLERY. ("BADGER BATTERY.")

Organized at Racine, Wis., and mustered in October 10, 1861. Ordered to Louisville, Ky., January 23, 1862, and duty there till March 10. Attached to Artillery, 5th Division, Army of the Ohio, to September, 1862. Artillery, 5th Division, 2nd Corps, Army of the Ohio, to November, 1862. Artillery, 3rd Division, Left Wing 14th Army Corps, Army of the Cumberland, to January, 1863. Artillery, 3rd Division, 21st Army Corps, Army of the Cumberland, to October, 1863. 2nd Division, Artillery Reserve, Dept. of the Cumberland, to March, 1864. Garrison Artillery, Chattanooga, Tenn., Dept. of the Cumberland, to April, 1865. Garrison Artillery, Murfreesboro, Tenn., Dept. of the Cumberland, to July, 1865.

SERVICE.—Ordered to Nashville, Tenn., March 10, 1862; thence march to Savannah, Tenn., March 29-April 9. Advance on and siege of Corinth, Miss., April 29-May 30. Pursuit to Booneville May 31-June 12. Buell's operations on line of Memphis & Charleston Railroad

in North Alabama and Middle Tennessee June to August. March to Louisville, Ky., in pursuit of Bragg August 21-September 26. Pursuit of Bragg into Kentucky October 1-20. Battle of Perryville, Ky., October 8 (Reserve). Pittman's Cross Roads October 18. March to Nashville, Tenn., October 22-November 7. Lebanon November 9. Rural Hill November 18. At Nashville, Tenn., till December 26. Advance on Murfreesboro, Tenn., December 26-30. Battle of Stone's River December 30-31, 1862, and January 1-3, 1863. Duty at Murfreesboro till July 5. Moved to McMinnville July 5, and duty there till September. Chickamauga (Ga.) Campaign September. Chickamauga September 13. Battle of Chickamauga September 19-20. Siege of Chattanooga September 24-November 23. Chattanooga-Ringgold Campaign November 23-27. Garrison duty in the Defences of Chattanooga; also duty by Detachments on transports on the Tennessee River till April, 1865. Moved to Murfreesboro and garrison duty there till July. Mustered out July 20, 1865.

Battery lost during service 6 Enlisted men killed and mortally wounded and 21 Enlisted men by disease. Total 27.

4th INDEPENDENT BATTERY LIGHT ARTILLERY.

Organized and mustered in at Racine, Wis., October 1, 1861. Ordered to Baltimore, Md., January 21, 1862; thence to Fortress Monroe, Va., and garrison duty there till September. Attached to District of Fortress Monroe, Va., Dept. of Virginia, to September, 1862. Camp Hamilton, Va., 7th Army Corps, Dept. of Virginia, to January, 1863. Artillery Division at Suffolk, Va., 7th Army Corps, Dept. of Virginia, to April, 1863. Artillery, 1st Division, 7th Army Corps, to May, 1863. 2nd Brigade, 2nd Division, 4th Army Corps, Dept. of Virginia, to July, 1863. Yorktown, Va., Dept. of Virginia and North Carolina, to December, 1863. Artillery Brigade, United States Forces, Norfolk and Portsmouth, Va., Dept. of Virginia and North Carolina, to April, 1864. Artillery, 1st Division, 18th Army Corps, Army of the James, Dept. of Virginia and North Carolina, to June, 1864. Artillery Brigade, 18th Army Corps, to June, 1864. Artillery Cavalry Division, Army of the James, Dept. of Virginia and North Carolina, to July, 1865.

SERVICE.—Fired gun "Union" during the Monitor and Merrimac engagement March 9, 1862. Moved to Camp Hamilton, Va., September, and duty there till January 11, 1863. Moved to Suffolk, Va., January 11. Siege of Suffolk April 11-May 4. Norfleet House April 15. Chuckatuck and Reed's Ferry May 3. Moved to Portsmouth, Va., May 5. To West Point, thence to Yorktown May 30. Keyes' Expedition up the Peninsula June 9-July 10. Garrison duty at Yorktown till August 25. Duty at Gloucester Point and Portsmouth till April, 1864. Butler's operations on south side of the James River and against Petersburg and Richmond May 4-28. Swift Creek or Arrowfield Church May 9-10. Operations against Fort Darling May 12-16. Battle of Drury's Bluff May 14-16. Bermuda Hundred May 16-June 4. Before Petersburg June 16-18. Siege operations against Petersburg and Richmond June 16, 1864, to April 3, 1865. At Bermuda Hundred, Va., till July 5, 1864, and at Jones' Landing till August 10. Moved to Light House Point August 10, thence to Prince George Court House and to Petersburg August 26. Duty in trenches till September 27. Chaffin's Farm, New Market Heights, September 28-30. Darbytown Road October 7 and 13. Battle of Fair Oaks October 27-28. Siege operations against Richmond till April, 1865. Before Richmond March 30-April 2. Occupation of Richmond April 3 and duty there till July. Mustered out July 3, 1865.

Battery lost during service 3 Enlisted men killed and mortally wounded and 22 Enlisted men by disease. Total 25.

5th INDEPENDENT BATTERY LIGHT ARTILLERY.

Organized at Racine, Wis., and mustered in October 10, 1861. Left State for St. Louis, Mo., March 15, 1862.

Moved to Sykestown March 19, thence to New Madrid, Mo., and report to Gen. Pope March 19. Attached to Artillery Division, Army of Mississippi, to May, 1862. Artillery, 4th Division, Army of Mississippi, to September, 1862. 30th Brigade, 9th Division, Army of the Ohio, October, 1862. 30th Brigade, 9th Division, 3rd Corps, Army of the Ohio, to November, 1862. 1st Brigade, 1st Division, Right Wing, 14th Army Corps, Army of the Cumberland, to January, 1863. Artillery, 1st Division, 20th Army Corps, Army of the Cumberland, to October, 1863. Artillery, 2nd Division, 14th Army Corps, to July 1864. Artillery Brigade, 14th Army Corps, to June, 1865.

SERVICE.—Duty in the fortifications of New Madrid and Island No. 10 till April 19, 1862. Moved to Hamburg Landing, Tenn., April 19-28. Advance on and siege of Corinth, Miss., April 29-May 30. Pursuit to Booneville May 30-June 12. Moved to Jacinto, thence to Ripley June 23-29, and duty there till August 14. Moved to Iuka, Miss., August 14, thence march to Nashville, Tenn., August 21-September 3. March to Louisville, Ky., in pursuit of Bragg September 23-26. Pursuit of Bragg to Crab Orchard, Ky., October 1-15. Battle of Perryville, Ky., October 8. March to Nashville, Tenn., October 19-November 6, and duty there till December 26. Wilson's Creek Pike December 25. Advance on Murfreesboro December 26-30. Nolensville December 26-27. Battle of Stone's River December 30-31, 1862, and January 1-3, 1863. Duty at Murfreesboro till June. Expedition to Franklin January 31-February 12. Reconnoissance from Salem to Versailles March 9-14. Operations on Edgefild Pike June 4. Middle Tennessee (or Tullahoma) Campaign June 23-July 7. Liberty Gap June 24-27. Occupation of Middle Tennessee till August 16. Passage of the Cumberland Mountains and Tennessee River and Chickamauga (Ga.) Campaign August 16-September 22. Battle of Chickamauga September 19-20. Siege of Chattanooga September 24-November 23. Battles of Chattanooga November 23-25. Duty in the Defences of Chattanooga till January, 1864. Re-enlisted January 2, 1864, and veterans on furlough January and February. Atlanta (Ga.) Campaign May 1 to September 8. Tunnel Hill May 6-7. Demonstrations on Rocky Faced Ridge May 8-11. Buzzard's Roost Gap May 8-9. Battle of Resaca May 14-15. Rome May 17-18. Advance on Dallas May 18-25. Operations on line of Pumpkin Vine Creek and battles about Dallas, New Hope Church and Allatoona Hills May 25-June 5. Operations about Marietta and against Kenesaw Mountain June 10-July 2. Pine Hill June 11-14. Lost Mountain June 15-17. Assault on Kenesaw June 27. Ruff's Station July 4. Chattahootchie River July 5-17. Peach Tree Creek July 19-20. Siege of Atlanta July 22-August 25. Utoy Creek August 5-7. Flank movement on Jonesboro August 25-30. Battle of Jonesboro August 31-September 1. Operations against Hood in North Georgia and North Alabama September 29-November 3. March to the sea November 15-December 10. Siege of Savannah December 10-21. Campaign of the Carolinas January to April, 1865. Battle of Bentonville, N. C., March 19-21. Occupation of Goldsboro March 24. Advance on Raleigh April 10-14. Occupation of Raleigh April 14. Bennett's House April 26. Surrender of Johnston and his army. March to Washington, D. C., via Richmond, April 29-May 17. Grand Review May 24. Mustered out June 6, 1865.

Battery lost during service 1 Officer and 5 Enlisted men killed and mortally wounded and 1 Officer and 18 Enlisted men by disease. Total 25.

6th INDEPENDENT BATTERY LIGHT ARTILLERY. —("BUENA VISTA ARTILLERY.")

Organized at Racine, Wis., and mustered in October 2, 1861. Moved to St. Louis, Mo., March 15-16, 1862, thence to New Madrid, Mo., March 19-20, and report to Gen. Pope. Attached to Artillery Division, Army of Mississippi, to September, 1862. Artillery, 3rd Division, Army of Mississippi, to November, 1862. Artillery, 7th Division, Left Wing, 13th Army Corps (Old), Dept. of the Tennessee, to December, 1862. Artillery, 7th Division, 16th Army Corps, to January, 1863. Artillery, 7th Divi-

sion, 17th Army Corps, to September, 1863. Artillery, 2nd Division, 17th Army Corps, to December, 1863. Artillery, 3rd Division, 15th Army Corps, to November, 1864. Garrison Artillery, Nashville, Tenn., Dept. of the Cumberland, to February, 1865. Artillery Reserve, Chattanooga, Tenn., Dept. of the Cumberland, to July, 1865.

SERVICE.—Duty in the fortifications of New Madrid, Mo., and Island No. 10, Missouri, till May 17, 1862. Moved to Hamburg Landing, Tenn., May 17-23. Siege of Corinth, Miss., May 23-30. Pursuit to Booneville May 30-June 12. Moved to Rienzi and duty there till October 1. Battle of Corinth, Miss., October 3-4. Duty at Corinth, Miss., till November 2. Moved to Grand Junction November 2. Grant's Central Mississippi Campaign November 2, 1862, to January 10, 1863. Moved to Memphis, Tenn., and duty there till March, 1863. Yazoo Pass Expedition and operations against Fort Pemberton and Greenwood March 13-April 5. Moved to Milliken's Bend, La., April 13. Movement on Bruinsburg and turning Grand Gulf April 25-30. Battle of Port Gibson, Miss., May 1 (Reserve). Jones' Cross Roads May 3. Battles of Raymond May 12; Jackson May 14; Champion's Hill May 16. Siege of Vicksburg, Miss., May 18-July 4. Assaults on Vicksburg May 19 and 22. Surrender of Vicksburg July 4 and duty there till September. Ordered to Helena, Ark., September 12, thence to Memphis, Tenn., September 27. March to Chattanooga, Tenn., October 5-November 20. Operations on the Memphis & Charleston Railroad in Alabama October 20-29. Chattanooga-Ringgold Campaign November 23-27. Tunnel Hill November 23-24. Mission Ridge November 25. Duty at Bridgeport, Ala., December 5-22. At Larkinsville, Ala., till January 7, 1864, and at Huntsville, Ala., till June 22. March to Kingston, Ga., June 22-30, and duty there till July 12. Stationed at Etowah River Bridge, near Cartersville, till November 10. Non-veterans mustered out October, 1864. Moved to Chattanooga, Tenn., November 10, thence to Nashville, Tenn., and garrison duty there till February 17, 1865. Battles of Nashville, Tenn., December 15-16, 1864 (not actively engaged). Ordered to Chattanooga February 17, 1865, and duty there till July. Mustered out at Madison, Wis., July 3, 1865.

Battery lost during service 1 Officer and 6 Enlisted men killed and mortally wounded and 22 Enlisted men by disease. Total 29.

7th INDEPENDENT BATTERY LIGHT ARTILLERY.— ("BADGER STATE FLYING ARTILLERY,")

Organized at Racine and mustered in October 4, 1861. Moved to St. Louis, Mo., March 15-16, 1862, thence to New Madrid, Mo., March 19-21. Attached to Artillery Division, Army of Mississippi, to July, 1862. Artillery, District of Columbus, Ky., Dept. of the Tennessee, to November, 1862. Artillery, District of Columbus, Ky., 13th Army Corps (Old), Dept. of the Tennessee, to December, 1862. Artillery, District of Jackson, Tenn., 16th Army Corps, to March, 1863. Artillery, 3rd Division, 16th Army Corps, to July, 1863. 4th Brigade, District of Memphis, Tenn., 5th Division, 16th Army Corps, to January, 1864. Artillery, District of Memphis, Tenn., 16th Army Corps, to June, 1864. 2nd Brigade, Cavalry Division, Sturgis' Expedition, June, 1864. 2nd Brigade, Memphis, Tenn., District of West Tennessee, to September, 1864. Unattached, District of Memphis, to December, 1864. Unattached, Artillery Reserve, District of West Tennessee, to July, 1865.

SERVICE.—Duty in the fortifications of New Madrid, Mo., and Island No. 10, Missouri, till June, 1862. Ordered to Union City, Tenn., June 13. Assigned to duty as railroad guard on Mobile & Ohio Railroad at Trenton and Humboldt, Tenn., till December. Action at Trenton and Humboldt December 20 (Detachments). Operations against Forest in West Tennessee December 18, 1862, to January 3, 1863. Action at Parker's Cross Roads December 30, 1862. Engagement at Red Mound or Parker's Cross Roads December 31. Moved to Jackson, Tenn., and duty there till June, 1863. At Corinth, Miss., till July 1. Moved to Memphis, Tenn., and garrison duty there till July, 1865. Sturgis' Expedition to Guntown,

Miss., June 1-13, 1864. Battle of Brice's or Tishamingo Creek, near Guntown, June 10. Repulse of Forest's attack on Memphis August 21, 1864. Mustered out July 6 and honorably discharged July 20, 1865.

Battery lost during service 1 Officer and 9 Enlisted men killed and mortally wounded and 19 Enlisted men by disease. Total 29.

8th INDEPENDENT BATTERY LIGHT ARTILLERY. —("LYONS' PINERY BATTERY.")

Organized at Racine and mustered in January 8, 1862. Ordered to St. Louis, Mo., March 18, and duty at Benton Barracks till April 4. Moved to Fort Leavenworth, Kansas, April 4, and attached to Dept. of Kansas to June, 1862. Artillery, 4th Division, Army of Mississippi, to August, 1862. Artillery, 2nd Division, Army of Mississippi, to September, 1862. 32nd Brigade, 9th Division, Army of the Ohio, September, 1862. 32nd Brigade, 9th Division, 3rd Corps, Army of the Ohio, to November, 1862. 3rd Brigade, 1st Division, Right Wing 14th Army Corps, Army of the Cumberland, to January, 1863. Artillery, 1st Division, 20th Army Corps, Army of the Cumberland, to October, 1863. 2nd Division, Artillery Reserve, Dept. of the Cumberland, to April, 1864. Post of Murfreesboro, Tenn., Dept. of the Cumberland, to July, 1864. 1st Brigade, Defences of Nashville and Chattanooga Railroad, Dept. of the Cumberland, to March, 1865. 1st Brigade, 1st Sub-District, District of Middle Tennessee, Dept. of the Cumberland, to August, 1865.

SERVICE.—March to Fort Scott with Lane's Southwestern Expedition April, 1862, thence to Fort Riley, Kansas, and return to Fort Leavenworth, Kansas. Moved to Columbus, Ky., May 10-June 4. Moved to Humboldt, Tenn., and guard duty on Mobile & Ohio Railroad till July. Movement to Corinth, Miss., thence to Iuka, Miss., July 9-August 14. Expedition from Jacinto to Bay Springs and skirmish August 4-7. Battle of Iuka, Miss., September 19 (Centre Section). Battle of Corinth, Miss., October 3-4 (Centre Section). Battery ordered to Nashville, Tenn., August 29-September 3. March to Nashville, Tenn., in pursuit of Bragg September 6-26. Pursuit of Bragg to Crab Orchard, Ky., October 2-16. Battle of Perryville October 8. Stanford, Ky., October 14. March to Bowling Green, Ky., thence to Nashville, Tenn., October 16-November 12. Tyree Springs November 7. Duty at Nashville till December 26. Action near Brentwood December 9. Advance on Murfreesboro December 26-30. Nolensville December 26-27. Battle of Stone's River December 30-31, 1862, and January 1-3, 1863. Duty at Murfreesboro till June. Reconnoissance from Salem to Versailles March 9-14. Operations on Edgefield Pike June 4. Middle Tennessee (or Tallahoma) Campaign June 23-July 7. Liberty Gap June 24-27. Occupation of Middle Tennessee till August 16. Passage of the Cumberland Mountains and Tennessee River and Chickamauga (Ga.) Campaign August 16-September 22. Battle of Chickamauga September 19-20. Siege of Chattanooga September 24-November 23. Chattanooga-Ringgold Campaign November 23-27. Lookout Mountain November 24. Moved to Nashville, Tenn., December 5, and duty there till March, 1864. Moved to Murfreesboro, Tenn., and garrison duty there till August, 1865. Mustered out August 10, 1865.

Battery lost during service 1 Officer and 1 Enlisted man killed and 26 Enlisted men by disease. Total 28.

9th INDEPENDENT BATTERY LIGHT ARTILLERY.

Organized at Burlington, Wis., and mustered in January 27, 1862. Moved to St. Louis, Mo., March 18-19, thence to Fort Leavenworth, Kansas, April 3. March to Denver City, Colo., via Fort Kearney and Julesburg, April 26-June 2. Right Section moved to Fort Union, N. M., June 3. Left Section moved to Fort Larned June 15 and garrison duty there till December, 1864. Right Section moved to Colorado Territory July 5, 1862, and duty there with Centre Section till April 26, 1864, then moved to Council Grove, Kansas, April 26-May 18, and duty there till August, 1864. Engaged in escorting trains and U. S. mail coaches on the Santa Fe Road. Moved to Fort Riley, Kansas, August, 1864. Action at

Smoky Hill Court House May 16, 1864. Defence of Fort Larned July 17, 18 and 19, 1863 (Left Section). Curtis' Campaign against Price in Missouri and Arkansas October, 1864. Big Blue and State Line October 22. Westport October 23. Engagement on the Marmiton (or Battle of Charlot) October 25. Mine Creek, Little Osage River, October 25. Battery consolidated at Fort Leavenworth, Kansas, December, 1864. Veteran Battery organized January 27, 1865. One section ordered to Fort Scott March 26, and duty there till June 18, then moved to Fort Riley and Fort Zarah. Battery mustered out at Fort Leavenworth, Kansas, September 30, 1865.

Battery lost during service 6 Enlisted men by disease.

10th INDEPENDENT BATTERY LIGHT ARTILLERY.

Organized at New Lisbon, Wis., and mustered in February 10, 1862. At Camp Utley, Racine, Wis., till March 18, 1862. Moved to St. Louis, Mo., March 18-20, and duty at Benton Barracks, Mo., till April 30. Moved to Pittsburg Landing, Tenn., April 30-May 5. Attached to Artillery Division, Army of Mississippi, to July, 1862. Artillery, 1st Division, Army of Mississippi, to September, 1862. Artillery, 13th Division, Army of the Ohio, to November, 1862. Artillery, 4th Division, Centre 14th Army Corps, Army of the Cumberland, to January, 1863. Artillery, 4th Division, 14th Army Corps, Army of the Cumberland, to June, 1863. Artillery, 2nd Division, Reserve Corps, Army of the Cumberland, to October, 1863. Unassigned, Dept. of the Cumberland to November, 1863. 2nd Division, Artillery Reserve, Dept. of the Cumberland, to April, 1864. Artillery, Kilpatrick's 3rd Division, Cavalry Corps, Army of the Cumberland, to November, 1864. Artillery, 3rd Division, Cavalry Corps, Military Division, Mississippi, to April, 1865.

SERVICE.—Advance on and siege of Corinth, Miss., May 5-30, 1862. Pursuit to Booneville May 31-June 6. Duty at Corinth till July 21. Moved to Iuka, Miss., July 21, thence march to Nashville, Tenn., August 12-September 14, and duty there till April 8, 1863. Siege of Nashville September 12-November 7, 1862. Action on Murfreesboro Pike November 6. Escort trains to Stone's River January 2-3, 1863. Battle of Stone's River January 3-5. Railroad guard duty at Brentwood April 3 to June 3. Moved to Nashville June 3, thence to Murfreesboro July 16, and duty there till August 19. Moved to Columbia August 19, thence to Athens August 26, and to Huntsville, Ala., September 1. To Stenson, Ala., September 3. Duty at Caperton's Ferry, Bridgeport, Anderson's Cross Roads and other points guarding line of the Tennessee River till April 27, 1864. Moved to Cleveland, Tenn., April 27, thence to Catoosa Springs and join 3rd Cavalry Division. Atlanta (Ga.) Campaign May to September. Battle of Resaca May 14-15. Gideon's Ferry May 15. Guard duty at Adairsville and Cartersville Ferry till August 3. Moved to Sandtown August 3. Kilpatrick's Raid around Atlanta August 18-22. Flint River August 19. Jonesboro and Lovejoy Station August 20. Flank movement on Jonesboro August 25-30. Red Oak August 28. Flint River Station August 30. Battle of Jonesboro August 31-September 1. Lovejoy Station September 2-6. Glass Bridge September 2. Jonesboro September 7. Operations in North Georgia and North Alabama against Hood September 29-November 3. Camp Creek September 30. Salt Springs October 1. Sweetwater and Noyes Creek October 1-3. Van Wert October 9-10. Silver Creek October 13. March to the sea November 15-December 10. Lovejoy Station November 16. Walnut Creek and East Macon November 20. Griswoldsville November 22. Sylvan Grove November 27. Waynesboro November 27-28. Buckhead Creek and Reynolds' Plantation November 28. Near Louisville November 29. Waynesboro December 4. Siege of Savannah December 10-21. Campaign of the Carolinas January to April, 1865. Near Barnwell, S. C., February 6. Williston February 8. Aiken and Blackville February 11. Gunter's Bridge February 14. Near Himsborough March 3. Phillips' Cross Roads March 4. Monroe's Cross Roads March 10. Scott's Mills, Black River, March 15. Taylor's Hole Creek, Averysboro, March 16. Battle of Bentonville March 19-21. Occupation of Goldsboro March 24. Advance on

Raleigh April 10-14. Non-veterans ordered to Madison, Wis., April 12, and there mustered out April 26. Veterans and recruits attached to 12th Wisconsin Battery April 20, 1865.

Battery lost during service 3 Enlisted men killed and mortally wounded and 25 Enlisted men by disease. Total 28.

11th INDEPENDENT BATTERY LIGHT ARTILLERY.

Organized with 17th Wisconsin Infantry at Madison, Wis., February 22, 1862. Transferred to 1st Illinois Light Artillery as Battery "L" February, 1862. (See Battery "L," 1st Illinois Light Artillery.)

12th INDEPENDENT BATTERY LIGHT ARTILLERY.

Organized at St. Louis, Mo., under authority of Governor Harvey, as a Company for the 1st Missouri Light Artillery, to be known as the 12th Wisconsin Battery February and March, 1862. Moved to Hamburg Landing, Tenn., May 6, 1862. Attached to Artillery Division, Army of Mississippi, to September, 1862. Artillery, 3rd Division, Army of Mississippi, to November, 1862. Artillery, 7th Division, Left Wing, 13th Army Corps (Old), Dept. of the Tennessee, to December, 1862. Artillery, 7th Division, 16th Army Corps, to January, 1863. Artillery, 7th Division, 17th Army Corps, to September, 1863. Artillery, 2nd Division, 17th Army Corps, to December, 1863. Artillery, 3rd Division, 15th Army Corps, to September, 1864. Artillery Brigade, 15th Army Corps, to June, 1865.

SERVICE.—Advance on and siege of Corinth, Miss., May 8-30, 1862. Pursuit to Booneville May 31-June 6. At Camp Clear Creek till August. Ordered to Jacinto August 14. Battle of Iuka, Miss., September 19. Battle of Corinth, Miss., October 3-4. Pursuit to Ripley October 5-12. At Corinth till November 8. Grant's Central Mississippi Campaign. Operations on the Mississippi Central Railroad November, 1862, to January, 1863. Duty at Germantown, Tenn., January 4 to February 8, 1863. Moved to Memphis, Tenn., February 8; thence to Grand Lake, Ark. Yazoo Pass Expedition and operations against Fort Pemberton and Greenwood March 13-April 5. Moved to Milliken's Bend, La., April 16. Movement on Bruinsburg and turning Grand Gulf April 25-30. Battle of Port Gibson, Miss., May 1 (Reserve). Battles of Raymond May 12. Jackson May 14. Champion's Hill May 16. Siege of Vicksburg, Miss., May 18-July 4. Assaults on Vicksburg May 19 and 22. Surrender of Vicksburg July 4. Duty at Vicksburg till September. Moved to Helena, Ark., September 12; thence to Memphis, Tenn., September 27. March to Chattanooga, Tenn., October 6-November 20. Operations on Memphis & Charleston Railroad in Alabama October 20-29. Chattanooga-Ringgold Campaign November 23-27. Tunnel Hill November 24-25. Mission Ridge November 25. Duty at Bridgeport, Ala., till December 22; at Larkinsville till January 7, 1864, and at Huntsville, Ala., till June 22. March to Kingston, Ga., June 22-30, and duty there till July 13. Moved to Allatoona, Ga., July 13, and duty there till November 12. Repulse of French's attack on Allatoona October 6. Reconnoissance from Rome on Cave Springs Road and skirmishes October 12-13. March to the sea November 15-December 10. Siege of Savannah December 10-21. Campaign of the Carolinas January to April, 1865. Combahee River, S. C., January 28. Hickory Hill February 1. South Edisto River February 9. North Edisto River February 12-13. Congaree Creek February 15. Columbia February 16-17. Battle of Bentonville, N. C., March 19-21. Near Falling Creek March 20. Mill Creek March 22. Occupation of Goldsboro March 24. Advance on Raleigh April 10-14. Occupation of Raleigh April 14. Bennett's House April 26. Surrender of Johnston and his army. March to Washington, D. C., via Richmond, Va., April 29-May 20. Grand Review May 24. Mustered out June 26, 1865.

Battery lost during service 1 Officer and 10 Enlisted men killed and mortally wounded and 23 Enlisted men by disease. Total 34.

13th INDEPENDENT BATTERY LIGHT ARTILLERY.

Organized at Milwaukee, Wis., and mustered in December 29, 1863. Moved to New Orleans, La., January 28-February 12, 1864; then to Baton Rouge, La., February 17, and garrison duty there till July, 1865. Mustered out July 20, 1865.

Lost during service 14 by disease.

COMPANY "G" 1st BERDAN SHARPSHOOTERS.

Organized at Camp Randall, Wis. Left State for Wehawken September 19, 1861. Mustered in September 23. Moved to Washington, D. C., September 24-25. Duty in the Defences of Washington till March, 1862. Moved to Fortress Monroe, Va., March 21. (See 1st United States Sharpshooters.)

1st REGIMENT INFANTRY.—(3 MONTHS.)

Organized at Milwaukee, Wis., and mustered into State service April 27, 1861. Mustered into United States service May 17, 1861. Left State for Harrisburg, Pa., June 9. Attached to Abercrombie's 6th Brigade, Negley's 2nd Division, Patterson's Army. Camp at Hagerstown till June 29. Moved to Williamsport, Md., June 29-July 1. Action at Falling Waters July 2. Moved to Martinsburg July 3. Duty at Charlestown, Harper's Ferry and guarding fords of the Monocacy River till August. Edwards' Ferry, Md., July 29. Mustered out August 21, 1861.

1st REGIMENT INFANTRY.—(3 YEARS.)

Organized at Camp Scott, Milwaukee, Wis., and mustered in October 19, 1861. Moved to Louisville, Ky., October 28-31, and duty there till November 14. Attached to Negley's 7th Brigade, Army of the Ohio, to December, 1861. 7th Brigade, 2nd Division, Army of the Ohio, to February, 1862. Negley's 7th Independent Brigade, Army of the Ohio, to August, 1862. 28th Brigade, 3rd Division, Army of the Ohio, to September, 1862. 28th Brigade, 3rd Division, 1st Army Corps, Army of the Ohio, to November, 1862. 3rd Brigade, 1st Division (Centre), 14th Army Corps, Army of the Cumberland, to January, 1863. 3rd Brigade, 1st Division, 14th Army Corps, Army of the Cumberland, to April, 1863. 2nd Brigade, 1st Division, 14th Army Corps, to October, 1863. 3rd Brigade, 1st Division, 14th Army Corps, to October, 1864.

SERVICE.—Ordered to West Point, Ky., November 14, 1861; thence to Elizabethtown, Ky., December 3, and to Bacon Creek December 11. Moved to Munfordsville, Ky., December 17, and duty at Camp Wood till February, 1862. Advance on Bowling Green, Ky., and Nashville, Tenn., February 14-March 3. Duty at Nashville till March 29. Action on Granny White Pike, near Nashville, March 8. Moved to Columbia March 29-April 2. Moved to Bigley's Creek, and duty guarding railroad at bridges till May 3. Rogersville May 13. Expedition to Chattanooga May 28-June 17 (Cos. "A," "B," "G" and "K"). Chattanooga June 7-8. Moved to Huntsville, Ala., and duty there till August. (Part of Regiment at Columbia and Mooresville till August 18.) March to Nashville, Tenn., thence to Louisville, Ky., in pursuit of Bragg August 18-September 26. Pursuit of Bragg to Crab Orchard, Ky., October 1-16. Battle of Perryville, Ky., October 8. Guard duty at Mitchellsville till December 7. Advance on Murfreesboro December 26-30. Jefferson December 30. Battle of Stone's River December 30-31, 1862, and January 1-3, 1863. Duty at Murfreesboro till June. Expedition to McMinnville April 20-30. Middle Tennessee (or Tullahoma) Campaign June 23-July 7. Hoover's Gap June 24-26. Jones' Ford July 2. Occupation of Middle Tennessee till August 16. Passage of the Cumberland Mountains and Tennessee River and Chickamauga (Ga.) Campaign August 16-September 22. Davis Cross Roads, near Dug Gap, September 11. Battle of Chickamauga September 19-21. Rossville Gap September 21. Siege of Chattanooga September 24-November 23. Chattanooga-Ringgold Campaign November 23-27. Orchard Knob November 23-24. Mission Ridge November 25. Reconnoissance to Cooper's Gap November 30-December 3. Scout to Harrison and Ootlewah January 21, 1864 (Detachment). Demonstration on Dalton, Ga., February 22-27, 1864. Tunnel Hill, Buzzard's Roost Gap and Rocky Faced Ridge February 23-25. Atlanta (Ga.) Campaign May 1 to September 8. Demonstrations on Rocky Faced Ridge May 8-11. Battle of Resaca May 14-15. Advance on Dallas May 18-25. Operations on line of Pumpkin Vine Creek and battles about Dallas, New Hope Church and Allatoona Hills May 25-June 5. Pickett's Mills May 27. Operations about Marietta and against Kenesaw Mountain June 10-July 2. Pine Hill June 11-14. Lost Mountain June 15-17. Assault on Kenesaw June 27. Ruff's Station July 4. Chattahoochie River July 5-17. Peach Tree Creek July 19-20. Siege of Atlanta July 22-August 25. Utoy Creek August 5-7. Flank movement on Jonesboro August 25-30. Battle of Jonesboro August 31-September 1. Non-Veterans ordered to Nashville, Tenn., September 21. Veterans and Recruits transferred to 21st Wisconsin Infantry. Regiment mustered out October 13, 1864.

Regiment lost during service 6 Officers and 151 Enlisted men killed and mortally wounded and 1 Officer and 142 Enlisted men by disease. Total 300.

2nd REGIMENT INFANTRY.

Organized at Madison, Wis., and mustered in June 11, 1861. Moved to Washington, D. C., June 20-25. Attached to Sherman's Brigade, Tyler's Division, McDowell's Army of Northeast Virginia, to August, 1861. Fort Corcoran, Division of the Potomac, to October, 1861. King's Brigade, McDowell's Division, Army of the Potomac, to March, 1862. 3rd Brigade, 3rd Division, 1st Army Corps, Army of the Potomac, to April, 1862. 3rd Brigade, King's Division, Dept. of the Rappahannock, to June, 1862. 4th Brigade, 1st Division, 3rd Army Corps, Army of Virginia, to September, 1862. 4th Brigade, 1st Division, 1st Army Corps, Army of the Potomac, to June, 1863. 1st Brigade, 1st Division, 1st Army Corps, to March, 1864. 1st Brigade, 4th Division, 5th Army Corps, to August, 1864. 3rd Brigade, 3rd Division, 5th Army Corps, to September, 1864. 1st Brigade, 3rd Division, 5th Army Corps, to October, 1864.

SERVICE.—Advance on Manassas, Va., July 16-21, 1861. Occupation of Fairfax Court House July 17. Action at Blackburn's Ford July 18. Battle of Bull Run July 21. Duty at Fort Corcoran, Defences of Washington, D. C., till August 27. Camp at Meridian Hill and duty at Fort Tillinghast till March, 1862. Reconnoissance to Lewinsville, Va., September 25, 1861. (Co. "K" transferred to 1st Wisconsin Heavy Artillery December 9, 1861. A new Co. "K" organized December 20, 1861.) Advance on Manassas, Va., March 10-16, 1862. Advance to Falmouth March 18-April 23. Woodstock April 1. McDowell's advance on Richmond May 25-29. Operations against Jackson June 2-11. Reconnoissance to Orange Court House July 24-26. Expedition to Frederick's Hall Station and Spottsylvania Court House August 5-8. Thornburg's Mills or Massapona Church August 5-6. Pope's Campaign in Northern Virginia August 16-September 2. Fords of the Rappahannock August 21-23. Catlett's Station August 21. Gainesville August 28. Battles of Groveton August 29. Bull Run August 30. Chantilly September 1 (Reserve). Maryland Campaign September 6-22. Battles of South Mountain, Md., September 14, and Antietam, Md., September 16-17. At Sharpsburg, Md., till October 30. Advance to Falmouth, Va., October 30-November 22. Battle of Fredericksburg, Va., December 12-15. "Mud March" January 20-24, 1863. At Belle Plains till April 27. Expedition from Belle Plains into Westmoreland County March 25-29. Chancellorsville Campaign April 27-May 6. Operations at Pollock's Mill Creek April 29-May 2. Fitzhugh's Crossing April 29-30. Battle of Chancellorsville May 2-5. Operations on Northern Neck May 20-26. Brandy Station and Beverly Ford June 9. Gettysburg (Pa.) Campaign June 11-July 24. Battle of Gettysburg, Pa., July 1-3. Pursuit of Lee to Manassas Gap, Va., July 5-24. Duty on line of the Rappahannock and Rapidan till October. Bristoe Campaign October

9-22. Haymarket October 19. Advance to line of the Rappahannock November 7-8. Mine Run Campaign November 26-December 2. Campaign from the Rapidan to the James River May 3-June 15, 1864. Battles of the Wilderness May 5-7; Laurel Hill May 8; Spottsylvania May 8-12. Detached from Brigade May 11 and assigned to duty as Provost Guard, 4th Division, 5th Army Corps. Spottsylvania Court House May 12-21. Assault on the Salient May 12. North Anna River May 23-26. On line of the Pamunkey May 26-28. Totopotomoy May 28-31. Cold Harbor June 1-12. Non-Veterans ordered to Madison, Wis., June 11, and there mustered out July 2, 1864. Veterans and Recruits consolidated to a Battalion of two Companies and assigned to duty as Provost Guard at Headquarters, 4th Division, 5th Army Corps, till September. Before Petersburg June 16-18. Siege of Petersburg June 16 to November 30. Weldon Railroad August 18-21. Boydton Plank Road, Hatcher's Run, October 27-28. Battalion consolidated with 6th Wisconsin Infantry as Companies "G" and "H" November 30, 1864.

Regiment lost during service 10 Officers and 228 Enlisted men killed and mortally wounded and 77 Enlisted men by disease. Total 315.

3rd REGIMENT INFANTRY.

Organized at Fond du Lac, Wis., and mustered in June 19, 1861. Ordered to Hagerstown, Md., July 12; thence to Harper's Ferry, W. Va., July 18. Attached to Hamilton's Brigade, Patterson's Army, to October, 1861. Stiles' Brigade, Banks' Division, Army of the Potomac, to March, 1862. 3rd Brigade, 1st Division, Banks' 5th Army Corps, to April, 1862. 3rd Brigade, 1st Division, Dept. of the Shenandoah, to June, 1862. 3rd Brigade, 1st Division, 2nd Corps, Army of Virginia, to September, 1862. 3rd Brigade, 1st Division, 12th Army Corps, Army of the Potomac, to October, 1863, and Army of the Cumberland, to April, 1864. 2nd Brigade, 1st Division, 20th Army Corps, Army of the Cumberland, to July, 1865.

SERVICE.—Moved to Darnestown August 18, 1861; thence to Frederick, Md., September 12, and duty there till February 25, 1862. Action at Harper's Ferry, W. Va., October 11, 1861 (Cos. "A," "C" and "H"). Bolivar Heights October 16 (Cos. "A," "C" and "H"). March to Sandy Hook February 25, 1862. Occupation of Winchester, Va., March 12. Advance toward Manassas March 22-25. Battle of Winchester March 23 (Co. "A"). Advance from Strasburg to Woodstock and Edenburg April 1-2. Edenburg April 1-2. Operations in the Shenandoah Valley till June 17. Buckton Station May 23 (Co. "G"). Middletown and Newtown May 24. Winchester May 25. Retreat to Martinsburg May 26-June 6. Duty at Front Royal till July 6, and at Little Washington till August 6. Battle of Cedar Mountain August 9. Pope's Campaign in Northern Virginia August 16-September 2. Guard trains of the army during Battles of Manassas August 27-30. Maryland Campaign September 6-22. Battle of Antietam September 16-17. Duty at Maryland Heights till October 30, and in the Defences of the Upper Potomac at Antietam Iron Works till December 10. March to Fairfax Station and duty there till January 3, 1863. Moved to Stafford Court House January 18, and duty there till April 27. Chancellorsville Campaign April 27-May 6. Germania Ford April 29. Battle of Chancellorsville May 1-5. Brandy Station and Beverly Ford June 9. Gettysburg (Pa.) Campaign June 11-July 24. Battle of Gettysburg July 1-3. Pursuit of Lee to Manassas Gap, Va., July 5-24. Duty in New York during draft disturbances August 16-September 5. Movement to Bridgeport, Ala., September 24-October 3. At Stevenson, Ala., and Decherd, Tenn., guarding railroad till December. Regiment veteranized December 21, 1863. Veterans on furlough December 25, 1863, to February 9, 1864. At Fayetteville, Tenn., till April 28. Atlanta (Ga.) Campaign May 1 to September 8. Demonstrations on Rocky Faced Ridge May 8-11. Battle of Resaca May 14-15. Cassville May 19. New Hope Church May 25. Operations on line of Pumpkin Vine Creek and battles about Dallas, New Hope Church and Allatoona Hills May 25-June 5. Operations about Marietta and against Kenesaw Mountain June 10-July 2. Pine Hill June 11-14. Lost Mountain June 15-17. Gilgal or Golgotha Church June 15. Muddy Creek June 17. Noyes Creek June 19. Kolb's Farm June 22. Assault on Kenesaw Mountain June 27. Ruff's Station July 4. Chattahoochie River July 5-17. Peach Tree Creek July 19-20. Siege of Atlanta July 22-August 25. Operations at Chattahoochie River Bridge August 26-September 2. Occupation of Atlanta September 2-November 15. March to the sea November 15-December 10. Montieth Swamp December 9. Siege of Savannah December 10-21. Campaign of the Carolinas January to April, 1865. Robertsville, S. C., January 29. Taylor's Hole Creek, Aversyboro, N. C., March 16. Battle of Bentonville March 19-21. Occupation of Goldsboro March 24. Advance on Raleigh April 10-14. Occupation of Raleigh April 14. Bennett's House April 26. Surrender of Johnston and his army. March to Washington, D. C., via Richmond, Va., April 29-May 19. Grand Review May 24. Moved to Louisville, Ky., June 11-16, and there mustered out July 18, 1865.

Regiment lost during service 9 Officers and 158 Enlisted men killed and mortally wounded and 2 Officers and 113 Enlisted men by disease. Total 282.

4th REGIMENT INFANTRY.

Organized at Racine, Wis., and mustered in July 2, 1861. Moved to Baltimore, Md., July 15-22. Designation changed to 4th Wisconsin Cavalry August 22, 1863. Service given under 4th Regiment Cavalry (which see).

5th REGIMENT INFANTRY.

Organized at Madison, Wis., and mustered in July 12, 1861. Ordered to Washington, D. C., July 24. Attached to King's Brigade, McDowell's Division, Army of the Potomac, to October, 1861. Hancock's Brigade, Smith's Division, Army of the Potomac, to March, 1862. 1st Brigade, 2nd Division, 4th Army Corps, Army of the Potomac, to May, 1862. 1st Brigade, 2nd Division, 6th Army Corps, Army of the Potomac, to February, 1863. Light Division, 6th Army Corps, to May, 1863. 3rd Brigade, 1st Division, 6th Army Corps, to January, 1864. 3rd Brigade, 2nd Division, 6th Army Corps, to February, 1864. 3rd Brigade, 1st Division, 6th Army Corps, Army of the Potomac, to August. Army of the Shenandoah, Middle Military Division, to December, 1864, and Army of the Potomac to July, 1865.

SERVICE.—Camp on Meridian Hill till September 3, 1861. Detached to construct Fort Marcy on north bank of the Potomac. At Camp Griffin, near Washington, D. C., till March 9, 1862. Lewinsville, Va., September 10, 1861. (Cos. "B," "C" and "G"). Reconnoissance to Lewinsville September 25. March to Flint Hill March 9, 1862, thence to near Alexandria March 16, and moved to Fortress Monroe March 23-25. Reconnoissance to Warwick Court House March 27. Advance from Newport News to Warwick River and toward Yorktown April 4-5. Siege of Yorktown April 5-May 4. Reconnoissance toward Yorktown April 16. Lee's Mills, Burnt Chimneys, April 16. Battle of Williamsburg May 5. Duty at White House till May 18. March to near Richmond May 24 and picket duty on the Chickahominy till June 5. Seven days before Richmond June 25-July 1. Garnett's Farm June 27. Savage Station June 29. White Oak Swamp and Glendale June 30. Malvern Hill July 1. At Harrison's Landing till August 16. Moved to Alexandria August 16-24, thence march to Centreville August 29-30. Maryland Campaign September 6-22. Sugar Loaf Mountain September 10-11. Crampton's Pass, South Mountain, September 14. Battle of Antietam September 16-17. At Williamsport September 18-22. Expedition to intercept Stuart's Cavalry October 11. At Hagerstown October 13-31. March to Aquia Creek November 3-18. Battle of Fredericksburg, Va., December 12-15. At White Oak Church till April, 1863. "Mud March" January 20-24. Chancellorsville Campaign April

27-May 6. Operations about Franklin's Crossing April 29-May 2. Maryes Heights, Fredericksburg, May 3. Salem Heights May 3-4. Banks' Ford May 4. Gettysburg (Pa.) Campaign June 11-July 24. Battle of Gettysburg, Pa., July 2-4. Near Fairfield, Pa., July 5. About Funkstown, Md., July 10-13. Detached duty at New York, Albany and Troy August-September during draft disturbances. Bristoe Campaign October 9-22. Advance to line of the Rappahannock November 7-8. Rappahannock Station November 7. Mine Run Campaign November 26-December 2. Duty at Brandy Station till April, 1864. Campaign from the Rapidan to the James River May 4-June 15. Battles of the Wilderness May 5-7; Spottsylvania May 8-12; Spottsylvania Court House May 12-21. Assault on the Salient, "Bloody Angle," May 12. North Anna River May 23-26. On line of the Pamunkey May 26-28. Totopotomoy May 28-31. Cold Harbor June 1-12. Before Petersburg June 17-18. Siege of Petersburg till July 9. Weldon Railroad June 22-23. Moved to Washington, D. C., July 9-12. Repulse of Early's attack on Washington July 12. Non-veterans ordered to Wisconsin July 16 and mustered out August 3, 1864. Veterans consolidated to a Battalion of three Companies. Sheridan's Shenandoah Valley Campaign August 7-November 28. Battle of Opequan, Winchester, September 19. Provost duty at Winchester, Va., and at Cedar Creek, Va., till December. Seven new companies organized September, 1864, and left State for Winchester, Va., October 2. At Alexandria till October 20, then joined Regiment at Cedar Creek. Moved to Petersburg, Va., October 1-4. Siege of Petersburg December 4, 1864, to April 2, 1865. Dabney's Mills, Hatcher's Run, February 5-7, 1865. Appomattox Campaign March 28-April 9. Assault on and fall of Petersburg April 2. Pursuit of Lee April 3-9. Sailor's Creek April 6. Appomattox Court House April 9. Surrender of Lee and his army. March to Danville April 23-27, thence to Richmond, Va., and Washington, D. C., May 18-June 2. Corps Review June 8. Mustered out June 24 (three Companies) and July 11, 1865 (Regiment).

Regiment lost during service 15 Officers and 180 Enlisted men killed and mortally wounded and 2 Officers and 132 Enlisted men by disease. Total 329.

6th REGIMENT INFANTRY.

Organized at Camp Randall, Madison, Wis., and mustered in July 16, 1861. Left State for Washington, D. C., July 28. At Harrisburg, Pa., till August 3, then moved to Washington. Attached to King's Brigade, McDowell's Division, Army of the Potomac, to March, 1862. 1st Brigade, 3rd Division, 1st Army Corps, Army of the Potomac, to April, 1862. 3rd Brigade, King's Division, Dept. of the Rappahannock, to June, 1862. 4th Brigade, 1st Division, 3rd Army Corps, Army of Virginia, to September, 1862. 4th Brigade, 1st Division, 1st Army Corps, Army of the Potomac, to June, 1863. 1st Brigade, 1st Division, 1st Army Corps, to March, 1864. 1st Brigade, 4th Division, 5th Army Corps, to August, 1864. 3rd Brigade, 3rd Division, 5th Army Corps, to September, 1864. 1st Brigade, 3rd Division, 5th Army Corps, to July, 1865.

SERVICE.—Camp on Meridian Hill and duty in the Defences of Washington, D. C., till March, 1862. Advance on Manassas, Va., March 10-16. Advance to Falmouth April 9-19. Duty at Falmouth and Fredericksburg till August. McDowell's advance on Richmond March 25-29. Operations against Jackson June 2-11. Reconnoissance to Orange Court House July 27. Reconnoissance to Frederick's Hall Station and Spottsylvania Court House August 5-8. Thornburg's Mills (or Massaponax Church) August 5-6. Battle of Cedar Mountain August 9. Pope's Campaign in Northern Virginia August 16-September 2. Fords of the Rappahannock August 21-23. Action at Gainesville August 28. Battles of Groveton August 29; Bull Run August 30; Chantilly September 1 (Reserve). Maryland Campaign September 6-22. Battles of South Mountain, Md., September 14; Antietam September 16-17. At Sharpsburg till October 30. Advance to Falmouth, Va., October 30-November 22. Battle of Fredericksburg December 12-15. "Mud March" January 20-24, 1863. At Belle Plain till April 27. Expedition to Heathville February 12-14. Chancellorsville Campaign April 27-May 6. Operations at Pollock's Mill Creek April 29-May 2. Fitzhugh's Crossing April 29-30. Battle of Chancellorsville May 2-5. Gettysburg (Pa.) Campaign June 11-July 24. Battle of Gettysburg, Pa., July 1-3. Pursuit of Lee to Manassas Gap, Va., July 5-24. Duty on line of the Rappahannock and Rapidan till October. Bristoe Campaign October 9-22. Haymarket October 19. Advance to line of the Rappahannock November 7-8. Mine Run Campaign November 26-December 2. Campaign from the Rapidan to the James River May 4-June 15, 1864. Battles of the Wilderness May 5-7; Laurel Hill May 8; Spottsylvania May 8-12; Spottsylvania Court House May 12-21. Assault on the Salient, "Bloody Angle," May 12. North Anna River May 23-26. Jericho Ford May 23. On line of the Totopotomoy May 28-31. Cold Harbor June 1-12. Bethesda Church June 1-3. Before Petersburg June 16-18. Siege of Petersburg June 16, 1864, to April 2, 1865. Weldon Railroad August 18-21, 1864. Boydton Road, Hatcher's Run, October 27-28. Dabney's Mills, Hatcher's Run, February 5-7, 1865. Appomattox Campaign March 28-April 9. Lewis Farm, near Gravelly Run, March 29. Boydton and White Oak Roads March 30-31. Five Forks April 1. Fall of Petersburg April 2. Pursuit of Lee April 3-9. Appomattox Court House April 9. Surrender of Lee and his army. March to Washington, D. C., May. Grand Review May 23. Moved to Louisville, Ky., June 17. Mustered out July 2, 1865.

Regiment lost during service 16 Officers and 228 Enlisted men killed and mortally wounded and 1 Officer and 112 Enlisted men by disease. Total 357.

7th REGIMENT INFANTRY.

Organized at Madison, Wis., and mustered in September 2, 1861. Left State for Washington, D. C., September 21. Attached to King's Brigade, McDowell's Division, Army of the Potomac, to March, 1862. 1st Brigade, 3rd Division, 1st Army Corps, Army of the Potomac, to April, 1862. 3rd Brigade, King's Division, Dept. of the Rappahannock, to June, 1862. 4th Brigade, 1st Division, 3rd Army Corps, Army of Virginia, to September, 1862. 4th Brigade, 1st Division, 1st Army Corps, Army of the Potomac, to June, 1863. 1st Brigade, 1st Division, 1st Army Corps, to March, 1864. 1st Brigade, 4th Division, 5th Army Corps, to August, 1864. 3rd Brigade, 3rd Division, 5th Army Corps, to September, 1864. 1st Brigade, 3rd Division, 5th Army Corps, to July, 1865.

SERVICE.—Duty in the Defences of Washington, D. C., till March, 1862. Advance on Manassas, Va., March 10-16. Advance to Falmouth, Va., April 9-19. Duty at Falmouth and Fredericksburg till August. McDowell's advance on Richmond May 25-29. Operations against Jackson June 2-11. Reconnoissance to Orange Court House July 24-27. Expedition to Frederick's Hall Station and Spottsylvania Court House August 5-8. Thornburg's Mills or Massaponax Church August 5-6. Battle of Cedar Mountain August 9. Pope's Campaign in Northern Virginia August 16-September 2. Fords of the Rappahannock August 21-23. Catlett's Station August 22. Gainesville August 28. Battles of Groveton August 29; Bull Run August 30; Chantilly September 1 (Reserve). Maryland Campaign September 6-22. Battles of South Mountain September 14; Antietam September 16-17. At Sharpsburg, Md., to October 30. Movement to Falmouth, Va., October 30-November 22. Battle of Fredericksburg, Va., December 12-15. "Mud March" January 20-24, 1863. At Belle Plain till April 27. Chancellorsville Campaign April 27-May 6. Operations at Pollock's Mill Creek April 29-May 2. Fitzhugh's Crossing April 29-30. Battle of Chancellorsville May 2-5. Gettysburg (Pa.) Campaign June 11-July 24. Battle of Gettysburg July 1-3. Pursuit of Lee to Manassas Gap, Va., July 5-24. Duty on line of the Rappahannock and Rapidan till October. Bristoe Campaign October 9-22. Haymarket October 19. Advance to line of the Rappahannock November 7-8. Mine Run Campaign November 26-December 2. Cam-

paign from the Rapidan to the James River May 4-June 15, 1864. Battles of the Wilderness May 5-7; Laurel Hill May 8; Spottsylvania May 8-12; Spottsylvania Court House May 12-21. Assault on the Salient, "Bloody Angle," May 12. North Anna River May 23-26. Jericho Ford May 23. On line of the Pamunkey May 26-28. Totopotomoy May 28-31. Cold Harbor June 1-12. Bethesda Church June 1-3. Before Petersburg June 16-18. Siege of Petersburg June 16, 1864, to April 2, 1865. Weldon Railroad August 18-21, 1864. Boydton Plank Road, Hatcher's Run, October 27-28. Dabney's Mills, Hatcher's Run, February 5-7, 1865. Appomattox Campaign March 28-April 9. Lewis Farm, near Gravelly Run, March 28. Boydton and White Oak Roads March 30-31. Five Forks April 1. Fall of Petersburg April 2. Appomattox Court House April 9. Surrender of Lee and his army. Moved to Washington. D. C., May. Grand Review May 23. Moved to Louisville, Ky., June 16 and mustered out July 2, 1865.

Regiment lost during service 10 Officers and 271 Enlisted men killed and mortally wounded and 143 Enlisted men by disease. Total 424.

8th REGIMENT INFANTRY.

Organized at Madison, Wis., and mustered in September 13, 1861. Left State for St. Louis, Mo., October 12; thence moved to Pilot Knob, Mo., October 14. Expedition to Fredericktown October 17-21. Action at Fredericktown October 21. Expedition against Thompson's Forces November 2-15. Moved to Sulphur Springs November 25, and duty there till January 17, 1862. Moved to Cairo, Ill., January 17, and duty there till March 4. (Co. "K" detached at Mound City till April. Rejoined Regiment April 14, 1862.) Attached to 3rd Brigade, District of Cairo, Ill., January to March, 1862. 1st Brigade, 5th Division, Army of Mississippi, to April, 1862. 1st Brigade, 3rd Division, Army of the Mississippi, to April, 1862. 2nd Brigade, 2nd Division, Army of the Mississippi, to November, 1862. 2nd Brigade, 8th Division, Left Wing 13th Army Corps (Old), Dept. of the Tennessee, to December, 1862. 2nd Brigade, 8th Division, 16th Army Corps, to April, 1863. 2nd Brigade, 3rd Division, 15th Army Corps, to December, 1863. 2nd Brigade, 1st Division, 16th Army Corps, to December, 1864. 2nd Brigade, 1st Division Detachment, Army of the Tennessee, Dept. of the Cumberland, to February, 1865. 2nd Brigade, 1st Division, 16th Army Corps (New), Military Division West Mississippi, to September, 1865.

SERVICE.—Operations against New Madrid, Mo., March 6-14, 1862. Siege and capture of Island No. 10, Mississippi River, March 15-April 8. Expedition to Fort Pillow, Tenn., April 13-17. Moved to Hamburg Landing, Tenn., April 18-22. Advance on and siege of Corinth, Miss., April 29-May 30. Reconnoissance toward Corinth May 8. Action at Farmington May 9. Occupation of Corinth and pursuit to Booneville May 30-June 12. Expedition to Rienzi June 30-July 1. At Camp Clear Creek till August. March to Tuscumbia, Ala., March 18-22. March to Iuka September 8-12. Actions near Iuka September 13-14. Battle of Iuka September 19. Battle of Corinth, Miss., October 3-4. Pursuit to Ripley October 5-12. Duty at Corinth till November 2. Moved to Grand Junction November 2. Grant's Central Mississippi Campaign. Operations on the Mississippi Central Railroad November 2, 1862, to January 10, 1863. Duty at LaGrange and Germantown, Tenn., January to March, 1863. Moved to Memphis, Tenn., March 14; thence to Young's Point, La., March 29. At Ducksport till May. Movement to join army in rear of Vicksburg, Miss., via Richmond and Grand Gulf May 2-14. Mississippi Springs May 13. Jackson May 14. Siege of Vicksburg, Miss., May 18-July 4. Assaults on Vicksburg May 19 and 22. Expedition to Mechanicsburg and Satartia June 2-8. Mechanicsburg, Satartia, June 4. Expedition to Richmond June 14-16. Richmond June 15. Advance on Jackson, Miss., July 4-10. Siege of Jackson July 10-17. Camp at Bear Creek till September 26. Expedition to Canton October 14-20.

Bogue Chitto Creek October 17. At Big Black River Bridge till November 7. Moved to Memphis, Tenn., November 7-13. Duty there, at LaGrange and at Salisbury till January 27, 1864. Expedition to Pocahontas December 2-4, 1863. Moved to Vicksburg, Miss., January 27-February 3. Meridian Campaign February 3-March 2. Red River Campaign March 10-May 22. Fort DeRussy March 14. Occupation of Alexandria March 16. Henderson's Hill March 21. Battle of Pleasant Hill April 9. About Cloutiersville April 22-24. At Alexandria April 26-May 13. Retreat to Morganza May 13-20. Mansura May 16. Yellow Bayou May 18. Moved to Vicksburg, Miss., May 20-22; thence moved to Memphis, Tenn. Old River Lake or Lake Chicot, Ark., June 6. Smith's Expedition to Tupelo, Miss., July 5-21. Camargo's Cross Roads, near Harrisburg, July 13. Tupelo July 14-15. Smith's Expedition to Oxford, Miss., August 1-30. Abbeville August 23 and 25. Expedition up White River to Brownsville, Ark., September 1-10. Pursuit of Price through Arkansas and Missouri September 17-November 16. Moved to Nashville, Tenn., November 23-December 1. Battle of Nashville December 15-16. Pursuit of Hood to the Tennessee River December 17-28. Moved to Clifton, Tenn., thence to Eastport, Miss., and duty there till February, 1865. Moved to New Orleans, La., February 6-19. Campaign against Mobile and its Defences March 17-April 12. Siege of Spanish Fort and Fort Blakely March 26-April 8. Assault and capture of Fort Blakely April 9. Occupation of Mobile April 12. March to Montgomery April 13-25. Duty at Montgomery and Uniontown till September. Mustered out at Demopolis, Ala., September 5, 1865.

Regiment lost during service 6 Officers and 53 Enlisted men killed and mortally wounded and 2 Officers and 219 Enlisted men by disease. Total 280.

9th REGIMENT INFANTRY.

Organized at Milwaukee, Wis., and mustered in October 26, 1861. Ordered to Fort Leavenworth, Kansas, January 22, 1862. Attached to Dept. of Kansas to August, 1862. 1st Brigade, Dept. of Kansas, to October, 1862. 1st Brigade, 1st Division, Army of the Frontier, Dept. of Missouri, to June, 1863. District of Rolla and District of St. Louis, Mo., Dept. of Missouri, to August, 1863. 2nd Brigade, 3rd Division, Arkansas Expedition, to January, 1864. 2nd Brigade, 3rd Division, 7th Army Corps, Dept. of Arkansas, to March, 1864. 1st Brigade, 3rd Division, 7th Army Corps, to May, 1864. 1st Brigade, 1st Division, 7th Army Corps, to August, 1865. Dept. of Arkansas to January, 1866.

SERVICE.—March to Fort Scott, Kansas, March 1-7, 1862, and duty there till May 27. (Cos. "A," "C," "F" and "K" at Carthage May 1-17.) March to Spring River May 27-June 6, thence to Baxter Springs June 13, and duty there till June 28. Expedition into Indian Country; march to Fort Gibson June 28-July 9, thence to Fort Scott July 10-August 11. March to Sarcoxie, Mo., September 18-22. Action at Newtonia September 30. Occupation of Newtonia October 4. Cane Hill November 28. Battle of Prairie Grove December 7. Expedition over Boston Mountains to Van Buren December 27-29. Guard and patrol duty at various points in Missouri till July, 1863. Ordered to St. Louis, Mo., July 8, and duty there till September 12. Ordered to Helena, Ark., September 12; thence moved to Little Rock October 10-22, and duty there till March, 1864. Reconnoissance to Burton October 26-November 1, 1863. Steele's Expedition to Camden March 23-May 3. Antoine or Terre Noir Creek April 2. Elkins' Ferry, Little Missouri River, April 3-4. Prairie D'Ann April 9-12. Jenkins' Ferry and Camden April 15. Liberty Postoffice April 15-16. Camden April 16-18. Evacuation of Camden April 26. Jenkins' Ferry April 30. Duty at Little Rock till June, 1865. Non-Veterans mustered out November 17, 1864. Veterans and Recruits consolidated to a Battalion of four Companies and moved to Camden June 15, 1865, and duty there till August 3. Duty at Little Rock till January, 1866. Mustered out January 30, 1866.

Regiment lost during service 77 Enlisted men killed and mortally wounded and 114 Enlisted men by disease. Total 191.

10th REGIMENT INFANTRY.

Organized at Milwaukee, Wis., and mustered in October 14, 1861. Moved to Louisville, Ky., November 9-11; thence to Shepherdsville and to Elizabethtown December 5. Attached to 9th Brigade, Army of the Ohio, December, 1861. 9th Brigade, 3rd Division, Army of the Ohio, to September, 1862. 9th Brigade, 3rd Division, 1st Corps, Army of the Ohio, to November, 1862. 1st Brigade, 1st Division, Centre 14th Army Corps, Army of the Cumberland, to January, 1863. 1st Brigade, 1st Division, 14th Army Corps, Army of the Cumberland, to October, 1864.

SERVICE.—Duty at Bacon Creek, Ky., till February, 1862. Advance on Bowling Green, Ky., February 13-15 and on Nashville, Tenn., February 22-25. Duty at Nashville till March 17. Advance on Murfreesboro March 17-19. Occupation of Shelbyville and Fayetteville and advance on Huntsville, Ala., April 5-11. Capture of Huntsville April 11. Paint Rock Bridge April 28 (Co. "H"). Pulaski May 4. Guard duty along Memphis & Charleston Railroad till August. Battle Creek June 21. March to Nashville, Tenn., thence to Louisville, Ky., in pursuit of Bragg August 31-September 26. Pursuit of Bragg to Crab Orchard, Ky., October 1-16. Battle of Perryville, Ky., October 8. March to Nashville, Tenn., October 17-November 7, and duty there till December 26. Advance on Murfreesboro December 26-30. Battle of Stone's River December 30-31, 1862, and January 1-3, 1863. Duty at Murfreesboro till June. Middle Tennessee (or Tullahoma) Campaign June 23-July 7. Hoover's Gap June 24-26. Occupation of Middle Tennessee till August 16. Passage of the Cumberland Mountains and Tennessee River and Chickamauga (Ga.) Campaign August 16-September 22. Davis' Cross Roads near Dug Gap September 11. Battle of Chickamauga September 19-21. Siege of Chattanooga September 24-November 23. Chattanooga-Ringgold Campaign November 23-27. Orchard Knob November 23. Mission Ridge November 25. Pea Vine Creek November 26. Demonstration on Dalton, Ga., February 22-27, 1864. Tunnel Hill, Buzzard's Roost Gap and Rocky Faced Ridge February 23-25. At Tyner's Station guarding East Tennessee & Georgia Railroad till May 24. Operations on line of Pumpkin Vine Creek and battles about Dallas, New Hope Church and Allatoona Hills May 26-June 5. Pickett's Mills May 27. Operations about Marietta and against Kenesaw Mountain June 10-July 2. Pine Hill June 11-14. Lost Mountain June 15-17. Assault on Kenesaw Mountain June 27. Ruff's Station July 4. Chattahoochie River July 5-17. Buckhead, Nancy's Creek, July 18. Peach Tree Creek July 19-20. Ordered to Marietta and duty there till October 3. Guard duty near Kenesaw Mountain till October 16. Mustered out October 25, 1864. Veterans and recruits transferred to 21st Wisconsin Infantry.

Regiment lost during service 5 Officers and 91 Enlisted men killed and mortally wounded and 1 Officer and 147 Enlisted men by disease. Total 244.

11th REGIMENT INFANTRY.

Organized at Madison, Wis., and mustered in October 18, 1861. Ordered to St. Louis, Mo., November 19, thence to Sulphur Springs and duty there and by detachments along Iron Mountain Railroad till March, 1862. Attached to Dept. of Missouri to March, 1862. District of Southeast Missouri, Dept. of Missouri, May, 1862. 1st Brigade, 1st Division, Army of Southwest Missouri, Dept. of Missouri, to July, 1862. District of Eastern Arkansas, Dept. of Missouri, to October, 1862. 1st Brigade, 1st Division, District of Southeast Missouri, Dept. of Missouri, to March 1863. 2nd Brigade, 14th Division, 13th Army Corps, Army of the Tennessee, to July, 1863. 2nd Brigade, 1st Division, 13th Army Corps, Army of the Tennessee, to August, 1863, and Dept. of the Gulf to May, 1864. District of La Fourche, Dept. of the Gulf, to February, 1865. 3rd Brigade, 2nd Division, 16th Army

Corps (New), Military Division West Mississippi, to September, 1865.

SERVICE.—Ordered to Pilot Knob, Mo., March 12, 1862, thence moved to Reeve's Station, Black River, March 23-27, and to White River April 19. March to Batesville, Ark., thence to Helena, Ark., May 25-July 13. Hill's Plantation, Cache River, July 7. Moved to Oldtown July 26 and duty there till September 20. Expedition after cotton July 30-August 4. Action at Totten's Plantation, near Oldtown, August 2 (Cos. "C," "E," "G," "H," "I" and "K"). Moved to Sugar Point September 20, thence to Pilot Knob, Mo., October 3, and duty there till November 2. Railroad guard and patrol duty at Patterson, Van Buren, West Plains and Middlebrook till March, 1863. Ordered to Helena, Ark., March 11, thence to Milliken's Bend, La. Movement on Bruinsburg and turning Grand Gulf April 25-30. Battle of Port Gibson May 1 (Reserve). Battle of Champion's Hill May 16. Big Black River May 17. Siege of Vicksburg, Miss., May 18-July 4. Assaults on Vicksburg May 19 and 22. Advance on Jackson, Miss., July 4-10. Siege of Jackson July 10-17. Ordered to Dept. of the Gulf August 13. Duty at Carrollton, Breasher City and Berwick till October. Western Louisiana Campaign October 3-November 10. Expedition to New Iberia October 3-6, and to Vermillionville Bayou October 8-30. Moved to Berwick City November 10. Expedition to Brazos Santiago, Texas, November 17-23. Duty at Matagorda Bay and Indianola till February, 1864. Regiment veteranized January, 1864, and remustered February 13. On furlough February 14-April 25. Moved to Memphis, Tenn., April 25-29. Sturgis' Expedition through Western Tennessee and Northern Mississippi May 2-9. Moved to Carrollton, La., May 11-15, thence to Brashear City May 19, and post and outpost duty at that point till February, 1865. Company "D" detached to Bayou Louis May 26, 1864; Company "E" to Tigerville May 31, 1864. Company "K" detached to Tigerville June 6; rejoined Regiment June 23. Companies "D" and "E" rejoined Regiment July 20. Expedition to Bayou Long June 30 (Cos. "A," "G" and "I"). Expedition to Grand Lake June 25 (Co. "F"). Expedition to Grand Lake July 27 (Cos. "E," "D" and "K"). Expedition to Grand River September 8 (Cos. "B" and "G") and again September 13 (Cos. "A," "C," "H" and "I"). Expedition to Grand River September 26-30. Non-veterans mustered out October 25, 1864. Expedition to Belle River October 22-24. Expedition to Bayou Portage November 17-19. Lake Fausse River November 18. Bayou La Fourche, Ash Bayou, November 18-19. Expedition from Brashear City to Bayou Sorrel January 21-22, 1865 (Co. "D"). Expedition from Brashear City to Lake Verret February 10-11 (Detachment). Moved to New Orleans, La., February 26. Campaign against Mobile and its Defences March 17-April 12. Siege of Spanish Fort and Fort Blakely March 26-April 8. Assault and capture of Fort Blakely April 9. Occupation of Mobile April 12. March to Montgomery April 13-25 and duty there till July. Moved to Mobile July 23 and duty there till September. Mustered out September 5, 1865.

Regiment lost during service 6 Officers and 80 Enlisted men killed and mortally wounded and 4 Officers and 253 Enlisted men by disease. Total 373.

12th REGIMENT INFANTRY.

Organized at Madison, Wis., October 18 to December 13, 1861. Left State for Fort Leavenworth, Kansas, January 11, 1862. At Weston, Mo., till February 15. Reach Fort Leavenworth February 16. Attached to Dept. of Kansas to June, 1862. District of Columbus, Ky., Dept. of the Tennessee, to October, 1862. 3rd Brigade, 4th Division, District of Jackson, Tenn., to November, 1862. 3rd Brigade, 4th Division, Right Wing 13th Army Corps (Old), Dept. of the Tennessee, to December, 1862. 3rd Brigade, 4th Division, 17th Army Corps, to January, 1863. 3rd Brigade, 4th Division, 16th Army Corps, to July, 1863. 3rd Brigade, 4th Division, 13th Army Corps, to August, 1863. 3rd Brigade, 4th Division, 17th Army Corps, to April, 1864. 1st Brigade,

4th Division, 17th Army Corps, to July, 1864. 1st Brigade, 3rd Division, 17th Army Corps, to July, 1865.

March from Fort Leavenworth to Fort Scott, Kansas, March 1-7, 1862, and duty there till March 27. Ordered to Lawrence, Kansas, March 27, thence to Fort Riley April 20 and to Fort Leavenworth May 27. Moved to St. Louis, Mo., thence to Columbus, Ky., May 29-June 2. Repairing Mobile & Ohio Railroad and duty at Union City and Humboldt, Tenn., till October 1. Moved to Bolivar October 1 and duty there till November 2. Grant's Central Mississippi Campaign, operations on the Mississippi Central Railroad, November 2, 1862, to January 10, 1863. Reconnoissance from La Grange toward Hilly Springs November 8, 1862. Moved to Lumpkin's Mills December 24, thence march to Colliersville, Tenn., via Holly Springs, Moscow and Lafayette, and guard duty along Memphis & Charleston Railroad till March 14, 1863. Moved to Memphis and duty there till May. Expedition to Coldwater River April 18-24. Hernando April 18. Perry's Ferry, Coldwater River, April 19. Ordered to Vicksburg, Miss., May 11. Siege of Vicksburg, Miss., May 22-July 4. Advance on Jackson, Miss., July 4-10. Siege of Jackson July 10-17. Duty at Vicksburg till August 15. Ordered to Natchez, Miss., August 15, and duty there till November 22. Expedition to Harrisonburg September 1-8. Near Harrisonburg and capture of Fort Beauregard September 4. Ordered to Vicksburg, Miss., November 22 and duty there till February, 1864. Meridian Campaign February 3-March 2. Champion's Hill and Bolton's Depot February 4. Canton February 29. Veterans on furlough till May. Non-veterans on duty at Vicksburg till April, then join Regiment at Cairo, Ill. Moved to Clifton, Tenn., May 5-14, thence march to Ackworth, Ga., via Huntsville and Decatur, Ala., and Rome, Ga., May 14-June 8. Atlanta (Ga.) Campaign May 8 to September 8. Operations about Marietta and against Kenesaw Mountain June 10-July 2. Assault on Kenesaw June 27. Nickajack Creek July 2-5. Howell's Ferry July 5. Chattahoochie River July 5-17. Nickajack Creek July 6-8. Leggett's or Bald Hill July 20-21. Battle of Atlanta July 22. Siege of Atlanta July 22-August 25. Ezra Chapel July 28. Flank movement on Jonesboro August 25-30. Battle of Jonesboro August 31-September 1. Lovejoy Station September 2-6. Operations against Hood in North Georgia and North Alabama September 30-November 3. March to the sea November 15-December 10. Siege of Savannah December 10-21. Campaign of the Carolinas January to April, 1865. Pocotaligo, S. C., January 14. Salkehatchie Swamp February 2-5. Binnaker's Swamp, South Edisto River, February 9. Orangeburg February 11-12. Columbia February 16-17. Battle of Bentonville, N. C., March 19-21. Occupation of Goldsboro March 24. Advance on Raleigh April 10-14. Occupation of Raleigh April 14. Bennett's House April 26. Surrender of Johnston and his army. March to Washington, D. C., via Richmond, Va., April 29-May 19. Grand Review May 24. Moved to Louisville, Ky., June. Mustered out July 20, 1865.

Regiment lost during service 3 Officers and 93 Enlisted men killed and mortally wounded and 3 Officers and 224 Enlisted men by disease. Total 323.

13th REGIMENT INFANTRY.

Organized at Janesville, Wis., and mustered in October 17, 1861. Left State for Leavenworth, Kansas, January 13, 1862. Attached to Dept. of Kansas to June, 1862. District of Columbus, Ky., Dept. of the Tennessee, to August, 1862. Garrison Forts Henry and Donelson, Tenn., to June, 1863. 1st Brigade, 3rd Division, Reserve Corps, Dept. of the Cumberland, to October, 1863. Post and District of Nashville, Tenn., Dept. of the Cumberland, to January, 1864. 1st Brigade, Rousseau's 3rd Division, 12th Army Corps, Army of the Cumberland, to April, 1864. 1st Brigade, 4th Division, 20th Army Corps, Dept. of the Cumberland, to March, 1865. 3rd Brigade, 3rd Division, 4th Army Corps, to August, 1865. Dept. of Texas to November, 1865.

SERVICE.—March to Fort Scott, Kansas, March 1-7, 1862, and duty there till March 26. Ordered to Lawrence, Kansas, March 26, thence to Fort Riley April 20 and to Fort Leavenworth May 27. Moved to St. Louis, Mo., thence to Columbus, Ky., May 29-June 2. Guard duty along Mobile & Ohio Railroad from Columbus, Ky., to Corinth, Miss., till August. Moved to Fort Henry, Tenn., thence to Fort Donelson, Tenn., September 2 and garrison duty there till November 11. Expedition to Clarksville September 5-10. Action at Rickett's Hill, Clarksville, September 7. Hopkinsville, Ky., November 6. Moved to Fort Henry November 11, and duty there as garrison and guarding supply steamers between the Fort and Hamburg Landing till February 3, 1863. Moved to relief of Fort Donelson February 3. Duty at Fort Donelson till August 27. March to Stevenson, Ala., August 27-September 14 and duty there guarding supplies till October. Moved to Nashville, Tenn., and duty there till February, 1864. Veterans on furlough February-March. Return to Nashville March 28. Garrison duty and guarding railroad trains from Louisville to Chattanooga till April 26. Guard duty along Tennessee River between Stevenson and Decatur till June. Moved to Claysville, Ala., June 4. Picket and patrol duty along Tennessee River till September. Scout from Gunter's Landing to Warrenton July 11 (Co. "C"). March to Woodville, thence to Huntsville, Ala., and guard Memphis & Charleston Railroad from Huntsville to Stevenson, Ala., with headquarters at Brownsboro till November. Repulse of Hood's attack on Decatur October 26-29. At Stevenson till December. At Huntsville till March, 1865. Paint Rock Ridge December 31, 1864 (Co. "G"). Operations in East Tennessee March 15-April 22. At Nashville, Tenn., till June. Ordered to New Orleans June 16, thence to Indianola, Texas, July 12. Duty at Green Lake and San Antonio, Texas, till November. Mustered out November 24, 1865.

Regiment lost during service 5 Enlisted men killed and mortally wounded and 188 Enlisted men by disease. Total 193.

14th REGIMENT INFANTRY.

Organized at Fond du Lac, Wis., and mustered in January 30, 1862. Left State for St. Louis, Mo., March 8, thence moved to Savannah, Tenn., March 23-28. Served unattached Army of the Tennessee to May, 1863. 2nd Brigade, 5th Division, Army of the Tennessee, May, 1862. Provost guard at Pittsburg Landing and Hamburg Landing, Tenn. Unattached, Army of the Tennessee, to August, 1862. 2nd Brigade, 6th Division, District of Corinth, Miss., Army of the Tennessee, to November, 1862. 2nd Brigade, 6th Division, Left Wing, 13th Army Corps (Old), Dept. of the Tennessee, to December, 1862. 2nd Brigade, 6th Division, 16th Army Corps, to January, 1863. 2nd Brigade, 6th Division, 17th Army Corps, to September, 1863. 2nd Brigade, 1st Division, 17th Army Corps, to March, 1864. 2nd Brigade, Provisional Divisional, 17th Army Corps, Dept. of the Gulf, to June, 1864. (Veterans attached to 3rd Brigade, 3rd Division, 17th Army Corps, Army of the Tennessee, April to November, 1864.) Detached Brigade, 17th Army Corps, and 4th Brigade, 1st Division, 16th Army Corps, to August, 1864. 1st Brigade, 3rd Division, 16th Army Corps, to December, 1864. 1st Brigade, 3rd Division, Detachment Army of the Tennessee, Dept. of the Cumberland, to February, 1865. 1st Brigade, 3rd Division, 16th Army Corps (New), Military Division of West Mississippi, to March, 1865. 2nd Brigade, 3rd Division, 16th Army Corps, to August, 1865. District of Alabama to October, 1865.

SERVICE.—Battle of Shiloh, Tenn., April 6-7, 1862. Advance on and siege of Corinth, Miss., April 29-May 30. Provost duty at Pittsburg Landing, Tenn., till July 23, and at Hamburg till August 23. Moved to Corinth August 23. Battle of Iuka, Miss., September 19. Battle of Corinth, Miss., October 3-4. Pursuit of Ripley October 5-12. At Corinth till November 2. Grant's Central Mississippi Campaign. Operations on the Mississippi Central Railroad November 2 to December 23. Moved to Moscow and duty along Memphis & Charleston Railroad till January 10, 1863. Moved to Memphis January 10, thence to Young's Point, La., January 17 and to Lake Providence, La., February 8. Duty there till April.

Movement on Bruinsburg and turning Grand Gulf April 25-30. Battle of Champion's Hill May 16. Siege of Vicksburg, Miss., May 18-July 4. Assaults on Vicksburg May 19 and 22. Expedition to Mechanicsville May 26-June 4. Moved to Natchez, Miss., July 12. Capture of Natchez July 13 and duty there till October 9. Moved to Vicksburg, Miss., October 9 and duty there till March, 1864. Regiment veteranized December 11, 1863, and Veterans on furlough January 3 to March 6 1864. (Company "E" and Veteran detachments from each Company joined 3rd Brigade, 3rd Division, 17th Army Corps, at Clifton, Tenn., thence march to Ackworth, Ga., via Huntsville and Decatur, Ala., and Rome, Ga., April 29-June 8. Atlanta (Ga.) Campaign June 8 to September 8. Operations about Marietta and against Kenesaw Mountain June 10-July 2. Assault on Kenesaw June 27. Nickajack Creek July 2-5. Chattahoochie River July 5-17. Howell's Ferry July 5. Leggett's or Bald Hill July 20-21. Battle of Atlanta July 22. Siege of Atlanta July 22-August 25. Flank movement on Jonesboro August 25-30. Battle of Jonesboro August 31-September 1. Lovejoy Station September 2-6. Pursuit of Hood into Alabama October 3-26. Rejoined Regiment at Nashville, Tenn., December, 1864, except Company "E," which went as a pontoon train guard to the sea November 15-December 10, and through the Carolinas to Washington, D. C., rejoining Regiment at Montgomery, Ala., July 16, 1865.) Non-veterans on Meridian Campaign February 3-March 2, 1864. Red River Campaign March 10-May 22, 1864. Fort De Russy March 14. Occupation of Alexandria March 16. Grand Ecore April 3. Pleasant Hill Landing April 12. About Cloutiersville April 22-24. About Alexandria April 26-May 13. Wells' Plantation May 6. Bayou Boeuf May 7. Retreat to Morganza May 13-20. Mansura May 16. Moved to Vicksburg, Miss., May 20-24, thence to Memphis, Tenn., May 28-30, and duty there till June 22. Moved to Moscow and LaGrange June 22-27. Smith's Expedition to Tupelo, Miss., July 5-21. Camargo's Cross Roads, near Harrisburg, July 13. Harrisburg, near Tupelo, July 14-15. Moved to St. Charles, Ark., August 3-6, thence to Devall's Bluff September 1, and to Brownsville September 8. March through Arkansas and Missouri in pursuit of Price September 17-November 17. Moved to Nashville, Tenn., November 23-30. Battle of Nashville December 15-16. Pursuit of Hood to the Tennessee River December 17-28. Moved to Eastport, Miss., and duty there till February 6, 1865. Moved to New Orleans, La., February 6-22. Campaign against Mobile and its Defences March 17-April 12. Fish River March 17. Siege of Spanish Fort and Fort Blakely March 26-April 8. Assault and capture of Fort Blakely April 9. Occupation of Mobile April 12. March to Montgomery April 13-25 and duty there till August. Moved to Mobile August 27 and duty there till October. Mustered out October 9, 1865.

Regiment lost during service 6 Officers and 116 Enlisted men killed and mortally wounded and 3 Officers and 194 Enlisted men by disease. Total 319.

15th REGIMENT INFANTRY.

Organized at Madison, Wis., and mustered in February 14, 1862. Ordered to St. Louis, Mo., March 2, thence to Bird's Point, Mo., March 5, and to Island No. 10 via Columbus and Hickman, Ky., March 14-17. Attached to Flotilla Brigade, Army of Mississippi, to April, 1862. Garrison at Island No. 10 to July, 1862. 2nd Brigade, 4th Division, Army of Mississippi, to September, 1862. 31st Brigade, 9th Division, Army of the Ohio, September, 1862. 31st Brigade, 9th Division, 3rd Army Corps, Army of the Ohio, to November, 1862. 2nd Brigade, 1st Division, Right Wing 14th Army Corps, Army of the Cumberland, to January, 1863. 2nd Brigade, 1st Division, 20th Army Corps, Army of the Cumberland, to March, 1863. 3rd Brigade, 1st Division, 20th Army Corps, to October, 1863. 1st Brigade, 3rd Division, 4th Army Corps, Army of the Cumberland, to November, 1864. 2nd Brigade, 1st Separate Division, District of the Etowah, Dept. of the Cumberland, to February, 1865.

SERVICE.—Operations against Island No. 10, Mississippi River, March 17-April 8, 1862. Expedition to

Union City, Tenn., March 30-April 2. Union City March 31. (Four Companies detached for duty at Bird's Point, Mo., March 5 to April 16; rejoined at Island No. 10.) Garrison duty at Island No. 10 till June (Cos. "G" and "I" till October, 1862). Moved to Union City, Tenn., June 12, thence to Humboldt and Corinth, Miss. Moved to Jacinto July 20, thence to Florence, Ala., August 21-24. March to Nashville, Tenn., thence to Louisville, Ky., in pursuit of Bragg August 26-September 26. Pursuit of Bragg to Crab Orchard, Ky., October 1-16. Battle of Perryville, Ky., October 8. Stanford October 14. Island No. 10 October 17 (Cos. "G" and "I"). March to Nashville, Tenn., October 19-November 7, and duty there till December 26. Expedition down the Cumberland River toward Clarksville after Morgan's guerrillas November 15-20. Wilson's Creek Pike December 25. Advance on Murfreesboro December 26-30. Nolinsville December 26-27. Battle of Stone's River December 30-31, 1862, and January 1-3, 1863. Duty at Murfreesboro till June. Reconnoissance from Murfreesboro March 6-7. Methodist Church, Shelbyville Pike, March 6. Reconnoissance to Versailles March 9-14. Operations on Edgefield Pike and Shelbyville Pike June 4. Middle Tennessee (or Tullahoma) Campaign June 23-July 7. Liberty Gap June 24-27. Occupation of Middle Tennessee till August 16. Passage of the Cumberland Mountains and Tennessee River and Chickamauga (Ga.) Campaign August 16-September 22. Caperton's Ferry, near Bridgeport, August 29. Battle of Chickamauga September 19-20. Siege of Chattanooga, Tenn., September 24-November 23. Chattanooga-Ringgold Campaign November 23-27. Orchard Knob November 23-24. Mission Ridge November 25. March to relief of Knoxville November 28-December 8. Charleston, Tenn., December 28. Operations in East Tennessee till April, 1864. Atlanta (Ga.) Campaign May 1 to September 8. Demonstrations on Rocky Faced Ridge and Dalton May 8-13. Battle of Resaca May 14-15. Near Cassville May 19. Operations on line of Pumpkin Vine Creek and battles about Dallas, New Hope Church and Allatoona Hills May 25-June 5. Pickett's Mills May 27. Operations about Marietta and against Kenesaw Mountain June 10-July 2. Pine Hill June 11-14. Lost Mountain June 15-17. Assault on Kenesaw June 27. Ruff's Station, Smyrna Camp Ground, July 4. Chattahoochie River July 5-17. Peach Tree Creek July 19-20. Siege of Atlanta July 22-August 25. Flank movement on Jonesboro August 25-30. Battle of Jonesboro August 31-September 1. Lovejoy Station September 2-6. Duty at Atlanta till September 29. Ordered to Chattanooga, Tenn., September 29, thence to Whiteside Station October 17 and guard bridge and railroad till February, 1865. Companies "A," "B" and "E" mustered out December 1, 1864; Company "C" January 1, Companies "F" and "G" January 14, Companies "I" and "K" February 11 and Companies "D" and "H" February 13, 1865.

Regiment lost during service 8 Officers and 86 Enlisted men killed and mortally wounded and 1 Officer and 241 Enlisted men by disease. Total 336.

16th REGIMENT INFANTRY.

Organized at Madison, Wis., and mustered in January 31, 1862. Left State for St. Louis, Mo., March 13, thence moved to Pittsburg Landing, Tenn., March 14-20. Attached to 1st Brigade, 6th Division, Army of the Tennessee, to July, 1862. 1st Brigade, 6th Division, District of Corinth, Miss., to November, 1862. 1st Brigade, 6th Division, Left Wing 13th Army Corps (Old), Dept. of the Tennessee, to December, 1862. 1st Brigade, 6th Division, 16th Army Corps, to January, 1863. 1st Brigade, 6th Division, 17th Army Corps, to September, 1863. 1st Brigade, 1st Division, 17th Army Corps, to April, 1864. 1st Brigade, 3rd Division, 17th Army Corps, to July, 1865.

SERVICE.—Battle of Shiloh, Tenn., April 6-7, 1862. Advance on and siege of Corinth, Miss., April 29-May 30. Duty at Corinth till September 17. Battle of Corinth, Miss., October 3-4. Pursuit to Ripley October 5-12. Ordered to Grand Junction November 2 and duty there till November 28. Grant's Central Mississippi Campaign.

Operations on the Mississippi Central Railroad to December 28. Moved to Moscow and duty along Memphis & Charleston Railroad till January 10, 1863. Moved to Memphis, Tenn., January 10, thence to Young's Point, La., January 17, and to Lake Providence March 8. Action at Old River, Lake Providence, February 10. Provost duty at Lake Providence till August. Pin Hook and Caledonia Bayou, Macon, May 10. Expedition to Mechanicsburg May 26-June 4. Near Lake Providence June 9. Moved to Red Bone Church August 1 and duty there till February 5, 1864. Garrison duty at Vicksburg till March 4. Veterans on furlough March and April. Non-veterans on duty at Vicksburg till April 5, then joined Regiment at Cairo, Ill. Veterans moved to Cairo, Ill., April 20-22. Moved to Clifton, Tenn., May 4, thence march to Ackworth, Ga. via Huntsville and Decatur, Ala., and Rome, Ga., May 5-June 8. Atlanta (Ga.) Campaign June 8-September 8. Operations about Marietta and against Kenesaw Mountain June 10-July 2. Brush Mountin June 15. Assault on Kenesaw Mountain June 27. Nickajack Creek July 2-5. Howell's Ferry July 5. Chattahoochie River July 5-17. Leggett's or Bald Hill July 20-21. Battle of Atlanta July 22. Siege of Atlanta July 22-August 25. Ezra Chapel July 28. Flank movement on Jonesboro August 25-30. Battle of Jonesboro August 31-September 1. Lovejoy Station September 2-6. Operations against Hood in North Georgia and North Alabama September 29-November 3. March to the sea November 15-December 10. Siege of Savannah December 10-21. Campaign of the Carolinas January to April, 1865. Pocotaligo, S. C., January 14. Reconnoissance to Salkehatchie River January 25. Barker's Mills, Whippy Swamp, February 1. Salkehatchie Swamp February 2-5. Binnaker's Bridge, South Edisto, February 9. Orangeburg February 11-12. Columbia February 16-17. Averysboro, N. C., March 16. Battle of Bentonville March 19-21. Occupation of Goldsboro March 24. Advance on Raleigh April 10-14. Occupation of Raleigh April 14. Bennett's House April 26. Surrender of Johnston and his army. March to Washington, D. C., via Richmond, Va., April 29-May 19. Grand Review May 24. Moved to Louisville, Ky., June 7. Mustered out July 12, 1865.

Regiment lost during service 6 Officers and 141 Enlisted men killed and mortally wounded and 4 Officers and 248 Enlisted men by disease. Total 399.

17th REGIMENT INFANTRY.

Organized at Madison, Wis., and mustered in March 15, 1862. Left State for St. Louis, Mo., March 23. At Benton Barracks till April 10. Moved to Pittsburg Landing, Tenn., April 10-14. Attached to 1st Brigade, 6th Division, Army of the Tennessee, to July, 1862. 1st Brigade, 6th Division, District of Corinth, Miss., to November, 1862. 1st Brigade, 6th Division, Left Wing 13th Army Corps (Old), Dept. of the Tennessee, to December, 1862. 2nd Brigade, 6th Division, 16th Army Corps, to January, 1863. 2nd Brigade, 6th Division, 17th Army Corps, to September, 1863. 2nd Brigade, 1st Division, 17th Army Corps, to April, 1864. 3rd Brigade, 3rd Division, 17th Army Corps, to November, 1864. 2nd Brigade, 3rd Division, 17th Army Corps, to July, 1865.

SERVICE.—Advance on and siege of Corinth, Miss., April 29-May 30, 1862. Duty at Corinth till November. Near Ramer's Crossing, Mobile & Ohio Railroad, October 2 (Co. "A"). Battle of Corinth October 3-4. Pursuit to Ripley October 5-12. Moved to Grand Junction November 2. Grant's Central Mississippi Campaign, operations on the Mississippi Central Railroad November 2, 1862, to January 3, 1863. Moved to Moscow, Tenn., January 3, thence to Memphis January 10, and to Young's Point, La., January 18. Moved to Lake Providence, La., February 8 and duty there till April 20. Movement on Bruinsburg and turning Grand Gulf April 20-30. Battle of Port Gibson, Miss., May 1 (Reserve). Battle of Champion's Hill May 16. Siege of Vicksburg, Miss., May 18-July 4. Assaults on Vicksburg May 19 and 22. Expedition to Mechanicsburg May 26-June 4. Moved to Natchez, Miss., July 12-13 and duty there till October 9. Expedition to Harrisonburg September 1-8.

Trinity September 2. Near Harrisonburg and capture of Fort Beauregard September 4. Cross Bayou September 10. Moved to Vicksburg October 9 and duty there till March, 1864. Veterans on furlough March 8-April 21. Moved to Cairo, Ill., April 21-22, thence moved to Clifton, Tenn., May 4, and march to Ackworth, Ga., via Huntsville and Decatur, Ala., and Rome, Ga., May 5-June 8. Atlanta (Ga.) Campaign June 8 to September 8. Operations about Marietta and against Kenesaw Mountain June 10-July 2. Brush Mountain June 15. Assault on Kenesaw June 27. Nickajack Creek July 2-5. Howell's Ferry July 5. Chattahoochie River July 5-17. Leggett's or Bald Hill July 20-21. Battle of Atlanta July 22. Siege of Atanta July 22-August 25. Ezra Chapel July 28. Flank movement on Jonesboro August 25-30. Battle of Jonesboro August 31-September 1. Lovejoy Station September 2-6. Operations against Hood in North Georgia and North Alabama September 29-November 3. March to the sea November 15-December 10. Siege of Savannah December 10-21. Campaigu of the Carolinas January to April, 1865. Pocotaligo, S. C., January 14. Barker's Mills, Whippy Swamp, February 1. Salkehatchie Swamp February 2-5. South Edisto River February 9. North Edisto River February 12-13. Columbia February 16-17. Battle of Bentonville, N. C., March 19-21. Occupation of Goldsboro March 24. Advance on Raleigh April 10-14. Occupation of Raleigh April 14. Bennett's House April 26. Surrender of Johnston and his army. March to Washington, D. C., via Richmond, Va., April 29-May 19. Grand Review May 24. Moved to Louisville, Ky., June, and there mustered out July 14, 1865.

Regiment lost during service 41 Enlisted men killed and mortally wounded and 228 Enlisted men by disease. Total 269.

18th REGIMENT INFANTRY.

Organized at Milwaukee, Wis., and mustered in March 15, 1862. Left State for St. Louis, Mo., March 30; thence moved to Pittsburg Landing, Tenn., March 31-April 5. Attached to 2nd Brigade, 6th Division, Army of the Tennessee, to July, 1862. 2nd Brigade, 6th Division, District of Corinth, Miss., to November, 1862. 2nd Brigade, 6th Division, Left Wing 13th Army Corps (Old), Dept. of the Tennessee, to December, 1862. 2nd Brigade, 6th Division, 16th Army Corps, to January, 1863. 2nd Brigade, 6th Division, 17th Army Corps, to May, 1863. 1st Brigade, 7th Division, 17th Army Corps, to September, 1863. 1st Brigade, 2nd Division, 17th Army Corps, to December, 1863. 1st Brigade, 3rd Division, 15th Army Corps, to April, 1865. 2nd Brigade, 4th Division, 15th Army Corps, to July, 1865. (Non-Veterans attached to 93rd Illinois Infantry November-December, 1864. Veterans attached to 1st Brigade, 1st Provisional Division, Dept. of the Cumberland, December, 1864, to February, 1865. District of New Berne, N. C., Dept. of North Carolina, to April, 1865.)

SERVICE.—Battle of Shiloh, Tenn., April 6-7, 1862. Advance on and siege of Corinth, Miss., April 29-May 30. Duty at Corinth till July 18. Moved to Bolivar, Tenn., July 18, and duty there till August 16. Return to Corinth, Miss., August 16. March to Iuka, Miss., September 7-19. Battle of Iuka September 19. Battle of Corinth October 3-4. Pursuit to Hatchie River July 5-12. Moved to Grand Junction November 2. Grant's Central Mississippi Campaign. Operations on the Mississippi Central Railroad November 2, 1862, to January 3, 1863. Moved to Moscow, Tenn., January 3; thence to Memphis, Tenn., January 10, and to Young's Point, La., January 17. Moved to Lake Providence, La., February 8, and duty there till April 20. Movement on Bruinsburg and turning Grand Gulf April 20-30. Battle of Port Gibson, Miss., May 1 (Reserve). Jackson May 14. Battle of Champion's Hill May 16. Siege of Vicksburg May 18-July 4. Assaults on Vicksburg May 19 and 22. Guard and patrol duty at Vicksburg till September. Moved to Helena, Ark., September 11; thence to Memphis and Corinth and march to Chattanooga, Tenn., October 6-November 20. Operations on

Memphis & Charleston Railroad in Alabama October 20-29. Chattanooga-Ringgold Campaign November 23-27. Tunnel Hill November 24-25. Mission Ridge November 25. Pursuit to Graysville November 26-27. Duty at Bridgeport, Ala., till December 21, and at Huntsville, Ala., till May 1, 1864. At Whitesburg, Ala., till June 19. Moved to Stevenson, Ala., June 19-25; thence to Allatoona, Ga., July 1-6, and garrison duty there till August 22. March to Chattanooga, Tenn. (7 Cos.), August 22-25. (Cos. "E," "F" and "I" remained on duty at Allatoona.) March into East Tennessee in pursuit of Wheeler August 25-30. Moved to Cowan, Tenn., and guard Nashville & Chattanooga Railroad till September 19. Moved to Allatoona, Ga., September 19-22, and garrison duty there till November. Repulse of French's attack on Allatoona October 5. Veterans on furlough November-December. Non-Veterans attached to 93rd Illinois Infantry November, 1864, to April, 1865, participating in march to the sea November 15-December 10. Siege of Savannah December 10-21. Campaign of the Carolinas January to April, 1865. Battle of Bentonville, N. C., March 19-21. Veterans ordered to Nashville, Tenn., December 28, 1864. Moved to Baltimore, Md., thence to Beaufort, N. C., January 5-February 2, 1865, and to New Berne, N. C., February 8. Duty at New Berne till March 28. Moved to Goldsboro, N. C., and rejoin command. Advance on Raleigh April 10-14. Occupation of Raleigh April 14. Bennett's House April 26. Surrender of Johnston and his army. March to Washington, D. C., via Richmond, Va., April 29-May 19. Grand Review May 24. Moved to Louisville, Ky., June, and mustered out July 18, 1865.

Regiment lost during service 4 Officers and 52 Enlisted men killed and mortally wounded and 2 Officers and 167 Enlisted men by disease. Total 225.

19th REGIMENT INFANTRY.

Organized at Madison, Wis., and mustered in April 30, 1862. Left State for Washington, D. C., June 2; thence moved to Hampton, Va., June 8, and to Norfolk, Va., June 29. Attached to District of Norfolk and Portsmouth, Va., 7th Army Corps, Dept. of Virginia, to April, 1863. Reserve Brigade, 3rd Division, 7th Army Corps, to June, 1863. Wistah's Independent Brigade, 7th Army Corps, to July, 1863. Yorktown, Va., Dept. of Virginia and North Carolina, to August, 1863. Newport News, Va., Dept. of Virginia and North Carolina, to October, 1863. New Berne, N. C., Dept. of Virginia and North Carolina, to April, 1864. 3rd Brigade, 1st Division, 18th Army Corps, Army of the James, Dept. of Virginia and North Carolina, to June, 1864. 2nd Brigade, 2nd Division, 18th Army Corps, to August, 1864. Norfolk, Va., to October, 1864. 3rd Brigade, 2nd Division, 18th Army Corps, to December, 1864. 1st Brigade, 3rd Division, 24th Army Corps, to July, 1865. 1st Independent Brigade, 24th Army Corps, to August, 1865.

SERVICE.—Garrison duty at Norfolk, Va., till April, 1863. Ordered to Suffolk, Va., April 14. Siege of Suffolk April 14-May 4. Action at Edenton Road, Suffolk, April 24. Operations on Norfolk & Petersburg Railroad May 15-18. Near Providence Church May 17. Moved to Norfolk June 17; thence to Yorktown June 18. Dix's Peninsula Campaign June 24-July 7. Garrison duty at Yorktown till August 16. At Newport News till October 8. Moved to New Berne, N. C., October 8-11. Outpost and picket duty there till April, 1864. Company "A" detached at Evans' Mills, Company "B" at Brier Creek, and Company "F" at Havelock Station till February, 1864. Operations about New Berne against Whiting January 18-February 10, 1864. Beech Grove and Batchelor's Creek, New Berne, February 1-3, 1864. Expedition to relief of Plymouth April 19-24 (Co. "A"). Moved to Yorktown April 26-28. Butler's operations on south side of the James River and against Petersburg and Richmond May 4-28. Occupation of Bermuda Hundred May 5. Operations against Fort Darling May 12-16. Battle of Drury's Bluff May 14-16. Bermuda Hundred June 16-July 20. Assaults on Petersburg June 15. Port Walthal June 16-17. In trenches before Petersburg till August. Veterans on furlough August 13 to October 10. Non-Veterans assigned to provost duty at Norfolk, Va., August to October. Regiment moved to Aiken's Landing, thence to Chaffin's Farm and operations against Richmond from north side of the James River till April, 1865. Battle of Fair Oaks October 27-28, 1864. Occupation of Richmond April 3, 1865, and provost duty there till April 28. Non-Veterans mustered out April 28, 1865. Provost duty at Fredericksburg, Va., till July 24, and at Warrenton, Va., till August 4. Moved to Richmond, Va., and mustered out August 9, 1865.

Regiment lost during service 2 Officers and 41 Enlisted men killed and mortally wounded and 3 Officers and 115 Enlisted men by disease. Total 161.

20th REGIMENT INFANTRY.

Organized at Madison, Wis., and mustered in August 23, 1862. Left State for St. Louis, Mo., August 30; thence moved to Benton Barracks September 2, and to Rolla, Mo., September 6. Attached to 1st Brigade, 3rd Division, Army of the Frontier, Dept. of Missouri, to June, 1863. 2nd Brigade, Herron's Division, 13th Army Corps, Army of the Tennessee, to August, 1863. 2nd Brigade, 2nd Division, 13th Army Corps, Dept. of the Gulf, to June, 1864. United States Forces, Texas, to August, 1864. United States Forces, Mobile Bay, to December, 1864. District of Southern Alabama, Dept. of the Gulf, to February, 1865. 1st Brigade, 2nd Division, Reserve Corps, Military Division West Mississippi, to February, 1865. 1st Brigade, 2nd Division, 13th Army Corps (New), Military Division West Mississippi, to July, 1865.

SERVICE.—March to Springfield, Mo., September 10-24, 1862; thence to Cassville October 11-14. Expedition to Cross Hollows over Boston Mountains October 17-24. March to Wilson's Creek November 4-22. Forced march to relief of General Blount December 3-6. Battle of Prairie Grove, Ark., December 7. Duty at Prairie Grove till December 27. Expedition over Boston Mountains to Van Buren December 27-29. Duty at various points in Missouri till March 31, 1863. At Lake Springs, Mo., till June. Moved to St. Louis, Mo., thence to Vicksburg, Miss., June 3-10. Siege of Vicksburg June 12-July 4. Expedition to Yazoo City July 12-21. Capture of Yazoo City July 13. Moved to Port Hudson, La., July 23, and duty there till August 28. Moved to Carrollton August 28, and duty there till September 5. Expedition to Morganza September 5-October 11. Atchafalaya September 8-9. Expedition to Rio Grande, Texas, October 24-November 10. Moved to Brownsville, Texas, November 5-6. Occupation of Brownsville November 6. Garrison duty at Fort Brown till July 28, 1864. Cross Rio Grande to Matamoras, Mexico, January 12, 1864, to protect American Consul and assist in the removal of property belonging to American citizens. Moved to Carrollton August 1-5, thence to Mobile Bay, Ala. Operations against Fort Morgan August 9-23. Capture of Fort Morgan August 23. Duty at Navy Cove, near Fort Morgan, till December 14. Expedition from Mobile Bay to Bonsecours and Fish River September 9-11. Moved to Pascagoula December 14, thence to Franklin Creek. Captured 8,000,000 feet of lumber and raft it through enemy's country to Griffin's Mills, where 7,000,000 feet more were captured. Moved to Navy Cove December 31, and duty there till March, 1865. Campaign against Mobile and its Defences March 17-April 12. Siege of Spanish Fort and Fort Blakely March 26-April 8. Assault and capture of Fort Blakely April 9. Duty at Spanish Fort and Fort Blakely collecting stores, ammunition and Artillery till May 6. Moved to Mobile May 6, and duty there till June 22. Ordered to Galveston, Texas, June 22, and duty there till July 14. Mustered out July 14, 1865.

Regiment lost during service 5 Officers and 100 Enlisted men killed and mortally wounded and 1 Officer and 145 Enlisted men by disease. Total 251.

21st REGIMENT INFANTRY.

Organized at Oshkosh, Wis., and mustered in September 5, 1862. Left State for Cincinnati, Ohio, September 11, thence to Covington, Ky., and to Louisville, Ky., September 15. Duty in the fortification of Louisville September 18-October 1. Attached to 28th Brigade, 3rd Division, Army of the Ohio, September, 1862. 28th Brigade, 3rd Division, 1st Army Corps, Army of the Ohio, to November, 1862. 3rd Brigade, 1st Division, Centre 14th Army Corps, Army of the Cumberland, to January, 1863. 3rd Brigade, 1st Division, 14th Army Corps, Army of the Cumberland, to April, 1863. 2nd Brigade, 1st Division, 14th Army Corps, to April, 1864. 1st Brigade, 1st Division, 14th Army Corps, to June, 1865.

SERVICE.—Pursuit of Bragg to Crab Orchard, Ky., October 1-16, 1862. Battle of Perryville, Ky., October 8. Guard duty at Mitchellsville till December 7. Moved to Nashville, Tenn., and duty there till December 26. Advance on Murfreesboro December 26-30. Jefferson December 30. Battle of Stone's River December 30-31, 1862, and January 1-3, 1863. Duty at Murfreesboro till June. Expedition to McMinnville April 20-30. Middle Tennessee (or Tullahoma) Campaign June 23-July 7. Hoover's Gap June 24-26. Occupation of Middle Tennessee till August 16. Passage of the Cumberland Mountains and Tennessee River and Chickamauga (Ga.) Campaign August 16-September 22. Davis Cross Roads, near Dug Gap, September 11. Battle of Chickamauga September 19-21. Rossville Gap September 21. Siege of Chattanooga September 24-November 23. Chattanooga-Ringgold Campaign November 23-27. Orchard Knob November 23-24. Mission Ridge November 25. Reconnoissance to Cooper's Gap November 30-December 3. Atlanta (Ga.) Campaign May 1 to September 8, 1864. Demonstrations on Rocky Faced Ridge May 8-11. Battle of Resaca May 14-15. Advance on Dallas May 18-25. Operations on line of Pumpkin Vine Creek and battles about Dallas, New Hope Church and Allatoona Hills May 25-June 5. Pickett's Mills May 27. Operations about Marietta and against Kenesaw Mountain June 10-July 2. Pine Hill June 11-14. Lost Mountain June 15-17. Assault on Kenesaw June 27. Ruff's Station July 4. Chattahoochie River July 5-17. Buckhead, Nancy's Creek, July 18. Peach Tree Creek July 19-20. Siege of Atlanta July 22-August 25. Utoy Creek August 5-7. Flank movement on Jonesboro August 25-30. Near Red Oak August 29. Battle of Jonesboro August 31-September 1. Operations against Hood in North Georgia and North Alabama September 30-November 3. March to the sea November 15-December 10. Siege of Savannah December 10-21. Campaign of the Carolinas January to April, 1865. Taylor's Hole Creek, Averysboro, N. C., March 16. Battle of Bentonville March 19-21. Occupation of Goldsboro March 24. Advance on Raleigh April 10-14. Occupation of Raleigh April 14. Bennett's House April 26. Surrender of Johnston and his army. March to Washington, D. C., via Richmond, Va., April 29-May 17. Grand Review May 24. Mustered out June 8 and discharged from service June 17, 1865.

Regiment lost during service 5 Officers and 117 Enlisted men killed and mortally wounded and 3 Officers and 180 Enlisted men by disease. Total 305.

22nd REGIMENT INFANTRY.

Organized at Racine, Wis., and mustered in September 2, 1862. Left State for Cincinnati, Ohio, September 16, thence moved to Covington, Ky., September 22. Attached to 2nd Brigade, 1st Division, Army of Kentucky, Dept. of the Ohio, to November, 1862. 1st Brigade, 3rd Division, Army of Kentucky, to February, 1863. Coburn's Brigade, Baird's Division, Army of Kentucky, Dept. of the Cumberland, to June, 1863. 3rd Brigade, 1st Division, Reserve Corps, Army of the Cumberland, to October, 1863. Coburn's Unattached Brigade, Dept. of the Cumberland, to December, 1863. Post of Murfreesboro, District of Nashville, Dept. of the Cumberland, to January, 1864. 2nd Brigade, 1st Division, 11th Army Corps, Army of the Cumberland, to April, 1864. 2nd Brigade, 3rd Division, 20th Army Corps, Army of the Cumberland, to June, 1865.

SERVICE.—March from Covington to Georgetown, Lexington, Sandersville and Nicholasville October 7-November 13, 1862. Duty at Nichclasville till December 12. Moved to Danville, Ky., December 12 and duty there till January 26, 1863. Moved to Louisville, Ky., thence to Nashville, Tenn., January 26-February 7, 1863, and to Brentwood Station February 21, thence to Franklin. Reconnoissance toward Thompson's Station, Spring Hill, March 3-5. Action at Thompson's Station March 4-5. (Nearly 200 of Regiment captured by Bragg's Cavalry forces under Van Dorn, nearly 18,000 strong.) Ordered to Brentwood Station March 8. Action at Little Harpeth, Brentwood, March 25. Regiment surrounded and surrendered to Forest. Exchanged May 5. Regiment reorganizing at St. Louis till June 12. Ordered to Nashville, Tenn., June 12, thence to Franklin June 22; to Murfreesboro, Tenn., July 3, and garrison duty there till February, 1864. Moved to Nashville, Tenn., February 24, and duty there till April. March to Lookout Valley, Tenn., April 19-28. Atlanta (Ga.) Campaign May 1 to September 8. Battle of Resaca May 14-15. Cassville May 19. New Hope Church May 25. Operations on line of Pumpkin Vine Creek and battles about Dallas, New Hope Church and Allatoona Hills May 25-June 5. Operations about Marietta and against Kenesaw Mountain June 10-July 2. Pine Hill June 11-14. Lost Mountain June 15-17. Gilgal or Golgotha Church June 15. Muddy Creek June 17. Noyes Creek June 19. Kolb's Farm June 22. Assault on Kenesaw June 27. Ruff's Station July 4. Chattahoochie River July 5-17. Peach Tree Creek July 19-20. Siege of Atlanta July 22-August 25. Operations at Chattahoochie River Bridge August 26-September 2. Occupation of Atlanta September 2-November 15. March to the sea November 15-December 10. Siege of Savannah December 10-21. Campaign of the Carolinas January to April 1865. Lawtonville, S. C., February 2. Taylor's Hole Creek, Averysboro, N. C., March 16. Battle of Bentonville March 19-21. Occupation of Goldsboro March 24. Advance on Raleigh April 10-14. Occupation of Raleigh April 14. Bennett's House April 26. Surrender of Johnston and his army. March to Washington, D. C., via Richmond, Va., April 29-May 19. Grand Review May 24. Mustered out June 12, 1865.

Regiment lost during service 2 Officers and 75 Enlisted men killed and mortally wounded and 3 Officers and 163 Enlisted men by disease. Total 243.

23rd REGIMENT INFANTRY.

Organized at Madison, Wis., and mustered in August 30, 1862. Left State for Cincinnati, Ohio, September 15. Attached to 2nd Brigade, 2nd Division, Army of Kentucky, Dept. of the Ohio, to October, 1862. 1st Brigade, 1st Division, Army of Kentucky, to November, 1862. 1st Brigade, 10th Division, Right Wing 13th Army Corps (Old), Dept. of the Tennessee, to December, 1862. 1st Brigade, 1st Division, Sherman's Yazoo Expedition, to January, 1863. 1st Brigade, 10th Division, 13th Army Corps, Army of the Tennessee, to August, 1863. 1st Brigade, 4th Division, 13th Army Corps, Dept. of the Gulf, to June, 1864. Defences of New Orleans, La., to August, 1864. 3rd Brigade, 2nd Division, 19th Army Corps, Dept. of the Gulf, August, 1864. Guppy's Brigade, Mobile Bay, Dept. of the Gulf, to October, 1864. District of Eastern Arkansas, 7th Army Corps, Dept. of Arkansas, to February, 1865. 3rd Brigade, 1st Division, Reserve Corps, Military Division West Mississippi, February, 1865. 3rd Brigade, 1st Division, 13th Army Corps (New), Military Division West Mississippi, to July, 1865. SERVICE.—Duty at Newport, Ky., till October 8, 1862. Moved to Paris, Ky., October 8-15, thence to Lexington and Nicholasville, Ky., October 22-31. Moved to Louisville, thence to Memphis, Tenn., November 8-27. Sherman's Yazoo Expedition December 20, 1862, to January 3, 1863. Expedition from Milliken's Bend to Louisiana & Shreveport Railroad December 25-26. Chickasaw Bayou December 26-28. Chickasaw Bluff December 29. Expedition to Arkansas Post, Ark., January 3-10, 1863. Assault on and capture of Fort Hindman, Arkansas Post, January 10-11. Moved to Young's Point, La., January

15, and duty there till March 8. Expedition to Cypress Bend, Ark., February 14-29. Moved to Milliken's Bend, La., March 8, and duty there till April 25. Movement on Bruinsburg and turning Grand Gulf April 25-30. Battle of Port Gibson May 1 (Reserve). Battle of Champion's Hill May 16. Big Black River May 17. Siege of Vicksburg, Miss., May 18-July 4. Assaults on Vicksburg May 19 and 22. Advance on Jackson, Miss., July 4-10. Siege of Jackson July 10-17. Camp at Vicksburg till August. Ordered to New Orleans, La., August 24. Expedition to New and Amite Rivers September 24-29. Western Louisiana Campaign October 3-November 30. Carrion Crow Bayou November 3. At New Iberia till December 7. Moved to Berwick December 7-10. Moved to Brashear City, thence to Algiers and to Matagorda Peninsula, Texas, December 13, 1863-January 1, 1864. Reconnoissance on Matagorda Peninsula January 21, 1864. Duty at DeCrow's Point till February 22. Moved to Algiers, La., February 22-26. Red River Campaign March 10-May 22. Advance from Franklin to Alexandria March 14-26. Bayou de Paul, Carroll's Mill, and battle of Sabine Cross Roads April 8. Monett's Ferry, Cane River Crossing, April 23. At Alexandria April 26-May 13. Construction of dam at Alexandria April 30-May 10. Retreat to Morganza May 13-20. Mansura May 16. Moved to Baton Rouge May 24, and duty there till July 8. Moved to Algiers, La., July 8, thence to Morganza July 26. Expedition to Mobile Bay August 18-September 2. Operations near Morganza September 16-25. Expedition to Bayou Sara October 3-6. Bayou Sara and Thompson's Creek, near Jackson, October 5. Moved to Helena, Ark., October 10, and duty there till February 23, 1865. Ordered to New Orleans, La., February 23. Campaign against Mobile, Ala., and its defences March 17-April 12. Siege of Spanish Fort and Fort Blakely March 26-April 8. Assault on and capture of Fort Blakely April 9. Occupation of Mobile April 12. Duty at and near Mobile till July. Mustered out July 4, 1865.

Regiment lost during service 1 Officer and 40 Enlisted men killed and mortally wounded and 5 Officers and 262 Enlisted men by disease. Total 308.

24th REGIMENT INFANTRY.

Organized at Milwaukee, Wis., and mustered in August 15, 1862. Left State for Louisville, Ky., September 5. Attached to 37th Brigade, 11th Division, Army of the Ohio, September, 1862. 37th Brigade, 11th Division, 3rd Corps, Army of the Ohio, to November, 1862. 1st Brigade, 3rd Division, Right Wing 14th Army Corps, Army of the Cumberland, to January, 1863. 1st Brigade, 3rd Division, 20th Army Corps, Army of the Cumberland, to October, 1863. 1st Brigade, 2nd Division, 4th Army Corps, Army of the Cumberland, to June, 1865.

SERVICE.—Camp at Jeffersonville, Ind., September 7-10, 1862. Moved to Cincinnati, Ohio, September 10, and duty at Covington, Ky., till September 18. Ordered to Louisville, Ky., September 18. Pursuit of Bragg to Crab Orchard, Ky., October 1-16. Battle of Perryville, Ky., October 8. March to Nashville, Tenn., October 16-November 7, and duty there till December 26. Advance on Murfreesboro December 26-30. Battle of Stone's River December 30-31, 1862, and January 1-3, 1863. Duty at Murfreesboro till June. Expedition toward Columbia March 4-14. Middle Tennessee (or Tullahoma) Campaign June 23-July 7. Passage of the Cumberland Mountains and Tennessee River and Chickamauga (Ga.) Campaign August 16-September 22. Battle of Chickamauga, Ga., September 19-20. Siege of Chattanooga, Tenn., September 24-November 23. Chattanooga-Ringgold Campaign November 23-27. Orchard Knob November 23-24. Mission Ridge November 25. March to relief of Knoxville, Tenn., November 28-December 8. Operations in East Tennessee till February, 1864. Duty at Division Headquarters at Loudon January 18 to April, 1864. Atlanta (Ga.) Campaign May 1 to September 8. Demonstrations on Rocky Faced Ridge and Dalton, Ga., May 8-11. Buzzard's Roost Gap May 8-9. Battle of Resaca May 14-15. Adairsville May 17. Near Kingston May 18-19. Near Cassville May 19. Operations on line of Pumpkin Vine Creek and battles about Dallas, New Hope Church and Allatoona Hills May 25-June 5. Operations about Marietta and against Kenesaw Mountain June 10-July 2. Pine Hill June 11-14. Lost Mountain June 15-17. Assault on Kenesaw June 27. Ruff's Station July 4. Chattahoochie River July 5-17. Buckhead, Nancy's Creek, July 18. Peach Tree Creek July 19-20. Siege of Atlanta July 22-August 25. Flank movement on Jonesboro August 25-30. Battle of Jonesboro August 31-September 1. Lovejoy Station September 2-6. Pursuit of Hood into Alabama October 1-26. Nashville Campaign November-December. In front of Columbia, Duck River, November 24-27. Spring Hill November 29. Battle of Franklin November 30. Battle of Nashville December 15-16. Pursuit of Hood to the Tennessee River December 17-28. Moved to Huntsville, Ala., and duty there till March, 1865. Operations in East Tennessee March 15-April 22. Moved to Nashville, Tenn., and duty there till June. Mustered out June 10, 1865.

Regiment lost during service 8 Officers and 103 Enlisted men killed and mortally wounded and 3 Officers and 87 Enlisted men by disease. Total 201.

25th REGIMENT INFANTRY.

Organized at LaCrosse, Wis., and mustered in September 14, 1862. Ordered to St. Paul, Minn., September 19, and assigned to duty on northwestern frontier at New Ulm and other points in Minnesota till November. March to Winona, Wis., 300 miles, November 27-December 13. Moved to Camp Randall, Wis., and duty there till February, 1863. Left State for Cairo, Ill., February 17, thence moved to Columbus, Ky., and duty there till April. Attached to' District of Columbus, Ky., 6th Division, 16th Army Corps, Army of the Tennessee, to May, 1863. 3rd Brigade, Kimball's Provisional Division, 16th Army Corps, to July, 1863. 3rd Brigade, Kimball's Division, District of Eastern Arkansas, to August, 1863. Helena, Ark., 2nd Brigade, 2nd Division, Army of Arkansas, to January, 1864. District of Eastern Arkansas, 7th Army Corps, Dept. of Arkansas, January, 1864. 1st Brigade, 4th Division, 16th Army Corps, Army of the Tennessee, to March, 1864. 2nd Brigade, 4th Division, 16th Army Corps, to September, 1864. 2nd Brigade, 1st Division, 17th Army Corps, to June, 1865.

SERVICE.—Moved to Cape Girardeau, Mo., April 27, 1863, thence to Memphis, Tenn., and to Young's Point, La., May 31-June 4. Moved to Haines' Bluff June 16, thence to Snyder's Bluff and duty there till July 25. Siege of Vicksburg, Miss., June 4 to July 4. Expedition to Greenville June 25-July 1. Gaines' Landing, Ark., June 28. Ordered to Helena, Ark., July 25, and duty there till February 1, 1864. Moved to Vicksburg February 1. Meridian Campaign February 3-March 2. Moved to Cairo, Ill., thence to Waterloo, Ala., and march to Decatur via Florence, Athens and Mooresville March 10-April 16. Operations against Forest March 16-April 14. Atlanta (Ga.) Campaign May 1 to September 8. Demonstrations on Resaca May 8-13. Sugar Valley near Resaca May 9. Battle of Resaca May 14-15. Advance on Dallas May 18-25. Operations on line of Pumpkin Vine Creek and battles about Dallas, New Hope Church and Allatoona Hills May 25-June 5. Operations about Marietta and against Kenesaw Mountain June 10-July 2. Assault on Kenesaw Mountain June 27. Nickajack Creek July 2-5. Ruff's Mills July 3-4. Chattahoochie River July 5-17. Decatur and battle of Atlanta July 22. Siege of Atlanta July 22-August 25. Flank movement on Jonesboro August 25-30. Battle of Jonesboro August 31-September 1. Lovejoy Station September 2-6. Operations against Hood in North Georgia and North Alabama September 29-November 3. March to the sea November 15-December 10. Montieth Swamp December 9. Siege of Savannah December 10-21. Campaign of the Carolinas January to April, 1865. Reconnoissance to Salkehatchie River, S. C., January 20. Rivers and Broxton Bridges, Salkehatchie River, S. C., February 2. Salkehatchie Swamp February 2-5. River's Bridge February 3. Columbia February 16-17. Battle of Ben-

tonville, N. C., March 19-21. Occupation of Goldsboro March 24. Advance on Raleigh April 10-14. Occupation of Raleigh April 14. Bennett's House April 26. Surrender of Johnston and his army. March to Washington, D. C., via Richmond, Va., April 29-May 19. Grand Review May 24. Mustered out June 7, 1865.

Regiment lost during service 3 Officers and 46 Enlisted men killed and mortally wounded and 7 Officers and 402 Enlisted men by disease. Total 460.

26th REGIMENT INFANTRY.

Organized at Milwaukee, Wis., and mustered in September 17, 1862. Left State for Washington, D. C., October 6, 1862. Attached to 2nd Brigade, 3rd Division, 11th Army Corps, Army of the Potomac, to October, 1863, and Army of the Cumberland, to April, 1864. 3rd Brigade, 3rd Division, 20th Army Corps, Army of the Cumberland, to June, 1865.

SERVICE.—Moved from Washington, D. C., to Fairfax Court House, Va., October 15, 1862. Movement to Gainesville November 2-9, and duty there till November 18. Moved to Centreville November 18, thence to Falmouth, Va., December 9-14. Battle of Fredericksburg, Va., December 15 (Reserve). At Stafford Court House till January 20, 1863. "Mud March" January 20-24. At Stafford Court House till April 27. Chancellorsville Campaign April 27-May 6. Battle of Chancellorsville May 1-5. Gettysburg (Pa.) Campaign June 11-July 24. Battle of Gettysburg July 1-3. Pursuit of Lee to Manassas Gap, Va., July 5-24. At Warrenton Junction till September 17. Moved to Rappahannock Station September 17, and to Bridgeport, Ala., September 24-October 3. Duty there till October 27. Re-opening Tennessee River October 27-29. Battle of Wauhatchie October 28-29. Duty in Lookout Valley till November 22. Chattanooga-Ringgold Campaign November 23-27. Orchard Knob November 23. Tunnel Hill November 24-25. Mission Ridge November 25. March to relief of Knoxville, Tenn., November 27-December 8. Duty in Lookout Valley till January 25, 1864, and at Whiteside, Ala., till April 23. Atlanta (Ga.) Campaign May 1 to September 8. Demonstration on Rocky Faced Ridge May 8-11. Buzzard's Roost Gap May 8-9. Battle of Resaca May 14-15. Cassville May 19. New Hope Church May 25. Operations on line of Pumpkin Vine Creek and battles about Dallas, New Hope Church and Allatoona Hills May 25-June 5. Operations about Marietta and against Kenesaw Mountain June 10-July 2. Pine Hill June 11-14. Lost Mountain June 15-17. Gilgal or Golgotha Church June 15. Muddy Creek June 17. Noyes Creek June 19. Kolb's Farm June 22. Assault on Kenesaw June 27. Ruff's Station July 4. Chattahoochie River July 5-17. Peach Tree Creek July 19-20. Siege of Atlanta July 22-August 25. Operations at Chattahoochie River Bridge August 26-September 2. Occupation of Atlanta September 2-November 15. March to the sea November 15-December 10. Siege of Savannah December 10-21. Campaign of the Carolinas January to April, 1865. Lawtonville, S. C., February 2. Reconnoissance on Goldsboro Road March 14. Taylor's Hole Creek, Averysboro, N. C., March 16. Battle of Bentonville March 19-21. Mill Creek March 22. Occupation of Goldsboro March 24. Advance on Raleigh April 10-14. Occupation of Raleigh April 14. Bennett's House April 26. Surrender of Johnston and his army. March to Washington, D. C., via Richmond, Va., April 29-May 17. Grand Review May 24. Mustered out June 17, 1865.

Regiment lost during service 12 Officers and 176 Enlisted men killed and mortally wounded and 77 Enlisted men by disease. Total 265.

27th REGIMENT INFANTRY.

Organized at Milwaukee, Wis., and mustered in March 7, 1863. Left State for Columbus, Ky., March 16. Attached to District of Columbus, Ky., 6th Division, 16th Army Corps, Dept. of the Tennessee, to May, 1863. 3rd Brigade, Kimball's Provisional Division, 16th Army Corps, to July, 1863. 3rd Brigade, Kimball's Division, District of Eastern Arkansas, to August, 1863. 2nd Brigade, 2nd Division, Arkansas Expedition, to January, 1864. 2nd Brigade, 2nd Division, 7th Army Corps, Dept. of Arkansas. to April, 1864. 3rd Brigade, 3rd Division, 7th Army Corps, to May, 1864. 2nd Brigade, 1st Division, 7th Army Corps, to February, 1865. 3rd Brigade, 3rd Division, Reserve Corps, Military Division West Mississippi, February, 1865. 3rd Brigade, 3rd Division, 13th Army Corps, Military Division West Mississippi, to August, 1865.

SERVICE.—Duty at Columbus, Ky., till May 30, 1863. Moved to Young's Point, La., May 30-June 3. Moved to Haines' Bluff June 11, thence to Snyder's Bluff June 16, and duty there till July 25. Siege of Vicksburg, Miss., June 4-July 4. Ordered to Helena, Ark., July 25, and duty there till August. Steele's Expedition against Little Rock, Ark., August 10-September 10. Bayou Fourche and capture of Little Rock September 10. Duty at Little Rock till March 23, 1864. Steele's Expedition to Camden March 23-May 3. Okolona April 2-3. Prairie D'Ann April 9-12. Occupation of Camden April 16. Evacuation of Camden April 26. Jenkins' Ferry, Saline River, April 30. Duty at Little Rock and Pine Bluff till February 7, 1865. Pine Bluff June 21, 1864. (Cos. "A," "D," "E" and "H" on guard duty along Little Rock & Memphis Railroad west of Brownsville.) Ordered to New Orleans, La., February 7, 1865, thence to Navy Cave, Mobile Bay. Campaign against Mobile and its defences March 17-April 12. Siege of Spanish Fort and Fort Blakely March 26-April 8. Assault and capture of Fort Blakely April 9. Occupation of Mobile April 12. Expedition to Manna Hubba Bluff April 19-25. Moved to McIntosh Bluff, and duty there till May 9. Moved to Mobile, thence to Brazos Santiago, Texas, June 1-6. Moved to Brownsville August 2 and there mustered out August 5, 1865. Discharged August 29, 1865.

Regiment lost during service 22 Enlisted men killed and mortally wounded and 5 Officers and 232 Enlisted men by disease. Total 259.

28th REGIMENT INFANTRY.

Organized at Milwaukee and mustered in October 14, 1862. Left State for Columbus, Ky., December 29, thence moved to Helena, Ark., January 5-7, 1863. Attached to 2nd Brigade, 13th Division, 13th Army Corps, Army of the Tennessee, to March, 1863. 1st Brigade, 13th Division, 13th Army Corps, to July, 1863. 1st Brigade, 13th Division, 16th Army Corps, to August, 1863. 2nd Brigade, 3rd Division, Arkansas Expedition, to January, 1864. 2nd Brigade, 3rd Division, 7th Army Corps, Dept. of Arkansas, to April, 1864. Post of Pine Bluff, Ark., 7th Army Corps, to May, 1864. 1st Brigade, 1st Division, 7th Army Corps, to February, 1865. 3rd Brigade, 3rd Division, Reserve Corps, Military Division West Mississippi, February, 1865. 3rd Brigade, 3rd Division, 13th Army Corps (New), Military Division West Mississippi, to June, 1865. Dept. of Texas to August, 1865.

SERVICE.—Expedition to Hickman, Ky., December 25-26, 1862. Expedition up White River, Ark., January 11-23, 1863. Yazoo Pass Expedition and operations against Fort Pemberton and Greenwood February 24-April 5. Duty at Helena till August. Repulse of Holmes' attack on Helena July 4. Steele's Expedition against Little Rock, Ark., August 11-September 10. Bayou Fourche and capture of Little Rock September 10. Duty at Little Rock till October 26. Pursuit of Marmaduke's forces to Rockport October 26-November 1. Moved to Pine Bluff, Ark., November 7 and garrison duty there till November 30, 1863. Expedition to Longview March 27-31, 1864. Actions at Mt. Elba March 28 and 30. Expedition to Mt. Elba April 28-30. Moved to Little Rock November 30, and duty there till February, 1865. Carr's Expedition to Mt. Elba January 22-February 4, 1865. Moved to New Orleans, La., February 11-16, thence to Mobile Point, Ala., February 22. Campaign against Mobile and its defences March 17-April 12. Siege of Spanish Fort and Fort Blakely March 26-April 8. Assault and capture of Fort Blakely April 9. Occupation of Mobile April 12. Expedition to

Manna Hubba Bluff April 15-26. At McIntosh Bluff till May 9. Moved to Mobile May 9, and duty there till May 31. Moved to New Orleans, La., thence to Brazos Santiago, Texas, May 31-June 6. Moved to Clarksville June 16, and to Brownsville August 3. Mustered out August 23, 1865.

Regiment lost during service 1 Officer and 12 Enlisted men killed and mortally wounded and 6 Officers and 221 Enlisted men by disease. Total 240.

29th REGIMENT INFANTRY.

Organized at Madison, Wis., and mustered in September 27, 1862. Moved to Cairo, Ill., thence to Helena, Ark., November 2-7, 1862. Attached to 3rd Brigade, 12th Division, District of Eastern Arkansas, Dept. of the Tennessee, to January, 1863. 3rd Brigade, 12th Division, 13th Army Corps, Dept. of the Tennessee, to February, 1863. 1st Brigade, 12th Division, 13th Army Corps, to July, 1863. 1st Brigade, 3rd Division, 13th Army Corps, Army of the Tennessee, to August, 1863, and Dept. of the Gulf, to June, 1864. District of Lafourche, Dept. of the Gulf, to August, 1864. 2nd Brigade, 2nd Division, 19th Army Corps, Dept. of the Gulf, to December, 1864. 1st Brigade, Reserve Corps, Military Division West Mississippi, to February, 1865. 1st Brigade, 1st Division, Reserve Corps, Military Division West Mississippi, February, 1865. 1st Brigade, 1st Division, 13th Army Corps (New), Military Division West Mississippi, to June, 1865.

SERVICE.—Expedition from Helena, Ark., to Arkansas Post, November 16-21, 1862. Duty opposite Helena till December 23. Action at Helena December 5. Moved to Helena December 23, thence to Friar's Point, and duty there till January 7, 1863. Expedition up White River to Devall's Bluff January 11-23. At Helena till April 10. Ordered to Milliken's Bend, La., April 10. Movement on Bruinsburg and turning Grand Gulf April 25-30. Battle of Port Gibson May 1 (Reserve). Battle of Champion's Hill May 16. Siege of Vicksburg, Miss., May 18-July 4. Assaults on Vicksburg May 19 and 22. Advance on Jackson, Miss., July 4-10. Siege of Jackson July 10-17. Ordered to New Orleans, La., August 6, thence to Brashear City September 15, and duty there till October 2. Western Louisiana Campaign October 3-November 30. Carrion Crow Bayou November 3. At New Iberia till December 19. March to Berwick December 19-21, thence to Algiers December 22-25. Moved to Pass Cavallo, Texas, January 5-12, 1864. Duty at DeCrow's Point till February 20. Moved to New Orleans February 20-23, and duty at Algiers till March 5. Red River Campaign March 10-May 22. Advance from Franklin to Alexandria March 14-26. Battle of Sabine Cross Roads April 8. Monett's Bluff, Cane River Crossing, April 23. At Alexandria April 26-May 13. Construction of dam at Alexandria April 30-May 10. Graham's Plantation May 5. Retreat to Morganza May 13-20. Duty at Morganza till June 13. Expedition to the Atchafalaya May 30-June 6. Moved to Carrollton June 13, thence to Kennersville June 21, and to Thibodeaux June 26, and duty there till July 9. Moved to Algiers July 9, and to Morganza July 26. Morgan's Ferry Road and Atchafalaya River July 28. Moved to Port Hudson August 23. Expedition to Clinton August 23-29. Moved to Morganza August 29, thence to St. Charles, Ark., September 3-11, and duty there till October 23. Expedition to Devall's Bluff October 23-November 12. Moved to Little Rock, Ark., November 12, thence to Memphis, Tenn., November 25, and duty there till January, 1865. Expedition to Moscow to assist Gen. Grierson December 21-31. Ordered to New Orleans, La., January 1, 1865, thence to Kennersville Station, and duty there till February 5. Moved to Dauphin Island near Mobile, Ala., February 5. Campaign against Mobile and its defences March 17-April 12. Siege of Spanish Fort and Fort Blakely March 26-April 8. Assault and capture of Fort Blakely April 9. Occupation of Mobile April 12 to May 26. Moved to New Orleans, La. thence to Shreveport May 26-June 8, and duty there till June 22. Mustered out June 22, 1865,

Regiment lost during service 1 Officer and 76 Enlisted men killed and mortally wounded and 3 Officers and 242 Enlisted men by disease. Total 322.

30th REGIMENT INFANTRY.

Organized at Camp Randall, Madison, Wis., and mustered in October 21, 1862.

SERVICE.—Duty at Green Bay, West Bay and other points in Wisconsin, enforcing draft, etc., till March, 1863. Headquarters of Regiment at Camp Randall till December 26, 1862, then at Camp Reno, Milwaukee, Wis. Companies "D" F," "I" and "K" ordered to St. Louis, Mo., May 2, 1863. Guard boats and supplies for Sully's Northwestern Indian Expedition up the Missouri River till August. Companies "I" and "K" ordered to Milwaukee. Companies "D' and "F" at Fann Island, and fatigue duty building Fort Sully till December, 1863. Companies "E" and "G" at Bayfield and Superior City, Wis., May 26-August 21, 1863, then report to Milwaukee. Company "G" ordered to Davenport, Iowa, December 5, 1863. Company "I" moved to St. Louis, Mo., April, 1864, and thence to Fort Union, D. T., and duty there till June, 1865. Rejoined Regiment at St. Louis, Mo., June 22, 1865. Companies "A," "C," "F" and "H" left Milwaukee, Wis., April 20, 1864, to join Sully's Northwestern Indian Expedition. Moved from St. Louis to Fort Sully, D. T., thence to Fort Rice, and duty there till October. Moved to Sioux City October 12-November 2. Company "D" join. Moved to Quincy, Ill., thence to Louisville, Ky., November 24-29. Companies "B," "E," "G" and "K" left Milwaukee for Dakota Territory April, 1864. Duty at Fort Wadsworth July 1-September 29. Ordered to St. Louis, Mo., thence to relief of Paducah, Ky., October 29. Moved to St. Louis December 6-10, and join balance of Regiment. Moved to Bowling Green, Ky., December 12 and assigned to 2nd Brigade, 2nd Division, Military District of Kentucky. Moved to Louisville, Ky., January 10, 1865, and provost duty there till September; also conducting prisoners to various points. Companies "B," "E" and "G" moved to Frankfort, Ky., February, 1865, and duty there till June. Mustered out September 20, 1865.

Regiment lost during service 2 Enlisted men killed and 2 Officers and 65 Enlisted men by disease. Total 69.

31st REGIMENT INFANTRY.

Companies "A," "B," "C," "D," "E" and "F" organized at Prairie du Chien, Wis., and mustered in October 9, 1862. Companies "G," "H," "I" and "K" organized at Camp Utley, Racine, Wis., and mustered in December 24, 1862. Companies "A," "D" and "F" ordered to Madison, Wis., November 14. Companies "B," "C" and "E" ordered to Racine, Wis., November 14, as guard for draft rendezvous. Companies "A," "D" and "F" moved to Racine December 20. Regiment ordered to Columbus, Ky., March 1, 1863. Attached to District of Columbus, Ky., 6th Division, 16th Army Corps, Dept. of the Tennessee, to October, 1863. Unattached, Dept. of the Cumberland, to November, 1863. Post of Murfreesboro, Tenn., Dept. of the Cumberland, to January, 1864. 2nd Brigade, Rousseau's 3rd Division, 12th Army Corps, Dept. of the Cumberland, to April, 1864. Unattached, 4th Division, 20th Army Corps, Dept. of the Cumberland, to July, 1864. 3rd Brigade, 1st Division, 20th Army Corps, Army of the Cumberland, to July, 1865.

SERVICE.—Duty at Columbus, Ky., March 6-September 24, 1863. Moved to Cairo, Ill., Louisville, Ky., and Nashville, Tenn., September 24-27, thence moved to Lavergne October 5, and railroad guard duty there till October 25. Moved to Murfreesboro, Tenn., October 25, and duty there till April, 1864. Companies "B," "G" and "K" detached at Stone's River Crossing, guarding railroad bridge and building fortifications, till April 2, 1864. Assigned to duty by Detachments, guarding Nashville & Chattanooga Railroad from Normandy to Murfreesboro, till June. Regiment ordered to Murfreesboro, thence to Nashville, Tenn., June 6-10, and provost and guard duty there till July 16. Moved to Atlanta, Ga., July 16-21. Atlanta (Ga.) Campaign July 21-September 8. Siege of Atlanta July 22-August 25. Operations at

Chattahoochie River Bridge August 26-September 2. Occupation of Atlanta September 2-November 15. Expedition from Atlanta to Tuckum's Cross Roads October 26-29. March to the sea November 15-December 10. Harrison's Field and Montieth Swamp December 9. Siege of Savannah December 10-21. Campaign of the Carolinas January to April, 1865. Taylor's Hole Creek, Averysboro, N. C., March 16. Battle of Bentonville March 19-21. Occupation of Goldsboro March 24. Advance on Raleigh April 10-14. Occupation of Raleigh April 14. Bennett's House April 26. Surrender of Johnston and his army. March to Washington, D. C., via Richmond, Va., April 29-May 17. Grand Review May 24. Companies "A" to "F" mustered out June 20, and Companies "G" to "K" mustered out July 8, 1865.

Regiment lost during service 23 Enlisted men killed and mortally wounded and 3 Officers and 86 Enlisted men by disease. Total 112.

32nd REGIMENT INFANTRY.

Organized at Oshkosh, Wis., and mustered in September 25, 1862. Left State for Memphis, Tenn., October 30. Attached to 5th Brigade, District of Memphis, Tenn., 13th Army Corps (Old), Dept. of the Tennessee, November, 1862. 3rd Brigade, 1st Division, District of Memphis, 13th Army Corps, to December, 1862. 3rd Brigade, 8th Division, 16th Army Corps, Army of the Tennessee, to March, 1863. 2nd Brigade, District of Memphis, 5th Division, 16th Army Corps, to December, 1863. 3rd Brigade, 1st Cavalry Division, 16th Army Corps, to January, 1864. 2nd Brigade, 4th Division, 16th Army Corps, to March, 1864. 3rd Brigade, 4th Division, 16th Army Corps, to September, 1864. 3rd Brigade, 1st Division, 17th Army Corps, to June, 1865.

SERVICE.—Grant's Central Mississippi Campaign; operations on the Mississippi Central Railroad November 18, 1862, to January 2, 1863. Moved to Memphis, Tenn., and provost duty there till November 26, 1863. Moved to Moscow, Tenn., November 26-30, and duty there till January 27, 1864. Repulse of Lee's attack on Moscow December 2, 1863. Moved to Memphis, Tenn., thence to Vicksburg, Miss., January 27-February 2, 1864. Meridian Campaign February 3-March 2. Meridian February 14-15. Laudersdale Springs February 16. Marion February 15-17. Operations against Forest in West Tennessee March 16-April 10. At Decatur, Ala., April 10-August 4, 1864. Expedition to Courtland, Ala., May 27-29. Pond Springs, near Courtland, May 27. Expedition from Decatur to Moulton July 25. Courtland July 25 and 27. Moved to Atlanta, Ga., August 4-8. Atlanta (Ga.) Campaign August 8-September 8. Siege of Atlanta August 8-25. Flank movement on Jonesboro August 25-30. Battle of Jonesboro August 31-September 1. Lovejoy Station September 2-6. Operations against Hood in North Georgia and North Alabama September 29-November 3. March to the sea November 15-December 10. Harrison's Field and Montieth Swamp December 9. Siege of Savannah December 10-21. Campaign of the Carolinas January to April, 1865. Reconnoissance to Salkehatchie River January 20. Salkehatchie Swamps February 2-5. Rivers' and Broxton Bridges, Salkehatchie River, February 2. Rivers' Bridge, South Edisto River, February 3. Binnaker's Bridge, South Edisto River, February 9. Orangeburg February 11-12. Columbia February 16-17. Averysboro, N. C., March 16. Battle of Bentonville March 19-21. Occupation of Goldsboro March 24. Advance on Raleigh April 10-14. Occupation of Raleigh April 14. Bennett's House April 26. Surrender of Johnston and his army. March to Washington, D. C., via Richmond, Va., April 29-May 20. Grand Review May 24. Mustered out June 12,• 1865.

Regiment lost during service 1 Officer and 26 Enlisted men killed and mortally wounded and 1 Officer and 253 Enlisted men by disease. Total 281.

33rd REGIMENT INFANTRY.

Organized at Racine, Wis., and mustered in October 18, 1862. Left State for Memphis, Tenn., November 12. Attached to Reserve Brigade, District of Memphis, Tenn., 13th Army Corps (Old), Dept. of the Tennessee, to December, 1862. 1st Brigade, 4th Division, 17th Army Corps, Army of the Tennessee, to January, 1863. 1st Brigade, 4th Division, 16th Army Corps, to July, 1863. 1st Brigade, 4th Division, 13th Army Corps, to August, 1863. 1st Brigade, 4th Division, 17th Army Corps, to March, 1864. 1st Brigade, Provisional Division, 17th Army Corps, Dept. of the Gulf, to June, 1864. Detached Brigade, 17th Army Corps, and 4th Brigade, 1st Division, 16th Army Corps, to December, 1864. 1st Brigade, 3rd Division, Detachment Army of the Tennessee, Dept. of the Cumberland, to February, 1865. 1st Brigade, 3rd Division, 16th Army Corps (New), Military Division West Mississippi, to August, 1865.

SERVICE.—Grant's Central Mississippi Campaign; operations on the Mississippi Central Railroad November 18, 1862, to January 10, 1863. Moved to Moscow, Tenn., and duty along Memphis & Charleston Railroad till March 9. Moscow February 13 (Detachment). Moved to Memphis, Tenn., March 9, and duty there till May 17. Expedition to the Coldwater April 18-24. Hernando April 18. Perry's Ferry, Coldwater, April 19. Ordered to Vicksburg, Miss., May 17. Siege of Vicksburg May 20-July 4. Advance on Jackson, Miss., July 4-10. Siege of Jackson July 10-17. Assault on Jackson July 12. Reconnoissance to Pearl River July 15. Duty at Vicksburg till August 18. Ordered to Natchez, Miss., and duty there till December 1. Expedition to Harrisonburg September 1-8. Moved to Vicksburg December 1, and duty at Camp Milldale till February, 1864. Meridian Campaign February 3-March 2. Pearl River, near Canton and Madisonville, February 27. Red River Campaign March 10-May 24. Fort DeRussy March 14. Occupation of Alexandria March 16. Pleasant Hill Landing April 12-13. About Cloutiersville April 22-24. About Alexandria April 26-May 13. Wells' Plantation May 6. Boyce's Plantation May 6. Bayou Boeuf May 7. Retreat to Morganza May 13-20. Mansura May 16. Moved to Vicksburg, Miss., May 22-24, thence to Memphis, Tenn., May 27-30, and duty there till June 22. Moved to LaGrange, Tenn., June 22-27. Smith's Expedition to Tupelo July 5-21. Camargo's Cross Roads, near Harrisburg, July 13. Harrisburg, near Tupelo, July 14-15. Smith's Expedition to Oxford August 1-3. Moved to St. Charles, Ark., August 3-6, thence to Devall's Bluff September 1, and to Brownsville, Ark., September 8. March through Arkansas and Missouri in pursuit of Price September 17-November 16. Moved to St. Louis, Mo., thence to Nashville, Tenn., November 23-30. Battle of Nashville December 15-16. Pursuit of Hood to the Tennessee River December 17-28. Moved to Clifton. Tenn., thence to Eastport, Miss., and duty there till February, 1865. Movement to New Orleans, La., February 6-22. Campaign against Mobile and its defences March 17-April 12. Expedition from Dauphin Island to Foul River Narrows March 18-22. Siege of Spanish Fort and Fort Blakely March 26-April 8. Assault on and capture of Fort Blakely April 9. Occupation of Mobile April 12. March to Montgomery April 13-25. Duty at Montgomery and Tuskegee till July. Moved to Vicksburg, Miss., July 23-31. Mustered out August 8, 1865.

Regiment lost during service 3 Officers and 30 Enlisted men killed and mortally wounded and 2 Officers and 167 Enlisted men by disease. Total 202.

34th REGIMENT INFANTRY.

Organized at Madison, Wis., December, 1862. Moved to Columbus, Ky., January 31-February 2, 1863. Attached to District of Columbus, Ky., 6th Division, 16th Army Corps, Dept. of the Tennessee, to August, 1863. (6 Companies attached to 4th Brigade, District of Memphis, Tenn., 5th Division, 16th Army Corps, May to August.)

SERVICE.—Garrison and fatigue duty at Fort Halleck, Columbus, Ky., till August, 1863. Company "E" detached at Paducah, Ky., March 3; Companies "I" and "G" at Cairo, Ill., April 25-June 1; Companies "B," "C," "D," "F," "H" and "K" at Memphis, Tenn., May 12. Regiment united at Cairo, Ill., August 14. Moved to Wisconsin August 16 and mustered out September 8, 1863.

Regiment lost during service 1 Officer and 18 Enlisted men by disease. Total 19.

35th REGIMENT INFANTRY.

Organized at Milwaukee, Wis., and mustered in February 27, 1864. Ordered to Alexandria, La., April 18. Moved to Benton Barracks, Mo., thence to New Orleans, La., April 26. Ordered to report to Gen. Williams at Port Hudson, La., arriving there May 7. Attached to 1st Brigade, 3rd Division, 19th Army Corps, Dept. of the Gulf, to December, 1864. 4th Brigade, Reserve Corps, Military Division West Mississippi, to February, 1865. 1st Brigade, 3rd Division, Reserve Corps, Military Division West Mississippi, February, 1865. 1st Brigade, 3rd Division, 13th Army Corps (New), Military Division West Mississippi, to July, 1865. Dept. of Texas to March, 1866.

SERVICE.—Duty at Port Hudson, La., till June 27, 1864. Moved to Morganza, La., June 27, and duty there till July 24. Moved to St. Charles, Ark., July 24, and duty there till August 6. Return to Morganza August 6-12. Expedition to Simsport October 1-10. Moved to Devall's Bluff, Ark., October 11-18. To Brownsville November 9, and guard Memphis & Little Rock Railroad till December 12. Moved to Devall's Bluff December 12, and duty there till February 7, 1865. Moved to Algiers, La., February 7, thence to Mobile Point, Ala., February 22. Campaign against Mobile and its defences March 17-April 12. Siege of Spanish Fort and Fort Blakely March 26-April 8. Assault on and capture of Fort Blakely April 9. Occupation of Mobile April 12. March to McIntosh Bluff April 13-26. Moved to Mobile May 9, and duty there till June 1. Moved to Brazos Santiago, Texas, June 1-8, thence to Clarksville June 20, and to Brownsville August 2. Duty at Brownsville till March, 1866. Mustered out March 15, 1866.

Regiment lost during service 2 Enlisted men killed and 3 Officers and 271 Enlisted men by disease. Total 276.

36th REGIMENT INFANTRY.

Organized at Madison, Wis., and mustered in March 23, 1864. Ordered to Washington, D. C., May 10, thence marched to Spottsylvania Court House and attached to 1st Brigade, 2nd Division, 2nd Army Corps, Army of the Potomac.

SERVICE.—Spottsylvania Court House May 18-21. North Anna River May 23-26. On line of the Pamunkey May 26-28. Totopotomoy May 28-31. Bethesda Church June 1. Cold Harbor June 1-12. Before Petersburg June 16-18. Siege of Petersburg June 16, 1864, to April 2, 1865. Weldon Railroad June 22-23, 1864. Demonstration north of the James River July 27-29. Deep Bottom July 27-28. Demonstration north of the James at Deep Bottom August 13-20. Strawberry Plains August 14-18. Ream's Station August 25. Boydton Plank Road, Hatcher's Run, October 27-28. Dabney's Mills, Hatcher's Run, February 5-7, 1865. Watkins' House March 25. Appomattox Campaign March 28-April 9. Hatcher's Run March 29. Boydton Plank Road and White Oak Road March 30-31. Crow's House March 31. Fall of Petersburg April 2. Pursuit of Lee April 3-9. Sailor's Creek April 6. High Bridge and Farmville April 7. Appomattox Court House April 9. Surrender of Lee and his army. Moved to Washington, D. C., May 2-12. Grand Review May 23. Moved to Louisville, Ky., June 17, and there mustered out July 12, 1865.

Regiment lost during service 7 Officers and 150 Enlisted men killed and mortally wounded and 3 Officers and 182 Enlisted men by disease. Total 342.

37th REGIMENT INFANTRY.

Organized at Madison, Wis., April 9, 1864. Left State for Washington, D. C., April 28 (Cos. "A" to "F"). Two more Companies, "H" and "I," join at Maryland Heights May 17. Duty at Washington, D. C., till May 30. Moved to White House, Va., May 30-June 1, and guard duty there till June 10. Guard supply train to Cold Harbor June 10. Attached to Casey's Brigade, 22nd Army Corps, to June, 1864. 1st Brigade, 3rd Division, 9th Army Corps, Army of the Potomac, to September,

1864. 1st Brigade, 1st Division, 9th Army Corps, to July, 1865.

SERVICE.—Movement across James River to Petersburg, Va., June 12-15. Assaults on Petersburg June 16-18. Siege of Petersburg June 16, 1864, to April 2, 1865. Mine Explosion, Petersburg, July 30, 1864. Weldon Railroad August 18-21. Poplar Springs Church September 29-October 2. Boydton Plank Road, Hatcher's Run, October 27-28. Fort Stedman, Petersburg, March 25, 1865. Appomattox Campaign March 28-April 9. Assault on and fall of Petersburg April 2. Occupation of Petersburg April 3. Pursuit of Lee April 3-9. Moved to Washington, D. C., April 21-24. Grand Review May 23. Provost duty at Washington and Alexandria till July. Mustered out July 26, 1865.

Regiment lost during service 7 Officers and 149 Enlisted men killed and mortally wounded and 2 Officers and 89 Enlisted men by disease. Total 247.

38th REGIMENT INFANTRY.

Companies "A," "B," "C" and "D" organized at Madison, Wis., and mustered in April 15, 1864. Moved to Washington, D. C., May 3-7. Attached to Casey's Provisional Brigade, 22nd Army Corps, May, 1864. 1st Brigade, 3rd Division, 9th Army Corps, Army of the Potomac, to September, 1864. 1st Brigade, 1st Division, 9th Army Corps, to July, 1865.

SERVICE.—Camp at Arlington, Va., till May 30, 1864. Moved to White House, Va., May 30-June 1. Battalion temporarily attached to 1st Minnesota Infantry. Guard supply train to Cold Harbor June 9. Cold Harbor June 10-12. Movement across James River to Petersburg June 12-15. Assaults on Petersburg June 16-18. Siege of Petersburg June 16, 1864, to April 2, 1865. (Co. "E" joined July 26, 1864.) Mine Explosion, Petersburg, July 30, 1864. Weldon Railroad August 18-21. Poplar Springs Church September 29-October 2. Boydton Plank Road, Hatcher's Run, October 27-28. (Companies "F," "G," "H," "I" and "K" joined October 1, 1864. Received Rebel Peace Commissioners Stephens, Hunter, Campbell and Hatch through lines under flag of truce January 29, 1865. Fort Stedman, Petersburg, March 25. Appomattox Campaign March 28-April 9. Assault on and fall of Petersburg April 2. Occupation of Petersburg April 3. Pursuit of Lee April 3-9. Moved to Washington, D. C., April 21-25. Grand Review May 23. 2nd Battalion mustered out June 6, 1865. 1st Battalion on duty at Arsenal, Washington, during trial and execution of President Lincoln's assassins. Mustered out July 26, 1865.

Regiment lost during service 1 Officer and 56 Enlisted men killed and mortally wounded and 56 Enlisted men by disease. Total 113.

39th REGIMENT INFANTRY.

Organized at Milwaukee, Wis., and mustered in June 3, 1864. Moved to Memphis, Tenn., June 13-17. Attached to 2nd Brigade, Post and Defences of Memphis, District of West Tennessee. Garrison, railroad guard and picket duty at and about Memphis, Tenn., till September. Repulse of Forest's attack on Memphis August 21. Mustered out September 22, 1864.

Regiment lost during service 3 Enlisted men killed and mortally wounded and 1 Officer and 27 Enlisted men by disease. Total 31.

40th REGIMENT INFANTRY.

Organized at Madison, Wis., and mustered in June 14, 1864. Moved to Memphis, Tenn., June 14-19. Attached to Post and Defences of Memphis, District of West Tennessee. Garrison, railroad guard and picket duty at and about Memphis, Tenn., till September. Repulse of Forest's attack on Memphis August 21. Mustered out September 16, 1864.

Regiment lost during service 1 Officer and 18 Enlisted men by disease. Total 19.

41st REGIMENT INFANTRY.

Organized at Milwaukee, Wis., and mustered in June 8, 1864. Moved to Memphis, Tenn., June 15-19. Attached to 2nd Brigade, Post of Memphis, Tenn., District of West Tennessee, to September. Garrison, railroad guard and picket duty at Memphis and in that vicinity till September. Repulse of Forest's attack on Memphis August 21. Mustered out September 24, 1864.

Regiment lost during service 18 by disease.

42nd REGIMENT INFANTRY.

Organized at Madison, Wis., and mustered in September 7, 1864. Moved to Cairo, Ill., September 20-22. Assigned to post and garrison duty at Cairo and provost duty by detachments at various points in Ilinois till June, 1865. Mustered out June 20, 1865.

Regiment lost during service 58 by disease.

43rd REGIMENT INFANTRY.

Organized at. Madison, Wis., and mustered in by Companies August 8 to September 30, 1864. Left State for Nashville, Tenn.. October 10. Attached to Defences of Nashville & Northwestern Railroad, Dept. of the Cumberland, to December, 1864. 3rd Brigade, Defences Nashville & Chattanooga Railroad, to March, 1865. 3rd Brigade, 1st Sub-District, District of Middle Tennessee, Dept. of the Cumberland, to June, 1865.

SERVICE.—Stationed at Johnsonville, Tenn., guarding railroad and supplies October 15-November 30. Repulse of attack on Johnsonville November 4-5. Moved to Clarksville, Tenn., November 30, thence to Nashville, Tenn., December 28, and to Dechard January 1, 1865. Guard duty at Elk River Bridge and along line of the Nashville & Chattanooga Railroad till June. Mustered out June 24, 1865.

Regiment lost during service 1 Enlisted man killed and 2 Officers and 72 Enlisted men by disease. Total 75.

44th REGIMENT INFANTRY.

Organized at Madison, Wis., by Companies October-November, 1864, and ordered to Nashville, Tenn., as fast as completed. Companies "A," "B," "C," "D" and "F" reached Nashville during October and November. Battle of Nashville December 15-16. Attached to Post and Defences of Nashville till March, 1865. Paducah, Ky., Dept. of Kentucky, to August, 1865.

SERVICE.—Garrison and guard duty at Nashville, Tenn., till March, 1865. Regimental organization completed February, 1865. Ordered to Paducah, Ky., April 3, and duty there till August. Mustered out August 28, 1865.

Regiment lost during service 1 Officer and 57 Enlisted men by disease. Total 58.

45th REGIMENT INFANTRY.

Organized at Madison, Wis., November 8, 1864. Companies as organized ordered to Nashville, Tenn. Attached to Post of Nashville, Tenn., Dept. of the Cumberland, to February, 1865. 2nd Brigade, 4th Division, 20th Army Corps, Dept. of the Cumberland, to March, 1865. Post of Nashville, Dept. of the Cumberland, to July, 1865.

SERVICE.—Garrison and guard duty at Nashville till July, 1865. Battle of Nashville December 15-16. Mustered out July 17, 1865.

Lost during service 34 by disease.

46th REGIMENT INFANTRY.

Organized at Madison, Wis., and mustered in March 2, 1865. Moved to Louisville, Ky., March 5-10, thence to Athens, Ala., April 22-24. Attached to 2nd Brigade, 1st Sub-District, District of Middle Tennessee, Dept. of the Cumberland.

SERVICE.—Duty along line of the Nashville & Decatur Railroad till September. Mustered out September 27, 1865.

Lost during service 20 by disease.

47th REGIMENT INFANTRY.

Organized at Madison, Wis., and mustered in February 27, 1865. Ordered to Louisville, Ky., thence to Nashville, Tenn., and Tullahoma, Tenn. Attached to 2nd Brigade, Defences Nashville & Chattanooga Railroad, Dept. of the Cumberland, to April, 1865. 2nd Brigade, 1st Sub-District, District Middle Tennessee, Dept. of the Cumberland, to September, 1865.

SERVICE—Railroad guard duty at Tullahoma and in District of Middle Tennessee till September. Mustered out September 4, 1865.

Lost during service 39 by disease.

48th REGIMENT INFANTRY.

Organized at Milwaukee, Wis., February-March, 1865. Left State for St. Louis, Mo., March 22, thence moved to Warrenton and to Paola, Kan., April 1-13. Assigned to provost duty in District of Kansas as follows: "C" at Lawrence, "B" at Olatho, "F" and "G" at Paola, "A," "B," "D" and "E" at Fort Scott (skirmish near Miami, Mo., April 24, 1865) till August. Companies "I" and "K" left Milwaukee, Wis., March 28, and reached Fort Scott April 28. Moved to Lawrence August 19-25. March to Fort Zarah September 6-26, and assigned to garrison duty as follows: "E" and "G" at Fort Zarah, "A" and "H" at Fort Larned, "B" and "I" at Fort Dodge, "D" and "F" at Fort Aubrey, "C" and "K" at Fort Lyon, Colo., till December, 1865. "A," "E," "G" and "H" ordered to Fort Leavenworth, Kan., December, 1865, and mustered out December 30, 1865. "B," "D," "F" and "I" moved to Fort Leavenworth, Kan., February, 1866, and mustered out February 19, 1866. "C" and "K" mustered out at Fort Leavenworth March 24, 1866.

Regiment lost during service 16 by disease.

49th REGIMENT INFANTRY.

Organized at Madison, Wis., December 24, 1864, to March 5, 1865. Left State for St. Louis, Mo., March 8, 1865, thence moved to Rolla, Mo., March 13. Garrison and guard duty at Rolla till August and at St. Louis, Mo., till November. Attached to 2nd Sub-District, District of St. Louis, Dept. of Missouri, March to August, and to 1st Sub-District to November. Mustered out November 8, 1865.

Regiment lost during service 54 by disease.

50th REGIMENT INFANTRY.

Organized at Madison, Wis., March and April, 1865. Moved to St. Louis, Mo., thence from Benton Barracks (skirmishes near Booneville, Mo., May 3, 1865, Detachment) to Fort Leavenworth, Kan., and to Fort Rice, D. T. Duty there till May, 1866. Mustered out April 19 to June 12, 1863.

Regiment lost during service 1 Enlisted man killed and 1 Officer and 43 Enlisted men by disease. Total 45.

51st REGIMENT INFANTRY.

Organized at Camp Washburn, Milwaukee, Wis., March 20-April 29, 1865. (Cos. "G," "H," "I" and "K" did not leave the State and were mustered out May 6, 1865.) Moved to St. Louis, Mo., May, 1865, and assigned to duty at St. Louis, Warrensburg and along Pacific Railroad from Hilden to Pleasant Hill May to August. Company "A" at Crawford River; "B" at Carondelet; "C" and "D" at Kingville; "E" and "F" at Pleasant Hill. Mustered out at Madison, Wis., August 16-30, 1865.

Regiment lost during service 16 by disease.

52nd REGIMENT INFANTRY.

Organized at Madison, Wis., April, 1865. Moved to St. Louis, Mo., thence to Holden, Mo., and guard workmen on the Pacific Railroad till June 21. Moved to Fort Leavenworth, Kan., and duty there till July 28. Mustered out July 28, 1865.

Regiment lost during service 9 by disease.

53rd REGIMENT INFANTRY.

Organized at Madison, Wis., March and April, 1865. Ordered to St. Louis, Mo., thence to Fort Leavenworth, Kan. Transferred to 51st Wisconsin Infantry June 10, 1865.

Regiment lost during service 8 by disease.

UNITED STATES—REGULAR ARMY.

1st REGIMENT CAVALRY.

On the Pacific Coast till November, 1861. Concentrated at Washington, D. C., November, 1861, to January, 1862. (Cos. "D" and "G" in New Mexico. Evacuation of Forts Breckenridge and Buchanan. Stationed at Fort Craig. Defence of Fort Craig January-February, 1862. Near Fort Craig February 19. Action at Valverde February 21. Apache Canon, near Santa Fe, March 26. Glorietta or Pigeon Ranch March 28. Albuquerque April 25. Peralta April 27.) Regiment attached to Cooke's Cavalry Reserve, Army Potomac, January to March, 1862. 2nd Brigade, Cavalry Reserve, Army Potomac, to July, 1862. Headquarters Army Potomac to February, 1863. Reserve Brigade, 1st Cavalry Division, Cavalry Corps, Army Potomac, to August, 1864. 3rd (Reserve) Brigade, 1st Division, Cavalry Corps, Army Shenandoah, Middle Military Division, to December, 1864. Headquarters Army Shenandoah to March, 1865. 3rd Brigade, 1st Division, Cavalry Corps, Army Potomac, to July, 1865.

SERVICE.—Advance on Manassas, Va., July 16-21, 1861 (Cos. "A" and "E"). Battle of Bull Run July 21 (Cos. "A" and "E"). Duty in the Defences of Washington, D. C., till March, 1862. Moved to Virginia Peninsula March. Siege of Yorktown, Va., April 5-May 4. Cheese Cake Church May 4. Reconnoissance to Hanover Court House May 26. Operations against Stuart June 13-15. Seven days before Richmond June 25-July 1. Gaines' Mill June 27. Malvern Hill July 1. Reconnoissance to Charlestown, W. Va., October 16-17. Charlestown October 16. Battle of Fredericksburg, Va., December 12-15. Expedition from Potomac Creek to Richards' and Ellis' Fords, Rappahannock River, December 29-30. Kelly's Ford March 17, 1863. Stoneman's Raid April 29-May 8. Brandy Station and Beverly Ford June 9. Middleburg June 19. Upperville June 21. Battle of Gettysburg, Pa., July 1-3. Williamsport, Md., July 6. Boonsboro July 8. Benevola or Beaver Creek July 9. About Funkstown July 10-13. Falling Waters July 14. Manassas Gap, Va., July 21-22. Wapping Heights and Chester Gap July 23. Kelly's Ford July 31-August 1. Brandy Station August 1-4. In Defences of Washington till September. Bristoe Campaign October 9-22. Manassas Junction October 17. Bristoe Station October 18. Advance to the Rappahannock November 7-8. Mine Run Campaign November 26-December 2. Demonstration on the Rapidan February 6-7, 1864. Barnett's Ford February 6-7. Custer's Raid in Albemarle County February 28-March 1. Near Charlottesville February 29. Stannardsville March 1. Rapidan Campaign May 4-June 12. Wilderness May 5-7. Todd's Tavern May 7-8. Sheridan's Raid to the James River May 9-24. Ground Squirrel Church and Yellow Tavern May 11. Mechanicsville May 12. On line of the Pamunkey May 26-28. Hanovertown Ferry and Hanovertown May 27. Totopotomoy May 28-31. Old Church and Mattadequin Creek May 30. Bethesda Church, Cold Harbor, May 31-June 1. Sheridan's Trevillian Raid June 7-24. Trevillian Station June 11-12. Mallory's Cross Roads June 12. Black Creek or Tunstall Station and White House or St. Peter's Church June 21. Jones' Bridge June 23. Siege of Petersburg till August. Deep Bottom July 27-28. Malvern Hill July 28. Sheridan's Shenandoah Valley Campaign August 7-November 28. Toll Gate, near White Post, and near Newtown, August 11. Near Strasburg August 14. Summit Point August 21. Halltown and near Kearneysville August 25. Leetown and Smithfield August 28. Smithfield, crossing of the Opequan, August 29. Locke's Ford, Opequan Creek, September 13. Sevier's Ford, Opequan Creek, September 15. Battle of Opequan, Winchester, September 19. Fisher's Hill September 21. Milford September 22. Front Royal September 23. Luray Valley September 24. Port Republic September 26-27. Rockfish Gap September 28. Mt. Crawford October 2. Tom's Brook, Woodstock Races, October 8-9. Expedition into Surrey County October 16-18. Battle of Cedar Creek October 19. Near Kernstown November 11. Expedition into Loudoun and Fauquier Counties November 28-December 3. Expedition from Winchester to near Gordonsville December 19-28. Liberty Mills December 22. Near Gordonsville December 23. Sheridan's Raid from Winchester February 27-March 25, 1865. Occupation of Staunton March 2. Action at Waynesborough March 2. Duguidsville March 8. Appomattox Campaign March 28-April 9. Dinwiddie Court House March 30-31. Five Forks April 1. Scott's Cross Roads April 2. Tabernacle Church or Beaver Pond Creek April 4. Sailor's Creek April 6. Appomattox Station April 8. Appomattox Court House April 9. Surrender of Lee and his army. Expedition to Danville April 23-29. Moved to Washington, D. C., May. Grand Review May 23. Ordered to New Orleans, La., and duty there till December, 1865.

Regiment lost during service 9 Officers and 73 Enlisted men killed and mortally wounded and 2 Officers and 91 Enlisted men by disease. Total 175.

2nd REGIMENT CAVALRY.

All Companies in Washington, D. C., by December, 1861, except "C," "G" and "I." Company "C" left Fort Leavenworth, Kan., June 11, 1861. At Springfield, Mo., August 6. Battle of Wilson's Creek, Mo., August 10. Moved to St. Louis, Mo., August 11-30, thence to Paducah, Ky. Attached to District of Paducah, Ky., to February, 1862. 2nd Division, District of West Tennessee, and Army Tennessee, to July, 1862. 2nd Division, District of Corinth, Miss., to November, 1862. District of Corinth, Miss., 13th Army Corps, Dept. Tennessee, to December, 1862. 2nd Division, District of Corinth, 17th Army Corps, to January, 1863. 2nd Division, District Corinth, 16th Army Corps, January, 1863. District of Memphis, Tenn., escort to Gen. Grant, Commanding Army Tennessee, to May, 1863.

SERVICE (Co. "C").—Operations against Fort Henry, Tenn., February 2-6, 1862. Investment and capture of Fort Donelson, Tenn., February 12-16. Expedition to Nashville, Tenn., February 19-25. Moved to Pittsburg Landing, Tenn., March 1-16. Battle of Shiloh, Tenn., April 6-7. Advance on and siege of Corinth, Miss., April 29-May 30. Duty at and about Corinth, Miss., till January, 1863. Battle of Corinth October 3-4, 1862. Grant's Central Mississippi Campaign November, 1862, to January, 1863. Reached Memphis, Tenn., January 15, 1863, and duty there as escort to Gen. Grant's Headquarters till May. Joined Regiment at Falmouth, Va., May, 1863.

Company "G."—Temporarily assigned to duty with McRae's Battery Artillery in New Mexico. Duty in New Mexico October, 1861, to September, 1862. Battle of Valverde February 21, 1862. Evacuation of Albuquerque and Santa Fe March 2-4. March to Fort Leavenworth, Kan., September and October, 1862, arriving there October 27. Arrive at Washington, D. C., November 23, and joined Regiment at Falmouth, Va., January 13, 1863.

Company "I."—At Taos, N. M., April to October, 1861. Moved to Fort Garland October 1-9, and duty there till September, 1862. Moved to Fort Leavenworth, Kan., arriving there October 27. Arrive at Washington, D. C., November 23, and join Regiment at Falmouth, Va., January 13, 1863.

Regiment attached to Thomas' Command, Patterson's Army, June, 1861. 1st Brigade, Banks' Division, Shenandoah, to August, 1861. Cavalry Reserve, Army Potomac, to March, 1862. Provost Guard, Army Potomac, to February, 1863. Reserve Brigade, 1st Division, Cavalry Corps, Army Potomac, to August, 1864. 3rd (Reserve) Brigade, 1st Division, Cavalry Corps, Army Shenandoah, Middle Military Division, March, 1865. Cavalry Brigade, Army Shenandoah, to July, 1865.

SERVICE.—Occupation of Arlington Heights, Va., May 24, 1861 (Detachment). Fairfax Court House June 1 (Co. "B"). Advance on Manassas, Va., July 16-21 (4 Cos.). Blackburn's Ford July 18. Battle of Bull Run July 21. Duty in the Defences of Washington, D. C., till March, 1862. Peninsula Campaign April to August. Siege of Yorktown, Va., April 5-May 4. Ellison's Mill near Mechanicsville May 23 (Detachment). New Bridge May 24 (Detachment). Seven days before Richmond June 25-July 1. Reconnoissance to Charlestown, W. Va.,

October 16-17. Charlestown October 16. Expedition from Potomac Creek to Richards and Ellis Fords, Rappahannock River, December 29-30. Chancellorsville Campaign April 27-May 8. Stoneman's Raid April 29-May 8. Brandy Station and Beverly Ford June 9. Expedition from Point Lookout, Md., to Pope's Creek June 11-21 (Detachment). Middleburg June 19. Upperville June 21. Battle of Gettysburg, Pa., July 1-3. Williamsport, Md., July 6. Boonesboro July town July 10-13. Falling Waters July 14. Manassas Gap July 21-22. Wapping Heights July 23. Kelly's Ford July 31-August 1. Brandy Station August 1-4. Advance from the Rappahannock to the Rapidan September 13-17. Bristoe Campaign October 9-22. Manassas Junction October 17. Bristoe Station October 18. Advance to line of the Rappahannock November 7-8. Mine Run Campaign November 26-December 2. Demonstration on the Rapidan February 6-7, 1864. Barnett's Ford February 6-7. Custer's Raid in Albemarle County February 28-March 1. Near Charlottesville February 29. Stannardsville March 1. Rapidan Campaign May 4-June 12. Wilderness May 5-7. Todd's Tavern May 7-8. Sheridan's Raid to the James River May 9-24. Ground Squirrel Church and Yellow Tavern May 11. Mechanicsville May 12. Line of the Pamunkey May 26-28. Hanovertown Ferry and Hanovertown May 27. Haw's Shop May 28. Totopotomoy May 28-31. Old Church and Mattadequin Creek May 30. Bethesda Church, Cold Harbor, May 31-June 1. Sheridan's Trevillian Raid June 7-24. Trevillian Station June 11-12. Mallory's Cross Roads June 12. Black Creek or Tunstall Station and White House or St. Peter's Church June 21. Jones' Bridge June 23. Siege of Petersburg till August. Deep Bottom July 27-28. Malvern Hill July 28. Sheridan's Shenandoah Valley Campaign August 7-November 28. Toll Gate near White Post and near Newtown August 11. Near Strasburg August 14. Halltown and near Kearneysville August 25. Leetown and Smithville August 28. Smithfield Crossing, Opequan, August 28. Locke's Ford, Opequan Creek, September 13. Sevier's Ford, Opequan Creek, September 15. Battle of Opequan, Winchester, September 19. Fisher's Hill September 21. Milford September 22. Front Royal September 23. Luray Valley September 24. Front Royal September 25. Port Republic September 26-27. Rockfish Gap September 28. Mt. Crawford October 2. Tom's Brook, Woodstock Races, October 8-9. Battle of Cedar Creek October 19. Near Kernstown November 11. Expedition into Loudoun and Faquier Counties, November 28-December 3. Expedition from Winchester to near Gordonsville December 19-28. Liberty Mills December 22. Near Gordonsville December 23. Duty in the Shenandoah Valley till July, 1865.

Regiment lost during service 5 Officers and 73 Enlisted men killed and mortally wounded and 3 Officers and 92 Enlisted men by disease. Total 173.

3rd REGIMENT CAVALRY, "1st MOUNTED RIFLES."

In New Mexico at outbreak of the Rebellion and duty there till September, 1862. Action at Mesilla July 25, 1861 (Cos. "B," "F"). Evacuation of Fort Fillmore July 26. San Augustine Springs July 27 (Cos. "B," "F," "I"). Near Fort Thorn September 26 (Cos. "C," "G," "K"). Battle of Valverde February 21, 1862 (Cos. "C," "D," "G," "I" and "K"). Comanche Canon March 3 (Cos. "C," "K"). Evacuation of Albuquerque and Santa Fe March 2-4 (Co. "E"). Apache Canon March 26 (Co. "C"). Glorietta or Pigeon Ranch March 28 (Co. "E"). Albuquerque April 9. Pursuit of Confederate forces April 13-22. Peralta April 15 (Cos. "D," "E," "G," "I," "K"). Parejie May 21. Near Fort Craig May 23. Operations in New Mexico till September. Moved from Fort Union to Jefferson Barracks, Mo., September 30-November 23 (1280 miles). Moved to Memphis, Tenn., December, 1862. Attached to District of Memphis, Tenn., 16th Army Corps, Dept. Tenn., to March, 1863. Unattached, District Memphis, 16th Corps, to May, 1863. 2nd Brigade, District of Memphis, 16th Corps, to October, 1863. Unattached, 15th Army Corps,

Army Tennessee, to March, 1864. St. Louis, Mo., Dept. Missouri, to May, 1864. Unattached, 7th Army Corps, Dept. Arkansas, to September, 1864. 2nd Brigade, Cavalry Division, 7th Army Corps, to February, 1865. Little Rock, Ark., 7th Corps, to July, 1865. Dept. of Arkansas to April, 1866.

SERVICE.—Duty in District of Memphis, Tenn., till October, 1863. Left Memphis for Corinth, Miss., October 8, thence moved to Cherokee, Ala. Operations on Memphis & Charleston Railroad in Alabama October 20-29. Barton Station, Cane Creek and Dickson's Station October 20. Cherokee Station October 21. Cane Creek October 26. Bear Creek, Tuscumbia, October 27. Chattanooga-Ringgold Campaign November 23-27. March to relief of Knoxville, Tenn., November 28-December 6. Near Loudon December 2 (Detachment). Expedition to Murphey, N. C., December 6-11 (Detachment). Moved to Huntsville, Ala., December 12-29, and duty there till March, 1864. Moved to St. Louis, Mo., March 6-7, thence to Devall's Bluff, Ark., May 20-26, and to Little Rock, Ark., June 4-9. Duty in the Dept. of Arkansas till April, 1866. Expedition from Little Rock to Little Red River August 6-16, 1864. Expedition from Little Rock to Fort Smith, Ark., September 25-October 13 (Detachment). Reconnoissance from Little Rock toward Monticello and Mt. Elba October 4-11. Reconnoissance from Little Rock to Princeton October 19-23. Expedition from Little Rock to Irving Station October 26-28. Expedition from Little Rock to Saline River November 17-18 (Detachment). Expedition from Little Rock to Benton November 27-30. Duty at Little Rock and other points in Arkansas till April, 1866.

Regiment lost during service 2 Officers and 30 Enlisted men killed and mortally wounded and 3 Officers and 105 Enlisted men by disease. Total 140.

4th REGIMENT CAVALRY (FORMERLY 1st CAVALRY).

On duty at Forts Washita, Wise and Kearney, Kan., at outbreak of the Rebellion. Moved to Fort Leavenworth, Kan., April 17-May 31, 1861. Companies "B," "C," "D" and "L" in Missouri with Lyons. Forsyth, Mo., July 27. Dug Springs August 2. Battle of Wilson's Creek August 10 (Cos. "D" and "I"). Fremont's Campaign against Springfield, Mo., September to November, 1861 (Cos. "B," "C," "D," "L"). Shawnee Mound, Milford, December 19 (Cos. "B," "C," "D"). Expedition to Camp Benyard and Viola, Ky., December 28-31 (Cos. "C," "I"). Investment and capture of Fort Donelson, Tenn., February 12-16, 1862 (Cos. "I," "K"). Company "K" joined Buell February, 1862. Operations about New Madrid and Island No. 10 February 29-April 8 (Cos. "B," "C," "D"). Battle of Shiloh, Tenn., April 6-7 (Co. "I"). Companies "B," "C," "D," "G," "I" and "K" attached to Cavalry Division, Army Mississippi, April, 1862. Advance on and siege of Corinth, Miss., April 29-May 30. Action at Farmington, Miss., May 9 (Detachment). Pursuit to Booneville May 30-June 12. Attached to Headquarters, Army of the Ohio, June, 1862 ("B," "C," "D," "G," "I," "K"). Buell's Campaign in North Alabama and Middle Tennessee June to August. March to Louisville, Ky., in pursuit of Bragg August 21-September 26. Pursuit of Bragg into Kentucky October 1-22. Battle of Perryville, Ky., October 8. March to Nashville, Tenn., October 22-November 7. Attached to Headquarters, Army Cumberland, November, 1862. At Nashville, Tenn., till December 26. Advance on Murfreesboro December 26-30. Overall's Creek December 30. Battle of Stone's River December 30-31, 1862-January 1-3, 1863. Manchester Pike January 5. Reconnoissance to Nolensville and Versailles January 13-15. Reconnoissance to Auburn, Liberty and Carnsville January 21-22 (Detachment). Attached to 1st Brigade, 2nd Division, Cavalry Corps, Army of the Cumberland, January, 1863. Unionville January 30. Expedition to Franklin January 31-February 13. Bradysville March 1. Expedition toward Columbia March 4-14. Union and River March 4. Rutherford Creek March 10-11. Franklin April 10. Expedition to McMinnville April 20-30. Expedition to Mid-

dleton May 21-22. Middleton May 21-22. Scout on Middleton and Edgeville Pike June 10. Expedition to Lebanon June 15-17. Lebanon June 16. Middle Tennessee or Tullahoma Campaign June 23-July 7. Fosterville and Guy's Gap June 27. Shelbyville June 27 and 30. Expedition to Huntsville July 13-22. Reconnoissance to Rock Island Ferry August 4-5. Sparta August 9. Chickamauga (Ga.) Campaign August 16-September 22. Calfkiller River near Sparta August 17. Ringgold, Ga., September 11. Pea Vine Ridge and Reed's Bridge, Chickamauga Creek, September 18. Battle of Chickamauga September 19-21. Chickamauga Creek September 25. Operations against Wheeler and Roddy September 30-October 17. Expedition from Maysville to Whitesburg and Decatur, Ala., November 14-17. Smith's Expedition from Nashville to Corinth, Miss., December 28, 1863-January 8, 1864. Smith's Expedition from Colliersville, Tenn., to Okolona, Miss., February 11-26. Ivy's Farm near Okolona, Miss., February 22. Tallahatchie River February 22. Atlanta (Ga.) Campaign May to September, 1864. Battle of Resaca May 14-15. Tanner's Bridge May 15. Near Rome May 15. Near Dallas May 24. About Dallas May 25-June 5. Near Big Shanty June 9. Operations against Kenesaw Mountain June 10-July 2. McAffee's Cross Roads June 11. Powder Springs, Lattimer's Mills and Noonday Creek June 20. Noonday Creek June 27. Assault on Kenesaw June 27. Nickajack Creek July 2-5. Chattahoochie River July 5-17. Siege of Atlanta July 22-August 25. Garrard's Raid to Covington July 22-24. Garrard's Raid to South River July 27-31. Flat Rock Bridge July 28. Kilpatrick's Raid around Atlanta August 18-22. Red Oak and Flint River August 19. Jonesboro August 19. Lovejoy Station August 20. Operations at Chattahoochie River Bridge August 26-September 2. Operations against Hood in North Georgia and North Alabama September 29-November 3. Near Lost Mountain October 4-7. New Hope Church October 5. Ordered to Cavalry Corps Headquarters, Nashville, Tenn., Nashville Campaign November-December. Battle of Nashville December 15-16. West Harpeth River December 17. At Headquarters, Cavalry Corps, Military Division Mississippi, till May, 1865. Wilson's Raid to Macon, Ga., March 22 to April 24, 1865. Capture of Selma April 2. Montgomery April 12 and Macon, Ga., April 20. Duty at Macon till November, 1865.

Companies "A" and "E" in the Defences of Washington, D. C., May, 1861. Attached to Heintzelman's Division, Army of Northeast Virginia, to August, 1861. Headquarters, Army Potomac, to November, 1862. Advance on Manassas, Va., July 16-21, 1861. Peninsula Campaign April to August, 1862. Siege of Yorktown April 5-May 4. Seven days before Richmond June 25-July 1. Gaines' Mill June 27. Malvern Hill July 1. Maryland Campaign September 6-22. Battle of Antietam September 16-17. Joined Regiment in Tennessee November, 1862.

Regiment lost during service 3 Officers and 59 Enlisted men killed and mortally wounded and 1 Officer and 108 Enlisted men by disease. Total 171.

5th REGIMENT CAVALRY.

Organized by direction of the President from 2nd Cavalry August 3, 1861. Attached to Cooke's Cavalry Reserve, Army Potomac, to March, 1862. 1st Brigade, Cooke's Cavalry Reserve, Army Potomac, to July, 1862. 1st Brigade, Cavalry Division, Army Potomac, to September, 1862. 1st Brigade, Pleasanton's Cavalry Division, Army Potomac, to November, 1862. Averill's Cavalry Brigade, Army Potomac, to February, 1863. Reserve Brigade, 1st Division, Cavalry Corps, Army Potomac, to August, 1864. 3rd (Reserve) Brigade, 1st Division, Cavalry Corps, Army Shenandoah, Middle Military Division, to March, 1865. 3rd Brigade, 1st Division, Cavalry Corps, Army Potomac, to June, 1865.

SERVICE.—Lewinsville, Va., September 11, 1861 (Co. "H"). Reconnoissance to Lewinsville September 25. Duty in Defences of Washington, D. C., till March, 1862. Reconnoissance to Cedar Run March 14-16. Siege of

Yorktown, Va., April 5-May 4. Battle of Williamsburg May 5. Hanover Court House May 27. Operations about Hanover Court House May 27-29. Ashland May 28. Operations against Stuart June 13-15. Old Church, Hanover Court House, and Haw's Shop, June 13. Haw's Shop June 15. Seven days before Richmond June 25-July 1. Operations at White House June 26-July 2. Sycamore Church and White Oak Swamp Bridge July 3. White Oak Swamp Bridge July 4. Malvern Hill July 5. Reconnoissance from Westover July 16. Maryland Campaign September 6-22. Sugar Loaf Mountain near Frederick September 10-11. Antietam September 16-17. Shepherdstown Ford September 19-20. Charlestown October 6 and 16. Kearneysville and Shepherdstown October 16-17 (Detachment). Bloomfield and Upperville November 2-3. Manassas Gap and Markham Station November 4. Manassas Gap, Barbee's Cross Roads, Chester Gap and Markham November 5-6. Waterloo Bridge November 7. Little Washington November 8. Reconnoissance from Sharpsburg to Smithfield, W. Va., November 24-25. Battle of Fredericksburg December 11-15. Expedition from Potomac Creek to Richards and Ellis Fords, Rappahannock River, December 29-30. Reconnoissance to Catlett's and Rappahannock Stations January 8-10, 1863 (Detachment). Near Grove Church January 9 (Detachment). Kelly's Ford March 17. Chancellorsville Campaign April 27-May 8. Stoneman's Raid April 29-May 8. Brandy Station April 29. Raccoon Ford April 30 (Detachment). Brandy Station and Beverly Ford June 9. Expedition from Point Lookout, Md., to Pope's Creek June 11-21 (Detachment). Middleburg June 19. Upperville June 21. Battle of Gettysburg, Pa., July 1-3. Williamsport, Md., July 6. Boonesboro July 8. Benevola or Beaver Creek July 9. At and near Funkstown July 10-13. Falling Waters July 14. Manassas Gap, Va., July 21-22. Wapping Heights July 23. Kelly's Ford July 31-August 1. Brandy Station August 1-4. Advance from the Rappahannock to the Rapidan September 13-17. Bristoe Campaign October 9-22. Manassas Junction October 17. Bristoe Station October 18. Advance to line of the Rappahannock November 7-8. Mine Run Campaign November 26-December 2. Demonstration on the Rapidan Februdan February 6-7, 1864. Barnett's Ford February 6-7. Custer's Raid in Albemarle County February 28-March 1. Charlottesville February 29. Stannardsville near Taylortown February 29. Stannardsville March 1. Rapidan Campaign May 4-June 12. Wilderness May 5-7. Todd's Tavern May 7-8. Sheridan's Raid to James River May 9-24. Davenport Bridge, North Anna River, May 10. Ground Squirrel Church and Yellow Tavern May 11. Mechanicsville May 12. Line of the Pamunkey May 26-28. Hanovertown Ferry and Hanovertown May 27. Haw's Shop May 28. Totopotomoy May 28-31. Old Church and Mattadequin Creek May 30. Cold Harbor May 31-June 1. Sheridan's Trevillian Raid June 7-24. Trevillian Station June 11-12. Mallory's Cross Roads June 12. Black Creek or Tunstall Station and White House or St. Peter's Church June 21. Jones' Bridge June 23. (Expedition from Point Lookout to Pope's Creek June 11-21, Detachment.) Siege of Petersburg till August. Deep Bottom July 27-28. Malvern Hill July 28. Sheridan's Shenandoah Valley Campaign August 7-November 28. Near Newtown August 11. Near Strasburg August 14. Near Kearneysville August 25. Locke's Ford, Opequan Creek, September 13. Sevier's Ford, Opequan Creek, September 15. Battle of Opequan, Winchester, September 19 Fisher's Hill September 21. Milford September 22. Front Royal September 23. Luray Valley September 24. Port Republic September 26-27. Rockfish Gap September 28. Mt. Crawford October 2. Tom's Brook, Woodstock Races, October 8-9. Expedition into Surrey County October 16-18. Battle of Cedar Creek October 19. Near Kernstown November 11. Expedition into Loudoun and Fauquier Counties November 28-December 3. Expedition from Winchester to near Gordonsville December 19-28. Liberty Mills December 22. Near Gordonsville December 23. Sheridan's Raid from Winchester February 27-

March 25, 1865. Occupation of Staunton March 2. Action at Waynesboro March 2. Duguidsville March 8. Appomattox Campaign March 28-April 9. Dinwiddie Court House March 30-31. Five Forks April 1. Scott's Cross Roads April 2. Tabernacle Church or Beaver Pond Creek April 4. Amelia Springs April 4-5. Sailor's Creek April 6. Appomattox Station April 8. Appomattox Court House April 9. Surrender of Lee and his army. Expedition to Danville April 23-29. March to Washington, D. C., May. Grand Review May 23.

Regiment lost during service 7 Officers and 60 Enlisted men killed and mortally wounded and 2 Officers and 90 Enlisted men by disease. Total 159.

6th REGIMENT CAVALRY.

Organized by direction of the President May 4, 1861, and confirmed by Act of Congress July 29, 1861. Regiment organized at Pittsburg, Pa. Moved to Washington, D. C., October 12, 1861. Attached to Stoneman's Cavalry Command, Army Potomac, to March, 1862. Emery's Brigade, Cavalry Reserve, Army Potomac, to July, 1862. 1st Brigade, Cavalry Division, Army Potomac, to September, 1862. 1st Brigade, Pleasanton's Cavalry Division, Army Potomac, to October, 1862. 2nd Brigade, Pleasanton's Cavalry Division, Army Potomac, to February, 1863. Reserve Brigade, 1st Division, Cavalry Corps, Army Potomac, to August, 1864. 3rd (Reserve) Brigade, 1st Division, Cavalry Corps, Army Shenandoah, Middle Military Division, to March, 1865. 3rd Brigade, 1st Division, Cavalry Corps, Army Potomac, to June, 1865. Frederick, Md., 8th Army Corps, Middle Dept., to October, 1865.

SERVICE.—Duty in the Defences of Washington, D. C., till March, 1862. Advance on Manassas, Va., March 10-15. Reconnoissance to Cedar Run March 14-16. Moved to Virginia Peninsula March 27-30. Siege of Yorktown April 5-May 4. Cheese Cake Church May 4. Slatersville May 9. New Kent Court House May 11. New Bridge May 20. Mechanicsville May 24. Hanover Court House May 27. Operations about Hanover Court House May 27-29. Destruction of bridges, South Anna River, May 28-29. Expedition to Wormsley Ferry June 2. Operations against Stuart June 13-15. Ashland June 16. Seven days before Richmond June 25-July 1. Operations about White House June 26-July 2. Black Creek June 26. Malvern Hill August 5. Movement to Alexandria August 15-26. Maryland Campaign September 6-22. Fall's Church September 5. Sugar Loaf Mountain, near Frederick, September 10-11. Petersville September 15. Antietam September 16-17. Shepherdstown Ford September 19-20. Charlestown September 28. Hillsboro September 29. Reconnoissance from Harper's Ferry to Leesburg October 1-2. Waterford October 1. Charlestown October 6. Reconnoissance to Charlestown October 16-17. Charlestown October 16. Philomont November 1. Union November 2-3. Upperville and Bloomfield November 2-3. Ashby's Gap November 3. Markham Station November 4. Barbee's Cross Roads, Chester Gap and Markham November 5-6. Amissville November 7-8. Little Washington November 8. Newby's Cross Roads November 9. Corbin's Cross Roads, near Amissville, November 10. Sulphur Springs November 17. Battle of Fredericksburg, Va., December 12-15. Chancellorsville Campaign April 27-May 8, 1863. Stoneman's Raid April 29-May 8. Stevensburg April 29. Brandy Station and Beverly Ford June 9. Middleburg June 19. Upperville June 21. Battle of Gettysburg, Pa., July 1-3. Williamsport, Md., July 6. Funkstown July 7. Boonesboro July 8. Benevola or Beaver Creek July 9. At and near Funkstown July 10-13. Falling Waters July 14. Manassas Gap, Va., July 21-22. Wapping Heights July 23. Kelly's Ford July 31-August 1. Brandy Station August 1-4. Advance from the Rappahannock to the Rapidan September 13-17. Bristoe Campaign October 9-22. Brandy Station October 11. Advance to line of the Rappahannock November 7-8. Mine Run Campaign November 26-December 2. Demonstration on the Rapidan February 6-7, 1864. Barnett's Ford February 6-7. Rapidan Campaign May 4-June 12. Wilderness May 5-7. Todd's

Tavern May 7-8. Sheridan's Raid to James River May 9-24. Ground Squirrel Church and Yellow Tavern May 11. Richmond fortifications May 12. Line of the Pamunkey May 26-28. Hanovertown Ferry and Hanovertown May 27. Haw's Shop May 28. Totopotomoy May 28-31. Old Church and Mattadequin Creek May 30. Cold Harbor May 31-June 1. Sheridan's Trevillian Raid June 7-24. Trevillian Station June 11-12. Mallory's Cross Roads June 12. Black Creek or Tunstall Station and White House or St. Peter's Church June 21. Siege of Petersburg till August. Deep Bottom July 27-28. Malvern Hill July 28. Sheridan's Shenandoah Valley Campaign August 7-November 28. Sevier's Ford, Opequan Creek, September 15. Battle of Opequan, Winchester, September 19. Fisher's Hill September 21-22. Luray Valley September 24. Battle of Cedar Creek October 19. Raid from near Winchester to Gordonsville December 19-28. Sheridan's Raid from Winchester February 27-March 25, 1865. Occupation of Staunton March 2. Action at Waynesboro March 2. Duguidsville March 8. Appomattox Campaign March 28-April 9. Dinwiddie Court House March 30-31. Five Forks April 1. Scott's Cross Roads April 2. Tabernacle Church or Beaver Pond Creek April 4. Amelia Springs April 4-5. Sailor's Creek April 6. Appomattox Station April 8. Appomattox Court House April 9. Surrender of Lee and his army. Expedition to Danville April 23-29. March to Washington, D. C., May. Grand Review May 23. At Frederick, Md., till October.

Regiment lost during service 2 Officers and 50 Enlisted men killed and mortally wounded and 1 Officer and 106 Enlisted men by disease. Total 159.

1st REGIMENT ARTILLERY.
BATTERY "A," 1st ARTILLERY.

Stationed at Fortress Monroe, Va., January, 1861. Fort Pickens and Pensacola, Fla., Dept. of the South, June, 1861, to September, 1862. Defences of New Orleans, La., Dept. Gulf, to February, 1863. Artillery, 1st Division, 19th Army Corps, Dept. Gulf, to August, 1863. Defences of New Orleans, La., to January, 1864. Artillery, 1st Division, 19th Army Corps, Dept. Gulf, to August, 1864.

SERVICE.—Embarked on Steamer "Brooklyn" for Fort Pickens, Fla., January 24, 1861, arriving in Pensacola Harbor February 6. Garrison duty at Fort Pickens till May, 1862. Action on Santa Rosa Island October 9, 1861. Bombardment of Forts McRae and Barrancas, Pensacola Harbor, November 22-23, 1861, and January 1, 1862. Capture of Forts McRee and Barrancas May 9. Moved to Pensacola May 13, and duty there till August. Moved to New Orleans, La., August 30-September 3, and duty in the defences of that city till January, 1863. Expedition up Bayou Teche January 11-18. Engagement with Steamer "Cotton" January 14. Moved to Baton Rouge, La. Expedition against Port Hudson March 7-27. Operations in Western Louisiana April 9-May 14. Teche Campaign April 11-20. Fort Bisland, near Centreville, April 12-13. Jeanerette April 14. Vermillion Bayou April 17. Expedition to Alexandria and Simsport May 5-16. Moved to Port Hudson, May 18-23. Siege of Port Hudson May 24-July 9. Assaults on Port Hudson May 27 and June 14. Surrender of Port Hudson July 9. Moved to Donaldsonville July 13, thence to Baton Rouge, La., August 2. Sabine Pass (Texas) Expedition September 2-12. Duty at New Orleans, La., till January, 1864. Expedition to Madisonville January 3. Garrison duty at New Orleans till July. Moved to New York July 27-August 3, thence to Washington, D. C. Consolidated with Battery "F," 1st Artillery, and remounted. Duty in the Defences of Washington, D. C., 22nd Corps, till September, 1865, when resumed separate organization.

BATTERY "B," 1st ARTILLERY.

Stationed at Fort Taylor, Key West, Fla., January, 1861, to June, 1862. Attached to District Key West, Fla., Dept. South, January to June, 1862. District Beaufort, S. C., Dept. South, to September, 1862. District of Beaufort, S. C., 10th Army Corps, Dept. South, to March, 1863.

District Hilton Head, S. C., 10th Corps, to July, 1863. Morris Island, S. C., 10th Corps, to September, 1863. Folly Island, S. C., Gordon's Division, 10th Corps, to January, 1864. District Hilton Head, S. C., 10th Corps, to February, 1864. Light Brigade, District Forida, Dept. South, to April, 1864. 2nd Division, 10th Army Corps, Army of the James, to May, 1864. Artillery Brigade, 10th Army Corps, to June, 1864. Kautz's Cavalry Division, Dept. Virginia and North Carolina, to July, 1864. Artillery Brigade, 18th Corps, to December, 1864. Artillery Brigade, 24th Army Corps, to August, 1865.

SERVICE.—Duty at Fort Taylor, Key West, Fla., till June, 1862. Moved to Hilton Head, S. C., thence to Beaufort, S. C., June 18-21, and duty there till March 20, 1863. Expedition to destroy Charleston & Savannah Railroad October 21-24. Battle of Pocotaligo, S. C., October 22. Moved to Hilton Head, S. C., March 20. Expedition against Charleston, S. C., April 5-13. Siege operations from Folly Island, S. C., against Morris Island, S. C., May to July. Attack on Morris Island July 10. Siege operations against Forts Wagner and Gregg, Morris Island, and against Fort Sumpter and Charleston, S. C., July 11-September 7. Capture of Forts Wagner and Gregg September 7. Moved to Folly Island, and duty there till November 26. Moved to Kiowah Island November 26, thence to Hilton Head, S. C., January 24, 1864. Expedition to Florida February 5-7. Capture of Jacksonville February 7. Expedition from Jacksonville to Lake City, Fla., April 7-22. Ten Mile Run, near Camp Finnegan, February 8. Barber's Place February 10. Lake City February 11. Battle of Olustee February 20. McGirt's Creek, Cedar Creek, March 1. Cedar Run April 2. Moved to Gloucester Point, Va., April 25-May 4. Butler's operations on south side of the James River and against Petersburg and Richmond May 5-28. Operations against Fort Darling May 12-16. Battle of Drury's Bluff May 14-16. Bermuda Hundred May 20-21. Duty in trenches at Bermuda Hundred till May 28. Moved to White House, thence to Cold Harbor May 28-June 1. Cold Harbor June 1-12. Before Petersburg June 15-19. Siege operations against Petersburg and Richmond June 16, 1864, to April 2, 1865. Wilson's Raid on Southside & Danville Railroad June 22-30. Staunton River Bridge or Roanoke Station June 25. Sappony Church or Stony Creek June 28-29. Ream's Station June 29. Duty at Point of Rocks, near Petersburg, till September. Demonstration on north side of the James September 28-30. Battle of Chaffin's Farm September 28-30. Johnson's Farm, Darbytown Road, October 7. Battle of Fair Oaks October 27-28. In trenches north of the James till March, 1865. Appomattox Campaign March 27-April 9. Hatcher's Run March 29-April 2. Fall of Petersburg April 2. Pursuit of Lee April 3-9. Rice's Station April 6. Appomattox Court House April 9. Surrender of Lee and his army. Duty at Richmond, Va., till October, 1865. Dismounted and ordered to Fort Hamilton, New York Harbor.

BATTERY "C" 1st ARTILLERY.

Stationed at Fortress Monroe, Va., January, 1861. Attached to District Fortress Monroe, Va., Dept. of Virginia, April, 1861, to February, 1862. Unattached, Burnside's North Carolina Expeditionary Corps, to April, 1862. Unattached. Dept. North Carolina, to December, 1862. Artillery Brigade, Dept. North Carolina, to January, 1863. Artillery Brigade, 18th Corps, Dept. of North Carolina and Dept. of the South, to April, 1863. District Hilton Head, S. C., 10th Corps. Dept. South, to June, 1863. Folly Island, S. C., 10th Corps, to July, 1863. Morris Island, S. C., 10th Corps, to December, 1863. Fort Macon, N. C., Dept. Virginia and North Carolina, to July, 1864. Artillery Brigade, 10th Army Corps, Army of the James, to October, 1864. Fort Independence, Boston Harbor, to October, 1865.

SERVICE.—Garrison at Fortress Monroe, Va., till February, 1862. Ordered to the field in North Carolina February 11. At Fort Hatteras, N. C., till March 12. Burnside's Expedition against New Berne March 12-14. Battle of New Berne February 14. Capture of Morehead City March 23. Operations against Fort Macon March 23-April 25. Capture of Fort Macon April 25. Garrison duty at Fort Macon till January, 1863. Foster's Expedition to Port Royal, S. C., January 26-February 5. At St. Helena Island and Hilton Head, S. C., till June. Expedition against Charleston April 3-13. Moved to Folly Island, S. C., June. Attacked on Morris Island, S. C., July 10. Siege of Fort Wagner and Battery Gregg, Morris Island, and operations against Fort Sumpter and Charleston, S. C., July 11-September 7. Capture of Forts Wagner and Gregg September 7. On Ordnance duty till January, 1864. At Fort Macon, N. C., and in the Dept. of North Carolina till July. Joined Battery "D," 1st Artillery, before Petersburg, Va., July 25, and temporarily consolidated with it. Siege of Petersburg, Va., till October. Demonstration north of the James August 13-20. Deep Bottom August 14. Deep Run August 15. Russell's Mills August 16. Strawberry Plains August 16-18. Battle of Chaffin's Farm, New Market Heights, September 28-30. Laurel Hill October 7. Duty north of the James before Richmond till October 31. Battle of Fair Oaks October 27-28. Detached from Battery "D" and moved to Concord, N. H., October 31-November 5, thence to Fort Independence, Boston Harbor, November 28, and duty there till October, 1865.

BATTERY "D" 1st ARTILLERY.

Stationed at Washington, D. C., February, 1861. Attached to Fort Washington, Md., April to December, 1861. Fort Taylor, Fla., Dept. of the South, to June, 1862. District of Beaufort, S. C., Dept. of the South, to September, 1862. District of Beaufort, S. C., 10th Army Corps, Dept. South, to April, 1864. Artillery, 2nd Division, 10th Army Corps, Army James, to August, 1864. Artillery Brigade, 10th Army Corps, to December, 1864. Artillery Brigade, 25th Army Corps, to November, 1865.

SERVICE.—Moved to Fort Washington, Md., April 15, 1861, and duty there till December. Ordered to Fort Taylor, Fla., December 21, and duty there till June 18, 1862. Moved to Hilton Head, thence to Beaufort, S. C., June 18-21, and duty there till April, 1864. Action at Port Royal Ferry July 4, 1862. Pocotaligo, S. C., October 22, 1862 (Detachment). Expedition against Charleston April 3-12. Moved to Gloucester Point, Va., April, 1864. Butler's operations on south side of James River and against Petersburg and Richmond, Va., May 4-June 15. Occupation of City Point May 5. Port Walthal May 7. Swift Creek May 9. Chester Station May 10. Proctor's Creek May 10. Operations against Fort Darling May 12-16. Battle of Drury's Bluff May 14-16. Defences of Bermuda Hundred May 20-21. Duty in the Defences of Bermuda Hundred till June 15. Petersburg June 9. Assaults on Petersburg June 15-19. Siege operations against Petersburg and Richmond June 16, 1864, to April 2, 1865. Demonstration north of the James River August 13-20, 1864. Deep Bottom, Strawberry Plains August 14-18. Russell's Mills August 16. Chaffin's Farm, New Market Heights, September 28-30. Darbytown Road October 7. Duty in trenches north of James before Richmond till April, 1865. Battle of Fair Oaks October 27-28, 1864. Occupation of Richmond April 3, 1865. Moved to Rio Grande, Texas, May, 1865. Duty at Ringgold Barracks till November, then ordered to Fort Hamilton, New York Harbor.

BATTERY "E" 1st ARTILLERY.

Stationed at Fort Sumpter, Charleston Harbor, S. C., January, 1861. Defence of Fort Sumpter, Charleston Harbor, April 12-13, 1861. Evacuation of Fort Sumpter April 13. Reached Fort Hamilton, N. Y. Harbor, April 19. Moved to Chambersburg, Pa., June 3, and joined Patterson's army. Attached to Patterson's army to October, 1861. Hooker's Division, Army Potomac, to March, 1862. Artillery Reserve, Army Potomac, to May, 1862. 2nd Brigade, Artillery Reserve, 5th Army Corps, Army Potomac, to September, 1862. Artillery, 2nd Division, 5th Army Corps, to October, 1862. Artillery, 3rd Division, 5th Army Corps, to May, 1863. 2nd Regular Brigade, Artillery Reserve, Army Potomac, to June,

1863. 2nd Brigade, Horse Artillery, Artillery Reserve, Army Potomac, to June, 1864. 3rd Brigade, DeRussy's Division, 22nd Army Corps, to July, 1864. 1st Brigade, DeRussy's Division, 22nd Army Corps, to October, 1865.

SERVICE.—Ordered to Washington, D. C., August 26, 1861. Duty at Arsenal and at Camp Duncan, Defences of Washington, till March, 1862. Moved to the Virginia Peninsula. Siege of Yorktown April 5-May 4. Battle of Fair Oaks, Seven Pines, May 31-June 1. Seven days before Richmond June 26-July 1. Savage Station and Peach Orchard June 29. White Oak Swamp and Glendale June 30. Malvern Hill July 1. At Harrison's Landing till August 16. Moved to Fortress Monroe, thence to Centreville August 16-28. Pope's Virginia Campaign August 28-September 2. Battles of Groveton August 29; Bull Run August 30. Maryland Campaign September 6-22. Battle of Antietam September 16-17. Shepherdstown Ford September 19-20. At Sharpsburg till October 30. Movement to Falmouth, Va., October 29-November 19. Battle of Fredericksburg, Va., December 11-15. At Falmouth, Va., till April, 1863. Chancellorsville Campaign April 27-May 6. Battle of Chancellorsville May 1-5. Gettysburg (Pa.) Campaign June 11-July 24. Aldie June 17. Middleburg June 19. Upperville June 21. Ashby's Gap June 21. Battle of Gettysburg, Pa., July 1-3. Near Harper's Ferry July 14. Shepherdstown July 16. Bristoe Campaign October 9-22. Advance to line of the Rappahannock November 7-8. Mine Run Campaign November 26-December 2. Custer's Raid into Albemarle County February 28-March 1, 1864. Near Charlottesville February 29. Stannardsville March 1. Rapidan Campaign May 4-June 8. Battles of the Wilderness May 5-7; Spottsylvania May 8-21; Milford Station May 21; Chesterfield May 23; North Anna River May 23-26. On line of the Pamunkey May 26-28. Totopotomoy May 28-31. Mechump's Creek May 31. Cold Harbor June 1-5. Sharp's Farm June 3. Moved to Washington, D. C., June 18. Garrison duty at Forts Willard and Strong, Defences of Washington, D. C., 22nd Army Corps, till October, 1865.

BATTERY "F" 1st ARTILLERY.

Stationed at Fort Duncan, Eagle Pass, Texas, January, 1861. Garrison Fort Taylor, Fla., till May, 1861. Moved to Fort Pickens, Fla., May 24, 1861, and duty there till May, 1862. Attached to District Fort Pickens and Pensacola, Fla., Dept. of the South, to August, 1862. Defences New Orleans, La., Dept. Gulf, to January, 1863. Artillery, 3rd Division, 19th Army Corps, Dept. Gulf, to March, 1864. Artillery, Cavalry Division, Dept. Gulf, to June, 1864. Defences of Washington, D. C., 22nd Army Corps, to October, 1865.

SERVICE.—Bombardment of Forts McRee and Barrancas, Pensacola Harbor, Fla., November 22-23, 1861, and January 1, 1862, Capture of Forts McRae and Barrancas May 9. Moved to Pensacola, Fla., May 13, and duty there till August. Moved to New Orleans, La., August 30-September 3, and duty in the defences of that city till February, 1863. Moved to Baton Rouge, La. Expedition to Port Hudson, La., March 7-27. Moved to Brashear City April 2-7. Operations in Western Louisiana April 9-May 14. Teche Campaign April 11-20. Fort Bisland April 12-13. Jeannette April 14. Vermillion Bayou April 17. Expedition from St. Martinsville to Breux Bridge and Opelousas April 17-21. Expedition to Alexandria and Simsport May 5-16. Moved to Port Hudson, La., May 18-23. Siege of Port Hudson May 24-July 9. Assaults on Port Hudson May 27 and June 14. Surrender of Port Hudson July 9. Moved to Baton Rouge July 13-August 2. Sabine Pass Expedition September 4-12. Western Louisiana ("Teche") Campaign October 3-November 17. At New Iberia till December. Moved to New Orleans and duty there till March, 1864. Red River Campaign. Moved to Alexandria on Red River March 30-April 3, and duty there till May 13. Retreat to Morganza May 13-22, with Lucas' Cavalry Brigade, Marksville May 15. Avoyelle's Prairie, Mansura, May 16. At Morganza till June. Expedition from Morganza to the Atchafalaya May 30-June 5. Moved to New

Orleans, thence to New York July 27-August 3, and to Washington, D. C., August 5. Duty in the Defences of that city till October, 1865. Moved to Fort Trumball, Conn.

BATTERY "G" 1st ARTILLERY.

Stationed at Fort Pickens, Fla., January to May, 1861. Moved to Fort Hamilton, N. Y. Harbor, May 13-26, thence to Washington, D. C., July 8. At Arlington Heights, Va., till July 16. Attached to Richardson's Brigade, Tyler's Division, McDowell's Army Northeast Virginia, to August, 1861. Richardson's Brigade, Division Potomac, to October, 1861. Artillery Reserve, Army Potomac (temporarily attached to Batteries "E" and "K," 1st Artillery, February, 1862), to May, 1862. 2nd Brigade, Artillery Reserve, 5th Army Corps, Army Potomac, to September, 1862. Artillery, 2nd Division, 5th Army Corps, to October, 1862. Artillery, 3rd Division, 5th Army Corps, to May, 1863. 2nd Regular Brigade, Artillery Reserve, Army Potomac, to June, 1863. 2nd Brigade, Horse Artillery, Army Potomac, to June, 1864.

SERVICE.—Reconnoissance from Alexandria on Fairfax, Richmond and Mt. Vernon Roads July 14. Advance on Manassas, Va., July 16-21. Occupation of Fairfax Court House July 17. Blackburn's Ford July 18. Battle of Bull Run July 21. Duty in the Defences of Washington, D. C., till March, 1862. Moved to the Virginia Peninsula. Siege of Yorktown April 5-May 4. Battle of Fair Oaks, Seven Pines, May 31-June 1. Seven days before Richmond June 26-July 1. Golding's Farm June 27. Savage Station and Peach Orchard June 29. White Oak Swamp and Glendale June 30. Malvern Hill July 1. At Harrison's Landing till August 16. Moved to Fortress Monroe, thence to Centreville August 16-28. Pope's Campaign in Virginia August 28-September 2. Battles of Groveton August 29. Bull Run August 30. Maryland Campaign September 6-22. Crampton's Pass September 14. Battle of Antietam September 16-17. Shepherdstown Ford September 19-20. At Sharpsburg, Md., till October 30. Movement to Falmouth October 30-November 19. Battle of Fredericksburg, Va., December 11-15. At Falmouth till April, 1863. Chancellorsville Campaign April 27-May 6. Battle of Chancellorsville May 1-6. Gettysburg (Pa.) Campaign June 11-July 24. Aldie June 17. Middleburg June 19. Upperville June 20-21. Ashby's Gap June 21. Battle of Gettysburg, Pa., July 1-3. Shepherdstown July 16. Bristoe Campaign October 9-22. Advance to line of the Rappahannock November 7-8. Mine Run Campaign November 26-December 2. Custer's Raid into Albemarle County February 28-March 1. Near Charlottesville February 29. Stannardsville March 1. Rapidan Campaign May 4-June 5. Wilderness May 5-7. Spottsylvania May 8-21. Milford Station May 21. Chesterfield May 23. North Anna May 23-26. Totopotomoy May 28-31. Machump's Creek May 31. Cold Harbor June 1-5. Sharp's Farm June 3. Moved to Washington, D. C., June 18, and garrison duty at Forts Willard and Strong, Defences of Washington, 22nd Corps, to October, 1865.

BATTERY "H" 1st ARTILLERY.

Stationed at Fort Sumpter, S. C., January, 1861. Duty there till April, 1861. Defence of Fort Sumpter April 12-13. Evacuation of Fort Sumpter April 13 and reached Fort Hamilton, N. Y. Harbor, April 19. Moved to Chambersburg, Pa., June 3, and joined Gen. Patterson's army. Ordered to Washington, D. C., arriving August 28. Attached to Reserve Artillery, Army Potomac, to March, 1862. 2nd Division, 3rd Army Corps, Potomac, to May, 1862. 1st Regular Brigade, Artillery Reserve, to October, 1863. 3rd Brigade, Artillery Reserve, to December, 1863. 2nd Brigade, Artillery Reserve, to March, 1864. Camp Barry, D. C., to April, 1864. Consolidated with Battery "I" April 20, 1864. 2nd Brigade, Horse Artillery, Potomac, to May, 1865. Dept. of Washington.

SERVICE.—Duty in the Defences of Washington, D. C., till March, 1862. Moved to Virginia Peninsula March. Siege of Yorktown, Va., April 5-May 4. Battle of Will-

iamsburg May 5. Battle of Fair Oaks, Seven Pines, May 31-June 1. Seven days before Richmond June 25-July 1. Oak Grove June 25. Glendale June 30. Malvern Hill July 1. Moved to Fortress Monroe, thence to Washington, D. C., August 16-23. Operations on Orange & Alexandria Railroad November 10-12. Battle of Fredericksburg, Va., December 11-15. "Mud March" January 20-24. Operations at Rappahannock Bridge and Grove Church February 5-7. At Falmouth till April. Rappahannock Bridge April 14. Chancellorsville Campaign April 27-May 6. Battle of Chancellorsville May 1-5. Gettysburg (Pa.) Campaign June 11-July 24. Battle of Gettysburg, Pa., July 1-3. Bristoe Campaign October 9-22. Advance to line of the Rappahannock November 7-8. Mine Run Campaign November 26-December 2. Rapidan Campaign May 4-June 12, 1864. Wilderness May 5-7. Spottsylvania May 8-21. North Anna May 23-26. Totopotomoy May 28-31. Cold Harbor June 1-7. Sheridan's Trevillian Raid June 7-24. Trevillian Station June 11-12. Black Creek or Tunstall Station and White House or St. Peter's Church June 21. St. Mary's Church June 24. At Light House Point June 29-July 27. At Camp Barry till September. Arthur's Swamp September 29. Poplar Springs Church September 29-October 1. Wyatt's Road October 1. Boydton Plank Road October 27-28. Warren's Raid on Weldon Railroad December 12. Dabney's Mills February 5-7, 1865. Appomattox Campaign March 28-April 9. Dinwiddie Court House March 30-31. Five Forks April 1. Namozine Church April 3. Paine's Cross Roads April 5. Sailor's Creek April 6. Appomattox Court House April 9. Surrender of Lee and his army. Moved to Washington, D. C., May. Grand Review May 23.

BATTERY "I" 1st ARTILLERY.

Stationed at Fort Leavenworth, Kan., January, 1861. Moved to Washington, D. C., January 7-29, 1861, and duty there till July. Attached to Willcox's Brigade, Heintzelman's Division, McDowell's Army Northeastern Virginia, to August, 1861. Stone's Brigade, Division Potomac, to October, 1861. Stone's (Sedgwick's) Division, Army Potomac, to March, 1862. Artillery, 2nd Division, 2nd Army Corps, Army Potomac, to November, 1862. Reserve Artillery, 2nd Army Corps, to May, 1863. Artillery Brigade, 2nd Army Corps, to November, 1863. 2nd Brigade, Horse Artillery, Artillery Reserve, Potomac, to May, 1865. Defences of Washington, D. C., 22nd Corps.

SERVICE.—Advance on Manassas, Va., July 16-21, 1861. Battle of Bull Run July 21. Moved to Poolesville, Md., August 7-15. Duty there and at Edward's Ferry till March, 1862. Ball's Bluff October 21, 1861. Edward's Ferry October 22. Ordered to the Virginia Peninsula March, 1862. Siege of Yorktown April 5-May 4. Battle of Fair Oaks, Seven Pines, May 31-June 1. Seven days before Richmond June 25-July 1. Peach Orchard and Savage Station July 29. White Oak Swamp and Glendale June 30. Malvern Hill July 1. Moved to Alexandria, Va., August 16-23. Maryland Campaign September 6-22. Battle of Antietam September 16-17. At Harper's Ferry till October 30. Movement to Falmouth, Va., October 30-November 17. Battle of Fredericksburg December 11-15. "Mud March" January 20-24, 1863. At Falmouth till April. Chancellorsville Campaign April 27-May 6. Battle of Chancellorsville May 1-5. Gettysburg (Pa.) Campaign June 11-July 24. Battle of Gettysburg July 1-3. Advance to line of the Rapidan September 13-17. Bristoe Campaign October 9-22. Bristoe Station October 14. Advance to line of the Rappahannock November 7-8. Mine Run Campaign November 26-December 2. Campaign from the Rapidan to the James. Battles of the Wilderness May 5-7; Spottsylvania Court House May 8-21; North Anna River May 23-26; Totopotomoy May 28-31; Cold Harbor June 1-7; Gaines' Mill, Salem Church and Haw's Shop June 2. Sheridan's Trevillian Raid June 7-24. Trevillian Station June 11-12. Black Creek or Tunstall Station and White House or St. Peter's Church June 21. St. Mary's Church June 24. At Light House Point June 29-July 27. At Camp

Barry, D. C., till September. Arthur's Swamp September 29. Poplar Springs Church September 29-October 1. Wyatt's Road October 1. Boydton Plank Road October 27-28. Warren's Raid on Weldon Railroad December 7-12. Dabney's Mills February 5-7, 1865. Appomattox Campaign March 28-April 9. Dinwiddie Court House March 30-31. Five Forks April 1. Namozine Church April 3. Paine's Cross Roads April 5. Sailor's Creek April 6. Appomattox Court House April 9. Surrender of Lee and his army. Moved to Washington, D. C., May. Grand Review May 23.

BATTERY "K" 1st ARTILLERY.

Stationed at Eagle Pass, Fort Duncan, Texas, January and February, 1861. Moved to Fort Taylor, Fla., and duty there till January, 1862. Moved to Washington, D. C. Attached to Artillery Reserve, Army Potomac, to May, 1862. 2nd Brigade, Artillery Reserve, 5th Army Corps, Army Potomac, to September, 1862. Reserve Artillery, 5th Army Corps, to December, 1862. Artillery Reserve, Army Potomac, to June, 1863, 2nd Brigade, Horse Artillery, Army Potomac, to June, 1864. Camp Barry, D. C., to August, 1864. Horse Artillery, Army Shenandoah, Middle Military Division, to December, 1864. Horse Artillery Reserve, Army Shenandoah, to April, 1865. Cavalry Brigade, Army Shenandoah.

SERVICE.—Moved to Virginia Peninsula March, 1862. Siege of Yorktown April 5-May 4. Battle of Williamsburg May 5. Battle of Fair Oaks, Seven Pines, May 31-June 1. Seven days before Richmond June 25-July 1. Malvern Hill July 1. Moved to Fortress Monroe, thence to Centreville August 16-28. Pope's Campaign in Northern Virginia August 28-September 2. Battles of Groveton August 29; Bull Run August 30; Chantilly September 1. Maryland Campaign September 6-22. Battle of Antietam September 16-17. Battle of Fredericksburg, Va., December 11-15. At Falmouth, Va., till April, 1863. Chancellorsville Campaign April 27-May 6. Battle of Chancellorsville May 1-5. Brandy Station or Fleetwood and Beverly Ford June 9. Upperville June 21. Battle of Gettysburg, Pa., July 1-3. Williamsburg and Hagerstown, Md., July 6. Boonsboro July 8. Benevola or Beaver Creek July 9. About Funkstown July 10-13. Brandy Station August 1-4. Advance from the Rappahannock to the Rapidan September 13-15. Culpeper Court House September 13. Robertson's Ford September 15. Bristoe Campaign October 9-22. Jefferson-ton October 12-13. Advance to line of the Rappahannock November 7-8. Mine Run Campaign November 26-December 2. Reconnoissance from Bealeton to Front Royal January 1-4, 1864. Rapidan Campaign May 4-June 12. Wilderness May 5-7. Spottsylvania Court House May 8-21. North Anna May 23-26. Totopotomoy May 28-31. Cold Harbor June 1-12. Ream's Station June 21. Wilson's Raid on Southside & Danville Railroad June 22-30. Nottaway Court House June 23. Sappony Church or Stony Creek June 28-29. Ream's Station June 29. Moved to Washington, D. C., July 12-14. Sheridan's Shenandoah Valley Campaign August 7-November 28. Near Kearneysville August 25. Leetown and Smithfield August 28. Smithfield Crossing, Opequan Creek, August 29. Sevier's Ford, Opequan Creek, September 15. Battle of Opequan, Winchester, September 19. Fisher's Hill September 21. Milford September 22. Mt. Jackson September 23-24. Port Republic September 26-27. Battle of Cedar Creek October 19. Duty in the Defences of Washington and Shenandoah Valley till August, 1865.

BATTERY "L" 1st ARTILLERY.

Duty at Fort Duncan, Eagle Pass, Texas, January, 1861. Moved to Fort Jefferson, Fla., February 20, 1861, and to Fort Pickens, Fla. May 24, 1861. Attached to District Fort Pickens and Pensacola, Fla., Dept. South, to September, 1862. Defences New Orleans, La., Dept. Gulf, to December, 1862. Grover's Division, Dept. of the Gulf, to January, 1863. Artillery, 4th Division, 19th Army Corps, Dept. Gulf, to August, 1863. Artillery Reserve, 19th Army Corps, to January, 1864. Artillery, 1st Di-

vision, 19th Army Corps, to August, 1864. Defences Washington, 22nd Army Corps, August, 1864. Horse Artillery, Army Shenandoah, Middle Military Division, to December, 1864. Horse Artillery (Reserve), Army Shenandoah, to April, 1865. Cavalry Brigade, Army Shenandoah.

SERVICE.—Duty at Fort Pickens, Fla., till May, 1862. Bombardment of Forts McRee and Barrancas, Pensacola Harbor, November 22-23, 1861, and January 1, 1862. Reconnoissance on Santa Rosa Island January 27-31, 1862. Capture of Forts McRee and Barrancas May 9. Moved to Pensacola May 13, and duty there till August. Moved to New Orleans, La., August 30-September 3, and duty there till December. Moved to Baton Rouge, La., and duty there till March, 1863. Expedition to Port Hudson March 7-27. Operations in Western Louisiana April 9-May 14. Teche Campaign April 11-20. Fort Bisland April 12-13. Porter's and McWilliams' Plantation at Indian Bend April 14. Irish Bend April 14. Bayou Vermillion April 17. Expedition to Breux Bridge and Opelousas April 17-21. Expedition to Alexandria and Simsport May 5-16. Moved to Port Hudson May 18-23. Siege of Port Hudson May 24-July 9. Assaults on Port Hudson May 27 and June 14. Surrender of Port Hudson July 9. Moved to Baton Rouge July 13-August 2. Sabine Pass Expedition September 4-12. Western Louisiana Campaign October 3-November 17. At New Iberia till December. Moved to New Orleans, La., and duty there till March, 1864. Red River Campaign March 10-May 22. Advance from Franklin to Alexandria March 14-26. Battle of Sabine Cross Roads April 8. Pleasant Hill April 9. Monett's Ferry, Cane River Crossing, April 23. At Alexandria during construction of dam April 30-May 10. Retreat to Morganza May 13-20. Marksville May 15. Avoyelle's Prairie, Mansura, May 16. At Morganza till June. Moved to New York, thence to Washington, D. C., July 27-August 5. Sheridan's Shenandoah Valley Campaign August to November. Near Kearneysville August 25. Leetown and Smithfield August 28. Smithfield Crossing, Opequan, August 29. Sevier's Ford, Opequan, September 15. Battle of Opequan, Winchester, September 19. Fisher's Hill September 21. Milford September 22. Mt. Jackson September 23-24. Port Republic September 26-27. Battle of Cedar Creek October 19. Duty in the Shenandoah Valley and in the Defences of Washington, D. C., till August, 1865.

BATTERY "M" 1st ARTILLERY.

Stationed at Fort Brown, Texas, till March, 1861. At Fort Jefferson, Fla., March 24, 1861, to June 16, 1862. Moved to Hilton Head, S. C., June 16-20; thence to Beaufort, S. C., June 21. Attached to District of Beaufort, S. C., Dept. of the South, to September, 1862. United States Forces, Port Royal Island, S. C., 10th Corps, Dept. of the South, to November, 1863. United States Forces, Hilton Head, S. C., 10th Army Corps, Dept. of the South, to February, 1864. Artillery, District of Florida to April, 1864. Artillery, 1st Division, 10th Army Corps, Army of the James, to May, 1864. Artillery, 3rd Division, 10th Army Corps, to August, 1864. Artillery Brigade, 10th Army Corps, to December, 1864. Artillery Brigade, 25th Army Corps, to May, 1865. Dept. of Texas to December, 1865.

SERVICE.—Duty at Beaufort, S. C., till November, 1863. Expedition to Pocotaligo, S. C., October 21-23, 1862. Action at Frampton's Plantation, Pocotaligo, October 22. Moved to Hilton Head, S. C., November, 1863, and duty there till February, 1864. Expedition to Jacksonville, Fla., February 5-7. Occupation of Jacksonville February 7. Expedition from Jacksonville to Lake City, Fla., February 7-22. Battle of Olustee February 20. Duty in District of Florida till April. Moved to Gloucester Point, Va., April 26-May 5. Butler's operations on south side of the James River and against Petersburg and Richmond May 5-28. Wier Bottom Church May 9. Proctor's Creek May 10. Operations against Fort Darling May 12-16. Battle of Drury's Bluff May 14-16. Bermuda Front May 16-June 16. Green

Plains May 20. Attack on Redoubt Dutton June 2. Siege operations against Petersburg and Richmond June 16, 1864, to April 2, 1865. Duty on the Bermuda front June 16 to August 28, 1864. Battle of Chaffin's Farm, New Market Heights, September 29-30. Darbytown Road October 7. Duty at New York during presidential election of 1864 November 2-17. Return to Army of the James November 17-22. Duty in trenches before Richmond till March 27, 1865. Appomattox Campaign March 27-April 9. Hatcher's Run March 28-April 2. Fall of Petersburg April 2. Pursuit of Lee April 3-9. Appomattox Court House April 9. Surrender of Lee and his army. At City Point till June 7. Moved to Brazos Santiago, Texas, June 7-July 1. At Brownsville till December. Moved to New Orleans, thence to New York December 31, 1861, to January 15, 1866.

1st Regiment Artillery lost during service 6 Officers and 75 Enlisted men killed and mortally wounded and 116 Enlisted men by disease. Total 197.

2nd REGIMENT ARTILLERY.
BATTERY "A" 2nd ARTILLERY.

At Washington, D. C., January, 1861. Expedition to relief of Fort Pickens, Fla., and return to Washington. Attached to Blenker's Brigade, Miles' Division, McDowell's Army of Northeast Virginia, June to August, 1861. Heintzelman's Brigade, Division of the Potomac, to October, 1861. Blenker's Brigade, Division of the Potomac, to October, 1861. Artillery Reserve, Army of the Potomac, to May, 1862. 1st Brigade, Horse Artillery, Artillery Reserve, 5th Army Corps, Army of the Potomac, to September, 1862. Artillery, Cavalry Division, Army of the Potomac, to February, 1863. Artillery Reserve, attached to 2nd Division, Cavalry Corps, Army of the Potomac, to June, 1863. 2nd Brigade, Horse Artillery, attached to 2nd Division, Cavalry Corps, Army of the Potomac, to May, 1865. Dept. of Washington, 22nd Corps.

SERVICE.—Advance on Manassas, Va., July 16-21, 1861. Battle of Bull Run July 21. Duty in the Defences of Washington, D. C., till March, 1862. Moved to the Virginia Peninsula. Siege of Yorktown April 5-May 4. Near Williamsburg May 4. Mechanicsville May 23-24. Seven days before Richmond June 25-July 1. Mechanicsville June 26. Gaines' Mill June 27. Malvern Hill July 1. At Harrison's Landing till August 16. Coggin's Point July 31-August 1. Moved to Fortress Monroe, thence to Alexandria August 16-24. Maryland Campaign September 6-22. Sugar Loaf Mountain September 11-12. Boonsborough September 15. Battle of Antietam September 16-17. Shepherdstown Ford September 19. Upperville and Bloomfield November 2-3. Snicker's Gap November 3-4. Markham Station November 4. Amissville November 10. Battle of Fredericksburg, Va., December 12-15. Operations at Rappahannock Bridge and Grove Church February 5-7, 1863. Stoneman's Raid April 29-May 8. Battle of Gettysburg July 1-3. Emmettsburg, Md., July 4. Williamsport and Hagerstown July 6. Boonsborough July 8. Old Antietam Forge July 10. Falling Waters July 14. Chester Gap July 21-22. Advance from the Rappahannock to the Rapidan September 13-17. Culpeper Court House September 13. Raccoon Ford September 14-16. Bristoe Campaign October 9-22. Groveton October 17-18. Gainesville and Buckland Mills October 19. Advance to line of the Rappahannock November 7-8. Mine Run Campaign November 26-December 2. New Hope Church November 27. Demonstration on the Rapidan February 6-7, 1864. Barnett's Ford February 6-7. Rapidan Campaign May 4-June 12. Wilderness May 5-7. Spottsylvania Court House May 8-21. Cold Harbor June 1-7. Gaines' Mill, Salem Church and Haw's Shop June 2. Sheridan's Trevillian Raid June 7-24. Trevillian Station June 11-12. Black Creek or Tunstall Station and White House or St. Peter's Church June 21. St. Mary's Church June 24. Siege operations against Petersburg and Richmond June 29, 1864, to April 2, 1865. Lee's Mills July 12, 1864. Demonstration north

of the James River July 27-29. Deep Bottom July 27-28. Malvern Hill July 29. Lee's Mills July 30. Demonstration north of the James August 13-20. Gravel Hill August 14. Deep Run August 16. Strawberry Plains August 16-18. Dinwiddie Road, near Ream's Station, August 23. Ream's Station August 23-25. Poplar Grove Church September 29-October 2. Arthur's Swamp September 30-October 1. Boydton Plank Road October 27-28. Reconnoissance toward Stony Creek November 7. Stony Creek Station December 1. Warren's Expedition to Weldon Railroad December 7-12. Dabney's Mills, Hatcher's Run, February 5-7, 1865. Appomattox Campaign March 28-April 9. Dinwiddie Court House March 30-31. Five Forks April 1. Namozine Church April 3. Payne's Cross Roads April 5. Amelia Springs April 5. Sailor's Creek April 6. Appomattox Station April 8. Appomattox Court House April 9. Surrender of Lee and his army. Expedition to Danville April 23-29. Moved to Washington, D. C. Grand Review May 23. Duty at Washington, D. C., till ———

BATTERY "B" 2nd ARTILLERY.

At Fortress Monroe, Va., January, 1861. Attached to Dept. of Virginia April, 1861, to September, 1861. Artillery Reserve, Army of the Potomac, to May, 1862. Consolidated with Battery "L" 2nd Artillery, May, 1862, and attached to 1st Brigade, Horse Artillery, Artillery Reserve, 5th Army Corps, Army of the Potomac, to September, 1862. Pleasanton's Cavalry Division, Army of the Potomac, to November, 1862. Averill's Cavalry Brigade, Right Grand Division, Army of the Potomac, to February, 1863. 1st Division, Cavalry Corps, Army of the Potomac, to June, 1863. 1st Brigade, Horse Artillery, Army of the Potomac and Shenandoah, to December, 1864. Reserve Artillery, Middle Military Division, to April, 1865. Horse Artillery Brigade, 22nd Corps, to August, 1865.

SERVICE.—Action at Big Bethel, Va., June 10, 1861. Capture of Forts Hatteras and Clark, Hatteras Inlet, N. C., August 28-29. Moved to Washington, D. C., September, and duty there till March, 1862. Moved to the Virginia Peninsula. Siege of Yorktown April 5-May 4. Near Williamsburg May 4. Slatersville, New Kent Court House, May 9. Seven days before Richmond June 25-July 1. Turkey Bridge June 30. Malvern Hill July 1. At Harrison's Landing till August 16. Moved to Fortress Monroe, thence to Alexandria August 16-24. Maryland Campaign September 6-22. Sugar Loaf Mountain September 10-11. Frederick, Md., September 12. Catoctin Mountain September 13. Battle of Antietam September 16-17. Shepherdstown Ford September 19. Markham Station November 4. Warrenton November 6. Battle of Fredericksburg, Va., December 12-15. Chancellorsville Campaign April 27-May 8. Stoneman's Raid April 29-May 8. Brandy Station or Fleetwood and Beverly Ford June 9. Gettysburg, Pa., July 1-3. Brandy Station August 1-4. Advance from the Rappahannock to the Rapidan September 13-17. Bristoe Campaign October 9-22. Raccoon Ford October 10. Morton's Ford, Stevensburg, and Kelly's Ford October 11. Brandy Station or Fleetwood October 11-12. Oak Hill October 15. Advance to line of the Rappahannock November 7-9. Mine Run Campaign November 26-December 2. New Hope Church November 27. Rapidan Campaign May 4-June 12. Wilderness May 5-7. Brock Road and the Furnaces May 6. Todd's Tavern May 7-8. Sheridan's Raid to the James River May 9-24. Ground Squirrel Church and Yellow Tavern May 11. Brook Church or Richmond fortifications May 12. On line of the Pamunkey May 26-28. Hanovertown May 27. Crump's Creek and Haw's Shop May 28. Totopotomoy May 28-31. Cold Harbor June 1-7. Siege of Petersburg June 16-August 5. Deep Bottom July 27-29. Sheridan's Shenandoah Valley Campaign August 7-November 28. Toll Gate, near White Post, and near Newtown August 11. Cedarville, Guard Hill or Front Royal August 16. Battle of Opequan, Winchester, September 19. Near Cedarville September 20. Front Royal September 21. Milford September 22. Waynesboro September 29.

54½

Tom's Brook October 8-9. Battle of Cedar Creek October 19. Expedition to Lacey Springs December 19-22. Duty in the Shenandoah Valley till April, 1865, and at Washington, D. C., till August, 1865.

BATTERY "C" 2nd ARTILLERY.

At Dry Tortugas, Fla., January, 1861, and duty there till September, 1861. At Fort Pickens, Fla., till May, 1862. Attached to District of Fort Pickens, Fla., Dept. of the South, to May, 1862. District of Pensacola, Fla., Dept. of the South, to September, 1862. New Orleans, La., Dept. of the Gulf, to December, 1862. Grover's Division, Dept. of the Gulf, to January, 1863. Artillery, 4th Division, 19th Army Corps. Dept. of the Gulf, to December, 1863. District of Baton Rouge, La., Dept. of the Gulf, to February, 1864. Artillery, 2nd Division, 19th Army Corps, to July, 1864. Defences of Washington, D. C., 22nd Army Corps, to August, 1865.

SERVICE.—Action on Santa Rosa Island, Fla., October 9, 1861. Engagement with Confederate Batteries at Barrancas November 22-23. Bombardment of Forts McRee and Barrancas, Pensacola Harbor, January 1, 1862. Moved to Pensacola May 13, and duty there till September. Moved to New Orleans, La., thence to Baton Rouge December, and duty there till March, 1863. Operations against Port Hudson March 7-27. Operations in Western Louisiana April 9-May 14. Teche Campaign April 11-20. Fort Bisland April 12-13. Irish Bend April 14. Bayou Vermillion April 17. Advance on Port Hudson May 12-24. Siege of Port Hudson May 24-July 9. Assaults on Port Hudson May 27 and June 14. Surrender of Port Hudson July 9. Moved to Baton Rouge, La., and duty there till March, 1864. Red River Campaign March to May. At Alexandria, La. Retreat to Morganza May 13-20. Moved to Washington, D. C., July, 1864, and duty there till August, 1865. Consolidated with Battery "E" 2nd Artillery August 24, 1864.

BATTERY "D" 2nd ARTILLERY.

Attached to Wilcox's Brigade, Heintzelman's Division, McDowell's Army of Northeast Virginia, June to August, 1861. Kearney's Brigade, Division of the Potomac, to October, 1861. Artillery, Franklin's Division, Army of the Potomac, to March, 1862. Artillery, 1st Division, 1st Army Corps, Army of the Potomac and Dept. of the Rappahannock, to May, 1862. Artillery, 1st Division, 6th Army Corps, Army of the Potomac, to May, 1863. Artillery Brigade, 6th Army Corps, to July, 1863. 1st Brigade, Horse Artillery, Army of the Potomac, to August, 1864. Horse Artillery, Army of the Shenandoah, Middle Military Division, to December, 1864. Reserve Horse Artillery, Army of the Shenandoah, to April, 1865. Horse Artillery, Defences of Washington, D. C., 22nd Army Corps, to October, 1865.

SERVICE.—Advance on Manassas, Va., July 16-21, 1861. Battle of Bull Run July 21. Duty in the Defences of Washington, D. C., till March, 1862. Advance on Manassas, Va., March 10-15. Advance to Falmouth, Va., April 9-19. Moved to the Virginia Peninsula. Peninsula Campaign May to August. West Point May 7. Seven days before Richmond June 25-July 1. Glendale June 30. Malvern Hill July 1. At Harrison's Landing till August 16. Moved to Alexandria August 16-24. Maryland Campaign September 6-22. Crampton's Pass, South Mountain, Md., September 14. Battle of Antietam September 16-17. Movement to Falmouth, Va., October 30-November 19. Battle of Fredericksburg, Va., December 12-15. At Falmouth till April, 1863. Chancellorsville Campaign April 27-May 6. Operations at Franklin's Crossing April 29-May 2. Battle of Maryes Heights, Fredericksburg, May 3. Salem Heights May 3-4. Battle of Gettysburg, Pa., July 2-4. Advance from the Rappahannock to the Rapidan September 13-17. Culpeper Court House September 13. Raccoon Ford September 14-16. Reconnoissance across the Rapidan September 21-23. Bristoe Campaign October 9-22. Raccoon Ford and Morton's Ford October 10. Morton's Ford, Stevensburg, and near Kelly's Ford October 11. Brandy Station or Fleetwood October 11-12. Oak Hill

October 15. Advance to line of the Rappahannock November 7-8. Mine Run Campaign November 26-December 2. Rapidan Campaign May 4-June 12, 1864. Wilderness May 5-7. Todd's Tavern May 7-8. Sheridan's Raid to the James River May 9-24. Ground Squirrel Church and Yellow Tavern May 11. On line of the Pamunkey May 26-28. Haw's Shop May 28. Totopotomoy May 28-31. Cold Harbor June 1-7. Sheridan's Trevillian Raid June 7-24. Trevillian Station June 11-12. Black Creek or Tunstall Station and White Horse or St. Peter's Church June 21. Siege of Petersburg June 29-August 2. Deep Bottom July 27-28. Malvern Hill July 28. Sheridan's Shenandoah Valley Campaign August 7-November 28. Toll Gate, near White Post, and near Newtown August 11. Near Kearneysville August 25. Leetown and Smithfield, W. Va., August 28. Smithfield Crossing, Opequan, August 29. Sevier's Ford, Opequan, September 15. Battle of Opequan September 19. Fisher's Hill September 21. Milford September 22. Tom's Brook October 8-9. Duty at Winchester and in the Shenandoah Valley till December, and at Pleasant Valley, Md., till April, 1865. At Washington, D. C., till October, 1865.

BATTERY "E" 2nd ARTILLERY.

At Washington, D. C., January, 1861. Attached to Schenck's Brigade, Tyler's Division, McDowell's Army, Northeast Virginia, June to August, 1861. Artillery Division, Army of the Potomac, to October, 1861. Porter's Division, Army of the Potomac, to March, 1862. Artillery Reserve, Potomac, to May, 1862. 5th Brigade, Artillery Reserve, 5th Army Corps, Army of the Potomac, to September, 1862. Artillery, 1st Division, 9th Army Corps, to December, 1862. Artillery, 3rd Division, 9th Army Corps, to February, 1863. Artillery, 1st Division, 9th Army Corps, Army of the Potomac, to April, 1863. District of Central Kentucky, Dept. of the Ohio, to June, 1863. Artillery Reserve, 9th Army Corps, Dept. of the Ohio, to August, 1863. Artillery, 1st Division, 9th Army Corps, Dept. of the Ohio, to March, 1864. Reserve Artillery, 9th Army Corps, Army of the Potomac, to June, 1864. Camp Barry, Washington, D. C., 22nd Army Corps, to November, 1864. Consolidated with Battery "C" 2nd Artillery August 24, 1864. 1st Separate Brigade, 22nd Army Corps, November, 1864, to October, 1865.

SERVICE.—Advance on Manassas, Va., July 16-21, 1861. Occupation of Fairfax Court House July 17. Battle of Bull Run July 21. Duty in the Defences of Washington till March, 1862. Moved to the Virginia Peninsula. Siege of Yorktown April 5-May 4. Near Williamsburg May 4. Seven days before Richmond June 25-July 1. Turkey Bridge June 30. Malvern Hill July 1. At Harrison's Landing till August 16. Movement to Centreville, Va., August 16-28. Battle of Groveton August 29. Battle of Bull Run August 30. Chantilly September 1. Maryland Campaign September 6-22. Battle of Antietam September 16-17. Warrenton or Sulphur Springs November 15. Battle of Fredericksburg, Va., December 12-15. "Mud March" January 20-24. Moved to Newport News February 10, and duty there till March 19. Movement to Kentucky March 19-23. Duty in District of Central Kentucky till June. Moved to Vicksburg, Miss., June 7-14. Siege of Vicksburg June 14-July 4. Advance on Jackson, Miss., July 4-10. Siege of Jackson July 10-17. Moved to Covington, thence to Crab Orchard, Ky., August 4-18. March to Knoxville, Tenn., September 10-26. Knoxville Campaign November 4-December 23. Action at Campbell's Station November 16. Siege of Knoxville November 17-December 5. Repulse of Longstreet's assault on Fort Saunders November 29. Operations in East Tennessee till March, 1864. Ordered to Annapolis, Md. Rapidan (Va.) Campaign May 4-June 7. Wilderness May 5-7. Spottsylvania May 8-21. Totopotomoy May 28-31. Cold Harbor June 1-7. Bethesda Church June 1-3. Ordered to Washington, D. C., and duty in the Defences of that city till October, 1865.

BATTERY "F" 2nd ARTILLERY.

At St. Louis, Mo., April, 1861. Attached to Army of the West and Dept. of Missouri to February, 1862. Artillery Division, Army of Mississippi, to April, 1862. Artillery, 2nd Division, Army of Mississippi, to November, 1862. Artillery, 8th Division, Left Wing 13th Army Corps, Dept. of Tennessee, to December, 1862. 1st Brigade, 8th Division, 16th Army Corps, Army of Tennessee, to March, 1863. Artillery, 2nd Division, District of Corinth, Miss., 16th Army Corps, to May, 1863. 3rd Brigade, District of Memphis, Tenn., 5th Division, 16th Army Corps, to November, 1863. Fuller's Brigade, 2nd Division, 16th Army Corps, to January, 1864. Artillery, 4th Division, 16th Army Corps, to September, 1864. Artillery, 1st Division, 17th Army Corps, to November, 1864. Artillery, District of Nashville, Tenn., Dept. of the Cumberland, to August, 1865.

SERVICE.—Expedition from St. Louis, Mo., to Booneville, Mo., June 13-17, 1861. Capture of Jefferson City June 14. Booneville June 17. Expedition from Springfield to Forsyth July 20-25. Forsyth July 22. Battle of Wilson's Creek August 10. Moved to Commerce, Mo., February, 1862. Operations against New Madrid, Mo., and Island No. 10, Mississippi River, February 28-April 8. Moved to Hamburg Landing, Tenn., April 18-23. Advance on and siege of Corinth, Miss., April 29-May 30. Reconnoissance toward Corinth May 8. Pursuit to Booneville May 30-June 12. Duty at Corinth till September. Battle of Iuka September 19. Battle of Corinth October 3-4. Pursuit to Hatchie River October 5-12. Grant's Central Mississippi Campaign. Operations on the Mississippi Central Railroad November 2, 1862, to January 10, 1863. Duty at Corinth, Miss., till May, 1863, and at Memphis, Tenn., till October. Movement to Prospect, Tenn., October 18-November 13. Duty there and at Decatur, Ala., till April, 1864. Atlanta (Ga.) Campaign May 1 to September 8. Demonstrations on Resaca May 8-13. Battle of Resaca May 13, 14 and 15. Battles about Dallas, New Hope Church and Allatoona Hills May 25-June 5. Operations about Marietta and against Kenesaw Mountain June 9-July 2. Assault on Kenesaw June 27. Nickajack Creek July 2-5. Ruff's Mills July 3-4. Chattahoochie River July 5-17. Battle of Atlanta July 22. Siege of Atlanta July 22-August 25. Ezra Chapel July 28. Flank movement on Jonesboro August 25-30. Battle of Jonesboro August 31-September 1. Lovejoy Station September 2-6. Operations against Hood in North Georgia and North Alabama September 29-November 3. Ordered to Nashville, Tenn. Duty at Nashville, Tenn., Bridgeport, Ala., and Chattanooga, Tenn., till August, 1865.

BATTERY "G" 2nd ARTILLERY.

At Washington, D. C., May, 1861. Attached to Davies' Brigade, Miles' Division, McDowell's Army, Northeast Virginia, June to August, 1861. Kearney's Brigade, Division of the Potomac, to October, 1861. Artillery, Franklin's Division, Army of the Potomac, to January, 1862. Artillery, Heintzelman's Division, Army of the Potomac, to March, 1862. Artillery, 3rd Division, 3rd Army Corps, Army of the Potomac, to August, 1862. Artillery, 1st Division, 4th Army Corps, Army of the Potomac, to September, 1862. Artillery, 3rd Division, 6th Army Corps, Army of the Potomac, to May, 1863. Artillery Brigade, 6th Army Corps, to August, 1863. 2nd Brigade, Horse Artillery, Army of the Potomac, to June, 1864. 1st Brigade, DeRussy's Division, 22nd Army Corps, Defences of Washington, D. C., south of the Potomac, to August, 1865.

SERVICE.—Advance on Manassas, Va., July 16-21, 1861. Near Fairfax Court House July 17. Battle of Bull Run July 21. Duty in the Defences of Washington till March, 1862. Moved to Virginia Peninsula. Siege of Yorktown April 5-May 4. Near Williamsburg May 4. Battle of Williamsburg May 5. Battle of Fair Oaks, Seven Pines, May 31-June 1. Seven days before Richmond June 25-July 1. Oak Grove June 25. Glendale June 30. Malvern Hill July 1. At Harrison's Landing till August 16. Moved to Alexandria, Va., August

16-24. Maryland Campaign September 6-22. Battle of Antietam September 16-17. Movement to Falmouth, Va., October 30-November 19. Battle of Fredericksburg, Va., December 12-15. "Mud March" January 20-24, 1863. At Falmouth till April. Chancellorsville Campaign April 27-May 6. Operations at Franklin's Crossing April 29-May 2. Battle of Maryes Heights, Fredericksburg, May 3. Salem Heights May 3-4. Battle of Gettysburg, Pa., July 1-3. Advance from the Rappahannock to the Rapidan September 13-17. Culpeper Court House September 13. Bristoe Campaign October 9-22. Advance to line of the Rappahannock November 7-8. Mine Run Campaign November 26-December 2. New Hope Church November 27. Demonstration on the Rapidan February 6-7, 1864. Barnett's Ford February 6-7. Rapidan Campaign May 4-June 2. Wilderness May 5-7. Spottsylvania Court House May 8-21. North Anna River May 23-26. On line of the Pamunkey May 26-28. Totopotomoy May 28-31. Cold Harbor May 31-June 2. Dismounted June 2 and ordered to Washington, D. C. Duty in the Defences of that city till August, 1865.

BATTERY "H" 2nd ARTILLERY.

At Washington, D. C., February, 1861. Ordered to Fort Pickens, Fla., April, 1861. Duty at Fort Pickens and Barrancas, Fla., District of Pensacola, Fla., till May, 1864. Action on Santa Rosa Island October 9, 1861. Engagement with Confederate Batteries at Pensacola November 22-23, 1861. Bombardment of Forts McRee and Barrancas, Pensacola Harbor, January 1, 1862. Moved to Baltimore, Md., May, 1864, and garrison duty at Fort McHenry till August, 1865.

BATTERY "I" 2nd ARTILLERY.

At Fort McHenry, Baltimore, Md., April, 1861. Attached to Dix's Command, Baltimore, Md., June, 1861, to July, 1862. Defences of Baltimore, Md., 8th Army Corps, Middle Department, to January, 1863. 1st Separate Brigade, 8th Army Corps, to May, 1864. 2nd Brigade, Haskins' Division, 22nd Army Corps, Defences of Washington, D. C., north of the Potomac, to July, 1864. 1st Brigade, Hardin's Division, 22nd Army Corps, to November, 1864. Fort Foote, Defences north of the Potomac, 22nd Army Corps, to April, 1865. Dept. of the Cumberland to August, 1865. Middle Department to August, 1865.

SERVICE.—On garrison duty at Fort McHenry, Baltimore, Md., till May, 1864, and in the Defences of Washington, D. C., till April, 1865. Moved to Alabama as Infantry April, 1865; to Chattanooga, Tenn., June, 1865, and to Fort McHenry, Baltimore, Md., August, 1865.

BATTERY "K" 2nd ARTILLERY.

At Washington, D. C., February, 1861. Ordered to Fort Pickens, Fla., April, 1861. Attached to District of Pensacola, Fla., Dept. of the South, to August, 1862. District of West Florida, Dept. of the Gulf, to May, 1864. New York, Dept. of the East, to August, 1864. Defences of Baltimore, Md., 8th Corps, Middle Department, to August, 1865.

SERVICE.—Garrison duty at Fort Pickens, Fla., till May, 1864. Engagement with Confederate Batteries at Pensacola November 22-23, 1861. Bombardment of Forts McRee and Barrancas, Pensacola Harbor, January 1, 1862. Moved to Fort Hamilton, N. Y., May, 1864, and to Fort McHenry, Baltimore, Md., August, 1864. Duty at Fort McHenry and at Federal Hill till August, 1865.

BATTERY "L" 2nd ARTILLERY.

At Fortress Monroe, Va., January, 1861. Attached to Dept. of Virginia to September, 1861. Artillery Reserve, Army of the Potomac, to May, 1862. Consolidated with Battery "B" May, 1862, and attached to 1st Brigade, Horse Artillery, Artillery Reserve, 5th Army Corps, Army of the Potomac, to September, 1862. Artillery, Pleasanton's Cavalry Division, Army of the Potomac, to November, 1862. Averill's Cavalry Brigade,

Right Grand Division, Army of the Potomac, to February, 1863. 1st Division, Cavalry Corps, Army of the Potomac, to June, 1863. 1st Brigade, Horse Artillery, Army of the Potomac, to August, 1864. Horse Artillery, Army of the Shenandoah, Middle Military Division, to December, 1864. Reserve Horse Artillery, Army of the Shenandoah, to April, 1865. Horse Artillery Brigade, 22nd Army Corps, to August, 1865.

SERVICE.—Duty at Fortress Monroe, Va., till September, 1861. Ordered to Washington, D. C., and duty there till March, 1862. Ordered to the Virginia Peninsula. Peninsula Campaign April to August. Seven days before Richmond June 25-July 1. Turkey Bridge June 30. Malvern Hill July 1. At Harrison's Landing till August 16. Moved to Fortress Monroe, thence to Alexandria August 16-24. Maryland Campaign September 7-22. Sugar Loaf Mountain September 10-11. Frederick September 12. Catoctin Mountain September 13. Battle of Antietam September 16-17. Shepherdstown Ford September 19. Markham Station November 4. Warrenton November 6. Battle of Fredericksburg December 12-15. Chancellorsville Campaign April 27-May 8. Stoneman's Raid April 29-May 6. Brandy Station or Fleetwood and Beverly Ford June 9. Battle of Gettysburg, Pa., July 1-3. Brandy Station August 1-4. Advance from the Rappahannock to the Rapidan September 13-17. Bristoe Campaign October 9-22. Raccoon Ford October 10. Morton's Ford, Stevensburg, and Kelly's Ford October 11. Brandy Station or Fleetwood October 11-12. Oak Hill October 15. Advance to line of the Rappahannock November 7-8. Mine Run Campaign November 26-December 2. New Hope Church November 27. Rapidan Campaign May 4-June 12, 1864. Wilderness May 5-7. Brock Road and the Furnaces May 6. Todd's Tavern May 7-8. Sheridan's Raid to the James River May 9-24. Ground Squirrel Church and Yellow Tavern May 11. Brook Church, Fortifications of Richmond, May 12. On line of the Pamunkey May 26-28. Hanovertown May 27. Crump's Creek and Haw's Shop May 28. Totopotomoy May 28-31. Cold Harbor June 1-7. Siege of Petersburg June 16-August 5. Sheridan's Shenandoah Valley Campaign August 7-November 28. Toll Gate, near White Post, and near Newtown August 11. Cedarville, Guard Hill or Front Royal August 16. Battle of Opequan, Winchester, September 19. Near Cedarville September 20. Front Royal September 21. Milford September 22. Waynesboro September 29. Tom's Brook October 8-9. Battle of Cedar Creek October 19. Expedition to Lacey Springs December 19-22. Duty in the Shenandoah Valley till April, 1865, and at Washington, D. C., till August. Moved to Fort McHenry, Baltimore, Md., August, 1865.

BATTERY "M" 2nd ARTILLERY.

In Texas January, 1861. Moved to New York April, 1861; thence to Fort Pickens, Fla. Ordered to Washington, D. C., June, 1861. Attached to Richardson's Brigade, Tyler's Division, McDowell's Army, Northeast Virginia, to August, 1861. Franklin's Brigade, Division of the Potomac, to October, 1861. Franklin's Division, Army of the Potomac, to March, 1862. Artillery Reserve, Army of the Potomac, to May, 1862. 1st Brigade, Horse Artillery, Artillery Reserve, 5th Army Corps, Army of the Potomac, to September, 1862. Artillery, Pleasanton's Cavalry Division, Army of the Potomac, to February, 1863. Reserve Brigade, 1st Division, Cavalry Corps, Army of the Potomac, to June, 1863. 1st Brigade, Horse Artillery, Army of the Potomac, to August, 1864. Horse Artillery, Army of the Shenandoah, Middle Military Division, to December, 1864. Reserve Horse Artillery, Army of the Shenandoah, to April, 1865. Horse Artillery Brigade, 22nd Army Corps, to August, 1865.

SERVICE.—Advance on Manassas, Va., July 16-21, 1861. Occupation of Fairfax Court House July 17. Battle of Bull Run July 21. Duty in the Defences of Washington, D. C., till March, 1862. Moved to the Virginia Peninsula. Siege of Yorktown April 5-May 4. Near Williamsburg May 4. Hanover Court House May 27.

Operations about Hanover Court House May 27-29. Seven days before Richmond June 25-July 1. Malvern Hill July 1. At Harrison's Landing till August 16. Action at Malvern Hill August 5. Moved to Fortress Monroe, thence to Alexandria August 16-23. Maryland Campaign September 6-22. Poolesville, Md., September 7. Barnesville September 9. Monocacy Church September 9. Sugar Loaf Mountain September 10-11. Frederick September 12. Catoctin Mountain September 13. Antietam September 16-17. Shepherdstown Ford September 19. Shepherdstown and Martinsburg October 1. Pursuit of Stuart into Pennsylvania October 9-12. Mouth of Monocacy and White's Ford October 12. Philomont November 1. Union, Bloomfield and Upperville November 2-3. Barbee's Cross Roads November 5. Waterloo Bridge November 7. Corbin's Cross Roads, near Amissville, November 10. Battle of Fredericksburg December 12-15. Chancellorsville Campaign April 27-May 6. Stevensburg May 9. Brandy Station or Fleetwood and Beverly Ford June 9. Upperville June 21. Hanover, Pa., June 30. Gettysburg, Pa., July 1-3. Hunterstown July 2. Smithburg July 5. Williamsport and Hagerstown July 6. Boonsboro July 8. Hagerstown July 12-13. Williamsport and Falling Waters July 14. Advance to the Rapidan September 13-17. Reconnoissance across the Rapidan September 21-23. Bristoe Campaign October 9-22. James City October 10. Bethesda Church and near Culpeper October 10. Morton's Ford October 11. Near Warrenton, White Sulphur Springs, October 11. Brandy Station October 11. Groveton October 17-18. Gainesville, Buckland's Mills and Catlett's Station October 19. Advance to line of the Rappahannock November 7-8. Mine Run Campaign November 26-December 2. Morton's Ford November 26. Rapidan Campaign May 4-June 12, 1864. Todd's Tavern May 5-6. Wilderness May 6-7. Alsop's Farm May 8. Sheridan's Raid to the James River May 9-24. Beaver Dam Station May 9-10. Ground Squirrel Church and Yellow Tavern May 11. Brook Church or Richmond fortifications May 12. On line of the Pamunkey May 26-28. Demonstration on Little River May 27. Hanovertown May 27. Haw's Shop May 28. Totopotomoy May 28-31. Cold Harbor June 1-7. Sheridan's Trevillian Raid June 7-24. Trevillian Station June 11-12. Mallory's Cross Roads June 12. Black Creek or Tunstall Station and White House or St. Peter's Church June 21. Siege of Petersburg June 29-August 5. Sheridan's Shenandoah Valley Campaign August 7-November 28. Winchester August 17. Near Kearneysville August 25. Abraham's Creek, near Winchester, September 18. Battle of Opequan, Winchester, September 19. Near Cedarville September 20. Front Royal September 21. Milford September 22. Waynesboro September 29. Tom's Brook October 8-9. Expedition to Lacey's Springs December 19-22. Sheridan's Expedition from Winchester February 27-March 25, 1865. Occupation of Staunton and action at Waynesboro March 2. Appomattox Campaign March 28-April 12. Dinwiddie Court House March 30-31. Five Forks April 1. Moved to Washington, D. C., and duty there till August. Moved to Fort McHenry, Baltimore, Md.

2nd Regiment of Artillery lost during service 5 Officers and 50 Enlisted men killed and mortally wounded and 1 Officer and 118 Enlisted men by disease. Total 174.

3rd REGIMENT ARTILLERY.
BATTERY "A" 3rd ARTILLERY.

In California at outbreak of the Rebellion. Carlton's Expedition from Southern California through Arizona to New Mexico April 13-September 20, 1862. Duty at various posts in New Mexico till 1865, then ordered to Boston, Mass.

BATTERY "B" 3rd ARTILLERY.

Stationed at San Francisco, Cal., during the entire war.

BATTERY "C" 3rd ARTILLERY.

At San Francisco, Cal., till October, 1861. Ordered to New York October 14, 1861; thence moved to Washington, D. C. Attached to Artillery Reserve, Army of the Potomac, to May, 1862. (Attached to Battery "G" May to October, 1862.) 1st Brigade, Horse Artillery, Artillery Reserve, 5th Army Corps, Army of the Potomac, to September, 1862. Artillery, Cavalry Division, Army of the Potomac, to November, 1862. (Battery "G" broken up October, 1862.) Bayard's Cavalry Brigade, Army of the Potomac, to February, 1863. Artillery Reserve, Army of the Potomac, to May, 1863. 2nd Regular Brigade, Artillery Reserve, Army of the Potomac, to June, 1863. 2nd Brigade, Horse Artillery, Army of the Potomac, to August, 1864. (Consolidated with Batteries "F" and "K" from March, 1864.) Horse Artillery, Army of the Shenandoah, Middle Military Division, to December, 1864. Horse Artillery, Reserve, Army of the Shenandoah, to April, 1865. Horse Artillery Brigade, 22nd Army Corps, to August, 1865.

SERVICE.—Duty in the Defences of Washington, D. C., till March, 1862. Moved to the Virginia Peninsula. Siege of Yorktown April 5-May 4. Seven days before Richmond June 25-July 1. Operations about White House June 26-July 2. Rejoined army via Gloucester Point. Malvern Hill August 5. Maryland Campaign September 6-22. Middletown, Md., September 13. Battle of Antietam, Md., September 16-17. Shepherdstown Ford September 19. Aldie October 31. Mountsville October 31. New Baltimore, Salem and Thoroughfare Gap November 4. Rappahannock Station November 7-9. Battle of Fredericksburg, Va., December 12-15. Chancellorsville Campaign April 27-May 6. Battle of Chancellorsville May 1-5. Aldie June 17. Middleburg June 19. Upperville June 22. Battle of Gettysburg, Pa., July 1-3. Smithburg, Md., July 5. Jones' Cross Roads, near Williamsport, July 10-13. Robertson's Ford September 23. Bristoe Campaign October 9-22. Advance to line of the Rappahannock November 7-8. Rappahannock Bridge November 7-8. Mine Run Campaign November 26-December 2. Kilpatrick's Raid on Richmond February 28-March 4, 1864. Fortifications of Richmond March 1. Rapidan Campaign May 4-June 12. Wilderness May 5-7. Spottsylvania Court House May 8-21. Salem Church May 27. Cold Harbor June 1-12. Siege of Petersburg June 16 to August 5. Deep Bottom July 27-28. Sheridan's Shenandoah Campaign August 7-November 28. Near Winchester August 11. Near Kearneysville August 25. Battle of Cedar Creek October 19. Duty in the Shenandoah Valley till April, 1865. In Defences of Washington till August, 1865.

BATTERY "D" 3rd ARTILLERY.

Stationed at San Francisco, Cal., during entire war.

BATTERY "E" 3rd ARTILLERY.

At Washington, D. C., May, 1861. Attached to Sherman's Brigade, Tyler's Division, McDowell's Army, Northeast Virginia, to August, 1861. Sherman's Brigade, Division of the Potomac, to October, 1861. Porter's Division, Army of the Potomac, to October, 1861. T. W. Sherman's South Carolina Expeditionary Corps to April, 1862. 2nd Brigade, 1st Division, Dept. of the South, to July, 1862. District of Hilton Head, S. C., Dept. of the South, to September, 1862. United States Forces, Hilton Head, S. C., 10th Army Corps, Dept. of the South, to June, 1863. United States Forces, Folly Island, S. C., 10th Army Corps, to July, 1863. United States Forces, Morris Island, S. C., 10th Army Corps, to January, 1864. Artillery, Folly Island, S. C., Northern District, 10th Army Corps, to February, 1864. Artillery, Ames' Division, District of Florida, Dept. of the South, to April, 1864. Artillery, 3rd Division, 10th Army Corps, Army of the James, to May, 1864. Artillery, 1st Division, 10th Army Corps, to June, 1864. Artillery, 2nd Division, 10th Army Corps, to August, 1864. Artillery Brigade, 10th Army Corps, to December, 1864. Artillery Brigade, 25th Army Corps, to January, 1865. Artillery, 3rd Division, Terry's Provisional Corps, Dept. of North Carolina, to March, 1865. Artillery, 3rd Division, 10th Army Corps, Dept. of North Carolina.

SERVICE.—Occupation of Arlington Heights, Va., May 24, 1861. Advance on Manassas, Va., July 16-21.

Blackburn's Ford July 18. Battle of Bull Run July 21. Expedition to Port Royal, S. C., October 21-November 7. Bombardment and capture of Forts Walker and Beauregard, Port Royal Harbor, November 7. Duty at Hilton Head, S. C., till February, 1862. Expedition to Florida February 25-March 5. At Hilton Head, S. C., till May. Operations on James Island, S. C., June 1-28. Action on James Island June 10. Battle of Secessionville June 16. At Hilton Head, S. C., till October. Expedition to Pocotaligo, S. C., October 21-23. Action at Pocotaligo October 22. At Hilton Head, S. C., till June, 1863. Moved to Folly Island, S. C. Attack on Morris Island, S. C., July 10. Operations on Morris Island against Forts Wagner and Gregg and against Fort Sumpter and Charleston July 10-September 7. Assault on Fort Wagner July 18. Capture of Forts Wagner and Gregg September 7. Operations on Morris and Folly Islands against Charleston till January, 1864. Expedition to Florida February 5-7. Expedition from Jacksonville to Lake City, Fla., February 8-22. Battle of Olustee February 20. Duty at Jacksonville till April. Moved to Gloucester Point, Va. Butler's operations on south side of the James River and against Petersburg and Richmond May 5-28. Siege operations against Petersburg and Richmond June 16 to December 7. Battle of Chaffin's Farm, New Market Heights, September 28-30. Darbytown Road October 7. Expedition to Fort Fisher, N. C., December 7-27. Second Expedition to Fort Fisher, N. C., January 3-15, 1865. Assault and capture of Fort Fisher January 15. Near Sugar Loaf Battery February 11. Occupation of Wilmington February 22. Northeast Ferry February 22. Campaign of the Carolinas March 1-April 26. Advance on Goldsboro March 6-21. Advance on Raleigh April 10-13. Bennett's House April 26. Surrender of Johnston and his army. Duty in Dept. of North Carolina till ———.

BATTERY "F" 3rd ARTILLERY.

Attached to Battery "K," Artillery Reserve, Army of the Potomac, October, 1861, to May, 1862. 5th Brigade, Artillery Reserve, 5th Army Corps, Army of the Potomac, to September, 1862. Artillery, 1st Division, 3rd Army Corps, Army of the Potomac, to May, 1863. 1st Regular Brigade, Artillery Reserve, Army of the Potomac, to November, 1863. Artillery Brigade, 5th Army Corps, Army of the Potomac, to March, 1864. (Consolidated with Battery "C" February, 1864.) Artillery Reserve, Army of the Potomac, to April, 1864. 1st Brigade, Horse Artillery, Army of the Potomac, to August, 1864. Horse Artillery, Army of the Shenandoah, Middle Military Division, to December, 1864. Reserve Horse Artillery, Army of the Shenandoah, to April, 1865. Horse Artillery Brigade, 22nd Army Corps, to August, 1865.

SERVICE.—Duty in the Defences of Washington, D. C., till March, 1862. Ordered to the Virginia Peninsula. Siege of Yorktown, Va., April 5-May 4. Seven days before Richmond June 25-July 1. Malvern Hill July 1. At Harrison's Landing till August 16. Moved to Alexandria August 16-23. Duty in the Defences of Washington till November. Movement to Falmouth, Va. Battle of Fredericksburg, Va., December 12-15. At Falmouth till April, 1863. Chancellorsville Campaign April 27-May 6. Battle of Chancellorsville May 1-5. Battle of Gettysburg, Pa., July 1-3. Bristoe Campaign October 9-22. Advance to line of the Rappahannock November 7-8. Rappahannock Station November 7. Mine Run Campaign November 26-December 2. Rapidan Campaign May 4-June 12, 1864. Wilderness May 5-7. Spottsylvania May 8-21. Cold Harbor June 1-12. Siege of Petersburg June 16 to August 5. Deep Bottom July 27-28. Sheridan's Shenandoah Valley Campaign August 7-November 28. Near Winchester August 11. Near Kearneysville August 25. Battle of Cedar Creek October 19. Duty in the Shenandoah Valley till April, 1865, and in the Defences of Washington till August, 1865.

BATTERY "G" 3rd ARTILLERY.

At San Francisco, Cal., till October, 1861. Ordered to New York October 14, thence moved to Washington, D. C. Attached to Artillery Reserve, Army of the Potomac (attached to Battery "C"), March to May, 1862. 1st Brigade, Horse Artillery, Artillery Reserve, 5th Army Corps, Army of the Potomac, to September, 1862. Cavalry Division, Army of the Potomac, to October, 1862. Ordered to Virginia Peninsula March, 1862. Siege of Yorktown April 5-May 4. Near Williamsburg May 4. Seven days before Richmond June 25-July 1. At White House rejoin army via Gloucester Point. Malvern Hill August 5. Maryland Campaign September 6-22. Middletown, Md., September 13. Battle of Antietam September 16-17. Shepherdstown Ford September 19. Broken up October, 1862.

Reorganized April, 1864. Attached to Artillery Reserve, 9th Army Corps, Army of the Potomac, to May, 1864. 3rd Brigade, Hardin's Division, 22nd Army Corps, to July, 1864. 1st Brigade, Hardin's Division, 22nd Army Corps, to December, 1864. Fort Foote, Defences of Washington north of the Potomac, 22nd Army Corps, to April, 1865. 2nd Brigade, Hardin's Division, 22nd Corps, to August, 1865.

SERVICE.—Rapidan Campaign May 4-14, 1864. Battles of the Wilderness May 5-7; Spottsylvania Court House May 8-14. Ordered to Washington May 14, and duty in the Defences of that city north of the Potomac till August, 1865.

BATTERY "H" 3rd ARTILLERY.

Battery on duty at San Francisco, Cal., during entire war.

BATTERY "I" 3rd ARTILLERY.

Battery on duty at San Francisco, Cal., till July, 1864, and in the Dept. of the East till

BATTERY "K" 3rd ARTILLERY.

(Attached to Battery "F".) Artillery Reserve, Army of the Potomac, October, 1861, to May, 1862. 5th Brigade, Artillery Reserve, 5th Army Corps, Army of the Potomac, to September, 1862. Artillery, 1st Division, 3rd Army Corps, Army of the Potomac, to May, 1863. 1st Regular Brigade, Artillery Reserve, Army of the Potomac, to November, 1863. Artillery Brigade, 5th Army Corps, Army of the Potomac, to February, 1864. (Consolidated with Battery "C" February, 1864.) 2nd Brigade, Horse Artillery, Army of the Potomac, to August, 1864. Horse Artillery, Army of the Shenandoah, Middle Military Division, to December, 1864. Horse Artillery Reserve, Army of the Shenandoah, to April, 1865. Horse Artillery Brigade, 22nd Army Corps, to August, 1865.

SERVICE.—Duty in the Defences of Washington, D. C., till March, 1862. Ordered to the Virginia Peninsula March, 1862. Siege of Yorktown April 5-May 4. Seven days before Richmond June 25-July 1. Malvern Hill July 1. At Harrison's Landing till August 16. Moved to Fortress Monroe, thence to Alexandria August 16-23. Duty in the Defences of Washington till November. Ashby's Gap September 22. Movement to Falmouth, Va. Battle of Fredericksburg, Va., December 12-15. At Falmouth till April, 1863. Chancellorsville Campaign April 27-May 6. Battle of Chancellorsville May 1-5. Battle of Gettysburg, Pa., July 1-3. Bristoe Campaign October 9-22. Advance to line of the Rappahannock November 7-8. Rappahannock Station November 7. Mine Run Campaign November 26-December 2. Rapidan Campaign May 4-June 12. Wilderness May 5-7. Spottsylvania Court House May 8-16. Cold Harbor June 1-12. Siege of Petersburg June 16 to August 5. Sheridan's Shenandoah Valley Campaign August 7-November 28. Near Winchester August 11. Near Kearneysville August 25. Battle of Cedar Creek October 19. Duty in the Shenandoah Valley till April, 1865, and in the Defences of Washington, D. C., till August, 1865.

BATTERY "L" 3rd ARTILLERY.

At San Francisco, Cal., till October, 1861. Ordered to New York October 14, thence to Washington, D. C.

Attached to Artillery Reserve, Army of the Potomac, March to May, 1862. Artillery, 2nd Division, 5th Army Corps, Army of the Potomac, to December, 1862. Artillery, 1st Division, 9th Army Corps, Army of the Potomac, to April, 1863, and Dept. of the Ohio to June, 1863. Artillery Reserve, 9th Army Corps, Army of the Tennessee, to August, 1863. Artillery, 1st Division, 9th Army Corps, to October, 1863. Artillery, 2nd Division, 9th Army Corps, to January, 1864. Artillery, 1st Division, 9th Army Corps, to April, 1864. Reserve Artillery, 9th Army Corps, Army of the Potomac, to June, 1864. Camp Barry, Defences of Washington, D. C., 22nd Army Corps, to February, 1865. District of Alexandria, Va., 22nd Army Corps, to August, 1865.

SERVICE.—Siege of Yorktown, Va., April 5-May 4, 1862. New Bridge June 19. Seven days before Richmond June 25-July 1. Mechanicsville June 26. Gaines' Mill June 27. Turkey Bridge June 30. Malvern Hill July 1. At Harrison's Landing till August 16. Moved to Fortress Monroe, thence to Alexandria, Va., August 16-23. Maryland Campaign September 6-22. Battle of Antietam September 16-17. At Sharpsburg till October 30. Movement to Falmouth, Va., October 30-November 19. Battle of Fredericksburg, Va., December 12-15. "Mud March" January 20-24, 1863. Moved to Newport News, Va., February 7; thence to Kentucky March 21-28. Duty in District of Central Kentucky till June. Moved to Vicksburg, Miss., June 4-14. Siege of Vicksburg, Miss., June 14-July 4. Advance on Jackson, Miss., July 4-10. Siege of Jackson July 10-17. Moved to Covington, thence to Crab Orchard, Ky., August 4-18. Moved to Knoxville, Tenn., September 10-26. Action at Philadelphia October 16. Knoxville Campaign November 4-December 23. Action at Campbell's Station November 16. Siege of Knoxville November 17-December 5. Blain's Cross Roads December 17. Strawberry Plains January 21-22, 1864. Duty in East Tennessee till March, 1864. Ordered to Annapolis, Md. Rapidan Campaign May 4-16. Wilderness May 5-7. Spottsylvania Court House May 8-16. Ordered to Washington, D. C., May 16, and duty in the Defences of that city and Alexandria till August, 1865.

BATTERY "M" 3rd ARTILLERY.

At San Francisco, Cal., till October, 1861. Ordered to New York October 14, thence to Washington, D. C. Attached to Battery "L," Artillery Reserve, Army of the Potomac, March to May, 1862. Artillery, 2nd Division, 5th Army Corps, Army of the Potomac, to December, 1862. Artillery, 1st Division, 9th Army Corps, Army of the Potomac, to April, 1863, and Dept. of the Ohio to June, 1863. Artillery Reserve, 9th Army Corps, Army of the Tennessee, to August, 1863. Artillery, 1st Division, 9th Army Corps, Dept. of the Ohio, to October, 1863. Artillery, 2nd Division, 9th Army Corps, to January, 1864. Artillery, 1st Division, 9th Army Corps, to April, 1864. Reserve Artillery, 9th Army Corps, Army of the Potomac, to June, 1864. Camp Barry, Defences of Washington, D. C., 22nd Army Corps, to February, 1865. District of Alexandria, 22nd Army Corps, to August, 1865.

SERVICE.—Siege of Yorktown, Va., April 5-May 4. New Bridge June 19. Seven days before Richmond June 25-July 1. Mechanicsville June 26. Gaines' Mill June 27. Turkey Bridge June 30. Malvern Hill July 1. At Harrison's Landing till August 16. Movement to Fortress Monroe, thence to Alexandria August 16-23. Maryland Campaign September 6-22. Battle of Antietam September 16-17. At Sharpsburg till October 30. Movement to Falmouth, Va., October 30-November 19. Battle of Fredericksburg, Va., December 12-15. "Mud March" January 20-24, 1863. Moved to Newport News February 7, thence to Kentucky March 21-28. Duty in District of Central Kentucky till June. Moved to Vicksburg, Miss., June 4-14. Siege of Vicksburg June 14-July 4. Advance on Jackson, Miss., July 4-10. Siege of Jackson July 10-17. Moved to Covington, thence to Crab Orchard, Ky., August 4-18. Moved to Knoxville, Tenn., September 10-26. Action at Philadelphia October 16. Knoxville Campaign November 4-December 23. Campbell's Station November 16. Siege of Knoxville November 17-December 5. Blain's Cross Roads December 17. Strawberry Plains January 21-22, 1864. Duty in East Tennessee till March. Moved to Annapolis, Md. Rapidan Campaign May 4-16. Battle of the Wilderness May 5-7. Spottsylvania Court House May 8-16. Ordered to Washington, D. C., May 16, and duty in the Defences of that city and Alexandria, Va., till August, 1865.

3rd Regiment Artillery lost during the war 2 Officers and 39 Enlisted men killed and mortally wounded and 3 Officers and 67 Enlisted men by disease. Total 111.

4th REGIMENT ARTILLERY.
BATTERY "A" 4th ARTILLERY.

Consolidated with Battery "C" at Washington, D. C., October, 1861. Attached to Sumner's Division, Army of the Potomac, to March, 1862. Artillery, 1st Division, 2nd Army Corps, Army of the Potomac, to November, 1862. (Batteries separated October 18, 1862.) Reserve Artillery, 2nd Army Corps, to May, 1863. Artillery Brigade, 2nd Army Corps, to July, 1863. 1st Brigade, Horse Artillery, Army of the Potomac, to June, 1864. 1st Brigade, Hardin's Division, 22nd Army Corps, to July, 1864. Camp Barry, Defences of Washington, D. C., 22nd Corps, to August, 1865.

SERVICE.—Duty in the Defences of Washington, D. C., till March, 1862. Moved to the Virginia Peninsula. Siege of Yorktown April 5-May 4. Battle of Seven Pines, Fair Oaks, May 31-June 1. Seven days before Richmond June 25-July 1. Peach Orchard and Savage Station June ·29. White Oak Swamp and Glendale June 30. Malvern Hill July 1. At Harrison's Landing till August 16. Movement to Alexandria and Centreville August 16-28. Cover Pope's retreat August 28-September 2. Maryland Campaign September 6-22. Battle of Antietam, Md., September 16-17. At Harper's Ferry September 22-October 30. Movement to Falmouth, Va., October 30-November 19. Battle of Fredericksburg December 12-15. At Falmouth, Va., till April, 1863. Chancellorsville Campaign April 27-May 6. Battle of Chancellorsville May 1-5. Gettysburg (Pa.) Campaign June 11-July 16. Battle of Gettysburg, Pa., July 1-3. Made a Horse Battery July 16, and attached to 1st Division, Cavalry Corps, Army of the Potomac. Advance to the Rapidan September 13-17. Culpeper Court House September 13. Reconnoissance across the Rapidan September 21-23. Bristoe Campaign October 9-22. White Sulphur Springs October 12. Bristoe Station October 14. St. Stephen's Church October 14. Advance to line of the Rappahannock November 7-8. Mine Run Campaign November 26-December 2. Parker's Store November 29. Rapidan Campaign May 4-June 4, 1864. Wilderness May 5-7. Sheridan's Raid to the James River May 9-24. North Anna River May 9. Ground Squirrel Church and Yellow Tavern May 11. Brook Church, Fortifications of Richmond, May 12. On line of the Pamunkey May 26-28. Totopotomoy May 28-31. Cold Harbor May 31-June 1. Dismounted and sent to Washington, D. C., June 4. Duty in the Defences of Washington, D. C., till August, 1865.

BATTERY "B" 4th ARTILLERY.

Reached Washington, D. C., October, 1861. Attached to McDowell's Division, Army of the Potomac, to March, 1862. Artillery, 1st Division, 1st Army Corps, Army of the Potomac, to April, 1862. Artillery, 3rd Division, Dept. of the Rappahannock, to June, 1862. Artillery, 1st Division, 3rd Corps, Army of Virginia, to September, 1862. Artillery, 1st Division, 1st Army Corps, Army of the Potomac, to May, 1863. Artillery Brigade, 1st Army Corps, to March, 1864. Artillery Brigade, 5th Army Corps, to May, 1865. Dept. of Washington, D. C., to August, 1865.

SERVICE.—Duty in the Defences of Washington, D. C., till March, 1862. Advance on Manassas, Va., March 10-15. Advance on Falmouth, Va., April 9-19. Duty at Falmouth and Fredericksburg till August. Reconnoissance from Fredericksburg to Orange Court House

July 24-27. Battle of Cedar Mountain August 9. Pope's Campaign in Northern Virginia August 16-September 2. Battles of Groveton August 29; Bull Run August 30. Maryland Campaign September 6-22. Battle of Antietam, Md., September 16-17. Movement to Falmouth, Va., October 30-November 19. Battle of Fredericksburg December 12-15. At Falmouth till April, 1863. Chancellorsville Campaign April 27-May 6. Operations at Pollock's Mill Crossing April 29-May 2. Battle of Chancellorsville May 2-5. Gettysburg (Pa.) Campaign June 11-July 24. Battle of Gettysburg July 1-3. Bristoe Campaign October 9-22. Advance to line of the Rappahannock November 7-8. Mine Run Campaign November 26-December 2. Demonstration on the Rapidan February 6-7, 1864. Rapidan Campaign May 4-June 12. Battles of the Wilderness May 5-7. Spottsylvania May 8-21. North Anna River May 22-26. Jericho Ford May 25. On line of the Pamunkey May 26-28. Totopotomoy May 28-31. Cold Harbor June 1-12. Bethesda Church June 1-3. Before Petersburg June 16-18. Siege of Petersburg June 16, 1864, to April 2, 1865. Boydton Plank Road, Hatcher's Run, October 27-28, 1864. Warren's Raid on Weldon Railroad December 7-12. Appomattox Campaign March 28-April 9, 1865. Junction, Quaker and Boydton Roads March 29. Lewis Farm, near Gravelly Run, March 29. White Oak Road March 31. Battle of Five Forks April 1. Appomattox Court House April 9. Surrender of Lee and his army. Moved to Washington, D. C., May. Grand Review May 23. Duty in the Defences of Washington, D. C., till August, 1865.

BATTERY "C" 4th ARTILLERY.

(Attached to Battery "A" till October, 1862.) Attached to Sumner's Division, Army of the Potomac, to March, 1862. Artillery, 1st Division, 2nd Army Corps, to May, 1863. 1st Regular Brigade, Artillery Reserve, Army of the Potomac, to November, 1863. Artillery Brigade, 6th Army Corps, to March, 1864. Artillery Reserve, Army of the Potomac, to April, 1864. (Consolidated with Battery "E" as a Horse Battery April 11, 1864.) 1st Brigade, Horse Artillery, Army of the Potomac, to August, 1864. Horse Artillery, Army of the Shenandoah, Middle Military Division, to December, 1864. Horse Artillery Reserve, Army of the Shenandoah, to May, 1865. Attached to 3rd Division, Cavalry Corps, Horse Artillery Brigade, 22nd Army Corps, to August, 1865.

SERVICE.—Duty in the Defences of Washington, D. C., till March, 1862. Operations on Orange & Alexandria Railroad March 28-31. Moved to the Virginia Peninsula. Siege of Yorktown April 5-May 4. Battle of Fair Oaks, Seven Pines, May 31-June 1. Seven days before Richmond June 25-July 1. Peach Orchard and Savage Station June 29. White Oak Swamp and Glendale June 30. Malvern Hill July 1. At Harrison's Landing till August 16. Movement to Alexandria and Centreville August 16-28. Cover Pope's retreat August 28-September 2. Maryland Campaign September 6-22. Battle of Antietam September 16-17. At Harper's Ferry September 22-October 30. Movement to Falmouth, Va., October 30-November 19. Battle of Fredericksburg December 12-15. At Falmouth till April, 1863. Chancellorsville Campaign April 27-May 6. Battle of Chancellorsville May 1-5. Gettysburg (Pa.) Campaign June 11-July 24. Battle of Gettysburg, Pa., July 1-3. Bristoe Campaign October 9-22. Advance to line of the Rappahannock November 7-8. Rappahannock Station November 7. Mine Run Campaign November 26-December 2. Rapidan Campaign May 4-June 12, 1864. Craig's Meeting House May 5. Todd's Tavern May 5-6. Wilderness May 6-7. Sheridan's Raid to the James River May 9-24. North Anna River May 9. Ground Squirrel Church and Yellow Tavern May 11. Brook Church, Richmond fortifications, May 12. Strawberry Hill May 12. On line of the Pamunkey May 26-28. Totopotomoy May 28-31. Cold Harbor June 1-12. Totopotomoy June 3. Long Bridge June 12. Riddell's Shop June 13. White Oak Swamp June 13. Siege of Petersburg June 16-August 5. Ream's Station June 22. Wilson's Raid on

Southside & Danville Railroad June 22-July 1. Nottaway Court House June 23. Staunton River Bridge June 25. Sappony Church, Stony Creek, June 28-29. Ream's Station June 29. Sheridan's Shenandoah Valley Campaign August 7-November 28. Expedition from Winchester into Faquier and Loudoun Counties November 28-December 3. Expedition to Gordonsville December 19-28. Liberty Mills December 22. Sheridan's Raid from Winchester February 27-March 25, 1865. Occupation of Staunton and action at Waynesboro March 2. Duguidsville March 8. Appomattox Campaign March 28-April 9. Dinwiddie Court House March 30-31. Five Forks April 1. Scott's Cross Roads April 2. Tabernacle Church or Beaver Pond Creek April 4. Sailor's Creek April 6. Appomattox Station April 8. Appomattox Court House April 9. Surrender of Lee and his army. Expedition to Danville April 23-29. March to Washington, D. C., May. Grand Review May 23. Duty at Washington till August.

BATTERY "D" 4th ARTILLERY.

At Fortress Monroe, Va., April, 1861. Attached to District Fortress Monroe, Va., Dept. of the Virginia, to July, 1862. Viele's Command, Norfolk, Va., 7th Army Corps, Dept. of Virginia, to April, 1863. Unattached, Artillery, 7th Army Corps, Dept. of Virginia, to June, 1863. Artillery, 1st Division, 7th Army Corps, to August, 1863. United States Forces, Norfolk and Portsmouth, Va., Dept. of Virginia and North Carolina, to December, 1863. Artillery Brigade, United States Forces, Norfolk and Portsmouth, Va., to April, 1864. Artillery, 2nd Division, 18th Army Corps, Army of the James, to June, 1864. Artillery, 2nd Division, 10th Army Corps, to August, 1864. Artillery Brigade, 10th Army Corps, to December, 1864. Artillery Brigade, 25th Army Corps, to August, 1865.

SERVICE.—Duty in District of Fortress Monroe, Va., till May, 1862. Capture of Norfolk, Va., May 10. Duty at Norfolk, Va., till April, 1863. Reconnoissance to Franklin on the Blackwater October 3, 1862. Franklin October 31. Action at Deserted House January 30, 1863. Siege of Suffolk April 11-May 4. Edenton Road April 24. Duty at Norfolk and Portsmouth, Va., till April, 1864. Butler's operations on south side of the James River and against Petersburg and Richmond May 4-June 16. Swift Creek May 9. Operations against Fort Darling May 12-16. Battle of Drury's Bluff May 14-16. Siege operations against Petersburg and Richmond June 16, 1864, to April 2, 1865. Darbytown Road October 7, 1864. Appomattox Campaign March 28-April 9, 1865. Appomattox Court House April 9. Surrender of Lee and his army. Moved to Texas May-June, and duty there.

BATTERY "E" 4th ARTILLERY.

Organized at Camp Monroe, Ohio, and joined Rosecrans in West Virginia. Attached to 2nd Brigade, Army of Occupation, West Virginia, to September, 1861. Scammon's Brigade, Dept. of West Virginia, to October, 1861. Kelly's Command, Railroad District, West Virginia, to January, 1862. Artillery, Lander's Division, Army of the Potomac, to March, 1862. Artillery, Shields' 2nd Division, Banks' 5th Army Corps, to April, 1862. Artillery, Shields' Division, Dept. of the Shenandoah, to May, 1862, and Dept. of the Rappahannock to June, 1862. Unattached Artillery, 3rd Corps, Army of Virginia, to September, 1862. Artillery, 2nd Division, 9th Army Corps, Army of the Potomac, to February, 1863. Reserve Brigade, 1st Cavalry Division, Cavalry Corps, Army of the Potomac, to May, 1863. 1st Brigade, Horse Artillery, Army of the Potomac, to August, 1864. Artillery, 1st Division, Cavalry Corps (Horse Artillery Reserve), Army of the Shenandoah, Middle Military Division, to March, 1865. Horse Artillery Reserve, attached to 3rd Division, Cavalry Corps, Army of the Shenandoah and Army of the Potomac, to May, 1865. Horse Artillery Brigade, 22nd Army Corps, to August, 1865.

SERVICE.—Duty in West Virginia till March, 1862. Advance on Winchester, Va., March 7-12. Battle of

Winchester March 23. Occupation of Mt. Jackson April 17. March to Fredericksburg May 10-21, and return to Front Royal May 25-30. Battle of Port Republic June 8-9. Pope's Campaign in Northern Virginia August 16-September 2. Fords of the Rappahannock August 20-23. Bristoe Station August 27. Maryland Campaign September 6-22. Battle of Antietam, Md., September 16-17. Reconnoissance to Charlestown October 16-17. Charlestown October 16. Movement to Falmouth, Va., October 30-November 19. Battle of Fredericksburg, Va., December 12-15. "Mud March" January 20-24, 1863. Operations at Welford's, Kelly's and Beverly Fords April 14-15. Chancellorsville Campaign April 27-May 6. Brandy Station and Beverly Ford June 9. Brandy Station and Beverly Ford June 9. Hanover, Pa., June 30. Battle of Gettysburg, Pa., July 1-3. Hunterstown, Pa., July 4. Boonsboro, Md., July 8. Hagerstown July 10-13. Falling Waters July 14. Expedition to Port Conway September 1-3. Advance from the Rappahannock to the Rapidan September 13-17. Culpeper Court House September 13. Bristoe Campaign October 9-22. James City, Bethesda Church and near Culpeper October 10. Brandy Station October 11. Gainesville October 14. Groveton October 17-18. Gainesville, New Baltimore, Buckland's Mills and Haymarket October 19. Advance to line of the Rappahannock November 7-8. Mine Run Campaign November 26-December 2. Rapidan Campaign May 4-June 12, 1864. Craig's Meeting House May 5. Todd's Tavern May 5-6. Wilderness May 6-7. Sheridan's Raid to the James River May 9-24. North Anna River May 9. Ground Squirrel Church and Yellow Tavern May 11. Brook Church and fortifications of Richmond May 12. Strawberry Hill May 12. On line of the Pamunkey May 26-28. Totopotomoy May 28-31. Cold Harbor June 1-12. Totopotomoy June 2. Long Bridge June 12. Riddell's Shop and White Oak Swamp June 13. Siege of Petersburg June 16-August 5. Ream's Station June 22. Wilson's Raid on Southside & Danville Railroad June 22-July 1. Nottaway Court House June 23. Staunton River Bridge June 25. Sappony Church, Stony Creek, June 28-29. Ream's Station June 29. Sheridan's Shenandoah Valley Campaign August 7-November 28. Expedition from Winchester into Faquier and Loudoun Counties November 28-December 3. Expedition to Gordonsville December 19-28. Liberty Mills December 22. Sheridan's Raid from Winchester February 27-March 25, 1865. Occupation of Staunton and action at Waynesboro March 2. Duguidsville March 8. Appomattox Campaign March 28-April 9. Dinwiddie Court House March 30-31. Five Forks April 1. Scott's Cross Roads April 2. Tabernacle Church or Beaver Pond Creek April 4. Sailor's Creek April 6. Appomattox Station April 8. Appomattox Court House April 9. Surrender of Lee and his army. Expedition to Danville April 23-29. Moved to Washington, D. C., May. Grand Review May 23. Duty at Washington, D. C., till August.

BATTERY "F" 4th ARTILLERY.

Arrived at Washington, D. C., April 18, 1861. Moved to Carlisle, Pa., June, 1861. Attached to Stone's Brigade, Patterson's Army, Shenandoah, July, 1861. Artillery, Banks' Division, Shenandoah, to October, 1861. Artillery, Banks' Division, Army of the Potomac, to March, 1862. Artillery, 1st Division, Banks' 5th Corps, to April, 1862, and Dept. of the Shenandoah, to June, 1862. Artillery, 1st Division, 2nd Corps, Army of Virginia, to September, 1862. Artillery, 1st Division, 12th Army Corps, Army of the Potomac, to May, 1863. Artillery Brigade, 12th Army Corps, Army of the Potomac, to October, 1863, and Army of the Cumberland, to March, 1864. 1st Division, Artillery Reserve, Dept. of the Cumberland, to August, 1865.

SERVICE.—Action at Falling Waters July 2, 1861. Operations on the Upper Potomac till March, 1862. Operations about Dams 4 and 5 December 17-20, 1861. Advance on Winchester, Va., March 7-12. Occupation of Winchester March 12. Operations in the Shenandoah Valley April 15-June 17. Actions at Middletown and Newtown May 24. Retreat to Williamsport May 24-26.

Battle of Winchester May 25. Battle of Cedar Mountain, Va., August 9. Pope's Campaign in Northern Virginia August 16-September 2. Battle of Bull Run August 30. Maryland Campaign September 6-22. Battle of Antietam, Md., September 16-17. At Maryland Heights till December. March to Fairfax Station December 10-14, and duty there till January 20, 1863. "Mud March" January 20-24. At Stafford Court House till April 27. Chancellorsville Campaign April 27-May 6. Battle of Chancellorsville May 1-5. Gettysburg (Pa.) Campaign June 11-July 24. Battle of Gettysburg, Pa., July 1-3. Movement to Bridgeport, Ala., September 24-October 3. Guard duty on Nashville & Chattanooga Railroad till March, 1864, and duty at Nashville, Tenn., till August, 1865.

BATTERY "G" 4th ARTILLERY.

Organized at Cincinnati, Ohio, and joined McClellan in West Virginia July, 1861. Attached to 3rd Brigade, Army of Occupation, West Virginia, to September, 1861. Cheat Mountain District, West Virginia, to December, 1861. Defences of Washington, D. C., to March, 1862. Artillery Reserve, Army of the Potomac, to May, 1862. 2nd Brigade, Horse Artillery, Artillery Reserve, 5th Army Corps, Potomac, to September, 1862. Artillery Reserve, 6th Army Corps, Army of the Potomac, to November, 1862. Artillery Reserve, Army of the Potomac, to May, 1863. 1st Regular Brigade, Artillery Reserve, Army of the Potomac, to June, 1863. Artillery Brigade, 11th Army Corps, Army of the Potomac, to October, 1863, and Army of the Cumberland to November, 1863. Artillery, 2nd Division, 4th Army Corps, Army of the Cumberland, to March, 1864. 1st Division, Artillery Reserve, Dept. of the Cumberland, to October, 1864.

SERVICE.—West Virginia Campaign July 6-17, 1861. Moved to Cheat Mountain and duty there till December, 1861. Action at Greenbrier River October 3-4. Blue's Gap January 7, 1862. Moved to Washington, D. C., and duty there till March, 1862. Ordered to the Virginia Peninsula. Siege of Yorktown April 5-May 4. Seven days before Richmond June 25-July 1. Bottom's Bridge June 28-29. Malvern Hill July 1. At Harrison's Landing till August 16. Movement to Fortress Monroe, thence to Alexandria August 16-23. Maryland Campaign September 6-22. Battle of Antietam September 16-17. Shepherdstown Ford September 19. Movement to Falmouth, Va., October 30-November 19. Battle of Fredericksburg, Va., December 12-15. Chancellorsville Campaign April 27-May 6. Battle of Chancellorsville May 1-6. Gettysburg (Pa.) Campaign June 11-July 24. Battle of Gettysburg July 1-3. Movement to Bridgeport, Ala., September 24-October 3. Reopening Tennessee River October 26-29. Battles of Chattanooga, Tenn., November 23-25; Bushy Knob November 23; Orchard Knob November 23-24; Mission Ridge November 25. Moved to Nashville, Tenn., February, 1864, and post duty there till October. Transferred to Battery "I" 4th Artillery October, 1864. Remounted as a Battery at Washington, D. C., February, 1865, and duty in the Defences of that city till August.

BATTERY "H" 4th ARTILLERY.

Arrived at Louisville, Ky., January, 1862. United with Battery "M" February, 1862, to January, 1863. Attached to 5th Division, Army of the Ohio, February to May, 1862. Artillery, 4th Division, Army of the Ohio, to September, 1862. 10th Brigade, 4th Division, 2nd Corps, Army of the Ohio, to November, 1862. Artillery, 2nd Division, Left Wing 14th Army Corps, Army of the Cumberland, to January, 1863. Artillery, 2nd Division, 21st Army Corps, Army of the Cumberland, to October, 1863. Artillery, 1st Division, 4th Army Corps, Army of the Cumberland, to March, 1864. 1st Division, Artillery Reserve, Dept. of the Cumberland, to October, 1864. Transferred to Battery "I" 4th Artillery October, 1864.

SERVICE.—Moved to Nashville, Tenn., February 14-25, 1862; thence march to Savannah, Tenn., to reinforce Army of the Tennessee March 20-April 6. Battle of Shiloh, Tenn., April 6-7. Advance on and siege of Corinth, Miss., April 29-May 30. Bridge Creek May 22. Tuscumbia Creek May 31. Buell's Campaign in North Alabama and Middle Tennessee June to August. March to Louisville, Ky., in pursuit of Bragg August 21-September 22. Pursuit of Bragg to Loudon October 1-22. Battle of Perryville, Ky., October 8. Danville October 11. March to Nashville, Tenn., October 22-November 9, and duty there till December 26. Advance on Murfreesboro December 26-30. Battle of Stone's River December 30-31 and January 1-3, 1863. At Murfreesboro till June. Middle Tennessee (or Tullahoma) Campaign June 23-July 7. Occupation of Middle Tennessee till August 16. Passage of Cumberland Mountains and Tennessee River and Chickamauga (Ga.) Campaign August 16-September 22. Battle of Chickamauga, Ga., September 19-20. Siege of Chattanooga, Tenn., September 24-November 23. Reopening Tennessee River October 26-29. Chattanooga-Ringgold Campaign November 23-27. Demonstration on Dalton, Ga., February 22-27, 1864. Near Dalton February 23. Tunnel Hill, Buzzard's Roost Gap and Rocky Faced Ridge February 23-25. Reserve Artillery at Nashville, Tenn., till October. Transferred to Battery "I" October, 1864. Reorganized at Washington, D. C., February, 1865, and duty in the Defences of that city till August, 1865.

BATTERY "I" 4th ARTILLERY.

Joined McClellan in West Virginia July, 1861, and served unattached, Army of Occupation, W. Va., to September, 1861. 3rd Brigade, Kanawha Division, West Virginia, to December, 1861. Artillery, 1st Division, Army Ohio, to September, 1862. Artillery, 1st Division, 3rd Army Corps, Army Ohio, to November, 1862. Artillery, 3rd Division, Centre 14th Army Corps, Army Cumberland, to January, 1863. Artillery, 3rd Division, 14th Army Corps, to April, 1864. Garrison Artillery, Nashville, Tenn., Dept. Cumberland, to October, 1864. 1st Division, Artillery Reserve, Army Cumberland, to November, 1864. Artillery, 6th Division, Cavalry Corps, Military Division Mississippi, to February, 1865. Artillery, 2nd Division, Cavalry Corps, Military Division Mississipp, to ——

SERVICE.—Campaign in West Virginia July 6-17, 1861. Rich Mountain July 11-12. Carnifex Ferry September 13. Operations in Kanawha Valley and New River Region October 19-November 16. New River November 5-11-12. Ordered to Kentucky December, 1861. Moved to Nashville, Tenn., February 10-March 2, 1862. March to Savannah, Tenn., March 20-April 8. Advance on and siege of Corinth, Miss., April 29-May 30. Buell's operations on the Memphis & Charleston Railroad in North Alabama and Middle Tennessee June to August, 1862. March to Louisville, Ky., in pursuit of Bragg August 21-September 26. Pursuit of Bragg into Kentucky October 1-15. Battle of Perryville, Ky., October 8. March to Nashville, Tenn., November 4-17. Duty there and at Murfreesboro till June, 1863. Expedition to Chapel Hill March 3-6. Expedition toward Columbia March 4-14. Harpeth River near Triune March 8. Action at Franklin June 4. Tullahoma Campaign June 23-July 7. Hoover's Gap June 24-26. Occupation of Middle Tennessee till August 16. Passage of Cumberland Mountains and Tennessee River and Chickamauga (Ga.) Campaign August 16-September 22. Battle of Chickamauga September 19-21. Siege of Chattanooga, Tenn., September 24-November 23. Chattanooga-Ringgold Campaign November 23-27. At Chattanooga till March, 1864, and garrison Artillery at Nashville till October. Nashville Campaign November-December. Battle of Nashville December 15-16. Spring Hill December 18. Richland Creek December 24. King's Gap near Pulaski December 25. Sugar Creek December 25. Wilson's Raid to Macon, Ga., March 22-April 24, 1865. Near Montevallo March 31. Ebenezer Church near Maysville April 1. Selma April 2. Montgomery April 12. Columbus, Ga., April 16. Capture of Macon April 20.

BATTERY "K" 4th ARTILLERY.

Attached to Artillery Reserve, Army Potomac, August, 1861, to June, 1862. Artillery Reserve, 3rd Army Corps, Army Potomac, to August, 1862. Artillery, 2nd Division, 3rd Army Corps, to May, 1863. Artillery Brigade, 3rd Army Corps, to March, 1864. Artillery Brigade, 2nd Army Corps, to June, 1865. Dept. of Washington, D. C., to August, 1865.

SERVICE.—Moved to Washington, D. C., August, 1861, and duty there till March, 1862. Ordered to the Virginia Peninsula March, 1862. Siege of Yorktown, Va., April 5-May 4. Seven days before Richmond June 25-July 1. Oak Grove June 25. Glendale and Brackett's June 30. Malvern Hill July 1 and August 5. Moved to Alexandria August 16-23, and duty there till November. Operations on Orange & Alexandria Railroad November 10-12. Battle of Fredericksburg, Va., December 12-15. Operations at Rappahannock Bridge and Grove Church February 5-7, 1863. Chancellorsville Campaign April 27-May 6. Battle of Chancellorsville May 1-5. Gettysburg (Pa.) Campaign June 11-July 24. Wapping Heights, Manassas Gap, July 23. Bristoe Campaign October 9-22. McLean's Ford, Bull Run, October 15. Advance to the Rappahannock November 7-8. Kelly's Ford November 7. Payne's Farm November 27. Demonstration on the Rapidan February 6-7, 1864. Rapidan Campaign May 4-June 12. Wilderness May 5-7. Spottsylvania Court House May 8-21. Assault on the Salient May 12. North Anna River May 22-26. On line of the Pamunkey May 26-28. Totopotomoy May 28-31. Cold Harbor June 1-12. Before Petersburg June 16-18. Siege of Petersburg June 16, 1864, to April 2, 1865. Jerusalem Plank Road June 22, 1864. Deep Bottom July 27-29. Strawberry Plains August 14-18. Hatcher's Run October 27-28. Warren's Raid on Weldon Railroad December 7-14. Dabney's Mills, Hatcher's Run, February 5-7, 1865. Watkins' House March 25. Appomattox Campaign March 28-April 9. Hatcher's Run, Boydton Road, March 30-31. White Oak Road March 31. Sutherland Station April 2. Sailor's Creek April 6. High Bridge April 7. Appomattox Court House April 9. Surrender of Lee and his army. March to Washington, D. C., May. Grand Review May 23. Duty in the Defences of Washington till August, 1865.

BATTERY "L" 4th ARTILLERY.

Stationed at Fortress Monroe, Va., July, 1861. Attached to District Fortress Monroe, Va., Dept. of Virginia, to July, 1862. Artillery Division at Suffolk, Va., 7th Army Corps, Dept. of Virginia, to April, 1863. Unattached, Artillery, 7th Army Corps, to June, 1863. Artillery, 1st Division, 7th Army Corps, to August, 1863. U. S. Forces, Norfolk and Portsmouth, Va., Dept. of Virginia and North Carolina, to December, 1863. U. S. Forces, Yorktown, Va., Dept. Virginia and North Carolina, to April, 1864. Artillery, 1st Division, 18th Army Corps, Army of the James, to June, 1864. Artillery Brigade, 18th Army Corps, to December, 1864. Artillery Brigade, 24th Army Corps, to August, 1865.

SERVICE.—Action at Newport News, Va., between "Monitor" and "Merrimac" March 8, 1862. Duty at Fortress Monroe till July, 1862, and at Suffolk, Va., to July, 1863. Expedition from Suffolk December 1-3, 1862. Franklin on the Blackwater December 2. Expedition toward the Blackwater January 8-10, 1863. Siege of Suffolk April 11-May 4. Providence Church Road May 3. Duty at Portsmouth, Va., till December, 1863. Expedition from Portsmouth to Jackson, N. C., July 25-August 3. Moved to Yorktown, Va., December, 1863, and duty there till April, 1864. Wistar's Expedition from Yorktown against Richmond February 6-8, 1864. Expedition into King and Queen County March 9-12. Butler's operations on south side of James River and against Petersburg and Richmond May 4-28. Port Walthal May 6. Chester Station June 6-7. Swift Creek May 9. Operations against Fort Darling May 12-16. Battle of Drury's Bluff May 14-16. Movement to Cold Harbor May 28-31. Battles about Cold Harbor June 1-12. Assault on Petersburg June 15. Siege operations against Petersburg and Richmond June 16, 1864, to April 2, 1865. Appomattox Campaign March 28-April 9, 1865. Fall of Petersburg and Richmond April 2-3. Duty in the Dept. of Virginia till August, 1865.

BATTERY "M" 4th ARTILLERY.

January, 1862. Louisville, Ky. (united with Battery "H," February, 1862, to January, 1863), February, 1862. Attached to Artillery, 5th Division, Army Ohio, to May, 1862. Artillery, 4th Division, Army Ohio, to September, 1862. 10th Brigade, 4th Division, 2nd Corps, Army Ohio, to November, 1862. Artillery, 2nd Division, Left Wing 14th Army Corps, Army Cumberland, to January, 1863. Artillery, 2nd Division, 21st Army Corps, Army Cumberland, to October, 1863. Artillery, 1st Division, 4th Army Corps, to March, 1864. 1st Division, Artillery Reserve, Dept. Cumberland, to October, 1864. Croxton's Cavalry Brigade to November, 1864. Artillery Brigade, 4th Army Corps, to February, 1865. Garrison Artillery, Bridgeport, Ala., to August, 1865.

SERVICE.—Moved to Nashville, Tenn., February 14-25, 1862, thence march to Savannah, Tenn., to reinforce Army Tennessee March 20-April 6. Battle of Shiloh, Tenn., April 6-7. Advance on and siege of Corinth, Miss., April 29-May 30. Bridge Creek near Corinth May 28. Tuscumbia Creek May 31. Buell's Campaign in North Alabama and Middle Tennessee June to August. March to Louisville, Ky., in pursuit of Bragg August 21-September 26. Pursuit of Bragg to Loudon, Ky., October 1-22. Battle of Perryville, Ky., October 8. Danville October 11. March to Nashville, Tenn., October 22-November 9, and duty there till December 26. Advance on Murfreesboro December 26-30. Battle of Stone's River December 30-31, 1862, and January 1-3, 1863. Duty at Murfreesboro till June. Middle Tennessee or Tullahoma Campaign June 23-July 7. Occupation of Middle Tennessee till August 16. Passage of the Cumberland Mountains and Tennessee River and Chickamauga (Ga.) Campaign August 16-September 22. Battle of Chickamauga, Ga., September 19-20. Siege of Chattanooga, Tenn., September 24-November 23. Reopening Tennessee River October 26-29. Battles of Chattanooga November 23-27. At Bridgeport, Ala., to March, 1864, and at Nashville, Tenn., till October, 1864. Attached to Croxton's Cavalry Brigade till November. Nashville Campaign November-December. Shoal Creek November 4. In front of Columbia November 24-27. Spring Hill November 29. Battle of Franklin November 30. Battle of Nashville December 15-16. Pursuit of Hood to the Tennessee River December 17-28. Moved to Huntsville, Ala., and duty there till February, 1865. Garrison Artillery at Bridgeport, Ala., till July.

The 4th Regiment of Artillery lost during service 6 Officers and 87 Enlisted men killed and mortally wounded and 4 Officers and 119 Enlisted men by disease. Total 216.

5th REGIMENT ARTILLERY.
BATTERY "A" 5th ARTILLERY.

Organized and equipped July, 1861. Attached to Artillery Reserve, Army Potomac, March to May, 1862. 2nd Brigade, Horse Artillery, Artillery Reserve, 5th Army Corps, Army Potomac, to September, 1862. Artillery, 3rd Division, 9th Army Corps, Army Potomac, to April, 1863. Artillery, 2nd Division, 7th Army Corps, Dept. of Virginia, to July, 1863. U. S. Forces, Portsmouth, Va., Dept. Virginia and North Carolina, to April, 1864. Artillery, 1st Division, 18th Army Corps, Army of the James, to June, 1864. Artillery Brigade, 18th Army Corps, to December, 1864. Artillery Brigade, 24th Army Corps, to May, 1864. Dept. of Virginia, to August, 1865.

SERVICE.—Duty in the Defences of Washington, D. C., till March, 1862. Mouth of Mattawoman Creek, Md., November 14, 1861. Ordered to the Virginia Peninsula March, 1862. Peninsula Campaign April to August. Siege of Yorktown April 5-May 4. Seven days before Richmond June 25-July 1. Gaines' Mill June 27. Golding's Farm June 28. Malvern Hill July 1. At Harrison's Landing till August 16. Moved to Alexandria, Va.,

August 16-23. Maryland Campaign September 6-22. Battle of Antietam, Md., September 16-17. Movement to Falmouth, Va., October 30-November 17. Battle of Fredericksburg, Va., December 12-15. "Mud March" January 20-24, 1863. Moved to Newport News, Va., February, thence to Suffolk, Va., March. Siege of Suffolk April 11-May 4. Norfleet House April 15. Dix's Peninsula Campaign June 24-July 8. Expedition from White House to South Anna River July 1-7. Duty at Portsmouth, Va., till April, 1864. Butler's operations on south side of the James River and against Petersburg and Richmond May 4-28. Swift Creek or Arrowfield Church May 9-10. Operations against Fort Darling May 12-16. Battle of Drury's Bluff May 14-16. On Bermuda Hundred front May 16-28. Movement to Cold Harbor May 28-June 1. Battles about Cold Harbor June 1-12. Assaults on Petersburg June 15-18. Siege operatoins against Petersburg and Richmond June 16, 1864, to April 2, 1865. Battle of Chaffin's Farm, New Market Heights, September 28-30. Occupation of Richmond April 3, 1865. Duty at Richmond and Lynchburg, Va., till August, 1865.

BATTERY "B" 5th ARTILLERY.

Organized November, 1862. Duty at Fort Hamilton, N. Y. Harbor, till June, 1863. Attached to 1st Division, Dept. of the Susquehanna, June-July, 1863. Unattached, Dept. West Virginia, to December, 1863. 3rd Brigade, 2nd Division, Dept. West Virginia, to May, 1864. Artillery Brigade, West Virginia, to December, 1864. Reserve Division, West Virginia, to January, 1865. 1st Separate Brigade, 3rd Division, Dept. West Virginia, to April, 1865. Artillery, 2nd Division, West Virginia, to July, 1865. Dept. of Washington, D. C., to ——

SERVICE.—Ordered to Dept. of the Susquehanna June, 1863, thence to Harper's Ferry, W. Va., July, 1863. Duty there and in the Dept. of West Virginia, till April, 1864. Sigel's Expedition from Martinsburg, W. Va., to New Market, Va., April 29-May 15, 1864. Battle of New Market May 15. Hunter's Raid to Lynchburg, Va., May 26-July 1. Lynchburg July 17-18. Catawba Mountains June 21. Sheridan's Shenandoah Valley Campaign August 7-November 28. Berryville September 3. Battle of Opequan, Winchester, September 19. Fisher's Hill September 22. Battle of Cedar Creek October 19. Duty in the Shenandoah Valley and in the Dept. of West Virginia, till July, 1865. At Washington, D. C., till ——

BATTERY "C" 5th ARTILLERY.

Organized September, 1861. Attached to Artillery, McCall's Division, Army Potomac, to March, 1862. Artillery, 2nd Division, 1st Army Corps, Army Potomac, to April, 1862, and Dept. of the Rappahannock, to June, 1862. Artillery, 3rd Division, 5th Army Corps, Army Potomac, to August, 1862. Artillery, 3rd Division, 3rd Corps, Army Virginia, to September, 1862. Artillery, 3rd Division, 1st Army Corps, Army Potomac, to February, 1863. Artillery, 2nd Division, 1st Army Corps, to May, 1863. 1st Regular Brigade, Artillery Reserve, Army Potomac, to July, 1863. Camp Barry, Washington, D. C., 22nd Army Corps, to November, 1863. Consolidated with Battery "I" November, 1863. Artillery Brigade, 2nd Army Corps, Army Potomac, to March, 1865. Artillery Reserve, Army Potomac, to June, 1865. Dept. of Washington, D. C., to ——

SERVICE.—Duty in the Defences of Washington, D. C,. till April, 1862. Advance on Falmouth, Va., April 9-19. McDowell's advance on Richmond May 25-28. Ordered to the Virginia Peninsula June. Seven days before Richmond June 25-July 1. Mechanicsville June 26. Gaines' Mill June 27. Glendale June 30. Malvern Hill July 1. At Harrison's Landing till August 16. Movement to Fort Monroe, thence to Centreville, Va., August 16-28. Pope's Campaign in Northern Virginia August 28-September 2. Battles of Groveton August 29; Bull Run August 30. Maryland Campaign September 6-22. South Mountain, Md., September 14. Antietam, Md., September 16-17. Movement to Falmouth, Va., October 30-November 19. Battle of Fredericksburg December 12-15. "Mud March" January 20-24, 1863. At Falmouth

till April. Chancellorsville Campaign April 27-May 6. Operations at Pollock's Mill Creek April 29-May 2. Fitzhugh's Crossing April 29-30. Battle of Chancellorsville May 1-5. Battle of Gettysburg, Pa., July 1-3. Draft riots in New York July 3-15. At Camp Barry, Washington, D. C., till November. Mine Run Campaign November 26-December 2. Rapidan Campaign May 4-June 12, 1864. Battles of the Wilderness May 5-7; Spottsylvania Court House May 8-21; Po River May 10. Assault on the Salient May 12. North Anna River May 22-26. On line of the Pamunkey May 26-29. Totopotomoy May 28-31. Cold Harbor June 1-12. Assaults on Petersburg June 16-18. Siege of Petersburg June 16, 1864, to April 2, 1865. Jerusalem Plank Road June 22, 1864. Deep Bottom July 27-29. Weldon Railroad August 18-21. Boydton Plank Road, Hatcher's Run, October 27-28. Fort Stedman March 25, 1865. Appomattox Campaign March 28-April 9. Assault on and fall of Petersburg April 2. Moved to Washington, D. C., May. Grand Review May 23. Duty at Washington, D. C., till

BATTERY "D" 5th ARTILLERY, "WEST POINT BATTERY."

Attached to Porter's Division, Army Potomac, October, 1861, to March, 1862. Artillery, 1st Division, 3rd Army Corps, Army Potomac, to May, 1862. Artillery, 1st Division, 5th Army Corps, Army Potomac, to May, 1863. Artillery Brigade, 5th Army Corps, to December, 1863. Camp Barry, Washington, D. C., 22nd Army Corps, to March, 1864. Artillery Brigade, 5th Army Corps, to November, 1864. Consolidated with Battery "G" November, 1864. Artillery Reserve, Army Potomac, to June, 1865. Dept. of Washington, D. C., 22nd Army Corps, to ——

SERVICE.—Rockville Expedition June 10-July 7, 1861. Duty in the Defences of Washington till March, 1862. Lewinsville, Va., September 11, 1861. Reconnoissance to Lewinsville September 25. Edward's Ferry October 22. Ordered to the Virginia Peninsula March, 1862. Howard's Mills April 4. Warwick Road April 5. Siege of Yorktown April 5-May 4. Hanover Court House May 27. Operations about Hanover Court House May 27-29. Seven days before Richmond June 25-July 1: Mechanicsburg June 26. Gaines Mill June 27. Turkey Bridge June 30. Malvern Hill July 1. At Harrison's Landing till August 16. Moved to Fortress Monroe, thence to Alexandria August 16-23. Maryland Campaign September 6-22. Battle of Antietam September 16-17. Shepherdstown Ford September 19. Reconnoissance to Smithfield, W. Va., October 16-17. Kearneysville and Shepherdstown October 16-17. Battle of Fredericksburg, Va., December 12-15. Expedition from Potomac Creek to Richards and Ellis Fords, Rappahannock River, December 29-30. Chancellorsville Campaign April 27-May 6. Battle of Chancellorsville May 1-5. Gettysburg (Pa.) Campaign June 11-July 24. Battle of Gettysburg July 1-3. Bristoe Campaign October 9-22. Advance to line of the Rappahannock November 7-8. Rappahannock Station November 7. Mine Run Campaign November 26-December 2. At Camp Barry, Washington, D. C., till March, 1864. Rapidan Campaign May 4-June 12. Battles of the Wilderness May 5-7; Spottsylvania Court House May 8-21; North Anna River May 22-26. On line of the Pamunkey May 26-28. Totopotomoy May 28-31. Cold Harbor June 1-12. Bethesda Church June 1-3. Siege of Petersburg June 16, 1864, to April 2, 1865. Weldon Railroad August 18-21, 1864. Appomattox Campaign March 28-April 9, 1865. Junction of Quaker and Boydton Roads and Lewis' Farm March 29. White Oak Road March 31. Battle of Five Forks April 1. Appomattox Court House April 9. Surrender of Lee and his army. Moved to Washington, D. C., May. Grand Review May 23. Duty at Washington, D. C., till ——

BATTERY "E" 5th ARTILLERY.

Organized May, 1862, and on duty at Fort Hamilton, N. Y. Harbor, till June, 1863. Ordered to Dept. of the Susquehanna, and duty in Pennsylvania till April, 1864. Ordered to Washington, and attached to 3rd Brigade,

SEE CORRECTION SHEET, PG. 1750

Artillery Reserve, Army Potomac, to May, 1864. Artillery Brigade, 6th Army Corps, Army Potomac, to July, 1864. Artillery Reserve, Army Potomac, to December, 1864. Artillery Brigade, 6th Army Corps, Army Potomac, to June, 1865. Dept. of Washington, D. C., to ——

SERVICE.—Rapidan Campaign May 4-June 12, 1864. Totopotomoy May 28-31. Cold Harbor June 1-12. Siege of Petersburg June 17, 1864, to April 2, 1865. Jerusalem Plank Road June 22, 1864. Fort Fisher, Petersburg, March 25, 1865. Appomattox Campaign March 28-April 9, 1865. Assaults on and fall of Petersburg April 2, 1865. Sailor's Creek April 6. Appomattox Court House April 9. Surrender of Lee and his army. March to Danville April 17-23, and duty there till May. Moved to Richmond, thence to Washington, D. C., May 18-June 3. Corps Review June 8. Duty in the Defences of Washington, D. C., till ——

BATTERY "F" 5th ARTILLERY.

Organized September, 1861. Attached to W. F. Smith's Division, Army Potomac, to March, 1862. Artillery, 2nd Division, 4th Army Corps, Army Potomac, to May, 1862. Artillery, 2nd Division, 6th Army Corps, Army Potomac, to May, 1863. Artillery Brigade, 6th Army Corps, to December, 1863. Camp Barry, Washington, D. C., 22nd Army Corps, to July, 1864. Artillery Brigade, 18th Army Corps, Army of the James, to December, 1864. Artillery Brigade, 24th Army Corps, to May, 1865. Dept. of Virginia, to ——

SERVICE.—Duty in the Defences of Washington, D. C., till March, 1862. Moved to the Virginia Peninsula March, 1862. Warwick Road April 5. Siege of Yorktown April 5-May 4. Lee's Mills April 16. Battle of Williamsburg May 5. Seven days before Richmond June 25-July 1. Gaines' Mill June 27. White Oak Swamp June 30. Malvern Hill July 1. Moved to Alexandria August 16-23. Maryland Campaign September 6-22. South Mountain September 14. Battle of Antietam September 16-17. Movement to Falmouth, Va., October 30-November 19. Battle of Fredericksburg, Va., December 12-15. "Mud March" January 20-24, 1863. Chancellorsville Campaign April 27-May 6. Operations at Franklin's Crossing April 29-May 2. Maryes Heights, Fredericksburg, May 3. Salem Heights May 3-4. Battle of Gettysburg, Pa., July 2-4. Bristoe Campaign October 9-22. Advance to line of the Rappahannock November 7-8. Rappahannock Station November 7. Mine Run Campaign November 26-December 2. At Camp Barry, Defences of Washington, D. C., till July, 1864. Joined 18th Army Corps, Army of the James, before Petersburg, Va. Siege of Petersburg and Richmond, Va., July, 1864, to April, 1865. Battle of Chaffin's Farm, New Market Heights, September 28-30, 1864. Chaffin's Farm October 29. Appomattox Campaign March 28-April 2, 1865. Fall of Petersburg and Richmond April 2. Duty at Richmond and in Dept. of Virginia, till ——

BATTERY "G" 5th ARTILLERY.

Organized and equipped June, 1862. Duty at Fort Hamilton, N. Y. Harbor, till December, 1862. Moved to New Orleans, La., and duty there till March, 1863. Attached to Defences of New Orleans, Dept. of the Gulf, to January, 1863. Artillery, 2nd Division, 19th Army Corps, Dept. of the Gulf, to May, 1863. Artillery, 1st Division, 19th Army Corps, to July, 1863. Garrison Artillery, Port Hudson, La., to August, 1863. Defences of New Orleans, La., to February, 1864. Cavalry Division, Dept. of the Gulf, to June, 1864. District of LaFourche, La., Dept. Gulf, to August, 1864. U. S. Forces, Mobile Bay, Dept. Gulf, to October, 1864. New York, Dept. of the East, to November, 1864. Consolidated with Battery "D" November, 1864. Attached to Artillery Brigade, 5th Army Corps, Army Potomac, to June, 1865. Dept. of Washington, D. C., to ——

SERVICE.—Operations against Port Hudson March 7-27, 1863. Advance on Port Hudson May 18-23. Action at Blain's Store May 21. Siege of Port Hudson May 24-July 9. Assaults on Port Hudson May 27 and June 14. Surrender of Port Hudson July 9, and garrison duty there till August. At Baton Rouge, La., and New Or-

leans, La., till February, 1864. Red River Campaign March 10-May 22. Advance from Franklin to Alexandria March 14-26. Henderson's Hill March 21. Monett's Ferry and Cloutiersville March 29-30. Natchitoches March 31. Crump's Hill, Piney Woods, April 2. Wilson's Farm April 7. Bayou de Paul, Carroll's Mills, and Battle of Sabine Cross Roads April 8. About Cloutiersville April 22-24. Monett's Ferry, Cane River Crossing, April 23. Retreat to Morganza May 13-22. Duty in the District of LaFourche till August. Operations in Mobile Bay, Ala., against Fort Gaines and Morgan August 2-23. Siege and capture of Fort Gaines August 3-5. Siege and capture of Fort Morgan August 5-23. Ordered to New York October, 1864. Moved to City Point, Va., November 1, 1864, and consolidated with Battery "D," 5th Artillery. Siege of Petersburg November, 1864, to April, 1865. Appomattox Campaign March 28-April 9, 1865. Junction Quaker and Boydton Roads and Lewis Farm near Gravelly Run March 29. White Oak Road March 31. Battle of Five Forks April 1. Appomattox Court House April 9. Surrender of Lee and his army. Moved to Washington, D. C., May. Grand Review May 23. Duty at Washington, D. C., till ——

BATTERY "H" 5th ARTILLERY.

Organized September, 1861. Moved to Louisville, Ky., November, 1861, thence to Munfordsville, Ky., and duty there till February, 1862. Attached to Artillery, 1st Division, Army Ohio, to May, 1862. Artillery, 4th Division, Army Ohio, to September, 1862. Artillery, 10th Brigade, 4th Division, 2nd Corps, Army Ohio, to November, 1862. Artillery, 2nd Division, Left Wing 14th Army Corps, Army of the Cumberland, to January, 1863. Artillery, 2nd Division, 21st Army Corps, Army of the Cumberland, to October, 1863. Artillery, 1st Division, 4th Army Corps, to March, 1864. 1st Division, Artillery Reserve, Dept. of the Cumberland, to November, 1864. Garrison Artillery, Nashville, Tenn., Dept. Cumberland, to April, 1865. Dept. of the East to ——

SERVICE.—Advance on Nashville, Tenn., February 14-25, 1862. March to Savannah, Tenn., to reinforce Army Tennessee March 20-April 8. Advance on and siege of Corinth, Miss., April 29-May 30. Buell's Campaign in North Alabama and Middle Tennessee June to August. March to Louisville, Ky., in pursuit of Bragg August 21-September 26. Pursuit of Bragg into Kentucky October 1-16. Lawrenceburg, Ky., October 8. Dog Walk October 9. March to Nashville, Tenn., October 16-November 7, and duty there till December 26. Kimbrough's Mills, Mill Creek, December 6. Advance on Murfreesboro, Tenn., December 26-30. Battle of Stone's River December 30-31, 1862, and January 1-3, 1863. Duty at Murfreesboro till June. Middle Tennessee or Tullahoma Campaign June 23-July 7. Hoover's Gap June 24-26. Occupation of Middle Tennessee till August 16. Passage of Cumberland Mountains and Tennessee River and Chickamauga (Ga.) Campaign August 16-September 22. Battle of Chickamauga, Ga., September 19-20. Siege of Chattanooga September 24-November 23. Chattanooga-Ringgold Campaign November 23-27. At Chattanooga till March 25, 1864, and at Nashville, Tenn., till August 31. Pulaski September 27. Moved to Tullahoma September 29. Operations against Wheeler October. Moved to Nashville, Tenn., October 31, and duty there till April, 1865. Moved to Fort Richmond, N. Y., April, 1865.

BATTERY "I" 5th ARTILLERY.

Organized September, 1861. Attached to Artillery Reserve, Army Potomac, to May, 1862. Artillery, 2nd Division, 5th Army Corps, Army Potomac, to May, 1863. Artillery Brigade, 5th Army Corps, to July, 1863. Camp Barry, Washington, D. C., 22nd Army Corps, to November, 1863. (Consolidated with Battery "C" November, 1863.) Artillery Brigade, 2nd Army Corps, Army Potomac, to March, 1865. Artillery Reserve, Army Potomac, to June, 1865. Dept. of Washington to ——

SERVICE.—Duty in the Defences of Washington, D. C., till March, 1862. Ordered to the Virginia Peninsula. Siege of Yorktown April 5-May 4. Near New Bridge June 20. Seven days before Richmond June 25-July 1. Mechanicsville June 26. Gaines' Mill June 27. Turkey Bend June 30. Malvern Hill July 1. Movement from Harrison's Landing to Centreville August 16-28. Pope's Campaign in Northern Virginia August 28-September 2. Battles of Groveton August 29; Bull Run August 30. Maryland Campaign September 6-22. Battle of Antietam September 16-17. Shepherdstown Ford September 19. Shepherdstown September 20. Movement to Falmouth, Va., October 30-November 19. Battle of Fredericksburg, Va., December 12-15. Chancellorsville Campaign April 27-May 6. Battle of Chancellorsville May 1-5. Gettysburg (Pa.) Campaign June 11-July 24. Battle of Gettysburg, Pa., July 1-3. At Camp Barry, Washington, D. C., till December, 1863. Consolidated with Battery "C" November, 1863. Rapidan Campaign May 4-June 12. Battles of the Wilderness May 5-7; Spottsylvania Court House May 8-21; Po River May 10. Assault on the Salient May 12. North Anna River May 22-26. On line of the Pamunkey May 26-28. Totopotomoy May 28-31. Cold Harbor June 1-12. Assaults on Petersburg June 16-18. Siege of Petersburg June 16, 1864, to April 2, 1865. Jerusalem Plank Road June 22, 1864. Deep Bottom July 27-29. Weldon Railroad August 18-21. Boydton Plank Road, Hatcher's Run, October 27-28. Fort Stedman March 25, 1865. Appomattox Campaign March 28-April 9. Assaults on and fall of Petersburg April 2. Moved to Washington, D. C., May. Grand Review May 23. Duty at Washington, D. C., till ——

BATTERY "K" 5th ARTILLERY.

Organized September, 1861. Attached to Provost Guard, Army Potomac, October, 1861, to March, 1862. Artillery Reserve, Army Potomac, to May, 1862. 2nd Brigade, Artillery Reserve, 5th Army Corps, Army Potomac. to September, 1862. Artillery, 2nd Division, 5th Army Corps, to October, 1862. Artillery Reserve, Army Potomac, to May, 1863. Artillery Brigade, 12th Army Corps, Army Potomac, to October, 1863, and Army of the Cumberland, October, 1863. Artillery, 2nd Division, 12th Army Corps, Army Cumberland, to March, 1864. 1st Division, Artillery Reserve, Dept. Cumberland, to August, 1864. Artillery Brigade, 20th Army Corps, Army Cumberland, to October, 1864. Garrison Artillery, Chattanooga, Tenn., Dept. of the Cumberland, to August, 1865.

SERVICE.—Duty in the Defences of Washington, D. C., till March, 1862. Ordered to the Virginia Peninsula. Siege of Yorktown, Va., April 5-May 4. Seven days before Richmond June 25-July 1. Mechanicsville June 26. Gaines' Mill June 27. Turkey Bridge June 30. Malvern Hill July 1. At Harrison's Landing till August 16. Movement to Centreville, Va., August 16-28. Pope's Campaign in Northern Virginia August 28-September 2. Battles of Groveton August 29; Bull Run August 30. Maryland Campaign September 6-22. Battle of Antietam September 16-17. Shepherdstown Ford September 19. Shepherdstown September 20. Movement to Falmouth, Va., October 30-November 19. Battle of Fredericksburg, Va., December 12-15. Chancellorsville Campaign April 27-May 6. Battle of Gettysburg, Pa., July 1-3. Movement to Bridgeport, Ala., September 24-October 3. Operations on line of Memphis & Charleston Railroad October-November. Chattanooga-Ringgold Campaign November 23-27. At Chattanooga, Tenn., till August, 1864. Atlanta (Ga.) Campaign. Siege of Atlanta August 25-September 2. Operations at Chattahoochie River Bridge August 26-September 2. Occupation of Atlanta to October. Garrison duty at Chattanooga, Tenn., till August, 1865.

BATTERY "L" 5th ARTILLERY.

Battery organized October, 1862, and duty at Baltimore, Md., till May, 1863. Attached to Defences of Baltimore, Md., 8th Army Corps, Middle Department, to January, 1863. 2nd Separate Brigade, 8th Army Corps, to February, 1863. 3rd Separate Brigade, 8th Army Corps, to March, 1863. 2nd Brigade, 2nd Division, 8th Army Corps, to June, 1863. 1st Brigade, 2nd Division, 8th Army Corps, to July, 1863. 3rd Separate Brigade, 8th Army Corps, to August, 1863. Camp Barry, Defences of Washington, D. C., 22nd Army Corps, to July, 1864. Artillery, 2nd Cavalry Division, West Virginia, to November, 1864. Horse Artillery, Cavalry Corps, Army Shenandoah, to December, 1864. Horse Artillery Reserve, Army Shenandoah, to April, 1865. Cavalry Division, 22nd Army Corps, to August, 1865.

SERVICE.—Joined Milroy at Winchester May, 1863. Actions at Middletown, Newtown and Winchester June 12, 1863. Battle of Winchester June 13-15. At Camp Barry, Washington, D. C., July, 1863, to July, 1864. Stephenson's Depot, Carter's Farm, July 20. Newtown July 22. Battle of Winchester July 24. Hagerstown, Md., July 29. Sheridan's Shenandoah Valley Campaign August 7-November 28. Williamsport August 26. Martinsburg, W. Va., August 31. Bunker Hill September 2-3. Darkesville September 10. Bunker Hill September 13. Near Berryville September 14. Battle of Opequan, Winchester, September 19. Fisher's Hill September 22. Mt. Jackson September 23-24. Forest Hill or Timberville, Brown's Gap, September 26. Weyer's Cave September 26-27. Milford October 25-26. Expedition to Gordonsville December 19-28. Liberty Mills December 22. Duty in the Shenandoah Valley till April, 1865, and in the Defences of Washington, D. C., till August, 1865.

BATTERY "M" 5th ARTILLERY.

Organized November, 1861. Attached to Artillery Reserve, Army Potomac, to June, 1862. Reserve Artillery, 4th Army Corps, Army Potomac, to December, 1862. Reserve Artillery, Yorktown, Va., 7th Army Corps, Dept. of Virginia, to May, 1863. Unattached Artillery, 4th Army Corps, Yorktown, Va., to July, 1863. Artillery Brigade, 6th Army Corps, Army Potomac, to July, 1864. Artillery, 3rd Division, 6th Army Corps, Army of the Shenandoah, Middle Military Division, to September, 1864. Artillery Brigade, 6th Army Corps, to December, 1864. Reserve Division, Harper's Ferry, W. Va., to January, 1865. Camp Barry, Defences of Washington, D. C., 22nd Army Corps, to August, 1865.

SERVICE.—Siege of Yorktown, Va., April 5-May 4, 1862. Duty at Yorktown, Va., till July, 1863. Dix's Peninsula Campaign June 24-July 7, 1863. Expedition from White House to Bottom's Bridge July 1-7. Joined 6th Army Corps, July, 1863. Bristoe Campaign October 9-22. Advance to line of the Rappahannock November 7-8. Rappahannock Station November 7. Mine Run Campaign November 26-December 2. Rapidan Campaign May 4-June 12. Battles of the Wilderness May 5-7; Spottsylvania Court House May 8-21. Assault on the Salient May 12. North Anna River May 22-26. On line of the Totopotomoy May 28-31. Cold Harbor June 1-12. Operations against Petersburg June 17 to July 9. Jerusalem Plank Road June 22. Movement to Washington, D. C., May 9-12. Sheridan's Shenandoah Valley Campaign August 6-November 28. Battle of Cedar Creek October 19. Duty at Harper's Ferry, W. Va., till April, 1865, and in the Defences of Washington, D. C., till August ——

The 5th Regiment of Artillery lost during service 7 Officers and 87 Enlisted men killed and mortally wounded and 1 Officer and 145 Enlisted men by disease. Total 240.

1st BATTALION ENGINEERS.

Attached to Engineer Brigade, Army Potomac, all through. Participated in the following service: Duty in the Defences of Washington till March, 1862. Peninsula Campaign April to August, 1862. Siege of Yorktown April 5-May 4. Seven days before Richmond June 25-July 1. Battles of Mechanicsville June 26; Gaines' Mill June 27; Turkey Bridge June 30; Malvern Hill July 1; Antietam, Md., September 16-17. Fredericksburg, Va., "Mud March," January 20-24, 1863. Chancellorsville Campaign April 27-May 6. Battle of Chancellorsville May 1-5. Gettysburg (Pa.) Campaign June 11-July 24. Battle of Gettysburg, Pa., July 1-4. Bristoe Campaign October 9-22. Advance to line of the Rappahannock November 7-8. Mine Run Campaign November 26-December 2. Rapidan Campaign May 4-June 12. Battles of the Wilderness May 5-7; Spottsylvania Court House May 8-21. North Anna River May 22-26. On line of the Pamunkey May 26-28. Totopotomoy May 28-31. Cold Harbor June 1-12. Before Petersburg June 16-18. Siege of Petersburg June 16, 1864, to April 2, 1865. Fall of Petersburg April 2.

1st REGIMENT INFANTRY.

Attached to Dept. of Missouri (6 Cos.) April, 1861, to March, 1862. Unassigned, Army of the Mississippi, to July, 1862. Post of Corinth, Miss., to November, 1862. Unattached, District of Corinth, Miss., 13th Army Corps, Dept. Tennessee, to December, 1862. Unattached, District of Corinth, 17th Army Corps, to January, 1863. Unattached, District of Corinth, 16th Army Corps, to March, 1863. 1st Brigade, 14th Division, 13th Army Corps, Army Tennessee, to July, 1863. 1st Brigade, 1st Division, 13th Army Corps, to August, 1863. Headquarters, 13th Army Corps, Dept. Gulf, to October, 1863. Defences of New Orleans, La., to February, 1864. 2nd Brigade, 4th Division, 13th Army Corps, to March, 1864. Defences of New Orleans, La., to April, 1865. District of LaFourche, La., Dept. Gulf, to October, 1865.

SERVICE.—Battle of Wilson's Creek, Mo., August 10, 1861 (Cos. "B," "C," "D"). Duty in the Dept. of Missouri till February, 1862. Operations against New Madrid, Mo., and Island Number 10, Mississippi River, February 28-April 8. Expedition to Fort Pillow, Tenn., April 13-17. Moved to Hamburg Landing, Tenn., April 18-22. Advance on and siege of Corinth, Miss., April 29-May 30. Duty at Corinth, Miss., till March, 1863. Battle of Corinth October 3-4, 1862. Pursuit to Ripley October 5-12. Grant's Central Mississippi Campaign November, 1862, to January, 1863. Moved to Milliken's Bend, La., March, 1863. Movement on Bruinsburg and turning Grand Gulf April 25-30. Battle of Port Gibson May 1. Big Black River Bridge May 17. Siege of Vicksburg, Miss., May 18-July 4. Assaults on Vicksburg May 19 and 22. Advance on Jackson, Miss., July 4-10. Siege of Jackson July 10-17. Moved to New Orleans, La., August, and on provost duty there till October, 1865. (Co. "E" engaged at Hickory Grove, Mo., August 13, 1862.)

Regiment lost during the war 2 Officers and 34 Enlisted men killed and mortally wounded and 3 Officers and 85 Enlisted men by disease. Total 124.

2nd REGIMENT INFANTRY.

In Kansas January, 1861. Companies "C" and "K" reached Washington, D. C., July, 1861. Attached to Porter's 1st Brigade, Hunter's Division, McDowell's Army of Northeast Virginia, to August, 1861. Porter's City Guard, Washington, D. C., to March, 1862. Regiment concentrated at Washington, December, 1861, except Company "H" at Fort Larned, Kan. Attached to Syke's Regular Infantry Brigade, Army Potomac, March to May, 1862. 2nd Brigade, 2nd Division, 5th Army Corps, Army Potomac, to September, 1863. 1st Brigade, 2nd Division, 5th Army Corps, to March, 1864. 4th Brigade, 1st Division, 5th Army Corps, to April, 1864. 1st Brigade, 1st Division, 5th Army Corps, to June, 1864. Provost Guard, 2nd Division, 5th Army Corps, to October, 1864. Newport Barracks, Ky., to October, 1865.

SERVICE.—Advance on Manassas, Va., July 16-21, 1861 (Cos. "C," "K"). Battle of Bull Run, Va., July 21. Duty as City Guard at Washington, D. C., till March, 1862. Moved to the Virginia Peninsula. Siege of Yorktown April 5-May 4. Seven days before Richmond June 25-July 1. Battles of Mechanicsville June 26; Gaines' Mill June 27; Turkey Bridge June 30; Malvern Hill July 1. At Harrison's Landing till August 16. Moved to Fortress Monroe, thence to Centreville August 16-28. Pope's Campaign in Northern Virginia August 28-September 2. Battles of Groveton August 29; Bull

Run August 30. Maryland Campaign September 6-22. Shepherdstown Ford September 19-20. At Sharpsburg till October 29. Movement to Falmouth, Va., October 29-November 19. Battle of Fredericksburg December 12-15. "Mud March" January 20-24, 1863. Chancellorsville Campaign April 27-May 6. Battle of Chancellorsville May 1-5. Gettysburg (Pa.) Campaign June 11-July 24. Battle of Gettysburg July 1-3. Pursuit of Lee, July 5-24. Bristoe Campaign October 9-22. Advance to line of the Rappahannock November 7-8. Mine Run Campaign November 26-December 2. Near Greenwich April 11, 1864 (Cos. "C," "H," "K"). Rapidan Campaign May 4-June 12. Battles of the Wilderness May 5-7; Spottsylvania Court House May 8-21; North Anna River May 22-26. On line of the Pamunkey May 26-28. Totopotomoy May 28-31. Cold Harbor June 1-12. Bethesda Church June 1-3. Before Petersburg June 16-18. Siege of Petersburg June 16 to October, 1864. Mine Explosion, Petersburg, July 30 (Reserve). Weldon Railroad August 18-21. Poplar Springs Church, Peeble's Farm, September 29-October 2. Moved to Newport Barracks, Ky., October, 1864, and duty there till October, 1865. Company "B" moved from Kansas to St. Louis, Mo., February, 1861. Expedition to Booneville June 13-17. Capture of Jefferson City June 13. Action at Booneville June 17. Company "E" moved to St. Louis, Mo., July, 1861. Lyon's Springfield Campaign July-August. Companies "B" and "E" action at Dug Springs August 2. Battle of Wilson's Creek August 10. Joined Regiment in Washington, D. C., December, 1861. Company "H" at Fort Laramie till June, 1863. Joined Regiment at Benson's Mills, Va., June 13, 1863.

Regiment lost during service 8 Officers and 88 Enlisted men killed and mortally wounded and 1 Officer and 58 Enlisted men by disease. Total 155.

3rd REGIMENT INFANTRY.

In Texas till March, 1861. Companies "C" and "E" moved to New York March, 1861, and Companies "B," "D," "G," "H" and "K" to New York March 19-April 25, 1861. Companies "C" and "E" moved to Fort Pickens, Fla., arriving there April 16, 1861, and duty there till June, 1862. Action on Santa Rosa Island, Fla., October 9, 1861. Bombardment of Fort Pickens November 22-23. Fort Barrancas January 1, 1862. Fort Pickens May 9-12. Rejoined Regiment in Army Potomac June, 1862. Companies "A," "F" and "I" surrendered at Mattagorda Bay, Texas, April 26, 1861. Companies "F" and "I" joined Regiment at Washington February, 1862. Companies "B," "D," "G," "H" and "K" moved from Fort Hamilton, N. Y. Harbor, to Washington, D. C., May 9, 1861, and duty there till March, 1862. Attached to Porter's Brigade, Hunter's Division, McDowell's Army of Northeast Virginia, to August, 1861. Porter's City Guard, Washington, D. C., to March, 1862. Sykes' Regular Infantry, Reserve Brigade, Army Potomac, to May, 1862. 1st Brigade, 2nd Division, 5th Army Corps, Army Potomac, to August, 1863. Dept. of the East, to October, 1864. Defences of Washington, D. C., 22nd Army Corps, to February, 1865. Headquarters Army Potomac, to May, 1865. Defences of Washington, 22nd Corps, to October, 1865.

SERVICE.—Advance on Manassas, Va., July 16-21, 1861. Battle of Bull Run July 21. Duty at Washington till March, 1862. Moved to the Virginia Peninsula March, 1862. Siege of Yorktown April 5-May 4. Seven days before Richmond June 25-July 1. Battles of Mechanicsville June 26; Gaines' Mill June 27; Turkey Bridge June 30; Malvern Hill July 1. At Harrison's Landing till August 16. Moved to Fortress Monroe, thence to Centreville August 16-28. Pope's Campaign in Northern Virginia August 28-September 2. Battles of Groveton August 29; Bull Run August 30. Maryland Campaign September 6-22. Battle of Antietam September 16-17. Shepherdstown Ford September 19-20. At Sharpsburg till October 29. Kearneysville and Shepherdstown October 16-17. Moved to Falmouth, Va., October 29-November 19. Battle of Fredericksburg, Va., December 12-15. "Mud March" January 20-24, 1863.

Chancellorsville Campaign April 27-May 6. Battle of Chancellorsville May 1-5. Gettysburg (Pa.) Campaign June 11-July 24. Battle of Gettysburg, Pa., July 1-3. Pursuit of Lee July 5-24. At New York City during draft disturbances August 21-September 14. Bristoe Campaign October 9-22. Advance to line of the Rappahannock November 7-8. Mine Run Campaign November 26-December 2. Ordered to New York December, 1863, and duty at Forts Richmond, Hamilton and Columbus, N. Y. Harbor, till October, 1864. Ordered to Washington, D. C., and duty there till February, 1865. Ordered to City Point, Va., and duty at Headquarters, Army of the Potomac, to May, 1865. Fall of Petersburg April 2. Moved to Washington, D. C., May, and duty there till October. 1865. Grand Review May 23.

Regiment lost during service 2 Officers and 39 Enlisted men killed and mortally wounded and 48 Enlisted men by disease. Total 89.

4th REGIMENT INFANTRY.

In California January, 1861. Ordered to Washington, D. C., and duty in the Defences of that city till March, 1862. Attached to Sykes' Regular Infantry (Reserve) Brigade, Army of the Potomac, to May, 1862. 1st Brigade, 2nd Division, 5th Army Corps, Army Potomac, to August, 1863. Dept. of the East, to April, 1864. 1st Brigade, 1st Division, 9th Army Corps, to June, 1864. 1st Brigade, 2nd Division, 5th Army Corps, June, 1864. City Point, Va., Headquarters. Army Potomac, to May, 1865. Dept. of Virginia to July, 1865.

SERVICE.—Moved to Virginia Peninsula March, 1862. Siege of Yorktown, Va., April 5-May 4. Seven days before Richmond June 25-July 1. Battles of Mechanicsville June 26; Gaines' Mill June 27; Turkey Bridge June 30; Malvern Hill July 1. At Harrison's Landing till August 16. Movement to Fortress Monroe, thence to Centreville August 16-28. Pope's Campaign in Northern Virginia August 28-September 2. Battles of Groveton August 29; Bull Run August 30. Maryland Campaign September 6-22. Battle of Antietam September 16-17. Shepherdstown Ford September 19-20. At Sharpsburg till October 29. Kearneysville and Shepherdstown October 16-17. Movement to Falmouth, Va., October 29-November 19. Battle of Fredericksburg, Va., December 12-15. "Mud March" January 20-24, 1863. Chancellorsville Campaign April 27-May 6. Battle of Chancellorsville May 1-5. Gettysburg (Pa.) Campaign June 11-July 24. Battle of Gettysburg July 1-3. Pursuit of Lee July 5-24. Moved to New York August 15. Duty at Forts Tompkins and Wood till April 25, 1864. Rejoined Army Potomac. Rapidan Campaign May 4-June 12. Battles of the Wilderness May 5-7; Spottsylvania Court House May 8-21; Ny River May 10; North Anna River May 22-26. On line of the Pamunkey May 26-28. Totopotomoy May 28-31. Cold Harbor June 1-12. Bethesda Church June 1-3. Before Petersburg June 16-18. Ordered to City Point, Va., June 22, and assigned to duty at headquarters of the army under Gen. Grant till April, 1865. Fall of Petersburg April 2, 1865. Duty at Richmond, Va., till July, 1865. Moved to N. Y. Harbor July 15, 1865.

Regiment lost during service 2 Officers and 58 Enlisted men killed and mortally wounded and 1 Officer and 61 Enlisted men by disease. Total 122.

5th REGIMENT INFANTRY.

Duty in the Dept. of New Mexico throughout the war, operating against Indians. Battle of Valverde, N. M., February 21, 1862 (Cos. "B," "D," "F," "I"). Evacuation of Albuqurque and Santa Fe March 2-4, 1862 (1 Co.). Action at Apache Canon March 28, 1862 (Cos. "A," "G"). Peralta April 15. Companies "D," "E," "F" and "G" joined Gen. Carlton's Command at Las Cruces August 10, 1862, Companies "A," "B," "I" and "K" at Fort Craig. Pecos River near Fort Sumner January 5, 1864 (Co. "D"). Expedition against Indians in Central Arizona December 26, 1864-January 1, 1865.

Regiment lost during service 2 Officers and 18 Enlisted men killed and mortally wounded and 2 Officers and 35 Enlisted men by disease. Total 57.

6th REGIMENT INFANTRY.

In California April, 1861. Regiment concentrated in Washington, D. C., October 31, 1861, to January 31, 1862. Attached to Sykes' Regular Infantry, Reserve Brigade, Army of the Potomac, to May, 1862. 2nd Brigade, 2nd Division, 5th Army Corps, Army Potomac, to June, 1863. 1st Brigade, 2nd Division, 5th Army Corps, to August, 1863. Dept. of the East, to May, 1865. District of Savannah, Ga., Dept. of the South, to October, 1865.

SERVICE.—Duty in the Defences of Washington, D. C., till March, 1862. Moved to the Virginia Peninsula. Siege of Yorktown, Va., April 5-May 4. Seven days before Richmond June 25-July 1. Battles of Mechanicsburg June 26; Gaines' Mill June 27; Turkey Bridge June 30; Malvern Hill July 1. At Harrison's Landing till August 16. Movement to Fortress Monroe, thence to Centreville August 16-28. Pope's Campaign in Northern Virginia August 28-September 2. Battle of Groveton August 29. Bull Run August 30. Maryland Campaign September 6-22. Battle of Antietam, Md., September 16-17. Shepherdstown Ford September 19-20. At Sharpsburg, Md., till October 29. Movement to Falmouth, Va., October 29-November 19. Snicker's Gap November 3. Battle of Fredericksburg, Va., December 12-15. "Mud March" January 20-24, 1863. Chancellorsville Campaign April 27-May 6. Battle of Chancellorsville May 1-5. Gettysburg (Pa.) Campaign June 11-July 24. Battle of Gettysburg July 1-3. Pursuit of Lee July 4-24. Moved to New York City August 16-21, thence to Fort Hamilton, N. Y. Harbor, and duty there till May 17, 1865. Moved to Savannah, Ga., May 17-21, and duty in District of Savannah, Ga., till October, 1865.

Regiment lost during service 2 Officers and 29 Enlisted men killed and mortally wounded and 1 Officer and 43 Enlisted men by disease. Total 75.

7th REGIMENT INFANTRY.

In New Mexico, January, 1861. Concentrated at Fort Fillmore. Action at Mesilla July 25, 1861. Evacuation of Fort Fillmore July 27. St. Augustine Springs July 27. Seven Companies surrendered by Major Lynde. Paroled and moved to Fort Union, thence ordered to Jefferson Barracks, Mo. Exchanged September 30, 1862, and ordered to join Army Potomac. (Cos. "C," "F," "H" at Valverde, N. M., February 21, 1862.) Attached to 2nd Brigade, 2nd Division, 5th Army Corps, Army Potomac, November, 1862, to August, 1863. Dept. of the East, to May, 1865. Moved to Florida May, 1865.

SERVICE.—Snicker's Gap, Va., November 3, 1862. Battle of Fredericksburg, Va., December 12-15. "Mud March" January 20-24, 1863. Chancellorsville Campaign April 27-May 6. Battle of Chancellorsville May 1-5. Gettysburg (Pa.) Campaign June 11-July 24. Battle of Gettysburg, Pa., July 1-3. Pursuit of Lee July 5-24. Moved to New York August 14, and duty there till May, 1865. Moved to Florida May, 1865.

Regiment lost during service 2 Officers and 50 Enlisted men killed and mortally wounded and 3 Officers and 56 Enlisted men by disease. Total 111.

8th REGIMENT INFANTRY.

In Texas January, 1861. Forced to surrender while en route north. "C" at San Antonio April 22, "A" and "D" at Indianola April 24, and Companies "B," "E," "F," "H," "I" and "K" at San Lucas Springs May 9, 1861. Company "G" attached to Porter's Brigade, Hunter's Division, McDowell's Army of Northeast Virginia, to August, 1861. Advance on Manassas, Va., July 16-21. Battle of Bull Run July 21. Company "F" reached Washington, D. C., July, 1861. Companies "F" and "G" attached to Porter's City Guard, Washington, D. C., to March, 1862. Provost Guard, Headquarters, Army Potomac, to July, 1863 (Cos. "A," "B," "D," "F," "G"). Dept. of the East to April, 1864. Provost Guard, 9th Army Corps, Army Potomac, to October, 1864. 1st Brigade, 2nd Division, 5th Army Corps, to November, 1864. Baltimore, Md., 8th Army Corps, Middle Department, to August, 1865.

SERVICE.—Duty in the Defences of Washington, D. C., till March, 1862. Moved to Virginia Peninsula. Siege of Yorktown April 5-May 4. Expedition up the Pamunkey May 17. Seven days before Richmond June 25-July 1. Mechanicsville June 26. Gaines' Mill June 27. Turkey Bridge June 30. Malvern Hill July 1. Movement to Alexandria August 16-23. Battle of Antietam September 16-17. (Co. "B" joined at Sharpsburg October 3, 1862.) At Sharpsburg, Md., till October 29. Movement to Falmouth, Va., October 29-November 19. Battle of Fredericksburg, Va., December 12-15. Chancellorsville Campaign April 27-May 6, 1863. (Co. "C" joined at Falmouth, Va., April 18, 1863.) Battle of Chancellorsville May 1-5. Gettysburg (Pa.) Campaign June 11-July 24. Battle of Gettysburg, Pa., July 1-3. Ordered to New York July 15. At City Hall Park, New York July 17-30, and on the Battery, New York, till August 22. At Forts in N. Y. Harbor till April 23, 1864. Moved to Washington, D. C., April 23. Rapidan Campaign May 4-June 12. Battles of the Wilderness May 5-7; Spottsylvania May 8-21; North Anna River May 22-26; Totopotomoy May 28-31; Cold Harbor June 1-12; Bethesda Church June 1-3. Before Petersburg June 16-18. Siege of Petersburg June 16-November 2. Mine Explosion, Petersburg, July 30. Boydton Plank Road, Hatcher's Run, October 27-28. Moved to Buffalo, N. Y., November 2, thence to Baltimore, Md., November 22, and duty there till August, 1865.

Companies "C" and "D" reached Washington, D. C., April, 1862. Attached to Defences of Washington, to May, 1862. Cooper's 1st Brigade, Sigel's Division, Dept. of the Shenandoah, to June, 1862. 2nd Brigade, 2nd Division, 2nd Corps, Army of Virginia, to September, 1862. 2nd Brigade, 2nd Division, 12th Army Corps, Army Potomac, September, 1862. Joined other Companies at Headquarters Army Potomac. Moved to Harper's Ferry, W. Va., May 24, 1862. Defence of Harper's Ferry May 24-30. Operations in the Shenandoah Valley till August. Battle of Cedar Mountain August 9. Pope's Virginia Campaign August 16-September 2. Fords of the Rappahannock August 20-23. Sulphur Springs August 26. Plains of Manassas August 27-29. Battle of Bull Run August 30. Battle of Antietam, Md., September 16-17.

Regiment lost during service 1 Officer and 15 Enlisted men killed and mortally wounded and 4 Officers and 47 Enlisted men by disease. Total 67.

9th REGIMENT INFANTRY.

On duty at posts about San Francisco, Cal., September, 1861, to November, 1865.

Lost during the war 2 Officers and 18 Enlisted men by disease. Total 20.

10th REGIMENT INFANTRY.

Companies "B," "E," "G" and "I" at Washington, D. C., January, 1862. Companies "D" and "K" at Fort Laramie, Neb., till June, 1862. Moved to Fort Kearney and duty there till April 7, 1863. Joined Regiment near Chancellorsville, Va., April 30, 1863. Companies "A" and "F" at Socorro, N. M., January, 1862. Company "H" at Pinos Ranch near Santa Fe, N. M., January, 1862. Concentrated at Fort Craig (Cos. "A," "F" and "H"). Battle of Valverde, N. M., February 21, 1862. Albuqurque April 8. Peralta April 15. Company "C" at Fort Wise, Colo., January, 1862. Companies "C," "F" and "H" march to Fort Leavenworth, Kan., September to November, arriving there November 7, and moved to Washington, D. C., November 24. Joined Regiment at Aquia Creek, Va., November 28, 1862. Regiment attached to Sykes' Regular Infantry (Reserve) Brigade, Army Potomac, to May, 1862. 2nd Brigade, 2nd Division, 5th Army Corps, Army Potomac, to August, 1863. Dept. of the East to April, 1864. 1st Brigade, 1st Division, 9th Army Corps, Army Potomac, to June, 1864. 1st Brigade, 2nd Division, 5th Army Corps, to October, 1864. Headquarters, Army Potomac, to November, 1864. Dept. of the East, to April, 1865. Headquarters, Army Potomac, to June, 1865. Dept. Washington, D. C., to October, 1865.

SERVICE.—Duty in Defences of Washington, D. C., till March, 1862. Moved to the Virginia Peninsula March, 1862. Siege of Yorktown, Va., April 5-May 4. Seven days before Richmond June 25-July 1. Battles of Mechanicsville June 26; Gaines' Mill June 27; Turkey Bridge June 30; Malvern Hill July 1. At Harrison's Landing till August 16. Movement to Fortress Monroe, thence to Centreville August 16-28. Pope's Campaign in Northern Virginia August 28-September 2. Battles of Groveton August 29; Bull Run August 30. Maryland Campaign September 6-22. Battle of Antietam September 16-17. Shepherdstown Ford September 19-20. At Sharpsburg, Md., till October 29. Movement to Falmouth, Va., October 29-November 19. Battle of Fredericksburg, Va., December 12-15. "Mud March" January 20-24, 1863. Chancellorsville Campaign April 27-May 6. Battle of Chancellorsville May 1-5. Gettysburg (Pa.) Campaign June 11-July 24. Battle of Gettysburg, Pa., July 1-3. Pursuit of Lee July 5-24. Moved to New York August 16-20. At Fort Hamilton, N. Y. Harbor, September 14, 1863, to April 23, 1864. Moved to front and joined 9th Army Corps at Bealeton Station, Va., April 29. Rapidan Campaign May 4-June 12. Battles of the Wilderness May 5-7; Spottsylvania Court House May 8-21; Ny River May 10. Assault on the Salient May 12. North Anna River May 22-26. On line of the Pamunkey May 26-28. Totopotomoy May 18-31. Cold Harbor June 1-12. Bethesda Church June 1-3. Transferred to 5th Army Corps June 11. Before Petersburg June 16-18. Siege of Petersburg June 16 to October 25. Weldon Railroad August 18-21. Poplar Springs Church, Peeble's Farm, September 29-October 2. Provost Guard, 2nd Division, 5th Army Corps, October 12 to 25. Moved to Fort Hamilton, N. Y. Harbor, October 25-29, and duty there till April, 1865. Moved to the field and joined Army Potomac, at Burkesville, Va., April 23. March to Washington, D. C., May 2-12. Grand Review May 23. Duty at Washington, D. C., till October. Moved to St. Louis, Mo., October 20-27, thence to St. Paul, Minn.

Regiment lost during service 3 Officers and 83 Enlisted men killed and mortally wounded and 3 Officers and 49 Enlisted men by disease. Total 138.

11th REGIMENT INFANTRY.

Organized by direction of the President May 4, 1861, and confirmed by Act of Congress July 29, 1861. Organized at Fort Independence, Boston Harbor, 1st Battalion ordered to Perryville, Md., October 10, 1861, and duty there till March, 1862. Ordered to Washington, D. C. Attached to Sykes' Regular Infantry, Reserve Brigade, Army Potomac, to May, 1862. 2nd Brigade, 2nd Division, 5th Army Corps, to September, 1863. 1st Brigade, 2nd Division, 5th Army Corps, to March, 1864. 4th Brigade, 1st Division, 5th Army Corps, to April, 1864. 1st Brigade, 1st Division, 5th Army Corps, to June, 1864. 1st Brigade, 2nd Division, 5th Army Corps, to November, 1864. Annapolis, Md., 8th Army Corps, Middle Department, to January, 1865. City Point, Va., Headquarters Army Potomac, to May, 1865. Dept. of Virginia, to October, 1865.

SERVICE.—Moved to Virginia Peninsula March, 1862. Siege of Yorktown April 5-May 4. Seven days before Richmond June 25-July 1. Battles of Mechanicsville June 26; Gaines' Mill June 27; Turkey Bridge June 30; Malvern Hill July 1. At Harrison's Landing till August 16. Movement to Fortress Monroe, thence to Centreville August 16-28. Pope's Campaign in Northern Virginia August 28-September 2. Battles of Groveton August 29; Bull Run August 30. Maryland Campaign September 6-22. Battle of Antietam, Md., September 16-17. Shepherdstown Ford September 19-20. At Sharpsburg, Md., till October 29. Movement to Falmouth, Va., October 29-November 19. Battle of Fredericksburg, Va., December 12-15. "Mud March" January 20-24, 1863. Chancellorsville Campaign April 27-May 6. Battle of Chancellorsville May 1-5. Gettysburg (Pa.) Campaign June 11-July 24. Battle of Gettysburg July 1-3. Pursuit of Lee July 5-24. On special duty at New York August 21-September 14. Rejoined army, Bristoe Campaign, October 9-22. Advance to line of the Rappahannock November 7-8. Mine Run Campaign November 26-December 2. Rapidan Campaign May 4-June 12, 1864. Battles of the Wilderness May 5-7; Spottsylvania Court House May 8-21; North Anna River May 22-26. On line of the Pamunkey May 26-28. Totopotomoy May 28-31. Cold Harbor June 1-12. Bethesda Church June 1-3. Before Petersburg June 16-18. Siege of Petersburg June 16-November 2. Mine Explosion, Petersburg, July 30 (Reserve). Weldon Railroad August 18-21. Poplar Springs Church, Peeble's Farm, September 29-October 2. Boydton Plank Road, Hatcher's Run, October 27-28. Moved to Fort Hamilton, N. Y. Harbor, November 2, thence to Baltimore, Md., November 18, and to Annapolis, Md., December 5. Duty at Camp Parole, Annapolis, Md., till January 26, 1865. Ordered to City Point, Va., January 26, and camp near Gen. Grant's Headquarters till March 8. Provost duty at Headquarters, Army Potomac, till May, and at Richmond, Va., till October, 1865.

Regiment lost during service 8 Officers and 117 Enlisted men killed and mortally wounded and 2 Officers and 86 Enlisted men by disease. Total, 213.

12th REGIMENT INFANTRY.

Organized by direction of the President May 4, 1861, and confirmed by Act of Congress July 29, 1861. Organized at Fort Hamilton, N. Y. Harbor. Moved to Washington, D. C., March 5, 1862. Attached to Sykes' Regular Infantry, Reserve Brigade, Army Potomac, to May, 1862. 1st Brigade, 2nd Division, 5th Army Corps, to August, 1863. Dept. of the East to September, 1863. 1st Brigade, 2nd Division, 5th Army Corps, to March, 1864. 4th Brigade, 1st Division, 5th Army Corps, to April, 1864. 1st Brigade, 1st Division, 5th Army Corps, to June, 1864. 1st Brigade, 2nd Division, 5th Army Corps, to November, 1864. Dept. of the East to July, 1865.

SERVICE.—Moved to the Virginia Peninsula March, 1862. Siege of Yorktown April 5-May 4. Seven days before Richmond June 25-July 1. Battles of Mechanicsville June 26; Gaines' Mill June 27; Turkey Bridge June 30; Malvern Hill July 1. At Harrison's Landing till August 16. Movement to Fortress Monroe, thence to Centreville August 16-28. Pope's Campaign in Northern Virginia August 28-September 2. Battles of Groveton August 29; Bull Run August 30. Maryland Campaign September 6-22. Battle of Antietam September 16-17. Shepherdstown Ford September 19-20. At Sharpsburg, Md., till October 29. Kearneysville and Shepherdstown October 16-17. Movement to Falmouth, Va., October 29-November 19. Battle of Fredericksburg, Va., December 12-15. "Mud March" January 20-24, 1863. Chancellorsville Campaign April 27-May 6. Battle of Chancellorsville May 1-5. Gettysburg (Pa.) Campaign June 11-July 24. Battle of Gettysburg, Pa., July 1-3. Pursuit of Lee July 5-24. Moved to New York August 16-19. (Cos. "F" and "H," 2nd Battalion, in N. Y. riots July, 1863.) Duty at New York till September 14. Rejoined army at Culpeper, Va., September 22. Bristoe Campaign October 9-22. Advance to line of the Rappahannock November 7-8. Mine Run Campaign November 26-December 2. Rapidan Campaign, battles of the Wilderness, May 5-7; Spottsylvania Court House May 8-21; North Anna River May 22-26. On line of the Pamunkey May 26-28. Totopotomoy May 28-31. Cold Harbor June 1-12. Bethesda Church June 1-3. Before Petersburg June 16-18. Siege of Petersburg June 16 to November 2. Mine Explosion, Petersburg, July 30 (Reserve). Weldon Railroad August 18-21. Poplar Springs Church, Peeble's Farm, September 29-October 2. Boydton Plank Road, Hatcher's Run, October 27-28. Moved to New York November 2-6. 1st Battalion on duty at Elmira, N. Y., and 2nd Battalion at Fort Hamilton, N. Y. Harbor, till July, 1865.

Regiment lost during service 8 Officers and 118 Enlisted men killed and mortally wounded and 3 Officers and 190 Enlisted men by disease. Total 319.

13th REGIMENT INFANTRY.

Created by direction of the President May 4, 1861, and confirmed by Act of Congress July 29, 1861. Organized at Jefferson Barracks, Mo. Company "A" organized October 8, 1861, "B," "C" and "G" November 13, 1861. "D," "E" and "F" April 1, 1862. Battalion ordered to Alton, Ill., February 12, 1862, and duty there till September 4, 1862. Moved to Newport News, Va., September 4, and duty there during Kirby Smith's threatened attack on Cincinnati, Ohio. Moved to Memphis, Tenn., October 14-22. Attached to District of Memphis, Tenn., Right Wing 13th Army Corps, Dept. Tennessee, to December, 1862. 1st Brigade, 2nd Division, Sherman's Yazoo Expedition to January, 1863. 1st Brigade, 2nd Division, 15th Army Corps, Army Tennessee, January, 1863. Headquarters, 15th Army Corps, to September, 1863. 1st Brigade, 2nd Division, 15th Army Corps, to December, 1863. District of Nashville, Tenn., Dept. Cumberland, to July, 1865.

SERVICE.—Duty at Memphis till November, 1862. Grant's Central Mississippi Campaign, "Tallahatchie March," November 26-December 12. Sherman's Yazoo Expedition December 20, 1862-January 3, 1863. Chickasaw Bayou December 26-28. Chickasaw Bluff December 29. Expedition to Arkansas Post, Ark., January 3-10, 1863. Assault and capture of Fort Hindman, Arkansas Post, January 10-11. Moved to Young's Point, La., January 17-22, and duty there till March. Expedition to Rolling Fork via Muddy, Steele's and Black Bayous March 14-27. Black Bayou March 21. Deer Creek, near Rolling Fork, March 22. At Young's Point till April 29. Demonstration on Haines and Drumgould's Bluffs April 29-May 2. Moved to join army in rear of Vicksburg via Richmond and Grand Gulf May 2-14. Jackson May 14. Battle of Champion's Hill May 16. Big Black May 17. Siege of Vicksburg, Miss., May 18-July 4. (1st at Vicksburg.) Assaults on Vicksburg May 19 and 22. Advance on Jackson, Miss., July 4-10. Siege of Jackson July 10-17. At Big Black till September, 1863. Moved to Memphis, Tenn., thence to Chattanooga, Tenn., September 27-November 21. Action at Colliersville October 11. Operations on the Memphis & Charleston Railroad in Alabama October 20-29. Bear Creek, Tuscumbia, October 27. Chattanooga-Ringgold Campaign November 23-27. Battles of Chattanooga November 23-25. Foot of Missionary Ridge November 24. March to relief of Knoxville, Tenn., November 28-December 17. At Bellefonte, Ala., till January 1, 1864, and at Huntsville, Ala., till April 4. Duty at Nashville, Tenn. Guard at Headquarters of General Sherman till July, 1865. Battle of Nashville December 15-16, 1864. Moved to St. Louis, Mo., July 13-20, 1865. To Jefferson Barracks August 8. To Fort Leavenworth, Kansas, August 24, thence moved to Fort Riley, Kansas. Company "E" at Newport Barracks, Ky., September 4, 1862, to May 4, 1863. At Dayton, Ohio, till June 6. Moved to Vicksburg, Miss., June 6-16.

Regiment lost during service 3 Officers and 55 Enlisted men killed and mortally wounded and 7 Officers and 121 Enlisted men by disease. Total 186.

14th REGIMENT INFANTRY.

Organized by direction of the President May 4, 1861, and confirmed by Act of Congress July 29, 1861. Organized at Fort Trumbull, Conn. Moved to Perryville, Md., October, 1861, and duty there till March, 1862. Moved to Washington, D. C. Attached to Sykes' Regular Infantry, Reserve Brigade, Army of the Potomac, to May, 1862. 1st Brigade, 2nd Division, 5th Army Corps, Army of the Potomac, to March, 1864. 4th Brigade, 1st Division, 5th Army Corps, to April, 1864. 1st Brigade, 1st Division, 5th Army Corps, to June, 1864. 1st Brigade, 2nd Division, 5th Army Corps, to November, 1864. Dept. of the East to April, 1865. Provost Guard, Army of the Potomac, to June, 1865. Dept. of Virginia to ———

SERVICE.—Moved to the Virginia Peninsula March, 1862. Siege of Yorktown, Va., April 5-May 4. Seven days before Richmond June 25-July 1. Battles of Mechanicsville June 26. Gaines' Mill June 27. Turkey Bridge June 30. Malvern Hill July 1. At Harrison's Landing till August 16. Movement to Fortress Monroe, thence to Centreville August 16-28. Pope's Campaign in Northern Virginia August 28-September 2. Battles of Groveton August 29. Bull Run August 30. Maryland Campaign September 6-22. Battle of Antietam September 16-17. Shepherdstown Ford September 19-20. At Sharpsburg, Md., till October 29. Kearneysville and Shepherdstown October 16-17. Movement to Falmouth, Va., October 29-November 19. Snicker's Gap November 3. Battle of Fredericksburg, Va., December 12-15. "Mud March" January 20-24, 1863. Chancellorsville Campaign April 27-May 6. Battle of Chancellorsville May 1-5. Gettysburg (Pa.) Campaign June 11-July 24. Battle of Gettysburg, Pa., July 1-3. Pursuit of Lee July 5-24. Moved to New York August 13-16, and duty there till September 14. Rejoined army at Culpeper, Va., September 24. Bristoe Campaign October 9-22. Advance to line of the Rappahannock November 7-8. Mine Run Campaign November 26-December 2. Rapidan Campaign May 4-June 12, 1864. Battles of the Wilderness May 5-7; Spottsylvania Court House May 8-21; North Anna River May 22-26. On line of the Pamunkey May 26-28. Totopotomoy May 28-31. Cold Harbor June 1-12. Bethesda Church June 1-3. Before Petersburg June 16-18. Siege of Petersburg June 16 to November 2. Mine Explosion, Petersburg, July 30 (Reserve). Weldon Railroad August 18-21. Poplar Springs Church, Peeble's Farm, September 29-October 2. Boydton Plank Road, Hatcher's Run, October 27-28. Ordered to New York November 1, thence to Elmira, N. Y., and duty there till March, 1865. Ordered to the field, arriving at City Point, Va., April 4. Provost duty till May, and at Richmond, Va., till ———

Regiment lost during service 8 Officers and 158 Enlisted men killed and mortally wounded and 2 Officers and 206 Enlisted men by disease. Total 374.

15th REGIMENT INFANTRY.

Organized by direction of the President May 4, 1861, and confirmed by Act of Congress July 29, 1861. Regiment organized at Wheeling, W. Va. Ordered to Kentucky October, 1861. Attached to Rousseau's Brigade, McCook's Command, at Nolin, Ky., Dept. of the Ohio, to November, 1861. 4th Brigade, Army of the Ohio, to December, 1861. 4th Brigade, 2nd Division, Army of the Ohio, to September, 1862. 4th Brigade, 2nd Division, 1st Corps, Army of the Ohio, to November, 1862. 3rd Brigade, 2nd Division, Right Wing 14th Army Corps, Army of the Cumberland, to December, 1862. 4th Brigade, 1st Division (Centre), 14th Army Corps, to January, 1863. 4th Brigade, 1st Division, 14th Army Corps, to April, 1863. 3rd Brigade, 1st Division, 14th Army Corps, to October, 1863. 2nd Brigade, 1st Division, 14th Army Corps, to October, 1864. Regular Brigade, Chattanooga, Tenn., Dept. of the Cumberland, to November, 1864. 1st Brigade, 1st Separate Division, District of the Etowah, Dept. of the Cumberland, to July, 1865.

SERVICE.—Camp at Bacon Creek and Green River, Ky., till February, 1862. March to Nashville, Tenn., February 14-25. Occupation of Nashville February 25. March to Duck River March 16-21, and to Savannah, Tenn., March 31-April 6. Battle of Shiloh, Tenn., April 6-7. Advance on and siege of Corinth, Miss., April 29-May 30. At Corinth till June 10. Buell's Campaign in North Alabama and Middle Tennessee June to August. March to Louisville, Ky., in pursuit of Bragg August 21-September 26. Pursuit of Bragg to Crab Orchard, Ky., October 1-15. Lawrenceburg-Dogwalk October 8. Perryville October 9. March to Nashville, Tenn., October 17-November 7, and duty there till December 26. Advance on Murfreesboro, Tenn., December 26-30. Battle of Stone's River December 30-31, 1862, and January 1-3, 1863. Duty near Murfreesboro till June. Middle Tennessee (or Tullahoma) Campaign June 23-July 7. Hoover's Gap June 24-26. Beech Grove June 26. Occupation of Middle Tennessee till August 16. Passage

of the Cumberland Mountains and Tennessee River and Chickamauga (Ga.) Campaign August 16-September 22. Battle of Chickamauga September 19-21. Rossville Gap September 21. Siege of Chattanooga, Tenn., September 24-November 23. Reopening Tennessee River October 26-29. Battles of Chattanooga November 23-25. Orchard Knob November 23-24. Mission Ridge November 25. Graysville November 26. Pea Vine Valley November 27. Reconnoissance of Dalton, Ga., February 22-27, 1864. Tunnel Hill, Buzzard's Roost Gap and Rocky Faced Ridge February 23-25. Atlanta (Ga.) Campaign May 1-September 8. Rocky Faced Ridge May 8-11. Battle of Resaca May 14-15. Advance on Dallas May 18-25. Operations on line of Pumpkin Vine Creek and battles about Dallas, New Hope Church and Allatoona Hills May 25-June 5. Pickett's Mills May 27. Operations about Marietta and against Kenesaw Mountain June 10-July 2. Pine Hill June 11-14. Lost Mountain June 15-17. Assault on Kenesaw June 27. Ruff's Station, Smyrna Camp Ground, July 4. Chattahoochie River July 5-17. Peach Tree Creek July 19-20. Siege of Atlanta July 22-August 25. Utoy Creek August 5-7. Flank movement on Jonesboro August 25-30. Battle of Jonesboro August 31-September 1. At Atlanta, Ga., till September 28. Moved to Chattanooga September 28-30, thence to Lookout Mountain and duty there till July, 1865.

Regiment lost during service 3 Officers and 131 Enlisted men killed and mortally wounded and 1 Officer and 228 Enlisted men by disease. Total 363.

16th REGIMENT INFANTRY.

Organized by direction of the President May 4, 1861, and confirmed by Act of Congress July 29, 1861. Organized at Chicago, Ill. Ordered to Kentucky October, 1861. Attached to 4th Brigade, Army of the Ohio, to December, 1861. 4th Brigade, 2nd Division, Army of the Ohio, to September, 1862. 4th Brigade, 2nd Division, 1st Corps, Army of the Ohio, to November, 1862. 3rd Brigade, 2nd Division, Right Wing 14th Army Corps, Army of the Cumberland, to December, 1862. 4th Brigade, 1st Division (Centre), 14th Army Corps, to January, 1863. 4th Brigade, 1st Division, 14th Army Corps, to April, 1863. 3rd Brigade, 1st Division, 14th Army Corps, to October, 1863. 2nd Brigade, 1st Division, 14th Army Corps, to October, 1864. Regular Brigade, Chattanooga, Tenn., Dept. of the Cumberland, to November, 1864. 1st Brigade, 1st Separate Division, District of the Etowah, Dept. of the Cumberland, to July, 1865.

SERVICE.—Camp at Bacon Creek and Green River, Ky., till February, 1862. March to Nashville, Tenn., February 14-25. Occupation of Nashville February 25. March to Duck River March 16-21, and to Savannah, Tenn., March 31-April 6. Battle of Shiloh, Tenn., April 6-7. Advance on and siege of Corinth, Miss., April 29-May 30. Buell's Campaign in North Alabama and Middle Tennessee June to August. March to Louisville, Ky., in pursuit of Bragg August 21-September 26. Pursuit of Bragg to Crab Orchard, Ky., October 1-15. Lawrenceburg-Dog Walk October 8. Perryville October 9. March to Nashville, Tenn., October 17-November 7, and duty there till December 26. Advance on Murfreesboro, Tenn., December 26-30. Battle of Stone's River December 30-31, 1862, and January 1-3, 1863. Duty at Murfreesboro till June. Middle Tennessee (or Tullahoma) Campaign June 23-July 7. Hoover's Gap June 24-26. Beech Grove June 26. Occupation of Middle Tennessee till August 16. Passage of the Cumberland Mountains and Tennessee River and Chickamauga (Ga.) Campaign August 16-September 22. Battle of Chickamauga September 19-21. Rossville Gap September 21. Siege of Chattanooga, Tenn., September 24-November 23. Reopening Tennessee River October 26-29. Battles of Chattanooga November 23-25. Orchard Knob November 23-24. Mission Ridge November 25. Graysville November 26. Pea Vine Valley November 27. Reconnoissance of Dalton, Ga., February 22-27, 1864. Tunnel Hill, Buzzard's Roost Gap and Rocky Faced

Ridge February 23-25. Atlanta (Ga.) Campaign May 1-September 8. Rocky Faced Ridge May 8-11. Battle of Resaca May 14-15. Advance on Dallas May 18-25. Operations on line of Pumpkin Vine Creek and battles about Dallas, New Hope Church and Allatoona Hills May 25-June 5. Pickett's Mills May 27. Operations about Marietta and against Kenesaw Mountain June 10-July 2. Pine Hill June 11-14. Lost Mountain June 15-17. Assault on Kenesaw June 27. Ruff's Station, Smyrna Camp Ground, July 4. Chattahoochie River July 5-17. Peach Tree Creek July 19-20. Siege of Atlanta July 22-August 25. Utoy Creek August 5-7. Flank movement on Jonesboro August 25-30. Battle of Jonesboro August 31-September 1. At Atlanta till September 28. Moved to Chattanooga, Tenn., September 28-30, thence to Lookout Mountain and duty there till July, 1865.

Regiment lost during service 7 Officers and 92 Enlisted men killed and mortally wounded and 2 Officers and 179 Enlisted men by disease. Total 280.

17th REGIMENT INFANTRY.

Organized by direction of the President May 4, 1861, and confirmed July 29, 1861, by Act of Congress. Regiment organized at Fort Preble, Maine. Moved to Washington, D. C., March 4, 1862. Attached to Sykes' Regular Infantry, Reserve Brigade, Army of the Potomac, to May, 1862. 2nd Brigade, 2nd Division, 5th Army Corps, to September, 1863. 1st Brigade, 2nd Division, 5th Army Corps, to March, 1864. 4th Brigade, 1st Division, 5th Army Corps, to April, 1864. 1st Brigade, 1st Division, 5th Army Corps, to June, 1864. 1st Brigade, 2nd Division, 5th Army Corps, to October, 1864. Dept. of the East to October, 1865.

SERVICE.—Moved to the Virginia Peninsula March, 1862. Siege of Yorktown, Va., April 5-May 4. Seven days before Richmond June 25-July 1. Battles of Mechanicsville June 26; Gaines' Mill June 27; Turkey Bridge June 30; Malvern Hill July 1. At Harrison's Landing till August 16. Movement to Fortress Monroe, thence to Centreville August 16-28. Pope's Campaign in Northern Virginia August 28-September 2. Battles of Groveton August 29. Bull Run August 30. Maryland Campaign September 6-22. Battle of Antietam, Md., September 16-17. Shepherdstown Ford September 19-20. At Sharpsburg, Md., till October 29. Movement to Falmouth, Va., October 29-November 19. Battle of Fredericksburg, Va., December 12-15. "Mud March" January 20-24, 1863. Chancellorsville Campaign April 27-May 6. Battle of Chancellorsville May 1-5. Gettysburg (Pa.) Campaign June 11-July 24. Battle of Gettysburg, Pa., July 1-3. Pursuit of Lee July 5-24. At New York on special duty August 14-September 21. Rejoined army at Culpeper, Va. Bristoe Campaign October 9-22. Advance to line of the Rappahannock November 7-8. Mine Run Campaign November 26-December 2. Rapidan Campaign May 4-June 12. Battles of the Wilderness May 5-7; Spottsylvania Court House May 8-21; North Anna River May 22-26. On line of the Pamunkey May 26-28. Totopotomoy May 28-31. Cold Harbor June 1-12. Bethesda Church June 1-3. Before Petersburg June 16-18. Siege of Petersburg June 16-October 13. Mine Explosion, Petersburg, July 30 (Reserve). Weldon Railroad August 18-21. Poplar Springs Church, Peeble's Farm, September 29-October 2. Ordered to New York October 13, 1864, and duty at Fort Lafayette, New York Harbor, till October, 1865.

Regiment lost during service 9 Officers and 92 Enlisted men killed and mortally wounded and 2 Officers and 100 Enlisted men by disease. Total 203.

18th REGIMENT INFANTRY.

Organized by direction of the President May 4, 1861, and confirmed by Act of Congress July 29, 1861. Regiment organized at Columbus, Ohio. Ordered to Louisville, Ky., December 2, 1861. Attached to 3rd Brigade, 1st Division, Army of the Ohio, to September, 1862. 3rd Brigade, 1st Division, 3rd Corps, Army of the Ohio, to November, 1862. 3rd Brigade, 3rd Division (Centre), 14th Army Corps, Army of the Cumberland, to December, 1862. 4th Brigade, 1st Division (Centre), 14th Army Corps, to January, 1863. 4th Brigade, 1st Division, 14th Army Corps, to April, 1863. 3rd Brigade, 1st Division, 14th Army Corps, to October, 1863. 2nd Brigade, 1st Division, 14th Army Corps, to October, 1864. Regular Brigade, Chattanooga, Tenn., Dept. of the Cumberland, to November, 1864. 1st Brigade, 1st Separate Division, District of the Etowah, Dept. of the Cumberland, to July, 1865.

SERVICE.—Operations in Southeast Kentucky December, 1861, to February, 1862. Advance to Camp Hamilton, Ky., January 1-17, 1862. Logan's Cross Roads, Mill Springs, January 19-20. Moved to Louisville, Ky., thence to Nashville, Tenn., February 10-March 2. March to Savannah, Tenn., March 20-April 6. Battle of Shiloh, Tenn., April 6-7. Advance on and siege of Corinth, Miss., April 29-May 30. Buell's Campaign in North Alabama and Middle Tennessee June to August. March to Louisville, Ky., in pursuit of Bragg August 21-September 26. Pursuit of Bragg into Kentucky October 1-22. Near Bardstown October 6. Battle of Perryville October 8. March to Nashville, Tenn., October 22-November 7, and duty there till December 26. Advance on Murfreesboro December 26-30. Battle of Stone's River December 30-31, 1862, and January 1-3, 1863. Duty near Murfreesboro till June. Eaglesville March 2 (Detachment). Middle Tennessee (or Tullahoma) Campaign June 23-July 7. Hoover's Gap June 24-26. Beech Grove June 26. Occupation of Middle Tennessee till August 16. Passage of the Cumberland Mountains and Tennessee River and Chickamauga (Ga.) Campaign August 16-September 22. Battle of Chickamauga, Ga., September 19-21. Rossville Gap September 21. Siege of Chattanooga, Tenn., September 24-November 23. Reopening Tennessee River October 26-29. Battles of Chattanooga November 23-27. Orchard Knob November 23-24. Mission Ridge November 25. Graysville November 26. Pea Vine Creek November 27. Reconnoissance of Dalton, Ga., February 22-27, 1864. Tunnel Hill, Buzzard's Roost Gap and Rocky Faced Ridge February 23-25. Atlanta (Ga.) Campaign May 1-September 8. Rocky Faced Ridge May 8-11. Battle of Resaca May 14-15. Advance on Dallas May 18-25. Operations on line of Pumpkin Vine Creek and battles about Dallas, New Hope Church and Allatoona Hills May 25-June 5. Pickett's Mills May 27. Operations about Marietta and against Kenesaw Mountain June 10-July 2. Pine Hill June 11-14. Lost Mountain June 15-17. Assault on Kenesaw Mountain June 27. Ruff's Station, Smyrna Camp Ground, July 4. Chattahoochie River July 5-17. Peach Tree Creek July 19-20. Siege of Atlanta July 22-August 25. Utoy Creek August 5-7. Flank movement on Jonesboro August 25-30. Battle of Jonesboro August 31-September 1. At Atlanta till September 28. Moved to Chattanooga, Tenn., September 28-30, thence to Lookout Mountain and duty there till July, 1865.

Regiment lost during service 9 Officers and 209 Enlisted men killed and mortally wounded and 6 Officers and 246 Enlisted men by disease. Total 470.

19th REGIMENT INFANTRY.

Organized by direction of the President May 4, 1861, and confirmed by Act of Congress July 29, 1861. Organized at Indianapolis, Ind. Ordered to Kentucky October, 1861. Attached to Rousseau's Brigade, McCook's Command, at Nolin, Ky., Army of the Ohio, to November, 1861. 4th Brigade, Army of the Ohio, to December, 1861. 4th Brigade, 2nd Division, Army of the Ohio, to September, 1862. 4th Brigade, 2nd Division, 1st Army Corps, Army of the Ohio, to November, 1862. 3rd Brigade, 2nd Division, Right Wing 14th Army Corps, Army of the Cumberland, to December, 1862. 4th Brigade, 1st Division (Centre), 14th Army Corps, to January, 1863. 4th Brigade, 1st Division, 14th Army Corps, to April, 1863. 3rd Brigade, 1st Division, 14th Army Corps, to October, 1863. 2nd Brigade, 1st Division, 14th Army Corps, to October, 1864. Regular Brigade, Chattanooga, Tenn., Dept. of the Cumberland, to November, 1864. 1st Brigade, 1st Separate Division, District of the Etowah, Dept. of the Cumberland, to July, 1862.

SERVICE.—Camp at Bacon Creek and Green River, Ky., till February, 1862. March to Nashville, Tenn., February 14-25. Occupation of Nashville February 25. March to Duck River March 16-21, and to Savannah, Tenn., March 31-April 6. Battle of Shiloh April 6-7. Advance on and siege of Corinth, Miss., April 29-May 30. Buell's Campaign in North Alabama and Middle Tennessee June to August. March to Louisville, Ky., in pursuit of Bragg August 21-September 26. Pursuit of Bragg to Crab Orchard, Ky., October 1-15. Lawrenceburg Dog Walk October 8. Perryville October 9. March to Nashville, Tenn., October 17-November 7, and duty there till November 26. Advance on Murfreesboro December 26-30. Battle of Stone's River December 30-31, 1862, and January 1-3, 1863. Duty at Murfreesboro till June. Middle Tennessee (or Tullahoma) Campaign June 23-July 7. Hoover's Gap June 24-26. Beech Grove June 26. Occupation of Middle Tennessee till August 16. Passage of the Cumberland Mountains and Tennessee River and Chickamauga (Ga.) Campaign August 16-September 22. Battle of Chickamauga, Ga., September 19-21. Rossville Gap September 21. Siege of Chattanooga, Tenn., September 24-November 23. Reopening Tennessee River October 26-29. Battles of Chattanooga November 23-27; Orchard Knob November 23-24; Mission Ridge November 25; Graysville November 26; Pea Vine Creek November 27. Reconnoissance to Dalton, Ga., February 22-27, 1864. Tunnel Hill, Buzzard's Roost Gap and Rocky Faced Ridge February 23-25. Atlanta (Ga.) Campaign May 1 to September 8. Rocky Faced Ridge May 8-11. Battle of Resaca May 14-15. Advance on Dallas May 18-25. Operations on line of Pumpkin Vine Creek and battles about Dallas, New Hope Church and Allatoona Hills May 25-June 5. Pickett's Mills May 27. Operations about Marietta and against Kenesaw Mountain June 10-July 2. Pine Hill June 11-14. Lost Mountain June 15-17. Assault on Kenesaw Mountain June 27. Ruff's Station, Smyrna Camp Ground, July 4. Chattahoochie River July 5-17. Peach Tree Creek July 19-20. Siege of Atlanta July 22-August 25. Utoy Creek August 5-7. Flank movement on Jonesboro August 25-30. Battle of Jonesboro August 31-September 1. At Atlanta till September 28. Moved to Chattanooga, Tenn., September 28-30, thence to Lookout Mountain and duty there till July, 1865.

Companies "G" and "H" 1st Battalion ordered from Indianapolis, Ind., to Washington, D. C., May, 1862. Attached to Sturgis' Command, Military District of Washington, to October, 1862. 2nd Brigade, 2nd Division, 5th Army Corps, Army of the Potomac, to December, 1862.

Provost guard duty in the Defences of Washington, D. C., till September, 1862. Maryland Campaign September 6-22. Battle of Antietam September 16-17. Movement to Falmouth, Va., October 29-November 19. Battle of Fredericksburg, Va., December 12-15. Rejoined Regiment in Dept. of the Cumberland January, 1863.

Regiment lost during service 3 Officers and 55 Enlisted men killed and mortally wounded and 2 Officers and 124 Enlisted men by disease. Total 184.

UNITED STATES VOLUNTEERS.

1st REGIMENT SHARPSHOOTERS.

Companies "A," "D" and "H" organized at New York City September, 1861; Company "B" at Albany, N. Y., September, 1861; Company "C" in Michigan August 21, 1861; Company "E" in New Hampshire September 9, 1861; Company "F" in Vermont September 13, 1861; Company "G" in Wisconsin September 19, 1861; Company "I" in Michigan March 4, 1862, and Company "K" in Michigan March 30, 1862. Most of Regiment concentrated at Weehawken, N. J., September, 1861, and moved to Washington, D. C., September 24-25. Mus-

tered in November 29, 1861. Served Unattached, Army of the Potomac, and Martindale's Brigade, Fitz John Porter's Division, Army of the Potomac, to March, 1862. Unassigned, 1st Division, 3rd Army Corps, Army of the Potomac, to May, 1862. 3rd Brigade, 1st Division, 5th Army Corps, to March, 1863. 3rd Brigade, 3rd Division, 3rd Army Corps, to June, 1863. 2nd Brigade, 1st Division, 3rd Army Corps, to September, 1863. 3rd Brigade, 1st Division, 3rd Army Corps, to March, 1864. 2nd Brigade, 3rd Division, 2nd Army Corps, to December, 1864.

SERVICE.—Duty in the Defences of Washington, D. C., till March, 1862. Moved to Fortress Monroe, Va., March 22. Advance on Yorktown April 1-5. Great Bethel and Howard's Bridge April 4. Warwick Road April 5. Siege of Yorktown April 5-May 4. Battle of Williamsburg May 5. Battle of Hanover Court House May 27. Operations about Hanover Court House April 27-29. Seven days before Richmond June 25-July 1. Battles of Mechanicsville June 26. Gaines' Mill June 27. Peach Orchard and Savage Station June 29. Turkey Bridge, White Oak Swamp, June 30. Malvern Hill July 1. Duty at Harrison's Landing till August 15. Movement to Centreville August 15-28. Pope's Campaign in Northern Virginia August 28-September 2. Battles of Groveton August 29; Bull Run August 30. Maryland Campaign September 6-22. Battle of South Mountain September 14. Battle of Antietam September 16-17. Sharpsburg, Shepherdstown Ford, September 19. Movement to Falmouth October 29-November 17. Battle of Fredericksburg, Va., December 12-15. Expedition from Potomac Creek to Richard's and Ellis' Fords, Rappahannock River, December 29-30. "Mud March" January 20-24, 1863. At Falmouth till April. Chancellorsville Campaign April 27-May 6. Battle of Chancellorsville May 1-5. Gettysburg (Pa.) Campaign June 11-July 24. Battle of Gettysburg, Pa., July 1-3. Pursuit of Lee to Manassas Gap, Va., July 5-24. Wapping Heights, Va., July 23. Bristoe Campaign October 9-22. Auburn and Bristoe October 14. Advance to line of the Rappahannock November 7-8. Kelly's Ford November 7. Mine Run Campaign November 26-December 2. Payne's Farm November 27. Demonstration on the Rapidan February 6-7, 1864. Campaign from the Rapidan to the James River May 4-June 15. Battles of the Wilderness May 5-7; Laurel Hill May 8; Spottsylvania May 8-12; Po River May 10; Spottsylvania Court House May 12-21. Assault on the Salient, "Bloody Angle," May 12. Harris Farm, Fredericksburg Road, May 19. North Anna River May 23-26. On line of the Pamunkey May 26-28. Totopotomoy May 28-31. Hanovertown May 30-31. Cold Harbor June 1-12. Before Petersburg June 16-19. Siege of Petersburg June 16 to December 31, 1864. Jerusalem Plank Road, Weldon Railroad, June 22-23. Demonstration north of the James July 27-29. Deep Bottom July 28-29. Demonstration north of the James at Deep Bottom August 13-20. Strawberry Plains August 14-18. Poplar Springs Church, Peeble's Farm, September 29-October 2. Boydton Plank Road, Hatcher's Run, October 27-28. Expedition to Weldon Railroad December 7-12. Company "A" mustered out August 19, Company "D" mustered out August 28, 1864. Veterans and Recruits assigned to Companies "I" and "K." Veterans of Company "H" to Company "D" September 15. Regiment consolidated with 2nd Regiment Sharpshooters December 31, 1864.

Regiment lost during service 10 Officers and 143 Enlisted men killed and mortally wounded and 1 Officer and 128 Enlisted men by disease. Total 282.

2nd REGIMENT SHARPSHOOTERS.

Organized by Companies as follows: Company "A" in Minnesota October 5, 1861; Company "B" in Michigan October 4, 1861; Company "C" in Pennsylvania October 4, 1861; Company "D" in Maine November 2, 1861; Company "E" in Vermont November 9, 1861; Company "F" in New Hampshire November 28, 1861; Company "G" in New Hampshire December 10, 1861; Company "H" in Vermont December 31, 1861. Companies moved to Washington, D. C., and duty in the Defences of that city till April, 1862. Attached to Augur's Brigade, King's 1st Division, McDowell's 1st Army Corps, Army of the Potomac, March to April, 1862. 1st Brigade, King's Division, Dept. of the Rappahannock, to June, 1862. 1st Brigade, 1st Division, 3rd Army Corps, Army of Virginia, to September, 1862. 1st Brigade, 1st Division, 1st Army Corps, Army of the Potomac, to March, 1863. 3rd Brigade, 3rd Division, 3rd Army Corps, Army of the Potomac, to June, 1863. 2nd Brigade, 1st Division, 3rd Army Corps, to September, 1863. 3rd Brigade, 1st Division, 3rd Army Corps, to March, 1864. 1st Brigade, 3rd Division, 2nd Army Corps, to February, 1865.

SERVICE.—Moved to Bristoe Station, Va., April 5-6; thence to Falmouth, Va., April 15-19. Duty at Falmouth till May 25. McDowell's advance on Richmond May 25-29. Operations against Jackson June 1-21. Duty at Falmouth till August. Blackburn's Ford July 19. Reconnoissance to Orange Court House July 24-26. Pope's Campaign in Northern Virginia August 16-September 2. Fords of the Rappahannock August 21-23. Sulphur Springs August 26. Battles of Groveton August 29; Bull Run August 30. Maryland Campaign September 6-22. Battles of South Mountain September 14; Antietam September 16-17. Camp near Sharpsburg till October 29. Movement to Falmouth, Va., October 29-November 17. Battle of Fredericksburg December 12-15. "Mud March" January 20-24, 1863. At Falmouth till April. Chancellorsville Campaign April 27-May 6. Battle of Chancellorsville May 1-5. Gettysburg (Pa.) Campaign June 11-July 24. Battle of Gettysburg, Pa., July 1-3. Pursuit of Lee July 5-24. Action at Wapping Heights, Va., July 23. Bristoe Campaign October 9-22. Auburn and Bristoe October 14. Advance to line of the Rappahannock November 7-8. Kelly's Ford November 7. Brandy Station November 8. Mine Run Campaign November 26-December 2. Payne's Farm November 27. Demonstration on the Rapidan February 6-7, 1864. Campaign from the Rapidan to the James River May 4-June 15. Battles of the Wilderness May 5-7; Laurel Hill May 8; Spottsylvania May 8-12; Po River May 10; Spottsylvania Court House May 12-21. Assault on the Salient, "Bloody Angle," May 12. Harris Farm, Fredericksburg Road, May 19. North Anna River May 23-26. On line of the Pamunkey May 26-28. Totopotomoy May 28-31. Cold Harbor June 1-12. Before Petersburg June 16-19. Siege of Petersburg June 16, 1864, to February 20, 1865. Jerusalem Plank Road, Weldon Railroad, June 22-23, 1864. Demonstration north of the James River July 27-29. Deep Bottom July 28-29. Demonstration north of the James August 13-20. Strawberry Plains, Deep Bottom, August 14-18. Poplar Springs Church, Peeble's Farm, September 29-October 2. Boydton Plank Road, Hatcher's Run, October 27-28. Expedition to Weldon Railroad December 7-12. Dabney's Mills, Hatcher's Run, February 5-7, 1865. Discontinued February 20, 1865. Company "A" transferred to 1st Minnesota Infantry, Company "B" to 5th Michigan Infantry, Company "C" to 105th Pennsylvania Infantry, Company "D" to 17th Maine Infantry, Company "F" to 5th New Hampshire Infantry, Company "G" to 5th New Hampshire Infantry, and Company "H" to 4th Vermont Infantry.

Regiment lost during service 8 Officers and 117 Enlisted men killed and mortally wounded and 2 Officers and 123 Enlisted men by disease. Total 250.

1st REGIMENT INFANTRY.

Organized at Point Lookout, Md., January 21 to April 22, 1864. Moved to Norfolk, Va., and provost duty there and at Portsmouth, Va., District of Eastern Virginia, Dept. of Virginia and North Carolina, to August, 1864. Ordered to Milwaukee, Wis., thence to St. Louis, Mo., arriving there August 22. (4 Cos. remained in Wisconsin till September, then ordered to Minnesota.) Six Companies moved from St. Louis to Fort Rice, Dakota Territory, arriving there October 17, and garrison duty there; at Fort Berthold and at Fort Union,

mouth of the Yellowstone, till October, 1865. Moved to St. Louis, Mo., and mustered out November 27, 1865. Four Companies on duty in District of Minnesota till May, 1866. Mustered out May 21, 1866.

2nd REGIMENT INFANTRY.

Organized at Rock Island, Ill., October, 1864. Ordered to Dept. of Missouri and assigned to duty in District of Upper Arkansas along the Santa Fe Road from Little Arkansas River to Fort Dodge and Cimaron Crossing. Stationed by Companies at Fort Riley, Salem, Fort Ellsworth, Fort Learned, Fort Zarah and Fort Scott, Kansas, on guard duty and operating against Indians till November, 1865. Mustered out November 7, 1865.

3rd REGIMENT INFANTRY.

Organized at Rock Island, Ill., October, 1864. Ordered to Dept. of Missouri, arriving at Fort Kearney, Neb., April 9, 1865, and assigned to duty in the District of Nebraska and Colorado. Stationed by Companies. "A" and "B" at Fort Kearney, "E" and "F" at Fort Rankin, "G" and "H" at Julesburg Junction, Colo., and "C" and "D" at Cottonwood protecting overland mail routes from Indian attacks. Skirmish at Elm Creek May 20, 1865. Mustered out November 29, 1865.

4th REGIMENT INFANTRY.

Organized at Point Lookout, Md., October 31, 1864. Duty at Portsmouth, Va., District of Eastern Virginia, Dept. of Virginia and North Carolina, and in District of the Northwest, Dept. of Missouri, till July, 1866. Mustered out July 2, 1866.

5th REGIMENT INFANTRY.

Organized at Alton and Camp Douglas, Ill., March to May, 1865. Ordered to Fort Leavenworth, Kansas, May 3, 1865. Assigned to duty in District of Upper Arkansas from Little Arkansas River to Fort Dodge and Cimaron Crossing. Duty in Districts of Nebraska, Colorado and Utah and the Plains till November, 1866. Mustered out November 13, 1866.

6th REGIMENT INFANTRY.

Organized at Columbus, Ohio, Camp Morton, Ind., and Camp Douglas, Ill., April 2, 1865. Ordered to Fort Leavenworth, Kansas, May, 1865, arriving there May 11. Moved to Fort Kearney, Neb., May 14; thence to Julesburg, Colo. Duty in District of the Plains and Utah till November, 1866. Mustered out November 3, 1866.

1st INDEPENDENT COMPANY INFANTRY.

Organized at Baltimore, Md., as Company "G" 1st Connecticut Cavalry. At Baltimore and in Middle Department till August, 1864. Ordered to Milwaukee, Wis., thence to Minnesota, and duty at various points in District of Minnesota operating against Indians till November, 1865. Designation changed to 1st Independent Company April 6, 1865. Mustered out November 16, 1865.

1st COMPANY PONTONEERS.

Organized at New Orleans, La., February 28, 1865. Mustered out May 12, 1865.

UNITED STATES VETERAN VOLUNTEERS.

1st REGIMENT ENGINEERS.

Organized in the Dept. of the Cumberland from Pioneer Brigade, Dept. of the Cumberland, July 8, 1864. Duty in the Dept. of the Cumberland repairing railroads, building block houses and bridges and in general engineering duties till September, 1865. Mustered out September 26, 1865.

1st REGIMENT INFANTRY.

Organized at Washington, D. C., December 24, 1864, to March 1, 1865. Attached to Hancock's 1st Veteran Corps March, 1865. 1st Brigade, 1st Veteran Corps, to April, 1865. 2nd Brigade, Provisional Division, Army of the Shenandoah, to June, 1865. Middle Department to July, 1866.

SERVICE.—Duty at Washington, D. C., in the Shenandoah Valley and in the Middle Department till July, 1866. Mustered out January 10 to July 21, 1866.

2nd REGIMENT INFANTRY.

Organized at Camp Stoneman, D. C., January to March, 1865. Attached to 2nd Brigade, 1st Division, 1st Veteran Corps, to June, 1865. District of New York, Dept. of the East, to August, 1866. Mustered out August 1, 1866.

3rd REGIMENT INFANTRY.

Organized at Camp Stoneman, D. C., February to March, 1865. Attached to 2nd Brigade, Provisional Division, Army of the Shenandoah, to June, 1865. Camp Butler, Ill., to July, 1866. Duty in the Defences of Washington, D. C., in the Shenandoah Valley, Va., and at Camp Butler, Ill. Mustered out July 20, 1866.

4th REGIMENT INFANTRY.

Organized at Camp Stoneman, D. C., December, 1864, to May, 1865. Mustered out August 6, 1866.

5th REGIMENT INFANTRY.

Organized at Camp Stoneman, D. C., January to April, 1865. Duty at Washington, D. C., Providence, R. I., Fort Wadsworth, N. Y., and Hart's Island, N. Y., till May, 1866. Mustered out May 28, 1866.

6th REGIMENT INFANTRY.

Organized at Camp Stoneman, D. C., March and April, 1865. Mustered out March 15 to July 27, 1866.

7th REGIMENT INFANTRY.

Organized at Camp Stoneman, D. C., January 25 to April 14, 1865. Attached to 3rd Brigade, 1st Division, 1st Veteran Corps, to June, 1865. Duty at Washington, D. C., Shenandoah Valley, Va., in Philadelphia, Pa., District and Schuylkill, Pa., District till July, 1866. Mustered out July 23, 1866.

8th REGIMENT INFANTRY.

Organized at Camp Stoneman, D. C., February to April, 1865. Mustered out July 28, 1866.

9th REGIMENT INFANTRY.

Organized at Camp Stoneman, D. C., March to June, 1865. Mustered out February 26 to July 1, 1866.

CORPS DE AFRIQUE.—UNITED STATES COLORED VOLUNTEERS.

1st REGIMENT CAVALRY.

Organized at New Orleans, La., September 12, 1863. Attached to Defences of New Orleans, La., to April, 1864. Designation of Regiment changed to 4th United States Colored Cavalry April 4, 1864 (which see).

1st REGIMENT HEAVY ARTILLERY.

Organized November 19, 1863, from 1st Louisiana Colored Heavy Artillery. Garrison Artillery in Defences of New Orleans to April, 1864. Designation of Regiment changed to 10th United States Colored Heavy Artillery May 21, 1864 (which see).

1st REGIMENT ENGINEERS.

Organized at Camp Parapet, La., April 28, 1863. Attached to 1st Division, 19th Army Corps, Dept. of the Gulf, to August, 1863. Engineer Brigade, Corps de Afrique, to October, 1863. Engineer Brigade, 13th Army Corps, Dept. of the Gulf, to April, 1864.

SERVICE.—Siege of Port Hudson, La., May 24-July 8, 1863. Assaults on Port Hudson May 27 and June 14. Surrender of Port Hudson July 9. Sabine Pass Expedition September 4-11. Western Louisiana ("Teche") Campaign October 3-27. Rio Grande Expedition and operations on Coast of Texas October 27-December 2. Arkansas Pass November 17. Expedition against and capture of Fort Esperanza, Mattagorda Island, November 22-30. Duty at Brazos Island, Point

Isabel and Brownsville, Texas, till April, 1864. Designation of Regiment changed to 95th United States Colored Troops April 4, 1864 (which see).

2nd REGIMENT ENGINEERS.

Organized at New Orleans, La., August 15, 1863. Attached to Engineer Brigade, Dept. of the Gulf, to October, 1863. Unattached, 13th Army Corps, Dept. of the Gulf, to March, 1864. Provisional Brigade, 2nd Division, 13th Army Corps, Texas, Dept. of the Gulf, to April, 1864.

SERVICE.—Duty at New Orleans, La., till December, 1863. Ordered to Mattagorda Bay, Texas, December 5. Engaged in engineering duty and erecting field works at De Crow's Point, Point Isabel, Fort Esperanza, Mattagorda Island, Indianola and Pass Cavallo, Texas, till April, 1864. Designation of Regiment changed to 96th United States Colored Troops April 4, 1864 (which see).

3rd REGIMENT ENGINEERS.

Organized at New Orleans, La., August 26, 1863. Attached to Engineer Brigade, Dept. of the Gulf, to October, 1863. Unattached, 13th Army Corps, Texas, Dept. of the Gulf, to March, 1864. Provisional Brigade, 13th Army Corps, Texas, Dept. of the Gulf, to April, 1864.

SERVICE.—Duty at New Orleans and Brashear City, La., till October, 1863. Ordered to Texas October, 1863, and duty there till March, 1864. Ordered to Berwick Bay, La., thence to Franklin, La. Red River Campaign March to May. In charge of Pontoon Train. Built bridge at Vermillionville Bayou March 18, and at Cane River March 30. Designation of Regiment changed to 97th United States Colored Troops April 4, 1864 (which see).

4th REGIMENT ENGINEERS.

Organized at New Orleans, La., September 3, 1863. Attached to Engineer Brigade, Dept. of the Gulf, to April, 1864. Stationed at New Orleans, Brashear City and Berwick City. Designation of Regiment changed to 98th United States Colored Troops April 4, 1864 (which see).

5th REGIMENT ENGINEERS.

Organized February 10, 1864, from 15th Corps de Afrique Infantry. Attached to Engineer Brigade, Dept. of the Gulf, to April, 1864.

SERVICE.—Stationed at Berwick City and Brashear City, La., till March, 1864. Red River Campaign March 10-May 22. Advance from Franklin to Alexandria March 14-26, with Pontoon Train. Built bridge at Vermillionville Bayou March 18, and at Cane River March 30. Designation of Regiment changed to 99th United States Colored Troops April 4, 1864 (which see).

1st REGIMENT INFANTRY.

Organized June 6, 1863, from 1st Louisiana Native Guard Infantry. Attached to Defences of New Orleans, La., to July, 1863. Port Hudson, La., to December, 1863. 1st Brigade, 1st Division, Corps de Afrique, Dept. of the Gulf, to April, 1864.

SERVICE.—Assault on Port Hudson June 14, 1863. Surrender of Port Hudson July 9. Duty at Port Hudson, La., till April, 1864. Skirmish at Jackson August 3, 1863, and at Tunica Bayou November 8. Designation of Regiment changed to 73rd United States Colored Troops April 4, 1864 (which see).

2nd REGIMENT INFANTRY.

Organized June 6, 1863, from 2nd Louisiana Native Guard Infantry. Attached to the Defences of New Orleans, Dept. of the Gulf, to September, 1863. 1st Brigade, 1st Division, Corps de Afrique, Dept. of the Gulf, to October, 1863. Defences of New Orleans to April, 1864. On garrison duty at Ship Island, Miss., June, 1863, to April, 1864. Designation of Regiment changed to 74th United States Colored Troops April 4, 1864 (which see).

3rd REGIMENT INFANTRY.

Organized June 6, 1863, from 3rd Louisiana Native Guard Infantry. Attached to 1st Division, 19th Army Corps, Dept. of the Gulf, to July, 1863. Port Hudson, La., to September, 1863. 1st Brigade, 1st Division, Corps de Afrique, Dept. of the Gulf, to April, 1864.

SERVICE.—Assault on Port Hudson, La., June 14, 1863. Surrender of Port Hudson July 9. Duty at Port Hudson till April, 1864. Skirmish at Jackson August 3, 1863. Designation of Regiment changed to 75th United States Colored Troops April 4, 1864 (which see).

4th REGIMENT INFANTRY.

Organized June 6, 1863, from 4th Louisiana Native Guard Infantry. Attached to 1st Division, 19th Army Corps, Dept. of the Gulf, to July, 1863. Defences of New Orleans to September, 1863. 2nd Brigade, 1st Division, Corps de Afrique, Dept. of the Gulf, to April, 1864.

SERVICE.—Assault on Port Hudson June 14, 1863. Surrender of Port Hudson July 9. Garrison duty at Forts St. Phillip and Jackson, Mississippi River, August 7, 1863, to February 20, 1864. Moved to Port Hudson, La., February 20-22, and duty there till April. Designation of Regiment changed to 76th United States Colored Troops April 4, 1864 (which see).

5th REGIMENT INFANTRY.

Organized at Fort St. Phillip December 8, 1863. Attached to Defences of New Orleans to January, 1864. 1st Brigade, 2nd Division, Corps de Afrique, Dept. of the Gulf, to April, 1864.

SERVICE.—Garrison duty at Fort St. Phillip, Defences of New Orleans, till April, 1864. Designation of Regiment changed to 77th United States Colored Troops April 4, 1864 (which see).

6th REGIMENT INFANTRY.

Organized at Port Hudson, La., September 4, 1863. Attached to Ullman's Brigade, Corps de Afrique, Dept. of the Gulf, to December, 1863. 2nd Brigade, 2nd Division, Corps de Afrique, to March, 1864. Garrison, Port Hudson, La., to April, 1864.

SERVICE.—Duty at Port Hudson, La., till April, 1864. Designation of Regiment changed to 78th United States Colored Troops April 4, 1864 (which see).

7th REGIMENT INFANTRY.

Organized at Port Hudson, La., August 31, 1863. Attached to Ullman's Brigade, Corps de Afrique, Dept. of the Gulf, to December, 1863. 2nd Brigade, 1st Division, Corps de Afrique, to April, 1864.

SERVICE.—Garrison duty at Port Hudson, La., till April, 1864. Skirmish at Vidalia February 7, 1864. Designation of Regiment changed to 79th United States Colored Troops April 4, 1864 (which see).

8th REGIMENT INFANTRY.

Organized at Port Hudson September 1, 1863. Attached to Ullman's Brigade, Corps de Afrique, Dept. of the Gulf, to December, 1863. 2nd Brigade, 1st Division, Corps de Afrique, to March, 1864. Garrison, Port Hudson, La., to April, 1864.

SERVICE.—Garrison duty at Port Hudson till April, 1864. Designation of Regiment changed to 80th United States Colored Troops April 4, 1864 (which see).

9th REGIMENT INFANTRY.

Organized at Port Hudson, La., September 2, 1863. Attached to Ullman's Brigade, Corps de Afrique, Dept. of the Gulf, to December, 1863. 2nd Brigade, 1st Division, Corps de Afrique, to March, 1864. Garrison, Port Hudson, to April, 1864.

SERVICE.—Garrison duty at Port Hudson, La., till April, 1864. Designation of Regiment changed to 81st United States Colored Troops April 4, 1864 (which see).

10th REGIMENT INFANTRY.

Organized at Port Hudson, La., September 1, 1863. Attached to Ullman's Brigade, Corps de Afrique, Dept. of the Gulf, to December, 1863. 2nd Brigade, 1st Division, Corps de Afrique, to April, 1864.

SERVICE.—Garrison duty at Port Hudson, La., till April, 1864. Designation of Regiment changed to 82nd United States Colored Troops April 4, 1864 (which see).

11th REGIMENT INFANTRY.

Organized at Port Hudson, La., August 17, 1863. Attached to Garrison, Port Hudson, La., to December, 1863. 1st Brigade, 1st Division, Corps de Afrique, Dept. of the Gulf, to April, 1864.

SERVICE.—Garrison duty at Port Hudson, La., till April, 1864. Skirmishes at Waterproof, La., February 14-15, 1864. Designation of Regiment changed to 83rd United States Colored Troops April 4, 1864 (which see).

12th REGIMENT INFANTRY.

Organized at Port Hudson, La., September 24, 1863. Attached to Garrison, Port Hudson, La., to December, 1863. 1st Brigade, 1st Division, Corps de Afrique, Dept. of the Gulf, to April, 1864.

SERVICE.—Garrison duty at Port Hudson till April, 1864. Expedition to Grand Gulf February 15-March 6, 1864. Designation of Regiment changed to 84th United States Colored Troops April 4, 1864 (which see).

13th REGIMENT INFANTRY.

Organized at New Orleans, La., September, 1863. Attached to 1st Brigade, 2nd Division, Corps de Afrique, Dept. of the Gulf, to December, 1863. Unattached, 13th Army Corps, Texas, to April, 1864.

SERVICE.—Garrison at Port Hudson till December, 1863. Ordered to Texas and duty at Brownsville and other points till April, 1864. Designation changed to 85th United States Colored Troops April 4, 1864 (which see).

14th REGIMENT INFANTRY.

Organized at New Orleans, La., August 12, 1863. Attached to Defences of New Orleans, Dept. of the Gulf, to September, 1863. 1st Brigade, 2nd Division, Corps de Afrique, Dept. of the Gulf, to October, 1863. District of West Florida, Dept. of the Gulf, to April, 1864.

SERVICE.—Duty at Port Hudson till October, 1863. Moved to Barrances, Fla., and duty there till April, 1864. Designation of Regiment changed to 86th U. S. Colored Troops April 4, 1864 (which see).

15th REGIMENT INFANTRY.

Organized at New Orleans, La., August 27, 1863. Attached to 1st Brigade, 2nd Division, Corps de Afrique, Dept. of the Gulf, to October, 1863. Engineer Brigade, Dept. of the Gulf, to February, 1864.

SERVICE.—Duty at New Orleans and Brashear City till February, 1864. Designation of Regiment changed to 5th Corps de Afrique Engineers, February 10, 1864 (which see).

16th REGIMENT INFANTRY.

Organized at New Orleans, La., October 8, 1863. Attached to 1st Brigade, 2nd Division, Corps de Afrique, Dept. of the Gulf, to October, 1863. Unattached 2nd Division, 13th Army Corps, Dept. of the Gulf, to April, 1864.

SERVICE.—Rio Grande Expedition, and operations on the coast of Texas October 27-December 2, 1863. At Brazos Island, Brownsville and Point Isabel, Texas, till April, 1864. Designation of Regiment changed to 87th United States Colored Troops April 4, 1864 (which see).

17th REGIMENT INFANTRY.

Organized at Port Hudson, La., September 24, 1863. Attached to 2nd Brigade, 1st Division, Corps de Afrique, Dept. of the Gulf, to April, 1864.

SERVICE.—Garrison duty at Port Hudson, La., till April, 1864. Designation of Regiment changed to 88th United States Colored Troops, April 4, 1864 (which see).

18th REGIMENT INFANTRY.

Organized at Port Hudson, La., October 9, 1863. Attached to 2nd Brigade, 2nd Division, Corps de Afrique, Dept. of the Gulf, to April, 1864.

SERVICE.—Duty at Port Hudson, La., till April, 1864. Designation of Regiment changed to 90th United States Colored Troops, April 4, 1864 (which see).

19th REGIMENT INFANTRY.

Organized at Madisonville, La., February 11, 1864. Duty at Madisonville and Lakeport, La., till March, and at Morganza, La., till May, 1864. Designation of Regiment changed to 91st United States Colored Troops, April 4, 1864 (which see).

20th REGIMENT INFANTRY.

Organized at Fort Pike, La., September 11, 1863. Attached to the Defences of New Orleans to April, 1864.

SERVICE.—Garrison Forts Pike, Macomb and Bienvenue till April, 1864. Designation of Regiment changed to 91st United States Colored Troops, April 4, 1864 (which see).

22nd REGIMENT INFANTRY.

Organized at New Orleans, La., September 30, 1863. Attached to District of La Fourche, Dept. of the Gulf, to February, 1864. 2nd Brigade, 2nd Division, Corps de Afrique, to March, 1864. 1st Brigade, 1st Division, Corps de Afrique, to April, 1864.

SERVICE.—Duty at New Orleans, Brashear City, New Iberia and in District of La Fourche till January, 1864. Ordered to Port Hudson January 4, and duty there till April, 1864. Moved to Brashear City and duty there till April, 1864. Designation of Regiment changed to 92nd United States Colored Troops, April 4, 1864 (which see).

25th REGIMENT INFANTRY.

Organized at New Iberia, La., November 21, 1863. Attached to 1st Brigade, 2nd Division, Corps de Afrique, Dept. of the Gulf, to March, 1864. District of La Fourche to April, 1864.

SERVICE.—Duty at New Iberia and in District of La Fourche till January, 1864. Moved to Franklin, La., January 5 and duty there till March 21. Moved to Brashear City and duty there till April. Designation of Regiment changed to 93rd United States Colored Troops April 4, 1864 (which see).

UNITED STATES COLORED TROOPS.

1st REGIMENT CAVALRY.

Organized at Camp Hamilton, Va., December 22, 1863. Attached to Fort Monroe, Va., Dept. of Virginia and North Carolina, to April, 1864. Unattached Williamsburg, Va., Dept. of Virginia and North Carolina, to June, 1864. 1st Brigade, 3rd Division, 18th Corps, Army of the James, to August, 1864. Defences of Portsmouth Va., District of Eastern Virginia, to May, 1865. Cavalry Brigade, 25th Corps, Dept. of Virginia and Dept. of Texas, to February, 1866.

SERVICE.—Duty at Fort Monroe and Williamsburg, Va., till May, 1864. Reconnoissance in Kings and Queens county February, 1864. Butler's operations on south side of James River and against Petersburg and Richmond May 4-28. Capture of Bermuda Hundred and City Point May 5. Swift Creek May 8-10. Operations against Fort Darling May 12-16. Actions at Drury's Bluff May 10-14-15 and 16. In trenches at Bermuda Hundred till June 18. Bayler's Farm June 15. Assaults on Petersburg June 16-19. Siege of Petersburg till August. Action at Deep Bottom July 27-28. Ordered to Fort Monroe August 3. Duty at Newport News and at Portsmouth and in District of Eastern Virginia till May, 1865. Cos. "E" and "I" Detached at Fort Powhatan and Harrison's Landing August, 1864, to May, 1865. Moved to City Point, Va.; thence sailed for Texas June 10. Duty on the Rio Grande and at various points in Texas till February, 1866. Mustered out February 4, 1866.

2nd REGIMENT CAVALRY.

Organized at Fort Monroe, Va., December 22, 1863. Attached to Fort Monroe, Va., Dept. of Virginia and North Carolina, to April, 1864. Unattached Williamsburg, Va., Dept. of Virginia and North Carolina, to June, 1864. 2nd Brigade, 3rd Division, 18th Corps, Army of the James, to August, 1864. Unattached 3rd Division, 18th Corps, to December, 1864. Unattached 25th Corps, Dept. of Virginia, to May, 1865. Cavalry Brigade, 25th Corps, Dept. of Virginia and Dept. of Texas, to February, 1866.

SERVICE.—Duty at Fort Monroe, Portsmouth and Williamsburg, Va., till May, 1864. Demonstration on Portsmouth March 4-5. Action near Suffolk March 10. Reconnoissance from Portsmouth to the Blackwater April 13-15. Butler's operations on the south side of James River and against Petersburg and Richmond May 4-28. Capture of Bermuda Hundred and City Point May 5. Swift Creek May 8-10. Operations against Fort Darling May 10-16. Actions at Drury's Bluff May 10-13-14-15 and 16. Near Drury's Bluff May 20. Duty in trenches at Bermuda Hundred till June 13. Point of Rocks June 10. Richmond Campaign June 13-July 31. Baylor's Farm June 15. Assaults on Petersburg June 16-19. Siege of Petersburg and Richmond June 16, 1864, to February 18, 1865. Duty before Petersburg till July, 1864. Moved to Deep Bottom July 25. Action at Deep Bottom July 27-28. Strawberry Plains, Deep Bottom, August 14-18. Actions at Deep Bottom September 2 and 6. Chaffin's Farm September 29-30. Barbytown Road October 7. Battle of Fair Oaks, Darbytown Road October 27-28. Near Richmond October 28-29. Duty in trenches north of James River till February, 1865. Ordered to Norfolk February 18. Duty in District of Eastern Virginia at Norfolk, Suffolk, etc., till May. Ordered to City Point, Va.; thence sailed for Texas June 10. Duty on the Rio Grande and at various points in Texas till February, 1866. Mustered out February 12, 1866.

3rd REGIMENT CAVALRY.

Organized from 1st Mississippi Cavalry (African Descent) March 11, 1864. Attached to 1st Brigade, United States Colored Troops, District of Vicksburg, Miss., Dept. of the Tennessee, to April, 1864. Winslow's Cavalry Brigade, District of Vicksburg, to December, 1864. 3rd Brigade, Cavalry Division, District of West Tennessee, to January, 1865. Unattached Cavalry, District of West Tennessee to June, 1865. 1st Brigade, Cavalry Division, District of West Tennessee, to January, 1866.

SERVICE.—Duty at Vicksburg, Miss., and in that District till December, 1864. Action at Roach's Plantation, Miss., March 30. Columbus, Ky., April 11 and 13 (Detachment). Expedition from Haines' Bluff up Yazoo River April 19-23. Near Mechanicsburg April 20. Expedition from Vicksburg to Yazoo City May 4-21. Benton May 7 and 9. Yazoo City May 13. Near Vicksburg June 4. Expedition from Vicksburg to Pearl River July 2-10. Jackson July 7. Utica July 13. Grand Gulf July 16. Bayou Tensas, La., August 26. Expedition from Goodrich Landing to Bayou Macon August 28-31. Expedition from Vicksburg to Deer Creek September 21-26. Near Rolling Fork September 22-23. Expedition from Vicksburg to Rodney and Fayette September 29-October 3. Expedition from Natchez to Woodville October 4-11. Fort Adams October 5. Woodville October 5-6. Operations in Issaqueena and Washington counties October 21-31. Steele's Bayou October 23. Expedition from Vicksburg to Gaines' Landing, Ark., and Bayou Macon, La., November 6-8. Rolling Fork November 11. Expedition from Vicksburg to Yazoo City November 23-December 4. Big Black River Bridge November 27. Moved to Memphis, Tenn. Grierson's Expedition from Memphis, Tenn., to destroy Mobile & Ohio Railroad December 21, 1864-January 5, 1865. Franklin Creek December 21-22, 1864. Okolona December 27. Egypt Station December 28. Franklin January 2, 1865. Moved to Memphis from Vicksburg, Miss., January 5-10. Duty there and in District of West Tennessee till April. Expedition from Memphis to Brownsville, Miss., April 23-26. Moved to Vicksburg April 29-May 1 and operating about Natchez for the capture of Jeff Davis May. Operations about Fort Adams May 3-6. Duty in District of West Tennessee and Dept. of Mississippi till January, 1866. Mustered out January 26, 1866.

4th REGIMENT CAVALRY.

Organized from 1st Corps de Afrique Cavalry April 4, 1864. Attached to Defences of New Orleans, La., Dept. of the Gulf, to August, 1864. District of Port Hudson, La., Dept. of the Gulf, to October, 1864. 1st Brigade, 2nd Division, United States Colored Troops, Dept. of the Gulf, to December, 1864. District of Port Hudson, La., Dept. of the Gulf, to July, 1865. Dept. of Mississippi to March, 1866.

SERVICE.—Duty in the Defences of New Orleans, La., at New Orleans, Carrollton, Camp Parapet and Donaldsonville, District of LaFourche, till August, 1864. Ordered to Baton Rouge, La., August 8, and duty in the Defences of that Post till July, 1865. Expedition to Clinton August 23-29, 1864. Action at Olive Branch, Comite River, August 25. Expedition from Port Hudson to Jackson April 11-13, 1865. Duty at various points in the Dept. of Mississippi till March, 1866. Mustered out March 20, 1866.

5th REGIMENT CAVALRY.

Organized at Camp Nelson, Ky., October 24, 1864. Attached to 1st Division, District of Kentucky, Dept. of Ohio, to February, 1865. Military District of Kentucky and Dept. of Arkansas, to March, 1866.

SERVICE.—Participated in Burbridge's Raid from Kentucky into Southwestern Virginia September 20-October 17, 1864. Action at Saltsville, Va., October 2. At Lexington, Ky., October 19. Harrodsburg, Ky., October 21. Stoneman's Raid into Southwestern Virginia December 10-29. Near Marion December 17-18. Capture of Saltsville and destruction of salt works December 20-21. Duty at Ghent, Paducah, LaGrange, Crab Orchard and Camp Nelson till August, 1865, and in the Dept. of Arkansas till March, 1866. Mustered out March 20, 1866.

Regiment lost during service 35 Enlisted men killed and mortally wounded and 1 Officer and 151 Enlisted men by disease. Total 187.

6th REGIMENT CAVALRY.

Organized at Camp Nelson, Ky., October 24, 1864. Attached to 1st Division, District of Kentucky, Dept. of Ohio, to February, 1865. Military District and Dept. of Kentucky to December, 1865, and Dept. of Arkansas to April, 1866.

SERVICE.—Stoneman's Raid into Southwestern Virginia December 10-29, 1864. Capture and destruction of lead mines December 17. Near Marion December 17-18. Saltsville December 20-21. At Camp Nelson and Paducah, Ky., till March, 1865. At LaGrange, Tenn., till May. At Camp Nelson, Wild Cat, and Danville, Ky., till July. At New Haven and Catlettsburg, Ky., till October. At Covington, Ky., till December. At Louisville, Ky., and Helena, Ark., till January, 1866. At Duvall's Bluff, Ark., till April 15, 1866. Mustered out April 15, 1866.

1st REGIMENT HEAVY ARTILLERY.

Organized at Knoxville, Tenn., February 20, 1864. Attached to 2nd Brigade, 4th Division, 23rd Corps, Dept. of Ohio, to February, 1865. 2nd Brigade, 4th Division, District of East Tennessee, Dept. of the Cumberland, to March, 1865. 1st Brigade, 4th Division, District of East Tennessee, to March, 1866.

SERVICE.—Duty at Knoxville, Tenn., till January, 1865. Operations against Wheeler in East Tennessee August 15-25, 1864. Operations in Northern Alabama and East Tennessee January 31-April 24, 1865. Stoneman's operations from East Tennessee into Southwestern Virginia and Western North Carolina February to April. At Greenville and in District of East Tennessee till March, 1866. Mustered out March 31, 1866.

3rd REGIMENT HEAVY ARTILLERY.

Organized from 1st Tennessee Heavy Artillery (African Descent). Designated 2nd United States Colored Heavy Artillery March 11, 1864, and 3rd Heavy Artillery April 26, 1864. Attached to District of Memphis, Tenn., Dept. of Tennessee, to June, 1864. Memphis, Tenn., District of West Tennessee, to July, 1865. 2nd Infantry Brigade, District of West Tennessee, to September, 1865. District of West Tennessee to April, 1866.

SERVICE.—Served as garrison at Fort Pickering, and in Defences of Memphis, Tenn., and in District of West Tennessee till April, 1866. Mustered out April 30, 1866.

4th REGIMENT HEAVY ARTILLERY.

Organized from 2nd Tennessee Heavy Artillery (African Descent). Designated 3rd Heavy Artillery March 11, 1864, and 4th Heavy Artillery April 26, 1864. Attached to District of Columbus, 16th Corps, Dept. of Tennessee, to August, 1864. District of Columbus, Dept. of Ohio, to June, 1865. Dept. of Arkansas to February, 1866.

SERVICE.—Garrison duty at Fort Halleck, Columbus, Ky., till June, 1865. Union City, Tenn., September 2, 1864. Near Fort Donelson, Tenn., October 11. Moved to Arkansas June, 1865, and duty at Pine Bluff, Ark., till February, 1866. Mustered out February 25, 1866.

5th REGIMENT HEAVY ARTILLERY.

Organized from 1st Mississippi Heavy Artillery (African Descent). Designated 4th Heavy Artillery March 11, 1864, and 5th Heavy Artillery April 26, 1864. Attached to 1st Division, United States Colored Troops, District of Vicksburg, Miss., to February, 1865. Unattached, Post of Vicksburg, Dept. of Mississippi, and Dept. of the Gulf to May, 1864.

SERVICE.—Garrison duty at Vicksburg, Miss., till May, 1866. Expedition from Vicksburg to Rodney and Fayette September 29-October 3, 1864. Expedition from Vicksburg to Yazoo City November 23-December 4, 1864. Mustered out May 20, 1866.

Lost during service 4 Officers and 124 Enlisted men killed and mortally wounded and 697 Enlisted men by disease. Total 829.

6th REGIMENT HEAVY ARTILLERY.

Organized from 2nd Mississippi Heavy Artillery (African Descent). Designated 5th Heavy Artillery March 11, 1864, and 6th Heavy Artillery April 26, 1864. Attached to Post of Natchez, Miss., District of Vicksburg, Miss., Dept. of Tennessee, and Dept. of Mississippi to February, 1865. Post of Natchez, Dept. of Mississippi, to April, 1865. Dept. of the Gulf to May, 1866.

SERVICE.—Duty at Natchez, Miss., and Vidalia, La., till May, 1866. Skirmish near Vidalia, La., July 22, 1864. Attack on Steamer "Clara Bell" July 24, 1864 (4 Cos.). Expedition from Natchez to Gillespie's Plantation, La., August 4-6, 1864. Concordia Bayou August 5. Expedition from Natchez to Buck's Ferry and skirmish September 19-22, 1864. Expedition from Natchez to Waterproof and Sicily Island September 26-30, 1864. Expedition from Natchez to Homichitto River October 5-8, 1864. Expedition from Vidalia to York Plantation, La., October 26-27, 1864. Skirmish at Black River October 31 and November 1, 1864. Mustered out May 18, 1866.

7th REGIMENT HEAVY ARTILLERY.

Organized from 1st Alabama Siege Artillery (African Descent). Designated 6th Heavy Artillery March 11, 1864, and 7th Heavy Artillery April 26, 1864. Attached to District of Memphis, Tenn., 16th Corps, Dept. of Tennessee, to June, 1864. Memphis, Tenn., District of West Tennessee, to January, 1865.

SERVICE.—Garrison duty at Fort Pickering and in Defences of Memphis, Tenn., till January, 1865. Companies "A," "B," "C" and "D" garrison at Fort Pillow, Tenn., and in massacre April 12, 1864. Skirmish at Pulaski May 18. Holly Springs, Miss., August 28, 1864.

Designated 11th United States Colored Troops (New) January 23, 1865.

8th REGIMENT HEAVY ARTILLERY.

Organized at Paducah, Ky., April 26, 1864. Attached to Paducah, Ky., District of Columbus, Ky., 16th Corps, Dept. of the Tennessee, to August, 1864. Paducah, Ky., District of Columbus, Ky., Dept. of the Ohio, to February, 1865, and Dept. of Kentucky to February, 1866.

SERVICE.—Garrison duty at Paducah, Ky., till February, 1866. Operations against Forest in Kentucky March 16 to April 14, 1864. Action at Fort Anderson, Paducah, Ky., March 25, 1864. Expedition from Paducah, Ky., to Haddix Ferry July 26-27, 1864. Skirmish near Haddix Ferry August 27, 1864. Mustered out February 10, 1866.

9th REGIMENT HEAVY ARTILLERY.

Organized at Clarksville and Nashville, Tenn., October 8 to November 1, 1864. Attached to District of Nashville, Dept. of the Cumberland, till May, 1865. Broken up May 5, 1865.

10th REGIMENT HEAVY ARTILLERY.

Organized from 1st Corps de Afrique Heavy Artillery. Designated 7th Regiment Heavy Artillery April 4, 1864, and 10th Regiment Heavy Artillery May 21, 1864. Attached to Defences of New Orleans, La., Dept. of the Gulf, to October, 1864. 1st Brigade, 3rd Division, United States Colored Troops, Dept. of the Gulf, to November, 1864. Defences of New Orleans, La., to February, 1867. Expedition to Lake Verret, Grand Bayou, and the Park April 2-10, 1865 (Co. "G").

SERVICE.—On garrison duty at New Orleans and in the Dept. of the Gulf entire term. Mustered out February 22, 1867.

11th REGIMENT HEAVY ARTILLERY.

Organized from 14th Rhode Island Colored Heavy Artillery. Designated 8th Heavy Artillery April 4, 1864, and 11th Heavy Artillery May 21, 1864. Attached to Defences of New Orleans, La., Dept. of the Gulf, to October, 1865.

SERVICE.—Garrison duty at New Orleans and other points in the Defences of that city till October, 1865 (see 14th Rhode Island Colored Heavy Artillery). Mustered out October 2, 1865.

12th REGIMENT HEAVY ARTILLERY.

Organized at Camp Nelson, Ky., July 15, 1864. Attached to 2nd Brigade, 1st Division, District of Kentucky, Dept. of the Ohio, to January, 1865. Military District of Kentucky and Dept. of Kentucky, to April, 1866.

SERVICE.—Garrison duty in District of Kentucky, at Bowling Green, Camp Nedson and other points till April, 1866. Mustered out April 24, 1866.

13th REGIMENT HEAVY ARTILLERY.

Organized at Camp Nelson, Ky., June 23, 1864. Attached to Military District of Kentucky, Dept. of the Ohio, to February, 1865, and to Dept. of Kentucky, to November, 1865.

SERVICE.—Garrison duty at Camp Nelson, Smithland, Lexington and other points in Kentucky till November-1865. Mustered out November 18, 1865.

14th REGIMENT HEAVY ARTILLERY.

Organized at New Berne and Morehead City, N. C., from 1st North Carolina Colored Heavy Artillery March 17, 1864. Attached to Defences of New Berne, N. C., Dept. of Virginia and North Carolina, to January, 1865. Sub-District of New Berne, Dept. of North Carolina, and Sub-District of Beaufort, N. C., Dept. of North Carolina, to December, 1865.

SERVICE.—Garrison duty at New Berne and other points in the Dept. of North Carolina till December, 1865. Mustered out December 11, 1865.

2nd REGIMENT LIGHT ARTILLERY.

BATTERY "A," 2nd REGIMENT LIGHT ARTILLERY.

Organized at Nashville, Tenn., April 30, 1864. Attached to Post and District of Nashville, Tenn., Dept. of the Cumberland, to March, 1865. District of Middle Tennessee, Dept. of the Cumberland, to January, 1866.

SERVICE.—Garrison duty at Nashville, Tenn., and in Middle Tennessee, till January, 1866. Battle of Nashville December 15-16, 1864. Mustered out January 13, 1866.

BATTERY "B," 2nd REGIMENT LIGHT ARTILLERY.

Organized at Fort Monroe, Va., January 8, 1864. Attached to Fort Monroe, Va., Dept. of Virginia and North Carolina, to April, 1864. Artillery, Hincks' Colored Division, 18th Corps, Army of the James, to May, 1864. Rand's Provisional Brigade, 18th Corps, to June, 1864. Artillery Brigade, 18th Corps, June, 1864. Unattached Artillery, Dept. of Virginia and North Carolina, to July, 1864. Defences of Norfolk and Portsmouth, Va., Dept. of Virginia and North Carolina, to May, 1865. Artillery 25th Corps and Dept. of Texas to March, 1866.

SERVICE.—Duty at Fort Monroe, Va., till April, 1864. Butler's operations south of James River and against Petersburg and Richmond, Va., May 4 to June 15, 1864. Action at Wilson's Wharf May 24. Petersburg, Va., June 9. Before Petersburg June 15-18. Siege operations against Petersburg and Richmond till July 7. Ordered to Portsmouth, Va., July 7, and duty there till May, 1865. Ordered to Texas May, 1865, and duty on the Rio Grande till March, 1866. Mustered out March 17, 1866.

BATTERY "C," 2nd REGIMENT LIGHT ARTILLERY.

Organized from 1st Louisiana Battery, African Descent. Designated Battery "A" March 11, 1864, and Battery "C" April 26, 1864. Attached to Post of Goodrich Landing, District of Vicksburg, Miss., to May, 1864. Post of Vicksburg, Miss., to July, 1864. Post of Milliken's Bend, La., District of Vicksburg, Miss., to December, 1864. Reserve Artillery, Post of Vicksburg, District of Vicksburg, Miss., to December, 1865.

SERVICE.—Post and garrison duty at Goodrich Landing, Vicksburg, and Milliken's Bend and in the Dept. of Mississippi till December, 1865. Mustered out December 28, 1865.

BATTERY "D," 2nd REGIMENT LIGHT ARTILLERY.

Organized from 2nd Louisiana Battery, African Descent. Designated Battery "B" March 11, 1864, and Battery "D" April 26, 1864. Attached to Post of Goodrich Landing, Dist. of Vicksburg, Miss., to December, 1864. Reserve Artillery, District of Vicksburg, Dept. of Mississippi, to December, 1865.

SERVICE.—Post and garrison duty at Goodrich Landing till December, 1864, and at Vicksburg, Miss., and in the Dept. of Mississippi till December, 1865. Mustered out December 28, 1865.

BATTERY "E," 2nd REGIMENT LIGHT ARTILLERY.

Organized from 3rd Battery Louisiana Artillery, African Descent. Designated Battery "C" March 11, 1864, and Battery "E" April 26, 1864. Attached to District of Eastern Arkansas, 7th Corps, Dept. of Arkansas, to September, 1865.

SERVICE.—Post and garrison duty at Helena, Ark., till muster out. Operations in Arkansas July 1-31, 1864. Action at Wallace's Ferry, Big Creek, July 26. Operations in Eastern Arkansas August 1-5, 1864. Lamb's Plantation, near Helena, August 1. Expedition from Helena to Kent's Landing August 11-14 (Detachment). Expedition up White River August 29-September 2, 1864. Mustered out September 26, 1865.

BATTERY "F," 2nd REGIMENT LIGHT ARTILLERY.

Organized from Memphis Light Battery, African Descent. Designated Battery "D" March 11, 1864, and Battery "F" April 26, 1864. Attached to 1st Colored Brigade, District of Memphis, Tenn., 16th Corps, Dept. of the Tennessee, to June, 1864. 3rd Brigade, Sturgis' Expedition, June, 1864. Post and Defences of Memphis, Tenn., District of West Tennessee, to December, 1864. Artillery Reserve, District of West Tennessee, to April, 1865. Bridgeport, Ala., Dept. of the Cumberland, to July, 1865. 2nd Infantry Brigade, District of West Tennessee, to December, 1865.

SERVICE.—Post and garrison duty at Memphis, Tenn., till April, 1865. Fort Pillow, Tenn., April 12, 1864 (Section). Sturgis' Expedition into Mississippi June 1-18. Battle of Ripley, Miss., June 7. Battle of Brice's Cross Roads, Guntown, June 10. Ripley June 11. Duty at Memphis till April, 1865. Repulse of Forest's attack on Memphis August 21, 1864. Moved to Bridgeport, Ala., April, 1865, and duty there till December,· Mustered out by consolidation with 3rd United States Colored Heavy Artillery December 28, 1865.

BATTERY "G," 2nd REGIMENT LIGHT ARTILLERY.

Organized at Hilton Head, S. C., May 24, 1864. Attached to District of Hilton Head, S. C., Dept. of the South, to August, 1864. District of Beaufort, S. C., Dept. of the South, to October, 1864. 2nd Separate Brigade, Dept. of the South, to June, 1865. Dept. of the South, to August, 1865.

SERVICE.—Post and garrison duty at Hilton Head and Beaufort, S. C., entire term. Mustered out August 12, 1865.

BATTERY "H," 2nd REGIMENT LIGHT ARTILLERY.

Organized from 1st Arkansas Battery, African Descent, December 13, 1864. Attached to Post of Pine Bluff, Ark., 7th Corps, Dept. of Arkansas, to September, 1865.

SERVICE.—Garrison duty at Pine Bluff, Ark., entire term. Expedition to Mount Elba, Ark., and skirmish at Saline River, January 22-February 4, 1865. Mustered out September 15, 1865.

BATTERY "I," 2nd REGIMENT LIGHT ARTILLERY.

Organized at Memphis, Tenn., April 19, 1864. Attached to District of Memphis, Tenn., 16th Corps, Dept. of the Tennessee, to June, 1864. Colored Brigade, District of Memphis, Tenn. District of West Tennessee to December, 1864. Artillery Reserve, District of West Tennessee, Dept. of the Cumberland, to January, 1866.

SERVICE.—Post and garrison duty at Memphis, Tenn., till April, 1865. Smith's Expedition to Tupelo, Miss., July 5-21. Battle of Tupelo July 14-15. Smith's Expedition to Oxford, Miss., August 1-30. Duty at Memphis and in District of West Tennessee till January, 1866. Mustered out January 10, 1866.

INDEPENDENT BATTERY.

Organized at Leavenworth, Kan., December 23, 1864. Attached to District of North Kansas, Dept. of Kansas, to July, 1865.

SERVICE.—Duty at Leavenworth and at Fort Leavenworth, Kan., till July, 1865. Mustered out July 22, 1865.

1st REGIMENT INFANTRY.

Organized in the District of Columbia May 19 to June 30, 1863. Ordered to Dept. of Virginia and attached to United States Forces, Norfolk and Portsmouth, Dept. of Virginia and North Carolina, July to October, 1863. United States Forces, Yorktown, Va., Dept. of Virginia and North Carolina, to April, 1864. 1st Brigade, Hincks' Colored Division, 18th Corps, Army of the James, Dept. of Virginia and North Carolina, to June, 1864. 1st Brigade, 3rd Division, 18th Corps, to December, 1864. 1st Brigade, 1st Division, 25th Corps, to December, 1864. 1st Brigade, 3rd Division, 25th Corps, to March, 1865. 1st Brigade, 3rd Division, 10th Corps, Dept. of North Carolina, to August, 1865. Dept. of North Carolina to muster out.

SERVICE.—Duty at Norfolk, Portsmouth and Yorktown, Va., till April, 1864. Expedition from Norfolk to South Mills, Camden Court House, etc., N. C., December 5-24, 1863. Butler's operations south of James River and against Petersburg and Richmond, Va., May 4-June 15. Action at Wilson's Wharf May 24. Assaults on Petersburg June 15-18. Siege of Petersburg and Richmond June 16 to December 7, 1864. Explosion of Mine, Petersburg, July 30. Demonstration on north side of the James River September 28-30. Battle of Chaffin's Farm, New Market Heights, September 28-30. Fort Harrison September 29. Battle of Fair Oaks October 27-28. Expedition to Fort Fisher, N. C., December 7-27. 2nd Expedition to Fort Fisher, N. C., January 7-15, 1865. Assault on and capture of Fort Fisher January 15. Sugar Loaf Hill January 19. Sugar Loaf Battery February 11. Fort Anderson February 18-20. Capture of Wilmington February 22. Northeast Ferry February 22. Campaign of the Carolinas March 1-April 26. Advance on Goldsboro March 6-21. Occupation of Goldsboro March 21. Cox's Bridge March 23-24. Advance on Raleigh April 9-13. Occupation of Raleigh April 13. Bennett's House April 26. Surrender of Johnston and his army. Duty in the Dept. of North Carolina till September. Mustered out September 29, 1865.

Regiment lost during service 4 Officers and 67 Enlisted men killed and mortally wounded and 1 Officer and 113 Enlisted men by disease. Total 185.

2nd REGIMENT INFANTRY.

Organized at Arlington, Va., June 20 to November 11, 1863. Ordered to the Dept. of the Gulf December, 1863. Attached to District of Key West, Fla., Dept. of the Gulf, February, 1864, to July, 1865. Dept. of Florida to January, 1866.

SERVICE.—Duty at New Orleans, La., and Ship Island, Miss., till February 13, 1864. Ordered to Key West, Fla., February 13. Affair at Tampa, Fla., May 5. Operations on West Coast of Florida July 1-31. Expedition from Fort Myers to Bayport July 1-4. Expedition from Cedar Key to St. Andrew's Bay July 20-29. Fort Taylor August 21. Station No. 4 February 13, 1865. Attack on Fort Myers February 20. Operations in the vicinity of St. Mark's February 21-March 7. East River Bridge March 4-5. Newport Bridge March 5-6. Natural Bridge March 6. Duty in District of Florida till January, 1866. Mustered out January 5, 1866.

Regiment lost during service 3 Officers and 24 Enlisted men killed and mortally wounded and 11 Officers and 135 Enlisted men by disease. Total 173.

3rd REGIMENT INFANTRY.

Organized at Camp William Penn, near Philadelphia, Pa., August 3-10, 1863. Ordered to Dept. of the South. Attached to 4th Brigade, Morris Island, S. C., 10th Corps, Dept. of the South, to November, 1863. 3rd Brigade, Morris Island, S. C., 10th Corps, to January, 1864. Montgomery's Brigade, District of Hilton Head, S. C., 10th Corps, to February, 1864. 2nd Brigade, Vodges' Division, District of Florida, Dept. of the South, to April, 1864. District of Florida, Dept. of the South, to October, 1864. 4th Separate Brigade, District of Florida, Dept. of the South, to July, 1865. Dept. of Florida to October, 1865.

SERVICE.—Siege of Forts Wagner and Gregg, Morris Island, S. C., August 20-September 7, 1863. Action at Forts Wagner and Gregg August 26. Capture of Forts Wagner and Gregg September 7. Operations against Charleston from Morris Island till January, 1864. Moved to Hilton Head, S. C., thence to Jacksonville, Fla., February 5-7, and duty there as Heavy Artillery till May, 1865. (1 Co. at Fernandina, Fla.) Expedition from Jacksonville to Camp Milton May 31-June 3, 1864. Front Creek July 15. Bryan's Plantation October 21. Duty at Tallahassee, Lake City and other points in Florida May to October, 1865. Mustered out October 31, 1865.

4th REGIMENT INFANTRY.

Organized at Baltimore, Md., July 15 to September 1, 1863. Moved to Fort Monroe, Va., October 1, 1863; thence moved to Yorktown, Va. Attached to 2nd Brigade, United States Forces, Yorktown, Va., 18th Corps, Dept. of Virginia and North Carolina, to April, 1864. 2nd Brigade, Hincks' Colored Division, 18th Corps, to June, 1864. 2nd Brigade, 3rd Division, 18th Corps, to December, 1864. 2nd Brigade, 1st Division, 25th Corps, to January, 1865. 2nd Brigade, 3rd Division, 25th Corps, to March, 1865. 2nd Brigade, 3rd Division, 10th Corps, Dept. of North Carolina, to August, 1865. Dept. of North Carolina to May, 1866.

SERVICE.—Duty at Yorktown till May, 1864. Expedition from Yorktown to Matthews County October 4-9, 1863. Wistar's Expedition against Richmond February

6-8, 1864. New Kent Court House February 8. Expedition to Bottom's Bridge in aid of Kilpatrick's Cavalry March 1-4. Expedition into King and Queen County March 9-12. Expedition into Matthews and Middlesex Counties March 17-21. Butler's operations south of the James River and against Petersburg and Richmond May 4-June 15. Skirmish at Bermuda Hundred May 4. Duty at Spring Hill on the Appomattox till June. (Built Fort Converse on the Bermuda Hundred line.) Attack on Fort Converse May 20. Before Petersburg June 15-18. Siege operations against Petersburg and Richmond June 16 to December 7. Mine Explosion, Petersburg, July 30. Dutch Gap September 7. Battle of Chaffin's Farm, New Market Heights, September 28-30. Battle of Fair Oaks October 27-28. 1st Expedition to Fort Fisher, N. C., December 7-27. 2nd Expedition to Fort Fisher, N. C., January 7-15. Assault and capture of Fort Fisher, N. C., January 15. Sugar Loaf Hill January 19. Sugar Loaf Battery February 11. Fort Anderson February 18-20. Capture of Wilmington February 22. Northeast Ferry February 22. Campaign of the Carolinas March 1-April 26. Advance on Goldsboro March 6-21. Occupation of Goldsboro March 21. Cox's Bridge March 23-24. Advance on Raleigh April 9-18. Occupation of Raleigh April 14. Bennett's House April 26. Surrender of Johnston and his army. Duty in the Dept. of North Carolina till May, 1866. Mustered out May 4, 1866.

Regiment lost during service 3 Officers and 102 Enlisted men killed and mortally wounded and 1 Officer and 186 Enlisted men by disease. Total 292.

5th REGIMENT INFANTRY.

Organized at Camp Delaware, Ohio, August to November, 1863. Moved to Norfolk, Va., November, 1863. Attached to United States Forces, Norfolk and Portsmouth, Va., Dept. of Virginia and North Carolina, to January, 1864. 2nd Brigade, United States Forces, Yorktown, Va., 18th Corps, Dept. of Virginia and North Carolina, to April, 1864. 2nd Brigade, Hincks' Colored Division, 18th Corps, Army of the James, Dept. of Virginia and North Carolina, to June, 1864. 2nd Brigade, 3rd Division, 18th Corps, to December, 1864. 3rd Brigade, 1st Division, 25th Corps, to December, 1864. 3rd Brigade, 3rd Division, 25th Corps, to March, 1865. 2nd Brigade, 3rd Division, 10th Corps, Dept. of North Carolina, to August, 1865. Dept. of North Carolina to September, 1865.

SERVICE.—Duty at Norfolk and Portsmouth, Va., till January, 1864. Wild's Expedition to South Mills and Camden Court House, N. C., December 5-24, 1863. Action at Sandy Swamp, N. C., December 8. Moved to Yorktown, Va., January, 1864, and duty there till May. Wistar's Expedition against Richmond February 6-8, 1864. Expedition to New Kent Court House in aid of Kilpatrick's Cavalry March 1-4. New Kent Court House March 2. Expedition into King and Queen County March 9-12. Expedition into Matthews and Middlesex Counties March 17-21. Butler's operations on south side of the James River and against Petersburg and Richmond May 4-June 15. Capture of City Point May 4. Fatigue duty at City Point and building Fort Converse on the Appomattox River till June 15. Attack on Fort Converse May 20. Before Petersburg June 15-18. Bailor's Farm June 15. Siege operations against Petersburg and Richmond June 16 to December 6. In trenches before Petersburg till August 27. Mine Explosion, Petersburg, July 30. Moved to Deep Bottom August 28. Battle of Chaffin's Farm, New Market Heights, September 28-30. Fort Harrison September 29. Battle of Fair Oaks October 27-28. In trenches before Richmond till December. 1st Expedition to Fort Fisher, N. C., December 7-27. 2nd Expedition to Fort Fisher, N. C., January 7-15. Assault and capture of Fort Fisher, N. C., January 15. Sugar Loaf Hill January 19. Federal Point February 11. Fort Anderson February 18-20. Capture of Wilmington February 22. Northeast Ferry February 22. Campaign of the Carolinas March 1-April 26. Advance on Kinston and Goldsboro March 6-21. Oc-

cupation of Goldsboro March 21. Cox's Bridge March 23-24. Advance on Raleigh April 9-14. Occupation of Raleigh April 14. Bennett's House April 26. Surrender of Johnston and his army. Duty at Goldsboro, New Berne and Carolina City, N. C., till September. Mustered out September 20, 1865.

Regiment lost during service 4 Officers and 77 Enlisted men killed and mortally wounded and 2 Officers and 166 Enlisted men by disease. Total 249.

6th REGIMENT INFANTRY.

Organized at Camp William Penn, near Philadelphia, Pa., July 28 to September 12, 1863. Moved from Philadelphia to Fort Monroe, Va., October 14; thence to Yorktown, Va. Attached to United States Forces, Yorktown, Va., Dept. of Virginia and North Carolina, to January, 1864. 2nd Brigade, United States Forces, Yorktown, Va., 18th Corps, Dept. of Virginia and North Carolina, to April, 1864. 2nd Brigade, Hincks' Colored Division, 18th Corps, Army of the James, to June, 1864. 2nd Brigade, 3rd Division, 18th Corps, to August, 1864. 3rd Brigade, 3rd Division, 18th Corps, to December, 1864. 2nd Brigade, 1st Division, 25th Corps, to December, 1864. 2nd Brigade, 3rd Division, 25th Corps, to March, 1865. 3rd Brigade, 3rd Division, 10th Corps, Dept. of North Carolina, to August, 1865. Dept. of North Carolina to September, 1865.

SERVICE.—Duty at Yorktown till May, 1864. Wild's Expedition to South Mills and Camden Court House, N. C., December 5-24, 1863. Wistar's Expedition against Richmond February 2-6, 1864. Expedition to New Kent Court House in aid of Kilpatrick's Cavalry March 1-4. New Kent Court House March 2. Williamsburg March 4. Expedition into King and Queen County March 9-12. Expedition into Matthews County March 17-21. Butler's operations south of the James River and against Petersburg and Richmond May 4-June 15. Capture of City Point May 4. Fatigue duty at City Point and building Fort Converse on Appomattox River till June 15. Attack on Fort Converse May 20. Before Petersburg June 15-18. Bailor's Farm June 15. Siege operations against Petersburg and Richmond June 15 to December 17. In trenches before Petersburg and fatigue duty at Dutch Gap Canal till August 27. Moved to Deep Bottom August 27. Battle of Chaffin's Farm, New Market Heights, September 29-30. Fort Harrison September 29. Battle of Fair Oaks October 27-28. In trenches before Richmond till December. 1st Expedition to Fort Fisher, N. C., December 7-27. 2nd Expedition to Fort Fisher, N. C., January 7-15. Bombardment of Fort Fisher January 13-15. Assault and capture of Fort Fisher January 15. Sugar Loaf Hill January 19. Sugar Loaf Battery February 11. Fort Anderson February 18-20. Capture of Wilmington February 22. Northeast Ferry February 22. Campaign of the Carolinas March 1-April 26. Advance on Kinston and Goldsboro March 6-21. Occupation of Goldsboro March 21. Cox's Bridge March 23-24. Advance on Raleigh April 9-14. Occupation of Raleigh April 14. Bennett's House April 26. Surrender of Johnston and his army. Duty in the Dept. of North Carolina till September. Mustered out September 20, 1865.

Regiment lost during service 8 Officers and 79 Enlisted men killed and mortally wounded and 5 Officers and 132 Enlisted men by disease. Total 224.

7th REGIMENT INFANTRY.

Organized at Baltimore, Md., September 26 to November 12, 1863. Duty at Camp Benedict, Md., till March, 1864. Ordered to Portsmouth, Va., March 4, thence to Hilton Head, S. C., March 7-10, and to Jacksonville, Fla., March 14-15. Attached to Post of Jacksonville, Fla., District of Florida, Dept. of the South, to July, 1864. District of Hilton Head, S. C., Dept. of the South, July, 1864. Jacksonville, Fla., District of Florida, Dept. of the South, to August, 1864. 1st Brigade, 3rd Division, 10th Corps, Army of the James, Dept. of Virginia and North Carolina, to December, 1864. 1st Brigade, 2nd Division, 25th Corps, to January, 1866. Dept. of Texas to October, 1866.

SERVICE.—Duty at Jacksonville, Fla., till June, 1864. Cedar Creek April 2. Near Jacksonville May 6. Near Camp Finnegan May 25. Near Jacksonville May 28. Expedition to Camp Milton May 31-June 3. Camp Milton June 2. Moved to Hilton Head, S. C., June 27. Expedition to North Edisto River and Johns and James Islands July 2-10. Near Winter's Point July 3. King's Creek July 3. Skirmishes on James Island July 5 and 7. Burden's Causeway, Johns Island, July 9. Moved to Jacksonville July 15. Expedition to Florida & Gulf Railroad July 22-August 5. Moved to Bermuda Hundred, Va., August 6-11. Siege operations against Petersburg and Richmond August, 1864, to April, 1865. Demonstration north of James River August 16-20. Russell's Mills August 16. Strawberry Plains August 16-18. Battle of Chaffin's Farm, New Market Heights, September 28-30. Darbytown Road October 13. Battle of Fair Oaks October 27-28. Near Richmond October 28. In trenches before Richmond till March 27, 1865. Appomattox Campaign March 27-April 9. Hatcher's Run March 29-31. Fall of Petersburg April 2. Pursuit of Lee April 3-9. Appomattox Court House April 9. Surrender of Lee and his army. Moved to Petersburg April 11, and duty there till May 24. Moved to Indianola, Texas, May 24-June 23. Duty on the Rio Grande and at various points in the Dept. of Texas, till October, 1866. Moved to Baltimore, Md., October 14-November 4. Mustered out October 13, 1866, and discharged at Baltimore, Md., November 15, 1866.

Regiment lost during service 1 Officer and 84 Enlisted men killed and mortally wounded and 1 Officer and 307 Enlisted men by disease. Total 393.

8th REGIMENT INFANTRY.

Organized at Camp William Penn, Philadelphia, Pa., September 22 to December 4, 1863. Left Philadelphia for Hilton Head, S. C., January 16, 1864. Attached to Howell's Brigade, District of Hilton Head, S. C., Dept. of the South, to February, 1864. Hawley's Brigade, Seymour's Division, District of Florida, Dept. of the South, to April, 1864. District of Florida, Dept. of the South, to August, 1864. 1st Brigade, 3rd Division, 10th Corps, Army of the James, Dept. of Virginia and North Carolina, to December, 1864. 2nd Brigade, 2nd Division, 25th Corps, to April, 1865. 1st Brigade, 2nd Division, 25th Corps, and Dept. of Texas, to November, 1865.

SERVICE.—Expedition from Hilton Head, S. C., to Jacksonville, Fla., February 5-6, 1864. Occupation of Jacksonville February 7. Advance into Florida February 8-20. Camp Finnegan February 8. Battle of Olustee February 20. Retreat to Jacksonville and duty there till April. Moved to St. John's Bluff April 17, and duty there till August. Raid on Baldwin July 23-28. Moved to Deep Bottom, Va., August 4-12. Action at Deep Bottom August 12. Duty at Deep Bottom and in trenches before Petersburg till September 27. Battle of Chaffin's Farm, New Market Heights, September 28-30. Fort Harrison September 29. Darbytown Road October 13. Battle of Fair Oaks October 27-28. In trenches before Richmond till March 27, 1865. Appomattox Campaign March 28-April 9. Hatcher's Run March 29-31. Fall of Petersburg April 2. Pursuit of Lee April 3-9. Appomattox Court House April 9. Surrender of Lee and his army. Moved to Petersburg April 11, and duty there till May 24. Sailed from City Point for Texas May 24. Duty at Ringgold Barracks and on the Rio Grande, Texas, till November, 1865. Mustered out November 10, 1865. Moved to Philadelphia, Pa., November 10-December 3. Discharged December 12, 1865.

Regiment lost during service 4 Officers and 115 Enlisted men killed and mortally wounded and 132 Enlisted men by disease. Total 251.

9th REGIMENT INFANTRY.

Organized at Camp Stanton, Md., November 11-30, 1863. Duty at Benedict, Md., till March, 1864. Moved to Port Royal, S. C., March 3-7. Attached to District of Hilton Head, S. C., Dept. of the South, to April, 1864. District of Beaufort, S. C., Dept. of the South, to August, 1864. 1st Brigade, 3rd Division, 10th Corps, Army

of the James, Dept. of Virginia and North Carolina, to December, 1864. 2nd Brigade, 3rd Division, 25th Corps, to January, 1865. 2nd Brigade, 1st Division, 25th Corps, to January, 1866. Dept. of Texas to November, 1866.

SERVICE.—Duty at Hilton Head, S. C., till April, 1864, and at Port Royal Island, S. C., till June. Ashepoo Expedition May 24-27. Expedition to Johns and James Islands June 30-July 10. Engaged July 7 and 9. Duty at Beaufort, S. C., till August. Moved to Bermuda Hundred, Va., August 4-8. Siege operations against Petersburg and Richmond August, 1864, to April, 1865. Demonstration on north side of James River August 13-18. Skirmishes at Deep Bottom August 14-15. Russell's Mills August 16. Moved to Bermuda Hundred front August 18, thence to Petersburg August 24, and duty in trenches till September 26. Demonstration on north side of James September 26-30. Battle of Chaffin's Farm, New Market Heights, September 28-30. Fort Gilmer September 29. Darbytown Road October 13. Battle of Fair Oaks October 27-28. In trenches before Richmond till April, 1865. Occupation of Richmond April 3. Duty at Richmond, Petersburg and City Point till June. Moved to Brazos Santiago, Texas, June 7-July 1, thence to Brownsville. Duty at Brownsville and on the Rio Grande, Texas, till October, 1866. Ordered to New Orleans, La., October 2. Mustered out November 20, 1866.

Regiment lost during service 1 Officer and 46 Enlisted men killed and mortally wounded and 2 Officers and 266 Enlisted men by disease. Total 315.

10th REGIMENT INFANTRY.

Organized in Virginia November 18, 1863. Attached to Drummondstown, Va., Dept. of Virginia and North Carolina, December, 1863, to April, 1864. 1st Brigade, Hincks' Colored Division, 18th Corps, Army James, Dept. of Virginia and North Carolina, to June, 1864. 1st Brigade, 3rd Division, 18th Corps, to July, 1864. Unattached, 18th Corps, to August, 1864. 3rd Brigade, 3rd Division, 18th Corps, to December, 1864. 3rd Brigade, 1st Division, 25th Corps, to January, 1865. 3rd Brigade, 3rd Division, 25th Corps, January, 1865. Attached Brigade, 1st Division, 25th Corps, to June, 1865. Dept. of Texas to May, 1866.

SERVICE.—Camp near Crany Island till January 12, 1864. Moved to Drummondstown, eastern shore of Virginia, and duty there till April. At Yorktown, Va., till May. Butler's operations on south side of James River and against Petersburg and Richmond May 4 to June 15. Capture of Fort Powhatan May 5. Wilson's Wharf May 24 (Detachment). At Fort Powhatan till July 6. On Bermuda front in operations against Petersburg and Richmond till August 27. At City Point, Va., till April 2, 1865. Moved to Bermuda Hundred, thence to Richmond April 2-3. Return to City Point April 6, and duty there till June 1. Moved to Texas, and duty at various points on the Rio Grande till May, 1866. Mustered out May 17, 1866. (A detachment at Plymouth, N. C., November 26, 1863, to April 20, 1864, participated in the siege of Plymouth April 17-20, 1864, and surrender April 20, 1864.)

11th REGIMENT INFANTRY (OLD).

Organized at Fort Smith, Ark., December 19, 1863, to March 3, 1864. Attached to 2nd Brigade, District of the Frontier, 7th Corps, Dept. of Arkansas, to January, 1865. Colored Brigade, 7th Corps, to February, 1865. 2nd Brigade, 1st Division, 7th Corps, to April, 1865.

SERVICE.—Post and garrison duty at Fort Smith, Ark., till November, 1864. Action at Fort Smith August 24. Moved to Little Rock, Ark., November, 1864. Action at Boggs' Mill January 24, 1865. Duty at Little Rock and at Lewisburg, Ark., till April, 1865. Consolidated with 112th and 113th to form new 113th U. S. Colored Troop April 22, 1865.

11th REGIMENT INFANTRY (NEW).

Organized from 7th U. S. Colored Heavy Artillery January 23, 1865. Attached to Post and Defences of Memphis, Tenn., District of West Tennessee, to July,

1865. 2nd Infantry Brigade, District of West Tennessee, to September, 1865. Dept. of the Tennessee to January, 1866.

SERVICE.—Duty at Memphis, Tenn., and in the District of West Tennessee, Dept. of the Tennessee, to January, 1866. Mustered out January 12, 1866.

12th REGIMENT INFANTRY.

Organized in Tennessee at large July 24 to August 14, 1863. Attached to Defences of Nashville & Northwestern Railroad, Dept. of the Cumberland, to October, 1864. 2nd Colored Brigade, District of the Etowah, Dept. of the Cumberland, to January, 1865. Defences of Nashville & Northwestern Railroad, District of Middle Tennessee, to May, 1865. 3rd Sub-District, District Middle Tennessee, Dept. of the Cumberland, to January, 1866.

SERVICE.—Railroad guard duty at various points in Tennessee and Alabama on line of the Nashville & Northwestern Railroad till December, 1864. Repulse of Hood's attack on Johnsonville November 2, 4 and 5. Action at Buford's Station, Section 37, Nashville & Northwestern Railroad, November 24. March to Clarksville, Tenn., and skirmish near that place December 2. Battle of Nashville December 15-16. Pursuit of Hood to the Tennessee River December 17-28. Action at Decatur, Ala., December 27-28. Railroad guard and garrison duty in the Dept. of the Cumberland till January, 1866.

Regiment lost during service 4 Officers and 38 Enlisted men killed and mortally wounded and 242 Enlisted men by disease. Total 284.

13th REGIMENT INFANTRY.

Organized at Nashville, Tenn., November 19, 1863. Attached to Defences Nashville & Northwestern Railroad, Dept. of the Cumberland, to November, 1864. 2nd Colored Brigade, District of the Etowah, Dept. of the Cumberland, to January, 1865. Defences Nashville & Northwestern Railroad, District Middle Tennessee, Dept. of the Cumberland, to May, 1865. 3rd Sub-District, District Middle Tennessee, Dept. of the Cumberland, to January, 1866.

SERVICE.—Railroad guard duty in Tennessee and Alabama on line of Nashville & Northwestern Railroad till December, 1864. Repulse of Hood's attack on Johnsonville, Tenn., September 25, and November 4 and 5. Eddyville, Ky., October 17 (Detachment). Battle of Nashville December 15-16. Pursuit of Hood to the Tennessee River December 17-18. Railroad guard and garrison duty in the Dept. of the Cumberland till January, 1866. Mustered out January 10, 1866.

Regiment lost during service 4 Officers and 86 Enlisted men killed and mortally wounded and 265 Enlisted men by disease. Total 355.

14th REGIMENT INFANTRY.

Organized at Gallatin, Tenn., November 16, 1863, to January 8, 1864. Attached to Post of Gallatin, Tenn., to January, 1864. Post of Chattanooga, Tenn., Dept. of the Cumberland, to November, 1864. Unattached, District of the Etowah, Dept. of the Cumberland, to December, 1864. 1st Colored Brigade, District of the Etowah, to May, 1865. District of East Tennessee, to August, 1865. Dept. of the Tennessee and Dept. of Georgia till March, 1866.

SERVICE.—Garrison duty at Chattanooga, Tenn., till November, 1864. March to relief of Dalton, Ga., August 14. Action at Dalton August 14-15. Siege of Decatur, Ala., October 27-30. Battle of Nashville, Tenn., December 15-16. Overton's Hill December 16. Pursuit of Hood to the Tennessee River December 17-28. Duty at Chattanooga and in District of East Tennessee till July, 1865. At Greenville and in the Dept. of the Tennessee till March, 1866. Mustered out March 26, 1866.

15th REGIMENT INFANTRY.

Organized at Nashville, Tenn., December 2, 1863, to March 11, 1864. Attached to Post and District of Nashville, Dept. of the Cumberland, to August, 1864. Post of Springfield, District of Nashville, Dept. of the Cumberland, to March, 1865. 5th Sub-District, District of Middle Tennessee, Dept. of the Cumberland, to April, 1866.

SERVICE.—Garrison and guard duty at Nashville, Columbia and Pulaski, Tenn., till June, 1864. Post duty at Springfield, Tenn., and in District of Middle Tennessee till April, 1866. Mustered out April 7, 1866.

16th REGIMENT INFANTRY.

Organized at Nashville, Tenn., December 4, 1863, to February 13, 1864. Attached to Post of Chattanooga, Dept. of the Cumberland, to November, 1864. Unattached, District of the Etowah, Dept. of the Cumberland, to December, 1864. 1st Colored Brigade, District of the Etowah, Dept. of the Cumberland, to January, 1865. Unattached, District of the Etowah, to March, 1865. 1st Colored Brigade, Dept. of the Cumberland, to April, 1865. 5th Sub-District, District of Middle Tennessee, to July, 1865. 2nd Brigade, 4th Division, District of East Tennessee and Dept. of the Cumberland, to April, 1866.

SERVICE.—Duty at Chattanooga, Tenn., till November, 1864. Battle of Nashville, Tenn., December 15-16. Overton Hill December 16. Pursuit of Hood to the Tennessee River December 17-28. Duty at Chattanooga and in Middle and East Tennessee till April, 1866. Mustered out April 30, 1866.

17th REGIMENT INFANTRY.

Organized at Nashville, Tenn., December 12 to 21, 1863. Attached to Post of Murfreesboro, Tenn., Dept. of the Cumberland, to April, 1864. Post and District of Nashville, Tenn., Dept. of the Cumberland, to December, 1864. 1st Colored Brigade, District of the Etowah, Dept. of the Cumberland, to January, 1865. Post and District of Nashville, Tenn., Dept. of the Cumberland, to April, 1866.

SERVICE.—Duty at McMinnville and Murfreesboro, Tenn., till November, 1864. Battle of Nashville, Tenn., December 15-16. Overton Hill December 16. Pursuit of Hood to the Tennessee River December 17-27. Decatur December 28-30. Duty at Post of Nashville, Tenn., and in the Dept. of Tennessee till April, 1866. Mustered out April 25, 1866.

18th REGIMENT INFANTRY.

Organized in Missouri at large February 1 to September 28, 1864. Attached to District of St. Louis, Mo., Dept. of Missouri, to December, 1864. Unassigned, District of the Etowah, Dept. of the Cumberland, December, 1864. 1st Colored Brigade, District of the Etowah, Dept. of the Cumberland, to January, 1865. Unassigned, District of the Etowah, Dept. of the Cumberland, to March, 1865. 1st Colored Brigade, Dept. of the Cumberland, to July, 1865. 2nd Brigade, 4th Division, District of East Tennessee and Dept. of the Tennessee, to February, 1866.

SERVICE.—Duty in District of St. Louis, Mo., and at St. Louis till November, 1864. Ordered to Nashville, Tenn., November 7. Moved to Paducah, Ky., November 7-11, thence to Nashville, Tenn. Occupation of Nashville during Hood's investment December 1-15. Battles of Nashville December 15-16. Pursuit of Hood to the Tennessee River December 17-28. At Bridgeport, Ala., guarding railroad till February, 1865. Action at Elrod's Tan Yard January 27. At Chattanooga, Tenn., and in District of East Tennessee till February, 1866. Mustered out February 21, 1866.

19th REGIMENT INFANTRY.

Organized at Camp Stanton, Md., December 25, 1863, to January 16, 1864. Duty at Camp Stanton, Benedict, Md., till March, 1864, and at Camp Birney till April. Attached to 2nd Brigade, 4th Division, 9th Corps, Army of the Potomac, April to September, 1864. 2nd Brigade, 3rd Division, 9th Corps, to December, 1864. 3rd Brigade, 3rd Division, 25th Corps, to January, 1865. 3rd Brigade, 1st Division, 25th Corps, to January, 1866. Dept. of Texas, to January, 1867.

SERVICE.—Campaign from the Rapidan to the James River, Va., May and June, 1864. Guard trains through the Wilderness. Before Petersburg, Va., June 15-18. Siege operations against Petersburg and Richmond, Va., June 16, 1864, to April 2, 1865. Mine Explosion, Petersburg, July 30, 1864. Weldon Railroad August 18-21. Fort Sedgwick September 28. Poplar Grove Church September 29-30. Hatcher's Run October 27-28. Actions on the Bermuda Hundred front November 17-18. Duty at Bermuda Hundred till March, 1865. Appomattox Campaign March 28-April 9. Hatcher's Run March 29-31. Assault and capture of Petersburg April 2. Pursuit of Lee April 3-9. Appomattox Court House April 9. Surrender of Lee and his army. Duty at Petersburg and City Point till June. Moved to Texas June 13-July 3. Duty at Brownsville and on the Rio Grande, Texas, till January, 1867. Mustered out January 15, 1867.

20th REGIMENT INFANTRY.

Organized at Riker's Island, New York Harbor, February 9, 1864. Attached to Dept. of the East to March, 1864. Defences of New Orleans, La., Dept. of the Gulf, to December, 1864. District of West Florida and Southern Alabama, Dept. of the Gulf, to February, 1865. Defences of New Orleans to June, 1865. District of La-Fourche, Dept. of the Gulf, to October, 1865.

SERVICE.—Ordered to the Dept. of the Gulf March, 1864, arriving at New Orleans March 20. Moved to Port Hudson, La., March 21 and to Pass Cavallo, Texas, April 21. In District of Carrollton, La., June. At Plaquemine July. At Camp Parapet and Chalmette August. 1866.
At Camp Parapet and in District of Carrollton till December. Ordered to West Pascagoula, Fla., December 26. Return to New Orleans February, 1865, and duty there till June. At Nashville, Tenn., August. Mustered out October 7, 1865.

21st REGIMENT INFANTRY.

Organized from 3rd and 4th Regiments, South Carolina Colored Infantry, March 14, 1864. Attached to 3rd Brigade, Vogdes' Division, District of Florida, Dept. of the South, to April, 1864. Morris Island, S. C., Northern District, Dept. of the South, to October, 1864. 1st Separate Brigade, Dept. of the South, to February, 1865. Garrison of Charleston, S. C., Dept. of the South, to August, 1865. Dept. of the South, to October, 1866.

SERVICE.—Duty at Jacksonville, Fla., till April, 1864. Moved to Hilton Head, S. C., thence to Folly Island, S. C., April 18. Duty on Folly Island, Morris Island and Coles Island operating against Charleston, S. C., till February, 1865. Expedition to James Island, S. C., June 30-July 10. Action on James Island July 2. Occupation of Charleston February 18. Garrison duty at Charleston and Mt. Pleasant, S. C., till August, 1865. and at various points in South Carolina and Georgia till October, 1866. Mustered out October 7, 1866.

22nd REGIMENT INFANTRY.

Organized at Philadelphia, Pa., January 10-29, 1864. Ordered to Yorktown, Va., January, 1864. Attached to U. S. Forces, Yorktown, Va., Dept. of Virginia and North Carolina, to April, 1864. 1st Brigade, Hincks' Division (Colored), 18th Corps, Army of the James, to June, 1864. 1st Brigade, 3rd Division, 18th Corps, June, 1864. 2nd Brigade, 3rd Division, 18th Corps, to August, 1864. 1st Brigade, 3rd Division, 18th Corps, August, 1864. 1st Brigade, 3rd Division, 10th Corps, to September, 1864. 1st Brigade, 3rd Division, 18th Corps, to December, 1864. 1st Brigade, 3rd Division, 25th Corps, December, 1864. 1st Brigade, 1st Division, 25th Corps, and Dept. of Texas, to October, 1865.

SERVICE.—Duty near Yorktown, Va., till May, 1864. Expedition to King and Queen County March 9-12. Butler's operations south of James River and against Petersburg and Richmond May 4-June 15. Duty at Wilson's Wharf, James River, protecting supply transports, then constructing works near Fort Powhatan till June. Attack on Fort Powhatan May 21. Before Petersburg June 15-18. Siege operations against Petersburg and Richmond June 16, 1864, to April 2, 1865. Deep Bottom

August 24. Dutch Gap August 24. Demonstration north of the James River September 28-30. Battle of Chaffin's Farm, New Market Heights, September 29-30. Fort Harrison September 29. Battle of Fair Oaks October 27-28. Chaffin's Farm November 4. In trenches before Richmond till April, 1865. Occupation of Richmond April 3. Moved to Washington, D. C., and participated in the obsequies of President Lincoln, and afterwards to eastern shore of Maryland and along lower Potomac in pursuit of the assassins. Rejoined Corps May, 1865. Moved to Texas May 24-June 6. Duty along the Rio Grande till October, 1865. Mustered out October 16, 1865.

Regiment lost during service 2 Officers and 70 Enlisted men killed and mortally wounded and 1 Officer and 144 Enlisted men by disease. Total 217.

23rd REGIMENT INFANTRY.

Organized at Camp Casey, Va., November 23, 1863, to June 30, 1864. Attached to 2nd Brigade, 4th Division, 9th Corps, Army of the Potomac, April to September, 1864. 2nd Brigade, 3rd Division, 9th Corps, to December, 1864. 3rd Brigade, 3rd Division, 25th Corps, December, 1865. 3rd Brigade, 1st Division, 25th Corps, and Dept. of Texas, to November, 1865.

SERVICE.—Campaign from the Rapidan to the James River, Va., May and June, 1864. Guarding wagon trains Army of the Potomac through the Wilderness. Before Petersburg June 15-18. Siege of Petersburg and Richmond June 16, 1864, to April 2, 1865. Mine Explosion, Petersburg, July 30, 1864. Weldon Railroad August 18-21. Fort Sedgwick September 28. Poplar Grove Church September 29-30. Boydton Plank Road, Hatcher's Run, October 27-28. Bermuda Hundred December 13. Duty on the Bermuda Hundred front till March, 1865. Appomattox Campaign March 28-April 9. Hatcher's Run March 29-31. Fall of Petersburg April 2. Pursuit of Lee April 3-9. Appomattox Court House April 9. Surrender of Lee and his army. Duty in Dept. of Virginia till May. Moved to Texas May-June. Duty at Brownsville and along the Rio Grande, Texas, till November. Mustered out November 30, 1865.

Regiment lost during service 4 Officers and 82 Enlisted men killed and mortally wounded and 1 Officer and 165 Enlisted men by disease. Total 252.

24th REGIMENT INFANTRY.

Organized at Camp William Penn, Philadelphia, Pa., January 30 to March 30, 1865. Moved to Washington, D. C., May 5, and duty at Camp Casey till June 1. At Point Lookout, Md., guarding prisoners till July 16. Moved to Richmond, Va., and duty in Sub-District of Roanoke, Headquarters at Burkesville, till September. Moved to Richmond, Va., and there mustered out October 1, 1865.

25th REGIMENT INFANTRY.

Organized at Philadelphia, Pa., January 3 to February 12, 1864. Sailed for New Orleans, La., on Steamer "Suwahnee" March 15, 1864 (Right Wing). Vessel sprung a leak off Hatteras and put into harbor at Beaufort, N. C. Duty there in the defences, under Gen. Wessells, till April, then proceeded to New Orleans, arriving May 1. Left Wing in camp at Carrollton. Attached to Defences of New Orleans, La., Dept. of the Gulf, May to July, 1864. District of Pensacola, Fla., Dept. of the Gulf, to October, 1864. 1st Brigade, 3rd Division, U. S. Colored Troops, Dept. Gulf, October, 1864. 1st Brigade, District of West Florida, to January, 1865. 3rd Brigade, 1st Division, U. S. Colored Troops, District of West Florida, to February, 1865. 1st Brigade, 1st Division, U. S. Colored Troops, District of West Florida, to April, 1865. Unattached, District of West Florida, to July, 1865. Dept. of Florida, to December, 1865.

SERVICE.—Duty in the Defences of New Orleans, La., till July, 1864. Garrison at Post of Barrancas, Fla. (6 Cos.), and at Fort Pickens, Pensacola Harbor (4 Cos.), till December, 1865. Mustered out December 6, 1865.

26th REGIMENT INFANTRY.

Organized at Riker's Island, New York Harbor, February 27, 1864. Ordered to Dept. of the South April,

1864. Attached to District of Beaufort, S. C., Dept. of the South, to October, 1864. 2nd Separate Brigade, Dept. of the South, to January, 1865. 1st Separate Brigade, Dept. of the South, to February, 1865. 2nd Separate Brigade, Dept. of the South, to June, 1865. Dept. of the South to August, 1865.

SERVICE.—Reported at Beaufort, S. C., April 13, 1864, and post duty there till November 27. Expedition to Johns and James Islands July 2-10. Operations against Battery Pringle July 4-9. Actions on Johns Island July 5 and 7. Burden's Causeway July 9. Battle of Honey Hill November 30. Demonstration on Charleston & Savannah Railroad December 6-9. Action at Devaux's Neck December 6. Tillifinny Station December 9. McKay's Point December 22. Ordered to Beaufort, S. C., January 2, 1865, and duty there till August. Mustered out August 28, 1865.

Regiment lost during service 2 Officers and 28 Enlisted men killed and mortally wounded and 3 Officers and 112 Enlisted men by disease. Total 145.

27th REGIMENT INFANTRY.

Organized at Camp Delaware, Ohio, January 16, 1864. Ordered to Annapolis, Md. Attached to 1st Brigade, 4th Division, 9th Corps, Army of the Potomac, to September, 1864. 1st Brigade, 3rd Division, 9th Corps, to December, 1864. 1st Brigade, 1st Division, 25th Corps, December, 1864. 1st Brigade, 3rd Division, 25th Corps, to January, 1865. 3rd Brigade, 3rd Division, 25th Corps, to March, 1865. 3rd Brigade, 3rd Division, 10th Corps, Dept. of North Carolina, to July, 1865. Dept. of North Carolina to September, 1865.

SERVICE.—Campaign from the Rapidan to the James River, Va., May-June, 1864. Guard trains of the Army of the Potomac through the Wilderness. Before Petersburg June 15-19. Siege of Petersburg and Richmond June 16 to December 7, 1864. Mine Explosion, Petersburg, July 30, 1864. Weldon Railroad August 18-21. Poplar Grove Church September 29-30, and October 1. Boydton Plank Road, Hatcher's Run, October 27-28. On the Bermuda front till December 1. 1st Expedition to Fort Fisher, N. C., December 7-27. 2nd Expedition to Fort Fisher, N. C., January 7-15, 1865. Bombardment of Fort Fisher January 13-15. Assault and capture of Fort Fisher January 15. Sugar Loaf Hill January 19. Federal Point February 11. Fort Anderson February 18-20. Capture of Wilmington February 22. Northeast Ferry February 22. Campaign of the Carolinas March 1-April 26. Advance on Kinston and Goldsboro March 6-21. Cox's Bridge March 23-24. Advance on Raleigh April 9-14. Occupation of Raleigh April 14. Bennett's House April 26. Surrender of Johnston and his army. Duty in the Dept. of North Carolina till September. Mustered out September 21, 1865.

28th REGIMENT INFANTRY.

Organized at Indianapolis, Ind., December 24, 1863, to March 31, 1864. Left Indianapolis, Ind., for Washington, D. C., April 24, thence moved to Alexandria, Va. Attached to Defences of Washington, D. C., 22nd Corps, April to June, 1864. White House, Va., Abercrombie's Command, to July, 1864. 2nd Brigade, 4th Division, 9th Corps, Army of the Potomac, to September, 1864. 2nd Brigade, 3rd Division, 9th Corps, to December, 1864. 3rd Brigade, 2nd Division, 25th Corps, to April, 1865. Attached Brigade, 1st Division, 25th Corps, to April, 1865. District of St. Mary's, 22nd Corps, to May, 1865. Dept. of Texas to November, 1865.

SERVICE.—Duty at Alexandria, Va., till June, 1864. Moved to White House, Va., June 2. Engaged June 21. Accompanied Gen. Sheridan's Cavalry through Chickahominy Swamps to Prince George Court House, with several skirmishes. Siege operations against Petersburg and Richmond July, 1864, to April, 1865. Mine Explosion, Petersburg, July 30, 1864. Weldon Railroad August 18-21. Poplar Grove Church September 29-30 and October 1. Boydton Plank Road, Hatcher's Run, October 27-28. On Bermuda front and before Richmond till April, 1865. Occupation of Richmond April 3. At City Point, Va., and St. Mary's, Md., in charge of

prisoners April 6-May 12. Moved to City Point, Va., thence to Texas June 10-July 1. Duty at Brazos Santiago and Corpus Christi, Texas, till November. Mustered out November 8, 1865.

Regiment lost during service 2 Officers and 45 Enlisted men killed and mortally wounded and 1 Officer and 164 Enlisted men by disease. Total 212.

29th REGIMENT INFANTRY.

Organized at Quincy, Ill., April 24, 1864. Ordered to Annapolis, Md., May 27, 1864, thence to Alexandria, Va. Attached to Defences of Washington, D. C., 22nd Corps, to June, 1864. 2nd Brigade, 4th Division, 9th Corps, Army of the Potomac, to September, 1864. 2nd Brigade, 3rd Division, 9th Corps, to December, 1864. 3rd Brigade, 2nd Division, 25th Corps, and Dept. of Texas, to November, 1865.

SERVICE.—Duty at Alexandria, Va., till June 15, 1864. Moved to White House, Va., thence to Petersburg, Va. Siege operations against Petersburg and Richmond June 19, 1864, to April 3, 1865. Mine Explosion, Petersburg, July 30, 1864. Weldon Railroad August 18-21. Poplar Grove Church September 29-30, and October 1. Boydton Plank Road, Hatcher's Run, October 27-28. On the Bermuda Hundred front and before Richmond till April, 1865. Appomattox Campaign March 28-April 9. Duty in the Dept. of Virginia till May. Moved to Texas May and June, and duty on the Rio Grande till November. Mustered out November 6, 1865.

Regiment lost during service 3 Officers and 43 Enlisted men killed and mortally wounded and 188 Enlisted men by disease. Total 234.

30th REGIMENT INFANTRY.

Organized at Camp Stanton, Md., February 12 to March 18, 1864. Attached to 1st Brigade, 4th Division, 9th Corps, Army of the Potomac, to September, 1864. 1st Brigade, 3rd Division, 9th Corps, to December, 1864. 1st Brigade, 1st Division, 25th Corps, December, 1864. 1st Brigade, 3rd Division, 25th Corps, to March, 1865. 1st Brigade, 3rd Division, 10th Corps, Dept. of North Carolina, to July, 1865. Dept. of North Carolina to December, 1865.

SERVICE.—Campaign from the Rapidan to the James River, Va., May-June, 1864. Guard trains of the Army of the Potomac through the Wilderness and to Petersburg. Before Petersburg June 15-18. Siege operations against Petersburg and Richmond June 16 to December 7, 1864. Mine Explosion, Petersburg, July 30. Weldon Railroad August 18-21. Poplar Grove Church September 29-October 1. Boydton Plank Road, Hatcher's Run, October 27-28. 1st Expedition to Fort Fisher, N. C., December 7-27. 2nd Expedition to Fort Fisher, N. C., January 7-15, 1865. Bombardment of Fort Fisher January 13-15. Assault and capture of Fort Fisher January 15. Sugar Loaf Hill January 19. Federal Point February 11. Fort Anderson February 18-20. Capture of Wilmington February 22. Northeast Ferry February 22. Campaign of the Carolinas March 1-April 26. Advance on Kinston and Goldsboro March 6-21. Action at Cox's Bridge March 23-24. Advance on Raleigh April 9-14. Occupation of Raleigh April 14. Bennett's House April 26. Surrender of Johnston and his army. Duty at various points in North Carolina till December. Mustered out December 10, 1865.

Regiment lost during service 3 Officers and 48 Enlisted men killed and mortally wounded and 2 Officers and 177 Enlisted men by disease. Total 225.

31st REGIMENT INFANTRY.

Organized at Hart's Island, N. Y., April 29, 1864. Attached to 2nd Brigade, 4th Division, 9th Corps, Army of the Potomac, to September, 1864. 2nd Brigade, 3rd Division, 9th Corps, to December, 1864. 3rd Brigade, 2nd Division, 25th Corps, and Dept. of Texas, to November, 1865.

SERVICE.—Campaign from the Rapidan to the James River, Va., May-June, 1864. Guard trains of the Army of the Potomac through the Wilderness. Battles about Cold Harbor June 2-12. Before Petersburg June 15-19.

Siege operations against Petersburg and Richmond June 16, 1864, to April 2, 1865. Mine Explosion, Petersburg, July 30, 1864. Weldon Railroad August 18-21. Fort Sedgwick September 28. Hatcher's Run October 27-28. On the Bermuda front till March, 1865. Moved to Hatcher's Run March 26-28. Appomattox Campaign March 28-April 9. Hatcher's Run March 29-31. Fall of Petersburg April 2. Pursuit of Lee April 3-9. Appomattox Court House April 9. Surrender of Lee and his army. Duty in the Dept. of Virginia till May. Moved to Texas May-June, and duty on the Rio Grande till November. Mustered out November 7, 1865.

Regiment lost during service 3 Officers and 48 Enlisted men killed and mortally wounded and 1 Officer and 123 Enlisted men by disease. Total 175.

32nd REGIMENT INFANTRY.

Organized at Camp William Penn, Philadelphia, Pa., February 7 to March 7, 1864. Ordered to Hilton Head, S. C., April, 1864, arriving April 27. Attached to Bailey's Brigade, District of Hilton Head, S. C., Dept. of the South, to June, 1864. Morris Island, S. C., Northern District, Dept. of the South, to October, 1864. 3rd Separate Brigade, Hilton Head, S. C., Dept. of the South, to November, 1864. 2nd Brigade, Coast Division, Dept. of the South, to December, 1864. 2nd Separate Brigade, Dept. of the South, to June, 1865. Dept. of the South to August, 1865.

SERVICE.—Ordered to Hilton Head, S. C., April, 1864, and duty there till June. Moved to Morris Island, S. C., and duty there operating against Charleston, S. C., till November. Expedition to Boyd's Neck November 28-30. Battle of Honey Hill November 30. Demonstration on Charleston & Savannah Railroad December 6-9. Devaux's Neck December 6. James Island February 14, 1865. Occupation of Charleston February 18. Potter's Expedition April 5-25. Dingle's Mills April 9. Statesboro April 15. Occupation of Camden April 17. Boydkin's Mills April 18. Beach Creek near Statesburg and Denken's Mills April 19. Garrison duty at Charleston, Beaufort and Hilton Head, S. C., till August. Mustered out August 22, 1865.

Regiment lost during service 2 Officers and 35 Enlisted men killed and mortally wounded and 113 Enlisted men by disease. Total 150.

33rd REGIMENT INFANTRY.

Organized February 8, 1864, from 1st South Carolina Colored Infantry. Attached to U. S. Forces, Port Royal Island, S. C., 10th Corps, Dept. of the South, to April, 1864. District of Beaufort, S. C., Dept. of the South, to July, 1864. Folly Island, S. C., Northern District, Dept. of the South, to October, 1864. 1st Separate Brigade, Dept. of the South, to March, 1865. District of Savannah, Ga., and Dept. of the South, to January, 1866.

SERVICE.—Duty at Port Royal Island, S. C., District of Beaufort, S. C., till July, 1864. Expedition to James Island, S. C., June 30-July 10. James Island near Secessionville July 2. Duty on Folly and Morris Islands operating against Charleston, S. C., to November. Demonstration on Charleston & Savannah Railroad December 6-9. Devaux's Neck December 6. Tillifinny Station December 9. Ordered to Folly Island December 9. Near Pocotaligo Road December 20. At Pocotaligo, S. C., till February, 1865. Occupation of Charleston till March 8. Moved to Savannah, Ga., March 8, and duty there till June 6. Moved to Augusta, Ga. Duty there and at various points in the Dept. of the South till January, 1866. Mustered out January 31, 1866.

34th REGIMENT INFANTRY.

Organized February 8, 1864, from 2nd South Carolina Colored Infantry. Attached to Montgomery's Brigade, District of Florida, Dept. of the South, February, 1864. 3rd Brigade, Vogdes' Division, District of Florida, Dept. of the South, to April, 1864. Morris Island, S. C., Northern District, Dept. of the South, to June, 1864. District of Beaufort, S. C., Dept. of the South, to August, 1864. District of Florida, Dept. of the South,

to October, 1864. 4th Separate Brigade, Dept. of the South, to November, 1864. 1st Brigade, Coast Division, Dept. of the South, to December, 1864. 2nd Brigade, Coast Division, Dept. of the South, to January, 1865. 4th Separate Brigade, District of Florida, Dept. of the South, and Dept. of Florida, to February, 1866.

SERVICE.—Provost duty at Jacksonville, Fla., till March 30, 1864. Moved to Palatka, Fla., March 30-31, and to Picolata April 12. Ordered to Folly Island, S. C., April 13, thence to Morris Island, S. C., and duty there, operating against Charleston till May 20. Moved to St. Augustine, Fla., May 20, thence to Tybee Island, S. C., May 22. Expedition to Ashepoo River May 24-27. Action at Ashepoo River May 26. Moved to Hilton Head, S. C., June 30. Expedition to James Island, S. C., July 1-10. Near Winter's Point July 3. King's Creek July 3. Actions on James Island July 3 and 9-10. Burden's Causeway July 9. Return to Jacksonville, Fla., July 31. Expedition to Enterprise August 2-5. Raid on Florida Railroad August 15-18. Action at Gainesville August 17. Duty at Jacksonville, Palatka and Magnolia Springs, Fla., till November. Ordered to Hilton Head, S. C., November 25. Expedition to Boyd's Neck, S. C., November 28-30. Battle of Honey Hill November 30. Expedition to Devaux's Neck December 1-6. Action at Devaux's Neck December 6. Moved to Hilton Head, thence return to Jacksonville, Fla., January, 1865. Duty at Jacksonville and at various points in Florida till February, 1866. Mustered out February 28, 1866.

35th REGIMENT INFANTRY.

Organized February 8, 1864, from 1st North Carolina Colored Infantry. Attached to Montgomery's Brigade, District of Florida, Dept. of the South, February, 1864. 2nd Brigade, Vogdes' Division, District of Florida, Dept. of the South, to April, 1864. District of Florida, Dept. of the South, to October, 1864. 4th Separate Brigade, Dept. of the South, to November, 1864. 2nd Brigade, Coast Division, Dept. of the South, to December, 1864. 4th Separate Brigade, Dept. of the South, to March, 1865. 1st Separate Brigade, Dept. of the South, to August, 1865. Dept. of the South, to June, 1866.

SERVICE.—Expedition to Lake City, Fla., February 14-22, 1864. Battle of Olustee February 20. Duty at Jacksonville, Fla., till November. Operations on St. Johns River May 19-27. Horse Head Landing May 23. (Four Companies detached on Expedition to James Island, S. C., July 1-10. King's Creek, S. C., July 3.) Raid from Jacksonville upon Baldwin July 23-28. South Fork, Black Creek, July 24. Black Creek near Whitesides July 27. Raid on Florida Railroad August 15-19. Ordered from Jacksonville to Hilton Head, S. C., November 25, Expedition to Boyd's Neck November 28-30. Battle of Honey Hill November 30. Return to Jacksonville, Fla., and duty there till March, 1865. Ordered to Charleston, S. C. Duty there and at various points in the Dept. of the South till June, 1866. Mustered out June 1, 1866.

Regiment lost during service 4 Officers and 49 Enlisted men killed and mortally wounded and 1 Officer and 151 Enlisted men by disease. Total 205.

36th REGIMENT INFANTRY.

Organized February 8, 1864, from 2nd North Carolina Colored Infantry. Attached to U. S. Forces, Norfolk and Portsmouth, Dept. of Virginia and North Carolina, to April, 1864. District of St. Marys, Dept. of Virginia and North Carolina to June, 1864. Unattached, Army of the James, to August, 1864. 2nd Brigade, 3rd Division, 18th Corps, to December, 1864. 1st Brigade, 3rd Division, 25th Corps, December, 1864. 1st Brigade, 1st Division, 25th Corps, and Dept. of Texas, to October, 1866.

SERVICE.—Duty at Norfolk and Portsmouth, Va., till April, 1864. At Point Lookout, Md., District of St. Marys, guarding prisoners till July, 1864. Expedition from Point Lookout to Westmoreland County April 12-14. Expedition from Point Lookout to Rappahannock River May 11-14, and to Pope's Creek June 11-21. Moved from Point Lookout to Bermuda Hundred, Va., July 1-3. Siege operations against Petersburg and Richmond, Va.,

July 3, 1864, to April 2, 1865. Battle of Chaffin's Farm, New Market Heights, September 29-30. Battle of Fair Oaks October 27-28. Dutch Gap November 17. Indiantown, Sandy Creek, N. C., December 18 (Detachment). Duty north of James River before Richmond till March 27, 1865. Appomattox Campaign March 27-April 9. Occupation of Richmond April 3. Duty in Dept. of Virginia till May. Moved to Texas May 24-June 6. Duty along the Rio Grande, Texas, and at various points in Texas till October, 1866. Mustered out October 28, 1866.

37th REGIMENT INFANTRY.

Organized February 8, 1864, from 3rd North Carolina Colored Infantry. Attached to U. S. Forces, Norfolk and Portsmouth, Va., Dept. of Virginia and North Carolina, to April, 1864. 1st Brigade, Hincks' Colored Division, 18th Corps, Army of the James, to June, 1864. 1st Brigade, 3rd Division, 10th Corps, to July, 1864. Unattached, Army of the James, to August, 1864. 1st Brigade, 3rd Division, 18th Corps, to December, 1864. 3rd Brigade, 3rd Division, 25th Corps, to January, 1865. 3rd Brigade, 3rd Division, Terry's Provisional Corps, Dept. of North Carolina, to March, 1865. 2nd Brigade, 3rd Division, 10th Corps, Dept. of North Carolina, to August, 1865. Dept. of North Carolina, to February, 1867.

SERVICE.—Duty at Norfolk and Portsmouth, Va., till April, 1864. Expedition to Westmoreland County April 12-14. Butler's operations on south side of James River and against Petersburg and Richmond May 4-June 15. Capture of Fort Powhatan May 5. Duty there and at Wilson's Wharf till September 28. Moved to Deep Bottom September 28-29. Battle of Chaffin's Farm, New Market Heights, September 29-30. Battle of Fair Oaks October 27-28. In trenches before Richmond till December 7. 1st Expedition to Fort Fisher, N. C., December 7-27. 2nd Expedition to Fort Fisher January 7-15, 1865. Bombardment of Fort Fisher January 13-15. Assault and capture of Fort Fisher January 15. Sugar Loaf Hill January 19. Federal Point February 11. Fort Anderson February 18-20. Capture of Wilmington February 22. Northeast Ferry February 22. Campaign of the Carolinas March 1-April 26. Advance on Kinston and Goldsboro March 6-21. Cox's Bridge March 23-24. Advance on Raleigh April 9-14. Occupation of Raleigh April 14. Bennett's House April 26. Surrender of Johnston and his army. Duty at various points in North Carolina and in the Dept. of the South till February, 1867. Mustered out February 11, 1867.

38th REGIMENT INFANTRY.

Organized in Virginia January 23, 1864. Attached to U. S. Forces, Norfolk and Portsmouth, Va., Dept. of Virginia and North Carolina, to June, 1864. Unattached, Dept. of Virginia and North Carolina, to August, 1864. 2nd Brigade, 3rd Division, 18th Corps, Army of the James, to December, 1864. 1st Brigade, 3rd Division, 25th Corps, to December, 1864. 1st Brigade, 1st Division, 25th Corps, and Dept. of Texas, to January, 1867.

SERVICE.—Duty at Norfolk and Portsmouth, Va., till June, 1864. Operations against Petersburg and Richmond June, 1864, to April, 1865. Battle of Chaffin's Farm, New Market Heights, September 29-30. Deep Bottom October 1. Battle of Fair Oaks October 27-28. Duty in trenches north of James River before Richmond till April, 1865. Occupation of Richmond April 3, 1865. Duty in the Dept. of Virginia till May. Moved to Texas May 24-June 6. Duty at Brownsville and at various points on the Rio Grande and at Brazos Santiago, Indianola and Galveston, Texas, till January, 1867. Mustered out January 25, 1867.

Regiment lost during service 1 Officer and 42 Enlisted men killed and mortally wounded and 2 Officers and 192 Enlisted men by disease. Total 237.

39th REGIMENT INFANTRY.

Organized at Baltimore, Md., March 22-31, 1864. Attached to 1st Brigade, 4th Division, 9th Corps, Army of the Potomac, to September, 1864. 1st Brigade, 3rd Division, 9th Corps, to December, 1864. 2nd Brigade,

1st Division, 25th Corps, to December, 1864. 2nd Brigade, 3rd Division, 25th Corps, January, 1865. 2nd Brigade, 3rd Division, Terry's Provisional Corps, Dept. of North Carolina, to March, 1865. 2nd Brigade, 3rd Division, 10th Corps. Dept. of North Carolina, to August, 1865. Dept. of North Carolina to December, 1865.

SERVICE.—Campaign from the Rapidan to the James River, Va., May-June, 1864. Guard trains of the Army of the Potomac through the Wilderness and to Petersburg. Before Petersburg June 15-19. Siege of Petersburg and Richmond June 16-December 7. Mine Explosion, Petersburg, July 30. Weldon Railroad August 18-21. Poplar Grove Church September 29-30 and October 1. Boydton Plank Road, Hatcher's Run, October 27-28. On the Bermuda Hundred front till December. 1st Expedition to Fort Fisher, N. C., December 7-27. 2nd Expedition to Fort Fisher, N. C., January 7-15, 1865. Bombardment of Fort Fisher January 13-15. Assault and capture of Fort Fisher January 15. Sugar Loaf Hill January 19. Federal Point February 11. Fort Anderson February 18-20. Capture of Wilmington February 22. Northeast Ferry February 22. Campaign of the Carolinas March 1-April 26. Advance on Kinston and Goldsboro March 6-21. Cox's Bridge March 23-24. Advance on Raleigh April 9-14. Occupation of Raleigh April 14. Bennett's House April 26. Surrender of Johnston and his army. Duty at various points in the Dept. of North Carolina till December. Mustered out December 4, 1865.

Regiment lost during service 38 Enlisted men killed and mortally wounded and 3 Officers and 239 Enlisted men by disease. Total 280.

40th REGIMENT INFANTRY.

Organized at Nashville, Tenn., February 29, 1864. Attached to Defences of Louisville & Nashville Railroad, Dept. of the Cumberland, to June, 1864. Defenses Nashville & Northwestern Railroad, Dept. of the Cumberland, to December, 1864. Defences of Louisville & Nashville Railroad, Dept. of the Cumberland, to April, 1865. 2nd Brigade, 4th Division, District of East Tennessee, Dept. of the Cumberland, to July, 1865. 1st Brigade, 4th Division, Dist. East Tennessee, to August, 1865, Dept. of the Tennessee to April, 1866.

SERVICE.—Railroad guard duty entire term, on Nashville & Louisville Railroad and Nashville & Northwestern Railroad, and in District of East Tennessee. Action at South Tunnel, Tenn., October 10, 1864. Mustered out April 25, 1866.

41st REGIMENT INFANTRY.

Organized at Camp William Penn, Philadelphia, Pa., September 30 to December 7, 1864. Ordered to join Army of the James, in Virginia, October 18, 1864. Attached to 1st Brigade, 3rd Division, 10th Corps, to December, 1864. 2nd Brigade, 3rd Division, 25th Corps, to January, 1865. 2nd Brigade, 1st Division, 25th Corps, January, 1865. 2nd Brigade, 2nd Division, 25th Corps, and Dept. of Texas, to December, 1865.

SERVICE.—Guard duty at Deep Bottom, Va., till October 20, 1864. Moved to Fort Burnham on line north of James River, before Richmond, October 27. Battle of Fair Oaks October 27-28. In trenches before Richmond, and picket duty on Chaffin's Farm, till January 1, 1865. Near Fort Burnham till March 27. Moved to Hatcher's Run March 27-28. Appomattax Campaign March 28-April 9. Hatcher's Run March 29-31. Fall of Petersburg April 2. Pursuit of Lee April 3-9. Appomattox Court House April 9. Surrender of Lee and his army. Moved to Petersburg April 11, and duty there till May 25. Embarked for Texas May 25, arriving at Brazos Santiago June 3. Moved to Edenburg and guard and provost duty there till November. Consolidated to a Battalion of four Companies September 30. Mustered out at Brownsville, Texas, November 10, 1865. Disbanded at Philadelphia, Pa., December 14, 1865.

42nd REGIMENT INFANTRY.

Organized at Chattanooga, Tenn., and Nashville, Tenn., April 20, 1864. Attached to District of Chattanooga, Dept. of the Cumberland, to November, 1864. Unattached, District of the Etowah, Dept. of the Cumberland, to December, 1864. 1st Colored Brigade, District of the Etowah, to January, 1865. Unattached, District of the Etowah, to March, 1865. 1st Colored Brigade, Dept. of the Cumberland, to July, 1865. 2nd Brigade, 4th Division, District of East Tennessee, July, 1865. Dept. of Georgia to January, 1866.

SERVICE.—Guard and garrison duty at Chattanooga, Tenn., in District of East Tennessee, and in Dept. of the Cumberland, and Dept. of Georgia during entire term. Mustered out January 31, 1866.

43rd REGIMENT INFANTRY.

Organized at Philadelphia, Pa., March 12 to June 3, 1864. Moved to Annapolis, Md., April 18. Attached to 1st Brigade, 4th Division, 9th Corps, Army of the Potomac, to September, 1864. 1st Brigade, 3rd Division, 9th Corps, to December, 1864. 3rd Brigade, 3rd Division, 25th Corps, to January, 1865. 3rd Brigade, 1st Division, 25th Corps and Dept. of Texas, to October, 1865.

SERVICE.—Campaign from the Rapidan to the James River, Va., May-June, 1864. Guard trains of the Army of the Potomac through the Wilderness and to Petersburg. Before Petersburg June 15-19. Siege operations against Petersburg and Richmond June 16, 1864, to April 2, 1865. Mine Explosion, Petersburg, July 30, 1864. Weldon Railroad August 18-21. Poplar Grove Church September 29-30 and October 1. Boydton Plank Road, Hatcher's Run, October 27-28. On the Bermuda Hundred front and before Richmond till March, 1865. Moved to Hatcher's Run March 27-28. Appomattox Campaign March 28-April 9. Hatcher's Run March 29-31. Fall of Petersburg April 2. Pursuit of Lee April 3-9. Appomattox Court House April 9. Surrender of Lee and his army. Duty at Petersburg and City Point till May 30. Moved to Texas May 30-June 10. Duty on the Rio Grande, opposite Mattamoras, Mexico, till October. Mustered out October 20, 1865, and discharged at Philadelphia, Pa., November 30, 1865.

Regiment lost during service 3 Officers and 48 Enlisted men killed and mortally wounded and 188 Enlisted men by disease. Total 239.

44th REGIMENT INFANTRY.

Organized at Chattanooga, Tenn., April 7, 1864. Attached to District of Chattanooga, Dept. of the Cumberland, to November, 1864. Unattached, District of the Etowah, Dept. of the Cumberland, to December, 1864. 1st Colored Brigade, District of the Etowah, Dept. of the Cumberland, to January, 1865. Unattached, District of the Etowah, to March, 1865. 1st Colored Brigade, Dept. of the Cumberland, to July, 1865. 2nd Brigade, 4th Division, District of East Tennessee, July, 1865. Dept. of the Cumberland and Dept. of Georgia to April, 1866.

SERVICE.—Post and garrison duty at Chattanooga, Tenn., till November, 1864. Action at Dalton, Ga., October 13, 1864. Battle of Nashville, Tenn., December 15-16. Pursuit of Hood to the Tennessee River December 17-28. Post and garrison duty at Chattanooga, Tenn., in District of East Tennessee, and in the Dept. of Georgia till April, 1866. Mustered out April 30, 1866.

45th REGIMENT INFANTRY.

Organized at Philadelphia, Pa., June 13 to August 19, 1864. Moved to Washington, D. C. (4 Cos.), July, 1864. Attached to Provisional Brigade, Casey's Division, 22nd Corps, and garrison duty at Arlington Heights, Va., till March, 1865. Rejoined Regiment at Chaffin's Farm, Va., March 14, 1865.

Six Companies moved to City Point, Va., September 20, 1864. Attached to 2nd Brigade, 3rd Division, 10th Corps, Army of the James, to December, 1864. 2nd Brigade, 2nd Division, 25th Corps, and Dept. of Texas, to November, 1865.

SERVICE.—Demonstration on north side of the James River and battle of Chaffin's Farm, New Market Heights, September 28-30, 1864. Fort Harrison September 29. Darbytown Road October 18. Battle of Fair Oaks October 27-28. In trenches before Richmond till March, 1865. Moved to Hatcher's Run March 27-28. Appomattox Campaign March 28-April 9. Hatcher's Run March 29-31. Fall of Petersburg April 2. Pursuit of Lee April 3-9. Appomattox Court House April 9. Surrender of Lee and his army. Duty at Petersburg and City Point till May. Moved to Texas May and June. Duty at Edinburg on Mexican Frontier till September 8, and at Brownsville, Texas, till November. Mustered out November 4, 1865.

46th REGIMENT INFANTRY.

Organized from 1st Arkansas Infantry, African Descent, May 11, 1864. Attached to Post of Milliken's Bend, La., District of Vicksburg, Miss., to November, 1864. 2nd Brigade, 1st Division, U. S. Colored Troops, District of Vicksburg, Miss., till January, 1865. 2nd Brigade, Post and Defences of Memphis, Tenn., District West Tennessee, to February, 1865. New Orleans, La., Dept. of the Gulf, to May, 1865. Dept. of Texas, to January, 1866.

SERVICE.—Post and garrison duty at Milliken's Bend, La., and at Haines' Bluff, Miss., till January, 1865. Actions at Mound Plantation, Miss., June 24 and 29, 1864. Ordered to Memphis, Tenn., January, 1865, and garrison duty there till February, 1865. Ordered to New Orleans, La., February 23, and duty there till May 4. Ordered to Brazos Santiago, Texas, May 4. Duty at Clarksville and Brownsville on the Rio Grande, Texas, till January, 1866. Mustered out January 30, 1866.

47th REGIMENT INFANTRY.

Organized March 11, 1864, from 8th Louisiana Infantry, African Descent. Attached to 2nd Brigade, 1st Division, U. S. Colored Troops, District of Vicksburg, Miss., to October, 1864. 2nd Brigade, 4th Division, 16th Corps, to November, 1864. 2nd Brigade, 1st Division, U. S. Colored Troops, District of Vicksburg, Miss., to February, 1865. 2nd Brigade, 1st Division, U. S. Colored Troops, Military Division West Mississippi, to June, 1865. Dept. of the Gulf to January, 1866.

SERVICE.—Post and garrison duty at Vicksburg, Miss., till October, 1864. Expedition from Haines Bluff up Yazoo River April 19-23. Near Mechanicsburg April 20. Lake Providence May 27. Moved to mouth of White River, Ark., October 15. Duty there and at Vicksburg, Miss., till February, 1865. Ordered to Algiers, La., February 26, thence to Barrancas, Fla. March from Pensacola, Fla., to Blakely, Ala., March 20-April 1. Siege of Fort Blakely April 1-9. Assault and capture of Fort Blakely April 9. Occupation of Mobile April 12. March to Montgomery April 13-25. Return to Mobile and duty there till June. Moved to New Orleans, La., thence to Texas, and duty on the Rio Grande and at various points in Texas, till January, 1866. Mustered out January 5, 1866.

Regiment lost during service 1 Officer and 30 Enlisted men killed and mortally wounded and 3 Officers and 398 Enlisted men by disease. Total 432.

48th REGIMENT INFANTRY.

Organized March 11, 1864, from 10th Louisiana Infantry (African Descent). Attached to 1st Colored Brigade, District of Vicksburg, Miss., to April, 1864. 1st Brigade, 1st Division, United States Colored Troops, District of Vicksburg, Miss., to February, 1865. 3rd Brigade, 1st Division, United States Colored Troops, Military Division West Mississippi, to May, 1865. 1st Brigade, 1st Division, United States Colored Troops, District of West Florida, to June, 1865. Dept. of the Gulf to January, 1866.

SERVICE.—Garrison duty at Vicksburg, Miss., till February, 1865. Expedition from Vicksburg to Rodney and Fayette September 29-October 3, 1864. Ordered to Algiers. La., February 26, 1865; thence to Barrancas, Fla. March from Pensacola, Fla., to Blakely, Ala.,

March 20-April 1. Siege of Fort Blakely April 1-9. Assault and capture of Fort Blakely April 9. Occupation of Mobile April 12. March to Montgomery April 13-25. Duty there and at Mobile till June. Moved to New Orleans, La., thence to Texas. Duty at various points on the Rio Grande till January, 1866. Mustered out January 4, 1866.

Regiment lost during service 3 Officers and 59 Enlisted men killed and mortally wounded and 1 Officer and 464 Enlisted men by disease. Total 527.

49th REGIMENT INFANTRY.

Organized March 11, 1864, from 11th Louisiana Infantry (African Descent). Attached to 1st Colored Brigade, District of Vicksburg, Miss., to April, 1864. 1st Brigade, 1st Division, United States Colored Troops, District of Vicksburg, Miss., April, 1864. 2nd Brigade, 1st Division, United States Colored Troops, District of Vicksburg, Miss., to October, 1864. 1st Brigade, 4th Division, 16th Corps, to November, 1864. 1st Brigade, 1st Division, United States Colored Troops, District of Vicksburg, Miss., to June, 1865. Dept. of Mississippi to March, 1866.

SERVICE.—Post and garrison duty at Vicksburg, Miss., and at various points in the Dept. of Mississippi entire term. Mustered out March 27, 1866.

50th REGIMENT INFANTRY.

Organized March 11, 1864, from 12th Louisiana Infantry (African Descent). Attached to 2nd Brigade, 1st Division, United States Colored Troops, District of Vicksburg, Miss., to October, 1864. 2nd Brigade, 4th Division, 16th Corps, to November, 1864. 2nd Brigade, 1st Division, United States Colored Troops, District of Vicksburg, Miss., to February, 1865. 2nd Brigade, 1st Division, United States Colored Troops, Military Division West Mississippi, to June, 1865. Dept. of the Gulf to March, 1866.

SERVICE.—Post and garrison duty at Vicksburg, Miss., till February, 1865. Expedition from Haines Bluff to Yazoo River April 19-23, 1864. Near Mechanicsburg April 20. Expedition from Vicksburg to Rodney and Fayette September 29-October 3. Ordered to Algiers, La., February 26, thence to Barrancas, Fla. March from Pensacola, Fla., to Blakely, Ala., March 20-April 1. Siege of Fort Blakely April 1-9. Assault and capture of Fort Blakely April 9. Occupation of Mobile April 12. March to Montgomery April 13-25. Duty there and at Mobile till June. Moved to New Orleans, La. At Greenville June 16. Duty at various points in Dept. of the Gulf till March, 1866. Mustered out March 20, 1866.

51st REGIMENT INFANTRY.

Organized March 11, 1864, from 1st Mississippi Infantry (African Descent). Attached to Post of Goodrich Landing, District of Vicksburg, Miss., to December, 1864. 1st Brigade, 1st Division, United States Colored Troops, District of Vicksburg, Miss., to February, 1865. 2nd Brigade, 1st Division, Steele's Command, Military District of West Mississippi, to June, 1865. Dept. of the Gulf to June, 1866.

SERVICE.—At Lake Providence till May, 1864. Post and garrison duty at Goodrich Landing, La., till December, 1864. Action at Langley's Plantation, Issaqueena County, March 22, 1864. Flod, La., July 2. Waterford August 16-17. Duty at Vicksburg, Miss., till February, 1865. Moved to Algiers, La., February 26; thence to Barrancas, Fla. March from Pensacola, Fla., to Blakely, Ala., March 20-April 1. Siege of Fort Blakely April 1-9. Assault and capture of Fort Blakely April 9. Occupation of Mobile April 12. March to Montgomery April 13-25. Duty there and at Mobile till June. Ordered to New Orleans, thence to Texas. Duty on the Rio Grande and at various points in Texas till June, 1866. Mustered out June 16, 1866.

52nd REGIMENT INFANTRY.

Organized March 11, 1864, from 2nd Mississippi Infantry (African Descent). Attached to 2nd Brigade,

1st Division, United States Colored Troops, District of Vicksburg, Miss., to October, 1864. 2nd Brigade, 4th Division, 16th Corps, to November, 1864. 2nd Brigade, 1st Division, United States Colored Troops, District of Vicksburg, Miss., to February, 1865. Maltby's Brigade, District of Vicksburg, Miss., and Dept. of Mississippi, to May, 1866.

SERVICE.—Post and garrison duty at Vicksburg, Miss., till June, 1865. Action at Coleman's Plantation, Port Gibson, July 4, 1864. Bayou Liddell October 15. Duty at various points in the Depts. of Mississippi and the Gulf till May, 1866. Mustered out May 5, 1866.

53rd REGIMENT INFANTRY.

Organized March 11, 1864, from 3rd Mississippi Infantry (African Descent). Attached to 1st Brigade, 1st Division, United States Colored Troops, District of Vicksburg, Miss., to October, 1864. 1st Brigade, 4th Division, 16th Corps, to November, 1864. Dept. of Arkansas to February, 1865. District of Vicksburg, Miss., and Dept. of Mississippi to March, 1866.

SERVICE.—Post and garrison duty at Haines Bluff, District of Vicksburg, Miss., till October, 1864. Expedition to Grand Gulf March 12-14. Action at Grand Gulf July 16. Moved to St. Charles, Ark., on White River October, 1864, and duty there till February, 1865. Action on White River, near St. Charles, October 22, 1864. Moved to Vicksburg, Miss., February, 1865, and duty there; at Macon, Meridian and other points in the Dept. of Mississippi till March, 1866. Mustered out March 8, 1866.

54th REGIMENT INFANTRY.

Organized March 11, 1864, from 2nd Arkansas Infantry (African Descent). Attached to 2nd Brigade, Frontier Division, 7th Corps, Dept. of Arkansas, to February, 1865. 2nd Brigade, 1st Division, 7th Corps, to August, 1865. Dept. of Arkansas to December, 1866.

SERVICE.—Duty at Helena, Ark., till May, 1864. Ordered to Fort Smith, Ark., and duty there till January, 1865. Actions at Fort Gibson September 16, 1864. Cabin Creek September 19. Cow Creek, Kansas, November 14 and 28. Ordered to Little Rock January, 1865. Action on Arkansas River January 18. Duty at Little Rock and at various points in Dept. of Arkansas till December, 1866. Mustered out August 8 to December 31, 1866.

55th REGIMENT INFANTRY.

Organized March 11, 1864, from 1st Alabama Infantry (African Descent). Attached to 1st Colored Brigade, District of Memphis, Tenn., 16th Corps, to April, 1864. Fort Pickering, Post and Defences of Memphis, District of West Tennessee, to June, 1864. 3rd Brigade, Infantry Division, Sturgis' Expedition, to June, 1864. 1st Colored Brigade, District of Memphis, Tenn., District of West Tennessee, to January, 1865. 2nd Brigade, Post and Defences of Memphis, Tenn., to February, 1865. 2nd Brigade, United States Colored Troops, District of Morganza, La., Dept. of the Gulf, to April, 1865. District of Port Hudson, La., Dept. of the Gulf, to December, 1865.

SERVICE.—Post and garrison duty at Memphis, Tenn., till June 1, 1864. Sturgis' Expedition from Memphis into Mississippi June 1-13. Battle of Brice's Cross Roads, near Guntown, June 10. Ripley June 11. Davis' Mills June 12. Duty at Memphis till August 1. Smith's Expedition to Oxford, Miss., August 1-30. Action at Waterford August 16-17. Garrison duty at Memphis, Tenn., till February, 1865. Ordered to New Orleans, La., February 23; thence to Morganza, La., February 28, and duty there till April. Garrison duty at Port Hudson, Baton Rouge and other points in Louisiana till December, 1865. Mustered out December 31, 1865.

56th REGIMENT INFANTRY.

Organized March 11, 1864, from 3rd Alabama Infantry (African Descent). Attached to District of Eastern Arkansas, 7th Corps, Dept. of Arkansas, to August, 1865. Dept. of Arkansas to September, 1866.

SERVICE.—Post and garrison duty at Helena, Ark., till February, 1865. Action at Indian Bay April 13, 1864. Muffleton Lodge June 29. Operations in Arkansas July 1-31. Wallace's Ferry, Big Creek, July 26. Expedition from Helena up White River August 29-September 3. Expedition from Helena to Friar's Point, Miss., February 19-22, 1865. Duty at Helena and other points in Arkansas till September, 1866. Mustered out September 15, 1866.

Regiment lost during service 4 Officers and 21 Enlisted men killed and mortally wounded and 2 Officers and 647 Enlisted men by disease. Total 674.

57th REGIMENT INFANTRY.

Organized March 11, 1864, from 4th Arkansas Infantry (African Descent). Attached to District of Eastern Arkansas, 7th Corps, Dept. of Arkansas, to May, 1864. 1st Brigade, 2nd Division, 7th Corps, to January, 1865. Colored Brigade, 7th Corps, to February, 1865. 2nd Brigade, 1st Division, 7th Corps, to August, 1865. Dept. of Arkansas to December, 1866.

SERVICE.—Garrison duty at Helena and Little Rock, Ark., till August, 1864. (A detachment on Steele's Camden Expedition March 23-May 3, 1864, as bridge train guard.) Skirmish near Little Rock April 26, 1864. Operations against Shelby north of Arkansas River May 13-31. Skirmishes near Little Rock May 24 and 28. March to Brownsville, Ark., August 23, and to Duvall's Bluff August 29. Duty there and at Little Rock till June, 1865; then at various points in the Dept. of Arkansas guarding property and on post duty till December, 1866. Companies "A" and "D" mustered out October 18-19, 1866. Regiment mustered out December 31, 1866.

58th REGIMENT INFANTRY.

Organized March 11, 1864, from 6th Mississippi Infantry (African Descent). Attached to Post of Natchez, Miss., District of Vicksburg, Miss., to April, 1866.

SERVICE.—Post and garrison duty at Natchez and in the Dept. of Mississippi entire term. Expedition from Natchez to Gillespie's Plantation, La., August 4-6, 1864. Mustered out April 30, 1866.

59th REGIMENT INFANTRY.

Organized March 11, 1864, from 1st Tennessee Infantry (African Descent). Attached to 1st Colored Brigade, District of Memphis, Tenn., Dept. of Tennessee, to June, 1864. 3rd Brigade, Infantry Division, Sturgis' Expedition, to June, 1864. 1st Colored Brigade, District of Memphis, District of West Tennessee, to February, 1865. Fort Pickering, Defences of Memphis, Tenn., District of West Tennessee, to July, 1865. 2nd Brigade, District of West Tennessee, to September, 1865. Dept. of Tennessee to January, 1866.

SERVICE.—Post and garrison duty at Memphis, Tenn., till June, 1864. Sturgis' Expedition from Memphis into Mississippi June 1-13. Battle of Brice's Cross Roads, Guntown, June 10. Ripley June 11. Davis Mill June 12. Smith's Expedition to Tupelo, Miss., July 5-21. Near Ripley July 7. Pontotoc July 11-12. Camargo's Cross Roads, Harrisburg, July 13. Tupelo July 14-15. Old Town Creek July 15. Post and garrison duty at Memphis, Tenn., and in District of West Tennessee till January, 1866. Repulse of Forest's attack on Memphis August 21, 1864. Mustered out January 31, 1866.

60th REGIMENT INFANTRY.

Organized March 11, 1864, from 1st Iowa Colored Infantry. Attached to District of Eastern Arkansas, 7th Corps, Dept. of Arkansas, to April, 1865. 2nd Brigade, 1st Division, 7th Corps, to August, 1865. Dept. of Arkansas to October, 1865.

SERVICE.—Post and garrison duty at Helena, Ark., till April, 1865. Expedition from Helena to Big Creek July 25, 1864. Action at Wallace's Ferry, Big Creek, July 26. Expedition to Kent's Landing August 11-13. Expedition up White River August 29-September 3 (Cos. "C" and "F"). Scout to Alligator Bayou September 9-14 (Detachment). Scouts to Alligator Bayou September 22-28 and October 1-4. Expedition to Harbert's Plantation, Miss., January 11-16, 1865 (Co. "C"). Moved to Little Rock April 8, 1865, and duty there till August 20. Moved to Duvall's Bluff, thence to Jacksonport, Ark. Duty there and at various points in Sub-District of White River, in White, Augusta, Franklin and Fulton Counties, Powhatan on Black River and at Batesville till September. Mustered out at Duvall's Bluff October 15, 1865. Discharged November 2, 1865.

61st REGIMENT INFANTRY.

Organized March 11, 1864, from 2nd Tennessee Infantry (African Descent). Attached to District of Memphis, Tenn., 16th Corps. Dept. of Tennessee, to June, 1864. 1st Colored Brigade, Memphis, Tenn., District of West Tennessee, to February, 1865. 1st Brigade, United States Colored Troops, District of Morganza, Dept. of the Gulf, to April, 1865. 1st Brigade, 1st Division, United States Colored Troops, District of West Florida, to June, 1865. Dept. of Alabama to December, 1865.

SERVICE.—Post and garrison duty at Memphis, Tenn., till July, 1864. Smith's Expedition to Tupelo, Miss., July 5-21. Camargo's Cross Roads July 13. Tupelo July 14-15. Old Town Creek July 15. Smith's Expedition to Oxford, Miss., August 1-30. Repulse of Forest's attack on Memphis, Tenn., August 21. Near Memphis August 24. Eastport October 10. Moscow Station December 2-3. Duty at Memphis till February, 1865. Ordered to New Orleans, La., February 23; thence to Morganza, La. Ordered to Barrancas, Fla., March 17. Ordered to Blakely, Ala., April 15. Duty there and in the District of Alabama till December. Mustered out December 30, 1865.

Regiment lost during service 1 Officer and 37 Enlisted men killed and mortally wounded and 2 Officers and 316 Enlisted men by disease. Total 356.

62nd REGIMENT INFANTRY.

Organized March 11, 1864, from 1st Missouri Colored Infantry. Attached to District of St. Louis, Dept. of Missouri, to March, 1864. District of Baton Rouge, La., Dept. of the Gulf, to June, 1864. Provisional Brigade, District of Morganza, Dept. of the Gulf, to September, 1864. 2nd Brigade, 1st Division, United States Colored Troops, District of Morganza, Dept. of the Gulf, to September, 1864. Port Hudson, La., Dept. of the Gulf, to September, 1864. Brazos Santiago, Texas, to October, 1864. 1st Brigade, 2nd Division, United States Colored Troops, Dept. of the Gulf, to December, 1864. Brazos Santiago, Texas, to June, 1865. Dept. of Texas to March, 1866.

SERVICE.—Ordered to Baton Rouge, La., March 23, 1864, and duty there till June. Ordered to Morganza, La., and duty there till September. Expedition from Morganza to Bayou Sara September 6-7. Ordered to Brazos Santiago, Texas, September, and duty there till May, 1865. Expedition from Brazos Santiago May 11-14. Action at Palmetto Ranch May 12-13, 1865. White's Ranch May 13. Last action of the war. Duty at various points in Texas till March, 1866. Ordered to St. Louis via New Orleans, La. Mustered out March 31, 1866.

63rd REGIMENT INFANTRY.

Organized March 11, 1864, from 9th Louisiana Infantry (African Descent). Attached to Post of Natchez, Miss., District of Vicksburg, Miss., to February, 1865. Sub-District of Vidalia, District of Natchez, Miss., Dept. of Mississippi, to January, 1866.

SERVICE.—Post and garrison duty at Natchez, Miss., till February, 1865. Skirmish at Waterproof, La., April 20, 1864. Ashwood, Miss., June 25. Camp Marengo September 4. Bullitt's Bayou September 14 (Cos. "B" and "G"). Post and garrison at Vidalia and Bullitt's Bayou till January, 1866. (A Detachment at Helena, Ark., District of Eastern Arkansas, Dept. of Arkansas, to February, 1865. Cos. "B" and "K" at Memphis, Tenn., February, 1865.) Mustered out January 9, 1866.

56

64th REGIMENT INFANTRY.

Organized March 11, 1864, from 7th Louisiana Infantry (African Descent). Attached to 1st Division, Unassigned, United States Colored Troops, District of Vicksburg, Miss., to May, 1864. District of Natchez, Miss., District of Vicksburg, Miss., to September, 1864. Davis' Bend, Miss., District of Vicksburg, Miss., to December, 1864. Unattached, 1st Division, United States Colored Troops, District of Vicksburg, Miss., to February, 1865. Post of Vicksburg and Dept. of Mississippi, to March, 1866.

SERVICE.—Post and garrison duty at Vicksburg, Miss., till May, 1864. Actions at Ashwood Landing, La., May 1 and 4. Post and garrison duty at Davis' Bend and Natchez, Miss., till February, 1865. Action at Davis' Bend June 2, 1864. Point Pleasant June 25. Davis' Bend June 29. (Pine Bluff, Ark., July 2, 1864. Helena, Ark., August 2, 1864, as a Detachment.) Duty at Vicksburg, Miss., till April, 1865. At Davis' Bend and in the Dept. of Mississippi till March, 1866. Mustered out March 13, 1866.

65th REGIMENT INFANTRY.

Organized March 11, 1864, from 2nd Missouri Colored Infantry. Attached to Dept. of Missouri to June, 1864. Provisional Brigade, District of Morganza, La., Dept. of the Gulf, to September, 1864. 2nd Brigade, 1st Division, United States Colored Troops, District of Morganza, Dept. of the Gulf, to February, 1865. 1st Brigade, 1st Division, United States Colored Troops, District of Morganza, La., Dept. of the Gulf, to May, 1865. Northern District of Louisiana and Dept. of the Gulf to January, 1867.

SERVICE.—Garrison duty at Morganza, La., till May, 1865. Ordered to Port Hudson, La. Garrison duty there and at Baton Rouge and in Northern District of Louisiana till January, 1867. Mustered out January 8, 1867.

Regiment lost during service 6 Officers and 749 Enlisted men by disease.

66th REGIMENT INFANTRY.

Organized March 11, 1864, from 4th Mississippi Infantry (African Descent). Attached to Post of Goodrich Landing, District of Vicksburg, Miss., Depts. of the Tennessee and Mississippi, to February, 1865. Little Rock, Ark., Unattached, 2nd Division, 7th Corps, Dept. of Arkansas, to February, 1865. Unattached, District of Vicksburg, Miss., and Dept. of Mississippi, to March, 1866.

SERVICE.—Post and garrison duty at Goodrich Landing and at Lake Providence, La., till February, 1865. Actions at Issaqueena County March 22, 1864. Goodrich Landing March 24. Bayou Mason July 2. Issaqueena County July 10. Goodrich Landing July 16. Bayou Tensas July 30. Issaqueena County August 17. Bayou Tensas August 26. Post and garrison duty at Little Rock, Ark., till March, 1865, and at Vicksburg, Miss., and in the Dept. of Mississippi till March, 1866. Mustered out March 20, 1866.

67th REGIMENT INFANTRY.

Organized March 11, 1864, from 3rd Missouri Colored Infantry. Attached to Dept. of Missouri to March, 1864. District of Port Hudson, La., Dept. of the Gulf, to June, 1864. Provisional Brigade, District of Morganza, Dept. of the Gulf, to September, 1864. 2nd Brigade, 1st Division, United States Colored Troops, District of Morganza, Dept. of the Gulf, to February, 1865. 1st Brigade, 1st Division, United States Colored Troops, District of Morganza, Dept. of the Gulf, to May, 1865. Northern District of Louisiana, Dept. of the Gulf, to July, 1865.

SERVICE.—Moved from Benton Barracks, Mo., to Port Hudson, La., arriving March 19, 1864, and duty there till June. Moved to Morganza, La., and duty there till June, 1865. Action at Mt. Pleasant Landing, La., May 15, 1864 (Detachment). Expedition from Morganza to Bayou Sara September 6-7, 1864. Moved to Port Hudson June 1, 1865. Consolidated with 65th Regiment, United States Colored Troops, July 12, 1865.

68th REGIMENT INFANTRY.

Organized March 11, 1864, from 4th Missouri Colored Infantry. Attached to District of Memphis, Tenn., 16th Corps, Dept. of the Tennessee, to June, 1864. 1st Colored Brigade, Memphis, Tenn., District of West Tennessee, to December, 1864. Fort Pickering, Defences of Memphis, Tenn., District of West Tennessee, to February, 1865. 3rd Brigade, 1st Division, United States Colored Troops, Military Division West Mississippi, to May, 1865. 1st Brigade, 1st Division, United States Colored Troops, District of West Florida, to June, 1865. Dept. of Texas to February, 1866.

SERVICE.—At St. Louis, Mo., till April 27, 1864. Ordered to Memphis, Tenn., and duty in the Defences of that city till February, 1865. Smith's Expedition to Tupelo, Miss., July 5-21, 1864. Camargo's Cross Roads, near Harrisburg, July 13. Tupelo July 14-15. Old Town Creek July 15. At Fort Pickering, Defences of Memphis, Tenn., till February, 1865. Ordered to New Orleans, La., thence to Barrancas, Fla. March from Pensacola, Fla., to Blakely, Ala., March 20-April 1. Siege of Fort Blakely April 1-9. Assault and capture of Fort Blakely April 9. Occupation of Mobile April 12. March to Montgomery April 13-25. Duty there and at Mobile till June. Moved to New Orleans, La., thence to Texas. Duty on the Rio Grande and at various points in Texas till February, 1866. Mustered out February 5, 1866.

69th REGIMENT INFANTRY.

Organized at Pine Bluff, Duvall's Bluff and Helena, Ark., and Memphis, Tenn., December 14, 1864, to March 17, 1865. On duty at these points in Dept. of Arkansas and District of West Tennessee till September, 1865. Discontinued September 20, 1865.

70th REGIMENT INFANTRY.

Organized at Natchez, Miss., April 23 to October 1, 1864. Attached to District of Natchez, Miss., District of Vicksburg, Miss., Depts. of the Tennessee and Mississippi, till March, 1867.

SERVICE.—Post and garrison duty at Natchez, Miss., till April, 1865, and at Rodney and other points in the Dept. of Mississippi till March, 1866. Mustered out March 7, 1866.

71st REGIMENT INFANTRY.

Organized at Black River Bridge and Natchez, Miss., and Alexandria, La., March 3 to August 13, 1864. Attached to District of Natchez, Miss., District of Vicksburg, Miss.

SERVICE.—Post and garrison duty at Natchez, Miss., till November, 1864. Expedition from Natchez to Buck's Ferry and skirmishes September 19-22. Consolidated with 70th Regiment United States Colored Troops November 8, 1864.

72nd REGIMENT INFANTRY.

Organized at Covington, Ky., April 18, 1865. Discontinued May 3, 1865.

73rd REGIMENT INFANTRY.

Organized April 4, 1864, from 1st Corps de Afrique Infantry. Attached to 1st Brigade, 1st Division, Corps de Afrique, Dept. of the Gulf, to March, 1865. 1st Brigade, 1st Division, United States Colored Troops, District of West Florida, to May, 1865. 3rd Brigade, 1st Division, United States Colored Troops, District of West Florida, to June, 1865. Dept. of the Gulf to September, 1865.

SERVICE.—Duty at Port Hudson, La., till March, 1864. Red River Campaign March 10-May 22. Advance from Franklin to Alexandria March 14-26. Retreat from Alexandria to Morganza May 13-20. Mansura May 16. Near Moreauville and Yellow Bayou May 17. Yellow Bayou May 18. Near Morganza May 24. Duty at Port Hudson till July, and at Morganza till February, 1865. Moved to Algiers, La., February 26; thence to Barrancas, Fla. March from Pensacola, Fla., to Blakely, Ala., March 20-April 1. Siege of Fort Blakely April

1-9. Assault and capture of Fort Blakely April 9. Occupation of Mobile April 12. March to Montgomery April 13-25. Detached as guard to transports April 28, and return to Mobile. Duty there till June. Moved to New Orleans, La., June 10; thence to Greenville, La. Duty there and in Dept. of the Gulf till September. Consolidated with 96th United States Colored Troops September 27, 1865.

Regiment lost during service 4 Officers and 42 Enlisted men killed and mortally wounded and 1 Officer and 173 Enlisted men by disease. Total 220.

74th REGIMENT INFANTRY.

Organized April 4, 1864, from 2nd Corps de Afrique Infantry. Attached to Defences of New Orleans, Dept. of the Gulf, to October, 1864. 3rd Brigade, 3rd Division, United States Colored Troops, Dept. of the Gulf, to November, 1864. Defences of New Orleans, Dept. of the Gulf, to October, 1864. Garrison duty at Ship Island, Miss., entire term. Expedition from Fort Pike to Pearl River September 9-12, 1864. Expedition from Fort Pike to Bayou Bonforica January 31-February 1, 1865 (Detachment). Expedition from Fort Pike to Bayou St. Louis March 28-30 (Detachment). Mustered out October 11, 1865.

75th REGIMENT INFANTRY.

Organized April 4, 1864, from 3rd Corps de Afrique Infantry. Attached to 1st Brigade, 1st Division, Corps de Afrique, Dept. of the Gulf, to February, 1865. District of LaFourche, Dept. of the Gulf, to November, 1865.

SERVICE.—Red River Campaign March 10-May 22, 1864. Advance from Franklin to Alexandria, La., March 14-26. Retreat from Alexandria to Morganza May 13-20. Mansura May 16. Near Moreauville May 17. Yellow Bayou May 18. Duty at Morganza till February, 1865. Ordered to Terre Bonne February 26. Duty there and in the District of LaFourche till November, 1865. Expedition to Lake Verret, Grand Lake and the Park April 2-10, 1865. Operations about Brashear City April 30-May 12. Mustered out November 25, 1865.

76th REGIMENT INFANTRY.

Organized April 4, 1864, from 4th Corps de Afrique Infantry. Attached to 2nd Brigade, 1st Division, Corps de Afrique, Dept. of the Gulf, to July, 1864. Post of Port Hudson, La., Dept. of the Gulf, to October, 1864. 1st Brigade, 2nd Division, United States Colored Troops, Dept. of the Gulf, to February, 1865. 3rd Brigade, 1st Division, United States Colored Troops, District of West Florida, to May, 1865. 1st Brigade, 1st Division, United States Colored Troops, District of West Florida, Dept. of the Gulf, to June, 1865. Dept. of the Gulf to December, 1865.

SERVICE.—Garrison duty at Port Hudson, La., till February, 1865. Ordered to Algiers, La., February 21; thence to Barrancas, Fla. March from Pensacola, Fla., to Blakely, Ala., March 20-April 1. Siege of Fort Blakely April 1-9. Assault and capture of Fort Blakely April 9. Occupation of Mobile April 12. March to Montgomery April 13-25. Duty there and at various points in Alabama to June, 1865. Ordered to New Orleans, La., thence to Texas, and duty on the Rio Grande till December. Mustered out December 31, 1865.

77th REGIMENT INFANTRY.

Organized April 4, 1864, from 5th Corps de Afrique Infantry. Attached to Defences of New Orleans, La., Dept. of the Gulf, to October, 1864. 3rd Brigade, 3rd Division, United States Colored Troops, Dept. of the Gulf, to November, 1864. Defences of New Orleans, La., Dept. of the Gulf, to October, 1865.

SERVICE.—Duty in the Defences of New Orleans at Fort St. Phillip, Jefferson City, and other points till October, 1865. Consolidated with 10th United States Colored Heavy Artillery October 18, 1865.

78th REGIMENT INFANTRY.

Organized April 4, 1864, from 6th Corps de Afrique Infantry. Attached to 2nd Brigade, 2nd Division, Corps de Afrique, Dept. of the Gulf, to July, 1864. Post of Port Hudson, La., Dept. of the Gulf, to October, 1864. 2nd Brigade, 2nd Division, United States Colored Troops, Dept. of the Gulf, to October, 1864. Post of Port Hudson, La., Dept. of the Gulf, to April, 1865. District of LaFourche, Dept. of the Gulf, to January, 1866.

SERVICE.—Post and garrison duty at Port Hudson, La., till April, 1865, and at Donaldsonville, Thibodeaux and other points in District of LaFourche, Dept. of the Gulf, to January, 1866. Mustered out January 6, 1866.

79th REGIMENT INFANTRY.—(OLD.)

Organized April 4, 1864, from 7th Corps de Afrique Infantry. Attached to 2nd Brigade, 1st Division, Corps de Afrique, Dept. of the Gulf, to June, 1864. 2nd Brigade, 2nd Division, Corps de Afrique, Dept. of the Gulf, to July, 1864.

SERVICE.—Post and garrison duty at Port Hudson, La., till April 17, 1864, and at Fort Pike and Fort Macomb, Defences of New Orleans, till July, 1864. Broken up July 28, 1864, and transferred to 75th United States Colored Troops. A new 79th United States Colored Troops ordered organized by consolidation of 80th and 83rd United States Colored Troops at New Orleans, La., July, 1864, but not completed.

79th REGIMENT INFANTRY.—(NEW.)

Organized from 1st Kansas Colored Infantry December 13, 1864. Attached to 2nd Brigade, District of the Frontier, 7th Corps, Dept. of Arkansas, to January, 1865. Colored Brigade, 7th Corps, to February, 1865. 2nd Brigade, 1st Division, 7th Corps, to August, 1865. Dept. of Arkansas to October, 1865.

SERVICE.—Duty at Fort Smith, Ark., till January, 1865. Skirmish at Ivey's Ford January 8. Ordered to Little Rock January 16. Skirmish at Clarksville, Ark., January 18. Duty at Little Rock, Ark., till July, and at Pine Bluff till October. Mustered out at Pine Bluff, Ark., October 1, 1865, and discharged at Fort Leavenworth, Kansas, October 30, 1865.

Regiment lost during service 5 Officers and 183 Enlisted men killed and mortally wounded and 1 Officer and 165 Enlisted men by disease. Total 354.

80th REGIMENT INFANTRY.

Organized April 4, 1864, from 8th Corps de Afrique Infantry. Attached to garrison at Port Hudson, La., Dept. of the Gulf, to April, 1864. District of Bonnet Carre, La., Dept. of the Gulf, to July, 1864. Transferred to 79th United States Colored Troops (New) July 6, 1864. Reorganized July, 1864, by consolidation of 90th, 96th and 98th United States Colored Troops. Attached to District of Bonnet Carre, Engineer Brigade, Dept. of the Gulf, to September, 1864. 2nd Brigade, 2nd Division, United States Colored Troops, Dept. of the Gulf, to February, 1865. District of Bonnet Carre, La., Dept. of the Gulf, to April, 1865. Defences of New Orleans to June, 1865. Northern District of Louisiana till January, 1866.

SERVICE.—Duty at Port Hudson, La., till April 17, 1864, and in District of Bonnet Carre till April, 1865. Scout from Bayou Goula to Grand River January 29-February 7, 1865. At Carrollton, Camp Parapet and New Orleans till June 16. At Shreveport and Alexandria, La., till January 1, 1866. Moved to Texas and garrison duty at various points in that State till March, 1867. Mustered out March 1, 1867.

81st REGIMENT INFANTRY.

Organized April 4, 1864, from 9th Corps de Afrique Infantry. Attached to 2nd Brigade, 1st Division, Corps de Afrique, Dept. of the Gulf, to July, 1864. Consolidated with 88th and 89th United States Colored Troops July 6, 1864, to form new 77th United States Colored Troops. Reorganized July, 1864, by consolidation of 87th and 95th United States Colored Troops. Attached to Engineer Brigade, Dept. of the Gulf, to September, 1864. 2nd Brigade, 2nd Division, United States Colored Troops, Dept. of the Gulf, to February, 1865. Garrison of Port Hudson, La., Dept. of the Gulf, to July, 1865. Dept. of the Gulf to January, 1866.

SERVICE.—Post and garrison duty at Port Hudson, La., and in the Dept. of the Gulf entire term. Mustered out January 30, 1866.

82nd REGIMENT INFANTRY.

Organized April 4, 1864, from 10th Corps de Afrique Infantry. Attached to 2nd Brigade, 1st Division, Corps de Afrique, Dept. of the Gulf, to July, 1864. Consolidated with 80th United States Colored Troops July 6, 1864, to form new 79th United States Colored Troops. Reorganized July, 1864, by consolidation of 97th and 99th United States Colored Troops. Attached to Pensacola, Fla., District of West Florida, Dept. of the Gulf, to October, 1864. 1st Brigade, 3rd Division, United States Colored Troops, Dept. of the Gulf, to October, 1864. 1st Brigade, District of West Florida, to January, 1865. 3rd Brigade, District of West Florida, to March, 1865. 1st Brigade, 1st Division, District of West Florida, to May, 1865. Pensacola, Fla., District of West Florida and Dept. of Florida, to muster out.

SERVICE.—Duty at Port Hudson, La., till April 17, 1864. Moved to Fort Barrancas, Fla., and duty there till March, 1865. Expedition toward Pollard, Ala., July 21-25, 1864. Camp Gonzales, Fla., July 22. Near Pollard, Ala., July 23. Expedition from Fort Barrancas August 15-19. Expedition to Marianna September 18-October 4. Euchee Anna Court House September 23. Marianna September 27. Expedition up Blackwater Bay October 25-28. Near Milton October 26. Expedition to Pollard, Ala., December 13-19. Mitchell's Creek December 15-16. Pine Barren Ford December 17-18. March from Pensacola to Blakely, Ala., March 20-April 1, 1865. Siege of Fort Blakely April 1-9. Assault and capture of Fort Blakely April 9. Occupation of Mobile April 12. March to Montgomery April 13-25. Duty there till May. Moved to Mobile, thence to Barrancas, Fla., May 23. Expedition to Appalachicola May 31-June 6. Duty at Appalachicola and in District of Florida till September, 1866. Mustered out September 10, 1866.

83rd REGIMENT INFANTRY.—(OLD.)

Organized April 4, 1864, from 11th Corps de Afrique Infantry. Attached to 1st Brigade, 1st Division, Corps de Afrique, Dept. of the Gulf, to July, 1864. Garrison duty at Port Hudson, La. Broken up July 28, 1864.

83rd REGIMENT INFANTRY.—(NEW.)

Organized from 2nd Kansas Colored Infantry December 13, 1864. Attached to 2nd Brigade, District of the Frontier, 7th Corps, Dept. of Arkansas, to January, 1865. Colored Brigade, 7th Corps, Dept. of Arkansas, to February, 1865. 2nd Brigade, 1st Division, 7th Corps, Dept. of Arkansas, to August, 1865. Dept. of Arkansas to October, 1865.

SERVICE.—Duty at Fort Smith, Ark., till January, 1865. Moved to Little Rock, Ark., January 15-February 4, and duty there till August. Moved to Camden, Ark., August 1-10, and duty there till October 9. Mustered out October 9, 1865. Discharged at Leavenworth, Kansas, November 27, 1865.

Regiment lost during service 2 Officers and 32 Enlisted men killed and mortally wounded and 211 Enlisted men by disease. Total 245.

84th REGIMENT INFANTRY.

Organized April 4, 1864, from 12th Corps de Afrique Infantry. Attached to 1st Brigade, 1st Division, Corps de Afrique, Dept. of the Gulf, to February, 1865. 2nd Brigade, 1st Division, United States Colored Troops, Dept. of the Gulf, to May, 1865. Northern District of Louisiana, Dept. of the Gulf, to March, 1866.

SERVICE.—Red River Campaign March 10-May 22. Advance from Franklin to Alexandria March 14-26. Retreat from Alexandria to Morganza May 13-20. Mansura May 16. Near Moreauville May 17. Yellow Bayou May 18. Duty at Morganza till May, 1865. Action near Morganza November 23, 1864. Duty in Northern District of Louisiana and Dept. of the Gulf to March, 1866. Mustered out March 14, 1866.

85th REGIMENT INFANTRY.

Organized April 4, 1864, from 13th Corps de Afrique Infantry. Attached to a Provisional Brigade, 13th Corps, Texas, Dept. of the Gulf, to May, 1864.

SERVICE.—Duty at Brownsville, Texas, and other points in Texas till May, 1864. Mustered out by consolidation with 77th United States Colored Troops May 24, 1864.

86th REGIMENT INFANTRY.

Organized April 4, 1864, from 14th Corps de Afrique Infantry. Attached to District of West Florida, Dept. of the Gulf, to October, 1864. 1st Brigade, 3rd Division, United States Colored Troops, Dept. of the Gulf, to November, 1864. 1st Brigade, District of West Florida, to January, 1865. 3rd Brigade, District of West Florida, to March, 1865. 1st Brigade, 1st Division, United States Colored Troops, Steele's Command, to May, 1865. District of West Florida to July, 1865. Dept. of Florida to April, 1866.

SERVICE.—Duty at Barrancas, Fla., till March, 1865. March from Pensacola, Fla., to Blakely, Ala., March 20-April 1. Siege of Fort Blakely April 1-9. Assault and capture of Fort Blakely April 9. Occupation of Mobile April 12. March to Montgomery April 13-25. Duty there and at Mobile till May 19. Garrison at Fort Morgan May 19 to July. Duty at Pensacola and other points in the Dept. of Florida till April, 1866. Mustered out April 10, 1866.

87th REGIMENT INFANTRY.—(OLD.)

Organized April 4, 1864, from 16th Corps de Afrique Infantry. Attached to 2nd Division, 13th Corps, to June, 1864. Colored Brigade, United States Forces, Texas, to July, 1864.

SERVICE.—Duty at Brazos Santiago, Point Isabel and Brownsville, Texas, till July, 1864. Consolidated with 95th United States Colored Troops July 6, 1864, to form new 81st United States Colored Troops. Redesignated 87th (New) December 10, 1864.

87th REGIMENT INFANTRY.—(NEW.)

Organized November 26, 1864, by consolidation of 87th (Old) and 96th United States Colored Troops. Attached to United States Forces, Texas, Dept. of the Gulf, to August, 1865. Duty at Brazos Santiago and other points in Texas till August, 1865. Consolidated with 84th United States Colored Troops August 14, 1865.

88th REGIMENT INFANTRY.—(OLD.)

Organized April 4, 1864, from 17th Corps de Afrique Infantry. Duty at Port Hudson, La., till July, 1864. Broken up July 28, 1864.

88th REGIMENT INFANTRY.—(NEW.)

Organized at Memphis, Tenn., February 20, 1865. Attached to Post and Defences of Memphis, Tenn., District of West Tennessee, to July, 1865. 2nd Infantry Brigade, District of West Tennessee, to September, 1865. Dept. of Tennessee to December, 1865.

SERVICE.—Duty at Memphis, Tenn., and in the District of West Tennessee till December, 1865. Consolidated with 3rd United States Colored Heavy Artillery December 16, 1865.

89th REGIMENT INFANTRY.

Organized April 4, 1864, from 18th Corps de Afrique Infantry. Duty at Port Hudson, La., till July, 1864. Broken up July 28, 1864.

90th REGIMENT INFANTRY.

Organized April 4, 1864, from 19th Corps de Afrique Infantry. Duty at Madisonville and Lakeport, La., till July. Broken up July 28, 1864.

91st REGIMENT INFANTRY.

Organized April 4, 1864, from 20th Corps de Afrique Infantry. Garrison duty at Fort Pike, Defences of

New Orleans, La., till July, 1864. Pearl River Expedition April 1-10 (Cos. "C," "D," "E" and "F"). Consolidated with 74th United States Colored Troops July 7, 1864.

92nd REGIMENT INFANTRY.

Organized April 4, 1864, from 22nd Corps de Afrique Infantry. Attached to 1st Brigade, 1st Division, Corps de Afrique, Dept. of the Gulf, to July, 1864. 1st Brigade, 1st Division, United States Colored Troops, District of Morganza, La., Dept. of the Gulf, to June, 1865. Northern District of Louisiana, Dept. of the Gulf, to December, 1865.

SERVICE.—Red River Campaign March 10-May 22, 1864. Advance from Franklin to Alexandria March 14-26. Retreat from Alexandria to Morganza May 18-20. Mansura May 16. Near Moreauville May 17. Yellow Bayou May 18. Duty at Morganza till June, 1865. Operations near Morganza September 16-25, 1864. Expedition from Morganza to the Atchafalaya River December 16-19, 1864. Duty in Northern District, Dept. of the Gulf, to December, 1865. Mustered out December 31, 1865.

93rd REGIMENT INFANTRY.

Organized April 4, 1864, from 26th Corps de Afrique Infantry. Attached to District of LaFourche, Dept. of the Gulf, to October, 1864. 2nd Brigade, 3rd Division, United States Colored Troops, Dept. of the Gulf, to November, 1864. District of LaFourche, Dept. of the Gulf, to June, 1865.

SERVICE.—Duty at Brashear City till June, 1864. At Brashear City and Berwick till June, 1865. Expedition from Berwick to Pattersonville August 2, 1864. Expedition from Brashear City to Belle River October 22-24, 1864 (Detachment). Expedition from Brashear City to Bayou Portage November 17-19 (Detachment). Skirmish at Lake Fausse Point November 18 (Detachment). Expedition from Brashear City to Lake Verret February 10-11, 1865 (Detachment). Expedition from Brashear City to Bayou Pigeon March 20-22 (Detachment). Bayou Teche March 21 (Detachment). Expedition from Brashear City to Indian Bend March 15-27 (Detachment). Expedition from Brashear City to Oyster Bayou March 25-28 (Detachment). Expedition to Lake Verret, Grand Bayou and the Park April 2-10 (Detachment). Operations about Brashear City April 30-May 2. Broken up June 23, 1865.

94th REGIMENT INFANTRY.

Failed to complete organization.

95th REGIMENT INFANTRY.

Organized April 4, 1864, from 1st Corps de Afrique Engineers. Attached to Engineers Brigade, 13th Corps, Dept. of the Gulf, to June, 1864. Colored Brigade, United States Forces, Texas, Dept. of the Gulf, to November, 1864.

SERVICE.—Duty at Brazos Santiago, Point Isabel, Brownsville, Arkansas Pass and other points in Texas till November, 1864. Consolidated with 87th United States Colored Troops November 26, 1864.

96th REGIMENT INFANTRY.

Organized April 4, 1864, from 2nd Corps de Afrique Engineers. Attached to a Provisional Brigade, 13th Corps, Dept. of the Gulf, to June, 1864. Engineer Brigade, Dept. of the Gulf, to October, 1864. United States Forces, Mobile Bay, Dept. of the Gulf, to October, 1864. 1st Brigade, 3rd Division, United States Colored Troops, Dept. of the Gulf, to November, 1864. United States Forces, Mobile Bay, Dept. of the Gulf, to December, 1864. District of Southern Alabama, Dept. of the Gulf, to March, 1865. Engineer Brigade, 13th Corps, Military Division West Mississippi, to June, 1865. Unassigned, Dept. of the Gulf, to January, 1866.

SERVICE.—Garrison at Fort Esperanza and engineer duty on Matagorda Peninsula, Texas, till May, 1864. Ordered to New Orleans, La., May 27; thence to Port Hudson, La., and duty there till July 27. Moved to New Orleans, thence to Mobile Bay, Ala. Siege opera-

tions against Fort Gaines and Morgan August 2-23. Duty at Mobile Point till November. At East Pascagoula till February, 1865. Campaign against Mobile and its Defences February to April. Siege of Spanish Fort and Fort Blakely March 17-April 9. Duty on the Fortifications at Mobile and at various points in the Dept. of the Gulf till January, 1866. Mustered out January 29, 1866.

97th REGIMENT INFANTRY.

Organized April 4, 1864, from 3rd Corps de Afrique Engineers. Attached to Provisional Brigade, 13th Corps, Texas, Dept. of the Gulf, to February, 1864. Engineer Brigade, Dept. of the Gulf, to October, 1864. United States Forces, Mobile Bay, Dept. of the Gulf, to November, 1st Brigade, District of West Florida, to February, 1865. 3rd Brigade, District of West Florida, to March, 1865. Engineer Brigade, Military Division West Mississippi, to June, 1865. Unattached, Dept. of the Gulf, to April, 1866.

SERVICE.—Red River Campaign to May 22, 1864. Built bridge over Red River at Grand Ecore April 12. Constructed rifle pits and Abatis about Grand Ecore April 13-19. Repair road from Grand Ecore to Cane River, and crossing over Cane River April 19-20. Lower Crossing of Cane River April 22. At Alexandria constructing works and dam April 25-May 13. Retreat to Morganza May 13-22. Marksville May 16. Operations about Yellow Bayou May 17-20. Fatigue duty at Morganza till June 20. Ordered to New Orleans, La., June 20. Duty in District of Carrollton till August. Moved to Mobile Bay, Ala., August 20. Duty at Mobile Point and Dauphin Island till February, 1865. In District of Florida till March, 1865. Campaign against Mobile and its Defences March 17-April 12. Siege of Spanish Fort and Fort Blakely March 26-April 9. Duty in the Fortifications of Mobile and at various points in the Dept. of the Gulf till April, 1866. Mustered out April 6, 1866.

98th REGIMENT INFANTRY.

Organized April 4, 1864, from 4th Corps de Afrique Engineers. Attached to Engineer Brigade, Dept. of the Gulf, to July, 1864. Defences of New Orleans, Dept. of the Gulf, to October, 1864. 2nd Brigade, 3rd Division, United States Colored Troops, Dept. of the Gulf, to November, 1864. District of LaFourche, Dept. of the Gulf, to August, 1865.

SERVICE.—Stationed at Brashear City, Berwick City and New Orleans till June, 1864. In District of Carrollton till July, 1864. At Greenville till September, 1864. At Plaquemine till February, 1865. At Brashear City and in the District of LaFourche till August, 1865. Consolidated with 78th United States Colored Troops August 26, 1865.

99th REGIMENT INFANTRY.

Organized April 4, 1864, from 5th Corps de Afrique Engineers. Attached to Engineer Brigade, Dept. of the Gulf, to October, 1864. 2nd Brigade, 1st Division, United States Colored Troops, Dept. of the Gulf, to February, 1865. District of Key West, Fla., to July, 1865. Dept. of Florida to April, 1866.

SERVICE.—Red River Campaign to May 22, 1864. Built bridges at Grand Ecore April 12. Built fortifications at Grand Ecore April 13-19. Repair road and crossing over Cane River April 19-20. Lower Crossing of Cane River April 22. At Alexandria constructing works and dam April 25-May 13. Retreat to Morganza May 18-22. Marksville May 16. Operations on Yellow Bayou May 17-20. Fatigue duty at Morganza till June 20. Ordered to New Orleans June 20. Duty at New Orleans and Plaquemine till December, 1864. At Key West and Tortugas, Fla., and in the Dept. of Florida till April, 1866. Operations near St. Marks, Fla., February 21-March 7, 1865. Newport Bridge March 5-6. Natural Bridge March 6. Mustered out April 23, 1866.

100th REGIMENT INFANTRY.

Organized in Kentucky at large May 3 to June 1, 1864. Attached to Defences of Nashville & Northwestern Railroad, Dept. of the Cumberland, to December, 1864. 2nd Colored Brigade, District of the Etowah, Dept. of the Cumberland, to January, 1865. Defences of Nashville & Northwestern Railroad, Dept. of the Cumberland, to December, 1865.

SERVICE.—Guard duty on Nashville & Northwestern Railroad in Tennessee till December, 1864. Skirmish on Nashville & Northwestern Railroad September 4. Action at Johnsonville November 4-5. Battle of Nashville, Tenn., December 15-16. Overton Hill December 16. Pursuit of Hood to the Tennessee River December 17-28. Again assigned to guard duty on Nashville & Northwestern Railroad January 16, 1865, and so continued till December, 1865. Mustered out December 26, 1865.

101st REGIMENT INFANTRY.

Organized in Tennessee at large September 16, 1864. Attached to Defences of Louisville & Nashville Railroad, Dept. of the Cumberland, to March, 1865. Dept. of the Tennessee to January, 1866.

SERVICE.—Duty at Nashville, Tenn., till October, 1864; then guard Louisville & Nashville Railroad, and duty in Tennessee and Alabama till muster out. Affairs at Scottsboro and Larkinsville, Ala., January 8, 1865. Mustered out January 21, 1866.

102nd REGIMENT INFANTRY.

Organized May 23, 1864, from 1st Michigan Colored Infantry. Attached to District of Hilton Head, S. C., Dept. of the South and District of Beaufort, S. C., Dept. of the South, to August, 1864. District of Florida, Dept. of the South, to October, 1864. 2nd Separate Brigade, Dept. of the South, to November, 1864. 2nd Brigade, Coast Division, Dept. of the South, to February, 1865. 2nd Separate Brigade, Dept. of the South, to March, 1865. 1st Separate Brigade and Dept. of the South to September, 1865.

SERVICE.—Garrison at Port Royal, S. C., till June 15. Moved to Beaufort, S. C., and garrison duty there till August 1. Moved to Jacksonville, Fla., August 1-3. Picket duty at Baldwin till August 15. Attack on Baldwin August 11-12. Raid on Florida Central Railroad August 15-19. At Magnolia till August 29. Moved to Beaufort, S. C., August 29-31, and duty there till January, 1865, engaged in outpost and picket duty on Port Royal, Lady and Coosa Islands. (A Detachment at Honey Hill November 30, 1864. Demonstration on Charleston & Savannah Railroad December 6-9. Deveaux's Neck, Tillifinny River, December 6 and 9.) Detachment at Beaufort; rejoined other Detachment at Deveaux's Neck, S. C., January 24, 1865. Moved to Pocotaligo February 28. Advance on Charleston February 7-23. Skirmish at Cuckwold Creek February 8 (Cos. "B," "E" and "I"). Duty at Charleston Neck till March 9. Moved to Savannah, Ga., March 9-16. Moved to Georgetown March 28-April 1. (Right wing of Regiment, under Chapman, moved to Charleston April 7-9, thence march to join Potter at Nelson's Ferry April 11-18.) Potter's Expedition from Georgetown to Camden April 5-29. Statesburg April 15. Occupation of Camden April 17. Boykin's Mills April 18. Bradford Springs April 18 (right wing). Dingle's Mills April 19. Singleton's Plantation April 19. Beech Creek, near Statesburg, April 19. Moved to Charleston April 29, thence to Summerville May 7-8; to Branchville May 18; to Orangeburg May 25, and provost duty there till July 28. March to Winsboro July 28-August 3, and duty there till September. Moved to Charleston and muster out September 30, 1865.

103rd REGIMENT INFANTRY.

Organized at Hilton Head, S. C., March 10, 1865. Attached to District of Savannah, Ga., Dept. of the South, to June, 1865. Dept. of the South to April, 1866.

SERVICE.—Garrison and guard duty at Savannah, Ga., and at various points in Georgia and South Carolina entire term. Mustered out April 15-20, 1866.

104th REGIMENT INFANTRY.

Organized at Beaufort, S. C., April 28 to June 25, 1865. Attached to Dept. of the South. Garrison and guard duty at various points in South Carolina till February. 1866. Mustered out February 5, 1866.

105th REGIMENT INFANTRY.

Failed to complete organization.

106th REGIMENT INFANTRY.

Organized May 16, 1864, from 4th Alabama Colored Infantry. Attached to District of North Alabama, Dept. of the Cumberland, to February, 1865. Defences of Nashville & Northwestern Railroad, Dept. of the Cumberland, to November, 1865.

SERVICE.—Garrison at Pulaski and railroad guard duty entire term. Forest's attack on Athens, Ala., September 23-24, 1864. Consolidated with 40th United States Colored Troops November 7, 1865.

107th REGIMENT INFANTRY.

Organized at Louisville, Ky., May 3 to September 15, 1864. Attached to Military District of Kentucky, Dept. of the Ohio, to October, 1864. Provisional Brigade, 3rd Division, 18th Corps, Army of the James, to December, 1864. 3rd Brigade, 1st Division, 25th Corps, to December, 1864. 3rd Brigade, 3rd Division, 25th Corps, to January, 1865. 1st Brigade, 3rd Division, 25th Corps, to March, 1865. 1st Brigade, 3rd Division, 10th Corps, Dept. of North Carolina, to August, 1865. Dept. of North Carolina and Dept. of the South to November, 1866.

SERVICE.—Duty in Kentucky till October, 1864. Ordered to Baltimore, Md., thence to City Point, Va., October 26. Siege of Petersburg November 3 to December 7. 1st Expedition to Fort Fisher, N. C., December 7-27. 2nd Expedition to Fort Fisher, N. C., January 7-15, 1865. Bombardment of Fort Fisher January 13-15. Assault and capture of Fort Fisher January 15. Sugar Loaf Hill January 19. Federal Point February 11. Fort Anderson February 18-20. Capture of Wilmington February 22. Northeast Ferry February 22. Campaign of the Carolinas March 1-April 26. March on Kinston and Goldsboro March 6-21. Action at Cox's Bridge March 23-24. Advance on Raleigh April 9-14. Occupation of Raleigh April 14. Bennett's House April 26. Surrender of Johnston and his army. Duty at various points in North Carolina and in the Dept. of the South till November, 1866. Mustered out November 22, 1866.

108th REGIMENT INFANTRY.

Organized at Louisville, Ky., June 20, 1864. Attached to 1st Brigade, 2nd Division, District of Kentucky, 5th Division, 23rd Corps, Dept. of the Ohio, to January, 1865. Military District of Kentucky to May, 1865. Dept. of Mississippi and the Gulf to March, 1866.

SERVICE.—Garrison and guard duty at various points in Kentucky till January, 1865. Action at Owensboro, Ky., October 22, 1864. Guard duty at Rock Island, Ill., January to May, 1865. Duty in the Dept. of Mississippi till March, 1866. Mustered out March 21, 1866.

109th REGIMENT INFANTRY.

Organized at Louisville, Ky., July 5, 1864. Attached to 3rd Brigade, 1st Division, District of Kentucky, 5th Division, 23rd Corps, Dept. of the Ohio, to October, 1864. Martindale's Provisional Brigade, 18th Corps, Army of the James, to December, 1864. 1st Brigade, 2nd Division, 25th Corps and Dept. of Texas, to March, 1866.

SERVICE.—Duty at Louisville and Louisa, Ky., till October. 1864. Ordered to join Army of the Potomac before Petersburg and Richmond, Va. Duty at Deep Bottom and in trenches before Richmond north of the James River till March, 1865. Actions at Fort Harrison December 10, 1864, and January 23, 1865. Moved to Hatcher's Run March 27-28. Appomattox Campaign March 28-April 9. Boydton Road, Hatcher's Run, March 29-31. Fall of Petersburg April 2. Pursuit of

Lee April 3-9. Appomattox Court House April 9. Surrender of Lee and his army. Duty at Petersburg and City Point till May. Embarked for Texas May 25, arriving at Indianola, Texas, June 25. Duty there and on the Rio Grande, Texas, till March, 1866. Mustered out March 21, 1866.

110th REGIMENT INFANTRY.

Organized June 25, 1864, from 2nd Alabama Colored Infantry. Attached to District of North Alabama, Dept. of the Cumberland, to February, 1865. Defences of Nashville & Northwestern Railroad to March, 1865. 3rd Sub-District, District of Middle Tennessee, to September, 1865. Dept. of the Tennessee to February, 1866.

SERVICE.—Garrison duty at Pulaski, Tenn., and guard duty on railroad in North Alabama till February, 1865. Forest's attack on Athens, Ala., September 23-24, 1864. Larkinsville, Ala., January 8, 1865 (Detachment of Co. "E"). Guard Nashville & Northwestern Railroad till June, 1865. At Gallatin, Tenn., and at various points in the Dept. of Tennessee till February, 1866. Mustered out February 6, 1866.

111th REGIMENT INFANTRY.

Organized June 25, 1864, from 3rd Alabama Colored Infantry. Attached to garrison at Pulaski, Tenn., District of North Alabama, Dept. of the Cumberland, to February, 1865. Defences of Nashville & Northwestern Railroad, Dept. of the Cumberland, to March, 1865. 3rd Sub-District, District of Middle Tennessee, to July, 1865. Dept. of the Tennessee to April, 1866.

SERVICE.—Duty at Pulaski, Tenn., and Athens, Ala., District of North Alabama, till September, 1864. Action at Athens with Forest September 23-24 (most of Regiment captured). Sulphur Branch Trestle September 25 (Detachment). Duty at Pulaski, Tenn., till January, 1865. Guard duty on Nashville & Northwestern Railroad and in Middle Tennessee till April, 1866. Mustered out April 30, 1866.

112th REGIMENT INFANTRY.

Organized at Little Rock, Ark., from 5th Arkansas Colored Infantry April 23 to November 8, 1864. Attached to 1st Division, 7th Corps, Dept. of Arkansas, June, 1864, to January, 1865. Colored Brigade, 7th Corps, to February, 1865. 2nd Brigade, 1st Division, 7th Corps, to April, 1865. Post and garrison duty at Little Rock, Ark., entire term. Transferred to 113th United States Colored Troops (New) April 1, 1865.

113th REGIMENT INFANTRY.—(OLD.)

Organized June 25, 1864, from 6th Arkansas Colored Infantry. Attached to 1st Division, 7th Corps, Dept. of Arkansas, to January, 1865. Colored Brigade, 7th Corps, to February, 1865. 2nd Brigade, 1st Division, 7th Corps, to April, 1865.

SERVICE.—Post and garrison duty at Little Rock, Ark., entire term. Consolidated with 11th United States Colored Troops (Old) and 112th United States Colored Troops to form 113th United States Colored Troops (New) April 1, 1865.

113th REGIMENT INFANTRY.—(NEW.)

Organized April 1, 1864, by consolidation of 11th United States Colored Troops (Old), 112th United States Colored Troops and 113th United States Colored Troops (Old). Attached to 2nd Brigade, 1st Division, 7th Corps, Dept. of Arkansas, to August, 1865, and Dept. of Arkansas to April, 1866. Duty in Dept. of Arkansas. Mustered out April 9, 1866.

114th REGIMENT INFANTRY.

Organized at Camp Nelson, Ky., July 4, 1864. Attached to Military District of Kentucky, Dept. of the Ohio, to January, 1865. 3rd Brigade, 1st Division, 25th Corps, Dept. of Virginia, to April, 1865. 2nd Brigade, 1st Division, 25th Corps and Dept. of Texas, to April, 1867.

SERVICE.—Duty at Camp Nelson and Louisa, Ky., till January, 1865. Ordered to Dept. of Virginia January 3, 1865. Siege operations against Petersburg and Richmond on the Bermuda Hundred Front till March, 1865. Appomattox Campaign March 28-April 9. Hatcher's Run March 29-31. Fall of Petersburg April 2. Pursuit of Lee April 3-9. Appomattox Court House April 9. Surrender of Lee and his army. Duty at Petersburg and City Point till June. Moved to Texas June and July. Duty at Brownsville and other points on the Rio Grande, Texas, till April, 1867. Mustered out April 2, 1867.

115th REGIMENT INFANTRY.

Organized at Bowling Green, Ky., July 15 to October 21, 1864. Attached to 2nd Brigade, 2nd Division, District of Kentucky, 5th Division, 23rd Corps, Dept. of the Ohio, to January, 1865. 1st Brigade, 2nd Division, 25th Corps, Dept. of Virginia, to March, 1865. 2nd Brigade, 1st Division, 25th Corps and Dept. of Texas, to February, 1866.

SERVICE.—Garrison duty at Lexington, Ky., till December, 1864. Ordered to Virginia. Siege operations against Petersburg and Richmond January to April, 1865. Occupation of Richmond April 3. Duty in the Dept. of Virginia till May. Sailed for Texas May 20. Duty in District of the Rio Grande till February, 1866. Mustered out February 10, 1866.

116th REGIMENT INFANTRY.

Organized at Camp Nelson, Ky., June 6 to July 12, 1864. Attached to Military District of Kentucky, Dept. of the Ohio, to September, 1864. Unattached, 10th Corps, Army of the James, to November, 1864. 1st Brigade, 3rd Division, 10th Corps, to December, 1864. 1st Brigade, 2nd Division, 25th Corps, to April, 1865. 3rd Brigade, 2nd Division, 25th Corps and Dept. of Texas, to September, 1866. Dept. of the Gulf to January, 1867.

SERVICE.—Duty at Camp Nelson till September, 1864. Defence of Camp Nelson and Hickman's Bridge against Forest's attack. Ordered to join Army of the James in Virginia, reporting to General Butler September 27. Duty at City Point, Va., till October. Moved to Deep Bottom October 23. Siege operations against Petersburg and Richmond October 23, 1864, to April 2, 1865. Operations on north side of the James River before Richmond October 27-28, 1864. Fatigue duty at Deep Bottom, Dutch Gap and in trenches before Richmond till March, 1865. Moved to Hatcher's Run March 27-28. Appomattox Campaign March 28-April 9. Boydton Road, Hatcher's Run, March 29-31. Fall of Petersburg April 2. Pursuit of Lee April 3-9. Appomattox Court House April 9. Surrender of Lee and his army. Duty at Petersburg till May 25. Embarked at City Point, Va., for Texas May 25, arriving at Brazos Santiago June 22. March to White's Ranch June 24. Duty at Rome, Texas, till February, 1866. In Sub-District, Lower Rio Grande, till September, 1866, and at New Orleans, La., till January, 1867. Mustered out at Louisville, Ky., January 17, 1867.

117th REGIMENT INFANTRY.

Organized at Covington, Ky., July 18 to September 27, 1864. Attached to Military District of Kentucky, Dept. of the Ohio, to October, 1864. Provisional Brigade, 18th Corps, Army of the James, to December, 1864. 1st Brigade, 1st Division, 25th Corps and Dept. of Texas, to August, 1867.

SERVICE.—Duty at Camp Nelson, Ky., till October, 1864. Ordered to Baltimore, Md., thence to City Point, Va., October 21. Siege operations against Petersburg and Richmond till March, 1865. Appomattox Campaign March 28-April 9. Hatcher's Run March 29-31. Fall of Petersburg April 2. Pursuit of Lee April 3-9. Appomattox Court House April 9. Surrender of Lee and his army. Duty at Petersburg and City Point till June. Moved to Brazos Santiago, Texas, June and July. Duty at Brownsville and on the Rio Grande, Texas, till August, 1867. Mustered out August 10, 1867.

118th REGIMENT INFANTRY.

Organized at Baltimore, Md., October 19, 1864. Moved to City Point, Va., October 26, 1864. Attached to Provisional Brigade, 3rd Division, 18th Corps, Army of the James, to December, 1864. 1st Brigade, 1st Division, 25th Corps and Dept. of Texas, to February, 1866.

SERVICE.—Siege operations against Petersburg and Richmond November, 1864, to April, 1865. Occupation of Richmond April 3, 1865. Duty in the Dept. of Virginia till June. Moved to Brazos Santiago, Texas, June and July. Duty at Brownsville and at various points on the Rio Grande till February, 1866. Mustered out February 6, 1866.

119th REGIMENT INFANTRY.

Organized at Camp Nelson, Ky., January 18 to May 16, 1865. Attached to Dept. of Kentucky and duty at various points in that State till April, 1866. Mustered out April 27, 1866.

120th REGIMENT INFANTRY.

Organized at Henderson, Ky., November, 1864. Garrison and guard duty at various points in Military District and Dept. of Kentucky till June, 1865. Discontinued June 21, 1865.

121st REGIMENT INFANTRY.

Organized at Maysville, Ky., October 8, 1864. Garrison and guard duty at various points in Military District and Dept. of Kentucky till June, 1865. Discontinued June 30, 1865.

122nd REGIMENT INFANTRY.

Organized at Louisville, Ky., December 31, 1864. Ordered to Virginia January 12, 1865. Attached to 25th Corps, Army of the James, Unassigned, to April, 1865. Dept. of Texas to February, 1866.

SERVICE.—Duty in the Defences of Portsmouth, Va., till February, 1865. Siege operations against Petersburg and Richmond, Va., February to April, 1865. Fall of Petersburg and Richmond April 2-3. Duty in the Dept. of Virginia till June, 1865. Moved to Brazos Santiago, Texas, June and July. Duty at Brownsville and at various points on the Rio Grande till February, 1866. Mustered out February 8, 1866.

123rd REGIMENT INFANTRY.

Organized at Louisville, Ky., December 2, 1864. Duty at Louisville, Ky., and other points in the Dept. of Kentucky till October, 1865. Mustered out October 24, 1865.

124th REGIMENT INFANTRY.

Organized at Camp Nelson, Ky., January 1 to April 27, 1865. Garrison and guard duty at various points in the Dept. of Kentucky till December, 1867. Mustered out December 20, 1867.

125th REGIMENT INFANTRY.

Organized at Louisville, Ky., February 12 to June 2, 1865. Garrison and guard duty at Louisville, Ky., and other points in the Dept. of Kentucky till December, 1867. Mustered out December 20, 1867.

126th REGIMENT INFANTRY.

Not organized.

127th REGIMENT INFANTRY.

Organized at Camp William Penn, Philadelphia, Pa., August 23 to September 10, 1864. Ordered to City Point, Va., September, 1864. Attached to 1st Brigade, 3rd Division, 10th Corps, Army of the James, to November, 1864. 2nd Brigade, 3rd Division, 10th Corps, to December, 1864. 2nd Brigade, 2nd Division, 25th Corps and Dept. of Texas, to October, 1865.

SERVICE.—Siege operations against Petersburg and Richmond, Va., September, 1864, to April, 1865. Chaffin's Farm, New Market Heights, September 29-30. Fort Harrison September 29. Darbytown Road October 13. Battle of Fair Oaks October 27-28. Duty in trenches north of the James River before Richmond till March, 1865. Moved to Hatcher's Run March 27-28. Appomattox Campaign March 28-April 9. Hatcher's Run March 29-31. Fall of Petersburg April 2. Pursuit of Lee April 3-9. Appomattox Court House April 9. Surrender of Lee and his army. Duty at Petersburg and City Point till June. Moved to Brazos Santiago, Texas, June and July. Duty at various points on the Rio Grande till October. Mustered out October 20, 1865.

128th REGIMENT INFANTRY.

Organized at Hilton Head, S. C., April, 1865. Duty in Dept. of the South till October, 1865. Mustered out October 20, 1865.

135th REGIMENT INFANTRY.

Organized at Goldsboro, N. C., March 28, 1865. Duty in Dept. of North Carolina till October, 1865. Mustered out October 23, 1865.

136th REGIMENT INFANTRY.

Organized at Atlanta, Ga., July 15, 1865. Duty in Dept. of Georgia. Mustered out January 4, 1866.

137th REGIMENT INFANTRY.

Organized at Selma, Ala., April 8, 1865. Mustered in at Macon, Ga., June 1, 1865. Duty in the Dept. of Georgia till January, 1866. Mustered out January 15, 1866.

138th REGIMENT INFANTRY.

Organized at Atlanta, Ga., July 15, 1865. Duty in the Dept. of Georgia. Mustered out January 6, 1866.

UNITED STATES VOLUNTEERS.—INDIAN TROOPS.

1st REGIMENT INDIAN HOME GUARD.

Organized at Leroy, Kansas, May 22, 1862. Attached to Dept. of Kansas to August, 1862. 3rd Brigade, Dept. of Kansas, to October, 1862. 3rd Brigade, 1st Division, Army of the Frontier, Dept. of Missouri, to February, 1863. District of Northwest Arkansas, Dept. of Missouri, to June, 1863. District of the Frontier, Dept. of Missouri, to December, 1863. 1st Brigade, District of the Frontier, Dept. of Missouri, to January, 1864. 1st Brigade, District of the Frontier, 7th Army Corps, Dept. of Arkansas, to February, 1864. Indian Brigade, District of the Frontier, Dept. of Arkansas, 7th Army Corps, to February, 1865. 3rd Brigade, 3rd Division, 7th Army Corps, to May, 1865.

SERVICE.—Expedition into Indian Territory May 25-July 28, 1862. Locust Grove, Cherokee Nation, July 3. Bayou Bernard July 27-28. Blount's Campaign in Missouri and Arkansas September 17 to December 3. Occupation of Newtonia October 4. Fort Gibson October 15. Old Fort Wayne or Beattie's Prairie, near Maysville, October 22. Between Fayetteville and Cane Hill November 9. Camp Babcock November 25. Cane Hill, Boston Mountains, November 28. Capture of Fort Davis December. Operations about Cane Hill December 4-6. Reed's Mountains December 6. Battle of Prairie Grove December 7. Expedition over Boston Mountains to Van Buren December 27-29. Capture of Van Buren December 29. Sent to Indian Territory January, 1863, and occupy line of the Arkansas River to protect friendly Indians, with Headquarters at Fort Gibson, I. T., and Fort Smith, Ark., till May, 1865. Action at Bentonville, Ark., February 20, 1863. Fort Blount April 30 and May 20. Fort Gibson, Cherokee Nation, May 22 and 25. Fort Blount June 9. Operations about Fort Gibson June 16-20. Greenlief Prairie June 16. Cabin Creek July 1-2. Elk Creek, near Honey Springs, July 17. Cabin Creek July 20. Creek Agency October 15 and 25. Repulse of Quantrell's attack on Fort Gibson December 16. Near Sheldon Place, Barren Fork, December 18. Operations in Indian Territory February 1-21, 1864. Cabin Creek September 19. Expedition from Fort Gibson to Little River and Hillabee March 18-20, 1865. Mustered out May 31, 1865.

2nd REGIMENT INDIAN HOME GUARD.

Organized on Big Creek and at Five-Mile Creek, Kansas, June 22 to July 18, 1862. Attached to Dept. of Kansas to August, 1862. 1st Brigade, Dept. of Kansas, to October, 1862. 3rd Brigade, 1st Division, Army of the Frontier, Dept. of Missouri, to February, 1863. District of Northwest Arkansas, Dept. of Missouri, to June, 1863. District of the Frontier, Dept. of Missouri, to December, 1863. 1st Brigade, District of the Frontier, Dept. of Missouri, to January, 1864. 1st Brigade, District of the Frontier, 7th Army Corps, Dept. of Arkansas, to February, 1864. Indian Brigade, District of the Frontier, 7th Army Corps, Dept. of Arkansas, to February, 1865. 3rd Brigade, 3rd Division, 7th Army Corps, to May, 1865.

SERVICE.—Expedition into Indian Territory May 25-July 28, 1862. Capture of Fort Gibson July 18. Bayou Bernard, I. T., July 28. Blount's Compaign in Missouri and Arkansas September 17-December 3. Shirley's Ford, Spring River, September 20. Expedition to Sarcoxie September 28-30. Occupation of Newtonia October 4. Old Fort Wayne or Beattie's Prairie, near Maysville, October 22. Cane Hill, Boston Mountains, November 28. Capture of Fort Davis December. Battle of Prairie Grove, Ark., December 7. Expedition over Boston Mountains to Van Buren December 27-29. Capture of Van Buren December 29. Sent to Indian Territory and occupy line of the Arkansas River and protect friendly Indians, with Headquarters at Fort Smith, Ark., and at Fort Gibson, I. T., till May, 1865. Near Fort Gibson, I. T., May 20, 1863. Fort Blount and Fort Gibson May 22. Operations near Fort Gibson June 6-20. Greenlief Prairie June 16. Cabin Creek July 1-2. Elk Creek, near Honey Springs, July 17. Operation in Cherokee Nation September 11-25. Repulse of Quantrell's attack on Fort Gibson December 16. Near Sheldon Place, Barren Fork, December 18. Cabin Creek December 19. Mustered out May 31, 1865.

3rd REGIMENT INDIAN HOME GUARD.

Organized at Carthage, Mo., September 16, 1862. Served Unattached, Dept. of Kansas, September, 1862. 1st Brigade, Dept. of Kansas, to October, 1862. 3rd Brigade, 1st Division, Army of the Frontier, Dept. of Missouri, to February, 1863. District of Northwest Arkansas, Dept. of Missouri, to June, 1863. District of the Frontier, Dept. of Missouri, to December, 1863. 1st Brigade, District of the Frontier, Dept. of Missouri, to January, 1864. 1st Brigade, District of the Frontier, 7th Army Corps, Dept. of Arkansas, to February, 1864. Indian Brigade, District of the Frontier, 7th Army Corps, Dept. of Arkansas, to February, 1865. 3rd Brigade, 3rd Division, 7th Army Corps, to May, 1865.

SERVICE.—Bayou Bernard, I. T., July 28, 1862. Neosho, Mo., September 1. Spring River September 1. Neosho September 3 and 5. Shirley's Ford, Spring River, September 20. Newtonia September 30. Occupation of Newtonia October 4. Newtonia October 5. Fort Gibson October 15. Old Fort Wayne or Beattie's Prairie, near Maysville, October 22. Cane Hill November 28. Capture of Fort Davis December. Salem December 2. Prairie Grove and Rhea's Mills December 7. Neosho December 15. Cane Hill December 20. Expedition over Boston Mountains and capture of Van Buren December 27-29. Sent to Indian Territory and occupy line of the Arkansas River and protect friendly Indians, with Headquarters at Fort Gibson, I. T., and Fort Smith, Ark., till May, 1865. Near Maysville January, 1863. Cherokee Country January 18. Fort Gibson February 28. Neosho March 2. Greenlief Priarie March 12. Fort Gibson March 27. Fort Blount March 27. Tahlequah March 30. Near Maysville May 8. Fort Smith, Ark., May 15. Near Fort Gibson and Fort Blount May 20. Fort Gibson May 22. Fort Blount May 25 and June 1. Operations about Fort Gibson June 6-20. Spring Creek June 6. Greenlief Prairie June 16. Fort Blount June 19. Cabin Creek July 1-2. Elk Creek, near Honey Springs, July 17. Operations in Cherokee Nation September 11-15. Fourteen-mile Creek October

30. Repulse of Quantrell's attack on Fort Gibson December 16. Near Sheldon Place, Barren Fork, December 18. Near Fort Gibson December 26. Operations in Indian Territory Februray 1-21, 1864. Scullyville April 16. Near Maysville May 8. Cabin Creek and Prior's Creek September 19. Cow Creek November 14 and 28. Expedition from Fort Gibson to Little River and Hillabee March 18-30, 1965. Skirmish on Snake River, Ark., April 28. Mustered out May 31, 1865.

4th REGIMENT INDIAN HOME GUARD.

Organization commenced but not completed. Men transferred to other organizations.

UNITED STATES VETERAN RESERVE CORPS.

1st REGIMENT.—Organized at Washington, D. C., October 10, 1863, by consolidation of the 17th, 34th, 97th, 103rd, 113th, 114th, 142nd, 144th, 145th and 151st Companies, 1st Battalion. Mustered out by detachments from June 25 to November 25, 1865.

2nd REGIMENT.—Organized at Detroit, Mich., October 10, 1863, by consolidation of the 38th, 52nd, 101st, 106th, 110th, 111th, 240th, 242nd and 247th Companies, 1st Battalion, and 6th Company, 2nd Battalion. Mustered out by detachments from July 3 to November 11, 1865.

3rd REGIMENT.—Organized October 10, 1863, by consolidation of the 8th, 10th, 16th, 28th, 50th, 54th, 168th, 172nd, 189th and 190th Companies, 1st Battalion. Mustered out by Detachments June 28 to December 15, 1865.

4th REGIMENT.—Organized at Rock Island, Ill., October 10, 1863, by consolidation of the 128th, 129th, 135th, 136th, 137th, 138th, 140th, 141st, 153rd and 166th Companies, 1st Battalion. Mustered out July 17, 1865, to January 23, 1866, by detachments.

5th REGIMENT.—Organized at Indianapolis, Ind., October 10, 1863, by consolidation of the 33rd, 35th, 36th, 40th, 44th, 45th, 109th, 149th, 152nd and 154th Companies, 1st Battalion. Mustered out July 2 to November 23, 1865, by detachments.

6th REGIMENT.—Organized at Washington, D. C., October 10, 1863, by consolidation of the 61st, 87th, 93rd, 95th, 100th, 112th, 164th, 167th, 169th and 170th Companies, 1st Battalion. Mustered out by detachments July 5 to November 25, 1865.

7th REGIMENT.—Organized October 10, 1863, by consolidation of the 46th, 56th, 62nd, 66th, 67th, 98th, 147th, 156th, 157th and 165th Companies, 1st Battalion. Mustered out by detachments June 30 to November 25, 1865.

8th REGIMENT.—Organized at Chicago, Ill., October 10, 1863, by consolidation of the 20th, 22nd, 23rd, 31st, 63rd, 78th, 81st, 83rd, 92nd and 96th Companies, 1st Battalion. Mustered out by detachments July 1 to November 20, 1865.

9th REGIMENT.—Organized at Washington, D. C., October 10, 1863, by consolidation of the 3rd, 53rd, 59th, 64th, 65th, 71st, 209th, 210th, 211th and 212th Companies, 1st Battalion. Mustered out by detachments July 1 to November 16, 1865.

10th REGIMENT.—Organized at New York City October 10, 1863, by consolidation of the 12th, 13th, 14th, 15th, 19th, 57th, 228th, 229th, 232nd and 233rd Companies, 1st Battalion. Mustered out by detachments July 1 to November 28, 1865.

11th REGIMENT.—Organized at Elmira, N. Y., October 10, 1863, by consolidation of the 177th, 178th, 179th, 180th, 193rd, 213th, 214th, 215th, 218th and 219th Companies, 1st Battalion. Mustered out by detachments June 29 to November 23, 1865.

12th REGIMENT.—Organized at Albany, N. Y., October 10, 1863, by consolidation of the 4th, 29th, 37th, 39th, 42nd, 51st, 222nd, 223rd, 224th and 225th Companies, 1st Battalion. Mustered out by detachments July 5 to November 25, 1865.

13th REGIMENT.—Organized October 10, 1863, by consolidation of the 7th, 9th, 11th, 27th, 32nd, 55th, 231st, 234th, 235th and 236th Companies, 1st Battalion. Mustered out by detachments July 1 to December 4, 1865.

14th REGIMENT.—Organized October 10, 1863, by consolidation of the 1st, 2nd, 5th, 30th, 41st, 88th, 186th,

200th, 201st and 202nd Companies, 1st Battalion. Mustered out by detachments July 14 to November 27, 1865.

15th REGIMENT.—Organized October 10, 1863, by consolidation of the 21st, 24th, 25th, 68th, 70th, 75th, 94th, 105th, 107th and 120th Companies, 1st Battalion. Mustered out by detachments June 28 to November 25, 1865.

16th REGIMENT.—Organized at Harrisburg, Pa., October 10, 1863, by consolidation of the 6th, 18th, 80th, 86th, 89th, 90th, 181st, 182nd, 217th and 221st Companies, 1st Battalion. Mustered out by detachments July 15 to November 26, 1865.

17th REGIMENT.—Organized January 12, 1864, by consolidation of the 26th, 76th, 102nd, 119th, 123rd, 124th, 131st, 132nd, 133rd and 139th Companies, 1st Battalion. Mustered out by detachments July 3 to November 14, 1865.

18th REGIMENT.—Organized at Washington, D. C., May 5, 1864, by consolidation of the 203rd, 204th, 205th, 206th, 207th, 208th, 216th, 220th, 227th and 237th Companies, 1st Battalion. Mustered out by detachments July 3 to November 21, 1865.

19th REGIMENT.—Organized at Washington, D. C., January 12, 1864, by consolidation of the 58th, 72nd, 79th, 85th, 108th, 115th, 194th, 196th, 197th and 198th Companies, 1st Battalion. Mustered out by detachments July 13 to November 16, 1865.

20th REGIMENT.—Organized at Baltimore, Md., January 12, 1864, by consolidation of the 60th, 69th, 82nd, 99th, 104th, 127th, 185th, 188th, 199th and 226th Companies, 1st Battalion. Mustered out by detachments June 15 to November 21, 1865.

21st REGIMENT.—Organized January 12, 1865, by consolidation of the 43rd, 47th, 48th, 49th, 73rd, 84th, 150th, 158th, 176th and 230th Companies, 1st Battalion. Mustered out by detachments July 7 to November 20, 1865.

22nd REGIMENT.—Organized at Washington, D. C., January 12, 1864, by consolidation of the 74th, 91st, 122nd, 126th, 130th, 134th, 175th, 183rd, 184th and 192nd Companies, 1st Battalion. Mustered out by detachments July 1 to November 19, 1865.

23rd REGIMENT.—Organized January 12, 1864, by consolidation of the 77th, 116th, 117th, 118th, 121st, 125th, 143rd, 155th, 162nd and 191st Companies, 1st Battalion. Mustered out by detachments July 1 to December 5, 1865.

24th REGIMENT.—Organized at Washington, D. C., February 24, 1864, by consolidation of the 146th, 148th, 159th, 160th, 161st, 163rd, 171st, 173rd, 174th and 195th Companies, 1st Battalion. Mustered out by detachments June 30 to November 27, 1865.

187th COMPANY, 1st BATTALION.—Organized at Convalescent Camp Smith, Tenn., February 23, 1864. Consolidated with 243rd Company, 1st Battalion, August 4, 1865.

238th COMPANY, 1st BATTALION.—Organized at Camp Stoneman, D. C., October 10, 1864. Consolidated with 243rd Company, 1st Battalion, August 4, 1865.

239th COMPANY, 1st BATTALION.—Organized at Camp Stoneman, D. C., October 10, 1864. Consolidated with 243rd Company, 1st Battalion, August 4, 1865.

243rd COMPANY, 1st BATTALION.—Formerly known as 1st Company, Provisional Cavalry, Veteran Reserve Corps, organized at Washington, D. C., June, 1864. Mustered out by detachments July 8 to November 13, 1865.

244th COMPANY, 1st BATTALION.—Organized at Knoxville, Tenn., February 7, 1865. Mustered out by detachments July 12 to November 27, 1865.

245th COMPANY, 1st BATTALION.—Organized at Knoxville, Tenn., February 24, 1865. Mustered out by detachments July 12 to November 27, 1865.

246th COMPANY, 1st BATTALION.—Organized at St. Albans, Vt., April, 1865. Mustered out by detachments July 8 to October 3, 1865.

1st COMPANY, 2nd BATTALION.—Formerly known as Company "G," 3rd Regiment, Veteran Reserve Corps. Organized at Convalescent Camp, Va., June 9, 1863. Des-

ignation changed to 1st Company, 2nd Battalion, May 20, 1864. Consolidated with 14th Company, 2nd Battalion, August 7, 1865.

2nd COMPANY, 2nd BATTALION.—Formerly known as Company "G," 11th Regiment, Veteran Reserve Corps. Organized at Washington, D. C., July 1, 1863. Designation changed to 2nd Company, 2nd Battalion, April 25, 1864. Mustered out by detachments July 19-November 21, 1865.

3rd COMPANY, 2nd BATTALION.—Formerly known as Company "H," 11th Regiment, Veteran Reserve Corps. Organized at Washington, D. C., July 1, 1863. Designation changed to 3rd Company, 2nd Battalion, April 25, 1864. Consolidated with 16th Company, 2nd Battalion, September 3, 1865.

4th COMPANY, 2nd BATTALION.—Formerly known as Company "G," 10th Regiment, Veteran Reserve Corps. Designation changed August 1, 1864. Transferred to 5th Independent Company January 4, 1866.

5th COMPANY, 2nd BATTALION.—Formerly known as Company "H," 10th Regiment, Veteran Reserve Corps. Organized at McDougall Gen. Hospital June 24, 1863. Designation changed August 1, 1864. Consolidated with 110th Company, 2nd Battalion, October 23, 1865.

6th COMPANY, 2nd BATTALION.—Formerly known as Company "G," 21st Regiment, Veteran Reserve Corps. Organized at Fort Schuyler, N. Y. Harbor, June 24, 1863. Designation changed May 16, 1864. Transferred to 2nd Regiment, Veteran Reserve Corps, as Company "H," December 27, 1864.

7th COMPANY, 2nd BATTALION.—Formerly known as Company "H," 1st Regiment, Veteran Reserve Corps. Organized at Convalescent Camp, Va., July 16, 1863. Designation changed to 7th Company, 2nd Battalion, March 7, 1864. Consolidated with 16th Company, 2nd Battalion, July 5, 1865.

8th COMPANY, 2nd BATTALION.—Formerly known as Company "I," 10th Regiment, Veteran Reserve Corps. Organized at New York City June 30, 1863. Designation changed August 1, 1864. Mustered out by detachments August 10 to September 14, 1866.

9th COMPANY, 2nd BATTALION.—Formerly known as Company "H," 2nd Regiment, Veteran Reserve Corps. Organized at Camp Joe Holt, Ind., September 30, 1863. Designation changed January 1, 1865. Mustered out August 7 to November 20, 1865.

10th COMPANY. 2nd BATTALION.—Formerly known as Company "G," 12th Regiment, Veteran Reserve Corps. Organized at Convalescent Camp, Va., July, 1863. Designation changed May 23, 1864. Consolidated with 58th Company, 2nd Battalion, July 5, 1865.

11th COMPANY, 2nd BATTALION.—Formerly known as Company "G," 7th Regiment, Veteran Reserve Corps. Organized at Nashville, Tenn., July 25, 1863. Designation changed March 7, 1864. Consolidated with 74th Company, 2nd Battalion, September 28, 1865.

12th COMPANY, 2nd BATTALION.—Formerly known as Company "H," 12th Regiment, Veteran Reserve Corps. Organized at Convalescent Camp, Va., July 16, 1863. Designation changed May 23, 1864. Consolidated with 58th Company, 2nd Battalion, July 5, 1865.

13th COMPANY, 2nd BATTALION.—Formerly known as Company "G," 8th Regiment, Veteran Reserve Corps. Organized at St. Louis, Mo., July 29, 1863. Designation changed April 25, 1864. Mustered out by detachments August 10 to December 2, 1865.

14th COMPANY, 2nd BATTALION.—Formerly known as Company "K," 6th Regiment, Veteran Reserve Corps. Organized at Washington, D. C., July, 1863. Designation changed March 7, 1864. Mustered out by detachments September 4, 1865, to February 1, 1866.

15th COMPANY, 2nd BATTALION.—Formerly known as Company "H," 8th Regiment, Veteran Reserve Corps. Organized at St. Louis, Mo., August 1, 1863. Designation changed April 25, 1864. Consolidated with 80th Company, 2nd Battalion, August 4, 1865.

16th COMPANY, 2nd BATTALION.—Formerly known as Company "G," 1st Regiment, Veteran Reserve Corps.

Organized at Convalescent Camp, Va., August, 1863. Designation changed March 7, 1864. Mustered out by detachments August 23, 1865, to January 29, 1866.

17th COMPANY, 2nd BATTALION.—Formerly known as Company "H," 21st Regiment, Veteran Reserve Corps. Organized at Newark, N. J., July 25, 1863. Designation changed May 13, 1864. Mustered out by detachments August 3, 1865, to October 22, 1866.

18th COMPANY, 2nd BATTALION.—Formerly known as Company "I," 13th Regiment, Veteran Reserve Corps. Organized at Lovett Gen. Hospital, Portsmouth Grove, R. I., October 7, 1863. Designation changed September 27, 1864. Consolidated with 138th Company, 2nd Battalion, September 29, 1865.

19th COMPANY, 2nd BATTALION.—Formerly known as Company "K," 13th Regiment, Veteran Reserve Corps. Organized at Lovett Gen. Hospital, Portsmouth Grove, R. I., October 7, 1863. Designation changed September 27, 1864. Consolidated with 117th Company, 2nd Battalion, September 29, 1865.

20th COMPANY, 2nd BATTALION.—Formerly known as Company "H," 5th Regiment, Veteran Reserve Corps. Organized at Nashville, Tenn., August 7, 1863. Designation changed March 7, 1864. Mustered out by detachments September 2 to November 14, 1865.

21st COMPANY, 2nd BATTALION.—Formerly known as Company "G," 6th Regiment, Veteran Reserve Corps. Organized at Convalescent Camp, Va., August 10, 1863. Designation changed March 7, 1864. Consolidated with 22nd Company, 2nd Battalion, September 21, 1865.

22nd COMPANY, 2nd BATTALION.—Formerly known as Company "K," 11th Regiment, Veteran Reserve Corps, Organized at Convalescent Camp, Va., August 17, 1863. Designation changed April 25, 1864. Mustered out by detachments August 9 to November 21, 1865.

23rd COMPANY, 2nd BATTALION.—Formerly known as Company "H," 6th Regiment, Veteran Reserve Corps. Organized at Convalescent Camp, Va., August 17, 1863. Designation changed March 7, 1864. Consolidated with 22nd Company, 2nd Battalion, August 19, 1865.

24th COMPANY, 2nd BATTALION.—Formerly known as Company "G," 13th Regiment, Veteran Reserve Corps. Organized at Brattleboro, Vt., August 11, 1863. Designation changed September 27, 1864. Mustered out by detachments August 9 to December 1, 1865.

25th COMPANY, 2nd BATTALION.—Formerly known as Company "G," 5th Regiment, Veteran Reserve Corps. Organized at Nashville, Tenn., August 15, 1863. Designation changed March 7, 1864. Mustered out August 15 to November 11, 1865, by detachments.

26th COMPANY, 2nd BATTALION.—Formerly known as Company "K," 10th Regiment, Veteran Reserve Corps. Organized at New York City July 16, 1863. Designation changed August 1, 1864. Mustered out by detachments July 7 to September 22, 1865.

27th COMPANY, 2nd BATTALION.—Formerly known as Company "K," 3rd Regiment, Veteran Reserve Corps. Organized at Washington, D. C., July, 1863. Designation changed May 20, 1864. Consolidated with 33rd Company, 2nd Battalion, July 28, 1865.

28th COMPANY, 2nd BATTALION.—Formerly known as Company "G," 15th Regiment, Veteran Reserve Corps. Organized at Balfour Gen. Hospital, Portsmouth, Va., August, 1863. Designation changed April 25, 1864. Mustered out by detachments July 19 to November 28, 1865.

29th COMPANY, 2nd BATTALION.—Formerly known as Company "H," 15th Regiment, Veteran Reserve Corps. Organized at Chesapeake Gen. Hospital, Fort Monroe, Va., August 1, 1863. Designation changed April 25, 1864. Mustered out by detachments August 31 to November 25, 1865.

30th COMPANY, 2nd BATTALION.—Formerly known as Company "I," 15th Regiment, Veteran Reserve Corps. Organized at Chesapeake Gen. Hospital, Fort Monroe, Va., August 1, 1863. Designation changed April 25, 1864. Mustered out by detachments August 12 to November 28, 1865.

31st COMPANY, 2nd BATTALION.—Formerly known as Company "K," 15th Regiment, Veteran Reserve Corps.

Organized at Hampton Gen. Hospital, Fort Monroe Va., August, 1863. Designation changed April 25, 1864. Mustered out by detachments August 12 to November 30, 1865.

32nd COMPANY, 2nd BATTALION.—Formerly known as Company "K," 20th Regiment, Veteran Reserve Corps. Organized at Hampton Gen. Hospital, Fort Monroe, Va., August, 1863. Designation changed May 25, 1864. Mustered out by detachments August 11 to September 28, 1865.

33rd COMPANY, 2nd BATTALION.—Formerly known as Company "G," 9th Regiment, Veteran Reserve Corps. Organized at Convalescent Camp, Va., August 24, 1864. Designation changed April 29, 1864. Consolidated with 36th Company, 2nd Battalion, September 21, 1865.

34th COMPANY, 2nd BATTALION.—Formerly known as Company "G," 18th Regiment, Veteran Reserve Corps, Organized at Nashville, Tenn., August, 1863. Designation changed April 25, 1864. Consolidated with 20th Company, 2nd Battalion, August 2, 1865.

35th COMPANY, 2nd BATTALION.—Formerly known as Company "I," 8th Regiment, Veteran Reserve Corps. Organized at St. Louis, Mo., August 18, 1863. Designation changed April 25, 1864. Consolidated with 62nd Company, 2nd Battalion, August 4, 1865.

36th COMPANY, 2nd BATTALION.—Formerly known as Company "H," 9th Regiment, Veteran Reserve Corps, Organized at Washington, D. C., August 24, 1863. Designation changed April 29, 1864. Mustered out by detachments September 4 to October 22, 1865.

37th COMPANY, 2nd BATTALION.—Formerly known as Company "I," 6th Regiment, Veteran Reserve Corps. Organized at Convalescent Camp, Va., August 28, 1863. Designation changed March 7, 1864. Consolidated with 14th Company, 2nd Battalion, July 5, 1865.

38th COMPANY, 2nd BATTALION.—Formerly known as Company "K," 9th Regiment, Veteran Reserve Corps. Organized at Washington, D. C., August, 1863. Designation changed April 29, 1864. Consolidated with 36th Company, 2nd Battalion, September 21, 1865.

39th COMPANY, 2nd BATTALION.—Formerly known as Company "I," 1st Regiment, Veteran Reserve Corps. Organized at Convalescent Camp, Va., September 1, 1863. Designation changed March 7, 1864. Consolidated with 14th Company, 2nd Battalion, September 21, 1865.

40th COMPANY, 2nd BATTALION.—Formerly known as Company "I," 5th Regiment, Veteran Reserve Corps. Organized at Nashville, Tenn., August 23, 1863. Designation changed March 7, 1864. Mustered out by detachments August 11 to September 2, 1865.

41st COMPANY, 2nd BATTALION.—Formerly known as Company "H," 13th Regiment, Veteran Reserve Corps. Organized at New Haven, Conn., August 8, 1863. Designation changed September 27, 1864. Consolidated with 159th Company, 2nd Battalion, August 18, 1865.

42nd COMPANY, 2nd BATTALION.—Formerly known as Company "G," 2nd Regiment, Veteran Reserve Corps. Organized at Nashville, Tenn., August 28, 1863. Designation changed January 1, 1865. Consolidated with 3rd Company, 2nd Battalion, September 5, 1865.

43rd COMPANY, 2nd BATTALION.—Formerly known as Company "I," 21st Regiment, Veteran Reserve Corps. Organized at Camp Dennison, Ohio, August 31, 1863. Designation changed May 23, 1864. Consolidated with 60th Company, 2nd Battalion, November 17, 1865.

44th COMPANY, 2nd BATTALION.—Formerly known as Company "I," 12th Regiment, Veteran Reserve Corps. Organized at Convalescent Camp, Va., September 4, 1863. Designation changed May 23, 1864. Consolidated with 22nd Company, 2nd Battalion, August 19, 1865.

45th COMPANY, 2nd BATTALION.—Formerly known as Company "K," 5th Regiment, Veteran Reserve Corps. Organized at Nashville, Tenn., September 2, 1863. Designation changed March 7, 1864. Consolidated with 74th Company, 2nd Battalion, August 5, 1865.

46th COMPANY, 2nd BATTALION.—Formerly known as Company "G," 16th Regiment, Veteran Reserve Corps. Organized at McClellan Gen. Hospital, Philadelphia, Pa., August 22, 1863. Designation changed April 29,

1864. Mustered out by detachments September 5 to October 2, 1865.

47th COMPANY, 2nd BATTALION.—Formerly known as Company "K," 12th Regiment, Veteran Reserve Corps. Organized at Depot Camp, Washington, D. C., September 9, 1863. Designation changed May 23, 1864. Consolidated with 33rd Company, 2nd Battalion, July 28, 1865.

48th COMPANY, 2nd BATTALION.—Formerly known as Company "H," 3rd Regiment, Veteran Reserve Corps. Organized at Convalescent Camp, Va., September 11, 1863. Designation changed May 20, 1864. Consolidated with 36th Company, 2nd Battalion, September 21, 1865.

49th COMPANY, 2nd BATTALION.—Formerly known as Company "I," 3rd Regiment, Veteran Reserve Corps. Organized at Convalescent Camp, Va., September 16, 1863. Designation changed May 20, 1864. Consolidated with 48th Company, 2nd Battalion, July 5, 1865.

50th COMPANY, 2nd BATTALION.—Formerly known as Company "I," 20th Regiment, Veteran Reserve Corps. Organized at Harrisburg, Pa., August, 1863. Designation changed May 25, 1864. Mustered out by detachments September 5, 1865, to February, 1866.

51st COMPANY, 2nd BATTALION.—Formerly known as Company "K," 14th Regiment, Veteran Reserve Corps. Organized at Satterlee Gen. Hospital, Philadelphia, Pa., August, 1863. Designation changed May 11, 1864. Mustered out by detachments August 14 to September 19, 1865.

52nd COMPANY, 2nd BATTALION.—Formerly known as Company "G," 14th Regiment, Veteran Reserve Corps. Organized at Mower Gen. Hospital, Philadelphia, Pa., August 24, 1863. Designation changed May 11, 1864. Mustered out by detachments July 7 to November 22, 1865.

53rd COMPANY, 2nd BATTALION.—Formerly known as Company "H," 14th Regiment, Veteran Reserve Corps. Organized at Mower Gen. Hospital, Philadelphia, Pa., August 24, 1863. Designation changed May 11, 1864. Mustered out by detachments July 8 to November 22, 1865.

54th COMPANY, 2nd BATTALION.—Formerly known as Company "H," 16th Regiment, Veteran Reserve Corps. Organized at Philadelphia September 10, 1863. Designation changed April 29, 1864. Transferred to 9th Regiment April 30, 1864.

55th COMPANY, 2nd BATTALION.—Formerly known as Company "I," 16th Regiment, Veteran Reserve Corps. Organized at Chester, Pa., October 10, 1863. Designation changed April 29, 1864. Consolidated with 50th Company, 2nd Battalion, October 18, 1865.

56th COMPANY, 2nd BATTALION.—Formerly known as Company "H," 7th Regiment, Veteran Reserve Corps. Organized at Louisville, Ky., September 16, 1863. Designation changed March 7, 1864. Consolidated with 79th Company, 2nd Battalion, August 5, 1865.

57th COMPANY, 2nd BATTALION.—Formerly known as Company "I," 14th Regiment, Veteran Reserve Corps. Organized at Satterlee Gen. Hospital, Philadelphia, Pa., September 9, 1863. Designation changed May 11, 1864. Consolidated with 50th Company, 2nd Battalion, October 18, 1865.

58th COMPANY, 2nd BATTALION.—Formerly known as Company "I," 11th Regiment, Veteran Reserve Corps. Organized at Washington, D. C., September, 1863. Designation changed April 25, 1864. Consolidated with 2nd Company, 2nd Battalion, July 5, 1865.

59th COMPANY, 2nd BATTALION.—Formerly known as Company "K," 16th Regiment, Veteran Reserve Corps. Organized at Philadelphia, Pa., August, 1863. Designation changed April 29, 1864. Mustered out by detachments August 2 to November 30, 1865.

60th COMPANY, 2nd BATTALION.—Organized at Nashville, Tenn., August 26, 1863. Mustered out by detachments September 5 to December 30, 1865.

61st COMPANY, 2nd BATTALION.—Formerly known as Company "G," 23rd Regiment, Veteran Reserve Corps. Organized at Cincinnati, Ohio, September 26,

1863. Designation changed May 13, 1864. Mustered out by detachments August 24 to September 12, 1865.

62nd COMPANY, 2nd BATTALION.—Formerly known as Company "K," 4th Regiment, Veteran Reserve Corps. Organized at Camp Alexander, St. Louis, Mo., September 12, 1863. Designation changed March 7, 1864. Mustered out by detachments July 17, 1865, to October 1, 1866.

63rd COMPANY, 2nd BATTALION.—Formerly known as Company "G," 20th Regiment, Veteran Reserve Corps. Organized at Convalescent Camp, Va., October 2, 1863. Designation changed May 25, 1864. Disbanded August 20, 1865.

64th COMPANY, 2nd BATTALION.—Formerly known as Company "H," 20th Regiment, Veteran Reserve Corps. Organized at Depot Camp, Washington, D. C., October 7, 1863. Designation changed May 25, 1864. Disbanded August 20, 1865.

65th COMPANY, 2nd BATTALION.—Formerly known as Company "I," 9th Regiment, Veteran Reserve Corps. Organized at Depot Camp, Washington, D. C., October 9, 1863. Designation changed April 29, 1864. Consolidated with 33rd Company, 2nd Battalion, July 28, 1865.

66th COMPANY, 2nd BATTALION.—Organized at Gallipolis, Ohio, September 30, 1863. Disbanded August 30, 1865.

67th COMPANY, 2nd BATTALION.—Formerly known as Company "H," 23rd Regiment, Veteran Reserve Corps. Organized at Louisville, Ky., October 2, 1863. Designation changed May 13, 1864. Consolidated with 61st Company, 2nd Battalion, August 5, 1865.

68th COMPANY, 2nd BATTALION.—Formerly known as Company "I," 23rd Regiment, Veteran Reserve Corps. Organized at Louisville, Ky., September 30, 1863. Designation changed May 13, 1864. Consolidated with 61st Company, 2nd Battalion, August 5, 1865.

69th COMPANY, 2nd BATTALION.—Formerly known as Company "K," 1st Regiment, Veteran Reserve Corps. Organized at Convalescent Camp, Va., July 16, 1863. Designation changed March 7, 1864. Consolidated with 39th Company, 2nd Battalion, July 5, 1865.

70th COMPANY, 2nd BATTALION.—Formerly known as Company "K," 8th Regiment, Veteran Reserve Corps. Organized at Camp Alexandria, St. Louis, Mo., October 1, 1863. Designation changed March 7, 1864. Disbanded August 10, 1865.

71st COMPANY, 2nd BATTALION.—Formerly known as Company "I," 7th Regiment, Veteran Reserve Corps. Organized at Baltimore, Md., September 29, 1863. Designation changed March 7, 1864. Mustered out by detachments July 31 to October 30, 1865.

72nd COMPANY, 2nd BATTALION.—Formerly known as Company "K," 7th Regiment, Veteran Reserve Corps. Organized at Baltimore, Md., October 1, 1863. Designation changed March 7, 1864. Mustered out by detachments July 31 to October 31, 1865.

73rd COMPANY, 2nd BATTALION.—Formerly known as Company "I," 2nd Regiment, Veteran Reserve Corps. Organized at Louisville, Ky., October 5, 1863. Designation changed January 1, 1865. Consolidated with 40th Company, 2nd Battalion, August 5, 1865.

74th COMPANY, 2nd BATTALION.—Formerly known as Company "K," 2nd Regiment, Veteran Reserve Corps. Organized at Camp Nelson, Ky., October 8, 1863. Designation changed January 1, 1865. Mustered out by detachments August 4 to November 20, 1865.

75th COMPANY, 2nd BATTALION.—Formerly known as Company "G," 19th Regiment, Veteran Reserve Corps. Organized at Convalescent Camp, Va., July —, 1863. Designation changed April 12, 1864. Consolidated with 36th Company, 2nd Battalion, August 27, 1865.

76th COMPANY, 2nd BATTALION.—Formerly known as Company "H," 19th Regiment, Veteran Reserve Corps. Organized at Convalescent Camp, Va., October 14, 1863. Designation changed April 12, 1864. Consolidated with 42nd Company, 2nd Battalion, August 27, 1865.

77th COMPANY, 2nd BATTALION.—Formerly known as Company "H," 18th Regiment, Veteran Reserve

Corps. Organized at Camp Joe Holt, Ind., October 3, 1863. Designation changed April 25, 1864. Consolidated with 11th Company, 2nd Battalion, August 5, 1865.

78th COMPANY, 2nd BATTALION.—Formerly known as Company "I," 19th Regiment, Veteran Reserve Corps. Organized at Convalescent Camp, Va., October 19, 1863. Designation changed April 12, 1864. Consolidated with 39th Company, 2nd Battalion, July 5, 1865.

79th COMPANY, 2nd BATTALION.—Formerly known as Company "I," 18th Regiment, Veteran Reserve Corps. Organized at Camp Joe Holt, Ind., September 30, 1863. Designation changed April 25, 1864. Mustered out by detachments August 22 to September 30, 1865.

80th COMPANY, 2nd BATTALION.—Organized at Alexander Barracks, St. Louis, Mo., October 15, 1863. Mustered out by detachments August 12 to November 30, 1865.

81st COMPANY, 2nd BATTALION.—Formerly known as Company "K," 19th Regiment, Veteran Reserve Corps. Organized at Washington, D. C., August, 1863. Designation changed April 12, 1864. Consolidated with 86th Company, 2nd Battalion, July 29, 1865.

82nd COMPANY, 2nd BATTALION.—Formerly known as Company "G," 22nd Regiment, Veteran Reserve Corps. Organized at Washington, D. C. Designation changed March 26, 1864. Consolidated with 86th Company, 2nd Battalion, July 29, 1865.

83rd COMPANY, 2nd BATTALION.—Formerly known as Company "K," 18th Regiment, Veteran Reserve Corps. Organized October 15, 1863. Designation changed April 25, 1864. Consolidated with 9th Company, 2nd Battalion, August 5, 1865.

84th COMPANY, 2nd BATTALION.—Formerly known as Company "K," 23rd Regiment, Veteran Reserve Corps. Organized October 15, 1864. Designation changed May 13, 1864. Consolidated with 61st Company, 2nd Battalion, August 5, 1865.

85th COMPANY, 2nd BATTALION.—Organized at Benton Barracks, Mo., September, 1863. Mustered out by detachments July 8 to November 30, 1865.

86th COMPANY, 2nd BATTALION.—Formerly known as Company "H," 22nd Regiment, Veteran Reserve Corps. Organized at Convalescent Camp, Va., November 14, 1863. Designation changed March 26, 1864. Consolidated with 8th Company, 2nd Battalion, September 21, 1865.

87th COMPANY, 2nd BATTALION.—Formerly known as Company "K," 21st Regiment, Veteran Reserve Corps. Organized at Camp Dennison, Ohio, October 31, 1863. Designation changed May 13, 1864. Consolidated with 43rd Company, 2nd Battalion, August 2, 1865.

88th COMPANY, 2nd BATTALION.—Organized at Camp Dennison, Ohio, October 31, 1863. Consolidated with 43rd Company, 2nd Battalion, August 2, 1865.

89th COMPANY, 2nd BATTALION.—Organized at Baltimore, Md., October 1, 1863. Disbanded August 30, 1865.

90th COMPANY, 2nd BATTALION.—Formerly known as Company "H," 4th Regiment, Veteran Reserve Corps. Organized at Rock Island Barracks, Ill., November 14, 1863. Designation changed March 7, 1864. Transferred to 4th Regiment, Veteran Reserve Corps, December 31, 1864.

91st COMPANY, 2nd BATTALION.—Formerly known as Company "G," 17th Regiment, Veteran Reserve Corps. Organized October 31, 1863. Designation changed April 25, 1864. Disbanded August 25, 1865.

92nd COMPANY, 2nd BATTALION.—Formerly known as Company "H," 17th Regiment, Veteran Reserve Corps. Organized October 31, 1863. Designation changed April 25, 1864. Consolidated with 43rd Company, 2nd Battalion, August 9, 1865.

93rd COMPANY, 2nd BATTALION.—Formerly Company "I," 17th Regiment, Veteran Reserve Corps. Organized October 31, 1863. Designation changed April 25, 1864. Consolidated with 20th Company, 2nd Battalion, August 2, 1865.

94th COMPANY, 2nd BATTALION.—Formerly known as Company "K," 17th Regiment, Veteran Reserve Corps.

Organized October 31, 1863. Designation changed April 25. 1864. Consolidated with 20th Company, 2nd Battalion, August 2, 1865.

95th COMPANY, 2nd BATTALION.—Formerly known as Company "I," 22nd Regiment, Veteran Reserve Corps. Organized at Harrisburg, Pa., September, 1863. Designation changed March 26, 1864. Mustered out by detachments August 14 to November 20, 1865.

96th COMPANY, 2nd BATTALION.—Formerly known as Company "K," 22nd Regiment, Veteran Reserve Corps. Organized at Convalescent Camp, Va., November 25, 1863. Designation changed March 26, 1864. Mustered out by detachments August 15 to November 20, 1865.

97th COMPANY, 2nd BATTALION.—Formerly known as Company "G," 4th Regiment, Veteran Reserve Corps. Organized at Alexander Barracks, St. Louis, Mo., October, 1863. Designation changed March 7, 1864. Transferred to 4th Regiment, Veteran Reserve Corps, December 31, 1864.

98th COMPANY, 2nd BATTALION.—Organized at Quincy, Ill., November 25, 1863. Consolidated with 59th Company, 2nd Battalion, August 2, 1865.

99th COMPANY, 2nd BATTALION.—Formerly known as Company "G," 24th Regiment, Veteran Reserve Corps. Organized at Washington, D. C., September, 1863. Designation changed March 26, 1864. Consolidated with 102nd Company, 2nd Battalion, June, 1864.

100th COMPANY, 2nd BATTALION.—Formerly known as Company "H," 24th Regiment, Veteran Reserve Corps. Organized at Convalescent Camp, Va., December 2, 1863. Designation changed March 26, 1864. Consolidated with 8th Company, 2nd Battalion, September 2, 1865.

101st COMPANY, 2nd BATTALION.—Organized at Cliffburne Barracks, Washington, D. C., November 25, 1863. Consolidated with 14th Company, 2nd Battalion, August 7, 1865.

102nd COMPANY, 2nd BATTALION.—Formerly known as Company "I," 24th Regiment, Veteran Reserve Corps. Organized at Convalescent Camp, Va., December 14, 1863. Designation changed March 26, 1864. Consolidated with 100th Company, 2nd Battalion, July 29, 1865.

103rd COMPANY, 2nd BATTALION.—Organized at Madison, Ind., November 22, 1863. Disbanded August 5, 1865.

104th COMPANY, 2nd BATTALION.—Formerly known as Company "K," 24th Regiment, Veteran Reserve Corps. Organized at Depot Camp, Washington, D. C., November 28, 1863. Designation changed March 26, 1864. Consolidated with 100th Company, 2nd Battalion, July 29, 1865.

105th COMPANY, 2nd BATTALION.—Organized at Madison, Ind., November 27, 1863. Mustered out by detachments August 19 to October 30, 1865.

106th COMPANY, 2nd BATTALION.—Organized at Evansville, Ind., December 3, 1863. Disbanded August 10, 1865.

107th COMPANY, 2nd BATTALION.—Organized at Camp Douglas, Chicago, Ill., November, 1863. Mustered out by detachments July 2 to November 30, 1865.

108th COMPANY, 2nd BATTALION.—Organized at York, Pa., December 8, 1863. Disbanded August 8, 1865.

109th COMPANY, 2nd BATTALION.—Organized at Pittsburg, Pa., December 1, 1863. Disbanded September 23, 1865.

110th COMPANY, 2nd BATTALION.—Organized at Madison Gen. Hospital, Ind., December 7, 1863. Mustered out by detachments August 5 to November 28, 1865.

111th COMPANY, 2nd BATTALION.—Organized at Camp Depot, Columbus, Ohio, December 1, 1863. Consolidated with 60th Company, 2nd Battalion, August 31, 1865.

112th COMPANY, 2nd BATTALION.—Organized at Convalescent Camp, Va., December 10, 1863. Consolidated with 86th Company, 2nd Battalion, August 22, 1865.

113th COMPANY, 2nd BATTALION.—Organized at Depot Camp, Washington, D. C., December 5, 1863. Consolidated with 2nd Regiment, Veteran Reserve Corps, December, 1864.

114th COMPANY, 2nd BATTALION.—Organized at Depot Camp, Washington, D. C., December 7, 1863. Consolidated with 21st Company, 2nd Battalion, July 26, 1865.

115th COMPANY, 2nd BATTALION.—Formerly known as Company "I," 4th Regiment, Veteran Reserve Corps. Organized at Camp Alexander, St. Louis, Mo., September 11, 1863. Designation changed March 7, 1864. Transferred back to 4th Regiment, Veteran Reserve Corps, December 31, 1864.

116th COMPANY, 2nd BATTALION.—Organized at Depot Camp, Washington, D. C., December 9, 1863. Consolidated with 100th Company, 2nd Battalion, July 29, 1865.

117th COMPANY, 2nd BATTALION.—Organized at Lovell Gen. Hospital, Portsmouth Grove, R. I., January 16, 1864. Consolidated with 110th Company, 2nd Battalion, October 28, 1865.

118th COMPANY, 2nd BATTALION.—Organized at Annapolis, Md., November 14, 1863. Mustered out by detachments July 29 to November 20, 1865.

119th COMPANY, 2nd BATTALION.—Organized at Annapolis, Md., November 14, 1863. Mustered out by detachments July 27 to December 31, 1865.

120th COMPANY, 2nd BATTALION.—Organized at Cincinnati, Ohio, December 15, 1863. Consolidated with 20th Company, 2nd Battalion, August 2, 1865.

121st COMPANY, 2nd BATTALION.—Organized at Satterlee Gen. Hospital, Philadelphia, Pa., November, 1863. Consolidated with 9th Regiment, Veteran Reserve Corps, April, 1864.

122nd COMPANY, 2nd BATTALION.—Organized at Satterlee Gen. Hospital, Philadelphia, Pa., November, 1863. Consolidated with 9th Regiment, Veteran Reserve Corps, April, 1864.

123rd COMPANY, 2nd BATTALION.—Organized at Satterlee Gen. Hospital, Philadelphia, Pa., November, 1863. Consolidated with 9th Regiment, Veteran Reserve Corps, April, 1864.

124th COMPANY, 2nd BATTALION.—Organized at Columbus, Ohio, December 22, 1863. Consolidated with 60th Company, 2nd Battalion, August 2, 1865.

125th COMPANY, 2nd BATTALION.—Organized December 18, 1863. Consolidated with 11th Company, 2nd Battalion, August 5, 1865.

126th COMPANY, 2nd BATTALION.—Organized at U. S. Gen. Hospital, Camp Dennison, Ohio, December 28, 1863. Consolidated with 43rd Company, 2nd Battalion, August 2, 1865.

127th COMPANY, 2nd BATTALION.—Organized at Cliffbourne Barracks, Washington, D. C., December 31, 1863. Disbanded April 26, 1864.

128th COMPANY, 2nd BATTALION.—Organized at New York City January 16, 1864. Consolidated with 36th Company, 2nd Battalion, August 27, 1865.

129th COMPANY, 2nd BATTALION.—Organized at Depot Camp, Washington, D. C., December 31, 1863. Consolidated with 38th Company, 2nd Battalion, August 28, 1865.

130th COMPANY, 2nd BATTALION.—Organized at McDougall Gen. Hospital, Fort Schuyler, N. Y. Harbor, December 28, 1863. Consolidated with 9th Regiment, Veteran Reserve Corps, April 28, 1864.

131st COMPANY, 2nd BATTALION.—Organized at Summit House Hospital, Philadelphia, Pa., December, 1863. Consolidated with 50th Company, 2nd Battalion, October 18, 1865.

132nd COMPANY, 2nd BATTALION.—Organized at Frederick, Md., December, 1863. Mustered out by detachments July 3 to September 15, 1865.

133rd COMPANY, 2nd BATTALION.—Organized at Mower Gen. Hospital, Philadelphia, Pa., January 20, 1864. Disbanded April 26, 1864.

134th COMPANY, 2nd BATTALION.—Organized at Mower Gen. Hospital, Philadelphia, Pa., January 20, 1864. Disbanded April 26, 1864.

135th COMPANY, 2nd BATTALION.—Organized at McClellan Gen. Hospital, Philadelphia, Pa., February 3, 1864. Consolidated with 42nd Company, 2nd Battalion, May 23, 1864.

136th COMPANY, 2nd BATTALION.—Organized at U. S. Gen. Hospital, Newark, N. J., January 12, 1864. Disbanded January, 1865.

137th COMPANY, 2nd BATTALION.—Organized at Detroit, Mich., August, 1863. Consolidated with 25th Company, 2nd Battalion, August 2, 1865.

138th COMPANY, 2nd BATTALION.—Organized at Alexander Barracks, St. Louis, Mo., February 9, 1864. Mustered out by detachments August 10 to December 31, 1865.

139th COMPANY, 2nd BATTALION.—Organized at Nashville, Tenn., January 25, 1864. Mustered out by detachments June 30 to September 7, 1865.

140th COMPANY, 2nd BATTALION.—Organized at New Orleans, La., February 5, 1864. Mustered out by detachments July 10 to November 20, 1865.

141st COMPANY, 2nd BATTALION.—Organized at Louisville, Ky., February 6, 1864. Consolidated with 61st Company, 2nd Battalion, August 5, 1865.

142nd COMPANY, 2nd BATTALION.—Organized at New Orleans, La., February 9, 1864. Mustered out by detachments August 8 to November 30, 1865.

143rd COMPANY, 2nd BATTALION.—Organized at West's Building, Gen. Hospital, Baltimore, Md., February 29, 1864. Mustered out by detachments August 1 to November 20, 1865.

144th COMPANY, 2nd BATTALION.—Organized at Seminary Hospital, Georgetown, D. C., February 22, 1864. Consolidated with 49th Company, 2nd Battalion, July 19, 1865.

145th COMPANY, 2nd BATTALION.—Organized at David's Island, N. Y. Harbor, February 22, 1864. Consolidated with 4th Company, 2nd Battalion, September 18, 1865.

146th COMPANY, 2nd BATTALION.—Organized at Camp Randall, Madison, Wis., January 9, 1864. Mustered out by detachments August 19 to October 31, 1865.

147th COMPANY, 2nd BATTALION.—Organized at U. S. Gen. Hospital, Cumberland, Md., February 1, 1864. Disbanded August 20, 1865.

148th COMPANY, 2nd BATTALION.—Organized January 22, 1864. Mustered out by detachments June 30 to October 18, 1865.

149th COMPANY, 2nd BATTALION.—Organized January 26, 1864. Mustered out by detachments June 30 and July 29, 1865.

150th COMPANY, 2nd BATTALION.—Organized at Nashville, Tenn., January 31, 1864. Disbanded July 2, 1865.

151st COMPANY, 2nd BATTALION.—Organized at Nashville, Tenn., January 31, 1864. Mustered out by detachments June 30 to September 7, 1865.

152nd COMPANY, 2nd BATTALION.—Organized at Nashville, Tenn., January 31, 1864. Mustered out by detachments June 30 to August 26, 1865.

153rd COMPANY, 2nd BATTALION.—Organized February 2, 1864. Disbanded July 22, 1865.

154th COMPANY, 2nd BATTALION.—Organized at Nashville, Tenn., January 31, 1864. Mustered out by detachments June 30 to September 7, 1865.

155th COMPANY, 2nd BATTALION.—Organized at Nashville, Tenn., February 2, 1864. Mustered out by detachments June 30 to September 7, 1865.

156th COMPANY, 2nd BATTALION.—Organized February 14, 1864. Consolidated with 13th Company, 2nd Battalion, August 4, 1865.

157th COMPANY, 2nd BATTALION.—Organized at Louisville, Ky., February 15, 1864. Consolidated with 74th Company, 2nd Battalion, August 5, 1865.

158th COMPANY, 2nd BATTALION.—Organized at New Albany, Ind., February 18, 1864. Consolidated with 11th Company, 2nd Battalion, August 5, 1865.

159th COMPANY, 2nd BATTALION.—Organized at Knight's Gen. Hospital, New Haven, Conn., February, 1864. Mustered out by detachments July 28 to November 30, 1865.

160th COMPANY, 2nd BATTALION.—Organized at Nashville, Tenn., January 31, 1864. Mustered out by detachments June 30 to September 7, 1865.

161st COMPANY, 2nd BATTALION.—Organized at New Orleans, La., December 16, 1863. Mustered out by detachments July 15 to November 30, 1865.

162nd COMPANY, 2nd BATTALION.—Organized at Cuyler Gen. Hospital, Germantown, Pa., March 20, 1864. Consolidated with 50th Company, 2nd Battalion, December 13, 1865.

163rd COMPANY, 2nd BATTALION.—Organized at New Orleans, La., March 9, 1864. Mustered out by detachments July 18 to November 30, 1865.

164th COMPANY, 2nd BATTALION.—Organized at New Orleans, La., March 19, 1864. Mustered out by detachments July 17 to November 30, 1865.

165th COMPANY, 2nd BATTALION.—Organized at Cincinnati, Ohio, March 20, 1864. Mustered out by detachments June 30 to September 13, 1865.

166th COMPANY, 2nd BATTALION.—Organized at Hamond Gen. Hospital, Point Lookout, Md., April 25, 1864. Mustered out August 24, 1865.

168th COMPANY, 2nd BATTALION.—Organized at Concord, N. H., April, 1864. Consolidated with 159th Company, 2nd Battalion, September 29, 1865.

169th COMPANY, 2nd BATTALION.—Organized at Keokuk, Iowa, April 29, 1864. Consolidated with 172nd Company, 2nd Battalion, August 21, 1865.

170th COMPANY, 2nd BATTALION.—Organized at Washington, D. C., June, 1864. Consolidated with 3rd Company, 2nd Battalion, July 5, 1865.

171st COMPANY, 2nd BATTALION.—Organized at Burlington, Vt., May 19, 1864. Consolidated with 4th Company, 2nd Battalion, September 8, 1865.

172nd COMPANY, 2nd BATTALION.—Organized at Davenport, Ia., June, 1864. Mustered out by detachments July 29 to November 25, 1865.

173rd COMPANY, 2nd BATTALION.—Organized at Hilton Head, S. C., September, 1864. Disbanded July 8, 1865.

174th COMPANY, 2nd BATTALION.—Organized at Knoxville, Tenn., February 7, 1865. Mustered out by detachments July 7 to November 6, 1865.

1st INDEPENDENT COMPANY.—Organized at Washington, D. C., December 4, 1865, by consolidation of enlisted men from 7th, 9th, 10th, 12th, 14th and 24th Regiments, Veteran Reserve Corps. Mustered out by detachments March 15 to October 22, 1866.

2nd INDEPENDENT COMPANY.—Organized at Harrisburg, Pa., December 15, 1865, by consolidation of enlisted men from 12th, 11th, 20th and 21st Regiments, Veteran Reserve Corps. Mustered out by detachments March 5 to August 30, 1866.

3rd INDEPENDENT COMPANY.—Organized at Columbus, Ohio, December 14, 1865, by consolidation of enlisted men from various Regiments and Companies, Veteran Reserve Corps. Mustered out by detachments April 15 to August 29, 1866.

4th INDEPENDENT COMPANY.—Organized at Camp Butler, Ill., February 17, 1866, by consolidation of enlisted men from 2nd, 4th, 6th, 8th, 15th and 23rd Regiments, Veteran Reserve Corps. Mustered out by detachments May 18 to August 26, 1866.

5th INDEPENDENT COMPANY.—Organized at David's Island, N. Y. Harbor, December 14, 1865, by consolidation of the enlisted men from various Regiments and Companies of the Veteran Reserve Corps. Mustered out by detachments May 15 to August 31, 1865.

6th INDEPENDENT COMPANY.—Organized at Gallop's Island, Boston Harbor, December 1, 1865, by consolidation of enlisted men from the 3rd, 11th and 13th Regiments, Veteran Reserve Corps. Mustered out by detachments June 1 to August 31, 1866.

7th INDEPENDENT COMPANY.—Organized at Elmira, N. Y., December 1, 1865, by consolidation of enlisted men from 1st, 19th and 21st Regiments, Veteran Reserve Corps. Mustered out by detachments June 15 to August 29, 1866.

INDEX

INDEX

Errata

Page 39—In summary of organizations, 1 Company of Heavy Arty. credited to Dakota Ter. should appear in Delaware.

Page 71—Harris, A. L. Credited to Cumberland. Should be Potomac.

Page 73—Hays, W. H., 1st Brigade should be 2nd Brigade and 2nd Brigade should be 3rd Brigade.

Page 74—Hills, S. G. 3rd Brig., 1st Div., Detachment A. T. Gulf, should be Cumberland.

Page 86—Miller, J. F. District of Nashville, should be Post Nashville.

Page 88—Mower, J. A., instead of 13th Corps Gulf, should read 1st and 3rd Divisions 16th Corps Gulf.

Page 91—Pease, W. R., instead of 3rd Brig., 3rd Div. Def. North Potomac should read 3rd Brig. Def. North Pomac.

Page 92—Pierson, G. N., instead of 2nd Brig.. 1st Div. 18th Corps Dept. Va. and N. C. read Dept. N. C.

Page 94—Reid, H. T., instead of Dist. of Cairo, Tenn., read Dist. Corinth 13th Corps.

Page 95—Robinson, J. C., instead of Robinson's Brig. Mountains, read Robinson's Brig. Dept. of Va.

Page 95—Rodgers, R. S., instead of 2nd Brig., 1st Div. W. Va., read 3rd Brig., 1st Div. W. Va.

Page 103—Stewart, Jas., Jr., instead of 1st Brig., 2nd Div. 18th Corps, Dept. N. C., read Dept. Va. and N. C.

Page 105—Tilson, John, should read Tillson, Davis, for all the Commands credited to Tilson, John.

Page 261—for Dept. of Northwestern Va. read Northeastern Va.

Page 271—for 52nd N. Y. (2nd S. M.) in 1st Brig. Stevens Div. read 82nd New York, (2nd S. M.).

Page 278—for 61st Penna. in 1st Brig. Sumner's Div., read 81st Penna.

Page 295—for 25th Indiana in 1st Brig., 1st Div., read 20th Indiana.

Page 313—for Light Division continued, at top of page, read Artillery Brigade cont'd.

Page 328—for 17th Maine, (1st H. A.) in Def. North Potomac, read 18th Maine.

Page 329—for 31st New York, in Prov'l Brig. Casey's Div., read 31st New Jersey.

Page 337—for Batty. D., 1st Ill. L. A. in Arty. R. R. District, read Batty. L. 1st Ill. L. A.

Page 356—for District of Beaufort, change from 1st Brig., 1st Div., 18th Corps, Dept. N. C. to 1st Brig., 1st Div., 18th Corps, Dept. South.

Page 364—for Batty. L., 1st N. Y. Arty. Fort Pickens and Pensacola, read Batty. L., 1st U. S. Arty.

Page 369—for 10th Indiana in Foster's 1st Brig., read 13th Indiana.

Page 427—for 34th Ohio in 20th Brig., read 64th Ohio.

Page 457—for 13th New Jersey in 3rd Brig., read 33rd New Jersey.

Page 457—for 149th Penna. in 1st Brig., 2nd Div., read 147th Penna.

Page 487—for 3rd Indiana in 4th Brig., Dist. Memphis, read 83rd Indiana.

Page 541, 542 and 544—for Welfey's Missouri, Batty., read Welfley's Batty.

Page 571—for 10th Illinois Infy. in 1st Brig., 1st Div., Cav. Corps W., Miss., read 10th Ill. Cav.

Page 583—for a Tabular Statement of the Battles, Skirmishes, etc., see page opposite 583, instead of page 581.

These errors have been corrected, as far as practical, in the Morningside Edition of Dyer's Compendium.

The Following Errors Have Been Discovered Since Publication, February 15, 1909, to Date, May 1, 1910:

Page   20—National Cemeteries.—For total known, read 176,397 instead of 17,397.

Page   25—Massachusetts Organizations.—Eliminate Devens' Cavalry Battalion. Mixed with Devens' 3d Battalion Rifles Infantry.

Page   29—New York Organizations.—For 24th Regiment Infantry. (3 months). See 24th Regt. Inf'y. (2 years). Regiment first started for three months but mustered for two years, dating back to first organization.

Page   156—Massachusetts Organizations.—Eliminate Devens' Battalion Mounted Rifles, Mixed with Deven's 3d Battalion Rifles, Infantry.

Page   243—Regimental Index.—Battery D. 5th U. S. Arty. Change to read as follows: June, 1861, Stone's expedition. July, 1861, 1st Brig. 2d Div. Army N. E. Va. August, 1861, W. F. Smith's Brig. Division of the Potomac. October, 1861, Arty. Porter's Div. Army Potomac. Balance as printed.

Page   271—To 1st Brig. 2d Div. Army N. E. Va., add Battery D 5th U. S. Arty., July, 1861, from Stone's Expedition, to W. F. Smith's Brig. Division of the Potomac, August, 1861.

Page   271—2d Brig. 3d Div. for Battery D 3d U. S. Arty., read Battery D 2d U. S. Arty.

Page   273—To W. F. Smith's Brigade Division of the Potomac, add Battery D 5th U. S. Arty, August, 1861, from 1st Brig. 2d Div. Army N. E. Va., to Porter's Div. Army Potomac, October, 1861.

Page   275—To Arty. Porter's Div. Army Potomac, add Battery D 5th U. S. Arty., from W. F. Smith's Brigade Division of the Potomac, to Arty. 1st Div. 3d Army Corps, Army Potomac, March, 1862.

Page   275—The transfers of King's Brigade (2d from top of page) should read, to 3rd Brig. 3d Div. 1st Corps Potomac, March, 1862, instead of, to 3d Brig. 1st Div. 1st Corps, Potomac, March, 1862.

Page   385—To Commanders 1st Brigade 3d Division West Va., add A. A. Tomlinson, Colonel 5th West Va. Infy. Temp'y at various times, December, 1863, to April, 1864.

Page   407—In Commanders 2d Brig. 1st Div. 19th Corps, change Samuel Thomas, Colonel 8th Vermont Infy. to Stephen Thomas, Col. 8th Vermont Infy.

Page   495—In Commanders 1st Brig. 2d Cav. Div., change Conrad Baker, from Col. 5th Illinois Cavalry, to Colonel 1st Indiana Cavalry.

Page   641—In Battle Index.—Change Pittinger's Raid to Andrews' Raid, and same on page 847, Tennessee.

Page   896—Engagement Dranesville, Va., December 20, 1861. Eliminate from troops engaged New York 49th Infantry. Only Ord's 3rd Brig. Penna, Reserve Division participated.

Page 1240—Massachusetts History.—Eliminate Devens' Battalion Mounted Rifles, mixed with Devens' Battalion Rifles Infy, which see.

Page 1334—30th Regiment Missouri Infy.—Change first four lines of service to read as follows: Moved to Pilot Knob, Mo., October 30, 1861, and duty there till December. Moved to St. Genevieve, thence to Helena, Ark., December 8-16, then as printed. Also change date of Muster-Out from August 31st to August 21st, and final discharge from September 11 to September 9, 1865.

Page 1423—History of 49th N. Y. Infantry, change action at Dranesville, Va., December 20, 1861 (2nd and 3rd lines of service), to skirmish at Lewinsville, Va., October 13, 1861.

Page 1542—In losses of 103rd Regiment, read as total, 248 instead of 148.

Page 1597—71st Regt. New York Infy.—In second line of service read Ball's Bluff instead of Hall's Bluff.

Page 1633—Battery F 1st Rhode Island Light Artillery. In 6th line from top of page, read "to Newport News, Va.," instead of to Norfolk, Va.

Pages 1693-1694-1696-1698-1699—Change Fort McRae, appearing in Histories of Batteries A., F. and L. 1st U. S. Arty., and Batteries C., F., H. and K., 2nd U. S. Arty. to Fort McRee.

Page 1694—Battery F 1st U. S. Arty.—In 3d line of service change January 1, 1863, to January 1, 1862.

Page 1696—History Battery K 1st U. S. Arty., in 8th line of organizations attached to, change date of line Arty. Reserve Army Potomac, from June, 1862, to June, 1863.

Page 1696—History Battery L 1st U. S. Arty.—In 4th line of service change Reconnoissance on Santa Rosa Island from January 27-31, 1861, to January 27-31, 1862.

Page 1697—1st Regiment U. S. Artillery.—Change total of losses from 175 to 197.

Page 1700—History Battery E. 3d U. S. Arty.—In 30th line from top of page, 2d column, change date of action near Warrenton White Sulphur Springs, from November 11 to October 11.

Page 1701—History Battery E. 3d U. S. Arty.—In 6th line of record, for W. T. Sherman read T. W. Sherman.

Page 1707—History Battery D. 5th U. S. Arty., add to beginning of history. Attached to Stone's Expedition, June, 1861. 1st Brig. 2d Div. Army of N. E. Va., to August, 1861. W. F. Smith's Brigade Division of the Potomac, to October, 1861, then as printed to service. After Rockville Expedition, June 10-July 7, 1861, insert the following: Advance on Manassas, Va., July 16-21, Battle of Bull Run, July 21, then read as printed.

Page 1712—History 10th U. S. Infy.—After line reading "moved to Fort Hamilton, N. Y. Harbor," insert thence to Fort Porter, Buffalo, N. Y., then read as printed.

CHANGES IN INDEX

Page 1752—In B for Denedict Lewis, read Benedict Lewis.

Page 1756—Devol, H. F. For page 290 read page 386.

Page 1768—Eliminate Devens' Cavalry Battalion and all page references thereto mixed with Deven's 3d Battalion Rifles, Infantry.

Page 1777—For 24 Regt. N. Y. Infy. (3 months), see 24th Rgt. N. Y. Infy. (3 years)

Page 1778—Sewell, W. J. For page 296 read page 297.

Page 1783—9th Rgt. Pa. Reserves Infy. for page 1580, read page 1581

Page 1790—Thomas, Stephen. For page 406, read page 407.

Index

C

I.

ILLINOIS.

M.

MAINE.

MICHIGAN.

NEW MEXICO.

NEW YORK.

NORTH CAROLINA.

OHIO.

U.

UNITED STATES REGULAR ARMY.

WISCONSIN.